Tenth Edition
TOYS & PRICES

2003

Edited by Sharon Korbeck & Dan Stearns

©2002 by Krause Publications

Published by

krause publications
An F&W Publications Company

700 East State Street • Iola, WI 54990-0001
715-445-2214 • 888-457-2873
www.krause.com

Please call or write for our free catalog of publications. Our toll-free number to place an order or obtain a free catalog is 800-258-0929 or please use our regular business telephone 715-445-2214.

Library of Congress Catalog Number: 93-77554
ISBN: 0-87349-468-7

Printed in the United States of America

Table of Contents

Foreword

**By Sharon Korbeck,
editorial director**
Toy Shop

The shelf life of toys are proportionately as short as our memories of them are long.

Buy a kid a toy, and he'll play with it until he wearies of its actions or colors . . . or until it wears out. Find that same kid 10 to 20 years later, and the man he has become will remember that toy like a lost love or a forgotten friend. When he sees it, he'll inhale excitedly and reach out to delicately handle that perfectly lithographed tin robot, pressed steel coupe, metal Erector set or Lone Ranger holster set. A tactile reminder of an innocent time.

That's all it takes to resuscitate a memory, reconstruct a childhood and renew a dream. *Toys have that power.* And like tens of thousands of enthusiasts worldwide, we at *Toys & Prices* realize that and share that dream.

That's why this 10th anniversary edition of this title is so special. For a decade, the editors of this book have sharpened our expertise by teaming up with toy titans everywhere . . . adding and refining listings, adding photos of those ever-elusive toys and consulting on everyone's best answer to the inevitable question -- what's it worth?

This revamped edition -- which includes more photos and a cleaner look -- will serve much in the way the Harry Potter's mirror did -- as a view of what you desire your life to be -- and what better than a happy existence filled with toys?

As youths, toys made us happy. They made us free.

They were our constant companions. What else could you ask for? This book allows you to reconnect with your Ponytail Barbie doll, your Howdy Doody lunch box or Wyandotte roadster much in the same way you'd reconnect with a long-lost cousin.

If you're anything like me, I'm certain that once you make that connection, you'll come back for more -- more toys, more friends, more memories. I know I have.

Toys have changed my life. They've taught me value -- both secondary market value and the intrinsic value of play. They've made me friends -- dealers and collectors who foster and feed my passion. They've brought me back to 8611 W. Cheyenne St. -- beating my sister at Mystery Date on the patio, rocking my Drowsy doll in the living room, playing with Malibu Barbie Colorforms on the school playground.

I hope this book will ignite such powerful memories for you. As those of us who love toys know, playthings are not mere road signs to our past. They are the crumbs we scattered on our way to adulthood . . . and we're all too happy to use them to find our way back.

Acknowledgments

Every year, it gets just a bit tougher to determine what should be in this book. We try out new sections, add from one, reconsider another, and ultimately, produce the edition you are now holding.

This tenth edition was a challenge. We wanted to make this book different, easier-to-use, and more "browse-worthy." Some categories stayed, some left, many were altered and updated. This book continues to be made for the general toy collector, and we plan on improving it more each year.

Naturally, many thanks go to our in-house team of experts: Merry Dudley, editor of *Toy Cars & Models*, Tom Bartsch, editor of *Toy Shop*, Karen O'Brien, Tom Michael, Angelo Van Bogart, Bonnie Tetzlaff, Sandra Morrison, Gena Pamperin, Guy Scudella, Gordon Ullom, Dean Parks, Sally Olson and Wendy Wendt. Without them, we simply wouldn't have a book.

Of course, plenty of help came from our outside experts as well: Leo Rishty, Jan Fennick, John K. Snyder, Jr., John Marshall, Mark Rich, Joe Soucy, Peter Gofton, Dr. Douglas Sadecky and Randy Prasse. With luck, we haven't forgotten anyone—thanks to all of you for excellent work!

Have a great year of collecting, and most importantly—have fun!

--Dan Stearns

Introduction

By Dan Stearns

This is the tenth year of *Toys & Prices*. Ten years, as any collector knows, is plenty of time to accumulate a lot of stuff. This new edition has been re-vamped, with a larger page size, more photos, updated prices and information and an easier-to-follow format.

Toy grading remains as elusive and subjective as ever. Our usual warning about not taking a stated value in this book as gospel still stands. To put it simply, if collecting is a source of joy and fun, it's worth doing. If it's a source of anxiety, it's time to find a new outlet and save some cash.

While the toy market has definitely seen bigger boom years compared to the last few, it's still a vibrant hobby. A quick perusal of shows and eBay can prove it. Probably the trend most noticeable in the past few years is specialization. Collectors are finding niches to concentrate on and might even pull back from ancillary areas. For example, a fan of pressed-steel vehicles might decide to only focus on Tonka and sell whatever Nylint items she has that caught her eye at a show. Barbie collectors might disregard any temptingly-priced Skipper dolls and instead save up for a harder-to-find accessory for their existing Barbie collection.

Another trend worth noting is the pull of newer, mint-in-pack toys. Many are easily found at major toy or discount stores, and are collected more for the love of the object itself rather than perceived investment value. These items, whether they are limited-edition die-cast, Barbie dolls, or G.I. Joe action figures will probably not increase dramatically in value. However, they are frequently well-made, exquisitely detailed, and a real joy just to contemplate.

Dengar from Empire Strikes Back. An early "everyman" bounty hunter.

The difference, of course, between current limited-edition models and vintage toys is simply that toys were meant, despite our insistence on mint condition, to be played with. So, anytime you find that perfect Corgi vehicle from the 1960s or that complete Major Matt Mason set, you know that it's definitely an unlikely treasure. On the other hand, the newer "collector" or "collectible" toys, nice as they are, probably won't appreciate unless they are a truly limited production run.

Be a kid again!

For those of you new to collecting, welcome! The next time you find yourself at a flea market saying longingly, "I had that doll," or "My brother and I played with the same truck in our sandbox," you'll know you've caught the toy-collecting bug.

Categories and how to use this book

Even after the revising and revamping, there will still be questions such as "where the heck do I find this toy?"

As a general rule, individual sections override character—if there is a section in the book for the type of toy you're looking for, try that section first. For instance, if you're looking up a Superman lunch box, first check out the lunch box section. Likewise, a Yogi Bear board game will most likely appear in the postwar games section rather than the character toys section. (The Character Toys section is somewhat of a catch-all for items that don't fit into other sections as easily.)

Bear in mind that the words "figure," "doll" and "action figure" are sometimes used interchangeably. So too, are words and phrases such as; "mint," "mint-in-pack" and "mint-in-box."

Overlapping categories are just part of the deal with toy classification, and finding a listing for a particular item can be a bit of a hunt. If you don't find what you're looking for in one place, try a related section.

Grading, pricing and all that...

Grading a toy is pretty subjective stuff. If you're a seller, than you naturally want to think of your items as being top-notch. The thing is, an item can be "mint-in-package" but have a dinged-up box with a gorgeous toy inside. The same item (sometimes selling for the same price) can be called "mint-in-package" with a perfect, crisp box. If you're a toy buyer, keep your eyes open.

The best bet for both buyer and seller is to try and grade toys as conservatively as possible, so that neither party will be surprised or disappointed.

Note that standards vary from class to class. Grading a Victorian board game is a different task than grading model kits or lunch boxes. Also bear in mind that most dealers will offer between forty and sixty percent of book value when buying—regardless of condition—as they obviously must be able to turn around and resell the toys at a profit in order to stay in business.

Ultimately, the market is driven by the twin demons of money and desire, or good, old-fashioned supply and demand. Pricing trends are established when a pattern of sales of the same or similar items sets up a range of prices to look back to and draw from. That's pretty much how the prices in guides like this are set. Various collectors, dealers and in-house experts compare prices on items, check out the shows, talk to contributors and finally settle on an average. That's what you'll find here.

Make no mistake: price guides can be helpful, but they can also be frustrating—both for the editor and the user. Prices for the same item can vary widely from place to place, even in this age of eBay and Internet sales. The value of a toy can range widely depending on geography, personal economics and target markets.

Three examples of condition shown here: Mint, Excellent and "well-loved."

ABBREVIATIONS

Common abbreviations seen around the biz...

MIB, MIP—(Mint-in-Box, Mint-in-Package, C10.) Considered the Holy Grail of toy collectors. This baby is just like new, in the original package. Picture yourself going back in a time machine and picking this one off the shelf. Factory-sealed boxes should preferably be unopened. Boxes that have been opened, (like Matchbox boxes, for example) should be crisp, include all flaps and be without pen or pencil marks. Blister packs, naturally, should be intact.

MNP or MNB—(Mint no package, Mint no Box, but still C10.) Perfect condition, but "loose." Perhaps it never came with a package at all, or the prospect of finding one still "in-pack" is so dim as to be like calculating stars in the galaxy. This category also includes prototypes or one-of-a-kind toys.

NM—(Near Mint, C9.) This toy appears like new overall, but might have some minor wear and doesn't have an original box. An exception to this would be a toy in kit form

EX—(Excellent, C8.) This toy is complete and has been played with. Some signs of minor wear may be evident, but the toy is very clean and well cared for.

VG—(Very Good, C6.) This is a toy that has obviously been played with and shows great general wear overall. Paint chipping is readily apparent. In metal toys, some minor rust may be evident. In sets, some minor pieces may be missing.

GD—(Good, C6.) The lower end of a "C6" condition. The toy has heavy evidence of play, with dents, chips in the paint and rust. The toy could be missing a replaceable part, such as a tailgate, a battery compartment door or something else easily restorable. It may be missing several pieces, if it's a set. At this condition, it may be advisable to consider restoration.

Action Figures

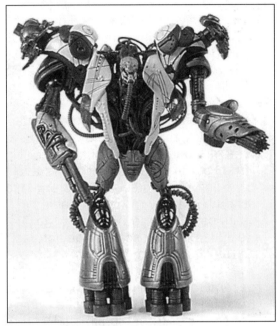

One of the most successful lines in action figure history is the McFarlane Spawn series. This Interlink TS2 figure has a $10 MIP value, making it an easy one to collect.

by Tom Bartsch

If you had to pick one of the most expansive, diverse and fastest-growing markets in the toy industry, you don't need to look any further than action figures. Want a piece of memorabilia from an overseas anime cartoon. It's available. Want a figure from your favorite show of the 1980s? Yep, it's out there, too. Want a boxed set of your favorite music group? Got it. And what about a figure of yourself? Not a problem. Someone will customize a figure for you.

Needless to say, today's toy market seems to be inundated with more and more figures every day. Can the market hold all these collectibles? Only time will tell. However, this is the best time to be alive if collecting figures is one of your passions. There certainly isn't a lack of products to choose from.

Evolving with the Times

When action figures first burst on the scene in 1964 with the introduction of G.I. Joe, boys finally had an answer to fashion dolls and Barbie. Once Joe hit the scene, the floodgates started to open on the male-orientated action figure genre. What we now know as the usual suspects of the 1960s came on strong soon afterward. The goal was to capture this new audience with the notion of fully articulated playthings holding precedence over sports and more stationary toys like Lincoln Logs and Monopoly. Marx, A.C. Gilbert and Ideal soon boarded the action figure train, producing figures of spy heroes (James Bond), comic life-savers (Captain Action) and legends of the West (Johnny West).

Ringo from the McFarlane Sgt. Pepper series. $8 MIP.

Using the foundations of comic books, TV series and movies, action figures had all the ammunition they needed to entice a buying public. The background stories were already laid out – all kids had to do was re-enact what they were watching and reading. Dialogue, movements and adventures were already ingrained in the minds of the fans who took these figures home and made the backyard their personal playground. Of course, once more and more figures entered the scene, the adventures could be intertwined, and G.I. Joe could be rounding up cattle with Johnny West or defeating the Joker with Batman. The storylines never ended.

Niche Needs

Today's figures don't necessarily have to have super-human strength or the ability to leap tall buildings to succeed in the eyes of eager boys and girls pulling at their parent's pants legs for a new toy. They simply need to fill a niche.

Let's take the military angle, shall we? No other category is currently exploding like this one. G.I. Joe, while still widely popular with fans across generations, has taken a back seat to the likes of Sideshow Toy, Dragon Models, Art Asylum and bbi, among others. Realism is the name of the games these days, and replica figures of soldiers fighting in the Civil

War to the current conflicts have found a buying audience. And can you blame them? Some of these figures are detailed down to the contents of their mess kit. Sausages for dinner anyone?

Or how about stars from the silver screen? These days any movie with a cult following or one heavy on special effects gets serious play in the action figure field. From *Reservoir Dogs* to the classic Universal Monsters films of the 1950s, movie figures have a strong following. If a manufacturer thinks a few hundred people will shell out money for a collectible based on a film, they'll produce it. And considering that limited-edition figures is the name of the game these days, manufacturers welcome this type of production schedule.

The figures produced today are a far cry from the same-body, different face scheme used by many companies in years past. With technologies like RealScan, a laser scan of the actor or actress from a film or TV series is scanned from head to toe, figures become eerily life-like. Every feature of that person, in the appearance of his or her character from the film or TV show, is reflected in the figure. Likeness is the key these days, and many companies are stepping up to the plate to make it happen.

Creature from the Black Lagoon by Sideshow Toys, $20 MIP.

Do It Again for the First Time

Even while all these young companies are producing recent stars in the action figures world, the old standbys are not forgotten. In fact, many are being reborn - getting an updated look in this new technology-mad world. Star Wars? Redone. Superheroes? Redone every day, or so it seems. G.I. Joe? All the time. If you can't beat the originals, sometimes it's best to just reproduce them.

But what does this do to the value of the originals? That depends. Sometimes, bringing back the old stuff in new editions draws more attention to the originals, thus driving up demand and price. In other cases, new editions crowd out the originals by sheer volume or because they are of better quality. Soon everyone is craving the newer items, sending the value for the originals down the tubes. And sometimes, re-issues are viewed almost as an entirely new line of figures, thereby having no impact on their predecessors.

For a general rule of thumb with re-issues and updated versions of originals, monitor their demand, see what the originals go for and don't expect the figures to pay for someone's college tuition. Actually, the latter is a pretty good rule of thumb for any collectible you seek.

Figuring Out a Trend

The action figure market is vast and fickle at the same time. Just because there seems to be a mad rush of attention toward a certain property doesn't always mean an action figure license will fly. In the past year, many lines have never seen the light of day even after they were announced as forthcoming because there wasn't enough long-term interest to make the lines a viable option. Other properties sell well early and sit on shelves a few months after their release. Action figure aficionados are a unique breed. Some will collect anything and everything, while others are fanatic about little-known properties and will scoop every related collect-ible they can find. So what do manufacturers do - hit the mass market that will buy early and then stop or target the select few who will gobble up everything they can get their hands on? That's where this vast world of action figures gets its ingredients to survive – diversity.

The manufacturer field is following this diversity. While there are still many hoping the bandwagon of major properties, others are seeking a niche. Companies like Art Asylum, Mezco and Palisades target specific audiences and are quite successful in doing so. Many of these companies are targeting a younger audience, one that grew up with video and computer games. Thus, there is a great demand for the characters from these games, opening up a whole new vault of collectors.

A blast from the past: Cheron, by Mego, part of the Star Trek Aliens series. $175 MIP. Corey LaChat photo.

What's Hot, What's Not?

With everything now being labeled a "collectible" these days in the action figure field, it's hard to say what will jump in value several years down the road. One way to envision what might pay a few bills down the road is to look at some of the toys that are hot today. These don't have to be "collectible" toys, but can be popular through all ages.

That's how toys of the 1960s and '70s have scored so well in the 1980s, - because baby boomers wanted the toys back they had as children and were willing to pay for it. So if today's kids and young adults like a particular toy, chances are they will be looking for it again down the road.

Here are a few to keep your eyes on:

The Simpsons figures by Playmates. These are, hands-down, one of the most popular series on the market today. Yes, there are a lot of them, but there are also many that are hard to get. This long-running TV series will not soon be forgotten by its legions of fans.

Sideshow Toy figures. All of Sideshow's offerings these days are limited in production and have some of the best depictions of characters on the market. The subjects are awesome as well.

Watch the niche properties. Yes, many of the niche properties only appeal to a select few. But those select few will pay big money for an Ozzy Osbourne figure or a Rudy from *Survivor* piece.

Don't Forget the Old Guys

All this talk about what will be valuable down the road, but what about the pieces that already are achieving great prices? That's where the classics come in. If you really want to get a glimpse of figures that empty wallets faster than children at a carnival, check out the vintage samples.

The royalty among action figures is still the Super Queens. Ideal unleashed these on the world in 1967, and their prices have been soaring ever since. Batgirl, Wonder Woman, Supergirl and Mera command several thousand dollars apiece.

For something a tad more affordable, yet still capable of turning a few heads with its price tag. Start with Mego. Sure these aren't the best-made or best-looking figures ever produced, but there's an endearing quality about them. Mego's American West, Buck Rogers Comic Action Heroes, StarTrek and World Greatest Superheroes series, among others, all command a good chunk of change.

If you need an overall rule of thumb of which figures carry a higher price tag, check their release date. Most figures from the 1960s through the mid-1970s will make you a very happy person if you have one.

Special thanks to John Marshall for contributing to this section. He can be reached at P.O. Box 340, Rancocas, NJ 08073 or by e-mail at jm@jmuniverse.com.

Did You Know?

Some larger action figures, such as G.I. Joe, have hair that is not rooted or molded, but is fuzzy. That style of hair is referred to as flocked hair.

Quite a few scheduled action figure lines were scheduled for release in 2002 but were canceled, including Jonny Quest and X-Files

Walton's truck, 1975, by Mego fits 8" figures. $80 MIP.

3D ANIMATION FROM JAPAN (McFARLANE, 2000)

AKIRA

❏ **Kaneda with Motorcycle**, 2000
MNP $3   MIP $13

❏ **Tetsuo**, 2000
MNP $3   MIP $13

TENCHI MUYO!

❏ **Ryoko**, 2000
MNP $3   MIP $15

TRIGUN

❏ **Vash with Stampede**, 2000
MNP $3   MIP $13

ACTION JACKSON (MEGO, 1974)

8" FIGURES

❏ **Action Jackson, Black version**, 1974, Mego
MNP $25   MIP $60

❏ **Action Jackson, blond, brown, or black beard**, 1974, Mego
MNP $15   MIP $30

❏ **Action Jackson, blond, brown, or black hair**, 1974, Mego
MNP $15   MIP $30

ACCESSORIES

❏ **Fire Rescue Pack**, 1984
MNP $5   MIP $15

❏ **Parachute Plunge**, 1974, Mego
MNP $5   MIP $15

❏ **Strap-On Helicopter**, 1974, Mego
MNP $5   MIP $15

❏ **Water Scooter**, 1974, Mego
MNP $5   MIP $15

OUTFITS

❏ **Air Force Pilot**, 1974, Mego
MNP $7   MIP $10

❏ **Army Outfit**, 1974, Mego
MNP $7   MIP $10

❏ **Aussie Marine**, 1974, Mego
MNP $7   MIP $10

❏ **Baseball**, 1974, Mego
MNP $7   MIP $10

❏ **Fisherman**, 1974, Mego
MNP $7   MIP $10

❏ **Football**, 1974, Mego
MNP $7   MIP $10

❏ **Frog Man**, 1974, Mego
MNP $7   MIP $10

❏ **Hockey**, 1974, Mego
MNP $7   MIP $10

❏ **Jungle Safari**, 1974, Mego
MNP $7   MIP $10

❏ **Karate**, 1974, Mego
MNP $7   MIP $10

❏ **Navy Sailor**, 1974, Mego
MNP $7   MIP $10

❏ **Rescue Squad**, 1974, Mego
MNP $7   MIP $10

❏ **Scramble Cyclist**, 1974, Mego
MNP $7   MIP $10

❏ **Secret Agent**, 1974, Mego
MNP $7   MIP $10

❏ **Ski Patrol**, 1974, Mego
MNP $7   MIP $10

❏ **Snowmobile Outfit**, 1974, Mego
MNP $7   MIP $10

❏ **Surf and Scuba Outfit**, 1974, Mego
MNP $7   MIP $10

❏ **Western Cowboy**, 1974, Mego
MNP $7   MIP $10

PLAY SETS

❏ **Jungle House**, 1974, Mego
MNP $75   MIP $150

❏ **Lost Continent Play Set**, 1974, Mego
MNP $75   MIP $150

VEHICLES

❏ **Adventure Set**, 1974, Mego
MNP $40   MIP $85

❏ **Campmobile**, 1974, Mego
MNP $40   MIP $85

❏ **Dune Buggy**, 1974, Mego
MNP $30   MIP $60

❏ **Formula Racer**, 1974, Mego
MNP $30   MIP $60

❏ **Mustang**, 1974, Mego
MNP $30   MIP $60

❏ **Rescue Helicopter**, 1974, Mego
MNP $40   MIP $85

❏ **Safari Jeep**, 1974, Mego
MNP $40   MIP $85

❏ **Scramble Cycle**, 1974, Mego
MNP $20   MIP $40

❏ **Snowmobile**, 1974, Mego
MNP $15   MIP $30

ADDAMS FAMILY (PLAYMATES, 1992)

FIGURES

❏ **Gomez**, 1992
MNP $4   MIP $15

❏ **Granny**, 1992
MNP $4   MIP $15

❏ **Lurch**, 1992
MNP $4   MIP $15

❏ **Morticia**, 1992
MNP $5   MIP $18

❏ **Pugsley**, 1992
MNP $4   MIP $15

❏ **Uncle Fester**, 1992
MNP $4   MIP $15

ADDAMS FAMILY (REMCO, 1964)

FIGURES

❏ **Lurch**, 1964
MNP $150   MIP $450

❏ **Morticia**, 1964
MNP $160   MIP $500

❏ **Uncle Fester**, 1964
MNP $160   MIP $500

ALICE COOPER (McFARLANE, 2000)

FIGURES

❏ **Alice Cooper**, 2000
MNP $3   MIP $13

ALIEN (KENNER, 1979)

18" FIGURE

❏ **Alien**, 1979, Kenner
MNP $200   MIP $500

ALIENS (KENNER, 1992-94)

ACCESSORIES

❏ **Evac Fighter**, Kenner
MNP $7   MIP $20

❏ **Hovertread**, Kenner
MNP $5   MIP $20

❏ **Power Loader**, Kenner
MNP $5   MIP $20

❏ **Stinger XT-37**, Kenner
MNP $5   MIP $20

SERIES 1, 1992

❏ **Apone**, 1992, Kenner
MNP $5   MIP $8

❏ **Bull Alien**, 1992, Kenner
MNP $7   MIP $8

❏ **Drake**, 1992, Kenner
MNP $5   MIP $8

❏ **Gorilla Alien**, 1992, Kenner
MNP $8   MIP $8

❏ **Hicks**, 1992, Kenner
MNP $5   MIP $8

❏ **Queen Alien**, 1992, Kenner
MNP $10   MIP $20

❏ **Ripley**, 1992, Kenner
MNP $5   MIP $15

❏ **Scorpion Alien**, 1992, Kenner
MNP $7   MIP $15

SERIES 2, 1993

(Toy Shop File Photo)

❑ **Alien vs. Predator,** 1993, Kenner, Billed as the "ultimate battle between beast and hunter.
    MNP $15   **MIP $30**

❑ **Flying Queen Alien,** 1993, Kenner
    MNP $5   **MIP $15**

❑ **Queen Face Hugger,** 1993, Kenner
    MNP $5   **MIP $15**

❑ **Snake Alien,** 1993, Kenner
    MNP $5   **MIP $15**

SERIES 3, 1994

❑ **Arachnid Alien,** 1994, Kenner
    MNP $4   **MIP $19**

❑ **Atax,** 1994, Kenner
    MNP $4   **MIP $15**

❑ **Clan Leader Predator,** 1994, Kenner
    MNP $4   **MIP $19**

❑ **Cracked Tusk Predator,** 1994, Kenner
    MNP $4   **MIP $11**

❑ **Hudson (foreign release),** 1994
    MNP $11   **MIP $30**

❑ **Invisible Predator (mail-in),** 1994, Kenner
    MNP $15   **MIP $30**

❑ **Kill Krab Alien,** 1994, Kenner
    MNP $4   **MIP $11**

❑ **King Alien,** 1994, Kenner
    MNP $8   **MIP $19**

❑ **Lasershot Predator (electronic),** 1994, Kenner
    MNP $11   **MIP $23**

❑ **Lava Predator,** 1994, Kenner
    MNP $4   **MIP $11**

❑ **Mantis Alien,** 1994, Kenner
    MNP $4   **MIP $11**

❑ **Night Cougar Alien,** 1994, Kenner
    MNP $4   **MIP $11**

❑ **Night Storm Predator,** 1994, Kenner
    MNP $4   **MIP $11**

❑ **O'Malley (foreign release),** 1994
    MNP $15   **MIP $30**

❑ **Panther Alien,** 1994, Kenner
    MNP $4   **MIP $11**

❑ **Rhino Alien,** 1994, Kenner
    MNP $5   **MIP $11**

❑ **Spiked Tail Predator,** 1994, Kenner
    MNP $3   **MIP $11**

❑ **Stalker Predator,** 1994, Kenner
    MNP $3   **MIP $11**

❑ **Swarm Alien (electronic),** 1994, Kenner
    MNP $11   **MIP $19**

❑ **Vasquez (foreign release),** 1994
    MNP $11   **MIP $30**

❑ **Wild Boar Alien,** 1994, Kenner
    MNP $3   **MIP $11**

ALPHA FIGHT (TOY BIZ, 1999)

5" FIGURES

❑ **Northstar & Aurora,** 1999
    MNP $3   **MIP $12**

❑ **Sasquatch & Vindicator,** 1999
    MNP $3   **MIP $12**

❑ **Snowabird & Puck,** 1999
    MNP $3   **MIP $12**

AMERICAN WEST (MEGO, 1973)

8" FIGURES

❑ **Buffalo Bill Cody, boxed,** 1973, Mego
    MNP $40   **MIP $75**

❑ **Buffalo Bill Cody, carded,** 1973, Mego
    MNP $40   **MIP $100**

❑ **Cochise, boxed,** 1973, Mego
    MNP $40   **MIP $75**

❑ **Cochise, carded,** 1973, Mego
    MNP $40   **MIP $100**

❑ **Davy Crockett, boxed,** 1973, Mego
    MNP $70   **MIP $110**

❑ **Davy Crockett, carded,** 1973, Mego
    MNP $70   **MIP $140**

❑ **Shadow (horse), boxed,** 1973, Mego
    MNP $70   **MIP $140**

❑ **Sitting Bull, boxed,** 1973, Mego
    MNP $45   **MIP $90**

❑ **Sitting Bull, carded,** 1973, Mego
    MNP $45   **MIP $125**

❑ **Wild Bill Hickok, boxed,** 1973, Mego
    MNP $40   **MIP $75**

❑ **Wild Bill Hickok, carded,** 1973, Mego
    MNP $40   **MIP $125**

❑ **Wyatt Earp, boxed,** 1973, Mego
    MNP $40   **MIP $75**

❑ **Wyatt Earp, carded,** 1973, Mego
    MNP $40   **MIP $125**

PLAY SETS

❑ **Dodge City Play Set, vinyl,** 1973, Mego
    MNP $100   **MIP $200**

ANTZ (PLAYMATES, 1998)

FIGURES

❑ **Colonel Cutter,** 1998
    MNP $2   **MIP $4**

❑ **General Mandible,** 1998
    MNP $2   **MIP $4**

❑ **Princess Bala,** 1998
    MNP $2   **MIP $4**

❑ **Weaver,** 1998
    MNP $2   **MIP $4**

(KP Photo)

❑ **Z,** 1998, Figure includes map and helmet. Interesting to note the World Trade Center Towers on the packaging
    MNP $2   **MIP $4**

ARCHIES (MARX, 1975)

FIGURES

(Toy Shop File Photo)

❑ **Archie,** 1975, Marx, seen here with Betty, Jughead and Archie
    MNP $15   **MIP $75**

❑ **Betty,** 1975, Marx, seen here with Jughead
    MNP $15   **MIP $75**

❑ **Jughead,** 1975, Marx, seen here with Veronica, Jughead and Archie
    MNP $15   **MIP $75**

(Toy Shop File Photo)

❑ **Veronica,** 1975, Marx, seen here with Betty, Archie and Jughead
MNP $15 MIP $75

ARMAGEDDON (MATTEL, 1998)

FIGURES

❑ **A.J. Frost,** 1998
MNP $3 MIP $10

❑ **Harry Stamper,** 1998
MNP $3 MIP $10

ASTRONAUTS (MARX, 1969)

FIGURES

(Toy Shop File Photo)

❑ **Jane Apollo Astronaut,** 1969, Marx, movable, includes helmet and a variety of plastic accessories, much in the style of the "Best of the West" series
MNP $65 MIP $125

❑ **Johnny Apollo Astronaut,** 1969, Marx, movable
MNP $125 MIP $200

❑ **Kennedy Space Center Astronaut,** 1969, Marx, movable
MNP $65 MIP $140

A-TEAM (GALOOB, 1984)

12" FIGURES

❑ **Mr. T, non-talking,** 1984
MNP $30 MIP $65

❑ **Mr. T, talking,** 1984
MNP $40 MIP $75

3-3/4" FIGURES AND ACCESSORIES

❑ **Armored Attack Adventure with B.A. Figure,** 1984, Galoob, vehicle with 3-3/4"
MNP $25 MIP $55

❑ **A-Team Four Figure Set,** 1984, Galoob, 3-3/4" figures
MNP $40 MIP $65

❑ **Bad Guys Figure Set: Viper, Rattler, Cobra, Python,** 1984, Galoob, 3-3/4" figures on card
MNP $35 MIP $60

❑ **Combat Headquarters with four A-Team figures,** 1984, Galoob, for 3-3/4" figures
MNP $30 MIP $60

❑ **Corvette with Face Figure,** 1984, Galoob, vehicle and 3-3/4" figure
MNP $25 MIP $50

❑ **Interceptor Jet Bomber with Murdock,** 1984, Galoob, vehicle with 3-3/4"
MNP $30 MIP $60

❑ **Motorized Patrol Boat,** 1984
MNP $15 MIP $35

❑ **Tactical Van Play Set,** 1984, Galoob
MNP $25 MIP $45

6-1/2" FIGURES AND ACCESSORIES

❑ **Amy Allen,** 1984, Galoob, 6-1/2" tall
MNP $10 MIP $30

❑ **B.A. Baracus,** 1984, Galoob, 6-1/2" tall
MNP $8 MIP $25

❑ **Cobra,** 1984, Galoob, 6-1/2" tall
MNP $6 MIP $15

❑ **Face,** 1984, Galoob, 6-1/2" tall
MNP $6 MIP $25

❑ **Hannibal,** 1984, Galoob, 6-1/2" tall
MNP $6 MIP $25

❑ **Murdock,** 1984, Galoob, 6-1/2" tall
MNP $8 MIP $25

❑ **Off Road Attack Cycle,** 1984, Galoob
MNP $8 MIP $20

❑ **Python,** 1984, Galoob, 6-1/2" tall
MNP $6 MIP $15

❑ **Rattler,** 1984, Galoob, 6-1/2" tall
MNP $6 MIP $15

❑ **Viper,** 1984, Galoob, 6-1/2" tall
MNP $6 MIP $15

AUSTIN POWERS (MCFARLANE, 1999-2000)

9" FIGURES

❑ **Austin Powers,** 2000
MNP $5 MIP $15

❑ **Dr. Evil,** 2000
MNP $5 MIP $15

(Toy Shop File Photo)

❑ **Fat Bastard,** 2000, In later versions, the name Bastard was removed.
MNP $5 MIP $20

SERIES 1

❑ **Austin in Union Jack underwear,** 1999, McFarlane
MNP $3 MIP $8

❑ **Austin in Union Jack Underwear, "dirty version",** 1999
MNP $5 MIP $10

❑ **Austin in velvet suit,** 1999, McFarlane
MNP $3 MIP $8

❑ **Austin in velvet suit, "dirty version",** 1999
MNP $5 MIP $10

❑ **Dr. Evil with Mr. Bigglesworth,** 1999, McFarlane
MNP $3 MIP $10

❑ **Dr. Evil with Mr. Bigglesworth, "dirty version",** 1999
MNP $5 MIP $10

❑ **Fat Bastard,** 1999
MNP $25 MIP $35

❑ **Felicity Shagwell,** 1999, McFarlane
MNP $3 MIP $8

❑ Felicity Shagwell, "dirty version," 1999
MNP $10   MIP $25

❑ Mini-Me, 1999
MNP $10   MIP $25

SERIES 2

❑ Austin Powers in striped suit, 2000
MNP $3   MIP $8

❑ Austin Powers, "dirty version", 2000
MNP $3   MIP $10

❑ Dr. Evil and Mini-Me with Mini-Mobile, 2000
MNP $8   MIP $20

❑ Dr. Evil, Moon Mission, 2000
MNP $4   MIP $12

❑ Fembot, 2000
MNP $3   MIP $8

❑ Mini-Me, Moon Mission, 2000
MNP $8   MIP $20

❑ Scott Evil, says "A trillion is worth more than a billion, numbnuts", 2000
MNP $3   MIP $10

❑ Scott Evil, says "Get away from me, you lazy-eyed psycho", 2000
MNP $3   MIP $8

❑ Vanessa Kensington, 2000
MNP $4   MIP $12

AUSTIN POWERS (TRENDMASTERS, 1999)

9" FIGURES

❑ Austin Powers, 1999
MNP $4   MIP $12

❑ Dr. Evil, 1999
MNP $4   MIP $12

❑ Fembot, 1999
MNP $8   MIP $20

AVENGERS (TOY BIZ, 1997-PRESENT)

12" COLLECTORS SERIES

❑ Captain America, 2000, 2000, Toy Biz
MNP $5   MIP $15

❑ Hawkeye, 2000, 2000, Toy Biz
MNP $5   MIP $15

❑ Tigra, 2000, 2000, Toy Biz
MNP $5   MIP $15

6" FIGURES

(Toy Shop File Photo)

❑ Iron Man, 1997, 1998, Toy Biz, 6" figure with "Power Converter"
MNP $4   MIP $8

❑ Loki, 1997, 1998, Toy Biz, 6" figure
MNP $4   MIP $8

❑ Scarlett Witch, 1997, 1998, Toy Biz, 6" figure
MNP $4   MIP $8

(Lenny Lee)

❑ The Mighty Thor, 1997, 1998, Toy Biz, 6" figure, with hammer
MNP $4   MIP $8

SERIES I, 5" FIGURES

❑ Ant-Man, 2000, 2000, Toy Biz
MNP $4   MIP $8

❑ Captain America, 2000, 2000, Toy Biz
MNP $4   MIP $8

❑ Ultron, 2000, 2000, Toy Biz
MNP $4   MIP $8

❑ Vision, 2000, 2000, Toy Biz
MNP $4   MIP $8

❑ Wasp, 2000, 2000, Toy Biz
MNP $4   MIP $8

SERIES II, 5" FIGURES

❑ Falcon, 2000, 2000, Toy Biz
MNP $4   MIP $8

❑ Hawkeye, 2000, 2000, Toy Biz
MNP $4   MIP $8

❑ Kang, 2000, 2000, Toy Biz
MNP $4   MIP $8

❑ Tigra, 2000, 2000, Toy Biz
MNP $4   MIP $8

❑ Wonder Man, 2000, 2000, Toy Biz
MNP $4   MIP $8

SERIES III, 5" FIGURES

❑ Ant-Man, 2000, 2000, Toy Biz
MNP $4   MIP $8

❑ Hawkeye, 2000, 2000, Toy Biz
MNP $4   MIP $8

❑ Iron Man, 2000, 2000, Toy Biz
MNP $4   MIP $8

❑ Remnant I, 2000, 2000, Toy Biz
MNP $4   MIP $8

❑ Thor, 2000, 2000, Toy Biz
MNP $4   MIP $8

SHAPE SHIFTERS

❑ Ant-Man transforms into Armored Ant, 2000, Toy Biz
MNP $4   MIP $8

❑ Captain America transform into American Eagle, 2000, Toy Biz
MNP $4   MIP $8

❑ Hawykeye transforms into Armored Hawk, 2000, Toy Biz
MNP $4   MIP $8

❑ Thor transforms into Flying Horse, 2000, Toy Biz
MNP $4   MIP $8

TEAM GIFT PACK

❑ Hulk, Iron Man, Thor, Ant-Man/Giant Man, The Wasp, 1999, Toy Biz
MNP $8   MIP $20

BABYLON 5 (EXCLUSIVE TOY PRODUCTS, 1997)

6" FIGURES

❑ Ambassador Juphar Trkider, 1997
MNP $3   MIP $7

❑ Ambassador Kosh, 1997
MNP $3   MIP $7

❑ Ambassador Londo Mollari, 1997
MNP $3   MIP $7

❑ Ambassador She'Lah, 1997
MNP $3   MIP $7

❑ Ambassador Vlur/Nhur, 1997
MNP $3   MIP $7

❏ **Captain Elizabeth Lochley**, 1997
MNP $3   MIP $7

❏ **Chief Garabaldi**, 1997
MNP $4   MIP $10

❏ **Delenn**, 1997
MNP $3   MIP $7

❏ **Delenn with Minbari, Diamond Exclusive**, 1997
MNP $5   MIP $15

❏ **G'Kar**, 1997
MNP $3   MIP $7

❏ **G'Kar, green outfit, Diamond Exclusive**, 1997
MNP $5   MIP $15

❏ **John Sheridan**, 1997
MNP $3   MIP $7

❏ **Lennier**, 1997
MNP $4   MIP $10

❏ **Lyta Alexander**, 1997
MNP $4   MIP $10

❏ **Marcus Cole**, 1997
MNP $4   MIP $10

❏ **PSI Cop Bester**, 1997
MNP $4   MIP $10

❏ **Shadow Sentient, Diamond Exclusive**, 1997
MNP $10   MIP $50

❏ **Stephen Franklin**, 1997
MNP $3   MIP $7

❏ **Susan Ivanova**, 1997
MNP $4   MIP $10

❏ **Susan Ivanova, White's Collecting Figures Exclusive**, 1997
MNP $5   MIP $20

❏ **Vir Cotto**, 1997
MNP $3   MIP $7

❏ **Vorlon Visitor, Diamond Exclusive**, 1997
MNP $5   MIP $20

9" FIGURES

❏ **Ambassador Delenn**, 1997
MNP $5   MIP $20

❏ **Ambassador G'Kar**, 1997
MNP $5   MIP $20

❏ **Ambassador G'Kar, Diamond Exclusive**, 1997
MNP $5   MIP $30

❏ **Chief Michael Girabaldi**, 1997
MNP $5   MIP $25

❏ **John Sheridan**, 1997
MNP $5   MIP $25

❏ **Lennier, Diamond Exclusive**, 1997
MNP $5   MIP $25

❏ **Londo**, 1997
MNP $5   MIP $25

❏ **Marcus Cole**, 1997
MNP $5   MIP $20

❏ **Michael Garibaldi**, 1997
MNP $5   MIP $20

❏ **Susan Ivanova**, 1997
MNP $5   MIP $25

❏ **Vir Cotta**, 1997
MNP $5   MIP $20

BANANA SPLITS (SUTTON, 1970)

FIGURES

❏ **Bingo the Bear**, 1970, Sutton
MNP $45   MIP $125

❏ **Drooper the Lion**, 1970, Sutton
MNP $45   MIP $125

❏ **Fleagle Beagle**, 1970, Sutton
MNP $45   MIP $125

❏ **Snorky the Elephant**, 1970, Sutton
MNP $45   MIP $125

BATMAN & ROBIN (KENNER, 1997-1998)

12" FIGURES

❏ **Batgirl**, 1997-98
MNP $15   MIP $35

❏ **Batman**, 1997-98
MNP $13   MIP $25

(Kenner)

❏ **Ice Battle Batman (WB Exclusive)**, 1997-98, Includes Batarang and Bat Laser
MNP $10   MIP $25

❏ **Mr. Freeze**, 1997-98
MNP $10   MIP $20

❏ **Robin**, 1997-98
MNP $13   MIP $23

❏ **Ultimate Batman**, 1997-98
MNP $8   MIP $20

❏ **Ultimate Robin**, 1997-98
MNP $8   MIP $20

5" FIGURES

❏ **Bane, Leather Impact**, 1997-98
MNP $3   MIP $8

(Toy Shop File Photo)

❏ **Batgirl**, 1997-98, on the right
MNP $3   MIP $5

❏ **Batman, Ambush Attack**, 1997-98
MNP $3   MIP $8

❏ **Batman, Battle Board with Ring**, 1997-98
MNP $3   MIP $8

❏ **Batman, Heat Scan**, 1997-98
MNP $3   MIP $8

❏ **Batman, Hover Attack**, 1997-98
MNP $3   MIP $8

❏ **Batman, Ice Blade**, 1997-98
MNP $3   MIP $8

❏ **Batman, Ice Blade with Ring**, 1997-98
MNP $3   MIP $13

❏ **Batman, Laser Cape with Ring**, 1997-98
MNP $3   MIP $8

❏ **Batman, Mail Away from Fuji**, 1997-98
MNP $23   MIP $40

❏ **Batman, Neon Armor**, 1997-98
MNP $3   MIP $8

❏ **Batman, Neon Armor with Ring**, 1997-98
MNP $3   MIP $13

❏ **Batman, Rotoblade with ring**, 1997-98
MNP $3   MIP $13

❏ **Batman, Sky Assault with ring**, 1997-98
MNP $3   MIP $13

❏ **Batman, Snow Tracker**, 1997-98
MNP $3   MIP $8

❏ **Batman, Thermal Shield with ring**, 1997-98
MNP $3   MIP $13

❏ **Batman, Wing Blast**, 1997-98
MNP $3   MIP $8

❏ **Batman, Wing Blast with ring**, 1997-98
MNP $3   MIP $13

❏ **Bruce Wayne, Battle Gear**, 1997-98
MNP $3   MIP $8

❏ **Frostbite**, 1997-98
MNP $3   MIP $8

ACTION FIGURES

(Toy Shop File Photo)

❑ **Jungle Venom Poison Ivy,** 1997-98, on the left
MNP $3   MIP $5

❑ **Mr. Freeze, Ultimate Armor,** 1997-98
MNP $5   MIP $13

❑ **Robin, Attack Wing,** 1997-98
MNP $3   MIP $8

❑ **Robin, Blade Blast,** 1997-98
MNP $3   MIP $8

❑ **Robin, Iceboard,** 1997-98
MNP $3   MIP $5

❑ **Robin, Razor Skate,** 1997-98
MNP $3   MIP $5

❑ **Robin, Talon Strike,** 1997-98
MNP $3   MIP $5

❑ **Robin, Talon Strike with ring,** 1997-98
MNP $3   MIP $13

❑ **Robin, Tripple Strike,** 1997-98
MNP $3   MIP $5

❑ **Robin, Tripple Strike with ring,** 1997-98
MNP $3   MIP $13

DELUXE FIGURES, 1997

❑ **Batgirl with Icestrike Cycle,** 1997
MNP $10   MIP $20

❑ **Batman,** 1998
MNP $5   MIP $10

❑ **Batman, Blast Wing,** 1997
MNP $5   MIP $8

❑ **Batman, Rooftop Pursuit,** 1997
MNP $5   MIP $8

❑ **Mr. Freeze, Ice Terror,** 1997
MNP $5   MIP $8

❑ **Robin,** 1998
MNP $5   MIP $10

❑ **Robin, Blast Wing,** 1997
MNP $5   MIP $8

❑ **Robin, Glacier Battle,** 1997
MNP $5   MIP $13

❑ **Robin, Redbird Cycle,** 1997
MNP $10   MIP $20

TWO PACK FIGURES, 1998

❑ **Batman vs Poison Ivy,** 1997-98
MNP $13   MIP $38

TWO-PACK FIGURES, 1998

❑ **A Cold Night At Gotham,** 1998
MNP $5   MIP $10

❑ **Batmobile,** 1998
MNP $8   MIP $20

❑ **Batmobile, Sonic,** 1998
MNP $8   MIP $15

❑ **Brain Vs. Brawn,** 1998
MNP $5   MIP $10

❑ **Changelers Of The Night,** 1998
MNP $10   MIP $15

❑ **Cryo Freeze Chamber,** 1998
MNP $3   MIP $8

❑ **Guardians Of Gotham,** 1998
MNP $5   MIP $10

❑ **Ice Fortress,** 1998
MNP $5   MIP $8

❑ **Ice Hammer,** 1998
MNP $10   MIP $20

❑ **Jet Blade,** 1998
MNP $8   MIP $20

❑ **Night Hunter Robin vs. Evil Entrapment Poison Ivy,** 1998
MNP $5   MIP $8

❑ **NightSphere,** 1998
MNP $10   MIP $25

❑ **Wayne Manor Batcave,** 1998
MNP $23   MIP $53

BATMAN 100TH EDITION FIGURE

FIGURES

(Toy Shop File Photo)

❑ **Batman,** 1996, Hasbro, With diorama display stand
n/a   MIP $15

BATMAN CRIME SQUAD (KENNER, 1995)

ACCESSORIES

❑ **Attack Jet,** 1995, Kenner
MNP $7   MIP $15

FIGURES

❑ **Air Assault Batman,** 1995, Kenner
MNP $5   MIP $15

❑ **Land Strike Batman,** 1995, Kenner
MNP $5   MIP $15

❑ **Piranha Blade Batman,** 1995, Kenner
MNP $5   MIP $15

❑ **Sea Claw Batman,** 1995, Kenner
MNP $5   MIP $15

❑ **Ski Blast Robin,** 1995, Kenner
MNP $5   MIP $15

❑ **Stealthwing Batman,** 1995, Kenner
MNP $5   MIP $15

❑ **Torpedo Batman,** 1995, Kenner
MNP $5   MIP $15

BATMAN DARK KNIGHT (KENNER, 1990-91)

FIGURES

❑ **Blast Shield Batman,** 1990-91, Kenner
MNP $12   MIP $25

(Toy Shop File Photo)

❑ **Bruce Wayne,** 1990-91, Kenner, shown on far left
MNP $7   MIP $20

❑ **Claw Climber Batman,** 1990-91, Kenner
MNP $12   MIP $25

❑ **Crime Attack Batman,** 1990-91, Kenner
MNP $7   MIP $15

❑ **Iron Winch Batman,** 1990-91, Kenner
MNP $7   MIP $15

❑ **Knockout Joker,** 1990-91, Kenner
MNP $25   MIP $75

❑ **Night Glider Batman,** 1990-91, Kenner
MNP $20   MIP $35

❑ **Power Wing Batman,** 1990-91, Kenner
MNP $12   MIP $25

❑ **Shadow Wing Batman,** 1990-91, Kenner
MNP $7   MIP $15

❑ **Sky Escape Joker,** 1990-91, Kenner
MNP $10   MIP $30

❑ **Thunder Whip Batman,** 1990-91, Kenner
MNP $12   MIP $25

❑ **Wall Scaler Batman,** 1990-91, Kenner
MNP $7   MIP $15

BATMAN FOREVER (KENNER, 1995)

FIGURES

❑ **Batman vs. The Riddler, Batman Forever, 1997,** 1997, Kenner
MNP $5   MIP $15

❑ **Blast Cape Batman,** 1995, Kenner
MNP $5   MIP $10

❏ **Fireguard Batman,** 1995, Kenner
MNP $5   MIP $10

❏ **Hydro Claw Robin,** 1995, Kenner
MNP $5   MIP $10

❏ **Manta Ray Batman,** 1995, Kenner
MNP $5   MIP $10

❏ **Night Hunter Batman,** 1995, Kenner
MNP $5   MIP $10

❏ **Riddler,** 1995, Kenner
MNP $10   MIP $15

❏ **Sonar Sensor Batman,** 1995, Kenner
MNP $4   MIP $10

❏ **Street Biker Robin,** 1995, Kenner
MNP $4   MIP $10

❏ **Talking Riddler,** Kenner
MNP $10   MIP $20

❏ **Transforming Bruce Wayne,** 1995, Kenner
MNP $4   MIP $10

❏ **Transforming Dick Grayson,** 1995, Kenner
MNP $4   MIP $10

❏ **Two Face,** 1995, Kenner
MNP $10   MIP $15

BATMAN RETURNS (KENNER, 1992-94)

FIGURES

❏ **Aerostrike Batman,** 1992-94, Kenner
MNP $5   MIP $15

❏ **Air Attack Batman,** 1992-94, Kenner
MNP $4   MIP $15

❏ **Arctic Batman,** 1992-94, Kenner
MNP $4   MIP $15

❏ **Batman vs. Catwoman, Batman Movie Collection, 1997,** 1997, Kenner
MNP $5   MIP $15

❏ **Batman, 12",** 1992-94, Kenner
MNP $25   MIP $75

❏ **Bola Strike Batman,** 1992-94, Kenner
MNP $4   MIP $15

❏ **Bruce Wayne,** 1992-93, Kenner
MNP $10   MIP $20

(Toy Shop File Photo)

❏ **Catwoman,** 1992-93, Kenner, On the right, shown here with Robin
MNP $5   MIP $15

❏ **Claw Climber Batman,** 1992-94, Kenner
MNP $4   MIP $15

❏ **Crime Attack Batman,** 1992-94, Kenner
MNP $4   MIP $15

❏ **Deep Dive Batman,** 1992-94, Kenner
MNP $5   MIP $15

❏ **Glider Batman,** 1992-94, Kenner
MNP $4   MIP $15

❏ **High Wire Batman,** 1992-94, Kenner
MNP $4   MIP $15

❏ **Hydrocharge Batman,** 1992-94, Kenner
MNP $4   MIP $15

❏ **Jungle Tracker Batman,** 1992-94, Kenner
MNP $4   MIP $15

❏ **Laser Batman,** 1992-94, Kenner
MNP $4   MIP $15

❏ **Night Climber Batman,** 1992-94, Kenner
MNP $4   MIP $15

❏ **Penguin,** 1992-93, Kenner
MNP $15   MIP $40

❏ **Penguin Commandos,** 1992-94, Kenner
MNP $10   MIP $25

❏ **Polar Blast Batman,** 1992-94, Kenner
MNP $4   MIP $15

❏ **Power Wing Batman,** 1992-94, Kenner
MNP $6   MIP $15

(Toy Shop File Photo)

❏ **Robin,** 1992-93, Kenner, On the left, shown here with Catwoman
MNP $10   MIP $25

❏ **Shadow Wing Batman,** 1992-94, Kenner
MNP $4   MIP $15

❏ **Sky Winch Batman,** 1992-94, Kenner
MNP $4   MIP $15

❏ **Thunder Strike Batman,** 1992-94, Kenner
MNP $4   MIP $15

❏ **Thunder Whip Batman,** 1992-94, Kenner
MNP $5   MIP $15

VEHICLES

❏ **B.A.T.V. Vehicle,** 1992-94, Kenner
MNP $5   MIP $15

❏ **Bat Cycle,** 1992-94, Kenner
MNP $5   MIP $25

❏ **Batmobile,** 1992-94, Kenner
MNP $20   MIP $70

❏ **Bat-Signal Jet,** 1992-94, Kenner
MNP $3   MIP $15

❏ **Bruce Wayne Custom Coupe,** 1992-94, Kenner
MNP $12   MIP $50

❏ **Camo Attack Batmobile,** 1992-94, Kenner
MNP $30   MIP $100

BATMAN: KNIGHT FORCE NINJAS (HASBRO, 1998-99)

FIGURES

❏ **Batman Ally Azrael,** 1998, Kenner
MNP $3   MIP $10

❏ **Batman vs. The Joker,** 1998, Kenner
MNP $8   MIP $20

❏ **Fist Fury Batman,** 1998, Kenner
MNP $3   MIP $10

❏ **Karate Chop Batman,** 1998, Kenner
MNP $3   MIP $10

❏ **Multi-Blast Batman,** 1998, Kenner
MNP $3   MIP $10

❏ **Power Kick Batman!,** 1998, Kenner
MNP $3   MIP $10

❏ **Side Strike Robin,** 1998, Kenner
MNP $3   MIP $10

❏ **Tail Whip Killer Croc,** 1998, Kenner
MNP $3   MIP $10

❏ **Thunder Kick Batman,** 1998, Kenner
MNP $3   MIP $10

❏ **Tornado Blade Riddler,** 1998, Kenner
MNP $3   MIP $10

VEHICLES

❏ **Knight Force Batmobile,** 1998, Kenner
MNP $5   MIP $15

BATMAN: LEGENDS OF THE DARK KNIGHT (KENNER, 1997-2000)

FIGURES

❏ **Assault Gauntlet Batman,** 1997-Present, Kenner
MNP $3   MIP $10

❏ **Bat Attack Batman,** 1997-Present, Kenner
MNP $3   MIP $10

❏ **Batgirl,** 1997-Present, Kenner
MNP $5   MIP $15

❏ **Batman The Dark Knight,** 1997-Present, Kenner
MNP $8   MIP $25

❏ **Clayface,** 1997-Present, Kenner
MNP $8   MIP $25

ACTION FIGURES

❏ **Dark Knight Detective Batman,** 1997-Present, Kenner
MNP $8   MIP $25

❏ **Dive Claw Robin,** 1997-Present, Kenner
MNP $5   MIP $15

❏ **Glacier Shield Batman,** 1997-Present, Kenner
MNP $3   MIP $10

❏ **Jungle Rage Robin,** 1997-Present, Kenner
MNP $3   MIP $10

❏ **Laughing Gas Joker,** 1997-Present, Kenner
MNP $5   MIP $15

❏ **Lava Fury Batman,** 1997-Present, Kenner
MNP $3   MIP $8

❏ **Lethal Impact Bane,** 1997-Present, Kenner
MNP $3   MIP $10

❏ **Man-Bat,** 1997-Present, Kenner
MNP $5   MIP $15

❏ **Neutral Claw Batman,** 1997-Present, Kenner
MNP $5   MIP $15

❏ **Panther Prowl Catwoman,** 1997-Present, Kenner
MNP $5   MIP $15

❏ **Penguin,** 1997-Present, Kenner
MNP $3   MIP $10

❏ **Shatter Blade Batman,** 1997-Present, Kenner
MNP $5   MIP $15

❏ **Spline Cape Batman,** 1997-Present, Kenner
MNP $5   MIP $15

❏ **Twister Strike Scarecrow,** 1997-Present, Kenner
MNP $3   MIP $10

❏ **Underwater Assault Batman,** 1997-Present, Kenner
MNP $3   MIP $8

BATMAN: THE ANIMATED SERIES (KENNER, 1993-95)

ACCESSORIES

❏ **Batcycle,** 1993-95, Kenner
MNP $10   MIP $20

❏ **Batmobile,** 1993-95, Kenner
MNP $10   MIP $65

❏ **Bat-Signal Jet,** 1993-95, Kenner
MNP $3   MIP $6

❏ **Hoverbat Vehicle,** 1993-95, Kenner
MNP $5   MIP $15

❏ **Joker Mobile,** 1993-95, Kenner
MNP $6   MIP $20

❏ **Robin Dragster,** 1993-95, Kenner
MNP $75   MIP $325

❏ **Street Jet,** 1993-95, Kenner
MNP $15   MIP $25

❏ **Turbo Batplane,** 1993-95, Kenner
MNP $6   MIP $20

FIGURES

❏ **Anti-Freeze Batman,** 1993-95, Kenner
MNP $4   MIP $15

(Lenny Lee)

❏ **Bane,** 1993-95, Kenner, With "Body Slam" action and venom tube
MNP $5   MIP $15

❏ **Bruce Wayne,** 1993-95, Kenner
MNP $10   MIP $20

❏ **Catwoman,** 1993-95, Kenner
MNP $7   MIP $25

❏ **Clay Face,** 1993-95, Kenner
MNP $5   MIP $20

❏ **Combat Belt Batman,** 1993-95, Kenner
MNP $7   MIP $40

❏ **Dick Grayson/Robin,** 1993-95, Kenner
MNP $5   MIP $15

❏ **Ground Assault Batman,** 1993-95, Kenner
MNP $5   MIP $10

❏ **Infrared Batman,** 1993-95, Kenner
MNP $5   MIP $10

❏ **Jet Pack Joker (green face),** 1993-95, Kenner
MNP $10   MIP $25

❏ **Jet Pack Joker (white face),** 1993-95, Kenner
MNP $10   MIP $25

❏ **Joker,** 1993-95, Kenner
MNP $7   MIP $15

❏ **Killer Croc,** 1993-95, Kenner
MNP $8   MIP $15

❏ **Knight Star Batman,** 1993-95, Kenner
MNP $4   MIP $10

❏ **Lightning Strike Batman,** 1993-95, Kenner
MNP $4   MIP $10

❏ **Manbat,** 1993-95, Kenner
MNP $7   MIP $25

❏ **Mechwing Batman,** 1993-95, Kenner
MNP $4   MIP $10

❏ **Mr. Freeze,** 1993-95, Kenner
MNP $8   MIP $15

❏ **Ninja Power Pack Batman and Robin,** 1993-95, Kenner
MNP $10   MIP $25

❏ **Ninja Robin,** 1993-95, Kenner
MNP $8   MIP $15

❏ **Parawing Robin,** 1993-95, Kenner
MNP $8   MIP $15

❏ **Penguin,** 1993-95, Kenner
MNP $12   MIP $85

❏ **Phantasm,** 1993-95, Kenner
MNP $15   MIP $30

(Toy Shop File Photo)

❏ **Poison Ivy,** 1993-95, Kenner, With crossbow and Venus Flytrap weapon
MNP $20   MIP $30

❏ **Power Vision Batman,** 1993-95, Kenner
MNP $8   MIP $15

❏ **Riddler,** 1993-95, Kenner
MNP $10   MIP $40

❏ **Scarecrow,** 1993-95, Kenner
MNP $7   MIP $20

❏ **Skydive Batman,** 1993-95, Kenner
MNP $5   MIP $10

❏ **Total Armor Batman,** 1993-95, Kenner
MNP $4   MIP $10

❏ **Turbojet Batman,** 1993-95, Kenner
MNP $7   MIP $15

❏ **Two Face,** 1993-95, Kenner
MNP $7   MIP $25

❏ **Ultimate Batman (15"),** 1993-95, Kenner
MNP $25   MIP $75

BATMAN: THE NEW BATMAN ADVENTURE (HASBRO, 1998-99)

12" FIGURES

❑ **Batgirl,** 1998-99, Hasbro, Batman's right-hand girl
MNP $10   MIP $30

❑ **Batman,** 1998-99, Hasbro
MNP $10   MIP $40

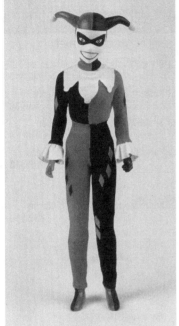

(Toy Shop File Photo)

❑ **Harley Quinn,** 1998-99, Hasbro, Popular female comic hero.
MNP $10   MIP $30

❑ **Joker,** 1998-99, Hasbro
MNP $10   MIP $40

❑ **Nightwing,** 1998-99, Hasbro
MNP $10   MIP $30

❑ **Robin,** 1998-99, Hasbro
MNP $10   MIP $40

FIGURES

❑ **Anti-Blaze Batman,** 1998-99, Hasbro
MNP $3   MIP $8

❑ **Arctic Blast Robin,** 1998-99, Hasbro
MNP $3   MIP $10

❑ **Cave Climber Batman,** 1998-99, Hasbro
MNP $3   MIP $8

❑ **Crime Fighter Robin,** 1998-99, Hasbro
MNP $4   MIP $12

❑ **Crime Solver Nightwing,** 1998-99, Hasbro
MNP $4   MIP $12

❑ **Dark Knight Detective Batman,** 1998-99, Hasbro
MNP $8   MIP $20

❑ **Desert Attack Batman,** 1998-99, Hasbro
MNP $3   MIP $8

❑ **Force Shield Nightwing,** 1998-99, Hasbro
MNP $3   MIP $8

❑ **Glider Strike Batman,** 1998-99, Hasbro
MNP $3   MIP $8

❑ **Heavy Artillery Batman,** 1998-99, Hasbro
MNP $3   MIP $8

❑ **Insect-Body Mr.Freese,** 1998-99, Hasbro
MNP $3   MIP $10

❑ **Jungle Tracker Batman,** 1998-99, Hasbro
MNP $3   MIP $10

❑ **Knight Glider Batman,** 1998-99, Hasbro
MNP $3   MIP $8

❑ **Mad Hatter,** 1998-99, Hasbro
MNP $5   MIP $15

❑ **Rumble Ready Riddler,** 1998-99, Hasbro
MNP $3   MIP $8

❑ **Shatter Blade Batman,** 1998-99, Hasbro
MNP $3   MIP $8

❑ **Slalom Racer Batman,** 1998-99, Hasbro
MNP $3   MIP $8

❑ **Speedboat Batman,** 1998-99, Hasbro
MNP $3   MIP $8

❑ **The Creeper,** 1998-99, Hasbro
MNP $3   MIP $8

❑ **Undercover Bruce Wayne,** 1998-99, Hasbro
MNP $3   MIP $10

❑ **Wildcard Joker,** 1998-99, Hasbro
MNP $5   MIP $15

BATTLESTAR GALACTICA (MATTEL, 1978-79)

12" FIGURES

(Toy Shop File Photo)

❑ **Colonial Warrior,** 1979, Mattel
MNP $30   MIP $85

❑ **Cylon Centurian,** 1979, Mattel, Silver armor, well-detailed figure
MNP $30   MIP $95

3-3/4" FIGURES, SERIES 1, 1978

(Toy Shop File Photo)

❑ **Commander Adama,** 1978, Mattel, With cloth robe and laser pistol. Also, limited painted facial detail
MNP $15   MIP $40

❑ **Cylon Centurian,** 1978, Mattel
MNP $15   MIP $40

❑ **Daggit (brown),** 1978, Mattel
MNP $15   MIP $30

❑ **Daggit (tan),** 1978, Mattel, Shown here with the reptilian-like Imperious Leader
MNP $15   MIP $30

(Toy Shop File Photo)

❑ **Imperious Leader,** 1978, Mattel, With red-purple cloth robe
MNP $15   MIP $30

(Toy Shop File Photo)

ACTION FIGURES

❏ **Ovion,** 1978, Mattel, Green insect-like alien that "harvests" humans. Hard to find out of pack with net-like robe still intact

MNP $12   MIP $35

(Toy Shop File Photo)

❏ **Starbuck,** 1978, Mattel, One of the show's male leads. Typically, the human action figures in this series had very limited facial detail, somewhat like the first 3-3/4" Star Trek figure released by Mego for "The Motion Picture"

MNP $15   MIP $40

3-3/4" FIGURES, SERIES 2, 1979

❏ **Baltar,** 1979, Mattel

MNP $30   MIP $75

❏ **Boray,** 1979, Mattel

MNP $30   MIP $75

❏ **Cylon Commander,** 1979, Mattel

MNP $55   MIP $110

(Toy Shop File Photo)

❏ **Lucifer,** 1979, Mattel, The creepy lieutenant of the Cylon Empire

MNP $55   MIP $110

BATTLESTAR GALACTICA (MATTEL 1978-79)

ACCESSORIES

(ToyShop File Photo)

❏ **Lasermatic Pistol,** 1978, Mattel, Barrel lights up when fired, has three different laser-firing sounds

MNP $35   MIP $75

SPACESHIPS

(ToyShop File Photo)

❏ **Colonial Scarab,** 1978, Mattel, Very imaginative vehicle, although it never appeared in the series. Originally, these toys had firing missiles, but due to safety, were replaced with projectiles that just sprang forward. The nice thing about the scarab, viper and colonial stellar probe was that all had interchangeable pieces, to make a kind of "expanded Galactica" universe

MNP $25   MIP $75

(Toy Shop File Photo)

❏ **Colonial Stellar Probe,** 1978, Mattel, Longer than the standard colonial viper, this vehicle had a different rear engine and included a small nose-cone satillite that could be re-combined with sections of the main toy to create something quite different

MNP $30   MIP $80

BEAVIS & BUTTHEAD (MOORE, 1998)

FIGURES

❏ **Beavis,** 1998

MNP $4   MIP $10

❏ **Butt-head,** 1998

MNP $4   MIP $10

❏ **Cornholio,** 1998

MNP $5   MIP $12

BEETLEJUICE (KENNER, 1989-90)

ACCESSORIES

❏ **Creepy Cruiser,** 1989-90, Kenner

MNP $3   MIP $13

❏ **Phantom Flyer,** 1989-90, Kenner

MNP $4   MIP $8

❏ **Snake Mask,** 1989-90, Kenner

MNP $4   MIP $8

❏ **Vanishing Vault,** 1989-90, Kenner

MNP $5   MIP $10

FIGURES

❏ **Adam Maitland,** 1989-90, Kenner

MNP $4   MIP $10

(Lenny Lee)

❏ **Exploding Beetlejuice,** 1989-90, Kenner, Body flies apart to reveal bug. Also includes smaller dragon figure

MNP $3   MIP $5

❏ **Harry the Haunted Hunter,** 1989-90, Kenner

MNP $4   MIP $10

❏ **Old Buzzard,** 1989-90, Kenner

MNP $4   MIP $10

❏ **Otho the Obnoxious,** 1989-90, Kenner

MNP $4   MIP $10

❏ **Shipwreck Beetlejuice,** 1989-90, Kenner

MNP $3   MIP $8

❏ **Shish Kabab Beetlejuice,** 1989-90, Kenner
MNP $3   MIP $8

❏ **Showtime Beetlejuice,** 1989-90, Kenner
MNP $3   MIP $8

❏ **Spinhead Beetlejuice,** 1989-90, Kenner
MNP $3   MIP $8

❏ **Street Rat,** 1989-90, Kenner
MNP $4   MIP $10

❏ **Talking Beetlejuice, 12" tall,** 1989-90, Kenner
MNP $18   MIP $38

❏ **Teacher Creature,** 1989-90, Kenner
MNP $5   MIP $10

BEST OF THE WEST (MARX, 1960s)

FIGURES

❏ **Bill Buck, 1967,** 1960s, Marx
MNP $300   MIP $475

(Toy Shop File Photo)

❏ **Buckboard with Horse and Harness,** 1960s, Marx, perfect vehicle for the "Best of the West" figures. The complete rig, (including horse) was over 34" long
MNP $100   MIP $225

(Toy Shop File Photo)

❏ **Chief Cherokee, 1965,** 1960s, Marx, in molded plastic buckskin outfit, included headress, rifle, spear, Bowie knife, ceremonial mask, pipe, and more
MNP $150   MIP $200

❏ **Daniel Boone, 1965,** 1960s, Marx
MNP $100   MIP $200

❏ **Davy Crockett,** 1960s, Marx
MNP $175   MIP $250

(Toy Shop File Photo)

❏ **Fighting Eagle, 1967,** 1960s, Marx, Fully poseable warrior figure includes a variety of accessories, including, spear, Bowie knife, hatchet, bear claw necklace, pouch and more
MNP $150   MIP $225

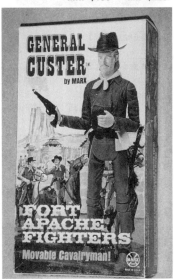

(Toy Shop File Photo)

❏ **General Custer, 1965,** 1960s, Marx, blue molded uniform, with yellow and dark blue plastic accessories
MNP $100   MIP $200

❏ **Geronimo and Pinto,** 1960s, Marx
MNP $150   MIP $200

(Toy Shop File Photo)

❏ **Geronimo, 1967,** 1960s, Marx, with tan molded buckskin uniform, darker brown, yellow and medium brown plastic accessories, including Bowie knife, headband, mask, spear, rifle and more
MNP $100   MIP $150

❏ **Jamie West, 1967,** 1960s, Marx
MNP $50   MIP $100

(Toy Shop File Photo)

❏ **Jane West, 1966,** 1960s, Marx, blue molded plastic clothing as part of figure. Included white plastic clothes and accessories
MNP $60   MIP $120

❑ **Janice West, 1967,** 1960s, Marx
MNP $50   MIP $100

❑ **Jay West, 1967,** 1960s, Marx
MNP $50   MIP $100

❑ **Johnny West Covered Wagon, with horse and harness,** 1960s, Marx, with horse and harness
MNP $100   MIP $225

❑ **Johnny West with Comanche,** 1960s, Marx, fully jointed
MNP $80   MIP $125

❑ **Johnny West, 1965,** 1960s, Marx
MNP $75   MIP $150

❑ **Josie West, 1967,** 1960s, Marx
MNP $50   MIP $100

(Toy Shop File Photo)

❑ **Pancho Horse, for 9" figures, 1968,** 1960s, Marx, for 9" figures, brown with off-white mane and tail. Includes black plastic saddle and bridle
MNP $50   MIP $75

❑ **Princess Wildflower, 1974,** 1960s, Marx, included 22 accessories and gear
MNP $100   MIP $175

(Toy Shop File Photo)

❑ **Sam Cobra, 1972,** 1960s, Marx, Black molded-plastic clothing and accessories. The perfect "bad guy" for the Johnny West universe
MNP $100   MIP $200

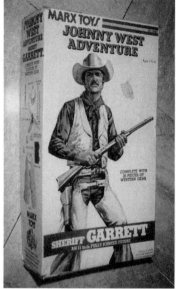

(Toy Shop File Photo)

❑ **Sheriff Garrett, 1973,** 1960s, Marx, now part of the re-released "Johnny West" series. Figure in blue-molded clothing with white and blue plastic clothing and accessories included. A fun toy to throw into the mix in a G.I. Joe adventure, just to shake things up a bit
MNP $150   MIP $200

❑ **Thunderbolt Horse,** 1960s, Marx
MNP $75   MIP $125

❑ **Zeb Zachary, 1967,** 1960s, Marx
MNP $200   MIP $300

BIG JIM (MATTEL, 1973-76)

ACCESSORIES

❑ **Baja Beast,** 1973
MNP $10   MIP $20

❑ **Boat and Buggy Set,** 1973
MNP $10   MIP $25

❑ **Camping Tent,** 1973
MNP $5   MIP $15

❑ **Devil River Trip,** 1974
MNP $15   MIP $30

❑ **Jungle Truck,** 1974
MNP $15   MIP $30

❑ **Motorcross Honda,** 1973
MNP $20   MIP $50

❑ **Rescue Rig,** 1973
MNP $20   MIP $50

❑ **Rugged Rider,** 1973
MNP $15   MIP $30

❑ **Sky Commander,** 1974
MNP $20   MIP $40

❑ **Sport Camper,** 1973
MNP $20   MIP $50

FIGURES

(Toy Shop File Photo)

❑ **Big Jack,** 1973, Mattel, The basic doll (accessories could be purchased separately) with karate-chop action
MNP $7   MIP $25

❑ **Big Jack,** 1973
MNP $7   MIP $25

❑ **Big Jeff,** 1973
MNP $7   MIP $25

❑ **Big Josh,** 1973
MNP $7   MIP $25

❑ **Dr. Steel,** 1975
MNP $10   MIP $30

BIG JIM'S P.A.C.K. (MATTEL, 1976-77)

ACCESSORIES

❑ **Beast,** 1976-77
MNP $45   MIP $100

❑ **BlitzRig,** 1976-77
MNP $60   MIP $120

❑ **Howler,** 1976-77
MNP $30   MIP $60

❑ **LazerVette,** 1976-77
MNP $45   MIP $100

FIGURES

❑ **Big Jim, window box**
MNP $40   MIP $90

❑ **Dr. Steel, window box**
MNP $30   MIP $75

❑ **Warpath, widow box**
MNP $35   MIP $80

❑ **Whip, The, window box**
MNP $35   MIP $80

BILL & TED'S EXCELLENT ADVENTURE (KENNER, 1991)

ACCESSORIES

☐ **Phone Booth**, 1991
MNP $10   MIP $20

☐ **Wild Stallyns Speaker and Tape**, 1991
MNP $7   MIP $20

FIGURES

☐ **Abe Lincoln**, 1991
MNP $15   MIP $30

☐ **Bill**, 1991
MNP $10   MIP $20

☐ **Bill & Ted Jam Session, two pack,** 1991
MNP $20   MIP $40

☐ **Billy The Kid**, 1991
MNP $10   MIP $25

☐ **Genghis Khan**, 1991
MNP $10   MIP $25

☐ **Grim Reaper**, 1991
MNP $25   MIP $50

☐ **Rufus**, 1991
MNP $10   MIP $25

☐ **Ted**, 1991
MNP $10   MIP $20

BIONIC SIX (LJN, 1986)

FIGURES

☐ **Bunji**, 1986
MNP $4   MIP $12

☐ **Chopper**, 1986
MNP $4   MIP $12

☐ **Dr. Scarab**, 1986
MNP $4   MIP $12

☐ **Eric**, 1986
MNP $4   MIP $12

☐ **FLUFFI**, 1986
MNP $8   MIP $20

☐ **Glove**, 1986
MNP $4   MIP $12

☐ **Helen**, 1986
MNP $4   MIP $12

☐ **J.D.**, 1986
MNP $4   MIP $12

☐ **Jack**, 1986
MNP $4   MIP $12

☐ **Klunk**, 1986
MNP $4   MIP $12

☐ **Madame O**, 1986
MNP $4   MIP $12

☐ **Mechanic**, 1986
MNP $4   MIP $12

☐ **Meg**, 1986
MNP $4   MIP $12

BIONIC WOMAN (KENNER, 1976-77)

12" FIGURES

☐ **Fembot**, 1977
MNP $70   MIP $225

☐ **Jamie Sommers**, 1976
MNP $40   MIP $150

(Toy Shop File Photo)

☐ **Jamie Sommers with purse**, 1976
MNP $50   MIP $175

ACCESSORIES

☐ **Beauty Salon**, 1976
MNP $30   MIP $70

☐ **Carriage House**, 1977
MNP $55   MIP $140

☐ **Classroom**, 1976-77
MNP $100   MIP $200

☐ **Dome House**, 1976-77
MNP $55   MIP $140

☐ **Sports Car**, 1976
MNP $40   MIP $100

BLACK HOLE (MEGO, 1979-80)

12" FIGURES

(Toy Shop File Photo)

☐ **Captain Holland**, 1979, Mego, Shown with other figures from the Black Hole
MNP $40   MIP $75

☐ **Dr. Alex Durant**, 1979, Mego
MNP $40   MIP $75

☐ **Dr. Hans Reinhardt**, 1979, Mego
MNP $40   MIP $75

☐ **Harry Booth**, 1979, Mego
MNP $45   MIP $85

☐ **Kate McCrae**, 1979, Mego
MNP $50   MIP $95

☐ **Pizer**, 1979, Mego
MNP $40   MIP $75

3-3/4" FIGURES

(Toy Shop File Photo)

☐ **Captain Holland, 1979,** 1979, Mego, Shown with other figures from the Black Hole
MNP $5   MIP $25

☐ **Dr. Alex Durant, 1979,** 1979, Mego
MNP $5   MIP $25

☐ **Dr. Hans Reinhardt, 1979,** 1979, Mego
MNP $5   MIP $25

☐ **Harry Booth, 1979,** 1979, Mego
MNP $5   MIP $25

☐ **Humanoid, 1980,** 1979, Mego
MNP $200   MIP $750

☐ **Kate McCrae, 1979,** 1979, Mego
MNP $5   MIP $25

☐ **Maximillian, 1979,** 1979, Mego
MNP $20   MIP $75

☐ **Old B.O.B., 1980,** 1979, Mego
MNP $60   MIP $200

☐ **Pizer, 1979,** 1979, Mego
MNP $10   MIP $50

☐ **S.T.A.R., 1980,** 1979, Mego
MNP $85   MIP $350

☐ **Sentry Robot, 1980,** 1979, Mego
MNP $15   MIP $75

☐ **V.I.N.cent., 1979,** 1979, Mego
MNP $15   MIP $70

BLACKSTAR (GALOOB, 1984)

ACCESSORIES

☐ **Ice Castle**, 1984
MNP $35   MIP $75

☐ **Triton**, 1984
MNP $25   MIP $50

☐ **Warlock**, 1984
MNP $25   MIP $50

FIGURES

☐ **Blackstar**, 1984
MNP $10   MIP $25

☐ **Blackstar with Laser Light**, 1984
MNP $10   MIP $35

☐ **Devil Knight with Laser Light**, 1984
MNP $25   MIP $45

☐ **Gargo**, 1984
MNP $10   MIP $35

ACTION FIGURES

❏ **Gargo with Laser Light**, 1984
MNP $10   MIP $35

❏ **Kadray**, 1984
MNP $10   MIP $35

❏ **Kadray with Laser Light**, 1984
MNP $10   MIP $35

❏ **Klone with Laser Light**, 1984
MNP $15   MIP $45

❏ **Lava Loc with Laser Light**, 1984
MNP $15   MIP $45

❏ **Mara**, 1984
MNP $30   MIP $60

❏ **Meuton**, 1984
MNP $10   MIP $35

❏ **Neptul**, 1984
MNP $15   MIP $50

❏ **Overlord**, 1984
MNP $15   MIP $45

❏ **Overlord with Laser Light**, 1984
MNP $15   MIP $40

❏ **Palace Guard**, 1984
MNP $15   MIP $40

❏ **Palace Guard with Laser Light**, 1984
MNP $10   MIP $35

❏ **Togo**, 1984
MNP $10   MIP $35

❏ **Togo with Laser Light**, 1984
MNP $10   MIP $35

❏ **Vizir with Laser Light**, 1984
MNP $10   MIP $35

❏ **White Knight**, 1984
MNP $10   MIP $35

BLADE (TOY BIZ, 1998)

6" FIGURES

❏ **Blade**, 1998, Toy Biz
MNP $10   MIP $30

❏ **Deacon Frost**, 1998, Toy Biz
MNP $10   MIP $30

❏ **Vampire Blade**, 1998, Toy Biz
MNP $8   MIP $20

❏ **Whistler**, 1998, Toy Biz
MNP $8   MIP $20

BLADE VAMPIRE HUNTER (TOY BIZ, 1998)

FIGURES

❏ **Blade**, 1998
MNP $2   MIP $8

❏ **Deacon Frost**, 1998
MNP $2   MIP $8

❏ **Vampire Blade**, 1998
MNP $2   MIP $8

❏ **Whistker**, 1998
MNP $2   MIP $8

BOB & DOUG MCKENZIE (MCFARLANE, 2000)

FIGURES

❏ **Bob McKenzie with half of Great White North stage set**, 2000, McFarlane
MNP $5   MIP $15

❏ **Doug McKenzie with half of Great White North stage set**, 2000, McFarlane
MNP $5   MIP $15

BONANZA (AMERICAN CHARACTER, 1966)

ACCESSOIRES

❏ **4 in 1 Wagon**, 1966
MNP $40   MIP $100

❏ **Ben's Palomino**, 1966
MNP $35   MIP $75

❏ **Hoss' Stallion**, 1966
MNP $35   MIP $75

❏ **Little Joe's Pinto**, 1966
MNP $35   MIP $75

FIGURES

❏ **Ben**, 1966
MNP $50   MIP $150

❏ **Ben with Palomino**, 1966
MNP $80   MIP $225

❏ **Hoss**, 1966
MNP $70   MIP $150

❏ **Hoss with Stallion**, 1966
MNP $70   MIP $200

❏ **Little Joe**, 1966
MNP $50   MIP $150

❏ **Little Joe with Pinto**, 1966
MNP $70   MIP $200

❏ **Outlaw**, 1966
MNP $50   MIP $150

BRAVESTARR (MATTEL, 1996)

FIGURES

❏ **BraveStarr and Thirty/Thirty, two-pack**, 1998, Mattel
MNP $15   MIP $50

❏ **Col. Borobot**, 1998, Mattel
MNP $7   MIP $25

❏ **Deputy Fuzz**, 1998, Mattel
MNP $7   MIP $25

❏ **Handle Bar**, 1998, Mattel
MNP $7   MIP $25

❏ **Laser-Fire BraveStarr**, 1998, Mattel
MNP $7   MIP $25

❏ **Laser-Fire Tex Hex**, 1998, Mattel
MNP $10   MIP $30

❏ **Marshal BraveStarr**, 1998, Mattel
MNP $7   MIP $25

❏ **Outlaw Skuzz**, 1998, Mattel
MNP $7   MIP $25

❏ **Sand Storm**, 1998, Mattel
MNP $7   MIP $25

❏ **Skull Walker**, 1998, Mattel
MNP $5   MIP $20

❏ **Tex Hex**, 1998, Mattel
MNP $10   MIP $30

❏ **Thunder Stick**, 1998, Mattel
MNP $10   MIP $30

BRUCE LEE (SIDESHOW TOYS, 1999-PRESENT)

8" FIGURES

(KP Photo)

❏ **Bruce Lee, bare chested**, 1999, With stand, nunchaku and staff
MNP $7   MIP $15

❏ **Bruce Lee, traditional outfit**, 1999
MNP $7   MIP $15

BUCK ROGERS (MEGO, 1979)

12" FIGURES

(Toy Shop File Photo)

❏ **Buck Rogers**, 1979, Mego
MNP $30   MIP $60

❏ **Doctor Huer**, 1979, Mego
MNP $30   MIP $60

❏ **Draco,** 1979, Mego
MNP $30   MIP $60

❏ **Draconian Guard,** 1979, Mego, With brown and silver uniform
MNP $30   MIP $60

❏ **Killer Kane,** 1979, Mego
MNP $30   MIP $60

(Toy Shop File Photo)

❏ **Tiger Man,** 1979, Mego, With tattooed face and head and tiger-skin vest and clothing
MNP $30   MIP $125

❏ **Twiki,** 1979, Mego
MNP $30   MIP $60

3-3/4" FIGURES

❏ **Ardella,** 1979, Mego
MNP $6   MIP $15

❏ **Buck Rogers,** 1979, Mego
MNP $35   MIP $60

❏ **Doctor Huer,** 1979, Mego
MNP $6   MIP $20

❏ **Draco,** 1979, Mego
MNP $6   MIP $20

❏ **Draconian Guard,** 1979, Mego
MNP $10   MIP $20

❏ **Killer Kane,** 1979, Mego
MNP $6   MIP $15

❏ **Tiger Man,** 1979, Mego
MNP $10   MIP $25

❏ **Twiki,** 1979, Mego
MNP $20   MIP $45

❏ **Wilma Deering,** 1979, Mego
MNP $12   MIP $25

3-3/4" PLAY SETS

❏ **Star Fighter Command Center,** 1979, Mego
MNP $35   MIP $100

3-3/4" VEHICLES

❏ **Draconian Marauder,** 1979, Mego
MNP $25   MIP $50

❏ **Land Rover,** 1979, Mego
MNP $20   MIP $40

❏ **Laserscope Fighter,** 1979, Mego
MNP $20   MIP $40

❏ **Star Fighter,** 1979, Mego
MNP $25   MIP $50

❏ **Star Searcher,** 1979, Mego
MNP $30   MIP $60

BUFFY THE VAMPIRE SLAYER (DIAMOND SELECT, 1999)

FIGURES

❏ **Prophecy Girl Buffy,** 1999, Diamond Select
MNP $5   MIP $15

❏ **Vampiric Angel,** 1999, Diamond Select
MNP $5   MIP $15

❏ **Willow,** 1999, Diamond Select
MNP $5   MIP $15

BUFFY THE VAMPIRE SLAYER (MOORE ACTION COLLECTIBLES, 1999-PRESENT)

SERIES I

❏ **Angel,** 1999, Moore Action Collectibles
MNP $5   MIP $15

❏ **Buffy,** 1999, Moore Action Collectibles
MNP $5   MIP $15

❏ **Buffy, blue shirt and black pants, Moore Action Collectibles Exclusive,** 1999, Moore Action Collectibles
MNP $10   MIP $30

❏ **Master, The,** 1999, Moore Action Collectibles
MNP $5   MIP $15

❏ **Willow,** 1999, Moore Action Collectibles
MNP $5   MIP $15

SERIES II

❏ **Buffy, red leather pants,** 2000
MNP $3   MIP $12

❏ **Giles,** 2000
MNP $3   MIP $12

❏ **Oz,** 2000
MNP $3   MIP $12

BUFFY THE VAMPIRE SLAYER (MOORE ACTION COLLECTIBLES)

SERIES II

(KP Photo)

❏ **Spike,** 2000, Moore Action Collectibles, In black trenchcoat. Includes gravesite stand
MNP $3   MIP $12

BUG'S LIFE, A   (MATTEL, 1998)

FIGURES

❏ **Enemy Hopper,** 1998, Mattel
MNP $2   MIP $5

❏ **Enemy Molt,** 1998, Mattel
MNP $2   MIP $5

❏ **Francis & Slim,** 1998, Mattel
MNP $2   MIP $5

❏ **Hang Glider Flik,** 1998, Mattel
MNP $2   MIP $5

❏ **Inventor Flik,** 1998, Mattel
MNP $2   MIP $5

❏ **Princess Atta,** 1998, Mattel
MNP $2   MIP $5

❏ **Tuck & Roll,** 1998, Mattel
MNP $2   MIP $5

❏ **Warrior Flik,** 1998, Mattel
MNP $2   MIP $5

BUTCH AND SUNDANCE: THE EARLY DAYS   (KENNER, 1979)

ACCESSORIES AND VEHICLES

❏ **Bluff, Butch's horse,** 1979, Kenner
MNP $20   MIP $50

❏ **Mint Wagon,** 1979, Kenner
MNP $25   MIP $60

❏ **Saloon Play Set,** 1979, Kenner
MNP $45   MIP $110

❏ **Spurs, Sundance's horse,** 1979, Kenner
MNP $20   MIP $50

FIGURES

❏ **Butch Cassidy,** 1979, Kenner
MNP $12   MIP $30

❏ **Marshall LeFors,** 1979, Kenner
MNP $12   MIP $30

❏ **O.C. Hanks,** 1979, Kenner
MNP $12   MIP $30

❏ **Sheriff Bledsoe,** 1979, Kenner
MNP $12   MIP $30

❏ **Sundance Kid,** 1979, Kenner
MNP $12   MIP $30

CADILLACS AND DINOSAURS (TYCO, 1994)

FIGURES

❏ **Hammer Terhune,** 1994, Tyco
MNP $2   MIP $5

❏ **Hannah Dundee,** 1994, Tyco
MNP $4   MIP $10

❏ **Hermes,** 1994, Tyco
MNP $2   MIP $5

ACTION FIGURES

❏ **Jack Cadillac Tenrec**, 1994, Tyco
MNP $2   MIP $5

❏ **Jungle Fighting Jack Tenrec**, 1994, Tyco
MNP $3   MIP $8

❏ **Kentrosaurus**, 1994, Tyco
MNP $5   MIP $15

❏ **Mustapha Cairo**, 1994, Tyco
MNP $2   MIP $5

❏ **Snake Eyes**, 1994, Tyco
MNP $5   MIP $15

❏ **Vice Terhune**, 1994, Tyco
MNP $3   MIP $8

❏ **Zeke**, 1994, Tyco
MNP $2   MIP $5

CAPTAIN & TENNILLE (MEGO, 1970s)

FIGURES

❏ **Daryl Dragon (Captain)**, Mego
MNP $40   MIP $75

(Toy Shop File Photo)

❏ **Toni Tennille**, 1977, Mego, Features a stand and "fully washable hair…wash and blow dry on cool setting. Interesting choice for an action figure, but after KISS, why not?
MNP $40   MIP $75

CAPTAIN ACTION (IDEAL, 1966-68)

12" FIGURES

❏ **Captain Action, parachute offer on box**, 1967, 1966-68, Ideal
MNP $275   MIP $700

❏ **Captain Action, photo box**, 1966, 1966-68, Ideal
MNP $300   MIP $900

❏ **Captain Action, with blue-shirted Lone Ranger on box**, 1966, 1966-68, Ideal
MNP $200   MIP $500

❏ **Captain Action, with red-shirted Lone Ranger on box**, 1966, 1966-68, Ideal
MNP $200   MIP $500

❏ **Dr. Evil**, 1967, 1966-68, Ideal
MNP $300   MIP $1200

9" FIGURES

❏ **Action Boy**, 1967, 1966-68, Ideal
MNP $275   MIP $900

❏ **Action Boy, with space suit**, 1968, 1966-68, Ideal
MNP $350   MIP $1100

ACCESSORIES

❏ **Action Cave Carrying Case, vinyl**, 1967, 1966-68, Ideal
MNP $400   MIP $700

❏ **Directional Communicator Set**, 1966, 1966-68, Ideal
MNP $110   MIP $300

❏ **Dr. Evil Sanctuary**, 1967, 1967, Ideal
MNP $2500   MIP $3500

❏ **Jet Mortar**, 1966, 1966-68, Ideal
MNP $110   MIP $300

❏ **Parachute Pack**, 1966, 1966-68, Ideal
MNP $100   MIP $225

❏ **Power Pack**, 1966, 1966-68, Ideal
MNP $125   MIP $250

❏ **Quick Change Chamber, Cardboard, Sears Exclusive**, 1967, 1966-68, Ideal, Sears Exclusive
MNP $750   MIP $900

❏ **Silver Streak Amphibian**, 1967, 1966-68, Ideal
MNP $800   MIP $1200

❏ **Silver Streak Garage (with Silver Streak Vehicle, Sears Exclusive)**, 1966-68, Ideal, Sears Exclusive
MNP $1500   MIP $2000

❏ **Survival Kit, twenty pieces**, 1967, 1966-68, Ideal
MNP $125   MIP $275

❏ **Vinyl Headquarters Carrying Case, Sears Exclusive**, 1967, 1966-68, Ideal, Sears Exclusive
MNP $200   MIP $500

❏ **Weapons Arsenal, ten pieces**, 1966, 1966-68, Ideal
MNP $110   MIP $225

ACTION BOY COSTUMES

❏ **Aqualad**, 1967, 1966-68, Ideal
MNP $300   MIP $900
(Toy Shop File Photo)

❏ **Robin**, 1967, 1966-68, Ideal, included gloves, Batarangs, boots, uniform, face mask, suction cups for climbing buildings
MNP $300   MIP $1200

❏ **Superboy**, 1967, 1966-68, Ideal
MNP $300   MIP $1000

CAPTAIN ACTION COSTUMES

❏ **Aquaman**, 1966, 1966-68, Ideal
MNP $160   MIP $600

❏ **Aquaman, with flasher ring**, 1967, 1966-68, Ideal
MNP $180   MIP $950

(Toy Shop File Photo)

❏ **Batman**, 1966, 1966-68, Ideal, Shown with other Superhero costumes
MNP $225   MIP $700

❏ **Batman, with flasher ring**, 1967, 1966-68, Ideal
MNP $250   MIP $1100

(Toy Shop File Photo)

❏ **Buck Rogers, with flasher ring**, 1967, 1967, Ideal
MNP $450   MIP $2700

❏ **Captain America**, 1966, 1966-68, Ideal
MNP $220   MIP $900

❏ **Captain America, with flasher ring**, 1967, 1966-68, Ideal
MNP $225   MIP $1200

❏ **Flash Gordon**, 1966, 1966-68, Ideal, white spacesuit with helmet, boots, space pistol, belt and mask
MNP $200   MIP $600

❑ **Flash Gordon, with flasher ring, 1967,** 1966-68, Ideal
 MNP $225   MIP $800

❑ **Green Hornet, with flasher ring, 1967,** 1967, Ideal
 MNP $2000   MIP $7500

❑ **Lone Ranger, blue shirt, with flasher ring, 1967,** 1966-68, Ideal
 MNP $500   MIP $1000

❑ **Lone Ranger, red shirt, 1966,** 1966-68, Ideal
 MNP $200   MIP $700

(Toy Shop File Photo)

❑ **Phantom, 1966,** 1966-68, Ideal, a neat set--includes uniform, boots, bayonet, rifle, two pistols and a mask
 MNP $200   MIP $750

❑ **Phantom, with flasher ring, 1967,** 1966-68, Ideal
 MNP $250   MIP $900

(Toy Shop File Photo)

❑ **Sgt. Fury, 1966,** 1966-68, Ideal
 MNP $200   MIP $800

❑ **Spider-Man, with flasher ring, 1967,** 1967, Ideal
 MNP $550   MIP $8000

❑ **Steve Canyon, 1966,** 1966-68, Ideal
 MNP $200   MIP $700

(Toy Shop File Photo)

❑ **Steve Canyon, with flasher ring, 1967,** 1966-68, Ideal, includes jumpsuit uniform, helmet, pistol, pack, ring and mask
 MNP $225   MIP $850

❑ **Superman, 1966,** 1966-68, Ideal
 MNP $200   MIP $700

❑ **Superman, with flasher ring, 1967,** 1966-68, Ideal
 MNP $225   MIP $1100

❑ **Tonto, with flasher ring, 1967,** 1966-68, Ideal
 MNP $375   MIP $1100

CAPTAIN ACTION (PLAYING MANTIS, 1998-99)

FIGURES AND COSTUMES

❑ **Captain Action,** 1998-99, Playing Mantis
 MNP $15   MIP $20

❑ **Dr. Evil,** 1998-99, Playing Mantis
 MNP $15   MIP $20

❑ **Flash Gordon,** 1998-99, Playing Mantis
 MNP $15   MIP $20

❑ **Green Hornet,** 1998-99, Playing Mantis
 MNP $15   MIP $25

❑ **Kato,** 1998-99, Playing Mantis
 MNP $15   MIP $20

(Playing Mantis)

❑ **Lone Ranger,** 1998-99, Playing Mantis, Shown with Tonto
 MNP $15   MIP $25

❑ **Ming the Merciless,** 1998-99, Playing Mantis
 MNP $15   MIP $35

(Playing Mantis)

❑ **Tonto,** 1998-99, Playing Mantis, Shown here with Lone Ranger. Playing Mantis has been able to hit just the right nostalgia buttons with their toys, and this series is just one example
 MNP $15   MIP $25

CAPTAIN POWER AND THE SOLDIERS OF THE FUTURE (MATTEL, 1987-88)

ACCESSORIES

❑ **Dread Stalker,** 1988
 MNP $8   MIP $15

❑ **Interlocker,** 1987
 MNP $10   MIP $20

❑ **Magna Cycle,** 1988
 MNP $12   MIP $25

❑ **Phantom Striker,** 1987
 MNP $12   MIP $25

❑ **Power Base,** 1987
 MNP $25   MIP $50

❑ **Power Jet XT-7,** 1987
 MNP $20   MIP $50

❑ **Power on Energizer with figure,** 1987
 MNP $5   MIP $15

❑ **Trans-Field Base Station,** 1988
 MNP $15   MIP $30

❑ **Trans-Field Communication Station,** 1988
 MNP $10   MIP $20

FIGURES, SERIES I

❑ **Blastarr Ground Guardian,** 1987
 MNP $5   MIP $15

❑ **Captain Power,** 1987
 MNP $10   MIP $20

❑ **Lord Dread,** 1987
 MNP $5   MIP $15

❑ **Lt. Tank Ellis,** 1987
 MNP $10   MIP $20

❑ **Major Hawk Masterson,** 1987
 MNP $5   MIP $15

❑ **Soaron Sky Sentry,** 1987
 MNP $5   MIP $15

ACTION FIGURES

FIGURES, SERIES II

❏ Col. Stingray Johnson, 1988
MNP $12   MIP $25

❏ Cpl. Pilot Chase, 1988
MNP $10   MIP $20

❏ Dread Commander, 1988
MNP $45   MIP $90

❏ Dread Trooper, 1988
MNP $45   MIP $90

❏ Sgt. Scout Baker, 1988
MNP $10   MIP $20

❏ Tritor, 1988
MNP $15   MIP $35

CAPTAIN SCARLETT (PEDIGREE, 1967)

12" FIGURE

❏ Captain Scarlet, 1967
MNP $300   MIP $600

CAPTAIN SCARLETT (VIVID IMAGINATIONS, 1993-94)

12" FIGURES

❏ Captain Black, 1993-94
MNP $25   MIP $50

❏ Captain Scarlett, 1993-94
MNP $25   MIP $50

3-3/4" FIGURES

❏ Captain Black, 1993-94
MNP $3   MIP $8

❏ Captain Blue, 1993-94
MNP $3   MIP $8

❏ Captain Scarlett, 1993-94
MNP $4   MIP $10

❏ Colonel White, 1993-94
MNP $3   MIP $8

❏ Destiny Angel, 1993-94
MNP $5   MIP $12

❏ Lieutenant Green, 1993-94
MNP $3   MIP $8

CHAOS! (MOORE ACTION COLLECTIBLES, 1997-PRESENT)

SERIES I, 12" FIGURES

❏ Lady Death, 1997-present
MNP $10   MIP $30

❏ Royal Lady Death, 1997-present
MNP $10   MIP $30

SERIES I, FIGURES

❏ Evil Earnie, 1997-present
MNP $3   MIP $12

❏ Evil Ernie, glow in the dark, 1997-present
MNP $8   MIP $25

❏ Lady Death, 1997-present
MNP $3   MIP $12

❏ Lady Death, chrome, 1997-present
MNP $10   MIP $30

❏ Lady death, glow in the dark, 1997-present
MNP $10   MIP $30

❏ Lady Demon, 1997-present
MNP $3   MIP $12

❏ Lady Demon, glow in the dark, 1997-present
MNP $10   MIP $30

❏ Purgatori, 1997-present
MNP $3   MIP $12

❏ Purgatori, metallic, 1997-present
MNP $8   MIP $25

SERIES II, FIGURES

❏ Cremator, 1997-present
MNP $8   MIP $20

❏ Cremator, 1997-present
MNP $3   MIP $12

❏ Lady Death in Battle Armor, 1997-present
MNP $3   MIP $12

❏ Lady Death, Azure, 1997-present
MNP $10   MIP $30

❏ Lady Death, bronze, 1997-present
MNP $10   MIP $30

CHARLIE'S ANGELS

FIGURES

(KP Photo)

❏ Dylan Sanders, 2000, JAKKS Pacific, Model of Drew Barrymore's character in "Charlie's Angels" movie
n/a   MIP $30

CHARLIE'S ANGELS (HASBRO, 1977)

8-1/2" FIGURES

(Toy Shop File Photo)

❏ Jill — Farrah Fawcett, 1977, Hasbro, Shown here with Sabrina and Kelly
MNP $50   MIP $100

❏ Kelly — Jaclyn Smith, 1977, Hasbro
MNP $40   MIP $75

❏ Kris — Cheryl Ladd, 1977, Hasbro
MNP $40   MIP $75

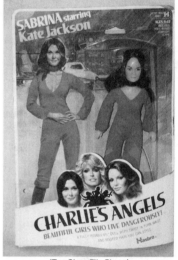

(Toy Shop File Photo)

❏ Sabrina — Kate Jackson, 1977, Hasbro
MNP $40   MIP $75

❏ Sabrina, Kris and Kelly Gift Set, 1977, Hasbro
MNP $75   MIP $200

CHIPs (MEGO, 1979)

3-3/4" FIGURES AND ACCESSORIES

❏ Jimmy Squeaks, 1979, Mego
MNP $5   MIP $15

❏ Jon, 1979, Mego
MNP $10   MIP $20

❏ Launcher with Motorcycle, 1979, Mego
MNP $25   MIP $50

❏ Motorcycle, boxed, 1979, Mego
MNP $5   MIP $30

❏ Ponch, 1979, Mego
MNP $8   MIP $20

❑ **Sarge,** 1979, Mego
　　　　MNP $10　　　MIP $30

❑ **Wheels Willie,** 1979, Mego
　　　　MNP $5　　　MIP $15

8" FIGURES AND ACCESSORIES

❑ **Jon,** 1979, Mego
　　　　MNP $20　　　MIP $50

❑ **Motorcycle,** 1979, Mego
　　　　MNP $30　　　MIP $75

❑ **Ponch,** 1979, Mego
　　　　MNP $15　　　MIP $40

❑ **Sarge,** 1979, Mego
　　　　MNP $25　　　MIP $50

CHUCK NORRIS (KENNER, 1986-87)

6" FIGURES

(Toy Shop File Photo)

❑ **Chuck Norris Battle Gear,** 1986
　　　　MNP $8　　　MIP $15

❑ **Chuck Norris Kung Fu Training,** 1986
　　　　MNP $6　　　MIP $12

❑ **Chuck Norris Undercover Agent,** 1986
　　　　MNP $8　　　MIP $15

❑ **Kimo,** 1986
　　　　MNP $6　　　MIP $12

❑ **Ninja Master,** 1986
　　　　MNP $6　　　MIP $12

❑ **Ninja Serpent,** 1986
　　　　MNP $6　　　MIP $12

❑ **Ninja Warrior,** 1986
　　　　MNP $6　　　MIP $12

❑ **Super Ninja,** 1986
　　　　MNP $6　　　MIP $12

❑ **Tabe,** 1986
　　　　MNP $6　　　MIP $12

CLASH OF THE TITANS (MATTEL, 1980)

FIGURES

❑ **Calibos,** 1980
　　　　MNP $20　　　MIP $50

❑ **Charon,** 1980
　　　　MNP $30　　　MIP $75

❑ **Kraken,** 1980
　　　　MNP $75　　　MIP $250

❑ **Pegasus,** 1980
　　　　MNP $25　　　MIP $75

❑ **Perseus,** 1980
　　　　MNP $20　　　MIP $50

❑ **Perseus and Pegasus, two-pack,** 1980
　　　　MNP $50　　　MIP $105

❑ **Thallo,** 1980
　　　　MNP $20　　　MIP $50

COMIC ACTION HEROES (MEGO, 1975)

3-3/4" FIGURES

❑ **Aquaman,** 1975, Mego
　　　　MNP $30　　　MIP $75

❑ **Batman,** 1975, Mego
　　　　MNP $20　　　MIP $75

❑ **Captain America,** 1975, Mego
　　　　MNP $20　　　MIP $75

❑ **Green Goblin,** 1975, Mego
　　　　MNP $22　　　MIP $125

❑ **Hulk,** 1975, Mego
　　　　MNP $20　　　MIP $50

❑ **Joker,** 1975, Mego
　　　　MNP $20　　　MIP $75

❑ **Penguin,** 1975, Mego, Shown here with Robin
　　　　MNP $20　　　MIP $75

(Toy Shop File Photo)

❑ **Robin,** 1975, Mego, Shown here with The Penguin.
　　　　MNP $20　　　MIP $65

❑ **Shazam,** 1975, Mego
　　　　MNP $20　　　MIP $75

❑ **Spider-Man,** 1975, Mego
　　　　MNP $20　　　MIP $75

❑ **Superman,** 1975, Mego
　　　　MNP $20　　　MIP $65

❑ **Wonder Woman,** 1975, Mego
　　　　MNP $20　　　MIP $65

ACCESSORIES

❑ **Collapsing Tower (with Invisible Plane & Wonder Woman),** 1975, Mego
　　　　MNP $100　　　MIP $200

❑ **Exploding Bridge with Batmobile,** 1975, Mego
　　　　MNP $100　　　MIP $200

❑ **Fortress of Solitude with Superman,** 1975, Mego
　　　　MNP $100　　　MIP $200

❑ **Mangler,** 1975, Mego
　　　　MNP $125　　　MIP $300

COMIC HEROINE POSIN' DOLLS (IDEAL, 1967)

12" BOXED FIGURES

(KP Photo, Joe Desris collection)

❑ **Batgirl, 1967,** Ideal, Purple gloves, boots, cape and mask. A highly-sought figure
　　　　MNP $1000　　MIP $5500

(Toy Shop File Photo)

❑ **Mera, 1967,** 1967, Ideal
　　　　MNP $600　　MIP $4500

❑ **Supergirl, 1967,** 1967, Ideal
　　　　MNP $600　　MIP $4500

ACTION FIGURES

(Toy Shop File Photo)

❑ **Wonder Woman, 1967,** Ideal, Very rare item from Ideal. Female action-hero dolls are in a strange lot for collectors. Typically, boys didn't buy or request them, and many girls either weren't interested, or just didn't receive them as gifts

| | MNP $600 | MIP $4500 |

COMMANDER POWER (MEGO, 1975)

FIGURE WITH VEHICLE

❑ **Commander Power with Lightning Cycle,** 1975, Mego

| | MNP $20 | MIP $40 |

COMMANDO (DIAMOND, 1985)

18" FIGURES

❑ **Arnold Schwarzenegger, black box,** 1985

| | MNP $80 | MIP $200 |

❑ **Arnold Schwarzenegger, red box,** 1985

| | MNP $80 | MIP $300 |

3-3/4" FIGURES

❑ **Blaster,** 1985

| | MNP $10 | MIP $25 |

❑ **Chopper,** 1985

| | MNP $10 | MIP $25 |

❑ **Lead Head,** 1985

| | MNP $10 | MIP $25 |

❑ **Matrix,** 1985

| | MNP $40 | MIP $150 |

❑ **Psycho,** 1985

| | MNP $10 | MIP $25 |

❑ **Sawbones,** 1985

| | MNP $10 | MIP $25 |

❑ **Spex,** 1985

| | MNP $10 | MIP $25 |

❑ **Stalker,** 1985

| | MNP $10 | MIP $25 |

6" FIGURES

❑ **Blaster,** 1985

| | MNP $15 | MIP $40 |

❑ **Chopper,** 1985

| | MNP $15 | MIP $40 |

❑ **Lead Head,** 1985

| | MNP $15 | MIP $40 |

❑ **Matrix,** 1985

| | MNP $35 | MIP $90 |

❑ **Pyscho,** 1985

| | MNP $15 | MIP $40 |

❑ **Sawbones,** 1985

| | MNP $15 | MIP $40 |

❑ **Spex,** 1985

| | MNP $15 | MIP $40 |

❑ **Stalker,** 1985

| | MNP $15 | MIP $40 |

CONAN (HASBRO, 1994)

FIGURES, ASST. I

❑ **Conan the Adventurer with Star Metal Slash,** 1994, Hasbro

| | MNP $10 | MIP $20 |

❑ **Conan the Warrior with Slashing Battle Action,** 1994, Hasbro

| | MNP $10 | MIP $20 |

❑ **Wrath-Amon with Serpent Slash,** 1994, Hasbro

| | MNP $10 | MIP $20 |

❑ **Zulu with Dart Firing Crossbow,** 1994, Hasbro

| | MNP $10 | MIP $20 |

FIGURES, ASST. II

❑ **Conan the Exlporer with Two-fisted Chopping Action,** 1994, Hasbro

| | MNP $10 | MIP $20 |

❑ **Greywolf with Cyclone Power Punch,** 1994, Hasbro

| | MNP $10 | MIP $35 |

❑ **Ninja Conan with Katana Chop,** 1994, Hasbro

| | MNP $10 | MIP $20 |

❑ **Skulkur with Zombie Tornado Slash,** 1994, Hasbro

| | MNP $10 | MIP $20 |

CONAN (REMCO, 1984)

FIGURES

❑ **Conan The Warrior,** 1984

| | MNP $15 | MIP $40 |

❑ **Devourer Of Souls,** 1984

| | MNP $15 | MIP $40 |

❑ **Jewel Man,** 1984

| | MNP $15 | MIP $40 |

❑ **Throth Amon,** 1984

| | MNP $15 | MIP $40 |

CONEHEADS (PLAYMATES, 1998)

FIGURES

(Playmates Toys)

❑ **Agent Seedling,** 1998, Playmates, Shown here with group of figures in the series

| | MNP $2 | MIP $4 |

❑ **Beldar in flight uniform,** 1998

| | MNP $2 | MIP $4 |

❑ **Beldar in street clothes,** 1998

| | MNP $2 | MIP $4 |

❑ **Connie,** 1998

| | MNP $2 | MIP $4 |

❑ **Prymaat in flight uniform,** 1998

| | MNP $2 | MIP $4 |

❑ **Prymaat in street clothes,** 1998

| | MNP $2 | MIP $4 |

CONGO (KENNER, 1995)

FIGURES

(KP Photo)

❑ **Amy,** 1995, Shown here with a group of Congo figures

| | MNP $3 | MIP $5 |

(KP Photo)

❏ **Blastface**, 1995, Shown here with Congo figure group
MNP $3   MIP $5

❏ **Bonecrucher, Deluxe**, 1995
MNP $4   MIP $8

❏ **Kahega**, 1995
MNP $2   MIP $4

❏ **Karen Ross**, 1995
MNP $2   MIP $4

❏ **Mangler**, 1995
MNP $2   MIP $4

❏ **Monroe**, 1995
MNP $2   MIP $4

❏ **Monroe, Deluxe**, 1995
MNP $4   MIP $8

❏ **Peter Elliot**, 1995
MNP $2   MIP $4

VEHICLES

❏ **Net trap Vehicle**, 1995
MNP $4   MIP $8

❏ **Trail Hacker Vehicle**, 1995
MNP $4   MIP $8

DANGER GIRL (McFARLANE, 1999)

FIGURES

❏ **Abbey Chase**, 1999
MNP $8   MIP $20

❏ **Major Maxim**, 1999
MNP $3   MIP $8

❏ **Natalia Kassle**, 1999
MNP $8   MIP $20

❏ **Sydney Savage**, 1999
MNP $8   MIP $20

DC COMICS SUPER HEROES (TOY BIZ, 1989)

FIGURES

❏ **Aquaman**, 1989, Toy Biz
MNP $5   MIP $8

❏ **Batman**, 1989, Toy Biz
MNP $3   MIP $5

❏ **Bob The Goon**, 1989, Toy Biz
MNP $5   MIP $10

❏ **Flash**, 1989, Toy Biz
MNP $4   MIP $8

❏ **Flash II with Turbo Platform**, 1989, Toy Biz
MNP $5   MIP $8

❏ **Green Lantern**, 1989, Toy Biz
MNP $8   MIP $15

❏ **Hawkman**, 1989, Toy Biz
MNP $8   MIP $15

❏ **Joker, no forehead curl**, 1989, Toy Biz
MNP $3   MIP $8

❏ **Joker, with forehead curl**, 1989, Toy Biz
MNP $5   MIP $8

❏ **Lex Luthor**, 1989, Toy Biz
MNP $3   MIP $5

❏ **Mr. Freeze**, 1989, Toy Biz
MNP $4   MIP $8

❏ **Penguin, long missile**, 1989, Toy Biz
MNP $8   MIP $13

❏ **Penguin, short missile**, 1989, Toy Biz
MNP $8   MIP $15

❏ **Penguin, umbrella-firing**, 1989, Toy Biz
MNP $3   MIP $8

❏ **Riddler**, 1989, Toy Biz
MNP $4   MIP $8

❏ **Superman**, 1989, Toy Biz
MNP $10   MIP $25

❏ **Two Face**, 1989, Toy Biz
MNP $15   MIP $20

❏ **Wonder Woman**, 1989, Toy Biz
MNP $8   MIP $15

DEFENDERS OF THE EARTH (GALOOB, 1985)

FIGURES

❏ **Flash Gordon**, 1985
MNP $8   MIP $25

❏ **Garaz**, 1985
MNP $8   MIP $25

❏ **Lothar**, 1985
MNP $8   MIP $25

❏ **Mandrake**, 1985
MNP $8   MIP $25

❏ **Ming**, 1985
MNP $8   MIP $20

❏ **Phantom, The**, 1985
MNP $10   MIP $30

VEHICLES

❏ **Claw Copter**, 1985
MNP $8   MIP $25

❏ **Flash Swordship**, 1985
MNP $8   MIP $25

❏ **Garax Swordship**, 1985
MNP $8   MIP $25

❏ **Phantom Skull Copter**, 1985
MNP $10   MIP $35

DICK TRACY (PLAYMATES, 1990)

FIGURES, LARGE

(Toy Shop File Photo)

❏ **Breathless Mahoney**, 1990, Based on the movie, shown here with the Dick Tracy figure
MNP $25   MIP $50

(Toy Shop File Photo)

❏ **Dick Tracy**, 1990, Shown here with "Breathless"
MNP $25   MIP $50

FIGURES, SMALL

❏ **Al "Big Boy" Caprice**, 1990
MNP $8   MIP $15

(Toy Shop File Photo)

❏ **Blank, The,** 1990
MNP $50   MIP $150

❏ **Brow, The,** 1990
MNP $6   MIP $12

❏ **Dick Tracy,** 1990
MNP $8   MIP $15

(Toy Shop File Photo)

❏ **Flattop,** 1990, Playmates, Includes Tommy gun and bullwhip
MNP $6   MIP $12

❏ **Influence,** 1990
MNP $6   MIP $12

❏ **Itchy,** 1990
MNP $8   MIP $15

❏ **Lips Manlis,** 1990
MNP $6   MIP $12

❏ **Mumbles,** 1990
MNP $6   MIP $12

❏ **Pruneface,** 1990
MNP $6   MIP $12

❏ **Rodent, The,** 1990
MNP $8   MIP $15

❏ **Sam Catchem,** 1990
MNP $6   MIP $12

(Toy Shop File Photo)

❏ **Shoulders,** 1990
MNP $6   MIP $12

❏ **Steve the Tramp,** 1990
MNP $6   MIP $12

DIE-CAST SUPER HEROES (MEGO, 1979)

6" FIGURES

❏ **Batman,** 1979, Mego
MNP $30   MIP $125

❏ **Hulk,** 1979, Mego
MNP $25   MIP $75

❏ **Spider-Man,** 1979, Mego
MNP $30   MIP $125

❏ **Superman,** 1979, Mego
MNP $30   MIP $95

DOCTOR WHO (DAPOL, 1988-95)

FIGURES

❏ **Ace with bat and pack,** 1988-95
MNP $4   MIP $8

❏ **Cyberman,** 1988-95
MNP $4   MIP $8

❏ **Dalek, black and gold, with friction drive,** 1988-95
MNP $5   MIP $10

❏ **Dalek, black and silver, with friction drive,** 1988-95
MNP $5   MIP $10

❏ **Dalek, gold, with friction drive,** 1988-95
MNP $5   MIP $10

❏ **Dalek, gray and black, with friction drive,** 1988-95
MNP $5   MIP $10

❏ **Dalek, gray and black, with friction drive,** 1988-95
MNP $5   MIP $10

❏ **Dalek, red and black, with friction drive,** 1988-95
MNP $5   MIP $10

❏ **Dalek, red and gold, with friction drive,** 1988-95
MNP $5   MIP $10

❏ **Dalek, white and gold, with friction drive,** 1988-95
MNP $5   MIP $10

❏ **Doctor Who (2nd) Pat Troughton,** 1988-95
MNP $5   MIP $10

❏ **Doctor Who (3rd), Jon Pertwee,** 1988-95
MNP $5   MIP $10

❏ **Doctor Who (4th), Tom Baker,** 1988-95
MNP $4   MIP $8

❏ **Doctor Who (7th) with brown coat,** 1988-95
MNP $5   MIP $10

❏ **Doctor Who (7th) with gray coat,** 1988-95
MNP $5   MIP $10

❏ **Early Cybermen,** 1988-95
MNP $5   MIP $10

❏ **Ice Warrior,** 1988-95
MNP $4   MIP $8

❏ **K9 with motor action,** 1988-95
MNP $5   MIP $10

❏ **Master, The,** 1988-95
MNP $4   MIP $8

❏ **Mel, blue shirt,** 1988-95
MNP $4   MIP $8

❏ **Mel, pink shirt,** 1988-95
MNP $4   MIP $8

❏ **Melkur,** 1988-95
MNP $5   MIP $10

❏ **Sea Devil with cloth outfit,** 1988-95
MNP $5   MIP $10

❏ **Silurian,** 1988-95
MNP $4   MIP $8

❏ **Silurian, armored,** 1988-95
MNP $4   MIP $8

❏ **Sontaran,** 1988-95
MNP $5   MIP $10

❏ **Sontaran Captain with helmet,** 1988-95
MNP $5   MIP $10

❏ **Tetrap,** 1988-95
MNP $5   MIP $10

❏ **Time Lords, brown,** 1988-95
MNP $5   MIP $10

❏ **Time Lords, burgundy,** 1988-95
MNP $5   MIP $10

❏ **Time Lords, gray,** 1988-95
MNP $5   MIP $10

❏ **Time Lords, off-white,** 1988-95
MNP $5   MIP $10

PLAY SETS

❏ **Doctor Who (3rd) Play Set,** 1988-95
MNP $20   MIP $55

VEHICLES AND ACCESSORIES

❏ **Dalek Play Set,** 1988-95
MNP $18   MIP $35

❏ **Tardis with flashing light,** 1988-95
MNP $12   MIP $25

DOCTOR WHO (DENYS FISHER, 1976)

FIGURES

(Corey LeChat)

❑ **Cyberman,** 1976, Denys Fisher, Very 1930s-looking robotic figure from the BBC-TV series. Called "The Threat from the Outerworld" on the box
MNP $250   MIP $600

❑ **Dalek,** 1976
MNP $250   MIP $600

❑ **Doctor Who (4th),** 1976
MNP $100   MIP $225

(Corey LeChat)

❑ **Giant Robot,** 1976, Denys Fisher, Gray plastic robot from the BBC-TV series
MNP $165   MIP $375

(Corey LeChat)

❑ **K-9,** 1976, Palitoy, Looking much like today's toy robot dogs, this Talking K-9 could say a variety of phrases by pressing the control panel on his back
MNP $150   MIP $300

❑ **Leela,** 1976, Denys Fisher
MNP $200   MIP $400

VEHICLES

(Corey LeChat)

❑ **Tardis play set,** 1976, Plastic model of the time-travelling police call box as seen in the popular BBC-TV series
MNP $150   MIP $300

DOCTOR WHO (PALITOY, 1976)

FIGURES

(Corey LeChat)

❑ **Dalek, Talking,** 1976, Palitoy, Shown on the right
MNP $250   MIP $475

(Corey LeChat)

❑ **K-9, Talking,** 1976, Palitoy
MNP $150   MIP $300

DUKES OF HAZZARD (MEGO, 1981-82)

3-3/4" CARDED FIGURES

❑ **Bo Duke,** 1981-82, Mego
MNP $8   MIP $15

❑ **Boss Hogg,** 1981-82, Mego
MNP $8   MIP $20

❑ **Cletus,** 1981-82, Mego
MNP $15   MIP $30

❑ **Cooter,** 1981-82, Mego
MNP $15   MIP $30

❑ **Coy Duke,** 1981-82, Mego
MNP $15   MIP $30

❑ **Daisy Duke,** 1981-82, Mego
MNP $12   MIP $25

❑ **Luke Duke,** 1981-82, Mego
MNP $8   MIP $20

❑ **Rosco Coltrane,** 1981-82, Mego
MNP $15   MIP $30

❑ **Uncle Jesse,** 1981-82, Mego
MNP $15   MIP $30

❑ **Vance Duke,** 1981-82, Mego
MNP $15   MIP $30

3-3/4" FIGURES WITH VEHICLES

❑ **Daisy Jeep with Daisy, 1981, boxed,** 1981-82, Mego
MNP $25   MIP $50

❑ **General Lee Car with Bo and Luke, 1981, boxed,** 1981-82, Mego
MNP $25   MIP $50

8" CARDED FIGURES

(Toy Shop File Photo)

❑ **Bo Duke,** 1981-82, Mego
MNP $15   MIP $30

❑ **Boss Hogg,** 1981-82, Mego
MNP $20   MIP $40

❑ **Coy Duke (card says Bo),** 1981-82, Mego
MNP $25   MIP $50

❑ **Daisy Duke,** 1981-82, Mego
MNP $25   MIP $50

(Lenny Lee)

❑ **Luke Duke,** 1981-82, Mego
MNP $15   MIP $30

❑ **Vance Duke (card says Luke),** 1981-82, Mego
MNP $25   MIP $50

DUNE (LJN, 1984)

FIGURES

❑ **Baron Harkonnen,** 1984
MNP $20   MIP $40

❑ **Feyd,** 1984
MNP $20   MIP $40

❑ **Paul Atreides,** 1984
MNP $20   MIP $40

❑ **Rabban,** 1984
MNP $20   MIP $40

❑ **Sardauker Warrior,** 1984
MNP $25   MIP $50

❑ **Stilgar the Freman,** 1984
MNP $20   MIP $40

VEHICLES

❑ **Sand Crawler,** 1984
MNP $20   MIP $40

❑ **Sand tracker,** 1984
MNP $20   MIP $40

❑ **Sandworm,** 1984
MNP $25   MIP $50

❑ **Spice Scout,** 1984
MNP $25   MIP $50

DUNGEONS & DRAGONS (LJN, 1983-84)

MONSTERS

❑ **Dragonne,** 1983
MNP $20   MIP $40

❑ **Hook Horror,** 1983
MNP $20   MIP $40

❑ **Timat,** 1983
MNP $90   MIP $200

MOUNTS

❑ **Bronze Dragon,** 1983
MNP $20   MIP $40

❑ **Destrier,** 1983
MNP $15   MIP $30

❑ **Nightmare,** 1983
MNP $15   MIP $30

PLAY SETS

❑ **Fortress of Fangs,** 1983
MNP $65   MIP $130

SERIES I, 3-3/4" FIGURES, 1983

❑ **Elkhorn,** 1983
MNP $15   MIP $30

❑ **Kelek,** 1983
MNP $15   MIP $30

❑ **Melf,** 1983
MNP $15   MIP $35

❑ **Mercion,** 1983
MNP $15   MIP $35

❑ **Peralay,** 1983
MNP $15   MIP $30

❑ **Ringlerun,** 1983
MNP $15   MIP $30

❑ **Strongheart,** 1983
MNP $15   MIP $30

❑ **Warduke,** 1983, LJN
MNP $15   MIP $30

❑ **Zarak,** 1983
MNP $15   MIP $30

SERIES I, 5" FIGURES, 1983

❑ **Northlord,** 1983
MNP $20   MIP $45

❑ **Ogre King,** 1983
MNP $20   MIP $45

❑ **Young Male Titan,** 1983
MNP $15   MIP $30

SERIES II, 3-3/4" FIGURES, 1984

❑ **Bowmarc,** 1984
MNP $40   MIP $90

❑ **Deeth,** 1984
MNP $55   MIP $120

❑ **Drex,** 1984
MNP $55   MIP $120

❑ **Elkhorn,** 1984
MNP $20   MIP $50

❑ **Grimsword,** 1984
MNP $30   MIP $70

❑ **Hawkler,** 1984
MNP $50   MIP $100

❑ **Strongheart,** 1984
MNP $20   MIP $45

❑ **Warduke,** 1984
MNP $20   MIP $45

❑ **Zarak,** 1984, LJN
MNP $20   MIP $45

❑ **Zorgar,** 1984, LJN
MNP $60   MIP $120

SERIES II, 5" FIGURES, 1984

❑ **Mandoom,** 1984
MNP $60   MIP $120

❑ **Mettaflame,** 1984
MNP $60   MIP $120

❑ **Northland,** 1984
MNP $50   MIP $100

❑ **Ogre King,** 1984
MNP $65   MIP $130

❑ **Young Male Titan,** 1984
MNP $50   MIP $100

E.T. THE EXTRA-TERRESTRIAL (LJN, 1982-83)

FIGURES

❑ **E.T and Elliot with bike,** 1982-83
MNP $10   MIP $20

❑ **E.T. with dress and hat,** 1982-83
MNP $6   MIP $12

❑ **E.T. with robe,** 1982-83
MNP $6   MIP $12

(Toy Shop File Photo)

❑ **E.T. with Speak and Spell,** 1982-83, Thumb-operated switch on E.T.'s back extends neck
MNP $6   MIP $12

❑ **E.T., talking,** 1982-83
MNP $15   MIP $35

❑ **E.T., walking,** 1982-83
MNP $12   MIP $25

EARTHWORM JIM (PLAYMATES, 1995)

FIGURES

❑ **Bob,** 1995, Playmates
MNP $5   MIP $12

❑ **Earthworm Jim with Battle Damage,** 1995, Playmates
MNP $5   MIP $8

(Playmates Toys)

❑ **Earthworm Jim with Pocket Rocket,** 1995, Playmates, Figure with small turbo-driven vehicle (looks a bit like a Gee-Bee racer)

MNP $5   MIP $8

❑ **Earthworm Jim with Snott,** 1995, Playmates

MNP $5   MIP $8

❑ **Hench Rat with Evil Cat,** 1995, Playmates

MNP $5   MIP $10

❑ **Monstrous Peter Puppy,** 1995, Playmates

MNP $5   MIP $8

❑ **Peter Puppy,** 1995, Playmates

MNP $5   MIP $8

❑ **Princess What's-Her-Name,** 1995, Playmates

MNP $7   MIP $12

❑ **Psycrow with Major Mucus,** 1995, Playmates

MNP $4   MIP $8

EMERGENCY (LJN, 1973)

FIGURES

❑ **John,** 1973

MNP $35   MIP $100

❑ **Roy,** 1973

MNP $35   MIP $100

VEHICLES

❑ **Rescue Truck,** 1973

MNP $75   MIP $200

EVEL KNIEVEL (IDEAL, 1973-74)

FIGURES

❑ **Evel Knievel, blue suit,** 1973-74, Ideal

MNP $20   MIP $50

❑ **Evel Knievel, red suit,** 1973-74

MNP $20   MIP $50

❑ **Evel Knievel, white suit,** 1973-74

MNP $20   MIP $50

❑ **Robby Knievel,** 1973-74, Ideal

MNP $25   MIP $60

VEHICLES AND ACCESSORIES

❑ **Arctic Explorer set,** 1973-74

MNP $35   MIP $75

❑ **Chopper,** 1973-74

MNP $35   MIP $75

❑ **Evel Knievel Canyon Stunt Cycle,** 1973-74

MNP $40   MIP $80

❑ **Evel Knievel Dragster,** 1973-74

MNP $50   MIP $110

❑ **Evel Knievel Stunt and Crash Car,** 1973-74

MNP $45   MIP $100

❑ **Evel Knievel Stunt Cycle,** 1973-74

MNP $35   MIP $75

❑ **Explorer Set,** 1973-74

MNP $20   MIP $40

❑ **Racing Set,** 1973-74

MNP $20   MIP $40

❑ **Rescue Set,** 1973-74

MNP $20   MIP $40

❑ **Road and Trail Set,** 1973-74

MNP $50   MIP $125

❑ **Scramble Van,** 1973-74

MNP $30   MIP $75

❑ **Skull Canyon Play Set,** 1973-74

MNP $50   MIP $125

❑ **Stunt Stadium,** 1973-74

MNP $40   MIP $100

❑ **Tail Bike,** 1973-74

MNP $35   MIP $60

EXOSQUAD (PLAYMATES, 1993-95)

EXOCONVERTING SERIES

❑ **J.T. Marsh with Exoconverting E-frame,** 1993-94

MNP $8   MIP $15

EXOWALKING SERIES

❑ **Marsala with ExoWalking E-frame,** 1993-94

MNP $8   MIP $15

GENERAL PURPOSE E-FRAMES WITH FIGURE, ORIGINAL SERIES

❑ **Alec DeLeon with Field Communications,** 1993-95

MNP $8   MIP $15

❑ **J.T. Marsh with Aerial Attack E-Frame,** 1993-95

MNP $8   MIP $15

❑ **Pheaton with Command E-Frame,** 1993-95

MNP $8   MIP $15

❑ **Typhonus with High Speed Stealth E-Frame,** 1993-95

MNP $8   MIP $15

GENERAL PURPOSE E-FRAMES WITH FIGURE, SECONDARY SERIES

❑ **Draconis with Interrogator E-frame,** 1994

MNP $8   MIP $15

❑ **Jinx Madison with Fire Warrior E-frame,** 1994

MNP $8   MIP $15

❑ **Jonas Simbacca with Pirate Captain E-frame,** 1994

MNP $8   MIP $15

❑ **Nara Burns with Reconnaissance E-frame,** 1994

MNP $8   MIP $15

❑ **Peter Tanaka with Samurai E-frame,** 1994

MNP $8   MIP $15

❑ **Rita Torres with Field Sergeant E-frame,** 1994

MNP $8   MIP $15

❑ **Sean Napier with police Enforcer E-frame,** 1994

MNP $8   MIP $15

❑ **Wolf Bronski with Ground Assault E-frame,** 1994

MNP $8   MIP $15

GENERAL PURPOSE E-FRAMES WITH FIGURE, THIRD SERIES

❑ **J.T. Marsh with Gridiron Command E-frame,** 1995

MNP $8   MIP $15

❑ **Kaz Takagi with Gorilla E-frame,** 1995

MNP $8   MIP $15

❑ **Marsala with Sub-Sonic Scout E-frame,** 1995

MNP $8   MIP $15

❑ **Wolf Bronski with Medieval Knight E-frames,** 1995

MNP $8   MIP $15

JUMPTROOPS

❑ **Captain Avery Butler,** 1993-94

MNP $4   MIP $8

❑ **Gunnery Sergeant Ramon Longfeather,** 1993-94

MNP $4   MIP $8

❑ **Lance Corporal Vince Pelligrino,** 1993-94

MNP $4   MIP $8

❑ **Lieutenant Colleen O'Reilly,** 1993-94

MNP $4   MIP $8

LIGHT ATTACK E-FRAMES

❑ **Livanus with Troop Transport E-frame,** 1993-94

MNP $12   MIP $25

❑ **Maggie Weston with Field Repair E-frame,** 1993-94

MNP $12   MIP $25

❑ **Marsala with rapid Assault E-frame,** 1993-94

MNP $12   MIP $25

❑ **Shiva with Amphibious Assault E-frame,** 1993-94

MNP $12   MIP $25

MINI EXO-COMMAND BATTLE SETS

❑ **Alec DeLeon and Phaeton with Vesta Space Port Battleset,** 1995

MNP $4   MIP $8

❑ **J.T. Marsh and Typhonus with Resolute II Hangar Battleset,** 1995

MNP $4   MIP $8

❑ **Phaeton and J.T. Marsh with Olympus Mons Command Ship Bridge Battleset,** 1995

MNP $4   MIP $8

ACTION FIGURES

NEO WARRIORS

❑ **Neo Cat**, 1993-94
  MNP $4   MIP $8

❑ **Neo Lord**, 1993-94
  MNP $4   MIP $8

ROBOTECH SERIES, 3" FIGURES

❑ **Excaliber**, 1995
  MNP $2   MIP $4

❑ **Gladiator**, 1995
  MNP $2   MIP $4

❑ **RaidarX**, 1995
  MNP $2   MIP $4

❑ **Spartan**, 1995
  MNP $2   MIP $4

ROBOTECH SERIES, 7" FIGURES

❑ **Excaliber MK VI**, 1995
  MNP $5   MIP $10

❑ **Gladiator Destroid**, 1995
  MNP $5   MIP $10

❑ **RaidarX**, 1995
  MNP $5   MIP $10

❑ **Spartan Destroid**, 1995
  MNP $5   MIP $10

❑ **Zentraedi Power Armor Botoru Battalion**, 1995
  MNP $5   MIP $10

❑ **Zentraedi Power Armor Quadrono Battalion**, 1995
  MNP $5   MIP $10

ROBOTECH SERIES, VEHICLES

❑ **VeriTech Hover Tank**, 1995
  MNP $12   MIP $24

❑ **VF-IS Veritech Fighter**, 1995, Playmates
  MNP $8   MIP $15

SPACE SERIES

❑ **Exocarrier Resolute II with Mini E-frames**, 1993-94
  MNP $12   MIP $25

❑ **Kaz Takagi with ExoFighter Space E-frame**, 1993-94
  MNP $12   MIP $25

❑ **Thrax with NeoFighter Space E-frame**, 1993-94
  MNP $12   MIP $25

SPECIAL MISSION E-FRAMES

❑ **Alec DeLeon with All-Terrain Special Mission E-frame**, 1993-94
  MNP $8   MIP $15

❑ **J.T. Marsh with Deep Space Special Mission E-frame**, 1993-94
  MNP $8   MIP $15

❑ **Typhonus with Deep Submergence Special Mission E-frame**, 1993-94
  MNP $8   MIP $15

❑ **Wolf Ronski with Subterranean Special Mission E-frame**, 1993-94
  MNP $8   MIP $15

EXTREME GHOSTBUSTERS (TRENDMASTERS, 1997-98)

FIGURES

❑ **Eduardo**, 1997
  MNP $2   MIP $4

❑ **Eduardo, Deluxe edition**, 1997
  MNP $2   MIP $4

❑ **Egon**, 1997
  MNP $2   MIP $4

❑ **Egon, Deluxe edition**, 1997
  MNP $2   MIP $4

❑ **House Ghost**, 1997
  MNP $2   MIP $4

❑ **Kylie**, 1997
  MNP $2   MIP $4

❑ **Kylie, Deluxe edition**, 1997
  MNP $2   MIP $4

❑ **Mouth Critter**, 1997
  MNP $2   MIP $4

❑ **Roland**, 1997
  MNP $2   MIP $4

❑ **Roland, Deluxe edition**, 1997
  MNP $2   MIP $4

❑ **Sam Hain**, 1997
  MNP $2   MIP $4

❑ **Slimer**, 1997
  MNP $2   MIP $4

VEHICLES AND ACCESSORIES

❑ **Ecto 1**, 1997
  MNP $12   MIP $24

❑ **Eduardo with Motorcycle**, 1998
  MNP $4   MIP $8

❑ **Roland and Gyro-Copter**, 1998
  MNP $4   MIP $8

FANTASTIC FOUR (TOY BIZ, 1995)

10" BOXED FIGURES

❑ **Dr. Doom**, 1995, Toy Biz
  MNP $6   MIP $12

❑ **Human Torch**, 1995, Toy Biz
  MNP $6   MIP $12

❑ **Silver Surfer**, 1995, Toy Biz
  MNP $10   MIP $15

5" FIGURES

❑ **Annihilus**, 1995, Toy Biz
  MNP $3   MIP $10

❑ **Attuma**, 1995, Toy Biz
  MNP $3   MIP $10

❑ **Black Bolt**, 1995, Toy Biz
  MNP $3   MIP $10

❑ **Blastaar**, 1995, Toy Biz
  MNP $3   MIP $10

❑ **Dr. Doom**, 1995, Toy Biz
  MNP $3   MIP $10

❑ **Dragon Man**, 1995, Toy Biz
  MNP $3   MIP $10

❑ **Firelord**, 1995, Toy Biz
  MNP $3   MIP $10

❑ **Gorgon**, 1995, Toy Biz
  MNP $3   MIP $10

❑ **Human Torch**, 1995, Toy Biz
  MNP $3   MIP $10

❑ **Invisible Woman**, 1995, Toy Biz
  MNP $10   MIP $20

❑ **Mole Man**, 1995, Toy Biz
  MNP $5   MIP $10

❑ **Mr. Fantastic**, 1995, Toy Biz
  MNP $3   MIP $10

❑ **Namor the Sub-Mariner**, 1995, Toy Biz
  MNP $3   MIP $10

❑ **Silver Surfer**, 1995, Toy Biz
  MNP $6   MIP $10

❑ **Super Skrull**, 1995, Toy Biz
  MNP $3   MIP $10

❑ **Terrax**, 1995, Toy Biz
  MNP $3   MIP $10

❑ **Thanos**, 1995, Toy Biz
  MNP $3   MIP $10

❑ **Thing**, 1995, Toy Biz
  MNP $5   MIP $10

❑ **Thing II**, 1995, Toy Biz
  MNP $5   MIP $10

❑ **Triton**, 1995, Toy Biz
  MNP $3   MIP $10

ELECTRONIC 14" FIGURES

❑ **Galactus**, 1995, Toy Biz
  MNP $10   MIP $40

❑ **Talking Thing**, 1995, Toy Biz
  MNP $10   MIP $20

VEHICLES

❑ **Fantasticar**, 1995, Toy Biz
  MNP $15   MIP $35

❑ **Mr. Fantastic Sky Shuttle**, 1995, Toy Biz
  MNP $7   MIP $15

❑ **The Thing's Sky Cycle**, 1995, Toy Biz
  MNP $7   MIP $15

FLASH GORDON (MEGO, 1976)

9" FIGURES

❑ **Dale Arden**, 1976, Mego
  MNP $35   MIP $85

❑ **Dr. Zarkow**, 1976, Mego
  MNP $55   MIP $110

❑ **Flash Gordon**, 1976, Mego
  MNP $55   MIP $110

❑ **Ming**, 1976, Mego
  MNP $30   MIP $85

PLAY SETS

❑ **Flash Gordon Play Set**, 1976, Mego
  MNP $55   MIP $125

FLINTSTONES (MATTEL, 1994)

FIGURES

❑ **Betty and Bamm Bamm,** 1994
MNP $4   MIP $8

❑ **Big Shot Fred,** 1994
MNP $3   MIP $6

❑ **Evil Cliff Vandercave,** 1994
MNP $4   MIP $8

❑ **Filling Station Barney,** 1994
MNP $3   MIP $6

❑ **Hard Hat Fred,** 1994
MNP $3   MIP $6

❑ **Lawn Bowling Barney,** 1994
MNP $3   MIP $6

❑ **Licking Dino,** 1994
MNP $4   MIP $8

❑ **Wilma and Pebbles,** 1994
MNP $4   MIP $8

GARGOYLES (KENNER, 1995)

ACCESSORIES

❑ **Gargoyle Castle,** 1995, Kenner
MNP $20   MIP $40

❑ **Night Striker,** 1995, Kenner
MNP $10   MIP $20

❑ **Rippin' Rider Cycle,** 1995, Kenner
MNP $7   MIP $12

FIGURES

❑ **Battle Goliath,** 1995, Kenner
MNP $3   MIP $15

❑ **Broadway,** 1995, Kenner
MNP $3   MIP $15

❑ **Bronx,** 1995, Kenner
MNP $3   MIP $15

❑ **Brooklyn,** 1995, Kenner
MNP $4   MIP $15

❑ **Claw Climber Goliath,** 1995, Kenner
MNP $3   MIP $15

❑ **Demona,** 1995, Kenner
MNP $4   MIP $15

❑ **Lexington,** 1995, Kenner
MNP $3   MIP $15

❑ **Mighty Roar Goliath,** 1995, Kenner
MNP $5   MIP $15

❑ **Power Wing Goliath,** 1995, Kenner
MNP $5   MIP $15

❑ **Quick Strike Goliath,** 1995, Kenner
MNP $3   MIP $15

❑ **Steel Clan Robot,** 1995, Kenner
MNP $3   MIP $15

❑ **Stone Armor Goliath,** 1995, Kenner
MNP $5   MIP $15

❑ **Strike Hammer Macbeth,** 1995, Kenner
MNP $3   MIP $15

❑ **Xanatos,** 1995, Kenner
MNP $3   MIP $15

GENERATION X (TOY BIZ, 1995-96)

FRESHMAN, 5" FIGURES

❑ **Chamber,** 1995
MNP $2   MIP $6

❑ **Emplate,** 1995, Toy Biz
MNP $2   MIP $6

❑ **Jubilee,** 1995, Toy Biz
MNP $2   MIP $6

❑ **Penance,** 1995, Toy Biz
MNP $2   MIP $6

❑ **Phalanx,** 1995, Toy Biz
MNP $2   MIP $6

❑ **Skin,** 1995, Toy Biz
MNP $2   MIP $7

SOPHOMORE, 5" FIGURES

❑ **Banshee,** 1996, Toy Biz
MNP $3   MIP $8

❑ **Marrow,** 1996, Toy Biz
MNP $3   MIP $8

❑ **Mondo,** 1996, Toy Biz
MNP $3   MIP $8

❑ **Protector, The,** 1996, Toy Biz
MNP $3   MIP $8

❑ **White Queen,** 1996, Toy Biz
MNP $3   MIP $8

GHOST RIDER (TOY BOZ, 1995)

10" FIGURES

❑ **Blaze,** 1995
MNP $4   MIP $8

❑ **Ghost Rider,** 1995
MNP $4   MIP $8

❑ **Vengence,** 1995
MNP $4   MIP $8

5" FIGURES

❑ **Blackout,** 1995
MNP $2   MIP $4

❑ **Blaze,** 1995
MNP $2   MIP $4

❑ **Ghost Rider,** 1995
MNP $2   MIP $4

❑ **Skinner,** 1995
MNP $2   MIP $4

❑ **Vengence,** 1995
MNP $2   MIP $4

❑ **Zarathos,** 1995
MNP $2   MIP $4

FLAMIN' STUNT CYCLES WITH MOLDED-ON FIGURES

❑ **Blaze,** 1995
MNP $4   MIP $8

❑ **Ghost Rider,** 1995
MNP $4   MIP $8

❑ **Vengeance,** 1995
MNP $4   MIP $8

PLAY SETS

❑ **Ghost Rider Play Set,** 1995
MNP $8   MIP $20

SPIRIT OF VENGEANCE MOTORCYCLES AND FIGURES

❑ **Blaze,** 1995, Toy Biz
MNP $4   MIP $8

❑ **Ghost Rider,** 1995, Toy Biz
MNP $4   MIP $8

❑ **Vengeance,** 1995
MNP $4   MIP $8

GHOSTBUSTERS (KENNER, 1986-91)

1986

❑ **Bad to the Bone Ghost,** 1986-91, Kenner
MNP $5   MIP $15

❑ **Banshee Bomber Gooper Ghost with Ecto-Plazm,** 1986-91, Kenner
MNP $5   MIP $15

❑ **Bug-Eye Ghost,** 1986-91, Kenner
MNP $5   MIP $15

❑ **Ecto-1,** 1986-91, Kenner
MNP $35   MIP $80

❑ **Egon Spengler & Gulper Ghost,** 1986-91, Kenner, 5-1/4" tall
MNP $6   MIP $15

❑ **Firehouse Headquarters,** 1986-91, Kenner
MNP $25   MIP $50

❑ **Ghost Pooper,** 1986-91, Kenner
MNP $5   MIP $10

❑ **Ghost Zapper,** 1986-91, Kenner
MNP $5   MIP $15

❑ **Gooper Ghost Sludge Bucket,** 1986-91, Kenner
MNP $5   MIP $15

❑ **Gooper Ghost Squisher with Ecto-Plazm,** 1986-91, Kenner
MNP $5   MIP $15

❑ **H2 Ghost,** 1986-91, Kenner
MNP $5   MIP $15

❑ **Peter Venkman & Grabber Ghost,** 1986-91, Kenner, 5-1/4" tall
MNP $6   MIP $15

❑ **Proton Pack,** 1986-91, Kenner
MNP $20   MIP $40

❑ **Ray Stantz & Wrapper Ghost,** 1986-91, Kenner, 5-1/4" tall
MNP $6   MIP $15

❑ **Slimer Plush Figure, 13",** 1986-91, Kenner, 13" tall
MNP $20   MIP $35

ACTION FIGURES

❏ **Slimer with Pizza,** 1986-91, Kenner
MNP $20   MIP $40

❏ **Stay-Puft Marshmallow Man Plush, 13",** 1986-91, Kenner, 13-3/4" tall plush
MNP $15   MIP $30

❏ **Winston Zeddmore & Chomper Ghost,** 1986-91, Kenner, 5-1/4" tall
MNP $7   MIP $18

1988

❏ **Brain Blaster Ghost Haunted Human,** 1986-91, Kenner
MNP $5   MIP $15

❏ **Ecto-2 Helicopter,** 1986-91, Kenner
MNP $5   MIP $15

❏ **Fright Feature Egon,** 1986-91, Kenner
MNP $5   MIP $15

❏ **Fright Feature Janine Melnitz,** 1986-91, Kenner
MNP $5   MIP $15

❏ **Fright Feature Peter,** 1986-91, Kenner
MNP $5   MIP $15

❏ **Fright Feature Ray,** 1986-91, Kenner
MNP $5   MIP $15

❏ **Fright Feature Winston,** 1986-91, Kenner
MNP $5   MIP $15

❏ **Gooper Ghost Slimer,** 1986-91, Kenner
MNP $12   MIP $25

❏ **Granny Gross Haunted Human,** 1986-91, Kenner
MNP $5   MIP $15

❏ **Hard Hat Horror Haunted Human,** 1986-91, Kenner
MNP $5   MIP $15

❏ **Highway Haunter,** 1986-91, Kenner
MNP $10   MIP $20

❏ **Mail Fraud Haunted Human,** 1986-91, Kenner
MNP $5   MIP $15

❏ **Mini Ghost Mini-Gooper,** 1986-91, Kenner
MNP $5   MIP $10

❏ **Mini Ghost Mini-Shooter,** 1986-91, Kenner
MNP $5   MIP $10

❏ **Mini Ghost Mini-Trap,** 1986-91, Kenner
MNP $5   MIP $10

❏ **Pull Speed Ahead Ghost,** 1986-91, Kenner
MNP $5   MIP $15

❏ **Terror Trash Haunted Human,** 1986-91, Kenner
MNP $5   MIP $15

❏ **Tombstone Tackle Haunted Human,** 1986-91, Kenner
MNP $5   MIP $15

❏ **X-Cop Haunted Human,** 1986-91, Kenner
MNP $5   MIP $15

1989

❏ **Dracula,** 1986-91, Kenner
MNP $5   MIP $15

❏ **Ecto-3,** 1986-91, Kenner
MNP $5   MIP $15

❏ **Fearsome Flush,** 1986-91, Kenner
MNP $5   MIP $10

❏ **Frankenstein,** 1986-91, Kenner
MNP $3   MIP $15

❏ **Hunchback,** 1986-91, Kenner
MNP $3   MIP $15

❏ **Mummy,** 1986-91, Kenner
MNP $3   MIP $15

❏ **Screaming Hero Egon,** 1986-91, Kenner
MNP $5   MIP $15

❏ **Screaming Hero Janine Melnitz,** 1986-91, Kenner
MNP $5   MIP $15

❏ **Screaming Hero Peter,** 1986-91, Kenner
MNP $5   MIP $15

❏ **Screaming Hero Ray,** 1986-91, Kenner
MNP $5   MIP $15

❏ **Screaming Hero Winston,** 1986-91, Kenner
MNP $5   MIP $15

❏ **Slimer with Proton Pack, red or blue,** 1986-91, Kenner, red or blue
MNP $15   MIP $35

❏ **Super Fright Egon with Slimy Spider,** 1986-91, Kenner
MNP $5   MIP $15

❏ **Super Fright Janine with Boo Fish Ghost,** 1986-91, Kenner
MNP $5   MIP $15

❏ **Super Fright Peter Venkman & Snake Head,** 1986-91, Kenner
MNP $5   MIP $15

❏ **Super Fright Ray,** 1986-91, Kenner
MNP $5   MIP $15

❏ **Super Fright Winston Zeddmore & Meanie Wienie,** 1986-91, Kenner
MNP $5   MIP $15

❏ **Wolfman,** 1986-91, Kenner
MNP $5   MIP $15

❏ **Zombie,** 1986-91, Kenner
MNP $5   MIP $15

1990

❏ **Ecto Bomber with Bomber Ghost,** 1986-91, Kenner
MNP $5   MIP $15

❏ **Ecto-1A with Ambulance Ghost,** 1986-91, Kenner
MNP $20   MIP $40

❏ **Ghost Sweeper,** 1986-91, Kenner, vehicle in box
MNP $5   MIP $15

❏ **Gobblin' Goblin Nasty Neck,** 1986-91, Kenner
MNP $6   MIP $15

❏ **Gobblin' Goblin Terrible Teeth,** 1986-91, Kenner, boxed action figure
MNP $6   MIP $15

❏ **Gobblin' Goblin Terror Tongue,** 1986-91, Kenner, boxed action figure
MNP $6   MIP $15

❏ **Slimed Hero Egon,** 1986-91, Kenner
MNP $5   MIP $15

❏ **Slimed Hero Louis Tully & Four Eyed Ghost,** 1986-91, Kenner
MNP $5   MIP $15

❏ **Slimed Hero Peter Venkman & Tooth Ghost,** 1986-91, Kenner
MNP $5   MIP $15

❏ **Slimed Hero Ray Stantz & Vapor Ghost,** 1986-91, Kenner
MNP $5   MIP $15

❏ **Slimed Hero Winston,** 1986-91, Kenner, boxed action figure
MNP $5   MIP $15

1991

❏ **Ecto-Glow Egon,** 1986-91, Kenner
MNP $10   MIP $30

❏ **Ecto-Glow Louis Tully,** 1986-91, Kenner
MNP $10   MIP $30

❏ **Ecto-Glow Peter,** 1986-91, Kenner
MNP $10   MIP $30

❏ **Ecto-Glow Ray,** 1986-91, Kenner
MNP $10   MIP $30

❏ **Ecto-Glow Winston Zeddmore,** 1986-91, Kenner
MNP $10   MIP $30

GHOSTBUSTERS, FILMATION (SCHAPER, 1986)

❏ **Time Hopper Vehicle,** 1986, Schaper
MNP $10   MIP $15

❏ **Tracy,** 1986, Schaper
MNP $10   MIP $15

FIGURES

❏ **Belfry and Brat-A-Rat,** 1986, Schaper
MNP $10   MIP $15

❏ **Bone Troller,** 1986, Schaper
MNP $10   MIP $15

❏ **Eddie,** 1986, Schaper
MNP $10   MIP $15

❏ **Fangster,** 1986, Schaper
MNP $10   MIP $15

❏ **Fib Face,** 1986, Schaper
MNP $10   MIP $15

❏ **Futura,** 1986, Schaper
MNP $10   MIP $15

❏ **Ghost Popper Ghost Buggy,** 1986, Schaper
MNP $20   MIP $40

❑ **Haunter,** 1986, Schaper
MNP $10 MIP $15

❑ **Jake,** 1986, Schaper
MNP $10 MIP $15

❑ **Jessica,** 1986, Schaper
MNP $10 MIP $15

❑ **Mysteria,** 1986, Schaper
MNP $10 MIP $15

❑ **Prime Evil,** 1986, Schaper
MNP $10 MIP $15

❑ **Scare Scooter Vehicle,** 1986, Schaper
MNP $10 MIP $20

❑ **Scared Stiff,** 1986, Schaper
MNP $6 MIP $15

❑ **Time Hopper Vehicle,** 1986, Schaper
MNP $10 MIP $15

❑ **Tracy,** 1986, Schaper
MNP $10 MIP $15

GODZILLA (TRENDMASTERS, 1998-PRESENT)

FIGURES

❑ **Baby X Baby Godzilla,** 1998-Present
MNP $3 MIP $8

❑ **Capture Net Phillipe,** 1996-Present
MNP $2 MIP $8

❑ **Claw Slashing Baby Godzilla,** 1996-Present
MNP $3 MIP $6

❑ **Combat Claw Godzilla,** 1996-Present
MNP $8 MIP $16

❑ **Double Blast O'Neil,** 1998-present
MNP $3 MIP $7

❑ **Fang Bite Godzilla,** 1998-present
MNP $3 MIP $7

❑ **Grapple Gear Nick,** 1998-present
MNP $3 MIP $7

❑ **Hammer Tail Baby Godzilla Hatchling,** 1998-present
MNP $3 MIP $7

❑ **Living Godzilla,** 1998-present
MNP $10 MIP $25

❑ **Monster Claw Baby Godzilla Hatching,** 1998-present
MNP $3 MIP $7

❑ **Nuclear Strike Godzilla vs. Hornet Jet,** 1998-present
MNP $3 MIP $7

❑ **Power Shield Jean-Luc,** 1998-present
MNP $3 MIP $7

❑ **Razor Bite Godzilla,** 1998-present
MNP $10 MIP $25

❑ **Razor Fang Baby Godzilla,** 1998-present
MNP $3 MIP $7

❑ **Shatter Blast Godzilla vs. Rocket Launcher,** 1998-present
MNP $3 MIP $7

❑ **Shatter Tail Godzilla,** 1998-present
MNP $7 MIP $15

❑ **Spike Jaw Baby Godzilla Hatchling,** 1998-present
MNP $3 MIP $7

❑ **Supreme Godzilla,** 1998-present
MNP $15 MIP $30

❑ **Tail Thrasher Baby Godzilla,** 1998-present
MNP $3 MIP $7

❑ **Thunder Tail Godzilla,** 1998-present
MNP $7 MIP $15

❑ **Ultimate Godzilla,** 1998-present
MNP $12 MIP $30

❑ **Ultra Attack Animal,** 1998-present
MNP $3 MIP $7

VEHICLES

❑ **All-Terrain Vehicle with figure,** 1998-present
MNP $7 MIP $15

❑ **Apache Attack Copter,** 1998-present
MNP $10 MIP $20

❑ **Battle Bike with figure,** 1998-present
MNP $7 MIP $15

❑ **Battle Blaster with figure,** 1998-present
MNP $7 MIP $15

❑ **Combat Cannon with figure,** 1998-present
MNP $7 MIP $15

❑ **Thunderblast Tank,** 1998-present
MNP $7 MIP $15

GODZILLA WARS (TRENDMASTERS, 1996)

FIGURES

❑ **Battra,** 1996
MNP $4 MIP $8

❑ **Biollante,** 1996
MNP $4 MIP $8

❑ **Gigan,** 1996
MNP $4 MIP $8

❑ **Moguera,** 1996
MNP $5 MIP $10

❑ **Space Godzilla,** 1996
MNP $5 MIP $10

❑ **Supercharged Godzilla,** 1996
MNP $4 MIP $8

GODZILLA: KING OF THE MONSTERS

10" FIGURES

❑ **Ghidorah,** 1995
MNP $4 MIP $10

❑ **Ghidorah, walking,** 1995
MNP $6 MIP $12

❑ **Godzilla,** 1995
MNP $4 MIP $10

❑ **Godzilla, walking,** 1995
MNP $7 MIP $15

❑ **Mecha-Ghidora,** 1995
MNP $6 MIP $12

❑ **Mecha-Godzilla,** 1995
MNP $6 MIP $12

❑ **Mothra,** 1995
MNP $8 MIP $16

❑ **Rodan,** 1995
MNP $4 MIP $10

FIGURES

❑ **Battra,** 1995
MNP $4 MIP $8

❑ **Biollante,** 1995
MNP $4 MIP $8

❑ **Ghidorah, boxed,** 1995
MNP $4 MIP $8

❑ **Ghidorah, carded,** 1995
MNP $5 MIP $10

❑ **Gigan,** 1995
MNP $5 MIP $10

❑ **Godzilla, boxed,** 1995
MNP $4 MIP $8

❑ **Mecha-Ghidorah, boxed,** 1995
MNP $4 MIP $8

❑ **Mecha-Ghidorah, carded,** 1995
MNP $3 MIP $6

❑ **Mecha-Godzilla, boxed,** 1995
MNP $4 MIP $8

❑ **Mecha-Godzilla, carded,** 1995
MNP $3 MIP $6

❑ **Moguera,** 1995
MNP $4 MIP $10

❑ **Mothra, boxed,** 1995
MNP $5 MIP $10

❑ **Mothra, carded,** 1995
MNP $4 MIP $8

❑ **Rodan, boxed,** 1995
MNP $4 MIP $8

❑ **Rodan, carded,** 1995
MNP $3 MIP $6

GREATEST AMERICAN HERO, THE (MEGO, 1981)

VEHICLES

❑ **Convertible Bug with Ralph and Bill figures,** 1981
MNP $150 MIP $450

HAPPY DAYS (MEGO, 1978)

FIGURES

❑ **Fonzie, boxed,** 1978, Mego
MNP $30 MIP $100

❑ **Fonzie, carded,** 1978, Mego
MNP $30 MIP $75

❑ **Potsie, carded,** 1978, Mego
MNP $30 MIP $75

ACTION FIGURES

(Lenny Lee)

❏ **Ralph, carded,** 1978, Mego, Interesting likeness of Ralph "The Mouth" by Mego. Of course, it's just amazing how many licenses Mego was able to secure. It seems as though every possible TV show and Movie had some toy representing it made by the company
  MNP $30 **MIP** $75

❏ **Richie, carded,** 1978, Mego
  MNP $30 **MIP** $75

PLAY SETS

❏ **Fonzie's Garage Play Set, 1978,** 1978, Mego
  MNP $60 **MIP** $150

VEHICLES

❏ **Fonzie's Jalopy, 1978,** 1978, Mego
  MNP $40 **MIP** $80

❏ **Fonzie's Motorcycle, 1978,** 1978, Mego
  MNP $40 **MIP** $80

HE-MAN (MATTEL, 1989-1991)

FIGURES

❏ **Artilla,** 1989-91
  MNP $7 **MIP** $15

❏ **Battle Blade Skelator,** 1989-91
  MNP $7 **MIP** $15

❏ **Battle Punch He-Man,** 1989-91
  MNP $7 **MIP** $15

❏ **Brakk,** 1989-91
  MNP $6 **MIP** $12

❏ **Butthead,** 1989-91
  MNP $7 **MIP** $15

❏ **Disks of Doom Skelator,** 1989-91
  MNP $6 **MIP** $14

❏ **Flipshot,** 1989-91
  MNP $6 **MIP** $12

❏ **Flogg,** 1989-91
  MNP $6 **MIP** $12

❏ **He-Man,** 1989-91
  MNP $6 **MIP** $12

❏ **He-Man with Flogg,** 1989-91
  MNP $7 **MIP** $18

❏ **He-Man with Skeletor,** 1989-91
  MNP $7 **MIP** $20

❏ **He-Man with Slush Head,** 1989-91
  MNP $7 **MIP** $20

❏ **Hoove,** 1989-91
  MNP $8 **MIP** $22

❏ **Hydron,** 1989-91
  MNP $6 **MIP** $12

❏ **Kalamarr,** 1989-91
  MNP $6 **MIP** $12

❏ **Karatti,** 1989-91
  MNP $6 **MIP** $12

❏ **Kayo,** 1989-91
  MNP $6 **MIP** $12

❏ **Lizorr,** 1989-91
  MNP $6 **MIP** $14

❏ **Nocturna,** 1989-91
  MNP $6 **MIP** $14

❏ **Optikk,** 1989-91
  MNP $6 **MIP** $14

❏ **Quakke,** 1989-91
  MNP $6 **MIP** $14

❏ **Skelator,** 1989-91
  MNP $6 **MIP** $12

❏ **Slush Head,** 1989-91
  MNP $6 **MIP** $12

❏ **Spin-Fist Hydron,** 1989-91
  MNP $6 **MIP** $14

❏ **Spinwit,** 1989-91
  MNP $6 **MIP** $14

❏ **Staghorn,** 1989-91
  MNP $6 **MIP** $14

❏ **Thunder Punch He-Man,** 1989-91
  MNP $8 **MIP** $20

❏ **Too-Tall hoove,** 1989-91
  MNP $15 **MIP** $35

❏ **Tuskador,** 1989-91
  MNP $6 **MIP** $14

❏ **Vizar,** 1989-91
  MNP $6 **MIP** $14

VEHICLES

❏ **AstroSub,** 1989-91
  MNP $6 **MIP** $14

❏ **Battle Bird,** 1989-91
  MNP $4 **MIP** $12

❏ **Bolajet,** 1989-91
  MNP $4 **MIP** $12

❏ **Doomcopter,** 1989-91
  MNP $4 **MIP** $12

❏ **Sagitar,** 1989-91
  MNP $6 **MIP** $14

❏ **Shuttle Pod,** 1989-91
  MNP $4 **MIP** $12

❏ **Starship Eterna,** 1989-91
  MNP $25 **MIP** $65

❏ **Terroclaw,** 1989-91
  MNP $6 **MIP** $14

❏ **Terrotread,** 1989-91
  MNP $6 **MIP** $14

HERCULES: THE LEGEND CONTINUES (TOY BIZ, 1995-97)

DELUXE 10" FIGURES

❏ **Hercules and Xena,** 1995-96
  MNP $20 **MIP** $40

FIGURES

❏ **Ares, Detachable Weapons of War,** 1995-96
  MNP $3 **MIP** $5

❏ **Centaur, Bug Horse Kick,** 1995-96
  MNP $3 **MIP** $5

❏ **Hercules I, Iron Spiked Spinning Mace,** 1995-96
  MNP $3 **MIP** $5

❏ **Hercules II, Archery Combat Set,** 1995-96
  MNP $3 **MIP** $5

❏ **Hercules III, Herculean Assault Blades,** 1995-96
  MNP $3 **MIP** $6

❏ **Hercules with Chain Breaking Strength,** 1995-96
  MNP $3 **MIP** $5

❏ **Hercules, Swash Buckling,** 1995-96
  MNP $3 **MIP** $5

❏ **Iolaus, Catapult Battle Gear,** 1995-96
  MNP $3 **MIP** $5

❏ **Minotaur, Immobilizing Sludge Mask,** 1995-96
  MNP $3 **MIP** $6

❏ **Mole-Man, Exploding Body,** 1995-96
  MNP $3 **MIP** $5

❏ **She-Demon, Stone Strike Tail,** 1995-96
  MNP $4 **MIP** $8

❏ **Xena, Warrior Princess Weaponry,** 1995-96
  MNP $5 **MIP** $25

MONSTERS

❏ **Cerberus,** 1995-96
  MNP $4 **MIP** $10

❏ **Echidna,** 1995-96
  MNP $4 **MIP** $10

❏ **Graegus,** 1995-96
  MNP $4 **MIP** $10

❏ **Hydra,** 1995-96
  MNP $4 **MIP** $10

❏ **Labyrinth Snake,** 1995-96
  MNP $4 **MIP** $10

❏ **Stymphalian Bird,** 1995-96
  MNP $4 **MIP** $10

PLAY SETS

❏ Hercules Tower of Power Play Set, 1995-96

  MNP $4 MIP $10

HERCULES: THE LEGENDARY JOURNEYS (TOY BIZ, 1995-97)

DELUXE 10" FIGURES

❏ Hercules with bladed shield and sword dagger, 1997

  MNP $8 MIP $20

❏ Xena with two sets of body armor, 1997

  MNP $8 MIP $20

LEGENDARY WARRIOR TWIN PACKS, 5" FIGURES

❏ Hercules and Iolaus, 1997

  MNP $8 MIP $20

❏ Hercules and Xena, 1997

  MNP $8 MIP $20

❏ Xena and Gabrielle, 1997

  MNP $10 MIP $40

LEGENDARY WARRIORS, 5" FIGURES

❏ Hercules, Mace Hurling Hercules, 1997

  MNP $3 MIP $8

❏ Iolaus, Catapult Back-pack Iolaus, 1997

  MNP $4 MIP $12

❏ Nessus, Leg Kicking Centaur, 1997

  MNP $3 MIP $8

❏ Xena, Temptress Costume Xena, 1997

  MNP $4 MIP $12

MONSTERS, 6" FIGURES

❏ Cerberus, 1997

  MNP $3 MIP $10

❏ Graegus, 1997

  MNP $3 MIP $10

❏ Hydra, 1997

  MNP $3 MIP $10

MT. OLYMPUS GAMES, 5" FIGURES

❏ Atlanta, Spear Shooting Weaponry Rack, 1997

  MNP $4 MIP $12

❏ Hercules, Discus Launcher, 1997

  MNP $3 MIP $8

❏ Mesomorph, Shield Attack Action, 1997

  MNP $3 MIP $8

❏ Salmoneus, Light-up Olympic Torch, 1997

  MNP $3 MIP $8

HONEY WEST (GILBERT, 1965)

ACCESSORIES

❏ Formal Outfit, Gilbert, 1965

  MNP $55 MIP $110

❏ Honey West Accessory Set: cap-firing pistol, binoculars, shoes and glasses, 1965, Gilbert

  MNP $45 MIP $85

❏ Honey West Accessory Set: telephone purse, lipstick, handcuffs and tele-scop, Gilbert, 1965

  MNP $45 MIP $85

❏ Karate Outfit, Gilbert, 1965

  MNP $50 MIP $100

❏ Pet Set with Ocelot, Gilbert, 1965

  MNP $60 MIP $100

❏ Secret Agent Outfit, Gilbert, 1965

  MNP $50 MIP $95

FIGURES

❏ Honey West Doll, 12", 1965, Gilbert

  MNP $175 MIP $325

HOOK (MATTEL, 1991-92)

DELUXE FIGURES

❏ Captain Hook, Skull Armor, 1991-92

  MNP $10 MIP $25

❏ Lost Boy Attack Croc, 1991-92

  MNP $8 MIP $18

❏ Pete Pan, Learn to Fly, 1991-92

  MNP $10 MIP $25

FIGURES

❏ Captain Hook, Multi-blade, 1991-92

  MNP $4 MIP $10

❏ Captain Hook, Swiss Army, 1991-92

  MNP $8 MIP $18

❏ Captain Hook, Tall Terror, 1991-92

  MNP $4 MIP $10

❏ Lost Boy Ace, 1991-92

  MNP $3 MIP $10

❏ Lost Boy Ruffio, 1991-92, Mattel

  MNP $3 MIP $10

❏ Lost Boy Thud Bud, 1991-92

  MNP $8 MIP $18

❏ Peter Pan, Air Attack, 1991-92

  MNP $4 MIP $10

❏ Peter Pan, Battle Swing, 1991-92

  MNP $5 MIP $15

❏ Peter Pan, Food Fighting, 1991-92

  MNP $5 MIP $15

❏ Peter Pan, Swashbuckling, 1991-92

  MNP $4 MIP $10

❏ Pirate Bill Jukes, 1991-92

  MNP $4 MIP $10

❏ Pirate Smee, 1991-92

  MNP $5 MIP $12

VEHICLES

❏ Lost Boy Attack Raft, 1991-92

  MNP $8 MIP $20

❏ Lost Boy Strike Tank, 1991-92

  MNP $8 MIP $20

INCREDIBLE HULK, THE (TOY BIZ, 1996-97)

6" FIGURES

❏ Abomination, Toxic Blaster, 1996

  MNP $5 MIP $12

❏ Gray Hulk Battle Damaged, 1996

  MNP $4 MIP $10

❏ Leader, Anti-Hulk Armor, 1996

  MNP $4 MIP $10

❏ Savage Hulk, Transforming Action, 1996

  MNP $4 MIP $10

❏ She Hulk, Gamma Cross Bow, 1996

  MNP $5 MIP $12

OUTCASTS, 5" FIGURES

❏ Battle Hulk, Mutant Outcast, 1997

  MNP $2 MIP $6

❏ Chainsaw, Gamma Outcast Bat, 1997

  MNP $3 MIP $7

❏ Leader-Hulk Metamorphosized, Gargoyle Sidekick, 1997

  MNP $3 MIP $7

❏ Two-Head, Gamma Outcast Kangaroo-Rat, 1997

  MNP $3 MIP $7

❏ Wendingo, Gamma Outcast Rattle-snake, 1997

  MNP $3 MIP $7

PLAY SETS

❏ Gamma Ray Trap, 1997

  MNP $3 MIP $10

❏ Steel Body Trap, 1997

  MNP $3 MIP $10

SMASH AND CRASH, 5" FIGURES

❏ Battle-Damaged Hulk with Restraints and Smash Out Action, 1997

  MNP $3 MIP $8

❏ Doc Samson, Omega with Missile Firing Action, 1997

  MNP $3 MIP $8

❏ Incredible Hulk, Crash out Action, 1997

  MNP $3 MIP $8

❏ Leader, Evil Robot Drone with Missile Firing Action, 1997

  MNP $3 MIP $8

❏ Zzzax with Energy Trap, 1997

  MNP $3 MIP $8

ACTION FIGURES

TRANSFORMATIONS, 6" FIGURES

(KP Photo)

❑ **Absorbing Man, Breakaway Safe and Wrecking Ball**, 1997, Includes accessories

MNP $3   MIP $8

❑ **Hulk 2099, Futuristic Clip-on Weapons**, 1997

MNP $3   MIP $8

(KP Photo)

❑ **Maestro, Fallen Hero Armor**, 1997, Includes Captain America's broken shield, and a belt featuring the masks of Iron Man and other Marvel characters

MNP $3   MIP $8

❑ **Smart Hulk, Gamma Blaster Backpack**, 1997

MNP $3   MIP $8

INDEPENDENCE DAY (TRENDMASTERS, 1996)

FIGURES

❑ **Alien Attacker Pilot**, 1996, Trendmasters

MNP $5   MIP $10

❑ **Alien in Bio Chamber**, 1996, Trendmasters

MNP $8   MIP $12

❑ **Alien Science Officer**, 1996, Trendmasters

MNP $5   MIP $10

❑ **Alien Shock Trooper**, 1996, Trendmasters

MNP $5   MIP $10

❑ **Alien Supreme Commander**, 1996, Trendmasters

MNP $15   MIP $25

❑ **David Levinson**, 1996, Trendmasters

MNP $5   MIP $10

❑ **President Thomas Whitmore**, 1996, Trendmasters

MNP $5   MIP $10

❑ **Steve Hiller**, 1996, Trendmasters

MNP $5   MIP $10

❑ **Ultimate Alien Commander**, 1996, Trendmasters, FAO Schwarz Exclusive

MNP $20   MIP $35

❑ **Weapons Expert**, 1996, Trendmasters

MNP $10   MIP $20

❑ **Zero Gravity**, 1996, Trendmasters

MNP $8   MIP $15

INDIANA JONES (TOYS MCCOY, 1999)

12" FIGURES

❑ **Arabian Horse**, 1999

MNP $150   MIP $450

❑ **Indiana Jones**, 1999

MNP $250   MIP $750

INDIANA JONES AND THE TEMPLE OF DOOM (LJN, 1984)

FIGURES

(Toy Shop File Photo)

❑ **Giant Thugee**, 1984, On the right

MNP $45   MIP $75

(Toy Shop File Photo)

❑ **Indiana Jones**, 1984, Shown in the center

MNP $65   MIP $150

(Toy Shop File Photo)

❑ **Mola Ram**, 1984, On the left. These figures didn't enjoy as much popularity at the time, probably reflecting the public's mood about the film

MNP $55   MIP $80

INDIANA JONES, THE ADVENTURES OF (KENNER, 1982-1983)

FIGURES

❑ **Belloq**, 1982-83

MNP $25   MIP $65

❑ **Belloq in Ceremonial Robe, mail away**, 1982-83

MNP $20   MIP $45

❑ **Belloq in Ceremonial Robe Carded**, 1982-83

MNP $20   MIP $500

❑ **Cairo Swordsman**, 1982-83

MNP $15   MIP $40

❑ **German Mechanic**, 1982-83

MNP $25   MIP $75

❑ **Indiana Jones in German Uniform**, 1982-83

MNP $25   MIP $90

(Toy Shop File Photo)

❑ **Indiana Jones with whip**, 1982-83, Includes fedora, leather jacket and pistol, too

MNP $50   MIP $250

(Toy Shop File Photo)

❑ **Indiana Jones, 12",** 1982-83, Includes leather jacket, fedora, bullwhip and pistol

    MNP $150   **MIP $450**

(Lenny Lee)

❑ **Marion Ravenwood,** 1982-83, Kenner, Includes small monkee

    MNP $100   **MIP $350**

❑ **Sallah,** 1982-83

    MNP $30   **MIP $90**

(Lenny Lee)

❑ **Toht,** 1982-83, Kenner, Fully poseable, black plastic overcoat and hat. Packaging has mail-in offer for ceremonial Beloq figure

    MNP $15   **MIP $40**

PLAY SETS

(Toy Shop File Photo)

❑ **Map Room Play Set,** 1982-83
    MNP $35   **MIP $90**

❑ **Streets of Cairo Play Set,** 1982-83
    MNP $35   **MIP $90**

❑ **Well of Souls Play Set,** 1982-83
    MNP $50   **MIP $125**

VEHICLES AND ACCESSORIES

❑ **Arabian Horse,** 1982-83
    MNP $75   **MIP $250**

❑ **Convoy Truck,** 1982-83
    MNP $35   **MIP $80**

INSPECTOR GADGET (GALOOB, 1984)

12" FIGURE

❑ **Inspector Gadget,** 1984
    MNP $55   **MIP $110**

INSPECTOR GADGET (TIGER TOYS, 1992)

FIGURES

❑ **Dr. Claw,** 1992
    MNP $8   **MIP $20**

❑ **Inspector Gadget that Falls Apart,** 1992
    MNP $5   **MIP $15**

❑ **Inspector Gadget that Squirts Water,** 1992
    MNP $5   **MIP $15**

❑ **Inspector Gadget with Expanding Arms,** 1992
    MNP $4   **MIP $12**

❑ **Inspector Gadget with Expanding Legs,** 1992
    MNP $5   **MIP $15**

❑ **Inspector Gadget with Snap Open Hat,** 1992
    MNP $5   **MIP $15**

❑ **Inspector Gadget with Telescopic Neck,** 1992
    MNP $5   **MIP $15**

❑ **MAD Agent with Bazooka,** 1992
    MNP $8   **MIP $20**

❑ **Penny and Brain,** 1992
    MNP $8   **MIP $20**

VEHICLES

❑ **Gadgetmoile,** 1992
    MNP $10   **MIP $30**

IRON MAN (TOY BIZ, 1995-96)

5" FIGURES, 1995

❑ **Backlash, Nunchaku and Whip-cracking Action,** 1995
    MNP $3   **MIP $8**

❑ **Blizzard, Ice-Fist Punch,** 1995
    MNP $7   **MIP $15**

❑ **Century, Cape and Battle Staff,** 1995
    MNP $3   **MIP $8**

❑ **Dreadknight, Firing Lance Action,** 1995
    MNP $3   **MIP $8**

❑ **Grey Gargoyle, Stone Hurling Action,** 1995
    MNP $3   **MIP $8**

❑ **Hawkeye, Bow and Arrow,** 1995
    MNP $7   **MIP $15**

❑ **Hulkbuster Iron Man, Removable Armor,** 1995
    MNP $3   **MIP $8**

❑ **Iron Man Arctic Armor, Removable Armor and Launching Claw Action,** 1995
    MNP $3   **MIP $8**

❑ **Iron Man Hologram,** 1995, Toy Biz
    MNP $3   **MIP $8**

❑ **Iron Man Space Armor, Power-lift Space Pack,** 1995, Toy Biz
    MNP $3   **MIP $8**

❑ **Iron Man Stealth Armor,** 1995, Toy Biz
    MNP $3   **MIP $8**

❑ **Iron Man, Hydro Armor,** 1995
    MNP $4   **MIP $10**

❑ **Iron Man, Plasma Cannon Missile Launcher,** 1995
    MNP $3   **MIP $8**

❑ **Mandarin, Light-up Power Rigs,** 1995
    MNP $3   **MIP $8**

❑ **Modok, Energy Brain Blasts,** 1995, Toy Biz
    MNP $3   **MIP $8**

❑ **Spider-Woman, Psisonic Web Hurling Action,** 1995
    MNP $7   **MIP $15**

❑ **Titanium Man, Retractable Blade Action,** 1995
    MNP $5   **MIP $12**

❑ **Tony Stark, Armor Carrying Suitcase,** 1995
    MNP $3   **MIP $8**

❑ **US Agent, Firing Shield Action,** 1995
    MNP $15   **MIP $35**

❏ **War Machine, Shoulder-Mount Cannons,** 1995
MNP $3   MIP $8

❏ **Whirlwind, Whirling Battle Action,** 1995
MNP $5   MIP $12

5" FIGURES, 1996

❏ **Crimson Dynamo,** 1996
MNP $3   MIP $8

❏ **Iron Man Inferno Armor,** 1996
MNP $3   MIP $8

❏ **Iron Man Lava Armor,** 1996
MNP $3   MIP $8

❏ **Iron Man Magnetic Armor,** 1996
MNP $3   MIP $8

❏ **Iron Man Radiation Armor,** 1996
MNP $3   MIP $8

❏ **Iron Man Samurai Armor,** 1996
MNP $3   MIP $8

❏ **Iron Man Subterranean Armor,** 1996
MNP $3   MIP $8

❏ **War Machine 2,** 1996
MNP $4   MIP $10

DELUXE 10" FIGURES

❏ **Iron Man,** 1995
MNP $4   MIP $12

❏ **Mandarin,** 1995
MNP $4   MIP $12

❏ **War Machine,** 1995
MNP $4   MIP $12

DELUXE DRAGONS

❏ **Argent,** 1995
MNP $7   MIP $15

❏ **Aureus,** 1995
MNP $7   MIP $15

❏ **FinFang Foom,** 1995
MNP $7   MIP $15

ISLAND OF MISFIT TOYS

FIGURES

❏ **Abominable Snowman,** 2002, Playing Mantis
n/a   MIP $8

(KP Photo)

❏ **Clarice,** 2002, Playing Mantis, Includes two racoons and two rabbits
n/a   MIP $8

(KP Photo)

❏ **Hermey,** 2002, Playing Mantis, With a hat, book, tools and two of Bumble's teeth
n/a   MIP $8

(KP Photo)

❏ **Rudolph,** 2002, Playing Mantis, Features a light-up nose and includes misfit doll
n/a   MIP $8

(KP Photo)

❏ **Sam,** 2002, Playing Mantis, With removeable hat, banjo and umbrella
n/a   MIP $8

(KP Photo)

❏ **Santa Claus,** 2002, Playing Mantis, Features a removeable hat, toy bag and spotted elephant
n/a   MIP $8

(KP Photo)

❏ **Yukon Cornelius,** 2002, Playing Mantis, In familiar bright orange hat, blue jacket and snowshoes. Includes knife, pick and hammer
n/a   MIP $8

JAMES BOND: MOONRAKER (MEGO, 1979)

12" FIGURES

❏ **Drax,** 1979, Mego
MNP $150   MIP $200

❏ **Holly,** 1979, Mego
MNP $150   MIP $200

❏ **James Bond,** 1979, Mego
MNP $125   MIP $150

❏ **James Bond, deluxe version,** 1979, Mego
MNP $350   MIP $500

❏ **Jaws,** 1979, Mego
MNP $300   MIP $500

FIGURES

❏ **Drax,** 1979
MNP $45   MIP $100

❏ **Holly Goodhead,** 1979
MNP $45   MIP $100

❏ **James Bond,** 1979
MNP $45   MIP $100

❏ **Jaws,** 1979
MNP $200   MIP $525

JAMES BOND: SECRET AGENT 007 (GILBERT, 1965-66)

FIGURES

❏ **James Bond,** 1965-66
MNP $190   MIP $400

❑ **Oddjob**, 1965-66
   MNP $200   MIP $550

JANIS JOPLIN (MCFARLANE, 2000)

FIGURES

❑ **Janis Joplin**, 2000
   MNP $5   MIP $15

JOHNNY HERO (ROSKO, 1965-68)

13" FIGURES

❑ **Johnny Hero**, 1965-68
   MNP $65   MIP $100

❑ **Johnny Hero, Olympic Hero**, 1965-68
   MNP $65   MIP $100

❑ **Outfits**, 1965-68
   MNP $40   MIP $75

JONNY QUEST (GALOOB, 1996)

ACCESSORIES

❑ **Cyber Copter**, 1996, Galoob
   MNP $5   MIP $15

❑ **Quest Porpoise with Deep Sea Jonny**, 1996, Galoob
   MNP $5   MIP $15

❑ **Quest Rover**, 1996, Galoob
   MNP $5   MIP $15

QUEST WORLD FIGURES

❑ **Cyber Cycle Jonny Quest**, 1996, Galoob
   MNP $5   MIP $10

❑ **Cyber Jet Race**, 1996, Galoob
   MNP $5   MIP $10

❑ **Cyber Suit Hadji**, 1996, Galoob
   MNP $5   MIP $10

❑ **Cyber Trax Surd**, 1996, Galoob
   MNP $5   MIP $10

REAL WORLD FIGURES

❑ **Deep Sea Race Bannon & Hadji**, 1996, Galoob
   MNP $4   MIP $8

❑ **Jungle Commando Dr. Quest & Ezekiel Rage**, 1996, Galoob
   MNP $4   MIP $8

❑ **Night Stryker Jonny Quest & Jessie**, 1996, Galoob
   MNP $5   MIP $10

❑ **Shuttle Pilot Jonny Quest & Race Bannon**, 1996, Galoob
   MNP $4   MIP $8

❑ **X-Treme Action Jonny Quest & Hadji**, 1996, Galoob
   MNP $4   MIP $8

KISS (MCFARLANE, 1997)

6" FIGURES

(McFarlane Toys)

❑ **Ace Frehley with album**, 1997, McFarlane, Shown with his other bandmates
   MNP $7   MIP $15

❑ **Ace Frehley with letter stand**, 1997, McFarlane
   MNP $5   MIP $10

❑ **Gene Simmons with album**, 1997, McFarlane
   MNP $7   MIP $15

❑ **Gene Simmons with letter base**, 1997, McFarlane
   MNP $5   MIP $10

❑ **Paul Stanley with album**, 1997, McFarlane
   MNP $7   MIP $15

❑ **Paul Stanley with letter stand**, 1997, McFarlane
   MNP $5   MIP $10

❑ **Peter Criss with album**, 1997, McFarlane
   MNP $7   MIP $15

❑ **Peter Criss with letter stand**, 1997, McFarlane
   MNP $5   MIP $10

KISS (MEGO, 1978)

12" BOXED FIGURES

❑ **Ace Frehley**, 1978, Mego
   MNP $100   MIP $260

(Toy Shop File Photo)

❑ **Gene Simmons**, 1978, Mego, With accurate face make-up and realistic "wild" hair
   MNP $110   MIP $260

(Toy Shop File Photo)

❑ **Paul Stanley**, 1978, Mego, Another in Mego's series--they wisely made the boxes interchangeable. The package shown appears to have been autographed. Face make-up is accurate, and figure also features realistic "wild" hair
   MNP $100   MIP $260

❑ **Peter Criss**, 1978, Mego
   MNP $100   MIP $260

KISS: ALIVE (MCFARLANE, 2000)

FIGURES

(KP Photo)

❑ **Ace**, 2000, McFarlane, Figure includes guitar and amp
   MNP $3   MIP $8

(KP Photo)

❑ **Gene**, 2000, McFarlane, Includes figure, amp, guitar and candleabra
   MNP $3   MIP $8

(KP Photo)

❏ **Paul,** 2000, McFarlane, Includes guitar and amp

MNP $3   **MIP** $8

(KP Photo)

❏ **Peter,** 2000, McFarlane, Includes drumkit

MNP $3   **MIP** $8

KISS: PSYCHO CIRCUS (McFARLANE, 1998)

FIGURES

(McFarlane Toys)

❏ **Ace Frehley with Stiltman,** 1998, McFarlane, Includes two figures, Stiltman with base and skull-topped stilts

MNP $5   **MIP** $10

(McFarlane Toys)

❏ **Gene Simmons with Ring Master,** 1998, McFarlane, Each poseable figure includes staff

MNP $5   **MIP** $10

(McFarlane Toys)

❏ **Paul Stanley with The Jester,** 1998, McFarlane

MNP $5   **MIP** $10

(McFarlane Toys)

❏ **Peter Criss with Animal Wrangler,** 1998, McFarlane

MNP $5   **MIP** $10

KISS: PSYCHO CIRCUS TOUR (McFARLANE, 1999)

FIGURES

❏ **Ace Frehley,** 1999, McFarlane

MNP $4   **MIP** $8

(McFarlane Toys)

❏ **Gene Simmons,** 1999, McFarlane, Fierce-looking Gene with black bass guitar

MNP $4   **MIP** $8

(McFarlane Toys)

❏ **Paul Stanley,** 1999, McFarlane, Paul includes flying-V guitar

MNP $4   **MIP** $8

❏ **Peter Criss,** 1999, McFarlane

MNP $4   **MIP** $8

LARA CROFT (PLAYMATES, 1999)

FIGURES

❏ **Lara in Area 51 outfit,** 1999, Playmates

MNP $10   **MIP** $20

❏ **Lara in jungle outfit,** 1999, Playmates

MNP $10   **MIP** $20

❏ **Lara in wet suit,** 1999, Playmates

MNP $10   **MIP** $20

❏ **talking Lara,** 1999, Playmates

MNP $15   **MIP** $30

LAVERNE AND SHIRLEY (MEGO, 1978)

12" BOXED FIGURES

❑ **Laverne and Shirley,** 1978, Mego
MNP $60   MIP $150

❑ **Lenny and Squiggy,** 1978, Mego
MNP $90   MIP $150

LEGENDS OF BATMAN (KENNER, 1994)

FIGURES

❑ **Catwoman,** 1994, Kenner
MNP $5   MIP $10

❑ **Crusader Batman,** 1994, Kenner
MNP $4   MIP $15

❑ **Crusader Robin,** 1994, Kenner
MNP $4   MIP $10

❑ **Cyborg Batman,** 1994, Kenner
MNP $4   MIP $10

❑ **Dark Rider Batman with Horse,** 1994, Kenner
MNP $10   MIP $25

❑ **Dark Warrior Batman,** 1994, Kenner
MNP $4   MIP $10

❑ **Desert Knight Batman,** 1994, Kenner
MNP $5   MIP $10

❑ **Flightpak Batman,** 1994, Kenner
MNP $5   MIP $10

❑ **Future Batman,** 1994, Kenner
MNP $5   MIP $10

❑ **Joker,** 1994, Kenner
MNP $5   MIP $10

❑ **Knightquest Batman,** 1994, Kenner
MNP $5   MIP $10

❑ **Knightsend Batman,** 1994, Kenner
MNP $4   MIP $10

❑ **Long Bow Batman,** 1994, Kenner
MNP $4   MIP $10

❑ **Nightwing Robin,** 1994, Kenner
MNP $5   MIP $10

❑ **Power Guardian Batman,** 1994, Kenner
MNP $5   MIP $10

❑ **Riddler,** 1994, Kenner
MNP $5   MIP $10

❑ **Samurai Batman,** 1994, Kenner
MNP $4   MIP $10

❑ **Silver Knight Batman,** 1994, Kenner
MNP $5   MIP $10

❑ **Viking Batman,** 1994, Kenner
MNP $4   MIP $10

VEHICLES

❑ **Batcycle,** 1994, Kenner
MNP $10   MIP $20

❑ **Batmobile,** 1994, Kenner
MNP $10   MIP $30

LONE RANGER RIDES AGAIN (GABRIEL, 1979)

FIGURES

(Toy Shop File Photo)

❑ **Butch Cavendish,** 1979, Gabriel, Figure shown here with Smoke, Butch's horse
MNP $40   MIP $75

❑ **Dan Reid,** 1979, Gabriel
MNP $25   MIP $60

❑ **Little Bear with Hawk,** 1979, Gabriel
MNP $25   MIP $60

(Toy Shop File Photo)

❑ **Lone Ranger,** 1979, Gabriel, Figure includes revolvers, hat, mask, scarf. Shown here with Silver
MNP $20   MIP $60

❑ **Red Sleeves,** 1979, Gabriel
MNP $25   MIP $60

(Toy Shop File Photo)

❑ **Tonto,** 1979, Gabriel, Includes buckskin cloth outfit. Shown here with Scout. The horses in this series were fully poseable and included stands
MNP $20   MIP $60

LONE RANGER, LEGEND OF (GABRIEL, 1982)

FIGURES

❑ **Buffalo Bill Cody,** 1982, Gabriel
MNP $10   MIP $25

❑ **Butch Cavendish,** 1982, Gabriel
MNP $10   MIP $20

❑ **General Custer,** 1982, Gabriel
MNP $10   MIP $20

❑ **Lone Ranger,** 1982, Gabriel
MNP $15   MIP $30

❑ **Lone Ranger with Silver,** 1982, Gabriel
MNP $25   MIP $50

❑ **Scout,** 1982, Gabriel
MNP $10   MIP $20

❑ **Silver,** 1982, Gabriel
MNP $15   MIP $30

❑ **Smoke,** 1982, Gabriel
MNP $10   MIP $25

❑ **Tonto,** 1982, Gabriel
MNP $7   MIP $15

❑ **Tonto with Scout,** 1982, Gabriel
MNP $25   MIP $50

LORD OF THE RINGS (TOY VAULT, 1998-99)

FIGURES

❑ **Balrog,** 1999, Toy Vault
MNP $7   MIP $13

(KP Photo)

ACTION FIGURES

❑ **Frodo in Lorien,** 1999, Toy Vault, Includes dagger, belt, pack walking stick and cloak. A nicely done toy, and interesting to see a version of Frodo that exists before release of the movies
MNP $7   MIP $13

(KP Photo)

❑ **Frodo in the Barrow Downs,** 1999, Toy Vault, In white cermonial cloak with gold highlights
MNP $8   MIP $18
(KP Photo)

❑ **Frodo the Hobbit,** 1999, Toy Vault, Includes cloak, sword, pack, belt and blanket
MNP $8   MIP $14

(KP Photo)

❑ **Gandalf the Wizard,** 1999, Toy Vault, In gray cloth robe, includes hat, food pouch, pipeweed pouch, staff, belt, sword and scabbard
MNP $7   MIP $13

❑ **Gimli in Battle,** 1999, Toy Vault
MNP $7   MIP $13

❑ **Gimli of the Fellowship,** 1999, Toy Vault
MNP $8   MIP $18

❑ **Gimli in Lorien,** 1999, Toy Vault
MNP $7   MIP $13

❑ **Gollum,** 1999, Toy Vault
MNP $7   MIP $13

❑ **Gollum the Fisherman,** 1999, Toy Vault
MNP $7   MIP $13

(KP Photo)

❑ **Ugluk at War,** 1999, Toy Vault, Fierce Orc with sword, helmet, dagger and shield
MNP $7   MIP $13

(KP Photo)

❑ **Ugluk on the Hunt,** 1999, Toy Vault
MNP $7   MIP $13

❑ **Ugluk the Orc,** 1999, Toy Vault, Figure in gold armor. Includes medicine bottle, sword, dagger and helmet
MNP $7   MIP $13

LOST IN SPACE (TRENDMASTERS, 1998)

FIGURES

(Lenny Lee)

❑ **Battle Armor Don West,** 1998, Trendmasters, Includes blaster rifle and magnet attack micro-spider
MNP $4   MIP $8

❑ **Cryo Chamber Judy Robinson,** 1998, Trendmasters
MNP $4   MIP $8

(Lenny Lee)

❑ **Cryo Chamber Will Robinson,** 1998, Trendmasters, With chamber, camera and magnet attack micro-spiders
MNP $4   MIP $8

(Lenny Lee)

❑ **Cryo-Suit Dr. Judy Robinson**, 1998, Trendmasters, With accessories and magnet attack micro-spider
    MNP **$4**   MIP **$8**

❑ **Cyclops**, 1998, Trendmasters
    MNP **$25**   MIP **$60**

(Lenny Lee)

❑ **Dr. Smith, sabotage action**, 1998, Trendmasters, Includes rifle, magnet attack micro-spider and accessories
    MNP **$7**   MIP **$15**

❑ **Judy Robinson**, 1998, Trendmasters
    MNP **$7**   MIP **$15**

(Lenny Lee)

❑ **Proteus Armor Dr. Smith**, 1998, Trendmasters, With rifle, and magnet attack micro-spider
    MNP **$4**   MIP **$8**

(Lenny Lee)

❑ **Proteus Armor John Robinson**, 1998, Trendmasters, Includes micro-spider and accessories
    MNP **$4**   MIP **$8**

❑ **Tybo the Carrot Man**, 1998, Trendmasters
    MNP **$20**   MIP **$45**

❑ **Will Robinson**, 1998, Trendmasters
    MNP **$7**   MIP **$15**

PLAY SETS

(Lenny Lee)

❑ **Jupiter 2 play set**, 1998, Trendmasters, Ship fits action figure in cockpit and features: pop-out hyperspace struts, missile launchers, "battle damage" and more magnet-attack micro spiders
    MNP **$25**   MIP **$75**

LOST IN SPACE (TRENDMASTERS, 1998)

PLAY SET

(Lenny Lee)

❑ **Bubble Fighter**, 1998, Trendmasters, Fighter ship as seen in the beginning of the movie. Features: swiveling cockpit, missile launchers, ejecting bubble section and breakaway battle damage
    MNP **$35**   MIP **$80**

LOST WORLD OF THE WARLORD (REMCO, 1983)

ACCESSORIES AND TEAMS

❑ **Warpult**, 1983
    MNP **$15**   MIP **$30**

❑ **Warteam with Arak**, 1983
    MNP **$25**   MIP **$75**

❑ **Warteam with Deimos**, 1983
    MNP **$25**   MIP **$75**

❑ **Warteam with Manchitse**, 1983
    MNP **$25**   MIP **$75**

❑ **Warteam with Mikola**, 1983
    MNP **$25**   MIP **$75**

FIGURES

❑ **Arak**, 1983
    MNP **$13**   MIP **$30**

❑ **Deimos**, 1983
    MNP **$15**   MIP **$38**

ACTION FIGURES

❑ **Hercules,** 1983
    MNP $13   MIP $30

❑ **Manchitse,** 1983
    MNP $15   MIP $38

❑ **Mikola,** 1983
    MNP $15   MIP $38

❑ **Warlord,** 1983
    MNP $8   MIP $25

LOVE BOAT (MEGO, 1981)

4" FIGURES

❑ **Captain Stubing,** 1981, Mego
    MNP $10   MIP $20

❑ **Doc,** 1981, Mego
    MNP $10   MIP $20

❑ **Gopher,** 1981, Mego
    MNP $10   MIP $20

❑ **Isaac,** 1981, Mego
    MNP $10   MIP $20

❑ **Julie,** 1981, Mego
    MNP $10   MIP $25

❑ **Vicki,** 1981, Mego
    MNP $10   MIP $25

M*A*S*H (TRISTAR, 1982)

3-3/4" FIGURES AND VEHICLES

❑ **B.J.,** 1982, Tristar, 3-3/4" tall
    MNP $5   MIP $15

❑ **Colonel Potter,** 1982, Tristar, 3-3/4" figure on car
    MNP $5   MIP $15

❑ **Father Mulcahy,** 1982, Tristar, 3-3/4" figure on car
    MNP $5   MIP $15

❑ **Hawkeye,** 1982, Tristar, 3-3/4" figure on car
    MNP $5   MIP $15

❑ **Hawkeye with Ambulance,** 1982, Tristar
    MNP $15   MIP $35

❑ **Hawkeye with Helicopter,** 1982, Tristar
    MNP $8   MIP $35

❑ **Hawkeye with Jeep,** 1982, Tristar
    MNP $10   MIP $35

❑ **Hot Lips,** 1982, Tristar, 3-3/4" figure on car
    MNP $10   MIP $20

❑ **Klinger,** 1982, Tristar, 3-3/4" figure on car
    MNP $5   MIP $15

❑ **Klinger in Drag,** 1982, Tristar, 3-3/4" figure on car
    MNP $15   MIP $35

❑ **M*A*S*H Figures Collectors Set,** 1982, Tristar
    MNP $26   MIP $65

❑ **Winchester,** 1982, Tristar, 3-3/4" tall
    MNP $5   MIP $15

8" FIGURES

❑ **B.J.,** 1982, Tristar, 8"
    MNP $35   MIP $75

❑ **Hawkeye,** 1982, Tristar, 8"
    MNP $20   MIP $50

❑ **Hot Lips,** 1982, Tristar, 8"
    MNP $20   MIP $50

M.A.S.K. (KENNER, 1985-87)

FIGURE SETS

❑ **Coast Patrol,** 1985-87
    MNP $8   MIP $20

❑ **Jungle Challenge,** 1985-87
    MNP $8   MIP $20

❑ **Rescue Mission,** 1985-87
    MNP $8   MIP $20

❑ **T-Bob,** 1985-87
    MNP $8   MIP $20

❑ **Venom's Revenge,** 1985-87
    MNP $8   MIP $20

M.A.S.K. VEHICLES

❑ **Billboard Blast with Dusty Hayes,** 1985-87
    MNP $10   MIP $30

❑ **Bulldog with Boris Bushkin,** 1985-87
    MNP $15   MIP $45

❑ **Bullet with Ali Bombay,** 1985-87
    MNP $15   MIP $45

❑ **Buzzard with Miles Mayhem and Maximus Mayhem,** 1985-87
    MNP $15   MIP $45

❑ **Condor with Brad Turner,** 1985-87
    MNP $10   MIP $30

❑ **Firecracker with Hondo Mac Lean,** 1985-87
    MNP $10   MIP $30

❑ **Firefly with Julio Lopez,** 1985-87
    MNP $10   MIP $30

❑ **Gator with Dirty Hayes,** 1985-87
    MNP $10   MIP $30

❑ **Goliath,** 1985-87
    MNP $15   MIP $45

❑ **Hurricane with Hondo Mac Lean,** 1985-87
    MNP $10   MIP $30

❑ **Iguana with Lester Sludge,** 1985-87
    MNP $10   MIP $30

❑ **Manta with Vanessa Warfield,** 1985-87
    MNP $15   MIP $45

❑ **Meteor with Ace Riker,** 1985-87
    MNP $10   MIP $25

❑ **Pit Stop Catapult with Sly Rax,** 1985-87
    MNP $10   MIP $30

❑ **Raven with Calhoun Burns,** 1985-87
    MNP $10   MIP $30

❑ **Razorback with Brad Turner,** 1985-87
    MNP $10   MIP $30

❑ **Rhino with Bruce Sato and Matt Tracker,** 1985-87
    MNP $15   MIP $45

❑ **Slingshot with Ace Riker,** 1985-87
    MNP $10   MIP $30

❑ **Thunder Hawk with Matt Tracker,** 1985-87
    MNP $15   MIP $45

❑ **Volcano with Matt Tracker and Jacques LaFleur,** 1985-87
    MNP $15   MIP $45

❑ **Wildcat with Clutch Hawks,** 1985-87
    MNP $10   MIP $35

PLAY SETS

❑ **Boulder Play Set,** 1985-87
    MNP $40   MIP $120

SPLIT SECONDS M.A.S.K. VEHICLES

❑ **Afterburner with Dusty Hanes,** 1985-87
    MNP $20   MIP $55

❑ **Detonator,** 1985-87
    MNP $10   MIP $30

❑ **Dynamo with Bruce Sato,** 1985-87
    MNP $15   MIP $55

❑ **Fireforce,** 1985-87
    MNP $10   MIP $30

SPLIT SECONDS V.E.N.O.M. VEHICLES

❑ **Barracuda with Bruno Shepherd,** 1985-87
    MNP $15   MIP $55

❑ **Vandal with Floyd Malloy,** 1985-87
    MNP $10   MIP $30

V.E.N.O.M. VEHICLES

❑ **Jackhammer with Cliffhanger,** 1985-87
    MNP $10   MIP $30

❑ **Outlaw with Miles Mayhem and Nash Gorey,** 1985-87
    MNP $15   MIP $50

❑ **Piranha with Sly Rax,** 1985-87
    MNP $10   MIP $25

❑ **Stinger with Bruno Shepherd,** 1985-87
    MNP $10   MIP $35

❑ **Switchblade with Miles Mayhem,** 1985-87
    MNP $15   MIP $50

❑ **Vampire with Floyd Malloy,** 1985-87
    MNP $10   MIP $30

MAD MONSTER SERIES (MEGO, 1974)

8" FIGURES

❑ **The Dreadful Dracula,** 1974, Mego
    MNP $80   MIP $160

ACTION FIGURES

❏ **The Horrible Mummy,** 1974, Mego
MNP $40   **MIP $90**

❏ **The Human Wolfman,** 1974, Mego
MNP $75   **MIP $150**

(Toy Shop File Photo)

❏ **The Monster Frankenstein,** 1974, Mego, With glow-in-the-dark eyes and hands
MNP $50   **MIP $100**

ACCESSORIES

❏ **Mad Monster Castle, vinyl,** 1974, Mego
MNP $300   **MIP $600**

MAJOR MATT MASON (MATTEL, 1967-70)

FIGURES

(Toy Shop Photo File)

❏ **Callisto, 6",** 1967-70, Mattel, 6" action figure
MNP $100   **MIP $250**

(Toy Shop File Photo)

❏ **Captain Lazer, 12",** 1967-70, Mattel, 12" action figure, knee-high boots
MNP $125   **MIP $300**

❏ **Doug Davis, 6",** 1967-70, Mattel, 6" yellow action fig
MNP $100   **MIP $300**

❏ **Jeff Long, 6",** 1967-70, Mattel, 6" action figure
MNP $150   **MIP $550**

❏ **Major Matt Mason, 6",** 1967-70, Mattel, 6" action figure
MNP $75   **MIP $225**

❏ **Mission Team Four-Pack,** 1967-70, Mattel
MNP $350   **MIP $625**

❏ **Scorpio, 7",** 1967-70, Mattel, 7" action figure
MNP $350   **MIP $850**

❏ **Sergeant Storm, 6",** 1967-70, Mattel, 6" red action figure
MNP $100   **MIP $400**

VEHICLES AND ACCESSORIES

❏ **Astro-Trak,** 1967-70, Mattel, vehicle
MNP $50   **MIP $150**

❏ **Firebolt Space Cannon,** 1967-70, Mattel, accessory
MNP $45   **MIP $125**

❏ **Gamma Ray Guard,** 1967-70, Mattel, accessory
MNP $30   **MIP $100**

❏ **Moon Suit Pak,** 1967-70, Mattel, accessory
MNP $35   **MIP $100**

❏ **Reconojet Pak,** 1967-70, Mattel, accessory
MNP $25   **MIP $75**

❏ **Rocket Launch,** 1967-70, Mattel, accessory
MNP $25   **MIP $75**

❏ **Satellite Launch Pak,** 1967-70, Mattel, accessory
MNP $25   **MIP $75**

❏ **Satellite Locker,** 1967-70, Mattel, carry case
MNP $30   **MIP $80**

❏ **Space Power Suit,** 1967-70, Mattel, accessory
MNP $30   **MIP $110**

❏ **Space Probe Pak,** 1967-70, Mattel, accessory
MNP $25   **MIP $75**

❏ **Space Shelter Pak,** 1967-70, Mattel, accessory
MNP $25   **MIP $75**

❏ **Space Station Set,** 1967-70, Mattel, three deck
MNP $150   **MIP $350**

❏ **Star Seeker,** 1967-70, Mattel, accessory
MNP $85   **MIP $180**

❏ **Supernaut Power Limbs,** 1967-70, Mattel, accessory
MNP $30   **MIP $110**

❏ **Uni-Tred & Space Bubble,** 1967-70, Mattel, vehicle
MNP $95   **MIP $175**

❏ **XRG-1 Reentry Glider,** 1967-70, Mattel, vehicle
MNP $150   **MIP $395**

MAN FROM U.N.C.L.E. (GILBERT, 1965)

FIGURES

❏ **Illya Kuryakin Doll: black sweater, pants and shoes, spring loaded arm for,** Gilbert, 1965
MNP $200   **MIP $400**

(Toy Shop File Photo)

ACTION FIGURES

❏ **Napoleon Solo Doll,** Gilbert, 1965, Plastic, white shirt, black pants and shoes

    MNP $145   MIP $325

MARS ATTACKS! (TRENDMASTERS, 1997)

FIGURES

❏ **Martian Ambassador,** 1997, Trendmasters, 6" figure

    MNP $6   MIP $12

❏ **Martian Leader,** 1997, Trendmasters, 6" figure

    MNP $6   MIP $12

❏ **Martian Spy Girl,** 1997, Trendmasters, 6" figure; talking version

    MNP $45   MIP $65

❏ **Martian Spy Girl,** 1997, Trendmasters, 6" figure

    MNP $35   MIP $70

❏ **Martian Trooper,** 1997, Trendmasters, 6" figure

    MNP $8   MIP $15

MARVEL FAMOUS COVERS (TOY BIZ, 1997-98)

8" FIGURES

(Toy Shop File Photo)

❏ **Aunt May,** 1997, Toy Biz, Mail-away exclusive, with tied bandana around neck

    MNP $15   MIP $40

❏ **Captain America,** 1998

    MNP $8   MIP $20

❏ **Cyclops,** 1999

    MNP $5   MIP $15

❏ **Dark Phoenix,** 1998

    MNP $4   MIP $12

❏ **Dr. Doom,** 1998

    MNP $4   MIP $12

❏ **Green Goblin,** 1997, Toy Biz, 8" figure

    MNP $15   MIP $35

❏ **Magneto,** 1999

    MNP $5   MIP $15

❏ **Nightcrawler,** 1999

    MNP $5   MIP $15

❏ **Rogue,** 1999

    MNP $5   MIP $15

❏ **Spider-Man, red and black costume,** 1997, Toy Biz, 8" figure

    MNP $15   MIP $40

❏ **Storm,** 1997, Toy Biz, 8" figure

    MNP $12   MIP $35

❏ **Thor,** 1998

    MNP $4   MIP $12

❏ **Wolverine,** 1997, Toy Biz, 8" figure

    MNP $10   MIP $35

MARVEL MILESTONE, 8" FIGURES

❏ **Black Widow,** 1998

    MNP $3   MIP $8

❏ **Daredevil,** 1998

    MNP $3   MIP $8

❏ **Falcon,** 1998

    MNP $3   MIP $8

❏ **Mr. Sinister,** 1998

    MNP $3   MIP $8

MARVEL FAMOUS COVERS AVENGERS ASSEMBLE (TOY BIZ, 1999)

8" FIGURES

❏ **Hawkeye,** 1999, Toy Biz

    MNP $5   MIP $15

❏ **Hulk,** 1999, Toy Biz

    MNP $5   MIP $15

❏ **Iron man,** 1999, Toy Biz

    MNP $5   MIP $15

❏ **Vision,** 1999, Toy Biz

    MNP $5   MIP $15

MARVEL GOLD (TOY BIZ, 1998)

FIGURES

❏ **Black Panther,** 1998, Toy Biz

    MNP $8   MIP $16

❏ **Captain Marvel,** 1998

    MNP $8   MIP $16

❏ **Iron Fist,** 1998

    MNP $10   MIP $20

❏ **Marvel Girl,** 1998, Toy Biz

    MNP $8   MIP $16

❏ **Moon Knight,** 1998, Toy Biz

    MNP $8   MIP $16

❏ **Power Man,** 1998, Toy Biz

    MNP $8   MIP $16

❏ **Vision,** 1998, Toy Biz

    MNP $8   MIP $16

MARVEL SHAPE SHIFTERS (TOY BIZ, 1999)

7" FIGURES

❏ **Hulk forms into Dino Beast,** 1999

    MNP $3   MIP $7

❏ **Rhino forms into Racing Rhino,** 1999

    MNP $3   MIP $7

❏ **Sabretooth forms into Sabretooth Tiger,** 1999

    MNP $3   MIP $7

❏ **Spider Sense Spider-Man forms into Spider-Bat,** 1999

    MNP $3   MIP $7

MARVEL SHAPE SHIFTERS II (TOY BIZ, 1999)

7" FIGURES

❏ **Captain America forms into American Eagle,** 1999

    MNP $3   MIP $7

❏ **Colossus forms into Cyborg Gorilla,** 1999

    MNP $3   MIP $7

❏ **Kraven forms into Mighty Lion,** 1999

    MNP $3   MIP $7

❏ **Thor forms into Winged Stallion,** 1999

    MNP $3   MIP $7

MARVEL SHAPE SHIFTERS WEAPONS (TOY BIZ, 1999)

DELUXE FIGURES

❏ **Apocalypse forms into Gattling Gun,** 1999

    MNP $3   MIP $7

❏ **Iron Man forms into Battle Axe,** 1999

    MNP $3   MIP $7

❏ **Punisher forms into Power Pistol,** 1999

    MNP $3   MIP $7

❏ **Spider-Man forms into Wrist Blaster,** 1999

    MNP $3   MIP $7

MARVEL SPECIAL EDITION SERIES (TOY BIZ, 1998)

12" FIGURES

❏ **Dr. Octopus,** 1998

    MNP $3   MIP $7

❏ **Punisher,** 1998

    MNP $3   MIP $7

❏ Spider-Woman, 1998
MNP $3   MIP $7

MARVEL SUPER HEROES (TOY BIZ, 1990-92)

SERIES 1, 1990

❏ **Captain America**, 1990-92, Toy Biz
MNP $10   MIP $20

❏ **Daredevil**, 1990-92, Toy Biz
MNP $15   MIP $40

❏ **Doctor Doom**, 1990-92, Toy Biz
MNP $10   MIP $25

❏ **Doctor Octopus**, 1990-92, Toy Biz
MNP $10   MIP $25

❏ **Hulk**, 1990-92, Toy Biz
MNP $5   MIP $15

❏ **Punisher (cap firing)**, 1990-92, Toy Biz
MNP $5   MIP $15

❏ **Silver Surfer**, 1990-92, Toy Biz
MNP $10   MIP $30

❏ **Spider-Man (suction cups)**, 1990-92, Toy Biz
MNP $5   MIP $20

SERIES 2, 1991

❏ **Green Goblin (back lever)**, 1990-92, Toy Biz
MNP $15   MIP $40

❏ **Green Goblin (no lever)**, 1990-92, Toy Biz
MNP $10   MIP $25

❏ **Iron Man**, 1990-92, Toy Biz
MNP $10   MIP $25

❏ **Punisher (machine gun sound)**, 1990-92, Toy Biz
MNP $5   MIP $15

❏ **Spider-Man (web climbing)**, 1990-92, Toy Biz
MNP $15   MIP $35

❏ **Spider-Man (web shooting)**, 1990-92, Toy Biz
MNP $10   MIP $30

❏ **Thor (back lever)**, 1990-92, Toy Biz
MNP $15   MIP $40

❏ **Thor (no lever)**, 1990-92, Toy Biz
MNP $10   MIP $25

❏ **Venom**, 1990-92, Toy Biz
MNP $10   MIP $20

SERIES 3, 1992

❏ **Annihilus**, 1990-92, Toy Biz
MNP $5   MIP $15

❏ **Deathlok**, 1990-92, Toy Biz
MNP $5   MIP $15

❏ **Human Torch**, 1990-92, Toy Biz
MNP $5   MIP $15

❏ **Invisible Woman, catapult**, 1990-92
MNP $5   MIP $15

(Toy Shop File Photo)

❏ **Invisible Woman, vanishing**, 1990-92, Toy Biz, turns from color uniform to translucent
MNP $75   MIP $150

❏ **Mister Fantastic**, 1990-92, Toy Biz
MNP $5   MIP $15

❏ **Silver Surfer (chrome)**, 1990-92, Toy Biz
MNP $5   MIP $15

❏ **Spider-Man (ball joints)**, 1990-92, Toy Biz
MNP $5   MIP $15

❏ **Spider-Man (web tracer)**, 1990-92, Toy Biz
MNP $5   MIP $15

❏ **Thing**, 1990-92, Toy Biz
MNP $5   MIP $15

❏ **Venom (tongue flicking)**, 1990-92, Toy Biz
MNP $15   MIP $20

TALKING HEROES

❏ **Cyclops**, 1990-92, Toy Biz
MNP $10   MIP $20

❏ **Hulk**, 1990-92, Toy Biz
MNP $10   MIP $20

❏ **Magneto**, 1990-92, Toy Biz
MNP $10   MIP $20

❏ **Punisher**, 1990-92, Toy Biz
MNP $10   MIP $20

❏ **Spider-Man**, 1990-92, Toy Biz
MNP $10   MIP $20

❏ **Venom**, 1990-92, Toy Biz
MNP $10   MIP $25

❏ **Wolverine**, 1990-92, Toy Biz
MNP $10   MIP $20

MARVEL SUPER HEROES COSMIC DEFENDERS (TOY BIZ, 1992-93)

FIGURES

❏ **Annihilus**, 1992-93, Toy Biz
MNP $5   MIP $15

❏ **Deathlok**, 1992-93, Toy Biz
MNP $5   MIP $15

❏ **Human Torch**, 1992-93, Toy Biz
MNP $5   MIP $15

❏ **Invisible Woman, vanishing color action**, 1992-93, Toy Biz
MNP $50   MIP $150

❏ **Mr. Fantastic**, 1992-93, Toy Biz
MNP $8   MIP $20

❏ **Silver Surfer**, 1992-93, Toy Biz
MNP $4   MIP $12

❏ **Spider-Man, enemy tracking tracer**, 1992-93, Toy Biz
MNP $8   MIP $20

❏ **Spider-Man, multi-jointed**, 1992-93, Toy Biz
MNP $5   MIP $15

MARVEL SUPER HEROES SECRET WARS (MATTEL, 1984-85)

4" FIGURES

❏ **Baron Zemo**, 1984-85, Mattel
MNP $15   MIP $35

(Lenny Lee)

❏ **Captain America, with secret shield**, 1984-85, Mattel, includes figure, shield and mini comic book
MNP $10   MIP $25

❏ **Constrictor (foreign release)**, 1984-85, Mattel
MNP $30   MIP $75

❏ **Daredevil**, 1984-85, Mattel
MNP $15   MIP $35

❏ **Doctor Doom**, 1984-85, Mattel
MNP $10   MIP $20

ACTION FIGURES

(Lenny Lee)

❑ **Doctor Octopus,** 1984-85, Mattel, Spidey's nemesis with mechanical arms and shield
MNP $10　　MIP $20

❑ **Electro (foreign release),** 1984-85, Mattel
MNP $30　　MIP $75

❑ **Falcon,** 1984-85, Mattel
MNP $20　　MIP $40

❑ **Hobgoblin,** 1984-85, Mattel
MNP $30　　MIP $60

❑ **Ice Man (foreign release),** 1984-85, Mattel
MNP $30　　MIP $75

❑ **Iron Man,** 1984-85, Mattel
MNP $20　　MIP $35

❑ **Kang,** 1984-85, Mattel
MNP $10　　MIP $20

❑ **Magneto,** 1984-85, Mattel
MNP $10　　MIP $20

❑ **Spider-Man, black outfit,** 1984-85, Mattel
MNP $25　　MIP $50

❑ **Spider-Man, red and blue outfit,** 1984-85, Mattel
MNP $20　　MIP $40

(Toy Shop File Photo)

❑ **Three-Figure Set,** 1984-85, Mattel, includes DareDevil, Spidey (in black costume) and Captain America
MNP $40　　MIP $90

❑ **Two-Figure Set,** 1984-85, Mattel
MNP $25　　MIP $50

❑ **Wolverine, black claws,** 1984-85, Mattel
MNP $25　　MIP $75

❑ **Wolverine, silver claws,** 1984-85, Mattel
MNP $25　　MIP $40

ACCESSORIES

❑ **Secret Messages Pack,** 1984-85, Mattel
MNP $1　　MIP $5

❑ **Tower of Doom,** 1984-85, Mattel
MNP $20　　MIP $35

VEHICLES

❑ **Doom Copter,** 1984-85, Mattel
MNP $10　　MIP $35

❑ **Doom Copter with Doctor Doom,** 1984-85, Mattel
MNP $15　　MIP $55

❑ **Doom Cycle,** 1984-85, Mattel
MNP $6　　MIP $20

❑ **Doom Cycle with Doctor Doom,** 1984-85, Mattel
MNP $10　　MIP $40

❑ **Doom Roller,** 1984-85, Mattel
MNP $10　　MIP $20

❑ **Doom Star Glider with Kang,** 1984-85, Mattel
MNP $15　　MIP $30

❑ **Freedom Fighter,** 1984-85, Mattel
MNP $10　　MIP $30

❑ **Star Dart with Spider-Man (black outfit),** 1984-85, Mattel
MNP $25　　MIP $50

❑ **Turbo Copter,** 1984-85, Mattel
MNP $10　　MIP $40

❑ **Turbo Cycle,** 1984-85, Mattel
MNP $5　　MIP $20

MARVEL'S MOST WANTED (TOY BIZ, 1998)

6" FIGURES

❑ **Blink,** 1998
MNP $3　　MIP $7

❑ **Spat and Grovel,** 1998
MNP $3　　MIP $7

❑ **X-Man,** 1998
MNP $3　　MIP $7

MASTERS OF THE UNIVERSE (MATTEL, 1981-1990)

12" FIGURES (ITALIAN)

❑ **Megator,** 1981-90
MNP $300　　MIP $1000

❑ **Tytus,** 1981-90
MNP $400　　MIP $1200

ACCESSORIES

❑ **Battle Bones Carrying Case,** 1981-90
MNP $10　　MIP $20

❑ **Battle Cat,** 1981-90
MNP $15　　MIP $50

❑ **Battle Cat with Battle Armor He-Man,** 1981-90
MNP $50　　MIP $125

❑ **Battle Cat with He-Man,** 1981-90
MNP $50　　MIP $150

❑ **Beam Blaster and Artillery,** 1981-90
MNP $25　　MIP $60

❑ **Jet Sled,** 1981-90
MNP $5　　MIP $15

❑ **Mantisaur,** 1981-90
MNP $15　　MIP $25

(Toy Shop File Photo)

❑ **Megalaser,** 1981-90, While this weapon didn't fire any projectiles, it had a blast-effect action and fit warriors in the series
MNP $5　　MIP $15

(Lenny Lee)

❑ **Monstroid Creature (The Evil Horde),** 1981-90, Mattel, Creature grabs warriors in pincers and whirls them around--pretty neat!
MNP $30　　MIP $75

❑ **Night Stalker,** 1981-90
MNP $15　　MIP $30

❑ **Night Stalker with Jitsu,** 1981-90
MNP $40   MIP $75

❑ **Panthor,** 1981-90
MNP $25   MIP $50

❑ **Panthor with Battle Armor Skeletor,** 1981-90
MNP $35   MIP $125

❑ **Panthor with Skeletor,** 1981-90
MNP $40   MIP $150

❑ **Screech,** 1981-90
MNP $15   MIP $40

❑ **Screech with Skeletor,** 1981-90
MNP $40   MIP $70

❑ **Stilt Stalkers,** 1981-90
MNP $5   MIP $20

❑ **Stridor Armored Horse,** 1981-90
MNP $10   MIP $30

❑ **Stridor with Fisto,** 1981-90
MNP $30   MIP $75

(Lenny Lee)

❑ **Weapons Pak,** 1981-90, Included laser guns, body armor, battle axe, shield, sword and more
MNP $5   MIP $15

❑ **Zoar,** 1981-90
MNP $15   MIP $30

❑ **Zoar with Teela,** 1981-90
MNP $40   MIP $120

FIFTH ANNIVERSARY FIGURES

❑ **Dragon Blaster Skeletor,** 1981-90
MNP $25   MIP $75

❑ **Flying Fists He-Man,** 1981-90
MNP $25   MIP $75

❑ **Hurricane Hordak,** 1981-90
MNP $15   MIP $60

❑ **Terror Claws Skeletor,** 1981-90
MNP $25   MIP $75

❑ **Thunder Punch He-man,** 1981-90
MNP $25   MIP $60

FIGURES

❑ **Battle Armor He-Man,** 1981-90
MNP $15   MIP $40

❑ **Battle Armor Skeletor,** 1981-90
MNP $15   MIP $40

❑ **Beast Man,** 1981-90
MNP $25   MIP $70

❑ **Blade,** 1981-90
MNP $25   MIP $70

(KP Photo)

❑ **Blast-Attack,** 1981-90, Limbs actually fly off the figure during battle
MNP $20   MIP $40

❑ **Buzz-Off,** 1981-90
MNP $25   MIP $40

❑ **Buzz-Saw Hordak,** 1981-90
MNP $15   MIP $40

❑ **Clamp Champ,** 1981-90
MNP $15   MIP $45

❑ **Clawful,** 1981-90
MNP $20   MIP $45

(KP Photo)

❑ **Dragstor (The Evil Horde),** 1981-90, Mattel, Ripcord (like the SST's series) makes this "transforming evil warrior vehicle" pursue the good guys
MNP $15   MIP $40

❑ **Evil-Lyn,** 1981-90
MNP $25   MIP $50

(KP Photo)

❑ **Extendar,** 1981-90, With extending arms, legs, head and torso
MNP $15   MIP $35

❑ **Faker,** 1981-90, Mattel
MNP $30   MIP $120

❑ **Faker II,** 1981-90
MNP $20   MIP $70

❑ **Fisto,** 1981-90
MNP $10   MIP $40

❏ **Grizzlor,** 1981-90
  MNP $15   MIP $40

❏ **Grizzlor, black,** 1981-90
  MNP $75   MIP $150

❏ **Gwildor,** 1981-90
  MNP $15   MIP $75

❏ **He-Man, original,** 1981-90
  MNP $40   MIP $130

❏ **Hordak,** 1981-90
  MNP $20   MIP $40

❏ **Horde Trooper,** 1981-90
  MNP $20   MIP $40

❏ **Jitsu,** 1981-90
  MNP $20   MIP $45

❏ **King Hiss,** 1981-90
  MNP $20   MIP $45

(KP Photo)

❏ **King Randor,** 1981-90, With scepter and mini comic book
  MNP $30   MIP $75

❏ **Kobra Kahn,** 1981-90
  MNP $10   MIP $35

❏ **Leech,** 1981-90
  MNP $10   MIP $35

❏ **Man-At-Arms,** 1981-90, Mattel
  MNP $20   MIP $40

❏ **Man-E-Faces,** 1981-90
  MNP $25   MIP $50

❏ **Man-E-Faces, five extra weapons,** 1981-90
  MNP $75   MIP $175

❏ **Mantenna,** 1981-90
  MNP $25   MIP $40

❏ **Mekaneck,** 1981-90
  MNP $20   MIP $40

❏ **Mer-Man,** 1981-90
  MNP $25   MIP $50

❏ **Modulok,** 1981-90
  MNP $15   MIP $35

❏ **Mosquitor,** 1981-90
  MNP $25   MIP $45

❏ **Moss Man,** 1981-90
  MNP $10   MIP $40

❏ **Multi-Bot,** 1981-90
  MNP $20   MIP $40

❏ **Ninjor,** 1981-90
  MNP $35   MIP $80

❏ **Orko,** 1981-90
  MNP $20   MIP $50

❏ **Prince Adam,** 1981-90
  MNP $20   MIP $60

❏ **Ram Man,** 1981-90
  MNP $20   MIP $60

(Toy Shop File Photo)

❏ **Rattlor,** 1981-90, With translucent plastic "snake staff" and mini comic book
  MNP $10   MIP $35

❏ **Rattlor, red neck,** 1981-90
  MNP $10   MIP $30

(Lenny Lee)

❏ **Rio Blast,** 1981-90, Mattel, An "old West" warrior with hidden weapons. Includes comic book
  MNP $25   MIP $40

❏ **Roboto,** 1981-90
  MNP $15   MIP $35

❏ **Rokkon,** 1981-90
  MNP $15   MIP $35

❏ **Rotar,** 1981-90
  MNP $35   MIP $70

❏ **Saurod,** 1981-90
  MNP $30   MIP $70

❏ **Scare Glow,** 1981-90
  MNP $35   MIP $75

❏ **Skeletor, original,** 1981-90
  MNP $35   MIP $110

❏ **Snake Face,** 1981-90
  MNP $25   MIP $45

❏ **Snout Spout,** 1981-90
  MNP $15   MIP $40

❏ **Sorceress,** 1981-90
  MNP $25   MIP $70

❏ **Spikor,** 1981-90
  MNP $15   MIP $40

(KP Photo)

❏ **Sssqueeze,** 1981-90, Mattel, Traps warriors in "slither-hold" grip. Includes serpent
  MNP $25   MIP $45

❏ **Stinkor,** 1981-90
  MNP $15   MIP $35

❏ **Stonedar,** 1981-90
  MNP $15   MIP $35

❏ **Stratos, blue wings,** 1981-90, Mattel
  MNP $25   MIP $75

❏ **Stratos, red wings,** 1981-90
  MNP $25   MIP $75

❏ **Sy-klone,** 1981-90
  MNP $20   MIP $40

❏ **Teela,** 1981-90
MNP $25   MIP $65

❏ **Trap Jaw,** 1981-90
MNP $30   MIP $85

❏ **Tri-Klops,** 1981-90
MNP $30   MIP $40

❏ **Tung Lashor,** 1981-90
MNP $10   MIP $45

❏ **Twistoid,** 1981-90
MNP $30   MIP $75

❏ **Two-Bad,** 1981-90
MNP $10   MIP $30

❏ **Webstor,** 1981-90
MNP $10   MIP $30

❏ **Whiplash,** 1981-90
MNP $10   MIP $25

❏ **Zodac,** 1981-90, Mattel
MNP $25   MIP $50

GRAYSKULL DINOSAUR SERIES

❏ **Bionatops,** 1981-90
MNP $35   MIP $75

❏ **Turbodaltyl,** 1981-90
MNP $25   MIP $50

❏ **Tyrantisaurus Rex,** 1981-90
MNP $75   MIP $125

LASER FIGURES

❏ **Laser Light Skeletor,** 1981-90
MNP $75   MIP $250

❏ **Laser Power He-Man,** 1981-90
MNP $75   MIP $250

MAIL AWAY FIGURES

❏ **Savage He-Man (Wonder Bread Exclusive),** 1981-90
n/a   MIP $500

METEORBS

❏ **Astro lion,** 1981-90
MNP $15   MIP $30

❏ **Comet Cat,** 1981-90
MNP $15   MIP $30

❏ **Cometroid,** 1981-90
MNP $15   MIP $30

❏ **Crocobite,** 1981-90
MNP $15   MIP $30

❏ **Dinosorb,** 1981-90
MNP $15   MIP $30

❏ **Gore-illa,** 1981-90
MNP $15   MIP $30

❏ **Orbear,** 1981-90
MNP $15   MIP $30

❏ **Rhinorb,** 1981-90
MNP $15   MIP $30

❏ **Tuskor,** 1981-90
MNP $15   MIP $30

❏ **Ty-Gyr,** 1981-90
MNP $15   MIP $30

OVERSEAS ACCESSORIES

❏ **Cliff Climber,** 1981-90
MNP $25   MIP $75

❏ **Scubattack,** 1981-90
MNP $25   MIP $75

❏ **Tower Tools,** 1981-90
MNP $25   MIP $75

PLAY SETS

❏ **Castle Grayskull,** 1981-90
MNP $75   MIP $165

❏ **Eternia,** 1981-90
MNP $350   MIP $700

❏ **Fright Zone,** 1981-90
MNP $45   MIP $125

(Lenny Lee)

❏ **Slime Pit,** 1981-90, Mattel, Slime oozes from top of pit to trap warriors. The set included real Slime, which actually must have made for a very cool effect on the figures.
MNP $25   MIP $75

(Toy Shop File Photo)

❏ **Snake Mountain,** 1981-90, Snake Pit went quite well with the Slime Pit for play value.
MNP $50   MIP $150

VEHICLES

❏ **Attack Trak,** 1981-90
MNP $25   MIP $75

❏ **Bashasaurus,** 1981-90
MNP $25   MIP $50

❏ **Battle Ram,** 1981-90
MNP $30   MIP $75

❏ **Blasterhawk,** 1981-90
MNP $25   MIP $60

(Lenny Lee)

❏ **Dragon Walker,** 1981-90, Open-cockpit vehicle that sideways "walks"
MNP $20   MIP $45

❏ **Fright Fighter,** 1981-90
MNP $15   MIP $45

❏ **Land Shark,** 1981-90
MNP $15   MIP $35

❏ **Laser Bolt,** 1981-90
MNP $15   MIP $40

❏ **Point Dread,** 1981-90
MNP $25   MIP $75

(KP Photo)

❏ **Road Ripper,** 1981-90, Mattel, He-Man's motorcycle-type vehicle, ripcord-powered
MNP $10   MIP $30

❏ **Roton,** 1981-90
MNP $10   MIP $30

❏ **Spydor,** 1981-90
MNP $25   MIP $50

❏ **Wind Raider,** 1981-90
MNP $15   MIP $60

METAL GEAR SOLID
(McFARLANE, 1998)

FIGURES

(McFarlane Toys)

❏ **Liquid Snake,** 1998, McFarlane, With pistol and machine gun rifle

MNP $4   MIP $8

(McFarlane Toys)

❏ **Meryl Silverburgh,** 1998, McFarlane, With pistol, bayonet, grappling hook and machine gun

MNP $4   MIP $8

(McFarlane Toys)

❏ **Ninja,** 1998, McFarlane, Multi-colored figure with sword

MNP $4   MIP $8

(McFarlane Toys)

❏ **Psycho Mantis,** 1998, McFarlane, Includes bust, vase, crystal ball and detailed figure

MNP $4   MIP $8

(McFarlane Toys)

❏ **Revolver Ocelot,** 1998, McFarlane, Detailed gunslinger figure includes two pistols

MNP $4   MIP $8

(KP Photo)

❏ **Sniper Wolf,** 1998, McFarlane, With rifle and snarling wolf figure

MNP $4   MIP $8

(McFarlane Toys)

❏ **Solid Snake,** 1998, McFarlane, Includes a variety of weapons and accessories; rifle, pistol, infra-red goggles and more

MNP $4   MIP $8

(McFarlane Toys)

❏ **Vulcan Raven,** 1998, McFarlane, With multi-barreled weapon and barrel-shaped pack

MNP $4   MIP $8

MICRONAUTS (MEGO, 1976-80)

ALIEN INVADERS CARDED

❏ **Antron,** 1979, 1976-80, Mego

MNP $15   MIP $30

❏ **Centaurus,** 1980, 1976-80, Mego

MNP $35   MIP $70

❏ **Karrio,** 1979, 1976-80, Mego

MNP $10   MIP $20

❏ **Kronos,** 1980, 1976-80, Mego

MNP $35   MIP $70

❏ **Lobros,** 1980, 1976-80, Mego

MNP $35   MIP $70

❏ **Membros,** 1979, 1976-80, Mego

MNP $15   MIP $30

❏ **Repto,** 1979, 1976-80, Mego

MNP $13   MIP $25

ALIEN INVADERS PLAY SETS

❏ **Rocket Tubes,** 1978, 1976-80, Mego

MNP $23   MIP $50

ALIEN INVADERS VEHICLES

❏ **Alphatron,** 1976-80, Mego

MNP $5   MIP $10

❏ **Aquatron,** 1977, 1976-80, Mego

MNP $10   MIP $20

❏ **Betatron,** 1976-80, Mego

MNP $5   MIP $10

❏ **Gammatron,** 1976-80, Mego

MNP $5   MIP $10

❏ **Hornetroid,** 1979, 1976-80, Mego

MNP $20   MIP $40

❏ **Hydra,** 1976, 1976-80, Mego

MNP $7   MIP $15

❏ **Mobile Exploration Lab,** 1976, 1976-80, Mego

MNP $17   MIP $35

❏ **Solarion,** 1978, 1976-80, Mego

MNP $15   MIP $30

❏ **Star Searcher,** 1978, 1976-80, Mego

MNP $15   MIP $40

❏ **Taurion,** 1978, 1976-80, Mego

MNP $11   MIP $22

❏ **Terraphant,** 1979, 1976-80, Mego

MNP $20   MIP $40

BOXED FIGURES

❏ **Andromeda,** 1977, 1976-80, Mego

MNP $10   MIP $25

❏ **Baron Karza,** 1977, 1976-80, Mego

MNP $15   MIP $30

❏ **Biotron,** 1976, 1976-80, Mego

MNP $10   MIP $25

❏ **Force Commander,** 1977, 1976-80, Mego

MNP $10   MIP $25

❏ **Giant Acroyear,** 1977, 1976-80, Mego

MNP $10   MIP $25

❏ **Megas,** 1981, 1976-80, Mego

MNP $10   MIP $25

❏ **Microtron,** 1976, 1976-80, Mego

MNP $5   MIP $20

❏ **Nemesis Robot,** 1978, 1976-80, Mego

MNP $7   MIP $15

❏ **Oberon,** 1977, 1976-80, Mego

MNP $10   MIP $25

❏ **Phobos Robot,** 1978, 1976-80, Mego

MNP $12   MIP $25

CARDED FIGURES

❏ **Acroyear II,** 1977, red, blue, orange, 1976-80, Mego

MNP $7   MIP $15

❏ **Acroyear,** 1976, red, blue, orange, 1976-80, Mego

MNP $10   MIP $20

❏ **Galactic Defender,** 1978, white, yellow, 1976-80, Mego

MNP $7   MIP $15

❏ **Galactic Warriors,** 1976, red, blue, orange, 1976-80, Mego

MNP $4   MIP $10

❏ **Pharoid with Time Chamber,** 1977, blue, red, gray, 1976-80, Mego

MNP $10   MIP $20

❏ **Space Glider,** 1976, blue, green, orange, 1976-80, Mego

MNP $5   MIP $10

❏ **Time Traveler,** 1976, clear plastic, yellow, orange, 1976-80, Mego

MNP $3   MIP $10

❏ **Time Traveler,** 1976, solid plastic, yellow, orange, 1976-80, Mego

MNP $5   MIP $15

MICROPOLIS PLAY SETS

❏ **Galactic Command Center,** 1978, 1976-80, Mego

MNP $20   MIP $40

❏ **Interplanetary Headquarters,** 1978, 1976-80, Mego

MNP $20   MIP $40

❏ **Mega City,** 1978, 1976-80, Mego

MNP $20   MIP $30

❏ **Microrail City,** 1978, 1976-80, Mego

MNP $20   MIP $40

PLAY SETS

❏ **Astro Station,** 1976, 1976-80, Mego

MNP $10   MIP $20

❏ **Stratstation,** 1976, 1976-80, Mego

MNP $15   MIP $30

VEHICLES

❏ **Battle Cruiser,** 1977, 1976-80, Mego

MNP $30   MIP $60

❏ **Crater Cruncher with figure,** 1976, 1976-80, Mego

MNP $5   MIP $15

❏ **Galactic Cruiser,** 1976, 1976-80, Mego

MNP $7   MIP $17

❏ **Hydro Copter,** 1976, 1976-80, Mego

MNP $10   MIP $25

❏ **Neon Orbiter,** 1977, 1976-80, Mego

MNP $6   MIP $20

❏ **Photon Sled with figure,** 1976, 1976-80, Mego

MNP $5   MIP $15

❏ **Rhodium Orbiter,** 1977, 1976-80, Mego

MNP $6   MIP $20

❏ **Thorium Orbiter,** 1977, 1976-80, Mego

MNP $6   MIP $20

❏ **Ultronic Scooter with figure,** 1976, 1976-80, Mego

MNP $5   MIP $15

❏ **Warp Racer with figure,** 1976, 1976-80, Mego

MNP $5   MIP $15

MIGHTY MORPHIN POWER RANGERS (BANDAI, 1993-95)

3" FIGURES

❏ **Black Ranger,** 1995, Bandai

MNP $5   MIP $15

❏ **Blue Ranger,** 1995, Bandai

MNP $5   MIP $15

❏ **Pink Ranger,** 1995, Bandai

MNP $5   MIP $15

❏ **Red Ranger,** 1995, Bandai

MNP $5   MIP $15

❏ **Yellow Ranger,** 1995, Bandai

MNP $5   MIP $15

5" FIGURES WITH THUNDER BIKES

❏ **Black Ranger,** 1995, Bandai

MNP $6   MIP $15

❏ **Blue Ranger,** 1995, Bandai

MNP $6   MIP $15

❏ **Pink Ranger,** 1995, Bandai

MNP $6   MIP $15

❏ **Red Ranger,** 1995, Bandai

MNP $6   MIP $15

❏ **Yellow Ranger,** 1995, Bandai

MNP $6   MIP $15

8" ALIENS, 1993

❏ **Baboo,** 1993, Bandai

MNP $10   MIP $20

❏ **Bones,** 1993, Bandai

MNP $10   MIP $20

ACTION FIGURES

❑ **Finster,** 1993, Bandai
MNP $10   MIP $20

❑ **Goldar,** 1993, Bandai
MNP $10   MIP $20

❑ **King Sphinx,** 1993, Bandai
MNP $10   MIP $20

❑ **Putty Patrol,** 1993, Bandai
MNP $10   MIP $20

❑ **Squatt,** 1993, Bandai
MNP $10   MIP $20

8" FIGURES, 1993

❑ **Black Ranger,** 1993, Bandai
MNP $7   MIP $20

❑ **Blue Ranger,** 1993, Bandai
MNP $7   MIP $20

❑ **Pink Ranger,** 1993, Bandai
MNP $10   MIP $20

❑ **Red Ranger,** 1993, Bandai
MNP $5   MIP $20

❑ **Yellow Ranger,** 1993, Bandai
MNP $10   MIP $20

8" MOVIE FIGURES, 1995

❑ **Black Ranger,** 1995, Bandai, metallic
MNP $6   MIP $15

❑ **Blue Ranger,** 1995, Bandai, metallic
MNP $6   MIP $15

❑ **Pink Ranger,** 1995, Bandai, metallic
MNP $6   MIP $15

❑ **Red Ranger,** 1995, Bandai, metallic
MNP $6   MIP $15

❑ **White Ranger,** 1995, Bandai, metallic
MNP $6   MIP $15

❑ **Yellow Ranger,** 1995, Bandai, metallic
MNP $6   MIP $15

ACTION FEATURE EVIL SPACE ALIENS, 5-1/2" FIGURES, 1994

❑ **Dark Knight,** 1994, Bandai
MNP $6   MIP $15

❑ **Eye Guy,** 1994, Bandai
MNP $6   MIP $15

❑ **Minotar,** 1994, Bandai
MNP $6   MIP $15

❑ **Mutaytus,** 1994, Bandai
MNP $6   MIP $15

❑ **Pudgy Pig,** 1994, Bandai
MNP $6   MIP $15

❑ **Rita Repulsa,** 1994, Bandai
MNP $6   MIP $15

❑ **Snizard Lips,** 1994, Bandai
MNP $6   MIP $15

❑ **Spidertron,** 1994, Bandai
MNP $6   MIP $15

AUTO-MORPHIN POWER RANGERS, 5-1/2" FIGURES, 1994

❑ **Black Ranger,** 1994, Bandai
MNP $3   MIP $15

❑ **Blue Ranger,** 1994, Bandai
MNP $3   MIP $15

❑ **Green Ranger,** 1994, Bandai
MNP $3   MIP $15

❑ **Pink Ranger,** 1994, Bandai
MNP $3   MIP $15

❑ **Red Ranger,** 1994, Bandai
MNP $2   MIP $15

❑ **Yellow Ranger,** 1994, Bandai
MNP $3   MIP $15

DELUXE EVIL SPACE ALIENS, 8" FIGURES, 1994

❑ **Evil Eye,** 1994, Bandai
MNP $7   MIP $15

❑ **Goo Fish,** 1994, Bandai
MNP $7   MIP $15

❑ **Guitardo,** 1994, Bandai
MNP $7   MIP $15

❑ **Lord Zedd,** 1994, Bandai
MNP $8   MIP $18

❑ **Pirantus Head,** 1994, Bandai
MNP $7   MIP $15

❑ **Pudgy Pig,** 1994, Bandai
MNP $7   MIP $15

❑ **Putty Patrol,** 1994, Bandai
MNP $7   MIP $15

❑ **Rhino Blaster,** 1994, Bandai
MNP $7   MIP $15

❑ **Socaddillo,** 1994, Bandai
MNP $7   MIP $15

KARATE ACTION FIGURES, 1994

❑ **Black Ranger,** 1994, Bandai
MNP $6   MIP $12

❑ **Blue Ranger,** 1994, Bandai
MNP $6   MIP $12

❑ **Pink Ranger,** 1994, Bandai
MNP $8   MIP $16

❑ **Red Ranger,** 1994, Bandai
MNP $5   MIP $10

❑ **Yellow Ranger,** 1994, Bandai
MNP $8   MIP $16

POWER RANGERS FOR GIRLS

❑ **Kimberly,** 1995, Bandai
MNP $10   MIP $20

❑ **Kimberly/Trini Set,** 1995, Bandai
MNP $20   MIP $40

❑ **Trini,** 1995, Bandai
MNP $10   MIP $20

ZORDS, 1993

❑ **Dragon Dagger,** 1993, Bandai
MNP $20   MIP $50

❑ **Dragon Zord with Green Ranger,** 1993, Bandai
MNP $25   MIP $55

❑ **MegaZord,** 1993, Bandai
MNP $15   MIP $30

❑ **MegaZord Deluxe,** 1993, Bandai
MNP $20   MIP $40

❑ **Titanus the Carrier Zord,** 1993, Bandai
MNP $35   MIP $75

ZORDS, 1994

❑ **MegaZord, black/gold, limit. ed.,** 1994, Bandai
MNP $50   MIP $100

❑ **Power Cannon,** 1994, Bandai
MNP $15   MIP $35

❑ **Power Dome Morphin Set,** 1994, Bandai
MNP $25   MIP $55

❑ **Red Dragon Thunder Zord,** 1994, Bandai
MNP $25   MIP $45

❑ **Saba (White Sword),** 1994, Bandai
MNP $15   MIP $30

❑ **Thunder Zord Assault Team,** 1994, Bandai
MNP $25   MIP $45

❑ **TOR the Shuttle Zord,** 1994, Bandai
MNP $30   MIP $60

❑ **Ultra Thunder Zord,** 1994, Bandai
MNP $35   MIP $70

❑ **White Tiger Zord with White Ranger,** 1994, Bandai
MNP $25   MIP $50

MONSTERS (MCFARLANE, 1998)

SERIES 1, PLAY SETS WITH 4" FIGURES

❑ **Dracula and Bat,** 1997, McFarlane, Includes Dracula, coffin, masouleum, "bat" figure and accessories
MNP $5   MIP $15

(McFarlane Toys)

❏ **Frankenstein and Igor,** 1997, McFarlane, Hunchbacked Igor in lab coat and monster figure on upright table
MNP $8   MIP $20

(McFarlane Toys)

❏ **Hunchback, Quasimodo and Gargoyle,** 1997, McFarlane, Includes catapult-topped bell tower and two figures
MNP $5   MIP $15

❏ **Werewolf and Victim,** 1997, Kenner
MNP $5   MIP $15

SERIES 2, PLAY SETS WITH 4" FIGURES

(McFarlane Toys)

❏ **Dr. Frankenstein,** 1998, McFarlane, Set includes re-animation bed, gruesome Frankenstein monster figure, Dr. F in lab coat. Includes various lab instruments
MNP $6   MIP $12

(McFarlane Toys)

❏ **The Mummy,** 1998, McFarlane, Includes sarcophogus, Anubis figure, jars, and Mummy
MNP $6   MIP $12

(McFarlane Toys)

❏ **The Phantom of the Opera,** 1998, McFarlane, Great detail--includes pipe organ, inspector and phantom figures
MNP $6   MIP $12

(McFarlane Toys)

❏ **The Sea Creature,** 1998, McFarlane, Set includes diver in old-fashioned dive suit and attacking sea creature
MNP $6   MIP $12

MORK AND MINDY

FIGURES

❏ **Mindy,** 1980, Mattel
MNP $20   MIP $45

❏ **Mork from Ork with egg,** 1980, Mattel
MNP $20   MIP $45

(Toy Shop File Photo)

❏ **Mork with Talking Spacepack, upside down,** 1980, Mattel, Talking Mork says, "Nano, Nano and 7 other crazy things"
MNP $20   MIP $50

MOVIE MANIACS (McFARLANE, 1998-PRESENT)

18" FIGURES

❏ **Freddy Krueger from "Nightmare on Elm Street",** 2000
MNP $10   MIP $25

❏ **Michael Myers from "Halloween",** 2000
MNP $10   MIP $25

SERIES 1

❏ **Eve, "Species II",** 1998, McFarlane
MNP $4   MIP $8

FREDDY®
from A NIGHTMARE ON ELM STREET®

(McFarlane Toys)

❏ **Freddy Krueger, "Nightmare on Elm Street"**, 1998, McFarlane, Classic Freddy with red-striped sweater, fedora and extended claws
  MNP $5   **MIP $15**

❏ **Freddy Krueger, gorey, "Nightmare on Elmstreet"**, 1998
  MNP $5   **MIP $15**

❏ **Jason, "Friday the 13th"**, 1998, McFarlane
  MNP $4   **MIP $8**

(McFarlane Toys)

❏ **Jason, gorey, "Friday the 13th"**, 1998, McFarlane, Detailed figure includes machete
  MNP $10   **MIP $30**

❏ **Leatherface, "The Texas Chainsaw Massacre"**, 1998, McFarlane
  MNP $15   **MIP $25**

❏ **Leatherface, gorey, "The Texas Chainsaw Massacre"**, 1998
  MNP $25   **MIP $45**

❏ **Patrick, "Species II"**, 1998, McFarlane
  MNP $4   **MIP $8**

SERIES 2

❏ **Chucky and Tiffany, "Bride of Chucky"**, 1999
  MNP $8   **MIP $20**

❏ **Chucky, "Child's Play"**, 1999
  MNP $5   **MIP $15**

(KP Photo)

❏ **Eric Draven, "The Crow"**, 1999, With black guitar and crow figure
  MNP $5   **MIP $15**

(KP Photo)

❏ **Ghostface, "Scream"**, 1999, McFarlane Toys, Detailed Scream figure with knife and cellphone, movie-poster stand
  MNP $5   **MIP $15**

(KP Photo)

❏ **Michael Myers, "Halloween"**, 1999, McFarlane, Michael Myers figure with knife and movie-poster stand
  MNP $5   **MIP $15**

(KP Photo)

❏ **Norman Bates, "Psycho"**, 1999, McFarlane, Norman in "mother" outfit and wig with knife, includes movie-poster stand
  MNP $5   **MIP $15**

(KP Photo)

❏ **Pumkinhead, "Pumpkinhead"**, 1999, McFarlane, Figure includes movie-poster stand
  MNP $5   **MIP $15**

SERIES 3

(KP Photo)

❏ **Ash from "The Army of Darkness"**, 2000, McFarlane, Great Bruce Campbell likeness with chainsaw hand, rifle and movie-poster stand
  MNP $5   **MIP $15**

(KP Photo)

❏ **Blair Monster from "The Thing"**, 2000, McFarlane, Highly detailed figure with movie stand
  MNP $5   **MIP $15**

(KP Photo)

❏ **Edward Scissorhands from "Edward Scissorhands"**, 2000, McFarlane, Very detailed likeness with movie-poster stand

    MNP $3   MIP $12

(KP Photo)

❏ **Fly, The from "The Fly"**, 2000, McFarlane, Brindle-pattern figure with movie-poster stand

    MNP $3   MIP $10

❏ **King Kong from "King Kong"**, 2000

    MNP $5   MIP $15

❏ **Norris Creature from "The Thing"**, 2000

    MNP $5   MIP $15

❏ **Norris Spider from "The Thing"**, 2000

    MNP $5   MIP $15

(KP Photo)

❏ **Shaft from "Shaft"**, 2000, McFarlane, Figures with "The Thing" movie stand

    MNP $3   MIP $10

(KP Photo)

❏ **Snake Plissken from the "Escape form L.A."**, 2000, McFarlane, Figure with rifle and movie-poster stand

    MNP $3   MIP $10

NIGHTMARE BEFORE CHRITSTMAS (HASBRO, 1993)

FIGURES

❏ **Behemouth**, 1993

    MNP $35   MIP $80

❏ **Evil Scientist**, 1993

    MNP $50   MIP $150

❏ **Jack Skellington**, 1993, Hasbro

    MNP $40   MIP $100

❏ **Jack Skellington as Santa**, 1993

    MNP $35   MIP $80

❏ **Lock, Shock and Barrel**, 1993

    MNP $75   MIP $250

❏ **Mayor**, 1993

    MNP $45   MIP $125

❏ **Oogie Boogie**, 1993

    MNP $75   MIP $250

❏ **Sally**, 1993, Hasbro

    MNP $40   MIP $100

❏ **Santa**, 1993

    MNP $75   MIP $250

❏ **Werewolf**, 1993

    MNP $40   MIP $100

NOBLE KNIGHTS (MARX, 1968)

❏ **Bravo Armor Horse**, 1968, Marx

    MNP $75   MIP $150

FIGURES

(Toy Shop File Photo)

❏ **Black Knight**, 1968, Marx, with removeable helmet, shield and accessories

    MNP $250   MIP $550

❏ **Bravo Armor Horse**, 1968, Marx

    MNP $75   MIP $150

(Toy Shop File Photo)

❏ **Gold Knight**, 1968, Marx, like the black knight, this figure had molded-on armor, but included a variety of plastic accessories such as shield, helmet and sword

    MNP $75   MIP $150

❏ **Silver Knight**, 1968, Marx

    MNP $75   MIP $150

❏ **Valiant Armor Horse**, 1968, Marx

    MNP $200   MIP $400

❏ **Valor Armor Horse**, 1968, Marx

    MNP $75   MIP $150

❏ **Victor Armor Horse**, 1968, Marx

    MNP $75   MIP $150

ONE MILLION YEARS, B.C. (MEGO, 1976)

FIGURES

❏ **Dimetrodon, 1976, boxed**, 1976, Mego

    MNP $100   MIP $250

❏ **Grok, 1976, carded**, 1976, Mego

    MNP $25   MIP $50

❏ **Hairy Rhino, 1976, boxed**, 1976, Mego

    MNP $125   MIP $300

❏ **Mada, 1976, carded**, 1976, Mego

    MNP $25   MIP $50

❏ **Orm, 1976, carded**, 1976, Mego

    MNP $25   MIP $50

❏ **Trag, 1976, carded**, 1976, Mego

    MNP $25   MIP $50

❏ **Tribal Lair Gift Set (five figures), 1976**, 1976, Mego

    MNP $70   MIP $180

❏ **Tribal Lair, 1976**, 1976, Mego

    MNP $60   MIP $120

ACTION FIGURES

❑ **Tyrannosaur, 1976, boxed,** 1976, Mego

    MNP $125   **MIP $300**

❑ **Zon, 1976, carded,** 1976, Mego

    MNP $25   **MIP $50**

OUTER SPACE MEN (COLORFORMS, 1968)

FIGURES

❑ **Alpha 7 / Man from Mars,** 1968, Colorforms

    MNP $150   **MIP $450**

(Toy Shop File Photo)

❑ **Astro-Nautilus / Man from Neptune,** 1968, Colorforms, A freaky-looking dude that is simliar to the work done on today's hit show Futurama.

    MNP $300   **MIP $750**

❑ **Colossus Rex / Man from Jupiter,** 1968, Colorforms

    MNP $300   **MIP $800**

❑ **Commander Comet / Man from Venus,** 1968, Colorforms

    MNP $200   **MIP $500**

(Toy Shop File Photo)

❑ **Electron / Man from Pluto,** 1968, Colorforms, A flexible figure that packs

heat, and by the looks of things, can shoot lightning from his head. Striking!

    MNP $200   **MIP $500**

(Toy Shop File Photo)

❑ **Orbitron / Man from Uranus,** 1968, Colorforms, An unfortunately-named, but neat toy nonetheless. Looking very much like the Metaluna Mutant in "This Island Earth," Orbitron was a bendable figure that included a blaster pistol

    MNP $200   **MIP $600**

❑ **Xodiac / Man from Saturn,** 1968, Colorforms

    MNP $200   **MIP $500**

OZZY OSBOURNE (MCFARLANE, 1999)

FIGURES

(KP Photo)

❑ **Ozzie Osbourne,** 1999, McFarlane, Fairly buff Ozzy figure holding cross and dead bat with dead bats and doves at his feet. Includes church window diorama backdrop

    MNP $5   **MIP $15**

PEE-WEE'S PLAYHOUSE

5" FIGURES

❑ **Chairry,** 1988

    MNP $9   **MIP $23**

❑ **Conky,** 1988

    MNP $11   **MIP $30**

❑ **Cowboy Curtis,** 1988

    MNP $9   **MIP $23**

❑ **Globey and Randy,** 1988

    MNP $9   **MIP $23**

❑ **Jambi and Puppetland Band,** 1988

    MNP $11   **MIP $26**

❑ **King of Cartoons,** 1988

    MNP $8   **MIP $19**

❑ **Magic Screen,** 1988

    MNP $6   **MIP $15**

❑ **Miss Yvonne,** 1988

    MNP $15   **MIP $30**

❑ **Pee-Wee Herman,** 1988

    MNP $6   **MIP $15**

❑ **Pee-Wee Herman with Scooter,** 1988

    MNP $9   **MIP $23**

❑ **Pterri,** 1988

    MNP $8   **MIP $19**

❑ **Reba,** 1988

    MNP $9   **MIP $26**

❑ **Ricardo,** 1988

    MNP $8   **MIP $19**

PLAY SETS

❑ **Pee-Wee's Playhouse,** 1988

    MNP $50   **MIP $175**

PLANET OF THE APES (HASBRO, 1998)

FIGURES

❑ **Cornelius,** 1998, Hasbro

    MNP $8   **MIP $20**

❑ **Dr. Zaius,** 1998, Hasbro

    MNP $8   **MIP $20**

❑ **General Ursus,** 1998, Hasbro

    MNP $8   **MIP $20**

PLANET OF THE APES (MEGO, 1973-75)

8" FIGURES

❑ **Astronaut Burke, 1975, boxed,** 1973-75, Mego

    MNP $50   **MIP $250**

❑ **Astronaut Burke, 1975, carded,** 1973-75, Mego

    MNP $50   **MIP $100**

❑ **Astronaut Verdon, 1975, boxed,** 1973-75, Mego

    MNP $50   **MIP $250**

❑ **Astronaut Verdon, 1975, carded,** 1973-75, Mego
　　　MNP $50　　**MIP $125**

❑ **Astronaut, 1973, boxed,** 1973-75, Mego
　　　MNP $50　　**MIP $250**

❑ **Astronaut, 1975, carded,** 1973-75, Mego
　　　MNP $50　　**MIP $100**

❑ **Cornelius, 1973, boxed,** 1973-75, Mego
　　　MNP $40　　**MIP $200**

❑ **Cornelius, 1975, carded,** 1973-75, Mego
　　　MNP $40　　**MIP $100**

❑ **Dr. Zaius, 1973, boxed,** 1973-75, Mego
　　　MNP $40　　**MIP $200**

❑ **Dr. Zaius, 1975, carded,** 1973-75, Mego
　　　MNP $40　　**MIP $100**

❑ **Galen, 1975, boxed,** 1973-75, Mego
　　　MNP $40　　**MIP $200**

❑ **Galen, 1975, carded,** 1973-75, Mego
　　　MNP $40　　**MIP $100**

❑ **General Urko, 1975, boxed,** 1973-75, Mego
　　　MNP $50　　**MIP $250**

❑ **General Urko, 1975, carded,** 1973-75, Mego
　　　MNP $50　　**MIP $100**

❑ **General Ursus, 1975, boxed,** 1973-75, Mego
　　　MNP $50　　**MIP $250**

❑ **General Ursus, 1975, carded,** 1973-75, Mego
　　　MNP $50　　**MIP $100**

❑ **Soldier Ape, 1973, boxed,** 1973-75, Mego
　　　MNP $50　　**MIP $250**

❑ **Soldier Ape, 1975, carded,** 1973-75, Mego
　　　MNP $50　　**MIP $100**

❑ **Zira, 1973, boxed,** 1973-75, Mego
　　　MNP $30　　**MIP $200**

❑ **Zira, 1975, carded,** 1973-75, Mego
　　　MNP $30　　**MIP $100**

ACCESSORIES

(Toy Shop File Photo)

❑ **Action Stallion, 1975,** 1973-75, Mego, brown, motorized, remote-controlled
　　　MNP $50　　**MIP $100**

❑ **Battering Ram, 1975, boxed,** 1973-75, Mego
　　　MNP $20　　**MIP $40**

❑ **Dr. Zaius' Throne, 1975, boxed,** 1973-75, Mego
　　　MNP $20　　**MIP $40**

❑ **Jail, 1975, boxed,** 1973-75, Mego
　　　MNP $20　　**MIP $40**

PLAY SETS

❑ **Forbidden Zone Trap, 1975,** 1973-75, Mego
　　　MNP $90　　**MIP $200**

❑ **Fortress, 1975,** 1973-75, Mego
　　　MNP $85　　**MIP $200**

❑ **Treehouse, 1975,** 1973-75, Mego
　　　MNP $75　　**MIP $200**

❑ **Village, 1975,** 1973-75, Mego
　　　MNP $85　　**MIP $200**

VEHICLES

❑ **Catapult and Wagon, 1975, boxed,** 1973-75, Mego
　　　MNP $75　　**MIP $150**

POCKET SUPER HEROES (MEGO, 1976-79)

3-3/4" FIGURES

❑ **Aquaman, 1976, white card,** 1979, Mego
　　　MNP $50　　**MIP $100**

❑ **Batman, 1976, red card,** 1979, Mego
　　　MNP $20　　**MIP $40**

❑ **Batman, 1976, white card,** 1979, Mego
　　　MNP $20　　**MIP $40**

❑ **Captain America, 1976, white card,** 1979, Mego
　　　MNP $50　　**MIP $100**

❑ **General Zod, 1979, red card,** 1979, Mego
　　　MNP $5　　**MIP $15**

❑ **Green Goblin, 1976, white card,** 1979, Mego
　　　MNP $50　　**MIP $100**

❑ **Hulk, 1976, white card,** 1979, Mego
　　　MNP $15　　**MIP $40**

(Toy Shop File Photo)

❑ **Hulk, 1979, red card,** 1979, Mego, Shown on right with Robin
　　　MNP $15　　**MIP $30**

❑ **Jor-El (Superman), 1979, red card,** 1979, Mego
　　　MNP $10　　**MIP $20**

❑ **Lex Luthor (Superman), 1979, red card,** 1979, Mego
　　　MNP $10　　**MIP $20**

❑ **Robin, 1976, white card,** 1979, Mego
　　　MNP $20　　**MIP $40**

(Toy Shop File Photo)

❑ **Robin, 1979, red card,** 1979, Mego, Shown on left with Hulk
　　　MNP $20　　**MIP $40**

❑ **Spider-Man, 1976, white card,** 1979, Mego
　　　MNP $15　　**MIP $40**

❑ **Spider-Man, 1979, red card,** 1979, Mego
　　　MNP $15　　**MIP $30**

❑ **Superman, 1976, white card,** 1979, Mego
　　　MNP $15　　**MIP $30**

❑ **Superman, 1979, red card,** 1979, Mego
　　　MNP $15　　**MIP $30**

❑ **Wonder Woman, 1979, white card,** 1979, Mego
　　　MNP $20　　**MIP $45**

ACCESSORIES

❑ **Batcave, 1981,** 1979, Mego
　　　MNP $120　　**MIP $300**

VEHICLES

❑ **Batmachine, 1979,** 1979, Mego
　　　MNP $40　　**MIP $100**

❑ **Batmobile, 1979, with Batman and Robin,** 1979, Mego
　　　MNP $80　　**MIP $200**

❑ **Spider-Car, 1979, with Spider-Man and Hulk,** 1979, Mego
　　　MNP $30　　**MIP $75**

❑ **Spider-Machine, 1979,** 1979, Mego
　　　MNP $40　　**MIP $100**

POWER RANGERS IN SPACE (BANDAI, 1998)

ACTION ZORDS, 5" FIGURES

❑ **Astro Megaship,** 1998, Bandai
　　　MNP $2　　**MIP $6**

❑ **Astro Megazord,** 1998, Bandai
　　　MNP $2　　**MIP $6**

❑ **Delta Megazord,** 1998, Bandai
　　　MNP $2　　**MIP $6**

ACTION FIGURES

❏ **Mega Tank,** 1998, Bandai
MNP $2   MIP $6

❏ **Mega Winger,** 1998, Bandai
MNP $2   MIP $6

ASTRO RANGER, 5" FIGURES

❏ **Black Ranger,** 1998, Bandai
MNP $2   MIP $6

❏ **Pink Ranger,** 1998, Bandai
MNP $2   MIP $6

❏ **Red Ranger,** 1998, Bandai
MNP $2   MIP $6

❏ **Red Ranger,** 1998, Bandai
MNP $2   MIP $6

❏ **Silver Ranger,** 1998, Bandai
MNP $2   MIP $6

❏ **Yellow Ranger,** 1998, Bandai
MNP $2   MIP $6

**BATTLIZED POWER RANGERS, 5"
FIGURES**

❏ **Black Ranger,** 1998, Bandai
MNP $2   MIP $6

❏ **Blue Ranger,** 1998, Bandai
MNP $2   MIP $6

❏ **Red ranger,** 1998, Bandai
MNP $2   MIP $6

❏ **Silver,** 1998, Bandai
MNP $2   MIP $6

EVIL SPACE ALIENS, 5" FIGURES

❏ **Craterite,** 1998, Bandai
MNP $2   MIP $6

❏ **Ecliptor,** 1998, Bandai
MNP $2   MIP $6

**STAR POWER RANGERS IN
SPACE, 5" FIGURES**

❏ **Blue Ranger,** 1998, Bandai
MNP $2   MIP $6

❏ **Green Ranger,** 1998, Bandai
MNP $2   MIP $6

❏ **Pink Ranger,** 1998, Bandai
MNP $2   MIP $6

❏ **Red Ranger,** 1998, Bandai
MNP $2   MIP $6

❏ **Yellow Ranger,** 1998, Bandai
MNP $2   MIP $6

**POWER RANGERS TURBO
(BANDAI, 1997)**

EVIL SPACE ALIENS, 5" FIGURES

❏ **Amphibitor,** 1997, Bandai
MNP $2   MIP $6

❏ **Chromite,** 1997, Bandai
MNP $2   MIP $6

❏ **Divatox,** 1997, Bandai
MNP $2   MIP $6

❏ **Elgar,** 1997, Bandai
MNP $2   MIP $6

❏ **Griller,** 1997, Bandai
MNP $2   MIP $6

❏ **Hammeron,** 1997, Bandai
MNP $2   MIP $6

❏ **Rygog,** 1997, Bandai
MNP $2   MIP $6

❏ **Visceron,** 1997, Bandai
MNP $2   MIP $6

**REPEAT TURBO RANGERS, 5"
FIGURES**

❏ **Blue Ranger,** 1997, Bandai
MNP $2   MIP $6

❏ **Green Ranger,** 1997, Bandai
MNP $2   MIP $6

❏ **Pink Ranger,** 1997, Bandai
MNP $2   MIP $6

❏ **Red Ranger,** 1997, Bandai
MNP $2   MIP $6

❏ **Yellow Ranger,** 1997, Bandai
MNP $2   MIP $6

TURBO CARTS WITH 4" FIGURE

❏ **Cart with Blue Turbo Ranger,** 1997,
Bandai
MNP $3   MIP $8

❏ **Cart with Green Turbo Ranger,** 1997,
Bandai
MNP $3   MIP $8

❏ **Cart with Pink Turbo Ranger,** 1997,
Bandai
MNP $3   MIP $8

❏ **Cart with Red Turbo Ranger,** 1997,
Bandai
MNP $3   MIP $8

❏ **Cart with Yellow Turbo Ranger,** 1997,
Bandai
MNP $3   MIP $8

**TURBO RANGERS, 5" FIGURES,
EACH ACTIVATED WITH KEY**

❏ **Blue Turbo Ranger,** 1997, Bandai
MNP $2   MIP $6

❏ **Green Turbo Ranger,** 1997, Bandai
MNP $2   MIP $6

❏ **Pink Turbo Ranger,** 1997, Bandai
MNP $2   MIP $6

❏ **Red Turbo Ranger,** 1997, Bandai
MNP $2   MIP $6

❏ **Yellow Turbo Ranger,** 1997, Bandai
MNP $2   MIP $6

TURBO SHIFTER, 5" FIGURES

❏ **Blue Ranger,** 1997, Bandai
MNP $2   MIP $6

❏ **Green Ranger,** 1997, Bandai
MNP $2   MIP $6

❏ **Pink Ranger,** 1997, Bandai
MNP $2   MIP $6

❏ **Red Ranger,** 1997, Bandai
MNP $2   MIP $6

❏ **Yellow Ranger,** 1997, Bandai
MNP $2   MIP $6

**POWER RANGERS ZEO
(BANDAI, 1996)**

AUTO MORPHIN, 5-1/2" FIGURES

❏ **Blue,** 1996, Bandai
MNP $2   MIP $6

❏ **Gold Warrior,** 1996, Bandai
MNP $2   MIP $6

❏ **Green,** 1996, Bandai
MNP $2   MIP $6

❏ **Pink,** 1996, Bandai
MNP $2   MIP $6

❏ **Red,** 1996, Bandai
MNP $2   MIP $6

❏ **Yellow,** 1996, Bandai
MNP $2   MIP $6

**EVIL SPACE ALIENS, 5-1/2"
FIGURES**

❏ **Cogs,** 1996, Bandai
MNP $2   MIP $6

❏ **Drill Master,** 1996, Bandai
MNP $2   MIP $6

❏ **Mechanizer,** 1996, Bandai
MNP $2   MIP $6

❏ **Quadfighter,** 1996, Bandai
MNP $2   MIP $6

❏ **Silo,** 1996, Bandai
MNP $2   MIP $6

ZEO JET CYCLES WITH FIGURE

❏ **Cycle with Blue Zeo Ranger III,** 1996,
Bandai
MNP $2   MIP $6

❏ **Cycle with Gold Zeo Ranger,** 1996,
Bandai
MNP $2   MIP $6

❏ **Cycle with Green Zeo Ranger IV,** 1996,
Bandai
MNP $2   MIP $6

❏ **Cycle with Pink Zeo Ranger I,** 1996,
Bandai
MNP $2   MIP $6

❏ **Cycle with Red Zeo Ranger V,** 1996,
Bandai
MNP $2   MIP $6

❏ **Cycle with Yellow Zeo Ranger II,** 1996,
Bandai
MNP $2   MIP $6

**ZEO POWER ZORDS, 5-1/2"
FIGURES**

❏ **1-2 Punching Action Red Battlezord,**
1996, Bandai
MNP $2   MIP $6

❏ **Auric the Conqueror Zord,** 1996, Bandai
MNP $2   MIP $6

❏ **Power Sword Action Zeo Megazord,** 1996, Bandai
MNP $2   MIP $6

❏ **Pyramidas,** 1996, Bandai
MNP $2   MIP $6

❏ **Super Zeo Megazord,** 1996, Bandai
MNP $2   MIP $6

❏ **Warrior Wheel,** 1996, Bandai
MNP $2   MIP $6

ZEO RANGERS, 5-1/2" FIGURES

❏ **Blue Zeo Ranger III,** 1996, Bandai
MNP $2   MIP $6

❏ **Gold Zeo Ranger,** 1996, Bandai
MNP $2   MIP $6

❏ **Green Zeo Ranger IV,** 1996, Bandai
MNP $2   MIP $6

❏ **Pink Zeo Ranger I,** 1996, Bandai
MNP $2   MIP $6

❏ **Red Zeo Ranger V,** 1996, Bandai
MNP $2   MIP $6

❏ **Yellow Zeo Ranger II,** 1996, Bandai
MNP $2   MIP $6

ZEO RANGERS, 8" FIGURES

❏ **Blue Zeo Ranger III,** 1996, Bandai
MNP $3   MIP $8

❏ **Gold Zeo Ranger,** 1996, Bandai
MNP $3   MIP $8

❏ **Green Zeo Ranger IV,** 1996, Bandai
MNP $3   MIP $8

❏ **Pink Zeo Ranger I,** 1996, Bandai
MNP $3   MIP $8

❏ **Red Zeo Ranger V,** 1996, Bandai
MNP $3   MIP $8

❏ **Yellow Zeo Ranger II,** 1996, Bandai
MNP $3   MIP $8

PUPPETMASTER (FULL MOON TOYS, 1997-PRESENT)

FIGURES

❏ **Blade,** 1997-present, Full Moon
MNP $8   MIP $20

❏ **Blade, blood splattered,** 1997-present, Full Moon
MNP $25   MIP $85

❏ **Blade, bullet-eyed (Troll & Joad),** 1997-present, Full Moon
MNP $15   MIP $40

❏ **Blade, gold,** 1997-present, Full Moon
MNP $8   MIP $20

❏ **Blade, red Japanese Exclusive,** 1997-present, Full Moon
MNP $15   MIP $40

❏ **Jester,** 1997-present, Full Moon
MNP $3   MIP $12

❏ **Jester, gold,** 1997-present, Full Moon
MNP $8   MIP $20

❏ **Jester, Japanese Exclusive, Carse of Jester,** 1997-present, Full Moon
MNP $3   MIP $12

❏ **Jester, Previews Exclusive,** 1997-present, Full Moon
MNP $8   MIP $20

❏ **Leech Woman,** 1997-present, Full Moon
MNP $3   MIP $12

❏ **Leech Woman, gold,** 1997-present, Full Moon
MNP $8   MIP $20

❏ **Leech Woman, Japanese Exclusive, Geisha Leech Woman,** 1997-present, Full Moon
MNP $3   MIP $12

❏ **Leech Woman, Previews Exclusive,** 1997-present, Full Moon
MNP $8   MIP $20

❏ **Mephisto,** 1997-present, Full Moon
MNP $3   MIP $12

❏ **Mephisto, clear,** 1997-present, Full Moon
MNP $5   MIP $15

❏ **Mephisto, Japanese Exclusive, death Mephisto,** 1997-present, Full Moon
MNP $8   MIP $20

❏ **Mephisto, Previews Exclusive,** 1997-present, Full Moon
MNP $8   MIP $20

❏ **Pinhead,** 1997-present, Full Moon
MNP $3   MIP $12

❏ **Pinhead, gold,** 1997-present, Full Moon
MNP $8   MIP $20

❏ **Pinhead, Halloween 1999,** 1999, Full Moon
MNP $8   MIP $20

❏ **Pinhead, Japanese Exclusive, Pinhead in the Dark,** 1997-present, Full Moon
MNP $8   MIP $25

❏ **Pinhead, Previews Exclusive,** 1997-present, Full Moon
MNP $8   MIP $20

❏ **Sixshooter,** 1997-present, Full Moon
MNP $8   MIP $20

❏ **Sixshooter,** 1997-present, Full Moon
MNP $8   MIP $20

❏ **Sixshooter, Japanese Exclusive, DOA Sixshooter,** 1997-present, Full Moon
MNP $10   MIP $30

❏ **Sixshooter, Troll & Joad edition,** 1997-present, Full Moon
MNP $10   MIP $30

❏ **Torch,** 1997-present, Full Moon
MNP $3   MIP $12

❏ **Torch, gold,** 1997-present, Full Moon
MNP $8   MIP $20

❏ **Torch, Japanese Exclusive, Camouflage Torch,** 1997-present, Full Moon
MNP $8   MIP $20

❏ **Torch, Previews Exclusive,** 1997-present, Full Moon
MNP $8   MIP $20

❏ **Totem,** 1997-present, Full Moon
MNP $3   MIP $12

❏ **Totem, 1998 San Diego Comicon,** 1997-present, Full Moon
MNP $15   MIP $45

❏ **Totem, gold,** 1997-present, Full Moon
MNP $5   MIP $15

❏ **Totem, Japanese Exclusive, Evil Spirit Totem,** 1997-present, Full Moon
MNP $10   MIP $35

❏ **Totem, Preview Exclusive,** 1997-present, Full Moon
MNP $8   MIP $20

❏ **Tunneler,** 1997-present, Full Moon
MNP $3   MIP $12

❏ **Tunneler, Australian Exclusive,** 1997-present, Full Moon
MNP $15   MIP $45

❏ **Tunneler, gold,** 1997-present, Full Moon
MNP $8   MIP $20

❏ **Tunneler, Japanese Exclusive, Cruel Sgt. Tunneler,** 1997-present, Full Moon
MNP $15   MIP $45

❏ **Tunneler, Previews Exclusive,** 1997-present, Full Moon
MNP $8   MIP $20

RAMBO (COLECO, 1985)

FIGURES

❏ **Black Dragon,** 1985, Coleco
MNP $4   MIP $10

❏ **Chief,** 1985, Coleco
MNP $8   MIP $15

❏ **Colonel Troutman,** 1985, Coleco
MNP $4   MIP $8

❏ **Dr. Hyde,** 1985, Coleco
MNP $10   MIP $23

❏ **General Warhawk,** 1985, Coleco
MNP $4   MIP $10

❏ **Gripper,** 1985, Coleco
MNP $4   MIP $10

❏ **K.A.T.,** 1985, Coleco
MNP $5   MIP $10

❏ **Mad Dog,** 1985, Coleco
MNP $4   MIP $10

❏ **Nomad,** 1985, Coleco
MNP $8   MIP $13

(Toy Shop File Photo)

❏ **Rambo,** 1985, Coleco, Popular '80s icon lives on.
MNP $5   MIP $13

❏ **Rambo with Fire Power,** 1985, Coleco
MNP $5   MIP $13

❏ **Sergeant Havoc,** 1985, Coleco
MNP $4   MIP $10

❏ **Turbo,** 1985, Coleco
MNP $4   MIP $10

❏ **White Dragon,** 1985, Coleco
MNP $4   MIP $10

RESIDENT EVIL

SERIES II

(KP Photo)

❏ **Alexia,** 2002, Palisades, Bug-winged figure with "leafy" hair
MNP $8   MIP $12

(KP Photo)

❏ **Claire Redfield,** 2002, Palisades, Figure includes dagger and pistol
MNP $8   MIP $12

(KP Photo)

❏ **Mr. X,** 2002, Palisades, Black jacket and uniform, dark gray skin, glowing eyes
MNP $8   MIP $12

(KP Photo)

❏ **Zombie Cop,** 2002, Palisades, Mauled policeman with terrifying ? on a leash…
MNP $8   MIP $12

RESIDENT EVIL (TOY BIZ, 1998)

5" FIGURES

❏ **Chris Redfield and Cerberus,** 1998
MNP $5   MIP $15

❏ **Hunter and Chimera,** 1998
MNP $3   MIP $8

❏ **Jill Valentine and Web Spinner,** 1998
MNP $3   MIP $8

❏ **Maggot Zombie and Forrest Speyer,** 1998
MNP $3   MIP $8

❏ **Tyrant,** 1998
MNP $3   MIP $8

ROB ZOMBIE (MCFARLANE, 2000)

FIGURES

(KP Photo)

❏ **Rob Zombie,** 2000, Figure with mechanical arms includes "Zombie" base
MNP $5   MIP $15

ROBIN HOOD AND HIS MERRY MEN (MEGO, 1974)

8" FIGURES

❏ **Friar Tuck,** 1974, Mego
MNP $25   MIP $75

(Toy Shop File Photo)

❑ **Little John,** 1974, Mego, With dagger and belt
    MNP $75   **MIP $150**

❑ **Robin Hood,** 1974, Mego
    MNP $75   **MIP $150**

❑ **Will Scarlett,** 1974, Mego
    MNP $75   **MIP $150**

FIGURES

❑ **Friar Tuck,** 1974
    MNP $25   **MIP $60**

❑ **Little John,** 1974
    MNP $65   **MIP $150**

❑ **Robin Hood,** 1974
    MNP $90   **MIP $300**

❑ **Will Scarlett,** 1974
    MNP $75   **MIP $275**

ROBIN HOOD PRINCE OF THIEVES (KENNER, 1991)

ACCESSORIES

❑ **Battle Wagon,** 1991, Kenner, accessory
    MNP $15   **MIP $30**

❑ **Bola Bomber,** 1991, Kenner, accessory
    MNP $5   **MIP $10**

❑ **Net Launcher,** 1991, Kenner, accessory
    MNP $5   **MIP $10**

❑ **Sherwood Forest Play Set,** 1991, Kenner, Play Set
    MNP $30   **MIP $60**

FIGURES

❑ **Azeem,** 1991, Kenner, action figure
    MNP $7   **MIP $15**

(Lenny Lee)

❑ **Friar Tuck, with Battle Staff,** 1991, Kenner, action figure, with fabric road
    MNP $15   **MIP $30**

❑ **Little John,** 1991, Kenner, action figure
    MNP $7   **MIP $15**

❑ **Robin Hood, Crossbow,** 1991, Kenner, action figure
    MNP $5   **MIP $18**

❑ **Robin Hood, Crossbow, Costner Head,** 1991, Kenner, action figure
    MNP $7   **MIP $20**

❑ **Robin Hood, Long Bow,** 1991, Kenner, action figure
    MNP $8   **MIP $17**

❑ **Robin Hood, Long Bow, Costner Head,** 1991, Kenner, action figure
    MNP $10   **MIP $20**

❑ **Sheriff of Nottingham,** 1991, Kenner, action figure
    MNP $5   **MIP $15**

❑ **The Dark Warrior,** 1991, Kenner, action figure
    MNP $8   **MIP $20**

❑ **Will Scarlett,** 1991, Kenner, action figure
    MNP $8   **MIP $20**

ROBOCOP AND THE ULTRA POLICE (KENNER, 1989-90)

FIGURES

❑ **Ace Jackson,** 1989-90, Kenner, action figure
    MNP $5   **MIP $15**

❑ **Anne Lewis,** 1989-90, Kenner, action figure
    MNP $5   **MIP $15**

❑ **Birdman Barnes,** 1989-90, Kenner, action figure
    MNP $8   **MIP $15**

❑ **Chainsaw,** 1989-90, Kenner, action figure
    MNP $5   **MIP $15**

❑ **Claw Callahan,** 1989-90, Kenner, action figure
    MNP $7   **MIP $15**

❑ **Dr. McNamara,** 1989-90, Kenner, action figure
    MNP $5   **MIP $15**

❑ **Ed-260,** 1989-90, Kenner, action figure
    MNP $10   **MIP $25**

❑ **Headhunter,** 1989-90, Kenner, action figure
    MNP $5   **MIP $15**

❑ **Nitro,** 1989-90, Kenner, action figure
    MNP $5   **MIP $15**

❑ **RoboCop,** 1989-90, Kenner, action figure
    MNP $9   **MIP $20**

❑ **RoboCop Night Fighter,** 1989-90, Kenner, action figure
    MNP $6   **MIP $20**

❑ **RoboCop, Gatlin' Gun,** 1989-90, Kenner, action figure
    MNP $15   **MIP $30**

❑ **Scorcher,** 1989-90, Kenner, action figure
    MNP $6   **MIP $15**

❑ **Sgt. Reed,** 1989-90, Kenner, action figure
    MNP $6   **MIP $15**

❑ **Toxic Waster,** 1989-90, Kenner, action figure
    MNP $10   **MIP $20**

❑ **Wheels Wilson,** 1989-90, Kenner, action figure
    MNP $6   **MIP $15**

VEHICLES

❑ **Robo-1,** 1989-90, Kenner, vehicle
    MNP $10   **MIP $25**

❑ **Robo-Command with figure,** 1989-90, Kenner, vehicle with figure
    MNP $10   **MIP $30**

❑ **Robo-Copter,** 1989-90, Kenner, vehicle
    MNP $15   **MIP $35**

❑ **Robo-Cycle,** 1989-90, Kenner, vehicle
    MNP $5   **MIP $10**

❑ **Robo-Hawk,** 1989-90, Kenner, vehicle
    MNP $10   **MIP $35**

❑ **Robo-Jailer,** 1989-90, Kenner, vehicle
    MNP $15   **MIP $40**

❑ **Robo-Tank,** 1989-90, Kenner, vehicle
    MNP $10   **MIP $35**

❑ **Skull-Hog,** 1989-90, Kenner, vehicle
    MNP $5   **MIP $10**

❑ **Vandal-1,** 1989-90, Kenner, vehicle
    MNP $5   **MIP $20**

ROBOTECH (MATCHBOX, 1986)

11-1/2" FIGURES

❑ **Dana Sterling,** 1986
    MNP $20   **MIP $50**

❑ **Lisa Heyes,** 1986
    MNP $20   **MIP $50**

❑ **Lynn Minemei,** 1986
    MNP $20   **MIP $50**

❑ **Rink Hunter,** 1986
    MNP $20   **MIP $50**

3-3/4" FIGURES

❑ **Bioroid Terminator,** 1986
    MNP $5   **MIP $15**

❑ **Corg,** 1986
    MNP $8   **MIP $20**

❑ **Dana Sterling,** 1986
    MNP $12   **MIP $30**

❑ **Lisa Hayes,** 1986, Center figure, shown with Roy Fokker and Zor Prime
    MNP $8   **MIP $20**

ACTION FIGURES

❑ **Lunk,** 1986
MNP $8   MIP $20

❑ **Max Sterling,** 1986
MNP $8   MIP $20

❑ **Miriya, black,** 1986
MNP $25   MIP $65

❑ **Miriya, red,** 1986
MNP $8   MIP $20

❑ **Rand,** 1986
MNP $5   MIP $12

❑ **Rick Hunter,** 1986
MNP $10   MIP $25

❑ **Robotech Master,** 1986
MNP $5   MIP $12

❑ **Rook Bartley,** 1986
MNP $20   MIP $50

❑ **Roy Fokker,** 1986, At left, shown with Lisa Hayes and Zor Prime
MNP $12   MIP $30

❑ **Scott Bernard,** 1986
MNP $12   MIP $37

❑ **Zor Prime,** 1986, Matchbox, At right, shown with Lisa Hayes and Roy Fokker
MNP $8   MIP $15

8" FIGURES

❑ **Armoured Zentraedi Warrior,** 1986
MNP $8   MIP $20

❑ **Breetai,** 1986
MNP $8   MIP $20

❑ **Dolza,** 1986
MNP $5   MIP $15

❑ **Exedore,** 1986
MNP $8   MIP $20

❑ **Khryon,** 1986
MNP $8   MIP $20

❑ **Miriya,** 1986
MNP $8   MIP $20

VEHICLES AND ACCESSORIES

❑ **Armoured Cyclone,** 1986
MNP $8   MIP $20

❑ **Bioroid Hover Craft,** 1986
MNP $10   MIP $25

❑ **Dana's Hover Cycle,** 1986
MNP $12   MIP $35

❑ **Invid Scout Ship,** 1986
MNP $12   MIP $30

❑ **Tactical Battle Pod,** 1986
MNP $12   MIP $30

❑ **Veritech Fighter,** 1986
MNP $15   MIP $40

❑ **Veritech Hover Tank,** 1986
MNP $15   MIP $40

❑ **Zentraedi Officer's Battle pod,** 1986
MNP $12   MIP $35

ROCKY HORROR PICTURE SHOW

FIGURES

(KP Photo)

❑ **Columbia, Series 1,** 2000, Vital Toys, Gold sequined hat and jacket, silver sequined top
MNP $3   MIP $10

(KP Photo)

❑ **Frank N Furter, Series 1,** 2000, Vital Toys, Very detailed likeness of Rocky Horror's famous character
MNP $3   MIP $10

ROCKY HORROW PICTURE SHOW

FIGURES

❑ **Riff Raff, Series 1,** 2000, Vital Toys, Detailed figure with yellow hair and face with proper white pallor
MNP $3   MIP $10

SHOGUN WARRIORS (MATTEL, 1979)

24" FIGURES

❑ **Daimos,** 1979, Mattel
MNP $75   MIP $150

FIGURES

❑ **Dragun,** 1979, Mattel
MNP $75   MIP $175

❑ **Dragun (2nd figure),** 1979, Mattel
MNP $75   MIP $150

❑ **Gaiking,** 1979, Mattel
MNP $75   MIP $150

❑ **Godzilla,** 1979, Mattel
MNP $100   MIP $200

❑ **Godzilla (2nd figure),** 1979, Mattel
MNP $150   MIP $200

❑ **Mazinga,** 1979, Mattel
MNP $85   MIP $175

❑ **Mazinga (2nd figure),** 1979, Mattel
MNP $75   MIP $150

❑ **Raydeen,** 1979, Mattel
MNP $75   MIP $150

❑ **Rodan,** 1979
MNP $150   MIP $300

SILVER SURFER (TOY BIZ, 1997-98)

COSMIC POWER ALIEN FIGHTERS

❑ **Adam Warlock with Cosmic Skull Space Racer,** 1998
MNP $3   MIP $8

❑ **Cosmic Silver Surfer and Pip the Troll,** 1998
MNP $3   MIP $8

❑ **Galactus with Silver Surfer in Cosmic Orb, 8" figure,** 1998
MNP $3   MIP $8

❑ **Ivar and Ant Warrior with Alien Annihilator,** 1998
MNP $3   MIP $8

❑ **Molten Lava Silver Surfer with Eyeball Alien Space Racer,** 1998
MNP $3   MIP $8

❏ **Ronan the Accussor with Tree Root Space Racer,** 1998
    MNP $3   MIP $8

❏ **Solar Silver Surfer & Draconian Warrior,** 1998
    MNP $3   MIP $8

❏ **Super Nova with Flaming Bird,** 1998
    MNP $3   MIP $8

FIGURES

❏ **Beta Ray Bull, Thunder Hammer,** 1997
    MNP $3   MIP $10

❏ **Classic Silver Surfer with Cosmetic Surf Board,** 1997
    MNP $3   MIP $10

❏ **Meegan Alien, Galactic Weapon Seeker,** 1997
    MNP $3   MIP $10

❏ **Nova, Poseable Flaming Hair,** 1997
    MNP $3   MIP $10

INFINITY GAUNTLET SERIES, 10" FIGURE

❏ **Silver Surfer,** 1997
    MNP $5   MIP $15

SIMPSONS (MATTEL, 1990)

FIGURES

❏ **Bart,** 1990, Mattel
    MNP $10   MIP $30

❏ **Bartman,** 1990, Mattel
    MNP $10   MIP $30

❏ **Homer,** 1990, Mattel
    MNP $10   MIP $35

❏ **Lisa,** 1990, Mattel
    MNP $15   MIP $40

❏ **Maggie,** 1990, Mattel
    MNP $15   MIP $40

❏ **Marge,** 1990, Mattel
    MNP $10   MIP $30

❏ **Nelson,** 1990, Mattel
    MNP $10   MIP $30

❏ **Sofa Set,** 1990, Mattel
    MNP $10   MIP $40

SIMPSONS (PLAYMATES, 2000-PRESENT)

ACCESSORIES

❏ **Kwiki Mart with Apu, interactive,** 2000-Present, Playmates
    MNP $8   MIP $20

❏ **Living Room with Marge and Maggie, interactive,** 2000-Present, Playmates
    MNP $10   MIP $25

❏ **Nuclear Power Plant with Homer, interactive,** 2000-Present, Playmates
    MNP $10   MIP $25

FIGURES

❏ **Barney,** 2000-Present, Playmates
    MNP $6   MIP $20

❏ **Bart,** 2000-Present, Playmates
    MNP $6   MIP $20

❏ **Chief Wiggum,** 2000-Present, Playmates
    MNP $6   MIP $16

❏ **Grandpa,** 2000-Present, Playmates
    MNP $10   MIP $30

❏ **Homer,** 2000-Present, Playmates
    MNP $8   MIP $24

❏ **Krusty,** 2000-Present, Playmates
    MNP $10   MIP $30

❏ **Lisa,** 2000-Present, Playmates
    MNP $10   MIP $30

❏ **Mr. Burns,** 2000-Present, Playmates
    MNP $10   MIP $30

❏ **Ned Flanders,** 2000-Present, Playmates
    MNP $6   MIP $20

❏ **Pinpal Homer,** 2000-Present, Playmates
    MNP $6   MIP $20

❏ **Radio Active Homer, ToyFare Exclusive,** 2000, Playmates
    MNP $50   MIP $200

❏ **Smithers,** 2000-Present, Playmates
    MNP $5   MIP $15

❏ **Sunday Best Bart,** 2000-Present, Playmates
    MNP $3   MIP $10

❏ **Treehouse of Horrors, Toys R Us Exclusive,** 2000, Playmates
    MNP $25   MIP $75

SIN CITY (MCFARLANE, 1999-PRESENT)

FIGURES

❏ **Death Row Marv,** 2000
    MNP $5   MIP $15

❏ **Marv,** 1999
    MNP $3   MIP $10

SIX MILLION DOLLAR MAN (KENNER, 1975-78)

ACCESSORIES

❏ **Backpack Radio,** 1975-78, Kenner
    MNP $10   MIP $25

❏ **Bionic Cycle,** 1975-78, Kenner
    MNP $10   MIP $20

❏ **Bionic Mission Vehicle,** 1975-78, Kenner
    MNP $25   MIP $25

❏ **Bionic Transport,** 1975-78, Kenner
    MNP $10   MIP $45

❏ **Bionic Video Center,** 1975-78, Kenner
    MNP $35   MIP $100

❏ **Critical Assignment Arms,** 1975-78, Kenner
    MNP $15   MIP $45

❏ **Critical Assignment Legs,** 1975-78, Kenner
    MNP $15   MIP $45

❏ **Dual Launch Drag Set with 4" Steve Austin Bionic Bigfoot figure,** 1975-78, Kenner
    MNP $45   MIP $80

❏ **Flight Suit,** 1975-78, Kenner
    MNP $15   MIP $30

❏ **Mission Control Center,** 1975-78, Kenner
    MNP $25   MIP $75

❏ **Mission to Mars Space Suit,** 1975-78, Kenner
    MNP $15   MIP $30

❏ **OSI Headquarters,** 1975-78, Kenner
    MNP $30   MIP $70

❏ **OSI Undercover Blue Denims,** 1975-78, Kenner
    MNP $15   MIP $30

❏ **Porta-Communicator,** 1975-78, Kenner
    MNP $20   MIP $50

❏ **Tower & Cycle Set,** 1975-78, Kenner
    MNP $25   MIP $50

❏ **Venus Space Probe,** 1975-78, Kenner
    MNP $125   MIP $275

FIGURES

(Toy Shop File Photo)

❏ **Bionic Bigfoot,** 1975-78, Kenner, A beast you wouldn't want to run into in the woods.
    MNP $75   MIP $175

(Toy Shop File Photo)

ACTION FIGURES

❏ **Maskatron,** 1975-78, Kenner
MNP $40   MIP $150

(Toy Shop File Photo)

❏ **Oscar Goldman,** 1975-78, Kenner, Wearing familiar checked jacket and carrying exploding briefcase, should Steve Austin's secrets fall into the wrong hands
MNP $50   MIP $100

❏ **Steve Austin,** 1975-78, Kenner
MNP $50   MIP $100

❏ **Steve Austin with biosonic arm,** 1975-78
MNP $75   MIP $300

❏ **Steve Austin with engine block,** 1975-78
MNP $50   MIP $150

❏ **Steve Austin with girder,** 1975-78
MNP $60   MIP $200

SLAP SHOT (MCFARLANE, 2000)

FIGURES

(KP Photo)

❏ **Jack Hanson,** 2000, From movie "Slap Shot." Includes detailed figure and rink diorama
MNP $5   MIP $10

❏ **Jeff Hanson,** 2000, Detailed figure with hockey rink base and background
MNP $5   MIP $10

(Toy Shop File Photo)

❏ **Steve Hanson,** 2000, McFarlane Toys, Part of the trio of figures from the movie "Slap Shot."
MNP $5   MIP $10

SLEEPY HOLLOW (MCFARLANE, 1999)

FIGURES

❏ **Crone,** 1999
MNP $3   MIP $10

❏ **Headless Horseman,** 1999
MNP $3   MIP $10

❏ **Headless Rider and Horse box set,** 1999
MNP $8   MIP $20

❏ **Ichabod Crane,** 1999
MNP $3   MIP $10

SPACE:1999 (MATTEL, 1976)

FIGURES

(Corey LeChat)

❏ **Commander Koenig,** 1976, Mattel, Shown at center with Bergman and Russell
MNP $30   MIP $60

(Corey LeChat)

❏ **Dr. Russell,** 1976, Mattel, Shown at right with Bergman and Koenig
MNP $30   MIP $60

(Corey LeChat)

❏ **Professor Bergman,** 1976, Mattel, Shown at left with Com. Koenig anf Dr. Russell
MNP $30   MIP $60

❏ **Zython Alien,** 1976, Mattel
MNP $75   MIP $200

PLAY SET

❏ **Eagle Playset with three 3" figures,** 1976, Mattel
MNP $150   MIP $300

❏ **Moonbase Alpha Deluxe Playset with three figures,** 1976, Mattel
MNP $75   MIP $200

❏ **Moonbase Alpha Playset,** 1976, Mattel
MNP $35   MIP $80

SPACE:1999 (PALITOY, 1975)

FIGURES

❏ **Alan Carter,** 1975, Palitoy
MNP $200   MIP $425

❏ **Captain Koenig,** 1975, Palitoy
MNP $150   MIP $250

❏ **Captain Zantor,** 1975, Palitoy
MNP $75   MIP $160

❏ **Mysterious Alien,** 1975, Palitoy
MNP $75   MIP $160

❏ **Paul Morrow,** 1975, Palitoy
MNP $175   MIP $300

SPAWN (MCFARLANE, 1994-PRESENT)

13" FIGURES

❏ **Angela,** 1996
MNP $10   MIP $25

□ **Medieval Spawn, Kay Bee Exclusive,** 1997
MNP $10   MIP $25

□ **Spawn,** 1996
MNP $10   MIP $25

ACCESSORIES

□ **Spawn Alley Play Set,** 1994-96, McFarlane
MNP $15   MIP $50

□ **Spawnmobile,** 1994-96, McFarlane
MNP $12   MIP $40

□ **Violator Monster Rig,** 1994-96, McFarlane
MNP $12   MIP $45

MCFARLANE TOYS COLLECTOR'S CLUB EXCLUSIVES

□ **Cogliosto**
MNP $5   MIP $15

□ **Terry Fitzgerald**
MNP $5   MIP $15

□ **Todd the Artist**
MNP $5   MIP $15

□ **Wanda and Cyan,** 2000
MNP $3   MIP $13

SERIES 1, 1994 (TODD TOYS PACKAGING)

□ **Clown,** clown head, 1994
MNP $6   MIP $20

□ **Clown, Kay Bee Exclusive,** 1994
MNP $3   MIP $10

□ **Clown,** monster head, 1994, McFarlane
MNP $6   MIP $10

□ **Medieval Spawn,** black armor, 1994
MNP $5   MIP $25

□ **Medieval Spawn, Kay Bee Exclusive,** 1994
MNP $5   MIP $15

□ **Medieval Spawn,** blue armor, 1994, McFarlane
MNP $5   MIP $20

□ **Overkill,** dark green, 1994
MNP $5   MIP $15

□ **Overkill, Kay Bee Exclusive,** 1996
MNP $3   MIP $12

□ **Overkill,** turquoise, 1994, McFarlane
MNP $7   MIP $20

□ **Spawn, Club Exclusive,** blue body, 1997
MNP $8   MIP $20

□ **Spawn, Club Exclusive,** green body, 1997
MNP $8   MIP $20

□ **Spawn, Diamond Exclusive,** 1994
MNP $45   MIP $120

□ **Spawn,** full mask, 1994, McFarlane
MNP $5   MIP $25

□ **Spawn, Kay Bee Exclusive,** 1995
MNP $10   MIP $30

□ **Spawn, Spawn No. 50 premium (Worm Head),** 1996
MNP $50   MIP $150

□ **Spawn,** unmasked (Hamburger Head), first card, 1994, McFarlane
MNP $15   MIP $40

□ **Tremor,** dark green costume, 1994
MNP $5   MIP $15

□ **Tremor, Kay Bee Exclusive,** 1996
MNP $3   MIP $12

□ **Tremor,** orange skin, 1994, McFarlane
MNP $8   MIP $15

□ **Violator,** 1994, McFarlane
MNP $5   MIP $20

□ **Violator,** chrome card, 1994
MNP $8   MIP $20

□ **Violator,** club version, 1997
MNP $8   MIP $20

□ **Violator,** green card, 1994
MNP $5   MIP $15

□ **Violator, Kay Bee Exclusive,** 1996
MNP $4   MIP $12

□ **Violator,** mail-order, 1995
MNP $20   MIP $75

□ **Violator,** red card, 1994
MNP $5   MIP $15

SERIES 10, MANGA, 1998

□ **Beast,** 1998, McFarlane
MNP $4   MIP $15

□ **Cyber Violator,** 1998, McFarlane
MNP $4   MIP $8

□ **Dead Spawn,** 1998, McFarlane
MNP $4   MIP $8

□ **Freak,** 1998, McFarlane
MNP $4   MIP $8

□ **Overkill,** 1998, McFarlane
MNP $4   MIP $8

□ **Samurai Spawn,** 1998, McFarlane
MNP $4   MIP $8

SERIES 11, DARK AGES, 1998

(KP Photo)

□ **Horrid, The,** 1998, McFarlane, Two figures; one winged human-type (larger) and the other, a small skeletal figure with weapon
MNP $3   MIP $8

(KP Photo)

□ **Ogre, The,** 1998, McFarlane, Large Ogre figure controlled by smaller figure riding on shoulders. Also includes war club
MNP $5   MIP $15

(KP Photo)

□ **Raider, The,** 1998, McFarlane, Centaur figure with battle armor, double-edged pike/axe, string of defeated skulls
MNP $3   MIP $8

(KP Photo)

□ **Skull Queen, The,** 1998, McFarlane, Figure includes battle axes, flying skeletal warrior
MNP $4   MIP $12

□ **Spawn-The Black Knight,** 1998, McFarlane
MNP $5   MIP $15

ACTION FIGURES

(KP Photo)

❏ **Spellcaster, The,** 1998, McFarlane,
Includes battle axe, shield and helmet
MNP $4 MIP $15

SERIES 12, 1998

❏ **Bottom Line,** 1998, McFarlane
MNP $5 MIP $15

❏ **Creech, The,** 1998, McFarlane
MNP $5 MIP $20

❏ **Cy-Gor,** 1998, McFarlane
MNP $5 MIP $25

❏ **Heap, The,** 1998, McFarlane
MNP $5 MIP $15

❏ **Reanimated Spawn,** 1998, McFarlane
MNP $5 MIP $15

❏ **Spawn IV,** 1998, McFarlane
MNP $5 MIP $15

❏ **Top Gun,** 1998, McFarlane
MNP $5 MIP $15

SERIES 14, DARK AGES, 1999

❏ **Iguantus and Tuskadon,** 1999
MNP $5 MIP $15

❏ **Necromancer,** 1999
MNP $5 MIP $15

(McFarlane Toys)

❏ **Scarlet Edge, The,** 1999, A double-
edged sword that is twice the size of the
figure. Who wants one? I do.
MNP $5 MIP $15

❏ **Spawn: The Black Heart,** 1999
MNP $5 MIP $15

❏ **Tormentor,** 1999
MNP $5 MIP $15

❏ **Viper King,** 1999
MNP $5 MIP $15

SERIES 15, TECHNO SPAWN, 1999

❏ **Code Red,** 1999
MNP $5 MIP $15

❏ **Cyber Spawn,** 1999
MNP $5 MIP $15

❏ **Gray thunder,** 1999
MNP $3 MIP $10

❏ **Iron Express,** 1999
MNP $3 MIP $10

❏ **Steel Trap,** 1999
MNP $3 MIP $10

❏ **Warzone,** 1999
MNP $3 MIP $10

SERIES 16, SPAWN NITRORIDERS, 2000

❏ **After Burner,** 2000
MNP $3 MIP $10

❏ **Eclipse 5000,** 2000
MNP $3 MIP $10

❏ **Flash point,** 2000
MNP $3 MIP $10

❏ **Green Vapor, the,** 2000
MNP $3 MIP $10

SERIES 17, SPAWN CLASSIC, 2001

(KP Photo)

❏ **Al Simmons,** 2001, McFarlane,
Includes stand, machine gun, pistol and
accessories
MNP $3 MIP $8

(KP Photo)

❏ **Clown III,** 2001, McFarlane, Includes
wrapped body and stretcher
MNP $3 MIP $8

(KP Photo)

❏ **Malebogia II,** 2001, McFarlane
MNP $3 MIP $8

(KP Photo)

❏ **Medieval Spawn II,** 2001, McFarlane,
Includes chain, sword and accessories
MNP $5 MIP $15

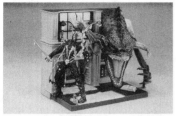

(KP Photo)

❑ **Spawn V,** 2001, McFarlane, With stand
MNP $5　　**MIP $15**

(KP Photo)

❑ **Tiffany II,** 2001, McFarlane, Includes swords, knives, pike, battle staff, accessories and stand
MNP $5　　**MIP $15**

SERIES 18, INTERLINK 6, 2001

(KP Photo)

❑ **HD1,** 2001, McFarlane
MNP $3　　**MIP $10**

(KP Photo)

❑ **LA6,** 2001, McFarlane
MNP $3　　**MIP $10**

(KP Photo)

❑ **LL4,** 2001, McFarlane
MNP $3　　**MIP $10**

(KP Photo)

❑ **RA5,** 2001, McFarlane
MNP $3　　**MIP $10**

(KP Photo)

❑ **RL3,** 2001, McFarlane
MNP $3　　**MIP $10**

(KP Photo)

❑ **TS2,** 2001, McFarlane
MNP $3　　**MIP $10**

SERIES 2, 1995

❑ **Angela,** 1995, McFarlane
MNP $5　　**MIP $25**

❑ **Angela, Club Exclusive, blue,** 1997, McFarlane
MNP $8　　**MIP $20**

❑ **Angela, Club Exclusive, pewter,** 1997, McFarlane
MNP $8　　**MIP $20**

(KP Photo)

❑ **Angela, gold headpiece with gold and purple costume,** 1995, McFarlane, Includes sword, belt and accessories
MNP $20　　**MIP $50**

❑ **Angela, Kay Bee Exclusive,** 1997, McFarlane
MNP $3　　**MIP $12**

❑ **Angela, McFarlane Toy Collector's Club Exclusive,** 1996, McFarlane
MNP $12　　**MIP $35**

❑ **Angela, silver headpiece with silver and blue costume,** 1995, McFarlane
MNP $10　　**MIP $25**

❑ **Badrock, blue,** 1995, McFarlane, With firing missiles
MNP $10　　**MIP $25**

❑ **Badrock, red pants,** 1995, McFarlane
MNP $3   MIP $12

(McFarlane Toys)

❑ **Chapel, blue/black pants,** 1995, McFarlane, Includes gun and jagged-edge sword
MNP $6   MIP $20

❑ **Chapel, green khaki pants,** 1995, McFarlane
MNP $3   MIP $12

(McFarlane Toys)

❑ **Commando Spawn,** 1995, McFarlane, Black and red uniform, includes weapons and headset
MNP $7   MIP $20

(McFarlane Toys)

❑ **Malebolgia,** 1995, McFarlane, Highly-detailed figure
MNP $30   MIP $60

❑ **Pilot Spawn, black costume,** 1995, McFarlane, Black uniform with red high-lights, includes jet pack and dagger
MNP $8   MIP $20

❑ **Pilot Spawn, Kay Bee Toys,** 1997, McFarlane
MNP $3   MIP $12

❑ **Pilot Spawn, white "Astronaut Spawn",** 1995, McFarlane
MNP $5   MIP $16

SERIES 3, 1995

❑ **Cosmic Angela,** 1995, McFarlane
MNP $5   MIP $15

❑ **Cosmic Angela, McFarlane Collector's Club Exclusive,** 1997, McFarlane
MNP $5   MIP $15

❑ **Cosmic Angela, No. 62 Spawn and No. 9 Curse of Spawn, Diamond Exclusive,** 1997, McFarlane
MNP $25   MIP $100

❑ **Curse, The,** 1995, McFarlane
MNP $5   MIP $15

❑ **Curse, The, McFarlane Collector's Club Exclusive,** 1997, McFarlane
MNP $5   MIP $15

❑ **Ninja Spawn,** 1995, McFarlane
MNP $7   MIP $15

❑ **Ninja Spawn, McFarlane Collector's Club Exclusive,** 1997, McFarlane
MNP $5   MIP $15

❑ **Redeemer,** 1995, McFarlane
MNP $5   MIP $15

❑ **Redeemer, McFarlane Collector's Club Exclusive,** 1997, McFarlane
MNP $5   MIP $15

❑ **Spawn II,** 1995, McFarlane
MNP $10   MIP $15

❑ **Spawn II, McFarlane Collector's Club Exclusive,** 1997, McFarlane
MNP $5   MIP $15

❑ **Vertebreaker,** 1995, McFarlane
MNP $10   MIP $25

❑ **Vertebreaker, gray or black body, Exclusive available through various store,** 1996, McFarlane
MNP $5   MIP $15

❑ **Vertebreaker, McFarlane Collector's Club Exclusive,** 1997, McFarlane
MNP $5   MIP $15

❑ **Violator II,** 1995, McFarlane
MNP $10   MIP $20

❑ **Violator II, McFarlane Collector's Club Exclusive,** 1997, McFarlane
MNP $5   MIP $15

SERIES 4, 1996

❑ **Clown II, black guns,** 1996, McFarlane
MNP $6   MIP $20

❑ **Clown II, neon orange guns,** 1996, McFarlane
MNP $3   MIP $12

❑ **Cy-Gor, gold trim,** 1996, McFarlane
MNP $4   MIP $15

❑ **Cy-Gor, purple trim,** 1996, McFarlane
MNP $4   MIP $15

❑ **Cy-Gor, Target Exclusive,** 1996, McFarlane
MNP $5   MIP $15

❑ **Exo-Skeleton Spawn, black and gray exo-skeleton,** 1996, McFarlane
MNP $5   MIP $20

❑ **Exo-Skeleton Spawn, Target Exclusive,** 1997, McFarlane
MNP $5   MIP $15

❑ **Exo-Skeleton Spawn, white and light gray bones and white costume,** 1996, McFarlane
MNP $8   MIP $20

❑ **Future Spawn, red trimmed,** 1996, McFarlane
MNP $10   MIP $15

❑ **Maxx, The, FAO Schwarz Exclusive,** 1996, McFarlane
MNP $15   MIP $40

❑ **Maxx, The, with black Isz,** 1996, McFarlane
MNP $15   MIP $40

❑ **Maxx, The, with white Isz,** 1996, McFarlane
MNP $10   MIP $35

❑ **Shadowhawk, black with silver trim,** 1996, McFarlane
MNP $4   MIP $15

❑ **Shadowhawk, gold with gray trim,** 1996, McFarlane
MNP $3   MIP $10

❑ **She-Spawn, black mask,** 1996, McFarlane
MNP $5   MIP $20

❑ **She-Spawn, red face mask,** 1996, McFarlane
MNP $5   MIP $20

SERIES 5, 1996

❑ **Nuclear Spawn, green skin,** 1996, McFarlane
MNP $3   MIP $10

❑ **Nuclear Spawn, orange skin,** 1996, McFarlane
MNP $4   MIP $15

❑ **Overtkill II, flesh colored with gray trim,** 1996, McFarlane
MNP $5   MIP $15

❑ **Overtkill II, silver with gold trim,** 1996, McFarlane
MNP $5   MIP $15

❑ **Tremor II, orange with red blood,** 1996, McFarlane
MNP $3   MIP $10

❏ **Tremor II, purple with green bloob,** 1996, McFarlane
MNP $3   MIP $10

❏ **Vandalizer, FAO Schwarz Exclusive,** 1996, McFarlane
MNP $10   MIP $25

❏ **Vandalizer, gray skinned with black trim,** 1996, McFarlane
MNP $3   MIP $10

❏ **Vandalizer, tan skinned with brown trim,** 1996, McFarlane
MNP $3   MIP $10

❏ **Viking Spawn,** 1996, McFarlane
MNP $5   MIP $25

❏ **Widow Maker, black and red with flesh-colored body,** 1996, McFarlane
MNP $5   MIP $15

❏ **Widow Maker, purple and rose outfit, gray body,** 1996, McFarlane
MNP $8   MIP $20

SERIES 6, 1996

❏ **Alien Spawn, black with white,** 1996, McFarlane
MNP $5   MIP $15

❏ **Alien Spawn, white with black,** 1996, McFarlane
MNP $3   MIP $10

❏ **Battleclad Spawn, black costume,** 1996, McFarlane
MNP $5   MIP $20

❏ **Battleclad Spawn, tan sections,** 1996, McFarlane
MNP $4   MIP $12

❏ **Freak, The, purplish flesh with brown and silver weapons,** 1996, McFarlane
MNP $3   MIP $10

❏ **Freak, The, tan flesh,** 1995, McFarlane
MNP $5   MIP $15

❏ **Sansker, black and yellow,** 1996, McFarlane
MNP $3   MIP $10

❏ **Sansker, brown and tan,** 1996, McFarlane
MNP $5   MIP $15

❏ **Superpatriot, metallic blue arms and legs,** 1996, McFarlane
MNP $3   MIP $10

❏ **Superpatriot, silver arms and legs,** 1996, McFarlane
MNP $3   MIP $10

❏ **Tiffany the Amazon, green trim,** 1996
MNP $5   MIP $15

❏ **Tiffany the Amazon, McFarlane Collector's Club Exclusive,** 1998
MNP $8   MIP $25

❏ **Tiffany the Amazon, red trim,** 1996, McFarlane
MNP $5   MIP $15

SERIES 7, 1997

❏ **Crutch, green goatee,** 1977, McFarlane
MNP $5   MIP $15

❏ **Crutch, purple goatee,** 1997
MNP $3   MIP $10

(McFarlane Toys)

❏ **Mangler, The,** 1997, McFarlane, Figure includes skull-topped staff
MNP $5   MIP $15

(McFarlane Toys)

❏ **No-Body,** 1997, McFarlane, Detailed robotic figure containing smaller "No-Body" inside
MNP $5   MIP $15

(McFarlane Toys)

❏ **Sam and Twitch,** 1997, McFarlane, Sam with donut and pistol, Twitch with rifle
MNP $5   MIP $15

❏ **Scourge,** 1997, McFarlane
MNP $5   MIP $15

❏ **Spawn III, with owl and bat,** 1997, McFarlane
MNP $8   MIP $25

(KP Photo)

❏ **Spawn III, with wolf and bat,** 1997, McFarlane, Figure also includes "spring up action cape"
MNP $8   MIP $25

(McFarlane Toys)

❏ **Zombie Spawn, tan skin with red tunic,** 1997, McFarlane, Figure includes chainsaw and large machine-gun rifle
MNP $3   MIP $10

SERIES 8, 1997

❏ **Curse of the Spawn,** 1997
MNP $5   MIP $15

❏ **Gate keeper,** 1997
MNP $4   MIP $12

❏ **Grave Digger,** 1997
MNP $4   MIP $12

❏ **Renegade, tan flesh,** 1997
MNP $4   MIP $12

❏ **Rotarr,** 1997
MNP $4   MIP $12

❏ **Sabre,** 1997
MNP $4   MIP $12

SERIES 9, 1997

❏ **Goddess, The,** 1997
MNP $4   MIP $12

❏ **Manga Clown,** 1997
MNP $4   MIP $12

❏ **Manga Curse,** 1997
MNP $4   MIP $12

❏ **Manga Ninja Spawn,** 1997
MNP $4   MIP $12

❏ **Manga Spawn,** 1997
MNP $5   MIP $15

❏ **Manga Violator,** 1997
MNP $4   MIP $12

ACTION FIGURES

SPAWN: THE MOVIE (McFARLANE, 1997)

DELUXE FIGURES

❏ **Attack Spawn,** 1997, McFarlane
  MNP $10   **MIP** $30

(McFarlane Toys)

❏ **Malebolgia,** 1997, McFarlane, Detailed figure includes skull-topped staff
  MNP $10   **MIP** $30

(McFarlane Toys)

❏ **Violator,** 1997, McFarlane, From the Spawn Deluxe Boxed Set, highly-detailed figure
  MNP $10   **MIP** $30

FIGURES

(McFarlane Toys)

❏ **Al Simmons,** 1997, McFarlane, With rifle and mobile rocket launcher
  MNP $4   **MIP** $10

(McFarlane Toys)

❏ **Burnt Spawn,** 1997, McFarlane, With rifle and femur-bone handled shovel
  MNP $4   **MIP** $10

(McFarlane Toys)

❏ **Clown,** 1997, McFarlane, Truly terrifying figure in referee shirt and pale blue face makeup
  MNP $4   **MIP** $10

(McFarlane Toys)

❏ **Jason Wynn,** 1997, McFarlane, With rifle, headset and accessories
  MNP $4   **MIP** $10

(McFarlane Toys)

❏ **Jessica Priest,** 1997, McFarlane, With rifle and accessories
  MNP $4   **MIP** $10

PLAY SETS

(McFarlane Toys)

❑ **Final Battle,** 1997, McFarlane, Spawn with creature crashing through house diorama

MNP $10   **MIP $20**

(McFarlane Toys)

❑ **Graveyard,** 1997, McFarlane, Includes two figures and open grave

MNP $10   **MIP $20**

(McFarlane Toys)

❑ **Spawn Alley,** 1997, McFarlane, Set includes Spawn, alley backdrop and creature

MNP $10   **MIP $20**

SPIDER-MAN ELECTRO-SPARK (TOY BIZ, 1997)

5" FIGURES

❑ **Captain America,** 1997

MNP $5   **MIP $15**

❑ **Electro,** 1997

MNP $3   **MIP $8**

❑ **Electro-Shock Spidey,** 1997

MNP $3   **MIP $8**

❑ **Electro-Spark Spider-Man,** 1997

MNP $3   **MIP $8**

❑ **Steel-Shock Spider-Man,** 1997

MNP $3   **MIP $8**

SPIDER-MAN SNEAK ATTACK (TOY BIZ, 1998)

BUG BUSTERS, 5" FIGURES

❑ **Jack O'Lantern and Bug Eye Blaster,** 1998

MNP $3   **MIP $8**

❑ **Silver Sable and Beetle Basher,** 1998

MNP $3   **MIP $8**

❑ **Spider-Man and Spider Stinger,** 1998

MNP $3   **MIP $8**

❑ **Vulture and Jaw Breaker,** 1998

MNP $3   **MIP $8**

SHAPE SHIFTERS, 7" FIGURES

❑ **Lizard forms into Mutant Alligator,** 1998

MNP $2   **MIP $6**

❑ **Spider-Man forms into Monster Spider,** 1998

MNP $2   **MIP $6**

❑ **Venom forms into 3-Headed Serpent,** 1998

MNP $2   **MIP $6**

STREET WARRIORS, 5" FIGURES

❑ **Scarecrow with Pitchfork Projectile,** 1998

MNP $2   **MIP $6**

❑ **Spider-Sense Peter Parker,** 1998

MNP $2   **MIP $6**

❑ **Street War Spider-Man,** 1998

MNP $2   **MIP $6**

❑ **Vermin with Rat-firing Fire Hydrant,** 1998

MNP $2   **MIP $6**

WEB FLYERS, 5" FIGURES

❑ **Carnage,** 1998

MNP $2   **MIP $6**

❑ **Copter Spider-Man,** 1998

MNP $2   **MIP $6**

❑ **Hobgoblin,** 1998

MNP $2   **MIP $6**

❑ **Spider-Man,** 1998

MNP $2   **MIP $6**

SPIDER-MAN SPECIAL EDITION SERIES (TOY BIZ, 1998)

12" FIGURES

❑ **Black Cat,** 1998

MNP $10   **MIP $30**

❑ **Spider-Man,** 1998

MNP $8   **MIP $25**

❑ **Venom,** 1998

MNP $8   **MIP $25**

SPIDER-MAN SPIDER FORCE (TOY BIZ, 1997)

5" FIGURES

❑ **Beetle with Transforming Beetle Armor,** 1997

MNP $2   **MIP $6**

❑ **Cybersect Spider-Man with Transforming Cyber Spider,** 1997

MNP $2   **MIP $6**

❑ **Swarm with Transforming Bee Action,** 1997

MNP $2   **MIP $6**

❑ **Tarantula with Transforming Tarantula Armor,** 1997

MNP $2   **MIP $6**

❑ **Wasp with Transforming Wasp Armor,** 1997

MNP $2   **MIP $6**

SPIDER-MAN SPIDER POWER (TOY BIZ, 1999)

SERIES I, 5" FIGURES

❑ **Slime Shaker Venom,** 1999

MNP $2   **MIP $6**

❑ **Spider Sense Spider-Man,** 1999

MNP $2   **MIP $6**

❑ **Street Warrior Spider-Man,** 1999

MNP $2   **MIP $6**

❑ **Triple Threat Spider-Man,** 1999

MNP $2   **MIP $6**

SERIES II, 5" FIGURES

❑ **Doctor Octopus,** 1999

MNP $2   **MIP $6**

❑ **Flip and Swing Spider-man,** 1999

MNP $2   **MIP $6**

❑ **J. Jonah Jameson,** 1999

MNP $2   **MIP $6**

❑ **Spider Sense Peter Parker,** 1999

MNP $2   **MIP $6**

SPIDER-MAN VAMPIRE WARS (TOY BIZ, 1996)

5" FIGURES

❑ **Air-Attack Spider-Man,** 1997

MNP $3   **MIP $8**

❑ **Anti-Vampire Apider-Man,** 1997

MNP $3   **MIP $8**

❑ **Blade-The Vampire Hunter,** 1997

MNP $3   **MIP $10**

❑ **Morbius Unbound,** 1997

MNP $3   **MIP $10**

❑ **Vampire Spider-Man,** 1997

MNP $3   **MIP $8**

SPIDER-MAN VENOM (TOY BIZ, 1996-97)

ALONG CAME A SPIDER, 6" FIGURES

❑ **Bride of Venom and Vile the Spider,** 1997

MNP $3   **MIP $10**

❑ **Phage and Pincer the Spider,** 1997

MNP $3   **MIP $8**

❑ **Spider-Carnage and Spit the Spider,** 1997

MNP $3   **MIP $8**

❑ **Venom the Symbiote and Riper the Spider,** 1997

MNP $3   **MIP $8**

ACTION FIGURES

PLANET OF THE SYMBIOTES, 6"
FIGURES

❏ **Hybrid, pincer Wing Action,** 1997
MNP $3   MIP $8

❏ **Lasher, Tentacle Whipping Action,**
1997
MNP $3   MIP $8

❏ **Riot, Launching Attack Arms,** 1997
MNP $3   MIP $8

❏ **Venom the Madness, Surprise Attack**
Heads, 1997
MNP $3   MIP $8

PLANET OF THE SYMBIOTES,
DELUXE 6" FIGURES

❏ **Hybrid, Pincer Wing Action,** 1996
MNP $3   MIP $8

❏ **Lasher, Tentacle Whipping Action,**
1996
MNP $3   MIP $8

❏ **Riot, Launcing Attack Arms,** 1996
MNP $3   MIP $8

❏ **Scream, Living Tendril Hair,** 1996
MNP $3   MIP $8

❏ **Venom the Madness, Surprise Attack**
Heads, 1996, Toy Biz
MNP $3   MIP $8

SPIDER-MAN WEB FORCE
(TOY BIZ, 1997)

5" FIGURES

❏ **Daredevil, Transforming Web Tank**
Armor, 1997
MNP $2   MIP $6

❏ **Lizard, Transforming Swamp Rider,**
1997
MNP $2   MIP $6

❏ **Vulture, Transforming Vuture-Bot,**
1997
MNP $2   MIP $6

❏ **Web Commando Spidey, Transform-**
ing Web Copter, 1997
MNP $2   MIP $6

❏ **Web Swamp Spidey, Transforming**
Web Swamp Seeker Armor, 1997
MNP $2   MIP $6

SPIDER-MAN WEB TRAPS
(TOY BIZ, 1997)

5" FIGURES

❏ **Future Spider-Man with Snapping**
Cacoon Trap, 1997
MNP $2   MIP $6

❏ **Monster Spider-Man with Grappling**
Spider Sidekick, 1997
MNP $2   MIP $6

❏ **Rhino with Rotating Web Snare,** 1997
MNP $2   MIP $6

❏ **Scorpion with Whipping Tail Attacker**
trap, 1997
MNP $3   MIP $8

❏ **Spider-Man with Pull-string Web Trap,**
1997
MNP $2   MIP $6

SPIDER-MAN: THE ANIMATED
SERIES (TOY BIZ, 1994-96)

15" TALKING FIGURES

❏ **Spider-Man,** 1994-96, Toy Biz
MNP $12   MIP $25

❏ **Venom,** 1994-96, Toy Biz
MNP $12   MIP $25

2-1/2" DIE-CAST FIGURES

❏ **Spider-Man vs. Carnage,** 1994-96, Toy
Biz
MNP $2   MIP $4

❏ **Spider-Man vs. Dr. Octopus,** 1994-96,
Toy Biz
MNP $2   MIP $4

❏ **Spider-Man vs. Hobgoblin,** 1994-96,
Toy Biz
MNP $2   MIP $4

❏ **Spider-Man vs. Venom,** 1994-96, Toy
Biz
MNP $2   MIP $4

5" FIGURES

❏ **Alien Spider Slayer,** 1994-96, Toy Biz
MNP $3   MIP $8

❏ **Battle-Ravaged Spider-Man,** 1994-96
MNP $3   MIP $10

❏ **Cameleon,** 1994-96
MNP $4   MIP $12

❏ **Carnage,** 1994-96, Toy Biz
MNP $5   MIP $15

❏ **Carnage II,** 1994-96
MNP $4   MIP $12

❏ **Dr. Octopus,** 1994-96, Toy Biz
MNP $4   MIP $12

❏ **Green Goblin,** 1994-96, Toy Biz
MNP $5   MIP $15

❏ **Hobgoblin,** 1994-96, Toy Biz
MNP $4   MIP $12

❏ **Kingpin,** 1994-96, Toy Biz
MNP $5   MIP $15

❏ **Kraven,** 1994-96, Toy Biz
MNP $4   MIP $12

❏ **Lizard,** 1994-96, Toy Biz
MNP $5   MIP $15

❏ **Morbius,** 1994-96
MNP $4   MIP $12

❏ **Mysterio,** 1994-96
MNP $3   MIP $12

❏ **Nick Fury,** 1994-96
MNP $3   MIP $12

❏ **Peter Parker,** 1994-96, Toy Biz
MNP $5   MIP $15

❏ **Prowler,** 1994-96
MNP $3   MIP $12

(Toy Shop File Photo)

❏ **Punisher,** 1994-96, The recognizable
man in black (and white)
MNP $3   MIP $12

❏ **Rhino,** 1994-96, Toy Biz
MNP $6   MIP $25

❏ **Scorpion,** 1994-96, Toy Biz
MNP $5   MIP $15

❏ **Shocker,** 1994-96, Toy Biz
MNP $4   MIP $15

❏ **Smythe,** 1994-96, Toy Biz
MNP $5   MIP $12

❏ **Spider-Man in Black Costume,** 1994-
96
MNP $3   MIP $12

❏ **Spider-Man Six Arm,** 1994-96
MNP $3   MIP $12

❏ **Spider-Man with Parachute Web,**
1994-96
MNP $3   MIP $12

❏ **Spider-Man with Spider Armor,** 1994-
96, Toy Biz
MNP $3   MIP $15

❏ **Spider-Man with Web Parachute,**
1994-96, Toy Biz
MNP $8   MIP $15

❏ **Spider-Man with Web Racer,** 1994-96,
Toy Biz
MNP $5   MIP $15

❏ **Spider-Man with Web Shooter,** 1994-
96, Toy Biz
MNP $5   MIP $15

❏ **Spider-Man, multi-jointed,** 1994-96,
Toy Biz
MNP $3   MIP $15

❏ **Spider-Sense Spider-Man,** 1994-96,
Toy Biz
MNP $3   MIP $12

❏ **Symbiotic Venom Attack,** 1994-96, Toy Biz
MNP $3   MIP $12

❏ **Venom,** 1994-96, Toy Biz
MNP $4   MIP $15

❏ **Venom II,** 1994-96, Toy Biz
MNP $3   MIP $12

❏ **Vulture,** 1994-96, Toy Biz
MNP $5   MIP $15

ACCESSORIES

❏ **Daily Bugle Play Set,** 1994-96, Toy Biz
MNP $10   MIP $15

DELUXE 10" FIGURES

❏ **Carnage,** 1994-96, Toy Biz
MNP $8   MIP $20

❏ **Dr. Octopus,** 1994-96, Toy Biz
MNP $7   MIP $15

❏ **Hobgoblin,** 1994-96, Toy Biz
MNP $7   MIP $15

❏ **Kraven,** 1994-96, Toy Biz
MNP $7   MIP $15

❏ **Lizard,** 1994-96, Toy Biz
MNP $7   MIP $15

❏ **Spider-Man Spider Sense,** 1994-96, Toy Biz
MNP $7   MIP $15

❏ **Spider-Man with suction cups,** 1994-96, Toy Biz
MNP $7   MIP $15

❏ **Spider-Man, wall hanging,** 1994-96, Toy Biz
MNP $7   MIP $15

❏ **Venom,** 1994-96, Toy Biz
MNP $7   MIP $15

❏ **Vulture,** 1994-96, Toy Biz
MNP $10   MIP $20

PROJECTORS

❏ **Hobgoblin,** 1994-96, Toy Biz
MNP $5   MIP $15

❏ **Lizard,** 1994-96
MNP $5   MIP $15

❏ **Spider-Man,** 1994-96, Toy Biz
MNP $5   MIP $15

❏ **Venom,** 1994-96, Toy Biz
MNP $5   MIP $15

VEHICLES

❏ **Hobgoblin Wing Bomber,** 1994-96, Toy Biz
MNP $10   MIP $25

❏ **Smythe Battle Chair Attack Vehicle,** 1994-96, Toy Biz
MNP $15   MIP $40

❏ **Spider-Man Wheelie Cycle,** 1994-96, Toy Biz
MNP $7   MIP $15

❏ **Spider-Man's Cycle (radio-controlled),** 1994-96, Toy Biz
MNP $15   MIP $30

❏ **Tri-Spider Slayer,** 1994-96, Toy Biz
MNP $10   MIP $25

SPORTS PICKS (MCFARLANE, 2000)

NHPLA FIGURES

❏ **Curtis Joseph,** 2000
MNP $3   MIP $10

❏ **Patrick Roy,** 2000
MNP $3   MIP $10

❏ **Paul Kariya,** 2000
MNP $3   MIP $10

❏ **Ray Bourque,** 2000
MNP $3   MIP $10

❏ **Steve Yzerman,** 2000
MNP $3   MIP $10

❏ **Tony Amonte,** 2000
MNP $3   MIP $10

STAR TREK (MEGO, 1974-80)

8" CARDED FIGURES

❏ **Andorian, 1976,** 1974-80, Mego
MNP $300   MIP $650

❏ **Captain Kirk, 1974,** 1974-80, Mego
MNP $25   MIP $50

❏ **Cheron, 1975,** 1974-80, Mego, Black and white face and uniform
MNP $85   MIP $175

❏ **Dr. McCoy, 1974,** 1974-80, Mego, Medical tricorder pack
MNP $35   MIP $75

❏ **Gorn, 1975,** 1974-80, Mego
MNP $80   MIP $180

(Corey LeChat)

❏ **Klingon, 1974,** 1974-80, Mego, Black boots, brown plastic body armor, brown tunic
MNP $25   MIP $50

❏ **Lt. Uhura, 1974,** 1974-80, Mego
MNP $50   MIP $135

❏ **Mr. Spock, 1974,** 1974-80, Mego
MNP $25   MIP $50

❏ **Mugato, 1976,** 1974-80, Mego
MNP $275   MIP $500

❏ **Neptunian, 1975,** 1974-80, Mego, Shown here with The Keeper
MNP $100   MIP $225

❏ **Romulan, 1976,** 1974-80, Mego
MNP $600   MIP $1000

❏ **Scotty, 1974,** 1974-80, Mego
MNP $35   MIP $80

❏ **Talos, 1976,** 1974-80, Mego
MNP $275   MIP $500

❏ **The Keeper, 1975,** 1974-80, Mego
MNP $75   MIP $175

PLAY SETS

❏ **Mission to Gamma VI,** 1974-80, Mego
MNP $700   MIP $1200

❏ **U.S.S. Enterprise Bridge,** 1974-80, Mego
MNP $100   MIP $275

STAR TREK ALIEN COMBAT (PLAYMATES, 1999)

FIGURES

❏ **Borg Drone,** 1999, Playmates
MNP $15   MIP $25

❏ **Klingon Warrior,** 1999, Playmates
MNP $15   MIP $25

STAR TREK COLLECTOR ASSORTMENT (PLAYMATES, 1999)

FIGURES

❏ **Andorian Ambassador,** 1999, Playmates
MNP $5   MIP $10

❏ **Captain Janeway,** 1999, Playmates
MNP $5   MIP $10

❏ **Counselor Troi,** 1999, Playmates
MNP $5   MIP $10

❏ **Dr. McCoy,** 1999, Playmates
MNP $5   MIP $10

❏ **Ensign Chekov,** 1999, Playmates
MNP $5   MIP $10

❏ **Geordi LaForge,** 1999, Playmates
MNP $5   MIP $10

❏ **Gorn Captain,** 1999, Playmates
MNP $5   MIP $10

❏ **Khan,** 1999, Playmates
MNP $5   MIP $10

❏ **Lieutenant Sulu,** 1999, Playmates
MNP $5   MIP $10

❏ **Lieutenant Uhura,** 1999, Playmates
MNP $5   MIP $10

❏ **Locutus of Borg,** 1999, Playmates
MNP $5   MIP $10

ACTION FIGURES

❏ **Mr. Spock,** 1999, Playmates
MNP $5　　MIP $10

❏ **Mugatu,** 1999, Playmates
MNP $5　　MIP $10

❏ **Q,** 1999, Playmates
MNP $5　　MIP $10

❏ **Scotty,** 1999, Playmates
MNP $5　　MIP $10

❏ **Seven of Nine,** 1999, Playmates
MNP $5　　MIP $10

STAR TREK COLLECTOR SERIES (PLAYMATES, 1994-95)

9-1/2" BOXED FIGURES

❏ **Borg,** 1995, Playmates
MNP $10　　MIP $25

❏ **Captain Benjamin Sisko (Command Edition),** 1994, Playmates
MNP $10　　MIP $25

❏ **Captain Jean-Luc Picard (Command Edition),** 1994, Playmates
MNP $10　　MIP $25

❏ **Captain Jean-Luc Picard (Movie Edition),** 1994, Playmates
MNP $10　　MIP $25

❏ **Captain Kirk (Command Edition),** 1994, Playmates
MNP $10　　MIP $25

❏ **Captain Kirk (Movie Edition),** 1994, Playmates
MNP $10　　MIP $25

❏ **Commander Riker,** 1995, Playmates
MNP $10　　MIP $25

❏ **Data (Movie Edition),** 1995, Playmates
MNP $10　　MIP $25

❏ **Dr. Beverly Crusher,** 1995, Playmates
MNP $10　　MIP $25

❏ **Geordi La Forge (Movie Edition),** 1994, Playmates
MNP $10　　MIP $25

STAR TREK ELECTRONIC DISPLAY ASSORTMENT (PLAYMATES, 1999)

FIGURES

❏ **Captain Kirk,** 1999, Playmates
MNP $20　　MIP $40

❏ **Captain Picard,** 1999, Playmates
MNP $20　　MIP $40

❏ **Commander Riker,** 1999, Playmates
MNP $20　　MIP $40

❏ **Lieutenant Commander Data,** 1999, Playmates
MNP $20　　MIP $40

❏ **Lieutenant Worf,** 1999, Playmates
MNP $20　　MIP $40

❏ **Mr. Spock,** 1999, Playmates
MNP $20　　MIP $40

STAR TREK MILLENNIUM COLLECTOR'S SET (PLAYMATES, 1999)

FIGURES

❏ **Captain Janeway/Commander Chakotay,** 1999, Playmates
MNP $15　　MIP $40

❏ **Captain Kirk/Mr. Spock,** 1999, Playmates
MNP $15　　MIP $40

❏ **Captain Picard/Commander Riker,** 1999, Playmates
MNP $15　　MIP $40

❏ **Captain Sisko/Commander Riker,** 1999, Playmates
MNP $15　　MIP $40

STAR TREK V (GALOOB, 1989)

BOXED FIGURES

❏ **Captain Kirk,** 1989, Galoob, action figure
MNP $10　　MIP $25

❏ **Dr. McCoy,** 1989, Galoob, action figure
MNP $10　　MIP $25

❏ **Klaa,** 1989, Galoob, action figure
MNP $10　　MIP $25

❏ **Mr. Spock,** 1989, Galoob, action figure
MNP $10　　MIP $25

❏ **Sybok,** 1989, Galoob, action figure
MNP $10　　MIP $25

STAR TREK: FIRST CONTACT (PLAYMATES, 1996)

FIGURES

❏ **Borg, 5" figure,** 1996, Playmates
MNP $8　　MIP $15

❏ **Data, 5" figure,** 1996, Playmates
MNP $5　　MIP $10

❏ **Data, 9" figure,** 1996, Playmates
MNP $12　　MIP $18

❏ **Deanna Troi, 5" figure,** 1996, Playmates
MNP $5　　MIP $10

❏ **Dr. Beverly Crusher, 5" figure,** 1996, Playmates
MNP $6　　MIP $12

❏ **Geordi LaForge, 5" figure,** 1996, Playmates
MNP $5　　MIP $10

❏ **Jean-Luc Picard in 21st century outfit, 9" figure,** 1996, Playmates
MNP $15　　MIP $23

❏ **Jean-Luc Picard in space suit, 5" figure,** 1996, Playmates
MNP $6　　MIP $12

❏ **Jean-Luc Picard, 5" figure,** 1996, Playmates
MNP $5　　MIP $10

❏ **Jean-Luc Picard, 9" figure,** 1996, Playmates
MNP $12　　MIP $18

❏ **Lily, 5" figure,** 1996, Playmates
MNP $8　　MIP $15

❏ **William Riker, 5" figure,** 1996, Playmates
MNP $5　　MIP $10

❏ **William Riker, 9" figure,** 1996, Playmates
MNP $12　　MIP $18

❏ **Worf, 5" figure,** 1996, Playmates
MNP $5　　MIP $10

❏ **Zefram Cochrane, 5" figure,** 1996, Playmates
MNP $5　　MIP $10

❏ **Zefram Cochrane, 9" figure,** 1996, Playmates
MNP $18　　MIP $25

STAR TREK: INSURRECTION (PLAYMATES, 1998)

FIGURES

❏ **Counselor Troi,** 1998, Playmates
MNP $8　　MIP $15

❏ **Data,** 1998, Playmates
MNP $8　　MIP $15

❏ **Geordi LaForge,** 1998, Playmates
MNP $8　　MIP $15

❏ **Jean-Luc Picard,** 1998, Playmates
MNP $8　　MIP $15

❏ **Ru' Afo,** 1998, Playmates
MNP $8　　MIP $15

❏ **Worf,** 1998, Playmates
MNP $8　　MIP $15

STAR TREK: SPACE TALK SERIES (PLAYMATES, 1995)

SPACE TALK SERIES

❏ **Borg,** 1995, Playmates
MNP $5　　MIP $20

❏ **Picard,** 1995, Playmates
MNP $5　　MIP $10

❏ **Q,** 1995, Playmates
MNP $5　　MIP $20

❏ **Riker,** 1995, Playmates
MNP $5　　MIP $10

STAR TREK: STARFLEET ACADEMY (PLAYMATES, 1996)

FIGURES

❏ **Cadet Geordi LaForge,** 1996, Playmates, 5" figure
MNP $8　　MIP $15

❏ **Cadet Jean-Luc Picard,** 1996, Playmates, 5" figure
      MNP $8   **MIP $15**

❏ **Cadet William Riker,** 1996, Playmates,
5" figure
      MNP $8   **MIP $15**

❏ **Cadet Worf,** 1996, Playmates, 5" figure
      MNP $8   **MIP $15**

STAR TREK: THE MOTION PICTURE (MEGO, 1980-81)

12" BOXED FIGURES

❏ **Arcturian, 1979,** 1974-80, Mego
      MNP $40   **MIP $125**

❏ **Captain Kirk, 1979,** 1974-80, Mego
      MNP $40   **MIP $75**

❏ **Decker, 1979,** 1974-80, Mego
      MNP $45   **MIP $115**

❏ **Ilia, 1979,** 1974-80, Mego
      MNP $40   **MIP $75**

❏ **Klingon, 1979,** 1974-80, Mego
      MNP $40   **MIP $125**

❏ **Mr. Spock, 1979,** 1974-80, Mego
      MNP $40   **MIP $75**

3-3/4" CARDED FIGURES

❏ **Acturian,** 1980-81, Mego, Light tan uniform
      MNP $75   **MIP $150**

❏ **Betelgeusian,** 1980-81, Mego
      MNP $75   **MIP $150**

❏ **Captain Kirk,** 1980-81, Mego
      MNP $12   **MIP $35**

❏ **Decker, 1979,** 1980-81, Mego
      MNP $12   **MIP $35**

❏ **Dr. McCoy,** 1980-81, Mego, White shirt,
gray pants
      MNP $12   **MIP $35**

❏ **Ilia,** 1980-81, Mego
      MNP $10   **MIP $20**

❏ **Klingon,** 1980-81, Mego
      MNP $75   **MIP $150**

❏ **Megarite,** 1980-81, Mego
      MNP $75   **MIP $150**

❏ **Mr. Spock,** 1980-81, Mego, Dark gray
uniform as seen in movie
      MNP $12   **MIP $35**

❏ **Rigellian,** 1980-81, Mego
      MNP $75   **MIP $150**

❏ **Scotty,** 1980-81, Mego
      MNP $12   **MIP $35**

❏ **Zatanite,** 1974-80, Mego
      MNP $75   **MIP $150**

PLAY SETS

❏ **U.S.S. Enterprise Bridge,** 1980-81,
Mego
      MNP $45   **MIP $105**

STAR TREK: THE NEXT GENERATION (GALOOB, 1988-89)

3-3/4" FIGURES, SERIES 1

❏ **Data, blue face,** 1988-89, Galoob, 3-
3/4" action figure
      MNP $70   **MIP $100**

❏ **Data, brown face,** 1988-89, Galoob, 3-
3/4" action figure
      MNP $30   **MIP $50**

❏ **Data, flesh face,** 1988-89, Galoob, 3-
3/4" action figure
      MNP $15   **MIP $30**

❏ **Data, spotted face,** 1988-89, Galoob,
3-3/4" action figure
      MNP $15   **MIP $30**

❏ **Geordi La Forge,** 1988-89, Galoob, 3-
3/4" action figure
      MNP $5   **MIP $15**

❏ **Jean-Luc Picard,** 1988-89, Galoob, 3-
3/4" action figure
      MNP $5   **MIP $15**

❏ **Lt. Worf,** 1988-89, Galoob, 3-3/4"
action figure
      MNP $5   **MIP $15**

❏ **Tasha Yar,** 1988-89, Galoob, 3-3/4"
action figure
      MNP $10   **MIP $25**

❏ **William Riker,** 1988-89, Galoob, 3-3/4"
action figure
      MNP $5   **MIP $15**

3-3/4" FIGURES, SERIES 2

❏ **Antican,** 1988-89, Galoob, 3-3/4" action
figure
      MNP $35   **MIP $75**

❏ **Ferengi,** 1988-89, Galoob, 3-3/4" action
figure
      MNP $35   **MIP $75**

❏ **Q,** 1988-89, Galoob, 3-3/4" action figure
      MNP $35   **MIP $75**

❏ **Selay,** 1988-89, Galoob, 3-3/4" action
figure
      MNP $35   **MIP $75**

ACCESSORIES

❏ **Enterprise,** 1988-89, Galoob, die-cast
vehicle
      MNP $10   **MIP $35**

❏ **Ferengi Fighter,** 1988-89, Galoob,
vehicle
      MNP $15   **MIP $50**

❏ **Galileo Shuttle,** 1988-89, Galoob, vehicle
      MNP $15   **MIP $50**

❏ **Phaser,** 1988-89, Galoob, role playing
toy
      MNP $20   **MIP $40**

STAR TREK: THE NEXT GENERATION (PLAYMATES, 1992-1996)

SERIES 1, 1992

❏ **Borg,** 1992, Playmates
      MNP $10   **MIP $20**

❏ **Commander Riker,** 1992, Playmates
      MNP $10   **MIP $18**

❏ **Data,** 1992, Playmates
      MNP $10   **MIP $20**

❏ **Deanna Troi,** 1992, Playmates
      MNP $15   **MIP $30**

❏ **Ferengi,** 1992, Playmates
      MNP $10   **MIP $25**

❏ **Geordi LaForge,** 1992, Playmates
      MNP $10   **MIP $25**

❏ **Gowron the Klingon,** 1992, Playmates
      MNP $12   **MIP $25**

❏ **Jean-Luc Picard,** 1992, Playmates
      MNP $10   **MIP $20**

❏ **Romulan,** 1992, Playmates
      MNP $15   **MIP $30**

❏ **Worf,** 1992, Playmates
      MNP $10   **MIP $20**

SERIES 2, 1993

❏ **Admiral McCoy,** 1993, Playmates
      MNP $5   **MIP $12**

❏ **Benzite,** 1993, Playmates
      MNP $7   **MIP $15**

❏ **Borg,** 1993, Playmates
      MNP $5   **MIP $10**

❏ **Captain Scott (Scotty),** 1993, Playmates
      MNP $5   **MIP $10**

❏ **Commander Riker,** 1993, Playmates
      MNP $6   **MIP $12**

❏ **Commander Sela,** 1993, Playmates
      MNP $6   **MIP $12**

❏ **Data,** 1993, Playmates
      MNP $6   **MIP $12**

❏ **Dathon,** 1993, Playmates
      MNP $7   **MIP $15**

❏ **Deanna Troi,** 1993, Playmates
      MNP $6   **MIP $12**

❏ **Dr. Beverly Crusher,** 1993, Playmates
      MNP $6   **MIP $12**

❏ **Geordi LaForge,** 1993, Playmates
      MNP $7   **MIP $15**

❏ **Guinan,** 1993, Playmates
      MNP $7   **MIP $15**

❏ **Jean-Luc Picard,** 1993, Playmates
      MNP $6   **MIP $12**

❏ **K'Ehleyr,** 1993, Playmates
      MNP $6   **MIP $12**

ACTION FIGURES

❑ **Locutus,** 1993, Playmates
MNP $6   MIP $12

❑ **Lore,** 1993, Playmates
MNP $7   MIP $15

(KP Photo)

❑ **Q, in judge's robe,** 1993, Playmates, Shows Q as he appears in "Mission to Farpoint," Next Gen's first episode, and "All Good Things," their last. Includes scroll, scepter, lion statue and gavel
MNP $6   MIP $12

❑ **Spock,** 1993, Playmates
MNP $6   MIP $12

❑ **Vorgon,** 1993, Playmates
MNP $10   MIP $20

❑ **Wesley Crusher,** 1993, Playmates
MNP $6   MIP $12

❑ **Worf,** 1993, Playmates
MNP $6   MIP $12

SERIES 3, 1994

❑ **Barclay,** 1994, Playmates
MNP $5   MIP $15

❑ **Beverly Crusher,** 1994, Playmates
MNP $5   MIP $15

❑ **Data as Romulan,** 1994, Playmates
MNP $5   MIP $15

❑ **Data, dress uniform,** 1994, Playmates
MNP $5   MIP $15

❑ **Data, Redemption outfit,** 1994, Playmates
MNP $75   MIP $300

(Lenny Lee)

❑ **Deanna Troi,** 1994, Playmates, One of many Deanna Troi figures, this one includes a stand, laptop computer, tricorder, PADD and accessories
MNP $3   MIP $15

❑ **Dr. Noonian Soong,** 1994, Playmates
MNP $5   MIP $15

❑ **Ensign Ro Laren,** 1994, Playmates
MNP $10   MIP $20

(Lenny Lee)

❑ **Esoqq,** 1994, Playmates, Fearsome-looking alien includes; knife, food ration, communicator, collector card
MNP $20   MIP $75

❑ **Geordi La Forge,** 1994, Playmates
MNP $5   MIP $15

❑ **Gowron,** 1994, Playmates
MNP $10   MIP $25

❑ **Guinan,** 1994, Playmates
MNP $5   MIP $15

❑ **Hugh Borg,** 1994, Playmates
MNP $5   MIP $15

❑ **Lore,** 1994, Playmates
MNP $3   MIP $15

❑ **Lwaxana Troi,** 1994, Playmates
MNP $3   MIP $15

❑ **Nausicaan,** 1994, Playmates
MNP $5   MIP $15

❑ **Picard as Dixon Hill,** 1994, Playmates
MNP $5   MIP $15

❑ **Picard as Romulan,** 1994, Playmates
MNP $3   MIP $15

❑ **Picard, red uniform,** 1994, Playmates
MNP $3   MIP $15

❑ **Q, judge's robes,** 1994, Playmates
MNP $5   MIP $15

❑ **Riker, Malcorian,** 1994, Playmates
MNP $3   MIP $15

❑ **Riker, red uniform,** 1994, Playmates
MNP $65   MIP $150

❑ **Sarek,** 1994, Playmates
MNP $5   MIP $15

❑ **Sela,** 1994, Playmates
MNP $5   MIP $15

❑ **Spock,** 1994, Playmates
MNP $5   MIP $15

❑ **Tasha Yar,** 1994, Playmates
MNP $5   MIP $15

❑ **Wesley Crusher,** 1994, Playmates
MNP $5   MIP $15

❑ **Worf,** 1994, Playmates
MNP $8   MIP $15

STAR TREK: VOYAGER (PLAYMATES, 1995-1996)

5" FIGURES

❑ **B'Elanna Torres,** 1996, Playmates, 5" figure
MNP $15   MIP $25

❑ **Chakotay,** 1996, Playmates, 5" figure
MNP $5   MIP $10

❑ **Chakotay as a Maquis,** 1996, Playmates, 5" figure
MNP $8   MIP $15

❑ **Doctor,** 1996, Playmates, 5" figure
MNP $8   MIP $15

❑ **Harry Kim,** 1996, Playmates, 5" figure
MNP $8   MIP $15

❑ **Kathryn Janeway,** 1995-19, Playmates, 5" figure
MNP $15   MIP $25

❑ **Kazon,** 1996, Playmates, 5" figure
MNP $5   MIP $10

❑ **Kes the Ocampa,** 1996, Playmates, 5" figure
MNP $12   MIP $18

❑ **Neelix,** 1996, Playmates, 5" figure
MNP $5   MIP $10

❑ **Seska,** 1996, Playmates, 5" figure
MNP $5   MIP $10

❑ **Tom Paris,** 1996, Playmates, 5" figure
MNP $5   MIP $10

❑ **Tuvok,** 1996, Playmates, 5" figure
MNP $5   MIP $10

STARGATE (HASBRO, 1994)

FIGURES

❏ **Anubis,** 1998
MNP $2   MIP $4

❏ **Col. O'Neil,** 1998
MNP $2   MIP $4

❏ **Daniel Jackson,** 1994, Hasbro
MNP $2   MIP $5

❏ **Horus, Attack Pilot,** 1998
MNP $2   MIP $4

❏ **Horus, Palace Guard,** 1998
MNP $2   MIP $4

❏ **Lt. Kawalsky,** 1998
MNP $2   MIP $4

❏ **Ra,** 1998
MNP $2   MIP $4

❏ **Skaara,** 1998
MNP $2   MIP $4

STARSKY AND HUTCH (MEGO, 1976)

8" FIGURES AND ACCESSORIES

❏ **Captain Dobey,** 1976, Mego
MNP $25   MIP $50

❏ **Car,** 1976, Mego
MNP $65   MIP $125

(Toy Shop File Photo)

❏ **Chopper,** 1976, Mego, In cable-knit sweater and dark pants
MNP $25   MIP $45

❏ **Huggy Bear,** 1976, Mego, Group shot
MNP $25   MIP $50

❏ **Hutch,** 1976, Mego
MNP $20   MIP $45

❏ **Starsky,** 1976, Mego
MNP $20   MIP $45

STREET FIGHTER (HASBRO, 1994)

12" FIGURES

❏ **Blanka,** 1994
MNP $15   MIP $25

❏ **Colonel Guile,** 1994, Hasbro
MNP $15   MIP $25

❏ **General Bison,** 1994, Hasbro
MNP $15   MIP $25

❏ **Ryu Hoshi,** 1994, Hasbro
MNP $15   MIP $25

SUPER HERO BENDABLES (MEGO, 1972)

5" FIGURES

❏ **Aquaman,** 1972, Mego
MNP $30   MIP $120

❏ **Batgirl,** 1972, Mego
MNP $50   MIP $120

❏ **Batman,** 1972, Mego
MNP $35   MIP $90

❏ **Captain America,** 1972, Mego
MNP $35   MIP $90

❏ **Catwoman,** 1972, Mego
MNP $70   MIP $175

❏ **Joker,** 1972, Mego
MNP $40   MIP $150

❏ **Mr. Mxyzptlk,** 1972, Mego
MNP $40   MIP $125

❏ **Penguin,** 1972, Mego
MNP $40   MIP $150

❏ **Riddler,** 1972, Mego
MNP $60   MIP $150

❏ **Robin,** 1972, Mego
MNP $30   MIP $75

❏ **Shazam,** 1972, Mego
MNP $50   MIP $125

❏ **Supergirl,** 1972, Mego
MNP $70   MIP $175

❏ **Superman,** 1972, Mego
MNP $30   MIP $75

❏ **Tarzan,** 1972, Mego
MNP $25   MIP $60

❏ **Wonder Woman,** 1972, Mego
MNP $50   MIP $100

SUPER POWERS (KENNER, 1984-86)

5" FIGURES

❏ **Aquaman, 1984,** 1984-86, Kenner, Shown with Cyclotron
MNP $15   MIP $45

❏ **Batman, 1984,** 1984-86, Kenner
MNP $35   MIP $75

(Lenny Lee)

❏ **Braniac, 1984,** 1984-86, Kenner, chrome plastic figure, includes free mini comic book
MNP $15   MIP $30

❏ **Clark Kent, mail-in figure, 1986,** 1984-86, Kenner
MNP $50   MIP $75

❏ **Cyborg, 1986,** 1984-86, Kenner
MNP $150   MIP $300

ACTION FIGURES

(Toy Shop File Photo)

❏ **Cyclotron, 1986,** 1984-86, Kenner, Shown with Aquaman
MNP $35   MIP $75

(Toy Shop File Photo)

❏ **Darkseid, 1985,** 1984-86, Kenner, gray and blue figure with "Power Action Raging Motion"
MNP $5   MIP $15

❏ **Desaad, 1985,** 1984-86, Kenner
MNP $10   MIP $30

❏ **Dr. Fate, 1985,** 1984-86, Kenner
MNP $35   MIP $80

❏ **Firestorm, 1985,** 1984-86, Kenner
MNP $15   MIP $35

(Lenny Lee)

❏ **Flash, 1984,** 1984-86, Kenner, figure has power action legs that simulate the Flash's lightning-speed running style
MNP $10   MIP $25

❏ **Golden Pharaoh, 1986,** 1984-86, Kenner
MNP $50   MIP $125

❏ **Green Arrow, 1985,** 1984-86, Kenner
MNP $25   MIP $55

❏ **Green Lantern, 1984,** 1984-86, Kenner
MNP $30   MIP $60

❏ **Hawkman, 1984,** 1984-86, Kenner
MNP $25   MIP $65

❏ **Joker, 1984,** 1984-86, Kenner
MNP $15   MIP $30

❏ **Kalibak, 1985,** 1984-86, Kenner
MNP $5   MIP $15

(Lenny Lee)

❏ **Lex Luthor, 1984,** 1984-86, Kenner, has "Power Action Nuclear Punch"
MNP $5   MIP $15

(Lenny Lee)

❏ **Mantis, 1985,** 1984-86, Kenner, figure has "Power Action Pincer Thrust" and includes a free comic book
MNP $10   MIP $30

❏ **Martian Manhunter, 1985,** 1984-86, Kenner
MNP $15   MIP $45

❏ **Mister Miracle, 1986,** 1984-86, Kenner
MNP $60   MIP $145

❏ **Mr. Freeze, 1986,** 1984-86, Kenner
MNP $25   MIP $65

(Lenny Lee)

❏ **Orion, 1986,** 1984-86, Kenner, with "Power Action Astro Punch"
MNP $25   MIP $65

(Lenny Lee)

❏ **Parademon, 1985,** 1984-86, Kenner, includes mini-comic book
MNP $15   MIP $35

(Lenney Lee)

❑ **Penguin, 1984,** 1984-86, Kenner, Shown with Plastic Man and Wonder Woman

MNP $20   MIP $40

(Lenny Lee)

❑ **Plastic Man, 1986,** 1984-86, Kenner, Shown with Wonder Woman and Penguin

MNP $65   MIP $150

❑ **Red Tornado, 1985,** 1984-86, Kenner
MNP $35   MIP $85

❑ **Robin, 1984,** 1984-86, Kenner
MNP $25   MIP $50

(Toy Shop File Photo)

❑ **Samurai, 1986,** 1984-86, Kenner, shown here with Tyr and Shazam figures
MNP $45   MIP $95

❑ **Shazam (Captain Marvel), 1986,** 1984-86, Kenner, bright-colored figure, very "cartoony" look
MNP $25   MIP $65

❑ **Steppenwolf, in mail-in bag, 1985,** 1984-86, Kenner
MNP $15   MIP $20

❑ **Steppenwolf, on card, 1985,** 1984-86, Kenner
MNP $15   MIP $75

❑ **Superman, 1984,** 1984-86, Kenner
MNP $20   MIP $35

❑ **Tyr, 1986,** 1984-86, Kenner, with yellow attached "Power Action Rocket Launcher"
MNP $40   MIP $75

(Lenny Lee)

❑ **Wonder Woman, 1984,** 1984-86, Kenner, Shown with Plastic Man and Penguin
MNP $15   MIP $40

ACCESSORIES

❑ **Collector's Case, 1984,** 1984-86, Kenner
MNP $20   MIP $40

PLAY SETS

❑ **Hall of Justice, 1984,** 1984-86, Kenner
MNP $75   MIP $175

VEHICLES

❑ **Batcopter, 1986,** 1984-86, Kenner
MNP $40   MIP $125

❑ **Batmobile, 1984,** 1984-86, Kenner
MNP $50   MIP $150

❑ **Darkseid Destroyer, 1985,** 1984-86, Kenner
MNP $25   MIP $50

❑ **Delta Probe One, 1985,** 1984-86, Kenner
MNP $15   MIP $30

❑ **Justice Jogger, wind-up, 1986,** 1984-86, Kenner
MNP $20   MIP $40

❑ **Kalibak Boulder Bomber, 1985,** 1984-86, Kenner
MNP $10   MIP $25

❑ **Lex-Soar 7, 1984,** 1984-86, Kenner
MNP $10   MIP $25

❑ **Supermobile, 1984,** 1984-86, Kenner
MNP $15   MIP $30

TEENAGE MUTANT NINJA TURTLES (PLAYMATES, 1988-92)

GIANT TURTLES, 13", 1991

❑ **Donatello,** 1988-92, Playmates, 13" tall
MNP $20   MIP $40

❑ **Leonardo,** 1988-92, Playmates, 13" tall
MNP $20   MIP $40

❑ **Michaelangelo,** 1988-92, Playmates, 13" tall
MNP $20   MIP $40

❑ **Raphael,** 1988-92, Playmates, 13" tall
MNP $20   MIP $40

GIANT TURTLES, 13", 1992

❑ **Bebop,** 1988-92, Playmates, 13" tall
MNP $20   MIP $40

❑ **Movie Don,** 1988-92, Playmates, 13" tall
MNP $20   MIP $40

❑ **Movie Leo,** 1988-92, Playmates, 13" tall
MNP $20   MIP $40

❑ **Movie Mike,** 1988-92, Playmates, 13" tall
MNP $20   MIP $40

❑ **Movie Raph,** 1988-92, Playmates, 13" tall
MNP $20   MIP $40

❑ **Rocksteady,** 1988-92, Playmates, 13" tall
MNP $20   MIP $40

SERIES 1, 1988

❑ **April O'Neil, no stripe,** 1988-92, Playmates
MNP $50   MIP $100

❑ **Bebop,** 1988-92, Playmates, 4-1/2" tall
MNP $3   MIP $8

❑ **Donatello,** 1988-92, Playmates, 4-1/2" tall
MNP $8   MIP $20

❑ **Donatello, with fan club form,** 1988-92, Playmates, 4-1/2" tall
MNP $12   MIP $50

❑ **Foot Soldier,** 1988-92, Playmates, 4-1/2" tall
MNP $8   MIP $20

❑ **Leonardo,** 1988-92, Playmates, 4-1/2" tall
MNP $8   MIP $20

❑ **Leonardo, with fan club form,** 1988-92, Playmates, 4-1/2" tall
MNP $12   MIP $50

❑ **Michaelangelo,** 1988-92, Playmates, 4-1/2" tall
MNP $8   MIP $20

❑ **Michaelangelo, with fan club form,** 1988-92, Playmates, 4-1/2" tall
MNP $12   MIP $50

❑ **Raphael,** 1988-92, Playmates, 4-1/2" tall
MNP $8   MIP $20

❑ **Raphael, with fan club form,** 1988-92, Playmates, 4-1/2" tall
MNP $12   MIP $50

❑ **Rocksteady,** 1988-92, Playmates, 4-1/2" tall
MNP $8   MIP $20

ACTION FIGURES

❏ **Shredder,** 1988-92, Playmates, 4-1/2" tall

MNP $8   MIP $20

❏ **Splinter,** 1988-92, Playmates, 4-1/2" tall

MNP $8   MIP $20

SERIES 10, 1991

❏ **Grand Slam Raph,** 1988-92, Playmates
MNP $5   MIP $15

❏ **Hose'em Down Don,** 1988-92, Playmates

MNP $5   MIP $15

❏ **Lieutenant Leo,** 1988-92, Playmates
MNP $5   MIP $15

❏ **Make My Day Leo,** 1988-92, Playmates
MNP $5   MIP $15

❏ **Midshipman Mike,** 1988-92, Playmates

MNP $5   MIP $15

❏ **Pro Pilot Don,** 1988-92, Playmates
MNP $5   MIP $15

❏ **Raph the Green Teen Beret,** 1988-92, Playmates
MNP $5   MIP $15

❏ **Slam Dunkin' Don,** 1988-92, Playmates
MNP $5   MIP $15

❏ **Slapshot Leo,** 1988-92, Playmates
MNP $5   MIP $15

❏ **T.D. Tossin' Leonardo,** 1988-92, Playmates
MNP $5   MIP $15

SERIES 11, 1992

❏ **Rahzer, black nose,** 1988-92, Playmates
MNP $5   MIP $15

❏ **Rahzer, red nose,** 1988-92, Playmates
MNP $7   MIP $25

❏ **Skateboard'n Mike,** 1988-92, Playmates
MNP $5   MIP $15

❏ **Super Shredder,** 1988-92, Playmates
MNP $5   MIP $15

❏ **Tokka, brown trim,** 1988-92, Playmates
MNP $9   MIP $25

❏ **Tokka, gray trim,** 1988-92, Playmates
MNP $5   MIP $15

SERIES 12, 1992

❏ **Movie Don,** 1988-92, Playmates
MNP $5   MIP $15

❏ **Movie Leo,** 1988-92, Playmates
MNP $5   MIP $15

❏ **Movie Mike,** 1988-92, Playmates
MNP $5   MIP $15

❏ **Movie Raph,** 1988-92, Playmates
MNP $5   MIP $15

❏ **Movie Splinter, no tooth,** 1988-92, Playmates
MNP $5   MIP $15

❏ **Movie Splinter, with tooth,** 1988-92, Playmates
MNP $25   MIP $75

SERIES 2, 1989

❏ **Ace Duck, hat off,** 1988-92, Playmates, 4-1/2" tall
MNP $5   MIP $40

❏ **Ace Duck, hat on,** 1988-92, Playmates, 4-1/2" tall
MNP $5   MIP $15

❏ **April O'Nei, blue stripe,** 1988-92, Playmates
MNP $12   MIP $30

(Toy Shop File Photo)

❏ **Baxter Stockman,** 1988-92, Playmates, 4-1/2" tall. A man who had a nasty run-in with a bug.
MNP $10   MIP $25

❏ **Genghis Frog, black belt,** 1988-92, Playmates, 4-1/2" tall
MNP $5   MIP $15

❏ **Genghis Frog, black belt, bagged weapons,** 1988-92, Playmates, 4-1/2" tall
MNP $5   MIP $30

❏ **Genghis Frog, yellow belt,** 1988-92, Playmates, 4-1/2" tall
MNP $30   MIP $75

❏ **Krang,** 1988-92, Playmates, 4-1/2" tall
MNP $5   MIP $15

SERIES 3, 1989

❏ **Casey Jones,** 1988-92, Playmates, 4-1/2" tall
MNP $5   MIP $15

❏ **General Traag,** 1988-92, Playmates, 4-1/2" tall
MNP $5   MIP $15

(Toy Shop File Photo)

❏ **Leatherhead,** 1988-92, Playmates, 4-1/2" tall. Way too much sun for this guy.
MNP $25   MIP $50

❏ **Metalhead,** 1988-92, Playmates, action figure, carded
MNP $5   MIP $15

❏ **Rat King,** 1988-92, Playmates, 4-1/2" action figure
MNP $5   MIP $15

❏ **Usagi Yojimbo,** 1988-92, Playmates, 4-1/2" tall
MNP $5   MIP $15

SERIES 4, 1990

❏ **Mondo Gecko,** 1988-92, Playmates, action figure, carded
MNP $5   MIP $15

❏ **Muckman and Joe Eyeball,** 1988-92, Playmates, action figure, carded
MNP $5   MIP $15

❏ **Scumbag,** 1988-92, Playmates, 4-1/2" action figure
MNP $5   MIP $15

❏ **Wingnut & Screwloose,** 1988-92, Playmates, 4-1/2" tall
MNP $5   MIP $15

SERIES 5, 1990

❏ **Fugitoid,** 1988-92, Playmates
MNP $5   MIP $15

❏ **Slash, black belt,** 1988-92, Playmates, action figure, carded
MNP $3   MIP $25

❏ **Slash, purple belt, red "S",** 1988-92, Playmates, action figure, carded
MNP $25   MIP $75

❏ **Triceraton,** 1988-92, Playmates, 4-1/2" tall
MNP $5   MIP $15

SERIES 6, 1990

❏ **Mutagen Man,** 1988-92, Playmates, 4-1/2" action figure
MNP $5   MIP $15

❏ **Napoleon Bonafrog,** 1988-92, Playmates, action figure, carded
MNP $5   MIP $15

❏ **Panda Khan,** 1988-92, Playmates, 4-1/2" action figure
MNP $5   MIP $15

SERIES 7, 1991

❏ **April O'Neil,** 1988-92, Playmates, 4-1/2" tall
MNP $25   MIP $125

❏ **April O'Neil, "Press",** 1988-92, Playmates, 4-1/2" tall
MNP $10   MIP $20

❏ **Pizza Face,** 1988-92, Playmates
MNP $5   MIP $15

❏ **Ray Fillet, purple body, red "V",** 1988-92, Playmates, purple torso, red V
MNP $10   MIP $25

❏ **Ray Fillet, red body, maroon "V",** 1988-92, Playmates, red torso, maroon V
MNP $10   MIP $30

❏ **Ray Fillet, yellow body, blue "V",** 1988-92, Playmates, yellow torso, blue V
MNP $10   MIP $15

SERIES 8, 1991

❏ **Don The Undercover Turtle,** 1988-92, Playmates
MNP $5   MIP $15

❏ **Leo the Sewer Samurai,** 1988-92, Playmates
MNP $5   MIP $15

❏ **Mike the Sewer Surfer,** 1988-92, Playmates
MNP $5   MIP $15

❏ **Raph the Space Cadet,** 1988-92, Playmates
MNP $5   MIP $15

SERIES 9, 1991

❏ **Chrome Dome,** 1988-92, Playmates, action figure, carded
MNP $5   MIP $15

❏ **Dirt Bag,** 1988-92, Playmates, action figure, carded
MNP $5   MIP $15

❏ **Ground Chuck,** 1988-92, Playmates
MNP $5   MIP $15

❏ **Storage Shell Don,** 1988-92, Playmates
MNP $5   MIP $15

❏ **Storage Shell Leo,** 1988-92, Playmates
MNP $5   MIP $15

❏ **Storage Shell Michaelangelo,** 1988-92, Playmates
MNP $5   MIP $15

❏ **Storage Shell Raphael,** 1988-92, Playmates
MNP $5   MIP $15

VEHICLES AND ACCESSORIES

❏ **Flushomatic,** 1988-92, Playmates
MNP $4   MIP $10

❏ **Foot Cruiser,** 1988-92, Playmates
MNP $14   MIP $35

❏ **Foot Ski,** 1988-92, Playmates
MNP $4   MIP $10

❏ **Mega Mutant Killer Bee,** 1988-92, Playmates
MNP $3   MIP $8

❏ **Mega Mutant Needlenose,** 1988-92, Playmates
MNP $8   MIP $20

❏ **Mike's Pizza Chopper Backpack,** 1988-92, Playmates
MNP $4   MIP $10

❏ **Mutant Sewer Cycle with Sidecar,** 1988-92, Playmates
MNP $4   MIP $10

❏ **Ninja Newscycle,** 1988-92, Playmates
MNP $5   MIP $12

❏ **Oozey,** 1988-92, Playmates
MNP $4   MIP $10

❏ **Pizza Powered Sewer Dragster,** 1988-92, Playmates
MNP $5   MIP $15

❏ **Pizza Thrower,** 1988-92, Playmates
MNP $14   MIP $35

❏ **Psycho Cycle,** 1988-92, Playmates
MNP $10   MIP $25

❏ **Raph's Sewer Dragster,** 1988-92, Playmates
MNP $6   MIP $16

❏ **Raph's Sewer Speedboat,** 1988-92, Playmates
MNP $5   MIP $12

❏ **Retrocatapult,** 1988-92, Playmates
MNP $4   MIP $10

❏ **Retromutagen Ooze,** 1988-92, Playmates
MNP $2   MIP $4

❏ **Sewer Seltzer Cannon,** 1988-92, Playmates
MNP $4   MIP $10

❏ **Sludgemobile,** 1988-92, Playmates
MNP $7   MIP $18

❏ **Technodrome, 22",** 1988-92, Playmates, 22"
MNP $24   MIP $60

❏ **Toilet Taxi,** 1988-92, Playmates
MNP $5   MIP $12

❏ **Turtle Blimp, green vinyl, 30",** 1988-92, Playmates, 30" green vinyl
MNP $12   MIP $30

❏ **Turtle Party Wagon,** 1988-92, Playmates
MNP $16   MIP $40

❏ **Turtle Trooper Parachute, 22",** 1988-92, Playmates, 22"
MNP $4   MIP $10

❏ **Turtlecopter,** 1988-92, Playmates
MNP $16   MIP $40

WACKY ACTION, 1991

❏ **Breakfightin' Raphael,** 1988-92, Playmates
MNP $5   MIP $15

❏ **Creepy Crawlin' Splinter,** 1988-92, Playmates, 4-1/2" tall
MNP $5   MIP $15

❏ **Headspinnin' Bebop,** 1988-92, Playmates, 4-1/2" tall
MNP $5   MIP $15

❏ **Machine Gunnin' Rocksteady,** 1988-92, Playmates
MNP $5   MIP $15

❏ **Rock & Roll Michaelangelo,** 1988-92, Playmates
MNP $5   MIP $15

❏ **Sewer Swimmin' Don,** 1988-92, Playmates
MNP $5   MIP $15

❏ **Slice 'n Dice Shredder,** 1988-92, Playmates, 4-1/2" tall
MNP $10   MIP $25

❏ **Sword Slicin' Leonardo,** 1988-92, Playmates
MNP $8   MIP $15

❏ **Wacky Walkin' Mouser,** 1988-92, Playmates
MNP $10   MIP $20

THIS IS SPINAL TAP (SIDESHOW TOYS, 2000)

FIGURES

❏ **David St. Hubbins,** 2000
MNP $10   MIP $25

❏ **Derek Smalls,** 2000
MNP $10   MIP $25

❏ **Nigel Tufnel,** 2000
MNP $10   MIP $25

THUNDERCATS (LJN, 1985-87)

6" FIGURES

❏ **Ben-Gali,** 1985-87
MNP $75   MIP $200

❏ **Capt. Cracker,** 1985-87
MNP $15   MIP $40

❏ **Capt. Shiner,** 1985-87
MNP $15   MIP $40

❏ **Cheetara,** 1985-87
MNP $30   MIP $70

❏ **Cheetara and Wilykit,** 1985-87
MNP $45   MIP $100

❏ **Grune the Destroyer,** 1985-87
MNP $10   MIP $30

❏ **Hachiman,** 1985-87
MNP $15   MIP $40

ACTION FIGURES

❏ Jackalman, 1985-87
MNP $15 MIP $35

❏ Lion-O, 1985-87
MNP $30 MIP $70

❏ Lion-O and Snarf, 1985-87
MNP $25 MIP $60

❏ Lynx-O, 1985-87
MNP $30 MIP $75

❏ Mongor, 1985-87
MNP $30 MIP $75

❏ Monkian, 1985-87
MNP $10 MIP $35

❏ Mumm-ra, 1985-87
MNP $10 MIP $35

❏ Panthro, 1985-87
MNP $30 MIP $70

❏ Pumyra, 1985-87
MNP $25 MIP $75

❏ Ratar-O, 1985-87
MNP $10 MIP $30

❏ Safari Joe, 1985-87
MNP $10 MIP $35

❏ Snowman of Hook Mountain, 1985-87
MNP $15 MIP $40

❏ S-S-Slithe, 1985-87
MNP $15 MIP $40

❏ Tuska Warrior, 1985-87
MNP $10 MIP $35

❏ Tygra, 1985-87
MNP $30 MIP $70

❏ Tygra and Wilykat, 1985-87
MNP $25 MIP $60

❏ Vultureman, 1985-87
MNP $10 MIP $30

BERSERKERS

❏ Cruncher, 1985-87
MNP $15 MIP $40

❏ Hammerhead, 1985-87
MNP $15 MIP $40

❏ Ram-Bam, 1985-87
MNP $15 MIP $40

❏ Top-Spinner, 1985-87
MNP $15 MIP $40

COMPANIONS

❏ Berbil Belle, 1985-87
MNP $15 MIP $50

❏ Berbil Bill, 1985-87
MNP $15 MIP $50

❏ Ma-Mut, 1985-87
MNP $10 MIP $45

❏ Snarf, 1985-87
MNP $10 MIP $45

❏ Wilykat, 1985-87
MNP $15 MIP $50

❏ Wilykit, 1985-87
MNP $15 MIP $50

RAM-PAGERS

❏ Driller, the, 1985-87
MNP $25 MIP $75

❏ Mad Bubbler, The, 1985-87
MNP $25 MIP $75

❏ Stinger, The, 1985-87
MNP $25 MIP $75

TICK, THE (BANDAI, 1994-95)

ACCESSORIES

(Bandai)

❏ Steel Box, 1994, Bandai, Figure-sized box with "Really, Really Dangerous!" and "Unsafe" in yellow type
MNP $8 MIP $20

SERIES I, 6" FIGURES

❏ Bounding Tick, 1994
MNP $8 MIP $20

❏ Death Hug Dean, 1994, Bandai
MNP $8 MIP $20

❏ Exploding Dyne-Mole, 1994, Bandai
MNP $6 MIP $15

❏ Fluttering Arthur, 1994
MNP $8 MIP $20

❏ Grasping El Seed, 1994, Bandai
MNP $8 MIP $20

❏ Growing Dinosaur Neil, 1994, Bandai
MNP $8 MIP $20

(KP Photo)

❏ Man Eating Cow, 1994, Bandai, Brown and white cow with moving jaw (and a set of teeth!)
MNP $15 MIP $50

❏ Pose Striking Die Fledermaus, 1994
MNP $15 MIP $50

❏ Projectile Human Bullet, 1994
MNP $8 MIP $20

❏ Sewer Spray Sewer Urchin, 1994
MNP $8 MIP $20

SERIES II, 6" FIGURES

❏ Color Changing Chameleon, 1995
MNP $15 MIP $45

❏ Hurling Stop Sign Tick, 1995
MNP $8 MIP $20

❏ Propellerized Skippy the Dog, 1995
MNP $8 MIP $20

❏ Sliming Mucus Tick, 1995
MNP $10 MIP $30

❏ Thrakkorzog, 1995
MNP $10 MIP $30

❏ Twist and Chop American Maid, 1995
MNP $10 MIP $35

TOMB RAIDER (PLAYMATES, 1999)

12" FIGURE

❏ Talking Lara Croft, 1999
MNP $8 MIP $25

9" FIGURES

❏ Lara Croft in Area 51 outfit with hand guns and an M-16, on base, 1999
MNP $8 MIP $20

❏ Lara Croft in jungle outfit with two guns, on base, 1999
MNP $8 MIP $20

(Playmates Toys)

❏ Lara Croft in wet suit with harpoon and two pistols, on base, 1999, Detailed figure with stand
MNP $8 MIP $20

ADVENTURES OF LARA CROFT, 6" FIGURES

❑ **Lara Croft escapes a Bengal, on diorama base,** 1999
    MNP $3   MIP $10

❑ **Lara Croft escapes the yeti, on diorama base,** 1999
    MNP $3   MIP $10

❑ **Lara Croft faces a Bengal, on diorama base,** 1999
    MNP $3   MIP $10

TOTAL CHAOS (MCFARLANE, 1996-97)

SERIES 1, FIGURES

❑ **Al Simmons,** 1996, McFarlane
    MNP $5   MIP $15

❑ **Al Simmons, blue uniform,** 1996
    MNP $3   MIP $12

❑ **Al Simmons, red uniform with "Spawn" on visor, available through convention,** 1997
    MNP $15   MIP $45

❑ **Conqueror,** 1996
    MNP $5   MIP $15

❑ **Dragon Blade vs. Conqueror, Puzzle Zoo Exclusive,** 1997
    MNP $6   MIP $18

❑ **Dragon Blade, black tunic,** 1996
    MNP $4   MIP $12

❑ **Dragon Blade, white tunic,** 1996, McFarlane
    MNP $5   MIP $15

(KP Photo)

❑ **Gore,** 1996, McFarlane, With harpoon-launching arm and bomb-dropping parrot figure
    MNP $5   MIP $15

❑ **Hoof, black body with khaki armor,** 1996
    MNP $3   MIP $12

(Lenny Lee)

❑ **Hoof, gray body with brown armor,** 1996, McFarlane, With rotating and firing missile launcher
    MNP $5   MIP $15

❑ **Thorax, black and yellow,** 1996
    MNP $3   MIP $12

❑ **Thorax, green and red,** 1996, McFarlane
    MNP $4   MIP $12

❑ **Thresher, light blue skin,** 1996, McFarlane
    MNP $5   MIP $15

❑ **Thresher, violet skin,** 1996
    MNP $3   MIP $10

SERIES 2, FIGURES

❑ **Blitz,** 1997
    MNP $3   MIP $10

❑ **Brain Drain,** 1997
    MNP $3   MIP $10

❑ **Corn Boy,** 1997
    MNP $3   MIP $10

❑ **Poacher,** 1997
    MNP $3   MIP $10

❑ **Quartz,** 1997
    MNP $3   MIP $10

❑ **Smuggler,** 1997
    MNP $3   MIP $10

TOTAL JUSTICE (KENNER, 1996)

5" FIGURES

❑ **Aquaman, black armor,** 1996, Kenner
    MNP $5   MIP $8

(Kenner)

❑ **Aquaman, with Hydro-Blasting Spear, gold armor,** 1996, Kenner
    MNP $7   MIP $8

(Kenner)

❑ **Batman,** 1996, Kenner, With flight armor and glider cape
    MNP $5   MIP $8

❑ **Black Lightning,** 1996, Kenner
    MNP $7   MIP $8

(Kenner)

❑ **Darkseid,** 1996, Kenner, With omega-effect capture claw
> MNP $5   MIP $8

(Kenner)

❑ **Despero,** 1996, Kenner, With galactic body blow attack
> MNP $5   MIP $8

(Kenner)

❑ **Flash, The,** 1996, Kenner, With velocity power suit
> MNP $5   MIP $8

❑ **Green Arrow,** 1996, Kenner
> MNP $5   MIP $8

(Kenner)

❑ **Green Lantern,** 1996, Kenner
> MNP $5   MIP $8

(Kenner)

❑ **Hawkman,** 1996, Kenner, With talon
> MNP $5   MIP $8

❑ **Huntress,** 1996, Kenner
> MNP $5   MIP $8

❑ **Parallax,** 1996, Kenner
> MNP $5   MIP $8

(Kenner)

❑ **Robin,** 1996, Kenner, With spinning razor disc and battle staff
> MNP $5   MIP $8

(Kenner)

❑ **Superman,** 1996, Kenner, With shield and kryptonite ray emitter
> MNP $5   MIP $8

TOY STORY (THINKWAY, 1996)

5" FIGURES

❑ **Alien,** 1996, Thinkway
> MNP $5   MIP $15

❑ **Boxer Buzz,** 1996, Thinkway
> MNP $4   MIP $8

❑ **Crawling Baby Face,** 1996, Thinkway
> MNP $3   MIP $9

❑ **Fighting Woody,** 1996, Thinkway
> MNP $3   MIP $9

❑ **Flying Buzz (Rocket),** 1996, Thinkway
MNP $4   MIP $8

❑ **Hamm,** 1996, Thinkway
MNP $4   MIP $8

❑ **Karate Buzz,** 1996, Thinkway
MNP $4   MIP $8

❑ **Kicking Woody,** 1996, Thinkway
MNP $4   MIP $8

❑ **Quick-Draw Woody,** 1996, Thinkway
MNP $4   MIP $8

❑ **Rex,** 1996, Thinkway
MNP $4   MIP $8

❑ **Super Sonic Buzz,** 1996, Thinkway
MNP $3   MIP $9

LARGE FIGURES

❑ **Talking Buzz Lightyear,** 1996, Thinkway
MNP $15   MIP $50

❑ **Talking Woody,** 1996, Thinkway
MNP $15   MIP $60

TRANSFORMERS (KENNER, 1984-1995)

GENERATION 1, SERIES 1, 1984

❑ **Bluestreak, blue,** 1984, Kenner
MNP $100   MIP $350

❑ **Bluestreak, silver,** 1984, Kenner
MNP $90   MIP $250

❑ **Brawn,** 1984, Kenner
MNP $10   MIP $40

❑ **Bumblebee, red,** 1984, Kenner
MNP $40   MIP $100

❑ **Bumblebee, yellow,** 1984, Kenner
MNP $20   MIP $50

❑ **Cliffjumper, red,** 1984, Kenner
MNP $10   MIP $40

❑ **Cliffjumper, yellow,** 1984, Kenner
MNP $20   MIP $50

❑ **Gears,** 1984, Kenner
MNP $10   MIP $40

❑ **Hound,** 1984, Kenner
MNP $100   MIP $275

❑ **Huffer,** 1984, Kenner
MNP $10   MIP $40

❑ **Ironhide,** 1984, Kenner
MNP $75   MIP $250

❑ **Jazz,** 1984, Kenner
MNP $75   MIP $250

(Lenny Lee)

❑ **Megatron,** 1984, Kenner, Deception Leader turns from handgun to robot
MNP $100   MIP $300

❑ **Mirage,** 1984, Kenner
MNP $90   MIP $250

❑ **Optimus Prime with gray or blue roller,** 1984, Kenner
MNP $100   MIP $300

❑ **Prowl,** 1984, Kenner
MNP $90   MIP $250

❑ **Ratchet with cross,** 1984, Kenner
MNP $75   MIP $150

❑ **Ratchet without cross,** 1984, Kenner
MNP $75   MIP $200

❑ **Sideswipe,** 1984, Kenner
MNP $100   MIP $275

❑ **Skywarp,** 1984, Kenner
MNP $50   MIP $120

❑ **Soundwave and Buzzsaw,** 1984, Kenner
MNP $50   MIP $120

❑ **Starscream,** 1984, Kenner
MNP $60   MIP $150

❑ **Sunstreaker,** 1984, Kenner
MNP $100   MIP $275

❑ **Thundercracker,** 1984, Kenner
MNP $50   MIP $120

❑ **Trailbreaker,** 1984, Kenner
MNP $75   MIP $150

❑ **Wheeljack,** 1984, Kenner
MNP $90   MIP $250

❑ **Windcharger,** 1984, Kenner
MNP $20   MIP $50

GENERATION 1, SERIES 2, 1985

❑ **Astrotrain,** 1985, Kenner
MNP $10   MIP $50

❑ **Barrage,** 1985, Kenner
MNP $20   MIP $55

❑ **Beachcomber,** 1985, Kenner
MNP $5   MIP $15

❑ **Blaster,** 1985, Kenner
MNP $20   MIP $50

❑ **Blitzwing,** 1985, Kenner
MNP $20   MIP $50

❑ **Bombshell,** 1985, Kenner
MNP $8   MIP $25

❑ **Bonecrusher,** 1985, Kenner
MNP $10   MIP $40

❑ **Brawn,** 1985, Kenner
MNP $8   MIP $20

❑ **Brawn with Minispy,** 1985, Kenner
MNP $10   MIP $40

❑ **Bumblebee with Minispy, yellow,** 1985, Kenner
MNP $20   MIP $50

❑ **Bumblebee, red,** 1985, Kenner
MNP $10   MIP $30

❑ **Bumblebee, yellow,** 1985, Kenner
MNP $10   MIP $30

❑ **Chop Shop,** 1985, Kenner
MNP $10   MIP $55

❑ **Cliffjumper with Minispy, red,** 1985, Kenner
MNP $50   MIP $125

❑ **Cliffjumper, red,** 1985, Kenner
MNP $8   MIP $20

❑ **Cliffjumper, yellow,** 1985, Kenner
MNP $10   MIP $30

❑ **Cosmos,** 1985, Kenner
MNP $8   MIP $20

❑ **Dirge,** 1985, Kenner
MNP $40   MIP $100

❑ **Gears,** 1985, Kenner
MNP $10   MIP $30

❑ **Gears with Minispy,** 1985, Kenner
MNP $10   MIP $30

❑ **Grapple,** 1985, Kenner
MNP $50   MIP $125

(Toy Shop File Photo)

❑ **Grimlock,** 1985, Kenner
MNP $20   MIP $125

❑ **Hoist,** 1985, Kenner
MNP $50   MIP $125

❑ **Hook,** 1985, Kenner
MNP $10   MIP $40

❑ **Huffer,** 1985, Kenner
MNP $10   MIP $30

❑ **Huffer with Minispy,** 1985, Kenner
MNP $10   MIP $40

❑ **Inferno,** 1985, Kenner
MNP $40   MIP $100

❑ **Jazz,** 1985, Kenner
MNP $5   MIP $40

(Lenny Lee)

❑ **Jetfire,** 1985, Kenner, Red and white pieces transform from folding-wing jet bomber to robot
MNP $100   MIP $325

ACTION FIGURES

Kickback, 1985, Kenner
MNP $8   MIP $25

Long Haul, 1985, Kenner
MNP $10   MIP $40

Mixmaster, 1985, Kenner
MNP $10   MIP $40

Omega Supreme, 1985, Kenner
MNP $75   MIP $200

Optimus Prime, 1985, Kenner
MNP $75   MIP $250

Perceptor, 1985, Kenner
MNP $40   MIP $100

Powerglide, 1985, Kenner
MNP $8   MIP $20

Ramjet, 1985, Kenner
MNP $40   MIP $80

Ransack, 1985, Kenner
MNP $20   MIP $55

Red Alert, 1985, Kenner
MNP $60   MIP $175

Roadbuster, 1985, Kenner
MNP $50   MIP $100

Scavenger, 1985, Kenner
MNP $10   MIP $40

Scrapper, 1985, Kenner
MNP $10   MIP $40

Seaspray, 1985, Kenner
MNP $8   MIP $20

Shockwave, 1985, Kenner
MNP $75   MIP $200

Shrapnel, 1985, Kenner
MNP $8   MIP $25

Skids, 1985, Kenner
MNP $60   MIP $175

Slag, 1985, Kenner
MNP $40   MIP $100

Sludge, 1985, Kenner
MNP $40   MIP $100

Smokescreen, 1985, Kenner
MNP $50   MIP $150

Snarl, 1985, Kenner
MNP $40   MIP $100

Thrust, 1985, Kenner
MNP $40   MIP $80

Tracks, 1985, Kenner
MNP $60   MIP $175

Venom, 1985, Kenner
MNP $20   MIP $55

Warpath, 1985, Kenner
MNP $8   MIP $20

Whirl, 1985, Kenner
MNP $50   MIP $150

Windcharger, 1985, Kenner
MNP $20   MIP $50

Windcharger with Minispy, 1985, Kenner
MNP $20   MIP $50

GENERATION 1, SERIES 3, 1986

Air Raid, 1986, Kenner
MNP $10   MIP $30

Air Raid with patch, 1986, Kenner
MNP $10   MIP $30

Beachcomber, 1986, Kenner
MNP $5   MIP $15

Beachcomber with patch, 1986, Kenner
MNP $8   MIP $20

Blades, 1986, Kenner
MNP $10   MIP $30

Blades, plastic chest, 1986, Kenner
MNP $10   MIP $30

Blast Off, metal treads, 1986, Kenner
MNP $10   MIP $30

Blast Off, plastic chest, 1986, Kenner
MNP $10   MIP $30

Blurr, 1986, Kenner
MNP $30   MIP $80

Blurr with poster, 1986, Kenner
MNP $20   MIP $60

Brawl, metal treads, 1986, Kenner
MNP $10   MIP $30

Brawl, plastic treads, 1986, Kenner
MNP $10   MIP $30

Breakdown, 1986, Kenner
MNP $10   MIP $30

Breakdown with patch, 1986, Kenner
MNP $10   MIP $30

Broadside, 1986, Kenner
MNP $20   MIP $60

Broadside with poster, 1986, Kenner
MNP $20   MIP $50

Bumblebee, 1986, Kenner
MNP $5   MIP $15

Bumblebee with patch, 1986, Kenner
MNP $20   MIP $50

Cosmos, 1986, Kenner
MNP $5   MIP $15

Cosmos with patch, 1986, Kenner
MNP $8   MIP $20

Dead End, 1986, Kenner
MNP $10   MIP $30

Dead End with patch, 1986, Kenner
MNP $10   MIP $30

Divebomb with poster, plastic body, 1986, Kenner
MNP $30   MIP $80

Divebomb, metal body, 1986, Kenner
MNP $30   MIP $80

Divebomb, plastic body, 1986, Kenner
MNP $40   MIP $100

Drag Strip, 1986, Kenner
MNP $10   MIP $30

Drag Strip with patch, 1986, Kenner
MNP $10   MIP $30

Fireflight, 1986, Kenner
MNP $10   MIP $30

Fireflight with patch, 1986, Kenner
MNP $10   MIP $30

First Aid, 1986, Kenner
MNP $10   MIP $30

First Aid, plastic chest, 1986, Kenner
MNP $10   MIP $30

Groove, 1986, Kenner
MNP $10   MIP $30

Groove, silver chest, 1986, Kenner
MNP $10   MIP $30

Headstrong, metal body, 1986, Kenner
MNP $40   MIP $100

Hot Rod with poster, plastic toes, 1986, Kenner
MNP $100   MIP $250

Hot Rod, metal toes, 1986, Kenner
MNP $50   MIP $150

Hot Spot, 1986, Kenner
MNP $10   MIP $40

Hubcap, 1986, Kenner
MNP $5   MIP $15

Hubcap with patch, 1986, Kenner
MNP $5   MIP $15

Kup, plastic tires and wheels, 1986, Kenner
MNP $20   MIP $60

Kup, rubber tires and metal wheels, 1986, Kenner
MNP $20   MIP $60

Motormaster, 1986, Kenner
MNP $10   MIP $40

Octane, 1986, Kenner
MNP $30   MIP $75

Octane with poster, 1986, Kenner
MNP $20   MIP $50

Onslaught, 1986, Kenner
MNP $10   MIP $40

Outback, 1986, Kenner
MNP $5   MIP $15

Outback with patch, 1986, Kenner
MNP $5   MIP $15

Pipes, 1986, Kenner
MNP $5   MIP $15

Pipes with patch, 1986, Kenner
MNP $5   MIP $15

Powerglide, 1986, Kenner
MNP $5   MIP $15

Powerglide with patch, 1986, Kenner
MNP $8   MIP $20

Rampage, metal body, 1986, Kenner
MNP $20   MIP $75

Rampage, plastic body, 1986, Kenner
MNP $20   MIP $75

Razorclaw, metal body, 1986, Kenner
MNP $20   MIP $75

❑ **Razorclaw, plastic body,** 1986, Kenner
MNP $20   MIP $75

❑ **Rodimus Prime, metal toes,** 1986, Kenner
MNP $50   MIP $130

❑ **Rodimus Prime, plastic toes,** 1986, Kenner
MNP $50   MIP $130

❑ **Sandstorm, metal or plastic toes,** 1986, Kenner
MNP $50   MIP $150

❑ **Sandstorm, plastic toes,** 1986, Kenner
MNP $30   MIP $75

❑ **Seaspray,** 1986, Kenner
MNP $5   MIP $15

❑ **Seaspray with patch,** 1986, Kenner
MNP $8   MIP $20

❑ **Silverbolt,** 1986, Kenner
MNP $10   MIP $40

❑ **Skydive,** 1986, Kenner
MNP $10   MIP $30

❑ **Skydive with patch,** 1986, Kenner
MNP $10   MIP $30

❑ **Slingshot,** 1986, Kenner
MNP $10   MIP $30

❑ **Slingshot with patch,** 1986, Kenner
MNP $10   MIP $30

❑ **Springer, metal or plastic front,** 1986, Kenner
MNP $50   MIP $100

❑ **Streetwise,** 1986, Kenner
MNP $10   MIP $30

❑ **Swerve,** 1986, Kenner
MNP $5   MIP $15

❑ **Swerve with patch,** 1986, Kenner
MNP $5   MIP $15

❑ **Swindle, gray plastic chest,** 1986, Kenner
MNP $10   MIP $30

❑ **Swindle, metal treads,** 1986, Kenner
MNP $10   MIP $30

❑ **Tailgate,** 1986, Kenner
MNP $5   MIP $15

❑ **Tailgate with patch,** 1986, Kenner
MNP $5   MIP $15

❑ **Tantrum with poster, plastic body,** 1986, Kenner
MNP $30   MIP $80

❑ **Tantrum, metal body,** 1986, Kenner
MNP $40   MIP $100

❑ **Tantrum, plastic body,** 1986, Kenner
MNP $30   MIP $80

❑ **Vortex, metal treads,** 1986, Kenner
MNP $10   MIP $30

❑ **Vortex, plastic chest,** 1986, Kenner
MNP $10   MIP $30

❑ **Warpath,** 1986, Kenner
MNP $5   MIP $15

❑ **Warpath with patch,** 1986, Kenner
MNP $8   MIP $20

❑ **Wheelie,** 1986, Kenner
MNP $5   MIP $15

❑ **Wheelie with patch,** 1986, Kenner
MNP $5   MIP $15

❑ **Wildrider,** 1986, Kenner
MNP $10   MIP $30

❑ **Wildrider with patch,** 1986, Kenner
MNP $10   MIP $30

❑ **Wreck-gar,** 1986, Kenner
MNP $20   MIP $60

❑ **Wreck-gar with poster,** 1986, Kenner
MNP $30   MIP $80

GENERATION 1, SERIES 3, 1987

❑ **Headstrong, plastic body,** 1987, Kenner
MNP $30   MIP $80

GENERATION 1, SERIES 4, 1987

❑ **Afterburner,** 1987, Kenner
MNP $8   MIP $25

❑ **Afterburner with decoy,** 1987, Kenner
MNP $10   MIP $30

❑ **Air Raid,** 1987, Kenner
MNP $5   MIP $15

❑ **Air Raid with decoy,** 1987, Kenner
MNP $10   MIP $35

❑ **Apeface,** 1987, Kenner
MNP $20   MIP $55

❑ **Battletrap,** 1987, Kenner
MNP $8   MIP $25

❑ **Blades with decoy, plastic chest,** 1987, Kenner
MNP $8   MIP $20

❑ **Blades, plastic chest,** 1987, Kenner
MNP $5   MIP $15

❑ **Blast Off with decoy, plastic chest,** 1987, Kenner
MNP $8   MIP $25

❑ **Blot with decoy,** 1987, Kenner
MNP $8   MIP $20

❑ **Blurr,** 1987, Kenner
MNP $50   MIP $150

❑ **Brainstorm,** 1987, Kenner
MNP $20   MIP $50

❑ **Brawl with decoy, plastic treads,** 1987, Kenner
MNP $8   MIP $20

❑ **Breakdown with decoy,** 1987, Kenner
MNP $8   MIP $20

❑ **Chase,** 1987, Kenner
MNP $8   MIP $20

❑ **Chase with decoy,** 1987, Kenner
MNP $8   MIP $35

❑ **Chromedome,** 1987, Kenner
MNP $30   MIP $75

❑ **Crosshairs,** 1987, Kenner
MNP $50   MIP $150

❑ **Cutthroat with decoy,** 1987, Kenner
MNP $8   MIP $35

❑ **Cyclonus,** 1987, Kenner
MNP $50   MIP $130

❑ **Dead End with decoy,** 1987, Kenner
MNP $8   MIP $20

❑ **Doublecross,** 1987, Kenner
MNP $20   MIP $45

❑ **Drag Strip with decoy,** 1987, Kenner
MNP $8   MIP $20

❑ **Fireflight,** 1987, Kenner
MNP $5   MIP $15

❑ **Fireflight with decoy,** 1987, Kenner
MNP $8   MIP $20

❑ **First Aid with decoy, plastic chest,** 1987, Kenner
MNP $8   MIP $20

❑ **First Aid, plastic chest,** 1987, Kenner
MNP $5   MIP $15

❑ **Flywheels,** 1987, Kenner
MNP $8   MIP $25

❑ **Fortess Maximus,** 1987, Kenner
MNP $300   MIP $900

❑ **Freeway,** 1987, Kenner
MNP $8   MIP $20

❑ **Freeway with decoy,** 1987, Kenner
MNP $10   MIP $35

❑ **Goldbug,** 1987, Kenner
MNP $8   MIP $20

❑ **Goldbug with decoy,** 1987, Kenner
MNP $10   MIP $35

❑ **Groove with decoy, silver chest,** 1987, Kenner
MNP $8   MIP $20

❑ **Groove, silver chest,** 1987, Kenner
MNP $5   MIP $15

❑ **Grotusque,** 1987, Kenner
MNP $20   MIP $45

❑ **Hardhead,** 1987, Kenner
MNP $20   MIP $50

❑ **Highbrow,** 1987, Kenner
MNP $20   MIP $50

❑ **Hot Rod,** 1987, Kenner
MNP $100   MIP $300

❑ **Kup,** 1987, Kenner
MNP $50   MIP $150

❑ **Lightspeed,** 1987, Kenner
MNP $8   MIP $20

❑ **Lightspeed with decoy,** 1987, Kenner
MNP $8   MIP $25

❑ **Mindwipe,** 1987, Kenner
MNP $20   MIP $50

❑ **Misfire,** 1987, Kenner
MNP $30   MIP $80

❑ **Nosecone,** 1987, Kenner
MNP $8   MIP $25

ACTION FIGURES

❑ **Nosecone with decoy,** 1987, Kenner
MNP $10   MIP $30

❑ **Pointblank,** 1987, Kenner
MNP $30   MIP $70

❑ **Repugnus,** 1987, Kenner
MNP $20   MIP $45

❑ **Rippersnapper with decoy,** 1987, Kenner
MNP $8   MIP $20

❑ **Rollbar,** 1987, Kenner
MNP $10   MIP $35

❑ **Rollbar with decoy,** 1987, Kenner
MNP $8   MIP $20

❑ **Scourge,** 1987, Kenner
MNP $50   MIP $130

❑ **Searchlight,** 1987, Kenner
MNP $8   MIP $20

❑ **Searchlight with decoy,** 1987, Kenner
MNP $10   MIP $35

❑ **Sinnertwin with decoy,** 1987, Kenner
MNP $8   MIP $20

❑ **Skullcruncher,** 1987, Kenner
MNP $20   MIP $50

❑ **Skydive,** 1987, Kenner
MNP $5   MIP $15

❑ **Skydive with decoy,** 1987, Kenner
MNP $10   MIP $35

❑ **Slingshot,** 1987, Kenner
MNP $5   MIP $15

❑ **Slingshot with decoy,** 1987, Kenner
MNP $10   MIP $35

❑ **Slugslinger,** 1987, Kenner
MNP $30   MIP $80

❑ **Snapdragon,** 1987, Kenner
MNP $20   MIP $55

❑ **Strafe,** 1987, Kenner
MNP $8   MIP $20

❑ **Strafe with decoy,** 1987, Kenner
MNP $10   MIP $35

❑ **Streetwise,** 1987, Kenner
MNP $5   MIP $15

❑ **Streetwise with decoy,** 1987, Kenner
MNP $8   MIP $20

❑ **Sureshot,** 1987, Kenner
MNP $30   MIP $70

❑ **Swindle with decoy, gray plastic chest,** 1987, Kenner
MNP $8   MIP $25

❑ **Triggerhappy,** 1987, Kenner
MNP $30   MIP $80

❑ **Vortex with decoy, plastic chest,** 1987, Kenner
MNP $8   MIP $25

❑ **Weirdwolf,** 1987, Kenner
MNP $20   MIP $50

❑ **Wideload,** 1987, Kenner
MNP $8   MIP $20

❑ **Wideload with decoy,** 1987, Kenner
MNP $10   MIP $35

❑ **Wildrider with decoy,** 1987, Kenner
MNP $8   MIP $20

GENERATION 1, SERIES 5, 1988

❑ **Afterburner,** 1988, Kenner
MNP $5   MIP $15

❑ **Backstreet,** 1988, Kenner
MNP $5   MIP $15

❑ **Blot,** 1988, Kenner
MNP $8   MIP $20

❑ **Bomb-burst, clear insert,** 1988, Kenner
MNP $20   MIP $60

❑ **Bugly,** 1988, Kenner
MNP $20   MIP $60

❑ **Carnivac,** 1988, Kenner
MNP $10   MIP $40

❑ **Catilla,** 1988, Kenner
MNP $20   MIP $50

❑ **Chainclaw,** 1988, Kenner
MNP $10   MIP $40

❑ **Cindersaur,** 1988, Kenner
MNP $4   MIP $10

❑ **Cloudburst, clear insert,** 1988, Kenner
MNP $20   MIP $50

❑ **Crankcase,** 1988, Kenner
MNP $5   MIP $15

❑ **Cutthroat,** 1988, Kenner
MNP $8   MIP $20

❑ **Darkwing,** 1988, Kenner
MNP $20   MIP $50

❑ **Dogfight,** 1988, Kenner
MNP $5   MIP $15

❑ **Dreadwind,** 1988, Kenner
MNP $20   MIP $50

❑ **Fangry,** 1988, Kenner
MNP $20   MIP $50

❑ **Finback,** 1988, Kenner
MNP $20   MIP $65

❑ **Fizzle,** 1988, Kenner
MNP $4   MIP $15

❑ **Flamefeather,** 1988, Kenner
MNP $4   MIP $10

❑ **Getaway,** 1988, Kenner
MNP $10   MIP $40

❑ **Groundbreaker,** 1988, Kenner
MNP $20   MIP $65

❑ **Gunrunner,** 1988, Kenner
MNP $20   MIP $55

❑ **Guzzle,** 1988, Kenner
MNP $4   MIP $15

❑ **Horri-bull,** 1988, Kenner
MNP $20   MIP $50

❑ **Hosehead,** 1988, Kenner
MNP $20   MIP $50

❑ **Iguanus,** 1988, Kenner
MNP $10   MIP $40

❑ **Joyride,** 1988, Kenner
MNP $10   MIP $40

❑ **Landfill,** 1988, Kenner
MNP $8   MIP $20

❑ **Landmine, clear insert,** 1988, Kenner
MNP $10   MIP $40

❑ **Lightspeed,** 1988, Kenner
MNP $5   MIP $15

❑ **Nautilator,** 1988, Kenner
MNP $10   MIP $30

❑ **Needlenose,** 1988, Kenner
MNP $10   MIP $30

❑ **Nightbeat,** 1988, Kenner
MNP $20   MIP $60

❑ **Nosecone,** 1988, Kenner
MNP $5   MIP $15

❑ **Overbite,** 1988, Kenner
MNP $10   MIP $30

❑ **Override,** 1988, Kenner
MNP $5   MIP $15

❑ **Quake,** 1988, Kenner
MNP $10   MIP $30

❑ **Quickmix,** 1988, Kenner
MNP $8   MIP $25

❑ **Rippersnapper,** 1988, Kenner
MNP $8   MIP $20

❑ **Roadgrabber,** 1988, Kenner
MNP $20   MIP $55

❑ **Ruckus,** 1988, Kenner
MNP $5   MIP $15

❑ **Scoop,** 1988, Kenner
MNP $8   MIP $25

❑ **Seawing,** 1988, Kenner
MNP $10   MIP $30

❑ **Sinnertwin,** 1988, Kenner
MNP $8   MIP $20

❑ **Siren,** 1988, Kenner
MNP $20   MIP $50

❑ **Sizzle,** 1988, Kenner
MNP $4   MIP $15

❑ **Skalor,** 1988, Kenner
MNP $10   MIP $30

❑ **Skullgrin, clear insert,** 1988, Kenner
MNP $20   MIP $50

❑ **Sky High,** 1988, Kenner
MNP $10   MIP $40

❑ **Slapdash,** 1988, Kenner
MNP $10   MIP $40

❑ **Snarler,** 1988, Kenner
MNP $20   MIP $50

❑ **Sparkstalker,** 1988, Kenner
MNP $4   MIP $10

❑ **Spinister,** 1988, Kenner
MNP $10   MIP $30

❑ **Splashdown,** 1988, Kenner
MNP $20   MIP $50

❏ **Squeezeplay,** 1988, Kenner
MNP $20   MIP $50

❏ **Strafe,** 1988, Kenner
MNP $5   MIP $15

❏ **Submarauder, clear insert,** 1988, Kenner
MNP $20   MIP $50

❏ **Tentakil,** 1988, Kenner
MNP $10   MIP $30

❏ **Waverider, clear insert,** 1988, Kenner
MNP $20   MIP $50

❏ **Windsweeper,** 1988, Kenner
MNP $5   MIP $15

GENERATION 1, SERIES 6, 1989

❏ **Air Strike Patrol,** 1989, Kenner
MNP $3   MIP $10

❏ **Airwave,** 1989, Kenner
MNP $8   MIP $20

❏ **Battle Patrol,** 1989, Kenner
MNP $3   MIP $10

❏ **Birdbrain,** 1989, Kenner
MNP $5   MIP $15

❏ **Bludgeon,** 1989, Kenner
MNP $10   MIP $30

❏ **Bomb-burst,** 1989, Kenner
MNP $10   MIP $30

❏ **Bristleback,** 1989, Kenner
MNP $5   MIP $15

❏ **Cloudburst,** 1989, Kenner
MNP $10   MIP $30

❏ **Crossblades,** 1989, Kenner
MNP $10   MIP $40

❏ **Doubleheader,** 1989, Kenner
MNP $8   MIP $20

❏ **Erector,** 1989, Kenner
MNP $5   MIP $15

❏ **Flattop,** 1989, Kenner
MNP $5   MIP $15

❏ **Greasepit,** 1989, Kenner
MNP $8   MIP $20

❏ **Groundshaker,** 1989, Kenner
MNP $10   MIP $30

❏ **Hot House,** 1989, Kenner
MNP $8   MIP $20

❏ **Ironworks,** 1989, Kenner
MNP $8   MIP $20

❏ **Landmine,** 1989, Kenner
MNP $20   MIP $50

❏ **Longtooth,** 1989, Kenner
MNP $8   MIP $20

❏ **Octopunch,** 1989, Kenner
MNP $8   MIP $20

❏ **Off Road Patrol,** 1989, Kenner
MNP $3   MIP $10

❏ **Overload,** 1989, Kenner
MNP $5   MIP $15

❏ **Pincher,** 1989, Kenner
MNP $8   MIP $20

❏ **Race Car Patrol,** 1989, Kenner
MNP $3   MIP $10

❏ **Rescue Patrol,** 1989, Kenner
MNP $3   MIP $10

❏ **Roadblock,** 1989, Kenner
MNP $20   MIP $50

❏ **Roughstuff,** 1989, Kenner
MNP $5   MIP $15

❏ **Scowl,** 1989, Kenner
MNP $5   MIP $15

❏ **Skullgrin,** 1989, Kenner
MNP $10   MIP $35

❏ **Skyhammer,** 1989, Kenner
MNP $20   MIP $50

❏ **Skyhopper,** 1989, Kenner
MNP $10   MIP $30

❏ **Slog,** 1989, Kenner
MNP $5   MIP $15

❏ **Sports Car Patrol,** 1989, Kenner
MNP $3   MIP $10

❏ **Stranglehold,** 1989, Kenner
MNP $8   MIP $20

❏ **Submarauder,** 1989, Kenner
MNP $10   MIP $30

❏ **Thunderwing,** 1989, Kenner
MNP $10   MIP $40

❏ **Vroom,** 1989, Kenner
MNP $10   MIP $40

❏ **Waverider,** 1989, Kenner
MNP $10   MIP $30

❏ **Wildfly,** 1989, Kenner
MNP $5   MIP $15

GENERATION 1, SERIES 7, 1990

❏ **Air Patrol,** 1990, Kenner
MNP $4   MIP $10

❏ **Astro Squad,** 1990, Kenner
MNP $5   MIP $15

❏ **Axer,** 1990, Kenner
MNP $8   MIP $20

❏ **Banzai-Tron,** 1990, Kenner
MNP $8   MIP $20

❏ **Battle Squad,** 1990, Kenner
MNP $5   MIP $15

❏ **Blaster,** 1990, Kenner
MNP $4   MIP $12

❏ **Bumblebee,** 1990, Kenner
MNP $4   MIP $12

❏ **Cannon Transport,** 1990, Kenner
MNP $8   MIP $20

❏ **Construction Patrol,** 1990, Kenner
MNP $4   MIP $10

❏ **Constructor Squad,** 1990, Kenner
MNP $5   MIP $15

❏ **Devastator,** 1990, Kenner
MNP $4   MIP $12

❏ **Erector,** 1990, Kenner
MNP $5   MIP $12

❏ **Flattop,** 1990, Kenner
MNP $5   MIP $12

❏ **Grimlock,** 1990, Kenner
MNP $4   MIP $12

❏ **Gutcruncher,** 1990, Kenner
MNP $10   MIP $45

❏ **Hot Rod Patrol,** 1990, Kenner
MNP $4   MIP $10

❏ **Inferno,** 1990, Kenner
MNP $8   MIP $20

❏ **Jackpot,** 1990, Kenner
MNP $4   MIP $12

❏ **Jazz,** 1990, Kenner
MNP $4   MIP $12

❏ **Kick-Off,** 1990, Kenner
MNP $8   MIP $20

❏ **Krok,** 1990, Kenner
MNP $4   MIP $12

❏ **Mainframe,** 1990, Kenner
MNP $4   MIP $12

❏ **Megatron,** 1990, Kenner
MNP $20   MIP $60

❏ **Metro Squad,** 1990, Kenner
MNP $5   MIP $15

❏ **Military Patrol,** 1990, Kenner
MNP $4   MIP $10

❏ **Missile Launcher,** 1990, Kenner
MNP $8   MIP $20

❏ **Monster Trucks Patrol,** 1990, Kenner
MNP $4   MIP $10

❏ **Overload,** 1990, Kenner
MNP $5   MIP $12

❏ **Over-Run,** 1990, Kenner
MNP $8   MIP $20

❏ **Prowl,** 1990, Kenner
MNP $8   MIP $20

❏ **Race Track Patrol,** 1990, Kenner
MNP $4   MIP $10

❏ **Rad,** 1990, Kenner
MNP $4   MIP $12

❏ **Rollout,** 1990, Kenner
MNP $4   MIP $12

❏ **Roughstuff,** 1990, Kenner
MNP $5   MIP $12

❏ **Shockwave,** 1990, Kenner
MNP $8   MIP $20

❏ **Skyfall,** 1990, Kenner
MNP $8   MIP $20

❏ **Snarl,** 1990, Kenner
MNP $8   MIP $20

❏ **Soundwave,** 1990, Kenner
MNP $5   MIP $15

❏ **Sprocket,** 1990, Kenner
MNP $10   MIP $35

ACTION FIGURES

❏ **Tanker Truck,** 1990, Kenner
 MNP $8   MIP $20

❏ **Treadshot,** 1990, Kenner
 MNP $4   MIP $12

❏ **Wheeljack,** 1990, Kenner
 MNP $10   MIP $35

GENERATION 2, SERIES 1, 1993

❏ **Afterburner,** 1993, Kenner
 MNP $3   MIP $12

❏ **Bonecrusher, orange,** 1993, Kenner
 MNP $5   MIP $17

❏ **Bonecrusher, yellow,** 1993, Kenner
 MNP $3   MIP $12

❏ **Bumblebee,** 1993, Kenner
 MNP $5   MIP $15

❏ **Deluge, changes colors,** 1993, Kenner
 MNP $5   MIP $15

❏ **Drench, changes colors,** 1993, Kenner
 MNP $5   MIP $15

❏ **Eagle Eye,** 1993, Kenner
 MNP $3   MIP $12

❏ **Gobots, changes colors,** 1993, Kenner
 MNP $5   MIP $15

❏ **Grimlock, dark blue,** 1993, Kenner
 MNP $8   MIP $20

❏ **Grimlock, silver,** 1993, Kenner
 MNP $20   MIP $65

❏ **Grimlock, turquoise,** 1993, Kenner
 MNP $35   MIP $100

❏ **Hook, orange,** 1993, Kenner
 MNP $5   MIP $15

❏ **Hook, yellow,** 1993, Kenner
 MNP $3   MIP $12

❏ **Hubcap,** 1993, Kenner
 MNP $5   MIP $15

❏ **Inferno,** 1993, Kenner
 MNP $8   MIP $25

❏ **Jazz,** 1993, Kenner
 MNP $35   MIP $100

❏ **Jetstorm, changes colors,** 1993, Kenner
 MNP $5   MIP $15

❏ **Long Haul, orange,** 1993, Kenner
 MNP $5   MIP $15

❏ **Long Haul, yellow,** 1993, Kenner
 MNP $3   MIP $12

❏ **Mixmaster, orange,** 1993, Kenner
 MNP $5   MIP $15

❏ **Mixmaster, yellow,** 1993, Kenner
 MNP $3   MIP $12

❏ **Ramjet, missiles grouped,** 1993, Kenner
 MNP $8   MIP $20

❏ **Ramjet, missiles separate,** 1993, Kenner
 MNP $10   MIP $35

❏ **Rapido,** 1993, Kenner
 MNP $3   MIP $12

❏ **Scavenger, orange,** 1993, Kenner
 MNP $5   MIP $15

❏ **Scavenger, yellow,** 1993, Kenner
 MNP $3   MIP $12

❏ **Scrapper, orange,** 1993, Kenner
 MNP $5   MIP $15

❏ **Scrapper, yellow,** 1993, Kenner
 MNP $5   MIP $15

❏ **Seaspray,** 1993, Kenner
 MNP $5   MIP $15

❏ **Sideswipe,** 1993, Kenner
 MNP $8   MIP $25

❏ **Skram,** 1993, Kenner
 MNP $5   MIP $15

❏ **Slag, green,** 1993, Kenner
 MNP $8   MIP $30

❏ **Slag, red,** 1993, Kenner
 MNP $20   MIP $55

❏ **Slag, silver,** 1993, Kenner
 MNP $20   MIP $55

❏ **Snarl, green,** 1993, Kenner
 MNP $20   MIP $55

❏ **Snarl, red,** 1993, Kenner
 MNP $8   MIP $30

❏ **Snarl, silver,** 1993, Kenner
 MNP $20   MIP $55

❏ **Starscream, missiles grouped,** 1993, Kenner
 MNP $8   MIP $20

❏ **Starscream, missiles separate,** 1993, Kenner
 MNP $10   MIP $35

❏ **Terradive,** 1993, Kenner
 MNP $5   MIP $15

❏ **Turbofire,** 1993, Kenner
 MNP $5   MIP $15

❏ **Windbreaker,** 1993, Kenner
 MNP $5   MIP $15

❏ **Windrazor,** 1993, Kenner
 MNP $5   MIP $15

GENERATION 2, SERIES 2, 1994

❏ **Air Raid,** 1994, Kenner
 MNP $5   MIP $15

❏ **Blast Off,** 1994, Kenner
 MNP $5   MIP $15

❏ **Brawl,** 1994, Kenner
 MNP $8   MIP $20

❏ **Electro,** 1994, Kenner
 MNP $5   MIP $15

❏ **Fireflight,** 1994, Kenner
 MNP $5   MIP $15

❏ **Jolt,** 1994, Kenner
 MNP $5   MIP $15

❏ **Leadfoot,** 1994, Kenner
 MNP $3   MIP $12

❏ **Manta Ray,** 1994, Kenner
 MNP $3   MIP $12

❏ **Megatron, purple and black camouflage,** 1994, Kenner
 MNP $5   MIP $15

❏ **Onslaught,** 1994, Kenner
 MNP $10   MIP $40

❏ **Optimus Prime, red and white,** 1994, Kenner
 MNP $10   MIP $30

❏ **Powerdive, black rotors,** 1994, Kenner
 MNP $8   MIP $20

❏ **Powerdive, red rotors,** 1994, Kenner
 MNP $3   MIP $12

❏ **Ransack, black rotors,** 1994, Kenner
 MNP $8   MIP $20

❏ **Ransack, red rotors,** 1994, Kenner
 MNP $3   MIP $12

❏ **Sizzle,** 1994, Kenner
 MNP $5   MIP $15

❏ **Skydive,** 1994, Kenner
 MNP $5   MIP $15

❏ **Slingshot,** 1994, Kenner
 MNP $5   MIP $15

❏ **Swindle,** 1994, Kenner
 MNP $5   MIP $15

❏ **Volt,** 1994, Kenner
 MNP $5   MIP $15

❏ **Vortex,** 1994, Kenner
 MNP $5   MIP $15

GENERATION 2, SERIES 3, 1995

❏ **Air Raid,** 1995, Kenner
 MNP $2   MIP $6

❏ **Blowout,** 1995, Kenner
 MNP $3   MIP $10

❏ **Bumblebee,** 1995, Kenner
 MNP $3   MIP $10

❏ **Dirtbag,** 1995, Kenner
 MNP $3   MIP $12

❏ **Double Clutch,** 1995, Kenner
 MNP $3   MIP $10

❏ **Firecracker,** 1995, Kenner
 MNP $3   MIP $10

❏ **Frenzy,** 1995, Kenner
 MNP $3   MIP $10

❏ **Gearhead, clear,** 1995, Kenner
 MNP $3   MIP $10

❏ **Gearhead, solid,** 1995, Kenner
 MNP $3   MIP $10

❏ **High Beam,** 1995, Kenner
 MNP $3   MIP $10

❏ **Hooligan,** 1995, Kenner
 MNP $2   MIP $6

❏ **Ironhide,** 1995, Kenner
 MNP $3   MIP $10

❏ **Jetfire,** 1995, Kenner
 MNP $2   MIP $6

❏ **Megatron,** 1995, Kenner
MNP $3   MIP $10

❏ **Mirage,** 1995, Kenner
MNP $3   MIP $10

❏ **Motormouth, clear,** 1995, Kenner
MNP $3   MIP $10

❏ **Motormouth, solid,** 1995, Kenner
MNP $3   MIP $10

❏ **Optimus Prime,** 1995, Kenner
MNP $3   MIP $10

❏ **Roadblock,** 1995, Kenner
MNP $3   MIP $12

❏ **Sideswipe,** 1995, Kenner
MNP $3   MIP $10

❏ **Skyjack,** 1995, Kenner
MNP $2   MIP $6

❏ **Soundwave,** 1995, Kenner
MNP $3   MIP $10

❏ **Space Case,** 1995, Kenner
MNP $2   MIP $6

❏ **Strafe,** 1995, Kenner
MNP $2   MIP $6

TRANSFORMERS: BEAST WARS (KENNER, 1996-1999)

BASIC BEAST, 1996

❏ **Airazor,** 1996, Kenner
MNP $10   MIP $30

❏ **Armordillo,** 1996, Kenner
MNP $5   MIP $15

❏ **Claw Jaw,** 1996, Kenner
MNP $8   MIP $25

❏ **Drill Bit,** 1996, Kenner
MNP $8   MIP $25

❏ **Iguanus,** 1996, Kenner
MNP $10   MIP $30

❏ **Insecticon,** 1996, Kenner
MNP $5   MIP $15

❏ **Lazorbeak,** 1996, Kenner
MNP $8   MIP $25

❏ **Rattrap,** 1996, Kenner
MNP $15   MIP $50

❏ **Razorbeast,** 1996, Kenner
MNP $15   MIP $45

❏ **Razorclaw,** 1996, Kenner
MNP $10   MIP $30

❏ **Snapper,** 1996, Kenner
MNP $8   MIP $20

❏ **Snarl,** 1996, Kenner
MNP $8   MIP $25

❏ **Terrorsaur,** 1996, Kenner
MNP $15   MIP $50

BASIC BEAST, 1997

❏ **Powerpinch,** 1997, Kenner
MNP $8   MIP $25

❏ **Spittor,** 1997, Kenner
MNP $8   MIP $25

BASIC FUZORS, 1998

❏ **Air Hammer,** 1998, Kenner
MNP $5   MIP $15

❏ **Bantor,** 1998, Kenner
MNP $3   MIP $8

❏ **Buzzclaw,** 1998, Kenner
MNP $3   MIP $8

❏ **Noctorro,** 1998, Kenner
MNP $3   MIP $8

❏ **Quickstrike,** 1998, Kenner
MNP $5   MIP $15

❏ **Terragator,** 1998, Kenner
MNP $4   MIP $12

BASIC TRANSMETAL 2, 1999

❏ **Optimus Minor,** 1999, Kenner
MNP $8   MIP $25

❏ **Scarem,** 1999, Kenner
MNP $3   MIP $8

❏ **Sonar,** 1999, Kenner
MNP $3   MIP $8

❏ **Spittor,** 1999, Kenner
MNP $3   MIP $10

COMIC 2-PACK, 1996

❏ **Megatron,** 1996, Kenner
MNP $15   MIP $50

❏ **Optimus Primal,** 1996, Kenner
MNP $15   MIP $50

DELUXE BEAST, 1996

❏ **Blackarachnia,** 1996, Kenner
MNP $40   MIP $115

❏ **Bonecrusher,** 1996, Kenner
MNP $15   MIP $50

❏ **Buzz Saw,** 1996, Kenner
MNP $25   MIP $75

❏ **Cheetor, blue eyes,** 1996, Kenner
MNP $50   MIP $150

❏ **Cheetor, red eyes,** 1996, Kenner
MNP $40   MIP $120

❏ **Cybershark,** 1996, Kenner
MNP $30   MIP $90

❏ **Dinobot,** 1996, Kenner
MNP $40   MIP $110

❏ **Jetstorm,** 1996, Kenner
MNP $15   MIP $45

❏ **Rhinox,** 1996, Kenner
MNP $40   MIP $110

❏ **Tarantulas,** 1996, Kenner
MNP $40   MIP $125

❏ **Tigatron,** 1996, Kenner
MNP $30   MIP $100

❏ **Waspinator,** 1996, Kenner
MNP $40   MIP $125

❏ **Wolfang,** 1996, Kenner
MNP $40   MIP $110

DELUXE BEAST, 1997

❏ **Grimlock,** 1997, Kenner
MNP $25   MIP $75

❏ **K-9,** 1997, Kenner
MNP $8   MIP $25

❏ **Manterror,** 1997, Kenner
MNP $15   MIP $50

❏ **Retrax,** 1997, Kenner
MNP $8   MIP $25

DELUXE FUZORS, 1998

❏ **Injector,** 1998, Kenner
MNP $4   MIP $12

❏ **Silverbolt,** 1998, Kenner
MNP $8   MIP $25

❏ **Sky Shadow,** 1998, Kenner
MNP $4   MIP $12

❏ **Torca,** 1998, Kenner
MNP $3   MIP $10

DELUXE TRANSMETAL 2, 1999

❏ **Iguanus,** 1999, Kenner
MNP $3   MIP $10

❏ **Jawbreaker,** 1999, Kenner
MNP $3   MIP $10

❏ **Ramulus,** 1999, Kenner
MNP $5   MIP $15

❏ **Scourge,** 1999, Kenner
MNP $4   MIP $12

DELUXE TRANSMETALS, 1998

❏ **Airazor,** 1998, Kenner
MNP $8   MIP $20

❏ **Cheetor,** 1998, Kenner
MNP $8   MIP $25

❏ **Rattrap,** 1998, Kenner
MNP $10   MIP $30

❏ **Rhinox,** 1998, Kenner
MNP $15   MIP $35

❏ **Tarantulas,** 1998, Kenner
MNP $8   MIP $20

❏ **Terrorsaur,** 1998, Kenner
MNP $5   MIP $15

❏ **Waspinator,** 1998, Kenner
MNP $8   MIP $25

MEGA BEAST, 1996

❏ **B'Boom,** 1996, Kenner
MNP $8   MIP $25

❏ **Polar Claw,** 1996, Kenner
MNP $20   MIP $65

❏ **Scorponok,** 1996, Kenner
MNP $15   MIP $45

MEGA BEAST, 1997

❏ **Inferno,** 1997, Kenner
MNP $15   MIP $45

❏ **Transquito,** 1997, Kenner
MNP $8   MIP $20

MEGA TRANSMETAL 2, 1999

❑ **Blackarachnia**, 1999, Kenner
MNP $15   MIP $45

❑ **Cybershark**, 1999, Kenner
MNP $5   MIP $15

MEGA TRANSMETALS, 1998

❑ **Megatron**, 1998, Kenner
MNP $8   MIP $20

❑ **Optimus Primal**, 1998, Kenner
MNP $8   MIP $25

❑ **Scavenger**, 1998, Kenner
MNP $5   MIP $15

SUPER BEAST, 1998

❑ **Optimal Optimus**, 1998, Kenner
MNP $8   MIP $20

ULTRA BEAST, 1996

❑ **Megatron**, 1996, Kenner
MNP $15   MIP $50

❑ **Optimus Primal**, 1996, Kenner
MNP $20   MIP $60

ULTRA TEAM, 1997

❑ **Magnaboss (Maximal Team)—Iron-hide, Silverbolt, Prowl**, 1997, Kenner
MNP $8   MIP $25

❑ **Tripredacus (Predacon Team)-Ram Horn, Sea Clamp, Cicadacon**, 1997, Kenner
MNP $8   MIP $25

ULTRA TRANSMETAL 2, 1999

❑ **Megatron**, 1999, Kenner
MNP $8   MIP $25

❑ **Tigerhawk**, 1999, Kenner
MNP $5   MIP $15

ULTRA TRANSMETALS, 1998

❑ **Depth Charge**, 1998, Kenner
MNP $8   MIP $20

❑ **Rampage**, 1998, Kenner
MNP $8   MIP $25

VIDEO PACK-IN, 1998

❑ **Airazor**, 1998, Kenner
MNP $8   MIP $25

❑ **Razorclaw**, 1998, Kenner
MNP $8   MIP $25

TUFF TALKIN' WRESTLERS (TOY BIZ, 1999)

FIGURES

❑ **Goldberg/Kevin Nash**, 1999, Toy Biz
MNP $20   MIP $40

❑ **Sting/Diamond Dallas Page**, 1999, Toy Biz
MNP $20   MIP $40

UNIVERSAL MONSTERS (REMCO, 1979)

8" FIGURES

❑ **Creature From the Black Lagoon**, 1979
MNP $75   MIP $200

❑ **Dracula**, 1979
MNP $40   MIP $100

❑ **Frankenstein**, 1979
MNP $20   MIP $40

❑ **Mummy, The**, 1979
MNP $20   MIP $40

❑ **Phantom of the Opera**, 1979
MNP $100   MIP $250

❑ **Wolfman, The**, 1979
MNP $55   MIP $130

UNIVERSAL MONSTERS (SIDESHOW TOYS, 1998-PRESENT)

12" FIGURES

❑ **Wolfman, The**, 2000
MNP $8   MIP $20

SERIES I, 8" FIGURES

❑ **Frankenstein**, 1998-Present
MNP $6   MIP $15

❑ **Mummy, The**, 1998-Present
MNP $8   MIP $20

(KP Photo)

❑ **Wolfman, The**, 1998-Present, With log base and trap. Packaged in movie-poster style box
MNP $8   MIP $20

SERIES II, 8" FIGURES

(KP Photo)

❑ **Bride of Frankenstein**, 1998-Present, Sideshow Toys, Detailed figure with stand
MNP $8   MIP $20

(KP Photo)

❑ **Creature From the Black Lagoon**, 1998-Present, Sideshow Toys, Realistic-looking gilled Creature with stand (showing abandoned harpoon gun)
MNP $8   MIP $20

(KP Photo)

❏ **Phantom of the Opera,** 1998-Present, Sideshow Toys, Highly-detailed figure with stand

    MNP $8   **MIP** $20

SERIES III, 8" FIGURES

(KP Photo)

❏ **Hunchback of Notredame,** 1998-present, Sideshow Toys, Detailed figure with purple cloak, scepter and green crown

    MNP $7   **MIP** $15

❏ **Invisible Man,** 1998-present
    MNP $7   **MIP** $15

(KP Photo)

❏ **Metaluna Mutant,** 1998-present, Sideshow Toys, Blue-gray detailed alien from "This Island Earth." A neat figure

    MNP $7   **MIP** $15

SERIES IV, 8" FIGURES

(KP Photo)

❏ **Mole People, The,** 2000, Fun-looking figure--even includes mushroom accessories!

    MNP $5   **MIP** $15

(KP Photo)

❏ **Son of Frankenstein,** 2000, Figure with fabric outer garment and replaceable arm

    MNP $5   **MIP** $15

(KP Photo)

❏ **Werewolf of London,** 2000, With cap, scarf and flower

    MNP $5   **MIP** $15

UNIVERSAL MONSTERS (SIDESHOW TOY, 2001)

FIGURES

(KP Photo)

ACTION FIGURES

❑ **Creature from the Black Lagoon,** special edition, 2001, Sideshow Toy, Fully poseable translucent figure
MNP $10   MIP $15

UNIVERSAL MONSTERS: HASBRO SIGNATURE SERIES (HASBRO, 1998)

FIGURES

❑ **Bride of Frankenstein, The,** 1998, Hasbro
MNP $10   MIP $25

❑ **Frankenstein,** 1998, Hasbro
MNP $10   MIP $25

❑ **Mummy, The,** 1998, Hasbro
MNP $10   MIP $25

❑ **Wolf Man, The,** 1998, Hasbro
MNP $10   MIP $25

UNIVERSAL MONSTERS: SILVER SCREEN EDITION (SIDESHOW TOYS, 1998-PRESENT)

SERIES I

❑ **Frankenstein,** 2000
MNP $5   MIP $15

❑ **Mummy, The,** 2000
MNP $5   MIP $15

❑ **Wolfman, The,** 2000
MNP $5   MIP $15

VAULT, THE (TOY BIZ, 1998)

6" FIGURES

❑ **Stegron,** 1998
MNP $3   MIP $6

❑ **Typhoid Mary,** 1998
MNP $3   MIP $6

❑ **Ultron,** 1998
MNP $3   MIP $6

VIKINGS (MARX, 1960s)

FIGURES

(Toy Shop File Photo)

❑ **Brave Erik the Viking,** 1960s, Marx, like many Marx figures, this too had a molded-uniform with other plastic accessories and clothing included in the package
MNP $150   MIP $300

❑ **Mighty Viking Horse,** 1960s, Marx
MNP $150   MIP $300

❑ **Odin the Viking Chieftan,** 1960s, Marx
MNP $150   MIP $300

VOLTRON (MATCHBOX, 1985-86)

3-3/4" FIGURES

❑ **Doom Commander,** 1985-86
MNP $5   MIP $15

❑ **Haggar the Witch,** 1985-86
MNP $5   MIP $15

❑ **Hunk,** 1985-86
MNP $8   MIP $20

❑ **Keith,** 1985-86
MNP $8   MIP $20

❑ **King Zarkon,** 1985-86
MNP $5   MIP $15

❑ **Lance,** 1985-86
MNP $5   MIP $15

❑ **Pidge,** 1985-86
MNP $5   MIP $15

❑ **Prince Lotor,** 1985-86
MNP $8   MIP $20

❑ **Princess Allura,** 1985-86
MNP $8   MIP $20

❑ **Robeast Mutilor,** 1985-86
MNP $4   MIP $10

❑ **Robeast Scorpious,** 1985-86
MNP $4   MIP $12

❑ **Voltron Robot,** 1985-86
MNP $10   MIP $30

ACCESSORIES

❑ **Coffin of Darkness,** 1985-86
MNP $8   MIP $20

❑ **Coffin of Doom,** 1985-86
MNP $8   MIP $20

❑ **Doom Blaster,** 1985-86
MNP $12   MIP $25

❑ **Skull Tank,** 1985-86
MNP $12   MIP $25

❑ **Zorkon Zapper,** 1985-86
MNP $12   MIP $25

GIFT SETS

❑ **Deluxe Gift Set I,** 1985-86
MNP $65   MIP $225

❑ **Deluxe Gift Set II,** 1985-86
MNP $55   MIP $200

❑ **Deluxe Gift Set III,** 1985-86
MNP $55   MIP $200

WALTONS (MEGO, 1975)

8" FIGURES

❑ **Grandma and Grandpa,** 1975, Mego
MNP $25   MIP $50

❑ **John Boy and Ellen,** 1975, Mego
MNP $25   MIP $50

❑ **Mom and Pop,** 1975, Mego
MNP $25   MIP $50

ACCESSORIES

❑ **Barn,** 1975, Mego
MNP $50   MIP $100

❑ **Country Store,** 1975, Mego
MNP $50   MIP $100

❑ **Truck,** 1975, Mego
MNP $40   MIP $80

PLAY SETS

❑ **Farm House,** 1975, Mego
MNP $75   MIP $150

❑ **Farm House with Six Figures,** 1975, Mego
MNP $150   MIP $300

WARRIOR BEASTS, THE (REMCO, 1983)

FIGURES

❑ **Craven,** 1983
MNP $15   MIP $50

❑ **Gecko,** 1983
MNP $15   MIP $60

❑ **Guana,** 1983
MNP $15   MIP $50

❑ **Hydraz,** 1983
MNP $15   MIP $60

❑ **Ramar,** 1983
MNP $15   MIP $50

❑ **Skullman,** 1983
MNP $25   MIP $90

❑ **Snake Man,** 1983
MNP $25   MIP $90

❑ **Stegos,** 1983
MNP $15   MIP $50

❑ **Wolf Warrior,** 1983
MNP $30   MIP $90

❑ **Zardus,** 1983
MNP $15   MIP $50

WCW BASH AT THE BEACH (TOY BIZ, 2000)

6" FIGURES

❑ **Diamond Dallas Page,** 2000, Toy Biz
MNP $3   MIP $8

❑ **Goldberg,** 2000, Toy Biz
MNP $3   MIP $8

❏ **Hulk Hogan**, 2000, Toy Biz
MNP $3   MIP $8

❏ **Lex Luger**, 2000, Toy Biz
MNP $3   MIP $8

❏ **Sting**, 2000, Toy Biz
MNP $3   MIP $8

WCW COLLECTOR SERIES (TOY BIZ, 2000)

12" FIGURES

❏ **Goldberg**, 2000, Toy Biz
MNP $5   MIP $15

❏ **Hulk Hogan**, 2000, Toy Biz
MNP $5   MIP $15

❏ **Sting**, 2000, Toy Biz
MNP $5   MIP $15

WCW CYBORG WRESTLERS (TOY BIZ, 2000)

6" FIGURES

❏ **Bret Hart**, 2000, Toy Biz
MNP $3   MIP $8

❏ **Goldberg**, 2000, Toy Biz
MNP $3   MIP $8

❏ **Kevin Nash**, 2000, Toy Biz
MNP $3   MIP $8

❏ **Sid Vicious**, 2000, Toy Biz
MNP $3   MIP $8

❏ **Sting**, 2000, Toy Biz
MNP $3   MIP $8

WCW NITRO ACTIVE WRESTLERS (TOY BIZ, 2000)

6" FIGURES

❏ **Buff Bagwell**, 2000, Toy Biz
MNP $3   MIP $8

❏ **Goldberg**, 2000, Toy Biz
MNP $3   MIP $8

❏ **Jeff Jarrett**, 2000, Toy Biz
MNP $3   MIP $8

❏ **Sid Vicious**, 2000, Toy Biz
MNP $3   MIP $8

❏ **Vampiro**, 2000, Toy Biz
MNP $3   MIP $8

WCW POWER SLAM WRESTLERS I (TOY BIZ, 2000)

6" FIGURES

❏ **Goldberg**, 2000, Toy Biz
MNP $3   MIP $8

❏ **Hak**, 2000, Toy Biz
MNP $3   MIP $8

❏ **Hulk Hogan**, 2000, Toy Biz
MNP $3   MIP $8

❏ **Rodman**, 2000, Toy Biz
MNP $3   MIP $8

❏ **Sid Vicious**, 2000, Toy Biz
MNP $3   MIP $8

WCW POWER SLAM WRESTLERS II (TOY BIZ, 2000)

6" FIGURES

❏ **Buff Bagwell**, 2000, Toy Biz
MNP $3   MIP $8

❏ **Kanyon**, 2000, Toy Biz
MNP $3   MIP $8

❏ **Kevin Nash**, 2000, Toy Biz
MNP $3   MIP $8

❏ **Roddy Piper**, 2000, Toy Biz
MNP $3   MIP $8

❏ **Sting**, 2000, Toy Biz
MNP $3   MIP $8

WCW S.L.A.M. FORCE (TOY BIZ, 2000)

6" FIGURES

❏ **Benoit with comic book**, 2000, Toy Biz
MNP $3   MIP $8

❏ **Bret Hart with comic book**, 2000, Toy Biz
MNP $3   MIP $8

❏ **Goldberg with comic book**, 2000, Toy Biz
MNP $3   MIP $8

❏ **Kevin Nash with comic book**, 2000, Toy Biz
MNP $3   MIP $8

❏ **Sting with comic book**, 2000, Toy Biz
MNP $3   MIP $8

WCW THUNDER SLAM TWIN PACKS (TOY BIZ, 2000)

6" FIGURES

❏ **Bam Bam Bigelow and Goldberg**, 2000, Toy Biz
MNP $3   MIP $10

❏ **Kevin Nash and Scott Hall**, 2000, Toy Biz
MNP $3   MIP $10

❏ **Sting and Bret Hart**, 2000, Toy Biz
MNP $3   MIP $10

WCW WORLD CHAMPIONSHIP WRESTLING RING FIGHTERS (TOY BIZ, 1999)

6" FIGURES

❏ **Booker T**, 1999
MNP $3   MIP $10

❏ **Bret Hart**, 1999
MNP $3   MIP $10

❏ **Chris Benoit**, 1999
MNP $3   MIP $10

❏ **Scott Steiner**, 1999
MNP $3   MIP $10

WCW WORLD CHAMPIONSHIP WRESTLING SMASH 'N SLAM (TOY BIZ, 1999)

6" FIGURES

❏ **Hollywood Hogan**, 1999
MNP $5   MIP $15

❏ **Kevin Nash**, 1999
MNP $5   MIP $15

❏ **Macho Man Randy Savage**, 1999
MNP $4   MIP $12

❏ **Scott Hall**, 1999
MNP $5   MIP $15

WCW WORLD CHAMPIONSHIP WRESTLING SMASH 'N SLAM II (TOY BIZ, 1999)

6" FIGURES

❏ **D.D.P.**, 1999
MNP $3   MIP $10

❏ **Giant & Rey Mysterio Jr.**, 1999
MNP $3   MIP $10

❏ **Goldberg & Masked Wrestler**, 1999
MNP $3   MIP $10

❏ **Lex Luger**, 1999
MNP $3   MIP $10

❏ **Sting**, 1999
MNP $3   MIP $10

WCW/NWO RING MASTERS (TOY BIZ, 1998)

6" FIGURES

❏ **Bret Hart**, 1999
MNP $3   MIP $10

❏ **Chris Jericho**, 1999
MNP $3   MIP $10

❏ **Goldberg**, 1999
MNP $3   MIP $10

❏ **Lex Luger**, 1999
MNP $3   MIP $10

WCW/NWO SLAM 'N CRUNCH (TOY BIZ, 1998)

6" FIGURES

❏ **Buff Bagwell**, 1999
MNP $3   MIP $10

❏ **Goldberg**, 1999
MNP $3   MIP $10

❏ **Konnan**, 1999
MNP $3   MIP $10

❏ **Sting**, 1999
MNP $3   MIP $10

ACTION FIGURES

WCW/NWO TWO PACKS (TOY BIZ, 1999)

BATTLE OF THE GIANTS, 6" FIGURES

❑ **Giant vs. Kevin Nash**, 1999
　　　　MNP $3　　　MIP $10

CLASH OF THE CHAMPIONS, 6" FIGURES

❑ **Sting vs. Hollywood Hogan**, 1999
　　　　MNP $5　　　MIP $15

GRIP 'N FLIP WRESTLERS II, 6" FIGURES

❑ **Kevin Nash vs. Bret Hart**, 1999
　　　　MNP $3　　　MIP $10

❑ **Scott Steiner vs. Rick Steiner**, 1999
　　　　MNP $3　　　MIP $10

❑ **Sting vs. Lex Luger**, 1999
　　　　MNP $3　　　MIP $10

GRIP 'N FLIP WRESTLERS, 6" FIGURES

❑ **Chris Jericho vs. Dean Malenko**, 1999, Toy Biz
　　　　MNP $3　　　MIP $10

❑ **Goldberg vs. Hollywood Hogan**, 1999, Toy Biz
　　　　MNP $5　　　MIP $15

❑ **Raven vs. Diamond Dallas Page**, 1999
　　　　MNP $3　　　MIP $10

POWER AND BEAUTY, 6" FIGURES

❑ **Macho Man & Elizabeth**, 1999
　　　　MNP $3　　　MIP $10

WELCOME BACK, KOTTER (MATTEL, 1976)

FIGURES

❑ **Barbarino**, 1976
　　　　MNP $40　　　MIP $80

❑ **Epstein**, 1976
　　　　MNP $20　　　MIP $50

❑ **Horshback**, 1976
　　　　MNP $20　　　MIP $50

❑ **Mr. Kotter**, 1976
　　　　MNP $20　　　MIP $50

❑ **Washington**, 1976
　　　　MNP $20　　　MIP $50

PLAY SETS

❑ **Welcome Back Kotter Play Set, Deluxe**, 1976
　　　　MNP $50　　　MIP $150

❑ **Welcome Back, Kotter Play Set**, 1976
　　　　MNP $40　　　MIP $100

WETWORKS (MCFARLANE, 1995-96)

SERIES 1

❑ **Dane**, 1995
　　　　MNP $3　　　MIP $10

❑ **Dozer**, 1995
　　　　MNP $3　　　MIP $10

❑ **Grail**, 1995
　　　　MNP $3　　　MIP $10

❑ **Mother-One**, 1995
　　　　MNP $5　　　MIP $15

❑ **Vampire, dark green**, 1995
　　　　MNP $5　　　MIP $15

❑ **Vampire, gray**, 1995
　　　　MNP $5　　　MIP $15

❑ **Werewolf, light blue**, 1995
　　　　MNP $5　　　MIP $15

❑ **Werewolf, reddish brown**, 1995
　　　　MNP $8　　　MIP $20

SERIES 2

❑ **Assasin One, blue**, 1996
　　　　MNP $3　　　MIP $10

❑ **Assasin One, red**, 1996
　　　　MNP $3　　　MIP $10

❑ **Blood Queen, all black**, 1996
　　　　MNP $8　　　MIP $20

❑ **Blood Queen, all black with red trim**, 1996
　　　　MNP $8　　　MIP $20

❑ **Delta Commander, flesh tones**, 1996
　　　　MNP $3　　　MIP $10

❑ **Delta Commander, gold**, 1996
　　　　MNP $3　　　MIP $10

❑ **Frankenstein, brown**, 1996
　　　　MNP $3　　　MIP $10

❑ **Frankenstein, green**, 1996
　　　　MNP $3　　　MIP $10

❑ **Mendoza, flesh colored**, 1996
　　　　MNP $3　　　MIP $10

❑ **Mendoza, half gold**, 1996
　　　　MNP $3　　　MIP $10

❑ **Pilgrim, flesh tones**, 1996
　　　　MNP $5　　　MIP $15

❑ **Pilgrim, gold**, 1996
　　　　MNP $8　　　MIP $20

WHERE THE WILD THINGS ARE (MCFARLANE, 2000)

FIGURES

❑ **Aaron**, 2000
　　　　MNP $4　　　MIP $15

❑ **Bernard**, 2000
　　　　MNP $4　　　MIP $15

❑ **Emil**, 2000
　　　　MNP $4　　　MIP $15

❑ **Max and Goatboy**, 2000
　　　　MNP $4　　　MIP $15

❑ **Moishe**, 2000
　　　　MNP $4　　　MIP $15

❑ **Tzippy**, 2000
　　　　MNP $4　　　MIP $15

WITCHBLADE (MOORE ACTION COLLECTIBLES, 1998-PRESENT)

SERIES I, FIGURES

❑ **Ian Nottingham**, 1998-present
　　　　MNP $3　　　MIP $12

❑ **Kenneth Irons**, 1998-present
　　　　MNP $3　　　MIP $12

❑ **Medieval Witchblade**, 1998-present
　　　　MNP $3　　　MIP $12

❑ **Sara Pezzini/Witchblade**, 1998-present
　　　　MNP $3　　　MIP $12

SERIES II, FIGURES

(Moore Action Collectibles)

❑ **Aspen Mathews/Fathom**, 1998-present, A ripped dude with a mutant right hand.
　　　　MNP $3　　　MIP $12

(Moore Action Collectibles)

❏ **Sara Pezzini,** 1998-present, In red dress, with matching boots.
MNP $3   MIP $12

WIZARD OF OZ   (MEGO, 1974)

4" BOXED FIGURES

❏ **Munchkin Dancer,** 1974, Mego
MNP $75   MIP $150

❏ **Munchkin Flower Girl,** 1974, Mego
MNP $75   MIP $150

❏ **Munchkin General,** 1974, Mego
MNP $75   MIP $150

❏ **Munchkin Lollipop Kid,** 1974, Mego
MNP $75   MIP $150

❏ **Munchkin Mayor,** 1974, Mego
MNP $75   MIP $150

8" BOXED FIGURES

❏ **Cowardly Lion,** 1974, Mego
MNP $25   MIP $50

❏ **Dorothy with Toto,** 1974, Mego
MNP $25   MIP $50

❏ **Glinda the Good Witch,** 1974, Mego
MNP $25   MIP $50

❏ **Scarecrow,** 1974, Mego
MNP $25   MIP $50

❏ **Tin Woodsman,** 1974, Mego
MNP $25   MIP $50

❏ **Wicked Witch,** 1974, Mego
MNP $50   MIP $100

❏ **Wizard of Oz,** 1974, Mego
MNP $35   MIP $250

PLAY SETS

❏ **Emerald City with eight 8" figures,** 1974, Mego
MNP $125   MIP $350

❏ **Emerald City with Wizard of Oz,** 1974, Mego
MNP $45   MIP $100

❏ **Munchkin Land,** 1974, Mego
MNP $150   MIP $300

❏ **Witch's Castle, Sears Exclusive,** 1974, Mego
MNP $250   MIP $450

WIZARD OF OZ   (MULTI-TOYS, 1989)

50TH ANNIVERSARY, 12" FIGURES

❏ **Cowardly Lion,** 1989, Multi-Toys
MNP $5   MIP $15

❏ **Dorothy and Toto,** 1989, Multi-Toys
MNP $5   MIP $15

❏ **Glinda,** 1989, Multi-Toys
MNP $5   MIP $15

(Toy Shop File Photo)

❏ **Scarecrow,** 1989, Multi-Toys
MNP $5   MIP $15

❏ **Tin Man,** 1989, Multi-Toys
MNP $5   MIP $15

(Toy Shop file Photo)

❏ **Wicked Witch,** 1989, Multi-Toys
MNP $5   MIP $15

❏ **Wizard,** 1989, Multi-Toys
MNP $5   MIP $15

WONDER WOMAN SERIES (MEGO, 1977-80)

FIGURES

(Toy Shop File Photo)

❏ **Major Steve Trevor, 1978,** 1977-80, Mego, Left, in white suit
MNP $26   MIP $65

❏ **Queen Hippolyte, 1978,** 1977-80, Mego
MNP $40   MIP $100

(Toy Shop File Photo)

❏ **Queen Nubia, 1978,** 1977-80, Mego
MNP $40   MIP $100

❏ **Wonder Woman with Diana Prince Outfit, 1978,** 1977-80, Mego
MNP $100   MIP $200

❏ **Wonder Woman with Fly Away Action,** 1977-80, Mego
MNP $125   MIP $250

WORLD'S GREATEST SUPER KNIGHTS   (MEGO, 1975)

8" FIGURES

❏ **Black Knight,** 1975
MNP $90   MIP $355

(Toy Shop File Photo)

❏ **Ivanhoe,** 1975, In full body armor
MNP $65   MIP $275

❏ **King Arthur,** 1975
MNP $60   MIP $200

❏ **Sir Galahad,** 1975
MNP $80   MIP $300

❏ **Sir Lancelot,** 1975
MNP $80   MIP $300

WORLD'S GREATEST SUPER PIRATES   (MEGO, 1974)

FIGURES

❏ **Blackbeard,** 1974
MNP $200   MIP $500

❏ **Captain Patch,** 1974
MNP $175   MIP $300

❏ **Jean Lafitte,** 1974
MNP $250   MIP $550

❏ **Long John Silver,** 1974
MNP $250   MIP $550

ACTION FIGURES

WORLD'S GREATEST SUPER-HEROES (MEGO, 1972-78)

12-1/2" FIGURES

❏ **Amazing Spider-Man, 1978**, 1972-78, Mego
MNP $40   MIP $100

❏ **Batman, 1978**, 1972-78, Mego
MNP $60   MIP $125

❏ **Batman, magnetic, 1978**, 1972-78
MNP $75   MIP $100

❏ **Captain America, 1978**, 1972-78, Mego
MNP $75   MIP $150

❏ **Hulk, 1978**, 1972-78, Mego
MNP $30   MIP $60

❏ **Robin, magnetic, 1978**, 1972-78
MNP $125   MIP $275

❏ **Spider-Man, web shooting**, 1972-78
MNP $75   MIP $150

❏ **Superman**, 1972-78, Mego
MNP $50   MIP $125

8" FIGURES

❏ **Aquaman, 1972, boxed**, 1972-78, Mego
MNP $50   MIP $150

❏ **Aquaman, 1972, carded**, 1972-78, Mego
MNP $50   MIP $150

❏ **Batgirl, 1973, boxed**, 1972-78, Mego
MNP $125   MIP $300

❏ **Batgirl, 1973, carded**, 1972-78, Mego
MNP $125   MIP $250

❏ **Batman, fist fighting, 1975, boxed**, 1972-78, Mego
MNP $150   MIP $350

❏ **Batman, painted mask, 1972, boxed**, 1972-78, Mego
MNP $60   MIP $150

❏ **Batman, painted mask, 1972, carded**, 1972-78, Mego
MNP $60   MIP $100

❏ **Batman, removable mask, 1972, boxed**, 1972-78, Mego
MNP $200   MIP $350

❏ **Batman, removable mask, 1972, Kresge card only**, 1972-78, Mego
MNP $200   MIP $450

❏ **Bruce Wayne, 1974, boxed, Montgomery Ward Exclusive**, 1972-78, Mego
MNP $1200   MIP $2000

❏ **Captain America, 1972, boxed**, 1972-78, Mego
MNP $60   MIP $200

❏ **Captain America, 1972, carded**, 1972-78, Mego
MNP $60   MIP $150

❏ **Catwoman, 1973, boxed**, 1972-78, Mego
MNP $150   MIP $350

❏ **Catwoman, 1973, carded**, 1972-78, Mego
MNP $150   MIP $450

❏ **Clark Kent, 1974, boxed, Montgomery Ward Exclusive**, 1972-78, Mego
MNP $1200   MIP $2000

❏ **Conan, 1975, boxed**, 1972-78, Mego
MNP $150   MIP $400

❏ **Conan, 1975, carded**, 1972-78, Mego
MNP $150   MIP $500

❏ **Dick Grayson, 1974, boxed, Montgomery Ward Exclusive**, 1972-78, Mego
MNP $1200   MIP $2000

❏ **Falcon, 1974, boxed**, 1972-78, Mego
MNP $60   MIP $150

❏ **Falcon, 1974, carded**, 1972-78, Mego
MNP $60   MIP $450

❏ **Green Arrow, 1973, boxed**, 1972-78, Mego, With hat, belt and bow and arrow accessories
MNP $150   MIP $450

❏ **Green Arrow, 1973, carded**, 1972-78, Mego
MNP $150   MIP $550

❏ **Green Goblin, 1974, boxed**, 1972-78, Mego
MNP $90   MIP $275

❏ **Green Goblin, 1974, carded**, 1972-78, Mego
MNP $90   MIP $650

❏ **Human Torch, Fantastic Four, 1975, boxed**, 1972-78, Mego
MNP $25   MIP $90

❏ **Human Torch, Fantastic Four, 1975, card**, 1972-78, Mego
MNP $25   MIP $50

❏ **Incredible Hulk, 1974, boxed**, 1972-78, Mego
MNP $20   MIP $100

❏ **Incredible Hulk, 1974, carded**, 1972-78, Mego
MNP $20   MIP $50

❏ **Invisible Girl, Fantastic Four, 1975, boxed**, 1972-78, Mego
MNP $30   MIP $150

❏ **Invisible Girl, Fantastic Four, 1975, card**, 1972-78, Mego
MNP $30   MIP $60

❏ **Iron Man, 1974, boxed**, 1972-78, Mego
MNP $75   MIP $125

❏ **Iron Man, 1974, carded**, 1972-78, Mego
MNP $75   MIP $450

❏ **Isis, 1976, boxed**, 1972-78, Mego
MNP $75   MIP $250

❏ **Isis, 1976, carded**, 1972-78, Mego
MNP $75   MIP $125

❏ **Joker, 1973, boxed**, 1972-78, Mego
MNP $60   MIP $150

❏ **Joker, 1973, carded**, 1972-78, Mego
MNP $60   MIP $150

❏ **Joker, fist fighting, 1975, boxed**, 1972-78, Mego
MNP $150   MIP $400

❏ **Lizard, 1974, boxed**, 1972-78, Mego
MNP $75   MIP $200

❏ **Lizard, 1974, carded**, 1972-78, Mego
MNP $75   MIP $450

❏ **Mr. Fantastic, Fantastic Four, 1975, boxed**, 1972-78, Mego
MNP $30   MIP $140

❏ **Mr. Fantastic, Fantastic Four, 1975, carded**, 1972-78, Mego
MNP $30   MIP $60

❏ **Mr. Mxyzptlk, open mouth, 1973, boxed**, 1972-78, Mego
MNP $50   MIP $75

❏ **Mr. Mxyzptlk, open mouth, 1973, carded**, 1972-78, Mego
MNP $50   MIP $150

❏ **Mr. Mxyzptlk, smirk, 1973, boxed**, 1972-78, Mego
MNP $60   MIP $150

❏ **Penguin, 1973, boxed**, 1972-78, Mego
MNP $60   MIP $150

❏ **Penguin, 1973, carded**, 1972-78, Mego
MNP $60   MIP $125

❏ **Peter Parker, 1974, boxed, Montgomery Ward Exclusive**, 1972-78, Mego
MNP $1200   MIP $2000

❏ **Riddler, 1973, boxed**, 1972-78, Mego
MNP $100   MIP $250

❏ **Riddler, 1973, carded**, 1972-78, Mego
MNP $100   MIP $400

❏ **Riddler, fist fighting, 1975, boxed**, 1972-78, Mego
MNP $150   MIP $400

❏ **Robin, fist fighting, 1975, boxed**, 1972-78, Mego
MNP $125   MIP $350

❏ **Robin, painted mask, 1972, boxed**, 1972-78, Mego
MNP $60   MIP $150

❏ **Robin, painted mask, 1972, carded**, 1972-78, Mego
MNP $60   MIP $90

❏ **Robin, removable mask, 1972, boxed**, 1972-78, Mego
MNP $250   MIP $400

❏ **Robin, removable mask, 1972, solid box**, 1972-78
MNP $250   MIP $1500

❏ **Shazam, 1972, boxed**, 1972-78, Mego
MNP $75   MIP $200

❏ **Shazam, 1972, carded**, 1972-78, Mego
MNP $75   MIP $150

❏ **Spider-Man, 1972, boxed**, 1972-78, Mego
MNP $20   MIP $100

❏ **Spider-Man, 1972, carded**, 1972-78, Mego
MNP $20   MIP $50

❏ **Supergirl, 1973, boxed,** 1972-78, Mego
MNP $300   MIP $450

❏ **Supergirl, 1973, carded,** 1972-78, Mego
MNP $300   MIP $450

❏ **Superman, 1972, boxed,** 1972-78, Mego
MNP $50   MIP $125

❏ **Superman, 1972, carded,** 1972-78, Mego
MNP $50   MIP $100

❏ **Tarzan, 1972, boxed,** 1972-78, Mego
MNP $50   MIP $150

❏ **Tarzan, 1976, Kresge card only,** 1972-78, Mego
MNP $60   MIP $225

❏ **Thing, Fantastic Four, 1975, boxed,** 1972-78, Mego
MNP $40   MIP $150

❏ **Thing, Fantastic Four, 1975, carded,** 1972-78, Mego
MNP $40   MIP $60

❏ **Thor, 1975, boxed,** 1972-78, Mego
MNP $150   MIP $300

❏ **Thor, 1975, carded,** 1972-78, Mego
MNP $150   MIP $300

❏ **Wonder Woman, boxed,** 1972-78, Mego
MNP $100   MIP $350

❏ **Wonder Woman, Kresge card only,** 1972-78, Mego
MNP $100   MIP $450

❏ **Wondergirl, carded,** 1972-78, Mego
MNP $125   MIP $400

ACCESSORIES

❏ **Super Hero Carry Case, 1973,** 1972-78
MNP $40   MIP $100

❏ **Supervator, 1974,** 1972-78
MNP $60   MIP $120

PLAY SETS

❏ **Aquaman vs. the Great White Shark, 1978,** 1972-78, Mego
MNP $300   MIP $750

❏ **Batcave Play Set, 1974, vinyl,** 1972-78, Mego
MNP $150   MIP $300

❏ **Batman's Wayne Foundation Penthouse, 1977, fiberboard,** 1972-78, Mego
MNP $600   MIP $1200

❏ **Hall of Justice, 1976, vinyl,** 1972-78, Mego
MNP $125   MIP $250

SUPERMAN SERIES

❏ **General Zod, 1978,** 1972-78, Mego
MNP $50   MIP $100

❏ **Jor-El, 1978,** 1972-78, Mego
MNP $50   MIP $100

❏ **Lex Luthor, 1978,** 1972-78, Mego
MNP $50   MIP $100

❏ **Superman, 1978,** 1972-78, Mego
MNP $50   MIP $125

TEEN TITANS, 6-1/2" FIGURES

❏ **Aqualad,** 1976, Mego
MNP $175   MIP $350

❏ **Kid Flash,** 1976, Mego
MNP $175   MIP $300

❏ **Speedy,** 1976, Mego
MNP $300   MIP $500

❏ **Wondergirl,** 1976, Mego
MNP $200   MIP $450

VEHICLES

❏ **Batcopter, 1974, boxed,** 1972-78, Mego
MNP $75   MIP $150

❏ **Batcopter, 1974, on display card,** 1972-78, Mego
MNP $55   MIP $110

❏ **Batcycle, black, 1975, boxed,** 1972-78, Mego
MNP $75   MIP $185

❏ **Batcycle, black, 1975, carded,** 1972-78, Mego
MNP $60   MIP $150

❏ **Batcycle, blue, 1974, boxed,** 1972-78, Mego
MNP $75   MIP $170

❏ **Batcycle, blue, 1974, carded,** 1972-78, Mego
MNP $75   MIP $135

❏ **Batmobile and Batman,** 1972-78, Mego
MNP $40   MIP $100

❏ **Batmobile, 1974, artwork box,** 1972-78
MNP $75   MIP $325

❏ **Batmobile, 1974, carded,** 1972-78, Mego
MNP $50   MIP $120

❏ **Batmobile, 1974, photo box,** 1972-78, Mego
MNP $75   MIP $395

❏ **Captain America,** 1976, 1972-78, Mego
MNP $125   MIP $275

❏ **Green Arrowcar,** 1976, 1972-78, Mego
MNP $175   MIP $350

❏ **Jokermobile,** 1976, 1972-78, Mego
MNP $150   MIP $300

❏ **Mobile Bat Lab, 1975,** 1972-78, Mego
MNP $125   MIP $250

❏ **Spidercar,** 1976, 1972-78, Mego
MNP $50   MIP $125

WWF (JAKKS PACIFIC, 1997-PRESENT)

2-TUFF, SERIES 1

❏ **D.O.A.,** 1997-present
MNP $4   MIP $12

❏ **Goldust and Marlena,** 1997-present
MNP $4   MIP $12

❏ **HHH and Chyna,** 1997-present
MNP $4   MIP $12

❏ **Truth Commission,** 1997-present
MNP $4   MIP $12

2-TUFF, SERIES 2

❏ **Brian Christopher and Jerry Lawler,** 1997-present
MNP $4   MIP $15

❏ **D-Lo Brown and Kama,** 1997-present
MNP $4   MIP $15

❏ **Kurrgan and Jackyl,** 1997-present
MNP $4   MIP $15

❏ **New Age Outlaws,** 1997-present
MNP $4   MIP $15

2-TUFF, SERIES 3

❏ **Kane and Mankind,** 1997-present
MNP $4   MIP $15

❏ **Legion of Doom 2000,** 1997-present
MNP $4   MIP $15

❏ **Rocky Maivia (The Rock) and Owen Hart,** 1997-present
MNP $8   MIP $20

❏ **Stone Cold Steve Austin/Undertaker,** 1997-present
MNP $4   MIP $15

2-TUFF, SERIES 4

❏ **Billy Gunn and Val Venis,** 1997-present
MNP $3   MIP $12

❏ **Mankind and The Rock,** 1997-present
MNP $3   MIP $12

❏ **Stone Cold Steve Austin and Big Bossman,** 1997-present
MNP $3   MIP $12

❏ **Undertaker and Kane,** 1997-present
MNP $3   MIP $12

2-TUFF, SERIES 5

❏ **Debra and Jarrett,** 1997-present
MNP $3   MIP $10

❏ **Road Dogg and Billy Gunn,** 1997-present
MNP $3   MIP $10

❏ **Stone Cold Steve Austin and The Rock,** 1997-present
MNP $8   MIP $20

❏ **Undertaker and Viscera,** 1997-present
MNP $3   MIP $10

BEST OF 1997, SERIES 1

- Ahmed Johnson, 1997-present
  MNP $3   MIP $10
- Bret Hart, 1997-present
  MNP $3   MIP $10
- British Bulldog, 1997-present
  MNP $3   MIP $10
- Owen Hart, 1997-present
  MNP $5   MIP $15
- Stone Cold Steve Austin, 1997-present
  MNP $3   MIP $12
- Undertaker, 1997-present
  MNP $3   MIP $10

BEST OF 1997, SERIES 2

- Crush, 1997-present
  MNP $3   MIP $10
- Goldust, 1997-present
  MNP $3   MIP $10
- HHH, 1997-present
  MNP $3   MIP $10
- Ken Shamrock, 1997-present
  MNP $3   MIP $10
- Marc Mero, 1997-present
  MNP $3   MIP $10
- Rocky Maivia (The Rock), 1997-present
  MNP $5   MIP $15
- Shawn Michaels, 1997-present
  MNP $3   MIP $10
- Undertaker, 1997-present
  MNP $3   MIP $10

BEST OF 1998, SERIES 1

- 8-Ball, 1997-present
  MNP $3   MIP $8
- Blackjack Bradshaw, 1997-present
  MNP $3   MIP $8
- Brian Christopher, 1997-present
  MNP $3   MIP $8
- Chyna, 1997-present
  MNP $3   MIP $8
- Shawn Michaels, 1997-present
  MNP $3   MIP $8
- Skull, 1997-present
  MNP $3   MIP $8
- Stone Cold Steve Austin, 1997-present
  MNP $4   MIP $10
- Vader, 1997-present
  MNP $3   MIP $8

BEST OF 1998, SERIES 2

- Dan Severn, 1997-present
  MNP $3   MIP $8
- Dude Love, 1997-present
  MNP $3   MIP $8
- HHH, 1997-present
  MNP $3   MIP $8

- Jeff Jarrett, 1997-present
  MNP $3   MIP $8
- Ken Shamrock, 1997-present
  MNP $3   MIP $8
- Mark Henry, 1997-present
  MNP $3   MIP $8
- Stone Cold Steve Austin, 1997-present
  MNP $4   MIP $10
- Undertaker, 1997-present
  MNP $3   MIP $8

BONE CRUNCHIN' BUDDIES, SERIES 1

- Dude Love, 1997-present
  MNP $5   MIP $15
- Shawn Michaels, 1997-present
  MNP $5   MIP $15
- Stone Cold Steve Austin, 1997-present
  MNP $5   MIP $15
- Undertaker, 1997-present
  MNP $5   MIP $15

BONE CRUNCHIN' BUDDIES, SERIES 2

- Animal, 1997-present
  MNP $5   MIP $15
- Hawk, 1997-present
  MNP $5   MIP $15
- Rock, The, 1997-present
  MNP $8   MIP $20
- Stone Cold Steve Austin, 1997-present
  MNP $5   MIP $15
- Undertaker, 1997-present
  MNP $5   MIP $15

BONE CRUNCHIN' BUDDIES, SERIES 3

- HHH, 1997-present
  MNP $5   MIP $15
- Kane, 1997-present
  MNP $5   MIP $15
- Rock, The, 1997-present
  MNP $8   MIP $20
- Stone Cold Steve Austin in shirt and pants, 1997-present
  MNP $5   MIP $15
- Stone Cold Steve Austin in tights and vest, 1997-present
  MNP $5   MIP $15
- Undertaker, 1997-present
  MNP $5   MIP $15

FULLY LOADED, SERIES 1

- Al Snow, 1997-present
  MNP $3   MIP $8
- Billy Gunn, 1997-present
  MNP $3   MIP $8
- Hunter Hearst Hemsley, 1997-present
  MNP $3   MIP $8

- Kane, 1997-present
  MNP $3   MIP $8
- Road Dog Jesse James, 1997-present
  MNP $3   MIP $8
- Rocky Maivia (The Rock), 1997-present
  MNP $5   MIP $15

FULLY LOADED, SERIES 2

- Road Dog Jesse James, 1997-present
  MNP $2   MIP $6
- Rock, The, 1997-present
  MNP $5   MIP $15
- Shane McMahon, 1997-present
  MNP $2   MIP $6
- Stone Cold Steve Austin, 1997-present
  MNP $3   MIP $10
- Test, 1997-present
  MNP $2   MIP $6
- X Pac, 1997-present
  MNP $3   MIP $8

GRUDGE MATCH

- Brian Christopher vs. TAKA, 1997-present
  MNP $5   MIP $15
- Dan Severn vs. Ken Shamrock, 1997-present
  MNP $5   MIP $15
- HHH vs. Owen Hart, 1997-present
  MNP $5   MIP $15
- HHHvs HBK, 1997-present
  MNP $5   MIP $15
- Jeff Jarrett vs. X Pac, 1997-present
  MNP $5   MIP $15
- Kane vs. Undertaker, 1997-present
  MNP $5   MIP $15
- Marc Mero vs. Steve Blackman, 1997-present
  MNP $5   MIP $15
- Mark Henry vs. Vader, 1997-present
  MNP $5   MIP $15
- McMahon vs. Stone Cold Steve Austin, 1997-present
  MNP $5   MIP $15
- Road Dog Jesse James vs. Al Snow, 1997-present
  MNP $5   MIP $15
- Sable vs. Luna Vachon, 1997-present
  MNP $5   MIP $15
- Shamrock vs. Billy Gunn, 1997-present
  MNP $5   MIP $15
- Shawn Michaels vs. Stone Cold Steve Austin, 1997-present
  MNP $8   MIP $20
- Stone Cold Steve Austin vs. The Rock, 1997-present
  MNP $8   MIP $20

LEGENDS, SERIES 1

❑ **Andre the Giant,** 1997-present
MNP $3   MIP $12

❑ **Captian Lou Albano,** 1997-present
MNP $3   MIP $12

❑ **Classie Freddie Blassie,** 1997-present
MNP $3   MIP $12

❑ **Jimmy Snuka,** 1997-present
MNP $3   MIP $12

LIVEWIRE, SERIES 1

❑ **Chyna,** 1997-present
MNP $3   MIP $8

❑ **Ken Shamrock,** 1997-present
MNP $3   MIP $8

❑ **Mankind,** 1997-present
MNP $3   MIP $8

❑ **Stone Cold Steve Austin,** 1997-present
MNP $4   MIP $10

❑ **Undertaker,** 1997-present
MNP $3   MIP $8

❑ **Vader,** 1997-present
MNP $3   MIP $8

LIVEWIRE, SERIES 2

❑ **Marc Mero,** 1997-present
MNP $2   MIP $6

❑ **Mark Henry,** 1997-present
MNP $2   MIP $6

❑ **Rock, The,** 1997-present
MNP $5   MIP $15

❑ **Shawn Michaels,** 1997-present
MNP $2   MIP $6

❑ **Val Venis,** 1997-present
MNP $2   MIP $6

❑ **X Pac,** 1997-present
MNP $2   MIP $6

MANAGER, SERIES 1

❑ **Backlund and Sultan,** 1997-present
MNP $3   MIP $12

❑ **Bearer and Mankind,** 1997-present
MNP $3   MIP $12

❑ **Mason and Crush,** 1997-present
MNP $3   MIP $12

❑ **Sable and Mero,** 1997-present
MNP $3   MIP $12

MAXIMUM SWEAT, SERIES 1

❑ **HHH,** 1997-present
MNP $3   MIP $8

❑ **Kane,** 1997-present
MNP $3   MIP $8

❑ **Rock, The,** 1997-present
MNP $5   MIP $15

❑ **Shawn Michaels,** 1997-present
MNP $3   MIP $8

❑ **Stone Cold Steve Austin,** 1997-present
MNP $3   MIP $10

❑ **Undertaker,** 1997-present
MNP $3   MIP $8

MAXIMUM SWEAT, SERIES 2

❑ **Billy Gunn,** 1997-present
MNP $2   MIP $6

❑ **Edge,** 1997-present
MNP $2   MIP $6

❑ **Ken Shamrock,** 1997-present
MNP $2   MIP $6

❑ **Road Dogg Jesse James,** 1997-present
MNP $2   MIP $6

❑ **Stone Cold Steve Austin,** 1997-present
MNP $3   MIP $10

❑ **Undertaker,** 1997-present
MNP $2   MIP $6

MAXIMUM SWEAT, SERIES 3

❑ **Big Bossman,** 1997-present
MNP $2   MIP $6

❑ **Billy Gunn,** 1997-present
MNP $2   MIP $6

❑ **Gangrel,** 1997-present
MNP $2   MIP $6

❑ **Mankind,** 1997-present
MNP $2   MIP $6

❑ **Rock, The,** 1997-present
MNP $5   MIP $15

❑ **Stone Cold Steve Austin,** 1997-present
MNP $3   MIP $10

RINGSIDE, SERIES 1

❑ **Referee,** 1997-present
MNP $3   MIP $8

❑ **Sable,** 1997-present
MNP $3   MIP $8

❑ **Sunny,** 1997-present
MNP $3   MIP $8

❑ **Vince McMahon,** 1997-present
MNP $3   MIP $8

RINGSIDE, SERIES 2

❑ **Honky Tonk Man,** 1997-present
MNP $2   MIP $6

❑ **Jim Cornette,** 1997-present
MNP $2   MIP $6

❑ **Jim Ross,** 1997-present
MNP $2   MIP $6

❑ **Referee,** 1997-present
MNP $2   MIP $6

❑ **Sgt. Slaughter,** 1997-present
MNP $2   MIP $6

❑ **Vince McMahon,** 1997-present
MNP $2   MIP $6

RIPPED AND RUTHLESS, SERIES 1

❑ **Goldust,** 1997-present
MNP $3   MIP $8

❑ **Mankind,** 1997-present
MNP $3   MIP $8

❑ **Stone Cold Steve Austin,** 1997-present
MNP $4   MIP $10

❑ **Undertaker,** 1997-present
MNP $3   MIP $8

RIPPED AND RUTHLESS, SERIES 2

❑ **HHH,** 1997-present
MNP $3   MIP $10

❑ **Kane,** 1997-present
MNP $5   MIP $15

❑ **Sable,** 1997-present
MNP $5   MIP $15

❑ **Shawn Michaels,** 1997-present
MNP $3   MIP $10

S.T.O.M.P., SERIES 1

❑ **Ahmed Johnson,** 1997-present
MNP $3   MIP $8

❑ **Brian Pillman,** 1997-present
MNP $3   MIP $8

❑ **Crush,** 1997-present
MNP $3   MIP $8

❑ **Ken Shamrock,** 1997-present
MNP $3   MIP $8

❑ **Stone Cold Steve Austin,** 1997-present
MNP $3   MIP $10

❑ **Undertaker,** 1997-present
MNP $3   MIP $8

S.T.O.M.P., SERIES 2

❑ **Chyna,** 1997-present
MNP $3   MIP $8

❑ **Mosh,** 1997-present
MNP $3   MIP $8

❑ **Owen Hart,** 1997-present
MNP $3   MIP $8

❑ **Rocky Maivia (The Rock),** 1997-present, Jakks Pacific
MNP $5   MIP $15

❑ **Stone Cold Steve Austin,** 1997-present
MNP $3   MIP $10

❑ **Thrasher,** 1997-present
MNP $3   MIP $8

S.T.O.M.P., SERIES 3

❑ **Animal,** 1997-present
MNP $3   MIP $8

❑ **Hawk,** 1997-present
MNP $3   MIP $8

❑ **Kane,** 1997-present
MNP $3   MIP $8

ACTION FIGURES

❏ **Marc Mero**, 1997-present
MNP $3   MIP $8

❏ **Sable**, 1997-present
MNP $3   MIP $8

❏ **Undertaker**, 1997-present
MNP $3   MIP $8

S.T.O.M.P., SERIES 4

❏ **Billy Gunn**, 1997-present
MNP $2   MIP $6

❏ **Chyna**, 1997-present
MNP $2   MIP $6

❏ **HHH**, 1997-present
MNP $2   MIP $6

❏ **Road Dog Jesse James**, 1997-present
MNP $2   MIP $6

❏ **Stone Cold Steve Austin**, 1997-present
MNP $3   MIP $8

❏ **X Pac**, 1997-present
MNP $2   MIP $6

SHOTGUN SATURDAY NIGHT, SERIES 1

❏ **Animal**, 1997-present
MNP $3   MIP $8

❏ **Hawk**, 1997-present
MNP $3   MIP $8

❏ **Henry O. Godwinn**, 1997-present
MNP $3   MIP $8

❏ **Phineas I. Godwinn**, 1997-present
MNP $3   MIP $8

❏ **Rocky Maivia (The Rock)**, 1997-present
MNP $5   MIP $15

❏ **Savio Vega**, 1997-present
MNP $3   MIP $8

❏ **Stone Cold Steve Austin**, 1997-present
MNP $3   MIP $10

❏ **Undertaker**, 1997-present
MNP $3   MIP $8

SHOTGUN SATURDAY NIGHT, SERIES 2

❏ **Billy Gunn**, 1997-present
MNP $2   MIP $6

❏ **Jeff Jarrett**, 1997-present
MNP $2   MIP $6

❏ **Kane**, 1997-present
MNP $2   MIP $6

❏ **Road Dog Jesse James**, 1997-present
MNP $2   MIP $6

❏ **Sable**, 1997-present
MNP $3   MIP $8

❏ **Shawn Michaels**, 1997-present
MNP $2   MIP $6

SIGNATURE, SERIES 1

❏ **Animal**, 1997-present
MNP $3   MIP $8

❏ **Goldust**, 1997-present
MNP $3   MIP $8

❏ **Hawk**, 1997-present
MNP $3   MIP $8

❏ **Hunter Hearst Hemsley**, 1997-present
MNP $3   MIP $8

❏ **Mankind**, 1997-present
MNP $3   MIP $8

❏ **Stone Cold Steve Austin**, 1997-present
MNP $5   MIP $15

SIGNATURE, SERIES 2

❏ **Billy Gunn**, 1997-present
MNP $3   MIP $8

❏ **Dude Love**, 1997-present
MNP $3   MIP $8

❏ **Kane**, 1997-present
MNP $3   MIP $8

❏ **Road Dog Jesse James**, 1997-present
MNP $3   MIP $8

❏ **Shawn Michaels**, 1997-present
MNP $3   MIP $8

❏ **Undertaker**, 1997-present
MNP $3   MIP $8

SIGNATURE, SERIES 3

❏ **Edge**, 1997-present
MNP $3   MIP $8

❏ **HHH**, 1997-present
MNP $2   MIP $6

❏ **Jackie**, 1997-present
MNP $3   MIP $8

❏ **Rock, The**, 1997-present
MNP $5   MIP $15

❏ **Stone Cold Steve Austin**, 1997-present
MNP $5   MIP $15

❏ **Undertaker**, 1997-present
MNP $3   MIP $8

SUNDAY NIGHT HEAT

❏ **Billy Gunn**, 1997-present
MNP $3   MIP $8

❏ **Road Dog Jesse James**, 1997-present
MNP $3   MIP $8

❏ **Rock, The**, 1997-present
MNP $5   MIP $15

❏ **Sable**, 1997-present
MNP $2   MIP $6

❏ **Stone Cold Steve Austin**, 1997-present
MNP $3   MIP $10

❏ **Undertaker**, 1997-present
MNP $3   MIP $8

SUPERSTARS, SERIES 1

❏ **Bret Hart**, 1997-present
MNP $8   MIP $20

❏ **Diesel**, 1997-present
MNP $10   MIP $40

❏ **Goldust**, 1997-present
MNP $8   MIP $20

❏ **Razor Ramon**, 1997-present
MNP $15   MIP $50

❏ **Shawn Michaels**, 1997-present
MNP $5   MIP $15

❏ **Undertaker**, 1997-present
MNP $8   MIP $20

SUPERSTARS, SERIES 2

❏ **Bret Hart**, 1997-present
MNP $5   MIP $15

❏ **Owen Hart**, 1997-present
MNP $8   MIP $30

❏ **Shawn Michaels**, 1997-present
MNP $5   MIP $15

❏ **Ultimate Warrior**, 1997-present
MNP $8   MIP $30

❏ **Undertaker**, 1997-present
MNP $10   MIP $30

❏ **Vader**, 1997-present
MNP $5   MIP $15

SUPERSTARS, SERIES 3

❏ **Ahmed Johnson**, 1997-present
MNP $3   MIP $10

❏ **Bret Hart**, 1997-present
MNP $3   MIP $10

❏ **British Bulldog**, 1997-present
MNP $5   MIP $15

❏ **Diesel, reissue**, 1997-present
MNP $5   MIP $15

❏ **Goldust, reissue**, 1997-present
MNP $5   MIP $15

❏ **Mankind**, 1997-present
MNP $3   MIP $10

❏ **Shawn Michaels**, 1997-present
MNP $3   MIP $10

❏ **Sycho Sid**, 1997-present
MNP $3   MIP $10

SUPERSTARS, SERIES 4

❏ **Farooq**, 1997-present
MNP $3   MIP $10

❏ **Hunter Hearst Hemsley**, 1997-present
MNP $3   MIP $10

❏ **Jerry The King Lawler**, 1997-present
MNP $3   MIP $10

❏ **Justin Hawk Bradshaw**, 1997-present
MNP $3   MIP $10

❏ **Stone Cold Steve Austin**, 1997-present
MNP $5   MIP $15

❏ **Vader**, 1997-present
MNP $3   MIP $10

SUPERSTARS, SERIES 5

❏ **Flash Funk**, 1997-present
MNP $3   MIP $10

❏ **Ken Shamrock,** 1997-present
MNP $3   MIP $10

❏ **Rocky Maivia,** 1997-present
MNP $3   MIP $10

❏ **Savio Vega,** 1997-present
MNP $3   MIP $10

❏ **Stone Cold Steve Austin,** 1997-present
MNP $5   MIP $15

❏ **Sycho Sid,** 1997-present
MNP $3   MIP $10

SUPERSTARS, SERIES 6

❏ **HHH,** 1997-present
MNP $3   MIP $10

❏ **Jeff Jarrett,** 1997-present
MNP $2   MIP $6

❏ **Marc Mero,** 1997-present
MNP $2   MIP $6

❏ **Mark Henry,** 1997-present
MNP $2   MIP $6

❏ **Owen Hart,** 1997-present, Jakks Pacific
MNP $5   MIP $15

❏ **Steve Blackman,** 1997-present
MNP $2   MIP $6

SUPERSTARS, SERIES 7

❏ **Dr. Death Steve Williams,** 1997-present
MNP $2   MIP $6

❏ **Edge,** 1997-present
MNP $2   MIP $6

❏ **Stone Cold Steve Austin,** 1997-present
MNP $3   MIP $10

❏ **Undertaker,** 1997-present
MNP $3   MIP $10

❏ **Val Venis,** 1997-present
MNP $2   MIP $6

❏ **X Pac,** 1997-present
MNP $3   MIP $8

SUPERSTARS, SERIES 8

❏ **Big Boss Man,** 1997-present
MNP $2   MIP $6

❏ **Ken Shamrock,** 1997-present
MNP $2   MIP $6

❏ **Rock, The,** 1997-present
MNP $5   MIP $15

❏ **Shane McMahon,** 1997-present
MNP $2   MIP $6

❏ **Shawn Michaels,** 1997-present
MNP $2   MIP $6

SUPERSTARS, SERIES 9

❏ **Bob Holly,** 1997-present
MNP $2   MIP $6

❏ **Christian,** 1997-present
MNP $2   MIP $6

❏ **Gangrel,** 1997-present
MNP $2   MIP $6

❏ **Paul Wright,** 1997-present
MNP $2   MIP $6

❏ **Undertaker with robe,** 1997-present
MNP $2   MIP $6

❏ **Vince McMahon,** 1997-present
MNP $2   MIP $6

TAG TEAM, SERIES 1

❏ **Godwinns,** 1997-present
MNP $4   MIP $15

❏ **Headbangers,** 1997-present
MNP $4   MIP $15

❏ **Legion of Doom,** 1997-present
MNP $4   MIP $15

❏ **New Blackjacks,** 1997-present
MNP $4   MIP $15

TITAN TRON LIVE

❏ **Kane,** 1997-present
MNP $2   MIP $6

❏ **Mankind,** 1997-present
MNP $2   MIP $6

❏ **Road Dogg Jesse James,** 1997-present
MNP $2   MIP $6

❏ **Rock, The,** 1997-present
MNP $5   MIP $15

❏ **Stone Cold Steve Austin,** 1997-present
MNP $3   MIP $10

❏ **Undertaker,** 1997-present
MNP $2   MIP $6

WWF WORLD WRESTLING FEDERATION (HASBRO, 1990-94)

FIGURES

❏ **1-2-3 Kid,** 1994, Hasbro
MNP $15   MIP $38

❏ **Adam Bomb,** 1994, Hasbro
MNP $10   MIP $18

❏ **Akeem,** 1990, Hasbro
MNP $15   MIP $38

❏ **Andre the Giant,** 1990, Hasbro
MNP $25   MIP $75

❏ **Ax,** 1990, Hasbro
MNP $5   MIP $15

❏ **Bam Bam Bigelow,** 1994, Hasbro
MNP $6   MIP $15

❏ **Bart Gunn,** 1994, Hasbro
MNP $10   MIP $18

❏ **Berzerker,** 1993, Hasbro
MNP $3   MIP $8

❏ **Big Bossman with Jailhouse Jam, 1992,** 1992, Hasbro
MNP $4   MIP $8

❏ **Big Bossman, 1990,** 1990, Hasbro
MNP $4   MIP $8

❏ **Billy Gunn,** 1994, Hasbro
MNP $10   MIP $18

❏ **Bret "Hitman" Hart with Hart Attack, 1992,** 1992, Hasbro
MNP $5   MIP $13

❏ **Bret Hart, 1993 mail-in,** 1993, Hasbro
MNP $38 n/a

❏ **Bret Hart, 1994,** 1994, Hasbro
MNP $4   MIP $8

❏ **British Bulldog with Bulldog Bash, 1992,** 1992, Hasbro
MNP $4   MIP $8

❏ **Brutus "The Barber" Beefcake with Beefcake Flattop, 1992,** 1992, Hasbro
MNP $6   MIP $13

❏ **Brutus the Barber, 1990,** 1990, Hasbro
MNP $6   MIP $13

❏ **Bushwackers, two-pack,** Hasbro
MNP $5   MIP $10

❏ **Butch Miller,** 1994, Hasbro
MNP $3   MIP $8

❏ **Crush, 1993,** 1993, Hasbro
MNP $6   MIP $13

(Hasbro)

❏ **Crush, 1994,** 1994, Hasbro, Made mincemeat out of his opponents.
MNP $3   MIP $8

❏ **Demolition, two-pack,** Hasbro
MNP $10   MIP $23

❏ **Doink the Clown,** 1994, Hasbro
MNP $4   MIP $8

❏ **Dusty Rhodes,** 1991, Hasbro
MNP $63   MIP $150

❏ **Earthquake,** 1991, Hasbro
MNP $8   MIP $15

❏ **Earthquake with Aftershock,** 1992, Hasbro
MNP $4   MIP $13

❏ **El Matador,** 1993, Hasbro
MNP $3   MIP $8

❏ **Fatu,** 1994, Hasbro
MNP $3   MIP $8

❏ **Giant Gonzales,** 1994, Hasbro
MNP $3   MIP $8

Greg "the Hammer" Valentine with Hammer Slammer (1992), 1992, Hasbro
MNP $5   MIP $15

Hacksaw Jim Duggan, 1991, 1991, Hasbro
MNP $3   MIP $8

Hacksaw Jim Duggan, 1994, 1994, Hasbro
MNP $3   MIP $8

Honky Tonk Man, 1991, Hasbro
MNP $13   MIP $25

Hulk Hogan with Hulkaplex, 1992, 1992, Hasbro
MNP $5   MIP $10

Hulk Hogan, 1990, 1990, Hasbro
MNP $6   MIP $13

Hulk Hogan, 1991, 1991, Hasbro
MNP $5   MIP $10

Hulk Hogan, 1993, mail-in, 1993, Hasbro
MNP $38   MIP $50

Hulk Hogan, 1993, no shirt, 1993, Hasbro
MNP $5   MIP $10

I.R.S., 1993, Hasbro
MNP $4   MIP $8

Jake the Snake Roberts, 1990, Hasbro
MNP $5   MIP $10

Jim Neidhart, 1993, Hasbro
MNP $3   MIP $8

Jimmy Superfly Snuka, 1991, Hasbro
MNP $6   MIP $13

Kamala, 1993, Hasbro
MNP $5   MIP $13

Koko B. Ware with Bird Man Bounce, 1992, 1992, Hasbro
MNP $10   MIP $30

Legion of Doom, two-pack, Hasbro
MNP $10   MIP $20

Lex Luger, 1994, Hasbro
MNP $8   MIP $15

Ludwig Borga, 1994, Hasbro
MNP $20   MIP $35

Luke Williams, 1994, Hasbro
MNP $5   MIP $15

Macho Man Randy Savage with Macho Masher, 1992, 1992, Hasbro
MNP $15   MIP $35

Macho Man, 1990, 1990, Hasbro
MNP $12   MIP $25

Macho Man, 1991, 1991, Hasbro
MNP $15   MIP $35

Macho Man, 1993, 1993, Hasbro
MNP $7   MIP $15

Marty Jannetty, 1994, Hasbro
MNP $5   MIP $15

Mountie, 1993, Hasbro
MNP $6   MIP $15

Mr. Perfect with Perfect Plex, 1992, 1992, Hasbro
MNP $8   MIP $20

Mr. Perfect with Texas Twister, 1992, 1992, Hasbro
MNP $15   MIP $35

Mr. Perfect, 1994, 1994, Hasbro
MNP $12   MIP $25

Nailz, 1993, Hasbro
MNP $12   MIP $25

Nasty Boys, two-pack, Hasbro
MNP $15   MIP $80

Owen Hart, 1993, Hasbro
MNP $15   MIP $45

Papa Shango, 1993, Hasbro
MNP $7   MIP $15

Razor Ramon, 1993, 1993, Hasbro
MNP $15   MIP $30

(Hasbro)

Razor Ramon, 1994, 1994, Hasbro, A bad dude who often sported toothpick in his mouth.
MNP $9   MIP $18

Repo Man, 1993, Hasbro
MNP $7   MIP $15

Ric Flair, 1993, Hasbro
MNP $7   MIP $15

Rick Martel, 1993, Hasbro
MNP $5   MIP $15

Rick Rude, 1990, Hasbro
MNP $15   MIP $30

Rick Steiner, 1994, Hasbro
MNP $9   MIP $18

Ricky "The Dragon" Steamboat with Steamboat Springer, 1992, 1992, Hasbro
MNP $7   MIP $15

Rockers, two-pack, Hasbro
MNP $10   MIP $20

Rowdy Roddy Piper, 1991, Hasbro
MNP $15   MIP $30

Samu, 1994, Hasbro
MNP $5   MIP $15

Scott Steiner, 1994, Hasbro
MNP $8   MIP $18

Sgt. Slaughter with Sgt.'s Salute, 1992, 1992, Hasbro
MNP $15   MIP $30

Shawn Michaels, 1993, 1993, Hasbro
MNP $10   MIP $25

(KP Photo)

Shawn Michaels, 1994, 1994, Hasbro, Shown here with group of figures from the series
MNP $6   MIP $15

Sid Justice, 1993, Hasbro
MNP $6   MIP $15

Skinner, 1993, Hasbro
MNP $6   MIP $15

Smash, 1990, Hasbro
MNP $12   MIP $25

Tatanka, 1993, 1993, Hasbro
MNP $7   MIP $15

Tatanka, 1994, 1994, Hasbro
MNP $7   MIP $15

Ted Diabiase, 1990, 1990, Hasbro
MNP $10   MIP $20

Ted Diabiase, 1991, 1991, Hasbro
MNP $7   MIP $15

Ted Diabiase, 1994, 1994, Hasbro
MNP $7   MIP $15

Texas Tornado with Texas Twister, 1992, 1992, Hasbro
MNP $10   MIP $50

Typhoon with Tidal Wave, 1992, 1992, Hasbro
MNP $15   MIP $30

Ultimate Warrior with Warrior Wham, 1992, 1992, Hasbro
MNP $20   MIP $40

Ultimate Warrior, 1990, 1990, Hasbro
MNP $12   MIP $25

Ultimate Warrior, 1991, 1991, Hasbro
MNP $10   MIP $20

Undertaker with Graveyard Smash, 1992, 1992, Hasbro
MNP $9   MIP $18

Undertaker, 1993, mail-in, 1993, Hasbro
MNP $25   MIP $50

Undertaker, 1994, 1994, Hasbro
MNP $15   MIP $25

Virgil, 1993, Hasbro
MNP $7   MIP $15

Warlord, 1993, Hasbro
MNP $6   MIP $15

❑ **Yokozuna**, 1994, Hasbro
MNP $15   MIP $30

XENA WARRIOR PRINCESS (TOY BIZ, 1998-99)

6" FIGURES

❑ **Callisto Warrior Goddess with Hope**, 1999
MNP $3   MIP $10

❑ **Grieving Gabrielle**, 1999
MNP $3   MIP $10

❑ **Xena Conqueror of Nations**, 1999
MNP $3   MIP $10

❑ **Xena Warrior Huntress**, 1999
MNP $3   MIP $10

SERIES I, 12" FIGURES

❑ **Callisto**, 1998
MNP $8   MIP $25

❑ **Gabrielle**, 1998
MNP $8   MIP $25

❑ **Xena**, 1998
MNP $8   MIP $25

SERIES II, 12" FIGURES

❑ **Ares**, 1999
MNP $8   MIP $25

❑ **Gabrielle Amazon Princess**, 1999
MNP $8   MIP $25

❑ **Roman Xena**, 1999
MNP $8   MIP $25

❑ **Warlord Xena**, 1999
MNP $8   MIP $25

SERIES III, 12" FIGURES

❑ **Empress Gabrielle**, 1999
MNP $8   MIP $25

❑ **Shamaness Xena**, 1999
MNP $8   MIP $25

❑ **Xena the Evil Warrior**, 1999
MNP $8   MIP $25

X-FILES (MCFARLANE, 1998)

FIGURES

❑ **Fireman with Cryolitter**, 1998, McFarlane
MNP $10   MIP $25

❑ **Mulder in Arctic wear**, 1998, McFarlane
MNP $4   MIP $8

❑ **Mulder with docile alien**, 1998, McFarlane
MNP $4   MIP $8

❑ **Mulder with Human Host and Cryopod Chamber**, 1998, McFarlane
MNP $4   MIP $8

❑ **Mulder with victim**, 1998, McFarlane
MNP $4   MIP $8

❑ **Primitive Man with Attack Alien**, 1998, McFarlane
MNP $4   MIP $8

❑ **Scully in Arctic wear**, 1998, McFarlane
MNP $4   MIP $8

❑ **Scully with docile alien**, 1998, McFarlane
MNP $4   MIP $8

(Lenny Lee)

❑ **Scully with Human Host and Cryopod Chamber**, 1998, McFarlane, Agent Scully in parka. Bases of human hosts snap together to form a row--just like in the movie
MNP $4   MIP $8

❑ **Scully with Victim**, 1998, McFarlane
MNP $4   MIP $8

X-MEN (TOY BIZ, 1991-96)

FIGURES

❑ **Ahab, 1994**, 1994, Toy Biz
MNP $5   MIP $15

❑ **Apocalypse I, 1991**, 1991, Toy Biz
MNP $7   MIP $15

❑ **Apocalypse I, 1993**, 1993, Toy Biz
MNP $4   MIP $15

❑ **Apocolypse, 1996**, 1996, Toy Biz
MNP $3   MIP $8

❑ **Archangel II, 1995**, 1995, Toy Biz
MNP $4   MIP $15

❑ **Archangel, 1991**, 1991, Toy Biz
MNP $7   MIP $15

❑ **Archangel, 1996**, 1996, Toy Biz
MNP $3   MIP $8

❑ **Banshee I, 1992**, 1992, Toy Biz
MNP $7   MIP $15

❑ **Battle Ravaged Wolverine, 1995**, 1995, Toy Biz
MNP $4   MIP $8

❑ **Beast, 1994**, 1994, Toy Biz
MNP $10   MIP $20

❑ **Bishop II, 1993**, 1993, Toy Biz
MNP $7   MIP $15

❑ **Bishop II, 1996**, 1996, Toy Biz
MNP $3   MIP $8

❑ **Blob, 1995**, 1995, Toy Biz
MNP $5   MIP $15

❑ **Cable Cyborg, 1995**, 1995, Toy Biz
MNP $4   MIP $15

❑ **Caliban, 1995**, 1995, Toy Biz
MNP $4   MIP $15

❑ **Cameron Hodge, 1995**, 1995, Toy Biz
MNP $4   MIP $15

❑ **Captive Sabretooth, 1995**, 1995, Toy Biz
MNP $4   MIP $15

❑ **Colossus, 1991**, 1991, Toy Biz
MNP $10   MIP $20

❑ **Colossus, 1993**, 1993, Toy Biz
MNP $6   MIP $15

❑ **Colossus, 1996**, 1996, Toy Biz
MNP $3   MIP $8

❑ **Corsair, 1995**, 1995, Toy Biz
MNP $3   MIP $15

❑ **Cyclops I, blue, 1991**, 1991, Toy Biz
MNP $10   MIP $20

❑ **Cyclops I, stripes, 1991**, 1991, Toy Biz
MNP $5   MIP $15

❑ **Cyclops II, 1993**, 1993, Toy Biz
MNP $5   MIP $15

❑ **Cyclops, 1996**, 1996, Toy Biz
MNP $3   MIP $8

❑ **Deadpool, 1995**, 1995, Toy Biz
MNP $6   MIP $15

❑ **Domino, 1995**, 1995, Toy Biz
MNP $5   MIP $15

❑ **Forge, 1992**, 1992, Toy Biz
MNP $10   MIP $25

❑ **Gambit, 1992**, 1992, Toy Biz
MNP $10   MIP $20

❑ **Gambit, 1993**, 1993, Toy Biz
MNP $7   MIP $15

❑ **Gladiator, 1995**, 1995, Toy Biz
MNP $3   MIP $15

❑ **Havok, 1995**, 1995, Toy Biz
MNP $4   MIP $15

❑ **Ice Man II, 1995**, 1995, Toy Biz
MNP $4   MIP $15

❑ **Ice Man, 1992**, 1992, Toy Biz
MNP $20   MIP $45

❑ **Juggernaut, 1991**, 1991, Toy Biz
MNP $10   MIP $25

❑ **Juggernaut, 1993**, 1993, Toy Biz
MNP $4   MIP $15

❑ **Lady Deathstrike, 1996**, 1996, Toy Biz
MNP $3   MIP $8

❑ **Magneto I, 1991**, 1991, Toy Biz
MNP $6   MIP $15

- Magneto II, **1992**, 1992, Toy Biz
  MNP $5   MIP $15

- Magneto, **1996**, 1996, Toy Biz
  MNP $3   MIP $8

- Morph, **1994**, 1994, Toy Biz
  MNP $10   MIP $20

- Mr. Sinister, **1992**, 1992, Toy Biz
  MNP $7   MIP $15

- Nightcrawler, **1993**, 1993, Toy Biz
  MNP $10   MIP $25

- Nimrod, **1995**, 1995, Toy Biz
  MNP $4   MIP $15

- Omega Red II, **1996**, Toy Biz
  MNP $3   MIP $8

- Omega Red, **1993**, 1993, Toy Biz
  MNP $6   MIP $15

- Phoenix, **1995**, 1995, Toy Biz
  MNP $10   MIP $25

- Polaris, **1996**, 1996, Toy Biz
  MNP $3   MIP $8

- Professor X, **1993**, 1993, Toy Biz
  MNP $6   MIP $15

- Raza, **1994**, 1994, Toy Biz
  MNP $3   MIP $15

- Sabretooth, **1996**, 1996, Toy Biz
  MNP $3   MIP $8

- Sauron, **1992**, 1992, Toy Biz
  MNP $3   MIP $15

- Savage Land Wolverine, **1996**, 1996, Toy Biz
  MNP $3   MIP $8

- Spiral, **1995**, 1995, Toy Biz
  MNP $4   MIP $15

- Storm, **1991**, 1991, Toy Biz
  MNP $20   MIP $40

- Strong Guy, **1993**, 1993, Toy Biz
  MNP $3   MIP $15

- Sunfire, **1995**, 1995, Toy Biz
  MNP $4   MIP $15

- Trevor Fitzroy, **1994**, 1994, Toy Biz
  MNP $3   MIP $15

- Tusk, **1992**, 1993, Toy Biz
  MNP $5   MIP $15

- Warstar, **1995**, 1995, Toy Biz
  MNP $6   MIP $15

- Weapon X, **1996**, 1996, Toy Biz
  MNP $3   MIP $8

- Wolverine Fang, **1995**, 1995, Toy Biz
  MNP $4   MIP $15

- Wolverine I, **1991**, 1991, Toy Biz
  MNP $10   MIP $20

- Wolverine I, **1993**, 1993, Toy Biz
  MNP $7   MIP $15

- Wolverine II, **1992**, 1992, Toy Biz
  MNP $7   MIP $15

- Wolverine III, **1992**, 1992, Toy Biz
  MNP $12   MIP $25

- Wolverine V, **1993**, 1993, Toy Biz
  MNP $7   MIP $15

- Wolverine, **1996**, 1996, Toy Biz
  MNP $3   MIP $10

- Wolverine, space armor, **1995**, 1995, Toy Biz
  MNP $6   MIP $15

- Wolverine, street clothes, **1994**, 1994, Toy Biz
  MNP $5   MIP $15

- X-Cutioner, **1995**, 1995, Toy Biz
  MNP $4   MIP $15

X-MEN (TOY BIZ, 1996-98)

AGE OF APOCALYPSE, 5" FIGURES, 1996

- Apocalypse, Removable Armor and Transforming Limbs, 1996
  MNP $3   MIP $8

- Cyclops, Cybernetic Guardian and Laser Blaster, 1996
  MNP $2   MIP $6

- Gambit, Blast-throwing Action, 1996
  MNP $2   MIP $6

- Magneto, Removable Helmet and Shrapnel, 1996
  MNP $2   MIP $6

- Sabretooth, Wild Child Sidekick Figure, 1996
  MNP $2   MIP $6

- Weapon X, Interchangeable Weaponry, 1996
  MNP $2   MIP $6

CLASSICS, LIGHT-UP WEAPONS, 5" FIGURES, 1996

- Gambit, Light-up Plasma Energy Weapon, 1996
  MNP $3   MIP $10

- Juggernaut, Light-up Jewel Weapon, 1996
  MNP $3   MIP $10

- Nightcrawler, Light-up Sword, 1996
  MNP $3   MIP $10

- Psylock, light-up Psychic Knife, 1996
  MNP $3   MIP $10

- Wolverine Stealth, Light-up Plasma Weapon, 1996
  MNP $3   MIP $10

MISSLE FLYERS, 5" FIGURES, 1997

- Apocalypse, Trap-door Chest, 1997
  MNP $3   MIP $8

- Bishop, Fold-out Armor Wing Blasters, 1997
  MNP $3   MIP $8

- Cable, Attack Wings, 1997
  MNP $3   MIP $8

- Shard, Spring Loaded Firing Wing Extensions, 1997
  MNP $3   MIP $8

- Wolverine, Head Launching Bird of Prey, 1997
  MNP $3   MIP $8

MONSTER ARMOR, 5" FIGURES, 1997

- Cyclops with Snap-on Cyclaw Armor, 1997
  MNP $2   MIP $6

- Mr. Sinister with Snap-on Cyber Tech Armor, 1997
  MNP $2   MIP $6

- Mystique with Snap-on She-Beast Armor, 1997
  MNP $2   MIP $6

- Rogue with Snap-on Leech Bat Armor, 1997
  MNP $2   MIP $6

- Wolverine with Snap-on Fangor Armor, 1997
  MNP $2   MIP $6

NEW MUTANTS, 5" FIGURES, 1998

- Magik, 1998
  MNP $2   MIP $6

- Warlock, 1998
  MNP $2   MIP $6

- Wolfsbane, 1998
  MNP $2   MIP $6

NINJA FORCE, 5" FIGURES, 1997

- Dark Nemesis with Spear Shooting Staff, 1997
  MNP $3   MIP $8

- Ninja Sabretooth with Clip-on Claw Armor, 1997
  MNP $3   MIP $8

- Ninja Wolverine with Warrior Assault Gear, 1997
  MNP $3   MIP $8

- Psylocke with Extending Power Sword, 1997
  MNP $3   MIP $8

- Space Ninja Deathbird with Fold-Out Ninja Wings, 1997
  MNP $3   MIP $8

ONSLAUGHT, 6" FIGURES, 1997

- Apocalypse Rising, Ozymandias, 1997
  MNP $3   MIP $11

- Jean Grey, Psychic Claw, 1997
  MNP $3   MIP $11

- Onslaught, Ultimate Power Armor, 1997
  MNP $3   MIP $10

- Wolverine Unleashed, Franklin Richards, 1997
  MNP $3   MIP $10

ROBOT FIGHTERS, 5" FIGURES, 1997

❑ Cyclops, Apocalypse Droid with Gattling Gun Arm, 1997
MNP $3   MIP $8

❑ Gambit, Attack Robot Droid with Projectile Missile, 1997
MNP $3   MIP $8

❑ Jubilee, Grabbing Sentinel Hand with Projectile Finger, 1997
MNP $4   MIP $12

❑ Storm, Spinning Weather Station with Lightning Projectile, 1997
MNP $4   MIP $12

❑ Wolverine, Slashing Sabretooth Droid with Missile Claw, 1997
MNP $3   MIP $8

SAVAGE LAND, 5" FIGURES, 1997

❑ Angel with Wing Flapping Sauron-Dino, 1997
MNP $2   MIP $6

❑ Kazar with Jumping Zabu Tiger, 1997
MNP $2   MIP $6

❑ Magneto with Water Spitting Amphibious, 1997
MNP $2   MIP $6

❑ Savage Storm with Head Ramming Colossus Dino, 1997
MNP $2   MIP $6

❑ Savage Wolverine with Jaw Chomping Crawler-Rex, 1997
MNP $2   MIP $6

SECRET WEAPON FORCE BATTLE BASES, 5" FIGURES, 1998

❑ Cyclops with War Tank Blaster, 1998
MNP $2   MIP $6

❑ Jean Grey with Catapult Tank Blaster, 1998
MNP $2   MIP $6

❑ Magneto Battle Base, 1998
MNP $2   MIP $6

❑ Omega with Spinning Rocket Blaster, 1998
MNP $2   MIP $6

❑ Wolverine Battle Base, 1998
MNP $2   MIP $6

❑ Wolverine with Claw Cannon Blaster, 1998
MNP $2   MIP $6

SECRET WEAPON FORCE FLYING FIGHTERS, 5" FIGURES, 1998

❑ Cyclops with High-Flying Hazard Gear, 1998
MNP $3   MIP $8

❑ Jean Grey with Fire Bird Flyer, 1998
MNP $3   MIP $8

❑ Maggot with Expanding Assault Wings, 1998
MNP $3   MIP $8

❑ Mr. Sinister with Bio-Tech Attack Wings, 1998
MNP $3   MIP $8

SECRET WEAPON FORCE POWER SLAMMERS, 5" FIGURES, 1998

❑ Gambit with Rapid Fire Card Cannon Slammer, 1998
MNP $2   MIP $6

❑ Master Mold with Rapid Fire Sentinels, 1998
MNP $2   MIP $6

❑ Rogue with Double Barrel Slammer, 1998
MNP $3   MIP $8

❑ Wolverine with Rapid Fire Disk Slammer, 1998
MNP $2   MIP $6

SECRET WEAPON FORCE SHAPE SHIFTERS, 7" FIGURES, 1998

❑ Juggernaut forms into Titanic Tank, 1998
MNP $2   MIP $6

❑ Morph forms into Mega Missile, 1998
MNP $2   MIP $6

❑ Wolverine forms into Mutant Wolf, 1998
MNP $2   MIP $6

SECRET WEAPON FORCE SUPER SHOOTER, 5" FIGURES, 1998

❑ Apocalypse, 1998
MNP $3   MIP $10

❑ Beast, 1998
MNP $3   MIP $8

❑ Colossus, 1998
MNP $3   MIP $8

❑ Wolverine, 1998
MNP $3   MIP $8

SHATTERSHOT, 5" FIGURES, 1996

❑ Age of Apocalypse Beast, Wind-up Chain Saw, 1996
MNP $2   MIP $6

❑ Archangel, Wing-flapping Action, 1996
MNP $2   MIP $6

❑ Colossus, Super Punch Gauntlets, 1996
MNP $2   MIP $6

❑ Lady Death Strike, Transforming Reaver Armor, 1996
MNP $2   MIP $6

❑ Patch Wolverine, Total Assault Arsenal, 1996
MNP $2   MIP $6

SPECIAL EDITION SERIES, 12" FIGURES, 1998

❑ Gambit, 1998
MNP $8   MIP $25

❑ Storm, 1998
MNP $8   MIP $25

❑ Wolverine, 1998
MNP $8   MIP $25

X-MEN 2099 (TOY BIZ, 1996)

5" FIGURES

❑ Bloodhawk, 1996
MNP $2   MIP $6

❑ Breakdown, Dominick Sidekick Figure, 1996
MNP $2   MIP $6

❑ Brimstone Love, 1996
MNP $2   MIP $6

❑ Halloween Jack, 1996
MNP $2   MIP $6

❑ Junkpile, Snap-on Battle Armor, 1996
MNP $2   MIP $6

❑ La Lunatica, Futuristic Jai-Lai, 1996
MNP $2   MIP $6

❑ Meanstreak, 1996
MNP $2   MIP $6

❑ Metalhead, 1996
MNP $2   MIP $6

❑ Shadow Dancer, 1996
MNP $2   MIP $6

❑ Skullfire, Glowing Fire Skeleton, 1996
MNP $2   MIP $6

X-MEN VS. STREET FIGHTER (TOY BIZ, 1998)

5" FIGURES

❑ Apocalypse vs. Dhalism, 1998
MNP $2   MIP $6

❑ Cyclops vs. M. Bison, 1998
MNP $5   MIP $15

❑ Gambit vs. Cammy, 1998
MNP $2   MIP $6

❑ Juggernaut vs. Chunu, 1998
MNP $2   MIP $6

❑ Magneto vs. Ryu, 1998
MNP $5   MIP $15

❑ Rogue vs. Zangief, 1998
MNP $2   MIP $6

❑ Sabretooth vs. Ken, 1998
MNP $5   MIP $15

❑ Wolverine vs. Akuma, 1998
MNP $5   MIP $15

X-MEN/X-FORCE (TOY BIZ, 1991-96)

DELUXE 10" FIGURES

❏ **Cable,** 1995
MNP $8   MIP $20

❏ **Kane,** 1995
MNP $8   MIP $20

❏ **Shatterstar,** 1995
MNP $8   MIP $20

FIGURES

❏ **Arctic Armor Cable, 1996,** 1996, Toy Biz
MNP $3   MIP $8

❏ **Avalanche, 1995,** 1995, Toy Biz
MNP $3   MIP $8

❏ **Black Tom, 1994,** 1994, Toy Biz
MNP $5   MIP $15

❏ **Black Tom, 1995,** 1994, Toy Biz
MNP $5   MIP $15

❏ **Blob, The, 1995,** 1995, Toy Biz
MNP $5   MIP $15

❏ **Bonebreaker, 1994,** 1994, Toy Biz
MNP $3   MIP $15

❏ **Bridge, 1992,** 1992, Toy Biz
MNP $5   MIP $15

❏ **Brood, 1993,** 1993, Toy Biz
MNP $4   MIP $15

❏ **Cable Cyborg, 1995,** 1995, Toy Biz
MNP $3   MIP $8

❏ **Cable I, 1992,** 1992, Toy Biz
MNP $6   MIP $15

❏ **Cable II, 1993,** 1993, Toy Biz
MNP $4   MIP $15

❏ **Cable III, 1993,** 1993, Toy Biz
MNP $4   MIP $15

❏ **Cable IV, 1994,** 1994, Toy Biz
MNP $3   MIP $15

❏ **Cable Stealth, 1996,** 1996, Toy Biz
MNP $3   MIP $8

❏ **Cable V, 1994,** 1995, Toy Biz
MNP $5   MIP $15

(KP Photo)

❏ **Cannonball, pink, 1993,** 1993, Toy Biz, How do muscles show so well through clothes?
MNP $15   MIP $35

❏ **Cannonball, purple, 1993,** 1993, Toy Biz
MNP $10   MIP $20

❏ **Commando, 1995,** 1995, Toy Biz
MNP $3   MIP $8

❏ **Deadpool, 1992,** 1992, Toy Biz
MNP $15   MIP $35

❏ **Deadpool, 1995,** 1995, Toy Biz
MNP $3   MIP $10

❏ **Domino, 1995,** 1995, Toy Biz
MNP $3   MIP $10

❏ **Exodus, 1995,** 1995, Toy Biz
MNP $3   MIP $8

❏ **Forearm, 1992,** 1992, Toy Biz
MNP $10   MIP $20

❏ **Genesis, 1995,** 1995, Toy Biz
MNP $3   MIP $8

❏ **Gideon, 1992,** 1992, Toy Biz
MNP $5   MIP $15

❏ **Grizzly, 1993,** 1993, Toy Biz
MNP $5   MIP $15

❏ **Kane I, 1992,** 1992, Toy Biz
MNP $7   MIP $15

❏ **Kane II, 1993,** 1993, Toy Biz
MNP $4   MIP $15

❏ **Killspree II, 1996,** 1995, Toy Biz
MNP $4   MIP $8

❏ **Killspree, 1994,** 1994, Toy Biz
MNP $7   MIP $15

❏ **Krule, 1993,** 1993, Toy Biz
MNP $3   MIP $15

❏ **Kylun, 1994,** 1994, Toy Biz
MNP $3   MIP $15

❏ **Longshot, 1994,** 1994, Toy Biz
MNP $7   MIP $15

❏ **Mojo, 1995,** 1995, Toy Biz
MNP $3   MIP $8

❏ **Nimrod, 1995,** 1995, Toy Biz
MNP $3   MIP $8

❏ **Pyro, 1994,** 1994, Toy Biz
MNP $5   MIP $15

❏ **Quark, 1994,** 1994, Toy Biz
MNP $3   MIP $15

❏ **Random, 1994,** 1994, Toy Biz
MNP $3   MIP $15

❏ **Rictor, 1994,** 1994, Toy Biz
MNP $3   MIP $15

❏ **Rogue, 1994,** 1994, Toy Biz
MNP $10   MIP $25

❏ **Sabretooth I, 1992,** 1992, Toy Biz
MNP $7   MIP $15

❏ **Sabretooth II, 1994,** 1994, Toy Biz
MNP $6   MIP $15

❏ **Shatterstar I, 1992,** 1992, Toy Biz
MNP $4   MIP $12

❏ **Shatterstar II, 1994,** 1994, Toy Biz
MNP $4   MIP $12

❏ **Shatterstar III, 1996,** 1996, Toy Biz
MNP $3   MIP $8

❏ **Silver Samurai, 1994,** 1994, Toy Biz
MNP $3   MIP $15

❏ **Slayback, 1994,** 1994, Toy Biz
MNP $3   MIP $15

❏ **Stryfe, 1992,** 1992, Toy Biz
MNP $10   MIP $25

❏ **Sunspot, 1994,** 1994, Toy Biz
MNP $3   MIP $15

❏ **Urban Assault, 1995,** 1995, Toy Biz
MNP $3   MIP $8

❏ **Warpath I, 1992,** 1992, Toy Biz
MNP $7   MIP $15

❏ **Warpath II, 1994,** 1994, Toy Biz
MNP $5   MIP $15

❏ **X-Treme, 1994,** 1994, Toy Biz
MNP $5   MIP $15

X-MEN: THE MOVIE (TOY BIZ, 2000)

FIGURES

❏ **Cyclops,** 2000, Toy Biz
MNP $3   MIP $10

❏ **Jean Grey,** 2000, Toy Biz
MNP $5   MIP $15

❏ **Logan,** 2000, Toy Biz
MNP $3   MIP $10

❏ **Magneto,** 2000, Toy Biz
MNP $3   MIP $10

❏ **Mystique,** 2000, Toy Biz
MNP $3   MIP $10

❏ **Professor X,** 2000, Toy Biz
MNP $4   MIP $12

❏ **Rogue,** 2000, Toy Biz
MNP $3   MIP $10

❏ **Sabretooth,** 2000, Toy Biz
MNP $3   MIP $10

❏ **Storm,** 2000, Toy Biz
MNP $4   MIP $12

❏ **Toad,** 2000, Toy Biz
MNP $3   MIP $10

❏ **Wolverine,** 2000, Toy Biz
MNP $3   MIP $10

TWO PACKS

❏ **Logan and Rogue,** 2000, Toy Biz
MNP $5   MIP $15

❏ **Magneto and Logan,** 2000, Toy Biz
MNP $5   MIP $15

❏ **Wolverine and Sabre,** 2000, Toy Biz
MNP $5   MIP $15

YELLOW SUBMARINE (McFARLANE, 1999-2000)

SERIES 1, 1999

❑ **George with Yellow Submarine,** 1999, McFarlane
MNP $3   MIP $10

❑ **John with Jeremy,** 1999, McFarlane
MNP $3   MIP $10

❑ **Paul with Glove and Love base,** 1999, McFarlane
MNP $4   MIP $12

❑ **Ringo with Blue Meanie,** 1999, McFarlane
MNP $3   MIP $10

SERIES 2, SGT. PEPPER'S LONELY HEARTS CLUB BAND, 2000

❑ **George with Snapping Turk,** 2000, McFarlane, Came with Snapping Turk
MNP $3   MIP $8

(McFarlane Toys)

❑ **John with Bulldog,** 2000, McFarlane, Came with Bulldog
MNP $3   MIP $8

(McFarlane Toys)

❑ **Paul with Sucking Monster,** 2000, McFarlane, Came with Sucking Monster
MNP $3   MIP $8

(McFarlane Toys)

❑ **Ringo with Apple Bonker,** 2000, McFarlane, Came with Apple Bonker
MNP $3   MIP $8

YOUNGBLOOD (McFARLANE, 1995)

FIGURES

❑ **Crypt,** 1995, McFarlane
MNP $5   MIP $10

❑ **Die Hard,** 1995, McFarlane
MNP $4   MIP $8

❑ **Dutch,** 1995, McFarlane
MNP $4   MIP $8

❑ **Sentinel,** 1995, McFarlane
MNP $4   MIP $8

❑ **Shaft,** 1995, McFarlane
MNP $4   MIP $8

❑ **Troll,** 1995, McFarlane
MNP $10   MIP $20

ZORRO (GABRIEL, 1982)

FIGURES

❑ **Amigo,** 1982, Gabriel
MNP $10   MIP $25

❑ **Captain Ramon,** 1982, Gabriel
MNP $10   MIP $25

❑ **Picaro,** 1982, Gabriel
MNP $15   MIP $35

❑ **Sergeant Gonzales,** 1982, Gabriel
MNP $10   MIP $25

❑ **Tempest,** 1982, Gabriel
MNP $10   MIP $25

❑ **Zorro,** 1982, Gabriel
MNP $15   MIP $25

ADVERTISING TOYS

Advertising Toys

Some of the most famous advertising toys of recent decades: The California Raisins. Prices for these can hover around $5-$10 a piece, depending on condition and rarity. This particular collectible crosses the boundary into fast food toys (Restaurant Premiums in this book).

by Dan Stearns

Advertising characters are probably the some of most recognizable man-made symbols on the planet. Star-Kist's Charlie the Tuna ("Sorry, Charlie"), the Michelin Man (now revived in the United States in recent commercials) and Ronald McDonald (even Grimace is making a reappearance at the time of this writing) are known virtually everywhere.

These great personas are part of what draws us to a brand, whether we want to admit it or not. Mascots and symbols like Elsie the Cow, Toucan Sam and Tony the Tiger bring back powerful memories.

After all, there's a reason so many of the things we pick up at the grocery store can be referred to as "comfort foods."

While cereal premiums are some of the most popular, they are certainly not the only favored product type out there. Speedy Alka Seltzer and the Pillsbury Doughboy are favorites. (The Doughboy has such appeal and lasting power, that the collecting sub-genre has cookie jars, figures, salt-and-pepper shakers and more devoted just to him and his extended family.)

The Douglas Oil Company issued this interestingly "retro" Freddy Fast figure in 1976. In perfect shape, it could fetch as much as $130.

Smokey the Bear toy from the 1950s, valued at about $50 in mint condition.

Kraft "Cheesasaurus Rex" mail-away figures from the 1990s. These have jumped to about $10 a piece in mint condition in the past couple of years.

7-ELEVEN

❑ **Big Bite Figures,** 1987, 7-Eleven, 3-1/2"
hot dog men holding snacks
EX $7   **NM** $10   **MIP** $12

7-UP

❑ **Spot Wind-Up,** 1990, 7-Up, 3" red circular figure w/sunglasses
EX $8   **NM** $12   **MIP** $15

AIR INDIA

❑ **Air India Man Figure,** 1973, Air India,
4-1/2" statue of man wearing turban
standing on flying carpet
EX $10   **NM** $20   **MIP** $25

ALKA-SELTZER

(Toy Shop File Photo)

❑ **Speedy Figure,** 1963, Alka-Seltzer, 5-
1/2" vinyl boy holding Alka-Seltzer figure
EX $280   **NM** $310   **MIP** $360

ALPO

❑ **Dan the Dog Cookie Jar,** 1980s, Alpo,
7" ceramic gray and white sheep dog
EX $35   **NM** $50   **MIP** $70

❑ **Dan the Dog Wind-Up,** 1979, Alpo, 3"
wind-up figure of shaggy gray dog walking on his front paws
EX $10   **NM** $15   **MIP** $25

AMERICAN HOME FOOD PRODUCTS

❑ **Marky Maypo Figure,** 1960, American
Home Food Products, 9" vinyl figure
EX $35   **NM** $45   **MIP** $55

AUNT JEMIMA SYRUP

❑ **Aunt Jemima Doll,** 1950s, Aunt
Jemima Syrup, 13" cloth doll wearing
red checkered dress
EX $60   **NM** $70   **MIP** $90

BASKIN ROBBINS

❑ **Pinky the Spoon Figure,** 1993, Baskin
Robbins, 5" bendable figure
EX $4   **NM** $5   **MIP** $10

BAZOOKA

❑ **Bazooka Joe Doll,** 1973, Bazooka, 19"
plush boy pirate
EX $20   **NM** $25   **MIP** $30

BEATRICE FOODS

❑ **Clark Bar Figure,** 1960s, Beatrice
Foods, 8-1/2" vinyl boy holding a Clark
bar wearing a striped shirt
EX $200   **NM** $225   **MIP** $275

BEECH-NUT

❑ **Fruit Stripe Gum Figure,** 1967, Beech-
Nut, 7-1/2" bendable man shaped like a
pack of gum riding a motorcycle
EX $150   **NM** $200   **MIP** $225

BOB'S BIG BOY

❑ **Dolly Doll,** 1978, Bob's Big Boy, 14"
cloth girl doll w/Dolly nametag
EX $15   **NM** $25   **MIP** $30

❑ **Nugget Doll,** 1978, Bob's Big Boy, 10"
cloth dog doll w/"Nugget" on collar
EX $15   **NM** $25   **MIP** $30

BORDEN'S

❑ **Elsie the Cow Cookie Jar,** 1950s, Borden's, 12" Elsie w/her head popping out
of barrel
EX $275   **NM** $300   **MIP** $350

(Toy Shop File Photo)

❑ **Elsie the Cow Doll,** 1950s, Borden's,
12" plush cow that moos when shaken
EX $55   **NM** $80   **MIP** $90

❑ **Elsie the Cow Lamp,** 1947, Borden's,
electric lamp, ceramic
EX $150   **NM** $175   **MIP** $225

BRADFORD HOUSE RESTAURANTS

(Toy Shop File Photo)

❑ **Bucky Bradford Figure,** 1960s, Bradford House Restaurants, 9-1/2" blond
pilgrim boy holding dish that reads "It's
Yum Yum Time"
EX $27   **NM** $33   **MIP** $40

CAMPBELL

❑ **Campbell's Kid Doll,** 1950s, Campbell,
9-1/2" vinyl jointed cheerleader wearing
a white shirt w/"C" in middle
EX $45   **NM** $65   **MIP** $80

❑ **Campbell's Kid Doll,** 1973, Campbell,
16" blonde girl w/red hair
EX $25   **NM** $35   **MIP** $40

❑ **Campbell's Kid Figure,** 1950s, Campbell, 7" boy chef doll w/"C" on hat and
spoon in his hand
EX $40   **NM** $50   **MIP** $65

❑ **Campbell's Kid Figure,** 1970s, Campbell, 7" vinyl Campbell boy w/blue overalls
EX $30   **NM** $40   **MIP** $50

❑ **Christmas Ornament,** 1989, Campbell,
ball ornament w/picture of Campbell Kid
dressed as Santa
EX $5   **NM** $10   **MIP** $15

❑ **Wizard of O's Figure,** 1978, Campbell,
7-1/2" vinyl wizard w/Spaghetti O's on
his hat and bow tie
EX $15   **NM** $25   **MIP** $30

CHAMPION AUTO STORES

❑ **Champ Man Figure,** 1991, Champion
Auto Stores, 6" bendable man; head is a
flag
EX $7   **NM** $10   **MIP** $15

CHICKEN DELIGHT INTERNATIONAL

❑ **Chicken Delight Bank,** 1960s, Chicken
Delight International, 6" yellow and red
chicken holding a tray of biscuits
EX $85   **NM** $125   **MIP** $150

CHIQUITA

❑ **Chiquita Banana Doll,** 1974, Chiquita,
16" plush dancing banana w/fruit on its
head
EX $18   **NM** $20   **MIP** $25

CRACKER JACK

❏ **Cracker Jack Doll,** 1974, Cracker Jack, 15" plush sailor holding small box of Cracker Jacks snacks
EX $15 **NM** $20 **MIP** $25

CREST TOOTHPASTE

(Toy Shop File Photo)

❏ **Sparkle Telephone,** 1980s, Crest Toothpaste, 11" blue and silver snow-man-type character
EX $27 **NM** $38 **MIP** $44

CURAD

❏ **Taped Crusader Figure,** 1977, Curad, 7-1/2" male cartoon superhero
EX $65 **NM** $75 **MIP** $85

CURITY

❏ **Miss Curity Display,** 1950s, Curity, 18" plastic store display of a nurse on a base
EX $125 **NM** $150 **MIP** $185

DEL MONTE

(Toy Shop File Photo)

❏ **Clown Bank,** Del Monte, colorful, smiling clown
EX $6 **NM** $11 **MIP** $22

DOUGLAS OIL COMPANY

❏ **Freddy Fast Figure,** 1976, Douglas Oil Company, 7" freckled face boy; hat says "Freddy Fast"
EX $90 **NM** $110 **MIP** $125

DOW BRANDS

❏ **Scrubbing Bubble Brush,** 1980s, Dow Brands, 3-1/2" light blue scrub brush
EX $8 **NM** $10 **MIP** $12

ESQUIRE MAGAZINE

❏ **Esky Store Display,** 1940s, Esquire Magazine, 11" old man dressed in a tuxedo standing on an Esquire magazine
EX $300 **NM** $350 **MIP** $375

ESSO

❏ **Esso Tiger Figure,** 1960s, Esso, 8-1/2" plastic tiger
EX $20 **NM** $25 **MIP** $30

❏ **Esso Tiger Garbage Can,** 1970s, Esso, 10" metal garbage can w/picture of the Esso tiger
EX $15 **NM** $20 **MIP** $30

EVEREADY BATTERIES

(Toy Shop File Photo)

❏ **Energizer Bunny Plush,** Eveready Batteries, 22" plush
EX $17 **NM** $42 **MIP** $68

❏ **Eveready Cat Bank,** 1981, Eveready Batteries, black cat w/Eveready battery on side
EX $10 **NM** $15 **MIP** $20

FACIT ADDING MACHINES

❏ **Facit Man Figure,** 1964, Facit Adding Machines, 4" man wearing yellow outfit w/black wizard hat
EX $20 **NM** $25 **MIP** $30

FLORIDA CITRUS DEPARTMENT

❏ **Florida Orange Bird Hat,** 1970s, Florida Citrus Department, child's-size hat w/visor, pictures Orange Bird on front and back
EX $10 **NM** $15 **MIP** $20

❏ **Florida Orange Bird Nodder,** 1970s, Florida Citrus Department, 7" plastic
EX $50 **NM** $60 **MIP** $75

❏ **Florida Orange Bird Stick Pin,** 1980s, Florida Citrus Department, metal, depicts the Florida Orange Bird
EX $5 **NM** $10 **MIP** $15

FUNNY FACE DRINK

(Toy Shop File Photo)

❏ **Choo Choo Cherry Ramp Walker,** 1971, Funny Face Drink, 3" round, red figure w/conductor's hat
EX $73 **NM** $95 **MIP** $120

(Toy Shop File Photo)

❏ **Funny Face Mugs,** 1969, Funny Face Drink, 3" mugs of Funny Face characters, each
EX $9 **NM** $13 **MIP** $17

❏ **Goofy Grape Pitcher,** 1973, Funny Face Drink, 10" pitcher of smiling, purple character wearing lime green captain's hat
EX $75 **NM** $95 **MIP** $125

❏ **Lefty Lemon Frisbee,** 1980s, Funny Face Drink, plastic w/picture of Lefty Lemon
EX $5 **NM** $10 **MIP** $12

GENERAL MILLS

(Toy Shop File Photo)

❏ **Boo Berry Figure,** 1975, General Mills, 7-1/2" white and light blue ghost w/hat and bow tie
EX $78 NM $97 MIP $124

❏ **Cereal Card Game,** 1981, General Mills, card game w/different cereal characters
EX $10 NM $15 MIP $20

❏ **Count Chocula Figure,** 1975, General Mills, 7-1/2" vinyl vampire
EX $70 NM $85 MIP $110

(Toy Shop File Photo)

❏ **Frankenberry Figure,** 1975, General Mills, 8" vinyl pink Frankenstein
EX $72 NM $100 MIP $140

❏ **Fruit Brute Figure,** 1975, General Mills, 8" vinyl werewolf w/striped shirt
EX $75 NM $90 MIP $120

❏ **Lucky Charms Leprechaun Doll,** 1978, General Mills, 17" plush
EX $20 NM $25 MIP $30

❏ **Monster Cereal Pencil Case,** 1980s, General Mills, 8" x 5", vinyl case featuring Count Chocula, Frankenberry and Boo Berry
EX $10 NM $15 MIP $20

(Toy Shop File Photo)

❏ **Trix Rabbit Figure,** 1977, General Mills, 9" vinyl white rabbit
EX $32 NM $44 MIP $56

GERBER PRODUCTS

❏ **Gerber Boy figure,** 1985, Gerber Products, 8" vinyl boy w/baseball cap turned sideways that reads "I'm a Gerber Kid"
EX $25 NM $27 MIP $30

GOOD HUMOR

❏ **Good Humor Bar,** 1975, Good Humor, 8" vinyl ice cream bar w/a bite out of it
EX $175 NM $200 MIP $275

GRANDMA'S COOKIES

❏ **Grandma Bank,** 1988, Grandma's Cookies, 7-1/2" hard plastic Grandma wearing a blue dress
EX $25 NM $30 MIP $35

H.P. HOOD

❏ **Harry Hood Figure,** 1981, H.P. Hood, 7-1/2" delivery man w/"Hood" inscription on chest
EX $55 NM $70 MIP $80

HEINZ

❏ **Aristocrat Tomato,** 1939, Heinz, 6" Aristocrat Tomato bust wearing top hat
EX $150 NM $200 MIP $225

HERSHEY'S

(Toy Shop File Photo)

❏ **Hershey's Chocolate Figure,** 1987, Hershey's, 4-1/2" bendable candy bar shaped like a man
EX $6 NM $9 MIP $12

HUSH PUPPIES

❏ **Hush Puppies Figure,** 1970s, Hush Puppies, 8" tan and brown basset hound
EX $20 NM $25 MIP $35

ICEE

❏ **ICEE Bear Figure,** 1970s, ICEE, 8" vinyl polar bear drinking an ICEE
EX $25 NM $30 MIP $35

INSTY-PRINTS

❏ **Insty-Prints Wizard Figure,** 1980s, Insty-Prints, 9" vinyl figure of wizard dressed in red outfit w/moons and stars
EX $75 NM $100 MIP $135

IRON FIREMAN FURNACE

❏ **Iron Fireman Figure,** 1943, Iron Fireman Furnace, 5" metal man shoveling coal
EX $65 NM $75 MIP $85

KAHN'S WIENERS

❏ **Beefy Frank Figure,** 1980, Kahn's Wieners, 5-1/2" vinyl figural hot dog mustard dispenser
EX $15 NM $18 MIP $22

KEEBLER COMPANY

(Toy Shop File Photo)

❑ **Ernie the Keebler Elf Figure,** 1974, Keebler Company, 7" figure of Ernie wearing oange and yellow hat and green jacket
EX $17   NM $27   MIP $33

❑ **Ernie the Keebler Elf Mug,** 1972, Keebler Company, 3" plastic figural mug
EX $8   NM $12   MIP $15

KELLOGG'S

❑ **Coppertone,** 1998, Kellogg's, Coppertone Beach Set: Coppertone girl, black dog, drawstring tote, suntan lotion, towel, radio and umbrella; Madame Alexander, the set
EX $25   NM $50   MIP $100

❑ **Dig 'Em Bendy Figure,** 1970, Kellogg's, 3-1/2" bendable frog figure w/"Dig 'Em" on shirt
EX $10   NM $15   MIP $25

❑ **Dig 'Em Doll,** 1973, Kellogg's, 16" smiling frog w/baseball hat wearing shirt that reads "Dig Em"
EX $15   NM $20   MIP $30

❑ **Dig 'Em Slide Puzzle,** 1979, Kellogg's, 4" plastic squares that make a scene when put together
EX $8   NM $10   MIP $15

❑ **Milton The Toaster Figure,** 1980, Kellogg's, 5" white, smiling toaster
EX $50   NM $70   MIP $90

❑ **Newton the Owl License Plate,** 1973, Kellogg's, 5" x 7" plastic license plate w/Newton the Owl; made in several colors
EX $5   NM $8   MIP $10

❑ **Rice Krispie Dolls,** 1998, Kellogg's, Snap, Crackle and Pop, the set
EX $100   NM $150   MIP $200

❑ **Rice Krispies Dolls,** 1998, Kellogg's, 8" Snap, Crackle, Pop; Madame Alexander, each
EX $20   NM $40   MIP $65

❑ **Rice Krispies Towel,** 1972, Kellogg's, 20 x 38" towel featuring Snap, Crackle and Pop!
EX $10   NM $20   MIP $25

❑ **Snap, Crackle and Pop Figures,** 1975, Kellogg's, 7-1/2" vinyl, arms at side, each
EX $20   NM $25   MIP $30

❑ **Snap, Crackle and Pop Figures,** 1975, Kellogg's, 7-1/2" vinyl, arms extended, each
EX $25   NM $30   MIP $35

❑ **Snap, Crackle and Pop Hand Puppets,** 1950s, Kellogg's, cloth body and vinyl head, each
EX $25   NM $35   MIP $40

❑ **Tony the Tiger Cookie Jar,** 1968, Kellogg's, 7" plastic
EX $70   NM $95   MIP $125

❑ **Tony the Tiger Figure,** 1974, Kellogg's, 7-1/2" vinyl tiger
EX $45   NM $60   MIP $75

❑ **Toucan Sam Backpack,** 1983, Kellogg's, 12" blue backpack that pictures Toucan Sam sitting on a schoolhouse
EX $15   NM $20   MIP $25

❑ **Toucan Sam Figure,** 1984, Kellogg's, 3" plastic jointed figure w/blue body and multi-colored beak
EX $12   NM $15   MIP $20

❑ **Toucan Sam Wallet,** 1984, Kellogg's, plastic w/picture of Toucan Sam
EX $10   NM $15   MIP $20

KENDALL COMPANY

❑ **Curad Taped Crusader Figure,** 1977, Kendall Company, 7-1/2" vinyl figure
EX $65   NM $75   MIP $85

KEN-L-RATION

❑ **Ken-L-Ration Wall Pockets,** 1960s, Ken-L-Ration, 3" pair of plastic wall pockets; cat's head and a dog's head
EX $40   NM $50   MIP $65

KENTUCKY FRIED CHICKEN

❑ **Colonel Sanders Nodder,** 1960s, Kentucky Fried Chicken, 7" plastic nodder of Colonel holding bucket of chicken
EX $70   NM $85   MIP $100

KIDDIE CITY TOY STORE

❑ **Kaycee Kangaroo Figure,** 1980s, Kiddie City Toy Store, vinyl kangaroo w/baby in pouch
EX $40   NM $55   MIP $65

KRAFT

(Toy Shop File Photo)

❑ **Cheesasaurus Rex Figure,** 1990s, Kraft, 5-1/2" orange dinosaur figures wearing different outfits
EX $4   NM $7   MIP $10

❑ **Mr. Wiggle Hand Puppet,** 1966, Kraft, 6" red rubber
EX $150   NM $185   MIP $225

(Toy Shop File Photo)

❑ **Vegetable Man Bank,** 1970s, Kraft, 8" vegetable man w/tomato for a head and a celery body
EX $205   NM $260   MIP $280

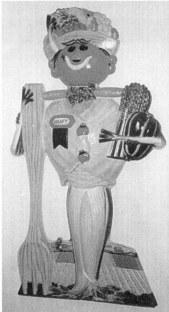

(Toy Shop File Photo)

❑ **Vegetable Man Display,** 1980, Kraft, 3' plastic vacuuform store display of Vegetable Man
EX $155   NM $230   MIP $280

LABATT'S BREWERY

(Toy Shop File Photo)

❏ **Labatt's Beer Man Figure**, 1972, Labatt's Brewery, 6" man standing next to wood barrel
EX $22   **NM** $30   **MIP** $38

MAGIC CHEF

(Toy Shop File Photo)

❏ **Magic Chef Figure**, 1980s, Magic Chef, 7" chef dressed in tuxedo and chef's hat
EX $10   **NM** $12   **MIP** $15

MICHELIN TIRES

❏ **Mr. Bib Figure**, 1980s, Michelin Tires, 12" plastic figure w/Michelin sash across chest
EX $30   **NM** $40   **MIP** $50

MOHAWK CARPET COMPANY

❏ **Mohawk Tommy Doll**, 1970, Mohawk Carpet Company, 16" stuffed doll of a little boy marked "Mohawk Tommy" across front
EX $10   **NM** $15   **MIP** $20

NABISCO

❏ **Barnum's Animal Crackers Cookie Jar**, 1972, Nabisco, ceramic, shaped like a box of animal crackers
EX $175   **NM** $225   **MIP** $275

❏ **Chips Ahoy Girl Figure**, 1983, Nabisco, 4-1/2" vinyl figure of girl w/Chips Ahoy cookie on her head and in her hand
EX $15   **NM** $18   **MIP** $20

(Toy Shop File Photo)

❏ **Fig Newton Girl Figure**, 1983, Nabisco, 4-1/2" girl w/Fig Newton on her head
EX $17   **NM** $21   **MIP** $25

❏ **Nabisco Thing**, 1996, Nabisco, 5" multi-colored bendable figure w/Nabisco logo for its head
EX $5   **NM** $10   **MIP** $15

❏ **Oreo Cookie Girl Figure**, 1983, Nabisco, 4-1/2" vinyl figure of girl w/Oreo Cookie on head and in her hand
EX $15   **NM** $18   **MIP** $20

NESTLE'S

(Toy Shop File Photo)

❏ **Quik Bunny Doll**, 1976, Nestle's, 24" plush rabbit w/letter "Q" on his chest
EX $27   **NM** $38   **MIP** $44

❏ **Quik Bunny Figure**, 1991, Nestle's, 6" bendable brown and tan rabbit w/the letter "Q" hanging from his neck
EX $3   **NM** $7   **MIP** $10

NOVOTEL HOTEL

❏ **Dophi Figure**, 1990s, Novotel Hotel, 4-1/2" bendable dolphin figures; set of four produced each year
EX $5   **NM** $8   **MIP** $10

OSCAR MAYER FOODS

❏ **Hot Wheels Wienermobile**, Oscar Mayer Foods, die-cast Wienermobile
EX $2   **NM** $4   **MIP** $6

(Toy Shop File Photo)

❏ **Little Oscar Puppet**, Oscar Mayer Foods, thin plastic, theme song on back
EX $5   **NM** $8   **MIP** $10

❏ **Wienermobile**, 1950s, Oscar Mayer Foods, 11" car; Little Oscar pops up when car is rolled
EX $75   **NM** $95   **MIP** $135

(Toy Shop File Photo)

❏ **Wienermobile Bank**, Oscar Mayer Foods, plastic
EX $3   **NM** $7   **MIP** $15

❏ **Wienermobile Beanbag**, 1998, Oscar Mayer Foods, 7" plush beanbag
EX $3   **NM** $5   **MIP** $8

PEPPERIDGE FARM

❏ **Goldfish Plush**, 1970s, Pepperidge Farm, 16" plush figure
EX $15   **NM** $20   **MIP** $25

PILLSBURY

❑ **Biscuit the Cat Puppet,** 1974, Pillsbury, 2-1/2" vinyl cat finger puppet
EX $18   NM $25   MIP $30

(Toy Shop File Photo)

❑ **Grandpopper & Grandmommer Figures,** 1974, Pillsbury, 5" vinyl pair of figures
EX $85   NM $128   MIP $155

❑ **Jolly Green Giant Figure,** 1970s, Pillsbury, 9-1/2" vinyl green man wearing loincloth of leaves
EX $85   NM $100   MIP $125

❑ **Little Sprout Figure,** 1970s, Pillsbury, 6-1/2" vinyl green figure w/leaves on head and body
EX $7   NM $10   MIP $15

❑ **Little Sprout Inflatable Figure,** 1976, Pillsbury, 24" vinyl
EX $25   NM $30   MIP $35

❑ **Little Sprout Salt and Pepper Shakers,** 1988, Pillsbury, 3" ceramic figural shakers
EX $25   NM $30   MIP $35

❑ **Poppin' Fresh Doll,** 1972, Pillsbury, white velour doll w/hat and scarf
EX $20   NM $25   MIP $30

❑ **Poppin' Fresh Figure,** 1971, Pillsbury, 6-1/2" vinyl white baker w/blue eyes and blue dot on hat
EX $5   NM $7   MIP $10

PIZZA HUT

❑ **Pizza Hut Pete Bank,** 1969, Pizza Hut, 7-1/2" plastic
EX $20   NM $35   MIP $50

PIZZA TIME THEATRE

❑ **Chuck E. Cheese Bank,** 1980s, Pizza Time Theatre, 6-1/2" plastic
EX $8   NM $12   MIP $15

PLANTERS PEANUTS

(Toy Shop File Photo)

❑ **Mr. Peanut Doll,** 1967, Planters Peanuts, 21" pillow doll
EX $15   NM $20   MIP $35

❑ **Mr. Peanut Figure,** 1930s, Planters Peanuts, 8-1/2" painted wood figure w/hat and cane
EX $275   NM $300   MIP $375

(Toy Shop File Photo)

❑ **Mr. Peanut Figure,** 1992, Planters Peanuts, 8-1/2" yellow and black plastic
EX $15   NM $20   MIP $27

❑ **Mr. Peanut Wind-Up,** 1984, Planters Peanuts, 3" yellow peanut man w/traditional hat and cane
EX $20   NM $25   MIP $30

POST CEREAL

❑ **California Raisins PVC Figure,** 1987, Post Cereal, 2" male raisin playing drums
EX $3   NM $5   MIP $8

❑ **California Raisins Wind-Up,** 1987, Post Cereal, 4" female raisin w/tambourine
EX $5   NM $7   MIP $10

❑ **Sugar Bear Doll,** 1970s, Post Cereal, 12" plush brown bear w/blue "Sugar Bear" shirt
EX $20   NM $25   MIP $30

❑ **Sugar Bear Doll,** 1988, Post Cereal, 12" plush bear w/blue "Sugar Bear" shirt
EX $15   NM $20   MIP $25

PROCTOR & GAMBLE

❑ **24 Hour Bug,** 1970s, Proctor & Gamble, 7" spotted green bug
EX $50   NM $65   MIP $80

❑ **Hawaiian Punch Doll,** 1983, Proctor & Gamble, 15" plush Punchy w/red hair and blue and white striped shirt
EX $20   NM $22   MIP $25

(Toy Shop File Photo)

❑ **Hawaiian Punch Radio,** 1970s, Proctor & Gamble, 6" figural radio of Punchy
EX $25   NM $35   MIP $45

❑ **Mr. Clean Figure,** 1961, Proctor & Gamble, 8" bald man wearing white clothes w/earring; arms are folded
EX $85   NM $100   MIP $135

PURINA CHUCK WAGON

❑ **Chuck Wagon,** 1975, Purina Chuck Wagon, 8" vinyl team of horses and checker board covered wagon
EX $25   NM $30   MIP $35

QUAKER OATS

❑ **Cap'n Crunch Bank,** 1969, Quaker Oats, 8" captain wearing blue outfit and sword
EX $45   NM $65   MIP $85

❏ **Jean LaFoote Bank,** 1975, Quaker Oats, 8" vinyl pirate wearing green suit and purple hat
EX $60 **NM** $85 **MIP** $125

❏ **Quake Cereal Doll,** 1965, Quaker Oats, 9" man w/raised arms and letter "Q" across chest
EX $85 **NM** $95 **MIP** $125

❏ **Quisp Bank,** 1960s, Quaker Oats, 6-1/2" papier-mâché
EX $500 **NM** $750 **MIP** $850

❏ **Quisp Cereal Doll,** 1965, Quaker Oats, 10" doll w/pink body, green clothes and letter "Q" across stomach
EX $70 **NM** $85 **MIP** $125

❏ **Quisp Powered Sugar Space Gun,** Quisp Cereal/Quaker, 7" long, red, mail away premium
EX $150 **NM** $250 **MIP** $400

R.J. REYNOLDS

(Toy Shop File Photo)

❏ **Joe Camel Can Cooler,** 1991, R.J. Reynolds, 4" vinyl
EX $7 **NM** $13 **MIP** $19

RAID

(Toy Shop File Photo)

❏ **Raid Bug,** 1989, Raid, plush green bug
EX $22 **NM** $30 **MIP** $40

❏ **Raid Bug Radio,** 1980s, Raid, Raid bug in standing position w/clock on one side and radio on the other
EX $70 **NM** $200 **MIP** $135

❏ **Raid Bug Wind-Up,** 1983, Raid, 4" yellow and green angry bug
EX $40 **NM** $50 **MIP** $70

RALSTON PURINA

❏ **Meow Mix Cat,** 1976, Ralston Purina, 4-1/2" vinyl yellow cat w/black stripes
EX $20 **NM** $25 **MIP** $30

RECKITT & COLMAN

❏ **Mr. Bubble Figure,** 1990, Reckitt & Colman, 8" pink vinyl
EX $20 **NM** $30 **MIP** $35

REDDY COMMUNICATIONS

❏ **Reddy Kilowatt Bobbin' Head,** 1960s, Reddy Communications, 6-1/2" Reddy wearing cowboy outfit
EX $225 **NM** $275 **MIP** $450

❏ **Reddy Kilowatt Figure,** 1961, Reddy Communications, 6" plastic figure w/lightbulb for head and lightning bolts for body
EX $150 **NM** $185 **MIP** $225

RITALIN

(Toy Shop File Photo)

❏ **Ritalin Man Statue,** 1970s, Ritalin, 7" smiling plastic statue w/hat
EX $58 **NM** $67 **MIP** $78

SEA HOST

❏ **Clem the Clam Push Puppets,** 1969, Sea Host, 4" fish push puppets; four different fish were issued
EX $15 **NM** $30 **MIP** $40

SHOP RITE

❏ **Scrunchy Bear Doll,** 1970s, Shop Rite, 16" plush bear w/Shop-Rite shirt
EX $20 **NM** $25 **MIP** $30

SMILE ORANGE DRINK

❏ **Drink Smile Statue,** 1930s, Smile Orange Drink, 8" plaster statue of char-

acter w/orange for head; "Drink Smile" written across base
EX $150 **NM** $200 **MIP** $250

SMITH KLINE & FRENCH LAB

❏ **Tagamet Figure,** 1989, Smith Kline & French Lab, 2-1/2" bendable pink figure standing on base
EX $15 **NM** $20 **MIP** $25

SONY

❏ **Sony Boy Figure,** 1960s, Sony, 4" vinyl boy wearing yellow "Sony" shirt
EX $150 **NM** $200 **MIP** $225

SQUIRT BEVERAGE

❏ **Squirt Doll,** 1961, Squirt Beverage, 17" vinyl boy w/blond hair and removable clothing; "Squirt" written across shirt
EX $100 **NM** $150 **MIP** $175

STARKIST

❏ **Charlie the Tuna Doll,** 1970, Starkist, 15" pull string talking doll
EX $40 **NM** $50 **MIP** $75

❏ **Charlie the Tuna Figure,** 1973, Starkist, 7-1/2" vinyl Charlie; arms pointed down
EX $50 **NM** $70 **MIP** $85

❏ **Charlie the Tuna Radio,** 1970, Starkist, 6" radio
EX $50 **NM** $60 **MIP** $90

❏ **Charlie the Tuna Scale,** 1972, Starkist, oval shaped bathroom scale w/Charlie the Tuna
EX $50 **NM** $65 **MIP** $80

STERLING DRUG

❏ **Diaparene Baby Doll,** 1980, Sterling Drug, 5" baby w/movable arms and legs; baby wears diaper
EX $35 **NM** $40 **MIP** $50

TASTYKAKE

❏ **Tastykake Baker Doll,** 1974, Tastykake, 13" pillow doll wearing chef outfit
EX $15 **NM** $20 **MIP** $25

TONY'S PIZZA

❏ **Mr. Tony Figure,** 1972, Tony's Pizza, 8" vinyl Italian pizza chef
EX $30 **NM** $35 **MIP** $40

TOYS R US

❏ **Geoffrey Doll,** 1967, Toys R Us, 2-1/2" plush Geoffrey wearing red and white striped shirt
EX $20 **NM** $25 **MIP** $35

❏ **Geoffrey Flashlight,** 1989, Toys R Us, 8-1/2" plastic figural flashlight of Geoffrey the Giraffe
EX $8 **NM** $10 **MIP** $12

TRAVELODGE

❏ **Sleepy Bear Squeeze Toy,** 1970s, Travelodge, 5-1/2" bear wearing pajamas
EX $25 **NM** $30 **MIP** $35

TROPICANA

❑ **Tropic-Ana Doll,** 1977, Tropicana, 17"
pillow doll of Hawaiian girl
EX $15   **NM** $20   **MIP** $25

U.S. FORESTRY DEPARTMENT

❑ **Woodsy Owl Bank,** 1970s, U.S. Forestry
Department, 8-1/2" ceramic figural bank
EX $100   **NM** $125   **MIP** $150

U.S. POSTAL SERVICE

❑ **Mr. ZIP Statue,** 1960s, U.S. Postal Service, 6-1/2" wood statue w/mailbag and
pop-up hat
EX $150   **NM** $180   **MIP** $225

WONDER BREAD

❑ **Fresh Guy Figure,** 1975, Wonder Bread,
4" smiling loaf of bread w/polka dots,
smiling face and "Wonder" on side
EX $100   **NM** $150   **MIP** $175

Barbie Dolls

The Barbie doll that started it all, Ponytail #1. Now valued at $6500 MIP.

By Sharon Korbeck
Toy Shop Editor

She's got a body to die for, and she goes by only one name.

Who is this superstar? Madonna? Cher?

It's none other than Mattel's Barbie doll.

Mattel's fashion doll icon still captures the essence of little girls' imaginations and dreams – and that's exactly what creator Ruth Handler intended.

Since the doll's inception in 1959, Barbie has seen cosmetic changes (like hairstyle, facial expression and slight changes in body style) and more major changes (literally dozens of careers, computer technological advances, etc.). Through it all, however, Barbie has come out ahead of the competitors. Today, Mattel sells close to $2 billion in Barbie dolls per year.

Rather Modest Beginnings

Barbie's beginnings are well-documented; her birth happened smack in the middle of a strong 1950s postwar economy.

It was then that the Barbie doll came as an inspiration to Mattel co-founder Handler as she watched her young daughter, Barbara, playing with paper dolls.

Barbara and her friends liked to play adult or teenage make-believe with the dolls, imagining them in roles as college students, cheerleaders and adults with careers.

Handler immediately recognized that playing and pretending about the future was an important part of growing up. In researching the marketplace, she discovered a void and was determined to fill the niche with a three-dimensional fashion doll. Her all-male design staff, however, harbored doubts.

Several designs later, Mattel introduced Barbie, the Teen-Age Fashion Model, to skeptical buyers at New York's annual Toy

Fair in 1959. Never before had they seen a doll so completely unlike the baby and toddler dolls popular at the time. A major point of controversy? Barbie's ample bosom. Actually, the contention was that the doll had breasts . . . period.

With fashion and teenage lifestyle trends evolving at a startling rate, the hundreds of people who have worked to keep Barbie current have had their hands full as styles changed from Paris couture to the inspired elegance of the Jacqueline Kennedy years to a more free-flowing, youthful look.

One of Barbie's first friends, Midge (the straight legged variety), shown with her various hair colors. $125 MIP.

Mattel's design and development staff have remained current by identifying trends that relate to the lives of American teenagers.

Barbie has been called an "evergreen" property, an adjective infrequently used in the toy industry. Far too often, toys and the whims of the fickle buying public are fleeting.

But unlike decades of toys lost in the attics of memory, Mattel's Barbie has surpassed probably even Ruth Handler's expectations.

A Collector's Dream

Barbie's charm as a children's toy may have been immediate, but it wasn't until decades later that collectors started paying more attention. Collectors who had grown up with Barbie wanted to reclaim her. There was, after all, plenty to recapture – the memories of playing with dolls with friends, Barbie's fabulous fancy out-

fits, dream dates with Ken and, who could forget, Barbie's dream house!

But since Barbie dolls were well-loved and played-with, many of the 1959 and early 1960s dolls were in less-than-perfect shape. That's why examples of the earliest Barbie dolls regularly command hundreds, even thousands, of dollars each. Having original boxes and clothing increases a doll's value.

Collectors today are interested in both vintage and newer, collector-edition dolls. Collecting is no small hobby. Full-time dealers make their livings off Barbie, and several publications exist solely what's new in Barbie's world.

Nostalgia and investment potential are perhaps the two biggest motivators for Barbie collectors. And investment potential has proven itself over the last decades.

Collecting Trends

Vintage dolls, particularly early 1960s issues, have consistently held their values. And auction prices have soared. A brunette #1 Ponytail Barbie (so called by collectors because of the early dolls' hairstyle) sold at a 2000 auction for more than $8,700.

The very first Barbie, known to collectors as Ponytail #1, has hovered around the $3,000 to $8,000 range for one in Mint in Box condition. Lesser condition

Mod Hair Ken was a nod to the times when he was released in 1972. $65 MIP.

#1 dolls, or those without original boxes, will bring only a fraction of that spectacular price.

Some limited-edition series dolls from the last 10 years are worthy of note since they have shown some appreciation in value. For example, the Harley-Davidson series of Barbie and Ken dolls has consistently held its value or increased over the past five years. The 100th anniversary of Harley-Davidson in 2003 may only serve to make the series even more desirable.

Bob Mackie designer dolls, known for their high-quality, quintessentially beautiful gowns, have remained collector favorites for more than 10 years.

Also in tune with Age of Aquarius, Live Action Barbie from 1970. $150 MIP.

Collector Alert: Not every doll in a series is a winner in collectors' eyes and not every series will maintain its popularity.

Tips for Collecting

Although many Barbie dolls do increase in value, others do not. Here are some tips for smart collecting:

- **Avoid regular issue (also known as pink box) dolls.** These are the ones that generally retail for less than $15. These have limited investment potential. Buy them because you like

them, not because you expect them to increase in value.

- **Look for limited-edition exclusives.** Certain dolls are "exclusives" because they are made only for one retail outlet, like Target or FAO Schwarz. Many of these dolls have increased in value; others, however, show less success. Harley-Davidson Barbie, exclusive to Toys R Us, for example, was next to impossible to find in stores. Its secondary market prices immediately soared to $250 or more.

- **Look for dolls in the best possible condition**. Dolls in top condition command higher prices than dolls in poor condition. And watch for original boxes, apparel and even tiny accessories. They can all add value to a doll.

- **Don't be fooled by dates!** Barbie dolls have distinct markings on their buttocks, but be aware that the date on a doll is likely the date the doll's body style was copyrighted, NOT necessarily the date the doll was made. Therefore, dolls with a 1960s date may actually be made in the 1990s. Plenty of books exist with photos of dolls and

Harley-Davidson Barbie #4, released in 2000. $100 MIP.

markings, making it more accurate to identify your doll.

- **Don't overlook licensed Barbie products.** Mattel licenses the Barbie name to companies which make paper dolls, clothing, cases, watches, lunch boxes and other collectibles. Anything with the Barbie name is collectible but not necessarily valuable.

Looking Out for #1

To the non-collector, the first Ponytail Barbie dolls all look similar. There are, however, subtle and important differences. The first Barbie (1959), known to collectors as Ponytail Barbie #1, featured:

- holes in the bottom of the feet with copper tubes inside the legs
- zebra-stripe one-piece swimsuit
- blond or brunette hair with soft curly bangs
- red fingernails, toenails and lips
- gold hoop earrings
- white irises and severely pointed black eyebrows
- heavy, black facial paint
- pale, almost white, ivory skin tone
- body markings: Barbie T.M./ Pats.Pend./[copyright mark]MCM-LVIII/by/Mattel/Inc.

Barbie as Wonder Woman, 2000, was a clever cross-collecting idea. $50 MIP.

BARBIE

ACCESSORIES

COLORFORMS SETS

Barbie Sport Fashion, 1975, Colorforms
EX n/a   NM $4   MIP $8

Barbie's 3-D Fashion Theatre, 1970, Colorforms
EX n/a   NM $9   MIP $20

Dress-Up Kit New Living Barbie, 1970, Colorforms
EX n/a   NM $10   MIP $38

Malibu Barbie, 1972, Colorforms
EX n/a   NM $7   MIP $20

MISCELLANEOUS

Barbie & Ken Wipe Away Cloths, 1964
EX n/a   NM $100   MIP $280

Barbie and Ken Hangers, 1960s, SPP, plastic hangers in bag w/cardboard backing
EX n/a   NM $20   MIP $35

Barbie Beauty Kit, 1961, Roclar
EX n/a   NM $100   MIP $200

Barbie Bubble Bath, 1961, Roclar
EX n/a   NM $45   MIP $100

Barbie Carry-All Wallet, 1963, SPP
EX n/a   NM $145   MIP $255

Barbie Disco Record Player, 1976
EX n/a   NM $85   MIP $160

Barbie Dresser Accessories, 1962
EX n/a   NM $175   MIP $300

Barbie Ge-Tar, 1963, Mattel
EX n/a   NM $200   MIP $400

Barbie Hair Fair, 1966, Mattel
EX n/a   NM $75   MIP $145

Barbie Mattel-A-Phone, 1968
EX n/a   NM $75   MIP $140

Barbie Nurse Kit, 1962, Pressman, tin litho box
EX n/a   NM $100   MIP $275

Barbie Powder Mitt, 1961
EX n/a   NM $75   MIP $140

Barbie Pretty Up Time, 1960s, brush/comb/mirror set
EX n/a   NM $50   MIP $125

Barbie Record, 1965, Columbia Records
EX n/a   NM $70   MIP $120

Barbie Store Display, 1980, Mattel
EX n/a   NM $10   MIP $30

Barbie Wig Wardrobe, 1960s, Mattel, doll head w/three wigs
EX n/a   NM $75   MIP $150

Barbie, Ken, Midge Pencil Case, 1964, SPP
EX n/a   NM $100   MIP $260

Barbie's Dog Snowball, 1990s, Arco/Mattel
EX n/a   NM $20   MIP $35

Francie Electric Drawing Table, 1966
EX n/a   NM $65   MIP $130

Jack and Jill magazine advertisements, 1960s
EX n/a   NM $15   MIP $35

Jigsaw Puzzle, 1963-65, Whitman
EX n/a   NM $30   MIP $60

Jumbo Trading Cards, 1962, Dynamic, complete set
EX n/a   NM $225   MIP $365

Record Player, 1961, Emenee
EX n/a   NM $700   MIP $950

Record Tote, 1961, Ponytail, vinyl, several colors
EX n/a   NM $75   MIP $180

Vanity Fair Transistor Radio, 1962, Vanity Fair
EX n/a   NM $700   MIP $1350

Wine Set, 1986
EX n/a   NM $40   MIP $75

PAPER DOLLS

Barbie and Ken Cut-Outs, 1962, Whitman, pink cover, Model No. 1971
EX n/a   NM $50   MIP $135

Barbie and Ken Paper Dolls, 1970, Whitman, Model No. 1986
EX n/a   NM $35   MIP $60

Barbie and Skipper, 1964, Whitman, Model No. 1957
EX n/a   NM $50   MIP $125

Barbie Costume Dolls, 1964, Whitman, Model No. 1976
EX n/a   NM $60   MIP $125

Barbie Cut-Outs, 1962, Model No. 1963
EX n/a   NM $55   MIP $125

Barbie Doll Cut-Outs, 1963, Whitman, Model No. 1962
EX n/a   NM $45   MIP $95

Barbie Dolls and Clothes, 1969, Model No. 1976
EX n/a   NM $35   MIP $70

Barbie Has a New Look Paper Dolls, 1967, Whitman, Model No. 1996
EX n/a   NM $40   MIP $100

Barbie Paper Dolls, boxed, 1967, Whitman, Model No. 4701
EX n/a   NM $20   MIP $60

Barbie, Christie and Stacey, 1968, Whitman, Model No. 1978
EX n/a   NM $35   MIP $80

Barbie, Ken and Midge Paper Dolls, 1963, Whitman, Model No. 1976
EX n/a   NM $50   MIP $90

Barbie, Two Magic Dolls w/stay-on clothes, 1969, Model No. 4763
EX n/a   NM $30   MIP $70

Barbie's Travel Wardrobe, boxed, 1964, Model No. 4616
EX n/a   NM $50   MIP $125

Francie and Casey Paper Dolls, 1967, Whitman, Model No. 1986
EX n/a   NM $30   MIP $60

Francie Paper Dolls, 1967, Whitman, Model No. 1094
EX n/a   NM $40   MIP $80

Malibu Barbie Paper Dolls, 1972, Whitman, Model No. 1994
EX n/a   NM $20   MIP $45

Meet Francie Paper Dolls, 1966, Whitman, Model No. 1980
EX n/a   NM $35   MIP $80

Midge Cut-Outs, 1963, Whitman, Model No. 1962
EX n/a   NM $45   MIP $90

P.J. Cover Girl Paper Dolls, 1971, Whitman, Model No. 1981
EX n/a   NM $20   MIP $40

Skipper Paper Dolls, 1965, Whitman, Model No. 1984
EX n/a   NM $25   MIP $50

Skooter Paper Dolls, 1965, Whitman, Model No. 1985
EX n/a   NM $35   MIP $95

Tutti, boxed, 1967, Model No. 4622
EX n/a   NM $30   MIP $60

Twiggy Paper Dolls, 1967, Whitman, Model No. 1999
EX n/a   NM $25   MIP $48

STRUCTURES

Barbie and Ken Little Theatre, 1964, Mattel, Model No. 4090
EX n/a   NM $200   MIP $400

Barbie Café Today, 1971, Model No. 4973
EX n/a   NM $200   MIP $400

Barbie Fashion Stage, 1971, Mattel, Model No. 1148
EX n/a   NM $60   MIP $100

Barbie Goes to College, 1964, Mattel, Model No. 4093
EX n/a   NM $250   MIP $600

Barbie's Dream House, 1962, Mattel, Model No. 816
EX n/a   NM $125   MIP $300

Barbie's Dream Kitchen, 1965, Mattel, Model No. 4095
EX n/a   NM $300   MIP $500

Barbie's New Dream House, 1964, Mattel, Model No. 4092
EX n/a   NM $100   MIP $250

Fashion Shop, 1962, Mattel, Model No. 817
EX n/a   NM $200   MIP $550

Francie and Casey Studio House, 1967, Model No. 1026
EX n/a   NM $75   MIP $150

Francie House, 1966, Model No. 3302
EX n/a   NM $90   MIP $140

Jamie's Penthouse (Sears), 1971, Model No. 31122
EX n/a   NM $220   MIP $475

❏ **Quick Curl Boutique,** 1973, Model No. 8665
EX n/a   NM $40   MIP $80

❏ **Skipper's Dream Room,** 1965, Mattel, Model No. 4094
EX n/a   NM $300   MIP $575

❏ **Skipper's Schoolroom,** 1965, Mattel
EX n/a   NM $375   MIP $600

❏ **Tutti Ice Cream Stand,** 1967, Model No. 3363
EX n/a   NM $130   MIP $225

❏ **Tutti's and Todd's Playhouse,** 1966
EX n/a   NM $75   MIP $125

TIMEPIECES

❏ **Barbie Personal Photo Clock,** 1964, Bradley/Elgin
EX n/a   NM $520   MIP $675

❏ **Barbie Starbright Boudoir Clock,** 1964, Bradley/Elgin
EX n/a   NM $640   MIP $775

❏ **Broken Heart Wristwatch,** 1964, Bradley/Elgin
EX n/a   NM $325   MIP $425

❏ **Brokn' Heart Pendant,** 1965, Bradley/Elgin
EX n/a   NM $425   MIP $575

❏ **Curly Bangs Pendant,** 1963-64, Bradley/Elgin
EX n/a   NM $200   MIP $450

❏ **Curly Bangs Wristwatch,** 1963-64, Bradley/Elgin
EX n/a   NM $150   MIP $375

❏ **Midge Wristwatch,** 1964, Bradley/Elgin
EX n/a   NM $350   MIP $500

❏ **Skipper Wristwatch,** 1964, Bradley/Elgin
EX n/a   NM $350   MIP $500

❏ **Swirl Ponytail Wristwatch,** 1964, Bradley/Elgin
EX n/a   NM $175   MIP $350

VEHICLES

❏ **Allan's Mercedes Roadster,** 1964, Irwin, Model No. 5348
EX n/a   NM $150   MIP $575

❏ **Barbie and Ken and Midge Convertible,** 1964, Irwin
EX n/a   NM $125   MIP $200

❏ **Barbie's Airplane,** 1964, Irwin
EX n/a   NM $1000   MIP $3500

❏ **Barbie's Austin-Healey,** 1964, Irwin, lavender, Montgomery Wards Exclusive
EX n/a   NM $800   MIP $1000

❏ **Barbie's Austin-Healey Convertible,** 1962, Irwin, coral
EX n/a   NM $125   MIP $450

(KP Photo)

❏ **Barbie's Speedboat,** 1964, Irwin, Shown with Ken at the helm
EX n/a   NM $100   MIP $1800

❏ **Barbie's Sport Plane,** 1964, Irwin
EX n/a   NM $1800   MIP $3500

❏ **Ken's Hot Rod,** 1963, Irwin, blue
EX n/a   NM $175   MIP $350

❏ **Skipper's Speedboat,** 1965, Irwin
EX n/a   NM $1450   MIP $1850

❏ **Skipper's Sports Car,** 1965, Irwin
EX n/a   NM $175   MIP $400

VINYL CASES

❏ **Barbie & Francie Case,** 1967, SPP
EX n/a   NM $35   MIP $50

❏ **Barbie & Stacey Sleep & Keep Case,** 1969, Sears Exclusive, Model No. 5023
EX n/a   NM $75   MIP $100

❏ **Barbie Double Case,** 1961, Ponytail, various illustrations/colors
EX n/a   NM $15   MIP $30

❏ **Barbie Double Case,** 1963, SPP, various illustrations/colors
EX n/a   NM $12   MIP $25

❏ **Barbie Goes Travelin' Case,** 1965, SPP
EX n/a   NM $100   MIP $325

❏ **Barbie Single Case,** 1961, Ponytail, various illustrations/colors
EX n/a   NM $10   MIP $20

❏ **Barbie Single Case,** 1963, SPP, various illustrations/colors
EX n/a   NM $7   MIP $15

❏ **Barbie Train Case,** 1961, SPP
EX n/a   NM $45   MIP $70

❏ **Fashion Queen Case,** 1963, SPP
EX n/a   NM $75   MIP $150

❏ **Hatbox-Style Cases,** 1961, Mattel, assorted styles
EX n/a   NM $20   MIP $50

❏ **Ken Cases (U.S. versions),** 1961, Ponytail
EX n/a   NM $12   MIP $25

❏ **Midge Cases (U.S. versions),** 1963
EX n/a   NM $20   MIP $45

❏ **Miss Barbie Case,** 1964, SPP
EX n/a   NM $75   MIP $150

❏ **Skipper Cases (U.S. versions),** 1964
EX n/a   NM $12   MIP $25

DOLLS

BARBIE & FRIENDS

❏ **All American Barbie,** 1991, Mattel, Model No. 9423
EX n/a   NM $4   MIP $20

❏ **All American Christie,** 1991, Mattel, Model No. 9425
EX n/a   NM $4   MIP $25

❏ **All American Ken,** 1991, Mattel, Model No. 9424
EX n/a   NM $4   MIP $15

❏ **All American Kira,** 1991, Mattel, Model No. 9427
EX n/a   NM $4   MIP $20

❏ **All American Teresa,** 1991, Mattel, Model No. 9426
EX n/a   NM $4   MIP $30

❏ **All Star Ken,** 1981, Mattel, Model No. 3553
EX n/a   NM $7   MIP $25

❏ **All Stars Barbie,** 1989, Mattel, Model No. 9099
EX n/a   NM $5   MIP $25

❏ **All Stars Christie,** 1989, Mattel, Model No. 9352
EX n/a   NM $5   MIP $20

❏ **All Stars Ken,** 1989, Mattel, Model No. 9361
EX n/a   NM $5   MIP $20

❏ **All Stars Midge,** 1989, Mattel, Model No. 9360
EX n/a   NM $5   MIP $30

❏ **All Stars Teresa,** 1989, Mattel, Model No. 9353
EX n/a   NM $5   MIP $30

(KP Photo)

❏ **Allan, bendable leg,** 1965, Mattel, Model No. 1010
EX n/a   NM $150   MIP $300

BARBIE

❏ **Allan, straight leg,** 1964, Mattel, Model No. 1000
EX n/a   **NM** $55   **MIP** $125

❏ **American Beauties Mardi Gras Barbie,** 1988, Mattel, Model No. 4930
EX n/a   **NM** $35   **MIP** $75

❏ **American Beauty Queen,** 1991, Mattel, Model No. 3137
EX n/a   **NM** $5   **MIP** $45

❏ **American Beauty Queen, black,** 1991, Mattel, Model No. 3245
EX n/a   **NM** $5   **MIP** $35

❏ **Angel Face Barbie,** 1982, Mattel, Model No. 5640
EX n/a   **NM** $8   **MIP** $40

❏ **Animal Lovin' Barbie, black,** 1989, Mattel, Model No. 4828
EX n/a   **NM** $5   **MIP** $75

❏ **Animal Lovin' Barbie, white,** 1989, Mattel, Model No. 1350
EX n/a   **NM** $5   **MIP** $40

❏ **Animal Lovin' Ken,** 1989, Mattel, Model No. 1351
EX n/a   **NM** $5   **MIP** $20

❏ **Animal Lovin' Nikki,** 1989, Mattel, Model No. 1352
EX n/a   **NM** $7   **MIP** $20

❏ **Astronaut Barbie, black,** 1985, Mattel, Model No. 1207
EX n/a   **NM** $25   **MIP** $40

❏ **Astronaut Barbie, white,** 1985, Mattel, Model No. 2449
EX n/a   **NM** $25   **MIP** $65

❏ **Babysitter Courtney,** 1991, Mattel, Model No. 9434
EX n/a   **NM** $4   **MIP** $15

❏ **Babysitter Skipper,** 1991, Mattel, Model No. 9433
EX n/a   **NM** $4   **MIP** $15

❏ **Babysitter Skipper, black,** 1991, Mattel, Model No. 1599
EX n/a   **NM** $4   **MIP** $10

❏ **Baggie Casey, blond (sold in plastic bag),** 1975, Mattel, Model No. 9000
EX n/a   **NM** $100   **MIP** $250

❏ **Ballerina Barbie on Tour, gold, 1st version,** 1976, Mattel, Model No. 9613
EX n/a   **NM** $45   **MIP** $125

❏ **Ballerina Barbie, 1st version,** 1976, Mattel, Model No. 9093
EX n/a   **NM** $20   **MIP** $65

❏ **Ballerina Cara,** 1976, Mattel, Model No. 9528
EX n/a   **NM** $25   **MIP** $65

❏ **Barbie & Her Fashion Fireworks,** 1976, Mattel, Model No. 9805
EX n/a   **NM** $20   **MIP** $60

❏ **Barbie & the Beat,** 1990, Mattel, Model No. 3751
EX n/a   **NM** $5   **MIP** $30

❏ **Barbie & the Beat Christie,** 1990, Mattel, Model No. 2752
EX n/a   **NM** $5   **MIP** $20

❏ **Barbie & the Beat Midge,** 1990, Mattel, Model No. 2754
EX n/a   **NM** $6   **MIP** $20

❏ **Barbie Hair Happenings (department store exclusive, red hair),** 1971, Mattel, Model No. 1174
EX n/a   **NM** $400   **MIP** $850

(KP Photo)

❏ **Barbie with Growin' Pretty Hair,** 1971, Mattel, Model No. 1144
EX n/a   **NM** $175   **MIP** $350

❏ **Bathtime Fun Barbie,** 1991, Mattel, Model No. 9601
EX n/a   **NM** $3   **MIP** $20

❏ **Bathtime Fun Barbie, black,** 1991, Mattel, Model No. 9603
EX n/a   **NM** $3   **MIP** $15

❏ **Beach Blast Barbie,** 1989, Mattel, Model No. 3237
EX n/a   **NM** $3   **MIP** $20

❏ **Beach Blast Christie,** 1989, Mattel, Model No. 3253
EX n/a   **NM** $4   **MIP** $15

❏ **Beach Blast Ken,** 1989, Mattel, Model No. 3238
EX n/a   **NM** $4   **MIP** $15

❏ **Beach Blast Miko,** 1989, Mattel, Model No. 3244
EX n/a   **NM** $4   **MIP** $15

❏ **Beach Blast Skipper,** 1989, Mattel, Model No. 3242
EX n/a   **NM** $4   **MIP** $15

❏ **Beach Blast Steven,** 1989, Mattel, Model No. 3251
EX n/a   **NM** $4   **MIP** $15

❏ **Beach Blast Teresa,** 1989, Mattel, Model No. 3249
EX n/a   **NM** $5   **MIP** $15

❏ **Beautiful Bride Barbie,** 1978, Mattel, Model No. 9907
EX n/a   **NM** $60   **MIP** $125

❏ **Beauty Secrets Barbie, 1st issue,** 1980, Mattel, Model No. 1290
EX n/a   **NM** $12   **MIP** $65

❏ **Beauty Secrets Christie,** 1980, Mattel, Model No. 1295
EX n/a   **NM** $12   **MIP** $65

❏ **Beauty, Barbie's Dog,** 1979, Mattel, Model No. 1018
EX n/a   **NM** $12   **MIP** $30

(KP Photo)

❏ **Bendable Leg "American Girl" Barbie, short hair,** 1965, Mattel, Model No. 1070
EX n/a   **NM** $500   **MIP** $1200

❏ **Bendable Leg "American Girl" Barbie, Color Magic Face,** 1966, Mattel, Model No. 1070
EX n/a   **NM** $850   **MIP** $1700

❏ **Bendable Leg "American Girl" Barbie, long hair,** 1965, Mattel, Model No. 1070
EX n/a   **NM** $850   **MIP** $1800

❏ **Bendable Leg "American Girl" Barbie, side-part long hair,** 1966, Mattel, Model No. 1070
EX n/a   **NM** $1700   **MIP** $2500

❏ **Bendable Leg "American Girl" Barbie, Swirl Ponytail or Bubblecut hairstyle,** 1965, Mattel, Model No. 1070
EX n/a   **NM** $1000   **MIP** $2800

❏ **Benetton Barbie,** 1991, Mattel, Model No. 9404
EX n/a   **NM** $10   **MIP** $45

❏ **Benetton Christie,** 1991, Mattel, Model No. 9407
EX n/a   **NM** $10   **MIP** $35

❏ **Benetton Marina,** 1991, Mattel, Model No. 9409
EX n/a   **NM** $10   **MIP** $35

(KP Photo)

❏ **Black Barbie,** 1980, Mattel, Model No. 1293
   EX n/a   **NM** $40   **MIP** $100

(KP Photo)

❏ **Brad, bendable leg,** 1970, Mattel, Model No. 1142
   EX n/a   **NM** $75   **MIP** $200

❏ **Brad, talking,** 1970, Mattel, Model No. 1114
   EX n/a   **NM** $65   **MIP** $200

❏ **Bubblecut Barbie Sidepart, all hair colors,** 1961, Mattel, Model No. 850
   EX n/a   **NM** $425   **MIP** $900

❏ **Bubblecut Barbie, blond, brunette, titian,** 1962, Mattel, Model No. 850
   EX n/a   **NM** $100   **MIP** $250

(KP Photo)

❏ **Bubblecut Barbie, brownette,** 1961, Mattel, Model No. 850
   EX n/a   **NM** $600   **MIP** $1000

❏ **Bubblecut Barbie, white ginger,** 1962, Mattel, Model No. 850
   EX n/a   **NM** $300   **MIP** $750

❏ **Busy Barbie,** 1971, Mattel, Model No. 3311
   EX n/a   **NM** $100   **MIP** $250

(KP Photo)

❏ **Busy Francie,** 1971, Mattel, Model No. 3313
   EX n/a   **NM** $175   **MIP** $375

(KP Photo)

❏ **Busy Ken,** 1971, Mattel, Model No. 3314
   EX n/a   **NM** $60   **MIP** $165

(KP Photo)

❏ **Busy Steffie,** 1971, Mattel, Model No. 3312
   EX n/a   **NM** $125   **MIP** $275

❏ **Calgary Olympic Skating Barbie,** 1987, Mattel, Model No. 4547
   EX n/a   **NM** $25   **MIP** $60

❏ **California Dream Barbie,** 1988, Mattel, Model No. 4439
   EX n/a   **NM** $5   **MIP** $20

❏ **California Dream Christie,** 1988, Mattel, Model No. 4443
   EX n/a   **NM** $6   **MIP** $15

BARBIE

❑ **California Dream Ken,** 1988, Mattel,
Model No. 4441
EX n/a   NM $8   MIP $15

❑ **California Dream Midge,** 1988, Mattel,
Model No. 4442
EX n/a   NM $3   MIP $15

❑ **California Dream Skipper,** 1988, Mattel, Model No. 4440
EX n/a   NM $13   MIP $20

❑ **California Dream Teresa,** 1988, Mattel,
Model No. 4403
EX n/a   NM $15   MIP $20

❑ **Carla, European exclusive,** 1976, Mattel, Model No. 7377
EX n/a   NM $65   MIP $140

❑ **Casey, Twist and Turn,** 1967, Mattel,
Model No. 1180
EX n/a   NM $100   MIP $300

❑ **Chris, titian, blond, brunette (Tutti's friend),** 1967, Mattel, Model No. 3570
EX n/a   NM $65   MIP $200

(KP Photo)

❑ **Christie, talking,** 1970, Mattel, Model
No. 1126
EX n/a   NM $100   MIP $250

❑ **Christie, Twist N Turn,** 1970, Mattel,
Model No. 1119
EX n/a   NM $125   MIP $350

❑ **Coach Ken & Tommy, white or black,** 2000, Mattel
EX n/a   NM $7   MIP $15

(KP Photo)

❑ **Color Magic Barbie, Golden Blonde,** 1966, Mattel, Model No. 1150
EX n/a   NM $450   MIP $1700

❑ **Color Magic Barbie, Midnight Black,** 1966, Mattel, Model No. 1150
EX n/a   NM $1300   MIP $3500

❑ **Cool City Blues: Barbie, Ken, Skipper,** 1989, Mattel, Model No. 4893
EX n/a   NM $20   MIP $45

❑ **Cool Shavin' Ken,** 1996, Mattel, Model
No. 15469
EX n/a   NM $10   MIP $15

❑ **Cool Times Barbie,** 1989, Mattel,
Model No. 3022
EX n/a   NM $5   MIP $25

❑ **Cool Times Christie,** 1989, Mattel,
Model No. 3217
EX n/a   NM $5   MIP $20

❑ **Cool Times Ken,** 1989, Mattel, Model
No. 3219
EX n/a   NM $5   MIP $20

❑ **Cool Times Midge,** 1989, Mattel, Model
No. 3216
EX n/a   NM $7   MIP $20

❑ **Cool Times Teresa,** 1989, Mattel,
Model No. 3218
EX n/a   NM $9   MIP $20

❑ **Cool Tops Courtney,** 1989, Mattel,
Model No. 7079
EX n/a   NM $7   MIP $20

❑ **Cool Tops Kevin,** 1989, Mattel, Model
No. 9351
EX n/a   NM $5   MIP $20

❑ **Cool Tops Skipper, black,** 1989, Mattel,
Model No. 5441
EX n/a   NM $5   MIP $15

❑ **Cool Tops Skipper, white,** 1989, Mattel, Model No. 4989
EX n/a   NM $7   MIP $15

❑ **Corduroy Cool Barbie,** 2000, Mattel,
Model No. 24658
EX n/a   NM $5   MIP $10

❑ **Costume Ball Barbie, black,** 1991,
Mattel, Model No. 7134
EX n/a   NM $6   MIP $15

❑ **Costume Ball Barbie, white,** 1991,
Mattel, Model No. 7123
EX n/a   NM $6   MIP $25

❑ **Costume Ball Ken, black,** 1991, Mattel,
Model No. 7160
EX n/a   NM $6   MIP $20

❑ **Costume Ball Ken, white,** 1991, Mattel,
Model No. 7154
EX n/a   NM $6   MIP $30

❑ **Crystal Barbie, black,** 1984, Mattel,
Model No. 4859
EX n/a   NM $10   MIP $25

❑ **Crystal Barbie, white,** 1984, Mattel,
Model No. 4598
EX n/a   NM $10   MIP $35

❑ **Crystal Ken, black,** 1983, Mattel, Model
No. 9036
EX n/a   NM $15   MIP $25

❑ **Crystal Ken, white,** 1983, Mattel, Model
No. 4898
EX n/a   NM $8   MIP $30

❑ **Dance Club Barbie,** 1989, Mattel,
Model No. 3509
EX n/a   NM $5   MIP $45

❑ **Dance Club Devon,** 1989, Mattel, Model
No. 3513
EX n/a   NM $5   MIP $40

❑ **Dance Club Kayla,** 1989, Mattel, Model
No. 3512
EX n/a   NM $5   MIP $85

❑ **Dance Club Ken,** 1989, Mattel, Model
No. 3511
EX n/a   NM $5   MIP $40

❑ **Dance Magic Barbie,** 1990, Mattel,
Model No. 4836
EX n/a   NM $7   MIP $25

❑ **Dance Magic Barbie, black,** 1990, Mattel, Model No. 7080
EX n/a   NM $7   MIP $25

❑ **Dance Magic Ken,** 1990, Mattel, Model
No. 7081
EX n/a   NM $6   MIP $20

❑ **Dance Magic Ken, black,** 1990, Mattel,
Model No. 7082
EX n/a   NM $6   MIP $20

❑ **Day-to-Night Barbie, black,** 1985, Mattel, Model No. 7945
EX n/a   NM $10   MIP $35

❑ **Day-to-Night Barbie, Hispanic,** 1985,
Mattel, Model No. 7944
EX n/a   NM $17   MIP $40

❑ **Day-to-Night Barbie, white,** 1985, Mattel, Model No. 7929
EX n/a   NM $10   MIP $40

(KP Photo)

❏ **Day-to-Night Ken, black,** 1984, Mattel, Model No. 9018
EX n/a   NM $8   MIP $20

❏ **Day-to-Night Ken, white,** 1984, Mattel, Model No. 9019
EX n/a   NM $8   MIP $25

❏ **Dentist Barbie,** 1997, Mattel, Model No. 17255
EX n/a   NM $15   MIP $30

❏ **Doctor Barbie,** 1988, Mattel, Model No. 3850
EX n/a   NM $8   MIP $45

❏ **Doctor Ken,** 1988, Mattel, Model No. 4118
EX n/a   NM $5   MIP $40

(Mattel Photo)

❏ **Dolls of the World Princess of China,** 2002, Mattel, Model No. 53368
EX n/a   NM $10   MIP $20

❏ **Dolls of the World Princess of India,** 2000, Mattel, Model No. 28374
EX n/a   NM $8   MIP $20

❏ **Dolls of the World Princess of Ireland,** 2002, Mattel, Model No. 53367
EX n/a   NM $10   MIP $20

(Mattel Photo)

❏ **Dolls of the World Princess of South Africa,** 2003, Mattel, Model No. 56218
EX n/a   NM $10   MIP $20

❏ **Dolls of the World Princess of the Danish Court,** 2003, Mattel, Model No. 56216
EX n/a   NM $10   MIP $20

❏ **Dolls of the World Princess of the French Court,** 2000, Mattel, Model No. 28372
EX n/a   NM $8   MIP $20

❏ **Dolls of the World Princess of the Incas,** 2000, Mattel, Model No. 28373
EX n/a   NM $8   MIP $20

(Mattel Photo)

❏ **Dolls of the World Princess of the Nile,** 2002, Mattel, Model No. 53369
EX n/a   NM $10   MIP $20

❏ **Dolls of the World Princess of the Portuguese Empire,** 2003, Mattel, Model No. 56217
EX n/a   NM $10   MIP $20

❏ **Dolls of the World/International Arctic,** 1997, Mattel, Model No. 16495
EX n/a   NM $20   MIP $30

❏ **Dolls of the World/International Australian, two box variations,** 1993, Mattel, Model No. 3626
EX n/a   NM $10   MIP $35

❏ **Dolls of the World/International Austrian,** 1999, Mattel, Model No. 21553
EX n/a   NM $15   MIP $25

❏ **Dolls of the World/International Brazilian,** 1990, Mattel, Model No. 9094
EX n/a   NM $15   MIP $60

❏ **Dolls of the World/International Canadian,** 1988, Mattel, Model No. 4928
EX n/a   NM $15   MIP $75

❏ **Dolls of the World/International Chilean,** 1998, Mattel, Model No. 18559
EX n/a   NM $10   MIP $20

❏ **Dolls of the World/International Chinese,** 1994, Mattel, Model No. 11180
EX n/a   NM $10   MIP $30

❏ **Dolls of the World/International Czechoslovakian,** 1991, Mattel, Model No. 7330
EX n/a   NM $30   MIP $110

❏ **Dolls of the World/International Dutch,** 1994, Mattel, Model No. 11104
EX n/a   NM $10   MIP $35

❏ **Dolls of the World/International English,** 1992, Mattel, Model No. 4973
EX n/a   NM $12   MIP $80

❏ **Dolls of the World/International Eskimo,** 1982, Mattel, Model No. 3898
EX n/a   NM $30   MIP $100

❏ **Dolls of the World/International Eskimo,** 1991, Mattel, Model No. 9844
EX n/a   NM $8   MIP $60

❏ **Dolls of the World/International French,** 1997, Mattel, Model No. 16499
EX n/a   NM $10   MIP $25

❏ **Dolls of the World/International German,** 1987, Mattel, Model No. 3188
EX n/a   NM $45   MIP $100

❏ **Dolls of the World/International German,** 1995, Mattel, Model No. 12598
EX n/a   NM $10   MIP $25

❏ **Dolls of the World/International Ghanaian,** 1996, Mattel, Model No. 15303
EX n/a   NM $15   MIP $25

❏ **Dolls of the World/International Gift Set (Chinese, Dutch, Kenyan),** 1994, Mattel, Model No. 12043
EX n/a   NM $30   MIP $70

❏ **Dolls of the World/International Gift Set (Irish, German, Polynesian),** 1995, Mattel, Model No. 13939
EX n/a   NM $30   MIP $65

❏ **Dolls of the World/International Gift Set (Japanese, Indian, Norwegian),** 1996, Mattel, Model No. 15283
EX n/a   NM $30   MIP $60

❏ **Dolls of the World/International Greek,** 1986, Mattel, Model No. 2997
EX n/a   NM $30   MIP $80

❏ **Dolls of the World/International Iceland,** 1987, Mattel, Model No. 3189
EX n/a   NM $30   MIP $100

❏ **Dolls of the World/International Indian,** 1982, Mattel, Model No. 3897
EX n/a   NM $50   MIP $75

❑ **Dolls of the World/International Indian,** 1995, Mattel, Model No. 14451
EX n/a NM $12 MIP $25

❑ **Dolls of the World/International Jamaican, silver earrings,** 1992, Mattel, Model No. 4647
EX n/a NM $12 MIP $55

❑ **Dolls of the World/International Malaysian,** 1991, Mattel, Model No. 7329
EX n/a NM $10 MIP $50

❑ **Dolls of the World/International Mexican,** 1989, Mattel, Model No. 1917
EX n/a NM $15 MIP $50

❑ **Dolls of the World/International Mexican,** 1995, Mattel, Model No. 14449
EX n/a NM $10 MIP $20

❑ **Dolls of the World/International Moroccan,** 1999, Mattel, Model No. 21507
EX n/a NM $15 MIP $25

❑ **Dolls of the World/International Native American #1, two box versions,** 1993, Mattel, Model No. 1753
EX n/a NM $12 MIP $35

❑ **Dolls of the World/International Native American #2,** 1994, Mattel, Model No. 11609
EX n/a NM $10 MIP $35

❑ **Dolls of the World/International Native American #3,** 1995, Mattel, Model No. 12699
EX n/a NM $10 MIP $30

(KP Photo)

(KP Photo)

❑ **Dolls of the World/International Irish,** 1984, Mattel, Model No. 7517
EX n/a NM $45 MIP $95

❑ **Dolls of the World/International Irish,** 1995, Mattel, Model No. 12998
EX n/a NM $10 MIP $40

❑ **Dolls of the World/International Japanese,** 1984, Mattel, Model No. 9481
EX n/a NM $55 MIP $90

❑ **Dolls of the World/International Japanese,** 1996, Mattel, Model No. 14163
EX n/a NM $10 MIP $20

(KP Photo)

❑ **Dolls of the World/International Nigerian,** 1990, Mattel, Model No. 7376
EX n/a NM $15 MIP $50

❑ **Dolls of the World/International Norwegian, pink flowers, limited to 3,000,** 1996, Mattel, Model No. 14450
EX n/a NM $12 MIP $65

❑ **Dolls of the World/International NW Coast Native American Barbie,** 2000, Mattel, Model No. 24671
EX n/a NM $12 MIP $25

❑ **Dolls of the World/International Oriental,** 1981, Mattel, Model No. 3262
EX n/a NM $55 MIP $95

❑ **Dolls of the World/International Parisian,** 1980, Mattel, Model No. 1600
EX n/a NM $50 MIP $95

(KP Photo)

(KP Photo)

❑ **Dolls of the World/International Italian,** 1980, Mattel, Model No. 1601
EX n/a NM $65 MIP $175

❑ **Dolls of the World/International Italian,** 1993, Mattel, Model No. 2256
EX n/a NM $10 MIP $50

❑ **Dolls of the World/International Kenyan,** 1994, Mattel, Model No. 11181
EX n/a NM $10 MIP $35

❑ **Dolls of the World/International Korean,** 1988, Mattel, Model No. 4929
EX n/a NM $15 MIP $75

❑ **Dolls of the World/International Parisian,** 1991, Mattel, Model No. 9843
EX n/a   **NM** $8   **MIP** $60

❑ **Dolls of the World/International Peruvian,** 1986, Mattel, Model No. 2995
EX n/a   **NM** $30   **MIP** $75

❑ **Dolls of the World/International Peruvian,** 1999, Mattel, Model No. 21506
EX n/a   **NM** $15   **MIP** $25

❑ **Dolls of the World/International Polish,** 1998, Mattel, Model No. 18560
EX n/a   **NM** $15   **MIP** $25

❑ **Dolls of the World/International Polynesian,** 1995, Mattel, Model No. 12700
EX n/a   **NM** $10   **MIP** $30

❑ **Dolls of the World/International Puerto Rican,** 1997, Mattel, Model No. 16754
EX n/a   **NM** $15   **MIP** $25

(KP Photo)

❑ **Dolls of the World/International Royal,** 1980, Mattel, Model No. 1602
EX n/a   **NM** $65   **MIP** $125

❑ **Dolls of the World/International Russian,** 1989, Mattel, Model No. 1916
EX n/a   **NM** $20   **MIP** $25

❑ **Dolls of the World/International Russian,** 1997, Mattel, Model No. 16500
EX n/a   **NM** $20   **MIP** $75

❑ **Dolls of the World/International Scottish,** 1981, Mattel, Model No. 3263
EX n/a   **NM** $50   **MIP** $110

❑ **Dolls of the World/International Scottish,** 1991, Mattel, Model No. 9845
EX n/a   **NM** $8   **MIP** $60

❑ **Dolls of the World/International Spanish,** 1983, Mattel, Model No. 4031
EX n/a   **NM** $40   **MIP** $75

❑ **Dolls of the World/International Spanish,** 1992, Mattel, Model No. 4963
EX n/a   **NM** $12   **MIP** $45

❑ **Dolls of the World/International Spanish,** 2000, Mattel, Model No. 24670
EX n/a   **NM** $12   **MIP** $25

❑ **Dolls of the World/International Swedish,** 1983, Mattel, Model No. 4032
EX n/a   **NM** $35   **MIP** $95

❑ **Dolls of the World/International Swedish,** 2000, Mattel, Model No. 24672
EX n/a   **NM** $12   **MIP** $25

❑ **Dolls of the World/International Swiss,** 1984, Mattel, Model No. 7451
EX n/a   **NM** $35   **MIP** $100

❑ **Dolls of the World/International Thai,** 1998, Mattel, Model No. 18561
EX n/a   **NM** $10   **MIP** $20

❑ **Dramatic New Living Barbie,** 1970, Mattel, Model No. 1116
EX n/a   **NM** $65   **MIP** $225

❑ **Dramatic New Living Skipper,** 1970, Mattel, Model No. 1117
EX n/a   **NM** $50   **MIP** $150

❑ **Dream Bride,** 1992, Mattel, Model No. 1623
EX n/a   **NM** $10   **MIP** $40

❑ **Dream Date Barbie,** 1983, Mattel, Model No. 5868
EX n/a   **NM** $10   **MIP** $25

❑ **Dream Date Ken,** 1983, Mattel, Model No. 4077
EX n/a   **NM** $10   **MIP** $25

❑ **Dream Glow Barbie, black,** 1986, Mattel, Model No. 2242
EX n/a   **NM** $12   **MIP** $25

❑ **Dream Glow Barbie, Hispanic,** 1986, Mattel, Model No. 1647
EX n/a   **NM** $25   **MIP** $50

❑ **Dream Glow Barbie, white,** 1986, Mattel, Model No. 2248
EX n/a   **NM** $12   **MIP** $45

❑ **Dream Glow Ken, black,** 1986, Mattel, Model No. 2421
EX n/a   **NM** $13   **MIP** $20

❑ **Dream Glow Ken, white,** 1986, Mattel, Model No. 2250
EX n/a   **NM** $13   **MIP** $15

❑ **Dream Time Barbie, pink,** 1985, Mattel, Model No. 9180
EX n/a   **NM** $10   **MIP** $25

❑ **Earring Magic Barbie, blond,** 1993, Mattel, Model No. 7014
EX n/a   **NM** $15   **MIP** $25

(KP Photo)

❑ **Earring Magic Ken,** 1993, Mattel, Model No. 2290
EX n/a   **NM** $15   **MIP** $40

❑ **Fabulous Fur Barbie,** 1983, Mattel, Model No. 7093
EX n/a   **NM** $20   **MIP** $65

❑ **Fashion Jeans Barbie,** 1981, Mattel, Model No. 5313
EX n/a   **NM** $15   **MIP** $65

❑ **Fashion Jeans Ken,** 1982, Mattel, Model No. 5316
EX n/a   **NM** $12   **MIP** $25

❑ **Fashion Photo Barbie, two versions,** 1978, Mattel, Model No. 2210
EX n/a   **NM** $20   **MIP** $75

❑ **Fashion Photo Christie,** 1978, Mattel, Model No. 2324
EX n/a   **NM** $20   **MIP** $75

❑ **Fashion Photo P.J.,** 1978, Mattel, Model No. 2323
EX n/a   **NM** $35   **MIP** $85

❑ **Fashion Play Barbie,** 1983, Mattel, Model No. 7193
EX n/a   **NM** $10   **MIP** $30

❑ **Fashion Play Barbie,** 1987, Mattel, Model No. 4835
EX n/a   **NM** $10   **MIP** $25

❑ **Fashion Play Barbie,** 1990, Mattel, Model No. 9429
EX n/a   **NM** $2   **MIP** $30

❑ **Fashion Play Barbie,** 1991, Mattel, Model No. 9629
EX n/a   **NM** $2   **MIP** $20

❑ **Fashion Play Barbie, black,** 1991, Mattel, Model No. 5953
EX n/a   **NM** $2   **MIP** $15

❑ **Fashion Play Barbie, Hispanic,** 1990, Mattel, Model No. 5954
EX n/a   **NM** $2   **MIP** $15

BARBIE

❑ **Fashion Queen Barbie,** 1963, Mattel, Model No. 870
EX n/a   NM $120   MIP $350

❑ **Feelin' Fun Barbie, two versions, white, 1st issue,** 1988, Mattel, Model No. 1189
EX n/a   NM $5   MIP $20

❑ **Flight Time Barbie, black,** 1990, Mattel, Model No. 9916
EX n/a   NM $5   MIP $20

❑ **Flight Time Barbie, white,** 1990, Mattel, Model No. 9584
EX n/a   NM $5   MIP $30

❑ **Flight Time Ken,** 1990, Mattel, Model No. 9600
EX n/a   NM $5   MIP $20

❑ **Fluff,** 1971, Mattel, Model No. 1143
EX n/a   NM $100   MIP $210

❑ **Francie with Growin' Pretty Hair,** 1971, Mattel, Model No. 1129
EX n/a   NM $75   MIP $200

❑ **Francie, bendable leg, blond, brunette,** 1966, Mattel, Model No. 1130
EX n/a   NM $95   MIP $350

❑ **Francie, Hair Happenins,** 1970, Mattel, Model No. 1122
EX n/a   NM $95   MIP $400

(KP Photo)

❑ **Francie, straight leg, brunette, blond,** 1966, Mattel, Model No. 1140
EX n/a   NM $95   MIP $400

❑ **Francie, Twist N Turn, "Black Francie" 1st issue, red hair,** 1967, Mattel, Model No. 1100
EX n/a   NM $750   MIP $1200

❑ **Francie, Twist N Turn, "Black Francie" 2nd issue, black hair,** Mattel, Model No. 1100
EX n/a   NM $900   MIP $1600

(KP Photo)

❑ **Francie, Twist N Turn, blond or brunette, "No Bangs",** 1967, Mattel, Model No. 1170
EX n/a   NM $650   MIP $1200

❑ **Francie, Twist N Turn, blond or brunette, long hair with bangs,** 1969, Mattel, Model No. 1170
EX n/a   NM $95   MIP $450

❑ **Francie, Twist N Turn, blond or brunette, short hair,** 1969, Mattel, Model No. 1170
EX n/a   NM $95   MIP $500

(KP Photo)

❑ **Free Moving Barbie,** 1974, Mattel, Model No. 7270
EX n/a   NM $50   MIP $100

❑ **Free Moving Cara,** 1974, Mattel, Model No. 7283
EX n/a   NM $65   MIP $125

❑ **Free Moving Ken,** 1974, Mattel, Model No. 7280
EX n/a   NM $50   MIP $75

❑ **Free Moving P.J.,** 1974, Mattel, Model No. 7281
EX n/a   NM $50   MIP $85

❑ **Funtime Barbie, black,** 1987, Mattel, Model No. 1739
EX n/a   NM $5   MIP $25

❑ **Funtime Barbie, white,** 1987, Mattel, Model No. 1738
EX n/a   NM $5   MIP $25

❑ **Funtime Ken,** 1987, Mattel, Model No. 7194
EX n/a   NM $7   MIP $20

❑ **Garden Party Barbie,** 1989, Mattel, Model No. 1953
EX n/a   NM $8   MIP $18

❑ **Gift Giving Barbie,** 1986, Mattel, Model No. 1922
EX n/a   NM $5   MIP $30

❑ **Gift Giving Barbie,** 1989, Mattel, Model No. 1205
EX n/a   NM $5   MIP $30

❑ **Gold Medal Olympic Barbie Skater,** 1975, Mattel, Model No. 7262
EX n/a   NM $20   MIP $75

❑ **Gold Medal Olympic Barbie Skier,** 1975, Mattel, Model No. 7264
EX n/a   NM $20   MIP $75

❑ **Gold Medal Olympic P.J. Gymnast,** 1975, Mattel, Model No. 7263
EX n/a   NM $20   MIP $85

❑ **Gold Medal Olympic Skier Ken,** 1975, Mattel, Model No. 7261
EX n/a   NM $20   MIP $65

❑ **Gold Medal Olympic Skipper,** 1975, Mattel, Model No. 7274
EX n/a   NM $20   MIP $65

❑ **Golden Dreams Barbie, two versions,** 1981, Mattel, Model No. 1974
EX n/a   NM $15   MIP $50

❏ **Golden Dreams Christie,** 1981, Mattel, Model No. 3249
EX n/a   NM $15   MIP $50

❏ **Great Shapes Barbie, black,** 1984, Mattel, Model No. 7834
EX n/a   NM $5   MIP $25

❏ **Great Shapes Barbie, w/Walkman,** 1984, Mattel, Model No. 7025
EX n/a   NM $12   MIP $40

❏ **Great Shapes Barbie, white,** 1984, Mattel, Model No. 7025
EX n/a   NM $5   MIP $35

❏ **Great Shapes Ken,** 1984, Mattel, Model No. 7310
EX n/a   NM $5   MIP $25

❏ **Great Shapes Skipper,** 1984, Mattel, Model No. 7417
EX n/a   NM $5   MIP $25

❏ **Groom Todd,** 1982, Mattel, Model No. 4253
EX n/a   NM $15   MIP $45

❏ **Growin' Pretty Hair Barbie,** 1971, Mattel, Model No. 1144
EX n/a   NM $150   MIP $350

❏ **Growing Up Ginger,** 1977, Mattel, Model No. 9222
EX n/a   NM $30   MIP $140

(KP Photo)

❏ **Growing Up Skipper,** 1977, Mattel, Model No. 7259
EX n/a   NM $30   MIP $150

❏ **Happy Birthday Barbie,** 1981, Mattel, Model No. 1922
EX n/a   NM $8   MIP $45

❏ **Happy Birthday Barbie,** 1984, Mattel, Model No. 1922
EX n/a   NM $8   MIP $35

❏ **Happy Birthday Barbie,** 1991, Mattel, Model No. 9561
EX n/a   NM $8   MIP $20

❏ **Happy Birthday Barbie, black,** 1991, Mattel, Model No. 9561
EX n/a   NM $8   MIP $30

❏ **Hawaiian Barbie,** 1975, Mattel, Model No. 7470
EX n/a   NM $25   MIP $68

❏ **Hawaiian Barbie,** 1977, Mattel, Model No. 7470
EX n/a   NM $30   MIP $80

❏ **Hawaiian Fun Barbie,** 1991, Mattel, Model No. 5040
EX n/a   NM $3   MIP $20

❏ **Hawaiian Fun Christie,** 1991, Mattel, Model No. 5044
EX n/a   NM $3   MIP $20

❏ **Hawaiian Fun Jazzie,** 1991, Mattel, Model No. 9294
EX n/a   NM $3   MIP $20

❏ **Hawaiian Fun Ken,** 1991, Mattel, Model No. 5041
EX n/a   NM $3   MIP $15

❏ **Hawaiian Fun Kira,** 1991, Mattel, Model No. 5043
EX n/a   NM $3   MIP $15

❏ **Hawaiian Fun Skipper,** 1991, Mattel, Model No. 5042
EX n/a   NM $3   MIP $15

❏ **Hawaiian Fun Steven,** 1991, Mattel, Model No. 5045
EX n/a   NM $3   MIP $15

❏ **Hawaiian Ken,** 1979, Mattel, Model No. 2960
EX n/a   NM $13   MIP $50

❏ **Hawaiian Ken,** 1984, Mattel, Model No. 7495
EX n/a   NM $7   MIP $30

❏ **High School Chelsie,** 1989, Mattel, Model No. 3698
EX n/a   NM $5   MIP $20

❏ **High School Dude, Jazzie's boyfriend,** 1989, Mattel, Model No. 3600
EX n/a   NM $5   MIP $20

❏ **High School Jazzie,** 1989, Mattel, Model No. 3635
EX n/a   NM $5   MIP $20

❏ **High School Stacie,** 1989, Mattel, Model No. 3636
EX n/a   NM $5   MIP $20

(KP Photo)

❏ **Hispanic Barbie,** 1980, Mattel, Model No. 1292
EX n/a   NM $15   MIP $75

❏ **Hollywood Nails Barbie, white or black,** 1999, Mattel
EX n/a   NM $7   MIP $15

❏ **Hollywood Nails Teresa, white or black,** 1999, Mattel
EX n/a   NM $7   MIP $15

❏ **Home Pretty Barbie,** 1990, Mattel, Model No. 2249
EX n/a   NM $8   MIP $18

❏ **Homecoming Queen Skipper, black,** 1988, Mattel, Model No. 2390
EX n/a   NM $8   MIP $20

❏ **Homecoming Queen Skipper, white,** 1988, Mattel, Model No. 1952
EX n/a   NM $12   MIP $25

❏ **Horse Lovin' Barbie,** 1983, Mattel, Model No. 1757
EX n/a   NM $10   MIP $40

❏ **Horse Lovin' Ken,** 1983, Mattel, Model No. 3600
EX n/a   NM $8   MIP $25

❏ **Horse Lovin' Skipper,** 1983, Mattel, Model No. 5029
EX n/a   NM $8   MIP $25

❏ **Hot Stuff Skipper,** 1984, Mattel, Model No. 7927
EX n/a   NM $5   MIP $18

❏ **Ice Capades Barbie, 50th Anniversary, black,** 1990, Mattel, Model No. 7348
EX n/a   NM $5   MIP $25

❏ **Ice Capades Barbie, 50th Anniversary, white,** 1990, Mattel, Model No. 7365
EX n/a   NM $5   MIP $35

❏ **Ice Capades Ken,** 1990, Mattel, Model No. 7375
EX n/a   NM $5   MIP $25

❏ **Inline Skating Barbie,** 1996, Mattel, Model No. 15473
EX n/a   NM $5   MIP $25

❏ **Inline Skating Ken,** 1996, Mattel, Model No. 15474
EX n/a   NM $5   MIP $25

❏ **Inline Skating Midge,** 1996, Mattel, Model No. 15475
EX n/a   NM $5   MIP $25

❏ **Island Fun Barbie,** 1988, Mattel, Model No. 4061
EX n/a   NM $3   MIP $20

❏ **Island Fun Christie,** 1988, Mattel, Model No. 4092
EX n/a   NM $3   MIP $20

❏ **Island Fun Ken,** 1988, Mattel, Model No. 4060
EX n/a   NM $3   MIP $15

❏ **Island Fun Skipper,** 1988, Mattel, Model No. 4064
EX n/a   NM $3   MIP $15

❏ **Island Fun Steven,** 1988, Mattel, Model No. 4093
EX n/a   NM $3   MIP $15

BARBIE

Island Fun Teresa, 1988, Mattel, Model No. 4117
EX n/a   NM $3   MIP $15

Jazzie Workout, 1989, Mattel, Model No. 3633
EX n/a   NM $5   MIP $12

Jewel Girl Barbie, Christie, Teresa (new body style, belly button), 2000, Mattel
EX n/a   NM $15   MIP $30

Jewel Secrets Barbie, black, two box versions, 1987, Mattel, Model No. 1756
EX n/a   NM $6   MIP $55

Jewel Secrets Barbie, white, two box versions, 1987, Mattel, Model No. 1737
EX n/a   NM $6   MIP $35

Jewel Secrets Ken, black, 1987, Mattel, Model No. 3232
EX n/a   NM $6   MIP $25

Jewel Secrets Ken, rooted hair, 1987, Mattel, Model No. 1719
EX n/a   NM $6   MIP $25

Jewel Secrets Skipper, 1987, Mattel, Model No. 3133
EX n/a   NM $6   MIP $25

Jewel Secrets Whitney, 1987, Mattel, Model No. 3179
EX n/a   NM $8   MIP $25

Julia, talking, first issue with straight hair, 1969, Mattel, Model No. 1128
EX n/a   NM $85   MIP $250

Julia, talking, second issue, Afro hair, 1969, Mattel, Model No. 1128
EX n/a   NM $85   MIP $250

Julia, Twist N Turn, one-piece nurse dress, 2nd issue, 1969, Mattel, Model No. 1127
EX n/a   NM $100   MIP $250

Julia, Twist N Turn, two-piece nurse outfit, 1st issue, 1969, Mattel, Model No. 1127
EX n/a   NM $125   MIP $300

Ken, bendable leg, brunette, 1965, Mattel, Model No. 750
EX n/a   NM $155   MIP $300

Ken, flocked hair, brunette, blond, 1961, Mattel, Model No. 750
EX n/a   NM $75   MIP $150

Ken, leg, talking, 1970, Mattel, Model No. 1124
EX n/a   NM $50   MIP $125

Ken, painted hair, brunette, blond, 1962, Mattel, Model No. 750
EX n/a   NM $50   MIP $175

Kevin, 1991, Mattel, Model No. 9325
EX n/a   NM $5   MIP $10

(KP Photo)

Kissing Barbie, 1979, Mattel, Model No. 2597
EX n/a   NM $8   MIP $65

Kissing Christie, 1979, Mattel, Model No. 2955
EX n/a   NM $10   MIP $65

Lights & Lace Barbie, 1991, Mattel, Model No. 9725
EX n/a   NM $4   MIP $30

Lights & Lace Christie, 1991, Mattel, Model No. 9728
EX n/a   NM $4   MIP $30

Lights & Lace Teresa, 1991, Mattel, Model No. 9727
EX n/a   NM $4   MIP $25

(KP Photo)

Live Action Barbie, 1970, Mattel, Model No. 1155
EX n/a   NM $60   MIP $150

Live Action Barbie Onstage, 1970, Mattel, Model No. 1152
EX n/a   NM $75   MIP $250

Live Action Christie, 1970, Mattel, Model No. 1175
EX n/a   NM $60   MIP $250

Live Action Ken, 1970, Mattel, Model No. 1159
EX n/a   NM $55   MIP $150

Live Action Ken on Stage, 1970, Mattel, Model No. 1172
EX n/a   NM $40   MIP $150

Live Action P.J., 1970, Mattel, Model No. 1156
EX n/a   NM $65   MIP $250

Live Action P.J. on Stage, 1970, Mattel, Model No. 1153
EX n/a   NM $75   MIP $175

Lovin' You Barbie, 1983, Mattel, Model No. 7072
EX n/a   NM $20   MIP $75

Magic Curl Barbie, black, 1982, Mattel, Model No. 3989
EX n/a   NM $8   MIP $25

Magic Curl Barbie, white, 1982, Mattel, Model No. 3856
EX n/a   NM $10   MIP $35

Magic Moves Barbie, black, 1985, Mattel, Model No. 3137
EX n/a   NM $15   MIP $35

Magic Moves Barbie, white, 1985, Mattel, Model No. 2126
EX n/a   NM $15   MIP $35

(KP Photo)

Malibu Barbie, 1971, Mattel, Model No. 1067
EX n/a   NM $15   MIP $60

Malibu Barbie (Sunset), 1975, Mattel, Model No. 1067
EX n/a   NM $15   MIP $40

Malibu Christie, 1975, Mattel, Model No. 7745
EX n/a   NM $10   MIP $40

Malibu Francie, 1971, Mattel, Model No. 1068
EX n/a   NM $15   MIP $45

❑ **Malibu Ken,** 1976, Mattel, Model No. 1088
EX n/a   **NM** $8   **MIP** $25

❑ **Malibu P.J.,** 1975, Mattel, Model No. 1087
EX n/a   **NM** $5   **MIP** $45

❑ **Malibu Skipper,** 1977, Mattel, Model No. 1069
EX n/a   **NM** $8   **MIP** $45

❑ **Midge, bendable leg, blond, brunette, titian,** 1965, Mattel, Model No. 1080
EX n/a   **NM** $250   **MIP** $425

❑ **Midge, straight leg, blond, brunette, titian,** 1963, Mattel, Model No. 860
EX n/a   **NM** $65   **MIP** $125

❑ **Miss Barbie (sleep eyes),** 1964, Mattel, Model No. 1060
EX n/a   **NM** $400   **MIP** $1200

(KP Photo)

❑ **Mod Hair Ken,** 1972, Mattel, Model No. 4224
EX n/a   **NM** $45   **MIP** $65

❑ **Music Lovin' Barbie,** 1985, Mattel, Model No. 9988
EX n/a   **NM** $15   **MIP** $45

❑ **Music Lovin' Ken,** 1985, Mattel, Model No. 2388
EX n/a   **NM** $15   **MIP** $45

❑ **Music Lovin' Skipper,** 1985, Mattel, Model No. 2854
EX n/a   **NM** $20   **MIP** $45

❑ **My First Barbie,** 1991, Mattel, Model No. 9942
EX n/a   **NM** $3   **MIP** $25

❑ **My First Barbie, aqua and yellow dress,** 1981, Mattel, Model No. 1875
EX n/a   **NM** $10   **MIP** $30

❑ **My First Barbie, black,** 1990, Mattel, Model No. 9943
EX n/a   **NM** $5   **MIP** $25

❑ **My First Barbie, Hispanic,** 1991, Mattel, Model No. 9944
EX n/a   **NM** $3   **MIP** $20

❑ **My First Barbie, pink checkered dress,** 1983, Mattel, Model No. 1875
EX n/a   **NM** $5   **MIP** $35

❑ **My First Barbie, pink tutu, black,** 1987, Mattel, Model No. 1801
EX n/a   **NM** $5   **MIP** $20

❑ **My First Barbie, pink tutu, white,** 1987, Mattel, Model No. 1788
EX n/a   **NM** $5   **MIP** $20

❑ **My First Barbie, white,** 1990, Mattel, Model No. 9942
EX n/a   **NM** $4   **MIP** $20

❑ **My First Barbie, white dress, black,** 1984, Mattel, Model No. 9858
EX n/a   **NM** $7   **MIP** $25

❑ **My First Barbie, white dress, white,** 1984, Mattel, Model No. 1875
EX n/a   **NM** $5   **MIP** $30

❑ **My First Barbie, white tutu, black,** 1988, Mattel, Model No. 1281
EX n/a   **NM** $6   **MIP** $15

❑ **My First Barbie, white tutu, Hispanic,** 1988, Mattel, Model No. 1282
EX n/a   **NM** $6   **MIP** $20

❑ **My First Barbie, white tutu, white,** 1988, Mattel, Model No. 1280
EX n/a   **NM** $5   **MIP** $20

❑ **My First Ken, 1st issue,** 1989, Mattel, Model No. 1389
EX n/a   **NM** $4   **MIP** $15

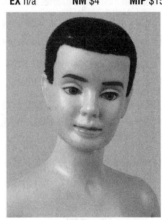

(KP Photo)

❑ **My First Ken, Prince,** 1990, Mattel, Model No. 9940
EX n/a   **NM** $4   **MIP** $15

❑ **New Look Ken,** 1976, Mattel, Model No. 9342
EX n/a   **NM** $23   **MIP** $65

❑ **Newport Barbie, two versions,** 1974, Mattel, Model No. 7807
EX n/a   **NM** $25   **MIP** $125

❑ **Nurse Whitney,** 1987, Mattel, Model No. 4405
EX n/a   **NM** $20   **MIP** $45

❑ **Ocean Friends Barbie,** 1996, Mattel, Model No. 15430
EX n/a   **NM** $5   **MIP** $17

❑ **Ocean Friends Ken,** 1996, Mattel, Model No. 15430
EX n/a   **NM** $5   **MIP** $17

❑ **Ocean Friends Kira,** 1996, Mattel, Model No. 15431
EX n/a   **NM** $5   **MIP** $17

❑ **Olympic Gymnast, blond,** 1996, Mattel, Model No. 15123
EX n/a   **NM** $10   **MIP** $25

❑ **P.J., talking,** 1970, Mattel, Model No. 1113
EX n/a   **NM** $65   **MIP** $250

❑ **P.J., Twist N Turn,** 1970, Mattel, Model No. 1118
EX n/a   **NM** $75   **MIP** $300

❑ **Party Treats Barbie,** 1989, Mattel, Model No. 4885
EX n/a   **NM** $8   **MIP** $25

❑ **Peaches n' Cream Barbie, black,** 1984, Mattel, Model No. 9516
EX n/a   **NM** $8   **MIP** $40

❑ **Peaches n' Cream Barbie, white,** 1984, Mattel, Model No. 7926
EX n/a   **NM** $8   **MIP** $45

❑ **Perfume Giving Ken, black,** 1989, Mattel, Model No. 4555
EX n/a   **NM** $6   **MIP** $25

❑ **Perfume Giving Ken, white,** 1989, Mattel, Model No. 4554
EX n/a   **NM** $6   **MIP** $25

❑ **Perfume Pretty Barbie, black,** 1989, Mattel, Model No. 4552
EX n/a   **NM** $8   **MIP** $25

❑ **Perfume Pretty Barbie, white,** 1989, Mattel, Model No. 4551
EX n/a   **NM** $8   **MIP** $25

❑ **Perfume Pretty Whitney,** 1987, Mattel, Model No. 4557
EX n/a   **NM** $8   **MIP** $35

❑ **Pink n' Pretty Barbie,** 1982, Mattel, Model No. 3551
EX n/a   **NM** $12   **MIP** $45

❑ **Pink n' Pretty Christie,** 1982, Mattel, Model No. 3554
EX n/a   **NM** $10   **MIP** $40

❑ **Playtime Barbie,** 1984, Mattel, Model No. 5336
EX n/a   **NM** $15   **MIP** $20

(KP Photo)

BARBIE

❑ **Ponytail Barbie #1, blond,** 1959, Mattel, Model No. 850
EX n/a   NM $2500   MIP $6000

(KP Photo)

❑ **Ponytail Barbie #1, brunette,** 1959, Mattel, Model No. 850
EX n/a   NM $3000   MIP $6500

❑ **Ponytail Barbie #2, blond,** 1959, Mattel, Model No. 850
EX n/a   NM $2500   MIP $5000

❑ **Ponytail Barbie #2, brunette,** 1959, Mattel, Model No. 850
EX n/a   NM $3000   MIP $6500

❑ **Ponytail Barbie #3, blond,** 1960, Mattel, Model No. 850
EX n/a   NM $400   MIP $900

❑ **Ponytail Barbie #3, brunette,** 1960, Mattel, Model No. 850
EX n/a   NM $500   MIP $1000

❑ **Ponytail Barbie #4, blond,** 1960, Mattel, Model No. 850
EX n/a   NM $250   MIP $575

❑ **Ponytail Barbie #4, brunette,** 1960, Mattel, Model No. 850
EX n/a   NM $350   MIP $400

❑ **Ponytail Barbie #5, blond,** 1961, Mattel, Model No. 850
EX n/a   NM $175   MIP $400

❑ **Ponytail Barbie #5, brunette,** 1961, Mattel, Model No. 850
EX n/a   NM $250   MIP $450

❑ **Ponytail Barbie #5, titian,** 1961, Mattel, Model No. 850
EX n/a   NM $250   MIP $500

❑ **Ponytail Barbie #6, blond,** 1962, Mattel, Model No. 850
EX n/a   NM $150   MIP $400

(KP Photo)

❑ **Ponytail Barbie #6, brunette,** 1962, Mattel, Model No. 850
EX n/a   NM $150   MIP $400

❑ **Ponytail Barbie #6, titian,** 1962, Mattel, Model No. 850
EX n/a   NM $150   MIP $400

❑ **Ponytail Swirl Style Barbie, blond,** 1964, Mattel, Model No. 850
EX n/a   NM $350   MIP $625

❑ **Ponytail Swirl Style Barbie, brunette,** 1964, Mattel, Model No. 850
EX n/a   NM $350   MIP $625

❑ **Ponytail Swirl Style Barbie, platinum,** 1964, Mattel, Model No. 850
EX n/a   NM $500   MIP $1200

❑ **Ponytail Swirl Style Barbie, titian,** 1964, Mattel, Model No. 850
EX n/a   NM $350   MIP $625

❑ **Pose n' Play Skipper (baggie),** 1973, Mattel, Model No. 1117
EX n/a   NM $20   MIP $55

❑ **Pretty Changes Barbie,** 1978, Mattel, Model No. 2598
EX n/a   NM $8   MIP $45

❑ **Pretty Party Barbie,** 1983, Mattel, Model No. 7194
EX n/a   NM $12   MIP $30

(KP Photo)

❑ **Quick Curl Barbie,** 1972, Mattel, Model No. 4220
EX n/a   NM $20   MIP $80

❑ **Quick Curl Cara,** 1974, Mattel, Model No. 7291
EX n/a   NM $20   MIP $60

❑ **Quick Curl Deluxe Barbie,** 1976, Mattel, Model No. 9217
EX n/a   NM $20   MIP $75

❑ **Quick Curl Deluxe Cara,** 1976, Mattel, Model No. 9219
EX n/a   NM $20   MIP $60

❑ **Quick Curl Deluxe P.J.,** 1976, Mattel, Model No. 9218
EX n/a   NM $20   MIP $50

❑ **Quick Curl Deluxe Skipper,** 1976, Mattel, Model No. 9428
EX n/a   NM $20   MIP $50

❑ **Quick Curl Francie,** 1972, Mattel, Model No. 4222
EX n/a   NM $20   MIP $55

❑ **Quick Curl Kelley,** 1972, Mattel, Model No. 4221
EX n/a   NM $20   MIP $75

(KP Photo)

❑ **Quick Curl Miss America, blond,** 1974, Mattel, Model No. 8697
EX n/a   NM $35   MIP $75

❑ **Quick Curl Miss America, brunette,** 1973, Mattel, Model No. 8697
EX n/a   NM $45   MIP $125

❑ **Quick Curl Skipper,** 1974, Mattel, Model No. 4223
EX n/a   NM $20   MIP $50

(KP Photo)

❏ **Ricky,** 1965, Mattel, Model No. 1090
  EX n/a   **NM** $55   **MIP** $125

❏ **Rocker Barbie, 1st issue,** 1986, Mattel, Model No. 1140
  EX n/a   **NM** $7   **MIP** $40

(KP Photo)

❏ **Rocker Barbie, 2nd issue,** 1987, Mattel, Model No. 3055
  EX n/a   **NM** $7   **MIP** $25

❏ **Rocker Dana, 1st issue,** 1986, Mattel, Model No. 1196
  EX n/a   **NM** $7   **MIP** $40

❏ **Rocker Dana, 2nd issue,** 1987, Mattel, Model No. 3158
  EX n/a   **NM** $7   **MIP** $20

❏ **Rocker Dee-Dee, 1st issue,** 1986, Mattel, Model No. 1141
  EX n/a   **NM** $7   **MIP** $30

❏ **Rocker Dee-Dee, 2nd issue,** 1987, Mattel, Model No. 3160
  EX n/a   **NM** $7   **MIP** $20

❏ **Rocker Derek, 1st issue,** 1986, Mattel, Model No. 2428
  EX n/a   **NM** $7   **MIP** $30

❏ **Rocker Derek, 2nd issue,** 1987, Mattel, Model No. 3173
  EX n/a   **NM** $7   **MIP** $20

❏ **Rocker Diva, 1st issue,** 1986, Mattel, Model No. 2427
  EX n/a   **NM** $7   **MIP** $30

❏ **Rocker Diva, 2nd issue,** 1987, Mattel, Model No. 3159
  EX n/a   **NM** $7   **MIP** $20

❏ **Rocker Ken, 1st issue,** 1986, Mattel, Model No. 3131
  EX n/a   **NM** $7   **MIP** $30

❏ **Rollerskating Barbie,** 1980, Mattel, Model No. 1880
  EX n/a   **NM** $8   **MIP** $60

❏ **Rollerskating Ken,** 1980, Mattel, Model No. 1881
  EX n/a   **NM** $8   **MIP** $40

❏ **Safari Barbie,** 1983, Mattel, Model No. 4973
  EX n/a   **NM** $8   **MIP** $30

❏ **Scott,** 1979, Mattel, Model No. 1019
  EX n/a   **NM** $15   **MIP** $60

❏ **Sea Lovin' Barbie,** 1984, Mattel, Model No. 9109
  EX n/a   **NM** $8   **MIP** $35

❏ **Sea Lovin' Ken,** 1984, Mattel, Model No. 9110
  EX n/a   **NM** $8   **MIP** $30

❏ **Secret Messages Barbie, white or black,** 2000, Model No. 26422
  EX n/a   **NM** $7   **MIP** $15

❏ **Sensations Barbie,** 1987, Mattel, Model No. 4931
  EX n/a   **NM** $5   **MIP** $12

❏ **Sensations Becky,** 1987, Mattel, Model No. 4977
  EX n/a   **NM** $5   **MIP** $12

❏ **Sensations Belinda,** 1987, Mattel, Model No. 4976
  EX n/a   **NM** $5   **MIP** $12

❏ **Sensations Bobsy,** 1987, Mattel, Model No. 4967
  EX n/a   **NM** $5   **MIP** $12

❏ **Sit 'n Style Barbie,** 2000, Mattel, Model No. 23421
  EX n/a   **NM** $7   **MIP** $15

❏ **Ski Fun Barbie,** 1991, Mattel, Model No. 7511
  EX n/a   **NM** $6   **MIP** $15

❏ **Ski Fun Ken,** 1991, Mattel, Model No. 7512
  EX n/a   **NM** $6   **MIP** $15

❏ **Ski Fun Midge,** 1991, Mattel, Model No. 7513
  EX n/a   **NM** $6   **MIP** $25

(KP Photo)

❏ **Skipper, bendable leg, brunette, blond, titian,** 1965, Mattel, Model No. 1030
  EX n/a   **NM** $65   **MIP** $175

❏ **Skipper, straight leg, brunette, blond, titian,** 1964, Mattel, Model No. 950
  EX n/a   **NM** $50   **MIP** $175

❏ **Skipper, straight leg, reissues, brunette, blond, titian,** 1971, Mattel, Model No. 950
  EX n/a   **NM** $125   **MIP** $400

❏ **Skipper, Twist N Turn, blonde or brunette, curl pigtails,** 1969, Mattel, Model No. 1105
  EX n/a   **NM** $95   **MIP** $275

❏ **Skipper, Twist N Turn, blonde, brunette, red hair, long straight hair,** 1968, Mattel, Model No. 1105
  EX n/a   **NM** $95   **MIP** $275

(KP Photo)

❏ **Skooter, bendable leg, brunette, blond, titian,** 1966, Mattel, Model No. 1120
  EX n/a   **NM** $100   **MIP** $300

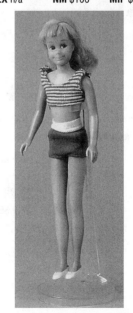

❏ **Skooter, straight leg, brunette, blond, titian,** 1965, Mattel, Model No. 1040
  EX n/a   **NM** $55   **MIP** $175

BARBIE

❑ **Snowboard Barbie,** 1996, Mattel, Model No. 15408
EX n/a   **NM** $10   **MIP** $20

❑ **Sparkle Barbie,** 1996, Mattel, Model No. 15419
EX n/a   **NM** $10   **MIP** $20

❑ **Sport n' Shave Ken,** 1980, Mattel, Model No. 1294
EX n/a   **NM** $8   **MIP** $40

❑ **Stacey, talking, blonde or red hair, side ponytail,** 1968, Mattel, Model No. 1125
EX n/a   **NM** $175   **MIP** $425

❑ **Stacey, Twist and Turn, blonde or red hair, long ponytail with spit curls,** 1968, Mattel, Model No. 1165
EX n/a   **NM** $150   **MIP** $425

❑ **Stacey, Twist N Turn, blonde or red hair, short rolled flip,** 1969, Mattel, Model No. 1165
EX n/a   **NM** $175   **MIP** $425

(KP Photo)

❑ **Standard Barbie, blond, brunette, long straight hair with bangs,** 1967, Mattel, Model No. 1190
EX n/a   **NM** $250   **MIP** $500

❑ **Standard Barbie, centered eyes,** 1971, Mattel, Model No. 1190
EX n/a   **NM** $350   **MIP** $700

❑ **Standard Barbie, titian, long straight hair with bangs,** 1967, Mattel, Model No. 1190
EX n/a   **NM** $300   **MIP** $500

❑ **Stars & Stripes Air Force Barbie,** 1990, Mattel, Model No. 3360
EX n/a   **NM** $15   **MIP** $75

(KP Photo)

❑ **Stars & Stripes Army Barbie, white or black,** 1993, Mattel, Model No. 1234/5618
EX n/a   **NM** $10   **MIP** $75

❑ **Stars & Stripes Marine Corps Barbie, white or black,** 1992, Mattel, Model No. 7549/7594
EX n/a   **NM** $10   **MIP** $75

(KP Photo)

❑ **Stars & Stripes Navy Barbie, white or black,** 1991, Mattel, Model No. 9693/9694
EX n/a   **NM** $10   **MIP** $75

❑ **Stars 'n Stripes Air Force Ken, white or black,** 1994, Mattel, Model No. 11554/11555
EX n/a   **NM** $15   **MIP** $75

❑ **Stars 'n Stripes Air Force Thunderbirds Barbie, white or black,** 1994, Mattel, Model No. 11552/11553
EX n/a   **NM** $15   **MIP** $75

❑ **Stars 'n Stripes Army Ken, white or black,** 1993, Mattel, Model No. 1237/5619
EX n/a   **NM** $15   **MIP** $75

❑ **Stars 'n Stripes Marine Corps Ken, black or white,** 1992, Mattel, Model No. 5352/7574
EX n/a   **NM** $20   **MIP** $75

❑ **Style Magic Barbie,** 1989, Mattel, Model No. 1283
EX n/a   **NM** $5   **MIP** $20

❑ **Style Magic Christie,** 1989, Mattel, Model No. 1288
EX n/a   **NM** $5   **MIP** $20

❑ **Style Magic Skipper,** 1989, Mattel, Model No. 1915
EX n/a   **NM** $10   **MIP** $20

❑ **Style Magic Whitney,** 1989, Mattel, Model No. 1290
EX n/a   **NM** $5   **MIP** $20

❑ **Summit Barbie, Asian,** 1990, Mattel, Model No. 7029
EX n/a   **NM** $10   **MIP** $25

❑ **Summit Barbie, black,** 1990, Mattel, Model No. 7028
EX n/a   **NM** $12   **MIP** $25

❑ **Summit Barbie, Hispanic,** 1990, Mattel, Model No. 7030
EX n/a   **NM** $10   **MIP** $28

❑ **Summit Barbie, white,** 1990, Mattel, Model No. 7027
EX n/a   **NM** $8   **MIP** $25

❑ **Sun Gold Malibu Barbie, black,** 1983, Mattel, Model No. 7745
EX n/a   **NM** $5   **MIP** $15

❑ **Sun Gold Malibu Barbie, Hispanic,** 1985, Mattel, Model No. 4970
EX n/a   **NM** $3   **MIP** $20
(KP Photo)

❑ **Sun Gold Malibu Barbie, white,** 1983, Mattel, Model No. 1067
EX n/a   **NM** $5   **MIP** $15

❑ **Sun Gold Malibu Ken, black,** 1983, Mattel, Model No. 3849
EX n/a   **NM** $3   **MIP** $15

❑ **Sun Gold Malibu Ken, Hispanic,** 1985, Mattel, Model No. 4971
EX n/a   **NM** $3   **MIP** $20

❑ **Sun Gold Malibu Ken, white,** 1983, Mattel, Model No. 1088
EX n/a   **NM** $3   **MIP** $15

❑ **Sun Gold Malibu P.J.,** 1983, Mattel, Model No. 1187
EX n/a   **NM** $5   **MIP** $15

❑ **Sun Gold Malibu Skipper,** 1983, Mattel, Model No. 1069
EX n/a   **NM** $5   **MIP** $15

❑ **Sun Lovin' Malibu Barbie,** 1978, Mattel, Model No. 1067
EX n/a   **NM** $5   **MIP** $20

❑ **Sun Lovin' Malibu Ken,** 1978, Mattel, Model No. 1088
EX n/a   **NM** $5   **MIP** $20

❏ **Sun Lovin' Malibu P.J.,** 1978, Mattel, Model No. 1187
EX n/a   **NM** $5   **MIP** $20

❏ **Sun Lovin' Malibu Skipper,** 1978, Mattel, Model No. 1069
EX n/a   **NM** $5   **MIP** $20

❏ **Sun Valley Barbie,** 1974, Mattel, Model No. 7806
EX n/a   **NM** $20   **MIP** $130

❏ **Sun Valley Ken,** 1974, Mattel, Model No. 7809
EX n/a   **NM** $20   **MIP** $100

❏ **Sunsational Malibu Barbie,** 1982, Mattel, Model No. 1067
EX n/a   **NM** $6   **MIP** $25

❏ **Sunsational Malibu Barbie, Hispanic,** 1982, Mattel, Model No. 4970
EX n/a   **NM** $8   **MIP** $25

❏ **Sunsational Malibu Christie,** 1982, Mattel, Model No. 7745
EX n/a   **NM** $6   **MIP** $20

(KP Photo)

❏ **Sunsational Malibu Ken, black,** 1981, Mattel, Model No. 3849
EX n/a   **NM** $15   **MIP** $35

❏ **Sunsational Malibu P.J.,** 1982, Mattel, Model No. 1187
EX n/a   **NM** $6   **MIP** $30

❏ **Sunsational Malibu Skipper,** 1982, Mattel, Model No. 1069
EX n/a   **NM** $5   **MIP** $35

❏ **Sunset Malibu Christie,** 1973, Mattel, Model No. 7745
EX n/a   **NM** $20   **MIP** $65

❏ **Sunset Malibu Francie,** 1971, Mattel, Model No. 1068
EX n/a   **NM** $25   **MIP** $65

❏ **Sunset Malibu Ken,** 1972, Mattel, Model No. 1088
EX n/a   **NM** $15   **MIP** $50

❏ **Sunset Malibu P.J.,** 1971, Mattel, Model No. 1187
EX n/a   **NM** $10   **MIP** $50

❏ **Sunset Malibu Skipper,** 1971, Mattel, Model No. 1069
EX n/a   **NM** $20   **MIP** $50

❏ **Super Hair Barbie, black,** 1987, Mattel, Model No. 3296
EX n/a   **NM** $8   **MIP** $20

❏ **Super Hair Barbie, white,** 1987, Mattel, Model No. 3101
EX n/a   **NM** $8   **MIP** $25

❏ **Super Sport Ken,** 1982, Mattel, Model No. 5839
EX n/a   **NM** $8   **MIP** $20

❏ **Super Talk Barbie,** 1994, Mattel, Model No. 12290
EX n/a   **NM** $10   **MIP** $20

❏ **Super Teen Skipper,** 1978, Mattel, Model No. 2756
EX n/a   **NM** $7   **MIP** $20

(KP Photo)

❏ **Supersize Barbie,** 1977, Mattel, Model No. 9828
EX n/a   **NM** $75   **MIP** $200

❏ **Supersize Bride Barbie,** 1977, Mattel, Model No. 9975
EX n/a   **NM** $150   **MIP** $295

❏ **Supersize Christie,** 1977, Mattel, Model No. 9839
EX n/a   **NM** $75   **MIP** $275

❏ **Supersize Super Hair Barbie,** 1979, Mattel, Model No. 2844
EX n/a   **NM** $85   **MIP** $175

❏ **Superstar Ballerina Barbie,** 1976, Mattel, Model No. 4983
EX n/a   **NM** $20   **MIP** $60

❏ **Superstar Barbie,** 1977, Mattel, Model No. 9720
EX n/a   **NM** $15   **MIP** $70

❏ **Superstar Barbie,** 1988, Mattel, Model No. 1604
EX n/a   **NM** $45   **MIP** $95

❏ **Superstar Barbie 30th Anniversary, black,** 1989, Mattel, Model No. 1605
EX n/a   **NM** $6   **MIP** $35

❏ **Superstar Barbie 30th Anniversary, white,** 1989, Mattel, Model No. 1604
EX n/a   **NM** $8   **MIP** $25

❏ **Superstar Christie,** 1977, Mattel, Model No. 9950
EX n/a   **NM** $20   **MIP** $75

❏ **Superstar Ken,** 1978, Mattel, Model No. 2211
EX n/a   **NM** $17   **MIP** $75

❏ **Superstar Ken, black,** 1989, Mattel, Model No. 1550
EX n/a   **NM** $5   **MIP** $30

❏ **Superstar Ken, white,** 1989, Mattel, Model No. 1535
EX n/a   **NM** $7   **MIP** $50

❏ **Superstar Malibu Barbie,** 1977, Mattel, Model No. 1067
EX n/a   **NM** $10   **MIP** $35

(KP Photo)

❏ **Sweet 16 Barbie,** 1974, Mattel, Model No. 7796
EX n/a   **NM** $25   **MIP** $125

❏ **Sweet Roses P.J.,** 1983, Mattel, Model No. 7455
EX n/a   **NM** $15   **MIP** $25

❏ **Swimming Champion Barbie,** 2000, Mattel, Model No. 24590
EX n/a   **NM** $7   **MIP** $15

❏ **Talk With Me Barbie,** 1997, Mattel, with software, Model No. 17350
EX n/a   **NM** $25   **MIP** $50

❏ **Talking Barbie, chignon with nape curls, blonde, brunette, titian,** 1970, Mattel, Model No. 1115
EX n/a   **NM** $175   **MIP** $500

BARBIE

(KP Photo)

❑ **Talking Barbie, side ponytail with spit curls, blonde or brunette,** 1968, Mattel, Model No. 1115
EX n/a   **NM** $125   **MIP** $425

(KP Photo)

❑ **Talking Busy Barbie,** 1972, Mattel, Model No. 1195
EX n/a   **NM** $125   **MIP** $300

❑ **Talking Busy Ken,** 1972, Mattel, Model No. 1196
EX n/a   **NM** $80   **MIP** $160

(KP Photo)

❑ **Talking Busy Steffie,** 1972, Mattel, Model No. 1186
EX n/a   **NM** $175   **MIP** $350

❑ **Talking Ken,** 1969, Mattel, Model No. 1111
EX n/a   **NM** $75   **MIP** $175

❑ **Teacher Barbie, painted on panties, black,** 1996, Mattel, Model No. 13915
EX n/a   **NM** $15   **MIP** $20

(KP Photo)

❑ **Teacher Barbie, painted on panties, white,** 1996, Mattel, Model No. 13914
EX n/a   **NM** $15   **MIP** $25

❑ **Teen Dance Jazzie,** 1989, Mattel, Model No. 3634
EX n/a   **NM** $7   **MIP** $35

❑ **Teen Fun Skipper Cheerleader,** 1987, Mattel, Model No. 5893
EX n/a   **NM** $5   **MIP** $15

❑ **Teen Fun Skipper Party Teen,** 1987, Mattel, Model No. 5899
EX n/a   **NM** $5   **MIP** $15

❑ **Teen Fun Skipper Workout,** 1987, Mattel, Model No. 5889
EX n/a   **NM** $5   **MIP** $15

❑ **Teen Jazzie (Teen Dance),** 1989, Mattel, Model No. 3634
EX n/a   **NM** $4   **MIP** $35

❑ **Teen Looks Jazzie Cheerleader,** 1989, Mattel, Model No. 3631
EX n/a   **NM** $4   **MIP** $20

❑ **Teen Looks Jazzie Workout,** 1989, Mattel, Model No. 3633
EX n/a   **NM** $4   **MIP** $20

❑ **Teen Scene Jazzie, two box versions,** 1991, Mattel, Model No. 5507
EX n/a   **NM** $5   **MIP** $35

❑ **Teen Sweetheart Skipper,** 1988, Mattel, Model No. 4855
EX n/a   **NM** $5   **MIP** $25

(KP Photo)

❑ **Teen Talk Barbie,** 1992, Mattel, Model No. 5745
EX n/a   **NM** $15   **MIP** $45

❑ **Teen Talk Barbie, "Math is Tough" variation,** 1992, Mattel, Model No. 5745
EX n/a   **NM** $50   **MIP** $275

❑ **Teen Time Courtney,** 1988, Mattel, Model No. 1950
EX n/a   **NM** $5   **MIP** $10

❑ **Teen Time Skipper,** 1988, Mattel, Model No. 1951
EX n/a   **NM** $5   **MIP** $10

❑ **Tennis Barbie,** 1986, Mattel, Model No. 1760
EX n/a   **NM** $5   **MIP** $25

❑ **Tennis Ken,** 1986, Mattel, Model No. 1761
EX n/a   **NM** $5   **MIP** $25

(KP Photo)

❑ **Todd,** 1967, Mattel, Model No. 3590
EX n/a   NM $95   MIP $200

❑ **Tracy Bride,** 1983, Mattel, Model No. 4103
EX n/a   NM $8   MIP $45

❑ **Tropical Barbie, black,** 1986, Mattel, Model No. 1022
EX n/a   NM $3   MIP $15

❑ **Tropical Barbie, white,** 1986, Mattel, Model No. 1017
EX n/a   NM $3   MIP $20

❑ **Tropical Ken, black,** 1986, Mattel, Model No. 1023
EX n/a   NM $3   MIP $15

❑ **Tropical Ken, white,** 1986, Mattel, Model No. 4060
EX n/a   NM $3   MIP $20

❑ **Tropical Miko,** 1986, Mattel, Model No. 2056
EX n/a   NM $3   MIP $20

❑ **Tropical Skipper,** 1986, Mattel, Model No. 4064
EX n/a   NM $3   MIP $20

❑ **Truly Scrumptious, standard,** 1969, Mattel, Model No. 1107
EX n/a   NM $200   MIP $500

❑ **Truly Scrumptious, talking,** 1969, Mattel, Model No. 1108
EX n/a   NM $175   MIP $475

❑ **Tutti, all hair colors, floral dress w/yellow ribbon,** 1967, Mattel, Model No. 3580
EX n/a   NM $45   MIP $150

(KP Photo)

❑ **Tutti, all hair colors, pink, white gingham suit, hat,** 1966, Mattel, Model No. 3550
EX n/a   NM $50   MIP $170

❑ **Tutti, Germany,** 1978, Mattel, Model No. 8128
EX n/a   NM $40   MIP $125

❑ **Twiggy,** 1967, Mattel, Model No. 1185
EX n/a   NM $125   MIP $300

❑ **Twirley Curls Barbie, black,** 1983, Mattel, Model No. 5723
EX n/a   NM $10   MIP $35

❑ **Twirley Curls Barbie, Hispanic,** 1982, Mattel, Model No. 5724
EX n/a   NM $10   MIP $40

❑ **Twirley Curls Barbie, white,** 1982, Mattel, Model No. 5579
EX n/a   NM $10   MIP $40

❑ **Twist N Turn Barbie, blonde, brunette, red hair with centered eyes,** 1971, Mattel, Model No. 1160
EX n/a   NM $200   MIP $600

❑ **Twist N Turn Barbie, flip hair, blonde or brunette,** 1969, Mattel, Model No. 1160
EX n/a   NM $125   MIP $450

❑ **Twist N Turn Barbie, light blonde, blonde, light brown, brunette,** 1967, Mattel, Model No. 1160
EX n/a   NM $95   MIP $450

❑ **Twist N Turn Barbie, long straight hair with bangs, red hair,** 1967, Mattel, Model No. 1160
EX n/a   NM $200   MIP $600

❑ **UNICEF Barbie, Asian,** 1989, Mattel, Model No. 4774
EX n/a   NM $17   MIP $30

❑ **UNICEF Barbie, black,** 1989, Mattel, Model No. 4770
EX n/a   NM $7   MIP $25

❑ **UNICEF Barbie, Hispanic,** 1989, Mattel, Model No. 4782
EX n/a   NM $7   MIP $30

❑ **UNICEF Barbie, white,** 1989, Mattel, Model No. 1920
EX n/a   NM $7   MIP $25

❑ **University Barbie,** 1997, Mattel, many schools offered
EX n/a   NM $12   MIP $18

(KP Photo)

❑ **Walk Lively Barbie,** 1971, Mattel, Model No. 1182
EX n/a   NM $75   MIP $200

❑ **Walk Lively Ken,** 1971, Mattel, Model No. 1184
EX n/a   NM $40   MIP $150

❑ **Walk Lively Miss America Barbie, brunette,** 1971, Mattel, Model No. 3200
EX n/a   NM $95   MIP $200

❑ **Walk Lively Steffie,** 1971, Mattel, Model No. 1183
EX n/a   NM $75   MIP $300

❑ **Walking Jamie,** 1970, Mattel, Model No. 1132
EX n/a   NM $175   MIP $400

❑ **Wedding Fantasy Barbie, black,** 1989, Mattel, Model No. 7011
EX n/a   NM $7   MIP $25

❑ **Wedding Fantasy Barbie, white,** 1989, Mattel, Model No. 2125
EX n/a   NM $7   MIP $40

❑ **Wedding Party Allan,** 1991, Mattel, Model No. 9607
EX n/a   NM $7   MIP $20

❑ **Wedding Party Barbie,** 1991, Mattel, Model No. 9608
EX n/a   NM $7   MIP $20

❑ **Wedding Party Kelly & Todd,** 1991, Mattel, Model No. 9852
EX n/a   NM $15   MIP $35

❑ **Wedding Party Ken,** 1991, Mattel, Model No. 9609
EX n/a   NM $7   MIP $20

❑ **Wedding Party Midge,** 1991, Mattel, Model No. 9606
EX n/a   NM $7   MIP $15

(KP Photo)

❑ **Western Barbie,** 1980, Mattel, Model No. 1757
EX n/a   NM $8   MIP $40

❑ **Western Fun Barbie, black,** 1989, Mattel, Model No. 2930
EX n/a   NM $5   MIP $15

❑ **Western Fun Barbie, white,** 1989, Mattel, Model No. 9932
EX n/a   NM $5   MIP $15

BARBIE

❑ **Western Fun Ken,** 1989, Mattel, Model No. 9934
EX n/a   **NM** $5   **MIP** $15

❑ **Western Fun Nia,** 1989, Mattel, Model No. 9933
EX n/a   **NM** $5   **MIP** $15

❑ **Western Ken,** 1981, Mattel, Model No. 3600
EX n/a   **NM** $7   **MIP** $40

❑ **Western Skipper,** 1982, Mattel, Model No. 5029
EX n/a   **NM** $8   **MIP** $30

❑ **Wet n' Wild Barbie,** 1990, Mattel, Model No. 4103
EX n/a   **NM** $8   **MIP** $35

❑ **Wet n' Wild Christie,** 1989, Mattel, Model No. 4121
EX n/a   **NM** $3   **MIP** $15

❑ **Wet n' Wild Ken,** 1989, Mattel, Model No. 4104
EX n/a   **NM** $3   **MIP** $15

❑ **Wet n' Wild Kira,** 1989, Mattel, Model No. 4120
EX n/a   **NM** $3   **MIP** $15

❑ **Wet n' Wild Skipper,** 1989, Mattel, Model No. 4138
EX n/a   **NM** $3   **MIP** $15

❑ **Wet n' Wild Steven,** 1989, Mattel, Model No. 4137
EX n/a   **NM** $3   **MIP** $15

❑ **Wet n' Wild Teresa,** 1989, Mattel, Model No. 4136
EX n/a   **NM** $3   **MIP** $15

❑ **Wig Wardrobe Midge,** 1965, Mattel, Model No. 1009
EX n/a   **NM** $200   **MIP** $500

❑ **Working Woman Barbie, black or white,** 1999, Mattel
EX n/a   **NM** $15   **MIP** $30

COLLECTORS' EDITIONS, STORE EXCLUSIVES, GIFT SETS

❑ **40th Anniversary Barbie, white or black,** 1999, Mattel, Model No. 21384/22336
EX n/a   **NM** $25   **MIP** $50

❑ **40th Anniversary Gala,** 1999, Mattel, "bumblebee"
EX n/a   **NM** $30   **MIP** $90

❑ **40th Anniversary Ken, black,** 2001, Mattel, Model No. 52967
EX n/a   **NM** $15   **MIP** $40

❑ **40th Anniversary Ken, white,** 2001, Mattel, Model No. 50722
EX n/a   **NM** $15   **MIP** $50

❑ **All American Barbie & Starstepper,** 1991, Mattel, Model No. 3712
EX n/a   **NM** $12   **MIP** $35

❑ **American Stories #1 American Indian,** 1996, Mattel, Model No. 14612
EX n/a   **NM** $10   **MIP** $20

❑ **American Stories #2 American Indian,** 1997, Mattel, Model No. 17313
EX n/a   **NM** $15   **MIP** $28

❑ **American Stories Civil War Nurse,** 1996, Mattel, Model No. 14612
EX n/a   **NM** $10   **MIP** $25

❑ **American Stories Colonial Barbie,** 1995, Mattel, Model No. 12578
EX n/a   **NM** $10   **MIP** $25

❑ **American Stories Patriot Barbie,** 1997, Mattel, Model No. 17312
EX n/a   **NM** $10   **MIP** $25

❑ **American Stories Pilgrim Barbie,** 1995, Mattel, Model No. 12577
EX n/a   **NM** $10   **MIP** $25

❑ **American Stories Pioneer Barbie,** 1995, Mattel, Model No. 12680
EX n/a   **NM** $10   **MIP** $25

❑ **American Stories Pioneer Shopkeeper,** 1996, Mattel, Model No. 14756
EX n/a   **NM** $15   **MIP** $25

❑ **Ames Country Looks Barbie,** 1993, Mattel, Model No. 5854
EX n/a   **NM** $12   **MIP** $25

❑ **Ames Denim 'N Lace Barbie,** 1992, Mattel, Model No. 2452
EX n/a   **NM** $10   **MIP** $30

❑ **Ames Hot Looks Barbie,** 1992, Mattel, Model No. 5756
EX n/a   **NM** $10   **MIP** $25

❑ **Ames Ice Cream Barbie,** 1998, Mattel, Model No. 19280
EX n/a   **NM** $8   **MIP** $15

❑ **Ames Lady Bug Fun Barbie,** 1997, Mattel, Model No. 17695
EX n/a   **NM** $5   **MIP** $20

❑ **Ames Party in Pink,** 1991, Mattel, Model No. 2909
EX n/a   **NM** $10   **MIP** $30

❑ **Ames Strawberry Party Barbie,** 1999, Mattel, Model No. 22895
EX n/a   **NM** $8   **MIP** $15

❑ **Angel Lights Barbie,** 1993, Mattel
EX n/a   **NM** $45   **MIP** $100

❑ **Angels of Music Harpist Angel, black or white,** 1998, Mattel
EX n/a   **NM** $35   **MIP** $75

❑ **Angels of Music Heartstring Angel, black or white,** 1999, Mattel
EX n/a   **NM** $40   **MIP** $85

❑ **Anne Klein Barbie,** 1997, Mattel, Model No. 17603
EX n/a   **NM** $35   **MIP** $70

❑ **Applause Barbie Holiday,** 1991, Mattel, Model No. 3406
EX n/a   **NM** $20   **MIP** $40

❑ **Applause Style Barbie,** 1990, Mattel, Model No. 5313
EX n/a   **NM** $10   **MIP** $35

❑ **Artist Series, Reflections of Light Barbie, Renoir,** 1999, Mattel, Model No. 23884
EX n/a   **NM** $40   **MIP** $65

❑ **Artist Series, Sunflower Barbie, Van Gogh,** 1998, Mattel, Model No. 19366
EX n/a   **NM** $40   **MIP** $65

❑ **Artist Series, Water Lily Barbie, Monet,** 1997, Mattel, Model No. 17783
EX n/a   **NM** $50   **MIP** $75

❑ **Avon Blushing Bride Barbie, white or black,** 2000, Mattel
EX n/a   **NM** $10   **MIP** $25

❑ **Avon Fruit Fantasy Barbie, blonde,** 1999, Mattel
EX n/a   **NM** $10   **MIP** $25

❑ **Avon Fruit Fantasy Barbie, brunette,** 1999, Mattel
EX n/a   **NM** $15   **MIP** $30

❑ **Avon Lemon-Lime Barbie,** 1999, Mattel, Model No. 20318
EX n/a   **NM** $10   **MIP** $25

❑ **Avon Mrs. P.F.E. Albee,** 1997, Mattel, Model No. 17690
EX n/a   **NM** $22   **MIP** $65

❑ **Avon Mrs. P.F.E. Albee #2,** 1998, Mattel, Model No. 20330
EX n/a   **NM** $30   **MIP** $75

❑ **Avon Representative Barbie, black, white, Hispanic,** 1999, Mattel
EX n/a   **NM** $20   **MIP** $50

❑ **Avon Snow Sensation, black or white,** 1999, Mattel
EX n/a   **NM** $15   **MIP** $40

❑ **Avon Spring Blossom, black,** 1996, Mattel, Model No. 15202
EX n/a   **NM** $10   **MIP** $20

❑ **Avon Spring Blossom, white,** 1996, Mattel, Model No. 15201
EX n/a   **NM** $10   **MIP** $25

❑ **Avon Spring Petals Barbie, black,** 1997, Mattel, Model No. 16871
EX n/a   **NM** $15   **MIP** $30

❑ **Avon Spring Petals Barbie, blond or brunette,** 1997, Mattel, Model No. 10746/16872
EX n/a   **NM** $15   **MIP** $30

❑ **Avon Spring Tea Party Barbie, black,** Mattel
EX n/a   **NM** $15   **MIP** $30

❑ **Avon Spring Tea Party Barbie, blond or brunette,** Mattel, Model No. 18658
EX n/a   **NM** $15   **MIP** $30

❑ **Avon Strawberry Sorbet Barbie,** 1999, Mattel, Model No. 20317
EX n/a   **NM** $10   **MIP** $25

❑ **Avon Timeless Silhouette Barbie, white or black,** 2001, Mattel
EX n/a   **NM** $10   **MIP** $25

❑ **Avon Victorian Skater Barbie, white or black,** 2000, Mattel
EX n/a   **NM** $10   **MIP** $35

❑ **Avon Winter Rhapsody Barbie, black,** Mattel, Model No. 16354
EX n/a   **NM** $15   **MIP** $30

❑ **Avon Winter Rhapsody Barbie, blond or brunette,** Mattel, Model No. 16353/16873
EX n/a   **NM** $15   **MIP** $30

❑ **Avon Winter Splendor Barbie, black,** 1998, Mattel, Model No. 19358
EX n/a　　**NM** $20　　**MIP** $40

❑ **Avon Winter Splendor Barbie, white,** 1998, Mattel, Model No. 19357
EX n/a　　**NM** $15　　**MIP** $35

❑ **Avon Winter Velvet, black,** 1996, Mattel, Model No. 15587
EX n/a　　**NM** $10　　**MIP** $85

❑ **Avon Winter Velvet, white,** 1996, Mattel, Model No. 15571
EX n/a　　**NM** $17　　**MIP** $75

❑ **B Mine Barbie,** 1993, Mattel, Model No. 11182
EX n/a　　**NM** $7　　**MIP** $25

❑ **Back To School,** 1993, Mattel, Model No. 3208
EX n/a　　**NM** $15　　**MIP** $35

❑ **Back to School,** 1997, Mattel
EX n/a　　**NM** $5　　**MIP** $10

❑ **Ballerina Dreams Barbie,** 2000, Mattel, Model No. 20676
EX n/a　　**NM** $5　　**MIP** $12

❑ **Ballerina on Tour Gift Set,** 1976, Mattel, Model No. 9613
EX n/a　　**NM** $25　　**MIP** $125

❑ **Ballet Lessons Barbie, black or white,** 2000, Mattel
EX n/a　　**NM** $5　　**MIP** $12

❑ **Ballroom Beauties, Midnight Waltz,** 1996, Mattel, Model No. 15685
EX n/a　　**NM** $35　　**MIP** $85

❑ **Ballroom Beauties, Moonlight Waltz Barbie,** 1997, Mattel, Model No. 17763
EX n/a　　**NM** $40　　**MIP** $80

❑ **Ballroom Beauties, Starlight Waltz Barbie,** 1995, Mattel, Model No. 14070
EX n/a　　**NM** $35　　**MIP** $85

❑ **Barbie 2000, white or black,** 2000, Mattel, Model No. 27409/27410
EX n/a　　**NM** $30　　**MIP** $60

❑ **Barbie 2001, black or white,** 2001, Mattel, Model No. 50842/50841
EX n/a　　**NM** $15　　**MIP** $50

❑ **Barbie 2002, (white or black),** 2002, Mattel, Model No. 53975/53976
EX n/a　　**NM** $20　　**MIP** $50

❑ **Barbie and Friends: Ken, Barbie, P.J.,** 1983, Mattel, Model No. 4431
EX n/a　　**NM** $25　　**MIP** $75

❑ **Barbie and Ken Camping Out,** 1983, Mattel
EX n/a　　**NM** $25　　**MIP** $65

❑ **Barbie and Ken Tennis Gift Set,** 1962, Mattel, Model No. 892
EX n/a　　**NM** $400　　**MIP** $900

❑ **Barbie and Krissy Magical Mermaids, black or white,** 2000, Mattel
EX n/a　　**NM** $15　　**MIP** $30

❑ **Barbie Beautiful Blues Gift Set,** 1967, Mattel, Model No. 3303
EX n/a　　**NM** $1600　　**MIP** $3000

❑ **Barbie Collector's Club Café Society,** 1998, Mattel, Model No. 18892
EX n/a　　**NM** $50　　**MIP** $200

❑ **Barbie Collector's Club Club Couture,** 2000, Mattel, Model No. 26068
EX n/a　　**NM** $25　　**MIP** $65

❑ **Barbie Collector's Club Embassy Waltz,** 1999, Mattel, Model No. 23386
EX n/a　　**NM** $45　　**MIP** $150

❑ **Barbie Collector's Club Grand Premiere,** 1997, Mattel, Model No. 16498
EX n/a　　**NM** $100　　**MIP** $225

❑ **Barbie Collector's Club Holiday Treasures 1999,** 1999, Mattel
EX n/a　　**NM** $75　　**MIP** $150

❑ **Barbie Collector's Club Holiday Treasures 2000,** 2000, Mattel, Model No. 27673
EX n/a　　**NM** $35　　**MIP** $75

❑ **Barbie Collector's Club Midnight Tuxedo, white or black,** 2001, Mattel
EX n/a　　**NM** $25　　**MIP** $65

❑ **Barbie Millicent Roberts Matinee Today,** 1996, Mattel, Model No. 16079
EX n/a　　**NM** $22　　**MIP** $60

❑ **Barbie Millicent Roberts Perfectly Suited,** 1997, Mattel, Model No. 17567
EX n/a　　**NM** $30　　**MIP** $45

❑ **Barbie Millicent Roberts Pinstripe Power,** 1998, Mattel, Model No. 19791
EX n/a　　**NM** $30　　**MIP** $50

❑ **Barbie's Round the Clock Gift Set, Bubblecut,** 1964, Mattel, Model No. 1013
EX n/a　　**NM** $1200　　**MIP** $3000

❑ **Barbie's Sparkling Pink Gift Set, Bubblecut,** 1964, Mattel, Model No. 1011
EX n/a　　**NM** $1000　　**MIP** $2400

❑ **Barbie's Wedding Party Gift Set,** 1964, Mattel, Model No. 1017
EX n/a　　**NM** $1000　　**MIP** $2400

❑ **Beauty Secrets Barbie Pretty Reflections Gift Set,** 1979, Mattel, Model No. 1702
EX n/a　　**NM** $40　　**MIP** $100

❑ **Best Buy Detective Barbie,** 2000, Mattel, Model No. 24189
EX n/a　　**NM** $8　　**MIP** $17

❑ **Bill Blass Barbie,** 1997, Mattel, Model No. 17040
EX n/a　　**NM** $35　　**MIP** $75

(KP Photo)

❑ **Billions of Dreams Barbie,** 1997, Mattel, Model No. 17641
EX n/a　　**NM** $150　　**MIP** $275

(KP Photo)

❑ **Billy Boy Feelin' Groovy Barbie,** 1986, Mattel, Model No. 3421
EX n/a　　**NM** $100　　**MIP** $175

(KP Photo)

❑ **Billy Boy Le Nouveau Theatre de la Mode Barbie,** 1985, Mattel, Model No. 6279
EX n/a　　**NM** $100　　**MIP** $200

❑ **Birds of Beauty #1 Peacock Barbie,** 1998, Mattel, Model No. 19365
EX n/a　　**NM** $32　　**MIP** $70

❑ **Birds of Beauty #2 Flamingo Barbie,** 1999, Mattel, Model No. 22957
EX n/a　　**NM** $40　　**MIP** $70

❑ **Birds of Beauty #3 Swan Barbie,** 2000, Mattel, Model No. 27682
EX n/a　　**NM** $40　　**MIP** $70

BARBIE

❏ **Birthday Fun at McDonald's Gift Set,**
1994, Mattel, Model No. 11589
EX n/a   **NM** $15   **MIP** $35

❏ **Birthday Wishes #1, black or white,**
1999, Mattel, Model No. 21128/21509
EX n/a   **NM** $15   **MIP** $35

❏ **Birthday Wishes #2, black or white,**
2000, Mattel, Model No. 24667/24668
EX n/a   **NM** $20   **MIP** $40

❏ **Birthday Wishes #3, black or white,**
2001, Mattel
EX n/a   **NM** $10   **MIP** $35

❏ **BJ's Fantastica Barbie,** 1993, Mattel,
Model No. 3196
EX n/a   **NM** $15   **MIP** $50

❏ **BJ's Festiva,** 1993, Mattel
EX n/a   **NM** $15   **MIP** $50

❏ **BJ's Golden Waltz, blonde or red,**
1999, Mattel
EX n/a   **NM** $10   **MIP** $25

❏ **BJ's Rose Bride Barbie,** 1996, Mattel,
Model No. 15987
EX n/a   **NM** $15   **MIP** $30

❏ **BJ's Sparkle Beauty,** 1997, Mattel
EX n/a   **NM** $15   **MIP** $30

❏ **Bloomingdale's Barbie at Bloom-
ingdale's,** 1996, Mattel, Model
No. 16290
EX n/a   **NM** $15   **MIP** $35

❏ **Bloomingdale's Calvin Klein Barbie,**
1996, Mattel
EX n/a   **NM** $20   **MIP** $55

❏ **Bloomingdale's Donna Karan, blond,**
1995, Mattel, Model No. 14452
EX n/a   **NM** $35   **MIP** $75

❏ **Bloomingdale's Donna Karan, brunette,** 1996, Mattel, Model No. 14452
EX n/a   **NM** $35   **MIP** $125

❏ **Bloomingdale's Oscar de la Renta,**
1998, Mattel, Model No. 20376
EX n/a   **NM** $35   **MIP** $80

❏ **Bloomingdale's Ralph Lauren,** 1997,
Mattel, Model No. 15950
EX n/a   **NM** $40   **MIP** $80

❏ **Bloomingdale's Savvy Shopper,
Nicole Miller,** 1994, Mattel, Model
No. 12152
EX n/a   **NM** $50   **MIP** $100

❏ **Bob Mackie Designer Gold,** 1990, Mattel, Model No. 5405
EX n/a   **NM** $350   **MIP** $500

❏ **Bob Mackie Empress Bride,** 1992, Mattel, Model No. 4247
EX n/a   **NM** $500   **MIP** $750

❏ **Bob Mackie Fantasy Goddess of Africa,**
1999, Mattel, Model No. 22044
EX n/a   **NM** $120   **MIP** $175

(Mattel Photo)

❏ **Bob Mackie Fantasy Goddess of Asia,**
1998, Mattel, Model No. SA415
EX n/a   **NM** $120   **MIP** $175

❏ **Bob Mackie Fantasy Goddess of the
Americas,** 2000, Mattel, Model
No. 25859
EX n/a   **NM** $125   **MIP** $175

❏ **Bob Mackie Fantasy Goddess of the
Arctic,** 2001, Mattel, Model No. 50840
EX n/a   **NM** $75   **MIP** $175

(KP Photo)

❏ **Bob Mackie Goddess of the Moon,**
1996, Mattel, Model No. 14105
EX n/a   **NM** $75   **MIP** $200

❏ **Bob Mackie Goddess of the Sun,** 1995,
Mattel, Model No. 14056
EX n/a   **NM** $75   **MIP** $200

❏ **Bob Mackie Jewel Essence Amethyst
Aura,** 1997, Mattel, Model No. 15522
EX n/a   **NM** $40   **MIP** $120

❏ **Bob Mackie Jewel Essence Diamond
Dazzle,** 1997, Mattel, Model No. 15519
EX n/a   **NM** $40   **MIP** $140

❏ **Bob Mackie Jewel Essence Emerald
Embers,** 1997, Mattel, Model
No. 15521
EX n/a   **NM** $40   **MIP** $120

❏ **Bob Mackie Jewel Essence Ruby Radi-
ance,** 1997, Mattel, Model No. 15520
EX n/a   **NM** $40   **MIP** $120

❏ **Bob Mackie Jewel Essence Sapphire
Splendor,** 1997, Mattel, Model
No. 15523
EX n/a   **NM** $40   **MIP** $120

❏ **Bob Mackie Madame du Barbie,** 1997,
Mattel, Model No. 17934
EX n/a   **NM** $100   **MIP** $225

❏ **Bob Mackie Masquerade Ball,** 1993,
Mattel, Model No. 10803
EX n/a   **NM** $250   **MIP** $375

(KP Photo)

❏ **Bob Mackie Neptune Fantasy,** 1992,
Mattel, Model No. 4248
EX n/a   **NM** $400   **MIP** $800

❏ **Bob Mackie Platinum,** 1991, Mattel,
Model No. 2703
EX n/a   **NM** $300   **MIP** $450

(Mattel Photo)

❏ **Bob Mackie Queen of Hearts,** 1994,
Mattel, Model No. 12046
EX n/a   **NM** $125   **MIP** $275

❑ **Bob Mackie Red Carpet, Brunette Brilliance,** 2003, Mattel, Model No. B0585
EX n/a   **NM** $50   **MIP** $200

❑ **Bob Mackie Red Carpet, Radiant Redhead,** 2002, Mattel, Model No. 55501
EX n/a   **NM** $100   **MIP** $200

❑ **Bob Mackie Starlight Splendor,** 1991, Mattel, Model No. 2704
EX n/a   **NM** $200   **MIP** $450

❑ **Bowling Champ Barbie,** 2000, Mattel, Model No. 25871
EX n/a   **NM** $15   **MIP** $30

❑ **Bridal Collection Millennium Wedding, white, black or Hispanic,** 2000, Mattel, Model No. 27674
EX n/a   **NM** $25   **MIP** $50

❑ **Burberry Barbie,** 2001, Mattel, Model No. 29421
EX n/a   **NM** $25   **MIP** $50

❑ **Byron Lars Cinnabar Sensation, black or white,** 1999, Mattel, Model No. 19848
EX n/a   **NM** $35   **MIP** $95

❑ **Byron Lars In the Limelight,** 1997, Mattel, Model No. 17031
EX n/a   **NM** $40   **MIP** $250

❑ **Byron Lars Indigo Obsession,** 2000, Mattel, Model No. 26935
EX n/a   **NM** $25   **MIP** $65

❑ **Byron Lars Moja Barbie,** 2001, Mattel, Model No. 50826
EX n/a   **NM** $40   **MIP** $100

❑ **Byron Lars Plum Royale,** 1998, Mattel, Model No. 23478
EX n/a   **NM** $40   **MIP** $95

❑ **Caroling Fun Barbie,** 1995, Mattel, Model No. 13966
EX n/a   **NM** $8   **MIP** $20

❑ **Casey Goes Casual Gift Set,** 1967, Mattel, Model No. 3304
EX n/a   **NM** $800   **MIP** $1650

❑ **Celebration Barbie 2000, white or black,** 2000, Mattel
EX n/a   **NM** $15   **MIP** $45

❑ **Celebration Teresa 2000,** 2000, Mattel, Model No. 29081
EX n/a   **NM** $15   **MIP** $45

❑ **Celestial Collection #1 Evening Star,** 2000, Mattel, Model No. 27690
EX n/a   **NM** $25   **MIP** $49

❑ **Celestial Collection #2 Morning Sun,** 2000, Mattel, Model No. 27688
EX n/a   **NM** $25   **MIP** $49

❑ **Celestial Collection #3 Midnight Moon Princess,** 2000, Mattel, Model No. 27689
EX n/a   **NM** $25   **MIP** $49

❑ **Children's Collector Series Belle (Beauty and the Beast),** 2000, Mattel, Model No. 24673
EX n/a   **NM** $20   **MIP** $40

❑ **Children's Collector Series Cinderella,** 1997, Mattel, Model No. 16900
EX n/a   **NM** $25   **MIP** $40

❑ **Children's Collector Series Little Bo Peep,** 1995, Mattel, Model No. 14960
EX n/a   **NM** $65   **MIP** $125

❑ **Children's Collector Series Rapunzel,** 1995, Mattel, Model No. 13016
EX n/a   **NM** $25   **MIP** $50

❑ **Children's Collector Series Sleeping Beauty,** 1998, Mattel
EX n/a   **NM** $20   **MIP** $45

❑ **Children's Collector Series Snow White,** 1999, Mattel, Model No. 21130
EX n/a   **NM** $20   **MIP** $40

❑ **Christian Dior 50th Anniversary,** 1997, Mattel, The New Look, Model No. 16013
EX n/a   **NM** $35   **MIP** $65

❑ **Christian Dior Barbie,** 1995, Mattel, Model No. 13168
EX n/a   **NM** $60   **MIP** $100

❑ **Chuck E. Cheese Barbie,** 1996, Mattel, Model No. 14615
EX n/a   **NM** $15   **MIP** $30

❑ **City Seasons Autumn in London,** 1999, Mattel, Model No. 22257
EX n/a   **NM** $20   **MIP** $50

❑ **City Seasons Autumn in Paris,** 1998, Mattel, Model No. 19367
EX n/a   **NM** $18   **MIP** $50

(KP Photo)

❑ **City Seasons Summer in Rome,** 1999, Mattel, Model No. 19431
EX n/a   **NM** $25   **MIP** $50

❑ **City Seasons Winter in Montreal,** 1999, Mattel, Model No. 22258
EX n/a   **NM** $20   **MIP** $50

(KP Photo)

❑ **City Seasons Spring in Tokyo,** 1999, Mattel, Model No. 19430
EX n/a   **NM** $25   **MIP** $50

❑ **City Seasons Spring in Tokyo, Internet Exclusive,** 1999, Mattel, Model No. 23499
EX n/a   **NM** $30   **MIP** $65

(KP Photo)

❑ **City Seasons Winter in New York,** 1998, Mattel, Model No. 19429
EX n/a   **NM** $18   **MIP** $50

❑ **Classic Ballet Flower Ballerina,** 2001, Mattel, Model No. 28375
EX n/a   **NM** $10   **MIP** $28

BARBIE

❑ **Classic Ballet Marzipan,** 1999, Mattel, Model No. 20581
EX n/a   **NM** $15   **MIP** $30

(Mattel Photo)

❑ **Classic Ballet Peppermint Candy Cane,** 2003, Mattel, Model No. 57578
EX n/a   **NM** $10   **MIP** $30

❑ **Classic Ballet Snowflake,** 2000, Mattel, Model No. 25642
EX n/a   **NM** $15   **MIP** $30

(KP Photo)

❑ **Classic Ballet Sugar Plum Fairy,** 1997, Mattel, Model No. 17056
EX n/a   **NM** $15   **MIP** $35

❑ **Classic Ballet Swan Ballerina,** 2002, Mattel, Model No. 53867
EX n/a   **NM** $10   **MIP** $30

❑ **Classic Ballet Swan Lake, black or white,** 1998, Mattel, Model No. 18509/18510
EX n/a   **NM** $15   **MIP** $30

❑ **Classique Benefit Ball Barbie,** 1992, Mattel, Model No. 1521
EX n/a   **NM** $50   **MIP** $125

❑ **Classique City Style Barbie,** 1993, Mattel, Model No. 10149
EX n/a   **NM** $30   **MIP** $100

❑ **Classique Evening Extravaganza,** 1994, Mattel, Model No. 11622
EX n/a   **NM** $25   **MIP** $65

❑ **Classique Evening Extravaganza, black,** 1994, Mattel, Model No. 11638
EX n/a   **NM** $25   **MIP** $75

❑ **Classique Evening Sophisticate,** 1998, Mattel, Model No. 19361
EX n/a   **NM** $18   **MIP** $50

❑ **Classique Midnight Gala,** 1995, Mattel, Model No. 12999
EX n/a   **NM** $25   **MIP** $60

❑ **Classique Opening Night Barbie,** 1993, Mattel, Model No. 10148
EX n/a   **NM** $30   **MIP** $95

❑ **Classique Romantic Interlude Barbie,** 1997, Mattel, Model No. 17136
EX n/a   **NM** $15   **MIP** $45

❑ **Classique Romantic Interlude Barbie, black,** 1997, Mattel, Model No. 17137
EX n/a   **NM** $15   **MIP** $45

❑ **Classique Starlight Dance,** 1996, Mattel, Model No. 15461
EX n/a   **NM** $20   **MIP** $45

❑ **Classique Starlight Dance, black,** 1996, Mattel, Model No. 15819
EX n/a   **NM** $20   **MIP** $45

❑ **Classique Uptown Chic Barbie,** 1994, Mattel, Model No. 11623
EX n/a   **NM** $25   **MIP** $70

❑ **Coca-Cola #5 (majorette),** 2002, Mattel, Model No. 53974
EX n/a   **NM** $20   **MIP** $60

❑ **Coca-Cola Barbie #1, carhop,** 1999, Mattel, Model No. 22831
EX n/a   **NM** $20   **MIP** $65

❑ **Coca-Cola Barbie #2,** 2000, Mattel, Model No. 24637
EX n/a   **NM** $25   **MIP** $59

❑ **Coca-Cola Cheerleader,** 2001, Mattel
EX n/a   **NM** $15   **MIP** $50

❑ **Coca-Cola Fashion Classic #1, Soda Fountain Sweetheart,** 1996, Mattel
EX n/a   **NM** $50   **MIP** $125

❑ **Coca-Cola Fashion Classic #2, After the Walk,** 1997, Mattel, Model No. 17341
EX n/a   **NM** $50   **MIP** $125

❑ **Coca-Cola Fashion Classic #3, Summer Daydreams,** 1998, Mattel, Model No. 19739
EX n/a   **NM** $50   **MIP** $100

❑ **Coca-Cola Ken,** 2000, Mattel, Model No. 25678
EX n/a   **NM** $25   **MIP** $59

❑ **Coca-Cola Party,** 1999, Mattel, Model No. 22964
EX n/a   **NM** $5   **MIP** $15

❑ **Coca-Cola Picnic,** 1998, Mattel, Model No. 19626
EX n/a   **NM** $5   **MIP** $15

❑ **Coca-Cola Splash,** 2000, Mattel, Model No. 22590
EX n/a   **NM** $5   **MIP** $15

❑ **Coca-Cola, Disney Teddy & Doll Convention, brunette, limited to 1,500,** Mattel
EX n/a   **NM** $45   **MIP** $95

❑ **Collectors' Request Commuter Set,** 1999, Mattel, Model No. 21510
EX n/a   **NM** $25   **MIP** $65

❑ **Collectors' Request Gay Parisienne,** 2003, Mattel, Model No. 57610
EX n/a   **NM** $25   **MIP** $50

❑ **Collectors' Request Gold 'N Glamour,** 2002, Mattel, Model No. 54185
EX n/a   **NM** $20   **MIP** $50

❑ **Collectors' Request Sophisticated Lady,** 1999, Mattel, Model No. 24930
EX n/a   **NM** $25   **MIP** $65

❑ **Collectors' Request Suburban Shopper,** 2000, Mattel
EX n/a   **NM** $15   **MIP** $45

❑ **Collectors' Request Twist N Turn Smasheroo, brunette,** 1998, Mattel, Model No. 18941
EX n/a   **NM** $25   **MIP** $40

❑ **Collectors' Request Twist N' Turn Smasheroo, red hair,** 1998, Mattel, Model No. 23258
EX n/a   **NM** $25   **MIP** $50

❑ **Cool Collecting Barbie,** 2000, Mattel, Nostalgic Toys, Model No. 25525
EX n/a   **NM** $25   **MIP** $40

❑ **Couture Collection Portrait in Taffeta Barbie,** 1996, Mattel, Model No. 15528
EX n/a   **NM** $65   **MIP** $100

❑ **Couture Collection Serenade in Satin Barbie,** 1997, Mattel, Model No. 17572
EX n/a   **NM** $65   **MIP** $100

❑ **Couture Collection Symphony in Chiffon,** 1998, Mattel, Model No. 21295
EX n/a   **NM** $65   **MIP** $100

❑ **Cracker Barrel Country Charm Barbie,** 2001, Mattel
EX n/a   **NM** $5   **MIP** $15

❑ **Dance Club Barbie Gift Set,** 1989, Mattel, Model No. 4917
EX n/a   **NM** $25   **MIP** $60

❑ **Dance Magic Gift Set Barbie & Ken,** 1990, Mattel, Model No. 5409
EX n/a   **NM** $15   **MIP** $35

❑ **Dance Sensation Barbie Gift Set,** 1984, Mattel, Model No. 9058
EX n/a   **NM** $15   **MIP** $40

❑ **Democratic National Convention Delegate Barbie,** 2000, Mattel
EX n/a   **NM** $25   **MIP** $150

❑ **Designer Spotlight, Katiana Jimenez,** 2003, Mattel, Model No. B0836
EX n/a   **NM** $20   **MIP** $50

❑ **Diva Collection, All that Glitters,** 2002, Mattel, Model No. 55426
EX n/a   **NM** $20   **MIP** $50

❑ **Diva Collection, Gone Platinum (white or black),** 2002, Mattel, Model No. 52739/53868
EX n/a   **NM** $20   **MIP** $50

(Mattel Photo)

❑ **Diva Collection, Red Hot (white or black),** 2003, Mattel, Model No. 56707/56708
EX n/a   NM $20   MIP $50

❑ **Empress Sissy, Barbie as,** 1996, Mattel, Model No. 15846
EX n/a   NM $35   MIP $80

❑ **Enchanted Mermaid,** 2002, Mattel, Model No. 53978
EX n/a   NM $100   MIP $300

❑ **Enchanted Seasons #1 Snow Princess,** 1994, Mattel, Model No. 11875
EX n/a   NM $40   MIP $125

❑ **Enchanted Seasons #2 Spring Bouquet,** 1995, Mattel, Model No. 12989
EX n/a   NM $40   MIP $125

❑ **Enchanted Seasons #3 Autumn Glory,** 1996, Mattel, Model No. 15204
EX n/a   NM $40   MIP $125

❑ **Enchanted Seasons #4 Summer Splendor,** 1997, Mattel, Model No. 15683
EX n/a   NM $40   MIP $125

❑ **Enchanted World of Fairies, Fairy of the Forest,** 2000, Mattel, Model No. 25639
EX n/a   NM $25   MIP $49

❑ **Enchanted World of Fairies, Fairy of the Garden,** 2001, Mattel
EX n/a   NM $15   MIP $45

❑ **Escada Barbie,** 1996, Mattel, Model No. 15948
EX n/a   NM $40   MIP $70

(KP Photo)

❑ **Essence of Nature #1 Water Rhapsody,** 1998, Mattel, Model No. 19847
EX n/a   NM $40   MIP $90

❑ **Essence of Nature #2 Whispering Wind,** 1999, Mattel, Model No. 22834
EX n/a   NM $40   MIP $80

❑ **Essence of Nature #3 Dancing Fire,** 2000, Mattel, Model No. 26327
EX n/a   NM $35   MIP $80

(Mattel Photo)

❑ **FAO Schwarz American Beauty, Barbie as George Washington,** 1996, Mattel, Model No. 17557
EX n/a   NM $35   MIP $65

(Mattel Photo)

❑ **FAO Schwarz American Beauty, Statue of Liberty,** 1996, Mattel, Model No. 14684
EX n/a   NM $40   MIP $65

❑ **FAO Schwarz Bob Mackie Lady Liberty,** 2000, Mattel, limited to 15,000
EX n/a   NM $75   MIP $125

❑ **FAO Schwarz Bob Mackie Le Papillon,** 1999, Mattel, Model No. 23276
EX n/a   NM $70   MIP $175

❑ **FAO Schwarz Circus Star Barbie,** 1995, Mattel, Model No. 13257
EX n/a   NM $35   MIP $80

❑ **FAO Schwarz City Seasons Summer in San Francisco, blond,** 1998, Mattel, Model No. 19363
EX n/a   NM $40   MIP $95

❑ **FAO Schwarz City Seasons Summer in San Francisco, red hair,** Mattel
EX n/a   NM $200   MIP $750

❑ **FAO Schwarz Fashion Model Fashion Editor,** 2000, Mattel
EX n/a   NM $50   MIP $90

❑ **FAO Schwarz Floral Signature #1 Antique Rose,** 1996, Mattel, limited to 10,000, Model No. 15814
EX n/a   NM $50   MIP $150

❑ **FAO Schwarz Floral Signature #2 Lily Barbie,** 1997, Mattel, limited to 10,000, Model No. 17556
EX n/a   NM $50   MIP $145

❑ **FAO Schwarz Golden Greetings Barbie,** 1989, Mattel, Model No. 7734
EX n/a   NM $65   MIP $225

❑ **FAO Schwarz Golden Hollywood Barbie, white or black,** 1999, Mattel
EX n/a   NM $55   MIP $100

❑ **FAO Schwarz Jeweled Splendor (125th Anniversary),** 1995, Mattel, Model No. 14061
EX n/a   NM $75   MIP $175

❑ **FAO Schwarz Madison Ave. Barbie,** 1992, Mattel, Model No. 1539
EX n/a   NM $75   MIP $175

❑ **FAO Schwarz Mann's Chinese Theatre Barbie, white or black,** 2000, Mattel, Model No. 24636/24998
EX n/a   NM $35   MIP $75

❑ **FAO Schwarz Night Sensation,** 1991, Mattel, Model No. 2921
EX n/a   NM $75   MIP $125

(KP Photo)

❑ **FAO Schwarz Phantom of the Opera Gift Set,** 1998, Mattel, Model No. 20377
EX n/a   NM $60   MIP $145

❑ **FAO Schwarz Rockettes Barbie,** 1993, Mattel, Model No. 2017
EX n/a   NM $75   MIP $175

❑ **FAO Schwarz Shopping Spree,** 1994, Mattel, Model No. 12749
EX n/a   NM $5   MIP $15

BARBIE

□ **FAO Schwarz Silver Screen Barbie,** 1994, Mattel, Model No. 11652
EX n/a   NM $65   MIP $150

□ **FAO Schwarz Winter Fantasy,** 1990, Mattel, Model No. 5946
EX n/a   NM $100   MIP $175

□ **FAO Schwarz, Barbie at FAO,** 1997, Mattel, Model No. 17298
EX n/a   NM $12   MIP $25

□ **Fashion Model, Capucine,** 2003, Mattel, Model No. B0146
EX n/a   NM $75   MIP $185

□ **Fashion Model, Continental Holiday Gift Set,** 2002, Mattel, Model No. 55497
EX n/a   NM $50   MIP $100

□ **Fashion Model, Delphine Barbie,** 2000, Mattel, Model No. 26929
EX n/a   NM $35   MIP $65

□ **Fashion Model, Dusk to Dawn,** 2001, Mattel, Model No. 29654
EX n/a   NM $50   MIP $125

□ **Fashion Model, In The Pink,** 2001, Mattel, Model No. 27683
EX n/a   NM $75   MIP $200

□ **Fashion Model, Lingerie #1, blond,** 2000, Mattel, Model No. 26930
EX n/a   NM $20   MIP $125

□ **Fashion Model, Lingerie #2, brunette,** 2000, Mattel, Model No. 26931
EX n/a   NM $20   MIP $150

□ **Fashion Model, Lingerie #3, black hair,** 2001, Mattel, Model No. 29651
EX n/a   NM $20   MIP $150

□ **Fashion Model, Lingerie #4,** 2002, Mattel, Model No. 55498
EX n/a   NM $20   MIP $50

(Mattel Photo)

□ **Fashion Model, Lingerie #5 (black),** 2002, Mattel, Model No. 56120
EX n/a   NM $20   MIP $50

□ **Fashion Model, Lingerie #6, redhead,** 2003, Mattel, Model No. 56948
EX n/a   NM $25   MIP $50

□ **Fashion Model, Lisette,** 2001, Mattel, Model No. 29650
EX n/a   NM $45   MIP $70

□ **Fashion Model, Maria Therese (bride),** 2002, Mattel, Model No. 55496
EX n/a   NM $50   MIP $100

□ **Fashion Model, Model Life Gift Set,** 2003, Mattel, Model No. B0147
EX n/a   NM $50   MIP $100

□ **Fashion Model, Provencale,** 2002, Mattel, Model No. 50829
EX n/a   NM $50   MIP $200

□ **Fashion Queen Barbie & Her Friends,** 1964, Mattel, Model No. 863
EX n/a   NM $1000   MIP $2400

□ **Fashion Queen Barbie & Ken Trousseau Gift Set,** 1964, Mattel, Model No. 864
EX n/a   NM $1200   MIP $2800

□ **Fashion Savvy #1 Tangerine Twist,** 1997, Mattel, Model No. 17860
EX n/a   NM $14   MIP $45

□ **Fashion Savvy #2 Uptown Chic,** 1998, Mattel, Model No. 19632
EX n/a   NM $20   MIP $45

□ **Ferrari Barbie #1, Scuderia, racing outfit,** 2001, Mattel, Model No. 25636
EX n/a   NM $30   MIP $75

□ **Ferrari Barbie #2, red dress,** 2001, Mattel, Model No. 29608
EX n/a   NM $15   MIP $45

□ **Festive Season,** 1998, Mattel
EX n/a   NM $5   MIP $15

□ **Fire and Ice (white or black),** 2002, Mattel, Model No. 53511/53863
EX n/a   NM $20   MIP $60

□ **Flowers in Fashion Orchid Barbie,** 2001, Mattel, Model No. 50319
EX n/a   NM $25   MIP $65

□ **Flowers in Fashion Rose Barbie,** 2001, Mattel
EX n/a   NM $25   MIP $65

□ **Francie Rise n' Shine Gift Set,** 1971, Mattel, Model No. 1194
EX n/a   NM $600   MIP $1200

□ **Francie Swingin' Separates Gift Set,** 1966, Mattel, Model No. 1042
EX n/a   NM $700   MIP $1500

□ **Fun to Dress Barbie Gift Set,** 1993, Mattel, Model No. 3826
EX n/a   NM $8   MIP $15

□ **Gap Barbie and Kelly Gift Set,** 1997, Mattel, Model No. 18547
EX n/a   NM $15   MIP $45

□ **Gap Barbie and Kelly Gift Set, black,** 1997, Mattel, Model No. 18548
EX n/a   NM $15   MIP $45

□ **Gap Barbie, black,** 1996, Mattel, Model No. 16450
EX n/a   NM $20   MIP $60

□ **Gap Barbie, white,** 1996, Mattel, Model No. 16449
EX n/a   NM $30   MIP $60

□ **Garden of Flowers Rose Barbie,** 1999, Mattel, Model No. 22237
EX n/a   NM $25   MIP $50

□ **General Mills Winter Dazzle, black,** 1997, Mattel
EX n/a   NM $5   MIP $20

□ **General Mills Winter Dazzle, white,** 1997, Mattel, Model No. 18456
EX n/a   NM $5   MIP $20

□ **Givenchy Barbie,** 2000, Mattel, Model No. 24635
EX n/a   NM $40   MIP $80

□ **Goddess of Beauty Barbie,** 2000, Mattel, Model No. 27286
EX n/a   NM $25   MIP $65

□ **Goddess of Spring Barbie,** 2000, Mattel, Model No. 28112
EX n/a   NM $25   MIP $65

□ **Goddess of Wisdom Barbie,** 2001, Mattel
EX n/a   NM $25   MIP $65

□ **Graduation Barbie Class of 1996,** 1996, Mattel
EX n/a   NM $5   MIP $15

□ **Graduation Barbie Class of 1997,** 1997, Mattel
EX n/a   NM $5   MIP $10

□ **Graduation Barbie Class of 1998, white or black,** 1998, Mattel
EX n/a   NM $5   MIP $10

□ **Graduation Barbie Class of 2000, black box,** 2000, Mattel
EX n/a   NM $5   MIP $15

□ **Graduation Barbie Class of 2000, blue box,** 2000, Mattel
EX n/a   NM $5   MIP $15

□ **Grand Entrance Barbie (white or black),** 2002, Mattel, Model No. 53841/53842
EX n/a   NM $20   MIP $50

□ **Grand Entrance Barbie, white or black,** 2001, Mattel
EX n/a   NM $25   MIP $65

□ **Grand Ole Opry #1 Country Rose Barbie,** 1997, Mattel, Model No. 17782
EX n/a   NM $40   MIP $80

□ **Grand Ole Opry #2 Rising Star Barbie,** 1998, Mattel, Model No. 17864
EX n/a   NM $50   MIP $100

□ **Grand Ole Opry Barbie and Kenny Country Duet,** 1999, Mattel, Model No. 23498
EX n/a   NM $55   MIP $75

□ **Great Eras #1, Gibson Girl,** 1993, Mattel, Model No. 3702
EX n/a   NM $25   MIP $125

□ **Great Eras #10, Chinese Empress,** 1997, Mattel, Model No. 16708
EX n/a   NM $35   MIP $50

□ **Great Eras #2, Flapper,** 1993, Mattel, Model No. 4063
EX n/a   NM $25   MIP $150

(Mattel Photo)

❏ **Great Eras #3, Egyptian Queen,** 1994, Mattel, Model No. 11397
EX n/a   NM $20   MIP $80

❏ **Great Eras #4, Southern Belle,** 1994, Mattel, Model No. 11478
EX n/a   NM $20   MIP $65

❏ **Great Eras #5, Medieval Lady,** 1995, Mattel, Model No. 12791
EX n/a   NM $25   MIP $60

❏ **Great Eras #6, Elizabethan Queen,** 1995, Mattel, Model No. 12792
EX n/a   NM $25   MIP $60

❏ **Great Eras #7, Grecian Goddess,** 1996, Mattel, Model No. 15005
EX n/a   NM $35   MIP $50

❏ **Great Eras #8, Victorian Lady,** 1996, Mattel, Model No. 14900
EX n/a   NM $35   MIP $50

❏ **Great Eras #9, French Lady,** 1997, Mattel, Model No. 16707
EX n/a   NM $35   MIP $50

❏ **Great Fashions of the 20th Century #1, Promenade in the Park,** 1998, Mattel, 1910s, Model No. 18630
EX n/a   NM $20   MIP $65

❏ **Great Fashions of the 20th Century #2, Dance 'til Dawn,** 1998, Mattel, 1920s, Model No. 19631
EX n/a   NM $30   MIP $65

❏ **Great Fashions of the 20th Century #3, Steppin Out Barbie,** 1999, Mattel, 1930s, Model No. 21531
EX n/a   NM $30   MIP $60

❏ **Great Fashions of the 20th Century #4, Fabulous Forties,** 2000, Mattel, 1940s, Model No. 22162
EX n/a   NM $25   MIP $50

(KP Photo)

❏ **Great Fashions of the 20th Century #5, Nifty Fifties,** 2000, Mattel, 1950s, Model No. 27675
EX n/a   NM $25   MIP $50

(KP Photo)

❏ **Great Fashions of the 20th Century #6, Groovy Sixties,** 2000, Mattel, 1960s, Model No. 27676
EX n/a   NM $25   MIP $50

❏ **Great Fashions of the 20th Century #7, Peace & Love 70s Barbie,** 2000, Mattel, 1970s, Model No. 27677
EX n/a   NM $15   MIP $50

❏ **Groliers Book Club The Front Window Barbie,** 2000, Mattel, Model No. 27968
EX n/a   NM $10   MIP $35

❏ **Hallmark Fair Valentine Barbie,** 1998, Mattel
EX n/a   NM $20   MIP $45

❏ **Hallmark Gold Crown #1, Victorian Elegance Barbie,** 1994, Mattel, Model No. 12579
EX n/a   NM $75   MIP $80

❏ **Hallmark Gold Crown #2, Holiday Memories Barbie,** 1995, Mattel, Model No. 14108
EX n/a   NM $20   MIP $50

❏ **Hallmark Holiday Sensation Barbie,** 1999, Mattel, Model No. 19792
EX n/a   NM $15   MIP $50

❏ **Hallmark Holiday Traditions Barbie,** 1997, Mattel, Model No. 17094
EX n/a   NM $25   MIP $50

❏ **Hallmark Holiday Voyage Barbie,** 1998, Mattel
EX n/a   NM $25   MIP $50

❏ **Hallmark Sentimental Valentine Barbie,** 1997, Mattel
EX n/a   NM $23   MIP $50

❏ **Hallmark Sweet Valentine Barbie,** 1996, Mattel, Model No. 14880
EX n/a   NM $20   MIP $50

❏ **Hallmark Yuletide Romance Barbie,** 1996, Mattel, Model No. 15621
EX n/a   NM $20   MIP $50

❏ **Hanae Mori Barbie,** 2000, Mattel
EX n/a   NM $50   MIP $75

❏ **Happy Birthday Barbie Gift Set,** 1985, Mattel
EX n/a   NM $20   MIP $40

(KP Photo)

❏ **Happy Holidays 1988,** 1988, Mattel, Model No. 1703
EX n/a   NM $75   MIP $700

(KP Photo)

❏ **Happy Holidays 1989,** 1989, Mattel, Model No. 3253
EX n/a   NM $50   MIP $175

BARBIE

(KP Photo)

❏ **Happy Holidays 1990,** 1990, Mattel, Model No. 4098
EX n/a   NM $25   MIP $110

❏ **Happy Holidays 1990, black,** 1990, Mattel, Model No. 4543
EX n/a   NM $20   MIP $85

(KP Photo)

❏ **Happy Holidays 1991,** 1991, Mattel, Model No. 1871
EX n/a   NM $40   MIP $125

❏ **Happy Holidays 1991, black,** 1991, Mattel, Model No. 2696
EX n/a   NM $40   MIP $75

(KP Photo)

❏ **Happy Holidays 1992,** 1992, Mattel, Model No. 1429
EX n/a   NM $30   MIP $100

❏ **Happy Holidays 1992, black,** 1992, Mattel, Model No. 2396
EX n/a   NM $30   MIP $75

(KP Photo)

❏ **Happy Holidays 1993,** 1993, Mattel, Model No. 10824
EX n/a   NM $30   MIP $95

❏ **Happy Holidays 1993, black,** 1993, Mattel, Model No. 10911
EX n/a   NM $30   MIP $60

(KP Photo)

❏ **Happy Holidays 1994,** 1994, Mattel, Model No. 12155
EX n/a   NM $30   MIP $100

❏ **Happy Holidays 1994, black,** 1994, Mattel, Model No. 12156
EX n/a   NM $30   MIP $75

(KP Photo)

❏ **Happy Holidays 1995,** 1995, Mattel, Model No. 14123
EX n/a   NM $20   MIP $65

❏ **Happy Holidays 1995, black,** 1995, Mattel, Model No. 14124
EX n/a   NM $20   MIP $55

(KP Photo)

❏ **Happy Holidays 1996, white or black,** 1996, Mattel, Model No. 15646
EX n/a   NM $30   MIP $55

(KP Photo)

❏ **Happy Holidays 1997,** 1997, Mattel, Model No. 17832
EX n/a   NM $5   MIP $25

❏ **Happy Holidays 1997, black,** 1997, Mattel, Model No. 17833
EX n/a   NM $5   MIP $25

(KP Photo)

❏ **Happy Holidays 1998, white or black,** 1998, Mattel, Model No. 20200/20201
EX n/a   NM $10   MIP $25

❏ **Harrods/Hamleys West End Barbie,** 1996, Mattel, Model No. 17590
EX n/a   NM $20   MIP $60

❏ **Harvey Nichols Special Edition (limited to 250),** 1995, Mattel, Model No. 0175
EX n/a   **NM** $500   **MIP** $900

❏ **Hawaiian Barbie,** 1982, Mattel, Model No. 7470
EX n/a   **NM** $25   **MIP** $100

❏ **Hills Blue Elegance Barbie,** 1992, Mattel, Model No. 1879
EX n/a   **NM** $12   **MIP** $40

❏ **Hills Evening Sparkle,** 1990, Mattel, Model No. 3274
EX n/a   **NM** $10   **MIP** $35

❏ **Hills Moonlight Rose,** 1991, Mattel, Model No. 3549
EX n/a   **NM** $7   **MIP** $30

❏ **Hills Party Lace Barbie,** 1989, Mattel, Model No. 4843
EX n/a   **NM** $15   **MIP** $35

❏ **Hills Polly Pocket Barbie,** 1994, Mattel, Model No. 12412
EX n/a   **NM** $12   **MIP** $25

❏ **Hills Sea Pearl Mermaid Barbie,** 1995, Mattel, Model No. 13940
EX n/a   **NM** $8   **MIP** $35

❏ **Hills Sidewalk Chalk Barbie,** 1998, Mattel, Model No. 19784
EX n/a   **NM** $10   **MIP** $25

❏ **Hills Teddy Fun Barbie,** 1996, Mattel, Model No. 15684
EX n/a   **NM** $10   **MIP** $25

❏ **Holiday Angel #1, black,** 2000, Mattel, Model No. 28080
EX n/a   **NM** $20   **MIP** $50

❏ **Holiday Angel #1, white,** 2000, Mattel, Model No. 26914
EX n/a   **NM** $20   **MIP** $50

❏ **Holiday Angel #2, black,** 2001, Mattel, Model No. 29770
EX n/a   **NM** $15   **MIP** $45

❏ **Holiday Angel #2, white,** 2001, Mattel, Model No. 29769
EX n/a   **NM** $15   **MIP** $45

❏ **Holiday Dreams Barbie,** 1994, Mattel, Model No. 12192
EX n/a   **NM** $10   **MIP** $20

❏ **Holiday Hostess Barbie,** 1993, Mattel, Model No. 10280
EX n/a   **NM** $25   **MIP** $50

❏ **Holiday Season,** 1996, Mattel, Model No. 15581
EX n/a   **NM** $5   **MIP** $15

❏ **Holiday Singing Sisters Gift Set,** 2000, Mattel
EX n/a   **NM** $15   **MIP** $50

❏ **Holiday Surprise Barbie, white or black,** 2000, Mattel
EX n/a   **NM** $5   **MIP** $15

❏ **Holiday Treats Barbie,** 1997, Mattel
EX n/a   **NM** $5   **MIP** $12

❏ **Hollywood Hair Deluxe Gift Set,** 1993, Mattel, Model No. 10928
EX n/a   **NM** $15   **MIP** $35

❏ **Hollywood Legends Dorothy (Wizard of Oz),** 1995, Mattel, Model No. 12701
EX n/a   **NM** $20   **MIP** $180

❏ **Hollywood Legends Eliza Doolittle (My Fair Lady), green coat,** 1996, Mattel, Model No. 15498
EX n/a   **NM** $30   **MIP** $50

❏ **Hollywood Legends Eliza Doolittle (My Fair Lady), lace ball gown,** 1996, Mattel, Model No. 15500
EX n/a   **NM** $30   **MIP** $95

❏ **Hollywood Legends Eliza Doolittle (My Fair Lady), pink,** 1996, Mattel, Model No. 15501
EX n/a   **NM** $30   **MIP** $75

❏ **Hollywood Legends Eliza Doolittle (My Fair Lady), white lace gown w/parasol,** 1996, Mattel, Model No. 15497
EX n/a   **NM** $30   **MIP** $75

❏ **Hollywood Legends Glinda (Wizard of Oz),** 1996, Mattel, Model No. 14901
EX n/a   **NM** $35   **MIP** $75

❏ **Hollywood Legends Ken as Cowardly Lion (Wizard of Oz),** 1996, Mattel, Model No. 16573
EX n/a   **NM** $35   **MIP** $75

❏ **Hollywood Legends Ken as Henry Higgins (My Fair Lady),** 1996, Mattel, Model No. 15499
EX n/a   **NM** $25   **MIP** $50

❏ **Hollywood Legends Ken as Rhett Butler,** 1994, Mattel, Gone With the Wind, Model No. 12741
EX n/a   **NM** $25   **MIP** $50

❏ **Hollywood Legends Ken as Scarecrow (Wizard of Oz),** 1996, Mattel, Model No. 16497
EX n/a   **NM** $35   **MIP** $50

❏ **Hollywood Legends Ken as Tin Man (Wizard of Oz),** 1996, Mattel, Model No. 14902
EX n/a   **NM** $35   **MIP** $40

❏ **Hollywood Legends Maria (Sound of Music),** 1995, Mattel, Model No. 13676
EX n/a   **NM** $20   **MIP** $50

❏ **Hollywood Legends Marilyn Monroe, pink,** 1997, Mattel, Gentlemen Prefer Blondes, Model No. 17451
EX n/a   **NM** $20   **MIP** $45

❏ **Hollywood Legends Marilyn Monroe, red,** 1997, Mattel, Gentlemen Prefer Blondes, Model No. 17452
EX n/a   **NM** $20   **MIP** $45

❏ **Hollywood Legends Marilyn Monroe, white,** 1997, Mattel, Seven Year Itch, Model No. 17155
EX n/a   **NM** $20   **MIP** $45

❏ **Hollywood Legends Scarlett O'Hara, black/white dress,** 1993, Mattel, Gone With the Wind, Model No. 13254
EX n/a   **NM** $25   **MIP** $65

(Mattel Photo)

❏ **Hollywood Legends Scarlett O'Hara, green velvet curtain,** 1994, Mattel, Gone With the Wind, Model No. 12045
EX n/a   **NM** $25   **MIP** $70

❏ **Hollywood Legends Scarlett O'Hara, green/white silk dress,** 1995, Mattel, Gone With the Wind, Model No. 12997
EX n/a   **NM** $25   **MIP** $50

❏ **Hollywood Legends Scarlett O'Hara, red velvet dress,** 1994, Mattel, Gone With the Wind, Model No. 12815
EX n/a   **NM** $25   **MIP** $50

(Mattel Photo)

❏ **Hollywood Movie Star, Between Takes,** 2000, Mattel, Model No. 27684
EX n/a   **NM** $25   **MIP** $50

❏ **Hollywood Movie Star, By the Pool,** 2000, Mattel, Model No. 27684
EX n/a   **NM** $25   **MIP** $50

❏ **Hollywood Movie Star, Day in the Sun,** 2000, Mattel, Model No. 2000
EX n/a   **NM** $25   **MIP** $50

❏ **Hollywood Movie Star, Hollywood Cast Party,** 2001, Mattel, Model No. 50825
EX n/a   **NM** $15   **MIP** $45

BARBIE

❑ **Hollywood Movie Star, Hollywood Premiere,** 2000, Mattel, Model No. 26914
EX n/a **NM** $25 **MIP** $50

❑ **Hollywood Movie Star, Publicity Tour,** 2001, Mattel
EX n/a **NM** $15 **MIP** $45

❑ **Home Shopping Club Evening Flame,** 1991, Mattel, Model No. 1865
EX n/a **NM** $70 **MIP** $125

❑ **Home Shopping Club Golden Allure Barbie,** 1999, Mattel
EX n/a **NM** $5 **MIP** $30

❑ **Home Shopping Club Premiere Night,** 1999, Mattel
EX n/a **NM** $5 **MIP** $30

❑ **I Dream of Jeannie Barbie,** 2001, Mattel
EX n/a **NM** $15 **MIP** $45

❑ **Japanese Living Eli,** 1970, Mattel, Foreign
EX n/a **NM** $700 **MIP** $1400

❑ **JCPenney Enchanted Evening,** 1991, Mattel, Model No. 2702
EX n/a **NM** $40 **MIP** $60

❑ **JCPenney Evening Elegance,** 1990, Mattel, Model No. 7057
EX n/a **NM** $40 **MIP** $50

❑ **JCPenney Evening Enchantment,** 1998, Mattel, Model No. 19783
EX n/a **NM** $25 **MIP** $55

❑ **JCPenney Evening Majesty,** 1997, Mattel, Model No. 17235
EX n/a **NM** $10 **MIP** $25

❑ **JCPenney Evening Sensation,** 1992, Mattel, Model No. 1278
EX n/a **NM** $12 **MIP** $50

❑ **JCPenney Golden Winter,** 1993, Mattel, Model No. 10684
EX n/a **NM** $12 **MIP** $50

❑ **JCPenney Night Dazzle,** 1994, Mattel, Model No. 12191
EX n/a **NM** $15 **MIP** $50

❑ **JCPenney Original Arizona Jean Co. Barbie #1,** 1996, Mattel, Model No. 15441
EX n/a **NM** $12 **MIP** $25

❑ **JCPenney Original Arizona Jean Co. Barbie #2,** 1997, Mattel, Model No. 18020
EX n/a **NM** $12 **MIP** $25

❑ **JCPenney Original Arizona Jean Co. Barbie #3,** 1998, Mattel, Model No. 19873
EX n/a **NM** $12 **MIP** $25

❑ **JCPenney Royal Enchantment,** 1995, Mattel, Model No. 14010
EX n/a **NM** $25 **MIP** $35

❑ **JCPenney Winter Renaissance,** 1996, Mattel, Model No. 15570
EX n/a **NM** $10 **MIP** $25

❑ **JCPenney/Sears Evening Recital Barbie, Stacie, Kelly and Tommy,** 2000, Mattel, Model No. 27954
EX n/a **NM** $15 **MIP** $42

❑ **Jubilee Series, Crystal Jubilee, limited to 20,000,** 1999, Mattel, Model No. 21923
EX n/a **NM** $150 **MIP** $275

❑ **Jubilee Series, Gold Jubilee, limited to 5,000,** 1994, Mattel, Model No. 12009
EX n/a **NM** $300 **MIP** $500

❑ **Jubilee Series, Pink Jubilee, limited to 1,200,** 1989, Mattel, Model No. 3756
EX n/a **NM** $800 **MIP** $2000

❑ **Julia Simply Wow Gift Set,** 1969, Mattel
EX n/a **NM** $400 **MIP** $1500

❑ **Just for You Barbie,** 2003, Mattel, Model No. B0151
EX n/a **NM** $10 **MIP** $35

❑ **K-B Fantasy Ball Barbie,** 1997, Mattel, Model No. 18594
EX n/a **NM** $10 **MIP** $20

❑ **K-B Fashion Avenue Barbie,** 1998, Mattel, Model No. 20782
EX n/a **NM** $8 **MIP** $15

❑ **K-B Glamour Barbie, black,** 1997, Mattel
EX n/a **NM** $10 **MIP** $20

❑ **K-B Starlight Carousel Barbie,** 1998, Mattel, Model No. 19708
EX n/a **NM** $10 **MIP** $20

❑ **Keepsake Treasures, Barbie and Curious George,** 2001, Mattel
EX n/a **NM** $15 **MIP** $30

❑ **Keepsake Treasures, Barbie and the Tale of Peter Rabbit,** 1998, Mattel, Model No. 19360
EX n/a **NM** $15 **MIP** $40

❑ **Keepsake Treasures, Peter Rabbit 100th Anniversary Barbie,** 2002, Mattel, Model No. 53872
EX n/a **NM** $20 **MIP** $40

❑ **Kissing Barbie Gift Set,** 1978, Mattel, Model No. 2977
EX n/a **NM** $25 **MIP** $65

❑ **Kmart March of Dimes Walk America Barbie & Kelly Gift Set,** 1999, Mattel, Model No. 20843
EX n/a **NM** $15 **MIP** $25

❑ **Kmart March of Dimes Walk America Barbie, black or white,** 1998, Mattel, Model No. 18506/18507
EX n/a **NM** $10 **MIP** $24

❑ **Kmart Peach Pretty Barbie,** 1989, Mattel, Model No. 4870
EX n/a **NM** $10 **MIP** $30

❑ **Kmart Pretty in Purple, black,** 1992, Mattel, Model No. 3121
EX n/a **NM** $12 **MIP** $25

❑ **Kmart Pretty in Purple, white,** 1992, Mattel, Model No. 3117
EX n/a **NM** $12 **MIP** $25

❑ **K-mart Route 66 Barbecue Bash,** 2000, Mattel
EX n/a **NM** $8 **MIP** $25

❑ **K-mart Very Berry Barbie, white or black,** 2000, Mattel
EX n/a **NM** $5 **MIP** $10

❑ **Kool-Aid Barbie,** 1996, Mattel
EX n/a **NM** $15 **MIP** $40

❑ **Kool-Aid Wacky Warehouse Barbie I,** 1993, Mattel, Model No. 10309
EX n/a **NM** $25 **MIP** $60

❑ **Kool-Aid Wacky Warehouse Barbie II,** 1994, Mattel, Model No. 11763
EX n/a **NM** $25 **MIP** $50

❑ **Kraft Treasures Barbie,** 1992, Mattel
EX n/a **NM** $30 **MIP** $55

❑ **L.E. Festival Holiday Barbie (540 made),** 1994, Mattel
EX n/a **NM** $500 **MIP** $900

❑ **Life Ball Barbie #1, Vivienne Westwood,** 1998, Mattel
EX n/a **NM** $200 **MIP** $400

❑ **Life Ball Barbie #2, Christian LaCroix,** 1999, Mattel
EX n/a **NM** $200 **MIP** $400

❑ **Little Debbie #1,** 1993, Mattel, Model No. 10123
EX n/a **NM** $25 **MIP** $60

❑ **Little Debbie #2,** 1996, Mattel, Model No. 14616
EX n/a **NM** $15 **MIP** $30

❑ **Little Debbie #3,** 1998, Mattel, Model No. 16352
EX n/a **NM** $15 **MIP** $25

❑ **Little Debbie #4,** 1999, Mattel, Model No. 24977
EX n/a **NM** $10 **MIP** $25

❑ **Living Barbie Action Accents Gift Set,** 1970, Mattel, Model No. 1585
EX n/a **NM** $500 **MIP** $1500

❑ **Loving You Barbie Gift Set,** 1983, Mattel, Model No. 7583
EX n/a **NM** $45 **MIP** $100

❑ **Macy's Anne Klein Barbie,** 1997, Mattel, Model No. 17603
EX n/a **NM** $30 **MIP** $70

❑ **Macy's City Shopper, Nicole Miller,** 1996, Mattel, Model No. 16289
EX n/a **NM** $25 **MIP** $70

❑ **Magic & Mystery, Morgan LeFay and Merlin,** 2000, Mattel, Model No. 27287
EX n/a **NM** $50 **MIP** $75

❑ **Magic & Mystery, Tales of the Arabian Nights,** 2001, Mattel, Model No. 50827
EX n/a **NM** $40 **MIP** $65

❑ **Major League Baseball Chicago Cubs,** 1999, Mattel, Model No. 23883
EX n/a **NM** $20 **MIP** $35

❑ **Major League Baseball Los Angeles Dodgers,** 1999, Mattel, Model No. 23882
EX n/a **NM** $20 **MIP** $11

❑ **Major League Baseball New York Yankees,** 1999, Mattel, Model No. 23881
EX n/a **NM** $20 **MIP** $11

❑ **Make-A-Valentine Barbie, white or black,** 1999, Mattel
EX n/a   NM $5   MIP $15

❑ **Malibu Barbie "The Beach Party," w/case,** 1979, Mattel, Model No. 1703
EX n/a   NM $17   MIP $35

❑ **Malibu Ken Surf's Up Gift Set,** 1971, Mattel, Model No. 1248
EX n/a   NM $75   MIP $200

❑ **Masquerade Gala #1, Illusion,** 1997, Mattel, Model No. 18667
EX n/a   NM $50   MIP $120

❑ **Masquerade Gala #2, Rendezvous,** 1998, Mattel, Model No. 20647
EX n/a   NM $50   MIP $85

❑ **Masquerade Gala #3, Venetian Opulence,** 2000, Mattel, Model No. 24501
EX n/a   NM $50   MIP $100

(Mattel Photo)

❑ **Mattel Festival 35th Anniversary (3,500 made),** 1994, Mattel
EX n/a   NM $100   MIP $175

❑ **Mattel Festival 35th Anniversary Gift Set (975 made),** 1994, Mattel, Model No. 11591
EX n/a   NM $250   MIP $400

❑ **Mattel Festival Banquet, blond,** 1994, Mattel
EX n/a   NM $100   MIP $175

❑ **Mattel Festival Banquet, brunette,** 1994, Mattel
EX n/a   NM $100   MIP $175

❑ **Mattel Festival Banquet, red hair,** 1994, Mattel
EX n/a   NM $100   MIP $175

❑ **Mattel Festival Doctor, brunette (1,500 made),** 1994, Mattel, Model No. 11160
EX n/a   NM $50   MIP $85

❑ **Mattel Festival Gymnast (1,500 made),** 1994, Mattel, Model No. 11921
EX n/a   NM $50   MIP $80

❑ **Mattel Festival Happy Holiday,** 1994, Mattel, Model No. 12155
EX n/a   NM $270   MIP $750

❑ **Mattel Festival Haute Couture, rainbow (500 made),** 1994, Mattel
EX n/a   NM $125   MIP $250

❑ **Mattel Festival Haute Couture, red velvet (480 made),** 1994, Mattel
EX n/a   NM $125   MIP $275

❑ **Mattel Festival Night Dazzle, brunette (420 made),** 1994, Mattel, Model No. 12191
EX n/a   NM $125   MIP $350

❑ **Mattel Festival Snow Princess, brunette (285 made),** 1994, Mattel, Model No. 12905
EX n/a   NM $500   MIP $1000

❑ **Meijers Hula Hoop,** 1997, Mattel, Model No. 18167
EX n/a   NM $10   MIP $20

❑ **Meijers Ice Cream,** 1998, Mattel, Model No. 19820
EX n/a   NM $10   MIP $20

❑ **Meijers Ladybug Fun,** 1997, Mattel, Model No. 17695
EX n/a   NM $10   MIP $20

❑ **Meijers Shopping Fun,** 1993, Mattel, Model No. 10051
EX n/a   NM $10   MIP $20

❑ **Meijers Something Extra,** 1992, Mattel, Model No. 0863
EX n/a   NM $10   MIP $20

❑ **Mervyns Ballerina Barbie,** 1983, Mattel, Model No. 4983
EX n/a   NM $30   MIP $75

❑ **Mervyns Fabulous Fur,** 1986, Mattel, Model No. 7093
EX n/a   NM $25   MIP $65

❑ **Midge's Ensemble Gift Set,** 1964, Mattel, Model No. 1012
EX n/a   NM $1200   MIP $3150

❑ **Millennium Bride, limited to 10,000,** 1999, Mattel, Model No. 24505
EX n/a   NM $150   MIP $300

❑ **Mix n' Match Gift Set,** 1962, Mattel, Model No. 857
EX n/a   NM $800   MIP $1850

(KP Photo)

❑ **Montgomery Wards (mail order box),** 1972, Mattel, Model No. 3210
EX n/a   NM $30   MIP $500

(KP Photo)

❑ **Montgomery Wards Barbie (pink box),** 1972, Mattel, Model No. 3210
EX n/a   NM $350   MIP $650

❑ **My First Barbie Gift Set,** 1991, Mattel, Model No. 2483
EX n/a   NM $8   MIP $20

❑ **My First Barbie Gift Set, pink tutu,** 1986, Mattel, Model No. 1979
EX n/a   NM $15   MIP $35

❑ **My First Barbie Gift Set, pink tutu,** 1987, Mattel, Model No. 5386
EX n/a   NM $18   MIP $40

❑ **My First Barbie, pink tutu, Zayre's Hispanic,** 1987, Mattel, Model No. 1875
EX n/a   NM $8   MIP $45

❑ **NASCAR Barbie #1, Kyle Petty #44,** 1998, Mattel, Model No. 20442
EX n/a   NM $20   MIP $25

❑ **NASCAR Barbie #2, Bill Elliott #94,** 1999, Mattel, Model No. 22954
EX n/a   NM $20   MIP $45

❑ **National Convention A Date with Barbie Doll in Atlanta,** 1998, Mattel
EX n/a   NM $100   MIP $350

❑ **National Convention Barbie in the Old West,** 2000, Mattel
EX n/a   NM $85   MIP $225

❑ **National Convention We Girls Can Do Anything Right Barbie,** 1999, Mattel
EX n/a   NM $85   MIP $225

❑ **National Convention, Barbie and the Bandstand,** 1996, Mattel, Pennsylvania
EX n/a   NM $225   MIP $450

❑ **National Convention, Barbie Around the World Festival,** 1985, Mattel, Michigan
EX n/a   NM $125   MIP $300

BARBIE

❑ **National Convention, Barbie Convention 1980,** 1980, Mattel, New York
EX n/a   NM $125   MIP $350

❑ **National Convention, Barbie Forever Young,** 1989, Mattel, California
EX n/a   NM $125   MIP $300

❑ **National Convention, Barbie Loves a Fairytale,** 1991, Mattel, Nebraska
EX n/a   NM $150   MIP $250

❑ **National Convention, Barbie Loves New York,** 1984, Mattel, New York
EX n/a   NM $125   MIP $275

❑ **National Convention, Barbie Ole,** 1995, Mattel, New Mexico
EX n/a   NM $225   MIP $400

❑ **National Convention, Barbie Wedding Dreams,** 1992, Mattel, New York
EX n/a   NM $50   MIP $200

❑ **National Convention, Barbie's Pow Wow,** 1983, Mattel, Arizona
EX n/a   NM $125   MIP $350

❑ **National Convention, Barbie's Reunion,** 1986, Mattel, Arizona
EX n/a   NM $125   MIP $275

❑ **National Convention, Beach Blanket Barbie,** 1997, Mattel, California
EX n/a   NM $225   MIP $375

❑ **National Convention, Christmas With Barbie,** 1987, Mattel, Oklahoma
EX n/a   NM $125   MIP $300

❑ **National Convention, Come Rain or Shine,** 1988, Mattel, Washington
EX n/a   NM $125   MIP $250

❑ **National Convention, Deep in the Heart of Texas,** 1990, Mattel, Texas
EX n/a   NM $125   MIP $250

❑ **National Convention, Michigan Entertains Barbie,** 1982, Mattel, Michigan
EX n/a   NM $125   MIP $275

❑ **National Convention, The Magic of Barbie,** 1994, Mattel, Alabama
EX n/a   NM $175   MIP $375

❑ **National Convention, You've Come a Long Way,** 1993, Mattel, Maryland
EX n/a   NM $225   MIP $450

❑ **New Lifestyles of the West Western Plains,** 1999, Mattel, Model No. 23205
EX n/a   NM $40   MIP $80

❑ **Nolan Miller #1, Sheer Illusion,** 1998, Mattel, Model No. 20662
EX n/a   NM $70   MIP $150

❑ **Nolan Miller #2, Evening Illusion,** 1999, Mattel, Model No. 23495
EX n/a   NM $70   MIP $110

❑ **Nostalgic 35th Anniversary Gift Set,** 1994, Mattel, Model No. 11591
EX n/a   NM $65   MIP $125

❑ **Nostalgic 35th Anniversary, blond,** 1994, Mattel, Model No. 11590
EX n/a   NM $25   MIP $50

❑ **Nostalgic 35th Anniversary, brunette,** 1994, Mattel, Model No. 11782
EX n/a   NM $40   MIP $65

❑ **Nostalgic Reproductions, Busy Gal Barbie,** 1995, Mattel, Model No. 13675
EX n/a   NM $25   MIP $55

❑ **Nostalgic Reproductions, Enchanted Evening Barbie, blond,** 1996, Mattel, Model No. 14992
EX n/a   NM $25   MIP $30

❑ **Nostalgic Reproductions, Enchanted Evening, brunette,** 1996, Mattel, Model No. 15407
EX n/a   NM $25   MIP $30

(KP Photo)

❑ **Nostalgic Reproductions, Fashion Luncheon,** 1997, Mattel, Model No. 17382
EX n/a   NM $25   MIP $55

❑ **Nostalgic Reproductions, Francie Wild Bunch,** 1997, Mattel, Model No. 17601
EX n/a   NM $20   MIP $55

(KP Photo)

❑ **Nostalgic Reproductions, Francie, 30th Anniversary,** 1996, Mattel, Model No. 14808
EX n/a   NM $20   MIP $45

❑ **Nostalgic Reproductions, Silken Flame, blond or brunette,** 1998, Mattel
EX n/a   NM $15   MIP $30

❑ **Nostalgic Reproductions, Solo in the Spotlight, blond or brunette,** 1995, Mattel, Model No. 13534/13820
EX n/a   NM $12   MIP $25

❑ **Nostalgic Reproductions, Wedding Day, blond,** 1997, Mattel
EX n/a   NM $10   MIP $25

❑ **Nursery Rhymes, Barbie Had a Little Lamb,** 1999, Mattel, Model No. 21740
EX n/a   NM $20   MIP $40

❑ **Nutcracker Barbie,** 1992, Mattel, Model No. 5472
EX n/a   NM $85   MIP $225

❑ **Ocean Friends Gift Set,** 1996, Mattel, Model No. 16442
EX n/a   NM $20   MIP $45

❑ **Olympic Barbie Gift Set,** 1996, Mattel, Model No. 16443
EX n/a   NM $15   MIP $30

❑ **On Parade Gift Set, Barbie, Ken, Midge,** 1964, Mattel, Model No. 1014
EX n/a   NM $800   MIP $2300

❑ **Osco Picnic Pretty,** 1993, Mattel, Model No. 3803
EX n/a   NM $15   MIP $25

❑ **Oshagatsu Barbie,** 1995, Mattel, Model No. 14024
EX n/a   NM $40   MIP $80

❑ **P.J.'s Swinging Silver Gift Set,** 1970, Mattel, Model No. 1588
EX n/a   NM $700   MIP $1500

❑ **Pace Party Sensations Barbie,** 1990, Mattel
EX n/a   NM $15   MIP $50

❑ **Pace Very Violet Barbie,** 1992, Mattel
EX n/a   NM $15   MIP $50

❑ **Paint 'N Dazzle Deluxe Gift Set,** 1993, Mattel, Model No. 10926
EX n/a   NM $17   MIP $35

(Mattel Photo)

❑ **Peanuts, Barbie and Snoopy,** 2002, Mattel, Model No. 55558
EX n/a   NM $15   MIP $35

❏ **Peppermint Princess Barbie, Winter Princess Collection,** 1995, Mattel, Model No. 13598
  EX n/a   NM $35   MIP $85

❏ **Picture Pockets Barbie, Christie, Kira or Teresa,** 2000, Mattel
  EX n/a   NM $5   MIP $11

❏ **Pink & Pretty Barbie Gift Set,** 1982, Mattel, Model No. 5239
  EX n/a   NM $35   MIP $90

(KP Photo)

❏ **Pink Splendor,** 1995, Mattel, Model No. 16091
  EX n/a   NM $175   MIP $350

❏ **Poodle Parade,** 1996, Mattel, Model No. 15280
  EX n/a   NM $25   MIP $55

(KP Photo)

❏ **Pop Culture Series, Barbie & Ken as Morticia & Gomez Addams,** 2000, Mattel, Model No. 27276
  EX n/a   NM $40   MIP $65

❏ **Pop Culture Series, Barbie and Ken as Lily and Herman Munster,** 2001, Mattel, Model No. 50544
  EX n/a   NM $25   MIP $75

(Mattel Photo)

❏ **Pop Culture Series, Barbie as Samantha from Bewitched,** 2002, Mattel, Model No. 53510
  EX n/a   NM $20   MIP $40

(Mattel Photo)

❏ **Pop Culture Series, Barbie as That Girl,** 2003, Mattel, Model No. 56705
  EX n/a   NM $20   MIP $40

❏ **Pop Culture Series, Barbie as Wonder Woman,** 2000, Mattel, Model No. 24638
  EX n/a   NM $25   MIP $50

❏ **Pop Culture Series, Barbie Loves Elvis Gift Set,** 1997, Mattel, Model No. 17450
  EX n/a   NM $30   MIP $55

❏ **Pop Culture Series, Barbie Loves Frankie Sinatra Gift Set,** 1999, Mattel, Model No. 22953
  EX n/a   NM $40   MIP $70

(Mattel Photo)

❏ **Pop Culture Series, James Bond 007 Ken and Barbie,** 2003, Mattel, Model No. B0150
  EX n/a   NM $30   MIP $75

(Mattel Photo)

❏ **Pop Culture Series, Malibu Barbie,** 2002, Mattel, Model No. 56061
  EX n/a   NM $10   MIP $20

(KP Photo)

❏ **Pop Culture Series, Star Trek Barbie and Ken,** 1996, Mattel, Model No. 15006
  EX n/a   NM $15   MIP $35

(Mattel Photo)

❏ **Pop Culture Series, Starring Barbie in King Kong,** 2003, Mattel, Model No. 56737
  EX n/a   NM $20   MIP $50

❏ **Pop Culture Series, X-Files Barbie and Ken,** 1998, Mattel
  EX n/a   NM $20   MIP $65

BARBIE

❏ **Pretty Changes Barbie Gift Set,** 1978, Mattel, Model No. 2598
EX n/a　　**NM** $35　　**MIP** $75

❏ **Pretty Hearts Barbie,** 1992, Mattel, Model No. 2901
EX n/a　　**NM** $7　　**MIP** $15

❏ **Pretty Pairs Angie N' Tangie,** 1970, Mattel, Foreign, Model No. 1135
EX n/a　　**NM** $125　　**MIP** $250

❏ **Pretty Pairs Lori N' Rori,** 1970, Mattel, Foreign, Model No. 1133
EX n/a　　**NM** $125　　**MIP** $250

❏ **Pretty Pairs Nan N' Fran,** 1970, Mattel, Foreign, Model No. 1134
EX n/a　　**NM** $125　　**MIP** $250

❏ **Princess and the Pea Barbie,** 2001, Mattel, Model No. 28800
EX n/a　　**NM** $15　　**MIP** $35

❏ **Princess Series, Rapunzel,** 2002, Mattel, Model No. 53973
EX n/a　　**NM** $20　　**MIP** $40

❏ **Radio Shack Earring Magic,** 1991, Mattel, came with software package, Model No. 25192
EX n/a　　**NM** $20　　**MIP** $40

❏ **Red Romance Barbie,** 1993, Mattel, Model No. 3161
EX n/a　　**NM** $7　　**MIP** $15

❏ **Republican National Convention Delegate Barbie,** 2000, Mattel
EX n/a　　**NM** $25　　**MIP** $150

❏ **Romantic Bride Barbie, black,** 2001, Mattel, Model No. 29439
EX n/a　　**NM** $15　　**MIP** $45

❏ **Romantic Bride Barbie, blond,** 2001, Mattel, Model No. 29438
EX n/a　　**NM** $15　　**MIP** $45

❏ **Royal Jewels Countess of Rubies,** 2001, Mattel
EX n/a　　**NM** $40　　**MIP** $100

❏ **Royal Jewels Duchess of Diamonds,** 2001, Mattel
EX n/a　　**NM** $40　　**MIP** $100

❏ **Royal Jewels Empress of Emeralds,** 2000, Mattel, Model No. 25680
EX n/a　　**NM** $50　　**MIP** $100

❏ **Royal Jewels Queen of Sapphires,** 2000, Mattel, Model No. 24924
EX n/a　　**NM** $50　　**MIP** $100

❏ **Russell Stover Easter,** 1996, Mattel, Model No. 14956
EX n/a　　**NM** $10　　**MIP** $25

❏ **Russell Stover Easter,** 1997, Mattel, Model No. 17091
EX n/a　　**NM** $5　　**MIP** $15

❏ **Russell Stover Easter (w/Easter basket),** 1996, Mattel, Model No. 14617
EX n/a　　**NM** $10　　**MIP** $25

❏ **Sam's Club 50s Fun Barbie,** 1996, Mattel, Model No. 15820
EX n/a　　**NM** $20　　**MIP** $40

❏ **Sam's Club 60s Fun Barbie, blond,** 1997, Mattel, Model No. 17252
EX n/a　　**NM** $15　　**MIP** $25

❏ **Sam's Club 60s Fun Barbie, red hair,** 1997, Mattel, Model No. 17693
EX n/a　　**NM** $10　　**MIP** $28

❏ **Sam's Club 70s Fun Barbie, blond,** 1998, Mattel, Model No. 19928
EX n/a　　**NM** $12　　**MIP** $25

❏ **Sam's Club 70s Fun Barbie, brunette,** 1998, Mattel, Model No. 19929
EX n/a　　**NM** $15　　**MIP** $30

❏ **Sam's Club Barbie Sisters' Celebration, Barbie and Krissy,** 2000, Mattel
EX n/a　　**NM** $10　　**MIP** $25

❏ **Sam's Club Bronze Sensation Barbie,** 1998, Mattel, Model No. 20022
EX n/a　　**NM** $25　　**MIP** $75

❏ **Sam's Club Dinner Date Barbie, blond,** 1998, Mattel, Model No. 19016
EX n/a　　**NM** $8　　**MIP** $15

❏ **Sam's Club Dinner Date Barbie, red hair,** 1998, Mattel, Model No. 19037
EX n/a　　**NM** $9　　**MIP** $20

❏ **Sam's Club Festiva Barbie,** 1993, Mattel, Model No. 10339
EX n/a　　**NM** $15　　**MIP** $35

❏ **Sam's Club Jewel Jubilee Barbie,** 1991, Mattel, Model No. 2366
EX n/a　　**NM** $25　　**MIP** $60

❏ **Sam's Club Party Sensation Barbie,** 1990, Mattel, Model No. 9025
EX n/a　　**NM** $20　　**MIP** $50

❏ **Sam's Club Peach Blossom Barbie,** 1992, Mattel, Model No. 7009
EX n/a　　**NM** $20　　**MIP** $40

❏ **Sam's Club Season's Greetings Barbie,** 1994, Mattel, Model No. 12384
EX n/a　　**NM** $25　　**MIP** $60

❏ **Sam's Club Sweet Moments Barbie,** 1997, Mattel, Model No. 17642
EX n/a　　**NM** $12　　**MIP** $20

❏ **Sam's Club Wedding Fantasy Barbie Gift Set,** 1993, Mattel, Model No. 10924
EX n/a　　**NM** $30　　**MIP** $70

❏ **Sam's Club Winter Fantasy Barbie, blond or brunette,** 1997, Mattel, Model No. 17249/17666
EX n/a　　**NM** $10　　**MIP** $20

❏ **Sam's Club Winter's Eve Barbie,** 1995, Mattel, Model No. 13613
EX n/a　　**NM** $12　　**MIP** $25

❏ **School Spirit Barbie,** 1996, Mattel
EX n/a　　**NM** $5　　**MIP** $10

❏ **Schooltime Barbie 1995,** 1995, Mattel
EX n/a　　**NM** $5　　**MIP** $10

❏ **Schooltime Barbie 1998,** 1998, Mattel
EX n/a　　**NM** $5　　**MIP** $10

❏ **Sears 100th Celebration Barbie,** 1986, Mattel, Model No. 2998
EX n/a　　**NM** $20　　**MIP** $75

❏ **Sears Barbie Twinkle Town Set,** 1969, Mattel, Model No. 1866
EX n/a　　**NM** $800　　**MIP** $1600

❏ **Sears Blossom Beautiful Barbie,** 1992, Mattel, Model No. 3817
EX n/a　　**NM** $100　　**MIP** $275

❏ **Sears Blue Starlight,** 1997, Mattel, Model No. 17125
EX n/a　　**NM** $15　　**MIP** $30

❏ **Sears Dream Princess,** 1992, Mattel, Model No. 2306
EX n/a　　**NM** $25　　**MIP** $50

❏ **Sears Enchanted Princess,** 1993, Mattel, Model No. 10292
EX n/a　　**NM** $35　　**MIP** $60

❏ **Sears Evening Enchantment,** 1989, Mattel, Model No. 3596
EX n/a　　**NM** $10　　**MIP** $40

❏ **Sears Evening Flame,** 1996, Mattel, Model No. 15533
EX n/a　　**NM** $15　　**MIP** $30

❏ **Sears Lavender Surprise,** 1990, Mattel, Model No. 9049
EX n/a　　**NM** $8　　**MIP** $35

❏ **Sears Lavender Surprise, black,** 1990, Mattel, Model No. 5588
EX n/a　　**NM** $8　　**MIP** $30

❏ **Sears Lilac and Lovely Barbie,** 1988, Mattel, Model No. 7669
EX n/a　　**NM** $10　　**MIP** $45

❏ **Sears Perfectly Plaid Gift Set,** 1971, Mattel, Model No. 1193
EX n/a　　**NM** $800　　**MIP** $1500

❏ **Sears Pink Reflections,** 1998, Mattel, Model No. 19130
EX n/a　　**NM** $10　　**MIP** $25

❏ **Sears Ribbons and Roses Barbie,** 1995, Mattel, Model No. 13011
EX n/a　　**NM** $10　　**MIP** $50

❏ **Sears Silver Sweetheart Barbie,** 1994, Mattel, Model No. 12410
EX n/a　　**NM** $17　　**MIP** $50

❏ **Sears Skooter Cut n' Button Gift Set,** 1967, Mattel, Model No. 1036
EX n/a　　**NM** $150　　**MIP** $650

❏ **Sears Southern Belle,** 1991, Mattel, Model No. 2586
EX n/a　　**NM** $10　　**MIP** $40

❏ **Sears Star Dream Barbie,** 1987, Mattel, Model No. 4550
EX n/a　　**NM** $10　　**MIP** $60

❏ **Sears Winter Sports,** 1975, Mattel, Model No. 9042
EX n/a　　**NM** $65　　**MIP** $115

❏ **Secret Hearts Gift Set,** 1993, Mattel, Model No. 10929
EX n/a　　**NM** $17　　**MIP** $35

❏ **See's Candy Barbie, white or black,** 2000, Mattel
EX n/a　　**NM** $15　　**MIP** $45

❏ **Service Merchandise Blue Rhapsody,** 1991, Mattel, Model No. 1364
EX n/a　　**NM** $75　　**MIP** $125

❑ **Service Merchandise City Sophisticate,** 1994, Mattel, Model No. 12005
EX n/a   **NM** $20   **MIP** $85

❑ **Service Merchandise Definitely Diamonds,** 1998, Mattel, Model No. 20204
EX n/a   **NM** $45   **MIP** $95

❑ **Service Merchandise Dream Bride, black or white,** 1997, Mattel, Model No. 17933/17153
EX n/a   **NM** $10   **MIP** $25

❑ **Service Merchandise Evening Symphony,** 1998, Mattel, Model No. 19777
EX n/a   **NM** $10   **MIP** $25

❑ **Service Merchandise Ruby Romance,** 1995, Mattel, Model No. 13612
EX n/a   **NM** $25   **MIP** $50

❑ **Service Merchandise Satin Nights, two earring versions,** 1992, Mattel, Model No. 1886
EX n/a   **NM** $20   **MIP** $80

❑ **Service Merchandise Sea Princess,** 1996, Mattel, Model No. 15531
EX n/a   **NM** $15   **MIP** $30

❑ **Service Merchandise Sparkling Splendor,** 1993, Mattel, Model No. 10994
EX n/a   **NM** $17   **MIP** $50

❑ **Sharin Sisters Gift Set,** 1992, Mattel, Model No. 5716
EX n/a   **NM** $12   **MIP** $25

❑ **Sharin Sisters Gift Set,** 1993, Mattel, Model No. 10143
EX n/a   **NM** $12   **MIP** $25

❑ **Shopko/Venture Blossom Beauty,** 1991, Mattel, Model No. 3142
EX n/a   **NM** $10   **MIP** $40

❑ **Shopko/Venture Party Perfect,** 1992, Mattel, Model No. 1876
EX n/a   **NM** $12   **MIP** $35

❑ **Skipper Party Time Gift Set,** 1964, Mattel, Model No. 1021
EX n/a   **NM** $100   **MIP** $550

❑ **Skipper Swing 'a' Rounder Gym Gift Set,** 1972, Mattel, Model No. 1172
EX n/a   **NM** $100   **MIP** $400

❑ **Snap 'N Play Gift Set (Snap 'N Play Deluxe),** 1992, Mattel, Model No. 2262
EX n/a   **NM** $12   **MIP** $35

❑ **Society Hound Barbie,** 2001, Mattel
EX n/a   **NM** $30   **MIP** $80

(Mattel Photo)

❑ **Sophisticated Wedding (white or black),** 2002, Mattel, Model No. 53370/53371
EX n/a   **NM** $20   **MIP** $50

❑ **Spiegel Golden Qi-Pao Barbie,** 1998, Mattel, Model No. 20866
EX n/a   **NM** $30   **MIP** $65

❑ **Spiegel Regal Reflections,** 1992, Mattel, Model No. 4116
EX n/a   **NM** $75   **MIP** $225

❑ **Spiegel Royal Invitation,** 1993, Mattel, Model No. 10969
EX n/a   **NM** $35   **MIP** $95

❑ **Spiegel Shopping Chic,** 1995, Mattel, Model No. 14009
EX n/a   **NM** $35   **MIP** $75

❑ **Spiegel Sterling Wishes,** 1991, Mattel, Model No. 3347
EX n/a   **NM** $45   **MIP** $115

❑ **Spiegel Summer Sophisticate,** 1996, Mattel, Model No. 15591
EX n/a   **NM** $20   **MIP** $45

❑ **Spiegel Theatre Elegance,** 1994, Mattel, Model No. 12077
EX n/a   **NM** $100   **MIP** $150

❑ **Spiegel Winner's Circle,** 1997, Mattel, Model No. 17441
EX n/a   **NM** $35   **MIP** $50

❑ **Splash 'N Color Barbie Gift Set,** 1997, Mattel
EX n/a   **NM** $10   **MIP** $20

❑ **Spring Bouquet Barbie,** 1993, Mattel, Model No. 3477
EX n/a   **NM** $10   **MIP** $20

❑ **Spring Parade Barbie,** 1992, Mattel, Model No. 7008
EX n/a   **NM** $15   **MIP** $25

❑ **Spring Parade Barbie, black,** 1992, Mattel, Model No. 2257
EX n/a   **NM** $15   **MIP** $25

(Mattel Photo)

❑ **Storybook Favorites, Alice and Mad Hatter (Kelly and Tommy),** 2003, Mattel, Model No. 57577
EX n/a   **NM** $10   **MIP** $20

❑ **Storybook Favorites, Goldilocks and the Three Bears (Kelly),** 2001, Mattel, Model No. 29605
EX n/a   **NM** $8   **MIP** $20

❑ **Storybook Favorites, Hansel & Gretel (Kelly and Tommy),** 2000, Mattel, Model No. 28535
EX n/a   **NM** $5   **MIP** $17

(Mattel Photo)

❑ **Storybook Favorites, Little Red Riding Hood (Kelly and Tommy),** 2002, Mattel, Model No. 52899
EX n/a   **NM** $10   **MIP** $20

(Mattel Photo)

❑ **Storybook Favorites, Mickey and Minnie Mouse (Kelly and Tommy),** 2002, Mattel, Model No. 55502
EX n/a   **NM** $10   **MIP** $20

❑ **Storybook Favorites, Raggedy Ann and Andy (Kelly and Tommy),** 2000, Mattel, Model No. 24639
EX n/a   **NM** $5   **MIP** $17

(Mattel Photo)

BARBIE

❏ **Style Set, Exotic Beauty,** 2003, Mattel, Model No. B0149
EX n/a **NM** $20 **MIP** $50

❏ **Style Set, Society Girl (white or black),** 2002, Mattel, Model No. 56203/56204
EX n/a **NM** $20 **MIP** $50

❏ **Sweet Spring Barbie,** 1992, Mattel, Model No. 3208
EX n/a **NM** $10 **MIP** $20

❏ **Sydney 2000 Olympic Pin Collector, black or white,** 2000, Mattel, Model No. 25644/26302
EX n/a **NM** $20 **MIP** $30

❏ **Target 35th Anniversary Barbie, black,** 1997, Mattel, Model No. 176608
EX n/a **NM** $10 **MIP** $24

❏ **Target 35th Anniversary Barbie, white,** 1997, Mattel, Model No. 16485
EX n/a **NM** $10 **MIP** $20

❏ **Target Baseball Date Barbie,** 1993, Mattel, Model No. 4583
EX n/a **NM** $10 **MIP** $30

❏ **Target City Style #1,** 1996, Mattel, Model No. 15612
EX n/a **NM** $8 **MIP** $15

❏ **Target City Style #2,** 1997, Mattel, Model No. 17237
EX n/a **NM** $10 **MIP** $20

❏ **Target Club Wedd Barbie, black,** 1998, Mattel, Model No. 20423
EX n/a **NM** $10 **MIP** $20

❏ **Target Club Wedd Barbie, blond or brunette,** 1998, Mattel, Model No. 19717/19718
EX n/a **NM** $10 **MIP** $20

❏ **Target Cute'n Cool,** 1991, Mattel, Model No. 2954
EX n/a **NM** $8 **MIP** $30

❏ **Target Dazzlin' Date Barbie,** 1992, Mattel, Model No. 3203
EX n/a **NM** $10 **MIP** $25

❏ **Target Easter Bunny Fun Barbie & Kelly,** 1999, Mattel, Model No. 21720
EX n/a **NM** $15 **MIP** $25

❏ **Target Easter Egg Hunt,** 1998, Mattel, Model No. 19014
EX n/a **NM** $15 **MIP** $25

❏ **Target Easter Egg Party, white or black,** 2000, Mattel
EX n/a **NM** $15 **MIP** $25

❏ **Target Easter Garden Hunt Barbie and Kelly,** 2001, Mattel
EX n/a **NM** $10 **MIP** $25

❏ **Target Gold and Lace Barbie,** 1989, Mattel, Model No. 7476
EX n/a **NM** $10 **MIP** $30

❏ **Target Golden Evening,** 1991, Mattel, Model No. 2587
EX n/a **NM** $6 **MIP** $45

❏ **Target Golf Date Barbie,** 1993, Mattel, Model No. 10202
EX n/a **NM** $10 **MIP** $25

❏ **Target Halloween Fun Barbie & Kelly, white or black,** 1999, Mattel, Model No. 23460
EX n/a **NM** $15 **MIP** $25

❏ **Target Halloween Fun Li'l Friends of Kelly,** 1999, Mattel, Model No. 23796
EX n/a **NM** $15 **MIP** $25

❏ **Target Halloween Party Barbie & Ken, pirates,** 1998, Mattel, Model No. 19874
EX n/a **NM** $20 **MIP** $40

❏ **Target Halloween Party Deidre (Pumpkin),** 2000, Mattel, Model No. 28310
EX n/a **NM** $5 **MIP** $15

❏ **Target Halloween Party Jenny (Pumpkin),** 2000, Mattel, Model No. 28308
EX n/a **NM** $5 **MIP** $15

❏ **Target Halloween Party Kayla (Ghost),** 2000, Mattel, Model No. 28307
EX n/a **NM** $5 **MIP** $15

❏ **Target Halloween Party Kelly (Alien),** 2000, Mattel, Model No. 28306
EX n/a **NM** $5 **MIP** $15

❏ **Target Halloween Party Tommy (Cowboy),** 2000, Mattel, Model No. 28309
EX n/a **NM** $5 **MIP** $15

(Mattel Photo)

❏ **Target Happy Halloween Barbie & Kelly,** 1997, Mattel, Model No. 17238
EX n/a **NM** $30 **MIP** $60

❏ **Target Party Pretty Barbie,** 1990, Mattel, Model No. 5955
EX n/a **NM** $6 **MIP** $25

❏ **Target Pet Doctor Barbie, brunette,** 1996, Mattel, Model No. 16458
EX n/a **NM** $15 **MIP** $30

❏ **Target Pretty in Plaid Barbie,** 1992, Mattel, Model No. 5413
EX n/a **NM** $15 **MIP** $30

❏ **Target Soccer Kelly & Tommy,** 1999, Mattel
EX n/a **NM** $8 **MIP** $20

❏ **Target Steppin' Out Barbie,** 1995, Mattel, Model No. 14110
EX n/a **NM** $8 **MIP** $20

❏ **Target Valentine Barbie,** 1996, Mattel, Model No. 15172
EX n/a **NM** $8 **MIP** $20

❏ **Target Valentine Date Barbie,** 1998, Mattel, Model No. 18306
EX n/a **NM** $8 **MIP** $20

❏ **Target Valentine Kelly and Friend,** 2001, Mattel
EX n/a **NM** $5 **MIP** $15

❏ **Target Valentine Romance Barbie,** 1997, Mattel, Model No. 16059
EX n/a **NM** $8 **MIP** $20

❏ **Target Valentine Style Barbie, black,** 1999, Mattel, Model No. 22150
EX n/a **NM** $8 **MIP** $18

❏ **Target Valentine Style Barbie, white,** 1999, Mattel, Model No. 20465
EX n/a **NM** $8 **MIP** $15

❏ **Target Wild Style Barbie,** 1992, Mattel, Model No. 0411
EX n/a **NM** $10 **MIP** $24

❏ **Target With Love Barbie,** 2000, Mattel
EX n/a **NM** $8 **MIP** $15

❏ **Target Xhilaration Barbie, white or black,** 1999, Mattel
EX n/a **NM** $15 **MIP** $35

❏ **Tennis Star Barbie & Ken,** 1988, Mattel, Model No. 7801
EX n/a **NM** $18 **MIP** $40

❏ **Tiff Pose N' Play,** 1972, Mattel, Foreign, Model No. 1199
EX n/a **NM** $125 **MIP** $350

❏ **Timeless Sentiments Angel of Hope,** 1999, Mattel, Model No. 22955
EX n/a **NM** $25 **MIP** $50

❏ **Timeless Sentiments Angel of Joy, white or black,** 1998, Mattel, Model No. 19633/20929
EX n/a **NM** $25 **MIP** $50

❏ **Timeless Sentiments Angel of Peace,** 1999, Mattel, Model No. 24240
EX n/a **NM** $25 **MIP** $50

❏ **Timeless Sentiments Angel of Peace, black,** 1999, Mattel, Model No. 24241
EX n/a **NM** $25 **MIP** $50

❏ **Todd Oldham (Designer),** 1999, Mattel
EX n/a **NM** $35 **MIP** $70

(KP Photo)

❏ **Together Forever, Romeo & Juliet,** 1998, Mattel, Model No. 19364
EX n/a   NM $50   MIP $100

(KP Photo)

❏ **Together Forever, King Arthur and Queen Guinevere,** 1999, Mattel, Model No. 23880
EX n/a   NM $50   MIP $100

❏ **Toys R Us 101 Dalmatians Barbie, black,** 1999, Mattel, Model No. 17601
EX n/a   NM $12   MIP $20

(KP Photo)

❏ **Toys R Us 101 Dalmatians Barbie, white,** 1997, Mattel, Model No. 17248
EX n/a   NM $15   MIP $28

❏ **Toys R Us 35th Anniversary Midge, Senior Prom,** 1998, Mattel, Model No. 18976
EX n/a   NM $25   MIP $40

❏ **Toys R Us Astronaut Barbie, black,** 1994, Mattel, Model No. 12150
EX n/a   NM $15   MIP $45

❏ **Toys R Us Astronaut Barbie, white,** 1994, Mattel, Model No. 12149
EX n/a   NM $15   MIP $45

(KP Photo)

❏ **Toys R Us Barbie for President,** 1992, Mattel, Model No. 3722
EX n/a   NM $17   MIP $65

❏ **Toys R Us Barbie for President,** 2000, Mattel, Model No. 3940
EX n/a   NM $5   MIP $18

❏ **Toys R Us Barbie Renaissance Rose Gift Set,** 2000, Mattel, Model No. 28633
EX n/a   NM $15   MIP $35

❏ **Toys R Us Bath Time Skipper,** 1992, Mattel, Model No. 7970
EX n/a   NM $12   MIP $25

❏ **Toys R Us Beauty Pagent Skipper,** 1991, Mattel, Model No. 9342
EX n/a   NM $10   MIP $25

❏ **Toys R Us Bicyclin' Barbie, black or white,** 1995, Mattel
EX n/a   NM $15   MIP $25

❏ **Toys R Us Birthday Fun Kelly Gift Set,** 1996, Mattel
EX n/a   NM $15   MIP $28

❏ **Toys R Us Cool 'N Sassy, black,** 1992, Mattel, Model No. 4110
EX n/a   NM $10   MIP $20

❏ **Toys R Us Cool 'N Sassy, white,** 1992, Mattel, Model No. 1490
EX n/a   NM $10   MIP $20

❏ **Toys R Us Crystal Splendor, black,** 1996, Mattel, Model No. 15137
EX n/a   NM $10   MIP $25

❏ **Toys R Us Crystal Splendor, white,** 1996, Mattel, Model No. 15136
EX n/a   NM $12   MIP $25

❏ **Toys R Us Dream Date Barbie,** 1982, Mattel, Model No. 9180
EX n/a   NM $7   MIP $30

❏ **Toys R Us Dream Date Ken,** 1982, Mattel, Model No. 4077
EX n/a   NM $5   MIP $30

❏ **Toys R Us Dream Date P.J.,** 1982, Mattel, Model No. 5869
EX n/a   NM $8   MIP $40

❏ **Toys R Us Dream Date Skipper,** 1990, Mattel, Model No. 1075
EX n/a   NM $10   MIP $25

❏ **Toys R Us Dream Time Barbie,** 1988, Mattel, Model No. 9180
EX n/a   NM $10   MIP $30

❏ **Toys R Us Dream Wedding Gift Set, black,** 1993, Mattel, Model No. 10713
EX n/a   NM $22   MIP $45

❏ **Toys R Us Dream Wedding Gift Set, white,** 1993, Mattel, Model No. 10712
EX n/a   NM $20   MIP $45

❏ **Toys R Us Fashion Brights Barbie, white or black,** 1992, Mattel, Model No. 1882/4112
EX n/a   NM $10   MIP $20

❏ **Toys R Us Fashion Fun Barbie Gift Set,** 1999, Mattel
EX n/a   NM $15   MIP $25

(KP Photo)

❏ **Toys R Us Firefighter Barbie, white or black,** 1995, Mattel, With yellow uniform and hat and dalmatian puppy, Model No. 13553/13472
EX n/a   NM $10   MIP $25

❏ **Toys R Us Gardening Fun Barbie & Kelly Gift Set,** 1997, Mattel, Model No. 17242
EX n/a   NM $12   MIP $23

❏ **Toys R Us Got Milk? Barbie, white or black,** 1996, Mattel, Model No. 15721/15122
EX n/a   NM $8   MIP $20

❏ **Toys R Us Gran Gala Teresa,** 1997, Mattel, Model No. 17239
EX n/a   NM $8   MIP $15

❏ **Toys R Us Harley-Davidson Barbie #3,** 1999, Mattel, Model No. 22256
EX n/a   NM $50   MIP $100

❏ **Toys R Us Harley-Davidson Barbie #1,** 1997, Mattel, Model No. 17692
EX n/a   NM $200   MIP $450

❏ **Toys R Us Harley-Davidson Barbie #2,** 1998, Mattel, Model No. 20441
EX n/a   NM $100   MIP $200

❏ **Toys R Us Harley-Davidson Barbie #4,** 2000, Mattel, Model No. 25637
EX n/a   NM $65   MIP $100

BARBIE

❑ **Toys R Us Harley-Davidson Barbie #5, black,** 2001, Mattel, Model No. 29208
EX n/a   NM $45   MIP $70

❑ **Toys R Us Harley-Davidson Barbie #5, white,** 2001, Mattel, Model No. 29207
EX n/a   NM $45   MIP $70

(KP Photo)

❑ **Toys R Us Harley-Davidson Ken #1,** 1999, Mattel, Model No. 22255
EX n/a   NM $50   MIP $90

❑ **Toys R Us Harley-Davidson Ken #2,** 2000, Mattel, Model No. 25638
EX n/a   NM $15   MIP $55

❑ **Toys R Us I'm A Toys R Us Kid Barbie, white or black,** 1998, Mattel, Model No. 18895/21040
EX n/a   NM $15   MIP $30

❑ **Toys R Us International Pen Friend Barbie,** 1995, Mattel, Model No. 13558
EX n/a   NM $7   MIP $16

❑ **Toys R Us Love to Read Barbie,** 1993, Mattel, Model No. 10507
EX n/a   NM $12   MIP $40

❑ **Toys R Us Malt Shop Barbie,** 1993, Mattel, Model No. 4581
EX n/a   NM $10   MIP $25

❑ **Toys R Us Moonlight Magic Barbie, black,** 1993, Mattel, Model No. 10609
EX n/a   NM $15   MIP $55

❑ **Toys R Us Moonlight Magic Barbie, white,** 1993, Mattel, Model No. 10608
EX n/a   NM $15   MIP $65

❑ **Toys R Us My Size Bride Barbie, red hair,** 1995, Mattel, Model No. 15649
EX n/a   NM $60   MIP $135

❑ **Toys R Us Olympic Gymnast Barbie, red hair, box w/o special edition marking,** 1996, Mattel, Model No. 15725
EX n/a   NM $15   MIP $30

❑ **Toys R Us Oreo Fun Barbie,** 1997, Mattel, Model No. 18511
EX n/a   NM $8   MIP $18

❑ **Toys R Us Paleontologist Barbie, white or black,** 1997, Mattel, Model No. 17240/17241
EX n/a   NM $12   MIP $24

❑ **Toys R Us Party Time Barbie, white or black,** 1994, Mattel, Model No. 12243
EX n/a   NM $10   MIP $20

❑ **Toys R Us Pepsi Spirit Barbie,** 1989, Mattel, Model No. 4869
EX n/a   NM $18   MIP $70

❑ **Toys R Us Pepsi Spirit Skipper,** 1989, Mattel, Model No. 4867
EX n/a   NM $15   MIP $65

❑ **Toys R Us POG Barbie,** 1995, Mattel, Model No. 13239
EX n/a   NM $7   MIP $15

(KP Photo)

❑ **Toys R Us Police Officer Barbie, black,** 1993, Mattel, Model No. 10689
EX n/a   NM $15   MIP $65

❑ **Toys R Us Police Officer Barbie, white,** 1993, Mattel, Model No. 10688
EX n/a   NM $15   MIP $70

❑ **Toys R Us Purple Passion, black,** 1995, Mattel, Model No. 13554
EX n/a   NM $10   MIP $30

❑ **Toys R Us Purple Passion, white,** 1995, Mattel, Model No. 13555
EX n/a   NM $10   MIP $30

❑ **Toys R Us Radiant in Red Barbie, black,** 1992, Mattel, Model No. 4113
EX n/a   NM $12   MIP $55

❑ **Toys R Us Radiant in Red Barbie, white,** 1992, Mattel, Model No. 1276
EX n/a   NM $12   MIP $55

❑ **Toys R Us Sapphire Sophisticate,** 1997, Mattel, Model No. 16692
EX n/a   NM $12   MIP $25

❑ **Toys R Us School Fun,** 1991, Mattel, Model No. 2721
EX n/a   NM $6   MIP $40

❑ **Toys R Us School Spirit Barbie, black,** 1993, Mattel, Model No. 10683
EX n/a   NM $10   MIP $30

❑ **Toys R Us School Spirit Barbie, white,** 1993, Mattel, Model No. 10682
EX n/a   NM $10   MIP $25

❑ **Toys R Us Share A Smile Barbie,** 1997, Mattel, Model No. 17247
EX n/a   NM $7   MIP $15

❑ **Toys R Us Share A Smile Becky,** 1997, Mattel, Model No. 15761
EX n/a   NM $15   MIP $28

❑ **Toys R Us Share A Smile Christie,** 1997, Mattel, Model No. 17372
EX n/a   NM $7   MIP $15

❑ **Toys R Us Show and Ride Barbie,** 1988, Mattel, Model No. 7799
EX n/a   NM $10   MIP $35

❑ **Toys R Us Sign Language Barbie, white or black,** 2000, Mattel
EX n/a   NM $8   MIP $20

❑ **Toys R Us Society Style Emerald Elegance,** 1994, Mattel, Model No. 12322
EX n/a   NM $15   MIP $40

❑ **Toys R Us Society Style Emerald Enchantment,** 1997, Mattel, Model No. 17443
EX n/a   NM $25   MIP $50

❑ **Toys R Us Society Style Sapphire Dream,** 1995, Mattel, Model No. 13256
EX n/a   NM $50   MIP $70

❑ **Toys R Us Space Camp Barbie, white or black,** 1999, Mattel, Model No. 22435/22246
EX n/a   NM $12   MIP $28

❑ **Toys R Us Spirit of the Earth Barbie,** 2001, Mattel
EX n/a   NM $25   MIP $75

❑ **Toys R Us Spots 'N Dots Barbie,** 1993, Mattel, Model No. 10491
EX n/a   NM $12   MIP $35

❑ **Toys R Us Spots 'N Dots Teresa,** 1993, Mattel, Model No. 10885
EX n/a   NM $12   MIP $40

❑ **Toys R Us Spring Parade Barbie, white or black,** 1992, Mattel, Model No. 7008/2257
EX n/a   NM $15   MIP $30

❑ **Toys R Us Sunflower Barbie,** 1995, Mattel, Model No. 13488
EX n/a   NM $9   MIP $20

❑ **Toys R Us Sunflower Teresa,** 1995, Mattel, Model No. 13489
EX n/a   NM $9   MIP $20

❑ **Toys R Us Sweet Romance,** 1991, Mattel, Model No. 2917
EX n/a   NM $8   MIP $30

❑ **Toys R Us Sweet Roses,** 1989, Mattel, Model No. 7635
EX n/a   NM $7   MIP $25

❑ **Toys R Us Totally Hair Courtney,** 1992, Mattel, Model No. 1433
EX n/a   NM $10   MIP $25

❑ **Toys R Us Totally Hair Skipper,** 1992, Mattel, Model No. 1430
EX n/a   NM $10   MIP $25

❑ **Toys R Us Totally Hair Whitney,** 1992, Mattel, Model No. 7735
EX n/a   NM $20   MIP $40

❑ **Toys R Us Travelin' Sisters Gift Set,** 1995, Mattel, Model No. 14073
EX n/a   **NM** $30   **MIP** $65

❑ **Toys R Us Vacation Sensation Barbie, blue,** 1986, Mattel, Model No. 1675
EX n/a   **NM** $10   **MIP** $40

❑ **Toys R Us Vacation Sensation Barbie, pink,** 1989, Mattel, Model No. 1675
EX n/a   **NM** $12   **MIP** $48

❑ **Toys R Us Wedding Fantasy Barbie & Ken Gift Set,** 1997, Mattel, Model No. 17243
EX n/a   **NM** $20   **MIP** $45

❑ **Toys R Us Winter Fun Barbie,** 1990, Mattel, Model No. 5949
EX n/a   **NM** $10   **MIP** $40

❑ **Toys R Us/FAO Schwarz Sea Holiday Barbie #1, with lip gloss,** 1993, Mattel
EX n/a   **NM** $15   **MIP** $30

❑ **Toys R Us/FAO Schwarz Sea Holiday Barbie #2, with lip gloss,** 1993, Mattel
EX n/a   **NM** $15   **MIP** $24

❑ **Toys R Us/FAO/JCPenney, Winter Sports Barbie,** 1995, Mattel
EX n/a   **NM** $15   **MIP** $30

❑ **Toys R Us/FAO/JCPenney, Winter Sports Ken,** 1995, Mattel
EX n/a   **NM** $15   **MIP** $30

❑ **Trail Blazin' Barbie,** 1991, Mattel, Model No. 2783
EX n/a   **NM** $10   **MIP** $25

❑ **Tree Trimming Barbie, white or black,** 1999, Mattel
EX n/a   **NM** $5   **MIP** $15

❑ **Trend Forecaster Barbie,** 1999, Mattel, Model No. 22833
EX n/a   **NM** $20   **MIP** $45

❑ **Tropical Barbie Deluxe Gift Set,** 1985, Mattel, Model No. 2996
EX n/a   **NM** $20   **MIP** $45

❑ **Tutti and Todd Sundae Treat Set,** 1966, Mattel, Model No. 3556
EX n/a   **NM** $150   **MIP** $350

❑ **Tutti Me n' My Dog,** 1966, Mattel, Model No. 3554
EX n/a   **NM** $150   **MIP** $350

❑ **Tutti Nighty Night Sleep Tight,** 1965, Mattel, Model No. 3553
EX n/a   **NM** $100   **MIP** $300

❑ **Twirley Curls Barbie Gift Set,** 1982, Mattel, Model No. 4097
EX n/a   **NM** $30   **MIP** $85

❑ **Twist and Turn Far Out Barbie,** 1999, Mattel, Model No. 21911
EX n/a   **NM** $20   **MIP** $40

❑ **Vera Wang #1, bride,** 1998, Mattel, Model No. 19788
EX n/a   **NM** $75   **MIP** $150

❑ **Vera Wang #2, lavender dress,** 1999, Mattel, Model No. 23027
EX n/a   **NM** $55   **MIP** $140

❑ **Very Violet Barbie,** 1992, Mattel, Model No. 1859
EX n/a   **NM** $10   **MIP** $20

❑ **Victorian Barbie with Cedric Bear,** 2000, Mattel
EX n/a   **NM** $25   **MIP** $59

❑ **Victorian Tea Orange Pekoe Barbie,** 2000, Mattel, Model No. 25507
EX n/a   **NM** $110   **MIP** $220

❑ **Walking Jamie Strollin' in Style Gift Set,** 1972, Mattel, Model No. 1247
EX n/a   **NM** $300   **MIP** $600

❑ **Wal-Mart 25th Year Pink Jubilee Barbie,** 1987, Mattel, Model No. 4589
EX n/a   **NM** $20   **MIP** $50

❑ **Wal-Mart 35th Anniversary Barbie, black or white,** Mattel, Model No. 17616/17245
EX n/a   **NM** $10   **MIP** $24

❑ **Wal-Mart 35th Anniversary Teresa,** 1997, Mattel, Model No. 17617
EX n/a   **NM** $12   **MIP** $25

❑ **Wal-Mart Anniversary Star Barbie,** 1992, Mattel, Model No. 2282
EX n/a   **NM** $15   **MIP** $30

❑ **Wal-Mart Ballroom Beauty,** 1991, Mattel, Model No. 3678
EX n/a   **NM** $8   **MIP** $30

❑ **Wal-Mart Bathtime Fun Barbie,** 1991, Mattel, Model No. 9601
EX n/a   **NM** $5   **MIP** $25

❑ **Wal-Mart Country Bride,** 1995, Mattel, Model No. 13014
EX n/a   **NM** $8   **MIP** $15

❑ **Wal-Mart Country Bride, black,** 1995, Mattel, Model No. 13015
EX n/a   **NM** $8   **MIP** $15

❑ **Wal-Mart Country Bride, Hispanic,** 1995, Mattel, Model No. 13016
EX n/a   **NM** $8   **MIP** $15

❑ **Wal-Mart Country Western Star Barbie, black or Hispanic,** 1994, Mattel, Model No. 12096
EX n/a   **NM** $12   **MIP** $30

❑ **Wal-Mart Country Western Star Barbie, white,** 1994, Mattel, Model No. 12097
EX n/a   **NM** $10   **MIP** $25

❑ **Wal-Mart Dream Fantasy,** 1990, Mattel, Model No. 7335
EX n/a   **NM** $8   **MIP** $35

❑ **Wal-Mart Frills and Fantasy Barbie,** 1988, Mattel, Model No. 1374
EX n/a   **NM** $7   **MIP** $45

❑ **Wal-Mart Jewel Skating Barbie,** 1999, Mattel, Model No. 23239
EX n/a   **NM** $6   **MIP** $12

❑ **Wal-Mart Lavender Look Barbie,** 1989, Mattel, Model No. 3963
EX n/a   **NM** $7   **MIP** $30

❑ **Wal-Mart Portrait in Blue Barbie, black,** 1998, Mattel, Model No. 19356
EX n/a   **NM** $10   **MIP** $20

❑ **Wal-Mart Portrait in Blue Barbie, white,** 1998, Mattel, Model No. 19355
EX n/a   **NM** $8   **MIP** $18

❑ **Wal-Mart Pretty Choices Barbie, black,** 1997, Mattel, Model No. 18018
EX n/a   **NM** $8   **MIP** $18

❑ **Wal-Mart Pretty Choices Barbie, blond or brunette,** 1997, Mattel, Model No. 17971/18019
EX n/a   **NM** $8   **MIP** $18

❑ **Wal-Mart Puzzle Craze Barbie, white or black,** 1998, Mattel, Model No. 20164/20165
EX n/a   **NM** $6   **MIP** $14

❑ **Wal-Mart Puzzle Craze Teresa,** 1998, Mattel, Model No. 20166
EX n/a   **NM** $6   **MIP** $14

❑ **Wal-Mart Shopping Time Barbie, black or white,** 1997, Mattel, Model No. 18231/18230
EX n/a   **NM** $7   **MIP** $15

❑ **Wal-Mart Shopping Time Teresa,** 1997, Mattel, Model No. 18232
EX n/a   **NM** $7   **MIP** $15

❑ **Wal-Mart Skating Star Barbie,** 1996, Mattel, Model No. 15510
EX n/a   **NM** $10   **MIP** $15

❑ **Wal-Mart Star Skater Barbie, white or black,** 2000, Mattel
EX n/a   **NM** $5   **MIP** $15

❑ **Wal-Mart Superstar Barbie, black,** 1993, Mattel, Model No. 10711
EX n/a   **NM** $15   **MIP** $40

❑ **Wal-Mart Superstar Barbie, white,** 1993, Mattel, Model No. 10592
EX n/a   **NM** $15   **MIP** $30

❑ **Wal-Mart Sweet Magnolia Barbie, black, white or Hispanic,** 1996, Mattel, Model No. 15653/15652/15654
EX n/a   **NM** $9   **MIP** $15

❑ **Wal-Mart Tooth Fairy #1,** 1994, Mattel, Model No. 11645
EX n/a   **NM** $7   **MIP** $20

❑ **Wal-Mart Tooth Fairy #2,** 1995, Mattel, Model No. 11645
EX n/a   **NM** $5   **MIP** $20

❑ **Wal-Mart Tooth Fairy #3,** 1998, Mattel, Model No. 17246
EX n/a   **NM** $6   **MIP** $14

❑ **Walt Disney World Animal Kingdom Barbie, white or black,** 1998, Mattel, Model No. 20363/20989
EX n/a   **NM** $15   **MIP** $30

❑ **Walt Disney World Barbie 25th Anniversary,** 1996, Mattel, Model No. 16525
EX n/a   **NM** $15   **MIP** $30

❑ **Walt Disney World Disney Fun 1994,** 1994, Mattel, Model No. 11650
EX n/a   **NM** $15   **MIP** $50

❑ **Walt Disney World Disney Fun 1995,** 1995, Mattel, Model No. 13533
EX n/a   **NM** $15   **MIP** $40

BARBIE

❏ **Walt Disney World Disney Fun 1997,** 1997, Mattel, Model No. 17058
EX n/a NM $8 MIP $20

❏ **Walt Disney World Millennium Barbie, white or black,** 2000, Mattel
EX n/a NM $5 MIP $15

❏ **Walt Disney World Resort Vacation Barbie, Ken, Tommy, Kelly,** 1998, Mattel, Model No. 20315
EX n/a NM $35 MIP $80

❏ **Walt Disney World Toontown Stacie,** 1994, Mattel, Model No. 11587
EX n/a NM $15 MIP $30

❏ **Warner Bros. Barbie Loves Tweety,** 1999, Mattel, Model No. 21632
EX n/a NM $8 MIP $22

❏ **Warner Bros. Scooby-Doo Barbie,** 2001, Mattel, Model No. 27966
EX n/a NM $5 MIP $15

❏ **Wedding Fantasy Gift Set,** 1993, Mattel, Model No. 10924
EX n/a NM $50 MIP $125

❏ **Wedding Flower Blushing Orchid Bride,** 1997, Mattel
EX n/a NM $100 MIP $200

❏ **Wedding Flower Romantic Rose Bride,** 1996, Mattel
EX n/a NM $100 MIP $220

❏ **Wedding Party Gift Set, six dolls,** 1991, Mattel, Model No. 9852
EX n/a NM $45 MIP $125

❏ **Wedgwood Barbie #1, blue dress,** 2000, Mattel, Model No. 25641
EX n/a NM $40 MIP $80

❏ **Wedgwood Barbie #2, pink dress, black,** 2001, Mattel, Model No. 50824
EX n/a NM $30 MIP $85

❏ **Wedgwood Barbie #2, pink dress, white,** 2001, Mattel, Model No. 50823
EX n/a NM $30 MIP $85

❏ **Wessco Carnival Cruise Barbie,** 1997, Mattel, Model No. 15186
EX n/a NM $25 MIP $40

❏ **Wessco International Traveler #1,** 1995, Mattel, Model No. 13912
EX n/a NM $35 MIP $60

❏ **Wessco International Traveler #2,** 1996, Mattel, Model No. 16158
EX n/a NM $25 MIP $50

❏ **Western Chic Barbie,** 2002, Mattel, Model No. 55487
EX n/a NM $20 MIP $50

❏ **Western Fun Gift Set Barbie & Ken,** 1989, Mattel, Model No. 5408
EX n/a NM $12 MIP $30

❏ **Western Fun Gift Set Barbie & Ken,** 1990, Mattel, Model No. 5408
EX n/a NM $12 MIP $30

❏ **Western Plains Barbie,** 2000, Mattel
EX n/a NM $40 MIP $95

❏ **Winn-Dixie Party Pink Barbie,** 1989, Mattel, Model No. 7637
EX n/a NM $7 MIP $25

❏ **Winn-Dixie Pink Sensation,** 1990, Mattel, Model No. 5410
EX n/a NM $6 MIP $20

❏ **Winn-Dixie Southern Beauty,** 1991, Mattel, Model No. 3284
EX n/a NM $10 MIP $25

❏ **Winter Princess #1 Winter Princess,** 1993, Mattel, Model No. 10655
EX n/a NM $35 MIP $175

❏ **Winter Princess #2 Evergreen Princess,** 1994, Mattel, Model No. 12123
EX n/a NM $35 MIP $100

❏ **Winter Princess #3 Peppermint Princess,** 1995, Mattel, Model No. 13598
EX n/a NM $35 MIP $175

❏ **Winter Princess #4 Jewel Princess,** 1996, Mattel, Model No. 15826
EX n/a NM $35 MIP $175

❏ **Winter Princess #5 Midnight Princess,** 1997, Mattel, Model No. 17780
EX n/a NM $35 MIP $175

❏ **Woolworth's Special Expressions, black, blue dress,** 1991, Mattel, Model No. 2583
EX n/a NM $4 MIP $10

❏ **Woolworth's Special Expressions, black, peach dress,** 1992, Mattel, Model No. 3200
EX n/a NM $5 MIP $30

❏ **Woolworth's Special Expressions, black, pink dress,** 1990, Mattel, Model No. 5505
EX n/a NM $4 MIP $10

❏ **Woolworth's Special Expressions, black, white dress,** 1989, Mattel, Model No. 7326
EX n/a NM $5 MIP $20

❏ **Woolworth's Special Expressions, blue dress, pastel print,** 1993, Mattel, Model No. 10048
EX n/a NM $5 MIP $15

❏ **Woolworth's Special Expressions, pink dress,** 1990, Mattel, Model No. 5504
EX n/a NM $3 MIP $20

❏ **Woolworth's Special Expressions, white,** 1989, Mattel, Model No. 4842
EX n/a NM $5 MIP $20

❏ **Woolworth's Special Expressions, white, blue dress,** 1991, Mattel, Model No. 2582
EX n/a NM $4 MIP $15

❏ **Woolworth's Special Expressions, white, peach dress,** 1992, Mattel, Model No. 3197
EX n/a NM $5 MIP $20

❏ **Woolworth's Sweet Lavender Barbie, black or white,** 1992, Mattel, Model No. 2523/2522
EX n/a NM $12 MIP $28

❏ **Workin' Out Barbie Gift Set,** 1997, Mattel
EX n/a NM $10 MIP $25

❏ **XXXOOO Barbie Doll,** 2000, Mattel
EX n/a NM $8 MIP $20

MATTEL DOLLS, NON-BARBIE

❏ **Audrey Hepburn, Breakfast At Tiffany's, black dress,** 1998, Mattel
EX n/a NM $40 MIP $75

❏ **Audrey Hepburn, Pink Princess,** 1998, Mattel
EX n/a NM $25 MIP $50

❏ **Betty Boop #1 Glamour Girl,** 2001, Mattel, Model No. 29733
EX n/a NM $15 MIP $40

❏ **Bob Mackie Cher,** 2001, Mattel, Model No. 29049
EX n/a NM $15 MIP $40

❏ **Buffy and Mrs. Beasley,** 1968, Mattel, Model No. 3577
EX n/a NM $125 MIP $275

❏ **Chatty Cathy, 1999 reissue,** 1999, Mattel, Model No. 23782
EX n/a NM $50 MIP $100

❏ **Chatty Cathy, Holiday,** 1999, Mattel, Model No. 23783
EX n/a NM $50 MIP $125

❏ **Coca-Cola Holiday Series, Santa Claus,** 1999, Mattel, Model No. 23288
EX n/a NM $25 MIP $60

❏ **Daytime Drama, Erica Kane #1,** 1998, Mattel
EX n/a NM $20 MIP $50

❏ **Daytime Drama, Erica Kane #2,** 1999, Mattel
EX n/a NM $20 MIP $45

❏ **Daytime Drama, Marlena Evans,** 1999, Mattel
EX n/a NM $20 MIP $45

❏ **Elizabeth Taylor as Cleopatra,** 1999, Mattel
EX n/a NM $35 MIP $60

❏ **Elizabeth Taylor in Father of the Bride,** 2000, Mattel, Model No. 26836
EX n/a NM $30 MIP $70

❏ **Elvis Presley #1,** 1998, Mattel, Model No. 20544
EX n/a NM $20 MIP $50

❏ **Elvis Presley #2 The Army Years,** 1999, Mattel, Model No. 21912
EX n/a NM $20 MIP $50

(Mattel Photo)

❏ **Elvis Presley #4 King of Rock 'N Roll,** 2002, Mattel, Model No. 53869
EX n/a   **NM** $20   **MIP** $40

❏ **Flapper Minnie Mouse,** 2001, Mattel, Model No. 29734
EX n/a   **NM** $30   **MIP** $60

❏ **Frank Sinatra The Recording Years,** 2001, Mattel
EX n/a   **NM** $15   **MIP** $35

(Mattel Photo)

❏ **Gone with the Wind, Clark Gable as Rhett Butler,** 2002, Mattel, Model No. 53854
EX n/a   **NM** $30   **MIP** $70

❏ **Great Villains, Captain Hook (Peter Pan),** 1999, Mattel
EX n/a   **NM** $30   **MIP** $75

❏ **Great Villains, Cruella DeVil, Power in Pinstripes,** 1996, Mattel, Model No. 16295
EX n/a   **NM** $35   **MIP** $75

❏ **Great Villains, Cruella DeVil, Ruthless in Red,** 1997, Mattel
EX n/a   **NM** $35   **MIP** $75

❏ **Great Villains, Evil Queen (Snow White),** 1998, Mattel, Model No. 18626
EX n/a   **NM** $30   **MIP** $75

❏ **Great Villains, Maleficent (Sleeping Beauty),** 1999, Mattel
EX n/a   **NM** $25   **MIP** $75

❏ **Great Villains, Ursula (Little Mermaid),** 1997, Mattel, Model No. 17575
EX n/a   **NM** $30   **MIP** $75

❏ **I Love Lucy, Be a Pal,** 2002, Mattel, Model No. 52737
EX n/a   **NM** $20   **MIP** $40

❏ **I Love Lucy, Job Switching,** 1999, Mattel, Model No. 21268
EX n/a   **NM** $20   **MIP** $35

❏ **I Love Lucy, Lucy and Ricky 50th Anniversary Dolls,** 2000, Mattel
EX n/a   **NM** $25   **MIP** $75

(Mattel Photo)

❏ **I Love Lucy, Lucy Gets a Paris Gown,** 2003, Mattel, Model No. B0313
EX n/a   **NM** $20   **MIP** $40

❏ **I Love Lucy, Lucy's Italian Movie,** 2000, Mattel, Model No. 25527
EX n/a   **NM** $20   **MIP** $40

❏ **I Love Lucy, Vitameatavegemin,** 1998, Mattel
EX n/a   **NM** $25   **MIP** $45

❏ **Jolly Holiday Mary Poppins,** 2000, Mattel
EX n/a   **NM** $20   **MIP** $40

❏ **Marilyn Monroe,** 2002, Mattel, Model No. 53873
EX n/a   **NM** $20   **MIP** $50

❏ **Rosie O'Donnell,** 1999, Mattel
EX n/a   **NM** $10   **MIP** $25

❏ **Tinker Bell,** 2001, Mattel, Model No. 29735
EX n/a   **NM** $20   **MIP** $40

❏ **Vivien Leigh Scarlett O'Hara #1 Barbecue at Twelve Oaks,** 2001, Mattel, Model No. 29910
EX n/a   **NM** $25   **MIP** $75

❏ **Vivien Leigh Scarlett O'Hara #2 Peachtree St. Drapery Dress,** 2001, Mattel, Model No. 29771
EX n/a   **NM** $25   **MIP** $75

PORCELAIN BARBIES

❏ **30th Anniversary Ken,** 1991, Mattel, Model No. 1110
EX n/a   **NM** $75   **MIP** $175

❏ **30th Anniversary Midge,** 1993, Mattel, Model No. 7957
EX n/a   **NM** $65   **MIP** $150

❏ **30th Anniversary Skipper,** 1994, Mattel, Model No. 11396
EX n/a   **NM** $50   **MIP** $150

❏ **Benefit Performance Barbie,** 1988, Mattel, Model No. 5475
EX n/a   **NM** $200   **MIP** $425

❏ **Blue Rhapsody, first porcelain Barbie,** 1986, Mattel, Model No. 1708
EX n/a   **NM** $300   **MIP** $600

❏ **Blushing Orchid Bride Barbie,** 1997, Mattel, Model No. 16962
EX n/a   **NM** $75   **MIP** $175

❏ **Bob Mackie Celebration of Dance Charleston,** 2001, Mattel
EX n/a   **NM** $100   **MIP** $300

❏ **Bob Mackie Celebration of Dance Tango,** 1999, Mattel, Model No. 23451
EX n/a   **NM** $150   **MIP** $200

❏ **Crystal Rhapsody, blond, Presidential Porcelain Barbie collection,** 1992, Mattel, Model No. 1553
EX n/a   **NM** $100   **MIP** $300

❏ **Crystal Rhapsody, brunette, Presidential Porcelain Barbie collection,** 1993, Mattel, Model No. 10201
EX n/a   **NM** $100   **MIP** $600

❏ **Enchanted Evening Barbie,** 1987, Mattel, Model No. 3415
EX n/a   **NM** $175   **MIP** $400

❏ **Faberge Imperial Elegance Barbie, limited to 15,000,** 1999, Mattel, Model No. 19816
EX n/a   **NM** $150   **MIP** $350

❏ **Gay Parisienne, blond,** 1991, Mattel, Model No. 9973
EX n/a   **NM** $225   **MIP** $625

❏ **Gay Parisienne, brunette,** 1991, Mattel, Model No. 9973
EX n/a   **NM** $150   **MIP** $225

❏ **Gay Parisienne, red hair,** 1991, Mattel, Model No. 9973
EX n/a   **NM** $225   **MIP** $625

❏ **Gold Sensation, Gold and Silver Porcelain Barbie Set,** 1993, Mattel, Model No. 10246
EX n/a   **NM** $175   **MIP** $350

❏ **Holiday Porcelain #1, Holiday Jewel,** 1995, Mattel, Model No. 14311
EX n/a   **NM** $55   **MIP** $225

❏ **Holiday Porcelain #2, Holiday Caroler,** 1996, Mattel, Model No. 15760
EX n/a   **NM** $60   **MIP** $200

❏ **Holiday Porcelain #3, Holiday Ball,** 1997, Mattel, Model No. 18326
EX n/a   **NM** $75   **MIP** $200

❏ **Holiday Porcelain #4, Holiday Gift,** 1998, Mattel, Model No. 20128
EX n/a   **NM** $100   **MIP** $200

❏ **Mattel's 50th Anniversary Barbie,** 1995, Mattel, Model No. 14479
EX n/a   **NM** $300   **MIP** $350

❏ **Mint Memories, Victorian Tea Porcelain Collection,** 1999, Mattel
EX n/a   **NM** $100   **MIP** $215

❏ **Plantation Belle, blond, Porcelain Treasures Collection,** 1992, Mattel, Model No. 7526
EX n/a   **NM** $100   **MIP** $575

❏ **Plantation Belle, red, Porcelain Treasures Collection,** 1992, Mattel, Model No. 5351
EX n/a   **NM** $100   **MIP** $200

❑ **Presidential Porcelain Evening Pearl Barbie,** 1996, Mattel
EX n/a   NM $95   MIP $225

❑ **Romantic Rose Bride,** 1995, Mattel, Model No. 14541
EX n/a   NM $75   MIP $175

❑ **Royal Splendor, Presidential Porcelain Collection,** 1993, Mattel, Model No. 10950
EX n/a   NM $100   MIP $250

❑ **Silken Flame Barbie, brunette, Porcelain Treasures Collection,** 1993, Mattel, Model No. 1249
EX n/a   NM $100   MIP $200

❑ **Silken Flame, blond,** 1993, Mattel, Model No. 11099
EX n/a   NM $250   MIP $500

❑ **Silver Starlight, Gold and Silver Porcelain Barbie Set,** 1994, Mattel, Model No. 11875
EX n/a   NM $175   MIP $350

❑ **Solo in the Spotlight,** 1990, Mattel, Model No. 7613
EX n/a   NM $100   MIP $200

❑ **Sophisticated Lady,** 1990, Mattel, Model No. 5313
EX n/a   NM $125   MIP $200

❑ **Star Lily Bride Barbie, Wedding Flower Collection,** 1995, Mattel, Model No. 12953
EX n/a   NM $125   MIP $250

❑ **Wedding Day Barbie,** 1989, Mattel, Model No. 2641
EX n/a   NM $300   MIP $400

(Mattel Photo)

❑ **Wizard of Oz Cowardly Lion,** 2002, Mattel, Model No. 54180
EX n/a   NM $50   MIP $150

❑ **Wizard of Oz Dorothy,** 2000, Mattel, Model No. 26834
EX n/a   NM $70   MIP $150

❑ **Wizard of Oz Scarecrow,** 2001, Mattel, Model No. 29190
EX n/a   NM $50   MIP $150

❑ **Wizard of Oz Tin Man,** 2001, Mattel, Model No. 29676
EX n/a   NM $50   MIP $150

❑ **Wizard of Oz Wicked Witch,** 2000, Mattel, Model No. 26835
EX n/a   NM $70   MIP $150

❑ **Wizard of Oz Winged Monkey,** 2001, Mattel, Model No. 29476
EX n/a   NM $50   MIP $150

FASHIONS

BARBIE VINTAGE FASHIONS 1959-1966

❑ **Aboard Ship,** Mattel, Model No. 1631
EX n/a   NM $245   MIP $475

❑ **After Five,** Mattel, Model No. 934
EX n/a   NM $68   MIP $135

❑ **American Airlines Stewardess,** Mattel, Model No. 984
EX n/a   NM $110   MIP $225

❑ **Apple Print Sheath,** Mattel, Model No. 917
EX n/a   NM $68   MIP $135

❑ **Ballerina,** Mattel, Model No. 989
EX n/a   NM $50   MIP $200

❑ **Barbie Arabian Nights,** Mattel, Model No. 0874
EX n/a   NM $275   MIP $410

❑ **Barbie Baby-Sits,** 1963, Mattel, Model No. 953
EX n/a   NM $200   MIP $325

❑ **Barbie in Hawaii,** Mattel, Model No. 1605
EX n/a   NM $140   MIP $275

❑ **Barbie in Holland,** Mattel, Model No. 0823
EX n/a   NM $85   MIP $200

❑ **Barbie in Japan,** Mattel, Model No. 0821
EX n/a   NM $350   MIP $475

❑ **Barbie in Mexico,** Mattel, Model No. 0820
EX n/a   NM $205   MIP $275

❑ **Barbie in Switzerland,** Mattel, Model No. 0822
EX n/a   NM $130   MIP $250

❑ **Barbie Learns to Cook,** Mattel, Model No. 1634
EX n/a   NM $195   MIP $500

❑ **Barbie Skin Diver,** Mattel, Model No. 1608
EX n/a   NM $45   MIP $110

❑ **Barbie-Q Outfit,** Mattel, Model No. 962
EX n/a   NM $72   MIP $155

❑ **Beau Time,** Mattel, Model No. 1651
EX n/a   NM $235   MIP $500

❑ **Beautiful Bride,** Mattel, Model No. 1698
EX n/a   NM $650   MIP $2100

❑ **Benefit Performance,** Mattel, Model No. 1667
EX n/a   NM $550   MIP $1375

❑ **Black Magic,** Mattel, Model No. 1609
EX n/a   NM $150   MIP $300

❑ **Bride's Dream,** Mattel, Model No. 947
EX n/a   NM $160   MIP $300

❑ **Brunch Time,** Mattel, Model No. 1628
EX n/a   NM $140   MIP $350

❑ **Busy Gal,** Mattel, Model No. 981
EX n/a   NM $225   MIP $400

❑ **Busy Morning,** Mattel, Model No. 956
EX n/a   NM $175   MIP $275

❑ **Campus Sweetheart,** Mattel, Model No. 1616
EX n/a   NM $615   MIP $1600

❑ **Candy Striper Volunteer,** Mattel, Model No. 0889
EX n/a   NM $200   MIP $365

❑ **Career Girl,** Mattel, Model No. 954
EX n/a   NM $120   MIP $275

❑ **Caribbean Cruise,** Mattel, Model No. 1687
EX n/a   NM $80   MIP $200

❑ **Cheerleader,** Mattel, Model No. 0876
EX n/a   NM $115   MIP $195

❑ **Cinderella,** Mattel, Model No. 0872
EX n/a   NM $265   MIP $460

❑ **Club Meeting,** Mattel, Model No. 1672
EX n/a   NM $145   MIP $375

❑ **Coffee's On,** Mattel, Model No. 1670
EX n/a   NM $70   MIP $150

(KP Photo)

❑ **Commuter Set,** Mattel, Model No. 916
EX n/a   NM $700   MIP $1500

❑ **Country Club Dance,** Mattel, Model No. 1627
EX n/a   NM $265   MIP $450

❑ **Country Fair,** Mattel, Model No. 1603
EX n/a   NM $55   MIP $165

❑ **Crisp'n Cool,** Mattel, Model No. 1604
EX n/a   NM $85   MIP $175

- **Cruise Stripes**, Mattel, Model No. 918
  EX n/a   **NM** $85   **MIP** $165
- **Dancing Doll**, Mattel, Model No. 1626
  EX n/a   **NM** $220   **MIP** $450
- **Debutante Ball**, Mattel, Model No. 1666
  EX n/a   **NM** $600   **MIP** $1200
- **Dinner At Eight**, Mattel, Model No. 946
  EX n/a   **NM** $90   **MIP** $225
- **Disc Date**, Mattel, Model No. 1633
  EX n/a   **NM** $155   **MIP** $295
- **Dog n' Duds**, Mattel, Model No. 1613
  EX n/a   **NM** $155   **MIP** $325
- **Dreamland**, Mattel, Model No. 1669
  EX n/a   **NM** $120   **MIP** $200
- **Drum Majorette**, Mattel, Model No. 0875
  EX n/a   **NM** $120   **MIP** $200

(KP Photo)

- **Easter Parade**, Mattel, Shown on a Ponytail #3 doll, Model No. 971
  EX n/a   **NM** $1500   **MIP** $4000

(KP Photo)

- **Enchanted Evening**, Mattel, Seen here on a Bubblecut Barbie, Model No. 983
  EX n/a   **NM** $207   **MIP** $385
- **Evening Enchantment**, Mattel, Model No. 1695
  EX n/a   **NM** $300   **MIP** $500
- **Evening Gala**, Mattel, Model No. 1660
  EX n/a   **NM** $130   **MIP** $350
- **Evening Splendor**, Mattel, Model No. 961
  EX n/a   **NM** $177   **MIP** $355
- **Fabulous Fashion**, Mattel, Model No. 1676
  EX n/a   **NM** $280   **MIP** $525
- **Fancy Free**, Mattel, Model No. 943
  EX n/a   **NM** $30   **MIP** $75
- **Fashion Editor**, Mattel, Model No. 1635
  EX n/a   **NM** $290   **MIP** $650
- **Fashion Luncheon**, Mattel, Model No. 1656
  EX n/a   **NM** $600   **MIP** $1200
- **Fashion Shiner**, Mattel, Model No. 1691
  EX n/a   **NM** $90   **MIP** $220
- **Floating Gardens**, Mattel, Model No. 1696
  EX n/a   **NM** $220   **MIP** $500
- **Floral Petticoat**, Mattel, Model No. 921
  EX n/a   **NM** $27   **MIP** $55
- **Formal Occasion**, Mattel, Model No. 1697
  EX n/a   **NM** $190   **MIP** $500
- **Fraternity Dance**, Mattel, Model No. 1638
  EX n/a   **NM** $240   **MIP** $610
- **Friday Night Date**, Mattel, Model No. 979
  EX n/a   **NM** $130   **MIP** $245
- **Fun At The Fair**, Mattel, Model No. 1624
  EX n/a   **NM** $140   **MIP** $285
- **Fun n' Games**, Mattel, Model No. 1619
  EX n/a   **NM** $135   **MIP** $300
- **Garden Party**, Mattel, Model No. 931
  EX n/a   **NM** $47   **MIP** $150
- **Garden Tea Party**, Mattel, Model No. 1606
  EX n/a   **NM** $70   **MIP** $175
- **Garden Wedding**, Mattel, Model No. 1658
  EX n/a   **NM** $240   **MIP** $500

(KP Photo)

- **Gay Parisienne**, Mattel, Shown here on a Ponytail #1, Model No. 964
  EX n/a   **NM** $1100   **MIP** $4000
- **Gold n' Glamour**, Mattel, Model No. 1647
  EX n/a   **NM** $775   **MIP** $1600
- **Golden Elegance**, Mattel, Model No. 992
  EX n/a   **NM** $225   **MIP** $350
- **Golden Evening**, Mattel, Model No. 1610
  EX n/a   **NM** $115   **MIP** $250
- **Golden Girl**, Mattel, Model No. 911
  EX n/a   **NM** $87   **MIP** $175
- **Golden Glory**, Mattel, Model No. 1645
  EX n/a   **NM** $230   **MIP** $425
- **Graduation**, Mattel, Model No. 945
  EX n/a   **NM** $48   **MIP** $95
- **Guinevere**, Mattel, Model No. 0873
  EX n/a   **NM** $190   **MIP** $300
- **Here Comes The Bride**, Mattel, Model No. 1665
  EX n/a   **NM** $440   **MIP** $995
- **Holiday Dance**, Mattel, Model No. 1639
  EX n/a   **NM** $325   **MIP** $595
- **Icebreaker**, Mattel, Model No. 942
  EX n/a   **NM** $60   **MIP** $120
- **International Fair**, Mattel, Model No. 1653
  EX n/a   **NM** $365   **MIP** $500
- **Invitation To Tea**, Mattel, Model No. 1632
  EX n/a   **NM** $285   **MIP** $525
- **It's Cold Outside, brown**, Mattel, Model No. 0819
  EX n/a   **NM** $45   **MIP** $110
- **It's Cold Outside, red**, Mattel, Model No. 0819
  EX n/a   **NM** $65   **MIP** $165

BARBIE

❏ **Junior Designer**, Mattel, Model No. 1620
EX n/a　　NM $200　　MIP $350

❏ **Junior Prom**, Mattel, Model No. 1614
EX n/a　　NM $375　　MIP $600

❏ **Knit Hit**, Mattel, Model No. 1621
EX n/a　　NM $165　　MIP $225

❏ **Knit Separates**, Mattel, Model No. 1602
EX n/a　　NM $70　　MIP $160

❏ **Knitting Pretty, blue**, Mattel, Model No. 957
EX n/a　　NM $80　　MIP $190

❏ **Knitting Pretty, pink**, Mattel, Model No. 957
EX n/a　　NM $200　　MIP $475

❏ **Let's Dance**, Mattel, Model No. 978
EX n/a　　NM $115　　MIP $230

❏ **Little Red Riding Hood & The Wolf**, Mattel, Model No. 0880
EX n/a　　NM $385　　MIP $585

❏ **London Tour**, Mattel, Model No. 1661
EX n/a　　NM $170　　MIP $400

❏ **Lunch Date**, Mattel, Model No. 1600
EX n/a　　NM $45　　MIP $125

❏ **Lunch On The Terrace**, Mattel, Model No. 1649
EX n/a　　NM $210　　MIP $325

❏ **Lunchtime**, Mattel, Model No. 1673
EX n/a　　NM $150　　MIP $285

❏ **Magnificence**, Mattel, Model No. 1646
EX n/a　　NM $350　　MIP $595

❏ **Masquerade**, Mattel, Model No. 944
EX n/a　　NM $75　　MIP $175

❏ **Matinee Fashion**, Mattel, Model No. 1640
EX n/a　　NM $320　　MIP $525

❏ **Midnight Blue**, Mattel, Model No. 1617
EX n/a　　NM $415　　MIP $800

(KP Photo)

❏ **Miss Astronaut**, Mattel, Shown here with re-constructed helmet, Model No. 1641
EX n/a　　NM $395　　MIP $650

❏ **Modern Art**, Mattel, Model No. 1625
EX n/a　　NM $360　　MIP $550

❏ **Mood For Music**, Mattel, Model No. 940
EX n/a　　NM $107　　MIP $190

❏ **Movie Date**, Mattel, Model No. 933
EX n/a　　NM $30　　MIP $50

❏ **Music Center Matinee**, Mattel, Model No. 1633
EX n/a　　NM $380　　MIP $600

❏ **Nighty Negligee**, Mattel, Model No. 965
EX n/a　　NM $46　　MIP $92

❏ **On The Avenue**, Mattel, Model No. 1644
EX n/a　　NM $245　　MIP $525

(KP Photo)

❏ **Open Road**, Mattel, The Mattel Road Map included with this outfit is especially hard to find, Model No. 985
EX n/a　　NM $225　　MIP $350

❏ **Orange Blossom,** 1961, Mattel, Model No. 987
EX n/a　　NM $55　　MIP $165

❏ **Outdoor Art Show**, Mattel, Model No. 1650
EX n/a　　NM $235　　MIP $500

❏ **Outdoor Life**, Mattel, Model No. 1637
EX n/a　　NM $115　　MIP $275

❏ **Pajama Party**, Mattel, Model No. 1601
EX n/a　　NM $20　　MIP $50

(KP Photo)

❏ **Pan Am Stewardess**, Mattel, Very rare fashion shown on American Girl doll, Model No. 1678
EX n/a　　NM $1500　　MIP $4000

❏ **Party Date**, Mattel, Model No. 958
EX n/a　　NM $85　　MIP $175

❏ **Patio Party**, Mattel, Model No. 1692
EX n/a　　NM $140　　MIP $325

❏ **Peachy Fleecy**, Mattel, Model No. 915
EX n/a　　NM $75　　MIP $150

❏ **Photo Fashion**, Mattel, Model No. 1648
EX n/a　　NM $150　　MIP $375

❏ **Picnic Set**, Mattel, Model No. 967
EX n/a　　NM $205　　MIP $410

❏ **Pink Moonbeams**, Mattel, Model No. 1694
EX n/a　　NM $110　　MIP $300

❏ **Plantation Belle**, Mattel, Model No. 966
EX n/a　　NM $240　　MIP $475

❏ **Poodle Parade**, Mattel, Model No. 1643
EX n/a　　NM $620　　MIP $950

❏ **Pretty As A Picture**, Mattel, Model No. 1652
EX n/a　　NM $225　　MIP $450

❏ **Print Aplenty**, Mattel, Model No. 1686
EX n/a　　NM $140　　MIP $275

❏ **Rain Coat**, Mattel, Model No. 949
EX n/a　　NM $50　　MIP $95

❏ **Reception Line**, Mattel, Model No. 1654
EX n/a　　NM $350　　MIP $500

❏ **Red Flare**, Mattel, Model No. 939
EX n/a　　NM $80　　MIP $165

(KP Photo)

❑ **Registered Nurse**, Mattel, Seen here on Midge, Model No. 991
EX n/a   NM $98   MIP $245

❑ **Resort Set**, Mattel, Model No. 963
EX n/a   NM $103   MIP $205

❑ **Riding In The Park**, Mattel, Model No. 1668
EX n/a   NM $300   MIP $595

(KP Photo)

❑ **Roman Holiday**, Mattel, Shown on Ponytail #4 Barbie doll, Model No. 968
EX n/a   NM $1500   MIP $4800

❑ **Satin n' Rose**, Mattel, Model No. 1611
EX n/a   NM $190   MIP $375

❑ **Saturday Matinee**, Mattel, Model No. 1615
EX n/a   NM $525   MIP $900

❑ **Senior Prom**, Mattel, Model No. 951
EX n/a   NM $115   MIP $225

❑ **Sheath Sensation**, Mattel, Model No. 986
EX n/a   NM $80   MIP $150

❑ **Shimmering Magic**, Mattel, Model No. 1664
EX n/a   NM $800   MIP $1600

❑ **Silken Flame**, Mattel, Model No. 977
EX n/a   NM $60   MIP $145

❑ **Singing In The Shower**, Mattel, Model No. 988
EX n/a   NM $65   MIP $130

❑ **Skater's Waltz**, Mattel, Model No. 1629
EX n/a   NM $180   MIP $395

❑ **Ski Queen**, Mattel, Model No. 948
EX n/a   NM $75   MIP $165

❑ **Sleeping Pretty**, Mattel, Model No. 1636
EX n/a   NM $100   MIP $350

❑ **Sleepytime Gal**, Mattel, Model No. 1674
EX n/a   NM $125   MIP $220

❑ **Slumber Party**, Mattel, Model No. 1642
EX n/a   NM $135   MIP $260

(KP Photo)

❑ **Solo In The Spotlight**, Mattel, Seen here on a Ponytail #4 doll, Model No. 982
EX n/a   NM $235   MIP $470

❑ **Sophisticated Lady**, Mattel, Model No. 993
EX n/a   NM $240   MIP $425

❑ **Sorority Meeting**, Mattel, Model No. 937
EX n/a   NM $120   MIP $240

❑ **Sporting Casuals**, Mattel, Model No. 1671
EX n/a   NM $60   MIP $165

❑ **Stormy Weather**, Mattel, Model No. 0949
EX n/a   NM $50   MIP $95

(KP Photo)

❑ **Student Teacher**, Mattel, Model No. 1622
EX n/a   NM $235   MIP $400

❑ **Studio Tour**, Mattel, Model No. 1690
EX n/a   NM $110   MIP $250

❑ **Suburban Shopper**, Mattel, Model No. 969
EX n/a   NM $180   MIP $360

❑ **Sunday Visit**, Mattel, Model No. 1675
EX n/a   NM $210   MIP $450

❑ **Sunflower**, Mattel, Model No. 1683
EX n/a   NM $140   MIP $245

❑ **Sweater Girl**, Mattel, Model No. 976
EX n/a   NM $75   MIP $175

❑ **Sweet Dreams, pink**, Mattel, Model No. 973
EX n/a   NM $240   MIP $425

❑ **Sweet Dreams, yellow**, Mattel, Model No. 973
EX n/a   NM $80   MIP $145

❑ **Swingin' Easy**, Mattel, Model No. 955
EX n/a   NM $125   MIP $245

❑ **Tennis Anyone**, Mattel, Model No. 941
EX n/a   NM $74   MIP $150

❑ **Theatre Date (1963),** 1963, Mattel, Model No. 1612
EX n/a   NM $100   MIP $175

❑ **Theatre Date (1964),** 1964, Mattel, Model No. 959
EX n/a   NM $75   MIP $200

❑ **Travel Togethers**, Mattel, Model No. 1688
EX n/a   NM $110   MIP $240

❑ **Under Fashions**, Mattel, Model No. 1655
EX n/a   NM $265   MIP $500

❑ **Undergarments**, Mattel, Model No. 919
EX n/a   NM $31   MIP $65

❑ **Underprints**, Mattel, Model No. 1685
EX n/a   NM $55   MIP $225

❑ **Vacation Time**, Mattel, Model No. 1623
EX n/a   NM $110   MIP $240

BARBIE

❑ **Wedding Day Set**, Mattel, Model
No. 972
EX n/a   **NM** $195   **MIP** $385

❑ **White Magic**, Mattel, Model No. 1607
EX n/a   **NM** $125   **MIP** $275

❑ **Winter Holiday**, Mattel, Model No. 975
EX n/a   **NM** $82   **MIP** $165

FRANCIE VINTAGE FASHIONS 1966

❑ **Checkmates**, Mattel, Model No. 1259
EX n/a   **NM** $85   **MIP** $140

❑ **Clam Diggers**, Mattel, Model No. 1258
EX n/a   **NM** $130   **MIP** $250

❑ **Concert In The Park**, Mattel, Model
No. 1256
EX n/a   **NM** $135   **MIP** $260

❑ **Dance Party**, Mattel, Model No. 1257
EX n/a   **NM** $180   **MIP** $250

❑ **First Formal**, Mattel, Model No. 1260
EX n/a   **NM** $100   **MIP** $175

❑ **First Things First**, Mattel, Model
No. 1252
EX n/a   **NM** $55   **MIP** $100

❑ **Fresh As A Daisy**, Mattel, Model
No. 1254
EX n/a   **NM** $85   **MIP** $140

❑ **Fur Out,** 1966, Mattel, Model No. 1262
EX n/a   **NM** $235   **MIP** $400

❑ **Gad-About**, Mattel, Model No. 1250
EX n/a   **NM** $120   **MIP** $220

❑ **Go Granny Go,** 1966, Mattel, Model
No. 1267
EX n/a   **NM** $110   **MIP** $200

❑ **Hip Knits,** 1966, Mattel, Model
No. 1265
EX n/a   **NM** $125   **MIP** $200

❑ **It's A Date**, Mattel, Model No. 1251
EX n/a   **NM** $70   **MIP** $125

❑ **Leather Limelight,** 1966, Mattel, Model
No. 1269
EX n/a   **NM** $110   **MIP** $255

❑ **Orange Cozy,** 1966, Mattel, Model
No. 1263
EX n/a   **NM** $170   **MIP** $235

❑ **Polka Dots N' Raindrops**, Mattel, Model
No. 1255
EX n/a   **NM** $55   **MIP** $100

❑ **Quick Shift,** 1966, Mattel, Model
No. 1266
EX n/a   **NM** $90   **MIP** $180

❑ **Shoppin' Spree**, Mattel, Model
No. 1261
EX n/a   **NM** $100   **MIP** $140

❑ **Style Setters,** 1966, Mattel, Model
No. 1268
EX n/a   **NM** $140   **MIP** $260

❑ **Swingin' Skimmy,** 1966, Mattel, Model
No. 1264
EX n/a   **NM** $140   **MIP** $245

❑ **Tuckered Out**, Mattel, Model No. 1253
EX n/a   **NM** $55   **MIP** $125

KEN VINTAGE FASHIONS 1961-1966

❑ **American Airlines Captain #1**, Mattel,
Model No. 0779
EX n/a   **NM** $205   **MIP** $300

❑ **Army and Air Force**, Mattel, Model
No. 797
EX n/a   **NM** $135   **MIP** $245

(KP Photo)

❑ **Best Man**, Mattel, Seen on Allan doll,
Model No. 1425
EX n/a   **NM** $700   **MIP** $1100

❑ **Business Appointment**, Mattel, Model
No. 1424
EX n/a   **NM** $800   **MIP** $1150

❑ **Campus Corduroys**, Mattel, Model
No. 1410
EX n/a   **NM** $20   **MIP** $65

❑ **Campus Hero**, Mattel, Model No. 770
EX n/a   **NM** $35   **MIP** $95

❑ **Casuals, striped shirt**, Mattel, Model
No. 0782
EX n/a   **NM** $70   **MIP** $100

❑ **Casuals, yellow shirt**, Mattel, Model
No. 782
EX n/a   **NM** $40   **MIP** $65

❑ **College Student**, Mattel, Model
No. 1416
EX n/a   **NM** $190   **MIP** $400

❑ **Country Clubbin'**, Mattel, Model
No. 1400
EX n/a   **NM** $40   **MIP** $85

❑ **Dr. Ken**, Mattel, Model No. 793
EX n/a   **NM** $55   **MIP** $130

❑ **Dreamboat**, Mattel, Model No. 785
EX n/a   **NM** $40   **MIP** $95

❑ **Drum Major**, Mattel, Model No. 0775
EX n/a   **NM** $75   **MIP** $175

❑ **Fountain Boy**, Mattel, Model No. 1407
EX n/a   **NM** $230   **MIP** $325

❑ **Fraternity Meeting**, Mattel, Model
No. 1408
EX n/a   **NM** $25   **MIP** $55

❑ **Fun On Ice**, Mattel, Model No. 791
EX n/a   **NM** $55   **MIP** $105

❑ **Going Bowling**, Mattel, Model No. 1403
EX n/a   **NM** $20   **MIP** $35

❑ **Going Huntin'**, Mattel, Model No. 1409
EX n/a   **NM** $50   **MIP** $100

❑ **Graduation**, Mattel, Model No. 795
EX n/a   **NM** $35   **MIP** $65

❑ **Here Comes The Groom**, Mattel, Model
No. 1426
EX n/a   **NM** $1000   **MIP** $1400

❑ **Hiking Holiday**, Mattel, Model No. 1412
EX n/a   **NM** $100   **MIP** $210

❑ **Holiday**, Mattel, Model No. 1414
EX n/a   **NM** $48   **MIP** $100

❑ **In Training**, Mattel, Model No. 780
EX n/a   **NM** $30   **MIP** $50

❑ **Jazz Concert**, Mattel, Model No. 1420
EX n/a   **NM** $135   **MIP** $250

(KP Photo)

❑ **Ken A Go Go**, Mattel, This outfit even
included a mod-hair wig to make the
rather staid Ken look hip, Model
No. 1423
EX n/a   **NM** $500   **MIP** $700

❑ **Ken Arabian Nights**, Mattel, Model
No. 0774
EX n/a   **NM** $100   **MIP** $200

❑ **Ken In Hawaii**, Mattel, Model No. 1404
EX n/a   **NM** $100   **MIP** $195

❑ **Ken In Holland**, Mattel, Model No. 0777
EX n/a   **NM** $155   **MIP** $250

❑ **Ken In Mexico**, Mattel, Model No. 0778
EX n/a   **NM** $150   **MIP** $250

❑ **Ken In Switzerland**, Mattel, Model
No. 0776
EX n/a   **NM** $150   **MIP** $200

❑ **Ken Skin Diver**, Mattel, Model No. 1406
EX n/a   **NM** $30   **MIP** $50

❑ **King Arthur**, Mattel, Model No. 0773
EX n/a   NM $225   MIP $375

❑ **Masquerade (Ken)**, Mattel, Model No. 794
EX n/a   NM $60   MIP $145

❑ **Mountain Hike**, Mattel, Model No. 1427
EX n/a   NM $150   MIP $300

❑ **Mr. Astronaut**, Mattel, Model No. 1415
EX n/a   NM $395   MIP $650

❑ **Off To Bed**, Mattel, Model No. 1413
EX n/a   NM $82   MIP $150

❑ **Play Ball**, Mattel, Model No. 792
EX n/a   NM $55   MIP $110

❑ **Rally Day**, Mattel, Model No. 788
EX n/a   NM $66   MIP $130

❑ **Roller Skate Date, w/hat**, Mattel, Model No. 1405
EX n/a   NM $40   MIP $125

❑ **Roller Skate Date, w/slacks**, Mattel, Model No. 1405
EX n/a   NM $40   MIP $150

❑ **Rovin' Reporter**, Mattel, Model No. 1417
EX n/a   NM $175   MIP $295

❑ **Sailor**, Mattel, Model No. 796
EX n/a   NM $65   MIP $120

❑ **Saturday Date**, Mattel, Model No. 786
EX n/a   NM $40   MIP $105

❑ **Seein' The Sights**, Mattel, Model No. 1421
EX n/a   NM $195   MIP $455

❑ **Ski Champion**, Mattel, Model No. 798
EX n/a   NM $85   MIP $155

❑ **Sleeper Set, blue**, Mattel, Model No. 0781
EX n/a   NM $60   MIP $120

❑ **Sleeper Set, brown**, Mattel, Model No. 781
EX n/a   NM $38   MIP $70

❑ **Special Date**, Mattel, Model No. 1401
EX n/a   NM $70   MIP $145

❑ **Sport Shorts**, Mattel, Model No. 783
EX n/a   NM $20   MIP $55

❑ **Summer Job**, Mattel, Model No. 1422
EX n/a   NM $290   MIP $475

❑ **Terry Togs**, Mattel, Model No. 784
EX n/a   NM $60   MIP $90

❑ **The Prince**, Mattel, Model No. 0772
EX n/a   NM $285   MIP $375

❑ **The Yachtsman, no hat**, Mattel, Model No. 789
EX n/a   NM $45   MIP $90

❑ **The Yachtsman, w/hat**, Mattel, Model No. 0789
EX n/a   NM $235   MIP $475

❑ **Time For Tennis**, Mattel, Model No. 790
EX n/a   NM $70   MIP $140

❑ **Time To Turn In**, Mattel, Model No. 1418
EX n/a   NM $80   MIP $175

❑ **Touchdown**, Mattel, Model No. 799
EX n/a   NM $55   MIP $125

❑ **Tuxedo**, Mattel, Model No. 787
EX n/a   NM $125   MIP $245

❑ **TV's Good Tonight**, Mattel, Model No. 1419
EX n/a   NM $110   MIP $250

❑ **Victory Dance**, Mattel, Model No. 1411
EX n/a   NM $60   MIP $135

RICKY FASHIONS 1965-1966

❑ **Let's Explore**, Mattel, Model No. 1506
EX n/a   NM $35   MIP $85

❑ **Lights Out**, Mattel, Model No. 1501
EX n/a   NM $55   MIP $100

❑ **Little Leaguer**, Mattel, Model No. 1504
EX n/a   NM $65   MIP $95

❑ **Saturday Show**, Mattel, Model No. 1502
EX n/a   NM $45   MIP $70

❑ **Skateboard Set**, Mattel, Model No. 1505
EX n/a   NM $55   MIP $100

❑ **Sunday Suit**, Mattel, Model No. 1503
EX n/a   NM $45   MIP $65

SKIPPER VINTAGE FASHIONS 1964-1966

❑ **Ballet Class**, Mattel, Model No. 1905
EX n/a   NM $60   MIP $135

❑ **Can You Play?**, Mattel, Model No. 1923
EX n/a   NM $60   MIP $125

❑ **Chill Chasers**, Mattel, Model No. 1926
EX n/a   NM $55   MIP $100

❑ **Cookie Time**, Mattel, Model No. 1912
EX n/a   NM $85   MIP $150

❑ **Country Picnic**, Mattel, Model No. 1933
EX n/a   NM $300   MIP $450

❑ **Day At The Fair**, Mattel, Model No. 1911
EX n/a   NM $120   MIP $200

❑ **Dog Show**, Mattel, Model No. 1929
EX n/a   NM $190   MIP $300

❑ **Dreamtime**, Mattel, Model No. 1909
EX n/a   NM $60   MIP $125

❑ **Dress Coat**, Mattel, Model No. 1906
EX n/a   NM $60   MIP $80

❑ **Flower Girl**, Mattel, Model No. 1904
EX n/a   NM $80   MIP $150

❑ **Fun Time**, Mattel, Model No. 1920
EX n/a   NM $100   MIP $200

❑ **Happy Birthday**, Mattel, Model No. 1919
EX n/a   NM $355   MIP $500

❑ **Junior Bridesmaid**, Mattel, Model No. 1934
EX n/a   NM $285   MIP $475

❑ **Land & Sea**, Mattel, Model No. 1917
EX n/a   NM $90   MIP $155

❑ **Learning To Ride**, Mattel, Model No. 1935
EX n/a   NM $185   MIP $275

❑ **Let's Play House**, Mattel, Model No. 1932
EX n/a   NM $125   MIP $250

❑ **Loungin' Lovelies**, Mattel, Model No. 1930
EX n/a   NM $55   MIP $125

❑ **Masquerade (Skipper)**, Mattel, Model No. 1903
EX n/a   NM $80   MIP $155

❑ **Me N' My Doll**, Mattel, Model No. 1913
EX n/a   NM $150   MIP $260

❑ **Outdoor Casuals**, Mattel, Model No. 1915
EX n/a   NM $85   MIP $135

❑ **Platter Party**, Mattel, Model No. 1914
EX n/a   NM $75   MIP $125

❑ **Rain Or Shine**, Mattel, Model No. 1916
EX n/a   NM $50   MIP $90

❑ **Rainy Day Checkers**, Mattel, Model No. 1928
EX n/a   NM $155   MIP $300

❑ **Red Sensation**, Mattel, Model No. 1901
EX n/a   NM $65   MIP $125

❑ **School Days**, Mattel, Model No. 1907
EX n/a   NM $60   MIP $130

❑ **School Girl**, Mattel, Model No. 1921
EX n/a   NM $200   MIP $295

❑ **Ship Ahoy**, Mattel, Model No. 1918
EX n/a   NM $155   MIP $275

❑ **Silk N' Fancy**, Mattel, Model No. 1902
EX n/a   NM $60   MIP $125

❑ **Skating Fun**, Mattel, Model No. 1908
EX n/a   NM $48   MIP $110

❑ **Sledding Fun**, Mattel, Model No. 1936
EX n/a   NM $155   MIP $275

❑ **Sunny Pastels**, Mattel, Model No. 1910
EX n/a   NM $60   MIP $125

❑ **Tea Party**, Mattel, Model No. 1924
EX n/a   NM $185   MIP $300

❑ **Town Togs**, Mattel, Model No. 1922
EX n/a   NM $95   MIP $170

❑ **Under-Pretties**, Mattel, Model No. 1900
EX n/a   NM $25   MIP $50

❑ **What's New At The Zoo?**, Mattel, Model No. 1925
EX n/a   NM $50   MIP $120

TUTTI FASHIONS 1966

❑ **Puddle Jumpers**, Mattel, Model No. 3601
EX n/a   NM $20   MIP $45

❑ **Sand Castles**, Mattel, Model No. 3603
EX n/a   NM $55   MIP $98

❑ **Ship Shape**, Mattel, Model No. 3602
EX n/a   NM $55   MIP $90

❑ **Skippin' Rope**, Mattel, Model No. 3604
EX n/a   NM $55   MIP $95

Battery-Operated Toys

Telephone Bear, or "VIP Busy Boss," from the 1950s. Mint value, $400.

Armies of colorful, playful tin toys are frequently found at toy shows and flea markets. Among the most popular are battery-operated toys.

The heyday of battery-operated toys began in the 1940s, with Japanese companies leading the charge. Popular wind-up and friction toys were soon replaced with longer-lasting battery-operated versions.

Thousands of designs were made with toys featuring a variety of creative characters—from bubble-blowing monkeys to robots to cigar-smoking clowns. Disney creations and other cartoon characters like Popeye were also popular. The ingenuity of the Japanese created some truly unique novelty toys, valued today for their motion, design and humorous appeal.

Toys were often complex and could replicate several motions, such as walking, lifting or drumming. Tin lithography was usually quite interesting and detailed.

It is often difficult to identify the manufacturer of a battery-operated toy. Many companies used only initials to mark toys; some didn't mark them at all. Major manufacturers of battery-operated toys from the 1940s-1960s include Marx, Linemar (Marx's Japanese subsidiary), Alps, Marusan, Yonezawa, Bandai, Asahi Toy and Modern Toy (MT).

Manufacture of tin toys dropped off in the 1960s in favor of cheaper methods and materials.

Determining Value

As in other collecting areas, toys with character ties generally command more money. Space-related battery-operated toys are also popular.

It's difficult to find most battery-operated toys in Mint condition in original boxes. Battery-operated toys are highly susceptible to rust, corrosion and yellowing of fabric or plush.

Having the original box greatly increases the toy's desirability. Instructions were often printed on the box, and the name of the toy on the box often didn't match the toy exactly.

Indian Joe by Alps Toy Company, 1960s. Mint value, $150.

The Cragstan Crapshooter (interesting choice for a toy!) was produced in the 1950s, and today carries a mint value of $250.

The complexity of the toy also determines value. A toy with three or more actions will generally be worth more than a toy that performs only one action. Even though they may be nice display pieces, toys that don't work command much less.

This book lists toys in Excellent, Near Mint and Mint in Pack conditions.

To be graded in Mint condition, a toy should be operational, clean, free of rust or corrosion, and have the original box. Note that those in Good condition will exhibit wear, but will still be operational. Lesser condition toys and those that are not operational are not graded here. Some collectors acquire them for parts.

Many Thanks to Leo Rishty for contributing the pricing information for this section.

BATTERY-OPERATED TOYS

❑ **ABC Fairy Train,** 1950s, MT, 14-1/2" long
EX $80   NM $95   MIP $160

❑ **Accordion Player Bunny,** 1950s, Alps, 12" tall
EX $200   NM $325   MIP $400

❑ **Air Cargo Prop-Jet Airplane,** 1960s, Marx, Seaboard World Airlines, 12" long
EX $150   NM $300   MIP $425

❑ **Air Control Tower,** 1960s, Bandai, 11" tall, 37" span
EX $210   NM $315   MIP $450

❑ **Air Defense Pom-Pom Gun,** 1950s, Linemar, 14" long
EX $115   NM $175   MIP $200

❑ **Aircraft Carrier,** 1950s, Marx, 20" long
EX $275   NM $450   MIP $625

❑ **Alley, the Exciting New Roaring Stalking Alligator,** 1960s, Marx, 17-1/2" long
EX $175   NM $250   MIP $350

❑ **American Airlines DC-7,** 1960s, Linemar, 17-1/2" long, 19" wingspan
EX $200   NM $325   MIP $450

❑ **American Airlines Electra,** 1950s, Linemar, 18" long, 19-1/2" wingspan
EX $175   NM $300   MIP $450

❑ **American Airlines Flagship Caroline,** 1950s, Linemar, 18" long, 19-1/2" wingspan
EX $175   NM $300   MIP $400

❑ **Anti-Aircraft Unit No. 1,** 1950s, Linemar, 12-1/2" long
EX $140   NM $225   MIP $310

❑ **Army Radio Jeep—J1490,** 1950s, Linemar, 7-1/4" long
EX $75   NM $125   MIP $165

(KP Photo)

❑ **Arthur A-Go-Go,** 1960s, Alps, 10" tall
EX $135   NM $200   MIP $295

❑ **Atomic Rocket X-1800,** 1960s, MT, 9" long
EX $145   NM $225   MIP $325

❑ **B-58 Hustler Jet,** 1950s, Marx, 21" long, 12" wingspan
EX $500   NM $750   MIP $1000

❑ **Ball Playing Dog,** 1950s, Linemar, 9"
EX $125   NM $200   MIP $250
(Don Hultzman)

❑ **Barber Bear,** 1950s, Linemar, 9-1/2" tall
EX $175   NM $300   MIP $400

❑ **Barking Boxer Dog,** 1950s, Marx, 7" long
EX $45   NM $65   MIP $100

❑ **Barney Bear Drummer,** 1950s, Alps, 11" tall
EX $110   NM $185   MIP $250

❑ **Barnyard Rooster,** 1950s, Marx, 10" tall
EX $100   NM $150   MIP $200

(KP Photo)

❑ **Bartender,** 1960s, TN, 11-1/2" tall
EX $50   NM $75   MIP $100

❑ **Bear the Cashier,** 1950s, MT, 7-1/2" tall
EX $250   NM $350   MIP $450

❑ **Bengali—The Exciting New Growling, Prowling Tiger,** 1961, Linemar, 18-1/2" tall
EX $100   NM $150   MIP $225

❑ **Big John,** 1960s, Alps, 12" tall
EX $55   NM $75   MIP $125

❑ **Big John the Indian Chief,** 1960s, TN, 12-1/2" tall
EX $100   NM $150   MIP $200

❑ **Big Max Robot,** 1958, Remco, 7" tall
EX $80   NM $125   MIP $175

❑ **Bimbo the Clown,** 1950s, Alps, 9-1/4" tall
EX $190   NM $325   MIP $400

❑ **Blushing Gunfighter,** 1960s, Y Co., 11" tall
EX $75   NM $100   MIP $125

❑ **Blushing Willie,** 1960s, Y Co., 10" tall
EX $65   NM $85   MIP $110

❑ **Bobby the Drumming Bear,** 1950s, Alps, 10" tall
EX $175   NM $275   MIP $380

❑ **Bongo Player,** 1960s, Alps, 10" tall
EX $75   NM $110   MIP $160

(KP Photo)

❑ **Bongo the Drumming Monkey,** 1960s, Alps, 9-1/2" tall
EX $75   NM $115   MIP $165

❑ **Brave Eagle,** 1950s, TN, 11" tall
EX $100   NM $150   MIP $200

❑ **Brewster the Rooster,** 1950s, Marx, 9-1/2" tall
EX $150   NM $200   MIP $275

❑ **Bubble Blowing Bear,** 1950s, MT, 9-1/2" tall
EX $150   NM $225   MIP $300

❑ **Bubble Blowing Boy**
EX $150   NM $175   MIP $250

(KP Photo)

❑ **Bubble Blowing Monkey,** 1950s, Alps, 10" tall
EX $150   NM $175   MIP $250

❑ **Bubble Blowing Popeye,** 1950s, Linemar, 11-3/4" tall
EX $750   NM $1200   MIP $2500

❑ **Bubbling Bull,** 1950s, Linemar, 8" tall
EX $100   NM $150   MIP $200

❑ **Bunny the Magician,** 1950s, Alps, 14-1/2" tall
EX $300   NM $400   MIP $500

❏ **Burger Chef,** 1950s, Y Co., 9" tall
EX $175   **NM** $250   **MIP** $350

❏ **Busy Housekeeper,** 1950s, Alps, 8-1/2" tall
EX $200   **NM** $325   **MIP** $400

❏ **Busy Secretary,** 1950s, Linemar, 7-1/2" tall
EX $125   **NM** $200   **MIP** $300

❏ **Busy Shoe Shining Bear,** 1950s, Alps, 10" tall
EX $125   **NM** $200   **MIP** $250

❏ **Cabin Cruiser with Outboard Motor,** 1950s, Linemar, 12" long
EX $100   **NM** $135   **MIP** $200

❏ **Calypso Joe,** 1950s, Linemar, 11" tall
EX $190   **NM** $310   **MIP** $400

❏ **Camera Shooting Bear,** 1950s, Linemar, 11" tall
EX $350   **NM** $475   **MIP** $700

❏ **Cappy the Baggage Porter Dog,** 1960s, Alps, 12" tall
EX $100   **NM** $150   **MIP** $200

❏ **Caterpillar,** 1950s, Alps, 16" long
EX $80   **NM** $125   **MIP** $175

❏ **Central Choo Choo,** 1960s, MT, 15" long
EX $30   **NM** $40   **MIP** $60

❏ **Charlie the Drumming Clown,** 1950s, Alps, 9-1/2" tall
EX $135   **NM** $200   **MIP** $275

(KP Photo)

❏ **Charlie Weaver,** 1962, TN, 12"
EX $75   **NM** $100   **MIP** $125

❏ **Charm the Cobra,** 1960s, Alps, 6" tall
EX $90   **NM** $130   **MIP** $175

❏ **Chee Chee Chihuahua,** 1960s, Mego, 8" tall
EX $50   **NM** $75   **MIP** $100

(KP Photo)

❏ **Chef Cook,** 1960s, Y Co., 11-1/2" tall
EX $100   **NM** $200   **MIP** $300

❏ **Chippy the Chipmunk,** 1950s, Alps, 12" long
EX $75   **NM** $120   **MIP** $155

❏ **Circus Fire Engine,** 1960s, MT, 11" long
EX $110   **NM** $175   **MIP** $235

❏ **Clancy the Great,** 1960s, Ideal, 19-1/2" tall
EX $85   **NM** $135   **MIP** $200

❏ **Climbing Donald Duck on Friction Fire Engine,** 1950s, Linemar, 12" long
EX $375   **NM** $600   **MIP** $800

❏ **Clown Circus Car,** 1960s, MT, 8-1/2" long
EX $100   **NM** $175   **MIP** $235

❏ **Clown on Unicycle,** 1960s, MT, 10-1/2" tall
EX $180   **NM** $280   **MIP** $375

❏ **Coney Island Penny Machine,** 1950s, Remco, 13" tall
EX $90   **NM** $130   **MIP** $300

❏ **Coney Island Rocket Ride,** 1950s, Alps, 13-1/2" tall
EX $300   **NM** $450   **MIP** $600

❏ **Cragstan Beep Beep Greyhound Bus,** 1950s, Cragstan, 20" long
EX $125   **NM** $175   **MIP** $250

(KP Photo)

❏ **Cragstan Crapshooter,** 1950s, Y Co., 9-1/2" tall
EX $125   **NM** $175   **MIP** $250

❏ **Cragstan Crapshooting Monkey,** 1950s, Alps, 9" tall
EX $125   **NM** $175   **MIP** $250

❏ **Cragstan Mother Goose,** 1960s, Y Co., 8-1/4" tall
EX $100   **NM** $150   **MIP** $200

❏ **Cragstan Playboy,** 1960s, Cragstan, 13" tall
EX $100   **NM** $150   **MIP** $200

❏ **Cragstan Roulette, A Gambling Man,** 1960s, Y Co., 9" tall
EX $150   **NM** $225   **MIP** $300

❏ **Crawling Baby,** 1940s, Linemar, 11" long
EX $45   **NM** $75   **MIP** $100

❏ **Daisy, the Jolly Drumming Duck,** 1950s, Alps, 9" tall
EX $125   **NM** $200   **MIP** $250

(KP Photo)

❏ **Dancing Merry Chimp,** 1960s, Kuramochi
EX $100   **NM** $150   **MIP** $200

❏ **Dandy, the Happy Drumming Pup,** 1950s, Alps, 8-1/2" tall
EX $100   **NM** $150   **MIP** $200

❏ **Dennis the Menace,** 1950s, Rosko, 9" tall, with xylophone
EX $120   **NM** $180   **MIP** $240

❏ **Disney Acrobats,** 1950s, Linemar, 9" tall; Mickey, Donald, and Pluto
EX $300   **NM** $625   **MIP** $800

❏ **Disney Fire Engine,** 1950s, Linemar, 11" long
EX $425   **NM** $650   **MIP** $870

❏ **Disneyland Fire Engine,** 1950s, Linemar, 18" long
EX $350   **NM** $550   **MIP** $750

❏ **Donald Duck,** 1960s, Linemar, 8" tall
EX $200   **NM** $300   **MIP** $400

❑ **Doxie the Dog,** 1950s, Linemar, 9" long
EX $20   NM $25   MIP $45

(KP Photo)

❑ **Drinking Captain,** 1960s, S & E
EX $100   NM $150   MIP $200

❑ **Drummer Bear,** 1950s, Alps, 10" tall
EX $130   NM $200   MIP $275

❑ **Drumming Mickey Mouse,** 1950s, Linemar, 10" tall
EX $1000   NM $1500   MIP $2000

❑ **Drumming Polar Bear,** 1960s, Alps, 12"
EX $75   NM $120   MIP $165

❑ **Ducky Duckling,** 1960s, Alps, 8"
EX $35   NM $55   MIP $85

❑ **El Toro, Cragstan Bullfighter,** 1950s, TN, 9-1/2" long
EX $90   NM $145   MIP $200

❑ **Feeding Bird Watcher,** 1950s, Linemar, 9" tall
EX $300   NM $350   MIP $600

❑ **Fido the Xylophone Player,** 1950s, Alps, 8-3/4" tall
EX $150   NM $200   MIP $250

❑ **Flintstone Yacht,** 1961, Remco, 17" long
EX $90   NM $145   MIP $200

❑ **Frankenstein Monster,** 1960s, TN, 14" tall
EX $175   NM $250   MIP $325

❑ **Frankie the Rollerskating Monkey,** 1950s, Alps, 12"
EX $90   NM $150   MIP $200

❑ **Fred Flintstone Bedrock Band,** 1962, Alps, 9-1/2" tall
EX $500   NM $650   MIP $1000

❑ **Fred Flintstone Flivver,** 1960s, Marx, 7" long
EX $400   NM $600   MIP $900

❑ **Fred Flintstone on Dino**
EX $500   NM $700   MIP $1000

❑ **Friendly Jocko, My Favorite Pet,** 1950s, Alps, 8" tall
EX $110   NM $175   MIP $245

(KP Photo)

❑ **Gino, Neapolitan Balloon Blower,** 1960s, Tomiyama, 10" tall
EX $100   NM $150   MIP $200

❑ **Girl with Baby Carriage,** 1960s, TN, 8" tall
EX $100   NM $150   MIP $200

❑ **Godzilla Monster,** 1970s, Marusan, 11-1/2" tall
EX $125   NM $160   MIP $250

(KP Photo)

❑ **Good Time Charlie,** 1960s, MT, 12" tall
EX $100   NM $150   MIP $200

❑ **Grandpa Panda Bear,** 1950s, MT, 9" tall
EX $100   NM $175   MIP $245

(KP Photo)

❑ **Great Garloo,** 1960s, Marx, 23" tall green monster
EX $300   NM $450   MIP $600

❑ **Green Caterpillar,** 1950s, Daiya, 19-1/2" long
EX $150   NM $250   MIP $350
(Don Hultzman and Ron Chojnacki)

❑ **Gypsy Fortune Teller,** 1950s, Ichida, 12" tall, twenty cards
EX $1500   NM $2000   MIP $2500

❑ **Happy & Sad Face Cymbal Clown,** 1960s, Y Co., 10" tall
EX $120   NM $180   MIP $200

❑ **Happy Fiddler Clown,** 1950s, Alps, 9-1/2" tall
EX $200   NM $300   MIP $425

❑ **Happy Naughty Chimp,** 1960s, Daishin, 9-1/2" tall
EX $75   NM $100   MIP $150

❑ **Happy Santa One-Man Band,** 1950s, Alps, 9" tall
EX $100   NM $185   MIP $245

❑ **Hippo Chef,** 1960s, Y Co., 10" tall
EX $100   NM $160   MIP $600

❑ **Hobo Clown with Accordion,** 1950s, Alps, 10-1/2" tall
EX $275   NM $425   MIP $525

❑ **Hoop Zing Girl,** 1950s, Linemar, 11-1/2" tall
EX $115   NM $185   MIP $245

❑ **Hoopy the Fishing Duck,** 1950s, Alps, 10" tall
EX $275   NM $375   MIP $525

❑ **Hooty the Happy Owl,** 1960s, Alps, 9" tall
EX $65   NM $100   MIP $145

❑ **Hungry Cat,** 1960s, Linemar, 9" tall
EX $250   NM $450   MIP $700

❑ **Hungry Hound Dog,** 1950s, Y Co., 9-1/2" tall
EX $150   NM $275   MIP $300

❑ **Ice Cream Baby Bear,** 1950s, MT
EX $200   NM $300   MIP $400

(KP Photo)

❑ **Indian Joe,** 1960s, Alps, 12" tall
   EX $75   **NM** $110   **MIP** $150

❑ **Jocko the Drinking Monkey,** 1950s, Linemar, 11" tall
   EX $100   **NM** $150   **MIP** $225

❑ **Jo-Jo the Flipping Monkey,** 1970s, TN, 10" tall
   EX $35   **NM** $55   **MIP** $80

❑ **Jolly Bambino,** 1950s, Alps, 9" tall
   EX $200   **NM** $300   **MIP** $400

❑ **Jolly Bear Peanut Vendor,** 1950s, TN, 8" tall
   EX $250   **NM** $285   **MIP** $500

❑ **Jolly Daddy,** 1950s, Marusan, 8-3/4" tall
   EX $165   **NM** $250   **MIP** $350

❑ **Jolly Drummer Chimpy,** 1950s, Alps, 9" tall
   EX $100   **NM** $125   **MIP** $150

❑ **Jolly Pianist,** 1950s, Marusan, 8" tall
   EX $90   **NM** $145   **MIP** $200

❑ **Jolly Santa on Snow,** 1950s, Alps, 12-1/2" tall
   EX $100   **NM** $200   **MIP** $300

❑ **Josie the Walking Cow,** 1950s, Daiya, 14" long
   EX $150   **NM** $200   **MIP** $250

❑ **Jumbo the Bubble Blowing Elephant,** 1950s, Y Co., 7-1/4" tall
   EX $100   **NM** $125   **MIP** $150

❑ **Jungle Trio,** 1950s, Linemar, 8" tall
   EX $400   **NM** $600   **MIP** $800

❑ **King Zor,** 1962, Ideal, blue plastic dinosaur, 30" long
   EX $100   **NM** $250   **MIP** $550

❑ **Kissing Couple,** 1950s, Ichida, 10-3/4" long
   EX $145   **NM** $200   **MIP** $300

❑ **Knitting Grandma,** 1950s, T-N, 8-1/2" tall
   EX $200   **NM** $275   **MIP** $400

❑ **Kooky-Spooky Whistling Tree,** 1950s, Marx, 14-1/4" tall
   EX $450   **NM** $760   **MIP** $1600

❑ **Lambo Elephant,** 1950s, Alps, 16" long with trailer
   EX $260   **NM** $385   **MIP** $525

❑ **Linemar Music Hall,** 1950s, Linemar, 8" tall
   EX $100   **NM** $120   **MIP** $200

❑ **Lion,** 1950s, Linemar, 9" long
   EX $100   **NM** $150   **MIP** $200

❑ **Loop the Loop Clown,** 1960s, T-N, 10" tall
   EX $60   **NM** $120   **MIP** $175
   (don Hultzman and Ron Chojnacki)

❑ **Mac the Turtle,** 1960s, Y Co., 8" tall
   EX $85   **NM** $135   **MIP** $185

❑ **Magic Man Clown,** 1950s, Marusan, 11" tall
   EX $250   **NM** $385   **MIP** $525

❑ **Magic Snowman,** 1950s, MT, 11-1/4" tall
   EX $125   **NM** $190   **MIP** $265

❑ **Main Street,** 1950s, Linemar, 19-1/2" long
   EX $1000   **NM** $1500   **MIP** $2000

❑ **Major Tooty,** 1960s, Alps, 14" tall
   EX $85   **NM** $130   **MIP** $175

❑ **Mambo the Jolly Drumming Elephant,** 1950s, Alps, 9-1/2" tall
   EX $90   **NM** $150   **MIP** $200

❑ **Marching Bear,** 1960s, Alps, 10" tall
   EX $150   **NM** $225   **MIP** $300

❑ **Marshal Wild Bill,** 1950s, Y Co., 10-1/2" tall
   EX $180   **NM** $280   **MIP** $375

❑ **Marvelous Mike,** 1950s, Saunders, 17" long
   EX $100   **NM** $175   **MIP** $245

❑ **Maxwell Coffee-Loving Bear,** 1960s, TN, 10" tall
   EX $100   **NM** $150   **MIP** $200

(KP Photo)

❑ **McGregor,** 1960s, Rosko, 12" tall
   EX $150   **NM** $200   **MIP** $250

❑ **Mickey the Magician,** 1960s, Linemar, 10" tall
   EX $785   **NM** $1200   **MIP** $2500

❑ **Mighty Kong,** 1950s, Marx, 11" tall
   EX $250   **NM** $325   **MIP** $500

❑ **Mischievous Monkey,** 1950s, MT, 18" tall
   EX $200   **NM** $300   **MIP** $400

❑ **Miss Friday the Typist,** 1950s, TN, 8" tall
   EX $200   **NM** $275   **MIP** $350

❑ **Motorcycle Cop**
   EX $450   **NM** $650   **MIP** $1000

❑ **Mr. MacPooch,** 1950s, SAN, 8" tall
   EX $150   **NM** $200   **MIP** $325

❑ **Mr. Traffic Policeman,** 1950s, A-I, 14" tall
   EX $175   **NM** $270   **MIP** $365

❑ **Mumbo Jumbo,** 1960s, Alps, 9-3/4" tall
   EX $85   **NM** $120   **MIP** $160

❑ **Musical Bear,** 1950s, Linemar, 10" tall
   EX $200   **NM** $300   **MIP** $400

❑ **Musical Jackal,** 1950s, Linemar, 10" tall
   EX $150   **NM** $225   **MIP** $600

❑ **Musical Marching Bear,** 1950s, Alps, 11" tall
   EX $115   **NM** $170   **MIP** $600

❑ **Nutty Mad Indian,** 1960s, Marx, 12" tall
   EX $100   **NM** $150   **MIP** $225

❑ **Nutty Nibs,** 1950s, Linemar, 11-1/2" tall
   EX $700   **NM** $850   **MIP** $1400

❑ **Odd Ogg,** 1962, Ideal, large plastic turtle-frog creature
   EX $75   **NM** $200   **MIP** $450

❑ **Ol' Sleepy Head RIP,** 1950s, Y Co., 9" tall
   EX $150   **NM** $250   **MIP** $320

❑ **Panda Bear,** 1970s, MT, 10" long
   EX $30   **NM** $45   **MIP** $65

❑ **Pat the Roaring Elephant,** 1950s, Y Co., 9" long
   EX $100   **NM** $160   **MIP** $225

❑ **Peppermint Twist Doll,** 1950s, Haji, 12" tall
   EX $150   **NM** $225   **MIP** $300

❑ **Peppy Puppy,** 1950s, Y Co., 8" long
   EX $45   **NM** $70   **MIP** $100

❑ **Pet Turtle,** 1960s, Alps, 7" long
   EX $65   **NM** $100   **MIP** $145

❑ **Pete the Space Man,** 1960s, Bandai, 5" tall
   EX $60   **NM** $90   **MIP** $130

❑ **Peter the Drumming Rabbit,** 1950s, Alps, 13" tall
   EX $145   **NM** $200   **MIP** $275

❑ **Phantom Raider,** 1963, Ideal, 33", freighter turned warship
   EX $35   **NM** $100   **MIP** $225

(KP Photo)

☐ **Picnic Bear,** 1950s, Alps, 10" tall
EX $100   NM $150   MIP $225

☐ **Picnic Bunny,** 1950s, Alps, 10" tall
EX $100   NM $150   MIP $225

☐ **Picnic Monkey,** 1950s, Alps, 10" tall
EX $100   NM $150   MIP $225

☐ **Picnic Poodle,** 1950s, STS, 7" long
EX $50   NM $75   MIP $100

☐ **Pierrot Monkey Cycle,** 1950s, M-T, 8" tall
EX $325   NM $460   MIP $650

☐ **Piggy Cook**
EX $175   NM $250   MIP $350

☐ **Pinkee the Farmer,** 1950s, MT, 9-1/2" long
EX $100   NM $155   MIP $200

☐ **Pipie the Whale,** 1950s, Alps, 12" long
EX $90   NM $100   MIP $180

☐ **Pistol Pete,** 1950s, Marusan, 10-1/4" tall
EX $250   NM $270   MIP $500

☐ **Playful Puppy,** 1950s, MT, 5" tall
EX $100   NM $150   MIP $200

☐ **Polar Bear,** 1970s, Alps, 8" long
EX $50   NM $75   MIP $100
(Don Hultzman and Ron Chojnacki)

☐ **Popcorn Eating Bear,** 1950s, MT, 9" tall
EX $100   NM $150   MIP $200

☐ **Rambling Ladybug,** 1960s, M-T, 8" long
EX $60   NM $90   MIP $125

☐ **Reading Bear,** 1950s, Alps, 9" tall
EX $100   NM $175   MIP $250

☐ **Rembrandt the Monkey Artist,** 1950s, Alps, 8" tall
EX $170   NM $240   MIP $365

☐ **Ricki the Begging Poodle,** 1950s, Rock Valley, 9" long
EX $35   NM $45   MIP $65

☐ **Roarin' Jungle Lion,** 1950s, Marx, 16" long
EX $175   NM $250   MIP $325

☐ **Rock 'N Roll Monkey,** 1950s, Rosko, 13" tall
EX $150   NM $225   MIP $300

☐ **Rocking Chair Bear,** 1950s, MT, 10" tall
EX $150   NM $200   MIP $250

☐ **Roller Skater,** 1950s, Alps, 12" tall
EX $100   NM $125   MIP $200

☐ **Root Beer Counter,** 1960s, K Co., 8" tall
EX $100   NM $160   MIP $230

☐ **Sam the Shaving Man,** 1960s, Plaything Toy, 11-1/2" tall
EX $125   NM $180   MIP $245

☐ **Sammy Wong the Tea Totaler,** 1950s, TN, 10" tall
EX $140   NM $200   MIP $285

☐ **Santa Claus on Handcar,** 1960s, MT, 10" tall
EX $100   NM $140   MIP $200

☐ **Santa Claus on Reindeer Sleigh,** 1950s, M-T, 17" long
EX $400   NM $600   MIP $825

☐ **Santa Claus on Scooter,** 1960s, MT, 10" tall
EX $100   NM $140   MIP $180

☐ **Santa Copter,** 1960s, MT, 8-1/2" high
EX $100   NM $150   MIP $200

☐ **Saxophone Playing Monkey,** 1950s, Alps, 9-1/2" tall
EX $200   NM $300   MIP $400

☐ **Serpent Charmer,** 1950s, Linemar, 7" tall
EX $225   NM $350   MIP $500

☐ **Shaggy the Friendly Pup,** 1960s, Alps, 8" long
EX $35   NM $45   MIP $65
(Don Hultzman and Ron Chojnacki)

☐ **Shoe Maker Bear,** 1960s, TN, 8-1/2" tall
EX $125   NM $200   MIP $250

☐ **Shoe Shine Bear,** 1950s, T-N, 9" tall
EX $175   NM $250   MIP $325

☐ **Shoe Shine Joe,** 1950s, Alps, 11" tall
EX $175   NM $250   MIP $325

☐ **Shoe Shine Monkey,** 1950s, TN, 9" tall
EX $175   NM $250   MIP $325

☐ **Shooting Gorilla,** 1950s, MT, 12" tall
EX $155   NM $235   MIP $325

☐ **Shutterbug Photographer,** 1950s, T-N
EX $550   NM $750   MIP $1000

☐ **Skating Circus Clown,** 1950s, TPS, 6" tall
EX $450   NM $595   MIP $800

☐ **Skiing Santa,** 1960s, MT, 12" tall
EX $160   NM $230   MIP $300
(Don Hultzman and Ron Chojnacki)

☐ **Skipping Monkey,** 1960s, TN, 9-1/2" tall
EX $45   NM $60   MIP $80

☐ **Slalom Game,** 1960s, T-N, 15-1/4" long
EX $100   NM $160   MIP $225

☐ **Sleeping Baby Bear,** 1950s, Linemar, 9" long
EX $200   NM $300   MIP $450

☐ **Sleeping Pup,** 1960s, Alps, 9" long
EX $45   NM $75   MIP $100

☐ **Slurpy Pup,** 1960s, TN, 6-1/2" long
EX $45   NM $60   MIP $100

☐ **Smokey Bear,** 1950s, SAN, 9" tall
EX $250   NM $300   MIP $500

☐ **Smoking Bunny,** 1950s, SAN, 10-1/2" tall
EX $125   NM $150   MIP $200
(Don Hultzman and Ron Chojnacki)

☐ **Smoking Elephant,** 1950s, Marusan, 8-3/4" tall
EX $115   NM $165   MIP $225

☐ **Smoking Spaceman,** 1950s, Linemar, 12" tall
EX $750   NM $1200   MIP $1600

☐ **Sneezing Bear,** 1950s, Linemar, 9" tall
EX $200   NM $300   MIP $400

☐ **Snoopy Sniffer,** 1960s, MT, 8" long
EX $50   NM $75   MIP $100

☐ **Spanking Bear,** 1950s, Linemar, 9" tall
EX $160   NM $200   MIP $320

☐ **Strutting Sam,** 1950s, Haji, 10-1/2" tall
EX $250   NM $350   MIP $450

☐ **Sunday Driver,** 1950s, MT, 10" long
EX $55   NM $90   MIP $125

☐ **Super Susie,** 1950s, Linemar, 9" tall
EX $500   NM $750   MIP $1000

☐ **Suzette the Eating Monkey,** 1950s, Linemar, 8-3/4" tall
EX $300   NM $450   MIP $625

☐ **Switchboard Operator,** 1950s, Linemar, 7-1/2" tall
EX $250   NM $380   MIP $800

☐ **Tarzan,** 1960s, Marusan, 13" tall
EX $480   NM $765   MIP $1000

☐ **Teddy Bear Swing,** 1950s, T-N, 17" tall
EX $300   NM $380   MIP $600

☐ **Teddy the Artist**
EX $350   NM $500   MIP $650

☐ **Teddy the Boxing Bear,** 1950s, Y Co., 9" tall
EX $115   NM $190   MIP $240

☐ **Teddy the Rhythmical Drummer,** 1960s, Alps, 11" tall
EX $100   NM $150   MIP $200

☐ **Teddy-Go-Kart,** 1960s, Alps, 10-1/2" long
EX $100   NM $150   MIP $200

(KP Photo)

☐ **Telephone Bear,** 1950s, Linemar, 7-1/2" tall
EX $200   NM $300   MIP $400

☐ **Telephone Bear with Rocking Chair**
EX $275   NM $375   MIP $500

☐ **Television Spaceman,** 1960s, Alps, 14-1/2" tall
EX $400   NM $600   MIP $825

☐ **Tinkling Trolley,** 1950s, M-T, 10-1/2" long
EX $150   NM $200   MIP $250

☐ **Tom and Jerry Choo Choo,** 1960s, M-T, 10-1/4" long
EX $150   NM $200   MIP $300

☐ **Tom and Jerry Handcar,** 1960s, M-T, 7-3/4" long
EX $150   NM $225   MIP $300

❏ **Tom-Tom Indian,** 1960s, Y Co., 10-1/2" tall
  EX $80   **NM** $120   **MIP** $160

❏ **Topo Gigio Playing the Xylophone,** 1960s, TN
  EX $265   **NM** $440   **MIP** $525

❏ **Traveler Bear,** 1950s, Linemar, 8" tall
  EX $100   **NM** $150   **MIP** $200

❏ **Trumpet Playing Bunny,** 1950s, Alps, 10" tall
  EX $150   **NM** $225   **MIP** $300

❏ **Trumpet Playing Monkey,** 1950s, Alps, 9" tall
  EX $150   **NM** $225   **MIP** $300

❏ **Tubby the Turtle,** 1950s, Y Co., 7" long
  EX $50   **NM** $75   **MIP** $100

❏ **Tumbles the Bear,** 1960s, Yanoman, 8-1/2" tall
  EX $100   **NM** $150   **MIP** $200

❏ **Twirly Whirly,** 1950s, Alps, 13-1/2" tall
  EX $290   **NM** $450   **MIP** $600
    (Don Hultzman and Ron Chojnacki)

❏ **Walking Bear with Xylophone,** 1950s, Linemar, 10" tall
  EX $175   **NM** $270   **MIP** $365

❏ **Walking Elephant,** 1950s, Linemar, 8-1/2" tall
  EX $80   **NM** $120   **MIP** $155

❏ **Walking Esso Tiger,** 1950s, Marx, 11-1/2" tall
  EX $300   **NM** $400   **MIP** $500

❏ **Walking Itchy Dog,** 1950s, Alps, 9" long
  EX $45   **NM** $75   **MIP** $100

❏ **Western Locomotive,** 1950s, MT, 10-1/2" long
  EX $45   **NM** $65   **MIP** $80

❏ **Windy the Elephant,** 1950s, TN, 9-3/4" tall
  EX $150   **NM** $200   **MIP** $250

❏ **Yeti the Abominable Snowman,** 1960s, Marx, 12" tall
  EX $250   **NM** $335   **MIP** $500

❏ **Yo-Yo Clown,** 1960s, Alps, 9" tall
  EX $150   **NM** $190   **MIP** $300

❏ **Yo-Yo Monkey,** 1960s, Alps, 9" tall
  EX $100   **NM** $185   **MIP** $245

❏ **Yo-Yo Monkey,** 1960s, YM, 12" tall
  EX $85   **NM** $135   **MIP** $180

❏ **Yummy Yum Kitty,** 1950s, Alps, 9-1/2" tall
  EX $170   **NM** $270   **MIP** $325

❏ **Zero Fighter Plane,** 1950s, Bandai, 15" wingspan
  EX $150   **NM** $230   **MIP** $300

Ty Beanie Baby Toys

Pounce the Cat, retired in 1999, an affordable $4 in mint condition.

by Tom Bartsch

If you ever needed a demonstration of a "craze," the beanbag toy market would be a perfect example. Start with a unique product idea, institute keen and secretive marketing tactics and then announce to your faithful following that production will cease on some of their favorite toys.

The result is a mad dash to snatch every collectible available at retail. And if the beanbag toys aren't available there, buy at ungodly prices via the Internet.

However, a craze ultimately means that whatever the attraction is eventually sees waning interest and falls far from the graceful position it once stood.

In a nutshell, that is what has happened with the beanbag toy market. What once was the talk of collectibles,

and the heavyweight seller at many retail outlets, has fallen to a general curiosity that still holds a few die-hard collectors that must grab every new Beanie baby that walks down the aisle.

Ty has made the move to "retire" many of its Beanie Babies, but there are still plenty out there for those who want to round out a collection. Toy shows remain a great place to find these collectibles, and now is a great time to pick them up because prices are far lower than five years ago. The days of a new Beanie, like Punchers the Lobster, attracting several hundred dollars in sales is gone.

In fact, few of the Beanies that have hit the market the past two years have created a stir among collectors. The only real hunting taking place for Beanie

Babies is for the first few generations, which continue to bring big.

Ty remains the leader in the beanbag market, and this edition of *Toys & Prices* reflects that by including only a Ty Beanie Babies section, opting to exclude other beanbag toys included in the past.

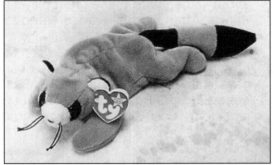

Ringo the Raccoon, retired in 1998, now valued at $30 in mint condition.

That said, there are still collectors looking for the other types of beanbag toys, but you won't find a high-priced secondary market. These toys still make great birthday and holiday presents, especially if the recipient collects a certain theme. There will always be a demand, but the days of searching stores daily and waiting for the next release has passed.

Big Hitters

While the picture isn't as rosy as in the past for beanbag toys, that doesn't mean there aren't samples out there that attract big bucks. How does $1,800 sound for a plush toy? That caught your attention, didn't it?

There are a few among the thousands produced that manage to bring a hefty payout. Most of these make up the initial offering of Ty Beanie Babies that were retired in the mid-1990s. These aren't the ones you will see in the discount racks at your local Hallmark store.

However, you should pay attention to the details of the valuable Beanies. There are variations that separate the high-dollar samples from the chump

change varieties. Yes, some research is needed in this hobby.

For instance, let's take a look at Peanut the Royal Blue Elephant. One version of the lovable character is valued at around $150 (for the its first introduction, third generation. Another rests at about $1,200. The difference? The expensive version is royal blue in color, while the other is light blue. Subtle differences are what set some Beanie babies apart from others. Another example is Quackers the Duck. Wingless, this little ducky can command $1,000. With wings, which is how most ducks wish to be, Quackers nets about $75.

You'll also want to check out the "tush tags" on the Beanie Babies. The older the tags (for instance, 1st generations vs. 3rd Generation), the more valuable it is. These are things you need to know so dishonest sellers don't dupe you.

There are some other Beanie Babies you want to be on the lookout for. Ty has given out special Beanie Babies to its employees in various years. Of course, these are quite limited in quantity and much sought after by collectors because

Spangle the American Bear (white face edition), retired in 1999, $10 in mint condition. This is truly a case where variation makes all the difference. A blue face edition of the same toy is valued at $22.

they were sold at retail outlets. Some of the names you want to remember of these employee-only beanies are #1 Bear, 1997 Employee Bear and any of the Billionaire the Bear samples. These can command anywhere from $900 to $4,700 for the #1 Bear.

Future Outlook

As hinted at above, the glory days for Ty's Beanie Babies have come and gone. Prices have been dropping the last couple of years – even the big dogs don't command what they used to.

However, don't look for a huge drop in prices for the already pricey ones out there. These are still rare, still command big bucks and this won't change in the next few years. It's like having a first edition novel. Everyone has the reprinted edition, but they all want that first one.

A lot of the new generation Beanie Babies won't shoot up in price. The reason their prices are low now is because many were produced and everyone has them. There's no real demand. These might even slide down to about $1 in the long run.

As for the new Beanie Babies that hit the market, they won't attract the attention of the older crop and shouldn't send prices anywhere near the roof, much less through it.

No Bean Counting

On a final note, don't be stressed about values with these great playthings. After all, they were created for fun and enjoyment. There's usually a story behind each one and you can see how they have evolved from their early days. Easy to display and pretty much nonbreakable, Beanie Babies are a collectible that can stand the test of time.

Fun facts

Nip the Cat is named after Ty Warner's (the founder of Ty Inc.) pet.

The Beanie Baby with the same name spelled forward and backward is Radar the Bat.

Very few Beanie babies are not a form of mammal, fish or bird. Two of them are Spooky the ghost and Snowball the Snowman.

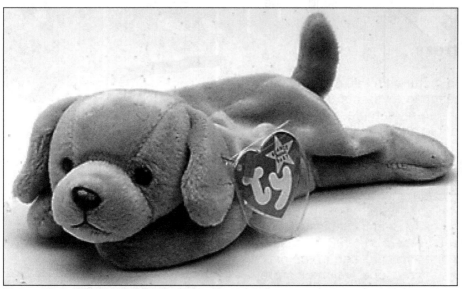

Fetch the Golden Retriever, an especially appealing Beanie, was retired in 1998. Mint value, $5.

BEANIE BABIES

❏ **#1 Bear,** Limited Edition, Ty, Employee-only Bear
EX n/a　　**NM** n/a　　**MIP** $4700

❏ **1997 Employee Bear,** Limited Edition, Ty, purple w/red or green ribbon, no hang tag
EX n/a　　**NM** n/a　　**MIP** $1250

(KP Photo)

❏ **1997 Holiday Teddy,** Retired 12/31/97, Ty, brown, red Santa hat
EX n/a　　**NM** n/a　　**MIP** $25

❏ **1998 Holiday Teddy,** Retired 12/31/98, Ty, white w/holly print
EX n/a　　**NM** n/a　　**MIP** $30

(KP Photo)

❏ **1999 Holiday Teddy,** Retired 12/31/99, Ty, blue w/snowflake print
EX n/a　　**NM** n/a　　**MIP** $15

(KP Photo)

❏ **1999 Signature Bear,** Retired 10/25/99, Ty, brown
EX n/a　　**NM** n/a　　**MIP** $10

❏ **2000 Signature Bear,** Current, Ty, white
EX n/a　　**NM** n/a　　**MIP** $15

(KP Photo)

❏ **Ally the Alligator,** Retired 10/1/97, Ty, two shades of green
EX n/a　　**NM** n/a　　**MIP** $15

❏ **Almond the Beige Bear,** Retired 12/23/99, Ty, beige
EX n/a　　**NM** n/a　　**MIP** $4

❏ **Amber the Gold Tabby,** Retired 12/23/99, Ty, gold with white streaks
EX n/a　　**NM** n/a　　**MIP** $3

❏ **America the Bear,** Ty, red, U.S. flag on chest
EX n/a　　**NM** n/a　　**MIP** $15

❏ **America the Bear,** Ty, blue, U.S. flag on chest
EX n/a　　**NM** n/a　　**MIP** $12

❏ **Ants the Anteater,** Retired 12/31/98, Ty, gray with black and white stripes
EX n/a　　**NM** n/a　　**MIP** $2

❏ **Aurora the Polar Bear: 6th and 7th Generations,** Current, Ty, tongue sticking out
EX n/a　　**NM** n/a　　**MIP** $4

(KP Photo)

❏ **B.B. Bear, the birthday Bear,** Retired 12/23/99, Ty, pastel colors
EX n/a　　**NM** n/a　　**MIP** $10

❏ **Baldy the Eagle: 4th and 5th Generations,** Retired 5/1/98, Ty, white head
EX n/a　　**NM** n/a　　**MIP** $5

❏ **Batty the Bat,** Retired 3/1/99, Ty, brown bat & tie-dyed
EX n/a　　**NM** n/a　　**MIP** $4

❏ **Beak the Kiwi,** Retired 12/23/99, Ty, brown
EX n/a　　**NM** n/a　　**MIP** $3

❏ **Beginning the Bear, The,** Current, Ty
EX n/a　　**NM** n/a　　**MIP** $20

❏ **Bernie the St. Bernard,** Retired 9/22/98, Ty, black eyes and ears
EX n/a　　**NM** n/a　　**MIP** $3

❏ **Bessie the Cow: Third and Fourth Generations,** Retired 10/1/97, Ty, brown and white
EX n/a　　**NM** n/a　　**MIP** $30

❏ **Billionaire 2 the Bear,** Limited Edition, Ty, employee-only bear, purple
EX n/a　　**NM** n/a　　**MIP** $1200

❏ **Billionaire 3 the Bear,** Ty, employee-only bear, orange
EX n/a　　**NM** n/a　　**MIP** $1100

❏ **Billionaire the Bear,** Limited Edition, Ty, employee-only bear, brown
EX n/a　　**NM** n/a　　**MIP** $900

❏ **Blackie the Bear: 1st Generation,** Ty, black bear
EX n/a　　**NM** n/a　　**MIP** $1000

❏ **Blackie the Bear: 2nd Generation,** Ty, black bear
EX n/a　　**NM** n/a　　**MIP** $170

❏ **Blackie the Bear: Open Production,** Retired 9/15/98, Ty, black bear
EX n/a　　**NM** n/a　　**MIP** $3

❏ **Blizzard the Snow Tiger: 4th and 5th Generations,** Retired 5/1/98, Ty, white w/black stripes
EX n/a　　**NM** n/a　　**MIP** $3

❏ **Bones the Dog, 1st generation,** Retired 5/1/98, Ty, brown w/black ears
EX n/a　　**NM** n/a　　**MIP** $1000

❏ **Bones the Dog, 2nd generation,** Ty, brown w/black ears
EX n/a　　**NM** n/a　　**MIP** $200

❏ **Bongo the Monkey: 3rd Generation,** Retired 12/31/98, Ty, brown tail
EX n/a　　**NM** n/a　　**MIP** $35

❏ **Bongo the Monkey: 4th Generation,** Retired 12/31/98, Ty, tan tail
EX n/a　　**NM** n/a　　**MIP** $4

❏ **Britannia the Bear,** Retired 7/26/99, Ty, European Exclusive, British flag
EX n/a　　**NM** n/a　　**MIP** $40

(KP Photo)

Bronty the Brontosaurus, Retired 6/15/96, Ty, tie-dyed
EX n/a　　**NM** n/a　　**MIP** $400

Brownie the Bear, Retired 1993, Ty, brown bear
EX n/a　　**NM** n/a　　**MIP** $1800

Bruno the Dog, Retired 9/18/98, Ty, brown and white
EX n/a　　**NM** n/a　　**MIP** $3

Bubbles the Beaver: 4th Generations, Retired 12/31/97, Ty, brown
EX n/a　　**NM** n/a　　**MIP** $9

Bubbles the Fish: 3rd and 4th Generations, Retired 5/11/97, Ty, yellow with black stripes
EX n/a　　**NM** n/a　　**MIP** $40

Buckingham the Bear, Ty, U.K. exclsuive
EX n/a　　**NM** n/a　　**MIP** $80

Bumble the Bee: 4th Generation, Retired 6/15/96, Ty, yellow and black
EX n/a　　**NM** n/a　　**MIP** $300

Bushy the Lion, Current, Ty, orange
EX n/a　　**NM** n/a　　**MIP** $3

Butch the Bull Terrier, Retired 12/23/99, Ty, white with black spot
EX n/a　　**NM** n/a　　**MIP** $3

Canyon the Cougar, Retired 8/16/9, Ty, white and brown
EX n/a　　**NM** n/a　　**MIP** $2

(KP Photo)

Caw the Crow, Retired 6/15/96, Ty, brown with orange beak and feet
EX n/a　　**NM** n/a　　**MIP** $300

Cheeks the Baboon, Retired 12/23/99, Ty, red face
EX n/a　　**NM** n/a　　**MIP** $3

Chilly the Polar Bear: 3rd Generation, Retired 1/7/96, Ty, white bear
EX n/a　　**NM** n/a　　**MIP** $500

Chinhook the Bear, Ty, Canadian exclusive
EX n/a　　**NM** n/a　　**MIP** $40

Chip the Calico Cat, Retired 3/31/99, Ty, black, white and brown
EX n/a　　**NM** n/a　　**MIP** $3

Chipper the Chipmunk, Retired 12/23/99, Ty, brown with black and white stripes
EX n/a　　**NM** n/a　　**MIP** $3

(KP Photo)

Chocolate the Moose: 5th Generation, Retired 12/31/98, Ty, tan antlers
EX n/a　　**NM** n/a　　**MIP** $55

(KP Photo)

Chops the Lamb: 4th Generation, Retired 1/1/97, Ty, black face, pink nose
EX n/a　　**NM** n/a　　**MIP** $60

Claude the Crab, Retired 12/31/98, Ty, tie-dyed
EX n/a　　**NM** n/a　　**MIP** $3

Clubby II the Bear, Retired 5/1/99, Ty, Official Collectors' Club Bear
EX n/a　　**NM** n/a　　**MIP** $7

Clubby III, Ty, Official Collectors' Club Bear
EX n/a　　**NM** n/a　　**MIP** $25

Clubby IV, Ty, Official Collectors' Club Bear
EX n/a　　**NM** n/a　　**MIP** $12

Clubby the Bear, Retired 3/15/99, Ty, Official Collectors' Club Bear
EX n/a　　**NM** n/a　　**MIP** $12

Congo the Gorilla, Retired 12/31/98, Ty, brown face
EX n/a　　**NM** n/a　　**MIP** $3

Coral the Fish: 3rd Generation, Retired 1/1/97, Ty, tie-dyed
EX n/a　　**NM** n/a　　**MIP** $60

Crunch the Shark, Retired 9/24/98, Ty, blue
EX n/a　　**NM** n/a　　**MIP** $3

Cubbie the Bear: 4th and 5th Generation, Retired 12/31/97, Ty, brown bear
EX n/a　　**NM** n/a　　**MIP** $5

Curly the Bear, Retired 12/31/98, Ty, brown bear with ribbon
EX n/a　　**NM** n/a　　**MIP** $3

Daisy the Cow: 4th and 5th Generations, Retired 9/15/98, Ty, white face
EX n/a　　**NM** n/a　　**MIP** $3

Derby the Horse, Retired 12/31/98, Ty, coarse mane, star
EX n/a　　**NM** n/a　　**MIP** $5

Derby the Horse, Retired 1995, Ty, fine mane
EX n/a　　**NM** n/a　　**MIP** $900

Derby the Horse, Retired 5/26/99, Ty, furry mane, star
EX n/a　　**NM** n/a　　**MIP** $5

Derby the Horse: 3rd Generation, Retired 12/15/97, Ty, coarse mane, no star
EX n/a　　**NM** n/a　　**MIP** $40

Digger the Crab: 1st Generation, Ty, orange
EX n/a　　**NM** n/a　　**MIP** $800

Digger the Crab: 2nd Generation, Ty, orange
EX n/a　　**NM** n/a　　**MIP** $350

(KP Photo)

Digger the Crab: 3rd Generation, Ty, red
EX n/a　　**NM** n/a　　**MIP** $60

Digger the Crab: 3rd Generation, Retired 6/3/95, Ty, orange
EX n/a　　**NM** n/a　　**MIP** $170

Digger the Crab: 4th Generation, Retired 5/11/97, Ty, red
EX n/a　　**NM** n/a　　**MIP** $30

Doby the Doberman, Retired 12/31/98, Ty, two shades of brown
EX n/a　　**NM** n/a　　**MIP** $4

(KP Photo)

❑ **Doodle the Rooster,** Retired 7/12/97, Ty, pink with red feathers
EX n/a   **NM** n/a   **MIP** $7

❑ **Dotty the Dalmatian,** Retired 12/31/98, Ty, white with black spots
EX n/a   **NM** n/a   **MIP** $3

❑ **Early the Robin,** Retired 12/23/99, Ty, red breast
EX n/a   **NM** n/a   **MIP** $2

❑ **Ears the Bunny: 3rds Generation,** Ty, brown and white
EX n/a   **NM** n/a   **MIP** $25

❑ **Ears the Bunny: 4th and 5th Generations,** Retired 5/1/98, Ty, brown and white
EX n/a   **NM** n/a   **MIP** $3

❑ **Echo the Dolphin,** Retired 5/1/98, Ty, blue and white
EX n/a   **NM** n/a   **MIP** $5

❑ **Echo the Dolphin,** Retired 5/1/98, Ty, w/"Waves" tags
EX n/a   **NM** n/a   **MIP** $6

❑ **Eggbert the Baby Chick,** Retired 7/28/99, Ty, bird emerging from egg
EX n/a   **NM** n/a   **MIP** $5

❑ **End the Bear, The,** Retired 12/23/99, Ty, "The End" on chest
EX n/a   **NM** n/a   **MIP** $20

❑ **Erin the Bear,** Retired 5/21/99, Ty, green w/shamrock on chest
EX n/a   **NM** n/a   **MIP** $5

(KP Photo)

❑ **Eucalyptus the Koala,** Retired 10/27/99, Ty, gray
EX n/a   **NM** n/a   **MIP** $5

❑ **Ewey the Lamb,** Retired 7/19/99, Ty, black feet
EX n/a   **NM** n/a   **MIP** $3

❑ **Fetch the Golden Retriever,** Retired 12/31/98, Ty, brown dog
EX n/a   **NM** n/a   **MIP** $5

❑ **Flash the Dolphin: 1st Generation,** Ty, gray and white
EX n/a   **NM** n/a   **MIP** $500

❑ **Flash the Dolphin: 2nd Generation,** Ty, gray and white
EX n/a   **NM** n/a   **MIP** $200

❑ **Flash the Dolphin: 3rd Generation,** Ty, gray and white
EX n/a   **NM** n/a   **MIP** $50

❑ **Flash the Dolphin: 4th Generation,** Retired 5/11/97, Ty, gray and white
EX n/a   **NM** n/a   **MIP** $30

❑ **Fleece the Lamb,** Retired 12/31/98, Ty, white with tan face
EX n/a   **NM** n/a   **MIP** $4

❑ **Fleecie the Lamb,** Current, Ty, yellow
EX n/a   **NM** n/a   **MIP** $5

❑ **Flip the Cat: 3rd Generation,** Ty, pink whiskers
EX n/a   **NM** n/a   **MIP** $40

(KP Photo)

❑ **Flip the Cat: 4th Generation,** Retired 10/1/97, Ty, pink whiskers
EX n/a   **NM** n/a   **MIP** $20

❑ **Flitter the Butterfly,** Retired 12/23/99, Ty, pink body, multi-colored wings
EX n/a   **NM** n/a   **MIP** $5

❑ **Floppity the Bunny,** Retired 5/1/98, Ty, lavender
EX n/a   **NM** n/a   **MIP** $7

❑ **Flutter the Butterfly,** Retired 6/15/96, Ty, black body, tie-dyed wings
EX n/a   **NM** n/a   **MIP** $350

❑ **Fortune the Panda,** Retired 8/24/99, Ty, red ribbon
EX n/a   **NM** n/a   **MIP** $4

❑ **Freckles the Leopard,** Retired 12/31/98, Ty, leopard spots
EX n/a   **NM** n/a   **MIP** $4

❑ **Frigid the Penguin,** Current, Ty, orange beak, pink feet
EX n/a   **NM** n/a   **MIP** $3

❑ **Fuzz the Bear,** Retired 12/23/99, Ty, tan bear
EX n/a   **NM** n/a   **MIP** $5

(KP Photo)

❑ **Garcia the Bear" 3rd Generation,** Ty, tie-dyed, old tag
EX n/a   **NM** n/a   **MIP** $120

❑ **Garcia the Bear: 4th Generation,** Retired 5/11/97, Ty, tie-dyed, old tag
EX n/a   **NM** n/a   **MIP** $100

❑ **Germania the Bear,** Retired 12/23/99, Ty, European Exclusive w/German flag
EX n/a   **NM** n/a   **MIP** $18

❑ **Gigi the Black Poodle,** Retired 12/23/99, Ty, black with ribbons
EX n/a   **NM** n/a   **MIP** $3

❑ **Glory the Bear,** Retired 12/31/98, Ty, U.S. flag on chest
EX n/a   **NM** n/a   **MIP** $15

❑ **Glow the Lightning Bug,** Current, Ty, orange wings
EX n/a   **NM** n/a   **MIP** $5

❑ **Goatee the Mountain Goat,** Retired 12/23/99, Ty, gray with black feet
EX n/a   **NM** n/a   **MIP** $4

(KP Photo)

❑ **Gobbles the Turkey,** Retired 3/1/99, Ty, red head, yellow beak
EX n/a   **NM** n/a   **MIP** $4

❑ **Goldie the Goldfish: 1st Generation,** Ty, all orange/gold
EX n/a   **NM** n/a   **MIP** $400

❑ **Goldie the Goldfish: 2nd Generation,** Ty, all orange/gold
EX n/a   **NM** n/a   **MIP** $200

❑ **Goldie the Goldfish: 3rd Generation,** Ty, all orange/gold
EX n/a   **NM** n/a   **MIP** $30

❑ **Goldie the Goldfish: 4th and 5th Generations,** Retired 12/31/97, Ty, all orange/gold
EX n/a   **NM** n/a   **MIP** $10

❑ **Goochy the Jellyfish,** Retired 12/23/99, Ty, tie-dyed
EX n/a   **NM** n/a   **MIP** $3

❑ **Grace the Bunny,** Current, Ty, sad-faced
EX n/a   **NM** n/a   **MIP** $6

❑ **Gracie the Swan,** Retired 5/1/98, Ty, orange beak and feet
EX n/a   **NM** n/a   **MIP** $3

❑ **Groovy the Ty-Dye Bear,** Retired 12/23/99, Ty, tie-dyed
EX n/a   **NM** n/a   **MIP** $6

❑ **Grunt the Razorback: 3rd Generation,** Ty, red with spine
EX n/a   **NM** n/a   **MIP** $70

❑ **Grunt the Razorback: 4th Generation,** Retired 5/11/97, Ty, red with spine
EX n/a   NM n/a   MIP $50

❑ **Halo II the Angel Bear,** Current, Ty, all white
EX n/a   NM n/a   MIP $4

❑ **Halo the Angel Bear,** Retired 11/19/99, Ty, white with gold wings
EX n/a   NM n/a   MIP $5

❑ **Happy the Hippo: 1st Generatioin,** Ty, gray
EX n/a   NM n/a   MIP $700

❑ **Happy the Hippo: 2nd Generatioin,** Ty, gray
EX n/a   NM n/a   MIP $300

❑ **Happy the Hippo: 3rd Generation,** Ty, lavender, old tag
EX n/a   NM n/a   MIP $60

❑ **Happy the Hippo: 3rd generation,** Retired 6/3/95, Ty, gray
EX n/a   NM n/a   MIP $250

❑ **Happy the Hippo: 4th and 5th Generations,** Retired 5/1/98, Ty, lavender, old tag
EX n/a   NM n/a   MIP $8

❑ **Hippie the Tie-Dyed Bunny,** Retired 7/12/99, Ty, tie-dyed
EX n/a   NM n/a   MIP $5

❑ **Hippity the Bunny,** Retired 5/1/98, Ty, mint green
EX n/a   NM n/a   MIP $5

❑ **Hissy the Snake,** Retired 3/31/99, Ty, blue and yellow
EX n/a   NM n/a   MIP $4

❑ **Honks the Goose,** Retired 12/23/99, Ty, orange beak and feet
EX n/a   NM n/a   MIP $3

❑ **Hoot the Owl: 3rd Generation,** Ty, two shades of brown
EX n/a   NM n/a   MIP $40

❑ **Hoot the Owl: 4th Generation,** Retired 10/1/97, Ty, two shades of brown
EX n/a   NM n/a   MIP $20

❑ **Hope the Prayer Bear,** Retired 12/23/99, Ty, hands clasped, eyes closed
EX n/a   NM n/a   MIP $5

❑ **Hoppity the Bunny,** Retired 5/1/98, Ty, pink
EX n/a   NM n/a   MIP $5

❑ **Humphrey the Camel: 1st Generation,** Ty, brown
EX n/a   NM n/a   MIP $1000

❑ **Humphrey the Camel: 2nd Generation,** Ty, brown
EX n/a   NM n/a   MIP $800

❑ **Humphrey the Camel: 3rd Generation,** Retired 6/15/95, Ty, brown
EX n/a   NM n/a   MIP $700

❑ **Iggy the Iguana,** Retired 3/31/99, Ty
EX n/a   NM n/a   MIP $5

❑ **Iggy the Iguana,** Retired 3/31/99, Ty, dark blue, spine
EX n/a   NM n/a   MIP $5

❑ **Iggy the Iguana,** Retired 3/31/99, Ty, tie-dyed
EX n/a   NM n/a   MIP $3

❑ **Inch the Worm,** Retired 5/1/98, Ty, yarn antenna
EX n/a   NM n/a   MIP $5

❑ **Inch the Worm: 3rd Generation,** Ty, felt antenna
EX n/a   NM n/a   MIP $80

(KP Photo)

❑ **Inch the Worm: 4th Generation,** Retired 10/15/97, Ty, felt antenna
EX n/a   NM n/a   MIP $70

❑ **Inky the Octopus: 1st Generation,** Ty, tan, no mouth
EX n/a   NM n/a   MIP $1000

❑ **Inky the Octopus: 2nd Generation,** Ty, tan, w/mouth
EX n/a   NM n/a   MIP $500

❑ **Inky the Octopus: 2nd generation,** Retired 9/12/94, Ty, tan, no mouth
EX n/a   NM n/a   MIP $700

(KP Photo)

❑ **Inky the Octopus: 3rd Generation,** Ty, pink
EX n/a   NM n/a   MIP $45

❑ **Inky the Octopus: 3rd Generation,** Retired 6/3/95, Ty, tan, w/mouth
EX n/a   NM n/a   MIP $300

❑ **Inky the Octopus: 4th and 5th Generations,** Retired 5/1/98, Ty, pink
EX n/a   NM n/a   MIP $7

❑ **Jabber the Parrot,** Retired 12/23/99, Ty, multicolored
EX n/a   NM n/a   MIP $3

❑ **Jake the Mallard Duck,** Retired 12/23/99, Ty, multicolored
EX n/a   NM n/a   MIP $3

(KP Photo)

❑ **Jolly the Walrus,** Retired 5/1/98, Ty, brown
EX n/a   NM n/a   MIP $4

(KP Photo)

❑ **Kicks the Soccer Bear,** Retired 12/23/99, Ty, green with soccer ball on chest
EX n/a   NM n/a   MIP $5

❑ **Kiwi the Toucan: 3rd Generation,** Ty, multicolored
EX n/a   NM n/a   MIP $75

❑ **Kiwi the Toucan: 4th Generation,** Retired 1/1/97, Ty, multicolored
EX n/a   NM n/a   MIP $60

❑ **Knuckles the Pig,** Retired 12/23/99, Ty, blue ribbon
EX n/a   NM n/a   MIP $3

❑ **Kuku the Cockatoo,** Retired 12/23/99, Ty, white
EX n/a   NM n/a   MIP $3

(KP Photo)

❑ **Lefty 2002 the Donkey,** Ty, flag on hind-quarters
EX n/a   NM n/a   MIP $3

(KP Photo)

❑ **Lefty the Donkey,** Retired 1/1/97, Ty, blue with U.S. flag, U.S. exclusive
EX n/a   NM n/a   MIP $100

❑ **Legs the Frog: 1st Generation**, Ty, green
EX n/a   NM n/a   MIP $500

❑ **Legs the Frog: 2nd Generation**, Ty, green
EX n/a   NM n/a   MIP $175

❑ **Legs the Frog: 3rd Generation**, Ty, green
EX n/a   NM n/a   MIP $30

❑ **Legs the Frog: 4th Generation,** Retired 10/1/97, Ty, green
EX n/a   NM n/a   MIP $5

❑ **Libearty the Bear,** Retired 1/1/97, Ty, white with U.S. flag, U.S. exclu.
EX n/a   NM n/a   MIP $225

❑ **Lips the Fish,** Retired 12/23/99, Ty, multicolored
EX n/a   NM n/a   MIP $5

❑ **Lizzy the Lizard,** Retired 1/7/96, Ty, tie-dyed
EX n/a   NM n/a   MIP $340

❑ **Lizzy the Lizard: 3rd Generation**, Ty, blue w/black spots, new tag
EX n/a   NM n/a   MIP $60

❑ **Lizzy the Lizard: 4th Generation**, Ty, blue w/black spots, new tag
EX n/a   NM n/a   MIP $10

❑ **Lizzy the Lizard: 5th Generation,** Retired 12/31/97, Ty, blue w/black spots, new tag
EX n/a   NM n/a   MIP $7

❑ **Loosy the Goose,** Retired 9/1/99, Ty, black face and neck
EX n/a   NM n/a   MIP $3

❑ **Lucky the Ladybug,** Retired 1997, Ty, 11 spots
EX n/a   NM n/a   MIP $10

❑ **Lucky the Ladybug,** Retired 5/1/98, Ty, 21 spots
EX n/a   NM n/a   MIP $300

❑ **Lucky the Ladybug: 1st Generation**, Ty, 7 felt dots
EX n/a   NM n/a   MIP $400

❑ **Lucky the Ladybug: 2nd Generation**, Ty, 7 felt dots
EX n/a   NM n/a   MIP $200

❑ **Lucky the Ladybug: 3rd Generation,** Retired 2/27/96, Ty, 7 felt spots
EX n/a   NM n/a   MIP $100

❑ **Luke the Black Labrador,** Retired 12/23/99, Ty, charcoal
EX n/a   NM n/a   MIP $8

❑ **Mac the Cardinal,** Retired 12/23/99, Ty, red
EX n/a   NM n/a   MIP $3

(KP Photo)

❑ **Magic the Dragon,** Retired 12/31/97, Ty, white, with wings
EX n/a   NM n/a   MIP $30

❑ **Manny the Manatee: 3rd Generation**, Ty, gray
EX n/a   NM n/a   MIP $50

❑ **Manny the Manatee: 4th Generation,** Retired 5/11/97, Ty, gray
EX n/a   NM n/a   MIP $40

❑ **Maple the Bear,** Retired 7/30/99, Ty, "Pride" tag
EX n/a   NM n/a   MIP $250

❑ **Maple the Bear,** Retired 7/30/99, Ty, Canadian Exclusive
EX n/a   NM n/a   MIP $50

❑ **Mel the Koala,** Retired 3/31/99, Ty, off brown with white ears
EX n/a   NM n/a   MIP $3

(KP Photo)

❑ **Millenium the Bear,** Retired 11/12/99, Ty, pink
EX n/a   NM n/a   MIP $5

❑ **Mooch the Spider Monkey,** Retired 12/23/99, Ty, black and white
EX n/a   NM n/a   MIP $3

❑ **Morrie the Eel,** Current, Ty, green
EX n/a   NM n/a   MIP $3

❑ **Mystic the Unicorn,** Retired 12/31/98, Ty, coarse mane, iridescent horn
EX n/a   NM n/a   MIP $5

❑ **Mystic the Unicorn,** Retired 5/18/99, Ty, rainbow mane, iridescent horn
EX n/a   NM n/a   MIP $5

❑ **Mystic the Unicorn: 1st Generation**, Ty, fine mane, tan horn
EX n/a   NM n/a   MIP $400

❑ **Mystic the Unicorn: 2nd Generation**, Ty, fine mane, tan horn
EX n/a   NM n/a   MIP $200

❑ **Mystic the Unicorn: 3rd Generation**, Ty, coarse mane, tan horn
EX n/a   NM n/a   MIP $40

❑ **Mystic the Unicorn: 3rd Generation,** Retired 1995, Ty, fine mane, tan horn
EX n/a   NM n/a   MIP $170

❑ **Mystic the Unicorn: 4th Generation,** Retired 10/23/97, Ty, coarse mane, tan horn
EX n/a   NM n/a   MIP $8

❑ **Nana the Monkey,** Retired 1995, Ty, brown
EX n/a   NM n/a   MIP $2000

❑ **Nanook the Husky,** Retired 3/31/99, Ty, gray and white
EX n/a   NM n/a   MIP $5

❑ **Neon the Seahorse,** Retired 12/23/99, Ty, tie-dyed
EX n/a   NM n/a   MIP $3

❑ **Nibbler the Rabbit,** Retired 7/9/99, Ty, white
EX n/a   NM n/a   MIP $5

❑ **Nibbly the Rabbit,** Retired 7/20/99, Ty, brown/gray
EX n/a   NM n/a   MIP $5

❑ **Niles the Camel,** Current, Ty, orange
EX n/a   NM n/a   MIP $5

❑ **Nip the Cat,** Retired 3/10/96, Ty, all gold
EX n/a   NM n/a   MIP $400

❑ **Nip the Cat: 2nd Generation**, Ty, white face and belly
EX n/a   NM n/a   MIP $370

❑ **Nip the Cat: 3rd Generation**, Ty, gold face, white paws
EX n/a   NM n/a   MIP $40

❑ **Nip the Cat: 3rd Generation,** Retired 1/7/96, Ty, white face and belly
EX n/a   NM n/a   MIP $300

❑ **Nip the Cat: 4th and 5th Generations,** Retired 12/31/97, Ty, gold face, white paws
EX n/a   NM n/a   MIP $5

❑ **Nipponia the Bear**, Ty, Japanese exclusive
EX n/a   NM n/a   MIP $40

❑ **Nuts the Squirrel,** Retired 12/31/98, Ty, brown and white
EX n/a   NM n/a   MIP $3

(KP Photo)

❏ **Osito the Mexican Bear,** Retired 11/30/99, Ty, U.S. exclusive, Mexican flag
EX n/a   NM n/a   **MIP** $4

❏ **Patti the Platypus,** Retired 2/28/95, Ty, dark magenta
EX n/a   NM n/a   **MIP** $800

❏ **Patti the Platypus,** Retired 5/1/98, Ty, light magenta
EX n/a   NM n/a   **MIP** $5

(KP Photo)

❏ **Paul the Walrus,** Retired 12/23/99, Ty, brown, white tusks
EX n/a   NM n/a   **MIP** $3

❏ **Peace the Tie-Dyed Bear,** Retired 7/14/99, Ty, Peace sign on chest
EX n/a   NM n/a   **MIP** $20

❏ **Peanut the Elephant,** Retired 10/2/95, Ty, royal blue
EX n/a   NM n/a   **MIP** $1200

❏ **Peanut the Elephant: 3rd Generation,** Retired 5/1/98, Ty, light blue
EX n/a   NM n/a   **MIP** $150

❏ **Pecan the Gold Bear,** Retired 12/23/99, Ty
EX n/a   NM n/a   **MIP** $7

❏ **Peking the Panda: 1st Generation,** Retired 1/7/96, Ty, black and white
EX n/a   NM n/a   **MIP** $900

❏ **Pinchers the Lobster: 1st Generation,** Ty, red
EX n/a   NM n/a   **MIP** $900

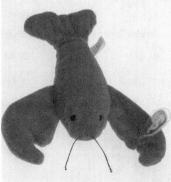

(KP Photo)

❏ **Pinchers the Lobster: 2nd Generation,** Retired 5/1/98, Ty, red
EX n/a   NM n/a   **MIP** $200

❏ **Pinky the Flamingo: 3rd Generation,** Retired 12/31/98, Ty, pink
EX n/a   NM n/a   **MIP** $30

❏ **Pouch the Kangaroo,** Retired 3/31/99, Ty
EX n/a   NM n/a   **MIP** $3

❏ **Pounce the Cat,** Retired 3/31/99, Ty
EX n/a   NM n/a   **MIP** $4

❏ **Prance the Cat,** Retired 3/31/99, Ty
EX n/a   NM n/a   **MIP** $3

❏ **Prickles the Hedgehog,** Retired 12/23/99, Ty
EX n/a   NM n/a   **MIP** $3

❏ **Princess the Bear: 5th Generation,** Retired 4/13/99, Ty, PE pellets
EX n/a   NM n/a   **MIP** $6

(KP Photo)

❏ **Princess the Bear: 5th Generation,** Retired 4/13/99, Ty, PVC pellets
EX n/a   NM n/a   **MIP** $20

❏ **Puffer the Puffin: 5th Generation,** Retired 9/18/98, Ty, black and white
EX n/a   NM n/a   **MIP** $3

❏ **Pugsly the Pug Dog: 4th and 5th Generations,** Retired 3/31/99, Ty, brown w/black face
EX n/a   NM n/a   **MIP** $4

❏ **Pumkin the Pumpkin: 5th Generation,** Retired 12/31/98, Ty, pumpkin body
EX n/a   NM n/a   **MIP** $8

(KP Photo)

❏ **Punchers the Lobster: 1st Generation,** Retired 1993, Ty, red
EX n/a   NM n/a   **MIP** $2000

❏ **Quackers the Duck: 1st Generation,** Retired 6/25/94, Ty, without wings
EX n/a   NM n/a   **MIP** $1000

❏ **Quackers the Duck: 2nd Generation,** Retired 5/1/98, Ty, w/wings
EX n/a   NM n/a   **MIP** $500

❏ **Radar the Bat: 3rd Generation,** Retired 5/11/97, Ty, black
EX n/a   NM n/a   **MIP** $70

❏ **Rainbow the Chameleon,** Retired 3/31/99, Ty, blue
EX n/a   NM n/a   **MIP** $3

❏ **Rainbow the Chameleon,** Retired 3/31/99, Ty, tie-dyed
EX n/a   NM n/a   **MIP** $3

❏ **Rex the Tyrannosaurus: 3rd Generation,** Retired 6/15/96, Ty, red
EX n/a   NM n/a   **MIP** $350

(KP Photo)

❏ **Righty 2000 the Elephant,** Ty, U.S. exclusive
EX n/a   NM n/a   **MIP** $5

(KP Photo)

❏ **Righty the Elephant: 4th Generation,** Retired 1/1/97, Ty, U.S. flag-colored
EX n/a   NM n/a   **MIP** $125

❏ **Ringo the Raccoon: 3rd Generation,** Retired 7/16/98, Ty, brown body
EX n/a   NM n/a   **MIP** $30

- **Roam the Buffalo,** Retired 12/23/99, Ty
  EX n/a   **NM** n/a   **MIP** $6

- **Roary the Lion,** Retired 12/31/98, Ty
  EX n/a   **NM** n/a   **MIP** $8

- **Rocket the Blue Jay,** Retired 12/23/99, Ty
  EX n/a   **NM** n/a   **MIP** $6

- **Rover the Dog: 5th Generation,** Retired 5/1/98, Ty, red
  EX n/a   **NM** n/a   **MIP** $5

- **Rufus the Dog,** Current, Ty
  EX n/a   **NM** n/a   **MIP** $10

- **Sakura the Bear: 6th generation,** Current, Ty, Japanese Exclusive
  EX n/a   **NM** n/a   **MIP** $120

- **Sammy the Bear Cub,** Retired 12/23/99, Ty
  EX n/a   **NM** n/a   **MIP** $9

- **Santa: 5th Generation,** Retired 12/31/98, Ty, typical Santa figure
  EX n/a   **NM** n/a   **MIP** $11

- **Sarge the German Shepherd,** Current, Ty
  EX n/a   **NM** n/a   **MIP** $8

- **Scaly the Lizard,** Retired 12/23/99, Ty
  EX n/a   **NM** n/a   **MIP** $9

- **Scat the Cat,** Retired 12/23/99, Ty
  EX n/a   **NM** n/a   **MIP** n/a

- **Schweetheart the Orangutan: 5th Generation,** Retired 12/23/99, Ty, brown
  EX n/a   **NM** n/a   **MIP** $3

- **Scoop the Pelican,** Retired 12/31/98, Ty, blue body, orange beak
  EX n/a   **NM** n/a   **MIP** $3

- **Scorch the Dragon,** Retired 12/31/98, Ty, brown w/colored wings
  EX n/a   **NM** n/a   **MIP** $5

- **Scottie the Terrier,** Retired 5/1/98, Ty, black
  EX n/a   **NM** n/a   **MIP** $7

- **Scurry the Beetle,** Current, Ty
  EX n/a   **NM** n/a   **MIP** n/a

- **Seamore the Seal: 1st Generation,** Retired 10/1/97, Ty, white
  EX n/a   **NM** n/a   **MIP** $700

- **Seamore the Seal: 2nd Generation,** Ty, white
  EX n/a   **NM** n/a   **MIP** $300

- **Seamore the Seal: 3rd Generation,** Ty, white
  EX n/a   **NM** n/a   **MIP** $50

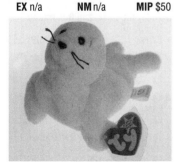

(KP Photo)

- **Seamore the Seal: 4th Generation,** Ty, white
  EX n/a   **NM** n/a   **MIP** $30

- **Seaweed the Otter: 3rd Generation,** Retired 9/19/98, Ty, dark brown
  EX n/a   **NM** n/a   **MIP** $40

- **Sheets the Ghost,** Retired 12/23/99, Ty
  EX n/a   **NM** n/a   **MIP** n/a

- **Silver the Grey Tabby,** Retired 12/23/99, Ty
  EX n/a   **NM** n/a   **MIP** n/a

- **Slippery the Seal,** Retired 12/23/99, Ty
  EX n/a   **NM** n/a   **MIP** n/a

- **Slither the Snake: 1st Generation,** Retired 6/15/95, Ty, green and yellow
  EX n/a   **NM** n/a   **MIP** $1000

- **Slither the Snake: 2nd Generation,** Ty, green and yellow
  EX n/a   **NM** n/a   **MIP** $800

- **Slither the Snake: 3rd Generation,** Ty, green and yellow
  EX n/a   **NM** n/a   **MIP** $700

- **Slowpoke the Sloth,** Retired 12/23/99, Ty
  EX n/a   **NM** n/a   **MIP** n/a

- **Sly the Fox: 4th Generation,** Retired 8/6/96, Ty, brown belly
  EX n/a   **NM** n/a   **MIP** $65

- **Sly the Fox: 4th Generation,** Retired 9/22/98, Ty, white belly
  EX n/a   **NM** n/a   **MIP** $3

- **Smoochy the Frog,** Retired 3/31/99, Ty, green with yellow feet
  EX n/a   **NM** n/a   **MIP** $3

- **Sneaky the Leopard,** Current, Ty
  EX n/a   **NM** n/a   **MIP** n/a

(KP Photo)

- **Snip the Cat,** Retired 12/31/98, Ty, Siamese
  EX n/a   **NM** n/a   **MIP** $3

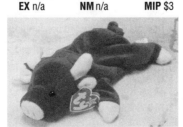

(KP Photo)

- **Snort the Bull,** Retired 9/15/98, Ty, red
  EX n/a   **NM** n/a   **MIP** $8

(KP Photo)

- **Snowball the Snowman,** Retired 12/31/97, Ty, red scarf, black hat
  EX n/a   **NM** n/a   **MIP** $11

- **Spangle the American Bear, 5th Generation,** Retired 12/23/99, Ty, blue face
  EX n/a   **NM** n/a   **MIP** $22

- **Spangle the American Bear, 5th Generation,** Retired 12/23/99, Ty, white face
  EX n/a   **NM** n/a   **MIP** $10

- **Spangle the American Bear, 5th Generation,** Retired 12/23/99, Ty, pink face
  EX n/a   **NM** n/a   **MIP** $11

(KP Photo)

- **Sparky the Dalmatian, 4th Generation,** Retired 5/11/97, Ty, white w/ black spots
  EX n/a   **NM** n/a   **MIP** $50

- **Speedy the Turtle, 1st Generation,** Retired 10/1/97, Ty, brown shell
  EX n/a   **NM** n/a   **MIP** $600

\(KP Photo)

❑ **Speedy the Turtle, 2nd Generation**, Ty, brown shell
EX n/a   NM n/a   MIP $200

❑ **Spike the Rhinoceros,** Retired 12/31/98, Ty
EX n/a   NM n/a   MIP n/a

❑ **Spinner the Spider,** Retired 9/18/98, Ty, w/"Creepy" tush tag
EX n/a   NM n/a   MIP $40

❑ **Spinner the Spider,** Retired 9/18/98, Ty
EX n/a   NM n/a   MIP n/a

❑ **Splash the Orca Whale, 1st Generation,** Retired 5/11/97, Ty, black w/white belly
EX n/a   NM n/a   MIP $400

❑ **Splash the Orca Whale, 2nd Generation,** Ty, black w/white belly
EX n/a   NM n/a   MIP $200

❑ **Spooky the Ghost, 3rd Generation,** Retired 12/31/97, Ty, white w/red ribbon
EX n/a   NM n/a   MIP $50

❑ **Spot the Dog, 1st Generation,** Retired 4/13/94, Ty, without spot
EX n/a   NM n/a   MIP $1000

❑ **Spot the Dog, 2nd Generation**, Ty, without spot
EX n/a   NM n/a   MIP $800

❑ **Spot the Dog, 2nd Generation,** Retired 10/1/97, Ty, w/spot
EX n/a   NM n/a   MIP $600

❑ **Springy the Lavender Bunny,** Current, Ty
EX n/a   NM n/a   MIP n/a

❑ **Spunky the Cocker Spaniel, 5th Generation,** Retired 3/31/99, Ty, light brown
EX n/a   NM n/a   MIP $5

❑ **Squealer the Pig, 1st Generation,** Ty, pink
EX n/a   NM n/a   MIP $200

❑ **Squealer the Pig, 1st Generation,** Retired 5/1/98, Ty, pink
EX n/a   NM n/a   MIP $550

❑ **Steg the Stegosaurus, 3rd Generation,** Retired 6/15/96, Ty, tie-dyed
EX n/a   NM n/a   MIP $300

❑ **Stilts the Stork,** Retired 5/31/99, Ty
EX n/a   NM n/a   MIP n/a

❑ **Sting the Stingray, 3rd Generation,** Retired 1/1/97, Ty, tie-dyed
EX n/a   NM n/a   MIP $65

❑ **Sting the Stingray, 4th Generation,** Ty, tie-dyed
EX n/a   NM n/a   MIP $50

❑ **Stinger the Scorpion,** Retired 12/31/98, Ty, purple
EX n/a   NM n/a   MIP $3

(KP Photo)

❑ **Stinky the Skunk, 3rd Generation,** Retired 9/28/98, Ty, black and white
EX n/a   NM n/a   MIP $30

(KP Photo)

❑ **Stretch the Ostrich,** Retired 3/31/99, Ty, brown coat
EX n/a   NM n/a   MIP $3

❑ **Stripes the Tiger,** Retired 5/1/98, Ty, light tan
EX n/a   NM n/a   MIP $5

❑ **Stripes the Tiger, 3rd Generation,** Retired 6/3/96, Ty, dark gold
EX n/a   NM n/a   MIP $120

❑ **Strut the Rooster,** Retired 3/31/99, Ty
EX n/a   NM n/a   MIP n/a

❑ **Swampy the Alligator,** Current, Ty
EX n/a   NM n/a   MIP n/a

❑ **Swirly the Snail,** Retired 12/23/99, Ty
EX n/a   NM n/a   MIP n/a

❑ **Swoop the Pterodactyl,** Current, Ty
EX n/a   NM n/a   MIP n/a

❑ **Tabasco the Bull, 3rd Generation,** Retired 1/1/97, Ty, red w/white horns
EX n/a   NM n/a   MIP $80

❑ **Tabasco the Bull, 4th Generation,** Ty, red w/white horns
EX n/a   NM n/a   MIP $60

❑ **Tank the Armadillo,** Retired 10/1/97, Ty, shell
EX n/a   NM n/a   MIP $25

❑ **Tank the Armadillo, 3rd Generation,** Retired 1/7/96, Ty, seven lines, no shell
EX n/a   NM n/a   MIP $170

❑ **Tank the Armadillo, 4th Generation,** Ty, seven lines, no shell
EX n/a   NM n/a   MIP $150

❑ **Tank the Armadillo, 4th Generation,** Retired 1/7/96, Ty, nine lines, no shell
EX n/a   NM n/a   MIP $200

❑ **Teddy the Bear, 1st Generation,** Retired 1/7/95, Ty, teal, old face
EX n/a   NM n/a   MIP $900

❑ **Teddy the Bear, 1st Generation,** Retired 1/7/95, Ty, magenta, old face
EX n/a   NM n/a   MIP $1000

❑ **Teddy the Bear, 1st Generation,** Retired 1/7/95, Ty, jade, old face
EX n/a   NM n/a   MIP $950

❑ **Teddy the Bear, 1st Generation,** Retired 1/7/95, Ty, cranberry, old face
EX n/a   NM n/a   MIP $900

❑ **Teddy the Bear, 1st Generation,** Retired 1/7/95, Ty, brown, old face
EX n/a   NM n/a   MIP $1100

❑ **Teddy the Bear, 1st Generation,** Retired 1/7/95, Ty, violet, old face
EX n/a   NM n/a   MIP $1000

❑ **Teddy the Bear, 2nd Generation,** Ty, teal, old face
EX n/a   NM n/a   MIP $700

❑ **Teddy the Bear, 2nd Generation,** Ty, violet, old face
EX n/a   NM n/a   MIP $700

❑ **Teddy the Bear, 2nd Generation,** Ty, magenta, old face
EX n/a   NM n/a   MIP $850

❑ **Teddy the Bear, 2nd Generation,** Ty, cranberry, old face
EX n/a   NM n/a   MIP $650

❑ **Teddy the Bear, 2nd Generation,** Ty, cranberry, new face
EX n/a   NM n/a   MIP $900

❑ **Teddy the Bear, 2nd Generation,** Ty, jade, old face
EX n/a   NM n/a   MIP $700

❑ **Teddy the Bear, 2nd Generation,** Retired 1/7/96, Ty, cranberry, new face
EX n/a   NM n/a   MIP $900

❑ **Teddy the Bear, 2nd Generation,** Retired 1/7/96, Ty, violet, new face
EX n/a   NM n/a   MIP $900

❑ **Teddy the Bear, 2nd Generation,** Retired 1/7/96, Ty, jade, new face
EX n/a   NM n/a   MIP $900

❑ **Teddy the Bear, 2nd Generation,** Retired 1/7/96, Ty, magenta, new face
EX n/a   NM n/a   MIP $900

❑ **Teddy the Bear, 2nd Generation,** Retired 1/7/96, Ty, teal, new face
EX n/a   NM n/a   MIP $900

❑ **Teddy the Bear, 2nd Generation,** Retired 10/1/97, Ty, brown, new face
EX n/a   NM n/a   MIP $350

❑ **Teddy the Bear, 3rd Generation,** Ty, magenta, new face
EX n/a   NM n/a   MIP $700

❑ **Teddy the Bear, 3rd Generation,** Ty, violet, new face
EX n/a   NM n/a   MIP $700

❑ **Teddy the Bear, 3rd Generation,** Ty, teal, new face
EX n/a   NM n/a   MIP $700

❑ **Teddy the Bear, 3rd Generation,** Ty, jade, new face
EX n/a   NM n/a   MIP $700

❑ **Teddy the Bear, 3rd Generation,** Ty, cranberry, new face
EX n/a   NM n/a   MIP $700

❑ **Teddy the Bear, 3rd Generation,** Ty, cranberry, new face
EX n/a   NM n/a   MIP $700

❑ **Teddy the Bear, 3rd Generation,** Ty, brown, new face
EX n/a   NM n/a   MIP $90

❑ **Teddy the Bear, 4th Generation,** Ty, brown, new face
EX n/a   NM n/a   MIP $60

❑ **Tiny the Chihuahua,** Retired 12/23/99, Ty
EX n/a   NM n/a   MIP n/a

❑ **Tiptoe the Mouse,** Retired 10/21/99, Ty
EX n/a   NM n/a   MIP n/a

❑ **Tracker the Basset Hound,** Retired 11/26/99, Ty
EX n/a   NM n/a   MIP n/a

❑ **Trap the Mouse, 1st Generation,** Retired 6/15/95, Ty, gray
EX n/a   NM n/a   MIP $850

❑ **Trap the Mouse, 2nd Generation,** Ty, gray
EX n/a   NM n/a   MIP $650

❑ **Trap the Mouse, 3rd Generation,** Ty, gray
EX n/a   NM n/a   MIP $400

❑ **Trumpet the Elephant,** Current, Ty
EX n/a   NM n/a   MIP n/a

❑ **Tuffy the Terrier,** Retired 12/31/98, Ty
EX n/a   NM n/a   MIP n/a

❑ **Tusk the Walrus, 3rd Generation,** Retired 1/1/97, Ty, brown
EX n/a   NM n/a   MIP $85

❑ **Tusk the Walrus, 4th Generation,** Retired 1/1/97, Ty, brown
EX n/a   NM n/a   MIP $50

❑ **Twigs the Giraffe, 3rd Generation,** Retired 5/1/98, Ty, yellow
EX n/a   NM n/a   MIP $40

❑ **Ty 2K the Bear,** Retired 12/23/99, Ty, confetti design
EX n/a   NM n/a   MIP $7

(KP Photo)

❑ **Valentina the Bear, 5th Generation,** Retired 12/23/99, Ty, red w/white heart
EX n/a   NM n/a   MIP $3

(KP Photo)

❑ **Valentino the Bear, 2nd Generation,** Retired 12/31/98, Ty, white w/red heart
EX n/a   NM n/a   MIP $800

❑ **Velvet the Panther, 3rd Generation,** Retired 10/1/97, Ty, black
EX n/a   NM n/a   MIP $40

❑ **Waddle the Penguin, 3rd Generation,** Retired 5/1/98, Ty, black and white w/yellow scarf
EX n/a   NM n/a   MIP $20

❑ **Wallace the Scottish Bear,** Retired 12/23/99, Ty, green
EX n/a   NM n/a   MIP $6

❑ **Waves the Whale,** Retired 5/1/98, Ty, w/"Echo" tags
EX n/a   NM n/a   MIP $5

❑ **Waves the Whale,** Retired 5/1/98, Ty
EX n/a   NM n/a   MIP n/a

❑ **Web the Spider, 1st Generation,** Retired 1/7/96, Ty, black
EX n/a   NM n/a   MIP $800

❑ **Web the Spider, 2nd Generation,** Ty, black
EX n/a   NM n/a   MIP $600

❑ **Web the Spider, 3rd Generation,** Ty, black
EX n/a   NM n/a   MIP $400

(KP Photo)

❑ **Weenie the Dog, 3rd Generation,** Retired 5/1/98, Ty, brown
EX n/a   NM n/a   MIP $40

❑ **Whisper the Deer,** Retired 12/23/99, Ty
EX n/a   NM n/a   MIP n/a

❑ **Wiggly the Octopus,** Current, Ty
EX n/a   NM n/a   MIP n/a

❑ **Wise the Owl,** Retired 12/31/998, Ty, brown w/graduation cap
EX n/a   NM n/a   MIP $3

(KP Photo)

❑ **Wiser the Owl,** Retired 8/27/99, Ty, gray w/graduation cap
EX n/a   NM n/a   MIP $4

❑ **Wisest the Owl,** Ty, brown w/bow tie and graduation cap
EX n/a   NM n/a   MIP $4

❑ **Wrinkles the Dog,** Retired 9/22/98, Ty
EX n/a   NM n/a   MIP n/a

❑ **Zero the Christmas Penguin,** Retired 12/31/98, Ty
EX n/a   NM n/a   MIP n/a

(KP Photo)

❑ **Ziggy the Zebra, 3rd Generation,** Retired 5/1/98, Ty, black and white stripes
EX n/a   NM n/a   MIP $35

❑ **Zip the Cat, 2nd Generation,** Retired 1/7/96, Ty, white face and belly
EX n/a   NM n/a   MIP $350

❑ **Zip the Cat, 3rd Generation,** Ty, white face and belly
EX n/a   NM n/a   MIP $300

❑ **Zip the Cat, 3rd Generation,** Retired 3/10/96, Ty, all black
EX n/a   NM n/a   MIP $500

❑ **Zip the Cat, 3rd Generation,** Retired 5/1/98, Ty, white paws
EX n/a   NM n/a   MIP $70

Character Toys

Neat stuff—this Dick Tracy Candid Camera was released in the 1950s, and is now valued at $175 in mint condition.

by Tom Bartsch

Ever meet someone and remark to a friend, "Wow, that was quite the character?" Well, toy collectors do that all the time, usually when referring to their character toys. From comic books, to television shows to movies and more, characters have been a part of our live for many years. And many times these same characters have appeared as toys. The sheer volume of character toys outweighs any other collecting category by far, simply because you can find the likeness of characters almost anywhere – soakies, clothes, books, glasses, costumes, ornaments, banks, etc. Because of these factors, character toys are among the most popular collectibles on the market, a major representation of which you will find in the following pages.

Looking at this mass of pages, it's a wonder where to begin collecting in this field. Easy. Most collectors pick a particular favorite character and focus on items bearing his or her likeness. With most of these characters, focusing on just one will more than fill a display case. Some characters have an unbelievable following – and licensing power. Other collectors will narrow their range to a group of characters from the same show or a band of superheroes. Your other challenge in all of this will be finding all the goodies that are out there. As you can see, some of the characters have a long history of entertaining the masses and being depicted on toys. The best course of action is to do your homework and always ask a lot of questions.

An Endless Array of Fun

The beauty of character toys is that they are not limited to action figures or die-cast vehicles. If you like Superman, you can pick up a comic book, a Superman member ring, candy or a million other things. Prices can range from under a dollar to several hundred thousand dollars for his first appearance in a comic book (*Action Comics #1*, 1938).

As a paper collectible, the Captain Marvel Buzz Bomb can be tough to find these days in mint condition, valued at $125.

However, many of the characters toys are very similar. The key to finding out which one is worth hundreds and which one is worth $50 is in the details. For starters, find out the name of the manufacturer. Then check out the details of the item. Sometimes the difference in valuable samples compared to average-priced ones is the color or an accessory. For instance, a 1970s Horsman Alice in Wonderland doll might fetch $65 Mint. A 1951 Duchess Alice in Wonderland doll can bring more than $200 Mint. Do your research before taking the plunge.

This Mickey Mouse set is just one Disney-licensed piece familiar to collectors. Colorforms are fun to collect—their mint value is rising, but examples in near-mint or excellent condition can still be found for bargain prices at flea markets. Mint price for this set? About $75. Excellent condition price? Only $10.

The massive amount of product seems to be on the upswing these days, with almost every film or movie bearing related collectibles to help fuel the marketing beast. The Simpsons, Buffy the Vampire Slayer and South Park are among the leading memorabilia from TV shows. In 2002, the characters receiving the biggest boosts were Spider-Man, Harry Potter and Lord of the Rings. Of course, you can't ignore the usual Disney favorites and the classics like Popeye and Batman.

Will these new toys on the block someday approach the prices of some of the older favorites? Maybe, but their popularity now is a good starting point to making that future a reality.

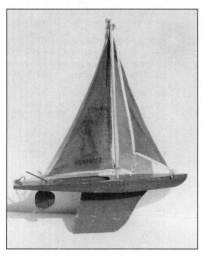

This Popeye Sailboat is a fun, affordable toy. First produced in 1976, it is still available in excellent condition for about $9.

Tom Bartsch is the Associate Editor of *Toy Shop* magazine, and was a huge help in putting together this book. He is also a big fan of action figures, blonde supermodels and work-related trade shows. His assistance is greatly appreciated.

101 DALMATIANS

ACCESSORIES

❑ **101 Dalmatians Snow Dome,** 1961, Marx, 3" x 5" x 3-1/2" tall
EX $35   **NM** $65   **MIP** $110

FIGURES

❑ **Dalmatian Pups Figures,** 1960s, Enesco, 4-1/2" tall, set of three
EX $25   **NM** $50   **MIP** $160

❑ **Lucky Figure,** 1960s, Enesco, 4" tall
EX $35   **NM** $65   **MIP** $100

TOY

❑ **101 Dalmatians Wind-Up,** 1959, Linemar
EX $70   **NM** $125   **MIP** $400

❑ **Lucky Squeeze Toy,** Dell, 7" tall, squeakers in the bottom
EX $10   **NM** $15   **MIP** $50

ALICE IN WONDERLAND

ACCESSORIES

❑ **Clock Radio,** 1970s, General Electric, features characters on face
EX $20   **NM** $40   **MIP** $75

❑ **Film Viewer,** 1950s, Tru-Vue, viewer and filmstrip
EX $30   **NM** $60   **MIP** $90

❑ **Handbag,** 1950s, ACME Briefcase, child's red leather shoulder bag
EX $30   **NM** $65   **MIP** $100

❑ **Handbag,** 1950s, Salient, child's pink vinyl shoulder bag, Alice w/rocking fly
EX $30   **NM** $65   **MIP** $100

❑ **Hatbox,** 1950s, Neevel, Caterpillar or Tea Party graphics
EX $55   **NM** $85   **MIP** $150

❑ **Picture Frame,** 1970s, Dexter-Mahnke, cloth picture frame, featuring Mad Tea Party
EX $20   **NM** $35   **MIP** $55

❑ **Record Player,** 1951, RCA Victor, 45 rpm
EX $75   **NM** $150   **MIP** $275

❑ **School Bag,** 1950s, ACME Briefcase, fabric and leather
EX $30   **NM** $70   **MIP** $120

❑ **Soap Set,** 1951
EX $30   **NM** $110   **MIP** $200

❑ **Wall Decor,** 1951, Dolly Toy, #260 contains Alice, Mad Hatter, March Hare and a lamp
EX $50   **NM** $100   **MIP** $200

❑ **Wall Plaque,** 1974, Leisuramics, bisque, oval shape, featuring Tweedle-Dee and TweedleDum
EX $20   **NM** $40   **MIP** $60

❑ **Wall Plaque,** 1974, Leisuramics, bisque, oval shape, featuring Mad Hatter
EX $20   **NM** $40   **MIP** $75

BANK

❑ **Alice Bank,** 1950s, Leeds, figural
EX $60   **NM** $115   **MIP** $210

BOOK

❑ **Alice in Wonderland and Cinderella Book,** 1950s, Collins, Great Britain version
EX $20   **NM** $50   **MIP** $85

❑ **Alice in Wonderland Book,** 1950s, Whitman, #2074 Cozy Corner Book, green endpapers
EX $10   **NM** $32   **MIP** $65

❑ **Alice in Wonderland Book,** 1950s, Whitman, #10426, without gold backing
EX $15   **NM** $40   **MIP** $80

❑ **Alice in Wonderland Book,** 1950s, Whitman, #10426, Big Golden Book, gold foil backing
EX $25   **NM** $65   **MIP** $130

❑ **Alice in Wonderland Book,** 1951, Whitman, Sandpiper Book w/dust jacket
EX $15   **NM** $60   **MIP** $125

❑ **Alice in Wonderland Book,** 1951, Dell Publishing, #331
EX $25   **NM** $50   **MIP** $125

❑ **Alice in Wonderland Book,** 1951, Whitman, #426, Big Golden Book
EX $20   **NM** $50   **MIP** $125

❑ **Alice in Wonderland Classic Series with Disney Book,** 1950s, Whitman, #2140 Lewis Carroll text w/Disney dust jacket
EX $20   **NM** $65   **MIP** $125

❑ **Alice in Wonderland Paint Book,** 1951, Whitman, #2167
EX $30   **NM** $75   **MIP** $150

❑ **Alice in Wonderland Punch-Out Book,** 1951, Whitman, #2164
EX $40   **NM** $110   **MIP** $225

❑ **Alice in Wonderland Sticker Fun,** 1950s, Whitman, #2193 stencil and coloring book
EX $15   **NM** $30   **MIP** $75

(KP Photo)

❑ **Alice Meets the White Rabbit Book,** 1951, Whitman, #D-19, Little Golden Book
EX $15   **NM** $30   **MIP** $75

(KP Photo)

❑ **Mad Hatter's Tea Party Book,** 1951, Whitman, #D-23 Little Golden Book
EX $15   **NM** $25   **MIP** $40

❑ **Unbirthday Party Book, The,** 1974, Whitman, #22, Walt Disney Showcase
EX $8   **NM** $15   **MIP** $30

CANDY TIN

❑ **Candy Tin,** 1950s, Edward Sharp and Sons, Great Britain English Toffee Tin
EX $60   **NM** $125   **MIP** $250

COLLECTIBLE

❑ **Alice Snow Dome,** 1961, Marx, 3" tall featuring Alice and the White Rabbit in front of tree
EX $15   **NM** $35   **MIP** $100

❑ **Caterpillar Figure,** 1956, Hagen-Renaker
EX $125   **NM** $300   **MIP** $500

❑ **Mad Hatter Snow Dome,** 1980s, New England Collectors Society, crystal, Mad Hatter, St. Patrick's Day
EX $15   **NM** $25   **MIP** $50

❑ **Mad Hatter Teapot,** 1950s, Regal
EX $500   **NM** $1000   **MIP** $1600

❑ **Pitcher,** 1950s, Regal, King of Hearts
EX $175   **NM** $350   **MIP** $575

❑ **Plaque,** 1970s, Disneyland, wooden, w/Alice and live flowers
EX $15   **NM** $25   **MIP** $50

❑ **Salt and Pepper Shakers,** 1950s, Regal, featuring TweedleDee and TweedleDum
EX $150   **NM** $300   **MIP** $525

❑ **Salt and Pepper Shakers,** 1950s, Regal, blue or white featuring Alice
EX $150   **NM** $300   **MIP** $500

❑ **Tea Cake Box,** 1980s, TDL, w/a Mad Tea Party lid
EX $10   **NM** $15   **MIP** $30

❑ **Tea Cup and Saucer,** 1986, TDL, ceramic, Mad Tea Party
EX $60   **NM** $120   **MIP** $200

❑ **Thimble,** 1980s, New England Collectors Society, Mad Hatter and Alice
EX $5   **NM** $15   **MIP** $25

❏ **Vase,** 1960s, Enesco, featuring Alice's head
EX $50   NM $100   MIP $210

❏ **White Rabbit Creamer,** 1950s, Regal
EX $110   NM $275   MIP $450

❏ **White Rabbit Sugar Bowl,** 1950s, Regal
EX $180   NM $360   MIP $550

COLORING BOOK

❏ **Alice in Wonderland Big Coloring Book,** 1951, Whitman, #301 Big Golden, Model No. 301
EX $25   NM $75   MIP $150

❏ **Alice in Wonderland Coloring Book,** 1974, Whitman, #1049
EX $5   NM $20   MIP $40

COOKIE JAR

❏ **Alice Cookie Jar,** Regal, 13-1/2" tall
EX $375   NM $1000   MIP $1600

❏ **Alice Cookie Jar,** 1950s, Leeds, printed in relief
EX $75   NM $175   MIP $350

❏ **Looking Glass Cookie Jar,** Fred Roberts, raised characters on the body of the jar w/a mirror lid
EX $150   NM $400   MIP $675

COSTUMES

❏ **Alice Costume,** 1950s, Ben Cooper, costume made until 1970s
EX $25   NM $65   MIP $125

❏ **Mad Hatter Costume,** 1950s, Ben Cooper, costume made until 1970s
EX $25   NM $35   MIP $85

❏ **March Hare Costume,** 1950s, Ben Cooper, costume made until 1970s
EX $20   NM $35   MIP $85

DOLLS

❏ **Alice Doll,** 1950s, Gund, flat vinyl, stuffed
EX $20   NM $75   MIP $150

❏ **Alice Doll,** 1951, Duchess, 12-1/2" tall
EX $60   NM $130   MIP $275

❏ **Alice Doll,** 1951, Duchess, #739, 7-1/2" tall
EX $40   NM $90   MIP $225

❏ **Alice Doll,** 1970s, Horsman, Alice has a castle on her apron
EX $20   NM $45   MIP $90

❏ **Alice Doll,** 1970s, Pedigree, Great Britain
EX $20   NM $40   MIP $75

❏ **Alice Doll,** 1970s, Horsman, #1071, Walt Disney Classics
EX $20   NM $35   MIP $75

❏ **Cheshire Cat Doll,** 1970s, Disneyland, plush
EX $10   NM $25   MIP $60

❏ **Dormouse Doll,** 1950s, Lars/Italy, stuffed
EX $160   NM $330   MIP $550

❏ **Mad Hatter Doll,** 1950s, Gund, flat vinyl, stuffed
EX $20   NM $45   MIP $90

❏ **Mad Hatter Doll,** 1950s, Gund, plush
EX $125   NM $275   MIP $400

❏ **March Hare Doll,** 1950s, Gund, plush
EX $175   NM $350   MIP $575

❏ **March Hare Doll,** 1950s, Gund, flat vinyl, stuffed
EX $25   NM $45   MIP $90

❏ **Queen of Hearts Doll,** 1950s, Gund, flat vinyl, stuffed
EX $25   NM $60   MIP $110

❏ **TweedleDee and TweedleDum Dolls,** 1950s, Gund, flat vinyl, stuffed, each
EX $35   NM $100   MIP $200

❏ **TweedleDee and TweedleDum Dolls,** 1980s, TDL, plush, each
EX $15   NM $30   MIP $55

❏ **Walrus Doll,** 1950s, Lars/Italy, stuffed
EX $150   NM $390   MIP $625

❏ **White Rabbit Doll,** 1950s, Gund, flat vinyl, stuffed
EX $20   NM $60   MIP $120

❏ **White Rabbit Doll,** 1950s, Gund
EX $110   NM $300   MIP $425

❏ **White Rabbit Doll,** 1970s, Sears, plush w/waistcoat and umbrella
EX $12   NM $20   MIP $40

❏ **White Rabbit Doll,** 1970s, Disneyland, large, plush w/yellow spectacles
EX $12   NM $20   MIP $40

❏ **White Rabbit Doll,** 1970s, Disneyland, small w/black spectacles
EX $10   NM $20   MIP $40

❏ **White Rabbit Doll,** 1974, Buena Vista/Disney, plush
EX $50   NM $100   MIP $150

❏ **White Rabbit Doll,** 1980s, TDL, plush
EX $10   NM $25   MIP $50

FIGURES

❏ **Alice Figure,** 1950s, Marx, painted w/"Holland" stamped on the bottom
EX $15   NM $45   MIP $85

❏ **Alice Figure,** 1950s, Aldon Industries, plastic, cut-out standup
EX $35   NM $90   MIP $135

❏ **Alice Figure,** 1951, Shaw
EX $120   NM $300   MIP $725

❏ **Alice Figure,** 1956, Hagen-Renaker
EX $150   NM $325   MIP $550

❏ **Alice Figure,** 1980s, Sears, Magic Kingdom Collection, bone china
EX $10   NM $15   MIP $35

❏ **Alice Figure,** 1984, Bully, Germany, PVC, wearing a blue or red dress, each
EX $10   NM $15   MIP $20

❏ **Disneyland Figures Set,** 1960s, United China, large set, each piece
EX $15   NM $30   MIP $60

❏ **Disneyland Figures Set,** 1970s, United China, small figures, each piece
EX $10   NM $15   MIP $30

❏ **Dormouse Figure,** 1951, Shaw
EX $130   NM $225   MIP $400

❏ **Mad Hatter Figure,** 1950s, Marx, painted w/"Holland" stamped on the bottom
EX $15   NM $20   MIP $40

❏ **Mad Hatter Figure,** 1950s, Sydney Pottery, large size, sold only in Australia
EX $200   NM $375   MIP $550

❏ **Mad Hatter Figure,** 1951, Shaw
EX $65   NM $200   MIP $350

❏ **Mad Hatter Figure,** 1956, Hagen-Renaker
EX $125   NM $275   MIP $400

❏ **Mad Hatter Figure,** 1980s, Schmid, playing xylophone
EX $20   NM $40   MIP $75

❏ **Mad Hatter/March Hare Figure,** 1980s, TDL, Mad Hatter, March Hare w/saxophone
EX $20   NM $40   MIP $60

❏ **March Hare Figure,** 1950s, Sydney Pottery, large size, sold only in Australia
EX $155   NM $330   MIP $550

❏ **March Hare Figure,** 1950s, Marx, painted w/"Holland" stamped on the bottom
EX $15   NM $25   MIP $50

❏ **March Hare Figure,** 1951, Shaw
EX $170   NM $320   MIP $500

❏ **March Hare Figure,** 1956, Hagen-Renaker
EX $110   NM $250   MIP $425

❏ **Queen of Hearts Figure,** 1950s, Marx, painted w/"Holland" stamped on the bottom
EX $10   NM $18   MIP $35

❏ **Queen of Hearts Figure,** 1980s, Sears, Magic Kingdom Collection, bone china
EX $15   NM $25   MIP $35

❏ **TweedleDee Figure,** 1950s, Sydney Pottery, large size, sold only in Australia
EX $175   NM $350   MIP $550

❏ **TweedleDee Figure,** 1951, Shaw
EX $70   NM $150   MIP $235

❏ **TweedleDum Figure,** 1950s, Sydney Pottery, large size, sold only in Australia
EX $175   NM $350   MIP $550

❏ **TweedleDum Figure,** 1951, Shaw
EX $70   NM $150   MIP $235

❏ **Walrus Figure,** 1950s, Sydney Pottery, large size, sold only in Australia
EX $160   NM $375   MIP $550

❏ **Walrus Figure,** 1951, Shaw
EX $110   NM $250   MIP $400

❏ **White Rabbit Figure,** Italy, 5-1/2" tall, ceramic
EX $15   NM $35   MIP $60

CHARACTER TOYS

□ **White Rabbit Figure,** 1950s, Marx, painted w/"Holland" stamped on the bottom
EX $10   NM $16   MIP $35

□ **White Rabbit Figure,** 1951, Shaw
EX $65   NM $140   MIP $250

□ **White Rabbit Figure,** 1980s, Sears, Magic Kingdom Collection, bone china
EX $12   NM $25   MIP $50

GAMES

□ **Adventures in Costumeland Game,** 1980s, Walt Disney World, created for Disney costume division members, game board and pieces in a small vinyl garment bag
EX $75   NM $125   MIP $200

□ **Alice in Wonderland Card Game,** 1980s, Thos. De LaRue
EX $4   NM $10   MIP $20

□ **Bridge Card Game,** 1950s, Whitman, two decks of cards
EX $35   NM $75   MIP $150

□ **Canasta Card Game,** 1950s, Whitman, two Canasta decks of White Rabbit cards
EX $30   NM $65   MIP $125

□ **Queen of Hearts Card Game,** 1975, Edu-Cards
EX $20   NM $30   MIP $50

GLASSWARE

□ **Alice and White Rabbit Mug,** 1991, TDL/Daiichi Seimei, promo piece
EX $25   NM $40   MIP $65

□ **Alice Mug,** 1970s, Disney
EX $12   NM $20   MIP $40

□ **Glass,** 1970s, Pepsi Cola, featuring Alice, part of Wonderful World of Disney set
EX $10   NM $20   MIP $35

□ **Glasses,** 1951, Libbey, eight styles released for film opening, each
EX $40   NM $60   MIP $120

□ **Mad Tea Party/Cheshire Cat Mug,** 1988, Applause, Cheshire Cat handle w/Tea Party on the mug
EX $12   NM $18   MIP $30

MUSIC BOX

□ **Music Box,** 1980s, Disneyland, Wooden box features Alice and White Rabbit "I'm Late"
EX $25   NM $50   MIP $100

□ **Music Box,** 1980s, TDL, plastic, tea cup rotates
EX $45   NM $70   MIP $150

□ **Music Box,** 1980s, TDL, ceramic teacup
EX $45   NM $70   MIP $150

PAPER DOLLS

□ **Alice Paper Dolls,** 1972, Whitman, #4712
EX $10   NM $25   MIP $60

□ **Alice Paper Dolls,** 1976, Whitman, #1948
EX $8   NM $20   MIP $50

PAPER GOODS

□ **Alice Stationery and Notepad,** 1970s, Pak-Well, #77065 w/a fan card cover
EX $10   NM $20   MIP $35

□ **Cheshire Cat Costume Pattern,** 1951, McCall's
EX $25   NM $40   MIP $75

□ **Fan Card,** 1951, Walt Disney, premium sent to fans who wrote letters to studio
EX $20   NM $40   MIP $70

□ **Fan Card,** 1951, Walt Disney, original release w/1973 invitation to studio screening
EX $30   NM $60   MIP $80

□ **Mad Hatter Costume Pattern,** 1951, McCall's
EX $20   NM $35   MIP $55

□ **March Hare Costume Pattern,** 1951, McCall's, pattern
EX $15   NM $30   MIP $60

□ **Poster,** 1958, Disneyland, Alice attraction
EX $300   NM $600   MIP $1000

□ **Poster,** 1980s, Walt Disney World, costume division poster featuring Cheshire Cat
EX $15   NM $30   MIP $65

□ **Ticket,** 1970s, Disneyland, employee screening ticket featuring Cheshire Cat
EX $5   NM $10   MIP $20

PREMIUMS

□ **Bread Labels,** 1950s, NBC, 12 different styles, each
EX $10   NM $40   MIP $80

□ **Bread Seal Poster,** 1950s, NBC
EX $20   NM $50   MIP $100

□ **Bread Stickers,** 1974, Continental Baking/Wonder, five styles, each
EX $5   NM $10   MIP $15

□ **Cards,** 1951, Royal Desserts, 16 different cards on the back of dessert packages, each
EX $10   NM $35   MIP $70

□ **Cereal Box with Record,** 1956, General Mills, Wheaties
EX $125   NM $300   MIP $500

□ **Magic Picture Kit Set,** 1974, Jiffy Pop, set of four
EX $12   NM $25   MIP $50

□ **Poster,** 1980, Kraft, Disneyland 25th Anniversary Family Reunion
EX $15   NM $30   MIP $65

RECORD

□ **Record/Little Nipper Giant Storybook,** 1951, RCA Victor, LY-437, 33, 45, or 78 rpm, each
EX $50   NM $100   MIP $150

TOY

□ **Alice Disneykin,** 1950s, Marx, unpainted, soft plastic
EX $10   NM $20   MIP $40

□ **Alice Disneykin,** 1950s, Marx, hard plastic
EX $10   NM $25   MIP $50

□ **Alice Marionette,** 1950s, Peter Puppet, comes in two different boxes, one "Alice in Wonderland" the other Peter Puppet Disney
EX $60   NM $160   MIP $375

□ **Balloons,** 1951, Oak Rubber, four different designs
EX $12   NM $20   MIP $50

□ **Balloons,** 1951, Eagle Rubber
EX $12   NM $20   MIP $50

□ **Blocks,** 1950s, Chad Valley, five cylindrical tin blocks w/color graphics
EX $60   NM $150   MIP $300

□ **Child's Vanity,** 1950s, Neevel, illustrated w/film scenes
EX $50   NM $100   MIP $200

□ **Disneykin Play Set,** 1950s, Marx
EX $175   NM $350   MIP $650

□ **Jingle Ball,** 1951, Vanguard
EX $12   NM $25   MIP $50

□ **Mad Hatter Disneykin,** 1950s, Marx, unpainted, soft plastic
EX $10   NM $16   MIP $30

□ **Mad Hatter Disneykin,** 1950s, Marx
EX $25   NM $45   MIP $85

□ **Mad Hatter Hand Puppet,** 1960s, hand puppet w/cloth body
EX $20   NM $50   MIP $85

□ **Mad Hatter Marionette,** 1950s, Peter Puppet
EX $50   NM $110   MIP $210

□ **Mad Hatter Nodder,** 1950s, Marx
EX $40   NM $150   MIP $300

□ **Mad Hatter Snap Eeze,** 1950s, Marx
EX $15   NM $30   MIP $50

□ **Make-Up Kit,** 1951, Hasbro
EX $25   NM $55   MIP $90

□ **March Hare Disneykin,** 1950s, Marx, unpainted and soft plastic
EX $12   NM $18   MIP $35

□ **March Hare Marionette,** 1950s, Peter Puppet
EX $50   NM $110   MIP $200

□ **March Hare Snap Eeze,** 1950s, Marx
EX $15   NM $20   MIP $40

□ **March Hare Twistoy,** 1950s, Marx
EX $15   NM $20   MIP $40

□ **Molding Set,** 1951, Model Craft
EX $50   NM $100   MIP $200

□ **Molding Set,** 1952, Great Britain, similar to Model Craft set
EX $60   NM $120   MIP $210

□ **Puppet Theatre,** 1950s, Peter Puppet
EX $85   NM $150   MIP $275

- ❏ **Puzzle,** 1951, Jaymar, Alice and Rabbit
  EX $30   **NM** $80   **MIP** $135

- ❏ **Puzzle,** 1951, Jaymar, Alice under a tree
  EX $20   **NM** $65   **MIP** $110

- ❏ **Puzzle,** 1951, Jaymar, Croquet cast scene
  EX $30   **NM** $80   **MIP** $135

- ❏ **Puzzle,** 1951, Jaymar, Tea Party scene
  EX $30   **NM** $80   **MIP** $135

- ❏ **Puzzle,** 1979, Stafford/England, wooden, Great Britain Tea Party
  EX $10   **NM** $25   **MIP** $40

- ❏ **Puzzle,** 1980s, TDL, #18, Mad Tea Party and Cast
  EX $5   **NM** $10   **MIP** $20

- ❏ **Queen of Hearts Disneykin,** 1950s, Marx
  EX $30   **NM** $55   **MIP** $85

- ❏ **Queen of Hearts Disneykin,** 1950s, Marx, unpainted, soft plastic
  EX $15   **NM** $20   **MIP** $35

- ❏ **Ramp Walker,** 1950s, Marx, Mad Hatter and White Rabbit
  EX $20   **NM** $40   **MIP** $80

- ❏ **Rubber Stamp Set,** 1970s, Multiprint, Italy, #177
  EX $20   **NM** $30   **MIP** $55

- ❏ **Rubber Stamp Set,** 1989, All Night Media
  EX $10   **NM** $15   **MIP** $25

(KP Photo)

- ❏ **Sewing Cards,** 1951, Whitman
  EX $25   **NM** $50   **MIP** $100

- ❏ **Sewing Kit,** 1951, Hasbro, 7" sewing machine and 5" doll, all plastic
  EX $35   **NM** $75   **MIP** $125

- ❏ **TV Scene, White Rabbit and March Hare,** 1950s, Marx
  EX $30   **NM** $65   **MIP** $100

- ❏ **View-Master Set,** 1970s, GAF, three reels, Disney
  EX $10   **NM** $20   **MIP** $35

- ❏ **Wallet,** 1950s, Salient, vinyl, featuring Mad Tea Party
  EX $20   **NM** $40   **MIP** $90

- ❏ **Wallet,** 1950s, Salient, vinyl, featuring White Rabbit
  EX $20   **NM** $40   **MIP** $90

- ❏ **White Rabbit Disneykin,** 1950s, Marx
  EX $30   **NM** $60   **MIP** $85

- ❏ **White Rabbit Disneykin,** 1950s, Marx, unpainted and soft plastic
  EX $10   **NM** $20   **MIP** $35

- ❏ **White Rabbit Ears,** 1980s, TDL
  EX $10   **NM** $20   **MIP** $35

- ❏ **White Rabbit Rolykin,** 1950s, Marx
  EX $20   **NM** $40   **MIP** $70

WATCH

- ❏ **Alice Wristwatch,** 1950s, U.S. Time, Alice peeking through pink flowers and a plastic statue
  EX $80   **NM** $300   **MIP** $550

- ❏ **Alice Wristwatch,** 1950s, U.S. Time, came w/ceramic statue
  EX $80   **NM** $300   **MIP** $550

- ❏ **Alice Wristwatch,** 1990s, Alba, Japan, gold tone face
  EX $15   **NM** $30   **MIP** $50

- ❏ **Tea Cup Wristwatch,** 1950s, U.S. Time, picture of Mad Hatter w/an overlay
  EX $175   **NM** $400   **MIP** $675

AMOS AND ANDY

ACCESSORIES

- ❏ **Amos and Andy Card Party,** 1930, A.M. Davis, 6" x 8", score pads and tallies
  EX $30   **NM** $80   **MIP** $175

- ❏ **Contest Winner Check,** 1936, Pepsodent, $2.00 winner's check for contest
  EX $700   **NM** $1000   **MIP** $1500

- ❏ **Stock Certificate,** 1930s, Bogus Taxi Company, premium
  EX $150   **NM** $300   **MIP** $400

TOY

- ❏ **Puzzle,** 1932, Pepsodent, 8-1/2" x 10", pictured Amos, Andy and other characters
  EX $40   **NM** $125   **MIP** $275

ANDY GUMP

ACCESSORIES

- ❏ **Brush and Mirror,** 4" diameter, red on ivory colored surface of brush
  EX $20   **NM** $75   **MIP** $175

TOY

- ❏ **Chester Gump Playstone Funnies Mold Set,** 1940s
  EX $55   **NM** $120   **MIP** $200

- ❏ **Chester Gump/Herby Nodders,** 1930s, ceramic 2-1/4" string nodders, each
  EX $75   **NM** $250   **MIP** $375

ARCHIES

ACCESSORIES

- ❏ **Archie Halloween Costume,** 1969, Ben Cooper
  EX $20   **NM** $55   **MIP** $85

TOY

- ❏ **Archies Paper Dolls,** 1969, Whitman
  EX $20   **NM** $40   **MIP** $90

- ❏ **Jalopy,** 1975, Marx, 12", plastic
  EX $40   **NM** $100   **MIP** $200

(KP Photo)

- ❏ **Puzzle,** 1960s, Jaymar, "Swinging Malt Shop"
  EX $20   **NM** $50   **MIP** $90

ATOM ANT AND FRIENDS

TOY

- ❏ **Atom Ant Kite,** 1960s, Roalex
  EX $25   **NM** $80   **MIP** $150

- ❏ **Atom Ant Punch-Out Set,** 1966, Whitman
  EX $50   **NM** $150   **MIP** $250

- ❏ **Atom Ant Push Puppet,** 1960s, Kohner
  EX $20   **NM** $50   **MIP** $75

- ❏ **Atom Ant Puzzle,** 1966, Whitman
  EX $15   **NM** $50   **MIP** $100

- ❏ **Atom Ant Soaky,** 1966, Purex
  EX $20   **NM** $65   **MIP** $85

- ❏ **Morocco Mole Bubble Club Soaky,** 1960s, Purex, 7" hard plastic
  EX $20   **NM** $60   **MIP** $100

- ❏ **Squiddly Diddly Bubble Club Soaky,** 1960s, Purex, 10-1/2" hard plastic
  EX $20   **NM** $60   **MIP** $100

- ❏ **Winsome Witch Bubble Club Soaky,** 1960s, Purex, 10-1/2" hard plastic
  EX $20   **NM** $60   **MIP** $100

BABES IN TOYLAND

DOLL

- ❏ **Cadet Doll,** Gund, 15-1/2" tall, fabric
  EX $30   **NM** $65   **MIP** $125

TOY

- ❏ **Babes in Toyland Go Mobile Friction Car,** 1961, Linemar, 4" x 5"x 6"
  EX $75   **NM** $200   **MIP** $400

- ❏ **Babes in Toyland Hand Puppets,** Gund, Silly Dilly Clown, Soldier, or Gorgonzo, each
  EX $35   **NM** $65   **MIP** $125

- ❏ **Babes in Toyland Twist 'N Bend Toy,** 1963, Marx, 4" tall flexible toy w/Private Valiant holding a baton
  EX $10   **NM** $25   **MIP** $50

CHARACTER TOYS

❏ **Babes in Toyland Wind-Up Toy,** 1950s, Linemar, tin
EX $80   NM $210   MIP $425

❏ **Puzzle,** 1961, Jaymar
EX $15   NM $30   MIP $50

BAMBI

ACCESSORIES

❏ **Bambi Prints,** 1947, New York Graphic Society, 11" x 14" framed
EX $25   NM $50   MIP $100

❏ **Lamp,** Bambi and Thumper
EX $50   NM $175   MIP $300

❏ **Throw Rug,** 1960s, 21" x 39", Bambi and Thumper
EX $25   NM $50   MIP $75

❏ **Thumper Ashtray,** 1950s, Goebel, 4" tall
EX $50   NM $100   MIP $175

BANK

❏ **Flower Bank,** 1940s, 5" x 5" x 7" tall, plaster
EX $50   NM $110   MIP $225

❏ **Thumper Bank,** 1950s, Leeds, ceramic, figural
EX $45   NM $85   MIP $165

BOOK

❏ **Bambi Book,** 1942, Grosset and Dunlap, black and white illustrations
EX $15   NM $35   MIP $75

❏ **Thumper Book,** 1942, Grosset and Dunlap, color and black/white illustrations
EX $15   NM $35   MIP $75

DOLL

❏ **Thumper Doll,** 16" tall, plush
EX $15   NM $30   MIP $50

TOY

❏ **Bambi Soaky,** Colgate-Palmolive
EX $15   NM $40   MIP $65

❏ **Thumper Pull Toy,** 1942, Fisher-Price, #533, 7-1/2" x 12", wood and metal, Thumper's tail rings the bell
EX $50   NM $125   MIP $250

❏ **Thumper Soaky,** 1960s, Colgate-Palmolive
EX $25   NM $60   MIP $85

BARNEY GOOGLE

DOLL

❏ **Barney Google Doll,** 1922, Schoenhut, 8-1/2" tall, wood and wood composition
EX $200   NM $600   MIP $1000

❏ **Spark Plug Doll,** 1922, Schoenhut, 9" long x 6-1/2" tall, jointed wood construction w/fabric
EX $200   NM $600   MIP $1000

FIGURE

❏ **Barney Google and Spark Plug Figurines,** 3" x 3", bisque, on white bisque pedestal
EX $75   NM $200   MIP $350

TOY

❏ **Barney Google and Spark Plug,** 1920s, Nifty, 7-1/2" tall, wind-up
EX $450   NM $950   MIP $1800

❏ **Spark Plug in Bathtub,** 1930, 5" long die-cast, white
EX $100   NM $225   MIP $400

❏ **Spark Plug Pull Toy,** 10" x 8" tall, wood
EX $80   NM $160   MIP $285

❏ **Spark Plug Squeaker Toy,** 1923, 5" long, rubber w/squeaker in mouth
EX $50   NM $125   MIP $185

❏ **Spark Plug Toy,** 1920s, 5" tall, wood, on wheels
EX $45   NM $150   MIP $235

BATMAN

ACCESSORIES

❏ **Batcoin Lot,** 1966, Space Magic Limited, Four 1-1/2" diameter metal coins, each depicting a scene featuring Batman and Robin battling villains
EX $30   NM $75   MIP $100

❏ **Batman and Robin Society Membership Button,** 1966, Button World, full color litho metal button featuring Batman and Robin and the words "Charter Member-Batman and Robin Society"
EX $15   NM $25   MIP $35

❏ **Batman Candy Box,** 1966, Phoenix Candy, 2-1/2" x 3-1/2" x 1", several color scenes
EX $40   NM $110   MIP $225

❏ **Batman Cereal Box,** 1966, Kellogg's, w/Yogi Bear on front
EX $300   NM $1000   MIP $1950

❏ **Batman Crazy Foam,** 1974
EX $20   NM $40   MIP $80

❏ **Batman Dinner Set,** 1966, ceramic; three pieces
EX $40   NM $70   MIP $150

❏ **Batman Fork,** 1966, Imperial, 6" stainless steel w/embossed figure of Batman, w/"Batman" engraved towards the bottom
EX $8   NM $25   MIP $50

❏ **Batman Halloween Costume,** 1965, Ben Cooper, plastic Halloween mask and purple and yellow cape, several versions, some feature logo on chest
EX $20   NM $50   MIP $110

(KP Photo)

❏ **Batman Helmet and Cape Set,** 1966, Ideal, blue hard plastic cowl shaped helmet and soft blue vinyl cape w/drawstring
EX $125   NM $350   MIP $600

❏ **Batman Lamp,** Vanity Fair, Made in Taiwan
EX $45   NM $75   MIP $160

(KP Photo)

❏ **Batman Pencil Box,** 1966, Empire Pencil, gun-shaped pencil box w/set of Batman pencils
EX $25   NM $55   MIP $125

❏ **Batman Pillow,** 1966, 10" x 12" w/1940s logo
EX $20   NM $40   MIP $75

❏ **Batman Wastepaper Basket,** 1966, 10" tall, color tin litho
EX $30   NM $60   MIP $125

❏ **Batmobile AM Radio,** 1970s, Bandai
EX $45   NM $90   MIP $185

❏ **Beach Towel,** 1966, 34" x 58" white, Batman hitting a crook
EX $40   NM $95   MIP $180

❏ **Cake Decoration,** 1960s, 2" hard plastic figure of Robin or Batman, each
EX $8   NM $15   MIP $25

❏ **Cake Decorations,** 1966, Space Magic Limited, 4" plastic one dimensional figures of Batman, Robin and old 1940s Batman logo
EX $15   NM $33   MIP $65

❏ **Catwoman Iron-On Patch,** 1966, Catwoman w/the words "Batkids Fan Club"
EX $10   NM $50   MIP $75

❏ **Charm Bracelet,** 1966, on card
EX $30   NM $60   MIP $125

❏ **Child's Dinner Plate,** 1966, Boontonware, 7" plastic w/image of Batman and Robin
EX $15   NM $30   MIP $50

❏ **Christmas Ornament,** 1989, Presents
EX $5   NM $10   MIP $20

❏ **Coins,** 1966, Transogram, plastic, set
EX $25   NM $55   MIP $110

❏ **Costume Patterns,** 1960s, McCalls, patterns for making Batman, Robin, and Superman costumes, paper envelope, each
EX $15   NM $35   MIP $75

❏ **Inflatable TV Chair,** 1982
EX $10   NM $20   MIP $35

❏ **Joker Cereal Bowl,** 1966, Sun Valley, 5" hard plastic
EX $12   NM $25   MIP $50

❏ **Lapel Pin,** 1966, Mamsell, 2" bat-shaped metal, black w/yellow eyes
EX $20   NM $35   MIP $50

❏ **Mug,** 1966, 5" clear plastic; color wrap around sheet
EX $30   NM $60   MIP $100

❏ **Paper Mask,** 1943, newspaper premium, announced first newspaper comic
EX $500   NM $1750   MIP $2500

❏ **Pennant,** 1966, 11 x 29" white felt, illustration of the Dynamic Duo swinging on ropes w/the Bat-signal in the background
EX $40   NM $150   MIP $225

❏ **Robin Character Sponge,** 1966, Epic, 5"
EX $10   NM $30   MIP $75

❏ **Robin Iron-on Patch,** 1966, 2-1/2" diameter patch, Batkids Fan Club
EX $8   NM $35   MIP $50

❏ **Robin Ornament,** 1989, Presents
EX $5   NM $13   MIP $20

❏ **Robin Placemat,** 1966, 13" x 18" vinyl
EX $20   NM $50   MIP $90

❏ **Sip-A-Drink Cup,** 1966, British, 6" tall, white plastic
EX $50   NM $100   MIP $200

(KP Photo)

❏ **Talking Alarm Clock,** 1975, Janex, plastic clock w/Bat logo on face
EX $40   NM $85   MIP $175

ACTION FIGURES

❏ **Batman Bendy Figure,** 1960s, Diener, on card
EX $35   NM $65   MIP $85

❏ **Batman Figure,** 1966, Ideal, 3" yellow plastic, detachable gray plastic cape
EX $12   NM $25   MIP $50

(KP Photo)

❏ **Batman Figure,** 1988, Applause, 15" tall w/stand
EX $15   NM $25   MIP $45

❏ **Batman Figure,** 1989, Bully, 7" bendy
EX $8   NM $15   MIP $25

❏ **Batman Figure,** 1989, Presents, 15-1/2" tall vinyl and cloth figure on base, 1970s logo, metal stand
EX $20   NM $40   MIP $75

❏ **Batman Figure,** 1989, Takara/Japan
EX $40   NM $80   MIP $150

❏ **Batman Figure,** 1989, Billiken, 8" on card
EX $8   NM $15   MIP $25

❏ **Batman Figure and Parachute,** 1966, CDC, 11" x 9" card, metallic blue figure of Batman and working parachute
EX $25   NM $50   MIP $100

❏ **Batman Flying Figure on String,** 1973, Ben Cooper, 6" rubber figure of Batman w/rubber cape
EX $10   NM $20   MIP $40

❏ **Batman Inflated Gliding Figure,** 1966, Ideal, 16" soft plastic inflatable Batman w/free flowing cape and hard plastic cable rail
EX $30   NM $60   MIP $125

❏ **Batman on a String Figure,** 1966, Fun Things, 4" rubber, flexible arms, legs and removable cape
EX $15   NM $30   MIP $60

❏ **Joker Figure,** Presents, 15" vinyl figure
EX $10   NM $20   MIP $40

❏ **Joker Figure,** 1966, Ideal, 3" blue plastic
EX $10   NM $20   MIP $45

❏ **Joker Figure,** 1988, Applause, vinyl w/stand
EX $10   NM $20   MIP $40

❏ **Robin Figure,** Presents, cloth and vinyl, on base
EX $10   NM $20   MIP $35

❏ **Robin Figure,** 1966, Ideal, 3" plastic, detachable yellow plastic cape
EX $10   NM $20   MIP $40

❏ **Robin Figure,** 1970s, Palitoy, 8" figure on card
EX $15   NM $40   MIP $80

❏ **Robin Figure,** 1988, Applause, vinyl w/stand
EX $10   NM $20   MIP $35

❏ **Robin on a String Figure,** Ben Cooper, 4" tall, rubber
EX $10   NM $25   MIP $40

BANK

❏ **Batman Bank,** 1966, 7" tall glazed china figural bank depicts Batman w/hands on hip
EX $45   NM $90   MIP $135

❏ **Batman Bank,** 1989, figural bank given away w/Batman Cereal
EX $6   NM $12   MIP $25

❏ **Joker Bank,** 1974, Mego, plastic
EX $30   NM $60   MIP $125

BOOK

❏ **Batman 3-D Comic Book,** 1966, DC Comics, 9" x 11" comic w/3-D pages and glasses
EX $100   NM $200   MIP $800

❏ **Batman Annual,** 1965-66, 8" x 10" hardback annual contains reprinted stories from 1950s Batman and Detective Comics
EX $20   NM $30   MIP $75

❏ **Batman Comic Book and Record Set,** 1966, Golden Records, 33-1/3 rpm record, full size Batman comic book, official Batman membership card w/secret Batman code on back
EX $30   NM $60   MIP $120

❏ **Batman vs. the Joker Book,** 1966, Signet, 160-page paperback
EX $5   NM $10   MIP $20

❏ **Dot-To-Dot and Coloring Book,** 1967, Vasquez Brothers, Batman w/Robin the Boy Wonder, printed in the Phillipines, 20 pages
EX $20   NM $40   MIP $90

❏ **From Alfred to Zowie! Book,** 1966, Golden Press
EX $10   NM $20   MIP $35

CHARACTER TOYS

❑ **Paint-By-Number Book,** 1966, Whitman
EX $20   NM $40   MIP $75

❑ **Sticker Fun with Batman Book,** 1966, Watkins-Strathmore, 8" x 11" softbound w/stickers
EX $15   NM $50   MIP $100

❑ **Three Villains of Doom Book,** 1966, Signet, 160 pages
EX $10   NM $40   MIP $75

CLOTHING

❑ **Child's Belt,** 1960s, elastic w/bronze logo buckle
EX $22   NM $40   MIP $85

❑ **Child's Mittens,** 1973, children's blue plastic vinyl, raised illustration of Batman and logo
EX $12   NM $25   MIP $50

❑ **Child's Pajamas,** 1966, Wormser, light blue, two piece pajamas, full color Batman logo on chest
EX $200   NM $450   MIP $900

FOOD PRODUCTS

❑ **Batman "Punch-O" Drink Mix,** 1966, small paper packet
EX $25   NM $40   MIP $75

❑ **Batman Cereal Box,** 1989, Ralston
EX $20   NM $55   MIP $80

❑ **Batman Crusader Sundae Fudgesicle,** 1966, Popsicle, 7" white and brown paper wrapper
EX $8   NM $15   MIP $25

❑ **Bread Wrapper,** 1966, New Century Bread, plastic
EX $20   NM $45   MIP $85

❑ **Candy Cigarettes,** 1960s, made in England
EX $15   NM $40   MIP $85

❑ **Chocolate Milk Carton,** 1966, Reiter and Hart, one-quart carton in yellow, red and brown, features front and back panels of Batman in action poses
EX $100   NM $200   MIP $400

❑ **Jelly Jar,** 1966, W.H. Marvin, 5"-6" glass jar w/color label, "Bat" Pure Apple Jelly
EX $200   NM $400   MIP $600

❑ **Slam Bang Ice Cream Carton,** 1966, Cabarrus Creamery, features Batman and Robin on side panels
EX $15   NM $40   MIP $55

GAMES

❑ **Batman Arcade Game,** 1989, Bluebox, electronic
EX $75   NM $120   MIP $165

❑ **Batman Pinball Game,** 1960s, Marx, tin litho w/plastic casing
EX $35   NM $80   MIP $175

❑ **Batman Target Game,** 1966, Hasbro, tin litho target w/plastic revolver and rubber-tipped darts
EX $40   NM $80   MIP $185

GLASSWARE

❑ **Batman Drinking Glass,** 1976, Pepsi, 7" tall glass tumbler, all Batman characters, each
EX $10   NM $20   MIP $30

❑ **Coffee Mug,** 1966, Anchor-Hocking, milk glass, action pose of Batman on one side and the Bat logo on the opposite side
EX $15   NM $30   MIP $50

❑ **Drinking Glass,** 1989, 5", made in France
EX $10   NM $25   MIP $40

MAGAZINE

❑ **Life Magazine,** 1966, March 11, 1966 issue, Adam West as Batman on cover
EX $25   NM $75   MIP $150

❑ **TV Guide,** 1966, TV Guide, March 26-April 1 issue, photo cover of Adam West as Batman
EX $75   NM $250   MIP $375

MODEL KIT

❑ **Catwoman Returns,** 1990s, Horizon, vinyl model kit
EX $10   NM $20   MIP $40

❑ **Penguin Returns Model Kit,** Horizon
EX $10   NM $20   MIP $40

PAINT SET

❑ **Batman Cast and Paint Set,** 1960s, plaster casting mold and paint set
EX $40   NM $80   MIP $160

❑ **Batman Paint by Number Set,** 1965, Hasbro, five pre-numbered sketches, ten oil paint vials and brush
EX $40   NM $85   MIP $175

❑ **Batman Super Powers Stain and Paint Set,** 1984
EX $10   NM $25   MIP $60

❑ **Sparkle Paint Set,** 1966, Kenner, paint and six pre-numbered sketches of Batman
EX $30   NM $75   MIP $150

PAPER GOODS

❑ **Batman and Robin Valentine,** 1966
EX $10   NM $30   MIP $60

❑ **Batman Lobby Display,** 1989, Warner Bros., Michael Keaton cardboard stand up
EX $50   NM $150   MIP $210

❑ **Batman Lucky Charm Display Card,** 1966, 4" x 4" paper display card used in bubble gum machines, card shows Bat logo and red "Be protected—Get your Batman lucky charm now"
EX $12   NM $30   MIP $60

❑ **Batman Postcards,** 1966, Dexter Press, set of eight postcards w/Carmine Infantino artwork
EX $30   NM $100   MIP $160

❑ **Batman Postcards,** 1966, Dexter Press, three full-color postcards, each taken from a comic panel from Batman comics, each
EX $8   NM $15   MIP $30

❑ **Batman Returns Display,** 1992, Warner Bros.
EX $25   NM $75   MIP $100

❑ **Batman Returns Lobby Display,** 1992, Warner Bros., Michael Keaton life-size cardboard stand up
EX $50   NM $150   MIP $210

❑ **Batmobile Display Sign,** 1969, Burry's, 34" x 48" die-cut 3-D plastic story display, raised images of Batman, Robin, and Batmobile, bright orange w/yellow lettering
EX $400   NM $1000   MIP $1500

❑ **Button Display Card,** 1966, full color display card used in bubble gum machines which offered Batman buttons
EX $20   NM $50   MIP $100

❑ **Costume Store Poster,** 1966, Ben Cooper, 12" x 24", yellow
EX $40   NM $150   MIP $210

❑ **Flicker Pictures Display Card,** 1966, bubble gum machine display card
EX $10   NM $25   MIP $45

❑ **Glow-in-the Dark Poster,** 1966, Ciro Art, 18" x 14" poster of Batman and Robin swinging across Gotham City
EX $30   NM $90   MIP $135

❑ **Official Bat-Signal Stickers,** 1966, Alan-Whitney
EX $10   NM $20   MIP $35

❑ **Party Hat,** 1972, Amscan/Canadian, 7" child's cardboard hat depicts Batman and Robin
EX $8   NM $15   MIP $25

PLAYSET

❑ **Batcave Play Set,** 1974, Mego, vinyl
EX $150   NM $250   MIP $500

(KP Photo)

❑ **Batman Play Set,** 1966, Ideal, eleven pieces including characters and vehicles
EX $1200   NM $4500   MIP $10000

(KP Photo)

❏ **Batman Switch and Go Play Set**, 1966, Mattel, 9" plastic Batmobile, forty feet of track, figures, etc.
EX $150   **NM** $325   **MIP** $650

❏ **Magic Magnetic Gotham City Play Set**, 1966, Remco, cardboard city, character figures
EX $200   **NM** $450   **MIP** $850

PUPPET

❏ **Batman and Robin Hand Puppets**, 1966, Ideal, 12" soft vinyl head, plastic body, each
EX $50   **NM** $160   **MIP** $300

(KP Photo)

❏ **Batman Push Puppet**, 1966, Kohner, 3" plastic w/push button on bottom
EX $20   **NM** $45   **MIP** $90

❏ **Batman String Puppet**, 1977, Madison
EX $35   **NM** $75   **MIP** $160

❏ **Robin Push Puppet**, 1966, Kohner, 3", plastic, push button on bottom
EX $30   **NM** $75   **MIP** $135

PUZZLE

(KP Photo)

❏ **Frame Tray Puzzle**, 1966, Whitman, 11" x 14", Batman and Robin thwarting the Joker
EX $15   **NM** $40   **MIP** $80

RECORD

❏ **Batman and Superman Record Album**, 1969-71, Wonderland, 45 rpm record Batman theme song from the 1966 television show and "The Superman Song"
EX $20   **NM** $75   **MIP** $100

❏ **Batman Soundtrack Record**, 1966, 20th Century Fox, mono and stereo versions, each
EX $50   **NM** $140   **MIP** $250

❏ **Catwoman's Revenge Record**, 1975, Power Records, 33-1/3 rpm story record
EX $5   **NM** $20   **MIP** $40

❏ **Joker Record**, 1966, SPC, 45 rpm, sleeve shaped like Joker's head
EX $20   **NM** $40   **MIP** $85

RECORDS

❏ **Batman Record**, 1966, SPC, 45 rpm, sleeve shaped like Batman's head; also available in Robin, Joker, Penguin, Riddler and Batmobile versions
EX $15   **NM** $50   **MIP** $100

RINGS

❏ **Bat Ring**, 1966, yellow plastic, originally for a gumball machine
EX $15   **NM** $40   **MIP** $65

❏ **Batman/Robin Flicker-Flasher Ring**, 1966, Vari-Vue, silver plastic base
EX $10   **NM** $20   **MIP** $25

❏ **Riddler/Batman Punching Riddler Flicker-Flasher Ring**, 1966, Vari-Vue, silver plastic base
EX $10   **NM** $25   **MIP** $45

❏ **Robin/Dick Grayson Flicker-Flasher Ring**, 1966, Vari-Vue, silver plastic base
EX $10   **NM** $25   **MIP** $45

TOY

❏ **Bat Bomb**, 1966, Mattel
EX $50   **NM** $100   **MIP** $185

❏ **Batman Cartoon Kit**, 1966, Colorforms
EX $25   **NM** $55   **MIP** $85

❏ **Batman Kite**, 1982, Hiflyer
EX $8   **NM** $15   **MIP** $30

❏ **Batman Radio Belt and Buckle**, 1966
EX $35   **NM** $100   **MIP** $175

❏ **Batman Superfriends Lite Brite Refill Pack**, 1980
EX $5   **NM** $15   **MIP** $25

❏ **Batman Superhero Stamp Set**, 1970s
EX $10   **NM** $25   **MIP** $60

(KP Photo)

❏ **Batman Trace-a-Graph**, 1966, Emenee
EX $30   **NM** $75   **MIP** $160

(KP Photo)

❏ **Batman Utility Belt**, 1960s, Ideal
EX $1200   **NM** $3200   **MIP** $5500

❏ **Batman Wind-Up**, 1989, Billiken, Tin litho
EX $25   **NM** $50   **MIP** $100

❏ **Batman Yo-Yo**, 1989, SpectraStar
EX $5   **NM** $20   **MIP** $35

(KP Photo)

❏ **Batphone**, 1966, Marx
EX $70   **NM** $150   **MIP** $275

❏ **Batscope Dart Launcher**, 1966, Tarco
EX $25   **NM** $45   **MIP** $85

❏ **Bat-Troll Doll**, 1966, Wish-Nik, vinyl, dressed in a blue felt Batman outfit w/cowl and cape
EX $75   **NM** $175   **MIP** $325

❏ **Cave Tun-L**, 1966, New York Toy, 26" x 26" x 2" tunnel
EX $600   **NM** $1200   **MIP** $2350

❏ **Escape Gun**, 1966, Lincoln, red plastic spring-loaded pistol w/Batman decal, two separate firing barrels
EX $50   **NM** $150   **MIP** $210

❏ **Give-A-Show Projector Cards**, 1960s, Kenner, four slide cards in box
EX $10   **NM** $25   **MIP** $50

❏ **Gotham City Stunt Set**, 1989, Tonka
EX $15   **NM** $55   **MIP** $85

(KP Photo)

❏ **Joker Wind-up,** 1989, Billiken
  EX $40   NM $100   MIP $185

❏ **Joker Yo-Yo,** 1989, SpectraStar
  EX $5   NM $20   MIP $45

❏ **Projector Gun,** 1989, Toy Biz
  EX $10   NM $20   MIP $60

❏ **Puppet Theater Stage,** 1966, Ideal,
  marketed by Sears, 19" x 11" x 20" cardboard stage w/hand puppets
  EX $80   NM $250   MIP $525

❏ **Ray Gun,** 1960s, 7" long blue and black
  futuristic space gun w/bat sights and
  bats on handgrip
  EX $80   NM $275   MIP $425

❏ **Rubber Stamp Set,** 1966, Kellogg's, 2"
  x 5" hard black plastic case, set of six
  plastic stamps plus ink pad: Batman,
  Robin, Batmobile, Joker, Riddler and
  Penguin
  EX $60   NM $100   MIP $200

❏ **Shooting Arcade,** 1970s, AHI, graphics
  of Joker, Catwoman and Penguin
  EX $35   NM $100   MIP $175

VEHICLES

❏ **Bat Cycle,** 1989, Toy Biz
  EX $10   NM $24   MIP $60

❏ **Bat Machine,** 1979, Mego
  EX $30   NM $55   MIP $120

(KP Photo)

❏ **Batboat,** 1987, Duncan
  EX $10   NM $25   MIP $60

❏ **Batboat Pullstring Toy,** Eidai, made in
  Japan
  EX $60   NM $120   MIP $200

❏ **Batman Flying Copter,** 1966, Remco,
  12" plastic w/guide-wire control
  EX $40   NM $100   MIP $200

❏ **Batman Road Race Set,** 1960s, slot car
  racing set
  EX $100   NM $275   MIP $475

❏ **Batman Slot Car,** 1966, Magicar
  (England), 5" long Batmobile being
  driven by Batman and Robin in illustrated display window box
  EX $150   NM $300   MIP $525

(KP Photo)

❏ **Batmobile,** Apollo (Japan), radio-controlled
  EX $60   NM $125   MIP $260

❏ **Batmobile,** Matsushiro, radio-controlled
  EX $60   NM $125   MIP $260

❏ **Batmobile,** 1960s, Simms, plastic car
  on card
  EX $20   NM $45   MIP $80

❏ **Batmobile,** 1972, AHI, 11" long tin litho
  battery-operated mystery action car
  w/blinking light and jet engine noise
  EX $75   NM $150   MIP $300

❏ **Batmobile,** 1974, Azrak-Hamway, battery operated
  EX $50   NM $100   MIP $210

❏ **Batmobile,** 1977, Duncan, 12" x 8" on
  card
  EX $25   NM $50   MIP $100

❏ **Batmobile,** 1980s, Bandai, pullback
  vehicle w/machine guns
  EX $25   NM $60   MIP $135

❏ **Batmobile,** 1980s, Aoshinu (Japan),
  motorized
  EX $30   NM $60   MIP $150

❏ **Batmobile,** 1989, Toy Biz, remote control
  EX $12   NM $30   MIP $65

❏ **Batmobile,** 1989, Rich Man's Toys,
  remote control
  EX $85   NM $160   MIP $350

❏ **Batmobile Motorized Kit,** 1980s,
  Aoshinu (Japan), smaller snap kit
  EX $20   NM $35   MIP $75

❏ **Batwing,** 1980s, Toy Biz
  EX $15   NM $30   MIP $60

(KP Photo)

❏ **Joker Van,** 1989, Ertl, die-cast vehicle
  on card
  EX $5   NM $10   MIP $25

❏ **Robin Shuttle,** 1979, Mego, sized for
  British-made Mego figures, in box
  EX $20   NM $40   MIP $90

❏ **Super Accelerator Batmobile,** 1970s,
  AHI, on card
  EX $15   NM $50   MIP $100

❏ **Turbine-Sound Batmobile,** 1989, Toy
  Biz
  EX $10   NM $15   MIP $25

WATCH

❏ **Batman Returns Watch,** 1989, Consort,
  gray or yellow Bat logo
  EX $10   NM $20   MIP $60

❏ **Batman Wristwatch,** 1991, Quintel,
  digital
  EX $8   NM $15   MIP $25

❏ **Catwoman Watch,** 1991, Quintel, digital
  EX $5   NM $15   MIP $40

❏ **Catwoman Watch,** 1991, Consort, Batman Returns
  EX $7   NM $20   MIP $50

❑ **Joker Wristwatch,** 1980s, Fossil
EX $25   **NM** $65   **MIP** $110

❑ **Joker Wristwatch,** 1989, Quintell, digital
EX $10   **NM** $20   **MIP** $50

❑ **Video Game Watch,** 1989, Tiger, w/alarm
EX $8   **NM** $20   **MIP** $35

BETTY BOOP

DOLL

❑ **Betty Boop Doll,** 1930s, wood w/composition head
EX $125   **NM** $450   **MIP** $800

❑ **Betty Boop Doll,** 1986, M-Toy, 12" vinyl jointed
EX $10   **NM** $20   **MIP** $50

❑ **Betty Boop Doll Clothing,** 1986, M-Toy, outfits for 12" dolls high fashion boutique, each
EX $5   **NM** $10   **MIP** $25

FIGURE

❑ **Betty Boop Figure,** 1980s, 3" PVC figure, eight different poses and outfits, each
EX $2   **NM** $4   **MIP** $10

❑ **Betty Boop Figure,** 1988, NJ Croce, 9" bendy
EX $5   **NM** $15   **MIP** $30

TOY

❑ **Betty Boop Delivery Truck,** 1990, Schylling, tin litho
EX $15   **NM** $30   **MIP** $60

BLONDIE AND DAGWOOD

ACCESSORIES

❑ **Blondie Paint Set,** 1946, American Crayon
EX $30   **NM** $110   **MIP** $250

❑ **Blondie's Peg Board Set,** 1934, King Features, 9" x 15-1/2", multi-colored pegs, hammer, cut-outs of Dagwood, Blondie, etc.
EX $45   **NM** $150   **MIP** $300

❑ **Blondie's Presto Slate,** 1944, Presto, 10" x 13" illustration of Blondie and Dagwood and other characters
EX $20   **NM** $60   **MIP** $90

❑ **Dagwood Marionette,** 1945, 14"
EX $75   **NM** $150   **MIP** $300

❑ **Dagwood's Solo Flight Airplane,** 1935, Marx, 12" wingspan, plane 9" in length
EX $300   **NM** $900   **MIP** $1450

❑ **Lucky Safety Card,** 1953, 2" x 4" cards, Dagwood offers safety tips
EX $10   **NM** $55   **MIP** $70

BOOK

❑ **Blondie Paint Book,** 1947, Whitman
EX $25   **NM** $100   **MIP** $225

DOLL

❑ **Blondie Paper Dolls,** 1944, Whitman
EX $80   **NM** $200   **MIP** $400

❑ **Blondie Paper Dolls,** 1955, Whitman
EX $35   **NM** $110   **MIP** $200

FIGURE

❑ **Blondie Figure,** 1940s, 2-1/2" tall, lead
EX $12   **NM** $65   **MIP** $135

❑ **Dagwood and Kids Figures,** 1944, King Features, Dagwood, Alexander, and Cookie, each
EX $30   **NM** $85   **MIP** $150

PUZZLE

❑ **Puzzle,** 1930s, Featured Funnies
EX $50   **NM** $125   **MIP** $175

BUGS BUNNY

ACCESSORIES

❑ **Bugs Bunny Charm Bracelet,** 1950s, brass charms of Bugs Bunny, Tweety, Sniffles, Fudd, etc.
EX $20   **NM** $60   **MIP** $125

❑ **Bugs Bunny Chatter Chum,** 1982, Mattel
EX $10   **NM** $25   **MIP** $50

❑ **Bugs Bunny Clock,** 1972, Litech, 12" x 14"
EX $35   **NM** $100   **MIP** $185

❑ **Bugs Bunny Mini Snow Dome,** 1980s, Applause
EX $5   **NM** $15   **MIP** $35

❑ **Bugs Bunny Musical Ge-Tar,** 1977, Mattel
EX $20   **NM** $45   **MIP** $90

❑ **Bugs Bunny Night Light,** 1980s, Applause
EX $5   **NM** $10   **MIP** $15

❑ **Bugs Bunny Talking Alarm Clock,** 1974, Janex, battery-operated
EX $40   **NM** $80   **MIP** $175

❑ **Bugs Bunny Wristwatch,** 1978, Lafayette
EX $30   **NM** $80   **MIP** $160

BANK

❑ **Bugs Bunny Bank,** 1940s, 5-3/4" x 5-1/2", pot metal, figure on base
EX $45   **NM** $130   **MIP** $250

❑ **Bugs Bunny Bank,** 1971, Dakin, on a basket of carrots
EX $15   **NM** $30   **MIP** $60

COSTUME

❑ **Bugs Bunny Costume,** 1960s, Collegeville, mask and costume
EX $9   **NM** $30   **MIP** $60

DOLL

❑ **Bugs Bunny Talking Doll,** 1971, Mattel
EX $30   **NM** $100   **MIP** $175

FIGURE

❑ **Bugs Bunny Bendy,** 1980s, Applause, 4" tall
EX $5   **NM** $15   **MIP** $30

❑ **Bugs Bunny Figure,** 1971, Dakin, 10" tall
EX $10   **NM** $35   **MIP** $70

❑ **Bugs Bunny Figure,** 1975, Warner Bros., 5-1/2" tall, ceramic, holding carrot
EX $20   **NM** $60   **MIP** $110

❑ **Bugs Bunny Figure,** 1975, Warner Bros., 2-3/4" tall, ceramic
EX $10   **NM** $25   **MIP** $60

❑ **Bugs Bunny Figure,** 1976, Dakin, yellow globes in "Cartoon Theater" box
EX $12   **NM** $30   **MIP** $60

❑ **Bugs Bunny in Uncle Sam Outfit,** 1976, Dakin, distributed through Great America Theme Park, Illinois
EX $20   **NM** $60   **MIP** $110

TOY

❑ **Bugs Bunny Colorforms Set,** 1958, Colorforms
EX $15   **NM** $50   **MIP** $90

❑ **Bugs Bunny Soaky,** soft rubber
EX $10   **NM** $25   **MIP** $50

CALIFORNIA RAISINS

ACCESSORIES

❑ **California Raisins Chalkboard,** 1988, Rose Art
EX $5   **NM** $10   **MIP** $30

❑ **California Raisins Clay Factory,** 1988, Rose Art
EX $10   **NM** $30   **MIP** $55

❑ **California Raisins Crayon By Number,** 1988, Rose Art
EX $10   **NM** $30   **MIP** $60

TOY

❑ **California Raisins Colorforms Play Set,** 1987, Colorforms
EX $10   **NM** $30   **MIP** $60

❑ **California Raisins Wind-Up Walkers,** 1987, Rasta
EX $4   **NM** $12   **MIP** $25

CAPTAIN AMERICA

ACCESSORIES

❑ **Captain America Club Kit,** 1941, includes two badges (copper and bronze), card, envelope
EX $700   **NM** $1750   **MIP** $3000

FIGURE

❑ **Captain America Bendy Figure,** 1966, Lakeside, 6", rubber
EX $50   **NM** $85   **MIP** $150

CHARACTER TOYS

TOY

❏ **Captain America Rocket Racer**, 1984, Buddy L, Secret Wars remote controlled battery operated car
EX $50   **NM** $125   **MIP** $175

(KP Photo)

❏ **Captain America Scooter**, 1967, Marx, 4", yellow plastic friction toy w/figure
EX $100   **NM** $225   **MIP** $350

CAPTAIN MARVEL

ACCESSORIES

❏ **Adventures of Captain Marvel Ink Blotter/Ruler**, 1940s, Republic/Fawcett, 6" blotter w/ruler advertises the 12-part serial, theatre premium
EX $150   **NM** $600   **MIP** $800

❏ **Captain Marvel Booklet**, 1940s, Fawcett
EX $35   **NM** $55   **MIP** $350

❏ **Captain Marvel Button**, 1940s, celluloid, pinback
EX $30   **NM** $90   **MIP** $130

❏ **Captain Marvel Club Button**, 1941, tin litho, showing Captain Marvel in bust 3/4 view, w/"Shazam" in lightning bolts at bottom
EX $30   **NM** $90   **MIP** $130

❏ **Captain Marvel Club Felt Shoulder Patches**, 1940s, Fawcett, Captain Marvel diving towards Earth, yellow
EX $125   **NM** $400   **MIP** $650

❏ **Captain Marvel Club Felt Shoulder Patches**, 1940s, Fawcett, Captain Marvel diving towards Earth, blue
EX $30   **NM** $100   **MIP** $200

❏ **Captain Marvel Club Membership Card**, 1940s, Fawcett
EX $25   **NM** $75   **MIP** $110

❏ **Captain Marvel Code Finder**, 1943
EX $150   **NM** $450   **MIP** $650

❏ **Captain Marvel Felt Pennant**, 1940s, Fawcett, yellow, shows Captain Marvel flying
EX $60   **NM** $160   **MIP** $285

❏ **Captain Marvel Felt Pennant**, 1940s, Fawcett, blue, shows Captain Marvel flying
EX $40   **NM** $100   **MIP** $200

❏ **Captain Marvel Film Viewer Gun**, 1940s, gun-shaped movie viewer w/film strips from Paramount series
EX $100   **NM** $200   **MIP** $375

❏ **Captain Marvel Flannel Patch**, 1940s, Fawcett
EX $25   **NM** $65   **MIP** $150

❏ **Captain Marvel Glow Pictures**, 1940s, Fawcett, set of four
EX $250   **NM** $650   **MIP** $1000

❏ **Captain Marvel Iron-Ons**, 1950s, Fawcett, sheet
EX $15   **NM** $40   **MIP** $85

❏ **Captain Marvel Jr. Wristwatch**, 1940s, blue band, round dial w/blue costumed Jr.
EX $300   **NM** $600   **MIP** $1000

❏ **Captain Marvel Key Chain**, 1940s, Fawcett
EX $40   **NM** $125   **MIP** $175

❏ **Captain Marvel Magic Dime Register Bank**, 1948, Fawcett, available in three colors
EX $100   **NM** $300   **MIP** $450

❏ **Captain Marvel Magic Flute**, 1940s, on die-cut card, shows Captain Marvel on side
EX $40   **NM** $100   **MIP** $150

(KP Photo)

❏ **Captain Marvel Magic Lightning Box**, 1940s, Fawcett
EX $50   **NM** $100   **MIP** $165

❏ **Captain Marvel Magic Membership Card**, 1940s, Fawcett
EX $20   **NM** $55   **MIP** $90

❏ **Captain Marvel Magic Picture**, 1940s, Reed and Associates, paper, shows Billy Batson "transforming" into Captain Marvel
EX $30   **NM** $75   **MIP** $150

❏ **Captain Marvel Magic Whistle**, 1948, Fawcett, seed company premium, picture of Captain Marvel on both sides, on card
EX $45   **NM** $120   **MIP** $175

❏ **Captain Marvel Neck Tie**, 1940s, Fawcett
EX $50   **NM** $150   **MIP** $250

❏ **Captain Marvel Overseas Cap**, 1940s, rare
EX $200   **NM** $600   **MIP** $800

❏ **Captain Marvel Paint Set**, 1940s, paint set w/five chalk figurines
EX $200   **NM** $600   **MIP** $1200

❏ **Captain Marvel Paper Horn**, 1940s, Fawcett
EX $20   **NM** $40   **MIP** $75

❏ **Captain Marvel Patch**, 1940s, Fawcett
EX $30   **NM** $75   **MIP** $150

❏ **Captain Marvel Pinback Pattern**, 1940s, Fawcett, pattern for original pinback
EX $15   **NM** $30   **MIP** $100

❏ **Captain Marvel Portrait**, 1940s, Whiz Comics/Fawcett
EX $50   **NM** $125   **MIP** $250

❏ **Captain Marvel Portrait**, 1940s, Republic, different version than Whiz Comics portrait
EX $50   **NM** $125   **MIP** $250

❏ **Captain Marvel Power Siren**, 1940s, Fawcett
EX $45   **NM** $125   **MIP** $175

❏ **Captain Marvel Secret Code Sheet**, 1940s, Fawcett
EX $15   **NM** $30   **MIP** $75

❏ **Captain Marvel Skull Cap**, 1940s
EX $85   **NM** $375   **MIP** $550

❏ **Captain Marvel Soap**, 1947, Fawcett, three illustrated bars in box
EX $100   **NM** $300   **MIP** $600

(KP Photo)

❏ **Captain Marvel Stationary**, 1940s, Fawcett, paper and envelopes in box
EX $100   **NM** $225   **MIP** $350

❏ **Captain Marvel Suspenders**, 1940s, Fawcett
EX $50   **NM** $125   **MIP** $185

❏ **Captain Marvel Sweater**, 1940s, white or off-white, red Captain Marvel logo
EX $60   **NM** $225   **MIP** $400

❏ **Captain Marvel Tattoo Transfers**, 1940s, Fawcett
EX $30   **NM** $110   **MIP** $200

❏ **Captain Marvel Tie Bar**, 1940s, on card
EX $35   **NM** $65   **MIP** $150

❏ **Captain Marvel Wristwatch**, 1948, in box, shows Captain Marvel holding an airplane
EX $200   **NM** $650   **MIP** $1250

❏ **Captain Marvel, Jr. Booklet**, 1940s, Fawcett
EX $25   **NM** $50   **MIP** $100

(KP Photo)

❏ **Fawcett's Comic Stars Christmas Tree Ornaments,** 1940s, Fawcett, metal star-shaped ornaments w/art of Captain Marvel and Hoppy
EX $25   NM $45   MIP $90

(KP Photo)

❏ **Mary Marvel Illustrated Soap,** 1947, Fawcett, three soap bars in box
EX $150   NM $350   MIP $500

❏ **Mary Marvel Patch,** 1940s, Fawcett
EX $100   NM $275   MIP $450

❏ **Mary Marvel Pin,** 1940s, Fawcett, fiberboard
EX $75   NM $175   MIP $350

❏ **Mary Marvel Stationery,** 1940s, Fawcett, boxed
EX $85   NM $200   MIP $375

(KP Photo)

❏ **Mary Marvel Wristwatch,** 1940s, in box
EX $250   NM $650   MIP $1200

❏ **Membership Secret Code Card,** 1940s, Fawcett
EX $20   NM $150   MIP $300

❏ **Rocket Raider,** 1940s, Fawcett, paper airplane in envelope
EX $12   NM $30   MIP $60

COMIC

❏ **Boy Who Never Heard of Captain Marvel Mini Comic,** 1940s, Bond Bread
EX $40   NM $100   MIP $200

❏ **Captain Marvel and Billy's Big Game Mini Comic,** 1940s
EX $90   NM $200   MIP $400

❏ **Captain Marvel Meets the Weatherman Mini Comic,** 1940s, Bond Bread, Bond Bread premium
EX $50   NM $110   MIP $175

❏ **Giveaway Comics #1, Captain Marvel and the Lt. of Safety,** 1950, Danger Flies a Kite
EX $125   NM $600   MIP $1250

❏ **Giveaway Comics #2, Captain Marvel and the Lt. of Safety,** 1950, Danger Takes to Climbing
EX $100   NM $500   MIP $1050

❏ **Giveaway Comics #3, Captain Marvel and the Lt. of Safety,** 1951, Danger Smashes Street Lights
EX $100   NM $500   MIP $1050

FIGURE

(Bruce Bergstrom-Artman Originals)

❏ **Captain Marvel Comic Hero Punch-Outs,** 1942, Lowe, cardboard figures
EX $75   NM $175   MIP $350

❏ **Captain Marvel Sirocco Figurine,** 1940s, Fawcett
EX $1000   NM $3000   MIP $4000

❏ **Mary Marvel Figurine,** 5"
EX $500   NM $1500   MIP $2500

PUZZLE

❏ **Captain Marvel Puzzle,** 1940s, Reed and Associates, in envelope
EX $50   NM $350   MIP $400

❏ **Captain Marvel Puzzle,** 1941, Fawcett, in box
EX $40   NM $200   MIP $350

TOY

❏ **Captain Marvel Beanbags,** 1940s, Captain Marvel, Mary Marvel or Hoppy, each
EX $50   NM $175   MIP $300

❏ **Captain Marvel Beanie,** 1940s, cap shows image of Captain Marvel flying toward word "Shazam," blue
EX $85   NM $275   MIP $450

❏ **Captain Marvel Beanie,** 1940s, girls' cap shows image of Captain Marvel flying toward word "Shazam," pink, rare
EX $300   NM $750   MIP $1000

(KP Photo)

❏ **Captain Marvel Buzz Bomb,** 1950s, Fawcett, paper airplane in envelope
EX $25   NM $85   MIP $125

(KP Photo)

❏ **Captain Marvel Jr. Ski Jump,** 1947, Reed and Associates, paper, in envelope
EX $10   NM $20   MIP $60

❏ **Captain Marvel Jr. Statuette,** 1940s, Fawcett, hand-painted plastic
EX $500   NM $1500   MIP $2500

❏ **Captain Marvel Lightning Wind-Up Race Car,** 1947, Fawcett, 4" long tin wind-up in green, yellow, orange or blue, four cars and box
EX $1000   NM $2500   MIP $3500

❏ **Captain Marvel Statuette,** 1940s, Fawcett, hand-painted plastic, shows Captain Marvel standing w/arms crossed, on base w/name engraved
EX $1000   NM $2500   MIP $4000

❏ **Mary Marvel Statuette,** 1940s, Fawcett, hand-painted plastic
EX $500   NM $2000   MIP $3500

CAPTAIN MIDNIGHT

ACCESSORIES

❏ **Captain Midnight Badge Brass,** 1930s, gold, wings and words "Flight Commander," fying cross
EX $90   NM $210   MIP $385

CHARACTER TOYS

(KP Photo)

❏ **Captain Midnight Cup**, plastic, 4" tall, "Ovaltine-The Heart of a Hearty Breakfast"
EX $30   NM $70   MIP $150

❏ **Captain Midnight Map**, 1940, Skelly Oil, 11" x 17"
EX $150   NM $650   MIP $1100

❏ **Captain Midnight Membership Manual**, 1930s, Secret Squadron official code and manual guide
EX $55   NM $125   MIP $250

❏ **Captain Midnight Secret Society Decoder**, 1949, w/key
EX $85   NM $180   MIP $350

CARTOON/COMIC CHARACTERS

ACCESSORIES

❏ **Beetle Bailey Comic Strip Stamper Set**, 1981, Ja-Ru, 7 stampers, book, crayon
EX $8   NM $25   MIP $50

❏ **Beetle Bailey Gun Set**, 1981, Ja-Ru, cord gun and target
EX $10   NM $40   MIP $75

❏ **Daffy Dog Poster**, 10" x 13", The Morning After
EX $10   NM $17   MIP $30

❏ **Dan Dunn Pinback Button**, 1930s, 1-1/4"
EX $50   NM $175   MIP $350

❏ **Doggie Daddy Metal Trivet**, 1960s, says "You have to work like a dog to live like one"
EX $15   NM $35   MIP $50

❏ **Dudley Do-Right Jigsaw Puzzle**, 1975, Whitman, Dudley and Snidley
EX $15   NM $35   MIP $65

❏ **Easy Show Movie Projector Films**, 1965, Kenner, numerous cartoon characters, each film
EX $8   NM $15   MIP $30

❏ **Favorite Funnies Printing Set**, 1930s, #4004, Orphan Annie, Herby, and Dick Tracy, six stamps, pad, paper and instructions
EX $50   NM $150   MIP $250

❏ **Geoffrey Jack-in-the-Box**, 1970s, Toys R Us, jack-in-the-box
EX $20   NM $40   MIP $75

❏ **Hair Bear Bunch Mug**, 1978, Square Bear figural mug
EX $5   NM $13   MIP $20

❏ **Hair Bear Bunch Wristwatch**, 1972, medium gold tone case, base metal back, articulated hands, red leather snap down band
EX $30   NM $70   MIP $125

❏ **Harold Teen Playstone Funnies Mold Set**, 1940s
EX $40   NM $100   MIP $200

❏ **Herman and Katnip Punch Out Kite**, 1960s, Saalfield, folds into a kite
EX $12   NM $30   MIP $60

❏ **Josie and the Pussycats Paper Doll Book**, 1971, Whitman, Model No. 1982
EX $22   NM $45   MIP $90

❏ **Little Audrey Dress Designer Kit**, 1962, Saalfield, die cut doll and accessories in illustrated box
EX $25   NM $75   MIP $150

❏ **Little Audrey Shoulder Bag Leathercraft Kit**, 1961, Jewel
EX $25   NM $75   MIP $150

❏ **Little Lulu Dish**, 1940s, 5-1/2" hand painted ceramic, pictures of Lulu, Tubby and her friends
EX $75   NM $150   MIP $250

❏ **Nancy Music Box**, 1968, United Feature, ceramic
EX $50   NM $125   MIP $175

❏ **Supercar Molding Color Kit**, 1960s, Sculptorcraft, set of rubber plaster casting models of vehicle and show characters, including Mike Mercury, Beaker and Popkiss, Jimmy and Mitch, Masterspy
EX $75   NM $200   MIP $275

❏ **Winnie Winkle Playstone Funnies Mold Set**, 1940s
EX $30   NM $75   MIP $150

BANK

❏ **Andy Panda Bank**, 1977, Walter Lantz, 7" tall, hard plastic
EX $12   NM $40   MIP $75

❏ **Little Lulu Bank**, 8" tall hard plastic w/black fire hydrant
EX $30   NM $75   MIP $150

❏ **Scrappy Bank**, 3" x 3-1/2" metal, embossed illustration of Scrappy and his dog
EX $75   NM $250   MIP $400

BOOK

❏ **Little Lulu Paint Book**, 1944, Whitman
EX $50   NM $125   MIP $250

DOLL

❏ **Bloom County Opus Doll**, 1986, 10" tall, plush, penguin Opus wearing a Santa Claus cap
EX $10   NM $30   MIP $50

❏ **Chilly Willy Doll**, 1982, Walter Lantz, plush
EX $7   NM $25   MIP $40

❏ **Dudley Do-Right Doll**, 1972, Wham-O, bendy
EX $15   NM $35   MIP $65

❏ **Hagar the Horrible Doll**, 1983, 12" tall
EX $12   NM $22   MIP $50

❏ **King Leonardo Doll**, 1960s, Holiday Fair, cloth plush dressed in royal robe
EX $35   NM $75   MIP $160

FIGURE

❏ **Alfred E. Neuman Figurine**, 1960s, base says "What Me Worry?"
EX $45   NM $100   MIP $200

❏ **Cadbury the Butler Figure**, 1981, DFC, 3-1/2" figure from Richie Rich
EX $7   NM $20   MIP $35

❏ **Wonder Woman Figure**, Presents, 14" tall cloth and vinyl figure on base
EX $9   NM $25   MIP $50

PUZZLE

❏ **Katzenjammer Kids Jigsaw Puzzle**, 1930s, 9-1/2" x 14", Featured Funnies
EX $50   NM $150   MIP $300

❏ **Little Lulu Puzzles**, 1973, Whitman, four frame tray puzzles
EX $25   NM $55   MIP $100

❏ **Rosie's Beau Puzzle**, 1930s, 9-1/2" x 14", Featured Funnies
EX $25   NM $75   MIP $100

❏ **Smilin' Jack Puzzle**, 1930s, 9-1/2" x 14", Featured Funnies
EX $35   NM $150   MIP $200

TOY

❏ **Breezley Soaky**, 1967, Purex, 9" tall, plastic
EX $25   NM $60   MIP $110

❏ **Henry on Trapeze Toy**, G. Borgfeldt, 6" x 9", celluloid, wind-up, jointed Henry suspended from trapeze
EX $200   NM $600   MIP $1000

❏ **Mush Mouse Pull Toy**, 1960s, Ideal, pull toy w/vinyl figure
EX $40   NM $100   MIP $180

❏ **Peter Potamus Soaky**, 11" tall
EX $20   NM $40   MIP $75

❏ **Touche Turtle Soaky**, 1960s, lying down
EX $15   NM $40   MIP $65

❏ **Touche Turtle Soaky,** 1960s, standing
EX $25   NM $60   MIP $110

❏ **Yipee Pull Toy,** 1960s, Ideal, w/vinyl figures of Yipee, Yapee and Yahooee
EX $40   NM $80   MIP $150

CASPER THE FRIENDLY GHOST

ACCESSORIES

❏ **Casper Figure Lamp,** 1950, Archlamp, 17" tall
EX $50   NM $125   MIP $200

❏ **Casper Light Shade,** 1960s
EX $35   NM $75   MIP $150

❏ **Casper Night Light,** 1975, Duncan, 6-1/2" tall
EX $15   NM $40   MIP $75

COSTUME

❏ **Casper Costume,** Collegeville, "Ghostland" costume, #216
EX $25   NM $40   MIP $85

❏ **Casper Halloween Costume,** 1960s, Collegeville, mask and costume
EX $12   NM $30   MIP $60

DOLL

❏ **Casper Doll,** 7-3/4" tall squeeze doll holds black spotted puppy
EX $25   NM $60   MIP $125

❏ **Casper Doll,** 1960s, 15" cloth
EX $25   NM $60   MIP $125

❏ **Casper Doll,** 1972, Sutton and Sons, rubber squeeze doll w/logo
EX $10   NM $20   MIP $40

❏ **Casper the Friendly Ghost Talking Doll,** 1961, Mattel, 15" tall, terry cloth, plastic head w/a pull string voice box
EX $50   NM $125   MIP $175

PUZZLE

❏ **Casper Jigsaw Puzzle,** 1988, Ja-Ru
EX $4   NM $10   MIP $20

TOY

❏ **Casper Hand Puppet,** 1960s, 8" tall, cloth and plastic head
EX $15   NM $40   MIP $85

❏ **Casper Soaky,** Colgate-Palmolive
EX $20   NM $55   MIP $85

❏ **Casper Spinning Top,** 1960s, blue top w/figure of Casper inside
EX $25   NM $60   MIP $85

❏ **Casper Wind-Up Toy,** 1950s, Linemar, tin
EX $175   NM $400   MIP $675

❏ **Wendy the Good Witch Soaky**
EX $20   NM $55   MIP $85

CHARLIE CHAPLIN

ACCESSORIES

❏ **Charlie Chaplin Pencil Case,** 8" long
EX $25   NM $75   MIP $150

❏ **Charlie Chaplin Wristwatch,** 1972, Bubbles/Cadeaux, Swiss, large chrome case, black and white dial, articulated sweep cane second hand, black leather band
EX $45   NM $100   MIP $225

❏ **Charlie Chaplin Wristwatch,** 1985, Bradley, oldies series, quartz, large black plastic case and band, sweep seconds, shows Chaplin as Little Tramp
EX $20   NM $50   MIP $100

DOLL

❏ **Charlie Chaplin Cloth Doll,** patterned fabric
EX $110   NM $225   MIP $450

❏ **Charlie Chaplin Doll,** 11-1/2" tall, wind-up
EX $300   NM $600   MIP $1200

FIGURE

❏ **Charlie Chaplin Figure,** 2-1/2" tall, lead
EX $40   NM $175   MIP $325

❏ **Charlie Chaplin Figure,** 8-1/2" tall, tin w/cast iron feet, wind-up
EX $360   NM $735   MIP $1450

TOY

❏ **Charlie Chaplin Toy,** 4" tall, spring mechanism tips his hat when string is pulled
EX $40   NM $130   MIP $275

CHARLIE'S ANGELS

ACCESSORIES

❏ **Charlie's Angels Pendant,** 1977, Fleetwood Toys, 4" plastic figure of Farrah hangs from pendant
EX $10   NM $25   MIP $45

❏ **River Race Outfits,** 1977, Palitoy
EX $15   NM $35   MIP $60

❏ **Slalom Caper Outfits,** Palitoy
EX $10   NM $25   MIP $50

(KP Photo)

❏ **Underwater Intrigue Outfits,** Palitoy
EX $10   NM $25   MIP $50

DOLL

❏ **Charlie's Angels Paper Dolls,** 1977, Toy Factory, Farrah, Kate or Jaclyn sets, each
EX $20   NM $50   MIP $90

❏ **Farrah Fawcett Doll,** 1977, Mattel, 12"
EX $50   NM $100   MIP $175

❏ **Kate Jackson Doll,** 1978, Mattel, 12"
EX $20   NM $40   MIP $85

❏ **Kelly Doll,** 1977, Hasbro, 8"
EX $12   NM $30   MIP $60

❏ **Kris Doll,** 1977, Hasbro, 8"
EX $10   NM $25   MIP $50

❏ **Sabrina Doll,** 1977, Hasbro, 8"
EX $15   NM $65   MIP $100

❏ **Sabrina, Kelly, and Kris Gift Set,** 1977, Hasbro
EX $20   NM $65   MIP $100

CHIPMUNKS

ACCESSORIES

❏ **Chipmunks Toothbrush,** 1984, battery-operated
EX $10   NM $25   MIP $45

❏ **Chipmunks Wallet,** 1959, vinyl
EX $15   NM $30   MIP $60

DOLL

❏ **Alvin Doll,** 1963, Knickerbocker, 14" tall plush w/vinyl head
EX $20   NM $50   MIP $85

TOY

❏ **Chipmunks Bean Bags,** 1998, three in set, talking
EX $20   NM $40   MIP $55

❏ **Chipmunks Soaky,** 1960s, 10" tall, Alvin, Simon, or Theodore, each
EX $10   NM $40   MIP $75

CINDERELLA

ACCESSORIES

❏ **Cinderella Alarm Clock,** Westclox, 2-1/2" x 4-1/2" x 4" tall
EX $50   NM $125   MIP $250

❏ **Cinderella Bank,** 1950s, ceramic, Cinderella holding magic wand
EX $30   NM $65   MIP $125

❏ **Cinderella Charm Bracelet,** 1950, golden brass link w/five charms, Cinderella, Fairy Godmother, slipper, pumpkin coach and Prince
EX $25   NM $50   MIP $85

❏ **Cinderella Molding Set,** 1950s, Model Craft, set of character molds in illustrated box
EX $40   NM $75   MIP $150

❏ **Cinderella Musical Jewelry Box,** mahogany music box plays "So This Is Love"
EX $15   NM $35   MIP $75

❏ **Cinderella Wristwatch,** 1950, US Time
EX $75   NM $175   MIP $400

❏ **Cinderella Wristwatch,** 1958, Timex, Cinderella and castle, pink leather band
EX $60   NM $125   MIP $250

❏ **Fairy Godmother Pitcher,** 7" tall figural pitcher
EX $22   NM $50   MIP $90

❏ **Gus/Jaq Serving Set,** 1960s, Westman, creamer, pitcher and sugar bowl
EX $50   NM $100   MIP $175

DOLL

❏ **Cinderella Doll**, 11" tall, blue stain ballgown w/white bridal gown, glass slippers, holding Little Little Golden Book
EX $20   **NM** $40   **MIP** $85

❏ **Cinderella Doll**, Horsman, 8" tall in illustrated box
EX $30   **NM** $75   **MIP** $150

❏ **Cinderella Paper Dolls**, 1965, Whitman
EX $35   **NM** $75   **MIP** $150

❏ **Gus Doll**, 1950s, Gund, 13" tall, gray doll w/dark red shirt and green felt hat
EX $55   **NM** $150   **MIP** $225

FIGURE

❏ **Cinderella Figurine**, 5" tall, plastic
EX $10   **NM** $20   **MIP** $40

❏ **Cinderella Figurine**, 5" tall, ceramic
EX $12   **NM** $40   **MIP** $90

PUZZLE

❏ **Cinderella Puzzle**, 1960s, Jaymar
EX $12   **NM** $25   **MIP** $50

TOY

❏ **Cinderella Soaky**, 1960s, 11" tall, blue
EX $15   **NM** $30   **MIP** $60

❏ **Cinderella Wind-Up Toy**, 1950, Irwin, 5" tall, Cinderella and Prince dancing
EX $50   **NM** $160   **MIP** $320

❏ **Prince Charming Hand Puppet**, 1959, Gund, 10" tall
EX $20   **NM** $45   **MIP** $90

CRUSADER RABBIT

ACCESSORIES

❏ **Crusader Rabbit Paint Set**, 1960s, 13" x 19"
EX $25   **NM** $75   **MIP** $150

BOOK

❏ **Crusader Rabbit Book**, 1958, Wonder Book
EX $15   **NM** $50   **MIP** $85

❏ **Crusader Rabbit in Bubble Trouble Book**, 1960, Whitman
EX $12   **NM** $45   **MIP** $75

❏ **Crusader Rabbit Trace and Color Book**, 1959, Whitman
EX $30   **NM** $85   **MIP** $135

TOY

❏ **Crusader Rabbit Soaky**, 1960s, Purex
EX $30   **NM** $80   **MIP** $150

DANGER MOUSE

ACCESSORIES

❏ **Danger Mouse ID Set**, 1985, Gordy
EX $7   **NM** $15   **MIP** $30

❏ **Danger Mouse Pendant Necklace**, 1986, Gordy
EX $7   **NM** $15   **MIP** $30

DOLL

❏ **Danger Mouse Doll**, 1988, Russ, 15" tall
EX $20   **NM** $50   **MIP** $90

DENNIS THE MENACE

ACCESSORIES

❏ **Dennis the Menace Giant Mischief Kit**, 1950s, Hasbro
EX $50   **NM** $110   **MIP** $210

❏ **Dennis the Menace Paint Set**, 1954, Pressman, paints, crayons, brush and trays
EX $30   **NM** $75   **MIP** $140

BOOK

❏ **Dennis the Menace and Ruff Book**, 1959, Whitman, Little Golden Book
EX $10   **NM** $18   **MIP** $40

❏ **Dennis the Menace and Ruff Book Ends**, 1974, ceramic
EX $30   **NM** $65   **MIP** $125

PUZZLE

❏ **Dennis the Menace TV Show Puzzle**, 1960, Whitman
EX $15   **NM** $30   **MIP** $60

TOY

❏ **Dennis the Menace Colorforms Set**, 1961, Colorforms
EX $15   **NM** $45   **MIP** $80

❏ **Dennis the Menace Tiddley Winks**, 1961, Whitman
EX $25   **NM** $45   **MIP** $80

DEPUTY DAWG

DOLL

❏ **Deputy Dawg Doll**, 1960s, Ideal, 14" tall, cloth w/plush arms and vinyl head
EX $25   **NM** $100   **MIP** $175

FIGURE

❏ **Deputy Dawg Figure**, 1977, Dakin, 6 " tall, plastic body w/vinyl head
EX $30   **NM** $55   **MIP** $100

TOY

❏ **Deputy Dawg Soaky**, 1966, 9-1/2" tall, plastic
EX $15   **NM** $45   **MIP** $75

DICK TRACY

ACCESSORIES

❏ **Air Detective Bracelet**, 1938
EX $300   **NM** $600   **MIP** $800

❏ **Air Detective Cap**, 1938, Quaker
EX $50   **NM** $275   **MIP** $500

❏ **Bonny Braids Store Contest Card**, 1951, 5-1/2" x 5-1/2"
EX $25   **NM** $65   **MIP** $125

❏ **Candy Box**, 1940s, Novel Package, box w/cartoons and story on back; comic strips on bottom
EX $50   **NM** $250   **MIP** $350

❏ **Christmas Tree Light Bulb**, 1930s, early painted figure of Dick Tracy
EX $40   **NM** $90   **MIP** $100

❏ **Detective Club Pin**, 1942, yellow, tab back
EX $25   **NM** $50   **MIP** $90

❏ **Dick Tracy Jr. Detective Agency Tie Clasp**, 1930s, silver or brass, each
EX $25   **NM** $60   **MIP** $125

(KP Photo)

❏ **Dick Tracy Lamp**, 1950s, painted ceramic bust of Tracy in black coat, yellow hat and red tie
EX $800   **NM** $1000   **MIP** $3250

❏ **Dick Tracy Mask**, 1933, Philadelphia Inquirer, paper
EX $100   **NM** $250   **MIP** $400

❏ **Dick Tracy Picture**, 1940s, Pillsbury, part of set of eight, each 7" x 10" in mat, shows Tracy and Junior
EX $60   **NM** $130   **MIP** $250

❏ **Dinnerware Set**, 1950s, Homer Laughlin, bowl, dinner plate, and mug
EX $70   **NM** $150   **MIP** $290

❏ **Dinnerware Set**, 1980s, Zak Designs, plate, cup, bowl
EX $10   **NM** $15   **MIP** $30

❏ **Hat**, 1940s, Miller Bros. Hat, wool fedora, blue/gray
EX $40   **NM** $100   **MIP** $175

❏ **Secret Service Patrol Bracelet**, 1938, Quaker, chain bracelet w/small head of Dick Tracy and Junior and four leaf clover
EX $70   **NM** $150   **MIP** $250

❏ **Sparkle Plenty Christmas Tree Lights**, 1940s, Mutual Equipment, seven-light set
EX $30   **NM** $65   **MIP** $125

❏ **Sparkle Plenty Christmas Tree Lights**, 1940s, Mutual Equipment, 15-light set
EX $40   **NM** $90   **MIP** $175

❏ **Super 8 Color Film**, 1965, Republic, b/w cartton "Trick or Treat"
EX $10   **NM** $25   **MIP** $50

❑ **Wall Clock,** 1990s, 16" x 20" battery power quartz, face shows Disney movie Tracy talking into wrist radio
EX $15   **NM** $20   **MIP** $40

❑ **Wallpaper Section,** 1950s, shows comic strip scenes of Tracy and seven other characters
EX $15   **NM** $40   **MIP** $75

BADGE

❑ **Air Detective Member Badge,** 1938, Quaker, brass, wing shape
EX $30   **NM** $100   **MIP** $150

❑ **Detective Club Crime Stoppers Badge,** 1940s, Guild
EX $25   **NM** $50   **MIP** $90

❑ **Dick Tracy Crime Stopper Badge,** 1960s, star shape giveaway badge from WGN "9 Official Dick Tracy Crimestopper" TV Badge
EX $30   **NM** $65   **MIP** $125

❑ **Dick Tracy Detective Club Belt Badge with belt,** premium
EX $35   **NM** $100   **MIP** $350

❑ **Secret Service Patrol Badge,** 1938, Quaker, Sergeant
EX $40   **NM** $100   **MIP** $225

❑ **Secret Service Patrol Badge,** 1938, Quaker, 2nd year chevron
EX $10   **NM** $25   **MIP** $60

❑ **Secret Service Patrol Badge,** 1938, Quaker, Lieutenant
EX $50   **NM** $185   **MIP** $350

❑ **Secret Service Patrol Badge,** 1938, Quaker, Inspector General, brass, 2-1/2"
EX $250   **NM** $600   **MIP** $900

❑ **Secret Service Patrol Badge,** 1938, Quaker, brass girl's division badge
EX $20   **NM** $50   **MIP** $100

❑ **Secret Service Patrol Badge,** 1938, Quaker, brass Captain badge
EX $75   **NM** $185   **MIP** $375

BANK

(KP Photo)

❑ **Sparkle Plenty Bank,** 1940s, Jayess, 12"tall, base features a medallion of Dick Tracy as Godfather
EX $120   **NM** $250   **MIP** $500

BOOK

❑ **Ace Detective Book,** 1943, Whitman
EX $15   **NM** $45   **MIP** $80

❑ **Adventures of Dick Tracy and Dick Tracy Jr. Book,** 1933, Whitman, 320 pages, hardcover Big Little Book
EX $150   **NM** $400   **MIP** $800

❑ **Adventures of Dick Tracy the Detective Book,** 1933, Whitman, first of Big Little Book series, hardcover
EX $350   **NM** $1000   **MIP** $1500

❑ **Booklet,** 1934, Big Thrill Chewing Gum, five different premium books, eight pages, each
EX $25   **NM** $60   **MIP** $120

❑ **Capture of Boris Arson Book, The,** 1935, Pleasure Books, pop-up book
EX $100   **NM** $350   **MIP** $600

❑ **Detective Dick Tracy and the Spider Gang Book,** 1937, Whitman, 240 pages, Big Little Book
EX $30   **NM** $75   **MIP** $150

❑ **Dick Tracy and His G-Men Book,** 1941, Whitman, 432 pages, Big Little Book, hardcover w/flip pictures
EX $30   **NM** $75   **MIP** $150

❑ **Dick Tracy and the Bicycle Gang Book,** 1948, Whitman, 288 pages, Big Little Book, hardcover
EX $25   **NM** $60   **MIP** $135

❑ **Dick Tracy and the Boris Arson Gang Book,** 1935, Whitman, 432 pages, Big Little Book, hardcover
EX $25   **NM** $70   **MIP** $145

❑ **Dick Tracy and the Hotel Murders Book,** 1937, Whitman, 432 pages, hardcover Big Little Book
EX $25   **NM** $70   **MIP** $145

❑ **Dick Tracy and the Invisible Man Book,** 1939, Whitman, Quaker premium, 132 pages, softcover Big Little Book
EX $50   **NM** $160   **MIP** $275

❑ **Dick Tracy and the Mad Killer Book,** 1947, Whitman, 288 pages, hardcover Big Little Book
EX $25   **NM** $65   **MIP** $120

❑ **Dick Tracy and the Mystery of the Purple Cross Book,** 1938, Whitman, 320 pages, Big Big Book, hardcover
EX $100   **NM** $400   **MIP** $800

❑ **Dick Tracy and the Phantom Ship Book,** 1940, Whitman, 432 pages, hardcover Big Little Book
EX $25   **NM** $60   **MIP** $135

❑ **Dick Tracy and the Racketeer Gang Book,** 1936, Whitman, 432 pages, hardcover Big Little Book
EX $25   **NM** $70   **MIP** $145

❑ **Dick Tracy and the Stolen Bonds Book,** 1934, Whitman, 320 pages, hardcover, Big Little Book
EX $25   **NM** $70   **MIP** $145

❑ **Dick Tracy and the Tiger Lilly Gang Book,** 1949, Whitman, 288 pages, hardcover Big Little Book
EX $20   **NM** $50   **MIP** $110

❑ **Dick Tracy and the Wreath Kidnapping Case Book,** 1945, Whitman, 432 pages, hardcover Big Little Book
EX $25   **NM** $60   **MIP** $120

❑ **Dick Tracy and Yogee Yamma Book,** 1946, Whitman, 352 pages, hardcover Big Little Book
EX $20   **NM** $50   **MIP** $110

❑ **Dick Tracy Encounters Facey Book,** 1967, Whitman, 260 pages, hardcover Big Little Book, cover price 39 cents
EX $10   **NM** $15   **MIP** $30

❑ **Dick Tracy From Colorado to Nova Scotia Book,** 1933, Whitman, 320 pages, hardcover Big Little Book
EX $25   **NM** $70   **MIP** $130

❑ **Dick Tracy in Chains of Crime Book,** 1936, Whitman, 432 pages, hardcover, Big Little Book
EX $25   **NM** $70   **MIP** $145

(KP Photo)

❑ **Dick Tracy Junior Detective Kit Book,** 1962, Golden Press, punchout book of Tracy tools, including badges, revolver, wrist radio
EX $25   **NM** $50   **MIP** $100

❑ **Dick Tracy Little Golden Book,** 1962, Golden Press, features characters from the TV show
EX $17   **NM** $25   **MIP** $50

❑ **Dick Tracy Meets a New Gang Book,** 1939, Whitman, Quaker premium, 132 pages, softcover Big Little Book
EX $60   **NM** $200   **MIP** $300

❑ **Dick Tracy on the High Seas Book,** 1939, Whitman, 432 pages, hardcover Big Little Book
EX $25   **NM** $70   **MIP** $150

❑ **Dick Tracy on the Trail of Larceny Lu Book,** 1935, Whitman, 432 pages, hardcover Big Little Book
EX $30   **NM** $75   **MIP** $150

CHARACTER TOYS

❑ **Dick Tracy on Voodoo Island Book,**
1944, Whitman, 352 pages, hardcover
Big Little Book
EX $22   **NM** $55   **MIP** $110

❑ **Dick Tracy Out West Book,** 1933, Whitman, 300 pages, hardcover, Big Little
Book
EX $30   **NM** $70   **MIP** $150

(KP Photo)

❑ **Dick Tracy Paint Book,** 1930s,
Saalfield, 96 pages
EX $60   **NM** $175   **MIP** $350

❑ **Dick Tracy Returns Book,** 1939, Whitman, 432 pages, hardcover Big Little
Book, Republic movie serial tie-in
EX $25   **NM** $70   **MIP** $150

❑ **Dick Tracy Solves the Penfield Mystery
Book,** 1934, Whitman, 320 pages, hardcover, Big Little Book
EX $25   **NM** $70   **MIP** $150

❑ **Dick Tracy Special FBI Operative Book,**
1943, Whitman, 432 pages, hardcover,
Big Little Book
EX $25   **NM** $55   **MIP** $120

❑ **Dick Tracy Super Detective Book,**
1941, Whitman
EX $25   **NM** $50   **MIP** $120

❑ **Dick Tracy the Man with No Face Book,**
1938, Whitman, 432 pages, hardcover,
Big Little Book
EX $25   **NM** $70   **MIP** $150

❑ **Dick Tracy the Super Detective Book,**
1939, Whitman, 432 pages, hardcover
Big Little Book
EX $25   **NM** $70   **MIP** $150

❑ **Dick Tracy vs. Crooks in Disguise
Book,** 1939, Whitman, 352 pages, hardcover, Big Little Book w/flip pictures
EX $25   **NM** $70   **MIP** $150

❑ **Dick Tracy's Ghost Ship Book,** 1939,
Whitman, Quaker premium, 132 pages,
softcover Big Little Book
EX $40   **NM** $175   **MIP** $300

❑ **Secret Code Book,** 1938, Quaker, premium
EX $35   **NM** $75   **MIP** $160

❑ **Secret Detective Methods and Magic
Tricks Book,** 1939, Quaker, cereal premium
EX $35   **NM** $100   **MIP** $225

BUTTON

❑ **Detective Button,** 1930s, celluloid pinback w/portrait, newspaper premium
EX $25   **NM** $50   **MIP** $90

❑ **Dick Tracy and Little Orphan Annie Button,** Genung Promo
EX $400   **NM** $1000   **MIP** $1800

❑ **Pep Flintheart Pin,** 1945, Kellogg's, tin
litho button
EX $10   **NM** $20   **MIP** $40

❑ **Secret Service Patrol Member Button,**
1938, Quaker, 1-1/4" blue and silver,
pinback
EX $20   **NM** $45   **MIP** $90

COMIC BOOK

❑ **Dick Tracy Comic Book,** 1947, Popped
Wheat Cereal, premium
EX $6   **NM** $10   **MIP** $20

❑ **Dick Tracy in 3-D Comic Book,** 1986,
Blackthorne, Ocean Death Trap
EX $4   **NM** $8   **MIP** $15

❑ **Motorola Presents Dick Tracy Comic
Book,** 1953, Motorola, premium comic
book w/paper mask and vest
EX $40   **NM** $80   **MIP** $150

DOLL

❑ **Bonny Braids Doll,** 1950s, 6" tall, plastic, walking wobble doll
EX $30   **NM** $75   **MIP** $150

❑ **Bonny Braids Doll,** 1951, Ideal, 14" tall
w/toothbrush
EX $90   **NM** $180   **MIP** $375

❑ **Bonny Braids Doll,** 1952, Ideal, 8" tall,
crawls when wound
EX $80   **NM** $170   **MIP** $325

❑ **Dick Tracy Doll,** 1930s, 13" tall, composition, grey trench coat w/moveable
head and mouth that operates w/back
pull string, gray or yellow coat
EX $150   **NM** $375   **MIP** $650

❑ **Little Honey Moon Doll,** 1965, Ideal,
16" space baby, bubble helmet and outfit
w/white pigtails, doll sitting on half a
moon w/stars in the background
EX $75   **NM** $170   **MIP** $350

❑ **Sparkle Plenty Doll,** 1947, Ideal, 12" tall
EX $125   **NM** $250   **MIP** $450

FIGURES

❑ **B.O. Plenty Figure,** 1950s, Marx,
Famous Comic Figures series, waxy
cream, pink, 60mm tall
EX $20   **NM** $40   **MIP** $65

❑ **Blank Figure, The,** 1990, Playmates,
figure w/gun and hat w/featureless face
attached
EX $60   **NM** $100   **MIP** $150

❑ **Breathless Mahoney Figure,** 1990,
Applause, 14" tall
EX $5   **NM** $10   **MIP** $20

❑ **Dick Tracy Figure,** 1940s, Professional
Art, 7" unpainted, detailed white chalk
figure or painted
EX $80   **NM** $175   **MIP** $375

❑ **Dick Tracy Figures,** 1950s, Marx,
Famous Comic Figures series, several
characters, each
EX $40   **NM** $75   **MIP** $150

❑ **Dick Tracy Nodder,** 1960s, 6-1/2" tall,
ceramic nodding head bust
EX $230   **NM** $650   **MIP** $1200

❑ **Gravel Gertie Figure,** 1950s, Marx,
Famous Comic Figures series
EX $10   **NM** $15   **MIP** $30

❑ **Sparkle Plenty Figure,** 1950s, Marx,
Famous Comic Figures series
EX $10   **NM** $15   **MIP** $40

❑ **Steve the Tramp Figure,** 1990, Playmates, discontinued
EX $5   **NM** $20   **MIP** $40

GAME

❑ **Dick Tracy Bingo, Lock Them Up in Jail
and Harmonize with Tracy Game,**
1940s, object of each is to roll BBs into
different holes on the face of a glass
framed game card for points
EX $45   **NM** $90   **MIP** $160

❑ **Dick Tracy Crime Stopper Game,** 1963,
Ideal, workstation contains crime indicator dial, decoder knobs, criminal buttons, clue cards and holders and clue
windows
EX $40   **NM** $90   **MIP** $180

❑ **Dick Tracy Pinball Game,** 1967, Marx,
14 x 24", shows characters from TV
show pilot
EX $40   **NM** $90   **MIP** $175

❑ **Dick Tracy Pop-Pop Game,** 1980s, Ja-Ru, Diet Smith and Flattop are targets
EX $10   **NM** $15   **MIP** $25

GUN

❑ **45 Special Water Handgun,** 1950s,
Tops Plastics, plastic
EX $30   **NM** $90   **MIP** $125

❑ **Automatic Target Range Gun,** 1967,
Marx, BB gun mounted in an enclosed
plastic shooting gallery
EX $55   **NM** $110   **MIP** $250

❑ **Dick Tracy Jr. Click Pistol #78,** 1930s,
Marx, aluminum
EX $50   **NM** $150   **MIP** $300

❑ **Luger Water Gun,** 1971, Larami
EX $15   **NM** $35   **MIP** $75

❑ **Pop Gun,** 1944, Tip Top Bread, 7-1/2" x
4-1/2" paper pop gun, premium
EX $35   **NM** $100   **MIP** $185

(KP Photo)

❑ **Power Jet Squad Gun,** 1962, Mattel, 29"
long cap and water rifle
EX $45   **NM** $100   **MIP** $210

❑ **Rapid Fire Tommy Gun,** 1940s, Parker
Johns, 20" long tommy gun w/Tracy on
stock
EX $75   **NM** $300   **MIP** $500

❑ **Siren Pistol,** 1930s, Marx, pressed steel, 8-1/2" long
EX $100   NM $300   MIP $500

❑ **Sub-Machine Gun,** 1950s, Tops Plastics, 12" long, red, green or blue, water gun "holds over 500 shots on one filling," Dick Tracy decal on magazine
EX $75   NM $150   MIP $300

PIN

❑ **Bonny Braids Pin,** 1951, Charmore, 1-1/4" figure plastic pin on full color card
EX $20   NM $60   MIP $100

❑ **Pep B.O. Plenty Pin,** 1945, Kellogg's, tin litho button
EX $20   NM $30   MIP $50

❑ **Pep Chief Brandon Pin,** 1945, Kellogg's, tin litho button
EX $10   NM $15   MIP $30

❑ **Pep Dick Tracy Pin,** 1945, Kellogg's, tin litho button
EX $25   NM $45   MIP $80

❑ **Pep Flattop Pin,** 1945, Kellogg's, tin litho button
EX $20   NM $35   MIP $60

❑ **Pep Gravel Gertie Pin,** 1945, Kellogg's, tin litho button
EX $20   NM $35   MIP $50

❑ **Pep Junior Tracy Pin,** 1945, Kellogg's, tin litho button
EX $10   NM $20   MIP $40

❑ **Pep Pat Patten Pin,** 1945, Kellogg's, tin litho button
EX $10   NM $20   MIP $35

❑ **Pep Tess Trueheart Pin,** 1945, Kellogg's, tin litho button
EX $12   NM $20   MIP $35

❑ **Secret Service Patrol Leader Pin,** 1938, Quaker, litho bar pin, Patrol Leader, rare
EX $450   NM $1200   MIP $1650

RECORD

❑ **Dick Tracy Original Radio Broadcast Album,** 1972, Coca-Cola, presents the cast from "The Case of the Firebug Murders" radio show
EX $20   NM $60   MIP $100

❑ **Flattop Story Double Record Set,** 1947, Mercury Records, record, book, comics
EX $55   NM $125   MIP $225

RING

❑ **Dick Tracy Monogram Ring,** 1938, Quaker, ring shows initials only, no Tracy name or picture
EX $150   NM $500   MIP $800

❑ **Dick Tracy Ring,** 1940s, Miller Bros. Hat, enameled portrait
EX $50   NM $100   MIP $200

❑ **Dick Tracy Service Patrol Ring,** 1966, premium
EX $20   NM $40   MIP $60

❑ **Secret Compartment Ring,** 1938, Quaker, removable cover picturing Tracy and good luck symbols
EX $90   NM $200   MIP $300

TOY

❑ **Auto Magic Picture Gun,** 1950s, 6-1/2" x 9" metal picture gun and filmstrip
EX $30   NM $75   MIP $150

(KP Photo)

❑ **Automatic Police Station,** 1950s, Marx, tin litho police station and car
EX $250   NM $750   MIP $1500
(Scott Smiles)

❑ **B.O. Plenty Walker,** 1940s, Marx, holds Sparkle Plenty
EX $175   NM $300   MIP $475

❑ **B.O. Plenty Wind-Up,** 1940s, Marx, 8-1/2" tall holding baby Sparkle, litho tin, walks, hat tips up and down when key is wound
EX $120   NM $250   MIP $500

(KP Photo)

❑ **Baby Sparkle Plenty Paper Dolls,** 1948, Saalfield, #1510, on cover, Baby Sparkle is standing by a clothes line
EX $22   NM $65   MIP $125

(KP Photo)

❑ **Baking Set,** 1937, Pillsbury, cookie cutter, six press-out sheets w/pictures of Dick Tracy and his pals
EX $50   NM $100   MIP $200

❑ **Big Boy Figure,** 1990, Playmates
EX $6   NM $12   MIP $25

❑ **Black Light Magic Kit,** 1952, Stroward, ultra-violet bulb, cloth, invisible pen, brushes and fluorescent dyes
EX $50   NM $100   MIP $200

(KP Photo)

❑ **Bonny Braids Paper Dolls,** 1951, Saalfield, #1559, Dick Tracy's new daughter and Tess
EX $25   NM $80   MIP $150

❑ **Bonny Braids Stroll Toy,** 1951, Charmore, tin litho, Bonny doll in carriage
EX $35   NM $80   MIP $160

❑ **Camera Dart Gun,** 1971, Larami, 8mm camera-shaped toy w/dart-shooting viewer
EX $30   NM $60   MIP $125

❑ **Coloring Set,** 1967, Hasbro, six pre-sketched, numbered pictures to color, w/pencils
EX $30   NM $65   MIP $110

❑ **Crimestopper Club Kit,** 1961, Chicago Tribune, premium kit containing badge, whistle, decoder, magnifying glass, fingerprinting kit, ID card, crimestopper textbook
EX $35   NM $60   MIP $100

(KP Photo)

❑ **Crimestopper Play Set,** 1970s, Hubley, Dick Tracy cap gun, holster, handcuffs, wallet, flashlight, badge and magnifying glass
EX $35   NM $70   MIP $50

❑ **Crimestoppers Set,** 1973, Larami, handcuffs, nightstick and badge
EX $12   NM $25   MIP $50

❑ **Decoder Card,** Post Cereal, cereal premium, red or green
EX $20   NM $50   MIP $100

❑ **Detective Club Belt,** 1937, leather w/secret pouch
EX $75   NM $225   MIP $400

❑ **Detective Kit,** 1944, Dick Tracy Junior Detective Manual, Secret Decoder, ruler, Certificate of Membership and badge
EX $175   NM $500   MIP $800

CHARACTER TOYS

❏ **Dick Tracy Braces**, 1940s, Deluxe, Chicago Tribune premium, suspenders on colorful card
  EX $25   NM $90   MIP $185

(KP Photo)

❏ **Dick Tracy Braces for Smart Boys and Girls**, 1950s, Deluxe, Police badge, metal handcuffs, whistle, suspenders w/a Dick Tracy badge as a holder and magnifying glass
  EX $35   NM $80   MIP $175

(KP Photo)

❏ **Dick Tracy Candid Camera**, 1950s, Seymour Sales, w/50mm lens, plastic carrying case and 127 film
  EX $45   NM $85   MIP $175

❏ **Dick Tracy Cartoon Kit**, 1962, Colorforms
  EX $20   NM $45   MIP $85

❏ **Dick Tracy Crime Lab**, 1980s, Ja-Ru, click pistol, fingerprint pad, badge and magnifying glass, available in orange and bright yellow
  EX $8   NM $15   MIP $30

❏ **Dick Tracy Crime Stoppers Laboratory**, 1955, Porter Chemical, 60 power microscope, fingerprint pack, glass slides and magnifying glass and textbook
  EX $100   NM $225   MIP $400

❏ **Dick Tracy Detective Club Wrist Radios**, 1945, Gaylord
  EX $85   NM $180   MIP $375

(KP Photo)

❏ **Dick Tracy Detective Set**, 1930s, Pressman, color graphics of Junior and Dick Tracy, ink roller, glass plate, and Dick Tracy fingerprint record paper
  EX $85   NM $170   MIP $350

❏ **Dick Tracy Figure**, Lakeside, bendy
  EX $15   NM $30   MIP $50

❏ **Dick Tracy Hand Puppet**, 1961, Ideal, 10-1/2", fabric and vinyl, w/record
  EX $35   NM $80   MIP $150

❏ **Dick Tracy Jr. Bombsight**, 1940s, Miller Bros. Hat, cardboard
  EX $40   NM $70   MIP $175

❏ **Dick Tracy Play Set**, 1973, Ideal, contains 18 cardboard figures that measure 3-1/2" to 5" tall, w/carrying case
  EX $50   NM $120   MIP $225

❏ **Dick Tracy Play Set**, 1982, Placo, plastic dart gun, targets of different villians and a set of handcuffs
  EX $10   NM $30   MIP $50

❏ **Dick Tracy Puzzle**, 1952, 11"x14" frame tray
  EX $25   NM $75   MIP $125

❏ **Dick Tracy Soaky**, 1965, Colgate-Palmolive, 10" tall
  EX $25   NM $60   MIP $100

❏ **Dick Tracy Sparkle Paints**, 1963, Kenner, paints, brushes and six pictures to paint
  EX $25   NM $50   MIP $100

❏ **Dick Tracy Target**, 1941, Marx, 10" square tin litho w/"Recovery" and "Rescuing" points on front and bullseye target on back
  EX $50   NM $150   MIP $300
  (CT012)

❏ **Dick Tracy Target Game**, 1940s, Marx, 17" circular cardboard target, w/dart gun and box
  EX $100   NM $275   MIP $500

❏ **Dick Tracy Target Set**, 1969, Larami, red, green or blue; shoots rubber bands
  EX $15   NM $35   MIP $75

❏ **Dick Tracy's Two-in-One Mystery Puzzle**, 1958, Jaymar, one puzzle shows the crime and the other the solution
  EX $30   NM $60   MIP $120

❏ **Famous Funnies Deluxe Printing Set**, 1930s, 14 stamps, paper and stamp pad, in illustrated box
  EX $45   NM $100   MIP $200

❏ **Favorite Funnies Printing Set**, 1935, Stampercraft, features Tracy and other cartoon characters
  EX $35   NM $852   MIP $160

❏ **Film Strip Viewer**, 1948, Acme, viewer and two films in colorful illustrated box
  EX $45   NM $90   MIP $185

(KP Photo)

❏ **Film Strip Viewer**, 1964, Acme, viewer w/two boxes of film, on card, jumbo movie style
  EX $20   NM $45   MIP $85

❏ **Film Viewer**, 1973, Larami, mini color televiewer w/two paper filmstrips
  EX $10   NM $20   MIP $45

❏ **Fingerprint Set**, 1933, Pressman, microscope, fingerprint pad, magnifying glass and badge
  EX $100   NM $250   MIP $450

❏ **Flashlight**, 1939, Quaker, red, green, and black; bullet shaped w/shield tag, pocket size
  EX $60   NM $150   MIP $300

❏ **Flashlight**, 1939, Quaker, 3" pen light, black
  EX $50   NM $110   MIP $200

❏ **Flashlight**, 1961, Bantam Lite, metal wrist light
  EX $25   NM $55   MIP $150

❏ **Handcuffs**, 1946, John Henry, metal toy handcuffs on display header card
  EX $25   NM $55   MIP $110

❏ **Hemlock Holmes Hand Puppet**, 1961, Ideal, includes record
  EX $40   NM $90   MIP $175

❏ **Hingees "Dick Tracy and his Friends to Life" Punch-outs**, 1944, Reed and Associates, 6-1/2" tall figures, Tess Trueheart, Chief Brandon, Junior, Pat Patton and Tracy
  EX $25   NM $60   MIP $115

❏ **Joe Jitsu Hand Puppet**, 1961, Ideal, 10-1/2", fabric and vinyl, includes record
  EX $45   NM $150   MIP $225

❏ **Junior Detective Kit**, 1944, Sweets Company, certificate, secret code dial, wall chart, file cards and tape measure
  EX $70   NM $200   MIP $425

❏ **Junior Dick Tracy Crime Detection Folio**, 1942, radio premium, contained detective's notebook, decoder w/three mystery sheets, and puzzle
  EX $70   NM $200   MIP $425

❏ **Mobile Commander**, 1973, Larami, toy telephone w/plastic connecting tube, plastic gun and badge
  EX $20   NM $40   MIP $85

❏ **Offical Holster Outfit**, 1940s, Classy Products, leather holster w/painted Tracy profile
  EX $60   NM $250   MIP $400

❏ **Playstone Funnies Kasting Kit**, 1930s, Allied, molds for casting figures of Tracy and other characters
EX $40 NM $80 MIP $35

❏ **Police Whistle No. 64**, Marx, tin
EX $20 NM $40 MIP $80

❏ **Puzzle, "Dick Tracy's New Daughter"**, 1951, Saalfield, tray puzzle of Bonny Braids
EX $22 NM $65 MIP $125

❏ **Puzzle, "The Bank Holdup"**, 1960s, Jaymar, triple-thick interlocking pieces featuring the TV cartoon
EX $20 NM $65 MIP $110

❏ **Puzzles, Dick Tracy Big Little Book Picture Puzzles**, 1938, Whitman, 8" x 10" x 2" contains two puzzles of BLB scenes
EX $55 NM $200 MIP $400

❏ **Secret Code Writer and Pencil**, 1939
EX $50 NM $150 MIP $275

❏ **Secret Detector Kit**, 1938, Quaker, Secret Formula Q-11 and negatives
EX $100 NM $325 MIP $600

❏ **Secret Service Phones**, 1938, Quaker, cardboard phones, walkie talkie type
EX $75 NM $200 MIP $340

❏ **Shoulder Holster Set**, 1950s, J. Hapern, leather holster w/Dick Tracy's profile
EX $45 NM $90 MIP $185

❏ **Sparkle Plenty Islander Ukette**, 1950, Styron, musical instrument, junior size, w/instruction book
EX $60 NM $130 MIP $275
(Lloyd W. Ralston Auctions)

❏ **Sparkle Plenty Washing Machine**, 1940s, Kalon Radio, 12" tall tin litho, pictured outside on tub is Gravel Gertie doing the wash as B.O. Plenty holds baby Sparkle
EX $70 NM $175 MIP $350

❏ **Talking Phone**, 1967, Marx, green w/ivory handle, battery-operated w/10 different phrases
EX $35 NM $75 MIP $125

❏ **Transistor Radio Receivers**, 1961, American Doll and Toy, shoulder holster and secret ear plug w/two transistor radio receivers
EX $40 NM $80 MIP $160

(KP Photo)

❏ **Two-Way Electronic Wrist Radios**, 1950s, Remco, 2-1/2" x 9 1/2" x 13-1/2", plastic battery-operated wrist radios
EX $60 NM $125 MIP $250

❏ **Two-Way Wrist Radios**, 1960s, American Doll and Toy, plastic w/power pack, battery-operated
EX $50 NM $100 MIP $185

❏ **Two-Way Wrist Radios**, 1990, Ertl, battery-operated
EX $15 NM $20 MIP $30

❏ **Wrist Band AM Radio**, 1976, Creative Creations, w/earphone and two mercury batteries; box shows Tracy and Flattop
EX $30 NM $65 MIP $135

(KP Photo)

❏ **Wrist Radio**, 1947, Da-Myco Products, crystal set w/receiver on a leather band, 30" wires and connectors for aerial and ground, no batteries, no tubes and no electric
EX $160 NM $325 MIP $650

❏ **Wrist TV**, 1980s, Ja-Ru, paper roll of cartoon strips are threaded through the TV viewer
EX $10 NM $20 MIP $40

VEHICLE

(KP Photo)

❏ **Convertible Squad Car**, 1948, Marx, 20", friction power w/flashing lights
EX $125 NM $350 MIP $800

❏ **Copmobile**, 1963, Ideal, 24" long, white and blue plastic, battery-operated w/a microphone w/amplified speaker on top
EX $55 NM $120 MIP $200

❏ **Dick Tracy Car**, 1950s, Marx, 6-1/2" long, light blue w/machine gun pointing out of the front window
EX $100 NM $275 MIP $450

❏ **Get Away Car**, 1990, Playmates
EX $15 NM $25 MIP $50

(KP Photo)

❏ **Space Coupe**, 1968, Aurora, assembly required, all plastic
EX $100 NM $275 MIP $600

WATCH

❏ **Dick Tracy Two-Way Wristwatch**, 1990, Playmates, watch w/no radio function
EX $4 NM $7 MIP $20

❏ **Dick Tracy Wristwatch**, 1937, New Haven, oblong, round, or square face, in box
EX $150 NM $450 MIP $900

❏ **Dick Tracy Wristwatch**, 1959, Bradley
EX $50 NM $100 MIP $210

❏ **Dick Tracy Wristwatch**, 1981, Omni, digital; police car box
EX $15 NM $40 MIP $90

❏ **Dick Tracy Wristwatch with Animated Gun**, 1951, New Haven
EX $90 NM $300 MIP $500

DISNEY

ACCESSORIES

❏ **Disney Figure Golf Balls**, set of twelve
EX $12 NM $23 MIP $35

❏ **Disney Filmstrips**, 1940s, Craftman's Guild, 13 color filmstrips
EX $95 NM $180 MIP $275

❏ **Disney Tin Tray**, Ohio Art, 8" x 10", pictures Mickey and Minnie Mouse, Goofy, Horace, Pluto, Donald Duck and Clarabelle
EX $25 NM $50 MIP $75

❏ **Disney World Globe**, 1950s, Rand McNally, 6-1/2" metal base, 8" diameter w/Disney characters
EX $50 NM $100 MIP $200

❏ **Disneyland Ashtray**, 1950s, 5" diameter, china, w/Tinker Bell and castle
EX $20 NM $65 MIP $150

❏ **Disneyland Electric Light**, 1950s, Econlite, picture of Disney characters leaving a bus on a drum base
EX $45 NM $80 MIP $235

❏ **Disneyland Felt Banner**, 1960s, Disney, "The Magic Kingdom," 24-1/2" red/white/blue coat of arms
EX $25 NM $60 MIP $85

(KP Photo)

❏ **Disneyland Give-A-Show Projector Color Slides**, 1960s, 112 color slides
EX $60 NM $115 MIP $200

❏ **Disneyland Metal Craft Tapping Set**, 1950s, Pressman
EX $25 NM $40 MIP $100

❏ **Disneyland Miniature License Plates**, 1966, Marx, 2" x 4" plates w/Mickey, Minnie and Pluto, or Snow White, Donald and Goofy, each
EX $12 NM $23 MIP $35

CHARACTER TOYS

❏ **Disneyland Pen,** 1960s, 6" long w/a picture of a floating riverboat
EX $15   NM $25   MIP $40

❏ **Duck Tales Travel Tote,** 1980s, travel agency premium
EX $5   NM $20   MIP $35

❏ **Fantasia Bowl,** 1940, Vernon Kilns, 12" diameter and 2-1/2" tall, pink bowl w/a winged nymph from Fantasia
EX $135   NM $275   MIP $450

❏ **Fantasia Cup and Saucer Set,** 1940, Vernon Kilns, 6-1/4" diameter saucer and 2" tall cup
EX $70   NM $140   MIP $225

❏ **Fantasia Musical Jewelry Box,** 1990, Schmid Bros., box features Mickey and plays "The Sorcerer's Apprentice"
EX $30   NM $55   MIP $85

❏ **Figural Light Switch Plates,** Monogram, hand-painted switch plates: Goofy, Donald, Mickey, on card, each
EX $6   NM $12   MIP $25

❏ **Happy Birthday/Pepsi Placemats,** 1978, Pepsi, set of four mats
EX $10   NM $25   MIP $50

❏ **Lap Trays,** 1960s, Hasko, set of four: Donald, Goofy and Pluto, Peter Pan, and the Seven Dwarfs
EX $35   NM $65   MIP $150

❏ **Silly Symphony Lights,** Noma, set of eight
EX $55   NM $100   MIP $350

BANK

❏ **Color Television Bank,** 1950s, Linemar, 4" x 4-1/2", tin, Mickey or Donald on side panels, litho screen rotates
EX $200   NM $400   MIP $600

❏ **Disneyland Haunted House Bank,** 1960s, Japanese
EX $35   NM $65   MIP $225

❏ **Second National Duck Bank,** Chein, 3-1/2" tall x 7" long
EX $100   NM $175   MIP $375

BOOK

❏ **Robin Hood of the Range Better Little Book,** 1942, Whitman
EX $10   NM $40   MIP $75

❏ **Toby Tyler Circus Playbook,** 1959, Whitman, punch-out character activity book
EX $25   NM $50   MIP $80

❏ **Walt Disney's Clock Cleaners Book,** 1938, Whitman, linen-like illustrated book
EX $60   NM $175   MIP $250

FIGURE

❏ **Fantasia Figure,** Vernon Kilns, half-woman, half-zebra centaur
EX $85   NM $180   MIP $400

FIGURES

❏ **Aristocats Thomas O'Malley Figure,** 1967, Enesco, 8" tall ceramic
EX $30   NM $65   MIP $125

❏ **Fantasia Unicorn Figure,** 1940s, Vernon Kilns, ceramic black-winged unicorn
EX $50   NM $110   MIP $230

❏ **Johnny Tremain Figure and Horse,** 1957, Marx, plastic, 9-1/2" tall horse and 5-1/2" tall Johnny
EX $60   NM $120   MIP $200

❏ **Jose Carioca Figure,** Marx, 2" tall, plastic
EX $30   NM $55   MIP $50

❏ **Jose Carioca Figure,** 1960s, Marx, 5-1/2" tall plastic, wire arms and legs
EX $50   NM $95   MIP $175

GAME

❏ **Disneyland Bagatelle,** 1970s, Wolverine, large game w/Disneyland graphics
EX $15   NM $25   MIP $100

❏ **Walt Disney's Game/Parade/Academy Award Winners,** American Toy Works, 15 games for all ages
EX $60   NM $120   MIP $185

PUZZLE

❏ **Black Hole Puzzle,** 1979, Whitman, jig-saw puzzle, V.I.N.C.E.N.T. or Cygnus
EX $8   NM $25   MIP $60

❏ **Disney "Sea Scouts" Puzzle,** 1930s, Williams Ellis
EX $30   NM $150   MIP $200

❏ **Disneyland Puzzle,** 1956, Whitman, frame tray
EX $15   NM $50   MIP $90

TOY

❏ **Carousel,** Linemar, 7" tall w/3" figures, wind-up
EX $150   NM $300   MIP $500

❏ **Casey Jr. Disneyland Express Train,** 1950s, Marx, 12" long, tin, wind-up
EX $80   NM $275   MIP $475

❏ **Character Molding and Coloring Set,** 1950s, red rubber molds of Bambi, Thumper, Dumbo, Goofy, Flower and Jose Carioca to make plaster figures
EX $35   NM $75   MIP $150

❏ **Disney Rattle,** 1930s, Noma, 4" tall w/Mickey and Minnie, Donald and Pluto carrying a Christmas tree
EX $60   NM $150   MIP $300

❏ **Disney Shooting Gallery,** 1950s, Welso Toys, 8" x 12" x 1-1/2" tin target w/molded figures of Mickey, Donald, Goofy and Pluto
EX $70   NM $135   MIP $275

❏ **Disney Treasure Chest Set,** 1940s, Craftman's Guild, red plastic film viewer and filmstrips in blue box designed like a chest
EX $65   NM $135   MIP $200

❏ **Disneyland Auto Magic Picture Gun and Theater,** 1950s, battery-operated metal gun w/oval filmstrip
EX $50   NM $90   MIP $150

❏ **Disneyland F.D. Fire Truck,** Linemar, 18" long, battery-operated, moveable, Donald Duck fireman climbs the ladder
EX $70   NM $175   MIP $325

❏ **Early Settlers Log Set,** 1960s, Halsam, log building set based on Disneyland's Tom Sawyer's Island
EX $25   NM $50   MIP $150

❏ **Horace Horsecollar Hand Puppet,** 1950s, Gund
EX $25   NM $65   MIP $140

❏ **Jose Carioca Wind-Up Toy,** 1940s, France, 3-1/2" x 5" x 7-1/2" tall
EX $100   NM $250   MIP $425

❏ **Nautilus Expanding Periscope,** 1954, Pressman, inspired by 20,000 Leagues Under the Sea, 19" long
EX $50   NM $160   MIP $250

(KP Photo)

❏ **Nautilus Wind-Up Submarine,** 1950s, Sutcliffe/England
EX $85   NM $175   MIP $375

❏ **Official Santa Fe and Disneyland R.R. Scale Model Train,** 1966, Tyco, HO scale, electric
EX $160   NM $300   MIP $525

❏ **Pecos Bill Wind-Up Toy,** 1950s, Marx, 10" tall, riding his horse Widowmaker and holding a metal lasso
EX $40   NM $120   MIP $275

❏ **Sand Pail and Shovel,** 1930s, Ohio Art, features pie-eyed Mickey selling cold drinks to Pluto, Minnie and Clarabelle
EX $35   NM $110   MIP $275

❏ **Walt Disney Movie Viewer and Cartridge,** 1972, Action Films, #9312 w/the cartridge "Lonesome Ghosts"
EX $9   NM $16   MIP $30

❏ **Walt Disney's Character Scramble,** 1940s, Plane Facts, 10 cardboard figures, 6" tall
EX $25   NM $70   MIP $175

❏ **Walt Disney's Realistic Noah's Ark,** 1940s, W.H. Greene, 6" x 7" x 18" Ark, 101 2" animals, and 4" human figures on cardboard
EX $130   NM $350   MIP $650

❏ **Walt Disney's Silly Symphony Bells,** Noma, Christmas tree bells
EX $40   NM $100   MIP $250

❏ **Walt Disney's Snap-Eeze Set,** 1963, Marx, 12-1/2" x 15" x 1" box w/12 flat plastic figures
EX $60   NM $115   MIP $275

❏ **Walt Disney's Television Car,** Marx, 8" long, friction toy lights up a picture on the roof when motor turns
EX $200   NM $650   MIP $1000

DOC SAVAGE

ACCESSORIES

- **Club Card,** 1930s
  EX $50   NM $75   MIP $150

- **Club Kit,** 1975, comics premium; includes card, button and mailer
  EX $10   NM $40   MIP $85

- **Club Mailer for Pin,** 1930s
  EX $100   NM $175   MIP $250

- **Club Pin,** 1930s, Pulp premium, brass
  EX $100   NM $225   MIP $375

- **Medal of Honor Award,** 1930s, brass
  EX $1100   NM $3600   MIP $5500

DONALD DUCK

ACCESSORIES

- **Donald Duck Alarm Clock,** 1950s, Glen Clock/Scotland, 5-1/2" x 5-1/2" x 2", Donald pictured w/blue bird on his hand
  EX $100   NM $275   MIP $600

- **Donald Duck Alarm Clock,** 1960s, Bayard, 2" x 4-1/2" x 5"
  EX $90   NM $275   MIP $575

- **Donald Duck Lamp,** 1940s, 9" tall, china, Donald holding an axe standing next to a tree trunk
  EX $80   NM $175   MIP $300

- **Donald Duck Lamp,** 1970s, Dolly Toy, Donald on a tug boat
  EX $50   NM $125   MIP $200

- **Donald Duck Light Switch Cover,** 1976, Dolly Toy, plastic, Donald on a boat
  EX $5   NM $10   MIP $15

- **Donald Duck Music Box,** 1971, Anri, Donald w/guitar, plays "My Way"
  EX $40   NM $80   MIP $160

- **Donald Duck Pinback,** 1930s, Wanna Fight movie premium
  EX $150   NM $650   MIP $850

- **Donald Duck Pinback,** 1935, Jackets premium, cello
  EX $150   NM $650   MIP $850

- **Donald Duck Soap,** Disney, figural castile soap
  EX $40   NM $70   MIP $110

- **Donald Duck Toothbrush Holder,** 1930s, bisque, figural
  EX $200   NM $450   MIP $700

- **Donald Duck Umbrella Handle,** 1930s, 3-1/4" tall
  EX $40   NM $100   MIP $200

- **Donald Duck WWI Pencil Box,** Dixon, 5" x 8-1/2" x 1-1/4" deep, Donald flying a plane, holding a tomahawk
  EX $40   NM $100   MIP $200

- **Ludwig Von Drake Wonderful World of Color Pencil Box,** 1961, Hasbro, box shows Ludwig and the nephews
  EX $25   NM $55   MIP $85

- **Uncle Scrooge Wallet,** 1970s, 3" x 4", Uncle Scrooge tossing coins
  EX $20   NM $40   MIP $85

BANK

- **Donald Duck Bank,** 1938, Crown Toy, 6" tall, composition, movable head
  EX $65   NM $200   MIP $500

- **Donald Duck Bank,** 1940s, 5-1/2" x 6" x 7-1/2" tall, china, Donald seated holding a coin in one hand
  EX $75   NM $175   MIP $300

- **Donald Duck Bank,** 1940s, 4-1/2" x 4-1/2" x 6-1/2" tall, ceramic, Donald holding a rope w/a large brown fish by his side
  EX $50   NM $75   MIP $250

- **Donald Duck Telephone Bank,** 1938, N.N. Hill Brass, 5" tall w/cardboard figure
  EX $75   NM $200   MIP $350

DOLL

- **Donald Duck Doll,** 1938, Knickerbocker, 17" tall, red jacket, black plush hat, Donald as drum major
  EX $100   NM $650   MIP $1250

- **Donald Duck Doll,** 1976, Mattel, talking doll
  EX $30   NM $175   MIP $375

- **Huey, Dewey and Louie Dolls,** 1950s, Gund, set of three 8" tall dolls
  EX $65   NM $125   MIP $350

- **Louie Doll,** 1940s, Gund, 8" tall, white/light green plush
  EX $40   NM $70   MIP $115

FIGURES

- **Donald Duck Figure,** Seiberling, 6" tall, hollow rubber w/squeaker in the base
  EX $100   NM $260   MIP $400

- **Donald Duck Figure,** Seiberling, 6" tall, solid rubber w/movable head
  EX $100   NM $260   MIP $400

- **Donald Duck Figure,** Seiberling, 5" tall, rubber
  EX $80   NM $210   MIP $350

- **Donald Duck Figure,** 1930s, Japanese, celluloid, long-billed Donald
  EX $100   NM $250   MIP $600

- **Donald Duck Figure,** 1950s, Dell, 7" tall, rubber
  EX $50   NM $110   MIP $250

- **Donald Duck Fun-E-Flex Figure,** 1930s, Fun-E-Flex, wooden Donald on red sled w/rope
  EX $50   NM $150   MIP $400

- **Donald Duck Nodder,** 1960s, 5-1/2" tall on green base
  EX $50   NM $125   MIP $200

- **Ludwig Von Drake Figure,** 1961, Marx, 3" tall, from the "Snap-Eeze" collection
  EX $10   NM $20   MIP $40

TOY

- **Carpet Sweeper,** 1930s, Ohio Art, 3" w/wooden handle, Donald Duck and Minnie Mouse
  EX $50   NM $125   MIP $250

- **Crayon Box,** 1946, Transogram, tin, pictures Donald and Mickey
  EX $30   NM $55   MIP $150

- **Donald,** 1930s, Fisher Price, Toy with Donna Duul
  EX $500   NM $2000   MIP $3500

- **Donald Duck and Pluto Car,** Sun Rubber, 6-1/2" long, hard rubber
  EX $50   NM $125   MIP $325

- **Donald Duck Bicycle,** 1949, Shelby
  EX $1000   NM $4500   MIP $9000

- **Donald Duck Camera,** 1950s, Herbert-George, 3" x 4" x 3"
  EX $40   NM $125   MIP $275

- **Donald Duck Car,** 1950s, Sun Rubber, 2-1/2" x 3-1/2" x 6-1/2", rubber
  EX $40   NM $110   MIP $325

- **Donald Duck Driving Pluto Toy,** 9" long, wind-up, celluloid
  EX $300   NM $750   MIP $1500

- **Donald Duck Dump Truck,** 1950s, Linemar
  EX $80   NM $150   MIP $500

- **Donald Duck Funee Movie Set,** 1940, Transogram, box features Donald, Mickey, and the nephews
  EX $50   NM $175   MIP $275

- **Donald Duck Funee Movie Set,** 1949, Irwin, hand-crank viewer and four films in box
  EX $85   NM $150   MIP $250

- **Donald Duck Marionette,** 1950s, Peter Puppet, 6-1/2" tall
  EX $50   NM $150   MIP $250

- **Donald Duck Paint Box,** 1938, Transogram
  EX $40   NM $120   MIP $275

- **Donald Duck Projector,** 1950s, Stephens, projector w/four films
  EX $55   NM $125   MIP $250

- **Donald Duck Puppet,** 1960s, Pelham Puppets, 10" tall, hollow composition
  EX $40   NM $75   MIP $200

- **Donald Duck Push Puppet,** 1950s, Kohner, sailor Donald
  EX $30   NM $100   MIP $160

- **Donald Duck Push Toy,** 1950s, Gong Bell
  EX $35   NM $60   MIP $100

- **Donald Duck Puzzle,** 1940s, Jaymar, frame tray
  EX $12   NM $60   MIP $100

- **Donald Duck Ramp Walker,** 1950s, Marx, 1-1/4" x 3-1/2" x 3" tall, Donald is pulling red wagon w/his nephews
  EX $110   NM $175   MIP $325

CHARACTER TOYS

❑ **Donald Duck Sand Pail,** 1939, Ohio Art, 4-1/2" tall, tin, Donald at beach playing tug-of-war w/his two nephews
EX $60   **NM** $120   **MIP** $225

❑ **Donald Duck Sand Pail,** 1950s, Ohio Art, 3-1/2" tall, tin, Donald in life pre-server fighting off seagulls
EX $40   **NM** $80   **MIP** $225

❑ **Donald Duck Scooter,** 1960s, Marx, tin wind-up, 4" x 4" x 2"
EX $90   **NM** $175   **MIP** $275

❑ **Donald Duck Skating Rink Toy,** 1950s, Mettoy, 4" diameter, Donald is skating while other Disney characters circle the rink
EX $40   **NM** $70   **MIP** $150

❑ **Donald Duck Sled,** 1935, S.L. Allen, 36" long wooden slat and metal runner sled w/character decals, Donald and neph-ews
EX $140   **NM** $400   **MIP** $800

❑ **Donald Duck Snow Shovel,** Ohio Art, wood, tin, litho
EX $60   **NM** $130   **MIP** $185

❑ **Donald Duck Soaky,** 1950s, 7" tall
EX $15   **NM** $50   **MIP** $95

❑ **Donald Duck Squeeze Toy,** 1960s, Dell, 8" tall, rubber
EX $15   **NM** $40   **MIP** $75

❑ **Donald Duck Tea Set**, Ohio Art, 7-1/2" tray, 2-1/4" diameter cups, saucers
EX $45   **NM** $95   **MIP** $210

❑ **Donald Duck the Drummer,** 1940s, Marx, 5" x" 7 x 10" tall, Donald beats on a metal drum
EX $175   **NM** $400   **MIP** $600

❑ **Donald Duck Toy**, Schuco, 5-1/2" tall, wind-up w/a bellows, quacking sound
EX $325   **NM** $625   **MIP** $925

❑ **Donald Duck Toy Raft,** 1950s, Ideal, 2" tall, blue plastic raft w/yellow sail w/Donald looking through a telescope
EX $400   **NM** $75   **MIP** $110

❑ **Donald Duck Trapeze Toy**, Linemar, 5" tall, celluloid, wind-up
EX $60   **NM** $200   **MIP** $600

❑ **Donald Duck Watering Can,** 1938, Ohio Art, 6" tall, tin litho
EX $25   **NM** $50   **MIP** $160

❑ **Donald Duck Wind-Up,** 1972, Durham Plastic, 6-1/2" tall, hard plastic
EX $15   **NM** $40   **MIP** $85

❑ **Donald Tricycle Toy,** 1950s, Linemar, tin
EX $300   **NM** $600   **MIP** $900

❑ **Ludwig Von Drake in Go Cart,** 1960s, Linemar, tin and plastic
EX $115   **NM** $250   **MIP** $500

❑ **Ludwig Von Drake Mug,** 1961, 3-1/2" white china
EX $15   **NM** $20   **MIP** $50

❑ **Ludwig Von Drake Squeeze Toy,** 1961, Dell, 8" tall, rubber
EX $10   **NM** $20   **MIP** $50

❑ **Ludwig Von Drake Tiddly Winks,** 1961, Whitman
EX $10   **NM** $20   **MIP** $50

WATCH

❑ **Daisy Duck Wristwatch,** 1948, US Time
EX $110   **NM** $350   **MIP** $700

❑ **Donald Duck Wristwatch,** 1940s, US Time
EX $150   **NM** $450   **MIP** $800

DR. DOOLITTLE

FIGURES

❑ **Dr. Doolittle Figure,** 1967, Mattel, 5" tall w/parrot
EX $15   **NM** $30   **MIP** $50

❑ **Dr. Doolittle Figure,** 1967, Mattel, 7" tall
EX $15   **NM** $35   **MIP** $75

TOY

❑ **Dr. Doolittle Giraffe-in-the-Box,** jack-in-the-box
EX $50   **NM** $100   **MIP** $200

DR. SEUSS

ACCESSORIES

❑ **Mattel-O-Phone,** 1970, Mattel
EX $40   **NM** $55   **MIP** $200

DOLL

❑ **Cat in the Hat Doll,** 1983, Coleco, plush
EX $10   **NM** $40   **MIP** $80

❑ **Grinch Doll,** 1983, Coleco
EX $50   **NM** $90   **MIP** $275

❑ **Horton the Elephant Doll,** 1983, Coleco
EX $25   **NM** $65   **MIP** $135

(KP Photo)

❑ **Lorax Doll,** 1983, Coleco
EX $25   **NM** $65   **MIP** $135

❑ **Star-Bellied Sneetch Doll,** 1983, Coleco
EX $40   **NM** $70   **MIP** $140

❑ **Talking Cat in the Hat Doll,** 1970, Mat-tel
EX $60   **NM** $150   **MIP** $300

❑ **Talking Hedwig Doll,** 1970, Mattel
EX $50   **NM** $125   **MIP** $250

❑ **Talking Horton Doll,** 1970, Mattel
EX $60   **NM** $175   **MIP** $350

(KP Photo)

❑ **Thidwick the Moose Doll,** 1983, Coleco
EX $15   **NM** $40   **MIP** $85

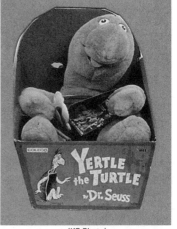

(KP Photo)

❑ **Yertle the Turtle Doll,** 1983, Coleco, 12" plush
EX $15   **NM** $45   **MIP** $85

TOY

❑ **Cat in the Hat Ge-Tar,** 1970, Mattel
EX $40   **NM** $110   **MIP** $200

❑ **Cat in the Hat Jack-in-the-Box,** 1969, Mattel
EX $50   **NM** $160   **MIP** $300

❑ **Cat in the Hat Riding Toy,** 1983, Coleco
EX $25   **NM** $50   **MIP** $125

❑ **Cat in the Hat Rocking Toy,** 1983, Coleco
EX $25   **NM** $50   **MIP** $125

❑ **Cat in the Hat Talking Puppet,** 1970, Mattel, vinyl head
EX $50   **NM** $125   **MIP** $275

DUMBO

ACCESSORIES

❑ **Dumbo Christmas Ornament**, 2" porcelain bisque, 50th anniversary
  EX $8   **NM** $15   **MIP** $30

❑ **Dumbo Milk Pitcher**, 1940s, 6" tall
  EX $30   **NM** $90   **MIP** $200

DOLL

❑ **Dumbo Doll**, 12" plush
  EX $10   **NM** $20   **MIP** $45

FIGURES

❑ **Dumbo Figure**, Dakin
  EX $12   **NM** $25   **MIP** $50

TOY

❑ **Dumbo Roll Over Wind-Up Toy**, 1941, Marx, 4" tall, tin w/tumbling action
  EX $150   **NM** $300   **MIP** $550

❑ **Dumbo Squeeze Toy**, 1950s, Dell, 5" tall
  EX $15   **NM** $30   **MIP** $75

ELMER FUDD

ACCESSORIES

❑ **Elmer Fudd Mini Snow Dome**, 1980s, Applause
  EX $10   **NM** $20   **MIP** $35

❑ **Elmer Fudd Mug**, 1980s, Applause, figural
  EX $5   **NM** $10   **MIP** $20

FIGURES

❑ **Elmer Fudd Figure**, 1950s, metal 5", on green base w/his name embossed, Elmer in hunting outfit
  EX $55   **NM** $120   **MIP** $235

❑ **Elmer Fudd Figure**, 1968, Dakin, 8" tall
  EX $20   **NM** $60   **MIP** $95

❑ **Elmer Fudd Figure**, 1971, Dakin, in a red hunting outfit
  EX $30   **NM** $70   **MIP** $125

❑ **Elmer Fudd Figure**, 1977, Dakin, Fun Farm
  EX $18   **NM** $33   **MIP** $65

TOY

❑ **Elmer Fudd Pull Toy**, 1940s, Brice Toys, 9", wooden, Elmer in fire chief's car
  EX $80   **NM** $200   **MIP** $350

FELIX THE CAT

ACCESSORIES

❑ **Felix Cartoon Lamp Shade**, 6" tall
  EX $50   **NM** $100   **MIP** $200

❑ **Felix Flashlight**, 1960s, contains whistle
  EX $50   **NM** $200   **MIP** $325

❑ **Felix Pencil Case**, 1950s
  EX $25   **NM** $75   **MIP** $120

(KP Photo)

❑ **Felix Sip-a-Drink Cup**, 5" tall
  EX $15   **NM** $25   **MIP** $50

DOLL

❑ **Felix Doll**, 1920s, 8" tall, wood, fully jointed
  EX $110   **NM** $300   **MIP** $610

❑ **Felix Doll**, 1920s, 13" tall, jointed arms
  EX $120   **NM** $290   **MIP** $600

FIGURES

❑ **Felix Figure**, 1920s, Schoenhut, 4" tall, wood, leather ears, stands on a white wood base
  EX $60   **NM** $270   **MIP** $550

GAME

❑ **Felix Manual Dexterity Game**, 1920s, German, 2", round, metal
  EX $80   **NM** $175   **MIP** $300

TOY

❑ **Felix on a Scooter**, 1924, Nifty, tin wind-up
  EX $250   **NM** $500   **MIP** $800

❑ **Felix Punching Bag**, 1960s, 11" tall inflatable bobber
  EX $25   **NM** $60   **MIP** $110

❑ **Felix Soaky**, 1960s, 10" tall, blue plastic
  EX $20   **NM** $60   **MIP** $100

❑ **Felix Soaky**, 1960s, 10" tall, red plastic
  EX $20   **NM** $60   **MIP** $100

❑ **Felix Soaky**, 1960s, 10" tall, black plastic
  EX $15   **NM** $50   **MIP** $90

❑ **Felix Squeak Toy**, 1930s, 6" tall, soft rubber
  EX $35   **NM** $110   **MIP** $175

❑ **Felix the Cat Pull Toy**, 1920s, Nifty, 5-1/2" tall, 8" long, tin, cat is chasing two red mice on the front of the cart, litho pictures of Felix on side
  EX $200   **NM** $400   **MIP** $725

WATCH

❑ **Felix Wristwatch**, 1960s
  EX $65   **NM** $150   **MIP** $275

FERDINAND THE BULL

BANK

❑ **Ferdinand Savings Bank**, Crown Toy, 5" tall, wood composition w/silk flower w/metal trap door
  EX $35   **NM** $70   **MIP** $220

BOOK

❑ **Ferdinand the Bull Book**, 1938, Whitman, linen picture book
  EX $35   **NM** $100   **MIP** $185

DOLL

❑ **Ferdinand Doll**, 1938, Knickerbocker, 5" x 9" x 8-1/2" tall, joint composition w/cloth tail and flower stapled in his mouth
  EX $100   **NM** $210   **MIP** $350

FIGURES

❑ **Ferdinand Figure**, 9" tall, plastic
  EX $20   **NM** $35   **MIP** $150

❑ **Ferdinand Figure**, 3-1/2" bisque
  EX $15   **NM** $40   **MIP** $110

❑ **Ferdinand Figure**, 1930s, Seiberling, 3" x 5-1/2" x 4" tall, rubber
  EX $50   **NM** $100   **MIP** $200

❑ **Ferdinand Figure**, 1938, Delco, 4-1/2" tall, ceramic, bull seated w/a purple garland around his neck
  EX $50   **NM** $100   **MIP** $200

❑ **Ferdinand Figure**, 1940s, Disney, composition
  EX $80   **NM** $175   **MIP** $325

TOY

❑ **Ferdinand Hand Puppet**, 1938, Crown Toy, 9-1/2" tall
  EX $60   **NM** $110   **MIP** $230

❑ **Ferdinand Toy**, 1940, Knickerbocker, wood composition w/jointed head and legs w/flower in his mouth
  EX $60   **NM** $120   **MIP** $300

FLIPPER

TOY

❑ **Flipper Halloween Costume**, 1964, Collegeville
  EX $20   **NM** $40   **MIP** $90

❑ **Flipper Magic Slate**, 1960s, Lowe
  EX $12   **NM** $24   **MIP** $50

❑ **Flipper Model Kit**, 1965, Revell
  EX $17   **NM** $35   **MIP** $80

❑ **Flipper Puzzle**, 1960s, Whitman, several variations, each
  EX $10   **NM** $21   **MIP** $34

❑ **Flipper Ukelele**, 1968, Mattel
  EX $12   **NM** $22   **MIP** $38

FOGHORN LEGHORN

FIGURES

❑ **Foghorn Leghorn Figure**, 1970, Dakin, 6-1/4" tall
  EX $22   **NM** $45   **MIP** $85

❑ **Foghorn Leghorn Figure**, 1980s, Applause, PVC
  EX $3   **NM** $50   **MIP** $75

TOY

❑ **Foghorn Leghorn Hand Puppet**, 1960s, 9", fabric w/vinyl head
  EX $20   **NM** $75   **MIP** $135

FONTAINE FOX

TOY

❑ **Powerful Katrinka Toy,** 1923, 5-1/2" tall, wind-up, pushing Jimmy in a wheel-barrow
EX $275   NM $650   MIP $1050

❑ **Toonerville Trolley,** Nifty, miniature, 2" tall
EX $95   NM $200   MIP $400

❑ **Toonerville Trolley,** 3" tall
EX $100   NM $200   MIP $400

❑ **Toonerville Trolley,** 4" tall, red pot metal
EX $200   NM $685   MIP $1250

❑ **Toonerville Trolley,** 1922, 7-1/2" tall, wind-up
EX $300   NM $675   MIP $1150

GARFIELD

BANK

❑ **Garfield Chair Bank,** 1981, Enesco
EX $12   NM $25   MIP $60

❑ **Garfield Figure Bank,** 1981, Enesco, 4-3/4"
EX $12   NM $24   MIP $45

FIGURES

❑ **Garfield Easter Figure,** 1978, Enesco
EX $7   NM $14   MIP $35

❑ **Garfield Figure,** 1978, Enesco, Garfield as graduate
EX $6   NM $12   MIP $25

MUSIC BOX

❑ **Garfield Music Box,** 1981, Enesco, Garfield dancing
EX $16   NM $42   MIP $80

GASOLINE ALLEY

ACCESSORIES

❑ **Skeezix Stationery,** 1926, 6" x 8-1/2"
EX $15   NM $30   MIP $60

❑ **Uncle Walt and Skeezix Pencil Holder,** F.A.S., 5" tall, bisque
EX $50   NM $200   MIP $300

FIGURES

❑ **Skeezix Comic Figure,** 1930s, 6" chalk statue
EX $10   NM $30   MIP $75

❑ **Uncle Walt and Skeezix Figure Set,** bisque, Uncle Walt, Skeezix, Herby and Smitty
EX $60   NM $175   MIP $320

GOOFY

ACCESSORIES

❑ **Goofy Night Light,** 1973, Horsman, green, figural
EX $16   NM $30   MIP $45

❑ **Goofy Toothbrush,** 1970s, Pepsodent
EX $5   NM $10   MIP $20

DOLL

❑ **Goofy Doll,** 1970s, 5" x 6" x 13" tall, fabric and vinyl, laughing doll
EX $30   NM $70   MIP $150

FIGURES

❑ **Goofy Figure,** Marx, Snap-Eeze figure
EX $12   NM $35   MIP $50

❑ **Goofy Figure,** Arco, bendy
EX $10   NM $15   MIP $25

❑ **Goofy Lil' Headbobber,** Marx
EX $30   NM $60   MIP $125

❑ **Goofy Rolykin,** Marx
EX $25   NM $50   MIP $75

❑ **Goofy Twist'N Bend Figure,** 1963, Marx, 4" tall
EX $11   NM $20   MIP $30

TOY

❑ **Goofy Car,** Spain, vinyl head Goofy drives tin litho car
EX $25   NM $45   MIP $85

❑ **Goofy Safety Scissors,** 1973, Monogram, on card
EX $5   NM $10   MIP $20

❑ **Goofy with Bump 'N Go Action Lawn Mower,** 1980s, Illfelder, 3-1/2" x 10" x 11", plastic figure pushing lawn mower w/silver handle
EX $40   NM $70   MIP $125

WATCH

❑ **Backwards Goofy Wristwatch,** Pedre, silver case 2nd edition
EX $35   NM $65   MIP $150

❑ **Backwards Goofy Wristwatch,** 1972, Helbros
EX $275   NM $520   MIP $820

GUMBY

ACCESSORIES

(KP Photo)

❑ **Gumby Adventure Costume,** 1960s, Lakeside, fireman, cowboy, knight and astronaut, each
EX $25   NM $50   MIP $85

FIGURE

❑ **Gumby Figure,** 1980s, large, foam rubber
EX $20   NM $30   MIP $60

FIGURES

❑ **Gumby Figure,** 1980s, Applause, 12" tall, poseable
EX $10   NM $20   MIP $35

❑ **Gumby Figure,** 1980s, Applause, 5-1/2" bendy, three styles
EX $5   NM $10   MIP $25

❑ **Pokey Figure,** 1960s, Lakeside
EX $20   NM $40   MIP $85

TOY

❑ **Gumby Colorforms Set,** 1988, Colorforms
EX $8   NM $12   MIP $30

❑ **Gumby Hand Puppet,** 1965, Lakeside, 9" tall w/vinyl head
EX $15   NM $40   MIP $80

❑ **Gumby Modeling Dough,** 1960s, Chemtoy
EX $25   NM $50   MIP $85

❑ **Gumby's Jeep,** 1960s, Lakeside, yellow tin litho, Gumby and Pokey's names are printed on seat
EX $90   NM $210   MIP $350

❑ **Pokey Modeling Dough,** 1960s, Chemtoy
EX $25   NM $50   MIP $90

TOYS

❑ **Adventures of Gumby Electric Drawing Set,** 1966, Lakeside
EX $22   NM $50   MIP $90

HAPPY HOOLIGAN

ACCESSORIES

❑ **Happy Hooligan Songsheet,** 1905, newspaper premium
EX $60   NM $150   MIP $250

TOY

❑ **Happy Hooligan Nesting Toys,** Anri, 4" tall, wooden set of four nesting pieces
EX $70   NM $130   MIP $260

❑ **Happy Hooligan Toy,** 1932, Chein, 6" tall, wind-up, walking figure
EX $150   NM $350   MIP $650

HECKLE AND JECKLE

BOOK

❑ **Heckle and Jeckle Story Book,** 1957, Wonder Book
EX $10   NM $30   MIP $50

FIGURES

❑ **Heckle and Jeckle Figures,** 7" soft foam figures
EX $15   NM $50   MIP $100

❑ **Little Roquefort Figure,** 1959, 8-1/2" tall, wood
EX $20   NM $40   MIP $70

TOY

❑ **Heckle and Jeckle Skooz-It Game,** 1963, Ideal, cylindrical container
EX $25   NM $60   MIP $105

HUCKLEBERRY HOUND

BANK

❏ **Huckleberry Hound Bank**, 1960, Knickerbocker, 10" tall, hard plastic figural
EX $18　　NM $40　　MIP $80

❏ **Huckleberry Hound Bank**, 1980, Dakin, 5" tall figural bank of Huck sitting
EX $15　　NM $30　　MIP $70

DOLL

❏ **Huckleberry Hound Doll**, 1959, Knickerbocker, 18" plush, vinyl hands and face
EX $30　　NM $70　　MIP $135

❏ **Mr. Jinks Doll**, 1959, Knickerbocker, 13" tall, plush, vinyl face
EX $25　　NM $110　　MIP $220

❏ **Pixie and Dixie Dolls**, 1960, Knickerbocker, 12" tall, each
EX $25　　NM $45　　MIP $75

FIGURES

❏ **Hokey Wolf Figure**, 1961, Marx, TV-Tinykin
EX $15　　NM $40　　MIP $75

❏ **Hokey Wolf Figure**, 1970, Dakin
EX $30　　NM $75　　MIP $140

❏ **Huckleberry Hound Figure**, Dakin, 8" tall
EX $25　　NM $50　　MIP $90

❏ **Huckleberry Hound Figure**, 1960s, 6" tall, glazed china
EX $20　　NM $40　　MIP $80

❏ **Huckleberry Hound Figure**, 1961, Marx, TV-Tinykins
EX $15　　NM $25　　MIP $50

❏ **Huckleberry Hound Figure Set**, 1961, Marx, TV-Tinykins
EX $30　　NM $70　　MIP $100

TOY

❏ **Huckleberry Hound Go-Cart**, 1960s, Linemar, 6-1/2" tall, friction
EX $100　　NM $200　　MIP $375

❏ **Huckleberry Hound Wind-Up Toy**, 1962, Linemar, 4" tall, tin
EX $90　　NM $180　　MIP $360

❏ **Mr. Jinks Soaky**, 1960s, Purex, 10" tall, Pixie and Dixie, hard plastic
EX $15　　NM $35　　MIP $65

❏ **Pixie and Dixie Magic Slate**, 1959
EX $15　　NM $30　　MIP $60

WATCH

❏ **Huckleberry Hound Wristwatch**, 1965, Bradley, chrome case, wind-up mechanism, gray leather band, face shows Huck in full view
EX $40　　NM $100　　MIP $200

HUMPTY DUMPTY

ACCESSORIES

❏ **Humpty Dumpty Bubble Bath**, 1960s, Avon, figural plastic container
EX $7　　NM $30　　MIP $75

❏ **Humpty Dumpty Figural Soap**, 1990s, Avon
EX $3　　NM $6　　MIP $12

❏ **Humpty Dumpty Magazine**, 1960s
EX $3　　NM $7　　MIP $15

❏ **Humpty Dumpty Potato Chip Tin**, 1990s, large blue and gold tin
EX $7　　NM $15　　MIP $35

FIGURE

❏ **Humpty Dumpty Figure**, 1950s, Marx, Fairy Tale series, plastic
EX $5　　NM $10　　MIP $25

❏ **Humpty Dumpty Game**, 1981, Orchard Toys, British matching game
EX $8　　NM $15　　MIP $30

PUZZLE

❏ **Humpty Dumpty Puzzle**, 1970s, wood frame tray puzzles, several varieties
EX $5　　NM $15　　MIP $30

TOY

❏ **Humpty Dumpty Crib Toy**, 1980s, Mattel, plastic, sits on crib rail
EX $4　　NM $8　　MIP $15

❏ **Humpty Dumpty Musical Toy**, 1960s, Alladin Plastics, plastic, record inside toy
EX $15　　NM $30　　MIP $60

❏ **Humpty Dumpty Pull Toy**, 1970s, Fisher-Price, plastic, several color variations
EX $5　　NM $10　　MIP $15

INDIANA JONES

ACCESSORIES

❏ **Indiana Jones Backpack**, Pepsi
EX $20　　NM $45　　MIP $90

❏ **Indiana Jones The Legend Mug**
EX $5　　NM $10　　MIP $15

❏ **Last Crusade Button**, Pepsi, retailer button
EX $5　　NM $12　　MIP $30

❏ **Patch**, 1990
EX $10　　NM $15　　MIP $30

❏ **Temple of Doom Calendar**
EX $5　　NM $10　　MIP $30

❏ **Temple of Doom Storybook**, hardbound
EX $7　　NM $20　　MIP $30

TOY

(KP Photo)

❏ **Indiana Jones 3-D View-Master Gift Set**, View-Master
EX $15　　NM $35　　MIP $75

JAMES BOND

ACCESSORIES

❏ **007 Flicker Rings**, 1967, set of 11
EX $50　　NM $110　　MIP $220

❏ **007 Video Disc Promo Kit**, 1980s, RCA, disc, poster, pamphlet
EX $15　　NM $30　　MIP $60

❏ **Bond Golf Tees**, 1987, British, six tees and pencil in leather pouch
EX $8　　NM $15　　MIP $30

❏ **James Bond Alarm Clock**, painting of Roger Moore in center
EX $20　　NM $40　　MIP $90

❏ **James Bond B.A.R.K. Attache Case With Box**, 1965, Multiple Toys, 007 luger, missles, hideaway pistol and rocket launching device, case and gun bears 007 logo
EX $350　　NM $750　　MIP $1200

❏ **James Bond Jr. Bath Towel**
EX $10　　NM $20　　MIP $20

❏ **James Bond Parachute Set**, 1984, Imperial, orange and green parachutist figures
EX $12　　NM $35　　MIP $70

❏ **James Bond Ring**, 1964, glass oval w/photo of Sean Connery
EX $10　　NM $25　　MIP $40

❏ **James Bond Wall Clock**, 1981, large clock w/painting of Roger Moore in action
EX $25　　NM $45　　MIP $90

❏ **View to a Kill Michelin Button**, Bond on large size pinback w/Midas man
EX $5　　NM $12　　MIP $25

ACTION FIGURES

❏ **James Bond Jr. Action Ninja Figure**, Hasbro
EX $8　　NM $15　　MIP $60

❏ **James Bond Jr. Buddy Mitchell Figure**, Hasbro
EX $5　　NM $10　　MIP $20

❏ **James Bond Jr. Capt. Walker D. Plank figure**, Hasbro
EX $3　　NM $6　　MIP $15

❏ **James Bond Jr. Dr. Derange figure**, Hasbro
EX $3　　NM $6　　MIP $15

❏ **James Bond Jr. Dr. No. figure**, Hasbro
EX $3　　NM $6　　MIP $20

❏ **James Bond Jr. Figure**, Hasbro, w/pistol
EX $3　　NM $8　　MIP $25

❏ **James Bond Jr. Figure**, Hasbro, w/scuba gear
EX $3　　NM $8　　MIP $25

❏ **James Bond Jr. Gordo Leiter figure**, Hasbro
EX $4　　NM $10　　MIP $30

CHARACTER TOYS

❏ **James Bond Jr. I.Q. figure**, Hasbro, w/weapon device
EX $3　　NM $6　　MIP $15

❏ **James Bond Jr. Jaws Figure**, Hasbro
EX $5　　NM $12　　MIP $30

❏ **James Bond Jr. Odd Job figure**, Hasbro
EX $6　　NM $15　　MIP $35

BOOK

❏ **Bond Pocket Diary**, 1988, British leather bound
EX $5　　NM $15　　MIP $30

❏ **James Bond Jr. Sticker Book**
EX $3　　NM $6　　MIP $15

COSTUME

❏ **Moonraker Halloween Costume**, 1979, mask of Roger Moore and space suit costume
EX $20　　NM $50　　MIP $125

DOLL

(KP Photo)

❏ **Odd Job Action Figure**, 1965, Gilbert, 12" doll in karate outfit, w/derby
EX $130　　NM $300　　MIP $600

FIGURES

❏ **Jaws Figure**, 1979, Mego
EX $135　　NM $275　　MIP $550

GAME

❏ **Goldfinger II Role Playing Game**
EX $6　　NM $15　　MIP $30

❏ **James Bond Computer Game "The Stealth Affair"**, 1990, based on Licence to Kill
EX $15　　NM $30　　MIP $60

❏ **James Bond Jr. Karate Punch Target Game**, gun w/boxing glove and targets of villain
EX $8　　NM $15　　MIP $35

(KP Photo)

❏ **James Bond Secret Service Game**, 1965, Spears
EX $60　　NM $230　　MIP $640

❏ **James Bond Tarot Game**, 1973
EX $15　　NM $30　　MIP $60

❏ **James Bond Video Game**, 1983, Coleco
EX $15　　NM $25　　MIP $50

❏ **Moonraker Spanish Card Game**, 33 cards w/different color stills
EX $15　　NM $30　　MIP $60

❏ **The James Bond Box**, 1965, rare game played w/dice
EX $40　　NM $75　　MIP $150

❏ **Thunderball Balloon Target Game**, 1965
EX $40　　NM $85　　MIP $170

GUN

(KP Photo)

❏ **James Bond Harpoon Gun (Thunderball)**, 1960s, Lone Star, box illustrated w/undersea fight scene graphics
EX $60　　NM $150　　MIP $300

PUPPETS

❏ **Odd Job Puppet**, Gilbert, plastic hand puppet
EX $75　　NM $340　　MIP $610

PUZZLE

❏ **Goldfinger Puzzle**, 1965, Milton Bradley, Bond and Golden Girl
EX $25　　NM $55　　MIP $110

(KP Photo)

❏ **Goldfinger Puzzle**, 1965, Milton Bradley, Bond's Bullets Blaze
EX $20　　NM $40　　MIP $85

❏ **Spy Who Loved Me Puzzle**, Milton Bradley, several scenes, each
EX $20　　NM $40　　MIP $80

STICKERS

❏ **007 Bullet Hole Stickers**, 1987, simulated bullet holes, magnetic license holder
EX $6　　NM $15　　MIP $25

TOY

(KP Photo)

❏ **007 Dart Gun**, 1984, Imperial, photo of Roger Moore
EX $10　　NM $25　　MIP $50

❏ **007 Exploding Cigarette Lighter**, Coibel
EX $6　　NM $20　　MIP $35

❏ **007 Exploding Coin**, Coibel, on blister pack
EX $6　　NM $20　　MIP $35

❏ **007 Exploding Pen**, Coibel, on blister pack
EX $6　　NM $20　　MIP $35

❏ **007 Exploding Spoon**, Coibel, on blister pack
EX $6　　NM $20　　MIP $35

❏ **007 Radio Trap**, 1966, Multiple Toys, radio w/secret business cards
EX $50　　NM $100　　MIP $200

❏ **007 Submachine Gun**, 1984, Imperial, photo of Roger Moore
EX $10　　NM $30　　MIP $60

❏ **007 Toy Pistol**, Edgemark
EX $5　　NM $15　　MIP $30

❏ **Electric Drawing Set**, 1965, Lakeside, plastic tracing board, pencils, sharpener, adventure sheets
EX $55　　NM $110　　MIP $225

❏ **James Bond Disguise Kit**, 1965, Gilbert
EX $40　　NM $85　　MIP $170

❏ **James Bond Disguise Kit #2**, 1965, Gilbert
EX $40　　NM $85　　MIP $170

❏ **James Bond Hand Puppet**, 1965, Gilbert
EX $45　　NM $90　　MIP $150

❏ **James Bond Hideaway Pistol**, 1985, Coibel
EX $20　　NM $50　　MIP $100

❏ **James Bond Jr. CD Player/Weapons Kit**, Hasbro
EX $10　　NM $20　　MIP $35

❏ **James Bond Jr. Crime Fighter Set**, includes handcuffs, watch and walkie-talkie
EX $5　　NM $15　　MIP $30

❏ **James Bond Jr. Ninja Play Set**, throw stars, nunchukas and badge
EX $8   NM $15   MIP $40

❏ **James Bond Jr. Ninja Wrist Weapon Set**
EX $5   NM $10   MIP $35

(KP Photo)

❏ **James Bond Secret Attache Case**, 1965, MPC
EX $160   NM $350   MIP $725

❏ **James Bond Sting Pistol**, Coibel, 8-shot cap pistol and booklet from On Her Majesty's Secret Service
EX $20   NM $40   MIP $85

❏ **Living Daylights German Pistol**, 1980s, Wicke, 25-shot cap gun
EX $12   NM $30   MIP $60

❏ **May Day Pistol**, 1985
EX $12   NM $25   MIP $50
EX $15   NM $40   MIP $80

(KP Photo)

❏ **Thunderball Puzzle**, 1965, Milton Bradley, several pictures, each
EX $20   NM $45   MIP $90

❏ **Thunderball Set**, 1965, Gilbert
EX $40   NM $105   MIP $210

❏ **Tuxedo Outfit**, 1965, Gilbert
EX $50   NM $110   MIP $220

VEHICLE

❏ **James Bond Aston Martin**, 1965, Gilbert, 12", battery operated
EX $150   NM $300   MIP $575

❏ **James Bond Aston Martin Slot Car**, 1965, Gilbert
EX $75   NM $150   MIP $300

VEHICLES

❏ **James Bond Jr. Corvette**
EX $15   NM $35   MIP $75

❏ **James Bond Jr. Scum Shark Mobile**
EX $10   NM $15   MIP $35

❏ **James Bond Jr. Sub Cycle**
EX $5   NM $14   MIP $32

❏ **James Bond Jr. Vehicles**, Ertl, S.C.U.M. Helicopter, Bond's car and van; set of three
EX $20   NM $65   MIP $125

❏ **James Bond Roadrace Set**, 1965, Gilbert, scenery tracks, Aston Martin and other cars
EX $175   NM $350   MIP $700

❏ **Licence to Kill Car Set**, Matchbox, jeep, seaplane, oil tanker, and copter
EX $25   NM $50   MIP $100

❏ **Living Daylights Record Mobile**, 1980s
EX $5   NM $20   MIP $40
EX $15   NM $40   MIP $75
EX $25   NM $60   MIP $165
EX $15   NM $35   MIP $70

(KP Photo)

EX $15   NM $35   MIP $70
EX $25   NM $50   MIP $125

❏ **Multi-Action Aston Martin**, 1960s, friction operated car for Agent 711
EX $70   NM $165   MIP $325

(KP Photo)

EX $35   NM $90   MIP $175
EX $10   NM $25   MIP $50
EX $25   NM $60   MIP $90

WATCHES

❏ **James Bond Pocket Watch**, 1981, Roger Moore on face
EX $30   NM $75   MIP $150

JUNGLE BOOK

ACCESSORIES

❏ **Jungle Book Dinner Set**, vinyl placemat, bowl, plate and cup
EX $10   NM $20   MIP $50

❏ **Jungle Book Utensils**, fork and spoon w/melamine handles
EX $5   NM $12   MIP $30

DOLL

❏ **Baloo Doll**, 12" tall, plush
EX $10   NM $50   MIP $110

FIGURES

❏ **Mowgli Figure**, 1967, Holland Hill, 8", vinyl
EX $20   NM $40   MIP $85

❏ **Shere Kahn Figure**, 1965, Enesco, 5" tall, ceramic
EX $15   NM $30   MIP $50

TOY

❏ **Jungle Book Carrying Case**, 1966, Ideal, 5" x 14" x 8"
EX $25   NM $60   MIP $120

❏ **Jungle Book Fun-L Tun-L**, 1966, New York Toy, 108" x 24"
EX $40   NM $70   MIP $125

❏ **Jungle Book Magic Slate**, 1967, Watkins-Strathmore
EX $10   NM $25   MIP $50

❏ **Jungle Book Sand Pail and Shovel**, 1966, Chein, tin litho, illustrated w/Jungle Book characters
EX $25   NM $60   MIP $100

❏ **Jungle Book Tea Set**, 1966, Chein, tin litho, plates, saucers, tea cups and serving tray
EX $25   NM $65   MIP $110

❏ **Mowgli's Hut Mobile and Figures**, 1968, Multiple Toymakers, 2" x 3" x 3" mobile w/Baloo and King Louis figures
EX $35   NM $70   MIP $135

WATCH

❏ **Mowgli/Baloo Wristwatch**, digital, clear plastic band
EX $5   NM $10   MIP $25

LADY AND THE TRAMP

DOLL

❏ **Lady Doll**, 1955, Woolikin, 5" x 8" x 8-1/2", light tank w/burnt orange accents on face, ears, stomach and tail, plastic eyes, nose and a white silk ribbon around neck
EX $50   NM $100   MIP $200

❏ **Perri Doll**, 1950s, Steiff, 6" tall, plush
EX $40   NM $85   MIP $175

❏ **Tramp Doll**, 1955, Schuco, 8" tall, brown w/a white underside and face, hard plastic eyes and nose
EX $75   NM $150   MIP $300

FIGURES

❏ **Lady and Tramp Figures**, 1955, Marx, Lady is 1-1/2" tall and white, Tramp is 2" tall and tan
EX $30   NM $65   MIP $125

TOY

□ **Modeling Clay,** 1955, Pressman
 EX $30 **NM** $120 **MIP** $185

□ **Puzzle,** 1954, Whitman, 11" x 15", frame tray
 EX $20 **NM** $35 **MIP** $75

□ **Toy Bus,** 1966, Modern Toys/Japan, 3-1/2" x 4" x 14" long
 EX $20 **NM** $40 **MIP** $75

LAUREL AND HARDY

BANK

(KP Photo)

□ **Oliver Hardy Bank,** 1974, Play Pal, 13-1/2" tall, plastic
 EX $15 **NM** $30 **MIP** $60

□ **Stan Laurel Bank,** 1972, 15" tall, vinyl figural bank
 EX $22 **NM** $50 **MIP** $85

(KP Photo)

□ **Stan Laurel Bank,** 1974, Play Pal, 13-1/2" tall, plastic
 EX $10 **NM** $30 **MIP** $50

FIGURES

□ **Oliver Hardy Figure,** 1974, Dakin, 7-1/2" tall
 EX $25 **NM** $90 **MIP** $175

□ **Stan Laurel Figure,** 1974, Dakin, 8" tall
 EX $30 **NM** $65 **MIP** $130

TOY

□ **Laurel and Hardy Die-Cut Puppets,** 1970s, Larry Harmon, moveable, each
 EX $25 **NM** $125 **MIP** $250

□ **Laurel and Hardy Die-Cut Puppets,** 1982, Dell, soft vinyl, each
 EX $20 **NM** $75 **MIP** $150

□ **Laurel and Hardy TV Set,** 1976, w/paper filmstrips
 EX $20 **NM** $40 **MIP** $80

□ **Oliver Hardy Doll,** Dakin, 5" tall wind-up dancing/shaking vinyl doll
 EX $35 **NM** $42 **MIP** $85

LITTLE MERMAID

ACCESSORIES

□ **Ariel Jewelry Box,** 5-3/4" x 4-1/2", musical
 EX $9 **NM** $16 **MIP** $30

□ **Ariel Toothbrush,** battery operated w/holder
 EX $9 **NM** $16 **MIP** $25

□ **Flounder and Ariel Faucet Cover,** plastic
 EX $5 **NM** $10 **MIP** $20

□ **Flounder Pillow,** 14" x 24" shaped like Flounder
 EX $7 **NM** $13 **MIP** $25

□ **Little Mermaid Purse,** 6" diameter, vinyl, canteen style purse
 EX $5 **NM** $12 **MIP** $20

□ **Little Mermaid Snow Globe,** 4" water globe
 EX $9 **NM** $16 **MIP** $30

□ **Under the Sea Jewelry Box,** 4" mahogany, musical
 EX $18 **NM** $35 **MIP** $65

DOLL

□ **Eric Doll,** 9-1/2" tall in full dress uniform
 EX $9 **NM** $16 **MIP** $30

□ **Flounder Doll,** 15" plush fish
 EX $9 **NM** $16 **MIP** $30

□ **Scuttle Doll,** 15" seagull, plush
 EX $12 **NM** $20 **MIP** $35

□ **Sebastian Doll,** 16" crab, plush
 EX $10 **NM** $16 **MIP** $30

FIGURES

□ **Little Mermaid Figures,** Applause, several PVC characters, each
 EX $2 **NM** $5 **MIP** $10

LITTLE ORPHAN ANNIE

ACCESSORIES

□ **Beetleware Mug,** 1933, Ovaltine
 EX $25 **NM** $70 **MIP** $110

□ **Beetleware Mug,** 1935, Ovaltine
 EX $35 **NM** $80 **MIP** $120

□ **ID Bracelet,** 1934, Ovaltine
 EX $25 **NM** $60 **MIP** $120

□ **Little Orphan Annie Altascope Ring,** 1942, Quaker, premium, only eight known to exist
 EX $1500 **NM** $5000 **MIP** $20000

□ **Little Orphan Annie and Sandy Ashtray,** 1930s, 3" tall, ceramic
 EX $50 **NM** $105 **MIP** $225

□ **Little Orphan Annie and Sandy Toothbrush Holder,** 1930s, bisque
 EX $60 **NM** $125 **MIP** $200

□ **Little Orphan Annie Clothespins,** 1938, Gold Medal, clothesline and pulley
 EX $20 **NM** $40 **MIP** $80

□ **Little Orphan Annie Glassips,** 1936, drinking straws
 EX $200 **NM** $500 **MIP** $700

□ **Little Orphan Annie Mug,** 1930, Ovaltine, Uncle Wiggily
 EX $30 **NM** $90 **MIP** $175

□ **Little Orphan Annie Music Box,** 1970, N.Y. News, figural
 EX $25 **NM** $60 **MIP** $100

□ **Little Orphan Annie Periscope,** 1942, Quaker, offered in handbook
 EX $100 **NM** $400 **MIP** $650

□ **Little Orphan Annie Stamper,** 1941, Quaker, premium, w/wood handle; secret guard
 EX $250 **NM** $600 **MIP** $800

□ **Round Decoder Pin,** 1936, Ovaltine
 EX $30 **NM** $130 **MIP** $210

□ **Secret Compartment Decoder Pin,** 1936, Ovaltine
 EX $20 **NM** $150 **MIP** $300

□ **Shake-Up Mug,** 1931, Ovaltine
 EX $30 **NM** $75 **MIP** $120

□ **Sunburst Decoder Pin,** 1937, Ovaltine
 EX $30 **NM** $75 **MIP** $160

BOOK

□ **Little Orphan Annie and Chizzler Book,** 1930s, Big Little Book
 EX $25 **NM** $75 **MIP** $130

□ **Little Orphan Annie and the Gooneyville Mystery Book,** 1947, Whitman
 EX $20 **NM** $100 **MIP** $160

□ **Little Orphan Annie and the Haunted House Comic Book,** 1928, Cupples and Leon
 EX $60 **NM** $150 **MIP** $300

□ **Little Orphan Annie Bucking the World Comic Book,** 1929, Cupples and Leon, hardcover
 EX $60 **NM** $150 **MIP** $310

□ **Little Orphan Annie in the Circus Comic Book,** 1927, Cupples and Leon, 9" x 7", 86 pages
 EX $60 **NM** $150 **MIP** $310

□ **Little Orphan Annie Shipwrecked Comic Book,** 1931, Cupples and Leon, 9" x 7", 86 pages
 EX $60 **NM** $120 **MIP** $310

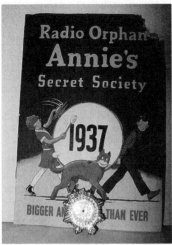

(KP Photo)

❑ **Radio Annie's Secret Society Booklet,** 1936, 6" x 9"
EX $30   NM $65   MIP $150

❑ **Radio Annie's Secret Society Manual,** 1938, 6" x 9", 12 pages
EX $50   NM $90   MIP $175

DOLL

❑ **Annie Doll,** 1982, Knickerbocker, 10" doll without locket
EX $2   NM $7   MIP $15

❑ **Annie Doll,** 1982, Knickerbocker, 10" tall, w/two dresses and removable heart locket
EX $5   NM $12   MIP $25

❑ **Daddy Warbucks Doll,** 1982, Knickerbocker
EX $10   NM $50   MIP $90

❑ **Little Orphan Annie and Sandy Dolls,** 1930, Famous Artists Syndicate, 9-3/4" tall, each
EX $60   NM $120   MIP $250

❑ **Little Orphan Annie Doll,** 1973, Well Toy, 7" tall
EX $15   NM $20   MIP $50

❑ **Miss Hannigan Doll,** 1982, Knickerbocker
EX $5   NM $10   MIP $25

❑ **Molly Doll,** 1982, Knickerbocker
EX $5   NM $10   MIP $25

❑ **Punjab Doll,** 1982, Knickerbocker
EX $5   NM $15   MIP $30

❑ **Snow White Paper Dolls,** 1938, rare red cover version; Ovaltine Annie premium
EX $500   NM $1000   MIP $1500

FIGURES

❑ **Annie Figures,** 1982, Knickerbocker, six figures, 2" tall, each
EX $2   NM $5   MIP $10

❑ **Little Orphan Annie Figure,** 1940s, 1-1/2" tall, lead
EX $20   NM $40   MIP $75

❑ **Sandy Figure,** 1940s, 3/4" tall, lead
EX $20   NM $55   MIP $100

GAME

❑ **Little Orphan Annie Light Up the Candles Game,** Ovaltine, 3-1/2" x 5", premium
EX $30   NM $150   MIP $300

❑ **Little Orphan Annie Rummy Cards,** 1937, Whitman, 5" x 6", colored silhouettes of Annie on the back
EX $20   NM $80   MIP $160

TOY

❑ **Little Orphan Annie Colorforms Set,** 1970s, Colorforms
EX $10   NM $20   MIP $40

❑ **Little Orphan Annie Costume,** 1930s, mask and slip-over paper dress w/belt
EX $125   NM $300   MIP $500

❑ **Little Orphan Annie Cut-Outs,** 1960s, Miller Toys, Sandy, Grunts the Pig, Pee Wee the Elephant
EX $20   NM $100   MIP $200

❑ **Little Orphan Annie Punch-Outs,** 1944, King, Larson, McMahon, 3-D punch-outs of Annie, Sandy, Punjab and Daddy Warbucks
EX $30   NM $60   MIP $125

❑ **Little Orphan Annie Stove,** 1930s, electric version, 8" x 9", gold metal, litho plates, functional oven doors and back burner
EX $70   NM $165   MIP $325

❑ **Little Orphan Annie Stove,** 1930s, non-electric model, gold-brass lithographed labels of Annie and Sandy, oven doors functional
EX $60   NM $150   MIP $300

❑ **Puzzle,** Novelty Dist., Famous Comics
EX $20   NM $75   MIP $150

LOONEY TUNES

BANK

❑ **Daffy Duck Bank,** 1980s, Applause, figural
EX $10   NM $20   MIP $40

(KP Photo)

❑ **Sylvester and Tweety Bank,** 1972, vinyl
EX $15   NM $25   MIP $60

❑ **Tasmanian Devil Bank,** 1980s, Applause
EX $5   NM $20   MIP $40

DOLL

❑ **Tasmanian Devil Doll,** 1971, Mighty Star, 13" tall, plush
EX $9   NM $40   MIP $75

❑ **Tweety Doll,** 1969, Dakin, 6", moveable head and feet
EX $10   NM $25   MIP $50

FIGURE

❑ **Daffy Duck Figure,** 1968, Dakin, 8-1/2" tall
EX $15   NM $25   MIP $60

❑ **Daffy Duck Figure,** 1970s, Dakin
EX $15   NM $30   MIP $70

❑ **Daffy Duck Figure,** 1980s, Applause, 4" bendy
EX $10   NM $20   MIP $40

❑ **Sylvester Figure,** 1971, Dakin, Sylvester on a fish crate
EX $15   NM $25   MIP $50

❑ **Sylvester Figure,** 1976, Dakin, Cartoon Theater
EX $11   NM $22   MIP $45

FIGURES

❑ **Pepe Le Pew Figure,** 1971, Dakin, 8" tall
EX $25   NM $50   MIP $100

❑ **Speedy Gonzales Figure,** Dakin, 5", vinyl
EX $10   NM $20   MIP $40

❑ **Speedy Gonzales Figure,** 1970, Dakin, 7-1/2" tall, vinyl
EX $15   NM $25   MIP $50

❑ **Sylvester and Tweety Figures,** 1975, Warner Bros., 6" tall
EX $10   NM $16   MIP $35

❑ **Sylvester Figure,** 1950, Oak Rubber, 6", rubber
EX $25   NM $60   MIP $125

❑ **Sylvester Figure,** 1969, Dakin
EX $15   NM $25   MIP $50

❑ **Tasmanian Devil Figure,** 1989, Superior, 7", plastic, on base
EX $5   NM $15   MIP $30

❑ **Tweety Figure,** 1971, Dakin, on bird cage
EX $14   NM $25   MIP $50

❑ **Tweety Figure,** 1971, Dakin, Goofy Gram, holding red heart
EX $15   NM $25   MIP $50

❑ **Tweety Figure,** 1976, Dakin, Cartoon Theater
EX $9   NM $22   MIP $45

TOY

❑ **Bugs Bunny Hand Puppet,** 1940s, Zany, rubber head
EX $35   NM $80   MIP $175

❑ **Elmer Fudd Hand Puppet,** 1940s, Zany, rubber head
EX $30   NM $70   MIP $150

❑ **Foghorn Leghorn Hand Puppet,** 1940s, Zany, rubber head
EX $30   NM $75   MIP $160

❑ **Pepe Le Pew Goofy Gram,** 1971, Dakin
EX $25   NM $50   MIP $100

❑ **Sylvester Hand Puppet,** 1940s, Zany, rubber head
EX $32   NM $80   MIP $160

❑ **Sylvester Soaky,** Colgate
EX $10   NM $30   MIP $60

❑ **Tweety Hand Puppet,** 1940s, Zany, rubber head
EX $30   NM $80   MIP $160

❑ **Tweety Soaky,** 1960s, Colgate, 8-1/2", plastic
EX $10   NM $30   MIP $60

MAGILLA GORILLA

ACCESSORIES

❑ **Magilla Gorilla Cereal Bowl,** MB Inc.
EX $10   NM $35   MIP $75

❑ **Magilla Gorilla Plate,** 1960s, 8" diameter, plastic
EX $7   NM $20   MIP $35

BOOK

❑ **Magilla Gorilla Book,** 1964, Golden, Big Golden Book
EX $12   NM $25   MIP $50

DOLL

❑ **Magilla Gorilla Doll,** 1960s, 11" tall, cloth body, hard arms and legs, hard plastic head
EX $30   NM $80   MIP $225

❑ **Magilla Gorilla Doll,** 1966, Ideal, 18-1/2" plush w/vinyl head
EX $50   NM $160   MIP $325

TOY

❑ **Droop-A-Long Coyote Soaky,** 1960s, Purex, 12", plastic
EX $20   NM $45   MIP $90

❑ **Droop-A-Long Hand Puppet,** Ideal, vinyl head
EX $25   NM $60   MIP $120

❑ **Magilla Gorilla Cannon,** 1964, Ideal
EX $30   NM $80   MIP $160

❑ **Magilla Gorilla Pull Toy,** 1960s, Ideal, w/vinyl figure
EX $40   NM $110   MIP $210

❑ **Magilla Gorilla Puppet,** Ideal
EX $40   NM $110   MIP $210

❑ **Magilla Gorilla Push Puppet,** 1960s, Kohner, brown plastic figure in pink shorts and shoes, yellow base
EX $25   NM $55   MIP $110

❑ **Punkin' Puss Soaky,** 1960s, Purex, 11-1/2" tall, plastic
EX $20   NM $50   MIP $85

❑ **Ricochet Rabbit Hand Puppet,** 1960s, Ideal, 11", vinyl head
EX $30   NM $45   MIP $90

❑ **Ricochet Rabbit Soaky,** 1960s, Purex, 10-1/2" tall, plastic
EX $30   NM $70   MIP $140

MARY POPPINS

ACCESSORIES

❑ **Mary Poppins Pencil Case,** 1964, vinyl w/zipper top
EX $10   NM $22   MIP $45

DOLL

❑ **Mary Poppins Doll,** 1964, Gund, 11-1/2" tall, bendable
EX $40   NM $100   MIP $210

FIGURES

❑ **Mary Poppins Figure,** 8" tall, ceramic
EX $20   NM $40   MIP $85

PUZZLE

❑ **Mary Poppins Puzzle,** 1964, Jaymar, frame tray
EX $8   NM $20   MIP $35

TOY

❑ **Mary Poppins Manicure Set,** 1964, Tre-Jur
EX $20   NM $45   MIP $90

❑ **Mary Poppins Paper Dolls,** 1973, Whitman, w/magic tote bag, Model No. 1977
EX $20   NM $45   MIP $90

❑ **Mary Poppins Tea Set,** 1964, Chein, tin, creamer, plates, place settings, cups, serving tray
EX $30   NM $80   MIP $160

MICKEY AND MINNIE MOUSE

ACCESSORIES

❑ **Mickey and Donald Alarm Clock,** 1960s, Jerger/Germany, 2-1/2" x 5" x 7"; metal case, dark brass finish, 3-D plastic figures of Mickey and Donald on either side
EX $60   NM $120   MIP $185

❑ **Mickey and Minnie and Donald Throw Rug,** 26" x 41", Mickey and Minnie in an airplane w/Donald parachuting
EX $60   NM $120   MIP $200

❑ **Mickey and Minnie Carpet,** 27" x 41", Peg Leg Pete is lassoed by Mickey; all characters in western outfits
EX $115   NM $225   MIP $350

❑ **Mickey and Minnie Snow Dome,** 1970s, Monogram, 3" x 4" x 3" tall, Mickey and Minnie w/a pot of gold at the end of the rainbow
EX $12   NM $25   MIP $50

❑ **Mickey and Minnie Toothbrush Holder,** 4-1/2" tall, bisque, toothbrush holes are located behind their heads
EX $90   NM $200   MIP $375

❑ **Mickey and Minnie Toothbrush Holder,** 2-1/2" x 4" x 3-1/2", Mickey and Minnie on sofa w/Pluto at their feet
EX $100   NM $210   MIP $400

❑ **Mickey and Minnie Trash Can,** 1970s, Chein, 13" tall tin litho, Mickey and Minnie fixing a flat tire on one side, other side shows Mickey feeding Minnie soup
EX $25   NM $80   MIP $160

❑ **Mickey and Pluto Ashtray,** 3" x 4" x 3" tall, ceramic, Mickey and Pluto playing banjos while sitting on the edge of the ashtray
EX $150   NM $300   MIP $500

❑ **Mickey Mouse Alarm Clock,** 1960s, Bayard, 2" x 4-1/2" x 4-1/2" tall, 1930s style Mickey w/movable head that ticks off the seconds
EX $100   NM $200   MIP $325

❑ **Mickey Mouse Alarm Clock,** 1975, Bradley, travel alarm, large red cube case, shut off button on top, separate alarm wind, in sleeve box
EX $30   NM $55   MIP $90

❑ **Mickey Mouse Alarm Clock,** 1988, House Martin, 5" x 7" x 2"
EX $11   NM $20   MIP $40

❑ **Mickey Mouse Ashtray,** 3-1/2" tall, wood composition figure of Mickey
EX $40   NM $110   MIP $225

❑ **Mickey Mouse Beanie,** 1950s, blue/yellow felt hat w/Mickey on front
EX $55   NM $200   MIP $375

❑ **Mickey Mouse Christmas Lights,** 1930s, Noma, eight lamps w/holiday decals of characters
EX $125   NM $225   MIP $350

❑ **Mickey Mouse Clock,** 1970s, Elgin, 10" x 15" x 3", electric wall clock
EX $12   NM $25   MIP $35

❑ **Mickey Mouse Club Coffee Tin,** 1950s, illustrated lid promotes the club, tin included MM badge
EX $35   NM $75   MIP $150

❑ **Mickey Mouse Club Mouseketeer Handbag,** Connecticut Leather, leather/vinyl crafting set
EX $45   NM $60   MIP $90

❑ **Mickey Mouse Club Plastic Plate,** 1960s, Arrowhead, 9" diameter, clubhouse w/Goofy, Pluto and Donald wearing mouse ears and sweaters w/club emblems
EX $16   NM $30   MIP $45

❑ **Mickey Mouse Club Toothbrush,** 1970s, Pepsodent
EX $4   NM $7   MIP $15

❑ **Mickey Mouse Cup,** 1950s, Cavalier, 3" tall, silver-plated cup w/a 2-1/2" opening
EX $25   NM $50   MIP $100

❑ **Mickey Mouse Electric Table Radio,** 1960s, General Electric, 4-1/2" x 10-1/2" x 6" tall
EX $30   NM $75   MIP $150

❑ **Mickey Mouse Lamp,** 1935, Soreng-Manegold, 10-1/2" tall
EX $100   NM $225   MIP $450

❏ **Mickey Mouse Map of the United States,** 1930s, Dixon, 9-1/4" x 14"
EX $40   NM $185   MIP $375

❏ **Mickey Mouse Night Light,** 1938, Disney, 4" tall, tin
EX $100   NM $200   MIP $300

❏ **Mickey Mouse Pencil Box,** 1930s, Dixon, 5-1/2" x 10-1/2" x 1-1/4", Mickey in a gymnasium
EX $60   NM $125   MIP $250

❏ **Mickey Mouse Pencil Box,** 1930s, Dixon, Mickey ready to hitch Horace to a carriage in which Minnie is sitting
EX $60   NM $125   MIP $250

❏ **Mickey Mouse Pencil Box,** 1937, Dixon, 5-1/2" x 9" x 3/4", Mickey, Goofy and Pluto riding a rocket
EX $60   NM $125   MIP $250

❏ **Mickey Mouse Pencil Box,** 1937, Dixon, 5" x 8-1/2" x 1-1/4", Mickey is a circus ringmaster and Donald riding a seal
EX $60   NM $125   MIP $250

❏ **Mickey Mouse Pencil Holder,** 1930s, Dixon, 4-1/2" tall
EX $65   NM $130   MIP $260

❏ **Mickey Mouse Pencil Sharpener,** 3" tall, celluloid, sharpener located on base
EX $65   NM $125   MIP $250

❏ **Mickey Mouse Pencil Sharpener,** 1960s, Hasbro, shape of Mickey's head, pencil goes into mouth
EX $12   NM $25   MIP $50

❏ **Mickey Mouse Pitcher,** 1930s, Germany, 2" x 3" diameter, china, white w/green shading around the base, Mickey on each side
EX $70   NM $135   MIP $270

❏ **Mickey Mouse Radio,** 1934, Emerson, wood composition cabinet w/designs of Mickey playing musical instruments
EX $750   NM $2000   MIP $4500

❏ **Mickey Mouse Radio,** 1970s, Philgee
EX $20   NM $40   MIP $70

❏ **Mickey Mouse Record Player,** 1970s, General Electric, playing arm is the design of Mickey's arm
EX $60   NM $125   MIP $175

❏ **Mickey Mouse Throw Rug,** 1935, Alex. Smith Carpet, 26" x 42"
EX $130   NM $250   MIP $375

❏ **Mickey Mouse Transistor Radio,** 1950s, Gabriel, 6-1/2" x 7" x 1-1/2"
EX $40   NM $80   MIP $160

❏ **Mickey Mouse Wall Clock,** 1978, Elgin, 9" diameter dial, 15" long, shaped like oversize watchband, "50 Happy Years" logo on dial
EX $30   NM $60   MIP $90

❏ **Minnie Mouse Alarm Clock,** 1970s, Bradley, pink metal electric two-bell clock w/articulated hands
EX $25   NM $50   MIP $85

❏ **Minnie Mouse Clock,** 1970s, Phinney-Walker, 8" diameter by 1-1/2" deep, plastic, "Behind Every Great Man, There is a Woman!"
EX $40   NM $70   MIP $125

BANK

❏ **Mickey Mouse Band Leader Bank,** Knickerbocker, 7-1/2" tall, plastic
EX $10   NM $25   MIP $50

❏ **Mickey Mouse Bank,** 1930s, 2" x 3" x 2-1/4", tin, shaped like a treasure chest w/Mickey and Minnie on the "Isle of the Thrift"
EX $180   NM $360   MIP $575

❏ **Mickey Mouse Bank,** 1930s, 2-1/2" x 6", shaped like a mailbox w/Mickey holding an envelope
EX $75   NM $200   MIP $400

❏ **Mickey Mouse Bank,** 1934, German, 2-1/2" x 3", tin, bright yellow bank shaped like a beehive, Mickey approaching door holding a honey jar in one arm and key to open the door in the other
EX $180   NM $375   MIP $750

❏ **Mickey Mouse Bank,** 1938, Crown Toy, 6" tall, composition, key locked trap door on base, w/figure standing next to treasure chest and head is movable
EX $75   NM $180   MIP $425

❏ **Mickey Mouse Bank,** 1950s, 5" x 5-1/2" x 6", china, shaped like Mickey's head w/slot between his ears
EX $30   NM $70   MIP $160

❏ **Mickey Mouse Bank,** 1960s, Wolverine, 1-1/2" x 5-1/2" x 1" tall, plastic
EX $50   NM $60   MIP $125

❏ **Mickey Mouse Bank,** 1970s, Transogram, 5" x 7-1/2" x 19" tall, plastic w/Mickey standing on a white chest
EX $15   NM $25   MIP $40

❏ **Mickey Mouse Bank,** 1978, Fricke and Nacke, 3" x 5" x 7" tall, embossed image of Mickey in front, side panels have Minnie, Goofy, Donald and Pluto
EX $15   NM $25   MIP $175

❏ **Mickey Mouse Club Bank,** 1970s, Play Pal Plastics, 4-1/2" x 6" x 11-1/2" tall, vinyl
EX $16   NM $30   MIP $60

❏ **Mickey Mouse Gumball Bank,** 1968, Hasbro
EX $15   NM $30   MIP $60

❏ **Mickey Mouse Telephone Bank,** 1938, N.N. Hill Brass, 5" tall w/cardboard figure of Mickey
EX $80   NM $165   MIP $325

BOOK

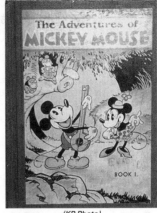

(KP Photo)

❏ **Adventures of Mickey Mouse Book,** 1931, David McKay, full color illustrations, softcover
EX $75   NM $225   MIP $500

❏ **Mickey Mouse Activity Book,** 1936, Whitman, 40 pages
EX $40   NM $120   MIP $200

❏ **Mickey Mouse Club Fun Box,** 1957, Whitman, box includes stamp book, club scrapbook, six coloring books and four small gameboards
EX $45   NM $85   MIP $160

❏ **Mickey Mouse Has a Busy Day Book,** 1937, Whitman, 16 pages
EX $25   NM $50   MIP $100

❏ **Mickey Mouse in Giantland Book,** 1934, David McKay, 45 pages, hardcover
EX $60   NM $112   MIP $225

❏ **Mickey Mouse Presents a Silly Symphony Book,** 1934, Whitman, Big Little Book
EX $35   NM $75   MIP $150

DOLL

❏ **Mickey and Minnie Dolls,** 1940s, Gund, 13" tall, each
EX $150   NM $325   MIP $750

(KP Photo)

❏ **Mickey Mouse Club Mouseketeer Doll,** 1960s, Horsman, 8" tall, denim outfit
EX $25 **NM** $65 **MIP** $125

❏ **Mickey Mouse Doll,** Knickerbocker, 5" x 7" x 12" tall, fabric, Mickey in checkered shorts and green jacket w/white felt flower stapled to it
EX $200 **NM** $375 **MIP** $650

❏ **Mickey Mouse Doll,** 1930s, 4" x 7" x 10-1/2" tall, movable arms and legs, swivel head, black velveteen body and red felt pants
EX $375 **NM** $750 **MIP** $1250

❏ **Mickey Mouse Doll,** 1935, Knicker-bocker, 11" tall, stuffed w/removable shoes and jointed head, red shorts
EX $120 **NM** $240 **MIP** $375

❏ **Mickey Mouse Doll,** 1950s, Schuco, 10" tall
EX $110 **NM** $225 **MIP** $400

❏ **Mickey Mouse Doll,** 1960s, Gund, 12", Mickey as fireman
EX $30 **NM** $55 **MIP** $90

❏ **Mickey Mouse Doll,** 1970s, Hasbro, 4" x 5-1/2" x 7-1/2" tall, talks
EX $20 **NM** $40 **MIP** $60

❏ **Mickey Mouse Doll,** 1972, Horsman, 3" x 10" x 12" tall, talking doll, says five different phrases
EX $20 **NM** $35 **MIP** $60

❏ **Minnie Mouse Doll,** 1935, Knicker-bocker, 14" tall, stuffed, cloth, polka-dot skirt and lace pantaloons
EX $150 **NM** $350 **MIP** $700

❏ **Minnie Mouse Doll,** 1940s, Petz, 10" tall
EX $125 **NM** $235 **MIP** $425

FIGURES

❏ **Mickey Mouse Figure,** 4" tall, bisque, dressed in a green nightshirt
EX $40 **NM** $80 **MIP** $140

❏ **Mickey Mouse Figure,** composition, part of the Lionel Circus Train Set
EX n/a **NM** n/a **MIP** n/a

❏ **Mickey Mouse Figure,** 1930s, Seiber-ling, 6-1/2" tall, rubber
EX $80 **NM** $175 **MIP** $250

❏ **Mickey Mouse Figure,** 1930s, Goebel, 3-1/2" tall, in a hunting outfit reading a book
EX $45 **NM** $90 **MIP** $150

❏ **Mickey Mouse Figure,** 1930s, Seiber-ling, 3-1/2" tall, black hard rubber
EX $60 **NM** $112 **MIP** $225

❏ **Mickey Mouse Figure,** 1930s, 3" tall, bisque, holding a parade flag and sword
EX $45 **NM** $100 **MIP** $185

❏ **Mickey Mouse Figure,** 1930s, 3" tall, bisque, plays saxophone
EX $45 **NM** $100 **MIP** $185

❏ **Mickey Mouse Figure,** 1930s, Seiber-ling, 3-1/2" tall, latex
EX $75 **NM** $150 **MIP** $200

❏ **Mickey Mouse Figure,** 1970, Marx, 6" tall, vinyl
EX $10 **NM** $20 **MIP** $40

❏ **Mickey Mouse Fun-E-Flex Figure,** 1930s, Fun-E-Flex, 7", bendy
EX $245 **NM** $455 **MIP** $750

❏ **Minnie Mouse Figure,** 1958, Ingersoll, 5-1/2" tall, plastic
EX $35 **NM** $60 **MIP** $100

❏ **Minnie Mouse Fun-E-Flex Figure,** 1930s, Fun-E-Flex, 5", bendy
EX $130 **NM** $250 **MIP** $375

GAME

❏ **Mickey Mouse Bean Bag Game,** 1930s, Marks Bros.
EX $100 **NM** $130 **MIP** $220

❏ **Mickey Mouse Club Magic Divider,** 1950s, Jacmar, arithmetic game
EX $30 **NM** $55 **MIP** $85

❏ **Mickey Mouse Club Magic Subtractor,** 1950s, Jacmar, arithmetic game
EX $11 **NM** $20 **MIP** $40

MUSIC BOX

❏ **Mickey Mouse Music Box,** 4-1/2" x 5" x 7", plays "It's a Small World," Mickey in conductor's uniform standing on cake
EX $20 **NM** $35 **MIP** $60

❏ **Mickey Mouse Music Box,** Schmid, 3" x 6" x 7-1/2" tall, bisque, Spirit of '76, plays "Yankee Doodle;" Mickey, Goofy and Donald are dressed as Revolution-ary War Minutemen
EX $60 **NM** $120 **MIP** $185

❏ **Mickey Mouse Music Box,** 1970s, Schmid, 3-1/2" x 5-1/2", plays "Mickey Mouse Club March," ceramic, Mickey in western clothes standing next to a cac-tus
EX $35 **NM** $60 **MIP** $90

❏ **Mickey Mouse Music Box,** 1970s, Japan, 4" x 6" tall, china, plays "Side by Side," Mickey is brushing a kitten in a washtub
EX $15 **NM** $25 **MIP** $60

❏ **Mickey Mouse Music Box,** 1971, Anri, 5" x 3-1/2", plays "If I Were Rich Man"
EX $50 **NM** $85 **MIP** $135

❏ **Minnie Mouse Music Box,** 1970s, Schmid, 3-1/2" diameter, plays "Love Story"
EX $12 **NM** $25 **MIP** $60

TOY

❏ **Crayons,** 1946, Transogram
EX $20 **NM** $45 **MIP** $85

❏ **Mickey and Donald Jack-in-the-Box,** 1966, Lakeside, Donald pops out
EX $30 **NM** $75 **MIP** $175

❏ **Mickey and Minnie Flashlight,** 1930s, Usalite Co., 6" long, Mickey leading Min-nie through the darkness guided by flashlight and Pluto
EX $50 **NM** $85 **MIP** $125

❏ **Mickey and Minnie Sand Pail,** Ohio Art, 5" x 5", tin, Mickey, Minnie, Pluto and Donald in boat looking across water at castle, w/swivel handle
EX $45 **NM** $120 **MIP** $310

❏ **Mickey and Minnie Sled,** 1935, S.L. Allen, 32" long, wooden slat sled, metal runners, "Mickey Mouse" decal on steer-ing bar
EX $140 **NM** $350 **MIP** $600

❏ **Mickey and Minnie Tea Set,** 1930s, Ohio Art, 5" x 8", pitcher pictures Mickey at piano and cups picture Mickey, Pluto and Minnie
EX $60 **NM** $150 **MIP** $300

❏ **Mickey and Minnie Tray,** 1930s, Ohio Art, 5-1/2" x 7-1/4", tin, Mickey and Min-nie in rowboat
EX $30 **NM** $90 **MIP** $185

❏ **Mickey and Three Pigs Spinning Top,** Lackawanna, 9" diameter, tin
EX $35 **NM** $85 **MIP** $175

❏ **Mickey Mouse Baby Gift Set,** 1930s, silver-plated cup, fork, spoon, cup and napkin holder
EX $100 **NM** $200 **MIP** $325

❏ **Mickey Mouse Band Drum,** 1936, 7" x 14" diameter, cloth mesh and paper drum heads
EX $75 **NM** $200 **MIP** $325

❏ **Mickey Mouse Band Sand Pail,** 1938, Ohio Art, 6" tall, tin, pictures of Mickey Mouse, Minnie, Horace, Pluto, and Clar-abelle the cow parading down street
EX $30 **NM** $100 **MIP** $260

❏ **Mickey Mouse Band Spinning Top,** 9" diameter
EX $30 **NM** $75 **MIP** $150

❏ **Mickey Mouse Boxed Lantern Slides,** 1930s, Ensign, 5" x 6" x 2", cartoons: Traffic Troubles, Gorilla Mystery, Cac-tus Kid, Castaway, Delivery Boy, Fishin' Around, Firefighters, Moose Hunt and Mickey Steps Out
EX $160 **NM** $325 **MIP** $475

❏ **Mickey Mouse Bubble Buster Gun,** 1936, Kilgore, 8" long, cork gun
EX $75 **NM** $150 **MIP** $225

❏ **Mickey Mouse Bump-N-Go Spaceship,** 1980s, Matsudaya, battery operated tin litho w/clear dome, has six flashing lights, rotating antenna
EX $35 **NM** $65 **MIP** $125

❏ **Mickey Mouse Camera,** 1960s, Ettel-son, 3" x 3" x 5"
EX $18 **NM** $40 **MIP** $60

❏ **Mickey Mouse Camera,** 1970s, Child Guidance, 4" x 7" x 7"
EX $12 **NM** $25 **MIP** $50

❏ **Mickey Mouse Camera,** 1970s, Helm Toy, 2" x 5" x 4-1/2", Mickey in engineer's uniform riding on top of the train
EX $13 **NM** $25 **MIP** $50

❏ **Mickey Mouse Car,** 1970s, Polistil, 2" x 4" x 1-1/2" tall plastic car w/rubber fig-ure, Mickey in driver's seat
EX $30 **NM** $55 **MIP** $85

❑ **Mickey Mouse Cardboard House,**
1930s, O.B. Andrews, 14" x 12" x 13" tall
EX $125   NM $250   MIP $400

❑ **Mickey Mouse Chatty Chums,** 1979,
Mattel
EX $8   NM $15   MIP $35

❑ **Mickey Mouse Club Magic Kit,** 1950s,
Mars Candy, two 8" x 20" punch-out
sheets
EX $30   NM $60   MIP $130

❑ **Mickey Mouse Club Marionette,**
1950s, 3" x 6-1/2" x 13-1/2" tall, composition figure of a girl w/black felt hat and
mouse ears
EX $160   NM $350   MIP $450

❑ **Mickey Mouse Club Mousketeer Ears,**
Kohner, 7" x 12-1/2"
EX $11   NM $20   MIP $40

❑ **Mickey Mouse Club Newsreel with
Sound,** 1950s, Mattel, 4" x 4-1/2" x 9"
tall, orange box, plastic projector w/two
short filmstrips, record, cardboard
screen, cartoons "Touchdown Mickey"
and "No Sail"
EX $75   NM $170   MIP $285

❑ **Mickey Mouse Club Rhythm Makers
Set,** Emenee
EX $65   NM $150   MIP $325

(KP Photo)

❑ **Mickey Mouse Colorforms Set,** 1976,
Colorforms, 8" x 12-1/2" x 1", Spirit of
'76
EX $10   NM $30   MIP $75

❑ **Mickey Mouse Dart Gun Target,** 1930s,
Marks Brothers, 10" target, dart gun and
suction darts
EX $85   NM $175   MIP $350

❑ **Mickey Mouse Dinner Set,** 1930s,
Empresa Electro, china, 2" creamer, 3-
4-1/2" plates and 3-5" plates, 7" long
dish, two oval platters
EX $150   NM $300   MIP $450

❑ **Mickey Mouse Dominoes,** Halsam,
Mickey and Pluto on dominoes
EX $80   NM $100   MIP $160
(Hakes Americana & Collectibles)

❑ **Mickey Mouse Drum,** 1930s, Ohio Art,
6" diameter
EX $60   NM $112   MIP $225

❑ **Mickey Mouse Electric Casting Set,**
1930s, Home Foundary, 9-1/2" x 16" x 2"
EX $65   NM $125   MIP $190

❑ **Mickey Mouse Fire Engine,** Sun Rubber, 7" long, rubber, push toy
EX $50   NM $100   MIP $200

(KP Photo)

❑ **Mickey Mouse Fire Truck with Figure,**
Sun Rubber, 2-1/2" x 6-1/2" x 4", Mickey
driving and mold-in image of Donald
standing on the back holding onto his
helmet
EX $50   NM $100   MIP $200

❑ **Mickey Mouse Jack-In-the-Box,**
1970s, 5-1/2" square tin litho box shows
Mickey, Pluto, Donald and Goofy,
Mickey pops out
EX $25   NM $50   MIP $75

❑ **Mickey Mouse Lionel Circus Train,**
1935, Lionel, five cars w/Mickey, 30"
train, 84 inches of track, circus tent,
Sunoco station, truck, tickets, Mickey
composition statue
EX $1000   NM $2500   MIP $5000

❑ **Mickey Mouse Lionel Circus Train
Handcar,** Lionel, metal, 9" long w/6" tall
composition/rubber figures of Mickey
and Minnie
EX $225   NM $450   MIP $900

❑ **Mickey Mouse Magic Slate,** 1950s,
Watkins-Strathmore, 8-1/2" x 14" tall
EX $15   NM $30   MIP $60

❑ **Mickey Mouse Marbles,** Monarch,
marbles and Mickey bag, on card
EX $5   NM $15   MIP $30

❑ **Mickey Mouse Mechanical Pencil,**
1930s, head of Mickey on one end and
decal of Mickey walking on other side of
pencil
EX $40   NM $80   MIP $160

❑ **Mickey Mouse Mechanical Robot,**
Gabriel
EX $70   NM $125   MIP $150

❑ **Mickey Mouse Mousegetar,** 1960s, 10"
x 30" x 2-1/2" black plastic
EX $40   NM $85   MIP $160

❑ **Mickey Mouse Movie Projector,** 1934,
Keystone, 5-1/2" x 11-1/2" x 11" tall for
8mm movies
EX $150   NM $300   MIP $600

❑ **Mickey Mouse Movie-Fun Shows,**
1940s, Mastercraft, 7-1/2" square by 4"
deep, animated action movies
EX $106   NM $212   MIP $325

❑ **Mickey Mouse Musical Money Box,**
1970s, 3" x 6", tin box w/Mickey, Pluto,
Donald and Goofy
EX $30   NM $55   MIP $90

❑ **Mickey Mouse Old Timers Fire Engine,**
1980s, Matsudaya, red, tin and plastic
fire truck w/Mickey at the wheel
EX $40   NM $70   MIP $125

❑ **Mickey Mouse Picture Gun,** 1950s,
Stephens, 6-1/2" x 9-1/2" x 3", metal,
lights to show filmstrips
EX $55   NM $100   MIP $250

❑ **Mickey Mouse Play Tiles,** 1964, Halsam, 336 tiles
EX $15   NM $25   MIP $50

❑ **Mickey Mouse Print Shop Set,** 1930s,
Fulton Specialty, 6-1/2" x 6-1/2", ink pad,
stamper, metal tweezers, wooden tray
EX $80   NM $160   MIP $285

❑ **Mickey Mouse Pull Toy,** Toy Kraft, 7" x
22" x 8" tall, horse cart drawn by wooden
horses
EX $300   NM $600   MIP $900

❑ **Mickey Mouse Pull Toy,** 1935, N.N. Hill
Brass, 14" tall, wood and metal
EX $135   NM $275   MIP $450

❑ **Mickey Mouse Puppet Forms,** 1960s,
Colorforms
EX $10   NM $25   MIP $60

❑ **Mickey Mouse Riding Toy,** 1930s,
Mengel, 6" x 17" x 16" tall
EX $400   NM $800   MIP $1500

❑ **Mickey Mouse Rodeo Rider,** 1980s,
Matsudaya, plastic wind-up, cowboy
Mickey rides a bucking bronco
EX $25   NM $45   MIP $75

❑ **Mickey Mouse Rolykin,** Marx, 1-1/2"
tall, ball bearing action
EX $12   NM $20   MIP $60

❑ **Mickey Mouse Rub 'N Play Magic
Transfer Set,** 1978, Colorforms
EX $15   NM $30   MIP $70

❑ **Mickey Mouse Safety Blocks,** 1930s,
Halsam, nine blocks
EX $100   NM $200   MIP $300

❑ **Mickey Mouse Sand Pail,** 1938, Ohio
Art, 6" tall, tin, Mickey, Donald and Goofy
playing golf
EX $33   NM $100   MIP $275

❑ **Mickey Mouse Sand Pail,** 1938, Ohio
Art, 3" tall, tin
EX $25   NM $80   MIP $185

❑ **Mickey Mouse Sand Shovel,** Ohio Art,
10" long, tin
EX $20   NM $65   MIP $150

❑ **Mickey Mouse Saxophone,** 1930s, 16"
tall
EX $125   NM $250   MIP $375

❑ **Mickey Mouse Scissors,** Disney, 3"
long, child's scissors w/Mickey figure
EX $20   NM $35   MIP $65

❑ **Mickey Mouse Serving Tray,** 1960s,
11" diameter, tin
EX $11   NM $20   MIP $60

❑ **Mickey Mouse Sewing Cards,** 1978,
Colorforms, 7-1/2" x 12" cut-out card
designs of Mickey, Minnie, Pluto, Clar-
abelle, Donald Duck and Horace
EX $10   NM $20   MIP $75

❑ **Mickey Mouse Sled,** 1930s, Flexible
Flyer, 18" x 30" x 6" tall, wood
EX $200   NM $600   MIP $1200

❏ **Mickey Mouse Squeeze Toy,** 1950s, Dell, rubber, Mickey as hitchhiking hobo
EX $35   NM $75   MIP $160

❏ **Mickey Mouse Squeeze Toy,** 1950s, Sun Rubber, 10" tall, rubber
EX $20   NM $45   MIP $90

❏ **Mickey Mouse Squeeze Toy,** 1960s, Dell, 8" tall
EX $15   NM $30   MIP $50

❏ **Mickey Mouse Stamp Pad,** 1930s, 3" long
EX $50   NM $100   MIP $200

❏ **Mickey Mouse Steamboat,** 1988, Matsudaya, wind-up plastic steamboat w/Mickey as Steamboat Willie, runs on floor as smokestacks go up and down, box says "60 Years w/You"
EX $30   NM $60   MIP $135

❏ **Mickey Mouse Tea Set,** Wolverine, plastic
EX $50   NM $175   MIP $175

❏ **Mickey Mouse Tea Set,** 1930s, 3" saucer, 2" pitcher, 2-1/2" sugar bowl each piece shows Mickey and Minnie in a rowboat
EX $44   NM $140   MIP $280

❏ **Mickey Mouse Tractor,** Sun Rubber, 5" long, rubber
EX $40   NM $100   MIP $200

❏ **Mickey Mouse Tricycle Toy,** 1932, Steiff, 8-1/2" x 7", wood and metal frame, action movement
EX $500   NM $1400   MIP $3800

❏ **Mickey Mouse Twirling Tail Toy,** 1950s, Marx, 3" x 5-1/2" x 5-1/2" tall, w/a built-in key, metal tail spins around as the toy vibrates
EX $120   NM $225   MIP $375

❏ **Mickey Mouse Utensils,** 1947, Wm. Rogers and Son, 6" fork and 5-1/2" spoon
EX $50   NM $100   MIP $175

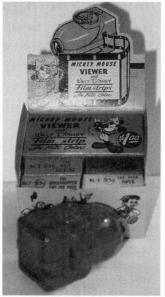

(KP Photo)

❏ **Mickey Mouse Viewer,** 1940s, Craftsmen's Guild, film viewer w/12 films
EX $70   NM $135   MIP $210

❏ **Mickey Mouse Wash Machine,** Ohio Art, 8" tin litho w/Mickey and Minnie Mouse pictured doing their wash
EX $50   NM $150   MIP $325

❏ **Mickey Mouse Water Globes,** 1970s, 3" x 4-1/2" x 5" tall, three dimensional plastic figures of Mickey seated w/a plastic water globe between his legs
EX $25   NM $50   MIP $100

❏ **Mickey Mouse Watering Can,** 1938, Ohio Art, 6" tin litho
EX $40   NM $135   MIP $260

❏ **Mickey Mouse Wind-Up Musical Toy,** 1970s, Illco, 6" tall, plays "Lullaby and Goodnight," 3-D figure of Mickey in red pants and yellow shirt
EX $25   NM $35   MIP $65

❏ **Mickey Mouse Wind-Up Toy,** 1978, Gabriel, plastic transparent figure of Mickey w/visible metal gears
EX $10   NM $20   MIP $50

❏ **Mickey Mouse Wind-Up Trike,** 1960s, Korean, tin litho trike w/plastic Mickey w/flag and balloon on handle, bell on back
EX $85   NM $150   MIP $250

❏ **Mickey Mouse Yarn Sewing Kit,** 1930s, Marks Bros., seven cards, yarn, needle
EX $40   NM $165   MIP $280

❏ **Mickey's Air Mail Plane,** 1940s, Sun Rubber, 3-1/2" x 6" long, 5" wingspan, rubber
EX $60   NM $175   MIP $325

❏ **Minnie Mouse Car,** 1979, Matchbox
EX $5   NM $15   MIP $35

❏ **Minnie Mouse Choo-Choo Train Pull Toy,** 1940s, Linemar, 3" x 8-1/2" x 7" tall, green metal base and green wooden wheels
EX $70   NM $175   MIP $350

❏ **Minnie Mouse Hand Puppet,** 1940s, 11" tall, white on red polka-dot, fabric hard cover and a pair of black and white felt hands
EX $55   NM $135   MIP $225

❏ **Minnie Mouse Rocker,** 1950s, Marx, tin wind-up, rocker moves back and forth w/gravity motion of her head and ears
EX $250   NM $480   MIP $720

❏ **Minnie with Bump-n-Go Action Shopping Cart,** 1980s, Illfelder, 4" x 9-1/2" x 11-1/2" tall, plastic, battery operated Minnie pushing cart
EX $30   NM $55   MIP $80

❏ **Mouseketeer Cut-Outs,** 1957, Whitman, figures and accessories
EX $35   NM $75   MIP $150

❏ **Mouseketeer Fan Club Typewriter,** 1950s, lithographed tin
EX $50   NM $100   MIP $185

❏ **Puzzle,** 1930s, Marks Brothers, 10" x 12", Mickey polishing the boiler on his "Mickey Mouse R.R." train engine and Minnie waving from the cab
EX $55   NM $110   MIP $225

❏ **Puzzle,** 1957, Whitman, Adventureland, 11" x 15" frame tray; Mickey, Minnie, Donald and his nephew in boat surrounded by jungle beasts
EX $15   NM $40   MIP $80

❏ **Puzzle,** 1960s, Jaymar, Pluto's Wash and Scrub Service
EX $15   NM $40   MIP $80

❏ **Spinning Top,** 1930s, Fritz Bueschel, 7" diameter, 7" tall, Mickey, Minnie, a nephew, Donald and Horace playing a musical instrument
EX $75   NM $150   MIP $300

❏ **Spinning Top,** 1950s, Chein, tin litho, features Mickey in cowboy outfit and other characters
EX $45   NM $130   MIP $260

WATCH

❏ **50 Years with Mickey Wristwatch,** 1983, Bradley, small round chrome case, inscription and serial number on back
EX $45   NM $85   MIP $175

❏ **Mickey and Pluto Wristwatch,** 1980, Bradley, LCD quartz, black vinyl band
EX $20   NM $45   MIP $100

❏ **Mickey Mouse Pocket Watch,** 1930s, Ingersoll, 2" diameter
EX $350   NM $1000   MIP $2000

❏ **Mickey Mouse Pocket Watch,** 1970s, Bradley
EX $40   NM $80   MIP $160

❏ **Mickey Mouse Pocket Watch,** 1976, Bradley, 3-1/2" x 4-1/2" x 3/4", Mickey in his Bicentennial outfit
EX $50   NM $100   MIP $200

❏ **Mickey Mouse Pocket Watch,** 1988, Lorus, #2202, quartz, small gold bezel, gold chain and clip fob, articulated hands
EX $25   NM $50   MIP $100

❏ **Mickey Mouse Wristwatch,** two-gun Mickey, saddle tan western style band
EX $25   NM $45   MIP $90

❏ **Mickey Mouse Wristwatch,** 1939, Ingersoll, rectangular w/standard second hand between Mickey's legs
EX $225   NM $425   MIP $850

(KP Photo)

❏ **Mickey Mouse Wristwatch**, 1958, Timex, electric
EX $120 **NM** $240 **MIP** $360

❏ **Mickey Mouse Wristwatch**, 1960s, Timex, large round case, stainless back, articulated hands, red vinyl band
EX $50 **NM** $80 **MIP** $125

❏ **Mickey Mouse Wristwatch**, 1970s, Bradley, white plastic case, watch on pendant, bubble crystal, articulated hands, gold chain
EX $25 **NM** $60 **MIP** $100

❏ **Mickey Mouse Wristwatch**, 1970s, Bradley, 2-1/2" x 6" x 2-1/2", plastic case, white dial w/Mickey playing tennis, the second hand has a tennis ball on the end of it
EX $35 **NM** $75 **MIP** $150

❏ **Mickey Mouse Wristwatch**, 1978, Bradley, commemorative edition
EX $65 **NM** $130 **MIP** $250

❏ **Mickey Mouse Wristwatch**, 1983, Bradley, medium black octagonal case, articulated hands, no numbers on face, in plastic window box
EX $25 **NM** $260 **MIP** $385

❏ **Mickey Mouse Wristwatch**, 1984, Bradley, medium white case, articulated hands, black face, sweep seconds, white vinyl band, in plastic window box
EX $20 **NM** $40 **MIP** $70

❏ **Minnie Mouse Wristwatch**, 1958, Timex, small round chrome case, stainless back, articulated hands, yellow vinyl band
EX $75 **NM** $150 **MIP** $250

❏ **Minnie Mouse Wristwatch**, 1978, Bradley, gold case, sweep seconds, red vinyl band, articulated hands
EX $16 **NM** $35 **MIP** $60

MIGHTY MOUSE

ACCESSORIES

❏ **Charm Bracelet**, 1950s, brass charms of Gandy Goose, Terry Bear, Mighty Mouse and other Terrytoon characters
EX $35 **NM** $75 **MIP** $150

(KP Photo)

❏ **Mighty Mouse Sneakers**, 1960s, Randy Co., children's, graphics on box, picture on sneakers
EX $25 **NM** $45 **MIP** $110

DOLL

❏ **Mighty Mouse Doll**, 1942, rubber head, yellow suit w/red cape
EX $300 **NM** $750 **MIP** $1050

❏ **Mighty Mouse Doll**, 1942, rubber head, wearing red suit
EX $325 **NM** $900 **MIP** $1200

❏ **Mighty Mouse Doll**, 1950s, Ideal, 14" tall, stuffed, cloth
EX $50 **NM** $100 **MIP** $200

FIGURES

❏ **Mighty Mouse Figure**, 1950s, 9-1/2" rubber, squeaks
EX $20 **NM** $60 **MIP** $120

❏ **Mighty Mouse Figure**, 1977, Dakin, hard and soft vinyl figure
EX $20 **NM** $50 **MIP** $90

❏ **Mighty Mouse Figure**, 1978, Dakin, Fun Farm
EX $20 **NM** $60 **MIP** $100

GAME

❏ **Mighty Mouse Ball Game**, 1981, Ja-Ru
EX $5 **NM** $12 **MIP** $30

TOY

❏ **Mighty Mouse Cinema Viewer**, 1979, Fleetwood, w/four strips
EX $7 **NM** $15 **MIP** $40

❏ **Mighty Mouse Dynamite Dasher**, 1981, Takara
EX $50 **NM** $110 **MIP** $250

❏ **Mighty Mouse Flashlight**, 1979, Dyno, 3-1/2" figural light
EX $20 **NM** $70 **MIP** $120

❏ **Mighty Mouse Hit the Claw Target Set**, Parks
EX $60 **NM** $125 **MIP** $250

❏ **Mighty Mouse Make-a-Face Sheet**, 1958, Towne, w/dials to change face parts
EX $20 **NM** $55 **MIP** $110

❏ **Mighty Mouse Mighty Money**, 1979, Fleetwood
EX $2 **NM** $55 **MIP** $85

❏ **Mighty Mouse Money Press**, 1981, Ja-Ru, stampers, pads and money
EX $8 **NM** $15 **MIP** $30

❏ **Mighty Mouse Movie Viewer**, 1980, Chemtoy
EX $8 **NM** $15 **MIP** $30

❏ **Mighty Mouse Picture Play Lite**, 1983, Janex
EX $8 **NM** $15 **MIP** $30

❏ **Mighty Mouse Wallet**, 1978, Larami
EX $15 **NM** $30 **MIP** $60

❏ **Puzzle**, tray puzzle; Mighty Mouse and his TV Pals
EX $10 **NM** $25 **MIP** $50

❏ **Puzzle**, 1979, Fleetwood, Mighty Mouse/Heckle and Jeckle
EX $20 **NM** $80 **MIP** $130

WATCH

❏ **Mighty Mouse Wristwatch**, 1979, Bradley, chrome case
EX $20 **NM** $40 **MIP** $80

MISCELLANEOUS CHARACTERS

ACCESSORIES

❏ **Amy Carter Paper Dolls**, 1970s, Toy Factory, 14" cardboard doll w/accessories
EX $15 **NM** $30 **MIP** $60

❏ **Holly Hobbie Wristwatch**, 1982, Bradley, small gold tone case, base metal back, yellow plastic band
EX $5 **NM** $10 **MIP** $35

❏ **Jimmy Carter Radio**, peanut-shaped transistor radio
EX $20 **NM** $45 **MIP** $90

❏ **Kennedy Kards**, 1960s, red, white, and blue playing cards w/cartoon artwork
EX $10 **NM** $20 **MIP** $35

❏ **Little King Lucky Safety Card**, 1953, New York Journal, 2" x 4" cards, Little King warns of safety
EX $15 **NM** $30 **MIP** $60

❏ **Mr. Potato Head Ice Pops**, 1950s, Hasbro, plastic molds for freezing treats, in box
EX $16 **NM** $35 **MIP** $70

❏ **Sandra Dee Paper Dolls**, 1959, Saalfield, two cardboard dolls w/outfits
EX $25 **NM** $50 **MIP** $100

❏ **Tuesday Weld Paper Dolls**, 1960, Saalfield, two cardboard dolls w/outfits
EX $25 **NM** $50 **MIP** $100

❏ **Uncle Don's "Puzzy and Sizzy" Membership Card**, 1950s
EX $10 **NM** $30 **MIP** $60

CHARACTER TOYS

❑ **Willie Whopper Pencil Case,** 1930s, green w/illustrations of Willie, Pirate and his gal
EX $45   NM $80   MIP $135

BANK

❑ **Sir Reginald Play-N-Save Bank,** 1960s, 7" tall plastic lion and hunter, on a 15" green plastic base, the hunter fires the coin into the lion's mouth
EX $45   NM $125   MIP $170

DOLL

❑ **Hardy Boys Dolls,** 1979, Kenner, 12" tall Joe Hardy (Shaun Cassidy) or Frank Hardy (Parker Stevenson)
EX $20   NM $40   MIP $80

FIGURES

❑ **Bruce Lee Figure,** 1986, Largo, 8" w/weapon
EX $20   NM $40   MIP $70

❑ **Diamond Jim Figure,** 1930s, 5-1/2" tall
EX $30   NM $80   MIP $160

❑ **George Bush Figure,** 7" tall
EX $8   NM $20   MIP $40

❑ **Lyndon Johnson Figure,** 1960s, Remco
EX $17   NM $35   MIP $60

❑ **Patton Figure,** Excel Toy, poseable doll w/clothing and accessories
EX $20   NM $40   MIP $80

❑ **Prince Charles of Wales Figure,** 1982, Goldberger, 13" tall, dressed in palace guard uniform
EX $18   NM $35   MIP $70

❑ **Sylvester Stallone Rambo Figure,** 1986, 18" tall, poseable figure
EX $10   NM $20   MIP $40

TOY

❑ **Bonzo Scooter Toy,** 7" scooter w/6" Bonzo, wind-up
EX $130   NM $260   MIP $520

❑ **Daktari Puzzle,** 1967, Whitman, 100 pieces
EX $10   NM $30   MIP $100

❑ **Evel Knievel Stunt Stadium,** 1974, Ideal, large vinyl case w/accessories
EX $40   NM $90   MIP $170

❑ **Jimmy Carter Wind-Up Walking Peanut,** 5" tall
EX $10   NM $22   MIP $45

❑ **Joan Palooka Stringless Marionette,** 1952, Nat'l Mask and Puppet, 12-1/2" tall "daughter of Joe Palooka" doll comes w/pink blanket and birth certificate
EX $55   NM $110   MIP $235

❑ **Komic Kamera Film Viewer Set,** 1950s, 5" long, Dick Tracy, Little Orphan Annie, Terry and the Pirates and The Lone Ranger
EX $40   NM $90   MIP $135

❑ **Mr. and Mrs. Potato Head Set,** 1960s, Hasbro, cars, boats, shopping trailer, etc.
EX $25   NM $55   MIP $110

❑ **Mr. Potato Head Frankie Frank,** 1966, Hasbro, companion to Mr. Potato Head, w/accessories
EX $20   NM $40   MIP $90

❑ **Mr. Potato Head Frenchy Fry,** 1966, Hasbro, companion to Mr. Potato Head, w/accessories
EX $20   NM $40   MIP $90

❑ **Red Ranger Ride 'Em Cowboy,** 1930s, Wyandotte, tin wind-up rocker
EX $125   NM $400   MIP $675

❑ **Ringling Bros. and Barnum and Bailey Circus Play Set,** 1970s, vinyl, w/animals, trapeze personnel, clowns and assorted circus equipment
EX $25   NM $50   MIP $100

❑ **Rin-Tin-Tin Magic Erasable Pictures,** 1955, Transogram
EX $50   NM $135   MIP $260

❑ **Space Ghost Puzzle,** 1967, Whitman
EX $20   NM $55   MIP $110

MOON MULLINS

ACCESSORIES

❑ **Moon Mullins and Kayo Toothbrush Holder,** 4" tall, bisque
EX $45   NM $100   MIP $185

❑ **Moon Mullins Playstone Funnies Mold Set,** 1940s
EX $40   NM $80   MIP $160

FIGURE

❑ **Moon Mullins Figure Set,** bisque, Uncle Willie, Kayo, Moon Mullins and Emmy, 2-1/4" to 3-1/2"
EX $85   NM $300   MIP $500

TOY

❑ **Moon Mullins and Kayo Railroad Handcar Toy,** 1930s, Marx, 6" long, wind-up, both figures bendable arms and legs
EX $250   NM $500   MIP $1000

❑ **Puzzle,** 1930s, 9-1/2" x 14", Featured Funnies
EX $20   NM $60   MIP $120

MR. MAGOO

ACCESSORIES

❑ **Mr. Magoo Drinking Glass,** 1962, 5-1/2" tall
EX $10   NM $25   MIP $50

DOLL

❑ **Mr. Magoo Doll,** 1962, Ideal, 5" tall, vinyl head w/cloth body
EX $55   NM $100   MIP $200

❑ **Mr. Magoo Doll,** 1970, Ideal, 12" tall
EX $25   NM $50   MIP $100

FIGURES

❑ **Mr. Magoo Figure,** Dakin, 7" tall
EX $40   NM $90   MIP $180

TOY

❑ **Mr. Magoo Car,** 1961, Hubley, 7-1/2" x 9" long, metal, battery-operated
EX $120   NM $360   MIP $500

❑ **Mr. Magoo Hand Puppet,** 1960s, vinyl head, cloth body
EX $35   NM $80   MIP $145

❑ **Mr. Magoo Puzzle,** 1978, Warren, frame tray
EX $10   NM $20   MIP $45

❑ **Mr. Magoo Soaky,** 1960s, Palmolive, 10" tall, vinyl and plastic
EX $20   NM $50   MIP $85

MUTT AND JEFF

BANK

❑ **Mutt and Jeff Bank,** 5" tall, cast iron, two piece construction held together by screw in the back
EX $55   NM $110   MIP $220

BOOK

❑ **Mutt and Jeff Caroon Book,** 1910, Ball Publications, 68 pages
EX $250   NM $900   MIP $1600

DOLL

❑ **Mutt and Jeff Dolls,** 1920s, 8" x 6-1/2" tall, composition hands and heads w/heavy cast iron feet, movable arms and legs, fabric clothing; pair
EX $130   NM $330   MIP $660

FIGURES

❑ **Mutt and Jeff Figures,** 1911, A. Steinhardt and Bros, ceramic, w/a coin inserted into base; pair
EX $90   NM $210   MIP $360

NIGHTMARE BEFORE CHRISTMAS

ACCESSORIES

❑ **Beach Towel,** Fashion Victim
EX $22   NM $29   MIP $40

❑ **Brass Keychain,** Disney, Jack Skellington's Tombstone
EX $3   NM $8   MIP $17

❑ **Buttons,** set of 12 featuring logo, characters, etc.
EX $15   NM $20   MIP $40

❑ **Comforter,** Wamsutta, twin size featuring Lock, Shock and Barrel
EX $45   NM $55   MIP $85

❑ **Drawstring Bag,** Jack Skellington on front
EX $10   NM $15   MIP $25

❑ **Jack Soaky,** glow head
EX $7   NM $30   MIP $60

❑ **Mug,** Selandia, 16 oz. acrylic mug w/floating snowflakes and glitter
EX $5   NM $10   MIP $25

❑ **Mug,** Selandia, 10 oz. acrylic mug w/floating snowflakes and glitter
EX $5   NM $10   MIP $25

❑ **Mylar Balloons**, Anagram, five variations, each
EX $10   NM $15   MIP $30

❑ **Pencil**, Whirly Sally or Whirly Jack
EX $4   NM $10   MIP $20

❑ **Purse**, multi-compartment w/mirror
EX $5   NM $25   MIP $50

❑ **PVC Figure on Drinking Straws**, Jack or Sally
EX $3   NM $7   MIP $10

❑ **Sunglasses**, Jet Vision Limited
EX $12   NM $15   MIP $30

❑ **Tumbler**, Selandia, 7 oz., acrylic
EX $10   NM $13   MIP $20

ACTION FIGURES

❑ **Magic Action Figures**, Applause, set of three; 4" figures has its own action when rolled
EX $20   NM $30   MIP $50

BOOK

❑ **Pop-Up Book**
EX $20   NM $45   MIP $90

CLOTHING

❑ **Bandanna**, Fashion Victim, two styles: Jack or Lock, Shock and Barrel
EX $5   NM $15   MIP $40

❑ **Baseball Caps**, Fashion Victim, three styles: Fishbone w/metal keychain; Lock, Shock and Barrel; or Jack "Bone Daddy"
EX $8   NM $10   MIP $20

❑ **Boxer Shorts**, Stanley DeSantis, Lock, Shock and Barrel or Jack styles; cotton
EX $6   NM $8   MIP $12

❑ **Silk Necktie**, many styles/patterns
EX $15   NM $22   MIP $45

❑ **Vest**, Fashion Victim, Lock, Shock and Barrel or Jack styles
EX $12   NM $15   MIP $35

DOLL

❑ **Lock, Shock and Barrel Dolls**, Applause, set of three; 6" cloth and vinyl dolls
EX $25   NM $60   MIP $110

❑ **Oogie Boogie Doll**, Applause, 16"; makes farting noise when squeezed
EX $15   NM $40   MIP $80

❑ **Sally Doll**, Hasbro, removable limbs
EX $55   NM $175   MIP $410

(KP Photo)

❑ **Santa Claus Doll**, Applause, 10" plush
EX $10   NM $30   MIP $60

❑ **Santa Puppet Doll**, Hasbro
EX $25   NM $50   MIP $85

❑ **Talking Jack Doll**, Hasbro
EX $50   NM $130   MIP $360

FIGURE

❑ **Glow Oogie Boogie Figure**, Applause, PVC figure
EX $7   NM $25   MIP $45

FIGURES

❑ **Jack Figure**, Hasbro, bendy on card
EX $6   NM $20   MIP $40

❑ **Jack in Coffin Figure**, Applause, 12"
EX $30   NM $100   MIP $275

❑ **Lock, Shock and Barrel Figures**, Applause, set of three, 3" PVC figures
EX $10   NM $30   MIP $60

❑ **Mayor Figure**, Hasbro, bendy on card
EX $10   NM $30   MIP $60

❑ **Sally Figure**, Hasbro, bendy on card
EX $15   NM $40   MIP $80

❑ **Sally in Coffin Figure**, Applause, 12"
EX $70   NM $200   MIP $475

❑ **Santa Jack Figure**, Hasbro, bendy on card
EX $6   NM $12   MIP $25

GAME

❑ **Handheld Video Game**, Tiger
EX $25   NM $35   MIP $75

GLASSWARE

❑ **Cookie Jar**, Treasure Craft, ceramic; Jack on Tombstone
EX $50   NM $100   MIP $200

JEWELRY

❑ **Pin**, Oopsa Daisy, several character styles, pewter
EX $10   NM $18   MIP $25

❑ **Rhinestone Pin**, Oopsa Daisy, red stones featuring Jack Skellington
EX $40   NM $65   MIP $85

❑ **Rhinestone Pin**, white stones featuring Jack Skellington
EX $30   NM $55   MIP $75

KITE

❑ **Sky Floater Kite**, Spectra Star
EX $5   NM $15   MIP $30

MUSIC BOX

❑ **Mayor Wind-Up Music Box**, Schmid, head spins while music plays "What's This?"
EX $40   NM $80   MIP $150

ORNAMENTS

❑ **Wooden Ornaments**, Kurt S. Adler, set of 10; 4" to 6" tall; individually packaged
EX $20   NM $65   MIP $80

PAPER GOODS

❑ **Bionic Airwalker Balloon**, Anagram, featuring Jack Skellington; over 7" tall
EX $15   NM $20   MIP $50

❑ **Bookmarks**, OSP Publishing, set of eight styles including wallet cards
EX $10   NM $15   MIP $30

❑ **Gift Bags**, Cleo, five styles available
EX $6   NM $10   MIP $20

❑ **Greeting Cards**, set of six featuring various characters
EX $15   NM $35   MIP $75

❑ **Notepad**, Beach, 75-sheet pad featuring Lock, Shock and Barrel
EX $3   NM $5   MIP $15

❑ **Partyware**, Beach, 65 pieces
EX $14   NM $16   MIP $30

❑ **Postcard Book**, 30 full-color postcards
EX $5   NM $16   MIP $35

❑ **Stickers**, Gibson, featuring movie characters
EX $2   NM $6   MIP $12

❑ **Video Release Poster**, Touchstone, 24" x 36"
EX $15   NM $50   MIP $70

STORE DISPLAY

❑ **Cardboard Store Display**, Applause, over 6" wide
EX $60   NM $120   MIP $180

TATTOOS

❑ **Temporary Tattoos**, US Kids
EX $2   NM $4   MIP $10

TOY

❑ **Kaleidoscope**, C. Bennett Scopes
EX $20   NM $35   MIP $70

WRISTWATCH

❑ **Wristwatch**, Timex, six styles available, each
EX $10   NM $40   MIP $75

YO-YO

❑ **Yo-Yo**, Spectra Star
EX $10   NM $25   MIP $50

PEANUTS

ACCESSORIES

❑ **Lucy Candlestick Holder**, Hallmark, 7-1/4" figural composition
EX $15   NM $21   MIP $30

❑ **Snoopy Snippers Scissors**, 1975, Mattel, plastic, Model No. 7410
EX $30   NM $45   MIP $60

Snoopy Toothbrush, 1972, Kenner, Snoopy on doghouse holder, Model No. 30301
EX $15   NM $30   MIP $40

Vaporizer/Humidifier, Milton Bradley, plastic, 13" x 16", Snoopy on doghouse
EX $45   NM $75   MIP $100

BANK

Peanuts Banks, 1970, United Features, set of five
EX $45   NM $80   MIP $150

Snoopy Bank, 1968, United Feature, 7" figural bank
EX $15   NM $35   MIP $75

BOOK

Peanuts Projects, 1963, Determined, activity book
EX $30   NM $45   MIP $60

Peanuts Trace and Color, 1960s, Saalfield, five book set, Model No. 6122
EX $35   NM $50   MIP $90

Speak Up, Charlie Brown Talking Storybook, 1971, Mattel, cardboard w/vinyl pages, Model No. 4812
EX $60   NM $120   MIP $170

BOOKS

Peanuts: A Book to Color, Saalfield, cover features Snoopy and Charlie Brown on skateboard, Model No. 4629
EX $25   NM $50   MIP $80

COSTUMES

Charlie Brown Costume, Collegeville, w/mask
EX $12   NM $25   MIP $50

Snoopy as Flying Ace Costume, Collegeville, w/mask
EX $15   NM $25   MIP $50

Snoopy Costume, Collegeville, w/mask
EX $12   NM $17   MIP $25

Woodstock Costume, Collegeville, w/mask
EX $10   NM $20   MIP $30

DOLL

Peppermint Patty Doll, 14" tall, cloth
EX $10   NM $20   MIP $40

Tub Time Snoopy Doll, 1980s, Knickerbocker, rubber, Model No. 0539
EX $15   NM $35   MIP $50

DOLLS

Charlie Brown Doll, 1958, Hungerford Plastics, 8-1/2" plastic
EX $60   NM $125   MIP $200

Charlie Brown Doll, 1970s, Determined, plastic; wearing baseball gear
EX $45   NM $90   MIP $150

Charlie Brown Doll, 1976, Ideal, removable clothing, Model No. 1412-6
EX $30   NM $60   MIP $100

Charlie Brown Pocket Doll, 1968, Boucher, 7", Model No. 800
EX $20   NM $32   MIP $70

Dolls, 1960s, Simon Simple, 7-1/2", Charlie Brown, Lucy, or Linus
EX $20   NM $50   MIP $85

Dress Me Belle Doll, 1983, Knickerbocker, Belle wearing pink dress w/blue dots, Model No. 1581
EX $15   NM $40   MIP $50

Dress Me Snoopy Doll, 1983, Knickerbocker, Snoopy wearing blue jeans and red/yellow shirt, Model No. 1580
EX $15   NM $40   MIP $50

Linus Doll, 1958, Hungerford Plastics, 8-1/2" plastic
EX $50   NM $85   MIP $175

Linus Doll, 1976, Ideal, removable clothing, Model No. 1414-2
EX $55   NM $90   MIP $195

Linus Pocket Doll, 1968, Boucher, 7", Model No. 801
EX $15   NM $25   MIP $40

Lucy Doll, 1958, Hungerford Plastics, 8-1/2" plastic
EX $50   NM $75   MIP $120

Lucy Doll, 1976, Ideal, removable clothing, Model No. 1411-8
EX $25   NM $50   MIP $90

Lucy Pocket Doll, 1968, Boucher, 7" open mouth, Model No. 802
EX $15   NM $25   MIP $45

Lucy Pocket Doll, 1968, Boucher, 7" smiling, Model No. 802
EX $15   NM $30   MIP $50

Peppermint Patty Doll, 1976, Ideal, removable clothing, Model No. 1413-4
EX $30   NM $45   MIP $60

Pigpen Doll, 1958, Hungerford Plastics, 8-1/2" plastic
EX $65   NM $100   MIP $150

Playmate Snoopy Doll, 1971, Determined, 6" plush, Model No. 819
EX $10   NM $20   MIP $50

Sally Doll, 1958, Hungerford Plastics, 6-1/2" plastic
EX $65   NM $100   MIP $160

Schroeder and Piano Doll, 1958, Hungerford Plastics, 7" plastic
EX $125   NM $250   MIP $375

Snoopy as Astronaut Doll, Knickerbocker, 5" vinyl
EX $35   NM $75   MIP $150

Snoopy as Astronaut Doll, 1969, Determined, 9", rubber head, plastic body, Model No. 808
EX $40   NM $80   MIP $160

Snoopy as Astronaut Doll, 1977, Ideal, 14" plush w/helmet and space suit, Model No. 1441-5
EX $90   NM $160   MIP $250

Snoopy as Magician Doll, 1977, Ideal, 14" plush w/cape, hat, and mustache, Model No. 1448-0
EX $95   NM $160   MIP $200

Snoopy as Rock Star Doll, 1977, Ideal, 14" plush w/wig, shoes and microphone, Model No. 1446-4
EX $90   NM $160   MIP $220

Snoopy Autograph Doll, 1971, Determined, 10-1/2", Model No. 838
EX $20   NM $25   MIP $40

Snoopy Doll, Ideal, 7" rag doll
EX $8   NM $20   MIP $40

Snoopy Doll, 1958, Hungerford Plastics, 7" plastic
EX $45   NM $75   MIP $160

Snoopy Doll, 1970s, Determined, plastic jointed
EX $25   NM $40   MIP $70

Snoopy Doll, 1971, Determined, 15" plush, felt eyes, eyebrows, and nose; red tag around neck
EX $25   NM $40   MIP $80

Snoopy Paper Dolls, 1976, Determined, w/10 outfits
EX $20   NM $40   MIP $60

Snoopy Pocket Doll, 1968, Boucher, 7" w/Flying Ace outfit, Model No. 803
EX $20   NM $35   MIP $75

GAME

Lucy Tea Party Game, 1972, Milton Bradley, Model No. 4129
EX $25   NM $35   MIP $60

Snoopy Snack Attack Game, 1980, Gabriel, Model No. 70345
EX $25   NM $40   MIP $60

Snoopy's Pound-A-Ball Game, 1980, Gabriel/Child Guidance, Model No. 51702
EX $35   NM $65   MIP $80

Table Top Snoopy Game, 1980s, Nintendo, Model No. SM-73
EX $65   NM $125   MIP $160

Tabletop Hockey, 1972, Munro Games
EX $65   NM $125   MIP $160

Tell Us a Riddle, Snoopy Game, 1974, Colorforms, Model No. 2397
EX $20   NM $55   MIP $90

MUSIC BOX

Linus Music Box, Anri, wood, Linus in pumpkin patch on cover, plays "Who Can I Turn To?"
EX $85   NM $130   MIP $175

Lucy and Charlie Brown Music Box, 1971, Anri, 4", each character beside large mushroom, plays "Rose Garden", Model No. 81973
EX $75   NM $150   MIP $200

Lucy Music Box, 1969, Anri, 6-1/2", Lucy behind psychiatrist booth, plays "Try to Remember", Model No. 819400
EX $80   NM $195   MIP $275

- **Lucy Music Box,** 1971, Anri, 5", Lucy w/mushrooms on ground, plays "Love Story", Model No. 81981
  EX $80   **NM** $195   **MIP** $275

- **Peanuts Music Box,** 1972, Schmid, 8" wooden ferris wheel box/bank, plays "Spinning Wheel", Model No. 277408
  EX $100   **NM** $245   **MIP** $325

- **Peanuts Music Box,** 1984, Schmid, 8", ceramic, characters revolve around Christmas tree, plays "Joy to the World", Model No. 253724
  EX $75   **NM** $175   **MIP** $250

- **Peanuts Music Box,** 1985, Schmid, ceramic, characters piled on car, "Clown Capers", plays "Be a Clown", Model No. 289052
  EX $75   **NM** $110   **MIP** $150

- **Schroeder Music Box,** 1971, Anri, 5", Schroeder at the piano, plays "Beethoven's Emperor's Waltz", Model No. 819030
  EX $90   **NM** $125   **MIP** $225

- **Snoopy as Astronaut Music Box,** 1970s, Schmid
  EX $25   **NM** $40   **MIP** $70

- **Snoopy Music Box,** 1974, Aviva, 6", Snoopy w/hobo pack w/Woodstock, plays "Born Free"
  EX $30   **NM** $45   **MIP** $70

- **Snoopy Music Box,** 1979, Aviva, 8", Snoopy on doghouse shaped box, roof is removable lid, plays "Candy Man", Model No. 214
  EX $35   **NM** $80   **MIP** $120

- **Snoopy Music Box,** 1982, Aviva, ceramic heart-shaped base w/Snoopy and Woodstock hugging on top, plays "Love Makes the World Go Round", Model No. 215
  EX $30   **NM** $60   **MIP** $75

- **Snoopy Music Box,** 1984, Schmid, 7" ceramic, Snoopy and Woodstock on seesaw, plays "Playmates", Model No. 253709
  EX $75   **NM** $110   **MIP** $140

- **Snoopy Music Box,** 1984, Quantasia, ceramic Snoopy and musical note on base, plays "Fur Elise", Model No. 141017
  EX $35   **NM** $45   **MIP** $65

- **Snoopy Music Box,** 1985, Quantasia, plastic, Snoopy in boat inside water-globe, plays "Blue Hawaii", Model No. 141020
  EX $20   **NM** $40   **MIP** $60

- **Snoopy Music Box,** 1986, Schmid, 6" ceramic, Snoopy as Lion Tamer, plays "Pussycat, Pussycat", Model No. 289053
  EX $45   **NM** $65   **MIP** $110

- **Snoopy Music Box,** 1986, Schmid, 7-1/2" ceramic, Snoopy next to Christmas tree, plays "O, Tannenbaum", Model No. 159101
  EX $95   **NM** $150   **MIP** $210

PUZZLES

- **Puzzle,** 1971, Determined, eight-panel cartoon strip, 1,000 pieces, Model No. 711-2
  EX $15   **NM** $25   **MIP** $40

- **Puzzle,** 1971, Determined, four "Love Is" scenes, 1,000 pieces, Model No. 711-4
  EX $25   **NM** $40   **MIP** $60

- **Puzzle,** 1973, Milton Bradley, Schroeder, Charlie Brown, Snoopy, and Lucy on baseball mound, Model No. 4383-3
  EX $10   **NM** $22   **MIP** $45

- **Puzzle,** 1979, Playskool, six pieces, Snoopy leaning on bat, Model No. 230-27
  EX $5   **NM** $10   **MIP** $20

RADIOS

- **Snoopy and Woodstock Radio,** 1970s, Determined, plastic, two-dimensional doghouse, Model No. 354
  EX $20   **NM** $35   **MIP** $75

- **Snoopy Bank Radio,** 1978, Concept 2000, plastic, Snoopy dancing, Model No. 4442
  EX $45   **NM** $70   **MIP** $100

- **Snoopy Doghouse Radio,** 1970s, Determined, plastic
  EX $35   **NM** $55   **MIP** $90

- **Snoopy Hi-Fi Radio,** 1977, Determined, three-dimensional Snoopy wearing headphones, plastic, Model No. 405
  EX $35   **NM** $75   **MIP** $150

- **Snoopy Radio,** 1970s, Determined, figural radio, Snoopy on green grass, plastic
  EX $20   **NM** $30   **MIP** $60

- **Snoopy Radio,** 1975, Determined, plastic two-dimensional, Model No. 351
  EX $30   **NM** $65   **MIP** $100

- **Snoopy Radio,** 1977, Determined, plastic square radio w/Snoopy pointing to dial
  EX $30   **NM** $65   **MIP** $100

- **Snoopy, Woodstock, and Charlie Brown Radio,** 1970s, Concept 2000, two-dimensional plastic, Model No. 4443
  EX $20   **NM** $35   **MIP** $50

- **Snoopy's Spaceship AM Radio,** 1978, Concept 2000, plastic, Model No. 4443
  EX $50   **NM** $100   **MIP** $185

TOY

- **Batter-Up Snoopy Colorforms,** 1979, Colorforms
  EX $10   **NM** $35   **MIP** $50

- **Big Quart-O-Snoopy Bubbles,** 1970s, Chemtoy
  EX $9   **NM** $13   **MIP** $15

- **Camp Kamp Play Set,** 1970s, Child Guidance, rubber camp building w/characters, Model No. 1683
  EX $30   **NM** $60   **MIP** $100

- **Charlie Brown Deluxe View-Master Gift Pak,** 1970s, GAF/View-Master, cylindrical container holds seven reels and viewer, Model No. 2380
  EX $20   **NM** $55   **MIP** $70

(KP Photo)

- **Charlie Brown Nodder,** 1960s, Japanese, 5-1/2" tall, bobbing head
  EX $60   **NM** $125   **MIP** $250

- **Charlie Brown Punching Bag,** 1970s, Determined
  EX $15   **NM** $30   **MIP** $50

- **Charlie Brown Push Puppet,** 1977, Ideal
  EX $20   **NM** $45   **MIP** $75

- **Charlie Brown's All-Star Dugout Play Set,** 1970s, Child Guidance, Model No. 1636
  EX $20   **NM** $40   **MIP** $50

- **Charlie Brown's Backyard Play Set,** 1970s, Child Guidance
  EX $20   **NM** $40   **MIP** $50

- **Chirping Woodstock,** 1977, Aviva, plastic w/electronic sound, Model No. 477
  EX $18   **NM** $25   **MIP** $50

- **Electronic Snoopy Playmate,** 1980, Romper Room/Hasbro, Model No. 830
  EX $60   **NM** $125   **MIP** $175

- **Express Station Set,** 1977, Aviva, Snoopy riding locomotive, Model No. 988
  EX $20   **NM** $50   **MIP** $80

- **Joe Cool Punching Bag,** 1976, Ideal, Model No. 5530-1
  EX $20   **NM** $30   **MIP** $50

- **Joe Cool Push Puppet,** 1977, Ideal
  EX $20   **NM** $40   **MIP** $80

- **Kaleidorama,** 1979, Determined, Model No. 4961
  EX $12   **NM** $20   **MIP** $40

- **Lucy Nurse Push Puppet,** 1977, Ideal
  EX $20   **NM** $35   **MIP** $60

❏ **Lucy's Winter Carnival Colorforms,** 1973, Colorforms, Model No. 7400
EX $20   NM $40   MIP $50

❏ **Official Peanuts Baseball,** 1969, Wilson, illustrated w/characters
EX $25   NM $95   MIP $130

❏ **Parade Drum,** 1969, Chein, large tin drum features characters in director's chairs, Model No. 1798
EX $90   NM $165   MIP $225

❏ **Peanuts Deluxe Play Set,** 1975, Determined, includes Lucy's psychiatrist booth and three action figures, Model No. 575
EX $90   NM $200   MIP $275

❏ **Peanuts Drum,** 1974, Chein, tin, features characters w/instruments, Model No. 1713
EX $75   NM $120   MIP $190

❏ **Peanuts Kindergarten Rhythm Set,** 1972, Chein, four percussion instruments, Model No. 327
EX $90   NM $160   MIP $220

❏ **Peanuts Magic Catch Puppets,** 1978, Synergistics, four characters w/Velcro balls
EX $10   NM $20   MIP $50

❏ **Peanuts Pelham Puppets,** 1979, Pelham/Tiderider, 7"-8" Charlie Brown, Snoopy or Woodstock
EX $45   NM $90   MIP $180

❏ **Peanuts Puppets Display,** 1979, Pelham/Tiderider, display theater
EX $110   NM $360   MIP $600

❏ **Peanuts Show Time Finger Puppets,** 1977, Ideal, several rubber character puppets, Model No. 5379-3
EX $25   NM $35   MIP $60

❏ **Peanuts Skediddler Clubhouse Set,** 1970, Mattel, three rubber skediddlers, Snoopy, Lucy, Charlie Brown, Model No. 3803
EX $125   NM $185   MIP $230

❏ **Peanuts Stackables,** 1979, Determined, four hard rubber figures, Model No. 8642
EX $18   NM $25   MIP $35

❏ **Peanuts Tea Set,** 1961, one tray, two plates, two cups, four small plates
EX $25   NM $50   MIP $100

❏ **Piano,** 1960s, Ely, wood w/characters on top
EX $165   NM $275   MIP $425

❏ **Picture Maker,** 1971, Mattel, plastic character stencils, Model No. 4153
EX $45   NM $65   MIP $90

❏ **Push and Play with the Peanuts Gang,** 1970s, Child Guidance, plastic w/rubber characters, Model No. 1700
EX $30   NM $50   MIP $90

❏ **Push 'N' Fly Snoopy,** 1980, Romper Room/Hasbro, pull toy featuring Snoopy the Flying Ace, Model No. 824
EX $12   NM $20   MIP $40

❏ **Rowing Snoopy,** 1981, Mattel, Model No. 3478
EX $20   NM $40   MIP $70

❏ **Schroeder's Piano,** 1970s, Child Guidance, Model No. 1701
EX $55   NM $110   MIP $175

❏ **See 'N' Say Snoopy Says,** 1969, Mattel, Model No. 4864
EX $40   NM $80   MIP $100

❏ **Snoopy Action Toys,** 1977, Aviva, wind-up Snoopy as drummer or boxer
EX $25   NM $45   MIP $60

❏ **Snoopy and Charlie Brown Copter,** 1979, Aviva/Hasbro, plastic, Model No. 600
EX $15   NM $25   MIP $50

❏ **Snoopy and his Flyin' Doghouse,** 1974, Mattel, Model No. 8263
EX $60   NM $100   MIP $150

❏ **Snoopy Color 'N' Recolor,** 1980, Avalon, Model No. 742
EX $30   NM $50   MIP $70

❏ **Snoopy Copter Pull Toy,** 1980, Romper Room, sound and action toy, Model No. 822
EX $6   NM $10   MIP $15

❏ **Snoopy Deep Diver Submarine,** 1980s, Knickerbocker, plastic, Model No. 0553
EX $35   NM $55   MIP $70

❏ **Snoopy Drive-In Movie Theater,** 1975, Kenner, Model No. 39570
EX $95   NM $160   MIP $250

❏ **Snoopy Express,** 1977, Aviva, mechanical wind-up train, wood, includes track, tunnel, and signs, Model No. 922
EX $20   NM $55   MIP $90

❏ **Snoopy Express,** 1982, Aviva, mechanical wind-up train, plastic, Model No. 70911
EX $20   NM $35   MIP $50

❏ **Snoopy Family Car,** 1978, Aviva, Model No. 2700
EX $40   NM $70   MIP $90

❏ **Snoopy Gravity Raceway,** 1977, Aviva, Model No. 990
EX $40   NM $70   MIP $90

❏ **Snoopy Gyro Cycle,** 1982, Aviva/Hasbro, plastic friction toy, Model No. 70440
EX $20   NM $50   MIP $80

❏ **Snoopy High Wire Act,** 1973, Monogram/Mattel, Model No. 6661
EX $25   NM $45   MIP $60

❏ **Snoopy in the Music Box,** 1969, Mattel, metal jack-in-the-box, Model No. 4747
EX $15   NM $30   MIP $80

❏ **Snoopy is Joe Cool Model Kit,** 1971, Monogram/Mattel, Snoopy rides surfboard, Model No. 7502
EX $40   NM $80   MIP $120

❏ **Snoopy Jack-in-the-Box,** 1980, Romper Room/Hasbro, plastic doghouse jack-in-the-box, Model No. 818
EX $8   NM $15   MIP $30

❏ **Snoopy Magician Push Puppet,** 1977, Ideal
EX $15   NM $35   MIP $70

❏ **Snoopy Marionette,** 1979, Pelham/Tiderider, 27", Pelham Puppets, Model No. DP10
EX $210   NM $475   MIP $600

❏ **Snoopy Movie Viewer,** 1975, Kenner, Model No. 35900
EX $15   NM $25   MIP $40

❏ **Snoopy Musical Ge-tar,** 1969, Mattel, crank handle, Model No. 4715
EX $25   NM $45   MIP $90

❏ **Snoopy Musical Guitar,** 1980, Aviva, plastic, crank handle, Model No. 444
EX $15   NM $35   MIP $60

❏ **Snoopy Nodder,** 1960s, Japanese, 5-1/2" tall, bobbing head
EX $30   NM $60   MIP $125

❏ **Snoopy Paint-by-Number Set,** 1980s, Craft House, 12" x 16"
EX $10   NM $20   MIP $35

❏ **Snoopy Phonograph,** 1979, Vanity Fair, features picture of dancing Snoopy, Model No. 66
EX $75   NM $110   MIP $150

❏ **Snoopy Playhouse,** 1977, Determined, plastic doghouse w/furniture, Snoopy, and Woodstock, Model No. 120
EX $40   NM $70   MIP $100

❏ **Snoopy Playland,** 1978, Aviva, Snoopy in bus and six other characters, Model No. 888
EX $45   NM $70   MIP $100

❏ **Snoopy Radio-Controlled Doghouse,** 1980, Aviva, Model No. 988
EX $35   NM $60   MIP $90

❏ **Snoopy Radio-Controlled Fire Engine,** 1980, Aviva, w/Woodstock transmitter, Model No. 988
EX $50   NM $75   MIP $100

❏ **Snoopy Sheriff Push Puppet,** 1977, Ideal
EX $20   NM $30   MIP $70

❏ **Snoopy Sign Mobile,** 1970s, Avalon, Model No. 262
EX $50   NM $80   MIP $120

❏ **Snoopy Skediddler and His Sopwith Camel,** 1969, Mattel, w/carrying case, Model No. 4954
EX $115   NM $270   MIP $360

❑ **Snoopy Slugger,** 1979, Playskool, ball, bat and cap, Model No. 411
EX $15　　**NM** $25　　**MIP** $60

(KP Photo)

❑ **Snoopy Soaper,** 1975, Kenner, gold soap dispenser w/Snoopy on top, Model No. 30700
EX $20　　**NM** $45　　**MIP** $60

❑ **Snoopy Tea Set,** 1970, Chein, metal, features tray, plate, cups, and saucers, Model No. 276
EX $50　　**NM** $150　　**MIP** $210

❑ **Snoopy the Critic,** 1977, Aviva, Snoopy and Woodstock on doghouse w/microphone, Model No. 222
EX $90　　**NM** $200　　**MIP** $260

❑ **Snoopy the Flying Ace Push Puppet,** 1977, Ideal
EX $20　　**NM** $30　　**MIP** $70

(KP Photo)

❑ **Snoopy-Matic Instant Load Camera,** 1970s, Helm Toy, uses 110 film, Model No. 975
EX $95　　**NM** $150　　**MIP** $182

❑ **Snoopy's Beagle Bugle,** 1970s, Child Guidance, plastic, Model No. 1730
EX $55　　**NM** $80　　**MIP** $110

❑ **Snoopy's Bubble Blowing Bubble Tub,** 1970s, Chemtoy
EX $20　　**NM** $45　　**MIP** $50

❑ **Snoopy's Dog House,** 1978, Romper Room/Hasbro, Snoopy walks on roof, Model No. 815
EX $20　　**NM** $45　　**MIP** $70

❑ **Snoopy's Dream Machine,** 1979, DCS, w/blinking lights
EX $95　　**NM** $155　　**MIP** $195

❑ **Snoopy's Dream Machine,** 1980, DCS, small version, no blinking lights, laminated cardboard, Model No. 417-M
EX $55　　**NM** $80　　**MIP** $110

❑ **Snoopy's Fantastic Automatic Bubble Pipe,** 1970s, Chemtoy, Model No. 126
EX $5　　**NM** $12　　**MIP** $20

❑ **Snoopy's Good Grief Glider,** 1970s, Child Guidance, spring load launcher, Model No. 1775
EX $35　　**NM** $65　　**MIP** $100

❑ **Snoopy's 'Lectric Comb and Brush,** 1975, Kenner, Model No. 30900
EX $35　　**NM** $50　　**MIP** $60

❑ **Snoopy's Pencil Sharpener,** 1974, Kenner, Model No. 3550
EX $15　　**NM** $40　　**MIP** $80

❑ **Snoopy's Shape Register,** 1980, Gabriel/Child Guidance, plastic cash register, Model No. 51740
EX $28　　**NM** $50　　**MIP** $80

❑ **Snoopy's Soft House,** 1980, Knickerbocker, soft cloth house, Model No. 0573
EX $25　　**NM** $40　　**MIP** $60

❑ **Snoopy's Stunt Spectacular,** 1978, Child Guidance, Snoopy on motorcycle, Model No. 1750
EX $35　　**NM** $50　　**MIP** $80

❑ **Snoopy's Swim and Sail Club,** 1970s, Child Guidance, characters and water vehicles, Model No. 1710
EX $45　　**NM** $75　　**MIP** $110

❑ **Snoopy's Take-a-Part Doghouse,** 1980, Gabriel/Child Guidance, Model No. 51705
EX $15　　**NM** $25　　**MIP** $50

❑ **Spinning Top**, Ohio Art, 5", Snoopy and the Gang
EX $10　　**NM** $20　　**MIP** $60

❑ **Spinning Top**, 1960s, Chein, faces of Snoopy, Charlie Brown, Lucy, and Linus, Model No. 263
EX $32　　**NM** $55　　**MIP** $120

❑ **Stack-Up Snoopy,** 1980, Romper Room/Hasbro, Model No. 818
EX $10　　**NM** $13　　**MIP** $20

❑ **Super Cartoon Maker,** 1970, Mattel, molds to make character figures, Model No. 4696
EX $65　　**NM** $120　　**MIP** $160

❑ **Swimming Snoopy,** 1970s, Concept 2000, Model No. 106
EX $15　　**NM** $40　　**MIP** $50

❑ **Talking Peanuts Bus,** 1967, Chein, metal, chracters seen in windows, Model No. 261
EX $150　　**NM** $350　　**MIP** $700

❑ **Tell Time Clock,** 1980s, Concept 2000, three styles: Snoopy, Woodstock or Charlie Brown
EX $15　　**NM** $25　　**MIP** $40

❑ **Woodstock Climbing String Action,** 1977, Aviva/Hasbro, plastic, Model No. 667
EX $15　　**NM** $28　　**MIP** $40

❑ **Yankee Doodle Snoopy,** 1975, Colorforms, Model No. 756
EX $20　　**NM** $35　　**MIP** $50

VEHICLE

❑ **Schroeder's Piano**, Aviva
EX $30　　**NM** $60　　**MIP** $90

❑ **Snoopy and Woodstock in Wagon,** Aviva, green die-cast w/white wheels, Model No. 72060
EX $10　　**NM** $15　　**MIP** $20

❑ **Snoopy and Woodstock on Skateboard,** Aviva
EX $10　　**NM** $15　　**MIP** $20

❑ **Snoopy as Beagle Scout in Bus,** 1983, Hasbro, die-cast
EX $4　　**NM** $10　　**MIP** $20

❑ **Snoopy as Flying Ace in Wagon,** Aviva, yellow die-cast w/red wheels, Model No. 72057
EX $10　　**NM** $20　　**MIP** $40

❑ **Snoopy as Joe Cool in Wagon,** Aviva, purple die-cast w/orange wheels, Model No. 72055
EX $10　　**NM** $15　　**MIP** $25

❑ **Snoopy Emergency Set,** Hasbro, Snoopy in three vehicles
EX $20　　**NM** $50　　**MIP** $75

❑ **Snoopy Handfuls,** Hasbro, twin pack; characters in die-cast racers
EX $15　　**NM** $35　　**MIP** $60

❑ **Snoopy in Tow Truck,** 1983, Hasbro, die-cast
EX $5　　**NM** $10　　**MIP** $25

❑ **Woodstock in Ice Cream Truck**, Aviva, friction vehicle
EX $6　　**NM** $9　　**MIP** $15

VEHICLES

❑ **Formula-1 Racing Car,** 1978, Aviva, 11-1/2" plastic w/Woodstock or Snoopy, Model No. 950
EX $80　　**NM** $125　　**MIP** $175

❑ **Snoopy Biplane,** 1977, Aviva, die-cast, Snoopy as Flying Ace, Model No. 2024
EX $15　　**NM** $30　　**MIP** $60

❑ **Snoopy Family Car,** 1977, Aviva, die-cast convertible, 2-1/4", Model No. 2028
EX $35　　**NM** $55　　**MIP** $80

❑ **Snoopy Racing Car Stickshifter,** 1978, Aviva, Model No. 975
EX $90 **NM** $150 **MIP** $210

❑ **Snoopy Slot Car Racing Set,** 1977, Aviva, Model No. XL500
EX $50 **NM** $100 **MIP** $180

WATCH

❑ **Lucy Wristwatch,** 1970s, Timex, small chrome case, articulated arms, sweep seconds, white vinyl band
EX $25 **NM** $70 **MIP** $140

❑ **Snoopy Wristwatch,** 1970s, Timex, gold bezel, tennis ball circles Snoopy on clear disk, articulated hands holding racket, denim background and band
EX $30 **NM** $55 **MIP** $100

WATCHES

❑ **Charlie Brown Wristwatch,** 1970s, Determined, Charlie Brown in baseball gear, yellow face, black band
EX $55 **NM** $180 **MIP** $275

❑ **Lucy's Watch Wardrobe,** 1970s, Determined, white face, comes w/blue, white, and pink bands
EX $60 **NM** $100 **MIP** $175

❑ **Snoopy Hero Time Watch,** 1970s, Determined, Snoopy in dancing pose, red band
EX $55 **NM** $110 **MIP** $200

❑ **Snoopy Wristwatch,** 1969, Determined, Snoopy in dancing pose, silver or gold case, various colors
EX $70 **NM** $110 **MIP** $175

❑ **Snoopy Wristwatch,** 1970s, Lafayette Watch, Snoopy dancing, Woodstock is the second hand, silver case w/red face and black band
EX $65 **NM** $120 **MIP** $180

PETER PAN

ACCESSORIES

❑ **Peter Pan Charm Bracelet,** 1974
EX $20 **NM** $30 **MIP** $75

❑ **Peter Pan Map of Neverland,** 1953, 18" x 24", collectors issue for users of Peter Pan Beauty Bar
EX $75 **NM** $175 **MIP** $350

❑ **Tinker Bell Pincushion,** 1960s, w/1-1/2" tall Tinker Bell figure, in clear plastic display can
EX $25 **NM** $40 **MIP** $90

DOLL

❑ **Peter Pan Doll,** 1953, Ideal, 18" tall
EX $100 **NM** $200 **MIP** $400

❑ **Peter Pan Doll,** 1953, Duchess Doll, 11-1/2" tall, brown trim fabric shoes, green mesh stockings w/flocked outfit, hat w/a large red feather, shiny silver white metal dagger in belt, eyes, arms and head move
EX $175 **NM** $350 **MIP** $600

❑ **Tinker Bell Doll,** 1953, Duchess Doll, 8" tall, flocked green outfit w/a pair of large white fabric wings w/gold trim, eyes open and close, jointed arms and head moves
EX $125 **NM** $250 **MIP** $500

❑ **Wendy Doll,** 1953, Duchess Doll, 8" tall, full purple length skirt w/purple bow in back of dress, eyes open and close, jointed arms and head moves
EX $112 **NM** $225 **MIP** $450

FIGURES

❑ **Captain Hook Figure,** 8" tall, plastic
EX $10 **NM** $20 **MIP** $40

❑ **Peter Pan Baby Figure,** 1950s, Sun Rubber
EX $40 **NM** $80 **MIP** $160

❑ **Peter Pan Paper Dolls,** 1952, Whitman, 11 die-cut cardboard figures
EX $35 **NM** $100 **MIP** $225

❑ **Tinker Bell Figure,** 1960s, Sutton, 7" tall, plastic and rubber figure
EX $25 **NM** $50 **MIP** $90

TOY

❑ **Captain Hook Hand Puppet,** 1950s, Gund, 9" tall
EX $35 **NM** $70 **MIP** $150

❑ **Peter Pan Hand Puppet,** 1953, Oak Rubber, rubber
EX $30 **NM** $60 **MIP** $120

❑ **Peter Pan Nodder,** 1950s, 6" tall
EX $75 **NM** $175 **MIP** $350

❑ **Peter Pan Push Puppet,** 1950s, Kohner, 6" tall, green and flesh colored beads, plastic head, light green plastic hat
EX $25 **NM** $50 **MIP** $100

❑ **Peter Pan Sewing Cards,** 1952, Whitman
EX $15 **NM** $30 **MIP** $60

❑ **Puzzle,** 1950s, Jaymar, frame tray puzzle shows Peter, Wendy, John and Michael flying over Neverland
EX $20 **NM** $42 **MIP** $85

PHANTOM

ACCESSORIES

❑ **Oil Paint by Numbers Set,** 1967, Hasbro
EX $225 **NM** $320 **MIP** $550

❑ **Phantom 2040 Rubber Ball,** 1995, Unice
EX $12 **NM** $17 **MIP** $30

❑ **Phantom Binoculars,** 1976, Larami
EX $120 **NM** $155 **MIP** $225

❑ **Phantom Candy Jar,** 1996, KFS, plastic w/figural lid
EX $12 **NM** $22 **MIP** $40

❑ **Phantom Club Rubber Stamper Skull Ring,** 1950s
EX $400 **NM** $800 **MIP** $1200

❑ **Phantom Costume,** 1950s, Ben Cooper
EX $175 **NM** $225 **MIP** $350

❑ **Phantom Costume,** 1970s, Collegeville
EX $70 **NM** $90 **MIP** $150

❑ **Phantom Puffy Magnet,** 1975, Hanna-Barbera
EX $40 **NM** $50 **MIP** $70

❑ **Phantom Squirt Camera,** 1976, Larami
EX $80 **NM** $120 **MIP** $185

❑ **Playing Cards,** 1990, Bulls Dist., Swedish
EX $16 **NM** $22 **MIP** $35

❑ **Playing Cards,** 1990, John Sands
EX $16 **NM** $22 **MIP** $35

❑ **Rub-On Transfer Set,** 1967, Hasbro
EX $100 **NM** $120 **MIP** $200

BOOK

❑ **Phantom Giant Games Book,** 1968, World Distributors
EX $80 **NM** $125 **MIP** $200

COSTUME

❑ **Phantom Costume,** 1989, Character Costumes
EX $40 **NM** $55 **MIP** $75

FIGURE

❑ **Phantom Figure,** 1980s, 6" dark blue PVC figure
EX $25 **NM** $35 **MIP** $60

❑ **Phantom Figure,** 1990s, 6" purple PVC figure
EX $12 **NM** $30 **MIP** $60

❑ **Phantom Figure,** 1996, Street Players, 4" action figure w/skull throne or horse
EX $10 **NM** $20 **MIP** $40

❑ **Phantom Figures,** 1990, Spain, 3-1/2", two pieces, purple PVC
EX $10 **NM** $20 **MIP** $35

❑ **Syrocco Figure,** 1944, Pillsbury Mills, brown
EX $800 **NM** $1300 **MIP** $1900

❑ **Syrocco Figure,** 1944, Pillsbury Mills, purple
EX $450 **NM** $900 **MIP** $1350

TOY

❑ **Phantom 2040 Carded Toys,** 1995, Ja-Ru, sword, crossbow, gun or whistle light
EX $8 **NM** $12 **MIP** $25

❑ **Phantom Archery Set,** 1976, Larami, bow, arrows, animals
EX $75 **NM** $125 **MIP** $200

❑ **Phantom Dagger Set,** 1976, Larami, knife and sheath
EX $100 **NM** $120 **MIP** $225

❑ **Phantom Desert Survival Kit,** 1976, Larami, canteen and Thermos bottle
EX $80 **NM** $120 **MIP** $200

❑ **Phantom Jungle Play Set,** 1976, Larami, figure, palm trees, animals
EX $110 **NM** $160 **MIP** $300

- ❑ **Phantom Pathfinder Set,** 1976, Larami, compass, canteen, binoculars, case
  EX $80   **NM** $120   **MIP** $185

- ❑ **Phantom Pinback,** 1940s, club member cello, Australia
  EX $150   **NM** $500   **MIP** $800

- ❑ **Phantom Safari Set,** 1976, Larami, figure, truck, trailer, animals
  EX $130   **NM** $180   **MIP** $275

- ❑ **Phantom Water Pistol,** 1974, Nasta, w/holster
  EX $70   **NM** $90   **MIP** $160

- ❑ **Phantom Water Pistol,** 1974, Nasta
  EX $80   **NM** $120   **MIP** $175

PINK PANTHER

ACCESSORIES

- ❑ **Pink Panther Memo Board,** write on/wipe off memo board
  EX $5   **NM** $10   **MIP** $15

BOOK

- ❑ **Pink Panther and The Fancy Party Book,** Golden
  EX $5   **NM** $10   **MIP** $20

- ❑ **Pink Panther and The Haunted House Book,** Golden
  EX $5   **NM** $10   **MIP** $20

- ❑ **Pink Panther at Castle Kreep Book,** Whitman
  EX $5   **NM** $10   **MIP** $20

- ❑ **Pink Panther at The Circus Sticker Book,** 1963, Golden
  EX $10   **NM** $20   **MIP** $40

- ❑ **Pink Panther Coloring Book,** 1976, Whitman, cover shows Pink Panther roasting hot dogs
  EX $10   **NM** $20   **MIP** $40

FIGURES

- ❑ **Pink Panther Figure,** 1971, Dakin, 8" tall, w/legs open
  EX $22   **NM** $45   **MIP** $90

- ❑ **Pink Panther Figure,** 1971, Dakin, 8" tall, w/legs closed
  EX $22   **NM** $45   **MIP** $90

GAME

- ❑ **Pink Panther Pool Game,** 1980s, Ja-Ru
  EX $4   **NM** $10   **MIP** $25

MUSIC BOX

- ❑ **Pink Panther Music Box,** 1982, Royal Orleans, Christmas limited edition
  EX $30   **NM** $70   **MIP** $120

- ❑ **Pink Panther Music Box,** 1983, Royal Orleans, Christmas limited edition
  EX $30   **NM** $70   **MIP** $120

- ❑ **Pink Panther Music Box,** 1984, Royal Orleans, Christmas limited edition
  EX $30   **NM** $70   **MIP** $120

TOY

- ❑ **Pink Panther Motorcycle,** 2-1/2" plastic
  EX $7   **NM** $15   **MIP** $30

- ❑ **Pink Panther One-Man Band,** 1980, Illco, 10" tall, battery-operated, plush body w/vinyl head
  EX $25   **NM** $55   **MIP** $100

- ❑ **Pink Panther Putty,** 1970s, Ja-Ru
  EX $4   **NM** $7   **MIP** $10

- ❑ **Pink Panther Wind-Up,** 3" tall, plastic, walking wind-up w/trench coat and glasses
  EX $10   **NM** $20   **MIP** $40

- ❑ **Puzzle,** 1960s, Whitman, 100 pieces, several pictures available, each
  EX $10   **NM** $25   **MIP** $50

PINOCCHIO AND JIMINY CRICKET

ACCESSORIES

- ❑ **Jiminy Cricket Toothbrush Set,** 1950s, Dupont, plastic wall hanging Jiminy holds a toothbrush
  EX $30   **NM** $55   **MIP** $85

- ❑ **Pinocchio Paperweight and Thermometer,** 1940, Plastic Novelties
  EX $30   **NM** $60   **MIP** $100

- ❑ **Pinocchio Plastic Cup,** 1939, Safetyware, 2-3/4" tall, plastic
  EX $25   **NM** $60   **MIP** $110

- ❑ **Pinocchio Snow Dome,** 1970s, Disney, 3" x 4-1/2" x 5" tall, Pinocchio holds plastic dome between hands and feet
  EX $20   **NM** $50   **MIP** $90

BANK

- ❑ **Pinocchio Bank,** 1939, Crown Toy, 5" tall, wood composition w/metal trap door on back
  EX $80   **NM** $60   **MIP** $320

- ❑ **Pinocchio Bank,** 1960s, Play Pal Plastics, 11-1/2" tall, plastic
  EX $15   **NM** $25   **MIP** $40

- ❑ **Pinocchio Bank,** 1970s, Play Pal Plastics, 7" x 7" x 10" tall, vinyl, 3-D molded head of Pinocchio
  EX $10   **NM** $20   **MIP** $50

BOOK

- ❑ **Pinocchio Book,** 1939, Whitman, 96 pages
  EX $22   **NM** $45   **MIP** $90

- ❑ **Pinocchio Book,** 1939, Grosset and Dunlap, 9-1/2" x 13", laminated cover
  EX $30   **NM** $60   **MIP** $120

- ❑ **Pinocchio Book,** 1940, Big Little Book
  EX $25   **NM** $70   **MIP** $130

- ❑ **Pinocchio Book Set,** 1940, Whitman, 8-1/2" x 11-1/2", set of six books, 24 pages each
  EX $100   **NM** $200   **MIP** $400

- ❑ **Pinocchio Cut-Out Book,** 1940, Whitman
  EX $50   **NM** $100   **MIP** $200

- ❑ **Pinocchio Paint Book,** 1939, Disney, 11" x 15", heavy paper cover
  EX $50   **NM** $100   **MIP** $200

- ❑ **Walt Disney Tells the Story of Pinocchio Book,** 1939, Whitman, 4-1/4" x 6-1/2" paperback, 144 pages
  EX $30   **NM** $60   **MIP** $90

- ❑ **Walt Disney's Pinocchio Book,** 1939, Random House, 8-1/2" x 11-1/2", hardcover
  EX $30   **NM** $60   **MIP** $120

DOLL

- ❑ **Jiminy Cricket Doll,** 1940, Ideal, wooden jointed
  EX $130   **NM** $275   **MIP** $550

- ❑ **Pinocchio and Jiminy Cricket Dolls,** 1962, Knickerbocker, 6" tall, vinyl, titled "Knixies", each
  EX $25   **NM** $50   **MIP** $100

- ❑ **Pinocchio Doll,** 1939, Ideal, 12" tall w/wire mesh arms and legs
  EX $100   **NM** $225   **MIP** $500

- ❑ **Pinocchio Doll,** 1940, Ideal, 8" tall, wood composition head, others are jointed wood
  EX $70   **NM** $140   **MIP** $325

- ❑ **Pinocchio Doll,** 1940, Ideal, 10" tall, wood composition head, jointed arms and legs attached to body
  EX $80   **NM** $150   **MIP** $400

- ❑ **Pinocchio Doll,** 1940, Ideal, 19-1/2" tall, composition
  EX $250   **NM** $500   **MIP** $900

- ❑ **Pinocchio Doll,** 1940, Knickerbocker, 3-1/2" x 4" x 9 1/2" tall, jointed composition doll w/movable arms and head
  EX $250   **NM** $500   **MIP** $900

FIGURES

- ❑ **Figaro Figure,** 1940, Multi-Wood Products, 3" tall, wood composition
  EX $32   **NM** $95   **MIP** $220

- ❑ **Figaro Figure,** 1940s, Knickerbocker, composition, movable limbs and head
  EX $95   **NM** $170   **MIP** $300

- ❑ **Gepetto Figure,** 1940, Multi-Wood Products, 5-1/2" tall, wood composition
  EX $55   **NM** $100   **MIP** $170

- ❑ **Gideon Figure,** Multi-Wood Products, 5" tall
  EX $40   **NM** $70   **MIP** $190

- ❑ **Honest John Figure,** Multi-Wood Products, 2-1/2" x 3" base w/a 7" tall figure
  EX $60   **NM** $110   **MIP** $270

- ❑ **Jiminy Cricket Figure,** Marx, 3-1/2" x 4-3/4" tall, Snap-Eeze, white plastic base w/movable arms and legs
  EX $30   **NM** $55   **MIP** $85

- ❑ **Jiminy Cricket Figure,** 1940s, Ideal, wood jointed, hand painted
  EX $160   **NM** $230   **MIP** $400

CHARACTER TOYS

❏ **Lampwick Figure,** 1940, Multi-Wood Products, 5-1/2" tall, wood composition
EX $50   NM $120   MIP $220

❏ **Pinocchio Figure,** Crown Toy, 9-1/2" tall, jointed arms
EX $45   NM $110   MIP $220

❏ **Pinocchio Figure,** 1940, Multi-Wood Products, 5" tall, wood composition
EX $45   NM $90   MIP $220

GAME

❏ **Pin the Nose on Pinocchio Game,** 1939, Parker Brothers, 15-1/2" x 20"
EX $35   NM $90   MIP $175

MUSIC BOX

❏ **Pinocchio Music Box,** plays "Puppet on a String"
EX $18   NM $35   MIP $75

TOY

❏ **Jiminy Cricket Hand Puppet,** 1950s, Gund, 11" tall
EX $30   NM $60   MIP $120

❏ **Jiminy Cricket Marionette,** 1950s, Pelham Puppets, 3" x 6" x 10" tall, dark green head with, large eyes, gray felt hat
EX $75   NM $160   MIP $325

❏ **Jiminy Cricket Ramp Walker,** 1960s, Marx, 1" x 3" x 3" tall, pushing a bass fiddle
EX $80   NM $140   MIP $270

❏ **Jiminy Cricket Soaky,** 7" tall bottle
EX $15   NM $50   MIP $75

❏ **Pinocchio and Jiminy Push Puppet,** 1960s, Marx, 2-1/2" x 5" x 4" tall, double puppet
EX $30   NM $45   MIP $100

❏ **Pinocchio Color Box,** Transogram, also known as paint box
EX $18   NM $35   MIP $75

❏ **Pinocchio Crayon Box,** 1940s, Transogram, 4-1/2" x 5-1/2" x 1/2" deep, tin
EX $18   NM $35   MIP $75

❏ **Pinocchio Hand Puppet,** Crown Toy, 9" tall, composition
EX $25   NM $45   MIP $60

❏ **Pinocchio Hand Puppet,** 1950s, Gund, 10" tall, w/squeaker
EX $25   NM $60   MIP $135

❏ **Pinocchio Hand Puppet,** 1962, Knickerbocker
EX $25   NM $50   MIP $85

❏ **Pinocchio Push Puppet,** 1960s, Kohner, 5" tall
EX $15   NM $25   MIP $65

❏ **Pinocchio Soaky**
EX $20   NM $40   MIP $75

❏ **Pinocchio Tea Set,** 1939, Ohio Art, tin tray, plates, saucers, serving platter, cups, bowls and smaller plates
EX $60   NM $125   MIP $275

❏ **Pinocchio Walker,** 1939, Marx, 9" tall, tin, animated eyes, rocking action
EX $225   NM $450   MIP $850

❏ **Pinocchio Wind-Up Toy,** Linemar, 6" tall, tin wind-up, arms and legs move
EX $100   NM $200   MIP $400

❏ **Puzzle,** 1960s, Jaymar, 5" x 7", "Pinocchio's Expedition"
EX $12   NM $22   MIP $35

WATCH

❏ **Jiminy Cricket Wristwatch,** 1948, US Time, Birthday Series
EX $80   NM $200   MIP $400

PLUTO

ACCESSORIES

❏ **Pluto Alarm Clock,** 1955, Allied, 4" x 5-1/2" x 10" tall, eyes and hands shaped like dog bones, glow in the dark
EX $60   NM $135   MIP $260

❏ **Pluto Purse,** 1940s, Gund, 9" x 14" x 2"
EX $25   NM $55   MIP $100

BANK

❏ **Pluto Bank,** 1940s, Disney, 4" x 4-1/2" x 6-1/2", ceramic
EX $40   NM $80   MIP $160

❏ **Pluto Bank,** 1970s, Animal Toys Plus, 9" tall vinyl, Pluto standing in front of a doghouse
EX $20   NM $35   MIP $70

FIGURE

❏ **Pluto Pop-Up Critter Figure,** 1936, Fisher-Price, wooden, Pluto standing on base 10-1/2" long
EX $80   NM $160   MIP $225

FIGURES

❏ **Pluto Figure,** 1930s, Seiberling, 7" tall, rubber
EX $40   NM $90   MIP $175

❏ **Pluto Figure,** 1930s, Seiberling, 3-1/2" long, rubber
EX $40   NM $90   MIP $175

❏ **Pluto Fun-E-Flex Figure,** 1930s, Fun-E-Flex, wood
EX $30   NM $75   MIP $160

TOY

❏ **Pluto Hand Puppet,** 1950s, Gund, 9" tall
EX $15   NM $35   MIP $80

❏ **Pluto Lantern Toy,** 1950s, Linemar
EX $130   NM $280   MIP $500

❏ **Pluto Pop-A-Part Toy,** 1965, Multiple Toymakers, 9" long, plastic
EX $20   NM $35   MIP $50

❏ **Pluto Push Toy,** 1936, Fisher-Price, 8" long, wood
EX $80   NM $180   MIP $320

❏ **Pluto Rolykin,** Marx, 1" x 1" x 1-1/2" tall, ball bearing action
EX $15   NM $35   MIP $70

❏ **Pluto Sports Car,** Empire, 2" long
EX $10   NM $20   MIP $40

❏ **Pluto the Acrobat Trapeze Toy,** Linemar, 10" tall, metal, celluloid, wind-up
EX $80   NM $250   MIP $320

❏ **Pluto the Drum Major,** 1950s, Marx/Linemar, tin, mechanical
EX $180   NM $350   MIP $750

POPEYE

ACCESORIES

❏ **Bowl,** 1971, Deka, oval, plastic
EX $10   NM $20   MIP $40

ACCESSORIES

❏ **60th Anniversary Candle Box,** 1989, Presents, metal, heart shaped, #P5979
EX $5   NM $12   MIP $25

❏ **Bell,** 1980, Vandor, Popeye on top, ceramic
EX $8   NM $15   MIP $35

❏ **Belt Buckle,** U.S. Spinach Growers, Strength thru Spinach
EX $8   NM $15   MIP $35

❏ **Belt Buckle,** 1973, Pyramid Belt, Popeye w/sailor hat
EX $10   NM $20   MIP $45

❏ **Belt Buckle,** 1980, Lee, Popeye w/spinach
EX $8   NM $15   MIP $35

❏ **Blinky Cup,** Beacon Plastics
EX $8   NM $15   MIP $25

❏ **Bookends,** 1980, Vandor, ceramic, Popeye and Brutus
EX $20   NM $45   MIP $80

❏ **Bowl,** 1979, National Home Products, plastic
EX $6   NM $12   MIP $25

❏ **Bowl,** 1980, Vandor, ceramic, 1 of 3
EX $8   NM $18   MIP $30

❏ **Cabinet,** mirrored
EX $35   NM $75   MIP $150

❏ **Candy,** 1980, Alberts, bonbons
EX $6   NM $10   MIP $15

❏ **Candy Box,** 1960, Phoenix Candy, Popeye and his pals
EX $20   NM $40   MIP $75

❏ **Candy Cigarettes,** 1959, Primrose Confectionery - England
EX $15   NM $35   MIP $70

❏ **Candy Sticks,** 1989, Hearst, red box
EX $6   NM $15   MIP $20

❏ **Candy Sticks,** 1990, World Candies, 48 count
EX $6   NM $15   MIP $20

❏ **Cereal Bowl,** 1979, National Home Products
EX $8   NM $20   MIP $40

❏ **Cereal Box,** 1987, Cocoa-Puffs, w/gum
EX $8   NM $20   MIP $40

❑ **Charm Bracelet,** 1990, Peter Brams, silver or gold
EX $10   NM $20   MIP $30

❑ **Chocolate Mold,** 1940s, metal, Popeye
EX $35   NM $80   MIP $150

❑ **Chocolate Mold,** 1991, Turmic Plastics, plastic, Popeye
EX $3   NM $6   MIP $10

❑ **Christmas Lamp Shades,** 1930s, General Electric, set of ten
EX $100   NM $200   MIP $400

❑ **Christmas Light Covers,** 1929, General Electric Textolite, "Cheers"
EX $60   NM $200   MIP $400

❑ **Christmas Ornament,** 1981, Bully, Bluto
EX $8   NM $15   MIP $30

❑ **Christmas Ornament,** 1981, Bully, Dufus
EX $8   NM $15   MIP $30

❑ **Christmas Ornament,** 1987, Presents, Alice the Goon, Swee'Pea, Wimpy, Popeye, Olive Oyl or Brutus, each
EX $8   NM $15   MIP $30

❑ **Christmas Ornament,** 1989, Presents, Season's Greetings
EX $8   NM $15   MIP $30

❑ **Christmas Tree Lamp Set,** 1935, General Electric
EX $80   NM $200   MIP $400

❑ **Circus Man Film,** 1950s, Brumberger, 8mm
EX $10   NM $25   MIP $50

❑ **Clothes Brush,** 1929, KFS, wooden, black or brown
EX $20   NM $80   MIP $175

❑ **Color Markers,** 1990, Sanrio, six
EX $2   NM $5   MIP $8

❑ **Comb and Brush,** 1979, KFS
EX $8   NM $25   MIP $50

❑ **Cookie Jar,** 1965, McCoy, ceramic white-suited Popeye
EX $80   NM $225   MIP $400

❑ **Cook's Catch-All,** 1980, KFS, ceramic, Wimpy
EX $10   NM $20   MIP $40

❑ **Cup,** 1940s, New Zealand, Popeye on skis, ceramic
EX $18   NM $40   MIP $70

❑ **Dice,** 1990, w/Popeye head
EX $2   NM $5   MIP $10

❑ **Dish,** 1940s, New Zealand, ceramic, Popeye and Olive
EX $20   NM $50   MIP $100

❑ **Dish Set,** 1964, Boontonware, three piece plastic
EX $20   NM $45   MIP $80

❑ **Egg Cup,** 1940s, Japan, Popeye sitting at table w/spinach
EX $30   NM $65   MIP $125

❑ **Egg Cup and Mug,** 1989, Magna, Great Britain
EX $15   NM $40   MIP $75

❑ **Film Card,** 1959, Tru-Vue, T-28
EX $8   NM $20   MIP $50

❑ **Freezicles,** 1980, Imperial
EX $5   NM $15   MIP $20

❑ **Indian Fighter Film,** Atlas Films, 8mm
EX $5   NM $10   MIP $20

❑ **Jackknife,** 1940s, Imperial, green Popeye on pearl handle
EX $75   NM $150   MIP $300

❑ **Jeep Wall Plaque,** ceramic
EX $6   NM $12   MIP $30

❑ **King of the Jungle Film,** 1960s, Atlas Films, 8mm
EX $5   NM $10   MIP $30

❑ **Knapsack,** 1979, Fabil
EX $10   NM $15   MIP $30

❑ **Kooky Straw,** 1980, Imperial
EX $4   NM $10   MIP $20

❑ **Lamp,** 1940s, boat w/Popeye light bulb
EX $350   NM $800   MIP $1100

❑ **Life Raft,** 1979, KFS, large, blue
EX $10   NM $20   MIP $40

❑ **Magic Eyes Film Card,** 1962, Tru-Vue, set of three
EX $15   NM $25   MIP $60

❑ **Mini Hurricane Lamp,** 1989, Presents, P5981-1993, 60th year
EX $4   NM $10   MIP $25

❑ **Mini Memo Board,** 1980, Freelance
EX $5   NM $10   MIP $15

❑ **Mirror,** 1978, Freelance, Popeye lifting weights
EX $7   NM $15   MIP $30

❑ **Mirror,** 1979, Freelance, Olive w/mirror
EX $7   NM $15   MIP $30

❑ **Mirror Rattle,** 1979, Cribmates
EX $8   NM $13   MIP $25

❑ **Mug,** 1950s, Schmid, ceramic
EX $10   NM $20   MIP $40

❑ **Music Lovers Film,** 1960s, Atlas Films, 8mm
EX $8   NM $15   MIP $20

❑ **Musical Mug,** 1982, KFS, ceramic
EX $10   NM $20   MIP $35

❑ **Musical Rattle,** 1979, Cribmates
EX $8   NM $15   MIP $25

❑ **Olive Oyl and Swee'Pea Hot Water Bottle,** 1970, Duarry
EX $30   NM $85   MIP $150

❑ **Olive Oyl and Swee'Pea Snow Globe,** 1989, Presents, several styles
EX $7   NM $15   MIP $30

❑ **Olive Oyl and Swee'Pea Telephone Shoulder Rest,** 1982, Comvu
EX $6   NM $15   MIP $30

❑ **Olive Oyl and Swee'Pea Thermometer,** 1981, KFS
EX $8   NM $13   MIP $18

❑ **Olive Oyl Cup,** 1977, Coke, Coke Kollect-A-Set
EX $4   NM $10   MIP $30

❑ **Olive Oyl Hairbrush,** 1979, Cribmates, musical
EX $8   NM $20   MIP $50

❑ **Olive Oyl Mug,** 1950s, Schmid, musical ceramic
EX $15   NM $40   MIP $80

❑ **Olive Oyl Mug,** 1980, Vandor, ceramic
EX $8   NM $15   MIP $25

❑ **Olive Oyl Wall Plaque,** ceramic
EX $3   NM $7   MIP $15

❑ **Paper Party Blowouts,** 1988, Gala/James River
EX $2   NM $4   MIP $10

❑ **Paperweight,** 1937, "Popeye Eats Del Monte Spinach"
EX $50   NM $100   MIP $200

❑ **Pencil Case,** 1936, Eagle, beige, #9027
EX $50   NM $100   MIP $200

❑ **Pencil Case,** 1950s, Hassenfeld Bros., red
EX $25   NM $50   MIP $100

❑ **Pencil Case,** 1990, Sanrio
EX $5   NM $10   MIP $20

❑ **Pencil Sharpener,** 1929, KFS, orange celluloid
EX $15   NM $30   MIP $85

❑ **Pig for a Friend Mug,** 1980, Vandor, ceramic
EX $6   NM $12   MIP $50

❑ **Playing Cards,** 1988, Presents, metal box, #P5998, two decks, 60th year
EX $4   NM $10   MIP $25

❑ **Popeye Alarm Clock,** 1967, Smiths, British
EX $80   NM $160   MIP $320

❑ **Popeye and Betty Boop Film,** 1935, Exclusive Films, 8mm film
EX $11   NM $25   MIP $45

❑ **Popeye and Cast Cigar Box**
EX $10   NM $25   MIP $60

❑ **Popeye and Olive Oyl Suspenders,** 1979, KFS, blue
EX $6   NM $12   MIP $20

❑ **Popeye and Swee'Pea Snow Globe,** 1989, Presents, several varieties
EX $5   NM $10   MIP $20

(KP Photo)

CHARACTER TOYS

Popeye Apron, 1990, Chester
EX $4   NM $8   MIP $15

Popeye Beach Set, 1950s, Peer Products/KFS, plastic rowboat, accessories
EX $15   NM $35   MIP $75

Popeye Charm, silver w/dangly parts
EX $10   NM $20   MIP $40

Popeye Charm, solid gold
EX $100   NM $150   MIP $200

Popeye Charm, 1930s, celluloid
EX $15   NM $30   MIP $70

Popeye Cup, 1979, Deca Plastics, plastic
EX $4   NM $7   MIP $20

Popeye Cup, 1989, Popeye Picnic, plastic
EX $1   NM $2   MIP $5

Popeye Cup and Saucer, 1930s, Japan
EX $40   NM $85   MIP $175

Popeye Glass, 1977, Coke, Coke Kollect-A-Set
EX $4   NM $7   MIP $20

Popeye Hot Water Bottle, 1970, Duarry
EX $40   NM $90   MIP $175

(KP Photo)

Popeye Lamp, 1940s, telescope w/Popeye at base
EX $65   NM $130   MIP $260

Popeye Lamp, 1959, Alan Jay, Popeye w/legs folded holding spinach
EX $50   NM $100   MIP $200

(KP Photo)

Popeye Mechanical Pencil, 1929, Eagle, 10-1/2" long illustrated pencil w/box
EX $30   NM $75   MIP $150

Popeye Night Light, Arrow Plastic
EX $8   NM $13   MIP $20

Popeye Picture, KFS-Sears, silver foil
EX $10   NM $20   MIP $40

Popeye Pin, Popeye at steering wheel, stick pin
EX $5   NM $12   MIP $25

Popeye Popcorn, 1949, Purity Mills, in can
EX $25   NM $50   MIP $100

Popeye Snow Globe, 1960s, KFS, Popeye holds globe between legs
EX $25   NM $45   MIP $90

Popeye Thimble, 1990
EX $4   NM $7   MIP $10

Popeye Toothbrush Holder, Vandor, 5" tall, figural
EX $10   NM $15   MIP $30

Popeye Toothbrush Set, 1980s, Nasta, holds two toothbrushes
EX $6   NM $15   MIP $25

Popeye Utensils, 1970s, Arrow Plastic, spoon and fork
EX $8   NM $15   MIP $30

Popeye Wall Hanging, 1979, Amscan, 42", jointed
EX $8   NM $13   MIP $20

Popeye Writing Tablet, 1929, KFS, Popeye w/spinach hypo
EX $30   NM $75   MIP $150

Popeye/Olive Oyl/Swee'Pea Lamp Shade, 1950s
EX $50   NM $75   MIP $150

Popeye/Olive Oyl/Wimpy Decals, 1935, IGS Stores
EX $15   NM $30   MIP $60

Punching Bag Film, 1950s, Brumberger, 8mm
EX $8   NM $15   MIP $25

Rain Boots, 1950s, KFS, spinach power
EX $13   NM $30   MIP $60

Record Player, 1960s, Emerson, Dynamite Music Machine
EX $35   NM $80   MIP $150

Secret Message Pen, 1981, Gordy
EX $6   NM $12   MIP $30

Sketchbook, 1960, Japan
EX $12   NM $25   MIP $50

Sleeping Bag, 1979, KFS
EX $15   NM $35   MIP $65

Soap Dispenser, 1970s, Woolfoam
EX $15   NM $25   MIP $35

Soap on a Rope, KFS, white, shaped like Popeye's head
EX $15   NM $25   MIP $45

Soap Set, 1930s, Kerk Guild, Olive Oyl, Swee'Pea, and Popeye soap figures
EX $75   NM $150   MIP $300

Stationery, 1989, Presents, metal box, heart-shaped note paper, #P5976
EX $6   NM $10   MIP $20

Storage Box, 1990, Sanrio, smoke colored
EX $6   NM $10   MIP $15

Sunday Funnies Soda Can, 1970s, Flavor Valley
EX $8   NM $15   MIP $25

Suspenders, 1970s, red, white and blue w/plastic emblems
EX $10   NM $20   MIP $35

Swee'Pea Cup, 1977, Coke, Coke Kollect-A-Cup
EX $4   NM $7   MIP $12

Swee'Pea Egg Cup, 1980, Vandor, ceramic
EX $10   NM $20   MIP $35

Swee'Pea Night Light, 1978, Presents, bone china
EX $10   NM $30   MIP $60

Swee'Pea Snow Globe, 1989, Presents, several styles
EX $5   NM $15   MIP $30

Swee'Pea Wall Plaque, 1950s, ceramic
EX $12   NM $35   MIP $70

Swee'Pea's Lemonade Stand Television Film, 1950s, Zaboly
EX $12   NM $25   MIP $50

Training Cup, 1971, Deka
EX $8   NM $13   MIP $30

Transistor Radio, 1960s, Philgee
EX $22   NM $45   MIP $85

Trash Can, 1980s, KFS
EX $10   NM $20   MIP $50

Trinket Box, 1980, Vandor, Popeye laying on top, ceramic
EX $10   NM $16   MIP $30

Trinket Box, 1980, Vandor, Popeye's head in preserver, ceramic
EX $10   NM $18   MIP $35

TV Tray, 1979, KFS
EX $8   NM $15   MIP $30

Umbrella, 1979, KFS, blue and white
EX $12   NM $25   MIP $50

Wagon Works Film, 1960s, Atlas Films, 8mm
EX $6   NM $10   MIP $20

Wallet, 1978, Larami
EX $8   NM $20   MIP $45

Wallet, 1990, Sanrio
EX $6   NM $10   MIP $20

Wallet, 1991, Presents, P-5432, tri-fold
EX $6   NM $10   MIP $20

Whistle Candy, 1989, Alberts
EX $6   NM $10   MIP $20

Wimpy Cup, 1977, Coke, Coke Kollect-A-Set
EX $4   NM $7   MIP $10

❑ **Wimpy Magnet**
EX $6　　NM $10　　MIP $15

❑ **Wimpy Thermometer,** 1981, KFS
EX $8　　NM $13　　MIP $20

❑ **Write on/Wipe Off Board,** 1979, Freelance
EX $6　　NM $12　　MIP $30

BADGE

❑ **Popeye and Swee'Pea Flicker Badge,** 1960s, Varivue
EX $8　　NM $15　　MIP $40

❑ **Popeye and Wimpy Flicker Badge,** 1960s, Varivue
EX $10　　NM $20　　MIP $40

BANK

❑ **60th Anniversary Bank,** 1988, Presents, metal, P5988
EX $5　　NM $20　　MIP $35

❑ **Brutus Mini Bank,** 1979, KFS
EX $10　　NM $20　　MIP $35

(KP Photo)

❑ **Daily Dime Bank,** 1956, KFS
EX $40　　NM $110　　MIP $225

(KP Photo)

❑ **Daily Quarter Bank,** 1950s, Kalon, 4-1/2" tall, metal
EX $100　　NM $175　　MIP $350

(KP Photo)

❑ **Dime Register Bank,** 1929, KFS, square, window shows total deposits
EX $110　　NM $250　　MIP $375

❑ **Knockout Bank,** 1935, Straits
EX $250　　NM $500　　MIP $1000

❑ **Olive Oyl Bank,** 1940s, cast iron
EX $90　　NM $200　　MIP $350

❑ **Olive Oyl Mini Bank,** 1979, KFS
EX $12　　NM $30　　MIP $60

❑ **Popeye Bank,** ceramic, Popeye in light blue cap
EX $5　　NM $10　　MIP $30

❑ **Popeye Bank,** 1940s, Popeye w/life preserver
EX $50　　NM $100　　MIP $200

❑ **Popeye Bank,** 1940s, 9" cast iron
EX $80　　NM $175　　MIP $350

❑ **Popeye Bank,** 1970s, Play Pal, plastic, Popeye sitting on rope
EX $10　　NM $30　　MIP $45

❑ **Popeye Bank,** 1972, Play Pal, shape of Popeye's head, plastic
EX $15　　NM $30　　MIP $60

❑ **Popeye Bank,** 1979, Renz, beige bust
EX $12　　NM $25　　MIP $55

❑ **Popeye Bank,** 1980, Leonard, silver, Popeye sitting
EX $15　　NM $30　　MIP $60

❑ **Popeye Bank,** 1980, Vandor, ceramic, Popeye sitting on rope
EX $12　　NM $25　　MIP $50

❑ **Popeye Bank,** 1980, Vandor, ceramic
EX $130　　NM $260　　MIP $525

❑ **Popeye Bank,** 1990, Sanrio, w/padlock
EX $5　　NM $10　　MIP $20

❑ **Popeye Bank,** 1990, Mexico, ceramic bust
EX $10　　NM $25　　MIP $50

❑ **Popeye Bank,** 1991, Presents, vinyl, Popeye w/removable pipe
EX $6　　NM $12　　MIP $20

❑ **Popeye Mini Bank,** 1979, KFS
EX $7　　NM $15　　MIP $30

❑ **Spinach Can Bank,** 1975, KFS, blue can w/raised characters
EX $15　　NM $30　　MIP $60

❑ **Swee'Pea Bank,** 1980, Vandor, 6-1/2" figural
EX $30　　NM $75　　MIP $150

❑ **Swee'Pea Mini Bank,** 1979, KFS
EX $10　　NM $25　　MIP $60

BOOK

❑ **60th Anniversary Collection Book,** 1990, Hawk Books
EX $20　　NM $40　　MIP $60

❑ **Adventures of Popeye Book,** 1934, Saalfield
EX $25　　NM $100　　MIP $300

❑ **Big Surprise Book,** 1976, Wonder Books
EX $5　　NM $15　　MIP $30

❑ **Captain George Presents Popeye Book,** 1970, Memory Lane
EX $10　　NM $25　　MIP $50

❑ **Danger Ahoy! Book,** 1969, Whitman, Big Little Book
EX $5　　NM $15　　MIP $30

❑ **Deep Sea Danger Book,** 1980, Whitman, Big Little Book
EX $2　　NM $6　　MIP $15

❑ **Fun Booklets,** 1980, Spot-O-Gold, set of 10
EX $20　　NM $40　　MIP $80

❑ **Ghost Ship to Treasure Island Book,** 1967, Whitman, Big Little Book
EX $8　　NM $15　　MIP $35

❑ **Giant 24 Big Picture Coloring Book,** 1981, Merrigold Press
EX $6　　NM $12　　MIP $30

❑ **Giant Paint Book,** 1937, Whitman, blue or red
EX $50　　NM $100　　MIP $200

❑ **Great Big Popeye Paint and Crayon Book,** 1937, McLoughlin Bros.
EX $75　　NM $150　　MIP $300

❑ **Hag of the Seven Seas Pop-Up Book,** 1935, Blue Ribbon Books
EX $100　　NM $300　　MIP $500

❑ **House that Popeye Built Book,** 1960, Wonder Books
EX $8　　NM $25　　MIP $50

❑ **In a Sock for Susan's Sake Book,** 1940, Whitman, Big Little Book
EX $30　　NM $75　　MIP $150

❑ **In Quest of Poopdeck Pappy Book,** 1937, Whitman, Big Little Book
EX $30　　NM $75　　MIP $150

❑ **Jiffy Pop Fun 'N Games Booklet,** 1980, Spot-O-Gold
EX $6　　NM $12　　MIP $30

❑ **Little Pops the Ghost Book,** 1981, Random House
EX $5　　NM $10　　MIP $30

❑ **Little Pops the Magic Flute Book,** 1981, Random House
EX $5　　NM $10　　MIP $30

❑ **Little Pops the Spinach Burgers Book,** 1981, Random House
EX $5　　NM $10　　MIP $30

❑ **Little Pops the Treasure Hunt Book,** 1981, Random House
EX $5　　NM $10　　MIP $30

❑ **Mix or Match Storybook,** 1981, Random House
EX $8　　NM $15　　MIP $30

❑ **Olive Oyl and Swee'Pea Wash Up Book,** 1980, Tuffy Books
EX $4　　NM $10　　MIP $25

❑ **Paint with Water Book,** 1981, Whitman
EX $3　　NM $6　　MIP $20

CHARACTER TOYS

❑ **Painting and Crayon Book,** 1960, England
EX $15　　NM $25　　MIP $60

❑ **Popeye Activity Pad,** 1982, Merrigold Press
EX $3　　NM $7　　MIP $13

❑ **Popeye All Picture Comic Book,** 1942, Whitman, Big Little Book
EX $20　　NM $60　　MIP $120

❑ **Popeye and his Jungle Pet Book,** 1937, Whitman
EX $30　　NM $75　　MIP $150

❑ **Popeye and Swee'Pea Coloring Book,** 1970, Whitman, 1056-31
EX $7　　NM $15　　MIP $30

❑ **Popeye and the Deep Sea Mystery Big Little Book,** 1939, Whitman
EX $25　　NM $75　　MIP $150

❑ **Popeye and the Jeep Book,** 1937, Whitman, Big Little Book
EX $25　　NM $75　　MIP $150

❑ **Popeye and the Pet Book,** 1987, Peter Haddock, book three of four
EX $3　　NM $5　　MIP $15

❑ **Popeye and the Time Machine Book,** 1990, Quaker, mini comic
EX $3　　NM $5　　MIP $15

❑ **Popeye Book,** 1980, Random House, hardcover, based on movie
EX $4　　NM $8　　MIP $20

❑ **Popeye Calls on Olive Oyl Book,** 1937, Whitman, 8-1/2" x 9-1/2"
EX $30　　NM $80　　MIP $160

❑ **Popeye Climbs a Mountain Book,** 1983, Wonder Books
EX $3　　NM $7　　MIP $15

❑ **Popeye Color and Recolor Book,** 1957, Jack Built, color, wipe and color again
EX $18　　NM $35　　MIP $100

❑ **Popeye How to Draw Cartoons Book,** 1939, Joe Musial/D. McKay
EX $60　　NM $125　　MIP $250

❑ **Popeye in Puddleburg Book,** 1934, Saalfield, Big Little Book
EX $25　　NM $75　　MIP $150

❑ **Popeye Learn and Play Activity Book,** 1985, Allen Canning
EX $2　　NM $5　　MIP $10

❑ **Popeye Meets his Rival Book,** 1937, Whitman, 8-1/2" x 11-1/2"
EX $30　　NM $75　　MIP $150

❑ **Popeye on Rocket Coloring Book,** 1980, Whitman - France
EX $8　　NM $15　　MIP $30

❑ **Popeye on Safari Book,** 1990, Quaker, mini comic
EX $2　　NM $4　　MIP $8

❑ **Popeye Paint Book,** 1932, McLoughlin Bros., blue
EX $50　　NM $100　　MIP $200

❑ **Popeye Paint Coloring Book,** 1951, Whitman
EX $25　　NM $50　　MIP $100

❑ **Popeye Pop-Up Book,** 1981, Random House
EX $6　　NM $12　　MIP $30

❑ **Popeye Punch-Out Play Book,** 1961, Whitman
EX $12　　NM $22　　MIP $45

❑ **Popeye Puppet Show Book,** 1936, Pleasure Books
EX $30　　NM $75　　MIP $150

❑ **Popeye Sees the Sea Book,** 1936, Whitman, Big Little Book
EX $30　　NM $75　　MIP $150

❑ **Popeye Song Folio Book,** 1936, Famous Music, Z
EX $25　　NM $80　　MIP $160

❑ **Popeye Stay in Shape Book,** 1980, Tuffy Books
EX $6　　NM $10　　MIP $20

❑ **Popeye Surprise Present Book,** 1987, Peter Haddock
EX $6　　NM $10　　MIP $20

❑ **Popeye the Movie Book,** 1980, Avon Printing
EX $6　　NM $10　　MIP $25

(KP Photo)

❑ **Popeye the Sailor Man Book,** 1942, Whitman, Big Little Book
EX $30　　NM $75　　MIP $150

❑ **Popeye vs. Bluto the Bad Book,** 1990, Quaker, mini comic
EX $2　　NM $4　　MIP $8

❑ **Popeye with his Friends Book,** 1937, Whitman
EX $20　　NM $75　　MIP $150

❑ **Popeye's Adventure Book,** 1958, Purnell, England
EX $15　　NM $30　　MIP $60

❑ **Popeye's Ark Book,** 1936, Saalfield, Big Little Book
EX $20　　NM $65　　MIP $130

❑ **Puzzle Party Book,** 1979, Cinnamon House
EX $6　　NM $12　　MIP $25

❑ **Quest for the Rainbird Book,** 1943, Whitman, Big Little Book
EX $20　　NM $65　　MIP $120

❑ **Race to Pearl Peak Book,** 1982, Golden
EX $6　　NM $10　　MIP $20

❑ **S.S. Funboat Coloring Book,** 1981, Merrigold Press
EX $4　　NM $7　　MIP $25

❑ **Sailor and the Spinach Stalk Coloring Book,** 1982, Whitman, 1150-1
EX $6　　NM $15　　MIP $30

❑ **Scott Fun 'N Games Booklet,** 1980, Spot-O-Gold, set of five
EX $10　　NM $20　　MIP $40

❑ **The Outer Space Zoo Book,** 1980, Golden
EX $6　　NM $12　　MIP $30

❑ **Thimble Theatre Book,** 1935, Whitman, Big Big Book
EX $100　　NM $300　　MIP $600

❑ **What! No Spinach? Book,** 1981, Golden
EX $6　　NM $10　　MIP $25

❑ **Wimpy in Back to his First Love Book,** eight pages
EX $6　　NM $10　　MIP $15

❑ **Wimpy the Hamburger Eater Book,** 1938, Whitman, Big Little Book
EX $25　　NM $75　　MIP $150

❑ **Wimpy Tricks Popeye and Roughhouse Book,** 1937, Whitman
EX $40　　NM $80　　MIP $160

❑ **Wimpy Tricks Popeye Book,** 1937, Whitman
EX $45　　NM $75　　MIP $130

❑ **Wimpy What's Good to Eat? Book,** 1980, Tuffy Books
EX $6　　NM $12　　MIP $30

BUTTON

❑ **Bluto Button,** 1979, Lisa Frank, 2", Bluto getting socked
EX $2　　NM $7　　MIP $15

❑ **Brutus Button,** 1980, Factors, 3", movie
EX $2　　NM $5　　MIP $10

❑ **Brutus Button,** 1983, Mini Media, 1", "I'm Mean"
EX $2　　NM $5　　MIP $10

❑ **Brutus Button,** 1985, Strand, 3", "Gonna Eat You for Breakfast"
EX $3　　NM $6　　MIP $12

❑ **Brutus Button,** 1985, Strand, 3", "Ya Little Runt"
EX $2　　NM $5　　MIP $10

❑ **Button,** 1930s, Offset Gravure, 1", New York Evening Journal
EX $25　　NM $60　　MIP $110

❑ **Button,** 1983, Mini Media, 1", "No Wimps"
EX $3　　NM $7　　MIP $15

❑ **Olive Oyl Button,** 1946, Pep
EX $8　　NM $22　　MIP $45

❑ **Olive Oyl Button,** 1980, Factors, 3"
EX $2　　NM $4　　MIP $8

❑ **Olive Oyl Button,** 1983, Mini Media, 1", "More than just a pretty face"
EX $2　　NM $4　　MIP $8

❏ **Popeye and Olive Oyl Button**, 1970s, 1-1/2", "I Love You"
EX $5　　NM $10　　MIP $22

❏ **Popeye and Olive Oyl Button**, 1980, Lisa Frank, 1", cowboy Popeye and Indian Olive
EX $5　　NM $10　　MIP $20

❏ **Popeye Button**, 1946, Pep
EX $15　　NM $35　　MIP $60

❏ **Popeye Button**, 1950s, KFS, 1", Famous Studios
EX $20　　NM $40　　MIP $80

(KP Photo)

❏ **Popeye Button**, 1959, Lowe, sew-on card
EX $12　　NM $20　　MIP $50

❏ **Popeye Button**, 1960s, KMOX TV, 1", S.S. Popeye
EX $5　　NM $15　　MIP $45

❏ **Popeye Button**, 1980, Factors, 3", movie
EX $2　　NM $4　　MIP $10

❏ **Popeye Button**, 1985, Strand, 3", several styles
EX $3　　NM $6　　MIP $20

❏ **Popeye Button**, 1989, KFS, 3", marine conservation
EX $2　　NM $4　　MIP $10

❏ **Popeye Button**, 1990, S. Cruz, 2", Santa Cruz boardwalk
EX $2　　NM $4　　MIP $10

❏ **Swee'Pea Button**, 1980, Lisa Frank, 1", Swee'Pea w/Jeep
EX $2　　NM $5　　MIP $12

❏ **Wimpy Button**, 1946, Pep
EX $10　　NM $20　　MIP $40

❏ **Wimpy Button**, 1979, Lisa Frank, 2"
EX $3　　NM $8　　MIP $15

❏ **Wimpy Button**, 1985, Strand, 3", "Must Go Home and Water the Ducks"
EX $3　　NM $8　　MIP $15

DOLL

❏ **Brutus Doll**, 1985, Presents, small
EX $12　　NM $25　　MIP $60

❏ **Brutus Doll**, 1985, Presents, large with tag
EX $20　　NM $50　　MIP $100

❏ **Chimes Doll**, 1950s, J. Swedlin, gray plush body, chimes
EX $20　　NM $50　　MIP $85

❏ **Jeep Doll**, 1985, Presents, two sizes
EX $8　　NM $20　　MIP $50

❏ **Olive Oyl Doll**, 9" vinyl sqeeze doll, Olive w/Swee'Pea
EX $15　　NM $40　　MIP $85

❏ **Olive Oyl Doll**, 1950s, Rempel, small
EX $25　　NM $50　　MIP $100

❏ **Olive Oyl Doll**, 1960s, Dakin, 8" tall
EX $25　　NM $50　　MIP $100

❏ **Olive Oyl Doll**, 1970s, Dakin, hard plastic w/removable clothes
EX $20　　NM $40　　MIP $80

❏ **Olive Oyl Doll**, 1970s, Dakin, Cartoon Theatre, in box
EX $25　　NM $50　　MIP $100

❏ **Olive Oyl Doll**, 1979, Uneeda, removable clothing
EX $15　　NM $30　　MIP $70

❏ **Olive Oyl Doll**, 1985, Presents, Christmas, large
EX $14　　NM $30　　MIP $50

❏ **Olive Oyl Doll**, 1985, Presents, small
EX $10　　NM $18　　MIP $30

❏ **Olive Oyl Doll**, 1990, Presents, small molded plastic, musical # P5948
EX $8　　NM $13　　MIP $25

❏ **Olive Oyl Doll**, 1990, Toy Toons
EX $4　　NM $9　　MIP $18

❏ **Olive Oyl Doll**, 1991, Presents, small molded plastic, # P5966
EX $4　　NM $8　　MIP $20

❏ **Olive Oyl Doll**, 1991, Presents, Christmas, small
EX $8　　NM $13　　MIP $25

❏ **Poopdeck Pappy Doll**, 1985, Presents, with tag
EX $35　　NM $75　　MIP $150

❏ **Popeye Doll**, 23" china
EX $110　　NM $225　　MIP $400

❏ **Popeye Doll**, 1935, Cameo
EX $150　　NM $300　　MIP $600

❏ **Popeye Doll**, 1936, Stack, 12" tall, wood jointed, w/pipe
EX $125　　NM $300　　MIP $550

❏ **Popeye Doll**, 1950s, Chicago Herald American
EX $30　　NM $85　　MIP $150

❏ **Popeye Doll**, 1950s, Rempel, small
EX $20　　NM $45　　MIP $90

❏ **Popeye Doll**, 1950s, Woolikin, white plush
EX $30　　NM $65　　MIP $130

❏ **Popeye Doll**, 1950s, Chad Valley, 7" tall, squeaks
EX $20　　NM $55　　MIP $110

❏ **Popeye Doll**, 1957, Sears/Cameo, 13" in box
EX $175　　NM $350　　MIP $750

❏ **Popeye Doll**, 1958, Gund, 20" tall
EX $50　　NM $100　　MIP $200

❏ **Popeye Doll**, 1960s, Quaker, 12" cloth
EX $20　　NM $40　　MIP $80

❏ **Popeye Doll**, 1960s, 9" vinyl squeeze doll, Popeye w/Swee'Pea
EX $15　　NM $30　　MIP $80

❏ **Popeye Doll**, 1968, Lakeside, 12" tall, sponge rubber
EX $15　　NM $30　　MIP $75

❏ **Popeye Doll**, 1970s, Dakin, Cartoon Theatre, in box
EX $30　　NM $60　　MIP $120

❏ **Popeye Doll**, 1970s, Dakin, hard plastic w/removable clothes
EX $20　　NM $60　　MIP $120

❏ **Popeye Doll**, 1974, Dakin, squeaks
EX $15　　NM $30　　MIP $75

❏ **Popeye Doll**, 1979, Uneeda
EX $20　　NM $40　　MIP $85

❏ **Popeye Doll**, 1979, Uneeda, 16" tall
EX $22　　NM $45　　MIP $90

❏ **Popeye Doll**, 1983, Etone, 8" plush
EX $7　　NM $15　　MIP $35

❏ **Popeye Doll**, 1985, Presents, small
EX $8　　NM $13　　MIP $30

❏ **Popeye Doll**, 1985, Presents, small doll w/pipe molded into hand
EX $10　　NM $15　　MIP $40

❏ **Popeye Doll**, 1990, Presents, small molded plastic, musical #P5949
EX $10　　NM $15　　MIP $30

❏ **Popeye Doll**, 1990, Toy Toons
EX $7　　NM $15　　MIP $35

❏ **Sea Hag Doll**, 1985, Presents
EX $30　　NM $75　　MIP $150

❏ **Swee'Pea Doll**, 1979, Uneeda
EX $10　　NM $20　　MIP $50

❏ **Swee'Pea Doll**, 1985, Presents, large
EX $15　　NM $30　　MIP $60

❏ **Swee'Pea Doll**, 1985, Presents, small
EX $12　　NM $25　　MIP $50

❏ **Swee'Pea Doll**, 1991, Presents, small molded plastic, # P5968
EX $10　　NM $15　　MIP $30

❏ **Swee'Pea Doll**, 1991, Presents, Christmas, small
EX $10　　NM $20　　MIP $50

❏ **Wimpy Doll**, 1950s, KFS, rubber
EX $25　　NM $50　　MIP $100

❏ **Wimpy Doll**, 1985, Presents, holding a hamburger
EX $35　　NM $75　　MIP $150

FIGURE

❏ **Popeye Galley Steward Figure**, 1980, KFS, ceramic
EX $10　　NM $22　　MIP $45

FIGURES

❏ **Bluto Figure**, Cristallerie Antonio, Italian crystal
EX $15　　NM $35　　MIP $75

CHARACTER TOYS

❑ **Brutus Figure,** 1962, Japan Olympics, wood, Brutus in barrel
EX $75   NM $180   MIP $340

❑ **Brutus Figure,** 1981, Bully, pink shirt
EX $7   NM $15   MIP $30

❑ **Brutus Figure,** 1984, Comic-Spain, Brutus w/club
EX $4   NM $7   MIP $12

❑ **Brutus Figure,** 1990, Presents, PVC
EX $2   NM $3   MIP $6

❑ **Brutus Figure,** 1991, KFS-Hearst, wood
EX $4   NM $7   MIP $12

❑ **Character Figures,** 1980, Spoontiques, two 1" figures: Jeep lifting tail, Swee'Pea w/feet showing, each
EX $10   NM $20   MIP $30

❑ **Character Figures,** 1980, Spoontiques, 2" figures: Popeye w/barbell, Popeye w/parrot, Olive walking, Popeye flexing muscles, Popeye w/spinach, each
EX $10   NM $20   MIP $35

❑ **Character Figures,** 1981, Spoontiques, pewter, three 1" figures: Olive w/hands clasped, Popeye w/muscles, Jeep standing, each
EX $10   NM $20   MIP $30

❑ **Character Figures,** 1991, Popeye's Chicken, blue plastic, several characters available
EX $2   NM $5   MIP $10

❑ **Dufus Figure,** 1981, Bully, w/hand on stomach
EX $8   NM $15   MIP $28

❑ **Jeep Figure,** 1991, KFS-Hearst, wood
EX $7   NM $14   MIP $35

❑ **Olive Oyl Figure,** Cristallerie Antonio, Italian crystal
EX $10   NM $15   MIP $40

❑ **Olive Oyl Figure,** 1940, KFS, 8" tall
EX $60   NM $120   MIP $240

❑ **Olive Oyl Figure,** 1940s, lead
EX $15   NM $30   MIP $75

❑ **Olive Oyl Figure,** 1940s, 5" wooden jointed
EX $75   NM $150   MIP $300

❑ **Olive Oyl Figure,** 1950s, Multiple Toy-makers, 2" tall
EX $7   NM $20   MIP $40

❑ **Olive Oyl Figure,** 1974, Ben Cooper, rubber
EX $15   NM $35   MIP $75

❑ **Olive Oyl Figure,** 1980, Amscan, large bendy
EX $6   NM $12   MIP $25

❑ **Olive Oyl Figure,** 1980, KFS, arms clamped together, hanging figure
EX $5   NM $10   MIP $25

❑ **Olive Oyl Figure,** 1981, Bully, w/hands clasp
EX $8   NM $15   MIP $25

❑ **Olive Oyl Figure,** 1981, Bully, holding flower
EX $8   NM $15   MIP $25

❑ **Olive Oyl Figure,** 1984, Comics Spain, PVC, Olive w/flower
EX $3   NM $7   MIP $15

❑ **Olive Oyl Figure,** 1986, Comics Spain, 6" bendy
EX $6   NM $10   MIP $18

❑ **Olive Oyl Figure,** 1988, Jesco, large bendy
EX $3   NM $6   MIP $18

❑ **Olive Oyl Figure,** 1988, Jesco, small bendy
EX $2   NM $4   MIP $12

❑ **Olive Oyl Figure,** 1990, Presents, 3" tall, plastic
EX $1   NM $3   MIP $6

❑ **Olive Oyl Figure,** 1990, Mexico, ceramic
EX $10   NM $20   MIP $40

❑ **Olive Oyl Figure,** 1990, Chester, 10", Olive w/rolling pin
EX $10   NM $20   MIP $40

❑ **Olive Oyl Figure,** 1990, Presents, PVC
EX $1   NM $3   MIP $6

❑ **Olive Oyl Figure,** 1991, KFS-Hearst, wood
EX $4   NM $8   MIP $15

❑ **Popeye Figure,** Cristallerie Antionio Imperatore, Italian crystal
EX $12   NM $25   MIP $50

❑ **Popeye Figure,** Dakin, 8" tall w/spinach can
EX $22   NM $45   MIP $90

❑ **Popeye Figure,** 1930s, 5" tall, wood jointed, held together w/string
EX $75   NM $150   MIP $300

❑ **Popeye Figure,** 1930s, 12" tall, chalk, w/pipe and hat, ashtray base
EX $60   NM $125   MIP $250

❑ **Popeye Figure,** 1940s, celluloid w/wooden feet
EX $40   NM $90   MIP $180

❑ **Popeye Figure,** 1940s, lead
EX $15   NM $30   MIP $60

❑ **Popeye Figure,** 1944, Sirocco-KFS, 5", wood
EX $40   NM $100   MIP $200

❑ **Popeye Figure,** 1950s, plastic, Popeye on four wheels w/telescope
EX $25   NM $50   MIP $100

❑ **Popeye Figure,** 1950s, Japan, celluloid
EX $25   NM $50   MIP $100

❑ **Popeye Figure,** 1950s, England, 7", bendy, yellow pants
EX $30   NM $60   MIP $160

❑ **Popeye Figure,** 1960s, Combex, rubber, Popey w/a can of spinach
EX $20   NM $40   MIP $80

❑ **Popeye Figure,** 1962, Japan Olympics, wood, Popeye at bat
EX $150   NM $300   MIP $550

❑ **Popeye Figure,** 1968, Lakeside, mini-flex
EX $10   NM $25   MIP $60

❑ **Popeye Figure,** 1969, Lakeside, super-flex
EX $10   NM $25   MIP $60

❑ **Popeye Figure,** 1970, Duncan, 8" tall
EX $20   NM $40   MIP $70

❑ **Popeye Figure,** 1970s, ceramic, removeable head Popeye
EX $30   NM $60   MIP $90

❑ **Popeye Figure,** 1974, Ben Cooper, rubber
EX $8   NM $15   MIP $40

❑ **Popeye Figure,** 1978, Bronco, bendy
EX $6   NM $10   MIP $25

❑ **Popeye Figure,** 1979, Imperial
EX $6   NM $10   MIP $20

❑ **Popeye Figure,** 1980, Amscan, small bendy
EX $4   NM $7   MIP $14

❑ **Popeye Figure,** 1980, Amscan, large bendy
EX $6   NM $12   MIP $20

❑ **Popeye Figure,** 1981, Bully, several variations
EX $9   NM $18   MIP $30

❑ **Popeye Figure,** 1984, Comics Spain, PVC, Popeye w/spinach
EX $4   NM $7   MIP $15

❑ **Popeye Figure,** 1986, Comics Spain, 6" bendy, white pants
EX $3   NM $6   MIP $20

❑ **Popeye Figure,** 1988, Jesco, small bendy
EX $2   NM $5   MIP $15

❑ **Popeye Figure,** 1988, Jesco, bendy
EX $6   NM $10   MIP $20

❑ **Popeye Figure,** 1990, Chester, 10", ceramic, Popeye w/spinach
EX $6   NM $10   MIP $25

❑ **Popeye Figure,** 1990, Presents, PVC
EX $1   NM $4   MIP $8

❑ **Popeye Figure,** 1990, Presents, 3" tall, plastic
EX $2   NM $3   MIP $6

❑ **Popeye Figure,** 1990, Mexico, ceramic
EX $7   NM $15   MIP $35

❑ **Popeye Figure,** 1991, KFS-Hearst, wood
EX $8   NM $12   MIP $25

❑ **Swee'Pea Figure,** Cristallerie Antionio Imperatore, Italian crystal
EX $15   NM $30   MIP $45

❑ **Swee'Pea Figure,** ceramic, one of five
EX $5   NM $15   MIP $35

❑ **Swee'Pea Figure,** 1984, Presents, PVC
EX $2   NM $4   MIP $10

❑ **Swee'Pea Figure,** 1984, Comics Spain, PVC, Swee'Pea w/cake
EX $4   NM $8   MIP $20

❑ **Swee'Pea Figure,** 1990, Presents, 3" tall, plastic
EX $5   **NM** $10   **MIP** $20

❑ **Wimpy Figure,** Cristallerie Antionio Imperatore, Italian crystal
EX $10   **NM** $30   **MIP** $60

❑ **Wimpy Figure,** 1940s, lead
EX $15   **NM** $30   **MIP** $60

❑ **Wimpy Figure,** 1944, Sirocco-KFS, 5", wood
EX $42   **NM** $85   **MIP** $200

❑ **Wimpy Figure,** 1950s, Buitoni, premium
EX $30   **NM** $70   **MIP** $140

❑ **Wimpy Figure,** 1981, Bully, yellow hat
EX $6   **NM** $12   **MIP** $25

❑ **Wimpy Figure,** 1984, Comics Spain, Wimpy w/hamburger
EX $7   **NM** $15   **MIP** $30

❑ **Wimpy Figure,** 1990, Presents, PVC
EX $2   **NM** $5   **MIP** $10

GAME

❑ **Adventures of Popeye Game,** 1957, Transogram
EX $35   **NM** $75   **MIP** $150

❑ **Boxing Game,** 1981, Harmony
EX $7   **NM** $15   **MIP** $30

❑ **Jumbo Card Game,** 1978, House of Games
EX $8   **NM** $17   **MIP** $35

❑ **Jumbo Trading Card Game,** 1960s, Dynamic Toy
EX $15   **NM** $30   **MIP** $60

❑ **Magic Play Around Game,** 1960s, Amsco
EX $20   **NM** $45   **MIP** $85

❑ **Pocket Pin Ball,** 1983, Nintendo/Ja-Ru, cups
EX $5   **NM** $10   **MIP** $15

❑ **Pocket Pin Ball,** 1983, Nintendo/Ja-Ru, holes
EX $5   **NM** $10   **MIP** $15

❑ **Popeye Arcade Game,** 1980, Parker Bros., card game
EX $5   **NM** $10   **MIP** $20

POPEYE
BALL TOSS GAME

(KP Photo)

❑ **Popeye Ball Toss Game,** 1950s, KFS
EX $40   **NM** $75   **MIP** $150

❑ **Popeye Bingo,** 1929, Bar Zim
EX $35   **NM** $75   **MIP** $150

❑ **Popeye Break-A-Plate Game,** 1963, Combex
EX $30   **NM** $80   **MIP** $150

❑ **Popeye Fishing Game,** 1962, Transogram, magnetic
EX $15   **NM** $30   **MIP** $65

❑ **Popeye Fishing Game,** 1980, Fleetwood
EX $5   **NM** $10   **MIP** $25

❑ **Popeye Games,** 1960s, Ed-U-Card, set of four games
EX $15   **NM** $30   **MIP** $60

❑ **Popeye Hammer Game,** 1960s, Holgate
EX $70   **NM** $140   **MIP** $280

❑ **Popeye Menu Pinball Game,** 1935, Durable Toy and Novelty
EX $60   **NM** $125   **MIP** $250

❑ **Popeye Mini Tennis Game,** 1970s, Nordic
EX $10   **NM** $15   **MIP** $30

❑ **Popeye Nail-On Game,** 1963, Colorforms
EX $20   **NM** $45   **MIP** $100

❑ **Popeye Party Game,** 1937, Whitman, posters, paper pipes, game box
EX $35   **NM** $75   **MIP** $150

❑ **Popeye Pinball Game,** 1983, Ja-Ru
EX $6   **NM** $10   **MIP** $25

(KP Photo)

❑ **Popeye Pipe Toss Game,** 1935, Rosebud Art, small version w/wooden pipe
EX $50   **NM** $100   **MIP** $200

❑ **Popeye Playing Card Game,** 1934, Whitman, 5" x 7", green box
EX $20   **NM** $60   **MIP** $130

❑ **Popeye Playing Card Game,** 1938, Whitman, blue box
EX $15   **NM** $55   **MIP** $120

❑ **Popeye Playing Card Game,** 1983, Parker Bros.
EX $6   **NM** $10   **MIP** $20

❑ **Popeye Ring Toss Game,** 1957, Transogram
EX $32   **NM** $65   **MIP** $135

❑ **Popeye Ring Toss Game,** 1980, Fleetwood
EX $6   **NM** $10   **MIP** $25

❑ **Popeye Shipwreck Game,** 1933, Einson-Freeman
EX $50   **NM** $100   **MIP** $200

❑ **Popeye Spinach Target Game,** 1960s, Gardner
EX $40   **NM** $75   **MIP** $110

❑ **Popeye the Juggler Bead Game,** 1929, Bar-Zim, 3-1/2" x 5", covered w/glass
EX $25   **NM** $50   **MIP** $100

❑ **Popeye Video Game,** 1983, Nintendo
EX $12   **NM** $20   **MIP** $30

❑ **Popeye/Olive Oyl/Wimpy Skill Games,** 1965, Lido
EX $10   **NM** $16   **MIP** $30

❑ **Popeye's Gang Pinball Game,** 1970s, MSS
EX $13   **NM** $25   **MIP** $50

❑ **Popeye's Lucky Jeep Game,** 1936, Northwestern Products
EX $50   **NM** $100   **MIP** $200

❑ **Popeye's Peg Board Game,** 1934, Bar Zim
EX $65   **NM** $150   **MIP** $300

❑ **Popeye's Sliding Boards and Ladders,** 1958, Warren Built-Rite
EX $12   **NM** $25   **MIP** $80

❑ **Popeye's Spinach Hunt Game,** 1976, Whitman
EX $11   **NM** $22   **MIP** $45

❑ **Popeye's Three Game Set,** 1956, Built-Rite
EX $20   **NM** $40   **MIP** $80

Popeye's Tiddly Winks, 1948, Parker Bros.
EX $20   NM $40   MIP $80

Popeye's Treasure Map Game, 1977, Whitman
EX $12   NM $25   MIP $50

Popeye's Where's Me Pipe Game
EX $30   NM $50   MIP $90

Puzzle Game, 1978, Waddington's House of Games
EX $10   NM $20   MIP $40

Ring the Bell with Hammer Game, 1960s, Harett-Gilmar
EX $25   NM $42   MIP $70

Ring Toss Stand-Up Game, 1958, Transogram
EX $15   NM $30   MIP $65

Roly Poly and Cork Gun Game, 1958, Knickbocker
EX $60   NM $120   MIP $200

Rub 'N Win Party Game, 1980, Spot-O-Gold
EX $5   NM $10   MIP $25

Skeet Shoot Game, 1950, Irwin
EX $50   NM $100   MIP $175

Skoozit Pick-A-Puzzle Game, 1966, Ideal
EX $15   NM $35   MIP $70

Water Ball Game, 1983, Nintendo, one basket
EX $6   NM $10   MIP $20

LUNCH BOX

Mini Lunch Box, 1990, Sanrio, plastic
EX $4   NM $10   MIP $25

MUSIC BOX

Brutus Music Box, 1980, KFS, Brutus dancing
EX $10   NM $15   MIP $30

Brutus Music Box, 1989, Presents, #P5984
EX $8   NM $17   MIP $35

Music Box, 1980, Vandor, revolving Popeye spanks Swee'Pea, ceramic
EX $20   NM $45   MIP $90

Music Box, 1980, Vandor, revolving Olive w/Popeye dancing, ceramic
EX $20   NM $45   MIP $90

Music Box, 1980, Vandor, Wimpy on top of hamburger, ceramic
EX $20   NM $45   MIP $90

Olive Oyl Music Box, 1980, KFS, Olive dancing
EX $8   NM $20   MIP $40

Olive Oyl Music Box, 1989, Presents, #P5983
EX $8   NM $20   MIP $40

Popeye and Olive Oyl Music Box, Schmid, 8-1/4" figural box
EX $50   NM $100   MIP $180

Swee'Pea Music Box, 1980, KFS, Swee'Pea dancing
EX $8   NM $13   MIP $30

Swee'Pea Music Box, 1989, Presents, #P5986
EX $8   NM $15   MIP $35

Wimpy Music Box, 1989, Presents, #P5985
EX $8   NM $15   MIP $30

PIN

Pin, 1935, JCPenney, Back to School Days w/Popeye
EX $15   NM $40   MIP $85

RECORD

Fleas A Crowd Record, 1962, Peter Pan, 78 rpm
EX $10   NM $25   MIP $50

Olive Oyl on Troubled Waters Record, 1976, Peter Pan, 45 rpm
EX $7   NM $20   MIP $40

Original Radio Broadcasts Record, 1977, Golden Age, 33 rpm
EX $7   NM $25   MIP $60

Picture Disc Record, 1948, Record of America, 78 rpm
EX $25   NM $50   MIP $100

Picture Disc Record, 1982, Peter Pan, 33 rpm
EX $6   NM $10   MIP $25

Pollution Solution Record, 1970s, Peter Pan, 45 rpm
EX $5   NM $10   MIP $35

Popeye and Friends Record, 1981, Merry Records, 33 rpm
EX $3   NM $10   MIP $25

Popeye French Record, 1981, Polygram, 45 rpm
EX $7   NM $15   MIP $35

Popeye in the Movies Record, Peter Pan, 33 rpm w/book
EX $6   NM $15   MIP $35

Popeye Launches His New Song Hits Record, 1958, Peter Pan, 45 rpm
EX $15   NM $30   MIP $60

Popeye on Parade/Strike Me Pink Record, 1950s, Cricket, 45 rpm
EX $12   NM $35   MIP $50

Popeye Record, 1977, Peter Pan, 33 rpm, four stories, #1114
EX $6   NM $15   MIP $30

Popeye the Ladies Man Record, 33 rpm
EX $8   NM $15   MIP $35

Popeye the Movie Soundtrack Record, 1980, Paramount
EX $6   NM $15   MIP $30

Popeye the Sailor Man and His Friends Record, 1960s, Golden, 33 rpm
EX $8   NM $15   MIP $30

Popeye the Sailor Man Record, 1959, Golden, 45 rpm
EX $7   NM $15   MIP $30

Popeye the Sailor Man Record, 1960, Diplomat Records, 33 rpm
EX $7   NM $15   MIP $35

Popeye the Sailor Man Record, 1976, Peter Pan, 33 rpm
EX $7   NM $15   MIP $35

Popeye's Favorite Sea Shanties Record, 1960, RCA Camden
EX $10   NM $25   MIP $50

Popeye's Favorite Sea Songs Record, 1959, Peter Pan, 45 rpm
EX $10   NM $25   MIP $50

Popeye's Favorite Stories Record, 1960, RCA Camden, 33 rpm
EX $10   NM $25   MIP $40

Popeye's Songs About...... Record, 1961, Golden, 33 rpm
EX $8   NM $18   MIP $35

Six Popeye Songs Record, 1950s, Wonderland Records, 45 rpm
EX $8   NM $30   MIP $60

Song and Story Skin Diver Record, 1964, KFS
EX $10   NM $20   MIP $40

Songs of Health Record, 1960s, Golden, 45 rpm
EX $6   NM $10   MIP $25

Songs of Safety Record, 1960s, Golden, 45 rpm
EX $6   NM $10   MIP $25

Whale of a Tale Record, 1981, Peter Pan, 45 rpm
EX $6   NM $10   MIP $20

RING

Candy Rings, 1989, Alberts
EX $6   NM $15   MIP $20

Popeye and Oscar Flicker Ring, blue
EX $8   NM $20   MIP $30

Popeye and Swee'Pea Flicker Ring, blue
EX $8   NM $15   MIP $30

Popeye and Wimpy Flicker Ring, blue
EX $8   NM $15   MIP $30

TOY

Apprentice Printer, 1970s, MSS
EX $6   NM $20   MIP $40

Ball and Jacks Set, MSS
EX $6   NM $12   MIP $25

Ball and Paddle, BC
EX $6   NM $15   MIP $30

Balloon Pump, 1957, inflato-pump
EX $25   NM $50   MIP $100

Barber Shop, 1970s, Larami
EX $5   NM $15   MIP $30

Baseball, 1983, Ja-Ru
EX $10   NM $20   MIP $40

Beach Boat, 1980, H.G. Industries, red or yellow
EX $5   NM $10   MIP $35

❑ **Biffbat-Fly Back Paddle,** 1935
EX $25   NM $50   MIP $100

❑ **Billion Bubbles,** 1984, Larami
EX $4   NM $8   MIP $15

❑ **Blackboard,** 1962, Bar Zim
EX $20   NM $40   MIP $85

❑ **Bop Bag,** 1981, Miner Industries
EX $8   NM $15   MIP $30

❑ **Boxing Gloves,** 1960s, Everlast
EX $25   NM $60   MIP $120

❑ **Brutus Dog Toy,** 1986, Petex
EX $6   NM $12   MIP $25

❑ **Brutus Figure Painting Kit,** 1980, Avalon
EX $8   NM $15   MIP $35

❑ **Brutus Hand Puppet,** 1960s, Gund
EX $25   NM $50   MIP $100

❑ **Brutus Hi-Pop Ball,** 1981, Ja-Ru
EX $6   NM $10   MIP $20

❑ **Brutus Hookies,** 1977, Tiger
EX $5   NM $18   MIP $50

❑ **Brutus Horse and Cart,** 1938, Marx, celluloid, w/Brutus, horse, and cart
EX $250   NM $600   MIP $900

❑ **Brutus in Jeep,** 1950s, tiny plastic car
EX $15   NM $35   MIP $70

❑ **Brutus in Steamroller,** 1980, Lesney/Matchbox, Matchbox
EX $8   NM $18   MIP $40

❑ **Brutus Jump-Up,** 1970s, Imperial
EX $8   NM $20   MIP $40

❑ **Brutus Painting Kit,** 1980, Avalon
EX $8   NM $15   MIP $25

❑ **Brutus Soaky,** 1960s, Colgate-Palmolive
EX $15   NM $35   MIP $75

❑ **Brutus Sports Car,** 1950s, tiny plastic car
EX $15   NM $35   MIP $70

❑ **Brutus Wind-Up Toy,** 1980, Durham
EX $5   NM $10   MIP $25

❑ **Bubble Blower,** 1958, Transogram
EX $15   NM $35   MIP $75

❑ **Bubble Blower Boat,** 1984, Larami
EX $7   NM $15   MIP $30

❑ **Bubble Blowing Popeye,** 1950s, Linemar
EX $325   NM $650   MIP $1300

❑ **Bubble Blowing Train,** 1970s, Hong Kong, pink
EX $10   NM $20   MIP $50

❑ **Bubble 'N Clean,** 1960s, Woolfoam
EX $20   NM $45   MIP $75

❑ **Bubble Pipe,** 1960s, KFS, yellow w/red end
EX $15   NM $30   MIP $60

❑ **Bubble Pipe,** 1985, Ja-Ru
EX $5   NM $12   MIP $25

❑ **Bubble Set,** 1936, Transogram, two wooden pipes, tray, soap in 5" x 7-1/2" box
EX $50   NM $100   MIP $200

❑ **Bubble Shooter,** 1980s, Ja-Ru, orange or yellow body
EX $5   NM $10   MIP $25

❑ **Bubbleblaster,** 1980, Carlin Playthings
EX $10   NM $15   MIP $30

❑ **Bubbles Blaster,** 1984, Larami
EX $5   NM $10   MIP $20

❑ **Bubbles with Dip Pow Bubbles,** 1986, MSS
EX $5   NM $10   MIP $20

❑ **Cap Gun,** 1981, Ja-Ru
EX $10   NM $25   MIP $50

❑ **Chain Bubbles Maker,** 1984, Larami, red Popeye
EX $6   NM $10   MIP $20

❑ **Chalk,** 1936, American Crayon, white, 18 pieces
EX $15   NM $50   MIP $100

❑ **Change Purse,** 1990, Sanrio
EX $5   NM $10   MIP $20

❑ **Checker Board,** 1959, Ideal
EX $15   NM $35   MIP $75

❑ **Chinese Jump Rope,** MSS
EX $4   NM $12   MIP $25

❑ **Colorforms Birthday Party Set,** 1961, Colorforms
EX $25   NM $70   MIP $110

❑ **Colorforms Movie Version,** 1980, Colorforms
EX $7   NM $15   MIP $30

❑ **Color-Me Stickers,** 1983, Diamond Toymakers
EX $5   NM $12   MIP $25

❑ **Color-Vue Pencil-by-Numbers,** 1979, Hasbro
EX $10   NM $20   MIP $35

❑ **Construction Trucks,** 1981, Larami
EX $6   NM $15   MIP $30

(KP Photo)

❑ **Crayons,** 1933, American Crayon, 12 giant crayons
EX $30   NM $60   MIP $125

❑ **Crayons,** 1950s, American Crayon
EX $15   NM $35   MIP $75

❑ **Crayons,** 1958, Dixon, 12 giant crayons
EX $15   NM $35   MIP $75

❑ **Dockside Presto Magix,** 1980, APC
EX $3   NM $6   MIP $12

❑ **Double Action Water Gun Set,** MSS
EX $10   NM $20   MIP $40

❑ **Drawing Board,** 1978, KFS, slate w/rope attached
EX $8   NM $16   MIP $30

❑ **Drawing Desk,** 1980, Carlin Playthings
EX $10   NM $25   MIP $50

❑ **Duck Shoot,** 1980s, Ja-Ru
EX $5   NM $15   MIP $30

❑ **Erase-O-Board and Magic Screen Set,** 1957, Hassenfeld Bros.
EX $30   NM $85   MIP $150

❑ **Film Projector,** Cinexin-Spain, 8mm w/13 movies
EX $65   NM $140   MIP $225

❑ **Finger Puppet Family,** 1960s, Denmark Plastics
EX $25   NM $50   MIP $100

❑ **Flashlight,** 1960s, Bantam-Lite, three color, wrist light
EX $10   NM $20   MIP $40

❑ **Flashlight,** 1983, Larami, blue, yellow, or red
EX $7   NM $15   MIP $30

❑ **Foto-Fun Printing Kit,** 1958, Fun Bilt
EX $32   NM $65   MIP $130

❑ **Funny Color Foam,** 1983, Creative Aerosol
EX $5   NM $15   MIP $60

(KP Photo)

❑ **Funny Face Maker,** 1962, Jaymar
EX $15   NM $30   MIP $65

CHARACTER TOYS

❏ **Funny Films Viewer,** 1940s, Acme
EX $20   NM $45   MIP $90

❏ **Funny Fire Fighters,** 1930s, Marx, celluloid figures, Popeye on ladder and Bluto drives fire truck--both figures wear boxing gloves
EX $400   NM $1250   MIP $2500

(KP Photo)

❏ **Give-A-Show Projector,** Kenner, projector w/slides
EX $35   NM $75   MIP $160

❏ **Gumball Dispenser,** 1983, Superior Toys, pocket pack
EX $5   NM $12   MIP $30

❏ **Gumball Machine,** 1968, Hasbro, 6", shape of Popeye's head
EX $10   NM $30   MIP $80

❏ **Gumball Machine,** 1983, Superior Toys, Popeye eating spinach
EX $7   NM $20   MIP $45

❏ **Gumball Machine,** 1983, Superior Toys, Popeye gives Olive flowers
EX $7   NM $20   MIP $45

❏ **Halloween Bucket,** 1979, Renz, shaped like Popeye's head, red, yellow or blue
EX $10   NM $15   MIP $35

❏ **Harmonica,** 1973, Larami
EX $15   NM $40   MIP $85

❏ **Hat and Pipe,** 1950s, Empire Plastics
EX $20   NM $50   MIP $100

❏ **Holster Set,** 1960s, Halco
EX $50   NM $100   MIP $200

❏ **Horseshoe Magnets,** 1984, Larami
EX $5   NM $15   MIP $30

❏ **Hunting Knife,** 1973, Larami
EX $20   NM $50   MIP $85

❏ **ID Set,** 1982, Gordy
EX $5   NM $15   MIP $35

❏ **Jack-in-the-Box,** 1961, Mattel
EX $50   NM $100   MIP $210

❏ **Jack-in-the-Box,** 1979, Nasta
EX $18   NM $40   MIP $85

❏ **Jack-in-the-Box,** 1983, Nasta
EX $12   NM $25   MIP $60

❏ **Jeep Lucky Spinner,** 1936, KFS
EX $75   NM $150   MIP $300

❏ **Kaleidoscope,** 1979, Larami
EX $10   NM $25   MIP $60

❏ **Kazoo and Harmonica,** 1979, Larami
EX $8   NM $20   MIP $35

❏ **Kazoo Pipe,** 1934, Northwestern Products
EX $30   NM $75   MIP $150

❏ **Kazoo Pipe,** 1960s, Peerless Playthings, yellow
EX $15   NM $30   MIP $60

❏ **Kite,** 1980, Sky-Way, inflatable
EX $6   NM $12   MIP $25

❏ **Kite,** 1980, Sky-Way, regular
EX $4   NM $8   MIP $20

❏ **Lantern,** 1950s, Linemar, 7-1/2" tall, battery operated, light in belly
EX $130   NM $250   MIP $500

❏ **Magic Glow Putty,** FC Famous Toys
EX $6   NM $10   MIP $15

❏ **Magic Slate,** 1959, Lowe
EX $12   NM $30   MIP $75

❏ **Magic Slate Paper Saver,** 1981, Whitman
EX $4   NM $8   MIP $20

❏ **Make-A-Picture Premium,** 1934, Quaker
EX $50   NM $100   MIP $200

❏ **Marble,** 1940s, 1" blue/white w/black/white or red Popeye
EX $8   NM $20   MIP $40

❏ **Marble Set,** 1935, Akro Agate, #116
EX $300   NM $750   MIP $1500

❏ **Marble Set,** 1980, Imperial
EX $12   NM $25   MIP $50

❏ **Marble Shooter,** 1940s, milk glass container
EX $20   NM $40   MIP $70

❏ **Metal Tapping Set,** 1950s, Carlton Dank
EX $25   NM $50   MIP $120

❏ **Metal Target Set,** 1983, Ja-Ru
EX $8   NM $18   MIP $40

❏ **Metal Whistle,** 1981, Ja-Ru
EX $5   NM $12   MIP $30

❏ **Micro-Movie,** 1990, Fascinations, Popeye-Ali Baba
EX $4   NM $8   MIP $15

❏ **Miniature Train Set,** 1980, Larami
EX $8   NM $15   MIP $35

❏ **Model Kit,** 1970s, Carto, Popeye and Olive Oyl
EX $25   NM $50   MIP $120

❏ **Modeling Clay,** 1936, American Crayon
EX $35   NM $90   MIP $185

❏ **Motor Friend,** 1976, Nasta
EX $10   NM $20   MIP $50

❏ **Muscle Builder Bluto,** 1980, Carlin Playthings
EX $6   NM $12   MIP $25

❏ **Muscle Builder Popeye,** 1980, Carlin Playthings
EX $6   NM $12   MIP $25

❏ **My Popeye Coloring Kit,** 1957, American Crayon
EX $37   NM $75   MIP $150

❏ **Official Popeye Pipe,** 1958, 5" stem w/2" bowl, battery operated, "It lites, it toots"
EX $45   NM $90   MIP $180

❏ **Old Time Wild West Train,** 1984, Larami
EX $5   NM $20   MIP $40

❏ **Olive Oyl Bike Bobbers,** 1960s, KFS
EX $15   NM $25   MIP $50

❏ **Olive Oyl Costume,** 1950s, Collegeville
EX $20   NM $50   MIP $110

❏ **Olive Oyl Costume,** 1976, Ben Cooper
EX $8   NM $20   MIP $60

❏ **Olive Oyl Figure Painting Kit,** 1980, Avalon
EX $6   NM $12   MIP $20

❏ **Olive Oyl Foam Toy,** 1979, Cribmates
EX $8   NM $15   MIP $35

❏ **Olive Oyl Hand Puppet,** 1960s, Gund, comic strip body
EX $30   NM $75   MIP $150

❏ **Olive Oyl Hi-Pop Ball,** 1981, Ja-Ru
EX $5   NM $10   MIP $40

❏ **Olive Oyl Hookies,** 1977, Tiger
EX $4   NM $10   MIP $30

❏ **Olive Oyl in a Sports Car,** 1980, Lesney/Matchbox
EX $12   NM $30   MIP $60
EX $12   NM $30   MIP $60

❏ **Olive Oyl Jump-Up,** Imperial
EX $5   NM $10   MIP $20

❏ **Olive Oyl Marionette,** 1950s, Gund, 11-1/2" tall
EX $40   NM $100   MIP $200

❏ **Olive Oyl Painting Kit,** 1980, Avalon
EX $5   NM $10   MIP $20

❏ **Olive Oyl Push Puppet,** 1960s, Kohner, 4" tall, plastic
EX $15   NM $35   MIP $65

❏ **Olive Oyl Sports Car,** 1950s, tiny plastic car
EX $15   NM $35   MIP $70

❏ **Olive Oyl Squeak Toy,** 1979, Cribmates, on a stick
EX $5   NM $13   MIP $20

❏ **Olive Oyl Squeeze Toy,** 1950s, Rempel, vinyl
EX $30   NM $60   MIP $120

❏ **Olive Oyl Swim Ring,** 1979, Wet Set-Zee Toys
EX $5   NM $10   MIP $20

❏ **Olive Oyl Tiles,** 1970s, Italy, 3" x 5" w/stand
EX $12   NM $25   MIP $45

❏ **Olive Oyl Toboggan,** 1979, KFS
EX $6   NM $15   MIP $30

❏ **Paint 'N Puff Set,** 1979, Art Award, two versions
EX $6   NM $12   MIP $25

❏ **Pick-Up Sticks,** 1957, Lido
EX $15   NM $40   MIP $80

❑ **Pirate Island Presto Magix**, 1980, American Pub.
EX $4   NM $10   MIP $25

❑ **Plane and Parachute**, 1980, Fleetwood
EX $8   NM $15   MIP $25

❑ **Play Money**, 1930s, color bucks- framed
EX $12   NM $35   MIP $75

❑ **Play Money**, 1970, The Toy House
EX $5   NM $10   MIP $30

❑ **Pool Table**, 1984, Larami
EX $5   NM $10   MIP $25

❑ **Pop Maker and Son**, 1987, Ja-Ru
EX $2   NM $4   MIP $15

❑ **Pop Pistol**, 1984, Larami
EX $4   NM $8   MIP $30

❑ **Popeye Air Mattress**, 1979, Zee Toys
EX $8   NM $20   MIP $25

❑ **Popeye and Brutus Punch Me Bop Bag**, 1960s, Dartmore
EX $15   NM $30   MIP $60

❑ **Popeye and Olive Oyl Sand Set**, 1950s, Peer Products, bucket, shovel
EX $20   NM $50   MIP $100

❑ **Popeye and Olive Oyl Toy Watch**, 1970s, Unknown, flicker
EX $6   NM $12   MIP $25

❑ **Popeye and Shark Swim Ring**, 1960s, Laurel Star-Japan
EX $10   NM $25   MIP $35

❑ **Popeye and Wimpy Walk-A-Way Toy**, 1964, Marx
EX $25   NM $50   MIP $100

❑ **Popeye Arcade**, 1980, Fleetwood
EX $6   NM $12   MIP $25

❑ **Popeye at the Wheel**, 1950s, Wool- nough, musical
EX $150   NM $300   MIP $600

❑ **Popeye Ball**, rubber kick ball
EX $7   NM $13   MIP $25

❑ **Popeye Bathtub Toy**, 1960s, Stahl- wood, floating boat
EX $20   NM $40   MIP $85

❑ **Popeye Bend-I-Face**, 1967, Lakeside
EX $15   NM $35   MIP $65

❑ **Popeye Bingo**, 1980, Nasta
EX $6   NM $10   MIP $20

❑ **Popeye Blow Me Down Airport**, 1935, Marx
EX $400   NM $800   MIP $1600

❑ **Popeye Bubble Liquid**, 1970s, M. Shimmel Sons, shaped like Popeye w/necktie similar to a sailor's knot
EX $8   NM $15   MIP $25

❑ **Popeye Car**, 1980, Vandor, Popeye and Olive in blue or pink car
EX $20   NM $45   MIP $100

❑ **Popeye Carnival**, 1965, Toymaster
EX $50   NM $100   MIP $225

❑ **Popeye Coloring Set**, 1960s, Hasbro, numbered, w/pencils
EX $12   NM $30   MIP $60

❑ **Popeye Costume**, 1950s, Collegeville
EX $15   NM $45   MIP $90

❑ **Popeye Costume**, 1980s, Collegeville
EX $9   NM $18   MIP $35

❑ **Popeye Costume**, 1984, Ben Cooper
EX $7   NM $15   MIP $30

❑ **Popeye Dog Toy**, 1986, Petex
EX $3   NM $6   MIP $10

❑ **Popeye Figure Painting Kit**, 1980, Ava- lon
EX $4   NM $8   MIP $20

❑ **Popeye Finger Rings**, 1949, Post Toasties
EX $20   NM $50   MIP $100

❑ **Popeye Flicker Badge**, 1960s, Varivue, Popeye eating spinach
EX $8   NM $15   MIP $35

❑ **Popeye Flickers**, 1960s, Sonwell
EX $8   NM $15   MIP $35

❑ **Popeye Ge-tar**, 1960s, Mattel, 14" long, shaped like Popeye's face, plays "I'm Popeye the Sailor Man"
EX $30   NM $60   MIP $120

❑ **Popeye Glow Putty**, 1984, Larami
EX $3   NM $6   MIP $10

❑ **Popeye Goes Swimming Colorforms**, 1963, Colorforms
EX $15   NM $35   MIP $65

❑ **Popeye Goes to School Television**, 1950s, Zaboly
EX $20   NM $45   MIP $90

❑ **Popeye Hand Puppet**, 1950s, Gund, plush
EX $15   NM $40   MIP $90

❑ **Popeye Hand Puppet**, 1960s, Gund, Popeye's head on cloth body
EX $20   NM $50   MIP $100

❑ **Popeye Hi-Pop Ball**, 1981, Ja-Ru
EX $4   NM $8   MIP $20

❑ **Popeye in a Spinach Truck**, 1980, Lesney/Matchbox
EX $8   NM $15   MIP $30
EX $8   NM $20   MIP $50

❑ **Popeye Jump-Up**, 1970s, Imperial
EX $8   NM $20   MIP $40

❑ **Popeye Magic Play Around**, 1950s, Amsco, characters w/magnetic bases that slide across play set
EX $35   NM $70   MIP $140

❑ **Popeye Marionette**, Create-Japan, wood
EX $100   NM $200   MIP $400

❑ **Popeye Marionette**, 1950s, Gund, 11-1/2" tall
EX $75   NM $150   MIP $300

❑ **Popeye Mini Winder**, 1980, Durham
EX $4   NM $10   MIP $25

❑ **Popeye Model Kit**, 1964, Tokyo Plamo, #808
EX $35   NM $80   MIP $180

❑ **Popeye on Tricycle**, Linemar, 4-1/2", tin wind-up w/celluloid arms and legs, bell rings behind Popeye
EX $175   NM $350   MIP $700

❑ **Popeye One Man Band**, 1980s, Larami
EX $6   NM $10   MIP $25

❑ **Popeye Paddle Ball**, 1984, Larami, w/color photo of Popeye
EX $7   NM $15   MIP $35

❑ **Popeye Paint and Crayon Set**, 1934, Milton Bradley
EX $50   NM $100   MIP $200

❑ **Popeye Paint By Numbers**, 1960s, Has- bro
EX $12   NM $25   MIP $60

❑ **Popeye Paint Set**, 1933, American Crayon, 6", tin
EX $50   NM $100   MIP $200

❑ **Popeye Paint-By-Numbers**, 1981, Has- bro
EX $8   NM $13   MIP $25

❑ **Popeye Painting Kit**, 1980, Avalon
EX $6   NM $10   MIP $20

❑ **Popeye Pencil-By-Numbers**, 1979, Hasbro
EX $10   NM $25   MIP $50

❑ **Popeye Peppy Puppet**, 1970, Kohner
EX $12   NM $25   MIP $40

❑ **Popeye Pipe**, 1940s, red wooden
EX $15   NM $25   MIP $50

❑ **Popeye Pipe**, 1958, Micro-Lite-KFS
EX $12   NM $30   MIP $75

❑ **Popeye Pipe**, 1970, Edmonton Pipe, figural head
EX $15   NM $25   MIP $50

❑ **Popeye Pipe**, 1970s, MSS, plastic, white
EX $8   NM $20   MIP $40

❑ **Popeye Pipe**, 1970s, KFS, plastic kazoo, red and blue
EX $6   NM $20   MIP $40

❑ **Popeye Pipe**, 1980, Harmony
EX $6   NM $10   MIP $20

❑ **Popeye Pistol**, Delcast, Super mini cap w/24 caps No. 807-BB
EX $15   NM $30   MIP $70

❑ **Popeye Pistol**, 1935, Marx
EX $150   NM $650   MIP $1100

❑ **Popeye Play Set**, 1979, Cribmates, Popeye, Olive Oyl, and Swee'Pea squeak toys, mirror, rattle and pillow
EX $15   NM $30   MIP $45

❑ **Popeye Presto Paints**, 1961, Kenner
EX $15   NM $50   MIP $65

❑ **Popeye Pull Toy**, 1950s, Metal Masters, 10-1/2" x 11-1/2", xylophone, wood w/paper litho labels, metal wheels
EX $100   NM $225   MIP $450

CHARACTER TOYS

Popeye Puppet, Kohner, pull string, Popeye jumps
EX $10   NM $15   MIP $25

Popeye Push Puppet, 1960, Kohner, 4" tall
EX $20   NM $45   MIP $85

(KP Photo)

Popeye Sailboat, 1976, KFS
EX $9   NM $15   MIP $40

Popeye Service Station, 1979, Larami
EX $8   NM $20   MIP $60

Popeye Soaky, 1960s, Colgate-Palmolive
EX $15   NM $40   MIP $70

(KP Photo)

Popeye Soaky, 1987, KFS, British
EX $12   NM $20   MIP $40

Popeye Sparkler, 1959, Chein
EX $90   NM $125   MIP $175

Popeye Speed Boat, 1981, Harmony
EX $10   NM $16   MIP $30

Popeye Speedboard Pull Toy, 1960s
EX $175   NM $350   MIP $675

Popeye Sports Car, 1950s, Linemar
EX $225   NM $400   MIP $700

Popeye Squeeze Toy, 1950s, Rempel, 8" tall, vinyl
EX $15   NM $40   MIP $90

Popeye Squeeze Toy, 1979, Cribmates, Popeye on a stick
EX $8   NM $15   MIP $30

Popeye Supergyro, 1980s, Larami
EX $6   NM $10   MIP $20

Popeye the Pilot, 1940s, Chein, tin wind-up airplane, 8" long, 8" wingspan
EX $400   NM $800   MIP $1350

Popeye the Weatherman Colorforms, 1959, Colorforms
EX $20   NM $50   MIP $110

Popeye Tiles, 1970s, Italy, 3" x 5" w/stand
EX $15   NM $35   MIP $65

Popeye Toboggan, 1979, KFS
EX $6   NM $10   MIP $25

Popeye Train Pull Toy, Larami
EX $135   NM $225   MIP $400

Popeye Train Set, 1973, Larami
EX $6   NM $15   MIP $30

Popeye Transit Company Moving Van, 1950, Linemar, tin
EX $300   NM $650   MIP $1200

Popeye Tricky Trapeze, 1970, Kohner
EX $15   NM $35   MIP $65

Popeye Tricky Walker, 1960s, Jaymar, plastic
EX $10   NM $25   MIP $55

Popeye Tricycling, 1950s, Linemar
EX $250   NM $500   MIP $900

Popeye Tug and Dingy Pull Toy, 1950s, Fisher-Price, wood
EX $135   NM $225   MIP $350

Popeye Tugboat, 1961, Ideal, inflatable
EX $15   NM $35   MIP $60

(KP Photo)

Popeye TV Cartoon Kit, 1966, Colorforms
EX $20   NM $40   MIP $75

Popeye TV Magic Putty, 1970s, MSS
EX $6   NM $10   MIP $15

Popeye Water Colors, 1933, American Crayon
EX $25   NM $50   MIP $100

Popeye Water Sprinkler, 1960s, KFS, w/rubbber head
EX $15   NM $25   MIP $40

Popeye's Official Wallet, 1959, KFS
EX $10   NM $25   MIP $70

Popeye's Submarine, 1973, Larami
EX $10   NM $25   MIP $45

Popsicle Harmonica, 1929, Czech
EX $60   NM $160   MIP $300

Punch Ball, 1970s, National Latex
EX $10   NM $20   MIP $40

Punch'Em Talking Rattle Toy, 1950s, Sanitoy
EX $15   NM $35   MIP $75

Punching Bag, 1960s, Dartmore
EX $15   NM $30   MIP $50

Puppetforms, 1950s, Colorforms
EX $25   NM $40   MIP $70

Puzzle, 1932, Saalfield, Popeye in Four
EX $40   NM $80   MIP $175

Puzzle, 1945, Jaymar, 22" x 13-1/2", Popeye
EX $35   NM $75   MIP $150

Puzzle, 1959, England, 120 pieces, "What a Catch"
EX $25   NM $55   MIP $80

Puzzle, 1960s, Roalex, tile
EX $20   NM $35   MIP $50

Puzzle, 1962, Tower Press, wood, Popeye
EX $10   NM $16   MIP $30

Puzzle, 1973, Larami, magnetic
EX $6   NM $15   MIP $30

Puzzle, 1976, American Pub. Corp., 5-1/2" round can
EX $10   NM $20   MIP $35

Puzzle, 1977, Opera Mundi, tile, "Popeye's Riddle"
EX $11   NM $18   MIP $25

Puzzle, 1978, Waddington's House of Games, 27" x 18" floor puzzle
EX $8   NM $15   MIP $30

Puzzle, 1981, Ja-Ru, comic
EX $6   NM $12   MIP $25

Puzzle, 1987, Illco, 11 pieces, Olive 3-D
EX $6   NM $10   MIP $20

Puzzle, 1987, Illco, 11 pieces, Popeye 3-D
EX $6   NM $10   MIP $20

Puzzle, 1987, Ja-Ru, Popeye and Son TV show
EX $5   NM $10   MIP $20

Puzzle, 1989, Ja-Ru, "Birthday Cake and Ice Cream"
EX $6   NM $10   MIP $20

❏ **Puzzle,** 1989, Ja-Ru, boating and dancing
EX $6　　NM $10　　MIP $20

❏ **Puzzle,** 1991, Jaymar, 63 pieces, jumbo, Popeye's boat
EX $6　　NM $12　　MIP $25

❏ **Puzzle,** 1991, Jaymar, 63 pieces, jumbo, Popeye rescues Olive
EX $6　　NM $10　　MIP $20

❏ **Puzzle,** 1991, Jaymar, 63 pieces, Popeye blowing candles
EX $6　　NM $10　　MIP $20

❏ **Puzzle,** 1991, Jaymar, 63 pieces, jumbo, Popeye and Olive surfing
EX $6　　NM $10　　MIP $20

❏ **Puzzle,** 1991, Jaymar, Christmas scene, inlaid, 12 pieces
EX $4　　NM $8　　MIP $15

❏ **Puzzle,** 1991, Jaymar, 12 pieces, Popeye holding turkey
EX $6　　NM $10　　MIP $20

❏ **Puzzle,** 1991, Jaymar, 12 pieces, Popeye gang swimming
EX $6　　NM $10　　MIP $20

❏ **Race Set,** 1989, Ja-Ru
EX $6　　NM $10　　MIP $20

❏ **Road Building Set,** 1979, Larami
EX $6　　NM $10　　MIP $20

❏ **Roller Skating Popeye,** 1950s, Linemar
EX $30　　NM $60　　MIP $125

❏ **Roly Poly Popeye,** 1940s, w/beaded arms and celluloid
EX $75　　NM $150　　MIP $250

❏ **Sailboats,** 1981, Larami
EX $6　　NM $10　　MIP $18

❏ **Sailor's Knife,** 1981, Ja-Ru
EX $10　　NM $20　　MIP $40

❏ **Screen-A Show Projector,** 1973, Denys Fisher
EX $35　　NM $90　　MIP $150

❏ **Sea Hag Hand Puppet,** 1987, Presents
EX $15　　NM $35　　MIP $75

❏ **Shaving Kit,** 1979, Larami
EX $6　　NM $10　　MIP $25

❏ **Sling Darts,** KFS
EX $20　　NM $35　　MIP $60

❏ **Soapy Popeye Boat,** 1950s, Kerk Guild
EX $50　　NM $100　　MIP $200

❏ **Squirt Face,** 1981, Ja-Ru
EX $6　　NM $10　　MIP $15

❏ **Stitch-A-Story,** KFS
EX $12　　NM $20　　MIP $35

❏ **Sun-Eze Pictures,** 1962, Tillman Toy
EX $10　　NM $25　　MIP $50

❏ **Sunglasses,** 1980s, Larami, red, yellow, or blue
EX $6　　NM $10　　MIP $20

❏ **Super Race with Launcher,** 1980, Fleetwood
EX $6　　NM $10　　MIP $20

❏ **Surf Rider,** 1979, Wet Set-Zee Toys
EX $10　　NM $22　　MIP $45

❏ **Swee'Pea Bean Bag,** 1974, Dakin
EX $10　　NM $20　　MIP $50

❏ **Swee'Pea Hand Puppet,** 1960s, Gund, bonnet on head, cloth body decorated w/baby lambs
EX $15　　NM $35　　MIP $80

❏ **Swee'Pea Hand Puppet,** 1987, Presents
EX $8　　NM $20　　MIP $50

❏ **Swee'Pea Hi-Pop Ball,** 1981, Ja-Ru
EX $6　　NM $12　　MIP $25

❏ **Swee'Pea Squeak Toy,** 1970s, frowning or smiling
EX $12　　NM $25　　MIP $60

❏ **Swirler Flying Barrel Toy,** 1980, Imperial
EX $8　　NM $15　　MIP $30

❏ **Talking View-Master Set,** 1962, GAF, old type
EX $12　　NM $25　　MIP $50

❏ **Tambourine,** 1980s, Larami
EX $6　　NM $10　　MIP $20

❏ **Tambourine,** 1990, Santa Cruz
EX $6　　NM $10　　MIP $15

❏ **Target Ball,** 1981, Ja-Ru
EX $6　　NM $10　　MIP $20

❏ **Telephone,** 1982, Comvu
EX $15　　NM $30　　MIP $50

❏ **Telescope,** 1973, Larami
EX $10　　NM $25　　MIP $50

❏ **Thimble Theatre Cut-Outs,** 1950s, Aldon
EX $25　　NM $60　　MIP $100

❏ **Toy Watch,** 1987, Sekonda-Japan, comic strip band
EX $30　　NM $50　　MIP $90

❏ **Trace and Color,** 1980, Fleetwood
EX $6　　NM $10　　MIP $20

❏ **Trumpet Bubble Blower,** 1984, Larami, pink or yellow pan
EX $6　　NM $12　　MIP $25

❏ **Tube-A-Loonies,** 1973, Larami, five small tubes on card
EX $6　　NM $12　　MIP $25

❏ **Turn-A-Scope,** 1979, Larami
EX $6　　NM $12　　MIP $35

❏ **TV Set with Three Film Scrolls,** 1957
EX $12　　NM $20　　MIP $45

❏ **View-Master Set,** 1959, Sawyers, three reels
EX $15　　NM $30　　MIP $60

❏ **View-Master Set,** 1959, GAF, "The Fish Story"
EX $8　　NM $15　　MIP $35

❏ **View-Master Set,** 1959, GAF, "The Hunting Bird"
EX $8　　NM $15　　MIP $30

❏ **View-Master Set,** 1962, GAF, three pack
EX $8　　NM $15　　MIP $30

❏ **Whistling Flashlights,** 1960s, Bantam-Lite, six w/display
EX $150　　NM $300　　MIP $600

❏ **Whistling Wing Ding,** 1950s, Mego
EX $20　　NM $40　　MIP $75

❏ **Wimpy Dog Toy,** 1986, Petex
EX $8　　NM $13　　MIP $20

❏ **Wimpy Hand Puppet,** 1950s, Gund, fabric hand cover, vinyl squeaker head and voice
EX $15　　NM $50　　MIP $100

❏ **Wimpy Hand Puppet,** 1960s, Gund, cloth body
EX $15　　NM $40　　MIP $80

❏ **Wimpy Hand Puppet,** 1987, Presents
EX $8　　NM $13　　MIP $35

❏ **Wimpy Ring,** 1949, Post Toasties
EX $12　　NM $35　　MIP $100

❏ **Wimpy Squeeze Toy,** 1950s, Rempel, vinyl
EX $20　　NM $40　　MIP $75

❏ **Wimpy Squeeze Toy,** 1979, Cribmates
EX $12　　NM $20　　MIP $40

❏ **Wimpy Tugboat,** 1961, Ideal, inflatable
EX $20　　NM $35　　MIP $60

❏ **Wood Slate,** 1983, Ja-Ru
EX $6　　NM $12　　MIP $30

WATCH

❏ **Popeye Wristwatch,** 1938, New Haven
EX $300　　NM $750　　MIP $1500

❏ **Popeye Wristwatch,** 1964, Bradley, #308, green case
EX $115　　NM $200　　MIP $325

❏ **Popeye Wristwatch,** 1979, Bradley
EX $60　　NM $110　　MIP $170

❏ **Popeye Wristwatch,** 1987, Unique, Popeye's head pops open, digital
EX $12　　NM $22　　MIP $50

❏ **Popeye Wristwatch,** 1990, KFS-Japan, Popeye in ship's wheel
EX $40　　NM $70　　MIP $120

❏ **Popeye Wristwatch,** 1991, Armitron
EX $20　　NM $35　　MIP $60

PORKY PIG

BANK

❏ **Porky Pig Bank,** 1930s, bisque, orange, blue, and yellow
EX $60　　NM $120　　MIP $200

DOLL

❏ **Porky Pig Doll,** 1950, Gund, 14" tall
EX $50　　NM $100　　MIP $180

❏ **Porky Pig Doll,** 1960s, Mattel, 17", cloth, vinyl head
EX $15　　NM $35　　MIP $70

❑ **Porky Pig Doll,** 1968, Dakin, 7-3/4" tall in black velvet jacket
EX $15　　NM $35　　MIP $70

FIGURES

❑ **Porky and Petunia Figures,** 1975, Warner Bros., 4-1/2" tall
EX $9　　NM $16　　MIP $35

TOY

❑ **Porky Pig Soaky**
EX $15　　NM $35　　MIP $70

❑ **Porky Pig Umbrella,** 1940s, hard plastic 3" figure on end, Porky and Bugs printed in red cloth
EX $40　　NM $90　　MIP $150

QUICK DRAW MCGRAW

ACCESSORIES

❑ **Cereal Box,** 1960, Kellogg's
EX $150　　NM $300　　MIP $425

BANK

❑ **Baba Looey Bank,** 1960s, Knickerbocker, 9" tall, vinyl, plastic head
EX $16　　NM $32　　MIP $65

❑ **Quick Draw McGraw Bank,** 1960, 9-1/2", plastic, orange, white, and blue
EX $25　　NM $50　　MIP $100

BOOK

❑ **Quick Draw McGraw Book,** 1960, Whitman
EX $15　　NM $30　　MIP $70

DOLL

❑ **Auggie Doggie Doll,** 1959, Knickerbocker, 10" tall, plush w/vinyl face
EX $20　　NM $50　　MIP $100

❑ **Baba Looey Doll,** 1959, Knickerbocker, 20" tall, plush w/vinyl donkey ears and sombrero
EX $50　　NM $100　　MIP $200

❑ **Blabber Doll,** 1959, Knickerbocker, 15" tall, plush w/vinyl face
EX $35　　NM $75　　MIP $150

❑ **Quick Draw McGraw Doll,** 1959, Knickerbocker, 16", plush w/vinyl face, cowboy hat
EX $60　　NM $125　　MIP $250

❑ **Scooper Doll,** 1959, Knickerbocker, 20", plush w/vinyl face
EX $35　　NM $70　　MIP $140

TOY

❑ **Auggie Doggie Soaky,** 1960s, Purex, 10" tall, plastic
EX $15　　NM $45　　MIP $80

❑ **Blabber Soaky,** 1960s, Purex, 10-1/2" tall, plastic
EX $18　　NM $45　　MIP $90

❑ **Quick Draw McGraw Moving Target Game,** 1960s, Knickerbocker
EX $95　　NM $125　　MIP $240

❑ **Quick Draw Mold and Model Cast Set,** 1960
EX $30　　NM $60　　MIP $90

RAGGEDY ANN AND ANDY

ACCESSORIES

❑ **Raggedy Ann/Andy Wastebasket,** 1972, tin
EX $8　　NM $20　　MIP $50

BANK

❑ **Raggedy Andy Bank,** Play Pal, 11"
EX $15　　NM $20　　MIP $30

❑ **Raggedy Ann Bank,** 1974, Play Pal, 11"
EX $15　　NM $20　　MIP $35

BOOK

❑ **Camel with the Wrinkled Knees Book,** 1924
EX $75　　NM $150　　MIP $275

❑ **Raggedy Ann Coloring Book,** 1968
EX $6　　NM $12　　MIP $35

❑ **Raggedy Ann/Andy Paper Doll Book,** 1974, Whitman, #1962
EX $15　　NM $25　　MIP $50

FIGURES

❑ **Raggedy Andy Figure,** 1970s, rubber/wire, 4" tall
EX $5　　NM $10　　MIP $20

TOY

❑ **Raggedy Andy Puppet,** 1975, Dakin, cloth
EX $15　　NM $25　　MIP $45

❑ **Raggedy Ann Puppet,** 1975, Dakin, cloth
EX $15　　NM $25　　MIP $45

❑ **Raggedy Ann/Andy Record Player,** square, cardboard
EX $45　　NM $65　　MIP $100

❑ **Raggedy Ann/Andy Record Player,** 1950s, plastic, heart shaped
EX $80　　NM $125　　MIP $185

ROAD RUNNER AND WILE E. COYOTE

ACCESSORIES

❑ **Road Runner and Coyote Lamp,** 1977, 12-1/2", figures standing on base
EX $40　　NM $100　　MIP $200

❑ **Road Runner Costume,** 1960s, Collegeville
EX $20　　NM $30　　MIP $65

❑ **Wile E. Coyote Night Light,** 1980s, Applause
EX $13　　NM $25　　MIP $50

BANK

❑ **Road Runner Bank,** standing on base
EX $8　　NM $15　　MIP $30

DOLL

❑ **Road Runner Doll,** 1971, Mighty Star, 13" tall
EX $12　　NM $30　　MIP $60

❑ **Wile E. Coyote Doll,** 1970, Dakin, on explosive box
EX $20　　NM $50　　MIP $100

❑ **Wile E. Coyote Doll,** 1971, Mighty Star, 18" tall, plush
EX $20　　NM $50　　MIP $100

FIGURES

❑ **Road Runner Figure,** Dakin, plastic, Cartoon Theater
EX $18　　NM $40　　MIP $85

❑ **Road Runner Figure,** 1968, Dakin, 8-3/4" tall
EX $15　　NM $35　　MIP $75

❑ **Road Runner Figure,** 1971, Dakin, Goofy Gram
EX $15　　NM $30　　MIP $60

❑ **Wile E. Coyote and Road Runner Figures,** 1979, Royal Crown, 7" tall, each
EX $15　　NM $30　　MIP $65

❑ **Wile E. Coyote Figure,** 1968, Dakin, 10" tall
EX $30　　NM $60　　MIP $120

❑ **Wile E. Coyote Figure,** 1971, Dakin, Goofy Gram, fused bomb in right hand
EX $20　　NM $40　　MIP $80

❑ **Wile E. Coyote Figure,** 1976, Dakin, Cartoon Theater
EX $18　　NM $30　　MIP $60

TOY

❑ **Road Runner Hand Puppet,** 1970s, Japanese, 10", vinyl head
EX $8　　NM $20　　MIP $40

❑ **Wile E. Coyote Hand Puppet,** 1970s, Japanese, 10" vinyl head
EX $10　　NM $20　　MIP $40

ROCKY

DOLL

❑ **Apollo Creed Doll,** 1983, Phoenix Toys, 8" tall
EX $5　　NM $10　　MIP $25

❑ **Clubber Lang Doll,** 1983, Phoenix Toys, 8" tall
EX $6　　NM $12　　MIP $30

❑ **Rocky Balboa Doll,** 1983, Phoenix Toys, 8" tall
EX $7　　NM $15　　MIP $35

ROGER RABBIT

ACCESSORIES

❑ **Baby Herman and Roger Rabbit Mug,** Applause
EX $5　　NM $8　　MIP $15

❑ **Jessica Zipper Pull**
EX $5　　NM $10　　MIP $15

❏ **Who Framed Roger Rabbit Game,**
1988, Milton Bradley low production run
EX $20　　NM $50　　MIP $110

BOOK

❏ **Paint with Water Book,** Golden, #1702
EX $6　　NM $12　　MIP $25

❏ **Trace and Color Book,** Golden, #2355
EX $5　　NM $10　　MIP $25

DOLL

❏ **Benny the Cab Doll,** 1988, Applause, 6"
long
EX $6　　NM $12　　MIP $25

❏ **Roger Rabbit Doll,** Applause, 8-1/2" tall
EX $7　　NM $15　　MIP $40

❏ **Roger Rabbit Doll,** Applause, 17" tall
EX $10　　NM $30　　MIP $85

FIGURES

❏ **Baby Herman Figure,** 1987, LJN, 6" figure on card
EX $9　　NM $20　　MIP $35

❏ **Baby Herman Figure,** 1988, LJN, ceramic
EX $9　　NM $15　　MIP $35

❏ **Boss Weasel Figure,** 1988, LJN, 4" bendable
EX $4　　NM $10　　MIP $20

❏ **Eddie Valiant Figure,** 1988, LJN, 4", flexible
EX $5　　NM $10　　MIP $20

❏ **Judge Doom Figure,** 1988, LJN, 4" bendable
EX $4　　NM $8　　MIP $24

❏ **Roger Rabbit Figure,** 1988, LJN, 4" bendable
EX $4　　NM $10　　MIP $20

FIGURESC

❏ **Smart Guy Figure,** 1988, LJN, flexible
EX $4　　NM $8　　MIP $15

GAME

❏ **Dip Flip Game,** LJN
EX $8　　NM $15　　MIP $30

TOY

❏ **Animates,** 1988, Doom, Roger, Eddie and Smart Guy, each
EX $5　　NM $8　　MIP $15

❏ **Benny the Cab,** LJN
EX $20　　NM $40　　MIP $75

❏ **Eddie Valiant Animate,** 1988, LJN, 6" tall, bendable
EX $4　　NM $8　　MIP $15

❏ **Jessica License Plate**
EX $6　　NM $12　　MIP $20

❏ **Judge Doom Animate,** 1988, LJN, 6" tall poseable
EX $6　　NM $12　　MIP $25

❏ **Paint-A-Cel Set,** Benny the Cab and Roger pictures
EX $8　　NM $15　　MIP $30

❏ **Roger Rabbit Animate,** 1988, LJN, 6" poseable
EX $4　　NM $10　　MIP $20

❏ **Roger Rabbit Blow-Up Buddy,** 36" tall
EX $6　　NM $12　　MIP $25

❏ **Roger Wacky Head Puppets,** Applause, hand puppets
EX $6　　NM $12　　MIP $30

❏ **Roger Wind-Up,** 1988, Matsudaya
EX $18　　NM $35　　MIP $60

❏ **Talking Roger in Benny the Cab,** 17" tall
EX $12　　NM $35　　MIP $75

WATCH

❏ **Roger Rabbit Bullet Hole Wristwatch,**
1987, Shiraka, white case and leather band, in plastic display box
EX $25　　NM $70　　MIP $140

❏ **Roger Rabbit Silhouette Wristwatch,**
1987, Shiraka, large gold case, black band
EX $20　　NM $70　　MIP $140

ROOTIE KAZOOTIE

BUTTON

❏ **Rootie Kazootie Club Button,** 1950s, 1" tin litho
EX $18　　NM $42　　MIP $70

TOY

❏ **Rootie Kazootie Drum,** 1950s, 8" diameter drum, Rootie on the drum head
EX $25　　NM $50　　MIP $90

❏ **Rootie Kazootie Fishing Tackle Box,**
1950s, RK Inc., tin litho, bright graphics
EX $15　　NM $30　　MIP $60

RUFF AND REDDY

BOOK

❏ **Ruff and Reddy Go To A Party Tell-A-Tale Book,** 1958, Whitman
EX $15　　NM $35　　MIP $65

TOY

❏ **Ruff and Reddy Draw Cartoon Set Color,** Wonder Art
EX $50　　NM $85　　MIP $150

❏ **Ruff and Reddy Magic Rub-Off Picture Set,** 1958, Transogram
EX $45　　NM $80　　MIP $150

SECRET SQUIRREL

TOY

❏ **Secret Squirrel Bubble Club Soaky,**
1960s, Purex
EX $20　　NM $35　　MIP $80

❏ **Secret Squirrel Push Puppet,** 1960s, Kohner, plastic figure in white coat, blue hat holding binoculars
EX $20　　NM $40　　MIP $75

❏ **Secret Squirrel Puzzle,** 1967, frame tray
EX $15　　NM $30　　MIP $60

❏ **Secret Squirrel Ray Gun**
EX $18　　NM $35　　MIP $70

SHIRLEY TEMPLE

ACCESSORIES

❏ **Doll Buggy,** 1935, F.A. Whitney Carriage, wicker, hubcaps are labeled Shirley Temple
EX $300　　NM $400　　MIP $500

❏ **Doll Trunk,** 18" tall w/"Our Little Girl" decal on the side, photo of Shirley
EX $100　　NM $200　　MIP $275

❏ **Doll Wardrobe Trunk,** 20" heavy cardboard/wood steamer trunk for 18" doll, leather strap, metal latch w/lock and key, two drawers, and four cardboard hangers
EX $120　　NM $200　　MIP $275

❏ **Hair Ribbon and Band,** 1934, Ribbon Mills, Several colors/styles
EX $15　　NM $30　　MIP $60

❏ **Hanger,** cardboard; picture of Shirley Temple, came w/all outfits
EX $15　　NM $25　　MIP $40

❏ **Pen and Pencil Set,** 1930s, David Kahn
EX $90　　NM $140　　MIP $220

❏ **Pin,** Reliable, "The World's Darling/Genuine Shirley Temple, A Reliable Doll"
EX $65　　NM $80　　MIP $90

❏ **Purse,** 1950s, red, white, and black w/Shirley Temple lettering
EX $30　　NM $40　　MIP $60

❏ **Stand Up and Cheer Doll Trunk,** 1934
EX $125　　NM $200　　MIP $275

❏ **Texas Ranger/Cowgirl Gun,** Came w/Texas Ranger outfit
EX $35　　NM $70　　MIP $135

BOOK

❏ **Composition Book,** 1935, Western
EX $25　　NM $30　　MIP $70

❏ **My Life and Times by Shirley Temple Book,** 1936, Saalfield, Big Little Book #116, Model No. 116
EX $30　　NM $85　　MIP $120

❏ **Scrap Book,** 1935, Saalfield, #1714, Model No. 1714
EX $60　　NM $85　　MIP $120

❏ **Shirley Temple at Play Book,** 1935, Saalfield, #1712, Model No. 1712
EX $40　　NM $50　　MIP $90

❏ **Shirley Temple Five Books About Me,**
1936, Saalfield, Just a Little Girl, Twinkletoes, On the Movie Lot, In Starring Roles, and Little Playmate, #1730, Model No. 1730
EX $90　　NM $130　　MIP $160

CHARACTER TOYS

□ **Shirley Temple in The Littlest Rebel,**
1935, Saalfield, Big Little Book, #1595,
Model No. 1595
EX $18 NM $30 MIP $75

□ **Shirley Temple My Book to Color,**
1937, Saalfield, #1768, Model No. 1768
EX $35 NM $45 MIP $70

□ **Shirley Temple Pastime Box,** 1937,
Saalfield, Four activity books: Favorite
Puzzles, Favorite Games, Favorite Sew-
ing Cards, and Favorite Coloring Book,
#1732, Model No. 1732
EX $55 NM $125 MIP $175

□ **Shirley Temple Scrap Book,** 1936,
Saalfield, #1722, Model No. 1722
EX $65 NM $85 MIP $125

□ **Shirley Temple Scrap Book,** 1937,
Saalfield, #1763, Model No. 1763
EX $50 NM $85 MIP $120

□ **Shirley Temple Story Book,** 1935,
Saalfield, #1726, Model No. 1726
EX $25 NM $40 MIP $75

□ **Shirley Temple Treasury Book,** 1959,
Random House
EX $20 NM $30 MIP $40

□ **Shirley Temple with Lionel Barrymore
in The Little Colonel,** 1935, Saalfield,
Big Little Book, #1095, Model No. 1095
EX $15 NM $35 MIP $70

□ **Shirley Temple's Blue Bird Coloring
Book,** 1939, Saalfield
EX $35 NM $65 MIP $100

□ **Shirley Temple's Busy Book,** 1958,
Saalfield, Activity book, #5326, Model
No. 5326
EX $40 NM $50 MIP $60

□ **Shirley Temple's Favorite Poems,**
1936, Saalfield, #1720, Model No. 1720
EX $20 NM $35 MIP $70

□ **The Story of Shirley Temple Book,**
1934, Saalfield, Big Little Book, #1089,
Model No. 1089
EX $18 NM $35 MIP $70

DOLL

□ **Blue Bird Doll,** 1939, 20" composition
EX $800 NM $1000 MIP $1275

□ **Blue Bird Doll,** 1939, 18", felt skirt and
vest, organdy blouse and apron w/blue
bird appliques
EX $910 NM $1025 MIP $1250

□ **Bright Eyes Doll,** 1936, 13" composition, plaid dress, leather shoes
EX $610 NM $700 MIP $850

□ **Captain January Doll,** Ideal, 22", dark
blue sailor suit w/white trim
EX $800 NM $910 MIP $1100

□ **Captain January Doll,** 1936, 16", green
pique w/silk ribbons
EX $650 NM $750 MIP $850

□ **Captain January Doll,** 1936, 13", white
sailor suit, red bow tie, white hat, original pin
EX $600 NM $700 MIP $900

□ **Captain January Doll,** 1936, 18", cotton
sailor suit w/anchor applique and red
silk tie
EX $650 NM $750 MIP $950

□ **Captain January Doll,** 1936, Ideal, 20",
blue floral print, cotton school dress
w/ruffled collar
EX $725 NM $800 MIP $1000

□ **Captain January Doll,** 1957, Ideal, 12",
vinyl head, dark blonde hair, plastic
body, arms and legs
EX $175 NM $225 MIP $350

□ **Curly Top Doll,** 1935, 16" composition;
different versions available
EX $675 NM $750 MIP $850

□ **Curly Top Doll,** 1935, Ideal, 11", pink
organdy dress
EX $875 NM $1050 MIP $1350

□ **Curly Top Doll,** 1935, 18" composition,
mohair hair, hazel eyes
EX $600 NM $685 MIP $850

□ **Curly Top Doll,** 1935, 11", dotted swiss
dress, blue silk ribbons
EX $600 NM $685 MIP $850

□ **Curly Top Doll,** 1935, 18", pleated dotted swiss w/blue silk ribbons, red or lavender
EX $600 NM $700 MIP $850

□ **Heidi Doll,** 1937, 18", striped cotton
skirt, black velveteen top w/red braid,
apron, mohair pigtails w/red ribbons
EX $950 NM $1075 MIP $1400

□ **Heidi Doll,** 1957, Ideal, 12", vinyl head,
dark blonde hair and plastic body, arms
and legs
EX $200 NM $285 MIP $340

□ **Heidi Doll,** 1960-61, 17"
EX $250 NM $325 MIP $400

□ **Little Colonel Doll,** 13", taffeta outfit,
variations in the collar, ruffles and pantaloons
EX $775 NM $900 MIP $1150

□ **Little Colonel Doll,** Alexander, 13", pink
hat w/ruffle, pink dress and bloomers
EX $475 NM $575 MIP $900

□ **Little Colonel Doll,** 20", blue organdy,
bonnet w/pink feather
EX $925 NM $1100 MIP $1500

□ **Little Colonel Doll,** 13", variations in
pantaloons, bonnets and shoes
EX $775 NM $900 MIP $1150

□ **Little Colonel Doll,** 1934, 13", light blue
dress w/bonnet, pantaloons and shoes
w/buckles
EX $775 NM $900 MIP $1150

□ **Little Colonel Doll,** 1934, 18", pink
organdy dress, bonnet, white pantaloons
EX $775 NM $900 MIP $1150

□ **Little Colonel Doll,** 1934, Ideal, 13",
smiling, pink hat w/feather and dress
and bloomers
EX $775 NM $900 MIP $1150

□ **Littlest Rebel Doll,** 1935, 13", yel-
low/brown dress, white ruffled collar,
yellow shoes
EX $775 NM $900 MIP $1150

□ **Littlest Rebel Doll,** 1935, 16", polka dot
outfit, pantaloons, gray felt hat
EX $625 NM $700 MIP $925

□ **Littlest Rebel Doll,** 1935, 18", cotton
and organdy outfit
EX $675 NM $725 MIP $950

□ **Littlest Rebel Doll,** 1935, 22", red/white
cotton dress w/organdy collar
EX $775 NM $900 MIP $1150

□ **Poor Little Rich Girl Doll,** 1936, 18",
pique sunsuit w/matching tam
EX $325 NM $750 MIP $950

□ **Poor Little Rich Girl Doll,** 1936, 13",
sailor dress w/white trim and matching
tam
EX $275 NM $375 MIP $750

□ **Poor Little Rich Girl Doll,** 1936, 13",
blue silk pajamas
EX $325 NM $750 MIP $950

□ **Rebecca of Sunnybrook Farm Doll,**
1957, 12" vinyl, blue bib overalls, blue
polka dot blouse, straw hat
EX $125 NM $230 MIP $325

□ **Rebecca of Sunnybrook Farm Doll,**
1957, 12" vinyl, red felt jumper and plastic purse
EX $175 NM $230 MIP $325

□ **Rebecca of Sunnybrook Farm Doll,**
1957, 12" vinyl, blue bib overalls w/plaid
blouse, black low shoes
EX $125 NM $185 MIP $220

□ **Rebecca of Sunnybrook Farm Doll,**
1957, Ideal, 12", vinyl head, dark blonde
hair, plastic body, arms and legs
EX $175 NM $230 MIP $325

□ **Shirley Temple Baby,** 16", mohair wig,
flirty eyes
EX $525 NM $800 MIP $1300

□ **Shirley Temple Baby,** 20", composition
head, arms and legs, cloth body
EX $700 NM $975 MIP $1450

□ **Shirley Temple Baby,** Ideal, 18",
painted hair, chubby toddler body
w/dimpled cheeks, flirty eyes, dressed
in pink organdy w/silk ribbons
EX $600 NM $925 MIP $1350

□ **Shirley Temple Doll,** Reliable
(Ideal/Canada), 13", yellow organdy
dress, silk ribbon
EX $460 NM $760 MIP $1000

□ **Shirley Temple Doll,** Made in Japan, 8"
composition w/pink silk undies
EX $175 NM $210 MIP $300

□ **Shirley Temple Doll,** 27" composition
w/pink taffeta, bonnet and pantaloons
EX $850 NM $1250 MIP $1850

□ **Shirley Temple Doll,** 22" composition
w/facial molding
EX $600 NM $800 MIP $950

❏ **Shirley Temple Doll**, 20" composition w/facial molding
EX $500   NM $750   MIP $950

❏ **Shirley Temple Doll**, 18" composition w/facial molding
EX $525   NM $700   MIP $900

❏ **Shirley Temple Doll**, 16", black velveteen coat and hat
EX $180   NM $350   MIP $850

❏ **Shirley Temple Doll**, 16", light blue organdy w/pink hemstitching and silk ribbons
EX $275   NM $575   MIP $850

❏ **Shirley Temple Doll**, 13", pleated pique w/white applique
EX $275   NM $550   MIP $800

❏ **Shirley Temple Doll**, Ideal, 22" jointed, composition body, blonde mohair, hazel glass eyes, open mouth, red/white polka dot dress
EX $225   NM $500   MIP $1000

❏ **Shirley Temple Doll**, Ideal, 19" vinyl, twinkle eyes, dressed in pink nylon, black purse
EX $180   NM $340   MIP $475

❏ **Shirley Temple Doll**, 16" composition
EX $375   NM $675   MIP $850

❏ **Shirley Temple Doll**, 1934, Ideal, 18", light pink organdy
EX $475   NM $650   MIP $950

❏ **Shirley Temple Doll**, 1934, Ideal, 18", pleated pale green, pink, or blue dress, embroidered collar and pink silk ribbon
EX $520   NM $675   MIP $750

❏ **Shirley Temple Doll**, 1935, 18" facial molding doll w/mohair wig (parted in the center), light complexion, outfit from "Curly Top"
EX $260   NM $525   MIP $1050

❏ **Shirley Temple Doll**, 1957, 12", vinyl, molded hands and feet, synthetic rooted wig, pink slip trimmed w/lace
EX $125   NM $225   MIP $400

❏ **Shirley Temple Doll**, 1957, 12" vinyl, molded hands and feet, synthetic rooted wig, two piece slip/undies
EX $110   NM $225   MIP $350

❏ **Shirley Temple Doll**, 1957, 12" vinyl, pink/blue nylon dress w/daisy appliques, hat, purse
EX $125   NM $250   MIP $375

❏ **Shirley Temple Doll**, 1958, 15" vinyl, red nylon dress w/floral detailing at collar, hair ribbon, purse
EX $110   NM $210   MIP $310

❏ **Shirley Temple Doll**, 1958, Ideal, 15" vinyl, yellow nylon dress trimmed w/lace and ribbon around skirt
EX $175   NM $320   MIP $425

❏ **Shirley Temple Doll**, 1958-59, Ideal, 17" vinyl, brown twinkle eyes, pink/blue dress
EX $210   NM $320   MIP $425

❏ **Shirley Temple Doll**, 1960, 15" vinyl, blue jumper w/red/white gingham blouse and pocket facing
EX $100   NM $200   MIP $310

❏ **Shirley Temple Doll**, 1960s, 17", yellow party dress, white purse w/Shirley Temple lettering
EX $225   NM $325   MIP $450

❏ **Shirley Temple Doll**, 1960s, Ideal, 17", yellow nylon dress and Twinkle Eyes wrist tag
EX $210   NM $320   MIP $450

❏ **Shirley Temple Doll**, 1972, Ideal/Hong Kong, 16", vinyl, red polka dot dress, Stand Up and Cheer
EX $155   NM $185   MIP $210

❏ **Shirley Temple Doll**, 1972, Ideal/Hong Kong, 15" vinyl manufactured for Montgomery Ward's
EX $190   NM $210   MIP $235

❏ **Stand Up and Cheer Doll**, 11" composition, short rayon dress w/blue polka dots
EX $675   NM $925   MIP $1050

❏ **Stand Up and Cheer Doll**, 1934, 11", dotted red, blue, or green organdy dress w/silk ribbon
EX $450   NM $675   MIP $950

❏ **Stand Up and Cheer Doll**, 1934, 13" composition, dotted organdy green dress
EX $150   NM $200   MIP $375

❏ **Stowaway Doll**, 1936, 20", two-piece linen w/brass buttons
EX $650   NM $825   MIP $1250

❏ **Stowaway Doll**, 1936, 25", pink taffeta, mohair hair
EX $700   NM $950   MIP $1300

❏ **Texas Ranger Doll**, 17", plaid shirt, leather vest w/trim
EX $550   NM $700   MIP $1050

❏ **Texas Ranger Doll**, 20", plaid shirt, leather vest w/trim, chaps, holster, and metal gun
EX $700   NM $950   MIP $1350

❏ **Texas Ranger/Cowgirl Doll**, 11", plaid cotton shirt, leather vest, chaps, holster, metal gun, felt 10 gallon hat w/"Ride 'Em Cowboy" printed band
EX $450   NM $750   MIP $1300

❏ **Wee Willie Winkie Doll**, 1937, 18", long sleeve cotton jacket, two pockets and six brass buttons, plaid wool skirt, tan belt w/brass buckle
EX $700   NM $1050   MIP $1450

❏ **Wee Willie Winkie Doll**, 1957, Ideal, 12", vinyl head, dark blonde hair, plastic body, arms and legs
EX $190   NM $250   MIP $375

DOLL CLOTHING

❏ **Baby Take A Bow Dress**, 1934, red cotton, red polka dots on collar and reverse on the bottom w/silk ribbons, fits 16" doll
EX $85   NM $95   MIP $120

❏ **Ballerina Outfit**, 1957-58, blue/green nylon and tulle, flower hair piece; fits 12" vinyl doll
EX $80   NM $85   MIP $100

❏ **Bright Eyes Dress**, 1934, fits 16" dolls, several colors variations
EX $85   NM $90   MIP $120

❏ **Bright Eyes Outfit**, white corduroy coat and hat w/original pin, fits 16" doll
EX $100   NM $150   MIP $200

❏ **Captain January Outfit**, 1936, red or green pleated pique, silk ribbons; fits a 16" doll
EX $85   NM $95   MIP $120

❏ **Coat and Hat**, velveteen coat and hat w/red buttons; fits 16" doll
EX $80   NM $90   MIP $100

❏ **Coat and Hat**, 1958, Ideal, red corduroy coat and hat, fits 12" doll
EX $60   NM $70   MIP $75

❏ **Curly Top Dress**, 1935, striped cotton dress, fits 20" doll
EX $85   NM $95   MIP $120

❏ **Dimples Outfit**, 1936, heavy felt jacket w/red trim; fits 16" doll
EX $85   NM $95   MIP $120

❏ **Dress**, light blue organdy; fits 16" doll
EX $85   NM $95   MIP $120

❏ **Dress**, 1958, Ideal, nylon w/loop details; fits 12" doll
EX $65   NM $80   MIP $90

❏ **Dress, Jacket, and Purse**, 1959, nylon
EX $65   NM $75   MIP $80

❏ **Jumper and Blouse**, 1959, Ideal, blue velveteen jumper w/floral applique, cotton blouse
EX $60   NM $70   MIP $80

❏ **Jumpsuit**, red w/white flowers
EX $80   NM $85   MIP $100

❏ **Jumpsuit**, red/white checkered
EX $35   NM $40   MIP $50

❏ **Littlest Rebel Dress**, 1935, yellow/brown, fits an 18" doll
EX $150   NM $185   MIP $300

❏ **Littlest Rebel Outfit**, checkered dress, rick rack ribbon on sleeves, lace collar and apron
EX $85   NM $110   MIP $200

❏ **Nightcoat and Cap**, 1958-59, Ideal, flannel; fits 12" doll
EX $60   NM $70   MIP $80

❏ **Our Little Girl Outfit**, 1935, blue or white pique, white dog appliques, fits 16" doll
EX $85   NM $100   MIP $175

❏ **Our Little Girl Outfit**, 1935, red or blue dress w/music appliques, matching hat, fits 16" doll
EX $85   NM $100   MIP $175

❏ **Polka Dot Dancing Dress**, 1935, blue organdy w/matching hat and sunsuit
EX $85   NM $90   MIP $110

❏ **Poor Little Rich Girl Outfit,** 1935, blue sailor dress, fits 16" doll
EX $90　　NM $100　　MIP $125

❏ **Poor Little Rich Girl Outfit,** 1935, pique and organdy dress, fits 16" doll
EX $90　　NM $100　　MIP $125

❏ **Poor Little Rich Girl Outfit,** 1936, pleated red plaid w/white collar, fits 16" doll
EX $90　　NM $100　　MIP $125

❏ **Rain Cape and Umbrella,** plaid red or blue rain cape w/hood and matching umbrella; fits 18" doll
EX $80　　NM $100　　MIP $150

❏ **Stowaway Outfit,** 1936, red or blue pique, fits 16" doll
EX $90　　NM $125　　MIP $210

❏ **Wee Willie Winkie Outfit,** 1937, pique outfit and tam, slip/undies; fits 16" doll
EX $125　　NM $160　　MIP $235

❏ **Wool Coat,** fits 18" dolls, from Little Miss Marker
EX $60　　NM $90　　MIP $145

PAPER DOLLS

❏ **Paper Doll Book,** 1976, Whitman, #1986, Model No. 1986
EX $8　　NM $15　　MIP $30

❏ **Paper Dolls,** 1934, Saalfield, four 8" dolls and 30 outfits; first licensed set, #2112, Model No. 2112
EX $75　　NM $215　　MIP $380

❏ **Paper Dolls,** 1958, Saalfield, #4435, Model No. 4435
EX $35　　NM $50　　MIP $125

❏ **Paper Dolls,** 1959, Saalfield, 18" folding doll w/easel, costumes, and accessories, #5110, Model No. 5110
EX $10　　NM $40　　MIP $80

❏ **Shirley Standing Doll,** 1935, Saalfield, cardboard doll on platform and different outfits, #1719, Model No. 1719
EX $35　　NM $90　　MIP $275

❏ **Shirley Temple Dolls and Dresses,** 1960, Saalfield, Two dolls w/different outfits, #1789, Model No. 1789
EX $12　　NM $18　　MIP $35

PHOTOGRAPH

❏ **Promo Photo,** 8" x 10" photo of Shirley w/facsimile autograph, came w/all composition dolls and outfits
EX $30　　NM $45　　MIP $60

PLAYING CARDS

❏ **Bridge Cards,** 1934, U.S. Playing Card
EX $35　　NM $45　　MIP $55

SLEEPING BEAUTY

ACCESSORIES

❏ **Sleeping Beauty Alarm Clock,** 1950s, Phinney-Walker, 2-1/2" x 4" x 4-1/2" tall, Sleeping Beauty surrounded by three birds and petting a rabbit
EX $50　　NM $90　　MIP $175

❏ **Sleeping Beauty Doll Crib Mattress,** 1960s, 9" x 17", Sleeping Beauty and the fairies
EX $15　　NM $25　　MIP $50

BOOK

❏ **Sleeping Beauty Sticker Fun Book,** 1959, Whitman
EX $15　　NM $30　　MIP $60

TOY

❏ **Fairy Godmother Hand Puppets,** 1958, set of three: 10-1/2" tall, Flora, Merryweather, and Fauna, each
EX $60　　NM $85　　MIP $225

❏ **King Huber/King Stefan Hand Puppets,** 1956, Gund, 10" tall, molded rubber heads w/fabric hand cover
EX $30　　NM $75　　MIP $150

❏ **Puzzle,** 1958, Whitman, 11-1/2" x 14-1/2", Three Good Fairies circling around a baby in a crib
EX $15　　NM $35　　MIP $60

❏ **Puzzle,** 1958, Whitman, 11-1/2" x 14-1/2", Sleeping Beauty w/Prince Phillip and Three Good Fairies circling
EX $15　　NM $35　　MIP $60

❏ **Puzzle,** 1958, Whitman, 11-1/2" x 14-1/2", Sleeping Beauty w/forest animals
EX $15　　NM $35　　MIP $60

❏ **Sleeping Beauty Jack-In-The-Box,** 1980s, Enesco, Princess Aurora, wooden box, plays "Once Upon A Dream"
EX $40　　NM $100　　MIP $185

❏ **Sleeping Beauty Magic Paint Set,** Whitman
EX $25　　NM $50　　MIP $80

❏ **Sleeping Beauty Squeeze Toy,** 1959, Dell, 4" x 4" x 5" tall, rubber, Sleeping Beauty w/rabbit
EX $25　　NM $60　　MIP $85

SMOKEY BEAR

BANK

❏ **Smokey Bank,** 6" tall, china
EX $20　　NM $60　　MIP $125

BOOK

❏ **Smokey Bear and the Campers Book,** 1961, Golden
EX $10　　NM $20　　MIP $40

❏ **Smokey Bear Coloring Book,** 1958, Whitman
EX $10　　NM $20　　MIP $50

DOLL

❏ **Smokey Doll,** 1950s, Ideal, 15" plush, vinyl face
EX $50　　NM $150　　MIP $275

FIGURES

❏ **Smokey Bobbing Head Figure,** 1960s, 6-1/4" tall
EX $40　　NM $175　　MIP $375

❏ **Smokey Figure,** 1971, Dakin, figure on a tree stump
EX $30　　NM $75　　MIP $150

TOY

❏ **Smokey Bear Record,** Peter Pan, 45 rpm
EX $5　　NM $15　　MIP $35

❏ **Smokey Soaky,** 1960s, 9" tall, plastic
EX $10　　NM $25　　MIP $50

WATCH

❏ **Smokey Wristwatch,** 1960s, Hawthorne
EX $45　　NM $100　　MIP $225

SNOW WHITE AND THE SEVEN DWARFS

ACCESSORIES

❏ **Doc Lamp,** 1938, LaMode Studios, 8" tall, plaster
EX $60　　NM $175　　MIP $325

❏ **Dopey Lamp,** 1940s, 9" tall, ceramic base w/Dopey
EX $75　　NM $150　　MIP $300

❏ **Pencil Box,** Venus Pencil, 3" x 8" x 1"
EX $75　　NM $125　　MIP $185

❏ **Radio,** 1938, Emerson, 8" x 8" w/characters on cabinet
EX $750　　NM $1500　　MIP $3600

❏ **Snow White Lamp,** 1938, LaMode Studios, 8-1/2" tall
EX $75　　NM $150　　MIP $375

❏ **Snow White Mirror,** 1940s, 9-1/2", plastic handle
EX $30　　NM $75　　MIP $150

❏ **Snow White Table Quoits,** 1930s, Chad Valley, 9-1/2" x 21" x 1-1/4" deep
EX $125　　NM $225　　MIP $350

BANK

❏ **Dime Register Bank,** 1938, Disney, holds up to five dollars
EX $65　　NM $200　　MIP $425

❏ **Dopey Bank,** 1938, Crown Toy, 7-1/2" tall, wood composition
EX $60　　NM $125　　MIP $275

❏ **Dopey Dime Register Bank,** 1938, Disney, holds up to $5
EX $50　　NM $175　　MIP $400

BOOK

❏ **Snow White and the Seven Dwarfs Book,** 1938, Whitman, Big Little Book
EX $25　　NM $75　　MIP $150

❏ **Snow White Paper Dolls,** 1938, Whitman, 10" x 15" x 1-1/2", blue
EX $100　　NM $375　　MIP $650

DOLL

❏ **Bashful Doll,** 1930s, Ideal
EX $65　　NM $150　　MIP $375

❑ **Doc Doll,** 1930s, Ideal
EX $65   NM $150   MIP $375

❑ **Dopey Doll,** Krueger, 14" tall
EX $100   NM $175   MIP $325

❑ **Dopey Doll,** 1930s, Ideal
EX $65   NM $150   MIP $325

❑ **Dopey Doll,** 1938, Knickerbocker, 11" tall composition
EX $125   NM $250   MIP $500

❑ **Dopey Doll,** 1938, Chad Valley, cloth body
EX $55   NM $110   MIP $275

❑ **Dopey Ventriloquist Doll,** 1938, Ideal, 18" tall
EX $160   NM $325   MIP $675

❑ **Grumpy Doll,** 1938, Knickerbocker, 11" tall, composition
EX $100   NM $310   MIP $625

❑ **Happy Doll,** 1930s, 5-1/2" tall, composition, holding a silver pick w/a black handle
EX $50   NM $100   MIP $275

❑ **Sneezy Doll,** Krueger, 14" tall
EX $125   NM $225   MIP $425

❑ **Snow White and the Seven Dwarfs Dolls,** 1940s, Deluxe, 22" Snow White and 7" dwarfs
EX $400   NM $800   MIP $1800

❑ **Snow White Doll,** Horsman, 8", in illustrated box
EX $25   NM $50   MIP $100

❑ **Snow White Doll,** 1938, Ideal, 3-1/2" x 6-1/2" x 16" tall, fabric face and arms, red/white dress w/dwarf and forest animal design
EX $300   NM $750   MIP $1050

❑ **Snow White Doll,** 1939, Knickerbocker, 3" x 7" x 3-1/2", composition w/movable arms and legs
EX $100   NM $350   MIP $700

❑ **Snow White Doll,** 1940, Knickerbocker, 12" tall, composition
EX $100   NM $300   MIP $675

FIGURES

❑ **Dopey Figure,** 1960s, ceramic figure and barrel
EX $15   NM $30   MIP $80

❑ **Seven Dwarfs Figures,** 1938, Seiberling, 5-1/2", rubber
EX $200   NM $425   MIP $750

GAME

❑ **Seven Dwarfs Target Game,** 1930s, Chad Valley, 6-1/2" x 11-1/2" target, spring locked gun
EX $125   NM $250   MIP $400

TOY

❑ **Baby Rattle,** 1938, Krueger, Snow White at piano, Dwarfs playing instruments
EX $150   NM $250   MIP $400

❑ **Dopey Rolykin,** Marx, 2"
EX $35   NM $75   MIP $125

❑ **Dopey Soaky,** 1960s, 10" tall
EX $11   NM $30   MIP $70

❑ **Dopey Walker,** 1938, Marx, 9" tall, tin, rocking walker
EX $300   NM $600   MIP $900

❑ **Happy Toy,** YS Toys (Taiwan), battery operated, Happy fries eggs
EX $50   NM $100   MIP $250

❑ **Ironing Board,** Wolverine, tin board and cover
EX $15   NM $25   MIP $60

❑ **Puzzle,** 1960s, Jaymar, 11" x 14"
EX $20   NM $35   MIP $60

❑ **Puzzles,** 1938, Whitman, set of two
EX $60   NM $120   MIP $200

(KP Photo)

❑ **Refrigerator,** 1970s, Wolverine, 15", tin, single door, white and yellow depicting Snow White
EX $25   NM $50   MIP $100

❑ **Safety Blocks,** 1938, Halsam, 7-1/2" x 14-1/2"
EX $50   NM $150   MIP $250

❑ **Sand Pail,** 1938, Ohio Art, 8", tin, Snow White plays hide-n-seek w/the dwarfs
EX $50   NM $125   MIP $300

❑ **Sled,** 1938, S. L. Allen, 40" long wood slat and metal runner sled w/character decals
EX $150   NM $300   MIP $550

❑ **Snow White Marionette,** 1930s, Tony Sarg/Alexander, 12-1/2" tall
EX $80   NM $200   MIP $425

❑ **Snow White Model Making Set,** 1930s, Sculptorcraft
EX $100   NM $225   MIP $425

❑ **Snow White Sewing Set,** 1940s, Ontex
EX $30   NM $55   MIP $100

❑ **Snow White Sink,** 1960s, Wolverine, tin
EX $15   NM $30   MIP $60

❑ **Snow White Soaky**
EX $15   NM $40   MIP $75

❑ **Tea Set,** 1930s, Wadeheath, white china, teapot, cups, saucers, and creamer
EX $130   NM $275   MIP $500

❑ **Tea Set,** 1937, Ohio Art, plates, cups, tray, saucers
EX $75   NM $200   MIP $400

❑ **Tea Set,** 1960s, Marx, teapot, five saucers, large plates and tea cups
EX $40   NM $70   MIP $150

SPORTS

DOLL

❑ **Dorothy Hamill Doll,** 1975, Ideal, 11-1/4" tall
EX $30   NM $55   MIP $90

❑ **Evel Knievel Doll,** Ideal, 6" tall
EX $20   NM $35   MIP $80

❑ **Julius Erving (Dr. J) Doll,** 1974
EX $20   NM $40   MIP $80

❑ **Wayne Gretzky Doll,** Mattel, 12" tall
EX $25   NM $50   MIP $75

WATCH

❑ **Muhammed Ali Wristwatch,** 1980, Bradley, chrome case, sweep seconds, brown leather band, face shows Ali in trunks and gloves, w/signature beneath
EX $35   NM $100   MIP $200

STEVE CANYON

BOOK

❑ **Steve Canyon's Interceptor Station Punch Out,** 1950s, Golden
EX $40   NM $90   MIP $160

TOY

❑ **Steve Canyon Costume,** 1959, Halco
EX $25   NM $60   MIP $175

❑ **Steve Canyon's Membership Card and Badge,** 1/2" x 4" Milton Caniff membership card for the Airagers, Morse code on back, 3" tin litho color badge w/gold feathers w/Steve's face centered
EX $70   NM $130   MIP $200

SUPERHEROES

ACCESSORIES

❑ **Aquaman Halloween Costume,** 1967, Ben Cooper
EX $20   NM $55   MIP $90

❑ **Captain America Halloween Costume,** 1967, Ben Cooper
EX $55   NM $150   MIP $250

❑ **Comic Book Tattoos,** 1967, Topps, Aquaman, Wonder Woman, Superman, or Batman
EX $20   NM $30   MIP $60

❑ **Flash Glass,** 1978, Pepsi
EX $20   NM $40   MIP $70

CHARACTER TOYS

❑ **Green Lantern Halloween Costume,** 1967, Ben Cooper
EX $80   NM $175   MIP $260

❑ **Hawkman Button,** 1966, Button World, 3", "Hawkman Superhero Club"
EX $20   NM $30   MIP $60

❑ **Justice League of America Display Card,** 1970, Fleer, cardboard display from inside gumball machine
EX $30   NM $45   MIP $85

❑ **Mr. Bubble Superfriends Box,** 1984, bubble bath box features Superman, Wonder Woman, Batman, and Robin
EX $20   NM $30   MIP $75

❑ **Spider-Man Button,** 1966, Button World, 3", "Superhero Club"
EX $15   NM $35   MIP $70

❑ **Spider-Man Crazy Foam,** 1974, American Aerosol
EX $10   NM $30   MIP $50

❑ **Wonder Woman Glass,** 1978, Pepsi, 6"
EX $10   NM $25   MIP $40

❑ **Wonder Woman Record,** 1977, Peter Pan Records, 33-1/3" rpm record w/comic book
EX $10   NM $30   MIP $50

BOOK

❑ **Aquaman Scourge of the Sea Book,** 1968, Whitman, Big Little Book
EX $15   NM $30   MIP $60

BOOKS

❑ **Spider-Man Coloring Book,** 1983, Marvel Books, oversized, "The Arms of Doctor Octopus"
EX $10   NM $20   MIP $40

GAMES

❑ **Marvel Superheroes Card Game,** 1978, Milton Bradley
EX $20   NM $30   MIP $75

TOY

❑ **Amazing Spider-Car,** 1976, Mego, 10" long, red plastic
EX $25   NM $50   MIP $100

❑ **Aquaman Jigsaw Puzzle,** 1968, Whitman, 100 pieces; Aquaman and Mera
EX $20   NM $40   MIP $70

❑ **Marvel Superheroes Colorforms Set,** 1983, Colorforms
EX $10   NM $20   MIP $50

❑ **Marvel Superheroes Easy Show Projector,** 1967, Kenner, projector and three cartridges
EX $60   NM $150   MIP $275

❑ **Marvel Superheroes Puzzle,** 1967, Milton Bradley, 100 pieces
EX $40   NM $80   MIP $175

❑ **Marvel Superheroes Sparkle Paint Set,** 1967, Kenner
EX $40   NM $80   MIP $175

❑ **Marvel World Adventure Play Set,** 1975, Amsco, w/stand-up scenes and figures
EX $60   NM $150   MIP $275

❑ **Spider-Man Hand Puppet,** 1976, Imperial, 9", vinyl head, plastic body
EX $15   NM $35   MIP $70

TOYS

❑ **Spider-Man Friction Vehicle,** 1968, Marx, tin litho w/Spider-Man figure at wheel
EX $90   NM $250   MIP $450

SUPERMAN

ACCESSORIES

❑ **Children's Dish Set,** 1966, Boontonware, 7" plate, 5-1/2" bowl, 3-1/2" cup, all white plastic w/Superman image
EX $50   NM $100   MIP $150

❑ **Fan Card,** 1942, 7" x 10", shows full color Superman in hands on hips pose, reads, "Best wishes from your friend Superman"
EX $250   NM $700   MIP $1000

❑ **Fan Card,** 1950s, National Comics, 5" x 7" promo b/w post card w/signature "Best Wishes, George Reeves"
EX $75   NM $150   MIP $200

❑ **Hair Brush,** 1940, Monarch, wood, full length decal of Superman, brush came in handle and no-handle styles w/box
EX $50   NM $150   MIP $300

❑ **Hair Brush,** 1976, Avon, Superman handle, illustrated box
EX $15   NM $25   MIP $50

❑ **Junior Defense League of America Membership Certificate,** 1940s, Superman, Inc., Superman Bread premium, red/blue print and Superman bust and logo on paper, "signed" by Clark Kent
EX $300   NM $600   MIP $1200

❑ **Membership Certificate,** 1965, last year of club
EX $100   NM $180   MIP $300

❑ **Original Radio Broadcasts Record,** 1977, Nostalgia Lane, old Superman radio teleplays, in illustrated sleeve showing chain breaking pose in color and b/w strip panels
EX $10   NM $25   MIP $50

❑ **Patch,** 1939, 5-1/2" diameter fabric premium patch, shows 3/4 profile of Superman breaking chains off chest, Supermen of America -- Action Comics
EX $1500   NM $5000   MIP $9000

❑ **Patch,** 1940s, 3-1/2" round patch shows chain breaking pose
EX $750   NM $2000   MIP $5700

❑ **Patch,** 1942, Superman Bread, cardboard shield
EX $300   NM $850   MIP $1600

❑ **Patch,** 1970s, cloth diamond-shaped patch of "S" logo in gold/red, several sizes, each
EX $5   NM $10   MIP $15

❑ **Patch,** 1970s, triangular orange cloth patch w/red border shows Superman flying over desert scene
EX $5   NM $10   MIP $15

❑ **Patch,** 1970s, rectangular white patch w/green border shows full color Superboy running toward viewer
EX $20   NM $40   MIP $65

❑ **Patch,** 1970s, rectangular white cloth patch w/green border shows full color Supergirl flying
EX $5   NM $10   MIP $15

❑ **Patch,** 1973, diamond-shaped cloth patch shows Superman standing against vertical red/white stripes, wide yellow border has stars and reads "Superman Junior Olympics"
EX $5   NM $10   MIP $15

❑ **Pen,** 1947, Jaffe, red/blue pen on illustrated card
EX $200   NM $400   MIP $700

❑ **Pencil Box,** 1966, Mattel
EX $25   NM $50   MIP $75

❑ **Pencil Holder,** 1940s, Superman, Inc., hollow holder in shape of large pencil, illustrated on shaft w/red and blue on white images and Superman-Tim Club logos
EX $400   NM $800   MIP $1200

❑ **Pennant,** 1940s, yellow pennant w/Superman image and raised logo
EX $300   NM $800   MIP $1500

❑ **Pennant,** 1973, 35th anniversary item, felt pennant has Amazing World of Superman logo and reads "Metropolis, Illinois, Home of Superman", came in two sizes, each
EX $12   NM $25   MIP $60

❑ **Pillow,** 1960s, 12" square felt pillow w/color art of flying Superman
EX $35   NM $65   MIP $100

❑ **Pin,** 1940s, Kellogg's, 7/8" round pin w/black/red/blue bust of Superman, most common pin in Pep Cereal series of late 1940s
EX $12   NM $25   MIP $50

❑ **Record and Club Membership Kit,** 1966, 33-1/3 rpm record of the original comic, Superman Club card, shoulder patch and 1" tin litho club button, in 12" square illustrated box
EX $100   NM $150   MIP $200

❑ **Super Candy and Toy,** 1967, Phoenix Candy, boxed candy w/a small toy inside each box
EX $50   NM $75   MIP $125

❑ **Superman 3-D Cut-Out Picture,** 1950s, Kellogg's, 4-1/2 x 6-1/2" premium framed cut-out of Superman from the back of cereal box, reads "Best Wishes From Your Friend Superman"
EX $60   NM $80   MIP $100

❏ **Superman Candy,** 1940, Leader Novelty Candy, boxed candy w/punch-out trading cards on box back and coupons redeemable for Superman items, red box, front shows chain-breaking pose
EX $500   **NM** $750   **MIP** $1500

❏ **Superman Christmas Card,** 1940s, 4" x 5", Superman Brings You Christmas Greetings, shows him flying w/small tree in hands
EX $50   **NM** $150   **MIP** $300

❏ **Superman Cigarette Lighter,** 1940s, Dunhill, battery-operated table-top lighter has chrome finish figure standing on black base
EX $500   **NM** $1000   **MIP** $1500

❏ **Superman Crazy Foam,** 1970s, American Aerosol, spray bath soap in full color illustrated can
EX $25   **NM** $50   **MIP** $75

❏ **Superman Cup,** 1984, Burger King, one of four in set w/figural handles, others are Batman, Wonder Woman and Darkseid
EX $5   **NM** $7   **MIP** $10

❏ **Superman Figurine,** 1966, Ideal, 3" tall hard plastic painted or unpainted figure on base, removable cape, part of Justice League series
EX $35   **NM** $65   **MIP** $85

❏ **Superman Figurine,** 1984, Craft Master, solid figurine and paint set, on illustrated card
EX $25   **NM** $50   **MIP** $80

❏ **Superman Hood Ornament,** 1940s, Lee, chrome finish, shows Superman in stylized running pose w/box
EX $500   **NM** $2000   **MIP** $3500

❏ **Superman Junior Defense League Pin,** 1940s, die cut pin in shape of flying Superman holding banner aloft, gold finish pin w/red/white/blue detailing
EX $75   **NM** $150   **MIP** $250

❏ **Superman Krypto-Raygun Filmstrips,** 1940s, Daisy, extra boxed films for Krypto-Raygun, each
EX $25   **NM** $50   **MIP** $100

❏ **Superman Mug,** 1950s, left handed mug, shows Superman on front and name across cape in back, handle has arrow and star
EX $75   **NM** $150   **MIP** $250

❏ **Superman Mug,** 1966, white glass, red and blue logo w/Superman image, reverse picture is Superman breaking chain
EX $20   **NM** $40   **MIP** $65

❏ **Superman of Metropolis Award Certificate,** 1973, premium given out during Metropolis, Illinois' 1973 35th anniversary of Superman celebration
EX $20   **NM** $40   **MIP** $70

❏ **Superman Phone Booth Radio,** 1978, Vanity Fair, battery operated AM radio of green British-style booth has color bas-relief Superman exiting
EX $35   **NM** $75   **MIP** $150

❏ **Superman Planter,** 1970s, 3" diameter painted ceramic
EX $5   **NM** $10   **MIP** $15

❏ **Superman Radio,** 1973, transistor radio made in punch-out shape of Superman from waist up
EX $50   **NM** $75   **MIP** $160

❏ **Superman Record Player,** 1978, latching box briefcase type record player illustrated on all sides in full color, also features b/w origin strip on back
EX $55   **NM** $100   **MIP** $160

❏ **Superman School Bag,** 1950s, Acme, red/blue fold-over clasp vinyl bag, screened full color Superman figure, black plastic handle and shoulder strap
EX $100   **NM** $200   **MIP** $400

❏ **Superman Soaky,** 1965, Colgate Palmolive, 10" soap bottle, shows him standing w/hands at sides
EX $20   **NM** $40   **MIP** $75

❏ **Superman Soaky,** 1978, Avon, 9-1/2" bubble bath bottle, Superman stands atop building
EX $30   **NM** $40   **MIP** $50

❏ **Superman Song Record,** 1950s, A.A. Records, 6" two-song, 45 rpm record in sleeve, other song is "Tarzan Song", Model No. 723
EX $25   **NM** $50   **MIP** $100

❏ **Superman Statue,** 1940s, 15" tall, crude painted plaster carnival prize
EX $75   **NM** $250   **MIP** $500

❏ **Superman Statue,** 1942, Syracuse Ornament, 5-1/2" tall composition statue of Superman in hands on hips pose, finished in brown patina w/red/black highlights
EX $750   **NM** $2000   **MIP** $4000

❏ **Superman Telephone,** 1979, ATE, plastic phone w/large figure of Superman in hands on hips pose standing over key pad, receiver hangs up into back of his cape, illustrated box
EX $150   **NM** $600   **MIP** $1200

❏ **Superman Toothbrush,** 1970s, Janex, figural, battery operated
EX $20   **NM** $35   **MIP** $65

❏ **Superman Towels,** 1970s, G.H. Wood, children's sponge towels, illustrated
EX $12   **NM** $25   **MIP** $50

❏ **Superman Wall Clock,** 1978, New Haven, plastic and cardboard battery operated framed wall clock showing Superman fighting alien shaceship
EX $30   **NM** $60   **MIP** $110

❏ **Superman Wallet,** 1950s, Croyden, brown, color embossed flying Superman and logo
EX $60   **NM** $175   **MIP** $350

❏ **Superman Wallet,** 1960s, brown leather
EX $25   **NM** $40   **MIP** $70

❏ **Superman's Christmas Adventure Record,** 1940s, Decca, set of three 78 rpm records in illustrated sleeves
EX $150   **NM** $500   **MIP** $900

❏ **Superman-Tim Club Membership Card,** 1940s, Superman, Inc., blue/red or red/black card
EX $750   **NM** $125   **MIP** $325

❏ **Superman-Tim Club Press Card,** 1940s, blue/red card for identifying self as an Official Reporter for club
EX $100   **NM** $150   **MIP** $350

❏ **Superman-Tim Club Redbacks,** 1940s, Superman, Inc., red on white imprinted coupons styled to look like money, denominations of $1, $5 and $10 "redbacks", each
EX $10   **NM** $20   **MIP** $35

❏ **Superman-Tim Magazine,** 1940s, 5" x 7" monthly store premium, each
EX $50   **NM** $75   **MIP** $150

❏ **Supermen of America Membership Certificate,** 1948, 8-1/2" x 11", signed by "Clark Kent"
EX $75   **NM** $150   **MIP** $350

❏ **Utensil Set,** 1966, Imperial Knife, stainless steel spoon and fork set w/Superman on the handles, on 4-1/2 x 10" illustrated card
EX $50   **NM** $100   **MIP** $200

❏ **Wall Banner,** 1966, 16" x 25" w/hanging rod at top, shows large central picture of Superman in front of city skyline and two lower panels of him smashing rocks and flying through space
EX $40   **NM** $85   **MIP** $175

ACTION FIGURE

❏ **Flying Superman,** 1950s, Kellogg's, plastic premium, 5" x 6-1/2", toy only
EX $50   **NM** $100   **MIP** $150

ACTION FIGURES

(KP Photo)

❏ **Energized Superman Figure,** 1979, Remco, 12" tall battery operated hard body figure, in box
EX $35   **NM** $65   **MIP** $150

❏ **Flying Superman,** 1950s, Kellogg's, premium, 5" x 6 1/2", rubber band propelled, w/instruction sheet and mailer
EX $100   **NM** $200   **MIP** $300

❏ **Flying Superman,** 1955, Transogram, 12-1/2" tall molded plastic figure propelled by "super flight launcher", a rub-

CHARACTER TOYS

ber band attached to a pistol grip holder, on illustrated card
EX $55   **NM** $100   **MIP** $200

❑ **Superman Figure**, Chemtoy, rubber, three different poses, on card, each
EX $25   **NM** $40   **MIP** $50

❑ **Superman Figure**, Fun Things, 6" rubber figure on card
EX $9   **NM** $16   **MIP** $30

❑ **Superman Figure**, Palitoy, 8" figure on card
EX $35   **NM** $65   **MIP** $120

❑ **Superman Figure**, 1979, Japan, plastic body w/soft vinyl head, movable arms and head, in illustrated window box
EX $40   **NM** $60   **MIP** $80

BANK

❑ **Superman Bank**, 1949, 9-1/2" painted ceramic shows youthful looking Superman standing on a cloud
EX $300   **NM** $500   **MIP** $1000

❑ **Superman Bank**, 1974, bust of Superman
EX $50   **NM** $75   **MIP** $100

❑ **Superman Dime Register Bank**, 1940s, 1/2" x 2-1/2" x 2 1/2" yellow tin, front shows full color Superman breaking chains off chest, held $5 in dimes
EX $100   **NM** $250   **MIP** $450

BOOKS

❑ **Adventures of Superman Book**, 1942, Random House, 4" x 5-1/2" armed services edition
EX $100   **NM** $225   **MIP** $425

❑ **Adventures of Superman Book**, 1942, Random House, 6-1/2" x 9" hardcover by George Lowther, no dust jacket
EX $100   **NM** $200   **MIP** $300

❑ **Adventures of Superman Book**, 1942, Random House, 6-1/2" x 9" hardcover, 220 pages, author George Lowther, full color dust jacket
EX $350   **NM** $800   **MIP** $1250

❑ **Book and Record Set**, 1947, Musette Records, The Magic Ring
EX $40   **NM** $100   **MIP** $150

❑ **Book and Record Set**, 1947, Musette Records, The Flying Train
EX $40   **NM** $100   **MIP** $150

❑ **Book, With Superman at the Gilbert Hall of Science**, 1948, Gilbert, 32-page promo catalog for Gilbert's Erector Sets and other toys, illustrated w/Superman
EX $75   **NM** $100   **MIP** $175

❑ **Superman Book and Record Set**, 1970s, Peter Pan, two stories w/record
EX $5   **NM** $10   **MIP** $15

❑ **Superman Cut-Outs**, 1940, Saalfield, red cover, lighter paper than blue book, non-perforated cut-outs
EX $750   **NM** $2000   **MIP** $3500

❑ **Superman Cut-Outs**, 1940, Saalfield, perforated figures, heavy stock paper, blue cover
EX $750   **NM** $2000   **MIP** $3500

❑ **Superman Paint-by-Number Book**, 1966, Whitman, 11" x 13-1/2", 40 pictures plus coloring guide on back cover
EX $15   **NM** $25   **MIP** $60

❑ **Superman Pop-Up Book**, 1979, Random House, hardcover, full color
EX $15   **NM** $30   **MIP** $60

❑ **Superman Press-Out Book**, 1966, Whitman, punch out, assemble and hang scenes and characters
EX $20   **NM** $35   **MIP** $70

(KP Photo)

❑ **Superman Scrap Book**, 1940, Saalfield, cover shows Superman flying over mountains toward stylized S.O.S. transmission
EX $75   **NM** $150   **MIP** $325

❑ **Superman To The Rescue Coloring Book**, 1964, Whitman, cover shows Superman rescuing woman, Model No. 1001
EX $25   **NM** $50   **MIP** $90

❑ **Superman Workbook**, 1940s, DC Comics, English grammar workbook
EX $100   **NM** $450   **MIP** $750

BUTTONS

❑ **Superman Button**, 1966, WABC Radio, radio premium button for "It's a Bird, It's a Plane..." production, shows faceless Superman w/"WABC 77" across chest
EX $100   **NM** $150   **MIP** $300

❑ **Superman Club Button**, 1966, 3-1/2" celluloid button, shows 3/4 profile thigh-up view of Superman in hands on hips pose, reads, "Official Member Superman Club"
EX $10   **NM** $20   **MIP** $30

❑ **Superman Muscle Building Club Button**, 1954, Peter Puppets Playthings, part of Golden Muscle Building set, full color bust in sunburst circle in white button, reads "Superman Muscle Building Club"
EX $50   **NM** $150   **MIP** $375

❑ **Superman-Tim Club Button**, 1940s, Superman, Inc., two different, both say

Superman-Tim Club and have red/blue lettering and images on white background
EX $50   **NM** $75   **MIP** $120

CLOTHING

❑ **Superman Beanie**, 1940s, hat w/two-color Superman embossed images on brim
EX $500   **NM** $750   **MIP** $1500

❑ **Superman Belt**, 1940s, Pioneer, clear plastic w/color images and round brass buckle in box
EX $300   **NM** $500   **MIP** $700

❑ **Superman Belt**, 1940s, Pioneer, brown leather w/Superman images and rectangular buckle, in box
EX $300   **NM** $500   **MIP** $750

❑ **Superman Belt**, 1950s, Kellogg's, 28" long red plastic, aluminum "S" symbol buckle in red/yellow
EX $100   **NM** $250   **MIP** $375

❑ **Superman Belt Buckle**, 1940s, square metal buckle shows red/blue chain breaking pose
EX $100   **NM** $150   **MIP** $400

❑ **Superman Moccasins**, 1940s, Penobscot Shoe, leather moccasins w/Superman chain breaking pose on toe upper
EX $250   **NM** $750   **MIP** $2000

❑ **Superman Necktie**, 1940s
EX $100   **NM** $200   **MIP** $350

❑ **Superman Necktie Set**, 1940s, boxed set of two ties, small tie shows Superman standing w/arms crosses, larger tie shows Superman landing
EX $500   **NM** $1000   **MIP** $1500

❑ **Superman Suspenders**, 1948, Pioneer, elastic, illustrated box
EX $350   **NM** $500   **MIP** $900

COMIC BOOKS

❑ **3-D Adventures of Superman Comic Book**, 1950s, DC Comics, w/3-D goggles
EX $100   **NM** $200   **MIP** $800

❑ **Action Comics #1**, 1938, DC Comics Top 9.2, first appearance of Superman
EX $40000 **NM** $115000 **MIP** $300000

❑ **Mini Comic Book**, 1955, Kellogg's, cereal premium, #1, The Superman Time Capsule
EX $75   **NM** $100   **MIP** $200

❑ **Mini Comic Book**, 1955, Kellogg's, cereal premium, #1-A, Duel in Space
EX $75   **NM** $100   **MIP** $200

❑ **Mini Comic Book**, 1955, Kellogg's, cereal premium, #1-B, Supershow of Metropolis
EX $75   **NM** $100   **MIP** $200

❑ **Superman's Christmas Adventure Comic Book**, 1940, Macy's, 1940 Macy's holiday premium
EX $700   **NM** $2500   **MIP** $4000

❑ **Superman's Christmas Play Book,**
1944, department store premium
EX $200 **NM** $500 **MIP** $1100

DOLLS

❑ **Super Babe Doll,** 1947, Imperial Crown
Toy, 15" tall, rubber skin, movable arms
and legs, sleep eyes, composition head
EX $500 **NM** $1000 **MIP** $2500

❑ **Superman Doll,** Knickerbocker, 20" tall
plush in box
EX $12 **NM** $25 **MIP** $40

❑ **Superman Doll,** 1940, Ideal, 13-1/2"
tall, wood jointed body w/composition
head, movable head, arms and legs, ball
knob hands
EX $500 **NM** $1000 **MIP** $2500

❑ **Superman Doll,** 1977, Toy Works, 25-
1/2" tall, cloth, w/cape
EX $12 **NM** $25 **MIP** $40

GAMES

❑ **Superman Action Game,** 1940s, American Toy Works, wood and cardboard
wartime game, Superman holds totter-
ing bridge and kids shoot darts at tanks
on bridge, Model No. 530
EX $750 **NM** $1500 **MIP** $2500

❑ **Superman City Game,** 1966, Remco,
board game w/magnetic figures and
buildings
EX $500 **NM** $750 **MIP** $1500

❑ **Superman Electronic Question and
Answer Quiz Machine,** 1966, Lisbeth
Whiting Co., battery operated quiz game
in full color illustrated box
EX $50 **NM** $100 **MIP** $225

❑ **Superman Official Eight-Piece Junior
Quoit Set,** 1940s, game in illustrated
box includes wood and rubber game
pieces, instruction booklet and membership card for "Superman Official
Sports Club"
EX $75 **NM** $100 **MIP** $150

❑ **Superman Pinball Game,** 1978, Bally,
full-sized arcade game
EX $200 **NM** $500 **MIP** $1000

❑ **Superman Tilt Track,** 1966, Kohner,
marble skill game, in illustrated window
box
EX $65 **NM** $95 **MIP** $175

PUZZLES

❑ **Puzzle,** 1940, set of two Superman puzzles
EX $300 **NM** $600 **MIP** $1200

❑ **Puzzle,** 1940, Saalfield, 300 pieces, 12
x 16", Superman w/Muscles Like Steel
EX $150 **NM** $350 **MIP** $500

❑ **Puzzle,** 1940, Saalfield, 300 pieces, 12
x 16", Superman the Man of Tomorrow
EX $150 **NM** $350 **MIP** $500

❑ **Puzzle,** 1940, Saalfield, 500 pieces, 16
x 20", Superman Stands Alone
EX $200 **NM** $500 **MIP** $750

❑ **Puzzle,** 1940, Saalfield, 300 pieces, 12
x 16", Superman Shows his Super
Strength
EX $150 **NM** $350 **MIP** $500

❑ **Puzzle,** 1940, Saalfield, 300 pieces, 12
x 16", Superman Saves the Streamliner
EX $150 **NM** $350 **MIP** $500

❑ **Puzzle,** 1940, Saalfield, 500 pieces, 16
x 20", Superman Saves a Life
EX $200 **NM** $500 **MIP** $750

❑ **Puzzle,** 1966, Whitman, 150 pieces, 14"
X 18", Superman
EX $12 **NM** $25 **MIP** $40

❑ **Puzzle,** 1966, Whitman, two frame tray
puzzles: one shows Superman fighting
space robot, other shows him flying
past manned rocket ship in outer space,
each
EX $25 **NM** $50 **MIP** $75

❑ **Puzzle,** 1973, APC
EX $10 **NM** $15 **MIP** $20

❑ **Puzzles,** 1940, Saalfield, set of six small
puzzles w/42 pieces each
EX $500 **NM** $1000 **MIP** $1500

RINGS

❑ **Superman Crusader Ring,** 1940s,
brass or silver finish ring shows forward
facing bust of Superman
EX $50 **NM** $120 **MIP** $250

❑ **Superman Member Ring,** 1940, red
paint on top of gold finish
EX $5000 **NM** $20000 **MIP** $70000

❑ **Superman Milk Defense Club Ring,**
1941, gold finish hidden compartment
ring, face is embossed milk companies
initial, different initials known, lightning
bolt and eyeball symbol, compartment
shows Superman decal image
EX $1300 **NM** $6000 **MIP** $20000

❑ **Superman Milk Defense Club Ring,**
1941, Different Milk Companies Spon-
sors, gold finish hidden compartment
ring, face is embossed w/"S", lightning
bolt and Superman bust, compartment
shows Superman image
EX $2500 **NM** $10000 **MIP** $25000

❑ **Superman Ring,** 1978, Nestle's, premium ring, gold finish w/white circle
center and yellow/red diamond "S" logo
in middle
EX $20 **NM** $40 **MIP** $70

❑ **Superman-Tim Club Ring,** 1940s,
bronze finish metal ring w/embossed
image of Superman in flight, w/initials
S and T near his feet
EX $800 **NM** $3500 **MIP** $7500

TOY

❑ **Bicycle Siren,** 1970s, Empire
EX $10 **NM** $20 **MIP** $40

❑ **Bubble Gum Badge,** 1948, Fo-Lee Gum
Corp., shield-shaped brass finish badge
shows a variant of the chain breaking
pose inside a sun burst pattern ringed
w/stars
EX $1500 **NM** $4000 **MIP** $6000

❑ **Cinematic Picture Pistol,** 1940, Daisy,
non-electric, film is viewed through view
in back of gun, metal gun w/one pre-
loaded 28 scene Superman film, Model
No. 96
EX $300 **NM** $750 **MIP** $1500

❑ **Crayon-by-Numbers Set,** 1954, Transogram, 16 crayons and 44 action
scenes
EX $100 **NM** $200 **MIP** $325

(KP Photo)

EX $20 **NM** $40 **MIP** $60

❑ **Dangle Dandies Mobile,** 1955,
Kellogg's, set of eight cut outs on boxes
of Rice Krispies and Corn Flakes
EX $75 **NM** $100 **MIP** $175

❑ **Film Viewer,** 1947, 1-1/2" x 4" x 6-1/2"
wide boxed set of hand-held viewer and
six films
EX $250 **NM** $500 **MIP** $725

❑ **Film Viewer,** 1947, Acme, 1-1/2" x 6-
1/2" wide boxed set of hand-held viewer
and two films
EX $100 **NM** $400 **MIP** $625

❑ **Film Viewer,** 1965, plastic hand viewer
w/two boxes of film, on illustrated card
EX $25 **NM** $40 **MIP** $65

❑ **Flying Noise Balloon,** 1966, Van Dam,
oversized balloon makes noise in flight,
Superman illustration on balloon and
card
EX $12 **NM** $23 **MIP** $40

❑ **Jumbo Movie Viewer,** 1950s, Acme,
blue/yellow plastic viewer w/35 mm
"theatre size" film, on illustrated card,
w/one filmstrip
EX $90 **NM** $165 **MIP** $250

❑ **Kryptonite Rock,** 1970s, glow-in-the-
dark rocks sold as kryptonite chunks, in
illustrated box
EX $10 **NM** $15 **MIP** $25
(Danny Fuchs)

❑ **Krypto-Raygun Film Viewer,** 1940,
Daisy, battery-operated metal projector
gun, seven Superman filmstrips, illustrated box, No. 94
EX $500 **NM** $1000 **MIP** $2500

❑ **Movie Viewer,** 1940, Acme Plastics,
tortoise shell plastic, and three individually boxed Superman films, in large full
color die-cut box
EX $200 **NM** $500 **MIP** $825

❑ **Movie Viewer,** 1947, Acme Plastics,
black plastic viewer, white knob and two
individually boxed Superman films, in
red/blue die-cut box
EX $100 **NM** $300 **MIP** $525

❑ **Movie Viewer,** 1948, Acme Plastics,
red plastic viewer and three individually
boxed Superman films, in small full
color die-cut box
EX $100 **NM** $300 **MIP** $525

❑ **Movie Viewer,** 1950s, Acme, black/red plastic viewer w/two individually boxed Superman films
EX $70 **NM** $130 **MIP** $200

❑ **Official Magic Kit,** 1956, Bar-Zim, magic balls, disappearing cards, multiplying corks, vanishing trick, shell game, balancing belt and directions, in illustrated box
EX $350 **NM** $750 **MIP** $1500

❑ **Official Superman Costume,** 1954, Ben Cooper, blue/red suit w/red/yellow monogram and belt, in box
EX $140 **NM** $260 **MIP** $400

❑ **Official Superman Krypto-Raygun Film Viewer,** 1940, Daisy, includes raygun, battery, bulb, lens and one film strip, in illustrated box
EX $500 **NM** $1000 **MIP** $1500

❑ **Official Superman Playsuit,** 1954, Funtime Playwear, rayon outfit, red cap w/screened Superman image, navy and red suit w/5" gold monogram and belt
EX $200 **NM** $400 **MIP** $600

❑ **Official Superman Playsuit,** 1970, Ben Cooper, cloth suit in illustrated box
EX $20 **NM** $40 **MIP** $60

❑ **Official Superman Two-Piece Kiddie Swim Set,** 1950s, set of rubber swim fins and goggles w/Superman's image or "S" symbol, in box
EX $50 **NM** $150 **MIP** $225

❑ **Paint-by-Numbers Watercolor Set,** 1954, Transogram, 16 watercolors and 44 action scenes
EX $75 **NM** $200 **MIP** $300

(KP Photo)

❑ **Super Heroes String Puppets,** 1978, Madison, string controlled cloth and vinyl marionette
EX $25 **NM** $75 **MIP** $100

❑ **Superman and Supergirl Push Puppets,** 1968, Kohner, set of two: 5-1/4" on bases, in window box
EX $200 **NM** $600 **MIP** $1000

❑ **Superman Back-a-Wack,** 1966, Dell, blue plastic paddle w/gold imprinted "S"

logo and name, elastic string and red ball, on illustrated card, Model No. 1194
EX $50 **NM** $100 **MIP** $150

❑ **Superman Balloon,** 1966, small balloon w/centered image
EX $5 **NM** $15 **MIP** $25

❑ **Superman Costume,** 1950s, red pants and tie-on cape, blue shirt w/red, blue and yellow "S" emblem on chest, yellow belt
EX $100 **NM** $260 **MIP** $400

❑ **Superman Figure,** Presents, 15" vinyl/cloth figure on base
EX $25 **NM** $40 **MIP** $60

❑ **Superman Golden Muscle Building Set,** 1954, Peter Puppets Playthings, handles, springs, hand grippers, jump rope, wall hooks, measuring tape, progress chart, membership certificate and button, illustrated box
EX $700 **NM** $1000 **MIP** $1500

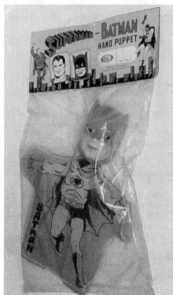

(KP Photo)

❑ **Superman Hand Puppet,** 1966, Ideal, 11", cloth body, vinyl head
EX $50 **NM** $75 **MIP** $100

❑ **Superman II View-Master Set,** three reels, based on film, Model No. L46
EX $5 **NM** $10 **MIP** $20

(KP Photo)

❑ **Superman III View-Master Set,** three reels, based on film, Model No. 4044
EX $5 **NM** $10 **MIP** $15

❑ **Superman Junior Horseshoe Set,** 1950s, Super Swim, four rubber horseshoes, two rubber bases and two wood pegs and Official Sports Club card and rules for sportsmanship
EX $50 **NM** $110 **MIP** $225

❑ **Superman Junior Swim Goggles,** 1950s, Super Swim, plastic lenses, rubber goggles w/red strap, "S" logo and membership card for Superman Safety Swim Club
EX $35 **NM** $90 **MIP** $200

❑ **Superman Kite,** 1966, Pressman
EX $50 **NM** $75 **MIP** $135

❑ **Superman Kite,** 1982, Hiflyer
EX $5 **NM** $10 **MIP** $20

❑ **Superman Krypton Rocket,** 1954, Kellogg's, 2" x 9" x 9-1/2" water powered rocket w/"Krypton generating pump," in mailer box
EX $150 **NM** $300 **MIP** $400

❑ **Superman Krypton Rocket,** 1956, Park Plastics, 2" x 9" x 9-1/2" water powered rocket w/Krypton generating pump, reserve fuel tank and Krypton Rocket, in illustrated box, same as Kellogg's rocket but in mass market packaging w/added fuel tank
EX $150 **NM** $300 **MIP** $400

❑ **Superman Paint Set,** 1940, American Toy Works, three brushes, small palette, water cup, 14 different paints and four b/w cartoon panels, in 11" x 14-1/2" color illustrated box
EX $250 **NM** $750 **MIP** $1200

❑ **Superman Paint Set,** 1940s, American Toy Works, larger version, shows Superman in front of pallet background
EX $250 **NM** $750 **MIP** $1200

❑ **Superman Paint Set,** 1940s, American Toy Works, box shows Superman flying up toward upper right corner of box, w/pallet and brushes at lower right, "Paint Set" inside pallet
EX $250 **NM** $750 **MIP** $1200

❑ **Superman Play Set,** 1973, Ideal, self-contained vinyl covered full color snap-close case opens to three backdrops, Fortress of Solitude, Daily Planet and villain's hideout, for staging action scenes w/supplied color punch-outs
EX $50 **NM** $75 **MIP** $150

❑ **Superman Playsuit,** 1940, Fishback, red and blue imprinted blue smock shirt and pants w/tie-on red cape
EX $150 **NM** $500 **MIP** $1200

❑ **Superman Pogo Stick,** 1977, 48" w/a vinyl bust on top
EX $50 **NM** $100 **MIP** $200

❑ **Superman Push Puppet,** 1966, Kohner, 5-1/4" on base, in window box
EX $50 **NM** $75 **MIP** $100

❑ **Superman Roller Skates,** 1975, Larami, plastic w/color bust of Super-

man shaped around front of each skate, in illustrated window box
EX $20   **NM** $50   **MIP** $75

❏ **Superman Rub-Ons**, 1966, Hasbro, magic picture transfers in box illustrated w/picture of Superman flying
EX $50   **NM** $100   **MIP** $150

❏ **Superman Senior Rubber Horseshoe Set**, 1950s, in box
EX $55   **NM** $100   **MIP** $150

❏ **Superman Senior Swim Goggles**, 1950s, Super Swim, plastic lenses, rubber goggles w/red strap, "S" logo on bridge, membership card for Superman Safety Swim Club
EX $40   **NM** $80   **MIP** $150

❏ **Superman Sky Hero**, 1977, Marx, rubber band glider w/color Superman image, on card, Model No. 9310
EX $25   **NM** $40   **MIP** $75

❏ **Superman Space Satellite Launcher Set**, 1950s, Kellogg's, premium set of generic plastic gun w/firing "satellite wheel" and illustrated instruction sheet, in mailer box
EX $150   **NM** $450   **MIP** $1000

❏ **Superman Stamp Set**, 1965, set of six wood-backed character stamps
EX $25   **NM** $50   **MIP** $150

❏ **Superman Super Watch**, 1967, Toy House, plastic toy watch w/moveable hands, watch "case" is large "S" chest symbol, on illustrated card
EX $15   **NM** $30   **MIP** $75

❏ **Superman Tank**, 1958, Linemar, large battery operated tin, 3-D Superman w/a cloth cape, in illustrated box
EX $350   **NM** $1750   **MIP** $3000

❏ **Superman the Movie View-Master Set**, 1979, three reels, based on film, Model No. J78
EX $5   **NM** $10   **MIP** $15

❏ **Superman Utility Belt**, 1979, Remco, illustrated window box, decoder glasses, kryptonite detector, nonworking watch, handcuffs, ring, decoder map, press card and secret message
EX $50   **NM** $150   **MIP** $250

❏ **Superman Water Gun**, 1967, Multiple Toymakers, 6" plastic, Model No. 484
EX $30   **NM** $100   **MIP** $185

❏ **Toy Wristwatch**, 1950s, Germany, non-working toy watch, blue plastic band, rectangular case w/full color full standing pose on white dial
EX $35   **NM** $65   **MIP** $150

❏ **Trick Picture Sun Camera**, 1950s, Made in Japan, when left in the sun for two minutes, the camera "develops" a picture of Superman fighting a space monster
EX $75   **NM** $150   **MIP** $225

TRADING CARDS

❏ **Superman II Trading Cards**, 1981, Costa Rican, set of 88 cards, complete set
EX $18   **NM** $35   **MIP** $50

❏ **Superman II Trading Cards**, 1981, Topps, set of 88 cards, complete set
EX $20   **NM** $30   **MIP** $40

❏ **Superman III Trading Cards**, 1983, Topps, set of 99 cards, complete set
EX $5   **NM** $10   **MIP** $15

❏ **Superman the Movie Trading Cards**, 1978, Topps, set of 77 cards, first issue
EX $7   **NM** $13   **MIP** $20

❏ **Superman the Movie Trading Cards**, 1979, Topps, set of 88 cards, second issue
EX $12   **NM** $25   **MIP** $35

❏ **Superman the Movie Trading Cards**, 1979, French, set of 180 cards
EX $18   **NM** $35   **MIP** $50

❏ **Superman the Movie Trading Cards**, 1979, OPC, set of 132 cards
EX $12   **NM** $25   **MIP** $35

❏ **Superman Trading Cards**, 1940, Gum Inc., 2-1/2" x 3-1/4" cards, set of 72
EX $2500   **NM** $8000   **MIP** $15000

❏ **Superman Trading Cards**, 1940, Gum Inc., 2-1/2" x 3-1/4" cards, each
EX $25   **NM** $50   **MIP** $100

❏ **Superman Trading Cards**, 1966, Topps, set of 66 cards, George Reeves TV series scenes
EX $90   **NM** $165   **MIP** $350

❏ **Superman Trading Cards**, 1966, Topps, set of 66 cards, shows George Reeves TV series scenes, each card
EX $5   **NM** $7   **MIP** $10

❏ **Superman Trading Cards Display Box**, 1966, Topps, 2" x 4" x 8" display box of 24 unopened packs, box shows George Reeves bust
EX $500   **NM** $750   **MIP** $1300

❏ **Superman Trading Cards Wrapper**, 1940, Gum Inc., 4-1/2" x 6" waxed paper
EX $300   **NM** $500   **MIP** $900

WATCHES

❏ **Superman Supertime Wristwatch**, 1950s, National Comics, gray band, stamped red "S" logo, silver western style buckle, full color hands on hips pose inside chrome finish case, second hand, even-hour numbers around face, in full color box
EX $250   **NM** $750   **MIP** $1500

❏ **Superman Wristwatch**, 1939, New Haven Clock Boxed, flattened oval face, shows color image of standing Superman from knees up, leather band
EX $1000   **NM** $1750   **MIP** $2500

❏ **Superman Wristwatch**, 1940s, New Haven Clock, squared-oval faced watch, leather band, dial shows Superman standing, hands on hips, in illustrated box
EX $1000   **NM** $1750   **MIP** $2500

❏ **Superman Wristwatch**, 1959, Bradley, dial shows Superman flying over city, second hand, chrome finish case
EX $600   **NM** $800   **MIP** $1400

❏ **Superman Wristwatch**, 1977, gold bezel, stainless back, blue leather band, face shows Superman flying upward from below
EX $35   **NM** $65   **MIP** $150

❏ **Superman Wristwatch**, 1986, Una-Donna, plastic case and band, several color and face illustrations, each
EX $10   **NM** $20   **MIP** $50

TARZAN

ACCESSORIES

❏ **Bracelet**, 1934, drink more milk radio premium
EX $1000   **NM** $2000   **MIP** $3400

❏ **Jungle Map**, 1933, radio premium
EX $150   **NM** $500   **MIP** $800

❏ **Poster**, 1933, Paper Mills, three masks; premium
EX $350   **NM** $1000   **MIP** $1600

❏ **Tarzan Flasher Ring**, 1960s, Vari-Vue
EX $10   **NM** $20   **MIP** $40

❏ **Tarzan Party Set**, 1977, Amscan
EX $10   **NM** $25   **MIP** $50

FIGURES

❏ **Figure**, 1950s, 2-1/2" tall, celluloid, French
EX $250   **NM** $500   **MIP** $1000

❏ **Kala Ape Figure**, 1984, Dakin, 3" tall
EX $10   **NM** $15   **MIP** $30

❏ **Young Tarzan Figure**, 1984, Dakin, 4", bendable
EX $10   **NM** $15   **MIP** $30

THREE LITTLE PIGS

ACCESSORIES

❏ **Three Little Pigs Bracelet**, 1930s, 1/2" x 2-1/4", wolf blowing down a house w/pig running away
EX $100   **NM** $225   **MIP** $400

GAME

❏ **Who's Afraid of the Big Bad Wolf Game**, 1930s, Parker Brothers
EX $65   **NM** $300   **MIP** $500

TOY

❏ **Puzzle**, 1940s, Jaymar, 7" x 10" x 2"
EX $50   **NM** $100   **MIP** $250

❏ **Three Little Pigs Sand Pail**, 1930s, Ohio Art, 4-1/2", tin
EX $50   **NM** $100   **MIP** $300

❏ **Three Little Pigs Soaky Set**, 1960s, Drew Chemical, 8" tall each: Three Little Pigs and the Big Bad Wolf
EX $70   **NM** $125   **MIP** $250

WATCH

❏ **Big Bad Wolf Pocket Watch Box**, 1934, Ingersoll
EX $500   **NM** $1500   **MIP** $3000

TOM AND JERRY

BANK

❏ **Tom and Jerry Bank,** 1980, Gorham, 6" tall
EX $20   NM $35   MIP $70

FIGURES

❏ **Jerry Figure,** 1973, Marx, 4" tall
EX $15   NM $25   MIP $60

❏ **Tom and Jerry Figure Set,** 1975, walking, Tom, Jerry, and Droopy
EX $25   NM $50   MIP $100

❏ **Tom Figure,** 1973, Marx, 6" tall
EX $15   NM $30   MIP $60

TOY

❏ **Puzzles,** Whitman, four frame tray puzzles
EX $20   NM $35   MIP $80

❏ **Tom and Jerry Go Kart,** 1973, Marx, plastic, friction drive
EX $30   NM $75   MIP $120

❏ **Tom and Jerry on Scooter,** 1971, Marx, plastic friction drive
EX $15   NM $25   MIP $60

WATCH

❏ **Tom and Jerry Wristwatch,** 1985, Bradley, quartz, oldies series, small white plastic case and band, sweep seconds, face shows Tom squirting Jerry w/hose
EX $15   NM $35   MIP $75

TONY THE TIGER

ACCESSORIES

❏ **Cookie Jar,** 1960s, Kellogg's, plastic, figural
EX $25   NM $70   MIP $110

❏ **Radio,** 1980s, plastic, figural
EX $20   NM $45   MIP $70

BANK

❏ **Figural Bank,** 1967, Kellogg's
EX $30   NM $45   MIP $70

FIGURES

❏ **Inflatable Tiger,** 1950s, Kellogg's
EX $7   NM $20   MIP $35

❏ **Plush Tiger,** 1970s, Kellogg's
EX $10   NM $25   MIP $50

TOP CAT

FIGURES

❏ **Top Cat Figure,** 1961, Marx, TV-Tinykins, plastic
EX $20   NM $35   MIP $50

TOY

❏ **Top Cat Soaky,** 1960s, 10" tall, vinyl
EX $25   NM $45   MIP $80

❏ **Viewmarx Micro-Viewer,** 1963, Marx, plastic
EX $20   NM $35   MIP $70

WINNIE THE POOH

ACCESSORIES

❏ **Lamp,** 1964, Dolly Toy, 7" tall
EX $35   NM $90   MIP $150

❏ **Radio,** 1970s, Thilgee, 5" x 6" x 1-1/2" tall
EX $45   NM $90   MIP $135

❏ **Winnie the Pooh Button,** 1960s, 3-1/2" celluloid
EX $10   NM $25   MIP $50

❏ **Winnie the Pooh Snow Globe,** 5-1/2", musical
EX $15   NM $35   MIP $60

DOLL

❏ **Winnie the Pooh and Christopher Robin Dolls,** 1964, Horsman, Winnie the Pooh 3-1/2" tall and Christopher 11" tall, set
EX $65   NM $135   MIP $275

❏ **Winnie the Pooh Doll,** 1960s, 12" tall
EX $25   NM $50   MIP $100

TOY

❏ **Jack-In-The-Box,** 1960s, Carnival Toys
EX $20   NM $40   MIP $75

❏ **Kanga and Roo Squeak Toy,** 1966, Holland Hill, vinyl
EX $15   NM $30   MIP $60

❏ **Magic Slate,** 1965, Western Publishing, 8-1/2" x 13-1/2"
EX $22   NM $45   MIP $75

❏ **Puzzle,** 1964, Whitman, frame tray
EX $10   NM $20   MIP $50

WIZARD OF OZ

ACCESSORIES

❏ **Christmas Ornaments,** 1977, Bradford Novelty, 4-1/2" tall, Dorothy, Scarecrow, Tin Man, Cowardly Lion, each
EX $5   NM $10   MIP $25

❏ **Christmas Ornaments,** 1989, Presents, cloth and vinyl: Dorothy, Scarecrow, Tin Man, Cowardly Lion, Glinda and Wicked Witch, each
EX $8   NM $10   MIP $15

❏ **Cookie Jar,** 1990, Clay Art, white w/relief figures of characters
EX $30   NM $75   MIP $150

❏ **Crayon Box,** 1975, Cheinco, rectangular, metal
EX $5   NM $10   MIP $20

❏ **Erasers,** 1989, Applause, set of six: figural, Scarecrow, Cowardly Lion, Dorothy, Wicked Witch, Tin Man, Glinda, set
EX $15   NM $20   MIP $30

❏ **Give-A-Show Projector Slides,** 1968, Kenner, 35 color slides, five different shows
EX $20   NM $40   MIP $80

❏ **Magnets,** 1987, Grynnen Barrett, six character magnets in box
EX $6   NM $10   MIP $15

❏ **Magnets,** 1989, Vanderbilt Products, several characters available, each
EX $2   NM $3   MIP $5

❏ **Pails,** 1950s, Swift and Company, Oz Peanut Butter, red and yellow and red, yellow and white tin
EX $25   NM $40   MIP $85

❏ **Scarecrow Night Light,** 1989, Hamilton Gifts, 7", unpainted bone china
EX $10   NM $15   MIP $25

❏ **Snack 'N Sip Pals,** 1989, Multi Toys, 12 red and white striped straws w/detachable character figures
EX $4   NM $7   MIP $20

❏ **Stationery,** 1939, Whitman, 10 sheets and envelopes, w/character illustrations
EX $100   NM $200   MIP $400

❏ **Tin,** 1989, Multi Toys, 8" x 10" x 2", illustrated w/Emerald City and characters
EX $8   NM $15   MIP $30

❏ **Trash Can,** 1975, Chein, oval metal
EX $20   NM $35   MIP $70

❏ **Wall Decorations,** 1967, Shepard Press, 20 punch-out decorations
EX $20   NM $35   MIP $60

BANK

❏ **Cowardly Lion Bank,** 1960s, ceramic, red nose
EX $30   NM $60   MIP $120

❏ **Dorothy Bank,** 1960s, ceramic, blue dress w/brown wicker basket
EX $30   NM $60   MIP $100

❏ **Scarecrow Bank,** 1960s, ceramic
EX $30   NM $50   MIP $100

❏ **Tin Man Bank,** 1960s, ceramic, silver
EX $30   NM $60   MIP $120

BOOK

❏ **Cut and Make Masks,** 1982, Dover, eight cut-out color masks
EX $5   NM $10   MIP $25

❏ **Dorothy and Friends Visit Oz Book,** 1967, Curtis Candy, candy premium
EX $8   NM $20   MIP $35

❏ **Dorothy Meets the Wizard Book,** 1967, Curtis Candy, candy premium
EX $10   NM $25   MIP $50

(KP Photo)

❏ **Jack Pumpkinhead and the Sawhorse of Oz Book,** 1939, Rand McNally, hardcover, also contains "Tik Tok and the Gnome King of Oz"
EX $60   NM $125   MIP $250

❏ **Little Dorothy and Toto of Oz Book,** 1939, Rand McNally, hardcover, also contains "The Cowardly Lion and the Hungry Tiger"
EX $65   NM $150   MIP $300

❏ **Little Golden Book Series,** 1951, The Road to Oz, The Emerald City of Oz, and The Tin Woodman of Oz, each
EX $8   NM $20   MIP $40

❏ **Mask Book,** 1990, Watermill Press, four paper masks
EX $3   NM $10   MIP $25

❏ **Return To Oz Little Golden Books,** 1985, Western, Dorothy Returns to Oz, Escape from the Witch's Castle, Dorothy in the Ornament Room, Dorothy Saves the Emerald City, each
EX $2   NM $5   MIP $10

❏ **Scarecrow and the Tin Man Book,** 1904, G. W. Dillingham
EX $150   NM $375   MIP $600

❏ **Scarecrow and the Tin Man Book,** 1946, Perks Publishing, black and yellow pictures
EX $20   NM $40   MIP $75

❏ **Tales of the Wizard of Oz Coloring Book,** 1962, Whitman, art from animated TV show
EX $15   NM $20   MIP $40

❏ **The Tin Woodsman and Dorothy Book,** 1967, Curtis Candy, candy premium
EX $12   NM $25   MIP $50

❏ **The Wonderful Cut-Outs of Oz Book,** 1985, Crown, 35 figures to cut out
EX $7   NM $15   MIP $30

❏ **Wizard of Oz Book,** 1975, Western, #310-32, Little Golden Book
EX $5   NM $10   MIP $20

❏ **Wizard of Oz Christmas Book,** 1968, Gimbel's, New York department store premium
EX $15   NM $25   MIP $70

❏ **Wizard of Oz Color-By-Number Book,** 1962, Karas Publishing, #A-116, Twinkle Books series
EX $10   NM $20   MIP $45

❏ **Wizard of Oz Paint Book,** 1939, Whitman
EX $80   NM $175   MIP $350

❏ **Wizard of Oz Paper Dolls,** 1976, Whitman
EX $7   NM $15   MIP $30

❏ **Wizard of Oz Sticker Fun Book,** 1976, Whitman
EX $6   NM $12   MIP $25

COMIC BOOK

❏ **Tales of the Wizard of Oz Comic Book,** 1962, Dell, #1306
EX $10   NM $15   MIP $35

❏ **Wizard of Oz Comic Book,** 1956, Dell, Dell Junior Treasury, #5
EX $12   NM $40   MIP $80

❏ **Wizard of Oz Comic Book,** 1957, Dell, Classic Illustrated Jr., #535
EX $6   NM $20   MIP $45

DOLL

❏ **Cowardly Lion Doll,** 1971, M-D Tissue, cloth, light brown body w/white snout
EX $10   NM $20   MIP $40

❏ **Cowardly Lion Doll,** 1984, Ideal, 9", Character Dolls series
EX $20   NM $40   MIP $70

❏ **Cowardly Lion Doll,** 1988, Presents, vinyl
EX $20   NM $40   MIP $70

❏ **Cowardly Lion Doll,** 1989, Largo Toys, rag doll
EX $8   NM $18   MIP $35

❏ **Dandy Lion Doll,** 1962, Artistic, 14" tall, cloth and vinyl
EX $35   NM $60   MIP $110

❏ **Doodle Dolls,** 1979, Whiting, three dolls: cardboard parts, yarn, Styrofoam balls, fabric
EX $8   NM $20   MIP $35

❏ **Dorothy and Toto Doll,** 1984, Ideal, 9", Character Dolls series
EX $20   NM $40   MIP $60

❏ **Dorothy Doll,** 1939, Ideal, 18", Judy Garland, blue checked jumper, open and close brown eyes
EX $500   NM $1000   MIP $2000

❏ **Dorothy Doll,** 1939, Sears, 15-1/2", Judy Garland, red or blue checked jumper w/black pin curls
EX $425   NM $850   MIP $1650

❏ **Dorothy Doll,** 1939, Ideal, 15-1/2", Judy Garland, blue checked jumper, open and close brown eyes
EX $375   NM $750   MIP $1500

❏ **Dorothy Doll,** 1939, Ideal, 13", Judy Garland, blue checked jumper, open and close brown eyes
EX $325   NM $550   MIP $1050

❏ **Dorothy Doll,** 1971, M-D Tissue, cloth, stuffed, yellow hair, orange jumper
EX $6   NM $20   MIP $40

❏ **Dorothy Doll,** 1984, Effanbee, 14-1/2" tall, vinyl, Judy Garland, blue dress and hair ribbons, ruby slippers, Legend Series
EX $45   NM $90   MIP $150

❏ **Dorothy Doll,** 1988, Presents, vinyl, blue checkered jumper, white blouse, red slippers, yellow brick road base
EX $20   NM $35   MIP $60

❏ **Dorothy Doll,** 1989, Largo Toys, Judy Garland
EX $8   NM $20   MIP $40

❏ **Dorothy Doll,** 1991, Madame Alexander, 8", blue checked jumper w/white blouse, basket w/Toto and red shoes, Storyland Dolls series
EX $20   NM $35   MIP $70

❏ **Glinda Doll,** 1989, Presents, vinyl, pink dress w/pink crown and wand, yellow brick road base
EX $20   NM $40   MIP $75

❏ **Jack Pumpkinhead Doll,** 1924, Oz Doll and Toy, 13"
EX $400   NM $750   MIP $1500

❏ **Lollipop Guild Boy Doll,** 1989, Presents, vinyl, plaid shirt, green shorts and striped socks, on a yellow brick road base
EX $20   NM $40   MIP $70

❏ **Lullabye League Girl Doll,** 1989, Presents, vinyl, pink ballerina dress and slippers w/hat on a yellow brick road base
EX $20   NM $40   MIP $70

❏ **Mayor of Munchkinland Doll,** 1989, Presents, vinyl, black suit and shoes on a yellow brick road base
EX $20   NM $40   MIP $70

❏ **Patchwork Girl Doll,** 1924, Oz Doll and Toy, 13"
EX $100   NM $200   MIP $400

❏ **Rusty the Tin Man Doll,** 1962, Artistic Toy Company, 14" tall, cloth and vinyl
EX $35   NM $60   MIP $100

❏ **Scarecrow Doll,** 1924, Oz Doll and Toy, 13"
EX $550   NM $1100   MIP $1650

❏ **Scarecrow Doll,** 1971, M-D Tissue, cloth, stuffed, frowning, blue pants and red and white plaid jacket
EX $10   NM $15   MIP $30

❏ **Scarecrow Doll,** 1984, Ideal, 9", Character Dolls series
EX $25   NM $40   MIP $70

❏ **Scarecrow Doll,** 1988, Presents, vinyl, brown pants, green shirt, and black hat and shoes, on a yellow brick road base
EX $25   NM $40   MIP $70

❏ **Scarecrow Doll,** 1989, Largo Toys, rag doll
EX $9   NM $15   MIP $40

❏ **Scarecrow Talkin' Patter Pillow Doll,** 1968, Mattel, cloth, pull-string, says 10

phrases, dark blue pants and sleeves, white gloves, black boots
EX $40   NM $75   MIP $150

❑ **Socrates the Scarecrow Doll,** 1962, Artistic, 14" tall, cloth and vinyl
EX $30   NM $60   MIP $120

❑ **Strawman Doll,** 1939, Ideal, 17", Ray Bolger, tan or pink pants, black or navy jacket
EX $300   NM $600   MIP $1050

❑ **Tin Man Doll,** 1924, Oz Doll and Toy, 13"
EX $400   NM $800   MIP $1400

❑ **Tin Man Doll,** 1971, M-D Tissue, cloth, stuffed, gray body, blue eyes, red heart
EX $8   NM $20   MIP $40

❑ **Tin Man Doll,** 1984, Ideal, 9", Character Dolls series
EX $20   NM $35   MIP $60

❑ **Tin Man Doll,** 1988, Presents, vinyl, silver body w/a heart clock on chaint, on a yellow brick road base
EX $20   NM $35   MIP $60

❑ **Tin Man Doll,** 1989, Largo Toys, rag doll
EX $10   NM $15   MIP $35

❑ **Toto Doll,** 1988, Presents, 5-1/2" plush
EX $15   NM $30   MIP $60

❑ **Wicked Witch Doll,** 1989, Presents, vinyl, black dress and hat, green face and hands holding broom on a yellow brick road base
EX $25   NM $40   MIP $80

❑ **Wizard of Oz Dolls,** 1985, Effanbee, 11-1/2", Dorothy, Scarecrow, Tin Man, Cowardly Lion, each
EX $15   NM $22   MIP $50

❑ **Wizard of Oz Live! Dolls**, Applause, cloth, three different sizes, each
EX $8   NM $15   MIP $30

FIGURES

❑ **Jack Pumpkinhead Figure,** 1985, Heart and Heart, Return to Oz, 3"-4" tall, plastic jointed
EX $35   NM $55   MIP $85

❑ **Munchkins Figures,** 1988, Presents, PVC, 1-3/4" to 2-3/4": Mayor, Lollipop Guild Boy, Sleepyhead Girl, Lady, Soldier and Ballerina, each
EX $5   NM $10   MIP $20

(KP Photo)

❑ **Oz-Kins Figures,** 1967, Aurora, plastic Burry Biscuit premium: set of 10
EX $40   NM $75   MIP $150

❑ **Scarecrow Figure,** 1939, Artisans Studio, 4", wood composition
EX $100   NM $200   MIP $375

❑ **Scarecrow Figure,** 1968, 15", ceramic, painted or unpainted
EX $20   NM $50   MIP $85

❑ **Scarecrow Figure,** 1984, Dalen Products, 6' inflatable
EX $12   NM $20   MIP $40

❑ **Scarecrow Figure,** 1985, Heart and Heart, Return to Oz, 3"-4" tall, plastic jointed
EX $30   NM $45   MIP $90

❑ **Tik Tok Figure,** 1985, Heart and Heart, Return to Oz, 3"-4" tall, plastic jointed
EX $35   NM $55   MIP $90

❑ **Tin Man Figure,** 1939, Artisans Studio, 4", wood composition
EX $100   NM $200   MIP $400

❑ **Tin Man Figure,** 1968, 15", ceramic, painted or unpainted
EX $20   NM $30   MIP $70

❑ **Tin Man Figure,** 1985, Return to Oz, 3"-4" tall, plastic jointed
EX $20   NM $35   MIP $75

❑ **Wizard of Oz Figures,** 1967, Multiple Toymakers, 6" tall, bendy, several characters, on card
EX $16   NM $30   MIP $60

❑ **Wizard of Oz Figures,** 1988, Presents, 3-3/4": Dorothy, Scarecrow, Tin Man, Cowardly Lion, Wicked Witch, Glinda, each
EX $4   NM $6   MIP $12

❑ **Wizard of Oz Figures,** 1989, Presents, six figures on musical bases, each
EX $10   NM $12   MIP $20

❑ **Wizard of Oz Figures,** 1989, Multi Toys, 4" poseable figures, set of six
EX $15   NM $25   MIP $45

❑ **Wizard of Oz Figures,** 1989, Just Toys, several characters, bendy, each
EX $4   NM $6   MIP $12

❑ **Wizard of Oz Squeak Toy,** 1939, Burnstein, 7" tall, hollow rubber, several characters
EX $90   NM $180   MIP $375

GAME

❑ **Game of The Wizard of Oz,** 1939, Whitman
EX $150   NM $300   MIP $500

❑ **Return to Oz Game,** 1985, Golden Press
EX $8   NM $13   MIP $30

❑ **Wizard of Oz Dart Game,** 1939, Dart Board Equipment, board illustrated w/yellow brick road and circular targets of Oz characters, w/three darts
EX $250   NM $500   MIP $1000

MUSIC BOX

❑ **Cowardly Lion Music Box,** 1983, Schmid
EX $20   NM $35   MIP $60

❑ **Dorothy Music Box,** 1983, Schmid, plays "Over the Rainbow"
EX $25   NM $40   MIP $60

❑ **Scarecrow Music Box,** 1983, Schmid
EX $20   NM $35   MIP $60

❑ **Tin Man Music Box,** 1983, Schmid
EX $20   NM $35   MIP $60

TOY

❑ **Carpet Sweeper,** 1939, Bissell, child-sized
EX $125   NM $200   MIP $300

❑ **Cast 'N Paint Set,** 1975, makes six 6" figures
EX $15   NM $25   MIP $60

❑ **Chalkboard,** 1975, Roth American, wood frame, steel stand w/chalk, chalk holder and eraser
EX $16   NM $27   MIP $60

❑ **Cowardly Lion Costume,** 1975, Ben Cooper, costume and mask
EX $15   NM $25   MIP $50

❑ **Cowardly Lion Costume,** 1989, Collegeville, plastic mask and vinyl bodysuit
EX $10   NM $15   MIP $20

❑ **Cowardly Lion Costume,** 1989, Collegeville, deluxe
EX $20   NM $40   MIP $60

❑ **Cowardly Lion Mask,** 1939, Newark Mask Company, linen, hand painted
EX $55   NM $90   MIP $150

❑ **Cowardly Lion Mask,** 1983, Don Post Studios, rubber
EX $35   NM $55   MIP $85

❑ **Cowardly Lion Wind-Up,** 1975, Durham Industries, on illustrated card
EX $15   NM $20   MIP $40

(KP Photo)

❑ **Decoupage Kit,** 1975, two wooden plaques, scenes based on film
EX $15   NM $25   MIP $40

❑ **Dorothy Costume,** 1975, Ben Cooper, costume and mask
EX $15   NM $25   MIP $40

Dorothy Costume, 1989, Collegeville, deluxe, includes red metallic glitter chips for shoes
EX $20   **NM** $40   **MIP** $60

Dorothy Costume, 1989, Collegeville, plastic mask and vinyl bodysuit
EX $8   **NM** $15   **MIP** $20

Dorothy Squeak Toy, 1939, Burnstein, 7", hollow rubber
EX $85   **NM** $175   **MIP** $400

Fun Shades, 1989, Multi Toys, children's sunglasses w/character images
EX $5   **NM** $8   **MIP** $15

Glinda Squeak Toy, 1939, Burnstein, 7", hollow rubber
EX $90   **NM** $180   **MIP** $375

Glinda's Magic Wand, 1989, Multi Toys, battery operated wand w/red glitter star on end, lights up, on illustrated card
EX $5   **NM** $10   **MIP** $25

Magic Picture Kit, 1968, Jiffy Pop Popcorn
EX $5   **NM** $25   **MIP** $50

Magic Slate, 1961, Lowe, art based on animated TV show
EX $12   **NM** $30   **MIP** $60

Magic Slate, 1976, Whitman
EX $6   **NM** $12   **MIP** $25

Magic Slate, 1985, Western, Return to Oz
EX $4   **NM** $10   **MIP** $20

Magic Slate, 1989, Western
EX $3   **NM** $6   **MIP** $15

Magic Story Cloth, 1978, Raco, 38" x 44" plastic sheet, eight crayons and sponge
EX $6   **NM** $12   **MIP** $25

Off to See the Wizard Colorforms, 1967, Colorforms
EX $25   **NM** $40   **MIP** $75

48-23391
MECH. OFF TO SEE THE WIZARD
DANCING TOYS
3 PCS. SET
MADE IN JAPAN

(KP Photo)

Off to See the Wizard Dancing Toys, 1967, Marx, mechanical, dancing Tin Man, the Cowardly Lion and the Scarecrow, Montgomery Ward's Exclusive, each
EX $50   **NM** $90   **MIP** $180

Off to See the Wizard Flasher Rings, 1967, Vari-Vue, gumball machine prizes, silver painted resin, gold painted, dark or light blue plastic, each
EX $6   **NM** $12   **MIP** $25

Off to See the Wizard Hand Puppet, 1968, Mattel, talking, four vinyl heads on finger tips, Toto and Cowardly Lion on thumb pad, ten phrases
EX $30   **NM** $45   **MIP** $90

Paint by Number 'N Frame Set, 1969, Hasbro, 16" x 18", two plastic frames, 18 watercolors, brush and eight pictures to paint
EX $20   **NM** $30   **MIP** $70

Paint by Number Set, 1968, Craft Master, six paints, brush, picture of Tin Man, Cowardly Lion, or the Scarecrow
EX $20   **NM** $35   **MIP** $75

Paint by Number Set, 1973, Hasbro, six oil paint vials and brush
EX $6   **NM** $12   **MIP** $30

Paint by Number Set, 1979, Craft House, two 10" x 14" panels, 15 colors, brush and instructions
EX $10   **NM** $15   **MIP** $35

Paint by Number Set, 1989, Art Award, three different versions
EX $6   **NM** $10   **MIP** $20

Paint with Crayons Set, 1989, Art Award, four pictures based on MGM film characters, in illustrated box
EX $5   **NM** $10   **MIP** $20

Paper Dolls, 1975, The Toy Factory, Dorothy, Tin Man, Scarecrow, Cowardly Lion and Toto, clothes and accessories
EX $10   **NM** $20   **MIP** $50

Playing Cards, 1988, Presents, tin holds two decks
EX $5   **NM** $10   **MIP** $30

Puppet Theatre, 1965, Proctor and Gamble, cardboard theater designed for P and G puppets
EX $40   **NM** $80   **MIP** $175

Puzzle, 1960s, Haret-Gilmar, 10" x 14" puzzle in canister
EX $7   **NM** $20   **MIP** $40

Puzzle, 1976, Whitman, frame tray
EX $4   **NM** $8   **MIP** $20

Puzzle, 1976, American Puzzle Company, 200 piece puzzle in canister
EX $8   **NM** $15   **MIP** $30

Puzzle, 1984, Effanbee, in canister
EX $8   **NM** $15   **MIP** $30

Puzzle, 1985, Crisco Oil, Return to Oz, mail away premium, 200 piece puzzle
EX $10   **NM** $20   **MIP** $40

Puzzle, 1989, Western, frame tray, 100 pieces, Glinda and Dorothy in Munchkinland
EX $5   **NM** $10   **MIP** $25

Puzzle, 1990, Milton Bradley, 1000 piece jigsaw featuring the 1989 Norman James Company poster
EX $6   **NM** $10   **MIP** $25

Puzzles, 1932, Reilly and Lee, set #2, two softcover editions of Tik-Tok and Jack Pumpkinhead and the Sawhorse, plus 25 piece puzzles
EX $200   **NM** $350   **MIP** $600

Puzzles, 1932, Reilly and Lee, #1, two softcover editions of the Scarecrow and the Tin Man, Ozma and the Little Wizard, plus two puzzles, in box
EX $200   **NM** $350   **MIP** $550

Puzzles, 1960s, Jaymar, set of four, 100 pieces each, each
EX $15   **NM** $30   **MIP** $60

Puzzles, 1960s, Jaymar, frame tray
EX $10   **NM** $20   **MIP** $40

Puzzles, 1967, Whitman, set of three: Peter Pan, Alice in Wonderland and The Wizard of Oz, in box
EX $12   **NM** $18   **MIP** $40

Puzzles, 1977, Doug Smith, 17" x 22" each, frame tray
EX $10   **NM** $20   **MIP** $30

Puzzles, 1985, Golden Press, frame tray, Return to Oz characters
EX $3   **NM** $5   **MIP** $10

Return to Oz Hand Puppets, 1985, Welch's Jelly, Scarecrow, Gump, or Tik-Tok, Return to Oz promotion
EX $12   **NM** $20   **MIP** $45

Rubber Stamps, 1989, set of 11 characters in plastic case
EX $10   **NM** $15   **MIP** $25

Rubber Stamps, 1989, Multi Toys, 12 figural stampers
EX $4   **NM** $6   **MIP** $10

Rubber Stamps, 1989, 18 chracter stamps
EX $12   **NM** $20   **MIP** $30

Scarecrow Costume, 1967, Ben Cooper
EX $20   **NM** $35   **MIP** $60

Scarecrow Costume, 1968, Ben Cooper, battery-operated light-up mask
EX $20   **NM** $35   **MIP** $60

Scarecrow Costume, 1989, Collegeville, plastic mask and vinyl bodysuit
EX $6   **NM** $12   **MIP** $20

Scarecrow Costume, 1989, Collegeville, deluxe, includes straw
EX $20   **NM** $35   **MIP** $50

Scarecrow Mask, 1939, Newark Mask, linen, hand painted
EX $55   **NM** $90   **MIP** $150

Scarecrow Mask, 1983, Don Post Studios, rubber
EX $40   **NM** $60   **MIP** $90

Scarecrow Wind-Up, 1975, Durham Industries, on illustrated card
EX $15   **NM** $20   **MIP** $50

Scarecrow-in-the-Box, 1967, Mattel, jack-in-the-box
EX $20   **NM** $35   **MIP** $80

Showboat Play Set, 1962, Remco, pink plastic showboat w/oversized central stage area, four different plays, scenery, players and scripts
EX $40   **NM** $62   **MIP** $125

❏ **Stand-Up Rub-Ons,** 1968, Hasbro, three full color transfer sheets, character outline sheets of 10 characters
EX $20   NM $30   MIP $60

❏ **Stitch a Story Set,** 1973, Hasbro, two framed pictures, thread and embroidery needle
EX $10   NM $15   MIP $25

❏ **Tea Set,** 1970s, Ohio Art, 30-piece set, red and yellow plastic
EX $30   NM $45   MIP $90

❏ **Tin Man Costume,** 1961, Halco, costume and mask
EX $20   NM $35   MIP $70

❏ **Tin Man Costume,** 1968, Ben Cooper
EX $20   NM $30   MIP $40

❏ **Tin Man Costume,** 1975, Ben Cooper, costume and mask
EX $15   NM $25   MIP $40

❏ **Tin Man Costume,** 1989, Collegeville, plastic mask and vinyl bodysuit
EX $6   NM $10   MIP $15

❏ **Tin Man Costume,** 1989, Collegeville, deluxe
EX $20   NM $35   MIP $60

❏ **Tin Man Mask,** 1939, Newark Mask, linen, hand painted
EX $60   NM $90   MIP $150

❏ **Tin Man Mask,** 1983, Don Post Studios, rubber
EX $35   NM $55   MIP $85

❏ **Tin Man Robot,** 1969, Remco, 21-1/2" tall, battery operated, lifts legs and swings arms as he walks
EX $75   NM $130   MIP $250

❏ **Tin Man Wind-Up,** 1975, Durham Industries
EX $15   NM $30   MIP $70

❏ **Toy Watch,** 1940s, tin, Scarecrow and the Tin Man on either side of non-working dial
EX $30   NM $60   MIP $120

❏ **Vinyl Stick-On Play Set,** 1989, Multi Toys, 10 vinyl stickers w/Emerald City background, on header card
EX $4   NM $6   MIP $10

❏ **Water Guns,** 1976, Durham, heads of Scarecrow, Tin Man, or Cowardly Lion, water squirts out of nose, each
EX $15   NM $30   MIP $60

❏ **Wicked Witch Mask,** 1975, Ben Cooper
EX $6   NM $12   MIP $20

❏ **Wicked Witch Squeak Toy,** 1939, Burnstein, 7", hollow rubber
EX $125   NM $275   MIP $450

❏ **Wizard of Oz Costume,** 1961, Halco, costume and mask
EX $20   NM $35   MIP $50

❏ **Wizard of Oz Hand Puppets,** 1965, Proctor and Gamble, plastic
EX $8   NM $15   MIP $30

❏ **Wizard of Oz Hand Puppets,** 1989, Presents, several characters available, each
EX $8   NM $15   MIP $30

❏ **Wizard of Oz Hand Puppets,** 1989, Multi Toys, set of six on blister cards, each
EX $6   NM $12   MIP $20

❏ **Wizard of Oz Wind-Ups,** 1989, Multi Toys, 50th anniversary editions, several characters, each
EX $4   NM $8   MIP $20

❏ **Wizard Squeak Toy,** 1939, Burnstein, 7", hollow rubber
EX $90   NM $180   MIP $375

WATCH

❏ **Oz Time Wristwatch,** 1989, Macy's, 50th anniversary premium, round face w/Emerald City, black plastic band
EX $30   NM $50   MIP $100

❏ **Wizard of Oz Pocket Watch,** 1980s, Westclock, silver finish case, four characters on dial
EX $20   NM $35   MIP $75

❏ **Wizard of Oz Wristwatch,** 1989, EKO, child's LCD, red face in round yellow case, plastic band shows yellow brick road and Emerald City
EX $15   NM $25   MIP $50

❏ **Wizard of Oz Wristwatch,** 1989, EKO, quartz, illustrated face showing Emerald City, black plastic band
EX $15   NM $25   MIP $50

WOODY WOODPECKER

❏ **Woody Woodpecker Nodder,** 1950s, plastic
EX $50   NM $125   MIP $175

ACCESSORIES

❏ **Alarm Clock,** 1959, Columbia Time, Woody's Cafe
EX $75   NM $135   MIP $350

❏ **Lamp,** 1971, 20" tall, plastic
EX $15   NM $50   MIP $100

❏ **Woody Woodpecker Nodder,** 1950s, plastic
EX $50   NM $125   MIP $175

BOOK

❏ **Woody Woodpecker Nodder,** 1950s, plastic
EX $50   NM $125   MIP $175

❏ **Woody Woodpecker's Fun-o-Rama Punch-Out Book,** 1972
EX $10   NM $20   MIP $35

TOY

❏ **Paper Dolls,** 1968, Saalfield, Woody Woodpecker and Andy Panda
EX $20   NM $35   MIP $70

❏ **Playing Cards,** 1950s, two decks in a carrying case
EX $30   NM $55   MIP $85

❏ **Woody Woodpecker Hand Puppet,** 1963, Mattel, pull-string voice box
EX $35   NM $70   MIP $100

❏ **Woody Woodpecker Nodder,** 1950s, plastic
EX $50   NM $125   MIP $175

YOGI BEAR

ACCESSORIES

❏ **Coat Rack,** 1979, Wolverine, 48", red wood, Yogi and Boo Boo cut out in front, growth chart on back
EX $40   NM $70   MIP $100

❏ **Hot Water Bottle,** 1966
EX $25   NM $50   MIP $75

❏ **Safety Scissors,** 1973, Monogram, on card
EX $4   NM $7   MIP $10

BANK

❏ **Yogi Bear Bank,** 1960s, Knickerbocker, 22", figural
EX $20   NM $45   MIP $90

❏ **Yogi Bear Bank,** 1980, Dakin, 7", figural
EX $6   NM $15   MIP $35

BOOK

❏ **Snagglepuss Sticker Fun Book,** 1963, Whitman
EX $15   NM $30   MIP $60

❏ **Yogi vs. Magilla for President Coloring Book,** 1964, Whitman, Model No. 1144
EX $20   NM $45   MIP $90

DOLL

❏ **Boo Boo Doll,** 1960s, Knickerbocker, 9-1/2" tall, plush
EX $30   NM $50   MIP $75

❏ **Cindy Bear Doll,** 1959, Knickerbocker, 16", plush w/vinyl face
EX $40   NM $70   MIP $90

❏ **Yogi Bear Doll,** 1959, Knickerbocker, 16" plush w/vinyl face
EX $45   NM $90   MIP $175

❏ **Yogi Bear Doll,** 1959, Knickerbocker, 10" tall
EX $60   NM $125   MIP $250

❏ **Yogi Bear Doll,** 1960s, Knickerbocker, 19" plush
EX $45   NM $90   MIP $175

❏ **Yogi Bear Doll,** 1962, 6", soft vinyl w/movable arms and head
EX $30   NM $60   MIP $125

❏ **Yogi Bear Stuff and Lace Doll,** 1959, Knickerbocker, items to make a 13" x 5" doll
EX $25   NM $45   MIP $80

❏ **Yogi Squeeze Doll,** 1979, Sanitoy, 12", vinyl
EX $10   NM $35   MIP $55

FIGURES

❏ **Character Figures,** 1960, 12" tall, Yogi, Boo Boo, and Ranger Smith, each
EX $30   NM $50   MIP $75

❑ **Snagglepuss Figure,** 1970, Dakin
EX $30   NM $60   MIP $100

❑ **Yogi Bear Figure,** 1960s, Knickerbocker, 9" tall, plastic
EX $25   NM $50   MIP $90

❑ **Yogi Bear Figure,** 1961, Marx, TV-
Tinykins
EX $20   NM $35   MIP $60

❑ **Yogi Bear Figure,** 1970, Dakin, 7-3/4"
tall
EX $20   NM $35   MIP $70

GAME

❑ **Yogi Bear and Pixie and Dixie Game
Car,** Whitman, 7-1/2" pile on game in car
EX $15   NM $35   MIP $75

❑ **Yogi Score-A-Matic Ball Toss Game,**
1960, Transogram
EX $45   NM $80   MIP $125

TOY

❑ **Bubble Pipe,** 1963, Transogram, Yogi
Bear figural pipe
EX $20   NM $35   MIP $50

❑ **Magic Slate,** 1963
EX $15   NM $30   MIP $60

❑ **Snagglepuss Soaky,** 1960s, Purex, 9"
tall, vinyl/plastic
EX $20   NM $40   MIP $80

❑ **Yogi Bear and Cindy Push Puppet Set,**
1960s, Kohner, boxed set of two
EX $60   NM $125   MIP $250

❑ **Yogi Bear Cartoonist Stamp Set,** 1961,
Lido
EX $30   NM $70   MIP $100

❑ **Yogi Bear Friction Toy,** 1960s, Yogi in
yellow tie and green hat, illustrated red
box
EX $50   NM $100   MIP $200

❑ **Yogi Bear Ge-Tar,** 1960s, Mattel
EX $55   NM $100   MIP $160

❑ **Yogi Bear Hand Puppet,** Knickerbocker
EX $20   NM $35   MIP $70

❑ **Yogi Bear Paint 'em Pals,** 1978, Craft
Master, paint-by-number set
EX $15   NM $30   MIP $60

❑ **Yogi Bear Push Puppet,** 1960s, Kohner
EX $25   NM $45   MIP $90

WATCH

❑ **Yogi Bear Wristwatch,** 1963
EX $40   NM $100   MIP $200

❑ **Yogi Wristwatch,** 1967, Bradley,
medium base metal case, shows Yogi
w/hobo sack on stick, black vinyl band
EX $45   NM $120   MIP $200

YOSEMITE SAM

ACCESSORIES

❑ **Mini Snow Dome,** 1980s, Applause
EX $9   NM $16   MIP $25

❑ **Musical Snow Dome,** 1980s, Applause
EX $15   NM $30   MIP $45

FIGURES

❑ **Yosemite Sam Figure,** 1968, Dakin, 7"
tall
EX $15   NM $30   MIP $60

❑ **Yosemite Sam Figure,** 1971, Dakin, on
treasure chest
EX $15   NM $40   MIP $65

❑ **Yosemite Sam Figure,** 1978, Dakin,
Fun Farm
EX $15   NM $25   MIP $40

TOY

❑ **Yosemite Sam Nodder,** 1960s, 6-1/4",
bobbing head and spring mounted head
EX $45   NM $150   MIP $250

A.C. Gilbert Erector Sets

The "Rocket Launcher" set from 1958 is a neat combination of industrial and atomic-age toy. Mint-in-package price, $135.

What adult doesn't recall the joy of using toys to vicariously experience adult tasks—whether it be driving a toy truck or playing house? Construction toys were designed to make kids "feel big" and exercise their imagination and creativity.

Those boxes of parts of many sizes, shapes, colors, and purpose taught basic mechanics, logic, fine motor coordination and a host of other skills—all while providing hours of fun.

Most boys can recall the colors, heft and smell of their first construction set, even if they may not remember when they received it or who gave it to them. Those unfortunates who never got one no doubt made do with sets of their own design—including wood scraps, string, old wheels and nails.

Few joys of childhood rival that of laboriously constructing some mechanical wonder, watching it work, and then gleefully tearing it all apart.

While many other construction sets have been made through the years, none has received the most collectors' attention and praise like the original A.C. Gilbert Erector sets.

A Set by Any Other Name isn't the Same

Alfred Carlton Gilbert, born in 1884, was both a product of and producer for his time, the industrial coming of age in America. He inspired legions of bright young tinkerers to grow up to become architects of the future—engineers, scientists and craftsmen of all types.

As a child, Gilbert loved magic tricks, a fascination that would later pay off almost like magic. Also an aspiring sports star, he decided on a career in health education, and worked his way through Yale medical school by performing magic shows. At Yale he also won a berth on the 1908 U.S.

Olympic team and won the gold medal in the pole vault.

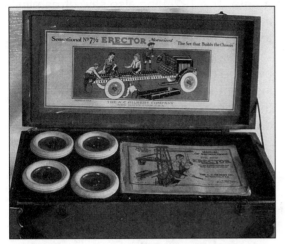

The "Sensational No. 7-1/2" from 1934 featured auto parts that built a motorized chassis. Mint value, $650.

While at Yale, Gilbert began giving magic lessons and became frustrated by the lack of available magic props for his students. A fellow amateur magician named John Petrie was also a mechanic, and he and Gilbert began making small magic kits and selling them.

After the Olympics, Gilbert returned to medical school and the magic business, which soon grew into a mail order magic company, supplying both amateurs and professionals. Gilbert and Petrie formed the Mysto Manufacturing Company.

By 1909, the newly-degreed Dr. Gilbert left his medical career to pursue his magic business—and business was good. In his promotional travels across America, Gilbert began selling to toy store buyers and soon realized the need for quality American-made toys. Deep in thought, he went home, and the result was the birth of the Erector set.

The origin of the first Erector set is the stuff of debate and myth, and even Gilbert told several versions of it during his life. What is fact is that Petrie was not impressed with Gilbert's new toy idea, and this eventually led Gilbert to buy out Petrie's interest in the Mysto Manufacturing Company.

Gilbert showed his new Mysto-Erector toy at the 1913 Toy Fair and retail orders poured in, threatening to swamp his new company. Gilbert rolled out a major national promotion for his new line, including an ingenious model building contest that provided him hundreds of new and free model configurations he promoted in future instruction manuals.

The 1913 holiday sales season was a resounding success, and Gilbert turned his sights on refining and improving the product line, upgrading the girders and providing factory-assembled motors for the 1914 kits. He also continued the model building contests with huge success, offering real cars as prizes, and those new model ideas were incorporated into instruction manuals.

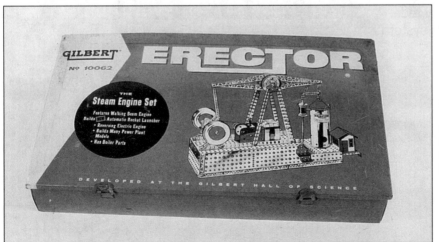

Also from 1958, the "Steam Engine Set" featured boiler parts but also build a rocket launcher. Mint value, $190.

A new plant in 1915 allowed Gilbert to expand the line into better motors for his Erector sets, tin toys and electric fans to fill the off-season work void.

In 1916, Gilbert renamed his firm The A.C. Gilbert Company, but kept the Mysto name for his magic sets. He also created the Gilbert Engineering Institute for Boys, a national club which became a highly successful promotional tool.

In 1917, World War I threatened to sideline the entire toy industry. Gilbert was called by the fledgling Toy Manufacturers Association, which he helped create, to lobby Congress for permission for the toy industry to continue making toys. Armed with his own toys, Gilbert triumphed and was hailed nationwide as the "Man Who Saved Christmas."

Gilbert introduced his now-famous chemistry sets in 1917 and proceeded to dramatically expand the Gilbert line in the years to come, introducing tool chests, a line of power tools and books.

It was a year of great change in 1920, with a near total overhaul of the Gilbert lines and the introduction of a series of more advanced scientific, mechanical and radio sets. That year also saw the introduction of the No. 10 Deluxe Erector sets, now by far the most highly desirable of all Gilbert construction sets.

A true overhaul came in 1924, when Gilbert introduced the new Erector line. He completely redesigned the Erector system

with thinner girders and debuted curved girders and numerous other advancements. The 1924 line also saw streamlining across all other divisions, with many toys dropped from production.

In 1927, Gilbert expanded his control over the construction toy market by buying Trumodel, a line of high quality toys that were redesigned and rolled into his deluxe Erector sets.

Gilbert's promotional activities took another turn in 1929 when he entered into a number of exclusive contracts with Sears, Macy's, J.C. Penney and other national retailers. Each company was allowed to market low-end Gilbert products, but not under the Erector name. They were sold under the names Trumodel, Steel-Tech and Little Jim among others, with each retailer having a different line. These sets have since become collectible in their own right.

Also in 1929, Gilbert essentially monopolized the American construction toy market by acquiring his chief rival, Meccano. For 1930, the Erector and Meccano lines were partially merged in the New American Meccano line, now commonly called Erector-Meccano.

The Great Depression finally hit the Gilbert company, but not before the Erector series hit its all-time pinnacle with the

A much newer set from the 1990s, still using metal parts. Mint value, about $10.

Erector Hudson Locomotive model, which was included in the top-of-the-line sets. In 1931, Gilbert's most expansive No. 10 set was produced. In addition to containing parts to build all models from lower numbered sets (which included the White Truck model, the Steam Shovel, and the Zeppelin), it also included parts for both the Hudson Locomotive and its tender. Gilbert would never offer an Erector set this grand again.

The Depression forced major downsizing at Gilbert, but the company would survive. The Erector line was acquired by Gabriel Industries in 1967. As previously noted, the Erector line has been revived with resounding success.

Trends

While still a relatively small subset of the toy collecting field, construction set collecting, particularly of Erector and Meccano products, is enjoying moderate and steady growth. Original Gilbert sets command the highest premiums, particularly the earliest ones bearing the company's previous Mysto Manufacturing name.

Not all collecting fields have their day in the sun, but this one, rich as it is in history and variety, presents a strong case for higher visibility.

Note: All sets listed are made by The A.C. Gilbert Company. Collectors tend to identify sets by number and year, rather than name; in this book, sets are listed by set number, then by year.

Erector sets are rarely found in Mint condition, especially with all the pieces and the box intact. This section lists two grades for sets collectors may likely find—Good and Excellent. Sets that have been refurbished and reassembled as a whole may be found and can command a price 40 to 75 percent higher than a similar, unrefurbished set.

Values given are averages for the time period noted. As a general rule, older sets are worth more than newer ones; larger sets are worth more than smaller.

ERECTOR JUNIOR

❏ **Erector Junior #1,** 1943-47, A.C. Gilbert, cardboard box
EX $40　　NM $115　　MIP n/a

❏ **Erector Junior #3,** 1943-47, A.C. Gilbert, cardboard box
EX $70　　NM $185　　MIP n/a

❏ **Erector Junior #5,** 1943-47, A.C. Gilbert, cardboard box
EX $100　　NM $225　　MIP n/a

JUNIOR ERECTOR

❏ **Junior Erector #10,** 1949-55, A.C. Gilbert, cardboard box
EX $85　　NM $225　　MIP n/a

❏ **Junior Erector #2,** 1949-55, A.C. Gilbert, cardboard box
EX $30　　NM $75　　MIP n/a

❏ **Junior Erector #4,** 1949-55, A.C. Gilbert, cardboard box
EX $45　　NM $100　　MIP n/a

POST 1957 SETS

❏ 1958, A.C. Gilbert, metal box, Model No. 10052
EX $55　　NM $95　　MIP n/a

❏ 1958, A.C. Gilbert, metal box, Model No. 10072
EX $185　　NM $290　　MIP n/a

❏ 1958, A.C. Gilbert, metal box, Model No. 10092
EX $785　　NM $1260　　MIP n/a

❏ 1958, A.C. Gilbert, metal box, Model No. 10082
EX $315　　NM $525　　MIP n/a

❏ 1958, A.C. Gilbert, metal box, Model No. 10062
EX $77　　NM $145　　MIP n/a

❏ 1958, A.C. Gilbert, metal box, Model No. 10041
EX $45　　NM $85　　MIP n/a

❏ 1958, A.C. Gilbert, cardboard box, Model No. 10026
EX $45　　NM $85　　MIP n/a

❏ 1958, A.C. Gilbert, cardboard box, Model No. 10031
EX $65　　NM $105　　MIP n/a

❏ 1958-61, A.C. Gilbert, cardboard tube box, Model No. 10011
EX $45　　NM $70　　MIP n/a

❏ 1958-61, A.C. Gilbert, cardboard tube box, Model No. 10021
EX $55　　NM $95　　MIP n/a

❏ 1959, A.C. Gilbert, metal box, Model No. 10083
EX $315　　NM $525　　MIP n/a

❏ 1959, A.C. Gilbert, metal box, Model No. 10073
EX $185　　NM $290　　MIP n/a

❏ 1959, A.C. Gilbert, metal box, Model No. 10093
EX $735　　NM $1265　　MIP n/a

❏ 1959-61, A.C. Gilbert, cardboard tube box, Model No. 10032
EX $70　　NM $115　　MIP n/a

❏ 1959-61, A.C. Gilbert, metal box, Model No. 10042
EX $45　　NM $85　　MIP n/a

❏ 1959-61, A.C. Gilbert, metal box, Model No. 10063
EX $80　　NM $150　　MIP n/a

❏ 1960, A.C. Gilbert, cardboard tube box, Model No. 10037
EX $135　　NM $210　　MIP n/a

❏ 1960-61, A.C. Gilbert, tube box, Model No. 18030
EX $80　　NM $115　　MIP n/a

❏ 1960-61, A.C. Gilbert, tube box, Model No. 18040
EX $105　　NM $150　　MIP n/a

❏ 1960-61, A.C. Gilbert, tube box, Model No. 18020
EX $65　　NM $95　　MIP n/a

❏ 1960-61, A.C. Gilbert, metal box, Model No. 10084
EX $160　　NM $295　　MIP n/a

❏ 1960-61, A.C. Gilbert, metal box, Model No. 10074
EX $85　　NM $150　　MIP n/a

❏ 1960-61, A.C. Gilbert, tube box, Model No. 18010
EX $55　　NM $80　　MIP n/a

❏ 1960-62, A.C. Gilbert, metal box, Model No. 10094
EX $420　　NM $685　　MIP n/a

❏ 1962, A.C. Gilbert, metal box, Model No. 10221
EX $100　　NM $185　　MIP n/a

❏ 1962, A.C. Gilbert, metal box, Model No. 10211
EX $85　　NM $160　　MIP n/a

❏ 1962, A.C. Gilbert, metal box, Model No. 10231
EX $210　　NM $315　　MIP n/a

❏ 1962, A.C. Gilbert, metal box, Model No. 10201
EX $60　　NM $95　　MIP n/a

❏ 1962-63, A.C. Gilbert, carton box, Model No. 10161
EX $55　　NM $85　　MIP n/a

❏ 1962-63, A.C. Gilbert, carton box, Model No. 10171
EX $65　　NM $105　　MIP n/a

❏ 1962-63, A.C. Gilbert, metal box, Model No. 10181
EX $50　　NM $80　　MIP n/a

❏ 1963-64, A.C. Gilbert, metal box, Model No. 10129
EX $210　　NM $315　　MIP n/a

❏ 1963-64, A.C. Gilbert, metal box, Model No. 10128
EX $120　　NM $160　　MIP n/a

❏ 1963-64, A.C. Gilbert, metal box, Model No. 10127
EX $95　　NM $135　　MIP n/a

❏ 1964, A.C. Gilbert, cardboard box, Model No. 10251
EX $22　　NM $35　　MIP n/a

❏ 1964, A.C. Gilbert, cardboard box, Model No. 10252
EX $30　　NM $40　　MIP n/a

❏ 1964, A.C. Gilbert, cardboard box, Model No. 10253
EX $35　　NM $45　　MIP n/a

❏ 1964, A.C. Gilbert, cardboard box, Model No. 10254
EX $40　　NM $55　　MIP n/a

❏ 1965-66, A.C. Gilbert, cardboard box, Model No. 10351
EX $22　　NM $35　　MIP n/a

❏ 1965-66, A.C. Gilbert, cardboard box, Model No. 10352
EX $30　　NM $40　　MIP n/a

❏ 1965-66, A.C. Gilbert, cardboard box, Model No. 10353
EX $35　　NM $45　　MIP n/a

❏ 1965-66, A.C. Gilbert, cardboard box, Model No. 10354
EX $45　　NM $55　　MIP n/a

❏ 1965-66, A.C. Gilbert, cardboard box, Model No. 10601
EX $115　　NM $210　　MIP n/a

❏ 1966, A.C. Gilbert, cardboard box, Model No. 10606
EX $180　　NM $265　　MIP n/a

SET #0

❏ 1913, A.C. Gilbert, cardboard box
EX $80　　NM $130　　MIP n/a

❏ 1914, A.C. Gilbert, cardboard box
EX $60　　NM $100　　MIP n/a

❏ **Toy Builder,** 1915, A.C. Gilbert, cardboard box
EX $120　　NM $290　　MIP n/a

SET #1

❏ 1913, A.C. Gilbert, cardboard box
EX $105　　NM $210　　MIP n/a

❏ 1914-34, A.C. Gilbert, cardboard box
EX $80　　NM $130　　MIP n/a

❏ 1945, A.C. Gilbert, cardboard box
EX $80　　NM $130　　MIP n/a

SET #10

❏ 1920-26, A.C. Gilbert, wood box
EX $4610　　NM $7875　　MIP n/a

❏ **Complete Erector in All Its Glory,** 1929-31, A.C. Gilbert, oak box
EX $4610　　NM $7875　　MIP n/a

❏ **Erector Deluxe In All Its Glory,** 1927, A.C. Gilbert, eight drawer oak chest box
EX $4610　　NM $7875　　MIP n/a

❏ **The Complete Deluxe Set,** 1928, A.C. Gilbert, nine-drawer oak chest box
EX $4610　　NM $7875　　MIP n/a

SET #10-1/2

- 1936-42, A.C. Gilbert, metal box
  EX $315   NM $470   MIP n/a

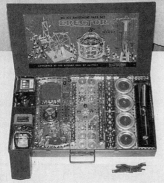

(Restored by William S Harrison)

- 1949-57, A.C. Gilbert, metal box
  EX $235   NM $395   MIP n/a

SET #1-1/2

- 1935-42, A.C. Gilbert, cardboard box
  EX $40   NM $55   MIP n/a
- 1950-56, A.C. Gilbert, cardboard box
  EX $40   NM $55   MIP n/a

SET #12-1/2

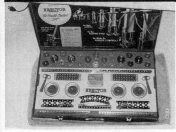

(Restored by William S Harrison III)

- 1948-50, A.C. Gilbert, metal box
  EX $735   NM $1365   MIP n/a
- 1956-57, A.C. Gilbert, metal box
  EX $735   NM $1365   MIP n/a

SET #2

- 1913, A.C. Gilbert, cardboard box
  EX $110   NM $220   MIP n/a
- 1914-21, A.C. Gilbert, cardboard box
  EX $75   NM $115   MIP n/a

SET #2-1/2

- 1936-42, A.C. Gilbert, cardboard box
  EX $45   NM $65   MIP n/a
- 1946-56, A.C. Gilbert, cardboard box
  EX $45   NM $65   MIP n/a

SET #3

- 1913, A.C. Gilbert, cardboard box
  EX $195   NM $315   MIP n/a
- 1914-34, A.C. Gilbert, cardboard box
  EX $95   NM $155   MIP n/a

- 1945, A.C. Gilbert, cardboard box
  EX $95   NM $155   MIP n/a

SET #3-1/2

- 1935, A.C. Gilbert, cardboard box
  EX $125   NM $165   MIP n/a
- 1936-42, A.C. Gilbert, cardboard box
  EX $65   NM $85   MIP n/a

SET #4

- 1913, A.C. Gilbert, cardboard box
  EX $220   NM $420   MIP n/a
- 1914, A.C. Gilbert, cardboard box
  EX $130   NM $210   MIP n/a
- 1915, A.C. Gilbert, wood box
  EX $130   NM $210   MIP n/a
- 1916-34, A.C. Gilbert, cardboard box
  EX $130   NM $210   MIP n/a
- 1945, A.C. Gilbert, metal box
  EX $105   NM $185   MIP n/a

SET #4-1/2

- 1935, A.C. Gilbert, metal box
  EX $140   NM $235   MIP n/a
- 1936-42, A.C. Gilbert, cardboard box
  EX $50   NM $85   MIP n/a
- 1946-57, A.C. Gilbert, metal box
  EX $140   NM $235   MIP n/a

SET #5

- 1913, A.C. Gilbert, cardboard box
  EX $220   NM $525   MIP n/a
- 1914, A.C. Gilbert, cardboard box
  EX $180   NM $290   MIP n/a
- 1915, A.C. Gilbert, wood box
  EX $145   NM $265   MIP n/a
- 1916, A.C. Gilbert, cardboard box
  EX $145   NM $265   MIP n/a
- **Meccano Super Power Outfit,** 1930,
  A.C. Gilbert, cardboard box
  EX $120   NM $290   MIP n/a
- **The Erector Machinery Outfit,** 1923,
  A.C. Gilbert, wood box
  EX $550   NM $895   MIP n/a

SET #5-1/2

- 1936-38, A.C. Gilbert, metal box
  EX $95   NM $140   MIP n/a

SET #6

- 1913, A.C. Gilbert
  EX $630   NM $840   MIP n/a
- 1914, A.C. Gilbert, wood box
  EX $185   NM $290   MIP n/a
- 1915-16, A.C. Gilbert, wood box
  EX $155   NM $260   MIP n/a
- 1920, A.C. Gilbert, wood box
  EX $155   NM $260   MIP n/a
- 1921, A.C. Gilbert, wood box
  EX $155   NM $260   MIP n/a

- 1945, A.C. Gilbert, metal box
  EX $190   NM $260   MIP n/a
- **The Wonderful No. 6 Erector,** 1931,
  A.C. Gilbert, cardboard box
  EX $100   NM $260   MIP n/a

SET #6-1/2

- 1935-42, A.C. Gilbert, metal, not made
  in 1936 or 1937 box
  EX $50   NM $95   MIP n/a
- 1946-57, A.C. Gilbert, metal box
  EX $50   NM $95   MIP n/a

SET #7

- 1913, A.C. Gilbert, wood box
  EX $315   NM $470   MIP n/a
- 1914-32, A.C. Gilbert, wood box
  EX $160   NM $260   MIP n/a
- 1933-34, A.C. Gilbert, metal box
  EX $160   NM $260   MIP n/a
- 1945, A.C. Gilbert, metal box
  EX $210   NM $315   MIP n/a

SET #7-1/2

- 1934-37, A.C. Gilbert, metal box
  EX $90   NM $155   MIP n/a

(Restored by William S Harrison III)

- 1938-57, A.C. Gilbert, metal box
  EX $75   NM $130   MIP n/a
- **Builds the Chassis,** 1928-32, Gilbert,
  wood box
  EX $260   NM $420   MIP n/a
- **Motorized Erector,** 1914, Gilbert, wood
  box
  EX $655   NM $1575   MIP n/a

SET #8

- 1913, A.C. Gilbert, wood box
  EX $575   NM $945   MIP n/a
- 1914-31, A.C. Gilbert, wood box
  EX $575   NM $945   MIP n/a
- 1933-34, A.C. Gilbert, metal box
  EX $575   NM $945   MIP n/a
- 1945, A.C. Gilbert, metal box
  EX $260   NM $350   MIP n/a

SET #8-1/2

- 1931-32, A.C. Gilbert, wood box
  EX $1900   NM $3150   MIP n/a
- 1933, A.C. Gilbert, metal box
  EX $190   NM $240   MIP n/a

(Restoration by William S Harrison III)

❑ 1935-57, A.C. Gilbert, metal box
EX $105 **NM** $180 **MIP** n/a

SET #9

❑ 1945, A.C. Gilbert, metal box
EX $210 **NM** $315 **MIP** n/a

❑ **Mechanical Wonders Set with 110 Volt Motor,** 1929-32, A.C. Gilbert, wood box
EX $2650 **NM** $4610 **MIP** n/a

SET #9-1/2

❑ 1935, A.C. Gilbert, metal box
EX $290 **NM** $390 **MIP** n/a

(Restored by William S Harrison)

❑ 1936-49, A.C. Gilbert, metal box
EX $210 **NM** $315 **MIP** n/a

Fisher Price Toys

The Nifty Station Wagon is a[n] excellent example of a "Little People" vehicle. The first versions of these wooden peg-li[ke] figures were fairly primitive ev[en] compared with later (and still wooden) models. Mint value, $375.

The familiar sturdy wood toys with paper lithography made by Fisher-Price are colorful remnants of how toys used to be made. Collectors especially value their quality and nostalgia.

While the rest of the world suffered through the Depression, Fisher-Price set up shop in 1930 in East Aurora, N.Y. Founded by Herman Fisher, Irving Price and Helen Schelle, the company hoped to bring toys of matchless charm and inherent quality to children.

Sixteen toys were introduced in 1931, the first production year, including Granny Doodle and Doctor Doodle, a pair of charming ducks.

Most collectors are familiar with the look of vintage Fisher-Price. Early toys featured unique, colorful, crisp paper lithography on wood. Finding such charm today is as rare as some of the early toys.

It didn't take long for Fisher-Price to realize the value of licensing. In 1935, the company issued the Walt Disney Mickey Mouse Band, featuring Mickey and Pluto. That piece alone can command around $2,000 in Mint in Box condition. Other Disney characters and Popeye also became popular Fisher-Price toys.

Musical toys, especially items featuring bells or xylophones, became perennial favorites.

By the late 1950s, plastic was beginning to appear as accents on toys, but by the late 1960s, most of the toys' bodies were made entirely of plastic.

The common Fisher-Price Play Family Little People appeared as early as 1959 in a yellow wooden Safety School Bus. Made of wood, they could be removed from their vehicles. Their body shapes and compositions have changed throughout the years. Today the Little People are about three times the size of the originals and are made of plastic.

Today, Fisher-Price is a subsidiary of toy giant Mattel. The company continues to make Little People play sets in a variety of themes, but has expanded its line to include outdoor playground and riding

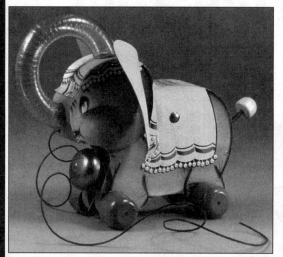

The Juggling Jumbo puts a more modern spin on old-fashioned pull toys: Jumbo's clear plastic trunk shoots around plastic balls, and the bell rings as he is pulled across the floor. Mint value, $425.

toys, apparel and books.

Trends

Collecting vintage Fisher-Price, especially pre-1950s pieces, can be costly, since it is difficult to find older pieces in premium condition. Many 1930s-1940s wooden toys can command $400-$2,000 or more in Mint in Box condition.

But collectors shouldn't pass on more modern, plastic Fisher-Price toys. Many toys from the 1960s and later are gaining

Fuzzy Fido is a great example of a fun, playful prewar Fisher-Price toy. It's simply a pull-toy, but its charming graphics make it irresistible to kids and collectors. Mint value, $550.

favor with younger collectors, especially Little People play sets and musical radios, clocks, and televisions. Adventure play sets featuring articulated figures and realistic vehicles and accessories will probably become even more popular in the next few years as crossover collecting from action figures takes hold. The musical toys are still fairly easy to find and can

A well-known early Disney-licensed toy, Donald and his Nephews is still a hot item for Fisher-Price and Donald Duck fans. However, its mint price could be a bit out of reach for some, at $1400.

range from $5-$30 in general.

Some of the more common and easy-to-find toys include the Chatter Telephone, Pull-a-Tune Xylophone, Corn Popper and numerous bees and Snoopy dogs. Because of their inherent play value and lengthy history, many were and still are used as toys and are often found in less than Mint condition.

Editor's Note: Many Fisher-Price toys had several variations, which often means several different values. Also, the date found on the toy may only be a copyright date, which may be earlier than the actual date of manufacture.

PLASTIC

ADVENTURE SETS

❏ **Aero-Marine Search Team,** 1979, Fisher-Price, Model No. 323
EX $40 **NM** $50 **MIP** $60

❏ **Alpha Probe,** 1980, Fisher-Price, Model No. 325
EX $40 **NM** $50 **MIP** $60

❏ **Alpha Star,** 1983, Fisher-Price, Model No. 326
EX $40 **NM** $50 **MIP** $60

❏ **Construction Workers,** 1976, Fisher-Price, Model No. 352
EX $30 **NM** $40 **MIP** $50

❏ **Cycle Racing Team,** 1977, Fisher-Price, Model No. 356
EX $20 **NM** $25 **MIP** $30

❏ **Dare Devil Sport Van,** 1978, Fisher-Price, Model No. 318
EX $40 **NM** $50 **MIP** $60

❏ **Daredevil Skydiver,** 1977, Fisher-Price, Model No. 354
EX $10 **NM** $15 **MIP** $20

❏ **Deep Sea Diver,** 1980, Fisher-Price, Model No. 358
EX $20 **NM** $30 **MIP** $40

❏ **Dune Buster,** 1979, Fisher-Price, Model No. 322
EX $30 **NM** $40 **MIP** $50

❏ **Firestar 1,** 1980, Fisher-Price, Model No. 357
EX $20 **NM** $25 **MIP** $30

❏ **Motocross Team,** 1983, Fisher-Price, Model No. 335
EX $40 **NM** $50 **MIP** $60

❏ **Mountain Climbers,** 1976, Fisher-Price, Model No. 351
EX $40 **NM** $50 **MIP** $60

❏ **Northwoods Trailblazer,** 1977, Fisher-Price, Model No. 312
EX $25 **NM** $30 **MIP** $40

❏ **Rescue Copter,** 1975, Fisher-Price, Model No. 305
EX $20 **NM** $25 **MIP** $30

❏ **Rescue Team,** 1976, Fisher-Price, Model No. 350
EX $15 **NM** $20 **MIP** $30

❏ **Rescue Truck,** 1975, Fisher-Price, Model No. 303
EX $25 **NM** $30 **MIP** $40

❏ **Safari,** 1975, Fisher-Price, Model No. 304
EX $60 **NM** $65 **MIP** $70

❏ **Scuba Divers,** 1976, Fisher-Price, Model No. 353
EX $20 **NM** $25 **MIP** $30

❏ **Sea Explorer,** 1977, Fisher-Price, Model No. 310
EX $40 **NM** $50 **MIP** $60

❏ **Sea Shark,** 1981, Fisher-Price, Model No. 334
EX $40 **NM** $50 **MIP** $60

❏ **Sport Plane,** 1975, Fisher-Price, Model No. 306
EX $20 **NM** $25 **MIP** $30

❏ **Super Speed Racer,** 1976, Fisher-Price, Model No. 308
EX $20 **NM** $25 **MIP** $30

❏ **T.V. Action Team,** 1977, Fisher-Price, Model No. 309
EX $60 **NM** $70 **MIP** $80

❏ **Wheelie Dragster,** 1981, Fisher-Price, Model No. 333
EX $15 **NM** $20 **MIP** $30

❏ **White Water Kayak,** 1977, Fisher-Price, Model No. 355
EX $20 **NM** $25 **MIP** $30

❏ **Wilderness Patrol,** 1976, Fisher-Price, Model No. 307
EX $50 **NM** $60 **MIP** $70

HUSKY PLAY SETS

❏ **Bulldozer,** 1980, Fisher-Price, Model No. 329
EX $10 **NM** $12 **MIP** $15

❏ **Farm Set,** 1981, Fisher-Price, Model No. 331
EX $15 **NM** $20 **MIP** $30

❏ **Fire Pumper,** 1983, Fisher-Price, Model No. 336
EX $10 **NM** $20 **MIP** $30

❏ **Firefighters,** 1979, Fisher-Price, Model No. 321
EX $20 **NM** $30 **MIP** $35

❏ **Highway Dump Truck,** 1980, Fisher-Price, Model No. 328
EX $20 **NM** $25 **MIP** $30

❏ **Hook & Ladder,** 1979, Fisher-Price, Model No. 319
EX $20 **NM** $25 **MIP** $30

❏ **Load Master Dump,** 1984, Fisher-Price, Model No. 327
EX $10 **NM** $15 **MIP** $20

❏ **Police Patrol Squad,** 1981, Fisher-Price, Model No. 332
EX $10 **NM** $15 **MIP** $20

❏ **Power & Light Service Rig,** 1983, Fisher-Price, Model No. 339
EX $20 **NM** $25 **MIP** $35

❏ **Power Tow Truck,** 1982, Fisher-Price, Model No. 338
EX $15 **NM** $20 **MIP** $30

❏ **Race Car Rig,** 1979, Fisher-Price, Model No. 320
EX $15 **NM** $20 **MIP** $30

❏ **Rescue Rig,** 1982, Fisher-Price, Model No. 337
EX $10 **NM** $15 **MIP** $20

❏ **Rodeo Rig,** 1980, Fisher-Price, Model No. 330
EX $10 **NM** $15 **MIP** $20

LITTLE PEOPLE

❏ **3-Car Circus Train,** 1979, Fisher-Price, three-car train, engine w/silver imprinted headlight, green or blue cage car w/lion litho, red caboose, light blue engineer, short ringmaster, and a red clown w/pointed yellow hat, Model No. 991
EX $25 **NM** $40 **MIP** $65

❏ **4-Car Circus Train,** 1973, Fisher-Price, four-car train, engine w/paper headlight litho, blue or green car w/giraffe litho, blue or green flat car w/lion litho, red caboose, elephant, monkey, lion, giraffe, tan bear, short, light blue engineer, red clown w/pointed yellow hat, and a short ringmaster, Model No. 991
EX $25 **NM** $40 **MIP** $60

❏ **A-Frame,** 1973, Fisher-Price, A-frame house w/removable door and sidewalk, three-rung white ladder, two sets of yellow bunk beds, two yellow lounge chairs, grill, two white picnic benches, white table w/steak litho, two yellow captain chairs, four-seat jeep, dad, mom, boy, girl and Lucky the dog, Model No. 990
EX $35 **NM** $50 **MIP** $80

❏ **Airport,** 1972, Fisher-Price, large fold out airport base, white/turquoise jet, orange/yellow helicopter, four-car tram front car, two luggage cars, fuel car, two white/green two seat cars w/luggage rack, two green hat boxes, two yellow pieces of luggage, cardboard hanger parts box, dad, mom, boy, girl, stewardess, African-American pilot w/turquoise base, Model No. 996
EX $35 **NM** $50 **MIP** $90

❏ **Airport,** 1986, Fisher-Price, airport building, blue and yellow copter, large blue and yellow plane, four captain chairs, two orange coffee tables, green and white two-seat car w/luggage rack, one brown and one blue suitcase, three-car tram, tan bald man, short light blue blond stewardess, short pilot, mom, boy and girl, Model No. 2502
EX $15 **NM** $25 **MIP** $45

❏ **Airport Crew,** Fisher-Price, green pilot, black pilot w/blue body, and a tall light blue stewardess, Model No. 678
EX $4 **NM** $7 **MIP** $15

❏ **Amusement Park,** 1963, Fisher-Price, large vinyl mat, tunnel/bridge, four-chair swing ride, single-seat swing ride, merry-go-round, four-piece train, two small single-seat cars (no holes for gas), two small single-seat boats, two small boats, straight-sided Little People including two blue boys, two mauve girls, two green boys and a black dog w/yellow or white ears, Model No. 932
EX $175 **NM** $250 **MIP** $425

❏ **Bath and Utility Sets,** 1972, Fisher-Price, toilet, sink, tub, captains chair, sewing machine, washer, dryer, all wooded family consisting of a dad, mom, boy and a girl; many color variations exist, Model No. 725
EX $12 **NM** $35 **MIP** $60

❑ **Beauty Salon,** 1990, Fisher-Price, small beauty salon connects w/No. 2454 and No. 2455; set comes w/one pink and white car w/a luggage rack and a girl, Model No. 2453
EX $7   **NM** $12   **MIP** $25

❑ **Boat Hauler,** 1981, Fisher-Price, blue and white truck and trailer w/snap on gray boat holder, blue and white speed-boat, one man w/white body and blue ca and one dark blue worker, Model No. 345
EX $5   **NM** $12   **MIP** $25

❑ **Brown Roof House,** 1980, Fisher-Price, fold-open house w/a garage, green and white car, one double bed, two twin beds, four captain chairs, one round table, two lounge chairs, one coffee table, dad, mom, boy, girl, and Lucky the dog, Model No. 952
EX $25   **NM** $35   **MIP** $45

❑ **Car and Camper,** 1979, Fisher-Price, white and red four-seat SUV, white and red pop-up camper w/yellow canvas tent inside, yellow clam carrier w/litho on top, green and yellow boat that sits on top of jeep, two green lounge chairs, grill, green table w/steak litho, motorcycle, dad, mom, boy and girl, Model No. 992
EX $25   **NM** $40   **MIP** $60

❑ **Castle,** 1975, Fisher-Price, castle w/attached flag, pink dragon, oone brown and one black horse, white or yellow horse armor, white or yellow scalloped horse harness, castle coach, two short red or yellow thrones, two tall red or yellow thrones, two red or yellow twin beds w/crown headboard, one red or yellow double bed w/crwon headboard, one red or yellow round table w/medievil-style litho, plastic knight, woodsman, king, queen, prince, princess and a cardboard parts box; reissued in 1987 w/no flag and all plastic people, Model No. 993
EX $90   **NM** $125   **MIP** $200

❑ **Change-a-Tune Carousel,** 1981, Fisher-Price, three records labeled A-B-C, two boys and a girl, Model No. 170
EX $25   **NM** $35   **MIP** $55

❑ **Choo-Choo Train,** 1963, Fisher-Price, small wood and plastic train engine w/three, three straight-sided Little People and a Lucky the dog, Model No. 719
EX $25   **NM** $35   **MIP** $60

❑ **Circus Clowns,** 1984, Fisher-Price, threee different clowns, on card, Model No. 675
EX $4   **NM** $7   **MIP** $15

❑ **Copter,** 1981, Fisher-Price, green and white truck and trailer w/gray snap-on compass, gold one-seat helicopter, one tall blue pilot and one worker w/tan base, Model No. 344
EX $5   **NM** $12   **MIP** $25

❑ **Crazy Clown Brigade,** 1983, Fisher-Price, large clown car, two white crooked hoses, two white crooked ladders, white hose reel, and small green bathtub w/wheels, clown feet, tall blue clown w/white or yellow tie, and a short

black clown w/a red fireman hat, Model No. 657
EX $35   **NM** $50   **MIP** $80

❑ **Cruise boat,** 1988, Fisher-Price, S.S. Tadpole, small ship, one-piece chair w/fishing pole, one yellow life preserver, short blue sea captain w/white beard, blond boy w/green base boy, Model No. 2524
EX $15   **NM** $25   **MIP** $35

❑ **Decorator Set,** 1970, Fisher-Price, double bed, two twin beds, T.V., checkerboard litho round table, two stuffed chairs, coffee table, all wooden family consisting of a dad, mom, boy and a girl; many color variations exist, Model No. 728
EX $13   **NM** $35   **MIP** $60

❑ **Drive In Movie,** 1990, Fisher-Price, small drive in movie building w/movie screen connects w/No. 2453 and No. 2455; set comes w/one white and yellow car w/a luggage rack and a boy, Model No. 2454
EX $7   **NM** $12   **MIP** $25

❑ **Dump Truckers,** 1965, Fisher-Price, dumping station w/three slots for trucks, three trucks of different shape and color, three balls in wood or plastic, three light or dark blue straight-sided boys (one smiling, one frowning, and one w/freckles), Model No. 979
EX $45   **NM** $70   **MIP** $120

❑ **Express Train,** 1987, Fisher-Price, three-car train, flat car, caboose, solid yellow one-seat car w/luggage rack, one yellow and one blue suitcase, dad, mom, light blue engineer and Lucky the dog, Model No. 2581
EX $10   **NM** $17   **MIP** $25

❑ **Farm,** 1986, Fisher-Price, barn base w/mooing door, silo, four pieces of fence, tractor, cart, white harness, white trough, red chicken, white chicken, horse, cow, pig, jointed dog, sheep, dad w/cowboy hat, mom, boy w/cowboy hat and a girl, Model No. 2501
EX $17   **NM** $25   **MIP** $45

❑ **Farm family on card,** 1984, Fisher-Price, dark red woman w/blond hair, tall green dad w/white hat and yellow scarf, and a blue girl w/blond hair, Model No. 677
EX $4   **NM** $7   **MIP** $15

❑ **Ferris Wheel,** 1966, Fisher-Price, ferris wheel base winds up plays music, three Little People and Lucky the dog; first year versions come w/straight-sided Little People, Model No. 969
EX $25   **NM** $45   **MIP** $80
(Sean and Debbie Craig)

❑ **Ferry Boat,** 1979, Fisher-Price, w/pull string and wheels, white and blue speed boat, two yellow life preservers, two two-seat cars, orange and black man w/o mustache, blue mom w/blond hair, tall blue captain, Model No. 932
EX $45   **NM** $60   **MIP** $100

❑ **Fire Engine,** Fisher-Price, large red and white truck w/cherry picker and attached yellow hose, red fire hydrant,

two firemen and one dalmatian, Model No. 2361
EX $7   **NM** $12   **MIP** $25

❑ **Fire Engine,** 1969, Fisher-Price, wooden truck and a fireman, Model No. 720
EX $7   **NM** $13   **MIP** $30

❑ **Fire Station,** 1979, Fisher-Price, fire house building, gray fire training tower, two yellow connecting ladders, two barricades, ambulance, fire truck w/ladder, fire chief car, two yellow truck braces, two black connecting fire hoses, two black rubber hoses, two yellow truck braces, three fireman and one dalmatian dog, Model No. 928
EX $45   **NM** $60   **MIP** $80

❑ **Fire Truck Rig,** 1983, Fisher-Price, long red fire engine w/two yellow braces, w/two firemen, Model No. 346
EX $5   **NM** $12   **MIP** $25

❑ **Floating Marina,** 1988, Fisher-Price, floating marina building w/two boats slips, orange seaplane, one yellow life preserver, detachable clear lighthouse dome, orange boat, red and white boat w/steering wheel, short blue captain w/white beard, boy and girl, Model No. 2582
EX $10   **NM** $17   **MIP** $25

❑ **Fun Jet,** 1970, Fisher-Price, plane w/red wings and tail, one green and one yellow suitcase, w/dad, mom, boy and a girl, Model No. 183
EX $5   **NM** $12   **MIP** $20

❑ **Fun Jet,** 1981, Fisher-Price, Green/white yellow plane, one brown and one blue suitcase, w/dad, mom, boy, and a girl, Model No. 182
EX $12   **NM** $18   **MIP** $25

❑ **Garage,** 1970, Fisher-Price, two-story building, elevator and car ramps, car grease rack, four single-seat cars in red, blue, green, yellow, and three little boys and one little girl, Model No. 930
EX $20   **NM** $25   **MIP** $30

❑ **Garage,** 1986, Fisher-Price, two-story building, elevator and car ramps, fire hydrant, pay phone, gas pump, three single-seat cars, and three little boys and one little girl, Model No. 2504
EX $15   **NM** $25   **MIP** $45

❑ **Garage Squad,** Fisher-Price, three workers, Model No. 679
EX $4   **NM** $7   **MIP** $15

❑ **Gas Station,** 1990, Fisher-Price, small gas station building connects w/No. 2453 and No. 2454; set comes w/one red and white car w/a luggage rack and a boy, Model No. 2455
EX $7   **NM** $12   **MIP** $25

❑ **Goldilocks,** 1967, Fisher-Price, playhouse w/yellow key attached, w/mama bear, papa bear, baby bear, and blue girl w/blond braids, Model No. 151
EX $35   **NM** $45   **MIP** $75

❑ **Happy Hoppers,** 1969, Fisher-Price, push toy playset w/three Little People that pop up and down as toy is pushed;

value may fluctuate depending on version of Little People, Model No. 121
EX $15   **NM** $25   **MIP** $40

❑ **Hospital,** 1976, Fisher-Price, building w/fold down door and elevator and white ambulance, turquoise plastic pieces include stretcher, x-ray, scale, two chairs, two beds, large sink, baby cradle; white plastic pieces include wheelchair, operating table, privacy screen; white baby without bib, white nurse w/white mask, doctor, African-American doctor, dad, mom and girl, Model No. 931
EX $65   **NM** $85   **MIP** $125
(Sean and Debbie Craig)

❑ **House,** 1969, Fisher-Price, fold-open house w/yellow roof and attached garage, car w/hook, one double bed, two twin beds, four captain chairs, one round table, two lounge chairs, one coffee table, yellow stairs w/closet and litho, blue cardboard moving van parts box, dad, mom, boy, girl and Lucky the dog; complete w/moving van add $100-200 to total value, Model No. 952
EX $25   **NM** $35   **MIP** $55

❑ **Houseboat,** 1972, Fisher-Price, blue base boat w/wheels and fold open lid, two yellow lounge chairs, two yellow life preservers, two red captain chairs, red lobster litho table, yellow grill, white/blue speedboat, white-bodied dad w/blue hat, mom, boy, girl and Lucky the dog, Model No. 985
EX $25   **NM** $40   **MIP** $65

❑ **Indy Race Rig,** 1983, Fisher-Price, yellow and white truck w/trailer, red Indy-type racecar, w/dad engineer and a driver w/a black body and helmet, Model No. 347
EX $5   **NM** $12   **MIP** $25

❑ **Jetliner,** 1986, Fisher-Price, large yellow and blue plane, one blue and one brown suitcase, dad, mom, boy and girl, Model No. 2360
EX $7   **NM** $12   **MIP** $25

❑ **Jetport,** 1981, Fisher-Price, airport building, blue and yellow copter, large blue and yellow plane, four captain chairs, two orange coffee tables, green and white two-seat car w/luggage rack, one brown and one blue suitcase, three-car tram, tan bald man, light blue short stewardess w/blond hair, short pilot, mom, boy and girl, Model No. 933
EX $25   **NM** $35   **MIP** $50

❑ **Kitchen Set,** 1971, Fisher-Price, stove, sink, fridge, litho table, four captain chairs, all wooden family consisting of a dad, mom, boy and a girl; many color variations exist, Model No. 729
EX $12   **NM** $35   **MIP** $60

❑ **Lacing Shoe,** 1970, Fisher-Price, shoe w/mostly brown litho and wheels, special lace, mom wearing glasses w/regular shaped body, two yellow triangle-shaped girls w/different faces, two square red boys w/different faces, and a dog w/marshmallow-shaped base, Model No. 146
EX $35   **NM** $45   **MIP** $75

❑ **Lift & Load Depot,** 1977, Fisher-Price, building, green and yellow dump truck, fork lift, scoop loader, yellow sling, four brown pallets, two brown crates, two gray crates, two black barrels, orange scoop bucket attached to building, and one African-American and two white workers w/light blue bodies and orange hardhats, Model No. 942
EX $35   **NM** $50   **MIP** $80

❑ **Lift & Load Lumber Yard,** 1978, Fisher-Price, small lumber yard building w/yellow ramp, green and yellow lift truck, truck and trailer, six pieces of wood lumber (two square, two long rectangular, two short rectangular), four brown pallets, one white and one African-American worker w/light blue bodies and orange hardhats, Model No. 944
EX $35   **NM** $45   **MIP** $70

❑ **Lift & Load Railroad,** 1978, Fisher-Price, train depot building w/track section, seven-piece track (makes a oval), two-piece train (engine winds up), orange sling, two gray crates, two black barrels, four brown pallets, orange ramp, green/yellow lift truck, one white and one African-American worker w/light blue body and orange hardhats, tall light blue train engineer w/mustache, Model No. 943
EX $35   **NM** $50   **MIP** $80

❑ **Little Mart,** 1987, Fisher-Price, small shopping mart building, red tow truck w/orange hook, orange shopping cart, brown bag of groceries, two-seat car w/solid greenback, yellow pay phone, dad, mom, policewoman and Lucky the dog, Model No. 2580
EX $10   **NM** $17   **MIP** $25

❑ **Little People Construction Set,** 1985, Fisher-Price, orange and yellow dump truck, scoop loader, bulldozer, two black barrels, one gold-cone barricade, one brown crate, two yellow w/black stripes road barricades, two white and one African-American construction workers, Model No. 2352
EX $7   **NM** $12   **MIP** $25

❑ **Little Riders,** 1976, Fisher-Price, plane, rocking horse, tricycle, wagon, train, w/boy and girl, Model No. 656
EX $4   **NM** $7   **MIP** $15

❑ **Little Trucks,** 1981, Fisher-Price, orange and yellow scoop loader, bulldozer, dump truck, lift truck, one brown pallet, one gray crate, w/two light blue construction workers and two green construction workers, Model No. 398
EX $12   **NM** $17   **MIP** $30

❑ **Main Street,** 1986, Fisher-Price, large building of main street w/a pull up background, two blue ramps, yellow two-seat taxi, blue mailbox, parking meter, pay phone, red fire hydrant, red stop sign, yellow turning stop light, yellow-and-black striped road diverter, mail truck, seven plastic letters, small one-seat fire truck, shopkeeper, fireman, mom, mailman, and a little girl, Model No. 2500
EX $17   **NM** $25   **MIP** $45

❑ **McDonald's,** 1990, Fisher-Price, McDonald's restaurant w/pull-out playground, one blue and white two-seat car, one brown trash can, one McDonald's sign, french fry cart, Ronald McDonald, Hamburglar, mom, yellow boy w/black molded hair and girl, Model No. 2552
EX $27   **NM** $45   **MIP** $80

❑ **Merry-Go-Round,** 1972, Fisher-Price, merry-go-round playset base, w/mom, two boys and a girl, Model No. 111
EX $35   **NM** $45   **MIP** $80

❑ **Mini Boat Set,** 1969, Fisher-Price, car w/hook, boat w/two holes in bottom, V-shaped trailer, straight yellow body boy w/cap, and a straight-sided Lucky, Model No. 685
EX $50   **NM** $80   **MIP** $120

❑ **Mini Camper Set,** 1969, Fisher-Price, car and trailer same as mini boat, wood camper marked "Fisher Price," straight yellow body boy w/cap, and a straight-sided Lucky the dog, Model No. 686
EX $50   **NM** $75   **MIP** $120

❑ **Mini Snowmobile,** 1970, Fisher-Price, snowmobile w/detachable sled, turquoise boy red cap, turquoise girl w/red hair and Lucky the dog, Model No. 705
EX $30   **NM** $50   **MIP** $80

❑ **Mini Van,** 1969, Fisher-Price, w/five Little People-dad, mom, girl, boy, and a dog, Model No. 141
EX $5   **NM** $10   **MIP** $25

❑ **Musical Shoe,** 1964, Fisher-Price, wind-up musical shoe w/wheels and special lace, and three straight-sided people w/red bases, all w/different facial imprints (girl, two different boys), Model No. 991
EX $45   **NM** $55   **MIP** $80

❑ **Neighborhood,** 1988, Fisher-Price, pull apart two-piece building connected by tree, attached basketball hoop w/ball, yellow five-rung ladder, two twin beds w/teddy bear imprint, one bed w/quilt imprint, one lounge chair, modular kitchen insert, modular bathroom insert, two-seat car, turquoise pool, one round table, two captain chairs, dad, mom, boy, girl and Lucky the dog, Model No. 2551
EX $17   **NM** $25   **MIP** $45

❑ **New School,** 1988, Fisher-Price, school house building w/pull-out playground, red stop sign, small school bus, yellow skateboard, white flag, chalk, orange and blue jump rope, white drum, red-bodied woman teacher w/glasses, boy, African-American girl, Asian-American boy, and orange-bodied girl w/glasses, Model No. 2550
EX $17   **NM** $25   **MIP** $45

(John Murray, Photo by Ross MacKearnin)

Nifty Station Wagon, 1960, Fisher-Price, wooden car w/wood top and two plastic braces on top, w/four large straight wooden figures, blue dad, green mom, yellow cone-shaped boy, and a black dog w/white ears and a ribbed body. The people from this set are similar in design to the people from the No. 990-984 Safety School Bus, Model No. 234

EX $175   NM $250   MIP $375

(Sean and Debbie Craig)

Nursery School, 1978, Fisher-Price, flat base w/dividing rooms and plastic edges, cardboard roof/play area, gold bus w/apple, double sink, stove, toilet, bathroom sink, slide, merry-go-round, blue easel, teeter totter, four captain chairs, round arts-and-craft table, dad, mom, African-American boy and two girls, Model No. 929

EX $35   NM $50   MIP $80

Nursery Sets, 1973, Fisher-Price, changing table, highchair, cradle, rocking horse, playpen, stroller, dad, mom, girl and a baby; many color variations exist, Model No. 761

EX $8   NM $13   MIP $20

Off-Shore Cargo Base, 1979, Fisher-Price, one large rectangular and square black floats, crane, tan cargo hold, helicopter landing pad, cargo hold cover, tug boat, helicopter, white and blue barge, two gold feed bags, two sections of pipe, two crates, mesh cargo net, two black tow chains, red diver, tall blue captain, and one white and one African-American worker w/light green bodies and yellow hardhats, Model No. 945

EX $55   NM $75   MIP $120

Pampers Promotional, 1988 only, Fisher-Price, yellow mini van w/family, green body boy and red cap exclusive to the set

EX $5   NM $10   MIP $25

Patio Set, 1971, Fisher-Price, flowered umbrella table, pool w/imprint, four captain chairs, BBQ grill, all wooden family consisting of a dad, mom, boy and a girl; many color variations exist, Model No. 726

EX $13   NM $35   MIP $60

Play Family Camper, 1972, Fisher-Price, green flatbed truck, white removable camper, green boat w/litho inside, boat sits on top of camper, yellow/red umbrella table, four red captain chairs, grill, yellow motorcycle, red table w/hot dog litho, toilet, sink, red ladder, dad, mom, boy, girl and Lucky the dog, Model No. 994

EX $25   NM $40   MIP $65

Play Family Circus, 1974, Fisher-Price, two yellow ladders, red hoop, yellow trapeze, blue tub (base w/clown on cardboard litho), yellow elephant stand, w/bear, monkey, lion, blue elephant, giraffe, short ringmaster and red clown, Model No. 135

EX $35   NM $45   MIP $80

Play Family Farm, 1968, Fisher-Price, barn base w/mooing door, silo, four pieces of fence, tractor, cart, white harness, white trough, red chicken, white chicken, horse, cow, pig, jointed dog, sheep, dad w/cowboy hat, mom, boy w/cowboy hat, and a girl; many variations exist, Model No. 915

EX $25   NM $40   MIP $60

Play Family Lacing Shoe, 1965, Fisher-Price, shoe w/mostly black litho and blue base, special lace, w/large all-wood mom wearing glasses, two-yellow triangle-shaped girls w/different faces, two square red boys w/different faces, and a dog w/marshmallow-shaped base, Model No. 136

EX $35   NM $50   MIP $75

Play Family Tow Truck and Car, 1969, Fisher-Price, tow truck, car w/hook, and a straight body yellow boy w/cap, Model No. 718

EX $35   NM $55   MIP $115

Playground, 1986, Fisher-Price, green base playground w/spring rides and a slide, orange and yellow swing, orange and yellow merry-go-round, blue climbing cube, boy and girl, Model No. 2525

EX $4   NM $7   MIP $15

Pool, 1986, Fisher-Price, swimming pool base, black stand-up grill, diving board, slide, lifeguard stand w/white life preserver, two lounge chairs (one orange and one yellow), umbrella table w/base shaped to fit in hole, boy, and a girl, Model No. 2526

EX $4   NM $7   MIP $15

Rooms—Sears Exclusive, 1971, Fisher-Price, flat base w/divided rooms, yellow fridge, yellow double sink, yellow stove w/litho, green table w/formal setting, four green captain chairs, white tub, scale, toilet, sink, red or blue couch, two red or blue twin beds, red or blue T.V. w/litho puppet, red or blue coffeetable, red and blue stuffed chair, turquoise umbrella table, two yellow captain chairs, turquoise or yellow grill, white cotton drawstring bag, all wooden family consisting of a green bald man, blue mom w/blond hair, orange bald boy, red girl w/blond hair and Lucky the dog, Model No. 909

EX $180   NM $250   MIP $350

Safety School Bus, 1959, Fisher-Price, First version-yellow school bus w/stop sign on the drivers side and a flat nose, wooden top piece reads "Fisher Price," six removable people w/litho on wooden bodies; Second version-four removable people and two that are fixed in the back, as the bus moves the fixed people bounce up and down, Model No. 983

EX $150   NM $225   MIP $375

Safety School Bus, 1961, Fisher-Price, yellow school bus w/stop sign on the drivers side and a flat nose, five tall wooden people, the people from this bus are similar in design to the people from the No. 990 Safety School Bus and the No. 234 Nifty Station wagon, Model No. 984

EX $150   NM $225   MIP $375

Safety School Bus, 1962, Fisher-Price, yellow school bus w/stop sign on the drivers side and a flat nose, five tall wooden people; the people from this bus and similar in design to the people from the No. 984 Safety School Bus and the No. 234 Nifty Station wagon, Model No. 990

EX $150   NM $225   MIP $375

School, 1971, Fisher-Price, schoolhouse building w/bell and pull down sidewall w/chalkboard, four green or yellow student desks, one green or yellow teachers desk w/chair, green and yellow swing, merry-go-round, green or yellow slide, numbers tray, letter tray w/letters A-Z and extra P, S, T, N, R, I, and E letters, chalk box, eraser, blue teacher w/blond hair, two boys and two girls, Model No. 923

EX $35   NM $50   MIP $80

School Bus, 1965, Fisher-Price, five Little People kids, and one dog. There have been many variations of the School bus over the years years; all brown dog from first issue is worth $30-50 in Excellent condition, Model No. 192

EX $12   NM $25   MIP $50

Sesame Street Clubhouse, 1977, Fisher-Price, clubhouse w/bird nest and shaker board and attached tire swing, yellow slide, three barrels (red, blue, yellow), yellow cable drum, black and red jump rope, two-seat wagon, Big Bird, Roosevelt Franklin, Grover, The Count, Bert, and Ernie, Model No. 937

EX $45   NM $60   MIP $100

Sesame Street Extras, 1976, Fisher-Price, boxed set showing Sesame Street scenes comes w/Ernie, Bert, Cookie Monster, Susan, Gordon, Mr. Hooper, Big Bird and Oscar in his can, Model No. 939

EX $25   NM $45   MIP $100

Sesame Street Extras, 1977, Fisher-Price, Boxed set showing Sesame Street scenes comes w/Roosevelt Franklin, Grover, Sherlock Hemlock, Prairie Dawn, The Count, Harry Monster, and Snuffleupagus, Model No. 940

EX $35   NM $55   MIP $125

Sesame Street House, 1975, Fisher-Price, brownstone fold-out building, Sesame Street lamppost, mailbox w/litho, garbage truck, five-rung white ladder, newsstand, fire hydrant on gray triangle, soda fountain stand, T.V. showing Grover, sofa, table w/pork chop litho, two captain chairs, two twin beds marked "B" and "E," chalk box, eraser, Big Bird's nest, coffeetable, Bert, Ernie, Mr. Hooper, Big Bird, Cookie Monster, Susan, Gordon, and Oscar in his can, Model No. 938

EX $45   NM $70   MIP $125

Snorkey Fire Engine, 1960, Fisher-Price, fire truck w/white base and blue wheels and yellow boom, w/four firemen w/green bases, red arms and hats, and a black dog exclusive to this set, Model No. 168

EX $150   NM $225   MIP $350

❑ **Snorkey Fire Engine,** 1961, Fisher-Price, fire truck w/red base, black wheels and a yellow boom, w/four fire-men w/white bases, red arms and hats, Model No. 168
EX $150 **NM** $225 **MIP** $350

❑ **Village,** 1973, Fisher-Price, large fold out village base, connecting bridge and traffic light, six letters, one yellow single bed, small fire engine, red and blue police car, mail truck, four yellow cap-tain chairs, umbrella table, green and white one-seat car w/luggage rack, white and green back-to-back two-seat car, phone booth, yellow grill, dentist chair, barber chair, yellow couch and coffeetable, African-American doctor, white doctor, fireman, mailman w/gray base, policewoman, mom, boy, girl and Lucky the dog, Model No. 997
EX $65 **NM** $75 **MIP** $100

❑ **Western Town,** 1982, Fisher-Price, building w/shaker board, tan or green buckboard, tan or green stagecoach w/removable red top, one brown and one black horse, two brown harnesses, brown saddle, gray crate, green hatbox luggage, four-pieces fence, blue sheriff w/star badge on chest, red sod-buster man w/black hat and mustache, Native American w/chest markings on front, yellow lady w/green hat, Model No. 934
EX $40 **NM** $50 **MIP** $85

❑ **Westerners,** 1984, Fisher-Price, tall ringmaster, Native American w/head-dress, and a green cowboy w/ten-gallon hat, on card, Model No. 676
EX $4 **NM** $7 **MIP** $15

❑ **Zoo,** 1984, Fisher-Price, zoo base, tree, orange and yellow parrots, vulture, black and orange monkeys, orange cabaña, black seal, blue elephant, yellow lion cub, hippo, gorilla, mountain goat, four food trays, two green benches, one green table, three car tram, dad, mom, girl, boy, and a zookeeper w/safari-style hat, Model No. 916
EX $20 **NM** $30 **MIP** $45

WOODEN

❑ **Allie Gator,** 1960, Fisher-Price, Model No. 653
EX $40 **NM** $80 **MIP** $160

❑ **Amusement Park,** 1963, Fisher-Price, Model No. 932
EX $50 **NM** $100 **MIP** $200

❑ **Baby Chick Tandem Cart,** 1953, Fisher-Price, Model No. 50
EX $45 **NM** $65 **MIP** $125

❑ **Barky,** 1958, Fisher-Price, Model No. 462
EX $45 **NM** $75 **MIP** $125

❑ **Barky Buddy,** 1934, Fisher-Price, Model No. 150
EX $400 **NM** $900 **MIP** $1800

❑ **Barky Puppy,** 1931, Fisher-Price, Model No. 103
EX $550 **NM** $1000 **MIP** $2000

❑ **Big Bill Pelican,** 1961, Fisher-Price, Model No. 794
EX $45 **NM** $75 **MIP** $125

❑ **Big Performing Circus,** 1932, Fisher-Price, Model No. 250
EX $450 **NM** $900 **MIP** $1800

❑ **Blackie Drummer,** 1939, Fisher-Price, Model No. 785
EX $400 **NM** $650 **MIP** $1000

❑ **Bonny Bunny Wagon,** 1959, Fisher-Price, Model No. 318
EX $30 **NM** $45 **MIP** $80

(John Murray, Photo by Ross MacKearnin)

❑ **Boom Boom Popeye,** 1937, Fisher-Price, Model No. 491
EX $550 **NM** $800 **MIP** $1600

❑ **Bossy Bell,** 1959, Fisher-Price, Model No. 656
EX $35 **NM** $45 **MIP** $70

❑ **Bouncing Bunny Wheelbarrow,** 1939, Fisher-Price, Model No. 727
EX $450 **NM** $750 **MIP** $1300

❑ **Bouncy Racer,** 1960, Fisher-Price, Model No. 8
EX $40 **NM** $65 **MIP** $90

(John Murray. Photo by Russ MacKearnin)

❑ **Bucky Burro,** 1955, Fisher-Price, Model No. 166
EX $95 **NM** $200 **MIP** $550

❑ **Buddy Bronc,** 1938, Fisher-Price, Model No. 430
EX $200 **NM** $400 **MIP** $800

❑ **Buddy Bullfrog,** 1959, Fisher-Price, Model No. 728
EX $40 **NM** $65 **MIP** $125

❑ **Bunny Basket Cart,** 1957, Fisher-Price, Model No. 301
EX $30 **NM** $45 **MIP** $80

❑ **Bunny Basket Cart,** 1960, Fisher-Price, Model No. 303
EX $30 **NM** $45 **MIP** $95

❑ **Bunny Bell Cart,** 1941, Fisher-Price, Model No. 520
EX $125 **NM** $250 **MIP** $550

❑ **Bunny Bell Cart,** 1954, Fisher-Price, Model No. 604
EX $45 **NM** $75 **MIP** $150

❑ **Bunny Cart,** 1948, Fisher-Price, Model No. 5
EX $75 **NM** $100 **MIP** $145

❑ **Bunny Drummer,** 1942, Fisher-Price, Model No. 512
EX $150 **NM** $225 **MIP** $550

❑ **Bunny Drummer,** 1946, Fisher-Price, Model No. 505
EX $150 **NM** $225 **MIP** $550

❑ **Bunny Egg Cart,** 1949, Fisher-Price, Model No. 404
EX $50 **NM** $70 **MIP** $125

❑ **Bunny Egg Cart,** 1950, Fisher-Price, Model No. 28
EX $50 **NM** $70 **MIP** $125

❑ **Bunny Engine,** 1954, Fisher-Price, Model No. 703
EX $45 **NM** $75 **MIP** $135

❑ **Bunny Racer,** 1942, Fisher-Price, Model No. 474
EX $125 **NM** $225 **MIP** $550

❑ **Busy Bunny Cart,** 1936, Fisher-Price, Model No. 719
EX $150 **NM** $300 **MIP** $750

❑ **Butch the Pup,** 1951, Fisher-Price, Model No. 333
EX $45 **NM** $75 **MIP** $125

❑ **Buzzy Bee,** 1950, Fisher-Price, Model No. 325
EX $40 **NM** $60 **MIP** $80

❑ **Cash Register,** 1960, Fisher-Price, Model No. 972
EX $35 **NM** $75 **MIP** $125

❑ **Chatter Monk,** 1957, Fisher-Price, Model No. 798
EX $45 **NM** $65 **MIP** $145

❑ **Chatter Telephone,** 1962, Fisher-Price, Model No. 747
EX $30 **NM** $45 **MIP** $65

❑ **Choo-Choo Local,** 1936, Fisher-Price, Model No. 517
EX $350 **NM** $700 **MIP** $1500

❑ **Chubby Chief,** 1932, Fisher-Price, Model No. 110
EX $450 **NM** $950 **MIP** $2000

❑ **Chuggy Pop-Up,** 1955, Fisher-Price, Model No. 616
EX $40 **NM** $65 **MIP** $135

(John Murray. Photo by Russ MacKearnin)

❑ **Circus Wagon,** 1942, Fisher-Price, Model No. 156
EX $125 **NM** $300 **MIP** $650

❑ **Concrete Mixer Truck,** 1959, Fisher-Price, Model No. 926
EX $150 **NM** $300 **MIP** $625

❑ **Corn Popper,** 1957, Fisher-Price, Model No. 785
EX $35 **NM** $50 **MIP** $115

❑ **Corn Popper,** 1963, Fisher-Price, Model No. 788
EX $35 **NM** $50 **MIP** $85

❑ **Cotton Tail Cart,** 1940, Fisher-Price, Model No. 525
EX $200 **NM** $400 **MIP** $800

❑ **Cowboy Chime,** 1951, Fisher-Price, Model No. 700
EX $150 **NM** $300 **MIP** $600

(John Murray. Photo by Russ MacKearnin)

❑ **Dandy Dobbin,** 1941, Fisher-Price, Model No. 765
EX $150 **NM** $325 **MIP** $675

❑ **Dashing Dobbin,** 1938, Fisher-Price, Model No. 742
EX $250 **NM** $400 **MIP** $850

❑ **Ding-Dong Duckey,** 1949, Fisher-Price, Model No. 724
EX $175 **NM** $225 **MIP** $575

❑ **Dinkey Engine,** 1959, Fisher-Price, Model No. 642
EX $35 **NM** $50 **MIP** $95

❑ **Dizzy Dino,** 1931, Fisher-Price, Model No. 407
EX $250 **NM** $400 **MIP** $800

(John Murray. Photo by Russ MacKearnin)

❑ **Dizzy Donkey,** 1939, Fisher-Price, Model No. 433
EX $45 **NM** $80 **MIP** $160

(John Murray, Photo by Ross MacKearnin)

❑ **Doc & Dopey Dwarfs,** 1938, Fisher-Price, Model No. 770
EX $550 **NM** $1000 **MIP** $2000

❑ **Doctor Doodle,** 1931, Fisher-Price, Model No. 100
EX $600 **NM** $1000 **MIP** $2000

❑ **Doctor Doodle,** 1940, Fisher-Price, Model No. 477
EX $150 **NM** $300 **MIP** $600

❑ **Dog Cart Donald,** 1936, Fisher-Price, Model No. 149
EX $600 **NM** $1000 **MIP** $2000

❑ **Doggy Racer,** 1942, Fisher-Price, Model No. 7
EX $150 **NM** $300 **MIP** $600

❑ **Donald Cart,** 1940, Fisher-Price, Model No. 469
EX $450 **NM** $900 **MIP** $1800

(John Murray, Photo by Ross MacKearnin)

❑ **Donald Duck & Nephews,** 1941, Fisher-Price, Model No. 479
EX $350 **NM** $700 **MIP** $1400

(John Murray, Photo by Ross MacKearnin)

❑ **Donald Duck Cart,** 1937, Fisher-Price, Model No. 500
EX $350 **NM** $600 **MIP** $1500

(John Murray. Photo by Russ MacKearnin)

❑ **Donald Duck Cart,** 1942, Fisher-Price, Model No. 544
EX $200 **NM** $350 **MIP** $750

❑ **Donald Duck Cart,** 1954, Fisher-Price, Model No. 605
EX $125 **NM** $250 **MIP** $500

❑ **Donald Duck Choo-Choo,** 1940, Fisher-Price, Model No. 450
EX $350 **NM** $600 **MIP** $1200

(John Murray, Photo by Ross MacKearnin)

❑ **Donald Duck Choo-Choo,** 1942, Fisher-Price, Model No. 450
EX $225 **NM** $450 **MIP** $900

❑ **Donald Duck Delivery,** 1936, Fisher-Price, Model No. 715
EX $350 **NM** $750 **MIP** $1500

❑ **Donald Duck Drum Major,** 1940, Fisher-Price, Model No. 550
EX $150 **NM** $300 **MIP** $600

❑ **Donald Duck Drum Major,** 1948, Fisher-Price, Model No. 432
EX $150 **NM** $300 **MIP** $600
(John Murray. Photo by Russ MacKearnin)

❏ **Donald Duck Drummer,** 1949, Fisher-Price, Model No. 454
  EX $175   **NM** $225   **MIP** $550

❏ **Donald Duck Pop-Up,** 1938, Fisher-Price, Model No. 425
  EX $325   **NM** $650   **MIP** $1200

❏ **Donald Duck Xylophone,** 1938, Fisher-Price, Model No. 185
  EX $325   **NM** $750   **MIP** $1000

(John Murray, Photo by Ross MacKearnin)

❏ **Donald Duck Xylophone,** 1946, Fisher-Price, Model No. 177
  EX $150   **NM** $350   **MIP** $700

❏ **Dopey Dwarf,** 1939, Fisher-Price, Model No. 770
  EX $350   **NM** $650   **MIP** $1700

❏ **Doughboy Donald,** 1942, Fisher-Price, Model No. 744
  EX $550   **NM** $1000   **MIP** $2000

❏ **Drummer Bear,** 1931, Fisher-Price, Model No. 102
  EX $550   **NM** $1000   **MIP** $2000

❏ **Ducky Cart,** 1948, Fisher-Price, Model No. 6
  EX $45   **NM** $85   **MIP** $145

❏ **Ducky Cart,** 1950, Fisher-Price, Model No. 51
  EX $45   **NM** $85   **MIP** $145

❏ **Ducky Daddles,** 1941, Fisher-Price, Model No. 14
  EX $35   **NM** $65   **MIP** $135

❏ **Ducky Daddles,** 1942, Fisher-Price, Model No. 148
  EX $175   **NM** $300   **MIP** $600

❏ **Dumbo Circus Racer,** 1941, Fisher-Price, Model No. 738
  EX $450   **NM** $1000   **MIP** $2000

❏ **Easter Bunny,** 1936, Fisher-Price, Model No. 490
  EX $165   **NM** $300   **MIP** $675

(John Murray, Photo by Ross MacKearnin)

❏ **Elsie's Dairy Truck,** 1948, Fisher-Price, Model No. 745
  EX $300   **NM** $700   **MIP** $1400

❏ **Farm Truck,** 1954, Fisher-Price, Model No. 845
  EX $145   **NM** $300   **MIP** $600

❏ **Farmer in Dell Music Box,** 1962, Fisher-Price, Model No. 763
  EX $30   **NM** $40   **MIP** $65

❏ **Farmer in the Dell TV Radio,** 1963, Fisher-Price, Model No. 166
  EX $25   **NM** $35   **MIP** $75

❏ **Fido Zilo,** 1955, Fisher-Price, Model No. 707
  EX $35   **NM** $65   **MIP** $135

❏ **Fire Truck,** 1959, Fisher-Price, Model No. 630
  EX $35   **NM** $50   **MIP** $95

(John Murray. Photo by Russ MacKearnin)

❏ **Fuzzy Fido,** 1941, Fisher-Price, Model No. 444
  EX $125   **NM** $200   **MIP** $550

❏ **Gabby Duck,** 1952, Fisher-Price, Model No. 767
  EX $55   **NM** $80   **MIP** $160

❏ **Gabby Goofies,** 1956, Fisher-Price, Model No. 775
  EX $25   **NM** $45   **MIP** $75

❏ **Gabby Goofies,** 1963, Fisher-Price, Model No. 777
  EX $35   **NM** $40   **MIP** $65

❏ **Gabby Goose,** 1936, Fisher-Price, Model No. 120
  EX $35   **NM** $65   **MIP** $95

❏ **Galloping Horse & Wagon,** 1948, Fisher-Price, Model No. 737
  EX $150   **NM** $350   **MIP** $750

(John Murray. Photo by Russ MacKearnin)

❏ **Gold Star Stagecoach,** 1954, Fisher-Price, Model No. 175
  EX $150   **NM** $425   **MIP** $975

❏ **Golden Gulch Express,** 1961, Fisher-Price, Model No. 191
  EX $65   **NM** $95   **MIP** $165

❏ **Go'N Back Jumbo,** 1931, Fisher-Price, Model No. 360
  EX $450   **NM** $900   **MIP** $1800

❏ **Granny Doodle,** 1931, Fisher-Price, Model No. 101
  EX $600   **NM** $1000   **MIP** $2000

❏ **Granny Doodle & Family,** 1933, Fisher-Price, Model No. 101
  EX $650   **NM** $1500   **MIP** $2000

❏ **Happy Helicopter,** 1953, Fisher-Price, Model No. 498
  EX $150   **NM** $225   **MIP** $425

❏ **Happy Hippo,** 1962, Fisher-Price, Model No. 151
  EX $35   **NM** $65   **MIP** $145

❏ **Hot Diggety,** 1934, Fisher-Price, Model No. 800
  EX $450   **NM** $900   **MIP** $1800

❏ **Howdy Bunny,** 1939, Fisher-Price, Model No. 757
  EX $300   **NM** $650   **MIP** $1100

❏ **Huckleberry Hound Xylo,** 1961, Fisher-Price, Model No. 711
  EX $175   **NM** $225   **MIP** $475

❏ **Huffy Puffy Train,** 1958, Fisher-Price, Model No. 999
  EX $55   **NM** $80   **MIP** $175

❏ **Humpty Dump Truck,** 1963, Fisher-Price, Model No. 145
  EX $40   **NM** $65   **MIP** $125

❏ **Humpty Dumpty,** 1957, Fisher-Price, Model No. 757
  EX $165   **NM** $225   **MIP** $550

❏ **Husky Dump Truck,** 1961, Fisher-Price, Model No. 145
  EX $30   **NM** $45   **MIP** $95

❏ **Jack-n-Jill TV Radio,** 1959, Fisher-Price, Model No. 148
  EX $25   **NM** $45   **MIP** $85

❏ **Jingle Giraffe,** 1956, Fisher-Price, Model No. 472
  EX $55   **NM** $175   **MIP** $375

❏ **Jolly Jumper,** 1954, Fisher-Price, Model No. 450
  EX $35   **NM** $75   **MIP** $165

❑ **Jolly Jumper,** 1963, Fisher-Price, Model No. 793
EX $25 **NM** $50 **MIP** $85

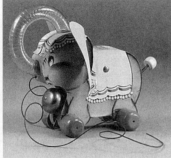

(John Murray, Photo by Ross MacKearnin)

❑ **Juggling Jumbo,** 1958, Fisher-Price, Model No. 735
EX $150 **NM** $225 **MIP** $425

❑ **Jumbo Jitterbug,** 1940, Fisher-Price, Model No. 422
EX $65 **NM** $150 **MIP** $325

❑ **Jumbo Rolo,** 1951, Fisher-Price, Model No. 755
EX $65 **NM** $150 **MIP** $295

❑ **Junior Circus,** 1963, Fisher-Price, Model No. 902
EX $75 **NM** $200 **MIP** $395

(John Murray. Photo by Russ MacKearnin)

❑ **Katy Kackler,** 1954, Fisher-Price, Model No. 140
EX $45 **NM** $80 **MIP** $160

❑ **Kicking Donkey,** 1937, Fisher-Price, Model No. 175
EX $175 **NM** $285 **MIP** $725

(John Murray, Photo by Ross MacKearnin)

❑ **Kitty Bell,** 1950, Fisher-Price, Model No. 499
EX $65 **NM** $150 **MIP** $275

❑ **Lady Bug,** 1961, Fisher-Price, Model No. 658
EX $30 **NM** $45 **MIP** $75

❑ **Leo the Drummer,** 1952, Fisher-Price, Model No. 480
EX $175 **NM** $225 **MIP** $450

❑ **Looky Chug-Chug,** 1949, Fisher-Price, Model No. 161
EX $75 **NM** $175 **MIP** $325

(John Murray, Photo by Ross MacKearnin)

❑ **Looky Fire Truck,** 1950, Fisher-Price, Model No. 7
EX $65 **NM** $100 **MIP** $250

(John Murray. Photo by Russ MacKearnin)

❑ **Lop-Ear Looie,** 1934, Fisher-Price, Model No. 415
EX $150 **NM** $300 **MIP** $600

❑ **Lucky Monk,** 1932, Fisher-Price, Model No. 109
EX $350 **NM** $850 **MIP** $1800

❑ **Merry Mousewife,** 1962, Fisher-Price, Model No. 662
EX $35 **NM** $50 **MIP** $80

❑ **Merry Mutt,** 1949, Fisher-Price, Model No. 473
EX $45 **NM** $75 **MIP** $145

❑ **Mickey Mouse Band,** 1935, Fisher-Price, Model No. 530
EX $750 **NM** $1500 **MIP** $2100
(John Murray. Photo by Russ MacKearnin)

❑ **Mickey Mouse Choo-Choo,** 1938, Fisher-Price, Model No. 432
EX $450 **NM** $850 **MIP** $1800

❑ **Mickey Mouse Drummer,** 1941, Fisher-Price, Model No. 476
EX $150 **NM** $300 **MIP** $625

❑ **Mickey Mouse Puddle Jumper,** 1953, Fisher-Price, Model No. 310
EX $150 **NM** $225 **MIP** $395

(John Murray, Photo by Ross MacKearnin)

❑ **Mickey Mouse Safety Patrol,** 1956, Fisher-Price, Model No. 733
EX $165 **NM** $300 **MIP** $625

❑ **Mickey Mouse Xylophone,** 1939, Fisher-Price, Model No. 798
EX $300 **NM** $600 **MIP** $975

❑ **Mickey Mouse Xylophone,** 1942, Fisher-Price, Model No. 798
EX $275 **NM** $500 **MIP** $925

❑ **Mickey Mouse Zilo,** 1963, Fisher-Price, Model No. 714
EX $165 **NM** $325 **MIP** $575

❑ **Molly Moo-Moo,** 1956, Fisher-Price, Model No. 190
EX $65 **NM** $200 **MIP** $400

❑ **Moo-oo Cow,** 1958, Fisher-Price, Model No. 155
EX $40 **NM** $80 **MIP** $160

❑ **Mother Goose Cart,** 1955, Fisher-Price, Model No. 784
EX $35 **NM** $70 **MIP** $145

❑ **Music Box Barn,** 1960, Fisher-Price, Model No. 764
EX $25 **NM** $45 **MIP** $90

❑ **Music Box Sweeper,** 1961, Fisher-Price, Model No. 131
EX $40 **NM** $65 **MIP** $165

(John Murray, Photo by Ross MacKearnin)

❑ **Musical Elephant,** 1948, Fisher-Price, Model No. 145
EX $165 **NM** $325 **MIP** $700

❑ **Musical Push Chime,** 1950, Fisher-Price, Model No. 722
EX $35 **NM** $50 **MIP** $95

❑ **Musical Sweeper,** 1950, Fisher-Price, Model No. 100
EX $65 **NM** $135 **MIP** $275

❑ **Musical Sweeper,** 1953, Fisher-Price, Model No. 225
EX $40   NM $65   MIP $170

❑ **Musical Tick Tock Clock,** 1962, Fisher-Price, Model No. 997
EX $25   NM $45   MIP $90

(John Murray. Photo by Russ MacKearnin)

❑ **Nosey Pup,** 1956, Fisher-Price, Model No. 445
EX $45   NM $75   MIP $155

❑ **Patch Pony,** 1963, Fisher-Price, Model No. 616
EX $25   NM $40   MIP $85

❑ **Perky the Pot,** 1958, Fisher-Price, Model No. 686
EX $40   NM $65   MIP $135

(John Murray, Photo by Ross MacKearnin)

❑ **Peter Bunny Cart,** 1939, Fisher-Price, Model No. 472
EX $150   NM $325   MIP $725

❑ **Peter Bunny Engine,** 1941, Fisher-Price, Model No. 715
EX $70   NM $225   MIP $475

❑ **Peter Bunny Engine,** 1949, Fisher-Price, Model No. 721
EX $75   NM $200   MIP $425

❑ **Peter Pig,** 1959, Fisher-Price, Model No. 479
EX $35   NM $50   MIP $110

❑ **Pinky Pig,** 1956, Fisher-Price, Model No. 695
EX $40   NM $70   MIP $160

❑ **Pinky Pig,** 1958, Fisher-Price, Model No. 695
EX $35   NM $65   MIP $145

(John Murray, Photo by Ross MacKearnin)

❑ **Pinocchio,** 1939, Fisher-Price, Model No. 494
EX $105   NM $400   MIP $975

❑ **Pinocchio,** 1939, Fisher-Price, Model No. 720
EX $200   NM $400   MIP $940

❑ **Playful Puppy,** 1961, Fisher-Price, Model No. 625
EX $35   NM $60   MIP $120

❑ **Playland Express,** 1962, Fisher-Price, Model No. 192
EX $40   NM $80   MIP $165

❑ **Pluto Pop-Up,** 1936, Fisher-Price, Model No. 440
EX $35   NM $75   MIP $160

❑ **Pony Chime,** 1962, Fisher-Price, Model No. 137
EX $30   NM $65   MIP $135

❑ **Pony Express,** 1941, Fisher-Price, Model No. 733
EX $65   NM $200   MIP $445

❑ **Poodle Zilo,** 1962, Fisher-Price, Model No. 739
EX $30   NM $65   MIP $145

❑ **Pop 'N Ring,** 1959, Fisher-Price, Model No. 809
EX $40   NM $65   MIP $125

❑ **Popeye,** 1935, Fisher-Price, Model No. 700
EX $700   NM $1500   MIP $2200

❑ **Popeye Cowboy,** 1937, Fisher-Price, Model No. 705
EX $650   NM $1000   MIP $2100

❑ **Popeye Spinach Eater,** 1939, Fisher-Price, Model No. 488
EX $225   NM $650   MIP $1300

❑ **Popeye Spinach Eater Pull Toy,** 1939, Fisher-Price, Model No. 488
EX $200   NM $400   MIP $600

(John Murray. Photo by Russ MacKearnin)

❑ **Popeye the Sailor,** 1936, Fisher-Price, Model No. 703
EX $600   NM $1200   MIP $2400

❑ **Prancing Horses,** 1937, Fisher-Price, Model No. 766
EX $175   NM $400   MIP $900

❑ **Pudgy Pig,** 1962, Fisher-Price, Model No. 478
EX $35   NM $50   MIP $110

❑ **Puffy Engine,** 1951, Fisher-Price, Model No. 444
EX $35   NM $75   MIP $145

❑ **Pull-A-Tune Xylophone,** 1957, Fisher-Price, Model No. 870
EX $30   NM $45   MIP $95

❑ **Pushy Doddle,** 1933, Fisher-Price, Model No. 507
EX $350   NM $800   MIP $1900

❑ **Pushy Elephant,** 1934, Fisher-Price, Model No. 525
EX $225   NM $600   MIP $1700

❑ **Pushy Piggy,** 1932, Fisher-Price, Model No. 500
EX $350   NM $800   MIP $1800

❑ **Quacko Duck,** 1939, Fisher-Price, Model No. 300
EX $135   NM $250   MIP $600

❑ **Quacky Family,** 1946, Fisher-Price, Model No. 799
EX $30   NM $50   MIP $85

(John Murray. Photo by Russ MacKearnin)

❑ **Queen Buzzy Bee,** 1962, Fisher-Price, Model No. 444
EX $25   NM $50   MIP $80

FISHER-PRICE

❏ **Rabbit Cart,** 1950, Fisher-Price, Model No. 52
EX $35   NM $70   MIP $140

❏ **Racing Bunny Cart,** 1938, Fisher-Price, Model No. 723
EX $150   NM $350   MIP $700

❏ **Racing Ponies,** 1936, Fisher-Price, Model No. 760
EX $200   NM $500   MIP $850

❏ **Racing Pony,** 1933, Fisher-Price, Model No. 705
EX $325   NM $1000   MIP $1475

(John Murray, Photo by Ross MacKearnin)

❏ **Racing Rowboat,** 1952, Fisher-Price, Model No. 730
EX $105   NM $225   MIP $475

❏ **Raggedy Ann & Andy,** 1941, Fisher-Price, Model No. 711
EX $400   NM $900   MIP $1975

❏ **Rattle Ball,** 1959, Fisher-Price, Model No. 682
EX $20   NM $30   MIP $50

❏ **Riding Horse,** 1940, Fisher-Price, Model No. 254
EX $400   NM $900   MIP $1475

❏ **Rock-A-Bye Bunny Cart,** 1940, Fisher-Price, Model No. 788
EX $175   NM $425   MIP $825

❏ **Rock-A-Stack,** 1960, Fisher-Price, Model No. 627
EX $15   NM $25   MIP $40

❏ **Roller Chime,** 1953, Fisher-Price, Model No. 123
EX $35   NM $70   MIP $140

❏ **Rolling Bunny Basket,** 1961, Fisher-Price, Model No. 310
EX $35   NM $65   MIP $135

❏ **Rooster Cart,** 1938, Fisher-Price, Model No. 469
EX $95   NM $225   MIP $575

❏ **Safety School Bus,** 1959, Fisher-Price, Model No. 983
EX $150   NM $300   MIP $600

❏ **Safety School Bus,** 1962, Fisher-Price, Model No. 990
EX $50   NM $100   MIP $175

❏ **Scotty Dog,** 1933, Fisher-Price, Model No. 710
EX $350   NM $850   MIP $1900

❏ **Shaggy Zilo,** 1960, Fisher-Price, Model No. 738
EX $40   NM $80   MIP $160

❏ **Skipper Sam,** 1934, Fisher-Price, Model No. 155
EX $650   NM $1300   MIP $2800

❏ **Sleepy Sue (Turtle),** 1962, Fisher-Price, Model No. 495
EX $25   NM $45   MIP $90

❏ **Smokie Engine,** 1960, Fisher-Price, Model No. 642
EX $30   NM $40   MIP $85

(John Murray, Photo by Ross MacKearnin)

❏ **Snoopy Sniffer,** 1938, Fisher-Price, Model No. 180
EX $65   NM $200   MIP $475

❏ **Snoopy Sniffer,** 1958, Fisher-Price, Model No. 180
EX $50   NM $100   MIP $195

❏ **Snorky Fire Engine,** 1960, Fisher-Price, Model No. 168
EX $50   NM $95   MIP $195

❏ **Sonny Duck Cart,** 1941, Fisher-Price, Model No. 410
EX $75   NM $200   MIP $475

❏ **Space Blazer,** 1953, Fisher-Price, Model No. 750
EX $175   NM $400   MIP $850

(John Murray. Photo by Russ MacKearnin)

❏ **Squeaky the Clown,** 1958, Fisher-Price, Model No. 777
EX $125   NM $225   MIP $550

❏ **Stake Truck,** 1960, Fisher-Price, Model No. 649
EX $40   NM $80   MIP $160

❏ **Streamline Express,** 1935, Fisher-Price, Model No. 215
EX $350   NM $700   MIP $1700

❏ **Strutter Donald Duck,** 1941, Fisher-Price, Model No. 510
EX $125   NM $300   MIP $700

❏ **Struttin' Donald Duck,** 1939, Fisher-Price, Model No. 900
EX $205   NM $450   MIP $875

❏ **Sunny Fish,** 1955, Fisher-Price, Model No. 420
EX $75   NM $200   MIP $425

❏ **Suzie Seal,** 1961, Fisher-Price, Model No. 460
EX $25   NM $40   MIP $85

❏ **Tabby Ding Dong,** 1939, Fisher-Price, Model No. 730
EX $200   NM $400   MIP $800

(David W Mapes Inc)

❏ **Tailspin Tabby,** 1931, Fisher-Price, Model No. 400
EX $125   NM $350   MIP $700

❏ **Tailspin Tabby Pop-Up,** 1947, Fisher-Price, Model No. 600
EX $100   NM $200   MIP $400

❏ **Talk-Back Telephone,** 1961, Fisher-Price, Model No. 747
EX $35   NM $70   MIP $140

(John Murray, Photo by Ross MacKearnin)

❏ **Talking Donald Duck,** 1955, Fisher-Price, Model No. 765
EX $35   NM $70   MIP $140

(John Murray, Photo by Ross MacKearnin)

❏ **Talky Parrot,** 1963, Fisher-Price, Model No. 698
EX $50   NM $100   MIP $195

❏ **Tawny Tiger,** 1962, Fisher-Price, Model No. 654
EX $30   NM $65   MIP $165

❏ **Teddy Bear Parade,** 1938, Fisher-Price, Model No. 195
EX $300   NM $700   MIP $1700

❏ **Teddy Choo-Choo,** 1937, Fisher-Price, Model No. 465
EX $200   NM $400   MIP $825

❏ **Teddy Drummer,** 1936, Fisher-Price, Model No. 775
EX $300   NM $600   MIP $1200

❏ **Teddy Station Wagon,** 1942, Fisher-Price, Model No. 480
EX $150   NM $300   MIP $650

❏ **Teddy Tooter,** 1940, Fisher-Price, Model No. 150
EX $200   NM $400   MIP $895

❏ **Teddy Tooter,** 1957, Fisher-Price, Model No. 712
EX $100   NM $225   MIP $525

❏ **Teddy Trucker,** 1949, Fisher-Price, Model No. 711
EX $100   NM $225   MIP $575

❏ **Teddy Xylophone,** 1948, Fisher-Price, Model No. 752
EX $175   NM $225   MIP $475

(John Murray. Photo by Russ MacKearnin)

❏ **Teddy Zilo,** 1950, Fisher-Price, Model No. 777
EX $35   NM $50   MIP $165

❏ **Ten Little Indians TV Radio,** 1961, Fisher-Price, Model No. 159
EX $25   NM $50   MIP $75

❏ **This Little Pig,** 1963, Fisher-Price, Model No. 910
EX $25   NM $40   MIP $45

❏ **Thumper Bunny,** 1942, Fisher-Price, Model No. 533
EX $225   NM $400   MIP $800

❏ **Timber Toter,** 1957, Fisher-Price, Model No. 810
EX $50   NM $100   MIP $175

❏ **Timmy Turtle,** 1953, Fisher-Price, Model No. 150
EX $40   NM $80   MIP $160

❏ **Tiny Teddy,** 1955, Fisher-Price, Model No. 634
EX $40   NM $75   MIP $145

❏ **Tiny Tim,** 1957, Fisher-Price, Model No. 496
EX $35   NM $70   MIP $135

❏ **Tip-Toe Turtle,** 1962, Fisher-Price, Model No. 773
EX $30   NM $45   MIP $95

❏ **Toot Toot Engine,** 1962, Fisher-Price, Model No. 641
EX $30   NM $45   MIP $90

❏ **Tow Truck,** 1960, Fisher-Price, Model No. 615
EX $45   NM $70   MIP $155

❏ **Toy Wagon,** 1951, Fisher-Price, Model No. 131
EX $125   NM $250   MIP $500

❏ **Trotting Donald Duck,** 1937, Fisher-Price, Model No. 741
EX $300   NM $650   MIP $1450

❏ **Tuggy Turtle,** 1959, Fisher-Price, Model No. 139
EX $45   NM $75   MIP $165

(John Murray, Photo by Ross MacKearnin)

❏ **Uncle Timmy Turtle,** 1956, Fisher-Price, Model No. 125
EX $50   NM $100   MIP $195

❏ **Waggy Woofy,** 1942, Fisher-Price, Model No. 437
EX $100   NM $250   MIP $500

❏ **Walt Disney's Carnival,** 1936, Fisher-Price, Model No. 207
EX $325   NM $600   MIP $1200

❏ **Walt Disney's Donald Duck,** 1936, Fisher-Price, Model No. 208
EX $250   NM $400   MIP $900

❏ **Walt Disney's Easter Parade,** 1936, Fisher-Price, Model No. 475
EX $450   NM $1000   MIP $1900

❏ **Walt Disney's Mickey Mouse,** 1936, Fisher-Price, Model No. 209
EX $250   NM $400   MIP $800

❏ **Walt Disney's Pluto-the-Pup,** 1936, Fisher-Price, Model No. 210
EX $225   NM $450   MIP $800

❏ **Whistling Engine,** 1957, Fisher-Price, Model No. 617
EX $40   NM $80   MIP $160

❏ **Wiggily Woofer,** 1957, Fisher-Price, Model No. 640
EX $40   NM $95   MIP $195

❏ **Winky Blinky Fire Truck,** 1954, Fisher-Price, Model No. 200
EX $45   NM $100   MIP $195

❏ **Woodsy-Wee Circus,** 1931, Fisher-Price, Model No. 201
EX $500   NM $900   MIP $2100

❏ **Woofy Wagger,** 1947, Fisher-Price, Model No. 447
EX $45   NM $75   MIP $185

❏ **Woofy Wowser,** 1940, Fisher-Price, Model No. 700
EX $100   NM $325   MIP $825

❏ **Ziggy Zilo,** 1958, Fisher-Price, Model No. 737
EX $50   NM $100   MIP $175

Games

The Charlie's Angels game in the Farrah Fawcett box shows how important star power can be. It's double the value of a non-Farrah edition, selling for $45 MIP.

Everybody remembers rainy Saturdays when the weather was too crummy outside to do anything, and cartoons were over for the day. At times like that, nothing beat dragging out a game like Stratego, Risk or Chutes and Ladders and challenging anyone within reach for a long afternoon. As you got older, maybe an Avalon Hill strategy game or Dungeons & Dragons would fit the bill. In any case, those great games (in great shape, of course) could be worth something.

Board games and tabletop games as we think of them really got their steam in the Victorian age. McLoughlin Bros. produced some of the best stuff of the era, with gorgeously lithographed packages and games. McLoughlin was purchased by the (now) much better-known Milton Bradley in 1920. Their re-issues of McLoughlin games don't command the same prices as the originals, as you would expect. Parker Brothers, too, is a venerable and recognized force in the world of games, producing them from 1883 until the present day.

Most collectors of games break the hobby into two segments: prewar and postwar. Of course, most postwar games have a common denominator—television. Games based on TV shows are probably one of the hottest segments in the field. For one thing, their box graphics are bright and recognizable, and the shows they represent are conjure up pure nostalgia. The market has fallen off a bit on these items in the past three years or so, but that just makes them easier for the collector to pick up.

These pop-culture games, along with early electronic games are likely to be best bets for collectors. Avoid word games like Scrabble—they just don't appreciate much.

Pricing:

Most experts agree that mint or mint-in-package examples of prewar games are virtually non-existent, so an "n/a" is indicated for that price range. On postwar games, though, three grades, excellent, near-mint, and mint-in-pack are given.

Another postwar TV-era game, "Wagon Train." This again is a case in which a toy overlaps a number of categories—TV toy, game, and character toy... Happily, many postwar games can be quite affordable. This one is valued at $65 MIP.

One of the first interactive games was "Winky Dink." It had a static cling "magic window" that fit over a TV screen and "magic crayons" and a "deluxe erasing mitt" that allowed kids to play along at home. This innovative kit is now valued at $100 MIP.

GAMES

POSTWAR GAMES

BOARD GAMES

❏ **$10,000 Pyramid Game, The,** 1974, Milton Bradley
EX $8   NM $20   MIP $30

❏ **$20,000 Pyramid Game, The,** 1975, Milton Bradley
EX $8   NM $20   MIP $30

❏ **$25,000 Pyramid,** 1980s, Cardinal Industries
EX $15   NM $35   MIP $50

❏ **$64,000 Question Quiz Game,** 1955, Lowell
EX $12   NM $30   MIP $45

❏ **1-2-3 Game Hot Spot!,** 1961, Parker Brothers
EX $6   NM $15   MIP $25

❏ **1863, Civil War Game,** 1961, Parker Brothers
EX $20   NM $40   MIP $65

❏ **2 For The Money,** 1955, Lowell
EX $10   NM $25   MIP $35

❏ **20,000 Leagues Under the Sea,** 1950s, Gardner
EX $25   NM $55   MIP $100

❏ **221 B Baker Street,** 1978, John Hansen
EX $2   NM $6   MIP $10

❏ **25 Ghosts,** 1969, Lakeside
EX $15   NM $25   MIP $40

❏ **3 Up,** 1972, Lakeside
EX $3   NM $7   MIP $12

❏ **300 Mile Race,** 1955, Warren
EX $15   NM $35   MIP $60

❏ **36 Fits,** 1966, Watkins-Strathmore
EX $12   NM $30   MIP $40

❏ **4 Alarm Game,** 1963, Milton Bradley
EX $18   NM $40   MIP $65

❏ **4000 A.D. Interstellar Conflict Game,** 1972, House of Games
EX $8   NM $20   MIP $35

(KP Photo)

❏ **77 Sunset Strip,** 1960, Lowell
EX $35   NM $50   MIP $75

❏ **99, The Game of,** 1969, Broman-Percepta Corp.
EX $8   NM $20   MIP $30

❏ **Abbott & Costello Who's On First?,** 1978, Selchow & Righter
EX $5   NM $10   MIP $15

❏ **ABC Monday Night Football Roger Staubach Edition,** 1973, Aurora
EX $8   NM $20   MIP $35

❏ **ABC Sports Winter Olympics,** 1987, Mindscape
EX $10   NM $15   MIP $25

❏ **Acquire (plastic tiles),** 1968, 3M
EX $12   NM $30   MIP $45

❏ **Acquire (wood tiles),** 1963, 3M
EX $35   NM $75   MIP $120

❏ **Across the Board Horse Racing Game,** 1975, MPH
EX $8   NM $20   MIP $35

❏ **Across the Continent (cars),** 1960, Parker Brothers
EX $20   NM $40   MIP $65

❏ **Across the Continent (trains),** 1952, Parker Brothers
EX $30   NM $50   MIP $80

❏ **Action Baseball,** 1965, Pressman
EX $35   NM $45   MIP $50

❏ **Addams Family,** 1965, Ideal
EX $65   NM $100   MIP $175

❏ **Addams Family,** 1973, Milton Bradley
EX $15   NM $35   MIP $50

❏ **Admirals,** 1973, Parker Brothers (U.K.)
EX $10   NM $25   MIP $35

❏ **Advance To Boardwalk,** 1985, Parker Brothers
EX $5   NM $15   MIP $20

❏ **Adventure in Science, An,** 1950, Jac-mar
EX $20   NM $30   MIP $50

❏ **Agent Zero-M Spy Detector,** 1964, Mattel
EX $30   NM $50   MIP $80

❏ **Aggravation,** 1970, Lakeside
EX $5   NM $10   MIP $15

❏ **Air Assault on Crete,** 1977, Avalon Hill
EX $3   NM $10   MIP $15

❏ **Air Charter,** 1970, Waddington
EX $10   NM $25   MIP $35

❏ **Air Empire,** 1961, Avalon Hill
EX $40   NM $100   MIP $160

❏ **Air Race Around the World,** 1950s, Lido
EX $12   NM $30   MIP $50

❏ **Air Traffic Controller,** 1974, Schaper
EX $12   NM $30   MIP $40

❏ **Airline,** 1985, Mulgara Products
EX $4   NM $10   MIP $15

❏ **Airline: The Jet Age Game,** 1977, MPH Games
EX $6   NM $15   MIP $25

❏ **Alfred Hitchcock "Why?",** 1965, Milton Bradley
EX $10   NM $20   MIP $30

❏ **Alfred Hitchcock Presents Mystery Game "Why",** 1958, Milton Bradley
EX $20   NM $35   MIP $55

(KP Photo)

❏ **Alien,** 1979, Kenner
EX $15   NM $45   MIP $70

❏ **All American Football,** 1969, Cadaco
EX $5   NM $10   MIP $20

(KP Photo)

❏ **All In The Family,** 1972, Milton Bradley
EX $10   NM $20   MIP $30

❏ **All My Children,** 1985, TSR
EX $5   NM $10   MIP $20

❏ **All Pro Baseball,** 1969, Ideal
EX $20   NM $35   MIP $55

❏ **All Pro Basketball,** 1969, Ideal
EX $10   NM $25   MIP $35

❏ **All Pro Football,** 1967, Ideal
EX $8   NM $20   MIP $30

❏ **All Star Baseball,** 1960s, Cadaco-Ellis
EX $20   NM $50   MIP $75

❏ **All Star Baseball,** 1970s, Cadaco-Ellis
EX $10   NM $25   MIP $45

❏ **All Star Baseball,** 1989, Cadaco
EX $5   NM $12   MIP $20

❏ **All Star Baseball Fame,** 1962, Cadaco-Ellis
EX $15   NM $25   MIP $40

❏ **All Star Basketball,** 1950s, Gardner
EX $55   NM $90   MIP $135

❏ **All Star Electric Baseball & Football,** 1955, Harett-Gilmar
EX $35   NM $60   MIP $90

❏ **All Star Football,** 1950, Gardner
EX $20   NM $45   MIP $65

❏ **All The King's Men,** 1979, Parker Brothers
EX $6   NM $10   MIP $15

❏ **All Time Greats Baseball Game,** 1971, Midwest Research
EX $15   NM $35   MIP $50

❏ **Alumni Fun,** 1964, Milton Bradley
EX $8   NM $20   MIP $30

❏ **Amazing Dunninger Mind Reading Game,** 1967, Hasbro
EX $12   NM $30   MIP $40

❏ **American Derby, The**, 1951, Cadaco-Ellis
EX $15   NM $35   MIP $50

❏ **American Dream, The**, 1979, Milton Bradley
EX $10   NM $25   MIP $35

❏ **Animal Crackers**, 1970s, Milton Bradley
EX $4   NM $7   MIP $11

❏ **Annette's Secret Passage**, 1958, Parker Brothers
EX $25   NM $55   MIP $80

❏ **Annie Oakley (larger)**, 1955, Milton Bradley
EX $20   NM $50   MIP $75

❏ **Annie Oakley (smaller game)**, 1950s, Milton Bradley
EX $12   NM $30   MIP $40

❏ **Annie, The Movie Game**, 1981, Parker Brothers
EX $4   NM $6   MIP $10

❏ **Anti-Monopoly**, 1973, Anti-Monopoly
EX $8   NM $20   MIP $30

❏ **APBA "Pro" League Football**, 1980s, APBA
EX $12   NM $20   MIP $30

❏ **APBA Baseball Master Game**, 1975, APBA
EX $20   NM $50   MIP $75

❏ **APBA Pro League Football**, 1964, APBA
EX $25   NM $60   MIP $85

❏ **APBA Saddle Racing Game**, 1970s, APBA
EX $15   NM $25   MIP $40

❏ **Apollo: A Voyage to the Moon**, 1969, Tracianne
EX $12   NM $30   MIP $40

❏ **Apple's Way**, 1974, Milton Bradley
EX $12   NM $30   MIP $40

❏ **Archies, The**, 1969, Whitman
EX $15   NM $35   MIP $50

❏ **Arena**, 1962, Lakeside
EX $6   NM $15   MIP $25

❏ **Arnold Palmer's Inside Golf**, 1961, D.B. Remson
EX $30   NM $70   MIP $100

❏ **Around the World**, 1962, Milton Bradley
EX $10   NM $25   MIP $35

❏ **Around The World in 80 Days**, 1957, Transogram
EX $15   NM $35   MIP $50

❏ **Art Lewis Football Game**, 1955, Morgantown Game
EX $70   NM $115   MIP $175

❏ **Art Linkletter's House Party**, 1968, Whitman
EX $8   NM $20   MIP $30

❏ **As The World Turns**, 1966, Parker Brothers
EX $12   NM $30   MIP $50

❏ **ASG Baseball**, 1989, 3W (World Wide Wargames)
EX $15   NM $35   MIP $50

❏ **ASG Major League Baseball**, 1973, Gerney Games
EX $35   NM $75   MIP $125

❏ **Assembly Line**, 1953, Selchow & Righter
EX $18   NM $45   MIP $65

❏ **Astro Launch**, 1963, Ohio Art
EX $18   NM $40   MIP $60

❏ **Astron**, 1955, Parker Prothers
EX $35   NM $75   MIP $100

(KP Photo)

❏ **A-Team**, 1984, Parker Brothers
EX $5   NM $10   MIP $15

❏ **Atom Ant Game**, 1966, Transogram
EX $25   NM $60   MIP $90

❏ **Aurora Pursuit! Game**, 1973, Aurora
EX $8   NM $25   MIP $40

❏ **Auto Dome**, 1967, Transogram
EX $18   NM $40   MIP $60

❏ **Autograph Baseball Game**, 1948, Philadelphia Inquirer
EX $110   NM $180   MIP $275

❏ **B.T.O. (Big Time Operator)**, 1956, Bettye-B
EX $20   NM $45   MIP $70

❏ **B-17 Queen of The Skies**, 1983, Avalon Hill
EX $6   NM $10   MIP $15

(KP Photo)

❏ **Babes in Toyland**, 1961, Whitman
EX $15   NM $35   MIP $50

❏ **Ballplayer's Baseball Game**, 1955, Jon Weber
EX $30   NM $50   MIP $75

❏ **Bamboozle**, 1962, Milton Bradley
EX $20   NM $45   MIP $65

❏ **Banana Tree**, 1977, Marx
EX $10   NM $15   MIP $25

❏ **Bang, A Game of the Old West**, 1956, Selchow & Righter
EX $35   NM $75   MIP $100

❏ **Bantu**, 1955, Parker Brothers
EX $18   NM $40   MIP $60

❏ **Barbapapa Takes A Trip**, 1977, Selchow & Righter
EX $3   NM $5   MIP $8

❏ **Barbie, Queen of The Prom**, 1960, Mattel
EX $30   NM $60   MIP $85

❏ **Barbie's Little Sister Skipper Game**, 1964, Mattel
EX $15   NM $40   MIP $60

(KP Photo)

❏ **Baretta**, 1976, Milton Bradley
EX $10   NM $25   MIP $40

❏ **Bargain Hunter**, 1981, Milton Bradley
EX $6   NM $15   MIP $25

(KP Photo)

❏ **Barnabas Collins Game**, 1969, Milton Bradley
EX $20   NM $50   MIP $80

(KP Photo)

❏ **Barney Miller**, 1977, Parker Brothers
EX $10   NM $15   MIP $25

❏ **Barnstormer**, 1970s, Marx
EX $20   NM $35   MIP $55

❏ **Bart Starr Quarterback Game**, 1960s
EX $175   NM $295   MIP $450

❏ **Bar-Teen Ranch Game**, 1950s, Warren Built-Rite
EX $10   NM $25   MIP $35

❏ **Baseball Challenge**, 1980, Tri-Valley Games
EX $15   NM $35   MIP $50

❏ **Baseball Game, Official**, 1969, Milton Bradley
EX $100   NM $165   MIP $250

❏ **Baseball Game, The**, 1988, Horatio
EX $12   NM $20   MIP $30

❏ **Baseball Strategy**, 1973, Avalon Hill
EX $6   NM $15   MIP $25

GAMES

❏ **Baseball, A Sports Illustrated Game,** 1971-73, Time
EX $60   **NM** $150   **MIP** $200

❏ **Baseball, Football & Checkers,** 1957, Parker Brothers
EX $20   **NM** $50   **MIP** $75

❏ **Basketball Strategy,** 1974, Avalon Hill
EX $10   **NM** $15   **MIP** $25

(KP Photo)

❏ **Bat Masterson,** 1958, Lowell
EX $45   **NM** $75   **MIP** $120

❏ **Batman,** 1978, Hasbro
EX $15   **NM** $30   **MIP** $50

❏ **Batman and Robin Game,** 1965, Hasbro
EX $30   **NM** $65   **MIP** $95

❏ **Batman Game,** 1966, Milton Bradley
EX $25   **NM** $60   **MIP** $90

❏ **Batter Up,** 1946, M. Hopper
EX $30   **NM** $50   **MIP** $75

❏ **Batter-Rou Baseball Game (Dizzy Dean),** 1950s, Memphis Plastic
EX $100   **NM** $165   **MIP** $250

❏ **Battle Cry,** 1962, Milton Bradley
EX $25   **NM** $60   **MIP** $85

(KP Photo)

❏ **Battle Line,** 1964, Ideal
EX $25   **NM** $50   **MIP** $75

❏ **Battle Masters,** 1992, Milton Bradley
EX $15   **NM** $40   **MIP** $60

(KP Photo)

❏ **Battle of the Planets,** 1970s, Milton Bradley
EX $15   **NM** $25   **MIP** $35

❏ **Battleboard,** 1972, Ideal
EX $10   **NM** $25   **MIP** $35

(KP Photo)

❏ **Battleship,** 1965, Milton Bradley
EX $10   **NM** $15   **MIP** $25

(KP Photo)

❏ **Battlestar Galactica,** 1978, Parker Brothers
EX $10   **NM** $15   **MIP** $25

❏ **Battling Tops Game,** 1968, Ideal
EX $20   **NM** $45   **MIP** $65

❏ **Bazaar,** 1967, 3M
EX $12   **NM** $30   **MIP** $40

❏ **Bazaar,** 1987, Discovery Toys
EX $8   **NM** $20   **MIP** $30

❏ **Beany & Cecil Match It,** 1960s, Mattel
EX $30   **NM** $50   **MIP** $80

❏ **Beat Inflation,** 1975, Avalon Hill
EX $8   **NM** $20   **MIP** $30

❏ **Beat the 8 Ball,** 1975, Ideal
EX $10   **NM** $25   **MIP** $35

❏ **Beat The Buzz,** 1958, Kenner
EX $10   **NM** $15   **MIP** $25

❏ **Beat The Clock,** 1954, Lowell
EX $15   **NM** $45   **MIP** $70

❏ **Beat The Clock,** 1960s, Milton Bradley
EX $6   **NM** $10   **MIP** $16

(KP Photo)

❏ **Beatles Flip Your Wig Game,** 1964, Milton Bradley
EX $60   **NM** $150   **MIP** $250

❏ **Beetle Bailey, The Old Army Game,** 1963, Milton Bradley
EX $40   **NM** $70   **MIP** $90

❏ **Behind the 8 Ball Game,** 1969, Selchow & Righter
EX $8   **NM** $20   **MIP** $35

(KP Photo)

❏ **Ben Casey MD Game,** 1961, Transogram
EX $15   **NM** $30   **MIP** $45

❏ **Bermuda Triangle,** 1976, Milton Bradley
EX $10   **NM** $15   **MIP** $25

❏ **Betsy Ross and the Flag,** 1950s, Transogram
EX $18   **NM** $45   **MIP** $70

(Toy Shop File Photo)

❏ **Beverly Hillbillies Game,** 1963, Standard Toykraft, "If you like the T.V. show… you'll love the game…"
EX $25   **NM** $55   **MIP** $80

❏ **Bewitched,** 1965
EX $50   **NM** $80   **MIP** $120

❏ **Beyond the Stars,** 1964, Game Partners
EX $20   **NM** $45   **MIP** $65

❏ **Bible Baseball,** 1950s, Standard
EX $50   **NM** $75   **MIP** $150

❏ **Big Boggle,** 1979, Parker Brothers
EX $15   **NM** $35   **MIP** $50

❏ **Big Foot,** 1977, Milton Bradley
EX $5   **NM** $12   **MIP** $20

❏ **Big League Baseball,** 1959, Saalfield
EX $20   **NM** $45   **MIP** $65

❏ **Big League Baseball Game,** 1966, 3M
EX $15   **NM** $25   **MIP** $40

❏ **Big League Manager Football,** 1965, BLM
EX $30   **NM** $75   **MIP** $100

❏ **Big Payoff,** 1984, Payoff Enterprises
EX $6   **NM** $10   **MIP** $15

❏ **Big Six Sports Game,** 1950s, Gardner
EX $125   **NM** $295   **MIP** $450

❏ **Big Time Colorado Football,** 1983, B.J. Tall
EX $6   **NM** $10   **MIP** $15

❏ **Big Town,** 1954, Lowell
EX $50   **NM** $80   **MIP** $125

❏ **Billionaire,** 1973, Parker Brothers
EX $5   **NM** $15   **MIP** $20

❏ **Bing Crosby's Game, Call Me Lucky,** 1954, Parker Brothers
EX $15   **NM** $35   **MIP** $50

❏ **Bingo-Matic,** 1954, Transogram
EX $5   NM $10   MIP $20

(KP Photo)

❏ **Bionic Crisis,** 1975, Parker Brothers
EX $6   NM $15   MIP $25

(KP Photo)

❏ **Bionic Woman,** 1976, Parker Brothers
EX $6   NM $15   MIP $25

❏ **Bird Brain,** 1966, Milton Bradley
EX $10   NM $25   MIP $40

❏ **Bird Watcher,** 1958, Parker Brothers
EX $15   NM $35   MIP $50

❏ **Birdie Golf,** 1964, Barris
EX $15   NM $35   MIP $50

❏ **Black Ball Express,** 1957, Schaper
EX $8   NM $25   MIP $40

❏ **Black Beauty,** 1957, Transogram
EX $15   NM $35   MIP $50

❏ **Black Box,** 1978, Parker Brothers
EX $5   NM $10   MIP $15

❏ **Blade Runner,** 1982
EX $25   NM $60   MIP $85

❏ **Blast Off,** 1953, Selchow & Righter
EX $35   NM $75   MIP $100

❏ **Blast, The Game of,** 1973, Ideal
EX $8   NM $20   MIP $35

❏ **Blitzkrieg,** 1965, Avalon Hill
EX $4   NM $10   MIP $16

❏ **Blockhead,** 1954, Russell
EX $10   NM $15   MIP $25

❏ **Blondie,** 1970s, Parker Brothers
EX $6   NM $10   MIP $15

❏ **Blondie and Dagwood's Race for the Office,** 1950, Jaymar
EX $30   NM $45   MIP $70

❏ **Blue Line Hockey,** 1968, 3M
EX $10   NM $25   MIP $40

❏ **Bluff,** 1964, Saalfield
EX $10   NM $25   MIP $40

❏ **BMX Cross Challenge Action Game,** 1988, Cross Challenge
EX $6   NM $10   MIP $15

❏ **Bob Feller's Big League Baseball,** 1949, Saalfield
EX $75   NM $150   MIP $200

❏ **Bobbsey Twins,** 1957, Milton Bradley
EX $8   NM $20   MIP $30

❏ **Bobby Shantz Baseball Game,** 1955, Realistic Games
EX $80   NM $150   MIP $225

❏ **Body Language,** 1975, Milton Bradley
EX $2   NM $5   MIP $10

❏ **Boggle,** 1976, Parker Brothers
EX $3   NM $8   MIP $12

(KP Photo)

❏ **Bonanza Michigan Rummy Game,** 1964, Parker Brothers
EX $30   NM $45   MIP $70

❏ **Bonkers!, This Game is,** 1978, Parker Brothers
EX $3   NM $10   MIP $15

❏ **Boom or Bust,** 1951, Parker Brothers
EX $60   NM $125   MIP $175

❏ **Booth's Pro Conference Football,** 1977, Sher-Co
EX $10   NM $15   MIP $25

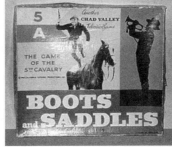

(KP Photo)

❏ **Boots and Saddles,** 1960, Chad Valley
EX $35   NM $65   MIP $100

❏ **Boris Karloff's Monster Game,** 1965, Gems
EX $75   NM $125   MIP $200

❏ **Boston Marathon Game, Official,** 1978, Perl Products
EX $15   NM $25   MIP $35

❏ **Bottoms Up,** 1970s
EX $3   NM $5   MIP $8

❏ **Boundary,** 1970, Mattel
EX $8   NM $20   MIP $30

❏ **Bowl & Score,** 1974, Lowe
EX $6   NM $10   MIP $15

❏ **Bowl And Score,** 1962, Lowe
EX $6   NM $10   MIP $15

❏ **Bowl Bound!,** 1973, Sports Illustrated
EX $15   NM $25   MIP $40

❏ **Brain Waves,** 1977, Milton Bradley
EX $6   NM $15   MIP $25

(KP Photo)

❏ **Branded,** 1966, Milton Bradley
EX $20   NM $50   MIP $90

❏ **Brass Monkey Game, The,** 1973, U.S. Game Systems
EX $6   NM $15   MIP $25

❏ **Break Par Golf Game,** 1950s, Warren/Built-Rite
EX $8   NM $20   MIP $30

❏ **Break The Bank,** 1955, Bettye-B
EX $12   NM $30   MIP $45

❏ **Breaker 1-9,** 1976, Milton Bradley
EX $5   NM $10   MIP $15

❏ **Breakthru,** 1965, 3M
EX $8   NM $20   MIP $30

❏ **Brett Ball,** 1981, 9th Inning
EX $15   NM $30   MIP $45

❏ **Bride Bingo,** 1957, Leister Game
EX $2   NM $5   MIP $8

❏ **Bride Game, The,** 1971, Selchow & Righter
EX $12   NM $30   MIP $40

❏ **Broadside,** 1962, Milton Bradley
EX $35   NM $75   MIP $100

❏ **Broadsides & Board Gameing Parties,** 1984, Milton Bradley
EX $50   NM $125   MIP $175

❏ **Bruce Jenner Decathlon Game,** 1979, Parker Brothers
EX $4   NM $7   MIP $11

❏ **Buck Fever,** 1984, L & D Robton
EX $12   NM $20   MIP $30

❏ **Buck Rogers Game,** 1979, Milton Bradley
EX $10   NM $25   MIP $35

❏ **Buck Rogers: Battle for the 25th Century,** 1988, TSR
EX $18   NM $45   MIP $65

❏ **Buckaroo,** 1947, Milton Bradley
EX $20   NM $35   MIP $55

❏ **Bucket Ball,** 1972, Marx
EX $10   NM $15   MIP $25

❏ **Bug-A-Boo,** 1968, Whitman
EX $6   NM $15   MIP $20

GAMES

(KP Photo)

❑ **Bugaloos**, 1971, Milton Bradley
EX $15   NM $35   MIP $60

❑ **Bugs Bunny Under the Cawit Game**,
1972, Whitman
EX $15   NM $25   MIP $40

❑ **Building Boom**, 1950s, Kohner
EX $10   NM $20   MIP $35

❑ **Built-Rite Swish Basketball Game**,
1950s, Warren/Built-Rite
EX $10   NM $20   MIP $35

(KP Photo)

❑ **Bullwinkle Hide & Seek Game**, 1961,
Milton Bradley
EX $15   NM $35   MIP $50

❑ **Bullwinkle's Super Market Game**,
1970s, Whitman
EX $15   NM $35   MIP $50

❑ **Buster Brown Game and Play Box**,
1950s, Buster Brown Shoes
EX $40   NM $75   MIP $125

❑ **Buy and Sell**, 1953, Whitman
EX $8   NM $20   MIP $30

❑ **Buy or Sell**, 1967, KMS Industries
EX $5   NM $12   MIP $18

❑ **C&O/B&O**, 1969, Avalon Hill
EX $20   NM $50   MIP $95

❑ **Cabbage Patch Kids**, 1984, Parker
Brothers
EX $5   NM $10   MIP $15

❑ **California Raisins Board Game**, 1987,
Decipher
EX $4   NM $16   MIP $25

❑ **Call it Golf**, 1966, Strauss
EX $15   NM $25   MIP $40

❑ **Call My Bluff**, 1965, Milton Bradley
EX $15   NM $20   MIP $30

❑ **Calling All Cars**, 1930s-40s, Parker
Brothers
EX $25   NM $60   MIP $85

❑ **Calling All Cars**, 1950s, Parker Brothers
EX $15   NM $35   MIP $50

❑ **Calvin & The Colonel High Spirits**,
1962, Milton Bradley
EX $12   NM $30   MIP $50

❑ **Camelot**, 1955, Parker Brothers
EX $20   NM $30   MIP $50

❑ **Camouflage**, 1961, Milton Bradley
EX $5   NM $20   MIP $35

❑ **Camp Granada Game, Allan Sherman's**, 1965, Milton Bradley
EX $30   NM $70   MIP $100

❑ **Camp Runamuck**, 1965, Ideal
EX $15   NM $30   MIP $65

❑ **Campaign**, 1966, Campaign Game
EX $8   NM $25   MIP $40

❑ **Campaign**, 1971, Waddington
EX $10   NM $30   MIP $45

❑ **Campaign: The American "Go" Game**,
1961, Saalfield
EX $15   NM $45   MIP $65

❑ **Can You Catch It Charlie Brown?**, 1976,
Ideal
EX $10   NM $25   MIP $35

❑ **Candid Camera Game**, 1963, Lowell
EX $15   NM $40   MIP $65

❑ **Candyland**, 1949, Milton Bradley
EX $25   NM $50   MIP $90

❑ **Candyland**, 1955, Milton Bradley
EX $10   NM $25   MIP $45

❑ **Cannonball Run, The**, 1981, Cadaco
EX $4   NM $16   MIP $25

❑ **Can't Stop**, 1980, Parker Brothers
EX $5   NM $12   MIP $20

❑ **Caper**, 1970, Parker Brothers
EX $30   NM $70   MIP $100

❑ **Capital Punishment**, 1981, Hammerhead
EX $25   NM $45   MIP $75

❑ **Captain America**, 1966, Milton Bradley
EX $40   NM $65   MIP $105

❑ **Captain America**, 1977, Milton Bradley
EX $10   NM $15   MIP $25

❑ **Captain Caveman and the Teen
Angels**, 1981, Milton Bradley
EX $8   NM $20   MIP $30

(KP Photo)

❑ **Captain Gallant Desert Fort Game**,
1956, Transogram
EX $20   NM $40   MIP $65

(KP Photo)

❑ **Captain Kangaroo**, 1956, Milton Bradley
EX $25   NM $85   MIP $125

(KP Photo)

❑ **Captain Video Game**, 1952, Milton Bradley
EX $55   NM $125   MIP $200

❑ **Car Travel Game**, 1958, Milton Bradley
EX $5   NM $16   MIP $25

❑ **Carapace**, 1970, Plan B Corp.
EX $5   NM $16   MIP $25

❑ **Cardino**, 1970, Milton Bradley
EX $10   NM $15   MIP $25

❑ **Careers**, 1957, Parker Brothers
EX $8   NM $20   MIP $30

❑ **Careers**, 1965, Parker Brothers
EX $6   NM $15   MIP $25

❑ **Cargoes**, 1958, Selchow & Righter
EX $15   NM $35   MIP $50

❑ **Carl Hubbell Mechanical Baseball**,
1950, Gotham
EX $100   NM $200   MIP $300

❑ **Carl Yastrzemski's Action Baseball**,
1968, Pressman
EX $90   NM $145   MIP $195

❑ **Carrier Strike**, 1977, Milton Bradley
EX $15   NM $25   MIP $45

❑ **Cars 'n Trucks Build-A-Game**, 1961,
Ideal
EX $15   NM $45   MIP $80

❑ **Cartel**, 1974, Gamut of Games
EX $18   NM $45   MIP $65

❑ **Case of the Elusive Assassin, The**,
1967, Ideal
EX $20   NM $50   MIP $75

❑ **Casey Jones,** 1959, Saalfield
EX $20   NM $45   MIP $65

(KP Photo)

❑ **Casper the Friendly Ghost Game,**
1959, Milton Bradley
EX $5   NM $10   MIP $20

❑ **Casper the Friendly Ghost Game,**
1974, Schaper
EX $8   NM $18   MIP $30

❑ **Castle Risk,** 1986, Parker Brothers
EX $15   NM $35   MIP $50

❑ **Cat & Mouse,** 1964, Parker Brothers
EX $7   NM $15   MIP $20

❑ **Catchword,** 1954, Whitman
EX $3   NM $10   MIP $15

❑ **Catfish Bend Storybook Game,** 1978,
Selchow & Righter
EX $15   NM $20   MIP $35

❑ **Cathedral,** 1986, Mattel
EX $10   NM $25   MIP $35

❑ **Cattlemen, The,** 1977, Selchow &
Righter
EX $10   NM $15   MIP $25

❑ **Cavalcade,** 1953, Selchow & Righter
EX $15   NM $45   MIP $65

❑ **Caveat Emptor,** 1971, Plan B
EX $5   NM $16   MIP $25

❑ **Centipede,** 1983, Milton Bradley
EX $6   NM $10   MIP $15

❑ **Century of Great Fights,** 1969,
Research Games
EX $40   NM $75   MIP $110

❑ **Challenge Golf at Pebble Beach,** 1972,
3M
EX $6   NM $15   MIP $25

❑ **Challenge the Yankees,** 1960s, Hasbro
EX $200   NM $500   MIP $700

❑ **Challenge Yahtzee,** 1974, Milton Bradley
EX $7   NM $15   MIP $20

❑ **Championship Baseball,** 1966, Championship Games
EX $8   NM $20   MIP $30

❑ **Championship Basketball,** 1966,
Championship Games
EX $8   NM $20   MIP $30

❑ **Championship Golf,** 1966, Championship Games
EX $8   NM $20   MIP $30

❑ **Changeover: The Metric Game,** 1976,
John Ladell
EX $8   NM $20   MIP $30

❑ **Changing Society,** 1981, Phil Carter
EX $5   NM $16   MIP $25

❑ **Chaos,** 1965, Amsco Toys
EX $5   NM $16   MIP $25

❑ **Chaos,** 1971, Lakeside
EX $8   NM $20   MIP $30

❑ **Charlie Brown's All Star Baseball
Game,** 1965, Parker Brothers
EX $18   NM $45   MIP $65

❑ **Charlie's Angels,** 1977, Milton Bradley
EX $6   NM $10   MIP $20

(KP Photo)

❑ **Charlie's Angels (Farrah Fawcett box),**
1977, Milton Bradley, Notice the price
difference between this version and the
non-Farrah edition? Star power really
brings up the price on this game
EX $10   NM $20   MIP $45

❑ **Charlotte's Web Game,** 1974, Hasbro
EX $10   NM $25   MIP $35

❑ **Chase, The,** 1966, Cadaco
EX $12   NM $30   MIP $45

❑ **Chaseback,** 1962, Milton Bradley
EX $5   NM $16   MIP $25

❑ **Checkpoint: Danger!,** 1978, Ideal
EX $5   NM $16   MIP $25

❑ **Cherry Ames' Nursing Game,** 1959,
Parker Brothers
EX $40   NM $90   MIP $135

❑ **Chess,** 1977, Milton Bradley
EX $3   NM $5   MIP $8

❑ **Chevyland Sweepstakes,** 1968, Milton
Bradley
EX $25   NM $50   MIP $100

❑ **Chex Ches Football,** 1971, Chex Ches
Games
EX $15   NM $25   MIP $40

❑ **Cheyenne,** 1958, Milton Bradley
EX $25   NM $60   MIP $95

❑ **Chicago Sports Trivia Game,** 1984,
Sports Trivia
EX $6   NM $10   MIP $15

❑ **Chicken In Every Pot, A,** 1980s, Animal
Town Game
EX $20   NM $30   MIP $50

❑ **Children's Hour, The,** 1946, Parker
Brothers
EX $10   NM $30   MIP $45

❑ **CHiPS,** 1981, Ideal
EX $7   NM $10   MIP $20

(KP Photo)

❑ **CHiPS Game,** 1977, Milton Bradley
EX $4   NM $7   MIP $10

❑ **Chit Chat Game,** 1963, Milton Bradley
EX $6   NM $10   MIP $15

❑ **Chopper Strike,** 1976, Milton Bradley
EX $10   NM $25   MIP $40

❑ **Chug-A-Lug,** 1969, Dynamic
EX $5   NM $16   MIP $25

❑ **Chute-5,** 1973, Lowe
EX $5   NM $12   MIP $20

❑ **Chutes & Ladders,** 1956, Milton Bradley
EX $10   NM $15   MIP $25

❑ **Chutzpah,** 1967, Cadaco
EX $10   NM $25   MIP $40

❑ **Chutzpah,** 1967, Middle Earth
EX $15   NM $35   MIP $50

❑ **Cimarron Strip,** 1967, Ideal
EX $35   NM $75   MIP $125

❑ **Circle Racer Board Game,** 1988, Sport
Games USA
EX $6   NM $10   MIP $15

❑ **Cities Game, The,** 1970, Psychology
Today
EX $5   NM $16   MIP $25

❑ **Civil War,** 1961, Avalon Hill
EX $15   NM $45   MIP $65

❑ **Civilization,** 1982, Avalon Hill
EX $7   NM $10   MIP $20

❑ **Clash of the Titans,** 1981, Whitman
EX $10   NM $25   MIP $45

❑ **Class Struggle,** 1978, Bernard Ollman
EX $10   NM $25   MIP $35

❑ **Clean Sweep,** 1960s, Schaper
EX $20   NM $50   MIP $75

❑ **Clean Water,** 1972, Urban Systems
EX $8   NM $25   MIP $40

❑ **Cloak & Dagger,** 1984, Ideal
EX $8   NM $25   MIP $40

GAMES

(KP Photo)

❏ **Close Encounters of the Third Kind,** 1977, Parker Brothers
EX $7   NM $15   MIP $20

❏ **Clue,** 1949, Parker Brothers
EX $25   NM $40   MIP $65

❏ **Clue,** 1972, Parker Brothers
EX $4   NM $7   MIP $11

❏ **Clue Master Detective,** 1988, Parker Brothers
EX $20   NM $55   MIP $75

❏ **Clue: The Great Museum Caper,** 1991, Parker Brothers
EX $8   NM $20   MIP $30

❏ **Code Name: Sector,** 1977, Parker Brothers
EX $10   NM $30   MIP $45

❏ **Collector, The,** 1977, Avalon Hill
EX $5   NM $16   MIP $25

❏ **College Basketball,** 1954, Cadaco-Ellis
EX $10   NM $25   MIP $35

(KP Photo)

❏ **Columbo,** 1973, Milton Bradley
EX $6   NM $10   MIP $15

❏ **Combat,** 1963, Ideal
EX $25   NM $45   MIP $70

❏ **Comin' Round The Mountain,** 1954, Einson-Freeman
EX $30   NM $50   MIP $80

❏ **Computer Baseball,** 1966, Epoch Playtime
EX $25   NM $40   MIP $65

❏ **Computer Basketball,** 1969, Electric Data
EX $10   NM $25   MIP $35

❏ **Computerized Pro Football,** 1971, Data Prog.
EX $15   NM $25   MIP $40

❏ **Concentration (25th Anniversary Ed.),** 1982, Milton Bradley
EX $6   NM $10   MIP $16

❏ **Concentration (3rd Ed.),** 1960, Milton Bradley
EX $12   NM $20   MIP $35

❏ **Conestoga,** 1964, Washburne Research
EX $25   NM $65   MIP $95

❏ **Coney Island, The Game of,** 1956, Selchow & Righter
EX $35   NM $75   MIP $125
(KP Photo)

❏ **Conflict,** 1960, Parker Brothers
EX $15   NM $45   MIP $65

❏ **Confucius Say,** 1960s, Pressman
EX $10   NM $30   MIP $45

❏ **Conquer,** 1979, Whitman
EX $8   NM $17   MIP $25

❏ **Conquest of the Empire,** 1984, Milton Bradley
EX $50   NM $105   MIP $150

❏ **Consetta and Her Wheel of Fate,** 1946, Selchow & Righter
EX $30   NM $75   MIP $110

❏ **Conspiracy,** 1982, Milton Bradley
EX $4   NM $9   MIP $11

❏ **Containment,** 1979, Shamus Gamus
EX $10   NM $25   MIP $35

❏ **Contigo,** 1974, 3M
EX $7   NM $20   MIP $35

❏ **Cootie,** 1949, Schaper
EX $10   NM $25   MIP $35

❏ **Count Coup,** 1979, Marcian Chronicles
EX $10   NM $30   MIP $45

❏ **Count Down Space Game,** 1960, Transogram
EX $15   NM $45   MIP $65

❏ **Countdown,** 1967, Lowe
EX $15   NM $40   MIP $60

❏ **Counter Point,** 1976, Hallmark
EX $10   NM $15   MIP $25

❏ **Cowboy Roundup,** 1952, Parker Brothers
EX $15   NM $25   MIP $40

❏ **Cracker Jack Game,** 1976, Milton Bradley
EX $5   NM $16   MIP $25

❏ **Creature Castle,** 1975, Whitman
EX $12   NM $30   MIP $40

❏ **Creature Features,** 1975, Athol
EX $20   NM $50   MIP $75

❏ **Creature From the Black Lagoon,** 1963, Hasbro
EX $150   NM $410   MIP $750

❏ **Cribb Golf,** 1980s
EX $10   NM $22   MIP $40

❏ **Crosby Derby, The,** 1947, Fishlove
EX $50   NM $90   MIP $135

❏ **Cross Up,** 1974, Milton Bradley
EX $2   NM $5   MIP $10

❏ **Crosswords,** 1954, National Games
EX $12   NM $20   MIP $32

(KP Photo)

❏ **Crusader Rabbit TV Game,** 1960s, Tryne
EX $50   NM $100   MIP $175

❏ **Cub Scouting, The Game of,** 1987, Cadaco
EX $5   NM $16   MIP $25

❏ **Curious George Game,** 1977, Parker Brothers
EX $4   NM $6   MIP $10

❏ **Curse of the Cobras Game,** 1982, Ideal
EX $10   NM $25   MIP $35

❏ **Cut Up Shopping Spree Game,** 1968, Milton Bradley
EX $8   NM $20   MIP $30

❏ **Dallas,** 1980, Yaquinto
EX $10   NM $25   MIP $35

❏ **Dallas,** 1985, Maruca Industries
EX $17   NM $35   MIP $55

❏ **Dallas (TV Role Playing),** 1980, SPI
EX $4   NM $7   MIP $11

❏ **Danger Pass,** 1964, Game Partners
EX $15   NM $45   MIP $65

❏ **Daniel Boone Trail Blazer,** 1964
EX $25   NM $60   MIP $85

❏ **Dark Crystal Game, The,** 1982, Milton Bradley
EX $7   NM $20   MIP $35

❏ **Dark Shadows Game,** 1968, Whitman
EX $18   NM $40   MIP $60

❏ **Dark Tower,** 1981, Milton Bradley
EX $90   NM $212   MIP $280

❏ **Dark World,** 1992, Mattel
EX $12   NM $25   MIP $35

❏ **Dastardly and Muttley,** 1969, Milton Bradley
EX $25   NM $45   MIP $65

❏ **Dating Game, The,** 1967, Hasbro
EX $15   NM $25   MIP $40

❏ **Davy Crockett Adventure Game**, 1956, Gardner
EX $45   NM $75   MIP $120

❏ **Davy Crockett Frontierland Game**, 1955, Parker Brothers
EX $20   NM $50   MIP $75

❏ **Davy Crockett Radar Action Game**, 1955, Ewing Mfg. & Sales
EX $40   NM $100   MIP $150

❏ **Davy Crockett Rescue Race Game**, 1950s, Gabriel
EX $20   NM $50   MIP $75

❏ **Dawn of the Dead**, 1978, SPI
EX $45   NM $95   MIP $135

❏ **Daytona 500 Race Game**, 1989, Milton Bradley
EX $10   NM $25   MIP $35

❏ **Dead Pan**, 1956, Selchow & Righter
EX $8   NM $20   MIP $30

❏ **Deadlock**, 1972, American Greetings
EX $8   NM $20   MIP $30

❏ **Dealer's Choice**, 1972, Parker Brothers
EX $10   NM $25   MIP $35

❏ **Dealer's Choice**, 1974, Gamut of Games
EX $18   NM $45   MIP $65

❏ **Dear Abby**, 1972, Ideal
EX $7   NM $20   MIP $35

❏ **Decathalon**, 1972, Sports Illustrated
EX $10   NM $25   MIP $35

❏ **Decoy**, 1956, Selchow & Righter
EX $12   NM $40   MIP $60

❏ **Deduction**, 1976, Ideal
EX $5   NM $9   MIP $12

❏ **Deluxe Wheel of Fortune**, 1986, Pressman
EX $5   NM $8   MIP $13

❏ **Dennis The Menace Baseball Game**, 1960
EX $22   NM $50   MIP $70

❏ **Denny McLain Magnetik Baseball Game**, 1968, Gotham
EX $115   NM $195   MIP $295

❏ **Deputy Dawg TV Lotto**, 1961, Ideal
EX $15   NM $35   MIP $60

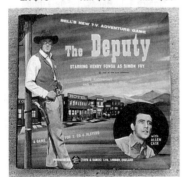

(Toy Shop File Photo)

❏ **Deputy Game, The**, 1960, Bell, "Starring Henry Fonda as Simon Fry"
EX $32   NM $50   MIP $85

❏ **Derby Day**, 1959, Parker Brothers
EX $18   NM $45   MIP $65

❏ **Derby Downs**, 1973, Great Games
EX $10   NM $30   MIP $45

(KP Photo)

❏ **Detectives Game, The**, 1961, Transogram
EX $30   NM $50   MIP $80

❏ **Dick Tracy Crime Stopper**, 1963, Ideal
EX $30   NM $70   MIP $95

(KP Photo)

❏ **Dick Tracy The Master Detective Game**, 1961, Selchow & Righter
EX $25   NM $65   MIP $90

❏ **Dick Van Dyke Board Game**, 1964, Standard Toykraft
EX $45   NM $100   MIP $175

❏ **Diet**, 1972, Dynamic
EX $5   NM $16   MIP $25

❏ **Diner's Club Credit Card Game, The**, 1961, Ideal
EX $15   NM $45   MIP $65

❏ **Dinosaur Island**, 1980, Parker Brothers
EX $5   NM $16   MIP $25

❏ **Diplomacy**, 1961, Games Research
EX $15   NM $35   MIP $50

❏ **Diplomacy**, 1976, Avalon Hill
EX $15   NM $25   MIP $40

❏ **Direct Hit**, 1950s, Northwestern Products
EX $40   NM $70   MIP $110

❏ **Dirty Water—The Water Pollution Game**, 1970, Urban Systems
EX $8   NM $20   MIP $30

❏ **Disney Mouseketeer**, 1964, Parker Brothers
EX $40   NM $65   MIP $100

(KP Photo)

❏ **Disneyland Game**, 1965, Transogram
EX $25   NM $60   MIP $85

❏ **Dispatcher**, 1958, Avalon Hill
EX $30   NM $70   MIP $100

❏ **Dobbin Derby**, 1950, Cadaco-Ellis
EX $8   NM $25   MIP $40

(KP Photo)

❏ **Doctor Who**, 1980s, Denys Fisher
EX $35   NM $75   MIP $100

❏ **Doctor, Doctor! Game**, 1978, Ideal
EX $8   NM $20   MIP $30

(KP Photo)

❏ **Dogfight**, 1962, Milton Bradley
EX $35   NM $75   MIP $100

❏ **Dollar A Second**, 1955, Lowell
EX $12   NM $30   MIP $45

❏ **Dollars & Sense**, 1946, Sidney Rogers
EX $100   NM $150   MIP $200

❏ **Domain**, 1983, Parker Brothers
EX $2   NM $3   MIP $5

❏ **Domination**, 1982, Milton Bradley
EX $8   NM $20   MIP $30

❏ **Don Carter's Strike Bowling Game**, 1964, Saalfield
EX $20   NM $55   MIP $75

❏ **Donald Duck Big Game Box**, 1979, Whitman
EX $10   NM $15   MIP $20

GAMES

❑ **Donald Duck Pins & Bowling Game,** 1955s, Pressman
EX $35   NM $60   MIP $90

❑ **Donald Duck Tiddley Winks Game,** 1950s
EX $6   NM $10   MIP $15

❑ **Donald Duck's Party Game,** 1950s, Parker Brothers
EX $10   NM $35   MIP $50

❑ **Dondi Potato Race Game,** 1950s, Hasbro
EX $15   NM $35   MIP $50

❑ **Donkey Party Game,** 1950, Saalfield
EX $4   NM $10   MIP $15

❑ **Donny & Marie Osmond TV Show Game,** 1977, Mattel
EX $8   NM $25   MIP $40

❑ **Don't Miss the Boat,** 1965, Parker Brothers
EX $12   NM $30   MIP $40

❑ **Doorways to Adventure VCR Game,** 1986, Pressman
EX $6   NM $15   MIP $25

❑ **Doorways to Horror VCR Game,** 1986, Pressman
EX $10   NM $25   MIP $35

❑ **Double Cross,** 1974, Lakeside
EX $5   NM $16   MIP $25

❑ **Double Crossing,** 1988, Lionel Games
EX $10   NM $25   MIP $35

❑ **Double Trouble,** 1987, Milton Bradley
EX $3   NM $5   MIP $8

❑ **Doubletrack,** 1981, Milton Bradley
EX $2   NM $7   MIP $12

(KP Photo)

❑ **Dr. Kildare,** 1962, Ideal
EX $25   NM $40   MIP $65

(KP Photo)

❑ **Dracula Mystery Game,** 1960s, Hasbro
EX $80   NM $160   MIP $225

❑ **Dracula's "I Vant To Bite Your Finger" Game,** 1981, Hasbro
EX $10   NM $20   MIP $30
(KP Photo)

❑ **Dragnet,** 1955, Transogram
EX $35   NM $60   MIP $95

❑ **Dragonlance,** 1988, TSR
EX $15   NM $35   MIP $50

❑ **Dragon's Lair,** 1983, Milton Bradley
EX $7   NM $10   MIP $20

❑ **Dream House,** 1968, Milton Bradley
EX $15   NM $35   MIP $50

❑ **Driver Ed,** 1973, Cadaco
EX $6   NM $10   MIP $20

❑ **Duell,** 1976, Lakeside
EX $5   NM $16   MIP $25

(KP Photo)

❑ **Dukes of Hazzard,** 1981, Ideal
EX $6   NM $15   MIP $25

❑ **Dunce,** 1955, Schaper
EX $7   NM $20   MIP $35

❑ **Dune,** 1984, Parker Brothers
EX $10   NM $25   MIP $35

❑ **Dune, Frank Herbert's,** 1979, Avalon Hill
EX $20   NM $50   MIP $75

❑ **Dungeon Dice,** 1977, Parker Brothers
EX $5   NM $8   MIP $15

❑ **Dungeon!,** 1981, TSR
EX $10   NM $25   MIP $35

❑ **Dungeons & Dragons, Electronic,** 1980, Mattel
EX $12   NM $30   MIP $40

❑ **Duplicate Ad-Lib,** 1976, Lowe
EX $5   NM $10   MIP $15

❑ **Duran Duran Game,** 1985, Milton Bradley
EX $15   NM $25   MIP $40

❑ **Dynomutt,** 1977, Milton Bradley
EX $10   NM $15   MIP $25

❑ **E.T. The Extra-Terrestrial,** 1982, Parker Brothers
EX $6   NM $10   MIP $15

❑ **Earl Gillespie Baseball Game,** 1961, Wei-Gill
EX $25   NM $40   MIP $65

❑ **Earth Satellite Game,** 1956, Gabriel
EX $30   NM $70   MIP $100

❑ **Easy Money,** 1956, Milton Bradley
EX $10   NM $25   MIP $35

❑ **Ecology,** 1970, Urban Systems
EX $7   NM $20   MIP $35

❑ **Egg and I, The,** 1947, Capex
EX $30   NM $50   MIP $80

❑ **El Dorado,** 1977, Invicta
EX $7   NM $20   MIP $35

❑ **Electra Woman and Dyna Girl,** 1977, Ideal
EX $10   NM $25   MIP $45

❑ **Electric Sports Car Race,** 1959, Tudor
EX $35   NM $60   MIP $90

(KP Photo)

❑ **Electronic Detective Game,** 1970s, Ideal
EX $12   NM $30   MIP $40

❑ **Electronic Lightfight,** 1981, Milton Bradley
EX $8   NM $20   MIP $30

❑ **Electronic Radar Search,** 1967, Ideal
EX $10   NM $15   MIP $25

❑ **Eliot Ness and the Untouchables,** 1961, Transogram
EX $30   NM $70   MIP $100

❑ **Ellsworth Elephant Game,** 1960, Selchow & Righter
EX $30   NM $45   MIP $70

❑ **Elmer Wheeler's Fat Boys Game,** 1951, Parker Brothers
EX $18   NM $40   MIP $60

❑ **Elvis Presley Game,** 1957, Teen Age Games
EX $300   NM $650   MIP $1000

❑ **Emenee Chocolate Factory,** 1966
EX $6   NM $10   MIP $15

❑ **Emergency,** 1974, Milton Bradley
EX $15   NM $35   MIP $50

❑ **Emily Post Popularity Game,** 1970, Selchow & Righter
EX $10   NM $25   MIP $40

❑ **Emperor of China,** 1972, Dynamic
EX $10   NM $25   MIP $40

❑ **Empire Auto Races,** 1950s, Empire Plastics
EX $20   NM $30   MIP $50

❑ **Empire Builder (1sy edition),** 1982, Mayfair Games
EX $20   NM $50   MIP $75

(KP Photo)

❑ **Empire Strikes Back, Hoth Ice World,** 1977, Kenner
EX $10   NM $20   MIP $30

❑ **Encore,** 1989, Parker Brothers
EX $8   **NM** $20   **MIP** $30

❑ **Enemy Agent,** 1976, Milton Bradley
EX $8   **NM** $20   **MIP** $30

❑ **Energy Quest,** 1977, Weldon
EX $5   **NM** $16   **MIP** $25

❑ **Engineer,** 1957, Selchow & Righter
EX $8   **NM** $25   **MIP** $40

❑ **Entertainment Trivia Game,** 1984, Lakeside
EX $5   **NM** $10   **MIP** $15

❑ **Entre's Fun & Games In Accounting,** 1988, Entrepreneurial Games
EX $4   **NM** $7   **MIP** $12

❑ **Ergo,** 1977, Invicta
EX $5   **NM** $16   **MIP** $25

(KP Photo)

❑ **Escape From New York,** 1980, TSR
EX $12   **NM** $30   **MIP** $40

❑ **Escape from the Casbah,** 1975, Selchow & Righter
EX $7   **NM** $20   **MIP** $35

❑ **Escape From the Death Star,** 1977, Kenner
EX $10   **NM** $20   **MIP** $30

❑ **Escort: Game of Guys and Gals,** 1955, Parker Brothers
EX $15   **NM** $35   **MIP** $50

❑ **Espionage,** 1973, MPH
EX $6   **NM** $18   **MIP** $30

❑ **Events,** 1974, 3M
EX $6   **NM** $15   **MIP** $25

❑ **Everybody's Talking!,** 1967, Watkins-Strathmore
EX $8   **NM** $25   **MIP** $40

❑ **Executive Decision,** 1971, 3M
EX $5   **NM** $16   **MIP** $25

❑ **Exit,** 1983, Milton Bradley
EX $2   **NM** $6   **MIP** $10

❑ **Expanse,** 1949, Milton Bradley
EX $15   **NM** $45   **MIP** $65

❑ **Extra Innings,** 1975, J. Kavanaugh
EX $30   **NM** $50   **MIP** $75

(KP Photo)

❑ **Eye Guess,** 1960s, Milton Bradley
EX $15   **NM** $20   **MIP** $35

❑ **F.B.I.,** 1958, Transogram
EX $35   **NM** $55   **MIP** $90

❑ **F.B.I. Crime Resistance Game,** 1975, Milton Bradley
EX $12   **NM** $30   **MIP** $40

❑ **F/11 Armchair Quarterback,** 1964, James R. Hock
EX $15   **NM** $25   **MIP** $40

❑ **Fact Finder Fun,** 1963, Milton Bradley
EX $10   **NM** $15   **MIP** $25

❑ **Fall Guy, The,** 1981, Milton Bradley
EX $10   **NM** $15   **MIP** $25

(KP Photo)

❑ **Family Affair,** 1967, Whitman
EX $25   **NM** $40   **MIP** $65

❑ **Family Feud,** 1977, Milton Bradley
EX $4   **NM** $12   **MIP** $20

❑ **Family Ties Game, The,** 1986, Apple Street
EX $10   **NM** $20   **MIP** $25

❑ **Famous 500 Mile Race,** 1988
EX $8   **NM** $13   **MIP** $20

❑ **Fang Bang,** 1966, Milton Bradley
EX $12   **NM** $25   **MIP** $35

❑ **Fangface,** 1979, Parker Brothers
EX $5   **NM** $8   **MIP** $13

❑ **Fantastic Voyage Game,** 1968, Milton Bradley
EX $15   **NM** $25   **MIP** $40

❑ **Fantasy Island Game,** 1978, Ideal
EX $7   **NM** $20   **MIP** $35

❑ **Farming Game, The,** 1979, Weekend Farmer Co.
EX $8   **NM** $20   **MIP** $30

❑ **Fast 111s,** 1981, Parker Brothers
EX $5   **NM** $16   **MIP** $25

❑ **Fastest Gun, The,** 1974, Milton Bradley
EX $10   **NM** $35   **MIP** $50

❑ **Fat Albert,** 1973, Milton Bradley
EX $15   **NM** $25   **MIP** $40

❑ **Fearless Fireman,** 1957, Hasbro
EX $30   **NM** $70   **MIP** $100

(KP Photo)

❑ **Felix the Cat Dandy Candy Game,** 1957, Warren/Built-Rite
EX $15   **NM** $35   **MIP** $50

❑ **Felix the Cat Game,** 1960, Milton Bradley
EX $10   **NM** $25   **MIP** $45

❑ **Felix the Cat Game,** 1968, Milton Bradley
EX $8   **NM** $20   **MIP** $30

❑ **Feudal,** 1967, 3M
EX $8   **NM** $20   **MIP** $30

❑ **Fighter Bomber,** 1977, Cadaco
EX $15   **NM** $25   **MIP** $40

❑ **Finance,** 1962, Parker Brothers
EX $10   **NM** $20   **MIP** $35

❑ **Finger Dinger Man,** 1969, Mattel
EX $10   **NM** $25   **MIP** $35

❑ **Fingers Harry,** 1967, Topper Toys
EX $20   **NM** $50   **MIP** $75

❑ **Fire Chief,** 1957, Selchow & Righter
EX $8   **NM** $25   **MIP** $40

❑ **Fire Fighters!,** 1957, Russell
EX $15   **NM** $25   **MIP** $40

❑ **Fire House Mouse Game,** 1967, Transogram
EX $10   **NM** $35   **MIP** $50

(KP Photo)

❑ **Fireball XL-5,** 1963, Milton Bradley
EX $40   **NM** $100   **MIP** $145

❑ **First Class Farmer,** 1965, F & W Publishing
EX $7   **NM** $20   **MIP** $35

❑ **First Down,** 1970, TGP Games
EX $50   **NM** $80   **MIP** $125

❑ **Fish Bait,** 1965, Ideal
EX $20   **NM** $50   **MIP** $75

❑ **Fish Pond,** 1950s, National Games
EX $10   **NM** $30   **MIP** $45

❑ **Flagship Airfreight: The Airplane Cargo Game,** 1946, Milton Bradley
EX $40   **NM** $70   **MIP** $115

❑ **Flash Gordon,** 1977, Waddington/House Of Games
EX $10   **NM** $25   **MIP** $35

❑ **Flash: The Press Photographer Game,** 1956, Selchow & Righter
EX $18   **NM** $50   **MIP** $75

❑ **Flight Captain,** 1972, Lowe
EX $5   **NM** $16   **MIP** $25

❑ **Flintstones,** 1971, Milton Bradley
EX $6   **NM** $15   **MIP** $25

GAMES

Flintstones, 1980, Milton Bradley
EX $15   NM $20   MIP $35

Flintstones Dino The Dinosaur Game, 1961, Transogram
EX $45   NM $75   MIP $120

Flintstones Hoppy The Hopperoo Game, 1964, Transogram
EX $45   NM $75   MIP $120

Flintstones Mitt-Full Game, 1962, Whitman
EX $40   NM $65   MIP $100

Flintstones Stone Age Game, 1961, Transogram
EX $20   NM $45   MIP $65

Flip Flop Go, 1962, Mattel
EX $6   NM $10   MIP $15

Flip 'N Skip, 1971, Little Kennys
EX $5   NM $10   MIP $15

(KP Photo)

Flipper Flips, 1960s, Mattel
EX $30   NM $50   MIP $80

Flying Nun Game, The, 1968, Milton Bradley
EX $20   NM $30   MIP $50

(KP Photo)

Fonz Game, The, 1976, Milton Bradley
EX $15   NM $25   MIP $40

Fooba-Roo Football Game, 1955, Memphis Plastic
EX $15   NM $35   MIP $50

Football Fever, 1985, Hansen
EX $20   NM $35   MIP $50

Football Strategy, 1962, Avalon Hill
EX $8   NM $25   MIP $40

Football Strategy, 1972, Avalon Hill
EX $3   NM $10   MIP $15

Football, Baseball, & Checkers, 1948, Parker Brothers
EX $15   NM $45   MIP $65

Fore, 1954, Artcraft Paper
EX $20   NM $35   MIP $50

Forest Friends, 1956, Milton Bradley
EX $5   NM $12   MIP $18

Formula One Car Race Game, 1968, Parker Brothers
EX $18   NM $40   MIP $60

Fortress America, 1986, Milton Bradley, Part of a series of intricate strategy games developed by Milton Bradley in the 1980s. Two others in the series were "Axis & Allies" and "Conquest of the Empire"
EX $35   NM $75   MIP $100

Fortune 500, 1979, Pressman
EX $5   NM $16   MIP $25

Foto-Electric Baseball, 1951, Cadaco-Ellis
EX $15   NM $35   MIP $65

(KP Photo)

Foto-Electric Football, 1965, Cadaco
EX $10   NM $25   MIP $35

Four Lane Road Racing, 1963, Transogram
EX $15   NM $45   MIP $65

Fox & Hounds, Game of, 1948, Parker Brothers
EX $10   NM $30   MIP $45

Frank Cavanaugh's American Football, 1955, F. Cavanaugh
EX $25   NM $60   MIP $90

Frankenstein Game, 1962, Hasbro
EX $80   NM $160   MIP $225

Frantic Frogs, 1965, Milton Bradley
EX $15   NM $35   MIP $50

Frisky Flippers Slide Bar Game, 1950s, Warren/Built-Rite
EX $5   NM $10   MIP $15

Frontier Fort Rescue Game, 1956, Gabriel
EX $10   NM $35   MIP $50

Frontier-6, 1980, Rimbold
EX $8   NM $25   MIP $40

F-Troop, 1965, Ideal
EX $40   NM $100   MIP $155

Fu Manchu's Hidden Hoard, 1967, Ideal
EX $20   NM $50   MIP $75

(KP Photo)

Fugitive, 1966, Ideal
EX $40   NM $90   MIP $130

Fun City, 1987, Parker Brothers
EX $8   NM $20   MIP $30

Funky Phantom Game, 1971, Milton Bradley
EX $10   NM $15   MIP $25

G.I. Joe, 1982, International Games
EX $15   NM $25   MIP $40

G.I. Joe Adventure, 1982, Hasbro
EX $20   NM $30   MIP $50

G.I. Joe Card Game, 1965, Whitman
EX $10   NM $15   MIP $25

G.I. Joe Marine Paratrooper, 1965, Hasbro
EX $20   NM $50   MIP $70

G.I. Joe Navy Frogman, 1965, Hasbro
EX $25   NM $60   MIP $85

Gambler, 1977, Parker Brothers
EX $6   NM $15   MIP $25

Gambler's Golf, 1975, Gammon Games
EX $4   NM $10   MIP $15

Games People Play Game, The, 1967, Alpsco
EX $7   NM $20   MIP $35

Gammonball, 1980, Fun-Time Products
EX $10   NM $16   MIP $25

Gang Way For Fun, 1964, Transogram
EX $25   NM $40   MIP $65

Gardner's Championship Golf, 1950s, Gardner
EX $10   NM $35   MIP $50

Garfield, 1981, Parker Brothers
EX $4   NM $6   MIP $10

Garrison's Gorillas, 1967, Ideal
EX $45   NM $75   MIP $120

Gay Puree, 1962
EX $25   NM $40   MIP $65

Gene Autry's Dude Ranch Game, 1950s, Warren/Built-Rite
EX $30   NM $70   MIP $100

General Hospital, 1974, Parker Brothers
EX $7   NM $15   MIP $25

General Hospital, 1980s, Cardinal
EX $15   NM $20   MIP $30

Generals, The, 1980, Ideal
EX $7   NM $20   MIP $35

Gentle Ben Animal Hunt Game, 1967, Mattel
EX $30   NM $70   MIP $100

Geo-Graphy, 1954, Cadaco-Ellis
EX $5   NM $15   MIP $25

George of the Jungle Game, 1968, Parker Brothers
EX $40   NM $90   MIP $125

Get Beep Beep: The Road Runner Game, 1975, Whitman
EX $15   NM $25   MIP $35

Get in That Tub, 1969, Hasbro
EX $15   NM $35   MIP $50

(KP Photo)

❑ **Get Smart Game,** 1966, Ideal
EX $40   **NM** $95   **MIP** $130

❑ **Get That License,** 1955, Selchow & Righter
EX $10   **NM** $35   **MIP** $50

❑ **Get the Message,** 1964, Milton Bradley
EX $5   **NM** $16   **MIP** $25

❑ **Get the Picture,** 1987, Worlds Of Wonder
EX $6   **NM** $10   **MIP** $15

❑ **Gettysburg,** 1960, Avalon Hill
EX $5   **NM** $16   **MIP** $25

❑ **Ghosts,** 1985, Milton Bradley
EX $8   **NM** $20   **MIP** $35

❑ **Giant Wheel Thrills 'n Spills Horse Race,** 1958, Remco
EX $15   **NM** $35   **MIP** $50

❑ **Gil Hodges' Pennant Fever,** 1970, Research Games
EX $35   **NM** $75   **MIP** $100

(KP Photo)

❑ **Gilligan, The New Adventures of,** 1974, Milton Bradley
EX $15   **NM** $35   **MIP** $50

(KP Photo)

❑ **Gilligan's Island,** 1965, Game Gems
EX $175   **NM** $350   **MIP** $600

❑ **Gingerbread Man,** 1964, Selchow & Righter
EX $10   **NM** $35   **MIP** $50

❑ **Globetrotter Basketball, Official,** 1950s, Meljak
EX $60   **NM** $100   **MIP** $150

❑ **Globe-Trotters,** 1950, Selchow & Righter
EX $8   **NM** $25   **MIP** $40

❑ **Go For Broke,** 1965, Selchow & Righter
EX $10   **NM** $15   **MIP** $25

❑ **Go for the Green,** 1973, Sports Illustrated
EX $10   **NM** $25   **MIP** $40

❑ **Goal Line Stand,** 1980, Game Shop
EX $12   **NM** $20   **MIP** $30

❑ **Godfather Game, The (violin case box),** 1971, Family Games
EX $25   **NM** $60   **MIP** $85

❑ **Godfather, The (white box),** 1971, Family Games
EX $8   **NM** $20   **MIP** $30

❑ **Godzilla,** 1960s, Ideal
EX $75   **NM** $250   **MIP** $400

❑ **Godzilla,** 1978, Mattel
EX $30   **NM** $50   **MIP** $80

❑ **Going to Jerusalem,** 1955, Parker Brothers
EX $15   **NM** $35   **MIP** $50

❑ **Going, Going, Gone!,** 1975, Milton Bradley
EX $6   **NM** $15   **MIP** $25

❑ **Gold!,** 1981, Avalon Hill
EX $5   **NM** $16   **MIP** $25

❑ **Golden Trivia Game,** 1984, Western
EX $6   **NM** $10   **MIP** $15

❑ **Goldilocks,** 1955, Cadaco-Ellis
EX $8   **NM** $25   **MIP** $40

❑ **Goldilocks and the Three Bears,** 1973, Cadaco
EX $2   **NM** $6   **MIP** $10

❑ **Gomer Pyle Game,** 1960s, Transogram
EX $20   **NM** $45   **MIP** $65

❑ **Gong Show Game,** 1975, Milton Bradley
EX $15   **NM** $25   **MIP** $40

❑ **Gong Show Game,** 1977, American Publishing
EX $15   **NM** $25   **MIP** $40

❑ **Good Guys 'N Bad Guys,** 1973, Cadaco
EX $5   **NM** $16   **MIP** $25

❑ **Good Ol' Charlie Brown Game,** 1971, Milton Bradley
EX $8   **NM** $20   **MIP** $30

❑ **Goodbye Mr. Chips Game,** 1969, Parker Brothers
EX $8   **NM** $20   **MIP** $30

❑ **Goofy's Mad Maze,** 1970s, Whitman
EX $6   **NM** $10   **MIP** $15

❑ **Goonies,** 1980s, Milton Bradley
EX $12   **NM** $30   **MIP** $40

❑ **Gooses Wild,** 1966, CO-5
EX $2   **NM** $7   **MIP** $12

(KP Photo)

❑ **Gotham Professional Basketball,** 1950s, Gotham
EX $35   **NM** $50   **MIP** $70

❑ **Grand Master of Martial Arts,** 1986, Hoyle
EX $6   **NM** $10   **MIP** $15

❑ **Gray Ghost, The,** 1958, Transogram
EX $30   **NM** $70   **MIP** $100

❑ **Great Escape, The,** 1967, Ideal
EX $8   **NM** $25   **MIP** $40

❑ **Great Grape Ape Game, The,** 1975, Milton Bradley
EX $15   **NM** $25   **MIP** $40

(KP Photo)

❑ **Green Acres Game, The,** 1960s, Standard Toykraft
EX $25   **NM** $65   **MIP** $90

(KP Photo)

❑ **Green Ghost Game,** 1965, Transogram
EX $40   **NM** $90   **MIP** $135

❑ **Green Ghost Game (re-issue),** 1997, Marx
EX $15   **NM** $35   **MIP** $50

❑ **Green Hornet Quick Switch Game,** 1966, Milton Bradley
EX $90   **NM** $225   **MIP** $300

❑ **Gremlins,** 1984, International Games
EX $10   **NM** $15   **MIP** $25

❑ **Greyhound Pursuit,** 1985, N/N Games
EX $8   **NM** $13   **MIP** $20

(KP Photo)

❑ **Grizzly Adams,** 1978, Waddington's House of Games
EX $15   **NM** $25   **MIP** $40

(KP Photo)

GAMES

❏ **Groucho's TV Quiz Game**, 1954, Pressman
EX $30   NM $65   MIP $100
(KP Photo)

❏ **Groucho's You Bet Your Life**, 1955, Lowell
EX $50   NM $100   MIP $140

❏ **Group Therapy**, 1969, Group Therapy Assn.
EX $3   NM $12   MIP $20

❏ **Guinness Book of World Records Game, The**, 1979, Parker Brothers
EX $5   NM $9   MIP $15

❏ **Gulf Strike**, 1983, Victory Games
EX $5   NM $16   MIP $25

(KP Photo)

❏ **Gunsmoke Game**, 1950s, Lowell
EX $40   NM $65   MIP $100

❏ **Gusher**, 1946, Carrom Industries
EX $40   NM $90   MIP $135

❏ **Half-Time Football**, 1979, Lakeside
EX $5   NM $9   MIP $15

❏ **Handicap Harness Racing**, 1978, Hall of Fame Games
EX $15   NM $25   MIP $35

❏ **Hang On Harvey**, 1969, Ideal
EX $15   NM $20   MIP $30

❏ **Hangman**, 1976, Milton Bradley
EX $5   NM $8   MIP $15

❏ **Hank Aaron Baseball Game**, 1970s, Ideal
EX $50   NM $80   MIP $125

❏ **Hank Aaron Bases Loaded**, 1976, Twentieth Century Enterprises
EX $45   NM $70   MIP $100

❏ **Hank Bauer's "Be a Manager"**, 1960s, Barco Games
EX $75   NM $125   MIP $175

❏ **Happiness**, 1972, Milton Bradley
EX $12   NM $30   MIP $45

❏ **Happy Days**, 1976, Parker Brothers
EX $8   NM $20   MIP $30

❏ **Happy Little Train Game, The**, 1957, Milton Bradley
EX $3   NM $12   MIP $20

(KP Photo)

❏ **Hardy Boys Mystery Game, Secret of Thunder Mountain**, 1978, Parker Brothers
EX $7   NM $15   MIP $25

❏ **Hardy Boys Mystery Game, The**, 1968, Milton Bradley
EX $6   NM $15   MIP $25

❏ **Hardy Boys Treasure**, 1960, Parker Brothers
EX $25   NM $50   MIP $85

❏ **Harlem Globetrotters Game**, 1971, Milton Bradley
EX $12   NM $30   MIP $50

❏ **Harlem Globetrotters Official Edition Basketball**, 1970s, Cadaco-Ellis
EX $45   NM $75   MIP $115

❏ **Harpoon**, 1955, Gabriel
EX $20   NM $45   MIP $65

❏ **Harry Lorayne Memory Game, The**, 1976, Reiss
EX $7   NM $20   MIP $35

❏ **Hashimoto San**, 1963, Transogram
EX $30   NM $45   MIP $70

❏ **Haul the Freight**, 1962, Bar-Zim
EX $15   NM $50   MIP $75

❏ **Haunted House Game**, 1963, Ideal
EX $120   NM $250   MIP $400

❏ **Haunted Mansion**, 1970s, Lakeside
EX $60   NM $150   MIP $200

❏ **Have Gun Will Travel Game**, 1959, Parker Brothers
EX $30   NM $75   MIP $100
(KP Photo)

❏ **Hawaii Five-O**, 1960s, Remco
EX $30   NM $90   MIP $120

❏ **Hawaiian Eye**, 1960, Transogram
EX $50   NM $120   MIP $160

❏ **Hawaiian Punch Game**, 1978, Mattel
EX $5   NM $16   MIP $25

❏ **Hector Heathcote**, 1963, Transogram
EX $35   NM $75   MIP $100

❏ **Hex: The Zig-Zag Game**, 1950, Parker Brothers
EX $10   NM $35   MIP $50

❏ **Hey Fatso**, 1969, Hasbro
EX $15   NM $35   MIP $50

❏ **Hey Pa, There's a Goat on the Roof!**, 1965, Parker Brothers
EX $20   NM $50   MIP $70

❏ **Hide 'N' Thief**, 1965, Whitman
EX $7   NM $20   MIP $35

❏ **Hide-N-Seek**, 1967, Ideal
EX $20   NM $50   MIP $75

❏ **High-Bid**, 1965, 3M
EX $7   NM $20   MIP $35

❏ **Highway Traffic Game**, 1957, John H Allison Jr.
EX $15   NM $35   MIP $50

❏ **Hi-Ho! Cherry-O**, 1960, Whitman
EX $6   NM $10   MIP $15

❏ **Hijacked**, 1973, Valley Games
EX $12   NM $30   MIP $40

❏ **Hip Flip**, 1968, Parker Brothers
EX $6   NM $15   MIP $25

❏ **Hippety Hop**, 1947, Corey Game
EX $25   NM $40   MIP $65

❏ **Hippopotamus**, 1961, Remco
EX $8   NM $25   MIP $40

❏ **Hispaniola, The Game of**, 1957, Schaper
EX $30   NM $70   MIP $100

❏ **Hit The Beach**, 1965, Milton Bradley
EX $45   NM $85   MIP $120

❏ **Hobbit Game, The**, 1978, Milton Bradley
EX $25   NM $60   MIP $85

❏ **Hock Shop**, 1975, Whitman
EX $3   NM $12   MIP $20

❏ **Hocus Pocus**, 1960s, Transogram
EX $30   NM $45   MIP $70

❏ **Hog Tied**, 1981, Selchow & Righter
EX $3   NM $12   MIP $20

❏ **Hogan's Heroes Game**, 1966, Transogram
EX $45   NM $85   MIP $120

❏ **Holiday**, 1958, Replogle Globes
EX $40   NM $65   MIP $100

❏ **Holiday**, 1973, RGI-Athol
EX $18   NM $40   MIP $60

❏ **Hollywood Awards Game**, 1976, Milton Bradley
EX $8   NM $25   MIP $40

❏ **Hollywood Go**, 1954, Parker Brothers
EX $10   NM $25   MIP $35

❏ **Hollywood Squares**, 1974, Ideal
EX $6   NM $10   MIP $15

❏ **Hollywood Squares**, 1980, Milton Bradley
EX $4   NM $6   MIP $10

❏ **Hollywood Stars, The Game of**, 1955, Whitman
EX $8   NM $20   MIP $30

❏ **Home Court Basketball**, 1954
EX $145   NM $250   MIP $375

❏ **Home Game**, 1960s, Pressman
EX $30   NM $50   MIP $80

❏ **Home Stretch Harness Racing**, 1967, Lowe
EX $15   NM $35   MIP $50

❏ **Home Team Baseball Game**, 1957, Selchow & Righter
EX $18   NM $45   MIP $65

❏ **Honey West**, 1965, Ideal
EX $50   NM $85   MIP $135
(KP Photo)

❏ **Honeymooners Game, The**, 1986, TSR
EX $7   NM $12   MIP $20

❏ **Hoodoo**, 1950, Tryne
EX $4   NM $10   MIP $15

❏ **Hookey Go Fishin'**, 1974, Cadaco
EX $8   NM $16   MIP $25

❏ **Hopalong Cassidy Chinese Checkers Game**, 1950s
EX $20   NM $50   MIP $75

(KP Photo)

❑ **Hopalong Cassidy Game,** 1950s, Milton Bradley
EX $40   NM $100   MIP $145

❑ **Horse Play,** 1962, Schaper
EX $10   NM $35   MIP $50

❑ **Horseshoe Derby Game,** 1950s, Built-Rite
EX $8   NM $20   MIP $30

❑ **Hot Property!,** 1980s, Take One Games
EX $8   NM $25   MIP $40

❑ **Hot Rod,** 1953, Harett-Gilmar
EX $15   NM $35   MIP $50

❑ **Hot Wheels Game,** 1982, Whitman
EX $8   NM $13   MIP $20

❑ **Hot Wheels Wipe-Out Game,** 1968, Mattel
EX $15   NM $35   MIP $50

❑ **Hotels,** 1987, Milton Bradley
EX $15   NM $35   MIP $50

❑ **Houndcats Game,** 1970s, Milton Bradley
EX $8   NM $15   MIP $25

❑ **House Party,** 1968, Whitman
EX $10   NM $25   MIP $35

❑ **Houston Astros Baseball Challenge Game,** 1980, Croque
EX $15   NM $25   MIP $35

❑ **How To Succeed In Business Without Really Trying,** 1963, Milton Bradley
EX $6   NM $15   MIP $25

❑ **Howard Hughes Game, The,** 1972, Family Games
EX $10   NM $35   MIP $50

❑ **Howdy Doody Adventure Game,** 1950s, Milton Bradley
EX $45   NM $75   MIP $100

❑ **Howdy Doody Quiz Show,** 1950s, Multiple Products
EX $20   NM $40   MIP $75

❑ **Howdy Doody's Electric Carnival Game,** Harrett-Gilmar
EX $15   NM $20   MIP $35

❑ **Howdy Doody's Own Game,** 1949, Parker Brothers
EX $40   NM $90   MIP $135

❑ **Howdy Doody's Three Ring Circus,** 1950, Harett-Gilmar
EX $45   NM $75   MIP $120

(KP Photo)

❑ **Howdy Doody's TV Game,** 1950s, Milton Bradley
EX $35   NM $50   MIP $100

❑ **Huckleberry Hound,** 1981, Milton Bradley
EX $10   NM $20   MIP $35

❑ **Huckleberry Hound Bumps,** 1960, Transogram
EX $20   NM $50   MIP $75

❑ **Huckleberry Hound Spin-O-Game,** 1959
EX $45   NM $75   MIP $120

❑ **Huckleberry Hound Tiddly Winks,** 1959, Milton Bradley
EX $15   NM $30   MIP $60

❑ **Huckleberry Hound Western Game,** 1959, Milton Bradley
EX $25   NM $40   MIP $65

❑ **Huff 'N Puff Game,** 1968, Schaper
EX $6   NM $15   MIP $25

❑ **Huggermugger,** 1989, Huggermugger Co.
EX $8   NM $20   MIP $30

(KP Photo)

❑ **Hullabaloo,** 1965, Remco
EX $25   NM $65   MIP $90

❑ **Humor Rumor,** 1969, Whitman
EX $10   NM $20   MIP $30

❑ **Humpty Dumpty Game,** 1950s, Lowell
EX $10   NM $25   MIP $35

❑ **Hunch,** 1956, Happy Hour
EX $7   NM $20   MIP $35

❑ **Hungry Ant, The,** 1978, Milton Bradley
EX $5   NM $16   MIP $25

❑ **Hunt For Red October,** 1988, TSR
EX $5   NM $15   MIP $25

❑ **Hurry Up,** 1971, Parker Brothers
EX $5   NM $16   MIP $25

❑ **Hurry Waiter! Game,** 1969, Ideal
EX $8   NM $20   MIP $30

❑ **Husker Du,** 1970, Regina Products
EX $10   NM $25   MIP $35

❑ **I Dream of Jeannie Game,** 1965, Milton Bradley
EX $30   NM $75   MIP $105

❑ **I Spy,** 1965, Ideal
EX $35   NM $75   MIP $100

❑ **I Vant to Bite Your Finger,** 1981, Hasbro
EX $12   NM $30   MIP $40

❑ **I Wanna Be President,** 1983, J.R. Mackey
EX $5   NM $16   MIP $25

❑ **Ice Cube Game, The,** 1972, Milton Bradley
EX $50   NM $125   MIP $175

(KP Photo)

❑ **Identipops,** 1969, Playvalue
EX $75   NM $175   MIP $250

❑ **I'm George Gobel, And Here's The Game,** 1955, Schaper
EX $12   NM $30   MIP $40

❑ **Image,** 1972, 3M
EX $3   NM $12   MIP $20

❑ **Incredible Hulk,** 1978, Milton Bradley
EX $6   NM $10   MIP $15

❑ **Indiana Jones: Raiders of The Lost Ark,** 1981, Kenner
EX $20   NM $35   MIP $55

❑ **Indianapolis 500 75th Running Race Game,** 1991, International Games
EX $8   NM $13   MIP $20

❑ **Input,** 1984, Milton Bradley
EX $4   NM $7   MIP $15

❑ **Inside Moves,** 1985, Parker Brothers
EX $3   NM $12   MIP $20

❑ **Inspector Gadget,** 1983, Milton Bradley
EX $15   NM $25   MIP $40

❑ **Instant Replay,** 1987, Parker Brothers
EX $8   NM $13   MIP $20

❑ **Intercept,** 1978, Lakeside
EX $7   NM $20   MIP $35

❑ **International Airport Game,** 1964, Magic Wand
EX $8   NM $20   MIP $30

❑ **International Grand Prix,** 1975, Cadaco
EX $8   NM $20   MIP $30

❑ **Interpretation of Dreams,** 1969, Hasbro
EX $7   NM $15   MIP $25

❑ **Interstate Highway,** 1963, Selchow & Righter
EX $20   NM $50   MIP $75

GAMES

(KP Photo)

❏ **Intrigue,** 1954, Milton Bradley
EX $12   NM $30   **MIP** $40

❏ **Inventors, The,** 1974, Parker Brothers
EX $5   NM $12   **MIP** $20

❏ **Ipcress File,** 1966, Milton Bradley
EX $20   NM $50   **MIP** $75

(KP Photo)

❏ **Ironside,** 1976, Ideal
EX $55   NM $95   **MIP** $150

(KP Photo)

❏ **Is the Pope Catholic?!,** 1986, Crowley Connections
EX $10   NM $25   **MIP** $45

❏ **Isolation,** 1978, Lakeside
EX $2   NM $7   **MIP** $12

❏ **It Takes Two,** 1970, NBC-Hasbro
EX $5   NM $12   **MIP** $18

❏ **Itinerary,** 1980, Xanadu Leisure
EX $3   NM $12   **MIP** $20

❏ **Jace Pearson's Tales of The Texas Rangers,** 1955, E.E. Fairchild
EX $20   NM $50   **MIP** $75

❏ **Jack and The Beanstalk,** 1946, National Games
EX $30   NM $45   **MIP** $75

❏ **Jack and The Beanstalk Adventure Game,** 1957, Transogram
EX $25   NM $50   **MIP** $75

❏ **Jack Barry's Twenty One,** 1956, Lowell
EX $20   NM $30   **MIP** $50

❏ **Jackie Gleason's and AW-A-A-A-Y We Go!,** 1956, Transogram
EX $75   NM $125   **MIP** $200
(KP Photo)

❏ **Jackie Gleason's Story Stage Game,** 1955, Utopia Enterprises
EX $100   NM $200   **MIP** $300

❏ **Jackpot,** 1975, Milton Bradley
EX $7   NM $11   **MIP** $20

❏ **Jacmar Big League Electric Baseball,** 1950s, Jacmar
EX $100   NM $175   **MIP** $250

❏ **James Bond 007 Goldfinger Game,** 1966, Milton Bradley
EX $35   NM $75   **MIP** $100

❏ **James Bond 007 Thunderball Game,** 1965, Milton Bradley
EX $35   NM $75   **MIP** $100

❏ **James Bond Message From M Game,** 1966, Ideal
EX $100   NM $250   **MIP** $350

❏ **James Bond Secret Agent 007 Game,** 1964, Milton Bradley
EX $15   NM $35   **MIP** $50

❏ **James Bond You Only Live Twice,** 1984, Victory Games
EX $5   NM $8   **MIP** $13

❏ **James Clavell's Noble House,** 1987, FASA
EX $6   NM $15   **MIP** $25

❏ **James Clavell's Shogun,** 1983, FASA
EX $6   NM $15   **MIP** $25

❏ **James Clavell's Tai-Pan,** 1987, FASA
EX $6   NM $15   **MIP** $25

❏ **James Clavell's Whirlwind,** 1986, FASA
EX $6   NM $15   **MIP** $25
(KP Photo)

❏ **Jan Murray's Charge Account,** 1961, Lowell
EX $25   NM $40   **MIP** $65

❏ **Jan Murray's Treasure Hunt,** 1950s, Gardner
EX $10   NM $25   **MIP** $35

❏ **JDK Baseball,** 1982, JDK Baseball
EX $20   NM $45   **MIP** $65

❏ **Jeanne Dixon's Game of Destiny,** 1968, Milton Bradley
EX $7   NM $12   **MIP** $20

❏ **Jeopardy,** 1964, Milton Bradley
EX $10   NM $15   **MIP** $25

❏ **Jerry Kramer's Instant Replay,** 1970, EMD Enterprises
EX $15   NM $25   **MIP** $40

❏ **Jet World,** 1975, Milton Bradley
EX $5   NM $16   **MIP** $25

❏ **Jetsons Fun Pad Game,** 1963, Milton Bradley
EX $40   NM $100   **MIP** $145

❏ **Jetsons Game,** 1985, Milton Bradley
EX $5   NM $10   **MIP** $15

❏ **Jetsons Out of this World Game,** 1963, Transogram
EX $40   NM $100   **MIP** $140

❏ **Jimmy the Greek Oddsmaker Football,** 1974, Aurora
EX $10   NM $25   **MIP** $35

❏ **Jockette,** 1950s, Jockette
EX $25   NM $40   **MIP** $60

❏ **Jockey,** 1976, Hallmark Games
EX $10   NM $25   **MIP** $35

❏ **Joe Palooka Boxing Game,** 1950s, Lowell
EX $35   NM $65   **MIP** $100

❏ **John Drake Secret Agent,** 1966, Milton Bradley
EX $30   NM $45   **MIP** $70

❏ **Johnny Ringo,** 1959, Transogram
EX $40   NM $90   **MIP** $135

❏ **Johnny Unitas Football Game,** 1970, Pro Mentor
EX $15   NM $35   **MIP** $50

❏ **Joker's Wild,** 1973, Milton Bradley
EX $5   NM $10   **MIP** $15

❏ **Jonathan Livingston Seagull,** 1973, Mattel
EX $8   NM $20   **MIP** $30

(KP Photo)

❏ **Jonny Quest Game,** 1964, Transogram
EX $200   NM $500   **MIP** $700

❏ **Jose Canseco's Perfect Baseball Game,** 1991, Perfect Game
EX $8   NM $13   **MIP** $20

❏ **Jubilee,** 1954, Cadaco-Ellis
EX $10   NM $25   **MIP** $35

❏ **Jumbo Jet,** 1963, Jumbo
EX $18   NM $45   **MIP** $65

❏ **Jumpin',** 1964, 3M
EX $7   NM $20   **MIP** $35

❏ **Jumping DJ,** 1962, Mattel
EX $15   NM $50   **MIP** $75

❏ **Junior Bingo-Matic,** 1968, Transogram
EX $6   NM $10   **MIP** $15

❏ **Junior Executive,** 1963, Whitman
EX $7   NM $15   **MIP** $30

❏ **Junior Quarterback Football,** 1950s, Warren/Built-Rite
EX $7   NM $20   **MIP** $35

❏ **Junk Yard Game,** 1975, Ideal
EX $8   NM $20   **MIP** $30

❏ **Jurisprudence,** 1974, James Vail
EX $8   NM $20   **MIP** $30

❏ **Justice,** 1954, Lowell
EX $25   NM $55   **MIP** $75

❏ **Justice League of America,** 1967, Hasbro
EX $70   NM $150   **MIP** $250

❑ **Ka Bala,** 1965, Transogram
EX $40 NM $75 MIP $120

❑ **Karate, The Game of,** 1964, Selchow & Righter
EX $7 NM $20 MIP $35

❑ **Karter Peanut Shell Game,** 1978, Morey & Neely
EX $7 NM $20 MIP $35

❑ **Kar-Zoom,** 1964, Whitman
EX $15 NM $20 MIP $35

❑ **Kennedys, The,** 1962, Transogram
EX $25 NM $60 MIP $90

❑ **Kentucky Derby,** 1960, Whitman
EX $15 NM $25 MIP $40

❑ **Kentucky Jones,** 1964, T. Cohn
EX $25 NM $40 MIP $65

❑ **Keyword,** 1954, Parker Brothers
EX $3 NM $7 MIP $10

❑ **Kick-Off Soccer,** 1978, Camden Products
EX $7 NM $20 MIP $35

❑ **King Kong Game,** 1963, Ideal
EX $75 NM $200 MIP $325

❑ **King Kong Game,** 1966, Milton Bradley
EX $8 NM $20 MIP $30

❑ **King Kong Game,** 1976, Ideal
EX $8 NM $20 MIP $30

❑ **King Leonardo and His Subjects Game,** 1960, Milton Bradley
EX $18 NM $45 MIP $65

❑ **King of the Hill,** 1965, Schaper
EX $25 NM $60 MIP $80

❑ **King of the Sea,** 1975, Ideal
EX $8 NM $25 MIP $40

❑ **King Oil,** 1974, Milton Bradley
EX $25 NM $55 MIP $75

❑ **King Tut's Game,** 1978, Cadaco
EX $5 NM $16 MIP $25

(KP Photo)

❑ **King Zor, The Dinosaur Game,** 1964, Ideal
EX $45 NM $85 MIP $120

❑ **Kismet,** 1971, Lakeside
EX $6 NM $15 MIP $25

❑ **KISS On Tour Game,** 1978, Aucoin
EX $25 NM $60 MIP $80

❑ **Klondike,** 1975, Gamma Two
EX $12 NM $30 MIP $40

❑ **Knight Rider,** 1983, Parker Brothers
EX $7 NM $12 MIP $20

(KP Photo)

❑ **Kojak,** 1975, Milton Bradley
EX $7 NM $12 MIP $20

❑ **Kommisar,** 1960s, Selchow & Righter
EX $12 NM $30 MIP $40

❑ **Koo Koo Choo Choo,** 1960s, Ohio Art
EX $12 NM $30 MIP $40

❑ **Kooky Carnival,** 1969, Milton Bradley
EX $10 NM $35 MIP $50

❑ **Korg 70,000 BC,** 1974, Milton Bradley
EX $7 NM $15 MIP $25

(KP Photo)

❑ **Kreskin's ESP,** 1966, Milton Bradley
EX $4 NM $10 MIP $18

❑ **Krull,** 1983, Parker Brothers
EX $6 NM $10 MIP $15

❑ **KSP Baseball,** 1983, Koch Sports Products
EX $25 NM $60 MIP $85

❑ **Kukla & Ollie,** 1962, Parker Brothers
EX $20 NM $45 MIP $65

❑ **Labyrinth (movie game),** 1986, Golden
EX $25 NM $60 MIP $85

❑ **Lancer,** 1968, Remco
EX $40 NM $90 MIP $135

(KP Photo)

❑ **Land of The Giants,** 1968, Ideal
EX $60 NM $125 MIP $175

❑ **Land of The Lost,** 1975, Milton Bradley
EX $10 NM $25 MIP $35

❑ **Landmarks, The Game of,** 1962, Selchow & Righter
EX $6 NM $15 MIP $25

❑ **Landslide,** 1971, Parker Brothers
EX $5 NM $16 MIP $25

❑ **Laramie,** 1960, Lowell
EX $50 NM $100 MIP $140

❑ **Las Vegas Baseball,** 1987, Samar Enterprises
EX $8 NM $13 MIP $20

❑ **Laser Attack Game,** 1978, Milton Bradley
EX $7 NM $20 MIP $35

❑ **Lassie Game,** 1965, Game Gems
EX $10 NM $35 MIP $50

❑ **Last Straw,** 1966, Schaper
EX $5 NM $10 MIP $15

(KP Photo)

❑ **Laugh-In's Squeeze Your Bippy Game,** 1968, Hasbro
EX $35 NM $75 MIP $100

❑ **Laurel & Hardy Game,** 1962, Transogram
EX $12 NM $30 MIP $40

(KP Photo)

❑ **Laverne & Shirley Game,** 1977, Parker Brothers
EX $9 NM $15 MIP $25

❑ **Leave It To Beaver Ambush Game,** 1959, Hasbro
EX $20 NM $45 MIP $70

❑ **Leave It To Beaver Money Maker,** 1959, Hasbro
EX $20 NM $45 MIP $70

(KP Photo)

❑ **Leave It To Beaver Rocket To The Moon,** 1959, Hasbro
EX $20 NM $45 MIP $70

❑ **Lee Vs Meade: Battle of Gettysburg,** 1974, Gamut of Games
EX $7 NM $15 MIP $25

❑ **Legend of Jesse James Game, The,** 1965, Milton Bradley
EX $30 NM $70 MIP $100

GAMES

LeMans, 1961, Avalon Hill
EX $25   NM $60   MIP $85

Let's Bowl a Game, 1960, DMR
EX $5   NM $12   MIP $20

Let's Drive, 1969, Milton Bradley
EX $8   NM $20   MIP $30

Let's Go to the Races, 1987, Parker Brothers
EX $7   NM $20   MIP $35

Let's Make a Deal, 1964, Milton Bradley
EX $12   NM $30   MIP $40

Let's Make A Deal, 1970s, Ideal
EX $10   NM $15   MIP $25

Let's Play Golf "The Hawaiian Open", 1968, Burlu
EX $8   NM $20   MIP $30

(KP Photo)

Let's Play Safe Traffic Game, 1960s, X-Acto
EX $25   NM $50   MIP $90

Let's Play Tag, 1958, Milton Bradley
EX $5   NM $16   MIP $25

Let's Take a Trip, 1962, Milton Bradley
EX $8   NM $20   MIP $30

Leverage, 1982, Milton Bradley
EX $4   NM $6   MIP $10

LF Baseball, 1980, Len Feder
EX $18   NM $45   MIP $65

Lie Detector Game, 1961, Mattel
EX $20   NM $50   MIP $75

Lie Detector Game, 1987, Pressman
EX $8   NM $20   MIP $30

Lieutenant, The, 1963, Transogram
EX $30   NM $70   MIP $100

Life, The Game of, 1960, Milton Bradley
EX $8   NM $20   MIP $30

Limit Up, 1980, Willem
EX $6   NM $18   MIP $30

Line Drive, 1953, Lord & Freber
EX $18   NM $45   MIP $65

Linebacker Football, 1990, Linebacker
EX $12   NM $20   MIP $30

Linkup, 1972, American Greetings
EX $5   NM $16   MIP $25

Linus the Lionhearted Uproarious Game, 1965, Transogram
EX $50   NM $85   MIP $135

Linx, 1972, American Greetings
EX $6   NM $15   MIP $25

Lion and the White Witch, The, 1983, David Cook
EX $5   NM $16   MIP $25

(KP Photo)

Lippy the Lion Game, 1963, Transogram
EX $25   NM $45   MIP $70

Little Black Sambo, 1952, Cadaco-Ellis
EX $50   NM $100   MIP $140

Little Boy Blue, 1955, Cadaco-Ellis
EX $6   NM $18   MIP $30

Little Creepies Monster Game, 1974, Toy Factory
EX $6   NM $10   MIP $15

Little House On The Prairie, 1978, Parker Brothers
EX $12   NM $30   MIP $40

Little League Baseball Game, 1950s, Standard Toykraft
EX $25   NM $45   MIP $70

Little Orphan Annie, 1981, Parker Brothers
EX $10   NM $20   MIP $30

Little Red Schoolhouse, 1952, Parker Brothers
EX $10   NM $25   MIP $35

Lobby, 1949, Milton Bradley
EX $8   NM $25   MIP $40

Long Shot, 1962, Parker Brothers
EX $45   NM $75   MIP $125

Longball, 1975, Ashburn Industries
EX $35   NM $75   MIP $100

Look All-Star Baseball Game, 1960, Progressive Research
EX $35   NM $60   MIP $90

Looney Tunes Game, 1968, Milton Bradley
EX $20   NM $40   MIP $65

Lord of the Rings, The, 1979, Milton Bradley
EX $40   NM $85   MIP $110

Los Angeles Dodgers Baseball Game, 1964, Ed-U-Cards
EX $10   NM $25   MIP $35

Lost Gold, 1975, Parker Brothers
EX $7   NM $20   MIP $35

(KP Photo)

Lost In Space Game, 1965, Milton Bradley
EX $45   NM $75   MIP $120

Lost Treasure, 1982, Parker Brothers
EX $7   NM $20   MIP $35

Lottery Game, 1972, Selchow & Righter
EX $6   NM $18   MIP $30

Louie the Electrician, ca. 1960, Hasbro
EX $20   NM $50   MIP $70

Love Boat World Cruise, 1980, Ungame
EX $5   NM $15   MIP $20

Loving Game, The, 1987, R.J.E. Enterprises
EX $4   NM $6   MIP $10

Lucan, The Wolf Boy, 1977, Milton Bradley
EX $5   NM $10   MIP $15

Lucky Break, 1975, Gabriel
EX $10   NM $20   MIP $30

Lucky Strike, 1972, International Toy
EX $5   NM $10   MIP $15

Lucky Town, 1946, Milton Bradley
EX $15   NM $50   MIP $75

Lucy Show Game, The, 1962, Transogram
EX $60   NM $100   MIP $160

Lucy's Tea Party Game, 1971, Milton Bradley
EX $20   NM $35   MIP $55

Ludwig Von Drake Ball Toss Game, 1960
EX $6   NM $10   MIP $15

Luftwaffe, 1971, Avalon Hill
EX $3   NM $8   MIP $15

M Squad, 1958, Bell Toys
EX $35   NM $75   MIP $125

M*A*S*H* Game, 1981, Milton Bradley
EX $15   NM $35   MIP $50

MacDonald's Farm, 1948, Selchow & Righter
EX $12   NM $30   MIP $40

(KP Photo)

❏ **MAD Magazine Game, The,** 1979, Parker Brothers
EX $4　　　NM $12　　　MIP $20

❏ **MAD, What Me Worry?,** 1987, Milton Bradley
EX $6　　　NM $10　　　MIP $15

❏ **Madame Planchette Horoscope Game,** 1967, Selchow & Righter
EX $6　　　NM $18　　　MIP $30

❏ **Magic Miles,** 1956, Hasbro
EX $10　　　NM $25　　　MIP $35

❏ **Magilla Gorilla,** 1964, Ideal
EX $40　　　NM $65　　　MIP $100

❏ **Magnetic Flying Saucers,** 1950s, Pressman
EX $21　　　NM $35　　　MIP $55

❏ **Magnificent Race,** 1975, Parker Brothers
EX $10　　　NM $25　　　MIP $40

❏ **Mail Run,** 1960, Quality Games
EX $35　　　NM $75　　　MIP $100

❏ **Main Street Baseball,** 1989, Main St. Toy
EX $20　　　NM $35　　　MIP $55

❏ **Major League Baseball,** 1965, Cadaco
EX $10　　　NM $20　　　MIP $30

❏ **Major League Baseball Magnetic Dart Game,** 1958, Pressman
EX $20　　　NM $45　　　MIP $65

(KP Photo)

❏ **Man from U.N.C.L.E. Napoleon Solo Game,** 1965, Ideal
EX $25　　　NM $45　　　MIP $70

❏ **Man from U.N.C.L.E. THRUSH Ray Gun Affair Game,** 1966, Ideal
EX $50　　　NM $85　　　MIP $135

❏ **Manage Your Own Team,** 1950s, Warren
EX $10　　　NM $30　　　MIP $40

❏ **Management,** 1960, Avalon Hill
EX $10　　　NM $25　　　MIP $40

❏ **Mandinka,** 1978, Lowe
EX $3　　　NM $12　　　MIP $20

❏ **Manhunt,** 1972, Milton Bradley
EX $5　　　NM $16　　　MIP $25

❏ **Maniac,** 1979, Ideal
EX $7　　　NM $15　　　MIP $20

❏ **Margie, The Game of Whoopie,** 1961, Milton Bradley
EX $12　　　NM $30　　　MIP $50

❏ **Marlin Perkins' Zoo Parade,** 1965, Cadaco-Ellis
EX $12　　　NM $30　　　MIP $40

❏ **Martin Luther King Jr.,** 1980, Cadaco
EX $6　　　NM $10　　　MIP $15

❏ **Mary Hartman, Mary Hartman,** 1976, Reiss Games
EX $10　　　NM $25　　　MIP $35

(KP Photo)

❏ **Mary Poppins Carousel Game,** 1964, Parker Brothers
EX $12　　　NM $30　　　MIP $50

❏ **Masquerade Party,** 1955, Bettye-B
EX $45　　　NM $75　　　MIP $100

❏ **Mastermind,** 1970s, Invicta
EX $5　　　NM $10　　　MIP $15

❏ **Masterpiece, The Art Auction Game,** 1971, Parker Brothers
EX $8　　　NM $20　　　MIP $30

❏ **Match Game (3rd Ed.), The,** 1963, Milton Bradley
EX $15　　　NM $25　　　MIP $40

❏ **Matchbox Traffic Game,** 1960s, Bronner
EX $25　　　NM $45　　　MIP $70

(KP Photo)

❏ **McDonald's Game, The,** 1975, Milton Bradley
EX $12　　　NM $30　　　MIP $40

(KP Photo)

❏ **McHale's Navy Game,** 1962, Transogram
EX $30　　　NM $50　　　MIP $80

❏ **McMurtle Turtle,** 1965, Cadaco-Ellis
EX $8　　　NM $25　　　MIP $40

❏ **Mechanic Mac,** 1961, Selchow & Richter
EX $15　　　NM $35　　　MIP $50

❏ **Meet The Presidents,** 1953, Selchow & Righter
EX $8　　　NM $20　　　MIP $30

❏ **Megiddo,** 1985, Global Games
EX $8　　　NM $20　　　MIP $30

(KP Photo)

❏ **Melvin The Moon Man,** 1960s, Remco
EX $30　　　NM $70　　　MIP $100

❏ **Men Into Space,** 1960, Milton Bradley
EX $20　　　NM $60　　　MIP $90

❏ **Merger,** 1965, Universal Games
EX $12　　　NM $30　　　MIP $40

(KP Photo)

❏ **Merry Milkman,** 1955, Hasbro
EX $35　　　NM $85　　　MIP $125

❏ **Merv Griffin's Word For Word,** 1963, Mattel
EX $5　　　NM $16　　　MIP $25

❏ **Miami Vice: The Game,** 1984, Pepperlane
EX $10　　　NM $25　　　MIP $35

❏ **Mickey Mantle's Action Baseball,** 1960, Pressman
EX $50　　　NM $125　　　MIP $175

(KP Photo)

❏ **Mickey Mantle's Big League Baseball,** 1958, Gardner
EX $125　　　NM $250　　　MIP $325

❏ **Mickey Mouse,** 1950, Jacmar
EX $35　　　NM $55　　　MIP $90

❏ **Mickey Mouse,** 1976, Parker Brothers
EX $6　　　NM $10　　　MIP $15

GAMES

Mickey Mouse Basketball, 1950s, Gardner
EX $55   NM $90   MIP $135

Mickey Mouse Lotto Game, 1950s, Jaymar
EX $10   NM $15   MIP $25

Mickey Mouse Pop Up Game, 1970s, Whitman
EX $7   NM $15   MIP $20

Mickey Mouse Slugaroo, 1950s
EX $20   NM $30   MIP $50

Mid Life Crisis, 1982, Gameworks
EX $5   NM $15   MIP $20

Mighty Comics Super Heroes Game, 1966, Transogram
EX $30   NM $70   MIP $100

(KP Photo)

Mighty Hercules Game, 1963, Hasbro
EX $125   NM $300   MIP $500

(KP Photo)

Mighty Heroes on the Scene Game, 1960s, Transogram
EX $35   NM $75   MIP $120

Mighty Mouse, 1978, Milton Bradley
EX $15   NM $20   MIP $30

(KP Photo)

Mighty Mouse Rescue Game, 1960s, Harett-Gilmar
EX $20   NM $50   MIP $75

(KP Photo)

Milton The Monster, 1966, Milton Bradley
EX $25   NM $45   MIP $70

Mind Over Matter, 1968, Transogram
EX $10   NM $15   MIP $25

Miss America Pageant Game, 1974, Parker Brothers
EX $12   NM $30   MIP $40

Miss Popularity Game, 1961, Transogram
EX $20   NM $35   MIP $55

Missing Links, 1964, Milton Bradley
EX $6   NM $18   MIP $35

Mission: Impossible, 1967, Ideal
EX $40   NM $100   MIP $135

(KP Photo)

Mission: Impossible, 1975, Berwick
EX $10   NM $15   MIP $25

Mister Ed Game, 1962, Parker Brothers
EX $20   NM $50   MIP $75

Mister Football, 1951, Alkay
EX $30   NM $75   MIP $100

Mob Strategy, 1969, NBC-Hasbro
EX $4   NM $10   MIP $15

Monday Morning Quarterback, 1963, Zbinden
EX $8   NM $25   MIP $35

Money Card: Amer. Express Travel Game, 1972, Schaper
EX $8   NM $20   MIP $30

Money! Money! Money!, 1957, Whitman
EX $15   NM $35   MIP $50

(KP Photo)

Monkees Game, 1968, Transogram
EX $30   NM $75   MIP $105

Monkeys and Coconuts, 1965, Schaper
EX $6   NM $15   MIP $20

Monopoly (large maroon box), 1964, Parker Brothers
EX $12   NM $30   MIP $40

(KP Photo)

Monopoly (train cover), 1958, Parker Brothers
EX $30   NM $70   MIP $100

Monster Game, 1977, Ideal
EX $25   NM $60   MIP $85

Monster Game, The, 1965, Milton Bradley
EX $15   NM $25   MIP $40

Monster Mansion, 1981, Milton Bradley
EX $20   NM $50   MIP $75

Monster Squad, 1977, Milton Bradley
EX $10   NM $25   MIP $40

Monsters of the Deep, 1976, Whitman
EX $5   NM $16   MIP $25

Moon Blast-Off, 1970, Schaper
EX $12   NM $30   MIP $40

Moon Shot, 1960s, Cadaco
EX $15   NM $35   MIP $60

Moon Tag, Game of, 1957, Parker Brothers
EX $40   NM $90   MIP $135

(KP Photo)

Mork and Mindy, 1978, Milton Bradley
EX $6   NM $15   MIP $25

Mostly Ghostly, 1975, Cadaco
EX $8   NM $20   MIP $30

Movie Moguls, 1970, RGI
EX $15   NM $35   MIP $50

Movie Studio Mogul, 1981, International Mktg.
EX $8   NM $25   MIP $40

❑ **Mr. Bug Goes To Town,** 1955, Milton Bradley
EX $8   NM $20   MIP $30

❑ **Mr. Doodle's Dog,** 1940s, Selchow & Righter
EX $20   NM $45   MIP $70

❑ **Mr. Machine Game,** 1961, Ideal
EX $40   NM $90   MIP $135

❑ **Mr. Magoo Maddening Misadventures Game, The,** 1970, Transogram
EX $45   NM $75   MIP $120

❑ **Mr. Magoo Visits The Zoo,** 1961, Lowell
EX $25   NM $45   MIP $70

❑ **Mr. President,** 1967, 3M
EX $8   NM $25   MIP $40

❑ **Mr. Ree,** 1957, Selchow & Righter
EX $10   NM $30   MIP $45

❑ **Mt. Everest,** 1955, Gabriel
EX $18   NM $40   MIP $60

❑ **Mug Shots,** 1975, Cadaco
EX $7   NM $12   MIP $20

❑ **Munsters Drag Race Game,** 1965, Hasbro
EX $250   NM $600   MIP $800

❑ **Munsters Masquerade Game,** 1965, Hasbro
EX $250   NM $600   MIP $800

❑ **Munsters Picnic Game,** 1965, Hasbro
EX $200   NM $500   MIP $700

(KP Photo)

❑ **Muppet Show,** 1977, Parker Brothers
EX $6   NM $15   MIP $25

❑ **Murder on the Orient Express,** 1967, Ideal
EX $20   NM $50   MIP $75

❑ **Murder She Wrote,** 1985, Warren
EX $4   NM $6   MIP $10

❑ **Mushmouse & Punkin Puss,** 1964, Ideal
EX $45   NM $75   MIP $120

❑ **MVP Baseball, The Sports Card Game,** 1989, Ideal
EX $8   NM $13   MIP $20

❑ **My Fair Lady,** 1960s, Standard Toykraft
EX $15   NM $35   MIP $50

(KP Photo)

❑ **My Favorite Martian,** 1963, Transogram
EX $50   NM $90   MIP $125

(KP Photo)

❑ **My First (Walt Disney Character) Game,** 1963, Gabriel
EX $20   NM $35   MIP $60

❑ **Mystery Checkers,** 1950s, Creative Designs
EX $15   NM $20   MIP $30

❑ **Mystery Date,** 1965, Milton Bradley
EX $60   NM $125   MIP $175

❑ **Mystery Date Game,** 1972, Milton Bradley
EX $30   NM $70   MIP $100

❑ **Mystery Mansion,** 1984, Milton Bradley
EX $10   NM $25   MIP $35

❑ **Mystic Skull The Game of Voodoo,** 1965, Ideal
EX $15   NM $40   MIP $60

❑ **Mystic Wheel of Knowledge,** 1950s, Novel Toy
EX $15   NM $25   MIP $40

❑ **Name That Tune,** 1959, Milton Bradley
EX $12   NM $30   MIP $50

❑ **Names and Faces,** 1960, Pressman
EX $6   NM $15   MIP $25

❑ **Nancy Drew Mystery Game,** 1957, Parker Brothers
EX $35   NM $75   MIP $110

❑ **NASCAR Daytona 500,** 1990, Milton Bradley
EX $10   NM $25   MIP $35

❑ **National Football League Quarterback, Official,** 1965, Standard Toykraft
EX $12   NM $30   MIP $40

❑ **National Inquirer,** 1991, Tyco
EX $10   NM $15   MIP $20

❑ **National Lampoon's Sellout,** 1970s, Cardinal
EX $6   NM $15   MIP $25

❑ **National Pro Football Hall of Fame Game,** 1965, Cadaco
EX $15   NM $25   MIP $40

❑ **National Pro Hockey,** 1985, Sports Action
EX $15   NM $25   MIP $40

(KP Photo)

❑ **National Velvet Game,** 1950s, Transogram
EX $20   NM $40   MIP $65

❑ **Naval Battle,** 1954, Coronet Products
EX $25   NM $60   MIP $85

❑ **NBA Basketball Game, Official,** 1970s, Gerney Games
EX $35   NM $75   MIP $100

❑ **NBC Game of the Week,** 1969, Hasbro
EX $10   NM $25   MIP $35

❑ **NBC Peacock,** 1966, Selchow & Righter
EX $20   NM $50   MIP $75

❑ **NBC Pro Playoff,** 1969, Hasbro
EX $10   NM $25   MIP $35

❑ **NBC TV News,** 1960, Dadan
EX $15   NM $35   MIP $50

❑ **Nebula,** 1976, Nebula
EX $4   NM $6   MIP $10

❑ **Neck & Neck,** 1981, Yaquinto
EX $8   NM $13   MIP $20

❑ **Negamco Basketball,** 1975, Nemadji Game
EX $10   NM $16   MIP $25

❑ **New Avengers Shooting Game,** 1976, Denys Fisher
EX $165   NM $275   MIP $440

❑ **New Frontier,** 1962, Colorful Products
EX $30   NM $50   MIP $80

❑ **New York World's Fair,** 1964, Milton Bradley
EX $20   NM $50   MIP $75

❑ **Newlywed Game (1st Ed.),** 1967, Hasbro
EX $8   NM $20   MIP $30

(KP Photo)

❑ **Newlywed Game (2nd Ed.),** 1967, Hasbro
EX $11   NM $22   MIP $35

❑ **Newtown,** 1972, Harwell Associates
EX $15   NM $35   MIP $50

❑ **Next President, The,** 1971, Reiss
EX $15   NM $35   MIP $50

GAMES

NFL Armchair Quarterback, 1986, Trade Wind
EX $8   NM $13   MIP $20

NFL Franchise, 1982, Rohrwood
EX $10   NM $16   MIP $25

NFL Game Plan, 1980, Tudor
EX $6   NM $10   MIP $15

NFL Quarterback, 1977, Tudor
EX $8   NM $20   MIP $30

NFL Strategy, 1976, Tudor
EX $15   NM $35   MIP $50

NHL All-Pro Hockey, 1969, Ideal
EX $12   NM $30   MIP $40

NHL Strategy, 1976, Tudor
EX $10   NM $35   MIP $50

Nieuchess, 1961, Avalon Hill
EX $12   NM $40   MIP $60

Nightmare, 1991, Chieftain Products
EX $8   NM $20   MIP $30

Nightmare II, III, IV (add-ons, each), mid-1990s, Chieftain Products
EX $15   NM $35   MIP $50

Nightmare On Elm Street, 1989, Cardinal
EX $15   NM $30   MIP $45

Nile, 1967, Lowe
EX $6   NM $18   MIP $30

Nirtz, The Game is, 1961, Ideal
EX $8   NM $20   MIP $30

No Respect, The Rodney Dangerfield Game, 1985, Milton Bradley
EX $2   NM $6   MIP $8

No Time for Sergeants Game, 1964, Ideal
EX $12   NM $40   MIP $60

Noah's Ark, 1953, Cadaco-Ellis
EX $8   NM $25   MIP $40

Nok-Hockey, 1947, Carrom
EX $20   NM $35   MIP $55

Noma Party Quiz, 1947, Noma Electric
EX $20   NM $35   MIP $50

Northwest Passage, 1969, Impact
EX $8   NM $20   MIP $30

Number Please TV Quiz, 1961, Parker Brothers
EX $15   NM $25   MIP $40

Numble, 1968, Selchow & Righter
EX $4   NM $10   MIP $15

Numeralogic, 1973, American Greetings
EX $6   NM $18   MIP $30

Nurses, The, 1963, Ideal
EX $10   NM $35   MIP $50

Nuts to You, 1969, Hasbro
EX $15   NM $35   MIP $50

O.J. Simpson See-Action Football, 1974, Kenner
EX $50   NM $125   MIP $175

Obsession, 1978, Mego
EX $5   NM $10   MIP $15

Obstruction, 1979, Whitman
EX $4   NM $10   MIP $15

Octopus, 1954, Norton Games
EX $12   NM $40   MIP $60

Off To See The Wizard, 1968
EX $10   NM $15   MIP $25

Oh Magoo Game, 1960s, Warren
EX $15   NM $30   MIP $45

Oh What a Mountain, 1980, Milton Bradley
EX $5   NM $16   MIP $25

Oh, Nuts! Game, 1968, Ideal
EX $10   NM $25   MIP $35

Oh-Wah-Ree, 1966, 3M
EX $8   NM $20   MIP $30

Oil Power, 1980s, Antfamco
EX $20   NM $45   MIP $65

Old Shell Game, The, 1974, Selchow & Righter
EX $7   NM $20   MIP $35

Oldies But Goodies, 1987, Orig. Sound Record
EX $6   NM $18   MIP $30

On Guard, 1967, Parker Brothers
EX $6   NM $10   MIP $15

Oodles, 1992, Milton Bradley
EX $8   NM $20   MIP $30

Operation, 1965, Milton Bradley
EX $5   NM $12   MIP $18

Opinion, 1970, Selchow & Righter
EX $6   NM $15   MIP $25

Option, 1983, Parker Brothers
EX $2   NM $7   MIP $12

Orbit, 1959, Parker Brothers
EX $10   NM $30   MIP $50

Organized Crime, 1974, Koplow Games
EX $6   NM $18   MIP $30

Orient Express, 1985, Just Games
EX $5   NM $16   MIP $25

Original Home Jai-Alai Game, The, 1984, Design Origin
EX $15   NM $25   MIP $35

Oscar Robertson's Pro Basketball Strategy, 1964, Research Games
EX $30   NM $70   MIP $100

Our Gang Bingo, 1958
EX $50   NM $85   MIP $135

Outdoor Survival, 1972, Avalon Hill
EX $2   NM $6   MIP $10

Outer Limits, 1964, Milton Bradley
EX $80   NM $180   MIP $275

Outlaw & Posse, 1978, Milton Bradley
EX $8   NM $20   MIP $30

Outlaw Trail, 1972, Dynamic
EX $6   NM $18   MIP $30

Outwit, 1978, Parker Brothers
EX $5   NM $10   MIP $15

Over the Rainbow See-Saw, 1949, Milton Bradley
EX $12   NM $30   MIP $40

Overboard, 1978, Lakeside
EX $3   NM $12   MIP $18

Overland Trail Board Game, 1960, Transogram
EX $35   NM $75   MIP $100

Ozark Ike's Complete 3 Game Set, 1956, Warren Built-Rite
EX $55   NM $90   MIP $135

P.T. Boat 109 Game, 1963, Ideal
EX $18   NM $45   MIP $65

Pac-Man, 1980, Milton Bradley
EX $5   NM $15   MIP $20

Pan American World Jet Flight Game, 1960, Hasbro
EX $10   NM $35   MIP $50

Panic Button, 1978, Mego
EX $7   NM $15   MIP $20

Panzer Blitz, 1970, Avalon Hill
EX $6   NM $12   MIP $20

Panzer Leader, 1974, Avalon Hill
EX $8   NM $15   MIP $25

Par '73, 1961, Big Top Games
EX $15   NM $25   MIP $40

Par Golf, 1950s, National Games
EX $20   NM $50   MIP $75

Parcheesi (Gold Seal Ed.), 1964, Selchow & Righter
EX $7   NM $12   MIP $20

Pari Horse Race Card Game, 1959, Pari Sales
EX $20   NM $35   MIP $50

❏ **Paris Metro,** 1981, Infinity Games
EX $10   NM $16   MIP $25

❏ **Park and Shop,** 1952, Traffic Game
EX $35   NM $75   MIP $100

❏ **Park and Shop Game,** 1960, Milton Bradley
EX $30   NM $70   MIP $110

❏ **Parker Brothers Baseball Game,** 1955, Parker Brothers
EX $25   NM $60   MIP $85

❏ **Parollette,** 1946, Selchow & Righter
EX $18   NM $40   MIP $60

(KP Photo)

❏ **Partridge Family,** 1974, Milton Bradley
EX $10   NM $25   MIP $40

❏ **Pass It On,** 1978, Selchow & Righter
EX $3   NM $12   MIP $20

❏ **Pass the Buck,** 1964, Transco Adult Games
EX $12   NM $30   MIP $40

(KP Photo)

❏ **Password,** 1963, Milton Bradley
EX $6   NM $15   MIP $25

❏ **Pathfinder,** 1977, Milton Bradley
EX $5   NM $15   MIP $20

❏ **Patty Duke Game,** 1963, Milton Bradley
EX $18   NM $45   MIP $65

❏ **Paul Brown's Football Game,** 1947, Trikilis
EX $110   NM $180   MIP $275

❏ **Payday,** 1975, Parker Brothers
EX $3   NM $7   MIP $12

❏ **Payday: The People's Game,** 1975, Payday Game Co/Barker
EX $12   NM $30   MIP $40

❏ **Paydirt,** 1979, Avalon Hill
EX $12   NM $30   MIP $40

❏ **Paydirt!,** 1973, Time, Inc., (Sports Illustrated)
EX $10   NM $25   MIP $35

❏ **Payoff Machine Game,** 1978, Ideal
EX $5   NM $16   MIP $25

❏ **Pazaz,** 1978, E.S.Lowe
EX $4   NM $10   MIP $15

❏ **Peanut Butter & Jelly Game,** 1971, Parker Brothers
EX $12   NM $30   MIP $40

(KP Photo)

❏ **Peanuts: The Game of Charlie Brown And His Pals,** 1959, Selchow & Righter
EX $20   NM $30   MIP $50

❏ **Pebbles Flintstone Game,** 1962, Transogram
EX $20   NM $35   MIP $55

❏ **Pee Wee Reese Marble Game,** 1956, Pee Wee Enterprises
EX $175   NM $295   MIP $450

❏ **Penetration,** 1968, Crea-Tek
EX $8   NM $20   MIP $30

❏ **Pennant Chasers Baseball Game,** 1946, Craig Hopkins
EX $25   NM $45   MIP $70

❏ **Pennant Drive,** 1980, Accu-Stat Game
EX $8   NM $13   MIP $20

❏ **People Trivia Game,** 1984, Parker Brothers
EX $7   NM $11   MIP $20

❏ **People's Court, The,** 1986, Pressman
EX $4   NM $10   MIP $15

❏ **Per Plexus,** 1976, Aladdin
EX $10   NM $25   MIP $35

❏ **Perils of Pauline,** 1964, Marx
EX $40   NM $90   MIP $135

❏ **Perquackey,** 1970, Lakeside
EX $4   NM $9   MIP $12

❏ **Perry Mason Case of The Missing Suspect Game,** 1959, Transogram
EX $20   NM $30   MIP $50

❏ **Personalysis,** 1957, Lowell
EX $15   NM $25   MIP $40

❏ **Pete the Plumber,** c. 1960, Hasbro
EX $20   NM $50   MIP $75

❏ **Peter Gunn Dectective Game,** 1960, Lowell
EX $25   NM $60   MIP $90

❏ **Peter Pan,** 1953, Transogram
EX $15   NM $35   MIP $60

❏ **Peter Potamus Game,** 1964, Ideal
EX $30   NM $50   MIP $80

❏ **Peter Principle Game,** 1973, Skor-Mor
EX $6   NM $18   MIP $30

❏ **Peter Principle Game,** 1981, Avalon Hill
EX $5   NM $16   MIP $25

❏ **Petropolis,** 1976, Pressman
EX $10   NM $35   MIP $50

❏ **Petticoat Junction,** 1963, Standard Toykraft
EX $25   NM $55   MIP $90

❏ **Phalanx,** 1964, Whitman
EX $10   NM $30   MIP $45

❏ **Phantom Game, The,** 1965, Transogram
EX $95   NM $160   MIP $255

❏ **Phantom's Complete Three Game Set, The,** 1955, Built-Rite
EX $30   NM $75   MIP $125

❏ **Phil Silvers' You'll Never Get Rich Game,** 1955, Gardner
EX $25   NM $60   MIP $85

(KP Photo)

❏ **Philip Marlowe,** 1960, Transogram
EX $20   NM $50   MIP $75

❏ **Phlounder,** 1962, 3M
EX $6   NM $18   MIP $30

❏ **Pig in the Garden,** 1960, Schaper
EX $20   NM $50   MIP $70

❏ **Pigskin Vegas,** 1980, Jokari/US
EX $6   NM $10   MIP $15

❏ **Pilgrimage,** 1984, Whitehall Games
EX $8   NM $20   MIP $30

❏ **Pinbo Sport-o-Rama,** 1950s
EX $35   NM $60   MIP $90

❏ **Pinhead,** 1959, Remco
EX $10   NM $35   MIP $50

❏ **Pink Panther Game,** 1977, Warren
EX $10   NM $25   MIP $40

❏ **Pink Panther Game,** 1981, Cadaco
EX $4   NM $7   MIP $12

❏ **Pinky Lee and the Runaway Frankfurters,** 1950s, Lisbeth Whiting
EX $30   NM $75   MIP $105

❏ **Pinocchio,** 1977, Parker Brothers
EX $5   NM $8   MIP $15

❏ **Pinocchio Board Game, Disney's,** 1960, Parker Brothers
EX $10   NM $15   MIP $25

❏ **Pinocchio, The New Adventures of,** 1961, Lowell
EX $25   NM $45   MIP $70

GAMES

(KP Photo)

Pirate and Traveller, 1953, Milton Bradley
EX $10   NM $25   MIP $40

Pirate Raid, 1956, Cadaco-Ellis
EX $8   NM $25   MIP $40

Pirate's Cove, 1956, Gabriel
EX $15   NM $35   MIP $65

Pizza Pie Game, 1974, Milton Bradley
EX $5   NM $16   MIP $25

Plane Parade, 1950s, Harett-Gilmar Inc.
EX $25   NM $60   MIP $85

Planet of the Apes, 1974, Milton Bradley
EX $18   NM $45   MIP $65

Play Ball! A Baseball Game of Skill, 1940s, Rosebud Art
EX $50   NM $75   MIP $150

Play Basketball with Bob Cousy, 1950s, National Games
EX $115   NM $195   MIP $295

Play Your Hunch, 1960, Transogram
EX $8   NM $25   MIP $40

Playoff Football, 1970s, Crestline
EX $20   NM $35   MIP $50

Plaza, 1947, Parker Brothers
EX $7   NM $20   MIP $35

Plot!, 1968, Cadaco
EX $10   NM $25   MIP $35

Ploy, 1970, 3M
EX $5   NM $16   MIP $25

Plus One, 1980, Milton Bradley
EX $6   NM $18   MIP $30

Pocket Size Bowling Card Game, 1950s, Warren/Built-Rite
EX $15   NM $25   MIP $40

Pocket Whoozit, 1985, Trivia
EX $4   NM $7   MIP $10

Point of Law, 1972, 3M
EX $4   NM $14   MIP $20

Pole Position, 1983, Parker Brothers
EX $8   NM $13   MIP $20

Police Patrol, 1955, Hasbro
EX $40   NM $100   MIP $150

Police State, 1974, Gameophiles Unltd.
EX $25   NM $60   MIP $85

Politics, Game of, 1952, Parker Brothers
EX $15   NM $45   MIP $65

Ponents, 1974, Dynamic
EX $6   NM $15   MIP $25

Pony Express, Game of, 1947, Polygon
EX $12   NM $40   MIP $60

Pooch, 1956, Hasbro
EX $10   NM $35   MIP $50

Pop Yer Top!, 1968, Milton Bradley
EX $15   NM $35   MIP $50

Popeye Spinach Flip, 1969, Whitman
EX $10   NM $25   MIP $35

Popeye, Adventures of, 1957, Transogram
EX $35   NM $75   MIP $100

Poppin Hoppies, 1968, Ideal
EX $10   NM $25   MIP $35

Population, 1970, Urban Systems
EX $6   NM $18   MIP $30

Pop-Up Store Game, 1950s, Milton Bradley
EX $12   NM $40   MIP $60

Post Office, 1968, Hasbro
EX $8   NM $20   MIP $30

Postman, 1957, Selchow & Righter
EX $8   NM $25   MIP $40

Pothole Game, The, 1979, Cadaco
EX $10   NM $25   MIP $40

Pow, The Frontier Game, 1955, Selchow & Righter
EX $12   NM $40   MIP $60

Power 4 Car Racing Game, 1960s, Manning
EX $15   NM $50   MIP $75

Power Play Hockey, 1970, Romac
EX $12   NM $35   MIP $50

Power: The Game, 1981, Power Games
EX $10   NM $25   MIP $35

Prediction Rod, 1970, Parker Brothers
EX $5   NM $16   MIP $25

Presidential Campaign, 1979, John Hansen
EX $6   NM $18   MIP $30

Prince Caspian, 1983, David Cook
EX $5   NM $16   MIP $25

Prince Valiant (Harold Foster's), 1950s, Transogram
EX $12   NM $40   MIP $60

Prize Property, 1974, Milton Bradley
EX $8   NM $25   MIP $40

Pro Draft, 1974, Parker Brothers
EX $15   NM $35   MIP $45

Pro Football, 1980s, Strat-O-Matic
EX $6   NM $10   MIP $15

Pro Foto-Football, 1977, Cadaco
EX $6   NM $15   MIP $25

Pro Franchise Football, 1987, Rohrwood
EX $10   NM $16   MIP $25

Pro Golf, 1982, Avalon Hill
EX $7   NM $11   MIP $17

Pro Quarterback, 1964, Tod Lansing
EX $20   NM $40   MIP $60

Pro Soccer, 1968, Milton Bradley
EX $12   NM $30   MIP $40

Probe, 1964, Parker Brothers
EX $2   NM $7   MIP $12

Products and Resources, Game of, 1962, Selchow & Righter
EX $6   NM $18   MIP $30

Profit Farming, 1979, Foster Enterprises
EX $6   NM $18   MIP $30

Prospecting, 1953, Selchow & Righter
EX $25   NM $65   MIP $90

Prospector, The, 1980, McJay Game Co.
EX $8   NM $20   MIP $30

Public Assistance, 1980, Hammerhead
EX $12   NM $40   MIP $60

Pug-i-Lo, 1960, Pug-i-Lo Games
EX $55   NM $90   MIP $135

Pure Greed, 1971, Crea-Tek
EX $12   NM $30   MIP $40

Pursue the Pennant, 1984, Pursue the Pennant
EX $30   NM $70   MIP $100

Pursuit!, 1973, Aurora
EX $8   NM $25   MIP $40

Push Over, 1981, Parker Brothers
EX $3   NM $12   MIP $18

Put and Take, 1956, Schaper
EX $5   NM $16   MIP $25

Puzzling Pyramid, 1960, Schaper
EX $6   NM $18   MIP $30

Pyramid, 1978, Hasbro
EX $6   NM $15   MIP $25

Pyramid Power, 1978, Castle Toy
EX $8   NM $20   MIP $30

Q*Bert, 1983, Parker Brothers
EX $4   NM $10   MIP $15

Quad-Ominos, 1978, Pressman
EX $2   NM $6   MIP $10

Quarterback Football Game, 1969, Transogram
EX $25   NM $40   MIP $65

Qubic, 1965, Parker Brothers
EX $3   NM $10   MIP $15

Quest, 1962, Lakeside
EX $12   NM $30   MIP $40

Quest, 1978, Gametime/Heritage Models
EX $10   NM $25   MIP $35

Quick Draw McGraw Game, 1981, Milton Bradley
EX $5   NM $12   MIP $18

❏ **Quick Draw McGraw Private Eye Game**, 1960
EX $10   NM $25   MIP $35

❏ **Quinto**, 1964, 3M
EX $6   NM $18   MIP $30

❏ **Quiz Panel**, 1954, Cadaco-Ellis
EX $6   NM $18   MIP $30

❏ **Race-A-Plane**, 1947, Phon-O-Game
EX $12   NM $40   MIP $60

❏ **Race-O-Rama**, 1960, Warren/Built-Rite
EX $10   NM $25   MIP $45

❏ **Raceway**, 1950s, B & B Toy
EX $30   NM $50   MIP $75

❏ **Radaronics**, 1946, ARC
EX $20   NM $65   MIP $90

❏ **Raggedy Ann**, 1956, Milton Bradley
EX $6   NM $18   MIP $30

❏ **Raiders of the Lost Ark**, 1981, Kenner
EX $8   NM $20   MIP $30

❏ **Rainy Day Golf**, 1980, Bryad
EX $6   NM $18   MIP $30

❏ **Raise the Titanic**, 1987, Hoyle
EX $12   NM $30   MIP $40

❏ **Rat Patrol Game**, 1966, Transogram
EX $40   NM $70   MIP $100

❏ **Rawhide**, 1959, Lowell
EX $75   NM $175   MIP $300

❏ **Raymar of The Jungle**, 1952, Dexter Wayne
EX $40   NM $100   MIP $135

❏ **Razzle**, 1981, Parker Brothers
EX $2   NM $6   MIP $10

❏ **Razzle Dazzle Football Game**, 1954, Texantics Unlimited
EX $50   NM $80   MIP $125

❏ **React-Or**, 1979
EX $15   NM $25   MIP $40

❏ **Real Action Baseball Game**, 1966, Real-Action Games
EX $20   NM $35   MIP $50

❏ **Real Baseball Card Game**, 1990, National Baseball
EX $110   NM $180   MIP $275

❏ **Real Ghostbusters, The**, 1986, Milton Bradley
EX $6   NM $18   MIP $30

❏ **Real Life Basketball**, 1974, Gamecraft
EX $20   NM $50   MIP $75

❏ **Realistic Football**, 1976, Match Play
EX $15   NM $25   MIP $35

(KP Photo)

❏ **Rebel, The**, 1961, Ideal
EX $50   NM $85   MIP $135

❏ **Rebound**, 1971, Ideal
EX $5   NM $16   MIP $25

❏ **Record Game, The**, 1984, The Record Game
EX $8   NM $25   MIP $40

❏ **Red Barber's Big League Baseball Game**, 1950s, G & R Anthony
EX $350   NM $575   MIP $900

❏ **Red Herring**, 1945, Cadaco-Ellis
EX $12   NM $40   MIP $60

❏ **Red Rover Game, The**, 1963, Cadaco-Ellis
EX $5   NM $16   MIP $25

❏ **Reddy Clown 3-Ring Circus Game**, 1952, Parker Brothers
EX $15   NM $35   MIP $55

❏ **Reese's Pieces Game**, 1983, Ideal
EX $5   NM $8   MIP $15

❏ **Reflex**, 1966, Lakeside
EX $5   NM $16   MIP $25

❏ **Regatta**, 1946
EX $40   NM $70   MIP $110

❏ **Regatta**, 1968, 3M
EX $8   NM $25   MIP $40

❏ **Replay Series Baseball**, 1983, Bond Sports
EX $6   NM $10   MIP $15

❏ **Restless Gun**, 1950s, Milton Bradley
EX $18   NM $40   MIP $60

❏ **Return To Oz Game**, 1985, Western
EX $10   NM $15   MIP $25

❏ **Reward**, 1958, Happy Hour
EX $10   NM $35   MIP $50

❏ **Rhyme Time**, 1969, NBC-Hasbro
EX $6   NM $15   MIP $25

❏ **Rich Farmer, Poor Farmer**, 1978, McJay Game
EX $5   NM $16   MIP $25

❏ **Rich Uncle The Stock Market Game**, 1955, Parker Brothers
EX $18   NM $40   MIP $60

(KP Photo)

❏ **Rich Uncle, Game of**, 1946, Parker Brothers
EX $18   NM $40   MIP $60

❏ **Richie Rich**, 1982, Milton Bradley
EX $3   NM $5   MIP $10

❏ **Rickenbacker Ace Game**, 1946, Milton Bradley
EX $60   NM $150   MIP $200

❏ **Ricochet Rabbit Game**, 1965, Ideal
EX $45   NM $75   MIP $120

❏ **Rifleman Game**, 1959, Milton Bradley
EX $20   NM $50   MIP $75

(KP Photo)

❏ **Rin Tin Tin Game**, 1950s, Transogram
EX $20   NM $50   MIP $65

❏ **Ringmaster**, 1947, Cadaco-Ellis
EX $12   NM $40   MIP $60

❏ **Ringmaster Circus Game**, 1947, Cadaco-Ellis
EX $15   NM $25   MIP $40

❏ **Rio, The Game of**, 1956, Parker Brothers
EX $10   NM $35   MIP $50

❏ **Ripley's Believe It Or Not**, 1979, Whitman
EX $6   NM $10   MIP $15

❏ **Risk**, 1959, Parker Brothers
EX $25   NM $50   MIP $75

❏ **Riverboat Game**, 1950s, Parker Brothers/Disney
EX $20   NM $35   MIP $55

❏ **Road Runner Game**, 1968, Milton Bradley
EX $10   NM $25   MIP $35

❏ **Road Runner Pop Up Game**, 1982, Whitman
EX $20   NM $30   MIP $50

❏ **Robert Schuller's Possibility Thinkers Game**, 1977, Selchow & Righter
EX $3   NM $5   MIP $10

❏ **Robin Hood**, 1955, Harett-Gilmar
EX $30   NM $50   MIP $80

❏ **Robin Hood Game**, 1970s, Parker Brothers
EX $7   NM $15   MIP $30

❏ **Robin Hood, Adventures of**, 1956, Bettye-B
EX $45   NM $75   MIP $120

❏ **Robin Roberts Sports Club Baseball Game**, 1960, Dexter Wayne
EX $100   NM $165   MIP $250

❏ **Robocop VCR Game**, 1988, Spinnaker
EX $7   NM $20   MIP $35

❏ **Robot Sam the Answer Man**, 1950, Jacmar
EX $15   NM $35   MIP $50

❏ **Rock 'N' Roll Replay**, 1984, Baron-Scott
EX $7   NM $20   MIP $35

❑ **Rock the Boat Game,** 1978, Milton Bradley
EX $6   NM $18   MIP $30

❑ **Rock Trivia,** 1984, Pressman
EX $5   NM $10   MIP $15

❑ **Rocket Race,** 1958, Stone Craft
EX $30   NM $70   MIP $95

❑ **Rocket Race To Saturn,** 1950s, Lido
EX $15   NM $20   MIP $35

❑ **Rodeo, The Wild West Game,** 1957, Whitman
EX $12   NM $40   MIP $60

(KP Photo)

❑ **Roger Maris' Action Baseball,** 1962, Pressman
EX $50   NM $125   MIP $175

❑ **Rol-A-Lite,** 1947, Durable Toy & Novelty
EX $45   NM $75   MIP $120

❑ **Rol-It,** 1954, Parker Brothers
EX $4   NM $12   MIP $20

❑ **Roll And Score Poker,** 1977, Lowe
EX $3   NM $7   MIP $12

❑ **Roll-A-Par,** 1964, Lowe
EX $8   NM $20   MIP $30

❑ **Roller Derby,** 1974, Milton Bradley
EX $70   NM $150   MIP $225

❑ **Roman X,** 1964, Selchow & Righter
EX $7   NM $20   MIP $35

❑ **Roscoe Turner Air Race Game,** 1960, Southern Games
EX $40   NM $90   MIP $135

❑ **Rose Bowl,** 1949, Keck Enterprises
EX $15   NM $35   MIP $50

❑ **Rose Bowl,** 1966, E.S.Lowe
EX $8   NM $20   MIP $30

❑ **Roundup,** 1952, Wales Game Systems
EX $15   NM $35   MIP $50

❑ **Route 66 Game,** 1960, Transogram
EX $75   NM $125   MIP $200

❑ **Roy Rogers Game,** 1950s
EX $20   NM $35   MIP $55

❑ **Rribit, Battle of the Frogs,** 1982, Genesis Enterprises
EX $6   NM $18   MIP $30

❑ **Ruffhouse,** 1980, Parker Brothers
EX $3   NM $10   MIP $15

❑ **Rules of the Road,** 1977, Cadaco
EX $5   NM $16   MIP $25

❑ **Run to Win,** 1980, Cabela
EX $6   NM $18   MIP $30

❑ **Russian Campaign, The,** 1976, Avalon Hill
EX $3   NM $5   MIP $10

(KP Photo)

❑ **S.O.S.,** 1947, Durable Toy & Novelty
EX $40   NM $70   MIP $110

(KP Photo)

❑ **S.W.A.T. Game,** 1970s, Milton Bradley
EX $10   NM $15   MIP $25

❑ **Sabotage,** 1985, Lakeside
EX $2   NM $6   MIP $10

❑ **Saddle Racing Game,** 1974, APBA
EX $20   NM $50   MIP $75

❑ **Safari,** 1950, Selchow & Righter
EX $12   NM $40   MIP $60

❑ **Safecrack,** 1982, Selchow & Righter
EX $4   NM $15   MIP $20

❑ **Sail Away,** 1962, Howard Mullen
EX $12   NM $30   MIP $40

❑ **Salvo,** 1961, Ideal
EX $15   NM $25   MIP $40

❑ **Samsonite Basketball,** 1969, Samsonite
EX $15   NM $35   MIP $60

❑ **Samsonite Football,** 1969, Samsonite
EX $12   NM $30   MIP $50

❑ **Sandlot Slugger,** 1960s, Milton Bradley
EX $35   NM $60   MIP $90

❑ **Save the President,** 1984, Jack Jaffe
EX $8   NM $20   MIP $30

❑ **Say When!,** 1961, Parker Brothers
EX $6   NM $18   MIP $30

❑ **Scavenger Hunt,** 1983, Milton Bradley
EX $3   NM $5   MIP $10

❑ **Scooby Doo and Scrappy Doo,** 1983, Milton Bradley
EX $3   NM $8   MIP $16

❑ **Scooby-Doo, Where are You?,** 1973, Milton Bradley
EX $18   NM $40   MIP $60

❑ **Scoop,** 1956, Parker Brothers
EX $35   NM $75   MIP $100

❑ **Scoop: The Newspaper Game,** 1976, Western Publishing
EX $18   NM $45   MIP $65

❑ **Score Four,** 1968, Funtastic
EX $3   NM $10   MIP $15

❑ **Scotland Yard,** 1985, Milton Bradley
EX $3   NM $10   MIP $15

❑ **Scrabble,** 1953, Selchow & Righter
EX $5   NM $12   MIP $20

❑ **Scrabble for Juniors,** 1968, Selchow & Righter
EX $2   NM $5   MIP $8

❑ **Scrabble RPM,** 1971, Selchow & Righter
EX $8   NM $20   MIP $30

❑ **Screaming Eagles,** 1987, Milton Bradley
EX $4   NM $15   MIP $20

❑ **Screwball The Mad Mad Mad Game,** 1960, Transogram
EX $30   NM $75   MIP $105

❑ **Scribbage,** 1963, Lowe
EX $3   NM $10   MIP $15

❑ **Scrimmage,** 1973, SPI
EX $5   NM $15   MIP $25

❑ **Scruples,** 1986, Milton Bradley
EX $5   NM $10   MIP $15

❑ **Scrutineyes,** 1992, Hersch & Co/Mattel
EX $12   NM $30   MIP $40

❑ **Sea World Treasure Key,** 1983, International Games
EX $4   NM $15   MIP $20

❑ **Sealab 2020 Game,** 1973, Milton Bradley
EX $6   NM $10   MIP $15

❑ **Seance,** 1972, Milton Bradley
EX $18   NM $60   MIP $80

❑ **Secrecy,** 1965, Universal Games
EX $12   NM $30   MIP $40

❑ **Secret Agent Man,** 1966, Milton Bradley
EX $25   NM $40   MIP $65

❑ **Secret of NIMH,** 1982, Whitman
EX $6　　NM $10　　MIP $15

❑ **Secret Weapon,** 1984, Selchow & Righter
EX $5　　NM $16　　MIP $25

❑ **Seduction,** 1966, Createk
EX $10　　NM $25　　MIP $35

❑ **See New York 'Round the Town,** 1964, Transogram
EX $8　　NM $25　　MIP $40

❑ **Sergeant Preston Game,** 1950s, Milton Bradley
EX $15　　NM $35　　MIP $50

❑ **Set Point,** 1971, XV Productions
EX $8　　NM $20　　MIP $30

❑ **Seven Keys,** 1961, Ideal
EX $12　　NM $30　　MIP $40

(KP Photo)

❑ **Seven Seas,** 1960, Cadaco-Ellis
EX $30　　NM $50　　MIP $80

(KP Photo)

❑ **Seven Up,** 1960s, Transogram
EX $7　　NM $12　　MIP $20

❑ **Shadowlord!,** 1983, Parker Brothers
EX $3　　NM $10　　MIP $15

❑ **Sha-ee, the Game of Destiny,** 1963, Ideal
EX $20　　NM $65　　MIP $90

(KP Photo)

❑ **Shazam, Captian Marvel's Own Game,** 1950s, Reed & Associates
EX $30　　NM $60　　MIP $95

❑ **Shenanigans,** 1964, Milton Bradley
EX $15　　NM $40　　MIP $60

❑ **Sheriff of Dodge City,** 1966, Parker Brothers
EX $8　　NM $25　　MIP $40

❑ **Sherlock Holmes,** 1950s, National Games
EX $30　　NM $75　　MIP $100

❑ **Sherlock Holmes,** 1980, Whitman
EX $5　　NM $16　　MIP $25

❑ **Sherlock Holmes Game, The,** 1974, Cadaco
EX $6　　NM $18　　MIP $30

❑ **Shifty Checkers,** 1973, Aurora
EX $8　　NM $25　　MIP $40

❑ **Shifty Gear Game,** 1962, Schaper
EX $5　　NM $16　　MIP $25

❑ **Shindig,** 1965, Remco
EX $25　　NM $65　　MIP $90

❑ **Shmo,** 1960s, Remco
EX $10　　NM $35　　MIP $50

❑ **Shogun,** 1976, Epoch Playthings
EX $6　　NM $15　　MIP $25

❑ **Shogun,** 1986, Milton Bradley
EX $18　　NM $45　　MIP $75

❑ **Shopping,** 1973, John Ladell
EX $5　　NM $16　　MIP $25

(KP Photo)

❑ **Shotgun Slade,** 1960, Milton Bradley
EX $20　　NM $45　　MIP $65

❑ **Show-Biz,** 1950s, Lowell
EX $15　　NM $50　　MIP $75

❑ **SI: The Sporting Word Game,** 1961, Time
EX $10　　NM $16　　MIP $25

❑ **Siege Game,** 1966, Milton Bradley
EX $20　　NM $50　　MIP $70

❑ **Silly Carnival,** 1969, Whitman
EX $7　　NM $12　　MIP $20

❑ **Silly Safari,** 1966, Topper
EX $30　　NM $70　　MIP $105

❑ **Silly Sidney,** 1963, Transogram
EX $12　　NM $30　　MIP $40

❑ **Simpsons Mystery of Life, The,** 1990, Cardinal
EX $5　　NM $7　　MIP $10

❑ **Sinbad,** 1978, Cadaco
EX $20　　NM $30　　MIP $50

❑ **Sinking of The Titanic, The,** 1976, Ideal
EX $25　　NM $55　　MIP $75

❑ **Sir Lancelot, Adventures of,** 1960s, Lisbeth Whiting
EX $40　　NM $70　　MIP $110

❑ **Situation 4,** 1968, Parker Brothers
EX $5　　NM $16　　MIP $25

❑ **Situation 7,** 1969, Parker Brothers
EX $8　　NM $25　　MIP $40
(KP Photo)

❑ **Six Million Dollar Man,** 1975, Parker Brothers
EX $5　　NM $10　　MIP $15

❑ **Skatebirds Game,** 1978, Milton Bradley
EX $7　　NM $20　　MIP $35

❑ **Skatterbug, Game of,** 1951, Parker Brothers
EX $30　　NM $50　　MIP $80

❑ **Skedaddle,** 1965, Cadaco-Ellis
EX $8　　NM $25　　MIP $40

❑ **Ski Gammon,** 1962, American Publishing
EX $8　　NM $20　　MIP $30

❑ **Skill-Drive,** 1950s, Sidney Tarrson
EX $10　　NM $35　　MIP $50

❑ **Skins Golf Game, Official,** 1985, O'Connor Hall
EX $12　　NM $20　　MIP $30

❑ **Skip-A-Cross,** 1953, Cadaco
EX $3　　NM $7　　MIP $10

❑ **Skipper Race Sailing Game,** 1949, Cadaco-Ellis
EX $25　　NM $60　　MIP $90

(KP Photo)

❑ **Skirmish,** 1975, Milton Bradley
EX $20　　NM $35　　MIP $55

❑ **Skirrid,** 1979, Kenner
EX $4　　NM $15　　MIP $20

❑ **Skudo,** 1949, Parker Brothers
EX $8　　NM $25　　MIP $40

❑ **Skully,** 1961, Ideal
EX $3　　NM $5　　MIP $10

❑ **Skunk,** 1950s, Schaper
EX $7　　NM $12　　MIP $20

❑ **Sky Lanes,** 1958, Parker Brothers
EX $35　　NM $75　　MIP $120

❑ **Sky's The Limit, The,** 1955, Kohner
EX $15　　NM $25　　MIP $40

❑ **Sla-lom Ski Race Game,** 1957, Cadaco-Ellis
EX $20　　NM $50　　MIP $75

❑ **Slap Trap,** 1967, Ideal
EX $8　　NM $25　　MIP $40

❑ **Slapshot,** 1982, Avalon Hill
EX $10　　NM $25　　MIP $35

Slip Disc, 1980, Milton Bradley
EX $5　　NM $16　　MIP $25

Smess, The Ninny's Chess, 1970,
Parker Brothers
EX $10　　NM $35　　MIP $50

Smog, 1970, Urban Systems
EX $8　　NM $20　　MIP $30

**Smokey: The Forest Fire Prevention
Bear,** 1961, Ideal
EX $30　　NM $65　　MIP $105

Smurf Game, 1984, Milton Bradley
EX $4　　NM $7　　MIP $12

Snafu, 1969, Gamescience
EX $7　　NM $20　　MIP $35

Snagglepuss Fun at the Picnic Game,
1961, Transogram
EX $40　　NM $60　　MIP $100

Snake Eyes, 1957, Selchow & Righter
EX $15　　NM $50　　MIP $75

Snakes & Ladders, 1974, Summmer-
ville/Canada
EX $4　　NM $7　　MIP $10

Snake's Alive, Game of, 1967, Ideal
EX $12　　NM $30　　MIP $40

Snakes In The Grass, 1960s, Kohner
EX $10　　NM $15　　MIP $25

**Snappet Catch Game with Harmon
Killebrew,** 1960, Killebrew
EX $55　　NM $90　　MIP $135

Sniggle!, 1980, Amway
EX $4　　NM $10　　MIP $15

Snob, A Fantasy Shopping Spree,
1983, Helene Fox
EX $7　　NM $20　　MIP $35

Snoopy & The Red Baron, 1970, Milton
Bradley
EX $15　　NM $35　　MIP $50

Snoopy Come Home Game, 1973, Milton Bradley
EX $5　　NM $16　　MIP $25

Snoopy Game, 1960, Selchow &
Righter
EX $25　　NM $45　　MIP $70

Snoopy's Doghouse Game, 1977, Milton Bradley
EX $5　　NM $16　　MIP $25

(KP Photo)

Snow White and the Seven Dwarfs,
1970s, Cadaco
EX $6　　NM $10　　MIP $15

Snuffy Smith Game, 1970s, Milton Bradley
EX $10　　NM $30　　MIP $45

Society Scandals, 1978, E.S.Lowe
EX $6　　NM $15　　MIP $25

Sod Buster, 1980, Santee
EX $10　　NM $16　　MIP $25

Solar Conquest, 1966, Atech Enterprises
EX $15　　NM $35　　MIP $50

Solarquest, 1986, Western
EX $6　　NM $10　　MIP $15

Solid Gold Music Trivia, 1984, Ideal
EX $6　　NM $10　　MIP $15

Solitaire (Lucille Ball), 1973, Milton
Bradley
EX $2　　NM $5　　MIP $10

Sons of Hercules Game, The, 1966,
Milton Bradley
EX $30　　NM $70　　MIP $100

Soupy Sales Sez Go-Go-Go Game,
1960s, Milton Bradley
EX $55　　NM $95　　MIP $150

Southern Fast Freight Game, 1970,
American Publishing
EX $8　　NM $25　　MIP $40

Space Angel Game, 1966, Transogram
EX $25　　NM $65　　MIP $85

Space Chase, 1967, United Nations
Constructors
EX $15　　NM $35　　MIP $50

Space Game, 1953, Parker Brothers
EX $25　　NM $65　　MIP $85

Space Pilot, 1951, Cadaco-Ellis
EX $35　　NM $75　　MIP $100

Space Shuttle 101, 1978, Media-
Ungame
EX $8　　NM $20　　MIP $30

Space Shuttle, The, 1981, Ungame
EX $8　　NM $20　　MIP $30

(KP Photo)

Space: 1999 Game, 1975, Milton Bradley
EX $10　　NM $15　　MIP $25

Special Agent, 1966, Parker Brothers
EX $10　　NM $25　　MIP $40

Special Detective/Speedway, 1959,
Saalfield
EX $15　　NM $40　　MIP $60

Speedorama, 1950s, Jacmar
EX $30　　NM $50　　MIP $80

Speedway, Big Bopper Game, 1961,
Ideal
EX $18　　NM $40　　MIP $60

Spider and the Fly, 1981, Marx
EX $12　　NM $20　　MIP $30

Spider-Man Game, The Amazing,
1967, Milton Bradley
EX $20　　NM $45　　MIP $85

(KP Photo)

Spider-Man with The Fantastic Four,
1977, Milton Bradley
EX $10　　NM $15　　MIP $25

Spider's Web Game, The, 1969, Multiple Plastics
EX $7　　NM $12　　MIP $20

Spin Cycle Baseball, 1965, Pressman
EX $25　　NM $40　　MIP $65

Spin The Bottle, 1968, Hasbro
EX $8　　NM $20　　MIP $30

Spin Welder, 1960s, Mattel
EX $7　　NM $12　　MIP $20

**Spiro T. Agnew American History Chal-
lenge Game,** 1971, Gabriel
EX $20　　NM $35　　MIP $55

Splat!, 1990, Milton Bradley
EX $8　　NM $20　　MIP $30

Sporting News: Baseroll, 1986, Mundo
Games
EX $8　　NM $13　　MIP $20

Sports Arena No. 1, 1954, Rennoc
Games & Toys
EX $35　　NM $60　　MIP $90

**Sports Illustrated All Time All Star
Baseball,** 1973, Sports Illustrated
EX $75　　NM $175　　MIP $250

Sports Illustrated Baseball, 1972,
Time, Inc. (Sports Illustrated)
EX $60　　NM $120　　MIP $175

Sports Illustrated College Football,
1971, Sports Illustrated
EX $8　　NM $25　　MIP $40

Sports Illustrated Decathlon, 1972,
Time
EX $8　　NM $25　　MIP $40

Sports Illustrated Handicap Golf,
1971, Sports Illustrated
EX $10　　NM $25　　MIP $35

Sports Illustrated Pro Football, 1970,
Time
EX $15　　NM $25　　MIP $40

Sports Trivia Game, 1984, Hoyle
EX $6　　NM $10　　MIP $15

Sports Yesteryear, 1977, Skor-Mor
EX $15　　NM $25　　MIP $35

Spot Cash, 1959, Milton Bradley
EX $7　　NM $15　　MIP $20

❑ **Spy vs. Spy,** 1986, Milton Bradley
EX $10   NM $15   MIP $25

❑ **Square Mile,** 1962, Milton Bradley
EX $12   NM $40   MIP $60

❑ **Square Off,** 1972, Parker Brothers
EX $8   NM $20   MIP $30

❑ **Square-It,** 1961, Hasbro
EX $5   NM $16   MIP $25

❑ **Squares,** 1950s, Schaper
EX $4   NM $15   MIP $20

❑ **Squatter: The Australian Wool Game,** 1960s, John Sands/Australia
EX $15   NM $25   MIP $45

❑ **St. Louis Cardinals Baseball Card Game,** 1964, Ed-U-Cards
EX $10   NM $25   MIP $35

❑ **Stadium Checkers,** 1954, Schaper
EX $7   NM $12   MIP $20

❑ **Stagecoach West Game,** 1961, Transogram
EX $35   NM $75   MIP $125

❑ **Stampede,** 1952, Wales Game Systems
EX $15   NM $35   MIP $50

❑ **Stampede,** 1956, Gabriel
EX $8   NM $25   MIP $40

❑ **Star Reporter,** 1950s, Parker Brothers
EX $50   NM $125   MIP $175

❑ **Star Team Battling Spaceships,** 1977, Ideal
EX $8   NM $20   MIP $30

(Toy Shop File Photo)

❑ **Star Trek,** 1979, Milton Bradley
EX $18   NM $40   MIP $60

❑ **Star Trek Adventure Game,** 1985, West End Games
EX $8   NM $20   MIP $30

(KP Photo)

❑ **Star Trek Game,** 1960s, Ideal
EX $35   NM $75   MIP $100

❑ **Star Trek: The Next Generation,** 1993, Classic Games
EX $15   NM $25   MIP $50

❑ **Star Wars Adventures of R2D2 Game,** 1977, Kenner
EX $12   NM $20   MIP $30

❑ **Star Wars Battle at Sarlacc's Pit,** 1983, Parker Brothers
EX $10   NM $15   MIP $25

❑ **Star Wars Escape from Death Star,** 1977, Kenner
EX $10   NM $15   MIP $25

❑ **Star Wars Monopoly,** 1997, Parker Brothers
EX $15   NM $20   MIP $35

(KP Photo)

❑ **Star Wars ROTJ Ewoks Save The Trees,** 1984, Parker Brothers
EX $10   NM $15   MIP $25

❑ **Star Wars Wicket the Ewok,** 1983, Parker Brothers
EX $7   NM $12   MIP $20

❑ **Star Wars X-Wing Aces Target Game,** 1978
EX $20   NM $30   MIP $50

❑ **Starship Troopers,** 1976, Avalon Hill
EX $5   NM $16   MIP $25

❑ **Starsky & Hutch,** 1977, Milton Bradley
EX $5   NM $16   MIP $25

❑ **State Capitals, Game of,** 1952, Parker Brothers
EX $4   NM $10   MIP $15

❑ **States, Game of the,** 1975, Milton Bradley
EX $4   NM $6   MIP $10

❑ **Statis Pro Football,** 1970s, Statis-Pro
EX $25   NM $40   MIP $65

❑ **Stay Alive,** 1971, Milton Bradley
EX $6   NM $15   MIP $25

❑ **Steps of Toyland,** 1954, Parker Brothers
EX $20   NM $35   MIP $55

❑ **Steve Allen's Qubila,** 1955, Lord & Freber
EX $8   NM $25   MIP $40

❑ **Steve Canyon,** 1959, Lowell
EX $20   NM $50   MIP $85

❑ **Steve Scott Space Scout Game,** 1952, Transogram
EX $30   NM $75   MIP $105

❑ **Stick the IRS!,** 1981, Courtland Playthings
EX $5   NM $16   MIP $25

❑ **Sting, The,** 1976, Ideal
EX $10   NM $25   MIP $40

❑ **Stock Car Race,** 1950s, Gardner
EX $20   NM $50   MIP $75

❑ **Stock Car Racing Game,** 1956, Whitman
EX $12   NM $30   MIP $40

❑ **Stock Car Racing Game (w/Petty/Yarborough),** 1981, Ribbit Toy
EX $17   NM $30   MIP $45

❑ **Stock Car Speedway, Game of,** 1965, Johnstone
EX $55   NM $90   MIP $135

❑ **Stock Market Game,** 1955, Gabriel
EX $8   NM $20   MIP $30

❑ **Stock Market Game,** 1963, 1968, Whitman
EX $15   NM $35   MIP $50

❑ **Stock Market Game,** 1970, Avalon Hill
EX $7   NM $12   MIP $20

❑ **Stock Market Specialist,** 1983, John Hansen
EX $6   NM $18   MIP $30

❑ **Stoney Burk,** 1963, Transogram
EX $30   NM $70   MIP $100

❑ **Stop Thief,** 1979, Parker Brothers
EX $15   NM $35   MIP $50

❑ **Straight Arrow,** 1950, Selchow & Righter
EX $25   NM $45   MIP $70

❑ **Straightaway,** 1961, Selchow & Righter
EX $45   NM $70   MIP $110

❑ **Strata 5,** 1984, Milton Bradley
EX $5   NM $16   MIP $25

❑ **Strategic Command,** 1950s, Transogram
EX $15   NM $35   MIP $50

❑ **Stratego (plastic pieces),** 1962-on, Milton Bradley
EX $6   NM $15   MIP $25

❑ **Stratego (wood pieces),** 1961, Milton Bradley
EX $30   NM $70   MIP $100

❑ **Strategy Manager Baseball,** 1967, McGuffin-Ramsey
EX $2   NM $6   MIP $12

❑ **Strato Tac-tics,** 1972, Strato-Various
EX $8   NM $25   MIP $40

❑ **Strat-O-Matic Baseball,** 1961, Strat-O-Matic
EX $100   NM $165   MIP $250

❑ **Strat-O-Matic College Football,** 1976, Strat-O-Matic
EX $25   NM $55   MIP $75

❑ **Strat-O-Matic Hockey,** 1978, Strat-O-Matic
EX $12   NM $30   MIP $50

❑ **Strat-O-Matic Sports "Know-How",** 1984, Strat-O-Matic
EX $6   NM $10   MIP $15

❑ **Strato-O-Matic Baseball,** 1970, Strat-O-Matic
EX $20   NM $50   MIP $70

❑ **Strato-O-Matic Baseball,** 1980, Strat-O-Matic
EX $15   NM $35   MIP $50

GAMES

- **Strato-O-Matic Baseball (varies by season of cards)**, 1960s, Strat-O-Matic
  EX $80   NM $150   MIP $225
- **Strato-O-Matic Football (varies by season of cards)**, 1967-74, Strat-O-Matic
  EX $50   NM $125   MIP $175
- **Strato-O-Matic Football (varies by season of cards)**, 1975-85, Strat-O-Matic
  EX $25   NM $60   MIP $85
- **Strato-O-Matic Football (varies by season of cards)**, 1986-90s, Strat-O-Matic
  EX $12   NM $30   MIP $40
- **Stretch Call**, 1986, Sevedeo A. Vigil
  EX $12   NM $20   MIP $30
- **Strike Three (Carl Hubbell's)**, 1948, Tone Products
  EX $275   NM $475   MIP $725
- **Stuff Yer Face**, 1982, Milton Bradley
  EX $6   NM $20   MIP $35
- **Stump the Stars**, 1962, Ideal
  EX $8   NM $25   MIP $40
- **Sub Attack Game**, 1965, Milton Bradley
  EX $7   NM $20   MIP $35
- **Sub Search**, 1973, Milton Bradley
  EX $8   NM $25   MIP $40
- **Sub Search**, 1977, Milton Bradley
  EX $6   NM $18   MIP $30
- **Sudden Death!**, 1978, Gabriel
  EX $5   NM $16   MIP $25
- **Suffolk Downs Racing Game**, 1947, Corey Game
  EX $40   NM $90   MIP $135
- **Sugar Bowl**, 1950s, Transogram
  EX $20   NM $45   MIP $65
- **Summit**, 1961, Milton Bradley
  EX $20   NM $45   MIP $65
- **Sunken Treasure**, 1948, Parker Brothers
  EX $15   NM $25   MIP $45
- **Sunken Treasure**, 1976, Milton Bradley
  EX $7   NM $12   MIP $20
- **Super Coach TV Football**, 1974, Coleco
  EX $5   NM $12   MIP $20
- **Super Market**, 1953, Selchow & Righter
  EX $10   NM $35   MIP $50
- **Super Powers**, 1984, Parker Brothers
  EX $15   NM $25   MIP $40
- **Super Spy**, 1971, Milton Bradley
  EX $15   NM $25   MIP $40

(KP Photo)

- **Superboy Game**, 1960s, Hasbro
  EX $45   NM $75   MIP $135
- **Supercar Road Race**, 1962, Standard Toykraft
  EX $45   NM $100   MIP $140

(KP Photo)

- **Supercar to the Rescue Game**, 1962, Milton Bradley
  EX $20   NM $50   MIP $75
- **Superman & Superboy**, 1967, Milton Bradley
  EX $40   NM $65   MIP $105
- **Superman Game**, 1965, Hasbro
  EX $45   NM $75   MIP $120
- **Superman Game**, 1966, Merry Manufacturing
  EX $35   NM $55   MIP $90
- **Superman II**, 1981, Milton Bradley
  EX $10   NM $20   MIP $35
- **Superman III**, 1982, Parker Brothers
  EX $4   NM $12   MIP $20
- **Superman, Adventures of**, 1940s, Milton Bradley
  EX $100   NM $250   MIP $375
- **Superstar Baseball**, 1966, Sports Illustrated
  EX $30   NM $50   MIP $75
- **Superstar Pro Wrestling Game**, 1984, Super Star Game
  EX $8   NM $13   MIP $20
- **Superstar TV Sports**, 1980, ARC
  EX $6   NM $10   MIP $15
- **Superstition**, 1977, Milton Bradley
  EX $12   NM $30   MIP $40
- **Sure Shot Hockey**, 1970, Ideal
  EX $15   NM $25   MIP $40

(KP Photo)

- **Surfside 6**, 1961, Lowell
  EX $30   NM $75   MIP $125
- **Surprise Package, Your**, 1961, Ideal
  EX $25   NM $60   MIP $85
- **Survive!**, 1982, Parker Brothers
  EX $12   NM $30   MIP $40
- **Swahili Game**, 1968, Milton Bradley
  EX $8   NM $20   MIP $30

- **Swap, the Wheeler-Dealer Game**, 1965, Ideal
  EX $7   NM $20   MIP $35
- **Swat Baseball**, 1948, Milton Bradley
  EX $20   NM $35   MIP $50

(KP Photo)

- **Swayze**, 1954, Milton Bradley
  EX $12   NM $30   MIP $40
- **Swish**, 1948, Jim Hawkers Games
  EX $45   NM $75   MIP $115
- **Swoop**, 1969, Whitman
  EX $7   NM $12   MIP $20
- **Sword In The Stone Game**, 1960s, Parker Brothers
  EX $18   NM $40   MIP $60
- **Swords and Shields**, 1970, Milton Bradley
  EX $10   NM $35   MIP $50
- **Syncron-8**, 1963, Transogram
  EX $18   NM $40   MIP $60
- **T.V. Bingo**, 1970, Selchow & Richter
  EX $3   NM $5   MIP $10
- **Tabit**, 1954, John Norton
  EX $25   NM $35   MIP $75
- **Tactics II**, 1984, Avalon Hill
  EX $6   NM $10   MIP $15
- **Taffy's Party Game**, 1960s, Transogram
  EX $10   NM $15   MIP $25
- **Taffy's Shopping Spree Game**, 1964, Transogram
  EX $10   NM $25   MIP $35
- **Tagalong Joe**, 1950, Wales Game Systems
  EX $8   NM $20   MIP $30
- **Tales of Wells Fargo**, 1959, Milton Bradley
  EX $40   NM $65   MIP $105
- **Talking Baseball**, 1971, Mattel
  EX $25   NM $60   MIP $85
- **Talking Football**, 1971, Mattel
  EX $20   NM $50   MIP $75
- **Talking Monday Night Football**, 1977, Mattel
  EX $10   NM $30   MIP $50
- **Tally Ho!**, 1950s, Whitman
  EX $8   NM $20   MIP $30
- **Tangle**, 1964, Selchow & Righter
  EX $6   NM $18   MIP $30
- **Tank Battle**, 1975, Milton Bradley
  EX $15   NM $35   MIP $50

❑ **Tank Command,** 1975, Ideal
EX $7   NM $20   MIP $35

❑ **Tantalizer,** 1958, Northern Signal
EX $10   NM $25   MIP $35

❑ **Tarzan,** 1984, Milton Bradley
EX $5   NM $10   MIP $15

(KP Photo)

❑ **Tarzan To The Rescue,** 1976, Milton Bradley
EX $10   NM $15   MIP $25

❑ **Taxi!,** 1960, Selchow & Righter
EX $15   NM $35   MIP $50

❑ **Tee Off by Sam Snead,** 1973, Glenn Industries
EX $18   NM $40   MIP $60

❑ **Teed Off!,** 1966, Cadaco
EX $6   NM $15   MIP $25

❑ **Teeko,** 1948, John Scarne Games
EX $10   NM $25   MIP $35

❑ **Teen Time,** 1960s, Warren-Built Rite
EX $6   NM $15   MIP $25

❑ **Telephone Game, The,** 1982, Cadaco
EX $7   NM $20   MIP $35

❑ **Television,** 1953, National Novelty
EX $35   NM $75   MIP $100

❑ **Tell It To The Judge,** 1959, Parker Brothers
EX $12   NM $35   MIP $60

❑ **Temple of Fu Manchu Game, The,** 1967, Pressman
EX $20   NM $30   MIP $50

❑ **Ten-Four, Good Buddy,** 1976, Parker Brothers
EX $5   NM $7   MIP $12

❑ **Tennessee Tuxedo,** 1963, Transogram
EX $75   NM $125   MIP $200

❑ **Tennis,** 1975, Parker Brothers
EX $10   NM $16   MIP $25

❑ **Tension,** 1970, Kohner
EX $7   NM $12   MIP $20

(KP Photo)

❑ **Terrytoons Hide N' Seek Game,** 1960, Transogram
EX $35   NM $75   MIP $100

❑ **Test Driver Game, The,** 1956, Milton Bradley
EX $25   NM $75   MIP $125

❑ **Texas Millionaire,** 1955, Texantics
EX $25   NM $55   MIP $75

❑ **Texas Rangers, Game of,** 1950s, All-Fair
EX $12   NM $40   MIP $60

❑ **That's Truckin',** 1976, Showker
EX $7   NM $20   MIP $35

❑ **They're at the Post,** 1976, MAAS Marketing
EX $12   NM $30   MIP $40

❑ **Thing Ding Robot Game,** 1961, Schaper
EX $35   NM $75   MIP $100

❑ **Think Twice,** 1974, Dynamic
EX $4   NM $15   MIP $20

❑ **Thinking Man's Football,** 1969, 3M
EX $6   NM $15   MIP $25

❑ **Thinking Man's Golf,** 1966, 3M
EX $5   NM $15   MIP $25

❑ **Think-Thunk,** 1973, Milton Bradley
EX $6   NM $18   MIP $30

❑ **Third Man,** 1969, Saalfield
EX $6   NM $15   MIP $25

❑ **Third Reich,** 1974, Avalon Hill
EX $3   NM $8   MIP $15

❑ **Thirteen,** 1955, Cadaco-Ellis
EX $3   NM $7   MIP $10

(KP Photo)

❑ **This Is Your Life,** 1954, Lowell
EX $15   NM $35   MIP $50

❑ **Three Little Pigs,** 1959, Selchow & Righter
EX $7   NM $20   MIP $35

❑ **Three Musketeers,** 1958, Milton Bradley
EX $35   NM $55   MIP $90

❑ **Three On a Match,** 1972, Milton Bradley
EX $10   NM $25   MIP $35

(KP Photo)

❑ **Three Stooges Fun House Game,** 1950s, Lowell
EX $100   NM $275   MIP $400

❑ **Thunder Road,** 1986, Milton Bradley
EX $10   NM $16   MIP $25

(KP Photo)

❑ **Thunderbirds Game,** 1965, Waddington/England
EX $40   NM $70   MIP $115

❑ **Tic-Tac Dough,** 1957, Transogram
EX $12   NM $30   MIP $45

❑ **Tiddle Flip Baseball,** 1949, Modern Craft
EX $20   NM $35   MIP $50

❑ **Tiddle-Tac-Toe,** 1955, Schaper
EX $3   NM $10   MIP $15

❑ **Tilt Score,** 1964, Schaper
EX $4   NM $15   MIP $20

❑ **Time Machine,** 1961, American Toy
EX $75   NM $150   MIP $250

(KP Photo)

❑ **Time Tunnel Game, The,** 1966, Ideal
EX $90   NM $150   MIP $240

❑ **Time: The Game,** 1983, Time/John Hansen
EX $2   NM $5   MIP $8

❑ **Tiny Tim Game of Beautiful Things, The,** 1970, Parker Brothers
EX $25   NM $65   MIP $90

(KP Photo)

❑ **Tom & Jerry,** 1977, Milton Bradley
EX $10   NM $15   MIP $25

❑ **Tom & Jerry Adventure In Blunderland,** 1965, Transogram
EX $25   NM $45   MIP $70

GAMES

Tom Seaver Game Action Baseball, 1969, Pressman
EX $50   NM $125   MIP $175

Tomorrowland Rocket To Moon, 1956, Parker Brothers
EX $20   NM $50   MIP $75

Toot! Toot!, 1964, Selchow & Righter
EX $8   NM $25   MIP $40

(KP Photo)

Tootsie Roll Train Game, 1969, Hasbro
EX $20   NM $30   MIP $50

Top Cat Game, 1962, Transogram
EX $50   NM $120   MIP $175

Top Cop, 1961, Cadaco-Ellis
EX $35   NM $65   MIP $105

Top Pro Basketball Quiz Game, 1970, Ed-U-Cards
EX $6   NM $15   MIP $25

Top Pro Football Quiz Game, 1970, Ed-U-Cards
EX $6   NM $15   MIP $25

Top Scholar, 1957, Cadaco-Ellis
EX $5   NM $16   MIP $25

Top Ten College Basketball, 1980, Top Ten Game
EX $30   NM $70   MIP $100

Top-ography, 1951, Cadaco-Ellis
EX $4   NM $15   MIP $20

Topper, 1962, Lakeside
EX $15   NM $35   MIP $50

Topple, 1979, Kenner
EX $4   NM $15   MIP $20

Tornado Bowl, 1971, Ideal
EX $5   NM $16   MIP $25

Tornado Rex, 1991, Parker Brothers
EX $10   NM $25   MIP $35

Total Depth, 1984, Orc Productions
EX $12   NM $30   MIP $40

Touche Turtle Game, 1964, Ideal
EX $45   NM $100   MIP $175

Town & Country Traffic Game, 1950s, Ranger Steel
EX $40   NM $90   MIP $135

Track Meet, 1972, Sports Illustrated
EX $10   NM $25   MIP $35

Trade Winds: The Caribbean Sea Pirate Treasure Hunt, 1960, Parker Brothers
EX $35   NM $75   MIP $125

Traffic Game, 1968, Matchbox
EX $35   NM $55   MIP $90

Traffic Jam, 1954, Harett-Gilmar
EX $15   NM $35   MIP $50

(KP Photo)

Trail Blazers Game, 1964, Milton Bradley
EX $10   NM $35   MIP $50

Trails to Tremble By, 1971, Whitman
EX $6   NM $18   MIP $30

Trap Door, 1982, Milton Bradley
EX $3   NM $10   MIP $15

Trap-em!, 1957, Selchow & Righter
EX $8   NM $25   MIP $40

Trapped (Ellery Queen's), 1956, Bettye-B
EX $30   NM $70   MIP $100

Traps, The Game of, 1950s, Traps
EX $75   NM $125   MIP $200

Travel America, 1950, Jacmar
EX $15   NM $25   MIP $40

Travel-Lite, 1946, Saxon Toy
EX $45   NM $75   MIP $120

Treasure Island, 1954, Harett-Gilmar
EX $30   NM $50   MIP $80

Tribulation, The Game of, 1981, Whitman
EX $3   NM $10   MIP $15

Tri-Ominoes, Deluxe, 1978, Pressman
EX $3   NM $5   MIP $10

Triple Play, 1978, Milton Bradley
EX $5   NM $10   MIP $15

Triple Yahtzee, 1972, Lowe
EX $4   NM $6   MIP $10

Tripoley Junior, 1962, Cadaco-Ellis
EX $5   NM $16   MIP $25

Trivial Pursuit, 1981, Selchow & Righter
EX $3   NM $10   MIP $15

Troke (Castle Checkers), 1961, Selchow & Righter
EX $6   NM $18   MIP $30

Tru-Action Electric Baseball Game, 1955, Tudor
EX $12   NM $30   MIP $40

Tru-Action Electric Sports Car Race, 1959, Tudor
EX $20   NM $50   MIP $75

True Colors, 1990, Milton Bradley
EX $20   NM $50   MIP $70

Trump, the Game, 1989, Milton Bradley
EX $5   NM $16   MIP $25

Trust Me, 1981, Parker Brothers
EX $5   NM $8   MIP $13

Truth or Consequences, 1955, Gabriel
EX $12   NM $40   MIP $60

Truth or Consequences, 1962, Lowell
EX $10   NM $35   MIP $50

TSG I: Pro Football, 1971, TSG
EX $35   NM $55   MIP $85

Tumble Bug, 1950s, Schaper
EX $6   NM $18   MIP $30

Turbo, 1981, Milton Bradley
EX $4   NM $15   MIP $20

TV Guide Game, 1984, Trivia
EX $8   NM $13   MIP $20

Twelve O'Clock High, 1965, Ideal
EX $25   NM $60   MIP $85

Twiggy, Game of, 1967, Milton Bradley
EX $18   NM $45   MIP $65

(KP Photo)

Twilight Zone Game, 1960s, Ideal
EX $75   NM $100   MIP $200

Twinkles Trip to the Star Factory, 1960, Milton Bradley
EX $45   NM $75   MIP $120

Twister, 1966, Milton Bradley
EX $5   NM $15   MIP $25

Twixt, 1962, 3M
EX $5   NM $16   MIP $25

Two For The Money, 1950s, Lowell
EX $10   NM $25   MIP $40

Tycoon, 1966, Parker Brothers
EX $12   NM $30   MIP $40

Tycoon, 1981, Wattson Games
EX $4   NM $10   MIP $15

Tycoon: The Real Estate Game, 1986, Ram Innovations
EX $6   NM $15   MIP $20

U.N. Game of Flags, 1961, Parker Brothers
EX $12   NM $20   MIP $30

U.S. Air Force, Game of, 1950s, Transogram
EX $25   NM $45   MIP $70

Ubi, 1986, Selchow & Righter
EX $6   NM $18   MIP $30

Ultimate Golf, 1985, Ultimate Golf
EX $6   NM $18   MIP $25

Uncle Milton's Ant Farm Game, 1969, Uncle Milton Industries
EX $15   NM $35   MIP $50

Uncle Wiggly, 1979, Parker Brothers
EX $8   NM $20   MIP $30

(KP Photo)

❏ **Undercover: The Game of Secret Agents,** 1960, Cadaco-Ellis
EX $20   NM $50   MIP $75

❏ **Underdog,** 1964, Milton Bradley
EX $20   NM $50   MIP $75

❏ **Underdog Save Sweet Polly,** 1972, Whitman
EX $25   NM $45   MIP $70

❏ **Undersea World of Jacques Cousteau,** 1968, Parker Brothers
EX $18   NM $40   MIP $60

❏ **Ungame,** 1975, Ungame
EX $4   NM $6   MIP $10

❏ **United Nations, A Game about the,** 1961, Payton Products
EX $12   NM $30   MIP $40

❏ **Universe,** 1966, Parker Brothers
EX $6   NM $18   MIP $30

❏ **Up for Grabs,** 1978, Mattel
EX $6   NM $15   MIP $20

❏ **Up! Against Time,** 1977, Ideal
EX $4   NM $10   MIP $15

❏ **Ur, Royal Game of Sumer,** 1977, Selchow & Righter
EX $3   NM $10   MIP $15

❏ **Uranium,** 1950s, Saalfield
EX $18   NM $40   MIP $60

(KP Photo)

❏ **Uranium Rush,** 1955, Gardner
EX $30   NM $70   MIP $100

❏ **USAC Auto Racing,** 1980, Avalon Hill
EX $18   NM $45   MIP $65

❏ **Vagabondo,** 1979, Invicta
EX $5   NM $16   MIP $25

❏ **Vallco Pro Drag Racing Game,** 1975, Zyla
EX $15   NM $25   MIP $35

❏ **Valvigi Downs,** 1985, Valvigi
EX $6   NM $18   MIP $30

❏ **Vaquero,** 1952, Wales Game Systems
EX $15   NM $50   MIP $75

❏ **Varsity,** 1955, Cadaco-Ellis
EX $12   NM $30   MIP $50

❏ **VCR Basketball Game,** 1987, Interactive VCR Games
EX $6   NM $10   MIP $15

❏ **VCR Quarterback Game,** 1986, Interactive VCR Games
EX $8   NM $13   MIP $20

(KP Photo)

❏ **Veda, The Magic Answer Man,** 1960s, Pressman
EX $20   NM $30   MIP $45

❏ **Vegas,** 1969, NBC-Hasbro
EX $6   NM $15   MIP $20

❏ **Vegas,** 1974, Milton Bradley
EX $4   NM $15   MIP $20

❏ **Venture,** 1970, 3M
EX $8   NM $20   MIP $30

❏ **Verbatim,** 1985, Lakeside
EX $3   NM $10   MIP $15

❏ **Verdict,** 1959, Avalon Hill
EX $15   NM $50   MIP $75

❏ **Verdict II,** 1961, Avalon Hill
EX $12   NM $40   MIP $60

❏ **Verne Gagne World Champion Wrestling,** 1950, Gardner
EX $40   NM $90   MIP $135

❏ **Vice Versa,** 1976, Hallmark Games
EX $5   NM $16   MIP $25

❏ **Video Village,** 1960, Milton Bradley
EX $10   NM $30   MIP $40

❏ **Vietnam,** 1984, Victory Games
EX $10   NM $15   MIP $25

❏ **Vince Lombardi's Game,** 1970, Research Games
EX $30   NM $65   MIP $85

❏ **Virginian, The,** 1962, Transogram
EX $35   NM $80   MIP $125

❏ **Visit To Walt Disney World Game,** 1970, Milton Bradley
EX $15   NM $20   MIP $35

❏ **Voice of The Mummy,** 1960s, Milton Bradley
EX $25   NM $60   MIP $90

❏ **Voodoo Doll Game,** 1967, Schaper
EX $12   NM $30   MIP $40

❏ **Voyage of the Dawn Treader,** 1983, David Cook
EX $5   NM $16   MIP $25

❏ **Voyage to Cipangu,** 1979, Heise-Cipangu
EX $25   NM $55   MIP $75

❏ **Wackiest Ship In The Army,** 1964, Ideal
EX $18   NM $45   MIP $65

❏ **Wacky Races Game,** 1970s, Milton Bradley
EX $15   NM $25   MIP $40

(KP Photo)

❏ **Wagon Train,** 1960, Milton Bradley
EX $25   NM $40   MIP $65

❏ **Wahoo,** 1947, Zondine
EX $15   NM $20   MIP $30

❏ **Wally Gator Game,** 1963, Transogram
EX $50   NM $85   MIP $130

❏ **Walt Disney's 101 Dalmatians,** 1960, Whitman
EX $20   NM $35   MIP $55

❏ **Walt Disney's 20,000 Leagues Under The Sea,** 1954, Jacmar
EX $45   NM $75   MIP $120

❏ **Walt Disney's Jungle Book,** 1967, Parker Brothers
EX $15   NM $25   MIP $45

(KP Photo)

❏ **Walt Disney's Official Frontierland,** 1950s, Parker Brothers
EX $15   NM $35   MIP $50

❏ **Walt Disney's Sleeping Beauty Game,** 1958, Whitman
EX $30   NM $50   MIP $80

❏ **Walt Disney's Swamp Fox Game,** 1960, Parker Brothers
EX $30   NM $50   MIP $80

(KP Photo)

❏ **Waltons,** 1974, Milton Bradley
EX $6   NM $15   MIP $25

(KP Photo)

GAMES

Wanted Dead or Alive, 1959, Lowell
EX $50   NM $75   MIP $125

War At Sea, 1976, Avalon Hill
EX $10   NM $20   MIP $30

War of the Networks, 1979, Hasbro
EX $6   NM $18   MIP $30

Watergate Scandal, The, 1973, American Symbolic
EX $8   NM $20   MIP $30

Waterloo, 1962, Avalon Hill
EX $10   NM $20   MIP $45

(KP Photo)

Weird-Ohs Game, The, 1964, Ideal
EX $85   NM $145   MIP $230

(KP Photo)

Welcome Back, Kotter, 1977, Ideal
EX $10   NM $25   MIP $40

Welfare, 1978, Jedco
EX $12   NM $40   MIP $60

(KP Photo)

Wendy, The Good Little Witch, 1966, Milton Bradley
EX $60   NM $135   MIP $175

West Point Story, The, 1950s, Transogram
EX $20   NM $50   MIP $75

What Shall I Be?, 1966, Selchow & Righter
EX $10   NM $15   MIP $25

What Shall I Wear?, 1969, Selchow & Righter
EX $5   NM $16   MIP $25

What's My Line Game, 1950s, Lowell
EX $15   NM $35   MIP $50

What's Up, Doc?, 1978, Milton Bradley
EX $6   NM $15   MIP $20

Whatzit?, 1987, Milton Bradley
EX $5   NM $16   MIP $25

Wheel of Fortune, 1985, Pressman
EX $5   NM $8   MIP $13

Where's The Beef?, 1984, Milton Bradley
EX $6   NM $10   MIP $15

Which Witch?, 1970, Milton Bradley
EX $35   NM $75   MIP $100

Whirl Out Game, 1971, Milton Bradley
EX $6   NM $18   MIP $30

Whirl-A-Ball, 1978, Pressman
EX $10   NM $15   MIP $25

Whirligig, 1963, Milton Bradley
EX $8   NM $20   MIP $30

Whirly Bird Play Catch, 1960s, Innovation Industries
EX $20   NM $35   MIP $50

White Shadow Basketball Game, The, 1980, Cadaco
EX $10   NM $25   MIP $40

Who Can Beat Nixon?, 1971, Dynamic
EX $10   NM $35   MIP $50

Who Framed Roger Rabbit?, 1987, Milton Bradley
EX $20   NM $35   MIP $55

Who What Or Where?, 1970, Milton Bradley
EX $5   NM $8   MIP $13

Who, Game of, 1951, Parker Brothers
EX $30   NM $50   MIP $80

Whodunit, 1972, Selchow & Righter
EX $10   NM $15   MIP $25

Whodunit?, 1959, Cadaco-Ellis
EX $8   NM $25   MIP $40

Whosit?, 1976, Parker Brothers
EX $6   NM $10   MIP $15

Wide World, 1957, 1962, Parker Brothers
EX $15   NM $25   MIP $40

Wide World of Sports Auto Racing, 1975, Milton Bradley
EX $12   NM $30   MIP $45

Wide World of Sports Golf, 1975, Milton Bradley
EX $12   NM $30   MIP $45

Wide World of Sports Tennis, 1975, Milton Bradley
EX $12   NM $30   MIP $45

Wide World Travel, 1957, Parker Brothers
EX $15   NM $35   MIP $50

Wil-Croft Baseball, 1971, Wil-Croft
EX $10   NM $16   MIP $25

(KP Photo)

Wild Bill Hickock, 1955, Built-Rite
EX $15   NM $35   MIP $50

Wild Kingdom Game, 1977, Teaching Concepts
EX $20   NM $35   MIP $50

Wild, Wild West, The, 1966, Transogram
EX $150   NM $350   MIP $500

Wildcatter, 1981, Kessler
EX $12   NM $30   MIP $40

Wildlife, 1971, Lowe
EX $15   NM $35   MIP $50

Willie Mays "Say Hey", 1954, Toy Development
EX $200   NM $350   MIP $525

Willie Mays "Say Hey" Baseball, 1958, Centennial Games
EX $190   NM $295   MIP $450

Willie Mays Push Button Baseball, 1965, Eldon
EX $175   NM $295   MIP $450

Willow, 1988, Parker Brothers
EX $10   NM $25   MIP $35

Win, Place & Show, 1966, 3M
EX $6   NM $20   MIP $30

Wine Cellar, 1971, Dynamic
EX $5   NM $16   MIP $25

Winko Baseball, 1940s, Milton Bradley
EX $45   NM $70   MIP $95

(KP Photo)

Winky Dink Official TV Game Kit, 1950s
EX $35   NM $75   MIP $100

Winnie The Pooh Game, 1959, Parker Brothers
EX $30   NM $50   MIP $80

Winnie The Pooh Game, 1979, Parker Brothers
EX $5   NM $8   MIP $13

Winning Ticket, The, 1977, Ideal
EX $6   NM $20   MIP $30

Wiry Dan's Electric Baseball Game, 1953, Harett-Gilmar
EX $8   NM $25   MIP $35

Wiry Dan's Electric Football Game, 1953, Harett-Gilmar
EX $8   NM $25   MIP $35

Witch Pitch Game, 1970, Parker Brothers
EX $15   NM $25   MIP $40

Wit's End, Game of, 1948, Parker Brothers
EX $15   NM $35   MIP $50

❏ **Wizard of Oz Game,** 1962, Lowe
EX $20   NM $30   MIP $50

(KP Photo)

❏ **Wizard of Oz Game,** 1974, Cadaco
EX $6   NM $15   MIP $25

(KP Photo)

❏ **Wolfman Mystery Game,** 1963, Hasbro
EX $80   NM $160   MIP $225

❏ **Woman & Man,** 1971, Psychology Today
EX $4   NM $15   MIP $20

❏ **Women's Lib,** 1970, Urban Systems
EX $12   NM $30   MIP $40

❏ **Wonder Woman Game,** 1967, Hasbro
EX $20   NM $35   MIP $65

❏ **Wonderbug Game,** 1977, Ideal
EX $8   NM $25   MIP $35

❏ **Woody Woodpecker Game,** 1959, Milton Bradley
EX $15   NM $35   MIP $50

(KP Photo)

❏ **Woody Woodpecker, Travel With,** 1950s, Cadaco-Ellis
EX $35   NM $65   MIP $100

❏ **Woody Woodpecker's Crazy Mixed Up Color Factory,** 1972, Whitman
EX $12   NM $20   MIP $30

❏ **Woody Woodpecker's Moon Dash Game,** 1976, Whitman
EX $12   NM $20   MIP $30

❏ **Word War,** 1978, Mattel
EX $6   NM $15   MIP $20

❏ **World Bowling Tour,** 1979, World Bowling Tour
EX $7   NM $20   MIP $35

❏ **World Champion Wrestling Official Slam O' Rama,** 1990, International Games
EX $5   NM $8   MIP $12

❏ **World of Micronauts,** 1978, Milton Bradley
EX $10   NM $15   MIP $25

❏ **World of Wall Street,** 1969, NBC-Hasbro
EX $4   NM $15   MIP $20

❏ **World's Greatest Baseball Game,** 1977, J. Woodlock
EX $35   NM $75   MIP $100

❏ **Wrestling Superstars,** 1985, Milton Bradley
EX $8   NM $13   MIP $20

❏ **WWF Wrestling Game,** 1991, Colorforms
EX $5   NM $8   MIP $12

❏ **Wyatt Earp Game,** 1958, Transogram
EX $35   NM $60   MIP $85

❏ **Xaviera's Game,** 1974, Dynamic
EX $7   NM $20   MIP $35

❏ **X-Men Alert! Adventure Game,** 1992, Pressman
EX $5   NM $16   MIP $25

❏ **Yacht Race,** 1961, Parker Brothers
EX $40   NM $85   MIP $125

(KP Photo)

❏ **Yahtzee,** 1956, Lowe
EX $6   NM $10   MIP $15

(KP Photo)

❏ **Yertle, The Game of,** 1960, Revell
EX $55   NM $95   MIP $150

❏ **Yogi Bear Break A Plate Game,** 1960s, Transogram
EX $50   NM $80   MIP $130

❏ **Yogi Bear Cartoon Game,** 1980, Milton Bradley
EX $3   NM $5   MIP $10

❏ **Yogi Bear Game,** 1971, Milton Bradley
EX $8   NM $20   MIP $30

❏ **Yogi Bear Go Fly A Kite Game,** 1961, Transogram
EX $25   NM $60   MIP $85

❏ **Your America,** 1970, Cadaco
EX $2   NM $7   MIP $12

❏ **Yours For a Song,** 1962, Lowell
EX $20   NM $35   MIP $55

❏ **Zaxxon,** 1982, Milton Bradley
EX $6   NM $10   MIP $15

❏ **Zig Zag Zoom,** 1970, Ideal
EX $10   NM $20   MIP $30

❏ **Ziggy Game, A Day With,** 1977, Milton Bradley
EX $4   NM $10   MIP $15

❏ **Zingo,** 1950s, Empire Plastics
EX $15   NM $20   MIP $30

(KP Photo)

❏ **Zip Code Game,** 1964, Lakeside
EX $40   NM $90   MIP $125

❏ **Zomax,** 1988, Zomax
EX $8   NM $25   MIP $40

❏ **Zoography,** 1972, Amway
EX $5   NM $16   MIP $25

GAMES

□ **Zorro Game, Walt Disney's,** 1966, Parker Brothers
EX $18   NM $40   MIP $65

□ **Zorro Target Game with Dart Gun,** 1950s, Knickerbocker
EX $20   NM $30   MIP $50

CARD GAMES

□ **Addams Family,** 1965, Milton Bradley
EX $25   NM $55   MIP $75

(KP Photo)

□ **Archie Bunker's Card Game,** 1972, Milton Bradley
EX $6   NM $15   MIP $25

□ **Art Linkletter's People are Funny Party Game,** 1954, Whitman
EX $5   NM $16   MIP $25

□ **Bali,** 1954, I-S Unlimited
EX $8   NM $20   MIP $30

□ **Baseball Card All Star Game,** 1987, Captoys
EX $5   NM $12   MIP $15

□ **Baseball Card Game,** 1950s, Ed-U-Cards
EX $8   NM $20   MIP $30

□ **Baseball Card Game, Official,** 1965, Milton Bradley
EX $20   NM $55   MIP $80

□ **Batman Card Game,** 1966, Ideal
EX $20   NM $65   MIP $85

□ **Batter Up Card Game,** 1949, Ed-U-Cards
EX $8   NM $20   MIP $30

(KP Photo)

□ **Beverly Hillbillies Game, "Set Back",** 1963, Milton Bradley
EX $10   NM $25   MIP $40

(KP Photo)

□ **Bewitched Stymie Game,** 1960s, Milton Bradley
EX $15   NM $40   MIP $60

□ **Bible Quiz Lotto,** 1949, Jack Levitz
EX $5   NM $12   MIP $20

□ **Boston Red Sox Game,** 1964, Ed-U-Cards
EX $15   NM $35   MIP $55

□ **Bullwinkle Card Game,** 1962, Ed-U-Cards
EX $10   NM $30   MIP $50

□ **Charge It!,** 1972, Whitman
EX $5   NM $15   MIP $25

□ **Combat,** 1964, Milton Bradley
EX $10   NM $25   MIP $40

□ **Cowboys & Indians,** 1949, Ed-U-Cards
EX $8   NM $20   MIP $35

□ **Dallas Game,** 1980, Mego
EX $3   NM $10   MIP $15

□ **Daniel Boone Wilderness Trail,** 1964, Transogram
EX $10   NM $40   MIP $65

□ **Dick Tracy Playing Card Game,** 1934, Whitman
EX $25   NM $60   MIP $100

□ **Dick Tracy Playing Card Game,** 1937, Whitman
EX $20   NM $45   MIP $75

□ **Dick Tracy Playing Card Game,** 1939, Esquire Novelty
EX $20   NM $45   MIP $75

□ **Dragonmaster,** 1981, Lowe
EX $8   NM $20   MIP $30

□ **Fast Golf,** 1977, Whitman
EX $8   NM $13   MIP $20

□ **Flintstones Animal Rummy,** 1960, Ed-U-Cards
EX $7   NM $25   MIP $45

□ **Flintstones Cut-Ups Game,** 1963, Whitman
EX $15   NM $45   MIP $75

□ **Funny Bones Game,** 1968, Parker Brothers
EX $5   NM $7   MIP $11

□ **Gidget,** 1966, Milton Bradley
EX $15   NM $35   MIP $50

□ **Go Go Go,** 1950s, Arco Playing Card
EX $6   NM $20   MIP $35

□ **Gong Hee Fot Choy,** 1948, Zondine Game
EX $20   NM $35   MIP $55

□ **Grabitz,** 1979, International Games
EX $2   NM $5   MIP $7

□ **Harry's Glam Slam,** 1962, Harry Obst
EX $35   NM $60   MIP $90

□ **Howdy Doody Card Game,** 1954, Russell
EX $20   NM $50   MIP $75

□ **I Survived New York!,** 1981, City Enterprises
EX $4   NM $7   MIP $12

□ **James Bond Live and Let Die Tarot Game,** 1973, US Games Systems
EX $20   NM $55   MIP $85

□ **Kardball,** 1946, Ajak
EX $20   NM $30   MIP $40

□ **Know Your States,** 1955, Garrard Press
EX $10   NM $25   MIP $45

□ **Let's Play Basketball,** 1965, D.M.R.
EX $12   NM $20   MIP $35

□ **Li'l Abner's Spoof Game,** 1950, Milton Bradley
EX $65   NM $95   MIP $135

□ **Man from U.N.C.L.E. Illya Kuryakin Card Game,** 1966, Milton Bradley
EX $10   NM $25   MIP $40

□ **Match,** 1953, Garrard Press
EX $10   NM $15   MIP $25

□ **Mickey Mouse Canasta Jr.,** 1950, Russell
EX $20   NM $55   MIP $85

□ **Mickey Mouse Jr. Royal Rummy,** 1970s, Whitman
EX $5   NM $15   MIP $30

□ **Mickey Mouse Library of Games,** 1946, Russell
EX $30   NM $65   MIP $125

□ **Mille Bornes,** 1962, Parker Brothers
EX $2   NM $7   MIP $12

(KP Photo)

□ **Monster Old Maid,** 1964, Milton Bradley
EX $10   NM $40   MIP $55

□ **Mr. T Game,** 1983, Milton Bradley
EX $5   NM $15   MIP $25

□ **Munsters Card Game,** 1966, Milton Bradley
EX $20   NM $45   MIP $65

□ **New York World's Fair Children's Game,** 1964, Ed-U-Cards
EX $15   NM $35   MIP $55

□ **Nuclear War,** 1965, Douglas Malewicki
EX $25   NM $40   MIP $75

□ **NY Mets Baseball Card Game, Official,** 1961, Ed-U-Cards
EX $20   NM $45   MIP $65

□ **Pro Baseball Card Game,** 1980s, Just Games
EX $6   NM $10   MIP $15

□ **Scan,** 1970, Parker Brothers
EX $3   NM $10   MIP $15

❏ **Scarne's Challenge,** 1947, John Scarne Games
EX $10   **NM** $25   **MIP** $35

❏ **Scott's Baseball Card Game,** 1989, Scott's Baseball Cards
EX $12   **NM** $20   **MIP** $30

❏ **Skeeter,** 1950s, Arco Playing Card
EX $6   **NM** $20   **MIP** $35

❏ **Strategy Poker Fine Edition,** 1967, Milton Bradley
EX $5   **NM** $12   **MIP** $18

❏ **Superheroes Card Game,** 1978, Milton Bradley
EX $15   **NM** $30   **MIP** $55

❏ **Superman Game,** 1966, Whitman
EX $35   **NM** $75   **MIP** $110

❏ **Syllable,** 1948, Garrard Press
EX $10   **NM** $15   **MIP** $25

❏ **Touch,** 1970, Parker Brothers
EX $5   **NM** $16   **MIP** $25

❏ **Trail Drive,** 1950s, Arco Playing Card
EX $15   **NM** $35   **MIP** $65

(KP Photo)

❏ **Twelve O'Clock High,** 1966, Milton Bradley
EX $20   **NM** $40   **MIP** $65

❏ **Waterworks,** 1972, Parker Brothers
EX $5   **NM** $12   **MIP** $18

❏ **Welcome Back, Kotter,** 1976, Milton Bradley
EX $5   **NM** $16   **MIP** $25

❏ **Wise Old Owl,** 1950s, Novel Toy
EX $20   **NM** $35   **MIP** $55

SKILL GAMES

❏ **Call It!,** 1978, Ideal
EX $5   **NM** $12   **MIP** $20

❏ **Calling Superman,** 1955, Transogram
EX $25   **NM** $85   **MIP** $125

❏ **Chicken Lotto,** 1965, Ideal
EX $8   **NM** $25   **MIP** $40

❏ **Chutes Away!,** 1978, Gabriel
EX $15   **NM** $45   **MIP** $65

❏ **Clickety-Clak,** 1950s, Milton Bradley
EX $10   **NM** $30   **MIP** $45

❏ **Clunk-A-Glunk,** 1968, Whitman
EX $8   **NM** $25   **MIP** $40

❏ **Don't Break the Ice,** 1960s, Schaper
EX $5   **NM** $16   **MIP** $25

❏ **Don't Spill the Beans,** 1967, Schaper
EX $5   **NM** $16   **MIP** $25

❏ **Feed the Elephant!,** 1952, Cadaco-Ellis
EX $10   **NM** $35   **MIP** $50

❏ **Gnip Gnop,** 1971, Parker Brothers
EX $5   **NM** $16   **MIP** $25

❏ **Hoc-Key,** 1958, Cadaco-Ellis
EX $10   **NM** $35   **MIP** $50

❏ **Hungry Henry,** 1969, Ideal
EX $7   **NM** $20   **MIP** $35

❏ **Jack & Jill Target Game,** 1948, Cadaco-Ellis
EX $7   **NM** $20   **MIP** $35

❏ **Jaws, The Game of,** 1975, Ideal
EX $5   **NM** $16   **MIP** $25

❏ **Kick Back,** 1965, Schaper
EX $5   **NM** $16   **MIP** $25

❏ **Leapin' Letters,** 1969, Parker Brothers
EX $5   **NM** $16   **MIP** $25

❏ **Marblehead,** 1969, Ideal
EX $5   **NM** $16   **MIP** $25

❏ **Mark "Three",** 1972, Ideal
EX $6   **NM** $18   **MIP** $30

❏ **Mentor,** 1960s, Hasbro
EX $18   **NM** $40   **MIP** $60

❏ **Mind Maze Game,** 1970, Parker Brothers
EX $5   **NM** $16   **MIP** $25

❏ **Mr. Mad Game,** 1970, Ideal
EX $12   **NM** $40   **MIP** $60

❏ **Nibbles 'N Bites,** 1964, Schaper
EX $5   **NM** $16   **MIP** $25

❏ **On Target,** 1973, Milton Bradley
EX $12   **NM** $40   **MIP** $60

❏ **Pitchin' Pal,** 1952, Cadaco-Ellis
EX $7   **NM** $20   **MIP** $35

(KP Photo)

❏ **Poosh-em-up Slugger Bagatelle,** 1946, Northwestern Products
EX $30   **NM** $75   **MIP** $105

❏ **Quick Shoot,** 1970, Ideal
EX $6   **NM** $18   **MIP** $30

❏ **Sharpshooter,** 1962, Cadaco-Ellis
EX $12   **NM** $40   **MIP** $60

❏ **Skip Bowl,** 1955, Transogram
EX $6   **NM** $18   **MIP** $30

❏ **Slap Stick,** 1967, Milton Bradley
EX $7   **NM** $20   **MIP** $35

❏ **Smack-A-Roo,** 1964, Mattel
EX $6   **NM** $18   **MIP** $30

(KP Photo)

❏ **Tight Squeeze,** 1967, Mattel
EX $7   **NM** $20   **MIP** $35

❏ **Tip-It,** 1965, Ideal
EX $5   **NM** $16   **MIP** $25

❏ **Topple Chairs,** 1962, Eberhard Faber
EX $6   **NM** $18   **MIP** $30

❏ **Wing-Ding,** 1951, Cadaco-Ellis
EX $8   **NM** $25   **MIP** $40

SKILL/ACTION GAME

❏ **Bandu,** 1991, Milton Bradley
EX $12   **NM** $30   **MIP** $40

❏ **Don't Dump the Daisy,** 1970, Ideal
EX $10   **NM** $25   **MIP** $35

❏ **Fascination Pool,** 1962, Remco
EX $8   **NM** $20   **MIP** $30

❏ **Grand Slam Game,** 1969, Ideal
EX $8   **NM** $20   **MIP** $30

❏ **Loopin' Louie,** 1992, Milton Bradley
EX $10   **NM** $25   **MIP** $35

❏ **Simon,** 1978, Milton Bradley
EX $6   **NM** $15   **MIP** $25

❏ **Space Strike,** 1980, Ideal
EX $12   **NM** $30   **MIP** $40

❏ **Tug Boat,** 1974, Parker Brothers
EX $10   **NM** $30   **MIP** $40

❏ **Whiplash,** 1966, Lakeside
EX $10   **NM** $25   **MIP** $35

SKILL/ACTION GAMES

❏ **Airways,** 1950s, Lindstrom Tool & Toy
EX $30   **NM** $50   **MIP** $75

❏ **Angry Donald Duck Game,** 1970s, Mexico
EX $40   **NM** $65   **MIP** $100

❏ **Baseball,** 1960s, Tudor
EX $25   **NM** $40   **MIP** $60

GAMES

(KP Photo)

❑ **Bash!,** 1967, Milton Bradley
EX $10 NM $15 MIP $25

❑ **Batman Batarang Toss,** 1966, Pressman
EX $150 NM $250 MIP $400

❑ **Batman Pin Ball,** 1966, Marx
EX $55 NM $95 MIP $150

❑ **Bats in the Belfry,** 1964, Mattel
EX $20 NM $55 MIP $80

(KP Photo)

❑ **Big 5 Poosh-M Up,** 1950s, Knickerbocker
EX $25 NM $40 MIP $60

❑ **Big Game Hunt, The,** 1947, Carrom Industries
EX $15 NM $25 MIP $40

❑ **Big Sneeze Game, The,** 1968, Ideal
EX $10 NM $25 MIP $40

❑ **Boob Tube Race,** 1962, Milton Bradley
EX $2 NM $80 MIP $30

❑ **Booby Trap,** 1965, Parker Brothers
EX $10 NM $15 MIP $25

❑ **Bop Bop 'N Rebop,** 1979, Hasbro
EX $12 NM $30 MIP $40

❑ **Bop The Beetle,** 1963, Ideal
EX $25 NM $60 MIP $85

❑ **Bowl-A-Matic,** 1963, Eldon
EX $100 NM $250 MIP $350

❑ **Bugs Bunny Game (Bagatelle),** 1975, Ideal
EX $15 NM $25 MIP $40

❑ **Candid Camera Target Shot,** 1950s, Lindstrom Tool & Toy
EX $35 NM $60 MIP $90

❑ **Careful: The Toppling Tower,** 1967, Ideal
EX $8 NM $20 MIP $30

❑ **Coney Island Penny Pitch,** 1950s, Novel Toy
EX $33 NM $55 MIP $88

(KP Photo)

❑ **Crazy Clock Game,** 1964, Ideal
EX $20 NM $50 MIP $75

❑ **Crazy Maze,** 1966, 1975, Lakeside
EX $8 NM $20 MIP $30

❑ **Deputy Dawg Hoss Toss,** 1973
EX $15 NM $25 MIP $40

(KP Photo)

❑ **Disney Dodgem Bagatelle,** 1960s, Marx
EX $30 NM $65 MIP $90

❑ **Dynamite Shack Game,** 1968, Milton Bradley
EX $10 NM $25 MIP $45

❑ **Facts In Five,** 1967, 3M
EX $3 NM $8 MIP $12

❑ **Fascination,** 1962, Remco
EX $15 NM $35 MIP $50

❑ **Feeley Meeley Game,** 1967, Milton Bradley
EX $20 NM $50 MIP $75

❑ **Fireball XL-5 Magnetic Dart Game,** 1963, Magic Wand
EX $75 NM $125 MIP $200

❑ **Flea Circus Magnetic Action Game,** 1968, Mattel
EX $15 NM $25 MIP $40

❑ **Flintstones Brake Ball,** 1962, Whitman
EX $45 NM $75 MIP $120

❑ **Flintstones Mechanical Shooting Gallery,** 1962, Marx
EX $75 NM $125 MIP $200

❑ **Flying Nun Marble Maze Game, The,** 1967, Hasbro
EX $20 NM $30 MIP $50

(KP Photo)

❑ **G.I. Joe Bagatelle Gun Action Game,** 1970s, Hasbro
EX $7 NM $12 MIP $15

(KP Photo)

❑ **Gotham's Ice Hockey,** 1960s, Gotham
EX $25 NM $60 MIP $85

❑ **Grab A Loop,** 1968, Milton Bradley
EX $7 NM $12 MIP $20

❑ **Hands Down,** 1965, Ideal
EX $10 NM $15 MIP $25

❑ **Hi Pop,** 1946, Advance Games
EX $20 NM $35 MIP $55

❑ **Hopalong Cassidy Bean Bag Toss Game,** 1950s
EX $20 NM $40 MIP $60

❑ **Hoppity Hooper Pin Ball Game,** 1965, Lido
EX $40 NM $75 MIP $115

❑ **Howdy Doody Dominoes Game,** 1950s, Ed-U-Cards
EX $60 NM $100 MIP $200

❑ **Huckleberry Hound's Huckle Chuck Target Game,** 1961, Transogram
EX $25   NM $50   MIP $100

(KP Photo)

❑ **Huggin' The Rail,** 1948, Selchow & Righter
EX $45   NM $65   MIP $100

❑ **I-Qubes,** 1948, Capex
EX $10   NM $15   MIP $25

❑ **Johnny Apollo Moon Landing Bagatelle,** 1969, Marx
EX $20   NM $35   MIP $55

❑ **KaBoom!,** 1965, Ideal
EX $10   NM $15   MIP $25

❑ **Ker-Plunk,** 1967, Ideal
EX $5   NM $10   MIP $15

❑ **Kimbo,** 1950s, Parker Brothers
EX $10   NM $15   MIP $25

❑ **King Arthur,** 1950s, Northwestern Products
EX $25   NM $40   MIP $65

❑ **King Pin Deluxe Bowling Alley,** 1947, Baldwin Mfg.
EX $10   NM $20   MIP $30

(KP Photo)

❑ **Knockout, Electronic Boxing Game,** 1950s, Northwestern Products
EX $90   NM $150   MIP $240

❑ **Krokay,** 1955, Transogram
EX $4   NM $10   MIP $15

❑ **Land of The Lost Pinball,** 1975, Larami
EX $10   NM $20   MIP $30

❑ **Lone Ranger and Tonto Spin Game, The,** 1967, Pressman
EX $15   NM $25   MIP $40

❑ **Magnetic Fish Pond,** 1948, Milton Bradley
EX $15   NM $25   MIP $65

❑ **Man from U.N.C.L.E. Pinball Game,** 1966
EX $80   NM $135   MIP $215

❑ **Man from U.N.C.L.E. Target Game,** 1966, Marx
EX $130   NM $275   MIP $550

❑ **Marathon Game,** 1978, Sports Games
EX $10   NM $20   MIP $35

(KP Photo)

❑ **Marx-O-Matic All Star Basketball,** 1950s, Marx
EX $150   NM $250   MIP $400

(KP Photo)

❑ **Mechanical Shooting Gallery,** 1950s, Wyandotte
EX $70   NM $135   MIP $195

(KP Photo)

❑ **Mickey Mouse Haunted House Bagatelle,** 1950s
EX $210   NM $350   MIP $550

(KP Photo)

❑ **Mighty Mouse Target Game,** 1960s, Parks
EX $30   NM $60   MIP $90

(KP Photo)

❑ **Monster Lab,** 1964, Ideal
EX $175   NM $275   MIP $450

❑ **Mouse Trap,** 1963, Ideal
EX $25   NM $45   MIP $70

❑ **NFL Football Game, Official,** 1968, Ideal
EX $12   NM $30   MIP $40

❑ **Nixon Ring Toss,** 1970s
EX $20   NM $30   MIP $50

❑ **Nutty Mads Bagatelle,** 1963, Marx
EX $25   NM $45   MIP $85

(KP Photo)

❑ **Nutty Mads Target Game,** 1960s, Marx
EX $35   NM $70   MIP $125

❑ **Par-A-Shoot Game,** 1947, Baldwin
EX $15   NM $25   MIP $40

(KP Photo)

GAMES

□ **Pony Polo,** 1960s, Remco
EX $10   NM $20   MIP $35

(KP Photo)

□ **Pro Bowl Live Action Football,** 1960s, Marx
EX $35   NM $65   MIP $95

□ **Rat Patrol Spin Game,** 1967, Pressman
EX $30   NM $65   MIP $85

(KP Photo)

□ **Rocket Patrol Magnetic Target Game,** 1950s, American Toy Products
EX $45   NM $75   MIP $120

(KP Photo)

□ **Rocket Sock-It Rifle and Target Game,** 1960s, Kenner
EX $20   NM $35   MIP $75

□ **Saratoga: 1777,** 1974, Gamut of Games
EX $10   NM $25   MIP $50

□ **Speed Circuit,** 1971, 3M
EX $15   NM $30   MIP $45

□ **Superman Spin Game,** 1967, Pressman
EX $40   NM $65   MIP $105

□ **Suspense,** 1950s, Northwestern Products
EX $15   NM $20   MIP $30

□ **Tickle Bee,** 1956, Schaper
EX $15   NM $20   MIP $35

(KP Photo)

□ **Time Bomb,** 1965, Milton Bradley
EX $35   NM $50   MIP $75

□ **Time Tunnel Spin-to-Win Game,** 1967, Pressman
EX $60   NM $100   MIP $160

□ **Tipp Kick,** 1970s, Top Set
EX $15   NM $25   MIP $40

□ **Tournament Labyrinth,** 1980s, Pressman
EX $10   NM $15   MIP $25

□ **Tru-Action Electric Basketball,** 1965, Tudor
EX $25   NM $50   MIP $75

□ **Tru-Action Electric Harness Race Game,** 1950s, Tudor
EX $15   NM $40   MIP $65

□ **Try-It Maze Puzzle Game,** 1965, Milton Bradley
EX $7   NM $12   MIP $20

□ **Untouchables, The,** 1950s, Marx
EX $95   NM $160   MIP $250

□ **Wow! Pillow Fight For Girls Game,** 1964, Milton Bradley
EX $12   NM $30   MIP $40

□ **Yogi Berra Pitch Kit,** 1963, Ross Products
EX $35   NM $50   MIP $100

□ **Zowie Horseshoe Game,** 1947, James L. Decker
EX $20   NM $35   MIP $55

PREWAR GAMES

BOARD GAMES

□ **21st Century Football,** 1930s, Kerger
EX $55   NM $90   MIP n/a

□ **400 Game, The,** 1890s, J.H. Singer
EX $100   NM $150   MIP n/a

□ **A&P Relay Boat Race Coast-to-Coast,** 1930s, A&P
EX $30   NM $40   MIP n/a

□ **ABC Baseball Game,** 1910s
EX $430   NM $715   MIP n/a

□ **ABC, Game of,** 1914
EX $60   NM $100   MIP n/a

□ **Abcdarian, The,** 1899, Chaffee & Selchow
EX $40   NM $100   MIP n/a

□ **Across the Channel,** 1926, Wolverine
EX $50   NM $85   MIP n/a

□ **Across the Continent,** 1892, Parker Brothers
EX $100   NM $175   MIP n/a

□ **Across the Continent,** 1922, Parker Brothers
EX $150   NM $300   MIP n/a

□ **Across the Sea Game,** 1930, Gabriel
EX $60   NM $100   MIP n/a

□ **Across the Yalu,** 1905, Milton Bradley
EX $75   NM $175   MIP n/a

□ **Add-Too,** 1940, All-Fair
EX $10   NM $15   MIP n/a

□ **Admiral Byrd's South Pole Game Little America,** 1930s, Parker Brothers
EX $125   NM $500   MIP n/a

□ **Admirals, The Naval War Game,** 1939, Merchandisers
EX $75   NM $120   MIP n/a

□ **ADT Delivery Boy,** 1890, Milton Bradley
EX $120   NM $200   MIP n/a

□ **ADT Messenger Boy (Small Version),** 1915, Milton Bradley
EX $40   NM $70   MIP n/a

□ **Advance And Retreat, Game of,** 1900s, Milton Bradley
EX $95   NM $175   MIP n/a

□ **Aero-Chute,** 1940, American Toy Works
EX $75   NM $200   MIP n/a

□ **Aeroplane Race,** 1922, Wolverine
EX $60   NM $95   MIP n/a

□ **After Dinner,** 1937, Frederick H. Beach (Beachcraft)
EX $10   NM $20   MIP n/a

□ **Air Base Checkers,** 1942, Einson-Freeman
EX $20   NM $30   MIP n/a

□ **Air Mail, The,** 1930, Archer Toy
EX $75   NM $125   MIP n/a

□ **Air Mail, The Game of,** 1927, Milton Bradley
EX $95   NM $100   MIP n/a

(KP Photo)

□ **Air Ship Game, The,** 1904, McLoughlin Bros.
EX $300   NM $700   MIP n/a

❑ **Air Ship Game, The,** 1912, McLoughlin Bros.
EX $300   **NM** $600   **MIP** n/a

❑ **Airplane Speedway Game,** 1941, Lowe
EX $20   **NM** $30   **MIP** n/a

(KP Photo)

❑ **Akins Real Baseball,** 1915, Akins
EX $450   **NM** $750   **MIP** n/a

❑ **Aldjemma,** 1944, Corey Games
EX $30   **NM** $45   **MIP** n/a

❑ **Alee-Oop,** 1937, Royal Toy
EX $15   **NM** $25   **MIP** n/a

❑ **Alexander's Baseball,** 1940s
EX $245   **NM** $400   **MIP** n/a

(KP Photo)

❑ **Alice in Wonderland,** 1930s, Parker Brothers
EX $60   **NM** $150   **MIP** n/a

❑ **Alice In Wonderland, Game of,** 1923, Stoll & Edwards
EX $50   **NM** $85   **MIP** n/a

❑ **All American Basketball,** 1941, Corey Games
EX $55   **NM** $65   **MIP** n/a

❑ **All American Football,** 1935
EX $35   **NM** $55   **MIP** n/a

❑ **All-American Big Boy Baseball Game,** 1920s, Rosensteel-Pulich
EX $200   **NM** $500   **MIP** n/a

❑ **All-American Football,** 1925, Parker Brothers
EX $100   **NM** $165   **MIP** n/a

❑ **All-Star Baseball Game,** 1935, Whitman
EX $100   **NM** $165   **MIP** n/a

❑ **Alpha Baseball Game,** 1930s, Redlich
EX $100   **NM** $150   **MIP** n/a

❑ **Alpha Football Game,** 1940s, Replica
EX $70   **NM** $115   **MIP** n/a

❑ **Amateur Golf,** 1928, Parker Brothers
EX $145   **NM** $245   **MIP** n/a

❑ **Ambuscade, Constellations And Bounce,** 1877, McLoughlin Bros.
EX $150   **NM** $200   **MIP** n/a

❑ **American Boy Game,** 1920s, Milton Bradley
EX $75   **NM** $125   **MIP** n/a

❑ **American Derby,** 1931, Henschel
EX $55   **NM** $90   **MIP** n/a

❑ **American Football Game,** 1930, Ace Leather Goods
EX $70   **NM** $115   **MIP** n/a

❑ **American Revolution, The New Game of The,** 1844, Lorenzo Burge
EX $960   **NM** $1600   **MIP** n/a

❑ **American Sports,** 1880s
EX $110   **NM** $180   **MIP** n/a

❑ **America's Football,** 1939, Trojan Games
EX $55   **NM** $90   **MIP** n/a

❑ **America's Yacht Race,** 1904, McLoughlin Bros.
EX $450   **NM** $750   **MIP** n/a

❑ **Amusing Game of Innocence Abroad, The,** 1888, Parker Brothers
EX $135   **NM** $300   **MIP** n/a

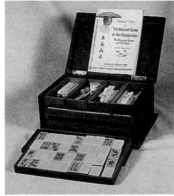

(KP Photo)

❑ **Ancient Game of the Mandarins, The,** 1923, Parker Brothers
EX $45   **NM** $75   **MIP** n/a

❑ **Andy Gump, His Game,** 1924, Milton Bradley
EX $60   **NM** $80   **MIP** n/a

❑ **Anex-A-Gram,** 1938, Embossing
EX $20   **NM** $40   **MIP** n/a

❑ **Animal & Bird Lotto,** 1926, All-Fair
EX $15   **NM** $20   **MIP** n/a

❑ **Arena,** 1896, Bliss
EX $120   **NM** $200   **MIP** n/a

❑ **Athletic Sports,** 1900, Parker Brothers
EX $145   **NM** $245   **MIP** n/a

❑ **Attack, Game of,** 1889, Bliss
EX $800   **NM** $1200   **MIP** n/a

❑ **Authors,** 1861, Whipple & Smith
EX $100   **NM** $300   **MIP** n/a

❑ **Authors,** 1890s, J.H. Singer
EX $40   **NM** $80   **MIP** n/a

❑ **Auto Game, The,** 1906, Milton Bradley
EX $100   **NM** $200   **MIP** n/a

❑ **Auto Race Electro Game,** 1929, Knapp Electric & Novelty
EX $125   **NM** $210   **MIP** n/a

❑ **Auto Race Game,** 1925, Milton Bradley
EX $200   **NM** $325   **MIP** n/a

❑ **Auto Race Jr.,** 1925, All-Fair
EX $150   **NM** $200   **MIP** n/a

❑ **Auto Race, Army, Navy, Game Hunt (four game set),** 1920s, Wilder
EX $90   **NM** $125   **MIP** n/a

❑ **Auto Race, Game Of,** 1920s, Orotech
EX $105   **NM** $175   **MIP** n/a

❑ **Automobile Race, Game of the,** 1904, McLoughlin Bros.
EX $500   **NM** $1000   **MIP** n/a

❑ **Auto-Play Baseball Game,** 1911, Auto-Play
EX $425   **NM** $700   **MIP** n/a

❑ **Aydelott's Parlor Baseball,** 1910
EX $195   **NM** $325   **MIP** n/a

❑ **Babe Ruth National Game of Baseball,** 1929, Keiser-Fry
EX $550   **NM** $910   **MIP** n/a

❑ **Babe Ruth's Baseball Game,** 1926, Milton Bradley
EX $400   **NM** $700   **MIP** n/a

❑ **Babe Ruth's Official Baseball Game,** 1940s, Toytown
EX $430   **NM** $715   **MIP** n/a

❑ **Baby Barn Yard,** 1940s, B.L. Fry Products
EX $15   **NM** $25   **MIP** n/a

❑ **Bagatelle, Game of,** 1898, McLoughlin Bros.
EX $350   **NM** $700   **MIP** n/a

❑ **Bagdad, The Game of The East,** 1940, Clover Games
EX $25   **NM** $40   **MIP** n/a

❑ **Bambino (Baseball, Chicago World's Fair),** 1933, Johnson Store Equipment
EX $295   **NM** $490   **MIP** n/a

❑ **Bambino Baseball Game,** 1940, Mansfield-Zesiger
EX $145   **NM** $250   **MIP** n/a

❑ **Bamboozle, or The Enchanted Isle,** 1876, Milton Bradley
EX $175   **NM** $250   **MIP** n/a

GAMES

Bang, Game of, 1903, McLoughlin Bros.
EX $100   NM $200   MIP n/a

Banner Lye Checkerboard, 1930s, Geo E. Schweig & Son
EX $15   NM $20   MIP n/a

Barage, 1941, Corey Games
EX $50   NM $100   MIP n/a

Barney Google and Spark Plug Game, 1923, Milton Bradley
EX $100   NM $200   MIP n/a

Baron Munchausen Game, The, 1933, Parker Brothers
EX $50   NM $75   MIP n/a

Base Hit, 1944, Games
EX $55   NM $90   MIP n/a

Baseball, 1942, Lowe
EX $15   NM $25   MIP n/a

Baseball & Checkers, 1925, Milton Bradley
EX $75   NM $150   MIP n/a

Baseball Dominoes, 1910, Evans
EX $250   NM $400   MIP n/a

Baseball Game, 1930, All-Fair
EX $100   NM $150   MIP n/a

Baseball Game & G-Man Target Game, 1940, Marks Brothers
EX $100   NM $165   MIP n/a

Baseball Game, New, 1885, Clark & Martin
EX $165   NM $275   MIP n/a

Baseball Wizard Game, 1916, Morehouse
EX $265   NM $450   MIP n/a

Baseball, Game of, 1886, J.H. Singer
EX $325   NM $550   MIP n/a

Basilinda, 1890, Horsman
EX $105   NM $175   MIP n/a

Basketball, 1942, Lowe
EX $15   NM $25   MIP n/a

Basketball Game, Official, 1940, Toy Creations
EX $55   NM $90   MIP n/a

Battle Checkers, 1925, Pen Man
EX $15   NM $50   MIP n/a

Battle Game, The, 1890s, Parker Brothers
EX $120   NM $200   MIP n/a

Battle of Ballots, 1931, All-Fair
EX $55   NM $125   MIP n/a

Battle of Manila, 1899, Parker Brothers
EX $400   NM $650   MIP n/a

Bear Hunt, Game of, 1923, Milton Bradley
EX $45   NM $70   MIP n/a

Beauty And The Beast, Game of, 1905, Milton Bradley
EX $45   NM $75   MIP n/a

Bee Gee Baseball Dart Target, 1935s, Bee Gee
EX $70   NM $115   MIP n/a

Bell Boy Game, The, 1898, Chaffee & Selchow
EX $425   NM $700   MIP n/a

Belmont Park, 1930, Marks Brothers
EX $75   NM $125   MIP n/a

Bengalee, 1940s, Advance Games
EX $20   NM $35   MIP n/a

Benny Goodman Swings, 1930s, Toy Creations
EX $65   NM $125   MIP n/a

Benson Football Game, The, 1930s, Benson
EX $85   NM $140   MIP n/a

Bible Boys, 1901, Zondervan
EX $10   NM $15   MIP n/a

Bible Characters, 1890s, Decker & Decker
EX $10   NM $25   MIP n/a

Bible Lotto, 1933, Goodenough and Woglom
EX $10   NM $15   MIP n/a

(KP Photo)

Bible Quotto, 1932, Goodenough and Woglom
EX $6   NM $10   MIP n/a

Bible Rhymes, 1933, Goodenough and Woglom
EX $10   NM $15   MIP n/a

Bicycle Game, 1896, Donaldson Brothers
EX $205   NM $350   MIP n/a

Bicycle Game, The New, 1894, Parker Brothers
EX $400   NM $700   MIP n/a

Bicycle Race, 1910, Milton Bradley
EX $125   NM $250   MIP n/a

Bicycle Race Game, The, 1898, Chaffee & Selchow
EX $430   NM $715   MIP n/a

(KP Photo)

Bicycle Race, A Game for the Wheelmen, 1891, McLoughlin Bros.
EX $600   NM $900   MIP n/a

Bicycling, The Merry Game of, 1900, Parker Brothers
EX $100   NM $165   MIP n/a

Big Apple, 1938, Rosebud Art
EX $20   NM $40   MIP n/a

Big Bad Wolf Game, 1930s, Parker Brothers
EX $100   NM $175   MIP n/a

Big Business, 1936, Parker Brothers
EX $75   NM $90   MIP n/a

Big Business, 1937, Transogram
EX $20   NM $50   MIP n/a

Big League Basketball, 1920s, Baumgarten
EX $145   NM $245   MIP n/a

Big Six: Christy Mathewson Indoor Baseball Game, 1922, Piroxloid
EX $500   NM $900   MIP n/a

Big Ten Football Game, 1936, Wheaties
EX $55   NM $90   MIP n/a

Bike Race Game, The, 1930s, Master Toy
EX $35   NM $100   MIP n/a

Bild-A-Word, 1929, Educational Card & Game
EX $10   NM $25   MIP n/a

Billy Whiskers, 1923, Saalfield
EX $45   NM $100   MIP n/a

Billy Whiskers, 1924, Russell
EX $45   NM $75   MIP n/a

Bilt-Rite Miniature Bowling Alley, 1930s, Atwood Momanus
EX $70   NM $115   MIP n/a

Bing Miller Base Ball Game, 1932, Ryan
EX $750   NM $2000   MIP n/a

Bingo, 1925, Rosebud Art
EX $15   NM $25   MIP n/a

Bingo or Beano, 1940s, Parker Brothers
EX $10   NM $15   MIP n/a

Bird Lotto, 1940s, Gabriel
EX $20   NM $35   MIP n/a

Black Beauty, 1921, Stoll & Edwards
EX $40   NM $65   MIP n/a

❏ **Black Falcon of The Flying G-Men, The,** 1939, Ruckelshaus
EX $400   NM $600   MIP n/a

❏ **Black Sambo, Game of,** 1939, Gabriel
EX $90   NM $200   MIP n/a

❏ **Blackout,** 1939, Milton Bradley
EX $60   NM $150   MIP n/a

❏ **Blockade,** 1941, Corey Games
EX $50   NM $95   MIP n/a

❏ **Blondie Goes To Leisureland,** 1935, Westinghouse
EX $20   NM $35   MIP n/a

❏ **Blow Football Game,** 1912
EX $30   NM $50   MIP n/a

❏ **Blox-O,** 1923, Lubbers & Bell
EX $15   NM $25   MIP n/a

❏ **Bluff,** 1944, Games of Fame
EX $15   NM $25   MIP n/a

❏ **Bo Bang & Hong Kong,** 1890, Parker Brothers
EX $275   NM $450   MIP n/a

❏ **Bo McMillan's Indoor Football,** 1939, Indiana Game
EX $60   NM $125   MIP n/a

❏ **Bo Peep Game,** 1895, McLoughlin Bros.
EX $195   NM $325   MIP n/a

❏ **Bo Peep, The Game of,** 1890, J.H. Singer
EX $200   NM $300   MIP n/a

❏ **Boake Carter's Star Reporter,** 1937, Parker Brothers
EX $105   NM $225   MIP n/a

❏ **Bomb The Navy,** 1940s, Pressman
EX $20   NM $50   MIP n/a

❏ **Bombardment, Game of,** 1898, McLoughlin Bros.
EX $100   NM $350   MIP n/a

❏ **Bombs Away,** 1944, Toy Creations
EX $75   NM $175   MIP n/a

❏ **Bookie,** 1931, Bookie Games
EX $55   NM $90   MIP n/a

❏ **Boston Baseball Game,** 1906, Boston Game
EX $495   NM $825   MIP n/a

❏ **Boston Globe Bicycle Game of Circulation,** 1895, Boston Globe
EX $55   NM $90   MIP n/a

❏ **Boston-New York Motor Tour,** 1920s, American Toy
EX $90   NM $150   MIP n/a

❏ **Bottle-Quoits,** 1897, Parker Brothers
EX $50   NM $85   MIP n/a

❏ **Bottoms Up,** 1934, Embossing
EX $20   NM $45   MIP n/a

❏ **Bowl 'em,** 1930s, Parker Brothers
EX $20   NM $35   MIP n/a

❏ **Bowling Board Game,** 1896, Parker Brothers
EX $350   NM $575   MIP n/a

❏ **Box Hockey,** 1941, Milton Bradley
EX $35   NM $60   MIP n/a

❏ **Boxing Game, The,** 1928, Stoll & Edwards
EX $85   NM $140   MIP n/a

❏ **Boy Scouts,** 1910s, McLoughlin Bros.
EX $125   NM $200   MIP n/a

❏ **Boy Scouts in Camp,** McLoughlin Bros.
EX $150   NM $300   MIP n/a

❏ **Boy Scouts Progress Game,** 1924, Parker Brothers
EX $200   NM $300   MIP n/a

❏ **Boy Scouts, The Game of,** 1926, Parker Brothers
EX $200   NM $350   MIP n/a

❏ **Boys Own Football Game,** 1900s, McLoughlin Bros.
EX $325   NM $750   MIP n/a

❏ **Bradley's Circus Game,** 1882, Milton Bradley
EX $60   NM $150   MIP n/a

❏ **Bradley's Telegraph Game,** 1900s, Milton Bradley
EX $85   NM $125   MIP n/a

❏ **Bradley's Toy Town Post Office,** 1910s, Milton Bradley
EX $90   NM $150   MIP n/a

❏ **Bringing Up Father Game,** 1920, Embee Distributing
EX $75   NM $175   MIP n/a

❏ **Broadway,** 1917, Parker Brothers
EX $150   NM $250   MIP n/a

❏ **Brownie Auto Race,** 1920s, Jeanette Toy & Novelty
EX $115   NM $195   MIP n/a

❏ **Brownie Horseshoe Game,** 1900s, M.H. Miller
EX $30   NM $50   MIP n/a

❏ **Brownie Ring Toss,** 1920s, M.H. Miller
EX $30   NM $50   MIP n/a

❏ **Buck Rogers and His Cosmic Rocket Wars Game,** 1934
EX $200   NM $350   MIP n/a

❏ **Buck Rogers Siege of Gigantica Game,** 1934
EX $400   NM $600   MIP n/a

❏ **Bucking Bronco,** 1930s, Transogram
EX $30   NM $50   MIP n/a

❏ **Buffalo Bill, The Game of,** 1898, Parker Brothers
EX $200   NM $400   MIP n/a

❏ **Buffalo Hunt,** 1898, Parker Brothers
EX $175   NM $250   MIP n/a

❏ **Bugle Horn or Robin Hood, Game of,** 1895, McLoughlin Bros.
EX $350   NM $650   MIP n/a

❏ **Bugville Games,** 1915, Animate Toy
EX $75   NM $125   MIP n/a

❏ **Bulls and Bears,** 1896, McLoughlin Bros.
EX $10000   NM $13000   MIP n/a

(KP Photo)

❏ **Bulls and Bears,** 1936, Parker Brothers
EX $150   NM $250   MIP n/a

❏ **Bunker Golf,** 1932
EX $115   NM $195   MIP n/a

❏ **Bunny Rabbit, or Cottontail & Peter, The Game of,** 1928, Parker Brothers
EX $85   NM $145   MIP n/a

❏ **Buried Treasure, The Game of,** 1930s, Russell
EX $35   NM $60   MIP n/a

❏ **Buster Brown at Coney Island,** 1890s, J. Ottmann Lith.
EX $225   NM $350   MIP n/a

❏ **Buster Brown Hurdle Race,** 1890s, J. Ottmann Lith.
EX $330   NM $550   MIP n/a

❏ **Buying and Selling Game,** 1903, Milton Bradley
EX $100   NM $200   MIP n/a

❏ **Cabby,** 1940, Selchow & Righter
EX $40   NM $75   MIP n/a

❏ **Cabin Boy,** 1910, Milton Bradley
EX $60   NM $100   MIP n/a

❏ **Cadet Game, The,** 1905, Milton Bradley
EX $100   NM $150   MIP n/a

❏ **Cake Walk Game, The,** 1900s, Parker Brothers
EX $750   NM $1500   MIP n/a

❏ **Cake Walk, The,** 1900s, Anglo American
EX $600   NM $1300   MIP n/a

❏ **Calling All Cars,** 1938, Parker Brothers
EX $25   NM $50   MIP n/a

❏ **Camelot,** 1950s, Parker Brothers
EX $20   NM $35   MIP n/a

❏ **Canoe Race,** 1910, Milton Bradley
EX $35   NM $60   MIP n/a

❏ **Capital Cities Air Derby, The,** 1929, All-Fair
EX $200   NM $350   MIP n/a

❏ **Captain and the (Katzenjammer) Kids,** 1940s, Milton Bradley
EX $50   NM $100   MIP n/a

❏ **Captain Hop Across Junior,** 1928, All-Fair
EX $100   NM $200   MIP n/a

❏ **Captain Kidd and His Treasure,** 1896, Parker Brothers
EX $195   NM $350   MIP n/a

❏ **Captain Kidd Junior,** 1926, Parker Brothers
EX $50   NM $75   MIP n/a

GAMES

(KP Photo)

❑ **Captive Princess,** 1880, McLoughlin Bros.
EX $135   **NM** $225   **MIP** n/a

(KP Photo)

❑ **Captive Princess,** 1899, McLoughlin Bros.
EX $65   **NM** $150   **MIP** n/a

❑ **Captive Princess, Tournament And Pathfinders, Games of,** 1888, McLoughlin Bros.
EX $100   **NM** $200   **MIP** n/a

❑ **Capture The Fort,** 1914, Valley Novelty Works
EX $45   **NM** $75   **MIP** n/a

❑ **Car Race and Game Hunt,** 1920s, Wilder
EX $100   **NM** $165   **MIP** n/a

❑ **Cargo For Victory,** 1943, All-Fair
EX $100   **NM** $150   **MIP** n/a

❑ **Cargoes,** 1934, Selchow & Righter
EX $50   **NM** $75   **MIP** n/a

❑ **Carl Hubbell Mechanical Baseball,** Gotham
EX $200   **NM** $500   **MIP** n/a

(KP Photo)

❑ **Carnival, The Show Business Game,** 1937, Milton Bradley
EX $50   **NM** $100   **MIP** n/a

❑ **Casey on the Mound,** 1940s, Kamm Games
EX $300   **NM** $400   **MIP** n/a

❑ **Cat,** 1915, Carl F. Doerr
EX $15   **NM** $25   **MIP** n/a

❑ **Cat, Game of,** 1900, Chaffee & Selchow
EX $270   **NM** $450   **MIP** n/a

❑ **Catching Mice, Game of,** 1888, McLoughlin Bros.
EX $200   **NM** $325   **MIP** n/a

❑ **Cats And Dogs,** 1929, Parker Brothers
EX $100   **NM** $225   **MIP** n/a

❑ **Cavalcade,** 1930s, Selchow & Righter
EX $40   **NM** $60   **MIP** n/a

❑ **Century Ride,** 1900, Milton Bradley
EX $100   **NM** $200   **MIP** n/a

❑ **Century Run Bicycle Game, The,** 1897, Parker Brothers
EX $210   **NM** $350   **MIP** n/a

❑ **Champion Baseball Game, The,** 1889, Schultz
EX $4100   **NM** $6800   **MIP** n/a

❑ **Champion Game of Baseball, The,** 1910s, Proctor Amusement
EX $60   **NM** $100   **MIP** n/a

❑ **Champion Road Race,** 1934, Champion Spark Plugs
EX $20   **NM** $25   **MIP** n/a

❑ **Championship Baseball Parlor Game,** 1914, Grebnelle Novelty
EX $150   **NM** $250   **MIP** n/a

❑ **Championship Fight Game,** 1940s, Frankie Goodman
EX $20   **NM** $50   **MIP** n/a

❑ **Champs, The Land of Brawno,** 1940, Selchow & Righter
EX $30   **NM** $50   **MIP** n/a

❑ **Characteristics,** 1845, Ives
EX $180   **NM** $300   **MIP** n/a

❑ **Charge, The,** 1898, E.O. Clark
EX $300   **NM** $500   **MIP** n/a

❑ **Charlie Chan, The Great Charlie Chan Detective Game,** 1937, Milton Bradley
EX $200   **NM** $350   **MIP** n/a

(KP Photo)

❑ **Charlie McCarthy Game of Topper,** 1938, Whitman
EX $30   **NM** $45   **MIP** n/a

❑ **Charlie McCarthy Put and Take Bingo Game,** 1938, Whitman
EX $30   **NM** $45   **MIP** n/a

❑ **Charlie McCarthy's Flying Hats,** 1938, Whitman
EX $25   **NM** $40   **MIP** n/a

❑ **Chasing Villa,** 1920, Smith, Kline & French
EX $65   **NM** $180   **MIP** n/a

❑ **Checkered Game of Life,** 1860, Milton Bradley
EX $200   **NM** $300   **MIP** n/a

❑ **Checkered Game of Life,** 1866, Milton Bradley
EX $130   **NM** $200   **MIP** n/a

❑ **Checkered Game of Life,** 1911, Milton Bradley
EX $100   **NM** $200   **MIP** n/a

❑ **Checkers & Avion,** 1925, American Toy Works
EX $30   **NM** $50   **MIP** n/a

❑ **Chee Chow,** 1939, Gabriel
EX $15   **NM** $25   **MIP** n/a

❑ **Cheerios Bird Hunt,** 1930s, General Mills
EX $15   **NM** $25   **MIP** n/a

❑ **Cheerios Hook The Fish,** 1930s, General Mills
EX $15   **NM** $25   **MIP** n/a

❑ **Chessindia,** 1895, Clark & Sowdon
EX $55   **NM** $95   **MIP** n/a

❑ **Chester Gump Game,** 1938, Milton Bradley
EX $65   **NM** $125   **MIP** n/a

❑ **Chester Gump Hops over the Pole,** 1930s, Milton Bradley
EX $75   **NM** $125   **MIP** n/a

❑ **Chevy Chase,** 1890, Hamilton-Myers
EX $75   **NM** $125   **MIP** n/a

❑ **Chicago Game Series Baseball,** 1890s, Doan
EX $1175   **NM** $1950   **MIP** n/a

❑ **China,** 1905, Wilkens Thompson
EX $50   **NM** $85   **MIP** n/a

❑ **Chin-Chow and Sum Flu,** 1925, Novitas Sales
EX $6   **NM** $10   **MIP** n/a

❑ **Ching Gong,** 1937, Gabriel
EX $20   **NM** $40   **MIP** n/a

❑ **Chiromagica, or The Hand of Fate,** 1901, McLoughlin Bros.
EX $300   **NM** $450   **MIP** n/a

❑ **Chivalrie Lawn Game,** 1875
EX $60   **NM** $100   **MIP** n/a

❑ **Chivalry,** 1925, Parker Brothers
EX $75   **NM** $125   **MIP** n/a

❑ **Chocolate Splash,** 1916, Willis G. Young
EX $51   **NM** $85   **MIP** n/a

❑ **Christmas Goose,** 1890, McLoughlin Bros.
EX $750   **NM** $1500   **MIP** n/a

❑ **Christmas Jewel, Game of the,** 1899, McLoughlin Bros.
EX $250   **NM** $400   **MIP** n/a

❑ **Christmas Mail,** 1890s, J. Ottmann Lith.
EX $390   **NM** $650   **MIP** n/a

❑ **Chutes And Ladders**, 1943, Milton Bradley
EX $15   **NM** $35   **MIP** n/a

❑ **Cinderella**, 1923, Stoll & Edwards
EX $40   **NM** $95   **MIP** n/a

❑ **Circus Game**, 1914
EX $75   **NM** $125   **MIP** n/a

❑ **Citadel**, 1940, Parker Brothers
EX $40   **NM** $60   **MIP** n/a

❑ **Cities**, 1932, All-Fair
EX $25   **NM** $40   **MIP** n/a

❑ **City of Gold**, 1926, Zulu Toy
EX $150   **NM** $250   **MIP** n/a

❑ **Classic Derby**, 1930s, Doremus Schoen
EX $30   **NM** $50   **MIP** n/a

❑ **Clipper Race**, 1930, Gabriel
EX $25   **NM** $75   **MIP** n/a

❑ **Clown Tenpins Game**, 1912
EX $60   **NM** $100   **MIP** n/a

❑ **Coast to Coast**, 1940s, Master Toy
EX $15   **NM** $25   **MIP** n/a

❑ **Cock-A-Doodle-Doo Game**, 1914
EX $60   **NM** $100   **MIP** n/a

❑ **Cocked Hat, Game of**, 1892, J.H. Singer
EX $150   **NM** $250   **MIP** n/a

❑ **College Baseball Game**, 1890s, Parker Brothers
EX $350   **NM** $700   **MIP** n/a

❑ **College Boat Race, Game of**, 1896, McLoughlin Bros.
EX $450   **NM** $750   **MIP** n/a

❑ **Colors, Game of**, 1888, McLoughlin Bros.
EX $150   **NM** $225   **MIP** n/a

❑ **Columbus**, 1892, Milton Bradley
EX $775   **NM** $1300   **MIP** n/a

(KP Photo)

❑ **Combination Board Games**, 1922, Wilder
EX $40   **NM** $50   **MIP** n/a

❑ **Comical Animals Ten Pins**, 1910, Parker Brothers
EX $185   **NM** $310   **MIP** n/a

❑ **Coney Island Playland Park**, 1940, Vitaplay Toy
EX $54   **NM** $90   **MIP** n/a

❑ **Conflict**, 1942, Parker Brothers
EX $75   **NM** $100   **MIP** n/a

❑ **Construction Game**, 1925, Wilder
EX $150   **NM** $300   **MIP** n/a

❑ **Coon Hunt Game, The**, 1903, Parker Brothers
EX $450   **NM** $1200   **MIP** n/a

❑ **Corn & Beans**, 1875, E.G. Selchow
EX $50   **NM** $85   **MIP** n/a

❑ **Corner The Market**, 1938, Whitman
EX $25   **NM** $40   **MIP** n/a

❑ **Cortella**, 1915, Atkins
EX $25   **NM** $45   **MIP** n/a

❑ **Cottontail and Peter, The Game of**, 1922, Parker Brothers
EX $75   **NM** $150   **MIP** n/a

❑ **Country Club Golf**, 1920s, Hustler Toy
EX $75   **NM** $125   **MIP** n/a

❑ **Country Store, The**, 1890s, J.H. Singer
EX $100   **NM** $200   **MIP** n/a

❑ **Covered Wagon**, 1927, Zulu Toy
EX $55   **NM** $85   **MIP** n/a

❑ **Cowboy Game, The**, 1898, Chaffee & Selchow
EX $400   **NM** $600   **MIP** n/a

❑ **Crash, The New Airplane Game**, 1928, Nucraft Toys
EX $30   **NM** $70   **MIP** n/a

❑ **Crazy Traveller**, 1908, Parker Brothers
EX $40   **NM** $60   **MIP** n/a

❑ **Crime & Mystery**, 1940s, Frederick H. Beach (Beachcraft)
EX $15   **NM** $25   **MIP** n/a

❑ **Criss Cross Words**, 1938, Alfred Butts
EX $90   **NM** $150   **MIP** n/a

❑ **Crooked Man Game**, 1914
EX $45   **NM** $75   **MIP** n/a

❑ **Cross Country**, 1941, Lowe
EX $20   **NM** $30   **MIP** n/a

❑ **Cross Country Marathon**, 1920s, Milton Bradley
EX $75   **NM** $150   **MIP** n/a

❑ **Cross Country Marathon Game**, 1930s, Rosebud Art
EX $100   **NM** $200   **MIP** n/a

❑ **Cross Country Racer**, 1940, Automatic Toy
EX $45   **NM** $75   **MIP** n/a

❑ **Cross Country Racer (w/wind-up cars)**, 1940s
EX $75   **NM** $130   **MIP** n/a

❑ **Crossing the Ocean**, 1893, Parker Brothers
EX $87   **NM** $175   **MIP** n/a

❑ **Crow Hunt**, 1904, Parker Brothers
EX $40   **NM** $60   **MIP** n/a

(KP Photo)

❑ **Crusade**, 1930s, Gabriel
EX $27   **NM** $45   **MIP** n/a

❑ **Crusaders, Game of the**, 1888, McLoughlin Bros.
EX $150   **NM** $300   **MIP** n/a

❑ **Cuckoo, A Society Game**, 1891, J.H. Singer
EX $40   **NM** $100   **MIP** n/a

❑ **Curly Locks Game**, 1910, United Game
EX $60   **NM** $100   **MIP** n/a

❑ **Cycling, Game of**, 1910, Parker Brothers
EX $100   **NM** $165   **MIP** n/a

❑ **Daisy Clown Ring Game**, 1927, Schacht Rubber
EX $9   **NM** $15   **MIP** n/a

❑ **Daisy Horseshoe Game**, 1927, Schacht Rubber
EX $9   **NM** $15   **MIP** n/a

❑ **Danny McFayden's Stove League Baseball Game**, 1920s, National Game
EX $295   **NM** $490   **MIP** n/a

❑ **Darrow Monopoly**, 1934, Charles Darrow
EX $3000   **NM** $7000   **MIP** n/a

❑ **Day at the Circus, Game of**, 1898, McLoughlin Bros.
EX $300   **NM** $400   **MIP** n/a

❑ **Deck Derby**, 1920s, Wolverine
EX $36   **NM** $60   **MIP** n/a

❑ **Decoy**, 1940, Selchow & Righter
EX $45   **NM** $75   **MIP** n/a

❑ **Defenders of The Flag Game**, 1920s
EX $24   **NM** $40   **MIP** n/a

❑ **Democracy**, 1940, Toy Creations
EX $50   **NM** $85   **MIP** n/a

❑ **Department Store, Game of Playing**, 1898, McLoughlin Bros.
EX $600   **NM** $1000   **MIP** n/a

❑ **Derby Day**, 1930, Parker Brothers
EX $45   **NM** $60   **MIP** n/a

❑ **Derby Steeple Chase**, 1888, McLoughlin Bros.
EX $150   **NM** $250   **MIP** n/a

❑ **Detective, The Game of**, 1889, Bliss
EX $1200   **NM** $2000   **MIP** n/a

GAMES

Dewey's Victory, 1900s, Parker Brothers
EX $120   NM $200   MIP n/a

Diamond Game of Baseball, The, 1894, McLoughlin Bros.
EX $1275   NM $2150   MIP n/a

Diamond Heart, 1902, McLoughlin Bros.
EX $150   NM $225   MIP n/a

Diceball, 1938, Ray-Fair
EX $90   NM $145   MIP n/a

Dicex Baseball Game, The, 1925, Chester S. Howland
EX $195   NM $325   MIP n/a

Dick Tracy Detective Game, 1933, Einson-Freeman
EX $45   NM $150   MIP n/a

Dick Tracy Detective Game, 1937, Whitman
EX $40   NM $100   MIP n/a

Discretion, 1942, Volume Sprayer
EX $30   NM $45   MIP n/a

District Messenger Boy, Game of, 1886, McLoughlin Bros.
EX $250   NM $500   MIP n/a

District Messenger Boy, Game of, 1904, McLoughlin Bros.
EX $80   NM $200   MIP n/a

Dog Race, 1937, Transogram
EX $20   NM $40   MIP n/a

Dog Show, 1890s, J.H. Singer
EX $85   NM $140   MIP n/a

Dog Sweepstakes, 1935, Stoll & Einson
EX $45   NM $75   MIP n/a

Donald Duck's Own Party Game, 1938, Parker Brothers
EX $80   NM $125   MIP n/a

(KP Photo)

Double Game Board (Baseball), 1925, Parker Brothers
EX $50   NM $75   MIP n/a

Double Header Baseball, 1935, Redlich
EX $145   NM $250   MIP n/a

Dreamland Wonder Resort Game, 1914, Parker Brothers
EX $275   NM $700   MIP n/a

Drive 'n Putt, 1940s, Carrom Industries
EX $50   NM $90   MIP n/a

Drummer Boy Game, The, 1890s, Parker Brothers
EX $100   NM $250   MIP n/a

Dubble Up, 1940s, Gabriel
EX $15   NM $25   MIP n/a

Dudes, Game of the, 1890, Bliss
EX $225   NM $375   MIP n/a

Durgin's New Baseball Game, 1885, Durgin & Palmer
EX $425   NM $700   MIP n/a

Eagle Bombsight, 1940s, Toy Creations
EX $100   NM $200   MIP n/a

East is East and West is West, 1920s, Parker Brothers
EX $80   NM $200   MIP n/a

Easy Money, 1936, Milton Bradley
EX $35   NM $55   MIP n/a

Ed Wynn The Fire Chief, 1937, Selchow & Righter
EX $45   NM $75   MIP n/a

Eddie Cantor's Tell It To The Judge, 1930s, Parker Brothers
EX $30   NM $50   MIP n/a

E-E-YAH Base Ball Game, 1900s, National Games
EX $600   NM $1800   MIP n/a

Election, 1896, Fireside
EX $20   NM $35   MIP n/a

Electric Baseball, 1935, Einson-Freeman
EX $35   NM $60   MIP n/a

Electric Football, 1930s, Electric Football
EX $55   NM $90   MIP n/a

Electric Magnetic Baseball, 1900
EX $175   NM $295   MIP n/a

Electric Questioner, 1920, Knapp Electric & Novelty
EX $20   NM $35   MIP n/a

Electric Speed Classic, 1930, Pressman
EX $390   NM $650   MIP n/a

Electro Gameset, 1930, Knapp Electric & Novelty
EX $30   NM $45   MIP n/a

Elementaire Musical Game, 1896, Theodore Presser
EX $20   NM $35   MIP n/a

Ella Cinders, 1944, Milton Bradley
EX $40   NM $80   MIP n/a

Elmer Layden's Scientific Football Game, 1936, Cadaco
EX $40   NM $80   MIP n/a

(KP Photo)

Elsie the Cow Game, The, 1941, Selchow & Righter
EX $50   NM $100   MIP n/a

Enchanted Forest Game, 1914
EX $120   NM $200   MIP n/a

Endurance Run, 1930, Milton Bradley
EX $60   NM $150   MIP n/a

Errand Boy, The, 1891, McLoughlin Bros.
EX $200   NM $350   MIP n/a

Ethan Allen's All-Star Baseball Game, 1942, Cadaco-Ellis
EX $150   NM $300   MIP n/a

Evening Parties, Game of, 1910s, Parker Brothers
EX $180   NM $300   MIP n/a

Fairyland Game, 1880s, Milton Bradley
EX $60   NM $95   MIP n/a

Fan-i-Tis, 1913, C.W. Marsh
EX $110   NM $180   MIP n/a

(KP Photo)

Fan-Tel, 1937, Schoenhut
EX $20   NM $30   MIP n/a

Farmer Jones' Pigs, 1890, McLoughlin Bros.
EX $165   NM $200   MIP n/a

Fashionable English Sorry Game, The, 1934, Parker Brothers
EX $20   NM $50   MIP n/a

Fast Mail Game, 1910, Milton Bradley
EX $105   NM $225   MIP n/a

Fast Mail Railroad Game, 1930s, Milton Bradley
EX $50   NM $85   MIP n/a

Favorite Steeple Chase, 1895, J.H. Singer
EX $200   NM $350   MIP n/a

Ferdinand The Bull Chinese Checkers Game, 1930s
EX $60   NM $100   MIP n/a

Fibber McGee, 1936, Milton Bradley
EX $25   NM $40   MIP n/a

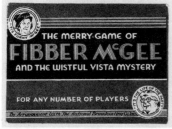

(KP Photo)

❑ **Fibber McGee and The Wistful Vista Mystery,** 1940, Milton Bradley
EX $30   NM $45   MIP n/a

❑ **Fig Mill,** 1916, Willis G. Young
EX $25   NM $80   MIP n/a

❑ **Finance,** 1937, Parker Brothers
EX $25   NM $40   MIP n/a

(KP Photo)

❑ **Finance And Fortune,** 1936, Parker Brothers
EX $35   NM $50   MIP n/a

❑ **Fire Alarm Game,** 1899, Parker Brothers
EX $1300   NM $2300   MIP n/a

❑ **Fire Department,** 1930s, Milton Bradley
EX $80   NM $125   MIP n/a

❑ **Fire Fighters Game,** 1909, Milton Bradley
EX $120   NM $200   MIP n/a

❑ **Flag Travelette,** 1895, Archarena
EX $45   NM $100   MIP n/a

❑ **Flapper Fortunes,** 1929, Embossing
EX $30   NM $45   MIP n/a

❑ **Flight To Paris,** 1927, Milton Bradley
EX $150   NM $250   MIP n/a

❑ **Fling-A-Ring,** 1930s, Wolverine
EX $20   NM $35   MIP n/a

❑ **Flip It,** 1925, American Toy Works
EX $40   NM $60   MIP n/a

❑ **Flip It,** 1940, Deluxe Game
EX $20   NM $30   MIP n/a

❑ **Flip It, Auto Race & Transcontinental Tour,** 1920s, Deluxe Game
EX $35   NM $90   MIP n/a

❑ **Flivver,** 1927, Milton Bradley
EX $150   NM $250   MIP n/a

❑ **Flowers, Game of,** 1899, Cincinnati Game
EX $45   NM $75   MIP n/a

❑ **Flying Aces,** 1940s, Selchow & Righter
EX $50   NM $100   MIP n/a

❑ **Flying the Beam,** 1941, Parker Brothers
EX $50   NM $100   MIP n/a

❑ **Flying the United States Airmail,** 1929, Parker Brothers
EX $200   NM $400   MIP n/a

❑ **Fobaga (football),** 1942, American Football
EX $50   NM $80   MIP n/a

❑ **Follow the Stars,** 1922, Watts
EX $225   NM $375   MIP n/a

❑ **Foot Race, The,** 1900s, Parker Brothers
EX $60   NM $100   MIP n/a

❑ **Football,** 1930s, Wilder
EX $50   NM $80   MIP n/a

❑ **Football Game,** 1898, Parker Brothers
EX $295   NM $495   MIP n/a

❑ **Football Knapp Electro Game Set,** 1929, Knapp Electric & Novelty
EX $125   NM $205   MIP n/a

❑ **Football, The Game of,** 1895, George A. Childs
EX $75   NM $125   MIP n/a

❑ **Football-As-You-Like-It,** 1940, Wayne W. Light
EX $85   NM $145   MIP n/a

❑ **Fore Country Club Game of Golf,** 1929, Wilder
EX $175   NM $295   MIP n/a

❑ **Fortune,** 1938, Parker Brothers
EX $40   NM $70   MIP n/a

❑ **Fortune Teller, The,** 1905, Milton Bradley
EX $20   NM $50   MIP n/a

❑ **Fortune Telling & Baseball Game,** 1889
EX $85   NM $140   MIP n/a

❑ **Fortune Telling Game,** 1934, Whitman
EX $50   NM $100   MIP n/a

❑ **Forty-Niners Gold Mining Game,** 1930s, National Games
EX $25   NM $40   MIP n/a

❑ **Foto World,** 1935, Cadaco
EX $90   NM $150   MIP n/a

❑ **Foto-Electric Football,** 1930s, Cadaco
EX $35   NM $50   MIP n/a

❑ **Foto-Finish Horse Race,** 1940s, Pressman
EX $30   NM $45   MIP n/a

❑ **Fox and Geese,** 1903, McLoughlin Bros.
EX $60   NM $100   MIP n/a

❑ **Fox and Hounds,** 1900, Parker Brothers
EX $85   NM $140   MIP n/a

❑ **Fox Hunt,** 1905, Milton Bradley
EX $40   NM $65   MIP n/a

❑ **Fox Hunt,** 1930s, Lowe
EX $20   NM $35   MIP n/a

❑ **Foxy Grandpa Hat Party,** 1906, Selchow & Righter
EX $55   NM $90   MIP n/a

❑ **Frisko,** 1937, Embossing
EX $20   NM $30   MIP n/a

❑ **Frog He Would a Wooing Go, The,** 1898, McLoughlin Bros.
EX $800   NM $1200   MIP n/a

❑ **Frog School Game,** 1914
EX $45   NM $75   MIP n/a

❑ **Frog Who Would a Wooing Go, The,** 1920s, United Game
EX $60   NM $125   MIP n/a

❑ **Fun at the Circus,** 1897, McLoughlin Bros.
EX $360   NM $600   MIP n/a

(KP Photo)

❑ **Fun at the Zoo, A Game,** 1902, Parker Brothers
EX $120   NM $200   MIP n/a

❑ **Fun Kit,** 1939, Frederick H. Beach (Beachcraft)
EX $15   NM $20   MIP n/a

❑ **Fut-Ball,** 1940s, Fut-Bal
EX $35   NM $60   MIP n/a

❑ **Game of Baseball,** 1886, McLoughlin Bros.
EX $750   NM $1600   MIP n/a

❑ **Game of Friendly Fun,** 1939, Milton Bradley
EX $50   NM $145   MIP n/a

(KP Photo)

❑ **Games You Like To Play,** 1920s, Parker Brothers
EX $75   NM $150   MIP n/a

❑ **Gang Busters Game,** 1938, Lynco
EX $150   NM $250   MIP n/a

❑ **Gang Busters Game,** 1939, Whitman
EX $50   NM $100   MIP n/a

❑ **General Headquarters,** 1940s, All-Fair
EX $75   NM $100   MIP n/a

❑ **Geographical Lotto Game,** 1921
EX $20   NM $30   MIP n/a

❑ **Geography Game,** 1910s, A. Flanagan
EX $15   NM $25   MIP n/a

GAMES

□ **Ges It Game,** 1936, Knapp Electric & Novelty
EX $20   NM $45   MIP n/a

□ **Get The Balls Baseball Game,** 1930
EX $20   NM $30   MIP n/a

(KP Photo)

□ **Glydor,** 1931, All-Fair
EX $75   NM $150   MIP n/a

□ **G-Men Clue Games,** 1935, Whitman
EX $60   NM $150   MIP n/a

□ **Go Bang,** 1898, Milton Bradley
EX $100   NM $300   MIP n/a

□ **Go to the Head of the Class,** 1938, Milton Bradley
EX $15   NM $35   MIP n/a

□ **Going To The Fire Game,** 1914, Milton Bradely
EX $90   NM $150   MIP n/a

□ **Gold Hunters, The,** 1900s, Parker Brothers
EX $105   NM $175   MIP n/a

□ **Goldenlocks & The Three Bears,** 1890, McLoughlin Bros.
EX $320   NM $800   MIP n/a

□ **Golf Tokalon Series, The Game of,** 1890s, E.O. Clark
EX $400   NM $700   MIP n/a

□ **Golf, A Game of,** 1930, Milton Bradley
EX $145   NM $245   MIP n/a

□ **Golf, Game of,** 1896, McLoughlin Bros.
EX $425   NM $715   MIP n/a

□ **Golf, The Game of,** 1898, J.H. Singer
EX $100   NM $300   MIP n/a

□ **Golf, The Game of,** 1905, Clark & Sowdon
EX $325   NM $550   MIP n/a

□ **Gonfalon Scientific Baseball,** 1930, Pioneer Game
EX $110   NM $180   MIP n/a

□ **Good Old Aunt, The,** 1892, McLoughlin Bros.
EX $150   NM $250   MIP n/a

□ **Good Old Game of Innocence Abroad, The,** 1888, Parker Brothers
EX $180   NM $300   MIP n/a

□ **Good Things To Eat Lotto,** 1940s, Gabriel
EX $15   NM $25   MIP n/a

□ **Goose Goslin Scientific Baseball,** 1935, Wheeler Toy
EX $600   NM $1000   MIP n/a

(KP Photo)

□ **Goose, The Jolly Game of,** 1851, J.P. Beach
EX $750   NM $1250   MIP n/a

□ **Goosey Gander, Or Who Finds the Golden Egg, Game of,** 1890, J.H. Singer
EX $675   NM $1150   MIP n/a

□ **Goosy Goosy Gander,** 1896, McLoughlin Bros.
EX $300   NM $500   MIP n/a

□ **Graham McNamee World Series Scoreboard Baseball Game,** 1930, Radio Sports
EX $250   NM $400   MIP n/a

□ **Grand National Sweepstakes,** 1937, Whitman
EX $20   NM $50   MIP n/a

□ **Grande Auto Race,** 1920s, Atkins
EX $75   NM $150   MIP n/a

□ **Graphic Baseball,** 1930s, Northwestern Products
EX $165   NM $275   MIP n/a

□ **Great American Baseball Game, The,** 1906, William Dapping
EX $145   NM $250   MIP n/a

□ **Great American Flag Game, The,** 1940, Parker Brothers
EX $50   NM $85   MIP n/a

□ **Great American Game,** 1910, Neddy Pocket Game
EX $145   NM $250   MIP n/a

□ **Great American Game of Baseball, The,** 1907, Pittsburgh Brewing
EX $145   NM $250   MIP n/a

□ **Great American Game, Baseball, The,** 1923, Hustler Toy
EX $150   NM $225   MIP n/a

(KP Photo)

□ **Great American Game, The,** 1925, Frantz
EX $110   NM $180   MIP n/a

□ **Great American War Game,** 1899, J.H. Hunter
EX $600   NM $1000   MIP n/a

□ **Great Family Amusement Game, The,** 1889, Einson-Freeman
EX $20   NM $35   MIP n/a

□ **Great Horse Race Game, The,** 1925, Selchow & Righter
EX $70   NM $115   MIP n/a

□ **Gregg Football Game,** 1924, Albert A. Gregg
EX $175   NM $285   MIP n/a

□ **Greyhound Racing Game,** 1938, Rex Manufacturing
EX $15   NM $25   MIP n/a

□ **Gumps at the Seashore, The,** 1930s, Milton Bradley
EX $65   NM $135   MIP n/a

□ **Gym Horseshoes,** 1930, Wolverine
EX $30   NM $45   MIP n/a

□ **Gypsy Fortune Telling Game, The,** 1895, Milton Bradley
EX $75   NM $125   MIP n/a

□ **Halma,** 1885, Horsman
EX $35   NM $60   MIP n/a

□ **Halma,** 1885, Milton Bradley
EX $30   NM $45   MIP n/a

□ **Hand of Fate,** 1901, McLoughlin Bros.
EX $1200   NM $2000   MIP n/a

□ **Happy Family, The,** 1910, Milton Bradley
EX $15   NM $25   MIP n/a

□ **Happy Hooligan Bowling Type Game,** 1925, Milton Bradley
EX $60   NM $200   MIP n/a

□ **Hardwood Ten Pins Wooden Game,** 1889
EX $60   NM $100   MIP n/a

□ **Hare & Hound,** 1895, Parker Brothers
EX $245   NM $400   MIP n/a

□ **Hare and Hounds,** 1890, McLoughlin Bros.
EX $200   NM $325   MIP n/a

□ **Harlequin, The Game of The,** 1895, McLoughlin Bros.
EX $150   NM $300   MIP n/a

□ **Harold Teen Game,** 1930s, Milton Bradley
EX $75   NM $150   MIP n/a

□ **Heedless Tommy,** 1893, McLoughlin Bros.
EX $240   NM $400   MIP n/a

□ **Hel-Lo Telephone Game,** 1898, J.H. Singer
EX $100   NM $200   MIP n/a

□ **Helps to History,** 1885, A. Flanagan
EX $20   NM $35   MIP n/a

❑ **Hen that Laid the Golden Egg, The,** 1900, Parker Brothers
EX $105   NM $175   MIP n/a

❑ **Hendrik Van Loon's Wide World Game,** 1935, Parker Brothers
EX $35   NM $65   MIP n/a

❑ **Hening's In-Door Game of Professional Baseball,** 1889, Inventor's
EX $525   NM $875   MIP n/a

❑ **Heroes of America,** 1920, Educational Card & Game
EX $20   NM $35   MIP n/a

❑ **Hialeah Horse Racing Game,** 1940s, Milton Bradley
EX $40   NM $65   MIP n/a

❑ **Hickety Pickety,** 1924, Parker Brothers
EX $20   NM $50   MIP n/a

❑ **Hide and Seek, Game of,** 1895, McLoughlin Bros.
EX $1500   NM $2000   MIP n/a

❑ **Hippodrome Circus Game,** 1895, Milton Bradley
EX $200   NM $300   MIP n/a

❑ **Hippodrome, The,** 1900s, E.O. Clark
EX $150   NM $200   MIP n/a

❑ **Hit and Run Baseball Game,** 1930s, Wilder
EX $150   NM $290   MIP n/a

❑ **Hit That Line,** 1930s, LaRue Sales
EX $100   NM $165   MIP n/a

❑ **Hi-Way Henry,** 1928, All-Fair
EX $600   NM $1500   MIP n/a

❑ **Hockey, Official,** 1940, Toy Creations
EX $50   NM $75   MIP n/a

❑ **Hold The Fort,** 1895, Parker Brothers
EX $125   NM $225   MIP n/a

❑ **Hold Your Horses,** 1930s, Klauber Novelty
EX $10   NM $20   MIP n/a

❑ **Home Baseball Game,** 1897, McLoughlin Bros.
EX $900   NM $1700   MIP n/a

❑ **Home Defenders,** 1941, Saalfield
EX $15   NM $25   MIP n/a

❑ **Home Diamond, The Great Baseball Game,** 1925, Phillips
EX $175   NM $295   MIP n/a

❑ **Home Games,** 1900s, Martin
EX $105   NM $175   MIP n/a

❑ **Home Run King,** 1930s, Selrite
EX $275   NM $450   MIP n/a

❑ **Home Run with Bases Loaded,** 1935, T.V. Morrison
EX $205   NM $350   MIP n/a

❑ **Honey Bee Game,** 1913, Milton Bradley
EX $50   NM $85   MIP n/a

❑ **Hood's Spelling School,** 1897, C.I. Hood
EX $20   NM $35   MIP n/a

❑ **Hoop-O-Loop,** 1930, Wolverine
EX $20   NM $30   MIP n/a

❑ **Hornet,** 1941, Lowe
EX $30   NM $45   MIP n/a

❑ **Horse Race,** 1943, Lowe
EX $10   NM $20   MIP n/a

❑ **Horse Racing,** 1935, Milton Bradley
EX $35   NM $60   MIP n/a

❑ **Horses,** 1927, Modern Makers
EX $45   NM $75   MIP n/a

❑ **Hounds & Hares,** 1894, J.W. Keller
EX $35   NM $60   MIP n/a

❑ **How Good Are You?,** 1937, Whitman
EX $10   NM $15   MIP n/a

❑ **Howard H. Jones Collegiate Football,** 1932, Municipal Service
EX $40   NM $100   MIP n/a

❑ **Huddle All-American Football Game,** 1931
EX $100   NM $165   MIP n/a

❑ **Hunting Hare, Game of,** 1891, McLoughlin Bros.
EX $205   NM $350   MIP n/a

❑ **Hunting the Rabbit,** 1895, Clark & Sowdon
EX $70   NM $115   MIP n/a

❑ **Hunting, The New Game of,** 1904, McLoughlin Bros.
EX $360   NM $600   MIP n/a

❑ **Hurdle Race,** 1905, Milton Bradley
EX $75   NM $150   MIP n/a

❑ **Hymn Quartets,** 1933, Goodenough and Woglom
EX $10   NM $15   MIP n/a

❑ **Ice Hockey,** 1942, Milton Bradley
EX $50   NM $75   MIP n/a

❑ **Improved Geographical Game, The,** 1890s, Parker Brothers
EX $60   NM $100   MIP n/a

❑ **In and Out the Window,** 1940s, Gabriel
EX $20   NM $35   MIP n/a

❑ **India,** 1940, Parker Brothers
EX $15   NM $20   MIP n/a

❑ **India Bombay,** 1910s, Cutler & Saleeby
EX $25   NM $40   MIP n/a

❑ **India, An Oriental Game,** 1890s, McLoughlin Bros.
EX $100   NM $125   MIP n/a

❑ **India, Game of,** 1910s, Milton Bradley
EX $15   NM $40   MIP n/a

❑ **Indianapolis 500 Mile Race Game,** 1938, Shaw
EX $350   NM $575   MIP n/a

❑ **Indians and Cowboys,** 1940s, Gabriel
EX $40   NM $65   MIP n/a

❑ **In-Door Baseball,** 1926, E. Bommer Foundation
EX $100   NM $180   MIP n/a

❑ **Indoor Football,** 1919, Underwood
EX $145   NM $250   MIP n/a

❑ **Indoor Horse Racing,** 1924, Man-O-War
EX $70   NM $115   MIP n/a

❑ **Inside Baseball Game,** 1911, Popular Games
EX $300   NM $500   MIP n/a

(KP Photo)

❑ **Intercollegiate Football,** 1923, Hustler Toy
EX $125   NM $245   MIP n/a

❑ **International Automobile Race,** 1903, Parker Brothers
EX $700   NM $1200   MIP n/a

❑ **International Spy, Game of,** 1943, All-Fair
EX $75   NM $125   MIP n/a

❑ **Jack and Jill,** 1890s, Parker Brothers
EX $55   NM $150   MIP n/a

❑ **Jack and Jill,** 1909, Milton Bradley
EX $60   NM $90   MIP n/a

❑ **Jack and the Bean Stalk,** 1895, Parker Brothers
EX $110   NM $175   MIP n/a

❑ **Jack and the Bean Stalk, The Game of,** 1898, McLoughlin Bros.
EX $550   NM $900   MIP n/a

❑ **Jack Spratt Game,** 1914
EX $45   NM $75   MIP n/a

❑ **Jack-Be-Nimble,** 1940s, Embossing
EX $20   NM $35   MIP n/a

❑ **Jackie Robinson Baseball Game,** 1940s, Gotham
EX $425   NM $900   MIP n/a

❑ **Jackpot,** 1943, B.L. Fry Products
EX $15   NM $25   MIP n/a

❑ **Japan, The Game of,** 1903, J. Ottmann Lith.
EX $180   NM $300   MIP n/a

❑ **Japanese Games of Cash and Akambo,** 1881, McLoughlin Bros.
EX $150   NM $250   MIP n/a

❑ **Jeep Board, The,** 1944, Lowe
EX $15   NM $35   MIP n/a

GAMES

Jeffries Championship Playing Cards, 1904
EX $35   NM $55   MIP n/a

Jig Chase, 1930s, Game Makers
EX $35   NM $50   MIP n/a

Jig Race, 1930s, Game Makers
EX $35   NM $50   MIP n/a

Jockey, 1920s, Carrom Industries
EX $35   NM $60   MIP n/a

John Gilpin, Rainbow Backgammon and Bewildered Travelers, 1875, McLoughlin Bros.
EX $175   NM $300   MIP n/a

Johnny Get Your Gun, 1928, Parker Brothers
EX $50   NM $75   MIP n/a

Jolly Pirates, 1938, Russell
EX $20   NM $35   MIP n/a

Journey to Bethlehem, The, 1923, Parker Brothers
EX $95   NM $160   MIP n/a

Jumpy Tinker, 1920s, Tinker Toys
EX $20   NM $30   MIP n/a

Jungle Hunt, 1940s, Rosebud Art
EX $30   NM $50   MIP n/a

Junior Baseball Game, 1915, Benjamin Seller
EX $100   NM $165   MIP n/a

Junior Basketball Game, 1930s, Rosebud Art
EX $55   NM $125   MIP n/a

Junior Bicycle Game, The, 1897, Parker Brothers
EX $250   NM $400   MIP n/a

Junior Combination Board, 1905, McLoughlin Bros.
EX $30   NM $50   MIP n/a

Junior Football, 1944, Deluxe Game
EX $30   NM $45   MIP n/a

Junior Motor Race, 1925, Wolverine
EX $40   NM $70   MIP n/a

Kan-Oo-Win-It, 1893, McLoughlin Bros.
EX $345   NM $575   MIP n/a

Kate Smith's Own Game America, 1940s, Toy Creations
EX $40   NM $75   MIP n/a

Keeping Up with the Jones', 1921, Parker Brothers
EX $50   NM $85   MIP n/a

Keeping Up with the Jones', The Game of, 1921, Phillips
EX $75   NM $100   MIP n/a

Kellogg's Baseball Game, 1936, Kellogg's
EX $25   NM $35   MIP n/a

Kellogg's Boxing Game, 1936, Kellogg's
EX $35   NM $55   MIP n/a

Kellogg's Football Game, 1936, Kellogg's
EX $25   NM $40   MIP n/a

Kellogg's Golf Game, 1936, Kellogg's
EX $25   NM $40   MIP n/a

Kentucky Derby Racing Game, 1938, Whitman
EX $20   NM $40   MIP n/a

Kilkenny Cats, The Amusing Game of, 1890, Parker Brothers
EX $100   NM $200   MIP n/a

Kings, 1931, Akro Agate
EX $55   NM $95   MIP n/a

King's Quoits, New Game of, 1893, McLoughlin Bros.
EX $300   NM $450   MIP n/a

Kitty Kat Cup Ball, 1930s, Rosebud Art
EX $50   NM $100   MIP n/a

Klondike Game, 1890s, Parker Brothers
EX $345   NM $575   MIP n/a

Knockout, 1937, Scarne Games
EX $55   NM $90   MIP n/a

Knute Rockne Football Game, Official, 1930, Radio Sports
EX $250   NM $400   MIP n/a

Ko-Ko the Clown, 1940, All-Fair
EX $20   NM $30   MIP n/a

Kriegspiel Junior, 1915, Parker Brothers
EX $50   NM $80   MIP n/a

La Haza, 1923, Supply Sales
EX $10   NM $20   MIP n/a

Lame Duck, The, 1928, Parker Brothers
EX $60   NM $100   MIP n/a

Land and Sea War Games, 1941, Lowe
EX $40   NM $65   MIP n/a

Lasso the Jumping Ring, 1912
EX $60   NM $100   MIP n/a

Le Choc, 1919, Milton Bradley
EX $50   NM $85   MIP n/a

League Parlor Base Ball, 1889, Bliss
EX $600   NM $1000   MIP n/a

Leap Frog Game, 1900, McLoughlin Bros.
EX $165   NM $275   MIP n/a

Leap Frog, Game of, 1910, McLoughlin Bros.
EX $45   NM $75   MIP n/a

Lee at Havana, 1899, Chaffee & Selchow
EX $150   NM $250   MIP n/a

Leslie's Baseball Game, 1909, Perfection Novelty
EX $145   NM $250   MIP n/a

Let's go to College, 1944, Einson-Freeman
EX $30   NM $45   MIP n/a

Let's Play Games, Golf, 1939, American Toy Works
EX $50   NM $80   MIP n/a

Let's Play Polo, 1940, American Toy Works
EX $45   NM $75   MIP n/a

Letter Carrier, The, 1890, McLoughlin Bros.
EX $100   NM $200   MIP n/a

Letters, 1878, Horsman
EX $30   NM $45   MIP n/a

Letters or Anagrams, 1890s, Parker Brothers
EX $30   NM $50   MIP n/a

Lew Fonseca Baseball Game, The, 1920s, Carrom Industries
EX $525   NM $875   MIP n/a

Library of Games, 1938, American Toy Works
EX $15   NM $25   MIP n/a

Life in the Wild West, 1894, Bliss
EX $300   NM $500   MIP n/a

Life of the Party, 1940s, Rosebud Art
EX $25   NM $35   MIP n/a

Life's Mishaps & Bobbing 'Round the Circle, 1891, McLoughlin Bros.
EX $300   NM $400   MIP n/a

Light Horse H. Cooper Golf Game, 1943, Trojan Games
EX $175   NM $295   MIP n/a

(KP Photo)

Limited Mail & Express Game, The, 1894, Parker Brothers
EX $200   NM $375   MIP n/a

Lindy Hop-Off, 1927, Parker Brothers
EX $200   NM $400   MIP n/a

Literature Game, 1897, L.J. Colby
EX $15   NM $25   MIP n/a

Little Black Sambo, Game of, 1934, Einson-Freeman
EX $75   NM $150   MIP n/a

Little Bo-Beep Game, 1914
EX $60   NM $100   MIP n/a

Little Boy Blue, 1910s, Milton Bradley
EX $50   NM $85   MIP n/a

Little Colonel, 1936, Selchow & Righter
EX $75   NM $125   MIP n/a

Little Cowboy Game, The, 1895, Parker Brothers
EX $200   NM $600   MIP n/a

Little Fireman Game, 1897, McLoughlin Bros.
EX $4000   NM $6000   MIP n/a

Little Jack Horner Golf Course, 1920s
EX $145   NM $250   MIP n/a

Little Jack Horner, A Game, 1910s, Milton Bradley
EX $45   NM $75   MIP n/a

Little Nemo Game, 1914
EX $500   NM $600   MIP n/a

(KP Photo)

Little Orphan Annie Game, 1927, Milton Bradley
EX $125   NM $250   MIP n/a

Little Red Riding Hood, 1900, McLoughlin Bros.
EX $200   NM $500   MIP n/a

Little Shoppers, 1915, Gibson Game
EX $150   NM $250   MIP n/a

Little Soldier, The, 1900s, United Game
EX $95   NM $160   MIP n/a

London Bridge, 1899, J.H. Singer
EX $100   NM $150   MIP n/a

London Game, The, 1898, Parker Brothers
EX $165   NM $275   MIP n/a

Lone Ranger Game, The, 1938, Parker Brothers
EX $40   NM $80   MIP n/a

Looping the Loop, 1940s, Advance Games
EX $25   NM $40   MIP n/a

Los Angeles Rams Football Game, 1930s, Zondine
EX $175   NM $295   MIP n/a

Lost Diamond, Game of, 1896, McLoughlin
EX $200   NM $300   MIP n/a

Lost in the Woods, 1895, McLoughlin Bros.
EX $660   NM $900   MIP n/a

(KP Photo)

Lotto, 1932, Milton Bradley
EX $6   NM $10   MIP n/a

Lou Gehrig's Official Playball, 1930s, Christy Walsh
EX $525   NM $875   MIP n/a

Lowell Thomas' World Cruise, 1937, Parker Brothers
EX $150   NM $400   MIP n/a

Luck, The Game of, 1892, Parker Brothers
EX $60   NM $100   MIP n/a

Lucky 7th Baseball Game, 1937, All-American
EX $100   NM $250   MIP n/a

Mac Baseball Game, 1930s, Mc Dowell
EX $145   NM $250   MIP n/a

Macy's Pirate Treasure Hunt, 1942, Einson-Freeman
EX $20   NM $35   MIP n/a

Madrap, The New Game of, 1914
EX $45   NM $75   MIP n/a

Magic Race, 1942, Habob
EX $55   NM $90   MIP n/a

Magnetic Jack Straws, 1891, Horsman
EX $27   NM $45   MIP n/a

Magnetic Treasure Hunt, 1930s, American Toy Works
EX $15   NM $25   MIP n/a

(KP Photo)

Mail, Express or Accommodation, Game of, 1895, McLoughlin Bros.
EX $600   NM $1200   MIP n/a

Mail, Express Or Accommodation, Game of, 1920s, Milton Bradley
EX $135   NM $225   MIP n/a

Major League Ball, 1921, National Game Makers
EX $325   NM $550   MIP n/a

Major League Base Ball Game, 1912, Philadelphia Game
EX $650   NM $1000   MIP n/a

Man Hunt, 1937, Parker Brothers
EX $150   NM $250   MIP n/a

Man in the Moon, 1901, McLoughlin Bros.
EX $2100   NM $3500   MIP n/a

Mansion of Happiness, 1843, Ives
EX $200   NM $300   MIP n/a

Mansion of Happiness, 1864, Ives
EX $100   NM $200   MIP n/a

Mansion of Happiness, The, 1895, McLoughlin Bros.
EX $510   NM $1000   MIP n/a

Marathon Game, The, 1930s, Rosebud Art
EX $75   NM $150   MIP n/a

Marriage, The Game of, 1899, J.H. Singer
EX $200   NM $300   MIP n/a

Match 'em, 1926, All-Fair
EX $12   NM $20   MIP n/a

Mathers Parlor Baseball Game, 1909, McClurg
EX $30   NM $50   MIP n/a

Meet the Missus, 1937, Fitzpatrick Brothers
EX $45   NM $75   MIP n/a

Mental Whoopee, 1936, Simon & Schuster
EX $10   NM $15   MIP n/a

Merry Hunt, The, Singer
EX $250   NM $400   MIP n/a

Merry Steeple Chase, 1890s, J. Ottmann Lith.
EX $45   NM $70   MIP n/a

Merry-Go-Round, 1898, Chaffee & Selchow
EX $2000   NM $2500   MIP n/a

Messenger Boy Game, 1910, J.H. Singer
EX $100   NM $200   MIP n/a

Messenger, The, 1890, McLoughlin Bros.
EX $75   NM $125   MIP n/a

Mexican Pete - I Got It, 1940s, Parker Brothers
EX $25   NM $50   MIP n/a

Mickey Mouse Baseball, 1936, Post Cereal
EX $55   NM $90   MIP n/a

Mickey Mouse Big Box of Games & Things To Color, 1930s
EX $45   NM $75   MIP n/a

Mickey Mouse Circus Game, 1930s, Marks Brothers
EX $180   NM $300   MIP n/a

Mickey Mouse Coming Home Game, 1930s, Marks Brothers
EX $80   NM $200   MIP n/a

Mickey Mouse Roll'em Game, 1930s, Marks Brothers
EX $90   NM $150   MIP n/a

Midget Auto Race, 1930s, Cracker Jack
EX $10   NM $15   MIP n/a

Midget Speedway, Game of, 1942, Whitman
EX $55   NM $90   MIP n/a

Miles at Porto Rico, 1899, Chaffee & Selchow
EX $100   NM $250   MIP n/a

Miniature Golf, 1930s, Miniature Golf
EX $35   NM $60   MIP n/a

Miss Muffet Game, 1914
EX $60   NM $100   MIP n/a

Mistress Mary, Quite Contrary, 1905, Parker Brothers
EX $60   NM $105   MIP n/a

GAMES

Modern Game Assortment, 1930s, Pressman
EX $25   NM $40   MIP n/a

Moneta: "Money Makes Money," Game of, 1889, F.A. Wright
EX $90   NM $150   MIP n/a

Monkey Shines, 1940, All-Fair
EX $20   NM $30   MIP n/a

Monopolist, Mariner's Compass And Ten Up, 1878, McLoughlin Bros.
EX $200   NM $500   MIP n/a

Monopoly, 1935, Parker Brothers
EX $35   NM $75   MIP n/a

Monopoly Jr. Edition, 1936, Parker Brothers
EX $15   NM $30   MIP n/a

Moon Mullins Automobile Race, 1927, Milton Bradley
EX $100   NM $200   MIP n/a

(KP Photo)

Mother Goose Bowling Game, 1884, Charles M. Crandall
EX $510   NM $850   MIP n/a

Mother Goose, Game of, 1921, Stoll & Edwards
EX $30   NM $50   MIP n/a

Mother Hubbard Game, 1914
EX $60   NM $100   MIP n/a

Motor Boat Race, An Exciting, 1930, American Toy Works
EX $110   NM $180   MIP n/a

(KP Photo)

Motor Cycle Game, 1905, Milton Bradley
EX $300   NM $600   MIP n/a

Motor Race, 1922, Wolverine
EX $90   NM $150   MIP n/a

Movie Inn, 1917, Willis G. Young
EX $45   NM $75   MIP n/a

Movie Millions, 1938, Transogram
EX $150   NM $300   MIP n/a

Movie-Land Lotto, 1920s, Milton Bradley
EX $45   NM $75   MIP n/a

Moving Picture Game, The, 1920s, Milton Bradley
EX $70   NM $120   MIP n/a

Mr. Ree, 1937, Selchow & Righter
EX $60   NM $100   MIP n/a

Mutuels, 1938, Mutuels
EX $85   NM $150   MIP n/a

My Word, Horse Race, 1938, American Toy Works
EX $60   NM $100   MIP n/a

Mythology, Game of, 1884, Peter G. Thompson
EX $65   NM $110   MIP n/a

Napoleon, Game of, 1895, Parker Brothers
EX $775   NM $1300   MIP n/a

National Derby Horse Race, 1938, Whitman
EX $20   NM $35   MIP n/a

National Game of Baseball, The, 1900s
EX $500   NM $875   MIP n/a

National Game of the American Eagle, The, 1844, Ives
EX $1600   NM $3500   MIP n/a

National Game, The, 1889, National Game
EX $875   NM $1450   MIP n/a

(KP Photo)

National League Ball Game, 1890, Yankee Novelty
EX $350   NM $575   MIP n/a

Naval Maneuvers, 1920, McLoughlin Bros.
EX $600   NM $900   MIP n/a

Navigator, 1938, Whitman
EX $45   NM $75   MIP n/a

Navigator Boat Race, 1890s, McLoughlin Bros.
EX $115   NM $195   MIP n/a

(KP Photo)

Nebbs on the Air, A Radio Game, 1930s, Milton Bradley
EX $50   NM $125   MIP n/a

Nebbs, Game of the, 1930s, Milton Bradley
EX $40   NM $75   MIP n/a

Neck and Neck, 1929, Embossing
EX $25   NM $40   MIP n/a

Neck and Neck, 1930, Wolverine
EX $50   NM $80   MIP n/a

Nellie Bly, 1898, J.H. Singer
EX $150   NM $300   MIP n/a

New Baseball Game, 1885, Clark & Martin
EX $165   NM $275   MIP n/a

New Parlor Game of Baseball, 1896, Sumner
EX $5000   NM $10000   MIP n/a

New York Recorder Newspaper Supplement Baseball Game, 1896
EX $430   NM $715   MIP n/a

Newsboy, Game of the, 1890, Bliss
EX $1200   NM $2000   MIP n/a

NFL Strategy, 1935, Tudor
EX $45   NM $70   MIP n/a

Nine Men Morris, 1930s, Milton Bradley
EX $15   NM $25   MIP n/a

Nineteenth Hole Golf Game, 1930s, Einson-Freeman
EX $85   NM $140   MIP n/a

Nip & Tuck Hockey, 1928, Parker Brothers
EX $115   NM $195   MIP n/a

No-Joke, 1941, Volume Sprayer
EX $12   NM $20   MIP n/a

Nok-Out Baseball Game, 1930, Dizzy & Daffy Dean
EX $350   NM $575   MIP n/a

North Pole Game, The, 1907, Milton Bradley
EX $200   NM $350   MIP n/a

Object Lotto, 1940s, Gabriel
EX $15   NM $25   MIP n/a

Obstacle Race, 1930s, Wilder
EX $70   NM $115   MIP n/a

Ocean to Ocean Flight Game, 1927, Wilder
EX $55   NM $125   MIP n/a

Office Boy, The, 1889, Parker Brothers
EX $150   NM $300   MIP n/a

Official Radio Baseball Game, 1930s, Toy Creations
EX $50   NM $75   MIP n/a

Official Radio Basketball Game, 1939, Toy Creations
EX $25   NM $50   MIP n/a

Official Radio Football Game, 1940, Toy Creations
EX $25   NM $50   MIP n/a

❑ **Old Hunter & His Game,** 1870
EX $175   NM $295   MIP n/a

❑ **Old Maid,** 1898, Chaffee & Selchow
EX $30   NM $75   MIP n/a

(KP Photo)

❑ **Old Maid & Old Bachelor, The Merry Game of,** 1898, McLoughlin Bros.
EX $180   NM $300   MIP n/a

❑ **Old Maid or Matrimony, Game of,** 1890, McLoughlin Bros.
EX $150   NM $250   MIP n/a

❑ **Old Mother Goose,** 1898, Chaffee & Selchow
EX $105   NM $175   MIP n/a

❑ **Old Mother Hubbard, Game of,** 1890s, Milton Bradley
EX $60   NM $100   MIP n/a

❑ **Old Mrs. Goose, Game of,** 1910, Milton Bradley
EX $50   NM $85   MIP n/a

❑ **Oldtimers,** 1940, Frederick H. Beach (Beachcraft)
EX $15   NM $20   MIP n/a

❑ **Ollo,** 1944, Games Of Fame
EX $15   NM $25   MIP n/a

❑ **Olympic Runners,** 1930, Wolverine
EX $125   NM $175   MIP n/a

❑ **On the Mid-Way,** 1925, Milton Bradley
EX $90   NM $150   MIP n/a

❑ **One Two Button Your Shoe,** 1940s, Master Toy
EX $15   NM $25   MIP n/a

❑ **Open Championship Golf Game,** 1930s, Beacon Hudson
EX $45   NM $75   MIP n/a

❑ **Opportunity Hour,** 1940, American Toy Works
EX $20   NM $35   MIP n/a

❑ **Ot-O-Win Football,** 1920s, Ot-O-Win Toys & Games
EX $55   NM $90   MIP n/a

❑ **Ouija, plywood,** 1920, William Fuld
EX $100   NM $150   MIP n/a

❑ **Our Defenders,** 1944, Master Toy
EX $40   NM $65   MIP n/a

❑ **Our National Ball Game,** 1887, McGill & DeLany
EX $425   NM $650   MIP n/a

❑ **Our No. 7 Baseball Game Puzzle,** 1910, Satisfactory
EX $110   NM $180   MIP n/a

❑ **Our Union,** 1896, Fireside Game
EX $25   NM $40   MIP n/a

❑ **Outboard Motor Race, The,** 1930s, Milton Bradley
EX $35   NM $75   MIP n/a

❑ **Overland Limited, The,** 1920s, Milton Bradley
EX $75   NM $125   MIP n/a

❑ **Owl and the Pussy Cat, The,** 1900s, E.O. Clark
EX $210   NM $350   MIP n/a

❑ **Pana Kanal, The Great Panama Canal Game,** 1913, Chaffee & Selchow
EX $65   NM $110   MIP n/a

❑ **Panama Canal Game,** 1910, Parker Brothers
EX $200   NM $400   MIP n/a

❑ **Pan-Cake Tiddly Winks,** 1920s, Russell
EX $55   NM $125   MIP n/a

❑ **Par Golf Card Game,** 1920, National Golf Services
EX $115   NM $195   MIP n/a

❑ **Par, The New Golf Game,** 1926, Russell
EX $115   NM $195   MIP n/a

❑ **Parcheesi,** 1880s, H.B. Chaffee
EX $50   NM $75   MIP n/a

❑ **Parker Brothers Post Office Game,** 1910s, Parker Brothers
EX $105   NM $175   MIP n/a

❑ **Parlor Base Ball, Game of,** 1892, McLoughlin
EX $1400   NM $1800   MIP n/a

❑ **Parlor Baseball Game,** 1908, Mathers
EX $200   NM $325   MIP n/a

❑ **Parlor Croquet,** 1940, Pressman
EX $20   NM $35   MIP n/a

❑ **Parlor Football Game,** 1890s, McLoughlin Bros.
EX $525   NM $950   MIP n/a

❑ **Parlor Golf,** 1897, Chaffee & Selchow
EX $55   NM $90   MIP n/a

❑ **Pat Moran's Own Baseball Game,** 1919, Smith, Kline & French
EX $325   NM $400   MIP n/a

❑ **Patent Parlor Bowling Alley,** 1899, Thomas Kochka
EX $70   NM $115   MIP n/a

❑ **Pedestrianism,** 1879
EX $350   NM $575   MIP n/a

❑ **Peg at my Heart,** 1914, Willis G. Young
EX $20   NM $45   MIP n/a

❑ **Peg Baseball,** 1915, Parker Brothers
EX $145   NM $250   MIP n/a

(KP Photo)

❑ **Peg Baseball,** 1924, Parker Brothers
EX $50   NM $100   MIP n/a

❑ **Peggy,** 1923, Parker Brothers
EX $35   NM $55   MIP n/a

❑ **Peg'ity,** 1925, Parker Brothers
EX $10   NM $25   MIP n/a

❑ **Pegpin, Game of,** 1929, Stoll & Edwards
EX $25   NM $45   MIP n/a

❑ **Pe-Ling,** 1923, Cookson & Sullivan
EX $25   NM $45   MIP n/a

❑ **Pennant Puzzle,** 1909, L.W. Hardy
EX $250   NM $400   MIP n/a

❑ **Pennant Winner,** 1930s, Wolverine
EX $175   NM $295   MIP n/a

❑ **Penny Post,** 1892, Parker Brothers
EX $150   NM $250   MIP n/a

❑ **Peter Pan,** 1927, Selchow & Righter
EX $100   NM $150   MIP n/a

❑ **Peter Peter Pumpkin Eater,** 1914, Parker Brothers
EX $60   NM $125   MIP n/a

❑ **Peter Rabbit Game,** 1910, Milton Bradley
EX $55   NM $95   MIP n/a

❑ **Peter Rabbit Game,** 1940s, Gabriel
EX $45   NM $75   MIP n/a

❑ **Philadelphia Inquirer Baseball Game, The,** 1896
EX $145   NM $250   MIP n/a

❑ **Philo Vance,** 1937, Parker Brothers
EX $100   NM $175   MIP n/a

(KP Photo)

❑ **Phoebe Snow, Game of,** 1899, McLoughlin Bros.
EX $150   NM $300   MIP n/a

❑ **Piggies, The New Game,** 1894, Selchow & Righter
EX $330   NM $550   MIP n/a

❑ **Pigskin,** 1940, Parker Brothers
EX $20   NM $50   MIP n/a

❑ **Pigskin, Tom Hamilton's Football Game,** 1934, Parker Brothers
EX $25   NM $60   MIP n/a

❑ **Pilgrim's Progress, Going To Sunday School, Tower of Babel,** 1875, McLoughlin Bros.
EX $120   NM $250   MIP n/a

❑ **Pinafore,** 1879, Fuller Upham
EX $45   NM $125   MIP n/a

GAMES

❏ **Pinch Hitter,** 1930s
EX $110   NM $180   MIP n/a

❏ **Pines, The,** 1896, Fireside Game
EX $15   NM $25   MIP n/a

❏ **Pinocchio Pitfalls Marble Game,** 1940
EX $30   NM $50   MIP n/a

❏ **Pinocchio Ring The Nose Game,** 1940
EX $20   NM $30   MIP n/a

❏ **Pioneers of the Santa Fe Trail,** 1935, Einson-Freeman
EX $25   NM $40   MIP n/a

❏ **Pirate & Traveller,** 1936, Milton Bradley
EX $20   NM $45   MIP n/a

❏ **Pirate Ship,** 1940, Lowe
EX $15   NM $25   MIP n/a

❏ **Pla-Golf Board Game,** 1938, Pla-Golf
EX $775   NM $1300   MIP n/a

❏ **Play Ball,** 1920, National Game
EX $145   NM $250   MIP n/a

❏ **Play Football,** 1934, Whitman
EX $55   NM $90   MIP n/a

❏ **Play Hockey Fun with Popeye & Wimpy,** 1935, Barnum
EX $205   NM $350   MIP n/a

❏ **Pocket Baseball,** 1940, Toy Creations
EX $15   NM $25   MIP n/a

❏ **Pocket Edition Major League Baseball Game,** 1943, Anderson
EX $85   NM $140   MIP n/a

❏ **Pocket Football,** 1940, Toy Creations
EX $25   NM $40   MIP n/a

❏ **Polar Ball Baseball,** 1940, Bowline Game
EX $90   NM $145   MIP n/a

❏ **Pool, Game of,** 1898
EX $700   NM $1175   MIP n/a

❏ **Posting, A Merry Game of,** 1890s, J.H. Singer
EX $180   NM $300   MIP n/a

❏ **Pro Baseball,** 1940
EX $70   NM $115   MIP n/a

❏ **Professional Game of Base Ball,** 1896, Parker Bros.
EX $500   NM $1000   MIP n/a

❏ **Psychic Baseball Game,** 1935, Parker Brothers
EX $175   NM $295   MIP n/a

❏ **Quarterback,** 1914, Littlefield
EX $100   NM $165   MIP n/a

❏ **Rabbit Hunt, Game of,** 1870, McLoughlin Bros.
EX $175   NM $400   MIP n/a

❏ **Race for the Cup,** 1910s, Milton Bradley
EX $125   NM $200   MIP n/a

❏ **Race, The Game of the,** 1860s
EX $425   NM $715   MIP n/a

❏ **Races, The Game of the,** 1844, William Crosby
EX $850   NM $1400   MIP n/a

❏ **Racing Stable, Game of,** 1936, D & H Games
EX $115   NM $195   MIP n/a

❏ **Radio Game,** 1926, Milton Bradley
EX $75   NM $150   MIP n/a

❏ **Raggedy Ann's Magic Pebble Game,** 1941, Milton Bradley
EX $50   NM $100   MIP n/a

❏ **Rainy Day Golf,** 1920, Selchow & Righter
EX $75   NM $150   MIP n/a

❏ **Rambles,** 1881, American
EX $195   NM $275   MIP n/a

❏ **Razz-O-Dazz-O Six Man Football,** 1938, Gruhn & Melton
EX $60   NM $100   MIP n/a

❏ **Realistic Baseball,** 1925, Realistic Game & Toy
EX $205   NM $350   MIP n/a

❏ **Realistic Golf,** 1898, Parker Brothers
EX $875   NM $1450   MIP n/a

❏ **Red Riding Hood, Game of,** 1898, Chaffee & Selchow
EX $200   NM $350   MIP n/a

❏ **Red Ryder Target Game,** 1939, Whitman
EX $75   NM $150   MIP n/a

❏ **Rex and the Kilkenny Cats Game,** 1892, Parker Brothers
EX $45   NM $75   MIP n/a

❏ **Ring-A-Peg,** 1885, Horsman
EX $25   NM $45   MIP n/a

❏ **Rip Van Winkle,** 1890s, Clark & Sowdon
EX $175   NM $225   MIP n/a

❏ **Rival Policemen,** 1896, McLoughlin Bros.
EX $2000   NM $4000   MIP n/a

❏ **Road Race, Air Race (Two-game set),** 1928, Wilder
EX $145   NM $250   MIP n/a

❏ **Robinson Crusoe, Game of,** 1909, Milton Bradley
EX $30   NM $75   MIP n/a

❏ **Roll-O Football,** 1923, Supply Sales
EX $35   NM $60   MIP n/a

❏ **Roll-O Golf,** 1923, Supply Sales
EX $35   NM $60   MIP n/a

❏ **Roll-O Junior Baseball Game,** 1922, Roll-O
EX $325   NM $550   MIP n/a

❏ **Roll-O-Motor Speedway,** 1922, Supply Sales
EX $65   NM $110   MIP n/a

❏ **Roly Poly Game,** 1910
EX $30   NM $50   MIP n/a

❏ **Rose Bowl Championship Football Game,** 1940s, Lowe
EX $40   NM $80   MIP n/a

❏ **Rough Riders, The Game of,** 1898, Clark & Sowdon
EX $400   NM $600   MIP n/a

❏ **Roulette Baseball Game,** 1929, W. Barthonomae
EX $115   NM $195   MIP n/a

❏ **Round the World Game,** 1914, Milton Bradley
EX $150   NM $200   MIP n/a

(KP Photo)

❏ **Round the World with Nellie Bly,** 1890, McLoughlin Bros.
EX $210   NM $350   MIP n/a

❏ **Royal Game of Kings and Queens,** 1892, McLoughlin Bros.
EX $375   NM $650   MIP n/a

❏ **Rube Bressler's Baseball Game,** 1936, Bressler
EX $130   NM $215   MIP n/a

❏ **Rube Walker & Harry Davis Baseball Game,** 1905
EX $875   NM $1450   MIP n/a

❏ **Rummy Football,** 1944, Milton Bradley
EX $35   NM $60   MIP n/a

❏ **Runaway Sheep,** 1892, Bliss
EX $165   NM $275   MIP n/a

❏ **Saratoga Horse Racing Game,** 1920, Milton Bradley
EX $40   NM $100   MIP n/a

❏ **Saratoga Steeple Chase,** 1900, J.H. Singer
EX $200   NM $500   MIP n/a

❏ **Scout, The,** 1900s, E.O. Clark
EX $105   NM $175   MIP n/a

(KP Photo)

❏ **Scouting, Game of,** 1930s, Milton Bradley
EX $200   NM $300   MIP n/a

❑ **Scrambles,** 1941, Frederick H. Beach (Beachcraft)
EX $15   **NM** $20   **MIP** n/a

❑ **Shadow Game, The,** 1940s, Toy Creations
EX $500   **NM** $1000   **MIP** n/a

❑ **Shopping, Game of,** 1891, Bliss
EX $1500   **NM** $2000   **MIP** n/a

❑ **Shufflebug, Game of,** 1921
EX $20   **NM** $30   **MIP** n/a

❑ **Siege of Havana, The,** 1898, Parker Brothers
EX $180   **NM** $300   **MIP** n/a

❑ **Sippa Fish,** 1936, Frederick H. Beach (Beachcraft)
EX $20   **NM** $30   **MIP** n/a

❑ **Skating Race Game, The,** 1900, Chaffee & Selchow
EX $700   **NM** $1200   **MIP** n/a

❑ **Skeezix and the Air Mail,** 1930s, Milton Bradley
EX $65   **NM** $125   **MIP** n/a

❑ **Skeezix Visits Nina,** 1930s, Milton Bradley
EX $65   **NM** $125   **MIP** n/a

❑ **Ski-Hi New York to Paris,** 1927, Cutler & Saleeby
EX $100   **NM** $150   **MIP** n/a

GAME OF
SKIPPY

LICENSED BY PERCY CROSBY
COPYRIGHT 1932

MILTON BRADLEY COMPANY
SPRINGFIELD MASS. MADE IN U.S.A.

(KP Photo)

❑ **Skippy, Game of,** 1932, Milton Bradley
EX $75   **NM** $150   **MIP** n/a

❑ **Skirmish at Harper's Ferry,** 1891, McLoughlin Bros.
EX $450   **NM** $750   **MIP** n/a

❑ **Skor-It Bagatelle,** 1930s, Northwestern Products
EX $145   **NM** $250   **MIP** n/a

❑ **Sky Hawks,** 1931, All-Fair
EX $120   **NM** $200   **MIP** n/a

❑ **Skyscraper,** 1937, Parker Brothers
EX $250   **NM** $400   **MIP** n/a

❑ **Slide Kelly! Baseball Game,** 1936, B.E. Ruth
EX $70   **NM** $115   **MIP** n/a

❑ **Slugger Baseball Game,** 1930, Marks Brothers
EX $110   **NM** $180   **MIP** n/a

❑ **Smitty Game,** 1930s, Milton Bradley
EX $200   **NM** $350   **MIP** n/a

❑ **Smitty Speed Boat Race Game,** 1930s, Milton Bradley
EX $50   **NM** $125   **MIP** n/a

❑ **Snake Game,** 1890s, McLoughlin Bros.
EX $2000   **NM** $3000   **MIP** n/a

❑ **Snap Dragon,** 1903, H.B. Chaffee
EX $135   **NM** $225   **MIP** n/a

❑ **Sniff,** 1940s, The Embossing Co.
EX $20   **NM** $30   **MIP** n/a

❑ **Snow White and the Seven Dwarfs,** 1938, Parker Brothers
EX $125   **NM** $200   **MIP** n/a

❑ **Snow White and the Seven Dwarfs,** 1938, Milton Bradley
EX $75   **NM** $150   **MIP** n/a

❑ **Snug Harbor,** 1930s, Milton Bradley
EX $50   **NM** $85   **MIP** n/a

❑ **Socko the Monk, The Game of,** 1935, Einson-Freeman
EX $15   **NM** $25   **MIP** n/a

❑ **Soldier Boy Game,** 1914, United Game
EX $60   **NM** $150   **MIP** n/a

❑ **Soldier's Cavalry,** McLouglin Bros.
EX $150   **NM** $300   **MIP** n/a

❑ **Soldiers on Guard**
EX $300   **NM** $500   **MIP** n/a

❑ **Speculation,** 1885, Parker Brothers
EX $40   **NM** $65   **MIP** n/a

❑ **Speed Boat,** 1920s, Parker Brothers
EX $85   **NM** $140   **MIP** n/a

❑ **Speed Boat Race,** 1926, Wolverine
EX $70   **NM** $115   **MIP** n/a

❑ **Speed King, Game Of,** 1922, Russell
EX $150   **NM** $250   **MIP** n/a

❑ **Speedem Junior Auto Race Game,** 1929, All-Fair
EX $70   **NM** $125   **MIP** n/a

❑ **Speedway Motor Race,** 1920s, Smith, Kline & French
EX $145   **NM** $250   **MIP** n/a

❑ **Spider's Web, Game of,** 1898, McLoughlin Bros.
EX $100   **NM** $200   **MIP** n/a

❑ **Squails,** 1870s, Adams
EX $100   **NM** $150   **MIP** n/a

❑ **Squails,** 1877, Milton Bradley
EX $50   **NM** $75   **MIP** n/a

❑ **Stanley in Africa,** 1891, Bliss
EX $1000   **NM** $2000   **MIP** n/a

❑ **Star Basketball,** 1926, Star Paper Products
EX $125   **NM** $205   **MIP** n/a

❑ **Star Ride,** 1934, Einson-Freeman
EX $100   **NM** $200   **MIP** n/a

❑ **Stars on Stripes Football Game,** 1941, Stars & Stripes Games
EX $55   **NM** $90   **MIP** n/a

❑ **Steeple Chase,** 1890, J.H. Singer
EX $200   **NM** $300   **MIP** n/a

❑ **Steeple Chase & Checkers,** 1910, Milton Bradley
EX $55   **NM** $90   **MIP** n/a

❑ **Steeple Chase, Game of,** 1900s, E.O. Clark
EX $60   **NM** $100   **MIP** n/a

❑ **Steeple Chase, Game of,** 1910s, Milton Bradley
EX $40   **NM** $65   **MIP** n/a

❑ **Steeple Chase, Improved Game of,** 1890s, McLoughlin Bros.
EX $195   **NM** $325   **MIP** n/a

❑ **Steps to Health Coke Game,** 1938, CDN
EX $40   **NM** $70   **MIP** n/a

❑ **Sto-Auto Race,** 1920s, Stough
EX $65   **NM** $110   **MIP** n/a

❑ **Stock Exchange,** 1936, Parker Brothers
EX $50   **NM** $100   **MIP** n/a

❑ **Stock Exchange, The Game of,** 1940s, Stox
EX $40   **NM** $65   **MIP** n/a

❑ **Stop & Go,** 1936, Einson-Freeman
EX $25   **NM** $50   **MIP** n/a

❑ **Stop and Go,** 1928, All-Fair
EX $100   **NM** $150   **MIP** n/a

❑ **Stop and Shop,** 1930, All-Fair
EX $75   **NM** $100   **MIP** n/a

❑ **Stop, Look, and Listen, Game of,** 1926, Milton Bradley
EX $40   **NM** $100   **MIP** n/a

❑ **Sto-Quoit,** 1920s, Stough
EX $10   **NM** $15   **MIP** n/a

❑ **Strat: The Great War Game,** 1915, Strat Game
EX $25   **NM** $45   **MIP** n/a

❑ **Strategy, Game of,** 1891, McLoughlin Bros.
EX $240   **NM** $400   **MIP** n/a

❑ **Strategy, Game of Armies,** 1938, Corey Games
EX $55   **NM** $100   **MIP** n/a

❑ **Stratosphere,** 1930s, Parker Brothers
EX $50   **NM** $125   **MIP** n/a

❑ **Stratosphere,** 1936, Whitman
EX $100   **NM** $200   **MIP** n/a

❑ **Street Car Game, The,** 1890s, Parker Brothers
EX $200   **NM** $400   **MIP** n/a

❑ **Strike Out,** 1920s, All-Fair
EX $175   **NM** $295   **MIP** n/a

❑ **Strike-Like,** 1940s, Saxon Toy
EX $55   **NM** $90   **MIP** n/a

❑ **Stubborn Pig, Game of the,** Milton Bradley
EX $100   **NM** $200   **MIP** n/a

❑ **Stunt Box,** 1941, Frederick H. Beach (Beachcraft)
EX $12   **NM** $20   **MIP** n/a

❑ **Submarine Drag,** 1917, Willis G. Young
EX $75   **NM** $125   **MIP** n/a

❑ **Substitute Golf,** 1906, John Wanamaker
EX $400   **NM** $700   **MIP** n/a

GAMES

Suffolk Downs, 1930s, Corey Game
EX $85   NM $140   MIP n/a

Susceptibles, The, 1891, McLoughlin Bros.
EX $325   NM $550   MIP n/a

Sweep, 1929, Selchow & Righter
EX $25   NM $40   MIP n/a

Sweeps, 1930s, E.E. Fairchild
EX $25   NM $60   MIP n/a

Sweepstakes, 1930s, Haras
EX $55   NM $90   MIP n/a

Swing A Peg, 1890s, Milton Bradley
EX $30   NM $50   MIP n/a

T.G.O. Klondyke, 1899, J.H. Singer
EX $150   NM $250   MIP n/a

Table Golf, 1909, McClurg
EX $15   NM $25   MIP n/a

Tackle, 1933, Tackle Game
EX $70   NM $115   MIP n/a

Tait's Table Golf, 1914, John Tait
EX $350   NM $575   MIP n/a

Take It And Double, 1943, Frederick H. Beach (Beachcraft)
EX $20   NM $35   MIP n/a

Take It or Leave It, 1942, Zondine Game
EX $25   NM $45   MIP n/a

Tak-Tiks, Basketball, 1939, Midwest Products
EX $15   NM $25   MIP n/a

Teddy's Bear Hunt, 1907, Bowers & Hard
EX $500   NM $750   MIP n/a

Teddy's Ride from Oyster Bay to Albany, 1899, Jesse Crandall
EX $3000   NM $5500   MIP n/a

Tee Off, 1935, Donogof
EX $115   NM $195   MIP n/a

Telegrams, 1941, Whitman
EX $50   NM $100   MIP n/a

Telegraph Boy, Game of the, 1888, McLoughlin Bros.
EX $250   NM $350   MIP n/a

Telepathy, 1939, Cadaco-Ellis
EX $65   NM $110   MIP n/a

Tell Bell, The, 1928, Knapp Electric & Novelty
EX $75   NM $100   MIP n/a

Ten Pins, 1920, Mason & Parker
EX $35   NM $60   MIP n/a

Tennis & Baseball, 1930
EX $70   NM $115   MIP n/a

Terry and the Pirates, 1930s, Whitman
EX $50   NM $100   MIP n/a

Tete-A-Tete, 1892, Clark & Sowdon
EX $40   NM $100   MIP n/a

They're Off, Race Horse Game, 1930s, Parker Brothers
EX $15   NM $30   MIP n/a

Thorobred, 1940s, Lowe
EX $55   NM $90   MIP n/a

Thorton W. Burgess Animal Game, 1925, Saalfield
EX $70   NM $115   MIP n/a

Three Bears, 1910s, Milton Bradley
EX $20   NM $50   MIP n/a

Three Blind Mice, Game of, 1930s, Milton Bradley
EX $25   NM $45   MIP n/a

Three Little Kittens, 1910s, Milton Bradley
EX $60   NM $100   MIP n/a

Three Little Pigs Game, 1933, Einson-Freeman
EX $55   NM $95   MIP n/a

Three Little Pigs, The Game of the, 1933, Kenilworth Press
EX $100   NM $165   MIP n/a

Three Men in a Tub, 1935, Milton Bradley
EX $40   NM $65   MIP n/a

Three Men on a Horse, 1936, Milton Bradley
EX $20   NM $50   MIP n/a

Three Point Landing, 1942, Advance Games
EX $35   NM $75   MIP n/a

Thrilling Indoor Football Game, 1933, Cronston
EX $70   NM $115   MIP n/a

Through The Clouds, 1931, Milton Bradley
EX $75   NM $150   MIP n/a

Through the Locks to the Golden Gate, 1905, Milton Bradley
EX $125   NM $225   MIP n/a

Ticker, 1929, Glow Products
EX $50   NM $100   MIP n/a

Tiddley Golf Game, 1928, Milton Bradley
EX $80   NM $135   MIP n/a

Tiddley Winks Game, 1920s, Wilder
EX $15   NM $35   MIP n/a

Tiger Hunt, Game of, 1899, Chaffee & Selchow
EX $270   NM $450   MIP n/a

Tiger Tom, Game of, 1920s, Milton Bradley
EX $30   NM $75   MIP n/a

Ting-A-Ling, The Game of, 1920, Stoll & Edwards
EX $25   NM $45   MIP n/a

Tinkerpins, 1916, Toy Creations
EX $55   NM $90   MIP n/a

Tipit, 1929, Wolverine
EX $15   NM $20   MIP n/a

Tip-Top Boxing, 1922, LaVelle
EX $200   NM $350   MIP n/a

Tit for Tat Indoor Hockey, 1920s, Lemper Novelty
EX $45   NM $75   MIP n/a

Tit-Tat-Toe, 1929, The Embossing
EX $15   NM $25   MIP n/a

Tit-Tat-Toe, Three in a Row, 1896, Austin & Craw
EX $45   NM $75   MIP n/a

To the Aid of your Party, 1942, Leister Game
EX $15   NM $25   MIP n/a

Tobagganing at Christmas, Game of, 1899, McLoughlin Bros.
EX $1200   NM $2000   MIP n/a

Toboggan Slide, 1890s, J.H. Singer
EX $200   NM $325   MIP n/a

Toboggan Slide, 1890s, Hamilton-Myers
EX $225   NM $385   MIP n/a

Toll Gate, Game of, 1890s, McLoughlin Bros.
EX $280   NM $700   MIP n/a

Tom Hamilton's Pigskin, 1935, Parker Brothers
EX $50   NM $75   MIP n/a

Tom Sawyer and Huck Finn, Adventures of, 1925, Stoll & Edwards
EX $70   NM $200   MIP n/a

Tom Sawyer on the Mississippi, 1935, Einson-Freeman
EX $100   NM $200   MIP n/a

Tom Sawyer, The Game of, 1937, Milton Bradley
EX $75   NM $150   MIP n/a

Toonerville Trolley Game, 1927, Milton Bradley
EX $175   NM $300   MIP n/a

Toonin Radio Game, 1925, All-Fair
EX $200   NM $400   MIP n/a

Top-Ography, 1941, Cadaco
EX $35   NM $45   MIP n/a

Topsy Turvey, Game of, 1899, McLoughlin Bros.
EX $150   NM $250   MIP n/a

Tortoise and the Hare, 1922, Russell
EX $45   NM $85   MIP n/a

Toto, The New Game, 1925, Baseball Toto Sales
EX $55   NM $90   MIP n/a

Touchdown, 1937, Cadaco
EX $65   NM $110   MIP n/a

Touchdown Football Game, 1920s, Wilder
EX $100   NM $165   MIP n/a

Touchdown or Parlor Football, Game of, 1897, Union Mutual Life
EX $85   NM $140   MIP n/a

Touchdown, The New Game, 1920, Hartford
EX $70   NM $115   MIP n/a

Tourist, A Railroad Game, 1900s, Milton Bradley
EX $150   NM $325   MIP n/a

Tournament, 1858, Mayhew & Baker
EX $180   NM $300   MIP n/a

❏ **Town Hall,** 1939, Milton Bradley
EX $20   **NM** $30   **MIP** n/a

❏ **Toy Town Bank,** 1910, Milton Bradley
EX $90   **NM** $150   **MIP** n/a

❏ **Toy Town Conductors Game,** 1910, Milton Bradley
EX $105   **NM** $175   **MIP** n/a

❏ **Toy Town Telegraph Office,** 1910s, Parker Brothers
EX $75   **NM** $150   **MIP** n/a

❏ **Trackle-Lite,** 1940s, Saxon Toy
EX $55   **NM** $90   **MIP** n/a

❏ **Traffic Hazards,** 1939, Trojan Games
EX $30   **NM** $75   **MIP** n/a

❏ **Trailer Trails,** 1937, Offset Gravure
EX $35   **NM** $60   **MIP** n/a

❏ **Train for Boston,** 1900, Parker Brothers
EX $400   **NM** $800   **MIP** n/a

❏ **Transatlantic Flight, Game of the,** 1925, Milton Bradley
EX $250   **NM** $400   **MIP** n/a

❏ **Transport Pilot,** 1938, Cadaco
EX $45   **NM** $90   **MIP** n/a

❏ **Trap-A-Tank,** 1920s, Wolverine
EX $40   **NM** $70   **MIP** n/a

❏ **Traps & Bunkers,** 1926?, Milton Bradley
EX $115   **NM** $195   **MIP** n/a

❏ **Travel, The Game of,** 1894, Parker Brothers
EX $225   **NM** $375   **MIP** n/a

❏ **Treasure Hunt,** 1940, All-Fair
EX $20   **NM** $50   **MIP** n/a

❏ **Treasure Island,** 1923, Stoll & Edwards
EX $75   **NM** $125   **MIP** n/a

❏ **Treasure Island,** 1934, Stoll & Einson
EX $60   **NM** $90   **MIP** n/a

❏ **Treasure Island, Game of,** 1923, Gem
EX $40   **NM** $65   **MIP** n/a

❏ **Triangular Dominoes,** 1885, Frank H. Richards
EX $35   **NM** $60   **MIP** n/a

❏ **Trilby,** 1894, E.I. Horsman
EX $270   **NM** $450   **MIP** n/a

❏ **Trip Around the World, A,** 1920s, Parker Brothers
EX $25   **NM** $45   **MIP** n/a

❏ **Trip Round the World, Game of,** 1897, McLoughlin Bros.
EX $400   **NM** $800   **MIP** n/a

❏ **Trip to Washington,** 1884, Milton Bradley
EX $100   **NM** $175   **MIP** n/a

❏ **Triple Play,** 1930s, National Games
EX $12   **NM** $20   **MIP** n/a

❏ **Trolley Ride, The Game of the,** 1890s, Hamilton-Myers
EX $210   **NM** $350   **MIP** n/a

❏ **Trunk Box Lotto Game,** 1890s, McLoughlin Bros.
EX $15   **NM** $35   **MIP** n/a

❏ **Tumblin Five Acrobats,** 1925, Doremus Schoen
EX $12   **NM** $20   **MIP** n/a

❏ **Turn Over,** 1908, Milton Bradley
EX $75   **NM** $100   **MIP** n/a

❏ **Turnover,** 1898, Chaffee & Selchow
EX $50   **NM** $85   **MIP** n/a

❏ **Tutoom, Journey to the Treasures of Pharoah,** 1923, All-Fair
EX $150   **NM** $225   **MIP** n/a

❏ **Twentieth Century Limited,** 1900s, Parker Brothers
EX $90   **NM** $150   **MIP** n/a

❏ **Ty Cobb's Own Game of Baseball,** 1920s, National Novelty
EX $350   **NM** $650   **MIP** n/a

❏ **U.S. Postman Game,** 1914
EX $60   **NM** $100   **MIP** n/a

❏ **U-Bat-It,** 1920s, Schultz Star
EX $70   **NM** $115   **MIP** n/a

❏ **Uncle Jim's Question Bee,** 1938, Kress
EX $20   **NM** $30   **MIP** n/a

❏ **Uncle Sam at War with Spain, Great Game of,** 1898, Rhode Island Game
EX $400   **NM** $600   **MIP** n/a

❏ **Uncle Sam's Baseball Game,** 1890, J.C. Bell
EX $525   **NM** $875   **MIP** n/a

(KP Photo)

❏ **Uncle Sam's Mail,** 1893, McLoughlin Bros.
EX $210   **NM** $400   **MIP** n/a

❏ **Uncle Wiggily's New Airplane Game,** 1920s, Milton Bradley
EX $50   **NM** $175   **MIP** n/a

❏ **Van Loon Story of Mankind Game, The,** 1931, Kerk Guild
EX $50   **NM** $85   **MIP** n/a

❏ **Vanderbilt Cup Race,** 1906, Bowers & Hard
EX $800   **NM** $1800   **MIP** n/a

❏ **Varsity Football Game,** 1942, Cadaco-Ellis
EX $45   **NM** $75   **MIP** n/a

❏ **Varsity Race,** 1899, Parker Brothers
EX $425   **NM** $725   **MIP** n/a

❏ **Vassar Boat Race, The,** 1899, Chaffee & Selchow
EX $500   **NM** $900   **MIP** n/a

❏ **Vest Pocket Checker Set,** 1929, Embossing
EX $15   **NM** $25   **MIP** n/a

❏ **Vest Pocket Quoits,** 1944, Colorful Creations
EX $25   **NM** $45   **MIP** n/a

❏ **Victo,** 1943, Spare Time
EX $15   **NM** $25   **MIP** n/a

❏ **Victory,** 1920s, Klak New Haven
EX $105   **NM** $175   **MIP** n/a

❏ **Vignette Author,** 1874, E.G. Selchow
EX $35   **NM** $75   **MIP** n/a

❏ **Visit of Santa Claus, Game of the,** 1899, McLoughlin Bros.
EX $600   **NM** $1000   **MIP** n/a

❏ **Visit to the Farm,** 1893, Bliss
EX $300   **NM** $500   **MIP** n/a

❏ **Vox-Pop,** 1938, Milton Bradley
EX $25   **NM** $45   **MIP** n/a

❏ **Voyage Around the World, Game of,** 1930s, Milton Bradley
EX $150   **NM** $250   **MIP** n/a

❏ **Wachter's Parlor Base Ball (bagatelle),** 1925, Wachter
EX $145   **NM** $250   **MIP** n/a

❏ **Walk the Plank,** 1925, Milton Bradley
EX $50   **NM** $95   **MIP** n/a

❏ **Walking the Tightrope,** 1897, McLoughlin Bros.
EX $125   **NM** $250   **MIP** n/a

❏ **Walking the Tightrope,** 1920, Milton Bradley
EX $50   **NM** $100   **MIP** n/a

❏ **Walt Disney's Game Parade,** 1930s
EX $30   **NM** $50   **MIP** n/a

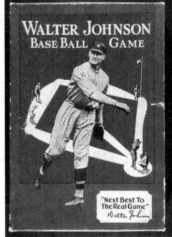

(KP Photo)

❏ **Walter Johnson Baseball Game,** 1930s
EX $195   **NM** $325   **MIP** n/a

❏ **Waner's Baseball Game,** 1930s, Waner's Baseball Game
EX $350   **NM** $650   **MIP** n/a

❏ **Wang, Game of,** 1892, Clark & Sowdon
EX $25   **NM** $65   **MIP** n/a

❏ **War of Nations,** 1915, Milton Bradley
EX $40   **NM** $65   **MIP** n/a

❏ **Ward Cuff's Football Game,** 1938, Continental Sales
EX $125   NM $200   MIP n/a

❏ **Watch on De Rind,** 1931, All-Fair
EX $300   NM $500   MIP n/a

(KP Photo)

❏ **Waterloo,** 1895, Parker Brothers
EX $325   NM $550   MIP n/a

❏ **Watermelon Frolic,** 1900, Horsman
EX $135   NM $225   MIP n/a

❏ **Watermelon Patch,** 1940s, Craig Hopkins
EX $25   NM $45   MIP n/a

❏ **Way to the White House, The,** 1927, All-Fair
EX $100   NM $200   MIP n/a

(KP Photo)

❏ **We, The Magnetic Flying Game,** 1928, Parker Brothers
EX $100   NM $200   MIP n/a

❏ **West Point,** 1902, Ottoman
EX $90   NM $150   MIP n/a

❏ **What's My Name?,** 1920s, Jaymar
EX $15   NM $25   MIP n/a

❏ **Whippet Race,** 1940s, Pressman
EX $20   NM $35   MIP n/a

❏ **Whirlpool Game,** 1890s, McLoughlin Bros.
EX $65   NM $150   MIP n/a

❏ **White Wings,** 1930s, Glevum Games
EX $45   NM $70   MIP n/a

❏ **Wide Awake, Game of,** 1899, McLoughlin Bros.
EX $200   NM $350   MIP n/a

❏ **Wide World and a Journey Round It,** 1896, Parker Brothers
EX $165   NM $275   MIP n/a

❏ **Wild West Cardboard Game,** 1914
EX $90   NM $150   MIP n/a

❏ **Wild West, Game of the,** 1889, Bliss
EX $1000   NM $1700   MIP n/a

❏ **Wilder's Football Game,** 1930s, Wilder
EX $100   NM $150   MIP n/a

❏ **Win, Place & Show,** 1940s, 3M
EX $25   NM $40   MIP n/a

❏ **Winko Baseball,** 1940, Milton Bradley
EX $45   NM $70   MIP n/a

(KP Photo)

❏ **Winnie Winkle Glider Race Game,** 1930s, Milton Bradley
EX $65   NM $150   MIP n/a

❏ **Winnie-The-Pooh Game,** 1933, Parker Brothers
EX $100   NM $200   MIP n/a

❏ **Winnie-The-Pooh Game, A. A. Milne's,** 1931, Kerk Guild
EX $50   NM $85   MIP n/a

❏ **Witzi-Wits,** 1926, All-Fair
EX $100   NM $200   MIP n/a

❏ **Wizard, The,** 1921, Fulton Specialty
EX $15   NM $25   MIP n/a

❏ **Wonderful Game of Oz (pewter pieces),** 1921, Parker Brothers
EX $600   NM $1300   MIP n/a

(KP Photo)

❏ **Wonderful Game of Oz (wooden pieces),** 1921, Parker Brothers
EX $200   NM $400   MIP n/a

❏ **Wordy,** 1938, Pressman
EX $25   NM $45   MIP n/a

❏ **World Flyers, Game of the,** 1926, All-Fair
EX $150   NM $300   MIP n/a

❏ **World Series Baseball Game,** 1940s, Radio Sports
EX $205   NM $350   MIP n/a

❏ **World Series Parlor Baseball,** 1916, Clifton E. Hooper
EX $150   NM $250   MIP n/a

❏ **World's Championship Baseball,** 1910, Champion Amusement
EX $175   NM $295   MIP n/a

❏ **World's Championship Golf Game,** 1930s, Beacon Hudson
EX $145   NM $250   MIP n/a

❏ **World's Columbian Exposition, Game of the,** 1893, Bliss
EX $450   NM $750   MIP n/a

❏ **World's Educator Game,** 1889, Reed
EX $45   NM $75   MIP n/a

❏ **World's Fair Game,** 1939
EX $90   NM $150   MIP n/a

❏ **World's Fair Game, The,** 1892, Parker Brothers
EX $800   NM $1400   MIP n/a

(KP Photo)

❏ **WPA, Work, Progress, Action,** 1935, All-Fair
EX $100   NM $200   MIP n/a

❏ **Wyntre Golf,** 1920s, All-Fair
EX $175   NM $400   MIP n/a

❏ **X-Plor-US,** 1922, All-Fair
EX $100   NM $150   MIP n/a

❏ **Yacht Race,** 1890s, Clark & Sowdon
EX $200   NM $350   MIP n/a

❏ **Yacht Race,** 1930s, Pressman
EX $150   NM $250   MIP n/a

❏ **Yachting,** 1890, J.H. Singer
EX $70   NM $115   MIP n/a

❏ **Yale Harvard Football Game,** 1922, LaVelle
EX $200   NM $300   MIP n/a

❏ **Yale Harvard Game,** 1890, McLoughlin Bros.
EX $1050   NM $1775   MIP n/a

❏ **Yale-Princeton Football Game,** 1895, McLoughlin Bros.
EX $575   NM $1100   MIP n/a

❏ **Ya-Lo Football Card Game,** 1930s
EX $85   NM $140   MIP n/a

❏ **Yankee Doodle!,** 1940, Cadaco-Ellis
EX $30   NM $50   MIP n/a

❏ **Yankee Doodle, A Game of American History,** 1895, Parker Brothers
EX $285   NM $475   MIP n/a

❏ **Yankee Trader,** 1941, Corey Games
EX $35   NM $80   MIP n/a

❏ **Young Athlete, The,** 1898, Chaffee & Selchow
EX $425   NM $700   MIP n/a

❏ **You're Out! Baseball Game,** 1941, Corey Games
EX $35   NM $65   MIP n/a

❏ **Yuneek Game,** 1889, McLoughlin Bros.
EX $450   NM $750   MIP n/a

❏ **Zimmer Baseball Game,** 1885, McLoughlin Bros.
EX $3000   NM $6000   MIP n/a

(KP Photo)

❏ **Zippy Zepps,** 1930s, All-Fair
EX $350 **NM** $600 **MIP** n/a

❏ **Zip-Top,** 1940, Deluxe Game
EX $35 **NM** $55 **MIP** n/a

❏ **Zoo Hoo,** 1924, Lubbers & Bell
EX $125 **NM** $200 **MIP** n/a

(KP Photo)

❏ **Zoom, Original Game of,** 1940s, All-Fair
EX $45 **NM** $85 **MIP** n/a

❏ **Zulu Blowing Game,** 1927, Zulu Toy
EX $50 **NM** $100 **MIP** n/a

CARD GAMES

❏ **ABC,** 1900s, Parker Brothers
EX $25 **NM** $40 **MIP** n/a

❏ **Airship Game, The,** 1916, Parker Brothers
EX $30 **NM** $50 **MIP** n/a

❏ **Allegrando,** 1884, Theodore Presser
EX $40 **NM** $60 **MIP** n/a

❏ **Allie-Patriot Game,** 1917, McDowell And Mellor
EX $30 **NM** $50 **MIP** n/a

❏ **American History, The Game of,** 1890s, Parker Brothers
EX $50 **NM** $90 **MIP** n/a

❏ **American League Fan Craze Card Game,** 1904, Fan Craze
EX $1950 **NM** $3250 **MIP** n/a

❏ **American National Game Baseball,** 1909, American National Game Co.
EX $75 **NM** $200 **MIP** n/a

❏ **Amusing Game of Conundrums,** 1853, John McLoughlin
EX $750 **NM** $1300 **MIP** n/a

❏ **Amusing Game of the Corner Grocery,** 1890s
EX $100 **NM** $150 **MIP** n/a

❏ **Anagrams,** 1885, Peter G. Thompson
EX $50 **NM** $90 **MIP** n/a

❏ **Apple Pie,** 1895, Parker Brothers
EX $40 **NM** $60 **MIP** n/a

❏ **Armstead's Play Ball,** 1910s, Austin
EX $200 **NM** $500 **MIP** n/a

❏ **Astronomy,** 1905, Cincinnati Game
EX $40 **NM** $60 **MIP** n/a

❏ **Auction Letters,** 1900, Parker Brothers
EX $40 **NM** $60 **MIP** n/a

❏ **Authors Illustrated,** 1893, Clark & Sowdon
EX $40 **NM** $60 **MIP** n/a

❏ **Authors, Game of Standard,** 1890s, McLoughlin Bros.
EX $25 **NM** $50 **MIP** n/a

❏ **Authors, The Game of,** 1890s, Parker Brothers
EX $15 **NM** $35 **MIP** n/a

❏ **Avilude,** 1873, West & Lee
EX $65 **NM** $100 **MIP** n/a

❏ **Balance The Budget,** 1938, Elten Game
EX $45 **NM** $75 **MIP** n/a

❏ **Bally Hoo,** 1931, Gabriel
EX $30 **NM** $65 **MIP** n/a

❏ **Baseballitis Card Game,** 1909, Baseballitis Card
EX $125 **NM** $205 **MIP** n/a

❏ **Basketball Card Game,** 1940s, Warren/Built-Rite
EX $20 **NM** $35 **MIP** n/a

❏ **Batter Up, Game of,** 1908, Fenner Game
EX $150 **NM** $200 **MIP** n/a

❏ **Betty Boop Coed Bridge,** 1930s
EX $50 **NM** $75 **MIP** n/a

❏ **Bible ABCs and Promises,** 1940s, Judson Press
EX $15 **NM** $25 **MIP** n/a

❏ **Bible Authors,** 1895, Evangelical Pub.
EX $20 **NM** $35 **MIP** n/a

❏ **Bible Cities,** 1920s, Nellie T. Magee
EX $15 **NM** $25 **MIP** n/a

❏ **Bicycle Cards,** 1898, Parker Brothers
EX $150 **NM** $200 **MIP** n/a

❏ **Big League Baseball Card Game,** 1940s, State College Game Lab
EX $35 **NM** $60 **MIP** n/a

❏ **Billy Bump's Visit To Boston,** 1888, Parker Brothers
EX $25 **NM** $55 **MIP** n/a

❏ **Bird Center Etiquette,** 1904, Home Game
EX $55 **NM** $90 **MIP** n/a

❏ **Birds, Game of,** 1899, Cincinnati Game
EX $55 **NM** $90 **MIP** n/a

❏ **Black Cat Fortune Telling Game, The,** 1897, Parker Brothers
EX $95 **NM** $150 **MIP** n/a

❏ **Block,** 1905, Parker Brothers
EX $15 **NM** $20 **MIP** n/a

❏ **Blondie Playing Card Game,** 1941, Whitman
EX $55 **NM** $90 **MIP** n/a

❏ **Botany,** 1900s, G.H. Dunston
EX $50 **NM** $100 **MIP** n/a

❏ **Bourse, or Stock Exchange,** 1903, Flinch Card
EX $25 **NM** $40 **MIP** n/a

❏ **Boy Scouts, The Game of,** 1912, Parker Brothers
EX $75 **NM** $125 **MIP** n/a

❏ **Buck Rogers in the 25th Century,** 1936, All-Fair
EX $300 **NM** $500 **MIP** n/a

❏ **Bugle Horn or Robin Hood,** 1850s, McLoughlin Bros.
EX $500 **NM** $800 **MIP** n/a

❏ **Bunco,** 1904, Home Game
EX $35 **NM** $55 **MIP** n/a

❏ **Buster Brown at the Circus,** 1900s, Selchow & Righter
EX $100 **NM** $250 **MIP** n/a

❏ **Camouflage, The Game of,** 1918, Parker Brothers
EX $35 **NM** $75 **MIP** n/a

❏ **Captain Jinks,** 1900s, Parker Brothers
EX $30 **NM** $55 **MIP** n/a

❏ **Characters, A Game of,** 1889, Decker & Decker
EX $20 **NM** $30 **MIP** n/a

❏ **Charlie Chan Game,** 1939, Whitman
EX $30 **NM** $75 **MIP** n/a

❏ **Charlie McCarthy Question and Answer Game,** 1938, Whitman
EX $40 **NM** $65 **MIP** n/a

❏ **Charlie McCarthy Rummy Game,** 1938, Whitman
EX $20 **NM** $35 **MIP** n/a

❏ **Chestnut Burrs,** 1896, Fireside Game
EX $35 **NM** $65 **MIP** n/a

❏ **Cinderella,** 1895, Parker Brothers
EX $55 **NM** $90 **MIP** n/a

❏ **Cinderella,** 1905, Milton Bradley
EX $50 **NM** $80 **MIP** n/a

❏ **Cinderella,** 1921, Milton Bradley
EX $15 **NM** $25 **MIP** n/a

❏ **Cinderella or Hunt the Slipper,** 1887, McLoughlin Bros.
EX $75 **NM** $105 **MIP** n/a

❏ **City Life, or The Boys of New York, The Game of,** 1889, McLoughlin Bros.
EX $65 **NM** $250 **MIP** n/a

❏ **Cock Robin,** 1895, Parker Brothers
EX $40 **NM** $75 **MIP** n/a

❏ **Cock Robin and His Tragical Death, Game of,** 1885, McLoughlin Bros.
EX $65 **NM** $105 **MIP** n/a

❏ **Columbia's Presidents and Our Country, Game of,** 1886, McLoughlin Bros.
EX $250 **NM** $400 **MIP** n/a

❏ **Comic Conversation Cards,** 1890, J. Ottmann Lith.
EX $100 **NM** $200 **MIP** n/a

GAMES

Comic Leaves of Fortune-The Sibyl's Prophecy, 1850s, Charles Magnus
EX $500   NM $900   MIP n/a

Comical Game of "Who," The, 1910s, Parker Brothers
EX $20   NM $40   MIP n/a

Comical Game of Whip, The, 1920s, Russell
EX $20   NM $45   MIP n/a

Comical History of America, 1924, Parker Brothers
EX $40   NM $75   MIP n/a

Comical Snap, Game of, 1903, McLoughlin Bros.
EX $40   NM $65   MIP n/a

Commanders of Our Forces, The, 1863, E.C. Eastman
EX $150   NM $225   MIP n/a

Commerce, 1900s, J. Ottmann Lith.
EX $60   NM $125   MIP n/a

Competition, or Department Store, 1904, Flinch Card
EX $25   NM $35   MIP n/a

Conquest of Nations, or Old Games With New Faces, The, 1853, Willis P. Hazard
EX $100   NM $175   MIP n/a

Costumes and Fashions, Game of, 1881, Milton Bradley
EX $80   NM $225   MIP n/a

County Fair, The, 1891, Parker Brothers
EX $45   NM $75   MIP n/a

Cousin Peter's Trip to New York, Game of, 1898, McLoughlin Bros.
EX $45   NM $75   MIP n/a

Crow Cards, 1910, Milton Bradley
EX $9   NM $15   MIP n/a

Defenders of the Flag, 1922, Stoll & Edwards
EX $35   NM $65   MIP n/a

Derby Day, 1900s, Parker Brothers
EX $30   NM $50   MIP n/a

Dewey at Manila, 1899, Chaffee & Selchow
EX $150   NM $225   MIP n/a

Dick Tracy Playing Card Game, 1934, Whitman
EX $50   NM $75   MIP n/a

Dick Tracy Super Detective Mystery Card Game, 1937, Whitman
EX $65   NM $90   MIP n/a

Din, 1905, Horsman
EX $25   NM $45   MIP n/a

Dixie Land, Game of, 1897, Fireside
EX $60   NM $90   MIP n/a

Doctor Busby Card Game, 1910
EX $35   NM $55   MIP n/a

Doctor Quack, Game of, 1922, Russell
EX $25   NM $40   MIP n/a

Doctors and the Quack, 1890s, Parker Brothers
EX $45   NM $75   MIP n/a

Donald Duck Game, 1930s, Whitman
EX $15   NM $30   MIP n/a

Donald Duck Playing Game, 1941, Whitman
EX $25   NM $40   MIP n/a

Double Eagle Anagrams, 1890, McLoughlin Bros.
EX $35   NM $75   MIP n/a

Double Flag Game, The, 1904, McLoughlin Bros.
EX $75   NM $125   MIP n/a

Down the Pike with Mrs. Wiggs at the St. Louis Exposition, 1904, Milton Bradley
EX $40   NM $75   MIP n/a

Dr. Busby, 1890s, J.H. Singer
EX $60   NM $75   MIP n/a

Dr. Busby, 1900s, J. Ottmann Lith.
EX $40   NM $60   MIP n/a

(KP Photo)

Dr. Busby, 1937, Milton Bradley
EX $20   NM $50   MIP n/a

Dr. Fusby, Game of, 1890s, McLoughlin Bros.
EX $65   NM $125   MIP n/a

Egerton R. Williams Popular Indoor Baseball Game, 1886, Hatch
EX $2500   NM $5000   MIP n/a

Elite Conversation Cards, 1887, McLoughlin Bros.
EX $35   NM $75   MIP n/a

Excursion to Coney Island, 1880s, Milton Bradley
EX $55   NM $75   MIP n/a

Excuse Me!, 1923, Parker Brothers
EX $15   NM $35   MIP n/a

Famous Authors, 1910, Parker Brothers
EX $40   NM $65   MIP n/a

Famous Authors, 1943, Parker Brothers
EX $10   NM $15   MIP n/a

Fan Craze Card Game, Generic, 1904, Fan Craze
EX $175   NM $295   MIP n/a

Fan Craze Card Game, Name Players, 1904, Fan Craze
EX $1500   NM $2000   MIP n/a

Favorite Art, Game of, 1897, Parker Brothers
EX $40   NM $65   MIP n/a

Ferdinand Card Game, 1938, Whitman
EX $25   NM $65   MIP n/a

Five Hundred, Game of, 1900s, Home Game
EX $20   NM $35   MIP n/a

Flags, 1899, Cincinnati Game
EX $55   NM $90   MIP n/a

Flinch, 1902, Flinch Card
EX $10   NM $15   MIP n/a

Foolish Questions, 1920s, Wallie Dorr
EX $50   NM $100   MIP n/a

Fortune Telling, 1920s, All-Fair
EX $40   NM $75   MIP n/a

Fortune Telling Game, 1930s, Stoll & Edwards
EX $35   NM $55   MIP n/a

Fortune Telling Game, The, 1890s, Parker Brothers
EX $40   NM $65   MIP n/a

Fortunes, Game of, 1902, Cincinnati Game
EX $55   NM $95   MIP n/a

Fox and Geese, The New, 1888, McLoughlin Bros.
EX $45   NM $75   MIP n/a

Foxy Grandpa at the World's Fair, 1904, J. Ottmann Lith.
EX $150   NM $200   MIP n/a

Fractions, 1902, Cincinnati Game
EX $25   NM $45   MIP n/a

Frank Buck's Bring 'em Back Alive Game, 1937, All-Fair
EX $50   NM $100   MIP n/a

Gamevelope, 1944, Morris Systems
EX $20   NM $35   MIP n/a

Gavitt's Stock Exchange, 1903, W.W. Gavitt
EX $35   NM $65   MIP n/a

Geographical Cards, 1883, Peter G. Thompson
EX $35   NM $65   MIP n/a

Geography up to Date, 1890s, Parker Brothers
EX $35   NM $55   MIP n/a

George Washington's Dream, 1900s, Parker Brothers
EX $45   NM $75   MIP n/a

G-Men, 1936, Milton Bradley
EX $35   NM $55   MIP n/a

Goat, Game of, 1916, Milton Bradley
EX $15   NM $35   MIP n/a

Gold Rush, The, 1930s, Cracker Jack
EX $20   NM $50   MIP n/a

Golden Egg, 1850s, McLoughlin Bros.
EX $450   NM $750   MIP n/a

Golden Egg, The, 1845, R.H. Pease
EX $165   NM $275   MIP n/a

- **Golliwogg,** 1907, Milton Bradley
  EX $200   **NM** $300   **MIP** n/a

- **Good Old Game of Corner Grocery, The,** 1900s, Parker Brothers
  EX $40   **NM** $60   **MIP** n/a

- **Good Old Game of Dr. Busby,** 1900s, Parker Brothers
  EX $55   **NM** $85   **MIP** n/a

- **Good Old Game of Dr. Busby,** 1920s, United Game
  EX $25   **NM** $50   **MIP** n/a

- **Grandmama's Improved Arithmetical Game,** 1887, McLoughlin Bros.
  EX $30   **NM** $50   **MIP** n/a

- **Grandmama's Improved Geographical Game,** 1887, McLoughlin Bros.
  EX $55   **NM** $90   **MIP** n/a

- **Grandmama's Sunday Game: Bible Questions, Old Testament,** 1887, McLoughlin Bros.
  EX $35   **NM** $65   **MIP** n/a

- **Grandma's Game of Useful Knowledge,** 1910s, Milton Bradley
  EX $20   **NM** $50   **MIP** n/a

- **Great Battlefields,** 1886, Parker Brothers
  EX $150   **NM** $250   **MIP** n/a

- **Great Composer, The,** 1901, Theodore Presser
  EX $35   **NM** $55   **MIP** n/a

- **Great Mails Baseball Game,** 1919, Walter Mails Baseball Game
  EX $2475   **NM** $4100   **MIP** n/a

- **Guess Again, The Game of,** 1890s, McLoughlin Bros.
  EX $75   **NM** $120   **MIP** n/a

- **Gypsy Fortune Telling Game,** 1909, McLoughlin Bros.
  EX $100   **NM** $175   **MIP** n/a

- **H.M.S. Pinafore,** 1880, McLoughlin Bros.
  EX $300   **NM** $500   **MIP** n/a

- **Have-U It?,** 1924, Selchow & Righter
  EX $15   **NM** $25   **MIP** n/a

- **Heads and Tails,** 1900s, Parker Brothers
  EX $30   **NM** $50   **MIP** n/a

- **Hens and Chickens, Game of,** 1875, McLoughlin Bros.
  EX $125   **NM** $175   **MIP** n/a

- **Hey What?,** 1907, Parker Brothers
  EX $20   **NM** $35   **MIP** n/a

- **Hidden Titles,** 1908, Parker Brothers
  EX $20   **NM** $35   **MIP** n/a

- **Historical Cards,** 1884, Peter G. Thompson
  EX $55   **NM** $75   **MIP** n/a

- **History up to Date,** 1900s, Parker Brothers
  EX $55   **NM** $65   **MIP** n/a

- **Hokum,** 1927, Parker Brothers
  EX $10   **NM** $20   **MIP** n/a

- **Hollywood Movie Bingo,** 1937, Whitman
  EX $50   **NM** $75   **MIP** n/a

- **Home Diamond,** 1913, Phillips
  EX $150   **NM** $225   **MIP** n/a

- **Home History Game,** 1910s, Milton Bradley
  EX $55   **NM** $75   **MIP** n/a

- **Hood's War Game,** 1899, C.I. Hood
  EX $40   **NM** $65   **MIP** n/a

- **Hoot,** 1926, Saalfield
  EX $75   **NM** $150   **MIP** n/a

- **House that Jack Built,** 1900s, Parker Brothers
  EX $55   **NM** $75   **MIP** n/a

- **House that Jack Built, The,** 1887, McLoughlin Bros.
  EX $55   **NM** $85   **MIP** n/a

- **Household Words, Game of,** 1916, Household Words Game
  EX $50   **NM** $85   **MIP** n/a

- **How Silas Popped the Question,** 1915, Parker Brothers
  EX $25   **NM** $40   **MIP** n/a

- **I Doubt It,** 1910, Parker Brothers
  EX $35   **NM** $55   **MIP** n/a

- **Illustrated Mythology,** 1896, Cincinnati Game
  EX $25   **NM** $50   **MIP** n/a

- **Improved Historical Cards,** 1900, McLoughlin Bros.
  EX $35   **NM** $55   **MIP** n/a

- **Industries, Game of,** 1897, A.W. Mumford
  EX $25   **NM** $55   **MIP** n/a

- **Ivanhoe,** 1886, Parker Brothers
  EX $55   **NM** $75   **MIP** n/a

- **Japanese Oracle, Game of,** 1875, McLoughlin Bros.
  EX $200   **NM** $325   **MIP** n/a

- **Joe "Ducky" Medwick's Big Leaguer Baseball Game,** 1930s, Johnson-Breier
  EX $125   **NM** $200   **MIP** n/a

- **Johnny's Historical Game,** 1890s, Parker Brothers
  EX $55   **NM** $95   **MIP** n/a

- **Jumping Frog, Game of,** 1890, J.H. Singer
  EX $75   **NM** $125   **MIP** n/a

- **Just Like Me, Game of,** 1899, McLoughlin Bros.
  EX $55   **NM** $95   **MIP** n/a

- **Kings, The Game of,** 1845, Josiah Adams
  EX $150   **NM** $250   **MIP** n/a

- **Komical Konversation Kards,** 1893, Parker Brothers
  EX $50   **NM** $75   **MIP** n/a

- **Lawson's Baseball Card Game,** 1910
  EX $100   **NM** $175   **MIP** n/a

- **Lawson's Patent Game of Baseball,** 1884, Lawson's Card
  EX $500   **NM** $1000   **MIP** n/a

- **Letters Improved for the Logomachist,** 1878, Noyes & Snow
  EX $50   **NM** $100   **MIP** n/a

- **Library of Games,** 1939, Russell
  EX $55   **NM** $75   **MIP** n/a

- **Lindy Flying Game,** 1927, Parker Brothers
  EX $35   **NM** $50   **MIP** n/a

- **Lindy Flying Game, The New,** 1927, Nucraft Toys
  EX $45   **NM** $75   **MIP** n/a

- **Lion & the Eagle, or the Days of '76,** 1883, E.H. Snow
  EX $75   **NM** $125   **MIP** n/a

- **Little Orphan Annie Rummy Cards,** 1937, Whitman
  EX $45   **NM** $75   **MIP** n/a

- **Lost Heir, Game of the,** 1910, Milton Bradley
  EX $30   **NM** $50   **MIP** n/a

- **Lost Heir, The Game of,** 1893, McLoughlin Bros.
  EX $65   **NM** $85   **MIP** n/a

- **Major League Baseball Game,** 1900s, Parker Brothers
  EX $50   **NM** $150   **MIP** n/a

- **Make A Million,** 1934, Rook Card
  EX $25   **NM** $50   **MIP** n/a

- **Mayflower, The,** 1897, Fireside Game
  EX $55   **NM** $85   **MIP** n/a

- **Mickey Mouse Bridge Game,** 1935, Whitman
  EX $35   **NM** $55   **MIP** n/a

- **Mickey Mouse Old Maid Game,** 1930s, Whitman
  EX $35   **NM** $65   **MIP** n/a

- **Mother Hubbard,** 1875, McLoughlin Bros.
  EX $75   **NM** $125   **MIP** n/a

- **Movie-Land Keeno,** 1929, Wilder
  EX $150   **NM** $250   **MIP** n/a

- **Musical Lotto,** 1936, Tudor Metal Products
  EX $35   **NM** $65   **MIP** n/a

- **Mythology,** 1900, Cincinnati Game
  EX $55   **NM** $75   **MIP** n/a

- **Napoleon LaJoie Baseball Game,** 1913, Parker Brothers
  EX $150   **NM** $500   **MIP** n/a

- **National American Baseball Game,** 1910, Parker Brothers
  EX $130   **NM** $200   **MIP** n/a

- **National Baseball Game, The,** 1913, National Baseball Playing Card
  EX $700   **NM** $1200   **MIP** n/a

- **Nations or Quaker Whist, Game of,** 1898, McLoughlin Bros.
  EX $75   **NM** $110   **MIP** n/a

GAMES

Nations, Game of, 1908, Milton Bradley
EX $25   NM $45   MIP n/a

Naughty Molly, 1905, McLoughlin Bros.
EX $75   NM $100   MIP n/a

Nosey, The Game of, 1905, McLoughlin Bros.
EX $250   NM $400   MIP n/a

(KP Photo)

Oh, Blondie!, 1940s
EX $30   NM $45   MIP n/a

Old Curiosity Shop, 1869, Novelty Game
EX $200   NM $300   MIP n/a

Old Maid, 1890s, J.H. Singer
EX $25   NM $75   MIP n/a

Old Maid Card Game, 1889
EX $20   NM $50   MIP n/a

Old Maid Fun Full Thrift Game, 1940s, Russell
EX $30   NM $50   MIP n/a

Old Maid, Game of, 1870, McLoughlin Bros.
EX $75   NM $125   MIP n/a

Old Maid, with Characters from Famous Nursery Rhymes, 1920s, All-Fair
EX $30   NM $50   MIP n/a

Oliver Twist, The Good Old Game of, 1888, Parker Brothers
EX $150   NM $225   MIP n/a

Our Bird Friends, 1901, Sarah H. Dudley
EX $20   NM $30   MIP n/a

Our National Life, 1903, Cincinnati Game
EX $35   NM $65   MIP n/a

Patch Word, 1938, All-Fair
EX $15   NM $20   MIP n/a

Paws & Claws, 1895, Clark & Sowdon
EX $60   NM $90   MIP n/a

Pepper, 1906, Parker Brothers
EX $20   NM $35   MIP n/a

Peter Coddle and his Trip to New York, 1890s, J.H. Singer
EX $35   NM $65   MIP n/a

(KP Photo)

Peter Coddle tells of his Trip to Chicago, 1890, Parker Brothers
EX $30   NM $50   MIP n/a

Peter Coddle, Improved Game of, 1900, McLoughlin Bros.
EX $35   NM $55   MIP n/a

Peter Coddles, 1890s, J. Ottmann Lith.
EX $25   NM $55   MIP n/a

Peter Coddle's Trip to New York, 1925, Milton Bradley
EX $20   NM $35   MIP n/a

Peter Coddle's Trip to New York, The Game of, 1888, Parker Brothers
EX $40   NM $50   MIP n/a

Peter Coddle's Trip to the World's Fair, 1939, Parker Brothers
EX $50   NM $85   MIP n/a

Pinocchio Playing Card Game, 1939, Whitman
EX $55   NM $95   MIP n/a

Psychic Baseball, 1927, Psychic Baseball
EX $60   NM $150   MIP n/a

Real Baseball Card Game, 1900, National Baseball
EX $180   NM $275   MIP n/a

Red Riding Hood and the Wolf, The New Game, 1887, McLoughlin Bros.
EX $75   NM $120   MIP n/a

Rex, 1920s, J. Ottmann Lith.
EX $35   NM $65   MIP n/a

Robinson Crusoe for Little Folks, Game of, 1900s, E.O. Clark
EX $35   NM $65   MIP n/a

Roodles, 1912, Flinch Card
EX $30   NM $50   MIP n/a

(KP Photo)

Rook, 1906, Rook Card
EX $10   NM $15   MIP n/a

Roosevelt at San Juan, 1899, Chaffee & Selchow
EX $150   NM $350   MIP n/a

Sabotage, 1943, Games Of Fame
EX $25   NM $45   MIP n/a

Skippy, A Card Game, 1936, All-Fair
EX $45   NM $75   MIP n/a

Skit Scat, 1905, McLoughlin Bros.
EX $50   NM $85   MIP n/a

Snap, 1883, Horsman
EX $20   NM $50   MIP n/a

Snap, Game of, 1892, McLoughlin Bros.
EX $40   NM $85   MIP n/a

Snap, Game of, 1910s, Milton Bradley
EX $20   NM $35   MIP n/a

Snap, The Game of, 1905s, Parker Brothers
EX $25   NM $40   MIP n/a

Stage, 1904, C.M. Clark
EX $100   NM $175   MIP n/a

Star Baseball Game, 1941, W.P. Ulrich
EX $70   NM $115   MIP n/a

Take-Off, 1930s, Russell
EX $25   NM $45   MIP n/a

Three Bears, The, 1922, Stoll & Edwards
EX $30   NM $50   MIP n/a

Three Merry Men, 1865, Amsdan
EX $75   NM $100   MIP n/a

Tom Barker Card Game, 1913
EX $1400   NM $2300   MIP n/a

Toot, 1905, Parker Brothers
EX $35   NM $65   MIP n/a

Totem, 1873, West & Lee
EX $45   NM $75   MIP n/a

Touring, 1906, Wallie Dorr
EX $35   NM $75   MIP n/a

Touring, 1926, Parker Brothers
EX $20   NM $40   MIP n/a

(KP Photo)

Traits, The Game of, 1933, Goodenough and Woglom
EX $20   NM $35   MIP n/a

Trip through our National Parks: Game of Yellowstone, A, 1910s, Cincinnati Game
EX $20   NM $45   MIP n/a

Trips of Japhet Jenkens & Sam Slick, 1871, Milton Bradley
EX $20   NM $35   MIP n/a

❑ **Trolley,** 1904, Snyder Brothers
EX $45   **NM** $75   **MIP** n/a

❑ **Trolley Came Off, The,** 1900s, Parker Brothers
EX $45   **NM** $75   **MIP** n/a

❑ **Twenty Five, Game of,** 1925, Milton Bradley
EX $10   **NM** $15   **MIP** n/a

❑ **United States History, The Game of,** 1903, Parker Brothers
EX $35   **NM** $65   **MIP** n/a

❑ **Venetian Fortune Teller, Game of,** 1898, Parker Brothers
EX $125   **NM** $165   **MIP** n/a

❑ **Verborum,** 1883, Peter G. Thompson
EX $35   **NM** $65   **MIP** n/a

❑ **Walt and Skeezix Gasoline Alley Game,** 1927, Milton Bradley
EX $100   **NM** $175   **MIP** n/a

❑ **War and Diplomacy,** 1899, Chaffee & Selchow
EX $85   **NM** $125   **MIP** n/a

❑ **War of Words,** 1910, McLoughlin Bros.
EX $35   **NM** $60   **MIP** n/a

❑ **What Would You Do?,** 1933, Geo E. Schweig & Son
EX $15   **NM** $25   **MIP** n/a

❑ **When My Ship Comes In,** 1888, Parker Brothers
EX $55   **NM** $75   **MIP** n/a

❑ **Where do you Live?,** 1890s, J.H. Singer
EX $55   **NM** $75   **MIP** n/a

❑ **Where's Johnny?,** 1885, McLoughlin Bros.
EX $65   **NM** $110   **MIP** n/a

❑ **Which is It? Speak Quick or Pay,** 1889, McLoughlin Bros.
EX $65   **NM** $110   **MIP** n/a

❑ **Whip, The Comical Game of,** 1930, Russell
EX $30   **NM** $50   **MIP** n/a

❑ **Who is the Thief?,** 1937, Whitman
EX $35   **NM** $55   **MIP** n/a

❑ **Wogglebug Game of Conundrums, The,** 1905, Parker Brothers
EX $200   **NM** $500   **MIP** n/a

❑ **Worth While,** 1907, Doan
EX $25   **NM** $40   **MIP** n/a

❑ **Wyhoo!,** 1906, Milton Bradley
EX $40   **NM** $60   **MIP** n/a

❑ **Yankee Pedlar, Or What Do You Buy,** 1850s, John McLoughlin
EX $725   **NM** $1200   **MIP** n/a

(KP Photo)

❑ **Yellowstone, Game of,** 1895, Fireside Game
EX $75   **NM** $100   **MIP** n/a

❑ **Young Folks Historical Game,** 1890s, McLoughlin Bros.
EX $45   **NM** $85   **MIP** n/a

❑ **Young Peddlers, Game of the,** 1859, Mayhew & Baker
EX $125   **NM** $175   **MIP** n/a

❑ **Young People's Geographical Game,** 1900s, Parker Brothers
EX $35   **NM** $55   **MIP** n/a

❑ **Zoom,** 1941, Whitman
EX $35   **NM** $55   **MIP** n/a

DEXTERITY

❑ **Golf,** 1900, Schoenhut
EX $2700   **NM** $5000   **MIP** n/a

SKILL/ACTION GAMES

❑ **400, Aristocrat of Games, The,** 1933, Morris Systems
EX $15   **NM** $25   **MIP** n/a

❑ **Aero Ball,** 1940s, Game Makers
EX $30   **NM** $75   **MIP** n/a

(KP Photo)

❑ **Animal Bingo,** Baldwin Manufacturing
EX $40   **NM** $125   **MIP** n/a

❑ **Bag of Fun,** 1932, Rosebud Art
EX $5   **NM** $10   **MIP** n/a

❑ **Balloonio,** 1937, Frederick H. Beach
EX $20   **NM** $40   **MIP** n/a

❑ **Bambino,** 1934, Bambino Products
EX $75   **NM** $125   **MIP** n/a

❑ **Bang Bird,** 1924, Doremus Schoen
EX $20   **NM** $30   **MIP** n/a

❑ **Barber Pole,** 1908, Parker Brothers
EX $75   **NM** $100   **MIP** n/a

❑ **Barn Yard Tiddledy Winks,** 1910s, Parker Brothers
EX $50   **NM** $85   **MIP** n/a

❑ **Bases Full,** 1930
EX $45   **NM** $70   **MIP** n/a

❑ **Basket Ball,** 1929, Russell
EX $150   **NM** $350   **MIP** n/a

❑ **Battles, or Fun For Boys, Game of,** 1889, McLoughlin Bros.
EX $600   **NM** $1000   **MIP** n/a

(KP Photo)

❑ **Bean-Em,** 1931, All-Fair
EX $400   **NM** $600   **MIP** n/a

❑ **Bingo,** 1929, All-Fair
EX $10   **NM** $15   **MIP** n/a

❑ **Bobb, Game of,** 1898, McLoughlin Bros.
EX $200   **NM** $400   **MIP** n/a

❑ **Bomber Ball,** 1940s, Game Makers
EX $75   **NM** $125   **MIP** n/a

❑ **Bottle Imps, Game of,** 1907, Milton Bradley
EX $300   **NM** $500   **MIP** n/a

❑ **Bowling Alley,** 1921, N.D. Cass
EX $20   **NM** $35   **MIP** n/a

❑ **Bow-O-Winks,** 1932, All-Fair
EX $100   **NM** $150   **MIP** n/a

❑ **Boy Hunter, The,** 1925, Parker Brothers
EX $60   **NM** $100   **MIP** n/a

❑ **Brownie Character Ten Pins Game,** 1890s
EX $125   **NM** $200   **MIP** n/a

❑ **Brownie Kick-In Top,** 1910s, M.H. Miller
EX $35   **NM** $60   **MIP** n/a

❑ **Bula,** 1943, Games Of Fame
EX $30   **NM** $45   **MIP** n/a

❑ **Bull in the China Shop,** 1937, Milton Bradley
EX $20   **NM** $40   **MIP** n/a

❑ **Buster Brown, Pin The Tail On The Tiger Game,** 1900s
EX $60   **NM** $100   **MIP** n/a

❑ **Busto,** 1931, All-Fair
EX $100   **NM** $200   **MIP** n/a

❑ **Buzzing Around,** 1924, Parker Brothers
EX $40   **NM** $65   **MIP** n/a

❑ **Cat and Witch,** 1940s, Whitman
EX $25   **NM** $65   **MIP** n/a

❑ **Cavalcade Derby Game,** 1930s, Wyandotte
EX $50   **NM** $85   **MIP** n/a

❑ **Chinaman Party,** 1896, Selchow & Righter
EX $75   **NM** $130   **MIP** n/a

❑ **Chivalry, The Game of,** 1888, Parker Brothers
EX $150   **NM** $225   **MIP** n/a

GAMES

□ **Click,** 1930s, Akro Agate
EX $50   NM $85   MIP n/a

□ **Clown Winks,** 1930s, Gabriel
EX $15   NM $25   MIP n/a

(KP Photo)

□ **Combination Tiddledy Winks,** 1910, Milton Bradley
EX $20   NM $40   MIP n/a

□ **Cones & Corns,** 1924, Parker Brothers
EX $39   NM $65   MIP n/a

□ **Conette,** 1890, Milton Bradley
EX $45   NM $65   MIP n/a

□ **Contack,** 1939, Parker Brothers
EX $5   NM $15   MIP n/a

□ **Cows In Corn,** 1889, Stirn & Lyon
EX $150   NM $250   MIP n/a

□ **Crazy Traveller,** 1920s, Parker Brothers
EX $40   NM $50   MIP n/a

□ **Crickets In The Grass,** 1920s, Madmar Quality
EX $35   NM $50   MIP n/a

□ **Crow Hunt,** 1930, Parker Brothers
EX $50   NM $85   MIP n/a

□ **Crows in the Corn,** 1930, Parker Brothers
EX $45   NM $75   MIP n/a

□ **Deck Ring Toss Game,** 1910
EX $30   NM $50   MIP n/a

□ **Dig,** 1940, Parker Brothers
EX $2   NM $5   MIP n/a

□ **Dim Those Lights,** 1932, All-Fair
EX $300   NM $600   MIP n/a

□ **Disk,** 1900s, Madmar Quality
EX $35   NM $55   MIP n/a

□ **Diving Fish,** 1920s, C.E. Bradley
EX $20   NM $30   MIP n/a

□ **Dodging Donkey, The,** 1920s, Parker Brothers
EX $45   NM $75   MIP n/a

□ **Donkey Party,** 1887, McLoughlin Bros.
EX $75   NM $150   MIP n/a

□ **Down and Out,** 1928, Milton Bradley
EX $50   NM $75   MIP n/a

□ **Faba Baga or Parlor Quiots,** 1883, Morton E. Converse
EX $40   NM $65   MIP n/a

□ **Fairies' Cauldron Tiddledy Winks Game, The,** 1925, Parker Brothers
EX $35   NM $50   MIP n/a

□ **Fascination,** 1890, Selchow & Righter
EX $35   NM $50   MIP n/a

□ **Fiddlestix,** 1937, Plaza
EX $10   NM $15   MIP n/a

□ **Fish Pond,** 1890, E.O. Clark
EX $50   NM $125   MIP n/a

□ **Fish Pond,** 1920s, Wilder
EX $25   NM $60   MIP n/a

□ **Fish Pond Game, Magnetic,** 1891, McLoughlin Bros.
EX $175   NM $300   MIP n/a

□ **Fish Pond, Game of,** 1910s, Wescott Brothers
EX $30   NM $50   MIP n/a

□ **Fish Pond, New and Improved,** 1890s, McLoughlin Bros.
EX $75   NM $125   MIP n/a

□ **Fish Pond, The Game of,** 1890, McLoughlin Bros.
EX $100   NM $175   MIP n/a

□ **Fishing Game,** 1899, Martin
EX $30   NM $65   MIP n/a

□ **Five Little Pigs,** 1890s, J.H. Singer
EX $50   NM $100   MIP n/a

□ **Five Wise Birds, The,** 1923, Parker Brothers
EX $25   NM $50   MIP n/a

□ **Flap Jacks,** 1931, All-Fair
EX $80   NM $225   MIP n/a

□ **Flash,** 1940s, Pressman
EX $20   NM $50   MIP n/a

□ **Flitters,** 1899, Martin
EX $45   NM $75   MIP n/a

□ **Floor Croquet Game,** 1912
EX $60   NM $100   MIP n/a

□ **Four and Twenty Blackbirds,** 1890s, McLoughlin Bros.
EX $750   NM $1500   MIP n/a

□ **Four Dare Devils, The,** 1933, Marx, Hess & Lee
EX $40   NM $65   MIP n/a

□ **Gee-Wiz Horse Race,** 1928, Wolverine
EX $50   NM $85   MIP n/a

□ **Genuine Steamer Quoits,** 1924, Milton Bradley
EX $15   NM $25   MIP n/a

(KP Photo)

□ **Happitime Bagatelle,** 1933, Northwestern Products
EX $30   NM $45   MIP n/a

□ **Happy Landing,** 1938, Transogram
EX $30   NM $45   MIP n/a

□ **Hop-Over Puzzle,** 1930s, Pressman
EX $20   NM $35   MIP n/a

□ **Hungry Willie,** 1930s, Transogram
EX $40   NM $70   MIP n/a

□ **Hunting in the Jungle,** 1920s, A. Gropper
EX $30   NM $45   MIP n/a

(KP Photo)

□ **Indoor Golf Dice,** 1920s, W.P. Bushell
EX $20   NM $35   MIP n/a

□ **Jack Straws, The Game of,** 1901, Parker Brothers
EX $25   NM $35   MIP n/a

□ **Jamboree,** 1937, Selchow & Righter
EX $75   NM $150   MIP n/a

□ **Japanese Ball Game,** 1930s, Girard
EX $35   NM $65   MIP n/a

❑ **Japanola,** 1928, Parker Brothers
EX $35   NM $60   MIP n/a

❑ **Jaunty Butler,** 1932, All-Fair
EX $75   NM $150   MIP n/a

❑ **Jav-Lin,** 1931, All-Fair
EX $105   NM $225   MIP n/a

❑ **Jolly Clown Spinette,** 1932, Milton Bradley
EX $30   NM $45   MIP n/a

❑ **Jolly Robbers,** 1929, Wilder
EX $50   NM $75   MIP n/a

❑ **Jumping Jupiter,** 1940s, Gabriel
EX $30   NM $50   MIP n/a

❑ **Jungle Hunt,** 1940, Gotham Pressed Steel
EX $30   NM $45   MIP n/a

❑ **Jungle Jump-Up Game,** 1940s, Judson Press
EX $30   NM $45   MIP n/a

❑ **Katzenjammer Kids Hockey,** 1940s, Jaymar
EX $40   NM $65   MIP n/a

❑ **Katzy Party,** 1900s, Selchow & Righter
EX $70   NM $120   MIP n/a

❑ **Kindergarten Lotto,** 1904, Strauss
EX $50   NM $80   MIP n/a

❑ **Knockout Andy,** 1926, Parker Brothers
EX $35   NM $75   MIP n/a

❑ **Kuti-Kuts,** 1922, Regensteiner
EX $20   NM $30   MIP n/a

❑ **Leaping Lena,** 1920s, Parker Brothers
EX $100   NM $200   MIP n/a

(KP Photo)

❑ **Lid's Off, The,** 1937, American Toy Works
EX $35   NM $75   MIP n/a

❑ **Little Orphan Annie Bead Game,** 1930s
EX $20   NM $35   MIP n/a

❑ **Little Orphan Annie Shooting Game,** 1930s, Milton Bradley
EX $30   NM $50   MIP n/a

❑ **Lone Ranger Hi-Yo Silver!! Target Game,** 1939, Marx
EX $70   NM $115   MIP n/a

❑ **Mammoth Conette,** 1898, Milton Bradley
EX $90   NM $150   MIP n/a

❑ **Marble Muggins,** 1920s, American Toy
EX $100   NM $200   MIP n/a

❑ **Mar-Juck,** 1923, Regensteiner
EX $20   NM $30   MIP n/a

❑ **Meteor Game,** 1916, A.C. Gilbert
EX $25   NM $45   MIP n/a

❑ **Mickey Mouse Miniature Pinball Game,** 1930s, Marks Brothers
EX $20   NM $35   MIP n/a

❑ **Mickey Mouse Shooting Game,** 1930s, Marks Brothers
EX $120   NM $200   MIP n/a

❑ **Mickey Mouse Skittle Ball Game,** 1930s, Marks Brothers
EX $60   NM $100   MIP n/a

❑ **Mickey Mouse Soldier Target Set,** 1930s, Marks Brothers
EX $60   NM $100   MIP n/a

❑ **Mumbly Peg,** 1920s, All-Fair
EX $25   NM $50   MIP n/a

❑ **Old Time Shooting Gallery,** 1940, Warren-Built-Rite
EX $15   NM $25   MIP n/a

❑ **Our Gang Tipple Topple Game,** 1930, All-Fair
EX $160   NM $300   MIP n/a

❑ **Peeza,** 1935, Toy Creations
EX $25   NM $45   MIP n/a

❑ **Pike's Peak or Bust,** 1890s, Parker Brothers
EX $75   NM $150   MIP n/a

❑ **Ping Pong,** 1902, Parker Brothers
EX $100   NM $175   MIP n/a

❑ **Pinocchio Target Game,** 1938, American Toy Works
EX $90   NM $150   MIP n/a

❑ **Pinocchio the Merry Puppet Game,** 1939, Milton Bradley
EX $55   NM $95   MIP n/a

(KP Photo)

❑ **Pitch Em, The Game of Indoor Horse Shoes,** 1929, Wolverine
EX $25   NM $35   MIP n/a

(KP Photo)

❑ **Pop the Hat,** 1930s, Milton Bradley
EX $35   NM $50   MIP n/a

❑ **Ranger Commandos,** 1942, Parker Brothers
EX $35   NM $60   MIP n/a

❑ **Red Ryder "Whirli-Crow" Target Game,** 1940s, Daisy
EX $150   NM $250   MIP n/a

❑ **Ride 'em Cowboy,** 1939, Gotham Pressed Steel
EX $25   NM $45   MIP n/a

❑ **Ring My Nose,** 1926, Milton Bradley
EX $60   NM $100   MIP n/a

❑ **Ring Scaling,** 1900, Martin
EX $25   NM $45   MIP n/a

❑ **Shuffle-Board, The New Game of,** 1920, Gabriel
EX $50   NM $85   MIP n/a

❑ **Simba,** 1932, All-Fair
EX $75   NM $150   MIP n/a

❑ **Smitty Target Game,** 1930s, Milton Bradley
EX $40   NM $75   MIP n/a

❑ **Snap-Jacks,** 1940s, Gabriel
EX $15   NM $25   MIP n/a

❑ **Snow White and the Seven Dwarfs,** 1938, American Toy Works
EX $150   NM $250   MIP n/a

❑ **Spin 'em Target Game,** 1930s, All Metal Product
EX $25   NM $40   MIP n/a

❑ **Spin It,** 1910s, Milton Bradley
EX $20   NM $50   MIP n/a

❑ **Stak, International Game of,** 1937, Marks Brothers
EX $30   NM $60   MIP n/a

❑ **Stax,** 1930s, Marks Brothers
EX $12   NM $20   MIP n/a

❑ **Superman Action Game,** 1940, American Toy Works
EX $60   NM $100   MIP n/a

❑ **Table Croquet,** 1890s, Milton Bradley
EX $30   NM $75   MIP n/a

GAMES

☐ **Tactics,** 1940, Northwestern Products
EX $25   NM $45   MIP n/a

☐ **Tiddledy Wink Tennis,** 1890, E.I. Horsman
EX $45   NM $75   MIP n/a

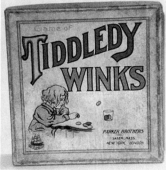

(KP Photo)

☐ **Tiddledy Winks, Game of,** 1910s, Parker Brothers
EX $35   NM $55   MIP n/a

☐ **Tinker Toss,** 1920s, Toy Creations
EX $25   NM $40   MIP n/a

☐ **Tip the Bellboy,** 1929, All-Fair
EX $120   NM $200   MIP n/a

☐ **Tip Top Fish Pond,** 1930s, Milton Bradley
EX $20   NM $45   MIP n/a

☐ **Toss-O,** 1924, Lubbers & Bell
EX $15   NM $35   MIP n/a

☐ **Touchdown,** 1930s, Milton Bradley
EX $150   NM $250   MIP n/a

☐ **Toy Town Target with Repeating Pistol,** 1911, Milton Bradley
EX $55   NM $95   MIP n/a

☐ **Traps and Bunkers, A Game of Golf,** 1930s, Milton Bradley
EX $25   NM $40   MIP n/a

☐ **United States Air Mail Game, The,** 1930s, Parker Brothers
EX $50   NM $85   MIP n/a

☐ **Wa-Hoo Pick-Em Up Sticks,** 1936, Doremus Schoen
EX $15   NM $25   MIP n/a

☐ **Walt Disney's Ski Jump Target Game,** 1930s, American Toy Works
EX $175   NM $295   MIP n/a

☐ **Walt Disney's Uncle Remus Game,** 1930s, Parker Brothers
EX $60   NM $125   MIP n/a

☐ **Washington's Birthday Party,** 1911, Russell
EX $55   NM $95   MIP n/a

☐ **Watermelon Patch Game,** 1896, McLoughlin Bros.
EX $900   NM $2000   MIP n/a

☐ **Wonder Tiddley Winks,** 1899, Martin
EX $20   NM $35   MIP n/a

TABLETOP GAMES

AUTO RACING

☐ **No. 300 Electric Auto Racing,** 1948-49, Tudor
EX $50   NM $100   MIP n/a

☐ **No. 530 Tru-Action Sports Car Race,** 1959-65, Tudor
EX $20   NM $40   MIP n/a

☐ **No. 590 Mickey Mouse Electric Treasure Hunt Game,** 1963-64, Tudor
EX $40   NM $80   MIP n/a

BASEBALL

☐ **No. 550 Tru-Action Baseball,** 1950-58, Tudor
EX $30   NM $60   MIP n/a

☐ **No. 550 Tru-Action Baseball,** 1958-63, Tudor
EX $25   NM $50   MIP n/a

☐ **No. 555 Tru-Action Baseball,** 1964-88, Tudor, square field
EX $22   NM $45   MIP n/a

BASKETBALL

☐ **No. 475 Magnetic Baseball,** 1964-67, Tudor
EX $20   NM $40   MIP n/a

☐ **No. 480 NBPA Game,** 1968-70, Tudor
EX $30   NM $60   MIP n/a

☐ **No. 480 NBPA Game,** 1971, Tudor
EX $15   NM $30   MIP n/a

☐ **No. 575 Tru-Action Electric Basketball,** 1957-58, Tudor
EX $30   NM $60   MIP n/a

☐ **No. 575 Tru-Action Electric Basketball,** 1959-63, Tudor
EX $25   NM $50   MIP n/a

FOOTBALL

☐ **G-890 Dick Butkus,** 1972, Gotham
EX $30   NM $60   MIP n/a

☐ **No. G-1400,** 1965-67, Gotham
EX $30   NM $60   MIP n/a

☐ **No. G-1440,** 1962-64, Gotham
EX $35   NM $70   MIP n/a

☐ **No. G-1503,** 1968, Gotham
EX $33   NM $65   MIP n/a

☐ **No. G-1503-S NFL Big Bowl,** 1965-67, Gotham
EX $50   NM $125   MIP n/a

☐ **No. G-1506 NFL Players Association,** Gotham
EX $25   NM $50   MIP n/a

☐ **No. G-1512 Super Dome,** 1969-71, Gotham
EX $45   NM $100   MIP n/a

☐ **No. G-1550 Yankee Stadium Grandstand,** 1962-64, Gotham
EX $40   NM $80   MIP n/a

☐ **No. G-812 Joe Namath,** 1969-71, Gotham
EX $35   NM $70   MIP n/a

☐ **No. G-812 Joe Namath,** 1972, Gotham
EX $35   NM $70   MIP n/a

☐ **No. G-818 Roman Gabriel Model,** 1969-71, Gotham
EX $25   NM $50   MIP n/a

☐ **No. G-818 Roman Gabriel Model,** 1972, Gotham
EX $25   NM $50   MIP n/a

☐ **No. G-880 Gotham All-Star Electric Football,** 1956-58, Gotham
EX $30   NM $60   MIP n/a

☐ **No. G-880 Gotham All-Star Electric Football,** 1959-61, Gotham
EX $25   NM $50   MIP n/a

☐ **No. G-882,** 1965-67, Gotham
EX $18   NM $35   MIP n/a

☐ **No. G-883,** 1968, Gotham
EX $15   NM $30   MIP n/a

☐ **No. G-883,** 1972, Gotham
EX $10   NM $20   MIP n/a

☐ **No. G-890 Gotham Official NFL Electric Football,** 1962-64, Gotham
EX $20   NM $40   MIP n/a

☐ **No. G-895 NFL Players Association,** 1969-71, Gotham
EX $22   NM $45   MIP n/a

☐ **No. G-940 Gotham Electro Magnetic Football,** 1954-55, Gotham
EX $38   NM $75   MIP n/a

HOCKEY

☐ **Bobby Hull,** 1960s, Munro
EX $125   NM $250   MIP n/a

☐ **Bobby Hull,** 1970s, Munro
EX $75   NM $150   MIP n/a

☐ **Bobby Orr,** late 1960s-early 1970s, Munro
EX $125   NM $250   MIP n/a

☐ **Canadian,** late 1960s, Eagle
EX $75   NM $135   MIP n/a

☐ **Canadian Hockey Master,** early 1960s, Munro
EX $100   NM $225   MIP n/a

☐ **City Series,** early 1970s, Coleco
EX $100   NM $200   MIP n/a

☐ **Foster Hewitt,** 1950s, Reliable
EX $125   NM $225   MIP n/a

☐ **Hockey games,** 1940s-50s, Cresta, various games
EX $200   NM $500   MIP n/a

☐ **Hot Shot,** late 1960s, Munro
EX $60   NM $110   MIP n/a

☐ **Hot Shot,** mid 1960s, Munro
EX $75   NM $150   MIP n/a

☐ **National,** early 1960s, Eagle
EX $125   NM $200   MIP n/a

☐ **NHPLA,** 1969, Tudor
EX $75   NM $125   MIP n/a

❏ **No. 5100 Pro Stars,** mid 1960s-early 1970s, Coleco
EX $65   NM $125   MIP n/a

❏ **No. 5160-80 Pro Stars,** late 1960s-early 1970s, Coleco
EX $75   NM $150   MIP n/a

❏ **No. G1200,** 1950s-1960s, Gotham
EX $75   NM $150   MIP n/a

❏ **No. G-200,** 1930s-1950s, Gotham
EX $125   NM $350   MIP n/a

❏ **Official Hockey Night,** early 1960s, Eagle
EX $150   NM $300   MIP n/a

❏ **Official NHL,** 1969-71, Coleco
EX $150   NM $500   MIP n/a

❏ **Olympic,** 1964, Eagle
EX $200   NM $500   MIP n/a

❏ **Pee Wee,** late 1950s, Eagle
EX $150   NM $250   MIP n/a

❏ **Playmaker,** early 1960s, Eagle
EX $150   NM $250   MIP n/a

❏ **Playoff,** early 1960s, Eagle
EX $125   NM $200   MIP n/a

❏ **Power Play,** early 1960s, Eagle
EX $125   NM $200   MIP n/a

❏ **Power Play,** late 1950s, Eagle
EX $125   NM $225   MIP n/a

❏ **Power Play,** late 1960s, Coleco
EX $100   NM $175   MIP n/a

❏ **Pro Series,** mid 1950s-early 1960s, Eagle
EX $125   NM $225   MIP n/a

❏ **Stanley Cup,** mid 1960s, Eagle
EX $150   NM $250   MIP n/a

❏ **Stanley Cup, Beliveau,** late 1960s, Coleco
EX $125   NM $225   MIP n/a

HORSE RACING

❏ **Horse and Harness Race Game,** 1963-64, Tudor, combined game
EX $20   NM $45   MIP n/a

❏ **No. 525 Horse Race Game,** 1950-58, Tudor
EX $25   NM $60   MIP n/a

❏ **No. 525 Horse Race Game,** 1959-61, Tudor, grooved plastic track
EX $22   NM $45   MIP n/a

❏ **No. 525 Horse Race Game,** 1962, Tudor, plastic track, no no grooves
EX $20   NM $40   MIP n/a

❏ **No. 526 Harness Race Game,** 1962, Tudor
EX $20   NM $40   MIP n/a

❏ **Tru-Action Races Game,** 1965-67, Tudor
EX $35   NM $70   MIP n/a

TRACK AND FIELD

❏ **No. 528 Track and Field Meet,** 1963-64, Tudor
EX $35   NM $75   MIP n/a

❏ **No. 528 Tru-Action Races,** 1965-67, Tudor
EX $35   NM $75   MIP n/a

❏ **No. 528 Tudor Track,** 1962, Tudor, plastic track
EX $15   NM $35   MIP n/a

G.I. Joe

A selection of "Joes." Boy, to have them in the box nowadays...

by Karen O'Brien

"G.I. Joe, G.I. Joe. Fighting man from head to toe. On the land, on the sea, in the air . . ."

To children in the 1960s, this familiar phrase signaled the arrival of a G.I. Joe television commercial. It is one of the few advertising slogans to stand the test of time, and still brings smiles to the grown-ups who remember dashing to the television to see the latest G.I. Joe figures.

G.I. Joe revolutionized the toy industry in the 1960s. A twelve-inch action figure made especially for boys had never been attempted and Hasbro's secret project had to overcome several challenges. Would the public embrace G.I. Joe as a military action figure? Or would it be perceived as a doll for boys? Hasbro decided that G.I. Joe was worth the gamble and launched an extensive advertising cam-

paign portraying G.I. Joe as "America's Movable Fighting Man."

Today, G.I. Joe is acknowledged as the first action figure and its articulated design set the standard for all action toys following in its boot tracks. Hasbro shattered the potential stigma of "boys playing with dolls" by offering boys a fully articulated, movable man of action, not a doll. G.I. Joe accomplished for boys in 1964 what Barbie accomplished five years earlier for girls—it allowed boys to role-play any situation their imaginations could dream up.

The 1960s

G.I. Joe rapidly moved through the development stages in 1963 at Hasbro's Pawtucket, Rhode Island facility in preparation for its debut at the 1964 International Toy Fair. Round-the-clock efforts to assemble figures, produce equipment, and prepare the dioramas culminated on February 9, 1964 when G.I. Joe was presented to toy buyers and the media. Merrill Hassenfeld, president of Hasbro, convinced the toy buyers that G.I. Joe was an action figure and not a doll, and their orders were enough to test the market. New York City was chosen as an initial test market for G.I. Joe and the figures sold out in a week. The same happened in stores across the country—G.I. Joe was a hit.

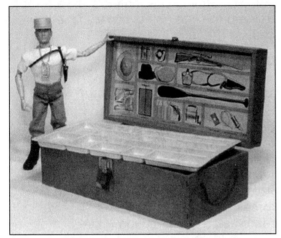

One of the first G.I. Joe figures shown here with a wooden footlocker.

Four figures were offered in 1964, Action Soldier, Action Sailor, Action Marine, and Action Pilot. Each figure was clothed in a branch-specific basic uniform with hat, boots, and dog tag. Uniform and equipment sets for all four branches were sold separately. Authenticity was one of Hasbro's goals with the line, and with 21 points of articulation and realistic equipment and uniforms, they produced a fighting man that was capable of real action poses and unlimited play value.

From its 1964 introduction through 1968, G.I. Joe was a military man of action. The Action Soldiers of the World were introduced in 1966, and the Talking G.I. Joe debuted in 1976. Dozens of uniform and equipment sets were added to the line so that G.I. Joe could participate in backyard battles through snow, desert, water, outer space, jungles or anywhere the imagination lead. Vehicles scaled-to-size for the figures included the Jeep, Space Capsule and Sea Sled. In 1967, Hasbro attempted to bring girls into the G.I. Joe marked by introducing the G.I. Nurse. Instead of a warm reception, she gathered dust on store shelves. She couldn't compete with Mattel's Barbie and boys weren't interested in adding girls to their adventures. Because so few were sold, the G.I. Nurse is one of the most valuable and sought-after G.I. Joe action figures.

Due to the escalation of the Vietnam conflict, G.I. Joe saw his last year of military service in 1968. Many anti-war activists protested Hasbro's production of a military figure. As public sentiment turned against the military action in Southeast Asia, many parents didn't want their children playing with "war" toys of any kind. Hasbro recognized the need for a change.

G.I. Joe became a civilian man of adventure in 1969. He was an Adventurer, Aquanaut, and an Astronaut. He became a Frogman, an Underwater Diver, lead missions to Spy Island, searched for sunken treasure, and even drove a dog sled in the Fight for Survival. Referred to as the Adventures of G.I. Joe, each figure came with a generic uniform consisting of a white t-shirt, green pants, boots, hat, dog tags, a shoulder holster with six-shot revolver, and a booklet outlining possible adventures.

The first Black Fighting Soldier was released in 1965. Mint-in-pack value, $800.

G.I. JOE

The 1970s

The Adventure Team was the next step for the G.I. Joe line. Using the same articulated body, Hasbro added "Life-Like" hair and a beard through a special flocking process to create the distinctive look of the new figures. The basic figures included the Land Adventurer, Sea Adventurer, Air Adventurer, the Man of Action, and the Black Adventurer. Each figure came with a distinctive uniform that included either a jumpsuit (for the Air Adventurers) or a shirt/pants combination. They also had boots, an "AT" dog tag, and shoulder holster with revolver.

The success of the Adventure Team prompted Hasbro to release a series of themed equipment sets including, Danger of the Depths, Hidden Missile Discovery, Fantastic Freefall, White Tiger Hunt, Capture of the Pigmy Gorilla, and Secret of the Mummy's Tomb among many others. Diversification of the tasks produced a variety of uniform sets including Karate, Smoke Jumper, Demolition, Jungle Survival, Secret Agent, and dozens more. Talking figures were still featured.

KUNG FU Grip was added in 1974 and the basic figures were packaged with rifles instead of the shoulder holster and revolver. Hasbro continued to add new equipment and vehicle sets for the popular lines.

The success of Kenner's Six Million Dollar Man action figures in 1975 prompted the expansion of the Adventure Team to include a part-man, part-machine character named Mike Powers: Atomic Man. Mike Powers featured an all-new body sculpt to accommodate his "Atomic" right arm and left leg, but retained a scar on his left cheek in homage to his military roots.

The G.I. Joe line began to fade in the mid-1970s prompted in part to the rising costs of plastic due to the OPEC oil shortage. A "New Life-Like" muscle-bodied G.I. Joe was introduced using only 15 points of articulation to keep the costs down. Eagle Eye Man of Action and Land Commander could move their eyes side

to side and talking versions were included. The Invaders were introduced to provide an intergalactic foe, and Bulletman was introduced to counter the popularity of super-hero toys throughout the decade. The Defenders were the last twelve-inch figures produced and in 1977, G.I. Joe was reduced to an eight-inch size and changed to the Super Joe Adventure Team. Super Joe fought for the safety of the universe and had interchangeable equipment sets, his own command center and villains including Gor, Luminos, and Terron, the Beast from Beyond. Super Joe was Steven Hassenfeld's last attempt to keep the line going, but G.I. Joe ceased production in 1978.

The 1980s

The phenomenal success of the 3-3/4" Star Wars figures in 1978 prompted Hasbro to re-introduce G.I. Joe in the small format as "G.I. Joe: A Real American Hero." The concept was changed to a team of individual characters assembled from all military ranks to combat the evil forces of Cobra. In 1982, G.I. Joe was reborn as a 3-3/4" action figure and no one could have predicted the amazing success of this new line. The figures were fully articulated in the arms, shoulders, waist, legs, and neck and were the most poseable figures ever created in this scale. A swivel-arm feature added in 1983 enhanced their mobility and enabled the figures to achieve any pose with their equipment.

The G.I. Joe team consisted of nine members in 1982, while Cobra had just two figures. Each figure was packaged with individual accessories and a file card that provided detailed information on that character's personal background, military specialties, vital statistics, and code name. Many of the characters were sculpted from the likenesses of Hasbro employees. Vehicles, play sets, and expanded equipment sets accompanied the line.

More than 500 characters were produced for the 3-3/4" line when it came to an end in 1994. The success of the line was bolstered by the Marvel comic book series that ran for twelve years and two television cartoon series.

The 1990s

The 3-3/4" G.I. Joe: A Real American Hero figures continued until 1994. A few special sets were released with much success in 1997, and 1998, receiving approval from collectors and a new generation of children. This prompted the return of the line in 2000.

In 1991, Hasbro created an exclusive twelve-inch figure, Duke: Master Sergeant. Its success prompted the release of the Hall of Fame figures. This combined well-known characters from the 3-3/4" line with the larger twelve-inch format and included four characters, Duke, Stalker, Cobra Commander, and Snake Eyes. The success of this new series prompted Hasbro to release additional characters, vehicles, and equipment. Electronic Talking Battle Command Duke was introduced in 1993, continuing a line of talking G.I. Joe figures that began in 1967.

G.I. Joe Action Soldier seen here in M.P. garb. Just the amount of "stuff" that was made for these action figures is staggering. The accessories are generally well-made and detailed, too, so collecting them can be a fun experience.

Hasbro celebrated G.I. Joe's 30th Anniversary in 1994 at New York's International Toy Fair by introducing a special line of 12- and 3-3/4-inch action figures. G.I. Joe Action Soldier, Action Sailor, Action Marine, Action Pilot, and an African-American Action Soldier were released to commemorate the anniversary and to honor the four branches of the military represented by the original G.I. Joe. The first G.I. Joe Collector's Convention was also held that year. Hasbro presented attendees and dealers with, among other items, limited-edition figures representing the entire G.I. Joe line.

The 1995 creation of the G.I. Joe Extreme, Sgt. Savage, and Mortal Kombat lines would never achieve the success of the 1996 Classic Collection. Hasbro released a nameless series of twelve-inch figures that, like their 1960s predecessors, focused on specific military branches, historical conflicts, and international military specialists. The Classic Collection enjoyed continued success through the late 1990s as the line expanded each year to include figures representing all service branches and virtually all U.S. military conflicts. Hasbro also released the Timeless Collection in 1998, a Target exclusive series featuring reproductions of 1960s figure favorites with an interesting assortment of reproduction equipment.

G.I. Joe turned 35-years-old in 1999 and the line expanded to include celebrity additions to the Classic Collections such as Ted Williams, Buzz Aldrin, and Lieutenant Col. Teddy Roosevelt. In 2000, the Adventures of G.I. Joe featured Save the Tiger and Peril of the Raging Inferno sets, and the Timeless Collection featured an Action Sailor and the popular Deep Sea Diver: Danger of the Depths set. Ever mindful that G.I. Joe is for kids, Hasbro also released two series at lower price-points, the G.I. Joe 2010 series featured futuristic equipment and the Alpha assortment offered military and paramilitary figures.

Today, both the 3 3/4- and 12-inch G.I. Joe lines enjoy considerable popularity.

G.I. JOE

The 2000 release of the Collector's Special Edition new "waves" of 3 3/4" figure favorites lead to an additional release of eight sets of figure two-packs for 2001. 2002 saw the release of the G.I. Joe v. Cobra resculpted figures that provided more detail, though less mobility due to the removal of the "o-ring" that enabled previous figures to pivot at the waist. Repaints of these figures also released in 2002 will send collectors scrambling. A full line of vehicles accompanies the new 3 3/4" releases and is available in the Collector's Special Edition series and the G.I. Joe v. Cobra series.

The 12" series is enjoying considerable popularity among collectors and kids alike. The authentic military figures are complimented by the rescue figures, historical releases, Adventure Team figure sets, equipment sets, vehicles, and even 12" G.I. Joe v. Cobra figures. No matter which era is your collecting preference, there are G.I. Joe figures for every mission and this hobby has a bright future. Yo Joe!

Karen O'Brien is the editor of numerous books on toy collecting, including; Pez, *The Complete Encyclopedia of G.I. Joe, A Universe of Star Wars Collectibles,* Warman's Flea Market Price Guides and numerous automotive books. She is currently working on her collection of vintage G.I. Joe figures and pressed steel trucks.

3-3/4" FIGURES (1980S)

SERIES #1, COBRA

□ **C.A.T.**, 1982, Hasbro, Motorized Crimson Attack Tank
EX n/a   **NM** $15   **MIP** $25

□ **Cobra**, 1982, Hasbro, Infantry Soldier, Model No. 6423
EX n/a   **NM** $25   **MIP** $55

□ **Cobra Commander**, 1982, Hasbro, mail order; Commanding Leader
EX n/a   **NM** $25   **MIP** $55

□ **Cobra Officer**, 1982, Hasbro, Infantry Officer, Model No. 6424
EX n/a   **NM** $25   **MIP** $55

□ **Major Bludd**, 1982, Hasbro, mail order; Mercenary with card, Model No. 6426
EX n/a   **NM** $10   **MIP** $25

SERIES #1, GI JOE

□ **Breaker**, 1982, Hasbro, Communications Officer, Model No. 6403
EX n/a   **NM** $20   **MIP** $35

□ **F.L.A.K.**, 1982, Hasbro, Attack Cannon, Model No. 6075
EX n/a   **NM** $20   **MIP** $45

□ **Flash**, 1982, Hasbro, Laser Rifle Trooper, Model No. 6406
EX n/a   **NM** $20   **MIP** $35

□ **Grunt**, 1982, Hasbro, Infantry Trooper, Model No. 6409
EX n/a   **NM** $20   **MIP** $35

□ **H.A.L.**, 1982, Hasbro, Heavy Artillery Laser with Grand Slam, Model No. 6052
EX n/a   **NM** $20   **MIP** $45

□ **J.U.M.P.**, 1982, Hasbro, Jet Pack with Platform, Model No. 6071
EX n/a   **NM** $20   **MIP** $45

□ **M.M.S.**, 1982, Hasbro, Mobile Missile System with Hawk, Model No. 6054
EX n/a   **NM** $20   **MIP** $45

□ **M.O.B.A.T.**, 1982, Hasbro, Motorized Battle Tank with Steeler, Model No. 6000
EX n/a   **NM** $30   **MIP** $65

□ **R.A.M.**, 1982, Hasbro, Rapid Fire Motorcycle, Model No. 6073
EX n/a   **NM** $15   **MIP** $25

□ **Rock 'n Roll**, 1982, Hasbro, Machine Gunner, Model No. 6408
EX n/a   **NM** $20   **MIP** $35

□ **Scarlett**, 1982, Hasbro, Counter Intelligence, Model No. 6407
EX n/a   **NM** $40   **MIP** $85

□ **Short Fuse**, 1982, Hasbro, Mortar Soldier, Model No. 6402
EX n/a   **NM** $20   **MIP** $35

□ **Snake Eyes**, 1982, Hasbro, Commando, Model No. 6404
EX n/a   **NM** $40   **MIP** $85

□ **Stalker**, 1982, Hasbro, Ranger, Model No. 6401
EX n/a   **NM** $25   **MIP** $35

□ **V.A.M.P.**, 1982, Hasbro, Multi-Purpose Attack Vehicle with Clutch, Model No. 6050
EX n/a   **NM** $20   **MIP** $35

□ **Zap**, 1982, Hasbro, Bazooka Soldier, Model No. 6405
EX n/a   **NM** $20   **MIP** $35

SERIES #2, COBRA

□ **Cobra**, 1983, Hasbro, Reissue, Model No. 6423
EX n/a   **NM** $25   **MIP** $50

□ **Cobra Commander**, 1983, Hasbro, Reissue, Model No. 6425
EX n/a   **NM** $25   **MIP** $50

□ **Cobra Glider**, 1983, Hasbro, Attack Glider with Viper, Model No. 6097
EX n/a   **NM** $35   **MIP** $75

□ **Cobra Officer**, 1983, Hasbro, Reissue, Model No. 6424
EX n/a   **NM** $25   **MIP** $50

□ **Destro**, 1983, Hasbro, Enemy Weapons Supplier, Model No. 6427
EX n/a   **NM** $25   **MIP** $50

□ **F.A.N.G.**, 1983, Hasbro, Fully Armed Negator Gyro Copter, Model No. 6077
EX n/a   **NM** $10   **MIP** $20

□ **H.I.S.S.**, 1983, Hasbro, High Speed Sentry Tank with H.I.S.S., Model No. 6051
EX n/a   **NM** $25   **MIP** $50

□ **Headquarters Missile-Command Center**, 1983, Hasbro, with three figures, Model No. 6200
EX n/a   **NM** $65   **MIP** $125

□ **Major Bludd**, 1983, Hasbro, Model No. 6426
EX n/a   **NM** $15   **MIP** $30

□ **S.N.A.K.E.**, 1983, Hasbro, One-Man Battle Armor, Model No. 6083
EX n/a   **NM** $10   **MIP** $25

SERIES #2, GI JOE

□ **A.P.C.**, 1983, Hasbro, Amphibious Personnel Carrier, Model No. 6093
EX n/a   **NM** $15   **MIP** $25

□ **Airborne**, 1983, Hasbro, Helicopter Assault Trooper, Model No. 6411
EX n/a   **NM** $15   **MIP** $35

□ **Battle Gear Accessory Pack #1**, 1983, Hasbro, Model No. 6088
EX n/a   **NM** $10   **MIP** $20

□ **Breaker**, 1983, Hasbro, Reissue, Model No. 6403
EX n/a   **NM** $15   **MIP** $30

□ **Doc**, 1983, Hasbro, Medic, Model No. 6415
EX n/a   **NM** $10   **MIP** $20

□ **Dragon Fly XH-1**, 1983, Hasbro, Assault Copter with Wild Bill, Model No. 4025
EX n/a   **NM** $25   **MIP** $50

□ **Duke**, 1983, Hasbro, mail order; Master Sergeant
EX n/a   **NM** $10   **MIP** $25

□ **Falcon**, 1983, Hasbro, Attack Glider with Grunt, Model No. 6097
EX n/a   **NM** $30   **MIP** $75

□ **Flash**, 1983, Hasbro, Reissue, Model No. 6406
EX n/a   **NM** $15   **MIP** $30

□ **Grunt**, 1983, Hasbro, Reissue, Model No. 6409
EX n/a   **NM** $15   **MIP** $30

□ **Gung-Ho**, 1983, Hasbro, Marine, Model No. 6414
EX n/a   **NM** $12   **MIP** $30

□ **Headquarters Command Center**, 1983, Hasbro, Model No. 6020
EX n/a   **NM** $40   **MIP** $85

□ **Jump**, 1983, Hasbro, Jet Pack and Platform with Grand Slam, Model No. 6065
EX n/a   **NM** $25   **MIP** $50

□ **Pac/Rats Flamethrower**, 1983, Hasbro, Remote Control Weapon, Model No. 6086-1
EX n/a   **NM** $10   **MIP** $25

□ **Pac/Rats Machine Gun**, 1983, Hasbro, Remote Control Weapon, Model No. 6086-2
EX n/a   **NM** $10   **MIP** $25

□ **Pac/Rats Missile Launcher**, 1983, Hasbro, Remote Control Weapon, Model No. 6086-3
EX n/a   **NM** $10   **MIP** $25

□ **Polar Battle Bear**, 1983, Hasbro, Sky Mobile, Model No. 6072
EX n/a   **NM** $15   **MIP** $25

□ **Rock 'n Roll**, 1983, Hasbro, Reissue, Model No. 6408
EX n/a   **NM** $15   **MIP** $30

□ **Scarlett**, 1983, Hasbro, Model No. 6407
EX n/a   **NM** $30   **MIP** $80

□ **Short Fuse**, 1983, Hasbro, Reissue, Model No. 6402
EX n/a   **NM** $15   **MIP** $30

□ **Sky Striker XP-14F**, 1983, Hasbro, F-14 Jet and Parachute with Ace, Model No. 6010
EX n/a   **NM** $35   **MIP** $75

□ **Snake Eyes**, 1983, Hasbro, Reissue, Model No. 6404
EX n/a   **NM** $40   **MIP** $80

□ **Snow Job**, 1983, Hasbro, Arctic Trooper, Model No. 6412
EX n/a   **NM** $15   **MIP** $25

□ **Stalker**, 1983, Hasbro, Reissue, Model No. 6401
EX n/a   **NM** $25   **MIP** $45

□ **Torpedo**, 1983, Hasbro, Navy S.E.A.L., Model No. 6413
EX n/a   **NM** $12   **MIP** $30

□ **Tripwire**, 1983, Hasbro, Mine Detector, Model No. 6410
EX n/a   **NM** $15   **MIP** $30

G. I. JOE

Whirlwind, 1983, Hasbro, Twin Battle Gun, Model No. 6074
EX n/a   **NM** $10   **MIP** $25

Wolverine, 1983, Hasbro, Armored Missile Vehicle with Cover Girl, Model No. 6048
EX n/a   **NM** $25   **MIP** $50

Zap, 1983, Hasbro, Reissue, Model No. 6405
EX n/a   **NM** $15   **MIP** $30

SERIES #3, COBRA

A.S.P., 1983, Hasbro, Assault System Pod, Model No. 6070
EX n/a   **NM** $15   **MIP** $30

Baroness, 1983-84, Hasbro, Intelligence Officer, Model No. 6428
EX n/a   **NM** $40   **MIP** $85

C.L.A.W., 1983, Hasbro, Cobra Covert Light Aerial Weapons, Model No. 6081-1
EX n/a   **NM** $15   **MIP** $30

Cobra Commander, 1983-84, Hasbro, mail order; Enemy Leader with Hood, Model No. 6425
EX n/a   **NM** $10   **MIP** $20

Fire Fly, 1983-84, Hasbro, Saboteur, Model No. 6432
EX n/a   **NM** $40   **MIP** $85

Rattler, 1983-84, Hasbro, Ground Attack Jet with Wild Weasel, Model No. 6027
EX n/a   **NM** $25   **MIP** $50

S.N.A.K.E., 1983, Hasbro, One-Man Armored Suit (white), Model No. 6081-2
EX n/a   **NM** $10   **MIP** $25

Scrap Iron, 1983-84, Hasbro, Anti-Armor Specialist, Model No. 6431
EX n/a   **NM** $15   **MIP** $30

Stinger, 1983-84, Hasbro, Night Attack Jeep with Cobra Officer, Model No. 6055
EX n/a   **NM** $20   **MIP** $40

Storm Shadow, 1983-84, Hasbro, Ninja, Model No. 6429
EX n/a   **NM** $35   **MIP** $75

Swamp Skier, 1983-84, Hasbro, Chameleon Vehicle with Zartan, Model No. 6064
EX n/a   **NM** $30   **MIP** $55

Water Moccasin, 1983-84, Hasbro, Swamp Boat with Copperhead, Model No. 6058
EX n/a   **NM** $20   **MIP** $40

SERIES #3, GI JOE

Attack Cannon (FLAK), 1983, Hasbro, Model No. 7444-3
EX n/a   **NM** $5   **MIP** $10

Attack Vehicle (VAMP), 1983, Hasbro, Model No. 7444-1
EX n/a   **NM** $15   **MIP** $35

Battle Gear Accessory Pack #2, 1983, Hasbro, Model No. 6092
EX n/a   **NM** $10   **MIP** $20

(ToyShop File Photo)

Battle Tank (MOBAT), 1983, Hasbro, Motorized, includes action figure, Model No. 7444-4
EX n/a   **NM** $15   **MIP** $25

Bivouac, 1983, Hasbro, Battle Station, Model No. 6125-1
EX n/a   **NM** $10   **MIP** $25

Blow Torch, 1983-84, Hasbro, Flamethrower, Model No. 6421
EX n/a   **NM** $10   **MIP** $20

Duke, 1983-84, Hasbro, First Sergeant, Model No. 6422
EX n/a   **NM** $15   **MIP** $25

(ToyShop File Photo)

Heavy Artillery Laser (HAL), 1983, Hasbro, swivel base, includes figure, Model No. 7444-2
EX n/a   **NM** $10   **MIP** $15

(ToyShop File Photo)

Killer W.H.A.L.E., 1983, Hasbro, Armored Hovercraft with Cutter, Model No. 6005
EX n/a   **NM** $30   **MIP** $65

Machine Gun Defense Unit, 1983, Hasbro, Model No. 6129-2
EX n/a   **NM** $10   **MIP** $20

Manta, 1983, Hasbro, mail order; Marine Assault Nautical Air Driven Transport
EX n/a   **NM** $10   **MIP** $20

Missile Defense Unit, 1983, Hasbro, Model No. 6129-1
EX n/a   **NM** $10   **MIP** $15

Mobile Missile System (MMS), 1983, Hasbro, Model No. 7444-5
EX n/a   **NM** $10   **MIP** $15

Mortar Defense Unit, 1983, Hasbro, Model No. 6129-3
EX n/a   **NM** $10   **MIP** $15

Mountain Howitzer, 1983, Hasbro, Model No. 6125-3
EX n/a   **NM** $10   **MIP** $15

Mutt, 1983-84, Hasbro, Dog Handler with Dog, Model No. 6416
EX n/a   **NM** $10   **MIP** $25

Parachute, 1983, Hasbro, mail order; Parachute Pack with Working Parachute
EX n/a   **NM** $5   **MIP** $10

RAM, HAL & VAMP, 1983, Hasbro, three-piece, die-cast set, Model No. 74450
EX n/a   **NM** $10   **MIP** $20

Rapid-Fire Motorcycle (RAM), 1983, Hasbro, Model No. 7444-6
EX n/a   **NM** $15   **MIP** $20

Recondo, 1983-84, Hasbro, Jungle Trooper, Model No. 6420
EX n/a   **NM** $15   **MIP** $25

Rip-Cord, 1983-84, Hasbro, H.A.L.O. Jumper, Model No. 6418
EX n/a   **NM** $10   **MIP** $25

Road Block, 1983-84, Hasbro, Heavy Machine Gunner, Model No. 6419
EX n/a   **NM** $15   **MIP** $25

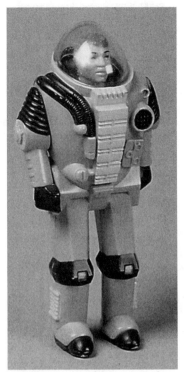

(KP Photo, Karen O'Brien collection)

❑ **S.H.A.R.C.**, 1983, Hasbro, Submersible High-Speed Attack & Recon Craft with Deep Six figure (shown), Model No. 6049
EX n/a　　NM $25　　MIP $50

❑ **Sky Hawk,** 1983, Hasbro, V.T.O.L. Jet, Model No. 6079
EX n/a　　NM $10　　MIP $15

❑ **Slugger,** 1983, Hasbro, Self-Propelled Cannon with Thunder, Model No. 6056
EX n/a　　NM $15　　MIP $25

❑ **Spirit,** 1983-84, Hasbro, Tracker with Eagle, Model No. 6417
EX n/a　　NM $15　　MIP $25

❑ **Vamp Jeep with H.A.L.,** 1983, Hasbro, Attack Vehicle with Heavy Artillery Laser Cannon, Model No. 6680
EX n/a　　NM $20　　MIP $35

❑ **Vamp Mark II,** 1983, Hasbro, Desert Jeep with Clutch, Model No. 6055
EX n/a　　NM $25　　MIP $40

❑ **Watchtower,** 1983, Hasbro, Model No. 6125-2
EX n/a　　NM $10　　MIP $15

SERIES #4, COBRA

❑ **Buzzer,** 1984, Hasbro, Mercenary, Model No. 6433
EX n/a　　NM $10　　MIP $25

❑ **Cobra Bunker,** 1984, Hasbro, Model No. 6125
EX n/a　　NM $5　　MIP $15

❑ **Crimson Guard,** 1984, Hasbro, Elite Trooper, Model No. 6450
EX n/a　　NM $15　　MIP $30

❑ **Eel,** 1984, Hasbro, Frogman, Model No. 6448
EX n/a　　NM $15　　MIP $30

❑ **Ferret,** 1984, Hasbro, All-Terrain Vehicle, Model No. 6069
EX n/a　　NM $10　　MIP $15

❑ **Flight Pod,** 1984, Hasbro, One-Man Bubble Pod, Model No. 6081
EX n/a　　NM $5　　MIP $15

❑ **Moray,** 1984, Hasbro, Hydrofoil with Lamprey, Model No. 6024
EX n/a　　NM $15　　MIP $25

❑ **Motorized Crimson Attack Tank,** 1984, Hasbro, MOBAT Tank, Model No. 6687
EX n/a　　NM $30　　MIP $60

❑ **Night Landing,** 1984, Hasbro, Mini Battlefield Vehicles Assortment, Model No. 6085
EX n/a　　NM $5　　MIP $15

❑ **Rifle Range,** 1984, Hasbro, Model No. 6129
EX n/a　　NM $5　　MIP $15

❑ **Ripper,** 1984, Hasbro, Mercenary, Model No. 6434
EX n/a　　NM $15　　MIP $30

❑ **Sentry and Missile System,** 1984, Hasbro, Sears, with H.I.S.S. Tank, Cobra Commander, Officer and Soldier, Model No. 6686
EX n/a　　NM $75　　MIP $150

❑ **Snow Serpent,** 1984, Hasbro, Polar Assault Trooper, Model No. 6449
EX n/a　　NM $15　　MIP $30

❑ **Tele-Viper,** 1984, Hasbro, Communications Trooper, Model No. 6447
EX n/a　　NM $15　　MIP $30

❑ **Tomax,** 1984, Hasbro, Crimson Guard Commander with Xamot, Model No. 6063
EX n/a　　NM $30　　MIP $65

❑ **Torch,** 1984, Hasbro, Mercenary, Model No. 6435
EX n/a　　NM $15　　MIP $30

SERIES #4, GI JOE

❑ **A.W.E. Striker,** 1984, Hasbro, All-Weather Environment Jeep with Crankcase, Model No. 6053
EX n/a　　NM $15　　MIP $25

❑ **Air Defense,** 1984, Hasbro, Model No. 6125-2
EX n/a　　NM $10　　MIP $15

❑ **Air Tight,** 1984, Hasbro, Hostile Environment Trooper, Model No. 6439
EX n/a　　NM $20　　MIP $40

❑ **Alpine,** 1984, Hasbro, Mountain Trooper, Model No. 6443
EX n/a　　NM $15　　MIP $25

❑ **Ammo Dump,** 1984, Hasbro, Model No. 6129-1
EX n/a　　NM $10　　MIP $15

❑ **Armadillo,** 1984, Hasbro, One-Man Mini-Tank, Model No. 6078
EX n/a　　NM $10　　MIP $15

❑ **Barbecue,** 1984, Hasbro, Fire Fighter, Model No. 6445
EX n/a　　NM $10　　MIP $25

❑ **Battle Gear Accessory Pack #3,** 1984, Hasbro, Model No. 6092
EX n/a　　NM $5　　MIP $10

❑ **Bazooka,** 1984, Hasbro, Missile Specialist, Model No. 6438
EX n/a　　NM $10　　MIP $25

❑ **Bomb Disposal,** 1984, Hasbro, Model No. 6085-2
EX n/a　　NM $10　　MIP $15

❑ **Bridge Layer,** 1984, Hasbro, Bridge Laying Trank with Toll Booth, Model No. 6023
EX n/a　　NM $15　　MIP $25

❑ **Check Point,** 1984, Hasbro, Model No. 6125-1
EX n/a　　NM $10　　MIP $15

❑ **Dusty,** 1984, Hasbro, Desert Trooper, Model No. 6442
EX n/a　　NM $10　　MIP $25

❑ **Flint,** 1984, Hasbro, Warrant Officer, Model No. 6436
EX n/a　　NM $10　　MIP $25

❑ **Footloose,** 1984, Hasbro, Infantry Trooper, Model No. 6444
EX n/a　　NM $10　　MIP $25

❑ **Forward Observer,** 1984, Hasbro, Model No. 6129-2
EX n/a　　NM $10　　MIP $15

❑ **Lady Jaye,** 1984, Hasbro, Covert Operations Officer, Model No. 6440
EX n/a　　NM $25　　MIP $50

❑ **Mauler,** 1984, Hasbro, Motorized Tank with Heavy Metal, Model No. 6015
EX n/a　　NM $15　　MIP $25

❑ **Quick Kick,** 1984, Hasbro, Silent Weapons Martial Artist, Model No. 6441
EX n/a　　NM $20　　MIP $40

❑ **Shipwreck,** 1984, Hasbro, Sailor and Parrot, Model No. 6446
EX n/a　　NM $15　　MIP $25

❑ **Silver Mirage,** 1984, Hasbro, Motorcycle with Sidecar, Model No. 6076
EX n/a　　NM $10　　MIP $15

❑ **Snake Eyes,** 1984, Hasbro, Commando and Wolf, Model No. 6437
EX n/a　　NM $30　　MIP $60

❑ **Snowcat,** 1984, Hasbro, Snow Half-Track Vehicle with Frost-Bite, Model No. 6057
EX n/a　　NM $15　　MIP $25

(ToyShop File Photo)

G.I. JOE

□ **Tactical Battle Platform,** 1984, Hasbro, With crane, heli-pad, swivel guns and missile launcher, Model No. 6021
EX n/a   **NM** $10   **MIP** $20

□ **Tripwire,** 1984, Hasbro, Mine Detector, Model No. 6102
EX n/a   **NM** $20   **MIP** $35

□ **U.S.S. Flagg,** 1984, Hasbro, Aircraft Carrier with Admiral Keel Haul, Model No. 6001
EX n/a   **NM** $125   **MIP** $250

□ **Weapon Transport,** 1984, Hasbro, Battlefield, Model No. 6085-1
EX n/a   **NM** $10   **MIP** $15

SERIES #5, COBRA

□ **Air Assault,** 1985, Hasbro, Air Vehicle
EX n/a   **NM** $10   **MIP** $15

□ **Air Chariot,** 1985, Hasbro, Vehicle with Serpentor "Cobra Emperor", Model No. 6062
EX n/a   **NM** $15   **MIP** $20

□ **B.A.T.,** 1985, Hasbro, Battle Android Trooper, Model No. 6456
EX n/a   **NM** $10   **MIP** $15

□ **Battle Gear Accessory Pack #4,** 1985, Hasbro, Model No. 6096
EX n/a   **NM** $5   **MIP** $10

□ **Dr. Mindbender,** 1985, Hasbro, Master of Mind Control, Model No. 6461
EX n/a   **NM** $10   **MIP** $15

□ **Ground Assault,** 1985, Hasbro, Land Vehicle
EX n/a   **NM** $10   **MIP** $20

□ **Hydro Sled,** 1985, Hasbro, Model No. 6099-2
EX n/a   **NM** $10   **MIP** $15

□ **Jet Pack,** 1985, Hasbro, One-Man Jet Set, Model No. 6099j-1
EX n/a   **NM** $10   **MIP** $15

□ **Monkey Wrench,** 1985, Hasbro, Mercenary, Model No. 6460
EX n/a   **NM** $10   **MIP** $15

□ **Night Raven S-3P,** 1985, Hasbro, Surveillance Jet with Drone Pod and Strato Viper, Model No. 6014
EX n/a   **NM** $20   **MIP** $35

□ **Stun,** 1985, Hasbro, Split Attack Vehicle with Motor Viper, Model No. 6041
EX n/a   **NM** $10   **MIP** $20

□ **Surveillance Port Playset,** 1985, Hasbro, Model No. 6130
EX n/a   **NM** $15   **MIP** $30

□ **Swamp Fire,** 1985, Hasbro, Air/Swamp Transforming Vehicle with Color-Change, Model No. 6068
EX n/a   **NM** $10   **MIP** $15

□ **Terror Drome,** 1985, Hasbro, Armored Headquarters with Fireball Jet and A.V.A.C., Model No. 6003
EX n/a   **NM** $75   **MIP** $150

□ **Thunder Machine,** 1985, Hasbro, Compilation Vehicle of Spare Parts with Thrasher, Model No. 6042
EX n/a   **NM** $10   **MIP** $20

□ **Viper,** 1985, Hasbro, Infantry Trooper, Model No. 6473
EX n/a   **NM** $10   **MIP** $15

□ **Zandar,** 1985, Hasbro, Zartan's Brother Mercenary, Model No. 6457
EX n/a   **NM** $10   **MIP** $15

□ **Zarana,** 1985, Hasbro, Zartan's Sister Mercenary, Model No. 6472
EX n/a   **NM** $10   **MIP** $15

□ **Zarana,** 1985, Hasbro, Reissue with earrings, Model No. 6472
EX n/a   **NM** $30   **MIP** $65

SERIES #5, GI JOE

□ **Beach Head,** 1985, Hasbro, Ranger, Model No. 6463
EX n/a   **NM** $10   **MIP** $15

□ **Conquest X-30,** 1985, Hasbro, Super-Sonic Jet with Slip Stream, Model No. 6031
EX n/a   **NM** $15   **MIP** $30

□ **Devil Fish,** 1985, Hasbro, High-Speed Attack Boat, Model No. 6066
EX n/a   **NM** $10   **MIP** $15

□ **Dial Tone,** 1985, Hasbro, Communications Expert, Model No. 6471
EX n/a   **NM** $10   **MIP** $15

□ **H.A.V.O.C.,** 1985, Hasbro, Heavy Artillery Vehicle Ordinance Carrier with Cross-Country, Model No. 6030
EX n/a   **NM** $10   **MIP** $15

□ **Hawk,** 1985, Hasbro, Commander, Model No. 6468
EX n/a   **NM** $10   **MIP** $15

□ **Ice Berg,** 1985, Hasbro, Snow Trooper, Model No. 6466
EX n/a   **NM** $10   **MIP** $15

□ **L.V.C. Recon Sled,** 1985, Hasbro, Low-Crawl Vehicle Cycle, Model No. 6067
EX n/a   **NM** $10   **MIP** $15

□ **Leather Neck,** 1985, Hasbro, Marine Gunner, Model No. 6458
EX n/a   **NM** $10   **MIP** $15

□ **Life Line,** 1985, Hasbro, Rescue Trooper, Model No. 6465
EX n/a   **NM** $10   **MIP** $15

□ **Low-Light,** 1985, Hasbro, Night Spotter, Model No. 6459
EX n/a   **NM** $10   **MIP** $15

□ **Main Frame,** 1985, Hasbro, Computer Specialist, Model No. 6462
EX n/a   **NM** $10   **MIP** $15

□ **Outpost Defender Mini Playset,** 1985, Hasbro, Model No. 6130
EX n/a   **NM** $5   **MIP** $10

□ **Road Block,** 1985, Hasbro, Heavy Machine Gunner, Model No. 6467
EX n/a   **NM** $10   **MIP** $15

□ **Sci-Fi,** 1985, Hasbro, Laser Trooper, Model No. 6469
EX n/a   **NM** $10   **MIP** $15

□ **Sgt. Slaughter,** 1985, Hasbro, Mail order; Drill Instructor
EX n/a   **NM** $10   **MIP** $15

□ **Tomahawk,** 1985, Hasbro, Troop Transit Helicopter with Lift Ticket, Model No. 6022
EX n/a   **NM** $15   **MIP** $30

□ **Triple T,** 1985, Hasbro, One-Man Tank with Sgt. Slaughter, Model No. 6061
EX n/a   **NM** $10   **MIP** $25

□ **Wet-Suit,** 1985, Hasbro, Navy S.E.A.L., Model No. 6470
EX n/a   **NM** $15   **MIP** $20

SERIES #6, COBRA

□ **Big Boa,** 1986-87, Hasbro, Troop Trainer, Model No. 6484
EX n/a   **NM** $5   **MIP** $10

□ **Buzz Boar,** 1986-87, Hasbro, Underground Attack Vehicle, Model No. 6087-3
EX n/a   **NM** $5   **MIP** $15

□ **Cobra Commander,** 1986-87, Hasbro, Cobra Leader with Battle Armor, Model No. 6474
EX n/a   **NM** $10   **MIP** $15

□ **Cobra-La Team,** 1986-87, Hasbro, Three-figure set, Model No. 6154
EX n/a   **NM** $20   **MIP** $40

□ **Crocmaster,** 1986-87, Hasbro, Reptile Trainer, Model No. 6487
EX n/a   **NM** $10   **MIP** $15

□ **Crystal Ball,** 1986-87, Hasbro, Hypnotist, Model No. 6479
EX n/a   **NM** $5   **MIP** $10

□ **Dreadnok Air Skiff,** 1986-87, Hasbro, Mini-set with Zanzibar, Model No. 6070
EX n/a   **NM** $10   **MIP** $20

□ **Dreadnok Cycle,** 1986-87, Hasbro, Compilation Cycle with Gunner Station, Model No. 6171
EX n/a   **NM** $5   **MIP** $10

□ **Earth Borer,** 1986, Hasbro, Model No. 6133-3
EX n/a   **NM** $5   **MIP** $10

□ **Maggot,** 1986-87, Hasbro, three-in-one tank vehicle with W.O.R.M.S. driver, Model No. 6029
EX n/a   **NM** $10   **MIP** $15

□ **Mamba,** 1986-87, Hasbro, Attack Copter with removable pods with Gyro-Viper, Model No. 6026
EX n/a   **NM** $10   **MIP** $15

□ **Mountain Climber,** 1986, Hasbro, Model No. 6133-7
EX n/a   **NM** $5   **MIP** $10

□ **Pogo,** 1986-87, Hasbro, Ballistic Battle Ball, Model No. 6170
EX n/a   **NM** $5   **MIP** $10

❑ **Pom-Pom Gun Pack,** 1986, Hasbro, Model No. 6133-8
EX n/a   **NM** $5   **MIP** $10

❑ **Raptor,** 1986-87, Hasbro, Falconer, Model No. 6485
EX n/a   **NM** $5   **MIP** $10

❑ **Rope Crosser,** 1986, Hasbro, Model No. 6133-5
EX n/a   **NM** $5   **MIP** $10

❑ **Sea Ray,** 1986-87, Hasbro, Combination Submarine/Jet with Sea Slug, Model No. 6040
EX n/a   **NM** $10   **MIP** $20

❑ **Techno-Viper,** 1986-87, Hasbro, Battlefield Technician, Model No. 6490
EX n/a   **NM** $5   **MIP** $10

❑ **Wolf,** 1986-87, Hasbro, Arctic Terrain Vehicle with Ice Viper, Model No. 6039
EX n/a   **NM** $10   **MIP** $20

SERIES #6, GI JOE

❑ **Antiaircraft Gun,** 1986, Hasbro, Model No. 6133-1
EX n/a   **NM** $5   **MIP** $10

❑ **Battle Gear Accessory Pack #5,** 1986, Hasbro, Model No. 6677
EX n/a   **NM** $5   **MIP** $10

❑ **Chuckles,** 1986-87, Hasbro, Undercover M.P., Model No. 6482
EX n/a   **NM** $3   **MIP** $5

❑ **Coastal Defender,** 1986-87, Hasbro, Mini-Vehicle with accessories, Model No. 6087-2
EX n/a   **NM** $5   **MIP** $10

❑ **Crazy Legs,** 1986-87, Hasbro, Air Assault Trooper, Model No. 6475
EX n/a   **NM** $10   **MIP** $15

❑ **Crossfire-Alfa,** 1986-87, Hasbro, Radio Control Vehicle with Rumbler, Model No. 6004-1
EX n/a   **NM** $25   **MIP** $50

❑ **Crossfire-Delta,** 1986-87, Hasbro, Radio Control Vehicle with Rumbler, Model No. 6004-2
EX n/a   **NM** $25   **MIP** $50

❑ **Defiant Space Shuttle Complex,** 1986-87, Hasbro, Space shuttle, space station, crawler, Model No. 6002
EX n/a   **NM** $75   **MIP** $350

❑ **Falcon,** 1986-87, Hasbro, Green Beret, Model No. 6476
EX n/a   **NM** $10   **MIP** $15

❑ **Fast Draw,** 1986-87, Hasbro, Mobile Missile Specialist, Model No. 6488
EX n/a   **NM** $10   **MIP** $15

❑ **Gung-Ho,** 1986-87, Hasbro, Marine in Dress Blues, Model No. 6486
EX n/a   **NM** $10   **MIP** $15

❑ **Helicopter Pack,** 1986, Hasbro, Model No. 6133-2
EX n/a   **NM** $5   **MIP** $10

❑ **Jinx,** 1986-87, Hasbro, Ninja Intelligence Officer, Model No. 6480
EX n/a   **NM** $10   **MIP** $15

❑ **Law & Order,** 1986-87, Hasbro, M.P. with Dog, Model No. 6478
EX n/a   **NM** $10   **MIP** $15

❑ **Mobile Command Center Play Set,** 1986, Hasbro, Model No. 6006
EX n/a   **NM** $25   **MIP** $50

❑ **Outback,** 1986-87, Hasbro, Survivalist, Model No. 6483
EX n/a   **NM** $5   **MIP** $10

❑ **Persuader,** 1986-87, Hasbro, Laser Tank with Backstop, Model No. 6038
EX n/a   **NM** $10   **MIP** $15

❑ **Psych-Out,** 1986-87, Hasbro, Deceptive Warfare Trooper, Model No. 6477
EX n/a   **NM** $5   **MIP** $10

❑ **Radar Station,** 1986-87, Hasbro, Model No. 6133-3
EX n/a   **NM** $5   **MIP** $10

❑ **Road Toad,** 1986-87, Hasbro, Tow Vehicle with accessories, Model No. 6087-1
EX n/a   **NM** $5   **MIP** $10

❑ **Rope Walker,** 1986, Hasbro, Model No. 6133-4
EX n/a   **NM** $5   **MIP** $10

❑ **S.L.A.M.,** 1986, Hasbro, Strategic Long-Range Artillery Machine, Model No. 6172
EX n/a   **NM** $10   **MIP** $15

❑ **Secret Mission: Brazil,** 1986-87, Hasbro, Toys R Us set with four figures
EX n/a   **NM** $75   **MIP** $150

❑ **Sgt. Slaughter Set,** 1986-87, Hasbro, Three-figure set, Model No. 6153
EX n/a   **NM** $10   **MIP** $25

❑ **Sneak Peek,** 1986-87, Hasbro, Advanced Recon Trooper, Model No. 6491
EX n/a   **NM** $10   **MIP** $15

❑ **Tunnel Rat,** 1986-87, Hasbro, Underground Explosive Expert, Model No. 6481
EX n/a   **NM** $5   **MIP** $10

❑ **Vehicle Gear Accessory Pack #1,** 1986, Hasbro, Model No. 6098
EX n/a   **NM** $5   **MIP** $10

COLLECTOR EDITIONS (1990S TO PRESENT)

12" HALL OF FAME FIGURES

❑ **Ace, Fighter Pilot,** 1993, Hasbro, Model No. 6837
EX n/a   **NM** $10   **MIP** $15

❑ **Cobra Commander, Cobra Leader,** 1992, Hasbro, Model No. 6827
EX n/a   **NM** $15   **MIP** $20

❑ **Destro, Weapons Manufacturer,** 1993, Hasbro, Model No. 6839
EX n/a   **NM** $10   **MIP** $15

❑ **Duke, Combat Camo,** 1994, Hasbro, Model No. 6044
EX n/a   **NM** $10   **MIP** $12

❑ **Duke, Master Sergeant,** 1991, Hasbro, Model No. 6019
EX n/a   **NM** $15   **MIP** $30

❑ **Duke, Master Sergeant,** 1992, Hasbro, Model No. 6826
EX n/a   **NM** $15   **MIP** $25

❑ **Flint, Battle Bazooka,** 1994, Hasbro, Model No. 6127
EX n/a   **NM** $10   **MIP** $12

❑ **Grunt, Infantry Squad Leader,** 1993, Hasbro, Model No. 6111
EX n/a   **NM** $10   **MIP** $20

❑ **Gung-Ho, Dress Marine,** 1993, Hasbro, Model No. 6849
EX n/a   **NM** $10   **MIP** $20

❑ **Heavy Duty, Heavy Ordinance Specialist,** 1993, Hasbro, Model No. 6114
EX n/a   **NM** $10   **MIP** $20

❑ **Major Budd, Battle-Pack,** 1994, Hasbro, Model No. 6159
EX n/a   **NM** $10   **MIP** $15

❑ **Rapid Fire, Commando,** 1993, Hasbro, Model No. 6924
EX n/a   **NM** $20   **MIP** $50

❑ **Roadblock, Combat Camo,** 1994, Hasbro, Model No. 6049
EX n/a   **NM** $10   **MIP** $12

❑ **Rock n Roll, Gatlin' Blastin',** 1994, Hasbro, Model No. 6128
EX n/a   **NM** $10   **MIP** $25

❑ **Rock 'n Roll, Heavy Weapons Gunner,** 1993, Hasbro, Model No. 6128
EX n/a   **NM** $10   **MIP** $20

❑ **Snake Eyes, Commando,** 1992, Hasbro, Model No. 6828
EX n/a   **NM** $15   **MIP** $30

❑ **Snake-Eyes, Karate Choppin',** 1994, Hasbro, Model No. 6089
EX n/a   **NM** $10   **MIP** $25

❑ **Stalker, Ranger,** 1992, Hasbro, Model No. 6829
EX n/a   **NM** $15   **MIP** $30

❑ **Storm Shadow, Ninja,** 1993, Hasbro, Model No. 6848
EX n/a   **NM** $10   **MIP** $20

❑ **Talking Duke, Talking Battle Commander,** 1993, Hasbro, Model No. 6117
EX n/a   **NM** $15   **MIP** $35

30TH SALUTE SERIES

❑ **30th Salute Black Action Soldier,** 1994, Hasbro, Model No. 81271
EX n/a   **NM** $55   **MIP** $100

❑ **35th Anniversary Gift Set,** 1999, Hasbro, Then and Now, 1964 figure, 1999 figure, set of two, 1999
EX n/a   **NM** $25   **MIP** $50
(Hasbro)

❑ **Action Marine,** 1994, Hasbro, Model No. 81047
EX n/a   **NM** $45   **MIP** $60
(Hasbro)

G. I. JOE

Action Pilot, 1994, Hasbro, Model No. 81046
EX n/a **NM** $50 **MIP** $75
(Hasbro)

Action Sailor, 1994, Hasbro, Model No. 81048
EX n/a **NM** $60 **MIP** $80

Action Soldier, 1994, Hasbro, Model No. 81045
EX n/a **NM** $25 **MIP** $50

Green Beret Lt. Joseph Colton, 1994, Hasbro, mail order
EX n/a **NM** $75 **MIP** $125

ACTION ASSORTMENT

Adventures of G.I. Joe: Peril of the Raging River, 1999, Hasbro
EX n/a **NM** $7 **MIP** $12

Delta Force, 1999, Hasbro
EX n/a **NM** $7 **MIP** $12

Salute to the Millennium Marine, 1999, Hasbro
EX n/a **NM** $7 **MIP** $12

ALPHA ASSORTMENT

Battle of the Bulge, 2000, Hasbro
EX n/a **NM** n/a **MIP** n/a

Demolitions Expert, 2000, Hasbro
EX n/a **NM** n/a **MIP** n/a

Navy Seal, 2000, Hasbro
EX n/a **NM** $7 **MIP** $12

WWII Pacific Marine, 2000, Hasbro
EX n/a **NM** n/a **MIP** n/a

ARMED FORCES ASSORTMENT

Army National Guard, 1998, Hasbro
EX n/a **NM** $10 **MIP** $12

U.S. Air Force Crew Chief, 1998, Hasbro
EX n/a **NM** $10 **MIP** $12

U.S. Marine Corps Korean Soldier, 1998, Hasbro
EX n/a **NM** $10 **MIP** $12

U.S. Marine Corps Recruit, 1998, Hasbro
EX n/a **NM** $10 **MIP** $12

U.S. Navy Serviceman, 1998, Hasbro
EX n/a **NM** $10 **MIP** $12

ARMED FORCES SERVICE COLLECTION

Police Officer, 1999, Hasbro
EX n/a **NM** $5 **MIP** $8

U.S. Army Infantry Desert Soldier, 1999, Hasbro
EX n/a **NM** $5 **MIP** $8

U.S. Army Pacific Forces, 1999, Hasbro
EX n/a **NM** $5 **MIP** $8

U.S. Army Vietnam Soldiers, 1998, Hasbro
EX n/a **NM** $5 **MIP** $8

U.S. Navy SEAL, 1999, Hasbro
EX n/a **NM** $5 **MIP** $8

USAF Fighter Pilot: Korean War, 1999, Hasbro
EX n/a **NM** $5 **MIP** $8

Vietnam Marine, 1999, Hasbro
EX n/a **NM** $5 **MIP** $10

ASTRONAUT ASSORTMENT

(Hasbro Photo)

Mercury Astronaut, 1997, Hasbro, In spacesuit and helmet
EX n/a **NM** $15 **MIP** $12

(Hasbro Photo)

Space Shuttle Astronaut, 1997, Hasbro, In orange spacesuit
EX n/a **NM** $15 **MIP** $12

BRAVO ASSORTMENT

Vietnam Combat Engineer, 2000, Hasbro
EX n/a **NM** n/a **MIP** n/a

Vietnam Jungle Recon Soldier, 2000, Hasbro
EX n/a **NM** $5 **MIP** $10

CORE FIGURE ASSORTMENT

Adventures of G.I. Joe: Save the Tiger, 1999, Hasbro
EX n/a **NM** $5 **MIP** $10

G.I. Joe: Challenge at Hawk River, 1999, Hasbro
EX n/a **NM** $5 **MIP** $10

U.S. Army Nurse: Vietnam, 1999, Hasbro
EX n/a **NM** $5 **MIP** $10

U.S. Coast Guard Boarding Party, 1999, Hasbro
EX n/a **NM** $5 **MIP** $10

DELTA ASSORTMENT

Navajo Code Talker, 2000, Hasbro
EX n/a **NM** $7 **MIP** $15

U.S. Marine Dog Unit, 2000, Hasbro
EX n/a **NM** $7 **MIP** $12

ECHO ASSORTMENT

John F. Kennedy, 2000, Hasbro
EX n/a **NM** $8 **MIP** $15

Vietnam Wall, 2000, Hasbro
EX n/a **NM** n/a **MIP** n/a

WWI Doughboy, 2000, Hasbro
EX n/a **NM** $7 **MIP** $12

WWII U.S. Army Airborne Normandy, 2000, Hasbro
EX n/a **NM** $7 **MIP** $15

FOREIGN ASSORTMENT

Japanese Zero pilot, 2000, Hasbro
EX n/a **NM** n/a **MIP** n/a

Red Infantry Pilot, 2000, Hasbro
EX n/a **NM** n/a **MIP** n/a

FOURTH OF JULY EDITION

(Hasbro Photo)

❏ **D-Day Salute,** 1997, Hasbro, With M-1 rifle, pack and camo-net helmet
EX n/a   **NM** $7   **MIP** $12

GREATEST HEROES

❏ **Buzz Aldrin,** 1999, Hasbro
EX n/a   **NM** $10   **MIP** $20

(KP Photo)

❏ **Lt. Colonel Theodore Roosevelt,** 1999, Hasbro, In Spanish-American War uniform, dark blue shirt, tan coat and pants. Includes American flag, pistol and other accessories
EX n/a   **NM** $10   **MIP** $20

❏ **Ted Williams,** 1999, Hasbro
EX n/a   **NM** $10   **MIP** $20

❏ **WWII Flame Thrower Soldier,** 1999, Hasbro
EX n/a   **NM** $7   **MIP** $12

HISTORICAL COMMANDERS ASSORTMENT

❏ **Colin Powell,** 1998, Hasbro
EX n/a   **NM** $10   **MIP** $20

❏ **Dwight Eisenhower,** 1997, Hasbro
EX n/a   **NM** $7   **MIP** $12

❏ **General Patton,** 1997, Hasbro
EX n/a   **NM** $7   **MIP** $12

❏ **Omar Bradley,** 1998, Hasbro
EX n/a   **NM** $7   **MIP** $12

HOLIDAY SALUTE

(Hasbro)

❏ **George Washington,** 1998, Hasbro
EX n/a   **NM** $7   **MIP** $12

HOLLYWOOD HEROES

❏ **Bob Hope,** 1998, Hasbro
EX n/a   **NM** $15   **MIP** $25

MILITARY SPORTS ASSORTMENT

❏ **Army Football,** 1998, Hasbro
EX n/a   **NM** $5   **MIP** $8

❏ **Navy Football,** 1998, Hasbro
EX n/a   **NM** $5   **MIP** $8

MODERN FORCES ASSORTMENT

❏ **82nd Airborne Division, female,** 1998, Hasbro
EX n/a   **NM** $5   **MIP** $8

❏ **Australian O.D.F.,** 1996, Hasbro
EX n/a   **NM** $5   **MIP** $8

❏ **Battle of the Bulge, Toys R Us Exlcusive,** 1996, Hasbro
EX n/a   **NM** $8   **MIP** $12

❏ **Belgium Para Commando,** 1997, Hasbro
EX n/a   **NM** $8   **MIP** $12

(Hasbro Photo)

❏ **British SAS,** 1996, Hasbro, Limited edition, with rifle, helmet and goggles
EX n/a   **NM** $8   **MIP** $15

❏ **Dress Marine, Toys R Us Exclusive,** 1996, Hasbro
EX n/a   **NM** $8   **MIP** $15

❏ **French Foreign Legion Legionnaire,** 1997, Hasbro
EX n/a   **NM** $8   **MIP** $12

❏ **U.S. Airborne Ranger HALO Parachutist,** 1996, Hasbro
EX n/a   **NM** $7   **MIP** $15

❏ **U.S. Army Coldweather Soldier,** 1998, Hasbro
EX n/a   **NM** $8   **MIP** $12

❏ **U.S. Army Drill Sergeant,** 1997, Hasbro
EX n/a   **NM** $5   **MIP** $10

❏ **U.S. Army Helicopter Pilot, female,** 1997, Hasbro
EX n/a   **NM** $10   **MIP** $20

(Hasbro Photo)

❏ **U.S. Army Infantry Soldier,** 1996, Hasbro, Limited edition, with goggles, machine and desert-pattern uniform
EX n/a   **NM** $8   **MIP** $12

❏ **U.S. Army M-1 Tank Commander,** 1997, Hasbro
EX n/a   **NM** $8   **MIP** $12

❏ **U.S. Marine Corp Force Recon,** 1998, Hasbro
EX n/a   **NM** $7   **MIP** $10

(Hasbro Photo)

❏ **U.S. Marine Corps Sniper,** 1996, Hasbro, Camouflaged rifle with scope, camo netting
EX n/a **NM** $10 **MIP** $20

❏ **U.S. Navy Blue Angel,** 1998, Hasbro
EX n/a **NM** $8 **MIP** $12

❏ **U.S. Navy Flight Deck Fuel Handler,** 1997, Hasbro
EX n/a **NM** $7 **MIP** $12

PEARL HARBOR COLLECTION

❏ **Army Defense Diorama Set,** Hasbro
EX n/a **NM** n/a **MIP** n/a

❏ **Battleship Row Defender,** 2000, Hasbro
EX n/a **NM** n/a **MIP** n/a

❏ **Diamond Head Lookout Invasion Alert,** 2000, Hasbro
EX n/a **NM** n/a **MIP** n/a

❏ **Hickam Field Army Defender,** 2000, Hasbro
EX n/a **NM** n/a **MIP** n/a

❏ **Vicker's Machine Gun,** 2000, Hasbro
EX n/a **NM** n/a **MIP** n/a

❏ **Wheeler Field Army Air Corp,** 2000, Hasbro
EX n/a **NM** n/a **MIP** n/a

WWII COMMEMORATIVE FIGURES, TARGET EXCLUSIVE

(Hasbro)

❏ **Action Marine,** 1995, Hasbro, In camo uniform with cap, rifle, canteen, grenades and pack
EX n/a **NM** $8 **MIP** $15

(Hasbro)

❏ **Action Pilot,** 1995, Hasbro, Khaki uniform, leather jacket and helmet, goggles, bayonet, .45 pistol, dog tags
EX n/a **NM** $5 **MIP** $10

(Hasbro)

❏ **Action Sailor,** 1995, Hasbro, Blue uniform, Shore Patrol armband, M-1 rifle, duffle bag
EX n/a **NM** $8 **MIP** $15
(Hasbro)

❏ **Action Soldier,** 1995, Hasbro
EX n/a **NM** $8 **MIP** $10

WWII FORCES ASSORTMENT

❏ **442nd Americans of Japanese Descent Combat Soldiers,** 1998, Hasbro
EX n/a **NM** $8 **MIP** $15

❏ **Congressional Medal of Honor, Platoon Sgt. Mitchell Paige,** 1998, Hasbro
EX n/a **NM** $8 **MIP** $12

❏ **Congressional Medal of Honor, Sgt. Francis S. Currey,** 1997, Hasbro
EX n/a **NM** $10 **MIP** $20

❏ **Tuskegee B-25 Bomber Pilot, African American,** 1997, Hasbro
EX n/a **NM** $8 **MIP** $10

❏ **Tuskegee Fighter Pilot, African American,** 1997, Hasbro
EX n/a **NM** $8 **MIP** $10

❏ **U.S. Air Force B-17 Bomber Crewman,** 1998, Hasbro
EX n/a **NM** $8 **MIP** $10

❏ **U.S. Navy PT-Boat Commander,** 1998, Hasbro
EX n/a **NM** $8 **MIP** $10

VINTAGE (1960-70s)

ACTION GIRL SERIES

❏ **G.I. Nurse,** 1967, Hasbro, Red Cross hat and arm band, white dress, stockings, shoes, crutches, medic bag, stethescope, plasma bottle, bandages and splints., Model No. 8060
EX n/a **NM** $1750 **MIP** $2000

ACTION MARINE SERIES

❏ **Action Marine,** 1964, Hasbro, fatigues, green cap, boots, dog tags, insignias and manual, Model No. 7700
EX n/a   NM $125   MIP $145

❏ **Beachhead Assault Field Pack Set,** 1964, Hasbro, M-1 rifle, bayonet, entrenching shovel and cover, canteen with cover, belt, mess kit with cover, field pack, flamethrower, first aid pouch, tent, pegs and poles, tent camo and camo, Model No. 7713
EX n/a   NM $100   MIP $175

(ToyShop File Photo)

❏ **Beachhead Assault Tent Set,** 1964, Hasbro, tent, flamethrower, pistol belt, first-aid pouch, mess kit with utensils and manual, Model No. 7711
EX n/a   NM $100   MIP $200

❏ **Beachhead Fatigue Pants,** 1964, Hasbro, Model No. 7715
EX n/a   NM $15   MIP $30

❏ **Beachhead Fatigue Shirt,** 1964, Hasbro, Model No. 7714
EX n/a   NM $20   MIP $30
(GICAT: Hasbro's 1965 Catalog)

❏ **Beachhead Field Pack,** 1964, Hasbro, cartridge belt, rifle, grenades, field pack, entrenching tool, canteen and manual, Model No. 7712
EX n/a   NM $40   MIP $65

❏ **Beachhead Flamethrower Set,** 1964, Hasbro, Model No. 7718
EX n/a   NM $15   MIP $30

❏ **Beachhead Flamethrower Set,** 1967, Hasbro, reissue, Model No. 7718
EX n/a   NM $15   MIP $30

❏ **Beachhead Mess Kit Set,** 1964, Hasbro, Model No. 7716
EX n/a   NM $25   MIP $40

❏ **Beachhead Rifle Set,** 1964, Hasbro, bayonet, cartridge belt, hand grenades and M-1 rifle, Model No. 7717
EX n/a   NM $30   MIP $50

❏ **Beachhead Rifle Set,** 1967, Hasbro, reissue, Model No. 7717
EX n/a   NM $30   MIP $50

❏ **Communications Field Radio/Telephone Set,** 1967, Hasbro, reissue, Model No. 7703
EX n/a   NM $35   MIP $60

❏ **Communications Field Set,** 1964, Hasbro, Model No. 7703
EX n/a   NM $35   MIP $50

❏ **Communications Flag Set,** 1964, Hasbro, flags for Army, Navy, Air Corps, Marines and United States, Model No. 7704
EX n/a   NM $200   MIP $250

❏ **Communications Poncho,** 1964, Hasbro, Model No. 7702
EX n/a   NM $35   MIP $50

❏ **Communications Post and Poncho Set,** 1964, Hasbro, field radio and telephone, wire roll, carbine, binoculars, map, case, manual, poncho, Model No. 7701
EX n/a   NM $125   MIP $175

❏ **Dress Parade Set,** 1964, Hasbro, Marine jacket, trousers, pistol belt, shoes, hat, M-1 rifle and manual, Model No. 7710
EX n/a   NM $125   MIP $225

❏ **Dress Parade Set,** 1968, Hasbro, reissue, Model No. 7710
EX n/a   NM $125   MIP $225

❏ **Jungle Fighter Set,** 1967, Hasbro, bush hat, jacket with emblems, pants, flamethrower, field telephone, knife and sheath, pistol belt, pistol, holster, canteen with cover and knuckle knife, Model No. 7732
EX n/a   NM $450   MIP $700

❏ **Jungle Fighter Set,** 1968, Hasbro, reissue, Model No. 7732
EX n/a   NM $450   MIP $700

❏ **Marine Automatic M-60 Machine Gun Set,** 1967, Hasbro, Model No. 7726
EX n/a   NM $35   MIP $75

❏ **Marine Basics Set,** 1966, Hasbro, Model No. 7722
EX n/a   NM $55   MIP $85

❏ **Marine Bunk Bed Set,** 1966, Hasbro, Model No. 7723
EX n/a   NM $55   MIP $80

❏ **Marine Bunk Bed Set,** 1967, Hasbro, reissue, Model No. 7723
EX n/a   NM $55   MIP $80

(ToyShop File Photo)

❏ **Marine Demolition Set,** 1966, Hasbro, mine detector and harness, land mine, Model No. 7730
EX n/a   NM $50   MIP $100

❏ **Marine Demolition Set,** 1968, Hasbro, reissue, Model No. 7730
EX n/a   NM $50   MIP $100

❏ **Marine First Aid Set,** 1964, Hasbro, first-aid pouch, arm band and helmet, Model No. 7721
EX n/a   NM $45   MIP $85

❏ **Marine First Aid Set,** 1967, Hasbro, reissue, Model No. 7721
EX n/a   NM $45   MIP $85

❏ **Marine Medic Series,** 1967, Hasbro, Red Cross helmet, flag and arm bands, crutch, bandages, splints, first aid pouch, stethoscope, plasma bottle, stretcher, medic bag, belt with ammo pouches, Model No. 90711
EX n/a   NM $325   MIP $425

❏ **Marine Medic Set,** 1965, Hasbro, with crutch, etc., Model No. 7720
EX n/a   NM $25   MIP $40

❏ **Marine Medic Set,** 1967, Hasbro, reissue, Model No. 7720
EX n/a   NM $25   MIP $40
(GICAT: Hasbro's 1965 Catalog)

❏ **Marine Medic Set with stretcher,** 1964, Hasbro, first-aid shoulder pouch, stretcher, bandages, arm bands, plasma bottle, stethoscope, Red Cross flag, and manual, Model No. 7719
EX n/a   NM $175   MIP $300

❏ **Marine Mortar Set,** 1967, Hasbro, Model No. 7725
EX n/a   NM $60   MIP $80

❏ **Marine Weapons Rack Set,** 1967, Hasbro, Model No. 7727
EX n/a   NM $75   MIP $145

❏ **Paratrooper Camouflage Set,** 1964, Hasbro, netting and foliage, Model No. 7708
EX n/a   NM $20   MIP $35

❏ **Paratrooper Helmet Set,** 1964, Hasbro, Model No. 7707
EX n/a   NM $20   MIP $40

❏ **Paratrooper Parachute Pack,** 1964, Hasbro, Model No. 7709
EX n/a   NM $30   MIP $80

❏ **Paratrooper Small Arms Set,** 1967, Hasbro, reissue, Model No. 7706
EX n/a   NM $30   MIP $75

❏ **Talking Action Marine,** 1967, Hasbro, Model No. 7790
EX n/a   NM $175   MIP $200

❏ **Talking Adventure Pack and Tent Set,** 1968, Hasbro, Model No. 90711
EX n/a   NM $275   MIP $325

❏ **Talking Adventure Pack with Field Pack Equipment,** 1968, Hasbro, Model No. 90712
EX n/a   NM $275   MIP $325

❏ **Tank Commander Set,** 1967, Hasbro, includes faux leather jacket, helmet and visor, insignia, radio with tripod,

G. I. JOE

machine gun, ammo box, Model
No. 7731
EX n/a   **NM** $325   **MIP** $500

❑ **Tank Commander Set,** 1968, Hasbro,
reissue, Model No. 7731
EX n/a   **NM** $325   **MIP** $500

ACTION PILOT SERIES

❑ **Action Pilot,** 1964, Hasbro, orange
jumpsuit, blue cap, black boots, dog
tags, insignias, manual, catalog and
club application, Model No. 7800
EX n/a   **NM** $130   **MIP** $165

❑ **Air Academy Cadet Set,** 1967, Hasbro,
deluxe set with figure, dress jacket,
shoes, and pants, garrison cap, saber
and scabbard, white M-1 rifle, chest
sash and belt sash, Model No. 7822
EX n/a   **NM** $225   **MIP** $450

❑ **Air Academy Cadet Set,** 1968, Hasbro,
reissue, Model No. 7822
EX n/a   **NM** $225   **MIP** $450

❑ **Air Force Basics Set,** 1966, Hasbro,
Model No. 7814
EX n/a   **NM** $30   **MIP** $55

❑ **Air Force Basics Set,** 1967, Hasbro,
reissue, Model No. 7814
EX n/a   **NM** $30   **MIP** $55

❑ **Air Force Mae West Air Vest & Equip-
ment Set,** 1967, Hasbro, Model
No. 7816
EX n/a   **NM** $85   **MIP** $125

❑ **Air Force Police Set,** 1965, Hasbro,
Model No. 7813
EX n/a   **NM** $70   **MIP** $150

❑ **Air Force Police Set,** 1967, Hasbro,
reissue, Model No. 7813
EX n/a   **NM** $70   **MIP** $150

❑ **Air Force Security Set,** 1967, Hasbro,
Air Security radio and helmet, cartridge
belt, pistol and holster, Model No. 7815
EX n/a   **NM** $275   **MIP** $350

❑ **Air/Sea Rescue Set,** 1967, Hasbro,
includes black air tanks, rescue ring,
buoy, depth gauge, face mask, fins,
orange scuba outfit, Model No. 7825
EX n/a   **NM** $325   **MIP** $550

❑ **Air/Sea Rescue Set,** 1968, Hasbro,
reissue, Model No. 7825
EX n/a   **NM** $325   **MIP** $550

❑ **Astronaut Set,** 1967, Hasbro, helmet
with visor, foil space suit, booties,
gloves, space camera, propellant gun,
tether cord, oxygen chest pack, silver
boots, white jumpsuit and cloth cap,
Model No. 7824
EX n/a   **NM** $100   **MIP** $200

❑ **Astronaut Set,** 1968, Hasbro, reissue,
Model No. 7824
EX n/a   **NM** $100   **MIP** $200

❑ **Communications Set,** 1964, Hasbro,
Model No. 7812
EX n/a   **NM** $55   **MIP** $100

(ToyShop File Photo)

❑ **Crash Crew Fire Truck Set,** 1967, Hasbro, Includes blue truck and fireproof
silver suit. Truck has working firehose,
Model No. 8040
EX n/a   **NM** $950   **MIP** $1700

❑ **Crash Crew Set,** 1966, Hasbro, fire
proof jacket, hood, pants and gloves, silver boots, belt, flashlight, axe, pliers, fire
extinguisher, stretcher, strap cutter,
Model No. 7820
EX n/a   **NM** $125   **MIP** $250

❑ **Dress Uniform Jacket Set,** 1964, Hasbro, Model No. 7804
EX n/a   **NM** $40   **MIP** $65

❑ **Dress Uniform Pants,** 1964, Hasbro,
Model No. 7805
EX n/a   **NM** $20   **MIP** $35

❑ **Dress Uniform Set,** 1964, Hasbro, Air
Force jacket, trousers, shirt, tie, cap and
manual, Model No. 7803
EX n/a   **NM** $225   **MIP** $450

❑ **Dress Uniform Shirt & Equipment Set,**
1964, Hasbro, Model No. 7806
EX n/a   **NM** $25   **MIP** $40

❑ **Fighter Pilot Set,** 1967, Hasbro, work-
ing parachute and pack, gold helmet,
Mae West vest, green pants, flash light,
orange jump suit, black boots, Model
No. 7823
EX n/a   **NM** $400   **MIP** $650

❑ **Fighter Pilot Set,** 1968, Hasbro, reissue, Model No. 7823
EX n/a   **NM** $400   **MIP** $650

❑ **Official Space Capsule Set,** 1966, Hasbro, space capsule, record, space suit,
cloth space boots, space gloves, helmet
with visor, Model No. 8020
EX n/a   **NM** $175   **MIP** $225

(ToyShop File Photo)

❑ **Official Space Capsule Set with flota-
tion,** 1966, Hasbro, Sears Exclusive
with collar, life raft and oars, Model
No. 5979
EX n/a   **NM** $200   **MIP** $325

❑ **Scramble Communications Set,** 1965,
Hasbro, poncho, field telephone and
radio, map with case, binoculars and
wire roll, Model No. 7812
EX n/a   **NM** $35   **MIP** $75

❑ **Scramble Communications Set,** 1967,
Hasbro, reissue, Model No. 7812
EX n/a   **NM** $35   **MIP** $75

❑ **Scramble Crash Helmet,** 1964, Hasbro, helmet, face mask, hose, tinted
visor, Model No. 7810
EX n/a   **NM** $65   **MIP** $90

❑ **Scramble Crash Helmet,** 1967, Hasbro, reissue, Model No. 7810
EX n/a   **NM** $65   **MIP** $90

❑ **Scramble Flight Suit,** 1964, Hasbro,
gray flight suit, Model No. 7808
EX n/a   **NM** $50   **MIP** $300

❑ **Scramble Flight Suit,** 1967, Hasbro,
Model No. 7808
EX n/a   **NM** $50   **MIP** $75

❑ **Scramble Parachute Set,** 1964, Hasbro, Model No. 7811
EX n/a   **NM** $20   **MIP** $40

❑ **Scramble Parachute Set,** 1967, Hasbro, reissue, Model No. 7809
EX n/a   **NM** $20   **MIP** $40

❑ **Scramble Set,** 1964, Hasbro, deluxe
set, gray flight suit, orange air vest,
white crash helmet, pistol belt with .45
pistol, holster, clipboard, flare gun and
parachute with insert, Model No. 7807
EX n/a   **NM** $125   **MIP** $225

❑ **Survival Life Raft Set,** 1964, Hasbro,
raft with oar and sea anchor, Model
No. 7802
EX n/a   **NM** $45   **MIP** $90

❑ **Survival Life Raft Set,** 1964, Hasbro,
raft with oar, flare gun, knife, air vest,

first-aid kit, sea anchor and manual, Model No. 7801
EX n/a   **NM** $75   **MIP** $125

❏ **Talking Action Pilot,** 1967, Hasbro, Model No. 7890
EX n/a   **NM** $190   **MIP** $245

ACTION SAILOR SERIES

❏ **Action Sailor,** 1964, Hasbro, white cap, denim shirt and pants, boots, dog tags, navy manual and insignias, Model No. 7600
EX n/a   **NM** $125   **MIP** $225

❏ **Annapolis Cadet,** 1967, Hasbro, garrison cap, dress jacket, pants, shoes, sword, scabbard, belt and white M-1 rifle, Model No. 7624
EX n/a   **NM** $275   **MIP** $375

❏ **Annapolis Cadet,** 1968, Hasbro, reissue, Model No. 7624
EX n/a   **NM** $275   **MIP** $375

❏ **Breeches Buoy,** 1967, Hasbro, yellow jacket and pants, chair and pulley, flare gun, blinker light, Model No. 7625
EX n/a   **NM** $325   **MIP** $425

❏ **Breeches Buoy,** 1968, Hasbro, reissue, Model No. 7625
EX n/a   **NM** $325   **MIP** $425

❏ **Deep Freeze,** 1967, Hasbro, white boots, fur parka, pants, snow shoes, ice axe, snow sled with rope and flare gun, Model No. 7623
EX n/a   **NM** $250   **MIP** $375

❏ **Deep Freeze,** 1968, Hasbro, reissue, Model No. 7623
EX n/a   **NM** $250   **MIP** $375

❏ **Deep Sea Diver Set,** 1965, Hasbro, underwater uniform, helmet, upper and lower plate, sledge hammer, buoy with rope, gloves, compass, hoses, lead boots and weight belt, Model No. 7620
EX n/a   **NM** $325   **MIP** $425

❏ **Deep Sea Diver Set,** 1968, Hasbro, reissue, Model No. 7620
EX n/a   **NM** $325   **MIP** $425

❏ **Frogman Scuba Bottoms,** 1964, Hasbro, Model No. 7604
EX n/a   **NM** $20   **MIP** $35

❏ **Frogman Scuba Tank Set,** 1964, Hasbro, Model No. 7606
EX n/a   **NM** $25   **MIP** $40

❏ **Frogman Scuba Top Set,** 1964, Hasbro, Model No. 7603
EX n/a   **NM** $25   **MIP** $45

❏ **Frogman Underwater Demolition Set,** 1964, Hasbro, headpiece, face mask, swim fins, rubber suit, scuba tank, depth gauge, knife, dynamite and manual, Model No. 7602
EX n/a   **NM** $175   **MIP** $250

❏ **Landing Signal Officer,** 1966, Hasbro, jumpsuit, signal paddles, goggles, cloth head gear, headphones, clipboard (complete), binoculars and flare gun., Model No. 7621
EX n/a   **NM** $225   **MIP** $350

❏ **Navy Attack Helmet Set,** 1964, shirt and pants, boots, yellow life vest, blue helmet, flare gun binoculars, signal flags, Model No. 7610
EX n/a   **NM** $35   **MIP** $75

❏ **Navy Attack Life Jacket,** 1964, Hasbro, Model No. 7611
EX n/a   **NM** $20   **MIP** $45

❏ **Navy Attack Set,** 1964, Hasbro, life jacket, field glasses, blinker light, signal flags, manual, Model No. 7607
EX n/a   **NM** $60   **MIP** $125

❏ **Navy Attack Work Pants Set,** 1964, Hasbro, Model No. 7609
EX n/a   **NM** $25   **MIP** $40

❏ **Navy Attack Work Shirt Set,** 1964, Hasbro, Model No. 7608
EX n/a   **NM** $25   **MIP** $40

❏ **Navy Basics Set,** 1966, Hasbro, Model No. 7628
EX n/a   **NM** $25   **MIP** $55

❏ **Navy Dress Parade Rifle Set,** 1965, Hasbro, Model No. 7619
EX n/a   **NM** $35   **MIP** $65

❏ **Navy Dress Parade Set,** 1964, Hasbro, billy club, cartridge belt, bayonet and white dress rifle, Model No. 7619
EX n/a   **NM** $45   **MIP** $80

❏ **Navy L.S.O. Equipment Set,** 1966, Hasbro, helmet, headphones, signal paddles, flare gun, Model No. 7626
EX n/a   **NM** $40   **MIP** $80

❏ **Navy Life Ring Set,** 1966, Hasbro, U.S.N. life ring, helmet sticker, Model No. 7627
EX n/a   **NM** $25   **MIP** $45

❏ **Navy Machine Gun Set,** 1965, Hasbro, MG and ammo box, Model No. 7618
EX n/a   **NM** $40   **MIP** $80

❏ **Navy Scuba Set,** 1968, Hasbro, Adventure Pack, Model No. 7643-83
EX n/a   **NM** $300   **MIP** $450

❏ **Official Sea Sled and Frogman Set,** 1966, Hasbro, without cave, Model No. 8050
EX n/a   **NM** $150   **MIP** $300

(ToyShop File Photo)

❏ **Official Sea Sled and Frogman Set,** 1966, Hasbro, Sears, with figure and underwater cave, orange scuba suit, fins, mask, tanks, sea sled in orange and black, Model No. 5979
EX n/a   **NM** $175   **MIP** $325

❏ **Sea Rescue Set,** 1964, Hasbro, life raft, oar, anchor, flare gun, first-aid kit, knife, scabbard, manual, Model No. 7601
EX n/a   **NM** $95   **MIP** $135

(ToyShop File Photo)

❏ **Sea Rescue Set,** 1966, Hasbro, reissued with life preserver, Model No. 7622
EX n/a   **NM** $95   **MIP** $135

❏ **Shore Patrol,** 1964, Hasbro, dress shirt, tie and pants, helmet, white belt, .45 and holster, billy club, boots, arm band, sea bag, Model No. 7612
EX n/a   **NM** $500   **MIP** $1000

❏ **Shore Patrol,** 1967, Hasbro, reissued with radio and helmet and shoes, Model No. 7612
EX n/a   **NM** $1000   **MIP** $2000

❏ **Shore Patrol Dress Jumper Set,** 1964, Hasbro, Model No. 7613
EX n/a   **NM** $75   **MIP** $125

❏ **Shore Patrol Dress Pant Set,** 1964, Hasbro, Model No. 7614
EX n/a   **NM** $40   **MIP** $75

❏ **Shore Patrol Helmet and Small Arms Set,** 1964, Hasbro, white belt, billy stick, white helmet, .45 pistol, Model No. 7616
EX n/a   **NM** $40   **MIP** $75

❏ **Shore Patrol Sea Bag Set,** 1964, Hasbro, Model No. 7615
EX n/a   **NM** $25   **MIP** $50

❏ **Talking Action Sailor,** 1967, Hasbro, Model No. 7690
EX n/a   **NM** $200   **MIP** $330

❏ **Talking Landing Signal Officer Set,** 1968, Hasbro, Talking Adventure Pack, Model No. 90621
EX n/a   **NM** $325   **MIP** $350

❏ **Talking Shore Patrol Set,** 1968, Hasbro, Talking Adventure Pack, Model No. 90612
EX n/a   **NM** $200   **MIP** $450

ACTION SOLDIER SERIES

(ToyShop File Photo)

❏ **Action Soldier,** 1964, Hasbro, fatigue cap, shirt, pants, boots, dog tags, army manual and insignias, helmet, belt with pouches, M-1 rifle, Model No. 7500
EX n/a   **NM** $100   **MIP** $175

❏ **Adventure Pack with fourteen pieces,** 1968, Hasbro, Adventure Pack Footlocker, Model No. 8008.83
EX n/a   **NM** $75   **MIP** $125

❏ **Adventure Pack with sixteen items,** 1968, Hasbro, Adventure Pack Footlocker, Model No. 8007.83
EX n/a   **NM** $75   **MIP** $125

❏ **Adventure Pack with twelve items,** 1968, Hasbro, Adventure Pack Footlocker, Model No. 8006.83
EX n/a   **NM** $75   **MIP** $125

❏ **Adventure Pack with twelve items,** 1968, Hasbro, Adventure Pack Footlocker, Model No. 8005.83
EX n/a   **NM** $75   **MIP** $125

❏ **Adventure Pack, Army Bivouac Series,** 1968, Hasbro, Model No. 7549-83
EX n/a   **NM** $225   **MIP** $450

❏ **Air Police Equipment,** 1964, Hasbro, gray field phone, carbine, white helmet and bayonet, Model No. 7813
EX n/a   **NM** $40   **MIP** $95

❏ **Amphibious Duck,** 1967, Irwin, 26" long, Model No. 5693
EX n/a   **NM** $175   **MIP** $375

❏ **Armored Car,** 1967, Irwin, friction powered, 20" long, Model No. 5397
EX n/a   **NM** $150   **MIP** $300
(GICAT: Hasbro's 1965 Catalog)

❏ **Basic Footlocker,** 1964, Hasbro, wood tray with cardboard wrapper, Model No. 8000
EX n/a   **NM** $35   **MIP** $75
(GICAT: Hasbro's 1965 Catalog)

❏ **Bivouac Deluxe Pup Tent Set,** 1964, Hasbro, M-1 rifle and bayonet, shovel and cover, canteen and cover, mess kit, cartridge belt, machine gun, tent, pegs, poles, camoflage, sleeping bag, netting, ammo box, Model No. 7513
EX n/a   **NM** $115   **MIP** $225

❏ **Bivouac Machine Gun Set,** 1964, Hasbro, machine gun set and ammo box, Model No. 7514
EX n/a   **NM** $25   **MIP** $40

❏ **Bivouac Machine Gun Set,** 1967, Hasbro, reissue, Model No. 7514
EX n/a   **NM** $25   **MIP** $40

❏ **Bivouac Sleeping Bag,** 1964, Hasbro, zippered bag, Model No. 7515
EX n/a   **NM** $20   **MIP** $30
(GICAT: Hasbro's 1965 Catalog)

❏ **Bivouac Sleeping Bag Set,** 1964, Hasbro, mess kit, canteen, bayonet, cartridge belt, M-1 rifle, manual, Model No. 7512
EX n/a   **NM** $25   **MIP** $30

❏ **Black Action Soldier,** 1965, Hasbro, Model No. 7900
EX n/a   **NM** $450   **MIP** $800

❏ **Canadian Mountie Set,** 1967, Hasbro, Sears Exclusive, Model No. 5904
EX n/a   **NM** $850   **MIP** $1500

(ToyShop File Photo)

❏ **Combat Camouflaged Netting Set,** 1964, Hasbro, foliage and posts, Model No. 7511
EX n/a   **NM** $25   **MIP** $40

❏ **Combat Construction Set,** 1967, Hasbro, orange safety helmet, work gloves, jack hammer, Model No. 7572
EX n/a   **NM** $325   **MIP** $400

❏ **Combat Demolition Set,** 1967, Hasbro, Model No. 7573
EX n/a   **NM** $65   **MIP** $100

❏ **Combat Engineer Set,** 1967, Hasbro, pick, shovel, detonator, dynamite, tripod and transit with grease gun, Model No. 7571
EX n/a   **NM** $125   **MIP** $175

❏ **Combat Fatigue Pants Set,** 1964, Hasbro, Model No. 7504
EX n/a   **NM** $15   **MIP** $25

❏ **Combat Fatigue Shirt Set,** 1964, Hasbro, Model No. 7503
EX n/a   **NM** $20   **MIP** $30

❏ **Combat Field Jacket,** 1964, Hasbro, Model No. 7505
EX n/a   **NM** $45   **MIP** $65
(GICAT: Hasbro's 1965 Catalog)

❏ **Combat Field Jacket Set,** 1964, Hasbro, jacket, bayonet, cartridge belt, hand grenades, M-1 rifle and manual, Model No. 7501
EX n/a   **NM** $65   **MIP** $100

❏ **Combat Field Pack & Entrenching Tool,** 1964, Hasbro, Model No. 7506
EX n/a   **NM** $25   **MIP** $45
(GICAT: Hasbro's 1965 Catalog)

❏ **Combat Field Pack Deluxe Set,** 1964, Hasbro, field jacket, pack, entrenching shovel with cover, mess kit, first-aid pouch, canteen with cover, Model No. 7502
EX n/a   **NM** $75   **MIP** $125

❏ **Combat Helmet Set,** 1964, Hasbro, with netting and foliage leaves, Model No. 7507
EX n/a   **NM** $20   **MIP** $35

❏ **Combat Mess Kit,** 1964, Hasbro, plate, fork, knife, spoon, canteen, etc., Model No. 7509
EX n/a   **NM** $20   **MIP** $45

❏ **Combat Rifle Set,** 1967, Hasbro, bayonet, M-1 rifle, belt and grenades, Model No. 7510
EX n/a   **NM** $55   **MIP** $100

❏ **Combat Sandbags Set,** 1964, Hasbro, three bags per set, Model No. 7508
EX n/a   **NM** $10   **MIP** $40

❏ **Command Post Field Radio and Telephone Set,** 1964, Hasbro, field radio, telephone with wire roll and map, Model No. 7520
EX n/a   **NM** $35   **MIP** $70

❏ **Command Post Field Radio and Telephone Set,** 1967, Hasbro, reissue, Model No. 7520
EX n/a   **NM** $35   **MIP** $70

❏ **Command Post Poncho,** 1964, Hasbro, on card, Model No. 7519
EX n/a   **NM** $30   **MIP** $45

❏ **Command Post Poncho Set,** 1964, Hasbro, poncho, field radio and telephone, wire roll, pistol, belt and holster, map and case and manual, Model No. 7517
EX n/a   **NM** $85   **MIP** $125

❏ **Command Post Small Arms Set,** 1964, Hasbro, holster and .45 pistol, belt, grenades, Model No. 7518
EX n/a   **NM** $30   **MIP** $60

❏ **Desert Patrol Attack Jeep Set,** 1967, Hasbro, Desert Fighter figure, jeep with steering wheel, spare tire, tan tripod, gun and gun mount and ring, black antenna, tan jacket and shorts, socks, goggles, Model No. 8030
EX n/a   **NM** $400   **MIP** $1250

❑ **Dress Parade Adventure Pack,** 1968, Hasbro, Adventure Pack with thirty-seven pieces, Model No. 8009.83
EX n/a   NM $750   MIP $1250

❑ **Forward Observer Set,** 1966, Hasbro, Sears Exclusive, Model No. 5969
EX n/a   NM $200   MIP $375

❑ **Green Beret,** 1966, Hasbro, field radio, bazooka rocket, bazooka, green beret, jacket, pants, M-16 rifle, grenades, camo scarf, belt pistol and holster, Model No. 7536
EX n/a   NM $275   MIP $400

❑ **Green Beret and Small Arms Set,** 1966, Hasbro, Model No. 7533
EX n/a   NM $85   MIP $110

❑ **Green Beret and Small Arms Set,** 1967, Hasbro, reissue, Model No. 7533
EX n/a   NM $85   MIP $100

(ToyShop File Photo)

❑ **Green Beret Machine Gun Outpost Set,** 1966, Hasbro, Sears Exclusive with two figures and equipment, Model No. 5978
EX n/a   NM $225   MIP $450

❑ **Heavy Weapons Set,** 1967, Hasbro, mortar launcher and shells, M-60 machine gun, grenades, flak jacket, shirt and pants, Model No. 7538
EX n/a   NM $175   MIP $325

❑ **Heavy Weapons Set,** 1968, Hasbro, reissue, Model No. 7538
EX n/a   NM $175   MIP $325

❑ **Helicopter,** 1967, Hasbro, Irwin, friction powered, 28" long, Model No. 5395
EX n/a   NM $150   MIP $300

❑ **Jet Fighter Plane,** 1967, Irwin, friction powered, 30" long, Model No. 5396
EX n/a   NM $225   MIP $475

❑ **Machine Gun Emplacement Set,** 1965, Hasbro, Sears Exclusive, Model No. 7531
EX n/a   NM $150   MIP $275

❑ **Military Police Duffle Bag Set,** 1964, Hasbro, Model No. 7523
EX n/a   NM $25   MIP $40

❑ **Military Police Helmet and Small Arms Set,** 1964, Hasbro, Model No. 7526
EX n/a   NM $35   MIP $75

❑ **Military Police Helmet and Small Arms Set,** 1967, Hasbro, reissue, Model No. 7526
EX n/a   NM $35   MIP $75

❑ **Military Police Ike Jacket,** 1964, Hasbro, jacket with red scarf and arm band, Model No. 7524
EX n/a   NM $40   MIP $60

(ToyShop File Photo)

❑ **Military Police Ike Pants,** 1964, Hasbro, matches Ike jacket, Model No. 7525
EX n/a   NM $20   MIP $30

❑ **Military Police Uniform Set,** 1964, Hasbro, includes Ike jacket and pants, scarf, boots, helmet, belt with ammo pouches, .45 pistol and holster, billy club, armband, duffle bag, Model No. 7521
EX n/a   NM $450   MIP $1650

❑ **Military Police Uniform Set,** 1967, Hasbro, includes green or tan uniform, black and gold MP Helmet, billy club, belt, pistol and holster, MP armband and red tunic, Model No. 7539
EX n/a   NM $450   MIP $1650

❑ **Military Police Uniform Set,** 1968, Hasbro, reissue, Model No. 7539
EX n/a   NM $450   MIP $900

❑ **Military Staff Car,** 1967, Irwin, friction powered, 24" long, Model No. 5652
EX n/a   NM $200   MIP $400

❑ **Motorcycle and Sidecar,** 1967, Irwin, 14" long, khaki, with decals, Model No. 5651
EX n/a   NM $75   MIP $150

(ToyShop File Photo)

❑ **Mountain Troops Set,** 1964, Hasbro, snow shoes, ice axe, ropes, grenades, camoflage pack, web belt, manual, Model No. 7530
EX n/a   NM $90   MIP $175

❑ **Official Combat Jeep Set,** 1965, trailer, steering wheel, spare tire, windshield, cannon, search light, shell, flag, guard rails, tripod, tailgate and hood, without Moto-Rev Sound, Model No. 7000
EX n/a   NM $200   MIP $375

❑ **Official Jeep Combat Set,** 1965, With Moto-Rev sound, Model No. 7000
EX n/a   NM $225   MIP $400

❑ **Personnel Carrier/Mine Sweeper,** 1967, Irwin, 26" long, Model No. 5694
EX n/a   NM $300   MIP $350

❑ **Sabotage Set,** 1967, Hasbro, dingy and oar, blinker light, detonator with strap, TNT, wool stocking cap, gas mask, binoculars, green radio and .45 pistol and holster, Model No. 7516
EX n/a   NM $125   MIP $250

❑ **Sabotage Set,** 1968, Hasbro, reissued in photo box, Model No. 7516
EX n/a   NM $125   MIP $250
(GICAT: Hasbro's 1965 Catalog)

❑ **Ski Patrol Deluxe Set,** 1964, Hasbro, White parka, boots, goggles, mittens, skis, poles and manual, Model No. 7531
EX n/a   NM $170   MIP $350

❑ **Ski Patrol Helmet and Small Arms Set,** 1965, Hasbro, Model No. 7527
EX n/a   NM $35   MIP $75

❑ **Ski Patrol Helmet and Small Arms Set,** 1967, Hasbro, reissue, Model No. 7527
EX n/a   NM $75   MIP $125

G. I. JOE

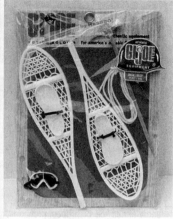

(ToyShop File Photo)

❏ **Snow Troop Set,** 1966, Hasbro, snow shoes, goggles and ice pick, Model No. 7529
   EX n/a   **NM** $20   **MIP** $45

❏ **Snow Troop Set,** 1967, Hasbro, reissue, Model No. 7529
   EX n/a   **NM** $20   **MIP** $45

❏ **Special Forces Bazooka Set,** 1966, Hasbro, Model No. 7528
   EX n/a   **NM** $35   **MIP** $45

❏ **Special Forces Bazooka Set,** 1967, Hasbro, reissue, Model No. 7528
   EX n/a   **NM** $35   **MIP** $45

❏ **Special Forces Uniform Set,** 1966, Hasbro, Model No. 7532
   EX n/a   **NM** $200   **MIP** $375

❏ **Talking Action Soldier,** 1967, Hasbro, Model No. 7590
   EX n/a   **NM** $85   **MIP** $135

❏ **Talking Adventure Pack, Bivouac Equipment,** 1968, Hasbro, Model No. 90513
   EX n/a   **NM** $275   **MIP** $325

❏ **Talking Adventure Pack, Command Post Equipt.,** 1968, Hasbro, Model No. 90517
   EX n/a   **NM** $275   **MIP** $375

❏ **Talking Adventure Pack, Mountain Troop Series,** 1968, Hasbro, Model No. 7557-83
   EX n/a   **NM** $375   **MIP** $650

❏ **Talking Adventure Pack, Special Forces Equip.,** 1968, Hasbro, Model No. 90532
   EX n/a   **NM** $275   **MIP** $500

❏ **West Point Cadet Uniform Set,** 1967, Hasbro, dress jacket, pants, shoes, chest and belt sash, parade hat with plume, saber, scabbard and white M-1 rifle, Model No. 7537
   EX n/a   **NM** $250   **MIP** $475

❏ **West Point Cadet Uniform Set,** 1968, Hasbro, reissue, Model No. 7537
   EX n/a   **NM** $250   **MIP** $375

ACTION SOLDIERS OF THE WORLD

❏ **Australian Jungle Fighter,** 1966, Hasbro, action figure with jacket, shorts, socks, boots, bush hat, belt, "Victoria Cross" medal, knuckle knife, flamethrower, entrenching tool, bush knife and sheath, Model No. 8105
   EX n/a   **NM** $250   **MIP** $400

❏ **Australian Jungle Fighter,** 1966, standard set with action figure uniform, no equipment, Model No. 8205
   EX n/a   **NM** $150   **MIP** $275

(ToyShop File Photo)

❏ **Australian Jungle Fighter Set,** 1966, Hasbro, basic set with flamethrower, machete, grenades, Victoria Cross medal, shovel, bayonet, Model No. 8305
   EX n/a   **NM** $25   **MIP** $50

❏ **British Commando,** 1966, Hasbro, standard set with no equipment, Model No. 8204
   EX n/a   **NM** $150   **MIP** $275

❏ **British Commando,** 1966, Hasbro, deluxe set with action figure, helmet, night raid green jacket, pants, boots, canteen and cover, gas mask and cover, belt, Sten sub machine gun, gun clip and "Victoria Cross" medal, Model No. 8104
   EX n/a   **NM** $300   **MIP** $425

❏ **British Commando Set,** 1966, Hasbro, Sten submachine gun, gas mask and carrier, canteen and cover, cartridge belt, rifle, "Victoria Cross" medal, manual, Model No. 8304
   EX n/a   **NM** $125   **MIP** $200

❏ **Foreign Soldiers of the World,** 1968, Hasbro, Talking Adventure Pack, Model No. 8111-83
   EX n/a   **NM** $750   **MIP** $825

❏ **French Resistance Fighter,** 1966, Hasbro, deluxe set with figure, beret, short black boots, black sweater, denim pants, "Croix de Guerre" medal, knife, shoulder holster, pistol, radio, sub machine gun and grenades, Model No. 8103
   EX n/a   **NM** $200   **MIP** $250

❏ **French Resistance Fighter,** 1966, Hasbro, Standard set with action figure and equipment, Model No. 8203
   EX n/a   **NM** $125   **MIP** $225

❏ **French Resistance Fighter Set,** 1966, Hasbro, shoulder holster, Lebel pistol, knife, grenades, radio, 7.65 submachine gun, "Croix de Guerra" medal, counter-intelligence manual, Model No. 8303
   EX n/a   **NM** $25   **MIP** $50

❏ **German Storm Trooper,** 1966, Hasbro, deluxe set with figure, helmet, jacket, pants, boots, Luger pistol, holster, cartridge belt, cartridges, "Iron Cross" medal, stick grenades, 9MM Schmeisser, field pack, Model No. 8100
   EX n/a   **NM** $275   **MIP** $425

❏ **German Storm Trooper,** 1966, Hasbro, Model No. 8300
   EX n/a   **NM** $125   **MIP** $175

❏ **German Storm Trooper,** 1966, Hasbro, Standard set with no equipment, Model No. 8200
   EX n/a   **NM** $275   **MIP** $325

❏ **Japanese Imperial Soldier,** 1966, Hasbro, deluxe set with figure, Arisaka rifle, belt, cartridges, field pack, Nambu pistol, holster, bayonet, "Order of the Kite" medal, helmet, jacket, pants, short brown boots, Model No. 8101
   EX n/a   **NM** $425   **MIP** $675

❏ **Japanese Imperial Soldier,** 1966, Hasbro, Standard set with equipment, Model No. 8201
   EX n/a   **NM** $300   **MIP** $325

❏ **Japanese Imperial Soldier Set,** 1966, Hasbro, field pack, Nambu pistol and holster, Arisaka rifle with bayonet, cartridge belt, "Order of the Kite" medal, counter-intelligence manual, Model No. 8301
   EX n/a   **NM** $175   **MIP** $275

❏ **Russian Infantry Man,** 1966, Hasbro, deluxe set with action figure, fur cap, tunic, pants, boots, ammo box, ammo rounds, anti-tank grenades, belt, bipod, DP light machine gun, "Order of Lenin" medal, field glasses and case, Model No. 8102
   EX n/a   **NM** $275   **MIP** $400

❏ **Russian Infantry Man,** 1966, Hasbro, standard set with no equipment, Model No. 8202
   EX n/a   **NM** $315   **MIP** $400

❏ **Russian Infantry Man Set,** 1966, Hasbro, DP light machine gun, bipod, field glasses and case, anti-tank grenades, ammo box, "Order of Lenin" medal, counter-intelligence medal, Model No. 8302
   EX n/a   **NM** $175   **MIP** $220

❏ **Uniforms of Six Nations,** 1967, Hasbro, Model No. 5038
   EX n/a   **NM** $750   **MIP** $950

ADVENTURE TEAM

❏ **Action Sea Sled,** 1973, Hasbro, J.C. Penney, 13", Adventure Pack
   EX n/a   **NM** $25   **MIP** $40

Action Figures

The Beatles Yellow Submarine figues, McFarlane Toys, $10 MIP.

Universal Monsters (Series Two) figures by Sideshow Toys. $20 MIP each.

Great selection of "Island of Misfit Toys" figures by Playing Mantis, 2002.

A selection of Hasbro's WWF series from 1994. Prices hover anywhere between $15 to $30 each, depending on the figure.

Mandarin Spawn from Dark Ages series. McFarlane Toys, $15 MIP.

Spawn Interlink figure RL3, from McFarlane Toys, 2001. $10 MIP.

Resident Evil "Mr. X" figure by Palisades Toys, 2002, $12 MIP.

Also from the Resident Evil series, Claire Redfield. $12 MIP.

Barbie

Battery-Operated Toys

Malibu Barbie, released by Mattel in 1971, set the style for Barbie dolls for years to come. $60 MIP.

Rocker Barbie and Ken, 1987. Barbie is $25 MIP, while Ken is $30 MIP.

A selection of battery-operated figures. Considering many of these toys were simply dimestore staples, their value has risen remarkably.

Cragstan Crapshooter, $250 MIP.

Telephone Bear, 1950s, $400 in mint condition.

Indian Joe, 1960s, $150 mint value.

Character Toys

Indiana Jones vehicles by Micro Machines, 1996. Included an Indiana Jones figure, too. About $35 MIP.

Board games

This Star Trek—The Motion Picture board game, valued at $60 in mint condition.

The "Bonanza" game "as played by the Cartwrights at their Ponderosa ranch..." from 1964 is valued at $70 MIP.

"The Flinstones" game from 1971 is popular with character toy collectors, too. $25 MIP.

"Benji Game" from the 1970s, $30 MIP.

"Charlies Angel's board game with Farrah Fawcett box, $45 MIP.

"The Six Million Dollar Man" game from 1975 is an affordable $15 MIP item.

Canadian version of "Battlestar Galactica" game, $25 MIP.

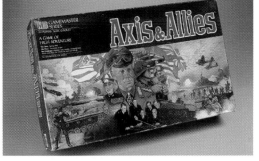

From the Milton Bradley "Gamemaster" series, "Axis & Allies," a great World War II board game with miniature planes, troops, tanks and ships. $47 MIP.

GI Joe

Covert Commando Team. 1997 $50 MIP.

Arctic Mission Team. 1997 $25 MIP.

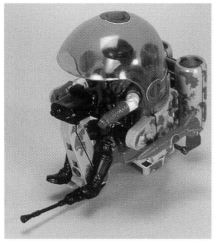

Cobra Viper Team, figure with flight pod. $50.

One of many styles of G.I. Joe Footlocker, $30.

G.I. Joe Action Soldier, blond, from 1965. C7 $90.

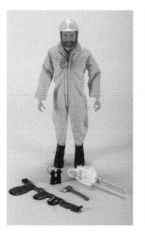

Flocked hair G.I. Joe, part of the new look for the "Adventure Team" starting in 1970. C8 $80.

U.S. Army Infantry Soldier, limited collectors' edition, 1996, $20 MIP.

British S.A.S. limited collectors' edition, 1996, $25 MIP.

A-10 Thunder Bolt, $30.

Slugger Tank with figure, $25 MIP.

G.I. Joe 3-3/4" Navy Seal Team, $30.

The Cobra Rage, $20.

Lunch Boxes

Three plastic lunch boxes, mint values (clockwise from the top) $30, $25 and $50.

Lone Ranger lunch box pictured here with a Yogi and Friends bottle. $600 mint value for lunch box, $100 mint value for bottle.

Peanuts bottle, $50 in mint condition.

Rat Patrol lunch box, steel, 1967, Aladdin, $225 in mint condition.

Brady Bunch lunch box, steel, 1970, $400 mint value.

Batman & Robin, steel, 1966, $225 in mint condition.

Beverly Hillbillies, steel, 1963, $225 mint value.

Porky's Lunch Wagon, steel dome style, 1959, $450 in mint condition.

Buccaneer steel dome style lunch box, 1957, $350 mint value.

Unique round Reese's lunch box, $60 in mint condition.

Candyland lunch box, $55 in mint condition.

Bonanza lunch box with black rim, $275 in mint condition.

G.I. Joe lunch box by King Seeley Thermos, 1967. $350 in mint condition.

Red Barn Dome lunch box by Thermos, 1972. $80 in mint condition.

Mork & Mindy lunch box, 1979, $65 in mint condition.

Star Trek Dome lunch box, 1968, $1150 in mint condition.

Man from U.N.C.L.E. steel lunch box, 1966, $275 in mint condition.

Land of the Lost steel lunch box, 1975, Aladdin. $150 in mint condition.

Julia lunch box, steel, 1969, King Seeley Thermos, $150 in mint condition.

COLOR GALLERY

Model Kits

Revell Sikorsky H-19 Rescue Helicopter Kit from the 1950s. About $40 MIP.

Guillow continues to make fun, flyable model kit airplanes. Happily, they've retained their older (now "retro") graphics on their packaging. $12 MIP.

Small Airfix military vehicles kits in poly bags from the 1960s. The instruction sheets were printed on the hang tags. About $13 each.

Great model kits are being produced all the time—the "Area 51 UFO" by Testors is one of them. It even includes aliens! About $30 MIP.

Restaurant Premiums

Jetsons and Flintstones toys from Denny's.

Robots

This Radar Robot toy from the 1950s tops off at a whopping $7000 MIP value.

Space and Science Fiction Toys

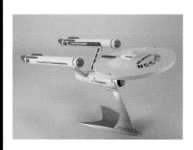

USS Enterprise NCC-1701 by Playmates, 1995, about $40 MIP.

Thunderbirds mountain hideout set by Matchbox, $60 MIP.

Galileo shuttlecraft with exclusive Kirk figure by Playmates Toys. $40 MIP.

Star Wars

Return of the Jedi Speeder Bike, 1983. Re-issues may have limited it's mint-in-pack price to only $25.

Scout Walker from Empire Strikes Back. Another vehicles that has been re-issued many times. $40 MIP.

The Obi-Wan Kenobi Coruscant Chase figure from Attack of the Clones, $8 MIP.

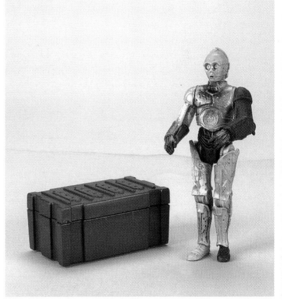

C3PO, Protocol Droid with removable outer plating and box. Pretty neat! $6 MIP.

Zam Wessell's speeder from Attack of The Clones featured "crush zones" to replicate her rough landing on Coruscant. About $17 (or less) MIP. The Zam figure is about $11 MIP.

Anakin's speeder with fly-off panels, about $16 (or less) MIP. The Anakin figure is about $7 MIP.

This classic action figure stand was a mail-order Star Wars item in 1978, $60.

Padme Amidala Arena Escape figure from Attack of the Clones. About $8 MIP.

"Imperial Cruiser" vehicle from Empire Strikes Back. This second version doesn't include sounds or any battery-driven features. $45 MIP.

Darth Maul Sith Speeder from Phantom Menace includes figure. $5 MIP.

Sneak Preview Clone Trooper figure, 2002, $11 MIP.

Sandtrooper figure from 1996. $12 MIP.

Grand Moff Tarkin, a 1997 release, $10 MIP.

Darth Maul figure by Applause, 1999. About $5 MIP.

Another Imperial officer, the AT-AT Commander (also known as General Veers figure) was packaged with the vehicle, and did not include a weapon. About $10 in mint condition.

R2D2 from Phantom Menace. Mint-in-pack value, $6.

The "Epic Force" series figures featured great detail and rotated on a plastic base. Mint-in-pack, $7.

Super Battle Droid from Attack of the Clones features laser blast damage and interchangeable arms. $6 MIP.

Rebel Fleet Trooper, 1997, $11 MIP.

"S.W.A.T." clicker gun and handcuffs set, a was a staple of dimestores in the 1970s, and is valued at about $20 today.

Vehicles

Tonka pickup with updated grille and body style from early 1970s, C-7 $50.

Tonka pickup with grille style used from late 1962 to 1964, C-5 $25.

Matchbox Superfast Range Rover Police vehicle, part of the "Rola-Matics" lineup, featured a rotating police light. This version of the car is valued at $8 MIP.

Tootsietoys Tow Trucks, the '35 and '34 Wreckers. Note the separately cast grille and wheels with tires on the earlier model on the right. Each about $70 MIP.

Matchbox Superfast Renault 5TL, otherwise known as "Le Car." Featured opening hatch, and was available in a variety of colors. $10 MIP.

Matchbox Datsun 260Z shown here with the more generic boxes that became more common toward the late 1970s and early 1980s. $10 MIP.

Matchbox Superfast Porsche 928. Available in a number of finishes, it looks pretty sharp in blue. About $11 MIP.

Hot Wheels Custom Barracuda, a great model with an opening hood. This was one of the "original sixteen" Hot Wheels cars in 1968. $400 MIP.

Hot Wheels Maserati Mistral, from 1969, $125 MIP.

Boss Hoss by Hot Wheels, 1971, $300 MIP. Early Hot Wheels models with decals are actually doing quite well on the market these days.

Later-era Boss Mustang by Matchbox. This Superfast model has been produced in a variety of color and decal versions. $9 MIP.

Classic Nomad, 1971, by Hot Wheels. This casting has been re-used many times by Mattel, but the first Redlines edition remains a favorite with collectors. $150 MIP.

Buddy L Coca-Cola truck, $200 MIP.

McClaren M6A by Hot Wheels, 1969, $65 MIP.

Hot Wheels Olds 442, 1971, $800 MIP.

Hot Wheels "Strip Teaser," 1971, $200 MIP.

GMC box truck by Tootsietoy. Postwar and prewar versions are shown here. Prewar models generally feature more painted detail and separate castings. About $40 each.

"Ice T" by Hot Wheels, 1973. $200 MIP.

Matchbox regular wheels, BRM racer, 1965. $25 MIP.

Cadillac 60 Special by Matchbox, 1960, $90 MIP.

Matchbox Superfast Lotus Europa, 1970. Produced in pink and blue versions, $20 MIP.

A selection of Dinky Toys. These heavy die-cast models are quite collectible, but their values seem to have leveled off a bit in recent years.

Ferrari 312P, 1970, by Hot Wheels. $60 MIP.

Matchbox regular wheels Compressor Lorry, 1959. Nicely detailed casting, $60 MIP.

Rolls Royce Silver Shadow by Matchbox, 1967. Model features opening trunk, and was carried over into the Superfast line in 1970. $25 MIP.

One of Hot Wheels' most famous Redlines, "Twin Mill" from 1969. $50 MIP.

Matchbox Mack Dump Truck, 1969. $25 MIP.

Honda Motorcycle with Trailer, 1967, by Matchbox. $40 MIP.

John Deere-Lanz tractor by Matchbox, 1964. The first versions of this model featured gray removable tires, later switched to black. $35 MIP.

The Matchbox Field Car has led to years of speculation over what brand vehicle it actually is: International Scout? Renault? Hard to tell, though it looks more like a Scout than anything. $18 MIP.

Matchbox Daimler Bus from 1966. $25 MIP.

Safari Land Rover by Matchbox, 1965. Two years later, the body color was switched from dark green to the medium blue shown. $25 MIP.

Dinky Toys Cadillac Ambulance, 1970s. The main body casting had been used for many years by the time this model was released. $60 MIP.

Bedford Coach by Matchbox, 1958. $95 MIP.

Iso Grifo by Matchbox, 1968, featured opening doors. $25 MIP.

Friction-powered Japanese police car, 1960s, $50 mint value.

Matchbox Superfast Safari Land Rover in bright gold, 1970. $25 MIP.

Volkswagen 1600 TL by Matchbox, 1967. $25 MIP.

Matchbox Superfast Mercury Fire Chief car, 1971, $16 MIP.

Power Pad by Hot Wheels, 1970, $125 MIP.

Hot Wheels' Sky Show Fleetside vehicle launched Mattel airplanes. 1970, $850 MIP.

Open Fire, 1972. A modified Hot Wheels AMC Gremlin, this model has a $400 MIP value.

Unusual vehicle by Hot Wheels, "What 4," from 1971. $150 MIP.

Super Chromes "Demon" by Hot Wheels, 1976. $75 MIP.

Scooper truck, part of the Heavyweights series by Hot Wheels, 1971. $325 MIP.

Moving Van, another Heavyweights vehicle by Hot Wheels, 1970. $125 MIP.

Hot Wheels Ambulance, 1970, $50 MIP.

Mercedes 280SL, 1969, a nice casting with an opening hood and detailed engine, but it was never a model that caught on with collectors. $70 MIP.

View-Master Toys

View-Master projector, 1970s, $25 MIP.

Discovery Channel projector/View-Master set, 1990s, $15 MIP.

Classic black Bakelite View-Master set, 1950s.

Charlie Brown View-Master set with reels, early 1970s, $50 MIP.

(ToyShop File Photo)

❏ **Adventure Team Headquarters Set,** 1972, Hasbro, Adventure Team playset, Model No. 7490
EX n/a   NM $50   MIP $125

❏ **Adventure Team Training Center Set,** 1973, Hasbro, rifle rack, logs, barrel, barber wire, rope ladder, three tires, two targets, escape slide, tent and poles, first aid kit, respirator and mask, snake, instructions, Model No. 7495
EX n/a   NM $75   MIP $125

❏ **Adventure Team Vehicle Set,** 1970, Hasbro, Model No. 7005
EX n/a   NM $50   MIP $75

❏ **Aerial Reconnaissance Set,** 1971, Hasbro, jumpsuit, helmet, aerial recon vehicle with built-in camera, Model No. 7345
EX n/a   NM $75   MIP $125

❏ **Air Adventurer,** 1970, Hasbro, includes figure with Kung Fu grip, orange flight suit, boots, insignia, dog tags, rifle, boots, warranty, club insert, Model No. 7403
EX n/a   NM $120   MIP $375

❏ **Air Adventurer,** 1974, Hasbro, with Kung Fu grip, Model No. 7282
EX n/a   NM $95   MIP $125

❏ **Air Adventurer,** 1976, Hasbro, life-like body figure, uniform and equipment, Model No. 7282
EX n/a   NM $75   MIP $100

❏ **All Terrain Vehicle,** 1973, Hasbro, 14" vehicle, Model No. 23528
EX n/a   NM $50   MIP $75

❏ **Amphicat,** 1973, Hasbro, Irwin, scaled to fit two figures, Model No. 59158
EX n/a   NM $35   MIP $55

❏ **Attack at Vulture Falls,** 1975, Hasbro, super deluxe set, Model No. 7420
EX n/a   NM $75   MIP $150

❏ **Avenger Pursuit Craft,** 1976, Hasbro, Sears Exclusive
EX n/a   NM $100   MIP $175

❏ **Big Trapper,** 1976, Hasbro, without action figure, Model No. 7498
EX n/a   NM $75   MIP $105

❏ **Big Trapper Adventure with Intruder,** 1976, Hasbro, with action figure, Model No. 7494
EX n/a   NM $100   MIP $150

❏ **Black Adventurer,** 1970, Hasbro, includes figure, shirt with insignia, pants, boots, dog tags, shoulder holster with pistol, Model No. 7404
EX n/a   NM $125   MIP $150

❏ **Black Adventurer,** 1976, Hasbro, with life-like body and Kung Fu grip, Model No. 7283
EX n/a   NM $85   MIP $125

❏ **Black Widow Rendezvous,** 1975, Hasbro, super deluxe set, Model No. 7414
EX n/a   NM $125   MIP $200

❏ **Bulletman,** 1976, Hasbro, Model No. 8026
EX n/a   NM $50   MIP $75

❏ **Buried Bounty,** 1975, Hasbro, deluxe set, Model No. 7328-5
EX n/a   NM $10   MIP $25

❏ **Capture Copter,** 1976, Hasbro, without action figure, Model No. 7480
EX n/a   NM $80   MIP $175

❏ **Capture Copter Adventure with Intruder,** 1976, Hasbro, with action figure, Model No. 7481
EX n/a   NM $110   MIP $200

❏ **Capture of the Pygmy Gorilla Set,** 1970, Hasbro, Model No. 7437
EX n/a   NM $100   MIP $175

❏ **Challenge of Savage River,** 1975, Hasbro, deluxe set, Model No. 8032
EX n/a   NM $100   MIP $175

❏ **Chest Winch Set,** 1972, Hasbro, Model No. 7313
EX n/a   NM $10   MIP $15

❏ **Chest Winch Set,** 1974, Hasbro, reissue, Model No. 7313
EX n/a   NM $10   MIP $15

❏ **Chopper Cycle,** 1973, Hasbro, 15" vehicle, J.C. Penney's, Model No. 59114
EX n/a   NM $30   MIP $50

❏ **Combat Action Jeep,** 1973, Hasbro, 18" vehicle, J.C. Penney's, Model No. 59751
EX n/a   NM $50   MIP $65

❏ **Combat Jeep and Trailer,** 1976, Hasbro, Model No. 7000
EX n/a   NM $80   MIP $135

❏ **Command Para Drop,** 1975, Hasbro, deluxe set, Model No. 8033
EX n/a   NM $200   MIP $300

❏ **Copter Rescue Set,** 1973, Hasbro, blue jumpsuit, red binoculars, Model No. 7308-3
EX n/a   NM $15   MIP $20

❏ **Danger of the Depths Set,** 1970, Hasbro, Model No. 7412
EX n/a   NM $100   MIP $175

❏ **Danger Ray Detection,** 1975, Hasbro, magnetic ray detector, solar communicator with headphones, two-piece uniform, instructions and comic, Model No. 7338-1
EX n/a   NM $45   MIP $90

❏ **Dangerous Climb Set,** 1973, Hasbro, Model No. 7309-2
EX n/a   NM $20   MIP $35

❏ **Dangerous Mission Set,** 1973, Hasbro, green shirt, pants, hunting rifle, Model No. 7608-5
EX n/a   NM $20   MIP $35

❏ **Demolition Set,** 1971, Hasbro, with land mines, mine detector and carrying case with metallic suit, Model No. 7371
EX n/a   NM $75   MIP $100

❏ **Demolition Set,** 1971, Hasbro, armored suit, face shield, bomb, bomb disposal box, extension grips, Model No. 7370
EX n/a   NM $20   MIP $45

❏ **Desert Explorer Set,** 1973, Hasbro, Model No. 7309-5
EX n/a   NM $20   MIP $40

❏ **Desert Survival Set,** 1973, Hasbro, Model No. 7308-6
EX n/a   NM $20   MIP $40

❏ **Devil of the Deep,** 1974, Hasbro, Model No. 7439
EX n/a   NM $80   MIP $135

❏ **Dive to Danger,** 1975, Hasbro, Mike Powers set, orange scuba suit, fins, mask, spear gun, shark, buoy, knife and scabbard, mini sled, air tanks, comic, Model No. 8031
EX n/a   NM $150   MIP $250

❏ **Diver's Distress,** 1975, Hasbro, Model No. 7328-6
EX n/a   NM $35   MIP $70

❏ **Drag Bike Set,** 1971, Hasbro, three-wheel motorcycle brakes down to backpack size, Model No. 7364
EX n/a   NM $25   MIP $65

❏ **Eagle Eye Black Commando,** 1976, Hasbro, Model No. 7278
EX n/a   NM $85   MIP $125

❏ **Eagle Eye Land Commander,** 1976, Hasbro, Model No. 7276
EX n/a   NM $65   MIP $80

❏ **Eagle Eye Man of Action,** 1976, Hasbro, Model No. 7277
EX n/a   NM $65   MIP $80

❏ **Eight Ropes of Danger Set,** 1970, Hasbro, Model No. 7422
EX n/a   NM $125   MIP $225

❏ **Emergency Rescue Set,** 1971, Hasbro, shirt, pants, rope ladder and hook, walkie talkie, safety belt, flashlight, oxygen tank, axe, first aid kit, Model No. 7374
EX n/a   NM $45   MIP $75

❏ **Equipment Tester Set,** 1972, Hasbro, Model No. 7319-5
EX n/a   NM $15   MIP $20

Escape Car Set, 1971, Hasbro, Model
No. 7360
EX n/a   NM $30   MIP $60

Escape Slide Set, 1972, Hasbro, Model
No. 7319-1
EX n/a   NM $15   MIP $25

Fangs of the Cobra, 1975, Hasbro,
deluxe set, Model No. 8028-2
EX n/a   NM $125   MIP $200

Fantastic Freefall Set, 1970, Hasbro,
Model No. 7423
EX n/a   NM $125   MIP $200

Fantastic Sea Wolf Submarine, 1975,
Hasbro, Model No. 7460
EX n/a   NM $60   MIP $100

(ToyShop File Photo)

Fate of the Troubleshooter, 1974, Hasbro, Includes vehicle, vulture, instructions and comic book, Model No. 7450
EX n/a   NM $50   MIP $125

Fight For Survival Set, 1970, Hasbro,
with blue parka, Model No. 7431
EX n/a   NM $300   MIP $550

Fight for Survival Set, 1973, Hasbro,
brown shirt and pants, machete, Model
No. 7308-2
EX n/a   NM $20   MIP $30

**Fight for Survival Set with Polar
Explorer,** 1969, Hasbro, Model
No. 7982
EX n/a   NM $250   MIP $450

Fire Fighter Set, 1971, Hasbro, Model
No. 7351
EX n/a   NM $20   MIP $30

(ToyShop File Photo)

Flying Rescue Set, 1971, Hasbro,
Model No. 7361
EX n/a   NM $35   MIP $60

Flying Space Adventure Set, 1970,
Hasbro, Model No. 7425
EX n/a   NM $400   MIP $600

Footlocker, 1974, Hasbro, green plastic
with cardboard wrapper, Model
No. 8000
EX n/a   NM $35   MIP $70

Giant Air-Sea Helicopter, 1973, Has-
bro, 28" vehicle, J.C. Penney's, Model
No. 59189
EX n/a   NM $50   MIP $125

Green Danger, 1975, Hasbro, Model
No. 7328-4
EX n/a   NM $30   MIP $45

Helicopter, 1973, Hasbro, 14", yellow,
with working winch, Model No. 7380
EX n/a   NM $50   MIP $90

Helicopter, 1976, Hasbro, Model
No. 7380
EX n/a   NM $50   MIP $90

Hidden Missile Discovery Set, 1970,
Hasbro, Model No. 7415
EX n/a   NM $100   MIP $200

Hidden Treasure Set, 1973, Hasbro,
shirt, pants, pick axe, shovel, Model
No. 7308-1
EX n/a   NM $15   MIP $25

(ToyShop File Photo)

High Voltage Escape Set, 1971, Hasbro, net, jumpsuit, hat, wrist meter, wire
cutters, wire, warning sign, Model
No. 7342
EX n/a   NM $40   MIP $75

(ToyShop File Photo)

Hurricane Spotter Set, 1971, Hasbro,
slicker suit, rain measure, portable
radar, map and case, binoculars, Model
No. 7343
EX n/a   NM $55   MIP $80

Intruder Commander, 1976, Hasbro,
Model No. 8050
EX n/a   NM $50   MIP $75

Intruder Warrior, 1976, Hasbro, Model
No. 8051
EX n/a   NM $50   MIP $75

Jaws of Death, 1975, Hasbro, super
deluxe set, Model No. 7421
EX n/a   NM $325   MIP $500

Jettison to Safety, 1975, Hasbro, infra-
red terrain scanner, mobile rocket pack,
two-piece flight suit, instructions and
comic, Model No. 7339-2
EX n/a   NM $85   MIP $200

Jungle Ordeal Set, 1973, Hasbro,
Model No. 7309-3
EX n/a   NM $15   MIP $25

Jungle Survival Set, 1971, Hasbro,
Model No. 7373
EX n/a   NM $15   MIP $25

Karate Set, 1971, Hasbro, Model
No. 7372
EX n/a   NM $35   MIP $70

(ToyShop File Photo)

Land Adventurer, 1970, Hasbro,
includes figure, camo shirt and pants,
boots, insignia, shoulder holster and
pistol, dog tags and team inserts, Model
No. 7401
EX n/a   NM $45   MIP $75

Land Adventurer, 1974, Hasbro, with
life-like body and Kung Fu grip and uniform set, Model No. 7280
EX n/a   NM $50   MIP $65

❑ **Land Adventurer,** 1976, Hasbro, Model No. 7280
EX n/a   NM $35   MIP $50

❑ **Land Adventurer,** 1976, Hasbro, Model No. 7270
EX n/a   NM $20   MIP $50

❑ **Laser Rescue Set,** 1972, Hasbro, handheld laser with backpack generator, Model No. 7311
EX n/a   NM $20   MIP $35

❑ **Laser Rescue Set,** 1974, Hasbro, reissue, Model No. 7311
EX n/a   NM $20   MIP $35

❑ **Life-Line Catapult Set,** 1971, Hasbro, Model No. 7353
EX n/a   NM $15   MIP $25

❑ **Long Range Recon,** 1975, Hasbro, deluxe set, Model No. 7328-3
EX n/a   NM $10   MIP $20

❑ **Magnetic Flaw Detector Set,** 1972, Hasbro, Model No. 7319-2
EX n/a   NM $10   MIP $20

❑ **Man of Action,** 1970, Hasbro, includes figure, shirt and pants, boots, insignia, dog tags, team inserts, Model No. 7500
EX n/a   NM $50   MIP $75

❑ **Man of Action,** 1974, Hasbro, figure with life-like body and Kung Fu grip, Model No. 7284
EX n/a   NM $45   MIP $75

❑ **Man of Action,** 1976, Hasbro, Model No. 7274
EX n/a   NM $25   MIP $45

❑ **Mike Powers/Atomic Man,** 1975, Hasbro, figure with "atomic" flashing eye, arm that spins hand-held helicopter, Model No. 8025
EX n/a   NM $20   MIP $45

❑ **Mine Shaft Breakout,** 1975, Hasbro, sonic rock blaster, chest winch, two-piece uniform, netting, instructions, comic, Model No. 7339-3
EX n/a   NM $70   MIP $125

❑ **Missile Recovery Set,** 1971, Hasbro, Model No. 7340
EX n/a   NM $40   MIP $55

❑ **Mobile Support Vehicle Set,** 1972, Hasbro, Model No. 7499
EX n/a   NM $85   MIP $150

❑ **Mystery of the Boiling Lagoon,** 1973, Hasbro, Sears, pontoon boat, diver's suit, diver's helmet, weighted belt and boots, depth gauge, air hose, buoy, nose cone, pincer arm, instructions
EX n/a   NM $150   MIP $200

❑ **Night Surveillance,** 1975, Hasbro, deluxe set, Model No. 7338-2
EX n/a   NM $35   MIP $45

❑ **Peril of the Raging Inferno,** 1975, Hasbro, fireproof suit, hood and boots, breathing apparatus, camera, fire extinguisher, detection meter, gaskets, Model No. 7416
EX n/a   NM $85   MIP $150

❑ **Photo Reconnaissance Set,** 1973, Hasbro, Model No. 7309-4
EX n/a   NM $20   MIP $30

❑ **Race for Recovery,** 1975, Hasbro, Model No. 8028-1
EX n/a   NM $20   MIP $35

❑ **Radiation Detection Set,** 1971, Hasbro, jumpsuit with belt, "uranium ore", goggles, container, pincer arm, Model No. 7341
EX n/a   NM $30   MIP $50

❑ **Raging River Dam Up,** 1975, Hasbro, Model No. 7339-1
EX n/a   NM $60   MIP $90

(ToyShop File Photo)

❑ **Recovery of the Lost Mummy Adventure Set,** 1971, Hasbro, Sears Exclusive
EX n/a   NM $125   MIP $250

❑ **Rescue Raft Set,** 1971, Hasbro, Model No. 7350
EX n/a   NM $15   MIP $20

❑ **Revenge of the Spy Shark,** 1975, Hasbro, super deluxe set, Model No. 7413
EX n/a   NM $50   MIP $175

❑ **Rock Blaster,** 1972, Hasbro, sonic blaster with tripod, backpack generator, face shield, Model No. 7312
EX n/a   NM $10   MIP $20

❑ **Rocket Pack Set,** 1972, Hasbro, Model No. 7315
EX n/a   NM $10   MIP $20

❑ **Rocket Pack Set,** 1974, Hasbro, reissue, Model No. 7315
EX n/a   NM $10   MIP $20

❑ **Sample Analyzer Set,** 1972, Hasbro, Model No. 7319-3
EX n/a   NM $10   MIP $20

❑ **Sandstorm Survival Adventure,** 1974, Hasbro, Model No. 7493
EX n/a   NM $125   MIP $200

(ToyShop File Photo)

❑ **Sea Adventurer,** 1970, Hasbro, includes figure, shirt, dungarees, insignia, boots, shoulder holster and pistol, Model No. 7402
EX n/a   NM $45   MIP $70

❑ **Sea Adventurer,** 1974, Hasbro, with life-like body and Kung Fu grip and uniform with equipment, Model No. 7281
EX n/a   NM $55   MIP $75

❑ **Sea Adventurer,** 1976, Hasbro, Model No. 7281
EX n/a   NM $55   MIP $85

❑ **Sea Adventurer,** 1976, Hasbro, Model No. 7271
EX n/a   NM $40   MIP $75

❑ **Search for the Abominable Snowman Set,** 1973, Hasbro, Sears, white suit, belt, goggles, gloves, rifle, skis and poles, show shoes, sled, rope, net, supply chest, binoculars, Abominable Snowman, comic book, Model No. 7439.16
EX n/a   NM $110   MIP $175

❑ **Search for the Stolen Idol Set,** 1971, Hasbro, Model No. 7418
EX n/a   NM $120   MIP $225

❑ **Secret Agent Set,** 1971, Hasbro, Model No. 7375
EX n/a   NM $30   MIP $55

❑ **Secret Courier,** 1975, Hasbro, Model No. 7328-1
EX n/a   NM $45   MIP $65

❑ **Secret Mission Set,** 1973, Hasbro, Model No. 7309-1
EX n/a   NM $45   MIP $65

❑ **Secret Mission Set,** 1975, Hasbro, deluxe set, Model No. 8030
EX n/a   NM $65   MIP $95

❑ **Secret Mission to Spy Island Set,** 1970, Hasbro, comic, inflatable raft with oar, binoculars, signal light, flare gun, TNT and detonator, wire roll, boots, pants, sweater, black cap, camera, radio with earphones, .45 submachine gun, Model No. 7411
EX n/a   NM $75   MIP $125

❑ **Secret Mountain Outpost,** 1975, Hasbro, Model No. 8040
EX n/a   NM $50   MIP $85

❑ **Secret of the Mummy's Tomb Set,** 1970, Hasbro, with Land Adventurer figure, shirt, pants, boots, insignia, pith helmet, pick, shovel, Mummy's tomb, net, gems, vehicle with winch, comic, Model No. 7441
EX n/a   NM $175   MIP $300

❑ **Secret Rendezvous Set,** 1973, Hasbro, parka, pants, flare gun, Model No. 7308-4
EX n/a   NM $10   MIP $20

❑ **Seismograph Set,** 1972, Hasbro, Model No. 7319-6
EX n/a   NM $10   MIP $20

❑ **Sharks Surprise Set with Sea Adventurer,** 1970, Hasbro, Model No. 7442
EX n/a   NM $175   MIP $325

G. I. JOE

Shocking Escape, 1975, Hasbro, escape slide, chest pack climber, jumpsuit with gloves and belt, high voltage sign, instructions and comic, Model No. 7338-3
EX n/a   NM $25   MIP $65

Signal All Terrain Vehicle, 1973, Hasbro, J.C. Penney's, 12" vehicle
EX n/a   NM $30   MIP $65

Signal Flasher Set, 1971, Hasbro, large back pack type signal flash unit, Model No. 7362
EX n/a   NM $15   MIP $30

Sky Dive to Danger, 1975, Hasbro, super deluxe set, Model No. 7440
EX n/a   NM $90   MIP $150

Sky Hawk, 1975, Hasbro, 5-3/4-foot wingspan, Model No. 7470
EX n/a   NM $65   MIP $100

Solar Communicator Set, 1972, Hasbro, Model No. 7314
EX n/a   NM $10   MIP $20

Solar Communicator Set, 1974, Hasbro, reissue, Model No. 7314
EX n/a   NM $10   MIP $20

Sonic Rock Blaster Set, 1972, Hasbro, Model No. 7312
EX n/a   NM $10   MIP $20

Sonic Rock Blaster Set, 1974, Hasbro, reissue, Model No. 7312
EX n/a   NM $10   MIP $20

Spacewalk Mystery Set with Astronaut, 1970, Hasbro, Model No. 7445
EX n/a   NM $225   MIP $300

Special Assignment, 1975, Hasbro, deluxe set, Model No. 8028-3
EX n/a   NM $30   MIP $55

Talking Adventure Team Black Commander, 1973, Hasbro, Model No. 7406
EX n/a   NM $150   MIP $225

Talking Adventure Team Black Commander, 1974, Hasbro, with Kung Fu grip, Model No. 7291
EX n/a   NM $85   MIP $350

(ToyShop File Photo)

Talking Adventure Team Commander, 1970, Hasbro, includes figure, two-pocket green shirt, pants, boots, insignia, instructions, dog tag, shoulder holster and pistol. With life-like hair and beard, Model No. 7400
EX n/a   NM $65   MIP $125

Talking Adventure Team Commander, 1974, Hasbro, with Kung Fu grip, Model No. 7290
EX n/a   NM $75   MIP $200

Talking Astronaut, 1970, Hasbro, Model No. 7590
EX n/a   NM $90   MIP $175

Talking Black Commander, 1976, Hasbro, Model No. 7291
EX n/a   NM $125   MIP $300

Talking Commander, 1976, Hasbro, Model No. 7290
EX n/a   NM $75   MIP $115

Talking Man of Action, 1970, Hasbro, shirt, pants, boots, dog tags, rifle, insignia, instructions, Model No. 7590
EX n/a   NM $75   MIP $125

Talking Man of Action, 1974, Hasbro, with life-like body and Kung Fu grip, Model No. 7292
EX n/a   NM $75   MIP $200

Talking Man of Action, 1976, Hasbro, Model No. 7292
EX n/a   NM $75   MIP $120

Thermal Terrain Scanner Set, 1972, Hasbro, Model No. 7319-4
EX n/a   NM $25   MIP $35

Three-in-One Super Adventure Set, 1971, Hasbro, Danger of the Depths, Secret Mission to Spy Island and Flying Space Adventure Packs, Model No. 7480
EX n/a   NM $550   MIP $975

Three-in-One Super Adventure Set, 1971, Hasbro, cold of the Arctic, Heat of the Desert and Danger of the Jungle, Model No. 7480
EX n/a   NM $250   MIP $400

Thrust into Danger, 1975, Hasbro, deluxe set, Model No. 7328-2
EX n/a   NM $45   MIP $55

Trapped in the Coils of Doom, 1974, Hasbro, J.C. Penney's Exclusive, Model No. 79-59301
EX n/a   NM $250   MIP $300

Trouble at Vulture Pass, 1975, Hasbro, Sears Exclusive, super deluxe set, Model No. 59289
EX n/a   NM $75   MIP $125

Turbo Copter Set, 1971, Hasbro, strap-on one man helicopter, Model No. 7363
EX n/a   NM $15   MIP $35

Undercover Agent Set, 1973, Hasbro, trenchcoat and belt, walkie-talkie, Model No. 7309-6
EX n/a   NM $15   MIP $30

Underwater Demolition Set, 1972, Hasbro, hand-held propulsion device,

breathing apparatus, dynamite, Model No. 7310
EX n/a   NM $15   MIP $20

Underwater Demolition Set, 1974, Hasbro, reissue, Model No. 7310
EX n/a   NM $10   MIP $20

Underwater Explorer Set, 1971, Hasbro, self propelled underwater device, Model No. 7354
EX n/a   NM $15   MIP $30

Volcano Jumper Set, 1971, Hasbro, jumpsuit with hood, belt, nylon rope, chest pack, TNT pack, Model No. 7344
EX n/a   NM $45   MIP $80

White Tiger Hunt Set, 1970, Hasbro, hunter's jacket and pants, hat, rifle, tent, cage, chain, campfire, white tiger, comic, Model No. 7436
EX n/a   NM $80   MIP $125

Windboat Set, 1971, Hasbro, back pack, sled with wheels, sail, Model No. 7353
EX n/a   NM $10   MIP $25

Winter Rescue Set, 1973, Hasbro, Replaced Photo Reconnaissance Set, Model No. 7309-4
EX n/a   NM $40   MIP $75

ADVENTURES OF G.I. JOE

Adventure Locker, 1969, Hasbro, Footlocker, Model No. 7940
EX n/a   NM $80   MIP $165

Aqua Locker, 1969, Hasbro, Footlocker, Model No. 7941
EX n/a   NM $90   MIP $180

Aquanaut, 1969, Hasbro, Model No. 7910
EX n/a   NM $175   MIP $550

Astro Locker, 1969, Hasbro, Footlocker, Model No. 7942
EX n/a   NM $90   MIP $180

Challenge at Hawk River, 1999, Hasbro, Recreations of Adventure Team series
EX n/a   NM $5   MIP $10

Danger of the Depths Underwater Diver Set, 1969, Hasbro, Model No. 7920
EX n/a   NM $140   MIP $275

Eight Ropes of Danger Set, 1969, Hasbro, diving suit, treasure chest, octopus, Model No. 7950
EX n/a   NM $110   MIP $225

Fantastic Freefall Set, 1969, Hasbro, includes figure with parachute and pack,

blinker light, air vest, flash light, crash helmet with visor and oxygen mask, dog tags, orange jump suit, black boots, Model No. 7951
EX n/a   **NM** $150   **MIP** $325

❑ **Flight for Survival Set with Polar Explorer,** 1969, Hasbro, reissue, Model No. 7982.83
EX n/a   **NM** $150   **MIP** $300

❑ **Hidden Missile Discovery Set,** 1969, Hasbro, Model No. 7952
EX n/a   **NM** $70   **MIP** $135

❑ **Mouth of Doom Set,** 1969, Hasbro, Model No. 7953
EX n/a   **NM** $125   **MIP** $250

(ToyShop File Photo)

❑ **Mysterious Explosion Set,** 1969, Hasbro, basic, Model No. 7921
EX n/a   **NM** $60   **MIP** $125

❑ **Negro Adventurer,** 1969, Hasbro, Sears Exclusive, includes painted hair figure, blue jeans, pullover sweater, shoulder holster and pistol, plus product letter from Sears, Model No. 7905
EX n/a   **NM** $450   **MIP** $750

❑ **Peril of the Raging Inferno,** 1999, Hasbro
EX n/a   **NM** $5   **MIP** $10

❑ **Perilous Rescue Set,** 1969, Hasbro, basic, Model No. 7923
EX n/a   **NM** $150   **MIP** $300

❑ **Save the Tiger,** 1999, Hasbro
EX n/a   **NM** $5   **MIP** $10

❑ **Secret Mission to Spy Island Set,** 1969, Hasbro, basic, Model No. 7922
EX n/a   **NM** $110   **MIP** $225

❑ **Sharks Surprise Set with Frogman,** 1969, Hasbro, Model No. 7980
EX n/a   **NM** $175   **MIP** $325

❑ **Sharks Surprise Set with Frogman,** 1969, Hasbro, with figure, orange scuba suit, blue sea sled, air tanks, harpoon, face mask, treasure chest, shark, instructions and comic, Model No. 7980
EX n/a   **NM** $125   **MIP** $300

❑ **Sharks Surprise Set without Frogman,** 1969, Hasbro, Model No. 7980.83
EX n/a   **NM** $150   **MIP** $300

❑ **Spacewalk Mystery Set with Spaceman,** 1969, Hasbro, Model No. 7981
EX n/a   **NM** $150   **MIP** $375

❑ **Spacewalk Mystery Set without Spaceman,** 1969, Hasbro, reissue, Model No. 7981.83
EX n/a   **NM** $125   **MIP** $275

❑ **Talking Astronaut,** 1969, Hasbro, hard-hand figure with white coveralls with insignias, white boots, dog tags, Model No. 7615
EX n/a   **NM** $85   **MIP** $275

GI JOE ACTION SERIES, ARMY, NAVY, MARINE AND AIR FORCE

❑ **Basic Footlocker,** 1965, Hasbro, Model No. 8000
EX n/a   **NM** $50   **MIP** $75

❑ **Footlocker Adventure Pack,** 1968, Hasbro, 22 pieces, Model No. 8002.83
EX n/a   **NM** $70   **MIP** $145

❑ **Footlocker Adventure Pack,** 1968, Hasbro, 15 pieces, Model No. 8001.83
EX n/a   **NM** $65   **MIP** $135

❑ **Footlocker Adventure Pack,** 1968, Hasbro, 16 pieces, Model No. 8000.83
EX n/a   **NM** $65   **MIP** $135

❑ **Footlocker Adventure Pack,** 1968, Hasbro, 15 pieces, Model No. 8002.83
EX n/a   **NM** $65   **MIP** $135

SUPER JOE

❑ **Aqua Laser,** 1977, Hasbro, Model No. 7528-1
EX n/a   **NM** $10   **MIP** $20

❑ **Edge of Adventure,** 1977, Hasbro, Model No. 7518-2
EX n/a   **NM** $10   **MIP** $20

❑ **Emergency Rescue,** 1977, Hasbro, Model No. 7518-3
EX n/a   **NM** $10   **MIP** $20

❑ **Fusion Bazooka,** 1977, Hasbro, Model No. 7528-3
EX n/a   **NM** $10   **MIP** $20

❑ **Gor,** 1977, Hasbro, Model No. 7510
EX n/a   **NM** $40   **MIP** $70

❑ **Helipak,** 1977, Hasbro, Model No. 7538-2
EX n/a   **NM** $10   **MIP** $20

❑ **Invisible Danger,** 1977, Hasbro, Model No. 7518-1
EX n/a   **NM** $10   **MIP** $20

❑ **Luminos,** 1977, Hasbro, Model No. 7506
EX n/a   **NM** $45   **MIP** $70

(ToyShop File Photo)

❑ **Magna Tools,** 1977, Hasbro, With uniform and rock-cutting drill and saw, Model No. 7538-1
EX n/a   **NM** $10   **MIP** $20

❑ **Path of Danger,** 1977, Hasbro, Model No. 7518-4
EX n/a   **NM** $10   **MIP** $20

❑ **Rocket Command Center,** 1977, Hasbro, Super Adventure Set including Gor, Model No. 7571
EX n/a   **NM** $60   **MIP** $115

❑ **Rocket Command Center,** 1977, Hasbro, Model No. 7570
EX n/a   **NM** $50   **MIP** $100

❑ **Sonic Scanner,** 1977, Hasbro, Model No. 7538-3
EX n/a   **NM** $10   **MIP** $20

❑ **Super Joe,** 1977, Hasbro, Model No. 7503
EX n/a   **NM** $20   **MIP** $35

❑ **Super Joe (Black),** 1977, Hasbro, Model No. 7504
EX n/a   **NM** $35   **MIP** $50

❑ **Super Joe Commander,** 1977, Hasbro, Model No. 7501
EX n/a   **NM** $25   **MIP** $45

❑ **The Shield,** 1977, Hasbro, Model No. 7505
EX n/a   **NM** $40   **MIP** $65

❑ **Treacherous Dive,** 1977, Hasbro, Model No. 7528-2
EX n/a   **NM** $10   **MIP** $20

Lunch Boxes

This Roy Rogers Chow Wagon dome-style lunch box is worth $400 in mint condition.

Remember carrying your lunch to school in a colorful metal lunch box?

Lunch kits have been manufactured since the 1920s, but the boxes that are most collectible today are those bearing illustrations of popular licensed characters.

It took the power of television to launch the lunch box industry out of the domed steel domain of workmen into the colorful art boxes generations of children carried to school each day.

As World War II ended, Aladdin Industries returned to providing millions of workmen with sturdy, if uninspired, lunch kits designed to take the beating of the workplace. Great change occurred in 1950 when Aladdin released a pair of rectangular steel boxes, one red and one blue, sporting scalloped color decals of the TV Western hero of the day, Hopalong Cassidy. Soon, 600,000 Hoppy boxes

were being carried to school by proud young owners. The youth market had been found, and it would never be ignored again.

The envious classmates of those first Hoppy boxers would not be denied. American Thermos, Aladdin's chief competitor, went one up on Aladdin by introducing the 1953 Roy Rogers box in full-color lithography. Aladdin responded by issuing a new 1954 Hoppy box in full color litho, and the lunch box era officially began.

Throughout the latter 1950s, the box wars were fought in earnest between Aladdin and American Thermos, with occasional challenges by Adco Liberty, Ohio Art and Okay Industries.

The smaller firms produced some classic boxes, notably Mickey Mouse and Donald Duck (1954), Howdy Doody (1954), and Davy Crockett (1955) from

Adco Liberty; and Captain Astro (1966), Bond XX (1967), Snow White (1980), and Pit Stop (1968) from Ohio Art. Okay Industries weighed in briefly later on with the now highly prized Wake Up America (1973) and Underdog (1974) boxes, but from the beginning it had always been a two-horse race.

Super-cool Johnny Lightning lunch box appeals to die-cast collectors and lunch box collectors alike. Released in 1970, it is currently valued at $110 in mint condition.

The popular boxes of each year mirrored the stars, heroes, and interests of the times. From the Westerns and space explorations of the late 1950s through the 1960s, Americans enjoyed a golden age of cartoon and film heroes such as the Flintstones (1962), Dudley Do-Right (1962), Bullwinkle and Rocky (1962) and Mary Poppins (1965). As the decade progressed, America grew more aggressive, turning toward such violent heroes as the Man From U.N.C.L.E. (1966), and G.I. Joe (1967) before Vietnam changed the national consciousness.

The early 1970s brought us such innocuous role models as H.R. Pufnstuf (1970), The Partridge Family (1971), and Bobby Sherman (1972), and by decade's end we were greeting both the promise and the threat from beyond in Close Encounters (1978) and Star Wars (1978).

The metal box reigned supreme through the mid-1980s when parental groups began calling for a ban on metal boxes as "deadly weapons." The industry capitulated, and by 1986, both Aladdin and American Thermos were producing all their boxes in plastic.

The switch to plastic was not nearly as abrupt as might be expected. Aladdin and Thermos had been making plastic and vinyl boxes since the late 1950s. These included many character boxes that had no counterparts in metal, which is presently their major saving grace in the collector market.

Neat graphics on this Tom Corbett Space Cadet lunch box and matching bottle make it a must for space toy collectors, too. Estimated value, $95 in mint condition.

Vinyl boxes were made of lower cost materials, consisting basically of cardboard sheathed in thin vinyl. They were not as popular as metal boxes, and their poor construction combined with lower unit sales have resulted in a field with higher rarity factors than the metal box arena. Additionally, vinyl was more affordable to small companies, which produced numerous limited-run boxes for sale or use as premiums.

Vinyl box collecting is an emerging field with few firmly established prices compared to the relative maturity of the metal box market, so any price guide such as this will be more open to debate. As the field matures, the pricing precedents of sales and time will build into a stronger body of knowledge. In this book, for ease of searching, boxes are listed alphabetically by box composition—plastic, steel, and vinyl.

Sports heroes are a natural on lunch boxes. You just wouldn't want to fill it up with junk food! This Wayne Gretzky lunch box was released in 1980, and is valued at $250 in mint condition.

Trends

Lunch boxes are still visible at toy and collectors' shows, but generalized dealers don't feature them quite as much. Specialized dealers still exist, however, dealing in good numbers. Character-related boxes—from Superman to Western heroes to the Munsters—remain popular, rounding out character toy collections. Boxes aren't made like they used to be, and vintage ones hold a true nostalgia and make great display items.

Editor's note: An "n/a" in the bottle column means the box did not come with a bottle.

Many thanks to Joe Soucy for providing pricing expertise for this chapter.

Television shows present a great palette of subject matter for lunch boxes. The Gentle Ben and Lance Link (Secret Chimp). Value in mint condition for each is about $150.

PLASTIC

- **101 Dalmatians,** 1990, Aladdin
  BOX $18   BOTTLE $8

- **18 Wheeler,** 1978, Aladdin
  BOX $30   BOTTLE $10

- **ALF,** unknown, red plastic
  BOX $20   BOTTLE n/a

- **Animalympics Dome,** 1979, Thermos
  BOX $35   BOTTLE $10

- **Astronauts,** 1986, Thermos
  BOX $30   BOTTLE $15

- **Atari Missile Command Dome,** 1983, Aladdin
  BOX $35   BOTTLE $10

- **Back to School,** 1980, Aladdin
  BOX $60   BOTTLE $20

- **Back to the Future,** 1989, Thermos
  BOX $30   BOTTLE $12

- **Bang Bang,** 1982, Thermos
  BOX $45   BOTTLE n/a

- **Barbie with Hologram Mirror,** 1990, Thermos
  BOX $25   BOTTLE $8

- **Batman (dark blue),** 1989, Thermos
  BOX $20   BOTTLE $10

- **Batman (light blue),** 1989, Thermos
  BOX $40   BOTTLE $10

- **Batman Returns,** 1991, Thermos
  BOX $15   BOTTLE $5

- **Beach Bronto,** 1984, Aladdin, no bottle
  BOX $40   BOTTLE n/a

- **Beach Party (blue/pink),** 1988, Deka, with generic plastic bottle
  BOX $15   BOTTLE $5

- **Bear with Heart (3-D),** 1987, Servo
  BOX $12   BOTTLE n/a

- **Beauty & the Beast,** 1991, Aladdin
  BOX $20   BOTTLE $5

- **Bee Gees,** 1978, Thermos
  BOX $40   BOTTLE $20

- **Beetlejuice,** 1980, Thermos
  BOX $10   BOTTLE $4

(KP Photo)

- **Big Jim,** 1976, Thermos
  BOX $80   BOTTLE $30

- **Bozostuffs,** 1988, Deka
  BOX $25   BOTTLE $10

- **C.B. Bears,** 1977, Thermos
  BOX $20   BOTTLE n/a

- **Care Bears,** 1986, Aladdin
  BOX $10   BOTTLE $5

- **Centurions,** 1986, Thermos
  BOX $15   BOTTLE $8

- **Chiclets,** 1987, Thermos, no bottle
  BOX $40   BOTTLE n/a

- **Chipmunks, Alvin and The,** 1983, Thermos
  BOX $20   BOTTLE $10

- **CHiPs,** 1977, Thermos
  BOX $45   BOTTLE $15

- **Cinderella,** 1992, Aladdin
  BOX $25   BOTTLE $10

- **Civil War, The,** 1961, Universal, generic "Thermax" bottle
  BOX $200   BOTTLE $25

- **Colonial Bread Van,** 1984, Moldmark Industries
  BOX $60   BOTTLE $20

- **Crestman Tubular!,** 1980, Taiwan
  BOX $50   BOTTLE $20

- **Days of Thunder,** 1988, Thermos
  BOX $30   BOTTLE $10

- **Deka 4 x 4,** 1988, Deka, generic plastic bottle
  BOX $25   BOTTLE $5

- **Dick Tracy,** 1989, Aladdin
  BOX $20   BOTTLE $10

- **Dino Riders,** 1988, Aladdin
  BOX $20   BOTTLE $10

- **Dinobeasties,** 1988, Thermos
  BOX $15   BOTTLE n/a

- **Dinorocker with Radio & Headset,** 1986, Fundes
  BOX $45   BOTTLE n/a

- **Disney on Parade,** 1970, Aladdin, plastic bottle, glass liner
  BOX $30   BOTTLE $15

- **Disney's Little Mermaid,** 1989, Thermos, w/generic plastic bottle
  BOX $10   BOTTLE $5

- **Duck Tales (4 X 4/Game),** 1986, Aladdin
  BOX $15   BOTTLE $5

- **Dukes of Hazzard,** 1981, Aladdin
  BOX $45   BOTTLE $10

- **Dukes of Hazzard Dome,** 1981, Aladdin
  BOX $45   BOTTLE $10

- **Dune,** 1984, Aladdin
  BOX $45   BOTTLE $20

- **Dunkin Munchkins,** 1972, Thermos
  BOX $25   BOTTLE $15

- **Ecology Dome,** 1980, Thermos
  BOX $45   BOTTLE $20

- **Ed Grimley,** 1988, Aladdin
  BOX $20   BOTTLE $5

- **Entenmann's,** 1989, Thermos
  BOX $15   BOTTLE n/a

- **Ewoks,** 1983, Thermos
  BOX $20   BOTTLE $5

- **Fame,** 1972, Thermos
  BOX $35   BOTTLE $15

- **Fievel Goes West,** 1991, Aladdin
  BOX $10   BOTTLE $4

- **Fire Engine Co. 7,** 1985, D.A.S., w/generic plastic bottle
  BOX $30   BOTTLE $5

- **Fisher-Price Mini Lunch Box,** 1962, Fisher-Price, red w/barnyard scenes, matching bottle
  BOX $20   BOTTLE $5

- **Flash Gordon Dome,** 1979, Aladdin
  BOX $60   BOTTLE $20

- **Flintstones,** unknown, premium, Denny's Restaurants
  BOX $30   BOTTLE n/a

- **Flintstones Kids,** 1987, Thermos
  BOX $40   BOTTLE $10

- **Food Fighters,** 1988, Aladdin
  BOX $20   BOTTLE $10

- **Fraggle Rock,** 1987, Thermos
  BOX $15   BOTTLE $5

- **Frito Lay's,** 1982, Thermos, no bottle
  BOX $50   BOTTLE n/a

- **G.I. Joe (Space Mission),** 1989, Aladdin
  BOX $25   BOTTLE $10

- **G.I. Joe, Live the Adventure,** 1986, Aladdin
  BOX $25   BOTTLE $10

- **Garfield (food fight),** 1979, Thermos
  BOX $25   BOTTLE $10

- **Garfield (lunch),** 1977, Thermos
  BOX $20   BOTTLE $10

(KP Photo)

- **Geoffrey,** 1981, Aladdin
  BOX $30   BOTTLE $10

- **Get Along Gang,** 1983, Aladdin
  BOX $10   BOTTLE $5

- **Ghostbusters,** 1986, Deka
  BOX $15   BOTTLE $5

- **Go Bots,** 1984, Thermos
  BOX $10   BOTTLE $5

- **Golden Girls,** 1984, Thermos
  BOX $10   BOTTLE $5

LUNCH BOXES

❑ **Goonies,** 1985, Aladdin
    BOX $20   **BOTTLE** $5

❑ **Gumby,** 1986, Thermos
    BOX $60   **BOTTLE** $20

❑ **Hot Wheels,** 1984, Thermos
    BOX $50   **BOTTLE** $20

(KP Photo)

❑ **Howdy Doody Dome,** 1977, Thermos
    BOX $80   **BOTTLE** $35

❑ **Incredible Hulk Dome,** 1980, Aladdin
    BOX $30   **BOTTLE** $10

(KP Photo)

❑ **Incredible Hulk, The,** 1978, Aladdin, plastic bottle
    BOX $30   **BOTTLE** $10

❑ **Inspector Gadget,** 1983, Thermos
    BOX $20   **BOTTLE** $8

❑ **It's Not Just the Bus - Greyhound,** 1980, Aladdin
    BOX $60   **BOTTLE** $20

(KP Photo)

❑ **Jabber Jaw,** 1977, Thermos
    BOX $50   **BOTTLE** $20

❑ **Jetsons (3-D),** 1987, Servo
    BOX $75   **BOTTLE** $30

❑ **Jetsons (paper picture),** 1987, Servo
    BOX $110   **BOTTLE** $30

❑ **Jetsons, The Movie,** 1990, Aladdin
    BOX $30   **BOTTLE** $15

❑ **Kermit the Frog, Lunch With,** 1988, Thermos
    BOX $18   **BOTTLE** $5

❑ **Kermit's Frog Scout Van,** 1989, Super-seal, no bottle
    BOX $15   **BOTTLE** n/a

❑ **Kool-Aid Man,** 1986, Thermos
    BOX $20   **BOTTLE** $10

❑ **Lisa Frank,** 1980, Thermos
    BOX $10   **BOTTLE** $5

❑ **Little Orphan Annie,** 1973, Thermos
    BOX $50   **BOTTLE** $20

❑ **Looney Tunes Birthday Party,** 1989, Thermos, blue or red
    BOX $20   **BOTTLE** $10

❑ **Looney Tunes Dancing,** 1977, Thermos
    BOX $20   **BOTTLE** $10

❑ **Looney Tunes Playing Drums,** 1978, Thermos
    BOX $20   **BOTTLE** $10

❑ **Looney Tunes Tasmanian Devil,** 1988, Thermos, w/generic plastic bottle
    BOX $15   **BOTTLE** $10

❑ **Los Angeles Olympics,** 1984, Aladdin
    BOX $20   **BOTTLE** $5

❑ **Lucy's Luncheonette,** 1981, Thermos, Peanuts characters
    BOX $15   **BOTTLE** $5

❑ **Lunch Man with Radio,** 1986, Fun Design, w/built-in radio, no bottle
    BOX $35   **BOTTLE** n/a

❑ **Lunch 'N Tunes Safari,** 1986, Fun Design, w/built-in radio, no bottle
    BOX $35   **BOTTLE** n/a

❑ **Lunch 'N Tunes Singing Sandwich,** 1986, Fun Design, w/built-in radio, no bottle
    BOX $35   **BOTTLE** n/a

❑ **Lunch Time with Snoopy Dome,** 1981, Thermos
    BOX $15   **BOTTLE** $5

❑ **Mad Balls,** 1986, Aladdin
    BOX $25   **BOTTLE** $10

❑ **Marvel Super Heroes,** 1990, Thermos
    BOX $20   **BOTTLE** $10

❑ **Max Headroom (Coca-Cola),** 1985, Aladdin
    BOX $50   **BOTTLE** $25

❑ **McDonald's Happy Meal,** 1986, Fisher-Price
    BOX $15   **BOTTLE** n/a

❑ **Menudo,** 1984, Thermos
    BOX $12   **BOTTLE** $5

❑ **Mickey & Minnie Mouse in Pink Car,** 1988, Aladdin
    BOX $10   **BOTTLE** $5

(ToyShop File Photo)

❑ **Mickey Mouse & Donald Duck,** 1984, Aladdin, Dome-style lunchbox with image of Mickey, Minnie, Donald and Daisy having a picnic
    BOX $10   **BOTTLE** $5

❑ **Mickey Mouse & Donald Duck See-Saw,** 1986, Aladdin
    BOX $10   **BOTTLE** $5

❑ **Mickey Mouse at City Zoo,** 1985, Aladdin
    BOX $10   **BOTTLE** $5

(KP Photo)

❑ **Mickey Mouse Head,** 1989, Aladdin
    BOX $20   **BOTTLE** $5

❑ **Mickey on Swinging Bridge,** 1987, Aladdin
    BOX $10   **BOTTLE** $5

❑ **Mickey Skateboarding,** 1980, Aladdin
    BOX $18   **BOTTLE** $5

❑ **Mighty Mouse,** 1979, Thermos
    BOX $35   **BOTTLE** $10

❑ **Miss Piggy's Safari Van,** 1989, Super-seal, no bottle
    BOX $15   **BOTTLE** n/a

❑ **Monster in My Pocket,** 1990, Aladdin
    BOX $30   **BOTTLE** $5

❑ **Movie Monsters,** 1979, Universal
    BOX $35   **BOTTLE** $12

❑ **Mr. T,** 1984, Aladdin
    BOX $20   **BOTTLE** $10

❑ **Munchie Tunes Bear with Radio,** 1986, Fun Design, w/built-in radio
    BOX $35   **BOTTLE** $5

❑ **Munchie Tunes Punchie Pup w/Radio,** 1986, Fun Design, w/built-in radio
BOX $35   BOTTLE $5

❑ **Munchie Tunes Robot with Radio,** 1986, Fun Design, w/built-in radio
BOX $35   BOTTLE $5

❑ **Muppets (blue),** 1982, Thermos
BOX $12   BOTTLE $5

❑ **Muppets Dome,** 1981, Thermos, plastic red box w/matching bottle
BOX $20   BOTTLE $5

❑ **New Kids on the Block (pink/orange),** 1990, Thermos
BOX $10   BOTTLE $5

❑ **Nosy Bears,** 1988, Aladdin
BOX $12   BOTTLE $5

❑ **Official Lunch Football,** 1974, unknown, football shaped box, red or brown
BOX $100   BOTTLE n/a

❑ **Peanuts, Wienie Roast,** 1985, Thermos
BOX $10   BOTTLE $4

❑ **Pee Wee's Playhouse,** 1987, Thermos, w/generic plastic bottle
BOX $20   BOTTLE $5

❑ **Peter Pan Peanut Butter,** 1984, Taiwan
BOX $85   BOTTLE $20

❑ **Pickle,** 1972, Fesco, no bottle
BOX $140   BOTTLE n/a

❑ **Popeye & Son,** 1987, Servo, plastic red box, flat paper label, w/matching bottle
BOX $65   BOTTLE $12

❑ **Popeye & Son (3-D),** 1987, Servo, plastic box, red or yellow, w/matching bottle
BOX $50   BOTTLE $12

❑ **Popeye Dome,** 1979, Aladdin
BOX $35   BOTTLE $15

❑ **Popeye, Truant Officer,** 1964, King Seeley Thermos, plastic red box, matching metal bottle (Canada)
BOX $150   BOTTLE $35

❑ **Punky Brewster,** 1984, Deka
BOX $20   BOTTLE $10

❑ **Q-Bert,** 1983, Thermos
BOX $15   BOTTLE $12

❑ **Race Cars,** 1987, Servo
BOX $20   BOTTLE n/a

❑ **Raggedy Ann & Andy,** 1988, Aladdin
BOX $45   BOTTLE $20

❑ **Rainbow Bread Van,** 1984, Moldmark Industries
BOX $60   BOTTLE $20

❑ **Rainbow Brite,** 1983, Thermos
BOX $10   BOTTLE $5

❑ **Robot Man and Friends,** 1984, Thermos
BOX $20   BOTTLE $10

❑ **Rocketeer,** 1990, Aladdin
BOX $10   BOTTLE $5

❑ **Rocky Roughneck,** 1977, Thermos
BOX $25   BOTTLE $10

❑ **Roller Games,** 1989, Thermos
BOX $25   BOTTLE $10

❑ **S.W.A.T. Dome,** 1975, Thermos
BOX $45   BOTTLE $15

❑ **Scooby Doo,** 1973, Thermos
BOX $30   BOTTLE $20

❑ **Scooby Doo,** 1984, Aladdin
BOX $40   BOTTLE $20

❑ **Scooby-Doo, A Pup Named,** 1988, Aladdin
BOX $20   BOTTLE $10

❑ **Sesame Street,** 1985, Aladdin/Canada
BOX $10   BOTTLE $5

❑ **Shirt Tales,** 1981, Thermos
BOX $10   BOTTLE $5

❑ **Sky Commanders,** 1987, Thermos, generic plastic bottle
BOX $15   BOTTLE $5

❑ **Smurfette,** 1984, Thermos
BOX $10   BOTTLE $5

❑ **Smurfs,** 1984, Thermos
BOX $15   BOTTLE $5

❑ **Smurfs Dome,** 1981, Thermos
BOX $20   BOTTLE $5

❑ **Smurfs Fishing,** 1984, Thermos
BOX $15   BOTTLE $5

❑ **Snak Shot Camera,** 1987, Hummer, camera-shaped box, blue or green, w/generic plastic bottle
BOX $30   BOTTLE $2

❑ **Snoopy Dome,** 1978, Thermos
BOX $20   BOTTLE $5

❑ **Snorks,** 1984, Thermos
BOX $12   BOTTLE $5

❑ **Snow White,** 1980, Aladdin
BOX $40   BOTTLE $15

❑ **Spare Parts,** 1982, Aladdin, w/generic plastic bottle
BOX $35   BOTTLE $10

❑ **Sport Billy,** 1982, Thermos
BOX $20   BOTTLE $10

❑ **Sport Goofy,** 1986, Aladdin
BOX $30   BOTTLE $10

❑ **Star Com. U.S. Space Force,** 1987, Thermos
BOX $20   BOTTLE $10

❑ **Star Trek Next Generation,** 1988, Thermos, blue box, group picture, matching bottle
BOX $35   BOTTLE $10

❑ **Star Trek Next Generation,** 1989, Thermos, red box, Picard, Data, Wesley, matching bottle
BOX $50   BOTTLE $20

❑ **Star Wars, Droids,** 1985, Thermos
BOX $30   BOTTLE $10

❑ **Strawberry Shortcake,** 1980, Aladdin
BOX $10   BOTTLE $5

❑ **Superman II Dome,** 1986, Aladdin
BOX $40   BOTTLE $20

❑ **Superman, This is a Job For,** 1980, Aladdin, no bottle
BOX $25   BOTTLE n/a

❑ **Tail Spin,** 1986, Aladdin
BOX $10   BOTTLE $5

❑ **Tang Trio,** 1988, Thermos, red or yellow box w/generic plastic bottle
BOX $35   BOTTLE $5

❑ **Teenage Mutant Ninja Turtles,** 1990, Thermos, w/generic plastic bottle
BOX $12   BOTTLE $5

❑ **Thundarr the Barbarian Dome,** 1981, Aladdin, plastic dome box w/matching bottle
BOX $25   BOTTLE $10

❑ **Timeless Tales,** 1989, Aladdin
BOX $10   BOTTLE $5

❑ **Tiny Toon Adventures,** 1990, Thermos
BOX $10   BOTTLE $5

❑ **Tom & Jerry,** 1989, Aladdin
BOX $30   BOTTLE $10

❑ **Transformers,** 1985, Aladdin
BOX $15   BOTTLE $5

❑ **Transformers Dome,** 1986, Aladdin/Canada, dome box, generic plastic bottle
BOX $35   BOTTLE $8

❑ **Tweety & Sylvester,** 1986, Thermos
BOX $45   BOTTLE $20

(KP Photo)

❑ **Wayne Gretzky,** 1980, Aladdin
BOX $100   BOTTLE $30

❑ **Wayne Gretzky Dome,** 1980, Aladdin
BOX $120   BOTTLE $30

❑ **Where's Waldo,** 1990, Thermos
BOX $10   BOTTLE $5

❑ **Who Framed Roger Rabbit,** 1987, Thermos, red or yellow, w/matching bottle
BOX $20   BOTTLE $10

❑ **Wild Fire,** 1986, Aladdin
BOX $15   BOTTLE $8

❑ **Wizard of Oz, 50th Anniversary,** 1989, Aladdin
BOX $60   BOTTLE $20

❑ **Woody Woodpecker,** 1972, Aladdin, yellow box, red bottle
BOX $50   BOTTLE $40

LUNCH BOXES

❏ **World Wrestling Federation,** 1986, Thermos
BOX $10   BOTTLE $5

❏ **Wrinkles,** 1984, Thermos
BOX $10   BOTTLE $5

❏ **Wuzzles,** 1985, Aladdin
BOX $10   BOTTLE $5

❏ **Yogi's Treasure Hunt,** 1987, Servo, flat paper label, w/matching bottle
BOX $25   BOTTLE $30

❏ **Yogi's Treasure Hunt (3-D),** 1987, Servo, 3-D box, green or pink, w/matching bottle
BOX $55   BOTTLE $30

STEEL

❏ **240 Robert,** 1978, Aladdin
BOX $3600   BOTTLE n/a

❏ **Action Jackson,** 1973, Okay Industries, matching steel bottle
BOX $950   BOTTLE $300

❏ **Adam-12,** 1973, Aladdin, matching plastic bottle
BOX $300   BOTTLE $125

(KP Photo)

❏ **Addams Family,** 1974, King Seeley Thermos, matching plastic bottle
BOX $225   BOTTLE $50

❏ **Airline,** 1969, Ohio Art, no bottle
BOX $150   BOTTLE n/a

❏ **All American,** 1954, Universal, steel/glass bottle
BOX $395   BOTTLE $95

❏ **America on Parade,** 1976, Aladdin, matching plastic bottle
BOX $75   BOTTLE $40

❏ **Americana,** 1958, King Seeley Thermos, steel/glass bottle
BOX $395   BOTTLE $150

❏ **Animal Friends,** 1978, Ohio Art, yellow or red background behind name
BOX $60   BOTTLE n/a

(KP Photo)

❏ **Annie Oakley & Tagg,** 1955, Aladdin, matching steel bottle, shown with Dukes of Hazzard & Magic Kingdom lunch boxes
BOX $425   BOTTLE $150

❏ **Annie, The Movie,** 1982, Aladdin, plastic bottle
BOX $50   BOTTLE $25

❏ **Apple's Way,** 1975, King Seeley Thermos, plastic bottle
BOX $95   BOTTLE $40

❏ **Archies,** 1969, Aladdin, matching plastic bottle
BOX $150   BOTTLE $65

❏ **Astronaut Dome,** 1960, King Seeley Thermos, steel/glass bottle
BOX $285   BOTTLE $75

❏ **Astronauts,** 1969, Aladdin, matching plastic bottle
BOX $150   BOTTLE $65

❏ **A-Team,** 1985, King Seeley Thermos, plastic bottle
BOX $50   BOTTLE $25

❏ **Atom Ant/Secret Squirrel,** 1966, King Seeley Thermos, matching steel bottle
BOX $265   BOTTLE $120

❏ **Auto Race,** 1967, King Seeley Thermos, matching steel bottle
BOX $100   BOTTLE $50

❏ **Back in '76,** 1975, Aladdin, plastic bottle
BOX $80   BOTTLE $40

❏ **Barbie Lunch Kit,** 1962, King Seeley Thermos, steel/glass bottle
BOX $275   BOTTLE $90

❏ **Basketweave,** 1968, Ohio Art, no bottle
BOX $75   BOTTLE n/a

(KP Photo)

❏ **Batman and Robin,** 1966, Aladdin, matching steel bottle
BOX $225   BOTTLE $100

❏ **Battle Kit,** 1965, King Seeley Thermos, matching steel bottle
BOX $125   BOTTLE $65

(KP Photo)

❏ **Battle of the Planets,** 1979, King Seeley Thermos, matching plastic bottle, shown with Chan Clan, The & Hot Wheels lunch boxes
BOX $90   BOTTLE $40

❏ **Battlestar Galactica,** 1978, Aladdin, matching plastic bottle
BOX $100   BOTTLE $35

❏ **Beatles,** 1966, Aladdin, blue, matching bottle
BOX $900   BOTTLE $275

❏ **Bedknobs & Broomsticks,** 1972, Aladdin, plastic bottle
BOX $75   BOTTLE $35

❏ **Bee Gees,** 1978, King Seeley Thermos, Robin on back, matching plastic bottle
BOX $125   BOTTLE $45

❏ **Bee Gees,** 1978, King Seeley Thermos, Maurice on back, matching plastic bottle
BOX $150   BOTTLE $45

❏ **Bee Gees,** 1978, King Seeley Thermos, Barry on back, matching plastic bottle
BOX $125   BOTTLE $45

❏ **Berenstain Bears,** 1983, American Thermos, matching plastic bottle
BOX $50   BOTTLE $25

(KP Photo)

❏ **Beverly Hillbillies,** 1963, Aladdin, matching steel bottle
BOX $225   BOTTLE $95

❏ **Bionic Woman, with Car,** 1977, Aladdin, plastic bottle
BOX $225   BOTTLE $95

❏ **Bionic Woman, with Dog,** 1978, Aladdin, matching plastic bottle
BOX $130   BOTTLE $40

❏ **Black Hole,** 1979, Aladdin, matching plastic bottle
BOX $95   BOTTLE $40

❏ **Blondie,** 1969, King Seeley Thermos, matching steel bottle
BOX $225   BOTTLE $75

❏ **Boating,** 1959, American Thermos, matching steel bottle
BOX $400   BOTTLE $125

❏ **Bobby Sherman,** 1972, King Seeley Thermos, matching steel bottle
BOX $125   BOTTLE $75

❏ **Bonanza,** 1963, Aladdin, green rim box, steel bottle
BOX $225   BOTTLE $95

❏ **Bonanza,** 1965, Aladdin, brown rim box, steel bottle
    BOX $160 **BOTTLE** $80

(KP Photo)

❏ **Bonanza,** 1968, Aladdin, black rim box, steel bottle
    BOX $275 **BOTTLE** $120

❏ **Bond XX,** 1967, Ohio Art, no bottle
    BOX $200 **BOTTLE** n/a

❏ **Boston Bruins,** 1973, Okay Industries, steel/glass bottle
    BOX $525 **BOTTLE** $250

❏ **Bozo the Clown Dome,** Aladdin, steel bottle
    BOX $325 **BOTTLE** $120

(KP Photo)

❏ **Brady Bunch,** 1970, King Seeley Thermos, matching steel bottle
    BOX $400 **BOTTLE** $150

❏ **Brave Eagle,** 1957, American Thermos, red, blue, gray or green band, matching steel bottle
    BOX $220 **BOTTLE** $150

❏ **Bread Box Dome,** 1968, Aladdin, Campbell's Soup bottle
    BOX $300 **BOTTLE** $175

(KP Photo)

❏ **Buccaneer Dome,** 1957, Aladdin, matching bottle, shown with Julia lunch box
    BOX $350 **BOTTLE** $125

❏ **Buck Rogers,** 1979, Aladdin, matching plastic bottle
    BOX $75 **BOTTLE** $35

❏ **Bugaloos,** 1971, Aladdin, matching plastic bottle
    BOX $125 **BOTTLE** $45

❏ **Bullwinkle & Rocky,** 1962, Universal, blue box, steel bottle
    BOX $800 **BOTTLE** $220

❏ **Cabbage Patch Kids,** 1984, King Seeley Thermos, matching plastic bottle
    BOX $15 **BOTTLE** $5

❏ **Cable Car Dome,** 1962, Aladdin, steel/glass bottle
    BOX $600 **BOTTLE** $125

❏ **Campbell's Kids,** 1973, Okay, matching steel bottle
    BOX $180 **BOTTLE** $100

❏ **Campus Queen,** 1967, King Seeley Thermos, matching steel bottle
    BOX $50 **BOTTLE** $25

❏ **Canadian Pacific Railroad,** 1970, Ohio Art, no bottle
    BOX $60 **BOTTLE** n/a

❏ **Captain Astro,** 1966, Ohio Art, no bottle
    BOX $325 **BOTTLE** n/a

❏ **Care Bear Cousins,** 1985, Aladdin, matching plastic bottle
    BOX $10 **BOTTLE** $5

❏ **Care Bears,** 1984, Aladdin, plastic bottle
    BOX $10 **BOTTLE** $5

❏ **Carnival,** 1959, Universal, matching steel bottle
    BOX $550 **BOTTLE** $250

❏ **Cartoon Zoo Lunch Chest,** 1962, Universal, steel/glass bottle
    BOX $325 **BOTTLE** $125

❏ **Casey Jones,** 1960, Universal, steel dome box, steel/glass bottle
    BOX $650 **BOTTLE** $125

(KP Photo)

❏ **Chan Clan, The,** 1973, King Seeley Thermos, plastic bottle, shown with Battle of the Planets & Hot Wheels lunch boxes
    BOX $110 **BOTTLE** $35

❏ **Charlie's Angels,** 1978, Aladdin, matching plastic bottle
    BOX $125 **BOTTLE** $40

❏ **Chavo,** 1979, Aladdin, matching plastic bottle
    BOX $150 **BOTTLE** $50

❏ **Children, blue,** 1974, Okay Industries, plastic bottle
    BOX $160 **BOTTLE** $40

❏ **Children, yellow,** 1974, Okay Industries, plastic bottle
    BOX $210 **BOTTLE** $40

❏ **Children's,** 1984, Ohio Art, no bottle
    BOX $60 **BOTTLE** n/a

❏ **Chitty Chitty Bang Bang,** 1969, King Seeley Thermos, matching steel bottle
    BOX $195 **BOTTLE** $60

❏ **Chuck Wagon Dome,** 1958, Aladdin, matching bottle
    BOX $295 **BOTTLE** $90

❏ **Circus Wagon Dome,** 1958, King Seeley Thermos, steel/glass bottle
    BOX $350 **BOTTLE** $150

❏ **Clash of the Titans,** 1981, King Seeley Thermos, matching plastic bottle
    BOX $95 **BOTTLE** $40

❏ **Close Encounters of the Third Kind,** 1978, King Seeley Thermos, plastic bottle
    BOX $125 **BOTTLE** $40

❏ **Color Me Happy,** 1984, Ohio Art, no bottle
    BOX $175 **BOTTLE** n/a

❏ **Corsage,** 1958, American Thermos, matching steel bottle
    BOX $95 **BOTTLE** $50

(KP Photo)

❏ **Cowboy in Africa, Chuck Connors,** 1968, King Seeley Thermos, matching steel bottle
    BOX $225 **BOTTLE** $75

❏ **Cracker Jack,** 1969, Aladdin, matching plastic bottle
    BOX $90 **BOTTLE** $35

❏ **Curiosity Shop,** 1972, King Seeley Thermos, matching steel bottle
    BOX $75 **BOTTLE** $45

❏ **Cyclist Dirt Bike,** 1979, Aladdin, plastic bottle
    BOX $80 **BOTTLE** $45

❏ **Daniel Boone,** 1955, Aladdin, matching steel bottle
    BOX $400 **BOTTLE** $110

❏ **Daniel Boone,** 1965, Aladdin, matching steel bottle
    BOX $195 **BOTTLE** $90

❏ **Dark Crystal,** 1982, King Seeley Thermos, matching plastic bottle
    BOX $35 **BOTTLE** $20

(ToyShop File Photo)

❏ **Davy Crockett,** 1955, Holtemp, matching steel bottle (shown)
BOX $225 **BOTTLE** $75

❏ **Davy Crockett,** 1955, Kruger, no bottle
BOX $475 **BOTTLE** n/a

❏ **Davy Crockett/Kit Carson,** 1955, Adco Liberty
BOX $290 **BOTTLE** n/a

❏ **Debutante,** 1958, Aladdin, matching steel bottle
BOX $110 **BOTTLE** $75

❏ **Denim Diner Dome,** 1975, Aladdin, matching plastic bottle
BOX $85 **BOTTLE** $30

(KP Photo)

❏ **Dick Tracy,** 1967, Aladdin, matching steel bottle
BOX $225 **BOTTLE** $80

❏ **Disco,** 1979, Aladdin, matching plastic bottle
BOX $90 **BOTTLE** $30

❏ **Disco Fever,** 1980, Aladdin, matching plastic bottle
BOX $110 **BOTTLE** $35

(KP Photo)

❏ **Disney Express,** 1979, Aladdin, matching plastic bottle, shown with Disney, Wonderful World & Mickey Mouse Club lunch boxes
BOX $35 **BOTTLE** $15

❏ **Disney Fire Fighters Dome,** 1974, Aladdin, matching plastic bottle
BOX $175 **BOTTLE** $60

❏ **Disney School Bus Dome,** 1968, Aladdin, steel/glass bottle
BOX $75 **BOTTLE** $30

❏ **Disney World,** 1972, Aladdin, matching plastic bottle
BOX $45 **BOTTLE** $25

(KP Photo)

❏ **Disney, Wonderful World of,** 1982, Aladdin, plastic bottle, shown with Mickey Mouse Club & Disney Express lunch boxes
BOX $50 **BOTTLE** $30

❏ **Disneyland (Castle),** 1957, Aladdin, matching steel bottle
BOX $220 **BOTTLE** $115

❏ **Disneyland (Monorail),** 1968, Aladdin, matching steel bottle
BOX $250 **BOTTLE** $115

(KP Photo)

❏ **Disney's Magic Kingdom,** 1980, Aladdin, plastic bottle
BOX $45 **BOTTLE** $25

❏ **Disney's Rescuers, The,** 1977, Aladdin, plastic bottle
BOX $55 **BOTTLE** $35

❏ **Disney's Robin Hood,** 1974, Aladdin, plastic bottle
BOX $65 **BOTTLE** $30

❏ **Donald Duck,** 1980, Cheinco, no bottle
BOX $50 **BOTTLE** n/a

❏ **Double Decker,** 1970, Aladdin, matching plastic bottle
BOX $75 **BOTTLE** $45

❏ **Dr. Dolittle,** Aladdin, steel/glass bottle
BOX $180 **BOTTLE** $65

❏ **Dr. Seuss,** 1970, Aladdin, matching plastic bottle
BOX $225 **BOTTLE** $75

(KP Photo)

❏ **Drag Strip,** 1975, Aladdin, matching plastic bottle
BOX $90 **BOTTLE** $35

❏ **Dragon's Lair,** 1983, Aladdin, matching plastic bottle
BOX $45 **BOTTLE** $25

❏ **Duchess,** 1960, Aladdin, steel/glass bottle
BOX $95 **BOTTLE** $40

❏ **Dudley Do-Right,** 1962, Universal, matching steel bottle
BOX $1800 **BOTTLE** $600

(KP Photo)

❏ **Dukes of Hazzard,** 1983, Aladdin, matching plastic bottle, shown with Annie & Magic Kingdom lunch boxes
BOX $125 **BOTTLE** $50

❏ **Dutch Cottage Dome,** 1958, King Seeley Thermos, steel/glass bottle
BOX $450 **BOTTLE** $150

❏ **Dyno Mutt,** 1977, King Seeley Thermos, plastic bottle
BOX $90 **BOTTLE** $40

❏ **E.T., The Extra-Terrestrial,** 1982, Aladdin, matching plastic bottle
BOX $45 **BOTTLE** $20

❑ **Early West Indian Territory,** 1982, Ohio Art
BOX $85 BOTTLE n/a

❑ **Early West Oregon Trail,** 1982, Ohio Art, no bottle
BOX $85 BOTTLE n/a

❑ **Early West Pony Express,** 1982, Ohio Art, no bottle
BOX $85 BOTTLE n/a

❑ **Emergency!,** 1973, Aladdin, plastic bottle
BOX $250 BOTTLE $50

❑ **Emergency! Dome,** 1977, Aladdin, plastic bottle
BOX $275 BOTTLE $50

❑ **Evel Knievel,** 1974, Aladdin, plastic bottle
BOX $140 BOTTLE $40

❑ **Exciting World of Metrics, The,** 1976, King Seeley Thermos, plastic bottle
BOX $65 BOTTLE $30

❑ **Fall Guy,** 1981, Aladdin, matching plastic bottle
BOX $35 BOTTLE $20

❑ **Family Affair,** 1969, King Seeley Thermos, matching steel bottle
BOX $125 BOTTLE $50

❑ **Fat Albert and the Cosby Kids,** 1973, King Seeley Thermos, plastic bottle
BOX $80 BOTTLE $30

❑ **Fess Parker,** 1965, King Seeley Thermos, matching steel bottle
BOX $200 BOTTLE $90

❑ **Fireball XL5,** 1964, King Seeley Thermos, steel/glass bottle
BOX $225 BOTTLE $85

❑ **Firehouse Dome,** 1959, American Thermos, steel/glass bottle
BOX $400 BOTTLE $150

❑ **Flag-O-Rama,** 1954, Universal, steel/glass bottle
BOX $475 BOTTLE $110

❑ **Flintstones,** 1962, Aladdin, orange, 1st issue, matching bottle
BOX $275 BOTTLE $80

❑ **Flintstones,** 1963, Aladdin, yellow, 2nd issue, matching bottle
BOX $300 BOTTLE $80

❑ **Flintstones,** 1973, Aladdin, matching plastic bottle
BOX $200 BOTTLE $50

(KP Photo)

❑ **Flipper,** 1966, King Seeley Thermos, matching steel bottle
BOX $200 BOTTLE $75

❑ **Floral,** 1970, Ohio Art, no bottle
BOX $40 BOTTLE n/a

❑ **Flying Nun,** 1968, Aladdin, matching steel bottle
BOX $250 BOTTLE $95

❑ **Fonz, The,** 1978, King Seeley Thermos, plastic bottle
BOX $120 BOTTLE $40

❑ **Fox and the Hound,** 1981, Aladdin, plastic bottle
BOX $45 BOTTLE $25

❑ **Fraggle Rock,** 1984, King Seeley Thermos, matching plastic bottle
BOX $45 BOTTLE $20

❑ **Fritos,** 1975, King Seeley Thermos, generic bottle
BOX $125 BOTTLE n/a

❑ **Frontier Days,** 1957, Ohio Art, no bottle
BOX $275 BOTTLE n/a

❑ **Frost Flowers,** 1962, Ohio Art, no bottle
BOX $70 BOTTLE n/a

❑ **Fruit Basket,** 1975, Ohio Art, no bottle
BOX $35 BOTTLE n/a

❑ **Funtastic World of Hanna-Barbera,** 1977, King Seeley Thermos, Huck Hound, plastic bottle
BOX $150 BOTTLE $45

❑ **Funtastic World of Hanna-Barbera,** 1978, King Seeley Thermos, Flintstones & Yogi, plastic bottle
BOX $175 BOTTLE $45

❑ **G.I. Joe,** 1967, King Seeley Thermos, steel/glass bottle
BOX $350 BOTTLE $90

❑ **G.I. Joe,** 1982, King Seeley Thermos, plastic bottle
BOX $65 BOTTLE $25

❑ **Gene Autry,** 1954, Universal, steel/glass bottle
BOX $600 BOTTLE $175

(KP Photo)

❑ **Gentle Ben,** 1968, Aladdin, plastic bottle, glass liner, shown here with Lance Link lunch box
BOX $150 BOTTLE $50

(KP Photo)

❑ **Get Smart,** 1966, King Seeley Thermos, steel/glass bottle
BOX $225 BOTTLE $95

❑ **Ghostland,** 1977, Ohio Art, spinner game, no bottle
BOX $50 BOTTLE n/a

(KP Photo)

❑ **Globe-Trotter Dome,** 1959, Aladdin, steel dome box, matching steel/glass bottle
BOX $265 BOTTLE $120

❑ **Gomer Pyle USMC,** 1966, Aladdin, matching steel bottle
BOX $250 BOTTLE $90

(KP Photo)

❑ **Goober and the Ghostchasers / Inch High,** 1974, King Seeley Thermos, matching plastic bottle
BOX $50 BOTTLE $25

❑ **Great Wild West,** 1959, Universal, matching steel bottle
BOX $550 BOTTLE $225

❑ **Green Hornet,** 1967, King Seeley Thermos, matching steel bottle
BOX $425 BOTTLE $150

(KP Photo)

❑ **Gremlins,** 1984, Aladdin, matching plastic bottle
BOX $45 BOTTLE $20

❑ **Grizzly Adams Dome,** 1977, Aladdin, plastic bottle
BOX $150 BOTTLE $40

❑ **Guns of Will Sonnett, The,** 1968, King Seeley Thermos, steel/glass bottle
BOX $195 BOTTLE $90

LUNCH BOXES

Gunsmoke, 1959, Aladdin, plastic bottle
BOX $250 **BOTTLE** $95

Gunsmoke, 1972, Aladdin, mule splashing box w/matching bottle
BOX $175 **BOTTLE** $65

Gunsmoke, 1973, Aladdin, stagecoach box, matching bottle
BOX $175 **BOTTLE** $65

Gunsmoke, Double L Version, 1959, Aladdin, double L error version, matching bottle
BOX $700 **BOTTLE** $95

(KP Photo)

Gunsmoke, Marshal Matt Dillon, 1962, Aladdin, matching steel bottle
BOX $250 **BOTTLE** $95

(KP Photo)

H.R. Pufnstuf, 1970, Aladdin, matching plastic bottle
BOX $225 **BOTTLE** $70

Hair Bear Bunch, The, 1972, King Seeley Thermos, plastic bottle
BOX $75 **BOTTLE** $35

Hansel and Gretel, 1982, Ohio Art, no bottle
BOX $80 **BOTTLE** n/a

Happy Days, 1977, American Thermos, matching plastic bottle
BOX $150 **BOTTLE** $40

Hardy Boys Mysteries, 1977, King Seeley Thermos, matching plastic bottle
BOX $65 **BOTTLE** $30

Harlem Globetrotters, 1971, King Seeley Thermos, steel bottle, blue or purple uniforms
BOX $95 **BOTTLE** $50

Have Gun, Will Travel, 1960, Aladdin, matching bottle, Paladin
BOX $375 **BOTTLE** $150

Heathcliff, 1982, Aladdin, matching plastic bottle
BOX $40 **BOTTLE** $20

Hector Heathcote, 1964, Aladdin, matching steel bottle
BOX $275 **BOTTLE** $90

(KP Photo)

Hee Haw, 1971, King Seeley Thermos, matching steel bottle
BOX $125 **BOTTLE** $65

He-Man & Masters of the Universe, 1984, Aladdin, matching plastic bottle
BOX $45 **BOTTLE** $20

Highway Signs, 1972, Ohio Art, no bottle
BOX $70 **BOTTLE** n/a

(KP Photo)

Hogan's Heroes Dome, 1966, Aladdin, steel/glass bottle
BOX $350 **BOTTLE** $125

Holly Hobbie, 1968, Aladdin, red rim, matching plastic bottle
BOX $40 **BOTTLE** $15

Holly Hobbie, 1973, Aladdin, matching plastic bottle
BOX $40 **BOTTLE** $15

Holly Hobbie, 1979, Aladdin, matching plastic bottle
BOX $40 **BOTTLE** $15

Home Town Airport Dome, 1960, King Seeley Thermos, steel/glass bottle
BOX $1000 **BOTTLE** $275

(KP Photo)

Hong Kong Phooey, 1975, King Seeley Thermos, steel/glass bottle
BOX $75 **BOTTLE** $40

(KP Photo)

Hopalong Cassidy, 1950, Aladdin, red or blue, steel/glass bottle
BOX $260 **BOTTLE** $90

Hopalong Cassidy, 1952, Aladdin, steel bottle
BOX $250 **BOTTLE** $90

Hopalong Cassidy, 1954, Aladdin, black rim, steel/glass bottle, full litho
BOX $400 **BOTTLE** $150

(ToyShop File Photo)

Hot Wheels, 1969, King Seeley Thermos, matching steel bottle
BOX $150 **BOTTLE** $65

How the West Was Won, 1979, King Seeley Thermos, matching plastic bottle
BOX $75 **BOTTLE** $40

Howdy Doody, 1954, Adco Liberty
BOX $575 **BOTTLE** n/a

Huckleberry Hound, 1961, Aladdin, steel/glass bottle
BOX $200 **BOTTLE** $90

Indiana Jones, 1984, King Seeley Thermos, matching plastic bottle
BOX $50 **BOTTLE** $25

Indiana Jones Temple of Doom, 1984, King Seeley Thermos, matching plastic bottle
BOX $50 **BOTTLE** $25

It's About Time Dome, 1967, Aladdin, matching bottle
BOX $275 **BOTTLE** $125

Jack and Jill, 1982, Ohio Art
BOX $400 **BOTTLE** n/a

James Bond 007, 1966, Aladdin, matching steel bottle
BOX $375 **BOTTLE** $150

Jet Patrol, 1957, Aladdin, matching steel bottle
BOX $400 **BOTTLE** $150

❑ **Jetsons Dome,** 1963, Aladdin, matching bottle
BOX $1450 **BOTTLE** $300

❑ **Joe Palooka,** 1949, Continental Can, no bottle
BOX $90 **BOTTLE** n/a

(KP Photo)

❑ **Johnny Lightning,** 1970, Aladdin, plastic bottle
BOX $110 **BOTTLE** $45

❑ **Jonathan Livingston Seagull,** 1973, Aladdin, matching plastic bottle
BOX $125 **BOTTLE** $50

(KP Photo)

❑ **Julia,** 1969, King Seeley Thermos, matching steel bottle, shown with Buccaneer Dome lunch box
BOX $150 **BOTTLE** $65

❑ **Jungle Book,** 1968, Aladdin, matching steel bottle
BOX $100 **BOTTLE** $75

❑ **Junior Miss,** 1978, Aladdin, matching plastic bottle
BOX $65 **BOTTLE** $30

❑ **Kellogg's,** 1969, Aladdin, plastic bottle
BOX $225 **BOTTLE** $75

❑ **King Kong,** 1977, King Seeley Thermos, plastic bottle
BOX $95 **BOTTLE** $40

❑ **KISS,** 1977, King Seeley Thermos, plastic bottle
BOX $225 **BOTTLE** $50

❑ **Knight in Armor,** 1959, Universal, matching steel bottle
BOX $950 **BOTTLE** $250

❑ **Knight Rider,** 1984, King Seeley Thermos, matching plastic bottle
BOX $45 **BOTTLE** $25

❑ **Korg,** 1975, King Seeley Thermos, matching plastic bottle
BOX $120 **BOTTLE** $45

❑ **Krofft Supershow,** 1976, Aladdin, matching plastic bottle
BOX $175 **BOTTLE** $50

❑ **Kung Fu,** 1974, King Seeley Thermos, matching plastic bottle
BOX $125 **BOTTLE** $40

(KP Photo)

❑ **Lance Link, Secret Chimp,** 1971, King Seeley Thermos, matching steel bottle, shown here with Gentle Ben lunch box
BOX $150 **BOTTLE** $75

(KP Photo)

❑ **Land of the Giants,** 1968, Aladdin, plastic bottle
BOX $195 **BOTTLE** $70

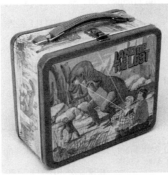

(KP Photo)

❑ **Land of the Lost,** 1975, Aladdin, matching plastic bottle
BOX $150 **BOTTLE** $45

❑ **Laugh-In (Helmet),** 1969, Aladdin, helmet on back, matching plastic bottle
BOX $150 **BOTTLE** $40

❑ **Laugh-In (Tricycle),** 1969, Aladdin, trike on back, matching plastic bottle
BOX $190 **BOTTLE** $50

❑ **Lawman,** 1961, King Seeley Thermos, generic bottle
BOX $195 **BOTTLE** $85

❑ **Legend of the Lone Ranger,** 1980, Aladdin, plastic bottle
BOX $125 **BOTTLE** $45

❑ **Lidsville,** 1971, Aladdin, matching plastic bottle
BOX $195 **BOTTLE** $60

❑ **Little Dutch Miss,** 1959, Universal, matching steel bottle
BOX $165 **BOTTLE** $75

❑ **Little Friends,** 1982, Aladdin, matching plastic bottle
BOX $850 **BOTTLE** $260

❑ **Little House on the Prairie,** 1978, King Seeley Thermos, matching plastic bottle
BOX $150 **BOTTLE** $45

❑ **Little Red Riding Hood,** 1982, Ohio Art, no bottle
BOX $50 **BOTTLE** n/a

❑ **Lone Ranger,** 1955, Adco Liberty, red rim, blue band, no bottle
BOX $600 **BOTTLE** n/a

❑ **Looney Tunes TV Set,** 1959, King Seeley Thermos, steel/glass bottle
BOX $275 **BOTTLE** $150

❑ **Lost in Space Dome,** 1967, King Seeley Thermos, steel/glass bottle
BOX $950 **BOTTLE** $90

❑ **Ludwig Von Drake,** 1962, Aladdin, steel/glass bottle
BOX $275 **BOTTLE** $90

❑ **Luggage Plaid,** 1955, Adco Liberty, no bottle
BOX $75 **BOTTLE** n/a

❑ **Luggage Plaid,** 1957, Ohio Art, no bottle
BOX $75 **BOTTLE** n/a

❑ **Magic of Lassie,** 1978, King Seeley Thermos, matching plastic bottle
BOX $95 **BOTTLE** $40

❑ **Major League Baseball,** 1968, King Seeley Thermos, matching bottle
BOX $125 **BOTTLE** $55

(KP Photo)

❑ **Man from U.N.C.L.E.,** 1966, King Seeley Thermos, matching steel bottle
BOX $275 **BOTTLE** $90

❑ **Marvel Super Heroes,** 1976, Aladdin, black rim, matching plastic bottle
BOX $95 **BOTTLE** $35

❑ **Mary Poppins,** 1965, Aladdin, steel/glass bottle
BOX $150 **BOTTLE** $75

❑ **Masters of the Universe,** 1983, Aladdin, matching plastic bottle
BOX $45 **BOTTLE** $15

❑ **Mickey Mouse & Donald Duck,** 1954, Adco Liberty, matching steel bottle
BOX $550 **BOTTLE** $600

LUNCH BOXES

(KP Photo)

❑ **Mickey Mouse Club,** 1963, Aladdin, yellow, steel/glass bottle, shown with Disney, Wonderful World & Mickey Mouse Club lunch boxes
BOX $150 BOTTLE $50

❑ **Mickey Mouse Club,** 1976, Aladdin, white, matching steel bottle
BOX $95 BOTTLE $40

❑ **Mickey Mouse Club,** 1977, Aladdin, red rim, sky boat, matching bottle
BOX $75 BOTTLE $30

❑ **Miss America,** 1972, Aladdin, matching plastic bottle
BOX $150 BOTTLE $50

❑ **Mod Floral Dome,** 1975, Okay Industries, matching steel bottle
BOX $350 BOTTLE $220

❑ **Monroes,** 1967, Aladdin, matching steel bottle
BOX $225 BOTTLE $110

(KP Photo)

❑ **Mork & Mindy,** 1979, American Thermos, matching plastic bottle
BOX $65 BOTTLE $30

❑ **Mr. Merlin,** 1982, King Seeley Thermos, matching plastic bottle
BOX $45 BOTTLE $20

❑ **Munsters,** 1965, King Seeley Thermos, matching steel bottle
BOX $450 BOTTLE $125

❑ **Muppet Babies,** 1985, King Seeley Thermos, matching plastic bottle
BOX $50 BOTTLE $20

❑ **Muppet Movie,** 1979, King Seeley Thermos, plastic bottle
BOX $90 BOTTLE $30

❑ **Muppet Show,** 1978, King Seeley Thermos, plastic bottle
BOX $75 BOTTLE $30

❑ **Muppets,** 1979, King Seeley Thermos, back shows Animal, Fozzie or Kermit, matching plastic bottle
BOX $75 BOTTLE $30

❑ **My Lunch,** 1976, Ohio Art, no bottle
BOX $45 BOTTLE n/a

❑ **Nancy Drew,** 1978, King Seeley Thermos, plastic bottle
BOX $65 BOTTLE $30

❑ **NFL,** 1962, Okay, black rim, steel/glass bottle
BOX $190 BOTTLE $130

❑ **NFL,** 1975, King Seeley Thermos, yellow rim, plastic bottle
BOX $65 BOTTLE $40

❑ **NFL,** 1976, King Seeley Thermos, red rim, matching plastic bottle
BOX $50 BOTTLE $40

❑ **NFL,** 1978, King Seeley Thermos, blue rim, matching plastic bottle
BOX $50 BOTTLE $40

❑ **NFL Quarterback,** 1964, Aladdin, matching steel bottle
BOX $195 BOTTLE $60

❑ **NHL,** 1970, Okay Industries, plastic bottle
BOX $525 BOTTLE $225

❑ **Orbit,** 1963, King Seeley Thermos, matching steel bottle
BOX $300 BOTTLE $90

❑ **Osmonds, The,** 1973, Aladdin, matching plastic bottle
BOX $100 BOTTLE $45

❑ **Our Friends,** 1982, Aladdin, matching plastic bottle
BOX $650 BOTTLE $225

❑ **Pac-Man,** 1980, Aladdin, matching plastic bottle
BOX $60 BOTTLE $25

❑ **Para-Medic,** 1978, Ohio Art, no bottle
BOX $65 BOTTLE n/a

❑ **Partridge Family,** 1971, King Seeley Thermos, plastic or steel bottle
BOX $150 BOTTLE $60

❑ **Pathfinder,** 1959, Universal, matching steel bottle
BOX $525 BOTTLE $180

❑ **Patriotic,** 1974, Ohio Art, no bottle
BOX $60 BOTTLE n/a

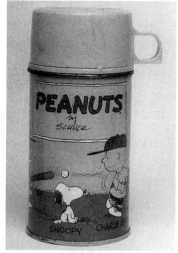

(KP Photo)

❑ **Peanuts,** 1966, King Seeley Thermos, orange rim, matching steel bottle (shown)
BOX $125 BOTTLE $50

❑ **Peanuts,** 1973, King Seeley Thermos, red rim psychiatric box, plastic bottle
BOX $100 BOTTLE $30

❑ **Peanuts,** 1976, King Seeley Thermos, red pitching box, plastic bottle
BOX $90 BOTTLE $25

❑ **Peanuts,** 1980, King Seeley Thermos, pitching box, yellow face, green band, matching bottle
BOX $90 BOTTLE $25

❑ **Pebbles & Bamm-Bamm,** 1971, Aladdin, matching plastic bottle
BOX $120 BOTTLE $60

❑ **Pele,** 1975, King Seeley Thermos, matching plastic bottle
BOX $110 BOTTLE $45

❑ **Pennant,** 1950, Ohio Art, basket type box, no bottle
BOX $50 BOTTLE n/a

❑ **Peter Pan,** 1969, Aladdin, matching plastic bottle, Disney
BOX $125 BOTTLE $50

❑ **Pete's Dragon,** 1978, Aladdin, matching plastic bottle
BOX $90 BOTTLE $35

❑ **Pets 'n Pals,** 1961, King Seeley Thermos, matching steel bottle
BOX $90 BOTTLE $45

❑ **Pigs In Space,** 1977, King Seeley Thermos, matching plastic bottle
BOX $60 BOTTLE $30

❑ **Pink Gingham,** 1976, King Seeley Thermos, matching plastic bottle
BOX $45 BOTTLE $20

❑ **Pink Panther & Sons,** 1984, King Seeley Thermos, matching plastic bottle
BOX $65 BOTTLE $30

❑ **Pinocchio,** 1938, unknown, steel round tin w/handle
BOX $150 BOTTLE n/a

❑ **Pinocchio,** 1938, unknown, square
BOX $150 BOTTLE n/a

❑ **Pinocchio,** 1971, Aladdin, plastic bottle
BOX $120 BOTTLE $50

❑ **Pit Stop,** 1968, Ohio Art
BOX $225 BOTTLE n/a

❑ **Planet of the Apes,** 1974, Aladdin, matching plastic bottle
BOX $190 BOTTLE $80

(KP Photo)

❏ **Play Ball,** 1969, King Seeley Thermos, game on back, steel bottle
BOX $125 **BOTTLE** $55

❏ **Police Patrol,** 1978, Aladdin, plastic bottle
BOX $165 **BOTTLE** $45

❏ **Polly Pal,** 1975, King Seeley Thermos, matching plastic bottle
BOX $45 **BOTTLE** $20

❏ **Pony Express,** 1982, Ohio Art
BOX $90 **BOTTLE** n/a

❏ **Popeye,** 1962, Universal, "Popeye socks Bluto" box, matching bottle
BOX $600 **BOTTLE** $300

❏ **Popeye,** 1964, King Seeley Thermos, "Popeye in boat" box w/matching steel bottle
BOX $175 **BOTTLE** $80

❏ **Popeye,** 1980, Aladdin, "arm wrestling" box, plastic bottle
BOX $90 **BOTTLE** $35

❏ **Popples,** 1986, Aladdin, plastic bottle
BOX $40 **BOTTLE** $20

(KP Photo)

❏ **Porky's Lunch Wagon Dome,** 1959, King Seeley Thermos, steel/glass bottle
BOX $450 **BOTTLE** $125

❏ **Pro Sports,** 1974, Ohio Art, no bottle
BOX $75 **BOTTLE** n/a

❏ **Psychedelic Dome,** 1969, Aladdin, plastic bottle
BOX $335 **BOTTLE** $85

❏ **Racing Wheels,** 1977, King Seeley Thermos, plastic bottle
BOX $75 **BOTTLE** $25

❏ **Raggedy Ann & Andy,** 1973, Aladdin, plastic bottle
BOX $80 **BOTTLE** $40

❏ **Rambo,** 1985, King Seeley Thermos, matching plastic bottle
BOX $50 **BOTTLE** $15

(KP Photo)

❏ **Rat Patrol,** 1967, Aladdin, steel/glass bottle
BOX $225 **BOTTLE** $90

❏ **Red Barn Dome,** 1957, King Seeley Thermos, closed door version, plain Holtemp bottle
BOX $80 **BOTTLE** $30

❏ **Red Barn Dome,** 1958, King Seeley Thermos, open door version, matching steel bottle
BOX $90 **BOTTLE** $50

❏ **Red Barn Dome,** 1972, Thermos, matching steel/glass bottle
BOX $80 **BOTTLE** $50

❏ **Rifleman, The,** 1961, Aladdin, steel/glass bottle
BOX $450 **BOTTLE** $140

❏ **Road Runner,** 1970, King Seeley Thermos, lavender or purple rim, steel or plastic bottle
BOX $95 **BOTTLE** $50

(KP Photo)

❏ **Robin Hood,** 1956, Aladdin, matching bottle
BOX $190 **BOTTLE** $120

❏ **Ronald McDonald, Sheriff,** 1982, Aladdin, plastic bottle
BOX $50 **BOTTLE** $20

❏ **Rose Petal Place,** 1983, Aladdin, plastic bottle
BOX $40 **BOTTLE** $15

❏ **Rough Rider,** 1973, Aladdin, plastic bottle
BOX $90 **BOTTLE** $40

(KP Photo)

❏ **Roy Rogers & Dale Double R Bar Ranch,** 1953, King Seeley Thermos, steel/glass bottle (shown)
BOX $190 **BOTTLE** $75

(KP Photo)

❏ **Roy Rogers & Dale Double R Bar Ranch,** 1954, American Thermos, blue or red band, woodgrain tall bottle
BOX $250 **BOTTLE** $75

(KP Photo)

❏ **Roy Rogers & Dale Double R Bar Ranch,** 1955, American Thermos, eight-scene box, red or blue band, matching bottle
BOX $200 **BOTTLE** $85

(KP Photo)

❏ **Roy Rogers & Dale Double R Bar Ranch,** 1955, American Thermos, cowhide back box, red or blue band, matching bottle
BOX $275 **BOTTLE** $80

❏ **Roy Rogers & Dale on Rail,** 1957, American Thermos, red or blue band, matching bottle
BOX $300 **BOTTLE** $80

(KP Photo)

❏ **Roy Rogers Chow Wagon Dome,** 1958, King Seeley Thermos, steel/glass bottle
BOX $400 **BOTTLE** $80

❏ **Saddlebag,** 1977, King Seeley Thermos, generic plastic bottle
BOX $150 **BOTTLE** $40

❏ **Satellite,** 1958, American Thermos, matching bottle, narrow band
BOX $150 **BOTTLE** $60

❏ **Satellite,** 1960, King Seeley Thermos, steel bottle
BOX $110 **BOTTLE** $60

❏ **Scooby Doo,** 1973, King Seeley Thermos, yellow rim, plastic bottle
BOX $225 **BOTTLE** $40

❑ **Scooby Doo,** 1973, King Seeley Thermos, orange rim, plastic bottle
BOX $275 **BOTTLE** $40

❑ **Secret Agent T,** 1968, King Seeley Thermos, matching bottle
BOX $120 **BOTTLE** $60

❑ **Secret of NIMH,** 1982, Aladdin, plastic bottle
BOX $90 **BOTTLE** $30

❑ **Secret Wars,** 1984, Aladdin, plastic bottle
BOX $90 **BOTTLE** $30

❑ **See America,** 1972, Ohio Art, no bottle
BOX $50 **BOTTLE** n/a

❑ **Sesame Street,** 1983, Aladdin, yellow or green rim, plastic bottle
BOX $55 **BOTTLE** $25

❑ **Sigmund and the Sea Monsters,** 1974, Aladdin, plastic bottle
BOX $180 **BOTTLE** $50

❑ **Six Million Dollar Man,** 1974, Aladdin, plastic bottle
BOX $90 **BOTTLE** $40

❑ **Six Million Dollar Man,** 1978, Aladdin, plastic bottle
BOX $90 **BOTTLE** $40

❑ **Skateboarder,** 1977, Aladdin, plastic bottle
BOX $70 **BOTTLE** $30

❑ **Sleeping Beauty,** 1960, General Steel Ware/Canada, generic steel bottle
BOX $450 **BOTTLE** $55

❑ **Smokey Bear,** 1975, Okay Industries, plastic bottle
BOX $425 **BOTTLE** $250

❑ **Smurfs,** 1983, King Seeley Thermos, blue box, plastic bottle
BOX $120 **BOTTLE** $30

❑ **Snoopy Dome,** 1968, King Seeley Thermos, yellow, "Have Lunch w/Snoopy", matching bottle
BOX $150 **BOTTLE** $50

❑ **Snow White, Disney,** 1975, Aladdin, orange rim, plastic bottle
BOX $75 **BOTTLE** $30

❑ **Snow White, with Game,** 1980, Ohio Art, no bottle
BOX $60 **BOTTLE** n/a

❑ **Space Explorer Ed McCauley,** 1960, Aladdin, matching steel bottle
BOX $400 **BOTTLE** $150

❑ **Space Ship,** 1950, unknown, Decoware, dark blue square
BOX $250 **BOTTLE** n/a

❑ **Space Shuttle Orbiter Enterprise,** 1977, King Seeley Thermos, plastic bottle
BOX $100 **BOTTLE** $45

❑ **Space: 1999,** 1976, King Seeley Thermos, plastic bottle
BOX $100 **BOTTLE** $35

❑ **Speed Buggy,** 1974, King Seeley Thermos, red rim, plastic bottle
BOX $80 **BOTTLE** $25

❑ **Spider-Man & Hulk,** 1980, Aladdin, Captain America on back, plastic bottle
BOX $100 **BOTTLE** $30

❑ **Sport Goofy,** 1983, Aladdin, yellow rim, plastic bottle
BOX $50 **BOTTLE** $25

❑ **Sport Skwirts,** 1982, Ohio Art, several variations
BOX $60 **BOTTLE** n/a

❑ **Sports Afield,** 1957, Ohio Art, no bottle
BOX $180 **BOTTLE** n/a

(KP Photo)

❑ **Star Trek Dome,** 1968, Aladdin, matching bottle
BOX $1150 **BOTTLE** $450

(ToyShop File Photo)

❑ **Star Trek, The Motion Picture,** 1980, King Seeley Thermos, matching bottle
BOX $150 **BOTTLE** $60

❑ **Star Wars,** 1978, King Seeley Thermos, cast or stars on band, matching plastic bottle
BOX $150 **BOTTLE** $40

❑ **Star Wars, Empire Strikes Back,** 1980, King Seeley Thermos, ship scene, plastic bottle
BOX $95 **BOTTLE** $30

❑ **Star Wars, Empire Strikes Back,** 1980, King Seeley Thermos, swamp scene, plastic bottle
BOX $125 **BOTTLE** $30

❑ **Star Wars, Return of the Jedi,** 1983, King Seeley Thermos, plastic bottle
BOX $65 **BOTTLE** $30

❑ **Stars and Stripes Dome,** 1970, King Seeley Thermos, matching plastic bottle
BOX $90 **BOTTLE** $40

❑ **Steve Canyon,** 1959, Aladdin, steel/glass bottle
BOX $350 **BOTTLE** $150

❑ **Strawberry Land**
BOX $75 **BOTTLE** n/a

❑ **Strawberry Shortcake,** 1980, Aladdin, plastic bottle
BOX $50 **BOTTLE** $15

❑ **Strawberry Shortcake,** 1981, Aladdin, plastic bottle
BOX $50 **BOTTLE** $15

❑ **Street Hawk,** 1985, Aladdin, plastic bottle
BOX $160 **BOTTLE** $90

❑ **Submarine,** 1960, King Seeley Thermos, steel/glass bottle
BOX $160 **BOTTLE** $80

❑ **Super Friends,** 1976, Aladdin, matching plastic bottle
BOX $110 **BOTTLE** $40

❑ **Super Powers,** 1983, Aladdin, plastic bottle
BOX $90 **BOTTLE** $40

❑ **Supercar,** 1962, Universal, steel/glass bottle
BOX $375 **BOTTLE** $150

❑ **Superman,** 1954, Universal, blue rim
BOX $6500 **BOTTLE** n/a

❑ **Superman,** 1967, King Seeley Thermos, red rim, "under fire" art on back, matching steel/glass bottle
BOX $300 **BOTTLE** $85

❑ **Superman,** 1978, Aladdin, red rim, Daily Planet Office on back, matching bottle
BOX $100 **BOTTLE** $45

❑ **Tapestry,** 1963, Ohio Art, no bottle
BOX $60 **BOTTLE** n/a

❑ **Tarzan,** 1966, Aladdin, steel/glass bottle
BOX $190 **BOTTLE** $65

❑ **Teenager,** 1957, King Seeley Thermos, generic bottle
BOX $85 **BOTTLE** $10

❑ **Teenager Dome,** 1957, King Seeley Thermos, generic bottle
BOX $140 **BOTTLE** $10

❑ **Three Little Pigs,** 1982, Ohio Art, red rim, generic/plastic bottle
BOX $70 **BOTTLE** n/a

❑ **Thundercats,** 1985, Aladdin, plastic bottle
BOX $100 **BOTTLE** $25

(KP Photo)

❏ **Tom Corbett Space Cadet,** 1952, Aladdin, blue or red paper decal box, steel/glass bottle
    BOX $250 **BOTTLE** $95

❏ **Tom Corbett Space Cadet,** 1954, Aladdin, full litho, matching bottle
    BOX $550 **BOTTLE** $110

❏ **Toppie Elephant,** 1957, American Thermos, yellow, matching bottle
    BOX $2800**BOTTLE** $800

❏ **Track King,** 1975, Okay Industries, matching steel bottle
    BOX $260 **BOTTLE** $180

❏ **Train,** 1971, Ohio Art, no bottle
    BOX $35 **BOTTLE** n/a

❏ **Transformers,** 1986, Aladdin, red box, matching plastic bottle
    BOX $50 **BOTTLE** $15

❏ **Traveler,** 1962, Ohio Art, no bottle
    BOX $85 **BOTTLE** n/a

❏ **Trigger,** 1956, King Seeley Thermos, no bottle
    BOX $300 **BOTTLE** n/a

(KP Photo)

❏ **U.S. Mail Dome,** 1969, Aladdin, plastic bottle
    BOX $90 **BOTTLE** $45

❏ **U.S. Space Corps,** 1961, Universal, plastic rocket bottle
    BOX $400 **BOTTLE** $125

❏ **UFO,** 1973, King Seeley Thermos, plastic bottle
    BOX $110 **BOTTLE** $40

❏ **Underdog,** 1974, Okay Industries, plastic bottle
    BOX $1800**BOTTLE** $550

❏ **Universal's Movie Monsters,** 1980, Aladdin, plastic bottle
    BOX $120 **BOTTLE** $40

(KP Photo)

❏ **Voyage to the Bottom of the Sea,** 1967, Aladdin, steel/glass bottle
    BOX $450 **BOTTLE** $140

❏ **VW Bus Dome,** 1960, Omni, plastic bottle
    BOX $500 **BOTTLE** $220

❏ **Wagon Train,** 1964, King Seeley Thermos, matching steel bottle
    BOX $275 **BOTTLE** $75

❏ **Wags 'n Whiskers,** 1978, King Seeley Thermos, matching plastic bottle
    BOX $45 **BOTTLE** $15

❏ **Wake Up America,** 1973, Okay Industries, matching steel bottle
    BOX $600 **BOTTLE** $250

❏ **Waltons, The,** 1973, Aladdin, plastic bottle
    BOX $125 **BOTTLE** $40

❏ **Washington Redskins,** 1970, Okay Industries, steel bottle
    BOX $260 **BOTTLE** $140

❏ **Wee Pals Kid Power,** 1974, American Thermos, matching plastic bottle
    BOX $65 **BOTTLE** $20

❏ **Welcome Back Kotter,** 1977, Aladdin, flat or embossed face, red rim, matching plastic bottle
    BOX $180 **BOTTLE** $40

❏ **Western,** 1963, King Seeley Thermos, tan band, steel/glass bottle
    BOX $250 **BOTTLE** $75

❏ **Western,** 1963, King Seeley Thermos, gear band, steel/glass bottle
    BOX $195 **BOTTLE** $75

(KP Photo)

❏ **Wild Bill Hickok,** 1955, Aladdin, steel/glass bottle
    BOX $250 **BOTTLE** $110

❏ **Wild Frontier,** 1977, Ohio Art, spinner game on back, no bottle
    BOX $90 **BOTTLE** n/a

❏ **Wild, Wild West,** 1969, Aladdin, plastic bottle
    BOX $375 **BOTTLE** $120

❏ **Winnie the Pooh,** 1976, Aladdin, blue rim, plastic bottle
    BOX $295 **BOTTLE** $80

❏ **Yankee Doodles,** 1975, King Seeley Thermos, plastic bottle
    BOX $60 **BOTTLE** $25

(KP Photo)

❏ **Yellow Submarine,** 1968, King Seeley Thermos, steel/glass bottle
    BOX $950 **BOTTLE** $275

❏ **Yogi Bear,** 1974, Aladdin
    BOX $180 **BOTTLE** $60

❏ **Yogi Bear & Friends,** 1961, Aladdin, black rim, matching steel bottle
    BOX $220 **BOTTLE** $100

❏ **Zorro,** 1958, Aladdin, black band, steel/glass bottle
    BOX $300 **BOTTLE** $120

❏ **Zorro,** 1966, Aladdin, red band, steel/glass bottle
    BOX $350 **BOTTLE** $180

VINYL

❏ **Alice in Wonderland,** 1972, Aladdin, matching plastic bottle
    BOX $200 **BOTTLE** $45

❏ **All American,** 1976, Bayville, Styrofoam bottle
    BOX $160 **BOTTLE** $20

❏ **All Dressed Up,** 1970s, Bayville, Styrofoam bottle
    BOX $90 **BOTTLE** $20

❏ **All Star,** 1960, Aladdin
    BOX $450 **BOTTLE** $60

❏ **Alvin and the Chipmunks,** 1963, King Seeley Thermos, matching plastic bottle
    BOX $400 **BOTTLE** $140

❏ **Annie 1,** 1981, Aladdin, matching plastic bottle
    BOX $75 **BOTTLE** $20

(KP Photo)

❏ **Bach's Lunch,** 1975, Volkwein Bros., red Styrofoam bottle
    BOX $130 **BOTTLE** $20

❏ **Ballerina,** 1960s, Universal, black, Thermax bottle
    BOX $800 **BOTTLE** $150

❏ **Ballerina,** 1962, Aladdin, pink, steel/glass bottle
BOX $200 **BOTTLE** $60

❏ **Ballet,** 1961, Universal, red, plastic generic bottle
BOX $500 **BOTTLE** $20

❏ **Banana Splits,** 1969, King Seeley Thermos, matching steel/glass bottle
BOX $500 **BOTTLE** $150

(KP Photo)

❏ **Barbarino Brunch Bag,** 1977, Aladdin, zippered bag, plastic bottle
BOX $300 **BOTTLE** $60

❏ **Barbie & Francie,** 1965, King Seeley Thermos, black, matching steel/glass bottle
BOX $120 **BOTTLE** $65

(KP Photo)

❏ **Barbie & Midge,** 1963, King Seeley Thermos, black, matching steel/glass bottle
BOX $110 **BOTTLE** $65

❏ **Barbie & Midge Dome,** 1964, King Seeley Thermos, matching glass/steel bottle
BOX $530 **BOTTLE** $65

❏ **Barbie Softy,** 1988, King Seeley Thermos, generic plastic bottle
BOX $45 **BOTTLE** $15

❏ **Barbie, World of,** 1971, King Seeley Thermos, pink box, matching steel/glass bottle
BOX $75 **BOTTLE** $25

❏ **Barbie, World of,** 1971, King Seeley Thermos, blue box, matching steel/glass bottle
BOX $90 **BOTTLE** $25

❏ **Barnum's Animals,** 1978, Adco Liberty, no bottle
BOX $60 **BOTTLE** n/a

(KP Photo)

❏ **Beany & Cecil,** 1963, King Seeley Thermos, steel/glass bottle
BOX $560 **BOTTLE** $150

❏ **Beatles,** 1965, Air Flite, no bottle
BOX $700 **BOTTLE** n/a

❏ **Beatles Brunch Bag,** 1966, Aladdin, zippered bag, matching bottle
BOX $750 **BOTTLE** $300

❏ **Beatles Kaboodles Kit,** 1965, Standard Plastic Products, no bottle
BOX $600 **BOTTLE** n/a

❏ **Betsey Clark,** 1977, King Seeley Thermos, yellow box, matching plastic bottle
BOX $110 **BOTTLE** $15

❏ **Betsey Clark Munchies Bag,** 1977, King Seeley Thermos, zippered bag, plastic bottle
BOX $90 **BOTTLE** $10

❏ **Blue Gingham Brunch Bag,** 1975, Aladdin, zippered box and plastic bottle
BOX $45 **BOTTLE** $30

❏ **Bobby Soxer,** 1959, Aladdin
BOX $575 **BOTTLE** n/a

(KP Photo)

❏ **Boston Red Sox,** 1960s, Universal
BOX $65 **BOTTLE** $20

❏ **Boy on the Swing,** Abeama Industries
BOX $80 **BOTTLE** $20

❏ **Buick 1910,** 1974, Bayville, Styrofoam bottle
BOX $90 **BOTTLE** $20

❏ **Bullwinkle,** 1963, King Seeley Thermos, blue steel/glass bottle
BOX $650 **BOTTLE** $200

❏ **Bullwinkle,** 1963, King Seeley Thermos, yellow, generic steel bottle
BOX $450 **BOTTLE** $60

❏ **Calico Brunch Bag,** 1980, Aladdin, zippered bag, plastic bottle
BOX $70 **BOTTLE** $30

❏ **Captain Kangaroo,** King Seeley Thermos, steel/glass bottle
BOX $500 **BOTTLE** $150

❏ **Captain Marvel Brunch Bag,** 1940s, red rectangular vinyl w/strap handle
EX $60 **BOX** $200 **BOTTLE** $400

❏ **Carousel,** 1962, Aladdin, matching steel/glass bottle
BOX $425 **BOTTLE** $130

❏ **Cars,** 1960, Universal
BOX $140 **BOTTLE** n/a

❏ **Casper the Friendly Ghost,** 1966, King Seeley Thermos, blue box, orange steel bottle
BOX $550 **BOTTLE** $150

❏ **Challenger, Space Shuttle,** 1986, Babcock, puffy box, no bottle
BOX $225 **BOTTLE** n/a

(KP Photo)

❏ **Charlie's Angels Brunch Bag,** 1978, Aladdin, zippered bag, plastic bottle
BOX $250 **BOTTLE** $50

(KP Photo)

❏ **Coca-Cola,** 1947, Aladdin, Styrofoam bottle
BOX $160 **BOTTLE** $20

❏ **Coco the Clown,** 1970s, Gary, Styrofoam bottle
BOX $90 **BOTTLE** $20

❏ **Combo Brunch Bag,** 1967, Aladdin, zippered bag, steel/glass bottle
BOX $200 **BOTTLE** $80

❏ **Corsage,** 1970, King Seeley Thermos, steel/glass bottle
BOX $90 **BOTTLE** $30

❏ **Cottage,** 1974, King Seeley Thermos
BOX $90 **BOTTLE** n/a

❏ **Cowboy,** 1960, Universal, plain plastic bottle
BOX $170 **BOTTLE** $20

❏ **Dateline Lunch Kit,** 1960, Hasbro, blue/pink, no bottle
BOX $250 **BOTTLE** n/a

❏ **Dawn,** 1971, Aladdin, matching plastic bottle
BOX $140 **BOTTLE** $35

❏ **Dawn,** 1972, Aladdin, matching plastic bottle
BOX $140 **BOTTLE** $35

❏ **Dawn Brunch Bag,** 1971, Aladdin, zippered bag, plastic bottle
BOX $180 **BOTTLE** $35

❏ **Denim Brunch Bag,** 1980, Aladdin, zippered bag, plastic bottle
BOX $80 **BOTTLE** $15

❏ **Deputy Dawg,** King Seeley Thermos, steel/glass bottle
BOX $550 **BOTTLE** $120

❏ **Deputy Dawg,** 1964, Thermos, no bottle
BOX $550 **BOTTLE** n/a

❏ **Donny & Marie,** 1977, Aladdin, long hair version, matching plastic bottle
BOX $110 **BOTTLE** $40

(KP Photo)

❏ **Donny & Marie,** 1978, Aladdin, short hair version, matching plastic bottle
BOX $120 **BOTTLE** $40

❏ **Donny & Marie Brunch Bag,** 1977, Aladdin, zippered bag, plastic bottle
BOX $125 **BOTTLE** $40

❏ **Dr. Seuss,** 1970, Aladdin, plastic bottle
BOX $575 **BOTTLE** $60

❏ **Dream Boat,** 1960, Feldco, dark brown, Styrofoam bottle
BOX $350 **BOTTLE** $20

❏ **Dream Boat,** 1960, Feldco, white, Styrofoam bottle
BOX $500 **BOTTLE** $20

❏ **Dream Boat,** 1960, Feldco, blue, Styrofoam bottle
BOX $700 **BOTTLE** $20

❏ **Eats 'n Treats,** King Seeley Thermos, blue or pink steel/glass bottle
BOX $200 **BOTTLE** $40

❏ **Fess Parker Kaboodle Kit,** 1960s, Aladdin, matching steel bottle
BOX $425 **BOTTLE** n/a

❏ **Fishing,** 1970, Universal, Styrofoam bottle
BOX $90 **BOTTLE** $20

❏ **Frog Flutist,** 1975, Aladdin, matching plastic bottle
BOX $75 **BOTTLE** $20

❏ **Fun to See'n Keep Tiger,** 1960, unknown, no bottle
BOX $350 **BOTTLE** n/a

❏ **G.I. Joe,** 1989, King Seeley Thermos, generic plastic bottle
BOX $55 **BOTTLE** $10

❏ **Gigi,** 1962, Aladdin, matching steel/glass bottle
BOX $280 **BOTTLE** $80

❏ **Girl & Poodle,** 1960, Universal, Styrofoam bottle
BOX $140 **BOTTLE** $20

❏ **Glamour Gal,** 1960, Aladdin, steel/glass bottle
BOX $100 **BOTTLE** $35

❏ **Goat Butt Mountain,** 1960, Universal, Styrofoam bottle
BOX $90 **BOTTLE** $20

❏ **Go-Go Brunch Bag,** 1966, Aladdin, plastic bottle
BOX $245 **BOTTLE** $60

❏ **Happy Powwow,** 1970s, Bayville, red, blue or yellow, w/Styrofoam bottle
BOX $90 **BOTTLE** $20

(KP Photo)

❏ **Highway Signs Snap Pack,** 1988, Avon
BOX $50 **BOTTLE** n/a

❏ **Holly Hobbie,** 1972, Aladdin, white bag, matching plastic bottle
BOX $100 **BOTTLE** $30

❏ **I Love a Parade,** 1970, Universal, Styrofoam bottle
BOX $130 **BOTTLE** $20

❏ **Ice Cream Cone,** 1975, Aladdin, matching plastic bottle
BOX $55 **BOTTLE** $20

❏ **It's a Small World,** 1968, Aladdin, matching steel/glass bottle
BOX $250 **BOTTLE** $110

❏ **Jonathan Livingston Seagull,** 1974, Aladdin, matching plastic bottle
BOX $160 **BOTTLE** $50

❏ **Junior Deb,** 1960, Aladdin, steel/glass bottle
BOX $175 **BOTTLE** $50

❏ **Junior Miss Safari,** 1962, Prepac, no bottle
BOX $140 **BOTTLE** n/a

❏ **Junior Nurse,** 1963, King Seeley Thermos, steel/glass bottle
BOX $320 **BOTTLE** $90

❏ **Kaboodle Kit,** 1960s, Aladdin, pink or white, no bottle
BOX $220 **BOTTLE** n/a

❏ **Kewtie Pie,** Aladdin, steel/glass bottle
BOX $200 **BOTTLE** $60

❏ **Kodak Gold,** 1970s, Aladdin
BOX $85 **BOTTLE** $20

❏ **Kodak II,** 1970s, Aladdin
BOX $85 **BOTTLE** $20

❏ **Lassie,** 1960s, Universal, Styrofoam bottle
BOX $120 **BOTTLE** $20

❏ **Liddle Kiddles,** 1969, King Seeley Thermos, matching steel/glass bottle
BOX $450 **BOTTLE** $60

❏ **L'il Jodie (Puffy),** 1985, Babcock
BOX $90 **BOTTLE** n/a

❏ **Linus the Lion-Hearted,** 1965, Aladdin, steel/glass bottle
BOX $550 **BOTTLE** $110

❏ **Little Ballerina,** 1975, Bayville, Styrofoam bottle
BOX $75 **BOTTLE** $20

❏ **Little Old Schoolhouse,** 1974, Dart
BOX $80 **BOTTLE** n/a

❏ **Love,** 1972, Aladdin, matching plastic bottle
BOX $160 **BOTTLE** $45

❏ **Lunch 'n Munch,** 1959, King Seeley Thermos, space theme, red, satellite botle
BOX $450 **BOTTLE** $60

(KP Photo)

❏ **Lunch 'n Munch,** 1959, American Thermos, boys on raft, tan, boating bottle
BOX $400 **BOTTLE** $125

❏ **Lunch 'n Munch,** 1959, American Thermos, boys on raft, red, boating bottle
BOX $450 **BOTTLE** $125

❏ **Lunch 'n Munch,** 1959, King Seeley Thermos, space theme, tan, satellite botle
BOX $450 **BOTTLE** $60

Mam'zelle, 1971, Aladdin, plastic bottle
BOX $180 BOTTLE $60

Mardi-Gras, 1971, Aladdin, matching plastic bottle
BOX $80 BOTTLE $20

Mary Ann, 1960, Aladdin, matching steel/glass bottle
BOX $75 BOTTLE $25

Mary Ann Lunch 'N Bag, 1960, Universal, no bottle
BOX $110 BOTTLE n/a

(KP Photo)

Mary Poppins, 1973, Aladdin, matching plastic bottle
BOX $175 BOTTLE $50

Mary Poppins Brunch Bag, 1966, Aladdin, steel/glass bottle
BOX $150 BOTTLE $50

Mod Miss Brunch Bag, 1969, Aladdin, plastic bottle
BOX $80 BOTTLE $30

(KP Photo)

Monkees, 1967, King Seeley Thermos, matching steel/glass bottle
BOX $450 BOTTLE $125

Moon Landing, 1960, Universal, Styrofoam bottle
BOX $250 BOTTLE $20

Mr. Peanut Snap Pack, 1979, Dart, snap close bag, no bottle
BOX $110 BOTTLE n/a

Mushrooms, 1972, Aladdin, matching plastic bottle
BOX $90 BOTTLE $45

(KP Photo)

New Zoo Revue, 1975, Aladdin, plastic bottle
BOX $250 BOTTLE $60

Pac-Man (Puffy), 1985, Aladdin
BOX $65 BOTTLE n/a

Peanuts, 1967, King Seeley Thermos, red "kite" box, steel/glass bottle
BOX $150 BOTTLE $50

Peanuts, 1969, King Seeley Thermos, red "baseball" box, steel bottle
BOX $150 BOTTLE $50

Peanuts, 1971, King Seeley Thermos, green "baseball" box, steel bottle
BOX $200 BOTTLE $50

Peanuts, 1973, King Seeley Thermos, white "piano" box, steel bottle
BOX $150 BOTTLE $50

Pebbles & Bamm-Bamm, 1973, Gary, matching plastic bottle
BOX $250 BOTTLE $55

Penelope & Penny, 1970s, Gary, yellow box w/Styrofoam bottle
BOX $80 BOTTLE $20

Peter Pan, 1969, Aladdin, white box, matching plastic bottle
BOX $210 BOTTLE $65

Pink Panther, 1980, Aladdin, matching plastic bottle
BOX $200 BOTTLE $50

Pony Tail, 1960s, Thermos, white box, original art w/gray border added, no bottle
BOX $200 BOTTLE n/a

Pony Tail, 1965, King Seeley Thermos, white box, fold over lid, steel/glass bottle
BOX $200 BOTTLE $30

Pony Tail Tid-Bit-Kit, 1962, King Seeley Thermos, steel/glass satellite bottle
BOX $200 BOTTLE $30

Ponytails Poodle Kit, 1960, King Seeley Thermos, steel/glass bottle
BOX $150 BOTTLE $20

Princess, 1963, Aladdin, steel/glass bottle
BOX $190 BOTTLE $55

Psychedelic, 1969, Aladdin, yellow, matching steel/glass bottle
BOX $150 BOTTLE $30

(KP Photo)

Pussycats, The, 1968, Aladdin, plastic bottle
BOX $220 BOTTLE $80

Ringling Bros. Circus, 1970, King Seeley Thermos, orange box w/matching steel/glass bottle
BOX $425 BOTTLE $140

Ringling Bros. Circus, 1971, King Seeley Thermos, puffy blue box, steel/glass bottle
BOX $175 BOTTLE $40

Robo Warriors, 1970, unknown, no bottle
BOX $35 BOTTLE n/a

Roy Rogers Saddlebag, 1960, King Seeley Thermos, cream, steel/glass bottle
BOX $650 BOTTLE $95

Roy Rogers Saddlebag, 1960, King Seeley Thermos, brown, steel/glass bottle
BOX $400 BOTTLE $95

Sabrina, 1972, Aladdin, yellow box w/matching plastic bottle
BOX $230 BOTTLE $85

Sesame Street, 1979, Aladdin, orange, matching plastic bottle
BOX $120 BOTTLE $30

Sesame Street, 1981, Aladdin, yellow, matching plastic bottle
BOX $150 BOTTLE $30

(KP Photo)

Shari Lewis, 1963, Aladdin, matching steel/glass bottle
BOX $470 BOTTLE $120

Sizzlers, Hot Wheels, 1971, King Seeley Thermos, matching steel/glass bottle
BOX $350 BOTTLE $60

Skipper, 1965, King Seeley Thermos, steel/glass bottle
BOX $220 BOTTLE $60

Sleeping Beauty, Disney, 1970, Aladdin, white box, matching plastic bottle
BOX $240 BOTTLE $80

Smokey the Bear, 1965, King Seeley Thermos, steel/glass bottle
BOX $450 BOTTLE $110

Snoopy Munchies Bag, 1977, King Seeley Thermos, plastic bottle
BOX $75 BOTTLE $20

❏ **Snoopy Softy,** 1988, King Seeley Thermos, matching plastic bottle
BOX $45 **BOTTLE** $20

❏ **Snow White,** 1975, Aladdin, white box w/matching plastic bottle
BOX $285 **BOTTLE** $45

❏ **Snow White, Disney,** 1967, unknown, fold-over lid, tapered box, no bottle
BOX $400 **BOTTLE** n/a

❏ **Soupy Sales,** 1966, King Seeley Thermos, blue box, no bottle
BOX $600 **BOTTLE** n/a

❏ **Spirit of '76,** unknown, red
BOX $110 **BOTTLE** n/a

❏ **Sports Kit,** 1960, Universal
BOX $350 **BOTTLE** $40

❏ **Stewardess,** 1962, Aladdin, steel/glass bottle
BOX $650 **BOTTLE** $110

❏ **Strawberry Shortcake,** 1980, Aladdin, matching plastic bottle
BOX $65 **BOTTLE** $15

❏ **Tammy,** 1964, Aladdin, matching steel/glass bottle
BOX $240 **BOTTLE** $85

❏ **Tammy & Pepper,** 1965, Aladdin, matching steel/glass bottle
BOX $240 **BOTTLE** $85

❏ **Tinker Bell, Disney,** 1969, Aladdin, plastic bottle
BOX $260 **BOTTLE** $90

❏ **Twiggy,** 1967, Aladdin, matching steel/glass bottle
BOX $225 **BOTTLE** $80

❏ **Twiggy,** 1967, King Seeley Thermos, steel/glass bottle
BOX $225 **BOTTLE** $80

❏ **U.S. Mail Brunch Bag,** 1971, Aladdin, zippered bag, plastic bottle
BOX $160 **BOTTLE** $80

❏ **Winnie the Pooh,** Aladdin, steel/glass bottle
BOX $450 **BOTTLE** $110

❏ **Wonder Woman (blue),** 1977, Aladdin, matching plastic bottle
BOX $150 **BOTTLE** $35

❏ **Wonder Woman (yellow),** 1978, Aladdin, matching plastic bottle
BOX $200 **BOTTLE** $35

❏ **Wrangler,** 1982, Aladdin, steel/glass bottle
BOX $325 **BOTTLE** $95

❏ **Yosemite Sam,** 1971, King Seeley Thermos, matching steel/glass bottle
BOX $560 **BOTTLE** $140

❏ **Ziggy's Munch Box,** 1979, Aladdin, plastic bottle
BOX $140 **BOTTLE** $40

Marx Play Sets

This Carry-All Play Set is a self-contained metal box that folds out into a miniature Fort Apache. The plastic blockhouses fit along the corners, and the usual cowboys, Indians and accessories are included. Mint value, $80.

For all practical purposes, play sets could have been invented by Louis Marx . . . at least as far as boys growing up in the 1950s and 1960s were concerned.

The words "Marx" and "play set" just went together, and they still go together today for many dedicated collectors.

A typical Marx play set included buildings, figures and lots of realistic accessories that helped bring the miniature world to life. The Fort Apache Stockade, for example, came with a hard plastic log fort, a colorful lithographed tin cabin, and, of course, pioneers and Indians locked in deadly combat. It was no wonder millions of kids had a burning desire for these toys. The play scenarios were almost endless.

This modern version of an age-old toy was a tribute to the marketing and manufacturing talents and whimsical genius of Louis Marx, the modern-day king of toys.

Not only was he responsible for developing the play set, but he popularized the yo-yo and produced some of the most innovative tin wind-ups, guns, dolls, trains, trikes, trucks and other toys that were commercially feasible. In 1955, Marx sold more than $30 million worth of toys, easily making it the largest toy manufacturer in the world.

What makes Marx's domination even more impressive was the fact that he rose from humble beginnings. He was born in Brooklyn in 1896 and didn't learn to speak English until he started school.

At age 16, Marx went to work for Ferdinand Strauss, a toy manufacturer who produced items for Abraham & Strauss Department Stores. By the age of 20, Marx was managing the company's New Jersey factory.

After being fired by Strauss, Marx contracted with manufacturers to produce toys he designed. By the mid-1920s,

Television tie-ins made up a big percentage of Marx toys. Although "Captain Gallant" was a short-lived series, it made for a great play set. The mint condition value reflects the rare nature of the toy–$1050.

Marx had three plants in the United States. By 1955, there were more than 5,000 items in the Marx toy line with plants worldwide.

Mass production and mass marketing through stores such as Sears and Montgomery Ward allowed Marx to keep prices low and quality high. Marx was also a master at producing new toys from the same basic components. Existing elements could be modified slightly, and new lithography would produce a new building from standard stock.

Part of Marx's repackaging genius included using popular TV or movie tie-ins to breathe new life into existing products. The Rifleman Ranch, Roy Rogers Ranch, Wyatt Earp and Wagon Train play sets were examples of repackaging existing parts to capture the fad of the day.

Marx sold his company to the Quaker Oats Company in 1972 for $31 million. Quaker Oats sold the company four years later for $15 million after losing money every year of its ownership.

The Marx Toy Company is in existence once again and making favorite Marx toys from original molds.

With the passing of a few short decades, once affordable children's toys have become highly prized collectibles. Play sets are among the price leaders in today's market for childhood treasures. And the figures that accompanied the play sets are also highly desired for their craftsmanship and detail.

A play set listed as MIB (Mint in Box) should be untouched and unassembled in the original box. Excellent condition means a complete set, but the buildings are assembled and the box may be worn or damaged. Good condition means the play set shows wear and may have a few minor pieces missing.

Trends

The play set market continues on a strong course, with several sets now commanding prices as high as some of their "classic" Marx tin wind-up counterparts. As it becomes increasingly difficult to find complete sets, individual pieces should sell well as collectors try to complete sets.

Service Station set by Marx. Another example of a set that re-used the pieces of many other sets. Valued at $255 in mint condition.

A more elaborate "Carry-All" play set, the Fighting Knights set. $230 mint value.

Operation Moon Base is a well sought-after play set. The pieces included come in a variety of scales, but it doesn't hurt the coolness of this toy one bit. Mint value, $465.

MINIATURE PLAY SETS

❑ **101 Dalmatians**, 1961, "The Barn Scene"
EX $75   NM $300   MIP $450

❑ **101 Dalmatians**, 1961, "The Wedding Scene"
EX $75   NM $300   MIP $450

(ToyShop File Photo)

❑ **20 Minutes to Berlin**, 1964, 174 hand-painted pieces
EX $110   NM $320   MIP $520

❑ **Alice in Wonderland**, New series, 1961
EX $100   NM $225   MIP $350

❑ **Attack on Fort Apache**, stable, cowboys, Indians, Model No. HK-8078
EX $85   NM $225   MIP $500

❑ **Babes In Toyland**, six different scenes, each
EX $25   NM $65   MIP $100

❑ **Battleground**, 1963, 170 pieces, Model No. HK-6111
EX $20   NM $60   MIP $200

(ToyShop File Photo)

❑ **Blue and Gray**, 1960s, 101 individual pieces, "Featured on T.V.", Model No. HK-6109
EX $95   NM $180   MIP $335

(ToyShop File Photo)

❑ **Border Battle**, Mexican-American War set with plastic Alamo, Mexican and Texan troops, horses and accessories
EX $150   NM $365   MIP $715

❑ **Charge of the Bengal Lancers**, British/Turks
EX $125   NM $325   MIP $500

❑ **Charge of the Light Brigade**, Sears, 216 pieces, Lancers/Cossacks
EX $175   NM $325   MIP $400

❑ **Charge of the Light Brigade**, 2nd version, photo box art, Lancers/Turks
EX $110   NM $300   MIP $400

❑ **Charge of the Light Brigade**, smaller version, Lancers/Russians
EX $75   NM $225   MIP $325

❑ **Cinderella**, New series
EX $100   NM $225   MIP $350

❑ **Covered Wagon Attack**
EX $85   NM $200   MIP $400

❑ **Custer's Last Stand**, 1964, 181 pieces
EX $125   NM $325   MIP $600

❑ **Disney 3-in-1 Set**, original series
EX $75   NM $225   MIP $350

❑ **Disney Circus Parade**, Super Circus performers, Disneykins
EX $85   NM $225   MIP $350

(ToyShop File Photo)

❑ **Disney See and Play Castle**, 1st and 2nd series Disneykins, Model No. 48-24388
EX $155   NM $360   MIP $465

❑ **Disney See and Play Doll House**, 1st series Disneykins
EX $100   NM $265   MIP $350

❑ **Donald Duck**, original series; Donald, Daisy, Louie, Goofy
EX $45   NM $100   MIP $150

❑ **Dumbo's Circus**, original series
EX $50   NM $100   MIP $150

❑ **Fairykin**, six different, each
EX $30   NM $80   MIP $125

❑ **Fairykin TV Scenes**, 12 different, each
EX $8   NM $20   MIP $30

❑ **Fairykin TV Scenes Gift Set**, two different, each w/six scenes, each
EX $65   NM $165   MIP $250

❑ **Fairykins 3-in-1 Diorama Set**
EX $100   NM $265   MIP $400

❑ **Fairykins Gift Set**, 34 in window box
EX $40   NM $175   MIP $250

❑ **Fairykins TV Scenes Boxed Set of Eight**
EX $45   NM $200   MIP $250

❑ **Fort Apache**, 1963, 90 pieces, Indians, Model No. HK-7526
EX $55   NM $80   MIP $165

❑ **Fort Apache**, large set, HQ bldg., cavalry/cowboys/Indians
EX $115   NM $295   MIP $375

❑ **Guerrilla Warfare**, 1960s, Viet Cong
EX $275   NM $350   MIP $450

❑ **Huckleberry Hound Presents**, two different, each
EX $75   NM $115   MIP $175

(ToyShop File Photo)

❑ **Invasion Day**, 1964, 304 pieces, miniature D-Day Invasion set
EX $70   NM $205   MIP $405

❑ **Jungle**, smaller than Jungle Safari
EX $50   NM $85   MIP $175

❑ **Jungle Safari**, 260 pieces, hunters/natives
EX $55   NM $100   MIP $200

❑ **Knights and Castle**, 1963, 132 pieces, Model No. HK-7563
EX $130   NM $200   MIP $300

❑ **Knights and Castle**, 1964, 64 pieces, Model No. HK-7562
EX $95   NM $175   MIP $275

❑ **Knights and Vikings**, 1964, 143 pieces
EX $145   NM $275   MIP $425

❑ **Lady and the Tramp**, New series, 1961
EX $100   NM $225   MIP $350

❑ **Lost Boys**, second series, 1961
EX $40   NM $120   MIP $200

❑ **Lost Boys**, New series
EX $100   NM $225   MIP $350

❑ **Ludwig Von Drake**, RCA premium set
EX $65   NM $130   MIP $200

❑ **Ludwig Von Drake**, 1962, "The Professor Misses"
EX $50   NM $100   MIP $150

❑ **Ludwig Von Drake**, 1962, "The Near-sighted Professor"
EX $50   NM $100   MIP $150

❑ **Mickey Mouse and Friends**, original series, display box
EX $50   NM $100   MIP $150

❑ **Munchville**, vegetable characters
EX $65   NM $165   MIP $250

(ToyShop File Photo)

❑ **Noah's Ark**, 1968, 100 pieces
EX $28   NM $70   MIP $110

❏ **Noah's Ark**, Ward's version, soft plastic figures
EX $20   NM $50   MIP $75

❏ **Over The Top**, WWI, Germans/Dough-boys
EX $200   NM $600   MIP $950

❏ **Panchito Western**, original series, display box
EX $50   NM $100   MIP $150

❏ **Pinocchio**, six different sets, each original series, display box
EX $65   NM $165   MIP $250

❏ **Pinocchio 3-in-1 Set**
EX $115   NM $295   MIP $450

❏ **Quick Draw McGraw**, two different, each
EX $75   NM $115   MIP $200

❏ **Revolutionary War**, British/Colonials
EX $95   NM $250   MIP $500

❏ **Sands of Iwo Jima**, 1964, 296 pieces
EX $150   NM $295   MIP $450

❏ **Sands of Iwo Jima**, 1963, 205 pieces
EX $115   NM $210   MIP $325

❏ **Sands of Iwo Jima**, 1963, 88 pieces
EX $75   NM $145   MIP $225

❏ **See and Play Dollhouse**, American Beauties/Campus Cuties
EX $75   NM $175   MIP $350

❏ **Sleeping Beauty**, new series, 1961
EX $75   NM $175   MIP $275

❏ **Snow White and the Seven Dwarfs**, original series, display box
EX $50   NM $100   MIP $150

❏ **Sunshine Farm Set**, farmers and animals
EX $45   NM $115   MIP $175

(ToyShop File Photo)

❏ **Sword in the Stone**, British only Disney release
EX $310   NM $1050   MIP $1560

❏ **Ten Commandments**, Montgomery Ward
EX $150   NM $395   MIP $600

❏ **Three Little Pigs**, new series
EX $100   NM $225   MIP $350

❏ **Tiger Town**, ENCO-like tigers, 1960s
EX $75   NM $175   MIP $300

❏ **Top Cat**, three different, each
EX $75   NM $115   MIP $200

(ToyShop File Photo)

❏ **Troll Village**, Includes hillside, troll figures, ox cart, trees, fence sections and accessories
EX $85   NM $220   MIP $360

❏ **TV-Tinykins Gift Set**, set of 34 figures
EX $115   NM $350   MIP $550

❏ **TV-Tinykins TV Scenes**, 12 different, each
EX $12   NM $35   MIP $50

(ToyShop File Photo)

❏ **Western Town**, over 170 pieces, hand painted buildings, stagecoach, fence sections, figures and accessories, Model No. 48-24398
EX $55   NM $160   MIP $265

❏ **Wooden Horse of Troy**, British only issue
EX $125   NM $600   MIP $800

PLAY SETS

❏ **Adventures of Robin Hood**, 1956, Richard Greene TV series, Model No. 4722
EX $250   NM $750   MIP $1250

❏ **Alamo**, 1960, for 54mm figures, Model No. 3534
EX $140   NM $250   MIP $400

❏ **Alamo**, only two cannons, Model No. 3546
EX $100   NM $300   MIP $500

(ToyShop File Photo)

❏ **Alaska Frontier**, 1959, 100 pieces including: igloos, polar bears, kayak, dog sled team, litho storefront, prospectors. Just in time for Alaskan statehood, this is a neat set, Model No. 3708
EX $280   NM $540   MIP $825

❏ **American Airlines Astro Jet Port**, Model No. 4822
EX $150   NM $250   MIP $450

❏ **American Airlines International Jet Port**, 1962, 98 pieces, Model No. 4810
EX $150   NM $250   MIP $450

❏ **Arctic Explorer**, 1960, Series 2000, Model No. 3702
EX $250   NM $450   MIP $700

❏ **Army Combat Set**, Sears, 411 pieces, Model No. 6019
EX $100   NM $300   MIP $500

❏ **Army Combat Training Center**, Model No. 2654
EX $20   NM $55   MIP $90

❏ **Babyland Nursery**, Model No. 3379
EX $125   NM $225   MIP $350

❏ **Bar-M Ranch**, Model No. 3956
EX $50   NM $100   MIP $150

❏ **Battle of Iwo Jima**, 1964, 247 pieces, Model No. 4147
EX $80   NM $240   MIP $400

❏ **Battle of Iwo Jima**, 1964, 128 pieces, Model No. 6057
EX $35   NM $105   MIP $175

(ToyShop File Photo)

❏ **Battle of Little Big Horn**, 1972, includes cavalrymen, Indians, horses, wagons, totem pole (?), and tepees, Model No. 4679MO
EX $130   NM $260   MIP $410

❏ **Battle of the Blue & Gray**, Series 1000, small set, no house, Model No. 2646
EX $80   NM $240   MIP $400

❏ **Battle of the Blue & Gray**, 1959, Series 2000, 54mm, Model No. 4745
EX $175   NM $375   MIP $600

❏ **Battle of the Blue & Gray**, Series 2000, large set, Model No. 4658
EX $250   NM $700   MIP $1200

❏ **Battle of the Blue & Gray**, 1963, Centennial edition, Model No. 4744
EX $200   NM $700   MIP $1200

❏ **Battlefield**, 1958, Series 5000, Model No. 4756
EX $25   NM $95   MIP $150

❏ **Battleground**, 1963, Montgomery Ward, Model No. 3745
EX $80   NM $240   MIP $400

❏ **Battleground**, U.S. and Nazi troops, Model No. 4169
EX $30   NM $90   MIP $150

❏ **Battleground**, 1971, Montgomery Ward Exclusive, Model No. 4752
EX $90   NM $275   MIP $450

❏ **Battleground**, 1962, 200 pieces, Model No. 4754
EX $35   NM $110   MIP $185

❏ **Battleground**, 1959, 180 pieces, Model No. 4751
EX $35   NM $110   MIP $185

❏ **Battleground**, 1958, largest of military sets, Model No. 4750
EX $130   NM $395   MIP $650

❏ **Battleground**, 1963, Sears, 160 pieces
EX $70   NM $210   MIP $350

❏ **Battleground**, 1970s, Model No. 4756
EX $40   NM $125   MIP $250

❏ **Beach Head Landing Set**, U.S. and Nazi Troops, Model No. 4939
EX $15   NM $65   MIP $100

(ToyShop File Photo)

❏ **Ben Hur**, 1959, Series 5000, large set, Model No. 4701
EX $355   NM $1085   MIP $1825

(ToyShop File Photo)

❏ **Ben Hur**, 1959, Series 2000, medium set, Model No. 4702
EX $255   NM $770   MIP $1300

❏ **Ben Hur**, 1959, 132 pieces, Model No. 4696
EX $170   NM $510   MIP $850

❏ **Ben Hur**, blister card, Model No. 2648
EX $25   NM $95   MIP $150

❏ **Big Inch Pipeline**, 1963, 200 pieces, Model No. 6008
EX $80   NM $240   MIP $400

❏ **Big Top Circus**, 1952, Model No. 4310
EX $80   NM $325   MIP $500

(ToyShop File Photo)

❏ **Boot Camp, Carry-All**, tin box set, with tank, half-track, jeep, artillery, figures and tents, Model No. 4645
EX $35   NM $135   MIP $215

❏ **Boy Scout**
EX $115   NM $600   MIP $900

❏ **Boys Camp**, 1956, Model No. 4103
EX $130   NM $395   MIP $650

❏ **Cape Canaveral**, 1960, Model No. 4524
EX $85   NM $195   MIP $300

❏ **Cape Canaveral**, 1959, Sears set, Model No. 5963
EX $80   NM $325   MIP $500

❏ **Cape Canaveral Missile Center**, 1959, Model No. 4528
EX $80   NM $240   MIP $400

(ToyShop File Photo)

❏ **Cape Canaveral Missile Center**, 1959, includes four-stage rocket, missile and launcher, flying saucer and launcher, scientists, and other accessories, Model No. 2656
EX $55   NM $160   MIP $255

❏ **Cape Canaveral Missile Center**, Model No. 4525
EX $50   NM $195   MIP $300

❏ **Cape Canaveral Missile Set**, 1958, Model No. 4526
EX $55   NM $225   MIP $350

❏ **Cape Kennedy Carry All**, 1968, tin box set, Model No. 4625
EX $35   NM $45   MIP $75

(ToyShop File Photo)

❏ **Captain Gallant of the Foreign Legion**, 1956, includes foreign legion soldiers,

sheiks, horses, camel and "Cuffy." A hard-to-find set, Model No. 4729/4730
EX $210   NM $620   MIP $1050

❏ **Captain Space Solar Academy**, 1954, Model No. 7018
EX $65   NM $260   MIP $400

❏ **Captain Space Solar Academy**, Model No. 7026
EX $80   NM $325   MIP $500

❏ **Castle and Moat Set**, Sears Exclusive, Model No. 4734
EX $65   NM $260   MIP $400

❏ **Cattle Drive**, mid-1970s, Model No. 3983
EX $60   NM $245   MIP $375

❏ **Civil War Centennial**, 1961, Model No. 5929
EX $400   NM $1200   MIP $2000

❏ **Comanche Pass**, 1976, Model No. 3416
EX $30   NM $130   MIP $200

❏ **Complete Happitime Dairy Farm**, Sears, Model No. 5957
EX $80   NM $325   MIP $500

❏ **Complete U.S. Army Training Center**, 1954, Model No. 4145
EX $70   NM $210   MIP $350

(ToyShop File Photo)

❏ **Construction Camp**, 1956, 54mm, Series 1000, includes: field office building, workmen, heavy duty equipment (friction-power dozer, road roller, high-lift loader), Model No. 4442
EX $120   NM $330   MIP $600

(ToyShop File Photo)

❏ **Construction Camp**, 1954, includes trucks, figures, buildings and accessories, Model No. 4439
EX $95   NM $280   MIP $455

❏ **Cowboy And Indian Camp**, 1953, Model No. 3950
EX $90   NM $275   MIP $450

❏ **Custer's Last Stand**, 1956, Series 500, Model No. 4779
EX $80   NM $325   MIP $500

❏ **Custer's Last Stand**, 1963, Sears, 187 pieces, Model No. 4670
EX $195   NM $1200   MIP $1800

❏ **D.E.W. Defense Line Arctic Satellite Base**, Model No. 4802
EX $100   NM $300   MIP $500

❏ **Daktari**, 1967, 110 pieces, Model No. 3717
EX $100   NM $300   MIP $500

❏ **Daktari**, 1967, 140 pieces, Model No. 3720
EX $130   NM $395   MIP $650

❏ **Daktari**, Model No. 3718
EX $80   NM $325   MIP $500

(ToyShop File Photo)

❏ **Daniel Boone Frontier**, 1958, includes covered wagon and horses with driver, Indians, Frontiersman, other accessories, Model No. 1393
EX $65   NM $235   MIP $365

❏ **Daniel Boone Wilderness Scout**, 1964, Model No. 0670
EX $75   NM $225   MIP $375

❏ **Daniel Boone Wilderness Scout**, 1964, Model No. 0631
EX $75   NM $225   MIP $375

❏ **Daniel Boone Wilderness Scout**, 1964, Model No. 2640
EX $120   NM $360   MIP $600

❏ **Davy Crockett at the Alamo**, Model No. 3442
EX $120   NM $360   MIP $600

(ToyShop File Photo)

❏ **Davy Crockett at the Alamo**, 1955, official Walt Disney, 100 pieces, first set, Model No. 3530
EX $70   NM $275   MIP $425

❏ **Davy Crockett at the Alamo**, 1955, official Walt Disney, biggest set, Model No. 3544
EX $160   NM $500   MIP $800

❏ **D-Day Army Set**, U.S. and Nazi troops, Model No. 6027
EX $100   NM $300   MIP $500

❏ **Desert Fox**, 1966, 244 pieces, Model No. 4177
EX $90   NM $275   MIP $450

❏ **Desert Patrol**, 1967, U.S., Nazi troops, Model No. 4174
EX $60   NM $175   MIP $300

❏ **Farm Set**, Model No. 6050
EX $45   NM $180   MIP $275

❏ **Farm Set**, deluxe, 1969, Model No. 3953
EX $75   NM $225   MIP $375

❏ **Farm Set**, Model No. 6006
EX $50   NM $195   MIP $300

❏ **Farm Set**, Model No. 5942
EX $40   NM $160   MIP $250

❏ **Farm Set**, 1958, 100 pieces, Series 2000, Model No. 3948
EX $80   NM $250   MIP $400

❏ **Farm Set**, Lazy Day, 1960, 100 pieces, Model No. 3945
EX $55   NM $165   MIP $275

(ToyShop File Photo)

❏ **Fighting Knights Carry All**, 1966-68, includes litho walls, plastic towers, metallic and solid color knights, catapults and horses, Model No. 4635
EX $50   NM $140   MIP $230

❏ **Fire House**, w/two friction vehicles, Model No. 4820
EX $500   NM $1500   MIP $2000

❏ **Fire House**, Model No. 4819
EX $180   NM $715   MIP $1100

❏ **Fort Apache**, Model No. 3616
EX $30   NM $90   MIP $150

❏ **Fort Apache**, 1965, Sears, 335 pieces, Model No. 6063
EX $105   NM $315   MIP $525

❏ **Fort Apache**, Model No. 3681A
EX $30   NM $90   MIP $150

❏ **Fort Apache**, 1965, Sears, 147 pieces
EX $40   NM $120   MIP $200

(ToyShop File Photo)

❏ **Fort Apache**, 1972, Sears, over 100 pieces including: plastic fort, U.S. flag,

Indians, tepee, horses, soldiers, cannon and accessories, Model No. 59093C
EX $35   NM $95   MIP $160

❏ **Fort Apache**, Model No. 6068
EX $35   NM $100   MIP $165

❏ **Fort Apache**, Sears, Model No. 6059
EX $11   NM $35   MIP $55

❏ **Fort Apache**, 1970s, Model No. 4202
EX $15   NM $50   MIP $80

❏ **Fort Apache**, giant set, Model No. 3685
EX $140   NM $425   MIP $700

❏ **Fort Apache**, Model No. 3682
EX $15   NM $50   MIP $85

❏ **Fort Apache**, 1967, Model No. 3681
EX $45   NM $135   MIP $225

❏ **Fort Apache**, 1976, Model No. 3681
EX $40   NM $120   MIP $200

(ToyShop File Photo)

❏ **Fort Apache Carry All**, with plastic block houses, cowboys, horses and Indians, Model No. 4685
EX $20   NM $50   MIP $80

❏ **Fort Apache Rin Tin Tin**, early, 60mm, Model No. 3627
EX $100   NM $300   MIP $450

❏ **Fort Apache Rin Tin Tin**, 54mm, Model No. 3658
EX $90   NM $275   MIP $350

❏ **Fort Apache Rin Tin Tin**, mixed scale set, Model No. 3957
EX $90   NM $275   MIP $350

❏ **Fort Apache Stockade**, 1951, Model No. 3610
EX $70   NM $210   MIP $350

(ToyShop File Photo)

❏ **Fort Apache Stockade**, 1961, Series 5000 includes: cavalry HQ building, stockade fence and gate blockhouses, cannon, cavarly men and horses, tepee, Indian figures, totem pole, canoe, horses and other accessories
EX $60   NM $170   MIP $285

❏ **Fort Apache Stockade**, 1960, Series 2000, 60mm figures, Model No. 3660
EX $75   NM $225   MIP $375

(ToyShop File Photo)

❑ **Fort Apache Stockade**, 1953, includes stockade, block house, ladders, cowboys and Indians, Model No. 3612
EX $55   NM $160   MIP $260

❑ **Fort Apache with Famous Americans**, Model No. 3636
EX $55   NM $165   MIP $270

❑ **Fort Dearborn**, 1952, w/metal walls, Model No. 3510
EX $85   NM $255   MIP $375

❑ **Fort Dearborn**, larger set, Model No. 3514
EX $20   NM $60   MIP $100

❑ **Fort Dearborn**, w/plastic walls, Model No. 3688
EX $80   NM $240   MIP $400

❑ **Fort Mohawk**, British, Colonials, Indians, 54mm, Model No. 3751
EX $80   NM $325   MIP $500

❑ **Fort Pitt**, 1959, Series 750, 54mm, Model No. 3741
EX $65   NM $260   MIP $400

❑ **Fort Pitt**, 1959, Series 1000, 54mm, Model No. 3742
EX $70   NM $290   MIP $450

❑ **Four-Level Allstate Service Station**, Model No. 6004
EX $80   NM $325   MIP $500

❑ **Four-Level Parking Garage**, Model No. 3502
EX $40   NM $120   MIP $200

❑ **Four-Level Parking Garage**, Model No. 3511
EX $40   NM $200   MIP $300

❑ **Freight Trucking Terminal**, plastic trucks, Model No. 5220
EX $30   NM $90   MIP $150

❑ **Freight Trucking Terminal**, friction trucks, Model No. 5422
EX $30   NM $90   MIP $150

❑ **Galaxy Command**, 1976, Model No. 4206
EX $10   NM $30   MIP $50

❑ **Gallant Men**, official set from TV series, Model No. 4634
EX $70   NM $290   MIP $450

❑ **Gallant Men Army**, U.S. troops, Model No. 4632
EX $65   NM $260   MIP $400

(ToyShop File Photo)

❑ **Gunsmoke Dodge City**, 1960, official, Series 2000, 80 pieces including: Gunsmoke characters, town building, ranch house, gold mine, stagecoach, wagon, oxen, horses, cowboys, trees, steers and other accessories, Model No. 4268
EX $250   NM $1210   MIP $2015

❑ **Happitime Army and Air Force Training Center**, 1954, 147 pieces, Model No. 4159
EX $50   NM $150   MIP $250

❑ **Happitime Civil War Centennial**, 1962, Sears, Model No. 5929
EX $115   NM $455   MIP $700

❑ **Happitime Farm Set**, Model No. 3480
EX $25   NM $95   MIP $150

❑ **Happitime Roy Rogers Rodeo Ranch**, 1953, Model No. 3990
EX $60   NM $180   MIP $300

❑ **Heritage Battle of the Alamo**, 1972, Heritage Series, Model No. 59091
EX $80   NM $240   MIP $400

❑ **History in the Pacific**, 1972, Model No. 4164
EX $90   NM $275   MIP $450

❑ **Holiday Turnpike**, battery-operated w/HO scale vehicles, Model No. 5230
EX $10   NM $30   MIP $45

(ToyShop File Photo)

❑ **I.G.Y. Arctic Satellite Base**, 1959, Series 1000, with quonset hut, missiles, launchers, explorer figures, eskimo figures, igloos, sleds, animals, weather station, skis, etc. A true "cold war" play set, for sure, Model No. 4800
EX $240   NM $710   MIP $1190

❑ **Indian Warfare**, Series 2000, Model No. 4778
EX $65   NM $260   MIP $400

❑ **Irrigated Farm Set**, working pump, Model No. 6021
EX $7   NM $20   MIP $35

❑ **Johnny Apollo Moon Launch Center**, 1970, Model No. 4630
EX $45   NM $135   MIP $225

❑ **Johnny Ringo Western Frontier Set**, 1959, Series 2000, Model No. 4784
EX $1200   NM $1800   MIP $2500

(ToyShop File Photo)

❑ **Johnny Tremain Revolutionary War**, 1957, official Walt Disney, Series 1000, Model No. 3402
EX $410   NM $1220   MIP $2100

❑ **Jungle**, metal trading post, Series 500, Model No. 3705
EX $110   NM $325   MIP $550

❑ **Jungle**, 1960, 48 pieces, Sears, large animals, Model No. 3716
EX $25   NM $95   MIP $150

(ToyShop File Photo)

❑ **Jungle Jim**, 1957, official, Series 1000, includes: HQ building, hunters, natives, wild animals, thatched huts, log fence and accessories, Model No. 3706
EX $290   NM $875   MIP $1450

❑ **Knights and Vikings**, 1972, Model No. 4743
EX $50   NM $150   MIP $250

(ToyShop File Photo)

❑ **Knights and Vikings**, 1973, includes plastic castle and mat with metallic silver knights fighting Vikings, Model No. 4733
EX $55   NM $155   MIP $260

❑ **Knights and Vikings**, Model No. 4773
EX $30   NM $90   MIP $150

❑ **Little Red School House**, 1956, Model No. 3381
EX $90   NM $270   MIP $450

MARX PLAY SETS

(ToyShop File Photo)

❑ **Lone Ranger Ranch**, 1957, Series 500, includes: Lone Ranger, Tonto, cabin, gateway, cowboys, horses, saddles, Indians and accessories, Model No. 3969
EX $90   **NM** $260   **MIP** $435

❑ **Lone Ranger Rodeo Set**, 1953, Model No. 3696
EX $30   **NM** $90   **MIP** $150
(ToyShop File Photo)

❑ **Medieval Castle**, 1960, metallic knights, castle, horses, tree and catapult, Model No. 4700
EX $80   **NM** $295   **MIP** $460

❑ **Medieval Castle**, Sears, w/knights and Vikings, Model No. 4734
EX $75   **NM** $290   **MIP** $450

❑ **Medieval Castle**, w/knights and Vikings, Model No. 4733
EX $30   **NM** $130   **MIP** $200

❑ **Medieval Castle**, 1954, Model No. 4709
EX $25   **NM** $95   **MIP** $150

❑ **Medieval Castle**, 1959, Sears, Series 2000, Model No. 4708
EX $120   **NM** $350   **MIP** $600

❑ **Medieval Castle**, 1964, gold knights, moat, Model No. 4704
EX $30   **NM** $90   **MIP** $150

❑ **Medieval Castle**, w/knights and Vikings, Model No. 4707
EX $35   **NM** $110   **MIP** $180

(ToyShop File Photo)

❑ **Medieval Castle Fort**, 1953, included: fortress, figures, horses, cannons and accessories, Model No. 4710
EX $30   **NM** $130   **MIP** $200

(ToyShop File Photo)

❑ **Midtown Service Station**, 1960, electric elevator, pumps with canopy, attendants, cars and accessories, Model No. 3420
EX $52   **NM** $155   **MIP** $255

❑ **Midtown Shopping Center**, Model No. 2644
EX $30   **NM** $90   **MIP** $150

❑ **Military Academy**, Model No. 4718
EX $90   **NM** $350   **MIP** $500

❑ **Modern Farm Set**, 1951, 54mm, Model No. 3931
EX $50   **NM** $150   **MIP** $250

(ToyShop File Photo)

❑ **Modern Farm Set**, 1967, Model No. 3932
EX $65   **NM** $185   **MIP** $310

❑ **Modern Service Center**, 1962, Model No. 3471
EX $70   **NM** $210   **MIP** $350

(ToyShop File Photo)

❑ **Modern Service Station**, 1966, plastic building with gray metal base, plastic vehicles, gas pumps, mechanics and attendants, Model No. 6044
EX $40   **NM** $115   **MIP** $180

(ToyShop File Photo)

❑ **Navarone Mountain Battleground Set**, 1976, included multi-level plastic mountain with two gun emplacements, German troops, ladders, communication and radio benches, tank, landing craft, halftrack, jeep, American soldiers. A great set from Marx, Model No. 3412
EX $45   **NM** $120   **MIP** $200

(ToyShop File Photo)

❑ **New Car Sales and Service**, With battery powered light, Model No. 3466, 3465
EX $80   **NM** $295   **MIP** $460

❑ **One Million, B.C.**, 1970s
EX $40   **NM** $115   **MIP** $195

(ToyShop File Photo)

❑ **Operation Moon Base**, 1962, includes vehicles, moon base structure, space man, moon ship and accessories, Model No. 4654
EX $95   **NM** $275   **MIP** $465

❑ **Pet Shop**, Model No. 4209
EX $60   **NM** $230   **MIP** $350

(ToyShop File Photo)

❑ **Pet Shop**, 1953, includes Shop building, fence, tree, cages, crates, dogs, monkees, rabbits, birds, aquarium and accessories, Model No. 4210
EX $65   **NM** $240   **MIP** $365

❑ **Prehistoric**, 1969, Model No. 3398
EX $35   **NM** $105   **MIP** $175

❑ **Prehistoric Dinosaur**, 1978, Model No. 4208
EX $35   **NM** $105   **MIP** $175

❑ **Prehistoric Times**, Model No. 3391
EX $20   **NM** $55   **MIP** $95

❑ **Prehistoric Times**, Model No. 2650
EX $30   **NM** $130   **MIP** $200

(ToyShop File Photo)

❏ **Prehistoric Times**, Series 500, plain box that reads, "Prehistoric Play Set Complete with Animals in Natural Setting", Model No. 3389
EX $40 NM $120 MIP $180

❏ **Prehistoric Times**, 1957, Series 1000, big set, includes: molded terrain base, cavemen, prehistoric animals, palm trees, ferns, tree stumps and accessories, Model No. 3390
EX $60 NM $230 MIP $350

❏ **Prehistoric Times**, Model No. 3388
EX $25 NM $75 MIP $125

❏ **Prince Valiant Castle**, 1955, Model No. 4705
EX $90 NM $270 MIP $450

(ToyShop File Photo)

❏ **Prince Valiant Castle**, 1955, has figures, Model No. 4706
EX $110 NM $320 MIP $515

❏ **Project Apollo Cape Kennedy**, Model No. 4523
EX $25 NM $75 MIP $125

❏ **Project Apollo Moon Landing**, Model No. 4646
EX $50 NM $150 MIP $250

❏ **Project Mercury Cape Canaveral**, 1959, Model No. 4524
EX $90 NM $270 MIP $450

❏ **Raytheon Missile Test Center**, 1961, Model No. 603-A
EX $60 NM $180 MIP $300

❏ **Real Life Western Wagon**, Model No. 4998
EX $15 NM $45 MIP $75

❏ **Red River Gang**, 1970s, mini set w/cowboys, Model No. 4104
EX $35 NM $105 MIP $175

(ToyShop File Photo)

❏ **Revolutionary War**, Series 1000, includes British Redcoats, stone wall section, shooting cannon, trees, litho building, Revolutionary troops and more, Model No. 3404
EX $125 NM $500 MIP $800

❏ **Revolutionary War**, 1959, 80 pieces, Sears, Model No. 3408
EX $100 NM $390 MIP $600

❏ **Revolutionary War**, 1957, Series 500, Model No. 3401
EX $200 NM $500 MIP $1000

(ToyShop File Photo)

❏ **Rex Mars Planet Patrol**, Model No. 7040
EX $105 NM $310 MIP $510

❏ **Rex Mars Space Drome**, 1954, Model No. 7016
EX $130 NM $395 MIP $650

❏ **Rifleman Ranch, The**, 1959, Model No. 3998
EX $130 NM $395 MIP $650

❏ **Rifleman Ranch, The**, 1959, Model No. 3997
EX $115 NM $455 MIP $700

❏ **Rin Tin Tin at Fort Apache**, 1956, Series 5000, Model No. 3686R
EX $240 NM $725 MIP $1200

❏ **Rin Tin Tin at Fort Apache**, 1956, Series 500, 60mm, Model No. 3628
EX $160 NM $475 MIP $800

❏ **Robin Hood Castle**, 60mm, Model No. 4717
EX $120 NM $360 MIP $600

❏ **Robin Hood Castle**, 1958, 54mm, Model No. 4718
EX $80 NM $325 MIP $500

❏ **Roy Rogers Double R Bar Ranch**, 1962, Model No. 3982
EX $100 NM $300 MIP $500

❏ **Roy Rogers Mineral City**, 1958, 95 pieces, Model No. 4227
EX $100 NM $300 MIP $500

❏ **Roy Rogers Ranch**, w/ranch kids, Model No. 3980
EX $200 NM $300 MIP $500

❏ **Roy Rogers Rodeo**, Model No. 3689
EX $20 NM $60 MIP $100

❏ **Roy Rogers Rodeo Ranch**, 1952, Model No. 3979
EX $55 NM $165 MIP $275

❏ **Roy Rogers Rodeo Ranch**, 1958, Model No. 3986R
EX $250 NM $750 MIP $1250

❏ **Roy Rogers Rodeo Ranch**, 54mm, Model No. 3988
EX $65 NM $195 MIP $325

❏ **Roy Rogers Rodeo Ranch**, Series 2000, Model No. 3996
EX $130 NM $395 MIP $650

(ToyShop File Photo)

❏ **Roy Rogers Rodeo Ranch**, 1952, 60mm, includes: bunk house, rodeo chute, cowboys, horses, steers, saddles, bridles, fence and accessories, Model No. 3985
EX $50 NM $140 MIP $235

❏ **Roy Rogers Western Town**, 1952, large set, Model No. 4258
EX $160 NM $475 MIP $800

❏ **Roy Rogers Western Town**, official, Series 5000, Model No. 4259
EX $80 NM $235 MIP $395

❏ **Roy Rogers Western Town**, Model No. 4216
EX $80 NM $240 MIP $400

❏ **Sears Store**, 1961, Allstate box, Model No. 5490
EX $350 NM $1200 MIP $1800

❏ **Service Station**, Model No. 5459
EX $15 NM $45 MIP $75

(ToyShop File Photo)

❏ **Service Station**, with parking garage, includes: service station, cars, attendants, high-level parking garage, Model No. 3485
EX $115 NM $325 MIP $540

❏ **Service Station**, w/elevator, Model No. 3495
EX $30 NM $90 MIP $150

❏ **Service Station**, deluxe, Model No. 3501
EX $50 NM $150 MIP $250

❏ **Shopping Center**, Model No. 3755
EX $40 NM $120 MIP $200

❑ **Silver City Western Town**, has Custer, Boone, Carson, Buffalo Bill, Sitting Bull, Model No. 4220
EX $50   **NM** $150   **MIP** $250

❑ **Skyscraper**, working elevator, Model No. 5449
EX $155   **NM** $800   **MIP** $1200

❑ **Skyscraper**, working elevator and light, Model No. 5450
EX $155   **NM** $800   **MIP** $1200

(ToyShop File Photo)

❑ **Sons of Liberty**, Sears Exclusive set includes: litho building, plastic figures and accessories, flag and stand, historic booklet, Model No. 4170
EX $55   **NM** $155   **MIP** $260

❑ **Star Station Seven**, 1970s
EX $10   **NM** $30   **MIP** $50

❑ **Strategic Air Command**, Model No. 6013
EX $130   **NM** $520   **MIP** $800

(ToyShop File Photo)

❑ **Super Circus**, 1952, over 70 pieces, including big top, Model No. 4319
EX $85   **NM** $245   **MIP** $420

❑ **Super Circus**, 1952, w/character figures, Model No. 4320
EX $75   **NM** $290   **MIP** $450

❑ **Tactical Air Command**, 1970s, Model No. 4106
EX $15   **NM** $40   **MIP** $65

❑ **Tales of Wells Fargo**, Model No. 4262
EX $150   **NM** $450   **MIP** $750

❑ **Tales of Wells Fargo**, Model No. 4263
EX $80   **NM** $240   **MIP** $400

(ToyShop File Photo)

❑ **Tales of Wells Fargo**, Series 1000, play set includes Wells Fargo office, western town building, stagecoach, horses and cowboys, Indians and accessories, Model No. 4264
EX $155   **NM** $465   **MIP** $760

❑ **Tales of Wells Fargo Train Set**, 1959, w/electric train, Model No. 54752
EX $240   **NM** $600   **MIP** $800

❑ **Tank Battle**, Sears, U.S., Nazi troops, Model No. 6056
EX $40   **NM** $120   **MIP** $200

❑ **Tank Battle**, U.S., Nazi troops, Model No. 6060
EX $40   **NM** $120   **MIP** $200

❑ **Turnpike Service Center**, 1961, Model No. 3460
EX $100   **NM** $300   **MIP** $500

❑ **U.S. Air Force**, Model No. 4807
EX $30   **NM** $90   **MIP** $160

❑ **U.S. Armed Forces**, Model No. 4151
EX $70   **NM** $210   **MIP** $350

(ToyShop File Photo)

❑ **U.S. Armed Forces Training Center**, 1955, Series 500, "Featuring Guided Missiles," and including: HQ building, flag, fence, jet plane, compass, helicopter, Air Force, Navy, Army and Marines figures, Model No. 4149
EX $90   **NM** $265   **MIP** $430

❑ **U.S. Armed Forces Training Center**, Marines, soldiers, sailors, airmen, tin litho building, Model No. 4144
EX $40   **NM** $160   **MIP** $250

(ToyShop File Photo)

❑ **U.S. Armed Forces Training Center**, 1956, includes barracks, tents, planes, soldiers, Marines, sailors, Air Force personnel, guns and accessories, Model No. 4158
EX $115   **NM** $340   **MIP** $600

❑ **U.S. Armed Forces Training Center**, Model No. 4150
EX $50   **NM** $150   **MIP** $250

(ToyShop File Photo)

❑ **U.S. Army Mobile Set**, 1956, flat figures, includes vehicles, Model No. 3655
EX $22   **NM** $60   **MIP** $110

❑ **U.S. Army Training Center**, Model No. 4153
EX $15   **NM** $55   **MIP** $85

(ToyShop File Photo)

❑ **U.S. Army Training Center**, 1954, 45mm, includes: HQ building, vehicle, soldiers and accessories, Model No. 4123
EX $30   **NM** $80   **MIP** $130

❑ **U.S. Army Training Center**, Model No. 4122
EX $20   **NM** $60   **MIP** $100

❑ **U.S. Army Training Center**, Model No. 3378
EX $20   **NM** $55   **MIP** $95

❑ **U.S. Army Training Center**, Model No. 3146
EX $20   **NM** $55   **MIP** $95

(ToyShop File Photo)

❑ **Untouchables**, 1961, 90 pieces including: buildings, figures, guns, street layout, furniture and accessories, Model No. 4676
EX $255   **NM** $985   **MIP** $1510

❑ **Vikings and Knights**, Model No. 6053
EX $60   **NM** $180   **MIP** $300

❑ **Wagon Train**, Series 1000, X Team, Model No. 4805
EX $160   **NM** $480   **MIP** $800

❑ **Wagon Train**, official, Series 5000, Model No. 4888
EX $245   **NM** $975   **MIP** $1500

❑ **Wagon Train**, official, Series 2000, Model No. 4788
EX $120 **NM** $360 **MIP** $600

❑ **Walt Disney Television Playhouse**, 1953, Model No. 4352
EX $120 **NM** $360 **MIP** $600

❑ **Walt Disney Television Playhouse**, 1953, Model No. 4350
EX $100 **NM** $300 **MIP** $500

❑ **Walt Disney Television Playhouse**, 1953, Peter Pan figures, Model No. 4352
EX $105 **NM** $420 **MIP** $650

(ToyShop File Photo)

❑ **Walt Disney's Zorro**, 1958, official, Series 1000, includes buildings, horses, figures and accessories, Model No. 3754
EX $265 **NM** $780 **MIP** $1325

❑ **Walt Disney's Zorro**, 1958, official, Series 500, Model No. 3753
EX $230 **NM** $695 **MIP** $1150

❑ **Walt Disney's Zorro**, 1958, official, Model No. 3758
EX $240 **NM** $725 **MIP** $1200

❑ **Walt Disney's Zorro**, 1972, official, Series 1000, Model No. 3758
EX $160 **NM** $500 **MIP** $800

(ToyShop File Photo)

❑ **Ward's Service Station**, 1959, included service station with elevator, water-filled gasoline pump, cars and attendents, Model No. 3488
EX $82 **NM** $245 **MIP** $410

❑ **Western Frontier Set**
EX $90 **NM** $275 **MIP** $450

❑ **Western Mining Town**, 1950s, Model No. 4265
EX $135 **NM** $400 **MIP** $675

❑ **Western Mining Town**, 1950s, Model No. 4266
EX $135 **NM** $405 **MIP** $675

❑ **Western Ranch Set**, Model No. 3954
EX $35 **NM** $105 **MIP** $175

❑ **Western Ranch Set**, Model No. 3980
EX $35 **NM** $105 **MIP** $175

❑ **Western Stagecoach**, 1965, Model No. 1395
EX $20 **NM** $60 **MIP** $100

❑ **Western Town**, 1952, bi-level town, Model No. 4229
EX $120 **NM** $490 **MIP** $650

❑ **Western Town**, single level, Model No. 2652
EX $60 **NM** $180 **MIP** $400

(ToyShop File Photo)

❑ **Westgate Auto Center**, 1968, nice-looking litho building and base, plastic accessories and "New, Fast Rolling Cars!"
EX $45 **NM** $125 **MIP** $205

❑ **White House**, house w/eight figures
EX $15 **NM** $40 **MIP** $70

❑ **White House & Presidents**, house & figures, 1/48 scale presidents, Model No. 3920
EX $15 **NM** $40 **MIP** $70

❑ **White House & Presidents**, house & figures, Model No. 3921
EX $15 **NM** $40 **MIP** $70

❑ **Wild Animal Jungle**, large animals, Model No. 3716
EX $10 **NM** $30 **MIP** $50

(ToyShop File Photo)

❑ **World War II Battleground**, 1970s, with U.S. and German troops, halftrack, landing craft, barbed wire, barricades, gun emplacements, tank and jeep, Model No. 4204
EX $35 **NM** $95 **MIP** $155

❑ **World War II European Theatre**, rare big set, Model No. 5949
EX $245 **NM** $1200 **MIP** $1500

❑ **World War II European Theatre**, Sears, Model No. 5939
EX $165 **NM** $470 **MIP** $780

❑ **World War II Set**, U.S., Nazi troops, Model No. 5938
EX $30 **NM** $80 **MIP** $135

❑ **Wyatt Earp Dodge City Western Town**, 1957, Series 1000, Model No. 4228
EX $165 **NM** $465 **MIP** $800

Model Kits

A Gigantic Frankenstein released by Aurora in 1964 now sells for a humongous price—over $1400 MIP.

by Karen O'Brien

Building model kits has been a popular hobby since the 1960s, and in recent years, unbuilt model kits have found a loyal following among collectors seeking to recapture a part of their youth. Plastic model kits were first produced shortly before World War II, but it wasn't until after the war that plastic kit building really began to take off as a hobby. Automobiles, aircraft, and ships all became the subject matter for miniature replicas popularized by companies including Aurora, Revell, Monogram, and Lindberg.

Each type of model kit has its own enthusiastic following, but probably the most collectible kits today are the figure and character kits produced in the 1960s. These kits continue to increase in value despite the up and down fluctuations of the model kit market over the last twelve years.

The Aurora Company is responsible for popularizing figure model kits, with its early 1960s representations of the Universal Pictures monsters. Aurora went into business in August of 1950 and ventured into the hobby business in 1952 with two plastic model airplanes. Aurora expanded its line through the 1950s to include ships, modern and historic aircraft, and trucks before issuing its first figure kits, the knights, starting with the Silver Knight in 1956.

The vision and tenacity of Aurora employee Bill Silverstein in 1961 would change Aurora forever. The remarkable popularity of the 1930s Universal monster films at Saturday matinees and on television prompted the idea of producing a Frankenstein model. Repeated rejections by the Aurora staff almost killed the project, but Silverstein won enough support for the model pattern to be displayed at the January 1962, HIAA show. No distributors placed orders and on the last day of the convention, two boys accompanying a wholesaler came to the table, ignored the popular Model Motoring layout and headed straight for Frankenstein. Orders trickled in, then poured in, and the rest is history. Frankenstein production began in earnest in 1962, followed by Dracula and the Wolfman. The Creature from the Black Lagoon, The Phantom of the Opera, and The Mummy were released in 1963. The Hunchback of Notre Dame, Godzilla, and King Kong followed in 1964, and Dr. Jekyll and Mr. Hyde joined the lineup in 1965. The Universal monster kits propelled Aurora to the top of the hobby and remain some of the most desired kits by collectors today.

This GMC 6x6 by Italeri (now picked up by Testors) is valued at about $16 MIP.

During the 1960s, Aurora also produced kits of more general monstrosities, such as its famous working guillotine kit. These toys offended the sensibilities of some groups, who brought about the political pressure that spelled the end of these kits. Aurora also produced kits based on popular television shows, comic book characters, and sports celebrities. Monogram and Revell reissued some of the popular Aurora kits, and resin copies of the harder-to-find Aurora kits are still being produced and sold today by independent "garage kit" makers. Recently, Polar Lights (a division of the Playing Mantis company) has enjoyed tremendous success with its award-winning reissues of old Aurora favorites, as well as

new releases of television and movie favorites.

A German tank destroyer Marder II by Tamiya, one of the premiere manufactures of military kits. Luckily for builders, they keep reissuing many of their best stuff, (although, apparently not this one—yet.) For collectors, it means that prices rise sporadically on their models. $14 MIP.

Other popular monster kits continued the fad of the 1960s. These kits weren't of traditional movie monsters; rather, they were an assortment of strange characters that often came in wild hot rods. Among the most popular were the Revell kits based on Ed "Big Daddy" Roth's Rat Fink concept. (The modern reissues of those classic kits are certain to be collectibles of the future.) Other companies, notably Hawk, also produced kits with this monstrous hot rod theme. Hawk's Weird-Ohs kits are still popular with collectors today. Even popular celebrities became model kit subjects. Airfix produced a series of historical figures, and Revell issued figure kits for each of the four Beatles.

An usual model kit on it's own, but perfectly sensible given the "Visible Woman" and "Visible Man" kits by Revell, and the "Visible Head" kits by Renwal. This Human Eye kit by Pyro is valued at about $65 MIP.

A nicely done two-in-one kit by Revell—the Mercury and Gemini capsules, about $40 MIP.

After a slow period in the late 1970s, (the OPEC oil shortage sent plastic costs soaring, which had a ripple-effect throughout the toy and hobby industry) figure kits enjoyed a renewed popularity in the 1980s as new large-scale kits of rather limited production runs were offered in vinyl and resin. Billiken, a Japanese company, produced vinyl kits of the classic movie monsters, some of which have become highly collectible. Screamin' and Horizon are two leaders in the burgeoning "garage kit" field of large-scale vinyl and resin kits of movie, monster, and comic book characters. This area continues to command collector's attention, as the limited runs of these "garage kits" will likely translate into future desirability.

The prices listed provide a general guideline as to the amount these kits would sell for today. MIB refers to a kit that is Mint in Box, in original condition in the original Mint condition box with instructions. The box may not be in the original factory seal, but if the kit pieces are contained within bags inside the box, those original bags have not been opened. Kits that remain in pristine condition and are still in their factory seals may command a slight premium over the MIB price. Near Mint (NM) refers to a kit that is like new, complete, and unassembled. The box may show some shelf wear and the interior bags may have been opened. "BT" refers to a kit that has been assembled, or "built up" and assumes a neatly built, cleanly painted, complete kit.

References
Graham, Thomas. *Greenberg's Guide To Aurora Model Kits.* (Waukesha, Wi: Kalmbach Publishing Co., 1998).

ADDAR

❏ **Caesar, Planet of the Apes,** 1974, Model No. 106
BT $15   **NM** $42   **MIP** $55

❏ **Cornelius, Planet of the Apes,** 1974, Planet of the Apes, Model No. 101
BT $12   **NM** $32   **MIP** $55

❏ **Cornfield Roundup, Planet of the Apes,** 1975, Planet of the Apes, Model No. 216
BT $15   **NM** $42   **MIP** $55

❏ **Dr. Zaius, Planet of the Apes,** 1974, Planet of the Apes, Model No. 102
BT $10   **NM** $26   **MIP** $44

❏ **Dr. Zira, Planet of the Apes,** 1974, Planet of the Apes, Model No. 105
BT $10   **NM** $26   **MIP** $44

❏ **Evil Knievel,** 1974, w/cycle, Model No. 152
BT $12   **NM** $26   **MIP** $55

❏ **Evil Knievel's Sky Cycle,** 1974, Model No. 154
BT $12   **NM** $26   **MIP** $85

❏ **Gen. Aldo, Planet of the Apes,** 1974, Planet of the Apes, Model No. 104
BT $10   **NM** $26   **MIP** $55

❏ **Gen. Ursus, Planet of the Apes,** 1974, Planet of the Apes, Model No. 103
BT $12   **NM** $32   **MIP** $39

❏ **Jail Wagon, Planet of the Apes,** 1975, Planet of the Apes, Model No. 217
BT $15   **NM** $42   **MIP** $50

❏ **Jaws,** 1975, Model No. 270
BT $35   **NM** $58   **MIP** $110

❏ **Jaws in a Bottle,** 1975, Jaws, Model No. 270
BT $20   **NM** $53   **MIP** $66

❏ **Spirit in a Bottle,** 1975, Model No. 227
BT $10   **NM** $21   **MIP** $50

❏ **Stallion & Soldier, Planet of the Apes,** 1974, Model No. 107
BT $25   **NM** $79   **MIP** $110

❏ **Tree House, Planet of the Apes,** 1975, Model No. 215
BT $15   **NM** $42   **MIP** $50

AIRFIX

❏ **10th British Hussar 1915,** 1976, Model No. 2551
BT $10   **NM** $18   **MIP** $28

❏ **2001: A Space Odyssey Orion,** 1970, Model No. 701
BT $60   **NM** $80   **MIP** $100

❏ **2001: A Space Odyssey Orion,** 1980, Model No. 5175
BT $10   **NM** $20   **MIP** $40

❏ **Anne Boleyn,** 1974, Model No. 3542
BT $7   **NM** $16   **MIP** $22

❏ **Anne Boleyn,** 1976, Model No. 3542
BT $10   **NM** $18   **MIP** $28

❏ **Black Prince,** 1973, Model No. 2502
BT $10   **NM** $26   **MIP** $33

❏ **Boy Scout,** 1965, Model No. 212
BT $7   **NM** $16   **MIP** $22

❏ **Charles I,** 1965, Model No. 211
BT $10   **NM** $21   **MIP** $28

❏ **Empire Strikes Back, Slave I,** 1982
BT $35   **NM** $45   **MIP** $55

❏ **English Muskateer 1642,** 1976, Model No. 1560
BT $10   **NM** $18   **MIP** $28

❏ **English Pikeman 1642,** 1976, Model No. 1559
BT $10   **NM** $18   **MIP** $28

❏ **Flying Saucer,** 1981, Model No. 7171
BT $10   **NM** $18   **MIP** $28

❏ **George Washington,** 1980, Model No. 2554
BT $10   **NM** $18   **MIP** $28

❏ **Henry VIII,** 1973, Model No. 2501
BT $4   **NM** $8   **MIP** $11

❏ **James Bond and Odd Job,** 1966, Model No. M401F
BT $30   **NM** $80   **MIP** $220

❏ **James Bond Autogyro,** 1996, Model No. 4401
BT $10   **NM** $18   **MIP** $28

❏ **James Bond's Aston Martin DB-5,** 1965, Model No. 823
BT $60   **NM** $210   **MIP** $250

❏ **Julius Caesar,** 1973, Model No. 2504
BT $10   **NM** $26   **MIP** $33

❏ **Napoleon,** 1978, Model No. 2508
BT $4   **NM** $8   **MIP** $11

❏ **Queen Elizabeth I,** 1980, Model No. 3546
BT $12   **NM** $22   **MIP** $35

❏ **Queen Victoria,** 1976, Model No. 3544
BT $12   **NM** $22   **MIP** $35

❏ **Richard I,** 1965, Model No. 203
BT $10   **NM** $27   **MIP** $33

(KP Photo)

❏ **Space: 1999 Eagle Transporter,** 1979, Model No. 6174
BT $10   **NM** $18   **MIP** $28

❏ **Space: 1999 Hawk Spaceship,** 1977, Model No. 5173
BT $80   **NM** $95   **MIP** $110

❏ **Yeoman of the Guard,** 1978, Model No. 2507
BT $4   **NM** $9   **MIP** $11

AMAZING FIGURE MODELER

❏ **London After Midnight,** 1998, London After Midnight
BT $30   **NM** $60   **MIP** $90

AMT

❏ **B.J. and the Bear "Big Rig" set,** 1980, Model No. 7705
BT $30   **NM** $40   **MIP** $50

❏ **B.J. and the Bear Kenworth cap,** 1980, Snap-together, Model No. 5025
BT $17   **NM** $25   **MIP** $35

❏ **Bigfoot,** 1978, Model No. 7701
BT $20   **NM** $63   **MIP** $83

❏ **Brute Farce,** 1960s, Model No. 611
BT $5   **NM** $11   **MIP** $17

❏ **Cliff Hanger,** 1960s, Model No. 610
BT $5   **NM** $11   **MIP** $17

❏ **Drag-U-La, Munsters,** 1965, Munsters, Model No. 905
BT $40   **NM** $185   **MIP** $275

❏ **Farrah's Foxy Vette,** 1977, Model No. 3101
BT $40   **NM** $50   **MIP** $60

❏ **Fireball 500 Plymouth by George Barris,** 1967, Model No. 911
BT $50   **NM** $65   **MIP** $80

❏ **Flintstones Rock Crusher,** 1974, Flintstones, Model No. 497
BT $20   **NM** $53   **MIP** $66

❏ **Flintstones Sports Car,** 1974, Model No. 495
BT $20   **NM** $58   **MIP** $73

❏ **Get Smart Sunbeam,** 1967, Model No. 925
BT $50   **NM** $65   **MIP** $80

❏ **Girl From U.N.C.L.E. Car,** 1974, Model No. 913
BT $75   **NM** $265   **MIP** $330

❏ **Graveyard Ghoul Duo (Munsters cars),** 1970, Graveyard Ghoul Duo, Model No. 309
BT $50   **NM** $105   **MIP** $165

❏ **Hero, 1966 Chrysler Imperial,** 1966, Model No. 914
BT $70   **NM** $85   **MIP** $100

❏ **KISS Custom Chevy Van,** 1977, KISS, Model No. 2501
BT $20   **NM** $53   **MIP** $83

❏ **Laurel & Hardy '27 T Roadster,** 1976, Model No. 462
BT $20   **NM** $53   **MIP** $66

❏ **Laurel & Hardy '27 T Touring Car,** 1976, Model No. 461
BT $20   **NM** $53   **MIP** $66

❏ **Man From U.N.C.L.E. Car,** 1966, Model No. 912
BT $75   **NM** $185   **MIP** $250

❏ **Matilda Custom Ford Van,** 1978, Model No. 2504
BT $25   **NM** $35   **MIP** $45

MODEL KITS

Mr. Spock, large box, 1973, Model No. 956
BT $15   NM $79   MIP $193

(KP Photo)

Mr. Spock, small box, 1973
BT $20   NM $105   MIP $165

Munster Koach, 1964, Munsters, Model No. 901
BT $50   NM $105   MIP $220

My Mother The Car, 1965, Model No. 904
BT $15   NM $38   MIP $44

Sonny & Cher Mustang, 1960s, Sonny & Cher, Model No. 907
BT $75   NM $265   MIP $330

Star Trek the Motion Picture, Klingon Cruiser, 1979, Model No. 971
BT $19   NM $28   MIP $40

Star Trek the Motion Picture, Mr. Spock, 1979, Model No. 973
BT $25   NM $38   MIP $50

Star Trek the Motion Picture, U.S.S. Enterprise, 1979, Model No. 970
BT $50   NM $65   MIP $80

Star Trek the Motion Picture, Vulcan Shuttle, 1979, Model No. 972
BT $25   NM $35   MIP $45

Star Trek, Command Bridge Model Kit, 1975, Model No. S950-601
BT $40   NM $50   MIP $85

Star Trek, Galileo Shuttle Model Kit, 1974, #S959-602, Model No. 959
BT $80   NM $95   MIP $175

Star Trek, K-7 Space Station, 1976, Model No. 955
BT $19   NM $28   MIP $40

Star Trek, Klingon Cruiser Model Kit, Model No. PK-5111
BT $45   NM $60   MIP $90

Star Trek, Klingon Cruiser Model Kit, 1968, Model No. S952-802
BT $135   NM $180   MIP $250

Star Trek, Romulan Bird of Prey Model Kit, 1975, Model No. S957-601
BT $100   NM $120   MIP $130

Star Trek, Space Ship Set, 1976, Snap-together, Model No. 953
BT $50   NM $65   MIP $80

T.h.e. Cat, 1967 Custom Corvette, 1967, Model No. 915
BT $50   NM $60   MIP $75

Threw'd Dude, 1960s, Model No. 612
BT $5   NM $11   MIP $17

Touchdown?, 1960s, Model No. 614
BT $10   NM $18   MIP $25

UFO Mystery Ship, UFO
BT $15   NM $63   MIP $83

USS Enterprise Bridge, Star Trek, 1975, Model No. 950
BT $10   NM $27   MIP $39

(KP Photo)

USS Enterprise w/lights, Star Trek, 1967, Model No. 921-200
BT $40   NM $210   MIP $275

USS Enterprise, Star Trek, 1966, Model No. 951-250
BT $40   NM $132   MIP $165

Vega$, 1957 Thunderbird, 1979, Model No. 3105
BT $35   NM $45   MIP $60

AURORA

Addams Family Haunted House, 1964, Addams Family, Model No. 805
BT $300   NM $630   MIP $880

Alfred E. Neuman (MAD), 1965, Model No. 802
BT $150   NM $175   MIP $200

(KP Photo)

American Astronaut, 1967, Astronaut, Model No. 409
BT $25   NM $71   MIP $90

American Buffalo, 1964, Model No. 402
BT $19   NM $37   MIP $52

American Buffalo, reissue, 1972, Model No. 402
BT $8   NM $13   MIP $17

Apache Warrior on Horse, 1960, Model No. 401
BT $180   NM $320   MIP $500

Aramis, Three Musketeers, 1958, Three Musketeers, Model No. K-10
BT $20   NM $79   MIP $110

Archie's Car, 1969, Model No. 582
BT $25   NM $89   MIP $110

Aston Martin Super Spy Car, 1965, Model No. 819
BT $40   NM $158   MIP $220

(KP Photo)

Athos, Three Musketeers, 1958, Three Musketeers, Model No. K-8
BT $20   NM $79   MIP $110

Banana Splits Banana Buggy, 1969, Banana Splits, Model No. 832
BT $150   NM $420   MIP $550

(KP Photo)

❑ **Batboat,** 1968, Batman, Model No. 811
BT $150   **NM** $315   **MIP** $495

❑ **Batcycle,** 1967, Batman, Model No. 810
BT $125   **NM** $263   **MIP** $440

❑ **Batman,** 1964, Batman, Model No. 467
BT $15   **NM** $79   **MIP** $275

(KP Photo)

❑ **Batman, Comic Scenes,** 1974, Batman, Model No. 187
BT $15   **NM** $42   **MIP** $66

❑ **Batmobile,** 1966, Batman, Model No. 486
BT $100   **NM** $205   **MIP** $358

❑ **Batplane,** 1967, Batman, Model No. 487
BT $50   **NM** $105   **MIP** $275

❑ **Black Bear and Cubs,** 1962, Model No. 407
BT $15   **NM** $32   **MIP** $44

❑ **Black Bear and Cubs, reissue,** 1969, Model No. 407
BT $17   **NM** $25   **MIP** $35

❑ **Black Fury,** 1958, Black Fury, Model No. 400
BT $10   **NM** $26   **MIP** $33

❑ **Black Fury, reissue,** 1969, Black Fury, Model No. 400
BT $10   **NM** $14   **MIP** $17

(KP Photo)

❑ **Black Knight,** 1956, Black Knight, Model No. K-3
BT $10   **NM** $32   **MIP** $39

❑ **Black Knight, reissue,** 1963, Black Knight, Model No. 473
BT $10   **NM** $14   **MIP** $17

❑ **Blackbeard,** 1965, Blackbeard, Model No. 463
BT $75   **NM** $210   **MIP** $248

(KP Photo)

❑ **Blue Knight,** 1956, Blue Knight, Model No. K-2
BT $10   **NM** $37   **MIP** $55

❑ **Blue Knight, reissue,** 1963, Model No. 472
BT $10   **NM** $18   **MIP** $22

❑ **Bond, James,** 1966, James Bond, Model No. 414
BT $250   **NM** $315   **MIP** $495

(KP Photo)

❑ **Bride of Frankenstein,** 1965, Bride of Frankenstein, Model No. 482
BT $300   **NM** $525   **MIP** $825

❑ **Brown, Jimmy,** 1965, Brown, Jimmy, Model No. 863
BT $75   **NM** $158   **MIP** $193

(KP Photo)

MODEL KITS

❏ **Canyon, Steve,** 1958, Canyon, Steve, Model No. 409
BT $75   **NM** $184   **MIP** $275

(KP Photo)

❏ **Captain Action,** 1966, Captain Action, Model No. 480
BT $100   **NM** $289   **MIP** $330

(KP Photo)

❏ **Captain America,** 1966, Captain America, Model No. 476
BT $85   **NM** $200   **MIP** $330

❏ **Captain America, Comic Scenes,** 1974, Captain America, Model No. 192
BT $30   **NM** $84   **MIP** $138

❏ **Captain Kidd,** 1965, Captain Kidd, Model No. 464
BT $25   **NM** $53   **MIP** $88

(KP Photo)

❏ **Cave Bear,** 1971, Cave Bear, Model No. 738
BT $15   **NM** $26   **MIP** $44

❏ **Chinese Girl,** 1957, Chinese Girl, Model No. 416
BT $15   **NM** $27   **MIP** $35

❏ **Chinese Junk,** 1962, Model No. 430
BT $100   **NM** $125   **MIP** $150

❏ **Chinese Mandarin,** 1957, Chinese Mandarin, Model No. 415
BT $12   **NM** $26   **MIP** $33

(KP Photo)

❏ **Chinese Mandarin & Girl,** 1957, Model No. 213
BT $75   **NM** $105   **MIP** $330

❏ **Chitty Chitty Bang Bang,** 1968, Chitty Chitty Bang Bang, Model No. 828
BT $30   **NM** $89   **MIP** $165

(KP Photo)

❏ **Confederate Raider,** 1959, Model No. 402
BT $150   **NM** $210   **MIP** $385

❏ **Creature From the Black Lagoon,** 1963, Creature, Model No. 426
BT $65   **NM** $315   **MIP** $468

❏ **Creature From The Black Lagoon, Glow Kit,** 1969, Creature, Model No. 483
BT $65   **NM** $105   **MIP** $248

❏ **Creature From The Black Lagoon, Glow Kit,** 1972, Creature, Model No. 483
BT $80   **NM** $130   **MIP** $240

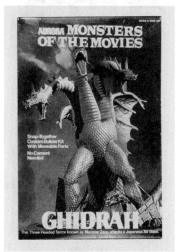

(KP Photo)

❏ **Creature, Monsters of Movies,** 1975, Creature, Model No. 653
BT $100   **NM** $145   **MIP** $265
(KP Photo)

❏ **Cro-Magnon Man,** 1971, Model No. 730
BT $10   **NM** $32   **MIP** $50

(KP Photo)

❏ **Cro-Magnon Woman,** 1971, Model No. 731
BT $7   **NM** $26   **MIP** $39

(KP Photo)

❑ **Crusader,** 1959, Model No. K-7
BT $75   **NM** $158   **MIP** $220

❑ **D'Artagnan, Three Musketeers,** 1966,
Three Musketeers, Model No. 410
BT $50   **NM** $158   **MIP** $193

❑ **Dempsey vs Firpo,** 1965, Dempsey,
Model No. 861
BT $40   **NM** $100   **MIP** $125

❑ **Dick Tracy in Action Model Kit,** 1968,
plastic
BT $85   **NM** $175   **MIP** $375

❑ **Dr. Deadly,** 1971, Dr. Deadly, Model
No. 631
BT $25   **NM** $74   **MIP** $88

❑ **Dr. Deadly's Daughter,** 1971, Dr.
Deadly Daughter, Model No. 632
BT $25   **NM** $68   **MIP** $83

(KP Photo)

❑ **Dr. Jekyll as Mr. Hyde,** 1964, Dr. Jekyll,
Model No. 460
BT $45   **NM** $263   **MIP** $385

❑ **Dr. Jekyll, Glow Kit,** 1969, Dr. Jekyll,
Model No. 482
BT $45   **NM** $105   **MIP** $193

❑ **Dr. Jekyll, Glow Kit,** 1972, Dr. Jekyll,
Model No. 482
BT $45   **NM** $68   **MIP** $88

❑ **Dr. Jekyll, Monster Scenes,** 1971, Dr.
Jekyll, Model No. 462
BT $40   **NM** $95   **MIP** $138

(KP Photo)

❑ **Dr. Jekyll, Monsters of Movies,** 1975,
Dr. Jekyll, Model No. 654
BT $25   **NM** $63   **MIP** $77

❑ **Dracula,** 1962, Dracula, Model No. 424
BT $25   **NM** $236   **MIP** $330

❑ **Dracula, Frightning Lightning,** 1969,
Dracula, Model No. 454
BT $30   **NM** $315   **MIP** $550

❑ **Dracula, Glow Kit,** 1969, Dracula,
Model No. 454
BT $20   **NM** $79   **MIP** $165

(KP Photo)

❑ **Dracula, Glow Kit,** 1972, Dracula,
Model No. 454
BT $20   **NM** $63   **MIP** $83

❑ **Dracula, Monster Scenes,** 1971, Dracula, Model No. 641
BT $75   **NM** $105   **MIP** $220

❑ **Dracula, Monsters of Movies,** 1975,
Dracula, Model No. 656
BT $75   **NM** $105   **MIP** $275

❑ **Dracula's Dragster,** 1966, Dracula,
Model No. 466
BT $125   **NM** $315   **MIP** $440

(KP Photo)

❑ **Dutch Boy,** 1957, Dutch Boy, Model
No. 413
BT $10   **NM** $26   **MIP** $33

❑ **Dutch Boy & Girl,** 1957, Model No. 209
BT $75   **NM** $210   **MIP** $330

(KP Photo)

MODEL KITS

❏ **Dutch Girl,** 1957, Dutch Girl, Model No. 414
BT $10   **NM** $21   **MIP** $28

❏ **Flying Sub,** 1968, Model No. 817
BT $35   **NM** $184   **MIP** $220

❏ **Flying Sub, reissue,** 1975, Model No. 254
BT $35   **NM** $89   **MIP** $110

❏ **Forgotten Prisoner,** 1966, Forgotten Prisoner, Model No. 422
BT $65   **NM** $368   **MIP** $440

❏ **Forgotten Prisoner, Frightning Lightning,** 1969, Forgotten Prisoner, Model No. 453
BT $65   **NM** $341   **MIP** $495

❏ **Forgotten Prisoner, Glow Kit,** 1969, Forgotten Prisoner, Model No. 453
BT $65   **NM** $184   **MIP** $220

❏ **Forgotten Prisoner, Glow Kit,** 1972, Forgotten Prisoner, Model No. 453
BT $65   **NM** $158   **MIP** $193

❏ **Frankenstein,** 1961, Frankenstein, Model No. 423
BT $30   **NM** $210   **MIP** $330

❏ **Frankenstein, Frightning Lightning,** 1969, Frankenstein, Model No. 449
BT $30   **NM** $315   **MIP** $440

❏ **Frankenstein, Gigantic 1:5 scale,** 1964, Frankenstein, Model No. 470
BT $300   **NM** $945   **MIP** $1430

❏ **Frankenstein, Glow Kit,** 1969, Frankenstein, Model No. 449
BT $20   **NM** $68   **MIP** $165

❏ **Frankenstein, Glow Kit,** 1972, Frankenstein, Model No. 449
BT $20   **NM** $53   **MIP** $83

❏ **Frankenstein, Monster Scenes,** 1971, Frankenstein, Model No. 633
BT $50   **NM** $79   **MIP** $110

❏ **Frankenstein, Monsters of Movies,** 1975, Frankenstein, Model No. 651
BT $100   **NM** $210   **MIP** $275

❏ **Frankie's Flivver,** 1964, Frankenstein, Model No. 465
BT $150   **NM** $368   **MIP** $440

❏ **Frog, Castle Creatures,** 1966, Frog, Model No. 451
BT $75   **NM** $210   **MIP** $275

❏ **Ghidrah,** 1975, Model No. 658
BT $95   **NM** $273   **MIP** $330

❏ **Giant Insect, Monster Scene,** 1971, Model No. 643
BT $95   **NM** $368   **MIP** $440

❏ **Godzilla,** 1964, Godzilla, Model No. 469
BT $85   **NM** $420   **MIP** $578

❏ **Godzilla, Glow Kit,** 1969, Godzilla, Model No. 466
BT $75   **NM** $236   **MIP** $358

❏ **Godzilla, Glow Kit,** 1972, Godzilla, Model No. 466
BT $75   **NM** $158   **MIP** $193

❏ **Godzilla's Go-Cart,** 1966, Godzilla, Model No. 485
BT $650   **NM** $2310   **MIP** $3520

❏ **Gold Knight of Nice,** 1957, Gold Knight, Model No. 475
BT $145   **NM** $280   **MIP** $350

❏ **Gold Knight of Nice,** 1965, Gold Knight, Model No. 475
BT $125   **NM** $263   **MIP** $303

❏ **Green Beret,** 1966, Green Beret, Model No. 413
BT $75   **NM** $158   **MIP** $193

❏ **Green Hornet Black Beauty,** 1966, Green Hornet, Model No. 489
BT $125   **NM** $368   **MIP** $550

❏ **Gruesome Goodies,** 1971, Model No. 634
BT $25   **NM** $84   **MIP** $110

❏ **Guillotine,** 1964, Guillotine, Model No. 800
BT $125   **NM** $368   **MIP** $440

❏ **Hanging Cage,** 1971, Model No. 637
BT $20   **NM** $84   **MIP** $110

❏ **Hercules,** 1965, Hercules, Model No. 481
BT $125   **NM** $235   **MIP** $340

(KP Photo)

❑ **Hulk, Comic Scenes,** 1974, Hulk, Model No. 184
BT $25   **NM** $79   **MIP** $94

❑ **Hulk, Original,** 1966, Hulk, Model No. 421
BT $75   **NM** $263   **MIP** $330

(KP Photo)

❑ **Hunchback of Notre Dame,** 1964, Hunchback, Model No. 460
BT $45   **NM** $210   **MIP** $330

❑ **Hunchback of Notre Dame, Glow Kit,** 1969, Hunchback, Model No. 481
BT $45   **NM** $95   **MIP** $165

❑ **Hunchback of Notre Dame, Glow Kit,** 1972, Hunchback, Model No. 481
BT $45   **NM** $68   **MIP** $83

❑ **Indian Chief,** 1957, Model No. 417
BT $40   **NM** $95   **MIP** $110

❑ **Indian Chief & Squaw,** 1957, Model No. 212
BT $60   **NM** $131   **MIP** $165

❑ **Indian Squaw,** 1957, Model No. 418
BT $15   **NM** $40   **MIP** $50

❑ **Infantryman,** 1957, Infantryman, Model No. 411
BT $20   **NM** $79   **MIP** $110

(KP Photo)

❑ **Invaders UFO,** 1968, Model No. 813
BT $35   **NM** $89   **MIP** $110

❑ **Invaders UFO,** 1975, Model No. 256
BT $25   **NM** $55   **MIP** $85

❑ **Iwo Jima,** 1966, Model No. 853
BT $75   **NM** $185   **MIP** $220

(KP Photo)

❑ **Jesse James,** 1966, Jesse James, Model No. 408
BT $60   **NM** $105   **MIP** $220

❑ **Kennedy, John F.,** 1965, Kennedy, John F., Model No. 851
BT $50   **NM** $75   **MIP** $165

❑ **King Arthur,** 1973, Model No. 885
BT $50   **NM** $105   **MIP** $220

❑ **King Arthur of Camelot,** 1967, King Arthur, Model No. 825
BT $30   **NM** $70   **MIP** $85

❑ **King Kong,** 1964, King Kong, Model No. 468
BT $75   **NM** $315   **MIP** $495

❑ **King Kong, Glow Kit,** 1969, King Kong, Model No. 468
BT $75   **NM** $185   **MIP** $275

❑ **King Kong, Glow Kit,** 1972, King Kong, Model No. 468
BT $75   **NM** $132   **MIP** $195

❑ **King Kong's Thronester,** 1966, King Kong, Model No. 484
BT $370   **NM** $840   **MIP** $1375

❑ **Land of the Giants Space Ship,** 1968, Land of Giants, Model No. 830
BT $150   **NM** $308   **MIP** $440

❑ **Land of the Giants, Diorama,** 1968, Land of the Giants, Model No. 816
BT $150   **NM** $368   **MIP** $495

❑ **Lone Ranger,** 1967, Lone Ranger, Model No. 808
BT $75   **NM** $105   **MIP** $196

❑ **Lone Ranger, Comic Scenes,** 1974, Lone Ranger, Model No. 188
BT $20   **NM** $42   **MIP** $55

❑ **Lost In Space, Large kit w/chariot,** 1966, Lost in Space, Model No. 420
BT $450   **NM** $1050   **MIP** $1485

(KP Photo)

❑ **Lost In Space, Small kit,** 1966, Lost in Space, Model No. 419
BT $300   **NM** $735   **MIP** $1012

(KP Photo)

❏ **Lost In Space, The Robot,** 1968, Model No. 418
BT $250   **NM** $630   **MIP** $880

❏ **Mad Barber,** 1972, Mad Barber, Model No. 455
BT $45   **NM** $105   **MIP** $165

❏ **Mad Dentist,** 1972, Model No. 457
BT $45   **NM** $105   **MIP** $165

❏ **Mad Doctor,** 1972, Model No. 456
BT $45   **NM** $105   **MIP** $165

(KP Photo)

❏ **Man From U.N.C.L.E., Illya Kuryakin,** 1966, Man From U.N.C.L.E., Model No. 412
BT $75   **NM** $105   **MIP** $220

❏ **Man From U.N.C.L.E., Napoleon Solo,** 1966, Man From U.N.C.L.E., Model No. 411
BT $75   **NM** $165   **MIP** $290

❏ **Marine,** 1959, Marine, Model No. 412
BT $20   **NM** $84   **MIP** $110

❏ **Mays, Willie,** 1965, Model No. 860
BT $100   **NM** $210   **MIP** $330

❏ **MBTican Caballero,** 1957, Model No. 421
BT $95   **NM** $100   **MIP** $175

❏ **MBTican Senorita,** 1957, MBTican Senorita, Model No. 422
BT $50   **NM** $96   **MIP** $170

(KP Photo)

❏ **Mod Squad Wagon,** 1970, Model No. 583
BT $35   **NM** $132   **MIP** $192

(KP Photo)

❏ **Monster Customizing Kit #1,** 1964, Model No. 463
BT $35   **NM** $117   **MIP** $140

❏ **Monster Customizing Kit #2,** 1964, Model No. 464
BT $65   **NM** $160   **MIP** $195

❏ **Moon Bus from 2001,** 1968, Model No. 828
BT $100   **NM** $250   **MIP** $330

(KP Photo)

❏ **Mr. Hyde, Monsters of Movies,** 1975, Mr. Hyde, Model No. 655
BT $40   **NM** $75   **MIP** $90

❏ **Mr. Spock,** 1972, Spock, Model No. 922
BT $40   **NM** $125   **MIP** $175

❏ **Mummy,** 1963, Mummy, Model No. 427
BT $30   **NM** $160   **MIP** $350

❏ **Mummy, Frightning Lightning,** 1969, Mummy, Model No. 452
BT $30   **NM** $210   **MIP** $440

❏ **Mummy, Glow Kit,** 1969, Mummy, Model No. 452
BT $20   **NM** $80   **MIP** $190

(KP Photo)

❏ **Mummy, Glow Kit,** 1972, Mummy, Model No. 452
BT $20   **NM** $42   **MIP** $66

(KP Photo)

❏ **Mummy's Chariot,** 1965, Mummy,
Model No. 459
BT $200   **NM** $340   **MIP** $550

❏ **Munsters, Living Room,** 1964, Munsters, Model No. 804
BT $400   **NM** $945   **MIP** $1430

(KP Photo)

❏ **Neanderthal Man,** 1971, Neanderthal
Man, Model No. 729
BT $15   **NM** $42   **MIP** $55

❏ **Neuman, Alfred E.,** 1965, Alfred E. Neuman, Model No. 802
BT $100   **NM** $289   **MIP** $440

(KP Photo)

❏ **Nutty Nose Nipper,** 1965, Nutty Nose
Nipper, Model No. 806
BT $45   **NM** $185   **MIP** $220

(KP Photo)

❏ **Odd Job,** 1966, Odd Job, Model No. 415
BT $200   **NM** $360   **MIP** $495

❏ **Pain Parlor,** 1971, Model No. 635
BT $25   **NM** $105   **MIP** $140

❏ **Pendulum,** 1971, Model No. 636
BT $25   **NM** $55   **MIP** $85

❏ **Penguin,** 1967, Penguin, Model
No. 416
BT $200   **NM** $420   **MIP** $570

❏ **Phantom of the Opera,** 1963, Phantom
of the Opera, Model No. 428
BT $30   **NM** $263   **MIP** $330

❏ **Phantom of the Opera, Frightning
Lightning,** 1969, Phantom of the Opera,
Model No. 451
BT $20   **NM** $263   **MIP** $385

(KP Photo)

❏ **Phantom of the Opera, Glow Kit,** 1969,
Phantom of the Opera, Model No. 451
BT $20   **NM** $75   **MIP** $165

❏ **Phantom of the Opera, Glow Kit,** 1972,
Phantom of the Opera, Model No. 451
BT $20   **NM** $63   **MIP** $88

❏ **Pilot USAF,** 1957, Model No. 409
BT $75   **NM** $145   **MIP** $190

❏ **Porthos, Three Musketeers,** 1958,
Three Musketeers, Model No. K-9
BT $25   **NM** $75   **MIP** $110

(KP Photo)

❏ **Pushmi-Pullyu, Dr. Dolittle,** 1968,
Model No. 814
BT $60   **NM** $110   **MIP** $160

❏ **Rat Patrol,** 1967, Rat Patrol, Model
No. 340
BT $30   **NM** $70   **MIP** $105

❏ **Red Knight,** 1957, Red Knight, Model
No. K-4
BT $15   **NM** $55   **MIP** $110

❏ **Red Knight,** 1963, Red Knight, Model
No. 474
BT $15   **NM** $40   **MIP** $55

MODEL KITS

(KP Photo)

❑ **Robin,** 1966, Robin, Model No. 488
  BT $40   **NM** $70   **MIP** $110

❑ **Robin, Comic Scenes,** 1974, Robin, Model No. 193
  BT $20   **NM** $70   **MIP** $110

❑ **Rodan,** 1975, Rodan, Model No. 657
  BT $125   **NM** $210   **MIP** $385

❑ **Roman Gladiator with sword,** 1959, Model No. 405
  BT $75   **NM** $130   **MIP** $200

❑ **Roman Gladiator with Trident,** 1964, Gladiator, Model No. 406
  BT $75   **NM** $140   **MIP** $200

❑ **Roman Gladiators,** 1959, Model No. 216
  BT $100   **NM** $210   **MIP** $275

❑ **Ruth, Babe,** 1965, Ruth, Babe, Model No. 862
  BT $100   **NM** $240   **MIP** $360

(KP Photo)

❑ **Scotch Lad,** 1957, Scoth Lad, Model No. 419
  BT $10   **NM** $26   **MIP** $35

❑ **Scotch Lad & Lassie,** 1957, Model No. 214
  BT $60   **NM** $95   **MIP** $110

(KP Photo)

❑ **Scotch Lassie,** 1957, Scotch Lassie, Model No. 420
  BT $10   **NM** $21   **MIP** $30

❑ **Seaview, Voyage to the Bottom of Sea,** 1966, Voyage to the Bottom, Model No. 707
  BT $100   **NM** $210   **MIP** $330

❑ **Seaview, Voyage to the Bottom of Sea,** 1975, Model No. 253
  BT $100   **NM** $168   **MIP** $209

(KP Photo)

❑ **Silver Knight,** 1956, Silver Knight, Model No. K-1
  BT $15   **NM** $42   **MIP** $55

❑ **Silver Knight,** 1963, Silver Knight, Model No. 471
  BT $15   **NM** $21   **MIP** $33

❑ **Sir Galahad,** 1973, Model No. 881
  BT $15   **NM** $42   **MIP** $55

❑ **Sir Galahad of Camelot,** 1967, Galahad, Model No. 826
  BT $25   **NM** $95   **MIP** $195

❑ **Sir Kay,** 1973, Model No. 882
  BT $20   **NM** $42   **MIP** $55

❑ **Sir Lancelot,** 1973, Model No. 883
  BT $20   **NM** $42   **MIP** $55

(KP Photo)

❑ **Sir Lancelot of Camelot,** 1967, Lancelot, Model No. 827
BT $25   **NM** $95   **MIP** $140

❑ **Sir Percival,** 1973, Model No. 884
BT $20   **NM** $30   **MIP** $55

(KP Photo)

❑ **Spartacus (Gladiator/sword reissue),**
1964, Spartacus, Model No. 405
BT $85   **NM** $150   **MIP** $275

❑ **Spider-Man,** 1966, Spider-Man, Model
No. 477
BT $85   **NM** $210   **MIP** $330

❑ **Spider-Man, Comic Scenes,** 1974, Spider-Man, Model No. 182
BT $50   **NM** $75   **MIP** $90

❑ **Star Trek, Klingon Cruiser,** 1972,
Model No. 923
BT $20   **NM** $50   **MIP** $85

❑ **Star Trek, USS Enterprise,** 1972, Model
No. 921
BT $20   **NM** $60   **MIP** $110

❑ **Superboy,** 1964, Superboy, Model
No. 478
BT $75   **NM** $210   **MIP** $275
(KP Photo)

❑ **Superboy, Comic Scenes,** 1974,
Superboy, Model No. 186
BT $35   **NM** $50   **MIP** $70

❑ **Superman,** 1963, Superman, Model
No. 462
BT $25   **NM** $180   **MIP** $374

(KP Photo)

❑ **Superman, Comic Scenes,** 1974,
Superman, Model No. 185
BT $20   **NM** $42   **MIP** $66

❑ **Tarpit,** 1972, Model No. 735
BT $65   **NM** $110   **MIP** $150

(KP Photo)

❑ **Tarzan,** 1967, Tarzan, Model No. 820
BT $25   **NM** $105   **MIP** $220

(KP Photo)

❑ **Tarzan, Comic Scenes,** 1974, Tarzan,
Model No. 181
BT $15   **NM** $26   **MIP** $39

❑ **Three Knights Set,** 1959, Model
No. 207
BT $50   **NM** $105   **MIP** $190

❑ **Three Musketeers Set,** 1958, Model
No. 398
BT $95   **NM** $210   **MIP** $385

❑ **Tonto,** 1967, Tonto, Model No. 809
BT $20   **NM** $105   **MIP** $220

❏ **Tonto, Comic Scenes,** 1974, Tonto, Model No. 183
BT $19   **NM** $25   **MIP** $37

❏ **Tracy, Dick,** 1968, Tracy, Dick, Model No. 818
BT $60   **NM** $105   **MIP** $275

❏ **Tracy, Dick, Space Coupe,** 1968, Tracy, Dick, Model No. 819
BT $50   **NM** $105   **MIP** $165

❏ **U.S. Marshal,** 1958, Model No. 408
BT $55   **NM** $78   **MIP** $115

❏ **Unitas, Johnny,** 1965, Unitas, Johnny, Model No. 864
BT $75   **NM** $132   **MIP** $195

(KP Photo)

❏ **United States Sailor,** 1957, Sailor, Model No. 410
BT $15   **NM** $31   **MIP** $38

❏ **Vampire, Castle Creatures,** 1966, Model No. 452
BT $60   **NM** $185   **MIP** $275

(KP Photo)

❏ **Vampirella,** 1971, Vampirella, Model No. 638
BT $75   **NM** $132   **MIP** $220

❏ **Victim,** 1971, Model No. 632
BT $20   **NM** $70   **MIP** $85

❏ **Viking,** 1959, Viking, Model No. K-6
BT $65   **NM** $105   **MIP** $275

❏ **Voyager, Fantastic Voyage,** 1969, Model No. 831
BT $125   **NM** $235   **MIP** $525

(KP Photo)

❏ **Wacky Back-Whacker,** 1965, Model No. 807
BT $50   **NM** $105   **MIP** $275

❏ **Washington, George,** 1965, Washington, Model No. 852
BT $25   **NM** $55   **MIP** $83

❏ **West, Jerry,** 1965, West, Jerry, Model No. 865
BT $50   **NM** $105   **MIP** $165

❏ **White Stallion,** 1964, Model No. 401
BT $10   **NM** $26   **MIP** $33

❏ **White Stallion, reissue,** 1969, Model No. 401
BT $10   **NM** $16   **MIP** $22

❏ **White-tailed Deer,** 1962, Model No. 403
BT $10   **NM** $26   **MIP** $33

❏ **White-tailed Deer, reissue,** 1969, Model No. 403
BT $10   **NM** $16   **MIP** $22

❏ **Whoozis, Alfalfa,** 1966, Whoozis, Model No. 204
BT $25   **NM** $53   **MIP** $83

❏ **Whoozis, Denty,** 1966, Whoozis, Model No. 203
BT $25   **NM** $53   **MIP** $83

❏ **Whoozis, Esmerelda,** 1966, Whoozis, Model No. 202
BT $25   **NM** $53   **MIP** $83

❏ **Whoozis, Kitty,** 1966, Whoozis, Model No. 205
BT $25   **NM** $53   **MIP** $83

❏ **Whoozis, Snuffy,** 1966, Whoozis, Model No. 206
BT $25   **NM** $53   **MIP** $83

❏ **Whoozis, Susie,** 1966, Whoozis, Model No. 201
BT $25   **NM** $53   **MIP** $83

❏ **Witch,** 1965, Witch, Model No. 483
BT $75   **NM** $210   **MIP** $330

❏ **Witch, Glow Kit,** 1969, Witch, Model No. 470
BT $50   **NM** $105   **MIP** $220

(KP Photo)

❏ **Witch, Glow Kit,** 1972, Witch, Model No. 470
BT $75   **NM** $105   **MIP** $138

❏ **Wolfman,** 1962, Wolfman, Model No. 425
BT $35   **NM** $210   **MIP** $330

❏ **Wolfman, Frightning Lightning,** 1969, Wolfman, Model No. 450
BT $35   **NM** $315   **MIP** $440

❏ **Wolfman, Glow Kit,** 1969, Wolfman, Model No. 450
BT $20   **NM** $53   **MIP** $165

❏ **Wolfman, Glow Kit,** 1972, Wolfman, Model No. 450
BT $20   **NM** $53   **MIP** $83

(KP Photo)

❏ **Wolfman, Monsters of Movies,** 1975, Wolfman, Model No. 652
BT $100   **NM** $210   **MIP** $275

❏ **Wolfman's Wagon,** 1965, Wolfman, Model No. 458
BT $175   **NM** $315   **MIP** $468

(KP Photo)

❑ **Wonder Woman,** 1965, Wonder Woman, Model No. 479
BT $150 **NM** $315 **MIP** $550

❑ **Zorro,** 1965, Zorro, Model No. 801
BT $125 **NM** $210 **MIP** $330

BILLIKEN

❑ **Batman, type A,** 1989, Batman
BT $35 **NM** $89 **MIP** $110

❑ **Batman, type B,** 1989, Batman
BT $35 **NM** $95 **MIP** $138

❑ **Bride of Frankenstein,** 1984, Bride of Frankenstein
BT $75 **NM** $105 **MIP** $248

❑ **Colossal Beast,** 1986, Colossal Beast
BT $20 **NM** $32 **MIP** $44

❑ **Creature From Black Lagoon,** 1991, Creature
BT $50 **NM** $89 **MIP** $138

❑ **Cyclops,** 1984
BT $75 **NM** $105 **MIP** $220

❑ **Dracula,** 1989, Dracula
BT $60 **NM** $105 **MIP** $165

❑ **Frankenstein,** 1988, Frankenstein
BT $60 **NM** $95 **MIP** $138

❑ **Joker,** 1989
BT $40 **NM** $95 **MIP** $165

❑ **Mummy,** 1990, Mummy
BT $60 **NM** $105 **MIP** $165

❑ **Phantom of the Opera,** 1980s, Phantom of the Opera
BT $100 **NM** $210 **MIP** $303

❑ **Predator,** 1991, Predator
BT $25 **NM** $53 **MIP** $72

❑ **Saucer Man**, Saucer Man
BT $20 **NM** $32 **MIP** $44

❑ **She-Creature,** 1989, She-Creature
BT $25 **NM** $42 **MIP** $55

❑ **Syngenor,** 1984, Syngenor
BT $100 **NM** $158 **MIP** $275

❑ **The Thing,** 1984, The Thing
BT $150 **NM** $210 **MIP** $330

❑ **Ultraman,** 1987, Ultraman
BT $25 **NM** $35 **MIP** $50

BOWEN DESIGNS

❑ **Kongzilla,** 1998, Kongzilla
BT $15 **NM** $30 **MIP** $50

GEOMETRIC DESIGN

❑ **Son of Frankenstein,** 1998, Son of Frankenstein
BT $15 **NM** $30 **MIP** $50

GEOMETRIC DESIGNS

❑ **Alien, Ripley,** 1998
BT $35 **NM** $45 **MIP** $60

❑ **Aliens, Alien Warrior,** 1996
BT $50 **NM** $65 **MIP** $80

❑ **Masters of the Universe, Talon Fighter,** 1984, Model No. 6015
BT $5 **NM** $10 **MIP** $15

❑ **Shogun Warriors, Raider,** 1978, Model No. 6023
BT $12 **NM** $18 **MIP** $25

HAWK

❑ **Beach Bunny,** 1964, Model No. 542
BT $25 **NM** $68 **MIP** $83

(KP Photo)

❑ **Daddy the Way-Out Suburbanite,** 1963, Daddy, Model No. 532
BT $30 **NM** $79 **MIP** $99

❑ **Davy the Way-Out Cyclist,** 1963, Davy, Model No. 531
BT $30 **NM** $79 **MIP** $99

❑ **Digger and Dragster,** 1963, Digger, Model No. 530
BT $30 **NM** $79 **MIP** $99

(KP Photo)

❑ **Drag Hag,** 1963, Drag Hag, Model No. 536
BT $30 **NM** $79 **MIP** $99

(KP Photo)

❑ **Endsville Eddie,** 1963, Endsville Eddie, Model No. 537
BT $20 **NM** $53 **MIP** $83

❑ **Francis The Foul,** 1963, Francis The Foul, Model No. 535
BT $15 **NM** $37 **MIP** $50

(KP Photo)

❑ **Frantic Banana,** 1965, Frantics, Model No. 548
BT $20 **NM** $84 **MIP** $138

❑ **Frantic Cats,** 1965, Frantics, Model No. 550
BT $20 **NM** $74 **MIP** $110

(KP Photo)

MODEL KITS

❏ **Frantics Steel Pluckers,** 1965, Frantics, Model No. 547
BT $20   NM $74   MIP $110

❏ **Frantics Totally Fab,** 1965, Frantics, Model No. 549
BT $20   NM $84   MIP $110

❏ **Freddy Flameout,** 1963, Freddy Flameout, Model No. 533
BT $20   NM $68   MIP $88

❏ **Hidad Silly Surfer,** 1964, Hidad Silly Surfer, Model No. 543
BT $20   NM $68   MIP $88

❏ **Hot Dogger Hangin' Ten,** 1964, Model No. 541
BT $20   NM $68   MIP $88

(KP Photo)

❏ **Huey's Hut Rod,** 1963, Huey's Hut Rod, Model No. 538
BT $20   NM $47   MIP $61

❏ **Killer McBash,** 1963, Killer McBash
BT $40   NM $131   MIP $165

(KP Photo)

❏ **Leaky Boat Louie,** 1963, Leaky Boat Louie, Model No. 534
BT $25   NM $84   MIP $105

❏ **Riding Tandem**
BT $25   NM $68   MIP $83

(KP Photo)

❏ **Sling Rave Curvette,** 1964, Sling Rave Curvette, Model No. 637
BT $15   NM $26   MIP $50

❏ **Steel Pluckers,** 1965, Frantics, Model No. 547
BT $20   NM $68   MIP $94

❏ **Totally Fab,** 1965, Frantics, Model No. 550
BT $25   NM $79   MIP $110

❏ **Wade A Minute,** 1963, Wade A Minute, Model No. 636
BT $45   NM $78   MIP $99

❏ **Weird-Oh Customizing Kit,** 1964, Weird-Oh
BT $75   NM $263   MIP $330

❏ **Wild Woodie Car,** Wild Woodie, Model No. 545
BT $20   NM $53   MIP $66

❏ **Woodie on a Surfari,** 1964, Model No. 540
BT $25   NM $89   MIP $110

LINDBERG

❏ **Baywatch Pickup,** 1995, Model No. 72598
BT $5   NM $10   MIP $15

❏ **Bert's Bucket,** 1971, Model No. 6422
BT $30   NM $84   MIP $110

❏ **Big Wheeler,** 1965, Lindberg Loony, Model No. 277
BT $30   NM $84   MIP $110

❏ **Blurp,** 1964, Lindy Loony Repulsive, Model No. 280
BT $10   NM $21   MIP $50

❏ **Creeping Crusher,** 1965, Model No. 273
BT $20   NM $42   MIP $61

❏ **Fat Max,** 1971, Model No. 6420
BT $30   NM $84   MIP $99

❏ **Flintstones, Flintmobile,** 1994, Model No. 72411
BT $10   NM $15   MIP $20

❏ **Flintstones, Le Sabertooth 5000,** 1994, Model No. 72412
BT $5   NM $10   MIP $15

❏ **Glob,** 1964, Lindy Loony Repulsive, Model No. 281
BT $10   NM $21   MIP $55

❏ **Godzilla,** 1995, Model No. 71344
BT $15   NM $22   MIP $30

❏ **Green Ghoul,** 1965, Model No. 274
BT $20   NM $37   MIP $55

❏ **Independence Day, Alien BTskeleton,** 1996, Model No. 77312
BT $5   NM $10   MIP $15

❏ **Independence Day, Capt. Hiller's F/A-18 Hornet,** 1996, Model No. 77313
BT $20   NM $30   MIP $40

❏ **Independence Day, Captured Alien Attacker,** 1996, Model No. 77311
BT $20   NM $30   MIP $40

❏ **Independence Day, Russell Casse's PT-17 Bi-Plane,** 1996, Model No. 77314
BT $20   NM $30   MIP $40

❏ **Krimson Terror,** 1965, Model No. 272
BT $20   NM $42   MIP $61

❏ **Mad Mangler,** 1965, Model No. 275
BT $20   NM $42   MIP $61

❏ **Road Hog,** 1964, Lindberg Loony, Model No. 276
BT $30   NM $84   MIP $99

❏ **Satan's Crate,** 1964, Lindberg Loony
BT $75   NM $131   MIP $165

❏ **Scuttle Bucket,** 1964, Lindberg Loony, Model No. 278
BT $30   NM $84   MIP $99

❏ **Shrieker, Glo-Monster,** 1971, Model No. 290
BT $35   NM $45   MIP $60

❏ **Sick Cycle,** 1971, Model No. 6421
BT $30   NM $84   MIP $99

❏ **UFO,** 1976, Model No. 1152
BT $35   NM $45   MIP $60

❏ **Voop,** 1964, Lindy Loony Repulsive, Model No. 283
BT $10   NM $21   MIP $55

❏ **Zopp,** 1964, Lindy Loony Repulsive, Model No. 282
BT $10   NM $21   MIP $55

MONOGRAM

❏ **Battlestar Galactica,** 1979, Model No. 6028
BT $15   NM $37   MIP $44

❏ **Battlestar Galactica, Colonial Viper Model Kit,** 1979
BT $15   NM $35   MIP $50

❏ **Battlestar Galactica, Cylon Base Star Model Kit,** 1979, Model No. 6029
BT $20   NM $40   MIP $55

❏ **Battlestar Galactica, Cylon Raider Model Kit,** 1979, Model No. 6026
BT $17   NM $35   MIP $50

❏ **Buck Rogers, Marauder,** 1979, Model No. 6031
BT $30   NM $50   MIP $65

❏ **Dracula,** 1983, Dracula, Model No. 6008
BT $20   NM $26   MIP $44

❏ **Elvira Macabre Mobile,** 1988, Model No. 2783
BT $10   NM $20   MIP $30

❏ **Flip Out,** 1965, Fred Flypogger, Model No. 105
BT $50   NM $158   MIP $220

❏ **Flying Sub, Voyage to the Bottom of the Sea,** 1979, Model No. 6011
BT $25   NM $45   MIP $55

❏ **Frankenstein,** 1983, Frankenstein, Model No. 6007
BT $20   NM $32   MIP $44

❏ **Godzilla,** 1978, Model No. 6300
BT $40   **NM** $68   **MIP** $88

❏ **Masters of the Universe, Roton Assault Vehicle,** 1984, Model No. 6016
BT $5   **NM** $10   **MIP** $15

❏ **Mummy,** 1983, Mummy, Model No. 6010
BT $20   **NM** $32   **MIP** $44

❏ **Skull, Lizard & Rat,** 1998, Model No. 5020
BT $10   **NM** $15   **MIP** $20

❏ **Sleepy Hollow, Headless Horseman,** 1999, Model No. 5022
BT $15   **NM** $20   **MIP** $25

❏ **Snoopy & Motorcycle,** 1971
BT $15   **NM** $26   **MIP** $33

❏ **Snoopy & Sopwith Camel,** 1971, Model No. 6779
BT $20   **NM** $32   **MIP** $39

❏ **Snoopy as Joe Cool,** 1971, Model No. 7502
BT $25   **NM** $53   **MIP** $110

❏ **Speed Racer Mach 5,** 2000, Model No. 6700
BT $10   **NM** $15   **MIP** $20

❏ **Speed Shift,** 1965, Fred Flypogger, Model No. MM106
BT $70   **NM** $105   **MIP** $220

❏ **Super Fuzz,** 1965, Fred Flypogger
BT $80   **NM** $105   **MIP** $248

❏ **Superman,** 1978, Superman, Model No. 6301
BT $25   **NM** $35   **MIP** $50

❏ **Three Stooges, Curly,** 1999, Model No. 5063
BT $10   **NM** $20   **MIP** $30

❏ **Three Stooges, Larry,** 1999, Model No. 5061
BT $10   **NM** $15   **MIP** $20

❏ **Three Stooges, Moe,** 1999, Model No. 5062
BT $10   **NM** $15   **MIP** $20

❏ **UFO, The Invaders,** 1979, UFO, Model No. 6012
BT $15   **NM** $37   **MIP** $44

❏ **Undertaker Dragster,** 1997, Model No. 5014
BT $10   **NM** $15   **MIP** $20

❏ **Vulture, Customizing Monster kit,** 1998, Model No. 5021
BT $10   **NM** $15   **MIP** $20

❏ **Witch,** 2000, Model No. 5092
BT $15   **NM** $20   **MIP** $25

❏ **Wolfman,** 1983, Wolfman, Model No. 6009
BT $20   **NM** $32   **MIP** $39

(KP Photo)

❏ **Wolfman's Wagon,** 1997, Model No. 5015
BT $10   **NM** $15   **MIP** $20

MPC

❏ **Alien,** 1979, Alien, Model No. 1-1961
BT $25   **NM** $79   **MIP** $110

❏ **Ape Man Haunted Glow Head,** 1975, Ape Man, Model No. 0303
BT $10   **NM** $32   **MIP** $55

❏ **AT-AT, Empire Strikes Back,** 1980, Model No. 190218
BT $15   **NM** $21   **MIP** $39

(KP Photo)

❏ **Barnabas Vampire Van,** 1969, Dark Shadows, Model No. 626
BT $75   **NM** $105   **MIP** $275

❏ **Barnabas, Dark Shadows,** 1968, Dark Shadows, Model No. 1550
BT $100   **NM** $341   **MIP** $440

❏ **Batman,** 1984, Batman, Model No. 1702
BT $20   **NM** $35   **MIP** $45

❏ **Beverly Hillbillies Truck,** 1968, Beverly Hillbillies, Model No. 612
BT $60   **NM** $105   **MIP** $220

❏ **Bionic Bustout, Six Million Dollar Man,** 1975, Model No. 0609
BT $15   **NM** $26   **MIP** $39

❏ **Bionic Repair, Bionic Woman,** 1976, Bionic Woman, Model No. 0610
BT $15   **NM** $26   **MIP** $39

❏ **Black Hole, Cygnus,** 1979, Model No. 1983
BT $75   **NM** $100   **MIP** $125

❏ **Black Hole, Maximillian,** 1979, Model No. 1982
BT $65   **NM** $85   **MIP** $110

❏ **Black Hole, V.I.N.CENT.,** 1979, Model No. 1915
BT $65   **NM** $85   **MIP** $110

❏ **Bloody Mama, Ma Barker Getaway Special,** 1970, Model No. 625
BT $30   **NM** $45   **MIP** $60

❏ **C-3PO, Structors Action Walker,** 1984, Model No. 1901
BT $5   **NM** $10   **MIP** $15

❏ **Cannonball Run, "Hawaiian Tropic" Malibu,** 1981, Model No. 681
BT $25   **NM** $38   **MIP** $50

❏ **Cannonball Run, Emergency Van,** 1981, Model No. 447
BT $11   **NM** $16   **MIP** $22

❏ **Cannonball Run, Lamborghini Countach,** 1981, Model No. 682
BT $18   **NM** $25   **MIP** $35

❏ **CB Freak,** 1975, Model No. 778
BT $10   **NM** $17   **MIP** $25

❏ **Condemned to Chains Forever,** 1974, Model No. 5003
BT $20   **NM** $42   **MIP** $61

❏ **Creepy T,** 1970, Model No. 631
BT $20   **NM** $35   **MIP** $50

❏ **Curl's Gurl,** 1960s, Model No. 103
BT $25   **NM** $68   **MIP** $88

❏ **Darth Vader Bust,** 1977, Model No. 1921
BT $20   **NM** $42   **MIP** $61

(KP Photo)

❏ **Darth Vader with Light Saber,** 1977, Model No. 1916
BT $15   **NM** $32   **MIP** $44

MODEL KITS

Dead Man's Raft, 1974, Model No. 5005
BT $20   NM $84   MIP $110

Dead Men Tell No Tales, 1972, Model No. 5001
BT $60   NM $100   MIP $125

Dukes of Hazzard, Cooter's Cruiser, 1980, Snap-together, Model No. 3220
BT $12   NM $17   MIP $25

Dukes of Hazzard, Cooter's Tow Truck, 1981, Model No. 441
BT $15   NM $20   MIP $25

Dukes of Hazzard, Daisy's Jeep CJ, 1980, Model No. 662
BT $17   NM $25   MIP $35

Dukes of Hazzard, Duke's Digger, 1980, Snap-together, Model No. 3219
BT $15   NM $20   MIP $25

Dukes of Hazzard, General Lee, 1979, Model No. 661
BT $17   NM $25   MIP $35

Dukes of Hazzard, General Lee, 1981, Model No. 3058
BT $10   NM $20   MIP $30

Dukes of Hazzard, Sheriff Rosco's Police Car, 1982, Model No. 663
BT $10   NM $17   MIP $25

Empire Strikes Back, Battle on Ice Planet Hoth, 1981, Snap-together, Model No. 1922
BT $10   NM $15   MIP $20

Empire Strikes Back, Luke Skywalker Snowspeeder, 1980, Model No. 1917
BT $20   NM $30   MIP $40

Empire Strikes Back, Rebel Base, 1981, Model No. 1924
BT $10   NM $15   MIP $20

Empire Strikes Back, Slave I, 1982, Model No. 1919
BT $10   NM $20   MIP $30

Empire Strikes Back, Star Destroyer, 1980, Model No. 1926
BT $20   NM $35   MIP $45

Encounter With Yoda Diorama, 1981, Model No. 1983
BT $15   NM $21   MIP $39

(KP Photo)

Escape From the Crypt, 1974, Model No. 5053
BT $60   NM $100   MIP $125

Evil Rider, Six Million Dollar Man, 1975, Model No. 604
BT $15   NM $21   MIP $44

Fate of the Mutineers, 1974, Model No. 5004
BT $20   NM $42   MIP $55

Fight for Survival, Six Million Dollar Man, 1975, Model No. 602
BT $15   NM $21   MIP $44

Fonzie & Dream Rod, 1976, Fonzie, Model No. 0635
BT $20   NM $35   MIP $50

Fonzie & Motorcycle, 1976, Fonzie, Model No. 0634
BT $20   NM $28   MIP $45

Freed in the Nick of Time, 1972, Model No. 5007
BT $20   NM $63   MIP $83

Ghost of America, Hot Rodder's, 1960s, Model No. 104
BT $50   NM $65   MIP $80

(KP Photo)

Ghost of the Treasure Guard, 1974, Model No. 5006
BT $20   NM $37   MIP $55

Grave Robber's Reward, 1974, Model No. 5051
BT $20   NM $42   MIP $55

Hardcastle & McCormick, GMC Truck, 1984, Model No. 450
BT $20   NM $32   MIP $45

Hogan's Heroes Jeep, 1968, Hogan's Heroes, Model No. 402
BT $30   NM $79   MIP $138

Hoist High the Jolly Roger, 1974, Model No. 5002
BT $20   NM $42   MIP $55

Hot Curl, 1960s, Hot Curl, Model No. 101
BT $20   NM $42   MIP $55

Hot Shot, Hot Shot
BT $20   NM $42   MIP $55

Hulk, 1978, Hulk, Model No. 1932
BT $20   NM $32   MIP $44

Jabba's Throne Room, 1983, Model No. 1928
BT $20   NM $32   MIP $50

Jaws of Doom, Six Million Dollar Man, 1975, Model No. 603
BT $15   NM $21   MIP $44

Knight Rider, Knight 2000 "KITT", 1982, Model No. 675
BT $15   NM $22   MIP $30

Mannix Roadster, 1968, Model No. 609
BT $35   NM $45   MIP $60

Millennium Falcon with Light, 1977, Model No. 1925
BT $35   NM $89   MIP $138

Monkeemobile, 1967, Monkees, Model No. 605
BT $70   NM $184   MIP $248

Muldowney, Shirley, Drag Kit, Muldowney, Shirley, Model No. 1-0702
BT $20   NM $53   MIP $72

Mummy Haunted Glow Head, 1975, Model No. 304
BT $20   NM $32   MIP $55

Mummy, Strange Changing, 1974, Model No. 902
BT $50   NM $75   MIP $100

Night Crawler Wolfman Car, 1971
BT $45   NM $79   MIP $138

Paul Revere & The Raiders Coach, 1970, Model No. 622
BT $40   NM $74   MIP $138

Play It Again Sam, 1974, Model No. 5052
BT $35   NM $84   MIP $110

Raiders of the Lost Ark Chase Scene, 1982, Model No. 1906
BT $15   NM $32   MIP $44

Raiders of the Lost Ark, Desert Chase, 1982, Snap-together, Model No. 1906
BT $10   NM $17   MIP $25

Return of the Jedi, AT-ST, 1984, Snap-together, Model No. 1903
BT $10   NM $15   MIP $22

Return of the Jedi, B-Wing Fighter, 1984, Snap-together, Model No. 1974
BT $15   NM $25   MIP $35

Return of the Jedi, C-3PO, 1983, Model No. 1935
BT $10   NM $20   MIP $30

Return of the Jedi, Millennium Falcon, 1983, Model No. 1933
BT $50   NM $65   MIP $80

Return of the Jedi, R2-D2, 1983, Model No. 1934
BT $15   NM $25   MIP $35

Return of the Jedi, Shuttle Tyridium, 1983, Model No. 1920
BT $15   NM $25   MIP $35

❏ **Return of the Jedi, Speeder Bike,** 1983, Model No. 1927
BT $10   NM $15   MIP $20

❏ **Return of the Jedi, TIE Interceptor,** 1983, Model No. 1972
BT $15   NM $25   MIP $35

❏ **Return of the Jedi, X-Wing Fighter,** 1983, Snap-together, Model No. 1971
BT $11   NM $18   MIP $25

❏ **Return of the Jedi, X-Wing Fighter,** 1983, Model No. 1930
BT $15   NM $22   MIP $30

❏ **Return of the Jedi, Y-Wing Fighter,** 1983, Snap-together, Model No. 1975
BT $11   NM $18   MIP $25

❏ **Road Runner Beep Beep,** Road Runner
BT $20   NM $53   MIP $83

❏ **Space: 1999 Hawk Spaceship,** 1977, Model No. 1904
BT $30   NM $50   MIP $65

❏ **Space: 1999, The Alien vehicle,** 1976, Model No. 1902
BT $30   NM $50   MIP $65

❏ **Space:1999, Eagle One Model Kit,** 1976
BT $50   NM $90   MIP $125

❏ **Space:1999, Moon Base Alpha Model Kit,** 1976
BT $20   NM $35   MIP $65

❏ **Spider-Man,** 1978, Spider-Man, Model No. 1931
BT $20   NM $26   MIP $39

❏ **Star Wars, C-3PO,** 1978, Model No. 1913
BT $10   NM $20   MIP $30

❏ **Star Wars, Darth Vader TIE Fighter,** 1978, Model No. 1915
BT $12   NM $20   MIP $30

❏ **Star Wars, Darth Vader Van,** 1979, Snap-together, Model No. 3209
BT $10   NM $15   MIP $20

❏ **Star Wars, Luke Skywalker Van,** 1977, Snap-together, Model No. 3210
BT $10   NM $15   MIP $20

❏ **Star Wars, Luke Skywalker's X-Wing Fighter,** 1978, Model No. 1914
BT $15   NM $25   MIP $35

❏ **Star Wars, R2-D2,** 1977, Model No. 1912
BT $20   NM $30   MIP $40

❏ **Star Wars, R2-D2 Van,** 1977, Snap-together, Model No. 3211
BT $15   NM $25   MIP $35

❏ **Strange Changing Mummy,** 1974, Model No. 0902
BT $15   NM $32   MIP $44

❏ **Strange Changing Time Machine,** 1974, Model No. 0903
BT $20   NM $42   MIP $55

❏ **Strange Changing Vampire,** 1974, Model No. 0901
BT $20   NM $42   MIP $55

❏ **Stroker McGurk & Surf Rod,** 1960s, Stroker McGurk, Model No. 100
BT $30   NM $84   MIP $138

❏ **Stroker McGurk Tall T,** 1964, Stroker McGurk, Model No. 102
BT $30   NM $84   MIP $138

❏ **Superman,** 1984, Superman, Model No. 1701
BT $15   NM $21   MIP $28

(KP Photo)

❏ **Sweathog Dream Machine,** 1976, Model No. 641
BT $15   NM $25   MIP $40

❏ **T.J. Hooker, Police Car,** 1982, Model No. 676
BT $10   NM $20   MIP $30

❏ **The Fall Guy, GMC Pickup,** 1982, Model No. 673
BT $15   NM $20   MIP $25

❏ **Time Machine, Strange Changing,** 1974, Model No. 903
BT $50   NM $75   MIP $100

❏ **Vampire Haunted Glow Head,** 1975, Model No. 301
BT $15   NM $21   MIP $50

❏ **Vampire, Strange Changin,** 1974, Model No. 901
BT $50   NM $75   MIP $100

❏ **Vampire's Midnight Madness,** 1974, Model No. 5050
BT $20   NM $47   MIP $55

❏ **Wacky Races, Compact Pussycat w/Penelope,** 1969, Model No. 901
BT $125   NM $160   MIP $200

❏ **Wacky Races, Mean Machine,** 1969, Model No. 900
BT $100   NM $145   MIP $175

❏ **Werewolf Haunted Glow Head,** 1975, Model No. 302
BT $20   NM $37   MIP $50

❏ **Werewolf, Dark Shadows,** 1969, Dark Shadows, Model No. 1552
BT $75   NM $200   MIP $275

❏ **Wile E. Coyote,** Wile E. Coyote, Model No. 2651
BT $20   NM $53   MIP $72

❏ **Yellow Submarine,** 1968, Beatles, Model No. 617
BT $70   NM $179   MIP $275

❏ **Automatic Baby Feeder,** 1965, Rube Goldberg, Model No. 955
BT $25   NM $63   MIP $83

❏ **Back Scrubber,** 1965, Rube Goldberg, Model No. 958
BT $25   NM $63   MIP $83

❏ **Iron Maiden,** 1966, Model No. 981
BT $35   NM $105   MIP $165

❏ **Painless Tooth BTtractor,** 1965, Rube Goldberg, Model No. 956
BT $25   NM $63   MIP $83

❏ **Signal for Shipwrecked Sailors,** 1965, Rube Goldberg, Model No. 957
BT $25   NM $63   MIP $83

❏ **Torture Chair,** 1966, Model No. 980
BT $35   NM $95   MIP $165

❏ **Torture Wheel,** 1966, Model No. 979
BT $35   NM $95   MIP $165

(KP Photo)

❏ **Castro, Born Losers,** 1965, Castro, Model No. 803
BT $35   NM $68   MIP $138

(KP Photo)

MODEL KITS

□ **Hitler, Born Losers,** 1965, Hitler, Model No. 802
BT $35   NM $68   MIP $193

(KP Photo)

□ **Napoleon, Born Losers,** 1965, Napoleon, Model No. 801
BT $35   NM $68   MIP $138

PLAYING MANTIS/POLAR LIGHTS

□ **Addams Family Haunted House,** 1995, Model No. 5002
BT $10   NM $20   MIP $30

(Playing Mantis)

□ **Bates Mansion from Psycho,** 1998, Model No. 5028
BT $10   NM $20   MIP $30

□ **Beatles Yellow Submarine, George,** 1999, Model No. 5071
BT $10   NM $15   MIP $20

□ **Beatles Yellow Submarine, John,** 2000, Model No. 5074
BT $10   NM $15   MIP $20

□ **Beatles Yellow Submarine, Paul,** 2000, Model No. 5073
BT $10   NM $15   MIP $20

□ **Beatles Yellow Submarine, Ringo,** 1999, Model No. 5072
BT $10   NM $15   MIP $20

□ **Bellringer of Notre Dame,** 2000, Model No. 5090
BT $10   NM $20   MIP $30

□ **Boris Karloff, The Mummy,** 1998
BT $35   NM $45   MIP $60

(Playing Mantis)

□ **Bride of Frankenstein,** 1997, Model No. 5005
BT $10   NM $20   MIP $30

□ **Cats, Bats, n' Rats,** 1998
BT $10   NM $20   MIP $30

□ **Chamber of Horrors, Guillotine,** 2000, Model No. 5091
BT $15   NM $20   MIP $25

□ **Clash of the Titans, Medusa,** 1994
BT $50   NM $65   MIP $80

□ **Crash Bandicoot on Jet Board,** 1999, Model No. 6026
BT $10   NM $15   MIP $20

□ **Creature From the Black Lagoon,** 1998, The Creature
BT $10   NM $20   MIP $30

□ **Creature from the Black Lagoon,** 1999
BT $35   NM $45   MIP $60

□ **Creepy Critters,** 1998
BT $10   NM $20   MIP $30

□ **Cyclops, The 7th Voyage of Sinbad,** 1990
BT $34   NM $45   MIP $60

□ **Demolition Man, Sandra Bullock,** 1990s
BT $25   NM $35   MIP $50

(Playing Mantis)

□ **Dick Tracy, Space Coupe,** 2000, Model No. 5097
BT $10   NM $15   MIP $20

□ **Dracula, Aurora box reissue,** 1999, Model No. 424
BT $20   NM $30   MIP $40

□ **Dracula's Dragster,** 1999, Model No. 5025
BT $10   NM $20   MIP $30

□ **Forgotten Prisoner of Castel-Mare',** 1999, Model No. 7509
BT $10   NM $20   MIP $30

□ **Frankenstein,** 1999, Model No. 423
BT $30   NM $45   MIP $60

□ **Frankenstein's Flivver,** 1997, Model No. 5006
BT $10   NM $20   MIP $30

□ **Fright Night, Amy,** 1990
BT $35   NM $45   MIP $60

□ **Ghost of Frankenstein, bust,** 1997
BT $35   NM $45   MIP $60

□ **Godzilla,** 2000, Model No. 7502
BT $15   NM $20   MIP $25

□ **Godzilla's Go-Cart,** 1999, Model No. 5029
BT $25   NM $35   MIP $50

□ **Green Hornet Black Beauty,** 1999, Model No. 5017
BT $10   NM $20   MIP $30

□ **H.P. Lovecraft's The UnNamable II,** 1999
BT $50   NM $60   MIP $70

(Playing Mantis)

□ **James Bond 007,** 1999, Model No. 5035
BT $10   NM $15   MIP $20

□ **King Ghidorah,** 2000, Model No. 6802
BT $10   NM $15   MIP $20

□ **King Kong,** 1990s
BT $50   NM $65   MIP $80

□ **King Kong,** 2000, Model No. 7507
BT $10   NM $15   MIP $20

□ **King Kong's Thronester,** 1998, Model No. 5016
BT $10   NM $15   MIP $20

□ **KISS, Ace Frehley,** 1998, Ace Frehley
BT $10   NM $20   MIP $30

□ **KISS, Gene Simmons,** 1998, Gene Simmons, Model No. 5058
BT $10   NM $20   MIP $30

□ **KISS, Paul Stanley,** 1998, Paul Stanley, Model No. 5055
BT $10   NM $20   MIP $30

❑ **KISS, Peter Criss,** 1998, Peter Criss, Model No. 5056
BT $10   **NM** $20   **MIP** $30

❑ **Lon Chaney, The Wolfman,** 1999
BT $35   **NM** $45   **MIP** $60

(KP Photo)

❑ **Lost in Space Cyclops w/Chariot,** 1998, Lost in Space Cyclops
BT $10   **NM** $20   **MIP** $30

(Playing Mantis)

❑ **Lost In Space, Cyclops,** 1997, Model No. 5031
BT $10   **NM** $15   **MIP** $20

❑ **Lost In Space, Cyclops w/ diorama and vehicle,** 1998, Model No. 5032
BT $10   **NM** $20   **MIP** $30

❑ **Lost In Space, Dr. Smith and Robot B-9,** 1999, Model No. 5019
BT $10   **NM** $20   **MIP** $30

❑ **Lost In Space, Jupiter 2,** 1998, Model No. 5033
BT $10   **NM** $20   **MIP** $30

(KP Photo)

❑ **Lost In Space, Jupiter 2 new box,** 2000, Model No. 5033
BT $15   **NM** $25   **MIP** $35

❑ **Lost In Space, Robot,** 1997, Model No. 5030
BT $10   **NM** $15   **MIP** $20

❑ **Michael Myers, Halloween,** 2000, Model No. 5095
BT $10   **NM** $20   **MIP** $30

❑ **Mummy,** 1999, Model No. 427
BT $30   **NM** $45   **MIP** $60

❑ **Mummy, 1999 movie version,** 1999, Model No. 5023
BT $20   **NM** $25   **MIP** $35

❑ **Mummy's Chariot,** 1995, Model No. 5003
BT $10   **NM** $15   **MIP** $20

❑ **Munsters Living Room diorama,** 1997, Model No. 5013
BT $10   **NM** $15   **MIP** $20

(Playing Mantis)

❑ **Mystery Machine,** 2000, Model No. 6808
BT $10   **NM** $15   **MIP** $20

❑ **Nosferatu,** 1998
BT $35   **NM** $45   **MIP** $60

❑ **Odd Job,** 1999, Model No. 5036
BT $10   **NM** $15   **MIP** $20

❑ **Phantom of the Opera,** 2000, Model No. 5027
BT $30   **NM** $45   **MIP** $60

❑ **Phantom of the Opera, bust,** 1997
BT $35   **NM** $45   **MIP** $60

❑ **Planet of the Apes, Cornelius, reissue,** 2000, Model No. 6803
BT $10   **NM** $15   **MIP** $20

❑ **Planet of the Apes, Dr. Zaius,** 2000, Model No. 6805
BT $10   **NM** $15   **MIP** $20

❑ **Planet of the Apes, Dr. Zira,** 2000, Model No. 6804
BT $10   **NM** $15   **MIP** $20

❑ **Planet of the Apes, General Ursus,** 2000, Model No. 6806
BT $10   **NM** $15   **MIP** $20

❑ **Predator,** 1997
BT $35   **NM** $45   **MIP** $60

❑ **Pumpkinhead the Metamorphosis,** 1994
BT $35   **NM** $45   **MIP** $60

(Playing Mantis)

❑ **Robby the Robot, Forbidden Planet,** 1999, Model No. 5025
BT $10   **NM** $20   **MIP** $30

❑ **Rodan, Aurora reissue,** 2000, Model No. 6801
BT $10   **NM** $15   **MIP** $20

❑ **Son of Frankenstein,** 1998
BT $35   **NM** $45   **MIP** $60

❑ **Star Trek the NBTt Generation, Ambassador Spock,** 1996
BT $50   **NM** $65   **MIP** $75

❑ **Star Trek the NBTt Generation, Capt. Picard,** 1992
BT $25   **NM** $35   **MIP** $50

❑ **Star Trek the NBTt Generation, Commander Riker,** 1993
BT $25   **NM** $35   **MIP** $50

❑ **Star Trek the NBTt Generation, Counselor Troi,** 1993
BT $25   **NM** $35   **MIP** $50

❑ **Star Trek the NBTt Generation, Ferengi,** 1995
BT $25   **NM** $35   **MIP** $50

❑ **Star Trek the NBTt Generation, Geordi La Forge,** 1993
BT $25   **NM** $35   **MIP** $50

❑ **Star Trek the NBTt Generation, Gowron the Klingon,** 1995
BT $25   **NM** $35   **MIP** $50

❑ **Star Trek the NBTt Generation, Lieutenant Worf,** 1992
BT $25   **NM** $35   **MIP** $50

❑ **Star Trek the NBTt Generation, Locutus of Borg,** 1994
BT $25   **NM** $35   **MIP** $50

❑ **Star Trek the NBTt Generation, Lt. Comdr. Data,** 1993
BT $25   NM $35   MIP $50

❑ **Star Trek the NBTt Generation, Romulan,** 1994
BT $25   NM $35   MIP $50

❑ **The Wolf Man,** 1998, cold-cast resin, Model No. 5018
BT $50   NM $100   MIP $200

❑ **Titan A.E., Drej Alien,** 2000, Model No. 5094
BT $10   NM $15   MIP $20

❑ **Tremors,** 1999
BT $35   NM $45   MIP $60

❑ **Ymir, 20 Million Miles to Earth,** 1990s
BT $50   NM $60   MIP $70

PRECISION

❑ **Cap'n Kidd the Pirate,** 1959, Captain Kidd, Model No. 402
BT $25   NM $63   MIP $83

❑ **Crucifix,** Jesus Christ, Model No. 501
BT $20   NM $42   MIP $55

PYRO

❑ **Der-Baron,** 1958, Model No. 166
BT $50   NM $79   MIP $110

❑ **Gladiator Show Cycle,** Gladiator, Model No. 175
BT $20   NM $42   MIP $55

❑ **Indian Chief,** Model No. 281
BT $20   NM $53   MIP $66

❑ **Indian Medicine Man,** 1960s, Model No. 282
BT $20   NM $53   MIP $66

❑ **Indian Warrior,** 1960, Model No. 283
BT $20   NM $53   MIP $66

❑ **Li'l Corporal,** 1970, Li'l Corporal, Model No. 168
BT $25   NM $68   MIP $83

(KP Photo)

❑ **Rawhide, Gil Favor,** 1958, Rawhide, Model No. 276
BT $20   NM $53   MIP $66

(KP Photo)

❑ **Restless Gun Deputy,** 1959, Restless Gun, Model No. 277
BT $20   NM $53   MIP $66

❑ **Surf's Up,** 1970, Surf's Up, Model No. 176
BT $15   NM $37   MIP $44

❑ **U.S. Marshal,** Model No. 286
BT $20   NM $53   MIP $66

(KP Photo)

❑ **Wyatt Earp,** 1958, Earp, Wyatt, Model No. 278
BT $20   NM $53   MIP $66

REMCO

❑ **Flintstones Motorized Paddy Wagon,** 1961, Model No. 452
BT $30   NM $105   MIP $220

❑ **Flintstones Motorized Sports Car & Trailer,** 1961, Model No. 450
BT $30   NM $105   MIP $220

❑ **Flintstones Motorized Yacht,** 1961, Model No. 451
BT $30   NM $105   MIP $220

REVELL

(KP Photo)

❑ **Angel Fink,** 1965, Big Daddy Roth, Model No. 1307
BT $40   NM $105   MIP $154

❑ **Apollo Astronaut on the Moon,** 1970, Model No. 1860
BT $115   NM $130   MIP $155

❑ **Apollo II Columbia and Eagle,** 1969, Model No. 1862
BT $115   NM $130   MIP $155

❑ **Apollo II Tranquility Base,** 1975, Model No. 714
BT $75   NM $100   MIP $125

❑ **Beatles, George Harrison,** 1965, Beatles, Model No. 1353
BT $75   NM $158   MIP $275

❑ **Beatles, John Lennon,** 1965, Beatles, Model No. 1352
BT $75   NM $158   MIP $275

❑ **Beatles, Paul McCartney,** 1965, Beatles, Model No. 1350
BT $75   NM $158   MIP $220

❑ **Beatles, Ringo Starr,** 1965, Beatles, Model No. 1351
BT $75   NM $158   MIP $220

(KP Photo)

❑ **Beatnik Bandit,** 1963, Model No. 1279
BT $70   NM $85   MIP $110

❑ **Billy Carter's Pickup,** 1978, Model No. 1385
BT $35   NM $50   MIP $65

❏ **Birthday Bird,** 1959, Dr. Seuss
BT $40   **NM** $158   **MIP** $275

(Toy Shop File Photo)

❏ **Bonanza,** 1965, Bonanza, Model
No. 1931
BT $50   **NM** $105   **MIP** $165

(KP Photo)

❏ **Brother Rat Fink,** 1963, Big Daddy
Roth, Model No. 1304
BT $20   **NM** $53   **MIP** $72

❏ **Busby the Tasselated Afghan Spaniel
Yak,** 1960, Dr. Seuss
BT $50   **NM** $131   **MIP** $275

❏ **Cat in the Hat,** 1960, Dr. Seuss, Model
No. 2000
BT $45   **NM** $105   **MIP** $165

❏ **Cat in the Hat with Thing 1 and Thing
2,** 1960s, Model No. 2050
BT $45   **NM** $105   **MIP** $248

❏ **Charlie's Angels Mobile Unit Van,**
1977, Model No. 1397
BT $30   **NM** $40   **MIP** $50

❏ **Charlie's Angels Van,** 1977, Model
No. 1397
BT $10   **NM** $21   **MIP** $33

❏ **ChiPs Helicopter,** 1980, Model
No. 6102
BT $20   **NM** $30   **MIP** $40

❏ **ChiPs Kawasaki Motorcycle,** 1980,
Model No. 7800
BT $20   **NM** $30   **MIP** $40

❏ **ChiPs Z-28 Chase Car,** 1980, Model
No. 6228
BT $10   **NM** $20   **MIP** $30

❏ **Dallas Cowboys Cheerleaders Van,**
1979, Snap-together, Model No. 6405
BT $10   **NM** $20   **MIP** $30

❏ **Dr. Seuss Zoo Kit #1,** 1959, three kits:
Gowdy, Tingo, Norval
BT $50   **NM** $236   **MIP** $440

❏ **Dr. Seuss Zoo Kit #2,** 1960, three kits:
Roscoe, Grickily, Busby
BT $50   **NM** $368   **MIP** $550

(KP Photo)

❏ **Drag Nut,** 1963, Big Daddy Roth, Model
No. 1303
BT $20   **NM** $53   **MIP** $72

❏ **Fink-Eliminator,** 1965, Big Daddy Roth,
Model No. 1310
BT $30   **NM** $105   **MIP** $220

❏ **Flash Gordon & Martian,** 1965, Flash
Gordon, Model No. 1450
BT $60   **NM** $105   **MIP** $165

❏ **Flipper,** 1965, Flipper, Model No. 1930
BT $75   **NM** $105   **MIP** $165

❏ **G.I. Joe Attack Vehicle,** 1982, Model
No. 8901
BT $10   **NM** $20   **MIP** $30

❏ **G.I. Joe Rapid Fire Motorcycle,** 1982,
Model No. 8900
BT $10   **NM** $20   **MIP** $30

❏ **Gowdy the Dowdy Grackle,** 1959, Dr.
Seuss
BT $40   **NM** $79   **MIP** $193

❏ **Grickily the Gractus,** 1960, Dr. Seuss
BT $50   **NM** $131   **MIP** $275

❏ **Hardy Boys Van,** 1977, Model No. 1398
BT $10   **NM** $20   **MIP** $30

❏ **Horton the Elephant,** 1960, Dr. Seuss
BT $150   **NM** $210   **MIP** $440

❏ **Jacques Cousteau Calypso,** 1976,
Model No. 575
BT $30   **NM** $45   **MIP** $60

❏ **Magnum P.I., 308 Ferrari GTS,** 1981,
Model No. 7378
BT $25   **NM** $35   **MIP** $50

❏ **Magnum P.I., T.C.'s Chopper,** 1981,
Model No. 4416
BT $25   **NM** $35   **MIP** $50

❏ **McHale's Navy PT-73,** 1965, McHale's
Navy, Model No. 323
BT $25   **NM** $63   **MIP** $83

❏ **Moonraker Space Shuttle,** 1979, Model
No. 4306
BT $10   **NM** $20   **MIP** $30

❏ **Mother's Worry,** 1963, Big Daddy Roth,
Model No. 1302
BT $20   **NM** $63   **MIP** $110

❏ **Mr. Gasser,** 1963, Big Daddy Roth,
Model No. 1301
BT $30   **NM** $79   **MIP** $110

(KP Photo)

❏ **Mr. Gasser BMR Racer,** 1964, Big
Daddy Roth, Model No. 3181
BT $30   **NM** $79   **MIP** $110

(KP Photo)

❏ **Norval the Bashful Blinket,** 1959, Dr.
Seuss
BT $40   **NM** $79   **MIP** $193

(KP Photo)

❏ **Peter Pan Pirate Ship,** 1960, Model
No. 377
BT $75   **NM** $85   **MIP** $100

❏ **Phantom & Voodoo Witch Doctor,**
1965, Phantom, Model No. 1451
BT $50   **NM** $105   **MIP** $220

(KP Photo)

MODEL KITS

Rat Fink, 1963, Big Daddy Roth, Model No. 1305
BT $95   NM $110   MIP $125

Rat Fink Lotus Racer, 1964, Big Daddy Roth
BT $25   NM $63   MIP $83

Red October Submarine, 1990, Model No. 4006
BT $45   NM $60   MIP $75

Robbin' Hood Fink, 1965, Big Daddy Roth
BT $200   NM $315   MIP $440

Robotech Defenders Aqualo, 1984, Model No. 1148
BT $10   NM $15   MIP $20

Robotech Defenders Robot Revovery Unit, 1984, Model No. 1194
BT $25   NM $40   MIP $50

Robotech Defenders Thoren, 1984, Model No. 1150
BT $10   NM $20   MIP $30

Robotech Defenders Zoltek, 1984, Model No. 1151
BT $20   NM $30   MIP $40

Robotech Nebo, 1984, Model No. 1400
BT $10   NM $20   MIP $30

Robotech SDF1, 1985, Model No. 1143
BT $25   NM $40   MIP $50

Robotech Trigon, 1985, Model No. 1405
BT $10   NM $20   MIP $30

Robotech VF-1A Fighter, 1985, Model No. 1409
BT $30   NM $40   MIP $50

Robotech VF-1D Fighter, 1985, Model No. 1408
BT $30   NM $40   MIP $50

Robotech VF-1J Fighter, 1985, Model No. 1406
BT $30   NM $40   MIP $50

Robotech, Condar, 1984, Model No. 1152
BT $10   NM $20   MIP $30

Robotech, Recon Team 2 in 1, 1984, Model No. 1135
BT $10   NM $15   MIP $20

Robotech, Tactical Unit 2 in 1, 1984, Model No. 1136
BT $10   NM $15   MIP $20

Roscoe the Many-Footed Lion, 1960s, Dr. Seuss, Model No. 2004
BT $30   NM $79   MIP $182

Saint's Jaguar XJS, 1979, Model No. 6402
BT $10   NM $20   MIP $30

Scuz-Fink with Dingbat, 1965, Big Daddy Roth, Model No. 1309
BT $275   NM $368   MIP $495

Superfink, 1964, Big Daddy Roth
BT $150   NM $263   MIP $385

Surfink, 1965, Big Daddy Roth, Model No. 1306
BT $35   NM $89   MIP $110

Tingo the Noodle-Topped Stroodle, 1960s, Dr. Seuss
BT $50   NM $79   MIP $193

Tweedy Pie with Boss-Fink, 1965, Big Daddy Roth, Model No. 1271
BT $200   NM $315   MIP $440

TOY BIZ

Ghost Rider, 1996, Model No. 48660
BT $7   NM $13   MIP $28

Hulk, 1996, Model No. 48656
BT $5   NM $11   MIP $22

Onslaught, 1997, Model No. 48640
BT $7   NM $13   MIP $28

Silver Surfer, 1996, Model No. 48653
BT $5   NM $11   MIP $22

Spider-Man, 1996, Model No. 48651
BT $5   NM $11   MIP $22

Spider-Man, with wall, 1996, Model No. 48658
BT $5   NM $11   MIP $22

Storm, 1996, Model No. 48659
BT $5   NM $11   MIP $22

Thing, 1996, Model No. 48652
BT $5   NM $11   MIP $22

Venom, 1996, Model No. 48654
BT $5   NM $11   MIP $22

Wolverine, 1996, Model No. 48657
BT $5   NM $11   MIP $22

Restaurant Premiums

Transformers from McDonald's—pretty neat toy, and you get a burger, too!

by Dan Stearns

Restaurant premiums, i.e., fast food toys, are probably one of the easiest and genuinely most fun items to collect. Plus, because they show up at almost every garage sale or flea market, you don't even have to watch your waistline while you amass your collection.

The thing is, because so many of these toys are so common, condition is a big determiner of price. There are two price grades shown here, excellent and mint. Even "excellent" toys are rarely played with and have no scratches or imperfections.

Rarity is, as always, a big factor as well. A toy's age, popularity and cross-collectibility play a crucial role here. A popular Disney tie-in, even a modern one, can be more valuable than older toys, though, because of the strong Disneyana collector market.

Sometimes toys are only distributed in certain regions, making them instantly rare for the rest of us. Understandably, these toys command higher prices than the usual national campaigns.

Several years back some of these toys had to be recalled, resulting in the design of special one-piece toys for younger children, commonly called "Under 3" or "U3" toys. (You'll see the "U3" designation scattered throughout the listings.) These toys are not produced for every campaign, and aren't normally advertised in the in-store displays. The lower number of these toys results in prices that are typically twenty percent higher than regular toys of the same campaign.

International toys are a fun subset of restaurant premiums. Often, a movie is released virtually everywhere, and there are no real differences to the toy other than some subtleties in packaging. However, every once in a while, there are

Most restaurant premiums are based on characters from television shows or movies. These *Ghostbusters* toys were offered by KFC in the 1990s.

items that just aren't released anywhere else. Right now, they can trade for a higher value than others, just because they're different. It'll take time to see if they hold value or not, though.

An older "fast food" toy, the cartoon "King Burger" doll from the 1970s.

"Hello Kitty" toys from McDonald's, 2000.

As you probably expect, McDonald's and Disney lead the way with restaurant premium toys. Although, their most successful promotion, as you'll probably recall, was the Teeny Beanie Baby Happy Meal promotion.

Another neat movie-based premium (neater than the movie) was this Puppy Dino Breakout toy from Burger King promoting *Viva Rock Vegas*.

Editor's note: Unless otherwise noted, prices listed are for ***each*** piece in a set, not the entire set.

ARBY'S

❑ **Babar's World Tour at the Beach Summer Sippers,** 1991, Arby's, set of three squeeze bottles: orange, yellow or purple top
EX n/a   NM $1   MIP $5

❑ **Babar's World Tour Finger Puppets,** 1990, Arby's, set of four: King Babar, Queen Celeste, Alexander & Zephyr, Pom
EX n/a   NM $3   MIP $5

❑ **Babar's World Tour License Plates,** 1990, Arby's, set of four: Paris, Brazil, USA, North Pole
EX n/a   NM $1   MIP $2

❑ **Babar's World Tour Puzzles,** 1990, Arby's, set of four: Cousin Arthur's New Camera, Babar's Gondola Ride, Babar, the Haunted Castle, Babar's Trip to Greece
EX n/a   NM $2   MIP $4

❑ **Babar's World Tour Racers,** 1992, Arby's, set of three pull-back racers: King Babar, Cousin Arthur, Queen Celeste
EX n/a   NM $2   MIP $4

❑ **Babar's World Tour Squirters,** Arby's, set of three
EX n/a   NM $1   MIP $3

❑ **Babar's World Tour Stampers,** 1990, Arby's, set of three: Babar, Flora, Arthur
EX n/a   NM $2   MIP $4

❑ **Babar's World Tour Storybooks,** 1991, Arby's, set of three: Read Get Ready, Set, Go, Calendar-Read and Have Fun-Read, Grow and Grow
EX n/a   NM $1   MIP $2

❑ **Babar's World Tour Vehicles,** 1990, Arby's, set of three vehicles: Babar in helicopter, Arthur on trike, Zephyr in car
EX n/a   NM $2   MIP $4

❑ **Classic Fairy Tales,** 1993, Arby's, set of three: Jack and the Beanstalk, The 3 Little Pigs, Hansel and Gretel
EX n/a   NM $4   MIP $5

❑ **Little Miss Figures,** 1981, Arby's, set of eight: Little Miss Giggles, Little Miss Helpful, Little Miss Shy, Little Miss Splendid, Little Miss Late, Little Miss Naughty, Little Miss Star, Little Miss Sunshine
EX n/a   NM $3   MIP $10

❑ **Little Miss Stencil,** 1985, Arby's
EX n/a   NM $2   MIP $4

❑ **Looney Tunes Car-Tunes,** 1989, Arby's, set of six: Sylvester's Cat-illac, Daffy's Dragster, Yosemite Sam's Rackin Frackin Wagon, Taz's Slush Musher, Bugs' Buggy, Road Runner's Racer
EX n/a   NM $3   MIP $6

❑ **Looney Tunes Christmas Ornament,** 1989, Arby's, set of three: Bugs as Santa, Porky Pig as toy soldier, Tweety as elf
EX n/a   NM $3   MIP $8

(Arby's Photo)

❑ **Looney Tunes Figures,** 1987, Arby's, set of seven figures on oval base: Tasmanian Devil, Tweetie, Porky, Bugs Bunny, Yosemite Sam, Sylvester, Pepe Le Pew
EX n/a   NM $4   MIP $10

❑ **Looney Tunes Figures,** 1988, Arby's, set of six free-standing figures: Bugs Bunny, Daffy Duck, Taz, Elmer Fudd, Road Runner, Wile E. Coyote
EX n/a   NM $3   MIP $6

❑ **Looney Tunes Flicker Rings,** 1987, Arby's, set of four rings: Bugs Bunny, Yosemite Sam, Porky Pig, Daffy Duck
EX n/a   NM $20   MIP $40

❑ **Looney Tunes Fun Figures,** 1989, Arby's, set of three: Tazmanian Devil as pilot, Daffy as student, Sylvester as fireman
EX n/a   NM $3   MIP $6

❑ **Looney Tunes Pencil Toppers,** 1988, Arby's, set of six: Sylvester, Yosemite, Porky Pig, Bugs Bunny, Taz, Daffy Duck, Tweety Bird
EX n/a   NM $5   MIP $10

❑ **Megaphone, Minnesota Twins 25th Anniversary,** 1986, Arby's
EX n/a   NM $1   MIP $2

❑ **Mr. Men Figures,** 1981, Arby's, set of ten: Mr. Bounce, Mr. Bump, Mr. Daydream, Mr. Funny, Mr. Greedy, Mr. Mischeif, Mr. Nosey, Mr. Rush, Mr. Strong, Mr. Tickle
EX n/a   NM $3   MIP $10

❑ **Polar Swirl Penguins,** 1987, Arby's, set of four: penguin with mask and snorkle, penguin with headphones, penguin with sunglasses, penguin with surfboard
EX n/a   NM $15   MIP $40

❑ **Yogi & Friends Fun Squirters,** 1994, Arby's, set of three: Yogi, Cindy, Boo-Boo
EX n/a   NM $4   MIP $5

❑ **Yogi & Friends Mini-Disk,** 1993, Arby's, set of four: Ranger Smith, Yogi, Cindy, Snagglepus
EX n/a   NM $1   MIP $2

❑ **Yogi & Friends Winter Wonderland Crazy Cruisers,** 1995, Arby's, Yogi, Snagglepuss, Cindy
EX n/a   NM $4   MIP $5

BIG BOY

❑ **Action Figures,** 1990, Big Boy, complete set of four: skater, pitcher, surfer, race driver
EX n/a   NM $2   MIP $4

❑ **Big Boy Bank, Large,** 1960s, Big Boy, produced from 1966-1976, 18" tall, full color
EX n/a   NM $125   MIP $300

❑ **Big Boy Bank, Medium,** 1960s, Big Boy, produced from 1966-1976, 9" tall, brown
EX n/a   NM $50   MIP $165

❑ **Big Boy Bank, Small,** 1960s, Big Boy, produced from 1966-1976, 7" tall, painted red/white
EX n/a   NM $40   MIP $100

❑ **Big Boy Board Game,** 1960s, Big Boy
EX n/a   NM $50   MIP $120

❑ **Big Boy Doll,** 1973, Bob's Big Boy, 8" plastic jointed doll holding a hamburger, made by Dakin, Model No. Dakin
EX n/a   NM $75   MIP $150

❑ **Big Boy Doll,** 1978, Bob's Big Boy, 14" cloth boy doll wearing checkerboard outfit
EX n/a   NM $25   MIP $30

❑ **Big Boy Kite,** 1960s, Big Boy, kite with image of Big Boy
EX n/a   NM $10   MIP $25

❑ **Big Boy Lamp,** 1960, Bob's Big Boy, 6-1/2" vinyl figural lamp
EX $40   NM $60   MIP $75

(Toy Shop File Photo)

❑ **Big Boy Nodder,** 1960s, Big Boy, papier-mâché
EX n/a   NM $900   MIP $1500

❑ **Big Boy Playing Cards,** 1960s, Big Boy, produced in four designs
EX n/a   NM $15   MIP $45

❑ **Big Boy Stuffed Dolls,** 1960s, Big Boy, set of three: Big Boy, girlfriend Dolly, both 12" tall, and dog Nuggets, 7" tall
EX n/a   NM $40   MIP $80

❑ **Helicopters,** 1991, Big Boy, set of plastic vehicles: Ambulance, Police, Fire Department
EX n/a   **NM** $1   **MIP** $3

❑ **Monster In My Pocket,** 1991, Big Boy, various secret monster packs
EX n/a   **NM** $2   **MIP** $4

❑ **Racers,** 1992, Big Boy, set of three cars: yellow, orange, purple
EX n/a   **NM** $2   **MIP** $5

❑ **Sport Poses,** 1990, Big Boy, set of four: surfing, baseball, racing, roller skating
EX n/a   **NM** $3   **MIP** $5

BURGER CHEF

❑ **Fun Village Funmeal Boxes,** 1973-74, Burger Chef, set of 24 featuring Burger Chef characters
EX n/a   **NM** $25   **MIP** $60

❑ **Funmeal Boxes,** 1975, Burger Chef, set of 24 village buildings: Antique Shop, Bakery Shop, Barn, Beauty Shop, Bike Shop, Burger Chef, Cape Cod, Castle, Cottage (2), Colonial, Gas Station, Grocery Shop, Hardware Store, Haunted House, Pirate Ship, Ranch (2), Toy Shop, Two Story (2), Shoe Shop
EX n/a   **NM** $20   **MIP** $30

❑ **Star Wars Funmeal Boxes,** 1978, Burger Chef, set of seven: Darth Vader's Card Game, Tie Fighter, X-Wing Fighter, Land Speeder, R2D2 Droid Puppet, C3PO Droid Puppet, Flight Game
EX n/a   **NM** $25   **MIP** $40

(Toy Shop File Photo)

❑ **Triple Play Funmeal Boxes,** 1978, Burger Chef, set of 24 featuring Major League Baseball teams: Astros, A's, Braves, Brewers, Cubs, Cards, Dodgers, Expos, Giants, Indians, Orioles, Padres, Rangers, Reds, Red Sox, Tigers, Twins, White Sox, Mets, Yankees, Angels, Phillies, Pirates, Royals
EX n/a   **NM** $20   **MIP** $90

❑ **Vacuform Race Cars,** 1981, Burger Chef
EX n/a   **NM** $20   **MIP** $30

BURGER KING

❑ **Adventure Kits,** 1991, Burger King, set of four activity kits with crayons; Passport, African Adventure, European Escapades, Worldwide Treasure Hunt
EX n/a   **NM** $1   **MIP** $3

(KP Photo)

❑ **Aladdin,** 1992, Burger King, set of five figures: Jafar and Iago, Genie in lamp, Jasmine and Rajah, Abu, Aladdin and the Magic Carpet
EX n/a   **NM** $1   **MIP** $3

❑ **Aladdin Hidden Treasures,** 1994, Burger King, set of four: Jasmine, Aladdin, Abu, Iago
EX n/a   **NM** $2   **MIP** $5

❑ **ALF,** 1987, Burger King, set of four: joke and riddle disk, door knob card, sand mold, refrigerator magnet
EX n/a   **NM** $1   **MIP** $2

❑ **ALF Puppets,** 1987, Burger King, set of four puppets with records: Sporting with Alf, Cooking with Alf, Born to Rock, Surfing with Alf
EX n/a   **NM** $3   **MIP** $8

❑ **Alvin and the Chipmunks,** 1987, Burger King, set of three: super ball, stickers, pencil topper
EX n/a   **NM** $1   **MIP** $2

❑ **Anastasia,** 1997, Burger King, set of six: Bouncing Bartok, Fiendish Flyer, Fall-Apart Rasputin, Beanie Bat Bartok, Collision Course Dimitri, Anya & Pooka
EX n/a   **NM** $2   **MIP** $5

❑ **Aquaman Tub Toy,** 1987, Burger King, green
EX n/a   **NM** $3   **MIP** $5

(KP Photo)

❑ **Archie Cars,** 1991, Burger King, set of four: Archie in red car, Betty in aqua car, Jughead in green car, Veronica in purple car
EX n/a   **NM** $1   **MIP** $3

❑ **Barnyard Commandos,** 1991, Burger King, set of four: Major Legger Mutton in boat, Sgt. Shoat & Sweet in plane, Sgt. Wooley Pullover in sub, Pvt. Side O'Bacon in truck
EX n/a   **NM** $1   **MIP** $2

❑ **Batman Toothbrush Holder,** 1987, Burger King
EX n/a   **NM** $4   **MIP** $10

(Toy Shop File Photo)

❑ **Beauty & the Beast,** 1991, Burger King, set of four PVC figures: Belle, Beast, Chip, Cogsworth
EX n/a   **NM** $2   **MIP** $5

(KP Photo)

❑ **Beetlejuice,** 1990, Burger King, set of six figures: Uneasy Chair, Head Over Heels, Ghost to Ghost TV, Charmer, Ghost Post, Peek A Boo Doo
EX n/a   **NM** $1   **MIP** $2

❑ **Bicycle Safety Fun Booklet,** Burger King
EX n/a   **NM** $1   **MIP** $2

❑ **BK Kids Club Action Figures,** 1991, Burger King, set of four: Boomer, I.Q., Jaws, Kid Vid
EX n/a   **NM** $1   **MIP** $3

❑ **BK Kids Club All-Stars,** 1994, Burger King, set of five: All-Stars Boomer, All-Stars I/Q, All-Stars Jaws, All-Stars Kid Vid, All-Stars Snaps
EX n/a   **NM** $2   **MIP** $5

❑ **BK Kids Club Bugs,** 1998, Burger King, set of five: I/Q Caterpillar, Snaps Cricket, Lingo Spider, Boomer Fire Eye, Kid Vid Scorpian
EX n/a   **NM** $1   **MIP** $3

(Burger King Photo)

❑ **BK Kids Club Coolers,** 1995, Burger King, set of five: Kid Vid, blue; Jaws, turquoise; Snaps, yellow; I/Q, red; Boomer, purple
EX n/a   **NM** $2   **MIP** $4

(Burger King Photo)

❑ **BK Kids Club Glo Force**, 1996, Burger King, set of five glow-in-the-dark figures with costumes: Jaws as scubdiver, Snaps with safari gear, I/Q as surgeon, Kid Vid as astronaut, Boomer with ski gear
EX n/a   NM $1   MIP $2

❑ **BK Kids Club Mini Sports Games**, 1993, Burger King, set of four games: two catcher mitts with ball, football, basketball hoop with ball, inflatable soccer ball
EX n/a   NM $1   MIP $2

❑ **BK Kids Club Planet Patrol**, 1997, Burger King, Space Commander Jaws, I.Q.'s Planet Pacer, Boomer's Lightspeed Spacetop, Kid Vid's Glo Chopper, J.D. Shuttle Launch
EX n/a   NM $2   MIP $1

❑ **BK Kids Club Pranks**, 1994, Burger King, set of five: Boomer's Joy Buzzer, Jaw's Spider, Kid Vid's Squirting Remote Control, Longo's Gumballs, I/Q's Whoopee Cushion
EX n/a   NM $3   MIP $5

❑ **BK Kids Club Transporters**, 1990, Burger King, set of six: Snaps and her Camera Car, Boomer and her Super Shoe, I/Q and his World Book Mobile, Kid Vid and his SEGA Video Gamester
EX n/a   NM $4   MIP $6

❑ **BK Kids Club World Travel Adventure Kits**, 1991, Burger King, set of four: Kid Vid's Mystery Treasure Map, Lingo's South American Quest, Jaw's African Adventure, Snap's Euproepan Escapade
EX n/a   NM $3   MIP $5

❑ **Bone Age Skeleton Kit**, 1989, Burger King, set of four dinos: T-Rex, Dimetron, Mastadon, Similodon
EX n/a   NM $3   MIP $6

❑ **Bonkers Crash-Apart Cars**, 1993, Burger King, set of five: Toots, Jitters, Fall-apart Rabbit, Piquel, Bonkers
EX n/a   NM $1   MIP $2

❑ **Burger King Clubhouse**, Burger King, full size for kids to play in
EX n/a   NM $15   MIP $35

❑ **Burger King Socks**, Burger King, rhinestone accents
EX n/a   NM $2   MIP $5

❑ **Calendar "20 Magical Years" Walt Disney World**, 1992, Burger King
EX n/a   NM $2   MIP $4

❑ **Capitol Critters**, 1992, Burger King, set of four: Hemmet for Prez in White House, Max at Jefferson Memorial,

Muggle at Lincoln Memorial, Presidential Cat
EX n/a   NM $1   MIP $2

❑ **Capitol Critters Cartons**, 1992, Burger King, punch-out masks: dog, chicken, duck, panda, rabbit, tiger, turtle
EX n/a   NM $2   MIP $4

(KP Photo)

❑ **Captain Planet**, 1991, Burger King, set of four flip-over vehicles: Captain Planet & Hoggish Greedily, Linka, Ma-Ti & Dr. Blight ecomobile, Verminous Skumm & Kwane helicopter, Wheeler and Duke Nukem snowmobile
EX n/a   NM $1   MIP $2

❑ **Captain Power**, 1988, Burger King, set of four plastic vacuform boxes: Powerjet Xt-7, Bio-Dread Patroller, Power Base, Phantom Striker
EX n/a   NM $8   MIP $10

(Toy Shop File Photo)

❑ **Cartoon King Doll**, 1972, Burger King, 16" tall; cloth
EX n/a   NM $20   MIP $30

❑ **Cartoon Network Racing Team**, 1997, Burger King, set of five: Speeding Bomber, Jeff Gordon Car, Scooby Doo Car, Burger King Race Car, Stoneage Rocker
EX n/a   NM $1   MIP $2

❑ **CatDog**, 1999, Burger King, set of five: Souped-up Skateboard, Crazy Catch Up, Gourmet Garbage Chaser, Key Catchin' Clock, Wacy Walker Upper
EX n/a   NM $1   MIP $3

❑ **Chicago Bull Bendies**, 1994, Burger King, set of four figures: Stacey King #21, John Paxson #5, Scotti Pippen #33, BJ Armstrong #10
EX n/a   NM $3   MIP $6

(KP Photo)

❑ **Chicken Run**, 2000, Burger King, set of four: Mac's Highwire Act, Ginger's Eggstream Eggscape, Rocky's Rooster Booster, Bunty Breaks Out
EX n/a   NM $1   MIP $3

❑ **Chipmunk Adventure**, 1987, Burger King, set of four: bicycle licence plate; Alvin pencil topper, Alvin rubber ball, Sick 'Ems
EX n/a   NM $4   MIP $6

❑ **Christmas Crayola Bear**, 1986, Burger King, set of four bears: blue, red, yellow, red
EX n/a   NM $5   MIP $8

❑ **Christmas Crayola Bear Plush Toys**, 1986, Burger King, set of four: red, yellow, blue or purple
EX n/a   NM $3   MIP $6

❑ **Christmas Sing-A-Long Cassette Tapes**, 1989, Burger King, set of three Christmas sing-a-long tapes: Joy to the World/Silent Night, We Three Kings/O Holy Night, Deck the Halls/Night Before Christmas
EX n/a   NM $2   MIP $4

❑ **Crayola Coloring Books**, 1990, Burger King, set of six books: Boomer's Color Chase, I.Q.'s Computer Code, Kids Club Poster, Jaws' Colorful Clue, Snaps' Photo Power, Kid Vid's Video Vision
EX n/a   NM $2   MIP $4

❑ **Crayola World Travel Adventure Kits**, 1991, Burger King, set of four: Kid Vid's Tresure Map, Lingo's South American Quest, Jaw's African Adventure, Snap's European Escape
EX n/a   NM $2   MIP $5

❑ **Dino Crawlers**, 1994, Burger King, set of five: blue, red, yellow, green, purple
EX n/a   NM $1   MIP $2

❑ **Dino Meals**, 1987, Burger King, punch-out sheets: Stegosaurus, Woolly Mammoth, T-Rex, Triceratops
EX n/a   NM $3   MIP $6

❑ **Disney 20th Anniversary Figures**, 1992, Burger King, set of four wind-up vehicles with connecting track: Minnie, Donald, Roger Rabbit, Mickey
EX n/a   NM $3   MIP $5

❑ **Disney Afternoon**, 1994, Burger King, set of four: Shovel, Treasure Chest, Sunshoes, Beach Balls
EX n/a   NM $2   MIP $5

❏ **Disney Collector Series Tumblers,** 1994, Burger King, set of eight: Snow White, Jungle Book, Lion King, Peter Pan, Beauty and the Beast, Pinocchio, Dumbo, Aladdin
EX n/a   **NM** $2   **MIP** $4

(KP Photo)

❏ **Disney Parade Figures,** 1991, Burger King, set of four: Mickey, Minnie, Donald, Roger Rabbit
EX n/a   **NM** $3   **MIP** $5

(Burger King Photo)

❏ **Dragonball Z,** 2000, Burger King, set of seven: Goku, Gohan, Vegeta, Frieza, Krillin, Piccolo, Super Saiyan Goku
EX n/a   **NM** $1   **MIP** $3

❏ **Fairy Tale Cassette Tapes,** 1989, Burger King, set of four fairy tale cassettes: Goldilocks, Jack and the Beanstalk, Three Little Pigs, Hansel and Gretel
EX n/a   **NM** $1   **MIP** $3

❏ **Food Miniatures,** 1983, Burger King
EX n/a   **NM** $3   **MIP** $5

❏ **Freaky Fellas,** 1992, Burger King, set of four: blue, green, red, yellow; each came with a roll of Life Savers candy
EX n/a   **NM** $2   **MIP** $4

❏ **Gargoyles I,** 1995, Burger King, set of four: Spin to Life Goliath, Color Mutation Broadway, Gargoyles Pop-up book
EX n/a   **NM** $3   **MIP** $5

❏ **Gargoyles II,** 1995, Burger King, set of five: Spectroscope, Sparkling Spinner, Mini-viewer, Spin-attack Broadway, Bronx Launcher
EX n/a   **NM** $4   **MIP** $5

❏ **Go-Go Gadget Gizmos,** 1992, Burger King, set of four: Copter Gadget, Inflated Gadget, Scuba Gadget, Surfer Gadget
EX n/a   **NM** $4   **MIP** $6

❏ **Golden Junior Classic Books,** Burger King, set of four: Roundabout Train, The Circus Train, Train to Timbucktoo, My Little Book of Trains
EX n/a   **NM** $1   **MIP** $2

❏ **Good Gobblin',** 1989, Burger King, set of three: Frankie Steen, Zelda Zoombroom, Gordy Goblin
EX n/a   **NM** $4   **MIP** $6

(Burger King Photo)

❏ **Goof Troop Bowlers,** 1992, Burger King, set of four total: Goofy, Pete, PJ, and Max
EX n/a   **NM** $3   **MIP** $4

❏ **Goofy and Max's Adventure Toys,** 1995, Burger King, set of five: Water Raft, Water Skis, Goofy on Bucking Bronco, Row Boat, Runaway Car
EX n/a   **NM** $2   **MIP** $5

(Burger King Photo)

❏ **Hunchback of Notre Dame,** 1996, Burger King, set of eight figures: Laverne, Clopin, Hugo, Frollo, Pheobus, Victor, Quasimodo, Esmerelda and Djali the Goat
EX n/a   **NM** $1   **MIP** $2

❏ **Hunchback of Notre Dame Puppets,** 1996, Burger King, four finger: Quasimodo, Esmeralda, Gargoyle, Jester
EX n/a   **NM** $2   **MIP** $4

❏ **It's Magic,** 1992, Burger King, set of four: Magic Trunk, Disappearing Food, Magic Frame, Remote Control
EX n/a   **NM** $1   **MIP** $2

❏ **Jet Age Meal,** 1982, Burger King, set of three: Widebody Glider, X-2000 Gilder, Magellan Glider
EX n/a   **NM** $10   **MIP** $12

❏ **Kid's Choice Awards,** 1999, Burger King, set of six: Slimed Again, Big Bold Blimp, Winning Wiggle Writer, Pop Goes the Rosie, Give the Winner a Hand, Heeeeere's Rosie
EX n/a   **NM** $1   **MIP** $3

❏ **Land Before Time,** 1997, Burger King, set of six: Littlefoot, Spike, Perle, Chomper, Cera, Duckey
EX n/a   **NM** $3   **MIP** $6

❏ **Lickety Splits,** 1990, Burger King, set of seven: Carbo Cooler, Carsan'which, Chicken Chassis, Expresstix, Flame Broiled Buggy, Indianapolis Racer, Spry Fries
EX n/a   **NM** $3   **MIP** $5

❏ **Lifesaver Funsters,** 1992, Burger King, set of four: red, yellow, green, blue
EX n/a   **NM** $2   **MIP** $5

❏ **Lion King Collectible Kingdom,** 1994, Burger King, set of seven figures: Mufasa, Young Nala, Young Simba, Scar, Rafiki, Ed the Hyena, Pumbaa and Timon
EX n/a   **NM** $2   **MIP** $3

❏ **Lion King Finger Puppets,** 1995, Burger King, set of six: Mufasa, Simba, Rafiki, Pumbaa and Timon, Ed the Hyena, Scar
EX n/a   **NM** $1   **MIP** $2

❏ **Lion King's Timon & Pumbaa,** 1996, Burger King, set of four: Timon, Pumbaa, Bug Munchin' Pumbaa, Super Secret Compass
EX n/a   **NM** $2   **MIP** $3

❏ **Little Mermaid Splash Collection,** 1993, Burger King, set of four: Ariel wind-up, Flounder squirter, Sebastian wind-up, Urchin squirter
EX n/a   **NM** $2   **MIP** $4

(Burger King Photo)

❏ **M & M's,** 1997, Burger King, set of five: red, orange, yellow, blue, green
EX n/a   **NM** $2   **MIP** $5

❏ **M & M's Minis,** 1997, Burger King, set of five: Chomping Teeth Swarm, Giggle Stick, Crazy Pull-back Swarm, Secret Swarm Squirter, Scoop & Shoot Buggy
EX n/a   **NM** $1   **MIP** $2

❏ **Masters of the Universe Cups,** 1985, Burger King, set of four: Thunder Punch He-Man Saves the Day, He-Man and Roboto to the Rescue, He-Man Takes on the Evil Horde, Spydor—Stalking Enemies of Skeletor
EX n/a   **NM** $3   **MIP** $5

❏ **Matchbox Cars,** 1987, Burger King, set of four vehicles: blue Mountain Man 4x4, yellow Corvette, red Ferrari, Ford LTD police car
EX n/a   **NM** $5   **MIP** $7

❏ **Meal Bots,** 1986, Burger King, paper masks with 3-D lenses: Broil Master, red; Winter Wizard, blue; Beta Burger, gray; Galactic Guardians, yellow
EX n/a   **NM** $4   **MIP** $8

❏ **Men in Black,** 1998, Burger King, set of twelve: Squishy Worm Guy, Squirting Worm Guy, Globe Space Spinner, Building Space Spinner, Split Apart Light Up Zed, Split Apart Rotating Zed, Red Button Building Blaster, Red Button Loop Blaster, Slimed Out Kay, Slimed Out Jay, MIB Alien Detector, MIB Neitralyzer
EX n/a   **NM** $1   **MIP** $3

❏ **Mickey's Toontown,** 1993, Burger King, set of four: Mickey and Minnie, Goofy, Donald, Chip 'n Dale; each comes with map section
EX n/a   **NM** $5   **MIP** $7

❏ **Mr. Potato Head,** 1998, Burger King, set of five: Speedster, Hats Off, Fry Flyer, Spinning Spud, Basket Shoot
EX n/a   **NM** $1   **MIP** $3

❏ **Mr. Potato Head,** 1999, Burger King, set of five: Fry Fighter, Gotta Get 'Em Mr. Potato Head, Fry Jumper, Smashed Potato, Light Up Mr. Potato Head
EX n/a   NM $1   MIP $3

❏ **Nerfuls,** 1989, Burger King, set of four: Bitsy Ball, Fetch, Officer Bob, Scratch; rubber characters, interchangeable
EX n/a   NM $1   MIP $7

❏ **Nickel-O-Zone,** 1998, Burger King, set of five: Action League Now, Hay Arnold Football, Alien Strange Pod, Cruising Skeeter, Thornberry Comvee
EX n/a   NM $1   MIP $3

❏ **Nightmare Before Christmas Wristwatches,** Burger King, set of four different styles
EX n/a   NM $15   MIP $30

❏ **Oliver & Co.,** 1996, Burger King, set of four: Dashing Dodger, Desot Launcher, Skateway Tito, Oliver Viewer; the second Oliver & Co. set was released to coincide with home video release
EX n/a   NM $2   MIP $5

(Burger King Photo)

❏ **Oliver & Company,** 1996, Burger King, set of four: Sneak-A-Peek Oliver, Dashing Dodger, Surprise Attack DeSoto, Skateaway Tito
EX n/a   NM $1   MIP $2

❏ **Pilot Paks,** 1988, Burger King, set of four Styrofoam airplanes: two-seater, sunburst, lightning, one unknown example
EX n/a   NM $4   MIP $8

❏ **Pinocchio Inflatables,** 1992, Burger King, set of four: Pinocchio, Jiminy Cricket, Monstro the Whale, Figaro
EX n/a   NM $3   MIP $5

❏ **Pocahontas Figures,** 1995, Burger King, set of eight: Meeko, Governor Radcliffe, Pocahontas, Flit, Captain John Smith, Grandmother Willow, Chief Powhatan, Percy
EX n/a   NM $1   MIP $3

(Burger King Photo)

❏ **Pocahontas Pop-Up Puppets,** 1996, Burger King, set of six: Peek-a-Boo Pocahontas, Meeko's Hideout, Pampered Percy, Ruthless Radcliffe, John Smith's Lookout, Busy Body Flit
EX n/a   NM $1   MIP $2

❏ **Pocahontas Tumblers,** 1995, Burger King, set of four: Chief Powhatan, Meeko, Governor Radcliffe, John Smith and Pocahontas
EX n/a   NM $3   MIP $5

(Burger King Photo)

❏ **Pokemon Mini Game Boys,** 2000, Burger King, set of twelve Mini Game Boys, each with a different play function; included are over 100 removable gold or silver cartidges featuring different Pokemon Gold or Silver characters
EX n/a   NM $1   MIP $4

❏ **Pokemon: The First Movie,** 1999, Burger King, set of six gold plated trading cards: No. 25 Pikachu, No. 151 Mewtwo, No. 39 Jigglypuff, No. 61 Poliwhirl, No. 06 Charizard, Togepi
EX n/a   NM $1   MIP $5

(Burger King Photo)

❏ **Pokemon: The First Movie,** 1999, Burger King, set of fifty-seven toys with 151 cards; each toy came in in Pokeball with a card
EX n/a   NM $1   MIP $4

❏ **Pokemon: The Movie 2000,** 2000, Burger King, set of twenty-four Power Cards. Each card features a a special power action
EX n/a   NM $1   MIP $3

❏ **Purrtenders,** 1988, Burger King, set of four: Free Wheeling Cheese Rider, Flip-Top Car, Radio Bank, Storybook
EX n/a   NM $2   MIP $5

❏ **Purrtenders Plush,** 1988, Burger King, set of four: Hop-purr, Flop-purr, Scamp-purr, Romp-purr
EX n/a   NM $2   MIP $4

❏ **Record Breakers,** 1990, Burger King, set of six cars: Aero, Indy, Dominator, Accelerator, Fastland, Shockwave
EX n/a   NM $3   MIP $6

(Burger King Photo)

❏ **Road to El Dorado, The,** 2000, Burger King, set of four: Swashbuckling Miguel and Prancing Altivo, Sabor Rattling Tulio and Headbutting Bull, Tzekel-Kan and Pouncing Jaguar, Bibo on the Go with Chel
EX n/a   NM $1   MIP $2

❏ **Rodney & Friends,** 1986, Burger King, set of four plush toys: Rodney, Rhonda, Romona, Randy
EX n/a   NM $5   MIP $8

❏ **Rugrats,** 1998, Burger King, set of five: Reptar Alive, Hero on the Move Tommy, Jumpin' Chuckle, Wind Blown Angelica, Tandem Phil & Lil
EX n/a   NM $1   MIP $3

(KP Photo)

❏ **Rugrats in Paris,** 2000, Burger King, set of eight: Tumbling Kimi Volcano, Daktar's Descent with Lil, Susie's Super Spiral, Raptar Rider, Dil's Ooey Gooey Roller Ride, Rumbling Robot Buggy, Phil's Snail Spinner, Angelica's Princess Castle Ride
EX n/a   NM $1   MIP $3

❏ **Rugrats, The Movie,** 1998, Burger King, set of twelve: Okeydokey Tommy; Reptar Wagon; Aqua Reptar; Monkey Mayhem; Phil & Lil: Reptar Mine!; Chuckie's Treasure Hunt; Spike to the Rescue; Shirley Lock Angelica; Dactar Glider; Scooting Susie; Baby Dil Awakened; Clip-On Tommy with Baby Dil
EX n/a   NM $1   MIP $3

❏ **Save the Animals,** 1993, Burger King, set of four: Mammals, Birds, Reptiles and Amphibians, Fish
EX n/a   NM $3   MIP $5

(Burger King Photo)

❑ **Scooby Doo,** 1996, Burger King, set of five: Scrappy-Doo, Scooby and Shaggy, Scooby Coffin, Scoby-Doo, Mystery Machine
EX n/a　　　NM $1　　　MIP $3

(KP Photo)

❑ **Scooby-Doo and the Alien Invaders,** 2000, Burger King, set of eight: Roll-Around Alien, Clip n' Glow Scooby-Doo, Scared Silly Shaggy, Fright in Glowing Armor, Speakin' Scooby, Alien Attack Mystery Machine, Scooby-Doo and Shaggy's Alienship Adventure, Scramblin' Scooby-Doo
EX n/a　　　NM $1　　　MIP $3

❑ **Sea Creatures,** 1989, Burger King, set of four terrycloth wash mitts: Stella Starfish, Dolly Dolphin, Sammy Seahorse, Ozzie Octopus
EX n/a　　　NM $2　　　MIP $3

❑ **Silverhawks,** 1987, Burger King, set of four: Sticker, Name Plate, Decoder Ring, Pencil Topper
EX n/a　　　NM $5　　　MIP $10

❑ **Simpsons Cups,** 1991, Burger King, set of four
EX n/a　　　NM $1　　　MIP $2

❑ **Simpsons Dolls,** 1990, Burger King, set of five soft plastic dolls: Bart, Homer, Lisa, Marge, Maggie
EX n/a　　　NM $2　　　MIP $4

(Burger King Photo)

❑ **Simpsons Figures,** 1991, Burger King, set of five: Bart with backpack, Homer with skunk, Lisa with saxaphone, Marge with birds, Maggie with turtle
EX n/a　　　NM $2　　　MIP $5

❑ **Small Soldiers,** 1998, Burger King, set of twelve: Chip Hazard, Slamfist Soft 'n Cuddly, Rip Roarin' Kip Killigan, Butch's Battle, Bobbling Insaniac, Levitating Lens Ocula, Morning Brake Brick Bazooka, Nick Nitro, Freedom Firing Archer, Laughing Insaniac, Boulder

Blasting Punchit & Scratchit, Crawling Link Static
EX n/a　　　NM $1　　　MIP $3

❑ **Spacebase Racers,** 1989, Burger King, set of five plastic vehicles: Moon Man Rover, Skylab Cruiser, StarshipViking, Super Shuttle, Cosmic Copter
EX n/a　　　NM $2　　　MIP $4

❑ **Spacebase Racers,** 1989, Burger King, set of four: Super Shuttle, Moonman Rover, Starship Viking, Cosmic Copter
EX n/a　　　NM $5　　　MIP $10

❑ **Super Hero Cups,** 1984, Burger King, set of four cups with figural handles: Batman, Wonder Woman, Darkseid, Superman
EX n/a　　　NM $4　　　MIP $8

❑ **Super Powers,** 1987, Burger King, set of four: Superman coin, Batman toothbrush holder, Aquaman toy, Super Powers door nameplate
EX n/a　　　NM $7　　　MIP $15

(KP Photo)

❑ **Teenage Mutant Ninja Turtles Bike Gear,** 1993, Burger King, set of eleven: pouch, horn, water bottle, four spike buttons, three license plates
EX n/a　　　NM $3　　　MIP $5

❑ **Teenage Mutant Ninja Turtles Poster,** 1991, Burger King
EX n/a　　　NM $2　　　MIP $4

❑ **Teenage Mutant Ninja Turtles Rad Badges,** 1990, Burger King, set of six: Michaelangelo, Leonardo, Raphael, Donatello, Heroes in a Half Shell, Shredder
EX n/a　　　NM $3　　　MIP $5

❑ **Teletubbies,** 1999, Burger King, set of six: Laa-Laa, Tinky Winky, Dipsy, Po, Bunny, Noo-Noo
EX n/a　　　NM $1　　　MIP $3

❑ **Thundercats,** 1986, Burger King, set of four: cup/bank, Snarf strawholder, light switch plate, secret message ring
EX n/a　　　NM $3　　　MIP $8

❑ **Toonsylvania,** 1998, Burger King, set of five: Gurney Getaway, Phil's Teddy Cruiser, Vic's Walkaway Bride, Monster Maker, Screaming Screetch
EX n/a　　　NM $1　　　MIP $3

❑ **Top Kids,** 1993, Burger King, set of four spinning tops with figural heads: Wheels, Kid Vid, Jaws, Boomer
EX n/a　　　NM $1　　　MIP $2

❑ **Toy Story,** 1995, Burger King, set of six: Hopping Mr. Potato Head, Woody, Action Wing Buzz, Racing R.C. Car,

Squash 'N Go Rex, Green Army Men Recon Squad
EX n/a　　　NM $2　　　MIP $4

(Burger King Photo)

❑ **Toy Story,** 1996, Burger King, set of eight: Stroll 'n Scope Lenny, Jawbreaker Scud, Speedy Deposit Hamm, Round 'em Up Woody, Spin-Top Bo Peep, Blast-away Buzz, Spaced Out Alien, Slinky Dog
EX n/a　　　NM $2　　　MIP $3

(Burger King Photo)

❑ **Toy Story Puppets,** 1995, Burger King, set of four: Woody, Buzz Lightyear, Rex, Hamm
EX n/a　　　NM $2　　　MIP $3

❑ **Toy Story Talking Puppets,** 1995, Burger King, set of four: R.C. Racer, Talking Woody, Talking Buzz
EX n/a　　　NM $3　　　MIP $5

❑ **Tricky Treaters Boxes,** 1989, Burger King, Monster Manor, Creepy Castle, Haunted House
EX n/a　　　NM $1　　　MIP $3

❑ **Tricky Treaters Figures,** 1989, Burger King, set of three PVC figures: Frankie Steen, Gourdy Goblin, Zelda Zoom Broom
EX n/a　　　NM $3　　　MIP $10

❑ **Trolls Dolls,** 1993, Burger King, set of four Kids Club characters with neon hair: Snaps, I.Q. Jaws, Kid Vid
EX n/a　　　NM $1　　　MIP $2

❑ **Universal Monsters,** 1997, Burger King, set of four: Wolf Man, Frankenstein, Dracula, Creature
EX n/a　　　NM $2　　　MIP $4

(KP Photo)

❑ **Viva Rock Vegas,** 2000, Burger King, set of four: Puppy Dino Breaks Out, The Great Gazoo's Close Encounter, Fred's Two-Heel Drive, Bronto King Dine & Drive
EX n/a　　　NM $1　　　MIP $2

❏ **Watermates,** 1991, Burger King, set of four: Lingo's Jet Ski, Snaps in Boat, Wheels on raft, I.Q. on dolphin
EX n/a   **NM** $1   **MIP** $2

❏ **Wild Wild West,** 1999, Burger King
EX n/a   **NM** $1   **MIP** $3

❏ **Z-bots,** 1994, Burger King, set of five: Bugeye, Buzzsaw, Jawbreaker, Skyviper, Turbine
EX n/a   **NM** $2   **MIP** $5

CARL'S JR.

❏ **50th Anniversary,** 1991, Carl's Jr., set of four: Happy Star baseball, Happy Star plastic puzzle, Cruisin booklet, Groovy 60's jigsaw puzzle
EX n/a   **NM** $3   **MIP** $5

❏ **Addams Family Figure,** 1993, Carl's Jr., set of five: Thing pencil topper, Lurch stamper, Cousin Itt Bubbles, The Addams Family Mansion and Stickers
EX n/a   **NM** $2   **MIP** $5

❏ **Camp California,** 1992, Carl's Jr., set of four: Bear Squirter, Lil' Bro Disk, Mini Volleyball, Spinner; similar to set issued by Hardee's
EX n/a   **NM** $3   **MIP** $5

❏ **Camping with Woody Woodpecker,** 1991, Carl's Jr., set of two: Andy Panda container, pen knife utensil kit
EX n/a   **NM** $5   **MIP** $10

❏ **Fender Bender 500,** 1990, Carl's Jr., set of five: Yogi and Boo Boo, Huckleberry Hound and Snagglepuss, Magilla Gorilla and Wally Gator, Quick Draw McGraw and Baba Looey, Dick Dasterdly and Muttley; also issued by Hardee's
EX n/a   **NM** $3   **MIP** $5

❏ **Life Savers Roll 'Em,** 1990, Carl's Jr., set of five: Pineapple, Cherry, Orange, Lemon, Lime
EX n/a   **NM** $4   **MIP** $8

❏ **Life Savers Roll 'Em,** 1995, Carl's Jr., set of five: Pineapple, Cherry, Orange, Lemon, Lime
EX n/a   **NM** $1   **MIP** $2

❏ **Muppet Parade of Stars,** 1995, Carl's Jr., set of four: Miss Piggy, Kermit Gonzo, Fozzy
EX n/a   **NM** $4   **MIP** $6

❏ **Starnaments,** 1990, Carl's Jr., set of seven: Yellow star, Reindeer star, Snowman star, Elf Star, Chimney Sweep star, Toy Soldier star
EX n/a   **NM** $4   **MIP** $6

❏ **Starnaments,** 1991, Carl's Jr., set of four: Anniversary star, Moose star, Holly star, Twinkle star
EX n/a   **NM** $4   **MIP** $6

❏ **Starnaments,** 1992, Carl's Jr., set of five: Angel star, Mouse star, Toy Soldier star, Caroler star, Snow star
EX n/a   **NM** $4   **MIP** $6

CHICK-FIL-A

❏ **Adventures in Odyssey Books,** 1991, Chick-Fil-A, set of seven: Mike Makes Right, The Treasure of La Monde, Isaac the Courageous, All's Well with Boswell, A Matter of Obedience, Last Great Adventure of Summer
EX n/a   **NM** $2   **MIP** $4

❏ **Adventures in Odyssey Cassette Tapes,** 1993, Chick-Fil-A, set of six: The Ill-Gotten Deed, This is Chad Pearson?, Wishful Thinking, A Test for Robin, Suspicious Minds, Father's Day
EX n/a   **NM** $3   **MIP** $6

❏ **On the Go,** 1993, Chick-Fil-A, set of six foam vehicles: car, airplane, train, truck, boat, helicopter
EX n/a   **NM** $1   **MIP** $2

❏ **Wonderful World of Kids,** 1995, Chick-Fil-A
EX n/a   **NM** $2   **MIP** $5

DAIRY QUEEN

❏ **Circus Train,** 1994, Dairy Queen
EX n/a   **NM** $4   **MIP** $5

❏ **Dennis the Menace,** 1993, Dairy Queen, set of four: Dennis in fire truck, Margaret in astronaut suit, Ruff in dinosaur costume, Joey in race car
EX n/a   **NM** $4   **MIP** $6

❏ **Dennis the Menace,** 1993, Dairy Queen, set of four: Dennis, Margaret, Joey, Ruff; each cup featured images of individual character and a 3-D molded plastic cup lid
EX n/a   **NM** $4   **MIP** $6

❏ **Funbunch Flyer,** Dairy Queen, each featured a different animal with the Dairy Queen logo
EX n/a   **NM** $3   **MIP** $5

❏ **Holiday Bendies,** 1993, Dairy Queen, set of four: Santa with open eyes, Santa with closed eyes, Reindeer with bell, Reindeer with scarf
EX n/a   **NM** $3   **MIP** $5

❏ **Rock-A-Doodles,** 1992, Dairy Queen, set of six: Chanticleer, Patou, Edmund, Peepers, Peepers, The Grand Duke of Owl
EX n/a   **NM** $6   **MIP** $10

❏ **Rockin' Toppers,** 1993, Dairy Queen, set of four pencil toppers: blue, yellow, green, red; rubber toppers with clingy surface allowing them to walk down walls
EX n/a   **NM** $1   **MIP** $2

❏ **Supersaurus Puzzles,** 1993, Dairy Queen, set of three
EX n/a   **NM** $2   **MIP** $3

❏ **Tom and Jerry figures,** 1993, Dairy Queen, set of six: Tom Squirter, Jerry Squirter, Tom Summer Cruiser, Jerry Summer Cruiser, Tom Stamper, Jerry Stamper
EX n/a   **NM** $4   **MIP** $6

DENNY'S

❏ **Dino-Makers,** 1991, Denny's, set of six: including blue dino, purple elephant, orange bird
EX n/a   **NM** $1   **MIP** $2

(Denny's Photo)

❏ **Flintstones Dino Racers,** 1991, Denny's, set of six: Fred, Bamm-Bamm, Dino, Pebbles, Barney, Wilma
EX n/a   **NM** $3   **MIP** $6

(Denny's Photo)

❏ **Flintstones Fun Squirters,** 1991, Denny's, set of six: Fred with telephone, Wilma with camera, Dino with flowers, Bam Bam with soda, Barney, Pebbles
EX n/a   **NM** $2   **MIP** $4

❏ **Flintstones Glacier Gliders,** 1990, Denny's, set of six: Bamm-Bamm, Barney, Fred, Dino, Hoppy, Pebbles
EX n/a   **NM** $2   **MIP** $4

❏ **Flintstones Mini Plush,** 1989, Denny's, set of four, in packages of two: Fred/Wilma, Betty/Barney, Dino/Hoppy, Pebbles/Bamm-Bamm
EX n/a   **NM** $2   **MIP** $4

❏ **Flintstones Rock 'n Rollers,** 1990, Denny's, set of six: Fred with guitar, Barney with sax, Bam Bam, Dino with piano, Elephant, Pebbles
EX n/a   **NM** $3   **MIP** $6

❏ **Flintstones Stone-Age Cruisers,** 1991, Denny's, set of six: Fred in green car, Wilma in red car, Dino in blue car, Pebbles in purple bird, Bam Bam in orange car, Barney in yellow car with sidecar
EX n/a   **NM** $2   **MIP** $4

❏ **Flintstones Vehicles,** 1990, Denny's, set of six: Fred, Wilma, Pebbles, Dino, Barney, Bamm-Bamm
EX n/a   **NM** $2   **MIP** $4

❏ **Jetsons Crayon Fun Game,** Denny's, set of six booklets with crayon game: George in Leisurly George, Jane in Jane Gets Decorated, Judy in Dream Date, Elroy What a Sport, Astro in Every Dog has his Daydream, Rosie in I Need Some Space
EX n/a   **NM** $2   **MIP** $4

❏ **Jetsons Game Packs,** 1992, Denny's, set of six: George, Elroy, Judy, Astro, Rosie, Jane
EX n/a   **NM** $2   **MIP** $4

❏ **Jetsons Go Back to School,** 1992, Denny's, set of six school tools: mini dictionary, folder, message board, pencil and topper, pencil box, triangle and curve
EX n/a   **NM** $2   **MIP** $4

❑ **Jetsons Puzzle Ornaments,** 1992, Denny's, set of six: Saturn with George, Earth with Jane, Jupiter with Judy, Mars with Elroy, Moon with Astro, Neptune with Rosie
EX n/a   NM $2   MIP $4

❑ **Jetsons Space Balls (Planets),** 1992, Denny's, set of six: Jupiter, Neptune, Earth, Saturn, Mars, glow-in-the-dark Moon
EX n/a   NM $2   MIP $4

❑ **Jetsons Space Cards,** 1992, Denny's, set of five: Spacecraft, Phenomenon, Astronomers, Constellations, Planets
EX n/a   NM $2   MIP $4

❑ **Jetsons Space Travel Coloring Books,** 1992, Denny's, set of six books: each with four crayons
EX n/a   NM $2   MIP $4

DOMINO'S PIZZA

(KP Photo)

❑ **Noids,** 1987, Domino's Pizza, set of seven figures: Boxer, Clown, He Man, Holding Bomb, Holding Jack Hammer, Hunchback, Magician
EX n/a   NM $2   MIP $4

❑ **Quarterback Challenge Cards,** 1991, Domino's Pizza, pack of four cards
EX n/a   NM $1   MIP $2

HARDEE'S

❑ **Apollo 13,** 1995, Hardee's
EX n/a   NM $2   MIP $5

❑ **Beach Bunnies,** 1989, Hardee's, set of four: girl with ball, boy with skateboard, girl with skates, boy with frisbee
EX n/a   NM $2   MIP $4

❑ **California Raisins,** 1987, Hardee's, set of four: dancer with blue and white shoes, singer with mike, sax player, raisin with sunglasses
EX n/a   NM $2   MIP $8

❑ **California Raisins,** 1988, Hardee's, set of six: Waves Weaver, F.F. Strings, Captain Toonz, Rollin' Rollo, Trumpy Tru-Note, S.B. Stuntz
EX n/a   NM $2   MIP $4

❑ **California Raisins,** 1991, Hardee's, third set: Alotta Stile in pink boots, Anita Break with package under her arm, Benny bowling, Buster with skateboard
EX n/a   NM $2   MIP $6

❑ **California Raisins,** 1991, Hardee's, set of four: Berry, Anita Break, Alotta Stile, Buster
EX n/a   NM $3   MIP $5

❑ **California Raisins Plush,** 1988, Hardee's, set of four: lady in yellow shoes, dancer in yellow hat, with mike in white shoes, in sunglasses with orange hat; each 6" tall
EX n/a   NM $3   MIP $6

❑ **Camp California,** 1993, Hardee's, set of four: Bear Squirter, Lil' Bro Disk, Mini Volleyball, Spinner; similar to set issued by Carl's Jr.
EX n/a   NM $3   MIP $5

❑ **Days of Thunder Racers,** 1990, Hardee's, set of four cars: Mello Yello #51, Hardee's #18 orange, City Chevrolet #46, Superflo #46 pink/white
EX n/a   NM $3   MIP $6

❑ **Dinosaur in My Pocket,** 1993, Hardee's, set of four: Stegosaurus, Triceratops, Bronotsaurus, Tyrannosaurus
EX n/a   NM $2   MIP $5

❑ **Disney's Animated Classics Plush Toys,** Hardee's, Pinocchio, Bambi
EX n/a   NM $3   MIP $5

❑ **Fender Bender 500,** 1990, Hardee's, set of five: Yogi and Boo Boo, Huckleberry Hound and Snagglepuss, Magilla Gorilla and Wally Gator, Quick Draw McGraw and Baba Looey, Dick Dasterdly and Muttley; also issued by Carl's Jr.
EX n/a   NM $2   MIP $3

❑ **Finger Crayons,** 1992, Hardee's, set of four: two Crayons included in each package; not marked Hardee's
EX n/a   NM $2   MIP $3

❑ **Flintstones First 30 Years,** 1991, Hardee's, set of five: Fred with TV, Barney with grill, Pebbles with phone, Dino with jukebox, Bamm Bamm with pinball
EX n/a   NM $3   MIP $6

(KP Photo)

❑ **Food Squirters,** 1990, Hardee's, set of four: cheeseburger, hot dog, shake, fries
EX n/a   NM $2   MIP $4

❑ **Ghostbuster Beepers,** 1989, Hardee's, set of four: red, white, black, gray
EX n/a   NM $10   MIP $12

❑ **Gremlin Adventures,** 1989, Hardee's, set of five book and record sets: Gift of the Mogwai, Gismo & the Gremlins, Escape from the Gremlins, Gremlins Trapped, The Late Gremlin
EX n/a   NM $2   MIP $4

❑ **Halloween Hideaways,** 1989, Hardee's, set of four: goblin in blue cauldron, ghost in yellow bag, cat in pumpkin, bat in stump
EX n/a   NM $3   MIP $6

❑ **Hardee's Racer,** Hardee's, blue or green
EX n/a   NM $4   MIP $6

❑ **Home Alone 2,** 1992, Hardee's, set of four cups: Kevin, The Pigeo Lady, Marv, Harry
EX n/a   NM $1   MIP $2

❑ **Homeward Bound,** Hardee's, set of five: Chance, Riley, Sassy, Delilah, Shadow
EX n/a   NM $2   MIP $5

❑ **Kazoo Crew Sailors,** 1991, Hardee's, set of four: bear, monkey, rabbit, rhino
EX n/a   NM $1   MIP $2

❑ **Little Little Golden Books,** 1987, Hardee's, set of four: The Poky Little Puppy, Little Red Riding Hood, The Three Little Pigs, The Little Red Hen
EX n/a   NM $5   MIP $7

❑ **Little Little Golden Books,** 1988, Hardee's, set of four: The Little Red Caboose, The Three Bears, Old MacDonald Had a Farm, Three Little Kittens
EX n/a   NM $2   MIP $4

(KP Photo)

❑ **Marvel Super Heroes,** 1990, Hardee's, set of three: She Hulk, Hulk, Captain America, Spider-Man
EX n/a   NM $3   MIP $6

❑ **Muppet Christmas Carol Finger Puppets,** 1994, Hardee's, set of four: Miss Piggy, Kermit, Gonzo, Fozzy Bear
EX n/a   NM $3   MIP $5

❑ **Nicktoons,** 1994, Hardee's, set of eight: Ren, Stimpy, Angelica Pickles, Tommy Pickles, Porkchop, Doug Funnie, Rocko, Spunky
EX n/a   NM $4   MIP $6

❑ **Pound Puppies,** 1986, Hardee's, set of four: black, white with black, tan with black, gray with black
EX n/a   NM $5   MIP $10

❑ **Pound Puppies and Pur-r-ries,** 1987, Hardee's, set of four: white cat with gray stripes, brown cat, gray bulldog, Damlatian
EX n/a   NM $5   MIP $10

❑ **Shirt Tales Plush Dolls,** Hardee's, set of five: Bogey, Pammy, Tyg, Digger, Rick; each 7" tall
EX n/a   NM $3   MIP $6

☐ **Smurfin' Smurfs,** 1990, Hardee's, set of four: Papa Smurf with red board, boy with orange board, girl with purple board, dog with blue board
EX n/a   NM $2   MIP $4

(KP Photo)

☐ **Smurfs figures,** 1987, Hardee's, Hardee's issued over 100 Smurfs in this promotion
EX n/a   NM $3   MIP $5

☐ **Speed Bunnies,** 1994, Hardee's, set of four: Cruiser, Dusty, Sunny, Stretch
EX n/a   NM $2   MIP $4

☐ **Super Bowl Cloisonné Pins,** 1991, Hardee's, set of twenty-five NFL Super Bowl pins
EX n/a   NM $2   MIP $6

☐ **Swan Princess,** 1994, Hardee's, set of four: Prince Derek, Princess Odette/Swan, Jean-Bob, Puffin, Rothbart
EX n/a   NM $3   MIP $5

☐ **Tang Mouth Figures,** 1989, Hardee's, set of four: Lance, Tag, Flap, Awesome Annie
EX n/a   NM $2   MIP $4

☐ **Waldo and Friends Holiday Ornaments,** 1991, Hardee's, in sets of three: Waldo with Woof, Waldo Watchers, Snowman; Waldo with camping gear, Wenda, Woof; Reindeer in sleigh, Wizard, Waldo with books
EX n/a   NM $3   MIP $5

☐ **Waldo's Straw Buddies,** 1990, Hardee's, set of four: Waldo, Wenda, Wizard, Woof
EX n/a   NM $2   MIP $3

☐ **Waldo's Travel Adventure,** 1992, Hardee's, set of four: Adventure Travel Journal, Postcards, Fold 'N Solve Travel Pictures, Space Puzzle
EX n/a   NM $2   MIP $3

☐ **X-Men,** 1995, Hardee's, set of three, in sets of two: Cyclops vs. Commando; Phantasia vs. Storm; The Blob vs. Wolverine; Rogue vs. Wolverine
EX n/a   NM $3   MIP $6

INTERNATIONAL HOUSE OF PANCAKES

☐ **Pancake Kid dolls,** 1992, International House of Pancakes, set of three cloth dolls: Bonnie Blueberry, Susie Strawberry, Chocolate Chip Charlie
EX n/a   NM $7   MIP $10

☐ **Pancake Kids,** 1991, International House of Pancakes, set of ten: Cynthis Cinnamon Apple, Susie Strawberry, Bonnie Blueberry, Harvey Harvest, Betty Buttermilk, Frenchy, Rosana Banana Nut, Peter Potato, Von der Gus
EX n/a   NM $4   MIP $6

☐ **Pancake Kids Cruisers,** 1993, International House of Pancakes, set of eight: Von der Gus, Bonnie Blueberry, Susie Strawberry, Harvey Harvest, Chocolate Chip Charlie, Frenchy, Cynthia Cinnamon Apple, Betty Buttermilk
EX n/a   NM $4   MIP $6

KENTUCKY FRIED CHICKEN

☐ **Alvin and the Chipmunks,** 1991, Kentucky Fried Chicken, Canadian issues; Alvin and Theodore
EX n/a   NM $3   MIP $5

☐ **Alvin and the Chipmunks,** 1992, Kentucky Fried Chicken, Canadian issues; Alvin and Simon
EX n/a   NM $2   MIP $4

(KP Photo)

☐ **Animorphs,** 1998, Kentucky Fried Chicken, set of five: Animorphs Puzzle Cube, DNA Transfer Cards, Animorphing Box, Tobias Hawk Glider, Thought Speak Revealer
EX n/a   NM $2   MIP $3

(KP Photo)

☐ **Beakman's World,** 1998, Kentucky Fried Chicken, set of six: Lester Reverser, Penguin TV, Optical Illusion Top, Diver Don, Beakman's Balancer, Dancing Liza
EX n/a   NM $2   MIP $3

☐ **Carmen Sandiego,** 1997, Kentucky Fried Chicken, set of six: Jr. Sleuth Pocket Pack, Carmen's Mystery Decoder, Carmen's World Map Puzzle, Carmen's Breakaway Escape Care, Carmen's Undercover Case with Stickers, Magic Answer Globe
EX n/a   NM $2   MIP $3

☐ **Colonel Sanders Figure,** 1960s, Kentucky Fried Chicken, 9" tall
EX n/a   NM $35   MIP $50

☐ **Colonel Sanders Nodder,** 1960s, Kentucky Fried Chicken, 7" tall; papier-mâché
EX n/a   NM $50   MIP $150

☐ **Colonel Sanders Nodder,** 1960s, Kentucky Fried Chicken, 7" tall; plastic
EX n/a   NM $15   MIP $40

☐ **Cool Summer Stuff featuring Chester Cheetah,** 1996, Kentucky Fried Chicken, set of five: Fast Flyin' Disk, Spotted Summer Shades, Mini Wrist-Pack, Totally Fun Visor, Inflatable Wobble Ball
EX n/a   NM $2   MIP $3

(KP Photo)

☐ **Extreme Ghostbusters,** 1997, Kentucky Fried Chicken, set of six: Haunted Cube, Ghost Trap Challenge, Screamin' Scrambler, Ecto1 Haunted Hauler, Ghostbusters Keychain Keeper, Slimer Squirter
EX n/a   NM $2   MIP $3

☐ **Garfield Catmobiles,** 1996, Kentucky Fried Chicken, set of six: Arlene finger puppet, Pookie finger puppet, Nermal Freewheeler, Jon Freewheeler, Garfield Pullback, Odie Pullback
EX n/a   NM $2   MIP $3

☐ **Garfield Racers,** 1996, Kentucky Fried Chicken, set of six
EX n/a   NM $2   MIP $4

☐ **Ghostly Glowing Squirters,** 1996, Kentucky Fried Chicken, set of six: Casper, Spooky, Stretch, Fatso, Poil, Stinkie
EX n/a   NM $2   MIP $3

☐ **Giga Pets,** 1997, Kentucky Fried Chicken, set of four: Digipooch, Cyberkitty, Micropup, Bitty Kitty; over the counter promotion
EX n/a   NM $2   MIP $3

☐ **Jim Henson's Scary Scary Monsters,** 1999, Kentucky Fried Chicken, set of five: Flip-A-Mungo, Super Stretch Norbert, Zuzu Zoomer, Monster Shoelace Munchers, Scary Scary Stick-Ons
EX n/a   NM $2   MIP $3

☐ **Koosh,** 1995, Kentucky Fried Chicken, set of three: Zipper Pull, Bookmark, Pencil Topper
EX n/a   NM $2   MIP $3

☐ **Linkbots,** 1995, Kentucky Fried Chicken, set of six Transformers
EX n/a   NM $2   MIP $3

☐ **Marvel Super Heroes,** 1997, Kentucky Fried Chicken, set of six: Spider-Man Symbol Clip, Invisible Woman Escape Launcher, Incredible Hulk Pencil Twirler, Spider-Man Wall Walker, Fantastic Four Terra Craft, Wolverine Press 'n Go
EX n/a   NM $2   MIP $3

☐ **Masked Rider to the Rescue,** 1997, Kentucky Fried Chicken, set of six: Masked Rider Super Gold, Magno the Super Car, Press & Go Super Chopper, Glow-in-the-Dark X-Ray Cyclopter, Ecto Viewer Wrist Band, Bump & Go Ferbus
EX n/a   NM $2   MIP $3

❑ **Matchbox,** 1995, Kentucky Fried Chicken, set of six: BMW, Ambulance, Fire Engine, Mustang, Jeep, Ferrari
EX n/a   **NM** $2   **MIP** $3

(KP Photo)

❑ **NCAA March Madness,** 1999, Kentucky Fried Chicken, set of three: 2-Hoop Game, Wacky Wrist Toss, Final Four Basketball
EX n/a   **NM** $2   **MIP** $3

(KP Photo)

❑ **Pokémon,** 1998, Kentucky Fried Chicken, set of six: Pokémon Monster Blocks, Go Pokémon Card Game, Pokémon Monster Matcher, Pokémon Tattoos, Ivysaur Squirter, Pikachu Treasure Keeper
EX n/a   **NM** $2   **MIP** $3

❑ **Pokémon Beanbags,** 1998, Kentucky Fried Chicken, set of four: Seel, Vulpix, Dratini, Zubat; over-the-counter promotion
EX n/a   **NM** $2   **MIP** $5

(KP Photo)

❑ **Secret Files of the Spy Dogs,** 1999, Kentucky Fried Chicken, set of five: The Evil Cat Astrophe, Fidgety Scribble, Mitzy Rolling Stamper, Eye Popping Space Slug, Agent Ralph's Marble Game
EX n/a   **NM** $2   **MIP** $3

(KP Photo)

❑ **SI for Kids,** 1998, Kentucky Fried Chicken, set of four: Dunk It In Fun Book,

Slam Dunk! Flipbook, Kick it in Fun Book, Kick! Flipbook
EX n/a   **NM** $2   **MIP** $3

(KP Photo)

❑ **Slimamander,** 1998, Kentucky Fried Chicken, set of six: Slimamander Wrist Squirter, Slimamander's Glowing Goo, Slimamander and Leap the Frog Tattoos, Leap the Frog Launcher, Slimamander Bubble Wand, Slimamander Spraying Top
EX n/a   **NM** $2   **MIP** $3

❑ **Timon and Pumbaa's World of Bugs,** 1997, Kentucky Fried Chicken, set of six: Snail Snackin' Timon, Bug Munchin' Pumbaa, Out-to-Lunch Timon, Hawaiian Luau Pumbaa, Jungle River-Riding Timon, Bug Bath Pumbaa
EX n/a   **NM** $2   **MIP** $3

❑ **Treeples,** 1999, Kentucky Fried Chicken, set of six: Dress-Up Rachel, Stevie's Acorn Searcher, Tangled Treeples, Othello Yo-Yo, Miranda's Banana-mated Theater, Linky Lurker
EX n/a   **NM** $2   **MIP** $3

❑ **Ultimate Eekstravaganza,** 1996, Kentucky Fried Chicken, set of five: Eek! Balancing Act, Sharky's Dog House Launcher, Ka-Boooom! Annabelle, Cool Moves Doc, Kutler Copter
EX n/a   **NM** $2   **MIP** $3

(KP Photo)

❑ **Wallace & Gromit,** 1998, Kentucky Fried Chicken, set of six: The Wrong Trousers, Gromit's Rollalong Sidecar, Wallace Bendable, Wallace & Gromit Character Card Set, Sheep-on-a-String, Blinking Feathers McGraw
EX n/a   **NM** $2   **MIP** $3

(KP Photo)

❑ **Winter Wonderpals,** 1999, Kentucky Fried Chicken, set of five: Wallace the

Walrus Paper Puncher, Roley Poley Polar Ball, Sippy the Penguin Play Straw, Slick the Sled Dog Igloo Launcher, Howl E. Wolf
EX n/a   **NM** $2   **MIP** $4

❑ **WWF Stampers,** Kentucky Fried Chicken, set of four: Canadian issues
EX n/a   **NM** $2   **MIP** $4

LEE'S FRIED CHICKEN

❑ **Cartoon Viewers,** 1980s, Lee's Fried Chicken, set of six: Mighty Mouse, Woody Woodpecker, Popeye, Superman, Bugs Bunny, Porky Pig
EX n/a   **NM** $20   **MIP** $50

LONG JOHN SILVER'S

❑ **Adventure on Volcano Island,** 1991, Long John Silver's, paint with water activity book
EX n/a   **NM** $2   **MIP** $4

❑ **Berenstain Bear books,** 1995, Long John Silver's
EX n/a   **NM** $2   **MIP** $5

❑ **Fish Cars,** 1986, Long John Silver's, fish-shaped cars done in red, yellow and blue, each with different peel-off stickers and details
EX n/a   **NM** $8   **MIP** $12

❑ **Once Upon a Forest,** 1993, Long John Silver's, set of five straw huggers: Abigail, Michelle, Cornelius, Edgar, Russell; done in two mold colors
EX n/a   **NM** $3   **MIP** $6

❑ **Sea Walkers,** 1990, Long John Silver's, set of four packaged with string: Parrot, Penguin, Turtle, Sylvia
EX n/a   **NM** $3   **MIP** $8

❑ **Sea Watchers Kaleidoscopes,** 1991, Long John Silver's, set of three: orange, yellow, pink
EX n/a   **NM** $2   **MIP** $4

❑ **Superstar Baseball Cards,** 1990, Long John Silver's, eight sets of five cards: Don Mattingly, Mark McGwire, Mark Grace, Wade Boggs, Darryl Strawberry, Nolan Ryan, Bobby Bonilla, Bret Saberhagen
EX n/a   **NM** $10   **MIP** $15

❑ **Treasure Trolls,** 1992, Long John Silver's, set of six: yellow hair, red hair, pink hair, blue hair, purple hair, green hair
EX n/a   **NM** $1   **MIP** $3

(KP Photo)

❑ **Water Blasters,** 1990, Long John Silver's, set of four: Billy Bones, Captain Flint, Ophelia Octopus, Parrot
EX n/a   **NM** $3   **MIP** $5

McDONALD'S

(KP Photo)

❏ **101 Dalmatians,** 1991, McDonald's, set of four: Lucky, Pongo, Sergeant Tibbs, Cruella
EX n/a   **NM** $1   **MIP** $2

❏ **101 Dalmatians,** 1996, McDonald's, 101 different PVC dogs. Premiums were randomly distributed in opaque bag and were un-named. Values for each dog can vary due to the haphazzard distribution.
EX n/a   **NM** $3   **MIP** $10

❏ **101 Dalmatians Snow Globes,** 1996, McDonald's, set of four: Snoman's Best Friend (snowman), Snow Furries (dome with red ribbon), Dog Sledding (sleigh), Dalmatian Celebration (number 101)
EX n/a   **NM** $2   **MIP** $5

❏ **101 Dalmatians the Series,** 1997, McDonald's, set of eight flip cars: Perdita/Scorch, Two-Tone/Lt. Pug, Lucky/Cruella, Rolly/Ed Pig, Steven/Sydney, Tripod/Dumpling, Cadpig/Spot, Pongo/Swamprat
EX n/a   **NM** $1   **MIP** $2

❏ **102 Dalmatians,** 2000, McDonald's, 102 different PVC dogs. Premiums were randomly distributed in opaque bag and were un-named. Values for each dog can vary due to the haphazzard distribution.
EX n/a   **NM** $3   **MIP** $8

❏ **3-D Happy Meal,** 1981, McDonald's, set of four cartons with 3-D designs and 3-D glasses inside: Bugsville, High Jinx, Loco Motion, Space Follies
EX n/a   **NM** $20   **MIP** $40

❏ **A Bug's Life Figures,** 1998, McDonald's, set of eight wind-ups: Dim, Rosie, Dot, Flik, Francis, Heimlich, Hopper, Atta
EX n/a   **NM** $1   **MIP** $2

❏ **A Bug's Life Watches,** 1998, McDonald's, set of three: Leafy Ant-icks with 3-D face, Pop Topper with flip-top lid, Bug Eye Spy with two floating characters
EX n/a   **NM** $2   **MIP** $3

❏ **Adventures of Ronald McDonald,** 1981, McDonald's, set of seven rubber figures: Ronald, Birdie, Big Mac, Captain Crook, Mayor McCheese, Hamburglar, Grimace
EX n/a   **NM** $5   **MIP** $10

❏ **Airport Happy Meal,** 1986, McDonald's, set of five: Birdie Bentwing Blazer, Fry Guy Flyer, Grimace Bi-Plane, Big Mac Helicopter, Ronald Sea Plane
EX n/a   **NM** $5   **MIP** $10

❏ **Airport Happy Meal,** 1986, McDonald's, set of two U3 toys: Fry Guy Friendly Flyer, Grimace Smiling Shuttle
EX n/a   **NM** $3   **MIP** $5

❏ **Aladdin and the King of Theives,** 1996, McDonald's, one U3 toy: Abu squirter
EX n/a   **NM** $2   **MIP** $5

❏ **Aladdin and the King of Thieves,** 1996, McDonald's, set of eight: Cassim, Abu, Jasmine, Iago, Genie, Sa'luk, Aladdin, Maitre d'Genie
EX n/a   **NM** $1   **MIP** $3

❏ **Alvin and The Chipmunks,** 1991, McDonald's, set of four figures: Simon with movie camera, Theodore with rap machine, Brittany with juke box, Alvin with guitar
EX n/a   **NM** $3   **MIP** $6

❏ **Alvin and The Chipmunks,** 1991, McDonald's, one U3 toy: Alvin leaning on jukebox
EX n/a   **NM** $10   **MIP** $20

❏ **Amazing Wildlife,** 1995, McDonald's, set of eight plush animals: Asiatic Lion, Chimpanzee, Koala Bear, African Elephant, Dromedary Camel, Galapagos Tortoise, Siberian Tiger, Polar Bear
EX n/a   **NM** $1   **MIP** $3

❏ **American Trio Teenie Beanie Babies,** 2000, McDonald's, set of three: Righty, Lefty, Libearty
EX n/a   **NM** $1   **MIP** $3

❏ **An American Tail,** 1986, McDonald's, set of four books: Fievel and Tiger, Fievel's Friends, Fievel's Boat Trip, Tony and Fievel
EX n/a   **NM** $2   **MIP** $3

❏ **Animal Kingdom,** 1998, McDonald's, set of thirteen: triceratops, toucan, gorilla and baby, elephant, dragon, iguanodon, lion, cheetah, zebra, rhino, crocodile, ringtail lemur, tortoise (only available at McDonald's in Wal-Mart stores); four special collector's cups were available with super sized combo meal
EX n/a   **NM** $1   **MIP** $2

❏ **Animal Pals,** 1997, McDonald's, set of six plush toys: Panda, Rhinoceros, Yak, Moose, Brown Bear, Gorilla
EX n/a   **NM** $1   **MIP** $2

❏ **Animal Riddles,** 1979, McDonald's, set of eight rubber figures: condor, snail, turtle, mouse, anteater, alligator, pelican, dragon, in various colors
EX n/a   **NM** $2   **MIP** $4

❏ **Animaniacs,** 1994, McDonald's, set of eight: Bicycle Built for Trio, Goodskate Goodfeathers, Upside-Down Wakko, Slappy and Skipper's Chopper, Dot's Ice Cream Machine, Midy and Buttons Wild Ride Yakko Ridin' Ralph, Pink and the Brain Mobile,
EX n/a   **NM** $2   **MIP** $3

❏ **Animaniacs,** 1995, McDonald's, set of eight: Pinky & the Brain, Goodfeathers, Dot & Ralph, Wacko & Yakko, Slappy & Skippy, Mindy & Buttons, Wakko, Yakko & Dot, Hip Hippos
EX n/a   **NM** $1   **MIP** $2

❏ **Animaniacs,** 1995, McDonald's, set of four U3 toys: Bicycle Built for Trio, Goodskate Goodfeathers, Yakko Ridin' Ralph, Mindy and Buttons Wild Ride
EX n/a   **NM** $3   **MIP** $5

❏ **Astrosnick Spacemobile,** 1984, McDonald's, 9-1/2" rocket ship available with four Happy Meal Cosmic Coupons
EX n/a   **NM** $30   **MIP** $60

(Toy Shop File Photo)

❏ **Astrosnicks I,** 1983, McDonald's, set of eight: eight different 3" rubber space creatures: Scout, Thirsty, Robo-Robot, Laser, Snickapotamus, Sport, Skater, Astralia
EX n/a   **NM** $4   **MIP** $20

❏ **Astrosnicks II,** 1984, McDonald's, set of six: Copter, Drill, Ski, Racing, Perfido, Commander
EX n/a   **NM** $5   **MIP** $20

❏ **Astrosnicks III,** 1985, McDonald's, set of eleven figures: C.B., Banner, Commander, Junior, Jet, Laser, Perfido, Pyramido, Robo-Robot, Astralia, Snikapotamus; regionally distributed in the Oklahoma area, many are the same as other Astroniks but without "m" marking
EX n/a   **NM** $5   **MIP** $40

❏ **Attack Pack/Polly Pocket,** 1995, McDonald's, set of four: Ruck, Battle Bird, Lunar Invader, Sea Creature; joint promotion with Polly Pocket
EX n/a   **NM** $1   **MIP** $2

❏ **Attack Pack/Polly Pocket,** 1995, McDonald's, one U3 toy: Truck
EX n/a   **NM** $2   **MIP** $3

❏ **Babe,** 1996, McDonald's, set of seven plush toys: Babe, Ferdinand, Fly, Maa, Cow, Mouse, Dutchess
EX n/a   **NM** $1   **MIP** $2

(KP Photo)

❑ **Back to the Future,** 1992, McDonald's, set of four: Doc's DeLorean, Verne's Jukebox, Marty's Hoverboard, Einstein's Traveling Train
EX n/a　　　**NM** $1　　　**MIP** $2

❑ **Bambi,** 1988, McDonald's, set of three U3 toys: Bambi with butterfly on tail, Bambi, Thumper
EX n/a　　　**NM** $5　　　**MIP** $10

(Copyright Museum of Science and Industry, Chicago)

❑ **Bambi,** 1988, McDonald's, set of four figures: Owl, Flower, Thumper, Bambi
EX n/a　　　**NM** $2　　　**MIP** $4

❑ **Barbie and Friends/World of Hot Wheels,** 1994, McDonald's, set of eleven: Bicyclin' Barbie, Jewel and Glitter Shani, Camp Barbie, Camp Teresa, Locket Surprise Ken, African-American or Caucasian, Locket Surprise Barbie, African-American or Caucasian, Jewel and Glitter Barbie, Bridesmaid Skipper; joint promotion with Hot Wheels
EX n/a　　　**NM** $2　　　**MIP** $5

❑ **Barbie/Hot Wheels,** 1990, McDonald's, set of four Barbie figures with dioramas: Movie Star with SuperStar Barbie; In Concert with Solo in the Spotlight Barbie; Tea Party with Enchanted Evening Barbie; Moonlight Ball with 1989 Happy Holiday Barbie. Test Market Happy Meal, regionally distributed in Savanah, Georgia; joint promotion with Hot Wheels
EX n/a　　　**NM** $90　　　**MIP** $125

❑ **Barbie/Hot Wheels,** 1991, McDonald's, set of two U3 toys: Costume Ball Barbie, Wedding Day Midge; joint promotion with Hot Wheels
EX n/a　　　**NM** $2　　　**MIP** $4

❑ **Barbie/Hot Wheels,** 1991, McDonald's, set of eight: Ice Capades, All American, Lights & Lace, Hawaiian Fun, Happy Birthday, Costume Ball, Wedding Day Midge, My First Barbie
EX n/a　　　**NM** $2　　　**MIP** $3

❑ **Barbie/Hot Wheels,** 1993, McDonald's, set of eight: My First Ballerina, Birthday Party, Western Stamping, Romantic Bride, Hollywood Hair, Paint 'n Dazzle, Twinkle Lights, Secret Hearts; joint promotion with Hot Wheels
EX n/a　　　**NM** $2　　　**MIP** $3

❑ **Barbie/Hot Wheels,** 1995, McDonald's, one U3 toy: figurine of blond girl wearing green dress
EX n/a　　　**NM** $2　　　**MIP** $3

❑ **Barbie/Hot Wheels,** 1995, McDonald's, set of ten: Hot Skatin' Barbie, Dance Moves Barbie, Butterfly Princess Teresa, Cool Country Barbie, Caucasian Lifeguard Ken, African-American Lifeguard Ken, Caucasian Lifeguard Barbie, African-American Lifeguard Barbie, Bubble Angel Barbie, Ice Skatin' Barbie; joint promotion with Hot Wheels
EX n/a　　　**NM** $2　　　**MIP** $3

❑ **Barbie/Hot Wheels,** 1996, McDonald's, set of five: Dutch Barbie, Kenyan Barbie, Japanese Barbie, Mexican Barbie, USA Barbie; joint promotion with Hot Wheels
EX n/a　　　**NM** $1　　　**MIP** $3

❑ **Barbie/Hot Wheels,** 1996, McDonald's, one U3 toy: Barbie slide puzzle
EX n/a　　　**NM** $2　　　**MIP** $3

❑ **Barbie/Hot Wheels,** 1997, McDonald's, set of five: Wedding Rapunzel Barbie, Rapunzel Barbie, Angel Princess Barbie, Blossom Beauty Barbie, Happy Holidays Barbie; joint promo with Hot Wheels
EX n/a　　　**NM** $1　　　**MIP** $3

❑ **Barbie/Hot Wheels,** 1998, McDonald's, set of four: Barbie, Teen Skipper, Eating Fun Kelly, Bead Blast Christie; joint promo with NASCAR Hot Wheels
EX n/a　　　**NM** $1　　　**MIP** $3

❑ **Barbie/Hot Wheels,** 1999, McDonald's, set of eight Barbies: Soccer Barbie, Sleeping Beauty Barbie, Happening Hair Barbie, Totally Yo-Yo Barbie, Birthday Party Barbie, Giggles 'n' Swing Barbie, Pet Loving Barbie, Bowling Party Barbie; joint promotion with Hot Wheels
EX n/a　　　**NM** $1　　　**MIP** $4

❑ **Barbie/Hot Wheels,** 2000, McDonald's, set of sixteen: Swimming Champion Barbie, Olympic Pin Barbie, Paralympic Barbie, Barbie Stopwatch, Rainbow Princess Barbie, Cool Clip Christie, Secret Message Teresa, Barbie Rainbow Horse, Birthday Party Barbie, Crew Barbie, Celebration Cake Barbie, Barbie Rock 'n Roll Radio, Cool Skating Barbie, Awesome Skateboard Stacie, Bicycling Barbie, Barbie Sports Water Bottle; joint promotion with Hot Wheels
EX n/a　　　**NM** $1　　　**MIP** $3

❑ **Barbie/Hot Wheels,** 2000, McDonald's, set of eighteen: Millenium Princess Barbie, Barbie No. 1, Solo in the Spotlight, Hollywood Nails Barbie, Malibu Barbie, Gymnast Barbie, Totally Hair Barbie, Sit 'n Style Barbie, Working Woman Barbie, Chic Barbie; joint promotion with Hot Wheels
EX n/a　　　**NM** $1　　　**MIP** $3

❑ **Barbie/Hot Wheels Mini-Streex,** 1992, McDonald's, one U3 toy: Sparkle Eyes Babie
EX n/a　　　**NM** $2　　　**MIP** $5

❑ **Barbie/Hot Wheels Mini-Streex,** 1992, McDonald's, set of eight dolls: Sparkle Eyes, Roller Blade, Rappin' Rockin', My First Ballerina, Snap 'N PLay, Sun Sensation, Birthday Surprise, Rose Bride; joint promotion with Hot Wheels Mini-Streex
EX n/a　　　**NM** $1　　　**MIP** $2

(KP Photo)

❑ **Batman,** 1992, McDonald's, set of four: Batmobile, Batmissle, Catwoman Cat Coupe, Penguin Roto-Roadster
EX n/a　　　**NM** $1　　　**MIP** $2

❑ **Batman Cups,** 1992, McDonald's, set of six cups; offered in conjunction with Happy Meal
EX n/a　　　**NM** $1　　　**MIP** $2

❑ **Batman, The Animated Series,** 1993, McDonald's, one U3 toy: Batman without removable cape
EX n/a　　　**NM** $2　　　**MIP** $5

❑ **Batman, The Animated Series,** 1993, McDonald's, set of eight: Batman with removable cape, Robin, Batgirl, Two Face, Poison Ivy, Joker, Catwoman with leopard, Riddler
EX n/a　　　**NM** $2　　　**MIP** $3

❑ **Beach Ball,** 1986, McDonald's, set of three inflatables: Ronald waving, red; Birdie with sandcastle, blue; Grimace with beach umbrella, yellow. Regionally distributed in Washington, New York and Colorado
EX n/a　　　**NM** $10　　　**MIP** $15

❑ **Beach Ball Characters,** 1985, McDonald's, set of three: Grimace in kayak, Ronald holding flag and beachball, Birdie in sailboat
EX n/a　　　**NM** $10　　　**MIP** $15

❑ **Beach Toy II,** 1990, McDonald's, set of eight: Ronald and Grimace sand pail with yellow lid and shovel, Birdie Seaside Submarine, Fry Kid Super Sailor, Fry Kids Sand Castle Pail, Grimace Beach Ball, Birdie Shovel, Ronald Squirt Gun Rake, Ronald Fun Flyer
EX n/a　　　**NM** $2　　　**MIP** $3

❑ **Beach Toys I,** 1989, McDonald's, set of four: Birdie Seaside Submarine, Grimace Bouncin' Beachball, Fry Kid Super Sailor, Ronald Fun Flyer; test market Happy Meal
EX n/a　　　**NM** $10　　　**MIP** $15

❑ **Beachcomber Happy Meal,** 1986, McDonald's, set of three sand pails with shovels: Grimace, Mayor McCheese, Ronald
EX n/a　　　**NM** $5　　　**MIP** $10

❑ **Bedtime,** 1989, McDonald's, set of four: Ronald toothbrush with tube of Crest toothpaste, Ronald bath mitt, Ronald Nite Stand Star Figure, Ronald cup
EX n/a　　　**NM** $4　　　**MIP** $8

❏ **BeetleBorgs Metallix,** 1997, McDonald's, set of six: Stinger Drill, Beetle Bonder, Hunter Claw, Platinum Purple BeetleBorg Covert Compact, Chromuim Gold BeetleBorg Covert Compact, Titanium Silver BeetleBorg Covert Compact
EX n/a   **NM** $1   **MIP** $2

❏ **Behind the Scenes,** 1992, McDonald's, set of four: Cartoon Wheel, Rainbow Viewer, Rub 'N' Draw, Balance Builder
EX n/a   **NM** $2   **MIP** $3

(KP Photo)

❏ **Berenstain Bears I,** 1986, McDonald's, set of four figures: Papa with wheelbarrow, Mama with shopping cart, Brother with scooter, Sister with sled; test market set, distributed in Evansville, Indiana
EX n/a   **NM** $30   **MIP** $75

❏ **Berenstain Bears II,** 1987, McDonald's, set of four figures with flocked heads: Papa with wheelbarrow, Mama with shopping cart, Brother with scooter, Sister with wagon
EX n/a   **NM** $2   **MIP** $4

❏ **Berenstain Bears II,** 1987, McDonald's, set of two U3 toys with paper punch outs: Mama, Papa
EX n/a   **NM** $5   **MIP** $10

❏ **Berenstain Bears Story Books,** 1990, McDonald's, set of eight books: Attic Treasure Story Book, Attic Treasure Activity Book, Substitute Teacher Story Book, Substitute Activity Book, Eager Beavers Story Book, Eager Beavers Activity Book, Life with Papa Story Book, Life with Papa Activity Book
EX n/a   **NM** $2   **MIP** $4

❏ **Bigfoot,** 1987, McDonald's, set of eight Ford trucks: Bronco, green or orange; Pickup, purple or orange; Ms. Pickup, turquoise or pink; Shuttle, red or black; without McDonald's "M" logo on back window
EX n/a   **NM** $5   **MIP** $10

❏ **Bigfoot,** 1987, McDonald's, set of eight Ford trucks: Bronco, green or orange; Pickup purple or orange; Ms. Pickup, turquoise or pink; Shuttle, red or black; each had McDonald's "M" logo on back window
EX n/a   **NM** $3   **MIP** $5

❏ **Birdie Bike Horn,** McDonald's, Japanese
EX n/a   **NM** $4   **MIP** $9

❏ **Birdie Magic Trick,** McDonald's, green or orange
EX n/a   **NM** $2   **MIP** $5

❏ **Black History,** 1988, McDonald's, two coloring books: Little Martin Jr. Coloring Book Volume One, Little Martin Jr. Coloring Book Volume Two; sold in six Detroit stores
EX n/a   **NM** $200   **MIP** $500

❏ **Boats 'n Floats,** 1987, McDonald's, set of four vaccuform boats with stickers: Chicken McNugget lifeboat, Birdie float, Fry Guys raft, Grimace ski boat
EX n/a   **NM** $5   **MIP** $10

❏ **Bobby's World,** 1994, McDonald's, one U3 toy: Bobby in intertube
EX n/a   **NM** $1   **MIP** $3

❏ **Bobby's World,** 1994, McDonald's, one U3 toy: inner tube
EX n/a   **NM** $2   **MIP** $3

❏ **Bobby's World,** 1994, McDonald's, set of four: Wagon-Race Car, Innertube-Submarine, Three Wheeler-Space Ship, Skates-Roller Coaster
EX n/a   **NM** $1   **MIP** $2

❏ **Breakfast Happy Meal,** 1991, McDonald's, squeeze bottle with Minute Maid logo
EX n/a   **NM** $1   **MIP** $3

❏ **Buzz Lightyear of Star Command,** 2001, McDonald's, set of six: Buzz Lightyear, Mira Nova, Booster, XR, The Evil Emporer Zurg, Commander Nebula
EX n/a   **NM** $1   **MIP** $3

❏ **Cabbage Patch,** 1992, McDonald's, one U3 toy: Anne Louise "Ribbons & Bows"
EX n/a   **NM** $1   **MIP** $2

❏ **Cabbage Patch Kids/Tonka,** 1992, McDonald's, set of five: Tiny Dancer, Holiday Pageant, Holiday Dreamer, Fun On Ice, All Dressed Up; joint promotion with Tonka
EX n/a   **NM** $2   **MIP** $3

❏ **Cabbage Patch Kids/Tonka,** 1994, McDonald's, one U3 toy: SaraJane
EX n/a   **NM** $2   **MIP** $3

❏ **Cabbage Patch Kids/Tonka,** 1994, McDonald's, set of four: Mimi Kristina, Abigail Lynn, Kimberly Katherine, Michelle Elyse; joint promotion with Tonka
EX n/a   **NM** $1   **MIP** $3

❏ **Camp McDonaldland,** 1990, McDonald's, set of four: Grimace Canteen, Birdie Mess Kit, Fry Kid Utensils, Ronald Collapsible Cup (also U3 premium)
EX n/a   **NM** $2   **MIP** $3

❏ **Captain Crook Bike Reflector,** 1988, McDonald's, blue plastic, Canada
EX n/a   **NM** $1   **MIP** $3

❏ **Castlemaker,** 1987, McDonald's, set of four vacuuform molds: dome, square, cylinder, rectangle; regionally distributed in Michigan and Houston, Texas
EX n/a   **NM** $20   **MIP** $40

❏ **Changeables,** 1987, McDonald's, set of six figures that change into robots: Big Mac, Milk Shake, Egg McMuffin, Quarter Pounder, French Fries, Chicken McNuggets
EX n/a   **NM** $4   **MIP** $8

❏ **Chip 'n Dale Rescue Rangers,** 1989, McDonald's, set of four figures: Chip's Whirly-Cuptor, Dale's Roto-Roadster, Gadgets Rescue Racer, Monteray Jack's Propel-A-Phone
EX n/a   **NM** $2   **MIP** $4

❏ **Chip 'n Dale Rescue Rangers,** 1989, McDonald's, set of two U3 toys: Gadget's Rockin', Chip's Rockin Racer
EX n/a   **NM** $2   **MIP** $4

❏ **Christmas Ornaments,** 1987, McDonald's, Fry Guy and Fry Girl, cloth, 3-1/2" tall
EX n/a   **NM** $3   **MIP** $6

❏ **Christmas Stocking,** 1981, McDonald's, plastic, "Merry Christmas to My Pal"
EX n/a   **NM** $3   **MIP** $6

❏ **Circus,** 1983, McDonald's, set of nine: Fun House Mirror with Ronald; Fun House Mirror with Hamburglar; Acrobatic Ronald, French Fry Faller; Strong Gong with Grimace; Punchout Midway: The Ronald Midway; Punchout Midaway: Fun House; Punchout Tent with Grimace; Punchout Tent with Birdie
EX n/a   **NM** $15   **MIP** $25

❏ **Circus Parade,** 1991, McDonald's, set of four: Ringmaster Ronald McDonald, Bareback Rider Birdie, Grimace Playing Caliope, Elephant Trainer Fry Guy
EX n/a   **NM** $2   **MIP** $4

❏ **Circus Wagon,** 1979, McDonald's, set of four rubber toys: poodle, chimp, clown, horse
EX n/a   **NM** $2   **MIP** $3

❏ **Colorforms Happy Meal,** 1986, McDonald's, set of five: Beach set, Grimace; Farm set, Ronald; Camping set, Professor; Play set, Birdie; Picnic, Hamburglar
EX n/a   **NM** $10   **MIP** $15

❏ **Colorforms Happy Meal,** 1986, McDonald's, two U3 sticker sets: Beach set, Grimace; Farm set, Ronald
EX n/a   **NM** $10   **MIP** $15

❏ **Colorful Puzzles-Japan,** McDonald's, set of three: Dumbo, Mickey & Minnie, Dumbo & Train
EX n/a   **NM** $5   **MIP** $10

❏ **Coloring Stand-Ups,** 1978, McDonald's, characters and backgrounds to color, punch out and stand
EX n/a   **NM** $4   **MIP** $8

❏ **Combs,** 1988, McDonald's, set of four: Capt. Crook, red; Grimace, yellow; Ronald, yellow, blue or purple; Grimace Groomer, green
EX n/a   **NM** $1   **MIP** $2

❏ **Commandrons,** 1985, McDonald's, set of four robots: Solardyn, Magna, Motron, Velocitor
EX n/a   **NM** $5   **MIP** $15

❏ **Connectables,** 1991, McDonald's, set of four: Birdie on tricycle, Grimace in wagon, Hamburglar in airplane, Ronald in soapbox racer
EX n/a   **NM** $3   **MIP** $5

❑ **Construx,** 1986, McDonald's, set of four: axle, wing, body cylinder, canopy; spaceship could be built from all four preiums
EX n/a   NM $10   MIP $25

❑ **CosMc Crayola,** 1988, McDonald's, one U3 toy: two fluorescent crayons with coloring page
EX n/a   NM $5   MIP $10

❑ **CosMc Crayola,** 1988, McDonald's, set of five coloring kits: four crayons with coloring page, thin red marker with coloring page, four chalk with chalkboard, washable thin marker with coloring page, three paints and brush with paint-by-number page
EX n/a   NM $5   MIP $10

❑ **Crayola Happy Meal,** 1986, McDonald's, set of three kits: triangle stencil with green marker, rectangular stencil with four fluorescent crayons, triangle stencil with orange marker, triangle stencil with thin blue marker, triangle stencil with thin red marker
EX n/a   NM $10   MIP $15

❑ **Crayola II,** 1987, McDonald's, one U3 stencil: Ronald on fire engine with four crayons
EX n/a   NM $5   MIP $10

❑ **Crayola II,** 1987, McDonald's, set of four stencils: Grimace with four fluorescent crayons, Hamburglar with four crayons, Birdie with thick orange or green marker, Ronald with thin blue or red marker
EX n/a   NM $2   MIP $5

❑ **Crayola Squeeze Bottle, Kay Bee,** McDonald's, set of four: regional promotion
EX n/a   NM $3   MIP $6

❑ **Crayon Squeeze Bottle,** 1992, McDonald's, set of four: blue, green, yellow, red; regionally distributed in New York state and Connecticut
EX n/a   NM $3   MIP $5

❑ **Crazy Creatures with Popoids,** 1985, McDonald's, set of four made up of two bellows and one connector: red and blue bellows with wheel joint; yellow and blue connectors with ball joint; yellow and red bellows with cube joint; red and yellow with seven-sided joint
EX n/a   NM $6   MIP $12

❑ **Crazy Vehicles,** 1991, McDonald's, set of four: Ronald in red car, Hamburglar in yellow train engine, Grimace in green car, Birdie in pink airplane
EX n/a   NM $3   MIP $5

❑ **Design-O-Saurs,** 1987, McDonald's, set of four: Ronald on Tyrannosaurus, Grimace on Pterodactyl, Fry Guy on Brontosaurus, Hamburglar on Triceratops
EX n/a   NM $5   MIP $10

❑ **Dink the Little Dinosaur,** 1990, McDonald's, set of six figures with diorama and description: Dink, Flapper, Amber, Crusty, Scat, Shyler
EX n/a   NM $4   MIP $8

❑ **Dino-Motion Dinosaurs,** 1993, McDonald's, set of six: Baby, Grandma, Robbie, Earl, Fran, Charlene
EX n/a   NM $1   MIP $2

❑ **Dino-Motion Dinosaurs,** 1993, McDonald's, one U3 toy: Baby squirter
EX n/a   NM $2   MIP $4

❑ **Dinosaur Days,** 1981, McDonald's, set of six rubber dinos: Pteranodon, Triceratops, Stegosaurus, Dimetrodon, T-Rex, Ankylosaurus
EX n/a   NM $1   MIP $2

❑ **Dinosaur Talking Storybook,** 1989, McDonald's, set of four books and tape: The Dinosaur Baby Boom, Danger Under the Lake, The Creature in the Cave, The Amazing Birthday Adventure
EX n/a   NM $5   MIP $10

❑ **Dinosaurs,** 2000, McDonald's, set of ten: Aladar Hand Puppet, Neera Hand Puppet, Carnotaur Hand Puppet, Kron Hand Puppet, Plio/Zini/Suri/Yar Talking Toy, Baylene Action Figure, Eema Action Figure, Bruton Action Figure
EX n/a   NM $1   MIP $3

❑ **Discover the Rain Forest,** 1991, McDonald's, set of four activity books with punch out figures: Sticker Safari, Wonders in the Wild, Paint It Wild, Ronald and the Jewel of the Amazon Kingdom
EX n/a   NM $2   MIP $4

❑ **Disney Favorites,** 1987, McDonald's, set of four activity books: Lady and the Tramp, Dumbo, Cinderella, The Sword in the Stone
EX n/a   NM $3   MIP $4

❑ **Disney Masterpiece Collection,** 1996, McDonald's, figures in video-shaped box
EX n/a   NM $1   MIP $2

❑ **Disney Video Favorites,** 1998, McDonald's, set of six: The Spirit of Mickey, Lady & the Tramp, Pocahontas: Journey to a New World, Mary Poppins, The Black Cauldron, Flubber
EX n/a   NM $1   MIP $3

❑ **Disney Video Showcase Collection,** 2000, McDonald's, set of six boxes and eighteen toys: A Bug's Life, Dinosaur, Little Mermaid II, Mickey's Once Upon a Christmas, Winnie the Pooh Season of Giving, Toy Story II
EX n/a   NM $1   MIP $3

❑ **Disneyland 40th Anniversary Viewers,** 1995, McDonald's, one U3 toy: Winnie the Pooh on Big Thunder Mountain without viewer (green cab)
EX n/a   NM $2   MIP $3

❑ **Disneyland 40th Anniversary Viewers,** 1995, McDonald's, set of nine: Brer on Space Mountain; Aladdin & Jasmine at Aladdin's Castle; Roger Rabbit in Mickey's Toontown; Winnie the Pooh on Big Thunder Mountain with viewer, green cab; Winnie the Pooh on Big Thunder Mountain with viewer, black cab; Simba in The Lion King Celebration; Mickey Mouse on Space Mountain; Peter Pan in Fantasmic!; King Louie on the Jungle Cruise
EX n/a   NM $2   MIP $3

❑ **Disney's House of Mouse,** 2001, McDonald's, set of six: Mickey Mouse, Minnie Mouse, Daisy Duck, Donald Duck, Goofy, Pluto
EX n/a   NM $1   MIP $3

❑ **Double Bell Alarm Clock,** McDonald's, wind-up alarm clock with silver bells, hammer ringer, silver feet, image of Ronald on face with head tilted over folded hands, as if asleep
EX n/a   NM $20   MIP $40

❑ **Doug's First Movie,** 1999, McDonald's, set of eight: Doug the Keychain, Doug the Pen Pal, Patti the Keychain Pal, Doug the Clip-on, Quilman the Bouncing Zipper Gripper, Skeeter the Keychain, Monster the Pocket Protector
EX n/a   NM $1   MIP $3

❑ **Duck Tales I,** 1988, McDonald's, set of four toys: Telescope, Duck Code Quacker, Magnifying Glass, Wrist Decoder
EX n/a   NM $2   MIP $4

❑ **Duck Tales I,** 1988, McDonald's, one U3 toy: Motion Magic Map
EX n/a   NM $2   MIP $5

❑ **Duck Tales II,** 1988, McDonald's, set of four toys: Uncle Scrooge in red car; Launchpad in plane; Huey, Dewey and Louie on jet ski; Webby on blue trike
EX n/a   NM $3   MIP $6

❑ **Duck Tales II,** 1988, McDonald's, one U3 toy: Huey on skates
EX n/a   NM $15   MIP $20

❑ **Dukes of Hazzard,** 1982, McDonald's, set of five vaccuform container vehicles, Boss Hogg's Caddy, Daisy's Jeep, Sheriff Roscoe's Police Car, Uncle Jesse's Pickup, General Lee; each container came with sticker sheet; regionally distributed in Missouri
EX n/a   NM $20   MIP $50

❑ **Dukes of Hazzard,** 1982, McDonald's, set of six white plastic cups: Luke, Boss Hogg, Bo, Sheriff Roscoe, Daisy, Uncle Jesse
EX n/a   NM $3   MIP $6

❑ **E.T.,** 1985, McDonald's, set of four posters: E.T. with boy and girl in front of spaceship, E.T. with boy and bike, E.T. with glowing finger, E.T. with radio
EX n/a   NM $8   MIP $12

❑ **Earth Days,** 1994, McDonald's, one U3 toy: tool carrier with shovel
EX n/a   NM $1   MIP $2

❑ **Earth Days,** 1994, McDonald's, one U3 toy: tool carrier with shovel
EX n/a   NM $1   MIP $2

❑ **Earth Days,** 1994, McDonald's, set of four: birdfeeder, globe terrarium, binoculars, tool carrier with shovel
EX n/a   NM $1   MIP $2

❑ **Emporer's New Groove, The,** 2000, McDonald's, set of six: Kuzco, Yzma the Kittycat, Kuzco as Llama, Kronk, Pacha, zma
EX n/a   NM $1   MIP $3

❏ **Eric Carle Finger Puppets,** 1996, McDonald's, set of six puppets: The Very Quiet Crickett, The Very Lonely Firefly, A House for Hermit Crab, The Grouchy Ladybug, The Very Hungry Caterpillar, The Very Busy Spider
EX n/a   **NM** $1   **MIP** $2

❏ **Extremely Goofy Movie, An,** 2000, McDonald's, set of eight: Goofy, Sylvia, Max, Bradley, PJ, Tank, Bobby, Slouch
EX n/a   **NM** $1   **MIP** $3

❏ **Fast Macs I,** 1984, McDonald's, set of four pull-back action cars: Big Mac in white police car, Ronald in yellow Jeep, Hamburglar in red racer, Birdie in pink convertible
EX n/a   **NM** $3   **MIP** $5

❏ **Fast Macs II,** 1985, McDonald's, set of four pull-back action cars: Big Mac in white police car, Ronald in yellow Jeep, Hamburglar in red racer, Birdie in pink convertible
EX n/a   **NM** $3   **MIP** $5

❏ **Favorite Friends,** 1978, McDonald's, set of seven character punch-out cards
EX n/a   **NM** $2   **MIP** $5

❏ **Feeling Good,** 1985, McDonald's, set of two U3 floating toys: Grimace in Tub, Fry Guys on Duck
EX n/a   **NM** $5   **MIP** $8

❏ **Feeling Good,** 1985, McDonald's, set of six grooming toys: Grimace soap dish, Fry Guy sponge, Birdie mirror, Ronald toothbrush, Hamburglar toothbrush, Captain Crook comb
EX n/a   **NM** $1   **MIP** $3

❏ **Field Trip,** 1993, McDonald's, one U3 toy: Nature Viewer
EX n/a   **NM** $1   **MIP** $2

❏ **Field Trip,** 1993, McDonald's, set of four: Kaleidoscope, Leaf Printer, Nature Viewer, Explorer Bag
EX n/a   **NM** $1   **MIP** $2

❏ **Fingerboard Pro Gear,** 2000, McDonald's, set of eight: Fingerboard w/Blue Ramp, Fingerboard w/Yellow Ramp, Fingerboard w/Light Blue Ramp, Fingerboard w/Green Ramp, Fingerboard w/Orange Clip, Fingerboard w/Pink Clip, Fingerboard w/purple Clip, Fingerboard w/Blue Clip
EX n/a   **NM** $1   **MIP** $2

❏ **Fisher-Price U3 Toys,** 1996, McDonald's, set of twenty-four: Balls in ball, Barn Puzzle, Bear in Train, Birdie in Poppity-Pop Car, Bus, Clock, Corn Popper, Cow Book, Dog Squeek, Dog Roll-A-Rounds, Dog in House, Dog on Red Wheels, Grimace Roll-A-Rounds, Horse, Jeep, Key Ring, Man in Poppity-Pop Car, Truck, Fun Sounds Ball, Puzzle Maze, Ronald McDonald in Drive-thru, Pig in Barrel, Radio Rattle, Chatter Telephone; In 1996, McDonald's began offering generic Fisher-Price toys as the U3 premium for Happy Meals.
EX n/a   **NM** $3   **MIP** $5

❏ **Flintstone Kids,** 1988, McDonald's, set of four figures in animal vehicles: Betty, Barney, Fred, Wilma
EX n/a   **NM** $4   **MIP** $8

❏ **Flintstone Kids,** 1988, McDonald's, one U3 toy: Dino figure
EX n/a   **NM** $10   **MIP** $15

❏ **Flintstones,** 1994, McDonald's, one U3 toy: Rocking Dino
EX n/a   **NM** $3   **MIP** $5

❏ **Flintstones,** 1994, McDonald's, set of five: Fred at Bedrock Bowl-O-Rama, Betty and Bamm Bamm at Roc Donald's, Wilma at the Flinstone's house, Barney at the Fossil Fill-Up, Pebbles and Dino at Toy-S-Aurus
EX n/a   **NM** $1   **MIP** $2

❏ **Florida Beach Ball,** 1985, McDonald's, set of three with Florida logo: Grimace in kayak, Ronald holding flag and beachball, Birdie in sailboat
EX n/a   **NM** $20   **MIP** $25

(Toy Shop Photo File)

❏ **Food Fundamentals,** 1993, McDonald's, set of four: Slugger the steak; Otis the sandwhich, Milly the milk carton, Ruby the apple
EX n/a   **NM** $1   **MIP** $2

❏ **Food Fundamentals,** 1993, McDonald's, one U3 toy: Dunkan the ear of corn
EX n/a   **NM** $1   **MIP** $2

❏ **Fraggle Rock I,** 1987, McDonald's, set of four: Gobo Fraggle, Bulldoozer and Friends, Cotterpin Doozer and Friends, Cotterpin Doozer; test market Happy Meal, regionally distributed in West Virginia
EX n/a   **NM** $20   **MIP** $30

(KP Photo)

❏ **Fraggle Rock II,** 1988, McDonald's, set of four: Gobo in carrot car, Red in radish car, Mokey in eggplant car, Wembly and Boober in pickle car
EX n/a   **NM** $1   **MIP** $2

❏ **Fraggle Rock II,** 1988, McDonald's, set of two U3 toys: Gobo holding carrot, Red holding radish
EX n/a   **NM** $4   **MIP** $6

❏ **French Fry Radio,** 1977, McDonald's, large red fry container with fries
EX n/a   **NM** $12   **MIP** $25

❏ **Friendly Skies,** 1991, McDonald's, set of two: Ronald in white plane, Grimace in white plane
EX n/a   **NM** $5   **MIP** $10

❏ **Friends of Barbie/World of Hot Wheels,** 1994, McDonald's, one U3 toy: Barbie Ball
EX n/a   **NM** $2   **MIP** $3

❏ **Fry Benders,** 1990, McDonald's, set of four figures: Grand Slam with baseball glove, Froggy with scuba tanks, Roadie with bicycle, Freestyle with rollerskates
EX n/a   **NM** $5   **MIP** $10

❏ **Fry Guy Cookie Cutter,** 1987, McDonald's, Fry Guy on unicycle, green or orange
EX n/a   **NM** $1   **MIP** $3

❏ **Fun Ruler,** 1983, McDonald's, white platic ruler featuring Mayor McCheese, Fry Guys, Birdie, Ronald, Grimace, Hamburglar
EX n/a   **NM** $3   **MIP** $5

❏ **Fun To Go,** 1977, McDonald's, set of seven cartons with games and activities
EX n/a   **NM** $2   **MIP** $4

❏ **Fun with Food,** 1989, McDonald's, set of four: Hamburger Guy, Fry Guy, Soft Drink Guy, Chicken McNugget Guys
EX n/a   **NM** $3   **MIP** $6

❏ **Funny Fry Friends,** 1990, McDonald's, two U3 toys: Lil' Chief, Little Darling
EX n/a   **NM** $3   **MIP** $5

(KP Photo)

❏ **Funny Fry Friends II,** 1990, McDonald's, set of eight: Too Tall, Tracker, Rollin' Rocker, Sweet Cuddles, Zzz's, Gadzooks, Matey, Hoops
EX n/a   **NM** $2   **MIP** $4

❏ **Funny Fry Guys,** 1989, McDonald's, set of four: Gadzooks, Matey, Zzz's, Tracker; test market Happy Meal, regionally distributed in California, Pennsylvania, Maryland
EX n/a   **NM** $15   **MIP** $25

❏ **Furby,** 1999, McDonald's, eight different designs done in ten different color combinations; there are a total of eighty diffferent Furby toys available. Each toy comes packaged in opage bags so the collector doesn't know which Furby they have
EX n/a   **NM** $5   **MIP** $10

Furby Keychains, 2000, McDonald's, set of twelve: Tiger, Elephant, Tree Frog, Raccoon, Giraffe, Monkey, Fox, Dinosaur, Snake, Lamb, Cow, Owl
EX n/a   **NM** $1   **MIP** $3

Garfield, 1988, McDonald's, set of four: Garfield on skateboard, Garfield on tricycle, Garfield in car, Garfield on scooter; test market Happy Meal, regionally distributed in Erie, Pennsylvania and Charlston, South Carolina
EX n/a   **NM** $20   **MIP** $50

Garfield II, 1989, McDonald's, set of two U3 toys: Garfield Skating, Garfield with Pooky
EX n/a   **NM** $2   **MIP** $5

(KP Photo)

Garfield II, 1989, McDonald's, set of four: Garfield on Scooter, Garfield on Skateboard, Garfield in Jeep, Garfield with Odie on Motorscooter
EX n/a   **NM** $3   **MIP** $6

Glo-Tron Spaceship, 1986, McDonald's, set of four vacuform spaceships: red, blue, green, gray; each spaceship came with set of glow-in-the-dark stickers
EX n/a   **NM** $25   **MIP** $50

Glow in the Dark Yo-Yo, 1978, McDonald's, no markings or dates
EX n/a   **NM** $2   **MIP** $5

Going Places/Hot Wheels, 1983, McDonald's, set of fourteen: Corvette Stingray, Jeep CJ-7, 3-Window '34, Baja Breaker, Chevy Citation, Firebird Funny Car, Land Lord, Malibu Grand Prix, 380-SEL, Minitrek, P-928, Sheriff Patrol, Split Window '63, Turismo
EX n/a   **NM** $12   **MIP** $15

Golf Ball, McDonald's, marked with McDonald's logo
EX n/a   **NM** $1   **MIP** $3

Good Morning, 1991, McDonald's, set of four: Ronald toothbrush, McDonaldland comb, Ronald clock, white plastic cup
EX n/a   **NM** $1   **MIP** $2

Good Sports, 1984, McDonald's, set of six puffy stickers: Hamburglar, Mayor McCheese, Ronald, Sam the Olympic Eagle, Birdie, Grimace
EX n/a   **NM** $8   **MIP** $12

Good Times Great Taste Record, McDonald's
EX n/a   **NM** $2   **MIP** $4

Gravedale High, 1991, McDonald's, set of four mechanical Halloween figures: Cleofatra, Frankentyke, Vinnie Stoker, Sid the Invisible Kid
EX n/a   **NM** $2   **MIP** $3

Gravedale High, 1991, McDonald's, one U3 toy: Cleofatra
EX n/a   **NM** $3   **MIP** $5

Grimace Bank, 1985, McDonald's, purple ceramic, 9" tall
EX n/a   **NM** $10   **MIP** $20

Grimace Pin, McDonald's, enamel
EX n/a   **NM** $6   **MIP** $12

Grimace Ring, 1970, McDonald's
EX n/a   **NM** $8   **MIP** $15

Grimace Sponge, McDonald's, Grimace, Grimace Car Wash
EX n/a   **NM** $2   **MIP** $4

Halloween, 1995, McDonald's, one U3 toy: pumpkin with pop-up Grimace
EX n/a   **NM** $2   **MIP** $3

Halloween, 1995, McDonald's, set of four figures: Hamburglar with witch costume, Grimace with ghost costume, Ronald with Frankenstein soctume, Birdie with pumpkin costume
EX n/a   **NM** $2   **MIP** $3

Halloween, 1995, McDonald's, set of four cassete tapes: Ronald Makes it Magic, Travel Tunes, Silly Sing-Along, Scary Sound Affects
EX n/a   **NM** $1   **MIP** $2

Halloween Buckets, 1986, McDonald's, set of three pumpkin-shaped pails: McGoblin, McPumpkin, McBoo
EX n/a   **NM** $2   **MIP** $4

Halloween Buckets, 1987, McDonald's, set of three pumpkin-shaped pails: McBoo, McGoblin, McPunk'n
EX n/a   **NM** $2   **MIP** $3

Halloween Buckets, 1989, McDonald's, set of three: Ghost, Witch, Pumpkin
EX n/a   **NM** $1   **MIP** $3

Halloween Buckets, 1990, McDonald's, set of threepumpkin-shaped pails: orange pumpkin, white glow-in-dark ghost, Green witch
EX n/a   **NM** $2   **MIP** $4

Halloween Buckets, 1992, McDonald's, set of three pumpkin-shaped pails with cut-out lids: Ghost, Witch, Pumpkin
EX n/a   **NM** $1   **MIP** $2

Halloween Buckets, 1994, McDonald's, set of three with cookie-cutter lids: Ghost, Whitch, Pumpkin
EX n/a   **NM** $1   **MIP** $3

Halloween Happy Meal, 1985, McDonald's, set of five pumpkin-shaped pails: McGoblin, McPunk'n, McPunky, McBoo, McBoo; regionally distributed in the northeast, marked with 1985 copyright
EX n/a   **NM** $12   **MIP** $15

Halloween McNugget Buddies, 1993, McDonald's, set of six: Pumpkin McNugget, McBoo McNugget, Monster McNugget, McNuggula McNugget, Witchie McNugget, Mummie McNugget
EX n/a   **NM** $1   **MIP** $3

Halloween McNugget Buddies, 1993, McDonald's, one U3 toy: McBoo McNugget
EX n/a   **NM** $3   **MIP** $5

Halloween McNugget Buddies, 1996, McDonald's, set of six: Dragon, Spider, Fairy Princess, Alien Monster, Rock Star, Ronald
EX n/a   **NM** $2   **MIP** $3

Halloween Pails, 1999, McDonald's, set of two: white bucket, orange bucket
EX n/a   **NM** $1   **MIP** $3

Halloween Pumpkin Ring, McDonald's, orange pumpkin face
EX n/a   **NM** $1   **MIP** $3

Hamburglar Doll, 1976, McDonald's, 7" stuffed doll by Remco; one of set of seven, sold on blister card
EX n/a   **NM** $12   **MIP** $25

Hamburglar Hockey, 1979, McDonald's
EX n/a   **NM** $2   **MIP** $4

Happy Holidays, 1984, McDonald's, set of two cards with stickers: Gingerbread House, Train
EX n/a   **NM** $15   **MIP** $20

Happy Meal From the Heart, 1990, McDonald's, set of two scratch-and-sniff Valentines: Grimace—Valentine Your Shake Me Up!; Ronald—Valentine You Warm My Heart!
EX n/a   **NM** $2   **MIP** $3

Happy Pail, 1983, McDonald's, set of three: pink pail with purple shovel, shows Ronald and Mayor McCheese under umbrella with purple shovel; white pail with yellow shovel, shows Ronald in intertube; white pail with slotted yellow shovel, shows airplane pulling banner; distributed in the New York state and New England area only
EX n/a   **NM** $25   **MIP** $35

Happy Pail III, 1986, McDonald's, set of five sand pails with either yellow shovel or red rake: Beach with blue lid, Parade with orange lid, Treasure Hunt with red lid, Vacation with green lid, Picnic with yellow lid
EX n/a   **NM** $5   **MIP** $10

Happy Pails, Olympics, 1984, McDonald's, set of four with shovels: Swimming, blue; Cycling, yellow; Athletics, beige; Olympic Games, white
EX n/a   **NM** $1   **MIP** $3

Happy Teeth, 1983, McDonald's, set of two: Reach toothbrush, tube of toothpaste
EX n/a   **NM** $15   **MIP** $20

Hat Happy Meal, 1990, McDonald's, set of four: Birdie green derby, Fry Guy orange safari hat, Grimace yellow construction hat, Ronald red fireman hat
EX n/a   **NM** $10   **MIP** $15

(KP Photo)

❏ **Hello Kitty/Transformers,** 2000, McDonald's, set of nine: Hello Kitty Crew Kid, Hello Kitty Charm Watch, Hello Kitty Sticker Art, Hello Kitty Pull String Toy, Helloe Kitty Wrap, Dear Daniel Stamp Mobile, Hello Kitty Kimono Clip, Hello Kitty Ballerina Scrunchy, Hello Kitty Apple Lock; joint promotion with Transformers
EX n/a   **NM** $1   **MIP** $4

❏ **Hercules,** 1997, McDonald's, set of ten: Wind Titan & Hermes, Rock Titan & Zeus, Hydra & Hercules, Lava Titan & Baby Pegasus, Cyclops & Pain, Fates & Panic, Pegasus & Megara, Ice Tita & Calliope, Nessus & Phil, Cerberus & Hades
EX n/a   **NM** $1   **MIP** $2

❏ **Hercules Plates,** 1997, McDonald's, set of six: Hercules, Megara, Pegasus, Zeus, Muses, Phil; offered by McDonald's for $1.99 with purchase and $2.99 without purchase
EX n/a   **NM** $3   **MIP** $5

❏ **Hercules Sports Toys,** 1998, McDonald's, set of eight: Zeus football, Hades stopwatch, Hercules sport bottle, Eye of Fates foot bag, Pain and Panic sound stick, Hercules medal, Phil megaphone, Whistling Discus
EX n/a   **NM** $1   **MIP** $2

❏ **High Flying Kite Happy Meal,** 1986, McDonald's, set of three kites: Hamburglar, Birdie, Ronald; regionally distributed in New England area
EX n/a   **NM** $200   **MIP** $225

❏ **Hobby Box,** 1985, McDonald's, set of four plastic boxes: yellow, green, red, blue; regionally distributed in the Southern United States
EX n/a   **NM** $10   **MIP** $15

❏ **Honey, I Shrunk the Kids Cups,** 1988, McDonald's, set of three white 20 oz. plastic cups: Giant Bee, On the Dog's Nose, Riding the Ant
EX n/a   **NM** $1   **MIP** $2

(Toy Shop File Photo)

❏ **Hook Figures,** 1991, McDonald's, set of four: Peter Pan, Mermaid, Rufio, Hook
EX n/a   **NM** $1   **MIP** $2

❏ **Hot Wheels Mini-Streex/Barbie,** 1992, McDonald's, one U3 toy: Orange Arrow car
EX n/a   **NM** $3   **MIP** $6

❏ **Hot Wheels Mini-Streex/Barbie,** 1992, McDonald's, set of eight: Flame-Out, Quick Flash, Turbo Flyer, Black Arrow, Hot Shock, Racer Tracer, Night Shadow, Blade Burner; joint promotion with Barbie
EX n/a   **NM** $2   **MIP** $4

❏ **Hot Wheels/Barbie,** 1988, McDonald's, set of twelve: Streat Beast, silver or red; P-911, white or black; Split Window '63, silver or black; '57 T-Bird, turquoise or white; 80's Firebird, blue or black; Sheriff Patrol; Fire Patrol
EX n/a   **NM** $10   **MIP** $15

❏ **Hot Wheels/Barbie,** 1990, McDonald's, set of four: Corvette, white; Ferrari, red; Hot Bird, silver; Camaro, turquoise; test market Happy Meal, regionally distributed in Savanah, Georgia; joint promotion with Barbie
EX n/a   **NM** $50   **MIP** $75

(Toy Shop File Photo)

❏ **Hot Wheels/Barbie,** 1991, McDonald's, set of eight cars: '55 Chevy, white or yellow; '63 Corvette, green or black; Camaro Z-28, purple or orange; '57 T-Bird, turquoise or red; joint promotion with Barbie
EX n/a   **NM** $2   **MIP** $3

❏ **Hot Wheels/Barbie,** 1991, McDonald's, one U3 tool set: yellow wrench and red hammer
EX n/a   **NM** $2   **MIP** $3

❏ **Hot Wheels/Barbie,** 1993, McDonald's, one U3 tool set: blue wrench and yellow hammer
EX n/a   **NM** $3   **MIP** $6

❏ **Hot Wheels/Barbie,** 1993, McDonald's, set of eight: Quaker State Racer #62, McDonald's Dragster, McDonald's Thunderbird #23, Hot Wheels Dragster, McDonald's Funny Car, Hot Wheels Funny Car, Hot Wheels Camaro #1, Duracell Racer #88; joint promotion with Barbie
EX n/a   **NM** $2   **MIP** $3

❏ **Hot Wheels/Barbie,** 1995, McDonald's, one U3 toy: Key Force car
EX n/a   **NM** $2   **MIP** $3

❏ **Hot Wheels/Barbie,** 1995, McDonald's, set of eight: Lightning Speed, Shock Force, Blue Bandit, Power Circuit, Twin Engine, Radar Racer, Back Burner, After Blast; joint promotion with Barbie
EX n/a   **NM** $2   **MIP** $3

❏ **Hot Wheels/Barbie,** 1996, McDonald's, set of five: Flame Series, Roarin' Road Series, Dark Rider Series, Hot Hubs Series, Krakel Car Series; joint promotion with Barbie
EX n/a   **NM** $1   **MIP** $2

❏ **Hot Wheels/Barbie,** 1996, McDonald's, one U3 toy: Hot Wheels squeek toy
EX n/a   **NM** $1   **MIP** $3

❏ **Hot Wheels/Barbie,** 1997, McDonald's, set of five: Tow Truck, Taxi, Police Car, Ambulance, Fire Truck; joint promotion with Barbie
EX n/a   **NM** $1   **MIP** $2

❏ **Hot Wheels/Barbie,** 1998, McDonald's, Ronald NASCAR, Mac Tonight NASCAR, Hot Wheels NASCAR, 50th Anniversary NASCAR; joint promo with Barbie
EX n/a   **NM** $1   **MIP** $2

❏ **Hot Wheels/Barbie,** 1999, McDonald's, set of eight: Double Cross, Maximizer, Lead Sled, Surf Boarder, Street Raptor, Black Track, Trail Runner, Innovator; joint promotion with Barbie
EX n/a   **NM** $1   **MIP** $4

❏ **Hot Wheels/Barbie,** 2000, McDonald's, set of sixteen: Lamborghini Diablo, Chevrolet Corvette, Lotus Elise, Key Clip Launcher, Jordan, Williamsf1 Car, Jaguar Racing, Hot Wheels Keychain, Motorcycle, BMX Bike, Sprint Car, Stop Watch, Helicopter, McDonald's Hot Rod, Airplane, Binocluars; joint promotion with Barbie
EX n/a   **NM** $1   **MIP** $3

❏ **Hot Wheels/Barbie,** 2000, McDonald's, set of eighteen: McDonald's NASCAR (current), McDonald's NASCAR (future), Hot Wheels NASCAR (current), Hot Wheels NASCAR (future), McLaren Grand Prix (current), McLaren Grand Prix (future), Del Worsham Funny Car (current), Del Worsham Funny Car (future), Champ Car (current), Champ Car (future)
EX n/a   **NM** $1   **MIP** $3

❏ **Hunchback of Notre Dame,** 1997, McDonald's, set of eight: Esmeralda Amulet, Scepter, Clopin Mask, Hugo Horn, Clopin Puppet Drum, Juggling Balls, Tambourine, Quasimodo Bird Catcher
EX n/a   **NM** $1   **MIP** $2

❏ **I Like Bikes,** 1990, McDonald's, set of four bike accessories: Ronald Basket, Grimace mirror, Birdie spinner, Fry Guy Horn
EX n/a   **NM** $10   **MIP** $20

❏ **Inspector Gadget,** 1999, McDonald's, set of eight: Navik 7 Sparker, Arm

Squirter, Watch Belt, Leg Tool, Leg Circuit Signaler, Leg Tool, Secret Communicator, Siren Hat
EX n/a   **NM** $2   **MIP** $5

(Toy Shop File Photo)

❑ **Jungle Book,** 1990, McDonald's, set of four wind-up figures: Baloo the bear, Shere Kahn the tiger, King Louie the orangutan, Kaa the snake
EX n/a   **NM** $1   **MIP** $3

❑ **Jungle Book,** 1990, McDonald's, set of two U3 toys: Junior, Mowgli
EX n/a   **NM** $3   **MIP** $6

❑ **Jungle Book,** 1997, McDonald's, set of six: Baloo, Junior, Bagheera, King Louie, Kaa, Mowgli
EX n/a   **NM** $1   **MIP** $2

❑ **Kissyfur,** 1987, McDonald's, set of four non-flocked figures: Floyd, Gus, Kissyfur, Jolene; the flocked and non-flocked figres make up one complete set
EX n/a   **NM** $5   **MIP** $10

❑ **Kissyfur,** 1987, McDonald's, set of four flocked figure: Beehonie, Duane, Toot, Lennie
EX n/a   **NM** $20   **MIP** $40

❑ **Lego,** 1999, McDonald's, set of eight: Ronald Helicopter, Sundae Water Vehicle, Birdie Airplane, McNugget Buddy Race Car, Grimmace Snow Plow, Yellow Fry Guy Seaplane, Hamburglar Airplane, Blue Fry Guy Speedplane
EX n/a   **NM** $1   **MIP** $3

❑ **Lego Building Set III,** 1986, McDonald's, four different sets: tanker boat, blue; airplane, green; roadster, red; helicopter, yellow
EX n/a   **NM** $3   **MIP** $5

❑ **Lego Building Sets,** 1983, McDonald's, set of four Duplo U3 toys: blue blocks, Bird, red blocks, green Duplo blocks
EX n/a   **NM** $5   **MIP** $10

❑ **Lego Building Sets,** 1983, McDonald's, set of four: ship, helicopter, truck, airplane
EX n/a   **NM** $25   **MIP** $40

❑ **Lego Building Sets II,** 1984, McDonald's, set of four: ship, truck, helicopter, airplane
EX n/a   **NM** $3   **MIP** $5

❑ **Lego Building Sets II,** 1984, McDonald's, set of two U3 toys: Duplo bird, Duplo boat with sailor
EX n/a   **NM** $4   **MIP** $8

❑ **Lego Building Sets III,** 1986, McDonald's, set of two U3 toys: Duplo bird, Duplo boat
EX n/a   **NM** $3   **MIP** $5

❑ **Lego Motion IV,** 1989, McDonald's, set of eight kits: Gyro Bird, Lightning Striker, Land Laser, Sea Eagle, Wind Whirler, Sea Skimmer, Turbo Force, Swamp Stinger
EX n/a   **NM** $3   **MIP** $6

❑ **Lego Motion IV,** 1989, McDonald's, set of two U3 Duplo toys: Giddy the Gator, Tuttle the Turtle
EX n/a   **NM** $2   **MIP** $5

❑ **Linkables,** 1993, McDonald's, set of four: Birdie on tricycle, Ronald in soapbox racer, Grimace in wagon, Hamburglar in airplane; regionally distributed in New England area
EX n/a   **NM** $2   **MIP** $4

❑ **Lion Circus,** 1979, McDonald's, set of four rubber figures: bear, elephant, hippo, lion
EX n/a   **NM** $2   **MIP** $3

❑ **Little Engineer,** 1987, McDonald's, set of five vacuform train engines: Birdie Sunshine Special, Fry Girl's Express, Fry Guy's Flyer, Grimace Streak, Ronald Railway
EX n/a   **NM** $4   **MIP** $8

❑ **Little Engineer,** 1987, McDonald's, set of four floating toys: Grimace Happy Taxi, green or yellow; Birdie, green or yellow
EX n/a   **NM** $2   **MIP** $6

❑ **Little Gardener,** 1989, McDonald's, one U3 toy: Birdie shovel
EX n/a   **NM** $5   **MIP** $10

❑ **Little Gardener,** 1989, McDonald's, set of four: Ronald Water Can, Birdie Shovel with Marigold seeds, Grimace Rake with radish seeds, Fry Guy Planter
EX n/a   **NM** $1   **MIP** $2

❑ **Little Golden Books,** 1982, McDonald's, set of five books: Country Mouse and City Mouse, Tom & Jerry, Pokey Little Puppy, Benji, Monster at the End of This Block
EX n/a   **NM** $2   **MIP** $4

❑ **Little Mermaid,** 1989, McDonald's, set of four: Flounder, Ursula, Prince Eric, Ariel with Sebastian
EX n/a   **NM** $1   **MIP** $2

❑ **Little Mermaid,** 1997, McDonald's, set of eight: Ursula, Flounder, Scuttle, Ariel, Max, Glut, Eric, Sebastian
EX n/a   **NM** $1   **MIP** $2

❑ **Little Mermaid, Gold,** 1997, McDonald's, set of eight: Ursula, Flounder, Scuttle, Ariel, Max, Glut, Eric, Sebastian; one out of every ten toys distributed with Happy Meal was a gold toy; compete sets of gold Little Mermaid premiums could be ordered for $12.99 plus

shipping with forms available at McDonald's
EX n/a   **NM** $5   **MIP** $10

❑ **Little Travelers with Lego Building Sets,** 1985, McDonald's, set of four: airplane, boat, helicopter, car; regionally distributed in Oklahoma; similar to Lego Building Set Happy Meal
EX n/a   **NM** $20   **MIP** $30

❑ **Littlest Pet Shop/Transformers Beast Wars,** 1996, McDonald's, one U3 toy: Hamster Wheel.
EX n/a   **NM** $1   **MIP** $2

❑ **Littlest Pet Shop/Transformers Beast Wars,** 1996, McDonald's, set of four: Swan, Unicorn, Dragon, Tiger; joint promotion with Transformers Beast Wars
EX n/a   **NM** $1   **MIP** $2

❑ **Looney Tunes Christmas Dolls-Canada,** McDonald's, set of four: Sylvester in nightgown and cap, Tasmanian Devil in Santa hat, Bugs in winter scarf , Tweetie dressed as Elf
EX n/a   **NM** $3   **MIP** $6

❑ **Looney Tunes Quack Up Cars,** 1993, McDonald's, one U3 toy: Bugs Bunny Swingin' Sedan in red or orange
EX n/a   **NM** $3   **MIP** $5

(KP Photo)

❑ **Looney Tunes Quack Up Cars,** 1993, McDonald's, set of five: Taz Tornado Tracker, Porky Ghost Catcher, Bugs Super Stretch Limo in red or orange, Daffy Splittin' Sportster
EX n/a   **NM** $3   **MIP** $5

❑ **Luggage Tags,** 1988, McDonald's, set of four: Birdie, Hamburglar, Grimace, Ronald
EX n/a   **NM** $3   **MIP** $5

❑ **Lunch Box,** 1987, McDonald's, set of four lunch boxes: Grimace at bat, Ronald playing football, Ronald on rainbow, Ronald flying spaceship
EX n/a   **NM** $5   **MIP** $10

(Toy Shop File Photo)

❑ **Mac Tonight,** 1988, McDonald's, set of six: Mac in Jeep, Mac in sports car, Mac on Surf Ski (with or without wheels), Mac on Motorcycle (red or black), Mac in Airplane (wearing blue or black sunglasses), Mac on Scooter; given out from 1988 to 1990, Surf Ski with wheels and Airplane with dark sunglasses were distributed in 1990
EX n/a   **NM** $8   **MIP** $15

☐ **Mac Tonight Pin,** 1988, McDonald's, Moonface and slogan enamel pin
EX n/a   NM $2   MIP $4

☐ **Mac Tonight Puppet,** 1988, McDonald's, Fingertronic foam puppet
EX n/a   NM $6   MIP $15

☐ **Mac Tonight Sunglasses,** 1988, McDonald's, adult size
EX n/a   NM $2   MIP $5

☐ **Magic School Bus,** 1994, McDonald's, set of four: Collector Card Kit, Space Tracer, Geo Fossil Finder, Undersea Adventure Game with yellow tab
EX n/a   NM $1   MIP $2

☐ **Magic School Bus,** 1994, McDonald's, one U3 toy: Undersea Adventure Game without yellow tab
EX n/a   NM $1   MIP $2

☐ **Magic Show,** 1985, McDonald's, set of five tricks: String Trick, Disappearing Hamburger Patch, Magic Tablet, Magic Picture—Ronald, Magic Picture—Grimace
EX n/a   NM $3   MIP $6

☐ **Makin' Movies,** 1994, McDonald's, one U3 toy: Sound Effects Machine
EX n/a   NM $1   MIP $2

☐ **Makin' Movies,** 1994, McDonald's, set of four: Sound Effects Machine, Movie Camera, Clapboard with chalk, Megaphone
EX n/a   NM $1   MIP $2

☐ **Marvel Super Heroes,** 1996, McDonald's, set of eight: Spider-Man, Storm, Wolverine, Jubilee, Color Change Invisible Woman, Thing, Hulk, Human Torch
EX n/a   NM $1   MIP $2

☐ **Marvel Super Heroes,** 1996, McDonald's, one U3 Toy: Spider-Man Ball
EX n/a   NM $1   MIP $2

☐ **Matchbox Mini-Flexies,** 1979, McDonald's, set of eight rubber cars: Cosmobile, Hairy Hustler, Planet Scout, Hi-Tailer, Datsun, Beach Hopper, Baja Buggy
EX n/a   NM $2   MIP $4

☐ **McBoo Bags,** 1991, McDonald's, set of six: three McBoo bags: Witch, Ghost, Monster; three pails: McBoo, McGoblin, witch
EX n/a   NM $3   MIP $5

☐ **McBunny Easter Pails,** 1989, McDonald's, set of three: Pinky, Fluffy, Whiskers
EX n/a   NM $3   MIP $6

☐ **McCharacters on Bikes,** 1991, McDonald's, set of four: Ronald on red tricycle, Grimace on blue tricycle, Hamburglar on yellow tricycle, Birdie on pink tricycle
EX n/a   NM $3   MIP $5

(KP Photo)

☐ **McDino Changeables,** 1991, McDonald's, set of eight: Happy Meal-o-don, Quarter Pounder Chees-o-saur, Big Mac-o-saurus Rex, McNugget-o-saurus, Hotcakes-o-dactyl, Large Fry-o-saur, Tri-shak-atops, McDino cone
EX n/a   NM $2   MIP $3

☐ **McDino Changeables,** 1991, McDonald's, set of three U3 toys: Bronto Cheeseburger, Small Fry Ceratops with yellow arches, Small Fry Ceratops with red arches
EX n/a   NM $2   MIP $3

☐ **McDonald Sun Glasses,** 1989, McDonald's, set of four: Grimace, Birdie, Ronald, Hamburglar; over-the-counter premium, sold for 99 cents, each
EX n/a   NM $5   MIP $7

☐ **McDonaldland Band,** 1987, McDonald's, set of eight music toys: Grimace saxophone, Fry Guy trumpet, Fry Guy boat whistle, Ronald harmonica, Ronald train whistle, Ronald pan pipes, Birdie kazoo, Hamburglar whistle
EX n/a   NM $1   MIP $3

☐ **McDonaldland Carnival,** 1990, McDonald's, set of four: Birdie on swing, Grimace in turn-around, Hamburglar on ferris wheel, Ronald on carousel
EX n/a   NM $3   MIP $5

☐ **McDonaldland Carnival,** 1990, McDonald's, one U3 floaty toy: Grimace
EX n/a   NM $10   MIP $15

☐ **McDonaldland Dough,** 1990, McDonald's, set of eight, each included can of modeling clay and mold: red with Ronald star mold, yellow with Ronald square mold, green with Fry Girl octagon mold, blue with Fry Guy hexagon mold, purple with Grimace square mold, orange with Grimace triangle mold, pink with Birdie heart mold, white with Birdie circle mold; sold in the Southern United States only
EX n/a   NM $3   MIP $5

☐ **McDonaldland Express,** 1982, McDonald's, set of four train car containers: Ronald engine, caboose, freight car, coach car
EX n/a   NM $25   MIP $50

☐ **McDonaldland Junction,** 1983, McDonald's, set of four snap-together train cars: red Ronald Engine, yellow Birdie Parlor car, green Hamburger Flat Car, purple Grimace caboose
EX n/a   NM $5   MIP $10

☐ **McDonaldland Junction,** 1983, McDonald's, set of four regionally distributed cars: blue Ronald Engine, pink Birdie Parlor Car, white Hamburger Flat Car, orange Grimace Caboose
EX n/a   NM $20   MIP $30

☐ **McDonaldland Play-Doh,** 1986, McDonald's, set of eight colors: white, orange, yellow, purple, pink, red, green, blue
EX n/a   NM $2   MIP $4

☐ **McDonaldland TV Lunch Box,** 1987, McDonald's, set of four lunch boxes: blue, green, yellow, red; each box came with a sheet of stickers; regionally distributed in New England area
EX n/a   NM $5   MIP $10

☐ **McDonald's All-Star Race Team (MAXX) '91,** 1991, McDonald's, complete set of cards
EX n/a   NM $4   MIP $5

☐ **McDonald's All-Star Race Team (MAXX) '92,** 1992, McDonald's, complete set of 36 cards
EX n/a   NM $4   MIP $5

☐ **McDonald's Playing Cards,** McDonald's, two decks to a set
EX n/a   NM $2   MIP $5

☐ **McDonald's Spinner Top-Holland,** McDonald's
EX n/a   NM $2   MIP $4

☐ **McDrive Thru Crew,** 1990, McDonald's, set of four: fries in potato roadster, shake in milk carton, McNugget in egg roadster, hamburger in ketchup bottle; regionally distributed in Ohio and Illinois
EX n/a   NM $20   MIP $40

(KP Photo)

☐ **McNugget Buddies,** 1988, McDonald's, set of ten: Cowpoke, First-Class, Sarge, Drummer, Corny, Sparky, Boomerang, Volley, Snorkel, Rocker
EX n/a   NM $4   MIP $6

☐ **McNugget Buddies,** 1989, McDonald's, set of two U3 toy: Slugger, Daisy
EX n/a   NM $1   MIP $2

☐ **McNugget Buddies,** 1989, McDonald's, set of ten rubber figures and accessories: Sparky, Volley, Corny, Drummer, Cowpoke, Sarge, Snorkel, First Class, Rocker, Boomerang
EX n/a   NM $1   MIP $2

Metrozoo Happy Meal, 1987, McDonald's, set of four: Elephant, Chimp, Flamingo, Tiger; distributed only in South Florida area
EX n/a   **NM** $25   **MIP** $250

Michael Jordan Fitness, 1992, McDonald's, set of eight toys: soccer ball, squeeze bottle, stopwatch, basketball, football, baseball, jump rope, flying disc
EX n/a   **NM** $2   **MIP** $4

Michael Jordan Fitness Fun Challenge, 1992, McDonald's, set of eight: baseball, basketball, flying disc, football, jump rope, soccer ball, squeeze bottle, stop watch; all premiums are marked with Michael Jordan logo
EX n/a   **NM** $2   **MIP** $4

Mickey and Friends Epcot Center '94 Adventure, 1994, McDonald's, set of eight: Donald in Mexico, Daisy in Germany, Mickey in U.S.A., Minnie in Japan, Chip in China, Pluto in France, Dale in Moroco, Goofy in Norway
EX n/a   **NM** $2   **MIP** $3

Mickey and Friends Epcot Center '94 Adventure, 1994, McDonald's, one U3 toy: Mickey in U.S.A.
EX n/a   **NM** $2   **MIP** $3

Mickey's Birthdayland, 1989, McDonald's, set of four U3 vehicles: Mickey's Convertible, Goofy's Car, Minnie's Convertible, Donald's Jeep
EX n/a   **NM** $5   **MIP** $10

Mickey's Birthdayland, 1989, McDonald's, set of five characters in vehicles: Minnie's Convertible, Donald's Train, Goofy's Jalopy, Mickey's Roadster, Pluto's Rumbler
EX n/a   **NM** $1   **MIP** $3

Micro Machines/Sky Dancers, 1997, McDonald's, set of four: Evac Copter, Polar Explorer, Ocean Flyer, Deep Sea Hunter; joint promotion with Sky Dancers
EX n/a   **NM** $1   **MIP** $2

Mighty Duck Pucks, 1997, McDonald's, set of four: Wildwing, Nosedive, Mallory, Duke L'Orange
EX n/a   **NM** $1   **MIP** $2

Mighty Mini 4x4s, 1991, McDonald's, set of four: Cargo Climber, Dune Buster, L'il Classic, Pocket Pickup
EX n/a   **NM** $1   **MIP** $2

Mighty Mini 4x4s, 1991, McDonald's, one U3 toy: Pocket Pickup
EX n/a   **NM** $3   **MIP** $5

Mighty Morphin Power Rangers, 1995, McDonald's, one U3 toy: Power Flute
EX n/a   **NM** $1   **MIP** $2

Mighty Morphin Power Rangers, 1995, McDonald's, set of four: Power Com, Powermorpher Buckle, Alien Detector, Power Siren
EX n/a   **NM** $1   **MIP** $2

Minnesota Twins Baseball Glove, 1984, McDonald's, Twins logo on side, Coca-Cola inside glove, McDonald's satin logo on back, given to the first 100 kids at 1984 Twins game
EX n/a   **NM** $40   **MIP** $75

Mix 'em Up Monsters, 1989, McDonald's, set of four: Thuggle, Blibble, Corkle, Gropple; regionally distributed in St. Louis, Missouri and Northern California
EX n/a   **NM** $2   **MIP** $5

Moster Crazy Bones, 2000, McDonald's, set of twelve: Funny Bone, Howler, Sweetie, Webs, Cool Dude, Haggy, Eggy, Punky, Boo, Menace, Goodie Goodie, Tut, Chef, Drac, Raskall, Wow, Music, Scraps, Fangs, Speedy, Doc, Top Hat, Luckey, Smiley
EX n/a   **NM** $1   **MIP** $3

Moveables, 1988, McDonald's, set of six vinyl bendies: Birdie, Captain Crook, Fry Girl, Hamburglar, Professor, Ronald; regionally distributed in St Louis, Missouri area
EX n/a   **NM** $4   **MIP** $12

M-Squad, 1993, McDonald's, one U3 toy: Spytracker watch
EX n/a   **NM** $1   **MIP** $2

M-Squad, 1993, McDonald's, set of four: Spystamper, Spytracker, Spynocular, Spycoder
EX n/a   **NM** $2   **MIP** $4

Mulan, 1998, McDonald's, set of eight: Mulan, Kahn, Little Brother, Shan-Yu, Mushi, Shang-Li, Cri-Kee, Chien-Po, Ling, Yao
EX n/a   **NM** $1   **MIP** $2

Mulan on Video, 1999, McDonald's, set of eight: Ling, Mulan, Kahn, Mushu, Shan-Yu, Chien-Po, Shang, Yao
EX n/a   **NM** $1   **MIP** $3

Muppet Babies holiday promotion, 1988, McDonald's, set of four stuffed toys: Miss Piggy, Kermit, Fozzie; over-the-counter premium sold with food purchase for for $1.99
EX n/a   **NM** $2   **MIP** $5

Muppet Babies I, 1986, McDonald's, set of four: Kermit with skateboard, Miss Piggy with car and flat hair ribbon, Gonzo with tricycle and no shoes, Fozzie with horse; test market Happy Meal, regionally distributed in Savannah, Georgia
EX n/a   **NM** $25   **MIP** $50

Muppet Babies II, 1987, McDonald's, set of two U3 toys: Kermit on skates, Miss Piggy on Skates
EX n/a   **NM** $3   **MIP** $5

Muppet Babies II, 1987, McDonald's, set of four: Kermit with skateboard, Miss Piggy with pink car, Gonzo with tricycle and shoes, Fozzie with horse
EX n/a   **NM** $2   **MIP** $4

(KP Photo)

Muppet Babies III, 1991, McDonald's, set of four: Miss Piggy on tricycle, Gonzo in airplane, Fozzie in wagon, Kermit on soapbox racer
EX n/a   **NM** $2   **MIP** $4

Muppet Kids, 1989, McDonald's, set of four: Kermit with red tricycle, Miss Piggy with pink tricycle, Gonzo with yellow tricycle, Fozzie with green tricycle
EX n/a   **NM** $15   **MIP** $25

Muppet Treasure Island, 1996, McDonald's, set of four: Miss Piggy, Kermit, Gonzo, Fozzy Bear
EX n/a   **NM** $2   **MIP** $3

Muppet Treasure Island, 1996, McDonald's, one U3 toy: Bath Book "The Muppet Treasure Island"
EX n/a   **NM** $1   **MIP** $2

Muppet Workshop, 1995, McDonald's, one U3 toy: What-Not
EX n/a   **NM** $1   **MIP** $2

Muppet Workshop, 1995, McDonald's, set of four: Bird, Dog, What-Not, Monster
EX n/a   **NM** $1   **MIP** $2

Music Happy Meal, 1985, McDonald's, set of four 33-1/3 RPM records: If You're Happy/Little Bunny Foo Foo; Do the Hokey Pokey/Eensy Weensy Spider; Boom, Boom, Ain't it Great to Be Crazy; She'll be Comin' 'Round the Mountain, Head, Shoulders, Knees and Toes
EX n/a   **NM** $3   **MIP** $5

My Little Pony (joint promotion w/Transformers), 1985, McDonald's, set of six: Minty, Snuzzle, Blossom, Cotton Candy, Blue Belle, Butterscotch; regionally distributed in St. Louis, Missouri area
EX n/a   **NM** $20   **MIP** $80

My Little Pony/Transformers, 1998, McDonald's, set of three: Ivy, Sundance, Light Heart; split promo with Transformers
EX n/a   **NM** $1   **MIP** $2

Mystery Happy Meal, 1983, McDonald's, set of five: Detective Kit, Crystal Ball, Ronald Magni-Finder, Birdie Mangi-Finder, Fry Guys Magni-Finder
EX n/a   **NM** $20   **MIP** $35

Mystery of the Lost Arches, 1992, McDonald's, set of four: mini-cassette, phone, telescope, camera
EX n/a   **NM** $1   **MIP** $2

Mystery of the Lost Arches, 1992, McDonald's, set of five: Phone/Periscope, Flashlight/Telescope in red and blue or red and yellow, Magic Lens Camera, Microcaste/Magnifier
EX n/a   **NM** $1   **MIP** $2

Mystic Knights of Tir na Nog, 1999, McDonald's, set of eight: Rohan, Queen Maeve, Angus. Tore, Deirdre, mider, Ivar, Lugad; a bonus toy can be built from Queen Maeve, Tore, Mider and Lugad
EX n/a   **NM** $1   **MIP** $3

❏ **NASCAR Hot Wheels/Barbie,** 1998, McDonald's, set of four: Ronald Happy Meal NASCAR, Mac Tonight, Hot Wheels, 50th Anniversary NASCAR; split promo with Barbie;
EX n/a **NM** $1 **MIP** $3

❏ **Nature's Helpers,** 1991, McDonald's, set of five: Double Digger with cucumber seeds, Bird Feeder, Watering Can, Terrarium with coleus seeds, Rake with marigold seeds
EX n/a **NM** $1 **MIP** $2

❏ **Nature's Watch,** 1992, McDonald's, one U3 toy: double shovel-rake
EX n/a **NM** $1 **MIP** $2

❏ **Nature's Watch,** 1992, McDonald's, set of four: Bird Feeder, Double Shovel-Rake, Greenhouse, Sprinkler
EX n/a **NM** $1 **MIP** $2

❏ **New Archies,** 1988, McDonald's, set of six figures in bumper cars: Moose, Reggie, Archie, Veronica, Betty, Jughead; regionally distributed in St. Louis, Missouri area
EX n/a **NM** $5 **MIP** $15

❏ **New Food Changeables,** 1989, McDonald's, set of eight: Krypto Cup, Fry Bot, Turbo Cone, Macro Mac, Gallacta Burger, Robo Cakes, C2 Cheeseburger, Fry Force
EX n/a **NM** $2 **MIP** $4

❏ **Nickelodeon,** 1993, McDonald's, one U3 toy: Blimp squirter
EX n/a **NM** $1 **MIP** $2

❏ **Nickelodeon,** 1993, McDonald's, set of four: Blimp Game, Loud-Mouth Mike, Gotcha Gusher, Applause Paws
EX n/a **NM** $1 **MIP** $2

❏ **Nickelodeon's Tangle Toy,** 1997, McDonald's, set of eight Twist-a-zoids
EX n/a **NM** $1 **MIP** $2

❏ **Norman Rockwell Brass Ornament,** 1983, McDonald's, 50th Annivesary Norman Rockwell design, gift packaged with McDonald and Coca-Cola logos
EX n/a **NM** $3 **MIP** $7

❏ **Norman Rockwell Ornament,** 1978, McDonald's, clear acrylic, "Christmas Trio," gift boxed
EX n/a **NM** $3 **MIP** $7

❏ **Old McDonald's Farm,** 1986, McDonald's, set of six figures: farmer, wife, rooster, pig, sheep, cow; regionally distributed in Missouri and Tennessee
EX n/a **NM** $10 **MIP** $15

❏ **Old West,** 1981, McDonald's, set of six rubber figures: cowboy, frontiersman, lady, Indian, Indian woman, sheriff
EX n/a **NM** $7 **MIP** $14

❏ **Oliver & Company,** 1988, McDonald's, set of four finger puppets: Oliver, Georgette, Francis, Dodger
EX n/a **NM** $3 **MIP** $5

❏ **Olympic Beach Ball,** 1984, McDonald's, set of three: Grimace in kayak, green; Ronald holding flag and beachball, red; Birdie in sailboat, blue
EX n/a **NM** $15 **MIP** $20

❏ **Olympic Sports,** 1984, McDonald's, set of five Guess'n'Glow puzzles: Guess Which Guy Comes in Under the Wire (Grimace and Hamburglar), Guess Who Makes the Biggest Splash (Ronald, Birdie and Captain); Guess Who Finished Smiles Ahead (Hamburglar and Birdie); Who Do You Know That Can Help them Row? (Ronald and Fry Guy); Guess Who Stole the Winning Goal (Grimace); this promotion replaced the original Olympics Sports Happy Meal
EX n/a **NM** $15 **MIP** $30

❏ **Olympic Sports,** 1984, McDonald's, set of five zip-action toys: Ronald on bicycle, roller skating Birdie, Grimace, Birdie and Captain rowing, running Grimace; prototypes only. The Olympic sports Happy Meal was cancelled after the toys failed safety tests. It was replaced by Guess'n'Glow puzzles
EX n/a **NM** $30 **MIP** $60

❏ **Olympic Sports II,** 1988, McDonald's, set of six clip-on buttons: Birdie/gymnastics, Hamburglar/track and field, CosMc/basketball, Fry Girl/diving, Ronald/bicyclling, Grimace/soccer
EX n/a **NM** $5 **MIP** $8

❏ **On the Go I,** 1985, McDonald's, set of five: On the Go Bead Game, Stop & Go Bead Game, Ronald Magic Slate, Hamburglar Magic Slate, On the Go Transfers
EX n/a **NM** $10 **MIP** $15

❏ **On the Go Lunch Box II,** 1988, McDonald's, set of four: red lunch box with bulliten board and stickers, green lunch box with bulletin board and stickers, yellow lunch bag with Ronald, white lunch bag with Grimace
EX n/a **NM** $2 **MIP** $4

❏ **Out of Fun Happy Meal,** 1993, McDonald's, set of four: Balloon Ball, Ronald Bubble Shoe Wand, Sunglasses, Sand Pail
EX n/a **NM** $1 **MIP** $2

❏ **Paint with Water,** 1978, McDonald's, paintless coloring board with self contained frame and easel
EX n/a **NM** $5 **MIP** $10

(Toy Shop File Photo)

❏ **Peanuts,** 1990, McDonald's, set of four: Snoopy's Hay Hauler, Charlie Brown's Seed Bag 'N Tiller, Lucy's Apple Cart, Linus' Milk Mover
EX n/a **NM** $2 **MIP** $4

❏ **Peanuts,** 1990, McDonald's, set of two U3 toys: Charlie Brown's egg basket or Snoopy's potato sack
EX n/a **NM** $2 **MIP** $4

❏ **Pencil Puppets,** 1978, McDonald's, six different pencil toppers in shapes of McDonaldland characters
EX n/a **NM** $2 **MIP** $4

❏ **Peter Pan,** 1998, McDonald's, set of seven: Peter Pan Glider, Tic Tock Croc, Captain Hook Spyglass, Tinker Bell Lantern Clip, Smee Light, Wendy & Michael Magnifier, Activity Tool
EX n/a **NM** $1 **MIP** $2

❏ **Peter Rabbit,** 1988, McDonald's, set of four books: The Tale of Benjamin Bunny, The Tale of Peter Rabbit, The Tale of the Flopsy Bunnies, The Tale of Squirrel Nutkin; regionally distributed in Pennsylvania and New York
EX n/a **NM** $10 **MIP** $25

❏ **Picture Perfect,** 1985, McDonald's, set of four Crayola products: coloring (thin) marker, red or blue; drawing (thick) marker, orange or green; box of three fluorescent Cayons; box of six Crayons
EX n/a **NM** $5 **MIP** $10

❏ **Piggsburg Pigs,** 1991, McDonald's, set of four: Rembrandt, Huff & Puff, Piggy & Crackers, Portly & Pighead; regionally distributed in Florida, Colorado and Ohio
EX n/a **NM** $3 **MIP** $5

❏ **Play-Doh,** 1983, McDonald's, set of four containers of Play-Doh: blue, red, yellow, white; regionally distributed in the New England area; containers did not have any McDonald's markings
EX n/a **NM** $15 **MIP** $20

❏ **Play-Doh II,** 1985, McDonald's, set of two containers of Play-Doh: pink and green
EX n/a **NM** $15 **MIP** $20

❏ **Play-Doh III,** 1986, McDonald's, set of eight containers of Play-Doh: pink, blue, purple, green, red, yellow, white, orange
EX n/a **NM** $5 **MIP** $8

❏ **Playmobile,** 1982, McDonald's, set of five toys and accesories: farmer, sheriff, Indian, umbrella girl, horse and saddle
EX n/a **NM** $10 **MIP** $20

❏ **Polly Pocket/Attack Pack,** 1995, McDonald's, one U3 toy: watch
EX n/a **NM** $2 **MIP** $3

❏ **Polly Pocket/Attack Pack,** 1995, McDonald's, set of four: Ring, Locket, Watch, Bracelet; joint promotion with Attack Pack
EX n/a **NM** $1 **MIP** $2

❏ **Popoids,** 1984, McDonald's, set of six made up of two to three bellows and one joint piece: blue and dark blue bellows with one ball joint; blue and white bellows with cube joint; blue and dark blue bellows with one cube joint; red and yellow bellows with pentahedron joint; red and yellow bellows with wheel joint; blue, dark blue and yellow bellows without joint; regionally distributed in the St. Louis, Missouri area
EX n/a **NM** $40 **MIP** $50

Potato Head Kids I, 1987, McDonald's, set of twelve: Lumpy, Potato Dumpling, Big Chip, Smarty Pants, Dimples, Spike, Potato Puff, Tulip, Spud, Lolly, Slugger, Slick; regionally distributed in Texas, Oklahoma and New Mexico

EX n/a   NM $5   MIP $25

Potato Head Kids II, 1992, McDonald's, set of eight: Dimples, Spike, Potato Dumpling, Slugger, Slick, Tulip, Potato Puff, Spud

EX n/a   NM $3   MIP $6

(KP Photo)

Power Rangers, 2000, McDonald's, set of eleven: Red Power Ranger, Yellow Power Ranger, Pink Power Ranger, Green Power Ranger, Blue Power Ranger, Silver Power Ranger, Yellow Rail Rescue, Blue Rail Rescue, Pink Rail Rescue, Green Rail Rescue

EX n/a   NM $1   MIP $3

Punkin' Makins, 1977, McDonald's, character cutouts to decorate pumpkins: Ronald, Goblin, Grimace

EX n/a   NM $7   MIP $15

Raggedy Ann and Andy, 1989, McDonald's, one U3 toy: Camel with Wrinkled Knees

EX n/a   NM $8   MIP $12

Raggedy Ann and Andy, 1989, McDonald's, set of four: Raggedy Andy with slide, Raggedy Ann with swing, Grouchy Bear merry-go-round, Camel with Wrinkled Knees with teeter totter

EX n/a   NM $5   MIP $10

Read Along with Ronald, 1989, McDonald's, set of four books and tapes: Grimace Goes to School, The Day Birdie the Early Bird Learned to Fly, The Mystery of the Missing French Fries, Dinosaur in McDonaldland

EX n/a   NM $5   MIP $10

Real Ghostbusters, 1987, McDonald's, set of five school tools: pencil case, notepad, ruler, pencil with pencil topper, pencil sharpener

EX n/a   NM $3   MIP $5

Real Ghostbusters II, 1992, McDonald's, one U3 toy: Slimer squirter

EX n/a   NM $3   MIP $5

Real Ghostbusters II, 1992, McDonald's, set of four: Ecto Siren, Egon Spinner, Slimer horn, water bottle; regionally distributed in Kansas City, Kansas

EX n/a   NM $3   MIP $5

Recess, 1998, McDonald's, set of seven: TJ, Spinelli, Vince, Mikey, Gretchen, Gus, School Teacher

EX n/a   NM $1   MIP $2

Records, 1985, McDonald's, set of four 45-RPM records in sleeves with different songs and colored labels

EX n/a   NM $3   MIP $6

Rescuers Down Under, 1990, McDonald's, One U3 toy: Bernard

EX n/a   NM $3   MIP $6

(KP Photo)

Rescuers Down Under, 1990, McDonald's, set of four slide-viewing movie camera toys: Jake, Wilbur, Bernard and Bianca, Cody

EX n/a   NM $2   MIP $4

Rescuers Down Under Christmas Ornament, 1990, McDonald's, set of two: Miss Bianca, Bernard

EX n/a   NM $3   MIP $6

Rings, 1977, McDonald's, set of five rings with character heads: Big Mac, Captain Crook, Grimace, Hamburglar, Ronald

EX n/a   NM $5   MIP $10

Robo-Chi Pets, 2001, McDonald's, set of eight, each in four different color schemes: Laydown Poo-Chi, Batting Meow-Chi, Dancing Poo-Chi, Lightup Meow-Chi, Predicting Poo-Chi, Singing Chirpy-Chi, Barking Poo-Chi, Flapping Chirpy-Chi

EX n/a   NM $1   MIP $3

Roger Rabbit Scarf-Japan, 1988, McDonald's, McDonald's logo, Japanese writing on scarf

EX n/a   NM $10   MIP $20

Ronald and Pals Haunted Halloween, 1998, McDonald's, set of six: Birdie, Gramace, Iam Hungry, Hamburglar, Ronald, McNugget Buddy

EX n/a   NM $1   MIP $2

Ronald McDonald Celebrates Happy Birthday, 1994, McDonald's, one U3 toy: Ronald McDonald

EX n/a   NM $3   MIP $5

Ronald McDonald Celebrates Happy Birthday, 1994, McDonald's, set of sixteen: Ronald McDonald, Barbie, Hot Wheels, E.T., Sonic the Hedgehog, Berenstain Bears, Tonka, Cabbage Patch Kids, 101 Dalmatians, Little Mermaid, Muppet Babies with white tie, Muppet Babies with or blue tie, Peanuts, The Little Mermaid, Tiny Toons, Happy Meal Guys

EX n/a   NM $3   MIP $5

Ronald McDonald Cookie Cutter, 1987, McDonald's, Ronald with balloons, green or orange

EX n/a   NM $1   MIP $3

Ronald McDonald Doll, McDonald's, 7" doll by Remco

EX n/a   NM $18   MIP $25

Ronald McDonald Doll, McDonald's, 14" vinyl head with a soft body by Dakin

EX n/a   NM $15   MIP $35

Ronald McDonald Maze, 1979, McDonald's, lift up mystery game

EX n/a   NM $4   MIP $10

Ronald McDonald Pin, McDonald's, enamel, Ronald in Christmas wreath

EX n/a   NM $6   MIP $12

Ronald McDonald Plastic Flyers, McDonald's, Ronald with legs and arms extended, red or yellow

EX n/a   NM $1   MIP $3

Ronald McDonald Shoe & Sock Game-Japan, McDonald's, plastic with ball and string, with Japanese writing

EX n/a   NM $5   MIP $10

Ronald McDonald Tote Bag-Japan, McDonald's, writing in Japanese

EX n/a   NM $5   MIP $10

Runaway Robots, 1987, McDonald's, set of six: Skull, Jab, Flame, Beak, bolt, Coil; regionally distributed in Nebraske, Maine, Massachusettes, Tenessee and Alabama

EX n/a   NM $15   MIP $20

Safari Adventure, 1980, McDonald's, six different rubber animals: alligator, monkey, gorilla, tiger, hippo, rhinoceros

EX n/a   NM $2   MIP $4

Sailors, 1988, McDonald's, set of four floating toys: Hamburglar Sailboat, Ronald Airboat, Grimace Submarine, Fry Kids Ferry

EX n/a   NM $5   MIP $10

Sailors, 1988, McDonald's, set of two U3 floating toys: Grimace in speedboat, Fry Guy on intertube

EX n/a   NM $4   MIP $8

Santa Claus: The Movie, 1985, McDonald's, set of four books: The Elves at the Top of the World, Sleighful of Surprises, Workshop of Surprises

EX n/a   NM $1   MIP $3

School Days, 1984, McDonald's, set of twelve: Ronald pencil, Grimace pencil, Hamburglar Pencil, Ronald eraser, Grimace eraser, Hamburglar eraser, Captain Crook eraser, Birdie eraser, Grimace pencil sharpener, Ronald pencil sharpener, Ronald and Birdie ruler, Ronald and Birdie pencil case

EX n/a   NM $5   MIP $10

Sea World of Ohio, 1988, McDonald's, set of three figures: Dolly Dolphin, Penny Penguin, Shamu the whale; regionally distributed in Clevland, Ohio area

EX n/a   NM $20   MIP $40

❏ **Sea World of Texas,** 1988, McDonald's, set of four stuffed toys: dolphin, penguin, walrus, whale; regionally distributed in San Antonio, Texas area
EX n/a　　**NM** $20　　**MIP** $30

❏ **Sea World of Texas II,** 1989, McDonald's, set of five: sea otter stuffed toy, dolphin stuffed toy, whale stuffed toy, penguin sunglasses, whale sunglasses
EX n/a　　**NM** $25　　**MIP** $50

❏ **Serving Trays,** McDonald's, set of six white plastic wedge-shaped trays: Ronald, Big Mac, Mayor McCheese, Hamburglar, Grimace, Captain Crook
EX n/a　　**NM** $3　　**MIP** $7

❏ **Ship Shape I,** 1983, McDonald's, set of four vacuform boat containers with stickers: Tubby Tugger, Splash Dasher, Rub-a-Dub Sub, Riverboat
EX n/a　　**NM** $10　　**MIP** $15

❏ **Ship Shape II,** 1985, McDonald's, set of two U3 floating toys: Grimace in Tub, Fry Guys on Duck
EX n/a　　**NM** $5　　**MIP** $8

❏ **Ship Shape II,** 1985, McDonald's, set of four vacuform boat containers with stickers: Tubby Tugger, Splash Dasher, Rub-a-Dub Sub, Riverboat; similar to 1983 Ship Shape Happy Meal but with redesigned stickers
EX n/a　　**NM** $10　　**MIP** $20

❏ **Sindy Doll,** 1970, McDonald's, dressed in older McDonald's uniform
EX n/a　　**NM** $4　　**MIP** $8

❏ **Sky Dancers/Micro Machines,** 1997, McDonald's, set of four dancing dolls: Rosemerry, Swan Shimmer, Princess Pegasus, Flutter Fly; split promo with Micro Machines
EX n/a　　**NM** $1　　**MIP** $2

❏ **Sky-Busters,** 1982, McDonald's, set of six rubber airplanes: Skyhawk AAF, Phantom, Mirage F1, United DC-10, MIG-21, Tornado
EX n/a　　**NM** $3　　**MIP** $5

❏ **Sleeping Beauty,** 1997, McDonald's, set of six: Sleeping Beauty, Maleficent, Prince Philip, Flora, Dragon, Raven
EX n/a　　**NM** $1　　**MIP** $2

❏ **Smart Duck,** 1979, McDonald's, set of six rubber figures: duck, cat, donkey, chipmunk, two rabbits
EX n/a　　**NM** $2　　**MIP** $3

❏ **Snow White and the Seven Dwarfs,** 1993, McDonald's, set of nine: Snow White with wishing well, Prince on horse with green base, Prince on horse without base, Queen/Witch, Bashful, Dopey and Sneezy, Doc, Happy and Grumpy, Sleepy
EX n/a　　**NM** $3　　**MIP** $6

❏ **Snow White and the Seven Dwarfs,** 1993, McDonald's, one U3 toy: Dopey and Sleepy
EX n/a　　**NM** $2　　**MIP** $3

❏ **Sonic 3 The Hedgehog,** 1994, McDonald's, set of four: Sonic the Hedgehog, Miles "Tails" Power, Knuckles & Dr. Ivo Robotnik
EX n/a　　**NM** $2　　**MIP** $4

❏ **Sonic 3 The Hedgehog,** 1994, McDonald's, one U3 toy: Sonic Ball
EX n/a　　**NM** $3　　**MIP** $6

❏ **Space Aliens,** 1979, McDonald's, set of eight rubber monsters: Lizard Man, Vampire Bat, Gill Face, Tree Monster, Winged Fish, Cyclops, Veined Brain, Insectman
EX n/a　　**NM** $2　　**MIP** $3

❏ **Space Jam,** 1996, McDonald's, set of eight interlocking pieces: Lola Bunny, Bugs Bunny, Taz, Marvin the Martian, Daffy Duck, Monstar, Sylvester & Tweety, Nerdlucks
EX n/a　　**NM** $2　　**MIP** $4

❏ **Space Jam Plush,** 1996, McDonald's, set of six: Lola Bunny, Bugs Bunny, Taz, Daffy Duck, Monstar, Nerdlucks
EX n/a　　**NM** $3　　**MIP** $5

❏ **Space Raiders,** 1979, McDonald's, set of eight rubber aliens: Drak, Dard, flying saucer, Rocket Kryoo-5, Horta, Zama, Rocket Ceti-3, Rocket Altair-2
EX n/a　　**NM** $2　　**MIP** $3

(KP Photo)

❏ **Space Rescue,** 1995, McDonald's, set of four: Astro Viewer, Tele-Communicator, Space Slate, Lunar Grabber
EX n/a　　**NM** $1　　**MIP** $2

❏ **Space Rescue,** 1995, McDonald's, one U3 toy: Astro-Viewer
EX n/a　　**NM** $1　　**MIP** $2

❏ **Spider-Man,** 1995, McDonald's, one U3 toy: The Amazing Spider-man
EX n/a　　**NM** $3　　**MIP** $5

❏ **Spider-Man,** 1995, McDonald's, set of eight: The Amazing Spider-Man, Dr. Octopus with moving tentacles, Mary Jane Watson with clip-on costumes, Spider-Sense Peter Parker, Scorpion Stingstriker, Spider-Man Webrunner, Venom Transport, Hobgoblin Landglider
EX n/a　　**NM** $3　　**MIP** $5

❏ **Spinner Baseball Game,** 1983, McDonald's, green plastic with four characters
EX n/a　　**NM** $2　　**MIP** $4

❏ **Spinner Bicycle Game,** 1984, McDonald's, pink or green game with two bicyclists
EX n/a　　**NM** $2　　**MIP** $5

❏ **Sports Ball,** 1991, McDonald's, set of gour: white baseball, brown football, orange basketball, red and yellow soccer ball; regionally distributed in Kansas City and Indiana
EX n/a　　**NM** $2　　**MIP** $5

❏ **Sports Balls,** 1988, McDonald's, set of four: basketball, baseball, football and tennis ball; test market Happy Meal, regionally distributed in Springfield, Missouri
EX n/a　　**NM** $20　　**MIP** $40

❏ **Sports Balls,** 1988, McDonald's, one U3 toy: hard plastic baseball
EX n/a　　**NM** $30　　**MIP** $40

❏ **Sports Balls,** 1990, McDonald's, set of four: baseball, football, basketball, soccer
EX n/a　　**NM** $2　　**MIP** $4

❏ **Star Trek,** 1979, McDonald's, set of four glitter iron-ons: Kirk, Spock, McCoy, Ilia; packaged in pairs
EX n/a　　**NM** $10　　**MIP** $20

❏ **Star Trek,** 1979, McDonald's, rings: Kirk, Spock, Starfleet insignia, Enterprise
EX n/a　　**NM** $15　　**MIP** $20

❏ **Star Trek,** 1979, McDonald's, Starfleet game
EX n/a　　**NM** $10　　**MIP** $15

❏ **Star Trek,** 1979, McDonald's, set of five video viewers, each with different story
EX n/a　　**NM** $15　　**MIP** $30

❏ **Star Trek,** 1979, McDonald's, navigation bracelet with decals
EX n/a　　**NM** $10　　**MIP** $25

❏ **Sticker Club,** 1985, McDonald's, set of five different sticker sheets: shiny, scratch and sniff, action stickers, puffy stickers, paper
EX n/a　　**NM** $5　　**MIP** $10

❏ **Stomper Mini 4x4 I,** 1985, McDonald's, set of six: Chevy S-10 Pick-Up, blue; Chevy S-10 Pick-up, white; Chevy Van; Dodge Rampage, white; Dodge Rampage, blue; Jeep Renegade
EX n/a　　**NM** $5　　**MIP** $10

❏ **Stomper Mini 4x4 I,** 1985, McDonald's, set of six push toys: Jeep Renegade, Dodge Rampage, white; Dodge Rampage, blue; Chevy S-10 Pick-up, blue; Chevy S-10 Pick-up, yellow; Chevy Van
EX n/a　　**NM** $5　　**MIP** $10

❏ **Stomper Mini 4x4 II,** 1986, McDonald's, set of sixteen: Toyota Tercel, blue or gray; AMC Eagle, black or orange; Chevy S-10 pickup, black or yellow; Chevy van, red or yellow; Chevy Blazer, yellow or red; Ford Ranger, orange or red; Jeep Renegade, maroon or orange; Dodge Rampage, blue or white
EX n/a　　**NM** $5　　**MIP** $10

RESTAURANT PREMIUMS

Story of Texas, 1986, McDonald's, set of eight books: Austin series—The Beginning, Independence, The Frontier, The 20th Century; Houston series—The Beginning, Independence, The Frontier, The 20th Century; regionally distributed in Texas
EX n/a　　**NM** $75　　**MIP** $100

Storybook Muppet Babies, 1988, McDonald's, set of three books: Baby Piggy, the Living Doll; The Legend of Gimmee Gulch; Just Kermit and Me!
EX n/a　　**NM** $2　　**MIP** $5

Super Looney Tunes, 1991, McDonald's, set of four figures with costumes: Super Bugs, Bat Duck, Taz Flash, Wonder Pig
EX n/a　　**NM** $2　　**MIP** $4

Super Looney Tunes, 1991, McDonald's, one U3 toy: Bat Duck in rocking boat
EX n/a　　**NM** $2　　**MIP** $4

Super Mario Brothers, 1990, McDonald's, set of four action figures: Mario, Luigi, Little Goomba, Koopa
EX n/a　　**NM** $2　　**MIP** $4

Super Mario Brothers, 1990, McDonald's, one U3 toy: Super Mario
EX n/a　　**NM** $2　　**MIP** $4

Super Sticker Squares, 1987, McDonald's, nine scenes and over 100 reusable stickers
EX n/a　　**NM** $1　　**MIP** $3

Super Summer, 1987, McDonald's, set of three: sailboat, watering can, beach-ball; test market Happy Meal, distributed in Fresno, California
EX n/a　　**NM** $20　　**MIP** $30

Super Summer II, 1988, McDonald's, set of six: sand castle pail with shovel, sand pail with rake, fish sand mold, inflatable sailboat, beach ball, watering can
EX n/a　　**NM** $2　　**MIP** $4

(KP Photo)

Tale Spin, 1990, McDonald's, set of four characters in airplanes: Wildcat's Flying Machine, Baloo's Seaplane, Molly's Biplane, Kit's Racing Plane
EX n/a　　**NM** $2　　**MIP** $4

Tale Spin, 1990, McDonald's, set of U3 toys: Baloo's seaplane, Wildcat's jet
EX n/a　　**NM** $2　　**MIP** $4

Tamagotchi Key Chains, 1998, McDonald's, set of nine: yellow, purple, green, red, blue with yellow figure inside, white with red figure inside, red/orange flip action, blue flashlight, purple #9 (only available at McDonald's in Wal-Mart stores)
EX n/a　　**NM** $2　　**MIP** $4

Tarzan, 1999, McDonald's, set of eight: Tarzan with Surf Branch, Terk, Jane, Tantor, Porter, Kala, Clayton, Sabor
EX n/a　　**NM** $1　　**MIP** $3

Tarzan on Video, 2000, McDonald's, set of eight: Tarzan, Sabor, Tantor, Young Tarzan, Terk, Kerchak, Kala & Baby Tarzan
EX n/a　　**NM** $1　　**MIP** $3

Teenie Beanie Babies, 1997, McDonald's, set of ten plush toys: Patti the Platypus, Pinky the Flamingo, Chops the Lamb, Chocolate the Moose, Goldie the Goldfish, Speed the Turtle, Seamore the Seal, Snort the Bull, Quack the Duck, Lizz the Lizard
EX n/a　　**NM** $10　　**MIP** $20

(KP Photo)

Teenie Beanie Babies, 1998, McDonald's, set of twelve plush toys: Doby the Doberman, Bongo the Monkey, Twigs the Giraffe, Inch the Worm, Pinchers the Lobster, Happy the Hippo, Mel the Koala, Scoop the Pelican, Bones the Dog, Zip the Cat, Waddle the Penguin, Peanut the Elephant
EX n/a　　**NM** $4　　**MIP** $8

Teenie Beanie Babies, 1999, McDonald's, set of twelve: Freckles the Leopard, Smoochy the Frog, Rocket the Blue Jay, Strut the Rooster, Claude the Crab, 'Nook the Husky, Antsy the Anteater, Spunk the Cocker Spaniel, Iggy the Iguana, Nuts the Squirrel, Stretchy the Ostrich, Chip the Cat
EX n/a　　**NM** $2　　**MIP** $4

(KP Photo)

Teenie Beanie Babies, 2000, McDonald's, set of twelve: Dotty the Fish, Lip the Fish, Slither the Snake, Flip the Cat, Tusk the Walrus, Blizz the White Tiger, Schweetheart the Orangutan, Spike the Rhino, Spinner the Spider, Bumble the Bee, Flitter the Butterfly, Lucky the Ladybug, Coral the Fish, Sting the Ray, Goochy the Jellyfish, Neon the Jellyfish
EX n/a　　**NM** $1　　**MIP** $3

Teenie Beanie Babies International Bears, 1999, McDonald's, set of four: Britania, Glory, Erin, Maple; over-the-counter promotion available for $1.99 with food purchase
EX n/a　　**NM** $1　　**MIP** $2

Teletubbies, 2000, McDonald's, set of four: Po, Laa-Laa, Tinky Winky, Dipsy
EX n/a　　**NM** $1　　**MIP** $3

The Busy World of Richard Scarry, 1995, McDonald's, one U3 toy: Lowly Worm, rubber
EX n/a　　**NM** $1　　**MIP** $2

The Busy World of Richard Scarry, 1995, McDonald's, set of four: Lowly Worm and Post Office, Huckle Cat and School, Mr. Fumble and Fire Station, Bananas Gorilla and Grocery Store
EX n/a　　**NM** $1　　**MIP** $2

The Legend of Mulan, 1998, McDonald's, set of ten figures: Mulan, Khan, Mushu, Shanyu, Shang, Chein Po, Ying, Yao, Little Brother, Cri-Kee
EX n/a　　**NM** $1　　**MIP** $2

The Lion King II Simba's Pride, 1998, McDonald's, set of eight: Kovu, Zazu, Timon, Simba, Kiara, Zira, Rafiki, Pumbaa
EX n/a　　**NM** $1　　**MIP** $2

Tic Toc Mac Game, 1981, McDonald's, yellow base, Grimace is X, Ronald is O
EX n/a　　**NM** $2　　**MIP** $5

Tigger Movie, The, 2000, McDonald's, set of six: Tigger, Roo, Pooh, Eeyore, Piglet, Owl
EX n/a　　**NM** $1　　**MIP** $3

Tinosaurs, 1986, McDonald's, set of eight figures: Link the Elf, Baby Jad, Merry Bones, Dinah, Time Traveller Fern, Tiny, Grumpy Spell, Kave Kolt Kobby; regionally distributed in St. Louis, Missouri
EX n/a　　**NM** $5　　**MIP** $10

Tiny Toon Adventures Flip Cars, 1991, McDonald's, set of two U3 toys: Gogo Dodo in bathtub, Plucky Duck in red boat
EX n/a　　**NM** $3　　**MIP** $5

(KP Photo)

Tiny Toon Adventures Flip Cars, 1991, McDonald's, set of four cars, each with two characters: Montana Max/Gobo Dodo, Babs/Plucky Duck, Hampton/Devil, Elmyra/Buster Bunny
EX n/a　　**NM** $1　　**MIP** $2

Tiny Toon Adventures Wacky Rollers, 1992, McDonald's, set of eight: Buster Bunny, Babs Bunny, Elmyra, Dizzy Devil, Gogo Dodo, Montana Max, Plucky Duck, Sweetie
EX n/a　　**NM** $1　　**MIP** $3

❏ **Tiny Toon Adventures Wacky Rollers**

❏ **Tiny Toons Adventures Wacky Rollers,** 1992, McDonald's, one U3 toy: Sweetie
EX n/a   NM $2   MIP $4

❏ **Tom & Jerry Band,** 1990, McDonald's, one U3 toy: Droopy
EX n/a   NM $5   MIP $8

❏ **Tom & Jerry Band,** 1990, McDonald's, set of four characters with musical instruments: Tom at keyboard, Jerry on drums, Spike on bass, Droopy at the mike
EX n/a   NM $4   MIP $8

❏ **Tonka/Cabbage Patch Kids,** 1992, McDonald's, set of five: Fire Truck, Loader, Cement Mixer, Dump Truck, Backhoe; joint promotion with Cabbage Patch Kids
EX n/a   NM $1   MIP $2

❏ **Tonka/Cabbage Patch Kids,** 1992, McDonald's, one U3 toy: Dump Truck
EX n/a   NM $1   MIP $2

❏ **Tonka/Cabbage Patch Kids,** 1992, McDonald's, set of four: Crane, Loader, Grader, Bulldozer; joint promotion with Cabbage Patch Kids
EX n/a   NM $1   MIP $3

❏ **Tonka/Cabbage Patch Kids,** 1994, McDonald's, one U3 toy: Dump Truck
EX n/a   NM $2   MIP $3

❏ **Toothbrush Happy Meal,** 1985, McDonald's, set of three Ronald toothbrushes: red, yellow, blue
EX n/a   NM $20   MIP $40

❏ **Tops,** 1978, McDonald's, set of three: red, blue and green
EX n/a   NM $3   MIP $7

❏ **Totally Toy Holiday,** 1993, McDonald's, set of three U3 toys: Keyforce Car, Magic Nursery Boy, Magic Nursery Boy
EX n/a   NM $2   MIP $3

❏ **Totally Toy Holiday,** 1993, McDonald's, Holiday Barbie snow dome; recalled
EX n/a   NM $25   MIP $50

❏ **Totally Toy Holiday,** 1993, McDonald's, set of eleven: Lil' Miss Candistripes, Magic Nursery Boy, Magic Nursery Girl, Polly Pocket, Key Force Truck, Key Force Car, Mighty Max, Tattoo Machines, Attack Pack Vehicles, Sally Secrets, Caucasian, Sally Sercets, African-American
EX n/a   NM $2   MIP $3

❏ **Totally Toy Holiday,** 1995, McDonald's, set of two U3 toys: Magic Nursery Boy, Magic Nursery Girl, Key Force Car
EX n/a   NM $3   MIP $5

❏ **Totally Toy Holiday,** 1995, McDonald's, set of eight: Great Adventures Knight figurine with green dragon, Holiday Barbie, Hot Wheels Vehicle with ramp (came with red or green vehicle), "Once Upon a Dream" Princess figurine, Polly Pocket Playset, Mighty Max Play-

set, Cabbage Patch Playset, South Pole Explorer Vehicle
EX n/a   NM $1   MIP $2

❏ **Toy Story 2,** 1999, McDonald's, set of twenty: Woody, Mr. And Mrs. Potatoe Head, Robot, Slinky Dog, Little Green Alien, Bo Peep, Hamm, Jessy, Rex, Lenny, Zurg, Prospector Pete, Marionette Woody, Barrel of Monekys, Buzz, Bullseye, Remote-controlled Car, Green Army Man, Tour Guide Barbie
EX n/a   NM $2   MIP $5

❏ **Toy Story 2 Candy Dispensers,** 1999, McDonald's, set of stx: Woody w/Nerds, Jesse w/Sprees, Rex w/Smarties, Mr./Mrs. Potato Head w/Tart n Tinys, Hamm, Buzz w/Nerds
EX n/a   NM $2   MIP $5

❏ **Transformers Beast Wars/Littlest Pet Shop,** 1996, McDonald's, set of four Transformer Beast Wars: Manta Ray, Beetle, Panther, Rhino; joint promotion with Littlest Pet Shop
EX n/a   NM $1   MIP $2

❏ **Transformers Beast Wars/Littlest Pet Shop,** 1996, McDonald's, one U3 toy: Lion's Head Transformer
EX n/a   NM $1   MIP $2

(KP Photo)

❏ **Transformers/Hello Kitty,** 2000, McDonald's, set of nine: Cheetor, Optimus Primal, Megatron, Jetstorm, Rattrap, Blackarachnia, Thrust, Nightsream, Tankor; Joint promotion with Hello Kitty
EX n/a   NM $1   MIP $3

❏ **Transformers/My Little Pony,** 1985, McDonald's, set of twenty-six: Brawn—green/blue, blue/yellow, red/green, red/blue, red/yellow, green/yellow; Cliffjumper—red/black, burgundy/black, yellow/black, black/green, violet/blue, teal/black, black/blue; Bumblebee—black/red, burgundy/black, teal/black, violet/blue, black/green, yellow/black; Gears—green/yellow, green/blue, red/yellow, red/green, blue/yellow, red/blue; joint promotion with My Little Pony; regionally distributed in St. Louis, Missouri area
EX n/a   NM $50   MIP $140

❏ **Transformers/My Little Pony,** 1998, McDonald's, set of three: Scorponok, Dinobot, Blackarachnia; split promo with My Little Pony
EX n/a   NM $1   MIP $2

❏ **Turbo Macs I,** 1988, McDonald's, set of four: Birdie in pink car, Hamburglar in yellow car, Grimace in white car, Ronald in red car; test market Happy Meal
EX n/a   NM $5   MIP $10

❏ **Turbo Macs I,** 1988, McDonald's, one U3 toy: Ronald in red car with yellow wheels
EX n/a   NM $5   MIP $10

❏ **Turbo Macs II,** 1990, McDonald's, set of four: Ronald in red car, Grimace in white car, Birdie in pink car, Hamburglar in yellow car
EX n/a   NM $3   MIP $6

❏ **Turbo Macs II,** 1990, McDonald's, one U3 toy: Ronald in red car with yellow wheels
EX n/a   NM $5   MIP $10

❏ **Under Sea,** 1980, McDonald's, set of six cartons with undersea art: Alligator, Dolphin, Hammerhead Shark, Sea Turtle, Seal, Walrus
EX n/a   NM $2   MIP $3

❏ **VR Troopers,** 1996, McDonald's, one U3 toy: Sphere
EX n/a   NM $1   MIP $2

❏ **VR Troopers,** 1996, McDonald's, set of four: Visor, Wrist Spinner, Virtualizer, Kaleidoscope
EX n/a   NM $1   MIP $2

❏ **Walt Disney Home Video Masterpiece Collection,** 1996, McDonald's, one U3 toy: Dumbo water squirter
EX n/a   NM $1   MIP $5

❏ **Walt Disney Home Video Masterpiece Collection,** 1996, McDonald's, set of eight: Cinderella, Robin Hood, Pocahontas, Return to Jafar, Snow White, Sword and the Stone, Alice in Wonderland, Aristocats
EX n/a   NM $1   MIP $2

❏ **Walt Disney Home Video Masterpiece Collection,** 1997, McDonald's, set of eight video cases with figure: Bambi with Bambi figure, The Lion King with Simba figure, Pete's Dragon with Elliot figure, Oliver and Company with Dodger figure, Toy Story with Woody figure, Sleeping Beauty with Sleeping Beauty figure, The Three Caballeros with Donald Duck figure, Winnie the Pooh with Tigger figure
EX n/a   NM $2   MIP $3

❏ **Water Friends,** 1992, McDonald's, one U3 toy: soft rubber Giant Panda
EX n/a   NM $3   MIP $5

❏ **Water Games,** 1992, McDonald's, one U3 toy: Grimace with squirting camera
EX n/a   NM $15   MIP $20

(Toy Shop File Photo)

❏ **Water Games,** 1992, McDonald's, set of four: Birdie sorts eggs, Grimace juggles shakes, Ronald catches fries, Hamburglar stacks burgers
EX n/a   NM $3   MIP $5

❏ **What is It?,** 1979, McDonald's, set of six rubber animals: Skunk, Squirrel, Bear, Owl, Baboon, Snake
EX n/a   NM $1   MIP $3

❏ **Wild Friends,** 1992, McDonald's, set of four animals on mini-comic books: Crocodile, Gorilla, Elephant, Panda; regionally distributed in Indiana and southern California
EX n/a   NM $3   MIP $5

❏ **Winnie the Pooh Sing a Song with Pooh Bear,** 1999, McDonald's, set of eight: Eeyore, Owl, Winnie the Pooh, Rabbit, Roo, Piglet, Gopher, Tigger
EX n/a   NM $5   MIP $10

❏ **Winter World,** 1983, McDonald's, set of five flat vinyl tree ornaments: Ronald, Hamburglar, Grimace, Mayor McCheese, Birdie
EX n/a   NM $5   MIP $10

❏ **World of Hot Wheels/Friends of Barbie,** 1994, McDonald's, set of eight: Turbine 4-2, Flame Rider, 2-Cool, Bold Eagle, Black Cat, Gas Hog, X21J Cruiser, Street Shocker; joint promotion with Barbie
EX n/a   NM $2   MIP $3

❏ **World of Hot Wheels/Friends of Barbie,** 1994, McDonald's, one U3 toy: Fast Forward
EX n/a   NM $2   MIP $3

❏ **Wrist Wallets,** 1977, McDonald's, set of four watch-type bands with coin-holding dial: Ronald, Captain Crook, Big Mac, Hamburglar
EX n/a   NM $5   MIP $10

❏ **Yo Yogi,** 1992, McDonald's, set of four: Yogi Bear on wave jumper, Cindy Bear on scooter, Huckleberry Hound in race car, Boo Boo Bear on skate board
EX n/a   NM $3   MIP $5

❏ **Young Astronauts,** 1986, McDonald's, set of four snap-together models: Apollo Command Module, Argo Land Shuttle, Space Shuttle, Cirrus Vtol
EX n/a   NM $5   MIP $20

❏ **Young Astronauts,** 1992, McDonald's, set of four vehicles: Space Shuttle & Space Walker, Command Module, Lunar Rover, Satalite Dish & Space Walker
EX n/a   NM $2   MIP $4

❏ **Young Astronauts,** 1992, McDonald's, one U3 toy: Ronald in lunar rover
EX n/a   NM n/a   MIP n/a

❏ **Yo-Yo,** 1979, McDonald's, half red, half yellow
EX n/a   NM $2   MIP $5

❏ **Zoo Face I,** 1987, McDonald's, set of four masks: Alligator, Monkey, Tiger, Toucan; test market Happy Meal, distributed in Evansville, Indiana
EX n/a   NM $20   MIP $30

❏ **Zoo Face II,** 1988, McDonald's, set of four rubber noses and makeup kits: Alligator, Monkey, Tiger, Toucan
EX n/a   NM $5   MIP $10

PIZZA HUT

❏ **Air Garfield,** 1993, Pizza Hut, figure of Garfield attached to either a parachute or suspended in a spaceball
EX n/a   NM $2   MIP $4

❏ **Air Garfield Cups,** 1993, Pizza Hut, set of two: each cup featured Garfield and Odie
EX n/a   NM $1   MIP $4

❏ **Beauty & the Beast Puppets,** 1992, Pizza Hut, set of four: Belle, Beast, Chip, Cogsworth
EX n/a   NM $4   MIP $8

❏ **Color Your World,** 1993, Pizza Hut, set includes erasable calendar board with four Crayons, poster with four Crayons; each meal came with plastic cup
EX n/a   NM $4   MIP $6

❏ **Dinosaurs!,** 1993, Pizza Hut, set of four 16 oz. cups with 3-D lids and sticker books: Brachiosaurus, Tyrannosaurus, Stegosaurus, Brachiosaurus
EX n/a   NM $4   MIP $8

(KP Photo)

❏ **Eureeka's Castle Puppets,** 1991, Pizza Hut, set of three: Batly, Eureeka, Magellan
EX n/a   NM $3   MIP $6

❏ **Fievel Goes West cups,** 1991, Pizza Hut, set of three: Fievel with cowboy hat, Cat R. Waul with red top hat, Wylie Burp with tan hat
EX n/a   NM $4   MIP $6

(KP Photo)

❏ **Land Before Time Puppets,** 1988, Pizza Hut, set of six: Spike, Sharptooth, Pteri, Little Foot, Cera, Ducky
EX n/a   NM $4   MIP $8

❏ **Marsupilami Houba Douba,** 1994, Pizza Hut, set of three: yo-yo, jump rope, glow ball
EX n/a   NM $4   MIP $6

❏ **Universal Monster Cups,** Pizza Hut, set of three: holographic cards with 3-D cups
EX n/a   NM $10   MIP $20

❏ **Young Indiana Jones Chronicles,** 1993, Pizza Hut
EX n/a   NM $4   MIP $6

ROY ROGERS

❏ **Critters,** 1990, Roy Rogers, set of eight: blue eyes-yellow; blue eyes-orange; blue eyes-purple; blue eyes-red; yellow eyes-orange; yellow eyes-yellow; pink eyes-orange; pink eyes-purple
EX n/a   NM $1   MIP $2

❏ **Cup Critters,** 1994, Roy Rogers, Elephant/Alligator/Frog/Bear/Pig/Beaver/Lion/Duck/Turtle
EX n/a   NM $2   MIP $5

❏ **Gator Tales,** 1989, Roy Rogers, set of four: AV Gator, Investi-Gator, Flora Gator, Skater Gator
EX n/a   NM $4   MIP $6

❏ **Hide 'n Keep Dinos,** 1989, Roy Rogers, set of three: Brontosaurus, Triceratops, Stegosaurus
EX n/a   NM $3   MIP $5

❏ **Ickky Stickky Bugs,** 1989, Roy Rogers, set of sixteen: Centipede, Grasshopper, Worm, Spider
EX n/a   NM $2   MIP $3

❏ **Skateboard Kids Figures,** 1989, Roy Rogers, set of four: Boy with red skateboard; Boy with orange skateboard, Boy with purple, Girl with blue skateboard
EX n/a   NM $3   MIP $5

❏ **Snorks,** 1988, Roy Rogers, set of thirty version of the four characters: Allstar, Case, Dimmy, Tooter
EX n/a   NM $3   MIP $5

❏ **Star Searchers,** 1990, Roy Rogers, set of four: Saucer, Robot, Vehicle, Shuttle
EX n/a   NM $2   MIP $5

❏ **Tatoo Heads,** 1995, Roy Rogers
EX n/a   NM $2   MIP $5

SONIC DRIVE-IN

❏ **Bag-A-Wag,** 1990, Sonic Drive-In, set of four: man with bag of burgers in hamburger car, man with bag of burgers walking, man with bag of burgers rollerblading, man with hamburger
EX n/a   NM $3   MIP $6

❏ **Brown Bag Bowlers,** 1994, Sonic Drive-In, set of four brown bag figures holding ball: yellow ball, red ball, blue ball, orange ball
EX n/a   NM $3   MIP $5

❏ **Brown Bag Buddies,** 1993, Sonic Drive-In, set of four brown bag figures with sports equipment: sled, skiis, surfboard, intertube
EX n/a   NM $2   MIP $5

(KP Photo)

- ❑ **Brown Bag Juniors,** 1989, Sonic Drive-In, set of four brown bag figures: Too Cool, Bookworm, Sure Shot, Marbles
  EX n/a   **NM** $4   **MIP** $6

- ❑ **Bump and Go,** 1993, Sonic Drive-In, series of 2" metal cars
  EX n/a   **NM** $2   **MIP** $5

- ❑ **Custom Cruisers,** 1993, Sonic Drive-In, set of four: Mercury, Chevy Convertible, Chevy Nomad, Cadillac Convertible
  EX n/a   **NM** $3   **MIP** $5

- ❑ **Dino Makers,** 1994, Sonic Drive-In
  EX n/a   **NM** $2   **MIP** $5

- ❑ **Sonic Super Kids,** 1989, Sonic Drive-In, set of four with comic book: Steve, Rick, Corky, Brin
  EX n/a   **NM** $5   **MIP** $8

- ❑ **Sonic Turbo Racers,** 1993, Sonic Drive-In, set of four: pink, yellow, orange, green
  EX n/a   **NM** $2   **MIP** $5

- ❑ **Wacky Sackers,** 1994, Sonic Drive-In, set of six: pink with bug-eyes, green with sunglasses, yelow, pink with three eyes, blue
  EX n/a   **NM** $3   **MIP** $5

TACO BELL

- ❑ **Chihuahua Plush,** 1999, Taco Bell, set of four talking dogs:standing, says "Yo Quiero Toca Bell"; sitting with Free Tacos sign, says "Here Lizard, Lizard"; sitting wearing beret, says: "Viva Gorditas"; lying down wearing Santa hat, says: "Feliz Navidad Amigos"
  EX n/a   **NM** $3   **MIP** $7

- ❑ **Happy Talk Sprites**, Taco Bell, set of two: Spark, yellow; Twink, white
  EX n/a   **NM** $2   **MIP** $4

- ❑ **Hugga Bunch Plush Dolls**, Taco Bell
  EX n/a   **NM** $2   **MIP** $4

TASTEE FREEZE

- ❑ **Roy Campanella Figure**, Tastee Freeze
  EX n/a   **NM** $20   **MIP** $35

WENDY'S

- ❑ **ALF Tales,** 1990, Wendy's, set of six: Sleeping Alf, Alf Hood, Little Red Riding Alf, Alf of Arabia, Three Little Pigs, Sir Gordon of Melmac
  EX n/a   **NM** $2   **MIP** $4

- ❑ **Alien Mix-Ups,** 1990, Wendy's, set of six: Crimsonoid, Bluezoid, Limetoid, Spotasoid, Yellowboid, Purpapoid
  EX n/a   **NM** $1   **MIP** $2

(KP Photo)

- ❑ **All Dogs Go To Heaven,** 1989, Wendy's, set of six: Anne Marie, Carface, Charlie, Flo, Itchy, King Gator
  EX n/a   **NM** $2   **MIP** $4

- ❑ **Definitely Dinosaurs,** 1988, Wendy's, set of four: blue Apatosaurus, gray T-Rex, yellow Anatosaurus, green Triceratops
  EX n/a   **NM** $3   **MIP** $6

- ❑ **Definitely Dinosaurs,** 1989, Wendy's, set of five: green Ankylosaurus, blue Parasaurolophus, green Ceratosaurus, yellow Stegosaurus, pink Apatosaurus
  EX n/a   **NM** $2   **MIP** $4

(KP Photo)

- ❑ **Fast Food Racers,** 1990, Wendy's, set of five: hamburger, fries, shake, salad, kid's meal
  EX n/a   **NM** $2   **MIP** $4

- ❑ **Felix the Cat,** 1995, Wendy's
  EX n/a   **NM** $2   **MIP** $5

- ❑ **Fun Flyers,** Wendy's, 3-1/2" wide in red, yellow or blue
  EX n/a   **NM** $1   **MIP** $3

- ❑ **Furskins Plush Dolls,** 1988, Wendy's, set of three: Boone in plaid shirt and red pants, Farrell in plaid shirt and blue jeans, Hattie in pink and white dress; all 7" tall
  EX n/a   **NM** $4   **MIP** $8

- ❑ **Glass Hangers**, Wendy's, set of four: yellow turtle, yellow frog, yellow penguin and purple gator
  EX n/a   **NM** $3   **MIP** $5

- ❑ **Glo Friends,** 1988, Wendy's, set of twelve: Book Bug, Bop Bug, Butterfly, Clutter Bug, Cricket, Doodle Bug, Globug, Granny Bug, Skunk Bug, Snail Bug, Snug Bug
  EX n/a   **NM** $2   **MIP** $4

- ❑ **Good Stuff Gang,** 1985, Wendy's, set of six: Cool Stuff, Cat, Hot Stuff, Over-stuffed, Bear, Penguin
  EX n/a   **NM** $2   **MIP** $4

- ❑ **Jetsons Figures,** 1989, Wendy's, set of six figures in spaceships: George, Judy, Jane, Elroy, Astro, Spacely
  EX n/a   **NM** $2   **MIP** $4

(KP Photo)

- ❑ **Jetsons: The Movie Space Gliders,** 1990, Wendy's, set of six PVC figures on wheeled bases: Astro, Elroy, Judy, Fergie, Grunchee, George
  EX n/a   **NM** $2   **MIP** $4

- ❑ **Micro Machines Super Sky Carriers,** 1990, Wendy's, set of six kits: connect to form Super Sky Carrier
  EX n/a   **NM** $2   **MIP** $4

- ❑ **Mighty Mouse,** 1989, Wendy's, set of six: Bat Bat, Cow, Mighty Mouse, Pearl Pureheart, Petey, Scrappy
  EX n/a   **NM** $3   **MIP** $5

- ❑ **Play-Doh Fingles,** 1989, Wendy's, set of three finger puppet molding kits: green dough with black mold, blue dough with green mold, yellow dough with white mold
  EX n/a   **NM** $3   **MIP** $6

- ❑ **Potato Head Kids,** 1987, Wendy's, set of six: Captain Kid, Daisy, Nurse, Policeman, Slugger, Sparky
  EX n/a   **NM** $4   **MIP** $8

(KP Photo)

- ❑ **Speed Writers,** 1991, Wendy's, set of six car-shaped pens: black, blue, fuchsia, green, orange, red
  EX n/a   **NM** $2   **MIP** $4

- ❑ **Summer Fun,** 1991, Wendy's, float pouch, sky saucer
  EX n/a   **NM** $1   **MIP** $2

- ❑ **Teddy Ruxpin,** 1987, Wendy's, set of five: Professor Newton Gimmick, Teddy, Wolly Whats-It, Fob, Grubby Worm
  EX n/a   **NM** $3   **MIP** $8

- ❑ **Too Kool for School**, Wendy's, set of five
  EX n/a   **NM** $2   **MIP** $4

- ❑ **Tricky Tints**, Wendy's, set of four
  EX n/a   **NM** $2   **MIP** $4

RESTAURANT PREMIUMS

(KP Photo)

❑ **Wacky Wind-Ups,** 1991, Wendy's, set of five: Milk Shake, Biggie French Fry, Stuff Potato, Hamburger, Hamburger in box
EX n/a   NM $2   MIP $3

❑ **Where's the Beef Stickers,** 1984, Wendy's, set of six
EX n/a   NM $1   MIP $3

❑ **World Wildlife Foundation,** 1988, Wendy's, set of four plush toys: Panda, Snow Leopard, Koala, Tiger
EX n/a   NM $5   MIP $10

❑ **World Wildlife Foundation,** 1988, Wendy's, set of four books: All About Koalas, All About Tigers, All About Snow Leopards, All About Pandas
EX n/a   NM $2   MIP $4

(KP Photo)

❑ **Yogi Bear & Friends,** 1990, Wendy's, set of six: Ranger Smith in kayak, Boo Boo on skateboard, Yogi on skates, Cindy on red scooter, Huckleberry in inner tube, Snagglepuss with surfboard
EX n/a   NM $2   MIP $4

WHITE CASTLE

❑ **Ballerina's Tiara,** White Castle
EX n/a   NM $3   MIP $6

❑ **Bendy Pens,** 1993, White Castle, set of five: Wilfred, Wobbles, Woofles, Woozy Wizard, Willis
EX n/a   NM $3   MIP $6

❑ **Camp White Castle,** White Castle
EX n/a   NM $2   MIP $4

❑ **Camp White Castle Bowls,** White Castle, orange plastic
EX n/a   NM $3   MIP $6

❑ **Castle Creatures,** White Castle
EX n/a   NM $2   MIP $5

❑ **Castle Friends Bubble Makers,** 1992, White Castle, set of four
EX n/a   NM $3   MIP $5

(KP Photo)

❑ **Castle Meal Family,** 1989, White Castle, set of six: Princess Wilhelmina, Wendell, Sir Wincelot, Willis, Woozy Wizard, Woofles
EX n/a   NM $4   MIP $6

❑ **Castle Meal Family,** 1992, White Castle, set of five: Wilfred, King Wooly and Queen Winnevere, Wally, Wobbles and Woody, Friar Wack
EX n/a   NM $4   MIP $6

❑ **Castle Meal Friends,** 1989-90, White Castle, set of six
EX n/a   NM $4   MIP $10

❑ **Castleburger Dudes Figures,** 1991, White Castle, set of four: Castleburger Dude, Castle Fry Dudette, Castle Drink Dude, Castle Cheeseburger Dude
EX n/a   NM $3   MIP $6

❑ **Castleburger Dudes Wind-Up Toys,** 1991, White Castle, set of four: Castleburger Dude, Castle Fry Dudette, Castle Drink Dude, Castle Cheeseburger Dude
EX n/a   NM $2   MIP $4

❑ **Easter Pals,** White Castle, set of two: rabbit with carrot, rabbit with purse
EX n/a   NM $3   MIP $5

(Copyright Museum of Science and Industry, Chicago)

❑ **Fat Albert and the Cosby Kids,** 1990, White Castle, set of four: Fat Albert, Dumb Donald, Russely, Weird Harold
EX n/a   NM $8   MIP $15

❑ **Food Squirters,** 1994, White Castle, set of three: Castle Fry Dudette, Castle Drink Dude, Castleburger Dude
EX n/a   NM $2   MIP $4

❑ **Glow in the Dark Monsters,** 1992, White Castle, set of three: Wolfman, Frankenstein, Mummy
EX n/a   NM $3   MIP $6

❑ **Godzilla Squirter,** White Castle
EX n/a   NM $3   MIP $6

❑ **Halloween PEZ,** 1990, White Castle, set of three PEZ dispensers: Pumpkin, Witch, Skull
EX n/a   NM $3   MIP $6

❑ **Holiday Huggables,** White Castle, Candy Canine, Kitty Lights, Holly Hog
EX n/a   NM $2   MIP $5

❑ **Nestle's Quik Rabbit,** 1990, White Castle, set of four: straw holder, spoon, cup, plush toy
EX n/a   NM $2   MIP $4

❑ **Puppy in My Pocket,** 1995, White Castle, set of twelve, two per package
EX n/a   NM $2   MIP $3

❑ **Silly Putty,** 1994, White Castle, set of three molds with Silly Putty: orange mold, yellow mold, green mold
EX n/a   NM $2   MIP $4

❑ **Stunt Grip Geckos,** 1992, White Castle, set of four figures: turquoise, pink, purple, blue
EX n/a   NM $2   MIP $4

❑ **Super Balls,** 1994, White Castle, set of four: Castleburger Dude, Castle Cheeseburger Dude, Castle Fry Dudette, Castle Drink Dude
EX n/a   NM $2   MIP $3

❑ **Swat Kats,** 1994, White Castle, set of three figures with launchers: Razor, T-Bone, Callie
EX n/a   NM $2   MIP $3

❑ **Tootsie Roll Express,** 1994, White Castle, set of four train cars: Engine, Gondola, Hopper, Caboose
EX n/a   NM $3   MIP $5

❑ **Totally U Back To School,** White Castle, set of two: pencil, pencil case
EX n/a   NM $2   MIP $4

❑ **Triastic Take-a-Parta,** 1994, White Castle, set of four: Megasaur, Spinasaur, Coolasaur, Sorasaur; also distributed by Carl's Jr.
EX n/a   NM $2   MIP $3

❑ **Water Balls,** 1993, White Castle, set of four: Castleburger Dude, Castle Cheeseburger Dude, Castle Fry Dudette, Castle Drink Dude
EX n/a   NM $2   MIP $3

❑ **Willis the Dragon,** White Castle, Christmas giveaway
EX n/a   NM $3   MIP $6

❑ **Willis the Dragon Sunglasses,** White Castle
EX n/a   NM $2   MIP $4

Robots

A collection of robots like this is fun and valuable. These playthings were once considered throw-away items by many adults (and kids). Boy, to have some of them in nice shape now…

by Dan Stearns

Watch any old sci-fi movie from the 1930s to the present, and you're gonna see robots. They're so much a part of the film and TV landscape that you'd be forgiven for thinking that these mechanical beings actually exist en masse right now (like videophones, flying cars—where is this stuff? It's already the 21st century, for crying out loud!)

More than any movie in recent decades, Star Wars probably did the most to re-popularize the robot to a new generation of audiences. Lucas spent plenty of time (and money) getting a complete new pantheon of droids on the screen—and not just C3PO and R2D2. Soon, entire living room floors were filled with toy representations of Power Droids, bug-headed humanoid-types, other "R2" units with differently colored bodies, and a whole slew of C3PO-almost look-alikes. *Editor's note*: Many of these fine toys can be found in our separate Star Wars chapter. This particular chapter is pretty-much "everything but."

In any event, most of the toy robots made in Japan in the 1950s have escalated to such a value that they are out of reach by any but the most determined (and well-funded) collector. Among the most popular robots of that era are the "gang-of-five." This series of skirted tin robots made by Masudaya have commanded five- to six-figure prices at auction.

Right before Star Wars hit the big screen, interest in robots really seemed on the wane. Most of the items being made had Hong Kong or Taiwanese origins, being that Japan didn't find it profitable to invest in toy making any longer.

However, if you're just interested in the aesthetics of the toy itself, there are plenty of good reproductions and modern takes on old robot toys, including some sharp remakes of the gang of five.

The Great Garloo from 1961 by Marx. At 22 inches tall, he was an impressive toy. His MIP value is about $650.

This Sparky Robot from KO-Japan is a wind-up toy valued at $515 MIP.

1950s

❑ **Ranger Robot,** Japan, 1950s, 11", battery-operated, clear body, w/smoke and sound
EX $500   **NM** $1200   **MIP** $2250

1960s

❑ **Raid "Bug" Robot,** Korea, 1960s, Large plastic, battery-operated, remote control, ad promo
EX $75   **NM** $150   **MIP** $250

ADVANCE TOYS

❑ **Mr. Atom,** 1960s, Advance Toys, 18", red and silver plastic, battery-operated. "The Electronic Walking Robot… Completely Harmless," according to the box
EX $135   **NM** $310   **MIP** $670

ALPS

❑ **Cragstan Great Astronaut,** 1960s, ALPS, 11", red tin, battery-operated, w/video scene, key in head
EX $500   **NM** $1250   **MIP** $2000

❑ **Mechanical Television Spaceman,** 1960s, ALPS, 7", tin and plastic, wind-up, w/chest scene and antenna
EX $95   **NM** $185   **MIP** $325

❑ **Television Space Man,** 1950s, Alps, 11", tin and plastic, battery-operated, chest video, key in head operates
EX $125   **NM** $350   **MIP** $800

AN-JAPAN

❑ **Astronaut Robot,** 1950s, AN-Japan, 8", tin, wind-up, tanks on back, gun in hand
EX $500   **NM** $1250   **MIP** $2000

ARCO

❑ **Ro-Gun "It's A Robot",** 1984, Arco, robot changes into a rifle
EX $11   **NM** $16   **MIP** $25

ASAK

❑ **Space Guard Pilot,** 1975, Asak, 8"
EX $20   **NM** $30   **MIP** $45

ASC JAPAN

❑ **Radar Robot,** 1950s, ASC Japan, 11", orange tin, wind-up, rotating antenna, chest sparks
EX $1500   **NM** $4000   **MIP** $7000

CRAGSTAN

❑ **Countdown-Y,** 1960s, Cragstan, 9"
EX $100   **NM** $145   **MIP** $225

(ToyShop File Photo)

❑ **Cragstan's Mr. Robot,** 1960s, Cragstan, 10-1/2" tin, battery-operated, red or white body, clear dome head
EX $310   **NM** $515   **MIP** $920

❑ **Magnor,** 1975, Cragstan, 9", plastic
EX $23   **NM** $35   **MIP** $50

❑ **Mr. Atomic,** 1960s, Cragstan, rare, 8", tin and plastic, battery-operated, bump and go action
EX n/a   **NM** n/a   **MIP** $15000

❑ **Mr. LEM Astronaut Robot,** 1970, Cragstan, 13", all plastic, battery-operated, rotates
EX $150   **NM** $310   **MIP** $475

(ToyShop File Photo)

❑ **Talking Robot,** 1960s, Cragstan, 10 1/2", battery-operated, tin and plastic, three functions
EX $380   **NM** $665   **MIP** $1100

DAIYA

❑ **Astro Captain,** 1970s, Daiya, 6", red/white/blue tin wind-up sparker, NASA on helmet
EX $35   **NM** $65   **MIP** $100

DURHAM

❑ **Robot 2500,** 1970s, Durham, 10", tin/plastic, battery-operated, "cyclops"
EX $25   **NM** $45   **MIP** $65

HONG KONG

❑ **See-Thru Robot,** 1970s, Hong Kong, 10", plastic, battery-operated, clear head and chest w/gears
EX $125   **NM** $325   **MIP** $600

HONG-KONG

❑ **Action Robot,** 1970s, Hong-Kong, 10", yellow/blue plastic, battery-operated, multiple functions
EX $15   **NM** $35   **MIP** $55

❑ **Radar Hunter,** 1970s, Hong-Kong, 5", plastic, wind-up, red/silver or orange
EX $15   **NM** $35   **MIP** $55

❑ **Robbie Robot,** 1970s, Hong-Kong, 9", blue/red/yellow, all plastic, battery-operated, blinks
EX $25   **NM** $45   **MIP** $85

❑ **Sounding Robot,** 1970s, Hong-Kong, 8", plastic, battery-operated, three push buttons on head
EX $25   **NM** $50   **MIP** $75

❑ **Sparking Robot,** 1970s, Hong-Kong, 6", black plastic, wind-up
EX $20   **NM** $35   **MIP** $50

❑ **Star Robot,** 1970s, Hong-Kong, 10", plastic, battery-operated, Star Wars Trooper head
EX $25   **NM** $45   **MIP** $70

HORIKAWA

❑ **Piston Robot,** 1960s, Horikawa, 10", tin/plastic, battery-operated, lighted pistons in square head
EX $200   **NM** $450   **MIP** $750

❑ **Space Explorer Robot,** 1960s, Horikawa, 11", tin and plastic, battery-operated, drop down chest cover reveals video
EX $95   **NM** $200   **MIP** $325

(ToyShop File Photo)

ROBOTS

❏ **Super Space Capsule**, 1960s, Horikawa, Blinking nosecone on top, opening panels with astronaut, rolling action
EX $220   **NM** $375   **MIP** $600

IDEAL

❏ **Maxx Steele Robot**, 1984, Ideal, 30", plastic, programmable servant, w/charger
EX $100   **NM** $250   **MIP** $425

❏ **Mighty Zogg the Leader Zeroid**, 1960s, Ideal, 6", plastic, battery-operated, w/Motorific motors
EX $60   **NM** $110   **MIP** $225

❏ **Mr. Machine**, 1961, Ideal, 18", plastic, wind-up, w/bell and key, disassembles
EX $85   **NM** $210   **MIP** $425

(ToyShop File Photo)

❏ **Mr. Machine**, 1977, Ideal, 18", plastic, wind-up, whistles, does not disassemble
EX $15   **NM** $30   **MIP** $60

(ToyShop File Photo)

❏ **Robert the Wonder Toy**, 1950s, Ideal, 14", plastic, battery-operated, remote "laser gun" styled control attached to toy
EX $220   **NM** $700   **MIP** $1300

(Edwin Price, Jr.)

❏ **Robot Commando**, 1960s, Ideal, 19", blue/red plastic, battery-operated, remote control, fires rockets and balls
EX $155   **NM** $465   **MIP** $810

(ToyShop File Photo)

❏ **Zerak the Blue Destroyer Zeroid**, 1968, Ideal, 6", plastic, battery-operated, w/Motorific motors
EX $60   **NM** $105   **MIP** $220

ZEROIDS

❏ **Zintar the Silver Explorer Zeroid**, 1960s, Ideal, 6", plastic, battery-operated, w/Motorific motors
EX $55   **NM** $110   **MIP** $210

❏ **Zobor the Bronze Transporter Zeroid**, 1960s, Ideal, 6", plastic, battery-operated, w/Motorific motors
EX $50   **NM** $100   **MIP** $200

IRWIN

❏ **Man from Mars**, 1950s, Irwin, 11", red tin, wind-up, "space boy"
EX $100   **NM** $250   **MIP** $450

JAPAN

❏ **Answer Game Machine**, 1960s, Japan, 14", tin, battery-operated, performs math tricks
EX $350   **NM** $675   **MIP** $950

❏ **Apollo 2000 Robot**, 1960s, Japan, 12", tin, battery-operated, red and blue, w/chest guns
EX $95   **NM** $175   **MIP** $300

❏ **Apollo 2000X**, 1970s, Japan, 6", blue and red tin wind-up w/spark
EX $45   **NM** $95   **MIP** $165

❏ **Atomic Robot Man**, 1948, Japan, 6", all tin, wind-up
EX $325   **NM** $900   **MIP** $1550

❏ **Construction Robot**, 1960s, Japan, 12", yellow tin, battery-operated, with forklift
EX $450   **NM** $100   **MIP** $1650

❏ **Door Robot**, 1950s, Japan, 9 1/2", tin, battery-operated, remote cont, revolving head
EX $700   **NM** $1650   **MIP** $3000

❏ **High-Wheel Robot**, 1950s, Japan, 9", blue, tin and plastic, battery-operated, remote control
EX $325   **NM** $750   **MIP** $1250

❏ **High-Wheel Ronot**, 1950s, Japan, 9", black, tin and plastic, wind-up, w/chest gears
EX $175   **NM** $425   **MIP** $700

❏ **Machine Robot,** 1960s, Japan, 11", tin and plastic, battery-operated, w/shoulder antennae
EX $145   **NM** $325   **MIP** $600

❏ **Mars Explorer,** 1950s, Japan, 9 1/2", red tin, battery-operated, w/wheels, face doors open
EX $450   **NM** $1000   **MIP** $1750

❏ **Mars King,** 1960s, Japan, 9", tin and plastic, battery-operated, w/video, siren and treads
EX $125   **NM** $350   **MIP** $650

❏ **Mr. Chief,** 1960s, Japan, 11-1/2", tin and plastic, battery-operated, smoking action
EX $475   **NM** $1000   **MIP** $1950

❏ **Mr. Patrol,** 1960s, Japan, 11", tin and plastic, battery-operated, meter in chest
EX $150   **NM** $350   **MIP** $575

❏ **New Astronaut Robot,** 1970s, Japan, 9", tin and plastic, battery-operated, w/three firing chest guns
EX $45   **NM** $85   **MIP** $135

❏ **Piston Action Robot,** 1950s, Japan, 8 1/2", tin and plastic, battery-operated, remote cont, "Robby" type
EX $500   **NM** $1200   **MIP** $2000

❏ **Piston Robot,** 1970s, Japan, 10", tin and plastic, battery-operated, lighted chest pistons
EX $60   **NM** $110   **MIP** $225

❏ **Piston Robot,** 1980s, Japan, 10", plastic, battery-operated, lighted chest pistons
EX $35   **NM** $65   **MIP** $125

(ToyShop File Photo)

❏ **R-35 Robot,** 1950s, Japan, 7 1/2", tin litho, battery-operated, remote cont, eyes lite up
EX $160   **NM** $450   **MIP** $700

(ToyShop File Photo)

❏ **Robot Mighty 8,** 1960s, Japan, Dark blue metal body, red feet, electric color display on chest
EX n/a   **NM** n/a   **MIP** n/a

❏ **Robot Tank - Mini,** Japan, 5-1/2" tall, tin and plastic, battery-operated, w/two guns
EX $85   **NM** $160   **MIP** $275

❏ **Roto-Robot,** 1960s, Japan, 9", tin and plastic, battery-operated, w/chest guns, rotates 360 degrees
EX $100   **NM** $205   **MIP** $335

❏ **Singing Robot,** 1970s, Japan, 10", plastic, battery-operated, missiles in head
EX $35   **NM** $75   **MIP** $100

❏ **Space Explorer Robot,** 1950s, Japan, 9", tin, wind-up, w/O2 gauge on chest
EX $450   **NM** $1000   **MIP** $1650

❏ **Space Explorer Robot,** 1960s, Japan, 12", tin and plastic, battery-operated, rotating shoulder antenna
EX $450   **NM** $1000   **MIP** $1650

❏ **Space Ranger,** 1970s, Japan, 10", battery-operated, all plastic, R/C, fires balls from chest
EX $50   **NM** $110   **MIP** $165

(ToyShop File Photo)

❏ **Space Robot X-70,** 1960s, Japan, 12", tin and plastic, battery-operated, lights, noise, and "Tulip Head"
EX $465   **NM** $1100   **MIP** $1700

❏ **Sparky Robot,** 1960s, Japan, 7", green cylindrical body, tin wind-up
EX $45   **NM** $65   **MIP** $100

❏ **Super Astronaut,** 1960s, Japan, 10", battery-operated, mostly tin, man's face, w/chest guns
EX $65   **NM** $145   **MIP** $250

❏ **Thunder Robot,** 1950s, Japan, 11", tin and plastic, battery-operated, w/antenna and guns in palms of hands
EX $1500   **NM** $5000   **MIP** $9000

❏ **Zoomer Robot,** 1950s, Japan, 7", blue or silver w/red, tin, battery-operated, w/wrench
EX $295   **NM** $525   **MIP** $900

KO-JAPAN

(ToyShop File Photo)

❏ **Chief Robotman,** 1960s, KO-Japan, 12", tin and plastic, battery-operated, bump and go
EX $460   **NM** $920   **MIP** $1600

❑ **Jupiter Robot,** 1970s, KO-Japan, 6 1/2", red plastic, wind-up, w/two antennae
EX $85 **NM** $175 **MIP** $310

(ToyShop File Photo)

❑ **Sparky Robot,** 1950s, KO-Japan, 8 1/2", silver and red, all tin, wind-up, w/head spring
EX $155 **NM** $300 **MIP** $515

(ToyShop File Photo)

❑ **Venus Robot,** 1960s, KO-Japan, 8", blue/red, tin and plastic, battery-operated, remote control
EX $105 **NM** $210 **MIP** $335

MARX

❑ **Big Loo,** 1960s, Marx, 36", plastic, battery-operated, water squirter, w/rockets and tools
EX $450 **NM** $1300 **MIP** $2600

❑ **Colonel Hap Hazard,** 1968, Marx, 11", tin and plastic, rotating antenna on head
EX $250 **NM** $575 **MIP** $1200

❑ **Electric Robot,** 1950s, Marx, 15", blk and red plastic, battery-operated, w/morse code
EX $130 **NM** $255 **MIP** $515

❑ **Frankenstein,** 1960s, Marx, 6", metal and plastic, wind-up walker
EX $100 **NM** $250 **MIP** $450

❑ **Frankenstein Robot,** 1960s, Marx, 14", tin and plastic, battery-operated, wired remote control
EX $575 **NM** $1250 **MIP** $2000

❑ **Moon Creature,** 1960s, Marx, 5 1/2", Bug-eyed, mechanical, tin, wind-up
EX $95 **NM** $165 **MIP** $275

❑ **Moon Scout,** 1968, Marx, 11", tin and plastic, shoots balls from chest
EX $500 **NM** $1050 **MIP** $2000

❑ **Mr. Mercury,** 1960s, Marx, 14", tin and plastic, battery-operated, bending action
EX $175 **NM** $450 **MIP** $1000

❑ **Mr. Smash,** 1970s, Marx, 6", red plastic, wind-up, Martian Mashed Potato promo
EX $45 **NM** $95 **MIP** $150

(ToyShop File Photo)

❑ **Rock 'Em, Sock 'Em Robots,** 1970s, Marx, Two plastic robots in boxing ring controlled by handles, when one is punched just right his head flies upward on a spring. Just plain goofy fun
EX $55 **NM** $120 **MIP** $200

❑ **Son of Garloo,** 1960s, Marx, 6", green metal and plastic, monster wind-up walker
EX $100 **NM** $225 **MIP** $425

MASUDAYA

❑ **Forbidden Planet Robby,** 1985, Masudaya, 5", plastic, wind-up
EX $10 **NM** $20 **MIP** $35

❑ **Forbidden Planet Robby,** 1985, Masudaya, 16", plastic, battery-operated, talks
EX $65 **NM** $125 **MIP** $200

(ToyShop File Photo)

❑ **Giant Sonic Robot (Train Robot),** 1950s, Masudaya, Red body, black arms and head, robot makes "trainlike" sound as it rolls along. Very hard to find
EX $4000 **NM** $7300 **MIP** $16000

(Sotheby's Photo)

❑ **Machine Man,** 1950s, Masudaya, The rarest robot from Masudaya's "Gang of Five" series, this robot sold for $42,550 at the Sotheby's auction of the Tin Toy Robot Collection of Matt Wyse in 1996
EX n/a **NM** n/a **MIP** $45000

❑ **Robot YM-3,** 1985, Masudaya, 5", wind-up, "Lost in Space B9" type
EX $10 **NM** $20 **MIP** $35

MEGO-JAPAN

❑ **Krome-Dome Robot,** 1960s, Mego-Japan, 11", plastic, battery-operated, disk-type head opes w/sound
EX $125 **NM** $295 **MIP** $525

MIKES TOY HOUSE

❏ **Mr. Atomic,** 1990s, Mikes Toy House, Limited reproduction
EX $95 **NM** $200 **MIP** $350

MTU-KOREA

❏ **Captain the Robot,** 1970s, MTU-Korea, 6", gray plastic wind-up, sparking
EX $15 **NM** $35 **MIP** $50

NAMURA

(ToyShop File Photo)

❏ **Robby Space Patrol,** 1957, Namura, Purple and silver metal body, battery operated with random running action. This is one of the most famous space toys, representing (in an unlicensed way) the robot and his transport from "The Forbidden Planet"
EX $7000 **NM** $17500 **MIP** $37000

N-JAPAN

❏ **Walking W Robot,** 1960s, N-Japan, 7", tin wind-up sparker, plastic antenna on head
EX $100 **NM** $225 **MIP** $350

NOMURA

❏ **Musical Drummer Robot R 57,** 1950s, Nomura, From the Matt Wyse collection, this robot sold for $17,250 at a Sotheby's auction in 1996
EX n/a **NM** n/a **MIP** $20000

ORIKAWA

❏ **Mr. Hustler,** 1960s, Orikawa, 11 1/2", tin and plastic, battery-operated, center chest light
EX $100 **NM** $225 **MIP** $400

PLAYING MANTIS

(ToyShop File Photo)

❏ **Robot B-9, Lost In Space,** 1990s, Playing Mantis, Die-cast metal with rolling wheels under base, sold individually, part of a series of four Lost-In-Space toys made by Playing Mantis Johnny Lightning
EX n/a **NM** n/a **MIP** $6

REMCO

❏ **Big Max & His Electronic Conveyor,** 1958, Remco, 8 x 7", battery-operated, plastic, w/truck and coins
EX $100 **NM** $185 **MIP** $300

❏ **Mr. Brain,** 1970, Remco, 13", plastic, battery-operated, programmable memory
EX $75 **NM** $150 **MIP** $250

(ToyShop File Photo)

❏ **Rudy the Robot,** 1967, Remco, 16", orange plastic, battery-operated. "He Walks Like a Man!"
EX $55 **NM** $170 **MIP** $385

S.H.

❏ **Attacking Martian,** 1960s, S.H., 12", tin, battery-operated, green lens on chest doors
EX $100 **NM** $200 **MIP** $300

❏ **Attacking Martian,** 1970s, S.H., 10", tin/plastic, battery-operated, guns in chest
EX $100 **NM** $250 **MIP** $425

❏ **Launching Robot,** 1975, S.H., 10"
EX $25 **NM** $35 **MIP** $55

(ToyShop File Photo)

❏ **Sky Robot,** 1970s, S.H., 8", yellow/red plastic, battery-operated
EX $25 **NM** $55 **MIP** $70

S.J.M.

(ToyShop File Photo)

❏ **Super Astronaut,** 1981, S.J.M., 10", battery-operated, tin and plastic, man's face, w/chest guns
EX $15 **NM** $25 **MIP** $35

SAUNDERS

❏ **Marvelous Mike,** 1950s, Saunders, battery-operated, plastic robot on tin bulldozer
EX $110 **NM** $225 **MIP** $395

ROBOTS

SCHAPER

❏ **Tobor,** 1978, Schaper, 7", black plastic, battery-operated, radio control
EX $15   NM $30   MIP $45

SH

❏ **Gear Robot,** 1960s, SH, 9", wind-up, visible gears
EX $125   NM $275   MIP $450

❏ **Gear Robot,** 1960s, SH, 11 1/2", battery-operated, tin w/plastic gears in chest, antennae on shoulders
EX $225   NM $500   MIP $850

❏ **Golden Gear Robot,** 1960s, SH, 9", gold tin, battery-operated, w/chest gears and lit dome
EX $225   NM $500   MIP $850

SH-JAPAN

❏ **Dino Robot,** 1960s, SH-Japan, 11", tin, battery-operated, head opens to reveal dinosaur
EX $450   NM $950   MIP $1600

❏ **Engine Robot,** 1960s, SH-Japan, 9", tin and plastic, battery-operated, w/chest gears
EX $125   NM $250   MIP $500

❏ **Engine Robot,** 1970s, SH-Japan, 10", plastic, battery-operated
EX $75   NM $150   MIP $300

❏ **Excavator Robot,** 1960s, SH-Japan, 10", tin and plastic, battery-operated, w/drill type hands
EX $275   NM $550   MIP $875

(ToyShop File Photo)

❏ **Fighting Robot,** 1960s, SH-Japan, 11", tin and plastic, battery-operated, single chest gun, flashing light on head. "Sounding and lighted rapid fire gun" on box
EX $135   NM $360   MIP $620

(ToyShop File Photo)

❏ **Mr. Zerox,** 1960s, SH-Japan, 9", tin and plastic, battery-operated, w/blinking, shooting actions. Interesting name
EX $110   NM $230   MIP $365

❏ **Radar Scope Space Scout,** 1960s, SH-Japan, 10", tin and plastic, battery-operated, TV screen w/noise
EX $65   NM $125   MIP $210

❏ **Smoking Engine Robot,** 1970s, SH-Japan, 10", plastic, battery-operated, piston action, w/sound and smoke
EX $45   NM $85   MIP $135

❏ **Space Commander Robot,** 1960s, SH-Japan, 10", tin and plastic, tank type base, bumpandgo, w/guns
EX $500   NM $1200   MIP $2000

❏ **Space Fighter,** 1960s, SH-Japan, 9", tin and plastic, battery-operated, w/chest doors andguns
EX $95   NM $200   MIP $325

(ToyShop File Photo)

❏ **Super Giant (Rotate-a-Matic) Robot,** 1970s, SH-Japan, 16", battery-operated, plastic, w/chest guns
EX $90   NM $160   MIP $265

❏ **Super Robot Tank,** 1950s, SH-Japan, 9" long, tin, friction powered w/two guns
EX $80   NM $175   MIP $295

❏ **Super Space Commander,** 1970s, SH-Japan, 10", blue plastic, battery-operated, chest video
EX $20   NM $40   MIP $60

❏ **Video Robot,** 1960s, SH-Japan, 9", blue tin and plastic, battery-operated, w/chest video
EX $75   NM $155   MIP $250

STRACO-JAPAN

❏ **Hysterical Robot,** 1970s, Straco-Japan, 13", black plastic, battery-operated, bump and go and laughing actions
EX $100   NM $250   MIP $400

SY JAPAN

❏ **Space Man Robot,** 1950s, SY Japan, 7 1/2" tin litho windup, w/floppy arms
EX $150   NM $400   MIP $700

❏ **Sparking Robot,** 1960s, SY Japan, 7", all tin, silver w/litho, keywound
EX $125   NM $275   MIP $450

TAIYO

❏ **Wheel-A-Gear Robot,** 1950s, Taiyo, 15", black, tin and plastic, battery-operated, w/mutli-chest gears and pullies
EX $425   NM $1000   MIP $1850

TN-JAPAN

❏ **Earthman Robot,** 1950s, TN-Japan, 9", tin, battery-operated, remote conttol, w/sound and blinking gun
EX $550   NM $1450   MIP $2500

❏ **Robot Tank-Z,** 1960s, TN-Japan, 10", battery-operated, tin and plastic, bumpandgo
EX $175   NM $395   MIP $575

❏ **Space Command Robot,** 1950s, TN-Japan, 7 1/2", all tin, wind-up, w/gun in hand
EX $375   NM $1000   MIP $1650

TOMY

❏ **Omnibot 2000,** 1980s, Tomy, 2 ft., plastic, battery-operated, remote control, programmable servant
EX $175   NM $400   MIP $675

❏ **Verbot,** 1984, Tomy, 8", plastic, battery-operated, radio control, programmable
EX $15   NM $35   MIP $60

TOPPER

(ToyShop File Photo)

❏ **King-Ding Robot,** 1970, Topper, 12", plastic, battery-operated, separate brain robot goes in head
EX $120   NM $285   MIP $510

WACO-JAPAN

❏ **Laughing Robot,** 1960s, Waco-Japan, 13", plastic, battery-operated, mouth opens, laughs loudly
EX $125   **NM** $275   **MIP** $500

YANOMAN

❏ **Rendezvous 7.8,** Yanoman, 15"
EX $170   **NM** $245   **MIP** $375

YONEZAWA

❏ **Directional Robot,** 1950s, Yonezawa, 10", blue tin, battery-operated, rotates, bump and go action
EX $225   **NM** $650   **MIP** $1200

❏ **Lunar Robot,** 1960s, Yonezawa, 7", wind-up, sparks, companion to Thunder Robot
EX $225   **NM** $550   **MIP** $800

❏ **Scare Mighty Robot,** 1960s, Yonezawa, 10", red and white metal and plastic, wind-up, sparking action
EX $175   **NM** $550   **MIP** $900

(ToyShop File Photo)

❏ **Smoking Spaceman,** 1960s, Yonezawa, Dark gray metal body, smoke puffs from mouth as robot walks
EX $1250   **NM** $1900   **MIP** $3750

YOSHIYA

❏ **Moon Explorer,** 1960s, Yoshiya, 12", tin, battery-operated, w/clock in chest
EX $475   **NM** $1000   **MIP** $1850

Space and Science Fiction Toys

These Remco Walkie Talkies were the generic version of the Buck Rogers models it made in the 1950s. $170 MIP.

by Dan Stearns

Although many writers consider Mary Shelley's Frankenstein (1818) to be the first true science fiction story, the genre would have to wait over 100 years before being recognized as an outcrop of "imaginative fiction." The toys, naturally, followed soon after.

Jules Verne and H.G. Wells come to mind as being the first modern originators of the science fiction motif, along with Frank Reade's pulps and other "Boys' Readers" of the late 19th century. Science fiction, though, is really a 20th century phenomenon.

After the First World War, the science fiction came into it's own. Buck Rogers' first appearance in 1928 in the magazine *Amazing Stories* set the standard for the swashbuckling, ray-gun toting hero, see

ever since in imitators from Flash Gordon to Han Solo.

Hugo Gernsback, considered the father of American science fiction, founded Amazing Stories in 1926. As a publisher and editor, he had an uncanny sense of timing.

The public was ready for these "scientifiction" stories, and although his first efforts found him publishing works by Edgar Allan Poe and Jules Verne, newer writers eventually came on board. Philip Nowlan, writer of "Argageddon—2419" (the story of Anthony "Buck" Rogers) was among them. Aided by illustrator Frank Paul, whose cover paintings are remembered today as some of the most vibrant in 20th century magazine publishing, the magazine became a huge hit.

Space and science fiction toys begin making their appearance during this period, notably the Tootsietoy Buck Rogers' series of ships in the late 1930s. These stylized die-cast vehicles were especially created to run on a string—better to create the appearance of flying. Ray guns, too, were an offshoot of this newly-created craze. While World War II put a dent in the toy making biz, it didn't dampen enthusiasm for the genre. With the new knowledge of atomic weapons, and the Roswell sighting in 1947, science fiction movies, magazines and toys were back in orbit.

Mystery Space Ship set by Marx, $260 MIP.

This *Space1999* model kit of the "Alien" vehicle is valued at $65 MIP.

In the 1950s, a war-recovering Japan made some of the best tin-litho robots ever. (Covered in our "Robots" chapter in this book.) Ray guns, robots, space ships and monsters were back in style. Flash Gordon and Buck Rogers serials were dusted off and put on television, creating a whole new generation of fans and toys. Monsters first seen in movies from the 1930s became everyday characters and the stuff of dreams and nightmares for boys and girls in the postwar world.

The 1960s saw it's own wave of science fiction and fantasy. Television shows such as *Lost in Space*, *Voyage to the Bottom of the Sea*, *Land of the Giants* and of course, *Star Trek*, helped create another

explosion of games, toys, comic books and accessories.

By the early 1970s, the grand "modernist" age of science fiction had pretty much run its course. In a way, reality set the big grounding on fantasy. Apollo 17 marked the last trip to the moon in 1972. The optimistic days when space exploration seemed around the corner appeared to be at an end. Science fiction was still around, but even popular (and fun-to-watch) movies like the *Planet of the Apes* series were more about a dystopian future (a messed-up present day) than they were about good and evil or the thrill of other worlds. Of course, the premiere of *Star Wars* changed all that.

In May 1977, the space age came back with a vengeance. Suddenly, a genre that seemed destined for a nostalgia dustbin had new life, new heroes and a slew of new villains. Science fiction hasn't been the same since.

(**Editor's note**: Of course, like the category of "Robots," this too, has it's own chapter, which pretty well illustrates the point of just how much stuff one idea and some good licensing agreements can generate.)

A grab bag of imitators immediately pounced on the scene, with television shows such as *Battlestar Galactica*, and re-issues of the Zeriod robots and Darth Vaderesque bad guys. Collecting the almost-rans—the stuff that looks a lot like Star Wars but isn't, can be as much if not more fun than the real deal.

In any event, the chapter that follows is a smattering—by no means a complete list—of some fun, collectible space and science fiction toys.

Space Patrol Rocket Lite Flashlight, $375 MIP.

ALIEN/ALIENS

❏ **Alien Blaster Target Game,** 1979, H.G. Toys, set features large free standing cardboard Alien target and plastic dart shooting rifle, gun has large block letters "Alien" on side, based on the movie
EX $65   NM $135   MIP $200

❏ **Alien Blaster Target Set**, HG Toys, larger set
EX $110   NM $220   MIP $300

❏ **Alien Chase Target Set**, HG Toys, dart pistol, cardboard target
EX $80   NM $190   MIP $225

❏ **Alien Costume**, Ben Cooper, black/white
EX $50   NM $65   MIP $100

❏ **Alien Model Kit,** 1980s, Tsukuda, vinyl, 1/6 scale
EX $60   NM $225   MIP $350

❏ **Alien Warrior Model Kit**, Halcyon, base and egg
EX $20   NM $30   MIP $50

❏ **Aliens Colorforms Set**, Colorforms
EX $10   NM $20   MIP $40

❏ **Aliens Computer Game,** 1985, Commodore
EX $5   NM $15   MIP $30

❏ **Glow Putty**, Laramie, unlicensed art, carded
EX $10   NM $15   MIP $20

❏ **Movie Viewer**, Kenner, "Alien Terror" film clip
EX $40   NM $75   MIP $100

BATTLESTAR GALACTICA

❏ **Colorforms Adventure Set**, 1978, Colorforms
EX $12   NM $25   MIP $35

❏ **Cylon Helmet Radio**, 1979, Vanity Fair
EX $25   NM $50   MIP $85

❏ **Cylon Warrior Costume**, 1978, boxed
EX $10   NM $15   MIP $30

❏ **Galactic Cruiser**, 1978, Larami, die-cast
EX $5   NM $10   MIP $15

❏ **Game of Starfighter Combat**, 1978, FASA, role playing game
EX $10   NM $17   MIP $30

❏ **L.E.M. Lander**, 1978, Larami, die-cast
EX $5   NM $10   MIP $15

❏ **Lasermatic Pistol**, 1978, Mattel
EX $15   NM $35   MIP $50

❏ **Lasermatic Rifle**, 1978, Mattel
EX $25   NM $50   MIP $75

❏ **Muffit the Daggit Halloween Costume,** 1978, Collegeville
EX $7   NM $15   MIP $35

❏ **Poster Art Set**, 1978, Craft Master
EX $6   NM $12   MIP $20

❏ **Puzzles,** 1978, Parker Brothers, The Rag-Tag Fleet, Starbuck, Interstellar Battle, price for each
EX $6   NM $12   MIP $20

❏ **Space Alert Game,** 1978, Mattel, hand-held electronic game
EX $10   NM $25   MIP $50

❏ **Viper Vertibird,** 1979, Mattel
EX $60   NM $120   MIP $220

BUCK ROGERS

❏ **25th Century Police Patrol Rocket,** 1935, Marx, tin wind-up, 12" long
EX $325   NM $950   MIP $1650

❏ **25th Century Scientific Laboratory,** 1934, Porter Chemical, w/three manuals
EX $800   NM $1300   MIP $2200

❏ **Adventures of Buck Rogers Book,** 1934, Whitman, All Pictures Comics edition, Big Big Book
EX $25   NM $100   MIP $200

❏ **Battle Cruiser Rocket,** 1937, Tootsietoy, two grooved wheels to run on string
EX $75   NM $225   MIP $350

❏ **Buck and Wilma Masks,** 1933, Einson-Freeman, paper litho, each
EX $120   NM $220   MIP $375

❏ **Buck Rogers 25th Century Rocket,** 1939, Marx, Buck and Wilma in window, 12" long, tin wind-up
EX $250   NM $650   MIP $1200

❏ **Buck Rogers and the Children of Hopetown Book,** 1980s, Golden Press, Little Golden Book
EX $4   NM $7   MIP $15

❏ **Buck Rogers and the Depth Men of Jupiter Book,** 1935, Whitman, Big Little Book
EX $50   NM $100   MIP $160

❏ **Buck Rogers and the Doom Comet Book,** 1935, Whitman, Big Little Book
EX $50   NM $100   MIP $160

❏ **Buck Rogers and the Overturned World Book,** 1941, Whitman, Big Little Book
EX $50   NM $85   MIP $130

❏ **Buck Rogers and the Planetoid Plot Book,** 1936, Whitman, Big Little Book
EX $50   NM $100   MIP $160

❏ **Buck Rogers and the Super Dwarf of Space Book,** 1943, Whitman, Big Little Book
EX $50   NM $85   MIP $130

❏ **Buck Rogers Battlecruiser,** Tootsietoy, 1937
EX $75   NM $110   MIP $165

❏ **Buck Rogers Figure,** 1937, Tootsietoy, 1-3/4" tall, cast, gray
EX $100   NM $150   MIP $250

❏ **Buck Rogers Films,** 1936, Irwin, set of six
EX $110   NM $190   MIP $285

❏ **Buck Rogers Flash Blast Attack Cruiser,** Tootsietoy, 1937
EX $50   NM $90   MIP $165

❏ **Buck Rogers Holster for U-238 Atomic Pistol,** 1946, Daisy, leather holster only
EX $40   NM $150   MIP $300

❏ **Buck Rogers Holster for XZ-35 Pop Gun,** 1934, Daisy, embossed leather, attached to belt by two short riveted straps
EX $50   NM $175   MIP $325

❏ **Buck Rogers in the 25th Century Book,** 1933, Whitman, Big Little Book, Cocomalt premium
EX $50   NM $90   MIP $160

❏ **Buck Rogers in the 25th Century Book,** 1933, Whitman, Big Little Book
EX $75   NM $130   MIP $210

❏ **Buck Rogers in the 25th Century Button,** 1935, pinback, color Buck bust profile on blue background, w/small ray gun and rocket ship at his shoulders
EX $30   NM $75   MIP $150

❏ **Buck Rogers in the 25th Century Pistol Set,** 1930s, Daisy, holster is red, yellow and blue leather gun is 9-1/2" pressed steel pop gun
EX $210   NM $425   MIP $750

❏ **Buck Rogers in the 25th Century Star Fighter,** 1979, Mego, vehicle for 3-3/4" figures
EX $20   NM $35   MIP $60

❏ **Buck Rogers in the 25th Century XZ-35 Rocket Pistol,** 1934, Daisy, holster is red, yellow and blue leather, gun is 9-1/2" pressed steel Rocket Pistol w/single cooling fin at barrel base
EX $180   NM $400   MIP $725

❏ **Buck Rogers in the City Below the Sea Book,** 1934, Whitman, Big Little Book
EX $75   NM $160   MIP $260

❏ **Buck Rogers in the City of Floating Globes Book,** 1935, Whitman, Cocomalt premium, paperback Big Little Book
EX $125   NM $250   MIP $500

❏ **Buck Rogers in the War With the Planet Venus Book,** 1938, Whitman, Big Little Book
EX $45   NM $80   MIP $130

❏ **Buck Rogers on the Moons of Saturn Book,** 1934, Whitman, premium, paperback Big Little Book
EX $75   NM $160   MIP $260

SPACE TOYS

Buck Rogers Rubber Band Gun, 1930s, Unknown, cut-out paper gun, on card, advertising premium item
EX $30   NM $60   MIP $100

Buck Rogers Sonic Ray Flashlight Gun, 1955, Norton-Honer, 7-1/4" black, green and yellow plastic w/code signal screw
EX $70   NM $150   MIP $300

Buck Rogers U-235 Atomic Pistol, 1946, Daisy, 9-1/2" long, pressed steel, makes pop noise and flash in window when trigger is pulled
EX $125   NM $275   MIP $550

Buck Rogers vs. The Fiend of Space Book, 1940, Whitman, Big Little Book
EX $45   NM $80   MIP $130

Buck Rogers Wristwatch, 1935, E. Ingraham
EX $400   NM $750   MIP $1500

Buck Rogers Wristwatch, 1970s, Huckleberry Time
EX $50   NM $125   MIP $250

Buck Rogers XZ-31 Rocket Pistol, 1934, Daisy, 10-1/2" long, heavy blued metal, grip pumps the action, gun pops when trigger is pulled
EX $140   NM $375   MIP $650

Buck Rogers XZ-35 Space Gun, 1934, Daisy, 7" long, heavy blued metal ray gun, the grip pumps the action and the gun pops when trigger is pulled, single cooling fin at barrel base, also called "Wilma Gun"
EX $125   NM $275   MIP $550

Buck Rogers XZ-38 Disintegrator Pistol, 1936, Daisy, 10-1/2" long, polished copper or blued finish, four flutes on barrel, spark is produced in the window on top of the gun when the trigger is pulled
EX $115   NM $400   MIP $600

Buck Rogers XZ-44 Liquid Helium Water Gun, 1936, Daisy, 7-1/2" long, red and yellow lightning bolt design stamped metal body w/a leather bladder to hold water; a later version was available in copper finish
EX $175   NM $500   MIP $800

Century of Progess Key Fob, 1934, metal, reverse shows Buck silhouette profile
EX $135   NM $275   MIP $500

Century of Progress Button, 1934, pin-back, I Saw Buck Rogers 25th Century Show, color litho
EX $135   NM $250   MIP $500

Chemistry Set, 1937, Grooper, advanced
EX $350   NM $800   MIP $1600

Chemistry Set, 1937, Grooper, beginners
EX $325   NM $775   MIP $1350

Chief Explorer Badge, 1936, gold
EX $150   NM $350   MIP $750

Chief Explorer Badge, 1936, red enamel
EX $90   NM $215   MIP $380

Chief Explorer Folder, 1936
EX $70   NM $125   MIP $250

Clock, 1970s, Huckleberry Time
EX $30   NM $60   MIP $100

Colorforms Set, 1979, Colorforms
EX $10   NM $15   MIP $40

Comet Socker Paddle Ball, 1935, Lee-Tex
EX $35   NM $100   MIP $200

Communicator Set, 1970s, w/silver Twiki figure
EX $10   NM $20   MIP $35

Costume, 1934, Sackman Bros.
EX $850   NM $1400   MIP $2500

Cut-Out Adventure Book, 1933, Cocomalt premium
EX $1250   NM $3500   MIP $6500

Electric Caster Rocket, 1930s, Marx
EX $125   NM $210   MIP $350

Flash Blast Attack Ship Rocket, 1937, Tootsietoy, Flash Blast Attack Ship 4-1/2", Venus Duo-Destroyer w/two grooved wheels to run on string
EX $90   NM $150   MIP $250

Galactic Play Set, 1980s, HG Toys
EX $17   NM $30   MIP $55

Helmet and Rocket Pistol Set, 1933, Einson-Freeman, set of paper partial-face "helmet" mask and paper pop gun, in envelope
EX $115   NM $275   MIP $550

Helmet XZ-34, 1935, Daisy, leather
EX $285   NM $500   MIP $750

Interplanetary Games Set, 1934, three game boards in box: Cosmic Rocket Wars, Secrets of Atlantis, Siege of Gigantica, set
EX $235   NM $425   MIP $700

Interplanetary Space Fleet Model Kit, 1935, six different kits, including instructions and poster, in box, each
EX $100   NM $200   MIP $350

Lite-Blaster Flashlight, 1936
EX $155   NM $285   MIP $500

Martian Wars Game, 1980s, TSR, role playing game
EX $15   NM $25   MIP $50

Official Utility Belt, 1970s, Remco, in window box, w/decoder glasses, wristwatch, disk-shooting ray gun, intruder detection badge, city decoder map, secret message
EX $20   NM $40   MIP $85

Paint By Number Set, 1980s, Craft Master
EX $8   NM $20   MIP $35

Pencil Box, 1930s, American Pencil
EX $75   NM $150   MIP $275

Pendant Watch, 1970s, Huckleberry Time
EX $115   NM $200   MIP $300

Pocket Knife, 1934, Adolph Kastor, red, green, blue
EX $450   NM $900   MIP $2000

Pocket Watch, 1935, E. Ingraham, round, face shows Buck and Wilma, lightning bolt hands
EX $500   NM $1800   MIP $3750

Pocket Watch, 1970s, Huckleberry Time
EX $90   NM $175   MIP $275

Punching Bag, 1942, Morton Salt, balloon w/characters
EX $50   NM $75   MIP $150

Puzzle, 1945, Puzzle Craft, Buck Rogers and His Atomic Bomber, three different each
EX $75   NM $150   MIP $300

Puzzle, 1979, Milton Bradley, two versions showing TV scenes, each
EX $6   NM $15   MIP $30

Puzzle with sleeve, 1952, Milton Bradley, space station scene, 14" x 10"
EX $75   NM $150   MIP $200

Repeller Ray Ring, 1936, brass w/inset green stone
EX $400   NM $1250   MIP $2500

Rocket Rangers Iron-On Transfers, 1940s, set of three
EX $30   NM $50   MIP $100

Rocket Rangers Membership Card,
EX $45   NM $75   MIP $150

Rocket Ship, 1934, Marx, 12" tall, wind-up
EX $250   NM $500   MIP $750

Roller Skates, 1935, Marx
EX $1400   NM $200   MIP $3000

Rubber Band Gun, 1930s, cut-out paper gun, on card
EX $35   NM $85   MIP $150

Satellite Pioneers Button, 1950s, green or blue
EX $20   NM $50   MIP $100

Satellite Pioneers Map of Solar System, 1958
EX $20   NM $40   MIP $85

Satellite Pioneers Membership Card, 1950s
EX $30   NM $60   MIP $110

Satellite Pioneers Starfinder, 1950s, paper
EX $20   NM $50   MIP $75

Saturn Ring, 1946, Post Corn Toasties, red stone, glow-in-the-dark white plastic on crocodile base
EX $150   NM $300   MIP $600

School Bag
EX $60   NM $100   MIP $200

Solar Scouts Member Badge, 1935, gold
EX $60   NM $100   MIP $160

❑ **Solar Scouts Patch,** 1936, Cream of Wheat, three colors
EX $1500   NM $5000   MIP $7000

❑ **Solar Scouts Radio Club Manual,** 1936
EX $125   NM $275   MIP $550

❑ **Space Glasses,** 1955, Norton-Honer
EX $40   NM $75   MIP $200

❑ **Space Ranger Halolight Ring,** 1953, Sylvania
EX $300   NM $750   MIP $1000

❑ **Space Ranger Kit,** 1952, Sylvania, 11" x 15" premium, envelope w/six punch-out sheets
EX $50   NM $100   MIP $200

❑ **Spaceship Commander,** 1930s, stationary
EX $50   NM $100   MIP $200

❑ **Spaceship Commander Banner,** 1936
EX $350   NM $1000   MIP $2000

❑ **Spaceship Commander Whistling Badge,** 1930s
EX $50   NM $110   MIP $225

❑ **Strange Adventures in the Spider Ship Pop-Up Book,** 1935
EX $110   NM $250   MIP $400

❑ **Strato-Kite,** 1946, Aero-Kite
EX $20   NM $35   MIP $75

❑ **Super Foto Camera,** 1955, Norton-Honer
EX $40   NM $70   MIP $150

❑ **Super Scope Telescope,** 1955, Norton-Honer, 9" plastic telescope
EX $40   NM $70   MIP $150

❑ **Superdreadnought SD51X Model Kit,** 1936, 6-1/2" long, balsa wood, one of Interplanetary Space Fleet kit set
EX $100   NM $200   MIP $350

❑ **Toy Watch,** 1978, GLJ Toys
EX $15   NM $30   MIP $60

❑ **Two-Way Transceiver,** 1948, DA Myco
EX $80   NM $130   MIP $200

❑ **View-Master Set,** 1979, View-Master, three-reel set, in envelope or on blister card
EX $5   NM $10   MIP $20

❑ **Walkie Talkies,** 1950s, Remco
EX $60   NM $150   MIP $200

❑ **Wilma Deering Figure,** 1937, Tootsietoy, 1-3/4" tall, cast, gold
EX $70   NM $125   MIP $185

CAPTAIN MIDNIGHT

❑ **Air Heroes Stamp Album,** 1930s, twelve stamps
EX $35   NM $75   MIP $150

❑ **Captain Midnight Medal,** 1930s, gold medal pin w/centered wings and words "Flight Commander"; Capt. is embossed on top w/medal dangling beneath
EX $65   NM $150   MIP $200

❑ **Cup,** Ovaltine, plastic, 4" tall, "Ovaltine-The Heart of a Hearty Breakfast"
EX $25   NM $50   MIP $80

❑ **Membership Manual,** 1930s, Secret Squadron official code and manual guide
EX $30   NM $55   MIP $110

❑ **Secret Society Decoder w/key,** 1949
EX $80   NM $185   MIP $325

CAPTAIN VIDEO

❑ **Captain Video and Ranger Photo,** 1950s, premium
EX $25   NM $50   MIP $85

❑ **Captain Video Game,** 1952, Milton Bradley
EX $75   NM $150   MIP $275

❑ **Captain Video Rite-O-Lite Flashlight Gun,** 1950s, Power House Candy, 3" long, red plastic gun w/bulb, space map, paper, directions and order form, in mailing envelope
EX $20   NM $60   MIP $100

❑ **Captain Video Rocket Launcher,** 1952, Lido
EX $65   NM $185   MIP $360

❑ **Comic Book, Captain Video No. 1,** 1951, Fawcett
EX $100   NM $375   MIP $1000

❑ **Flying Saucer Ring,** 1950s, w/two saucers and papers
EX $500   NM $1000   MIP $1500

❑ **Galaxy Spaceship Riding Toy,** 1950s
EX $250   NM $425   MIP $650

❑ **Interplantary Space Men Figures,** 1950s, in die-cut box
EX $55   NM $110   MIP $175

❑ **Kukla, Fran and Ollie Puppet Show,** 1962, Milton Bradley, cardboard stage, puppets, props
EX $50   NM $200   MIP $375

❑ **Mysto-Coder,** 1950s, w/photo
EX $65   NM $200   MIP $400

❑ **Rite-O-Lite Flashlight Gun,** 1950s, Power House Candy
EX $40   NM $90   MIP $185

❑ **Rocket Tank,** 1952, Lido
EX $55   NM $95   MIP $145

❑ **Secret Seal Ring,** 1950s, w/initials CV, gold or copper
EX $250   NM $400   MIP $600

(ToyShop File Photo)

❑ **Space Port Play Set,** 1950s, Superior, All tin set, including rocket (not shown)
EX $250   NM $430   MIP $660

❑ **Troop Transport Ship,** 1950s, Lido, in box
EX $55   NM $95   MIP $145

DEFENDERS OF THE EARTH

❑ **Gripjaw Vehicle,** 1985, Galoob
EX $11   NM $16   MIP $25

❑ **Mongor Figure,** 1985, Galoob
EX $16   NM $23   MIP $35

❑ **Puzzle,** frame tray
EX $9   NM $15   MIP $25

DEFENDERS OF THE UNIVERSE

❑ **Battling Black Lion Voltron Vehicle,** 1986, LJN
EX $9   NM $13   MIP $20

❑ **Coffin of Darkness Voltron Vehicle,** 1986, LJN
EX $7   NM $10   MIP $15

❑ **Doom Blaster Voltron Vehicle,** 1986, LJN, mysterious flying machine
EX $9   NM $13   MIP $20

❑ **Doom Commander Figure,** 1985, Matchbox
EX $5   NM $7   MIP $10

❑ **Green Lion Voltron Vehicle,** 1986, LJN
EX $9   NM $13   MIP $20

❑ **Hagar Figure,** 1985, Matchbox
EX $5   NM $7   MIP $10

❑ **Hunk Figure,** 1985, Matchbox
EX $5   NM $7   MIP $10

❑ **Keith Figure,** 1985, Matchbox
EX $5   NM $7   MIP $10

❑ **King Zarkon Figure,** 1985, Matchbox
EX $5   NM $7   MIP $10

❑ **Lance Figure,** 1985, Matchbox
EX $5   NM $7   MIP $10

❑ **Motorized Lion Force Voltron Vehicle Set,** 1986, LJN, black lion w/blazing sound
EX $9   NM $13   MIP $20

❑ **Pidge Figure,** 1985, Matchbox
EX $5   NM $7   MIP $10

❑ **Prince Lothar Figure,** 1985, Matchbox
EX $5   NM $7   MIP $10

❑ **Princess Allura Figure,** 1985, Matchbox
EX $5   NM $7   MIP $10

❑ **Robeast Mutilor Figure,** 1985, Matchbox
EX $5   NM $7   MIP $10

❑ **Robeast Scorpious Figure,** 1985, Matchbox
EX $5   NM $7   MIP $10

❑ **Skull Tank Voltron Vehicle,** 1986, LJN
EX $9   NM $13   MIP $20

❑ **Vehicle Team Assembler,** 1986, LJN, forms Voltron
EX $9   NM $13   MIP $20

❑ **Voltron Lion Force & Vehicle Team Assemblers Gift Set,** 1986, LJN
EX $9   NM $13   MIP $20

SPACE TOYS

❑ **Voltron Motorized Giant Commander,** 1984, LJN, plastic 36", multicolor body w/movable head, arms and wings, wire remote control, battery operated
EX $15   NM $25   MIP $40

❑ **Zarkon Zapper Voltron Vehicle,** 1986, LJN, w/galactic sound
EX $11   NM $16   MIP $25

DOCTOR WHO

❑ **Cyberman Robot Doll,** 1970s, Denys Fisher, 10"
EX $250   NM $350   MIP $550

❑ **Dalek Bagatelle,** 1976, Denys Fisher
EX $70   NM $110   MIP $160

❑ **Dalek Shooting Game,** 1965, Marx, 8" x 20", four-color tin litho stand up target and generic cork rifle
EX $225   NM $325   MIP $525

❑ **Dalek's Oracle Question & Answer Board Game,** 1965, magnetized Dalek that spins
EX $115   NM $165   MIP $250

❑ **Davros Figure,** 1986, Dapol, villain w/left arm
EX $11   NM $16   MIP $45

❑ **Doctor Who Card Set,** 1970s, 12 octagon cards
EX $14   NM $20   MIP $35

❑ **Doctor Who Card Set,** 1976, Denys Fisher, 24 cards
EX $18   NM $26   MIP $45

❑ **Doctor Who Trump Card Game,** 1970s
EX $9   NM $13   MIP $20

(ToyShop File Photo)

❑ **Doctor Who...Dodge the Daleks Board Game,** 1965
EX $120   NM $175   MIP $280

FLASH GORDON

❑ **Adventure on the Moons of Mongo Game,** 1977, House of Games
EX $15   NM $25   MIP $40

❑ **Arak Figure,** 1979, Mattel, 3-3/4", carded
EX $17   NM $30   MIP $50

❑ **Battle Rocket with Space Probing Action,** 1976
EX $6   NM $10   MIP $20

❑ **Beastman Figure,** 1979, Mattel, 3-3/4", carded
EX $15   NM $25   MIP $45

❑ **Book Bag,** 1950s, 12" wide, three-color art on flap
EX $17   NM $35   MIP $75

❑ **Candy Box,** 1970s, eight illustrated boxes, each
EX $4   NM $10   MIP $20

❑ **Dr. Zarkov Figure,** 1979, Mattel, 3-3/4" figure, on card
EX $15   NM $35   MIP $50

❑ **Flash and Ming Button,** 1970s, shows Flash and Ming crossing swords
EX $4   NM $10   MIP $20

❑ **Flash Gordon Air Ray Gun,** 1950s, Budson, 10" unusual air blaster, handle on top cocks mechanism, pressed steel
EX $215   NM $350   MIP $700

❑ **Flash Gordon and Martian,** 1965, Revell, #1450
EX $60   NM $125   MIP $175

❑ **Flash Gordon and the Ape Men of Mor Book,** 1942, Dell, 196 pages, Fast Action Story
EX $75   NM $150   MIP $250

❑ **Flash Gordon and the Fiery Desert of Mongo Book,** 1948, Whitman, Big Little Book
EX $30   NM $60   MIP $90

❑ **Flash Gordon and the Monsters of Mongo Book,** 1935, Whitman, hardback Big Little Book
EX $50   NM $90   MIP $135

❑ **Flash Gordon and the Perils of Mongo Book,** 1940, Whitman, Big Little Book
EX $35   NM $70   MIP $100

❑ **Flash Gordon and the Power Men of Mongo Book,** 1943, Whitman, Big Little Book
EX $35   NM $65   MIP $95

❑ **Flash Gordon and the Red Sword Invaders Book,** 1945, Whitman, Big Little Book
EX $30   NM $60   MIP $90

❑ **Flash Gordon and the Tournaments of Mongo Book,** 1935, Whitman, paperback Big Little Book
EX $45   NM $80   MIP $120

❑ **Flash Gordon and the Tyrant of Mongo Book,** 1941, Whitman, Big Little Book, w/flip pictures
EX $35   NM $70   MIP $105

❑ **Flash Gordon and the Witch Queen of Mongo Book,** 1936, Whitman, Big Little Book
EX $45   NM $80   MIP $120

❑ **Flash Gordon Arresting Ray Gun,** 1939, Marx, picture of Flash on handle, 12" long
EX $200   NM $500   MIP $1000

❑ **Flash Gordon Costume,** 1951, Esquire Novelty
EX $90   NM $145   MIP $225

❑ **Flash Gordon Figure,** 1944, wood composition, 5" tall
EX $115   NM $195   MIP $300

❑ **Flash Gordon Game,** 1970s, House of Games
EX $15   NM $30   MIP $40

❑ **Flash Gordon Hand Puppet,** 1950s, rubber head
EX $90   NM $145   MIP $250

❑ **Flash Gordon in the Forest Kingdom of Mongo Book,** 1938, Whitman, Big Little Book
EX $40   NM $75   MIP $110

❑ **Flash Gordon in the Ice World of Mongo Book,** 1942, Whitman, Big Little Book, w/flip pictures
EX $35   NM $70   MIP $100

❑ **Flash Gordon in the Jungles of Mongo Book,** 1947, Whitman, Big Little Book
EX $35   NM $65   MIP $95

❑ **Flash Gordon in the Water World of Mongo Book,** 1937, Whitman, Big Little Book
EX $35   NM $70   MIP $105

❑ **Flash Gordon Kite,** 1950s, 21" x 17", paper
EX $55   NM $90   MIP $135

❑ **Flash Gordon on the Planet Mongo Book,** 1934, Whitman, Big Little Book
EX $55   NM $105   MIP $155

❑ **Flash Gordon Paint Book,** 1930s
EX $60   NM $125   MIP $200

❑ **Flash Gordon Radio Repeater Clicker Pistol,** Marx, 10" long, 1930s
EX $250   NM $750   MIP $1500

❑ **Flash Gordon Signal Pistol,** 1930s, Marx, 7", siren sounds when trigger is pulled, tin/pressed steel, green w/red trim
EX $250   NM $600   MIP $1200

❑ **Flash Gordon Space Water Gun,** 1976, Nasta, water ray gun on illustrated card
EX $10   NM $25   MIP $50

❑ **Flash Gordon Three Color Ray Gun,** 1976, Nasta, battery-operated
EX $8   NM $35   MIP $75

❑ **Flash Gordon vs. the Emperor of Mongo Book,** 1936, Dell, 244 pages, Fast Action Story
EX $70   NM $140   MIP $225

❑ **Flash Gordon Water Pistol,** 1940s, Marx, plastic w/whistle in handle, 7-1/2" long
EX $80   NM $250   MIP $500

❑ **Flash Gordon Wristwatch,** 1979, Bradley, medium chrome case, back and sweep seconds, Flash in foreground w/city behind
EX $70   NM $115   MIP $175

❑ **Flash Gordon, The Movie Buttons,** 1980, set of five, each
EX $2   NM $4   MIP $8

❑ **Home Foundry Casting Set,** 1935, lead casting set w/molds of Flash and other characters
EX $575   NM $975   MIP $1500

❑ **Lizard Woman Figure,** 1979, Mattel, 3-3/4", carded
EX $15   NM $25   MIP $40

❏ **Medals and Insignia,** 1978, Larami, set of five on blister card
EX $10   **NM** $25   **MIP** $50

❏ **Ming Figure,** 1979, Mattel, 3-3/4", carded
EX $12   **NM** $20   **MIP** $35

❏ **Ming's Space Shuttle,** Mattel
EX $15   **NM** $25   **MIP** $40

❏ **Pencil Box,** 1951
EX $75   **NM** $150   **MIP** $200

❏ **Puzzle,** 1930s, Featured Funnies
EX $55   **NM** $110   **MIP** $160

❏ **Puzzle,** 1951, Milton Bradley, frame tray
EX $45   **NM** $80   **MIP** $120

❏ **Puzzles,** 1951, Milton Bradley, set of three
EX $105   **NM** $200   **MIP** $300

❏ **Rocket Fighter,** 1939, Marx, tin wind-up, 12" long
EX $175   **NM** $350   **MIP** $600

❏ **Rocket Ship,** 1975, 3" die-cast metal
EX $10   **NM** $20   **MIP** $35

❏ **Rocket Ship,** 1979, Mattel, inflatable, 3' long, w/plastic nose, rocket and gondola attachments
EX $20   **NM** $40   **MIP** $60

❏ **Solar Commando Set,** 1950s, Premier Products
EX $65   **NM** $115   **MIP** $175

❏ **Space Compass,** 1950s, ornately housed compass on illustrated watchband
EX $25   **NM** $40   **MIP** $75

❏ **Space Water Gun,** 1976, Nasta, water ray gun on illustrated card
EX $6   **NM** $15   **MIP** $30

❏ **Sunglasses,** 1981, Ja-Ru, plastic w/emblem on bridge, carded
EX $3   **NM** $5   **MIP** $10

❏ **Three-Color Ray Gun,** 1976, Nasta
EX $8   **NM** $15   **MIP** $30

❏ **Thun, Lion Man Figure,** 1979, Mattel, 3-3/4", carded
EX $15   **NM** $25   **MIP** $45

❏ **Two-Way Telephone,** 1940s, Marx
EX $60   **NM** $110   **MIP** $185

❏ **View-Master Set,** 1963, View-Master, three reels in envelope
EX $20   **NM** $35   **MIP** $60

❏ **View-Master Set,** 1976, View-Master, three reels, In the Planet Mongo
EX $6   **NM** $10   **MIP** $20

❏ **Vultan Figure,** 1979, Mattel, 3-3/4", carded
EX $15   **NM** $30   **MIP** $50

❏ **Wallet,** 1949, w/zipper
EX $70   **NM** $115   **MIP** $175

❏ **Water Pistol,** 1950s, Marx, 7-1/2" plastic
EX $155   **NM** $275   **MIP** $500

LAND OF THE GIANTS

❏ **Annual Book,** 1969, World Dist./UK, two volumes, set
EX $30   **NM** $50   **MIP** $75

❏ **Colorforms Set,** 1968, Colorforms
EX $30   **NM** $50   **MIP** $75

❏ **Costumes,** 1968, Ben Cooper, Steve Burton, Giant Witch, or Scientist, each
EX $35   **NM** $60   **MIP** $150

❏ **Deluxe Numbered Pencil Coloring Set,** 1969, Hasbro
EX $60   **NM** $100   **MIP** $150

❏ **Double Action Bagatelle Game,** 1969, Hasbro, pinball game, cardboard back
EX $35   **NM** $75   **MIP** $160

❏ **Flight of Fear Book,** Whitman, hardcover
EX $8   **NM** $15   **MIP** $35

❏ **Flying Saucer,** 1968, Remco, flying disk
EX $60   **NM** $100   **MIP** $150

❏ **Land of the Giants Book,** Pyramid, paperback by Murray Leinster
EX $8   **NM** $13   **MIP** $25

❏ **Land of the Giants Comic Book #1,** 1968, Gold Key
EX $10   **NM** $15   **MIP** $30

❏ **Land of the Giants Comic Books #2-#5,** 1968, Gold Key, each
EX $8   **NM** $13   **MIP** $22

❏ **Motorized Flying Rocket,** 1968, Remco, plastic airplane w/motor, LOTG logo on wings
EX $80   **NM** $130   **MIP** $200

❏ **Movie Viewer,** 1968, Acme, film strip viewer, on card
EX $30   **NM** $45   **MIP** $75

❏ **Painting Set,** 1969, Hasbro
EX $40   **NM** $65   **MIP** $100

❏ **Puzzle,** 1968, Whitman, round floor puzzle w/cartoon illustration
EX $35   **NM** $55   **MIP** $85

❏ **Rub-Ons,** 1969, Hasbro
EX $30   **NM** $50   **MIP** $75

❏ **Shoot & Stick Target Rifle Set,** 1968, Remco, western rifle w/logo decals
EX $90   **NM** $145   **MIP** $225

❏ **Signal Ray Space Gun,** 1968, Remco, ray gun w/logo decals
EX $70   **NM** $115   **MIP** $175

❏ **Space Sled,** 1968, Remco, Supercar refitted w/LOTG decals—Mike Mercury still sits behind the wheel
EX $200   **NM** $350   **MIP** $525

❏ **Spaceship Control Panel,** 1968, Remco, Firebird 99 dashboard w/a cardboard cut-out of logo on top
EX $200   **NM** $300   **MIP** $525

❏ **Spindrift Interior Model Kit,** 1989, Lunar Models, #Sf029, interior for 16" model shell
EX $35   **NM** $55   **MIP** $85

❏ **Spindrift Toothpick Kit,** 1968, Remco, box of toothpicks w/a few cardboard pieces to build ship
EX $35   **NM** $60   **MIP** $85

❏ **Target Set,** 1969, Hasbro, small guns w/darts
EX $60   **NM** $100   **MIP** $160

❏ **The Hot Spot Book,** Pyramid, paperback, #2 in series, by Leinster
EX $12   **NM** $20   **MIP** $35

❏ **Trading Card Wrapper,** 1968, Topps/A & BC
EX $60   **NM** $100   **MIP** $160

❏ **Trading Cards,** 1968, A & BC/England, 55 cards
EX $275   **NM** $450   **MIP** $710

❏ **Trading Cards,** 1968, Topps USA, 55 cards
EX $275   **NM** $450   **MIP** $710

❏ **Trading Cards Box,** 1968, Topps/A & BC, display box only
EX $395   **NM** $650   **MIP** $1000

❏ **Unknown Danger Book,** Pyramid, paperback #3 by Leinster
EX $12   **NM** $20   **MIP** $35

❏ **View-Master Set,** 1968, GAF, three reels, first episode
EX $20   **NM** $35   **MIP** $50

❏ **Walkie Talkies,** 1968, Remco, generic walkie talkies w/LOTG decals added
EX $80   **NM** $130   **MIP** $210

❏ **Wrist Flashlight,** 1968, Bantam Lite
EX $30   **NM** $50   **MIP** $80

LOST IN SPACE

❏ **Chariot Model Kit,** Marusan/Japanese, figures and motor
EX $625   **NM** $975   **MIP** $1500

❏ **Chariot Model Kit,** 1987, Lunar Models, #SF009, 1:35 scale, w/clear vacuform canopy and dome, plastic body, treads, roof rack
EX $35   **NM** $50   **MIP** $80

❏ **Costume,** 1965, Ben Cooper, silver spacesuit w/logo
EX $85   **NM** $150   **MIP** $225

❏ **Doll Set,** Marusan/Japanese, dressed in spacesuits w/their own freezing tubes w/a cardboard insert w/color photos and description
EX $2900   **NM** $4500   **MIP** $7000

❏ **Fan Cards,** 1960s, promo cards mailed to fans; color photo
EX $20   **NM** $35   **MIP** $60

❏ **Fan Cards,** 1960s, promo cards mailed to fans; black/white photo
EX $15   **NM** $25   **MIP** $40

❏ **Helmet and Gun Set,** 1967, Remco, child size helmet w/blue flashing light and logo decals, blue and red molded gun
EX $300   **NM** $530   **MIP** $880

❏ **Jupiter Model Kit,** 1966, Marusan/Japanese, large version
EX $425   **NM** $650   **MIP** $1000

SPACE TOYS

❑ **Jupiter-2 Model Kit**, Comet/England, 2" diameter, solid metal
EX $8　　NM $13　　MIP $25

❑ **Jupiter-2 Model Kit**, 1966, Maru-san/Japanese, 6" molded in green plastic w/wheels and wind-up motor
EX $425　　NM $650　　MIP $1000

❑ **Laser Water Pistol**, Unknown, 5" long, first season pistol style
EX $30　　NM $50　　MIP $80

(ToyShop File Photo)

❑ **Lost In Space 3-D Action Fun Game**, 1966, Remco, three levels w/small card-board figures
EX $530　　NM $785　　MIP $1220

❑ **Note Pad**, June Lockhart on front
EX $25　　NM $40　　MIP $65

❑ **Puzzles**, 1966, Milton Bradley, frame tray; three poses w/Cyclops
EX $40　　NM $65　　MIP $110

❑ **Robot**, 1966, Remco, 12" high, motor-ized w/blinking lights
EX $180　　NM $365　　MIP $680

❑ **Robot**, 1968, Aurora, 6" high w/base
EX $150　　NM $400　　MIP $1100

❑ **Robot**, 1977, K-mart/Ahi, 10", plastic w/green dome, battery-operated
EX $85　　NM $200　　MIP $325

❑ **Robot YM-3**, 1985, Masudaya, 4" high, wind-up
EX $20　　NM $30　　MIP $50

❑ **Robot YM-3**, 1986, Masudaya, 16" high, speaks English and Japanese
EX $85　　NM $150　　MIP $250

❑ **Roto-Jet Gun Set**, 1966, Mattel, TV tie-in, modular gun can be reconfigured into different variations, shoots discs
EX $775　　NM $1300　　MIP $2600

❑ **Saucer Gun**, 1977, Ahi, disk shooting gun
EX $30　　NM $60　　MIP $125

❑ **Space Family Robinson Comic Book**, 1960s, Gold Key
EX $15　　NM $25　　MIP $45

❑ **Switch-and-Go Set**, 1966, Mattel, fig-ures, Jupiter and chariot that ran around track
EX $975　　NM $1500　　MIP $2400

❑ **Trading Cards**, 1966, Topps, 55 black and white cards, no wrappers or box
EX $175　　NM $260　　MIP $400

❑ **Tru-Vue Magic Eyes Set**, 1967, GAF, rectangular reels
EX $30　　NM $50　　MIP $80

❑ **View-Master Set**, 1967, GAF, Con-demned of Space
EX $25　　NM $40　　MIP $65

❑ **Walkie Talkies**, 1977, AHI, small card
EX $30　　NM $50　　MIP $80

MISCELLANEOUS

❑ **Astro Base**, 1960, Ideal, 22" tall, red/white astronaut base, control panel opens lock door, extends crane and low-ers astronaut in scout car
EX $225　　NM $325　　MIP $525

❑ **Astro Boy Mask/Glasses**, 1960s, blue glasses w/Astro boy hair on top
EX $25　　NM $50　　MIP $75

❑ **Astronaut Costume**, 1960, Collegeville
EX $18　　NM $25　　MIP $50

❑ **Astronaut Costume**, 1962, Ben Cooper
EX $18　　NM $25　　MIP $50

❑ **Astronaut Space Commander Play Suit**, 1950s, Yankeeboy, green outfit and cap (military style) w/gold piping on collar and pants
EX $35　　NM $50　　MIP $85

❑ **Fireball XL-5 Space City Play Set**, 1963, MPC, includes ship, base and fig-ures
EX $550　　NM $1100　　MIP $2200

❑ **Fireball XL-5 Spaceship**, 1963, MPC, plastic, 20" ship w/figures
EX $200　　NM $500　　MIP $1300

❑ **Martian Bobbing Head**, 1960s, 7" tall, blue vinyl martian w/bobbing eyes and exposed brain
EX $23　　NM $35　　MIP $60

❑ **Men into Space Astronaut Space Hel-met**, 1960s, Ideal, plastic helmet w/visor
EX $35　　NM $50　　MIP $80

❑ **Puzzle**, 1970, Selchow & Righter, 10" x 14", picture of the moon's surface
EX $14　　NM $20　　MIP $35

❑ **Rex Mars Atomix Pistol Flashlight**, 1950s, Marx, plastic
EX $50　　NM $80　　MIP $125

❑ **Space Safari Planetary Play Set**, 1969, four battery operated space vehicles, 3" tall astronaut figures in silver plastic, 2" hard plastic aliens
EX $45　　NM $65　　MIP $100

❑ **TV Space Riders Coloring Book**, 1952, Abbott, 14" X 15"
EX $7　　NM $12　　MIP $25

❑ **V-Enemy Visitor Doll**, 1984, LJN, 12"
EX $16　　NM $30　　MIP $60

❑ **Voyage to the Bottom of the Sea Scout Play Set**, 1964, Remco, includes mini-sub, sea crawler and divers
EX $250　　NM $650　　MIP $1300

❑ **Voyage to the Bottom of the Sea Sea-view Play Set**, 1964, Remco, includes plastic sub, sea monster and divers
EX $320　　NM $675　　MIP $1625

MONSTERS

❑ **Creature From the Black Lagoon Aquarium Figure**, 1950s, Japan, 3 1/2" Lead figure
EX $85　　NM $150　　MIP n/a

❑ **Creature from the Black Lagoon Aquar-ium Figure**, 1971, Penn-Plax, 6" Moving Figure
EX $150　　NM $250　　MIP $450

❑ **Creature From the Black Lagoon Fig-ure**, 1963, Marx, 5", hard plastic blue or orange
EX $10　　NM $20　　MIP $40

❑ **Creature From the Black Lagoon Fig-ure**, 1973, 74, AHI, 5", hard rubber like bendy
EX $40　　NM $65　　MIP $100

❑ **Creature From the Black Lagoon Fig-ure**, 1974, AHI, 8", plastic, bendable joints
EX $295　　NM $425　　MIP $700

❑ **Creature From the Black Lagoon Hal-loween Costume**, 1973, Ben Cooper, Child's Mask and Costume
EX $35　　NM $80　　MIP $120

❑ **Creature From the Black Lagoon Motionette**, 1992, Telco, 24", Electric, w/sound
EX $100　　NM $200　　MIP $350

❑ **Creature From the Black Lagoon Motionette**, 1992, Telco, 17", Batt op, w/sound
EX $10　　NM $15　　MIP $30

❑ **Creature From the Black Lagoon Robot**, 1991, Robot House, 9", tin/plas-tic, wind-up
EX $35　　NM $65　　MIP $110

❑ **Creature From the Black Lagoon Soaky**, 1960s, Colgate-Palmolive, 10", plastic, bubble bath bottle
EX $45　　NM $85　　MIP $125

❑ **Creature From the Black Lagoon Sparky**, 1970s, Hong Kong, 3 1/2", plas-tic, wind-up
EX $10　　NM $20　　MIP $35

❑ **Creature From the Black Lagoon Wig-gle Ick Figure**, 1960s, Japan, 7", rub-bery plastic, bobbin' head
EX $50　　NM $85　　MIP $150

❑ **Deadly Grell Figure**, 1983, LJN, bend-able
EX $5　　NM $7　　MIP $10

❑ **Dracula Action Figure**, AHI, w/Aurora head
EX $65　　NM $125　　MIP $200

❑ **Dracula Glow-in-the-Dark Mini Mon-sters**, Remco
EX $23　　NM $30　　MIP $45

❑ **Dwarves of the Mountain Human/Mon-ster Figure**, 1983, LJN
EX $5　　NM $7　　MIP $10

❏ **Evil Monster Figure Bugbear & Goblin,** 1983, LJN, Orcs of the Broken Bone
EX $5   **NM** $7   **MIP** $10

❏ **Frankenstein Figure,** AHI, w/Aurora head
EX $65   **NM** $125   **MIP** $200

❏ **Frankenstein Figure,** 1978, Remco, poseable, glow-in-the-dark features and removable cloth costumes
EX $23   **NM** $35   **MIP** $50

❏ **Godzilla Combat Joe Set,** 1984, vinyl, w/12" tall Combat Joe figure, poseable
EX $450   **NM** $650   **MIP** $1000

❏ **Godzilla Figure,** 1977, Mattel, 19" tall
EX $20   **NM** $30   **MIP** $60

❏ **Godzilla Figure,** 1985, Imperial, 6-1/2" tall, arms, legs and tail movable
EX $5   **NM** $10   **MIP** $20

❏ **Godzilla Figure,** 1985, Imperial, 13" tall, arms, legs and tail movable
EX $15   **NM** $23   **MIP** $40

MOON McDARE

❏ **Action Communication Set,** 1966, Gilbert
EX $25   **NM** $35   **MIP** $60

❏ **Moon Explorer Set,** 1966, Gilbert
EX $35   **NM** $50   **MIP** $80

❏ **Moon McDare Figure,** 1966, Gilbert, 12" tall astronaut w/blue jumpsuit
EX $55   **NM** $80   **MIP** $150

❏ **Moon McDare Space Gun Set,** 1966, Gilbert
EX $25   **NM** $50   **MIP** $125

❏ **Space Accessory Pack,** 1966, Gilbert
EX $25   **NM** $35   **MIP** $60

❏ **Space Gun Set,** 1966, Gilbert
EX $30   **NM** $40   **MIP** $70

❏ **Space Mutt Set,** 1966, Gilbert
EX $30   **NM** $45   **MIP** $75

OTHER WORLDS, THE

❏ **Castle Zendo,** 1983, Arco
EX $20   **NM** $30   **MIP** $50

❏ **Fighting Glowgons Figure Set,** 1983, Arco
EX $18   **NM** $25   **MIP** $40

❏ **Fighting Terrans Figure Set,** 1983, Arco
EX $20   **NM** $30   **MIP** $50

❏ **Kamaro Figure,** 1983, Arco
EX $8   **NM** $12   **MIP** $18

❏ **Sharkoss Figure,** 1983, Arco
EX $8   **NM** $12   **MIP** $18

PLANET OF THE APES

❏ **Color-Vue Set,** 1970s, Hasbro, eight pencils and nine 12" x 13" pictures to color
EX $30   **NM** $45   **MIP** $70

❏ **Dr. Zaius Bank,** 1967, Play Pal, figural, vinyl, 11"
EX $20   **NM** $30   **MIP** $60

❏ **Fun-Doh Modeling Molds,** 1974, Chemtoy, molds of Zira, Cornelius, Zaius, and Aldo
EX $20   **NM** $30   **MIP** $50

❏ **Galen Bank,** 1960s, Play Pal
EX $25   **NM** $35   **MIP** $60

❏ **Planet of the Apes Activity Book,** 1974, Saalfield, #C3031
EX $15   **NM** $30   **MIP** $45

❏ **Puzzles,** H.G. Toys, 96-piece canister puzzles, each
EX $7   **NM** $12   **MIP** $25

❏ **Wagon,** AHI, friction powered prison wagon
EX $20   **NM** $45   **MIP** $70

❏ **Wastebasket,** 1967, Chein, oval, tin
EX $25   **NM** $35   **MIP** $60

❏ **Zaius, Zera, or Cornelius Walkers,** 1970s, Hong Kong, 3 1/2" plastic, wind-up
EX $20   **NM** $40   **MIP** $80

ROCKY JONES, SPACE RANGER

❏ **Rocky Jones, Space Ranger Coloring Book,** 1951, Whitman, 14" x 16"
EX $25   **NM** $50   **MIP** $75

❏ **Space Ranger Button,** 1954
EX $17   **NM** $35   **MIP** $60

❏ **Wings Pin,** 1954
EX $17   **NM** $40   **MIP** $75

❏ **Wristwatch,** 1954, in illustrated box
EX $80   **NM** $150   **MIP** $300

SPACE GUNS

❏ **4-Barrel Waist Space Dart Gun Belt,** 1950s, Knickerbocker, 11" wide gun system on belt, designed to be worn on waist or chest and aimed w/periscope sight, red plastic belt
EX $30   **NM** $50   **MIP** $85

❏ **888 Space Gun,** 1955, Japan, 3" long, tin, shoots caps, painted blue body and grip w/stars, planets and spaceship, red barrel w/"888" above grip
EX $30   **NM** $60   **MIP** $120

❏ **Astro Ray Gun,** 1960s, Shudo/Japan, 5-7/8" long, silver finish body w/red, yellow and black detailing, friction sparkling action, single large spark window near muzzle, prominent "Astro Ray Gun" in center of body
EX $15   **NM** $30   **MIP** $60

❏ **Astro Ray Gun,** 1968, Shudo/Japan, 9" long, friction spark action, tin litho body w/clear red plastic barrel, red on yellow "ASTRO RAY GUN" lettering
EX $25   **NM** $40   **MIP** $75

❏ **Astro Ray Laser Lite Beam Dart Gun,** 1960s, Ohio Art, 10" red and white plastic flashlight lights target w/four darts
EX $70   **NM** $120   **MIP** $185

❏ **Astro-Ray Space Gun,** 10"
EX $20   **NM** $30   **MIP** $50

❏ **Atom Bubble Gun,** 1940s, Unknown, red tubular barrel w/handle attached, two sets of silver finish fins--at barrel base and muzzle, wire loop projects from muzzle for bubble blowing, handle embossed "Atom Trade Mark"
EX $75   **NM** $150   **MIP** $250

❏ **Atom Buster Mystery Gun,** 1950s, Webb Electric, 11" long yellow plastic gun w/inner bladder, fires blast of air at tissue paper atomic mushroom target, w/instructions, atomic explosion cover art on box
EX $105   **NM** $200   **MIP** $300

❏ **Atom Ray Gun,** 1949, Hiller, 5-1/2" long, sleek red body gun of aluminum and brass w/bulbous water reservoir on top of gun, reads "Atom Ray Gun" between two lightning bolts on reservoir
EX $135   **NM** $300   **MIP** $500

❏ **Atomee Water Pistol,** 1960s, Park Plastics, 4-1/4" black plastic
EX $15   **NM** $25   **MIP** $40

❏ **Atomic Disintegrator Ray Gun,** 1954, Hubley, 8" in long, die-cast metal w/red handles, ornately embellished w/dials and other equipment outcroppings, shoots caps
EX $150   **NM** $325   **MIP** $675

❏ **Atomic Flash Gun,** 1955, Chein, 7-1/2" long, tin, sparkling action seen through tinted elongated oval plastic muzzle, w/yellow and red on turquoise body w/red lettered "Atomic Flash" over trigger
EX $40   **NM** $70   **MIP** $135

❏ **Atomic Gun,** 1960s, Japan, 5" long, gold, blue, white and red tin litho, friction sparkling action, "Atomic Gun" on body sides
EX $20   **NM** $40   **MIP** $75

❏ **Atomic Gun,** 1969, Haji, 9" long, red, gray and yellow tin litho gun w/plastic muzzle, friction sparkling action, large hollow letter "ATOMIC GUN" on body
EX $15   **NM** $35   **MIP** $70

❏ **Atomic Jet Gun,** 1954, Stevens, 8-1/2" long, gold chromed die-cast metal, cap shooting, "Atomic Jet" and large circular "S" logo on grip
EX $90   **NM** $160   **MIP** $275

❏ **Atomic Ray Gun,** 1957, Marx, 30" long, "Captain Space Solar Scout," blue plastic w/oversized telescope sight flashlight and "electric buzzer" sound
EX $75   **NM** $175   **MIP** $300

❏ **Baby Space Gun,** 1950s, Daiya/Japan, 6" friction siren and spark action
EX $35   **NM** $60   **MIP** $135

❏ **Batman Ray Gun,** 1960s, Unknown, cap pistol w/bat symbol for the sight
EX $35   **NM** $65   **MIP** $140

❏ **Battlestar Galactica Lasermatic Pistol,** 1978, Mattel
EX $15   **NM** $30   **MIP** $60

❏ **Battlestar Galactica Lasermatic Rifle,** 1978, Mattel
EX $25   **NM** $40   **MIP** $80

Bee-Vo Bell Gun, 1950s, Beaver Toys, #204, 6-1/2" long, red plastic, fires trapped marble at bell in muzzle, in box
EX $25 NM $40 MIP $80

Bicycle Water Cannon Ray Gun, 1950s, Unknown, 10", red plastic, swivel mount attached to bicycle handles, fired by lever
EX $30 NM $75 MIP $125

Cherilea Space Gun, Marx, miniature scale, die-cast
EX $27 NM $40 MIP $65

Clicker Ray Gun, 1950s, Unknown, 5" red, blue or gray hard plastic, no boxes, sold loose
EX $15 NM $25 MIP $50

Clicker Ray Gun, 1960, Irwin, 9" long, red plastic w/deep blue cooling fins on barrel base
EX $30 NM $45 MIP $75

Clicker Whistle Ray Gun, 1950s, Unknown, 5" plastic, blue/green or olive/green swirl plastic, imprinted spacemen and rocket ships, back of gun is a whistle
EX $15 NM $25 MIP $50

Daisy Rocket Dart Pistol, 1954, Daisy, 7" long, red, blue and yellow sheet metal gun w/blue body, blue grips w/yellow trim, blue and yellow barrel stripes, same body as Zooka Pop Pistol but w/connecting rod from gun to barrel
EX $80 NM $175 MIP $350

Daisy Zooka Pop Pistol, 1954, Daisy, 7" long, colorful red, blue and yellow sheet metal gun w/blue body, red grips w/yellow trim and litho star reading "It's a Daisy Play Gun," yellow barrel w/red stripes, and wide red muzzle, handle cock
EX $80 NM $175 MIP $350

Dan Dare & the Aliens Ray Gun, 1950s, 21", tin litho gun
EX $105 NM $175 MIP $300

Dune Fremen Tarpel Gun, 1984, LJN, 8" long, battery-operated w/internal light, light beam and chirping sound, plastic
EX $25 NM $40 MIP $70

Dune Sardaukar Laser Gun, 1984, LJN, 7" black plastic w/flashing lights, battery-operated
EX $20 NM $35 MIP $55

Flash-O-Matic, The Safe Gun, 1950s, Royal Plastics, 7" long red and yellow plastic battery-operated light beam gun
EX $60 NM $100 MIP $160

Floating Satellite Target Game, 1958, S. Horikawa/Japan, 6-1/2" x 9", battery-operated, includes a pistol and three rubber tipped darts, a blower supports the styrofoam ball on a column of air and the players shoot darts to knock it down
EX $175 NM $300 MIP $475

Ideal Flash Gun, 1957, Ideal, 9" long, plastic three-color flashlight gun w/red or blue body and bulbous contrasting-color blue or red rimmed flash unit, trig-

ger switch and tail battery compartment cover, w/color switch at top of flash unit
EX $80 NM $150 MIP $220

Jack Dan Space Gun, 1959, Metamol/Spain, 7-1/2" long, in black, red or blue painted die-cast metal cap gun w/"Jack Dan" over trigger
EX $105 NM $200 MIP $300

Jet Gun, 1957, Japan, 6" long, tin, sparkling action, red body w/three small red tinted spark windows near muzzle, grip shows silver-suited astronaut in modern helmet and wording "JET GUN" at top of grip near trigger
EX $35 NM $60 MIP $130

Jet Jr. Cap Gun, 1950s, Stevens, 6-1/2" long, fires roll caps, side loading door, silver finish, rear jet "Blast Off Fins"
EX $135 NM $250 MIP $375

Jet Plane Missile Gun, 1968, Hasbro, jet shaped handgun shoots darts, targets supplied on box back
EX $35 NM $60 MIP $100

Jupiter 4 Color Signal Gun, 1950s, Remco, 9" long black, red and yellow plastic gun that lights up in four colors, red telescoping sight
EX $35 NM $55 MIP $90

Over and Under Ray Gun, 1960s, Haji, 8-1/2" long, red, yellow, white and black tin litho gun w/two over and under reciprocating plastic muzzles, friction sparkling action
EX $30 NM $50 MIP $80

Planet Clicker Bubble Gun, 1953, Mercury Toys, 8" long, plastic, red body w/yellow accents, dip the barrel in bubble solution and pull trigger to make bubbles and produce click sound, in illustrated box
EX $40 NM $65 MIP $110

Planet Patrol Saucer Gun, 1950s, Unknown, w/spaceman motif
EX $40 NM $70 MIP $120

Pop Gun, 1967, Chemtoy, 4-1/2" long red hard plastic gun w/space designs on handle
EX $25 NM $35 MIP $80

Pop Ray Gun, 1930s, Wyandotte, red pressed steel body w/five widely spaced vertical round fins, unpainted trigger and muzzle w/large gunsight, rod connects body to pop mechanism in muzzle
EX $70 NM $125 MIP $200

Radar Gun, 1956, Unknown, 5-1/2" long, mauve or silver/gray swirl plastic body w/green or yellow spaceman sight and trigger, Saturn and star embossed above grip and "Radar Gun" embossed above that
EX $20 NM $35 MIP $60

Ratchet Sound Space Gun, 1950s, Ideal, 7" long, red plastic w/silver trim, flywheel ratchet on top of gun
EX $30 NM $50 MIP $80

Ratchet Water Pistol Ray Gun, 1960s, Hong Kong, 6-1/2" unusual pull back mechanism loads pistol, ratchet forces water out when trigger is pulled
EX $25 NM $40 MIP $70

Ray Dart Gun, 1968, Tarrson, 9-1/2" long, blue plastic body w/yellow muzzle, w/three darts, storage compartment in red handle base
EX $15 NM $27 MIP $55

Ray Gun, 1936, Wyandotte, 7" stamped metal pop gun that uses a captive cork to make the pop, red body, unpainted muzzle, w/connecting rod from body to barrel tip
EX $50 NM $100 MIP $175

Ray Gun, 1957, Japan, 6-1/2" long, tin, sparkling action w/two red tinted plastic tapered rectangle windows at muzzle, "Ray Gun" in red at top of body w/rocket exhaust encircling green/blue planet against deep blue star studded background
EX $32 NM $65 MIP $130

Ray Gun Water Pistol, 1950s, Palmer Plastics, 5-1/2" many color variations: green, orange, translucent blue, royal blue, black, yellow and red
EX $10 NM $15 MIP $30

Ray Gun Water Pistols, 1950s, Palmer Plastics, 5-1/2" many color variations green, orange, translucent blue, royal blue, black, yellow and red
EX $10 NM $15 MIP $30

Razer Ray Gun, 1972, H.Y. Mfg./Hong Kong, plastic bronze finish body w/five large cooling fins near red plastic barrel,friction sparkling action, chrome finish muzzle tip, "Razer Ray Gun" embossed on rear of barrel
EX $10 NM $15 MIP $30

Rex Mars Planet Patrol 45 Caliber Machine Gun, 1950s, Marx, 22" long, tin and plastic, wind-up
EX $60 NM $150 MIP $300

Robot Raiders Space Signal Gun, 1980s, TNT/Hong Kong, 6" long flashlight gun w/interchangeable lenses and click sound
EX $6 NM $10 MIP $20

Robotech Water Pistol, 1985, Matchbox
EX $6 NM $10 MIP $20

Rocket Gun, 1958, Jak-Pak, 7" hard yellow/green plastic w/spring loaded plunger that shoots corks up to 50 feet
EX $10 NM $15 MIP $30

Rocket Jet Water Pistol, 1957, U.S. Plastics, 5" long, red, orange or yellow clear plastic body, fill plug at top of gun, large integral gunsight fin at rear, small sight fin at front
EX $12 NM $30 MIP $60

Rocket Pop Gun, 1955, Unknown, wood, green and red horizontal striped body w/black tri-fin pump base, cork and string stopper in nose, pump fins into body to make it pop
EX $25 NM $40 MIP $75

Rocket Signal Pistol, 1930s, Marx, same bulbous teardrop metal body as Flash Gordon Signal Pistol and Siren sparkling Airplane Pistol but without siren hole or wings; same rear fin, red w/litho of three horizontally stacked finned orange/yellow bombs
EX $135 NM $275 MIP $525

Ro-Gun "It's A Robot", 1984, Arco, Shogun-type robot transforms into a rifle, in window box
EX $8   NM $13   MIP $25

S-58 Space Gun, 1957, Japan, 12" long, tin litho, deep metallic blue body w/friction sparkling action, "S-58" on muzzle, w/ringed planet graphic on front sight
EX $35   NM $70   MIP $135

Satellite & Rocket Pistol, 1960s, Hong Kong, 5" long, green plastic gun fires either yellow plastic darts or saucers, on card
EX $12   NM $20   MIP $60

Secret Squirrel Ray Gun, 1960s, Unknown
EX $25   NM $50   MIP $100

Signal Flash Gun, 1957, Unknown, 6" long, plastic flashlight, black body w/translucent white plastic light housing at muzzle and pearl finish plastic grip plates, modern missile type sight on top of barrel, large "SIGNAL FLASH" above trigger
EX $20   NM $40   MIP $75

Smoke Ring Gun, 1950s, Nu-Age Products, large, sleek gray finished breakfront pistol w/red barrel and muzzle ring, used rocket shaped matches to produce smoke, trigger fired smoke rings, small engraved "Smoke Ring Gun" logo on gunsight fin
EX $175   NM $295   MIP $450

Space Atomic Gun, 1955, Japan, 5-1/2" long, tin, sparkling action seen through red tinted plastic window, two-tone blue body w/red/white atomic symbol on grip, "Space Atomic Gun" letters around oval spaceship-and-stars logo above trigger
EX $32   NM $65   MIP $130

Space Atomic Gun, 1960, T/Japan, 4" long, tin litho, friction sparkling action, silver gray finish w/yellow and red trim, w/"SPACE" on body in white small all caps and large yellow lower caps "atomic gun," small "T/Made in JAPAN" logo above trigger
EX $25   NM $40   MIP $70

Space Atomic Gun, 1960s, Unknown, 4" silver, orange/red tin litho, sparking action
EX $25   NM $40   MIP $70

Space Control Ray Gun, 1956, Unknown, 5-1/2" long, red plastic w/yellow trigger, clicks
EX $25   NM $42   MIP $85

Space Control Space Gun, 1954, Nomura/Japan, 3" long, tin sparkling gun w/green body, red sights, decorated all over w/stars and planets, red and yellow "Space Control" letters over trigger and spacemen firing gun and rocket flying overhead on grips
EX $30   NM $50   MIP $85

Space Dart Gun, 1950s, Unknown, 6" long, gun has one white side and one black side, both w/star and lightning motif, eight thin cooling fins on barrel
EX $30   NM $50   MIP $90

Space Dart Gun, 1950s, Arliss, 4" solid color plastic gun, shoots standard rubber tipped darts
EX $12   NM $35   MIP $70

Space Gun, 1955, San/Japan, 3-1/4" long, tin, sparkling action, aqua blue body w/red and yellow highlights and "Space" in script lettering over grip, grip shows rocket shooting toward planets, circular San/Japan logo behind trigger
EX $30   NM $50   MIP $85

Space Gun, 1957, Yoshiya/Japan, 7" long, tin w/sparkling action, shows a realistic white rocket blasting off over lunar terrain on side of body and atomic symbol on grip center w/diamond-shaped "SY" logo and "Made in Japan" at bottom of grip
EX $40   NM $65   MIP $120

Space Gun, 1957, Daiya/Japan, 6" long, tin, sparkling action, metallic teal finish w/red grooves and muzzle, green spaceship on body above "Space Gun," small Daiya logo inside red/yellow burst on grip w/"577001" at bottom of grip
EX $35   NM $75   MIP $150

Space Gun, 1957, Japan, 9" long, friction sparkling action w/three red tinted plastic spark windows and clear red plastic barrel, body in metallic blue w/large red "SPACE GUN" letters on yellow background
EX $35   NM $65   MIP $140

Space Gun, 1960, Hero Toy/Japan, 7" long, tin litho, friction sparkling action, yellow body w/blue and red trim, small Hero Toy logo by trigger
EX $35   NM $60   MIP $95

Space Gun, 1960s, TN/Japan, 8" long, battery-operated, reciprocating spark shaft has red and blue lenses that flash when fired, makes rat-a-tat noise, large circular "8" over handgrip, winged eagle over trigger, large block letter "SPACE GUN" on barrel
EX $70   NM $115   MIP $185

Space Gun, 1967, Shudo/Japan, 4" tin litho, friction sparkling action, red body w/blue inset and grips, yellow block letter "SPACE GUN," large yellow and white vertical painted fins, six red tinted plastic sparkling windows, oval Shudo logo by grip
EX $20   NM $35   MIP $70

Space Jet Gun, 1957, KO/Japan, 9" long, tin, sparkling action w/black body, orange "Space Jet" on body w/orange and red atomic symbol on grip, clear green plastic finned barrel base, clear blue plastic finned muzzle
EX $35   NM $60   MIP $120

Space Jet Water Pistol, 1957, Knickerbocker, 4" long, black plastic w/white "Space Jet" lettering and spaceship line art on sides, fill plug in gunsight
EX $15   NM $30   MIP $65

Space Navigator Gun, 1953, Asahitoy/Japan, 3-1/2" long, tin, looks like sawed off military .45, colorfully trimmed blue body w/smiling spaceman, blasting winged rocketship and

"Space Navigator" logo on grips, planets and star on body
EX $35   NM $60   MIP $135

Space Outlaw Ray Gun, 1965, B.C.M., 10" long, chrome plated, die-cast metal, recoiling barrel action, "Cosmic", "Sonic" or "Gamma" power levels, large red clear plastic teardrop shaped window
EX $115   NM $250   MIP $450

Space Rocket Gun, 1950s, M & L Toy, 9" gray plastic, modern police-style pistol grip and shell chamber body w/oversized barrel and muzzle sights, spring loaded, shoots rocket projectiles, in box w/two "rockets"
EX $55   NM $95   MIP $185

Space Scout Spud Gun, 1960s, Mil Jo, 7" black and white plastic
EX $15   NM $30   MIP $50

Space Ship Flashlight Gun, 1950s, Irwin, 7-1/4", blue plastic ray gun has cockpit w/orange spaceman, nose unscrews for AAA batteries, pulling trigger lights nose and moves guns and spaceman
EX $60   NM $110   MIP $165

Space Target Game, 1952, T. Cohn, 24" tall, metal target w/rubber tipped darts and dartgun to shoot down all the jet rockets and missiles
EX $40   NM $80   MIP $175

Space Water Gun, 1957, Palmer Plastics, 5-1/2" long, clear red plastic body w/embossed Ringed planet and star, four cooling fins at barrel base, hollow telescope sight, yellow plastic trigger, white plastic stopper attached by loop to red knob at gun back
EX $15   NM $30   MIP $50

Space Water Gun, 1960, Park Plastics, 6" long, red transparent plastic, stopper at rear of gun, finned trigger guard, zeppelin-shaped reservoir w/single embossed lightning bolt running its length, tiny "Park Plastics" imprinted along lateral reservoir fin
EX $15   NM $25   MIP $40

Space Water Pistol, 1976, Nasta
EX $7   NM $10   MIP $20

Space X-Ray Gun, 1970s, Lido, #46598, 8-1/2" long, plastic, friction sparkling action, same body as Razer Ray Gun but w/more futuristic handgrip and noisemaker at rear, sold in bag w/header card
EX $15   NM $25   MIP $40

Sparking Atom Buster Pistol, Marx, aluminum
EX $30   NM $50   MIP $85

Sparking Space Gun Rifle, Marx
EX $50   NM $100   MIP $175

Sparkling Ray Gun, 1976, Nasta
EX $6   NM $10   MIP $20

Star Team Ionization Nebulizer, 1969, Ideal, 9" water gun fires water mist, red, white, blue and black plastic, Star Team decal
EX $30   NM $50   MIP $85

SPACE TOYS

- **Strato Gun,** 1950s, Futuristic Products, 9" long, gray finish die-cast, cap firing, internal hammer, top of gun lifts to load
  EX $70   NM $125   MIP $200

- **Strato Gun,** 1950s, Futuristic Products, 9" long, chrome finish die-cast, red cooling fins, cap firing, internal hammer, top of gun lifts to load
  EX $100   NM $175   MIP $325

- **Super Sonic Gun,** 1957, Endoh/Japan, 9" long, tin, sparkling action w/three red plastic spark windows and clear red plastic barrel, blue body w/red lightning bolt beneath yellow "Super Sonic" on rounded gun body, small ENDOH logo printed above grips
  EX $40   NM $80   MIP $160

- **Super Sonic Space Gun,** 1957, Daiya/Japan, 7-1/2" long, tin litho, metallic gray body w/red gunsight fin, friction siren and sparkling action, large oval center art w/outstanding lunar scene of rockets, mountains and Earth in sky, red helmeted spaceman on grip
  EX $40   NM $80   MIP $160

- **Super Space Gun,** 1960, Japan, 6" long, tin litho, friction sparkling action, blue on blue body w/white/yellow/red highlights, large red on white "SUPER SPACE" lettering on side
  EX $25   NM $50   MIP $100

- **Superior Rocket Gun,** 1956, Unknown, 8" long, dark gray plastic, embossed "Superior Rocket Gun" on grip
  EX $30   NM $50   MIP $85

- **Tomi Space Gun,** 1950s, Shawnee, solid red plastic w/yellow barrel plug, modelled after modern .45 caliber pistol w/rounded reservoir lined w/two horizontal fins over grip; embossed logo and circular Shawnee logos on grip
  EX $50   NM $90   MIP $135

- **Universe Gun,** 1960s, T/Japan, 4" long, blue, yellow and red tin litho gun w/friction sparkling action, large all caps italic "Universe" on body side, sold in bag w/header card
  EX $15   NM $25   MIP $40

- **Visible Sparkling Ray Gun,** Hong Kong, 8-1/2" long, plastic, mechanism visible, bagged w/header card
  EX $15   NM $32   MIP $65

- **Wham-O Air Blaster,** 1960s, Wham-O, 10" long plastic gun uses rubber diaphragm to shoot air; styling is reminiscent of Budson Flash Gordon Air Ray Gun
  EX $70   NM $120   MIP $185

- **X100 Mystery Dart Gun,** 1956, Arliss, 3-3/4" long, yellow or gray plastic gun on cardboard display card, w/two yellow and blue talcum impregnated darts which create a smoke effect when striking any target
  EX $25   NM $45   MIP $80

SPACE PATROL

- **Atomic Pistol Flashlight Gun,** 1950s, Marx, plastic
  EX $85   NM $160   MIP $275

- **Cosmic Cap,** 1950s
  EX $125   NM $200   MIP $400

- **Cosmic Gun,** 1970, Nomura/Japan, 12" long, plastic, battery-operated w/a small electric motor that runs reciprocating light in clear red plastic barrel, dark blue body, red and orange lettered "COSMIC GUN" decal
  EX $35   NM $55   MIP $90

- **Cosmic Ray Gun,** 1954, Ranger Steel Products, 9" long, tin body w/plastic barrel, boldly painted in blue, yellow and red lightning bolts
  EX $50   NM $90   MIP $150

- **Cosmic Ray Gun #249,** 1953, Ranger Steel Products, 8" long, plastic, blue body, yellow barrel, red tip, in box showing two space kids in bubble helmets and backpacks shooting at spaceships
  EX $40   NM $75   MIP $135

- **Cosmic Rocket Launcher Set,** 1950s
  EX $300   NM $525   MIP $850

- **Cosmic Smoke Gun,** 1950s, red
  EX $110   NM $170   MIP $325

- **Cosmic Smoke Gun,** 1950s, green
  EX $120   NM $325   MIP $675

- **Drink Mixer,** 1950s, boxed
  EX $60   NM $100   MIP $200

- **Emergency Kit,** 1950s, w/rations, plastic w/yellow insert
  EX $600   NM $1350   MIP $2500

- **Handbook,** 1950s
  EX $55   NM $125   MIP $200

- **Interplanetary Space Patrol Credits Coins,** different denominations and colors: Terra, Moon and Saturn, each
  EX $10   NM $16   MIP $35

- **Jet Glow Code Belt,** 1950s, gold-finish metal, spaceship-shaped buckle, decoder ring behind buckle
  EX $120   NM $200   MIP $375

- **Lunar Fleet Base,** 1950s, premium punch-outs in mailing envelope
  EX $500   NM $1700   MIP $3200

- **Man From Mars Totem Head Mask,** 1950s, paper, several styles
  EX $65   NM $105   MIP $175

- **Monorail Set,** 1950s, Toys of Tomorrow
  EX $1650   NM $3000   MIP $4200

- **Non-Fall Space Patrol X-16,** 1950s, Masudaya
  EX $50   NM $150   MIP $300

- **Outer Space Helmet Mask,** 1950s, paper helmet w/plastic one-way visor
  EX $110   NM $170   MIP $300

- **Project-O-Scope,** 1950s, rocket-shaped film viewer w/filmstrips
  EX $175   NM $350   MIP $800

- **Puzzle,** 1950s, Milton Bradley, frame tray w/sleeve
  EX $40   NM $75   MIP $175

- **Rocket Gun and Holster Set,** 1950s, w/darts
  EX $200   NM $300   MIP $525

- **Rocket Gun Set,** 1950s, w/darts, without holster
  EX $110   NM $185   MIP $360

- **Rocket Lite Flashlight,** 1950s, Rayovac, in box
  EX $140   NM $250   MIP $375

- **Rocket Port Set,** 1950s, Marx
  EX $125   NM $200   MIP $350

- **Rocket-Shaped Pen,** 1950s
  EX $120   NM $185   MIP $350

- **Space Binoculars,** 1950s, black plastic, logo on sides
  EX $80   NM $125   MIP $200

- **Space Binoculars,** 1950s, green plastic, large logo on top
  EX $120   NM $190   MIP $300

- **Space Holster with oval badge,** 1950, w/unmarked blue gun
  EX $200   NM $500   MIP $800

- **Space Patrol Atomic Flashlight Pistol,** 1950s, Marx, gold/bronze finish pistol w/seven large cooling fins on barrel and three smaller ones at back of gun, large clear plastic diffuser on muzzle, white "Official Space Patrol" on handgrip
  EX $135   NM $225   MIP $525

- **Space Patrol Badge,** 1950s, plastic, w/ship and crest
  EX $75   NM $150   MIP $300

- **Space Patrol Badge,** 1950s, metal oval on card
  EX $125   NM $400   MIP $800

- **Space Patrol Cadet Membership Card,** 1950s
  EX $25   NM $75   MIP $175

- **Space Patrol Cereal Box,** 1953, Wheat Chex Magic Picture Offer
  EX $125   NM $275   MIP $450

- **Space Patrol Commander Helmet,** 1950s, plastic, in box
  EX $140   NM $275   MIP $425

- **Space Patrol Cosmic Glow Ring,** 1950s, red and blue
  EX $450   NM $900   MIP $1800

- **Space Patrol Cosmic Smoke Gun,** 1950s, Unknown, solid color red or green plastic w/"Space Patrol" on body above grip, TV show tie-in, shoots baking powder, on card
  EX $135   NM $375   MIP $750

- **Space Patrol Hydrogen Ray Gun Ring,** 1950s, Unknown, glow-in-the-dark ring
  EX $70   NM $125   MIP $275

- **Space Patrol Mobile Store Display,** Wheat Chex, 1953
  EX $400   NM $1200   MIP $1600

- **Space Patrol Periscope,** 1950s, paper w/mirrors
  EX $75   NM $200   MIP $400

- **Space Patrol Printing Ring,** 1950s
  EX $200   NM $400   MIP $800

- **Space Patrol Wristwatch,** 1950s, illustrated box w/"Terra" compass
  EX $275   NM $500   MIP $750

Space-A-Phones, 1950s
EX $175   NM $500   MIP $750

SPACE:1999

Astro Popper Gun, 1976, Larami, on card
EX $6   NM $10   MIP $40

Colorforms Adventure Set, 1975, Colorforms
EX $10   NM $16   MIP $25

Cut and Color Book, 1975, Saalfield
EX $6   NM $12   MIP $25

Dr. Russell, 1976, Mattel
EX n/a   NM $30   MIP $60

Dr. Russell Figure, 1976, Mattel
EX $17   NM $30   MIP $45

Eagle Freighter, 1975, Dinky, No. 360, die-cast
EX $25   NM $80   MIP $160

Eagle One Spaceship, 1976, Mattel
EX $125   NM $325   MIP $525

Eagle Transport, 1975, Dinky, No. 359, die-cast
EX $25   NM $55   MIP $110

Eagle Transporter Model Kit, 1976, Airfix
EX $12   NM $20   MIP $80

Film Viewer TV Set, 1976, Larami
EX $8   NM $20   MIP $55

Galaxy Time Meter, 1976, Larami
EX $6   NM $10   MIP $20

Puzzle, 1976, HG Toys
EX $8   NM $15   MIP $30

Space Expedition Dart Set, 1976, Larami, carded
EX $6   NM $10   MIP $20

(ToyShop File Photo)

Space: 1999 Adventure Play Set, 1976, Amsco/Milton Bradley, Paper color and cut-out construction, included two Eagle Spacecraft, Moonbase Alpha with moving antenna, six-wheeled moon buggy, complete cast
EX $40   NM $55   MIP $85

Space:1999 Astro Popper Gun, 1976, Mattel, on card
EX $6   NM $10   MIP $20

Space:1999 Utility Belt Set, 1976, Remco, w/disc shooting stun gun, watch and compass
EX $12   NM $30   MIP $60

Stamping Set, 1976, Larami
EX $8   NM $13   MIP $25

Superscope, 1976, Larami
EX $6   NM $10   MIP $18

Utility Belt Set, 1976, Remco
EX $12   NM $40   MIP $110

Walking Spaceman, 1975, Azrak Hamway
EX $50   NM $175   MIP $425

Zython Figure, 1976, Mattel
EX $40   NM $80   MIP $100

SPACESHIPS

Eagle Lunar Module, 1960s, 9"
EX $80   NM $115   MIP $185

Friendship 7, 9-1/2", friction
EX $35   NM $50   MIP $80

Inter-Planet Toy Rocketank Patrol, 1950, Macrey, 10"
EX $30   NM $45   MIP $75

Jupiter Space Station, 1960s, TN/Japan, 8"
EX $90   NM $135   MIP $225

Moon-Rider Spaceship, 1930s, Marx, tin wind-up
EX $125   NM $200   MIP $275

(ToyShop File Photo)

Mystery Spaceship, 1960s, Marx, 35mm astronauts and moonmen, rockets, launchers
EX $80   NM $165   MIP $260

Rocket Fighter, 1950s, Marx, w/tail fin and sparking action, tin wind-up
EX $250   NM $375   MIP $525

Rocket Fighter Spaceship, 1930s, Marx, celluloid window, tin wind-up, 12" long
EX $125   NM $225   MIP $300

Satellite X-107, 1965, Cragstan, 9"
EX $90   NM $130   MIP $200

Sky Patrol Jet, 1960s, TN/Japan, 5" x 13" x 5", battery operated, working taillights
EX $295   NM $425   MIP $650

Solar-X Space Rocket, TN/Japan, 15"
EX $45   NM $65   MIP $100

Space Bus, tin helicopter, battery operated w/wired remote
EX $350   NM $500   MIP $750

Space Pacer, 1978, 7", battery operated
EX $20   NM $29   MIP $50

Space Survey X-09, battery operated, tin and plastic flying saucer w/clear bubble
EX $175   NM $375   MIP $550

Space Train, 1950s, 9" long, engine and three metallic cars
EX $18   NM $26   MIP $50

Spaceship, Marx, bronze plastic
EX $40   NM $60   MIP $100

Super Space Capsule, 1960s, 9-1/2"
EX $70   NM $100   MIP $160

X-3 Rocket Gyro, 1950s
EX $25   NM $35   MIP $60

STAR TREK

Action Toy Book, 1976, Random House
EX $7   NM $10   MIP $20

Beanbag Chair, ST:TMP
EX $25   NM $35   MIP $55

Bowl, ST:TMP, 1979, Deka, plastic
EX $3   NM $7   MIP $15

Bridge Punch-Out Book, ST:TMP, 1979, Wanderer
EX $7   NM $10   MIP $20

Bulletin Board, ST:TMP, 1979, Milton Bradley, w/four pens
EX $6   NM $8   MIP $15

Clock, 1986, white wall clock, red 20th anniversary logo on face, Official Star Trek Fan Club
EX $14   NM $20   MIP $40

Clock, 1989, Enterprise orbiting planet, rectangular
EX $23   NM $33   MIP $60

Colorforms Set, 1975, Colorforms
EX $15   NM $20   MIP $40

Comb & Brush Set, 1977, 6" x 3", blue, oval brush
EX $14   NM $20   MIP $35

Communicators, 1976, Mego, blue plastic walkie talkies
EX $70   NM $125   MIP $200

Communicators, 1989, McNerney, black plastic walkie talkies
EX $35   NM $50   MIP $85

Communicators, ST:TMP, 1980, Mego, plastic wristband walkie talkies belt pack, battery operated
EX $90   NM $150   MIP $250

Controlled Space Flight, 1976, Remco, plastic Enterprise, battery operated
EX $80   NM $125   MIP $225

Digital Travel Alarm, Lincoln Enterprises
EX $15   NM $20   MIP $35

Dinnerware Set, ST:TMP, 1979, Deka, plate, bowl, glass and cup
EX $15   NM $25   MIP $40

Enterprise Make-A-Model, ST:TNG, 1990, Chatham River Press
EX $4   NM $5   MIP $10

SPACE TOYS

Enterprise Model Kit, 1980, Mego/Grand Toys, #91232/B, Canadian issue, ST:TMP
EX $90   NM $100   MIP $150

Enterprise Punch-Out Book, ST:TMP, 1979, Wanderer
EX $9   NM $15   MIP $30

Enterprise Wristwatch, ST:TMP, Bradley
EX $20   NM $30   MIP $50

Enterprise Wristwatch, ST:TMP, 1989, Rarities Mint, gold-plated silver
EX $55   NM $80   MIP $125

Enterprise, ST:III, 1984, Ertl, 4" long, die-cast w/black plastic stand
EX $10   NM $15   MIP $30

Enterprise, ST:IV, 1986, Sterling, 24", silver plastic, inflatable
EX $20   NM $30   MIP $45

Enterprise, ST:TMP, 1979, South Bend, 20" long, white plastic, battery powered lights and sound w/stand
EX $80   NM $120   MIP $185

Excelsior, ST:III, 1984, Ertl, 4" long, die-cast w/black plastic stand
EX $7   NM $10   MIP $30

Ferengi Costume, ST:TNG, 1988, Ben Cooper
EX $7   NM $10   MIP $25

Figurine Paint Set, 1979, Milton Bradley
EX $14   NM $25   MIP $40

Flashlight, 1976, battery operated, small phaser shape
EX $6   NM $10   MIP $15

Flashlight, ST:TMP, 1979, Larami
EX $6   NM $10   MIP $15

Giant in the Universe Pop-Up Book, 1977, Random House
EX $14   NM $20   MIP $35

Golden Trivia Game, 1985, Western
EX $20   NM $30   MIP $50

Helmet, 1976, Remco, plastic, w/sound and red lights
EX $55   NM $80   MIP $130

Kirk & Spock Wristwatch, ST:TMP, Bradley, LCD rectangular face display, Enterprise on blue face w/Kirk and Spock
EX $25   NM $35   MIP $60

Kirk Bank, 1975, Play Pal, 12" plastic
EX $25   NM $35   MIP $60

Kirk Costume, 1975, Ben Cooper, plastic mask, one-piece jumpsuit
EX $9   NM $13   MIP $25

Kirk Doll, ST:TMP, 1979, Knickerbocker, 13" tall, soft body w/plastic head
EX $16   NM $23   MIP $50

Kirk or Spock Costumes, 1967, Ben Cooper, tie-on jumpsuit, mask
EX $11   NM $16   MIP $30

Kirk Puzzle, ST:TMP, 1979, Larami, fifteen-piece sliding puzzle
EX $5   NM $7   MIP $12

Kite, 1975, Hi-Flyer, TV Enterprise or Spock
EX $14   NM $20   MIP $35

Kite, ST:III, 1984, Lever Bros., pictures Enterprise
EX $14   NM $20   MIP $35

Kite, ST:TMP, 1976, Aviva, picture of Spock
EX $17   NM $22   MIP $38

Klingon Bird of Prey, ST:III, 1984, Ertl, 3-1/2", die-cast w/black plastic stand
EX $7   NM $10   MIP $30

Klingon Costume, 1975, Ben Cooper, plastic mask, one piece jumpsuit
EX $9   NM $13   MIP $30

Klingon Costume, ST:TNG, 1988, Ben Cooper
EX $7   NM $10   MIP $20

Light Switch Cover, 1985, American Tack & Hardware, ST:TMP
EX $6   NM $8   MIP $15

Magic Slates, 1979, Whitman, four designs: Spock, Kirk, Kirk and Spock
EX $7   NM $10   MIP $20

Make-a-Game Book, 1979, Wanderer
EX $7   NM $10   MIP $20

Metal Detector, 1976, Jetco, U.S.S. Enterprise decal
EX $100   NM $145   MIP $225

Mirror, 1966, 2" x 3" metal, w/black and white photo of crew
EX $2   NM $5   MIP $10

Mix 'N Mold, 1975, Kirk, Spock or McCoy, molding compound, paint and brush
EX $35   NM $50   MIP $75

Movie Viewer, 1967, Chemtoy, 3" red and black plastic
EX $10   NM $16   MIP $35

Needlepoint Kit, 1980, Arista, Kirk
EX $16   NM $23   MIP $35

Needlepoint Kit, 1980, Arista, 14" x 18", "Live Long and Prosper"
EX $16   NM $23   MIP $35

Paint-By-Numbers Set, 1972, Hasbro, small
EX $20   NM $35   MIP $55

Paint-By-Numbers Set, 1972, Hasbro, large
EX $35   NM $50   MIP $80

Pen & Poster Kit, 1976, Open Door, four versions; each
EX $11   NM $16   MIP $30

Pen & Poster Kit, ST:III, 1984, Placo, 3-D poster "Search for Spock" w/overlay, 3-D glasses and four felt tip pens
EX $10   NM $20   MIP $40

Pennant, 1982, Image Products, 12" x 30" triangular, black, yellow and red on white w/"Spock Lives"
EX $6   NM $10   MIP $15

Pennant, 1982, Image Products, 12" x 30" triangle, The Wrath of Khan
EX $6   NM $10   MIP $15

Pennant, 1988, Universal Studios, Paramount Pictures Adventure
EX $6   NM $10   MIP $15

Phaser, 1975, Remco, black plastic, shaped like pistol, electronic sound, flashlight projects target
EX $35   NM $65   MIP $100

Phaser Battle Game, 1976, Mego, black plastic, 13" high battery operated electronic target game, LED scoring lights, sound effects and adjustable controls
EX $195   NM $275   MIP $450

Phaser Gun, 1967, Remco, Astro Buzz-Ray Gun w/three-color flash beam
EX $80   NM $150   MIP $250

Phaser Gun, ST:III, 1984, Daisy, white and blue plastic gun w/light and sound effects
EX $35   NM $60   MIP $100

Phaser Gun, ST:TNG, 1988, Galoob, gray plastic light and sound hand phaser
EX $14   NM $20   MIP $40

Pinball Game, ST:TMP, Azrak-Hamway, 12", plastic, Kirk or Spock
EX $23   NM $35   MIP $80

Pinball Game, ST:TMP, 1979, Bally, electronic
EX $200   NM $350   MIP $650

Pocket Flix, 1978, Ideal, battery operated movie viewer and film cartridge
EX $18   NM $25   MIP $50

Pop-Up Book, ST:TMP, 1980, Wanderer
EX $10   NM $20   MIP $40

Puzzle, 1974, H.G. Toys, 150 pieces, Attempted Hijacking of U.S.S. Enterprise
EX $4   NM $8   MIP $15

Puzzle, 1974, H.G. Toys, 150 pieces, Battle on the Planet Klingon
EX $3   NM $7   MIP $12

Puzzle, 1974, H.G. Toys, 150 pieces, Kirk and officers beaming down
EX $3   NM $7   MIP $12

Puzzle, 1974, H.G. Toys, 150 pieces, Battle on the Planet Romulon
EX $5   NM $7   MIP $15

Puzzle, 1976, H.G. Toys, 150 pieces, "Force Field Capture"
EX $4   NM $8   MIP $15

Puzzle, 1976, H.G. Toys, 150 pieces; Kirk, Spock, and McCoy
EX $4   NM $8   MIP $12

Puzzle, 1978, Whitman, 8-1/2" x 11" tray, Spock in spacesuit
EX $2   NM $5   MIP $10

❏ **Puzzle,** 1979, Milton Bradley, ST:TMP, 50 pieces
EX $3   **NM** $7   **MIP** $12

❏ **Puzzle,** 1979, Aviva, 551 pieces
EX $8   **NM** $15   **MIP** $25

❏ **Puzzle,** 1979, Larami, ST:TMP, 15-piece sliding puzzle
EX $3   **NM** $7   **MIP** $12

❏ **Puzzle,** 1986, Mind's Eye Press, 551 pieces, ST:IV, "The Voyage Home"
EX $10   **NM** $20   **MIP** $30

❏ **Role Playing Game, 2001 Deluxe Edition,** FASA, Star Trek Basic Set and the Star Trek III Combat Game
EX $20   **NM** $30   **MIP** $50

❏ **Role Playing Game, 2004 Basic Set,** FASA, three books outlining Star Trek Universe
EX $7   **NM** $10   **MIP** $20

❏ **Role Playing Game, Second Deluxe Edition,** FASA
EX $14   **NM** $20   **MIP** $35

❏ **Space Design Center, ST:TMP,** 1979, Avalon, blue plastic tray, paints, pens, crayons, project book and crew member cut-outs
EX $70   **NM** $110   **MIP** $175

❏ **Spock & Enterprise Wristwatch, ST:TMP,** 1986, Lewco, 20th anniversary, digital
EX $9   **NM** $20   **MIP** $40

❏ **Spock Bank,** 1975, Play Pal, 12" plastic
EX $25   **NM** $35   **MIP** $60

❏ **Spock Bop Bag,** 1975, plastic, inflatable
EX $55   **NM** $80   **MIP** $125

❏ **Spock Chair, ST:TMP,** 1979, inflatable
EX $16   **NM** $23   **MIP** $40

❏ **Spock Costume,** 1973, Ben Cooper, plastic mask, one-piece jumpsuit
EX $11   **NM** $16   **MIP** $30

❏ **Spock Doll, ST:TMP,** 1979, Knickerbocker, 13" tall, soft body, plastic head
EX $16   **NM** $25   **MIP** $50

❏ **Spock Ears, ST:TMP,** 1979, Aviva
EX $7   **NM** $10   **MIP** $20

❏ **Spock Tray,** 1979, Aviva, 17-1/2" metal lap tray
EX $9   **NM** $13   **MIP** $20

❏ **Spock Wristwatch,** Bradley, ST:TMP
EX $20   **NM** $30   **MIP** $50

❏ **Star Trek Cartoon Puzzle,** 1978, Whitman
EX $4   **NM** $5   **MIP** $10

❏ **Star Trek Costume,** 1979, Collegeville, one-piece outfit, Spock, Kirk, Ilia or Klingon, each
EX $11   **NM** $16   **MIP** $25
EX $9   **NM** $13   **MIP** $25

❏ **Star Trek Tracer Gun,** 1966, Rayline, 6-1/2" plastic firing tracer gun
EX $40   **NM** $65   **MIP** $125

❏ **Star Trek Tracer Scope,** 1968, Rayline, rifle w/disks
EX $50   **NM** $80   **MIP** $150

❏ **Star Trek Water Pistol,** 1976, Azrak-Hamway, white plastic, shaped like U.S.S. Enterprise
EX $15   **NM** $30   **MIP** $60

❏ **Star Trek:TMP Water Pistol,** 1979, Aviva, gray plastic, early pistol-grip phaser design
EX $10   **NM** $20   **MIP** $60

❏ **Telescreen,** 1976, Mego, plastic, battery operated target game w/light and sound effects
EX $70   **NM** $100   **MIP** $160

❏ **Tracer Gun,** 1966, Rayline, plastic pistol w/colored plastic discs
EX $45   **NM** $65   **MIP** $135

❏ **Tricorder,** 1976, Mego, blue plastic tape recorder, battery operated w/shoulder strap
EX $70   **NM** $110   **MIP** $160

❏ **Trillions of Trilligs Pop-Up Book,** 1977, Random House
EX $16   **NM** $25   **MIP** $40

❏ **Utility Belt,** 1975, Remco, black plastic phaser miniature, tricorder, communicator and belt w/Star Trek buckle
EX $45   **NM** $65   **MIP** $120

❏ **Vulcan Shuttle Model Kit,** 1980, Mego/Grand Toy, #91231, ST:TMP
EX $100   **NM** $120   **MIP** $145

❏ **Vulcan Shuttle Model Kit,** 1984, Ertl, #6679, ST:III
EX $20   **NM** $25   **MIP** $50

❏ **Vulcan Shuttle Model Kit,** 1984, Ertl, #6679, ST:TMP
EX $18   **NM** $20   **MIP** $35

❏ **Wastebasket,** 1977, Chein, black metal
EX $35   **NM** $50   **MIP** $80

❏ **Wastebasket, ST:TMP,** 1979, Chein, 13" high, metal rainbow painting w/photograph of Enterprise surrounded by smaller pictures
EX $11   **NM** $16   **MIP** $35

❏ **Water Pistol,** 1976, Azrak-Hamway, white plastic, shaped like U.S.S. Enterprise
EX $20   **NM** $30   **MIP** $50

❏ **Water Pistol, ST:TMP,** 1979, Aviva, gray plastic, early phaser
EX $11   **NM** $16   **MIP** $30

❏ **Writing Tablet,** 1967, 8" x 10"
EX $11   **NM** $16   **MIP** $30

❏ **Yo-Yo,** 1979, Aviva, ST:TMP, blue sparkle plastic
EX $10   **NM** $20   **MIP** $40

TOM CORBETT

❏ **Binoculars**
EX $60   **NM** $100   **MIP** $150

❏ **Flash X-1,** 1967, Shudo/Japan, 4" long, tin litho, friction sparkling action, red body w/blue and yellow inset and grips, large white "Flash X-1" on body, four red tinted plastic sparkling windows
EX $15   **NM** $25   **MIP** $50

❏ **Flash X-1 Space Gun,** 5" long
EX $55   **NM** $110   **MIP** $160

❏ **Model Craft Molding and Coloring Set,** 1950s, Kay Standley, various characters
EX $150   **NM** $350   **MIP** $500

❏ **Official Sparking Space Gun,** Marx, 21" long, w/numerous apparatus on body
EX $80   **NM** $150   **MIP** $250

❏ **Polaris Wind-Up Spaceship,** 1952, Marx, 12" long, 1952
EX $200   **NM** $375   **MIP** $600

❏ **Push-Outs Book,** 1952, Saalfield
EX $30   **NM** $60   **MIP** $100

❏ **Puzzles,** 1950s, Saalfield, frame tray, three versions, each
EX $17   **NM** $30   **MIP** $50

❏ **Rocket Scout Ring,** 1950s
EX $10   **NM** $20   **MIP** $35

❏ **Signal Siren Flashlight,** 1950s, Usalite
EX $70   **NM** $115   **MIP** $175

❏ **Space Cadet Belt,** 1950s
EX $65   **NM** $105   **MIP** $165

❏ **Space Gun,** 1950s, 9-1/2" long light blue and black sparking
EX $70   **NM** $130   **MIP** $200

❏ **Space Suit Ring,** 1950s
EX $10   **NM** $16   **MIP** $25

❏ **Tom Corbett Coloring Book,** 1950s, Saalfield, two versions, each
EX $25   **NM** $40   **MIP** $80

❏ **Tom Corbett Official Space Cadet Gun,** 1950s, Marx, poorly designed composite rifle w/modern military plastic stock and front grip at ends of long tin litho gun body w/litho bombs and "Ray Adjuster" scale
EX $135   **NM** $300   **MIP** $500

❏ **Tom Corbett Portrait Ring,** 1950s
EX $20   **NM** $35   **MIP** $50

❏ **Tom Corbett Space Academy Play Set,** 1950s, Marx, #7020
EX $195   **NM** $550   **MIP** $600

(ToyShop File Photo)

❏ **Tom Corbett Space Academy Play Set,** 1952, Marx, #7010, 45mm figures
EX $205   **NM** $360   **MIP** $515

❏ **Tom Corbett Space Cadet Atomic Flashlight Pistol,** 1950s, Marx, identical to Space Patrol Atomic Flashlight Pistol except for body colors and "Tom Corbett Space Cadet" printed upside down on handgrip
EX $135   **NM** $300   **MIP** $500

❏ **Tom Corbett Space Cadet Gun,** 1952, Marx, 10-1/2" long, sheet metal clicker based on Flash Gordon Radio repeater molds, red body, blue barrel reads "Space Cadet," handgrips show bust of Tom in front of planet w/rocket ship symbol above

EX $150 **NM** $400 **MIP** $700

❏ **Tom Corbett Wristwatch,** 1950s, Ingraham, round dial, embossed band w/ship and planets, on illustrated rocket shaped card

EX $250 **NM** $450 **MIP** $700

Star Wars

*Quite menacing…
Darth Maul seen here
in Sith robe from the
accessory pack
released in 1999. MIP
value,*

By Merry Dudley

It's a good time to be a Star Wars collector.

Ten years go, Star Wars fans had little to gloat about. The Power of the Force figures of the mid-1980s were easy to find, and the second round wouldn't come until the late 1990s.

All we had were the usual rumors that someday George Lucas would go back and make the first three movies. But being a skeptical and cynical toy collector, I believed these rumors were part of a cruel hoax perpetuated by the legions of fans who couldn't bear to see the series die with only the eerie memory of furry Ewoks dancing and singing in our heads.

Those were dark times indeed.

But at least we had the vintage market. While the Holy Grails of Star Wars collection were still pricey — think telescoping lightsaber Luke, vinyl cape Jawa or blue Snaggletooth — there were plenty of bargains to be had.

All that changed by the end of the 1990s with the advent of *The Phantom Menace*.

Expanded Universe speeder bike—still pretty easy to find, it's a neat representation of some of the concept sketches for the original speeder bikes used by Luke, Leia and the Empire in Jedi.

I'm not complaining. New movies meant new toys to collect. But even today, nearly four years after *Menace* debuted, plenty of collectors are still complaining about the glut of toys produced for Episode I. But I assert that too much product is not a problem. I like variety, and I'm not in the game to make money — I just like toys!

Star Wars Lego sets have become almost as varied as the movies' universe—this Naboo Swamp set was released just before *The Phantom Menace* in April 1999.

Lucasfilm was much more savvy with its licensing choices for *Attack of the Clones* in 2002. Hasbro and Lego practically cornered the market, and each company pro-

duced the most amazing Star Wars product to date. Mace Windu with a magnet in his hand that allows him to hold a lightsaber? Why didn't we have this technology 20 years ago!

Remember waiting that first summer for Boba Fett? All you had to do was send in four proofs of purchase, a shipping and handling check, and a whole new action figure was yours. A few of us remember being vaguely disappointed that his missile wasn't made to fire after all, but...

Grand Moff Tarkin may have been in the first movie back in 1977, but he didn't have an action figure until 20 years later with the re-release of the films. Part of the "Power of the Force 2" series, this toy is valued at $10 MIP.

For the new or uninitiated collector, I will say only this — if increasing the future value of your collection is your main objective, then save your *Clones* product and pare down your *Menace* items. And keep your eyes open for the sneak preview figures and Yoda items for Episode II. These items are sure to be hard to find as the years go on.

Some of the store exclusive vehicles released in recent years have been especially well-done. This TIE Interceptor is a Toys R Us exclusive, and is already selling on the secondary market for around $60, even though it is a 2002 release.

For a long time, die-cast vehicles from the Star Wars movies were an overlooked segment of the collector's market. No more, though. This particular model is selling for about $550 MIP. Dang.

Merry Dudley is the editor of Toy Cars & Models *magazine, and is a great fan of die-cast vehicles, classic American cars, virtually all things Star Wars and the actor Sean Bean. One of her next major projects is a* Standard Catalog of 1:18-scale Vehicles.

This Clone Trooper Sneak Preview figure is equipped with a blaster rifle complete with blue blast. The development of the Clone Trooper "look" is well documented in the book, The Art of Star Wars—Attack of the Clones.

ACTION FIGURES, 03-3/4"

ATTACK OF THE CLONES

❏ **Anakin Skywalker w/Lightsaber Slashing Action**, 2002, Hasbro, Includes two lightsabers and an easily-sliced Geonosian warrior
EX n/a   **NM** n/a   **MIP** $19

❏ **Anakin Skywalker, Hangar Duel**, 2002, Hasbro, Includes two lightsabers, has fighting action
EX n/a   **NM** n/a   **MIP** $13

(KP Photo)

❏ **Anakin Skywalker, Outland Peasant Disguise**, 2002, Hasbro, Includes cloak, lightsaber, and cargo
EX n/a   **NM** n/a   **MIP** $6

(KP Photo)

❏ **Battle Droid**, 2002, Hasbro, With orange laser blast
EX n/a   **NM** n/a   **MIP** $6

❏ **Boba Fett, Kamino Escape**, 2002, Hasbro, Two blaster pistols, flame effect, missile pack
EX n/a   **NM** n/a   **MIP** $12

(KP Photo)

❏ **C-3PO, Protocol Droid**, 2002, Hasbro, Comes with removeable outer plating and box for storage
EX n/a   **NM** n/a   **MIP** $6

❏ **Captain Typho**, 2002, Hasbro, With removeable helmet, blaster with blast effect
EX n/a   **NM** n/a   **MIP** $18

(KP Photo)

❏ **Clone Trooper**, 2002, Hasbro, With rifle and tripod-style gun. This figure also lacks the painted-on sand and grime that the preview model features
EX n/a   **NM** n/a   **MIP** $9

(KP Photo)

❏ **Clone Trooper**, 2002, Hasbro, With laser rifle and blue "blast" attachment. This model shows painted-on battlefield "dirt" detail
EX n/a   **NM** n/a   **MIP** $11

❏ **Count Dooku**, 2002, Hasbro, Includes lightsaber and smaller Darth Sidious hologram figure
EX n/a   **NM** n/a   **MIP** $18

❏ **Darth Tyranus w/Force Flipping Attack**, 2002, Hasbro, Like the Obi-Wan version, pushing a button on the launch pad makes Tyranus leap, flip and land on his feet
EX n/a   **NM** n/a   **MIP** $11

(KP Photo)

❏ **Dexter Jetster**, 2002, Hasbro, Detailed sculpt with four moving arms. Includes cutlery
EX n/a   **NM** n/a   **MIP** $9

(KP Photo)

❏ **Geonosian Warrior**, 2002, Hasbro, Poseable wings
EX n/a   **NM** n/a   **MIP** $9

❏ **Jango Fett**, 2002, Hasbro
EX n/a   **NM** n/a   **MIP** $14

❏ **Jango Fett, Final Battle**, 2002, Hasbro, Includes pack, two blasters, and plastic "flame"
EX n/a   **NM** n/a   **MIP** $18

(KP Photo)

❑ **Jango Fett, Kamino Escape,** 2002, Hasbro, With two pistols, grappling hook, and firing missile pack
EX n/a　　**NM** n/a　　**MIP** $12

(KP Photo)

❑ **Jango Fett, w/Electronic Attack and Snap-On Armor,** 2002, Hasbro, Another incredibly detailed Jango figure
EX n/a　　**NM** n/a　　**MIP** $11

(KP Photo)

❑ **Jar Jar Binks, Gungan Senator,** 2002, Hasbro, With staff and blue energy bolts
EX n/a　　**NM** n/a　　**MIP** $6

(KP Photo)

❑ **Kit Fisto, Jedi Master,** 2002, Hasbro, With "laser blast" attachment for lightsaber
EX n/a　　**NM** n/a　　**MIP** $9

(KP Photo)

❑ **Luminara Unduli, Jedi Master,** 2002, Hasbro, Extremely detailed sculpt. Figure includes lightsaber with blaster deflect attachement
EX n/a　　**NM** n/a　　**MIP** $14

(KP Photo)

❑ **Mace Windu w/Blast-Apart Battle Droid,** 2002, Hasbro, Battle droid breaks apart as Mace stikes with saber
EX n/a　　**NM** n/a　　**MIP** $11

(KP Photo)

❑ **Mace Windu, Geonosian Rescue,** 2002, Hasbro, Pushing a button on Mace's back moves arm with lightsaber in a "slashing attack." These newest Star Wars figures probably have the most detail and moving parts of any series yet--and this is just one example
EX n/a　　**NM** n/a　　**MIP** $18

❑ **Massiff with Geonosian Warrior,** 2002, Hasbro, Includes Geonosian warrior with Massiff on chain leash
EX n/a　　**NM** n/a　　**MIP** $14

❑ **Nexu w/Snapping Jaw and Attack Roar,** 2002, Hasbro, Well detailed with snapping jaw and roaring sound
EX n/a　　**NM** n/a　　**MIP** $19

(KP Photo)

❑ **Nikto, Jedi Knight,** 2002, Hasbro, With lightsaber and "force blast effect"
EX n/a　　**NM** n/a　　**MIP** $7

(KP Photo)

❑ **Obi-Wan Kenobi w/Force Flipping Attack,** 2002, Hasbro, Includes platform and launcher that makes Obi-Wan figure flip over and then land on his feet (after a few tries, usually). A neat idea that easily lends itself to "I betcha can't make him land this time" games
EX n/a　　**NM** n/a　　**MIP** $9

(KP Photo)

❏ **Obi-Wan Kenobi, Coruscant Chase,** 2002, Hasbro, With flying droid that magnetically attaches to Obi-Wan's hand
EX n/a   **NM** n/a   **MIP** $8

(KP Photo)

❏ **Orn Free Taa,** 2002, Hasbro, With floating camera droid
EX n/a   **NM** n/a   **MIP** $14

(KP Photo)

❏ **Padme Amidala, Arena Escape,** 2002, Hasbro, Swinging arm with blaster pistol and column
EX n/a   **NM** n/a   **MIP** $8

❏ **Plo Koon, Arena Battle,** 2002, Hasbro, With lightsaber
EX n/a   **NM** n/a   **MIP** $13

(KP Photo)

❏ **R2-D2, Coruscant Sentry,** 2002, Hasbro, With two plastic assassin bugs. Probably the best R2 sculpt yet, with lights and sound, to boot
EX n/a   **NM** n/a   **MIP** $8

(KP Photo)

❏ **R3-T7,** 2002, Hasbro, Detailed astromech droid with blue engergy bolts that wrap around body
EX n/a   **NM** n/a   **MIP** $11

(KP Photo)

❏ **Royal Guard, Coruscant Security,** 2002, Hasbro, Red figure with staff and blue "energy bolts." Definitely the prototype for the Imperial Guard after the fall of the Republic
EX n/a   **NM** n/a   **MIP** $14

(KP Photo)

❏ **Saesee Tiin, Jedi Master,** 2002, Hasbro, With lightsaber and force-repelled blast effect
EX n/a   **NM** n/a   **MIP** $8

(KP Photo)

❏ **Shaak Ti, Jedi Master,** 2002, Hasbro, With "blast effect" lightsaber. Very well-detailed figure
EX n/a   **NM** n/a   **MIP** $12

(KP Photo)

❏ **Super Battle Droid,** 2002, Hasbro, With laser blast battle damage and attachments
EX n/a   **NM** n/a   **MIP** $6

(KP Photo)

❏ **Taun We, Kamino Cloner,** 2002, Hasbro, With cloning pod
EX n/a   **NM** n/a   **MIP** $14

❏ **Tusken Raider, Female w/Tusken Child,** 2002, Hasbro, Child figure can be freestanding or fit in pack
EX n/a   **NM** n/a   **MIP** $11

❏ **Yoda, Jedi Master,** 2002, Hasbro, Includes lightsaber, walking stick, and base
EX n/a   **NM** n/a   **MIP** $17

(KP Photo)

❏ **Zam Wessell,** 2002, Hasbro, With long gun, human face partially covered by scarf
EX n/a   **NM** n/a   **MIP** $11

(KP Photo)

❏ **Zam Wessell,** 2002, Hasbro, Shorter blaster than preview edition, removable changeling face
EX n/a   **NM** n/a   **MIP** $11

DROIDS

(ToyShop File Photo)

❏ **A-Wing Pilot,** 1985, Kenner
EX n/a   **NM** $40   **MIP** $150

❏ **Boba Fett,** 1985, Kenner
EX n/a   **NM** $20   **MIP** $800

❏ **C-3PO,** 1985, Kenner, Solid, multicolored plastic body (not gold chromed) with painted eyes
EX n/a   **NM** $70   **MIP** $130

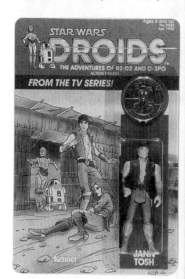

(KP Photo)

❏ **Jann Tosh,** 1985, Kenner
EX n/a   **NM** $15   **MIP** $20

❏ **Jord Dusat,** 1985, Kenner
EX n/a   **NM** $12   **MIP** $20

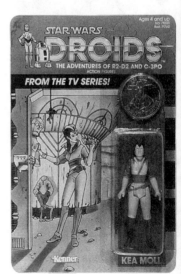

(KP Photo)

❏ **Kea Moll,** 1985, Kenner, Light tan and darker brown clothing, includes blaster pistol
EX n/a   **NM** $12   **MIP** $30

STAR WARS

(KP Photo)

(KP Photo)

(KP Photo)

❑ **Kez-Iban,** 1985, Kenner, Purple body, tan clothing, standard-issue blaster (same as early Stormtroopers)
EX n/a   **NM** $12   **MIP** $30

❑ **Thall Joben,** 1985, Kenner
EX n/a   **NM** $15   **MIP** $20

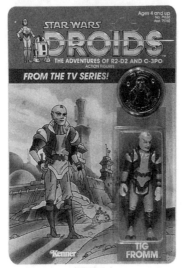

(KP Photo)

❑ **R2-D2,** 1985, Kenner, Simplified body markings and head--same sculpt and legs as regular (vintage) R2, though
EX n/a   **NM** $60   **MIP** $105

❑ **Sise Fromm,** 1985, Kenner, Large-headed, green skinned figure with purple cloth robe
EX n/a   **NM** $50   **MIP** $130

❑ **Tig Fromm,** 1985, Kenner, Blue and gray figure
EX n/a   **NM** $45   **MIP** $90

❑ **Uncle Gundy,** 1985, Kenner, Short, portly figure with white hair and mustache. Includes blaster pistol
EX n/a   **NM** $15   **MIP** $20

EMPIRE STRIKES BACK

❑ **2-1B,** 1981, Kenner, The medical droid who assists Luke's recovery after his duel with Vader. In the movie, you actually never see his legs
EX n/a   **NM** $6   **MIP** $80

❑ **4-LOM,** 1982, Kenner, Tan plastic cloak with brown belt worn over the top, unique blaster rifle
EX n/a   **NM** $10   **MIP** $115

❑ **AT-AT Commander,** 1982, Kenner, Available with Sears Exclusive Hoth Rebel base set, or individually. Includes blaster pistol
EX n/a   **NM** $6   **MIP** $40

❑ **AT-AT Driver,** 1981, Kenner, White and gray uniform, includes blaster rifle
EX n/a   **NM** $8   **MIP** $75

(KP Photo)

❑ **Bespin Security Guard, black,** 1982, Kenner, Includes blaster pistol
EX n/a   **NM** $10   **MIP** $40

❑ **Bespin Security Guard, white,** 1980, Kenner, With blaster pistol
EX n/a   **NM** $8   **MIP** $50

(KP Photo)

❑ **Bossk,** 1980, Kenner, Includes blaster rifle with forward grip so rifle body rests against arm
EX n/a   NM $8   MIP $65

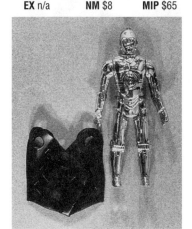

(KP Photo)

❑ **C-3PO w/Removable Limbs,** 1982, Kenner, Included pouch for Chewbacca to carry the disassembled 3PO
EX n/a   NM $6   MIP $65

❑ **Cloud Car Pilot,** 1982, Kenner, White uniform, orange and yellow helmet. Style of figure reminiscent of rebel troops
EX n/a   NM $15   MIP $65

(KP Photo)

❑ **Dengar,** 1980, Kenner, One of the bounty hunters hired by Vader ("we don't need their scum…"). This figure originally came with a long rifle
EX n/a   NM $8   MIP $65

❑ **FX-7,** 1980, Kenner, Also called the "medical droid," this model had a series of spindly arms that pivoted up from the cylindrical body
EX n/a   NM $7   MIP $50

❑ **Han in Bespin Outfit,** 1981, Kenner, Includes blaster pistol
EX n/a   NM $7   MIP $95

❑ **Han in Hoth Gear,** 1980, Kenner, In dark blue parka, khaki pants, includes small blaster pistol
EX n/a   NM $8   MIP $75

(KP Photo)

❑ **Hoth Rebel Soldier,** 1980, Kenner, Light brown and off-white uniform, small blaster pistol looking a bit like a Star Trek phaser
EX n/a   NM $6   MIP $45

❑ **IG-88,** 1980, Kenner, One of the most highly-collected ESB figures, very classic robot look. According to Star Wars lore, IG88's head was one of the props behind the bar in the Cantina scene from the first movie. Includes two blasters
EX n/a   NM $8   MIP $120

❑ **Imperial Commander,** 1981, Kenner, The packaging showed General Veers in a green uniform, but the figure was an anonymous black-uniformed officer. Some variation in hair color paint exists. Included standard-issue Stormtrooper blaster
EX n/a   NM $8   MIP $45

❑ **Imperial TIE Fighter Pilot,** 1982, Kenner, Black uniform, gray gloves and boots, included gray blaster pistol
EX n/a   NM $10   MIP $90

❑ **Lando Calrissian,** 1981, Kenner, Two-tone blue clothing with gray plastic cloak and blaster pistol
EX n/a   NM $8   MIP $55

❑ **Leia in Bespin Gown,** 1980, Kenner, Brown outfit with printed plastic cloak. Included blaster pistol
EX n/a   NM $17   MIP $140

❑ **Leia in Hoth Gear,** 1981, Kenner, White uniform with light tan vest and brown boots, included small blaster pistol
EX n/a   NM $16   MIP $95

No. 39349
ASST #39300   Ages 4 and up

STAR WARS EMPIRE STRIKES BACK

Lobot

Kenner

(KP Photo)

❑ **Lobot,** 1981, Kenner, Includes blaster pistol
EX n/a   NM $6   MIP $50

(ToyShop File Photo)

❑ **Luke in Bespin Fatigues,** 1980, Kenner, Included blaster pistol and stand-alone lightsaber (not part of the figure)
EX n/a   NM $16   MIP $130

❑ **Luke in Hoth Gear,** 1982, Kenner, White uniform with brown vest and gray boots. Included blaster rifle
EX n/a   NM $8   MIP $75

❑ **R2-D2 with Sensorscope,** 1982, Kenner, Available first with Sears Exclusive Hoth Rebel Base play set, or individually. Essentially the same as the standard R2, but with a blue plastic sensorscope that could be raised or lowered from his head
EX n/a   NM $11   MIP $60

❑ **Rebel Commander,** 1980, Kenner, Off-white uniform, brown boots, blaster rifle
EX n/a   NM $6   MIP $75

❑ **Snowtrooper,** 1980, Kenner, Plastic cloak along belt, included heavy laser rifle
EX n/a   NM $10   MIP $65

❑ **Ugnaught,** 1981, Kenner, With blue cloth apron and white toolkit
EX n/a   NM $8   MIP $65

(ToyShop File Photo)

❏ **Yoda,** 1981, Kenner, With cloth cloak, plastic belt, snake and walking stick. The plastic accessories were produced in varying colors
EX n/a   **NM** $18   **MIP** $160

❏ **Zuckuss,** 1982, Kenner
EX n/a   **NM** $12   **MIP** $80

EWOKS

(KP Photo)

❏ **Dulok Scout,** 1985, Kenner, Medium-green figure with club
EX n/a   **NM** $8   **MIP** $22

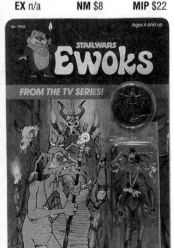

(KP Photo)

❏ **Dulok Shaman,** 1985, Kenner, Bright green figure with skull-topped staff
EX n/a   **NM** $10   **MIP** $22

(KP Photo)

❏ **King Gorneesh,** 1985, Kenner, Fear-some bright green figure with staff
EX n/a   **NM** $10   **MIP** $22

(KP Photo)

❏ **Logray,** 1985, Kenner, With bright blue plastic robe and staff
EX n/a   **NM** $10   **MIP** $22

(KP Photo)

❏ **Urgah Lady Gorneesh,** 1985, Kenner, Green figure with red-brown poncho, blue highlights on head and face
EX n/a   **NM** $10   **MIP** $18

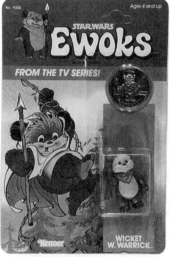

(KP Photo)

❏ **Wicket,** 1985, Kenner, Fittingly, a more "cartoony" simplified version of the Wicket from ROTJ. Included spear
EX n/a   **NM** $12   **MIP** $35

POTF

❏ **Amanaman, w/coin,** 1985
EX n/a   **NM** $95   **MIP** $200

❏ **Anakin Skywalker, w/coin,** 1985
EX n/a   **NM** $20   **MIP** $1950

❏ **AT-AT Driver, w/coin,** 1985
EX n/a   **NM** $9   **MIP** $550

(KP Photo)

❑ **AT-ST Driver, w/coin,** 1985
   EX n/a   **NM** $9   **MIP** $45

(KP Photo)

❑ **A-Wing Pilot, w/coin,** 1985
   EX n/a   **NM** $40   **MIP** $95

(KP Photo)

❑ **Barada, w/coin,** 1985
   EX n/a   **NM** $40   **MIP** $95
❑ **Biker Scout, w/coin,** 1985
   EX n/a   **NM** $12   **MIP** $90

(KP Photo)

❑ **B-Wing Pilot, w/coin,** 1985
   EX n/a   **NM** $9   **MIP** $30
❑ **C-3PO w/Removable Limbs, w/coin,**
   1985
   EX n/a   **NM** $6   **MIP** $65
❑ **Chewbacca, w/coin,** 1985
   EX n/a   **NM** $9   **MIP** $100
❑ **Darth Vader, w/coin,** 1985
   EX n/a   **NM** $12   **MIP** $135
❑ **Emperor Palpatine, w/coin,** 1985
   EX n/a   **NM** $6   **MIP** $60

(KP Photo)

❑ **EV-9D9, w/coin,** 1985
   EX n/a   **NM** $65   **MIP** $120
❑ **Gamorrean Guard, w/coin,** 1985
   EX n/a   **NM** $5   **MIP** $300

(ToyShop File Photo)

❑ **Han in Carbonite, w/coin,** 1985
   EX n/a   **NM** $70   **MIP** $195
❑ **Han in Trenchcoat, w/coin,** 1985
   EX n/a   **NM** $9   **MIP** $330

(KP Photo)

❑ **Imperial Dignitary, w/coin,** 1985
   EX n/a   **NM** $35   **MIP** $70
❑ **Imperial Gunner, w/coin,** 1985
   EX n/a   **NM** $55   **MIP** $105
❑ **Jawa, w/coin,** 1985
   EX n/a   **NM** $11   **MIP** $75

STAR WARS

(ToyShop File Photo)

❏ **Lando as General Pilot, w/coin,** 1985
EX n/a   NM $50   MIP $90

❏ **Leia in Battle Poncho,** 1985
EX n/a   NM $16   MIP $70

❏ **Luke as Jedi Knight w/Green Saber, w/coin,** 1985
EX n/a   NM $20   MIP $185

❏ **Luke as X-Wing Pilot, w/coin,** 1985
EX n/a   NM $12   MIP $100

❏ **Luke in Battle Poncho, w/coin,** 1985
EX n/a   NM $60   MIP $105

(ToyShop File Photo)

❏ **Luke in Stormtrooper Disguise, w/coin,** 1985
EX n/a   NM $105   MIP $275

❏ **Lumat, w/coin,** 1985
EX n/a   NM $18   MIP $50

❏ **Nikto, w/coin,** 1985
EX n/a   NM $10   MIP $650

❏ **Obi-Wan Kenobi, w/coin,** 1985
EX n/a   NM $13   MIP $110

❏ **Paploo, w/coin,** 1985
EX n/a   NM $16   MIP $60

❏ **R2-D2 with pop-up Lightsaber, w/coin,** 1985
EX n/a   NM $70   MIP $130

(KP Photo)

❏ **Romba, w/coin,** 1985
EX n/a   NM $30   MIP $40

❏ **Stormtrooper, w/coin,** 1985
EX n/a   NM $10   MIP $145

❏ **Teebo, w/coin,** 1985
EX n/a   NM $13   MIP $120

(KP Photo)

❏ **Warok, w/coin,** 1985
EX n/a   NM $35   MIP $55

❏ **Wicket, w/coin,** 1985
EX n/a   NM $10   MIP $110

❏ **Yak Face, w/coin,** 1985
EX n/a   NM $175   MIP $1325

(ToyShop File Photo)

❏ **Yoda, w/coin,** 1985
EX n/a   NM $17   MIP $325

POTF2

(Hasbro Photo)

❏ **2-1B Medic Droid,** 1997, Series 5
EX n/a   NM $2   MIP $8

❏ **4-LOM,** 1997, Series 7
EX n/a   NM $3   MIP $10

❏ **8-D8 Droid,** 1998, Series 14
EX n/a   NM $3   MIP $10

❏ **Admiral Ackbar,** 1997, Series 7
EX n/a   NM $3   MIP $10

❏ **Admiral Motti,** 2000, Series 20
EX n/a   NM $5   MIP $9

❏ **Anakin Skywalker,** 1999, Series 17
EX n/a   NM $3   MIP $12

❏ **ASP-7 Droid,** 1997, Series 7
EX n/a   NM $3   MIP $8

❏ **AT-AT Driver,** 1998
EX n/a   NM $3   MIP $20

❏ **AT-ST Driver**, 1997, Series 5
  EX n/a   **NM** $3   **MIP** $10

❏ **Aunt Beru**, 1999, Series 17
  EX n/a   **NM** $3   **MIP** $14

❏ **Ben (Obi-Wan) Kenobi**, 1997
  EX n/a   **NM** $5   **MIP** $9

❏ **Bib Fortuna**, 1997, Series 6
  EX n/a   **NM** $3   **MIP** $10

(Hasbro Photo)

❏ **Biggs Darklighter**, 1998, Series 11
  EX n/a   **NM** $3   **MIP** $14

❏ **Boba Fett**, 1996, Series 2
  EX n/a   **NM** $4   **MIP** $15

❏ **Boba Fett**, 1997
  EX n/a   **NM** $5   **MIP** $10

❏ **Boba Fett vs. IG-88**, 1996, Packaged
  with comic book
  EX n/a   **NM** $6   **MIP** $25

❏ **B'omarr Monk**, Internet exclusive offer.
  Moving spider-like legs and brain
  encased in plastic bubble
  EX n/a   **NM** $10   **MIP** $15

(Hasbro Photo)

❏ **Bossk**, 1997, Series 5
  EX n/a   **NM** $3   **MIP** $10

❏ **C-3PO**, 1995, Series 1
  EX n/a   **NM** $3   **MIP** $10

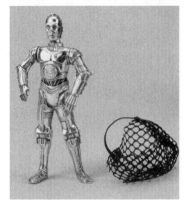

(Hasbro Photo)

❏ **C-3PO w/Removable Limbs and Backpack**, 1998, Series 13
  EX n/a   **NM** $3   **MIP** $16

❏ **C-3PO, Shop Worn**, 1999, Series 17
  EX n/a   **NM** $3   **MIP** $8

❏ **C-3PO, w/Millennium Minted Coin**
  EX n/a   **NM** $5   **MIP** $10

❏ **Cantina Aliens—Labria, Nabrun
  Leids, Takeel**
  EX n/a   **NM** $6   **MIP** $12

❏ **Cantina Greedo**, 1999, Series 18
  EX n/a   **NM** $3   **MIP** $5

❏ **Cantina Han Solo**, 1999, Series 18
  EX n/a   **NM** $3   **MIP** $5

❏ **Cantina Showdown—Obi-Wan
  Kenobi, Ponda Baba, Dr. Evazan**
  EX n/a   **NM** $6   **MIP** $12

❏ **Captain Piett**, 1998, Series 12
  EX n/a   **NM** $3   **MIP** $14

❏ **Chewbacca**, 1995, Series 1
  EX n/a   **NM** $3   **MIP** $12

❏ **Chewbacca (Hoth)**, 1998, Series 16,
  with painted "snow" on face
  EX n/a   **NM** $3   **MIP** $8

❏ **Chewbacca as Boushh's Bounty**, 1998,
  Series 15
  EX n/a   **NM** $3   **MIP** $18

❏ **Chewbacca in Bounty Hunter Disguise**,
  1996
  EX n/a   **NM** $3   **MIP** $6

❏ **Chewbacca, w/Millennium Minted
  Coin**
  EX n/a   **NM** $5   **MIP** $10

❏ **Clone Emperor**, 1998
  EX n/a   **NM** $3   **MIP** $18

❏ **Crowd Control Stormtrooper**, 1996
  EX n/a   **NM** $5   **MIP** $9

❏ **Dagobah w/Yoda**, 1998
  EX n/a   **NM** $6   **MIP** $12

❏ **Darktrooper**, 1998
  EX n/a   **NM** $3   **MIP** $30

❏ **Darth Vader**, 1995, Series 1
  EX n/a   **NM** $4   **MIP** $13

❏ **Darth Vader**, 1997
  EX n/a   **NM** $5   **MIP** $9

❏ **Darth Vader**, 1998, Series 16
  EX n/a   **NM** $3   **MIP** $8

❏ **Darth Vader w/Interrogation Droid**,
  1999, Series 19
  EX n/a   **NM** $5   **MIP** $5

(KP Photo)

❏ **Darth Vader w/Removable Helmet**,
  1998, Series 12
  EX n/a   **NM** $4   **MIP** $24

❏ **Dash Rendar**, 1996
  EX n/a   **NM** $3   **MIP** $8

❏ **Death Star Droid w/Mouse Droid**, 1998
  EX n/a   **NM** $3   **MIP** $20

❏ **Death Star Escape—Luke and Han in
  Stormtrooper Disguise, Chewbacca**
  EX n/a   **NM** $6   **MIP** $22

❏ **Death Star Gunner**, 1996, Series 3
  EX n/a   **NM** $3   **MIP** $18

❏ **Death Star Trooper**, 1998, Series 15
  EX n/a   **NM** $3   **MIP** $26

❏ **Death Star w/Darth Vader**, 1998
  EX n/a   **NM** $6   **MIP** $12

❏ **Dengar**, 1997, Series 7
  EX n/a   **NM** $3   **MIP** $10

❏ **Droopy McCool and Barquin D'an**
  EX n/a   **NM** $6   **MIP** $20

❏ **Emperor Palpatine**, 1997, Series 6
  EX n/a   **NM** $3   **MIP** $10

❏ **Emperor Palpatine**, 1998, Series 16
  EX n/a   **NM** $3   **MIP** $8

❏ **Emperor Palpatine, w/Millennium
  Minted Coin**
  EX n/a   **NM** $5   **MIP** $10

❏ **Emperor's Royal Guard**, 1997, Series 8
  EX n/a   **NM** $3   **MIP** $12

❏ **Emporer Palpatine**, 1997
  EX n/a   **NM** $5   **MIP** $9

STAR WARS

(Hasbro Photo)

❏ **Endor Rebel Soldier,** 1998, Series 10
EX n/a   NM $3   MIP $14

❏ **Endor w/Wicket,** 1998
EX n/a   NM $10   MIP $22

(Hasbro Photo)

❏ **EV-9D9,** 1997, Series 9
EX n/a   NM $3   MIP $10

❏ **Falcon w/Han Solo,** 1998
EX n/a   NM $6   MIP $8

❏ **Falcon w/Luke Skywalker,** 1998
EX n/a   NM $6   MIP $8

❏ **Figrin D'an (Cantina Band Member)**
EX n/a   NM $10   MIP $15

❏ **Final Jedi Duel—Darth Vader, Luke, Emperor Palpatine**
EX n/a   NM $6   MIP $24

(Hasbro Photo)

❏ **Gamorrean Guard,** 1997, Series 9
EX n/a   NM $3   MIP $10

❏ **Garindan (Long Snoot),** 1997, Series 7
EX n/a   NM $3   MIP $10

❏ **Grand Admiral Thrawn,** 1998
EX n/a   NM $3   MIP $20

(KP Photo)

❏ **Grand Moff Tarkin,** 1997, Series 7, surprisingly not produced until the release of the first three movies
EX n/a   NM $3   MIP $10

❏ **Greedo,** 1996, Series 3
EX n/a   NM $3   MIP $18

❏ **Han in Bespin Outfit,** 1997, Series 8
EX n/a   NM $3   MIP $10

❏ **Han in Bespin Outfit, w/Millennium Minted Coin**
EX n/a   NM $5   MIP $10

❏ **Han in Carbonite,** 1996
EX n/a   NM $3   MIP $6

❏ **Han in Endor Gear,** 1997, Series 6
EX n/a   NM $3   MIP $12

❏ **Han in Hoth Gear,** 1996, Series 2
EX n/a   NM $3   MIP $12

❏ **Han in Stormtrooper Disguise**
EX n/a   NM $10   MIP $20

(KP Photo)

❏ **Han Solo,** 1995, Series 1
EX n/a   NM $3   MIP $12

❏ **Han Solo w/Smuggler's Flight Pack,** 1996
EX n/a   NM $5   MIP $9

❏ **Hoth Rebel Soldier,** 1997, Series 5
EX n/a   NM $3   MIP $10

❏ **Imperial Probe Droid,** 1997
EX n/a   NM $5   MIP $9

❏ **Imperial Sentinel,** 1998
EX n/a   NM $3   MIP $18

(Hasbro Photo)

❑ **Ishi Tib,** 1998, Series 12
EX n/a   NM $3   MIP $14

❑ **Jabba the Hutt's Dancers—Rystall, Greeata, Lyn Me**
EX n/a   NM $6   MIP $16

(KP Photo)

❑ **Jabba's Skiff Guards - Klaatu, Barada, Nikto,** 1999, Well-detailed figures with stand. Keeping them in-pack, the box doubles as a diorama background
EX n/a   NM $8   MIP $35

❑ **Jawa & Gonk Droid,** 1999, Series 18, Droid also known as "power droid," a walking generator. Called "Gonk" because of the noise it makes when walking around on the Jawas' Sand-crawer in Episode IV
EX n/a   NM $3   MIP $5

(Hasbro Photo)

❑ **Jawas,** 1996, Series 4
EX n/a   NM $3   MIP $20

❑ **Jedi Knight Luke Skywalker,** 1997
EX n/a   NM $5   MIP $9

❑ **Jedi Spirits—Anakin Skywalker, Yoda, Obi-Wan Kenobi**
EX n/a   NM $6   MIP $10

❑ **Kyle Katarn,** 1998
EX n/a   NM $3   MIP $35

(Hasbro Photo)

❑ **Lak Sivrak,** 1998, Series 11
EX n/a   NM $3   MIP $12

(Hasbro Photo)

❑ **Lando as General,** 1998, Series 10
EX n/a   NM $3   MIP $14

❑ **Lando as Skiff Guard,** 1997, Series 6
EX n/a   NM $3   MIP $10

(Hasbro Photo)

❑ **Lando Calrissian,** 1996, Series 2
EX n/a   NM $3   MIP $10

❑ **Leia and Han,** 1998
EX n/a   NM $6   MIP $12

(Hasbro Photo)

❑ **Leia and Luke,** 1998
EX n/a   NM $6   MIP $12

❑ **Leia and R2-D2,** 1998
EX n/a   NM $6   MIP $12

(Hasbro Photo)

❑ **Leia and Wicket the Ewok,** 1998
EX n/a   NM $6   MIP $12

❑ **Leia as Jabba's Prisoner,** 1997, Series 8
EX n/a   NM $3   MIP $10

❑ **Leia in Boushh Disguise,** 1996
EX n/a   NM $3   MIP $6

❑ **Leia in Endor Gear, w/Millennium Minted Coin**
EX n/a   NM $5   MIP $10

(Hasbro Photo)

❑ **Leia in Ewok Celebration Outfit**, 1998, Series 10
EX n/a   NM $3   MIP $14

❑ **Leia in Hoth Gear**, 1998
EX n/a   NM $3   MIP $22

❑ **Leia w/All-New Likeness**, 1998, Series 13, a much better sculpt than the first re-release
EX n/a   NM $3   MIP $16

❑ **Lobot**, 1998, Series 15
EX n/a   NM $3   MIP $14

(Hasbro Photo)

❑ **Luke as X-Wing Pilot**, 1996, Series 2
EX n/a   NM $3   MIP $14

❑ **Luke in Battle Poncho, w/Millennium Minted Coin**
EX n/a   NM $5   MIP $10

❑ **Luke in Bespin Outfit**, 1998, Series 10
EX n/a   NM $3   MIP $16

❑ **Luke in Ceremonial Garb**, 1997, Series 10
EX n/a   NM $3   MIP $12

❑ **Luke in Dagobah Fatigues**, 1996, Series 3
EX n/a   NM $3   MIP $12

(Hasbro Photo)

❑ **Luke in Hoth Gear**, 1997, Series 5
EX n/a   NM $3   MIP $11

❑ **Luke in Imperial Guard Disguise**, 1996
EX n/a   NM $3   MIP $8

(KP Photo)

❑ **Luke in Stormtrooper Disguise**, 1996, Series 4
EX n/a   NM $4   MIP $24

❑ **Luke Skywalker**, 1995, Series 1
EX n/a   NM $4   MIP $12

❑ **Luke Skywalker**, 1998, Series 16
EX n/a   NM $3   MIP $8

❑ **Luke Skywalker (Dark Empire)**, 1998
EX n/a   NM $3   MIP $18

❑ **Luke Skywalker w/T16**, 1999, Series 18
EX n/a   NM $3   MIP $5

❑ **Luke Skywalker's Desert Sport Skiff**, 1996
EX n/a   NM $5   MIP $10

❑ **Luke w/Blast Shield Helmet**, 1998, Series 13
EX n/a   NM $3   MIP $16

❑ **Mace Windu**
EX n/a   NM $5   MIP $10

(Hasbro Photo)

❑ **Malakili (Rancor Keeper)**, 1997, Series 9
EX n/a   NM $3   MIP $8

❑ **Mara Jade**, 1998
EX n/a   NM $3   MIP $35

❑ **Max Rebo and Doda Bodonawieedo**
EX n/a   NM $6   MIP $25

❑ **Momaw Nadon (Hammerhead)**, 1996, Series 4
EX n/a   NM $2   MIP $16

❑ **Mon Mothma**, 1998, Series 15
EX n/a   NM $3   MIP $16

❑ **Muftak and Kabe**
EX n/a   NM $10   MIP $16

❑ **Mynock Hunt—Han, Leia, Chewbacca**
EX n/a   NM $6   MIP $32

(Hasbro Photo)

❏ **Nien Nunb**, 1997, Series 9
EX n/a **NM** $3 **MIP** $10

❏ **Obi-Wan Kenobi**, 1995, Series 1
EX n/a **NM** $4 **MIP** $12

❏ **Obi-Wan Kenobi**, 1998, Series 16
EX n/a **NM** $3 **MIP** $8

(KP Photo)

❏ **Obi-Wan Kenobi Spirit**, Figure was a mail-in offer from Frito Lay. Made of translucent blue plastic
EX n/a **NM** $10 **MIP** $10

❏ **Oola and Salacious Crumb**
EX n/a **NM** $10 **MIP** $14

❏ **Orrimaarko (Prune Face)**, 1998, Series 15, with brown plastic cloak
EX n/a **NM** $3 **MIP** $22

❏ **Ponda Baba**, 1997, Series 7
EX n/a **NM** $3 **MIP** $10

❏ **Pote Snitkin**, 1998
EX n/a **NM** $3 **MIP** $20

❏ **Prince Xizor**, 1996
EX n/a **NM** $3 **MIP** $6

❏ **Prince Xizor vs. Darth Vader**, 1996
EX n/a **NM** $6 **MIP** $15

❏ **Princess Leia**, 1995, Series 1
EX n/a **NM** $3 **MIP** $13

❏ **Princess Leia**, 1998, Series 16
EX n/a **NM** $3 **MIP** $8

❏ **Princess Leia (Hood Up)**, 2000, Series 20
EX n/a **NM** $5 **MIP** $9

❏ **Princess Leia Organa Solo**, 1998
EX n/a **NM** $3 **MIP** $18

❏ **Purchase of the Droids—Luke, C-3PO, Uncle Owen**
EX n/a **NM** $6 **MIP** $18

❏ **R2-D2**, 1995, Series 1
EX n/a **NM** $3 **MIP** $12

❏ **R2-D2**, 1997
EX n/a **NM** $5 **MIP** $9

❏ **R2-D2**, 1998, Series 16
EX n/a **NM** $3 **MIP** $8

❏ **R2-D2 w/Datalink and Sensorscope**, 1998, Series 13
EX n/a **NM** $3 **MIP** $14

❏ **R2-D2 w/Holographic Princess Leia**, 1999, Series 20
EX n/a **NM** $12 **MIP** $27

❏ **R5-D4**, 1996, Series 4
EX n/a **NM** $3 **MIP** $11

❏ **Rebel Fleet Trooper**, 1997, Series 7
EX n/a **NM** $3 **MIP** $11

❏ **Rebel Pilots—Wedge Antilles, B-Wing Pilot (Ten Nunb), Y-Wing Pilot**
EX n/a **NM** $6 **MIP** $26

❏ **Ree-Yees**, 1998, Series 15
EX n/a **NM** $3 **MIP** $26

(Hasbro Photo)

❏ **Saelt-Marae (Yak Face)**, 1997, Series 9
EX n/a **NM** $3 **MIP** $10

(KP Photo)

❏ **Sandtrooper**, 1996, Series 3, with blaster rifle and backpack
EX n/a **NM** $3 **MIP** $12

(KP Photo)

❏ **Snowtrooper**, 1997, Series 8, nicely detailed sculpt
EX n/a **NM** $3 **MIP** $10

❏ **Snowtrooper (Deluxe)**, 1997, With tripod laser cannon
EX n/a **NM** $5 **MIP** $9

❏ **Snowtrooper, w/Millennium Minted Coin**
EX n/a **NM** $5 **MIP** $10

❏ **Spacetrooper**, 1998
EX n/a **NM** $3 **MIP** $25

(KP Photo)

STAR WARS

☐ **STAP and Battle Droid**
EX n/a   NM $10   MIP $12

☐ **Stormtrooper,** 1995, Series 1
EX n/a   NM $3   MIP $11

☐ **Stormtrooper,** 1999, Series 19
EX n/a   NM $5   MIP $5

☐ **Sy Snootles and Joh Yowza**
EX n/a   NM $6   MIP $20

☐ **Tatooine w/Luke Skywalker,** 1998
EX n/a   NM $10   MIP $25

☐ **Theater Edition Jedi Knight Luke Skywalker,** 1996
EX n/a   NM $10   MIP $65

(KP Photo)

☐ **TIE Fighter Pilot,** 1996, Series 2, equipped with two blaster rifles
EX n/a   NM $3   MIP $11

☐ **Tie Fighter w/Darth Vader,** 1998
EX n/a   NM $6   MIP $15

(KP Photo)

☐ **Tusken Raider,** 1996, Series 4
EX n/a   NM $3   MIP $13

☐ **Ugnaught,** 1998, Series 13
EX n/a   NM $3   MIP $10

☐ **Weequay Skiff Guard,** 1997, Series 7
EX n/a   NM $3   MIP $10

(Hasbro Photo)

☐ **Wicket and Logray,** 1998, Series 11
EX n/a   NM $3   MIP $10

☐ **Yoda,** 1996, Series 2
EX n/a   NM $3   MIP $11

☐ **Yoda,** 1998, Series 16
EX n/a   NM $3   MIP $12

☐ **Zuckuss,** 1998, Series 12
EX n/a   NM $3   MIP $14

POTJ

☐ **Aurra Sing,** 2001, Hasbro
EX n/a   NM $3   MIP $6

☐ **Boba Fett,** Hasbro
EX n/a   NM $3   MIP $6

☐ **Boss Nass, Gungan Sacred Place,** Hasbro
EX n/a   NM $3   MIP $6

☐ **Chewbacca, Dejarik Challenge,** 2000, Hasbro
EX n/a   NM $3   MIP $6

☐ **Coruscant Guard,** 2001, Hasbro
EX n/a   NM $3   MIP $6

☐ **Darth Maul w/Sith Attack Droid,** Hasbro
EX n/a   NM $3   MIP $6

☐ **Darth Maul, Final Duel,** 2000, Hasbro
EX n/a   NM $3   MIP $6

☐ **Darth Maul, Sith Apprentice,** 2001, Hasbro
EX n/a   NM $3   MIP $6

☐ **Darth Vader, Dagobah,** Hasbro
EX n/a   NM $3   MIP $6

☐ **Destroyer Droid, Battle Damaged,** 2000, Hasbro
EX n/a   NM $3   MIP $8

☐ **Eeth Koth,** Hasbro
EX n/a   NM $3   MIP $6

☐ **Ellorrs Madak,** 2001, Hasbro
EX n/a   NM $3   MIP $6

☐ **Gungan Warrior,** Hasbro
EX n/a   NM $3   MIP $6

(KP Photo)

☐ **Han Solo, Bespin Capture,** 2002, Includes blaster pistol, cuffs and 8-page "Jedi Force File"
EX n/a   NM n/a   MIP $6

☐ **Jar Jar Binks, Tatooine,** Hasbro
EX n/a   NM $3   MIP $6

☐ **Ketwol,** 2001, Hasbro
EX n/a   NM $3   MIP $6

☐ **Mas Amedda,** 2000, Hasbro
EX n/a   NM $3   MIP $6

☐ **Obi-Wan Kenobi, Cold Weather Gear,** 2001, Hasbro
EX n/a   NM $3   MIP $6

☐ **Obi-Wan Kenobi, Jedi Training Gear,** Hasbro
EX n/a   NM $3   MIP $6

☐ **Plo Koon,** 2000, Hasbro
EX n/a   NM $3   MIP $6

☐ **Queen Amidala, Decoy,** Hasbro
EX n/a   NM $3   MIP $6

☐ **Qui-Gon Jinn, Mos Espa Disguise,** Hasbro, Includes gray cloth poncho and lightsaber
EX n/a   NM $3   MIP $6

☐ **R2-D2, Naboo Escape,** 2000, Hasbro
EX n/a   NM $3   MIP $6

☐ **Red Throne Queen,** 2001, Hasbro
EX n/a   NM $3   MIP $6

☐ **Sabe,** 2001, Hasbro, With blaster pistol
EX n/a   NM $3   MIP $6

☐ **Saesae Tiin,** 2001, Hasbro
EX n/a   NM $3   MIP $6

☐ **Sandtrooper,** 2001, With binoculars and pistol
EX n/a   NM n/a   MIP $12

☐ **Sebulba,** Hasbro, Includes removeable helmet and goggles
EX n/a   NM $3   MIP $6

☐ **Shmi Skywalker,** Hasbro
EX n/a   NM $3   MIP $6

❏ **Tusken Raider, Desert Sniper,** 2000, Hasbro
EX n/a   **NM** $3   **MIP** $6

RETURN OF THE JEDI

❏ **8D8,** 1983, Kenner
EX n/a   **NM** $6   **MIP** $35

(KP Photo)

(KP Photo)

(KP Photo)

❏ **Emperor Palpatine,** 1983, Kenner
EX n/a   **NM** $6   **MIP** $30

❏ **Emperor's Royal Guard,** 1984
EX n/a   **NM** $9   **MIP** $40

❏ **Bib Fortuna,** 1983, Kenner, "Pay Jabba no bother…" This figure is the original sculpt of Jabba's major domo who apparently, was weak-minded enough to allow Luke's Jedi mind trick to work on him
EX n/a   **NM** $8   **MIP** $20

❏ **Biker Scout,** 1983, Kenner
EX n/a   **NM** $11   **MIP** $40

❏ **B-Wing Pilot,** 1984, Kenner
EX n/a   **NM** $9   **MIP** $20

(KP Photo)

❏ **Admiral Ackbar,** 1983, Kenner
EX n/a   **NM** $8   **MIP** $20

(KP Photo)

❏ **AT-ST Driver,** 1983
EX n/a   **NM** $9   **MIP** $20

❏ **Chief Chirpa,** 1983, Kenner
EX n/a   **NM** $7   **MIP** $20

❏ **Gamorrean Guard,** 1983, Kenner
EX n/a   **NM** $5   **MIP** $30

❏ **General Madine,** 1983
EX n/a   **NM** $8   **MIP** $30

❏ **Han in Trenchcoat,** 1984
EX n/a   **NM** $11   **MIP** $35

STAR WARS

❑ **Klaatu,** 1983
EX n/a   NM $8   MIP $20

(KP Photo)

❑ **Klaatu in Skiff Guard Outfit,** 1983
EX n/a   NM $9   MIP $20

❑ **Lando Calrissian, Skiff Guard Outfit,**
1983, Kenner
EX n/a   NM $9   MIP $35

(KP Photo)

❑ **Leia in Battle Poncho,** 1984, Green
camo pattern cloth poncho, removeable
helmet, ammo belt and blaster pistol
EX n/a   NM $16   MIP $35

❑ **Leia in Boushh Disguise,** 1983
EX n/a   NM $10   MIP $40

❑ **Logray,** 1983
EX n/a   NM $6   MIP $20

❑ **Luke as Jedi Knight, Blue Saber,** 1983
EX n/a   NM $35   MIP $115

❑ **Luke as Jedi Knight, Green Saber,**
1983, Kenner
EX n/a   NM $20   MIP $60

❑ **Lumat,** 1983, Kenner
EX n/a   NM $20   MIP $35

❑ **Nien Nunb,** 1983
EX n/a   NM $6   MIP $30

❑ **Nikto,** 1984
EX n/a   NM $11   MIP $20

(KP Photo)

❑ **Paploo,** 1984
EX n/a   NM $20   MIP $35

(ToyShop File Photo)

❑ **Prune Face,** 1984
EX n/a   NM $8   MIP $25

❑ **Rancor Keeper,** 1984
EX n/a   NM $9   MIP $20

❑ **Rebel Commando,** 1983, Kenner
EX n/a   NM $8   MIP $30

(ToyShop File Photo)

❑ **Ree-Yees,** 1983, Kenner
EX n/a   NM $8   MIP $20

(ToyShop File Photo)

❏ **Squid Head,** 1983
   EX n/a   **NM** $7   **MIP** $25

❏ **Sy Snootles and the Rebo Band,** 1984, Kenner
   EX n/a   **NM** $40   **MIP** $110

(ToyShop File Photo)

❏ **Teebo,** 1984
   EX n/a   **NM** $12   **MIP** $25

(ToyShop File Photo)

❏ **Weequay,** 1984, Kenner
   EX n/a   **NM** $8   **MIP** $30

❏ **Wicket,** 1984, Kenner
   EX n/a   **NM** $11   **MIP** $45

STAR WARS

❏ **Boba Fett,** 1978, Kenner
   EX n/a   **NM** $20   **MIP** $750

❏ **C-3PO,** 1977, Kenner
   EX n/a   **NM** $9   **MIP** $155

❏ **Chewbacca,** 1977, Kenner
   EX n/a   **NM** $9   **MIP** $250

❏ **Darth Vader,** 1977, Kenner
   EX n/a   **NM** $12   **MIP** $350

(ToyShop File Photo)

❏ **Death Squad Commander,** 1977, Kenner
   EX n/a   **NM** $11   **MIP** $200

(ToyShop File Photo)

❏ **Death Star Droid,** 1978, Kenner
   EX n/a   **NM** $10   **MIP** $140

❏ **Early Bird Figures — Luke, Leia, R2-D2, Chewbacca,** 1977, Kenner
   EX n/a   **NM** $195   **MIP** $425

(ToyShop File Photo)

❏ **Greedo,** 1978, Kenner
   EX n/a   **NM** $7   **MIP** $170
   (KP Photo)

❏ **Hammerhead,** 1978, Kenner
   EX n/a   **NM** $9   **MIP** $170

(ToyShop File Photo)

❏ **Han Solo, Large Head,** 1977, Kenner
   EX n/a   **NM** $18   **MIP** $475

STAR WARS

(ToyShop File Photo)

❑ **Han Solo, Small Head,** 1977, Kenner
EX n/a   NM $25   MIP $500

(ToyShop File Photo)

❑ **Jawa, Cloth Cape,** 1977, Kenner
EX n/a   NM $11   MIP $170

(ToyShop File Photo)

❑ **Jawa, Vinyl Cape,** 1977, Kenner
EX n/a   NM $200   MIP $2125

(ToyShop File Photo)

❑ **Luke as X-Wing Pilot,** 1978, Kenner
EX n/a   NM $11   MIP $200

❑ **Luke Skywalker,** 1977, Kenner
EX n/a   NM $20   MIP $450

❑ **Luke w/Telescoping Saber,** 1977, Kenner
EX n/a   NM $185   MIP $3450

❑ **Obi-Wan Kenobi,** 1977, Kenner
EX n/a   NM $14   MIP $325

(KP Photo)

❑ **Power Droid,** 1978, Kenner, Dark blue body with stocky legs. These robots are also called "Gonk" droids, based on the sound they make as seen in Star Wars Episode IV, "A New Hope." Very reminiscent of the robots in the movie "Silent Running"
EX n/a   NM $7   MIP $155

❑ **Princess Leia,** 1977, Kenner
EX n/a   NM $25   MIP $325

❑ **R2-D2,** 1977, Kenner
EX n/a   NM $10   MIP $170

❑ **R5-D4,** 1978, Kenner
EX n/a   NM $9   MIP $170

(ToyShop File Photo)

❑ **Sand People (Tusken Raider),** 1977, Kenner
EX n/a   NM $9   MIP $200

❑ **Snaggletooth, Blue Body, Sears Exclusive,** 1978, Kenner
EX n/a   NM $165   MIP n/a

(KP Photo)

❑ **Snaggletooth, Red Body,** 1978, Kenner
EX n/a   NM $7   MIP $175

(ToyShop File Photo)

❑ **Stormtrooper,** 1977, Kenner
EX n/a   **NM** $11   **MIP** $200

(ToyShop File Photo)

❑ **Walrus Man,** 1978, Kenner
EX n/a   **NM** $8   **MIP** $155

THE PHANTOM MENACE

(KP Photo)

❑ **Adi Gallia,** 1999, Hasbro, With removeable cloak and lightsaber
EX n/a   **NM** n/a   **MIP** $8

❑ **Anakin Skywalker, Mechanic,** 2000, Hasbro, Includes pit droid figure
EX n/a   **NM** n/a   **MIP** $6

(KP Photo)

❑ **Anakin Skywalker, Naboo,** 1999, Hasbro, With removable plastic cloak
EX n/a   **NM** n/a   **MIP** $8

❑ **Anakin Skywalker, Naboo Pilot,** 2000, Hasbro, Includes helmet and ship controls
EX n/a   **NM** n/a   **MIP** $8

(KP Photo)

❑ **Anakin Skywalker, Tatooine,** 1999, Hasbro, With backpack and blaster pistol
EX n/a   **NM** n/a   **MIP** $8

(KP Photo)

❑ **Battle Droid w/Federation Issue Blaster,** 1999, Hasbro, These droids came in variety of paint finishes--some pristine, others with battle damage
EX n/a   **NM** n/a   **MIP** $6

(KP Photo)

❑ **Battle Droid, Battle Damage,** Hasbro, Variations on this model include: "star" blast point on chest, silver lines on body, and lighter and darker sand marks
EX n/a   **NM** $3   **MIP** $6

❑ **Battle Droid, Security,** 2000, Hasbro, Fairly plain light tan with dark brown. Includes blaster rifle
EX n/a   **NM** n/a   **MIP** $8

(KP Photo)

❏ **Boss Nass,** 1999, Hasbro, With staff
EX n/a   **NM** n/a   **MIP** $8

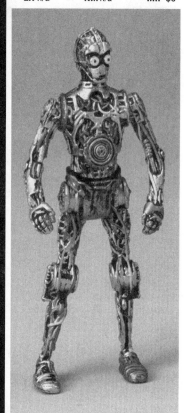

(KP Photo)

❏ **C-3PO,** 1999, Hasbro, Skeletal-looking version of 3PO before he had metal "skin"
EX n/a   **NM** n/a   **MIP** $8

(KP Photo)

❏ **Captain Panaka,** 2000, Hasbro, With blaster rifle
EX n/a   **NM** n/a   **MIP** $9

(KP Photo)

❏ **Captain Tarpals,** 1999, Hasbro, With "electropole" staff
EX n/a   **NM** n/a   **MIP** $8

(KP Photo)

❏ **Chancellor Valorum,** 1999, Hasbro, Includes staff
EX n/a   **NM** n/a   **MIP** $8

(KP Photo)

❏ **Darth Maul,** 1999, Hasbro
EX n/a   **NM** n/a   **MIP** $10

❏ **Darth Maul, Jedi Duel,** 1999, Hasbro, The first release of a 3-3/4" Darth Maul figure
EX n/a   **NM** n/a   **MIP** $9

(KP Photo)

❏ **Darth Maul, Sith Lord,** 2000, Hasbro, With double-edged lightsaber, second stand-alone release of figure
EX n/a   **NM** n/a   **MIP** $8

❏ **Darth Maul, Tatooine,** 1999, Hasbro, With black cloth cloak--the cloak and other weapons were also available in an accessory set
EX n/a   **NM** n/a   **MIP** $8

(KP Photo)

❏ **Darth Sidious,** 1999, Hasbro, Black-robed figure with Commtech chip
EX n/a　　**NM** n/a　　**MIP** $8

❏ **Darth Sidious, Holograph,** 2000, Hasbro, Translucent purple figure with Commtech chip
EX n/a　　**NM** n/a　　**MIP** $8

❏ **Destroyer Droid,** 1999, Hasbro, Includes Commtech chip
EX n/a　　**NM** n/a　　**MIP** $8

(KP Photo)

❏ **Gasgano, w/pit droid,** 1999, Hasbro, Mult-armed figure packaged with pit droid and Commtech chip
EX n/a　　**NM** n/a　　**MIP** $8

(KP Photo)

❏ **Jar Jar Binks,** 1999, Hasbro, Figure included Gungan Battle Staff and comtech chip stand
EX n/a　　**NM** n/a　　**MIP** $8

❏ **Jar Jar Binks, Swamp,** 2000, Hasbro, Specially made to be posed in swimming motion, includes fish
EX n/a　　**NM** n/a　　**MIP** $18

(KP Photo)

❏ **Ki-Adi-Mundi,** 1999, Hasbro, With lightsaber
EX n/a　　**NM** n/a　　**MIP** $8

(KP Photo)

❏ **Mace Windu,** 1999, Hasbro, With lightsaber and removeable plastic cloak
EX n/a　　**NM** n/a　　**MIP** $8

❏ **Mace Windu, Sneak Preview,** 1998, Hasbro, Includes different cloak and has a more stoic, less active pose and expression than the regular-issue Mace Windu
EX n/a　　**NM** n/a　　**MIP** $6

❏ **Mosespa Encounter - Sebulba, Jar Jar, Anakin,** 1999, Hasbro
EX n/a　　**NM** n/a　　**MIP** $12

❏ **Naboo Royal Guard,** 2000, Hasbro, Includes removeable helmet and blaster pistol
EX n/a　　**NM** n/a　　**MIP** $8

❏ **Naboo Royal Security,** 2000, Hasbro, Included two blaster rifles
EX n/a　　**NM** n/a　　**MIP** $9

(KP Photo)

❏ **Nute Gunray,** 1999, Hasbro, A good likeness--includes Commtech chip
EX n/a　　**NM** $3　　**MIP** $6

❏ **Obi-Wan Kenobi,** 1999, Hasbro
EX n/a　　**NM** n/a　　**MIP** $10

(KP Photo)

❑ **Obi-Wan Kenobi, Jedi Duel,** 1999, Hasbro, Includes lightsaber
EX n/a   **NM** n/a   **MIP** $8

❑ **Obi-Wan Kenobi, Jedi Knight,** 2000, Hasbro, In plain white robe, much like the Jedi Duel figure, but includes extra belt and gear, along with lightsaber
EX n/a   **NM** n/a   **MIP** $8

❑ **Obi-Wan Kenobi, Naboo,** 1999, Hasbro, In dark robe--has two lightsabers, one activated, the other not
EX n/a   **NM** n/a   **MIP** $8

❑ **Ody Mandrell w/Pit Droid,** 1999, Hasbro, Another two-figure pack with Commtech chip
EX n/a   **NM** n/a   **MIP** $8

❑ **OOM-9,** 1999, Hasbro, Yellow markings on head and body. This figure includes binoculars and blaster rifle
EX n/a   **NM** n/a   **MIP** $8

(KP Photo)

❑ **Padme Naberrie,** 1999, Hasbro, Figure included viewscreen to watch the pod race
EX n/a   **NM** n/a   **MIP** $8

(KP Photo)

❑ **Pit Droids,** 2000, Hasbro, Highly-detailed sculpts of the ubiquitous droids seen in Episode 1
EX n/a   **NM** $3   **MIP** $8

❑ **Queen Amidala, Battle,** 2000, Hasbro, In dark robe, includes blaster pistol and grappling hook crossbow
EX n/a   **NM** n/a   **MIP** $23

❑ **Queen Amidala, Coruscant,** 1999, Hasbro, In full royal outfit and makeup
EX n/a   **NM** n/a   **MIP** $10

(KP Photo)

❑ **Queen Amidala, Naboo w/Blaster Pistols,** 1999, Hasbro, Figure included two sleek blaster pistols and comtech chip stand
EX n/a   **NM** n/a   **MIP** $8

❑ **Qui-Gon Jinn,** 1999, Hasbro
EX n/a   **NM** n/a   **MIP** $10

❑ **Qui-Gon Jinn, Jedi Duel,** 1999, Hasbro, In plain-colored robe. Includes lightsaber
EX n/a   **NM** n/a   **MIP** $8

❑ **Qui-Gon Jinn, Jedi Master,** 2000, Hasbro, With lightsaber and Commtech chip
EX n/a   **NM** n/a   **MIP** $8

❑ **Qui-Gon Jinn, Naboo,** 1999, Hasbro, Includes two lightsabers: one activated, the other not
EX n/a   **NM** n/a   **MIP** $8

❑ **R2-B1 Astromech Droid,** 2000, Hasbro, Dark blue with light green body, includes harness pod
EX n/a   **NM** n/a   **MIP** $8

(KP Photo)

❑ **R2-D2,** 1999, Hasbro, With retractable middle "foot"
EX n/a   **NM** n/a   **MIP** $6

(KP Photo)

❑ **Ric Olie,** 1999, Hasbro, Removeable helmet and two blaster pistols
EX n/a   **NM** n/a   **MIP** $8

❑ **Rune Haako,** Hasbro, Includes Commtech chip
EX n/a   **NM** n/a   **MIP** $6

(KP Photo)

❑ **Senator Palpatine,** 1999, Hasbro, With cam droid and Commtech chip
EX n/a   NM n/a   MIP $8

❑ **Sio Bibble,** 2000, Hasbro, Includes blaster pistol and Commtech chip
EX n/a   NM n/a   MIP $8

❑ **Tatooine Showdown - Darth Maul, Qui-Gon, Anakin,** 1999, Hasbro
EX n/a   NM n/a   MIP $15

❑ **TC-14,** 2000, Hasbro, Silver-plated, includes serving tray and Commtech chip. Somewhat harder to find, almost exlusively available from dealers
EX n/a   NM n/a   MIP $8

(KP Photo)

❑ **Watto,** 1999, Hasbro, Highly-detailed figure
EX n/a   NM n/a   MIP $9

❑ **Watto's Box - Watto, Graxol Kelvyyn, Shakka,** 2000, Hasbro
EX n/a   NM n/a   MIP $20

❑ **Yoda, w/Jedi Council Chair,** 1999, Hasbro, Includes blue chair and Commtech chip
EX n/a   NM n/a   MIP $8

ACTION FIGURES, 12"

ATTACK OF THE CLONES

(KP Photo)

❑ **Anakin Skywalker,** 2002, Hasbro, In black robe, includes lightsaber
EX n/a   NM n/a   MIP $25

❑ **Clone Trooper,** 2002, Hasbro, Includes blaster rifle
EX n/a   NM n/a   MIP $25

❑ **Mace Windu, Jedi Master,** 2002, Hasbro, In light tan cloak, includes lightsaber
EX n/a   NM n/a   MIP $30

(KP Photo)

❑ **Obi-Wan Kenobi,** 2002, Hasbro, Includes lightsaber
EX n/a   NM n/a   MIP $25

COLLECTOR'S SERIES

❑ **Admiral Ackbar,** 1997
EX n/a   NM $15   MIP $15

❑ **AT-AT Driver,** 1998
EX n/a   NM $15   MIP $25

❑ **Barquin D'an,** 1998
EX n/a   NM $7   MIP $15

❑ **Boba Fett,** 1997
EX n/a   NM $15   MIP $55

❑ **C-3PO,** 1997
EX n/a   NM $15   MIP $27

❑ **Cantina Band Aliens, six members,** six different members
EX n/a   NM $15   MIP $35

❑ **Chewbacca,** 1997
EX n/a   NM $15   MIP $35

❑ **Chewbacca (Chained),** 1998
EX n/a   NM $15   MIP $35

(KP Photo)

❑ **Darth Vader,** 1996
EX n/a   NM $15   MIP $25

❑ **Emperor Palpatine,** 1998
EX n/a   NM $7   MIP $12

❑ **Grand Moff Tarkin and Imperial Gunner**
EX n/a   NM $45   MIP $80

❑ **Grand Moff Tarkin w/Interrogation Droid,** 1998
EX n/a   NM $15   MIP $22

❑ **Greedo,** 1998
EX n/a   NM $15   MIP $22

❑ **Han and Luke in Stormtrooper Disguise**
EX n/a   NM $30   MIP $55

❑ **Han in Carbonite,** 1998
EX n/a   NM $10   MIP $15

❑ **Han in Hoth Gear,** 1998
EX n/a   NM $15   MIP $18

❑ **Han in Hoth Gear w/Tauntaun**
EX n/a   NM $25   MIP $50

(KP Photo)

❏ **Han Solo,** 1996
   EX n/a   NM $15   MIP $20

❏ **Jawa,** 1998
   EX n/a   NM $15   MIP $12

❏ **Lando Calrissian,** 1997
   EX n/a   NM $5   MIP $10

❏ **Leia as Jabba's Prisoner and R2-D2**
   EX n/a   NM $25   MIP $43

❏ **Leia in Hoth Gear,** 1999
   EX n/a   NM $15   MIP $22

❏ **Luke as Jedi Knight,** 1998
   EX n/a   NM $5   MIP $12

❏ **Luke as Jedi Knight and Bib Fortuna**
   EX n/a   NM $30   MIP $60

(KP Photo)

❏ **Luke as X-Wing Pilot,** 1997
   EX n/a   NM $15   MIP $30

❏ **Luke in Bespin Outfit,** 1997
   EX n/a   NM $11   MIP $21

❏ **Luke in Ceremonial Garb,** 1998
   EX n/a   NM $15   MIP $15

❏ **Luke in Hoth Gear,** 1998
   EX n/a   NM $8   MIP $12

❏ **Luke in Hoth Gear w/Wampa**
   EX n/a   NM $30   MIP $80

(KP Photo)

❏ **Luke Skywalker,** 1996
   EX n/a   NM $8   MIP $15

❏ **Luke w/Poncho (Tatooine), Han w/Flight Jacket, Leia in Boushh Disguise**
   EX n/a   NM $20   MIP $50

(KP Photo)

❏ **Obi-Wan Kenobi,** 1996
   EX n/a   NM $10   MIP $20

❏ **Princess Leia,** 1997
   EX n/a   NM $10   MIP $25

❏ **R2-D2,** 1998
   EX n/a   NM $15   MIP $12

❏ **R2-D2 (Wal-Mart Exclusive),** 1998
   EX n/a   NM $10   MIP $15

❏ **R5-D4,** 1998
   EX n/a   NM $10   MIP $15

❏ **Sandtrooper,** 1998
   EX n/a   NM $15   MIP $15

❏ **Snowtrooper,** 1998
   EX n/a   NM $5   MIP $8

❏ **Stormtrooper,** 1997
   EX n/a   NM $10   MIP $18

❏ **TIE Fighter Pilot,** 1997
   EX n/a   NM $10   MIP $18

❏ **Tusken Raider,** 1997
   EX n/a   NM $10   MIP $18

❏ **Wedge Antilles and Biggs Darklighter**
   EX n/a   NM $30   MIP $70

❏ **Wicket,** 1998
   EX n/a   NM $10   MIP $15

❏ **Yoda,** 1998
   EX n/a   NM $15   MIP $20

EMPIRE STRIKES BACK

❏ **Boba Fett,** 1979, Empire Strikes Back Box
   EX n/a   NM $155   MIP $525

(ToyShop File Photo)

❏ **IG-88,** 1980, Empire Strikes Back Box
   EX n/a   NM $250   MIP $700

STAR WARS

(ToyShop File Photo)

❏ **Boba Fett,** 1979, Star Wars Box
   EX n/a   NM $155   MIP $450

(ToyShop File Photo)

❏ **C-3PO**, 1979
    EX n/a   **NM** $35   **MIP** $150

❏ **Chewbacca**, 1979
    EX n/a   **NM** $50   **MIP** $155

(ToyShop File Photo)

❏ **Darth Vader**, 1978
    EX n/a   **NM** $60   **MIP** $240
(ToyShop File Photo)

❏ **Han Solo**, 1979
    EX n/a   **NM** $140   **MIP** $450

(ToyShop File Photo)

❏ **Jawa**, 1979
    EX n/a   **NM** $55   **MIP** $200

(ToyShop File Photo)

❏ **Luke Skywalker**, 1979
    EX n/a   **NM** $95   **MIP** $325

(ToyShop File Photo)

❏ **Obi-Wan Kenobi**, 1979
    EX n/a   **NM** $100   **MIP** $250

❏ **Princess Leia**, 1979
    EX n/a   **NM** $90   **MIP** $225

❏ **Princess Leia in Ceremonial Gown**, 1999
    EX n/a   **NM** $10   **MIP** $25

❏ **R2-D2**, 1979
    EX n/a   **NM** $35   **MIP** $185

(ToyShop File Photo)

❏ **Stormtrooper**, 1979
    EX n/a   **NM** $75   **MIP** $225

THE PHANTOM MENACE

❏ **Anakin Skywalker**, 1999, Hasbro
    EX n/a   **NM** n/a   **MIP** $10

❏ **Anakin Skywalker, w/Theed Hangar Droid**, Hasbro
    EX n/a   **NM** n/a   **MIP** $15

❏ **Aurra Sing**, Hasbro
    EX n/a   **NM** n/a   **MIP** $15

❏ **Battle Droid**, 1999, Hasbro
    EX n/a   **NM** n/a   **MIP** $15

❏ **Battle Droid Commander w/electrob-inoculars**, Hasbro
    EX n/a   **NM** n/a   **MIP** $15

❏ **Boss Nass**, Hasbro
    EX n/a   **NM** n/a   **MIP** $15

(KP Photo)

❏ **Darth Maul**, 1999, Hasbro
    EX n/a   **NM** n/a   **MIP** $25

(KP Photo)

STAR WARS

- ❏ **Jar Jar Binks,** 1999, Hasbro
  EX n/a   NM n/a   MIP $20

- ❏ **Luke Skywalker, 100th figure,** Hasbro
  EX n/a   NM n/a   MIP $15

- ❏ **Mace Windu w/lightsaber,** Hasbro
  EX n/a   NM n/a   MIP $15

- ❏ **Obi-Wan Kenobi,** 1999, Hasbro
  EX n/a   NM n/a   MIP $20

- ❏ **Padme, Beautiful Braids,** 2000, Hasbro
  EX n/a   NM n/a   MIP $16

- ❏ **Pit Droid,** 1999, Hasbro
  EX n/a   NM n/a   MIP $10

(KP Photo)

- ❏ **Queen Amidala, Black Travel Dress,** 1999, Hasbro
  EX n/a   NM n/a   MIP $40

(KP Photo)

- ❏ **Queen Amidala, Hidden Majesty,** 1999, Hasbro
  EX n/a   NM n/a   MIP $16

- ❏ **Queen Amidala, Red Senate Gown,** 1999, Hasbro
  EX n/a   NM n/a   MIP $40

- ❏ **Queen Amidala, Return to Naboo,** 2000, Hasbro
  EX n/a   NM n/a   MIP $45

- ❏ **Queen Amidala, Royal Elegance,** 1999, Hasbro
  EX n/a   NM n/a   MIP $16

- ❏ **Queen Amidala, Ultimate Hair,** 1999, Hasbro
  EX n/a   NM n/a   MIP $16

- ❏ **Qui-Gon Jimm w/Tatooine Poncho,** Hasbro
  EX n/a   NM n/a   MIP $15

(KP Photo)

- ❏ **Qui-Gon Jinn,** 1999, Hasbro
  EX n/a   NM n/a   MIP $20

- ❏ **Qui-Gon Jinn and Queen Amidala, Entertainment Earth exclusive,** Hasbro, Entertainment Earth exclusive
  EX n/a   NM n/a   MIP $25

- ❏ **R2-A6,** 1999, Hasbro
  EX n/a   NM n/a   MIP $10

- ❏ **R2-D2,** Hasbro
  EX n/a   NM n/a   MIP $15

- ❏ **TC-14 Protocol Droid, electronic,** Hasbro
  EX n/a   NM n/a   MIP $15

- ❏ **Watto,** 1999, Hasbro
  EX n/a   NM n/a   MIP $15

CARRYING CASES

EMPIRE STRIKES BACK

(KP Photo)

- ❏ **Darth Vader,** 1982
  EX n/a   NM $11   MIP $40

(KP Photo)

- ❏ **Mini Figure,** 1980
  EX n/a   NM $13   MIP $30

RETURN OF THE JEDI

(ToyShop File Photo)

- ❏ **C-3PO,** 1983
  EX n/a   NM $11   MIP $30

- ❏ **Darth Vader (w/three figs.),** 1983, w/three figures
  EX n/a   NM $11   MIP $225

- ❏ **Laser Rifle,** 1984
  EX n/a   NM $11   MIP $25

STAR WARS

- ❏ **24-Figure**
  EX n/a   NM $18   MIP $30

COINS

- ❏ **2-1B,** 1985, Kenner
  EX n/a   NM $125   MIP n/a

- ❏ **63rd Coin, lightsaber,** 1985, Kenner
  EX n/a   NM $1200   MIP n/a

- ❏ **Amanaman,** 1985, Kenner
  EX n/a   NM $4   MIP n/a

- ❏ **Anakin Skywalker,** 1985, Kenner
  EX n/a   NM $70   MIP n/a

- ❏ **AT-AT,** 1985, Kenner
  EX n/a   NM $55   MIP n/a

- ❏ **AT-ST Driver,** 1985, Kenner
  EX n/a   NM $9   MIP n/a

- ❏ **A-Wing Pilot,** 1985, Kenner
  EX n/a   NM $4   MIP n/a

- ❏ **Barada,** 1985, Kenner
  EX n/a   NM $4   MIP n/a

❏ **Bib Fortuna,** 1985, Kenner
EX n/a   **NM** $105   **MIP** n/a

❏ **Biker Scout,** 1985, Kenner
EX n/a   **NM** $9   **MIP** n/a

❏ **Boba Fett,** 1985, Kenner
EX n/a   **NM** $225   **MIP** n/a

❏ **B-Wing Pilot,** 1985, Kenner
EX n/a   **NM** $9   **MIP** n/a

❏ **C-3PO,** 1985, Kenner
EX n/a   **NM** $9   **MIP** n/a

❏ **Chewbacca,** 1985, Kenner
EX n/a   **NM** $9   **MIP** n/a

❏ **Chief Chirpa,** 1985, Kenner
EX n/a   **NM** $35   **MIP** n/a

❏ **Creatures,** 1985, Kenner
EX n/a   **NM** $55   **MIP** n/a

❏ **Darth Vader,** 1985, Kenner
EX n/a   **NM** $18   **MIP** n/a

❏ **Droids,** 1985, Kenner
EX n/a   **NM** $50   **MIP** n/a

❏ **Emperor,** 1985, Kenner
EX n/a   **NM** $12   **MIP** n/a

❏ **Emperor's Royal Guard,** 1985, Kenner
EX n/a   **NM** $50   **MIP** n/a

❏ **EV-9D9,** 1985, Kenner
EX n/a   **NM** $4   **MIP** n/a

❏ **FX-7,** 1985, Kenner
EX n/a   **NM** $165   **MIP** n/a

❏ **Gamorrean Guard,** 1985, Kenner
EX n/a   **NM** $20   **MIP** n/a

❏ **Greedo,** 1985, Kenner
EX n/a   **NM** $175   **MIP** n/a

❏ **Han Hoth,** 1985, Kenner
EX n/a   **NM** $75   **MIP** n/a

❏ **Han in Carbonite,** 1985, Kenner
EX n/a   **NM** $4   **MIP** n/a

❏ **Han Original,** 1985, Kenner
EX n/a   **NM** $145   **MIP** n/a

❏ **Han Rebel (trenchcoat),** 1985, Kenner
EX n/a   **NM** $9   **MIP** n/a

❏ **Hoth Stormtrooper,** 1985, Kenner
EX n/a   **NM** $225   **MIP** n/a

❏ **Imperial Commander,** 1985, Kenner
EX n/a   **NM** $65   **MIP** n/a

❏ **Imperial Dignitary,** 1985, Kenner
EX n/a   **NM** $4   **MIP** n/a

❏ **Imperial Gunner,** 1985, Kenner
EX n/a   **NM** $4   **MIP** n/a

❏ **Jawas,** 1985, Kenner
EX n/a   **NM** $9   **MIP** n/a

❏ **Lando General,** 1985, Kenner
EX n/a   **NM** $4   **MIP** n/a

❏ **Lando with Cloud City,** 1985, Kenner
EX n/a   **NM** $70   **MIP** n/a

❏ **Logray,** 1985, Kenner
EX n/a   **NM** $35   **MIP** n/a

❏ **Luke Jedi,** 1985, Kenner
EX n/a   **NM** $16   **MIP** n/a

❏ **Luke on Dagobah,** 1985, Kenner
EX n/a   **NM** $120   **MIP** n/a

❏ **Luke original,** 1985, Kenner
EX n/a   **NM** $75   **MIP** n/a

❏ **Luke Poncho,** 1985, Kenner
EX n/a   **NM** $4   **MIP** n/a

❏ **Luke Stormtrooper,** 1985, Kenner
EX n/a   **NM** $4   **MIP** n/a

❏ **Luke with Taun Taun,** 1985, Kenner
EX n/a   **NM** $75   **MIP** n/a

❏ **Luke X-Wing,** 1985, Kenner
EX n/a   **NM** $5   **MIP** n/a

❏ **Luke X-Wing, small,** 1985, Kenner
EX n/a   **NM** $45   **MIP** n/a

❏ **Lumat,** 1985, Kenner
EX n/a   **NM** $9   **MIP** n/a

❏ **Millennium Falcon,** 1985, Kenner
EX n/a   **NM** $65   **MIP** n/a

❏ **Millennium Falcon,** 1994, Bend Ems
EX n/a   **NM** $5   **MIP** n/a

❏ **Obi-Wan Kenobi,** 1985, Kenner
EX n/a   **NM** $16   **MIP** n/a

❏ **Paploo,** 1985, Kenner
EX n/a   **NM** $9   **MIP** n/a

❏ **Princess Leia Rebel Leader (poncho),** 1985, Kenner
EX n/a   **NM** $9   **MIP** n/a

❏ **Princess Leia, Boushh,** 1985, Kenner
EX n/a   **NM** $145   **MIP** n/a

❏ **Princess Leia, Original,** 1985, Kenner
EX n/a   **NM** $85   **MIP** n/a

❏ **R2-D2 Pop-Up Lightsaber,** 1985, Kenner
EX n/a   **NM** $4   **MIP** n/a

❏ **Romba,** 1985, Kenner
EX n/a   **NM** $4   **MIP** n/a

❏ **Sail Skiff,** 1985, Kenner
EX n/a   **NM** $250   **MIP** n/a

❏ **Star Destroyer Commander,** 1985, Kenner
EX n/a   **NM** $60   **MIP** n/a

❏ **Stormtrooper,** 1985, Kenner
EX n/a   **NM** $16   **MIP** n/a

❏ **Teebo,** 1985, Kenner
EX n/a   **NM** $18   **MIP** n/a

❏ **TIE Fighter,** 1994, Bend Ems
EX n/a   **NM** $5   **MIP** n/a

❏ **TIE Fighter Pilot,** 1985, Kenner
EX n/a   **NM** $50   **MIP** n/a

❏ **Tusken Raider,** 1985, Kenner
EX n/a   **NM** $145   **MIP** n/a

❏ **Warok,** 1985, Kenner
EX n/a   **NM** $4   **MIP** n/a

❏ **Wicket,** 1985, Kenner
EX n/a   **NM** $9   **MIP** n/a

❏ **X-Wing,** 1994, Bend Ems
EX n/a   **NM** $5   **MIP** n/a

❏ **Yak Face,** 1985, Kenner
EX n/a   **NM** $85   **MIP** n/a

❏ **Yoda,** 1985, Kenner
EX n/a   **NM** $16   **MIP** n/a

❏ **Zuckuss,** 1985, Kenner
EX n/a   **NM** $145   **MIP** n/a

CREATURES

ATTACK OF THE CLONES

❏ **Reek, Arena Battle Beast w/Attack Sounds,** 2002, Hasbro
EX n/a   **NM** $4   **MIP** $18

EMPIRE STRIKES BACK

❏ **Hoth Wampa**
EX n/a   **NM** $15   **MIP** $40

(KP Photo)

❏ **Taun Taun, solid belly**
EX n/a   **NM** $9   **MIP** $35

❏ **Taun Taun, split belly**
EX n/a   **NM** $9   **MIP** $40

RETURN OF THE JEDI

(ToyShop File Photo)

❏ **Rancor**
EX n/a   **NM** $30   **MIP** $60

STAR WARS

(ToyShop File Photo)

❑ **Patrol Dewback**
EX n/a   NM $20   MIP $75

THE PHANTOM MENACE

(KP Photo)

❑ **Kaadu w/Jar Jar Binks**, 1999, Hasbro
EX n/a   NM $2   MIP $5

LEGO SETS

ATTACK OF THE CLONES

❑ **Bounty Hunter Pursuit w/Obi-Wan Kenobi, Anakin Skywalker, Zam Wessell**, LEGO, 7133
EX n/a   NM n/a   MIP $25

❑ **Jango Fett**, LEGO, 8011
EX n/a   NM n/a   MIP $30

❑ **Jango Fett's Slave I w/Jango Fett, Boba Fett**, LEGO, 7153
EX n/a   NM n/a   MIP $40

(KP Photo)

❑ **Jedi Duel w/Yoda, Count Dooku**, LEGO, 7103
EX n/a   NM n/a   MIP $10

❑ **Jedi Starfighter w/Obi-Wan Kenobi, R4-P17**, LEGO, 7143
EX n/a   NM n/a   MIP $15

❑ **Republic Gunship w/Jedi Clone Troopers, Battle Droids, Destroyer Droids**, LEGO, 7163
EX n/a   NM n/a   MIP $75

❑ **Super Battle Droid**, LEGO, 8012
EX n/a   NM n/a   MIP $30

❑ **Tusken Raider Encounter w/Anakin Skywalker, two Tusken Raiders**, LEGO, 7113
EX n/a   NM n/a   MIP $10

EMPIRE STRIKES BACK

❑ **Boba Fett's Slave I**, LEGO, 7144
EX n/a   NM n/a   MIP $20

❑ **Luke Skywalker, Han Solo, Boba Fett**, LEGO, 3341
EX n/a   NM n/a   MIP $5

❑ **Twin-Pod Cloud Car w/Lobot**, LEGO, 7119
EX n/a   NM n/a   MIP $10

❑ **Yoda**, LEGO, 7194
EX n/a   NM n/a   MIP $100

RETURN OF THE JEDI

❑ **B-Wing at Rebel Control Center w/pilot, droid, mechanic**, LEGO, 7180
EX n/a   NM n/a   MIP $30

❑ **Chewbacca, two Biker Scouts**, LEGO, 3342
EX n/a   NM n/a   MIP $5

❑ **Desert Skiff w/Luke Skywalker, Han Solo**, LEGO, 7104
EX n/a   NM n/a   MIP $6

❑ **Ewok Attack w/Biker Scout, Stormtrooper, two Ewoks**, LEGO, 7139
EX n/a   NM n/a   MIP $13

❑ **Final Duel I w/Emperor, Darth Vader**, LEGO, 7200
EX n/a   NM n/a   MIP $10

❑ **Final Duel II w/Luke Skywalker, Imperial Officer, Stormtrooper**, LEGO, 7201
EX n/a   NM n/a   MIP $7

❑ **Imperial AT-ST w/Chewbacca**, LEGO, 7127
EX n/a   NM n/a   MIP $10

❑ **Imperial Shuttle w/Emperor, Pilot, two Royal Guards**, LEGO, 7166
EX n/a   NM n/a   MIP $35

STAR WARS

❑ **C-3PO**, LEGO, 8007
EX n/a   NM n/a   MIP $35

❑ **Dark Side Developer**, LEGO, 9754
EX n/a   NM n/a   MIP $100

❑ **Darth Vader**, LEGO, 8010
EX n/a   NM n/a   MIP $40

❑ **Droid Escape w/R2-D2, C-3PO**, LEGO, 7106
EX n/a   NM n/a   MIP $7

❑ **Emperor Palpatine, Darth Maul, Darth Vader**, LEGO, 3340
EX n/a   NM n/a   MIP $5

(KP Photo)

❑ **Landspeeder w/Luke Skywalker, Obi-Wan Kenobi**, 1999, LEGO, 7110
EX n/a   NM n/a   MIP $6

❑ **Millennium Falcon w/Han Solo, Leia, Luke, Chewbacca, R2-D2, C-3PO**, LEGO, 7190
EX n/a   NM n/a   MIP $100

❑ **R2-D2**, LEGO, 8009
EX n/a   NM n/a   MIP $20

❑ **Rebel Blockade Runner - Tantive IV Corellian Corvette**, LEGO, 10019
EX n/a   NM n/a   MIP $150

❑ **Stormtrooper**, LEGO, 8008
EX n/a   NM n/a   MIP $35

❑ **TIE Fighter w/Pilot, Stormtrooper**, LEGO, 7146
EX n/a   NM n/a   MIP $20

❑ **TIE Interceptor**, LEGO, 7181
EX n/a   NM n/a   MIP $20

(LEGO Photo)

❑ **X-Wing Fighter**, LEGO, 7140
EX n/a   NM n/a   MIP $45

THE PHANTOM MENACE

❑ **Battle Droid**, LEGO, 8001
EX n/a   NM n/a   MIP $25

❑ **Command Officer, two Battle Droids**, LEGO, 3343
EX n/a   NM $2   MIP $5

❑ **Darth Maul (bust)**, LEGO, 10018
EX n/a   NM n/a   MIP $125

❑ **Destroyer Droid**, LEGO, 8002
EX n/a   NM n/a   MIP $45

❑ **Droid Fighter**, LEGO, 7111
EX n/a   NM n/a   MIP $6

❑ **Flash Speeder w/Royal Naboo Security Force**, LEGO, 7121
EX n/a   NM n/a   MIP $10

❑ **Gungan Patrol w/Jar Jar Binks, Gungan Warrior**, LEGO, 7115
EX n/a   NM n/a   MIP $10

❏ **Gungan Sub w/Qui-Gon Jinn, Obi-Wan Kenobi, Jar Jar Binks,** 1999, LEGO, 7161
EX n/a   NM n/a   MIP $45

❏ **Jedi Defense I w/Obi-Wan Kenobi, two Destroyer Droids,** LEGO, 7203
EX n/a   NM n/a   MIP $7

❏ **Jedi Defense II w/Qui-Gon Jinn, two Battle Droids,** LEGO, 7204
EX n/a   NM n/a   MIP $7

❏ **Lightsaber Duel w/Qui-Gon Jinn, Darth Maul,** 1999, LEGO, 7101
EX n/a   NM n/a   MIP $5

❏ **Mos Espa Podrace w/Padme, Anakin, R2-D2, Qui-Gon, Jar Jar, Sebulba, Gasgano,** LEGO, 7171
EX n/a   NM n/a   MIP $85

(KP Photo)

❏ **Naboo Fighter w/Anakin Skywalker, two Battle Droids,** 1999, LEGO, 7141
EX n/a   NM n/a   MIP $25

(KP Photo)

❏ **Naboo Swamp w/Qui-Gon Jinn, Jar Jar Binks, two Battle Droids,** 1999, LEGO, 7121
EX n/a   NM n/a   MIP $10

❏ **Pit Droid,** LEGO, 8000
EX n/a   NM n/a   MIP $20

❏ **Podracer,** 1999, LEGO, 7131
EX n/a   NM n/a   MIP $20

❏ **Sith Infiltrator w/Darth Maul,** LEGO, 7151
EX n/a   NM n/a   MIP $30

❏ **Trade Federation MTT,** LEGO, 7184
EX n/a   NM n/a   MIP $45

MICRO COLLECTION

❏ **Bespin Control Room,** 1982, Kenner
EX n/a   NM $10   MIP $20

❏ **Bespin Freeze Chamber,** 1982, Kenner
EX n/a   NM $22   MIP $45

❏ **Bespin Gantry,** 1982, Kenner
EX n/a   NM $11   MIP $30

❏ **Bespin World,** 1982, Kenner
EX n/a   NM $35   MIP $85

❏ **Death Star Compactor,** 1982, Kenner
EX n/a   NM $30   MIP $55

❏ **Death Star Escape,** 1982, Kenner
EX n/a   NM $30   MIP $50

❏ **Death Star World,** 1982, Kenner
EX n/a   NM $60   MIP $130

❏ **Hoth Generator Attack,** 1982, Kenner
EX n/a   NM $15   MIP $20

(ToyShop File Photo)

❏ **Hoth Ion Cannon,** 1982, Kenner
EX n/a   NM $14   MIP $30

❏ **Hoth Turret Defense,** 1982, Kenner
EX n/a   NM $18   MIP $30

❏ **Hoth Wampa Cave,** 1982, Kenner
EX n/a   NM $14   MIP $25

(ToyShop File Photo)

❏ **Hoth World,** 1982, Kenner
EX n/a   NM $40   MIP $90

❏ **Imperial TIE Fighter,** 1982, Kenner
EX n/a   NM $25   MIP $60

(ToyShop File Photo)

❏ **Millennium Falcon,** 1982, Kenner
EX n/a   NM $90   MIP $225

(ToyShop File Photo)

❏ **Snowspeeder,** 1982, Kenner
EX n/a   NM $50   MIP $100

(ToyShop File Photo)

❏ **X-Wing Fighter,** 1982, Kenner
EX n/a   NM $18   MIP $40

MICRO MACHINES

THE PHANTOM MENACE

(KP Photo)

❏ **Anakin Skywalker & Ratts Tyerell,** 1999, Galoob
EX n/a   NM $3   MIP $8

❏ **Anakin Skywalker's Podracer w/figure,** 1999, Galoob
EX n/a   NM $2   MIP $6

❏ **Arch Canyon Adventure,** 1999, Galoob
EX n/a   NM $2   MIP $6

STAR WARS

❑ **Battle Droid/Trade Federation Droid Control Ship,** 1999, Galoob
EX n/a   NM $2   MIP $6

❑ **Beggar's Canyon Challenge,** 1999, Galoob
EX n/a   NM $2   MIP $6

❑ **Boles Roor & Neva Kee,** 1999, Galoob
EX n/a   NM $3   MIP $8

❑ **Boonta Eve Challenge Deluxe Podracing Track Set,** 1999, Galoob
EX n/a   NM $2   MIP $6

❑ **Build Your Own Podracer Pack I,** 1999, Galoob
EX n/a   NM $2   MIP $6

❑ **Destroyer Droid Ambush,** 1999, Galoob
EX n/a   NM $3   MIP $8

❑ **Dud Bolt & Mars Guo,** 1999, Galoob
EX n/a   NM $3   MIP $8

❑ **Fambaa,** 1999, Galoob
EX n/a   NM $4   MIP $18

❑ **Flash Speeder w/figure,** 1999, Galoob
EX n/a   NM $2   MIP $6

❑ **Galactic Dogfight,** 1999, Galoob
EX n/a   NM $2   MIP $5

❑ **Galactic Senate,** 1999, Galoob
EX n/a   NM $2   MIP $5

❑ **Generator Core Duel,** 1999, Galoob
EX n/a   NM $3   MIP $8

(KP Photo)

❑ **Gian Speeder,** 1999, Galoob, A nicely detailed, heavy model with pivoting cannon and slide-open canopy
EX n/a   NM $3   MIP $8

❑ **Gian Speeder & Theed Palace Sneak Preview Set,** 1999, Galoob
EX n/a   NM $2   MIP $6

❑ **Gungan Sub (Bonto)/Otoh Gunga,** 1999, Galoob
EX n/a   NM $3   MIP $8

❑ **Gungan Sub w/figure,** 1999, Galoob
EX n/a   NM $2   MIP $6

(KP Photo)

❑ **Jar Jar Binks/Naboo,** 1999, Galoob
EX n/a   NM $3   MIP $8

❑ **Mars Guo's Podracer w/figure,** 1999, Galoob
EX n/a   NM $2   MIP $6

❑ **Naboo Fighter w/figure,** 1999, Galoob
EX n/a   NM $2   MIP $6

❑ **Naboo Temple Ruins,** 1999, Galoob
EX n/a   NM $2   MIP $5

❑ **Podrace Arena,** 1999, Galoob
EX n/a   NM $2   MIP $5

❑ **Podracer Launchers,** 1999, Galoob
EX n/a   NM $2   MIP $6

❑ **Republic Cruiser,** 1999, Galoob
EX n/a   NM $3   MIP $8

❑ **Republic Cruiser w/figure,** 1999, Galoob
EX n/a   NM $2   MIP $6

❑ **Royal Starship,** 1999, Galoob
EX n/a   NM $3   MIP $8

❑ **Royal Starship Repair Deluxe Platform Action Set,** 1999, Galoob
EX n/a   NM $2   MIP $5

❑ **Sebulba & Clegg Holdfast,** 1999, Galoob
EX n/a   NM $3   MIP $8

❑ **Sebulba's Podracer,** 1999, Galoob
EX n/a   NM $3   MIP $8

❑ **Sebulba's Podracer w/figure,** 1999, Galoob
EX n/a   NM $2   MIP $6

❑ **Sith Infiltrator,** 1999, Galoob
EX n/a   NM $3   MIP $8

❑ **Tatooine Desert,** 1999, Galoob
EX n/a   NM $2   MIP $5

❑ **Theed Palace Assault,** 1999, Galoob
EX n/a   NM $4   MIP $18

❑ **Theed Rapids,** 1999, Galoob
EX n/a   NM $2   MIP $5

❑ **Trade Federation Battleship,** 1999, Galoob
EX n/a   NM $3   MIP $8

❑ **Trade Federation Droid Fighter,** 1999, Galoob, The wings of this model slide open into "firing" mode
EX n/a   NM $3   MIP $8

❑ **Trade Federation Droid Fighter w/figure,** 1999, Galoob
EX n/a   NM $2   MIP $6

❑ **Trade Federation Landing Ship w/figure,** 1999, Galoob
EX n/a   NM $2   MIP $6

❑ **Trade Federation MTT w/figure,** 1999, Galoob
EX n/a   NM $2   MIP $6

❑ **Trade Federation MTT/Naboo Battlefield Mega Deluxe Action Set,** 1999, Galoob
EX n/a   NM $3   MIP $8

❑ **Trade Federation Tank,** 1999, Galoob
EX n/a   NM $4   MIP $18

❑ **Trade Federation Tank,** 1999, Galoob
EX n/a   NM $3   MIP $8

❑ **Turbo Blast Podracers,** 1999, Galoob
EX n/a   NM $2   MIP $6

MINI RIGS

❑ **AST-5,** 1983
EX n/a   NM $7   MIP $16

❑ **CAP-2 Captivator,** 1982, Bubble-topped vehicle with room for one figure. Roller wheels on bottom with tank tread façade and two laser moveable laser cannon in front
EX n/a   NM $7   MIP $20

❑ **Desert Sail Skiff,** 1984
EX n/a   NM $8   MIP $18

❑ **Endor Forest Ranger,** 1984
EX n/a   NM $12   MIP $22

❑ **INT-4 Interceptor,** 1982
EX n/a   NM $8   MIP $20

❑ **ISP-6 Imperial Shuttle Pod,** 1983
EX n/a   NM $8   MIP $25

❑ **MLC-3 Mobile Laser Cannon,** 1981
EX n/a   NM $7   MIP $25

(KP Photo)

❑ **MTV-7 Multi-Terrain Vehicle,** 1981, Off-white with room for one 3-3/4" figure (most likely a snowtrooper, if the box is a guide). Features two spring-loaded roller wheels and a pivoting front blaster. The Mini Rigs were, in a way, the first "expanded universe" toys for Star Wars
EX n/a   NM $6   MIP $25

❑ **PDT-8 Personal Deployment Transport,** 1981
EX n/a   NM $8   MIP $20

❑ **Radar Laser Cannon,** 1982
EX n/a   NM $5   MIP $17

❑ **Tri-Pod Laser Cannon,** 1982, Cannon with "ammo box" and three folding legs
EX n/a   NM $5   MIP $12

❑ **Vehicle Maintenance Energizer,** 1982, Generator for vehicles
EX n/a   NM $6   MIP $15

PLAY SETS

EMPIRE STRIKES BACK

(ToyShop File Photo)

❑ **Cloud City Play Set, Sears Exclusive, 1981**
EX n/a   NM $100   MIP $275

(ToyShop File Photo)

❑ **Dagobah, 1982**
EX n/a   NM $19   MIP $90

(ToyShop File Photo)

❑ **Darth Vader's Star Destroyer**
EX n/a   NM $30   MIP $100

(ToyShop File Photo)

❑ **Hoth Ice Planet, 1980**
EX n/a   NM $30   MIP $90

(ToyShop File Photo)

❑ **Imperial Attack Base, 1980**
EX n/a   NM $20   MIP $55

(ToyShop File Photo)

❑ **Rebel Command Center, 1980**
EX n/a   NM $55   MIP $130

❑ **Turret and Probot, 1980**
EX n/a   NM $30   MIP $80

EWOKS

❑ **Ewoks Treehouse, 1985**
EX n/a   NM $16   MIP $35

RETURN OF THE JEDI

(ToyShop File Photo)

❑ **Ewok Village, 1983**
EX n/a   NM $35   MIP $100

(ToyShop File Photo)

❑ **Jabba the Hutt, 1983**
EX n/a   NM $20   MIP $65

(ToyShop File Photo)

❑ **Jabba the Hutt Dungeon, w/EV-9D9, Amanaman, Barada, 1983**
EX n/a   NM $180   MIP $250

❑ **Jabba the Hutt Dungeon, w/Nikto, 8D8, Klaatu, 1983**
EX n/a   NM $30   MIP $65

STAR WARS

❑ **Cantina Adventure Set, Sears Exclusive, 1977**
EX n/a   NM $120   MIP $350

(ToyShop File Photo)

❑ **Creature Cantina, 1977**
EX n/a   NM $30   MIP $100

(ToyShop File Photo)

❑ **Death Star Space Station, 1977**
EX n/a   NM $75   MIP $350

(ToyShop File Photo)

❑ **Droid Factory, 1977**
EX n/a   NM $40   MIP $90

STAR WARS

(ToyShop File Photo)

❑ **Land of the Jawas**, 1977
EX n/a   NM $40   MIP $95

VEHICLES

ATTACK OF THE CLONES

(KP Photo)

❑ **Anakin Skywalker Speeder**, 2002, Hasbro, With blast-off panels. Apparently, Lucas made a last-minute color change to this model (for the movie) making the speeder yellow as an homage to John Milner's 132 Coupe in "American Graffiti"
EX n/a   NM $3   MIP $16

(KP Photo)

❑ **Jango Fett's Slave I**, 2002, Hasbro, Launches four missiles, has more vibrant color as a new ship than it does by the time Boba inherits it
EX n/a   NM $5   MIP $25

❑ **Obi-Wan Kenobi Jedi Starfighter**, 2002, Hasbro
EX n/a   NM $5   MIP $25

❑ **Republic Gunship**, 2002, Hasbro, Fits one pilot, carries troops in main body, pivoting laser cannon
EX n/a   NM n/a   MIP $30

(KP Photo)

❑ **Zam Wessell Coruscant Speeder**, 2002, Hasbro, With flexible "crush zones" to emulate Zam's rough landing on Coruscant. A nice-looking vehicle
EX n/a   NM $3   MIP $17

DIE-CAST

❑ **Darth Vader's TIE Fighter**, 1979
EX n/a   NM $17   MIP $60

❑ **Land Speeder**, 1979
EX n/a   NM $18   MIP $70

❑ **Millennium Falcon**, 1979
EX n/a   NM $25   MIP $110

❑ **Naboo Starfighter**, 1999, Hasbro
EX n/a   NM $4   MIP $10

(ToyShop File Photo)

❑ **Slave I**, 1979
EX n/a   NM $400   MIP $550

❑ **Snowspeeder**, 1979
EX n/a   NM $15   MIP $50

❑ **Star Destroyer**, 1979
EX n/a   NM $20   MIP $70

❑ **TIE Bomber**, 1979
EX n/a   NM $20   MIP $90

❑ **TIE Fighter**, 1979
EX n/a   NM $20   MIP $65

(ToyShop File Photo)

❑ **Twin-Pod Cloud Car**, 1979
EX n/a   NM $18   MIP $60

❑ **X-Wing Fighter**, 1979
EX n/a   NM $30   MIP $125

❑ **Y-Wing Fighter**, 1979
EX n/a   NM $25   MIP $115

DROIDS

❑ **ATL Interceptor**, 1985
EX n/a   NM $25   MIP $75

(ToyShop File Photo)

❑ **A-Wing Fighter**, 1983
EX n/a   NM $180   MIP $320

(ToyShop File Photo)

❑ **Side Gunner**, 1985
EX n/a   NM $16   MIP $60

EMPIRE STRIKES BACK

(ToyShop File Photo)

❑ **AT-AT**, 1980, All-Terrain Armored Transport
EX n/a   NM $70   MIP $170

(ToyShop File Photo)

❑ **Rebel Transport**, 1980
EX n/a   NM $35   MIP $105

(KP Photo)

❏ **Scout Walker**, 1982, Two-legged vehicle with "walking" legs operated by button behind cockpit. A lever allowed the legs to remain locked so the vehicle could stand in place. Opening flip-up top to place figures, and opening turret allowing stormtroopers to fire weapons
EX n/a   **NM** $20   **MIP** $40

❏ **Slave I**, 1980
EX n/a   **NM** $30   **MIP** $80

(ToyShop File Photo)

❏ **Snowspeeder**, 1980
EX n/a   **NM** $25   **MIP** $65

❏ **Twin-Pod Cloud Car**, 1980
EX n/a   **NM** $18   **MIP** $70

EWOKS

❏ **Ewoks Fire Cart**, 1985
EX n/a   **NM** $6   **MIP** $17

❏ **Ewoks Woodland Wagon**, 1985
EX n/a   **NM** $7   **MIP** $30

EXPANDED UNIVERSE

(KP Photo)

❏ **Speeder Bike**, 1998, Based on previous concept drawing for speeder bike. Includes figure unique to vehicle, like other Expanded Universe vehicles. Fires missile, and outriggers move to sides when in "battle mode"
EX n/a   **NM** n/a   **MIP** $11

POTF

(ToyShop File Photo)

❏ **Ewok Battle Wagon**, 1985
EX n/a   **NM** $70   **MIP** $180

❏ **Imperial Sniper Vehicle**, 1985
EX n/a   **NM** $35   **MIP** $55

❏ **One-Man Sand Skimmer**, 1985
EX n/a   **NM** $30   **MIP** $55

❏ **Security Scout Vehicle**, 1985
EX n/a   **NM** $35   **MIP** $75

(ToyShop File Photo)

❏ **Tatooine Skiff**, 1985
EX n/a   **NM** $200   **MIP** $375

POTF2

❏ **Speeder Bike**, 1997, Includes Scout Trooper figure. Bike pieces and trooper fall off when "battle damage" button is pushed on bike
EX n/a   **NM** n/a   **MIP** $11

POTJ

(KP Photo)

❏ **TIE Interceptor**, 2002, Includes figure, wings pop off simulating battle damage. A Toys R Us exclusive, these toys are now exclusively found in the secondary market, doubling the price collectors pay to get their hands on one
EX n/a   **NM** n/a   **MIP** $60

RETURN OF THE JEDI

❏ **B-Wing Fighter**, 1984
EX n/a   **NM** $65   **MIP** $130

❏ **Ewok Combat Glider**, 1984
EX n/a   **NM** $13   **MIP** $30

(ToyShop File Photo)

❏ **Imperial Shuttle**, 1984
EX n/a   **NM** $180   **MIP** $450

❏ **Speeder Bike**, 1983
EX n/a   **NM** $9   **MIP** $25

❏ **TIE Interceptor**, 1984
EX n/a   **NM** $50   **MIP** $105

(ToyShop File Photo)

❏ **Y-Wing Fighter**, 1983
EX n/a   **NM** $55   **MIP** $125

STAR WARS

(ToyShop File Photo)

❏ **Darth Vader's TIE Fighter**, 1977, Kenner, Fly-apart panels, battery-powered laser cannon lights up in front
EX n/a   **NM** $30   **MIP** $80

STAR WARS

(KP Photo)

❏ **Imperial Cruiser**, 1982, Kenner, Second version of this vehicle. What was once the compartment for a 9-volt battery was now a "weapons storage bin." This vehicle had no battery-powered sounds, but did have opening doors, rotating turret and antenna and opening tailgate
EX n/a　　NM n/a　　MIP $45

❏ **Imperial TIE Fighter**, 1977, Kenner, Fly-apart panels
EX n/a　　NM $25　　MIP $110

❏ **Imperial Trooper Transport**, 1977, Kenner, First version was a Sears Exclusive, with battery-powered laser sounds. Later model released with "Empire Strikes Back" didn't include sounds or require battery power
EX n/a　　NM $20　　MIP $70

(ToyShop File Photo)

❏ **Jawa Sandcrawler, battery-operated**, 1977, Kenner, battery-operated
EX n/a　　NM $280　　MIP $550

(ToyShop File Photo)

❏ **Land Speeder**, 1977, Kenner, Retractable hovering wheels, opening hood
EX n/a　　NM $5　　MIP $50

❏ **Land Speeder, battery-operated**, 1977, Kenner, battery-operated
EX n/a　　NM $16　　MIP $50

❏ **Millennium Falcon**, 1977, Kenner
EX n/a　　NM $65　　MIP $375

❏ **Sonic Land Speeder, JC Penney Exclusive**, 1977, Kenner
EX n/a　　NM $120　　MIP $550

❏ **X-Wing Fighter**, 1977, Kenner, Pushing R2 head into vehicle would put foils in "X-wing" position. Opening canopy, light-up laser cannon on front
EX n/a　　NM $20　　MIP $85

THE PHANTOM MENACE

❏ **Ammo Wagon and Falumpaset**, Hasbro
EX n/a　　NM $5　　MIP $30

❏ **Anakin Skywalker's Podracer**, Hasbro
EX n/a　　NM $3　　MIP $11

❏ **Armored Scout Tank w/Battle Droid**, Hasbro
EX n/a　　NM $2　　MIP $7

(KP Photo)

❏ **Flash Speeder**, 1999, Hasbro, Hovercraft much in the style of other Star Wars speeders. Shown here with unloaded gun turret, this model actually fires a missle (a pretty fair distance, too)
EX n/a　　NM $3　　MIP $11

❏ **Gungan Assault Cannon w/Jar Jar Binks**, Hasbro
EX n/a　　NM $3　　MIP $16

❏ **Gungan Mini-Sub w/Obi-Wan Kenobi**, Hasbro
EX n/a　　NM $3　　MIP $19

❏ **Naboo Starfighter**, 1999, Hasbro
EX n/a　　NM $3　　MIP $16

❏ **Sebulba's Pod Racer w/Sebulba**, Hasbro
EX n/a　　NM $3　　MIP $17

(KP Photo)

❏ **Sith Speeder w/Darth Maul**, 1999, Hasbro
EX n/a　　NM $2　　MIP $5

❏ **STAP w/Battle Droid**, Hasbro
EX n/a　　NM $2　　MIP $5

❏ **Trade Federation Droid Fighter**, Hasbro
EX n/a　　NM $5　　MIP $30

❏ **Trade Federation Tank**, Hasbro
EX n/a　　NM $5　　MIP $30

WEAPONS

ATTACK OF THE CLONES

❏ **Anakin Skywalker Lightsaber**, 2002, Hasbro
EX n/a　　NM $5　　MIP $25

❏ **Count Dooku Lightsaber**, 2002, Hasbro
EX n/a　　NM $5　　MIP $25

❏ **Lightsaber, blue**, 2002, Hasbro
EX n/a　　NM $3　　MIP $9

❏ **Lightsaber, green**, 2002, Hasbro
EX n/a　　NM $3　　MIP $9

❏ **Lightsaber, purple**, 2002, Hasbro
EX n/a　　NM $4　　MIP $14

❏ **Lightsaber, red**, 2002, Hasbro
EX n/a　　NM $4　　MIP $14

❏ **Obi-Wan Kenobi Lightsaber**, 2002, Hasbro
EX n/a　　NM $5　　MIP $25

DROIDS

❏ **Droids Lightsaber**, 1985
EX n/a　　NM $85　　MIP $225

EMPIRE STRIKES BACK

❏ **Laser Pistol**, 1980
EX n/a　　NM $18　　MIP $65

❏ **Lightsaber, red or green**, 1980, red or green
EX n/a　　NM $30　　MIP $60

RETURN OF THE JEDI

❏ **Biker Scout's Laser Pistol**, 1984
EX n/a　　NM $18　　MIP $60

❏ **Lightsaber, red or green**, red or green plastic
EX n/a　　NM $20　　MIP $30

STAR WARS

❏ **Han Solo's Laser Pistol**
EX n/a　　NM $20　　MIP $90

❏ **Inflatable Lightsaber**, 1977
EX n/a　　NM $25　　MIP $120

❏ **Three-Position Laser Rifle**, 1980
EX n/a　　NM $65　　MIP $250

BANKS

❑ **C-3PO, ceramic,** 1977, Roman, ceramic
EX n/a   **NM** $50   **MIP** $65

❑ **Chewbacca,** 1983, Sigma
EX n/a   **NM** $25   **MIP** $35

❑ **Darth Vader,** 1983, Adam Joseph
EX n/a   **NM** $9   **MIP** $13

❑ **Darth Vader, ceramic,** 1977, Roman, ceramic
EX n/a   **NM** $50   **MIP** $75

❑ **Darth Vader, silver plated,** 1981, Leonard Silver, silver plated
EX n/a   **NM** $45   **MIP** $65

❑ **Emperor's Royal Guard,** 1983, Adam Joseph
EX n/a   **NM** $9   **MIP** $13

❑ **Gamorrean Guard,** 1983, Adam Joseph
EX n/a   **NM** $75   **MIP** $100

❑ **Jabba the Hutt,** 1983, Sigma
EX n/a   **NM** $25   **MIP** $35

❑ **Kneesaa Bank,** 1983, Adam Joseph
EX n/a   **NM** $7   **MIP** $10

❑ **R2-D2,** 1983, Adam Joseph
EX n/a   **NM** $7   **MIP** $10

❑ **R2-D2, ceramic,** 1977, Roman, ceramic
EX n/a   **NM** $25   **MIP** $35

❑ **Wicket,** 1983, Adam Joseph
EX n/a   **NM** $7   **MIP** $10

❑ **Yoda,** 1983, Sigma
EX n/a   **NM** $25   **MIP** $35

❑ **Yoda, lithographed tin w/combination dials,** lithographed tin with combination dials
EX n/a   **NM** $11   **MIP** $16

BISQUE FIGURES

❑ **Boba Fett, bisque,** 1983, Towle/Sigma, bisque
EX n/a   **NM** $30   **MIP** $45

❑ **Darth Vader, bisque,** 1983, Towle/Sigma, bisque
EX n/a   **NM** $30   **MIP** $45

❑ **Galactic Emperor, bisque,** 1983, Towle/Sigma, bisque
EX n/a   **NM** $20   **MIP** $30

❑ **Gamorrean Guard, bisque,** 1983, Towle/Sigma, bisque
EX n/a   **NM** $20   **MIP** $30

❑ **Han Solo, bisque,** 1983, Towle/Sigma, bisque
EX n/a   **NM** $25   **MIP** $35

❑ **Lando Calrissian, bisque,** 1983, Towle/Sigma, bisque
EX n/a   **NM** $30   **MIP** $45

❑ **Luke Skywalker, bisque,** 1983, Towle/Sigma, bisque
EX n/a   **NM** $30   **MIP** $45

BOARD GAMES

❑ **Star Wars Adventures of R2D2 Game,** 1977, Kenner
EX n/a   **NM** $10   **MIP** $20

❑ **Star Wars Battle at Sarlacc's Pit,** 1983, Parker Brothers
EX n/a   **NM** $10   **MIP** $20

❑ **Star Wars Escape from Death Star,** 1977, Kenner
EX n/a   **NM** $15   **MIP** $25

❑ **Star Wars Monopoly,** 1997, Parker Brothers
EX n/a   **NM** $15   **MIP** $25

❑ **Star Wars ROTJ Ewoks Save The Trees,** 1984, Parker Brothers
EX n/a   **NM** $10   **MIP** $15

❑ **Star Wars Wicket the Ewok,** 1983, Parker Brothers
EX n/a   **NM** $10   **MIP** $15

❑ **Star Wars X-Wing Aces Target Game,** 1978
EX n/a   **NM** $150   **MIP** $500

BOOKS

❑ **Burger Chef Fun Book,** 1978
EX n/a   **NM** $3   **MIP** $3

❑ **Chewbacca and C-3PO Coloring Book,** Kenner
EX n/a   **NM** $2   **MIP** $4

❑ **Chewbacca and Leia Coloring Book,** Kenner
EX n/a   **NM** $2   **MIP** $4

❑ **Chewbacca, Han, Leia and Lando Coloring Book,** Kenner
EX n/a   **NM** $2   **MIP** $4

❑ **Chewbacca's Activity Book,** Random House
EX n/a   **NM** $3   **MIP** $5

❑ **Darth Vader and Stormtroopers Coloring Book,** Kenner
EX n/a   **NM** $2   **MIP** $4

❑ **Empire Strikes Back Coloring Book,** 1980
EX n/a   **NM** $5   **MIP** $7

❑ **Empire Strikes Back Panorama Book,** Random House
EX n/a   **NM** $15   **MIP** $20

❑ **Empire Strikes Back Pop-Up Book,** 1980, Random House
EX n/a   **NM** $10   **MIP** $15

❑ **Empire Strikes Back Sketchbook,** 1980, Ballantine
EX n/a   **NM** $14   **MIP** $20

❑ **Escape from the Monster Ship Book,** 1985, Random House
EX n/a   **NM** $6   **MIP** $8

❑ **Ewoks Coloring Book,** 1983, Kenner
EX n/a   **NM** $7   **MIP** $10

❑ **Fuzzy as an Ewok,** 1985, Random House
EX n/a   **NM** $6   **MIP** $8

❑ **How the Ewoks Saved the Trees,** 1985, Random House
EX n/a   **NM** $6   **MIP** $8

❑ **Jedi Master's Quiz,** 1985, Random House
EX n/a   **NM** $6   **MIP** $8

❑ **Lando Fighting Skiff Guard Coloring Book,** 1983, Kenner
EX n/a   **NM** $2   **MIP** $4

❑ **Lando in Falcon Cockpit Coloring Book,** 1983, Kenner
EX n/a   **NM** $2   **MIP** $4

❑ **Learn-to-Read Activity Book,** 1985, Random House
EX n/a   **NM** $6   **MIP** $8

❑ **Luke Skywalker Coloring Book,** 1983, Kenner
EX n/a   **NM** $2   **MIP** $4

❑ **Max Rebo Coloring Book,** 1983, Kenner
EX n/a   **NM** $3   **MIP** $5

❑ **My Jedi Journal,** Ballantine
EX n/a   **NM** $7   **MIP** $10

❑ **R2-D2 Coloring Book,** Kenner
EX n/a   **NM** $2   **MIP** $4

❑ **Return of the Jedi Activity Book,** 1983, Happy House
EX n/a   **NM** $5   **MIP** $7

❑ **Return of the Jedi Coloring Book,** 1984
EX n/a   **NM** $2   **MIP** $4

❑ **Return of the Jedi Maze Book,** 1983, Happy House
EX n/a   **NM** $2   **MIP** $4

❑ **Return of the Jedi Monster Activity Book,** 1983, Happy House
EX n/a   **NM** $2   **MIP** $4

❑ **Return of the Jedi Picture Puzzle Book,** 1983, Happy House
EX n/a   **NM** $2   **MIP** $4

❑ **Return of the Jedi Pop-Up Book,** 1983, Random House
EX n/a   **NM** $10   **MIP** $12

❑ **Return of the Jedi Punch-Out Book,** Random House
EX n/a   **NM** $10   **MIP** $12

❑ **Return of the Jedi Sketchbook,** 1983, Ballantine
EX n/a   **NM** $11   **MIP** $16

❑ **Return of the Jedi Word Puzzle Book,** 1983, Happy House
EX n/a   **NM** $5   **MIP** $7

❑ **Star Wars Pop-Up Book,** 1978, Random House
EX n/a   **NM** $10   **MIP** $16

❑ **Star Wars Poster Art Coloring Set,** 1978, Craft Master
EX n/a   **NM** $9   **MIP** $13

❑ **Star Wars Questions and Answers About Space Book,** 1979, Random House
EX n/a   **NM** $5   **MIP** $7

STAR WARS (NON-ACTION FIGURES)

❏ **Star Wars Sketchbook**, 1977, Ballantine
EX n/a   NM $10   MIP $12

❏ **Sticker Book, 256 stickers**, 1977, Panini
EX n/a   NM $23   MIP $35

❏ **Yoda Coloring Book**, Kenner
EX n/a   NM $2   MIP $4

CANDLES

❏ **Chewbacca Birthday Candle**, Wilton
EX n/a   NM $6   MIP $8

❏ **Darth Vader Birthday Candle**, Wilton
EX n/a   NM $6   MIP $8

❏ **R2-D2 Birthday Candle**, Wilton
EX n/a   NM $6   MIP $8

CAST & CREW ITEMS

❏ **"The Star Wars" large sticker**, 1977
EX n/a   NM n/a   MIP $10

❏ **Blue Harvest cap**, 1983
EX n/a   NM n/a   MIP $250

❏ **Blue Harvest stationery**, 1983
EX n/a   NM n/a   MIP $10

❏ **Blue Harvest t-shirt**, 1983
EX n/a   NM n/a   MIP $75

❏ **Dancing Probot T-shirt**, 1980
EX n/a   NM n/a   MIP $50

❏ **Empire Srikes Back Norwegian unit patch**, 1980
EX n/a   NM n/a   MIP $75

❏ **Empire Strikes Back logo coaster**, 1980
EX n/a   NM n/a   MIP $20

❏ **Empire Strikes Back lucite star**, 1980
EX n/a   NM n/a   MIP $200

❏ **Empire Strikes Back paperweight**, 1980
EX n/a   NM n/a   MIP $150

❏ **Empire Strikes Back R2-D2 coaster**, 1980
EX n/a   NM n/a   MIP $20

❏ **Empire Strikes Back Vader flames patch**, 1980
EX n/a   NM n/a   MIP $75

❏ **Intergalactic Passport, stamped**, 1980
EX n/a   NM n/a   MIP $150

❏ **Intergalactic Passport, unstamped**, 1980
EX n/a   NM n/a   MIP $75

❏ **May the Force Be With You lucite star**, 1977
EX n/a   NM n/a   MIP $200

❏ **McQuarrie lettering Star Wars patch**, 1977
EX n/a   NM n/a   MIP $75

❏ **Revenge of the Jedi paperweight**, 1983
EX n/a   NM n/a   MIP $150

❏ **Revenge of the Jedi t-shirt**, 1983
EX n/a   NM n/a   MIP $50

❏ **Revenge of the Jedi Yoda patch**, 1983
EX n/a   NM n/a   MIP $50

❏ **Revenge of the Jedi Yoda sticker**, 1983
EX n/a   NM n/a   MIP $10

❏ **Star Wars lucite star**, 1977
EX n/a   NM n/a   MIP $200

CEREAL BOXES

❏ **Apple Jacks, w/Droids comic**, 1995, Kellogg's
EX n/a   NM n/a   MIP $15

❏ **Apple Jacks, w/Star Wars comic**, 1995, Kellogg's
EX n/a   NM n/a   MIP $10

❏ **Boo Berry, w/card offer**, 1978, General Mills
EX n/a   NM n/a   MIP $150

❏ **Boo Berry, w/sticker offer**, 1978, General Mills
EX n/a   NM n/a   MIP $150

❏ **C-3PO's, w/C-3PO mask**, 1984, Kellogg's
EX n/a   NM n/a   MIP $30

❏ **C-3PO's, w/Chewbacca mask**, 1984, Kellogg's
EX n/a   NM n/a   MIP $30

❏ **C-3PO's, w/Darth Vader mask**, 1984, Kellogg's
EX n/a   NM n/a   MIP $30

❏ **C-3PO's, w/Luke mask**, 1984, Kellogg's
EX n/a   NM n/a   MIP $30

❏ **C-3PO's, w/Rebel Rocket**, 1984, Kellogg's
EX n/a   NM n/a   MIP $30

❏ **C-3PO's, w/Stick R Card**, 1984, Kellogg's
EX n/a   NM n/a   MIP $30

❏ **C-3PO's, w/Stormtrooper mask**, 1984, Kellogg's
EX n/a   NM n/a   MIP $30

❏ **Cheerios, w/poster offer**, 1978, General Mills
EX n/a   NM n/a   MIP $50

❏ **Cheerios, w/tumbler offer**, 1979, General Mills
EX n/a   NM n/a   MIP $50

❏ **Chocolate Crazy Cow, w/card offer**, 1978, General Mills
EX n/a   NM n/a   MIP $150

❏ **Cocoa Puffs, w/card offer**, 1978, General Mills
EX n/a   NM n/a   MIP $75

❏ **Cocoa Puffs, w/sticker offer**, 1978, General Mills
EX n/a   NM n/a   MIP $75

❏ **Corn Pops, w/Making of Star Wars**, 1995, Kellogg's
EX n/a   NM n/a   MIP $10

❏ **Count Chocula, w/card offer**, 1978, General Mills
EX n/a   NM n/a   MIP $150

❏ **Count Chocula, w/sticker offer**, 1978, General Mills
EX n/a   NM n/a   MIP $150

❏ **Franken Berry, w/card offer**, 1978, General Mills
EX n/a   NM n/a   MIP $150

❏ **Franken Berry, w/sticker offer**, 1978, General Mills
EX n/a   NM n/a   MIP $150

❏ **Froot Loops, w/Han Stormtrooper offer**, 1995, Kellogg's
EX n/a   NM n/a   MIP $10

❏ **Lucky Charms, w/hang glider offer**, 1978, General Mills
EX n/a   NM n/a   MIP $75

❏ **Lucky Charms, w/sticker offer**, 1978, General Mills
EX n/a   NM n/a   MIP $75

❏ **Raisin Bran, w/Star Wars video ad**, 1995, Kellogg's
EX n/a   NM n/a   MIP $10

❏ **Strawberry Crazy Cow, w/card offer**, 1978, General Mills
EX n/a   NM n/a   MIP $150

❏ **Trix, w/hang glider offer**, 1978, General Mills
EX n/a   NM n/a   MIP $75

❏ **Trix, w/sticker offer**, 1978, General Mills
EX n/a   NM n/a   MIP $75

CEREAL PREMIUMS

❏ **Card, set of eighteen**, 1978, General Mills
EX n/a   NM n/a   MIP $3

❏ **Han Stormtrooper**, 1995, Kellogg's
EX n/a   NM n/a   MIP $10

❏ **Hang glider, set of four**, 1978, General Mills
EX n/a   NM n/a   MIP $8

❏ **Kite**, 1978, General Mills
EX n/a   NM n/a   MIP $30

❏ **Making of Star Wars video**, 1995, Kellogg's
EX n/a   NM n/a   MIP $5

❏ **Micro Collection figures**, 1984, Kellogg's
EX n/a   NM n/a   MIP $10

❏ **Poster, set of four**, 1978, General Mills
EX n/a   NM n/a   MIP $2

❏ **Rebel Rocket, set of four**, 1984, Kellogg's
EX n/a   NM n/a   MIP $10

❏ **Star Wars comic**, 1995, Kellogg's
EX n/a   NM n/a   MIP $5

❏ **Stick R Card, set of ten**, 1984, Kellogg's
EX n/a   NM n/a   MIP $2

❏ **Stickers, set of sixteen**, 1978, General Mills
EX n/a   NM n/a   MIP $4

❏ **Tumbler**, 1978, General Mills
EX n/a   NM n/a   MIP $15

CLOCKS

❏ **3-D, electronic, quartz**, 1982, Bradley
EX n/a   **NM** $16   **MIP** $23

❏ **C-3PO and R2-D2 Alarm Clock**, 1980, Bradley
EX n/a   **NM** $15   **MIP** $25

❏ **Droid, wall clock**, Bradley
EX n/a   **NM** $20   **MIP** $30

❏ **Empire Strikes Back, wall clock**, Bradley
EX n/a   **NM** $20   **MIP** $30

❏ **Portable Clock/Radio**, 1984, Bradley
EX n/a   **NM** $11   **MIP** $16

CLOTHING

❏ **Chewbacca Bandolier Strap**, 1983
EX n/a   **NM** n/a   **MIP** $15

❏ **Darth Vader Belt Buckle**, 1977, Leather Shop
EX n/a   **NM** $14   **MIP** $20

❏ **R2-D2 and C-3PO Belt Buckles**, 1977, Leather Shop
EX n/a   **NM** $14   **MIP** $20

❏ **R2-D2 Belt Buckle**, 1977, Leather Shop
EX n/a   **NM** $14   **MIP** $20

❏ **Return of the Jedi Belt**, 1977, Leather Shop
EX n/a   **NM** $5   **MIP** $7

❏ **Yoda Backpack**, Sigma
EX n/a   **NM** $14   **MIP** $20

COOKIE JARS

❏ **C-3PO Cookie Jar, ceramic**, 1977, Roman
EX n/a   **NM** $150   **MIP** $250

❏ **Darth Vader, R2-D2 and C-3PO Cookie Jar, hexagon**, Sigma
EX n/a   **NM** $55   **MIP** $80

❏ **R2-D2 Cookie Jar, ceramic**, 1977, Roman
EX n/a   **NM** $90   **MIP** $150

DISPLAYS

EMPIRE STRIKES BACK

❏ **Empire Strikes Back Display Arena**, 1980
EX n/a   **NM** n/a   **MIP** $105

STAR WARS

❏ **Star Wars Action Figure Display Stand**, 1977, Mail-In Premium
EX n/a   **NM** n/a   **MIP** $300

ELECTRONICS

❏ **Darth Vader Speaker Phone**, 1983, ATC
EX n/a   **NM** $40   **MIP** $60

❏ **Duel Racing Set**, 1978, Lionel
EX n/a   **NM** $40   **MIP** $75

❏ **Give-A-Show Projector, w/filmstrips**, 1979, Kenner
EX n/a   **NM** $25   **MIP** $35

❏ **Luke Skywalker AM Headset Radio**
EX n/a   **NM** $95   **MIP** $150

❏ **Movie Viewer**, 1978, Kenner
EX n/a   **NM** $15   **MIP** $20

FAST FOOD

❏ **Boba Fett Toy**, 1997, Taco Bell
EX n/a   **NM** $1   **MIP** $2

❏ **Cloud City Toy**, 1997, Taco Bell
EX n/a   **NM** $1   **MIP** $2

❏ **Death Star Spinner toy**, 1997, Taco Bell
EX n/a   **NM** $1   **MIP** $2

❏ **Empire Strikes Back glasses**, 1980, Burger King
EX n/a   **NM** $3   **MIP** $8

❏ **Empire Strikes Back Sticker Album**, 1980, Burger King
EX n/a   **NM** $5   **MIP** $20

❏ **Fun Trays**, Burger Chef
EX n/a   **NM** $3   **MIP** $10

❏ **Glasses**, 1977, Burger King
EX n/a   **NM** $3   **MIP** $10

❏ **Millennium Falcon toy**, 1997, Taco Bell
EX n/a   **NM** $1   **MIP** $2

❏ **Mirror Cube toy**, 1997, Taco Bell
EX n/a   **NM** $1   **MIP** $2

❏ **Puzzle Cube**, 1997, Taco Bell
EX n/a   **NM** $1   **MIP** $2

❏ **R2-D2 toy**, 1997, Taco Bell
EX n/a   **NM** $1   **MIP** $2

❏ **Return of the Jedi glasses**, 1983, Burger King
EX n/a   **NM** $2   **MIP** $5

❏ **Star Wars poster**, 1997, Pizza Hut, three in all
EX n/a   **NM** $2   **MIP** $5

❏ **Transforming playsets, small, set of sixteen**, 1998, Pizza Hut
EX n/a   **NM** $1   **MIP** $3

❏ **Yoda toy**, 1997, Taco Bell
EX n/a   **NM** $1   **MIP** $2

FIGURAL BANKS

THE PHANTOM MENACE

❏ **Darth Maul**, 1999, Thinkway
EX n/a   **NM** n/a   **MIP** $20

❏ **Jar Jar Binks**, 1999, Thinkway
EX n/a   **NM** n/a   **MIP** $15

❏ **Obi-Wan Kenobi**, 1999, Thinkway
EX n/a   **NM** n/a   **MIP** $20

❏ **Qui-Gon Jinn**, 1999, Thinkway
EX n/a   **NM** n/a   **MIP** $15

FRAMES

❏ **Darth Vader Picture Frame**, Sigma
EX n/a   **NM** $30   **MIP** $45

❏ **R2-D2 Picture Frame**, Sigma
EX n/a   **NM** $30   **MIP** $45

HALLOWEEN COSTUME

❏ **Admiral Ackbar**, 1983, Ben Cooper
EX n/a   **NM** n/a   **MIP** $10

❏ **Boba Fett**, 1979, Ben Cooper
EX n/a   **NM** n/a   **MIP** $10

❏ **C-3PO**, 1977, Ben Cooper
EX n/a   **NM** n/a   **MIP** $10

❏ **Chewbacca**, 1977, Ben Cooper
EX n/a   **NM** n/a   **MIP** $10

❏ **Darth Vader**, 1977, Ben Cooper
EX n/a   **NM** n/a   **MIP** $10

❏ **Gamorrean Guard**, 1983, Ben Cooper
EX n/a   **NM** n/a   **MIP** $10

❏ **Klaatu**, 1983, Ben Cooper
EX n/a   **NM** n/a   **MIP** $10

❏ **Leia**, 1977, Ben Cooper
EX n/a   **NM** n/a   **MIP** $10

❏ **Luke**, 1977, Ben Cooper
EX n/a   **NM** n/a   **MIP** $10

❏ **Luke X-Wing pilot**, 1977, Ben Cooper
EX n/a   **NM** n/a   **MIP** $10

❏ **R2-D2**, 1977, Ben Cooper
EX n/a   **NM** n/a   **MIP** $10

❏ **Stormtrooper**, 1977, Ben Cooper
EX n/a   **NM** n/a   **MIP** $10

❏ **Wicket**, 1983, Ben Cooper
EX n/a   **NM** n/a   **MIP** $10

❏ **Yoda**, 1980, Ben Cooper
EX n/a   **NM** n/a   **MIP** $10

KITS

❏ **Flying R2-D2 Rocket Kit**, 1978, Estes
EX n/a   **NM** $9   **MIP** $13

❏ **TIE Fighter Rocket Kit**, 1978, Estes
EX n/a   **NM** $11   **MIP** $16

❏ **X-Wing Fighter Rocket Kit**, 1978, Estes
EX n/a   **NM** $11   **MIP** $16

❏ **X-Wing with Maxi-Brutel Rocket Kit**, 1978, Estes
EX n/a   **NM** $18   **MIP** $25

MEDALS

❏ **Chewbacca**, 1980, W. Berrie
EX n/a   **NM** $6   **MIP** $8

❏ **X-Wing**, 1980, W. Berrie
EX n/a   **NM** $6   **MIP** $8

MISCELLANEOUS

❏ **Chewbacca/Darth Vader Bookends**, Sigma
EX n/a   **NM** $25   **MIP** $35

❏ **Darth Vader Duty Roster**, school supplies
EX n/a   **NM** $5   **MIP** $7

❏ **Darth Vader SSP Van**, 1978, Kenner, black
EX n/a   **NM** $20   **MIP** $25

❏ **Empire Strikes Back Dinnerware Set**
EX n/a   **NM** $15   **MIP** $25

❏ **Intergalactic Passport and Stickers,** 1983, Ballantine
EX n/a   NM $7   MIP $10

❏ **Original Fan Club Kit,** 1977
EX n/a   NM $10   MIP $15

❏ **Original Press Kit,** 1977
EX n/a   NM $25   MIP $45

❏ **Return of the Jedi Candy Containers,** figural, set of eighteen, 1983, Topps
EX n/a   NM $25   MIP $35

❏ **Star Wars Dinnerware Set**
EX n/a   NM $20   MIP $30

❏ **Sticker Set and Album,** Burger King
EX n/a   NM $7   MIP $10

❏ **Yoda Hand Puppet**
EX n/a   NM $14   MIP $20

❏ **Yoda Jedi Master Fortune Teller Ball**
EX n/a   NM $20   MIP $30

MUGS

❏ **C-3PO,** ceramic, Sigma
EX n/a   NM $16   MIP $23

❏ **Chewbacca,** ceramic, Sigma
EX n/a   NM $18   MIP $25

❏ **Darth Vader,** ceramic, Sigma
EX n/a   NM $16   MIP $23

❏ **Gamorrean Guard,** ceramic, Sigma
EX n/a   NM $10   MIP $20

❏ **Han Solo,** ceramic, Sigma
EX n/a   NM $23   MIP $35

❏ **Lando Calrissian,** ceramic, Sigma
EX n/a   NM $16   MIP $23

❏ **Leia,** ceramic, Sigma
EX n/a   NM $20   MIP $30

❏ **Luke Skywalker,** ceramic, Sigma
EX n/a   NM $20   MIP $30

PAINTS

❏ **Admiral Ackbar Figurine Paint Set,** Craft Master
EX n/a   NM $9   MIP $13

❏ **C-3PO Figurine Paint Set,** Craft Master
EX n/a   NM $9   MIP $13

❏ **Darth Vader Paint Set, glow-in-the-dark**
EX n/a   NM $9   MIP $13

❏ **Han Solo Figurine Paint Set,** Craft Master
EX n/a   NM $16   MIP $23

❏ **Leia and Han Solo Paint Set, glow-in-the-dark**
EX n/a   NM $9   MIP $13

❏ **Leia Figurine Paint Set,** Craft Master
EX n/a   NM $11   MIP $16

❏ **Luke and Tauntaun Figurine Paint Set,** Craft Master
EX n/a   NM $14   MIP $20

❏ **Luke Skywalker Paint Set, glow-in-the-dark**
EX n/a   NM $9   MIP $13

❏ **Wicket Figurine Paint Set,** Craft Master
EX n/a   NM $9   MIP $13

❏ **Yoda Figurine Paint Set,** Craft Master
EX n/a   NM $9   MIP $13

❏ **Yoda Paint Set, glow-in-the-dark**
EX n/a   NM $9   MIP $13

PEZ

❏ **Boba Fett,** 1999, PEZ
EX n/a   NM $1   MIP $2

❏ **C-3PO,** 1997, PEZ
EX n/a   NM $1   MIP $3

❏ **Chewbacca,** 1997, PEZ
EX n/a   NM $1   MIP $3

❏ **Darth Vader,** 1997, PEZ
EX n/a   NM $1   MIP $3

❏ **Ewok,** 1999, PEZ
EX n/a   NM $1   MIP $3

❏ **Luke Skywalker,** 1999, PEZ
EX n/a   NM $1   MIP $3

❏ **Princess Leia,** 1999, PEZ
EX n/a   NM $1   MIP $3

❏ **Stormtrooper,** 1997, PEZ
EX n/a   NM $1   MIP $3

❏ **Yoda,** 1997, PEZ
EX n/a   NM $1   MIP $3

PLAY-DOH

❏ **Ewoks Play-Doh Set**
EX n/a   NM $11   MIP $16

❏ **Ice Planet Hoth Play-Doh Set**
EX n/a   NM $16   MIP $23

❏ **Jabba the Hutt Play-Doh Set**
EX n/a   NM $11   MIP $16

❏ **Star Wars Action Play-Doh Set**
EX n/a   NM $20   MIP $30

POSTERS

❏ **Ben Kenobi/Darth Vader,** 1978, Proctor & Gamble
EX n/a   NM $9   MIP $13

❏ **Chewbacca,** 1978, Burger King
EX n/a   NM $5   MIP $7

❏ **Dagobah,** 1980, Burger King
EX n/a   NM $5   MIP $7

❏ **Darth Vader,** 1978, Burger King
EX n/a   NM $5   MIP $7

❏ **Darth Vader,** 1980, Proctor & Gamble
EX n/a   NM $5   MIP $8

❏ **Darth Vader,** 1980, Nestea
EX n/a   NM $5   MIP $7

❏ **Death Star,** 1978, Proctor & Gamble
EX n/a   NM $5   MIP $8

❏ **Empire Strikes Back 1981 re-release**
EX n/a   NM n/a   MIP $40

❏ **Empire Strikes Back 1982 re-release**
EX n/a   NM n/a   MIP $40

❏ **Empire Strikes Back advance**
EX n/a   NM n/a   MIP $65

❏ **Empire Strikes Back Poster Album Vol. 1**
EX n/a   NM $10   MIP $15

❏ **Empire Strikes Back Radio Program Poster**
EX n/a   NM $15   MIP $20

❏ **Empire Strikes Back Special Edition**
EX n/a   NM n/a   MIP $20

❏ **Hoth Poster,** 1980, Burger King
EX n/a   NM $5   MIP $7

❏ **Luke Skywalker,** 1978, Burger King
EX n/a   NM $5   MIP $7

❏ **Luke Skywalker,** 1980, Proctor & Gamble
EX n/a   NM $5   MIP $8

❏ **Luke Skywalker,** 1980, Nestea
EX n/a   NM $5   MIP $7

❏ **R2-D2 and C-3PO Poster,** 1980, Proctor & Gamble
EX n/a   NM $5   MIP $8

❏ **R2-D2 Poster,** 1978, Burger King
EX n/a   NM $5   MIP $7

❏ **Return of the Jedi 1985 re-release**
EX n/a   NM n/a   MIP $40

❏ **Return of the Jedi Special Edition**
EX n/a   NM n/a   MIP $20

❏ **Revenge of the Jedi w/date**
EX n/a   NM n/a   MIP $175

❏ **Revenge of the Jedi without date**
EX n/a   NM n/a   MIP $250

❏ **Star Destroyer,** 1978, General Mills
EX n/a   NM $5   MIP $10

❏ **Star Wars 1982 re-release**
EX n/a   NM n/a   MIP $65

❏ **Star Wars Birthday,** first anniversary
EX n/a   NM n/a   MIP $700

❏ **Star Wars Mylar Advance**
EX n/a   NM n/a   MIP $750

❏ **Star Wars Radio Program,** Golden
EX n/a   NM $23   MIP $35

❏ **Star Wars second advance**
EX n/a   NM n/a   MIP $100

❏ **Star Wars Special Edition**
EX n/a   NM n/a   MIP $20

❏ **Star Wars: Episode I — The Phantom Menace**
EX n/a   NM n/a   MIP $20

❏ **TIE Fighter and X-Wing Poster,** 1978, General Mills
EX n/a   NM $30   MIP $40

PUNCHING BAGS

❏ **Chewbacca,** 1977, Kenner, 50"
EX n/a   NM $20   MIP $40

❏ **Darth Vader,** 1977, Kenner, 50"
EX n/a   NM $15   MIP $30

❏ **Jawa,** 1977, Kenner, 50"
EX n/a   NM $45   MIP $65

❏ **R2-D2,** 1977, Kenner, 50"
EX n/a   NM $15   MIP $30

PUZZLES

❏ **Attack of the Sand People, 140 pieces**, Kenner
EX n/a   **NM** $5   **MIP** $7

❏ **Cantina Band, 500 pieces**, Kenner
EX n/a   **NM** $6   **MIP** $8

❏ **Han Solo and Chewbacca, 140 pieces**, Kenner
EX n/a   **NM** $6   **MIP** $8

❏ **Jabba the Hutt,** 1983, Craft Master
EX n/a   **NM** $4   **MIP** $7

❏ **Jabba the Hutt,** 1983, Craft Master
EX n/a   **NM** $4   **MIP** $7

❏ **Jawas capture R2-D2, 140 pieces**, Kenner
EX n/a   **NM** $4   **MIP** $6

❏ **Luke and Leia leap for their lives, 500 pieces**, Kenner
EX n/a   **NM** $6   **MIP** $8

❏ **Luke Skywalker, 500 pieces**, Kenner
EX n/a   **NM** $6   **MIP** $10

❏ **Space Battle, 500 pieces**, Kenner
EX n/a   **NM** $7   **MIP** $10

❏ **Stormtroopers stop the Landspeeder, 140 pieces**, Kenner
EX n/a   **NM** $5   **MIP** $7

❏ **Trapped in the Trash Compactor, 140 pieces**, Kenner
EX n/a   **NM** $5   **MIP** $7

❏ **Victory Celebration, 500 pieces**, Kenner
EX n/a   **NM** $6   **MIP** $8

❏ **X-Wing Fighters Prepare to Attack, 500 pieces**, Kenner
EX n/a   **NM** $6   **MIP** $8

RINGS

❏ **Darth Vader,** 1980, W. Berrie
EX n/a   **NM** $6   **MIP** $8

SCHOOL SUPPLIES

❏ **C-3PO Pencil Tray**, Sigma
EX n/a   **NM** $23   **MIP** $35

❏ **C-3PO Tape Dispenser**, Sigma
EX n/a   **NM** $23   **MIP** $35

❏ **R2-D2 String Dispenser with Scissors**, Sigma
EX n/a   **NM** $20   **MIP** $30

❏ **Yoda Tumbler/Pencil Cup**, Sigma
EX n/a   **NM** $20   **MIP** $30

STAR WARS BUDDIES

❏ **C-3PO**, 1998, Hasbro
EX n/a   **NM** n/a   **MIP** $6

❏ **Cantina Band Member**, 1998, Hasbro
EX n/a   **NM** n/a   **MIP** $6

❏ **Chewbacca, first version**, 1998, Hasbro, first version
EX n/a   **NM** n/a   **MIP** $10

❏ **Chewbacca, second version**, 1998, Hasbro, second version
EX n/a   **NM** n/a   **MIP** $6

❏ **Darth Vader Pillow**, 1983
EX n/a   **NM** $9   **MIP** $13

❏ **Jabba the Hutt**, 1998, Hasbro
EX n/a   **NM** n/a   **MIP** $6

❏ **Jawa**, 1998, Hasbro
EX n/a   **NM** n/a   **MIP** $6

❏ **Max Rebo**, 1998, Hasbro
EX n/a   **NM** n/a   **MIP** $6

❏ **R2-D2**, 1998, Hasbro
EX n/a   **NM** n/a   **MIP** $6

❏ **Salacious Crumb**, 1998, Hasbro
EX n/a   **NM** n/a   **MIP** $6

❏ **Wampa**, 1998, Hasbro
EX n/a   **NM** n/a   **MIP** $6

❏ **Wicket**, 1998, Hasbro
EX n/a   **NM** n/a   **MIP** $6

❏ **Yoda**, 1998, Hasbro
EX n/a   **NM** n/a   **MIP** $6

❏ **Yoda Sleeping Bag**
EX n/a   **NM** $16   **MIP** $23

TOOTHBRUSHES & ACC.

❏ **Electric Toothbrush**, 1978, Kenner
EX n/a   **NM** $16   **MIP** $23

❏ **Snow Speeder Toothbrush Holder**, Sigma
EX n/a   **NM** $25   **MIP** $35

❏ **Wicket Toothbrush, battery-operated**, 1984
EX n/a   **NM** $9   **MIP** $13

WATCHES

❏ **C-3PO and R2-D2, digital**, 1970s, Bradley
EX n/a   **NM** $55   **MIP** $80

❏ **C-3PO and R2-D2, digital, rectangular**, 1970s, Bradley
EX n/a   **NM** $30   **MIP** $45

❏ **C-3PO and R2-D2, digital, round face**, 1970s, Bradley
EX n/a   **NM** $45   **MIP** $65

❏ **C-3PO and R2-D2, digital, round, musical**, 1970s, Bradley
EX n/a   **NM** $70   **MIP** $100

❏ **C-3PO and R2-D2, vinyl band**, 1970s, Bradley
EX n/a   **NM** $45   **MIP** $60

❏ **C-3PO and R2-D2, vinyl band, photo**, 1970s, Bradley
EX n/a   **NM** $30   **MIP** $45

❏ **C-3PO and R2-D2, white border, photo**, 1970s, Bradley
EX n/a   **NM** $45   **MIP** $65

❏ **Darth Vader, digital**, 1970s, Bradley
EX n/a   **NM** $30   **MIP** $45

❏ **Darth Vader, star and planet on face**, 1970s, Bradley
EX n/a   **NM** $45   **MIP** $65

❏ **Darth Vader, vinyl band**, 1970s, Bradley
EX n/a   **NM** $30   **MIP** $45

❏ **Droids, digital**, 1970s, Bradley
EX n/a   **NM** $30   **MIP** $45

❏ **Ewoks, vinyl band**, 1970s, Bradley
EX n/a   **NM** $30   **MIP** $45

❏ **Jabba the Hutt, digital**, 1970s, Bradley
EX n/a   **NM** $30   **MIP** $45

❏ **Wicket the Ewok Wristwatch**, 1970s, Bradley
EX n/a   **NM** $30   **MIP** $45

❏ **Yoda**, 1970s, Bradley
EX n/a   **NM** $30   **MIP** $45

❏ **Yoda**, 1970s, Bradley
EX n/a   **NM** $30   **MIP** $45

Tin Toys

Another toy produced by Unique Art, the Motorcycle Cop, with a mint value of $500.

Yesterday's tin creations are some of today's priciest collectible toys. Many of the metal toys produced before World War I can be considered true works of art, especially since tin toys were often painstakingly hand painted.

The advent of chromolithography changed all that. The technology was actually developed late in the 19th century, but first applied to tin toys in the 1920s. The technique allowed multicolor illustrations to be printed on flat tin plates which were molded into toys. American manufacturers could produce these colorful toys more inexpensively than the classic European toys that had dominated the toy market until this time.

With mass production came mass appeal, and these new tin mechanical toys were often based on the characters and celebrities that were popular at the time. Comic strip characters and Walt Dis-

ney movies provided most of the already-popular subject matter for toy marketers.

Among the most well-known makers of mechanical tin toys were Marx, Chein, Lehmann and Strauss. Others included Courtland, Girard, Ohio Art, Schuco, Unique Art and Wolverine.

Many of these manufacturers had business relationships with each other. Over the years, some would be found working together, producing or distributing other's toys or being absorbed by other companies. Of course, there appeared to be some occasoinal pilfering and reproducing others' ideas as well.

One of the advantages of lithography was that it allowed old toys to be recycled in many ways. When a character's public appeal began to wane, a new image could be printed on the same body to produce a new toy. Or when a toy company was absorbed by another, older models could be dusted off and dressed up with new lithography. Many of the mechanical tin wind-up toys show up in surprisingly similar versions with another manufacturer's name on them.

Clown playing violin, 1950s, by Schuco. This is considered one of the more affordable tin toys at a $350 mint value.

Of the companies listed here, Marx was no doubt the most prolific. The company's founder, Louis Marx, at one time was employed by another leading toy maker, Ferdinand Strauss. He left Strauss in 1918 to start his own company. Some of his first successes were new versions of old Strauss toys like the (still reproduced and quite famous) Climbing Monkey.

Many of the popular Marx tin wind-ups were also based on popular characters. Not surprisingly, some of the other highly valued character toys are the Amos 'N Andy Walkers, the Donald Duck Duet,

Popeye the Champ, Li'l Abner and his Dogpatch Band, and the Superman Roll-over Airplane.

While Marx went on to produce many different kinds of toys, other companies, such as Chein, specialized in inexpensive lithographed tin. And like Marx, Chein also capitalized on popular cartoon characters, producing several Popeye toys, among others. J. Chein and Company, which was founded in 1903, was best known for its carnival-themed mechanical toys. Its Ferris wheel is fairly well known among toy collectors and was made in several lithographed versions, including one with a Disneyland theme. Chein also produced a number of affordable tin banks.

Girard was founded shortly after Chein, but didn't start producing toys until 1918. It subcontracted toys for Marx and Strauss in the 1920s. In fact, several Girard and Marx toys are identical, having been produced in the same plant with different names on them. Marx later took over the company in the 1930s.

New Jersey-based Unique Art isn't known for an extensive line of toys, but

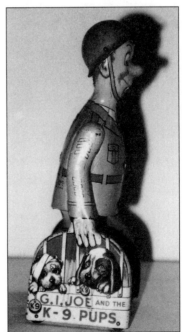

In an era before the famous action figure, this toy, known as "G.I. Joe and his K-9 Pups" was produced by Unique Art in the 1940s. Mint value, $300.

it produced some that are favorites among tin toy collectors. It, too, reportedly was acquired by Marx at some point.

There are many other companies that produced lithographed tin toys not included in this section, particularly German and Japanese companies. Lehmann and Schuco, both German firms, are the only non-American toy makers listed in this guide. More lithographed tin toys can be found in the vehicles section of this book.

Prices listed are for toys in Good, Excellent and Mint conditions. Toys will usually command a premium over the listed price if they are in their original boxes.

This neat Elephant Bank by Chein was produced in the 1950s. Collectors can still find this beauty at flea markets and toy shows for under $100 in excellent condition.

Trends

Tin toys have kept their values over the years, and the trade still pretty healthy. However, there are number of quality reproductions for fairly low prices for the collector who just wants the toy without it being an investment.

BANKS

❏ **2nd National Duck Bank,** 1954, Chein, Disney characters
EX $90   NM $145   MINT $225

❏ **Cash Box,** 1930, Chein, round trap
EX $30   NM $50   MINT $75

❏ **Child's Safe Bank,** 1900s, Chein
EX $40   NM $65   MINT $100

❏ **Child's Safe Bank,** 1910, Chein, sailboat on front of door
EX $35   NM $60   MINT $90

❏ **Child's Safe Bank,** 1910, Chein, dog on front of door
EX $35   NM $60   MINT $95

❏ **Church,** 1930s, Chein
EX $35   NM $60   MINT $90

❏ **Church,** 1954, Chein
EX $70   NM $115   MINT $175

❏ **Clown,** 1931, Chein
EX $70   NM $115   MINT $175

(Toy Shop File Photo)

❏ **Clown,** 1949, Chein, says bank on front
EX $35   NM $60   MINT $95

❏ **Drum,** 1930s, Chein
EX $35   NM $60   MINT $95

(Toy Shop File Photo)

❏ **Elephant,** 1950s, Chein
EX $55   NM $90   MINT $135

❏ **God Bless America,** 1930s, Chein, drum shaped
EX $30   NM $50   MINT $75

❏ **Happy Days Cash Register,** 1930s, Chein
EX $45   NM $80   MINT $120

❏ **Humpty Dumpty,** 1934, Chein
EX $60   NM $100   MINT $150

❏ **Log Cabin,** 1930s, Chein
EX $80   NM $130   MINT $200

❏ **Mascot Safe,** 1914, Chein
EX $35   NM $60   MINT $95

❏ **Mascot Safe,** 1914, Chein
EX $35   NM $55   MINT $85

(Toy Shop File Photo)

❏ **Monkey,** 1950s, Chein
EX $55   NM $90   MINT $135

❏ **New Deal,** 1930s, Chein
EX $50   NM $80   MINT $125

❏ **Prosperity Bank,** 1930s, Chein, pail shaped, w/band
EX $35   NM $60   MINT $95

❏ **Prosperity Bank,** 1930s, Chein, pail shaped, without band
EX $30   NM $50   MINT $75

❏ **Roly Poly,** 1940s, Chein
EX $135   NM $230   MINT $350

❏ **Scout,** 1931, Chein, cylinder
EX $100   NM $165   MINT $250

❏ **Three Little Pigs,** 1930s, Chein
EX $60   NM $100   MINT $150

❏ **Treasure Chest,** 1930s, Chein
EX $35   NM $60   MINT $90

❏ **Uncle Sam,** 1934, Chein, hat shaped
EX $50   NM $75   MINT $100

❏ **Uncle Wiggly,** 1950s, Chein
EX $50   NM $75   MINT $100

BUILDINGS AND ROOMS

❏ **Airport,** 1930s, Marx
EX $125   NM $200   MINT $300

❏ **Automatic Car Wash,** Marx
EX $135   NM $225   MINT $350

❏ **Automatic Firehouse with Fire Chief Car,** 1940s, Marx, friction car, firehouse w/plastic doors
EX $125   NM $200   MINT $300

❏ **Automatic Garage,** Marx, family car
EX $150   NM $245   MINT $375

❏ **Blue Bird Garage,** 1937, Marx
EX $150   NM $225   MINT $350

❏ **Brightlite Filling Station,** 1930s, Marx, pump w/round top says "Fresh Air"
EX $250   NM $425   MINT $650

❏ **Brightlite Filling Station,** 1930s, Marx, bottle-shaped gas pumps, battery-operated
EX $255   NM $425   MINT $650

❏ **Brightlite Filling Station,** late 1930s, Marx, rectangular shaped pumps, battery-operated
EX $255   NM $425   MINT $650

❏ **Bus Terminal,** 1937, Marx
EX $175   NM $295   MINT $450

❏ **Busy Airport Garage,** 1936, Marx
EX $195   NM $325   MINT $500

❏ **Busy Parking Lot,** 1937, Marx, five heavy gauge streamline autos
EX $235   NM $390   MINT $600

❏ **Busy Street,** 1935, Marx, six vehicles
EX $150   NM $300   MINT $475

❏ **City Airport,** 1938, Marx, w/two metal planes
EX $125   NM $200   MINT $300

❏ **Crossing Gate House,** Marx
EX $125   NM $200   MINT $300

❏ **Crossover Speedway,** 1938, Marx, litho buildings on bridge, two cars, litho drivers
EX $125   NM $200   MINT $295

❏ **Crossover Speedway,** 1941, Marx
EX $100   NM $175   MINT $250

❏ **Dick Tracy Automatic Police Station,** Marx, station and car
EX $375   NM $625   MINT $950

❏ **Gas Pump Island,** Marx
EX $125   NM $200   MINT $300

❏ **General Alarm Fire House,** 1938, Marx, wind-up alarm bell, steel chief car and patrol truck
EX $175   NM $295   MINT $450

❏ **Greyhound Bus Terminal,** 1938, Marx
EX $125   NM $200   MINT $300

❏ **Gull Service Station,** 1940s, Marx
EX $200   NM $300   MINT $475

❏ **Hollywood Bungalow House,** 1935, Marx
EX $175   NM $275   MINT $425

❏ **Home Town Drug Store,** 1930s, Marx
EX $175   NM $300   MINT $450

❏ **Home Town Favorite Store,** 1930s, Marx
EX $175   NM $300   MINT $450

❑ **Home Town Fire House,** 1930s, Marx
EX $175   NM $300   MINT $450

❑ **Home Town Grocery Store,** 1930s, Marx
EX $165   NM $275   MINT $425

❑ **Home Town Meat Market,** 1930s, Marx
EX $180   NM $300   MINT $465

❑ **Home Town Movie Theatre,** 1930s, Marx
EX $150   NM $250   MINT $375

❑ **Home Town Police Station,** 1930s, Marx
EX $150   NM $250   MINT $375

❑ **Home Town Savings Bank,** 1930s, Marx
EX $150   NM $250   MINT $375

❑ **Honeymoon Garage,** 1935, Marx
EX $165   NM $275   MINT $425

❑ **Lincoln Highway Set,** 1933, Marx, pumps, oil-grease rack, traffic light and car
EX $350   NM $600   MINT $900

❑ **Loop-the-Loop Auto Racer,** 1931, Marx
EX $150   NM $295   MINT $400

❑ **Magic Garage,** 1934, Marx, w/friction town car
EX $150   NM $250   MINT $375

❑ **Magic Garage,** 1934, Marx, litho garage, wind-up car
EX $150   NM $250   MINT $375

❑ **Main Street Station,** Marx, litho garage, 4" wind-up steel vehicles
EX $175   NM $275   MINT $425

❑ **Metal Service Station,** 1949-1950, Marx
EX $175   NM $275   MINT $425

❑ **Military Airport,** Marx
EX $100   NM $180   MINT $275

❑ **Model School House,** 1960s, Marx
EX $50   NM $80   MINT $125

❑ **Mot-O-Run 4 Lane Hi-Way,** 1949, Marx, cars, trucks, buses move on 27" electric track
EX $100   NM $180   MINT $275

❑ **New York World's Fair Speedway,** 1939, Marx, litho track, two red cars
EX $300   NM $500   MINT $750

❑ **Newlyweds' Bathroom,** 1920s, Marx
EX $100   NM $165   MINT $500

❑ **Newlyweds' Bedroom,** 1920s, Marx
EX $100   NM $165   MINT $500

❑ **Newlyweds' Dining Room,** 1920s, Marx
EX $100   NM $165   MINT $500

❑ **Newlyweds' Kitchen,** 1920s, Marx
EX $100   NM $165   MINT $500

❑ **Newlyweds' Library,** 1920s, Marx
EX $100   NM $165   MINT $500

❑ **Roadside Rest Service Station,** 1935, Marx, Laurel and Hardy at counter, w/stools in front
EX $625   NM $1050   MINT $1600

❑ **Roadside Rest Service Station,** 1938, Marx, Laurel and Hardy at counter, no stool in front
EX $550   NM $950   MINT $1450

❑ **Service Station,** 1929, Marx, two pumps, two friction vehicles
EX $300   NM $500   MINT $750

❑ **Service Station Gas Pumps,** Marx, wind-up
EX $125   NM $200   MINT $325

❑ **Sky Hawk Flyer,** Marx, wind-up, two planes, tower
EX $125   NM $200   MINT $325

❑ **Stunt Auto Racer,** 1931, Marx, two blue racers
EX $135   NM $225   MINT $350

❑ **Sunnyside Garage,** 1935, Marx
EX $255   NM $425   MINT $650

❑ **TV and Radio Station,** Marx
EX $150   NM $225   MINT $350

❑ **Universal Motor Repair Shop,** 1938, Marx, tin
EX $250   NM $425   MINT $650

❑ **Used Car Market,** 1939, Marx, base, several vehicles and signs
EX $250   NM $425   MINT $650

❑ **Whee-Whiz Auto Racer,** 1925, Marx, four 2" multicolored racers w/litho driver
EX $300   NM $500   MINT $750

JACK IN THE BOXES

(Toy Shop File Photo)

❑ **Flipper,** 1967, Mattel
EX $45   NM $75   MINT $125

❑ **Mother Goose,** Mattel
EX $10   NM $15   MINT $25

(Toy Shop File Photo)

❑ **Porky Pig,** 1965, Mattel
EX $40   NM $75   MINT $150

(Toy Shop File Photo)

❑ **Super Chief,** 1964, Mattel
EX $50   NM $200   MINT $300

(Toy Shop File Photo)

❑ **Tom & Jerry,** 1966, Mattel
  EX $25   **NM** $45   **MINT** $100

(Toy Shop File Photo)

❑ **Woody Woodpecker,** 1965, Mattel
  EX $40   **NM** $75   **MINT** $150

MISCELLANEOUS TOYS

❑ **1917 Ford,** Schuco
  EX $50   **NM** $80   **MINT** $125

❑ **Aha Truck,** Lehmann
  EX $470   **NM** $780   **MINT** $1200

❑ **Airplane and Pilot,** 1930s, Schuco, friction toy, oversized pilot
  EX $135   **NM** $225   **MINT** $350

❑ **Airplane Carousel,** 1930s, Wyandotte
  EX $100   **NM** $200   **MINT** $375

❑ **Ajax Acrobat,** Lehmann, does somersaults
  EX $850   **NM** $1425   **MINT** $2200

(Toy Shop File Photo)

❑ **Alabama Jigger,** 1920s, Lehmann, wind-up tap dancer on square base
  EX $500   **NM** $825   **MINT** $1500

❑ **Arithmetic Quiz Toy,** 1950s, Wolverine, math quiz machine
  EX $30   **NM** $50   **MINT** $75

❑ **Army Code Sender,** Marx, pressed steel
  EX $20   **NM** $35   **MINT** $50

❑ **Army Drummer,** 1930s, Chein, plunger-activated
  EX $70   **NM** $115   **MINT** $175

❑ **Artie the Clown in his Crazy Car,** Unique Art
  EX $250   **NM** $400   **MINT** $595

❑ **Automatic Airport,** Ohio Art, two planes circle tower
  EX $200   **NM** $325   **MINT** $500

❑ **Auton Boy & Cart,** Lehmann
  EX $200   **NM** $325   **MINT** $495

❑ **Baby Grand Piano,** Marx, w/piano-shaped music books
  EX $50   **NM** $100   **MINT** $250

❑ **Battleship,** 1930s, Wolverine
  EX $75   **NM** $125   **MINT** $200

❑ **Bavarian Boy,** 1950s, Schuco, tin and cloth boy w/beer mug
  EX $100   **NM** $200   **MINT** $300

❑ **Bavarian Dancing Couple,** Schuco, tin and cloth
  EX $105   **NM** $180   **MINT** $275

❑ **Big Shot,** Marx
  EX $75   **NM** $100   **MINT** $150

❑ **Black Man,** Schuco, tin and cloth
  EX $250   **NM** $425   **MINT** $650

❑ **Bombo the Monk,** Unique Art
  EX $125   **NM** $200   **MINT** $300

❑ **Capitol Hill Racer,** 1930s, Unique Art
  EX $125   **NM** $225   **MINT** $325

❑ **Captain of Kopenick,** early 1900s, Lehmann
  EX $625   **NM** $1050   **MINT** $1600

(Toy Shop File Photo)

❑ **Carnival Set,** 1930s, Wyandotte, diorama w/several rides on tin base
  EX $300   **NM** $500   **MINT** $1000

❑ **Casey the Cop,** Unique Art
  EX $350   **NM** $575   **MINT** $900

❑ **Cat Pushing Ball,** 1938, Marx, lever action, wood ball
  EX $75   **NM** $100   **MINT** $150

❑ **Circus Shooting Gallery,** 1960s, Ohio Art, w/gun and darts
  EX $50   **NM** $100   **MINT** $200

(Toy Shop File Photo)

❑ **Clown Playing Violin,** 1950s, Schuco, tin and cloth
  EX $135   **NM** $225   **MINT** $350

❑ **Coast Guard Plane,** 1960s, Ohio Art
  EX $50   **NM** $75   **MINT** $100

❑ **Combinato Convertible,** 1950s, Schuco
  EX $100   **NM** $175   **MINT** $250

❑ **Coney Island Roller Coaster,** 1950s, Ohio Art
  EX $125   **NM** $200   **MINT** $300

❑ **Crane,** Wolverine, red and blue
  EX $40   **NM** $65   **MINT** $100

❏ **Crocodile**, Lehmann, walks, mouth opens
EX $300　　NM $475　　MINT $725

❏ **Curvo Motorcycle,** 1950s, Schuco
EX $150　　NM $225　　MINT $350

❏ **Dancing Boy and Girl,** 1930s, Schuco, tin and cloth
EX $125　　NM $200　　MINT $300

❏ **Dancing Mice,** 1950s, Schuco, large and small mouse, tin and cloth
EX $135　　NM $225　　MINT $350

❏ **Dancing Monkey with Mouse,** 1950s, Schuco, tin and cloth
EX $125　　NM $210　　MINT $325

(Toy Shop File Photo)

❏ **Dancing Sailor**, Lehmann
EX $600　　NM $975　MINT $1500

(Toy Shop File Photo)

❏ **Dandy Jim**, Unique Art
EX $500　　NM $750　MINT $1000

❏ **Daredevil Motor Cop**, Unique Art
EX $300　　NM $450　　MINT $600

❏ **Delivery Van**, Lehmann, "Huntley & Palmers Biscuits"
EX $650　　NM $1075　MINT $1650

❏ **Disneyland Tea Set,** 1954, Chein, fifteen-piece set featuring Disney characters
EX $100　　NM $175　　MINT $500

❏ **Doll Stroller,** 1950s, Ohio Art, teddy bear design
EX $40　　NM $60　　MINT $80

❏ **Dolly's Washer,** 1930s, Chein, washing machine
EX $65　　NM $100　　MINT $300

❏ **Donald Duck Carpet Sweeper,** 1940s, Ohio Art, red w/Disney litho
EX $60　　NM $100　　MINT $250

❏ **Drum Major,** Wolverine, round base
EX $100　　NM $175　　MINT $250

❏ **Drum Major,** 1950, Wolverine
EX $100　　NM $150　　MINT $300

❏ **Drummer,** 1930s, Schuco, tin and cloth
EX $125　　NM $210　　MINT $325

❏ **Easter Basket**, Chein, nursery rhyme figures
EX $35　　NM $55　　MINT $100

❏ **Easter Egg,** 1938, Chein, tin, chicken on top, opens to hold candy
EX $35　　NM $55　　MINT $85
(Don Hultzman. Photo by Ron Chojnacki)

❏ **Examico 4001 Convertible,** 5-1/2", Schuco, maroon tin wind-up
EX $175　　NM $250　　MINT $375

❏ **Express Bus**, Wolverine
EX $125　　NM $210　　MINT $325

(Toy Shop File Photo)

❏ **Express Man & Cart**, Lehmann
EX $350　　NM $550　　MINT $850

❏ **Finnegan the Porter**, Unique Art
EX $200　　NM $300　　MINT $400

❏ **Flic 4520**, Schuco, traffic cop-type figure
EX $135　　NM $225　　MINT $350

❏ **Flying Bird**, Lehmann
EX $300　　NM $475　　MINT $750

❏ **Flying Circus**, Unique Art
EX $490　　NM $825　MINT $1250

❏ **Fox And Goose,** 1950s, Schuco, tin and cloth, fox holding goose in cage
EX $150　　NM $250　　MINT $375

(Scott Smiles. Photo by Mike Adams)

❏ **G.I. Joe and His Jouncing Jeep,** 1940s, Unique Art, wind-up
EX $200　　NM $275　　MINT $375

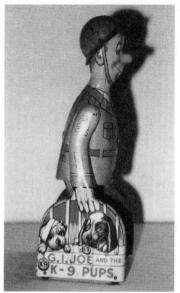

(Toy Shop File Photo)

❏ **G.I. Joe and His K-9 Pups**, Unique Art
EX $150　　NM $225　　MINT $300

❏ **Galop Race Car,** 1920s, Lehmann
EX $250　　NM $400　　MINT $600

❏ **Gertie the Galloping Goose**, Unique Art
EX $125　　NM $200　　MINT $300

❏ **Gustav The Climbing Miller**, Lehmann
EX $400　　NM $650　MINT $1000

❏ **Hee Haw**, Unique Art, donkey pulling milk cart
EX $150　　NM $225　　MINT $300

❏ **Helicopter, Toy Town Airways**, 1950s, Chein, friction drive
EX $55　　NM $90　　MINT $135

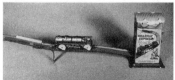

(Toy Shop File Photo)

❏ **Hillbilly Express,** 1930s, Unique Art
EX $150   NM $225   MINT $350

(Toy Shop File Photo)

❏ **Hobo Train**, Unique Art
EX $175   NM $295   MINT $450
(Scott Smiles)

❏ **Hoky Poky,** 1930s, Wyandotte, clowns on railcar
EX $200   NM $300   MINT $400

❏ **Hopping Rabbit,** 1950s, Marx, metal and plastic
EX $40   NM $65   MINT $100

❏ **Hott and Trott**, Unique Art
EX $900   NM $1500   MINT $2300

❏ **Howdy Doody & Buffalo Bob at Piano**, Unique Art
EX $750   NM $1300   MINT $2000

❏ **Indian in Headdress**, 1930s, Chein
EX $75   NM $125   MINT $200

❏ **Ito Sedan and Driver**, Lehmann
EX $525   NM $875   MINT $1350

(Bill Bertoia Auctions)

❏ **Jazzbo Jim**, Unique Art
EX $375   NM $625   MINT $1200

❏ **Jet Roller Coaster**, Wolverine
EX $125   NM $200   MINT $300

❏ **Juggling Clown**, Schuco, tin and cloth
EX $135   NM $225   MINT $350

❏ **Jumping Frog**, Marx
EX $40   NM $65   MINT $100

❏ **Jungle Eyes Shooting Gallery,** 1960s, Ohio Art, w/gun and darts
EX $50   NM $75   MINT $150

❏ **Jungle Man Spear**, Marx
EX $100   NM $150   MINT $200

(Bill Bertoia Auctions)

❏ **KADI**, Lehmann, Chinese men carrying box
EX $600   NM $975   MINT $2000

❏ **Kiddy Go-Round**, Unique Art
EX $175   NM $250   MINT $400

❏ **Kid-Go-Round**, Unique Art
EX $175   NM $250   MINT $400

❏ **King Kong**, Marx, on wheels, w/spring-loaded arms
EX $35   NM $60   MINT $95

❏ **Krazy Kar**, Unique Art
EX $200   NM $350   MINT $500

(Toy Shop File Photo)

❏ **Lehmann's Autobus**, Lehmann
EX $975   NM $1625   MINT $2500

(Toy Shop File Photo)

❏ **Li'l Abner and His Dogpatch Band**, Unique Art
EX $400   NM $700   MINT $1000

❏ **Li-La Car**, Lehmann, driver in rear, women passengers
EX $725   NM $1200   MINT $1850

(Toy Shop File Photo)

❏ **Lincoln Tunnel**, Unique Art
EX $250   NM $375   MINT $575

❏ **Little Red Riding Hood Tea Set,** 1920s, Ohio Art, seven-piece set
EX $100   NM $200   MINT $350

❏ **Marine**, Chein, hand on belt
EX $60   NM $100   MINT $150

❏ **Mauswagen**, Schuco, tin and cloth mice and wagon
EX $200   NM $325   MINT $500

❏ **Melody Organ Player**, Chein
EX $75   NM $125   MINT $175

❏ **Mercer Car No. 1225,** 1950s, Schuco
EX $100   NM $150   MINT $225

❏ **Merry-Go-Round**, Wolverine
EX $250   NM $400   MINT $600

❏ **Mexican Boy Tea Set,** 1940s, Ohio Art, nine-piece set
EX $75   NM $100   MINT $200

❏ **Mickey & Minnie Dancing**, Schuco, tin and cloth
EX $700   NM $1200   MINT $1800

❏ **Mickey Mouse Tray**, 1930s, Ohio Art
EX $50   NM $100   MINT $200

❏ **Mikado Family**, Lehmann
EX $1525   NM $2550   MINT $3900

❏ **Minstrel Man**, early 1900s, Lehmann
EX $350   NM $550   MINT $1000

❏ **Model Shooting Gallery**, 1930s, Wyandotte
EX $85   NM $200   MINT $300

❏ **Monk Drinking Beer**, Schuco, tin and cloth
EX $125   NM $200   MINT $300

❏ **Monkey Drummer,** 1950s, Schuco, tin and cloth
EX $125   NM $200   MINT $300

❏ **Monkey in Car,** 1930s, Schuco
EX $335   NM $550   MINT $850

❏ **Monkey on Scooter,** 1930s, Schuco, tin and cloth
EX $125   NM $200   MINT $300

❏ **Monkey Playing Violin,** 1950s, Schuco, tin and cloth
EX $125   NM $210   MINT $325

❏ **Mother Duck with Baby Ducks,** 1950s, Wyandotte, two baby ducks on wheels pulled behind mother ducks
EX $50   NM $100   MINT $125

❏ **Mother Goose Tea Set,** 1931, Ohio Art, seven-piece set
EX $90   NM $150   MINT $250

(Toy Shop File Photo)

TIN TOYS

❏ **Motorcycle Cop**, Unique Art
EX $300 NM $400 MINT $500

❏ **Musical Sail-Way Carousel**, Unique Art
EX $175 NM $300 MINT $450

❏ **Musical Top Clown**, 1950s, Chein, clown head handle
EX $75 NM $125 MINT $195

❏ **Mysterious Woodpecker**, Marx
EX $50 NM $80 MINT $125

❏ **Mystery Car**, Wolverine
EX $100 NM $165 MINT $250

❏ **New Century Cycle**, Lehmann, driver and black man w/umbrella
EX $700 NM $1175 MINT $1800

❏ **Ostrich Cart**, Lehmann
EX $380 NM $650 MINT $975

❏ **Paddy and the Pig**, Lehmann
EX $750 NM $1400 MINT $2000

❏ **Pathe Movie Camera**, 1930s, Marx
EX $55 NM $90 MINT $135

❏ **Pecking Goose, Witch and Cat**, Unique Art
EX $175 NM $300 MINT $450

❏ **Player Piano**, Chein, eight rolls
EX $195 NM $325 MINT $500

❏ **Quack Quack**, Lehmann, duck pulling babies
EX $300 NM $500 MINT $750

❏ **Rodeo Joe Crazy Car**, 1950s, Unique Art
EX $150 NM $250 MINT $400

❏ **Rollover Motorcycle Cop**, Unique Art
EX $300 NM $400 MINT $500

❏ **Rooster**, Marx
EX $60 NM $100 MINT $150
(Bill Bertoia Auctions)

❏ **Rooster and Rabbit**, Lehmann, rooster pulls rabbit on cart
EX $400 NM $625 MINT $975

❏ **Sand Toy**, Chein, monkey bends and twists
EX $30 NM $50 MINT $75

❏ **Sand Toy Set**, Chein, duck mold, sifter, frog on card
EX $30 NM $45 MINT $70

❏ **Sandy Andy Fullback**, Wolverine, kicking fullback
EX $175 NM $295 MINT $450

❏ **Schuco Turn Monkey on Suitcase**, 1950s, Schuco, tin and cloth
EX $125 NM $195 MINT $300

❏ **Scuba Diver**, Chein
EX $70 NM $120 MINT $185

❏ **Sea Lion**, Lehmann
EX $150 NM $250 MINT $375

❏ **Searchlight**, Marx
EX $40 NM $65 MINT $100

❏ **Sedan and Garage**, Lehmann
EX $350 NM $550 MINT $850

(Toy Shop File Photo)

❏ **See-Saw Sand Toy**, 1930s, Chein, bright colors, boy and girl on see-saw move
EX $55 NM $90 MINT $135

❏ **See-Saw Sand Toy**, 1930s, Chein, pastel colors, boy and girl on see-saw move
EX $70 NM $120 MINT $185

❏ **Shenandoah Zeppelin**, Lehmann
EX $155 NM $255 MINT $395

❏ **Skier**, 1920s, Lehmann, wind-up
EX $500 NM $850 MINT $1300

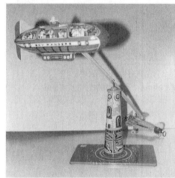

(Toy Shop File Photo)

❏ **Sky Rangers**, Unique Art
EX $300 NM $400 MINT $625

❏ **Snow White Stove**, 1960s, Wolverine
EX $20 NM $35 MINT $50

❏ **Space Ride**, Chein, tin litho, boxed, lever action w/music
EX $135 NM $230 MINT $350

❏ **Sparkler Toy**, Chein, on original card
EX $30 NM $50 MINT $75

❏ **Studio No. 1050 Race Car**, Schuco
EX $125 NM $175 MINT $250

❏ **Submarine**, Wolverine
EX $100 NM $165 MINT $250

❏ **Sunny and Tank**, Wolverine, yellow and green
EX $75 NM $130 MINT $200

❏ **Sunny Suzy Deluxe Washing Machine**, 1930s, Wolverine
EX $50 NM $95 MINT $200

❏ **Taxi**, 1920s, Lehmann
EX $450 NM $750 MINT $1150

❏ **Ten Little Indians Spinning Top**, Ohio Art
EX $15 NM $25 MINT $35

❏ **Three Little Pigs Spinning Top**, Ohio Art
EX $15 NM $25 MINT $35

❏ **Three Little Pigs Wind-Up Toy**, 1930s, Schuco, 4-1/2" pigs playing fiddle, fife and drum
EX $250 NM $500 MINT $775

❏ **Toto the Acrobat**, Marx
EX $100 NM $165 MINT $250

❏ **Trapeze Artist**, 1930s, Wyandotte
EX $125 NM $200 MINT $325

❏ **Tumbling Boy**, 1950s, Schuco, tin and cloth
EX $100 NM $165 MINT $250

❏ **Tut-Tut Car**, Lehmann, driver has horn
EX $850 NM $1300 MINT $2000

❏ **Watering Cans**, Ohio Art, many variations, value is for each
EX $25 NM $30 MINT $40

❏ **Wild West Bucking Bronco**, Lehmann
EX $575 NM $900 MINT $1400

❏ **Yellow Taxi**, 1940s, Wolverine
EX $150 NM $225 MINT $350

❏ **Yes-No Monkey**, Schuco
EX $175 NM $275 MINT $425

❏ **Zebra Cart "Dare Devil"**, 1920s, Lehmann
EX $400 NM $600 MINT $800

❏ **Zig-Zag**, Lehmann, handcar-type vehicle on oversized wheels
EX $800 NM $1300 MINT $2000

(Toy Shop File Photo)

❏ **Zilotone**, 1920s, Wolverine, clown on xylophone, w/three musical discs
EX $450 NM $700 MINT $900

MUSICAL TOYS

❑ **Hickory Dickory Dock Clock**, Mattel, crank; mouse climbs clock
EX $10   NM $25   MINT $40

❑ **Man on the Flying Trapeze**, Mattel, tin base, two metal rods holding trapeze man on top
EX $75   NM $100   MINT $145

❑ **Sing a Song of Sixpence**, Mattel, pie-shaped tin music box
EX $20   NM $35   MINT $65

TRAINS

❑ **Commodore Vanderbilt Train**, Marx, track, wind-up
EX $75   NM $125   MINT $190

❑ **Crazy Express Train,** 1960s, Marx, plastic and litho, wind-up
EX $115   NM $195   MINT $300

❑ **Disneyland Express,** 1950s, Marx, locomotive and three tin cars, wind-up
EX $255   NM $425   MINT $650

❑ **Disneyland Express, Casey Jr. Circus Train**, Marx, wind-up
EX $100   NM $165   MINT $250

❑ **Disneyland Train,** 1950, Marx, Goofy drives locomotive w/three tin cars, wind-up
EX $135   NM $225   MINT $350

❑ **Engine Train,** 1960s, Marx, ten cars, no track, HO-scale
EX $65   NM $110   MINT $170

❑ **Flintstones Choo Choo Train "Bedrock Express",** 1950s, Marx, wind-up
EX $235   NM $390   MINT $600

❑ **Glendale Depot Railroad Station Train,** 1930s, Marx
EX $235   NM $390   MINT $600

❑ **Mickey Mouse Express Train Set,** 1952, Marx
EX $235   NM $390   MINT $900

❑ **Mickey Mouse Meteor Train,** 1950s, Marx, four cars/engine, wind-up
EX $255   NM $425   MINT $650

❑ **Musical Choo-Choo,** 1966, Marx
EX $50   NM $75   MINT $100

❑ **Mystery Tunnel**, Marx, wind-up
EX $90   NM $145   MINT $225

❑ **New York Central Engine Train**, Marx, four cars
EX $200   NM $325   MINT $500

❑ **New York Circular with Train, with airplane**, 1928, Marx, wind-up
EX $490   NM $825   MINT $1250

❑ **New York Circular with Train, without airplane**, 1928, Marx, wind-up
EX $400   NM $700   MINT $1050

❑ **Popeye Express,** 1936, Marx, version of Honeymoon Express, w/airplane
EX $925   NM $1550   MINT $2400

❑ **Railroad Watch Tower**, Marx, electric light
EX $35   NM $60   MINT $90

❑ **Scenic Express Train Set,** 1950s, Marx, wind-up
EX $60   NM $105   MINT $160

(Toy Shop File Photo)

❑ **Subway Express,** 1954, Marx, w/plastic tunnel
EX $185   NM $310   MINT $475

❑ **Train Set,** 1950s, Marx, plastic locomotive, tin cars, wind-up
EX $60   NM $100   MINT $150

❑ **Trolley No. 200,** 1920s, Marx, headlight, bell, tin wind-up
EX $195   NM $325   MINT $500

WAGONS AND CARTS

❑ **Busy Delivery,** 1939, Marx, open three-wheel cart, wind-up
EX $300   NM $475   MINT $650

❑ **Farm Wagon,** 1940s, Marx, horse pulling wagon
EX $60   NM $100   MINT $150

❑ **Horse and Cart,** 1934, Marx, wind-up
EX $80   NM $130   MINT $200

❑ **Horse and Cart,** 1950s, Marx, w/driver
EX $50   NM $75   MINT $125

❑ **Horse and Cart with Clown Driver,** 1923, Marx, wind-up
EX $135   NM $225   MINT $350

❑ **Pinocchio Busy Delivery,** 1939, Marx, on unicycle facing two-wheel cart, wind-up
EX $275   NM $475   MINT $750

❑ **Popeye Horse and Cart**, Marx, wind-up
EX $335   NM $550   MINT $850

❑ **Rooster Pulling Wagon,** 1930s, Marx
EX $135   NM $225   MINT $350

❑ **Toyland's Farm Products Milk Wagon,** 1930s, Marx, wind-up
EX $145   NM $245   MINT $375

❑ **Two Donkeys Pulling Cart,** 1940s, Marx, w/driver, wind-up
EX $150   NM $225   MINT $300

❑ **Wagon with Two-Horse Team,** late 1940s, Marx, wind-up
EX $90   NM $145   MINT $225

WIND-UP TOYS

(Don Hultzman)

❑ **Acrobatic Marvel Monkey,** 1930s, Marx, balances on two chairs
EX $100   NM $175   MINT $250

❑ **Airplane, square-winged**, Chein, early tin
EX $100   NM $150   MINT $225

❑ **Amos 'n Andy Fresh Air Taxi,** 1930s, Marx, 5" x 8" long
EX $550   NM $1200   MINT $1800

(Toy Shop File Photo)

❑ **Amos 'n Andy Walkers,** 1930, Marx, values are for each
EX $650   NM $1000   MINT $1500

❑ **Army Cargo Truck,** 1920s, Chein
EX $235   NM $390   MINT $600

❑ **Army Plane**, Chein
EX $135   NM $230   MINT $350

❑ **Army Sergeant**, Chein
EX $70   NM $120   MINT $185

❑ **Army Truck**, Chein, open bed
EX $50   NM $75   MINT $100

❑ **Army Truck**, Chein, cannon on back
EX $50   NM $80   MINT $125

(Scott Smiles. Photo by Mike Adams)

TIN TOYS

❏ **Balky Mule,** 1948, Marx
EX $100   NM $175   MINT $250

❏ **Ballerina,** Marx
EX $90   NM $145   MINT $225

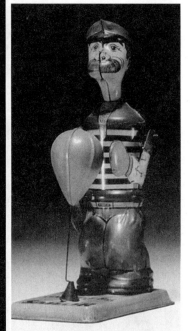

(Christie's East)

❏ **Barnacle Bill,** 1930s, Chein, looks like Popeye, waddles
EX $330   NM $550   MINT $850

❏ **Barney Rubble Riding Dino,** 1960s, Marx
EX $185   NM $310   MINT $475

(Toy Shop File Photo)

❏ **Bear,** 1938, Chein, w/hat, pants, shirt, bow tie
EX $55   NM $90   MINT $135

❏ **Bear Cyclist,** 1934, Marx
EX $70   NM $115   MINT $175

❏ **Bear Waddler,** 1960s, Marx
EX $50   NM $80   MINT $125

❏ **Beat It! The Komikal Kop,** 1930s, Marx
EX $200   NM $350   MINT $550

❏ **Big Parade,** 1928, Marx
EX $400   NM $700   MINT $1000

❏ **Big Three Aerial Acrobats,** 1920, Marx
EX $235   NM $390   MINT $600

❏ **Boy on Trapeze,** Marx
EX $90   NM $145   MINT $225

❏ **Bunny,** 1940s, Chein
EX $35   NM $60   MINT $100

❏ **Busy Bridge,** 1937, Marx, vehicles on bridge
EX $350   NM $575   MINT $895

(Toy Shop File Photo)

❏ **Busy Miners,** 1930s, Marx, miner's car
EX $200   NM $300   MINT $450

❏ **Butter and Egg Man,** Marx, wind-up walker
EX $700   NM $1000   MINT $1400

❏ **Cabin Cruiser,** 1940s, Chein
EX $35   NM $55   MINT $85

❏ **Captain America Wind-up Toy,** 1968, Marx, tin
EX $55   NM $90   MINT $140

❏ **Carter Climbing Monkey,** 1921, Marx
EX $115   NM $190   MINT $290

(Toy Shop File Photo)

❏ **Cat,** Chein, w/wood wheels
EX $40   NM $65   MINT $100

❏ **Charleston Trio,** 1926, Marx, man, boy and dog dancers on roof,
EX $525   NM $875   MINT $1350

❏ **Charlie McCarthy Bass Drummer,** 1939, Marx
EX $450   NM $750   MINT $1150

❏ **Charlie McCarthy Walker,** 1930s, Marx
EX $335   NM $550   MINT $850

❏ **Chick,** Chein, bright colored clothes, polka dot bow tie
EX $35   NM $55   MINT $85

❏ **Chicken Pushing Wheelbarrow,** 1930s, Chein
EX $35   NM $60   MINT $100

❏ **China Clipper,** Chein
EX $150   NM $250   MINT $350

❏ **Chipmunk,** Marx
EX $50   NM $80   MINT $125

❏ **Chompy the Beetle,** 1960s, Marx, w/action and sound
EX $60   NM $100   MINT $150

❏ **Clancy,** 1931, Marx, walker
EX $195   NM $325   MINT $500

(Toy Shop File Photo)

❏ **Climbing Fireman,** 1950s, Marx, tin and plastic
EX $135   NM $225   MINT $350

❏ **Clown Boxing,** Chein, tin
EX $235   NM $390   MINT $600

(Toy Shop File Photo)

❏ **Clown in Barrel,** 1930s, Chein, waddles
EX $175   NM $295   MINT $450

❏ **Clown with Parasol,** 1920s, Chein
  EX $105   NM $180   MINT $275

❏ **Coast Defense Revolving Airplane,**
  1929, Marx, circular w/three cannons
  EX $400   NM $600   MINT $900

❏ **Cowboy on Horse,** 1925, Marx
  EX $75   NM $125   MINT $175

❏ **Cowboy Rider,** 1930s, Marx, black
  horse version
  EX $165   NM $275   MINT $425

❏ **Cowboy Rider,** 1941, Marx, w/lariat on
  black horse
  EX $145   NM $245   MINT $375

❏ **Crazy Dora,** Marx
  EX $165   NM $275   MINT $425

❏ **Dan-Dee Dump Truck,** Chein
  EX $115   NM $195   MINT $300

(Toy Shop File Photo)

❏ **Dapper Dan Coon Jigger,** 1922, Marx
  EX $600   NM $900   MINT $1300

❏ **Dippy Dumper,** Marx
  EX $135   NM $225   MINT $350

(Toy Shop File Photo)

❏ **Disneyland Ferris Wheel,** 1940s, Chein
  EX $400   NM $650   MINT $1000

❏ **Disneyland Roller Coaster,** Chein
  EX $400   NM $600   MINT $900

❏ **Donald Duck and Scooter,** 1960s, Marx
  EX $90   NM $145   MINT $225

(Toy Shop File Photo)

❏ **Donald Duck Duet,** 1946, Marx, Donald
  and Goofy
  EX $500   NM $800   MINT $1100

❏ **Donald Duck Walker,** Marx, w/three
  nephews
  EX $100   NM $165   MINT $250

❏ **Donald the Skier,** 1940s, Marx, plastic,
  metal skis
  EX $175   NM $275   MINT $425

❏ **Dopey,** 1938, Marx, walker
  EX $310   NM $525   MINT $1000

❏ **Doughboy,** 1920s, Chein, tin litho, WWI
  soldier w/rifle
  EX $150   NM $250   MINT $375

❏ **Doughboy Walker,** Marx
  EX $225   NM $350   MINT $550

❏ **Drummer Boy,** 1930s, Chein, w/shako
  EX $100   NM $150   MINT $225

❏ **Drummer Boy,** 1939, Marx
  EX $275   NM $475   MINT $725

❏ **Duck,** 1930, Chein, waddles
  EX $50   NM $75   MINT $100

❏ **Duck,** 1930, Chein, waddles
  EX $50   NM $80   MINT $150

❏ **Dumbo,** 1941, Marx, rollover action
  EX $175   NM $295   MINT $450

❏ **Easter Rabbit,** Marx, holds Easter basket
  EX $70   NM $115   MINT $175

(Toy Shop File Photo)

❏ **Ferris Wheel,** 1930s, Chein, six compartments, ringing bell
  EX $250   NM $425   MINT $1000

(Toy Shop File Photo)

❏ **Ferris Wheel, The Giant Ride,** Chein
  EX $100   NM $250   MINT $500

❏ **Figaro (Pinocchio),** 1940, Marx, roll-
  over action
  EX $135   NM $225   MINT $350

❏ **Fireman on Ladder,** Marx
  EX $200   NM $300   MINT $450

❏ **Flipping Monkey,** Marx
  EX $80   NM $130   MINT $200

❏ **Flippo the Jumping Dog,** 1940, Marx
  EX $175   NM $275   MINT $425

❏ **Flutterfly,** 1929, Marx
  EX $90   NM $145   MINT $225

❏ **George the Drummer Boy,** 1930s,
  Marx, moving eyes
  EX $200   NM $325   MINT $500

(Toy Shop File Photo)

❏ **George the Drummer Boy,** 1930s, Marx, stationary eyes
EX $175   **NM** $300   **MINT** $450

❏ **Gobbling Goose,** 1940s, Marx, lays golden eggs
EX $125   **NM** $210   **MINT** $325

❏ **Golden Pecking Goose,** 1924, Marx
EX $135   **NM** $225   **MINT** $350

❏ **Goofy,** 1950s, Marx, tail spins, plastic
EX $125   **NM** $210   **MINT** $325

❏ **Goofy the Walking Gardener,** 1960, Marx, holds a wheelbarrow
EX $250   **NM** $425   **MINT** $650

❏ **Greyhound Bus,** Chein, wood tires
EX $90   **NM** $155   **MINT** $235

❏ **Handstand Clown,** Chein
EX $75   **NM** $125   **MINT** $200

(Scott Smiles)

❏ **Handstand Clown,** 1930s, Chein
EX $75   **NM** $125   **MINT** $200

❏ **Hap/Hop Ramp Walker,** 1950s, Marx
EX $40   **NM** $65   **MINT** $100

❏ **Happy Hooligan,** 1932, Chein, tin litho
EX $195   **NM** $325   **MINT** $500

❏ **Harold Lloyd Funny Face,** 1928, Marx, walker
EX $275   **NM** $475   **MINT** $600

❏ **Hercules Ferris Wheel,** Chein
EX $150   **NM** $250   **MINT** $400

❏ **Hey Hey the Chicken Snatcher,** 1926, Marx, black man w/chicken
EX $850   **NM** $1250   **MINT** $200

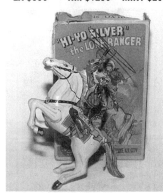

(Toy Shop File Photo)

❏ **Hi-Yo Silver and the Lone Ranger,** 1938, Marx
EX $200   **NM** $325   **MINT** $575

❏ **Honeymoon Cottage, Honeymoon Express 7,** Marx, square base
EX $125   **NM** $200   **MINT** $300

❏ **Honeymoon Express,** 1927, Marx, old-fashioned train on circular track
EX $225   **NM** $375   **MINT** $575

❏ **Honeymoon Express,** 1940s, Marx, circular train and plane
EX $225   **NM** $375   **MINT** $550

(Continental Hobby House)

❏ **Honeymoon Express,** 1947, Marx, streamlined train on circular track
EX $200   **NM** $300   **MINT** $475

(Toy Shop File Photo)

❏ **Hop-A-Long Cassidy Rocker,** 1950s, Marx
EX $90   **NM** $150   **MINT** $325

❏ **Hoppo the Monkey,** 1925, Marx, plays cymbals
EX $100   **NM** $165   **MINT** $250

(Toy Shop File Photo)

❏ **Howdy Doody,** 1950, Marx, does jig and Clarabell sits at piano
EX $525   **NM** $875   **MINT** $1350

❏ **Howdy Doody,** 1950, Marx, plays banjo and moves head
EX $250   **NM** $425   **MINT** $625

❏ **Indian in Headdress,** 1930s, Chein, red
EX $50   **NM** $80   **MINT** $125

❏ **Jazzbo Jim,** 1920s, Marx
EX $375   **NM** $625   **MINT** $1000

❏ **Jetsons Figure,** 1960s, Marx
EX $75   **NM** $150   **MINT** $200

❏ **Jiminy Cricket Pushing Bass Fiddle,** Marx, walker
EX $100   **NM** $175   **MINT** $225

(Toy Shop File Photo)

❏ **Jiving Jigger,** 1950, Marx
EX $135   **NM** $225   **MINT** $350

(Toy Shop File Photo)

❑ **Joe Penner and His Duck Goo-Goo,** 1934, Marx
EX $375   NM $625   MINT $900

❑ **Jumbo The Climbing Monkey,** 1923, Marx
EX $135   NM $225   MINT $425

❑ **Jumping Rabbit,** 1925, Chein
EX $100   NM $165   MINT $250

❑ **Junior Bus,** Chein, yellow
EX $70   NM $115   MINT $175

❑ **Knockout Champs Boxing Toy,** 1930s, Marx
EX $175   NM $300   MINT $450

❑ **Leopard,** 1950, Marx, growls and walks
EX $65   NM $105   MINT $165

❑ **Little King Walkers,** 1963, Marx, 3" tall
EX $50   NM $80   MINT $125

❑ **Little Orphan Annie and Sandy,** 1930s, Marx
EX $275   NM $475   MINT $725

❑ **Little Orphan Annie Skipping Rope,** Marx
EX $200   NM $300   MINT $425

❑ **Little Orphan Annie's Dog Sandy,** Marx, tin litho
EX $125   NM $200   MINT $275

❑ **Mack Hercules Motor Express,** Chein, tin litho
EX $235   NM $385   MINT $595

❑ **Mack Hercules Truck,** Chein
EX $165   NM $275   MINT $425

❑ **Mad Russian Drummer,** Marx
EX $225   NM $375   MINT $500

❑ **Main Street,** 1929, Marx, street scene w/moving cars, traffic cop
EX $300   NM $500   MINT $700

❑ **Mammy's Boy,** 1929, Marx, wind-up walker
EX $310   NM $525   MINT $795

❑ **Mark 1 Cabin Cruiser,** 1957, Chein
EX $35   NM $60   MINT $95

❑ **Mechanical Aquaplane, No. 39,** 1932, Chein, boat-like pontoons
EX $100   NM $165   MINT $250

❑ **Mechanical Fish,** 1940s, Chein
EX $30   NM $50   MINT $75

❑ **Merry-Go-Round,** Chein, 11" w/swan chairs
EX $475   NM $775   MINT $1200

❑ **Merrymakers Band,** 1931, Marx, without marquee, mouse band
EX $600   NM $1000   MINT $1600
(Scott Smiles)

❑ **Merrymakers Band,** 1931, Marx, w/marquee, mouse band
EX $700   NM $1200   MINT $1800

❑ **Mickey Mouse,** Marx
EX $200   NM $400   MINT $600

❑ **Minnie Mouse,** Marx
EX $200   NM $400   MINT $600

❑ **Minnie Mouse in Rocker,** 1950s, Marx
EX $275   NM $450   MINT $650

❑ **Minstrel Figure,** Marx
EX $175   NM $295   MINT $450

❑ **Monkey Cyclist,** 1923, Marx
EX $100   NM $175   MINT $275

❑ **Moon Creature,** Marx
EX $135   NM $225   MINT $350

❑ **Moon Mullins and Kayo on Handcar,** 1930s, Marx
EX $335   NM $550   MINT $850

❑ **Mortimer Snerd Bass Drummer,** 1939, Marx
EX $850   NM $1450   MINT $2200

❑ **Mortimer Snerd Hometown Band,** 1935, Marx
EX $800   NM $1200   MINT $2000

❑ **Mortimer Snerd Walker,** 1939, Marx
EX $185   NM $300   MINT $475

❑ **Mother Goose,** 1920s, Marx
EX $150   NM $250   MINT $400

❑ **Mother Penguin with Baby Penguin on Sled,** 1950s, Marx
EX $35   NM $55   MINT $85

❑ **Motorboat,** 1950s, Chein
EX $40   NM $65   MINT $100

❑ **Motorboat,** 1950s, Chein, crank action
EX $35   NM $60   MINT $90

(Toy Shop File Photo)

❑ **Musical Aero Swing,** 1940s, Chein
EX $300   NM $500   MINT $750

❑ **Musical Circus Horse,** 1939, Marx, pull toy, metal drum rolls w/chimes
EX $80   NM $130   MINT $200

❑ **Musical Merry-Go-Round,** Chein, small version
EX $155   NM $260   MINT $400

❑ **Musical Toy Church,** 1937, Chein, crank music box
EX $90   NM $145   MINT $225

❑ **Mystery Cat,** 1931, Marx
EX $100   NM $165   MINT $250

❑ **Mystery Pluto,** 1948, Marx
EX $100   NM $165   MINT $250

❑ **Nodding Goose,** Marx
EX $75   NM $120   MINT $150

❑ **Pecos Bill,** 1950s, Marx, twirls rope, plastic
EX $100   NM $200   MINT $300

❑ **Peggy Jane Speedboat,** Chein
EX $50   NM $75   MINT $100

❑ **Pelican,** Chein
EX $100   NM $165   MINT $250

❑ **Penguin in Tuxedo,** 1940s, Chein
EX $50   NM $100   MINT $125

(Scott Smiles)

❑ **Pig,** Chein
EX $35   NM $60   MINT $95

❑ **Pikes Peak Mountain Climber,** Marx, vehicle on track
EX $325   NM $525   MINT $800

❑ **Pinched,** 1927, Marx, square based, open circular track
EX $350   NM $500   MINT $775

❑ **Pinocchio,** 1938, Marx
EX $275   NM $450   MINT $700

❑ **Pinocchio,** 1950s, Marx
EX $250   NM $425   MINT $650

❑ **Pinocchio the Acrobat,** 1939, Marx
EX $335   NM $550   MINT $850

❏ **Pinocchio Walker,** 1930s, Marx, stationary eyes
EX $250   NM $425   MINT $650

❏ **Pinocchio Walker,** 1930s, Marx, animated eyes
EX $275   NM $450   MINT $700

(Toy Shop File Photo)

❏ **Playland Merry-Go-Round,** 1930s, Chein
EX $500   NM $850   MINT $1200

❏ **Playland Whip, No. 340,** Chein, four bump cars, driver's head wobbles
EX $500   NM $700   MINT $1100

(Ed Hayes Antique Toys)

❏ **Pluto Drum Major,** Marx
EX $235   NM $390   MINT $595

❏ **Pluto Watch Me Roll-Over,** 1939, Marx
EX $165   NM $275   MINT $425

❏ **Poor Fish,** 1936, Marx
EX $70   NM $115   MINT $175

(Toy Shop File Photo)

❏ **Popeye Acrobat,** Marx
EX $2000   NM $3500   MINT $5500

❏ **Popeye and Olive Oyl Jiggers,** 1936, Marx
EX $700   NM $1175   MINT $1800

❏ **Popeye Express,** 1932, Marx, w/trunk and wheelbarrow
EX $200   NM $500   MINT $800

❏ **Popeye Handcar,** 1935, Marx
EX $775   NM $1300   MINT $2000

❏ **Popeye in Barrel,** Chein
EX $400   NM $650   MINT $1000

❏ **Popeye the Champ,** 1936, Marx, tin and celluloid
EX $1800   NM $2800   MINT $4000

❏ **Popeye the Heavy Hitter,** Chein, bell and mallet
EX $2550   NM $4225   MINT $6500

(Toy Shop File Photo)

❏ **Popeye the Pilot,** 1936, Marx
EX $575   NM $775   MINT $1175

(Toy Shop File Photo)

❏ **Popeye with Punching Bag,** Chein
EX $1000   NM $1625   MINT $2500

❏ **Porky Pig Cowboy with Lariat,** 1949, Marx
EX $280   NM $475   MINT $725

❏ **Porky Pig with Rotating Umbrella,** 1939, Marx, w/or without top hat
EX $300   NM $525   MINT $800

❏ **Red Cap Porter,** Marx
EX $375   NM $625   MINT $950

(Toy Shop File Photo)

❏ **Red the Iceman,** Marx
EX $1350   NM $2275   MINT $3500
(Don Hultzman)

❏ **Ride 'Em Cowboy,** Marx
EX $90   NM $145   MINT $225

❏ **Ride-A-Rocket Carnival Ride,** 1950s, Chein, four rockets
EX $450   NM $750   MINT $1000

(Toy Shop File Photo)

❏ **Ring-A-Ling Circus,** 1925, Marx
EX $1100   NM $1700   MINT $2200

❏ **Roadster,** 1925, Chein
EX $50   NM $80   MINT $125

❏ **Rodeo Joe,** 1933, Marx
EX $200   NM $300   MINT $450

❏ **Roller Coaster,** 1938, Chein, includes two cars
EX $250   NM $400   MINT $600
(Don Hultzman. Photo by Ron Chojnacki)

❏ **Roller Coaster,** 1950s, Chein, includes two cars
EX $300   NM $450   MINT $700

❏ **Royal Blue Line Coast to Coast Service,** Chein
EX $800   NM $685   MINT $1050

❏ **Running Scottie,** 1938, Marx
EX $70   NM $115   MINT $175

❏ **Sandmill,** Chein, beach scene on side
EX $90   NM $145   MINT $225

❏ **Santa's Elf,** 1925, Chein, boxed
EX $235   NM $390   MINT $600

❏ **Sea Plane,** 1930s, Chein, silver, red, and blue
EX $115   NM $195   MINT $300

❏ **Seal,** Chein, balancing barbells
EX $90   NM $145   MINT $225

❏ **Ski-Boy,** 1930s, Chein
EX $200   NM $300   MINT $450

❏ **Smitty Riding a Scooter,** 1932, Marx
EX $500   NM $850   MINT $1300

❏ **Smokey Joe the Climbing Fireman,** 1930s, Marx
EX $325   NM $475   MINT $575

❏ **Smokey Sam the World Fireman,** 1950s, Marx
EX $125   NM $210   MINT $325

❏ **Snappy the Miracle Dog,** 1931, Marx, w/dog house
EX $80   NM $130   MINT $200

❑ **Speedboat**, Chein
EX $90   NM $145   MINT $225

❑ **Spic and Span,** 1924, Marx, black
drummer and dancer
EX $500   NM $850   MINT $1300

❑ **Stop, Look and Listen,** 1927, Marx, circular track toy
EX $300   NM $500   MINT $750

❑ **Streamline Speedway**, Marx, two racers on track
EX $80   NM $130   MINT $200

❑ **Subway Express,** 1950s, Marx
EX $65   NM $110   MINT $170

(Toy Shop File Photo)

❑ **Superman Holding Airplane,** 1940,
Marx
EX $875   NM $1450   MINT $2250

❑ **Superman Turnover Tank,** 1940, Marx,
2-1/2 x 3" x 4" long tin wind-up
EX $500   NM $1200   MINT $2500

❑ **Tidy Tim Streetcleaner,** 1933, Marx,
pushes wagon
EX $175   NM $295   MINT $450

(Ed Hyers Antique Toys)

❑ **Tom Tom Jungle Boy**, Marx
EX $100   NM $150   MINT $200

❑ **Touring Car**, Chein
EX $60   NM $100   MINT $150

(Scott Smiles)

❑ **Tumbling Monkey,** 1942, Marx
EX $75   NM $125   MINT $190

❑ **Tumbling Monkey and Trapeze,** 1932,
Marx
EX $135   NM $225   MINT $350

❑ **Turtle with Native on Its Back,** 1940s,
Chein
EX $165   NM $275   MINT $425

❑ **Walking Popeye,** 1932, Marx, carrying
parrots in cages
EX $400   NM $600   MINT $800

❑ **Walking Porter,** 1930s, Marx, carries
two suitcases
EX $205   NM $340   MINT $525

❑ **Wee Running Scottie,** 1930s, Marx
EX $125   NM $175   MINT $250

❑ **Wee Running Scottie,** 1952, Marx
EX $100   NM $150   MINT $225

❑ **Wise Pluto**, Marx
EX $100   NM $165   MINT $250

❑ **Woody Car,** 1940s, Chein, red
EX $100   NM $165   MINT $250

❑ **WWI Soldier**, Marx, prone position
w/rifle
EX $50   NM $75   MINT $125

❑ **Xylophonist**, Marx
EX $75   NM $125   MINT $200

(Toy Shop File Photo)

❑ **Yellow Cab**, Chein
EX $200   NM $300   MINT $400

❑ **Yellow Taxi**, Chein, orange and black
EX $135   NM $225   MINT $350

❑ **Zippo Monkey,** 1938, Marx
EX $100   NM $150   MINT $200

TV Toys

From the show, "The Fall Guy," a slot car set by Aurora, about $90 MIP.

By Dan Stearns

If you have a favorite television show (or, if you're like me, more than one) chances are there's a toy to commemorate it. Like radio, TV was a medium of advertising and marketing—and there was no better way to tie that in with a program than with toys.

Traditionally, the TV show came first—Hopalong Cassidy, The Lone Ranger, Dragnet, The Brady Bunch, etc… and toy followed. Not always, though. By the 1980s, more toys were being produced with a cartoon that acted as a combination adventure/advertisement for an already existing item. G.I. Joe, Transformers, Smurfs, Masters of the Universe, to name just a few, are Saturday morning cartoon shows that didn't exist until the release of the toy made it possible.

By the 1990s, TV toys were also being produced as restaurant premiums—often toys were made to represent shows that the audience never saw in first-run form. The Cartoon Network, for instance, made the great old Hanna-Barbera cartoons of the 1960s popular to a much younger crowd. Contemporary shows weren't left in the cold at all, though. Plenty of X-Files, Simpsons and Buffy the Vampire Slayer tie-ins made it to store shelves.

These days, nostalgia (and curiosity from younger fans) fuels an ever-growing market of toys and TV-show tie-ins. Corgi and Johnny Lightning, for instance, have both released Black Beauty car models from the Green Hornet series. Another Playing Mantis company, Polar Lights, does a great job of making model kits for Lost In Space, the Jetsons and Batman (series) vehicles.

It might have been "farm living," but that was no reason the Douglas's couldn't dress well, as this paper doll set proves.

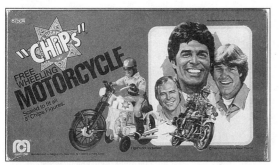

Perfectly set for Ponch and Jon to set off on patrol, a CHiPs motorcycle by Mego, late 1970s.

Plush Drooper doll from "The Banana Splits" was released in the 1960s and has a $95 mint value.

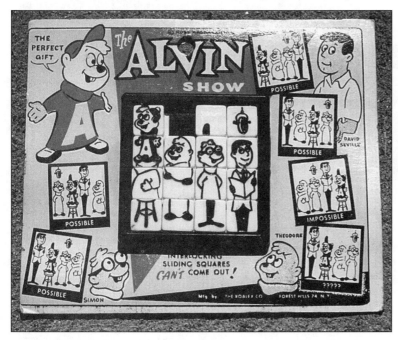

This Alvin puzzle game is almost as difficult as the little chipmunk himself.

ADDAMS FAMILY

❑ **Gomez Hand Puppet,** 1965, Ideal
EX $50   NM $120   MIP $250

❑ **Lurch Figure,** 1964, Remco
EX $80   NM $175   MIP $350

❑ **Morticia Figure,** 1964, Remco
EX $100   NM $200   MIP $675

❑ **Morticia Halloween Costume,** 1964,
Ben Cooper, painted hair
EX $40   NM $100   MIP $200

❑ **Morticia Halloween Costume,** 1964,
Ben Cooper, w/hair
EX $50   NM $125   MIP $250

❑ **Morticia Hand Puppet,** 1965, Ideal
EX $50   NM $130   MIP $260

❑ **Thing Bank,** 1964, plastic, battery-
operated
EX $40   NM $150   MIP $225

❑ **Uncle Fester Figure,** 1964, Remco
EX $100   NM $250   MIP $600

ALVIN SHOW

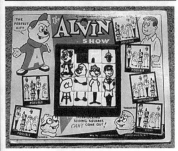

(Toy Shop File Photo)

❑ **Sliding Squares Game,** 1960s, Roalex
Co., Sliding squares form a variety of
"possible" solutions
EX $25   NM $45   MIP n/a

A-TEAM

(Toy Shop File Photo)

❑ **A-Team Combat Headquarters Set,**
1980s, Galoob, Includes 3-3/4" figures
of Hannibal, Face, B.A. Baracus, Murdock and gear, including inflatable raft,
machine guns, flag and tent
EX $40   NM $85   MIP n/a

❑ **A-Team Rocket Ball Target Set,** 1983,
gumballs w/gun and target
EX $5   NM $10   MIP $20

❑ **A-Team Shrinky Dinks Set,** 1980s
EX $5   NM $10   MIP $20

AVENGERS

(Toy Shop File Photo)

❑ **Shooting Game,** 1960s, Merit
EX $20   NM $45   MIP n/a

(Toy Shop File Photo)

❑ **Steed Sword Stick,** 1960s, Lone Star,
Toy of John Steed's secret cane/sword
combo
EX $35   NM $70   MIP n/a

BANANA SPLITS

(Toy Shop File Photo)

❑ **4 The Banana Splits Puzzle,** 1969,
Whitman, frame tray
EX $25   NM $55   MIP $85

❑ **Banana Band,** 1973, Larami, horn, sax,
mouth harp
EX $25   NM $60   MIP $120

❑ **Banana Buggy Model Kit,** 1968, Aurora
EX $60   NM $200   MIP $325

❑ **Banana Splits Bingo Costume,** 1968,
Ben Cooper
EX $60   NM $175   MIP $300

(Toy Shop File Photo)

❑ **Banana Splits Doll,** 1960s, Sutton, 12"
tall plush Drooper
EX $45   NM $95   MIP $200

❑ **Banana Splits Kut-Up Kit,** 1973, Larami
EX $20   NM $40   MIP $75

❑ **Banana Splits Mug,** 1969, plastic yellow dog mug
EX $20   NM $40   MIP $65

❑ **Banana Splits Record,** 1969, Kellogg's
EX $20   NM $90   MIP $175

❑ **Paint-By-Number Set,** 1969, Hasbro
EX $45   NM $80   MIP $150

❑ **Talking Telephone,** 1969, Hasbro
EX $70   NM $175   MIP $350

BEANY AND CECIL

❑ **Beany and Cecil and Their Pals Record
Player,** 1961, Vanity Fair
EX $80   NM $200   MIP $375

❑ **Beany and Cecil Carrying Case,** 1960s,
9" diameter w/strap, vinyl-covered cardboard
EX $40   NM $85   MIP $100

❑ **Beany and Cecil Gun,** 1961, Mattel,
w/propeller disks
EX $30   NM $150   MIP $200

❑ **Beany and Cecil Puzzle,** 1961, Playskool, wooden frame tray
EX $25   NM $65   MIP $100

❑ **Beany and Cecil Skill Ball,** 1960s, colorful tin w/wood frame
EX $30   NM $80   MIP $120

❑ **Beany and Cecil Travel Case,** 1960s,
8" tall, round, red vinyl w/zipper and
strap
EX $25   NM $55   MIP $95

❑ **Beany and Cecil Travel Case,** 1960s,
square, 4-1/2" x 3-1/2" x 3" red vinyl, carrying strap, illustrated w/characters
EX $30   NM $70   MIP $100

❑ **Beany and His Magic Set Book,** 1953,
Tell-a-Tale Book
EX $10   NM $20   MIP $50

❑ **Beany Doll,** 1963, Mattel, 15", non-talking
EX $20   NM $100   MIP $150

❑ **Beany Figure,** 1984, Caltoy, 8" tall
EX $8   NM $20   MIP $40

❑ **Beany Talking Doll,** 1950s, Mattel, 17"
tall, stuffed cloth, vinyl head w/pull
string
EX $90   NM $250   MIP $425

❑ **Bob Clampetts' Beany Coloring Book,**
1960s, Whitman
EX $15   NM $75   MIP $150

❑ **Captain Huffenpuff Puzzle,** 1961, large
EX $25   NM $85   MIP $120

❑ **Cecil and His Disguise Kit,** 1962, Mattel, 17" tall plush Cecil w/disguise wigs,
mustaches, etc.
EX $30   NM $90   MIP $175

❑ **Cecil in the Music Box,** 1961, Mattel,
jack-in-the-box
EX $80   NM $225   MIP $375

❏ **Cecil Soaky**, 8-1/2" tall, plastic
EX $25   NM $85   MIP $150

❏ **Leakin' Lena Boat**, 1962, Irwin, plastic and wood
EX $50   NM $110   MIP $225

❏ **Leakin' Lena Pound 'N Pull Toy**, 1960s, Pressman, wood
EX $60   NM $125   MIP $250

BEN CASEY

❏ **Ben Casey Pencils**, 1962, Hassenfeld Bros., ten red/white pencils on card
EX $15   NM $30   MIP $65

BEN CASEY, M.D.

(Toy Shop File Photo)

❏ **Play Hosptial Set**, 1960s, Transogram, Includes doctor bag, microscope, stethascope and more
EX $50   NM $100   MIP n/a

BEVERLY HILLBILLIES

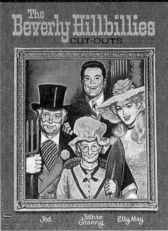

(Toy Shop File Photo)

❏ **Paper cut-outs**, 1960s, Whitman, Includes Jed, Jethro, Granny and Elly May
EX $40   NM $80   MIP n/a

BEWITCHED

(Toy Shop File Photo)

❏ **Bewitched Samantha Doll**, 1967, Ideal, 12-1/2" tall
EX $180   NM $395   MIP $750

❏ **Bewitched Tabitha Paper Doll Set**, 1966, Magic Wand, 11" cardboard doll, clothes
EX $30   NM $75   MIP $150

BIONIC WOMAN

(Toy Shop File Photo)

❏ **Play-Doh Action Play Set**, 1970s, Kenner, Includes molds for making Play-Doh characters from the show, 3 containers of Play-Doh, plastic mat and six-wheeled vehicle
EX $25   NM $40   MIP n/a

BOZO

(Toy Shop File Photo)

❏ **Bozo Record Player**
EX $45   NM $90   MIP n/a

❏ **Bozo the Clown Beach Towel**, 1960s, 16" x 24"
EX $8   NM $15   MIP $35

❏ **Bozo the Clown Doll**, 1970s
EX $10   NM $30   MIP $60

❏ **Bozo the Clown Figure**, 1970s, vinyl, 5" tall
EX $5   NM $15   MIP $30

❏ **Bozo the Clown Push Button Marionette**, 1962, Knickerbocker
EX $25   NM $45   MIP $85

❏ **Bozo the Clown Puzzle**, 1965, Whitman, #4516, Model No. 4516
EX $10   NM $25   MIP $50

❏ **Bozo the Clown Slide Puzzle**, 1960s
EX $15   NM $40   MIP $75

❏ **Bozo the Clown Soaky**, 1960s, Palmolive
EX $15   NM $45   MIP $75

❏ **Bozo Trick Trapeze**, 1960s, red base
EX $15   NM $35   MIP $65

BRADY BUNCH

❏ **Brady Bunch Halloween Costume**, 1970s, Collegeville, smock reads "One of The Brady Bunch"
EX $40   NM $90   MIP $150

❏ **Brady Bunch Kite Fun Book**, 1976, Pacific Gas and Electric
EX $15   NM $35   MIP $75

❏ **Brady Bunch Paper Dolls Cut-Out Book**, 1973, Whitman
EX $30   NM $85   MIP $150

❏ **Brady Bunch Puzzle**, frame tray
EX $25   NM $45   MIP $80

❏ **Brady Bunch Trading Cards**, 1971, Topps, 55 cards
EX $250   NM $550   MIP $800

❏ **Kitty Karry-All Doll**, 1969, Remco
EX $80   NM $160   MIP $325

CAPTIAN KANGAROO

(Toy Shop File Photo)

❏ **Captain Kangaroo Duck Pin Game**, 1950s, Gardner, With self returning ball
EX $35   NM $75   MIP n/a

❑ **Captain Kangaroo Presto Slate,** 1960s, Fairchild, slate on illustrated card, several versions
  EX $12   NM $30   MIP $40

❑ **Captain Kangaroo Puzzle,** 1960, Whitman, #4446, frame tray, Model No. 4446
  EX $10   NM $30   MIP $60

CHARLIE'S ANGELS

❑ **Hide-A-Way House,** 1970s, Hasbro, Revolving five-sided dollhouse for Charlie's Angels figures
  EX $80   NM $150   MIP n/a

❑ **Target Set,** 1970s, Placo Toys, Includes 2 safety guns, 6 safety darts and a knockdown target
  EX $40   NM $85   MIP n/a

CHiPs

❑ **Colorforms Play Set,** 1970s, Colorforms
  EX $30   NM $55   MIP n/a

❑ **Free Wheeling Motorcycle,** 1970s, Mego, Made to fit Mego's 8" figures from the series
  EX $35   NM $50   MIP n/a

❑ **Police Set,** 1970s, HG Toys, Includes snub-nose revolver, badge, sunglasses (of course!), handcuffs and holster
  EX $27   NM $60   MIP n/a

COMBAT!

❑ **Official Play Set,** 1960s, Marx, Supercool toy soldier set includes tanks, howitzers, army trucks, tanks, personnel carriers, soldiers and landing craft. This same set was re-packaged in the 1970s without the "Combat" TV-show name or tie-in
  EX $40   NM $85   MIP n/a

DOBIE GILLIS

❑ **Paint-N-Press Art Set,** 1960s, Includes watercolors and instructions
  EX $15   NM $25   MIP n/a

DR. KILDARE

❑ **Dr. Kildare Photo Scrapbook,** 1962
  EX $10   NM $25   MIP $50

DRAGNET

❑ **Dragnet Badge 714,** 1955, Knickerbocker, 2-1/2" bronze finish badge in yellow box w/illustration of Jack Webb, box bottom has ID card
  EX $45   NM $90   MIP $80

(Toy Shop File Photo)

❏ **Dragnet Badge 714 Target Game,** 1950s, Includes 3 guns, corks and darts and litho metal target. $2.98 original price!
EX $75   NM $150   MIP n/a

(Toy Shop File Photo)

❏ **Dragnet Crime Lab,** 1950s, Transogram, "A complete crime detection outfit for the junior detective"
EX $120   NM $225   MIP n/a

DUKES OF HAZZARD

(Toy Shop File Photo)

❏ **Daisy's Jeep,** 1970s, Includes "Dixie," a white and brown CJ5 Jeep and one Daisy Duke figure
EX $35   NM $50   MIP n/a

FAMILY AFFAIR

(Toy Shop File Photo File)

❏ **5 Family Affair Paper Dolls,** Whitman
EX $30   NM $45   MIP $55

❏ **Buffy Halloween Costume,** 1970, Ben Cooper
EX $20   NM $40   MIP $80

❏ **Buffy Make-Up and Hairstyling Set,** 1971, Amsco
EX $20   NM $40   MIP $80

❏ **Buffy with Mrs. Beasley Dolls,** 1967, Mattel, 6" Buffy w/smaller Mrs. Beasley
EX $30   NM $65   MIP $115

❏ **Family Affair Cartoon Kit,** 1970, Colorforms
EX $12   NM $25   MIP $50

❏ **Family Affair Puzzle,** 1970, Whitman
EX $12   NM $30   MIP $60

❏ **Mrs. Beasley Paper Dolls,** 1970s, Whitman, several variations
EX $12   NM $30   MIP $60

❏ **Mrs. Beasley Rag Doll,** 1973, Mattel, 14"
EX $12   NM $25   MIP $45

❏ **Talking Mrs. Beasley Doll,** 1967, Mattel
EX $50   NM $95   MIP $210

FLINTSTONES

❏ **Baby Puss Figure,** 1961, Knickerbocker, 10" tall, vinyl
EX $35   NM $75   MIP $135

❏ **Bamm-Bamm Bank,** 1960s, 11" tall, hard plastic figure sitting on turtle
EX $20   NM $45   MIP $75

❏ **Bamm-Bamm Bubble Pipe,** 1963, Transogram, figural pipe on illustrated card
EX $12   NM $25   MIP $50

❏ **Bamm-Bamm Doll,** 1962, Ideal, 15" tall
EX $50   NM $115   MIP $225

❏ **Bamm-Bamm Figure,** 1970, Dakin, 7" tall
EX $20   NM $40   MIP $75

❏ **Bamm-Bamm Finger Puppet,** 1972, Knickerbocker
EX $5   NM $15   MIP $25

❏ **Bamm-Bamm Soaky,** 1960s, Purex
EX $20   NM $40   MIP $70

❏ **Barney Bank,** 1973, solid plastic, Barney holding a bowling ball
EX $15   NM $35   MIP $60

❏ **Barney Doll,** 1962, 6" tall, soft vinyl doll, movable arms and head
EX $25   NM $45   MIP $80

❏ **Barney Figure,** 1961, Knickerbocker, 10" tall, vinyl
EX $40   NM $55   MIP $160

❏ **Barney Figure,** 1970, Dakin, 7-1/4" tall
EX $20   NM $40   MIP $75

❏ **Barney Figure,** 1986, Flintoys
EX $5   NM $10   MIP $15

❏ **Barney Finger Puppet,** 1972, Knickerbocker
EX $8   NM $15   MIP $25

❏ **Barney Night Light,** 1979, Electricord, figural
EX $8   NM $15   MIP $25

❏ **Barney Policeman Figure,** 1986, Flintoys
EX $4   NM $8   MIP $12

❏ **Barney Riding Dino Toy,** 1960s, Marx, 8" long, metal and vinyl, wind-up
EX $110   NM $300   MIP $550

❏ **Barney Soaky,** 1970s, Roclar
EX $6   NM $15   MIP $35

❏ **Barney Wind-Up Toy,** 1960s, Marx, 3-1/2" tall figure, tin
EX $85   NM $190   MIP $375

❏ **Barney's Car,** 1986, Flintoys
EX $8   NM $15   MIP $30

❏ **Betty Figure,** 1961, Knickerbocker, 10" tall, vinyl
EX $50   NM $100   MIP $200

❏ **Betty Figure,** 1986, Flintoys
EX $4   NM $7   MIP $10

❏ **Dino Bank,** china, Dino carrying a golf bag
EX $45   NM $95   MIP $185

❏ **Dino Bank,** 1973, hard vinyl, blue w/Pebbles on his back
EX $18   NM $35   MIP $75

❏ **Dino Bath Puppet Sponge,** 1973, bath mitt
EX $10   NM $18   MIP $35

❏ **Dino Doll,** movable head and arms
EX $15   NM $25   MIP $45

❏ **Dino Figure,** 1970, Dakin, 7-3/4" tall
EX $25   NM $50   MIP $100

❏ **Dino Figure,** 1986, Flintoys
EX $4   NM $7   MIP $15

❏ **Dino Wind-Up Toy,** 1960s, Marx, 3-1/2" tall, tin
EX $90   NM $180   MIP $360

❏ **Fang Figure,** 1970, Dakin, 7" tall
EX $25   NM $50   MIP $95

❏ **Flintmobile,** 1986, Flintoys
EX $10   NM $18   MIP $40

❏ **Flintmobile with Fred Figure,** 1986, Flintoys
EX $18   NM $33   MIP $60

❏ **Flintstones Ashtray,** 1960, ceramic w/Wilma
EX $25   NM $70   MIP $100

❏ **Flintstones Bank,** 1971, 19" tall w/Barney and Bamm Bamm
EX $25   NM $50   MIP $85

❏ **Flintstones Car,** 1964, Remco, battery operated car w/Barney, Fred, Wilma and Betty
EX $85   NM $200   MIP $385

❏ **Flintstones Figure Set,** 1981, Spoontiques, eight figures
EX $35   NM $50   MIP $90

❏ **Flintstones Figures,** 1976, Empire, three-inch solid figures of Fred, Barney, Wilma and Betty
EX $10　　NM $40　　MIP $85

❏ **Flintstones Figures,** 1976, Imperial, eight acrylic figures: Fred, Barney, Wilma, Betty, Pebbles, Bamm Bamm, Dino and Baby Puss
EX $15　　NM $35　　MIP $65

❏ **Flintstones House,** 1986, Flintoys
EX $12　　NM $25　　MIP $35

❏ **Flintstones Lamp,** 9-1/2" tall, plastic Fred w/lampshade picturing characters
EX $50　　NM $120　　MIP $210

❏ **Flintstones Paint Box,** 1961, Transogram
EX $18　　NM $35　　MIP $60

❏ **Flintstones Party Place Set,** 1969, Reed, tablecloth, napkins, plates, cups
EX $10　　NM $20　　MIP $40

❏ **Flintstones Roto Draw,** 1969, British
EX $30　　NM $70　　MIP $100

❏ **Flintstones Tru-Vue Film Card,** 1962, Tru-Vue, #T-37, w/strips of Fred
EX $30　　NM $70　　MIP $100

❏ **Fred Bubble Blowing Pipe,** soft vinyl w/curved stem
EX $6　　NM $12　　MIP $20

❏ **Fred Doll,** 1960, 13" soft vinyl doll w/movable head
EX $45　　NM $100　　MIP $225

❏ **Fred Doll,** 1972, Perfection Plastic, 11" tall
EX $15　　NM $35　　MIP $60

❏ **Fred Figure,** 1960, Knickerbocker, 15" tall
EX $40　　NM $85　　MIP $200

❏ **Fred Figure,** 1961, Knickerbocker, 10" tall, vinyl
EX $32　　NM $75　　MIP $150

❏ **Fred Figure,** 1970, Dakin, 8-1/4" tall
EX $22　　NM $45　　MIP $85

❏ **Fred Figure,** 1986, Flintoys
EX $4　　NM $8　　MIP $12

❏ **Fred Finger Puppet,** 1972, Knickerbocker
EX $8　　NM $15　　MIP $22

❏ **Fred Flintstone's Bedrock Bank,** 1962, Alps, 9", tin and vinyl, battery operated
EX $175　　NM $310　　MIP $325

❏ **Fred Flintstone's Lithograph Wind-Up,** 1960s, Marx, 3-1/2" tall figure, metal
EX $85　　NM $170　　MIP $385

❏ **Fred Gumball Machine,** 1960s, plastic, shaped like Fred's head
EX $20　　NM $32　　MIP $60

❏ **Fred Loves Wilma Bank,** ceramic
EX $50　　NM $110　　MIP $185

❏ **Fred Night Light,** 1970, figural
EX $6　　NM $12　　MIP $25

❏ **Fred Policeman Figure,** 1986, Flintoys
EX $4　　NM $8　　MIP $15

❏ **Fred Push Puppet,** 1960s, Kohner
EX $10　　NM $25　　MIP $45

❏ **Fred Riding Dino,** 1962, Marx, 18" long battery operated w/Fred in Howdah
EX $175　　NM $350　　MIP $675

❏ **Fred Riding Dino,** 1962, Marx, 8" long, tin and vinyl, wind-up
EX $175　　NM $350　　MIP $675

❏ **Great Big Punch-Out Book,** 1961, Whitman
EX $20　　NM $50　　MIP $125

❏ **Motorbike,** 1986, Flintoys
EX $6　　NM $12　　MIP $20

❏ **Pebbles Bank,** 9" tall vinyl w/Pebbles sitting in chair
EX $10　　NM $25　　MIP $50

❏ **Pebbles Doll,** 1963, Ideal, 15" tall
EX $55　　NM $115　　MIP $225

❏ **Pebbles Doll,** 1982, Mighty Star, vinyl head, arms and legs, cloth stuffed body 12" tall
EX $15　　NM $25　　MIP $45

❏ **Pebbles Figure,** 1970, Dakin, 8" tall w/blonde hair and purple velvet shirt
EX $25　　NM $45　　MIP $85

❏ **Pebbles Finger Puppet,** 1972, Knickerbocker
EX $5　　NM $13　　MIP $20

❏ **Pebbles Flintstone Cradle,** 1963, Ideal, for a 15" doll
EX $40　　NM $75　　MIP $150

❏ **Pebbles Soaky,** 1960s, Purex
EX $20　　NM $35　　MIP $65

❏ **Police Car,** 1986, Flintoys
EX $8　　NM $15　　MIP $30

❏ **Wilma Figure,** 1961, Knickerbocker, 10" tall, vinyl
EX $50　　NM $100　　MIP $190

❏ **Wilma Figure,** 1986, Flintoys
EX $4　　NM $7　　MIP $15

❏ **Wilma Friction Car,** 1962, Marx, metal
EX $90　　NM $175　　MIP $375

FLIPPER

(Toy Shop File Photo)

❏ **Flipper Game,** 1970s, Koide, Japanese issue
EX $40　　NM $65　　MIP n/a

(Toy Shop File Photo)

❏ **Flipper Numbered Pencil Coloring Set,** 1960s, Includes colored pencils, sharpener and pre-sketched pictures to color
EX $20　　NM $40　　MIP n/a

(Toy Shop File Photo)

❏ **Puncho,** 1960s, Coleco, Inflatable 40" toy with weighted bottom, so he appears to be swimming upright in a pool or lake
EX $25　　NM $45　　MIP n/a

FLYING NUN

❏ **Flying Nun Chalkboard,** 1967, Screen Gems
EX $22　　NM $45　　MIP $80

❏ **Flying Nun Doll,** 1960s, Hasbro, 4"
EX $22　　NM $125　　MIP $200

❏ **Flying Nun Doll,** 1967, Hasbro, 11"
EX $30　　NM $85　　MIP $175

❏ **Flying Nun Halloween Costume,** 1967, Ben Cooper
EX $20　　NM $60　　MIP $100

(Toy Shop File Photo)

❏ **Flying Nun Paint-By-Number Set,** 1960s, Hasbro, two scenes and 10 paint vials
EX $15   NM $30   MIP $60

❏ **Flying Nun Paper Doll Set,** 1969, Saalfield, five dolls and costumes
EX $16   NM $40   MIP $80

GET SMART

(Toy Shop File Photo)

❏ **Secret Agent 86 Pen Radio,** 1960s, Miner Industries, Functioning crystal radio set in shape of pen, included earphone and contact clip. Received AM radio stations
EX $35   NM $70   MIP n/a

(Toy Shop File Photo)

❏ **Secret Agent 99 Spy Purse,** 1960s, Miner Industries, Includes secret compartment, two-way mirror, secret micro-film holder (inside rose), ID card
EX $55   NM $105   MIP n/a

GILLIGAN'S ISLAND

❏ **Gilligan's Floating Island Play Set,** 1977, Playskool
EX $75   NM $190   MIP $350

❏ **Gilligan's Island Notepad,** 1965, Whitman, Gilligan and Skipper on cover
EX $12   NM $30   MIP $60

❏ **Gilligan's Island Trading Cards,** 1965, Topps, set of 55 cards
EX $400   NM $800   MIP $1550

❏ **New Adventures of Gilligan Dip Dots Painting Set,** 1975, Kenner, book w/paints and brush
EX $220   NM $570   MIP $1200

GIRL FROM U.N.C.L.E.

❏ **1967 British Annual Book,** 1967, World Distributors, hardcover, 95 pages, photo cover
EX $10   NM $30   MIP $60

❏ **1968 British Annual Book,** 1968, World Distributors, hardcover, 95 pages, photo cover
EX $10   NM $30   MIP $60

❏ **1969 British Annual Book,** 1969, World Distributors, hardcover, 95 pages, photo cover
EX $10   NM $30   MIP $60

❏ **Costume,** 1967, Halco, transparent or painted mask, dress-style costume has show logo and silhouette image of Girl spy holding smoking gun, in illustrated window box
EX $55   NM $115   MIP $250

❏ **Garter Holster,** 1966, Lone Star, metal pistol fires small plastic bullets from metal shells, checker design vinyl holster and bullet pouch, on card
EX $60   NM $125   MIP $275

❏ **Girl From U.N.C.L.E. Doll,** 1967, Marx, 11" tall w/30 accessories in illustrated box
EX $250   NM $500   MIP $1000

❏ **Music from the Television Series,** 1966, M.G.M. Records, photo cover shows Stephanie against a wall
EX $9   NM $20   MIP $40

❏ **Secret Agent Wristwatch,** 1966, Bradley, watch has pink face w/April Dancer image, in case
EX $85   NM $200   MIP $400

GREEN ACRES

(Toy Shop File Photo)

❏ **2 Magic Stay-On Dolls,** 1960s, Includes Oliver and Lisa figures, plus complete wardrobes
EX $25   NM $40   MIP n/a

GREEN HORNET

❏ **Assistant Badge,** 1966, Don Howard Associates
EX $45   NM $95   MIP $200

❏ **Bike Badge,** 1966, Burry Cookies, premium; w/Vari-Vue flasher
EX $85   NM $175   MIP $350

❏ **Black Beauty Balloon Toy,** 1966, Oak Rubber
EX $70   NM $145   MIP $275

❏ **Black Beauty Slot Car,** 1966, Aurora, clear box w/insert
EX $85   NM $200   MIP $400

❏ **Black Beauty Slot Car,** 1966, BZ Industries, large scale
EX $160   NM $380   MIP $775

❏ **Captain Action Flasher Ring,** 1966, Vari-Vue, chrome
EX $13   NM $25   MIP $40

❏ **Captain Action Flasher Ring,** 1966, Vari-Vue, blue
EX $10   NM $18   MIP $30

❏ **Charm,** 1966, Cracker Jack, hornet-shaped
EX $10   NM $30   MIP $50

❏ **Charms,** 1966, Folz Vending, hornet-shaped
EX $10   NM $15   MIP $25

❏ **Comic Strip Stickers,** 1966, Folz Vending, 7" long, from vending machines, each
EX $25   NM $50   MIP $100

❏ **Electric Drawing Set,** 1966, Lakeside
EX $90   NM $190   MIP $275

❏ **Fan Club Photos,** 1938, Golden Jersey Milk, set of four; radio premium
EX $400   NM $800   MIP $1200

❏ **Flasher Button,** 1966, Vari-Vue, pin-back, 3"
EX $15   NM $30   MIP $45

❏ **Flasher Button,** 1966, Vari-Vue, no pin-back, 3"
EX $10   NM $20   MIP $35

❏ **Flasher Button,** 1966, Vari-Vue, no pin-back, 7"
EX $25   NM $45   MIP $80

❏ **Flasher Rings,** 1960s, Vari-Vue, blue plastic base, each
EX $5   NM $10   MIP $30

❏ **Flasher Rings,** 1960s, Vari-Vue, chrome base, each
EX $10   NM $20   MIP $40

❏ **Flashlight Whistle,** 1966, Bantamlight
EX $40   NM $90   MIP $175

❏ **Frame Tray Puzzles,** 1966, Whitman, box of four
EX $40   NM $90   MIP $175

TV TOYS

❏ **Green Hornet Bendy Figure,** 1966, Lakeside
EX $40   NM $80   MIP $175

❏ **Green Hornet Bubble Gum Ring**, Frito Lay, rubber ring, in cello pack
EX $25   NM $45   MIP $90

❏ **Green Hornet Candy/Toy Box,** 1966, Phoenix Candy, several variations
EX $40   NM $90   MIP $150

❏ **Green Hornet Charm Bracelet,** 1966, gold finish chain w/five charms: Hornet, Van, Kato, Pistol, Black Beauty, on 3" x 7-1/2" illustrated card
EX $50   NM $125   MIP $200

❏ **Green Hornet Colorforms Set,** 1966, Colorforms
EX $60   NM $125   MIP $250

❏ **Green Hornet Dashboard,** 1966, Remco
EX $300   NM $1000   MIP $2000

❏ **Green Hornet Mini Walkie Talkies,** 1966, Remco
EX $75   NM $150   MIP $300

❏ **Green Hornet Print Putty,** 1966, Colorforms
EX $20   NM $50   MIP $95

❏ **Green Hornet Seal Ring,** 1940, General Mills, cereal premium
EX $225   NM $780   MIP $1650

❏ **Green Hornet Soundtrack Record,** 1966, 20th Century Fox
EX $25   NM $100   MIP $200

❏ **Green Hornet Troll Figure,** 1966, Uneeda Wishnik, 7" tall
EX $55   NM $100   MIP $250

❏ **Green Hornet Troll Figure,** 1966, Damm, 3" tall
EX $45   NM $75   MIP $150

❏ **Green Hornet TV Guide,** 1966, Cover features Van Williams and Bruce Lee
EX $50   NM $125   MIP $250

❏ **Green Hornet Utensils,** 1966, Imperial Knife, fork and spoon
EX $30   NM $75   MIP $150

❏ **Green Hornet Walkie Talkies,** 1966, Remco
EX $50   NM $100   MIP $175

❏ **Green Hornet Wallet,** 1966, green vinyl, Hornet or Kato
EX $25   NM $50   MIP $100

❏ **Green Hornet Wrist Radios,** 1966, Remco, battery-operated
EX $150   NM $250   MIP $525

❏ **Halloween Costume,** 1966, Ben Cooper, several variations
EX $100   NM $200   MIP $350

❏ **Hand Puppet,** 1966, Ideal, w/hat
EX $80   NM $175   MIP $300

❏ **Inflatable Raft,** 1966, Ideal
EX $160   NM $350   MIP $700

❏ **Instant Squeeze Candy,** 1966, Dre's Inc., toothpaste-type container w/hornet-shaped plug
EX $40   NM $90   MIP $175

❏ **Kato and Black Beauty Glass,** 1938, Golden Jersey Milk, radio premium
EX $100   NM $300   MIP $500

❏ **Kite,** 1966, Roalex
EX $30   NM $75   MIP $150

❏ **Magic Eyes Movie Viewer Slides,** 1966, Sawyers
EX $75   NM $150   MIP $300

❏ **Magic Rub-On Set,** 1966, Whitman
EX $70   NM $150   MIP $275

❏ **Magic Slate,** 1966, Watkins-Strathmore, three variations
EX $35   NM $90   MIP $175

❏ **Mini Movie Viewer,** 1966, Acme/Chemtoy, w/filmstrips
EX $50   NM $100   MIP $200

❏ **Mini Movie Viewer,** 1971, Chemtoy, w/filmstrips
EX $25   NM $45   MIP $90

❏ **Numbered Pencil and Paint Set,** 1966, Hasbro
EX $75   NM $160   MIP $300

❏ **Paint By Number Set,** 1966, Hasbro
EX $65   NM $130   MIP $260

❏ **Pencil Case,** 1966, Hasbro
EX $30   NM $65   MIP $120

❏ **Pencils,** 1966, Empire Pencil, five on card
EX $30   NM $80   MIP $150

❏ **Pennant,** 1966, RMS, blue or orange
EX $35   NM $100   MIP $175

❏ **Playing Cards,** 1966, Ed-U-Cards
EX $10   NM $75   MIP $150

❏ **Postcard,** 1936, Golden Jersey Milk, radio premium
EX $150   NM $300   MIP $400

❏ **Punch-Out Book,** 1966, Whitman
EX $100   NM $200   MIP $375

❏ **Secret Agent Badge,** 1966, Don Howard Associates
EX $20   NM $35   MIP $50

❏ **Stardust Craft Kit,** 1966, Hasbro
EX $35   NM $75   MIP $150

❏ **The Case of the Disappearing Doctor Book,** 1966, Whitman
EX $20   NM $30   MIP $45

❏ **The Green Hornet Cracks Down Book,** 1942, Whitman, Better Little Books
EX $25   NM $60   MIP $120

❏ **The Green Hornet Returns Book,** 1941, Whitman, Better Little Books
EX $25   NM $60   MIP $120

❏ **The Green Hornet Strikes Book,** 1940, Whitman, Better Little Books
EX $25   NM $60   MIP $120

❏ **Thingmaker Mold and Accessories,** 1966, Mattel
EX $100   NM $175   MIP $325

❏ **Trading Cards,** 1966, Donruss, set of 44
EX $85   NM $100   MIP $325

❏ **Trading Cards Display Box,** 1966, Donruss
EX $100   NM $250   MIP $500

❏ **Trading Cards Wrapper,** 1966, Donruss
EX $15   NM $30   MIP $60

❏ **Trading Stickers,** 1966, Topps, set of 44
EX $85   NM $160   MIP $325

❏ **Trading Stickers Display Box,** 1966, Topps
EX $100   NM $250   MIP $500

❏ **Trading Stickers Wrapper,** 1966, Topps
EX $10   NM $25   MIP $50

❏ **Wrist Signal Light,** 1966, Bantamlight
EX $40   NM $80   MIP $175

HOGAN'S HEROES

(Toy Shop File Photo)

❏ **Peri-Peeper,** 1977, Continental Plastics, Includes Periscope, ID card and pinback button
EX $15   NM $30   MIP n/a

HOWDY DOODY

❏ **Cereal Box,** 1954, Kellogg's, Rice Krispies, Howdy Mask on back
EX $250   NM $650   MIP $1000

❏ **Clarabell Bank,** 1976, Strauss, flocked plastic, 9"
EX $20   NM $40   MIP $85

- ❏ **Clarabell Jumping Toy,** 1950s, Linemar, 7" tall tin litho, squeeze lever to make figure hop forward and squeak
  EX $200 **NM** $450 **MIP** $825

- ❏ **Clarabell Marionette,** 1950s, Peter Puppet
  EX $100 **NM** $210 **MIP** $425

- ❏ **Flub-a-Dub Figure,** 1950s, TeeVee Toys, 4" x 4" painted plastic, movable mouth
  EX $40 **NM** $90 **MIP** $150

- ❏ **Flub-a-Dub Flip A Ring Game,** 1950s, Flip-A-Ring, 9", ring toss game
  EX $25 **NM** $45 **MIP** $75

- ❏ **Flub-a-Dub Marionette,** 1950s, Peter Puppet
  EX $100 **NM** $225 **MIP** $450

- ❏ **Flub-a-Dub Puppet,** 1950s, Gund
  EX $40 **NM** $75 **MIP** $150

- ❏ **Howdy Doody Acrobat,** 1950s, Arnold, tin, plastic, Howdy swings on high bar
  EX $15 **NM** $25 **MIP** $60

- ❏ **Howdy Doody Air Doodle Beanie,** 1950s, Kellogg's, Rice Krispies premium
  EX $75 **NM** $200 **MIP** $300

- ❏ **Howdy Doody Air-O-Doodle Circus Train,** 1950s, Plasticraft/Kagran, red/yellow plastic train, boat and plane toy on card w/cut out character passengers
  EX $40 **NM** $100 **MIP** $160

- ❏ **Howdy Doody and Clarabell Book,** 1952, Simon and Schuster, Little Golden Book
  EX $12 **NM** $22 **MIP** $50

- ❏ **Howdy Doody and Clarabell Coloring Book,** 1955, Whitman, Model No. 1188
  EX $15 **NM** $75 **MIP** $185

- ❏ **Howdy Doody and Clarabell Puppet Mitten Kit,** 1950s, Connecticut Leather
  EX $30 **NM** $75 **MIP** $110

- ❏ **Howdy Doody and his Magic Hat Book,** 1953, Whitman, Little Golden Book
  EX $10 **NM** $22 **MIP** $40

- ❏ **Howdy Doody and Mr. Bluster Book,** 1954, Whitman, Little Golden Book
  EX $10 **NM** $22 **MIP** $40

- ❏ **Howdy Doody and the Musical Forest Record,** 1950s, RCA, 45 rpm
  EX $20 **NM** $50 **MIP** $80

- ❏ **Howdy Doody and the Princess Book,** 1952, Whitman, Little Golden Book
  EX $10 **NM** $25 **MIP** $45

- ❏ **Howdy Doody and You Record,** 1950s, RCA, 45 rpm
  EX $18 **NM** $40 **MIP** $65

- ❏ **Howdy Doody Bank,** Vandor, ceramic figural head
  EX $25 **NM** $55 **MIP** $100

- ❏ **Howdy Doody Bank,** 1950s, ceramic bank, all color, bust of Howdy
  EX $300 **NM** $500 **MIP** $850

- ❏ **Howdy Doody Bank,** 1950s, 7" tall, ceramic, Howdy riding a pig
  EX $70 **NM** $160 **MIP** $300

- ❏ **Howdy Doody Bank,** 1976, Strauss, flocked plastic, 9"
  EX $20 **NM** $40 **MIP** $85

- ❏ **Howdy Doody Bubble Pipe,** 1950s, Lido, 4" long, Howdy or Clarabell
  EX $30 **NM** $160 **MIP** $285

- ❏ **Howdy Doody Button,** 1949, New York Sunday News, reads "New Color Comic—Sunday News"
  EX $30 **NM** $55 **MIP** $100

- ❏ **Howdy Doody Coin,** 1950s, Kellogg's, plastic, silver, raised bust on Howdy on front
  EX $20 **NM** $40 **MIP** $75

- ❏ **Howdy Doody Color TV Set,** American Plastic, plastic, w/films
  EX $130 **NM** $275 **MIP** $500

- ❏ **Howdy Doody Coloring Books,** 1955, Whitman, boxed set of six
  EX $42 **NM** $150 **MIP** $300

- ❏ **Howdy Doody Comic Book,** 1949, Dell, Issue No. 1
  EX $110 **NM** $420 **MIP** $1200

- ❏ **Howdy Doody Cookbook,** 1952, Welch's
  EX $30 **NM** $110 **MIP** $225

- ❏ **Howdy Doody Cookie-Go-Round,** 1950s, Luce/Krispy Kan, lithographed cookie tin
  EX $75 **NM** $160 **MIP** $285

- ❏ **Howdy Doody Costume,** 1950s, Collegeville
  EX $50 **NM** $100 **MIP** $200

- ❏ **Howdy Doody Crayon Set,** 1950, Milton Bradley, 16 crayons w/pictures
  EX $45 **NM** $100 **MIP** $200

- ❏ **Howdy Doody Doll,** 1950s, Ideal, eyes and mouth move
  EX $40 **NM** $90 **MIP** $160

- ❏ **Howdy Doody Doll,** 1950s, 7" tall vinyl squeeze toy, Howdy in blue pants and red shirt
  EX $40 **NM** $90 **MIP** $160

- ❏ **Howdy Doody Doll,** 1970s, Goldberger, 30", vinyl ventriloquist doll
  EX $40 **NM** $90 **MIP** $160

- ❏ **Howdy Doody Doll,** 1976, Goldberger, 12" vinyl ventriloquist doll
  EX $25 **NM** $50 **MIP** $95

- ❏ **Howdy Doody Doll,** 1988, Applause, 11" cloth doll
  EX $10 **NM** $40 **MIP** $75

- ❏ **Howdy Doody Dominoes,** 1950s
  EX $20 **NM** $40 **MIP** $80

- ❏ **Howdy Doody Figure,** Stahlwood, 5" x 7" rubber squeeze figure on airplane
  EX $175 **NM** $360 **MIP** $725

- ❏ **Howdy Doody Fingertronic Puppet Theater,** 1970s, Sutton
  EX $25 **NM** $45 **MIP** $85

- ❏ **Howdy Doody Flasher Rings,** 1950s, Nabisco, set of eight plastic character rings
  EX $90 **NM** $175 **MIP** $400

- ❏ **Howdy Doody Flicker Ring,** 1950s, Nabisco
  EX $10 **NM** $20 **MIP** $50

- ❏ **Howdy Doody in Funland Book,** 1953, Whitman, Little Golden Book
  EX $10 **NM** $25 **MIP** $50

- ❏ **Howdy Doody Kiddie Pool,** 1950s, Ideal, 40" diameter, yellow/blue vinyl
  EX $80 **NM** $150 **MIP** $275

- ❏ **Howdy Doody Marionette,** 1950s, Peter Puppet
  EX $85 **NM** $190 **MIP** $375

- ❏ **Howdy Doody Mug,** 1950s, Ovaltine, red plastic w/Howdy decal (Be Keen, Drink Chocolate Flavored Ovaltine)
  EX $35 **NM** $50 **MIP** $100

- ❏ **Howdy Doody Music Box,** Vandor, Howdy playing piano
  EX $40 **NM** $55 **MIP** $90

- ❏ **Howdy Doody Newspaper #1,** 1950, Poll Parrot, premium
  EX $200 **NM** $400 **MIP** $500

- ❏ **Howdy Doody Night Light,** 1950s, Leco, figural, Howdy's face
  EX $35 **NM** $75 **MIP** $140

- ❏ **Howdy Doody Outdoor Sports Box,** 1950s, tin litho box w/colorful graphics
  EX $30 **NM** $60 **MIP** $110

- ❏ **Howdy Doody Paint Set,** 1950s, Milton Bradley
  EX $40 **NM** $80 **MIP** $160

- ❏ **Howdy Doody Paint Set,** 1950s, Marx, plaster figures, paint
  EX $35 **NM** $100 **MIP** $185

- ❏ **Howdy Doody Pencil Case,** 1950s, vinyl; smiling Howdy on front
  EX $20 **NM** $90 **MIP** $160

- ❏ **Howdy Doody Periscope,** 1950s, Wonder Bread premium
  EX $350 **NM** $700 **MIP** $1000

- ❏ **Howdy Doody Phono Doodle,** Sharatone Products
  EX $120 **NM** $260 **MIP** $350

- ❏ **Howdy Doody Pumpmobile,** Nylint, tin vehicle
  EX $110 **NM** $275 **MIP** $525

- ❏ **Howdy Doody Puppet Show Set,** 1950s, includes plastic figures of Howdy, Clarabell, Mr. Bluster, Flub, Dilly Dally
  EX $80 **NM** $170 **MIP** $325

- ❏ **Howdy Doody Puzzle,** 1950s, Whitman, frame tray, Howdy Goes Fishing
  EX $25 **NM** $45 **MIP** $90

- ❏ **Howdy Doody Puzzle Set,** 1950s, Milton Bradley, set of three
  EX $40 **NM** $75 **MIP** $150

- ❏ **Howdy Doody Ranch House Tool Box,** 1950s, Liberty Steel, 14" x 6" x 3" illustrated steel box w/handle
  EX $45 **NM** $110 **MIP** $185

❏ **Howdy Doody Salt and Pepper Shakers,** 1950s, Peter Puppet, shape of Howdy's head; removable blue vinyl neckerchief
EX $75 **NM** $160 **MIP** $300

❏ **Howdy Doody Sand Forms,** 1952, Ideal/Kagran, on card
EX $40 **NM** $80 **MIP** $150

❏ **Howdy Doody Songs Record,** 1974, Take Two, record, cut-outs, coloring book
EX $20 **NM** $50 **MIP** $75

❏ **Howdy Doody Sticker Fun Book,** 1952, Whitman
EX $15 **NM** $30 **MIP** $60

❏ **Howdy Doody Swim Ring,** 1950s, Ideal, inflatable, 20" diameter
EX $20 **NM** $40 **MIP** $75

❏ **Howdy Doody Talking Alarm Clock,** 1974, Janex
EX $30 **NM** $90 **MIP** $185

❏ **Howdy Doody Television,** 1950s, Lido, filmstrips w/TV box
EX $25 **NM** $110 **MIP** $250

❏ **Howdy Doody Ukulele,** 1950s, Emenee, plastic, white or yellow, 17"
EX $40 **NM** $65 **MIP** $110

❏ **Howdy Doody Umbrella,** 1950s, Holllander, Howdy head for handle
EX $30 **NM** $80 **MIP** $160

❏ **Howdy Doody Wall Walker,** Tigrett
EX $25 **NM** $50 **MIP** $100

❏ **Howdy Doody Wristwatch,** 1950s, Ever Tick/Kagran, glow-in-the-dark
EX $100 **NM** $300 **MIP** $600

❏ **Howdy Doody Wristwatch,** 1954, Ingraham, deep blue band w/blue and white dial showing character faces
EX $140 **NM** $350 **MIP** $750

❏ **Howdy Doody Xylo-Doodle,** 1950s, yellow plastic piano/xylophone w/colorful graphics
EX $75 **NM** $375 **MIP** $675

❏ **Howdy Doody's Animal Friends Book,** 1956, Whitman, Little Golden Book
EX $10 **NM** $20 **MIP** $50

❏ **Howdy Doody's Circus Book,** 1950, Whitman, Little Golden Book
EX $10 **NM** $20 **MIP** $50

❏ **Howdy Doody's Electric Carnival Game,** 1950s, Harett-Gilmar
EX $60 **NM** $120 **MIP** $225

❏ **Howdy Doody's Laughing Circus Record Set,** 1950s, RCA, two 78 rpm records
EX $35 **NM** $70 **MIP** $135

❏ **Howdy Doody's Lucky Trip Book,** 1953, Whitman, Little Golden Book
EX $12 **NM** $25 **MIP** $50

❏ **Howdy Doody's One-Man Band,** Trophy Products/Kagran, musical instruments
EX $100 **NM** $225 **MIP** $500

❏ **Merchandise Manual,** 1954, list of toys
EX $150 **NM** $450 **MIP** $650

❏ **Merchandise Manual,** 1955, list of toys
EX $100 **NM** $350 **MIP** $600

❏ **Mr. Bluster Bank,** 1976, Strauss, flocked plastic, 9"
EX $20 **NM** $35 **MIP** $65

❏ **Princess Summerfall Winterspring Doll,** 1950s, Beehler Arts, 8", hard plastic, braided black hair
EX $100 **NM** $190 **MIP** $350

❏ **Princess Summerfall Winterspring Sewing Cards,** 1950s, Milton Bradley, four cards, thread, plastic needle
EX $30 **NM** $65 **MIP** $135

❏ **Puppets,** 1950s, Gund, Howdy, Bluster, Clarabell, Dilly or Princess
EX $20 **NM** $50 **MIP** $90

❏ **Sparkle Gun,** 1987, Ja-Ru, plastic gun
EX $6 **NM** $20 **MIP** $45

❏ **Spinning Top,** 1970s, Lorenz Bolz, tin top w/characters
EX $30 **NM** $60 **MIP** $110

I DREAM OF JEANNIE

❏ **I Dream of Jeannie Costume,** 1970s, Ben Cooper
EX $8 **NM** $20 **MIP** $50

❏ **I Dream of Jeannie Doll,** 1965, Ideal, 18"
EX $45 **NM** $120 **MIP** $225

❏ **I Dream of Jeannie Doll,** 1977, Remco, 6"
EX $25 **NM** $50 **MIP** $110

❏ **I Dream of Jeannie Play Set,** 1977, Remco, w/6" doll
EX $40 **NM** $120 **MIP** $250

I SPY

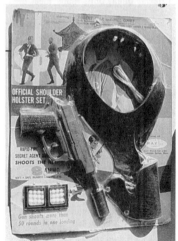

(Toy Shop File Photo)

❏ **Official Shoulder Holster Set,** 1960s, Ray Line, Inc., Includes rapid fire pistol ("shoots more than 50 rounds in one loading"), shoulder holster and ammo
EX $40 **NM** $65 **MIP** n/a

JETSONS

BOOK

❏ **Jetsons Birthday Surprise Book,** 1963, Whitman, Tell-A-Tale Book
EX $12 **NM** $25 **MIP** $65

FIGURES

❏ **Jetson Figures,** 1990, Applause, 10" tall; Judy, George, Elroy, Rosie, each
EX $50 **NM** $100 **MIP** $185

TOY

❏ **Elroy Toy,** 1963, Transogram
EX $10 **NM** $20 **MIP** $40

❏ **Jetsons Colorforms Kit,** 1963, Colorforms
EX $40 **NM** $75 **MIP** $150

❏ **Puzzle,** 1962, Whitman, 70 pieces
EX $25 **NM** $95 **MIP** $175

KNIGHT RIDER

❏ **Knight Rider Impossibles Stunt Set,** 1982, LJN
EX $45 **NM** $95 **MIP** $150

❏ **Knight Rider Wrist Communicator,** 1982, Larami
EX $10 **NM** $20 **MIP** $40

LASSIE

(Toy Shop File Photo)

❏ **Lassie's Pups,** 1950s, Set including plastic toy dogs, blanket, tub and puppy bed
EX $25 **NM** $45 **MIP** n/a

(Toy Shop File Photo)

❏ **Original Lassie Stuffed Toy,** 1950s, Smile Novelty Toy Co., Reddish-brown and white stuffed toy with plastic face
EX $80 **NM** $120 **MIP** n/a

LAUGH-IN

(Toy Shop File Photo)

❑ **"Sock It To Me" Plastic Purse,** 1970s,
Yellow with black lettering and strap
EX $17   **NM** $30   **MIP** n/a

(Toy Shop File Photo)

❑ **Laugh-In Electric Drawing Set,** 1960s,
Lakeside Toys, Included an "electric"
drawing set, color pencils, Laugh-In
cartoon guides, drawing paper, eraser,
sharpener and instructions
EX $30   **NM** $65   **MIP** n/a

LOVE BOAT

(Toy Shop File Photo)

❑ **Love Boat Playset,** 1970s, Boat-shaped
dollhouse with figures of the cast, furniture and accessories. Over two feet
long
EX $45   **NM** $90   **MIP** n/a

MAN FROM U.N.C.L.E.

❑ **1966 British Annual,** 1966, World Distributors, hardcover, 95 pages, photo
cover
EX $20   **NM** $50   **MIP** $75

❑ **1967 British Annual Book,** 1967, World
Distributors, hardcover, 95 pages,
photo cover
EX $15   **NM** $35   **MIP** $65

❑ **1968 British Annual Book,** 1968, World
Distributors, hardcover, 95 pages,
photo cover
EX $15   **NM** $30   **MIP** $60

❑ **1969 British Annual,** 1969, World Distributors, hardcover, 95 pages, photo
cover
EX $15   **NM** $25   **MIP** $55

❑ **Action Figure Apparel Set,** 1965, Gilbert, bullet proof vest, three targets,
three shells, binoculars, and bazooka
EX $50   **NM** $100   **MIP** $210

❑ **Action Figure Armament Set,** 1965, Gilbert, for 12" figures: jacket, cap firing
pistol w/barrel extension, bipod stand,
telescopic sight, grenade belt, binoculars, accessory pouch and beret
EX $50   **NM** $90   **MIP** $180

❑ **Action Figure Arsenal Set #1,** 1965,
Gilbert, tommy gun, bazooka, three
shells, cap firing pistol and attachments,
in shallow window box
EX $40   **NM** $80   **MIP** $175

❑ **Action Figure Arsenal Set #2,** 1965,
Gilbert, cap firing THRUSH rifle w/tele-
scopic sight, grenade belt and four grenades, on wrapped header card
EX $40   **NM** $80   **MIP** $175

❑ **Action Figure Jumpsuit Set,** 1965, Gilbert, for 12" figures: jumpsuit w/boots,
helmet w/chin strap, 28" parachute and
pack, cap firing tommy gun w/scope,
instructions
EX $50   **NM** $100   **MIP** $225

❑ **Action Figure Pistol Conversion Kit,**
1965, Gilbert, binoculars and pistol
w/attachments, for 12" figures, on
wrapped header card
EX $22   **NM** $45   **MIP** $90

❑ **Action Figure Scuba Set,** 1965, Gilbert,
for 12" Gilbert dolls: swim trunks, air
tanks, tank bracket, tubes, scuba jacket
and knife
EX $65   **NM** $130   **MIP** $260

❑ **Affair of the Gentle Saboteur Book,**
1966, Whitman, hardcover
EX $8   **NM** $15   **MIP** $35

❑ **Affair of the Gunrunners' Gold Book,**
1967, Whitman, hardcover
EX $8   **NM** $15   **MIP** $35

❑ **Alexander Waverly Figure,** 1966,
Marx, blue plastic, 5-3/4" tall, stamped
w/character's name and U.N.C.L.E. logo
on the bottom of base
EX $8   **NM** $15   **MIP** $30

❑ **Arcade Cards,** 1960s, postcards w/b/w
photo fronts, Napoleon or Illya
EX $5   **NM** $10   **MIP** $30

❑ **Attache Case,** 1966, Lone Star, small
cardboard briefcase, contains die-cast
Mauser and parts to assemble
U.N.C.L.E. Special
EX $130   **NM** $230   **MIP** $500

❑ **Attache Case, British,** 1965, Lone Star,
15" x 8" x 2" vinyl case w/a pistol, holster,
walkie talkie, cigarette box gun,
U.N.C.L.E. badge, international passport, invisible cartridge pen and handcuffs
EX $225   **NM** $450   **MIP** $900

❑ **Attache Case, British,** 1966, Lone Star,
cardboard covered in vinyl, 9mm automatic luger, shoulder stock, sight,
silencer, belt, holster, secret wrist holster and pistol that fires cap and cork,
grenade, wallet w/passport, play money
EX $250   **NM** $500   **MIP** $950

❑ **Bagatelle Game,** 1966, Hong Kong, 8"
x 14" pinball game
EX $75   **NM** $155   **MIP** $325

❑ **Bicycle License Plates,** 1967, Marx,
four different, metal: Man from
U.N.C.L.E., The Girl from U.N.C.L.E.,
Napoleon Solo, Illya Kuryakin, each
EX $15   **NM** $30   **MIP** $50

❑ **Calcutta Affair Book,** 1967, Whitman,
254 pages, Big Little Book
EX $5   **NM** $10   **MIP** $30

❑ **Candy Cigarette Box,** 1966, Cadet
Sweets, candy and trading card, illus-
trated box
EX $25   **NM** $60   **MIP** $125

❑ **Candy Cigarette Counter Display Box,**
1966, Cadet Sweets, holds 72 candy cigarette boxes, illustrated
EX $30   **NM** $90   **MIP** $200

❑ **Coin of El Diablo Affair Book,** 1965,
Wonder Books, softcover, 48 pages
EX $10   **NM** $20   **MIP** $40

❑ **Counter Spy Water Gun,** 1960s, Hong
Kong, luger water gun w/unlicensed
Napoleon Solo illustration header card
EX $5   **NM** $15   **MIP** $40

❑ **Counterspy Outfit,** 1966, Marx, contains trench coat w/secret pockets, pistol, shoulder holster, launcher barrel,
silencer, scope sight, two pair of
glasses, beards, eye patch, badge case,
etc., in box
EX $125   **NM** $230   **MIP** $475

❑ **Counterspy Outfit Store Display,** 1966,
Marx, 35" x 36" wide cardboard display
w/one piece of each item in Counterspy
Outfit
EX $320   **NM** $650   **MIP** $1250
EX $275   **NM** $525   **MIP** $1050

❑ **Die-Cast Car,** 1968, Playart, 2-3/4"
long, die-cast metal, metallic purple
EX $90   **NM** $200   **MIP** $425

❑ **Die-Cast Metal Gun,** 1965, Lone Star,
die-cast automatic cap pistol w/plastic
grips, plus cut-out badge, on card
EX $75   **NM** $150   **MIP** $325

❑ **Diving Dames Affair Book,** 1967, Souvenir Press/England, #10 in series
EX $4   **NM** $8   **MIP** $20

❑ **Doomsday Affair Book,** 1965, Souvenir
Press, #2 in series
EX $4   **NM** $8   **MIP** $20

TV TOYS

❏ **Fingerprint Kit,** 1966, ink pad, roller, code book, magnifier, fingerprint records and pressure plate, in illustrated window box
EX $125   NM $250   MIP $500

❏ **Flicker Ring,** 1965, silver plastic ring w/b/w photos, each
EX $10   NM $20   MIP $50

❏ **Flicker Ring,** 1966, blue plastic w/"changing portrait" of Napoleon or Illya, each
EX $10   NM $20   MIP $40

❏ **Foto-Fantastiks Coloring Set,** 1965, Eberhard Faber, six colored pencils, paint brush, and six 8" x 10" photos, came in four different versions, each
EX $40   NM $85   MIP $175

❏ **Generic Spies Figures,** 1966, Marx, six different solid plastic, unpainted figures 5-3/4" tall, each
EX $8   NM $15   MIP $20

❏ **Handkerchief,** 1966, England, U.N.C.L.E. logo, Illya and Napoleon
EX $30   NM $65   MIP $150

❏ **Headquarters Transmitter,** 1965, Cragstan, molded gold colored plastic transmitter, amplifier and under cover case, silver ID card, 20-foot wire, in box
EX $80   NM $160   MIP $325

❏ **Illya Kuryakin Action Figure,** 1965, Gilbert, 12" tall, plastic, black sweater, pants and shoes, spring loaded arm for firing cap pistol, folding badge, ID card and instruction sheet, in photo box
EX $80   NM $225   MIP $425

❏ **Illya Kuryakin Action Puppet,** 1965, Gilbert, 13" tall, soft vinyl hand puppet of Illya holding a communicator, on 10" x 16" card
EX $80   NM $175   MIP $375

❏ **Illya Kuryakin Costume,** 1967, Halco, painted mask, rayon costume in three colors showing Illya holding a gun, in illustrated window box
EX $45   NM $90   MIP $200

❏ **Illya Kuryakin Figure,** 1966, Marx, blue or gray plastic figure, 5-3/4" tall, stamped w/character's name and U.N.C.L.E. logo on the bottom of base
EX $15   NM $30   MIP $70

❏ **Illya, That Man From U.N.C.L.E. Book,** 1966, Pocket Books, 6" x 9" paperback, 100 pages of David McCallum
EX $10   NM $30   MIP $70

❏ **Invisible Writing Cartridge Pen,** 1965, Platinum/England, pen, two vials of ink and two invisible ink vials
EX $125   NM $230   MIP $475

❏ **Magic Slates,** 1965, Watkins-Strathmore, 9" x 14" slate w/two punch-out figures of either Napoleon or Illya, each
EX $45   NM $100   MIP $200

❏ **Man from the U.N.C.L.E. Record,** 1965, Capitol Records, 45 rpm w/The Man from U.N.C.L.E. theme song and "The Vagabond"
EX $25   NM $60   MIP $120

❏ **Man from U.N.C.L.E. and other TV Themes Record,** 1965, Metro Records, photo cover, has three songs from U.N.C.L.E. plus theme songs from Dr. Kildare, Mr. Novak, Bonanza and other shows
EX $8   NM $25   MIP $50

❏ **Man from U.N.C.L.E. Button,** 1965, Button World, 3-1/2" diam. round button w/portrait of Napoleon or Illya, each
EX $10   NM $17   MIP $30

❏ **Man from U.N.C.L.E. Card Game,** 1966, Japan, small artwork cards in illustrated box
EX $40   NM $75   MIP $160

❏ **Man from U.N.C.L.E. Code Board,** 1966, chalkboard w/line art illustrations
EX $70   NM $150   MIP $300

❏ **Man from U.N.C.L.E. Finger Puppets,** 1966, Dean, vinyl; THRUSH agent, Solo, Kuryakin, Waverly and two female agents; window box
EX $140   NM $300   MIP $600

❏ **Man from U.N.C.L.E. Playing Cards,** 1965, Ed-U-Cards, standard 54-card deck w/action photo illustrations, on card
EX $20   NM $35   MIP $70

❏ **Man from U.N.C.L.E. Playing Cards Display Box,** 1965, Ed-U-Cards, holds 12 packs
EX $130   NM $250   MIP $525

❏ **Man from U.N.C.L.E. Puzzles,** 1965, Jaymar, frame tray; three versions; each
EX $25   NM $40   MIP $75

❏ **Man from U.N.C.L.E. Record,** 1965, Crescendo Records, by the Challengers, cover shows blonde female spy w/gun
EX $5   NM $15   MIP $35

❏ **Man from U.N.C.L.E. Record,** 1966, Union/Japan, 45 rpm w/photo sleeve
EX $35   NM $75   MIP $150

❏ **Man from U.N.C.L.E. Sheet Music,** 1964, Hastings Music Corp., six pages, theme song and a brief description of the TV show
EX $15   NM $50   MIP $100

❏ **Man from U.N.C.L.E. Trading Cards,** 1965, Topps, set of 55 b/w photo cards
EX $45   NM $90   MIP $160

❏ **Man from U.N.C.L.E. Trading Cards,** 1966, Cadet Sweets, set of 50 cards, color photos, set
EX $22   NM $45   MIP $90

❏ **Man from U.N.C.L.E. Trading Cards,** 1966, ABC/England, 25 cards
EX $22   NM $45   MIP $90

❏ **Mystery Jigsaw Series Puzzles,** 1965, Milton Bradley, 14" x 24" puzzle, 250 pieces plus story booklet, The Loyal Groom, The Vital Observation, The Impossible Escape, The Micro-Film Affair, each
EX $25   NM $50   MIP $100

❏ **Napoleon Solo Costume,** 1965, Halco, transparent plastic "mystery mask," costume has line art shirt, tie, shoulder holster and U.N.C.L.E. logo, in illustrated box
EX $50   NM $95   MIP $185

❏ **Napoleon Solo Credentials and Passport Set,** 1965, Ideal, silver ID card, badge, identification wallet, slide window passport, on header card
EX $35   NM $65   MIP $150

❏ **Napoleon Solo Credentials and Secret Message Sender,** 1965, Ideal, message sender, badge, and silver ID, on card
EX $40   NM $80   MIP $175

❏ **Napoleon Solo Doll,** 1965, Gilbert, 11" tall, plastic, white shirt, black pants and shoes, spring loaded arm for firing cap pistol, folding badge, ID card and instruction sheet
EX $70   NM $145   MIP $350

❏ **Napoleon Solo Figure,** 1966, Marx, blue or gray plastic figure, 5-3/4" tall stamped w/character's name and U.N.C.L.E. logo on the bottom of base
EX $10   NM $25   MIP $65

❏ **Pinball Affair Game,** 1966, Marx, 12" x 24" tin litho pinball game
EX $75   NM $150   MIP $300

❏ **Pistol Cane Gun,** 1966, Marx, 25" long, cap firing, bullet shooting aluminum cane w/eight bullets and one metal shell, on illustrated card
EX $125   NM $250   MIP $600

❏ **Power Cube Affair Book,** 1968, Souvenir, #15 in series, British
EX $5   NM $10   MIP $25

❏ **Puzzle,** 1966, Milton Bradley, 10" x 19", 100 pieces, Illya's Battle Below
EX $15   NM $35   MIP $70

❏ **Puzzle,** 1966, Milton Bradley, 10" x 19", 100 pieces, Illya Crushes THRUSH
EX $15   NM $40   MIP $70

❏ **Puzzles,** 1966, England, four 11" x 17" puzzles, each w/340 pieces: The Getaway, Solo in Trouble, The Frogman Affair, Secret Plans, each
EX $40   NM $80   MIP $165

❏ **Secret Agent Wristwatch,** 1966, Bradley, gray watch face shows Solo holding a communicator, came w/either plain "leather" or "mod" watch band, in case
EX $115   NM $250   MIP $500

❏ **Secret Code Wheel Pinball,** 1966, Marx, 10" x 22" x 6" tin litho pinball game
EX $80   NM $170   MIP $325

❏ **Secret Message Pen,** 1966, American Character, 6-1/2" long double tipped pen for writing invisible messages, on header card
EX $100   NM $200   MIP $325

❏ **Secret Print Putty,** 1965, Colorforms, putty in a gun shaped container, print paper, display cards of Kuryakin and Solo and a book of spy and weapons illustrations, on card
EX $20   NM $45   MIP $95

❏ **Secret Service Gun,** 1965, Ideal, pistol, holster, badge and silver ID card, in window box
EX $160   NM $310   MIP $650

❏ **Secret Service Pop Gun,** 1960s, bagged Luger pop gun on header card

w/unlicensed illustration of Illya and Napoleon on header
EX $10   **NM** $15   **MIP** $50

❏ **Secret Weapon Set,** 1965, Ideal, clip loading cap firing pistol, holster, ID wallet, silver ID card, U.N.C.L.E. badge, two demolition grenades and holster, in window box
EX $190   **NM** $400   **MIP** $775

❏ **Shirt,** 1965, has secret pocket, glow-in-the-dark badge and ID, photo package
EX $190   **NM** $375   **MIP** $725

❏ **Shoot Out! Game,** 1965, Milton Bradley, skill and action game for two players, plastic marble game in illustrated box
EX $80   **NM** $160   **MIP** $325

❏ **Shooting Arcade Game,** 1966, Marx, tin litho arcade w/mechanical wind-up THRUSH agent targets for pellet shooting pistol, scope and stock attachments
EX $200   **NM** $400   **MIP** $850

❏ **Shooting Arcade Game,** 1966, Marx, smaller version w/THRUSH spinner targets
EX $150   **NM** $275   **MIP** $525

❏ **Spy Magic Tricks,** 1965, Gilbert, mystery gun, Illya playing cards, tricks
EX $125   **NM** $250   **MIP** $525

❏ **Television Picture Story Book,** 1968, P.B.S. Limited, hardcover, 62 pages, Gold Key reprints
EX $15   **NM** $20   **MIP** $60

❏ **THRUSH Agent Figures,** 1966, Marx, three different blue plastic figures, 5-3/4" tall stamped w/titles and U.N.C.L.E. logo on the bottom of each base, each
EX $10   **NM** $20   **MIP** $35

❏ **THRUSH Ray-Gun Affair Game,** 1966, Ideal, four U.N.C.L.E. agent pieces, Area Decoder cards, 3-D THRUSH hideouts,THRUSH vehicles, crayons, dice and a rotating "ray gun," in illustrated box
EX $55   **NM** $110   **MIP** $225
EX $170   **NM** $330   **MIP** $700

❏ **U.N.C.L.E. Badges Store Display,** 1965, Lone Star, illustrated card holds 12 triangular black plastic badges w/gold lettering, w/badges
EX $50   **NM** $120   **MIP** $225

McHALE'S NAVY

(Toy Shop File Photo)

❏ **McHale's Navy Signal Sender,** 1960s, Gabriel-Bell, Inc., Megaphone sends amplifies voice, sends light signal and includes a Morse code button
EX $25   **NM** $55   **MIP** n/a

MONKEES

❏ **Flip Movies,** 1967, Topps, each
EX $5   **NM** $10   **MIP** $20

❏ **Halloween Costumes,** 1967, Bland Charnas, each
EX $60   **NM** $125   **MIP** $250

❏ **Jigsaw Puzzle,** 1967, Fairchild
EX $15   **NM** $25   **MIP** $45

❏ **Monkees Dolls,** 1967, Remco, 4", rubber, each
EX $35   **NM** $80   **MIP** $175

❏ **Monkees Finger Puppets,** 1969, Remco
EX $15   **NM** $25   **MIP** $45

❏ **Talking Hand Puppet,** 1966, Mattel, cloth w/heads of Monkees on fingertips
EX $50   **NM** $100   **MIP** $200

❏ **Tambourine,** 1967, Raybert
EX $45   **NM** $100   **MIP** $200

❏ **Toy Guitar,** 1966, Mattel, 20"
EX $60   **NM** $125   **MIP** $250

(Toy Shop File Photo)

❏ **Toy Guitar,** 1966, Mattel, 14", wind-up crank
EX $40   **NM** $90   **MIP** $175

MORK AND MINDY

❏ **Mork and Mindy Colorforms,** 1979, Colorforms
EX $10   **NM** $15   **MIP** $30

MR. ED

(Toy Shop File Photo)

❏ **Mr. Ed Talking Horse Puppet,** 1962, Mattel
EX $40   **NM** $80   **MIP** $150

MUNSTERS, THE

❏ **Grandpa Doll,** 1964, Remco
EX $150   **NM** $325   **MIP** $610

❏ **Herman Munster Doll,** 1964, Remco
EX $155   **NM** $350   **MIP** $720

❏ **Lily Baby Doll,** 1965, Ideal, unlicensed "monster baby"
EX $45   **NM** $85   **MIP** $170

❏ **Lily Doll,** 1964, Remco
EX $150   **NM** $325   **MIP** $625

❏ **Puzzle,** 1960s, Whitman, frame tray
EX $30   **NM** $50   **MIP** $100

❏ **Puzzle,** 1965, Whitman, 100 pieces, boxed
EX $35   **NM** $60   **MIP** $150

❏ **The Last Resort Book,** 1964, Whitman
EX $13   **NM** $30   **MIP** $50

PARTRIDGE FAMILY

❏ **David Cassidy Dress-Up Kit,** 1972, Colorforms
EX $20   **NM** $40   **MIP** $75

❏ **Laurie Partridge Doll,** 1973, Remco, 20" tall
EX $55   **NM** $120   **MIP** $225

❏ **Partridge Family Bus,** 1973, Remco, plastic, 14" long
EX $55   **NM** $160   **MIP** $300

❏ **Partridge Family Guitar,** 1970s, Carnival, 19" plastic, decal of David Cassidy on body
EX $35   **NM** $75   **MIP** $150

❏ **Partridge Family Paper Dolls,** 1970s, Saalfield, several styles
EX $20   **NM** $40   **MIP** $75

❏ **Patti Partridge Doll,** 1971, Ideal
EX $50   **NM** $110   **MIP** $200

PEE WEE HERMAN

❏ **Ball Dart Set**
EX $5   NM $10   MIP $15

❏ **Billy Baloney Doll,** 1988, Matchbox, 18" tall
EX $12   NM $20   MIP $45

❏ **Chairry Figure**, Matchbox, 15" tall
EX $12   NM $20   MIP $45

❏ **Conky Wacky Wind-Up,** 1988, Matchbox
EX $3   NM $5   MIP $10

❏ **Cowboy Curtis Figure**, Matchbox
EX $8   NM $15   MIP $35

❏ **Globey with Randy,** 1988, Matchbox
EX $8   NM $15   MIP $35

❏ **King of Cartoons Figure,** 1988, Matchbox, 5" tall
EX $8   NM $15   MIP $35

❏ **Magic Screen Figure,** 1988, Matchbox, 5" tall poseable
EX $8   NM $15   MIP $35

❏ **Magic Screen Wacky Wind-Up,** 1988, Matchbox, 6" tall
EX $3   NM $5   MIP $10

❏ **Miss Yvonne Doll,** 1988, Matchbox, poseable 5" tall
EX $8   NM $15   MIP $45

❏ **Pee Wee Herman Deluxe Colorforms,** 1980s, Colorforms
EX $7   NM $10   MIP $35

❏ **Pee Wee Herman Doll**, Matchbox, 15" tall, non talking
EX $10   NM $20   MIP $65

❏ **Pee Wee Herman Doll,** 1988, Matchbox, poseable 5" tall
EX $4   NM $10   MIP $25

❏ **Pee Wee Herman Play Set,** 1989, Matchbox, 20" x 28" x 8" for use w/5" figures, Pee Wee's bike, folds into large carrying case
EX $12   NM $28   MIP $60

❏ **Pee Wee Herman Slumber Bag,** 1988, Matchbox
EX $10   NM $20   MIP $35

❏ **Pee Wee Herman Ventriloquist Doll,** 1980s, Matchbox
EX $30   NM $65   MIP $135

❏ **Pee Wee with Scooter and Helmet,** 1988, Matchbox
EX $4   NM $7   MIP $10

❏ **Pee Wee Yo-Yo**
EX $3   NM $10   MIP $20

❏ **Pterri Doll**, Matchbox, 13" tall
EX $15   NM $25   MIP $45

❏ **Pterri Wacky Wind-Ups,** 1988, Matchbox
EX $3   NM $5   MIP $10

❏ **Reba Figure,** 1988, Matchbox, poseable
EX $5   NM $10   MIP $30

❏ **Ricardo Figure,** 1988, Matchbox
EX $5   NM $10   MIP $30

❏ **Vance the Talking Pig Figure,** 1987, Matchbox
EX $20   NM $40   MIP $85

RAT PATROL

(Toy Shop File Photo)

❏ **Rat Patrol Diorama Kit,** 1960s, Aurora, includes 15 figures, 2 Rat Patrol Jeeps, 1 German Panzer Tank, 1 German Panther Tank, dimensional battlefield with sandbags, bunkers, dunes and palm trees
EX $40   NM $65   MIP n/a

ROCKY AND BULLWINKLE

ACCESSORIES

❏ **Bullwinkle and Rocky Wastebasket,** 1961, 11" tall, metal w/Jay Ward cast pictured
EX $35   NM $65   MIP $135

❏ **Bullwinkle for President Bumper Sticker,** 1972
EX $10   NM $16   MIP $40

❏ **Bullwinkle Jewelry Hanger,** 1960s, 5" tall, suction cup on back
EX $15   NM $25   MIP $50

❏ **Bullwinkle Stickers,** 1984, Bullwinkle, Sherman and Peabody, Snidely Whiplash
EX $5   NM $10   MIP $20

❏ **Rocky and Bullwinkle Toothpaste Holder,** 1960s, glazed china
EX $80   NM $190   MIP $375

BANK

❏ **Bullwinkle and Rocky Clock Bank,** 1969, Larami, 4-1/2" tall, plastic
EX $30   NM $60   MIP $120

❏ **Bullwinkle Bank,** 1960s, 6" tall, glazed china
EX $75   NM $125   MIP $400

❏ **Bullwinkle Bank,** 1972, Play Pal, 11-1/2", plastic
EX $35   NM $50   MIP $100

❏ **Mr. Peabody Bank,** 1960s, 6" tall, glazed china
EX $90   NM $190   MIP $385

❏ **Rocky and Bullwinkle Bank,** 1960, 5" tall, glazed china
EX $90   NM $190   MIP $385

❏ **Rocky Bank,** 1950s, 5" tall, slot in large tail, glazed china
EX $80   NM $225   MIP $425

BOOK

❏ **Bullwinkle Paintless Paint Book,** 1960, Whitman
EX $15   NM $35   MIP $80

❏ **Rocky and His Friends Book,** 1960s, Whitman, Little Golden Book
EX $20   NM $50   MIP $80

❏ **Rocky the Flying Squirrel Coloring Book,** 1960, Whitman
EX $20   NM $40   MIP $80

DOLL

❏ **Bullwinkle Talking Doll,** 1970, Mattel
EX $30   NM $75   MIP $150

FIGURES

❏ **Bullwinkle Figure,** 1976, Dakin, Cartoon Theater, 7-1/2" tall, plastic
EX $25   NM $50   MIP $90

❏ **Dudley Do-Right Figure,** 1972, Wham-O, 5" tall, flexible
EX $12   NM $40   MIP $80

❏ **Dudley Do-Right Figure,** 1976, Dakin, Cartoon Theater
EX $15   NM $40   MIP $80

❏ **Mr. Peabody Figure,** 1972, Wham-O, 4" tall, flexible
EX $10   NM $30   MIP $70

❏ **Natasha Figure,** 1972, Wham-O
EX $10   NM $30   MIP $70

❏ **Rocky Figure,** 1976, Dakin, Cartoon Theater, 6-1/2" tall, plastic
EX $30   NM $60   MIP $125

❏ **Sherman Figure,** 1972, Wham-O, 4" tall, flexible
EX $15   NM $35   MIP $70

❏ **Snidely Whiplash Figure,** 1972, Wham-O, 5" tall, flexible
EX $15   NM $40   MIP $80

GAME

❏ **Bullwinkle Travel Adventure Board Game,** 1960s, Transogram
EX $30   NM $70   MIP $135

❏ **Bullwinkle Travel Game,** 1971, Larami, magnetic
EX $15   NM $30   MIP $60

TOY

❏ **Bullwinkle and Rocky Movie Viewer,** 1960s, #225, red and white plastic viewer w/three movies
EX $25   NM $50   MIP $75

❏ **Bullwinkle Cartoon Kit,** 1962, Colorforms
EX $35   NM $50   MIP $160

❏ **Bullwinkle Dinner Set,** 1960s, Boonton Molding, plate and cup pictures Bullwinkle and the Cheerios Kid
EX $25   NM $50   MIP $85

❏ **Bullwinkle Flexy Figure,** 1970, Larami
EX $10   NM $35   MIP $70

❏ **Bullwinkle Magic Slate,** 1963
EX $15 **NM** $40 **MIP** $85

❏ **Bullwinkle Make Your Own Badge Set,** 1960s, Larami
EX $20 **NM** $40 **MIP** $85

❏ **Bullwinkle Spell and Count Board,** 1969
EX $12 **NM** $25 **MIP** $50

❏ **Bullwinkle Stamp Set,** 1970, Larami
EX $12 **NM** $25 **MIP** $40

❏ **Bullwinkle's Circus Time Toy,** 1969, Rocky on a circus horse
EX $20 **NM** $40 **MIP** $90

❏ **Bullwinkle's Circus Time Toy,** 1969, Bullwinkle on a elephant
EX $20 **NM** $40 **MIP** $90

❏ **Bullwinkle's Double Boomerangs,** 1969, Larami, set of two on illustrated card
EX $15 **NM** $25 **MIP** $50

❏ **Dudley Do-Right Puzzle,** 1975, Whitman
EX $12 **NM** $30 **MIP** $60

❏ **Rocky and Bullwinkle Presto Sparkle Painting Set,** 1962, Kenner, six cartoon pictures and two comic strip panels
EX $30 **NM** $70 **MIP** $135

❏ **Rocky and Bullwinkle Puzzle,** 1972, Whitman, boxed
EX $15 **NM** $30 **MIP** $75

❏ **Rocky Flexy Figure,** 1970, Larami
EX $10 **NM** $25 **MIP** $50

❏ **Rocky Soaky,** 10-1/2" tall, plastic
EX $15 **NM** $45 **MIP** $80

ROMPER ROOM

(Toy Shop File Photo)

❏ **Bop-A-Loop Toy (MIB),** Hasbro, Shown here with Romper Room Rhythm set
EX n/a **NM** $8 **MIP** $10

❏ **Build & Play Discs,** Hasbro
EX n/a **NM** $6 **MIP** $12

❏ **Can You Guess? Wonder Book,** Hasbro
EX n/a **NM** $4 **MIP** $8

❏ **Ceramic Mug – Jack-in-the-Box,** Hasbro
EX n/a **NM** $15 **MIP** $34

❏ **Chalkboard,** Hasbro
EX n/a **NM** $7 **MIP** $15

❏ **Digger the Dog (MIB),** Hasbro
EX n/a **NM** $15 **MIP** $32

❏ **Do Bee Dough Machine,** Hasbro
EX n/a **NM** $15 **MIP** $34

❏ **Do Bee Iron On Transfer,** Hasbro
EX n/a **NM** $3 **MIP** $5

❏ **Do Bee Rider,** Hasbro
EX n/a **NM** $20 **MIP** $55

❏ **Do Bees Little Golden Book of Manners,** Hasbro
EX n/a **NM** $9 **MIP** $18

❏ **Dump Truck (Do Bee hubcaps),** Hasbro
EX n/a **NM** $3 **MIP** $6

❏ **Fitness Fun 45 RPM,** Hasbro
EX n/a **NM** $2 **MIP** $4

❏ **Fun Time Puzzle Clock,** Hasbro
EX n/a **NM** $5 **MIP** $10

❏ **G.E. Show 'N Tell Phonoviewer,** Hasbro
EX n/a **NM** $14 **MIP** $28

❏ **G.E. Show 'N Tell Picturesound Refill Programs (each),** Hasbro
EX n/a **NM** $2 **MIP** $4

❏ **Happy Jack and Mr. Do Bee hand puppets,** Hasbro
EX n/a **NM** $20 **MIP** $40

❏ **Happy Jack Magnetic Puzzle,** Hasbro
EX n/a **NM** $8 **MIP** $16

❏ **Happy Jack Punching Clown,** Hasbro
EX n/a **NM** $9 **MIP** $18

❏ **Inchworm,** Hasbro
EX n/a **NM** $30 **MIP** $60

❏ **Moe the Monkey Game,** Hasbro
EX n/a **NM** $5 **MIP** $10

❏ **Mr. Do Bee Bank,** Hasbro
EX n/a **NM** $15 **MIP** $35

❏ **Mr. Do Bee Miniature Poly-Blocks,** Hasbro
EX n/a **NM** $5 **MIP** $10

❏ **Mr. Stacking Man,** Hasbro
EX n/a **NM** $8 **MIP** $15

❏ **Musical Block Clock,** Hasbro
EX n/a **NM** $20 **MIP** $45

❏ **Musical Jack in the Box,** Hasbro
EX n/a **NM** $35 **MIP** $75

❏ **Official TV Bo Dee Dance Record,** Hasbro
EX n/a **NM** $8 **MIP** $16

❏ **Peg Town Railroad,** Hasbro
EX n/a **NM** $5 **MIP** $10

❏ **Preschool Super Fun Pad,** Hasbro
EX n/a **NM** $3 **MIP** $6

❏ **Rhythm Set,** Hasbro
EX n/a **NM** $9 **MIP** $22

❏ **Sew Easy Sewing Machine,** Hasbro
EX n/a **NM** $6 **MIP** $12

❏ **Snoopy Counting Camera,** Hasbro
EX n/a **NM** $10 **MIP** $20

❏ **Snoopy Play Telephone,** Hasbro
EX n/a **NM** $5 **MIP** $10

❏ **Squirt, Squirt, Squirt the Animals Tub Toy,** Hasbro
EX n/a **NM** $5 **MIP** $10

❏ **Super Mr. Potato Head,** Hasbro
EX n/a **NM** $7 **MIP** $14

❏ **Talk 'N Chalk Board,** Hasbro
EX n/a **NM** $15 **MIP** $30

❏ **Toy Ring – Gold Plated Plastic,** Hasbro
EX n/a **NM** $20 **MIP** $40

❏ **Weebles Playground,** Hasbro
EX n/a **NM** $55 **MIP** $110

❏ **Willie the Weather Man,** Hasbro
EX n/a **NM** $20 **MIP** $45

ROOKIES

(Toy Shop File Photo)

❏ **Special Forces Set,** 1975, Fleetwood Toys, Includes target pistol, silencer, rocket grenade, official ID and six plastic bullets
EX $15 **NM** $25 **MIP** n/a

ROOKIES, THE

❏ **Rookie Chris Doll,** 1973, LJN, 8" tall
EX $10 **NM** $20 **MIP** $40

❏ **Rookie Mike Doll,** 1973, LJN, 8" tall
EX $10 **NM** $20 **MIP** $40

❏ **Rookie Terry Doll,** 1973, LJN, 8" tall
EX $10 **NM** $20 **MIP** $40

❏ **Rookie Willy Doll,** 1973, LJN, 8" tall
EX $10 **NM** $20 **MIP** $40

TV TOYS

S.W.A.T.

(Toy Shop File Photo)

❏ **Clicker Gun & Handcuffs Set,** 1975, Fleetwood Toys
EX $12   **NM** $20   **MIP** n/a

SCOOBY DOO

❏ **Scooby Doo and the Pirate Treasure Book,** 1974, Golden, Little Golden Book
EX $5   **NM** $10   **MIP** $15

❏ **Scooby Doo Hand Puppet,** 1970s, Ideal, vinyl head
EX $20   **NM** $40   **MIP** $75

❏ **Scooby Doo Paint with Water Book,** 1984
EX $5   **NM** $10   **MIP** $20

❏ **Scooby Doo Squeak Toy,** 1970s, Sani-toy, 6" tall
EX $20   **NM** $35   **MIP** $50

SGT. PRESTON

❏ **Sgt. Preston of the Yukon Punch-Out Cards,** 1950s, Quaker, "Big Game Tro-phy" cardboard cut-outs, set of nine
EX $30   **NM** $100   **MIP** $175

SIX MILLION DOLLAR MAN

(Toy Shop File Photo)

❏ **Porta-Communicator,** 1970s, Kenner, Walkie-talkie device that attaches to Colonel Austin like a backpack. You transmit your voice on one end, and it's broadcasted from the receiver on the other. Included a 10-foot cord
EX $20   **NM** $45   **MIP** n/a

SOUPY SALES

❏ **Soupy Sales Card Game,** 1960s, Jay-mar, Slap Jack, Old Maid, Funny Rummy, or Hearts/Crazy 8s
EX $20   **NM** $40   **MIP** $60

❏ **Soupy Sales Doll,** 1960s, Remco, 5" doll
EX $40   **NM** $150   **MIP** $250

❏ **Soupy Sales Doll,** 1966, Knicker-bocker, 12" plush, vinyl head
EX $25   **NM** $60   **MIP** $150

STARSKY & HUTCH

❏ **Deluxe Police Set,** 1970s, HG Toys, Includes badges, service revolver, Colt .45, shoulder holster, cuffs, whistle and poster
EX $30   **NM** $60   **MIP** n/a

STARSKY AND HUTCH

❏ **Starsky and Hutch Puzzle,** 1970s, HG Toys
EX $15   **NM** $30   **MIP** $50

❏ **Starsky and Hutch Shoot-Out Target Set,** 1970s, Berwick
EX $25   **NM** $45   **MIP** $95

STINGRAY

(Toy Shop File Photo)

❏ **Puzzle,** 1960s, Whitman
EX $15   **NM** $35   **MIP** n/a

(Toy Shop File Photo)

❏ **Stingray Atomic Submarine**, Doyusha, With electonic lights and sounds
EX $40   **NM** $90   **MIP** n/a

(Toy Shop File Photo)

❏ **Stingray Hand Puppet, Titan,** 1960s
EX $15   **NM** $30   **MIP** n/a

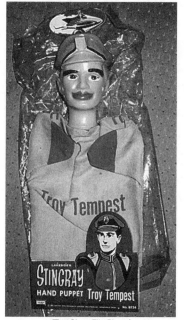

(Toy Shop File Photo)

❏ **Stingray Hand Puppet, Troy Tempest,** 1960s
EX $15   **NM** $30   **MIP** n/a

(Toy Shop File Photo)

❏ **Stingray Hand Puppet, X2-Zero,** 1960s
EX $17　　**NM** $35　　**MIP** n/a

(Toy Shop File Photo)

❏ **Stingray Underwater Maze Game,**
1960s, Transogram
EX $35　　**NM** $70　　**MIP** n/a

THE FALL GUY

(Toy Shop File Photo)

❏ **Fall Guy Bounty Hunter HO Scale Race
set,** 1970s, Aurora, Includes Fall Guy
truck, passenger car, figure 8 track
EX $50　　**NM** $90　　**MIP** n/a

THUNDERBIRDS

(Toy Shop File Photo)

❏ **"The Mole" vehicle,** Bandai, Tracked
vehicle with rotating drill section, from
the Gerry Anderson series "Thunderbirds"
EX $22　　**NM** $45　　**MIP** n/a

UNDERDOG

❏ **Kite Fun Book,** 1970s, Pacific Gas and
Electric
EX $10　　**NM** $35　　**MIP** $85

❏ **Puzzle,** 1975, Whitman, 100 pieces
EX $10　　**NM** $20　　**MIP** $30

❏ **Underdog Costume,** 1969, Ben Cooper
EX $55　　**NM** $85　　**MIP** $125

❏ **Underdog Dot Funnies Kit,** 1974, Whitman
EX $10　　**NM** $20　　**MIP** $40

❏ **Underdog Figure,** 1976, Dakin, plastic,
Cartoon Theater
EX $35　　**NM** $100　　**MIP** $150

WELCOME BACK, KOTTER

❏ **Halloween Costume,** 1976, Collegeville, several styles
EX $10　　**NM** $20　　**MIP** $25

❏ **Sweathogs Dolls,** 1976, Mattel,
Epstein, Washington, Barbarino, Kotter,
Horshack; each
EX $10　　**NM** $25　　**MIP** $60

❏ **Sweathogs Grease Machine Cars,**
1977, Ahi, 3" long, plastic cars; various
styles, each
EX $15　　**NM** $30　　**MIP** $60

❏ **Welcome Back, Kotter Classroom,**
1976, Mattel, play set
EX $25　　**NM** $45　　**MIP** $100

❏ **Welcome Back, Kotter Colorforms Set,**
1976, Colorforms
EX $10　　**NM** $20　　**MIP** $50

WINKY DINK AND YOU

❏ **When Winky Winks at You Record,**
1956, Decca
EX $45　　**NM** $60　　**MIP** $80

❏ **Winky Dink Book,** 1956, Golden, Little
Golden Book
EX $9　　**NM** $16　　**MIP** $25

❏ **Winky Dink Comic Book,** 1950s, Dell,
#663
EX $20　　**NM** $40　　**MIP** $90

❏ **Winky Dink Magic Crayons,** 1960s
EX $20　　**NM** $35　　**MIP** $50

❏ **Winky Dink Official TV Game Kit,**
1950s
EX $30　　**NM** $50　　**MIP** $100

❏ **Winky Dink Secret Message Game,**
1950s, Lowell
EX $75　　**NM** $130　　**MIP** $225

❏ **Winky Dink Winko Magic Kit,** 1950s
EX $20　　**NM** $35　　**MIP** $50

Vehicles

The Hot Wheels Deora, #6210, a 1968 release. Many are found sans surf-boards, MIP examples are valued at $375.

by Dan Stearns

Toy cars let us drive into an imaginary world of low (or no) gas prices, perfect traffic and ideal road conditions. Collect them, and you suddenly own a fleet of Ferraris, a squad of Shelbys or a battalion of Beetles.

After World War II, there was an explosion of die-cast and pressed steel vehicles. Venerable companies like Buddy L, Dinky and Hubley continued to make new replicas, sometimes reusing older prewar castings. And, new firms sprang up everywhere. Matchbox, Eska, Ertl, Tonka—all have honored places in the Baby Boomer childhood and beyond.

Of course, one of the most famous makers of steel cars and trucks was Buddy L. Spanning both pre- and postwar worlds, some of Buddy L's offerings were over two feet long! These prewar toys are highly prized by collectors, but many of

the 1950s and 1960s vehicles have been coming into their own in recent years as later-era Tonkas climb in price.

Tonka collector opinion tends to split about which era Tonkas are worth bothering about. Some see the company's best work as occurring before 1963 when Tonka trucks lost the "Ford" grille and went to more generic (or "Chevy") front end. Others prefer the vintage rounded fenders of the pre-1958 New Generation models. And still others, (this editor included) like them all, but are more partial to the later 1960s and early 1970s trucks and cars they had as a kid. (Those Jeep Wagoneers and Gladiator pickups are just plain fun!) In any event, we've started adding a smattering of later-era vehicles to our listings but plan to keep adding more in the future.

Die-cast cars on our side of the Atlantic made an appearance by Tootsietoy in the early 20th century. The company dates back to the turn of the nineteenth century to Samuel Dowst of Chicago. The trade name, which eventually became the company's mainstay, originated with Dowst's daughter, Tootsie. Although a few cars were produced even before the First World War, by the 1920s and 30s, the company produced a veritable car show of vehicles, including the Grahams and LaSalles that are so highly sought today.

The Matchbox response to Hot Wheels: Superfast. Many of the first cars, released in 1970, were simply updates to older "regular wheels" castings. The new wheels and axles were lighter, and the cars lost their slower speed, but some would say they lost much of their appealing realism as well.

In the past decade, the number one small-scale vehicle for collectors has been Mattel's Hot Wheels. Dreamt up in the late 1960s to compete with Matchbox cars, these beauties debuted in 1968 and immediately became the line to beat. The "original sixteen" as the first releases have come to be known were a combination of realistic customized street machines and a few outrageous concept vehicles. The craze for Redlines—named

so for the "redwall" tires the cars sported until about 1977—keeps driving prices to ever-higher summits. Just when you think you're going to get a deal on a 1968 Custom Barracuda, you realize you have no groceries left at home. To think how many of these cars I personally sent to their orange-tracked destruction…well, best not to think of it, I guess.

Topper Toys had the fastest response to the new Hot Wheels in the form of Johnny Lightning cars. Many were obviously modeled after Mattel's breakthrough vehicles, but these cars boasted better axles and faster wheels, making them capable of "400 scale miles per hour." Because Topper went under in 1971, these vehicles have become real collector favorites, and their mint-in-pack values reflect it.

None of this is to say that Matchbox cars have dropped off of the collecting radar screen—areas to look for include mint-in-box Superfast, King-Size and their later cousin, Superkings vehicles. Right now, some of these vehicles can be had for a bargain, but that could change shortly.

Japanese tin cars, once the mainstay of Woolworth's toy departments and various five-and-dime stores, have become extremely popular during the past fifteen years. The colorful lithography and colors, combined with the vehicles size (pre-dating the huge current popularity of 1:18-scale cars by about 30 years) make them attractive pieces to acquire. The cars you see in this book under the generic "Japanese" heading include various, and sometimes unmarked, manufacturers.

Foden 8-Wheel Diesel Wagon by Dinky, part of the "Supertoys" range. $435 MIP.

In 1968, kids everywhere saw the appearance of the "Tiny-Tonka" trucks. The #655 Bottom Dump seen here is in great shape and a real bargain for entry-level Tonka collectors. Figure about $25 MIP, but about $12 or less for the model shown.

Grading and pricing...

The galaxy of toy vehicles is so diverse that grading can be tough to pin down to a few general guidelines. Older pre-war vehicles are more than likely to have chipped paint, split tires and missing parts.

While any imperfections or scratches always lessen the values of a vehicle, they are going to really pull away from the price on smaller die-cast such as Matchbox, Hot Wheels and Dinky vehicles. Consider about 25% of the vehicle's value reduced from a mint condition when you see signs of playwear on the car.

Editing, research and all that...

By Merry Dudley

As the editor of *Toy Cars & Models* magazine, I have many reference books on my desk. However, many of them languish on my back shelf, collecting dust and doing nothing but impeding the growth of my die-cast collection.

Very few reference books make the cut to assume its place on my front shelf, which is easily accessible as I sit in my chair writing and researching stories.

But *Toys & Prices* is one of them.

With its significantly different look, this reference book will be especially invaluable to those who search for favorite items from the Baby Boomer years.

For instance, I'm a fan of cars with fins — the bigger, the better. I'm currently concentrating on researching, finding and purchasing models of the 1959-60 Chevy Impalas along with old DeSotos and Chryslers. While I'm not too concerned about scale, I'm limiting myself to die-cast toys, which means that most of the items I seek were made during the post-war years. This edition of *Toys & Prices* has been expanded to include more photos which helps me find the models and toys that appeal to the fin-lover in me.

The only problem is that I can spend hours poring over this book, and for some reason, my boss doesn't like that. Hey, I'm researching!

What do you think of the new look of this special 10th anniversary edition? Let us know because we'd love to hear your thoughts. I know I'll be consulting this edition quite often . . . for both business and pleasure.

Many thanks to: Merry Dudley, Tom Michael, George Cuhaj, Angelo Van Bogart, Karen O'Brien, Dr. Douglas Sadecky, Peter Gofton, (check out his web site for great deals on die-cast, vintage toys, antiques and more at www.greatfinds.com), Randy Prasse, Mark Rich, John Brown, Sr., Ron Smith and Ron O'Brien for their invaluable contributions to this section.

BUDDY L

AIRPLANES

❑ **5000 Monocoupe "The Lone Eagle"**, Buddy L, orange wing, black fuselage and tail w/tailskid, all steel high wind cabin monoplane, 9-7/8" wingspan, 1929
EX $250 **NM** $300 **MIP** $400

❑ **Army Tank Transport Plane**, Buddy L, low-wing monoplane, two small four-wheel tanks that clip beneath wings, 27" wingspan, 1941
EX $250 **NM** $350 **MIP** $400

❑ **Catapult Airplane and Hangar**, Buddy L, 5000 Monocoupe w/tailwheel, 9-7/8" wingspan, olive/gray hangar, black twin-spring catapult, 1930
EX $955 **NM** $1210 **MIP** $1520

❑ **Four Motor Air Cruiser**, Buddy L, white, red engine cowlings, yellow fuselage and twin tails, four engine monoplane, 27" wingspan, 1952
EX $200 **NM** $310 **MIP** $350

❑ **Four-Engine Transport**, Buddy L, green wings, white engine cowlings, yellow fuselage and twin tails, four engine monoplane, 27" wingspan, 1949
EX $205 **NM** $300 **MIP** $405

❑ **Hangar and Three 5000 Monocoupes**, Buddy L, olive/gray hangar, windows outlined in red or orange, planes 9-7/8" wingspan, all steel high wing cabin monoplanes, 1930
EX $750 **NM** $1000 **MIP** $2000

❑ **Transport Airplane**, Buddy L, white wings and engine cowlings, red fuselage and twin tails, four engine monoplane, 27" wingspan, 1946
EX $205 **NM** $310 **MIP** $410

CARS

❑ **Army Staff Car**, Buddy L, olive drab body, 15-3/4" long, 1964
EX $100 **NM** $150 **MIP** $200

❑ **Bloomin' Bus**, Buddy L, chartreuse body, white roof and supports, similar to VW minibus, 10-3/4" long, 1969
EX $90 **NM** $135 **MIP** $180

❑ **Buddywagon**, Buddy L, red body w/white roof, 10-3/4" long, 1966
EX $100 **NM** $150 **MIP** $200

❑ **Buddywagon**, Buddy L, red body w/white roof, no chrome on front, 10-3/4" long, 1967
EX $100 **NM** $155 **MIP** $195

❑ **Colt Sportsliner**, Buddy L, red open body, white hardtop, off-white seats and interior, 10-1/4" long, 1967
EX $35 **NM** $50 **MIP** $70

❑ **Colt Sportsliner**, Buddy L, light blue-green open body, white hardtop, pale tan seats and interior, 10-1/4" long, 1968
EX $30 **NM** $45 **MIP** $65

❑ **Colt Utility Car**, Buddy L, red open body, white plstic seats, floor and luggage space, 10-1/4" long, 1967
EX $45 **NM** $60 **MIP** $75

❑ **Colt Utility Car**, Buddy L, light orange body, tan interior, 10-1/4" long, 1968
EX $35 **NM** $45 **MIP** $65

❑ **Country Squire Wagon**, Buddy L, off-white hood fenders, end gate and roof, brown woodgrain side panels, 15-1/2" long, 1963
EX $85 **NM** $130 **MIP** $175

❑ **Country Squire Wagon**, Buddy L, red hood fenders, end gate and roof, brown woodgrain side panels, 15" long, 1965
EX $75 **NM** $115 **MIP** $150

❑ **Deluxe Convertible Coupe**, Buddy L, metallic blue enamel front, sides and deck, cream top retracts into rumble seat, 19" long, 1949
EX $310 **NM** $455 **MIP** $605

❑ **Desert Rats Command Car**, Buddy L, light tan "Colt" open body, light beige interior, black .50-caliber machine gun swivels on post between seats, 10-1/4" long, blackwall tires, 1968
EX $45 **NM** $65 **MIP** $90

❑ **Desert Rats Command Car**, Buddy L, light tan "Colt" open body, light beige interior, black .50-caliber machine gun swivels on post between seats, 10-1/4" long, 1967
EX $60 **NM** $85 **MIP** $110

❑ **Flivver Coupe**, Buddy L, black w/red eight-spoke wheels, black hubs, aluminum tires, flat, hardtop roof on enclosed glass-window-style body, 11" long, 1924
EX $775 **NM** $1100 **MIP** $1550

❑ **Flivver Roadster**, Buddy L, black w/red eight-spoke wheels, black hubs, aluminum tires, simulated soft, folding top, 11" long, 1924
EX $750 **NM** $1000 **MIP** $1500

❑ **Jr. Camaro**, Buddy L, metallic blue body, white racing stripes across hood nose, 9" long, 1968
EX $50 **NM** $75 **MIP** $100

❑ **Jr. Flower Power Sportster**, Buddy L, purple hood, fenders and body, white roof and supports, white plastic seats, lavender and orange five-petal blossom decals on hood top, roof, and sides, 6" long, 1969
EX $35 **NM** $55 **MIP** $75

❑ **Jr. Sportster**, Buddy L, blue hood and open body, white hardtop and upper sides, 6" long, 1968
EX $35 **NM** $55 **MIP** $75

❑ **Mechanical Scarab Automobile**, Buddy L, red radically streamlined body, bright metal front and rear bumpers, 10-1/2" long, 1936
EX $200 **NM** $300 **MIP** $500

❑ **Police Colt**, Buddy L, deep blue open body, white hardtop, "POLICE" across top of hood, "POLICE 1" on sides, 10-1/4" long, 1968
EX $50 **NM** $75 **MIP** $100

❑ **Ski Bus**, Buddy L, white body and roof, similar to VW minibus, 10-3/4" long, 1967
EX $75 **NM** $115 **MIP** $150

❑ **Station Wagon**, Buddy L, light blue/green body and roof, 15-1/2" long, 1963
EX $75 **NM** $115 **MIP** $150

❑ **Streamline Scarab**, Buddy L, red, radically streamlined body, non-mechanical, 10-1/2" long, 1941
EX $145 **NM** $225 **MIP** $290

❑ **Suburban Wagon**, Buddy L, powder blue or white body and roof, 15-1/2" long, 1963
EX $75 **NM** $115 **MIP** $150

❑ **Suburban Wagon**, Buddy L, gray/green body and roof, 15-3/4" long, 1964
EX $70 **NM** $100 **MIP** $140

❑ **Town and Country Convertible**, Buddy L, maroon front, hood, rear deck and fenders, gray top retracts into rumble seat, 19" long, 1947
EX $300 **NM** $450 **MIP** $600

(Toy Shop File Photo)

❑ **Travel Trailer and Station Wagon**, Buddy L, red station wagon, two-wheel trailer w/red lower body and white steel camper-style upper body, 27-1/4" long, 1965
EX $155 **NM** $230 **MIP** $310

❑ **Yellow Taxi with Skyview**, Buddy L, yellow hood, roof and body, red radiator front and fenders, 18-1/2" long, 1948
EX $200 **NM** $400 **MIP** $600

EMERGENCY VEHICLES

❑ **Aerial Ladder and Emergency Truck**, Buddy L, red w/white ladders, bumper and steel disc wheels, three eight-rung steel ladders, no rear step, no siren or SIREN decal, 22-1/4" long, 1953
EX $225 **NM** $345 **MIP** $450

❑ **Aerial Ladder and Emergency Truck**, Buddy L, red w/white ladders, bumper and steel disc wheels, three eight-rung steel ladders, 22-1/4" long, 1952
EX $200 **NM** $300 **MIP** $400

❑ **Aerial Ladder Fire Engine**, Buddy L, red tractor, wraparound bumper and semi-trailer, two aluminum thirteen-rung extension ladders on sides, swivel-base aluminum central ladder, 26-1/2" long, 1960
EX $125 **NM** $185 **MIP** $250

❑ **Aerial Ladder Fire Engine**, Buddy L, red tractor and semi-trailer, white plastic bumper w/integral grille guard, two aluminum thirteen-rung extension ladders on sides, swivel-base aluminum central ladder, 26-1/2" long, 1961
EX $125 **NM** $185 **MIP** $250

VEHICLES

❑ **Aerial Ladder Fire Engine**, Buddy L, red tractor and semi-trailer, chrome one-piece wraparound bumper, slotted grille, two aluminum thirteen-rung extension ladders on sides, swivel-base aluminum central ladder, 26-1/2" long, 1966
EX $125   NM $185   MIP $250

❑ **Aerial Ladder Fire Engine**, Buddy L, red cab-over-engine tractor and semi-trailer units, two thirteen-rung white sectional ladders and swivel-mounted aerial ladder w/side rails, 25-1/2" long, 1968
EX $100   NM $150   MIP $200

❑ **Aerial Ladder Fire Engine**, Buddy L, snub-nose red tractor and semi-trailer, white swivel-mounted aerial ladder w/side rails, two white thirteen-rung sectional ladders, 27-1/2" long, 1970
EX $100   NM $150   MIP $200

❑ **Aerial Truck**, Buddy L, red w/nickel ladders, black hand wheel, brass bell, and black hubs, 39" long w/ladder down, 1925
EX $850   NM $1300   MIP $1700

❑ **American LaFrance Aero-Chief Pumper**, Buddy L, red cab-over-engine and body, white underbody, rear step and simulated hose reels, black extension ladders on right side, 25-1/2" long, 1972
EX $90   NM $150   MIP $200

❑ **Brute Fire Pumper**, Buddy L, red cab-over-engine body and frame, two yellow five-rung sectional ladders on sides of open body, 5-1/4" long, 1969
EX $35   NM $60   MIP $85

❑ **Brute Hook-N-Ladder**, Buddy L, red cab-over-engine tractor and detachable semi-trailer, white elevating, swveling aerial ladder w/side rails, 10" long, 1969
EX $30   NM $40   MIP $55

❑ **Extension Ladder Fire Truck**, Buddy L, red w/silver ladders and yellow removable rider seat, enclosed cab, 35" long, 1945
EX $200   NM $300   MIP $400

❑ **Extension Ladder Rider Fire Truck**, Buddy L, duo-tone slant design, tractor has white front, lower hood sides and lower doors, red hood top, cab and frame, red semi-trailer, white ten-rung and eight-rung ladders, 32-1/2" long, 1949
EX $150   NM $225   MIP $300

❑ **Extension Ladder Trailer Fire Truck**, Buddy L, red tractor w/enclosed cab, boxy fenders, red semi-trailer w/fenders, two white eight-rung side ladders, ten-rung central extension ladder, 29-1/2" long, 1955
EX $200   NM $300   MIP $400

❑ **Extension Ladder Trailer Fire Truck**, Buddy L, red tractor unit and semi-trailer, enclosed cab, two white thirteen-rung side extension ladders on sides, white central ladder on swivel base, 29-1/2" long, 1956
EX $125   NM $185   MIP $250

❑ **Fire and Chemical Truck**, Buddy L, duo-tone slant design, white front, lower hood sides and lower doors, rest is red, bright-metal or white eight-rung ladder on sides, 25" long, 1949
EX $125   NM $185   MIP $250

❑ **Fire Department Emergency Truck**, Buddy L, red streamlined body, enclosed cab, chrome one-piece grille, bumper, and headlights, 12-3/4" long, 1953
EX $100   NM $150   MIP $200

❑ **Fire Engine**, Buddy L, red w/nickel-plated upright broiler, nickel rims and flywheels on dummy water pump, brass bell, 23-1/4" long, 1925-29
EX $500   NM $800   MIP $1600

❑ **Fire Engine**, Buddy L, red w/nickel rim flywheels on dummy pump, brass bell, dim-or-bright electric headlights, 25-1/2" long, 1933
EX $500   NM $750   MIP $1500

❑ **Fire Hose and Water Pumper**, Buddy L, red w/two white five-rung ladders, one red/white removable fire extinguisher, enclosed cab, 12-1/2" long, 1952
EX $100   NM $150   MIP $200

❑ **Fire Hose and Water Pumper**, Buddy L, red w/two white five-rung ladders, two removable fire extinguishers, enclosed cab, 12-1/2" long, 1950
EX $105   NM $155   MIP $200

❑ **Fire Pumper**, Buddy L, red cab-over-engine and open body, eleven-rung white 10" ladder on each side, 16-1/4" long, 1968
EX $100   NM $150   MIP $200

❑ **Fire Pumper with Action Hydrant**, Buddy L, red wraparound bumper, hood cab and cargo section, aluminum nine-rung ladders, white hose reel, 15" long, 1960
EX $75   NM $115   MIP $150

❑ **Fire Truck**, Buddy L, bright red w/black inverted L-shaped crane mounted in socket on seat back, red floor, open driver's seat, 26" long, 1925
EX $450   NM $800   MIP $1600

❑ **Fire Truck**, Buddy L, red w/two white ladders, enclosed cab, bright metal grille and headlights, 25" long, 1948
EX $125   NM $200   MIP $250

❑ **Fire Truck**, Buddy L, duo-tone slant design, yellow front, bumper, hood sides and skirted fenders, rest is red, nickel ladders, 28-1/2" long, 1939
EX $500   NM $700   MIP $1000

❑ **Fire Truck**, Buddy L, duo-tone slant design, yellow front, single-bar bumper, hood sides and removable rider seat, rest is red, 25-1/2" long, 1936
EX $170   NM $250   MIP $500

❑ **Fire Truck**, Buddy L, red w/nickel or white ladders, bright-metal radiator grille and black removable rider saddle, 25-1/2" long, 1935
EX $255   NM $385   MIP $510

❑ **Fire Truck**, Buddy L, bright red, red floor, open driver's seat, 26" long, 1928
EX $450   NM $800   MIP $1200

❑ **Fire Truck**, Buddy L, bright red w/black inverted L-shaped crane mounted in socket on seat back, open driver's seat, 26" long, 1924
EX $500   NM $900   MIP $1850

❑ **Fire Truck**, Buddy L, duo-tone slant design, tractor has white front, lower hood sides and lower doors, red hood top, cab and frame, red semi-trailer, rubber wheels w/black tires, 32-1/2" long, 1953
EX $200   NM $300   MIP $400

❑ **Fire Truck**, Buddy L, red w/white ladders, black rubber wheels, enclosed cab, 12" long, 1945
EX $75   NM $115   MIP $150

❑ **Fire Truck**, Buddy L, red w/black solid-rubber Firestone tires on red seven-spoke embossed metal wheels, two 18-1/2" red steel sectional ladders, 26" long, 1930
EX $800   NM $1000   MIP $1600

❑ **GMC Deluxe Aerial Ladder Fire Engine**, Buddy L, white tractor and semi-trailer units, golden thirteen-rung extension ladder on sides, golden central aerial ladder, black and white DANGER battery case w/two flashing lights, 28" long, 1959
EX $225   NM $345   MIP $450

(Calvin L. Chaussee Photo)

❑ **GMC Extension Ladder Trailer Fire Engine**, Buddy L, red tractor w/chrome GMC bar grille, red semi-trailer, white thirteen-rung extension ladders on sides, white swiveling central ladder w/side rails, 27-1/4" long, 1957
EX $110   NM $260   MIP $405

❑ **GMC Fire Pumper with Horn**, Buddy L, red w/aluminum-finish eleven-rung side ladders and white reel of black plastic hose in open cargo section, chrome GMC bar grille, 15" long, 1958
EX $150   NM $200   MIP $300

❑ **GMC Hydraulic Aerial Ladder Fire Engine**, Buddy L, red tractor unit w/chrome GMC bar grille, red semi-trailer, white thirteen-rung extension ladders on sides, white swiveling central ladder, 26-1/2" long, 1958
EX $125   NM $185   MIP $250

❑ **GMC Red Cross Ambulance**, Buddy L, all white, removable fabric canopy w/a red cross and "Ambulance" in red, 14-1/2" long, 1960
EX $150   NM $250   MIP $400

❑ **Hook & Ladder Fire Truck**, Buddy L, medium-dark red, w/black inverted L-shaped crane mounted in socket on seat back, open driver's seat, 26" long, 1923
EX $1200   NM $1800   MIP $2400

(Joe & Sharon Freed Photo)

❑ **Hose Truck**, Buddy L, red w/two white hose pipes, white cord hose on reeland brass nozzle, electric headlights w/red bulbs, 21 3/4" long, 1933
EX $495   NM $760   MIP $1100

❑ **Hydraulic Aerial Truck**, Buddy L, duo-tone slant design, yellow front, single-bar bumper, chassis, radiator, front fender, lower sides and removable rider saddle, rest is red, 40" long w/ladders down, 1936
EX $550   NM $825   MIP $1100

❑ **Hydraulic Aerial Truck**, Buddy L, red w/brass bell on cowl, nickel ladders mounted on 5-1/2" turntable rotated by black hand wheel, 39" long, 1927
EX $850   NM $1300   MIP $1700

❑ **Hydraulic Snorkel Fire Pumper**, Buddy L, red cab-over-engine and open rear body, white eleven-rung 10" ladder on each side, snorkel pod w/solid sides, 21" long, 1969
EX $105   NM $155   MIP $210

❑ **Hydraulic Water Tower Truck**, Buddy L, red w/nickel water tower, dim/bright electric headlights, brass bell, added-on bright-metal grille, 44-7/8" long w/tower down, 1935
EX $600   NM $900   MIP $1500

❑ **Hydraulic Water Tower Truck**, Buddy L, duo-tone slant design, yellow bumper, hood sides, front fenders, rest is red, electric headlights, added-on bright-metal grille, 44-7/8" long w/tower down, 1936
EX $600   NM $1000   MIP $1500

❑ **Hydraulic Water Tower Truck**, Buddy L, red w/nickel water tower, dim/bright electric headlights, brass bell, 44-7/8" long w/tower down, 1933
EX $800   NM $1000   MIP $1700

❑ **Hydraulic Water Tower Truck**, Buddy L, duo-tone slant design, yellow front, single-bar bumper and hood sides, red hood top, enclosed cab and water tank, brass bell, nickel water tower, 46" long w/tower down, 1939
EX $900   NM $1200   MIP $1700

❑ **Jr. Fire Emergency Truck**, Buddy L, red cab-over-engine and body, one-piece chrome wraparound narrow bumper and twenty-four-hole grille w/plastic vertical-pair headlights, 6-3/4" long, 1968
EX $55   NM $80   MIP $105

❑ **Jr. Fire Emergency Truck**, Buddy L, red cab-over-engine and body, wider one-piece chrome wraparound narrow bumper and four-slot grille w/two square plastic headlights, 6-3/4" long, 1969
EX $50   NM $75   MIP $100

❑ **Jr. Fire Snorkel Truck**, Buddy L, red cab-over-engine and body, chrome one-piece narrow wraparound bumper and twenty-four-hole grille w/plastic vertical-pair headlights, 11-1/2" long, 1968
EX $100   NM $150   MIP $200

❑ **Jr. Fire Snorkel Truck**, Buddy L, red cab-over-engine and body, full-width chrome one-piece bumper and four-slot grille w/two square plastic headlights, 11" long, 1969
EX $60   NM $150   MIP $200

❑ **Jr. Hook-n-Ladder Aerial Truck**, Buddy L, red cab-over-engine tractor w/one-piece four-slot grille and two square plastic headlights, red semi-trailer, white high-sides ladder, plastic vertical-pair headlights, 17" long, 1969
EX $75   NM $115   MIP $150

❑ **Jr. Hook-n-Ladder Aerial Truck**, Buddy L, red cab-over-engine tractor and semi-trailer, white high-sides ladder, chrome one-piece wraparound bumper and twenty-four-hole grille, plastic veritcal-pair headlights, 17" long, 1967
EX $100   NM $150   MIP $200

❑ **Jr. Hook-n-Ladder Aerial Truck**, Buddy L, red cab-over-engine tractor and semi-trailer, white high-sides ladder, one-piece chrome four-slot grille, two square plastic headlights, 17" long, 1969
EX $75   NM $115   MIP $150

❑ **Ladder Fire Truck**, Buddy L, red w/bright-metal V-nose radiator, head-lights and ladder, black wooden wheels, 12" long, 1941
EX $125   NM $200   MIP $250

❑ **Ladder Truck**, Buddy L, modified duo-tone slant design, white front, front fenders and lower doors, white ladders, bright-metal grille, no bumper, 17-1/2" long, 1941
EX $200   NM $300   MIP $400

❑ **Ladder Truck**, Buddy L, red w/two yellow sectional ladders, enclosed square cab, 22-3/4" long, 1933
EX $120   NM $250   MIP $500

❑ **Ladder Truck**, Buddy L, red w/two white ladders, bright-metal radiator grille and headlights, 24" long, 1941
EX $125   NM $200   MIP $250

❑ **Ladder Truck**, Buddy L, red w/yellow severely streamlined, skirted fenders and lower doors, white ladders, bright-metal grille, no bumper, 17-1/2" long, 1940
EX $200   NM $300   MIP $400

❑ **Ladder Truck**, Buddy L, red w/bright-metal grille and headlights, two white ladders, 24" long, 1939
EX $100   NM $200   MIP $300

❑ **Ladder Truck**, Buddy L, duo-tone slant design, white front, hood sides, fenders and two ladders, rest is red, square enclosed cab w/sharply protruding visor, no headlights, 22-3/4" long, 1937
EX $135   NM $200   MIP $275

❑ **Ladder Truck**, Buddy L, duo-tone slant design, white front, hood sides, fenders and two ladders, rest is red, square enclosed cab w/sharply protruding visor, 22-3/4" long, 1936
EX $150   NM $225   MIP $300

❑ **Ladder Truck**, Buddy L, red w/two yellow ladders, enclosed square cab w/sharply protruding visor, bright-metal radiator front, 22-3/4" long, 1935
EX $255   NM $380   MIP $510

❑ **Ladder Truck**, Buddy L, red w/two yellow ladders, enclosed square cab w/sharply protruding visor, 22-3/4" long, 1934
EX $200   NM $300   MIP $400

❑ **Police Squad Truck**, Buddy L, yellow front and front fenders, dark blue-green body, yellow fire extinguisher, 21-1/2" long over ladders, 1947
EX $150   NM $300   MIP $550

❑ **Pumping Fire Engine**, Buddy L, red w/nickel stack on boiler, nickel rims on pump flywheels, nickel-rim headlights and searchlight, 23-1/2" long, 1929
EX $3000   NM $3500   MIP $4000

❑ **Rear Steer Trailer Fire Truck**, Buddy L, red w/two white ten-rung ladders, chrome one-piece grille, headlights and bumper, 20" long, 1952
EX $65   NM $100   MIP $200

❑ **Red Cross Ambulance**, Buddy L, all white, removable fabric canopy w/a red cross and "Ambulance" in red, 14-1/2" long, 1958
EX $60   NM $95   MIP $125

❑ **Suburban Pumper**, Buddy L, red station wagon body, white plastic wraparound bumpers, one-piece grille and double headlights, 15" long, 1964
EX $100   NM $150   MIP $175

❑ **Texaco Fire Chief American LaFrance Pumper**, Buddy L, promotional piece, red rounded-front enclosed cab and body, white one-pice underbody, running boards and rear step, 25" long, 1962
EX $210   NM $305   MIP $410

❑ **Trailer Ladder Truck**, Buddy L, duo-tone slant design, tractor unit has yellow front, lower hood sides and lower doors, red hood top, enclosed cab and semi-trailer, nickel ten-rung ladders, 30" long w/ladders, 1940
EX $200   NM $300   MIP $400

❑ **Trailer Ladder Truck**, Buddy L, all red w/cream removable rider saddle, three bright metal ten-rung ladders, 20" long over ladders, 1941
EX $150   NM $225   MIP $300

❑ **Water Tower Truck**, Buddy L, red w/nickel two-bar front bumper, red nickel-rim headlights on cowl, nickel latticework water tower, 45-1/2" long w/tower down, 1929
EX $3000   NM $4500   MIP $6000

VEHICLES

FARM AND CONSTRUCTION EQUIPMENT

❑ **Aerial Tower Tramway**, Buddy L, two tapering dark green 33-1/2" tall towers and 12" square bases, black hand crank, 1928
EX $1000 **NM** $1300 **MIP** $2700

❑ **Big Derrick**, Buddy L, red mast and 20" boom, black base, 24" tall, 1921
EX $600 **NM** $900 **MIP** $1200

❑ **Brute Articulated Scooper**, Buddy L, yellow front-loading scoop, cab, articulated frame and rear power unit, black radiator, exhaust, steering wheel and driver's seat, 5-1/2" long, 1970
EX $50 **NM** $75 **MIP** $100

❑ **Brute Double Dump Train**, Buddy L, yellow hood, fenders and back on tractor unit, yellow coupled bottom-dumping earth carriers, 9-1/2" long, 1969
EX $50 **NM** $75 **MIP** $100

❑ **Brute Dumping Scraper**, Buddy L, yellow hood, fenders and back on two-wheel tractor unit, yellow scraper-dump unit, 7" long, 1970
EX $50 **NM** $75 **MIP** $100

❑ **Brute Farm Tractor-n-Cart**, Buddy L, bright blue tractor body and rear fenders, green plastic radiator, engine, exhaust and driver's seat, bright blue detachable, square, two-wheel open cart, 6-1/4" long, 1969
EX $30 **NM** $45 **MIP** $60

❑ **Brute Road Grader**, Buddy L, yellow hood, cab, frame and adjustable blade, black radiator, driver's seat and steering wheel, 6-1/2" long, 1970
EX $50 **NM** $75 **MIP** $100

❑ **Cement Mixer on Treads**, Buddy L, medium gray w/black treads and water tank, 16" tall, 1929-31
EX $2500 **NM** $3500 **MIP** $4500

❑ **Cement Mixer on Wheels**, Buddy L, medium gray w/black cast steel wheels and water tank, 14-1/2" tall, 1926-29
EX $700 **NM** $900 **MIP** $1500

❑ **Concrete Mixer**, Buddy L, green w/black cast-steel wheels, crank, gears, and band mixing drum, 10-1/2" long, 1930
EX $175 **NM** $265 **MIP** $350

❑ **Concrete Mixer**, Buddy L, yellow/orange frame and base, red hopper and drum, black crank handle, 10-1/2" long, 1936
EX $110 **NM** $175 **MIP** $225

❑ **Concrete Mixer**, Buddy L, red frame and base, cream/yellow hopper, drum and crank handle, 10-1/2" long, 1941
EX $135 **NM** $195 **MIP** $255

❑ **Concrete Mixer**, Buddy L, green frame, base, crank, crank handle and bottom of mixing drum, gray hopper and top of drum, 9-5/8" long, 1949
EX $100 **NM** $150 **MIP** $200

❑ **Concrete Mixer**, Buddy L, medium gray w/black cast-steel wheels, black water tank, w/wood-handle, steel-blade scoop shovel, 17-3/4" long w/tow bar up, 1926
EX $500 **NM** $700 **MIP** $1000

❑ **Concrete Mixer with Motor Sound**, Buddy L, green frame, base, crank, crank handle and bottom of mixing drum, gray hopper and top of drum, w/sound when crank rotates drum, 9 5/8" long, 1950
EX $75 **NM** $115 **MIP** $150

❑ **Dandy Digger**, Buddy L, yellow main frame, operators, seat and boom, brown shovel, arm, under frame and twin skids, 27" long, 1941
EX $95 **NM** $145 **MIP** $195

❑ **Dandy Digger**, Buddy L, yellow seat, lower control lever and main boom, black underframe, skids, shovel, arm and control lever, 38-1/2" long w/shovel arm extended, 1953
EX $75 **NM** $115 **MIP** $150

❑ **Dandy Digger**, Buddy L, yellow main frame, operators, seat and boom, green shovel, arm, under frame and twin skids, 27" long, 1936
EX $85 **NM** $130 **MIP** $175

❑ **Dandy Digger**, Buddy L, yellow seat lower control lever and main boom, black underframe, skids, shovel and arm, 38-1/2" long w/shovel arm extended, 1953
EX $75 **NM** $115 **MIP** $150

❑ **Dandy Digger**, Buddy L, red main frame, operators, seat and boom, black shovel, arm, under frame and twin skids, 27" long, 1931
EX $100 **NM** $160 **MIP** $215

❑ **Digger**, Buddy L, red main frame, operators, seat and boom, black shovel, arm, lower frame and twin skids, curved connecting rod, boom tilts down for digging, 11-1/2" long w/shovel arm extended, 1935
EX $100 **NM** $150 **MIP** $200

❑ **Dredge**, Buddy L, red corrugated roof and base w/four wide black wheels, red hubs, black boiler, floor, frame boom and clamshell bucket, 19" long, 1924
EX $750 **NM** $1000 **MIP** $1500

❑ **Giant Digger**, Buddy L, red main frame, operators, seat and boom, black shovel, arm, lower frame and twin skids, boom tilts down for digging, 42" long w/shovel arm extended, 1931
EX $275 **NM** $415 **MIP** $550

❑ **Giant Digger**, Buddy L, red main frame, operators, seat and boom, black shovel, arm, lower frame and twin skids, curved connecting rod, boom tilts, 31" long w/shovel arm extended, 1933
EX $265 **NM** $395 **MIP** $525

❑ **Giant Digger**, Buddy L, yellow main frame, operators, seat and boom, green shovel, arm, lower frame and twin skids, boom tilts, 11-1/2" long w/shovel arm extended, 1936
EX $85 **NM** $130 **MIP** $175

❑ **Giant Digger**, Buddy L, yellow main frame, operators, seat and boom, brown shovel, arm, lower frame and twin skids, boom tilts, 11-1/2" long w/shovel arm extended, 1941
EX $75 **NM** $115 **MIP** $155

❑ **Gradall**, Buddy L, bright yellow truck and superstructure, black plastic bumper and radiator, 32" long w/digging arm extended, 1965
EX $350 **NM** $750 **MIP** $1000

❑ **Hauling Rig with Construction Derrick**, Buddy L, duo-tone slant design tractor, yellow bumper, lower hood and cab sides, white upper hood and cab, white trailer w/yellow loading ramp, overall 38-1/2" long, 1953
EX $175 **NM** $250 **MIP** $400

❑ **Hauling Rig with Construction Derrick**, Buddy L, yellow tractor unit, green semi-trailer, winch on front of trailer makes sound, 36-3/4" long, 1954
EX $110 **NM** $175 **MIP** $225

❑ **Hoisting Tower**, Buddy L, dark green, hoist tower and three distribution chutes, 29" tall, 1928-31
EX $1500 **NM** $2000 **MIP** $2500

❑ **Husky Tractor**, Buddy L, bright blue body with white wheels and large rear fenders, black engine block, exhaust, steering wheel and driver's seat, 13" long, 1969
EX $40 **NM** $60 **MIP** $80

❑ **Husky Tractor**, Buddy L, bright yellow body, red large rear fenders and wheels, black engine block, exhaust, steering wheel and driver's seat, 13" long, 1970
EX $30 **NM** $45 **MIP** $65

❑ **Husky Tractor**, Buddy L, bright yellow body and large rear fenders, black engine block, exhaust, steering wheel and driver's seat, 13" long, 1966
EX $50 **NM** $80 **MIP** $105

❑ **Improved Steam Shovel**, Buddy L, black w/red roof and base, 14" tall, 1927-29
EX $100 **NM** $150 **MIP** $200

❑ **Junior Excavator**, Buddy L, red shovel, arm, underframe, control lever and twin skids, yellow boom, rear lever, frame and seat, 28" long, 1945
EX $75 **NM** $115 **MIP** $150

❑ **Mechanical Crane**, Buddy L, orange removable roof, boom and wheels in black cleated rubber crawler treads, olive green enclosed cab and base, hand crank w/rat-tat motor noise, 20" tall, 1950
EX $175 **NM** $265 **MIP** $350

❑ **Mechanical Crane**, Buddy L, orange removable roof, boom, yellow wheels in white rubber crawler treads, olive green enclosed cab and base, hand crank w/rat-tat motor noise, 20" tall, 1952
EX $150 **NM** $225 **MIP** $300

❑ **Mobile Construction Derrick**, Buddy L, orange laticework main mast, swiveling base, yellow latticework boom, green clamshell bucket and main platform base, 25-1/2" long w/boom lowered, 1953
EX $155 **NM** $250 **MIP** $355

❑ **Mobile Construction Derrick**, Buddy L, orange laticework main mast, swiveling base, yellow latticework boom, gray clamshell bucket, green main platform base, 25-1/2" long w/boom lowered, 1955
EX $160 **NM** $260 **MIP** $355

❑ **Mobile Construction Derrick**, Buddy L, orange laticework main mast, swiveling base, yellow latticework boom, gray clamshell bucket, orange main platform base, 25-1/2" long w/boom lowered, 1956
EX $150   NM $250   MIP $350

❑ **Mobile Power Digger Unit**, Buddy L, clamshell dredge mounted on 10-wheel truck, orange truck, yellow dredge cab on swivel base, 31-3/4" long w/boom lowered, 1955
EX $125   NM $185   MIP $250

❑ **Mobile Power Digger Unit**, Buddy L, clamshell dredge mounted on six-wheel truck, orange truck, yellow dredge cab on swivel base, 31-3/4" long w/boom lowered, 1956
EX $100   NM $150   MIP $250

❑ **Overhead Crane**, Buddy L, black folding end frames and legs, braces, red cross-beams and platform, 45" long, 1924
EX $1500   NM $2000   MIP $3000

❑ **Pile Driver on Wheels**, Buddy L, black w/red roof and base, 22-1/2" tall, 1924-27
EX $800   NM $1800   MIP $2600

❑ **Polysteel Farm Tractor**, Buddy L, orange molded plastic four-wheel tractor, silver radiator front, headlights, and motor parts, 12" long, 1961
EX $80   NM $120   MIP $155

❑ **Pull-n-Ride Horse-Drawn Farm Wagon**, Buddy L, red four-wheel steel hopper-body wagon, detailed litho horse, 22-3/4" long, 1952
EX $150   NM $225   MIP $300

❑ **Road Roller**, Buddy L, dark green w/red roof and rollers, nickel plated steam cylinders, 20" long, 1929-31
EX $3000   NM $4000   MIP $5000

❑ **Ruff-n-Tuff Tractor**, Buddy L, yellow grille, hood and frame, black plastic engine block and driver's seat, 10-1/2" long, 1971
EX $50   NM $75   MIP $100

❑ **Sand Loader**, Buddy L, warm gray w/twelve black buckets, 21" long, 18" high, 1924
EX $150   NM $210   MIP $450

❑ **Sand Loader**, Buddy L, warm gray w/twelve black buckets, chain-tension adjusting device at bottom of elevator side frames, 21" long, 1929
EX $175   NM $305   MIP $500

❑ **Sand Loader**, Buddy L, yellow w/twelve black buckets, chain-tension adjusting device at bottom of elevator side frames, 21" long, 1931
EX $200   NM $250   MIP $350

❑ **Scoop-n-Load Conveyor**, Buddy L, cream body frame, red loading scoop and chute, bright-plated circular crank operates black rubber cleated conveyor belt, "PORTABLE" decal in white, 18" long, 1955
EX $60   NM $95   MIP $125

❑ **Scoop-n-Load Conveyor**, Buddy L, cream body frame, red loading scoop and chute, bright-plated circular crank operates black rubber cleated conveyor belt, "PORTABLE" decal in yellow, 18" long, 1956
EX $55   NM $85   MIP $115

❑ **Scoop-n-Load Conveyor**, Buddy L, cream body frame, green loading scoop, black circular crank operates black rubber cleated conveyor belt, "PORTABLE" decal in red, 18" long, 1954
EX $65   NM $105   MIP $140

❑ **Scoop-n-Load Conveyor**, Buddy L, cream body frame, green loading scoop, black circular crank operates black rubber cleated conveyor belt, 18" long, 1953
EX $75   NM $115   MIP $150

❑ **Side Conveyor Load-n-Dump**, Buddy L, all steel yellow cab, hood, bumper and frame, white dump body and tailgate, red conveyor frame w/chute, 21-1/4" long, 1954
EX $65   NM $100   MIP $135

❑ **Side Conveyor Load-n-Dump**, Buddy L, all steel yellow cab, hood, bumper and frame, deep blue dump body, white tailgate, red conveyor frame w/chute, 21-1/4" long, 1955
EX $60   NM $95   MIP $125

❑ **Side Conveyor Load-n-Dump**, Buddy L, yellow plastic front end including cab, yellow steel bumper, green frame and dump body, red conveyor frame w/chute, 20-1/2" long, 1953
EX $80   NM $130   MIP $150

❑ **Small Derrick**, Buddy L, red 20" movable boom and three angle-iron braces, black base and vertical mast, 21-1/2" tall, 1921
EX $500   NM $750   MIP $1000

❑ **Steam Shovel**, Buddy L, black w/red roof and base, 25-1/2" tall, 1921-22
EX $125   NM $250   MIP $500

❑ **Traveling Crane**, Buddy L, red crane, carriage, and long cross beams, hand wheel rotates crane boom, 46" long, 1928
EX $1275   NM $1900   MIP $2550

❑ **Trench Digger**, Buddy L, yellow main frame, base, and motor housing, red elevator and conveyor frame and track frames, 20" tall, 1928-31
EX $2000   NM $3500   MIP $5000

MISCELLANEOUS

(Toy Shop File Photo)

❑ **49 LST**, Buddy L, Gray landing craft with swivel guns on deck, opening ramp door, includes tank and army truck
EX $20   NM $40   MIP $85

(Toy Shop File Photo)

❑ **Fill-R-Up Gas Pump**, Buddy L, White plastic gas pump, 4" wide, 7" high, 2-3/4" deep. Magnetic pump holds to metal vehicles, two "C" batteries power the pump register and bell. According to the 1970 catalog, it "totals price automatically--up to 39 gallons at $9.75."
EX $12   NM $25   MIP $40

SETS

❑ **Army Combination Set**, Buddy L, searchlight repair-it truck, transport truck and howitzer, ammunition conveyor, stake delivery truck, ammo, soldiers, 1956
EX $300   NM $400   MIP $500

❑ **Army Commando Set**, Buddy L, 14-1/2" truck, searchlight unit, two-wheel howitzer, soldiers, 1957
EX $125   NM $185   MIP $250

❑ **Big Brute 3-Piece Highway Set**, Buddy L, bulldozer, dump truck, yellow four-wheel trailer, 1971
EX $95   NM $155   MIP $210

❑ **Big Brute 3-Piece Road Set**, Buddy L, cement mixer truck, scooper, dump truck, 1971
EX $125   NM $185   MIP $250

❑ **Big Brute 4-Piece Freeway Set**, Buddy L, scraper, grader, scooper and dump truck, 1971
EX $125   NM $185   MIP $250

❑ **Brute Fire Department Set**, Buddy L, semi-trailer aerial ladder truck, fire pumper, fire wrecker, brute tow truck, 1970
EX $75   NM $115   MIP $150

❑ **Brute Five-Piece Highway Set**, Buddy L, bulldozer, grader, scraper, dumping scraper and double dump train, 1970
EX $50   NM $80   MIP $105

❑ **Brute Fleet Set**, Buddy L, car carrier w/two plastic coupes, dump truck, pickup truck, cement mixer truck, tow truck, 1969
EX $85   NM $130   MIP $175

❑ **Delivery Set Combination**, Buddy L, 16-1/2" long wrigley express truck, 15" long sand and stone dump truck, 14-1/4" long freight conveyor and 14-1/4" long stake delivery truck, 1955
EX $175   NM $265   MIP $350

❑ **Family Camping Set**, Buddy L, Camper/cruiser truck, 15-1/2" long maroon suburban wagon, and brown/light gray/beige folding teepee camping trailer, 1963
EX $60   NM $95   MIP $130

VEHICLES

❏ **Family Camping Set**, Buddy L, blue camping trailer and suburban wagon, blue camper-n-cruiser, 1964
EX $50   NM $75   MIP $100

❏ **Farm Combination Set**, Buddy L, cattle transport stake truck w/six plastic steers, hydraulic farm supplies trailer dump truck, trailer and three farm machines and farm machinery trailer hauler truck, 1956
EX $100   NM $155   MIP $210

❏ **Fire Department Set**, Buddy L, aerial ladder fire engine, fire pumper w/action hydrant that squirts water, two plastic hoses, two plastic firemen, fire chief's badge, 1960
EX $250   NM $375   MIP $505

❏ **Freight Conveyor and Stake Delivery Truck**, Buddy L, blue frame 14-1/4" long conveyor, red, white and yellow body 14-3/4" long truck, 1955
EX $125   NM $185   MIP $250

❏ **GMC Air Defense Set**, Buddy L, 15" long, GMC army searchlight truck, 15" long, GMC signal corps truck, two four-wheel trailers, plastic soliders, 1957
EX $300   NM $500   MIP $700

❏ **GMC Brinks Bank Set**, Buddy L, silver gray, barred windows on sides and in double doors, coin slot and hole in roof, brass padlock w/two keys, pouch, play money, two gray plastic guard figures, 16" long, 1959
EX $305   NM $360   MIP $455

❏ **GMC Fire Department Set**, Buddy L, red GMC extension ladder trailer and GMC pumper w/ladders and hose reel, four-wheel red electric searchlight trailer, warning barrier, red plastic helmet, firemen, policeman, 1958
EX $300   NM $500   MIP $750

❏ **GMC Highway Maintenance Fleet**, Buddy L, orange maintenance truck w/trailer, sand and stone dump truck, scoop-n-load conveyor, sand hopper, steel scoop shovel, four white steel road barriers, 1957
EX $310   NM $505   MIP $710

❏ **GMC Livestock Set**, Buddy L, red fenders, hood, cab and frame, white flatbed cargo section , six sections of brown plastic rail fencing, five black plastic steers, 14-1/2" long, 1958
EX $300   NM $400   MIP $500

❏ **GMC Western Roundup Set**, Buddy L, blue fenders, hood, cab and frame, white flatbed cargo section, plastic six sections of rail fencing w/swinging gate, rearing and standing horse, cowboys, calf, steer, 1959
EX $300   NM $400   MIP $500

❏ **Highway Construction Set**, Buddy L, orange and black bulldozer and driver, truck w/orange pickup body, orange dump truck, 1962
EX $200   NM $300   MIP $400

❏ **Highway Maintenance Mechanical Truck & Concrete Mixer**, Buddy L, 20" truck plus movable ramp, w/duo-tone slant design, blue lower hood sides, yel-low hood top and cab, 10-3/4" blue and yellow mixer, overall 36" long, 1949
EX $160   NM $245   MIP $325

❏ **Interstate Highway Set**, Buddy L, orange, parks department dumper, landscape truck, telephone truck, accessories include trees, drums, workmen and traffic cones, scoop shovel, 1959
EX $260   NM $410   MIP $505

❏ **Interstate Highway Set**, Buddy L, orange, husky dumper, contractor's truck and ladder, utility truck, plastic pickaxe, spade, shovel, nail keg, 1960
EX $250   NM $350   MIP $500

❏ **Jr. Animal Farm Set**, Buddy L, 6-1/2" long Jr. Giraffe Truck, 6-1/4" long Jr. Kitty Kennel, 11-1/4" long Jr. Pony Trailer w/Sportster, 1968
EX $120   NM $185   MIP $250

❏ **Jr. Fire Department**, Buddy L, 17" long Jr. hook-n-ladder aerial truck, 11-1/2" long Jr. fire snorkel, 6-3/4" long truck, all have twenty-four-hole chrome grilles, 1968
EX $120   NM $190   MIP $255

❏ **Jr. Fire Department**, Buddy L, 17" long Jr. hook-n-ladder aerial truck, 11-1/2" long Jr. fire snorkel, 6-3/4" long truck, all have four-slot grilles and two square plastic headlights, 1969
EX $120   NM $185   MIP $250

❏ **Jr. Highway Set**, Buddy L, yellow and black Jr. scooper tractor, yellow and white Jr. cement mixer truck, yellow Jr. dump truck, 1969
EX $200   NM $300   MIP $400

❏ **Jr. Sportsman Set**, Buddy L, Jr. camper pickup w/red cab and body and yellow camper, towing 6" plastic runabout on yellow two-wheel boat trailer, 1971
EX $50   NM $80   MIP $105

❏ **Loader, Dump Truck, and Shovel Set**, Buddy L, conveyor, green body sand and gravel dump truck, 8-3/4" long green-enameled steel scoop shovel, 1954
EX $100   NM $150   MIP $200

❏ **Loader, Dump Truck, and Shovel Set**, Buddy L, conveyor, blue body sand and gravel dump truck, 8-3/4" long blue-enameled steel scoop shovel, 1955
EX $85   NM $130   MIP $175

❏ **Mechanical Hauling Truck and Concrete Mixer**, Buddy L, truck w/duo-tone slant design, red/orange lower hood sides, dark green upper hood, cab, ramp, yellow trailer, 9-5/8" green mixer, gray hopper, 38" long w/ramps, 1951
EX $150   NM $225   MIP $300

❏ **Mechanical Hauling Truck and Concrete Mixer**, Buddy L, truck w/duo-tone slant design, red-orange lower hood sides, dark green upper hood, cab, trailer and ramp, 9-5/8" green mixer, gray hopper, 38" long w/ramps, 1950
EX $160   NM $245   MIP $325

❏ **Polysteel Farm Set**, Buddy L, blue milk-man truck w/rack and nine milk bottles,red and gray milk tanker, orange farm tractor, 1961
EX $70   NM $115   MIP $160

❏ **Road Builder Set**, Buddy L, green/white cement mixer truck, yellow/black bulldozer, red dump truck, husky dumper, 1963
EX $200   NM $300   MIP $400

❏ **Truck with Concrete Mixer Trailer**, Buddy L, 22" truck w/duo-tone slant design, green fenders and lower sides, yellow squarish cab and body, 10" mixer w/yellow frame and red hopper, overall 34-1/2" long, 1937
EX $175   NM $265   MIP $350

❏ **Truck with Concrete Mixer Trailer**, Buddy L, 22" truck w/duo-tone slant design, green front and lower hood sides, yellow upper hood, cab and body, 10" mixer w/yellow frame and red hopper, overall 32-1/2" long, 1938
EX $165   NM $250   MIP $330

❏ **Warehouse Set**, Buddy L, Coca-Cola truck, two hand trucks, eight cases Coke bottles, store-door delivery truck, lumber, sign, two barrels, forklift, 1958
EX $175   NM $265   MIP $350

❏ **Warehouse Set**, Buddy L, Coca-Cola truck, two hand trucks, eight cases Coke bottles, store-door delivery truck, sign, two barrels, forklift, 1959
EX $150   NM $225   MIP $300

❏ **Western Roundup Set**, Buddy L, turquoise fenders, hood, cab and frame, white flatbed cargo section, six sections of rail fencing w/swinging gate, rearing and standing horse, cowboys, calf, steer, 1960
EX $175   NM $250   MIP $400

TRUCKS

❏ **Air Force Supply Transport**, Buddy L, blue w/blue removable fabric canopy, rubber wheels, decals on cab doors, 14-1/2" long, 1957
EX $125   NM $250   MIP $355

❏ **Air Mail Truck**, Buddy L, black front, hood fenders, enclosed cab and opening doors, red enclosed body and chassis, 24" long, 1930
EX $675   NM $1000   MIP $1400

❏ **Allied Moving Van**, Buddy L, tractor and semi-trailer van, duo-tone slant design, black front and lower sides, orange hood top, cab and van body, 29-1/2" long, 1941
EX $600   NM $900   MIP $1200

❏ **Army Electric Searchlight Unit**, Buddy L, shiny olive drab flatbed truck, battery-operated searchlight, 14-3/4" long, 1957
EX $125   NM $230   MIP $330

❏ **Army Half-Track and Howitzer**, Buddy L, olive drab w/olive drab carriage, 12-1/2" truck, 9-3/4" gun, overall 22-1/2" long, 1953
EX $105   NM $150   MIP $200

❏ **Army Half-Track with Howitzer**, Buddy L, olive drab steel, red firing knob on

gun, 17" truck, 9-3/4" gun, overall 27" long, 1955
EX $100   **NM** $150   **MIP** $200

❏ **Army Medical Corps Truck**, Buddy L, white, black rubber tires on white steel disc wheels, 29-1/2" long, 1941
EX $125   **NM** $185   **MIP** $250

❏ **Army Searchlight Repair-It Truck**, Buddy L, shiny olive drab truck and flat-bed cargo section, 15" long, 1956
EX $125   **NM** $175   **MIP** $225

❏ **Army Supply Truck**, Buddy L, shiny olive drab truck and removable fabric cover, 14-1/2" long, 1956
EX $100   **NM** $150   **MIP** $175

❏ **Army Transport Truck and Trailer**, Buddy L, olive drab truck, 20-1/2" long, trailer 34-1/2" long, 1940
EX $250   **NM** $350   **MIP** $450

❏ **Army Transport with Howitzer**, Buddy L, olive drab steel, 17" truck, 9-3/4" gun, overall 27" long, 1955
EX $150   **NM** $250   **MIP** $350

❏ **Army Transport with Howitzer**, Buddy L, olive drab steel, re-firing knob on gun, 17" truck, 9-3/4" gun, overall 27" long, 1954
EX $115   **NM** $175   **MIP** $230

❏ **Army Transport with Howitzer**, Buddy L, olive drab, 12" truck, 9-3/4" gun, over-all 28" long, 1953
EX $100   **NM** $150   **MIP** $200

❏ **Army Transport with Tank**, Buddy L, olive drab, 15-1/2" long truck, 11-1/2" long detachable two-wheel trailer, over-all 26-1/2" long, 7-1/2" long tank, 1959
EX $100   **NM** $150   **MIP** $200

❏ **Army Troop Transport with Howitzer**, Buddy L, dark forest green truck and gun, canopy mixture of greens, 14" long truck, 12" long, gun, overall 25-3/4" long, 1965
EX $100   **NM** $150   **MIP** $200

❏ **Army Truck**, Buddy L, olive drab, 20-1/2" long, 1939
EX $110   **NM** $175   **MIP** $225

❏ **Army Truck**, Buddy L, olive drab, 17" long, 1940
EX $150   **NM** $200   **MIP** $250

❏ **Atlas Van Lines**, Buddy L, green tractor unit, chrome one-piece toothed grille and headlights, green lower half of semi-trailer van body, cream upper half, silvery roof, 29" long, 1956
EX $200   **NM** $300   **MIP** $400

❏ **Auto Hauler**, Buddy L, yellow cab-over-engine tractor unit and double-deck semi-trailer, three 8" long vehicles, 25-1/2" long, 1968
EX $75   **NM** $115   **MIP** $150

❏ **Auto Hauler**, Buddy L, snub-nose medium blue tractor unit and double-deck semi-truck trailer, three plastic coupes, overall 27-1/2" long, 1970
EX $65   **NM** $95   **MIP** $130

❏ **Baggage Rider**, Buddy L, duo-tone horizontal design, green bumper, fenders

and lower half of truck, white upper half, 28" long, 1950
EX $250   **NM** $175   **MIP** $500

❏ **Baggage Truck**, Buddy L, green hood, fenders, and cab, yellow cargo section, no bumper, 17-1/2" long, 1945
EX $175   **NM** $265   **MIP** $350

❏ **Baggage Truck**, Buddy L, duo-tone slant design, yellow skirted fenders and cargo section, green hood top, enclosed cab, 27-3/4" long, 1938
EX $300   **NM** $600   **MIP** $1000

❏ **Baggage Truck**, Buddy L, black front, hood, and fenders, enclosed cab w/opening doors, nickel-rim, red-shell headlights, yellow stake body, 26-1/2" long, 1930-32
EX $3000   **NM** $5000   **MIP** $7000

❏ **Baggage Truck**, Buddy L, green front, hood, and fenders, non-open doors, yellow cargo section slat or solid sides, metal grille, 26-1/2" long, 1935
EX $350   **NM** $500   **MIP** $650

❏ **Baggage Truck**, Buddy L, black front, hood, and fenders, doorless cab, yellow four-post stake sides, two chains across back, 26-1/2" long, 1927
EX $805   **NM** $1020   **MIP** $2100

❏ **Baggage Truck**, Buddy L, duo-tone slant design, yellow fenders, green hood top, cab, and removable rider seat, 26-1/2" long, 1936
EX $350   **NM** $750   **MIP** $1000

❏ **Big Brute Dumper**, Buddy L, yellow cab-over-engine, frame and tiltback dump section w/cab shield, striped black and yellow bumper, black grille, 8" long, 1971
EX $50   **NM** $75   **MIP** $100

❏ **Big Brute Mixer Truck**, Buddy L, yellow cab-over-engine, body and frame, white plastic mixing drum, white plastic seats, 7" long, 1971
EX $35   **NM** $50   **MIP** $70

❏ **Big Fella Hydraulic Rider Dumper**, Buddy L, duo-tone slant design, yellow front and lower hood, red upper cab, dump body and upper hood, rider seat has large yellow sunburst-style decal, 26-1/2" long, 1950
EX $110   **NM** $175   **MIP** $225

❏ **Big Mack Dumper**, Buddy L, off-white front, hood cab and chassis, blue-green tiltback dump section, white plastic bumper, 20-1/2" long, 1964
EX $75   **NM** $115   **MIP** $150

❏ **Big Mack Dumper**, Buddy L, yellow front, hood cab, chassis and tiltback dump section, black plastic bumper, 20-1/2" long, 1967
EX $70   **NM** $100   **MIP** $140

❏ **Big Mack Dumper**, Buddy L, yellow front, hood cab, chassis and tiltback dump section, black plastic bumper, single rear wheels, 20-1/2" long, 1968
EX $65   **NM** $95   **MIP** $130

❏ **Big Mack Dumper**, Buddy L, yellow front, hood cab, chassis and tiltback dump section, black plastic bumper, heavy-duty

black balloon tires on yellow plastic five-spoke wheels, 20-1/2" long, 1971
EX $60   **NM** $90   **MIP** $120

❏ **Big Mack Hydraulic Dumper**, Buddy L, red hood, cab and tiltback dump section w/cab shield, white plastic bumper, short step ladder on each side, 20-1/2" long, 1968
EX $50   **NM** $75   **MIP** $100

❏ **Big Mack Hydraulic Dumper**, Buddy L, white hood, cab and tiltback dump section w/cab shield, white plastic bumper, short step ladder on each side, 20-1/2" long, 1969
EX $45   **NM** $65   **MIP** $90

❏ **Big Mack Hydraulic Dumper**, Buddy L, red hood, cab and tiltback dump section w/cab shield, dump body sides have a large circular back, white plastic bumper, short step ladder on each side, 20-1/2" long, 1970
EX $40   **NM** $60   **MIP** $80

❏ **Boat Transport**, Buddy L, blue flatbed truck carrying 8" litho metal boat, boat deck white, hull red, truck 15" long, 1959
EX $300   **NM** $550   **MIP** $750

❏ **Borden's Milk Delivery Van**, Buddy L, white upper cab-over-engine van body and sliding side doors, yellow lower body, metal-handle yellow plastic tray and six white milk bottle w/yellow caps, 11-1/2" long, 1965
EX $125   **NM** $200   **MIP** $275

❏ **Brute Car Carrier**, Buddy L, bright blue cab-over-engine tractor unit and detachable double-deck semi-trailer, two plastic cars, 10" long, 1969
EX $60   **NM** $95   **MIP** $125

❏ **Brute Cement Mixer Truck**, Buddy L, sand-beige cab-over-engine body and frame, white plastic mixing drum, white plastic seats, 5-1/4" long, 1968
EX $35   **NM** $55   **MIP** $75

❏ **Brute Cement Mixer Truck**, Buddy L, blue cab-over-engine body and frame, white plastic mixing drum, white plastic seats, white-handled crank rotates drum, 5-1/4" long, 1969
EX $30   **NM** $50   **MIP** $70

❏ **Brute Dumper**, Buddy L, red cab-over-engine body and cab shield on tiltback dump section, wide chrome wrap-around bumper, 5" long, 1968
EX $35   **NM** $55   **MIP** $75

❏ **Brute Monkey House**, Buddy L, yellow cab-over-engine body, striped orange and white awning roof, cage on back, two plastic monkeys, 5" long, 1968
EX $50   **NM** $75   **MIP** $100

❏ **Brute Monkey House**, Buddy L, yellow cab-over-engine body, red and white awning roof, cage on back, two plastic monkeys, 5" long, 1969
EX $40   **NM** $60   **MIP** $80

❏ **Brute Sanitation Truck**, Buddy L, lime green cab-over-engine and frame, white open-top body, wide chrome wrap-around bumper, 5-1/4" long, 1969
EX $50   **NM** $75   **MIP** $100

VEHICLES

❑ **Buddy L Milk Farms Truck**, Buddy L, white body, black roof, short hood w/black wooden headlights, 13-1/2" long, 1945
EX $150   NM $300   MIP $450

❑ **Buddy L Milk Farms Truck**, Buddy L, light cream body, red roof, nickel glide headlights, sliding doors, 13" long, 1949
EX $170   NM $300   MIP $500

❑ **Camper**, Buddy L, bright medium blue steel truck and camper body, 14-1/2" long, 1964
EX $60   NM $95   MIP $125

❑ **Camper**, Buddy L, medium blue truck and back door, white camper body, 14-1/2" long, 1965
EX $50   NM $75   MIP $100

❑ **Camper-N-Cruiser**, Buddy L, bright medium blue camper w/matching boat trailer and 8-1/2" long plastic sport cruiser, overall 27" long, 1964
EX $50   NM $75   MIP $100

❑ **Camper-N-Cruiser**, Buddy L, powder blue pickup truck and trailer, pale blue camper body, 24-1/2" long, 1963
EX $60   NM $95   MIP $125

❑ **Campers Truck**, Buddy L, turquoise pickup truck, pale turquoise plastic camper, 14-1/2" long, 1961
EX $55   NM $85   MIP $110

❑ **Campers Truck with Boat**, Buddy L, green/turquoise pickup truck, lime green camper body, red plastic runabout boat on camper roof, 14-1/2" long, 1962
EX $50   NM $100   MIP $150

❑ **Campers Truck with Boat**, Buddy L, green/turquoise pickup, no side mirror, lime green camper body w/red plastic runabout boat on top, 14-1/2" long, 1963
EX $50   NM $100   MIP $150

❑ **Camping Trailer and Wagon**, Buddy L, bright medium blue suburban wagon, matching teepee trailer, overall 24-1/2" long, 1964
EX $60   NM $95   MIP $125

❑ **Cattle Transport Truck**, Buddy L, red w/yellow stake sides, 15" long, 1956
EX $75   NM $115   MIP $150

❑ **Cattle Transport Truck**, Buddy L, green and white w/white stake sides, 15" long, 1957
EX $75   NM $115   MIP $150

❑ **Cement Mixer Truck**, Buddy L, red body, tank ends, and chute, white side ladder, water tank, mixing drum and loading hopper, 15-1/2" long, 1965
EX $75   NM $115   MIP $150

❑ **Cement Mixer Truck**, Buddy L, snub-nosed yellow body, cab, frame and chute, white plastic mixing drum, loading hopper and water tank w/yellow ends, 16" long, 1970
EX $35   NM $50   MIP $70

❑ **Cement Mixer Truck**, Buddy L, red body, tank ends, and chute, white water

tank, mixing drum and loading hopper, black wall tires, 15-1/2" long, 1967
EX $60   NM $95   MIP $125

❑ **Cement Mixer Truck**, Buddy L, turquoise body, tank ends, and chute, white side ladder, water tank, mixing drum and loading hopper, 16-1/2" long, 1964
EX $60   NM $95   MIP $125

❑ **Cement Mixer Truck**, Buddy L, red body, tank ends, and chute, white water tank, mixing drum and loading hopper, whitewall tires, 15-1/2" long, 1968
EX $50   NM $75   MIP $100

❑ **Charles Chip Delivery Truck Van**, Buddy L, tan/beige body, decal on sides has brown irregular center resembling a large potato chip, 1966
EX $125   NM $200   MIP $275

❑ **City Baggage Dray**, Buddy L, duo-tone slant design, green front and skirted fenders, yellow hood top, enclosed cab and cargo section, 20-3/4" long, 1938
EX $150   NM $200   MIP $350

❑ **City Baggage Dray**, Buddy L, green front, hood, and fenders, non-open doors, yellow stake-side cargo section, 19" long, 1934
EX $150   NM $300   MIP $400

❑ **City Baggage Dray**, Buddy L, cream w/aluminum-finish grille, no bumper, black rubber wheels, 20-3/4" long, 1940
EX $100   NM $200   MIP $300

❑ **City Baggage Dray**, Buddy L, light green w/aluminum-finish grille, no bumper, black rubber wheels, 20-3/4" long, 1939
EX $95   NM $250   MIP $300

❑ **City Baggage Dray**, Buddy L, duo-tone slant design, green front and fenders, yellow hood top and cargo section, dummy headlights, 19" long, 1937
EX $150   NM $300   MIP $400

❑ **City Baggage Dray**, Buddy L, green front, hood, and fenders, non-open doors, yellow stake-side cargo section, bright metal grille, 19" long, 1935
EX $150   NM $300   MIP $400

❑ **City Baggage Dray**, Buddy L, duo-tone slant design, green front and fenders, yellow hood top and cargo section, 19" long, 1936
EX $150   NM $300   MIP $400

❑ **Coal Truck**, Buddy L, black hopper body and fully enclosed cab w/opening doors, red wheels, 25" long, 1930
EX $900   NM $1500   MIP $2000

❑ **Coal Truck**, Buddy L, black front, hood, fenders, doorless cab, red chassis and disc wheels, 25" long, 1926
EX $700   NM $1000   MIP $2000

❑ **Coal Truck**, Buddy L, black front, hood, fenders, sliding discharge door on each side of hopper body, red chassis and disc wheels, 25" long, 1927
EX $800   NM $1000   MIP $2000

❑ **Coca-Cola Bottling Route Truck**, Buddy L, bright yellow, w/small metal hand truck,

six or eight yellow cases of miniature green Coke bottles, 14-3/4" long, 1955
EX $125   NM $175   MIP $250

❑ **Coca-Cola Bottling Route Truck**, Buddy L, bright yellow, w/two small metal hand trucks and eight yellow cases of miniature green Coke bottles, 14-3/4" long, 1957
EX $110   NM $175   MIP $225

❑ **Coca-Cola Delivery Truck**, Buddy L, orange/yellow cab and double-deck, open-side cargo, two small hand trucks, four red and four green cases of bottles, 15" long, 1963
EX $75   NM $100   MIP $150

❑ **Coca-Cola Delivery Truck**, Buddy L, orange/yellow cab and double-deck, open-side cargo, two small hand trucks, four red and four green cases of bottles, 15" long, 1964
EX $62   NM $100   MIP $130

(KP Photo)

❑ **Coca-Cola Delivery Truck**, Buddy L, red lower cab-over-engine and van body, white upper cab, left side of van lifts to reveal 10 miniature bottle cases, 9-1/2" long, 1971
EX $30   NM $45   MIP $60

❑ **Coca-Cola Delivery Truck**, Buddy L, orange/yellow cab and double-deck, open-side cargo, two small hand trucks, four red and four green cases of bottles, 15" long, 1960
EX $100   NM $150   MIP $200

❑ **Coke Coffee Co. Delivery Truck Van**, Buddy L, black lower half of body, orange upper half, roof and sliding side doors, 1966
EX $85   NM $130   MIP $175

❑ **Colt Vacationer**, Buddy L, blue/white Colt sportsliner w/trailer carrying 8-1/2" long red/white plastic sport cruiser, overall 22-1/2" long, 1967
EX $60   NM $95   MIP $125

❑ **Curtiss Candy Trailer Van**, Buddy L, blue tractor and bumper, white semi-trailer van, blue hood, chrome one-piece toothed grille and headlights, white drop-down rear door, 32-3/4" long w/tailgate/ramp lowered, 1955
EX $250   NM $400   MIP $500

❑ **Dairy Transport Truck**, Buddy L, duo-tone slant design, red front and lower hood sides, white hood top, cab and semi-trailer tank body, tank opens in back, 26" long, 1939
EX $150   NM $225   MIP $300

❑ **Deluxe Auto Carrier**, Buddy L, turquoise tractor unit, aluminum loading ramps, three plastic cars, overall 34" long including, 1962
EX $100   NM $175   MIP $250

❏ **Deluxe Camping Outfit**, Buddy L, turquoise pickup truck and camper, and 8-1/2" long plastic boat on pale turquoise boat trailer, overall 24" long, 1961
EX $60   NM $95   MIP $125

❏ **Deluxe Hydraulic Rider Dump Truck**, Buddy L, duo-tone slant design, red front and lower hood sides, white upper cab, dump body and chassis, red or black removable rider saddle, 26" long, 1948
EX $175   NM $265   MIP $350

❏ **Deluxe Motor Market**, Buddy L, duo-tone slant design, red front, curved bumper, lower hood and cab sides, white hood top, body and cab, 22-1/4" long, 1950
EX $250   NM $350   MIP $500

❏ **Deluxe Rider Delivery Truck**, Buddy L, duo-tone horizontal design, deep blue lower half, gray upper half, red rubber disc wheels, black barrel skid, 22-3/4" long, 1945
EX $135   NM $200   MIP $270

(Joe and Sharon Freed Photo)

❏ **Deluxe Rider Delivery Truck**, Buddy L, duo-tone horizontal design, gray lower half, blue upper half, red rubber disc wheels, black barrel skid, 22-3/4" long, 1945
EX $135   NM $200   MIP $270

❏ **Deluxe Rider Dump Truck**, Buddy L, various colors, dual rear wheels, no bumper, 25-1/2" long, 1945
EX $75   NM $115   MIP $150

❏ **Double Hydraulic Self-Loader-N-Dump**, Buddy L, green front loading scoop w/yellow arms attached to cab sides, yellow hood and enclosed cab, orange frame and wide dump body, 29" long w/scoop lowered, 1956
EX $85   NM $130   MIP $175

❏ **Double Tandem Hydraulic Dump and Trailer**, Buddy L, truck has red bumper, hood, cab and frame, four-wheel trailer w/red tow and frame, both w/white tilt-back dump bodies, 38" long, 1957
EX $85   NM $130   MIP $175

❏ **Double-Deck Boat Transport**, Buddy L, light blue steel flatbed truck carrying three 8" white plastic boats w/red decks, truck 15" long, 1960
EX $150   NM $250   MIP $400

❏ **Dr. Pepper Delivery Truck Van**, Buddy L, red, white, and blue, 1966
EX $85   NM $130   MIP $175

❏ **Dump Body Truck**, Buddy L, black front, hood, open driver's seat and dump section, red chassis, crank windlass w/ratchet raises dump bed, 25" long, 1921
EX $800   NM $1400   MIP $2000

❏ **Dump Body Truck**, Buddy L, black front, hood, open driver's seat and dump section, red chassis, chain drive dump mechanism, 25" long, 1923
EX $1200   NM $1800   MIP $2500

❏ **Dump Truck**, Buddy L, duo-tone slant design, red front, fenders and lower doors, white upper, bright radiator grille and headlights, no bumper, 22-1/4" long, 1939
EX $250   NM $375   MIP $500

❏ **Dump Truck**, Buddy L, duo-tone slant design, red front, fenders and dump body, yellow hood top, upper sides, upper cab and chassis, no bumper, 22-1/2" long, 1948
EX $125   NM $185   MIP $250

❏ **Dump Truck**, Buddy L, various colors, black rubber wheels, 12" long, 1945
EX $50   NM $75   MIP $100

❏ **Dump Truck**, Buddy L, black enclosed cab and opening doors, front and hood, red dump body and chassis, crank handle lifts dump bed, 24" long, 1931
EX $750   NM $1125   MIP $1500

❏ **Dump Truck**, Buddy L, red hood top and cab, white or cream dump body and frame, no bumper, 17-1/2" long, 1945
EX $75   NM $115   MIP $150

❏ **Dump Truck**, Buddy L, white upper hood, enclosed cab, wide-skirt fenders and open-frame chassis, orange dump body, bright-metal grille, no bumper, 17-3/8" long, 1941
EX $85   NM $135   MIP $180

❏ **Dump Truck**, Buddy L, green w/cream hood top and upper enclosed cab, no bumper, bright-metal headlights and grille, 22-1/4" long, 1941
EX $85   NM $130   MIP $175

❏ **Dump Truck**, Buddy L, duo-tone slant design, yellow enclosed cab and hood, red front and dump body, no bumper, dummy headlights, 20" long, 1937
EX $250   NM $375   MIP $505

❏ **Dump Truck**, Buddy L, duo-tone slant design, yellow enclosed cab and hood, red front and dump body, no bumper, bright-metal headlights, 20" long, 1936
EX $250   NM $375   MIP $500

❏ **Dump Truck**, Buddy L, yellow enclosed cab, front and hood, red dump section, no bumper, bright-metal radiator, 20" long, 1935
EX $325   NM $485   MIP $650

❏ **Dump Truck**, Buddy L, yellow enclosed cab, front and hood, red dump section, no bumper, 20" long, 1934
EX $275   NM $415   MIP $550

❏ **Dump Truck**, Buddy L, yellow upper hood and enclosed cab, red wide-skirt fenders and open-frame chassis, blue dump body, no bumper, 17-1/4" long, 1940
EX $85   NM $130   MIP $175

❏ **Dump Truck**, Buddy L, black enclosed cab and opening doors, front and hood, red dump body and chassis, simple

lever arrangement lifts dump bed, 24" long, 1930
EX $650   NM $975   MIP $1300

❏ **Dump Truck**, Buddy L, duo-tone slant design, red lower cab, lower hood, front and dump body, yellow upper hood, upper cab and chassis, no bumper, 22-1/4" long, 1939
EX $250   NM $375   MIP $500

❏ **Dump Truck-Economy Line**, Buddy L, dark blue dump body, remainder is yellow, bright-metal grille and headlights, no bumper or running boards, 12" long, 1941
EX $75   NM $125   MIP $150

❏ **Dumper with Shovel**, Buddy L, medium green body, frame and dump section, white one-piece bumper and grille guard, no side mirror, large white steel scoop shovel, spring suspension on front axle only, 15" long, 1964
EX $75   NM $115   MIP $150

❏ **Dumper with Shovel**, Buddy L, orange body, frame and dump section, chrome one-piece grille, no bumper guard, no side mirror, large white steel scoop shovel, no spring suspension, 15-3/4" long, 1965
EX $75   NM $115   MIP $150

❏ **Dumper with Shovel**, Buddy L, medium green body, frame and dump section, white one-piece bumper and grille guard, no side mirror, large white steel scoop shovel, 15" long, 1963
EX $75   NM $115   MIP $150

❏ **Dumper with Shovel**, Buddy L, turquoise body, frame and dump section, white one-piece bumper and grille guard, large white steel scoop shovel, 15" long, 1962
EX $75   NM $115   MIP $150

❏ **Dump-n-Dozer**, Buddy L, orange husky dumper truck and orange flatbed four-wheel trailer carrying orange bulldozer, 23" long including trailer, 1962
EX $75   NM $115   MIP $150

❏ **Express Trailer Truck**, Buddy L, red tractor unit, hood, fenders and enclosed cab, green semi-trailer van w/removable roof and drop-down rear door, bright-metal dummy headlights, 23-3/4" long, 1934
EX $350   NM $525   MIP $700

❏ **Express Trailer Truck**, Buddy L, red tractor unit, hood, fenders and enclosed cab, green semi-trailer van w/removable roof and drop-down rear door, 23-3/4" long, 1933
EX $350   NM $525   MIP $700

❏ **Express Truck**, Buddy L, all black except red frame, enclosed cab w/opening doors, nickel-rim, red-shell headlights, six rubber tires, double bar front bumper, 24-1/2" long, 1930-32
EX $3000   NM $4500   MIP $6000

❏ **Farm Machinery Hauler Trailer Truck**, Buddy L, blue tractor unit, yellow flatbed semi-trailer, 31-1/2" long, 1956
EX $125   NM $185   MIP $250

❑ **Farm Supplies Automatic Dump**, Buddy L, duo-tone slant design, blue curved bumper, front, lower hood sides and cab, yellow upper hood, cab and rest of body, 22-1/2" long, 1950
EX $125   **NM** $190   **MIP** $250

❑ **Farm Supplies Dump Truck**, Buddy L, duo-tone slant design, red front, fenders and lower hood sides, yellow upper hood, cab and body, 22-3/4" long, 1949
EX $125   **NM** $185   **MIP** $250

❑ **Farm Supplies Hydraulic Dump Trailer**, Buddy L, green tractor unit, long cream body on semi-trailer, fourteen rubber wheels, 26-1/2" long, 1956
EX $100   **NM** $150   **MIP** $200

❑ **Fast Delivery Pickup**, Buddy L, yellow hood and cab, red open cargo body, removable chain across open back, 13-1/2" long, 1949
EX $105   **NM** $155   **MIP** $200

❑ **Finger-Tip Steering Hydraulic Dumper**, Buddy L, powder blue bumper, fenders, hood, cab and frame, white tilt-back dump body, 22" long, 1959
EX $75   **NM** $115   **MIP** $150

❑ **Fisherman**, Buddy L, light tan pickup truck w/tan steel trailer carrying plastic 8-1/2" long sport crusier, overall 24-1/4" long, 1962
EX $80   **NM** $120   **MIP** $160

❑ **Fisherman**, Buddy L, sage gray/green and white pickup truck w/steel trailer carrying plastic 8-1/2" long sport cruiser, overall 25" long, 1965
EX $65   **NM** $100   **MIP** $135

❑ **Fisherman**, Buddy L, metallic sage green pickup truck w/boat trailer carrying plastic 8-1/2" long sport cruiser, overall 25" long, 1964
EX $70   **NM** $100   **MIP** $140

❑ **Fisherman**, Buddy L, pale blue/green station wagon w/four-wheel boat trailer carrying plastic 8-1/2" long boat, overall 27-1/2" long, 1963
EX $75   **NM** $115   **MIP** $150

❑ **Flivver Dump Truck**, Buddy L, black w/red eight-spoke wheels, black hubs, aluminum tires, flat, open dump section w/squared-off back w/latching, drop-down endgate, 11" long, 1926
EX $700   **NM** $1000   **MIP** $1500

❑ **Flivver Scoop Dump Truck**, Buddy L, black w/red eight-spoke wheels, 12-1/2" long, 1926-27, 1929-30
EX $1500   **NM** $2500   **MIP** $3500

❑ **Flivver Truck**, Buddy L, black w/red eight-spoke wheels w/aluminum tires, black hubs, 12" long, 1924
EX $800   **NM** $1000   **MIP** $1500

❑ **Ford Flivver Dump Cart**, Buddy L, black w/red eight-spoke wheels, black hubs, aluminum tires, flat, short open dump section tapers to point on each side, 12-1/2" long, 1926
EX $1500   **NM** $2500   **MIP** $3500

❑ **Frederick & Nelson Delivery Truck Van**, Buddy L, medium green body, roof and sliding side doors, 1966
EX $125   **NM** $200   **MIP** $275

❑ **Freight Delivery Stake Truck**, Buddy L, red hood, bumper, cab and frame, white cargo section, yellow three-post, three-slat removable stake sides, 14-3/4" long, 1955
EX $75   **NM** $125   **MIP** $150

❑ **Front Loader Hi-Lift Dump Truck**, Buddy L, red scoop and arms attached to white truck at rear fenders, green dump body, 17-3/4" long w/scoop down and dump body raised, 1955
EX $85   **NM** $130   **MIP** $175

❑ **Giant Hydraulic Dumper**, Buddy L, overall color turquoise, dump lever has a red plastic tip, 22-3/4" long, 1961
EX $135   **NM** $200   **MIP** $275

❑ **Giant Hydraulic Dumper**, Buddy L, red bumper, frame, hood and cab, light tan tiltback dump body and cab shield 23-3/4" long, 1960
EX $125   **NM** $185   **MIP** $250

❑ **Giraffe Truck**, Buddy L, powder blue hood, white cab roof, high-sided open-top cargo section, two orange/yellow plastic giraffes, 13-1/4" long, 1968
EX $60   **NM** $95   **MIP** $125

❑ **GMC Air Force Electric Searchlight Unit**, Buddy L, all blue flatbed, off white battery-operated searchlight swivel mount, decals on cab doors, 14-3/4" long, 1958
EX $200   **NM** $300   **MIP** $410

❑ **GMC Airway Express Van**, Buddy L, green hood, cab and van body, latching double rear doors, shiny metal drum coin bank and metal hand truck, 17-1/2" long w/rear doors open, 1957
EX $250   **NM** $350   **MIP** $450

❑ **GMC Anti-Aircraft Unit with Search-light**, Buddy L, 15" truck w/four-wheel trailer, battery-operated, over 25-1/4" long, 1957
EX $240   **NM** $345   **MIP** $460

❑ **GMC Army Hauler with Jeep**, Buddy L, shiny olive drab tractor unit and flatbed trailer, 10" long jeep, overall 31-1/2" long, 1958
EX $200   **NM** $300   **MIP** $400

❑ **GMC Army Transport with Howitzer**, Buddy L, shiny olive drab, 14-1/2" long, truck, overall w/gun 22-1/2" long, 1957
EX $200   **NM** $300   **MIP** $400

❑ **GMC Brinks Armored Truck Van**, Buddy L, silver gray, barred windows on sides and in double doors, coin slot and hole in roof, brass padlock w/two keys, pouch, play money, three gray plastic guard figures, 16" long, 1958
EX $300   **NM** $350   **MIP** $450

❑ **GMC Coca-Cola Route Truck**, Buddy L, lime/yellow, w/small metal hand truck and eight cases of miniature green Coke bottles, 14-1/8" long, 1957
EX $200   **NM** $305   **MIP** $410

❑ **GMC Coca-Cola Route Truck**, Buddy L, orange/yellow, w/two small metal hand trucks and eight cases of miniature green Coke bottles, 14-1/8" long, 1958
EX $200   **NM** $300   **MIP** $400

❑ **GMC Construction Company Dumper**, Buddy L, pastel blue including control lever on left and dump section w/cab shield, hinged tailgate, chrome GMC bar grille, four wheels, 16" long, 1959
EX $150   **NM** $250   **MIP** $350

❑ **GMC Construction Company Dumper**, Buddy L, pastel blue including control lever on left and dump section w/cab shield, hinged tailgate, chrome GMC bar grille, six wheels, 16" long, 1958
EX $200   **NM** $305   **MIP** $410

❑ **GMC Highway Giant Trailer**, Buddy L, blue tractor, blue and white van, chrome GMC bar grille and headlights, blue roof on semi-trailer, white tailgate doubles as loading ramp, eighteen-wheeler, 31-1/4" long, 1957
EX $250   **NM** $350   **MIP** $450

❑ **GMC Highway Giant Trailer Truck**, Buddy L, blue tractor, blue and white van, chrome GMC bar grille and head-lights, blue roof on semi-trailer, white tailgate doubles as loading ramp, four-teen-wheeler, 30-3/4" long, 1958
EX $200   **NM** $300   **MIP** $400

❑ **GMC Husky Dumper**, Buddy L, red hood, bumper, cab and chassis, chrome GMC bar grille and nose emblem, white oversize dump body, red control lever on right side, 17-1/2" long, 1957
EX $150   **NM** $250   **MIP** $350

❑ **GMC Self-Loading Auto Carrier**, Buddy L, yellow tractor and double-deck semi trailer, three plastic cars, overall 33-1/4" long, 1959
EX $200   **NM** $300   **MIP** $410

❑ **GMC Signal Corps Unit**, Buddy L, both olive drab, 14-1/4" long truck w/remov-able fabric canopy, 8" long four-wheel trailer, 1957
EX $150   **NM** $200   **MIP** $255

❑ **Grocery Motor Market Truck**, Buddy L, duo-tone slant design, yellow front, lower hood sides, fenders and lower doors, white hood top, enclosed cab and body, no bumper, 20-1/2" long, 1937
EX $275   **NM** $415   **MIP** $550

❑ **Grocery Motor Market Truck**, Buddy L, duo-tone slant design, yellow front, lower hood sides, skirted fenders and lower doors, white hood top, cab and body, no bumper, 21-1/2" long, 1938
EX $275   **NM** $420   **MIP** $560

❑ **Heavy Hauling Dumper**, Buddy L, red hood, bumper, cab and frame, cream tiltback dump body, 20-1/2" long, 1955
EX $75   **NM** $125   **MIP** $150

❑ **Heavy Hauling Dumper**, Buddy L, red hood, bumper, cab and frame, cream oversize dump body, hinged tailgate, 21-1/2" long, 1956
EX $75   **NM** $125   **MIP** $140

❑ **Heavy Hauling Hydraulic Dumper**, Buddy L, green hood, cab and frame, cream tiltback dump body, and cab shield, raising dump body almost to vertical, 23" long, 1956
EX $70   **NM** $105   **MIP** $140

❑ **Hertz Auto Hauler**, Buddy L, bright yellow tractor and double-deck semi-trailer, three plastic vehicles, 27" long, 1965
EX $100   **NM** $150   **MIP** $200

❑ **Highway Hawk Trailer Van**, Buddy L, bronze cab tractor, chrome metallized plastic bumper, grille, air cleaner and exhaust, 19-3/4" long, 1985
EX $50   **NM** $80   **MIP** $100

❑ **Highway Maintenance Truck with Trailer**, Buddy L, orange w/black rack of four simulated floodlights behind cab, 19-1/2" long including small two-wheel trailer, 1957
EX $100   **NM** $150   **MIP** $200

❑ **Hi-Lift Farm Supplies Dump**, Buddy L, red plastic front end including hood and enclosed cab, yellow dump body, cab shield and hinged tailgate, 21-1/2" long, 1953
EX $100   **NM** $175   **MIP** $225

❑ **Hi-Lift Farm Supplies Dump**, Buddy L, all steel, red front end including hood and enclosed cab, yellow dump body, cab shield and hinged tailgate, 23-1/2" long, 1954
EX $100   **NM** $175   **MIP** $225

❑ **Hi-Lift Scoop-n-Dump Truck**, Buddy L, orange truck w/deeply fluted sides, dark green scoop on front rises to empty load into hi-lift light cream dump body, 16" long, 1953
EX $80   **NM** $125   **MIP** $175

❑ **Hi-Lift Scoop-n-Dump Truck**, Buddy L, orange truck w/deeply fluted sides, dark green scoop on front rises to empty load into deep hi-lift slightly orange dump body, 16" long, 1955
EX $75   **NM** $115   **MIP** $155

❑ **Hi-Lift Scoop-n-Dump Truck**, Buddy L, orange hood, fenders and cab, yellow front loading scoop and arms attached to fenders, white frame, dump body and cab shield, 17-3/4" long, 1956
EX $70   **NM** $135   **MIP** $145

❑ **Hi-Lift Scoop-n-Dump Truck**, Buddy L, blue hood, fenders and cab, yellow front loading scoop and arms attached to fenders, white frame, dump body, cab shield, and running boards, 17-3/4" long, 1957
EX $65   **NM** $100   **MIP** $135

❑ **Hi-Lift Scoop-n-Dump Truck**, Buddy L, orange truck w/deeply fluted sides, dark green scoop on front rises to empty load into hi-lift cream/yellow dump body, 16" long, 1952
EX $85   **NM** $130   **MIP** $175

❑ **Hi-Tip Hydraulic Dumper**, Buddy L, orange hood, cab and frame, cream tiltback dump body, and cab shield, raising dump body almost to vertical, 23" long, 1957
EX $70   **NM** $115   **MIP** $150

❑ **Husky Dumper**, Buddy L, white plastic wraparound bumper, tan body, frame and dump section, hinged tailgate, plated dump lever on left side, 15-1/4" long, 1961
EX $75   **NM** $125   **MIP** $140

❑ **Husky Dumper**, Buddy L, snub-nose red body, tiltback dump section, cab shield, full-width chrome bumperless grille, deep-tread whitewall tires, 14-1/2" long, 1970
EX $45   **NM** $70   **MIP** $90

❑ **Husky Dumper**, Buddy L, snub-nose red body, tiltback dump section snda cab shield, full-width chrome bumperless grille, white-tipped dump-control lever on left, deep-tread whitewall tires, 14-1/2" long, 1971
EX $40   **NM** $60   **MIP** $80

❑ **Husky Dumper**, Buddy L, yellow hood, cab, fram and tiltback dump section w/cab shield, crome one-piece wraparound bumper, 14-1/2" long, 1969
EX $55   **NM** $75   **MIP** $105

❑ **Husky Dumper**, Buddy L, orange wraparound bumper, body, frame and dump section, hinged tailgate, plated dump lever on left side, 15-1/4" long, 1960
EX $75   **NM** $115   **MIP** $150

❑ **Husky Dumper**, Buddy L, red hood, cab, chassis and dump section, chrome one-piece bumper and slotted grille w/double headlights, 14-1/2" long, 1968
EX $60   **NM** $95   **MIP** $125

❑ **Husky Dumper**, Buddy L, bright yellow, chrome one-piece bumper, slotted rectangular grille and double headlights, 14-1/2" long, 1966,
EX $75   **NM** $115   **MIP** $150

❑ **Hydraulic Auto Hauler with Four GMC Cars**, Buddy L, powder blue GMC tractor, 7" long plastic cars, overall 33-1/2" long including loading ramp, 1958
EX $250   **NM** $350   **MIP** $450

❑ **Hydraulic Construction Dumper**, Buddy L, red front, cab and chassis, large green dump section w/cab shield, 15-1/4" long, 1962
EX $65   **NM** $100   **MIP** $135

❑ **Hydraulic Construction Dumper**, Buddy L, tan/beige front, cab and chassis, large green dump section w/cab shield, 15-1/4" long, 1963
EX $60   **NM** $95   **MIP** $125

❑ **Hydraulic Construction Dumper**, Buddy L, bright blue front, cab and chassis, large green dump section w/cab shield, 15-1/2" long, 1964
EX $50   **NM** $75   **MIP** $100

❑ **Hydraulic Construction Dumper**, Buddy L, bright green front, cab and chassis, large green dump section w/cab shield, 14" long, 1965
EX $50   **NM** $75   **MIP** $100

❑ **Hydraulic Construction Dumper**, Buddy L, medium blue front, cab and chassis, large green dump section w/cab shield, 15-1/4" long, 1967
EX $50   **NM** $75   **MIP** $100

❑ **Hydraulic Dump Truck**, Buddy L, black front, hood, fenders, dark reddish maroon dump body, red chassis and disc wheels w/seven embossed spokes, black hubs, 25" long, 1931
EX $665   **NM** $885   **MIP** $1300

❑ **Hydraulic Dump Truck**, Buddy L, black front, hood, fenders and enclosed cab, red dump body, chassis and wheels w/six embossed spokes, bright hubs, 24-3/4" long, 1933
EX $325   **NM** $485   **MIP** $650

❑ **Hydraulic Dump Truck**, Buddy L, black front, hood, fenders, open seat, and dump body, red chassis and disc wheels w/aluminum tires, 25" long, 1926
EX $510   **NM** $800   **MIP** $1000

❑ **Hydraulic Dump Truck**, Buddy L, duo-tone slant design, red hood sides, dump body and chassis, white upper hood, cab and removable rider seat, electric headlights, 24-3/4" long, 1936
EX $300   **NM** $500   **MIP** $700

❑ **Hydraulic Dumper**, Buddy L, green, plated dump lever on left side, large hooks on left side hold yellow or off-white steel scoop shovel, white plastic side mirro and grille guard, 17" long, 1961
EX $125   **NM** $180   **MIP** $245

❑ **Hydraulic Dumper with Shovel**, Buddy L, green, plated dump lever on left side, large hooks on left side hold yellow or off-white steel scoop shovel, 17" long, 1960
EX $120   **NM** $185   **MIP** $250

❑ **Hydraulic Highway Dumper**, Buddy L, orange w/row of black square across scraper edges, one-piece chrome eight-hole grille and double headlights, no scraper blade, 17-3/4" long over blade and raised dump body, 1959
EX $55   **NM** $80   **MIP** $105

(Toy Shop File Photo)

❑ **Hydraulic Highway Dumper with Scraper Blade**, Buddy L, orange w/row of black square across scraper edges, one-piece chrome eight-hole grille and double headlights, 17-3/4" long over blade and raised dump body, 1958
EX $75   **NM** $105   **MIP** $155

❑ **Hydraulic Hi-Lift Dumper**, Buddy L, duo-tone slant design, green hood nose and lower cab sides, remainder white w/chrome grille, enclosed cab, 24" long, 1953
EX $75   **NM** $115   **MIP** $150

❑ **Hydraulic Hi-Lift Dumper**, Buddy L, green hood, fenders, cab, and dump-body supports, white dump body w/cab shield, 22-1/2" long, 1954
EX $85   **NM** $130   **MIP** $175

VEHICLES

❏ **Hydraulic Hi-Lift Dumper**, Buddy L, blue hood, fenders, cab, and dump-body supports, white dump body w/cab shield, 22-1/2" long, 1955
EX $75   **NM** $115   **MIP** $150

❏ **Hydraulic Husky Dumper**, Buddy L, red body, white one-piece bumper and grille guard, heavy side braces on dump section, 14" long, 1963
EX $50   **NM** $75   **MIP** $100

❏ **Hydraulic Husky Dumper**, Buddy L, red body, frame, dump section and cab shield, 15-1/4" long, 1962
EX $65   **NM** $100   **MIP** $135

❏ **Hydraulic Rider Dumper**, Buddy L, duo-tone slant design, yellow front and lower hood, red upper cab, dump body and upper hood, 26-1/2" long, 1949
EX $175   **NM** $265   **MIP** $360

❏ **Hydraulic Sturdy Dumper**, Buddy L, yellow hood, cab, fram and tiltback dump section, green lever on left side controls hydraulic dumping, 14-1/2" long, 1969
EX $50   **NM** $75   **MIP** $100

❏ **Hydraulic Sturdy Dumper**, Buddy L, snub-nose green/yellow body, cab and tiltback dump section, white plastic seats, 14-1/2" long, 1970
EX $45   **NM** $60   **MIP** $80

❏ **Hydraulic Sturdy Dumper**, Buddy L, lime green hood, cab, frame and tiltback dump section, green lever on left side controls hydraulic dumping, 14-1/2" long, 1969
EX $50   **NM** $75   **MIP** $100

(Tim Oei Photo)

❏ **Hy-Way Maintenance Mechanical Truck and Concrete Mixer**, Buddy L, Yellow and dark blue cab, silver wheels, yellow flatbed with dark blue and yellow mixer, 36" long, 1949
EX $345   **NM** $530   **MIP** $690

(Tim Oei Photo)

❏ **Ice Truck**, Buddy L, black front, hood, fenders and doorless cab, yellow open cargo section, canvas sliding cover, 26-1/2" long, 1926
EX $700   **NM** $900   **MIP** $1600

❏ **Ice Truck**, Buddy L, black front, hood, fenders and enclosed cab, yellow open cargo section, canvas, ice cakes, miniature tongs, 26-1/2" long, 1930
EX $700   **NM** $900   **MIP** $1500

❏ **Ice Truck**, Buddy L, black front, hood, fenders and enclosed cab, yellow ice compartment, canvas, ice cakes, tongs, 26-1/2" long, 1933-34
EX $700   **NM** $900   **MIP** $1300

❏ **Ice Truck**, Buddy L, black front, hood, fenders and enclosed cab, yellow ice compartment, 26-1/2" long, 1933
EX $700   **NM** $900   **MIP** $1500

❏ **IHC "Red Baby" Express Truck**, Buddy L, red doorless roofed cab, open pickup body, chassis and fenders, 24-1/4" long, 1928
EX $750   **NM** $1000   **MIP** $2000

❏ **IHC "Red Baby" Express Truck**, Buddy L, red w/black hubs and aluminum tires, 24-1/4" long, 1929
EX $800   **NM** $1300   **MIP** $1900

❏ **Insurance Patrol**, Buddy L, red w/open driver's seat and body, brass bell on cowl and full-length handrails, no CFD decal, 27" long, 1928
EX $625   **NM** $950   **MIP** $1250

❏ **Insurance Patrol**, Buddy L, red w/open driver's seat and body, brass bell on cowl and full-length handrails, 27" long, 1925
EX $650   **NM** $1000   **MIP** $1300

❏ **International Delivery Truck**, Buddy L, duo-tone slant design, red front, bumper and lower hood sides, yellow hood top, upper sides, cab and open cargo body, bright metal dummy headlights, 24-1/2" long, 1938
EX $150   **NM** $225   **MIP** $300

❏ **International Delivery Truck**, Buddy L, red w/removable black rider saddle, black-edged yellow horizontal strip on cargo body, 24-1/2" long, 1935
EX $225   **NM** $350   **MIP** $450

❏ **International Delivery Truck**, Buddy L, duo-tone slant design, red front, bumper and lower hood sides, yellow hood top, upper sides, cab and open cargo body, 24-1/2" long, 1936
EX $205   **NM** $320   **MIP** $410

❏ **International Dump Truck**, Buddy L, red w/bright-metal radiator grille, and black removable rider saddle, 25-3/4" long, 1935
EX $325   **NM** $485   **MIP** $650

❏ **International Dump Truck**, Buddy L, duo-tone slant design, yellow radiator, fenders, lower hood and detachable rider seat, rest of truck is red, 25-3/4" long, 1936
EX $315   **NM** $475   **MIP** $630

❏ **International Dump Truck**, Buddy L, red, w/red headlights on radiator, black removable rider saddle, 25-3/4" long, 1938
EX $125   **NM** $185   **MIP** $250

❏ **International Railway Express Truck**, Buddy L, duo-tone slant design, yellow front, lower hood sides and removable top, green hood top, enclosed cab and van body, electric headlights, 25" long, 1937
EX $350   **NM** $525   **MIP** $700

❏ **International Railway Express Truck**, Buddy L, duo-tone slant design, yellow front, lower hood sides and removable top, green hood top, enclosed cab and van body, dummy headlights, 25" long, 1938
EX $345   **NM** $525   **MIP** $690

❏ **International Wrecker Truck**, Buddy L, duo-tone slant design, yellow upper cab, hood, and boom, red lower cab, fenders, grille and body, rubber tires, removable rider seat, 32" long, 1938
EX $600   **NM** $900   **MIP** $1800

❏ **Jewel Home Service Truck Van**, Buddy L, dark brown body and sliding side doors, 1967
EX $135   **NM** $205   **MIP** $275

❏ **Jewel Home Shopping Truck Van**, Buddy L, pale mint green upper body and roof, darker mint green lower half, no sliding doors, 1968
EX $125   **NM** $200   **MIP** $275

❏ **Jolly Joe Ice Cream Truck**, Buddy L, white w/black roof, black tires and wooden wheels, 17-1/2" long, 1947
EX $225   **NM** $350   **MIP** $455

❏ **Jolly Joe Popsicle Truck**, Buddy L, white w/black roof, black tires and wooden wheels, 17-1/2" long, 1948
EX $275   **NM** $430   **MIP** $555

❏ **Jr. Animal Ark**, Buddy L, fuschia lap-strake hull, four black tires, 10 pairs of plastic animals, 5" long, 1970
EX $40   **NM** $60   **MIP** $80

❏ **Jr. Auto Carrier**, Buddy L, yellow cab-over-engine tractor unit and double-deck semi-trailer, two red plastic cars, 15-1/2" long, 1967
EX $50   **NM** $75   **MIP** $100

❏ **Jr. Auto Carrier**, Buddy L, bright blue cab-over-engine tractor unit and double-deck semi-trailer, two plastic cars, 17-1/4" long, 1969
EX $60   **NM** $95   **MIP** $125

❏ **Jr. Beach Buggy**, Buddy L, yellow hood, fenders and topless jeep body, red plastic seats, white plastic surfboard that clips to roll bar and windshield, truck 6" long, 1969
EX $45   **NM** $65   **MIP** $90

❏ **Jr. Beach Buggy**, Buddy L, lime green hood, fenders and topless jeep body, red plastic seats, lime green plastic surfboard that clips to roll bar and windshield, truck 6" long, 1971
EX $35   **NM** $50   **MIP** $70

❏ **Jr. Buggy Hauler**, Buddy L, fuschia jeep body w/orange seats, orange two-wheel trailer tilts to unload sandpiper beach buggy, 12" long including jeep and trailer, 1970
EX $35   **NM** $55   **MIP** $75

❏ **Jr. Camper**, Buddy L, red cab and pickup body wih yellow camper body, 7" long, 1971
EX $50   **NM** $75   **MIP** $100

❑ **Jr. Canada Dry Delivery Truck**, Buddy L, green/lime cab-over-engine body, hand truck, 10 cases of green bottles, 9-1/2" long, 1968
EX $100   **NM** $150   **MIP** $200

❑ **Jr. Canada Dry Delivery Truck**, Buddy L, green/lime cab-over-engine body, hand truck, 10 cases of green bottles, 9-1/2" long, 1969
EX $85   **NM** $130   **MIP** $170

❑ **Jr. Cement Mixer Truck**, Buddy L, blue cab-over-engine body, frame and hopper, white plastic mixing drum, white plastic seats, wide one-piece chrome bumper, 7-1/2" long, 1969
EX $35   **NM** $50   **MIP** $70

❑ **Jr. Cement Mixer Truck**, Buddy L, blue cab-over-engine body, frame and hopper, white plastic mixing drum, white plastic seats, 7-1/2" long, 1968
EX $60   **NM** $85   **MIP** $120

❑ **Jr. Dump Truck**, Buddy L, red cab-over-engine, frame and tiltback dump section, plastic vertical headlights, 7-1/2" long, 1967
EX $50   **NM** $75   **MIP** $100

❑ **Jr. Dumper**, Buddy L, avocado cab-over-engine, frame and tiltback dump section w/cab shield, one-piece chrome bumper and four-slot grille, 7-1/2" long, 1969
EX $335   **NM** $55   **MIP** $75

❑ **Jr. Giraffe Truck**, Buddy L, turquoise cab-over-engine body, white cab roof, plastic giraffe, 6-1/2" long, 1968
EX $50   **NM** $75   **MIP** $100

❑ **Jr. Giraffe Truck**, Buddy L, turquoise cab-over-engine body, white cab roof, plastic giraffe, 6-1/4" long, 1969
EX $40   **NM** $60   **MIP** $80

❑ **Jr. Kitty Kennel**, Buddy L, pink cab-over-engine body, white cab roof, four white plastic cats, 6-1/4" long, 1969
EX $55   **NM** $85   **MIP** $115

❑ **Jr. Kitty Kennel**, Buddy L, pink cab-over-engine body, white cab roof, four colored plastic cats, 6-1/4" long, 1968
EX $60   **NM** $95   **MIP** $125

❑ **Jr. Sanitation Truck**, Buddy L, blue cab-over-engine, white frame, refuse body and loading hopper, 10" long, 1968
EX $75   **NM** $115   **MIP** $150

❑ **Jr. Sanitation Truck**, Buddy L, yellow cab-over-engine and underframe, refuse body and loading hopper, full width bumper and grille, 10" long, 1969
EX $75   **NM** $115   **MIP** $150

❑ **Junior Line Air Mail Truck**, Buddy L, black enclosed cab, red chassis and body, headlights and double bar bumper, six rubber tires, 24" long, 1930-32
EX $400   **NM** $650   **MIP** $1200

❑ **Kennel Truck**, Buddy L, red/orange pickup body and cab, yellow roof, six section kennel w/six plastic dogs fits in cargo box, 13-1/4" long, 1969
EX $65   **NM** $100   **MIP** $135

❑ **Kennel Truck**, Buddy L, cream/yellow pickup body and cab, clear plastic twelve-section kennel w/twelve plastic dogs fits in cargo box, 13-1/4" long, 1968
EX $80   **NM** $120   **MIP** $160

❑ **Kennel Truck**, Buddy L, medium blue pickup body and cab, clear plastic twelve-section kennel w/twelve plastic dogs fits in cargo box, 13-1/2" long, 1964
EX $60   **NM** $90   **MIP** $120

❑ **Kennel Truck**, Buddy L, bright blue pickup body and cab, clear plastic twelve-section kennel w/twelve plastic dogs fits in cargo box, 13-1/4" long, 1966
EX $95   **NM** $145   **MIP** $190

❑ **Kennel Truck**, Buddy L, turquoise pickup body and cab, clear plastic twelve-section kennel w/twelve plastic dogs fits in cargo box, 13-1/2" long, 1965
EX $60   **NM** $95   **MIP** $125

❑ **Kennel Truck**, Buddy L, snub-nosed red/orange body and cab, plastic kennel section in back, six kennels w/six plastic dogs, 13-1/4" long, 1970
EX $60   **NM** $95   **MIP** $125

❑ **Kennel Truck**, Buddy L, bright blue pickup body and cab, clear plastic twelve-section kennel w/twelve plastic dogs fits in cargo box, 13-1/4" long, 1967
EX $85   **NM** $130   **MIP** $175

❑ **Lumber Truck**, Buddy L, black front, hood, fenders, cabless open seat and low-sides cargo bed, red bumper, chassis and a pair of removable solid stake sides, load of lumber pieces, 24" long, 1924
EX $750   **NM** $1000   **MIP** $1500

❑ **Lumber Truck**, Buddy L, black front, hood, fenders, doorless cab and low-sides cargo bed, red bumper, chassis and a pair of removable solid stake sides, load of lumber, 25-1/2" long, 1926
EX $650   **NM** $1300   **MIP** $2700

❑ **Mack Hydraulic Dumper**, Buddy L, red front, hood, cab, chassis and tiltback dump section w/cab shield, white plastic bumper, short step ladder on each side, 20-1/2" long, 1967
EX $50   **NM** $75   **MIP** $100

❑ **Mack Hydraulic Dumper**, Buddy L, red front, hood, cab, chassis and tiltback dump section w/cab shield, white plastic bumper, 20-1/2" long, 1965
EX $60   **NM** $95   **MIP** $125

❑ **Mack Quarry Dumper**, Buddy L, orange front, hood cab and chassis, blue-green tiltback dump section, white plastic bumper, 20-1/2" long, 1965
EX $75   **NM** $115   **MIP** $150

❑ **Mammoth Hydraulic Quarry Dumper**, Buddy L, deep green hood, red cab, chassis and tiltback dump section, black plastic bumper, 22-1/2" long, 1963
EX $60   **NM** $90   **MIP** $125

❑ **Mammoth Hydraulic Quarry Dumper**, Buddy L, deep green hood, cab and chassis, red tiltback dump section, black plastic bumper, 23" long, 1962
EX $60   **NM** $105   **MIP** $175

❑ **Marshall Field's Delivery Truck Van**, Buddy L, hunter green body, sliding doors and roof, 1966
EX $125   **NM** $200   **MIP** $275

❑ **Milkman Truck**, Buddy L, deep cream hood, cab and flatbed body, white side rails, 14 3" white plastic milk bottles w/red caps, 14-1/4" long, 1962
EX $100   **NM** $150   **MIP** $200

❑ **Milkman Truck**, Buddy L, lime yellow hood, cab and flatbed body, white side rails, 14 3" white plastic milk bottles, 14-1/4" long, 1964
EX $75   **NM** $115   **MIP** $150

❑ **Milkman Truck**, Buddy L, light blue hood, cab and flatbed body, white side rails, 14 3" white plastic milk bottles, 14-1/4" long, 1963
EX $85   **NM** $130   **MIP** $175

❑ **Milkman Truck**, Buddy L, deep cream hood, cab and flatbed body, white side rails, fourteen 3" white plastic milk bottles w/red caps, 14-1/4" long, 1962
EX $50   **NM** $105   **MIP** $200

❑ **Milkman Truck**, Buddy L, medium blue hood, cab and flatbed body, white side rails, eight 3" white plastic milk bottles, 14-1/4" long, 1961
EX $110   **NM** $175   **MIP** $225

❑ **Milkman Truck**, Buddy L, light blue hood, cab and flatbed body, white side rails, 14 3" white plastic milk bottles, 14-1/4" long, 1963
EX $85   **NM** $130   **MIP** $175

❑ **Milkman Truck**, Buddy L, medium blue hood, cab and flatbed body, white side rails, eight 3" white plastic milk bottles, 14-1/4" long, 1961
EX $50   **NM** $100   **MIP** $200

❑ **Milkman Truck**, Buddy L, light yellow hood, cab and flatbed body, white side rails, 14 3" white plastic milk bottles, 14-1/4" long, 1964
EX $75   **NM** $125   **MIP** $155

(Toy Shop File Photo)

❑ **Mister Buddy Ice Cream Truck**, Buddy L, white cab-over-engine van body, pale blue or off-white plastic underbody and floor, 11-1/2" long, 1964
EX $55   **NM** $85   **MIP** $250

❑ **Mister Buddy Ice Cream Truck**, Buddy L, white cab-over-engine van body, red plastic underbody and floor, 11-1/2" long, 1966
EX $45   **NM** $75   **MIP** $100

VEHICLES

❑ **Mister Buddy Ice Cream Truck**, Buddy L, white cab-over-engine van body, red plastic underbody and floor, red bell knob, 11-1/2" long, 1967
EX $55   **NM** $85   **MIP** $115

❑ **Model T Flivver Truck**, Buddy L, black w/red eight-spoke wheels w/aluminum tires, black hubs, 12" long, 1924
EX $1000   **NM** $1500   **MIP** $2000

❑ **Motor Market Truck**, Buddy L, duo-tone horizontal design, white hood top, upper cab and high partition in cargo section, yellow-orange grille, fenders, lower hood and cab sides, 21-1/2" long, 1941
EX $200   **NM** $350   **MIP** $550

❑ **Moving Van**, Buddy L, black front, hood and seat, red chassis and disc wheels w/black hubs, green van body, roof extends forward above open driver's seat, 25" long, 1924
EX $1200   **NM** $2000   **MIP** $3000

❑ **Overland Trailer Truck**, Buddy L, duo-tone horizontal design, red and white tractor has red front, lower half chassis, chassis, enclosed cab, 40", 1939
EX $350   **NM** $560   **MIP** $710

❑ **Overland Trailer Truck**, Buddy L, yellow tractor, enclosed cab, red semi-trailer and four-wheel full trailer w/removable roofs, 39-3/4" long, 1935
EX $350   **NM** $525   **MIP** $700

❑ **Overland Trailer Truck**, Buddy L, duo-tone slant design, green and yellow semi-streamlined tractor and green hood sides, yellow hood, chassis, enclosed cab, 40", 1939
EX $350   **NM** $550   **MIP** $700

❑ **Overland Trailer Truck**, Buddy L, duo-tone slant design, green and yellow tractor unit w/yellow cab, red semi-trailer and four-wheel full trailer w/yellow removable roofs, 39-3/4" long, 1936
EX $325   **NM** $485   **MIP** $650

❑ **Pepsi Delivery Truck**, Buddy L, powder blue hood and lower cab, white upper cab and double-deck cargo section, two hand trucks, four blue cases of red bottles, four red cases of blue bottles, 15" long, 1970
EX $60   **NM** $95   **MIP** $125

❑ **Polysteel Boat Transport**, Buddy L, medium blue soft plastic body, steel flat-bed carrying 8" white plastic runabout boat w/red deck, truck 12-1/2" long, 1960
EX $75   **NM** $115   **MIP** $150

❑ **Polysteel Coca-Cola Delivery Truck**, Buddy L, yellow plastic truck, slanted bottle racks, eight red Coke cases w/green bottles, small metal hand truck, 12-1/2" long, 1961
EX $50   **NM** $75   **MIP** $100

❑ **Polysteel Coca-Cola Delivery Truck**, Buddy L, yellow plastic truck, slanted bottle racks, eight green Coke cases w/red bottles, small metal hand truck, 12-1/4" long, 1962
EX $60   **NM** $90   **MIP** $120

❑ **Polysteel Dumper**, Buddy L, green soft molded plastic front, cab and frame, yellow steel dump body w/sides rounded at back, hinged tailgate, 13" long, 1959
EX $100   **NM** $150   **MIP** $200

❑ **Polysteel Dumper**, Buddy L, medium blue soft molded plastic front, cab and frame, off-white steel dump body w/sides rounded at back, hinged tailgate, 13" long, 1960
EX $87   **NM** $130   **MIP** $175

❑ **Polysteel Dumper**, Buddy L, orange plastic body and tiltback dump section w/cab shield, "Come-Back Motor," 13" long, 1961
EX $75   **NM** $115   **MIP** $150

❑ **Polysteel Dumper**, Buddy L, orange plastic body and tiltback dump section w/cab shield, no "Come-Back Motor," no door decals, 13-1/2" long, 1962
EX $60   **NM** $95   **MIP** $125

❑ **Polysteel Highway Transport**, Buddy L, red soft plastic tractor, cab roof lights, double horn, radio antenna and side fuel tanks, white steel semi-trailer van, 20-1/2" long, 1960
EX $100   **NM** $150   **MIP** $200

❑ **Polysteel Hydraulic Dumper**, Buddy L, beige soft molded-plastic front, cab and frame, off-white steel dump section w/sides rounded at rear, 13" long, 1959
EX $60   **NM** $95   **MIP** $125

❑ **Polysteel Hydraulic Dumper**, Buddy L, red soft plastic body, frame and tiltback ribbed dump section w/cab shield, 13" long, 1962
EX $65   **NM** $100   **MIP** $130

❑ **Polysteel Hydraulic Dumper**, Buddy L, red soft molded-plastic front, cab and frame, light green steel dump section w/sides rounded at rear, 13" long, 1960
EX $80   **NM** $120   **MIP** $160

❑ **Polysteel Hydraulic Dumper**, Buddy L, yellow soft plastic body, frame and tilt-back ribbed dump section w/cab shield, 13" long, 1961
EX $75   **NM** $125   **MIP** $150

❑ **Polysteel Milk Tanker**, Buddy L, red soft plastic tractor unit, light blue/gray semi-trailer tank w/red ladders and five dooms, 22" long, 1961
EX $60   **NM** $95   **MIP** $125

❑ **Polysteel Milk Tanker**, Buddy L, turquoise soft plastic tractor unit, light blue/gray semi-trailer tank w/red ladders and five dooms, 22" long, 1961
EX $60   **NM** $95   **MIP** $125

❑ **Polysteel Milkman Truck**, Buddy L, light blue soft plastic front, cab and frame, light yellow steel open cargo section w/nine oversized white plastic milk bottles, 11-3/4" long, 1960
EX $65   **NM** $100   **MIP** $130

❑ **Polysteel Milkman Truck**, Buddy L, light blue soft plastic front, cab and frame, light blue steel open cargo section w/nine oversized white plastic milk bottles, 11-3/4" long, 1961
EX $60   **NM** $95   **MIP** $125

❑ **Polysteel Milkman Truck**, Buddy L, turquoise soft plastic front, cab and frame, light blue steel open cargo section w/nine oversized white plastic milk bottles w/red caps, 11-3/4" long, 1962
EX $35   **NM** $50   **MIP** $70

❑ **Polysteel Supermarket Delivery**, Buddy L, medium blue soft molded-plastic front, hood, cab and frame, steel off-white open cargo section, 13" long, 1959
EX $75   **NM** $115   **MIP** $150

❑ **Pull-N-Ride Baggage Truck**, Buddy L, duo-tone horizontal design, light cream upper half, off-white lower half and bumper, 24-1/4" long, 1953
EX $150   **NM** $225   **MIP** $300

❑ **R E A Express Truck**, Buddy L, dark green cab-over-engine van body, sliding side doors, double rear doors, white plastic one-piece bumper, 11-1/2" long, 1964
EX $200   **NM** $300   **MIP** $400

❑ **R E A Express Truck**, Buddy L, dark green cab-over-engine van body, sliding side doors, double rear doors, white plastic one-piece bumper, no spring suspension, 11-1/2" long, 1965
EX $130   **NM** $195   **MIP** $260

❑ **R E A Express Truck**, Buddy L, dark green cab-over-engine van body, sliding side doors, double rear doors, white plastic one-piece bumper, no spring suspension, side doors are embossed "BUDDY L," 11-1/2" long, 1966
EX $125   **NM** $185   **MIP** $250

❑ **Railroad Transfer Rider Delivery Truck**, Buddy L, duo-tone horizontal design, yellow upper half, hood top, cab and slatted caro sides, green lower half, small hand truck, two milk cans w/removable lids, 23-1/4" long, 1949
EX $70   **NM** $100   **MIP** $140

❑ **Railroad Transfer Store Door Delivery**, Buddy L, duo-tone horizontal design, yellow hood top, cab and upper body, red lower half of hood and body, small hand truck, two metal drums w/coin slots, 23-1/4" long, 1950
EX $90   **NM** $135   **MIP** $180

❑ **Railway Express Truck**, Buddy L, green all-steel hood, cab, frame and high-sides open bady, sides have three horizontal slots in upper back corners, 22" long, 1954
EX $75   **NM** $115   **MIP** $150

❑ **Railway Express Truck**, Buddy L, red tractor unit, enclosed square cab, green 12-1/4" long two-wheel semi-trailer van w/removable roof, "Wrigley's Spearmint Gum" poster on trailer sides, 23" long, 1935
EX $375   **NM** $565   **MIP** $750

❑ **Railway Express Truck**, Buddy L, duo-tone slant design, tractor unit has white skirted fenders and hood sides, green hood top, enclosed cab and chassis, green semi-trailer w/white removable roof, 25" long, 1939
EX $350   **NM** $475   **MIP** $700

(Toy Shop File Photo)

(Thomas G. Nefos Photo)

❏ **Railway Express Truck**, Buddy L, duo-tone slant design, tractor has silvery and hood sides, green hood top, enclosed cab, green semi-trailer, "Wrigley's Spearmint Gum" poster on trailer sides, 23" long, 1935
EX $400   **NM** $600   **MIP** $800

❏ **Railway Express Truck**, Buddy L, black front hood, fenders, seat and low body sides, dark green van body, red chassis, 25" long, 1926
EX $400   **NM** $800   **MIP** $1600

❏ **Railway Express Truck**, Buddy L, dark green or light green screen body, double-bar nickel front bumper, brass radiator knob, red wheels, 25" long, 1930
EX $500   **NM** $1000   **MIP** $2000

❏ **Railway Express Truck**, Buddy L, yellow and green tractor unit has white skirted fenders and hood sides, green hood top, enclosed cab and chassis, green semi-trailer w/yellow removable roof, 25" long, 1940
EX $330   **NM** $495   **MIP** $660

❏ **Railway Express Truck**, Buddy L, duo-tone horizontal design, tractor unit has yellow front, lower door and chassis, green hood top and enclosed upper cab, semi-trailer has yellow lower sides, 25" long, 1941
EX $325   **NM** $485   **MIP** $650

❏ **Railway Express Truck**, Buddy L, deep green plastic "Diamond T" hood and cab, deep green steel frame and van body w/removable silvery roof, small two-wheel hand truck, steel four-rung barrel skid, 21" long, 1952
EX $200   **NM** $300   **MIP** $400

❏ **Railway Express Truck**, Buddy L, green plastic hood and cab, green steel high-sides open body, frame and bumper, small two-wheel hand truck, steel four-rung barrel skid, 20-3/4" long, 1953
EX $125   **NM** $185   **MIP** $250

❏ **Ranchero Stake Truck**, Buddy L, medium green, white plastic one-piece bumper and grille guard, four-post, four-slat fixed stake sides and cargo section, 14" long, 1963
EX $50   **NM** $75   **MIP** $100

❏ **Rider Dump Truck**, Buddy L, duo-tone horizontal design, yellow hood top, upper cab and upper dump body, red front, hood sides, lower doors and lower dump body, no bumper, 23" long, 1947
EX $75   **NM** $115   **MIP** $150

❏ **Rider Dump Truck**, Buddy L, duo-tone horizontal design, yellow hood top, upper cab and upper dump body, red front, hood sides, lower doors and lower dump body, no bumper, 21-1/2" long, 1945
EX $160   **NM** $245   **MIP** $325

❏ **Riding Acedemy Truck**, Buddy L, Blue body, white roof over bed, side and rear opening ramps, three plastic horses, "Riding Acedemy" in white type along sides
EX $55   **NM** $78   **MIP** $125

❏ **Rival Dog Food Delivery Van**, Buddy L, cream front, cab and boxy van body, metal drum coin bank w/"RIVAL DOG FOOD" label in blue, red, white and yellow, 16-1/2" long, 1956
EX $160   **NM** $245   **MIP** $325

❏ **Robotoy**, Buddy L, black fenders and chassis, red hood and enclosed cab w/small visor, green dump body's front and back are higher than sides, 21-5/8" long, 1932
EX $575   **NM** $900   **MIP** $1200

❏ **Rockin' Giraffe Truck**, Buddy L, powder blue hood, cab, and high-sided open-top cargo section, two orange and yellow plastic giraffes, 13-1/4" long, 1967
EX $75   **NM** $115   **MIP** $150

❏ **Ruff-n-Tuff Cement Mixer Truck**, Buddy L, yellow snub-nosed cab-over-engine body, frame and water-tank ends, white plastic water tank and mixing drum, white seats, 16" long, 1971
EX $40   **NM** $60   **MIP** $85

❏ **Ruff-n-Tuff Log Truck**, Buddy L, yellow snub-nose cab-over-engine, frame and shallow truck bed, black full-width grille, 16" long, 1971
EX $50   **NM** $75   **MIP** $100

❏ **Ryder City Special Delivery Truck Van**, Buddy L, duo-tone horizontal design, yellow upper half including hood top and cab, brown removable van roof, warm brown front and lower half of van body, 24-1/2" long, 1949
EX $150   **NM** $225   **MIP** $300

❏ **Ryder Van Lines Trailer**, Buddy L, duo-tone slant design, black front and lower hood sides and doors, deep red hood top, enclosed cab and chassis, 35-1/2" long, 1949
EX $350   **NM** $525   **MIP** $700

❏ **Saddle Dump Truck**, Buddy L, duo-tone slant design, yellow front, fenders, lower hood and cab, and removable rider seat, rest of body red, no bumper, 21-1/2" long, 1939
EX $125   **NM** $185   **MIP** $250

❏ **Saddle Dump Truck**, Buddy L, duo-tone horizontal design, deep blue hood top, upper cab and upper dump body, orange fenders radiator front lower two-thirds of cab and lower half of dump body, 21-1/2" long, 1941
EX $85   **NM** $130   **MIP** $175

❏ **Saddle Dump Truck**, Buddy L, duo-tone slant design, yellow front, fenders and removable rider seat, red enclosed square cab and dump body, no bumper, 19-1/2" long, 1937
EX $200   **NM** $300   **MIP** $400

❏ **Sand and Gravel Rider Dump Truck**, Buddy L, duo-tone horizontal design, blue lower half, yellow upper half including hoop top and enclosed cab, 24" long, 1950
EX $350   **NM** $525   **MIP** $700

❏ **Sand and Gravel Truck**, Buddy L, black body, doorless roofed cab and steering wheel, red chassis and disc wheels w/black hubs, 25-1/2" long, 1926
EX $600   **NM** $1000   **MIP** $1200

❏ **Sand and Gravel Truck**, Buddy L, dark or medium green hood, cab, roof lights and skirted body, white or cream dump section, 13-1/2" long, 1949
EX $100   **NM** $150   **MIP** $200

❏ **Sand and Gravel Truck**, Buddy L, duo-tone horizontal design, red front, bumper, lower hood, cab sides, chassis and lower dump body sides, white hood top, enclosed cab and upper dump body, 23-3/4" long, 1949
EX $350   **NM** $525   **MIP** $700

❏ **Sand and Gravel Truck**, Buddy L, black w/red chassis and wheels, nickel-rim, red-shell headlights, enclosed cab w/opening doors, 25-1/2" long, 1930-32
EX $2000   **NM** $3000   **MIP** $5000

❏ **Sand Loader and Dump Truck**, Buddy L, duo-tone horizontal design, yellow hood top and upper dump blue cab sides, frame and lower dump body, red loader on dump w/black rubber conveyor belt, 24-1/2" long, 1950
EX $175   **NM** $265   **MIP** $350

❏ **Sand Loader and Dump Truck**, Buddy L, duo-tone horizontal design, yellow hood top and upper dump blue cab sides, frame and lower dump body, red loader on dump w/black rubber conveyor belt, 24-1/2" long, 1952
EX $60   **NM** $95   **MIP** $125

❏ **Sanitation Service Truck**, Buddy L, blue front fenders, hood, cab and chassis, white encllosed dump section and hinged loading hopper, one-piece chrome bumper, plastic windows in garbage section, 16-1/2" long, 1967
EX $75   **NM** $150   **MIP** $200

❏ **Sanitation Service Truck**, Buddy L, blue front fenders, hood, cab and chassis, white encllosed dump section and hinged loading hopper, one-piece chrome bumper, no plastic windows in garbage section, 16-1/2" long, 1968
EX $75   **NM** $115   **MIP** $150

❏ **Sanitation Service Truck**, Buddy L, blue snub-nose hood, cab and frame, white cargo dump body and rear loading unit, two round plastic headlights, 17" long, 1972
EX $75   **NM** $115   **MIP** $150

VEHICLES

❑ **Sears Roebuck Delivery Truck Van**, Buddy L, gray/green and off-white, no side doors, 1967, Model No. *
EX $125   **NM** $200   **MIP** $280

❑ **Self-Loading Auto Carrier**, Buddy L, medium tan tractor unit, three plastic cars, overall 34" long including loading ramp, 1960
EX $85   **NM** $130   **MIP** $175

❑ **Self-Loading Boat Hauler**, Buddy L, pastel blue tractor and semi-trailer w/three 8-1/2" long boats, overall 26-1/2" long, 1962
EX $150   **NM** $225   **MIP** $350

❑ **Self-Loading Boat Hauler**, Buddy L, pastel blue tractor and semi-trailer w/three 8-1/2" long boats, no side mirror on truck, overall 26-1/2" long, 1963
EX $150   **NM** $225   **MIP** $350

❑ **Self-Loading Car Carrier**, Buddy L, lime green tractor unit, three plastic cars, overall 33-1/2" long including, 1963
EX $75   **NM** $115   **MIP** $150

❑ **Self-Loading Car Carrier**, Buddy L, beige/yellow tractor unit, three plastic cars, overall 33-1/2" long including, 1964
EX $60   **NM** $95   **MIP** $125

❑ **Shell Pickup and Delivery**, Buddy L, reddish orange hood and body, open cargo section w/solid sides, chain across back, red coin-slot oil drum w/Shell emblem and lettering, 13-1/4" long, 1950
EX $135   **NM** $200   **MIP** $275

❑ **Shell Pickup and Delivery**, Buddy L, yellow/orange hood and body, open cargo section, three curved slots toward rear in sides, chains across back, red coin-slot oil drum w/Shell emblem and lettering, 13-1/4" long, 1952
EX $125   **NM** $185   **MIP** $250

❑ **Shell Pickup and Delivery**, Buddy L, yellow/orange hood and body, open cargo section w/three curved slots toward rear in sides, red coin-slot oil drum w/Shell emblem and lettering, 13-1/4" long, 1953
EX $110   **NM** $175   **MIP** $225

❑ **Smoke Patrol**, Buddy L, lemon yellow body, six wheels, garden hose attaches and water squirts through large chrome swivel-mount water cannon on rear deck, 7" long, 1970
EX $50   **NM** $75   **MIP** $100

❑ **Sprinkler Truck**, Buddy L, black front, hood, fenders and cabless open driver's seat, red bumper and chassis, bluish/gray/green water tank, 25" long, 1929
EX $800   **NM** $1500   **MIP** $2000

❑ **Stake Body Truck**, Buddy L, black cabless open driver's seat, hood, front fenders and flatbed body, red chassis and five removable stake sections, 25" long, 1921
EX $1000   **NM** $1500   **MIP** $2000

❑ **Stake Body Truck**, Buddy L, black cabless open driver's seat, hood, front

fenders and flatbed body, red chassis and five removable stake sections, cargo bed w/low sidesboards, drop-down tailgate, 25" long, 1924
EX $1000   **NM** $1500   **MIP** $2000

❑ **Standard Coffee Co. Delivery Truck Van**, Buddy L, 1966
EX $125   **NM** $200   **MIP** $275

❑ **Standard Oil Tank Truck**, Buddy L, duo-tone slant design, white upper cab and hood, red lower cab, grille, fenders and tank, rubber wheels, electric headlights, 26" long, 1936-37
EX $350   **NM** $500   **MIP** $1000

❑ **Stor-Dor Delivery**, Buddy L, red hood and body, open cargo body w/four horizontal slots in sides, plated chains across open back, 14-1/2" long, 1955
EX $65   **NM** $100   **MIP** $175

❑ **Street Sprinkler Truck**, Buddy L, black front, hood, front fenders and cabless open driver's seat, red bumper and chassis, bluish/gray/green water tank, 25" long, 1929
EX $700   **NM** $900   **MIP** $1800

❑ **Street Sprinkler Truck**, Buddy L, black front, hood, and fenders, open cab, nickel-rim, red-shell headlights, double bar front bumper, bluish/gray/green water tank, six rubber tires, 25" long, 1930-32
EX $800   **NM** $1000   **MIP** $1900

(Joe and Sharon Freed Photo)

❑ **Sunshine Biscuits Van**, Buddy L, Dark yellow body, light gray chassis, white-wall tires, Sunshine chef decals along sides, with Sunshine Biscuits photo decal showing Krispy, Cheez-It crackers and Hydrox and HiHo cookies
EX $145   **NM** $260   **MIP** $330

❑ **Sunshine Delivery Truck Van**, Buddy L, bright, yellow cab-over-engine van body and opening double rear doors, off-white plastic bumper and under body, 11-1/2" long, 1967
EX $125   **NM** $200   **MIP** $275

❑ **Super Motor Market**, Buddy L, duo-tone horizontal design, white hood top, upper cab and high partition in cargo section, yellow/orange lower hood and cab sides, semi-trailer carrying supplies, 21-1/2" long, 1942
EX $300   **NM** $500   **MIP** $700

❑ **Supermarket Delivery**, Buddy L, all white w/rubber wheels, enclosed cab, pointed nose, bright metal one-piece grille, 13-3/4" long, 1950
EX $125   **NM** $185   **MIP** $250

❑ **Supermarket Delivery**, Buddy L, blue bumper, front, hood, cab and frame,

one-piece chrome four-hole grille and headlights, 14-1/2" long, 1956
EX $75   **NM** $115   **MIP** $150

❑ **Tank and Sprinkler Truck**, Buddy L, black front, hood, fenders, doorless cab and seat, dark green tank and side racks, black or dark green sprinkler attachment, 26-1/4" long w/sprinkler attachment, 1924
EX $700   **NM** $900   **MIP** $1700

❑ **Teepee Camping Trailer and Wagon**, Buddy L, maroon suburban wagon, two-wheel teepee trailer and its beige plastic folding tent, overall 24-1/2" long, 1963
EX $75   **NM** $180   **MIP** $260

(Calvin L. Chaussee Photo)

❑ **Texaco Tank Truck**, Buddy L, red steel GMC 550-series blunt-nose tractor and semi-trailer tank, 25" long, 1959
EX $175   **NM** $250   **MIP** $400

(Toy Shop File Photo)

❑ **Texaco Tanker, Promotional Piece**, Buddy L, White rounded cabover with red tanker section, black plastic hose. "Texaco" logo stickers on cab, "Texaco" on tanker sides, 25" long
EX $78   **NM** $130   **MIP** $205

❑ **Tom's Toasted Peanuts Delivery Truck Van**, Buddy L, light tan/beige body, no seat or sliding doors, blue bumpers, floor and underbody, 11-1/2" long, 1973
EX $125   **NM** $200   **MIP** $275

❑ **Trail Boss**, Buddy L, red, square-corner body w/sloping sides, open cockpit, white plastic seat, 7" long, 1970
EX $35   **NM** $65   **MIP** $80

❑ **Trail Boss**, Buddy L, lime green, square-corner body w/sloping sides, open cockpit, yellow plastic seat, 7" long, 1971
EX $35   **NM** $55   **MIP** $75

❑ **Trailer Dump Truck**, Buddy L, cream tractor unit w/enclosed cab, dark blue semi-trailer dump body w/high sides and top-hinged opening endgate, no bumper, 20-3/4" long, 1941
EX $75   **NM** $115   **MIP** $155

❑ **Trailer Van Truck**, Buddy L, red tractor and van roof, blue bumper, white semi-trailer van, chrome one-piece toothed grille and headlights, white drop-down rear door, 29" long w/tailgate/ramp lowered, 1956
EX $145   **NM** $225   **MIP** $300

❑ **Trailer Van with Tailgate Loader**, Buddy L, green steel tractor, bumper, chrome one-piece toothed grille and headlights, cream van w/green roof and tailgate loader, 31-3/4" long, w/tailgate down, 1954
EX $125   NM $185   MIP $250

❑ **Trailer Van with Tailgate Loader**, Buddy L, green high-impacted styrene plastic tractor on steel frame, cream steel detachable semi-trailer van w/green roof and crank operated tailgate, 33" long w/tailgate lowered, 1953
EX $125   NM $185   MIP $250

❑ **Traveling Zoo**, Buddy L, red high side pickup w/yellow plastic triple-cage unit, six compartments w/plastic animals, 13-1/4" long, 1965
EX $85   NM $130   MIP $175

❑ **Traveling Zoo**, Buddy L, red high side pickup w/yellow plastic triple-cage unit, six compartments w/plastic animals, 13-1/4" long, 1967
EX $70   NM $115   MIP $150

❑ **Traveling Zoo**, Buddy L, yellow high side pickup w/red plastic triple-cage unit, six compartments w/plastic animals, 13-1/4" long, 1969
EX $65   NM $95   MIP $130

❑ **Traveling Zoo**, Buddy L, snub-nosed yellow body and cab, six red plastic cages w/six plastic zoo animals, 13-1/4" long, 1970
EX $60   NM $95   MIP $125

❑ **U.S. Army Half-Track and Howitzer**, Buddy L, olive drab, 12-1/2" truck, 9-3/4" gun, overall 22-1/2" long, 1952
EX $125   NM $200   MIP $275

❑ **U.S. Mail Delivery Truck**, Buddy L, blue cab, hood, bumper, frame and removable roof on white van body, 23-1/4" long, 1956
EX $150   NM $300   MIP $510

(Toy Shop File Photo)

❑ **U.S. Mail Delivery Truck**, Buddy L, white upper cab-over-engine, sliding side doors and double rear doors, red belt-line stripe on sides and front, blue lower body, 11-1/2" long, 1964
EX $70   NM $105   MIP $205

(Calvin L. Chaussee Photo)

❑ **U.S. Mail Truck**, Buddy L, shiny olive green body and bumper, yellow-cream removable van roof, enclosed cab, 22-1/2" long, 1953
EX $215   NM $410   MIP $580

❑ **United Parcel Delivery Van**, Buddy L, duo-tone horizontal design, deep cream upper half w/brown removable roof, chocolate brown front and lower half, 25" long, 1941
EX $250   NM $450   MIP $650

❑ **Utility Delivery Truck**, Buddy L, duo-tone horizontal design, green upper half including hood top, dark cream lower half, green wheels, red and yellow horizontal stripe, 22-3/4" long, 1941
EX $125   NM $185   MIP $250

❑ **Utility Delivery Truck**, Buddy L, duo-tone slant design, blue front and lower hood sides, gray hood top, cab and open body w/red and yellow horizontal stripe, 22-3/4" long, 1940
EX $250   NM $450   MIP $650

❑ **Utility Dump Truck**, Buddy L, duo-tone slant design, red front, lower doord and fenders, gray chassis and enclosed upper cab, royal blue dump body, yellow removable rider seat, 25-1/2" long, 1940
EX $125   NM $185   MIP $250

❑ **Utility Dump Truck**, Buddy L, duo-tone slant design, red front, lower door and fenders, gray chassis, red upper hood, upper enclosed cab and removable rider seat, yellow body, 25-1/2" long, 1941
EX $85   NM $130   MIP $175

❑ **Van Freight Carriers Trailer**, Buddy L, bright blue streanlined tractor and enclosed cab, cream/yellow semi-trailer van, removable silvery roof, 22" long, 1949
EX $65   NM $100   MIP $135

❑ **Van Freight Carriers Trailer**, Buddy L, red streamlined tractor, bright blue enclosed cab, cream/yellow semi-trailer van, white removable van roof, 22" long, 1952
EX $55   NM $85   MIP $115

❑ **Van Freight Carriers Trailer**, Buddy L, red streamlined tractor, bright blue enclosed cab, light cream/white semi-trailer van w/removable white roof, 22" long, 1953
EX $125   NM $185   MIP $250

(Thomas G. Nefos Photo)

❑ **Wild Animal Circus**, Buddy L, red tractor unit and semi-trailer, three cages w/plastic elephant, lion, tiger, 26" long, 1966
EX $150   NM $225   MIP $300

❑ **Wild Animal Circus**, Buddy L, red tractor unit and semi-trailer, three cages w/six plastic animals, 26" long, 1967
EX $110   NM $185   MIP $235

❑ **Wild Animal Circus**, Buddy L, red tractor unit and semi-trailer, trailer cage doors lighter than body, 26" long, 1970
EX $100   NM $150   MIP $200

❑ **Wrecker Truck**, Buddy L, black front, hood, and fenders, open cab, four rubber tires, red wrecker body, 26-1/2" long, 1930
EX $800   NM $1000   MIP $2500

❑ **Wrecker Truck**, Buddy L, duo-tone slant design, red upper cab, hood, and boom, white lower cab, grille, fenders, body, rubber wheels, electric headlights, removable rider seat, 31" long, 1936
EX $250   NM $450   MIP $700

❑ **Wrecker Truck**, Buddy L, black open cab, red chassis and bed, disc wheels, 26-1/2" long, 1928-29
EX $700   NM $1000   MIP $2000

❑ **Wrigley Express Truck**, Buddy L, forest green w/chrome one-piece, three-bar grille and headlights, "Wrigley's Spearmint Gum" poster on sides, 16-1/2" long, 1955
EX $135   NM $215   MIP $295

❑ **Zoo-A-Rama**, Buddy L, sand yellow four-wheel trailer cage, matching Colt Sportsliner w/white top, three plastic animals, 20-3/4" long, 1968
EX $100   NM $155   MIP $205

❑ **Zoo-A-Rama**, Buddy L, greenish yellow four-wheel trailer cage, matching Colt Sportsliner w/white top, three plastic animals, 20-3/4" long, 1969
EX $85   NM $130   MIP $185

❑ **Zoo-A-Rama**, Buddy L, lime green Colt Sportsliner w/four-wheel trailer cage, cage contains plastic tree, monkeys and bears, 20-3/4" long, 1967
EX $100   NM $160   MIP $205

CORGI

AGRICULTURAL

❑ **Agricultural Set,** 1962-66, 1962-64 issue: No. 55 Fordson Tractor, No. 51 Tipping Trailer, No. 438 Land Rover, No. 101 Flat Trailer w/No. 1487 Milk Churns; 1965-66 issue: No. 60 Fordson Tractor, No. 62 Tipping Trailer, No. 438 Land Rover, red No. 100 Dropside Trailer w/No. 1487 Milk Churns, Model No. 22-A
EX $280   NM $450   MIP $1000

❑ **Agricultural Set,** 1967-72, No. 69 Massey-Ferguson tractor, No. 62 trailer, No. 438 Land Rover, No. 484 Livestock Truck w/pigs, No. 71 harrow, No. 1490 skip and churns; w/accessories: four calves, farmhand, dog and six sacks, Model No. 5-B
EX $120   NM $180   MIP $400

❑ **Agricultural Set,** 1978-80, No. 55 Tractor, No. 56 Tipping Trailer, Silo and mustard yellow conveyor, Model No. 42-A
EX $60   NM $90   MIP $130

❑ **Beast Carrier Trailer,** 1965-71, red chassis, yellow body and tailgate, four plastic calves, red plastic wheels, black rubber tires, Model No. 58-A
EX $24   NM $36   MIP $60

❑ **Bedford Articulated Horse Box,** 1973-76, cast cab, lower body and three working ramps, yellow interior, plastic upper body, w/horse and Newmarket Racing Stables labels, dark metallic green or light green body w/orange or yellow upper, four horses, Model No. 1104-B
EX $32   NM $48   MIP $80

❑ **Berliet Articulated Horse Box,** 1976-80, bronze cab and lower semi body, cream chassis, white upper body, black interior, three working ramps, National Racing Stables decals, horse figures, chrome wheels, Model No. 1105-B
EX $30   NM $45   MIP $75

❑ **Combine, Tractor and Trailer,** 1959-62, set of three: No. 1111 combine, No. 50 Massey-Ferguson tractor, and No. 51 trailer, Model No. 8-A
EX $110   NM $185   MIP $350

❑ **Country Farm Set,** 1974-75, No. 50 Massey Ferguson tractor, red No. 62 hay trailer w/load, fences, figures, Model No. 4-B
EX $30   NM $45   MIP $75

❑ **Country Farm Set,** 1976, same as 4-B but without hay load on trailer, Model No. 5-C
EX $30   NM $45   MIP $75

❑ **David Brown Combine,** 1978-79, No. 55 Tractor, red and yellow combines, white JF labels, Model No. 1112-B
EX $30   NM $45   MIP $75

❑ **David Brown Tractor,** 1977-82, white body w/black/white David Brown No. 1412 labels, red chassis and plastic engine, Model No. 55-B
EX $15   NM $25   MIP $45

❑ **David Brown Tractor & Trailer,** 1976-79, two-piece set; No. 55 tractor and No. 56 trailer, Model No. 34-A
EX $30   NM $45   MIP $75

❑ **Dodge Livestock Truck,** 1967-72, tan cab and hood, green body, working tailgate and ramp, five pigs, Model No. 484-A
EX $34   NM $51   MIP $85

❑ **Ford 5000 Super Major Tractor,** 1967-73, blue body/chassis w/Ford Super Major 5000 decals, gray cast fenders and rear wheels, gray plastic front wheels, black plastic tires, driver, Model No. 67-A
EX $30   NM $45   MIP $75

❑ **Ford 5000 Tractor with Scoop,** 1969-72, blue body/chassis, gray fenders, yellow scoop arm and controls, chrome scoop, black control lines, Model No. 74-A
EX $55   NM $80   MIP $130

(KP Photo by Dr. Douglas Sadecky)

❑ **Ford Tractor and Beast Carrier,** 1966-72, Gift Set included No. 67 Ford 5000 tractor and No. 58 Beast Carrier, Model No. 1-B
EX $60   NM $90   MIP $150

❑ **Ford Tractor and Conveyor,** 1966-69, No. 67 tractor, conveyor w/trailer, figures and accessories, Model No. 47-A
EX $60   NM $90   MIP $175

❑ **Ford Tractor with Trencher,** 1970-74, blue body/chassis, gray fenders, cast yellow trencher arm and controls, chrome trencher, black control lines, Model No. 72-A
EX $50   NM $75   MIP $125

(KP Photo by Dr. Douglas Sadecky)

❑ **Fordson Power Major Halftrack Tractor,** 1962-64, blue body/chassis, silver steering wheel, seat and grille, three versions: orange cast wheels, gray treads, lights in radiator or on sides of radiator. This bizarre little model can be quite difficult to find--especially with original tracks, Model No. 54-A
EX $90   NM $135   MIP $225

(KP Photo by Dr. Douglas Sadecky)

❑ **Fordson Power Major Tractor,** 1961-63, blue body/chassis w/Fordson Power Major decals, silver steering wheel, seat, exhaust, grille and lights. The 61-A Four Furrow Plough makes a nice companion piece to the model, Model No. 55-A
EX $45   NM $65   MIP $110

❑ **Fordson Power Major Tractor,** 1964-66, blue body w/Fordson Power Major decals, driver, blue chassis and steering wheel, silver seat, hitch, exhaust, Model No. 60-A
EX $50   NM $75   MIP $125

❑ **Fordson Tractor and Plow,** 1961-64, No. 55 Fordson Tractor and No. 56 Four Furrow plow, Model No. 18-A
EX $55   NM $85   MIP $140

❑ **Fordson Tractor and Plow,** 1964-66, No. 60 tractor and No. 61 four-furrow plow, Model No. 13-A
EX $55   NM $85   MIP $140

❑ **Four Furrow Plow,** 1961-63, red frame, yellow plastic parts, Model No. 56-A
EX $15   NM $20   MIP $35

❑ **Four Furrow Plow,** 1964-70, blue frame w/chrome plastic parts, Model No. 61-A
EX $15   NM $20   MIP $35

❑ **Jeep FC-150 Pickup with Conveyor Belt,** 1965-69, red body, yellow interior, orange grille, two black rubber belts, shaped wheels, black rubber tires; accessories include farmland figure and sacks, Model No. 64-A
EX $45   NM $65   MIP $130

❑ **Land Rover & Horse Box,** 1968-77, blue/white Land Rover w/horse trailer in two versions: cast wheels (1968-74) and Whizz Wheels (1975-77); accessories include a mare and a foal; value is for each individual complete set, Model No. 15-B
EX $50   NM $75   MIP $125

❑ **Land Rover and Pony Trailer,** 1958-62, two versions: green No. 438 Land Rover and a red and black No. 102 Pony trailer (1958-62); tan/cream No. 438 Land Rover and a pony trailer (1963-68); value given is for each individual complete set, Model No. 2-A
EX $50   NM $90   MIP $175

❑ **Massey-Ferguson 165 Tractor,** 1966-72, gray engine and chassis, red hood and fenders w/black/white Massey Ferguson 165 decals, white grille, red cast wheels; makes engine sound, Model No. 66-A
EX $35   NM $55   MIP $90

(KP Photo by Dr. Douglas Sadecky)

❏ **Massey-Ferguson 165 Tractor with Saw,** 1969-73, red hood and fenders, gray engine and seat, cast yellow arm and control, chrome circular saw, Model No. 73-A
EX $55   **NM** $85   **MIP** $140

(KP Photo by Dr. Douglas Sadecky)

❏ **Massey-Ferguson 165 Tractor with Shovel,** 1967-73, gray chassis, red hood, fenders and shovel arms, unpainted shovel and cylinder, red cast wheels, black plastic tires, w/figure. This tractor even featured engine noises!, Model No. 69-A
EX $45   **NM** $65   **MIP** $120

❏ **Massey-Ferguson 50B Tractor,** 1973-77, yellow body, black interior and roof, red plastic wheels w/black plastic tires, widows, Model No. 50-B
EX $15   **NM** $18   **MIP** $75

❏ **Massey-Ferguson 65 Tractor,** 1959-66, silver metal or plastic steering wheel, seat and grille, red engine hood, red metal or plastic wheels w/black rubber tires, Model No. 50-A
EX $40   **NM** $60   **MIP** $100

❏ **Massey-Ferguson 65 Tractor And Shovel,** 1960-66, two versions: red bonnet w/either cream or gray chassis, red metal or orange plastic wheels; value is for each, Model No. 53-A
EX $55   **NM** $85   **MIP** $140

❏ **Massey-Ferguson Combine,** 1959-63, red body w/yellow metal blades, metal tines, black/white decals, yellow metal wheels, Model No. 1111-A
EX $70   **NM** $105   **MIP** $175

❏ **Massey-Ferguson Combine,** 1968-73, red body, plastic yellow blades, red wheels, Model No. 1111-B
EX $60   **NM** $90   **MIP** $150

❏ **Massey-Ferguson Tipping Trailer,** 1959-65, two versions: red chassis w/either yellow or gray tipper and tailgate, red metal or plastic wheels, value is for each, Model No. 51-A
EX $10   **NM** $18   **MIP** $35

❏ **Massey-Ferguson Tractor and Tipping Trailer,** 1959-63, No. 50 tractor and No. 51 trailer, no driver, Model No. 7-A
EX $50   **NM** $75   **MIP** $125

❏ **Massey-Ferguson Tractor and Tipping Trailer,** 1965, No. 50 Massey-Ferguson tractor w/driver, No. 51 trailer, Model No. 29-A
EX $50   **NM** $75   **MIP** $125

(KP Photo by Dr. Douglas Sadecky)

❏ **Massey-Ferguson Tractor with Fork,** 1963-67, red cast body and shovel, arms, cream chassis, red plastic wheels, black rubber tires, Massey-Ferguson 65 decals, w/driver, Model No. 57-A
EX $60   **NM** $90   **MIP** $150

❏ **Massey-Ferguson Tractor with Shovel,** 1974-81, two versions: either yellow and red or red and white body colors; value is for each, Model No. 54-B
EX $20   **NM** $30   **MIP** $50

❏ **Massey-Ferguson Tractor with Shovel & Trailer,** 1965-66, No. 54 MF tractor w/driver and shovel, No. 62 trailer, Model No. 32-A
EX $30   **NM** $75   **MIP** $150

❏ **Pony Club Set,** 1978-80, brown/white No. 421 Land Rover w/Corgi Pony Club labels, horse box, horse and rider, Model No. 47-B
EX $30   **NM** $45   **MIP** $75

❏ **Rice Beaufort Double Horse Box,** 1969-72, long, blue body and working gates, white roof, brown plastic interior, two horses, cast wheels, plastic tires, Model No. 112-A
EX $15   **NM** $30   **MIP** $50

(KP Photo by Dr. Douglas Sadecky)

❏ **Rice Pony Trailer,** 1958-65, cast body and chassis w/working tailgate, horse, in six variations, smooth or shaped hubs, cast or wire drawbar. Shown here

is the harder-to-find two-tone cream/red variation, Model No. 102-A
EX $20   **NM** $30   **MIP** $50

❏ **Silo & Conveyor Belt,** 1978-80, w/yellow conveyor and Corgi Harvesting Co. label on silo, Model No. 43-A
EX $35   **NM** $50   **MIP** $85

❏ **Tandem Disc Harrow,** 1967-72, yellow main frame, red upper frame, working wheels linkage, unpainted linkage and cast discs, black plastic tires, Model No. 71-A
EX $15   **NM** $20   **MIP** $45

❏ **Tipping Farm Trailer,** 1965-72, red working tipper and tailgates, yellow chassis, red plastic wheels, black tires, w/detachable raves, Model No. 62-A
EX $10   **NM** $15   **MIP** $30

❏ **Tipping Farm Trailer,** 1977-80, cast chassis and tailgate, red plastic tipper and wheels, black tires, in two versions, Model No. 56-B
EX $10   **NM** $15   **MIP** $25

❏ **Tractor and Beast Carrier,** 1965-66, No. 55 Fordson tractor, figures and No. 58 beast carrier, Model No. 33-A
EX $65   **NM** $100   **MIP** $165

❏ **Tractor with Shovel and Trailer,** 1968-73, standard colors, No. 69 Massey-Ferguson Tractor and No. 62 Tipping Trailer, Model No. 9-B
EX $65   **NM** $100   **MIP** $165

AIRCRAFT

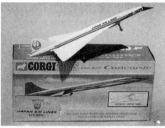

(KP Photo by Dr. Douglas Sadecky)

❏ **Concorde-First Issues,** 1969-72, Japan Airlines decals. This rare model was probably an import issue. Ironically, the real Concorde was never part of the Japan Air Lines livery, Model No. 653-A
EX $280   **NM** $420   **MIP** $700

❏ **Concorde-First Issues,** 1969-72, Air Canada decals, Model No. 652-A
EX $80   **NM** $120   **MIP** $200

❏ **Concorde-First Issues,** 1969-72, Air France decals, Model No. 651-A
EX $20   **NM** $45   **MIP** $85

❏ **Concorde-First Issues,** 1969-72, BOAC decals, Model No. 650-A
EX $20   **NM** $30   **MIP** $50

❏ **Concorde-Second Issue,** 1976-82, Air France model on display stand, Model No. 651-B
EX $15   **NM** $20   **MIP** $35

❏ **Concorde-Second Issues,** 1976-82, BOAC model on display stand, Model No. 650-B
EX $15   **NM** $20   **MIP** $35

VINTAGE

❑ **Corgi Flying Club Set,** 1972-77, blue/orange No. 438 Land Rover w/red dome light, blue trailer w/either orange/yellow or orange/white plastic airplane, Model No. 19-B
EX $24 **NM** $45 **MIP** $90

❑ **Flying Club Set,** 1978-80, green and white No. 419 Jeep w/Corgi Flying Club labels, green trailer, blue/white airplane, Model No. 49-A
EX $36 **NM** $55 **MIP** $90

❑ **Glider Set,** 1981-83, two versions: white No. 345 Honda, 1981-82; yellow Honda, 1983, value is for individual complete sets, Model No. 12-C
EX $30 **NM** $45 **MIP** $75

❑ **Lunar Bug,** 1970-72, white body w/red roof, blue interior and wings, clear and amber windows, red working ramp, Lunar Bug labels, Model No. 806-A
EX $25 **NM** $40 **MIP** $95

❑ **NASA Space Shuttle,** 1980, white body, two opening hatches, black plastic interior, jets and base, unpainted retracting gear castings, black plastic wheels, w/satalite, Model No. 648-A
EX $30 **NM** $45 **MIP** $75

❑ **Stromberg Jet Ranger Helicopter,** 1978-79, black body w/yellow trim and interior, clear windows, black plastic rotors, white/blue labels, Model No. 926-A
EX $30 **NM** $45 **MIP** $85

AUTOMOBILE

❑ **AMC Pacer,** 1977-78, metallic red body, white Pacer X decals, working hatch, clear windows, light yellow interior, chrome bumpers and wheels, Model No. 291-A
EX $15 **NM** $20 **MIP** $50

❑ **Aston Martin DB4,** 1960-65, red or yellow body w/working hood, detailed engine, clear windows, plastic interior, silver lights, grille, license plate and bumpers, red taillights, rubber tires, smooth or cast spoked wheels; working scoop on early models, Model No. 218-A
EX $45 **NM** $65 **MIP** $110

(KP Photo by Dr. Douglas Sadecky)

❑ **Austin A40,** 1959-62, one-piece light blue body with dark blue roof or red body w/black roof and clear windows, smooth wheels, rubber tires, Model No. 216-A
EX $35 **NM** $50 **MIP** $100

❑ **Austin A40-Mechanical,** 1959-60, friction motor, red body w/black roof, Model No. 216-M
EX $55 **NM** $75 **MIP** $170

(KP Photo by Dr. Douglas Sadecky)

❑ **Austin A60 Driving School,** 1964-68, medium blue body w/silver trim, left-hand drive steering wheel, steering control on roof; came w/five language leaflet (US version of No. 236), Model No. 255-A
EX $45 **NM** $65 **MIP** $160

(KP Photo by Dr. Douglas Sadecky)

❑ **Austin A60 Motor School,** 1964-69, light blue body w/silver trim, red interior, single body casting, right-hand drive steering wheel, two figures, steering control on roof; came w/Highway Patrol leaflet, Model No. 236-A
EX $45 **NM** $65 **MIP** $120

(KP Photo by Dr. Douglas Sadecky)

❑ **Austin Cambridge,** 1956-61, available in gray, green/gray, silver/green, aqua, green/cream, two-tone green, smooth wheels, shown here with Austin Cambridge-Mechanical, Model No. 201-A
EX $40 **NM** $60 **MIP** $120

❑ **Austin Cambridge-Mechanical,** 1956-59, fly-wheel motor, available in orange, cream, light or dark gray, or silver over metallic blue, smooth wheels, Model No. 201M
EX $50 **NM** $75 **MIP** $150

❑ **Austin Mini Countryman,** 1965-69, turquoise body, jeweled headlights, opening rear doors, chrome roofrack w/two surfboards, shaped or cast wheels, w/surfer figure, Model No. 485-A
EX $55 **NM** $80 **MIP** $150

❑ **Austin Mini-Metro,** 1981, blue or red body w/plastic interior, working rear hatch and doors, clear windows, folding seats, chrome headlights, orange taillights, black plastic base, grille, bumpers, Whizz Wheels, Model No. 275-B
EX $18 **NM** $27 **MIP** $45

❑ **Austin Seven Mini,** 1961-67, primrose yellow, red interior, rare, Model No. 225-A2, second issue
EX $100 **NM** $200 **MIP** $325

❑ **Austin Seven Mini,** 1961-67, red or yellow body, yellow interior, silver bumpers, grille and headlights, orange taillights, Model No. 225-A1
EX $50 **NM** $75 **MIP** $125

❑ **Bentley Continental,** 1961-66, two-tone green or black and silver bodies, w/red interior, clear windows, chrome grille and bumpers, jewel headlights, red jeweled taillights, suspension, shaped wheels, gray rubber tires, Model No. 224-A
EX $45 **NM** $65 **MIP** $110

❑ **Bentley T Series,** 1970-72, red body, cream interior, working hood, trunk and doors, clear windows, folding seats, chrome bumper/grille, jewel headlights, Whizz Wheels, Model No. 274-A
EX $36 **NM** $55 **MIP** $90

❑ **Buick and Cabin Cruiser,** 1965-68, two versions: light blue or dark metallic blue, No. 245 Buick, red boat trailer, dolphin cabin cruiser w/two figures, Model No. 31-A
EX $80 **NM** $120 **MIP** $280

❑ **Buick Riviera,** 1964-68, metallic gold, dark blue, pale blue or gold body, red interior, gray steering wheel, and tow hook, clear windshield, chrome grille and bumpers, suspension, Tan-o-lite headlights, spoked wheels and rubber tires, Model No. 245-A
EX $30 **NM** $45 **MIP** $75

❑ **Chevrolet Caprice Classic,** 1981-82, working doors and trunk, whitewall tires, two versions: light metallic green body w/green interior or silver on blue body w/brown interior, Model No. 325-B
EX $24 **NM** $36 **MIP** $60

(KP Photo by Dr. Douglas Sadecky)

❑ **Chevrolet Corvair,** 1961-66, either blue or pale-blue body w/yellow interior and working rear hood, detailed engine, clear windows, silver bumpers, headlights and trim, red taillights, rear window blind, shaped wheels, rubber tires, Model No. 229-A
EX $36 **NM** $55 **MIP** $90

(KP Photo by Dr. Douglas Sadecky)

❑ **Chevrolet Impala,** 1960-62, pink body, yellow plastic interior, clear windows, silver headlights, bumpers, grille and trim, suspension, die-cast base w/rubber tires; a second version has a blue body w/red or yellow interior and smooth or shaped hubs, Model No. 220-A
EX $50 **NM** $75 **MIP** $125

❑ **Chevrolet Impala,** 1965-67, tan body, cream interior, gray steering wheel, clear windshields, chrome bumpers, grille, headlights, suspension, red taillights, shaped wheels and rubber tires, Model No. 248-A
EX $50 **NM** $75 **MIP** $125

(KP Photo by Dr. Douglas Sadecky)

❑ **Chevrolet Kennel Club Van,** 1967-69, white upper, red lower body, working tailgate and rear windows, green interior, four dog figures, kennel club decals; shaped spun or detailed cast wheels, rubber tires, Model No. 486-A
EX $56 **NM** $84 **MIP** $140

❑ **Chrysler Imperial Convertible,** 1965-66, red body w/gray base, working hood, trunk and doors, golf bag in trunk, detailed engine, clear windshield, aqua interior, driver, chrome bumpers, Model No. 246-A1
EX $45 **NM** $65 **MIP** $110

❑ **Chrysler Imperial Convertible,** 1967-68, metallic blue body w/gray base, working hood, trunk and doors, golf bag in trunk, detailed engine, clear windshield, aqua interior, driver, chrome bumpers, Model No. 246-A2
EX $50 **NM** $90 **MIP** $160

❑ **Citroen 2CV Charleston,** 1981, yellow/black or maroon/black body versions w/opening hood, Model No. 346-A
EX $15 **NM** $18 **MIP** $30

❑ **Citroen DS19,** 1957-65, one-piece body in several colors, clear windows, silver lights, grille and bumpers, smooth wheels, rubber tires; colors: red, metallic green w/black roof, yellow w/red roof, Model No. 210-A
EX $56 **NM** $84 **MIP** $140

❑ **Citroen Dyane,** 1974-78, metallic yellow or green body, black roof and interior, working rear hatch, clear windows, black base and tow bar, silver bumpers, grille and headlights, red taillights, marching duck and French flag decals, suspension, chrome wheels, Model No. 287-A
EX $15 **NM** $18 **MIP** $30

❑ **Citroen ID-19 Safari,** 1963-65, orange body w/red/brown or red/green luggage on roof rack, green/brown interior, working hatch, two passengers, Wildlife Preservation decals, Model No. 436-A
EX $40 **NM** $60 **MIP** $100

❑ **Citroen Le Dandy Coupe,** 1966, metallic maroon body and base, yellow interior, working trunk and two doors, clear windows, plastic interior, folding seats, chrome grille and bumpers, jewel headlights, red taillights, suspension, spoked wheels, rubber tires, Model No. 259-A1
EX $50 **NM** $75 **MIP** $125

(KP Photo by Dr. Douglas Sadecky)

❑ **Citroen Le Dandy Coupe,** 1967-69, metallic dark blue hood, sides and base, plastic aqua interior, white roof and trunk lid, clear windows, folding seats, chrome grille and bumpers, jewel headlights, red taillights, suspension, spoked wheels, rubber tires, Model No. 259-A2
EX $70 **NM** $105 **MIP** $175

❑ **Citroen SM,** 1971-75, metallic lime gold w/chrome wheels or mauve body w/spoked wheels, pale blue interior and lifting hatch cover, working rear hatch and two doors, chrome inner drs., window frames, bumpers, grille, amber headlights, red taillights, Whizz Wheels, Model No. 284-A
EX $16 **NM** $24 **MIP** $40

❑ **Citroen Tour de France Car,** 1970-72, red body, yellow interior and rear bed, clear windshield and headlights, driver, black plastic rack w/four bicycle wheels, swiveling team manager figure w/megaphone in back of car, Paramount and Tour de France decals, Whizz Wheels, Model No. 510-A
EX $40 **NM** $60 **MIP** $100

❑ **Citroen Winter Olympics Car,** 1967-69, white body, blue roof and hatch, blue interior, red roof rack w/yellow skis, gold sled w/rider, skier, gold Grenoble Olympiade decals on car roof, Model No. 499-A
EX $70 **NM** $105 **MIP** $200

❑ **Citroen Winter Sports Safari,** 1964-67, white body in three versions: two w/Corgi Ski Club decals and either w/or without roof ski rack, or one w/1964 Winter Olympics decals, Model No. 475-A
EX $56 **NM** $84 **MIP** $140

(KP Photo by Dr. Douglas Sadecky)

❑ **Fiat 1800,** 1960-63, one-piece body in several colors, clear windows, plastic interior, silver lights, grille and bumpers, red taillights, smooth wheels, rubber tires, colors: blue body w/light or bright yellow interior, light tan, mustard, light blue or two-tone blue body, Model No. 217-A
EX $24 **NM** $40 **MIP** $80

❑ **Fiat 2100,** 1961-64, light two-tone mauve body, yellow interior, purple roof, clear windows w/rear blind, silver grille, license plates and bumpers, red taillights, shaped wheels, rubber tires, Model No. 232-A
EX $22 **NM** $33 **MIP** $75

(KP Photo by Dr. Douglas Sadecky)

❑ **Ford Consul,** 1956-61, one-piece body in several colors, clear windows, silver grille, lights and bumpers, smooth wheels, rubber tires, Model No. 200-A
EX $45 **NM** $65 **MIP** $120

❑ **Ford Consul Classic,** 1961-65, cream or gold body and base, yellow interior, pink roof, clear windows, gray steering wheel, silver bumpers, grille, opening hood, Model No. 234-A
EX $35 **NM** $55 **MIP** $90

❑ **Ford Consul-Mechanical,** 1956-59, same as model 200-A but w/friction motor and blue or green body, Model No. 200-M
EX $55 **NM** $85 **MIP** $160

❑ **Ford Cortina Estate Car,** 1966-68, 3-1/2" metallic dark blue body and base, brown and cream simulated wood panels, cream interior, chrome bumpers and grille, jewel headlights, Model No. 440-A
EX $35 **NM** $55 **MIP** $90

❑ **Ford Cortina Estate Car,** 1966-69, red body and base or metallic charcoal gray body and base, cream interior, chrome bumpers and grille, jewel headlights, Model No. 491-A
EX $35 **NM** $55 **MIP** $90

❏ **Ford Escort 13 GL,** 1980, red, blue or yellow body, opening doors, Model No. 334-B
EX $8   **NM** $15   **MIP** $25

❏ **Ford Torino Road Hog,** 1981, orange-red body, yellow and gray chassis, gold lamps, chrome radiator shell, windows and bumpers, one-piece body, working horn, Model No. 1003-A
EX $15   **NM** $20   **MIP** $35

❏ **Ford Zephyr Estate Car,** 1960-65, light blue one-piece body, dark blue hood and stripes, red interior, silver bumpers, grille and headlights, red taillights, Model No. 424-A
EX $30   **NM** $45   **MIP** $75

(KP Photo by Dr. Douglas Sadecky)

❏ **Ghia L64 Chrysler V8,** 1963-69, metallic light blue, green, copper or yellow, plastic interior, hood, trunk and two doors working, detailed engine, clear windshield, shaped or detailed cast wheels, Model No. 241-A
EX $25   **NM** $40   **MIP** $75

❏ **Ghia-Fiat 600 Jolly,** 1963-65, light or dark blue body, red and silver canopy, red seats, two figures, windshield, chrome dash, floor, steering wheels, Model No. 240-A
EX $45   **NM** $75   **MIP** $130

❏ **Golden Guinea Set,** 1961-63, three vehicle set, gold plated No. 224 Bentley Continental, No. 229 Chevy Corvair and No. 234 Ford Consul, Model No. 20-A
EX $90   **NM** $150   **MIP** $325

(KP Photo by Dr. Douglas Sadecky)

❏ **Hillman Husky,** 1956-60, one-piece tan or metallic blue/silver body, clear windows, silver lights, grille and bumpers, smooth wheels. The car on the left is the more rare two-tone version, while the car on the right is the mechanical flywheel version that was only produced for one year in 1959, Model No. 206-A
EX $40   **NM** $70   **MIP** $125

❏ **Hillman Husky-Mechanical,** 1956-59, same as 206-A but w/friction motor, black base and dark blue, gray or cream body, Model No. 206-M
EX $50   **NM** $90   **MIP** $125

❏ **Hillman Imp,** 1963-67, metallic copper, blue, dark blue or gold one-piece bodies, w/white/yellow interior, silver bumpers, headlights, Model No. 251-A
EX $30   **NM** $45   **MIP** $85

❏ **Honda Ballade Driving School,** 1982-83, red body/base, tan interior, clear windows, tow hook, mirrors, bumpers, Model No. 273-B
EX $10   **NM** $15   **MIP** $25

❏ **Honda Prelude,** 1981-82, dark metallic blue body, tan interior, clear windows, folding seats, sunroof, chrome wheels, Model No. 345-B
EX $8   **NM** $15   **MIP** $20

❏ **Jaguar 2.4 Litre,** 1957-63, one-piece white body w/no interior 1957-59, or yellow body w/red interior 1960-63, clear windows, smooth hubs, Model No. 208-A
EX $50   **NM** $80   **MIP** $130

(KP Photo by Dr. Douglas Sadecky)

❏ **Jaguar 2.4 Litre-Mechanical,** 1957-59, same as 208-A but w/friction motor and metallic blue body, Model No. 208-M
EX $60   **NM** $90   **MIP** $180

(KP Photo by Dr. Douglas Sadecky)

❏ **Jaguar Mark X Saloon,** 1962-67, several different color versions w/working front and rear hood castings, clear windshields, plastic interior, gray steering wheel. Shown here in silver and blue versions, pictured at the left are the two suitcases that were included with each car, Model No. 238-A
EX $35   **NM** $55   **MIP** $110

❏ **Lincoln Continental,** 1967-69, metallic gold or light blue body, black roof, maroon plastic interior, working hood, trunk and doors, clear windows; accessories include TV w/picture strips for TV, Model No. 262-A
EX $60   **NM** $90   **MIP** $150

❏ **Mercedes-Benz 220SE Coupe,** 1962-64, cream, black or dark red body, red plastic interior, clear windows, working trunk, silver bumpers, grille and plate, spare wheel in boot, Model No. 230-A
EX $40   **NM** $60   **MIP** $100

(KP Photo by Dr. Douglas Sadecky)

❏ **Mercedes-Benz 220SE Coupe,** 1967-68, metallic maroon or blue body, cream plastic interior, medium gray base, clear windows, silver bumpers, headlights, grille and license; accessories include plastic luggage and spare wheel in boot. Except for different exterior colors and the inclusion of luggage, this was exactly the same car as the 230-A, Model No. 253-A
EX $40   **NM** $60   **MIP** $100

❏ **Mercedes-Benz 240D,** 1975-81, silver, blue or copper/beige body, working trunk, two doors, clear windows, plastic interior, two hook, chrome bumpers, grille and headlights, Whizz Wheels, Model No. 285-A
EX $10   **NM** $15   **MIP** $25

❏ **Mercedes-Benz 600 Pullman,** 1964-69, metallic maroon body, cream interior and steering wheel, clear windshields, chrome grille, trim and bumpers, working windshield operators; includes instruction sheet, Model No. 247-A
EX $40   **NM** $60   **MIP** $100

(KP Photo by Dr. Douglas Sadecky)

❏ **Morris Cowley,** 1959-60, long, one-piece body in several colors, clear windows, silver lights, grille and bumper, smooth wheels, rubber tires. The model on the left is the rare blue version, and the car on the right is the 202-M mechanical flywheel version, Model No. 202-A
EX $45   **NM** $75   **MIP** $140

❏ **Morris Cowley-Mechanical,** 1956-59, same as 202-A but w/friction motor, available in off-white or green body, Model No. 202-M
EX $55   **NM** $95   **MIP** $170

❏ **Oldsmobile Super 88,** 1962-68, three versions: light blue, light or dark metallic blue body w/white stripes, red interior, single body casting, Model No. 235-A
EX $40   **NM** $60   **MIP** $100

❏ **Oldsmobile Toronado,** 1967-68, metallic medium or dark blue body, cream interior, one-piece body, clear windshield, chrome bumpers, grille, headlight covers, shaped or cast spoked wheels, Model No. 264-A
EX $35   **NM** $55   **MIP** $90

❑ **Oldsmobile Toronado,** 1968-70, metallic copper, metallic blue or red one-piece body, cream interior, Golden jacks, gray tow hook, clear windows, bumpers, grille, headlights, Model No. 276-A
EX $35   **NM** $55   **MIP** $90

❑ **Opel Senator Doctor's Car,** 1980-81, Model No. 332-B
EX $10   **NM** $15   **MIP** $25

❑ **OSI DAF City Car,** 1971-74, orange/red body, light cream interior, textured black roof, sliding left door, working hood, hatch and two right doors, Whizz Wheels, Model No. 283-A
EX $18   **NM** $25   **MIP** $45

❑ **Plymouth Sports Suburban,** 1959-63, dark cream body, tan roof, red interior, die-cast base, red axle, silver bumpers, trim and grille and rubber tires, Model No. 219-A
EX $40   **NM** $60   **MIP** $100

(KP Photo by Dr. Douglas Sadecky)

❑ **Plymouth Sports Suburban,** 1963-65, pale blue body w/silver trim, red roof, yellow interior, gray die-cast base without rear axle bulge, shaped wheels, Model No. 445-A
EX $40   **NM** $60   **MIP** $100

❑ **Plymouth Suburban Mail Car,** 1963-66, white upper, blue lower body w/red stripes, gray die-cast base without rear axle bulge, silver bumpers and grille, U.S. Mail decals, Model No. 443-A
EX $55   **NM** $85   **MIP** $140

❑ **Rambler Marlin Fastback,** 1966-69, red body, black roof and trim, cream interior, clear windshield, folding seats, chrome bumpers, grille and headlights, opening doors, Model No. 263-A
EX $35   **NM** $55   **MIP** $90

❑ **Rambler Marlin with Kayak and Trailer,** 1968-69, blue No. 263 Marlin w/roof rack, blue/white trailer, w/two kayaks, Model No. 10-A
EX $100   **NM** $150   **MIP** $250

❑ **Renault 16,** 1969, metallic maroon body, dark yellow interior, chrome base, grille and bumpers, clear windows, opening bonnet and hatch cover, Renault decal, Model No. 260-A
EX $25   **NM** $35   **MIP** $60

❑ **Renault 16TS,** 1970-72, metallic blue body w/Renault decal on working hatch, clear windows, detailed engine, yellow interior, Model No. 202-B
EX $20   **NM** $25   **MIP** $50

❑ **Renault 5TS,** 1980-81, light blue body, red plastic interior, dark blue roof, dome light, S.O.S. Medicine lettering, working

hatch and two doors, French issue, Model No. 293-A
EX $20   **NM** $35   **MIP** $70

❑ **Renault Alpine 5TS,** 1980, dark blue body, off white interior, red and chrome trim, clear windows and headlights, gray base and bumpers, black grille, opening doors and hatchback, Model No. 294-A
EX $15   **NM** $25   **MIP** $40

❑ **Renault Floride,** 1959-65, one-piece dark red, maroon or lime green body, clear windows, silver bumper, grille, lights and plates, red taillights, smooth or shaped hubs, rubber tires, Model No. 222-A
EX $35   **NM** $55   **MIP** $95

(KP Photo by Dr. Douglas Sadecky)

❑ **Riley Pathfinder,** 1956-61, red or dark blue one-piece body, clear windows, silver lights, grille and bumpers, smooth wheels, rubber tires, Model No. 205-A
EX $45   **NM** $65   **MIP** $125

❑ **Riley Pathfinder-Mechanical,** 1956-59, w/friction motor and either red or blue body, Model No. 205-M
EX $60   **NM** $95   **MIP** $170

❑ **Rolls-Royce Corniche,** 1979, different color versions w/light brown interior, working hood, trunk and two doors, clear windows, folding seats, chrome bumpers, Model No. 279-A
EX $10   **NM** $20   **MIP** $40

❑ **Rolls-Royce Silver Shadow,** 1970, metallic white upper/dusty blue lower body, working hood, trunk and two doors, clear windows, folding seats, chrome bumpers, Golden Jacks wheels, Model No. 273-A
EX $30   **NM** $50   **MIP** $95

❑ **Rolls-Royce Silver Shadow,** 1971-73, metallic silver upper and metallic blue lower body, light brown interior, may or may not include hole in trunk for spare tire, Whizz Wheels, Model No. 280-A1
EX $25   **NM** $40   **MIP** $65

❑ **Rolls-Royce Silver Shadow,** 1974-78, metallic blue or gold body, bright blue interior, working hood, trunk and two doors, clear windows, folding seats, spare wheel, Model No. 280-A2
EX $25   **NM** $40   **MIP** $65

❑ **Rover 2000,** 1963-66, metallic blue w/red interior or maroon body w/yellow interior, gray steering wheel, clear windshields, Model No. 252-A
EX $30   **NM** $45   **MIP** $75

❑ **Rover 2000TC,** 1968-70, metallic olive green or maroon one-piece body, light

brown interior, chrome bumpers/grille, jewel headlights, red taillights, Golden Jacks wheels, Model No. 275-A
EX $30   **NM** $45   **MIP** $75

❑ **Rover 2000TC,** 1971-73, metallic purple body, light orange interior, black grille, one-piece body, amber windows, chrome bumpers and headlights, Whizz Wheels, Model No. 281-A
EX $25   **NM** $35   **MIP** $60

❑ **Rover 3500,** 1979, three different body and interior versions, plastic interior, opening hood, hatch and two doors, lifting hatch cover, Model No. 338-B
EX $8   **NM** $15   **MIP** $25

(KP Photo by Dr. Douglas Sadecky)

❑ **Rover 90,** 1956-60, one-piece body, silver headlights, grille and bumpers, smooth wheels, rubber tires; multiple colors available. The car on the left is the rare two-tone color scheme and the vehicle on the right is the mechanical version in metallic green, Model No. 204-A
EX $50   **NM** $75   **MIP** $145

❑ **Rover 90-Mechanical,** 1956-59, w/friction motor and red, green, gray or metallic green body, Model No. 204-M
EX $60   **NM** $90   **MIP** $170

(KP Photo by Dr. Douglas Sadecky)

❑ **Standard Vanguard,** 1957-61, one-piece red and pale green body, clear windows, silver lights, grille and bumpers, smooth wheels, rubber tires. Pictured with the 207M, the attractive two-tone 207-A version is on the left, and the mechanical version is on the right, Model No. 207-A
EX $50   **NM** $75   **MIP** $125

❑ **Standard Vanguard-Mechanical,** 1957-59, w/friction motor and yellow or off-white body w/black or gray base, or cream body w/red roof, Model No. 207-M
EX $55   **NM** $90   **MIP** $170

❑ **Studebaker Golden Hawk,** 1958-60, one-piece body in blue and gold or white and gold, clear windows, silver lights, grille and bumpers, smooth wheels, rubber tires, Model No. 211-A
EX $55   **NM** $85   **MIP** $140

VINTAGE

(KP Photo by Dr. Douglas Sadecky)

❑ **Studebaker Golden Hawk,** 1960-65, second issue: gold painted body, shaped hubs. The "S" after the catalog number stood for "suspension" which was a new Corgi innovation at the time of the model's release, Model No. 211S2
EX $60   **NM** $180   **MIP** $180

❑ **Studebaker Golden Hawk,** 1960-65, first issue: gold plated body, white flashing, shaped hubs, Model No. 211S1
EX $55   **NM** $85   **MIP** $140

❑ **Studebaker Golden Hawk-Mechanical,** 1958-59, w/friction motor and white body w/gold trim, Model No. 211-M
EX $70   **NM** $105   **MIP** $175

❑ **Tour de France Set,** 1968-72, white and black body, Renault w/Paramount Film roof sign, rear platform w/cameraman and black camera on tripod, plus bicycle and rider, Model No. 13-B
EX $60   **NM** $90   **MIP** $200

❑ **Tour de France Set,** 1981-82, w/white No. 373 Peugeot, red and yellow Raleigh and Total logos, Racing cycles, includes manager figures, Model No. 13-C
EX $25   **NM** $45   **MIP** $90

❑ **Triumph Acclaim Driving School,** 1982, dark yellow body w/black trim, black roof mounted steering wheel steers front wheels, clear windows, mirrors, bumpers, Model No. 277-A
EX $15   **NM** $25   **MIP** $40

❑ **Triumph Acclaim Driving School,** 1982-83, yellow or red body/base, Corgi Motor School labels, black roof mounted steering wheel steers front wheels, clear windows, Model No. 278-B
EX $15   **NM** $25   **MIP** $50

❑ **Triumph Acclaim HLS,** 1981-83, metallic peacock blue body/base, black trim, light brown interior, clear windows, mirrors, bumpers, vents, tow hook, Model No. 276-B
EX $15   **NM** $18   **MIP** $30

❑ **Triumph Herald Coupe,** 1961-66, blue or gold top and lower body, white upper body, red interior, clear windows, silver bumpers, grille, headlights, shaped hubs, Model No. 231-A
EX $35   **NM** $65   **MIP** $110

(KP Photo by Dr. Douglas Sadecky)

❑ **Trojan Heinkel,** 1962-72, issued in mauve, red, orange or lilac body, plastic interior, silver bumpers and headlights, red taillights, suspension, smooth, spun, or detailed cast wheels, Model No. 233-A
EX $35   **NM** $55   **MIP** $95

(KP Photo by Dr. Douglas Sadecky)

❑ **Vauxhall Velox,** 1956-60, one-piece body in red, cream, yellow or yellow and red body, clear windows, silver lights, grille and bumpers, smooth wheels, rubber tires, Model No. 203-A
EX $50   **NM** $75   **MIP** $150

❑ **Vauxhall Velox-Mechanical,** 1956-59, w/friction motor; orange, red, yellow or cream body, Model No. 203-M
EX $60   **NM** $90   **MIP** $170

❑ **Volkswagen 1200 Driving School,** 1974-75, metallic red or blue body, yellow interior, gold roof mounted steering wheel that steers, silver headlights, red taillights, Model No. 400-A
EX $25   **NM** $35   **MIP** $60

❑ **Volkswagen 1500 Karmann-Ghia,** 1963-68, cream, red or gold body, plastic interior and taillights, front and rear working hoods, clear windshields, silver bumpers; includes spare wheel and plastic suitcase in trunk, Model No. 239-A
EX $35   **NM** $55   **MIP** $90

❑ **Volkswagen Driving School,** 1975-77, metallic blue body, yellow interior, gold roof mounted steering wheel that steers, silver headlights, red taillights, Model No. 401-A
EX $25   **NM** $40   **MIP** $70

❑ **Volkswagen Polo,** 1976-79, apple green or bright yellow body, black DBP and posthorn (German Post Office) labels, off white interior, black dash, Model No. 289-A
EX $25   **NM** $40   **MIP** $65

❑ **Volkswagen Polo,** 1979-81, metallic light brown body, off-white interior, black dash, clear windows, silver bumpers, grille and headlights, Model No. 302-C
EX $15   **NM** $18   **MIP** $30

❑ **Volkswagen Polo Auto Club Car,** 1977-79, yellow body, white roof, yellow dome light, ADAC Strassenwacht labels, Model No. 489-B
EX $15   **NM** $25   **MIP** $40

❑ **Volkswagen Polo German Auto Club Car,** 1977-79, yellow body, off-white interior, black dash, silver bumpers, grille and headlights, white roof, yellow dome light, Model No. 489-A2
EX $25   **NM** $35   **MIP** $60

❑ **Volkswagen Polo Mail Car,** 1976-80, bright yellow body, black DBP and Posthorn labels, German issue, Model No. 289-B
EX $25   **NM** $35   **MIP** $60

❑ **Volvo P-1800,** 1962-65, one-piece body light brown, dark red, pink or dark red body, clear windows, plastic interior, shaped wheels, rubber tires, Model No. 228-A
EX $40   **NM** $60   **MIP** $100

BOAT

(KP Photo by Dr. Douglas Sadecky)

❑ **Dolphin Cabin Cruiser,** 1965-68, white hull, blue deck plastic boat w/red/white stripe labels, driver, blue motor w/white cover, gray prop, cast trailer w/smooth wheels, rubber tires, Model No. 104-A
EX $24   **NM** $36   **MIP** $70

❑ **Fiat X 1/9 & Powerboat,** 1979-82, green and white automobile, w/white and gold boat, Carlsberg labels, Model No. 37-B
EX $30   **NM** $45   **MIP** $75

❑ **HDL Hovercraft SR-N1,** 1960-62, blue superstructure, gray base and deck, clear canopy, red seats, yellow SR-N1 decals, Model No. 1119-A
EX $60   **NM** $90   **MIP** $150

❑ **Olds Toronado and Speedboat,** 1967-70, blue No. 276 Toronado, blue and yellow boat and chrome trailer, w/swordfish decals and three figures, Model No. 36-A
EX $60   **NM** $90   **MIP** $165

❑ **Powerboat Team,** 1980-81, white/red No. 319 Jaguar w/red/white boat on silver trailer, Team Corgi Carlsberg, Union Jack and #1 labels on boat, Model No. 38-C
EX $25   **NM** $35   **MIP** $60

BUS

❑ **Beep Beep London Bus,** 1981, battery-operated working horn, red body, black windows, BTA decals, Model No. 1004-A
EX $26   **NM** $39   **MIP** $65

❑ **Green Line Bus,** 1983, green body, white interior and stripe, TDK labels, six spoked wheels, Model No. 470-C
EX $10   **NM** $15   **MIP** $25

❑ **Inter-City Mini Bus,** 1973-79, orange body w/brown interior, clear windows, green/yellow/black decals, Whizz Wheels, Model No. 701-A
EX $8   **NM** $15   **MIP** $25

(KP Photo by Dr. Douglas Sadecky)

❑ **London Set,** 1964-68, No. 418 taxi and No. 468 bus w/policeman, in two versions: "Corgi Toys" on bus (1964-66); "Outspan Oranges" on bus (1967-68); values for each individual complete set, Model No. 35-A
EX $55   **NM** $85   **MIP** $150

❑ **London Set,** 1971-75, orange No. 226 Mini, Policeman, No. 418 London Taxi and No. 468 Outspan Routemaster bus, Whizz Wheels, Model No. 11-B
EX $50   **NM** $75   **MIP** $125

❑ **London Set,** 1980-82, No. 425 London Taxi and No. 469 Routemaster B.T.A. bus in two versions: w/mounted Policeman (1980-81); without Policeman, (1982-on); value is for each individual complete set, Model No. 11-C
EX $25   **NM** $35   **MIP** $60

(KP Photo by Dr. Douglas Sadecky)

❑ **London Transport Routemaster Bus,** 1964-75, clear windows w/driver and conductor, released w/numerous advertiser logos, shaped or cast spoked wheels, Model No. 468-A
EX $35   **NM** $50   **MIP** $85

❑ **London Transport Routemaster Bus,** 1975, long, clear windows, interior, some models have driver and conductor, released w/numerous advertiser logos, Whizz Wheels, Model No. 469-A
EX $25   **NM** $35   **MIP** $60

(KP Photo by Dr. Douglas Sadecky)

❑ **Midland Red Express Coach,** 1961-62, red one-piece body, black roof w/shaped or smooth wheels, yellow interior, clear windows, silver grille and headlights. Two box variations shown in this photo, Model No. 1120-A
EX $70   **NM** $105   **MIP** $225

❑ **National Express Bus,** 1983, variety of colors and label variations, Model No. 1168-A
EX $8   **NM** $15   **MIP** $25

❑ **Open Top Disneyland Bus,** 1977-78, yellow body, red interior and stripe, Disneyland labels, eight-spoked wheels or orange body, white interior and stripe, Model No. 470-B
EX $30   **NM** $50   **MIP** $95

❑ **Routemaster Bus-Promotionals,** 1977, different body and interior versions and promotional labels, Model No. 467-A
EX $15   **NM** $25   **MIP** $40

❑ **Silver Jubilee London Transport Bus,** 1977, silver body w/red interior, no passengers, labels read "Woolworth Welcomes the World" and "The Queen's Silver, Model No. 471-B
EX $15   **NM** $18   **MIP** $30

CHARACTER

❑ **1927 Bentley "World of Wooster",** 1967-69, green body, metallic black chassis, cast spoked wheels, figures of Jeeves & Bertie Wooster, Model No. 9004-A
EX $50   **NM** $100   **MIP** $150

❑ **Avengers Set,** 1966-69, white Lotus, red or green Bentley; Jonathan Steed and Emma Peel figures w/three umbrellas, Model No. 40-A
EX $260   **NM** $390   **MIP** $800

(KP Photo by Dr. Douglas Sadecky)

❑ **Basil Brush's Car,** 1971-73, red body, dark yellow chassis, gold lamps and dash, Basil Brush figure, red plastic wheels, plastic tires; w/"Laugh Tapes" and soundbox. Basil Brush could be heard laughing with the aid of laugh tapes and a soundbox that were included with the car, Model No. 808-A
EX $70   **NM** $105   **MIP** $200

❑ **Batbike,** 1978-83, black body, one-piece body, black and red plastic parts, gold engine and exhaust pipes, clear windshield, chrome stand, black plastic five-spoked wheels, Batman figure and decals, Model No. 268-B
EX $40   **NM** $60   **MIP** $125

❑ **Batboat,** 1967-72, black plastic boat, red seats, fin and jet, blue windshield, Batman and Robin figures, gold cast trailer, tinplate fin cover, cast wheels, plastic tires, w/plastic towhook for Batmobile, Model No. 107-A1
EX $60   **NM** $90   **MIP** $175

❑ **Batboat,** 1976-80, black plastic boat w/Batman and Robin figures, small Bat logo labels on fin and on side of boat, chain link labels, Whizz Wheels on trailer, Model No. 107-A2
EX $30   **NM** $45   **MIP** $100

❑ **Batcopter,** 1976-81, black body w/yellow/red/black decals, red rotors, Batman figure, operable winch, Model No. 925-A
EX $26   **NM** $39   **MIP** $95

❑ **Batman Set,** 1976-81, three vehicle set: No. 267 Batmobile, No. 107 Batboat w/trailer and No. 925 Batcopter, Whizz Wheels on trailer, Model No. 40-B
EX $150   **NM** $300   **MIP** $800

(KP Photo by Dr. Douglas Sadecky)

❑ **Batmobile,** 1966, matte black (rare) or gloss black body, gold hubs, bat logos on door and hubs, maroon interior, black body, plastic rockets, yellow headlights and gold rocket control, blue tinted canopy, working front chain cutter, no tow hook, rubber tires. Although it's difficult to tell from this photo, this is the rare first issue matte black finish with no towhook version of the famous Batmobile, Model No. 267-A1
EX $200   **NM** $300   **MIP** $550

❑ **Batmobile,** 1967-69, gloss black body, light red interior, gold towhook, Whizz-wheels with 8-spoke chrome hubs, Model No. 267-D
EX $110   **NM** $80   **MIP** $175

❑ **Batmobile,** 1967-72, same as first issue except for gloss black body, gold towhook, Model No. 267-A2
EX $200   **NM** $300   **MIP** $500

(KP Photo by Dr. Douglas Sadecky)

VINTAGE

❑ **Batmobile,** 1973, chrome hubs w/red bat logos on door, maroon interior, red plastic tires, gold tow hook, plastic rockets, yellow headlight and gold rocket control, tinted blue canopy w/chrome support, chain cutter. Made for only one year, this version featured red plastic tires and chrome wheels. Also pictured is the back of the rare first-issue window box for this model, Model No. 267-C1
EX $140   **NM** $200   **MIP** $400

❑ **Batmobile,** 1974-79, chrome hubs w/black plastic tires, red bat logos on door, light red interior, gold tow hook, plastic rockets, yellow headlights and gold rocket control, tinted blue canopy w/chrome support, Model No. 267-C2
EX $80   **NM** $120   **MIP** $200

❑ **Batmobile, Batboat and Trailer,** 1967-72, first and second versions: red bat hubs on wheels, 1967-72; red tires and chrome wheels, Model No. 3-B1
EX $240   **NM** $360   **MIP** $650

❑ **Batmobile, Batboat and Trailer,** 1973-81, third and fourth versions: 1973; black tires, big labels on boat, 1974-76; chrome wheels, boat labels, Whizz Wheels on trailer, Model No. 3-B2
EX $120   **NM** $175   **MIP** $350

❑ **Beatles' Yellow Submarine,** 1969, yellow and white hatches, red pinstripes, first issue, Model No. 803-A1
EX $200   **NM** $500   **MIP** $1000

❑ **Beatles' Yellow Submarine,** 1969-70, second issue, yellow and white body, working red hatches w/two Beatles in each, Model No. 803-A2
EX $180   **NM** $270   **MIP** $700

❑ **Buck Rogers Starfighter,** 1980, white body w/yellow plastic wings, amber windows, blue jets, color decal, Buck and Wilma figures, Model No. 647-A
EX $32   **NM** $48   **MIP** $90

❑ **Captain America Jetmobile,** 1979-80, 6" white body, metallic blue chassis, black nose cone, red shield and jet, red-white-blue Captain America decals, light blue seats and driver, chrome wheels, red tires, Model No. 263-B
EX $24   **NM** $36   **MIP** $60

❑ **Captain Marvel Porsche,** 1979-80, white body, gold parts, red seat, driver, red/yellow/blue Captain Marvel decals, black plastic base, gold wheels, Model No. 262-B
EX $20   **NM** $30   **MIP** $60

❑ **Chevrolet Charlie's Angels Van,** 1977-80, light rose-mauve body w/Charlie's Angels decals, in two versions: either solid or spoked chrome wheels, Model No. 434-B
EX $15   **NM** $30   **MIP** $55

❑ **Chevrolet Spider-Van,** 1978-80, dark blue body w/Spider-Man decals, in two versions: w/either spoke or solid wheels, Model No. 436-B
EX $26   **NM** $39   **MIP** $65

❑ **Chitty Chitty Bang Bang,** 1968-72, metallic copper body, dark red interior and spoked wheels, four figures, black

chassis w/silver running boards, silver hood, horn, brake, dash, tail and headlights, gold radiator, red and orange wings, handbrake operates side wings, Model No. 266-A
EX $180   **NM** $270   **MIP** $425

❑ **Daily Planet Helicopter,** 1979-81, red and white body, rocket launcher w/ten spare missiles, Model No. 929-A
EX $24   **NM** $36   **MIP** $60

❑ **Daktari Set,** 1967-75, two versions: No. 438 Land Rover, green w/black stripes, cast wheels, 1968-73; Whizz Wheels, 1974-75, each set, Model No. 7-B
EX $50   **NM** $75   **MIP** $150

❑ **Dick Dastardly's Racing Car,** 1973-76, dark blue body, yellow chassis, chrome engine, red wings, Dick and Muttley figures, Model No. 809-A
EX $40   **NM** $60   **MIP** $150

(KP Photo by Dr. Douglas Sadecky)

❑ **Dougal's Magic Roundabout Car,** 1971-74, yellow body, red interior, clear windows, dog and snail figures, red wheels w/gold trim, Magic Roundabout labels, Model No. 807-A
EX $70   **NM** $105   **MIP** $175

❑ **Drax Jet Helicopter,** 1979-81, white body, yellow rotors and fins, yellow/black Drax labels, Model No. 930-A
EX $24   **NM** $36   **MIP** $75

❑ **Giant Daktari Set,** 1969-73, black and green No. 438 Land Rover, tan No. 503 Giraffe truck, blue and brown No. 484 Dodge Livestock truck, figures, Model No. 14-B
EX $225   **NM** $350   **MIP** $650

❑ **Green Hornet's Black Beauty,** 1967-72, black body, green window/interior, two figures, working chrome grille and panels w/weapons, green headlights, red taillights, Model No. 268-A
EX $175   **NM** $275   **MIP** $550

❑ **Hardy Boys' Rolls-Royce,** 1970, red body w/yellow hood, roof and window frames, band figures on roof on removable green base, Model No. 805-A
EX $70   **NM** $105   **MIP** $200

❑ **Incredible Hulk Mazda Pickup,** 1979-80, metallic light brown body, gray or red plastic cage, black interior, Hulk label on hood, chrome wheels; includes green and red Hulk figure, Model No. 264-B
EX $20   **NM** $30   **MIP** $75

(KP Photo by Dr. Douglas Sadecky)

❑ **James Bond Aston Martin,** 1968-77, metallic silver body, red interior, two figures, working roof hatch, ejector seat, bullet shield and guns, chrome bumpers, spoked wheels. Orginally issued in a rare bubble-pack, the subsequent issues were sold in window boxes. On the left, the rare first issue window box; on the right, the more commonly seen version, Model No. 270-A
EX $100   **NM** $150   **MIP** $325

❑ **James Bond Aston Martin,** 1978, metallic silver body and die-cast base, red interior, two figures, clear windows, passenger seat raises to eject, Model No. 271-B
EX $30   **NM** $45   **MIP** $90

❑ **James Bond Aston Martin DB5,** 1965-68, metallic gold body, red interior, working roof hatch, clear windows, two figures, left seat ejects, spoked wheels, accessory pack, Model No. 261-A
EX $70   **NM** $105   **MIP** $275

(KP Photo by Dr. Douglas Sadecky)

❑ **James Bond Citroen 2CV6,** 1981-86, dark yellow body and hood, red interior, clear windows, chrome headlights, red taillights, black plastic grille. This model was available in a window box, or the more difficult to find photo box shown here, Model No. 272-A
EX $15   **NM** $35   **MIP** $70

❑ **James Bond Lotus Esprit,** 1977, white body and base, black windshield, grille and hood panel, white plastic roof device that triggers fins and tail, rockets, Model No. 269-B
EX $30   **NM** $45   **MIP** $95

❑ **James Bond Moon Buggy,** 1972-73, white body w/blue chassis, amber canopy, yellow tanks, red radar dish, arms and jaws, yellow wheels, Model No. 811-A
EX $175   **NM** $275   **MIP** $525

(KP Photo by Dr. Douglas Sadecky)

VINTAGE

❏ **James Bond Mustang Mach 1,** 1972-73, red and white body w/black hood and opening doors. Because using this model as a Bond vehicle was a last-minute decision, a label was adhered to the right side of the window box. Without this label, no one would know this was a James Bond issue, Model No. 391-A
EX $100   **NM** $150   **MIP** $300

❏ **James Bond Set,** 1979-81, set of three: No. 271 Lotus Esprit, No. 649 Space Shuttle and No. 269 Aston Martin, Model No. 22-B
EX $80   **NM** $135   **MIP** $295

❏ **James Bond Space Shuttle,** 1979-81, white body w/yellow/black Moonraker labels, Model No. 649-A
EX $30   **NM** $45   **MIP** $75

❏ **James Bond Toyota 2000GT,** 1967-69, white body, black interior w/Bond and female driver, working trunk and gun rack, spoked wheels, plastic tires, accessory pack, Model No. 336-A
EX $115   **NM** $180   **MIP** $375

❏ **Kojak's Buick Regal,** 1976-81, metallic bronze brown body, off-white interior, two opening doors, clear windows, chrome bumpers, grille and headlights, red taillights; accessories include Kojak and Crocker figures, Model No. 290-A
EX $25   **NM** $55   **MIP** $95

❏ **Lions of Longleat,** 1968-74, black/white No. 438 Land Rover pickup w/lion cages and accessories, two versions: cast wheels, 1969-73; Whizz Wheels, 1974, each, Model No. 8-B
EX $60   **NM** $90   **MIP** $200

❏ **Magic Roundabout Musical Carousel,** 1973, plastic roundabout w/Swiss musical movement, w/Dylan, Rosalie, Paul, Florence and Basil figures, rare, Model No. 852-A
EX $275   **NM** $425   **MIP** $750

❏ **Magic Roundabout Playground,** 1973, contains No. 851 Train, No. 852 Carousel, six figures, seesaw, park bench, shrubs and fowers, rare, Model No. 853-A
EX $295   **NM** $500   **MIP** $900

❏ **Magic Roundabout Train,** 1973, red and blue plastic three-piece train; accessories include figures of Mr. Rusty, Basil, Rosaile, Paul and Dougal, Model No. 851-A
EX $70   **NM** $195   **MIP** $350

❏ **Man From U.N.C.L.E. THRUSH-Buster,** 1966-68, plastic interior, blue windows, two figures, two spotlights, dark metallic blue body, w/3-D Waverly ring, Model No. 497-A1
EX $80   **NM** $120   **MIP** $250

(KP Photo by Dr. Douglas Sadecky)

❏ **Man From U.N.C.L.E. THRUSH-Buster,** 1968-69, plastic interior, blue windows, two figures, two spotlights, cream body, w/3-D Waverly ring, RARE, Model No. 497-A2
EX $100   **NM** $350   **MIP** $550

❏ **Monkeemobile,** 1968-70, red body/base, white roof, yellow interior, clear windows, four figures, chrome grille, headlights, engine, orange taillights, Model No. 277-A
EX $145   **NM** $225   **MIP** $450

❏ **Mr. McHenry's Trike,** 1972-74, red and yellow trike and trailer; accessories include Mr. McHenry and Zebedee figures, Model No. 859-A
EX $70   **NM** $105   **MIP** $175

❏ **Muppet Vehicles,** Fozzie Bear's Truck, Model No. 2031-A
EX $15   **NM** $30   **MIP** $50

❏ **Muppet Vehicles,** Animal's Percussion-mobile, Model No. 2033-A
EX $15   **NM** $30   **MIP** $50

❏ **Muppet Vehicles,** Miss Piggy's Sports Coupe, Model No. 2032-A
EX $15   **NM** $30   **MIP** $50

❏ **Muppet Vehicles,** Kermit's Car, Model No. 2030-A
EX $15   **NM** $35   **MIP** $60

❏ **Noddy's Car,** yellow body, red chassis, Noddy alone, closed trunk w/spare wheel, Model No. 804-A
EX $60   **NM** $90   **MIP** $175

❏ **Noddy's Car,** 1969-71, first issue: yellow body, red chassis and fenders, figures of Noddy, Big-Ears, and black, gray, or light tan face Golliwog, Model No. 801-A1
EX $200   **NM** $400   **MIP** $600

❏ **Noddy's Car,** 1972-73, second issue: same as first issue except Master Tubby is substituted for Golliwog, Model No. 801-A2
EX $100   **NM** $200   **MIP** $350

❏ **Penguinmobile,** 1979-80, white body, black and white lettering on orange-yellow-blue labels, gold body panels, seats, air scoop, chrome engine, w/penguin figure, Model No. 259-B
EX $20   **NM** $30   **MIP** $65

(KP Photo by Dr. Douglas Sadecky)

❏ **Popeye's Paddle Wagon,** 1969-72, yellow and white body, red chassis, blue rear fenders, bronze and yellow stacks, white plastic deck, blue lifeboat w/Swee' Pea; includes figures of Popeye, Olive Oyl, Bluto and Wimpey. Produced for a short period, the colorful Paddle-Wagon had multiple working features and contained all of the main characters, Model No. 802-A
EX $195   **NM** $300   **MIP** $525

❏ **Professionals Ford Capri,** 1980-82, metallic silver body and base, red interior, black spoiler, grille, bumpers, tow hook and trim, blue windows, chrome wheels; includes figures of Cowley, Bodie and Doyle, Model No. 342-B
EX $30   **NM** $45   **MIP** $85

❏ **Saint's Jaguar XJS,** 1978-81, white body, red interior, black trim, Saint figure hood label, opening doors, black grille, bumpers and tow hook, chrome headlights, Model No. 320-B
EX $30   **NM** $45   **MIP** $85

(KP Photo by Dr. Doug Sadecky)

❏ **Saint's Volvo P-1800,** 1965-69, three versions of white one-piece body w/silver trim and different colored Saint decals on hood, driver. Pictured here with the 201-B. Note the wheel and hood logo variation between the two cars, Model No. 258-A
EX $55   **NM** $85   **MIP** $175

❏ **Saint's Volvo P-1800,** 1970-72, one-piece white body w/red Saint decal on hood, gray base, clear windows, black interior w/driver, Whizz Wheels, Model No. 201-B
EX $55   **NM** $95   **MIP** $200

❏ **Silver Jubilee Landau,** 1977-80, Landua w/four horses, two footmen, two riders, Queen and Prince figures, and Corgi dog, in two versions, Model No. 41-B
EX $15   **NM** $25   **MIP** $40

❏ **Spider-Bike,** 1979-83, medium blue body, one-piece body, dark blue plastic front body and seat, blue and red Spider-Man figure, amber windshield, black or white wheels, Model No. 266-B
EX $40   **NM** $60   **MIP** $85

□ **Spider-Buggy,** 1979-81, red body, blue hood, clear windows, dark blue dash, seat and crane, chrome base w/bumper and steps, silver headlights; includes Spider-Man and Green Goblin figures, Model No. 261-B
EX $50　　**NM** $75　　**MIP** $150

□ **Spider-Copter,** 1979-81, blue body w/Spider-Man labels, red plastic legs, tongue and tail rotor, black windows and main rotor, Model No. 928-A
EX $30　　**NM** $45　　**MIP** $85

□ **Spider-Man Set,** 1980-81, set of three: No. 266 Spider-Bike, No. 928 Spider-Copter and No. 261 Spider-Buggy, Model No. 23-B
EX $80　　**NM** $160　　**MIP** $350

□ **Starsky and Hutch Ford Torino,** 1977-81, red one-piece body, white trim, light yellow interior, clear windows, chrome bumpers, grille and headlights, orange taillights; includes Starsky, Hutch and Bandit figures, Model No. 292-A
EX $35　　**NM** $55　　**MIP** $100

□ **Superman Set,** 1979-81, set of three: No. 265 Supermobile, No. 925 Daily Planet Helicopter and No. 260 Metropolis Police Car, Model No. 21-C
EX $70　　**NM** $120　　**MIP** $225

□ **Supermobile,** 1979-81, blue body, red, chrome or gray fists, red interior, clear canopy, Superman figure, chrome arms w/removable "striking fists", Model No. 265-A
EX $30　　**NM** $45　　**MIP** $75

□ **Supervan,** 1978-81, silver van w/Superman labels, working rear doors, chrome spoked wheels, Model No. 435-B
EX $15　　**NM** $25　　**MIP** $50

□ **Tarzan Set,** 1976-78, metallic green No. 421 Land Rover w/trailer and Dinghy; cage, five figures and other accessories, Model No. 36-B
EX $100　　**NM** $150　　**MIP** $275

□ **Vegas Ford Thunderbird,** 1980-81, orange/red body and base, black interior and grille, opening hood and trunk, amber windshield, white seats, driver, chrome bumper, Model No. 348-B
EX $25　　**NM** $40　　**MIP** $75

CIRCUS

□ **Chipperfield Circus Bedford Giraffe Transporter,** 1964-71, red "TK" Bedford truck w/blue giraffe box w/Chipperfield decal, two giraffes, shaped, cast or detailed wheels, Model No. 503-A
EX $60　　**NM** $90　　**MIP** $175

□ **Chipperfield Circus Cage Wagon,** 1961-68, red body, yellow chassis, smooth or spun hubs; includes lions, tigers or polar bears, Model No. 1123-A
EX $56　　**NM** $84　　**MIP** $140

□ **Chipperfield Circus Chevrolet Performing Poodles Van,** 1970-72, blue upper body and tailgate, red lower body and base, clear windshield, pale blue interior w/poodles in back and ring of poodles and trainer, plastic tires, Model No. 511-A
EX $160　　**NM** $240　　**MIP** $550

□ **Chipperfield Circus Crane and Cage,** 1970-72, No. 1144 crane truck, cage w/rhinoceros, red and blue trailer w/three animal cages and animals; very rare gift set, Model No. 21-B
EX $400　　**NM** $700　　**MIP** $2000

□ **Chipperfield Circus Crane and Cage Wagon,** 1961-65, No. 1121 crane truck, No. 1123 cage wagon and accessories, Model No. 12-A
EX $150　　**NM** $225　　**MIP** $375

(KP Photo by Dr. Douglas Sadecky)

□ **Chipperfield Circus Crane Truck,** 1960-68, red body, embossed Chipperfield blue logo, tinplate boom, blue wheels. Pictured here with Chipperfield Circus Cage Wagon 1123-A, that included a set of polar bears or lions and their appropriate label transfers, Model No. 1121-A
EX $80　　**NM** $120　　**MIP** $225

(KP Photo by Dr. Douglas Sadecky)

□ **Chipperfield Circus Horse Transporter,** 1962-72, red Bedford "TK" cab, blue upper/red lower horse trailer, three wheel variations; includes six horses, Model No. 1130-A
EX $80　　**NM** $120　　**MIP** $235

(KP Photo by Dr. Douglas Sadecky)

□ **Chipperfield Circus Karrier Booking Office,** 1962-64, red body, light blue roof, clear windows, tin lithographed interior, circus decals, smooth or shaped wheels, rubber tires, Model No. 426-A
EX $105　　**NM** $165　　**MIP** $325

□ **Chipperfield Circus Land Rover and Elephant Cage,** 1962-68, red No. 438 Range Rover w/blue canopy, Chipperfields Circus decal on canopy, burnt orange No. 607 elephant cage on red bed trailer, Model No. 19-A
EX $90　　**NM** $135　　**MIP** $275

(KP Photo by Dr. Douglas Sadecky)

□ **Chipperfield Circus Land Rover Parade Vehicle,** 1967-69, red body, yellow interior, blue rear and speakers, revolving clown, chimp figures, Chipperfield decals, Model No. 487-A
EX $60　　**NM** $90　　**MIP** $175

□ **Chipperfield Circus Menagerie Transporter,** 1968-72, Scammell Handyman MKIII red/blue cab, blue trailer w/three animal cages, two lions, two tigers and two bears, Model No. 1139-A
EX $120　　**NM** $180　　**MIP** $350

□ **Chipperfield Circus Scammell Crane Truck,** 1969-72, red upper cab and rear body, light blue lower cab, crane base and winch crank housing, red interior, tow hook, jewel headlights, Model No. 1144-A
EX $175　　**NM** $275　　**MIP** $450

□ **Chipperfield Circus Set, 1st Version,** 1963-65, vehicle and accessory set in two versions: w/No. 426 Booking Office, Model No. 23-A1
EX $380　　**NM** $600　　**MIP** $1300

□ **Chipperfield Circus Set, 2nd Version,** 1966, vehicle and accessory set w/#503 Giraffe Truck, Model No. 23-A2
EX $340　　**NM** $500　　**MIP** $1000

□ **Circus Human Cannonball Truck,** 1978-81, red and blue body; w/Marvo figure, Model No. 1163-A
EX $30　　**NM** $45　　**MIP** $75

□ **Circus Land Rover and Trailer,** 1978-81, yellow/red No. 421 Land Rover w/Pinder-Jean Richard decals; accessories include blue loudspeakers and figures, Model No. 30-B
EX $30　　**NM** $50　　**MIP** $90

□ **Jean Richard Circus Set,** 1978-81, yellow and red Land Rover and cage trailer w/Pinder-Jean Richard decals, No. 426 office van and trailer, No. 1163 Human Cannonball truck, ring and cut-out "Big Top" circus tent, Model No. 48-C
EX $90　　**NM** $135　　**MIP** $275

CLASSICS

□ **1910 Renault 12/16,** 1965-69, pale yellow body & spoked wheels, light black chassis, black ragtop, Model No. 9032-A
EX $25　　**NM** $50　　**MIP** $80

❏ **1910 Renault 12/16,** 1965-69, light purple body & spoked wheels, light black chassis, Model No. 9031-A
EX $25   **NM** $50   **MIP** $80

(KP Photo by Dr. Douglas Sadecky)

❏ **1927 Bentley,** 1964-69, red body, metallic black chassis, brown interior, black ragtop, red spoked wheels, driver. The red Bentley is slightly harder to find than the green version, Model No. 9002-A
EX $30   **NM** $60   **MIP** $90

❏ **1927 Bentley,** 1964-69, green body, metallic black chassis, brown interior, black ragtop, spoked wheels, driver, Model No. 9001-A
EX $35   **NM** $50   **MIP** $75

(KP Photo by Dr. Douglas Sadecky)

❏ **Daimler 38 1910,** 1964-69, orange-red body, gray and yellow chassis, yellow spoked wheels; w/four figures, Model No. 9021-A
EX $20   **NM** $30   **MIP** $50

❏ **Model T Ford,** 1964-69, blue body, black chassis, black ragtop, yellow wheels, one figure, Model No. 9013-A
EX $20   **NM** $40   **MIP** $65

❏ **Model T Ford,** 1964-69, black body & chassis, spoked wheels, two figures, Model No. 9011-A
EX $20   **NM** $40   **MIP** $65

(KP Photo by Dr. Douglas Sadecky)

❏ **Model T Ford,** 1964-69, yellow body & spoked wheels, black chassis, two figures, Model No. 9012-A
EX $20   **NM** $40   **MIP** $65

❏ **Rolls-Royce Silver Ghost,** 1966-69, silver body/hood, charcoal and silver chassis, bronze interior, gold lights, box and tank, clear windows, dash lights, radiator, Model No. 9041-A
EX $15   **NM** $30   **MIP** $60

CONSTRUCTION

❏ **Allis-Chalmers AFC 60 Fork Lift,** 1981, yellow body, white engine hood, w/driver, tan pallets and red containers, Model No. 409-C
EX $15   **NM** $20   **MIP** $45

(KP Photo by Dr. Douglas Sadecky)

❏ **Bedford TK Tipper Truck,** 1968-72, red cab and chassis w/yellow tipper, side mirrors, Model No. 494-A
EX $26   **NM** $39   **MIP** $65

❏ **Berliet Fruehauf Dumper,** 1974-76, yellow cab, fenders and dumper; black cab and semi chassis; plastic orange or dark orange dumper body; black interior, Model No. 1102-B
EX $30   **NM** $45   **MIP** $75

❏ **Caterpillar Tractor,** 1960-64, lime green body w/black or gray rubber treads, gray plastic seat, driver figure, controls, stacks, Model No. 1103-B
EX $70   **NM** $105   **MIP** $250

(KP Photo by Dr. Douglas Sadecky)

❏ **ERF 64G Earth Dumper,** 1958-67, red cab, yellow tipper, clear windows, unpainted hydraulic cylinder, spare tire, smooth wheels, rubber tires, Model No. 458-A
EX $30   **NM** $45   **MIP** $85

❏ **Euclid Caterpillar Tractor,** 1960-63, TC-12 lime green body w/black or pale gray rubber treads, gray plastic seat, driver figure, controls, stacks, silver grille, painted blue engine sides and Euclid decals, Model No. 1103-A
EX $50   **NM** $100   **MIP** $190

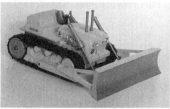

(KP Photo by Dr. Douglas Sadecky)

❏ **Euclid TC-12 Bulldozer,** 1958-62, lime green body w/black or pale gray treads, silver blade surface, gray plastic seat, controls, and stacks; silver grille and lights, painted blue engine sides, black sheet metal base, rubber treads and Euclid decals, Model No. 1102-A
EX $80   **NM** $120   **MIP** $225

❏ **Euclid TC-12 Bulldozer,** 1963-66, yellow or pale lime-green body, metal control rod, driver, black rubber treads, Model No. 1107-A
EX $80   **NM** $120   **MIP** $200

❏ **Ford Transit Tipper,** 1983, orange cab and chassis, tan tipper, chrome wheels, Model No. 1121-B
EX $10   **NM** $15   **MIP** $25

❏ **Giant Tower Crane,** 1981-82, white body, orange cab and chassis, Model No. 1154-B
EX $35   **NM** $50   **MIP** $85

❏ **Hyster 800 Stacatruck,** 1977, clear windows, black interior w/driver, Model No. 1113-B
EX $35   **NM** $50   **MIP** $85

❏ **JCB 110B Crawler Loader,** 1976-80, white cab, yellow body, working red shovel, red interior w/driver, clear windows, black treads, JCB labels, Model No. 1110-B
EX $20   **NM** $30   **MIP** $50

❏ **Mack-Priestman Crane Truck,** 1972-76, red truck, yellow crane cab, red interior, black engine, Hi Lift and Long Vehicle or Hi-Grab labels, Model No. 1154-A
EX $50   **NM** $75   **MIP** $125

❏ **Mercedes-Benz Unimog & Dumper,** 1969-76, yellow cab and tipper, red fenders and tipper chassis, charcoal gray cab chassis, black plastic mirrors or without, Model No. 1145-A
EX $25   **NM** $35   **MIP** $60

❏ **Priestman Cub Crane,** 1972-74, orange body, red chassis and two-piece bucket, unpainted bucket arms, lower boom, knobs, gears and drum castings, clear window, Hi-Grab labels, Model No. 1153-A
EX $50   **NM** $75   **MIP** $125

(KP Photo by Dr. Douglas Sadecky)

VINTAGE

❏ **Priestman Cub Power Shovel,** 1963-76, orange upper body and panel, yellow lower body, lock rod and chassis, rubber or plastic treads, pulley panel, gray boom, w/figure of driver, Model No. 1128-A
EX $40   **NM** $60   **MIP** $100

❏ **Priestman Shovel and Carrier,** 1963-72, No. 1128 cub shovel and No. 1131 low loader machinery carrier, Model No. 27-A
EX $90   **NM** $135   **MIP** $225

❏ **Raygo Rascal Roller,** 1973-78, dark yellow body, base and mounting, green interior and engine, orange and silver roller mounting and castings, clear windshield, Model No. 459-B
EX $15   **NM** $25   **MIP** $45

❏ **Road Repair Unit,** 1982, dark yellow Land Rover w/battery hatch and trailer w/red plastic interior w/sign and open panels, stripe and Roadwork labels, Model No. 1007-A
EX $15   **NM** $25   **MIP** $40

❏ **Scania Dump Truck,** 1983, white cab w/green tipper, black/green Barratt labels, black exhaust and hydraulic cylinders, six-spoked Whizz Wheels, Model No. 1152-B
EX $7   **NM** $15   **MIP** $30

❏ **Scania Dump Truck,** 1983, yellow truck and tipper w/black Wimpey labels, in two versions: either clear or green windows; six-spoked Whizz Wheels, Model No. 1153-B
EX $7   **NM** $15   **MIP** $30

❏ **Skyscraper Tower Crane,** 1975-79, red body w/yellow chassis and booms, gold hook, gray loads of block, black/white Skyscraper labels, black tracks, Model No. 1155-A
EX $30   **NM** $45   **MIP** $75

❏ **Thwaites Tusker Skip Dumper,** 1974-79, yellow body, chassis and tipper, driver and seat, hydraulic cylinder, red wheels, black tires two sizes, name labels, Whizz Wheels, Model No. 403-B
EX $10   **NM** $20   **MIP** $40

❏ **Unimog Dump Truck,** 1971-73, first issue, blue cab, yellow tipper, fenders and bumpers, metallic charcoal gray chassis, red interior, black mirrors, gray tow hook, Model No. 409-B1
EX $20   **NM** $30   **MIP** $50

❏ **Unimog Dump Truck,** 1976-77, second issue, yellow cab, chassis, rear frame and blue tipper, fenders and bumpers, red interior, no mirrors, gray tow hook, hydraulic cylinders, Model No. 409-B2
EX $20   **NM** $30   **MIP** $50

❏ **Unimog Dumper & Priestman Cub Shovel,** 1971-73, standard colors, #1145 Mercedes-Benz unimog w/Dumper and 1128 Priestman Cub Shovel, Model No. 2-B
EX $70   **NM** $105   **MIP** $175

❏ **Volvo Concrete Mixer,** 1977-81, yellow or orange cab, red or white mixer w/yellow and black stripes, rear chassis, chrome chute and unpainted hitch casings, Model No. 1156-A
EX $30   **NM** $45   **MIP** $75

❏ **Warner & Swasey Crane,** 1975-81, yellow cab and body, blue chassis, blue/yellow stripe labels, red interior, black steering wheel, silver knob, gold hook, Model No. 1101-B
EX $30   **NM** $45   **MIP** $75

EMERGENCY

❏ **AMC Pacer Rescue Car,** 1978-80, chrome roll bars and red roof lights, white w/black engine hood; w/or without Secours decal, Model No. 484-B
EX $10   **NM** $15   **MIP** $30

(KP Photo by Dr. Douglas Sadecky)

❏ **American LaFrance Ladder Truck,** 1968-81, first issue: red cab, trailer, ladder rack and wheels; chrome decks and chassis, yellow plastic three-piece operable ladder, rubber tires, six firemen figures, issued 1968-70; second issue: same as first issue except for unpainted wheels, issued 1970-72; third issue: same as earlier issues except for white decks and chassis, silver wheels, plastic tires, issued 1973-81; later issues only had four firemen, Model No. 1143-A
EX $60   **NM** $90   **MIP** $150

(KP Photo by Dr. Douglas Sadecky)

❏ **Austin Police Mini Van,** 1964-69, dark blue body w/policeman and dog figures, white police decals, opening rear doors, gray plastic antenna, Model No. 448-A
EX $50   **NM** $75   **MIP** $175

(KP Photo by Dr. Douglas Sadecky)

❏ **Bedford Fire Tender,** 1956-61, divided windshield, red or green body, each w/different decals, smooth or shaped hubs, Model No. 405-A
EX $60   **NM** $90   **MIP** $175

❏ **Bedford Fire Tender,** 1960-62, single windshield version, red body w/either black ladders and smooth wheels or unpainted ladders and shaped wheels, Model No. 423-A
EX $60   **NM** $90   **MIP** $150

❏ **Bedford Fire Tender-Mechanical,** 1956-59, friction motor, red body w/Fire Dept. decals, divided windshield, silver or black ladder, smooth or shaped hubs, Model No. 405M
EX $70   **NM** $105   **MIP** $175

(KP Photo by Dr. Douglas Sadecky)

❏ **Bedford Utilecon Ambulance,** 1957-60, divided windshield, cream body w/red/white/blue decals, smooth wheels, Model No. 412-A
EX $50   **NM** $75   **MIP** $125

❏ **Belgian Police Range Rover,** 1976-77, white body, working doors, red interior, Belgian Police decal; includes policeman, Emergency signs, Model No. 483-B
EX $22   **NM** $33   **MIP** $55

❏ **Bell Rescue Helicopter,** 1976-80, two-piece blue body w/working doors, red interior, yellow plastic floats, black rotors, white N428 decals, Model No. 924-A
EX $20   **NM** $30   **MIP** $50

❏ **Buick Police Car,** 1977-78, metallic blue body w/white stripes and Police decals, chrome light bar w/red lights, orange taillights, chrome spoke wheels, w/two policemen, Model No. 416-B
EX $18   **NM** $27   **MIP** $45

(KP Photo by Dr. Douglas Sadecky)

❏ **Cadillac Superior Ambulance,** 1962-68, battery-operated warning lights, red lower/cream upper body or white lower body/blue upper body, Model No. 437-A
EX $60   **NM** $90   **MIP** $150

❏ **Canadian Mounted Police Set,** 1978-80, blue No. 421 Land Rover w/Police sign on roof and RCMP decals, No. 102 trailer; includes mounted Policeman, Model No. 45-B
EX $30   **NM** $50   **MIP** $100

❏ **Chevrolet Caprice Fire Chief Car,** 1982, red body, red-white-orange decals, chrome roof bar, opaque black windows, red dome light, chrome bumpers, grille and headlights, orange taillights, Fire Dept. and Fire Chief decals, chrome wheels; includes working siren and dome light, Model No. 1008-A
EX $28   **NM** $42   **MIP** $70

❏ **Chevrolet Caprice Police Car,** 1980-81, black body w/white roof, doors and trunk, red interior, silver light bar, Police decals, Model No. 326-A
EX $20   **NM** $30   **MIP** $50

❏ **Chevrolet Impala Fire Chief Car,** 1963-65, red body, yellow interior, w/four white doors, w/round either shield or rectangular decals on two doors; includes two fireman, Model No. 439-A
EX $55   **NM** $80   **MIP** $130

(KP Photo by Dr. Douglas Sadecky)

❏ **Chevrolet Impala Fire Chief Car,** 1965-69, w/Fire Chief decal on hood, yellow interior w/driver, red on white body w/either round or rectangular "Fire Chief" decals on doors, spun or cast wheels, Model No. 482-A
EX $55   **NM** $80   **MIP** $130

(KP Photo by Dr. Douglas Sadecky)

❏ **Chevrolet Impala Police Car,** 1965-69, black lower body and roof, white upper body, yellow interior w/two policemen, Police and Police Patrol decals on doors and hood, Model No. 481-A
EX $55   **NM** $80   **MIP** $130

❏ **Chevrolet State Patrol Car,** 1959-61, black body, State Patrol decals, smooth wheels w/hexagonal panel or raised lines and shaped wheels, yellow plastic interior, gray antenna, clear windows, silver bumpers, grille, headlights and trim, rubber tires, Model No. 223-A
EX $50   **NM** $75   **MIP** $125

❏ **Chevrolet Superior Ambulance,** 1978-80, white body, orange roof and stripes, two working doors, clear windows, red interior w/patient on stretcher and attendant, Red Cross decals, Model No. 405-B
EX $30   **NM** $45   **MIP** $75

❏ **Chopper Squad Helicopter,** 1978-79, blue and white body, Sure Rescue decals, Model No. 927-A
EX $20   **NM** $30   **MIP** $50

❏ **Chopper Squad Rescue Set,** 1978-79, blue No. 919 Jeep w/Chopper Squad decal and red/white boat w/Surf Rescue decal, No. 927 Helicopter, Model No. 35-B
EX $40   **NM** $60   **MIP** $100

❏ **Chubb Pathfinder Crash Tender,** 1981-83, red body, Emergency Unit decals, working water pump, Model No. 1118-B
EX $45   **NM** $65   **MIP** $110

❏ **Chubb Pathfinder Crash Truck,** 1974-80, red body w/either "Airport Fire Brigade" or "New York Airport" decals, upper and lower body, gold water cannon unpainted and sirens, clear windshield, yellow interior, black steering wheel, chrome plastic deck, silver lights; w/working pump and siren, Model No. 1103-B
EX $60   **NM** $90   **MIP** $150

(KP Photo by Dr. Douglas Sadecky)

❏ **Citroen Alpine Rescue Safari,** 1970-72, white body, light blue interior, red roof and rear hatch, yellow roof rack and skis, clear windshield, man and dog, gold die-cast bobsled, Alpine Rescue decals, Model No. 513-A
EX $80   **NM** $150   **MIP** $375

❏ **Coast Guard Jaguar XJ12C,** 1975-77, blue and white body, Coast Guard labels, Model No. 414-B
EX $18   **NM** $27   **MIP** $45

(KP Photo by Dr. Douglas Sadecky)

❏ **Commer 3/4 Ton Police Van,** 1963-68, battery operated working dome light, in several color combinations of dark or light metallic blue or green bodies, various foreign issues. The van on the left

has "County Police" labels, horizontal cast bars on the rear side windows, and a metallic blue paint finish. The van on the right has an embossed "Police" logo cast in the sides, vertical lines on the rear side windows, and a dark blue paint finish. Both models have a battery-operated flashing roof light, Model No. 464-A
EX $45   **NM** $65   **MIP** $110

(KP Photo by Dr. Douglas Sadecky)

❏ **Commer 3/4-Ton Ambulance,** 1964-66, in either white or cream body, red interior, blue dome light, red Ambulance decals, shaped wheels, Model No. 463-A
EX $36   **NM** $55   **MIP** $90

❏ **Emergency Set,** 1976-77, three-vehicle set w/figures and accessories, No. 402 Ford Cortina Police car, No. 921 Police Helicopter, No. 481 Range Rover Ambulance, Model No. 18-B
EX $40   **NM** $60   **MIP** $100

❏ **Emergency Set,** 1979-81, No. 339 Land Rover Police Car and No. 921 Police Helicopter w/figures and accessories, Model No. 19-C
EX $30   **NM** $50   **MIP** $80

❏ **Fire Bug,** 1972-73, orange body, Whizz Wheels, Model No. 395-A
EX $20   **NM** $30   **MIP** $50

❏ **Ford Cortina Police Car,** 1972-76, white body, red or pink and black stripe labels, red interior, folding seats, blue dome light, clear windows, chrome bumpers, Police labels, opening doors, Model No. 402-A
EX $15   **NM** $25   **MIP** $45

❏ **Ford Escort Police Car,** 1982, blue body and base, tan interior, white doors, blue dome lights, red Police labels, black grille and bumpers, Model No. 297-A
EX $8   **NM** $15   **MIP** $30

(KP Photo by Dr. Douglas Sadecky)

❏ **Ford Zephyr Patrol Car,** 1960-65, white or cream body, blue and white Police red interior, blue dome light, silver bumpers. The car on the left has the common "Police" label, the car on the

right, 419-A2, has the Dutch "Politie" label on the hood, Model No. 419-A1
EX $35   NM $50   MIP $85

❏ **Ford Zephyr Patrol Car,** 1960-65, white or cream body, blue and white Politie/Rijkspolitie decals, red interior, blue dome light, silver bumpers; import, Model No. 419-A2
EX $60   NM $125   MIP $225

❏ **German Life Saving Set,** 1980-82, red/white No. 421 Land Rover and lifeboat, white trailer, German labels, Model No. 33-B
EX $30   NM $45   MIP $75

❏ **HGB-Angus Firestreak,** 1980, chrome plastic spotlight and ladders, black hose reel, red dome light, white water cannon, in two interior versions, electronic siren and lights, Model No. 1001-A
EX $35   NM $50   MIP $85

❏ **Hi-Speed Fire Engine,** 1975-78, red body, yellow plastic ladder, Model No. 703-A
EX $16   NM $24   MIP $40

❏ **Hughes Police Helicopter,** 1975-80, red interior, dark blue rotors, in several international imprints, Netherlands, German, Swiss, in white or yellow, Model No. 921-A
EX $20   NM $30   MIP $50

❏ **Jaguar 2.4 Litre Fire Chief's Car,** 1959-61, red body w/unpainted roof signal/siren, red/white fire and shield decals on doors, in two versions, smooth or spun hubs, Model No. 213-A
EX $60   NM $90   MIP $150

❏ **Jaguar XJ12C Police Car,** 1978-80, white body w/blue and pink stripes, light bar w/blue dome light, tan interior, police labels, Model No. 429-A
EX $15   NM $18   MIP $45

❏ **Jet Ranger Police Helicopter,** 1980, white body w/chrome interior, red floats and rotors, amber windows, Police labels, Model No. 931-A
EX $25   NM $40   MIP $65

❏ **Mercedes-Benz Ambulance,** 1980-81, four different foreign versions, white interior, opening rear and two doors, blue windows and dome lights, chrome bumpers, grille and headlights, various labels; accessories include two attendant figures, Model No. 406-C
EX $15   NM $20   MIP $35

❏ **Mercedes-Benz Ambulance,** 1981, white body and base, red stripes and taillights, Red Cross and black and white

ambulance labels, open rear door, white interior, no figures, Model No. 407-B
EX $15   NM $20   MIP $35

❏ **Mercedes-Benz Fire Chief,** 1982-83, light red body, black base, tan plastic interior, blue dome light, white Notruf 112 labels, red taillights, no tow hook, German export model, Model No. 284-B
EX $15   NM $25   MIP $40

❏ **Mercedes-Benz Police Car,** 1975-80, white body w/two different hood versions, brown interior, polizei or police lettering, blue dome light, Model No. 412-B
EX $15   NM $18   MIP $30

❏ **Metropolis Police Car,** 1979-81, metallic blue body, off white interior, white roof/stripes, two working doors, clear windows, chrome bumpers, grille and headlights, two roof light bars, City of Metropolis labels, Model No. 260-B
EX $20   NM $30   MIP $50

❏ **Motorway Ambulance,** 1973-79, white body, dark blue interior, red-white-black Accident and Red Cross labels, dark blue windows, clear headlights, red die-cast base and bumpers, Model No. 700-A
EX $10   NM $15   MIP $30

CORGI TOYS

OLDSMOBILE "SHERIFF" CAR

(KP Photo by Dr. Douglas Sadecky)

❏ **Oldsmobile Sheriff's Car,** 1962-66, black upper body w/white sides, red interior w/red dome light and County Sheriff decals on doors, single body casting, Model No. 237-A
EX $50   NM $75   MIP $125

❏ **Police Land Rover,** 1981, white body, red and blue police stripes, black lettering, open rear door, opaque black windows, blue dome light, working roof light and siren, Model No. 1005-A
EX $15   NM $25   MIP $50

❏ **Police Land Rover and Horse Box,** 1978-80, white No. 421 Land Rover w/police labels and mounted policeman, No. 112 Horse Box, Model No. 44-A
EX $30   NM $45   MIP $75

❏ **Police Vigilant Range Rover,** 1972-79, white body, red interior, black shutters, blue dome light, two chrome and amber spotlights, black grille, silver headlights, Police labels, w/police figure, Model No. 461-A
EX $25   NM $35   MIP $60

❏ **Porsche 924 Police Car,** 1978-80, white body w/different hood and door color versions, blue and chrome light, Polizei white on green panels or Police labels, "1" or "20" labels, Model No. 430-B
EX $15   NM $25   MIP $40

❏ **Porsche Targa Police Car,** 1970-75, white body and base, red doors and hood, black roof and plastic interior also comes w/an orange interior, unpainted siren, Polizei labels, Model No. 509-A
EX $25   NM $35   MIP $60

❏ **Range Rover Ambulance,** 1975-77, two different versions of body sides, red interior, raised roof, open upper and lower doors, black shutters, blue dome light, Ambulance label; includes stretcher and two ambulance attendants, Model No. 482-B
EX $20   NM $30   MIP $50

❏ **Renault 5 Police Car,** 1978-79, white body, red interior, blue dome light, black hood, hatch and doors w/white Police labels, orange taillights, aerial, Model No. 428-B
EX $15   NM $20   MIP $35

❏ **Renault 5TS,** 1977-80, metallic golden orange body, black trim, tan plastic interior, working hatch and two doors, clear windows and headlights, Model No. 293-A
EX $15   NM $18   MIP $30

❏ **Renault 5TS Fire Chief,** 1982, red body, tan interior, amber headlights, gray antenna, black/white Sapeurs Pompiers labels, blue dome light, French export issue, Model No. 295-A
EX $15   NM $25   MIP $40

❏ **Riley Pathfinder Police Car,** 1958-61, black body w/blue/white Police lettering, unpainted roof sign, gray antenna, Model No. 209-A
EX $50   NM $75   MIP $135

❏ **Riot Police Quad Tractor,** 1977-80, white body and chassis, brown interior, red roof w/white panel, gold water cannons, gold spotlight w/amber lens, Riot Police and No. 6 labels, Model No. 422-B
EX $15   NM $20   MIP $35

❏ **Rover 3500 Police Car,** 1980, white body, light red interior, red stripes, white plastic roof sign, blue dome light, red and blue Police and badge label, Model No. 339-B
EX $8   NM $15   MIP $25

❏ **Sikorsky Skycrane Casualty Helicopter,** 1975-78, red and white body, black rotors and wheels, orange pipes, working rear hatch, Red Cross decals, Model No. 922-A
EX $15   NM $20   MIP $40

❏ **Simon Snorkel Fire Engine,** 1964-76, red body w/yellow interior, two snorkel arms, rotating base, five firemen in cab and one in basket, various styles of wheels, Model No. 1127-A
EX $35   NM $55   MIP $90

❏ **Simon Snorkel Fire Engine,** 1977-81, red body w/yellow interior, blue windows and dome lights, chrome deck, black hose reels and hydraulic cylinders, Model No. 1126-B
EX $30   NM $45   MIP $75

(KP Photo by Dr. Douglas Sadecky)

❑ **Sunbeam Imp Police Car,** 1968-72, three versions, white or light blue body, tan interior, driver, black or white hood and lower doors, dome light, Police decals, cast wheels. Shown here are two color and box variations, Model No. 506-A
EX $25   **NM** $45   **MIP** $85

❑ **Volkswagen 1200,** 1970-76, seven different color and label versions, plastic interior, one-piece body, silver headlights, red taillights, die-cast base and bumpers, Model No. 383-A2
EX $20   **NM** $45   **MIP** $85

❑ **Volkswagen 1200,** 1970-76, dark yellow body, white roof, red interior and dome light, unpainted base and bumpers, black and white ADAC Strassenwacht labels, Whizz Wheels, Model No. 383-A1
EX $60   **NM** $90   **MIP** $150

(KP Photo by Dr. Douglas Sadecky)

❑ **Volkswagen 1200 Police Car,** 1966-69, two different body versions made for Germany, Netherlands and Switzerland, blue dome light in chrome collar, Polizei or Politie decals. Note the opening hood and trunk on this attractive car. The front wheels turn via the roof warning light, Model No. 492-A
EX $40   **NM** $60   **MIP** $100

❑ **Volkswagen Police Car/Foreign Issues,** 1970-76, five different versions, one-piece body, red interior, dome light, silver headlights, red taillights, clear windows, Whizz Wheels, Model No. 373-A
EX $60   **NM** $90   **MIP** $150

❑ **Volkswagen Polo Police Car,** 1976-80, white body, green hood and doors, black dash, silver bumpers, grille and headlights, white roof, blue dome light, Model No. 489-A1
EX $15   **NM** $25   **MIP** $40

JEEP

❑ **Golden Eagle Jeep,** 1979-82, tan and brown or white and gold body, tan plastic top, chrome plastic base, bumpers and steps, chrome wheels, Model No. 441-B
EX $8   **NM** $15   **MIP** $25

❑ **Jeep & Horse Box,** 1981-83, metallic painted No. 441 Jeep and No. 112 trailer; accessories include girl on pony, three jumps and three hay bales, Model No. 29-C
EX $15   **NM** $30   **MIP** $50

❑ **Jeep and Motorcycle Trailer,** 1982-83, red working No. 441 Jeep w/two blue/yellow bikes on trailer, Model No. 10-C
EX $15   **NM** $20   **MIP** $40

❑ **Jeep CJ-5,** 1977-79, dark metallic green body, removable white top, white plastic wheels, spare tire, Model No. 419-B
EX $8   **NM** $15   **MIP** $30

(KP Photo by Dr. Douglas Sadecky)

❑ **Jeep FC-150 Covered Truck,** 1965-72, four versions: blue body, rubber tires (1965-67); yellow/brown body; rubber tires w/spun hubs (1965-67); blue or yellow/brown body, plastic tires w/cast spoked hubs. The two major color and wheel variations are pictured here, Model No. 470-A
EX $30   **NM** $45   **MIP** $75

❑ **Jeep FC-150 Pickup,** 1959-65, blue body, clear windows, sheet metal tow hook, in two wheel versions: smooth or shaped wheels, Model No. 409-A
EX $35   **NM** $55   **MIP** $90

(KP Photo by Dr. Douglas Sadecky)

❑ **Jeep FC-150 Tower Wagon,** 1965-69, metallic green body, yellow interior and basket w/workman figure, clear windows, w/either rubber or plastic tires. This was the updated version of the previously released GS14-A which had a red Jeep, smooth wheels and a lamp post, Model No. 478-A
EX $40   **NM** $60   **MIP** $100

❑ **Off Road Set,** 1983, No. 5 label on No. 447 Jeep, blue boat, trailer, Model No. 36-C
EX $15   **NM** $20   **MIP** $45

❑ **Renegade Jeep,** 1983, dark blue body w/no top, white interior, base and bumper, white plastic wheels and rear mounted spare, Model No. 447-B
EX $8   **NM** $15   **MIP** $25

❑ **Renegade Jeep with Hood,** 1983, yellow body w/removable hood, red interior, base, bumper, white plastic wheels, side mounted spare, No. 8, Model No. 448-B
EX $8   **NM** $15   **MIP** $25

❑ **Tower Wagon and Lamp Standard,** 1961-65, red No. 409 Jeep Tower wagon w/yellow basket, workman figure and lamp post, Model No. 14-A
EX $40   **NM** $60   **MIP** $120

LAND ROVER

(KP Photo by Dr. Douglas Sadecky)

❑ **Land Rover 109 WB Pickup,** 1957-62, yellow, green or metallic blue body, spare wheel on hood, clear windows, sheet metal tow hook, smooth hubs, rubber tires, Model No. 406-A
EX $45   **NM** $70   **MIP** $100

❑ **Land Rover 109WB,** 1977-79, working rear doors, tan interior, spare wheel on hood, plastic tow hook, Model No. 421-B
EX $15   **NM** $18   **MIP** $30

❑ **Land Rover Breakdown Truck,** 1960-65, red body w/silver boom and yellow canopy, revolving spotlight, Breakdown Service labels, Model No. 417-A
EX $35   **NM** $55   **MIP** $90

❑ **Land Rover Breakdown Truck,** 1965-77, red body, yellow canopy, chrome revolving spotlight, Breakdown Service labels, shaped hubs or Whizz Wheels, Model No. 477-A
EX $25   **NM** $35   **MIP** $60

❑ **Land Rover with Canopy,** 1963-77, long, one-piece body w/clear windows, plastic interior, spare wheel on hood, issued in numerous colors, Model No. 438-A
EX $35   **NM** $55   **MIP** $90

(KP Photo by Dr. Douglas Sadecky)

❑ **Public Address Land Rover,** 1964-66, green No. 438 Land Rover body, yellow plastic rear body and loudspeakers, red interior, clear windows, silver bumper, grille and headlights; includes figure

w/microphone and girl figure w/pamphlets, Model No. 472-A
EX $50 **NM** $75 **MIP** $145

(KP Photo by Dr. Douglas Sadecky)

❏ **RAC Land Rover,** 1959-64, light or dark blue body, plastic interior and rear cover, gray antenna, RAC and Radio Rescue decals, Model No. 416-A
EX $60 **NM** $90 **MIP** $150

❏ **Safari Land Rover and Trailer,** 1976-80, black and white No. 341 Land Rover in two versions: w/chrome wheels, 1976; w/red wheels, 1977-80; came w/Warden and Lion figures, Model No. 31-B
EX $20 **NM** $30 **MIP** $60

LARGE TRUCK

❏ **Bedford Car Transporter,** 1957, first issue, black die-cast cab base w/blue "S" cab, yellow semi trailer, blue lettering decals, RARE, Model No. 1101-A1
EX $100 **NM** $200 **MIP** $350

❏ **Bedford Car Transporter,** 1957-62, second issue, red cab, pale green upper and blue lower semi-trailer, white decals, working ramps, clear windshield, Model No. 1101-A2
EX $70 **NM** $105 **MIP** $175

❏ **Bedford Car Transporter,** 1962-66, red "TK" cab w/blue lower and light green upper trailer, working ramp, yellow interior, clear windows, white lettering and Corgi dog decals, Model No. 1105-A
EX $60 **NM** $90 **MIP** $150

(KP Photo by Dr. Douglas Sadecky)

❏ **Bedford Carrimore Low Loader,** 1958-62, red or yellow "S" cab, metallic blue semi trailer and tailgate; smooth and/or shaped wheels, Model No. 1100-A
EX $60 **NM** $90 **MIP** $150

(KP Photo by Dr. Douglas Sadecky)

❏ **Bedford Carrimore Low Loader,** 1963-65, yellow "TK" cab, red trailer with working ramp, clear windows, red interior, suspension, shaped wheels, rubber tires, Model No. 1132-A
EX $90 **NM** $190 **MIP** $325

(KP Photo by Dr. Douglas Sadecky)

❏ **Bedford Milk Tanker,** 1962-65, light blue "S" cab and lower semi, white upper tank, w/blue/white milk decals, shaped wheels, rubber tires, Model No. 1129-A
EX $100 **NM** $150 **MIP** $275

❏ **Bedford Milk Tanker,** 1966-67, light blue "TK" cab and lower semi, white upper tank w/blue/white milk decals, Model No. 1141-A
EX $110 **NM** $165 **MIP** $375

(KP Photo by Dr. Douglas Sadecky)

❏ **Bedford Mobilgas Tanker,** 1959-65, red "S" cab and tanker w/Mobilgas decals, shaped wheels, rubber tires, Model No. 1110-A
EX $100 **NM** $150 **MIP** $250

❏ **Bedford Mobilgas Tanker,** 1965-66, red "TK" cab and tanker w/red, white and blue Mobilgas decals, shaped wheels, rubber tires, Model No. 1140-A
EX $100 **NM** $175 **MIP** $350

❏ **Bedford Tanker,** 1983, red cab w/black chassis, plastic tank w/chrome catwalk, Corgi Chemco decals, Model No. 1130-B
EX $15 **NM** $20 **MIP** $35

❏ **Berliet Container Truck,** 1978, blue cab and semi fenders; white cab chassis and semi flatbed; each w/United States Lines label, Model No. 1107-B
EX $30 **NM** $45 **MIP** $75

❏ **Berliet Dolphinarium Truck,** 1980-83, yellow and blue cab and trailer, clear plastic tank; includes two dolphins and a girl trainer, Model No. 1164-A
EX $56 **NM** $84 **MIP** $175

❏ **Berliet Holmes Wrecker,** 1975-78, red cab and bed, blue rear body, white chassis, black interior, two gold booms and hooks, yellow dome light, driver, amber lenses and red/white/blue stripes, Model No. 1144-B
EX $30 **NM** $45 **MIP** $75

❏ **BL Roadtrain and Trailers,** 1981, white and orange cab, dark blue freighter semi body w/Yorkie Chocolate labels and tanker semi body w/Gulf label; includes playmat, Model No. 1002-A
EX $16 **NM** $24 **MIP** $40

❏ **Car Transporter & Cars,** 1970-73, Scammell tri-deck transporter w/six cars: Ford Capri, the Saint's Volvo, Pontiac Firebird, Lancia Fulvia, MGC GT, Marcos 3 Litre, each w/Whizz Wheels; value is for complete set, Model No. 20-B
EX $200 **NM** $400 **MIP** $900

❏ **Car Transporter and Four Cars,** 1963-66, two versions: No. 1105 Bedford TK Transporter w/Fiat 1800, Renault Floride, Mercedes 230SE and Ford Consul, 1963-65; No. 1105 Bedford TK Transporter w/Chevy Corvair, VW Ghia, Volvo P-1800 and Rover 2000, 1966 only; value is for each individual complete set, Model No. 28-A
EX $200 **NM** $300 **MIP** $700

❏ **Carrimore Car Transporter and Cars,** 1966, Ford "H" series Transporter and six cars; there are several car variations; sold by mail order only, Model No. 41-A
EX $240 **NM** $360 **MIP** $700

❏ **Carrimore Car Transporter and Four Cars,** 1957-62, three versions: No. 1101 Bedford Carrimore Transporter w/Riley, Jaguar, Austin Healey and Triumph, 1957-60; No. 1101 Bedford Carrimore Transporter w/four American cars, 1959; No. 1101 Bedford Carrimore Transporter w/Triumph, Mini, Citroen and Plymouth, 1961-62; value is for individual complete sets, Model No. 1-A
EX $300 **NM** $450 **MIP** $800

(KP Photo by Dr. Douglas Sadecky)

❏ **Ecurie Ecosse Transporter,** 1961-65, in dark blue body w/either blue or yellow lettering, or light blue body w/red or yellow lettering, working tailgate and sliding door, yellow interior, shaped wheels, rubber tires, Model No. 1126-A
EX $70 **NM** $105 **MIP** $200

❏ **Ford Aral Tank Truck,** 1977-80, light blue cab and chassis, white tanker body, Aral labels, Model No. 1161-A
EX $20 **NM** $30 **MIP** $50

❏ **Ford Car Transporter,** 1976-79, metallic lime green or metallic cab and semi, cream cab chassis, deck and ramp, Model No. 1159-A
EX $20 **NM** $30 **MIP** $60

❑ **Ford Car Transporter,** 1982, white cab, red chassis and trailer, white labels and ramps, Model No. 1170-A
EX $20   **NM** $30   **MIP** $50

❑ **Ford Covered Semi-Trailer,** 1979-80, blue cab and trailer, black cab chassis and trailer fenders, yellow covers, Model No. 1109-B
EX $15   **NM** $25   **MIP** $50

❑ **Ford Esso Tank Truck,** 1976-81, white cab and tank, red tanker chassis and fenders, chrome wheels, Esso labels, Model No. 1157-A
EX $15   **NM** $30   **MIP** $60

❑ **Ford Express Semi-Trailer,** 1965-70, metallic blue cab and trailer, silver roof on trailer, chrome doors marked "Express Service," shaped or detailed cast wheels, Model No. 1137-A
EX $60   **NM** $110   **MIP** $225

❑ **Ford Exxon Tank Truck,** 1976-81, white cab and tank, red tanker chassis and fenders, chrome wheels, Exxon labels, Model No. 1158-A
EX $15   **NM** $30   **MIP** $60

❑ **Ford Guinness Tanker,** 1982, orange, tan, black cab, tan tanker body, Guinness labels, Model No. 1169-A
EX $20   **NM** $30   **MIP** $50

❑ **Ford Gulf Tank Truck,** 1976-78, white cab w/orange chassis, blue tanker body, Gulf labels, chrome wheels, Model No. 1160-A
EX $15   **NM** $25   **MIP** $40

❑ **Ford Holmes Wrecker,** 1967-74, white upper cab, black roof, red rear body and lower cab, mirrors, unpainted or gold booms, Model No. 1142-A
EX $60   **NM** $90   **MIP** $200

❑ **Ford Michelin Container Truck,** 1981, blue cab and trailer, white cab chassis and trailer fenders, yellow containers; includes Michelin Man figure, Model No. 1108-B
EX $15   **NM** $25   **MIP** $50

❑ **Ford Transit Wrecker,** 1981, white cab and rear body, red roof, silver bed, "24-hour Service" labels, Model No. 1140-B
EX $25   **NM** $35   **MIP** $60

❑ **Mack Container Truck,** 1972-78, yellow cab, red interior, white engine, red suspension, white ACL labels, Model No. 1106-B
EX $30   **NM** $50   **MIP** $80

❑ **Mack Esso Tank Truck,** 1971-75, white cab and tank w/Esso labels, red tank chassis and fenders, Model No. 1152-A
EX $20   **NM** $40   **MIP** $80

❑ **Mack Exxon Tank Truck,** 1974-75, white cab and tank, red tank chassis and fenders, red interior, chrome catwalk, Exxon labels, Model No. 1151-B
EX $15   **NM** $35   **MIP** $75

❑ **Mack Trans Continental Semi,** 1971-73, orange cab body and semi chassis and fenders, metallic light blue semi body, unpainted trailer rests, Model No. 1100-B
EX $35   **NM** $55   **MIP** $90

❑ **Mercedes-Benz Refrigerator,** 1983, yellow cab and tailgate, red semi-trailer, two-piece lowering tailgate and yellow spare wheel base, red interior, clear window, Model No. 1131-B
EX $15   **NM** $18   **MIP** $30

❑ **Mercedes-Benz Semi-Trailer,** 1983, red cab and trailer, black chassis, Model No. 1144-C
EX $15   **NM** $18   **MIP** $30

❑ **Mercedes-Benz Semi-Trailer Van,** 1983, black cab and plastic semi trailer, white chassis and airscreen, red doors, red-blue and yellow stripes, white Corgi lettering, Model No. 1129-B
EX $15   **NM** $18   **MIP** $30

❑ **Mercedes-Benz Tanker,** 1983, two different versions, white cab and tank, green chassis, chrome or black plastic catwalk, red/white/green 7-Up labels or Corgi Chemo labels, Model No. 1167-A
EX $15   **NM** $18   **MIP** $30

❑ **Mercedes-Benz Tanker,** 1983, tan cab, plastic tank body, black chassis, black and red Guinness labels, w/chrome or black plastic catwalk, clear windows, Model No. 1166-A
EX $15   **NM** $18   **MIP** $30

❑ **Scammell Carrimore Tri-deck Car Transporter,** 1970-73, orange lower cab, chassis and lower deck, white upper cab and middle deck, blue top deck, red interior, black hydraulic cylinders, detachable rear ramp, Model No. 1146-A
EX $35   **NM** $60   **MIP** $130

❑ **Scammell Coop Semi-Trailer Truck,** 1970, white cab and trailer fenders, light blue semi-trailer, red interior, gray bumper base, jewel headlights, black hitch lever, spare wheel, Model No. 1151-A
EX $135   **NM** $210   **MIP** $350

❑ **Scammell Ferrymasters Semi-Trailer Truck,** 1969-72, white cab, red interior, yellow chassis, black fenders, clear windows, jewel headlights, cast wheels, plastic tires, Model No. 1147-A
EX $60   **NM** $90   **MIP** $150

❑ **Scania Bulk Carrier,** 1983, white cab, blue and white silos, ladders and catwalk, amber windows, blue British Sugar labels, Whizz Wheels, Model No. 1150-B
EX $7   **NM** $15   **MIP** $30

❑ **Scania Bulk Carrier,** 1983, white cab, orange and white silos, clear windows, orange screen, black/orange Spillers Flour labels, Whizz Wheels, Model No. 1151-C
EX $7   **NM** $15   **MIP** $30

❑ **Scania Container Truck,** 1983, yellow truck and box w/red Ryder Truck rental labels, clear windows, black exhaust stack, red rear doors, six-spoke Whizz Wheels, Model No. 1147-B
EX $7   **NM** $15   **MIP** $30

❑ **Scania Container Truck,** 1983, blue cab w/blue and white box and rear doors, white deck, Securicor Parcels labels, in red or white rear door colors, Model No. 1148-B
EX $7   **NM** $15   **MIP** $30

❑ **Scania Container Truck,** 1983, white cab and box w/BRS Truck Rental labels, blue windows, red screen, roof and rear doors, Model No. 1149-A
EX $7   **NM** $15   **MIP** $30

❑ **Transporter & Six Cars,** 1970-73, Scammell transporter w/six cars: No. 180 Mini DeLuxe, No. 204 Mini, No. 339 Mini Rally, No. 201 The Saint's Volvo, No. 340 Sunbeam Imp, No. 378 MGC GT; includes bag of cones and leaflet, Model No. 48-B
EX $250   **NM** $450   **MIP** $900

(KP Photo by Dr. Douglas Sadecky)

❑ **Transporter and Six Cars,** 1966-69, first issue: No. 1138 Ford 'H' Series Transporter w/six cars, No. 252 Rover 2000, blue No. 251 Hillman Imp, No. 440 Ford Cortina Estate, No. 180 Mini w/'wickerwork', metallic maroon No. 204 Mini, and No. 321 Mini Rally ('1966 Monte Carlo Rally') racing No. 2; second issue: same as first issue except No. 251 Hillman is metallic gold, No. 204 Mini is blue, No. 321 Mini is substituted for No. 333 SUN/RAC Rally Mini w/autographs on roof. The Car Transporter gift sets were a good way for Corgi to get rid of their excess stock of automobile models, Model No. 48-A
EX $225   **NM** $365   **MIP** $700

MILITARY

❑ **AMX 30D Recovery Tank,** 1976-80, olive body w/black plastic turret and gun, accessories and three figures, Model No. 908-A
EX $35   **NM** $50   **MIP** $80

❑ **Army Heavy Equipment Transporter,** 1964-65, olive cab and trailer w/white U.S. Army decals w/red interior and driver, Model No. 1135-A
EX $70   **NM** $105   **MIP** $325

❑ **Army Troop Transporter,** 1964-65, olive w/white U.S. Army decals, Model No. 1133-A
EX $70   **NM** $105   **MIP** $175

(KP Photo by Dr. Douglas Sadecky)

❑ **Bedford Army Fuel Tanker,** 1964-65, olive cab and tanker, w/white "U.S. Army" and "No Smoking" decals, Model No. 1134-A
EX $140   NM $210   MIP $375

❑ **Bedford Military Ambulance,** 1961-64, clear front and white rear windows, olive body w/Red Cross decals, w/or without suspension, Model No. 414-A
EX $56   NM $84   MIP $140

❑ **Bell Army Helicopter,** 1975-80, two-piece olive/tan camouflage body, clear canopy, olive green rotors, U.S. Army decals, Model No. 920-A
EX $24   NM $36   MIP $60

❑ **Bloodhound Launching Ramp,** 1959-62, military green ramp, Model No. 1116-A
EX $34   NM $51   MIP $85

❑ **Bloodhound Loading Trolley,** 1959-62, military green working lift, red rubber nose cone, Model No. 1117-A
EX $40   NM $60   MIP $100

❑ **Bloodhound Missile,** 1959-62, white and yellow missile, red rubber nose cone, Model No. 1115-A
EX $70   NM $105   MIP $175

(KP Photo by Dr. Douglas Sadecky)

❑ **Bloodhound Missile and Launching Platform,** 1958-61, white and yellow missile, red rubber nose cone; military green ramp, Model No. 1108-A
EX $110   NM $165   MIP $275

❑ **Bloodhound Missile on Trolley,** 1959-62, white and yellow missile, red rubber nose cone; military green trolley, rubber tires, Model No. 1109-A
EX $120   NM $180   MIP $300

❑ **Centurion Mark III Tank,** 1974-78, tan and brown camouflage or olive drab body, rubber tracks; includes twelve shells, Model No. 901-A
EX $30   NM $45   MIP $75

❑ **Centurion Tank and Transporter,** 1973-78, No. 901 olive tank and No. 1100 transporter, Model No. 10-B
EX $55   NM $80   MIP $130

❑ **Chieftain Medium Tank,** 1974-80, olive drab body, black tracks, Union Jack labels; includes twelve shells, Model No. 903-A
EX $30   NM $45   MIP $75

❑ **Commer Military Ambulance,** 1964-66, olive drab body, blue rear windows and dome light, driver, Red Cross decals, Model No. 354-A
EX $50   NM $75   MIP $125

❑ **Commer Military Police Van,** 1964-65, olive drab body, barred rear windows, white MP decals, driver, Model No. 355-A
EX $55   NM $80   MIP $130

(KP Photo by Dr. Douglas Sadecky)

❑ **Corporal Missile & Erector Vehicle,** 1959-62, white missile, red rubber-nose cone, olive green body on erector body, Model No. 1113-A
EX $240   NM $360   MIP $600

❑ **Corporal Missile Launching Ramp,** 1960-61, sold in temporary pack, Model No. 1124-A
EX $36   NM $55   MIP $90

❑ **Corporal Missile on Launching Ramp,** 1959-62, white missile, red rubber-nose cone, Model No. 1112-A
EX $80   NM $120   MIP $200

❑ **Corporal Missile Set,** 1959-62, No. 1112 missile and No. 1113 ramp, erector vehicle and No. 1118 army truck, Model No. 9-A
EX $340   NM $510   MIP $850

❑ **Decca Airfield Radar Van,** 1959-60, cream body w/four or five orange vertical bands, working rotating scanner and aerial, Model No. 1106-A
EX $120   NM $180   MIP $350

❑ **Decca Radar Scanner,** 1959-60, w/either orange or custard colored scanner frame, silver scanner face, w/gear on base for turning scanner, Model No. 353-A
EX $34   NM $51   MIP $85

❑ **Half Track Rocket Launcher & Trailer,** 1975-80, two rocket launchers and single trailer castings, gray plastic roll cage, man w/machine gun, front wheels and hubs, Model No. 907-A
EX $20   NM $35   MIP $55

❑ **International 6x6 Army Truck,** 1959-63, olive drab body w/clear windows, red/blue decals, six cast olive wheels w/rubber tires, Model No. 1118-A
EX $70   NM $105   MIP $225

(KP Photo by Dr. Douglas Sadecky)

❑ **Karrier Field Kitchen,** 1964-66, olive body, white decals, w/figure, Model No. 359-A
EX $60   NM $90   MIP $175

❑ **King Tiger Heavy Tank,** 1974-78, tan and rust body, working turret and barrel, tan rollers and treads, German labels, Model No. 904-A
EX $30   NM $45   MIP $75

❑ **M60 A1 Medium Tank,** 1974-80, green/tan camouflage body, working turret and barrel, green rollers, white decals, Model No. 902-A
EX $30   NM $45   MIP $75

❑ **Military Set,** 1975-80, set of three, No. 904 Tiger tank, No. 920 Bell Helicopter, No. 906 Saladin Armored Car, Model No. 17-B
EX $60   NM $90   MIP $150

❑ **Oldsmobile 88 Staff Car,** 1964-66, olive drab body, four figures, white decals, Model No. 358-A
EX $50   NM $75   MIP $125

❑ **RAF Land Rover,** 1958-62, blue body and cover, sheet metal rear cover, RAF rondel label, w/or without suspension, silver bumper, Model No. 351-A
EX $60   NM $90   MIP $150

❑ **RAF Land Rover & Bloodhound,** 1958-61, set of three standard colored, No, 351 RAF Land Rover, No. 1115 Bloodhound Missile, No. 1116 Ramp and No. 1117 Trolley, Model No. 4-A
EX $150   NM $300   MIP $600

❑ **RAF Land Rover and Thunderbird Missile,** 1958-63, Standard colors, No. 350 Thunderbird Missile on Trolley and 351 RAF Land Rover, Model No. 3-A
EX $100   NM $150   MIP $300

❑ **Rocket Age Set,** 1959-60, set of eight standard models including: No. 350 Thunderbird Missile on Trolley, No. 351 RAF Land Rover, No. 352 RAF Staff Car, No. 353 Radar Scanner, No. 1106 Decca Radar Van and No. 1108 Bloodhound missile w/ramp, Model No. 6-A
EX $325   NM $650   MIP $1400

❑ **Rocket Launcher and Trailer,** 1975-80, steel blue and red launcher, fires rocket, Model No. 907-A
EX $25   NM $35   MIP $60

❑ **Saladin Armored Car,** 1974-77, olive drab body, swiveling turret and raising barrel castings, black plastic barrel end and tires, olive cast wheels, w/twelve shells, fires shells, Model No. 906-A
EX $30   NM $45   MIP $75

❑ **Sikorsky Skycrane Army Helicopter,** 1975-78, olive drab and yellow body w/Red Cross and Army labels, Model No. 923-A
EX $15   NM $20   MIP $40

❑ **Standard Vanguard RAF Staff Car,** 1958-62, blue body, RAF labels, Model No. 352-A
EX $55   NM $85   MIP $140

❑ **SU-100 Medium Tank,** 1974-77, olive and cream camouflage upper body, gray lower, working hatch and barrel, black

treads, red star and #103 labels; twelve shells included, fires shells, Model No. 905-A
EX $30   **NM** $50   **MIP** $80

❑ **Thunderbird Missile and Trolley,** 1958-62, ice blue or silver missile, RAF blue trolley, red rubber nose cone, plastic tow bar, steering front and rear axles, Model No. 350-A
EX $55   **NM** $85   **MIP** $165

❑ **Tiger Mark I Tank,** 1973-78, tan and green camouflage finish, German emblem, swiveling turret and raising barrel castings, black plastic barrel end, antenna; includes twelve shells, fires shells, Model No. 900-A
EX $30   **NM** $45   **MIP** $75

❑ **Tractor, Trailer and Field Gun,** 1976-80, tan tractor body and chassis, trailer body, base and opening doors, gun chassis and raising barrel castings, brown plastic interior; twelve shells included, fires shells, Model No. 909-A
EX $30   **NM** $50   **MIP** $80

(KP Photo by Dr. Douglas Sadecky)

❑ **Volkswagen Military Personnel Carrier,** 1964-66, olive drab body, white decals, driver, Model No. 356-A
EX $55   **NM** $95   **MIP** $180

MISCELLANEOUS

❑ **Service Ramp,** 1958-60, metallic blue and silver operable ramp, Model No. 1401-A
EX $30   **NM** $45   **MIP** $95

❑ **Shell or BP Garage Gift Set,** 1963-65, gas station/garage w/pumps and other accessories including five different cars; in two versions: Shell or B.P., rare; value is for each set, Model No. 25-A
EX $295   **NM** $550   **MIP** $1200

❑ **Touring Caravan,** 1975-79, white body w/blue trim, white plastic opening roof and door, pale blue interior, red plastic hitch and awning, Model No. 490-B
EX $15   **NM** $25   **MIP** $40

MOTORCYCLE

❑ **Cafe Racer Motorcycle,** 1983, Model No. 173-A
EX $15   **NM** $18   **MIP** $30

❑ **Matra & Motorcycle Trailer,** 1980-81, red No. 57 Talbot Matra Rancho w/two yellow and blue bikes on trailer, Model No. 25-C
EX $15   **NM** $20   **MIP** $35

❑ **Red Wheelie Motorcycle,** 1982, red plastic body and fender w/black/white/yellow decals, black handlebars, kickstand and seat, chrome engine, pipes, flywheel-powered rear wheel, Model No. 171-A
EX $10   **NM** $15   **MIP** $25

❑ **Stunt Motorcycle,** 1971-72, made for Corgi Rockets race track, gold cycle, blue rider w/yellow helmet, clear windshield, plastic tires, Model No. 681-A
EX $70   **NM** $105   **MIP** $175

❑ **White Wheelie Motorcycle,** 1982, white body w/black/white police decals, Model No. 172-A
EX $15   **NM** $20   **MIP** $35

RACING

❑ **Adams Drag-Star,** 1972-74, orange body, red nose, gold engines, chrome pipes and hood panels, Whizz Wheels, Model No. 165-A
EX $20   **NM** $30   **MIP** $45

❑ **Adams Probe 16,** 1970-73, one-piece body, blue sliding canopy; metallic burgundy, or metallic lime/gold w/and without racing stripes, Whizz Wheels, Model No. 384-A
EX $15   **NM** $25   **MIP** $40

❑ **All Winners Set,** 1966-69, first issue: No. 310 Corvette, No. 312 Jaguar XKE, No. 314 Ferrari 250LM, No. 324 Marcos, No. 325 Mustang; second issue: No. 312 Jaguar XKE, No. 314 Ferrari 250LM, No. 264 Toronado, No. 327 MGB, No. 337 Corvette, Model No. 46-A
EX $100   **NM** $240   **MIP** $450

(KP Photo by Dr. Douglas Sadecky)

❑ **Aston Martin DB4,** 1962-65, white top w/aqua green sides, yellow plastic interior, racing Nos. 1, 3 or 7, Model No. 309-A
EX $50   **NM** $75   **MIP** $125

❑ **Austin Mini-Metro Datapost,** 1982-83, white body, blue roof, hood and trim, red plastic interior, hepolite and #77 decals, working hatch and doors, clear windows, folding seats, chrome headlights, orange taillights, Whizz Wheels, Model No. 281-B
EX $15   **NM** $18   **MIP** $30

❑ **Bertone Barchetta Runabout,** 1971-73, yellow and black body, black interior, amber windows, die-cast air foil, suspension, red/yellow Runabout decals, Whizz Wheels, Model No. 386-A
EX $15   **NM** $22   **MIP** $45

❑ **BMC Mini-Cooper,** 1971-74, white body, black working hood, trunk, two

doors, red interior, clear windows, orange/black stripes and #177 decals, suspension, Whizz Wheels, Model No. 282-A
EX $30   **NM** $45   **MIP** $95

(KP Photo by Dr. Douglas Sadecky)

❑ **BMC Mini-Cooper S "Sun/RAC" Rally Car,** 1967, red body, white roof w/six jewel headlights, RAC Rally and No. 21 decals, Model No. 333-A
EX $90   **NM** $180   **MIP** $350

❑ **BMC Mini-Cooper S Rally,** 1967-72, red body, white roof, chrome roof rack w/two spare tires, Monte Carlo Rally and No. 177 decals, w/shaped wheels/rubber tires or cast detailed wheels/plastic tires, Model No. 339-A
EX $40   **NM** $90   **MIP** $180

(KP Photo by Dr. Douglas Sadecky)

❑ **BMC Mini-Cooper S Rally Car,** 1965-66, red body, white roof, five jewel headlights, Monte Carlo Rally decals w/either No. 52 (1965) or No. 2 (1966); rare w/drivers' autographs on roof, Model No. 321-A
EX $100   **NM** $275   **MIP** $500

❑ **BMW M1,** 1981, yellow body, black plastic base, rear panel and interior, white seats, clear windshield, multicolored stripes, lettering and #25 decal, Goodyear label, Model No. 308-B
EX $15   **NM** $20   **MIP** $35

❑ **BMW M1 BASF,** 1983, red body, white trim w/black/white BASF and No. 80 decals, Model No. 380-B
EX $15   **NM** $18   **MIP** $30

❑ **British Leyland Mini 1000,** 1978, red interior, chrome lights, grille and bumper, #8 decal; three variations: silver body w/decals, 1978-82; silver body, no decals; orange body w/extra hood stripes, 1983, Model No. 201-C
EX $16   **NM** $24   **MIP** $40

❑ **British Racing Cars,** 1959-63, set of three cars, three versions: blue No. 152 Lotus, green No. 151 BRM, green No. 150 Vanwall, all w/smooth wheels, 1959; same cars w/shaped wheels, 1960-61; red Vanwall, green BRM and blue Lotus, 1963, each set, Model No. 5-A
EX $140   **NM** $210   **MIP** $475

❑ **BRM Racing Car,** 1958-65, silver seat, dash and pipes, smooth wheels, rubber tires, in three versions: dark green body, 1958-60; light green body w/driver and various number decals 1961-65; light green body, no driver, Model No. 152-A
EX $50   **NM** $75   **MIP** $145

❑ **Campbell Bluebird,** 1960-65, blue body, red exhaust, clear windshield, driver, in two versions: black plastic wheels, 1960; metal wheels and rubber tires, Model No. 153-A
EX $56   **NM** $84   **MIP** $175

❑ **Chevrolet Caprice Classic,** 1981, white upper body, red sides w/red/white/blue stripes and No. 43 decals, tan interior, STP labels, Model No. 341-B
EX $24   **NM** $36   **MIP** $60

(KP Photo by Dr. Douglas Sadecky)

❑ **Citroen DS 19 Rally,** 1965-66, light blue body, white roof, yellow interior, four jewel headlights, Monte Carlo Rally and No. 75 decals, w/antenna, Model No. 323-A
EX $70   **NM** $105   **MIP** $175

❑ **Commuter Dragster,** 1971-73, maroon body w/Ford Commuter, Union Jack and #2 decals, cast silver engine, chrome plastic suspension and pipes, clear windshield, driver, spoke wheels, Model No. 161-A
EX $30   **NM** $45   **MIP** $75

❑ **Cooper-Maserati Racing Car,** 1967-69, blue body w/red/white/blue Maserati and #7 decals, unpainted engine and suspension, chrome plastic steering wheel, roll bar, mirrors and pipes, driver, cast eight-spoke wheels, plastic tires, Model No. 156-A
EX $26   **NM** $39   **MIP** $65

❑ **Cooper-Maserati Racing Car,** 1969-72, yellow/white body w/yellow/black stripe and #3 decals, driver tilts to steer car, Model No. 159-A
EX $18   **NM** $27   **MIP** $45

(KP Photo by Dr. Douglas Sadecky)

❑ **Corvette Sting Ray,** 1967-69, yellow body, red interior, suspension, No. 13 decals. This car's decorative appear-

ance definitely places it in the 1960's, Model No. 337-A
EX $30   **NM** $55   **MIP** $95

❑ **Corvette Sting Ray,** 1970-73, metallic gray body w/black hood, Go-Go-Go labels, Whizz Wheels, Model No. 376-A
EX $40   **NM** $65   **MIP** $100

❑ **Datsun 240Z,** 1973-76, white body w/red hood and roof, No. 46 and John Morton labels, Whizz Wheels, Model No. 396-A
EX $15   **NM** $20   **MIP** $35

❑ **Datsun 240Z,** 1973-76, red body w/No. 11 and other labels, two working doors, white interior, orange roll bar and tire rack; one version also has East Africa Rally labels, Model No. 394-A
EX $15   **NM** $20   **MIP** $35

❑ **Ecurie Ecosse Racing Set,** 1961-66, metallic dark or light blue No. 1126 transporter w/three cars in two versions: BRM, Vanwall and Lotus XI, 1961-64; BRM, Vanwall and Ferrari, 1964-66, value is for individual complete set, Model No. 16-A
EX $140   **NM** $210   **MIP** $450

❑ **Ferrari 206 Dino,** 1969-73, black interior and fins, in either red body w/No. 30 label and gold hubs or Whizz Wheels, or yellow body w/No. 23 label and gold hubs or Whizz Wheels, Model No. 344-A
EX $24   **NM** $36   **MIP** $60

❑ **Ferrari 312 B2 Racing Car,** 1973-75, red body, white fin, gold engine, chrome suspension, mirrors and wheels, Ferrari and #5 labels, Model No. 152-B
EX $16   **NM** $24   **MIP** $40

(KP Photo by Dr. Douglas Sadecky)

❑ **Ferrari Berlinetta 250LM,** 1965-72, red body w/yellow stripe, blue windshields, chrome interior, grille and exhaust pipes, detailed engine, #4 Ferrari logo and yellow stripe decals, spoked wheels and spare, rubber tires, Model No. 314-A
EX $30   **NM** $45   **MIP** $75

❑ **Ferrari Daytona,** 1973-78, white body w/red roof and trunk, black interior, two working doors, amber windows and headlights, No. 81 and other labels, Model No. 323-B
EX $15   **NM** $30   **MIP** $55

❑ **Ferrari Daytona,** 1979, apple green body, black tow hook, red-yellow-silver-black Daytona #5 and other racing labels, amber windows, headlights, black plastic interior, base, four spoke chrome wheels, Model No. 300-C
EX $15   **NM** $20   **MIP** $35

❑ **Ferrari Daytona and Racing Car,** 1975-77, blue/yellow No. 323 Ferrari and No. 150 Surtees on yellow trailer, Model No. 29-B
EX $25   **NM** $40   **MIP** $85

❑ **Ferrari Daytona JCB,** 1973-74, orange body w/No. 33, Corgi and other labels, chrome spoked wheels, Model No. 324-B
EX $15   **NM** $25   **MIP** $50

❑ **Ferrari Racing Car,** 1963-72, red body, chrome plastic engine, roll bar and dash, driver, silver cast base and exhaust, Ferrari and No. 36 decals, shaped or spoked wheels, Model No. 154-A
EX $24   **NM** $36   **MIP** $75

❑ **Fiat X1/9,** 1980-81, metallic blue body and base, white Fiat #3, multicolored lettering and stripe labels, black roof, trim, interior, rear panel, grille, bumpers and tow hook, chrome wheels and detailed engine, Model No. 306-B
EX $15   **NM** $20   **MIP** $35

❑ **Ford Capri 3 Litre GT,** 1973-76, white and black body, racing number 5 label, Model No. 331-A
EX $15   **NM** $20   **MIP** $35

❑ **Ford Capri S,** 1982, white body, red lower body and base, red interior, clear windshield, black bumpers, grille and tow hook, chrome headlights and wheels, red taillights, #6 and other racing labels, Model No. 312-C
EX $15   **NM** $20   **MIP** $35

❑ **Ford Capri Santa Pod Gloworm,** 1971-76, white and blue body w/red, white and blue lettering and flag decals, red chassis, amber windows, gold-based black engine, gold scoop, pipes and front suspension, w/driver, plastic wheels, Model No. 163-A
EX $18   **NM** $27   **MIP** $45

❑ **Ford GT 70,** 1972-73, green and black body, white interior, No. 32 label, Model No. 316-B
EX $10   **NM** $25   **MIP** $45

❑ **Grand Prix Racing Set,** 1968-72, four vehicle set includes: No. 490 Volkswagen Breakdown Truck w/No. 330 Porsche (1969), Porsche No. 371(1970-72), No. 155 Lotus, No. 156 Cooper-Maserati, red trailer, Model No. 12-B
EX $135   **NM** $210   **MIP** $425

❑ **Grand Prix Set,** 1973, sold by mail order only; kit version of No. 151 Yardley, No. 154 JPS, No. 152 Surtees and No. 153 Surtees, Model No. 30-A
EX $60   **NM** $125   **MIP** $275

❑ **Hesketh-Ford Racing Car,** 1975-78, white body w/red/white/blue Hesketh, stripe and #24 labels, chrome suspension, roll bar, mirrors and pipes, Model No. 160-A
EX $15   **NM** $18   **MIP** $30

❑ **Hillman Hunter,** 1969-72, blue body, gray interior, black hood, white roof, unpainted spotlights, clear windshield, red radiator screen, black equipment,

Golden Jacks wheels; came w/Kangaroo figure, Model No. 302-B
EX $45　　　**NM** $65　　　**MIP** $125

(KP Photo by Dr. Douglas Sadecky)

❏ **Hillman Imp Rally,** 1966, in various metallic body colors, w/cream interior, Monte Carlo Rally and No. 107 decals, Model No. 328-A
EX $30　　　**NM** $65　　　**MIP** $110

❏ **Jaguar E Type Competition,** 1964-68, gold or chrome plated body, black interior, blue and white stripes and black #2 decals, no top, clear windshield, headlights, w/driver, Model No. 312-A
EX $45　　　**NM** $65　　　**MIP** $110

❏ **Jaguar XJS Motul,** 1983, black body w/red/white Motul and No. 4, chrome wheels, Model No. 318-B
EX $8　　　**NM** $15　　　**MIP** $25

❏ **JPS Lotus Racing Car,** 1974-77, black body, scoop and wings w/gold John Player Special, Texaco and #1 labels, gold suspension, pipes and wheels, Model No. 190-A
EX $30　　　**NM** $45　　　**MIP** $75

❏ **Lamborghini Miura,** 1973-74, silver body, black interior, yellow/purple stripes and No. 7 label, Whizz Wheels, Model No. 319-B
EX $30　　　**NM** $45　　　**MIP** $75

❏ **Land Rover and Ferrari Racer,** 1963-67, red and tan No. 438 Land Rover and red No. 154 Ferrari F1 on yellow trailer, Model No. 17-A
EX $60　　　**NM** $90　　　**MIP** $150

(KP Photo by Dr. Douglas Sadecky)

❏ **Lotus Elan S2 Roadster,** 1965-67, working hood, plastic interior w/folding seats, shaped wheels and rubber tires, issued in metallic blue, Exxon "I've got a Tiger in my tank" label on trunk. The ordinary model is metallic blue, but shown here is the rare white version of the car, Model No. 318-A
EX $30　　　**NM** $50　　　**MIP** $110

(KP Photo by Dr. Douglas Sadecky)

❏ **Lotus Eleven,** 1958-64, red, silver, or light blue/green body, clear windshield and plastic headlights, smooth wheels, rubber tires, racing decals, Model No. 151-A
EX $60　　　**NM** $95　　　**MIP** $160

❏ **Lotus Racing Car,** 1973-82, black body and base, gold cast engine, roll bar, pipes, dash and mirrors, driver, gold cast wheels, in two versions, Model No. 154-B
EX $25　　　**NM** $35　　　**MIP** $60

❏ **Lotus Racing Set,** 1976-79, three versions: "3" on No. 301 Elite and "JPS" on No. 154 Lotus racer; "7" on No. 301 Elite and "JPS" on racer; "7" on No. 301 Elite and "Texaco" on No. 154 Lotus racer; value is for each individual complete set, Model No. 32-B
EX $30　　　**NM** $45　　　**MIP** $95

❏ **Lotus Racing Team Set,** 1966-69, 490 VW Breakdown Truck, red trailer w/#318 Lotus Elan Open Top, #319 Lotus Elan Hard Top, #155 Lotus Climax; includes pack of cones, sheet of racing number labels, Model No. 37-A
EX $125　　　**NM** $200　　　**MIP** $375

❏ **Lotus-Climax Racing Car,** 1964-69, green body and base w/black/white #1 and yellow racing stripe labels, unpainted engine and suspension, w/driver, Model No. 155-A
EX $25　　　**NM** $35　　　**MIP** $65

(KP Photo by Dr. Douglas Sadecky)

❏ **Lotus-Climax Racing Car,** 1969-72, orange/white body w/black/white stripe and #8 labels, unpainted cast rear wing, cast eight-spoke wheels, w/driver, Model No. 158-A
EX $15　　　**NM** $25　　　**MIP** $50

❏ **Matra and Racing Car,** 1983, black/yellow No. 457 Talbot Matra Rancho and No. 160 Hesketh yellow car w/Team Corgi trailer and labels, Model No. 26-B
EX $15　　　**NM** $35　　　**MIP** $65

❏ **McLaren M19A Racing Car,** 1972-77, white body, orange stripes, chrome

engine, exhaust and suspension, black mirrors, driver, Yardley McLaren #55 labels, Whizz Wheels, Model No. 151-B
EX $15　　　**NM** $25　　　**MIP** $40

❏ **McLaren M23 Racing Car,** 1974-77, large 1:18-scale red and white body and wings w/red, white and black Texaco-Marlboro #5 labels, chrome pipes, suspension and mirrors, removable wheels, Model No. 191-A
EX $30　　　**NM** $60　　　**MIP** $110

❏ **Mercedes-Benz 240D Rally,** 1982, cream or tan body, black, red and blue lettering, "dirt," red plastic interior, clear windows, black radiator guard and roof rack, opening doors, racing #5 label, Model No. 291-B
EX $10　　　**NM** $15　　　**MIP** $25

(KP Photo by Dr. Douglas Sadecky)

❏ **Mercedes-Benz 300SL Coupe,** 1959-65, chrome body, red hardtop, red stripe, clear windows, 1959-60 smooth wheels no suspension, 1961-65 racing stripes, Model No. 304-A
EX $45　　　**NM** $65　　　**MIP** $130

❏ **Mercedes-Benz 300SL Roadster,** 1958-66, blue or white body, yellow interior, plastic interior, smooth, shaped or cast wheels, racing stripes and number, driver, Model No. 303-A
EX $45　　　**NM** $75　　　**MIP** $140

❏ **Mini-Marcos GT850,** 1972-73, white body, red-white-blue racing stripe and #7 labels, clear headlights, Whizz Wheels, opening doors and hood, Model No. 305-B
EX $20　　　**NM** $30　　　**MIP** $50

(KP Photo by Dr. Douglas Sadecky)

❏ **Monte Carlo Rally Set,** 1965-67, three vehicle set, No. 326 Citroen, No. 318 Mini and No. 322 Land Rover rally cars, Model No. 38-A
EX $295　　　**NM** $450　　　**MIP** $900

(KP Photo by Dr. Douglas Sadecky)

❏ **Morris Mini-Cooper,** 1962-65, yellow or blue body and base and/or hood, white roof and/or hood, two versions, red plastic interior, jewel headlights, flag, numbers decals. Even though there are various paint and decal versions of this model, any one of them is valuable, Model No. 227-A

EX $80   NM $150   MIP $300

❏ **Morris Mini-Cooper,** 1964-65, red body and base, white roof, yellow interior, chrome spotlight, No. 37 and Monte Carlo Rally decals, Model No. 317-A

EX $60   NM $125   MIP $250

❏ **Mustang Organ Grinder Dragster,** 1971-74, yellow body w/green/yellow name, #39 and racing stripe labels, black base, green windshield, red interior, roll bar, w/driver, Model No. 166-A

EX $20   NM $30   MIP $50

❏ **Porsche 924,** 1978-81, red or metallic light brown or green body, dark red interior, opening two doors and rear window, chrome headlights, black plastic grille, racing No. 2, Model No. 321-B

EX $10   NM $25   MIP $50

❏ **Porsche Carrera 6,** 1967-69, white body, red or blue trim, blue or amber tinted engine covers, black interior, clear windshield and canopy, red jewel taillights, No. 1 or No. 20 decals, Model No. 330-A

EX $30   NM $45   MIP $75

❏ **Porsche Carrera 6,** 1970-73, white upper body, red front hood, doors, upper fins and base, black interior, purple rear window, tinted engine cover, racing No. 60 decals, Model No. 371-A

EX $25   NM $35   MIP $60

❏ **Porsche-Audi 917,** 1973-78, white body, red and black No. 6, L and M, Porsche Audi and stripe labels or orange body, orange, two-tone green, white No. 6, racing driver, Model No. 397-A

EX $15   NM $20   MIP $35

(KP Photo by Dr. Douglas Sadecky)

❏ **Psychedelic Ford Mustang,** 1968, light blue body and base, aqua interior, red-orange-yellow No. 20 and flower decals, cast eight spoke wheels, plastic tire, Model No. 348-A

EX $30   NM $45   MIP $95

❏ **Quartermaster Dragster,** 1971-73, long, dark metallic green upper body w/green/yellow/black #5 and Quartermaster labels, light green lower body, w/driver, Model No. 162-A

EX $30   NM $45   MIP $75

❏ **Radio Luxembourg Dragster,** 1972-76, long, blue body w/yellow, white and blue John Wolfe Racing, Radio Luxembourg and #5 labels, silver engine, w/driver, Model No. 170-A

EX $30   NM $45   MIP $85

❏ **Renault 5 Turbo,** 1981, bright yellow body, red plastic interior, black roof and hood, working hatch and two doors, black dash, chrome rear engine, racing #8 Cibie and other sponsor labels, Model No. 307-B

EX $15   NM $18   MIP $25

❏ **Renault 5 Turbo,** 1983, white body, red roof, red and blue trim painted on, No. 5 lettering, blue and white label on windshield, facom decal, Model No. 381-B

EX $15   NM $18   MIP $25

❏ **Roger Clark's Capri,** 1970-72, white body, black hood, grille and interior, open doors, folding seats, chrome bumpers, clear headlights, red taillights, Racing #73, label sheet, Whizz Wheels, Model No. 303-B

EX $15   NM $25   MIP $55

(KP Photo by Dr. Douglas Sadecky)

❏ **Rover 2000 Rally,** 1965-66, white body, red interior, black bonnet, No. 21 decal, cast spoked wheels, Model No. 322-A2

EX $55   NM $100   MIP $200

❏ **Rover 2000 Rally,** 1965-66, metallic dark red body, white roof, shaped wheels, No. 136 and Monte Carlo Rally decals, Model No. 322-A1

EX $50   NM $95   MIP $175

❏ **Rover 3500 Triplex,** 1981, white sides and hatch, blue roof and hood, red plastic interior and trim, detailed engine, red-white-black No. 1 label, Model No. 340-B

EX $8   NM $15   MIP $20

❏ **Shadow-Ford Racing Car,** 1974-76, black body and base w/white/black #17, UOP and American flag labels, cast chrome suspension and pipes, Embassy Racing label, Model No. 155-B

EX $10   NM $20   MIP $50

❏ **Shadow-Ford Racing Car,** 1974-77, white body, red stripes, driver, chrome plastic pipes, mirrors and steering wheel, in two versions, Jackie Collins driver figure, Model No. 156-B

EX $10   NM $20   MIP $45

❏ **Silver Streak Jet Dragster,** 1973-76, metallic blue body w/Firestone and flag labels on tank, silver engine, orange plastic jet and nose cone, Model No. 169-A

EX $15   NM $25   MIP $45

❏ **Silverstone Racing Layout,** 1963-66, seven-vehicle set w/accessories; Vanwall, Lotus XI, Aston Martin, Mercedes 300SL, BRM, Ford Thunderbird, Land Rover Truck; second version has a No. 154 Ferrari substituted for Lotus XI, rare, Model No. 15-A

EX $400   NM $700   MIP $1500

(KP Photo by Dr. Douglas Sadecky)

❏ **Simca 1000,** 1964-66, chrome plated body, No. 8 and red-white-blue stripe decals, one-piece body, clear windshield, red interior, Model No. 315-A

EX $30   NM $45   MIP $75

❏ **STP Patrick Eagle Racing Car,** 1974-77, red body w/red, white and black STP and #20 labels, chrome lower engine and suspension, black plastic upper engine; includes Patrick Eagle driver figure, Model No. 159-B

EX $20   NM $30   MIP $50

❏ **Sunbeam Imp Rally,** 1967-68, metallic blue body w/white stripes, Monte Carlo Rally and No. 77 decals, cast wheels, Model No. 340-A

EX $20   NM $45   MIP $85

❏ **Super Karts,** 1982, two carts, orange and blue, Whizz Wheels in front, slicks on rear, silver and gold drivers, Model No. 46-B

EX $15   NM $18   MIP $30

❏ **Surtees TS9 Racing Car,** 1972-74, black upper engine, chrome lower engine, pipes and exhaust, driver, Brook Bond Oxo-Rob Walker labels, eight-spoke Whizz Wheels, Model No. 150-B

EX $15   NM $20   MIP $40

❏ **Surtees TS9B Racing Car,** 1972-74, red body w/white stripes and wing, black plastic lower engine, driver, chrome upper engine, pipes, suspension, eight-spoke wheels, Model No. 153-B

EX $15   NM $20   MIP $40

❏ **Tyrrell P34 Racing Car,** 1977, dark blue body and wings w/yellow stripes, #4 and white Elf and Union Jack decals, chrome plastic engine, w/driver in red or blue helmet, Model No. 161-B

EX $20   NM $30   MIP $55

❏ **Tyrrell P34 Racing Car,** 1978-79, without yellow labels, First National Bank labels, w/driver in red or orange helmet, Model No. 162-B
EX $20   NM $30   MIP $55

❏ **Tyrrell-Ford Racing Car,** 1974-78, dark blue body w/blue/black/white Elf and #1 labels, chrome suspension, pipes, mirrors, Jackie Stewart driver figure, Model No. 158-B
EX $18   NM $25   MIP $50

❏ **U.S. Racing Buggy,** 1972-74, white body w/red/white/blue stars, stripes and USA #7 labels, red base, gold engine, red plastic panels, driver, Model No. 167-A
EX $18   NM $25   MIP $50

(KP Photo by Dr. Douglas Sadecky)

❏ **Vanwall Racing Car,** 1957-65, clear windshield, unpainted dash, silver pipes and decals, smooth wheels, rubber tires, in three versions: green body or red body w/silver or yellow seats, Model No. 150-A
EX $35   NM $55   MIP $120

❏ **Volkswagen 1200 Rally,** 1976-77, light blue body, off-white plastic interior, silver headlights, red taillights, suspension, Whizz Wheels, Model No. 384-B
EX $20   NM $30   MIP $50

(KP Photo by Dr. Douglas Sadecky)

❏ **Volkswagen East African Safari,** 1965-69, light red body, brown interior, working front and rear hood, clear windows, spare wheel on roof steers front wheels, jewel headlights, w/rhinoceros figure. Although never issued as a gift set, this spectacular little toy could easily have been made into one. A rhinoceros was added as a charging menace to the racing VW, Model No. 256-A
EX $60   NM $130   MIP $285

❏ **Volkswagen Racing Tender and Cooper,** 1967-69, white No. 490 VW breakdown truck w/racing labels, blue No. 156 Cooper on trailer, Model No. 6-B
EX $50   NM $75   MIP $150

❏ **Volkswagen Racing Tender and Cooper Maserati,** 1970-71, two versions:

tan or white No. 490 VW breakdown truck, and No. 159 Cooper-Maserati on trailer; value is for each set, Model No. 25-B
EX $50   NM $75   MIP $150

❏ **Wild Honey Dragster,** 1971-73, yellow body w/red/yellow Wild Honey and Jaguar Powered labels, green windows and roof, black grille, driver, Whizz Wheels, Model No. 164-A
EX $25   NM $40   MIP $65

SMALL TRUCK

❏ **Breakdown Truck,** 1975-79, red body, black plastic boom w/gold hook, yellow interior, amber windows, black/yellow decals, Whizz Wheels, Model No. 702-A
EX $15   NM $18   MIP $30

❏ **Commer 3/4-Ton Pickup,** 1963-66, red cab w/orange canopy, yellow interior, Trans-o-Lites, Model No. 465-A
EX $30   NM $45   MIP $75

❏ **Commer 5-Ton Dropside Truck,** 1956-62, either blue or red cab, both w/cream rear body, sheet metal tow hook, smooth or shaped wheels, rubber tires, Model No. 452-A
EX $40   NM $60   MIP $110

❏ **Commer 5-Ton Platform Truck,** 1957-62, either yellow or metallic blue cab w/silver body, smooth or shaped wheels, Model No. 454-A
EX $40   NM $60   MIP $120

(KP Photo by Dr. Douglas Sadecky)

❏ **Commer Refrigerator Van,** 1956-60, either light or dark blue cab (pictured here), both w/cream bodies and red/white/blue Wall's Ice Cream decals, smooth wheels, Model No. 453-A
EX $80   NM $120   MIP $225

(KP Photo by Dr. Douglas Sadecky)

❏ **Constructor Set,** 1963-68, one red and one white cab bodies, w/four different interchangeable rear units; van, pickup, milk truck, and ambulance; various accessories include a milkman figure, Model No. 24-A
EX $48   NM $72   MIP $140

(KP Photo by Dr. Douglas Sadecky)

❏ **Dodge Kew Fargo Tipper,** 1967-72, white cab and working hood, blue tipper, red interior, clear windows, black hydraulic cylinders, cast wheels, plastic tires, Model No. 483-A
EX $34   NM $51   MIP $85

❏ **ERF 44G Dropside Truck,** 1961-64, yellow cab and chassis, metallic blue bed, smooth or shaped wheels, Model No. 456-A
EX $36   NM $55   MIP $110

(KP Photo by Dr. Douglas Sadecky)

❏ **ERF 44G Moorhouse Van,** 1958-60, yellow cab, red body, Moorhouse Lemon Cheese decals, smooth wheels, rubber tires, Model No. 459-A
EX $100   NM $150   MIP $295

(KP Photo by Dr. Douglas Sadecky)

❏ **ERF 44G Platform Truck,** 1958-64, light blue cab w/dark blue flatbed body or yellow cab and blue flatbed, smooth hubs, Model No. 457-A
EX $36   NM $55   MIP $110

❏ **ERF Dropside Truck and Trailer,** 1960-64, No. 456 truck and No. 101 trailer w/No. 1488 cement sack load and No. 1485 plank load, Model No. 11-A
EX $60   NM $90   MIP $200

(KP Photo by Dr. Douglas Sadecky)

VINTAGE

❏ **ERF Neville Cement Tipper,** 1959-66, yellow cab, gray tipper, cement decal, plastic or metal filler caps, w/either smooth or shaped wheels, Model No. 460-A
EX $32　　**NM** $48　　**MIP** $80

❏ **Ford Transit Milk Float,** 1982, white one-piece body, blue hood and roof, tan interior, chrome and red roof lights, open compartment door and milk cases, Model No. 405-C
EX $15　　**NM** $25　　**MIP** $40

❏ **Mazda 4X4 Open Truck,** 1983, blue body, white roof, black windows, no interior, white plastic wheels, Model No. 495-A
EX $15　　**NM** $20　　**MIP** $35

❏ **Mazda B-1600 Pickup Truck,** 1975-78, issued in either blue and white or blue and silver bodies w/working tailgate, black interior, chrome wheels, Model No. 493-A
EX $15　　**NM** $20　　**MIP** $35

❏ **Mazda Camper Pickup,** 1976-78, red truck and white camper w/red interior and folding supports, Model No. 415-A
EX $15　　**NM** $25　　**MIP** $451

❏ **Mazda Custom Pickup,** 1979-80, orange body w/red roof, United States flag label, Model No. 440-B
EX $15　　**NM** $18　　**MIP** $30

❏ **Mazda Motorway Maintenance Truck,** 1976-78, deep yellow body w/red base, black interior and hydraulic cylinder, yellow basket w/workman figure, Model No. 413-B
EX $18　　**NM** $25　　**MIP** $45

❏ **Mazda Pickup and Dinghy,** 1975-78, two versions: red No. 493 Mazda w/"Ford" labels; or w/"Sea Spray" labels, dinghy and trailer, Model No. 28-B
EX $25　　**NM** $35　　**MIP** $60

❏ **Mercedes-Benz and Caravan,** 1975-81, truck and trailer in two versions: w/blue No. 285 Mercedes truck and No. 490 Caravan (1975-79); w/brown No. 285 Mercedes and No. 490 Caravan (1980-81); value is for each set, Model No. 24-B
EX $15　　**NM** $30　　**MIP** $50

❏ **Mercedes-Benz Unimog 406,** 1970-76, yellow body, red and green front fenders and bumpers, metallic charcoal gray chassis w/olive or tan rear plastic covers, red interior, Model No. 406-B
EX $18　　**NM** $25　　**MIP** $45

❏ **Mercedes-Faun Street Sweeper,** 1980, orange body w/light orange or brown figure, red interior, black chassis and unpainted brushing housing and arm castings, Model No. 1117-B
EX $15　　**NM** $25　　**MIP** $40

(KP Photo by Dr. Douglas Sadecky)

❏ **Milk Truck and Trailer,** 1962-66, blue and white ERF No. 456 milk truck w/No. 101 trailer and milk churns, Model No. 21-A
EX $60　　**NM** $130　　**MIP** $250

❏ **Shelvoke and Drewry Garbage Truck,** 1979, long, orange or red cab, silver body w/City Sanitation decals, black interior, grille and bumpers, clear windows, Model No. 1116-B
EX $15　　**NM** $25　　**MIP** $40

❏ **Unimog with Snowplow (Mercedes-Benz),** 1971-76, 6" four different body versions, red interior, cab, rear body, fender-plow mounting, lower and charcoal upper chassis, rear fenders, Model No. 1150-A
EX $30　　**NM** $45　　**MIP** $75

❏ **Volkswagen Breakdown Truck,** 1966-72, tan or white body, red interior and equipment boxes, clear windshield, chrome tools, spare wheels, red VW emblem, no lettering, Model No. 490-A
EX $50　　**NM** $75　　**MIP** $125

❏ **Volkswagen Pickup,** 1964-66, dark yellow body, red interior and rear plastic cover, silver bumpers and headlights, red VW emblem, shaped wheels, Model No. 431-A
EX $45　　**NM** $65　　**MIP** $110

SPORTS CAR

❏ **Alfa Romeo P33 Pininfarina,** 1970-74, white body, gold or black spoiler, red seats, Whizz Wheels, Model No. 380-A
EX $16　　**NM** $24　　**MIP** $45

❏ **Austin Healey,** 1956-63, blue body w/cream seats, shaped hubs, rare, Model No. 300-A2
EX $75　　**NM** $125　　**MIP** $250

(KP Photo by Dr. Douglas Sadecky)

❏ **Austin-Healey,** 1956-63, cream body w/red seats or red body w/cream seats, Model No. 300-A1
EX $50　　**NM** $75　　**MIP** $125

❏ **Beach Buggy & Sailboat,** 1971-76, purple No. 381 buggy, yellow trailer and red/white boat, Model No. 26-A
EX $20　　**NM** $30　　**MIP** $55

❏ **Bertone Shake Buggy,** 1972-74, clear windows, green interior, gold engine, four variations: yellow upper/white lower body or metallic mauve upper/white lower body w/spoked or solid chrome wheels, Model No. 392-A
EX $15　　**NM** $22　　**MIP** $45

❏ **BMC Mini-Cooper Magnifique,** 1966-70, metallic blue or olive green body w/working doors, hood and trunk, clear

windows and sunroof, cream interior w/folding seats, jewel headlights, cast detailed wheels, plastic tires, Model No. 334-A
EX $34　　**NM** $65　　**MIP** $115

❏ **BMC Mini-Cooper S,** 1972-76, bright yellow body, red plastic interior, chrome plastic roof rack w/two spare wheels, clear windshield, one-piece body silver grille, bumpers, headlights, red taillights, suspension, Whizz Wheels, Model No. 308-A
EX $45　　**NM** $65　　**MIP** $110

❏ **British Leyland Mini 1000,** 1976-78, metallic blue body, working doors, black base, clear windows, white interior, silver lights, grille and bumper, Union Jack decal on roof, Whizz Wheels, Model No. 200-B
EX $18　　**NM** $27　　**MIP** $45

❏ **Chevrolet Astro I,** 1969-74, dark metallic green/blue body w/working rear door, cream interior w/two passengers, in two versions: gold wheels w/red plastic hubs or Whizz wheels, Model No. 347-A
EX $18　　**NM** $40　　**MIP** $85

❏ **Chevrolet Camaro SS,** 1968-70, metallic gold body w/two working doors, black roof and stripes, red interior, take-off wheels, Model No. 338-A
EX $30　　**NM** $45　　**MIP** $75

❏ **Chevrolet Camaro SS,** 1972-73, blue or turquoise body w/white stripe, cream interior, working doors, white plastic top, clear windshield, folding seats, silver air intakes, red taillights, black grille and headlights, suspension, Whizz Wheels, Model No. 304-B
EX $30　　**NM** $45　　**MIP** $95

(KP Photo by Dr. Douglas Sadecky)

❏ **Corvette Sting Ray,** 1963-68, metallic silver, bronze or red body, two working headlights, clear windshield, yellow interior, silver hood panels, four rotating jewel headlights, suspension, chrome bumpers, w/spoked or shaped wheels, rubber tires. The swivelling jeweled headlights and spoked wheels added real pizzaz to this cool toy, Model No. 310-A
EX $60　　**NM** $90　　**MIP** $175

❏ **Corvette Sting Ray,** 1970-72, metallic green or metallic red body, yellow interior, black working hood, working headlights, clear windshield, amber roof panel, gold dash, chrome grille and bumpers, decals, gray die-cast base, Golden jacks, cast wheels, plastic tires, Model No. 300-B
EX $40　　**NM** $90　　**MIP** $185

❏ **Corvette Sting Ray,** 1972, either dark metallic blue or metallic mauve-rose body, chrome dash, Whizz Wheels, Model No. 387-A
EX $40 **NM** $65 **MIP** $100

❏ **De Tomaso Mangusta,** 1969, white upper/light blue lower body/base, black interior, clear windows, silver engine, black grille, amber headlights, red taillights, gray antenna, spare wheel, gold stripes and black logo decal on hood, suspension, removable gray chassis, Model No. 271-A
EX $32 **NM** $48 **MIP** $80

❏ **De Tomaso Mangusta,** 1970-73, metallic dark green body w/gold stripes and logo on hood, silver lower body, clear front windows, cream interior, amber rear windows and headlights, gray antenna, spare wheel, Whizz Wheels, Model No. 203-B
EX $26 **NM** $39 **MIP** $65

❏ **Ferrari 308GTS,** 1982, red or black body w/working rear hood, black interior w/tan seats, movable chrome headlights, detailed engine, Model No. 378-B
EX $15 **NM** $20 **MIP** $35

❏ **Ferrari 308GTS Magnum,** 1982, red body w/solid chrome wheels, Model No. 298-A
EX $24 **NM** $36 **MIP** $60

❏ **Fiat X1/9,** 1975-79, metallic light green or silver body w/black roof, trim and interior, two working doors, rear panel, grille, tow hook and bumpers, detailed engine, suspension, chrome wheels, Model No. 314-B
EX $15 **NM** $20 **MIP** $35

❏ **Ford Capri,** 1970-72, orange-red or dark red body, gold wheels w/red hubs or Whizz Wheels, two working doors, clear windshield and headlights, black interior, folding seats, black grille, silver bumpers, Model No. 311-A
EX $40 **NM** $80 **MIP** $145

❏ **Ford Capri 30 S,** 1980-81, Silver or yellow body, black markings, opening doors and hatchback, Model No. 343-B
EX $15 **NM** $20 **MIP** $35

❏ **Ford Cobra Mustang,** 1982, white, black, red and blue body and chassis, Mustang decal, Model No. 370-A
EX $15 **NM** $18 **MIP** $30

❏ **Ford Cortina GXL,** 1970-73, tan or metallic silver blue body, black roof and stripes, red plastic interior, working doors, clear windshield, Model No. 313-A
EX $30 **NM** $45 **MIP** $75

❏ **Ford Mustang Fastback,** 1965-66, metallic lilac, metallic dark blue, silver or light green body, spoked or detailed cast wheels, Model No. 320-A
EX $30 **NM** $45 **MIP** $95

(KP Photo by Dr. Douglas Sadecky)

❏ **Ford Mustang Fastback,** 1965-69, white body w/double red stripe, blue interior, spun, detailed cast, wire or cast alloy wheels. Shown in the foreground of this photo is an unused number sheet to help jazz up the model, Model No. 325-A
EX $25 **NM** $45 **MIP** $85

❏ **Ford Mustang Mach 1,** 1973-76, green upper body, white lower body and base, cream interior, folding seat backs, chrome headlights and rear bumper, Model No. 329-A
EX $25 **NM** $35 **MIP** $60

❏ **Ford Sierra,** 1982, many body color versions w/plastic interior, working hatch and two doors, clear windows, folding seat back, lifting hatch cover, Model No. 299-A
EX $8 **NM** $15 **MIP** $25

❏ **Ford Sierra and Caravan Trailer,** 1983, blue #299 Sierra, two-tone blue/white #490 Caravan, Model No. 1-C
EX $15 **NM** $20 **MIP** $35

❏ **Ford Thunderbird 1957,** 1982, cream body, dark brown, black or orange plastic hardtop, black interior, open hood and trunk, chrome bumpers, Model No. 801-B
EX $10 **NM** $20 **MIP** $35

❏ **Ford Thunderbird 1957,** 1983, white body, black interior and plastic top, amber windows, white seats, chrome bumpers, headlights and spare wheel cover, Model No. 810-B
EX $10 **NM** $20 **MIP** $35

(KP Photo by Dr. Douglas Sadecky)

❏ **Ford Thunderbird Hardtop,** 1959-65, light green body, cream roof, clear windows, silver lights, grille and bumpers, red taillights, rubber tires, Model No. 214-A
EX $50 **NM** $80 **MIP** $130

(KP Photo by Dr. Douglas Sadecky)

❏ **Ford Thunderbird Hardtop-Mechanical,** 1959, same as 214-A but w/friction motor and pink body and black roof. This model is fairly hard to find, Model No. 214-M
EX $70 **NM** $105 **MIP** $195

❏ **Ford Thunderbird Roadster,** 1959-65, clear windshield, silver seats, lights, grille and bumpers, red taillights, rubber tires, white body, Model No. 215-A
EX $50 **NM** $75 **MIP** $125

(KP Photo by Dr. Douglas Sadecky)

❏ **Ghia-Fiat 600 Jolly,** 1965-66, dark yellow body, red seats, two figures and a dog, clear windshield, silver bumpers and headlights, red taillights, Model No. 242-A
EX $80 **NM** $175 **MIP** $325

❏ **GP Beach Buggy,** 1970-76, metallic blue or orange-red body, two surfboards, flower label, Whizz Wheels, Model No. 381-A
EX $15 **NM** $20 **MIP** $35

❏ **Iso Grifo 7 Litre,** 1970-73, metallic blue body, light blue interior, black hood and stripe, clear windshield, black dash, folding seats, chrome bumpers, Whizz Wheels, Model No. 301-B
EX $15 **NM** $18 **MIP** $30

❏ **Jaguar 1952 XK120 Rally,** 1983, cream body w/black top and trim, red interior, Rally des Alps and #414 decals, Model No. 803-A
EX $8 **NM** $15 **MIP** $25

(KP Photo by Dr. Douglas Sadecky)

❏ **Jaguar E Type,** 1962-64, maroon or metallic dark gray body, tan interior, red and clear plastic removable hardtop, clear windshield, folded top, spun hubs, Model No. 307-A
EX $45 **NM** $65 **MIP** $110

VINTAGE

❑ **Jaguar E Type 2+2,** 1968-69, red or blue body and chassis, working hood, doors and hatch, black interior w/folding seats, copper engine, pipes and suspension, spoked wheels, Model No. 335-A
EX $40   **NM** $60   **MIP** $120

❑ **Jaguar E Type 2+2,** 1970-76, in five versions: red or yellow w/nonworking doors; or w/V-12 engine in yellow body or metallic yellow body, Whizz Wheels, Model No. 374-A
EX $35   **NM** $55   **MIP** $90

❑ **Jaguar XJ12C,** 1974-79, five different metallic versions, working hood and two doors, clear windows, tow hook, chrome bumpers, grille and headlights, Model No. 286-A
EX $10   **NM** $15   **MIP** $35

❑ **Jaguar XJS,** 1978-81, metallic burgundy body, tan interior, clear windows, working doors, spoked chrome wheels, Model No. 319-C
EX $10   **NM** $15   **MIP** $25

❑ **Jaguar XJS-HE Supercat,** 1982-83, black body w/silver stripes and trim, red interior, dark red taillights, light gray antenna, no tow hook, clear windshield, Model No. 314-C
EX $8   **NM** $15   **MIP** $25

❑ **Jaguar XK120 Hardtop,** 1983, red body, black hardtop, working hood and trunk, detailed engine, cream interior, clear windows, chrome wheels, Model No. 803-B
EX $8   **NM** $15   **MIP** $25

❑ **Lamborghini Miura P400,** 1970-72, w/red or yellow body, working hood, detailed engine, clear windows, jewel headlights, bull figure, Whizz Wheels, Model No. 342-A
EX $40   **NM** $60   **MIP** $100

❑ **Lancia Fulvia Zagato,** 1967-69, metallic blue body, metallic green or yellow and black body, light blue interior, working hood and doors, folding seats, amber lights, cast wheels, Model No. 332-A
EX $25   **NM** $35   **MIP** $70

❑ **Lancia Fulvia Zagato,** 1970-72, orange body, black working hood and interior, Whizz Wheels, Model No. 372-A
EX $15   **NM** $25   **MIP** $40

❑ **Lotus Elan S2 Hardtop,** 1967-68, cream interior w/folding seats and tan dash, working hood, separate chrome chassis, issued in blue body w/white top or red body w/white top, Model No. 319-A
EX $30   **NM** $45   **MIP** $75

❑ **Lotus Elite,** 1976-78, red body, white interior, two working doors, clear windshield, black dash, hood panel, grille, bumpers, base and tow hook, Model No. 315-C
EX $15   **NM** $18   **MIP** $35

❑ **Lotus Elite 22,** 1970-75, dark blue body w/silver trim, Whizz Wheels, Model No. 382-B
EX $15   **NM** $18   **MIP** $35

❑ **Marcos 3 Litre,** 1970-73, working hood, detailed engine, black interior, Marcos label, Whizz Wheels, issued in orange or metallic blue-green, Model No. 377-A
EX $20   **NM** $30   **MIP** $55

❑ **Marcos Mantis,** 1971-73, metallic red body, opening doors, cream interior and headlights, silver gray lower body base, bumpers, hood panel, spoked wheels, Model No. 312-B
EX $20   **NM** $35   **MIP** $55

(KP Photo by Dr. Douglas Sadecky)

❑ **Marcos Volvo 1800 GT,** 1966-69, issued w/either white body w/two green stripes or blue body w/two white stripes, plastic interior w/driver, spoked wheels, rubber tires. The blue version is shown here--the common version is white with racing stripes, Model No. 324-A
EX $25   **NM** $40   **MIP** $70

❑ **Mercedes-Benz 300SC Convertible,** 1983, black body, black folded top, white interior, folding seat backs, detailed engine, chrome grille and wheels, lights, bumpers, Model No. 806-B
EX $8   **NM** $12   **MIP** $25

❑ **Mercedes-Benz 300SC Hardtop,** 1983, maroon body, tan top and interior, open hood and trunk, clear windows, folding seat backs, top w/chrome side irons, Model No. 805-B
EX $8   **NM** $15   **MIP** $25

❑ **Mercedes-Benz 300SL,** 1982, red body and base, tan interior, open hood and two gullwing doors, black dash, detailed engine, clear windows, chrome bumpers, Model No. 802-B
EX $8   **NM** $15   **MIP** $25

❑ **Mercedes-Benz 300SL,** 1983, silver body, tan interior, black dash, clear windows, open hood and two gullwing doors, detailed engine, chrome bumpers, Model No. 811-B
EX $8   **NM** $15   **MIP** $25

❑ **Mercedes-Benz 350SL,** 1972-79, white body, spoke wheels or metallic dark blue body solid wheels, pale blue interior, folding seats, detailed engine, Model No. 393-A
EX $15   **NM** $30   **MIP** $60

❑ **Mercedes-Benz C-111,** 1971-74, orange main body w/black lower and base, black interior, vents, front and rear grilles, silver headlights, red taillights, Whizz Wheels, Model No. 388-A
EX $15   **NM** $20   **MIP** $45

❑ **MG Maestro,** 1983, yellow body, black trim, opaque black windows, black plastic grille, bumpers, spoiler, trim and battery hatch, clear headlights, AA Service label, Model No. 1009-A
EX $15   **NM** $20   **MIP** $35

❑ **MGA,** 1957-65, red or metallic green body, cream seats, black dash, clear windshield, silver bumpers, grille and headlights, smooth or shaped wheels, Model No. 302-A
EX $60   **NM** $90   **MIP** $150

❑ **MGB GT,** 1967-69, dark red body, pale blue interior, opening hatch and two doors, jewel headlights, chrome grille and bumpers, orange taillights, spoked wheels, w/suitcase, Model No. 327-A
EX $50   **NM** $75   **MIP** $110

❑ **MGC GT,** 1969, bright yellow body and base, black interior, hood and hatch, folding seats, luggage, jewel headlights, red taillights, Model No. 345-A
EX $50   **NM** $75   **MIP** $125

❑ **MGC GT,** 1970-73, red body, black hood and base, black interior, opening hatch and two doors, folding seat backs, luggage, orange taillights, Whizz Wheels, Model No. 378-A
EX $50   **NM** $75   **MIP** $125

❑ **Mini Camping Set,** 1977-78, cream Mini, w/red/blue tent, grille and two figures, Model No. 38-B
EX $25   **NM** $40   **MIP** $65

❑ **Mini-Marcos GT850,** 1966-70, metallic maroon body, white name and trim decals, cream interior, open hood and doors, clear windows and headlights, Golden Jacks wheels, Model No. 341-A
EX $30   **NM** $45   **MIP** $75

❑ **Minissima,** 1975-79, cream upper body, metallic lime green lower body w/black stripe centered, black interior, clear windows, headlights, Model No. 288-A
EX $15   **NM** $20   **MIP** $35

❑ **Morris Marina 1.8 Coupe,** 1971-73, metallic dark red or lime green body, cream interior, working hood and two doors, clear windshield, chrome grille and bumpers, Whizz Wheels, Model No. 306-A
EX $15   **NM** $30   **MIP** $60

❑ **Morris Mini-Cooper Deluxe,** 1965-68, black body/base, red roof, yellow and black wicker work decals on sides and rear, yellow interior, gray steering wheel, jewel headlights, Model No. 249-A
EX $45   **NM** $65   **MIP** $120

(KP Photo by Dr. Douglas Sadecky)

❏ **Morris Mini-Minor,** 1960-71, light blue or red body w/shaped or smooth wheels, plastic interior, silver bumpers, grille and headlights, Model No. 226-A1
EX $40 **NM** $60 **MIP** $100

❏ **Morris Mini-Minor,** 1960-71, sky blue body w/shaped and/or smooth wheels, plastic interior, silver bumpers, grille and headlights, Model No. 226-A2
EX $100 **NM** $175 **MIP** $350

❏ **Morris Mini-Minor,** 1972-73, one-piece body in dark or metallic blue or orange body, plastic interior, silver lights, grille and bumpers, red taillights, Whizz Wheels, Model No. 204-B
EX $30 **NM** $45 **MIP** $75

(KP Photo by Dr. Douglas Sadecky)

❏ **NSU Sport Prinz,** 1963-66, metallic burgundy or maroon body, yellow interior, one-piece body, silver bumpers, headlights and trim, shaped wheels, Model No. 316-A
EX $30 **NM** $45 **MIP** $75

❏ **Pontiac Firebird,** 1969-72, metallic silver body and base, red interior, black hood, stripes and convertible top, doors open, clear windows, folding seats, Golden Jacks wheels, Model No. 343-A
EX $50 **NM** $75 **MIP** $125

(KP Photo by Dr. Douglas Sadecky)

❏ **Pop Art Mini-Mostest,** 1969, light red body and base, yellow interior, jewel headlights, orange taillights, yellow-blue-purple pop art and "Mostest" decals; very rare. This rare Mini is one of the Holy Grails of any Corgi collection. Very few of these cars were produced in 1969, possibly due to the fact that psychedelia had already passed its prime, Model No. 349-A
EX $1000 **NM** $1500 **MIP** $2700

❏ **Porsche 917,** 1970-76, red or metallic blue body, black or gray base, blue or amber tinted windows and headlights, opening hood, headlights, Whizz Wheels, Model No. 385-A
EX $15 **NM** $20 **MIP** $45

❏ **Porsche 92 Turbo,** 1982, black body w/gold trim, yellow interior, four

chrome headlights, clear windshield, taillight-license plate decal, opening doors and hatchback, Model No. 310-B
EX $15 **NM** $20 **MIP** $35

❏ **Porsche 924,** 1980-81, bright orange body, dark red interior, black plastic grille, multicolored stripes, swivel roof spotlight, Model No. 303-C
EX $10 **NM** $15 **MIP** $25

❏ **Porsche Targa 911S,** 1970-75, metallic blue, silver-blue or green body, black roof w/or without stripe, orange interior, opening hood and two doors, chrome engine and bumpers, Whizz Wheels, Model No. 382-A
EX $25 **NM** $35 **MIP** $60

❏ **Reliant Bond Rug 700 E.S.,** 1971-74, bright orange or lime green body, off white seats, black trim, silver headlights, red taillights, Bug label, Model No. 389-A
EX $15 **NM** $25 **MIP** $50

❏ **Renault 11 GTL,** 1983, light tan or maroon body and base, red interior, opening doors and rear hatch, lifting hatch cover, folding seats, grille, Model No. 384-C
EX $15 **NM** $25 **MIP** $40

❏ **Talbot-Matra Rancho,** 1981-84, red and black, green and black or white and blue body, working tailgate and hatch, clear windows, plastic interior, black bumpers, grille and tow hook, Model No. 457-B
EX $10 **NM** $15 **MIP** $25

❏ **Toyota 2000 GT,** 1970-72, metallic dark blue or purple one-piece body, cream interior, red gear shift and antenna, two red and two amber taillights, Whizz Wheels, Model No. 375-A
EX $15 **NM** $30 **MIP** $55

❏ **Triumph TR2,** 1956-59, cream one-piece body w/red seats, light green body w/white or cream seats, clear windshield, silver grille, Model No. 301-A
EX $70 **NM** $105 **MIP** $175

(KP Photo by Dr. Douglas Sadecky)

❏ **Triumph TR3,** 1960-62, metallic olive or cream one-piece body, red seats, clear windshield, silver grille, bumpers and headlights, smooth or shaped hubs, Model No. 305-A
EX $60 **NM** $90 **MIP** $150

❏ **Volkswagen Polo Turbo,** 1982, cream body, red interior w/red and orange trim, working hatch and two door castings, clear windshield, black plastic dash, Model No. 309-B
EX $15 **NM** $18 **MIP** $30

TAXI

❏ **Austin London Taxi,** 1960-65, black body w/yellow plastic interior, w/or without driver, shaped or smooth hubs or rubber tires, Model No. 418-A1
EX $36 **NM** $55 **MIP** $90

❏ **Austin London Taxi,** 1978-83, black body w/two working doors, light brown interior, Whizz Wheels, Model No. 425-A
EX $15 **NM** $20 **MIP** $35

❏ **Austin London Taxi/Reissue,** 1971-74, updated version w/Whizz Wheels, black or maroon body, Model No. 418-A2
EX $15 **NM** $20 **MIP** $35

❏ **Chevrolet Caprice Taxi,** 1979-81, orange body w/red interior, white roof sign, Taxi and TWA decals, Model No. 327-B
EX $20 **NM** $30 **MIP** $50

❏ **Chevrolet Impala Taxi,** 1960-65, light orange body, base w/hexagonal panel under rear axle and smooth wheels, or two raised lines and shaped wheels, one-piece body, clear windows, plastic interior, silver grille, headlights and bumpers; smooth or shaped spun wheels w/rubber tires, Model No. 221-A
EX $50 **NM** $75 **MIP** $125

(KP Photo by Dr. Douglas Sadecky)

❏ **Chevrolet Impala Yellow Cab,** 1965-67, red lower body, yellow upper, red interior w/driver, white roof sign, red decals, Model No. 480-A
EX $80 **NM** $120 **MIP** $200

❏ **Ford Sierra Taxi,** 1983, cream body, Model No. 451-A
EX $8 **NM** $15 **MIP** $20

❏ **Mercedes-Benz 240D Taxi,** 1975-80, orange body, orange interior, black roof sign w/red and white Taxi labels, black on door, Model No. 411-B
EX $15 **NM** $18 **MIP** $30

❏ **Peugeot 505 STI,** 1981-82, red body and base, red interior, blue-red-white Taxi labels, black grille, bumpers, tow hook, chrome headlights and wheels, opening doors, Model No. 373-B
EX $8 **NM** $15 **MIP** $25

❏ **Peugeot 505 Taxi,** 1983, cream body, red interior, red, white and blue taxi decals, Model No. 450-B
EX $8 **NM** $15 **MIP** $25

❏ **Thunderbird Bermuda Taxi,** 1962-65, white body w/blue, yellow or green plastic canopy w/red fringe, yellow interior, driver, yellow and black labels, Model No. 430-A
EX $50 **NM** $75 **MIP** $125

VINTAGE

TRAILER

❏ **Dropside Trailer,** 1957-65, cream body, red chassis in five versions: smooth wheels 1957-61; shaped wheels, 1962-1965; white body, cream or blue chassis; or silver gray body, blue chassis, each, Model No. 100-A
EX $10   **NM** $21   **MIP** $45

❏ **Pennyburn Workmen's Trailer,** 1968-69, blue body w/working lids, red plastic interior, three plastic tools, shaped wheels, plastic tires, Model No. 109-A
EX $15   **NM** $35   **MIP** $50

(KP Photo by Dr. Douglas Sadecky)

❏ **Platform Trailer,** 1958-64, in five versions: silver body, blue chassis; silver body, yellow chassis; blue body, red chassis; blue body, yellow chassis, Model No. 101-A
EX $10   **NM** $20   **MIP** $45

VANS

(KP Photo by Dr. Douglas Sadecky)

❏ **Austin Mini Van,** 1964-67, metallic deep green body w/two working rear doors, clear windows, Model No. 450-A
EX $40   **NM** $60   **MIP** $100

(KP Photo by Dr. Douglas Sadecky)

❏ **Bedford AA Road Service Van,** 1957-62, dark yellow body in two versions: first version with divided windshield, 1957-59 shown; single windshield, 1960-62, Model No. 408-A
EX $50   **NM** $75   **MIP** $125

(KP Photo by Dr. Douglas Sadecky)

❏ **Bedford Corgi Toys Van,** 1960-62, Corgi Toys decals, w/either yellow body/blue roof or blue body/yellow roof, Model No. 422-A2
EX $60   **NM** $90   **MIP** $175

❏ **Bedford Corgi Toys Van,** 1962, yellow upper/blue lower body, Corgi Toy decals, Model No. 422-A1
EX $100   **NM** $225   **MIP** $400

❏ **Bedford Daily Express Van,** 1956-59, dark blue body w/white Daily Express decals, divided windshield, smooth wheels, rubber tires, Model No. 403-A
EX $60   **NM** $90   **MIP** $150

(KP Photo by Dr. Douglas Sadecky)

❏ **Bedford Dormobile,** 1956-62, two versions and several colors: divided windshield w/cream, green or metallic maroon body; or single windshield w/yellow body/blue roof w/shaped or smooth wheels. Pictured here; the 404-A on the left and the 404M on the right with a mechanical friction motor, Model No. 404-A
EX $50   **NM** $75   **MIP** $125

❏ **Bedford Dormobile-Mechanical,** 1956-59, friction motor, dark metallic red or turquoise body, smooth wheels, Model No. 404M
EX $60   **NM** $90   **MIP** $175

(KP Photo by Dr. Douglas Sadecky)

❏ **Bedford Evening Standard Van,** 1960-62, black body/silver roof or black lower body/silver upper body and roof, Evening Standard decals, smooth wheels, Model No. 421-A
EX $55   **NM** $80   **MIP** $130

❏ **Bedford KLG Van-Mechanical,** 1956-59, w/friction motor, red body w/KLG Spark Plugs decals, smooth hubs, Model No. 403M
EX $70   **NM** $125   **MIP** $285

❏ **Chevrolet Coca-Cola Van,** 1978-80, red body, white trim, w/Coca Cola logos, Model No. 437-B
EX $15   **NM** $20   **MIP** $35

❏ **Chevrolet Rough Rider Van,** 1977-78, yellow body w/working rear doors, cream interior, amber windows, Rough Rider decals, Model No. 423-B
EX $15   **NM** $18   **MIP** $30

❏ **Chevrolet Vantastic Van,** 1977-80, off white body w/Vantastic decals, Model No. 431-B
EX $10   **NM** $15   **MIP** $25

❏ **Chevrolet Vantastic Van,** 1977-80, black body w/Vantastic decals, Model No. 432-A
EX $10   **NM** $15   **MIP** $25

❏ **Commer 3/4-Ton Milk Float,** 1964-65, white cab w/light blue body, Model No. 466-A1
EX $32   **NM** $48   **MIP** $80

❏ **Commer 3/4-Ton Milk Float,** 1970, white cab w/light blue body, w/CO-OP decals, Model No. 466-A2
EX $40   **NM** $80   **MIP** $160

❏ **Commer 3/4-Ton Van,** 1970-71, either dark blue body with green roof and Hammonds decals (1971) or white body with light blue roof and CO-OP labels (1970), both w/cast spoked wheels w/plastic tires, Model No. 462-A
EX $45   **NM** $90   **MIP** $180

❏ **Commer Holiday Mini Bus,** 1968-69, white upper body w/orange lower body, white interior, clear windshield, silver bumpers, grille and headlights, Holiday Camp Special decal, roof rack, two working rear doors. With bathing suits packed in the roof luggage, a trip to the shore was inevitable in this mod van, Model No. 508-A
EX $30   **NM** $60   **MIP** $110

(KP Photo by Dr. Douglas Sadecky)

❏ **Commer Mobile Camera Van,** 1967-72, metallic blue lower body and roof rack, white upper body, two working rear doors, black camera on gold tripod, cameraman, Model No. 479-A
EX $60   **NM** $90   **MIP** $175

(KP Photo by Dr. Douglas Sadecky)

❏ **Ford Thames Airborne Caravan,** 1962-67, various color versions of body and plastic interior w/table, white blinds, silver bumpers, grille and headlights, two doors, Model No. 420-A
EX $35 **NM** $55 **MIP** $95

(KP Photo by Dr. Douglas Sadecky)

❏ **Ford Thames Wall's Ice Cream Van,** 1965-68, light blue body, cream pillar, chimes, chrome bumpers and grille, no figures. This wonderful toy played the Wall's Ice Cream musical tune by turning the hand crank on the rear of the van, Model No. 474-A
EX $55 **NM** $110 **MIP** $225

❏ **Ford Wall's Ice Cream Van,** 1965-67, light blue body, dark cream pillars, plastic striped rear canopy, white interior, silver bumpers, grille and headlights. A sidewalk/street display plus a salesman and small boy dress up this non-musical version of the van, Model No. 447-A
EX $80 **NM** $160 **MIP** $325

❏ **Karrier Bantam Two Ton Van,** 1957-60, blue body, red chassis and bed, clear windows, smooth wheels, rubber tires, Model No. 455-A
EX $35 **NM** $55 **MIP** $95

(KP Photo by Dr. Douglas Sadecky)

❏ **Karrier Butcher Shop,** 1960-64, white body, blue roof, butcher shop interior, Home Service labels, in two versions: w/or without suspension, smooth hubs. Note the meat hanging in the side windows, Model No. 413-A
EX $65 **NM** $100 **MIP** $165

(KP Photo by Dr. Douglas Sadecky)

❏ **Karrier Dairy Van,** 1962-64, light blue body w/Drive Safely on Milk decals, white roof, w/either smooth or shaped wheels, Model No. 435-A
EX $50 **NM** $75 **MIP** $145

(KP Photo by Dr. Douglas Sadecky)

❏ **Karrier Ice Cream Van,** 1963-66, cream upper, blue lower body and interior, clear windows, sliding side windows, Mister Softee decals, figure inside, Model No. 428-A
EX $90 **NM** $150 **MIP** $275

(KP Photo by Dr. Douglas Sadecky)

❏ **Karrier Lucozade Van,** 1958-62, yellow body w/gray rear door, Lucozade decals, rubber tires, w/either smooth or shaped wheels, Model No. 411-A
EX $70 **NM** $120 **MIP** $225

(KP Photo by Dr. Douglas Sadecky)

❏ **Karrier Mobile Canteen,** 1965-66, blue body, white interior, amber windows, roof knob rotates figure, working side panel counter, Joe's Diner label. In this photo, the model on the left has the common "Joe's Diner" label, while the van on the right (471-A2) features the rare

Belgian-issued "patates frites" label, Model No. 471-A1
EX $60 **NM** $90 **MIP** $150

❏ **Karrier Mobile Canteen,** 1965-66, blue body, white interior, amber windows, roof knob rotates figure, working side panel counter, Patates Frites label, Belgium issue, Model No. 471-A2
EX $90 **NM** $150 **MIP** $325

❏ **Karrier Mobile Grocery,** 1957-61, light green body, grocery store interior, red/white Home Service labels, smooth hubs, rubber tires, Model No. 407-A
EX $70 **NM** $110 **MIP** $185

❏ **Radio Roadshow Van,** 1982, white body, red plastic roof and rear interior, opaque black windows, red-white-black Radio Tele Luxembourg labels, gray plastic loudspeakers and working radio in van, Model No. 1006-A
EX $25 **NM** $35 **MIP** $60

❏ **Security Van,** 1976-79, black body, blue mesh windows and dome light, yellow/black Security labels, Whizz Wheels, Model No. 424-B
EX $7 **NM** $15 **MIP** $25

❏ **Volkswagen Delivery Van,** 1962-64, white upper and red lower body, plastic red or yellow interior, silver bumpers and headlights, red VW emblem, shaped wheels, Model No. 433-A
EX $55 **NM** $85 **MIP** $140

❏ **Volkswagen Kombi Bus,** 1962-66, off-green upper and olive green lower body, red interior, silver bumpers and headlights, red VW emblem, shaped wheels, Model No. 434-A
EX $50 **NM** $75 **MIP** $125

(KP Photo by Dr. Douglas Sadecky)

❏ **Volkswagen Tobler Van,** 1963-67, light blue body, plastic interior, silver bumpers, Trans-o-lite headlights and roof panel, shaped wheels, rubber tires, Model No. 441-A
EX $55 **NM** $85 **MIP** $140

VINTAGE

DINKY

AIRCRAFT

❏ **A.W. Ensign,** 1940, camouflaged, dark variation, Model No. 68a
EX $150   **NM** $300   **MIP** $450

❏ **A.W. Ensign,** 1945-49, A.W. Airliner, silver, G-ADSV, Model No. 62P
EX $65   **NM** $145   **MIP** $175

❏ **A.W. Ensign,** 1945-49, forty-seat airliner, olive/dark green, G-AZCA, Model No. 62x
EX $95   **NM** $275   **MIP** $350

❏ **Airspeed Envoy,** 1938-40, King's Aeroplane, red, blue, and silver, G-AEXX, Model No. 62k
EX $70   **NM** $200   **MIP** $300

❏ **Airspeed Envoy,** 1938-41, silver, G-ACVI, Model No. 62m
EX $55   **NM** $175   **MIP** $250

❏ **Airspeed Envoy,** 1945-49, light transport, red, G-ATMH, Model No. 62m
EX $40   **NM** $125   **MIP** $200

❏ **Amiot 370,** 1939-48, Model No. 64a
EX $70   **NM** $130   **MIP** $200

❏ **Arc-en-Ciel,** 1935-40, Model No. 60a
EX $200   **NM** $375   **MIP** $450

❏ **Armstrong Whitworth Ensign,** 1938-41, silver, G-ADSR, Model No. 62p
EX $90   **NM** $175   **MIP** $250

❏ **Atalanta,** 1940, camouflaged, dark variation, Model No. 66a
EX $200   **NM** $450   **MIP** $650

❏ **Atalanta (Imperial Airways Liner),** 1934-41, gold, G-ABTI, Model No. 60a
EX $150   **NM** $375   **MIP** $500

❏ **Autogyro,** 1934-41, gold, blue rotor, w/pilot, Model No. 60f
EX $90   **NM** $180   **MIP** $250

❏ **Autogyro,** 1940, Army cooperation, silver, RAF roundels, Model No. 66f
EX $125   **NM** $250   **MIP** $350

❏ **Avro Vulcan Delta Wing Bomber,** 1955-56, Model No. 749/992
EX $800   **NM** $1500   **MIP** $4500

❏ **Avro York,** 1946-59, silver, G-AGJC, Model No. 70a/704
EX $45   **NM** $155   **MIP** $200

❏ **Beechcraft Baron,** 1968-76, Model No. 715
EX $25   **NM** $60   **MIP** $90

❏ **Beechcraft Bonanza,** 1965-76, Model No. 710
EX $20   **NM** $55   **MIP** $80

❏ **Beechcraft T42A,** 1972-77, Model No. 712
EX $30   **NM** $75   **MIP** $110

❏ **Bell 47 Police Helicopter,** 1974-80, Model No. 732
EX $10   **NM** $30   **MIP** $55

❏ **Bloch 220,** 1939-48, Model No. 64b
EX $75   **NM** $150   **MIP** $250

❏ **Boeing 737,** 1970-75, Model No. 717
EX $20   **NM** $45   **MIP** $90

❏ **Boeing Flying Fortress,** 1939-41, silver, USAAC stars on wings, Model No. 62g
EX $100   **NM** $200   **MIP** $300

❏ **Boeing Flying Fortress,** 1945-48, "Long Range Bomber" under wings, Model No. 62g
EX $50   **NM** $125   **MIP** $225

❏ **Breguet Corsair,** 1935-40, Model No. 60d
EX $100   **NM** $200   **MIP** $300

❏ **Bristol 173 Helicopter,** 1956-63, turquoise, red rotors, G-AUXR, Model No. 715
EX $20   **NM** $60   **MIP** $95

❏ **Bristol Blenheim,** Model No. 62B
EX $60   **NM** $85   **MIP** $130

❏ **Bristol Blenheim,** 1940-41, silver, roundels w/outer yellow ring, Model No. 62b/62d
EX $60   **NM** $140   **MIP** $175

❏ **Bristol Blenheim,** 1945-48, medium bomber; silver, red, and blue roundels, Model No. 62B
EX $35   **NM** $95   **MIP** $120

(KP Photo by Dr. Douglas Sadecky)

❏ **Bristol Brittania,** 1959-65, silver, blue line, CF-CZA. Canadian Pacific shown, Model No. 998
EX $50   **NM** $250   **MIP** $500

(KP Photo by Dr. Douglas Sadecky)

❏ **Caravelle S.E. 210,** 1959-62, Model No. 60f/891
EX $45   **NM** $170   **MIP** $230

❏ **Cierva Autogyro,** 1935-40, Model No. 60f
EX $100   **NM** $250   **MIP** $250

❏ **Clipper III Flying Boat,** 1938-41, silver, NC16736, Model No. 60w
EX $150   **NM** $250   **MIP** $400

❏ **Clipper III Flying Boat,** 1945-49, silver, no registration, Model No. 60w
EX $75   **NM** $175   **MIP** $250

❏ **D.H. Albatross,** 1939-41, Frobisher Class Liner, silver, G-AFDI, Model No. 62w
EX $75   **NM** $275   **MIP** $400

❏ **D.H. Albatross,** 1939-41, silver, G-AEVV, Model No. 62r
EX $75   **NM** $275   **MIP** $400

❏ **D.H. Albatross,** 1940, camouflaged, dark variation, Model No. 68b
EX $150   **NM** $300   **MIP** $450

❏ **D.H. Albatross,** 1945-49, four-engine liner; gray, G-ATPV, Model No. 62R
EX $75   **NM** $170   **MIP** $250

(KP Photo by Dr. Douglas Sadecky)

❏ **D.H. Comet Airliner,** 1954-65, silver wings, G-ALYX, wingspan 7-1/8", Model No. 702/999
EX $45   **NM** $105   **MIP** $200

❏ **D.H. Comet Racer,** 1935-40, silver, G-ACSR, Model No. 60g
EX $60   **NM** $125   **MIP** $225

❏ **D.H. Comet Racer,** 1946-49, yellow, G-RACE, Model No. 60g
EX $50   **NM** $110   **MIP** $155

❏ **D.H. Sea Vixen,** 1960-65, gray, white undersides, Model No. 738
EX $30   **NM** $65   **MIP** $110

❏ **Dewoitine 500,** 1935-40, Model No. 60e
EX $100   **NM** $200   **MIP** $300

❏ **Dewoitine D338,** 1937-46, Model No. 61a/64
EX $225   **NM** $350   **MIP** $500

❏ **Douglas DC3,** 1938-41, silver, PH-ALI, Model No. 60t
EX $125   **NM** $300   **MIP** $650

❏ **Empire Flying Boat,** 1937-41, silver, G-ADUV, solid front to hull, Model No. 60r
EX $150   **NM** $325   **MIP** $450

❏ **Empire Flying Boat,** 1937-41, MAIA, silver, G-AVKW, Model No. 700
EX $150   **NM** $275   **MIP** $350

❏ **Empire Flying Boat,** 1938-40, Atlantic Flying Boat, blue, cream wings, G-AZBP, Model No. 60x
EX $350   **NM** $600   **MIP** $1000

❏ **Empire Flying Boat,** 1945-49, silver, G-ADUV, hollowed out front to hull, Model No. 60r
EX $90   **NM** $175   **MIP** $250

❏ **Fairy Battle,** 1937-41, camouflaged, one roundel, light variation, Model No. 60s
EX $50   **NM** $125   **MIP** $200

❏ **Fairy Battle,** 1937-41, silver, "Fairy Battle Bomber" under wing, Model No. 60n
EX $40   **NM** $100   **MIP** $140

❏ **General Monospar,** 1934-41, silver, blue wing tips, Model No. 60e
EX $75   **NM** $225   **MIP** $300

❏ **General Monospar,** 1940, camouflaged, dark, Model No. 66e
EX $90   **NM** $300   **MIP** $350

❏ **Gloster Gladiator,** 1937-40, silver, RAF roundels, no words under wing, Model No. 60p
EX $90   **NM** $175   **MIP** $225

❏ **Gloster Javelin,** 1956-65, green/gray camouflage, wingspan, 3-1/4", Model No. 735
EX $15   **NM** $50   **MIP** $90

(KP Photo)

❏ **Gloster Meteor,** 1946-62, silver, RAF roundels, Model No. 70e/732
EX $10   **NM** $25   **MIP** $35

❏ **Hanriot 180M,** 1937-40, Model No. 61e
EX $90   **NM** $150   **MIP** $225

❏ **Hawker Harrier,** 1970-80, Model No. 722
EX $25   **NM** $65   **MIP** $95

❏ **Hawker Hunter,** 1955-63, green/gray camouflage, Model No. 736
EX $15   **NM** $45   **MIP** $85

❏ **Hawker Hurricane,** 1939-41, silver, no undercarriage, Model No. 62h
EX $30   **NM** $70   **MIP** $115

❏ **Hawker Hurricane,** 1945-49, three-blade prop; red, white, and blue roundels, Model No. 62S
EX $40   **NM** $95   **MIP** $130

❏ **Hawker Hurricane IIc,** 1972-75, Model No. 718
EX $50   **NM** $95   **MIP** $155

❏ **Hawker Siddeley HS 125,** 1970-75, Model No. 723/728
EX $20   **NM** $50   **MIP** $75

❏ **Hawker Tempest II,** 1946-55, silver, RAF roundels, flat spinner, Model No. 70b/730
EX $15   **NM** $45   **MIP** $75

❏ **Henriot 180T,** 1935-40, Model No. 60c
EX $110   **NM** $170   **MIP** $225

❏ **Junkers JU87B Stuka,** 1969-80, Model No. 721
EX $40   **NM** $75   **MIP** $145

❏ **Junkers JU89,** 1938-41, high speed monoplane, green/dark green, D-AZBK, Model No. 62y
EX $100   **NM** $275   **MIP** $350

❏ **Junkers JU89,** 1945-49, high speed monoplane, silver, G-ATBK, Model No. 62Y
EX $70   **NM** $160   **MIP** $225

❏ **Junkers JU89 Heavy Bomber,** 1941, black, German cross, Model No. 67a
EX $100   **NM** $400   **MIP** $600

❏ **Junkers JU90 Airliner,** 1938-40, silver, D-AIVI, Model No. 62n
EX $90   **NM** $250   **MIP** $325

❏ **Leopard Moth,** 1934-41, light green, G-ACPT, Model No. 60b
EX $50   **NM** $140   **MIP** $180

❏ **Leopard Moth,** 1940, camouflaged, dark, Model No. 66b
EX $70   **NM** $225   **MIP** $300

❏ **Lockheed P-80 Shooting Star,** 1947-62, silver, USAF stars, Model No. 701/733
EX $10   **NM** $20   **MIP** $30

❏ **M.D. F-4 Phantom,** 1972-77, Model No. 725/727/73
EX $70   **NM** $125   **MIP** $175

❏ **Mayo Composite,** 1939-41, Model No. 63
EX $200   **NM** $450   **MIP** $750

❏ **ME BI 109,** 1972-76, motorized, Model No. 726
EX $50   **NM** $100   **MIP** $175

❏ **Mercury Seaplane,** 1939-41, silver, G-ADHJ, Model No. 63b
EX $50   **NM** $100   **MIP** $175

❏ **Mercury Seaplane,** 1949-57, silver, G-AVKW, Model No. 700
EX $35   **NM** $75   **MIP** $110

❏ **Mitsubishi A65M Zero,** 1975-78, motorized, Model No. 739
EX $75   **NM** $150   **MIP** $225

❏ **MRCA Tornado,** 1974-76, Model No. 729
EX $35   **NM** $90   **MIP** $155

❏ **Mystere IV,** 1957-63, Model No. 60a/800
EX $30   **NM** $75   **MIP** $110

❏ **Nord Noratlas,** 1960-64, Model No. 804
EX $125   **NM** $250   **MIP** $400

❏ **P1B Lightning,** 1959-69, silver, RAF roundels, Model No. 737
EX $20   **NM** $55   **MIP** $100

❏ **Percival Gull,** 1934-41, white, blue wing tips, Model No. 60c
EX $70   **NM** $150   **MIP** $225

❏ **Percival Gull,** 1940, camouflaged, dark, Model No. 66c
EX $100   **NM** $225   **MIP** $275

❏ **Percival Gull,** 1945-48, Light Tourer, light green, Model No. 66c
EX $65   **NM** $125   **MIP** $150

❏ **Potez 56,** 1937-40, Model No. 61b
EX $125   **NM** $200   **MIP** $270

❏ **Potez 58,** 1935-40, Model No. 60b/61d
EX $100   **NM** $260   **MIP** $350

❏ **Potez 58 Sanitaire,** 1937-40, Model No. 61d
EX $110   **NM** $175   **MIP** $250

❏ **Potez 63,** 1939-48, Model No. 64c
EX $150   **NM** $250   **MIP** $400

❏ **Potez 662,** 1939-40, Model No. 64d
EX $125   **NM** $250   **MIP** $400

❏ **Republic P47 Thunderbolt,** 1975-78, motorized, Model No. 734
EX $75   **NM** $175   **MIP** $250

❏ **S.E. Caravelle Airliner,** 1962-69, Air France, F-BGNY, starboard wing, Model No. 997
EX $70   **NM** $150   **MIP** $250

❏ **Sea King Helicopter,** 1971-79, motorized, Model No. 724/736
EX $15   **NM** $35   **MIP** $85

❏ **SEPCAT Jaguar,** 1973-76, Model No. 731
EX $25   **NM** $70   **MIP** $115

❏ **Short Shetland Flying Boat,** 1947-49, silver, G-AGVD, Model No. 701
EX $200   **NM** $550   **MIP** $750

❏ **Sikorsky S58 Helicopter,** 1957-61, Model No. 60d/802
EX $45   **NM** $135   **MIP** $190

❏ **Singapore Flying Boat,** 1936-41, four-engine, silver, G-EUTG, Model No. 60m
EX $125   **NM** $400   **MIP** $550

❏ **Singapore Flying Boat,** 1936-41, silver, RAF roundels, Model No. 60h
EX $100   **NM** $300   **MIP** $400

❏ **Spitfire,** 1940-41, silver, small canopy, roundels red, white, and blue, Model No. 62e/62a
EX $35   **NM** $150   **MIP** $200

❏ **Spitfire,** 1945-49, silver, large canopy, roundels red, white, and blue, Model No. 62A
EX $30   **NM** $75   **MIP** $125

❏ **Spitfire II,** 1978-80, non-motorized, Model No. 741
EX $40   **NM** $80   **MIP** $135

❏ **Spitfire II,** 1979, chrome, Model No. 700
EX $65   **NM** $165   **MIP** $250

(KP Photo by Dr. Douglas Sadecky)

❏ **Super G Constellation Lockheed,** 1956-63, Wingspan, 7-3/4", Model No. 60c/892
EX $90   **NM** $200   **MIP** $350

❏ **Supermarine Spitfire II,** 1969-78, motorized, Model No. 719
EX $60   **NM** $95   **MIP** $175

❑ **Supermarine Swift,** 1955-63, green/gray camouflage, Model No. 734
EX $10   **NM** $45   **MIP** $85

❑ **Trident Star Fighter,** French-made, Model No. 362
EX $15   **NM** $30   **MIP** $60

❑ **Twin Engined Fighter,** 1946-55, silver, no registration, Model No. 70d/731
EX $10   **NM** $25   **MIP** $35

❑ **Vautour,** 1957-63, Model No. 60b/801
EX $30   **NM** $80   **MIP** $125

❑ **Vickers Jockey,** 1934-41, red, cream wing tips, Model No. 60d
EX $75   **NM** $110   **MIP** $150

❑ **Vickers Jockey,** 1940, camouflaged, dark, Model No. 66d
EX $75   **NM** $175   **MIP** $225

❑ **Vickers Viking,** 1947-63, silver, G-AGOL, flat spinners, Model No. 70c/705
EX $15   **NM** $40   **MIP** $65

(KP Photo by Dr. Douglas Sadecky)

❑ **Vickers Viscount,** 1956-65, British European Airways, G-AOJA, wingspan 5-7/8", Model No. 708
EX $40   **NM** $125   **MIP** $200

❑ **Vickers Viscount,** 1956-65, Air France, F-BGNL, Model No. 708
EX $40   **NM** $125   **MIP** $200

❑ **Viscount,** 1957-60, Model No. 60e/803
EX $75   **NM** $125   **MIP** $195

❑ **Vulcan Bomber,** 1955-56, silver, RAF roundels, Model No. 749/707/99
EX $500   **NM** $1500   **MIP** $4000

❑ **Westland Sikorsky Helicopter,** 1957-63, red/cream, G-ATWX, Model No. 716
EX $30   **NM** $75   **MIP** $125

❑ **Whitley Bomber,** 1937-41, silver, RAF roundels, Model No. 60v
EX $95   **NM** $150   **MIP** $225

❑ **Whitley Bomber,** 1937-41, camouflaged, light variation, Model No. 62t
EX $95   **NM** $300   **MIP** $350

BUSES AND TAXIS

(KP Photo)

❑ **Austin Taxi with Driver,** 1951-62, Pictured here with Robot Traffic Signal, 773 (which is 2-3/4" H and approx. $35 MIP), Model No. 40H/254
EX $65   **NM** $95   **MIP** $140

❑ **Austin/London Taxi,** 1972-79, Model No. 284
EX $25   **NM** $35   **MIP** $75

❑ **Autobus Parisien,** 1948-51, Model No. F29D
EX $80   **NM** $135   **MIP** $200

❑ **Autocar Chausson,** 1956-60, Model No. F29F/571
EX $70   **NM** $120   **MIP** $200

(ToyShop File Photo)

❑ **B.O.A.C. Coach,** 1956-63, Dark blue and white with "BOAC" lettering and symbol in yellow, Model No. 283
EX $55   **NM** $80   **MIP** $115

❑ **Continental Touring Coach,** 1963-66, Model No. 953
EX $135   **NM** $200   **MIP** $350

❑ **Ford Vedette Taxi,** 1956-59, Model No. F24XT
EX $60   **NM** $95   **MIP** $150

❑ **Observation Coach,** 1954-60, Model No. 29F/280
EX $50   **NM** $75   **MIP** $100

❑ **Peugeot 404 Taxi,** 1967-71, Model No. F1400
EX $50   **NM** $75   **MIP** $100

❑ **Plymouth Plaza Taxi,** 1960-67, Model No. 266
EX $65   **NM** $100   **MIP** $155

(D. Klein Photo)

❑ **Plymouth USA Taxi,** 1970s, Model No. 265
EX $15   **NM** $70   **MIP** $140

❑ **Routemaster Bus,** 1964-80, Tern Shirts, Model No. 289
EX $75   **NM** $100   **MIP** $150

❑ **Silver Jubilee Bus,** 1977, Model No. 297
EX $25   **NM** $35   **MIP** $70

CARS

❑ **Armstrong Siddeley,** 1937-40, blue or brown, Model No. 36A
EX $85   **NM** $130   **MIP** $225

❑ **Aston Martin DB5,** Model No. 110
EX $25   **NM** $60   **MIP** $120

❑ **Austin Atlantic Convertible,** 1954-58, blue, Model No. 106/140A
EX $60   **NM** $95   **MIP** $150

❑ **Austin Healey "100",** Model No. 109
EX $25   **NM** $60   **MIP** $120

❑ **Austin Mini-Moke,** 1967-75, Model No. 342
EX $20   **NM** $30   **MIP** $55

❑ **Beach Buggy,** Model No. 227
EX $5   **NM** $20   **MIP** $40

❑ **Big Cat Jaguar,** Model No. 219
EX $5   **NM** $12   **MIP** $40

❑ **Cabriolet 404 Peugeot Pininfarina,** Model No. 528
EX $25   **NM** $100   **MIP** $200

❑ **Cadillac 1962,** Model No. 147
EX $25   **NM** $60   **MIP** $120

❑ **Cadillac Eldorado,** 1956-62, Model No. 131
EX $60   **NM** $95   **MIP** $135

❑ **Chrysler Airflow,** 1935-40, Model No. 32/30A
EX $130   **NM** $250   **MIP** $450

❑ **Chrysler Royal Saloon,** Note that some colors are worth more than values shown, Model No. 39e
EX $45   **NM** $150   **MIP** $300

❑ **Chrysler Saratoga,** 1961-66, Model No. F550
EX $70   **NM** $100   **MIP** $190

❑ **Chrysler Simca 1308/GT,** Model No. 11542
EX $25   **NM** $60   **MIP** $120

❑ **Citroen 2 CV,** 1959-63, Model No. F535/24T
EX $50   **NM** $70   **MIP** $90

❑ **Citroen DS-19,** 1959-68, Model No. F522/24C
EX $60   **NM** $90   **MIP** $135

❑ **Cooper-Bristol Racer,** Model No. 233
EX $20   **NM** $40   **MIP** $170

❑ **Corvette Stingray,** Model No. 221
EX $10   **NM** $25   **MIP** $50

❑ **Cunningham C-5R Racer,** Model No. 133
EX $20   **NM** $50   **MIP** $100

❑ **Custom Land Rover,** Model No. 202
EX $5   **NM** $15   **MIP** $60

❑ **Custom Stingray,** Model No. 206
EX $5   **NM** $15   **MIP** $60

❑ **Customized Freeway Cruiser,** Model No. 390
EX $5   **NM** $15   **MIP** $40

❑ **Customized Range Rover,** Model No. 203
EX $5   **NM** $15   **MIP** $40

❑ **De Tomaso-Mangusta,** Model No. 137
EX $5   **NM** $10   **MIP** $40

❑ **DeSoto Diplomat,** 1960-63, orange, Model No. F545
EX $25   **NM** $85   **MIP** $160

❏ **DeSoto Diplomat,** 1960-63, green, Model No. F545
EX $70   NM $100   MIP $190

❏ **DeSoto Fireflite,** Model No. 192
EX $25   NM $70   MIP $140

(KP Photo)

❏ **Dodge Royal Sedan,** 1959-64, available in various color schemes, Model No. 191
EX $80   NM $120   MIP $160

❏ **E Type Jaguar,** Model No. 120
EX $20   NM $60   MIP $120

❏ **Estate Car,** 1954-61, Model No. 27D/344
EX $45   NM $70   MIP $115

❏ **Ferrari Racer,** Model No. 242
EX $15   NM $30   MIP $60

❏ **Ford Cortina Rally Car,** 1967-69, Model No. 212
EX $35   NM $55   MIP $75

❏ **Ford Escort,** Model No. 168
EX $30   NM $60   MIP $120

❏ **Ford Fairlane,** Model No. 149
EX $25   NM $50   MIP $100

❏ **Ford Fairlane,** 1962-66, South African Issue, bright blue, Model No. 148
EX $150   NM $300   MIP $700

❏ **Ford Fairlane,** 1962-66, pale green, Model No. 148
EX $30   NM $55   MIP $80

❏ **Ford Thunderbird,** South African Issue, blue, Model No. F565
EX $120   NM $250   MIP $600

❏ **Ford Thunderbird,** 1965-67, (Hong Kong), Model No. 57/005
EX $50   NM $70   MIP $100

❏ **Ford Thunderbird Coupe,** Model No. 1419
EX $25   NM $70   MIP $140

❏ **Hesketh 308E Racing Car,** Model No. 222
EX $20   NM $40   MIP $75

❏ **Hillman Minx,** Model No. 40f
EX $20   NM $75   MIP $150

❏ **Hudson Commodore Sedan,** Cream and blue body, Model No. 171
EX $25   NM $100   MIP $200

❏ **Hudson Commodore Sedan,** Hi-Line, Model No. 171
EX $50   NM $200   MIP $400

(ToyShop File Photo)

❏ **Hudson Hornet Sedan,** Yellow and brown, white tires, Model No. 174
EX $25   NM $80   MIP $160

❏ **Humber Hawk,** Model No. 165
EX $25   NM $80   MIP $160

❏ **HWM Racer,** Model No. 235
EX $25   NM $70   MIP $140

❏ **Jaguar 3.4 Saloon,** Model No. 195
EX $25   NM $80   MIP $160

❏ **Jaguar D-Type,** 1957-65, Model No. 238
EX $60   NM $86   MIP $125

❏ **Jaguar SS 100 Sports Car,** Model No. 38f
EX $30   NM $100   MIP $200

❏ **Jaguar XK 120,** 1954-62, yellow/gray, Model No. 157
EX $80   NM $125   MIP $250

❏ **Jaguar XK 120,** 1954-62, white, Model No. 157
EX $120   NM $200   MIP $400

❏ **Jaguar XK 120,** 1954-62, turquoise, cerise, Model No. 157
EX $80   NM $125   MIP $250

(KP Photo by Dr. Douglas Sadecky)

❏ **Jaguar XK 120,** 1959-62, gray-green, yellow or red, Model No. 157
EX $95   NM $210   MIP $375

❏ **Jensen FF,** Model No. 188
EX $15   NM $50   MIP $100

❏ **Lamborghini Marzal,** Model No. 189
EX $10   NM $20   MIP $60

❏ **Lotus F1 Racing Car,** Model No. 225
EX $10   NM $20   MIP $40

❏ **Lotus Racing Car,** 1963-70, Model No. 241
EX $20   NM $30   MIP $50

❏ **Maserati Race Car,** 1954-64, Model No. 231
EX $45   NM $75   MIP $110

❏ **McLaren M8A Can Am Racer,** Model No. 223
EX $10   NM $20   MIP $40

❏ **Mercedes 190 SL,** Model No. 526
EX $25   NM $100   MIP $200

❏ **Mercedes-Benz C111,** Model No. 224
EX $5   NM $20   MIP $50

❏ **MG Midget Sports Car,** Model No. 108
EX $25   NM $100   MIP $200

❏ **MGB Sports Car,** Model No. 113
EX $25   NM $60   MIP $130

❏ **Mustang Fastback,** 1965-73, Model No. 161
EX $35   NM $55   MIP $75

❏ **Nash Rambler,** Model No. 173
EX $20   NM $70   MIP $140

❏ **Packard Convertible,** Model No. 132
EX $25   NM $80   MIP $160

❏ **Packard Super 8 Tourer,** Model No. 39a
EX $25   NM $80   MIP $160

❏ **Panhard PL17,** 1960-68, Model No. F547
EX $45   NM $80   MIP $120

❏ **Pathe News Camera Car,** 1967-70, Model No. 281
EX $70   NM $105   MIP $180

❏ **Peugeot 203 Berline Saloon,** Model No. 24r
EX $25   NM $100   MIP $200

❏ **Peugeot 403 Sedan,** 1959-61, Model No. F521/24B
EX $50   NM $90   MIP $135

❏ **Plymouth Belvedere,** Model No. 24D
EX $35   NM $150   MIP $300

❏ **Plymouth Estate Car,** Model No. 27F
EX $20   NM $70   MIP $140

❏ **Plymouth Fury Convertible,** Model No. 137G
EX $20   NM $60   MIP $120

❏ **Plymouth Fury Sports,** 1965-69, Model No. 115
EX $35   NM $55   MIP $80

❏ **Plymouth Plaza,** white roof, harder-to-find version, Model No. 178
EX $25   NM $150   MIP $300

❏ **Plymouth Plaza,** Model No. 178
EX $25   NM $75   MIP $150

❏ **Plymouth Stock Car,** Model No. 201
EX $10   NM $20   MIP $40

❏ **Pontiac Parisienne,** Model No. 173
EX $20   NM $50   MIP $100

❏ **Rambler Cross Country Station Wagon,** Model No. 193
EX $20   NM $70   MIP $140

❏ **Range Rover,** Model No. 192
EX $5   NM $20   MIP $60

❏ **Renault Dauphine,** 1959-62, Model No. F524/24E
EX $50   NM $80   MIP $125

Rolls Royce Phantom V, Model No. 194
EX n/a   NM n/a   MIP n/a

Rolls Royce Silver Wraith, Model No. 150
EX $20   NM $60   MIP $120

Rolls-Royce, 1946-50, Model No. 30B
EX $65   NM $100   MIP $125

Rolls-Royce Phantom V, 1962-69, Model No. 198
EX $50   NM $75   MIP $100

Rover 3500, Model No. 180
EX $5   NM $20   MIP $60

Singer Vogue, 1962-67, Model No. 145
EX $50   NM $75   MIP $100

Standard Vanguard, 1954-60, Model No. 153
EX $60   NM $85   MIP $120

Streamline Racer, harder to find and subsequently, worth more, in red finish, Model No. 23s
EX $20   NM $40   MIP $80

(KP Photo)

Studebaker Commander, 1959-61, another in the line of French-made Dinky toys, Model No. F24Y/540
EX $75   NM $95   MIP $160

Studebaker Golden Hawk, Model No. 169
EX $25   NM $80   MIP $160

Studebaker Land Cruiser, single color body, Model No. 172
EX $25   NM $80   MIP $160

Studebaker Land Cruiser, two-toned version, harder-to-find, Model No. 172
EX $25   NM $150   MIP $300

Studebaker President, Model No. 179
EX $25   NM $80   MIP $160

Sunbeam Alpine, Model No. 107
EX $20   NM $80   MIP $160

Town Sedan, 1934-40, Model No. 24C
EX $85   NM $130   MIP $200

Triumph Spitfire, Model No. 114
EX $20   NM $75   MIP $150

Triumph TR2, Model No. 111
EX $20   NM $100   MIP $200

(KP Photo)

Triumph TR-2, 1957-60, yellow, pictured here with 773 Robot Traffic Signal, Model No. 105
EX $75   NM $120   MIP $200

Triumph TR-2, 1957-60, gray, Model No. 105
EX $60   NM $85   MIP $135

Universal Jeep, green or red body, Model No. 405
EX $25   NM $60   MIP $120

Vanguard, Model No. 40e
EX $25   NM $75   MIP $150

Vanwall Race Car, Model No. 239
EX $20   NM $60   MIP $130

Vauxhall, Model No. 151
EX $20   NM $50   MIP $100

Volkswagen 1300 Sedan, 1965-76, Model No. 129
EX $20   NM $35   MIP $75

Volkswagen Karmann-Ghia, 1959-64, Model No. 187
EX $45   NM $80   MIP $125

Volkswagen VW 1600 TL, Model No. 163
EX $15   NM $40   MIP $100

Volkswagen VW Beetle, green body, Model No. 181
EX $20   NM $50   MIP $100

Volvo 1800S, Model No. 116
EX $20   NM $60   MIP $120

(KP Photo)

Volvo 265 DL Estate, 1977-79, Blue, with opening rear hatch and brown plastic interior, black grille, Model No. 122
EX $12   NM $22   MIP $45

VW Porsche 914, Model No. 208
EX $15   NM $30   MIP $80

CHARACTER & TV RELATED

"Emergency" Rescue Paramedic Truck, Model No. 267
EX $10   NM $45   MIP $90

Galactic War Chariot, 1979-80, Model No. 361
EX $30   NM $45   MIP $70

Joe's Car, 1969-75, Model No. 102
EX $60   NM $90   MIP $140

Klingon Battle Cruiser, 1976-79, Model No. 357
EX $30   NM $45   MIP $70

Lady Penelope's Fab 1, 1966-76, shocking pink version, Model No. 100
EX $115   NM $200   MIP $340

(ToyShop File Photo)

Lady Penelope's Fab 1, 1966-76, pink version, Model No. 100
EX $80   NM $135   MIP $220

(KP Photo by Dr. Douglas Sadecky)

Parsley's Car Morris Oxford, 1970-72, Cut-out stand-up figures of Parsley's friends were included for additional play, Model No. 477
EX $65   NM $115   MIP $145

Prisoner Mini-Moke, 1967-70, Model No. 106
EX $120   NM $210   MIP $345

Renault Sinpar, 1968-71, Model No. F1406
EX $80   NM $135   MIP $220

Santa Special Model T Ford, 1964-68, Model No. 485
EX $65   NM $100   MIP $150

Tiny's Mini-Moke, 1970-73, Model No. 350
EX $60   NM $85   MIP $120

(KP Photo)

U.S.S. Enterprise, 1980, Model No. 371/803
EX $30   NM $45   MIP $70

CONSTRUCTION

Atlas Digger, Model No. 984
EX $30   NM $45   MIP $70

Bedford Tipper, orange, Model No. 410
EX $20   NM $75   MIP $150

Blaw Knox Bulldozer, Model No. 561
EX $45   NM $75   MIP $115

Coles Crane, Model No. 972
EX $10   NM $40   MIP $80

❏ **Coles Hydra Crane Truck 150T**, Yellow with black chassis, swivel crane section with working boom and hook, working levellers. 210mm, Model No. 980
EX $10   **NM** $40   **MIP** $80

❏ **Coles Mobile Crane**, 1955-66, Model No. 971
EX $40   **NM** $70   **MIP** $110

❏ **Conventry Climax Fork Lift**, Model No. 401
EX $15   **NM** $40   **MIP** $80

❏ **Conveyancer Fork Lift Truck**, Includes driver and pallet. Rear wheels turn, Model No. 404
EX $15   **NM** $30   **MIP** $60

❏ **Dinky Shovel Dozer**, Yellow body, red-roofed cab, rolling treads, lifting and dumping bucket, Model No. 977
EX $10   **NM** $40   **MIP** $80

❏ **Dumper Truck**, Model No. 382
EX $5   **NM** $10   **MIP** $20

❏ **Eaton Yale Articulated Tractor Shovel**, Model No. 973
EX $10   **NM** $40   **MIP** $80

(KP Photo)

❏ **Euclid Dump Truck**, 1955-69, with lever-operated tipping bed. Part of the "Dinky Supertoys" range, Model No. 965
EX $55   **NM** $80   **MIP** $125

❏ **Ford D800 Snow Plow Tipper**, Blue cab with opening doors, silver tipping section with opening tailgate, yellow plow raises and lowers. 194mm, Model No. 439
EX $10   **NM** $40   **MIP** $80

❏ **Johnson 2-Ton Dumper**, Yellow open-cab articulated body with driver, red tipper section, 106mm, Model No. 430
EX $5   **NM** $30   **MIP** $60

❏ **Lorry Mounted Concrete Mixer**, Model No. 960
EX $10   **NM** $50   **MIP** $100

❏ **Michigan 180-111 Tractor Dozer**, Yellow body, silver engine, red blade raises and lowers, cab is removeable, Model No. 976
EX $10   **NM** $40   **MIP** $80

❏ **Muir Hill Dumper Truck**, Model No. 962
EX $15   **NM** $30   **MIP** $60

❏ **Muir Hill Loader & Trencher**, Yellow tractor body with working loader and backhoe. 163mm, Model No. 967
EX $5   **NM** $30   **MIP** $60

❏ **Muir Hill Two-Wheel Loader**, 1962-78, Model No. 437
EX $30   **NM** $40   **MIP** $60

❏ **Richier Road Roller**, 1959-69, Model No. F830
EX $75   **NM** $100   **MIP** $150

(ToyShop File Photo)

❏ **Road Grader**, 1973-75, Yellow and red with swivel blade, Model No. 963
EX $30   **NM** $45   **MIP** $70

❏ **Salev Crane**, 1959-61, Model No. F595
EX $65   **NM** $100   **MIP** $175

❏ **Simca Tipper Dump Truck**, French-made, Model No. 33
EX $30   **NM** $90   **MIP** $180

EMERGENCY VEHICLES

❏ **Airport Fire Engine**, Model No. 263
EX $10   **NM** $40   **MIP** $80

(KP Photo by Dr. Douglas Sadecky)

❏ **Airport Fire Tender with Flashing Light**, 1962-69, Model No. 276
EX $32   **NM** $65   **MIP** $100

❏ **Ambulance**, Model No. 30F
EX $100   **NM** $160   **MIP** $275

❏ **Bedford Fire Escape**, 1969-74, Model No. 956
EX $75   **NM** $110   **MIP** $175

(KP Photo by Dr. Douglas Sadecky)

❏ **Berliet Fire Pumper**, Included two detachable hose reels as accessories. French-made Dinky toy, Model No. 32E
EX $75   **NM** $95   **MIP** $120

❏ **Citroen DS19 Police Car**, 1967-70, Model No. F501
EX $75   **NM** $95   **MIP** $175

❏ **Citroen Fire Van**, 1959-63, Model No. F25D/562
EX $80   **NM** $110   **MIP** $250

❏ **Commer Fire Engine**, 1955-69, Model No. 955
EX $60   **NM** $85   **MIP** $135

❏ **Convoy Rescue Fire Truck**, Model No. 384
EX $5   **NM** $20   **MIP** $40

❏ **Crash Squad set**, With Bell Helicopter and Plymouth Police Car, Model No. 299
EX $10   **NM** $40   **MIP** $80

❏ **Daimler Ambulance**, Model No. 254
EX $15   **NM** $60   **MIP** $120

(KP Photo by Dr. Douglas Sadecky)

❏ **Delahaye Fire Truck**, 1955-70, the white tires really enhance this French-made Dinky toy, Model No. F32D/899
EX $120   **NM** $190   **MIP** $375

❏ **DeSoto USA Police Car**, Model No. 258
EX $10   **NM** $60   **MIP** $120

❏ **ERF Fire Tender**, Red body, removable extending escape ladder with wheels, Model No. 266
EX $15   **NM** $50   **MIP** $100

❏ **Fire Chief Land Rover**
EX $35   **NM** $50   **MIP** $85

❏ **Fire Chief's Range Rover**, Red body, opening hood, tailgate and doors, Model No. 195
EX $5   **NM** $30   **MIP** $60

❏ **Fire Engine**, Model No. 555
EX $25   **NM** $65   **MIP** $130

❏ **Ford Escort Panda Police Car**, Model No. 270
EX $5   **NM** $30   **MIP** $60

❏ **Ford Police Car**, 1960s, Model No. F551
EX $50   **NM** $100   **MIP** $150

❏ **Ford Transit Ambulance**, Model No. 274
EX $5   **NM** $25   **MIP** $50

(ToyShop File Photo)

❏ **Ford Transit Fire Appliance**, Red with silver ladder and sliding door, Model No. 286
EX $5   **NM** $25   **MIP** $50

☐ **Ford Transit Police Accident Unit**, Model No. 269
EX $5   NM $30   MIP $60

☐ **Merryweather Marquis Fire Tender**, 1970s, Red body with removeable silver ladder and working fire pump, Model No. 285
EX $5   NM $50   MIP $100

(KP Photo)

☐ **Mersey Tunnel Police Land Rover**, 1955-61, Model No. 255
EX $60   NM $85   MIP $135

☐ **Motorway Services Ford Transit Van**, 1970s, Yellow body with "Motorway Services" on panel sides, Model No. 417
EX $5   NM $25   MIP $50

☐ **Nash Rambler Canadian Fire Chief's Car**, Model No. 257
EX $10   NM $40   MIP $80

☐ **Plymouth Police Car**, Model No. 244
EX $5   NM $30   MIP $60

☐ **Plymouth Police Car**, 1977-80, Model No. 244
EX $25   NM $35   MIP $50

☐ **Police Accident Unit**, Model No. 287
EX $5   NM $30   MIP $60

☐ **Police Land Rover**, Model No. 277
EX $5   NM $30   MIP $60

☐ **Police Mini Clubman**, 1976, Light blue with opening white doors and "Police" on sides, Model No. 255
EX $5   NM $30   MIP $60

☐ **Police Range Rover**, White body, orange stripe on sides, opening hood, doors and tailgate. 109mm, Model No. 254
EX $5   NM $30   MIP $60

(ToyShop File Photo)

☐ **Range Rover Ambulance**, 1974-78, With opening hood, doors and tailgate. Includes patient on stretcher, Model No. 268
EX $25   NM $35   MIP $50

☐ **RCMP Ford Fairlane**, Model No. 264
EX $10   NM $60   MIP $120

☐ **Rover 3500 Police**, Model No. 264
EX $5   NM $30   MIP $60

☐ **Streamline Fire Engine**, Model No. 250
EX $15   NM $60   MIP $120

☐ **Streamlined Fire Engine**, 1946-53, Model No. 25H/25
EX $75   NM $100   MIP $175

(KP Photo)

☐ **Superior Cadillac Ambulance**, 1971-79, opening rear hatch with plastic patient on stretcher, Model No. 288
EX $15   NM $28   MIP $60

☐ **Superior Criterion Ambulance**, 1962-68, Model No. 263
EX $50   NM $75   MIP $100

(KP Photo by Dr. Douglas Sadecky)

☐ **Superior Criterion Ambulance**, 1962-68, The roof beacon warning light actually flashed with the aid of a small battery, Model No. 277
EX $40   NM $75   MIP $110

☐ **USA Police Car (Pontiac)**, Model No. 251
EX $35   NM $50   MIP $85

☐ **Vauxhall Victor Ambulance**, 1964-70, Model No. 278
EX $55   NM $85   MIP $115

☐ **Volvo Police Car**, 1970s, Same body as 265 Estate, but in white with orange stripes, Model No. 243
EX $5   NM $30   MIP $60

FARM

☐ **Convoy Farm Truck**, Model No. 381
EX $5   NM $15   MIP $30

☐ **David Brown Tractor**, 1966-75, Model No. 305
EX $35   NM $50   MIP $75

☐ **Field Marshall Tractor**, 1954-65, Model No. 37N/301
EX $60   NM $85   MIP $150

(KP Photo)

☐ **Garden Roller**, 1948-54, Model No. 105A
EX $15   NM $25   MIP $35

☐ **Halesowen Harvest Trailer**, Model No. 320
EX $10   NM $30   MIP $60

☐ **Hayrake**, 1954-71, Model No. 324
EX $30   NM $40   MIP $60

☐ **Massey-Harris Tractor**, Model No. 27A/300
EX $50   NM $75   MIP $120

☐ **Moto-Cart**, 1954-60, Model No. 27G/342
EX $35   NM $50   MIP $75

☐ **Wheelbarrow**, Model No. 382
EX $10   NM $20   MIP $40

MILITARY

☐ **1 Ton Cargo Truck**, Model No. 641
EX $20   NM $40   MIP $80

☐ **10 Ton Army Truck**, 1954-63, Model No. 622
EX $20   NM $40   MIP $80

☐ **105mm U.S. Howitzer with Crew**, Model No. 609
EX $20   NM $40   MIP $80

☐ **155mm Mobile Gun**, Model No. 654
EX $25   NM $50   MIP $100

☐ **155mm self-propelled gun**, French-made toy, Model No. 813
EX $45   NM $90   MIP $180

☐ **25-pounder Field Gun**, Model No. 686
EX $20   NM $40   MIP $85

☐ **25-pounder Field Gun with Tractor and Trailer**, Model No. 697
EX $55   NM $110   MIP $220

☐ **25-pounder gun trailer**, Model No. 687
EX $15   NM $30   MIP $60

(KP Photo)

☐ **5.5 Medium Gun**, 1955, Model No. 692
EX $15   NM $30   MIP $50

❏ **6-pounder anti-tank gun**, Model No. 625
EX $16   NM $32   MIP $65

❏ **7.2 Howitzer**, Model No. 693
EX $25   NM $50   MIP $100

❏ **88mm gun**, Model No. 656
EX $25   NM $50   MIP $100

❏ **AEC Arctic Transport with Helicopter**, Model No. 618
EX $50   NM $85   MIP $125

❏ **Alvis Scorpion**, 1970s, Turret fires plastic shells, includes camo netting. 1:40-scale, Model No. 690
EX $10   NM $40   MIP $80

❏ **AML Panhard Armored Car**, French-made Dinky Toy, Model No. 814
EX $30   NM $60   MIP $120

❏ **AMX 13 T Tank**, Model No. 801/80c
EX $35   NM $70   MIP $140

❏ **AMX Bridge Layer**, Lever extends folding bridge set on AMX tank chassis, Model No. F883
EX $75   NM $110   MIP $200

(KP Photo)

❏ **AMX Tank**, Model No. F80C/817
EX $50   NM $75   MIP $100

❏ **Armored Car**, Model No. 670
EX $25   NM $50   MIP $100

❏ **Armored Personnel Carrier**, Model No. 676
EX $25   NM $50   MIP $100

(KP Photo)

❏ **Armoured Command Vehicle**, Squared, longer bodied six-wheeled vehicle. Shown here with #641 Cargo Truck, Model No. 677
EX $50   NM $85   MIP $125

❏ **Army Covered Wagon**, Model No. 623
EX $40   NM $85   MIP $150

❏ **Army Field Kitchen Cuisine Roulante**, Trailer with two boilers/kettles, stovepipe, spare tire, Model No. 823
EX $30   NM $60   MIP $120

❏ **Army Jeep**, Model No. 669
EX $20   NM $40   MIP $80

❏ **Army Water Tanker**, Model No. 643
EX $25   NM $50   MIP $100

❏ **Austin Champ**, Model No. 674
EX $20   NM $40   MIP $80

❏ **Austin Champ**, Model No. 674
EX $20   NM $40   MIP $80

❏ **Austin Covered Truck**, Model No. 30SM/625
EX $85   NM $135   MIP $275

❏ **Austin Paramoke**, Includes parachute, vehicle holder and vehicle, Model No. 601
EX $25   NM $35   MIP $50

❏ **Bedford Military Truck**, Model No. 25WM/60
EX $80   NM $125   MIP $250

(ToyShop File Photo)

❏ **Berliet All Terrain 6x6 Truck**, Green body with canopy top over bed. Shown here with 80E/819 Howitzer, Model No. 80D/818
EX $40   NM $80   MIP $150

(KP Photo)

❏ **Berliet Missile Launcher**, Green six-wheeled truck with Nord R20 winged missile, Model No. 620
EX $75   NM $100   MIP $175

(ToyShop File Photo)

❏ **Berliet Tank Transporter**, Another French-made Dinky Toy, shown here with Panhard Armored Car, #815, Model No. 890
EX $65   NM $130   MIP $250

(ToyShop File Photo)

❏ **Berliet Wrecker**, Crane hook and swivel base, six-wheels, Model No. F826
EX $60   NM $120   MIP $240

❏ **Bren Gun Carrier**, Green body, working treads. Two figures included, 1:32-scale, Model No. 622
EX $10   NM $40   MIP $80

❏ **Bren Gun Carrier and Anti-Tank Gun**, Includes #622 Bren Gun Carrier with #625 6-pounder anti-tank gun that fires shells, Model No. 619
EX $15   NM $50   MIP $100

❏ **Centurian Tank**, Model No. 651
EX $30   NM $50   MIP $75

❏ **Centurion Tank**, Rolling rubber treads, swivel turret, raising and lowering gun barrel, Model No. 683
EX $45   NM $90   MIP $180

❏ **Chieftain Tank**, 1970s, With rolling treads, swivel turret, gun barrel that raises and lowers, white numbers on front, gold square emblem on turret. Fires shells, 1:50-scale, Model No. 683
EX $15   NM $50   MIP $100

❏ **Commando Jeep**, Model No. 612
EX $25   NM $35   MIP $50

❏ **Commando Squad Gift Set**, Model No. 303
EX $25   NM $70   MIP $140

❏ **Convoy Army Truck**, Green body with removeable plastic canopy. "Available Later" in 1977 catalog, Model No. 687
EX $5   NM $20   MIP $40

❏ **Cooker Trailer**, Model No. 151c
EX $25   NM $50   MIP $100

(ToyShop File Photo)

□ **Covered Army Transport Wagon,** 1937-41, Prewar toy, six-wheeled truck with black plastic tires. Molded driver, metal canopy, Model No. 151B
EX $50 NM $100 MIP $200

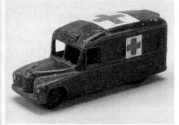

(KP Photo)

□ **Daimler Ambulance**, a popular casting available in military and civilian variations, Model No. 30HM/624
EX $80 NM $125 MIP $250

□ **Dodge Command Car**, Model No. F810
EX $40 NM $60 MIP $85

□ **DUKW Amphibian**, Green, open-topped body, 1:76-scale, Model No. 681
EX $10 NM $30 MIP $60

□ **EBR Panhard Armored Car**, 8-wheeled vehicle, 2 sets of road wheels, front and back, with two sets of floating all-terrain wheels in the center. Rotating turret, Model No. 80A/815
EX $30 NM $60 MIP $120

□ **Ferret Armored Car**, Green scout car with open turret, 1:48-scale, Model No. 680
EX $5 NM $20 MIP $40

□ **Ferret Armoured Car**, Model No. 630
EX $25 NM $35 MIP $50

□ **Field Artillery Tractor**, Model No. 688
EX $25 NM $50 MIP $90

□ **Foden Army Truck**, Model No. 668
EX $5 NM $30 MIP $60

□ **Ford U.S. Army Staff Car**, Model No. 170
EX $65 NM $130 MIP $250

□ **GMC Military Truck**, French-made, Model No. 809
EX $50 NM $100 MIP $200

□ **GMC Tanker**, Model No. F823
EX $125 NM $250 MIP $500

□ **Hanomag Tank Destroyer**, German Hanomag half-track with pivoting anti-tank gun that fires plastic shells. 1:35-scale, Model No. 694
EX $10 NM $40 MIP $80

(ToyShop File Photo)

□ **Honest John Missile Launcher**, Green truck with rubber-band powered plastic missile, Model No. 665
EX $45 NM $90 MIP $180

□ **Jeep**, Model No. F816
EX $50 NM $75 MIP $115

(ToyShop File Photo)

□ **Jeep**, Model No. 153a
EX $25 NM $50 MIP $100

□ **Jeep**, French-made, Model No. 80b
EX $30 NM $60 MIP $120

□ **Jeep avec Canon de 106**, French-made, Model No. 829
EX $25 NM $50 MIP $100

□ **Jeep Hotchkiss-Willys**, French-made, Model No. 816
EX $25 NM $50 MIP $100

□ **Jeep with Rocket Launcher**, French-made, Model No. 828
EX $35 NM $75 MIP $140

□ **Land Rover Bomb Disposal Unit,** 1976, Green Land-Rover Safari with orange quarter panels, blue dome light and "Explosive Disposal" sign on roof. Has opening doors and hood, and includes remote bomb-finding tank. 1:42-scale, Model No. 604
EX $20 NM $40 MIP $80

□ **Leopard Recovery Tank**, 1970s, Green with rolling treads, pivoting boom, raising and lowering blade, West German Bundeswehr markings. 1:50-scale, Model No. 699
EX $15 NM $50 MIP $100

□ **Leopard Tank**, Swivel turret, pivoting gun fires plastic shells, West German Army markings, Model No. 692
EX $15 NM $50 MIP $100

□ **Light Dragon Field Gun Set**, Model No. 162
EX $75 NM $150 MIP $300

□ **Light Dragon Tractor**, Model No. 162a
EX $40 NM $80 MIP $150

(ToyShop File Photo)

□ **Light Tank**, Green, metal treads, rolling tread wheels, Model No. 152A
EX $50 NM $100 MIP $200

□ **Light Tank Set**, Model No. 152
EX $125 NM $250 MIP $500

(ToyShop File Photo)

□ **M3 Halftrack**, Olive body, working treads, AA gun in turret, Model No. 822
EX $50 NM $100 MIP $200

(ToyShop File Photo)

□ **Medium Artillery Tractor**, Part of the Dinky Supertoys line, this model was 5-1/2" long. Shown here at bottom with #622 truck at top, Model No. 689
EX $25 NM $50 MIP $100

(ToyShop File Photo)

□ **Mercedes-Benz Military Unimog**, French-made toy, dark olive with canopy top over bed, shown here with 823 Field Kitchen trailer, Model No. 821
EX $30 NM $60 MIP $120

□ **Military Ambulance**, With Red Cross decals and opening rear doors, Model No. 626
EX $25 NM $45 MIP $75

□ **Military Ambulance**, Model No. F80F/820
EX $50 NM $75 MIP $100

(KP Photo by Dr. Douglas Sadecky)

❏ **Missile Erecting Vehicle,** 1959, with Corporal Missile and Launching Platform, Model No. 666
EX $100   **NM** $155   **MIP** $240

(KP Photo by Dr. Douglas Sadecky)

❏ **Missile Servicing Platform,** 1960, this vehicle made a nice companion to the 666 Missile Erecting Vehicle. A nicely detailed toy, it had a short production run, Model No. 667
EX $95   **NM** $130   **MIP** $270

❏ **Obusier 155mm Cannon,** French Dinky toy, four-wheeled chassis under cannon, Model No. 80E/819
EX $40   **NM** $80   **MIP** $160

(ToyShop File Photo)

❏ **RAF Pressure Refueller,** Dark gray body, part of the Dinky Supertoys line, 5-1/2" long. Shown here (top) in photo with #661 recovery tractor, Model No. 642
EX $40   **NM** $80   **MIP** $160

(KP Photo)

❏ **Reconnaisance Car,** This model was produced in pre- and post-war periods, Model No. 152B
EX $40   **NM** $60   **MIP** $100

(KP Photo)

❏ **Recovery Tractor,** 1957, Tow hook has working reel, Model No. 661
EX $60   **NM** $90   **MIP** $140

(ToyShop File Photo)

❏ **Scout Car,** Open-turret scout car, shown here at right with Austin Para-Moke, #601. 2-5/8", Model No. 673
EX $5   **NM** $40   **MIP** $80

(ToyShop File Photo)

❏ **Searchlight,** prewar, Model No. 161A
EX $125   **NM** $250   **MIP** $500

❏ **Sinpar 4x4 Military Police Vehicle,** Model No. 815
EX $30   **NM** $60   **MIP** $120

❏ **Stalwart Load Carrier,** Model No. 682
EX $10   **NM** $30   **MIP** $60

(ToyShop File Photo)

❏ **Static 88mm Gun with Crew,** Includes shells and three soldiers, Model No. 662
EX $10   **NM** $40   **MIP** $80

❏ **Stiker Anti-Tank Vehicle,** Angluar armored vehicle with 5-missile launcher that fires all rockets individually or at once
EX n/a   **NM** n/a   **MIP** n/a

❏ **Tank Transporter,** Model No. 660
EX $75   **NM** $100   **MIP** $175

(ToyShop File Photo)

❏ **Tank Transporter and Centurion Tank,** Includes #660 Tank Transporter with

#651 Centurion Tank. Shown here with single box for tank, Model No. 698
EX $45   **NM** $70   **MIP** $140

❏ **Tank Transporter with Chieftain Tank,** Model No. 616
EX $20   **NM** $60   **MIP** $120

❏ **Task Force Set,** Model No. 677
EX $20   **NM** $50   **MIP** $100

❏ **Three Ton Army Wagon,** 1954-63, Model No. 621
EX $50   **NM** $85   **MIP** $125

❏ **U.S. Jeep with 105mm Howitzer set,** Includes firing gun, Model No. 615
EX $20   **NM** $50   **MIP** $100

(ToyShop File Photo)

❏ **VW KDF (Kubelwagen) and PAK Anti-Tank gun,** Excellent two-piece set--the gun actually fires plastic shells, Model No. 617
EX $20   **NM** $50   **MIP** $100

MISCELLANEOUS

(KP Photo by Dr. Douglas Sadecky)

❏ **Healey Sports Boat on Trailer,** 1960-62, Model No. 796
EX $25   **NM** $35   **MIP** $55

❏ **Land Rover Trailer,** Model No. 341
EX $15   **NM** $40   **MIP** $80

❏ **Large Trailer,** Model No. 428
EX $15   **NM** $25   **MIP** $50

❏ **Loading ramp for Pullmore Car Transporter,** Model No. 994
EX $10   **NM** $20   **MIP** $40

MOTORCYCLES AND CARAVANS

❏ **4-Berth Caravan w/ Transparent Roof,** 1963-69, Model No. 188
EX $25   **NM** $45   **MIP** $85

(KP Photo by Dr. Douglas Sadecky)

VINTAGE

A.A. Motorcycle Patrol, 1946-64, the decal on the sidecar changed depending in which country the motorcycle was sold, Model No. 270/44B
EX $30   NM $45   MIP $70

Caravan, postwar, Model No. 30G
EX $40   NM $60   MIP $85

Caravan, prewar, Model No. 30G
EX $55   NM $85   MIP $150

Caravan, 1956-64, Model No. 190
EX $30   NM $45   MIP $60

Caravane Caravelair
EX $75   NM $150   MIP $250

Police Motorcycle Patrol, 1936-40, Model No. 42B
EX $50   NM $75   MIP $125

Police Motorcycle Patrol, 1946-53, Model No. 42B
EX $30   NM $45   MIP $70

Police Motorcyclist, 1938-40, Model No. 37B
EX $50   NM $75   MIP $125

Police Motorcyclist, 1946-48, Model No. 37B
EX $30   NM $45   MIP $70

Touring Secours Motorcycle Patrol, 1960s, Swiss version, Model No. 271
EX $70   NM $110   MIP $200

SHIPS

Coastguard Amphibious Missile Launch, White-hulled amphibious vehicle launches missiles from hood, 155mm, Model No. 674
EX $5   NM $20   MIP $40

Cunard White-Star No 534 Queen Mary, Model No. 52
EX $25   NM $50   MIP $100

MK 1 Corvette, White, black and gray camo hull, gray conning tower, brown deck, Model No. 671
EX $5   NM $20   MIP $40

Motor Patrol Boat, Model No. 1050
EX $5   NM $20   MIP $40

OSA Missile Boat, White and black, fires four missiles, runs on concealed wheels, Model No. 672
EX $5   NM $20   MIP $40

RAF Air/Sea Rescue Launch, Black hull, orange cabin, silver deck. Includes figure and raft, Model No. 678
EX $5   NM $20   MIP $40

Submarine Chaser, 1976, White and gray with launching depth charges, Model No. 673
EX $5   NM $20   MIP $40

TRUCKS

A.E.C. Hoynor Transporter, 1969-75, Model No. 974
EX $60   NM $90   MIP $130

A.E.C. Shell Chemicals Tanker, Model No. 991
EX $35   NM $80   MIP $160

B.E.V. Truck, 1954-60, Model No. 14A/400
EX $15   NM $30   MIP $70

Bedford Garbage Truck, brown, Model No. 252
EX $15   NM $50   MIP $100

Berliet Flat Truck with Container, French-made Dinky Toy truck, Model No. 34b
EX $30   NM $60   MIP $120

Berliet Transformer Carrier, 1961-65, Model No. F898
EX $100   NM $200   MIP $450

Big Bedford, blue, yellow, Model No. 408/922
EX $90   NM $135   MIP $210

Big Bedford, maroon, fawn, Model No. 408/922
EX $80   NM $120   MIP $185

Breakdown Truck "Dinky Service", Model No. 25x
EX $20   NM $80   MIP $160

Chevrolet El Camino, 1961-68, Model No. 449
EX $35   NM $65   MIP $100

Citroen Milk Truck, 1961-65, Model No. F586
EX $145   NM $275   MIP $600

Citroen Wrecker, 1959-71, Model No. F35A/582
EX $75   NM $120   MIP $250

Covered Wagon, Carter Paterson, Model No. 25B
EX $150   NM $300   MIP $750

Covered Wagon, green, gray, Model No. 25B
EX $65   NM $115   MIP $160

Electric Articulated Vehicle, Model No. 30W/421
EX $60   NM $85   MIP $120

Esso Gas Tanker, Model No. 442
EX $40   NM $90   MIP $180

(KP Photo)

Foden Diesel 8-Wheel Wagon, 1948-52, Dark cab and bed, red fenders and chassis. Various color variations were available. Pictured here is the first-version cab, updated in 1952. Part of the Dinky Supertoy range, Model No. 501
EX $160   NM $220   MIP $435

Foden Flat Truck w/ Tailboard 1, red/black, Model No. 503/903
EX $140   NM $210   MIP $450

(ToyShop File Photo)

Foden Flat Truck w/ Tailboard 2, blue/yellow, orange or blue, Model No. 503/903
EX $90   NM $150   MIP $275

Foden Flat Truck w/Tailboard 1, gray/blue, Model No. 503/903
EX $140   NM $210   MIP $450

Foden Mobilgas Tanker, 1954-57, Model No. 941
EX $145   NM $350   MIP $750

Foden Regent Tanker, Model No. 942
EX $135   NM $300   MIP $550

Forward Control Wagon, 1948-53, Model No. 25R
EX $45   NM $65   MIP $90

Guy Flat Truck, common variations, Model No. 513
EX $80   NM $250   MIP $500

Guy Truck, "Eveready" decals, Model No. 918
EX $80   NM $200   MIP $400

Guy Warrior 4 Ton, 1958-64, Model No. 431
EX $150   NM $270   MIP $450

Guy Warrior Snow Plow, Model No. 958
EX $60   NM $150   MIP $300

Hindle Smart Helecs, Model No. 30w
EX $20   NM $50   MIP $100

Horse Box, Model No. 981
EX $30   NM $60   MIP $120

Johnson Road Sweeper, Opening doors on cab, moving brushes on sweeper section, Model No. 449
EX $15   NM $50   MIP $100

(KP Photo by Dr. Douglas Sadecky)

Johnston Road Sweeper, 1970s, as the toy was pushed forward, a spring coil turned the brushes in a sweeping motion, Model No. 449/451
EX $25   NM $50   MIP $75

Leland Tanker, Corn Products
EX $700   NM $1200   MIP $3000

Leland Tanker, 1963-69, Shell/BP, Model No. 944
EX $125   NM $215   MIP $450

(KP Photo)

❏ **Leyland Cement Wagon,** 1956-59, one of Dinky's foreign vehicles, this toy was made in Argentina, Model No. 419/933
EX $90   NM $130   MIP $220

❏ **Leyland Eight-Wheeled Test Chassis,** 1964-69, Model No. 936
EX $65   NM $125   MIP $175

❏ **Leyland Octapus Flat Truck w/ Chassis,** 1964-66, Model No. 935
EX $500   NM $1000   MIP $1600

❏ **Leyland Octopus Esso Tanker,** Model No. 943
EX $100   NM $300   MIP $600

❏ **Market Gardeners Wagon,** yellow, Model No. 25F
EX $65   NM $115   MIP $160

(KP Photo by Dr. Douglas Sadecky)

❏ **McLean Tractor-Trailer,** 1961-67, Model No. 948
EX $95   NM $190   MIP $280

❏ **Mechanical Horse,** 1935-41, Model No. 33a
EX $35   NM $60   MIP $100

❏ **Midland Bank,** 1966-68, Model No. 280
EX $60   NM $85   MIP $120

(KP Photo)

❏ **Mighty Antar With Propeller,** 1959-64, the propeller included with this model is made of plastic, Model No. 986
EX $150   NM $300   MIP $425

❏ **Motor Truck,** red, green, blue, Model No. 22C
EX $80   NM $120   MIP $200

❏ **Motor Truck,** red, blue, Model No. 22C
EX $150   NM $350   MIP $650

❏ **National Benzole Tanker,** Model No. 443
EX $30   NM $75   MIP $150

(KP Photo)

❏ **Panhard Esso Tanker,** 1954-59, this toy was a French-made vehicle as part of the Dinky Supertoys line, Model No. F32C
EX $75   NM $120   MIP $170

❏ **Panhard Kodak Semi Trailer,** 1952-54, Model No. F32AJ
EX $140   NM $250   MIP $450

❏ **Panhard SNCF Semi Trailer,** 1954-59, Model No. F32AB
EX $100   NM $165   MIP $280

❏ **Petrol Wagon,** Power, Model No. 25D
EX $150   NM $300   MIP $500

(KP Photo by Dr. Douglas Sadecky)

❏ **Pinder Circus Peugeot and Caravan,** 1969-71, The Peugeot and Caravan are the only other vehicles produced in the Pinder Circus livery by Dinky. It would have been interesting to see what other circus vehicles would have been produced had sales been better. Again, this is a French-produced model, Model No. 882
EX $110   NM $240   MIP $380

(KP Photo by Dr. Douglas Sadecky)

❏ **Pinder Circus Truck and Wagon,** 1969-71, A French-made Dinky toy. This photo shows the animals and decorative labels still in the package, Model No. 881
EX $110   NM $235   MIP $375

❏ **Pullmore Car Transporter,** light blue, Model No. 583
EX $25   NM $70   MIP $140

(KP Photo by Dr. Douglas Sadecky)

❏ **Pullmore Car Transporter with 994 Loading Ramp,** 1954-63, the 784 loading ramp cam separately packaged in the Transporter box and was used to unload the cars, Model No. 982
EX $85   NM $140   MIP $190

❏ **Renault Estafette,** Model No. F561
EX $50   NM $85   MIP $150

❏ **Simca Glass Truck,** gray, green, Model No. F33C/579
EX $75   NM $120   MIP $170

❏ **Simca Glass Truck,** yellow, green, Model No. F33C/579
EX $100   NM $150   MIP $250

❏ **Studebaker Mobilgas Tanker,** 1954-61, Model No. 440
EX $70   NM $100   MIP $175

❏ **Thames Flat Truck,** 1951-60, Model No. 422/30R
EX $45   NM $75   MIP $110

(KP Photo by Dr. Douglas Sadecky)

❏ **Unic Auto Transporter,** 1959-68, French-made Dinky toy, part of the Supertoys line. Ramp raises and lowers with a lever on the side of the trailer, Model No. F39A/984
EX $100   NM $200   MIP $300

❏ **Unic Bucket Truck,** 1957-65, Model No. F38A/895
EX $75   NM $120   MIP $225

❏ **Willeme Log Truck,** 1956-71, Model No. F36A/897
EX $75   NM $120   MIP $200

(KP Photo)

❑ **Willeme Semi Trailer Truck,** 1959-71, another French-made Dinky toy, Model No. F36B/896
EX $95   **NM** $140   **MIP** $235

VANS

(KP Photo by Dr. Douglas Sadecky)

❑ **ABC-TV Mobile Control Room,** 1962-69, A camera and cameraman was also included with this van, Model No. 987
EX $65   **NM** $130   **MIP** $210

(KP Photo by Dr. Douglas Sadecky)

❑ **ABC-TV Transmitter Van,** 1962-69, this was the companion vehicle to the 987 ABC TV Mobile Control Room, Model No. 988
EX $65   **NM** $130   **MIP** $210

❑ **Atco Delivery Van,** 1935-40, type 2, Model No. 28N
EX $200   **NM** $375   **MIP** $850

❑ **Atco Delivery Van,** 1935-40, type 3, Model No. 28N
EX $135   **NM** $200   **MIP** $350

❑ **Austin Van,** 1954-56, Shell/BP, Model No. 470
EX $60   **NM** $110   **MIP** $175

❑ **Austin Van,** 1955-63, Nestle's, Model No. 471
EX $60   **NM** $110   **MIP** $175

❑ **Austin Van,** 1957-60, Raleigh, Model No. 472
EX $60   **NM** $110   **MIP** $175

(KP Photo by Dr. Douglas Sadecky)

❑ **BBC TV Extending Mast Vehicle,** 1959-64, Model No. 969
EX $60   **NM** $125   **MIP** $185

(KP Photo by Dr. Douglas Sadecky)

❑ **BBC-TV Camera Truck,** 1959-64, Model No. 968
EX $60   **NM** $125   **MIP** $185

❑ **BBC-TV Control Room,** 1959-64, Model No. 967
EX $60   **NM** $125   **MIP** $185

❑ **Bedford 10 cwt Van, Ovaltine,** Model No. 481
EX $25   **NM** $100   **MIP** $200

❑ **Bedford AA Van,** Model No. 412
EX $5   **NM** $30   **MIP** $60

❑ **Bedford Van,** 1955-59, Heinz, Model No. 923
EX $100   **NM** $165   **MIP** $300

❑ **Bedford Van,** 1956-58, Dinky Toys, Model No. 482
EX $60   **NM** $115   **MIP** $200

❑ **Citroen Cibie Delivery Van,** 1960-63, Model No. F561
EX $90   **NM** $150   **MIP** $350

❑ **Dairy Van,** Model No. 490
EX $20   **NM** $50   **MIP** $100

❑ **Ensign Delivery Van,** 1934, type 1, Model No. 28E
EX $300   **NM** $500   **MIP** $1000

❑ **Ford Transit Van,** 1978-80, Model No. 417
EX $15   **NM** $20   **MIP** $30

❑ **Guy Van,** Spratts, Model No. 514
EX $135   **NM** $300   **MIP** $575

(KP Photo)

❑ **Guy Van,** Slumberland, Model No. 514
EX $145   **NM** $315   **MIP** $590

❑ **Guy Van,** Lyons, Model No. 514
EX $275   **NM** $550   **MIP** $1600

❑ **Mini Minor Van,** Joseph Mason Paints, Model No. 274
EX $150   **NM** $300   **MIP** $500

❑ **Mini Minor Van,** 1960s, R.A.C., Model No. 273
EX $65   **NM** $115   **MIP** $150

❑ **Pickfords Delivery Van,** 1934-35, type 2, Model No. 28B
EX $200   **NM** $375   **MIP** $600

❑ **Pickfords Delivery Van,** 1934-35, type 1, Model No. 28B
EX $300   **NM** $500   **MIP** $1000

❑ **Royal Mail Bedford Van,** Model No. 410
EX $5   **NM** $15   **MIP** $40

(KP Photo by Dr. Douglas Sadecky)

❑ **Royal Mail Van,** 1955-61, Model No. 260
EX $75   **NM** $125   **MIP** $180

❑ **Saviem Race Horse Van,** 1969-71, Model No. F571
EX $125   **NM** $225   **MIP** $400

❑ **Telephone Service Van,** Model No. 261
EX $25   **NM** $75   **MIP** $150

❑ **Trojan Dunlop Van,** 1952-57, Model No. 31B/451
EX $70   **NM** $110   **MIP** $185

❑ **Trojan OXO Van,** Model No. 31D
EX $40   **NM** $160   **MIP** $320

HOT WHEELS

REDLINES

❏ **Alive '55,** 1973, assorted, Model No. 6968
EX n/a   NM $125   MIP $600

❏ **Alive '55,** 1974, blue, Model No. 6968
EX n/a   NM $90   MIP $350

❏ **Alive '55,** 1974, green, Model No. 6968
EX n/a   NM $50   MIP $110

❏ **Alive '55,** 1977, chrome, redline, Model No. 9210
EX n/a   NM $15   MIP $55

(KP Photo)

❏ **Ambulance,** 1970, assorted, Model No. 6451
EX n/a   NM $30   MIP $50

(KP Photo)

❏ **American Hauler,** 1976, blue metal cab, white plastic box with American-flag style graphics and "American Hauler" lettering, Model No. 9118
EX n/a   NM $30   MIP $70

(KP Photo)

❏ **American Tipper,** 1976, red metal cab, white plastic tipper bed with American flag graphics, Model No. 9089
EX n/a   NM $25   MIP $65

(KP Photo)

❏ **American Victory,** 1975, light blue with American flag design and number "9" on sides, silver interior and exposed engine, Model No. 7662
EX n/a   NM $20   MIP $60

(KP Photo)

❏ **AMX/2,** 1971, assorted colors, rear engine covers lift up. Name changed to "Xploder" in 1973, Model No. 6460
EX n/a   NM $40   MIP $150

(KP Photo)

❏ **Backwoods Bomb,** 1975, Light blue body with green striping along the sides, plastic camper shell on bed, silver base, Model No. 7670
EX n/a   NM $40   MIP $125

❏ **Baja Bruiser,** 1974, yellow, magenta in tampo, Model No. 8258
EX n/a   NM $300   MIP $1200

❏ **Baja Bruiser,** 1974, orange, Model No. 8258
EX n/a   NM $30   MIP $75

❏ **Baja Bruiser,** 1974, yellow, blue in tampo, Model No. 8258
EX n/a   NM $300   MIP $1200

❏ **Baja Bruiser,** 1976, light green, Model No. 8258
EX n/a   NM $400   MIP $1300

❏ **Baja Bruiser,** 1977, blue, redline or blackwall, Model No. 8258
EX n/a   NM $25   MIP $85

(KP Photo)

❏ **Beatnik Bandit,** 1968, assorted, Model No. 6217
EX n/a   NM $15   MIP $45

(KP Photo)

❏ **Boss Hoss,** 1970, chrome, Club Kit, Model No. 6499
EX n/a   NM $50   MIP $160

(KP Photo)

❏ **Boss Hoss,** 1971, assorted, Model No. 6406
EX n/a   NM $125   MIP $300

(KP Photo)

❏ **Brabham-Repco F1,** 1969, assorted colors, long tailpipe on silver engine, Model No. 6264
EX n/a   NM $20   MIP $65

❏ **Breakaway Bucket,** 1974, dark blue with orange designs, Model No. 8263
EX n/a   NM n/a   MIP n/a

(KP Photo)

VEHICLES

❑ **Bugeye,** 1971, assorted, Model No. 6178
EX n/a   NM $30   MIP $75

❑ **Buzz Off,** 1973, assorted, Model No. 6976
EX n/a   NM $110   MIP $500

❑ **Buzz Off,** 1974, blue, Model No. 6976
EX n/a   NM $30   MIP $90

❑ **Buzz Off,** 1977, gold plated, redline or blackwall, Model No. 6976
EX n/a   NM $15   MIP $30

(KP Photo)

❑ **Bye-Focal,** 1971, assorted, with opening hood. Called "Show-Off" in 1973, Model No. 6187
EX n/a   NM $125   MIP $400

(KP Photo)

❑ **Carabo,** 1970, assorted, Model No. 6420
EX n/a   NM $35   MIP $80

❑ **Carabo,** 1974, yellow, Model No. 7617
EX n/a   NM $500   MIP $1400

(KP Photo)

❑ **Carabo,** 1974, Light green with blue and red stripes, opening gull-wing style doors, Model No. 7617
EX n/a   NM $35   MIP $100

(KP Photo)

❑ **Cement Mixer,** 1970, assorted colors for cab and chassis, orange plastic cement mixer with Hot Wheels logo. Part of the "Heavyweights" series, Model No. 6452
EX n/a   NM $30   MIP $60

(KP Photo)

❑ **Chaparral 2G,** 1969, assorted, Model No. 6256
EX n/a   NM $20   MIP $45

❑ **Chief's Special Cruiser,** 1977, red, redline, Model No. 7665
EX n/a   NM $25   MIP $65

(KP Photo)

❑ **Classic '31 Ford Woody,** 1969, assorted, Model No. 6251
EX n/a   NM $30   MIP $90

(KP Photo)

❑ **Classic '32 Ford Vicky,** 1969, assorted, Model No. 6250
EX n/a   NM $30   MIP $95

❑ **Classic '36 Ford Coupe,** 1969, blue, Model No. 6253
EX n/a   NM $20   MIP $60

(KP Photo)

❑ **Classic '36 Ford Coupe,** 1969, assorted, Model No. 6253
EX n/a   NM $35   MIP $100

(KP Photo)

❑ **Classic '57 T-Bird,** 1969, assorted, Model No. 6252
EX n/a   NM $30   MIP $100

(KP Photo)

❑ **Classic Cord,** 1971, assorted colors, opening hood, detachable plastic soft-top roof (often missing), Model No. 6472
EX n/a   NM n/a   MIP n/a

(KP Photo)

❑ **Classic Nomad,** 1970, assorted, Model No. 6404
EX n/a   NM $55   MIP $150

(KP Photo)

❑ **Cockney Cab,** 1971, assorted, Model No. 6466
EX n/a   NM $50   MIP $160

(KP Photo)

❏ **Cool One,** 1976, Magenta body, "Cool One" letting on front, lightning tampo on body. Available as blackwalls variation, Model No. 9120
EX n/a   **NM** $30   **MIP** $60

❏ **Custom AMX,** 1969, assorted, Model No. 6267
EX n/a   **NM** $100   **MIP** $225

(KP Photo)

❏ **Custom Barracuda,** 1968, assorted, Model No. 6211
EX n/a   **NM** $80   **MIP** $400

(KP Photo)

❏ **Custom Camaro,** 1968, assorted, Model No. 6208
EX n/a   **NM** $100   **MIP** $450

(KP Photo)

❏ **Custom Charger,** 1969, Assorted body colors, white plastic interior, opening hood, Model No. 6268
EX n/a   **NM** $100   **MIP** $250

(KP Photo)

❏ **Custom Continental Mark III,** 1969, assorted, Model No. 6266
EX n/a   **NM** $20   **MIP** $60

❏ **Custom Corvette,** 1968, assorted, Model No. 6215
EX n/a   **NM** $90   **MIP** $300

(KP Photo)

❏ **Custom Cougar,** 1968, assorted, Model No. 6205
EX n/a   **NM** $80   **MIP** $275

❏ **Custom El Dorado,** 1968, assorted, Model No. 6218
EX n/a   **NM** $40   **MIP** $140

(KP Photo)

❏ **Custom Firebird,** 1968, assorted, Model No. 6212
EX n/a   **NM** $50   **MIP** $250

(KP Photo)

❏ **Custom Fleetside,** 1968, assorted, Model No. 6213
EX n/a   **NM** $60   **MIP** $250

(KP Photo)

❏ **Custom Mustang,** 1968, assorted, Model No. 6206
EX n/a   **NM** $80   **MIP** $425

❏ **Custom Mustang,** 1968, assorted w/open hood scoops or louvered windows, Model No. 6206
EX n/a   **NM** $400   **MIP** $1200

(KP Photo)

❏ **Custom Police Cruiser,** 1969, Black and white paint scheme on a Plymouth with "Police" and star tampos, red dome light. A nice companion car to the the 6469 Fire Chief Cruiser, Model No. 6269
EX n/a   **NM** $65   **MIP** $205

(KP Photo)

❏ **Custom T-Bird,** 1968, assorted, with opening hood, Model No. 6207
EX n/a   **NM** $50   **MIP** $165

(KP Photo)

❏ **Custom VW Bug,** 1968, Beetle with oversized engine, sunroof, assorted colors, Model No. 6220
EX n/a   NM $30   MIP $125

(KP Photo)

❏ **Demon,** 1970, assorted colors. Called "Demon" in 1973, Model No. 6401
EX n/a   NM $25   MIP $50

(KP Photo)

❏ **Deora,** 1968, assorted, Model No. 6210
EX n/a   NM $60   MIP $375

(KP Photo)

❏ **Double Header,** 1973, assorted, Model No. 5880
EX n/a   NM $120   MIP $450

(KP Photo)

❏ **Double Vision,** 1973, assorted finishes, flip-up plastic canopy over the seats, rear engine, Model No. 6975
EX n/a   NM $110   MIP $400

(KP Photo)

❏ **Dump Truck,** 1970-72, metal cab and chassis, unpainted base, plastic dump truck bed, part of the Heavyweights series, Model No. 6453
EX n/a   NM $25   MIP $50

(KP Photo)

❏ **Dune Daddy,** 1973, assorted, Model No. 6967
EX n/a   NM $110   MIP $400

(KP Photo)

❏ **El Rey Special,** 1974, Green with yellow and red "Dunlop" and number "1" tampos. Silver metal base, Model No. 8273
EX n/a   NM $40   MIP $75

❏ **El Rey Special,** 1974, light green, Model No. 8273
EX n/a   NM $75   MIP $175

❏ **El Rey Special,** 1974, dark blue, Model No. 8273
EX n/a   NM $225   MIP $900

(KP Photo)

❏ **Evil Weevil,** 1971, assorted, Model No. 6471
EX n/a   NM $75   MIP $150

(KP Photo)

❏ **Ferrari 312P,** 1970, assorted, Model No. 6417
EX n/a   NM $30   MIP $60

❏ **Ferrari 312P,** 1973, assorted, Model No. 6973
EX n/a   NM $300   MIP $1100

(KP Photo)

❏ **Ferrari 512-S,** 1972, assorted, featured opening rear hood and cockpit, Model No. 6021
EX n/a   NM $75   MIP $250

(KP Photo)

❏ **Fire Chief Cruiser,** 1970, red Plymouth Fury--matches Custom Police Cruiser, #6269, Model No. 6469
EX n/a   NM $15   MIP $45

(KP Photo)

❏ **Fire Engine,** 1970, red, Model No. 6454
EX n/a   NM $25   MIP $100

(KP Photo)

❏ **Ford J-Car,** 1968, assorted, Model No. 6214
EX n/a   **NM** $20   **MIP** $70

(KP Photo)

❏ **Ford MK IV,** 1969, assorted, Model No. 6257
EX n/a   **NM** $15   **MIP** $60

(KP Photo)

❏ **Fuel Tanker,** 1971, White cab and chassis, with plastic fuel tanker section and removable fuel hoses. Part of the "Heavyweights" series, Model No. 6018
EX n/a   **NM** $75   **MIP** $200

(KP Photo)

❏ **Funny Money,** 1972, gray armored car body on funny car chassis, orange plastic bumper (usually missing), "Funny Money" labels, Model No. 6005
EX n/a   **NM** $70   **MIP** $335

(KP Photo)

❏ **Grass Hopper,** 1971, assorted, shown here without white plastic canopy, Model No. 6461
EX n/a   **NM** $45   **MIP** $100

(KP Photo)

❏ **Grass Hopper,** 1974, light green, Model No. 7621
EX n/a   **NM** $40   **MIP** $100

❏ **Grass Hopper,** 1975, light green, no engine, Model No. 7622
EX n/a   **NM** $90   **MIP** $350

❏ **Gremlin Grinder,** 1975, green, Model No. 7652
EX n/a   **NM** $35   **MIP** $75

(KP Photo)

❏ **Gremlin Grinder,** 1976, chrome, Model No. 9201
EX n/a   **NM** $20   **MIP** $40

(KP Photo)

❏ **Gun Bucket,** 1976, Olive green body with redlines wheels in front, white "Army," star and number tampos on hood, black plastic anti-aircraft gun and

treads. Also comes in blackwalls wheels variation, Model No. 9090
EX n/a   **NM** $25   **MIP** $60

❏ **Gun Slinger,** 1975, olive, Model No. 7664
EX n/a   **NM** $25   **MIP** $50

(KP Photo)

❏ **Hairy Hauler,** 1971, assorted, with lifting front canopy, Model No. 6458
EX n/a   **NM** $20   **MIP** $65

(KP Photo)

❏ **Heavy Chevy,** 1970, chrome, Club Kit, Model No. 6189
EX n/a   **NM** $75   **MIP** $300

❏ **Heavy Chevy,** 1970, assorted, Model No. 6408
EX n/a   **NM** $65   **MIP** $200

❏ **Heavy Chevy,** 1974, light green, Model No. 7619
EX n/a   **NM** $200   **MIP** $750

❏ **Heavy Chevy,** 1974, yellow, Model No. 7619
EX n/a   **NM** $90   **MIP** $200

❏ **Heavy Chevy,** 1977, chrome, redline or blackwall, Model No. 9212
EX n/a   **NM** $40   **MIP** $120

(KP Photo)

❏ **Hiway Robber,** 1973, assorted, Model No. 6979
EX n/a   **NM** $75   **MIP** $250

(KP Photo)

❑ **Hood,** 1971, assorted, Model No. 6175
  EX n/a   **NM** $25   **MIP** $110

(KP Photo)

❑ **Hot Heap,** 1968, assorted, Model No. 6219
  EX n/a   **NM** $20   **MIP** $65

(KP Photo)

❑ **Ice T,** 1971, yellow, with "Ice T" on plastic roof, Model No. 6184
  EX n/a   **NM** $40   **MIP** $200

(KP Photo)

❑ **Ice T,** 1973, Body in assorted colors, black plastic interior, plastic roof (mostly in white), silver base. Blackwall wheels variations also produced at the same time, Model No. 6980
  EX n/a   **NM** $200   **MIP** $650

❑ **Ice T,** 1974, yellow with hood tampo, Model No. 6980
  EX n/a   **NM** $200   **MIP** $525

❑ **Ice T,** 1974, light green, Model No. 6980
  EX n/a   **NM** $25   **MIP** $75

❑ **Indy Eagle,** 1969, gold, Model No. 6263
  EX n/a   **NM** $75   **MIP** $240

(KP Photo)

❑ **Indy Eagle,** 1969, assorted colors with tinted plastic windshield and silver rear engine and tailpipes, Model No. 6263
  EX n/a   **NM** $15   **MIP** $40

(KP Photo)

❑ **Jack Rabbit Special,** 1970, white, Model No. 6421
  EX n/a   **NM** $15   **MIP** $55

❑ **Jack-in-the-Box Promotion,** 1970, white, Jack Rabbit w/decals, Model No. 6421
  EX n/a   **NM** $300   **MIP** n/a

(KP Photo)

❑ **Jet Threat,** 1971, assorted, Model No. 6179
  EX n/a   **NM** $45   **MIP** $160

❑ **King Kuda,** 1970, chrome, Club Kit, Model No. 6411
  EX n/a   **NM** $75   **MIP** $300

(KP Photo)

❑ **King 'Kuda,** 1970, assorted, Model No. 6411
  EX n/a   **NM** $25   **MIP** $100

(KP Photo)

❑ **Large Charge,** 1975, green, Model No. 8272
  EX n/a   **NM** $25   **MIP** $60

❑ **Letter Getter,** 1977, white, redline, Model No. 9643
  EX n/a   **NM** $175   **MIP** $550

(KP Photo)

❑ **Light My Firebird,** 1970, Convertible in assorted finishes, with decal number on doors and exposed silver engine in front. Brown plastic interior, Model No. 6412
  EX n/a   **NM** $35   **MIP** $75

(KP Photo)

❑ **Lola GT 70,** 1969, assorted, Model No. 6254
  EX n/a   **NM** $20   **MIP** $60

(KP Photo)

❑ **Lotus Turbine,** 1969, Assorted colors, plastic interior, Model No. 6262
  EX n/a   **NM** $20   **MIP** $60

❑ **Lowdown,** 1976, light blue, Model No. 9185
  EX n/a   **NM** $30   **MIP** $75

❏ **Lowdown,** 1977, gold plated, redline or blackwall, Model No. 9185
EX n/a   NM $15   MIP $30

❏ **Mantis,** 1970, assorted, Model No. 6423
EX n/a   NM $20   MIP $60

❏ **Maserati Mistral,** 1969, assorted, Model No. 6277
EX n/a   NM $50   MIP $125

(KP Photo)

❏ **Maxi Taxi,** 1976, Oldsmobile 442 body in yellow with checkboard and "Maxi Taxi" tampo on sides, black plastic interior. Also in a blackwalls variation, Model No. 9184
EX n/a   NM $25   MIP $60

(KP Photo)

❏ **McClaren M6A,** 1969, assorted, Model No. 6255
EX n/a   NM $20   MIP $65

(KP Photo)

❏ **Mercedes 280SL,** 1969, assorted, Model No. 6275
EX n/a   NM $25   MIP $70

❏ **Mercedes 280SL,** 1973, assorted, Model No. 6962
EX n/a   NM $100   MIP $450

❏ **Mercedes C-111,** 1972, assorted, Model No. 6169
EX n/a   NM $80   MIP $250

❏ **Mercedes C-111,** 1973, assorted, Model No. 6978
EX n/a   NM $300   MIP $1200

(KP Photo)

❏ **Mercedes C-111,** 1974, red, with stars and stripes tampo, Model No. 6978
EX n/a   NM $55   MIP $100

(KW6414)

❏ **Mighty Maverick,** 1970, assorted, Model No. 6414
EX n/a   NM $45   MIP $130

(KP Photo)

❏ **Mighty Maverick,** 1975, light green, Model No. 9209
EX n/a   NM $300   MIP $750

❏ **Mighty Maverick,** 1975, blue, Model No. 7653
EX n/a   NM $50   MIP $100

(KP Photo)

❏ **Mighty Maverick,** 1976, chrome, part of the "Super Chromes" series. Called "Street Snorter" in 1973, Model No. 9209
EX n/a   NM $25   MIP $50

(KP Photo)

❏ **Mod-Quad,** 1970, assorted, Model No. 6456
EX n/a   NM $20   MIP $60

❏ **Mongoose,** 1973, red/blue, Model No. 6970
EX n/a   NM $400   MIP $1400

(KP Photo)

❏ **Mongoose Funny Car,** 1970, red, Model No. 6410
EX n/a   NM $50   MIP $160

(KP Photo)

❏ **Mongoose II,** 1971, metallic blue, Model No. 5954
EX n/a   NM $75   MIP $350

❏ **Mongoose Rail Dragster,** 1971, blue, two pack, Model No. 5952
EX n/a   NM $75   MIP n/a

❏ **Monte Carlo Stocker,** 1975, yellow, Model No. 7660
EX n/a   NM $45   MIP $90

(KP Photo)

VEHICLES

❏ **Motocross I,** 1975, red plastic seat and tank, unpainted gray die-cast body, Model No. 7668
EX n/a   **NM** $100   **MIP** $200

(KP Photo)

❏ **Moving Van,** 1970, assorted, another vehicle in the "Heavyweights" series, Model No. 6455
EX n/a   **NM** $50   **MIP** $125

❏ **Mustang Stocker,** 1975, yellow w/red in tampo, Model No. 9203
EX n/a   **NM** $300   **MIP** $900

❏ **Mustang Stocker,** 1975, white, Model No. 7664
EX n/a   **NM** $400   **MIP** $1200

❏ **Mustang Stocker,** 1975, yellow with magenta and orange tampo with "Ford" and "450 HP", Model No. 7664
EX n/a   **NM** $80   **MIP** $135

❏ **Mustang Stocker,** 1976, chrome, Model No. 9203
EX n/a   **NM** $40   **MIP** $90

❏ **Mustang Stocker,** 1977, chrome, redline or blackwall, Model No. 9203
EX n/a   **NM** $40   **MIP** $90

(KP Photo)

❏ **Mutt Mobile,** 1971, assorted. The dogs in back are an especially nice touch, Model No. 5185
EX n/a   **NM** $80   **MIP** $185

❏ **Neet Streeter,** 1976, blue, Model No. 9244
EX n/a   **NM** $30   **MIP** $75

(KP Photo)

❏ **Nitty Gritty Kitty,** 1970, assorted, Model No. 6405
EX n/a   **NM** $25   **MIP** $65

(KP Photo)

❏ **Noodle Head,** 1971, assorted, Model No. 6000
EX n/a   **NM** $55   **MIP** $165

❏ **Odd Job,** 1973, assorted, Model No. 6981
EX n/a   **NM** $100   **MIP** $600

(KP Photo)

❏ **Odd Rod,** 1977, yellow plastic bucket around seats, clear plastic hood with flame graphics, redline or blackwall version available, Model No. 9642
EX n/a   **NM** $30   **MIP** $50

❏ **Odd Rod,** 1977, plum, blackwall or redline, Model No. 9642
EX n/a   **NM** $200   **MIP** $400

❏ **Olds 442,** 1971, assorted, Model No. 6467
EX n/a   **NM** $400   **MIP** $800

(KP Photo)

❏ **Open Fire,** 1972, modified AMC Gremlin with oversized engine and six wheels, assorted colors, Model No. 5881
EX n/a   **NM** $100   **MIP** $400

(KP Photo)

❏ **Paddy Wagon,** 1970, blue, with plastic covering over bed, Model No. 6402
EX n/a   **NM** $20   **MIP** $35

❏ **Paddy Wagon,** 1973, blue, Model No. 6966
EX n/a   **NM** $30   **MIP** $120

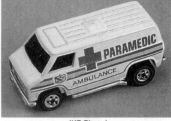

(KP Photo)

❏ **Paramedic,** 1975, white with yellow and red stripes and "Paramedic" lettering, Model No. 7661
EX n/a   **NM** $30   **MIP** $65

(KP Photo)

❏ **Peepin' Bomb,** 1970, assorted, Model No. 6419
EX n/a   **NM** $20   **MIP** $50

(KP Photo)

❏ **Pit Crew Car,** 1971, white, Model No. 6183
EX n/a   **NM** $30   **MIP** $350

(KP Photo)

❏ **Poison Pinto,** 1976, Light green body with Skull and Crossbones and "Poison Pinto" lettering tampo on side panels. A late-era redlines, also available with blackwalls wheels, Model No. 9240
EX n/a   **NM** $25   **MIP** $65

❏ **Police Cruiser,** 1974, white, Model
No. 6963
EX n/a   **NM** $45   **MIP** $125

(KP Photo)

❏ **Porsche 911,** 1975, yellow, with blue
and red stripes on hood and roof, Model
No. 7648
EX n/a   **NM** $40   **MIP** $75

❏ **Porsche 911,** 1975, orange, Model
No. 6972
EX n/a   **NM** $25   **MIP** $65

❏ **Porsche 911,** 1977, chrome, redline or
blackwall, Model No. 9206
EX n/a   **NM** $20   **MIP** $40

❏ **Porsche 917,** 1970, assorted, Model
No. 6416
EX n/a   **NM** $25   **MIP** $65

❏ **Porsche 917,** 1973, assorted, Model
No. 6972
EX n/a   **NM** $300   **MIP** $950

❏ **Porsche 917,** 1974, red, Model
No. 6972
EX n/a   **NM** $175   **MIP** $500

❏ **Porsche 917,** 1974, orange, Model
No. 6972
EX n/a   **NM** $40   **MIP** $75

(KP Photo)

❏ **Power Pad,** 1970, assorted, Model
No. 6459
EX n/a   **NM** $30   **MIP** $125

❏ **Prowler,** 1973, assorted, Model
No. 6965
EX n/a   **NM** $200   **MIP** $1000

❏ **Prowler,** 1974, light green, Model
No. 6965
EX n/a   **NM** $500   **MIP** $1000

(KP Photo)

❏ **Python,** 1968, assorted, Model
No. 6216
EX n/a   **NM** $20   **MIP** $75

(KP Photo)

❏ **Racer Rig,** 1971, red/white, part of the
"Heavyweights" series, Model No. 6194
EX n/a   **NM** $100   **MIP** $375

(KP Photo)

❏ **Ranger Rig,** 1975, medium green with
yellow lettering and design, Model
No. 7666
EX n/a   **NM** $20   **MIP** $65

❏ **Rear Engine Mongoose,** 1972, red,
Model No. 5699
EX n/a   **NM** $200   **MIP** $600

(KP Photo)

❏ **Rear Engine Snake,** 1972, yellow,
Model No. 5856
EX n/a   **NM** $200   **MIP** $600

(KP Photo)

❏ **Red Baron,** 1970, red, Model No. 6400
EX n/a   **NM** $15   **MIP** $40

(KP Photo)

❏ **Red Baron,** 1973, red, note no Iron
Cross on the helmet, Model No. 6964
EX n/a   **NM** $30   **MIP** $200

❏ **Rock Buster,** 1976, yellow, Model
No. 9088
EX n/a   **NM** $20   **MIP** $35

(KP Photo)

❏ **Rocket Bye Baby,** 1971, assorted,
Model No. 6186
EX n/a   **NM** $60   **MIP** $200

(KP Photo)

❏ **Rodger Dodger,** 1974, Magenta Dodge
Charger with flame tampos on hood and
roof, exposed silver engine, red plastic
exhaust pipes, Model No. 8259
EX n/a   **NM** $40   **MIP** $90

❏ **Rodger Dodger,** 1974, blue, Model
No. 8259
EX n/a   **NM** $200   **MIP** $550

❏ **Rodger Dodger,** 1977, gold plated,
blackwall or redline, Model No. 8259
EX n/a   **NM** $30   **MIP** $80

(KP Photo)

VEHICLES

Rolls-Royce Silver Shadow, 1969, assorted, opening hood shows detailed engine, Model No. 6276
EX n/a   NM $30   MIP $125

(KP Photo)

Sand Crab, 1970, assorted, Model No. 6403
EX n/a   NM $20   MIP $60

Sand Drifter, 1975, green, Model No. 7651
EX n/a   NM $150   MIP $375

(KP Photo)

Sand Drifter, 1975, yellow, with flame tampo on hood, black plastic interior and covering over bed, Model No. 7651
EX n/a   NM $45   MIP $85

(KP Photo)

Sand Witch, 1973, assorted, Model No. 6974
EX n/a   NM $125   MIP $400

(KP Photo)

S'Cool Bus, 1971, yellow, with lift-up funny car body and silver chassis, Model No. 6468
EX n/a   NM $175   MIP $750

(KP Photo)

Scooper, 1971, assorted, Model No. 6193
EX n/a   NM $100   MIP $325

(KP Photo)

Seasider, 1970, assorted, Model No. 6413
EX n/a   NM $60   MIP $135

(KP Photo)

Second Wind, 1977, white with yellow and red striping and number "5" on hood. Can feature either blackwall or redline wheels, Model No. 9644
EX n/a   NM $35   MIP $75

(KP Photo)

Shelby Turbine, 1969, assorted, Model No. 6265
EX n/a   NM $20   MIP $55

(KP Photo)

Short Order, 1971, assorted, with extending plastic tailgate, Model No. 6176
EX n/a   NM $50   MIP $125

(KP Photo)

Show Hoss II, 1977, yellow funny car Mustang II body lifts up over silver base, black plastic rollcage, redline or black-walls versions available, Model No. 9646
EX n/a   NM $300   MIP $600

Show-Off, 1973, assorted, Model No. 6982
EX n/a   NM $140   MIP $400

Sidekick, 1972, assorted, Model No. 6022
EX n/a   NM $80   MIP $200

(KP Photo)

Silhouette, 1968, Body in assorted colors, plastic dome canopy over seats, exposed front engine, Model No. 6209
EX n/a   NM $20   MIP $90

Sir Sidney Roadster, 1974, yellow, Model No. 8261
EX n/a   NM $50   MIP $90

Sir Sidney Roadster, 1974, light green, Model No. 8261
EX n/a   NM $325   MIP $650

(KP Photo)

Sir Sidney Roadster, 1974, Orange body with brown plastic roof and exposed silver engine. Red flame tampos, silver metal base, Model No. 8261
EX n/a   NM $375   MIP $700

(KP Photo)

❏ **Six Shooter,** 1971, assorted, Model No. 6003
EX n/a **NM** $75 **MIP** $225

(KP Photo)

❏ **Sky Show Fleetside (Aero Launcher),** 1970, assorted, Model No. 6436
EX n/a **NM** $400 **MIP** $850

❏ **Snake,** 1973, white/yellow, Model No. 6969
NM $600 **MIP** $1500

(KP Photo)

❏ **Snake Funny Car,** 1970, assorted, Model No. 6409
EX n/a **NM** $60 **MIP** $300

❏ **Snake II,** 1971, white, Model No. 5953
EX n/a **NM** $60 **MIP** $275

(KP Photo)

❏ **Snake Rail Dragster,** 1971, white, part of a two-pack, Model No. 5951
EX n/a **NM** $75 **MIP** n/a

(KP Photo)

❏ **Snorkel,** 1971, assorted, Model No. 6020
EX n/a **NM** $90 **MIP** $200

(KP Photo)

❏ **Special Delivery,** 1971, blue, Model No. 6006
EX n/a **NM** $45 **MIP** $150

(KP Photo)

❏ **Splittin' Image,** 1969, assorted, Model No. 6261
EX n/a **NM** $15 **MIP** $50

(KP Photo)

❏ **Spoiler Sport,** 1977, light green van with tropical island scene on side panels, redline wheels. Blackwalls variations also exist, Model No. 9641
EX n/a **NM** $25 **MIP** $50

(KP Photo)

❏ **Steam Roller,** 1974, white body with stars and stripes graphics, three stars reversed out of red stripe on hood; the more common model, Model No. 8260
EX n/a **NM** $25 **MIP** $70

❏ **Steam Roller,** 1974, white body with red white and blue graphics, seven stars on front, Model No. 8260
EX n/a **NM** $100 **MIP** $300

❏ **Street Rodder,** 1976, black, Model No. 9242
EX n/a **NM** $40 **MIP** $85

❏ **Street Snorter,** 1973, assorted, Model No. 6971
EX n/a **NM** $110 **MIP** $400

(KP Photo)

❏ **Strip Teaser,** 1971, assorted, Model No. 6188
EX n/a **NM** $65 **MIP** $200

❏ **Sugar Caddy,** 1971, assorted, Model No. 6418
EX n/a **NM** $45 **MIP** $120

❏ **Super Van,** 1975, Toys-R-Us, Model No. 7649
EX n/a **NM** $100 **MIP** $350

(KP Photo)

❏ **Super Van,** 1975, Magenta body with dirt bike in yellow circel tampo on side panels, Model No. 7649
EX n/a **NM** $110 **MIP** $270

❏ **Superfine Turbine,** 1973, assorted, Model No. 6004
EX n/a **NM** $400 **MIP** $1100

❏ **Sweet 16,** 1973, assorted, Model No. 6007
EX n/a **NM** $125 **MIP** $650

(KP Photo)

VEHICLES

❑ **Swingin' Wing,** 1970, assorted, Model No. 6422
EX n/a **NM** $25 **MIP** $75

(KP Photo)

❑ **T-4-2,** 1971, assorted, Model No. 6177
EX n/a **NM** $50 **MIP** $175

(KP Photo)

❑ **Team Trailer,** 1971, white/red, detailed plastic interior and opening door on trailer, Model No. 6019
EX n/a **NM** $95 **MIP** $225

(KP Photo)

❑ **TNT-Bird,** 1970, assorted, Model No. 6407
EX n/a **NM** $60 **MIP** $125

(KP Photo)

❑ **Top Eliminator,** 1974, blue lift-up funny car body on silver chassis, with green light tan and orange "Hot Wheels" graphics and stripes on sides, Model No. 7630
EX n/a **NM** $50 **MIP** $165

(KP Photo)

❑ **Torero,** 1969, assorted, Model No. 6260
EX n/a **NM** $15 **MIP** $60

(KP Photo)

❑ **Torino Stocker,** 1975, red, Model No. 7647
EX n/a **NM** $35 **MIP** $70

(KP Photo)

❑ **Tough Customer,** 1975, olive, with rotating turret and white numbering tampos, Model No. 7655
EX n/a **NM** $30 **MIP** $60

(KP Photo)

❑ **Tow Truck,** 1970, assorted, Model No. 6450
EX n/a **NM** $30 **MIP** $80

(KP Photo)

❑ **Tri-Baby,** 1970, assorted, interesting engine casting under opening rear hood, Model No. 6424
EX n/a **NM** $20 **MIP** $55

❑ **T-Totaller,** 1977, black, Red Line, six-pack only, Model No. 9648
EX n/a **NM** $500 **MIP** $1000

❑ **Turbofire,** 1969, assorted, Model No. 6259
EX n/a **NM** $15 **MIP** $50

(KP Photo)

❑ **Twinmill,** 1969, assorted, Model No. 6258
EX n/a **NM** $15 **MIP** $50

❑ **Twinmill II,** 1976, orange, Model No. 8240
EX n/a **NM** $10 **MIP** $35

❑ **Vega Bomb,** 1975, green, Model No. 7658
EX n/a **NM** $250 **MIP** $800

(KP Photo)

❑ **Vega Bomb,** 1975, orange, this model is right on the cusp of the Redlines era--blackwall versions (like this one as #7654) were becoming a more common sight, Model No. 7658
EX n/a **NM** $40 **MIP** $85

(KP Photo)

❑ **Volkswagen,** 1974, orange enamel with bug graphic on roof, Model No. 7620
EX n/a **NM** $30 **MIP** $60

❑ **Volkswagen,** 1974, orange w/stripes on roof, Model No. 7620
EX n/a **NM** $100 **MIP** $400

(KP Photo)

❑ **Volkswagen Beach Bomb,** 1969, surf boards on side raised panels, Model No. 6274
EX n/a **NM** $115 **MIP** $310

❑ **Volkswagen Beach Bomb,** 1969, surf boards in rear window, Model No. 6274
EX n/a **NM** $7000 **MIP** n/a

(KP Photo)

❑ **Warpath,** 1975, white, with stars and stripes tampo, opening plastic engine covers, Model No. 7654
EX n/a **NM** $60 **MIP** $115

(KP Photo)

❑ **Waste Wagon,** 1971, assorted, part of the "Heavyweights" series of highly-detailed trucks, Model No. 6192
EX n/a **NM** $90 **MIP** $325

(KP Photo)

❑ **What-4,** 1971, assorted, Model No. 6001
EX n/a **NM** $50 **MIP** $150

(KP Photo)

❑ **Whip Creamer,** 1970, assorted, with slide-back plastic canopy, Model No. 6457
EX n/a **NM** $25 **MIP** $60

❑ **Xploder,** 1973, assorted, Model No. 6977
EX n/a **NM** $100 **MIP** $500

❑ **Z Whiz,** 1977, white, redline, Model No. 9639
EX n/a **NM** $1500 **MIP** n/a

❑ **Z Whiz,** 1977, gray, redline, Model No. 9639
EX n/a **NM** $35 **MIP** $70

VEHICLES

JAPANESE

(Ron Smith)

❏ **1949 Ford Sedan**, Japanese, wind-up, Guntherman, 11" (J93)
EX $150　　**NM** $300　　**MIP** $400

(Ron Smith)

❏ **1950 Cadillac**, Japanese, battery-op, Marusan, 11" (J18)
EX $400　　**NM** $800　　**MIP** $1800

(Ron Smith)

❏ **1950 Champion No.15 Racer**, Japanese, friction, German, 18" (J289)
EX $500　　**NM** $750　　**MIP** $1500

(Ron Smith)

❏ **1950 Champion No.42 Racer**, Japanese, friction, German, 18" (J288)
EX $500　　**NM** $750　　**MIP** $1500

(Ron Smith)

❏ **1950 Volkswagen Convertible**, Japanese, friction, T.N., 9-1/2" (J258)
EX $100　　**NM** $150　　**MIP** $225

(Ron Smith)

❏ **1950's Agajanian Racer No.98**, Japanese, friction, "Y" Co., 18" (J286)
EX $500　　**NM** $1000　　**MIP** $2000

(Ron Smith)

❏ **1950's Atom Car**, Japanese, Yonezawa, 17" (J284)
EX $200　　**NM** $400　　**MIP** $900

(Ron Smith)

❏ **1950's Buick Futuristic LeSabre**, Japanese, friction, Yonezawa, 7-1/2" (J276)
EX $200　　**NM** $300　　**MIP** $500

(Ron Smith)

❏ **1950's Champion No.98 Racer**, Japanese, friction, "Y" Co., 18" (J287)
EX $500　　**NM** $800　　**MIP** $1100

(Ron Smith)

❏ **1950's Mazda Auto Tricycle**, Japanese, friction, Bandai, 8" (J274)
EX $75　　**NM** $125　　**MIP** $250

(Ron Smith)

❏ **1950's Porsche Speedster**, Japanese, battery-op, Distler, 10-1/2" (J235)
EX $200　　**NM** $300　　**MIP** $600

(Toy Shop File Photo)

❏ **1950's Porsche Speedster**, Japanese, battery-op, Distler, 10-1/2" (J235)
EX $200　　**NM** $300　　**MIP** $600

(Toy Shop File Photo)

❏ **1950's Volvo**, Japanese, wind-up, Sweden, 11" (J265A)
EX $600　　**NM** $1000　　**MIP** $2000

(Ron Smith)

❏ **1952 Cadillac**, Japanese, friction, Alps, 11-1/2" (J20)
EX $250　　**NM** $400　　**MIP** $800

(Toy Shop File Photo)

❏ **1952 Oldsmobile**, Japanese, friction, "Y" Co., 11" (J207A)
EX $150　　**NM** $350　　**MIP** $500

(Ron Smith)

❏ **1953 Chevrolet Corvette**, Japanese, friction, Bandai, 7" (J37)
EX $100　　**NM** $200　　**MIP** $400

(Toy Shop File Photo)

❑ **1953 Packard Convertible/Sedan**, Japanese, friction, Alps, 16" (J222)
EX $500   **NM** $800   **MIP** $1600

(Ron Smith)

❑ **1954 Cadillac**, Japanese, battery-op, Joustra, 12" (J23)
EX $100   **NM** $200   **MIP** $450

(Ron Smith)

❑ **1954 Chevrolet**, Japanese, friction, Marusan, 11" (J49)
EX $300   **NM** $800   **MIP** $1500

(Ron Smith)

❑ **1954 Pontiac**, Japanese, Minister, friction, Minister, 11" (J218A)
EX $10   **NM** $20   **MIP** $30

(Ron Smith)

❑ **1954 Studebaker**, Japanese, friction, Yoshiva, 9" (J243)
EX $150   **NM** $200   **MIP** $375

(Ron Smith)

❑ **1955 Buick Roadmaster**, Japanese, friction, Yoshiya, 11" (J5)
EX $125   **NM** $250   **MIP** $500

(Ron Smith)

❑ **1955 Chevrolet**, Japanese, battery-op, Marusan, 10-3/4" (J50)
EX $300   **NM** $800   **MIP** $1500

(Ron Smith)

❑ **1955 Chrysler**, Japanese, friction, Yonezawa, 8" (J71)
EX $100   **NM** $200   **MIP** $300

(Ron Smith)

❑ **1955 Ford Ambulance**, Japanese, friction, Bandai, 12" (J98)
EX $150   **NM** $200   **MIP** $250

(Ron Smith)

❑ **1955 Ford Convertible**, Japanese, friction, Bandai, 12" (J100)
EX $200   **NM** $400   **MIP** $700

(Ron Smith)

❑ **1955 Ford Panel Truck**, Japanese, "Flowers," friction, Bandai, 12" (J99)
EX $200   **NM** $400   **MIP** $600

(Ron Smith)

❑ **1955 Ford Pickup**, Japanese, friction, Bandai, 12" (J96)
EX $150   **NM** $250   **MIP** $300

(Ron Smith)

❑ **1955 Ford Station Wagon**, Japanese, friction, Bandai, 12" (J97)
EX $150   **NM** $250   **MIP** $300

(Toy Shop File Photo)

❑ **1955 Ford Thunderbird**, Japanese, friction, Bandai, 7" (J126A)
EX $75   **NM** $100   **MIP** $150

(Ron Smith)

❑ **1955 Lincoln Sedan**, Japanese, friction, Yonezawa, 12" (J163)
EX $250   **NM** $600   **MIP** $1200

(Ron Smith)

❑ **1956 Ford Convertible**, Japanese, friction, Haji, 11-1/2" (J102)
EX $400   **NM** $600   **MIP** $900

(Ron Smith)

❑ **1956 Ford Sedan**, Japanese, friction, Marusan, 13" (J103)
EX $500   **NM** $1000   **MIP** $3000

(Ron Smith)

VEHICLES

❑ **1956 Ford Thunderbird**, Japanese, friction, T.N., 11" (J127)
EX $200   NM $300   MIP $400

(Ron Smith)

❑ **1956 Ford Thunderbird**, Japanese, battery-op, T.N., 11" (J129)
EX $200   NM $300   MIP $400

(Ron Smith)

❑ **1956 Ford Wagon**, Japanese, friction, Nomura, 10-1/2" (J104)
EX $100   NM $150   MIP $300

(Ron Smith)

❑ **1956 Lincoln**, Japanese, friction, Ichiko, 16-1/2" (J165)
EX $150   NM $250   MIP $375

(Ron Smith)

❑ **1956 Lincoln Continental Mark II**, Japanese, friction, Linemar, 12" (J164)
EX $600   NM $1200   MIP $2500

(Ron Smith)

❑ **1956 Mercury Hardtop**, Japanese, friction, Alps, 9-1/2" (J193)
EX $600   NM $800   MIP $1400

(Ron Smith)

❑ **1956 Oldsmobile Sedan**, Japanese, friction, Ichiko/Kanto, 10-1/2" (J208)
EX $200   NM $400   MIP $600

(Ron Smith)

❑ **1956 Oldsmobile Super 88 Sedan**, Japanese, friction, Masudaya, 16" (J209)
EX $200   NM $300   MIP $500

(Ron Smith)

❑ **1956 Plymouth Hardtop**, Japanese, friction, unknown manufacturer, 8-1/2" (J224)
EX $150   NM $200   MIP $400

(Ron Smith)

❑ **1956 Plymouth Hardtop**, Japanese, battery-op, Alps, 12" (J225)
EX $300   NM $400   MIP $600

(Toy Shop File Photo)

❑ **1957 Chrysler New Yorker**, Japanese, friction, Alps, 14" (J72)
EX $500   NM $700   MIP $1500

(Ron Smith)

❑ **1957 Ford Fairlane Sedan**, Japanese, friction, Ichiko, 10" (J105)
EX $100   NM $200   MIP $300

(Ron Smith)

❑ **1957 Ford Hardtop**, Japanese, friction, T.N., 12" (J106)
EX $100   NM $200   MIP $300

(Ron Smith)

❑ **1957 Ford Sedan/Convertible/Wagon/Pickup**, Japanese, friction, Joustra, 12" (J107)
EX $200   NM $250   MIP $300

(Ron Smith)

❑ **1957 Packard Hawk Convertible**, Japanese, battery-op, Schuco, 10-3/4" (J223)
EX $300   NM $400   MIP $900

(Ron Smith)

❑ **1957 Plymouth Fury Hardtop**, Japanese, friction, "Y" Co., 11-1/2" (J226)
EX $300   NM $400   MIP $600

(Ron Smith)

❏ **1958 Buick Century**, Japanese, friction, Yonezawa, 12" (J6)
EX $400 **NM** $650 **MIP** $1500

(Ron Smith)

❏ **1958 Buick Century**, Japanese, friction, Bandai, 8" (J7)
EX $80 **NM** $100 **MIP** $150

(Ron Smith)

❏ **1958 Chevrolet Corvette**, Japanese, friction, Yonezawa, 9-1/2" (J38)
EX $200 **NM** $300 **MIP** $600

(Toy Shop File Photo)

❏ **1958 Chevrolet Station Wagon**, Japanese, friction, Bandai, 8" (J57)
EX $50 **NM** $65 **MIP** $125

(Ron Smith)

❏ **1958 Chrysler**, Japanese, battery-op, unknown manufacturer, 13" (J73)
EX $300 **NM** $400 **MIP** $800

(Ron Smith)

❏ **1958 Dodge Sedan**, Japanese, friction, T.N., 11" (J82)
EX $300 **NM** $400 **MIP** $800

(Ron Smith)

❏ **1958 Edsel Convertible/Sedan**, Japanese, friction, Haji, 10-1/2" (J86)
EX $300 **NM** $500 **MIP** $1000

(Ron Smith)

❏ **1958 Edsel Convertible/Sedan**, Japanese, friction, Haji, 10-1/2" (J86)
EX $300 **NM** $500 **MIP** $1000

(Ron Smith)

❏ **1958 Edsel Hardtop**, Japanese, friction, Asahi, 10-3/4" (J91)
EX $100 **NM** $200 **MIP** $350

(Ron Smith)

❏ **1958 Edsel Station Wagon**, Japanese, friction, T.N., 11" (J89)
EX $150 **NM** $200 **MIP** $300

(Ron Smith)

❏ **1958 Edsel Wagon**, Japanese, friction, Haji, 10-1/2" (J87)
EX $200 **NM** $300 **MIP** $600

(Toy Shop File Photo)

❏ **1958 Ford Fairlane Hardtop/Convertible**, Japanese, friction, Sankei Gangu, 9" (J114)
EX $90 **NM** $115 **MIP** $125

(Ron Smith)

❏ **1958 Mercury Hardtop**, Japanese, friction, Yonezawa, 11-1/2" (J195)
EX $250 **NM** $325 **MIP** $400

(Ron Smith)

❏ **1958 Oldsmobile Sedan**, Japanese, friction, A.T.C., 12" (J210)
EX $200 **NM** $300 **MIP** $400

(Ron Smith)

❏ **1958 Plymouth Fury**, Japanese, friction, Bandai, 8" (J227)
EX $75 **NM** $90 **MIP** $165

(Ron Smith)

❏ **1959 Buick**, Japanese, friction, T.N., 11" (J8)
EX $90 **NM** $150 **MIP** $300

(Ron Smith)

❏ **1959 Cadillac Convertible**, Japanese, friction, Bandai, 12" (J25)
EX $50 **NM** $100 **MIP** $185

(Ron Smith)

❏ **1959 Cadillac Convertible**, Japanese, friction, Bandai, 12" (J25)
EX $50   **NM** $100   **MIP** $185

(Ron Smith)

❏ **1959 Chevrolet Sedan/Convertible/Wagon**, Japanese, friction, SY, 11-1/2" (J59)
EX $200   **NM** $400   **MIP** $800

(Ron Smith)

❏ **1959 Chrylser Imperial Convertible**, Japanese, friction, Bandai, 8" (J74)
EX $50   **NM** $100   **MIP** $175

(Ron Smith)

❏ **1959 Dodge Pickup**, Japanese, friction, unknown manufacturer, 18-1/2" (J84)
EX $350   **NM** $500   **MIP** $1200

(Ron Smith)

❏ **1959 Ford Retractable**, Japanese, friction, T.N., 11" (J117)
EX $80   **NM** $100   **MIP** $165

(Ron Smith)

❏ **1959 Ford Station Wagon**, Japanese, friction, T.N., 12" (J116)
EX $100   **NM** $150   **MIP** $200

(Ron Smith)

❏ **1959 Lincoln Continental Mark III Convertible**, Japanese, friction, Bandai, 12" (J166)
EX $90   **NM** $125   **MIP** $175

(Ron Smith)

❏ **1959 Lincoln Continental Mark III Sedan**, Japanese, friction, Bandai, 12" (J167)
EX $90   **NM** $125   **MIP** $175

(Ron Smith)

❏ **1959 Oldsmobile Sedan**, Japanese, friction, Ichiko, 12-1/2" (J213)
EX $75   **NM** $125   **MIP** $175

(Ron Smith)

❏ **1959 Plymouth Hardtop**, Japanese, friction, A.T.C., 10-1/2" (J228)
EX $200   **NM** $400   **MIP** $600

(Ron Smith)

❏ **1960 Chevrolet**, Japanese, friction, Marusan, 11-1/2" (J60)
EX $200   **NM** $400   **MIP** $800

(Toy Shop File Photo)

❏ **1960 Citroen 2 CV**, Japanese, friction, Daiya, 8" (J269A)
EX $100   **NM** $150   **MIP** $250

(Toy Shop File Photo)

❏ **1960 Citroen DS 19 Sedan**, Japanese, friction, Bandai, 12" (J68)
EX $300   **NM** $600   **MIP** $900

(Ron Smith)

❏ **1960 Ford**, Japanese, friction, Haji, 11" (J119)
EX $125   **NM** $200   **MIP** $350

(Ron Smith)

❏ **1960 Lincoln Hardtop/Convertible**, Japanese, friction, Yonezawa, 11" (J168)
EX $100   **NM** $150   **MIP** $300

(Toy Shop File Photo)

❏ **1960 Renault**, Japanese, friction, Bandai, 7-1/2" (J241)
EX $95   **NM** $150   **MIP** $200

(Toy Shop File Photo)

❏ **1960 Rolls Royce**, Japanese, friction, T.N., 10-1/2" (J239)
EX $200   **NM** $300   **MIP** $500

(Ron Smith)

❏ **1960 Rolls Royce Silver Coupe Convertible**, Japanese, friction, Bandai, 12" (J236)
EX $100 **NM** $150 **MIP** $300

(Ron Smith)

❏ **1960 Volkswagen Karmann-Ghia**, Japanese, friction, Bandai, 7" (J252)
EX $100 **NM** $150 **MIP** $300

(Ron Smith)

❏ **1960's Aston-Martin DB5**, Japanese, (James Bond), friction, Gilbert, 11-1/2" (J1)
EX $75 **NM** $150 **MIP** $350

(Ron Smith)

❏ **1960's Aston-Martin DB6**, Japanese, friction, Asahi Toy Co., 11" (J2)
EX $200 **NM** $400 **MIP** $600

(Toy Shop File Photo)

❏ **1960's Ford Taunus 17M**, Japanese, friction, Bandai, 8" (J145)
EX $20 **NM** $40 **MIP** $60

(Toy Shop File Photo)

❏ **1960's Jaguar XKE Convertible**, Japanese, friction, T.T., 10-1/2" (J155)
EX $75 **NM** $100 **MIP** $250

(Ron Smith)

❏ **1960's Mercedes-Benz 219 Convertible**, Japanese, friction, Bandai, 8" (J177)
EX $50 **NM** $80 **MIP** $120

(Ron Smith)

❏ **1960's Mercedes-Benz 219 Sedan**, Japanese, friction, Bandai, 8" (J176)
EX $50 **NM** $80 **MIP** $120

(Ron Smith)

❏ **1960's Ramgler Rebel Station Wagon**, Japanese, friction, Bandai, 12" (J240)
EX $60 **NM** $90 **MIP** $150

(Ron Smith)

❏ **1960's Rolls Royce Silver Sedan Coupe**, Japanese, friction, Bandai, 12" (J237)
EX $100 **NM** $150 **MIP** $250

(Ron Smith)

❏ **1960's Studebaker Avanti**, Japanese, friction, Bandai, 8" (J242)
EX $125 **NM** $175 **MIP** $350

(Ron Smith)

❏ **1960's Volkswagen**, Japanese, battery-op, Bandai, 11" (J264)
EX $25 **NM** $50 **MIP** $75

(Ron Smith)

❏ **1960's Volkswagen Convertible**, Japanese, battery-op, Bandai, 11" (J260)
EX $110 **NM** $145 **MIP** $200

(Ron Smith)

❏ **1960's Volkswagen with or without Sun Roof**, Japanese, friction, Bandai, 15" (J265)
EX $60 **NM** $90 **MIP** $125

(Ron Smith)

❏ **1961 Cadillac Fleetwood**, Japanese, friction, SSS, 17-1/2" (J29)
EX $100 **NM** $200 **MIP** $350

(Ron Smith)

VEHICLES

❑ **1961 Chevrolet Impala Convertible**, Japanese, friction, Bandai, 11" (J63)
EX $100   NM $150   MIP $300

(Ron Smith)

❑ **1961 Chevrolet Impala Sedan**, Japanese, friction, Bandai, 11" (J62)
EX $100   NM $150   MIP $300

(Ron Smith)

❑ **1961 Ford Country Sedan**, Japanese, friction, Bandai, 10-1/2" (J120)
EX $125   NM $150   MIP $250

(Ron Smith)

❑ **1961 Oldsmobile Convertible**, Japanese, friction, Yonezawa, 12" (J214)
EX $75   NM $125   MIP $200

(Ron Smith)

❑ **1961 Plymouth Sedan**, Japanese, friction, Ichiko, 12" (J230)
EX $150   NM $300   MIP $550

(Ron Smith)

❑ **1961 Plymouth Station Wagon**, Japanese, friction, Ichiko, 12" (J231)
EX $150   NM $250   MIP $500

(Ron Smith)

❑ **1961 Plymouth T.V. Car**, Japanese, battery-op, Ichiko, 12" (J232)
EX $100   NM $150   MIP $300

(Ron Smith)

❑ **1962 Chevrolet**, Japanese, friction, unknown manufacturer, 11" (J65)
EX $125   NM $250   MIP $350

(Ron Smith)

❑ **1962 Chevrolet Secret Agent**, Japanese, battery-op, unknown manufacturer, 14" (J64)
EX $50   NM $75   MIP $150

(Ron Smith)

❑ **1962 Chrysler Imperial**, Japanese, 16", friction, black, red (white: add 20% to value)
EX $600   NM $1200   MIP $2200

(Ron Smith)

❑ **1962 Ford Country Sedan**, Japanese, friction, Asahi, 12" (J121)
EX $200   NM $350   MIP $700

(Ron Smith)

❑ **1963 Buick Wildcat**, Japanese, friction, Ichiko, 15" (J13)
EX $200   NM $400   MIP $800

(Ron Smith)

❑ **1963 Chevrolet Impala**, Japanese, friction, Bandai (?), 18" (J66)
EX $200   NM $300   MIP $400

(Ron Smith)

❑ **1963 Ford Thunderbird Retractable**, Japanese, battery-op, Yonezawa, 11" (J134)
EX $80   NM $150   MIP $200

(Ron Smith)

❑ **1963 Ford Thunderbird Retractable**, Japanese, battery-op, Yonezawa, 11" (J134)
EX $80   NM $150   MIP $200

(Ron Smith)

❑ **1964 Chevrolet Corvette**, Japanese, battery-op, Ichida, 12" (J41)
EX $150   NM $225   MIP $350

(Ron Smith)

❑ **1964 Ford Hardtop**, Japanese, friction, Ichiko, 13" (J122)
EX $200   NM $450   MIP $700

(Ron Smith)

❑ **1964 Ford Thunderbird**, Japanese, friction, Ichiko, 16" (J137)
EX $100   NM $200   MIP $400

(Ron Smith)

❏ **1964 Ford Thunderbird Hardtop**, Japanese, friction, Asahi, 12" (J136)
EX $150   **NM** $200   **MIP** $400

(Toy Shop File Photo)

❏ **1964 Lincoln**, Japanese, friction, unknown manufacturer, 10-1/2" (J169)
EX $90   **NM** $175   **MIP** $275

(Ron Smith)

❏ **1964 Lincoln**, Japanese, friction, unknown manufacturer, 10-1/2" (J169)
EX $90   **NM** $175   **MIP** $275

(Ron Smith)

❏ **1965 Ford Galaxie Hardtop**, Japanese, friction, MT, 11" (J125)
EX $125   **NM** $150   **MIP** $300

(Ron Smith)

❏ **1965 Ford Mustang Fastback**, Japanese, friction, Bandai, 11" (J139)
EX $45   **NM** $65   **MIP** $90

(Ron Smith)

❏ **1965 Ford Mustang Hardtop/Convertible**, Japanese, friction/battery-op, Bandai, 11" (J140)
EX $75   **NM** $125   **MIP** $150

(Ron Smith)

❏ **1965 Ford Thunderbird Hardtop**, Japanese, friction, Bandai, 10-3/4" (J138)
EX $60   **NM** $90   **MIP** $175

❏ **1966 Ford Mustang Fastback**, Japanese, friction, T.N., 17" (J143)
EX $120   **NM** $200   **MIP** $325

(Ron Smith)

❏ **1966 Oldsmobile Toronado**, Japanese, battery-op, Bandai, 11" (J215)
EX $65   **NM** $110   **MIP** $150

(Ron Smith)

❏ **1967 Cadillac**, Japanese, friction, K.O., 10-1/2" (J34)
EX $100   **NM** $150   **MIP** $250

(Toy Shop File Photo)

❏ **1967 Chevrolet Camaro**, Japanese, battery-op, T.N., 14" (J46)
EX $100   **NM** $150   **MIP** $300

(Ron Smith)

❏ **1967 Chevrolet Camaro**, Japanese, battery-op, T.N., 14" (J46)
EX $100   **NM** $150   **MIP** $300

(Ron Smith)

❏ **1967 Mercury Cougar Hardtop**, Japanese, friction, Asakusa Toys, 15" (J197)
EX $200   **NM** $400   **MIP** $800

(Ron Smith)

❏ **1967 Pontiac Firebird**, Japanese, friction, Akasura, 15-1/2" (J219)
EX $200   **NM** $400   **MIP** $900

(Ron Smith)

❏ **1967 Pontiac Firebird**, Japanese, friction, Bandai, 10" (J220)
EX $30   **NM** $55   **MIP** $100

(Ron Smith)

❏ **1968 Chevrolet Corvette**, Japanese, battery-op, Taiyo, 9-1/2" (J42)
EX $20   **NM** $40   **MIP** $80

(Ron Smith)

❏ **1968 Ford Torino**, Japanese, friction, S.T., 16" (J126)
EX $175   **NM** $300   **MIP** $600

(Ron Smith)

❏ **1968 Oldsmobile Toronado**, Japanese, friction, Ichiko, 17-1/2" (J216)
EX $300   **NM** $400   **MIP** $500

(Ron Smith)

VEHICLES

❏ **1971 Chevrolet Camaro Rusher**, Japanese, battery-op, Taiyo, 9-1/2" (J48)
EX $10   NM $20   MIP $25

(Toy Shop File Photo)

❏ **Dream Car**, Japanese, friction, "Y" Co., 17" (J278A)
EX $600   NM $800   MIP $1500

(Toy Shop File Photo)

❏ **Electrospecial No. 21**, Japanese, battery-op, "Y" Co., 10" (J290)
EX $300   NM $600   MIP $1200

(Toy Shop File Photo)

❏ **Midget Special No. 6**, Japanese, friction, "Y" Co., 7" (J291)
EX $300   NM $500   MIP $1000

CARS

❏ **1935 Pontiac Four-Door Sedan**, Japanese, 8", maroon, friction
EX $30   NM $65   MIP $90

(Ron Smith)

❏ **1949 Ford Sedan**, Japanese, wind-up, Guntherman, 11" (J93)
EX $150   NM $300   MIP $400

(Ron Smith)

❏ **1950 Cadillac**, Japanese, battery-op, Marusan, 11" (J18)
EX $400   NM $800   MIP $1800

(Ron Smith)

❏ **1950 Champion No.15 Racer**, Japanese, friction, German, 18" (J289)
EX $500   NM $750   MIP $1500

(Ron Smith)

❏ **1950 Champion No.42 Racer**, Japanese, friction, German, 18" (J288)
EX $500   NM $750   MIP $1500

(Ron Smith)

❏ **1950 Volkswagen Convertible**, Japanese, friction, T.N., 9-1/2" (J258)
EX $100   NM $150   MIP $225

(Ron Smith)

❏ **1950's Agajanian Racer No.98**, Japanese, friction, "Y" Co., 18" (J286)
EX $500   NM $1000   MIP $2000

(Ron Smith)

❏ **1950's Atom Car**, Japanese, Yonezawa, 17" (J284)
EX $200   NM $400   MIP $900

(Ron Smith)

❏ **1950's Buick Futuristic LeSabre**, Japanese, friction, Yonezawa, 7-1/2" (J276)
EX $200   NM $300   MIP $500

(Ron Smith)

❏ **1950's Champion No.98 Racer**, Japanese, friction, "Y" Co., 18" (J287)
EX $500   NM $800   MIP $1100

❏ **1950s Cunningham Roadster**, Japanese, 7-1/2", light blue, friction
EX $40   NM $90   MIP $125

❏ **1950s DeSoto**, Japanese, Asahi Toy, 8", green, friction
EX $40   NM $90   MIP $125

❏ **1950s DeSoto**, Japanese, 6", green, friction
EX $20   NM $45   MIP $65

❏ **1950s Jaguar XKE Convertible**, Japanese, Tomiyama, 12", white, friction
EX $195   NM $455   MIP $650

❏ **1950s Jeep Station Wagon**, Japanese, Yonezawa, 7-1/2", two-tone brown, friction
EX $100   NM $210   MIP $300

❏ **1950s Kaiser Darren Convertible**, Japanese, 6-1/2", red, friction
EX $300   NM $70   MIP $100

(Ron Smith)

❏ **1950's Mazda Auto Tricycle**, Japanese, friction, Bandai, 8" (J274)
EX $75   NM $125   MIP $250

❏ **1950s Mercedes Convertible**, Japanese, Alps, 9", red, friction
EX $105   NM $245   MIP $350

(Ron Smith)

❏ **1950's Porsche Speedster**, Japanese, battery-op, Distler, 10-1/2" (J235)
EX $200   **NM** $300   **MIP** $600

(Toy Shop File Photo)

❏ **1950's Porsche Speedster**, Japanese, battery-op, Distler, 10-1/2" (J235)
EX $200   **NM** $300   **MIP** $600

❏ **1950s Studebaker Lark**, Japanese, 5-1/2", blue, friction
EX $20   **NM** $45   **MIP** $65

❏ **1950s Volvo**, Japanese, 5-1/2", red, friction
EX $20   **NM** $38   **MIP** $55

(Toy Shop File Photo)

❏ **1950's Volvo**, Japanese, wind-up, Sweden, 11" (J265A)
EX $600   **NM** $1000   **MIP** $2000

❏ **1950s Volvo PV-544**, Japanese, HoKu, 7-1/2", black, friction
EX $165   **NM** $385   **MIP** $550

❏ **1950s VW Convertible**, Japanese, 9-1/2", dark blue, maroon, or light metallic blue, friction w/battery-operated engine light
EX $85   **NM** $195   **MIP** $275

❏ **1950s VW Sedan**, Japanese, 7-1/2", gray, oval window, friction
EX $45   **NM** $105   **MIP** $150

❏ **1950s Zephyr Deluxe Convertible**, Japanese, 11", maroon/yellow/blue, friction
EX $120   **NM** $280   **MIP** $400

❏ **1951 Cadillac Four-Door Sedan**, Japanese, Marusan, 12-1/2", gray, battery-operated, remote control, working headlights
EX $480   **NM** $1120   **MIP** $1600

❏ **1951 Cadillac Four-Door Sedan**, Japanese, Marusan, 12-1/2", gray, black, white, or red, friction
EX $300   **NM** $700   **MIP** $1000

❏ **1951 Ford Sedan**, Japanese, 7", tan, battery-operated
EX $30   **NM** $70   **MIP** $100

❏ **1951 Futuristic Buick LeSabre**, Japanese, Yonezawa, 7-1/2", black, friction
EX $240   **NM** $560   **MIP** $800

(Ron Smith)

❏ **1952 Cadillac**, Japanese, friction, Alps, 11-1/2" (J20)
EX $250   **NM** $400   **MIP** $800

(Toy Shop File Photo)

❏ **1952 Ford Yellow Cab**, Japanese, Marusan, 10-1/2", yellow, friction, working money meter
EX $165   **NM** $385   **MIP** $550

(Toy Shop File Photo)

❏ **1952 Oldsmobile**, Japanese, friction, "Y" Co., 11" (J207A)
EX $150   **NM** $350   **MIP** $500

(Ron Smith)

❏ **1953 Chevrolet Corvette**, Japanese, friction, Bandai, 7" (J37)
EX $100   **NM** $200   **MIP** $400

❏ **1953 Chrysler Orion Convertible**, Japanese, 6-1/2", blue/green, friction
EX $25   **NM** $60   **MIP** $85

(Toy Shop File Photo)

❏ **1953 Packard Convertible/Sedan**, Japanese, friction, Alps, 16" (J222)
EX $500   **NM** $800   **MIP** $1600

❏ **1953 Studebaker Coupe**, Japanese, 9", yellow, friction, working wipers
EX $45   **NM** $100   **MIP** $140

(Ron Smith)

❏ **1954 Cadillac**, Japanese, battery-op, Joustra, 12" (J23)
EX $100   **NM** $200   **MIP** $450

(Ron Smith)

❏ **1954 Chevrolet**, Japanese, friction, Marusan, 11" (J49)
EX $300   **NM** $800   **MIP** $1500

❏ **1954 Chevrolet Bel Air**, Japanese, Marusan and Linemar, 11", gray/black, friction
EX $400   **NM** $840   **MIP** $1200

❏ **1954 Chevrolet Bel Air**, Japanese, Marusan and Linemar, 11", rare orange/yellow, friction
EX $660   **NM** $1550   **MIP** $2200

(Ron Smith)

❏ **1954 Pontiac**, Japanese, Minister, friction, Minister, 11" (J218A)
EX $10   **NM** $20   **MIP** $30

(Ron Smith)

❏ **1954 Studebaker**, Japanese, friction, Yoshiva, 9" (J243)
EX $150   **NM** $200   **MIP** $375

(Ron Smith)

❏ **1955 Buick Roadmaster**, Japanese, friction, Yoshiya, 11" (J5)
EX $125   **NM** $250   **MIP** $500

❏ **1955 Buick Special**, Japanese, 8-1/2", two-tone blue, battery-operated, working headlights
EX $55   **NM** $122   **MIP** $175

(Ron Smith)

❏ **1955 Chevrolet**, Japanese, battery-op, Marusan, 10-3/4" (J50)
EX $300   **NM** $800   **MIP** $1500

❏ **1955 Chevrolet Bel Air**, Japanese, Asahi Toy, 7" light green, friction
EX $50   **NM** $105   **MIP** $150

(Ron Smith)

❏ **1955 Chrysler**, Japanese, friction, Yonezawa, 8" (J71)
EX $100   **NM** $200   **MIP** $300

(Ron Smith)

❏ **1955 Ford Ambulance**, Japanese, friction, Bandai, 12" (J98)
EX $150   **NM** $200   **MIP** $250

(Ron Smith)

❏ **1955 Ford Convertible**, Japanese, friction, Bandai, 12" (J100)
EX $200   **NM** $400   **MIP** $700

❏ **1955 Ford Convertible**, Japanese, Haji, 6-1/2", two-tone blue or red/white, friction
EX $60   **NM** $140   **MIP** $200

(Ron Smith)

❏ **1955 Ford Panel Truck**, Japanese, "Flowers," friction, Bandai, 12" (J99)
EX $200   **NM** $400   **MIP** $600

(Ron Smith)

❏ **1955 Ford Pickup**, Japanese, friction, Bandai, 12" (J96)
EX $150   **NM** $250   **MIP** $300

(Ron Smith)

❏ **1955 Ford Station Wagon**, Japanese, friction, Bandai, 12" (J97)
EX $150   **NM** $250   **MIP** $300

(Toy Shop File Photo)

❏ **1955 Ford Thunderbird**, Japanese, friction, Bandai, 7" (J126A)
EX $75   **NM** $100   **MIP** $150

❏ **1955 Ford Thunderbird Convertible**, Japanese, 8", orange, friction
EX $45   **NM** $100   **MIP** $140

(Ron Smith)

❏ **1955 Lincoln Sedan**, Japanese, friction, Yonezawa, 12" (J163)
EX $250   **NM** $600   **MIP** $1200

❏ **1955 Mercedes 300 SL Coupe**, Japanese, 9", metallic red, opening gull-wing doors, battery-operated
EX $105   **NM** $245   **MIP** $350

(Ron Smith)

❏ **1956 Ford Convertible**, Japanese, friction, Haji, 11-1/2" (J102)
EX $400   **NM** $600   **MIP** $900

(Ron Smith)

❏ **1956 Ford Sedan**, Japanese, friction, Marusan, 13" (J103)
EX $500   **NM** $1000   **MIP** $3000

(Ron Smith)

❏ **1956 Ford Thunderbird**, Japanese, friction, T.N., 11" (J127)
EX $200   **NM** $300   **MIP** $400

(Ron Smith)

❏ **1956 Ford Thunderbird**, Japanese, battery-op, T.N., 11" (J129)
EX $200   **NM** $300   **MIP** $400

❏ **1956 Ford Two-Door HT**, Japanese, Ichiko, 10", two-tone blue or orange/white, friction
EX $165   **NM** $385   **MIP** $550

❏ **1956 Ford Two-Door Sedan**, Japanese, Marusan, 13", orange/white or blue/white
EX $1050   **NM** $2450   **MIP** $3500

(Ron Smith)

❏ **1956 Ford Wagon**, Japanese, friction, Nomura, 10-1/2" (J104)
EX $100   **NM** $150   **MIP** $300

❏ **1956 GM Gas Turbine Firebird II**, Japanese, 8-1/2", red, friction
EX $240   **NM** $560   **MIP** $800

(Ron Smith)

❑ **1956 Lincoln**, Japanese, friction, Ichiko, 16-1/2" (J165)
EX $150 **NM** $250 **MIP** $375

(Ron Smith)

❑ **1956 Lincoln Continental Mark II**, Japanese, friction, Linemar, 12" (J164)
EX $600 **NM** $1200 **MIP** $2500

❑ **1956 Lincoln Premiere Two-Door HT**, Japanese, 7-1/2", orange, friction
EX $30 **NM** $70 **MIP** $100

(Ron Smith)

❑ **1956 Mercury Hardtop**, Japanese, friction, Alps, 9-1/2" (J193)
EX $600 **NM** $800 **MIP** $1400

(Ron Smith)

❑ **1956 Oldsmobile Sedan**, Japanese, friction, Ichiko/Kanto, 10-1/2" (J208)
EX $200 **NM** $400 **MIP** $600

❑ **1956 Oldsmobile Super 88**, Japanese, Modern Toys, 14", orange, battery-operated, working headlights and signal lights
EX $225 **NM** $525 **MIP** $750

(Ron Smith)

❑ **1956 Oldsmobile Super 88 Sedan**, Japanese, friction, Masudaya, 16" (J209)
EX $200 **NM** $300 **MIP** $500

(Ron Smith)

❑ **1956 Plymouth Hardtop**, Japanese, friction, unknown manufacturer, 8-1/2" (J224)
EX $150 **NM** $200 **MIP** $400

(Ron Smith)

❑ **1956 Plymouth Hardtop**, Japanese, battery-op, Alps, 12" (J225)
EX $300 **NM** $400 **MIP** $600

❑ **1956 Plymouth HT**, Japanese, Alps, 8-1/2", two-tone green, friction
EX $165 **NM** $385 **MIP** $550

(Toy Shop File Photo)

❑ **1957 Chrysler New Yorker**, Japanese, friction, Alps, 14" (J72)
EX $500 **NM** $700 **MIP** $1500

❑ **1957 Chrysler New Yorker**, Japanese, 6-1/2", red/black, friction
EX $25 **NM** $60 **MIP** $85

❑ **1957 Ford Convertible**, Japanese, HTC, 12", orange/pink, friction
EX $115 **NM** $265 **MIP** $375

❑ **1957 Ford Fairlane 500 HT**, Japanese, ToyMaster, 9-1/2", green/yellow, friction
EX $45 **NM** $100 **MIP** $140

(Ron Smith)

❑ **1957 Ford Fairlane Sedan**, Japanese, friction, Ichiko, 10" (J105)
EX $100 **NM** $200 **MIP** $300

(Ron Smith)

❑ **1957 Ford Hardtop**, Japanese, friction, T.N., 12" (J106)
EX $100 **NM** $200 **MIP** $300

(Ron Smith)

❑ **1957 Ford Sedan/Convertible/Wagon/Pickup**, Japanese, friction, Joustra, 12" (J107)
EX $200 **NM** $250 **MIP** $300

(Ron Smith)

❑ **1957 Packard Hawk Convertible**, Japanese, battery-op, Schuco, 10-3/4" (J223)
EX $300 **NM** $400 **MIP** $900

(Ron Smith)

❑ **1957 Plymouth Fury Hardtop**, Japanese, friction, "Y" Co., 11-1/2" (J226)
EX $300 **NM** $400 **MIP** $600

(Ron Smith)

❑ **1958 Buick Century**, Japanese, friction, Bandai, 8" (J7)
EX $80 **NM** $100 **MIP** $150

VEHICLES

(Ron Smith)

❑ **1958 Buick Century**, Japanese, friction, Yonezawa, 12" (J6)
EX $400   **NM** $650   **MIP** $1500

(Ron Smith)

❑ **1958 Chevrolet Corvette**, Japanese, friction, Yonezawa, 9-1/2" (J38)
EX $200   **NM** $300   **MIP** $600

(Toy Shop File Photo)

❑ **1958 Chevrolet Station Wagon**, Japanese, friction, Bandai, 8" (J57)
EX $50   **NM** $65   **MIP** $125

(Ron Smith)

❑ **1958 Chrysler**, Japanese, battery-op, unknown manufacturer, 13" (J73)
EX $300   **NM** $400   **MIP** $800

❑ **1958 Dodge Four-Door HT**, Japanese, 8-1/2", orange/white, friction
EX $55   **NM** $125   **MIP** $175

(Ron Smith)

❑ **1958 Dodge Sedan**, Japanese, friction, T.N., 11" (J82)
EX $300   **NM** $400   **MIP** $800

(Ron Smith)

❑ **1958 Edsel Convertible/Sedan**, Japanese, friction, Haji, 10-1/2" (J86)
EX $300   **NM** $500   **MIP** $1000

(Ron Smith)

❑ **1958 Edsel Convertible/Sedan**, Japanese, friction, Haji, 10-1/2" (J86)
EX $300   **NM** $500   **MIP** $1000

(Ron Smith)

❑ **1958 Edsel Hardtop**, Japanese, friction, Asahi, 10-3/4" (J91)
EX $100   **NM** $200   **MIP** $350

(Ron Smith)

❑ **1958 Edsel Station Wagon**, Japanese, friction, T.N., 11" (J89)
EX $150   **NM** $200   **MIP** $300

❑ **1958 Edsel Station Wagon**, Japanese, 11", red/black, friction
EX $225   **NM** $525   **MIP** $750

(Ron Smith)

❑ **1958 Edsel Wagon**, Japanese, friction, Haji, 10-1/2" (J87)
EX $200   **NM** $300   **MIP** $600

(Toy Shop File Photo)

❑ **1958 Ford Fairlane Hardtop/Convertible**, Japanese, friction, Sankei Gangu, 9" (J114)
EX $90   **NM** $115   **MIP** $125

❑ **1958 Ford HT Convertible**, Japanese, 11", orange/white, battery-operated
EX $60   **NM** $140   **MIP** $200

❑ **1958 Ford HT Convertible**, Japanese, 9-1/2", blue/white, battery-operated
EX $85   **NM** $195   **MIP** $275

(Ron Smith)

❑ **1958 Mercury Hardtop**, Japanese, friction, Yonezawa, 11-1/2" (J195)
EX $250   **NM** $325   **MIP** $400

❑ **1958 Oldsmobile**, Japanese, Asahi Toy, 12", gold/black, friction
EX $540   **NM** $1260   **MIP** $1800

(Ron Smith)

❑ **1958 Oldsmobile Sedan**, Japanese, friction, A.T.C., 12" (J210)
EX $200   **NM** $300   **MIP** $400

❑ **1958 Oldsmobile Station Wagon**, Japanese, 7-1/2", red/black, friction
EX $30   **NM** $70   **MIP** $100

(Ron Smith)

❑ **1958 Plymouth Fury**, Japanese, friction, Bandai, 8" (J227)
EX $75   **NM** $90   **MIP** $165

❑ **1958 Pontiac Four-Door HT**, Japanese, Asahi Toy, 8", green/pink, friction
EX $45   **NM** $105   **MIP** $150

(Ron Smith)

❑ **1959 Buick**, Japanese, friction, T.N., 11" (J8)
EX $90   **NM** $150   **MIP** $300

❑ **1959 Buick Convertible**, Japanese, 11", orange/yellow, friction, dog and driver figures
EX $115   **NM** $245   **MIP** $350

❑ **1959 Buick HT Convertible**, Japanese, Linemar, 9-1/2" red/white, friction
EX $50   **NM** $105   **MIP** $150

❏ **1959 Buick Station Wagon**, Japanese, Yonezawa, 9", two-tone green, friction
EX $50　　NM $105　　MIP $150

(Ron Smith)

❏ **1959 Cadillac Convertible**, Japanese, friction, Bandai, 12" (J25)
EX $50　　NM $100　　MIP $185

(Ron Smith)

❏ **1959 Cadillac Convertible**, Japanese, friction, Bandai, 12" (J25)
EX $50　　NM $100　　MIP $185

❏ **1959 Chevrolet Highway Patrol Car**, Japanese, ASC, 10", black/white, friction
EX $55　　NM $125　　MIP $175

❏ **1959 Chevrolet HT**, Japanese, 7", green, friction
EX $30　　NM $70　　MIP $100

(Ron Smith)

❏ **1959 Chevrolet Sedan/Convertible/Wagon**, Japanese, friction, SY, 11-1/2" (J59)
EX $200　　NM $400　　MIP $800

(Ron Smith)

❏ **1959 Chrylser Imperial Convertible**, Japanese, friction, Bandai, 8" (J74)
EX $50　　NM $100　　MIP $175

(Ron Smith)

❏ **1959 Dodge Pickup**, Japanese, friction, unknown manufacturer, 18-1/2" (J84)
EX $350　　NM $500　　MIP $1200

❏ **1959 Dodge Two-Door HT**, Japanese, 9", blue/white, friction
EX $135　　NM $315　　MIP $450

❏ **1959 Ford HT Convertible**, Japanese, 11", blue/white, red/white, or green/white, battery-operated
EX $70　　NM $160　　MIP $225

(Ron Smith)

❏ **1959 Ford Retractable**, Japanese, friction, T.N., 11" (J117)
EX $80　　NM $100　　MIP $165

❏ **1959 Ford Station Wagon**, Japanese, 10-1/2", green/white, friction
EX $40　　NM $90　　MIP $125

(Ron Smith)

❏ **1959 Ford Station Wagon**, Japanese, friction, T.N., 12" (J116)
EX $100　　NM $150　　MIP $200

(Ron Smith)

❏ **1959 Lincoln Continental Mark III Convertible**, Japanese, friction, Bandai, 12" (J166)
EX $90　　NM $125　　MIP $175

(Ron Smith)

❏ **1959 Lincoln Continental Mark III Sedan**, Japanese, friction, Bandai, 12" (J167)
EX $90　　NM $125　　MIP $175

(Toy Shop File Photo)

❏ **1959 Oldsmobile Highway Patrol Car**, Japanese, Ichiko, 12-1/2", black/white, friction, working speed meter on trunk
EX $75　　NM $175　　MIP $250

(Ron Smith)

❏ **1959 Oldsmobile Sedan**, Japanese, friction, Ichiko, 12-1/2" (J213)
EX $75　　NM $125　　MIP $175

❏ **1959 Oldsmobile Two-Door HT**, Japanese, Ichiko, 12-1/2", two-tone blue, two-tone green, or brown/white, friction
EX $135　　NM $315　　MIP $450

❏ **1959 Plymouth Convertible**, Japanese, Asahi Toy, 11", red/white, friction
EX $330　　NM $770　　MIP $1100

(Ron Smith)

❏ **1959 Plymouth Hardtop**, Japanese, friction, A.T.C., 10-1/2" (J228)
EX $200　　NM $400　　MIP $600

❏ **1960 Cadillac Four-Door Sedan**, Japanese, Yonezawa, 18" black or maroon, friction
EX $300　　NM $630　　MIP $900

(Ron Smith)

❏ **1960 Chevrolet**, Japanese, friction, Marusan, 11-1/2" (J60)
EX $200　　NM $400　　MIP $800

❏ **1960 Chevrolet Impala HT**, Japanese, Alps, 9", red/white, friction
EX $105　　NM $245　　MIP $350

(Toy Shop File Photo)

❏ **1960 Citroen 2 CV**, Japanese, friction, Daiya, 8" (J269A)
EX $100　　NM $150　　MIP $250

VEHICLES

(Toy Shop File Photo)

❑ **1960 Citroen DS 19 Sedan**, Japanese, friction, Bandai, 12" (J68)
EX $300   **NM** $600   **MIP** $900

(Ron Smith)

❑ **1960 Ford**, Japanese, friction, Haji, 11" (J119)
EX $125   **NM** $200   **MIP** $350

❑ **1960 Ford Gyron**, Japanese, Ichida, 11", red/white, battery-operated
EX $135   **NM** $315   **MIP** $450

❑ **1960 Ford Gyron**, Japanese, Ichida, 11", red/black, remote control, battery-operated
EX $85   **NM** $195   **MIP** $275

❑ **1960 Ford Gyron**, Japanese, Ichida, red/black, friction
EX $45   **NM** $100   **MIP** $140

(Ron Smith)

❑ **1960 Lincoln Hardtop/Convertible**, Japanese, friction, Yonezawa, 11" (J168)
EX $100   **NM** $150   **MIP** $300

(Toy Shop File Photo)

❑ **1960 Renault**, Japanese, friction, Bandai, 7-1/2" (J241)
EX $95   **NM** $150   **MIP** $200

(Toy Shop File Photo)

❑ **1960 Rolls Royce**, Japanese, friction, T.N., 10-1/2" (J239)
EX $200   **NM** $300   **MIP** $500

(Ron Smith)

❑ **1960 Rolls Royce Silver Coupe Convertible**, Japanese, friction, Bandai, 12" (J236)
EX $100   **NM** $150   **MIP** $300

(Ron Smith)

❑ **1960 Volkswagen Karmann-Ghia**, Japanese, friction, Bandai, 7" (J252)
EX $100   **NM** $150   **MIP** $300

(Ron Smith)

❑ **1960's Aston-Martin DB5**, Japanese, (James Bond), friction, Gilbert, 11-1/2" (J1)
EX $75   **NM** $150   **MIP** $350

(Ron Smith)

❑ **1960's Aston-Martin DB6**, Japanese, friction, Asahi Toy Co., 11" (J2)
EX $200   **NM** $400   **MIP** $600

❑ **1960s BMW Coupe**, Japanese, Yonezawa, 11" tan, battery-operated
EX $50   **NM** $105   **MIP** $150

(Toy Shop File Photo)

❑ **1960s Ferrari Berlinetta 250 LeMans**, Japanese, Asahi Toy, 11", red, friction
EX $115   **NM** $265   **MIP** $375

❑ **1960s Ford Falcon**, Japanese, Marusan, 9", red/white, friction
EX $25   **NM** $55   **MIP** $75

(Toy Shop File Photo)

❑ **1960's Ford Taunus 17M**, Japanese, friction, Bandai, 8" (J145)
EX $20   **NM** $40   **MIP** $60

(Toy Shop File Photo)

❑ **1960's Jaguar XKE Convertible**, Japanese, friction, T.T., 10-1/2" (J155)
EX $75   **NM** $100   **MIP** $250

❑ **1960s Jaguar XKE Coupe**, Japanese, 10-1/2", red, friction
EX $55   **NM** $125   **MIP** $175

❑ **1960s Mercedes Convertible**, Japanese, HTC, 8", red, opening door w/swing-out driver, friction
EX $45   **NM** $105   **MIP** $150

(Ron Smith)

❏ **1960's Mercedes-Benz 219 Convertible**, Japanese, friction, Bandai, 8" (J177)
EX $50   **NM** $80   **MIP** $120

(Ron Smith)

❏ **1960's Mercedes-Benz 219 Sedan**, Japanese, friction, Bandai, 8" (J176)
EX $50   **NM** $80   **MIP** $120

(Toy Shop File Photo)

❏ **1960s Porsche 911 Rally**, Japanese, 11", red, friction
EX $70   **NM** $160   **MIP** $225

❏ **1960s Porsche 914 Rally**, Japanese, Daiya, 9", blue, battery-operated
EX $25   **NM** $55   **MIP** $75

(Ron Smith)

❏ **1960's Ramgler Rebel Station Wagon**, Japanese, friction, Bandai, 12" (J240)
EX $60   **NM** $90   **MIP** $150

(Ron Smith)

❏ **1960's Rolls Royce Silver Sedan Coupe**, Japanese, friction, Bandai, 12" (J237)
EX $100   **NM** $150   **MIP** $250

(Ron Smith)

❏ **1960's Studebaker Avanti**, Japanese, friction, Bandai, 8" (J242)
EX $125   **NM** $175   **MIP** $350

(Ron Smith)

❏ **1960's Volkswagen**, Japanese, battery-op, Bandai, 11" (J264)
EX $25   **NM** $50   **MIP** $75

(Ron Smith)

❏ **1960's Volkswagen Convertible**, Japanese, battery-op, Bandai, 11" (J260)
EX $110   **NM** $145   **MIP** $200

(Ron Smith)

❏ **1960's Volkswagen with or without Sun Roof**, Japanese, friction, Bandai, 15" (J265)
EX $60   **NM** $90   **MIP** $125

❏ **1961 Buick Fire Department Car**, Japanese, 16", red, friction, working wipers, revolving emergency light
EX $50   **NM** $105   **MIP** $150

(Ron Smith)

❏ **1961 Cadillac Fleetwood**, Japanese, friction, SSS, 17-1/2" (J29)
EX $100   **NM** $200   **MIP** $350

(Ron Smith)

❏ **1961 Chevrolet Impala Convertible**, Japanese, friction, Bandai, 11" (J63)
EX $100   **NM** $150   **MIP** $300

(Ron Smith)

❏ **1961 Chevrolet Impala Sedan**, Japanese, friction, Bandai, 11" (J62)
EX $100   **NM** $150   **MIP** $300

(Ron Smith)

❏ **1961 Ford Country Sedan**, Japanese, friction, Bandai, 10-1/2" (J120)
EX $125   **NM** $150   **MIP** $250

❏ **1961 Mercedes 220-S**, Japanese, 12", black, jack-up feature, friction
EX $75   **NM** $175   **MIP** $250

(Ron Smith)

❏ **1961 Oldsmobile Convertible**, Japanese, friction, Yonezawa, 12" (J214)
EX $75   **NM** $125   **MIP** $200

❏ **1961 Oldsmobile Rally Car**, Japanese, Asahi Toy, 15", red, friction
EX $55   **NM** $125   **MIP** $175

(Ron Smith)

❏ **1961 Plymouth Sedan**, Japanese, friction, Ichiko, 12" (J230)
EX $150   **NM** $300   **MIP** $550

(Ron Smith)

❏ **1961 Plymouth Station Wagon**, Japanese, friction, Ichiko, 12" (J231)
EX $150   **NM** $250   **MIP** $500

VEHICLES

(Ron Smith)

❏ **1961 Plymouth T.V. Car**, Japanese, battery-op, Ichiko, 12" (J232)
EX $100   **NM** $150   **MIP** $300

❏ **1962 Cadillac Polic Car**, Japanese, Ichiko, 6-1/2" black/white, friction w/siren
EX $30   **NM** $65   **MIP** $90

(Ron Smith)

❏ **1962 Chevrolet**, Japanese, friction, unknown manufacturer, 11" (J65)
EX $125   **NM** $250   **MIP** $350

(Ron Smith)

❏ **1962 Chevrolet Secret Agent**, Japanese, battery-op, unknown manufacturer, 14" (J64)
EX $50   **NM** $75   **MIP** $150

(Ron Smith)

❏ **1962 Chrysler Imperial**, Japanese, 16", friction, black, red (white: add 20% to value)
EX $600   **NM** $1200   **MIP** $2200

(Ron Smith)

❏ **1962 Ford Country Sedan**, Japanese, friction, Asahi, 12" (J121)
EX $200   **NM** $350   **MIP** $700

❏ **1962 Ford Thunderbird HT Convertible**, Japanese, Yonezawa, 11-1/2", red, battery-operated
EX $105   **NM** $245   **MIP** $350

(Ron Smith)

❏ **1963 Buick Wildcat**, Japanese, friction, Ichiko, 15" (J13)
EX $200   **NM** $400   **MIP** $800

(Ron Smith)

❏ **1963 Chevrolet Impala**, Japanese, friction, Bandai (?), 18" (J66)
EX $200   **NM** $300   **MIP** $400

❏ **1963 Corvette Coupe**, Japanese, 12", metallic red or white, battery-operated, working headlights
EX $180   **NM** $420   **MIP** $600

❏ **1963 Ford Fire Chief Car**, Japanese, Taiyo, 12-1/2", red, battery-operated
EX $23   **NM** $55   **MIP** $75

❏ **1963 Ford Stock Car**, Japanese, Taiyo, 10-1/2", red/silver/blue, friction
EX $25   **NM** $60   **MIP** $85

(Ron Smith)

❏ **1963 Ford Thunderbird Retractable**, Japanese, battery-op, Yonezawa, 11" (J134)
EX $80   **NM** $150   **MIP** $200

(Ron Smith)

❏ **1963 Ford Thunderbird Retractable**, Japanese, battery-op, Yonezawa, 11" (J134)
EX $80   **NM** $150   **MIP** $200

(Ron Smith)

❏ **1964 Chevrolet Corvette**, Japanese, battery-op, Ichida, 12" (J41)
EX $150   **NM** $225   **MIP** $350

(Ron Smith)

❏ **1964 Ford Hardtop**, Japanese, friction, Ichiko, 13" (J122)
EX $200   **NM** $450   **MIP** $700

(Ron Smith)

❏ **1964 Ford Thunderbird**, Japanese, friction, Ichiko, 16" (J137)
EX $100   **NM** $200   **MIP** $400

(Ron Smith)

❏ **1964 Ford Thunderbird Hardtop**, Japanese, friction, Asahi, 12" (J136)
EX $150   **NM** $200   **MIP** $400

❏ **1964 Ford Thunderbird HT Convertible**, Japanese, Ichiko, 15-1/2", red, working side windows, friction
EX $120   **NM** $280   **MIP** $400

❏ **1964 Lincoln**, Japanese, 11", burgundy, battery-operated
EX $165   **NM** $385   **MIP** $550

(Ron Smith)

❏ **1964 Lincoln**, Japanese, friction, unknown manufacturer, 10-1/2" (J169)
EX $90   **NM** $175   **MIP** $275

(Toy Shop File Photo)

❏ **1964 Lincoln**, Japanese, friction, unknown manufacturer, 10-1/2" (J169)
EX $90   **NM** $175   **MIP** $275

❑ **1965 Ford Country Squire Wagon**, Japanese, 9", white, friction
EX $30   **NM** $70   **MIP** $100

(Ron Smith)

❑ **1965 Ford Galaxie Hardtop**, Japanese, friction, MT, 11" (J125)
EX $125   **NM** $150   **MIP** $300

(Ron Smith)

❑ **1965 Ford Mustang Fastback**, Japanese, friction, Bandai, 11" (J139)
EX $45   **NM** $65   **MIP** $90

❑ **1965 Ford Mustang GT**, Japanese, 15-1/2", red, friction
EX $85   **NM** $195   **MIP** $275

(Ron Smith)

❑ **1965 Ford Mustang Hardtop/Convertible**, Japanese, friction/battery-op, Bandai, 11" (J140)
EX $75   **NM** $125   **MIP** $150

(Ron Smith)

❑ **1965 Ford Thunderbird Hardtop**, Japanese, friction, Bandai, 10-3/4" (J138)
EX $60   **NM** $90   **MIP** $175

❑ **1966 Dodge Charger Sonic Car**, Japanese, 16", red, battery-operated
EX $145   **NM** $335   **MIP** $475

(Ron Smith)

❑ **1966 Ford Mustang Fastback**, Japanese, friction, T.N., 17" (J143)
EX $120   **NM** $200   **MIP** $325

(Ron Smith)

❑ **1966 Oldsmobile Toronado**, Japanese, battery-op, Bandai, 11" (J215)
EX $65   **NM** $110   **MIP** $150

(Ron Smith)

❑ **1967 Cadillac**, Japanese, friction, K.O., 10-1/2" (J34)
EX $100   **NM** $150   **MIP** $250

(Ron Smith)

❑ **1967 Chevrolet Camaro**, Japanese, battery-op, T.N., 14" (J46)
EX $100   **NM** $150   **MIP** $300

(Toy Shop File Photo)

❑ **1967 Chevrolet Camaro**, Japanese, battery-op, T.N., 14" (J46)
EX $100   **NM** $150   **MIP** $300

(Ron Smith)

❑ **1967 Mercury Cougar Hardtop**, Japanese, friction, Asakusa Toys, 15" (J197)
EX $200   **NM** $400   **MIP** $800

(Ron Smith)

❑ **1967 Pontiac Firebird**, Japanese, friction, Akasura, 15-1/2" (J219)
EX $200   **NM** $400   **MIP** $900

(Ron Smith)

❑ **1967 Pontiac Firebird**, Japanese, friction, Bandai, 10" (J220)
EX $30   **NM** $55   **MIP** $100

(Ron Smith)

❑ **1968 Chevrolet Corvette**, Japanese, battery-op, Taiyo, 9-1/2" (J42)
EX $20   **NM** $40   **MIP** $80

(Ron Smith)

❑ **1968 Ford Torino**, Japanese, friction, S.T., 16" (J126)
EX $175   **NM** $300   **MIP** $600

(Ron Smith)

❑ **1968 Oldsmobile Toronado**, Japanese, friction, Ichiko, 17-1/2" (J216)
EX $300   **NM** $400   **MIP** $500

❑ **1970s VW Rabbit Rally Team Car**, Japanese, Asahi Toy, 8", yellow, battery-operated
EX $20   **NM** $45   **MIP** $65

(Ron Smith)

❑ **1971 Chevrolet Camaro Rusher**, Japanese, battery-op, Taiyo, 9-1/2" (J48)
EX $10   **NM** $20   **MIP** $25

VEHICLES

(Toy Shop File Photo)

❏ **Dream Car**, Japanese, friction, "Y" Co., 17" (J278A)
EX $600   **NM** $800   **MIP** $1500

(Toy Shop File Photo)

❏ **Electrospecial No. 21**, Japanese, battery-op, "Y" Co., 10" (J290)
EX $300   **NM** $600   **MIP** $1200

❏ **Ford Model-T**, Japanese, 9", red, hard top, friction
EX $25   **NM** $55   **MIP** $75

❏ **Ford Model-T**, Japanese, 9", black, open top, friction
EX $25   **NM** $55   **MIP** $75

(Toy Shop File Photo)

❏ **Midget Special No. 6**, Japanese, friction, "Y" Co., 7" (J291)
EX $300   **NM** $500   **MIP** $1000

JOHNNY LIGHTNING / TOPPER

(KP Photo)

❑ **'32 Roadster,** 1969, Varied chromed color body, rumble seat in back flips up. This model has missing windshield, common to play worn examples
EX $25 **NM** $60 **MIP** $125

❑ **A.J. Foyt Indy Special,** 1970, blackwall tires
EX $40 **NM** $60 **MIP** $250

(KP Photo, Tom Michael collection)

❑ **Al Unser Indy Special,** 1970, Chrome blue finish, Lightning number "2" decal, black wall tires
EX $100 **NM** $200 **MIP** $500

❑ **Baja,** 1970, Marx
EX $45 **NM** $125 **MIP** $200

(KP Photo, Tom Michael collection)

❑ **Big Rig,** 1971, Originally included add on extras called "Customs;" prices reflect fully accessorized car. Called the "Track Bac" in the 1970 Topper Toys catalog
EX $65 **NM** $150 **MIP** $275

❑ **Bubble,** 1970, Jet Powered
EX $45 **NM** $75 **MIP** $150

(Photo courtesy Dennis Seleman)

❑ **Bug Bomb,** 1970, Various chromed color schemes, two silver engines, blackwall tires. This example is missing the rear engine
EX $40 **NM** $90 **MIP** $225

❑ **Condor,** 1970, blackwall tires
EX $150 **NM** $200 **MIP** $1200

❑ **Custom Camaro,** 1968-69, Prototype, only one known to exist
EX n/a **NM** $6000 **MIP** n/a

❑ **Custom Charger,** 1968-69, Prototype, only one known to exist. A Version of this car is now available by Playing Mantis as part of the "Lost Toppers" series
EX n/a **NM** $6000 **MIP** n/a

❑ **Custom Continental,** 1968-69, Prototype, only six known to exist. Another casting re-released by Playing Mantis
EX n/a **NM** $4000 **MIP** n/a

❑ **Custom Dragster,** 1969, Without canopy
EX $35 **NM** $75 **MIP** $125

❑ **Custom Dragster,** 1969, Mirror finish
EX $150 **NM** $250 **MIP** $1000

(KP Photo)

❑ **Custom Dragster,** 1969, Version with a plastic canopy, Topper-style redlines wheels, unpainted base. While versions were made without a canopy, the example here is simply missing one
EX $60 **NM** $150 **MIP** $200

❑ **Custom El Camino,** 1969, With sealed doors
EX $100 **NM** $300 **MIP** $500

(Photo courtesy Dennis Seleman)

❑ **Custom El Camino,** 1969, With opening doors, surfboards on back, Topper-style redlines wheels
EX $150 **NM** $275 **MIP** $475

❑ **Custom El Camino,** 1969, Mirror finish
EX $200 **NM** $350 **MIP** $1125

❑ **Custom Eldorado,** 1969, With sealed doors
EX $150 **NM** $300 **MIP** $1000

❑ **Custom Eldorado,** 1969, With opening doors
EX $150 **NM** $275 **MIP** $275

❑ **Custom Ferrari,** 1969, With opening doors, mirror finish
EX $300 **NM** $450 **MIP** $1000

(KP Photo)

❑ **Custom Ferrari,** 1969, With sealed doors
EX $35 **NM** $80 **MIP** $125

❑ **Custom Ferrari,** 1969, With opening doors
EX $150 **NM** $275 **MIP** $500

❑ **Custom GTO,** 1969, Mirror finish
EX $200 **NM** $475 **MIP** $1000

❑ **Custom GTO,** 1969, With sealed doors
EX $200 **NM** $350 **MIP** $1700

❑ **Custom GTO,** 1969, With opening doors
EX $200 **NM** $350 **MIP** $1500

❑ **Custom Mako Shark,** 1969, With sealed doors
EX $40 **NM** $75 **MIP** $225

(Photo Courtesy Dennis Seleman)

❑ **Custom Mako Shark,** 1969, With opening doors, mirror finish
EX $200 **NM** $500 **MIP** $2000

❑ **Custom Mako Shark,** 1969, With opening doors
EX $125 **NM** $350 **MIP** $500

❑ **Custom Mustang,** 1968-69, Prototype, only one known to exist
EX n/a **NM** $6000 **MIP** n/a

❑ **Custom Spoiler,** 1970, Blackwall tires
EX $35 **NM** $65 **MIP** $150

❑ **Custom T-Bird,** 1969, With opening doors
EX $100 **NM** $250 **MIP** $475

❑ **Custom T-Bird,** 1969, Mirror finish
EX $200 **NM** $400 **MIP** $5000

❑ **Custom T-Bird,** 1969, With sealed doors
EX $150 **NM** $300 **MIP** $700

❑ **Custom Toronado,** 1969, With opening doors
EX $225 **NM** $400 **MIP** $1000

❑ **Custom Toronado,** 1969, Mirror finish
EX $450 **NM** $600 **MIP** $2000

❑ **Custom Toronado,** 1969, With sealed doors
EX $300 **NM** $500 **MIP** $1500

❑ **Custom Turbine,** 1969, Red, black, white painted interior
EX $50　　NM $150　　MIP $200

(KP Photo, Tom Michael collection)

❑ **Custom Turbine,** 1969, With unpainted interior, Topper redline-style wheels
EX $25　　NM $45　　MIP $125

❑ **Custom Turbine,** 1969, Mirror finish
EX $150　　NM $225　　MIP $500

❑ **Custom XKE,** 1969, With opening doors, mirror finish
EX $300　　NM $450　　MIP $800

(KP Photo, Tom Michael collection)

❑ **Custom XKE,** 1969, With sealed doors, unpainted base, full window plastic all-around, opening hood, blackwalls tires
EX $35　　NM $80　　MIP $100

(KP Photo, Tom Michael collection)

❑ **Custom XKE,** 1969, With opening doors, unpainted base, opening hood, blackwalls tires
EX $150　　NM $275　　MIP $400

❑ **Double Trouble,** 1970, Blackwall tires
EX $75　　NM $100　　MIP $1500

❑ **Flame Out,** 1970, Black wall tires
EX $60　　NM $125　　MIP $350

❑ **Flying Needle,** 1970, Jet Powered
EX $45　　NM $100　　MIP $225

(KP Photo)

❑ **Frantic Ferrari,** 1970, Unpainted base, silver exposed engine, various finishes
EX $35　　NM $45　　MIP $90

❑ **Glasser,** 1970, Jet Powered
EX $40　　NM $75　　MIP $150

❑ **Hairy Hauler,** 1971, Came with add-on extras called "Customs;" prices reflect fully accessorized cars
EX $65　　NM $150　　MIP $275

❑ **Jumpin' Jag,** 1970, Blackwall tires
EX $35　　NM $80　　MIP $175

(KP Photo)

❑ **Leapin' Limo,** 1970, Blackwall tires, large silver and black plastic engine. Example here shows Topper packaging, duplicated to an extent by Playing Mantis with the Commemorative series
EX $50　　NM $125　　MIP $400

❑ **Mad Maverick,** 1970, Blackwall tires
EX $75　　NM $150　　MIP $450

❑ **Monster,** 1970, Jet Powered
EX $40　　NM $74　　MIP $150

❑ **Movin' Van,** 1970, Blackwall tires
EX $35　　NM $65　　MIP $90

(KP Photo, Tom Michael collection)

❑ **Nucleon,** 1970, Blackwall tires
EX $35　　NM $80　　MIP $225

❑ **Parnelli Jones Indy Special,** 1970, Blackwall tires
EX $40　　NM $60　　MIP $250

❑ **Pipe Dream,** 1971, Came with add-on extras called "Customs;" prices reflect fully accessorized cars
EX $65　　NM $150　　MIP $275

❑ **Sand Stormer,** 1970, Blackwall tires
EX $20　　NM $35　　MIP $90

❑ **Sand Stormer,** 1970, Black roof, blackwall tires
EX $50　　NM $100　　MIP $200

❑ **Screamer,** 1970, Jet Powered
EX $45　　NM $75　　MIP $200

❑ **Sling Shot,** 1970, Blackwall tires
EX $50　　NM $95　　MIP $250

❑ **Smuggler,** 1970, Blackwall tires
EX $35　　NM $75　　MIP $150

(KP Photo)

❑ **Stiletto,** 1970, Blackwall tires, various paint schemes. The example shown is pretty rough. The casting was re-released by Playing Mantis as part of the "Topper Series"
EX $60　　NM $85　　MIP $300

❑ **TNT,** 1970, Blackwall tires
EX $40　　NM $75　　MIP $175

❑ **Triple Threat,** 1970, Blackwall tires
EX $40　　NM $90　　MIP $200

❑ **Twin Blaster,** 1971, Came with add-on extras called "Customs;" prices reflect fully accessorized cars
EX $65　　NM $150　　MIP $275

(KP Photo)

❑ **Vicious Vette,** 1970, Blackwall tires
EX $35　　NM $80　　MIP $225

❑ **Vulture w/wing,** 1970, Blackwall tires
EX $75　　NM $130　　MIP $500

❑ **Wasp,** 1970, Blackwall tires
EX $80　　NM $100　　MIP $400

❑ **Wedge,** 1970, Jet Powered
EX $45　　NM $75　　MIP $200

❑ **Whistler,** 1970, Blackwall tires
EX $75　　NM $125　　MIP $300

❑ **Wild Winner,** 1971, Came w/add on extras called "Customs;" prices reflect fully accessorized cars
EX $60　　NM $125　　MIP $250

(KP Photo, Tom Michael collection)

MARX

AIRPLANES

❑ **727 Riding Jet**, Marx, jet engine sound
EX $150   **NM** $225   **MIP** $300

❑ **Airmail Biplane**, Marx, four engines, tin wind-up, 18" wingspan, 1936
EX $225   **NM** $325   **MIP** $450

❑ **Airmail Monoplane**, Marx, two engines, tin wind-up, 1930
EX $100   **NM** $150   **MIP** $225

❑ **Airplane**, Marx, mail biplane, tin wind-up, 9-3/4" wingspan, 1926
EX $150   **NM** $225   **MIP** $300

❑ **Airplane**, Marx, monoplane, pressed steel, 9" wingspan, 1942
EX $110   **NM** $165   **MIP** $300

❑ **Airplane**, Marx, no engines, tin wind-up, 9-1/2" wingspan
EX $135   **NM** $200   **MIP** $300

❑ **Airplane**, Marx, two propellers, tin wind-up, 9 7/8" wingspan, 1927
EX $200   **NM** $300   **MIP** $400

❑ **Airplane**, Marx, tin wind-up, 9-1/4" wingspan, 1926
EX $150   **NM** $225   **MIP** $300

❑ **Airplane**, Marx, adjustable rudder, tin wind-up, 10" wingspan, 1926
EX $150   **NM** $225   **MIP** $300

❑ **Airplane**, Marx, monoplane, adjustable rudder, tin wind-up, 9-1/4" wingspan
EX $150   **NM** $225   **MIP** $300

❑ **Airplane**, Marx, medium fuselage, tin wind-up
EX $125   **NM** $150   **MIP** $250

❑ **Airplane**, Marx, light fuselage, tin wind-up
EX $125   **NM** $175   **MIP** $250

❑ **Airplane**, Marx, twin engine, tin wind-up, 9-1/2" wingspan
EX $100   **NM** $150   **MIP** $200

❑ **Airplane #90**, Marx, tin wind-up, 5" wingspan, 1930
EX $240   **NM** $360   **MIP** $480

❑ **Airplane with Parachute**, Marx, monoplane, tin wind-up, 13" wingspan, 1929
EX $115   **NM** $170   **MIP** $325

❑ **Air-Sea Power Bombing Set**, Marx, 12" wingspan, 1940s
EX $325   **NM** $450   **MIP** $650

❑ **Airways Express Plane**, Marx, tin wind-up, 13" wingspan, 1929
EX $200   **NM** $300   **MIP** $400

❑ **American Airlines Airplane**, Marx, passenger plane, tin wind-up, 27" wingspan, 1940
EX $130   **NM** $190   **MIP** $400

(Toy Shop File Photo)

❑ **American Airlines Flagship**, Marx, pressed steel, wood wheels, 27" wingspan, 1940
EX $200   **NM** $300   **MIP** $500

❑ **Army Airplane**, Marx, biplane, tin wind-up, 25-3/4" wingspan, 1930
EX $225   **NM** $340   **MIP** $450

❑ **Army Airplane**, Marx, 18" wingspan, 1951
EX $150   **NM** $225   **MIP** $300

❑ **Army Airplane**, Marx, two engines, tin wind-up, 18" wingspan, 1938
EX $125   **NM** $190   **MIP** $250

❑ **Army Airplane**, Marx, tin, mechanical fighter, 7" wingspan
EX $125   **NM** $170   **MIP** $230

❑ **Army Bomber**, Marx, two engines, tin wind-up, 18" wingspan, 1940s
EX $250   **NM** $375   **MIP** $500

❑ **Army Bomber**, Marx, monoplane, litho machine gun and pilot, 25-1/2" wingspan, 1935
EX $300   **NM** $450   **MIP** $600

❑ **Army Bomber**, Marx, tri-motor, 25-1/2" wingspan, 1935
EX $250   **NM** $375   **MIP** $500

❑ **Army Bomber with Bombs**, Marx, camouflage pattern, metal, wind-up, 12" wingspan, 1930s
EX $100   **NM** $150   **MIP** $250

❑ **Army Fighter Plane**, Marx, tin wind-up, 5" wingspan, 1940s
EX $100   **NM** $150   **MIP** $250

❑ **Autogyro**, Marx, tin wind-up, 27" wingspan, 1940s
EX $150   **NM** $225   **MIP** $375

❑ **Blue and Silver Bomber**, Marx, two engines, tin wind-up, 18" wingspan, 1940
EX $190   **NM** $280   **MIP** $375

❑ **Bomber**, Marx, four propellers, metal, wind-up, 14-1/2" wingspan
EX $100   **NM** $150   **MIP** $300

❑ **Bomber with Tricycle Landing Gear**, Marx, four engine, tin wind-up, 18" wingspan, 1940
EX $225   **NM** $325   **MIP** $425

❑ **Camouflage Airplane**, Marx, four engines, 18" wingspan, 1942
EX $125   **NM** $200   **MIP** $295

❑ **China Clipper**, Marx, four engines, tin wind-up, 18-1/4" wingspan, 1938
EX $100   **NM** $150   **MIP** $250

❑ **City Airport**, Marx, extra tower and planes, 1930s
EX $125   **NM** $190   **MIP** $250

❑ **Crash-Proof Airplane**, Marx, monoplane, tin wind-up, 11-3/4" wingspan, 1933
EX $100   **NM** $150   **MIP** $200

❑ **Cross Country Flyer**, Marx, 19" tall, 1929
EX $375   **NM** $550   **MIP** $725

❑ **Dagwood's Solo Flight Airplane**, Marx, wind-up, 9" wingspan, 1935
EX $200   **NM** $300   **MIP** $950

❑ **Daredevil Flyer**, Marx, tin wind-up, 1929
EX $115   **NM** $170   **MIP** $325

❑ **Daredevil Flyer**, Marx, Zeppelin-shaped, 1928
EX $225   **NM** $350   **MIP** $475

❑ **DC-3 Airplane**, Marx, aluminum, wind-up, 9-1/2" wingspan, 1930s
EX $125   **NM** $190   **MIP** $300

❑ **Eagle Air Scout**, Marx, monoplane, tin wind-up, 26-1/2" wingspan, 1929
EX $200   **NM** $300   **MIP** $400

❑ **Fighter Jet, USAF**, Marx, battery-operated, 7" wingspan
EX $90   **NM** $135   **MIP** $250

❑ **Fighter Plane**, Marx, battery-operated, remote controlled, 1950s
EX $90   **NM** $135   **MIP** $250

❑ **Fix All Helicopter**, Marx
EX $275   **NM** $400   **MIP** $600

❑ **Flip-Over Airplane**, Marx, tin wind-up
EX $200   **NM** $300   **MIP** $450

❑ **Floor Zeppelin**, Marx, 9-1/2" long, 1931
EX $225   **NM** $340   **MIP** $500

❑ **Floor Zeppelin**, Marx, 16-1/2" long, 1931
EX $350   **NM** $525   **MIP** $750

(RLM MacNary Collection)

❑ **Flying Fortress 2095**, Marx, sparking, four engines, 1940
EX $150   **NM** $245   **MIP** $400

❑ **Flying Zeppelin**, Marx, wind-up, 9" long, 1930
EX $225   **NM** $340   **MIP** $475

❑ **Flying Zeppelin**, Marx, wind-up, 17" long, 1930
EX $350   **NM** $525   **MIP** $750

❑ **Flying Zeppelin**, Marx, wind-up, 10" long
EX $275   **NM** $400   **MIP** $600

❑ **Four-Motor Transport Plane**, Marx, friction, tin litho
EX $120   **NM** $180   **MIP** $325

❑ **Golden Tricky Airplane**, Marx
EX $75   NM $115   MIP $225

❑ **Hangar with One Plane**, Marx, 1940s
EX $150   NM $225   MIP $500

❑ **International Airline Express**, Marx, monoplane, tin wind-up, 17-1/2" wingspan, 1931
EX $200   NM $300   MIP $425

❑ **Jet Plane**, Marx, friction, 6" wingspan, 1950s
EX $65   NM $90   MIP $195

❑ **Little Lindy Airplane**, Marx, friction, 2-1/4" wingspan, 1930
EX $200   NM $300   MIP $500

❑ **Looping Plane**, Marx, silver version, tin wind-up, 7" wingspan, 1941
EX $225   NM $325   MIP $525

❑ **Lucky Stunt Flyer**, Marx, tin wind-up, 6" long, 1928
EX $150   NM $225   MIP $350

❑ **Mammoth Zeppelin, 1st Mammoth**, Marx, pull toy, 28" long, 1930
EX $400   NM $600   MIP $900

❑ **Mammoth Zeppelin, 2nd Mammoth**, Marx, pull toy, 28" long, 1930
EX $375   NM $575   MIP $775

❑ **Municipal Airport Hangar**, Marx, 1929
EX $100   NM $150   MIP $425

❑ **Overseas Biplane**, Marx, three propellers, tin wind-up, 9-7/8" wingspan, 1928
EX $150   NM $275   MIP $395

❑ **PAA Clipper Plane**, Marx, pressed steel, 27" wingspan, 1952
EX $125   NM $175   MIP $525

(Toy Shop File Photo)

❑ **PAA Passenger Plane**, Marx, tin litho, 14" wingspan, 1950s
EX $120   NM $175   MIP $275

❑ **Pan American**, Marx, pressed steel, four motors, 27" wingspan, 1940
EX $90   NM $150   MIP $525

❑ **Piggy Back Plane**, Marx, tin wind-up, 9" wingspan, 1939
EX $100   NM $150   MIP $350

❑ **Pioneer Air Express Monoplane**, Marx, tin litho, pull toy, 25-1/2" wingspan
EX $125   NM $190   MIP $300

❑ **Popeye Flyer**, Marx, Popeye and Olive Oyl in plane, tin litho tower, wind-up, 1936
EX $475   NM $700   MIP $1250

❑ **Popeye Flyer**, Marx, Wimpy and Swee'Pea litho on tower, 1936
EX $600   NM $900   MIP $1600

❑ **Pursuit Planes**, Marx, one propeller, 8" wingspan, 1930s
EX $125   NM $200   MIP $300

❑ **Rollover Airplane**, Marx, tin wind-up, forward and reverse, 6" wingspan, 1947
EX $200   NM $300   MIP $575

(Toy Shop File Photo)

❑ **Rollover Airplane**, Marx, tin wind-up, 1920s
EX $200   NM $300   MIP $575

❑ **Rookie Pilot**, Marx, tin litho, wind-up, 7" long, 1930s
EX $225   NM $340   MIP $550

❑ **Seversky P-35**, Marx, single-engine plane, 16" wingspan, 1940s
EX $125   NM $200   MIP $350

❑ **Sky Bird Flyer**, Marx, two planes, 9-1/2" tower, 1947
EX $275   NM $400   MIP $550

❑ **Sky Cruiser Two-Motored Transport Plane**, Marx, 18" wingspan, 1940s
EX $125   NM $175   MIP $325

❑ **Sky Flyer**, Marx, biplane and Zeppelin, 8-1/2" tall tower, 1927
EX $225   NM $340   MIP $450

❑ **Sky Flyer**, Marx, 9" tall tower, 1937
EX $150   NM $225   MIP $375

❑ **Spirit of America**, Marx, monoplane, tin wind-up, 17-1/2" wingspan, 1930
EX $325   NM $500   MIP $650

❑ **Spirit of St. Louis**, Marx, tin wind-up, 9-1/4" wingspan, 1929
EX $150   NM $225   MIP $595

❑ **Stunt Pilot**, Marx, tin wind-up
EX $175   NM $250   MIP $425

❑ **Tower Flyers**, Marx, 1926
EX $175   NM $250   MIP $350

❑ **TP-816 USAF**, Marx, twin engine, tin, made in Japan, 3-3/4" wingspan, 1960s
EX $5   NM $10   MIP $15

❑ **Trans-Atlantic Zeppelin**, Marx, wind-up, 10" long, 1930
EX $225   NM $350   MIP $450

❑ **TWA Biplane**, Marx, four-engine, 18" wingspan
EX $225   NM $350   MIP $450

❑ **U.S. Marines Plane**, Marx, monoplane, tin wind-up, 17-7/8" wingspan, 1930
EX $200   NM $300   MIP $400

❑ **Zeppelin**, Marx, friction pull toy, steel, 6" long
EX $100   NM $200   MIP $250

❑ **Zeppelin**, Marx, flies in circles, wind-up, 17" long, 1930
EX $350   NM $525   MIP $700

❑ **Zeppelin**, Marx, all metal, pull toy, 28" long, 1929
EX $400   NM $600   MIP $800

BOATS AND SHIPS

❑ **Battleship USS Washington**, Marx, friction, 14" long, 1950s
EX $50   NM $75   MIP $225

❑ **Caribbean Luxury Liner**, Marx, sparkling, friction, 15" long
EX $50   NM $75   MIP $225

❑ **Luxury Liner Boat**, Marx, tin, friction
EX $100   NM $150   MIP $250

❑ **Mosquito Fleet Putt Putt Boat**, Marx
EX $40   NM $55   MIP $95

❑ **River Queen Paddle Wheel Station**, Marx, plastic
EX $50   NM $75   MIP $150

❑ **Sparkling Warship**, Marx, tin friction motor, 14" long
EX $50   NM $75   MIP $195

(Toy Shop File Photo)

❑ **Tugboat**, Marx, plastic, battery-operated, 6" long, 1966
EX $50   NM $75   MIP $195

BUSES

❑ **American Van Lines Bus**, Marx, cream and red, tin wind-up, 13-1/2" long
EX $65   NM $100   MIP $130

❑ **Blue Line Tours Bus**, Marx, tin litho, wind-up, 9-1/2" long, 1930s
EX $150   NM $225   MIP $425

(RLM MacNary Collection)

❑ **Bus**, Marx, red, 4" long, 1940
EX $35   NM $50   MIP $95

(RLM MacNary Collection)

❏ **Coast to Coast Bus**, Marx, tin litho, wind-up, 10" long, 1930s
EX $125 **NM** $200 **MIP** $325

❏ **Greyhound Bus**, Marx, tin litho, wind-up, 6" long, 1930s
EX $100 **NM** $150 **MIP** $200

❏ **Liberty Bus**, Marx, tin litho, wind-up, 5" long, 1931
EX $75 **NM** $125 **MIP** $200

❏ **Mystery Speedway Bus**, Marx, tin litho, wind-up, 14" long, 1938
EX $200 **NM** $300 **MIP** $550

❏ **Royal Bus Lines Bus**, Marx, tin litho, wind-up, 10-1/4" long, 1930s
EX $135 **NM** $200 **MIP** $450

(David W Mapes Inc)

❏ **Royal Van Co. Truck "We Haul Anywhere"**, Marx, tin wind-up, 9" long, 1920s-30's
EX $140 **NM** $225 **MIP** $500

❏ **School Bus**, Marx, steel body, wooden wheels, pull toy, 11-1/2" long
EX $125 **NM** $200 **MIP** $325

CARS

❏ **Anti-Aircraft Gun on Car**, Marx, 5-1/4" long
EX $50 **NM** $75 **MIP** $225

❏ **Army Car**, Marx, battery-operated
EX $65 **NM** $100 **MIP** $200

❏ **Army Staff Car**, Marx, litho steel, tin wind-up, 1930s
EX $125 **NM** $200 **MIP** $425

❏ **Army Staff Car**, Marx, w/flasher and siren, tin wind-up, 11" long, 1940s
EX $75 **NM** $125 **MIP** $400

(Toy Shop File Photo)

❏ **Automatic Brake Car**, Marx, plastic w/tin litho base, 8-1/2" long
EX $20 **NM** $30 **MIP** $60

❏ **Big Lizzie Car**, Marx, tin wind-up, 7-1/4" long, 1930s
EX $75 **NM** $125 **MIP** $235

(Bill Bertoia Auctions)

❏ **Blondie's Jalopy**, Marx, tin litho, 16" long, 1941
EX $325 **NM** $500 **MIP** $850

❏ **Boat Tail Racer #2**, Marx, litho, 13" long, 1948
EX $125 **NM** $200 **MIP** $425

❏ **Boat Tail Racer #3**, Marx, tin wind-up, 5" long, 1930s
EX $40 **NM** $55 **MIP** $200

❏ **Bouncing Benny Car**, Marx, pull toy, 7" long, 1939
EX $325 **NM** $500 **MIP** $750

❏ **Bumper Auto**, Marx, large bumpers front and rear, tin wind-up, 1939
EX $60 **NM** $100 **MIP** $225

❏ **Cadillac Coupe**, Marx, 8-1/2" long, 1931
EX $175 **NM** $275 **MIP** $400

❏ **Cadillac Coupe**, Marx, trunk w/tools on luggage carrier, tin wind-up, 11" long, 1931
EX $200 **NM** $300 **MIP** $525

❏ **Camera Car**, Marx, heavy gauge steel car, 9-1/2" long, 1939
EX $850 **NM** $1300 **MIP** $1900

❏ **Careful Johnnie**, Marx, plastic driver, 6-1/2" long, 1950s
EX $100 **NM** $150 **MIP** $350

(Bill Bertoia Auctions)

❏ **Charlie McCarthy "Benzine Buggy" Car**, Marx, w/white wheels, tin wind-up, 7" long, 1938
EX $450 **NM** $625 **MIP** $950

❏ **Charlie McCarthy "Benzine Buggy" Car**, Marx, w/red wheels, tin wind-up, 7" long, 1938
EX $600 **NM** $900 **MIP** $1450

(Bill Bertoia Auctions)

❏ **Charlie McCarthy and Mortimer Snerd Private Car**, Marx, tin wind-up, 16" long, 1939
EX $600 **NM** $900 **MIP** $1500

❏ **Charlie McCarthy Private Car**, Marx, wind-up, 1935
EX $1450 **NM** $2200 **MIP** $3500

❏ **Convertible Roadster**, Marx, nickel-plated tin, 11" long, 1930s
EX $175 **NM** $275 **MIP** $395

(Don Hultzmann)

❏ **Coo Coo Car**, Marx, 8" long, tin wind-up, 1931
EX $375 **NM** $575 **MIP** $825

❏ **Crazy Dan Car**, Marx, tin wind-up, 6" long, 1930s
EX $140 **NM** $225 **MIP** $395

❏ **Dagwood the Driver**, Marx, 8" long, tin wind-up, 1941
EX $200 **NM** $300 **MIP** $900

❏ **Dan Dipsy Car**, Marx, nodder, tin wind-up, 5-3/4" long, 1950s
EX $250 **NM** $375 **MIP** $450

❏ **Dick Tracy Police Car**, Marx, 9" long
EX $150 **NM** $225 **MIP** $350

❏ **Dick Tracy Police Station Riot Car**, Marx, friction, sparkling, 7-1/2" long, 1946
EX $130 **NM** $200 **MIP** $375

❏ **Dick Tracy Squad Car**, Marx, yellow flashing light, tin litho, wind-up, 11" long, 1940s
EX $250 **NM** $375 **MIP** $525

(Toy Shop File Photo)

❏ **Dick Tracy Squad Car**, Marx, battery-operated, tin litho, 11-1/4" long, 1949
EX $170 **NM** $275 **MIP** $475

(The Toy Collector News)

❑ **Dick Tracy Squad Car**, Marx, friction, 20" long, 1948
EX $125 NM $170 MIP $300

(Toy Shop File Photo)

❑ **Dippy Dumper**, Marx, Brutus or Popeye, celluloid figure, tin wind-up, 9", 1930s
EX $350 NM $525 MIP $900

(Toy Shop File Photo)

❑ **Disney Parade Roadster**, Marx, tin litho, wind-up, 1950s
EX $100 NM $150 MIP $900

(Toy Shop File Photo)

❑ **Donald Duck Disney Dipsy Car**, Marx, plastic Donald, tin wind-up, 5-3/4" long, 1953
EX $425 NM $650 MIP $895

❑ **Donald Duck Go-Kart**, Marx, plastic and metal, friction, rubber tires, 1960s
EX $75 NM $130 MIP $325

❑ **Donald the Driver**, Marx, plastic Donald, tin car, wind-up, 6-1/2" long, 1950s
EX $200 NM $300 MIP $595

❑ **Dora Dipsy Car**, Marx, nodder, tin wind-up, 5-3/4" long, 1953
EX $400 NM $600 MIP $725

❑ **Dottie the Driver**, Marx, nodder, tin wind-up, 6-1/2" long, 1950s
EX $150 NM $225 MIP $450

❑ **Driver Training Car**, Marx, tin wind-up, 1950s, "Safe Driving School"
EX $80 NM $120 MIP $225

(Bill Bertoia Auctions)

❑ **Drive-Up Self Car**, Marx, turns left, right or straight, 1940
EX $100 NM $150 MIP $225

❑ **Electric Convertible**, Marx, tin and plastic, 20" long
EX $65 NM $100 MIP $295

❑ **Falcon**, Marx, plastic bubble top, black rubber tires
EX $50 NM $75 MIP $175

❑ **Funny Fire Fighters**, Marx, 7" long, tin wind-up, 1941
EX $800 NM $1200 MIP $1600

(Bill Bertoia Auctions)

❑ **Funny Flivver Car**, Marx, tin litho, wind-up, 7" long, 1926
EX $275 NM $425 MIP $675

❑ **Gang Buster Car**, Marx, tin wind-up, 14-1/2" long, 1938
EX $200 NM $300 MIP $800

❑ **Giant King Racer**, Marx, dark blue, tin wind-up, 12-1/4" long, 1928
EX $250 NM $375 MIP $725
(Toy Shop File Photo)

❑ **G-Man Pursuit Car**, Marx, sparks, 14-1/2" long, 1935
EX $190 NM $285 MIP $750

❑ **Hot Rod #23**, Marx, friction motor, tin, 8" long, 1967
EX $45 NM $75 MIP $90

❑ **Huckleberry Hound Car**, Marx, friction
EX $125 NM $200 MIP $250

❑ **Instant Speedway Action Set**, Marx, plastic track, hanging hook, die-cast car, 1968-69
EX $10 NM $20 MIP $45
(Toy Shop File Photo)

❑ **International Agent Car**, Marx, friction, tin litho, 1966
EX $60 NM $100 MIP $195

❑ **International Agent Car**, Marx, tin wind-up
EX $30 NM $55 MIP $125

❑ **Jaguar**, Marx, battery-operated, 13" long
EX $225 NM $325 MIP $450

❑ **Jalopy**, Marx, tin driver, friction, 1950s
EX $125 NM $200 MIP $250

❑ **Jalopy Car**, Marx, tin driver, motor sparks, crank, wind-up
EX $140 NM $225 MIP $280

❑ **Jolly Joe Jeep**, Marx, tin litho, 5-3/4" long, 1950s
EX $150 NM $225 MIP $375

❑ **Joy Riders Crazy Car**, Marx, tin litho, wind-up, 8" long, 1928
EX $340 NM $500 MIP $675

❑ **Jumping Jeep**, Marx, tin litho, 5-3/4" long, 1947
EX $210 NM $325 MIP $425

❑ **King Racer**, Marx, yellow body, red trim, tin wind-up, 8-1/2" long, 1925
EX $375 NM $575 MIP $750

❑ **King Racer**, Marx, yellow w/black outlines, 8-1/2" long, 1925
EX $250 NM $430 MIP $575

(Bill Bertoia Auctions)

❑ **Komical Kop**, Marx, black car, tin litho, wind-up, 7-1/2" long, 1930s
EX $450 NM $675 MIP $900

❑ **Leaping Lizzie Car**, Marx, tin wind-up, 7" long, 1927
EX $250 NM $375 MIP $500

❑ **Learn To Drive Car**, Marx, wind-up
EX $110 NM $165 MIP $225

❑ **Lola Climax Racer**, Marx, plastic, make in Hong Kong, 6-1/2" long, 1960s
EX $8 NM $12 MIP $18

(Bill Bertoia Auctions)

❑ **Lonesome Pine Trailer and Convertible Sedan**, Marx, 22" long, 1936
EX $375 NM $600 MIP $795

❑ **Machine Gun on Car**, Marx, hand crank activation on gun, 3" long
EX $75 NM $130 MIP $225

❑ **Magic George and Car**, Marx, litho, 1940s
EX $170 **NM** $250 **MIP** $350

❑ **Mechanical Speed Racer**, Marx, tin wind-up, 12" long, 1948
EX $125 **NM** $200 **MIP** $275

(Toy Shop File Photo)

❑ **Mickey Mouse Disney Dipsy Car**, Marx, plastic Mickey, tin wind-up, 5-3/4" long, 1953
EX $425 **NM** $655 **MIP** $875

❑ **Mickey the Driver**, Marx, plastic Mickey, tin car, wind-up, 6-1/2" long, 1950s
EX $170 **NM** $250 **MIP** $450

(RLM MacNary Collection)

❑ **Midget Racer "Midget Special" #2**, Marx, miniature car, clockwork-powered, 5" long, 1930s
EX $125 **NM** $200 **MIP** $250

(RLM MacNary Collection)

❑ **Midget Racer "Midget Special" #7**, Marx, miniature car, tin wind-up, 5" long, 1930s
EX $125 **NM** $200 **MIP** $250

(Toy Shop File Photo)

❑ **Milton Berle Crazy Car**, Marx, tin litho, wind-up, 6" long, 1950s
EX $250 **NM** $375 **MIP** $595

❑ **Mini Marx Super Speed Car**, Marx, various models, die-cast racing cars, late 1960s
EX $5 **NM** $10 **MIP** $15

❑ **Miniature Sports Cars**, Marx, set of 8, 4" long, hard plastic with metal tires, five plastic service station attendants, 1950s
EX $20 **NM** $50 **MIP** $80

(Toy Shop File Photo)

❑ **Mortimer Snerd's Tricky Auto**, Marx, tin litho, wind-up, 7-1/2" long, 1939
EX $400 **NM** $600 **MIP** $750

❑ **Mystery Car**, Marx, press down activation, 9" long, 1936
EX $125 **NM** $200 **MIP** $275

❑ **Mystery Taxi**, Marx, press down activation, steel, 9" long, 1938
EX $160 **NM** $250 **MIP** $375

(Toy Shop File Photo)

❑ **Nutty Mad Car**, Marx, blue car w/goggled driver, friction, hard plastic, 1960s
EX $75 **NM** $130 **MIP** $200

(Toy Shop File Photo)

❑ **Nutty Mad Car**, Marx, red tin car, vinyl driver, friction, 4" long, 1960s
EX $100 **NM** $150 **MIP** $225

(Toy Shop File Photo)

❑ **Nutty Mad Car**, Marx, w/driver, battery-operated, 1960s
EX $100 **NM** $150 **MIP** $225

(Toy Shop File Photo)

❑ **Old Jalopy**, Marx, tin wind-up, driver, "Old Jalopy" on hood, 7" long, 1950
EX $225 **NM** $325 **MIP** $425

❑ **Old Jalopy**, Marx, blue car w/yellow trim, college boys, hood reads "Queen of the Campus," tin wind-up, 8" long, 1930s
EX $300 **NM** $450 **MIP** $525

❑ **Parade Roadster**, Marx, w/Disney characters, tin litho, wind-up, 11" long, 1950
EX $225 **NM** $325 **MIP** $900

❑ **Peter Rabbit Eccentric Car**, Marx, tin wind-up, 5-1/2" long, 1950s
EX $250 **NM** $375 **MIP** $500

(Toy Shop File Photo)

❑ **Queen of the Campus**, Marx, w/four college students' heads, 1950
EX $250 **NM** $400 **MIP** $525

❑ **Race 'N Road Speedway**, Marx, HO scale racing set, 1950s
EX $60 **NM** $100 **MIP** $125

❑ **Racer #12**, Marx, tin litho, wind-up, 16" long, 1942
EX $225 **NM** $325 **MIP** $625

VEHICLES

(RLM MacNary Collection)

❑ **Racer #3**, Marx, miniature car, tin wind-up, 5" long
EX $75   NM $125   MIP $195

(RLM MacNary Collection)

❑ **Racer #4**, Marx, miniature car, tin wind-up, 5" long
EX $75   NM $125   MIP $195

(RLM MacNary Collection)

❑ **Racer #5**, Marx, miniature car, tin wind-up, 5" long, 1948
EX $75   NM $125   MIP $195

❑ **Racer #61**, Marx, miniature car, tin wind-up, 4-3/4" long, 1930
EX $75   NM $125   MIP $195

(RLM MacNary Collection)

❑ **Racer #7**, Marx, miniature car, tin wind-up, 5" long, 1948
EX $75   NM $125   MIP $195

❑ **Racing Car**, Marx, plastic driver, tin wind-up, 27" long, 1950
EX $100   NM $175   MIP $450

❑ **Racing Car**, Marx, two man team, tin litho, wind-up, 12" long, 1940
EX $125   NM $200   MIP $425

❑ **Roadster**, Marx, 11-1/2" long, 1949
EX $100   NM $150   MIP $225

❑ **Roadster and Cannon Ball Keeper**, Marx, wind-up, 9" long
EX $175   NM $250   MIP $350

❑ **Roadster Convertible with Trailer and Racer**, Marx, mechanical, 1950
EX $125   NM $200   MIP $275

❑ **Rocket Racer**, Marx, tin litho, 1935
EX $275   NM $425   MIP $550

❑ **Rolls-Royce**, Marx, black plastic, friction, 6" long, 1955
EX $40   NM $60   MIP $80

❑ **Royal Coupe**, Marx, tin litho, wind-up, 9" long, 1930
EX $175   NM $275   MIP $375

❑ **Secret Sam Agent 012 Car**, Marx, tin litho, friction, 5" long, 1960s
EX $40   NM $65   MIP $165

❑ **Sedan**, Marx, battery-operated, plastic, 9-1/2" long
EX $175   NM $275   MIP $350

❑ **Sheriff Sam and His Whoopee Car**, Marx, plastic, tin wind-up, 5-3/4" long, 1949
EX $200   NM $300   MIP $475

(Toy Shop File Photo)

❑ **Siren Police Car**, Marx, 15" long, 1930s
EX $75   NM $125   MIP $395

❑ **Smokey Sam the Wild Fireman Car**, Marx, 6-1/2" long, 1950
EX $125   NM $200   MIP $395

❑ **Smokey Stover Whoopee Car**, Marx, 1940s
EX $175   NM $275   MIP $525

❑ **Snoopy Gus Wild Fireman**, Marx, 7" long, 1926
EX $500   NM $750   MIP $1150

❑ **Space Car**, Marx, gray plastic w/clear cockpit cover, 5-3/4" long, sold with play sets, 1950s
EX $30   NM $60   MIP $80

(Toy Shop File Photo)

❑ **Speed Cop**, Marx, two 4" all tin wind-up cars, track, 1930s
EX $175   NM $275   MIP $795

❑ **Speed King Racer**, Marx, tin litho, wind-up, 16" long, 1929
EX $325   NM $500   MIP $650

❑ **Speed Racer**, Marx, 13" long, 1937
EX $250   NM $375   MIP $500

❑ **Speedway Coupe**, Marx, tin wind-up, battery-operated headlights, 8" long, 1938
EX $200   NM $300   MIP $400

❑ **Speedway Set**, Marx, two wind-up sedans, figure eight track, 1937
EX $250   NM $375   MIP $500

❑ **Sports Coupe**, Marx, tin, 15" long, 1930s
EX $125   NM $200   MIP $250

(Toy Shop File Photo)

❑ **Sportster**, Marx, 20" long, 1950s
EX $50   NM $80   MIP $125

❑ **Station Wagon**, Marx, friction, 11" long, 1950
EX $125   NM $200   MIP $325

❑ **Station Wagon**, Marx, green w/woodgrain pattern, wind-up, 7" long, 1950
EX $50   NM $75   MIP $250

❑ **Station Wagon**, Marx, litho family of four w/dogs on back windows, 6-3/4" long
EX $60   NM $100   MIP $275

❑ **Station Wagon**, Marx, light purple w/woodgrain pattern, wind-up, 7-1/2" long
EX $60   NM $100   MIP $275

❑ **Streamline Speedway**, Marx, two tin wind-up racing cars, 1936
EX $175   NM $275   MIP $395

❑ **Stutz Roadster**, Marx, driver, 15" long, wind-up, 1928
EX $325   NM $500   MIP $750

❑ **Super Hot Rod**, Marx, "777" on rear door, 11" long, 1940s
EX $200   NM $300   MIP $400

❑ **Super Streamlined Racer**, Marx, tin wind-up, 17" long, 1950s
EX $125   NM $200   MIP $400

❑ **The Marvel Car, Reversible Coupe**, Marx, tin wind-up, 1938
EX $125   NM $200   MIP $400

❑ **Tricky Safety Car**, Marx, 6-1/2" long, 1950
EX $100   NM $150   MIP $200

(Toy Shop File Photo)

❑ **Tricky Taxi**, Marx, red, black, and white, tin wind-up, 4-1/2" long, 1940s
EX $175   NM $275   MIP $375

(Toy Shop File Photo)

❑ **Tricky Taxi**, Marx, black/white version, tin wind-up, 4-1/2" long, 1935
EX $160   NM $250   MIP $375

❑ **Uncle Wiggly, He Goes A Ridin' Car**, Marx, rabbit driving, tin wind-up, 7-1/2" long, 1935
EX $425   NM $650   MIP $850

❑ **Walt Disney Television Car**, Marx, friction, 7-1/2" long, 1950s
EX $125   NM $200   MIP $425

❑ **Western Auto Track**, Marx, steel, 24" long
EX $75   NM $125   MIP $225

(Bill Bertoia Auctions)

❑ **Whoopee Car**, Marx, witty slogans, tin litho, wind-up, 7-1/2" long, 1930s
EX $375   NM $580   MIP $775

(Bill Bertoia Auctions)

❑ **Whoopee Cowboy Car**, Marx, bucking car, cowboy driver, tin wind-up, 7-1/2" long, 1930s
EX $400   NM $600   MIP $800

❑ **Woody Sedan**, Marx, tin friction, 7-1/2" long
EX $60   NM $100   MIP $225

(Toy Shop File Photo)

❑ **Yellow Taxi**, Marx, wind-up, 7" long, 1927
EX $275   NM $425   MIP $575

❑ **Yogi Bear Car**, Marx, friction, 1962
EX $50   NM $85   MIP $195

EMERGENCY VEHICLES

❑ **Ambulance**, Marx, 13-1/2" long, 1937
EX $225   NM $350   MIP $650

❑ **Ambulance**, Marx, tin litho, 11" long
EX $125   NM $175   MIP $375

(David W Mapes Inc)

❑ **Ambulance with Siren**, Marx, tin wind-up
EX $100   NM $150   MIP $400

❑ **Army Ambulance**, Marx, 13-1/2" long, 1930s
EX $250   NM $375   MIP $750

❑ **Chief-Fire Department No. 1 Truck**, Marx, friction, 1948
EX $60   NM $90   MIP $195

❑ **Chrome Racer**, Marx, miniature racer, 5" long, 1937
EX $85   NM $125   MIP $250

❑ **City Hospital Mack Ambulance**, Marx, tin litho, wind-up, 10" long, 1927
EX $190   NM $280   MIP $500

❑ **Electric Car**, Marx, runs on electric power, license #A7132, 1933
EX $225   NM $325   MIP $500

❑ **Electric Car**, Marx, wind-up, 1933
EX $175   NM $250   MIP $475

❑ **Fire Chief Car**, Marx, wind-up, 6-1/2" long, 1949
EX $75   NM $125   MIP $275

❑ **Fire Chief Car**, Marx, battery-operated headlights, wind-up, 11" long, 1950
EX $100   NM $150   MIP $325

❑ **Fire Chief Car**, Marx, friction, loud fire siren, 8" long, 1936
EX $150   NM $250   MIP $425

❑ **Fire Chief Car**, Marx, working lights, 16" long
EX $125   NM $200   MIP $295

❑ **Fire Chief Car with Bell**, Marx, 10-1/2" long, 1940
EX $175   NM $250   MIP $450

❑ **Fire Engine**, Marx, sheet iron, 9" long, 1920s
EX $100   NM $175   MIP $335

❑ **Fire Truck**, Marx, friction, all metal, 14" long, 1945
EX $90   NM $135   MIP $295

❑ **Fire Truck**, Marx, battery-operated, two celluloid firemen, 12" long
EX $50   NM $75   MIP $300

❑ **Giant King Racer**, Marx, pale yellow, tin wind-up, 12-1/2" long, 1928
EX $225   NM $325   MIP $575

❑ **Giant King Racer**, Marx, red, 13" long, 1941
EX $200   NM $300   MIP $550

❑ **Giant Mechanical Racer**, Marx, tin litho, 12-3/4" long, 1948
EX $100   NM $175   MIP $350

❑ **H.Q. - Staff Car**, Marx, 14-1/2" long, 1930s
EX $325   NM $500   MIP $750

❑ **Hook and Ladder Fire Truck**, Marx, three tin litho firemen, 13-1/2" long
EX $90   NM $135   MIP $225

(Toy Shop File Photo)

❑ **Hook and Ladder Fire Truck**, Marx, plastic ladder on top, 24" long, 1950
EX $90   NM $135   MIP $225

❑ **Plastic Racer**, Marx, 6" long, 1948
EX $50   NM $75   MIP $150

❑ **Racer with Plastic Driver**, Marx, tin litho car, 16" long, 1950
EX $150   NM $225   MIP $375

❑ **Rocket-Shaped Racer #12**, Marx, 1930s
EX $275   NM $425   MIP $600

(Toy Shop File Photo)

VEHICLES

❑ **Siren Fire Chief Car**, Marx, red car w/siren, 1934
EX $225   NM $325   MIP $495

❑ **Siren Fire Chief Truck**, Marx, battery-operated, 15" long, 1930s
EX $100   NM $175   MIP $325

❑ **Tricky Fire Chief Car**, Marx, 4-1/2" long, 1930s
EX $250   NM $375   MIP $625

❑ **V.F.D. Emergency Squad**, Marx, w/ladder, metal, electrically powered, 14" long, 1940s
EX $70   NM $125   MIP $200

❑ **V.F.D. Fire Engine**, Marx, w/hoses and siren, 14" long, 1940s
EX $120   NM $180   MIP $295

❑ **V.F.D. Hook and Ladder Fire Truck**, Marx, 33" long, 1950
EX $140   NM $225   MIP $325

❑ **War Department Ambulance**, Marx, 1930s
EX $100   NM $150   MIP $695

FARM AND CONSTRUCTION EQUIPMENT

❑ **Aluminum Bulldog Tractor Set**, Marx, tin wind-up, 9-1/2" long tractor, 1940
EX $250   NM $375   MIP $500

❑ **American Tractor**, Marx, w/accessories, tin wind-up, 8" long, 1926
EX $150   NM $225   MIP $300

❑ **Army Design Climbing Tractor**, Marx, tin wind-up, 7-1/2" long, 1932
EX $80   NM $120   MIP $300

❑ **Automatic Steel Barn and Mechanical Plastic Tractor**, Marx, tin wind-up, 7" long red tractor, 1950
EX $85   NM $125   MIP $475

❑ **Bulldozer Climbing Tractor**, Marx, bumper auto, large bumpers, tin wind-up, 1939
EX $50   NM $75   MIP $325

(Toy Shop File Photo)

❑ **Bulldozer Climbing Tractor**, Marx, caterpillar type, tin wind-up, 10-1/2" long, 1950s
EX $45   NM $75   MIP $295

❑ **Caterpillar Climbing Tractor**, Marx, orange tractor, tin wind-up, 9-1/2" long, 1942
EX $100   NM $175   MIP $325

❑ **Caterpillar Climbing Tractor**, Marx, yellow tractor, tin wind-up, 9-1/2" long, 1942
EX $75   NM $125   MIP $300

❑ **Caterpillar Tractor and Hydraulic Lift**, Marx, tin wind-up, 1948
EX $50   NM $75   MIP $295

❑ **Climbing Tractor**, Marx, tin wind-up, 8-1/4" long, 1930
EX $100   NM $150   MIP $325

❑ **Climbing Tractor**, Marx, w/driver, tin wind-up, 1920s
EX $50   NM $100   MIP $275

❑ **Climbing Tractor with Chain Pull**, Marx, tin wind-up, 7-1/2" long, 1929
EX $150   NM $225   MIP $350

❑ **Construction Tractor**, Marx, reversing, tin wind-up, 14" long, 1950s
EX $100   NM $150   MIP $465

❑ **Co-Op Combine**, Marx, tin friction, 6"
EX $30   NM $45   MIP $95

❑ **Covered Wagon**, Marx, friction, tin litho, 9" long
EX $20   NM $30   MIP $195

❑ **Crawler**, Marx, w/or without blades and drivers, litho, 1/25 scale, 1950
EX $75   NM $125   MIP $150

❑ **Crawler with Stake Bed**, Marx, litho, 1/25 scale, 1950
EX $75   NM $130   MIP $175

❑ **Farm Tractor and Implement Set**, Marx, tin wind-up, tractor mower, hayrake, three-gang plow, 1948
EX $200   NM $300   MIP $400

❑ **Farm Tractor Set**, Marx, 40 pieces, tin wind-up, 1939
EX $325   NM $500   MIP $650

❑ **Farm Tractor Set and Power Plant**, Marx, 32 pieces, tin wind-up, 1938
EX $200   NM $300   MIP $400

❑ **Hill Climbing Dump Truck**, Marx, tin wind-up, 13-1/2" long, 1932
EX $140   NM $210   MIP $375

❑ **Industrial Tractor Set**, Marx, orange and red heavy gauge plate tractor, 7-1/2" long, 1930
EX $145   NM $225   MIP $395

❑ **International Harvester Tractor**, Marx, diesel, driver and set of tools, 1/12 scale, 1954
EX $75   NM $125   MIP $150

(Toy Shop File Photo)

❑ **Magic Barn and Tractor**, Marx, plastic tractor, tin litho barn, 1950s
EX $70   NM $100   MIP $375

❑ **Mechanical Tractor**, Marx, tin wind-up, 5-1/2" long, 1942
EX $125   NM $200   MIP $275

❑ **Midget Climbing Tractor**, Marx, tin wind-up, 5-1/4" long, 1935
EX $125   NM $200   MIP $250

❑ **Midget Road Building Set**, Marx, tin wind-up, 5-1/2" long tractor, 1939
EX $200   NM $300   MIP $400

❑ **Midget Tractor**, Marx, copper color metal, tin wind-up, 5-1/4" long, 1940
EX $40   NM $60   MIP $125

❑ **Midget Tractor**, Marx, red metal, tin wind-up, 5-1/4" long, 1940
EX $30   NM $45   MIP $125

❑ **Midget Tractor and Plow**, Marx, tin wind-up, 1937
EX $70   NM $100   MIP $225

❑ **Midget Tractor with Driver**, Marx, red metal, tin wind-up, 5-1/4" long, 1940
EX $40   NM $60   MIP $220

❑ **No. 2 Tractor**, Marx, red w/black wheels, tin wind-up, 8-1/2" long, 1940
EX $95   NM $150   MIP $225

❑ **Plastic Sparkling Tractor Set**, Marx, tin wind-up, 6-1/2" long tractor w/10-1/2" long wagon, 1950
EX $40   NM $60   MIP $195

❑ **Plastic Tractor with Scraper**, Marx, tin wind-up, 8" long w/road scraper, 1949
EX $50   NM $75   MIP $195

(Toy Shop File Photo)

❑ **Power Grader**, Marx, black or white wheels, 17-1/2" long
EX $50   NM $100   MIP $125

(Toy Shop File Photo)

❑ **Power Shovel**, Marx
EX $50   NM $75   MIP $100

❑ **Reversible Six-Wheel Farm Tractor-Truck**, Marx, tin wind-up, 13-3/4" steel tractor, 7-1/2" stake truck, 1950
EX $80   NM $125   MIP $425

(Toy Shop File Photo)

❑ **Reversible Six-Wheel Tractor**, Marx, red steel tractor, tin wind-up, 11-3/4" long, 1940
EX $200   NM $300   MIP $475

(Toy Shop File Photo)

❑ **Self-Reversing Tractor**, Marx, tin wind-up, 10" long, 1936
EX $125   NM $200   MIP $350

(Toy Shop File Photo)

❑ **Sparkling Climbing Tractor**, Marx, tin wind-up, 8-1/2" long, 1950s
EX $100   NM $150   MIP $300

(Toy Shop File Photo)

❑ **Sparkling Climbing Tractor**, Marx, tin wind-up, 10" long, 1940s
EX $175   NM $275   MIP $350

❑ **Sparkling Heavy Duty Bulldog Tractor**, Marx, w/road scraper, tin wind-up, 11" long, 1950s
EX $40   NM $60   MIP $225

❑ **Sparkling Hi-Boy Climbing Tractor**, Marx, 10-1/2" long, 1950s
EX $25   NM $40   MIP $195

❑ **Sparkling Tractor**, Marx, w/plow blade, tin wind-up, 1939
EX $50   NM $75   MIP $235

❑ **Sparkling Tractor**, Marx, w/driver and trailer, tin wind-up, 16" long, 1950s
EX $60   NM $90   MIP $295

❑ **Sparkling Tractor and Trailer Set**, Marx, "Marborook Farms," tin wind-up, 21" long, 1950s
EX $55   NM $75   MIP $255

❑ **Steel Farm Tractor and Implements**, Marx, tin wind-up, 15" long steel bulldozer tractor, 1947
EX $160   NM $240   MIP $325

❑ **Super Power Reversing Tractor**, Marx, tin wind-up, 12" long, 1931
EX $100   NM $150   MIP $325

❑ **Super Power Tractor and Trailer Set**, Marx, tin wind-up, 8-1/2" tractor, 1937
EX $125   NM $200   MIP $375

❑ **Super-Power Bulldog Tractor with V-Shaped Plow**, Marx, aluminum finish, tin wind-up, 1938
EX $75   NM $130   MIP $200

❑ **Super-Power Climbing Tractor and Nine-Piece Set**, Marx, tin wind-up, 9-1/2" long tractor, 1942
EX $160   NM $240   MIP $395

❑ **Super-Power Giant Climbing Tractor**, Marx, tin wind-up, 13" long, 1939
EX $180   NM $270   MIP $450

❑ **Tractor**, Marx, red tractor, tin wind-up, 8-1/2" long, 1941
EX $100   NM $175   MIP $300

❑ **Tractor**, Marx, tin wind-up, 8-1/2" long, 1941
EX $100   NM $175   MIP $315

❑ **Tractor and Equipment Set**, Marx, five pieces, tin wind-up, 16" long tractor, 1949
EX $160   NM $240   MIP $320

❑ **Tractor and Mower**, Marx, tin wind-up, 5" long litho steel tractor, 1948
EX $50   NM $75   MIP $215

❑ **Tractor and Six Implement Set**, Marx, tin wind-up, 8-1/2" long aluminum tractor, 1948
EX $160   NM $240   MIP $425

❑ **Tractor and Trailer**, Marx, tin wind-up, 16-1/2" long, 1950s
EX $40   NM $60   MIP $115

❑ **Tractor Road Construction Set**, Marx, thirty-six pieces, tin wind-up, 8-1/2" long tractor, 1938
EX $200   NM $325   MIP $595

❑ **Tractor Set**, Marx, two-pieces, tin wind-up, 19" long steel tractor, 1950
EX $65   NM $100   MIP $215

❑ **Tractor Set**, Marx, seven pieces, tin wind-up, 8-1/2" long tractor, 1932
EX $125   NM $200   MIP $400

❑ **Tractor Set**, Marx, five pieces, tin wind-up, 8-1/2" long tractor, 1935
EX $70   NM $100   MIP $220

❑ **Tractor Set**, Marx, four pieces, tin wind-up, 8-1/2" long, 1936
EX $100   NM $150   MIP $325

❑ **Tractor Set**, Marx, thirty-two pieces, tin wind-up, 1937
EX $180   NM $270   MIP $450

❑ **Tractor Set**, Marx, five pieces, tin wind-up, 8-1/2" tractor, 1938
EX $90   NM $135   MIP $295

❑ **Tractor Set**, Marx, forty pieces, tin wind-up, 8-1/2" long, 1942
EX $300   NM $450   MIP $800

❑ **Tractor Trailer and Scraper**, Marx, tin wind-up, 8-1/2" long tractor, 1946
EX $80   NM $120   MIP $200

❑ **Tractor Train with Tractor Shed**, Marx, tin wind-up, 8-1/2" long, 1936
EX $100   NM $150   MIP $220

❑ **Tractor with Airplane**, Marx, wind-up, 5-1/2" long tractor, 27" wingspan on airplane, 1941
EX $250   NM $375   MIP $675

❑ **Tractor with Driver**, Marx, wind-up, 1940s
EX $100   NM $150   MIP $300

❑ **Tractor with Earth Grader**, Marx, tin wind-up, mechanical, 21-1/2" long, 1950s
EX $40   NM $60   MIP $190

❑ **Tractor with Plow and Scraper**, Marx, aluminum tractor, tin wind-up, 1938
EX $70   NM $125   MIP $295

❑ **Tractor with Plow and Wagon**, Marx, tin wind-up, 1934
EX $70   NM $125   MIP $295

❑ **Tractor with Road Scraper**, Marx, tin wind-up, 8-1/2" long climbing tractor, 1937
EX $90   NM $125   MIP $325

❑ **Tractor with Scraper**, Marx, tin wind-up, 8-1/2" long, 1933
EX $70   NM $125   MIP $295

❑ **Tractor with Trailer and Plow**, Marx, tin wind-up, 8-1/2" long, 1940
EX $80   NM $120   MIP $295

❑ **Tractor, Trailer, and V-Shaped Plow**, Marx, tin wind-up, 8-1/2" steel tractor, 1939
EX $85   NM $125   MIP $325

❑ **Tractor-Trailer Set**, Marx, tin wind-up, 8-1/2" long copper-colored tractor, 1939
EX $70   NM $125   MIP $295

❑ **Yellow and Green Tractor**, Marx, tin wind-up, 8-1/2" long, 1930
EX $90   NM $135   MIP $335

MOTORCYCLES

❑ **Motorcycle Cop**, Marx, tin litho, mechanical, siren, 8-1/4" long
EX $75   NM $125   MIP $235

VEHICLES

❑ **Motorcycle Delivery Toy**, Marx, "Speedy Boy Delivery Toy" on rear of cart, tin wind-up, 1932
EX $175 **NM** $275 **MIP** $500

❑ **Motorcycle Delivery Toy**, Marx, "Speedy Boy Delivery Toy" on side of cart, tin wind-up, 1930s
EX $175 **NM** $280 **MIP** $525

❑ **Motorcycle Police**, Marx, red uniform on cop, tin wind-up, 8" long, 1930s
EX $125 **NM** $200 **MIP** $275

❑ **Motorcycle Police #3**, Marx, tin wind-up, 8-1/2" long
EX $100 **NM** $150 **MIP** $250

❑ **Motorcycle Policeman**, Marx, orange/blue, tin wind-up, 8" long, 1920s
EX $100 **NM** $150 **MIP** $325

❑ **Motorcycle Trooper**, Marx, tin litho, wind-up, 1935
EX $80 **NM** $120 **MIP** $275

❑ **Mystery Police Cycle**, Marx, yellow, tin wind-up, 4-1/2" long, 1930s
EX $75 **NM** $125 **MIP** $225

❑ **Mystic Motorcycle**, Marx, tin litho, wind-up, 4-1/4" long, 1936
EX $75 **NM** $130 **MIP** $235

❑ **P.D. Motorcyclist**, Marx, tin wind-up, 4" long
EX $40 **NM** $60 **MIP** $195

❑ **Pinched Roadster Motorcycle Cop**, Marx, in circular track, tin wind-up, 1927
EX $125 **NM** $200 **MIP** $365

❑ **Pluto Motorcycle with Siren**, Marx, 1930s
EX $150 **NM** $225 **MIP** $550

❑ **Police Motorcycle with Sidecar**, Marx, tin wind-up, 3-1/2" long, 1930s
EX $300 **NM** $450 **MIP** $750

❑ **Police Motorcycle with Sidecar**, Marx, tin litho, wind-up, 8" long, 1950
EX $175 **NM** $280 **MIP** $425

❑ **Police Motorcycle with Sidecar**, Marx, tin wind-up, 8" long, 1930s
EX $425 **NM** $650 **MIP** $950

❑ **Police Patrol Motorcycle with Sidecar**, Marx, tin wind-up, 1935
EX $110 **NM** $165 **MIP** $400

❑ **Police Siren Motorcycle**, Marx, tin litho, wind-up, 8" long, 1938
EX $150 **NM** $225 **MIP** $350

❑ **Police Squad Motorcycle Sidecar**, Marx, tin litho, wind-up, 8" long, 1950
EX $100 **NM** $150 **MIP** $375

❑ **Police Tipover Motorcycle**, Marx, tin litho, wind-up, 8" long, 1933
EX $200 **NM** $300 **MIP** $525

❑ **Rookie Cop**, Marx, yellow w/driver, tin litho, wind-up, 8" long, 1940
EX $175 **NM** $275 **MIP** $425

❑ **Sparkling Soldier Motorcycle**, Marx, tin litho, wind-up, 8" long, 1940
EX $175 **NM** $275 **MIP** $425

❑ **Speeding Car and Motorcycle Policeman**, Marx, tin litho, wind-up, 1939
EX $90 **NM** $150 **MIP** $350

❑ **Tricky Motorcycle**, Marx, tin wind-up, 4-1/2" long, 1930s
EX $100 **NM** $150 **MIP** $250

TANKS

❑ **Anti-Aircraft Tank Outfit**, Marx, three cardboard tanks
EX $150 **NM** $225 **MIP** $350

❑ **Anti-Aircraft Tank Outfit**, Marx, four flat metal soldiers, tank, anti-aircraft gun, 1941
EX $90 **NM** $135 **MIP** $300

❑ **Army Tank**, Marx, sparking climbing tank, tin wind-up, 1940s
EX $150 **NM** $225 **MIP** $375

❑ **Climbing Fighting Tank**, Marx, tin wind-up
EX $90 **NM** $135 **MIP** $250

❑ **Climbing Tank**, Marx, tin wind-up, 9-1/2" long, 1930
EX $125 **NM** $200 **MIP** $325

❑ **Doughboy Tank**, Marx, doughboy pops out, tin litho, wind-up, 9-1/2" long, 1930
EX $150 **NM** $225 **MIP** $425

❑ **Doughboy Tank**, Marx, sparking tank, tin wind-up, 10" long, 1937
EX $125 **NM** $200 **MIP** $400

❑ **Doughboy Tank**, Marx, tin wind-up, 10" long, 1942
EX $150 **NM** $225 **MIP** $450

❑ **E12 Tank**, Marx, makes rat-a-tat-tat or rumbling noise, tin wind-up, 1942
EX $100 **NM** $150 **MIP** $375

(Bill Holt)

❑ **E12 Tank**, Marx, green tank, 9-1/2" long, tin wind-up, 1942
EX $150 **NM** $225 **MIP** $375

❑ **M48T Tank**, Marx, battery-operated, 1960s
EX $50 **NM** $100 **MIP** $225

❑ **Midget Climbing Fighting Tank**, Marx, 5-1/2" long, 1937
EX $100 **NM** $175 **MIP** $375

❑ **Midget Climbing Fighting Tank**, Marx, tin litho, wind-up, 5-1/4" long, 1931
EX $90 **NM** $135 **MIP** $235

(Harvey K Rainess)

❑ **Midget Climbing Fighting Tank**, Marx, wide plastic wheels, supergrid tread, 5-1/4" long, 1951
EX $100 **NM** $150 **MIP** $300

❑ **Refrew Tank**, Marx, tin wind-up
EX $75 **NM** $125 **MIP** $200

❑ **Rex Mars Planet Patrol Tank**, Marx, tin wind-up, 10" long, 1950s
EX $150 **NM** $225 **MIP** $375

❑ **Sparkling Army Tank**, Marx, tan or khaki hull, tin litho, wind-up, 1938
EX $95 **NM** $150 **MIP** $235

❑ **Sparkling Army Tank**, Marx, yellow hull, E12 Tank, tin litho, wind-up, 1942,
EX $100 **NM** $150 **MIP** $300

❑ **Sparkling Army Tank**, Marx, camouflage hull, two olive guns, tin wind-up, 5-1/2" long
EX $100 **NM** $150 **MIP** $275

❑ **Sparkling Army Tank**, Marx, camouflage hull, two khaki guns, tin wind-up, 5-1/2" long
EX $125 **NM** $200 **MIP** $325

❑ **Sparkling Climbing Tank**, Marx, tin wind-up, 10" long, 1939
EX $110 **NM** $165 **MIP** $310

❑ **Sparkling Space Tank**, Marx, tin wind-up, 1950s
EX $250 **NM** $375 **MIP** $600

❑ **Sparkling Super Power Tank**, Marx, tin wind-up, 9-1/2" long, 1950s
EX $75 **NM** $125 **MIP** $250

(Toy Shop File Photo)

❏ **Sparkling Tank**, Marx, tin wind-up, 4"
long, 1948
EX $75　　NM $130　　MIP $195

❏ **Superman Turnover Tank**, Marx,
Superman lifts tank, 4" long, tin wind-
up, 1940
EX $250　　NM $375　　MIP $600

❏ **Tank**, Marx, pop-up army man shooting
EX $150　　NM $225　　MIP $400

❏ **Turnover Army Tank**, Marx, camouflage, tan or khaki hull, tin wind-up, 1938
EX $175　　NM $275　　MIP $450

❏ **Turnover Army Tank**, Marx, tin wind-up,
9" long, 1930
EX $150　　NM $225　　MIP $375

❏ **Turnover Tank**, Marx, tin litho, wind-up,
4" long, 1942
EX $100　　NM $150　　MIP $275

TRUCKS

(Toy Shop File Photo)

❏ **A & P Supermarket Truck**, Marx,
pressed steel, rubber tires, litho, 19"
long
EX $50　　NM $100　　MIP $275

(Bob Smith)

❏ **Aero Oil Co. Mack Truck**, Marx, tin litho,
friction, 5-1/2" long, 1930
EX $125　　NM $200　　MIP $350

❏ **Air Force Truck**, Marx, 32" long
EX $75　　NM $125　　MIP $300

❏ **American Railroad Express Agency
Inc. Truck**, Marx, open cab, 7" long,
1930s
EX $100　　NM $150　　MIP $325

❏ **American Truck Co. Mack Truck**, Marx,
friction, 5" long
EX $100　　NM $150　　MIP $225

❏ **Armored Trucking Co. Mack Truck**,
Marx, black cab, yellow printing, wind-
up, 9-3/4" long
EX $200　　NM $300　　MIP $400

❏ **Armored Trucking Co. Truck**, Marx, tin
litho, wind-up, 10" long, 1927
EX $100　　NM $150　　MIP $325

❏ **Army Transport Truck**, Marx, 19" long,
1960s
EX $25　　NM $45　　MIP $65

❏ **Army Truck**, Marx, tin, 12" long, 1950
EX $60　　NM $90　　MIP $150

❏ **Army Truck**, Marx, olive drab truck, 4-
1/2" long, 1930s
EX $125　　NM $200　　MIP $350

❏ **Army Truck**, Marx, 20" long
EX $50　　NM $75　　MIP $125

❏ **Army Truck**, Marx, canvas top, 20" long,
1940s
EX $150　　NM $225　　MIP $325

❏ **Army Truck with Rear Benches and
Canopy**, Marx, olive drab paint, 10" long
EX $75　　NM $125　　MIP $225

❏ **Artillery Set**, Marx, three-piece set,
1930
EX $100　　NM $150　　MIP $225

❏ **Auto Carrier**, Marx, two yellow plastic
cars, two ramp tracks, 14" long, 1950
EX $125　　NM $200　　MIP $295

❏ **Auto Hauler**, Marx, hard plastic, 14:
long; 1950
EX $25　　NM $50　　MIP $75

❏ **Auto Mack Truck**, Marx, yellow/red, 12"
long, 1950
EX $50　　NM $75　　MIP $175

❏ **Auto Transport Mack Truck and Trailer**,
Marx, dark blue cab, wind-up, 11-1/2"
long, 1932
EX $150　　NM $225　　MIP $400

❏ **Auto Transport Mack Truck and Trailer**,
Marx, medium blue cab, friction, 11-1/2"
long, 1932
EX $150　　NM $225　　MIP $425

❏ **Auto Transport Mack Truck and Trailer**,
Marx, dark blue cab, dark green trailer,
wind-up, 11-1/2" long, 1932
EX $150　　NM $225　　MIP $375

❏ **Auto Transport Truck**, Marx, w/three
cars, 21" long, 1940
EX $250　　NM $375　　MIP $575

❏ **Auto Transport Truck**, Marx, w/three
wind-up cars, 22-3/4" long, 1931
EX $250　　NM $375　　MIP $525

❏ **Auto Transport Truck**, Marx, w/two tin
litho cars, 34" long, 1950s
EX $60　　NM $90　　MIP $200

❏ **Auto Transport Truck**, Marx, pressed
steel, w/two plastic cars, 14" long, 1940
EX $75　　NM $125　　MIP $225

❏ **Auto Transport Truck**, Marx, double
decker transport truck, 24-1/2" long,
1935
EX $275　　NM $425　　MIP $575

❏ **Auto Transport Truck**, Marx, w/three
racing coupes, 22" long, 1933
EX $250　　NM $375　　MIP $525

❏ **Auto Transport Truck**, Marx, 21" long,
1947
EX $175　　NM $250　　MIP $400

❏ **Auto Transport Truck**, Marx, w/two
plastic sedans, wooden wheels, 13-3/4"
long, 1950
EX $75　　NM $130　　MIP $225

❏ **Auto Transport Truck**, Marx, w/dump
truck, roadster and coupe, 30 1/2" long,
1938
EX $275　　NM $425　　MIP $575

❏ **Auto Transwalk Truck**, Marx, w/three
cars, 1930s
EX $175　　NM $250　　MIP $395

❏ **Bakery Van**, Marx, plastic, clear top,
"Bakery," 10" long, 1950s
EX $20　　NM $30　　MIP $45

❏ **Bamberger Mack Truck**, Marx, dark
green, wind-up, 5" long, 1920s
EX $200　　NM $300　　MIP $525

❏ **Big Boss Car Carrier**, Marx, plastic, battery-operated, 1963
EX $50　　NM $80　　MIP $125

❏ **Big Bruiser Highway Service Truck**,
Marx, plastic, 24: long, battery-oper-
ated, w/large plastic pickup to tow, 1964
EX $35　　NM $55　　MIP $85

❏ **Big Job Dump Truck**, Marx, plastic,
1970s
EX $15　　NM $25　　MIP $35

❏ **Big Load Van Co. Hauler and Trailer**,
Marx, w/little cartons of products, 12-
3/4" long, 1927
EX $200　　NM $300　　MIP $525

❏ **Big Load Van Co. Mack Truck**, Marx,
wind-up, 13" long, 1928
EX $225　　NM $350　　MIP $600

❏ **Big Shot Cannon Truck**, Marx, battery-
operated, 23" long, 1960s
EX $150　　NM $250　　MIP $325

❏ **Cannon Army Mack Truck**, Marx, 9"
long, 1930s
EX $175　　NM $250　　MIP $325

❏ **Carpenter's Truck**, Marx, stake bed
truck, pressed steel, 14" long, 1940s
EX $175　　NM $250　　MIP $350

❏ **Carrier with Three Racers**, Marx, tin
litho, wind-up, 22-3/4" long, 1930
EX $150　　NM $225　　MIP $425

❏ **Cement Mixer Truck**, Marx, red cab, tin
finish mixing barrel, 6" long, 1930s
EX $100　　NM $150　　MIP $300

❏ **City Coal Co. Mack Dump Truck**, Marx,
14" long, 1934
EX $225　　NM $350　　MIP $525

❏ **City Delivery Van**, Marx, yellow steel
truck, 11" long
EX $140　　NM $210　　MIP $280

(Calvin L Chaussee)

❏ **City Sanitation Dept. "Help Keep Your
City Clean" Truck**, Marx, 12-3/4" long,
1940
EX $60　　NM $90　　MIP $250

VEHICLES

❑ **Coal Truck**, Marx, battery-operated, automatic dump, forward and reverse, tin
EX $75   NM $125   MIP $175

❑ **Coal Truck**, Marx, 3rd version, Lumar Co. truck, 10" long, 1939
EX $150   NM $250   MIP $310

❑ **Coal Truck**, Marx, 2nd version, light blue truck, 12" long
EX $140   NM $225   MIP $280

❑ **Coal Truck**, Marx, 1st version, red cab, litho blue and yellow dumper, 12" long
EX $140   NM $225   MIP $280

(Toy Shop File Photo)

❑ **Coca-Cola Truck**, Marx, stamped steel, 20" long, 1940s, Sprite boy, stake body
EX $175   NM $250   MIP $350

❑ **Coca-Cola Truck**, Marx, red steel, 11-1/2" long, 1940s
EX $100   NM $175   MIP $250

❑ **Coca-Cola Truck**, Marx, tin, 17" long, 1940s
EX $125   NM $200   MIP $250

❑ **Coca-Cola Truck**, Marx, yellow, 20" long, 1950
EX $150   NM $225   MIP $300

❑ **Construction Set, 3-piece**, Marx, set of mini trucks, 7" long, futuristic cabover style, electric headlights; cement, tow and dump trucks, 1968
EX $25   NM $35   MIP $55

❑ **Contractors and Builders Truck**, Marx, 10" long
EX $125   NM $200   MIP $250

(Taylor's Toys John Taylor)

❑ **Cunningham's Drug Store Truck**, Marx, plastic, 1950s
EX $40   NM $60   MIP $80

(Toy Shop File Photo)

❑ **Curtiss Candy Truck**, Marx, red plastic truck, 10" long, 1950
EX $125   NM $200   MIP $250

❑ **Dairy Farm Pickup Truck**, Marx, 22" long
EX $60   NM $100   MIP $150

❑ **Delivery Truck**, Marx, blue truck, 4" long, 1940
EX $100   NM $175   MIP $225

❑ **Deluxe Delivery Stake Truck**, Marx, plastic cab, metal bed, 12" long, 1950s
EX $40   NM $60   MIP $90

(Toy Shop File Photo)

❑ **Deluxe Delivery Truck**, Marx, w/six delivery boxes, stamped steel, 13-1/4" long, 1948
EX $100   NM $150   MIP $200

❑ **Deluxe Fire Truck**, Marx, red plastic ladder truck, open cab, keywind motor, 13-1/2" long
EX $30   NM $50   MIP $75

(Taylor's Toys John Taylor)

❑ **Deluxe Trailer Truck**, Marx, tin and plastic, 14" long, 1950s
EX $70   NM $100   MIP $145

❑ **Dodge Salerno Engineering Department Truck**, Marx
EX $600   NM $900   MIP $1200

(Toy Shop File Photo)

❑ **Dump Truck**, Marx, 4-1/2" long, 1930s
EX $100   NM $175   MIP $325

❑ **Dump Truck**, Marx, motor, tin friction, 12" long, 1950s
EX $50   NM $75   MIP $100

❑ **Dump Truck**, Marx, 6" long, 1930s
EX $100   NM $150   MIP $250

❑ **Dump Truck**, Marx, red cab, green body, 6-1/4" long
EX $50   NM $75   MIP $100

❑ **Dump Truck**, Marx, various colors, 18" long, 1950s
EX $100   NM $150   MIP $200

❑ **Dump Truck**, Marx, red cab, green dump bed, 12" long, 1940s
EX $50   NM $90   MIP $150

❑ **Dump Truck**, Marx, red cab, gray bumper, yellow bed, 18" long, 1950
EX $100   NM $150   MIP $200

❑ **Emergency Service Truck**, Marx, friction, tin
EX $125   NM $200   MIP $275

(Toy Shop File Photo)

❑ **Emergency Service Truck**, Marx, friction, tin, searchlight behind car and siren
EX $150   NM $225   MIP $300

❑ **Farm Truck**, Marx, red plastic, chicken cage on stake bed, battery-operated, 11-1/2" long, 1960s
EX $10   NM $18   MIP $25

❑ **Firestone Truck**, Marx, metal, 14" long, 1950s
EX $50   NM $75   MIP $150

❑ **Ford Heavy Duty Express Truck**, Marx, cab w/canopy, 1950s
EX $60   NM $100   MIP $175

❑ **Gas Truck**, Marx, green truck, 4" long, 1940
EX $60   NM $90   MIP $165

❑ **Giant Reversing Tractor Truck**, Marx, w/tools, tin wind-up, 14" long, 1950s
EX $75   NM $130   MIP $350

❑ **Go-Cart, "Letters"**, Marx, Magic Marxie vehicle with mailbox figure, plastic w/rubber tires, 5-1/2" long, 1969
EX $20   NM $30   MIP $45

❑ **Gravel Truck**, Marx, 1st version, pressed steel cab, red tin dumper, 10" long, 1930
EX $100   NM $150   MIP $250

❑ **Gravel Truck**, Marx, 2nd version, metal, 8-1/2" long, 1940s
EX $75   NM $125   MIP $200

(Taylor's Toys John Taylor)

❑ **Gravel Truck**, Marx, 3rd version, metal w/"Gravel Mixer" drum, 10" long, 1930s
EX $100   NM $150   MIP $250

❑ **Grocery Truck**, Marx, cardboard boxes, tinplate and plastic, 14-1/2" long
EX $90   NM $150   MIP $225

❑ **Guided Missile Truck**, Marx, blue, red and yellow body, friction, 16" long, 1958
EX $75   NM $125   MIP $225

❑ **Hi Way Express Truck**, Marx, metal, 15-1/2" long, 1940s
EX $100   NM $150   MIP $225

❑ **Hi Way Express Truck**, Marx, "Nationwide Delivery," 1950s
EX $100   NM $150   MIP $225

❑ **Hi Way Express Truck**, Marx, tin, tin tires, 16" long, 1940s
EX $50   NM $75   MIP $185

❑ **Hi Way Express Truck**, Marx, pressed steel
EX $95   NM $150   MIP $185

❑ **Hydraulic Dump Truck**, Marx, steel, made "motor noise," hydraulic lift, 20-14" long, early 1970s
EX $20   NM $30   MIP $50

❑ **Jalopy Pickup Truck**, Marx, tin wind-up, 7" long
EX $60   NM $90   MIP $175

❑ **Jeep**, Marx, 11" long, 1946-50
EX $75   NM $130   MIP $200

❑ **Jeepster**, Marx, mechanical, plastic
EX $110   NM $165   MIP $250

❑ **Lazy Day Dairy Farm Pickup Truck and Trailer**, Marx, 22" long
EX $45   NM $75   MIP $275

❑ **Lincoln Transfer and Storage Co. Mack Truck**, Marx, wheels have cut-out spokes, tin litho, wind-up, 13" long, 1928
EX $350   NM $525   MIP $750

❑ **Lone Eagle Oil Co. Mack Truck**, Marx, bright blue cab, green tank, wind-up, 12" long, 1930
EX $225   NM $350   MIP $550

❑ **Lumar concrete Co. Truck**, Marx, plastic, 5-1/2" long, 1950s
EX $10   NM $16   MIP $22

❑ **Lumar Contractors Scoop/Dump Truck**, Marx, 17-1/2" long, 1940s
EX $75   NM $125   MIP $200

❑ **Lumar Hydraulic Dump Truck**, Marx, "Mechanical Action Hydraulic Dump Truck," 19" long, 1950s
EX $50   NM $80   MIP $125

❑ **Lumar Lines and Gasoline Set**, Marx, 1948
EX $250   NM $375   MIP $725

❑ **Lumar Lines Truck**, Marx, red cab, aluminum finished trailer, 14" long
EX $125   NM $200   MIP $300

❑ **Lumar Log Truck**, Marx, die-cast tractor-trailer, made in England, 7" long
EX $20   NM $30   MIP $40

❑ **Lumar Motor Transport Truck**, Marx, litho, 13" long, 1942
EX $75   NM $130   MIP $250

❑ **Lumar Stake Truck**, Marx, die-cast tractor-trailer, made in England, 7" long
EX $20   NM $30   MIP $40

(Bob Smith)

❑ **Lumar Van Lines Coast to Coast**, Marx, red/white cab; blue, red and white trailer; 15" long, 1950s
EX $50   NM $90   MIP $150

(Taylor's Toys John Taylor)

❑ **Lumar Wrecker Truck**, Marx, black and white, "Nite-Day Service," 18" long, 1950s
EX $50   NM $90   MIP $150

❑ **Machinery Moving Truck**, Marx
EX $60   NM $90   MIP $200

❑ **Mack Army Truck**, Marx, pressed steel, wind-up, 7-1/2" long
EX $70   NM $100   MIP $250

❑ **Mack Army Truck**, Marx, 13-1/2" long, 1929
EX $225   NM $350   MIP $600

❑ **Mack Army Truck**, Marx, khaki brown body, wind-up, 10-1/2" long
EX $125   NM $225   MIP $400

❑ **Mack Army Truck**, Marx, friction, 5" long, 1930
EX $125   NM $200   MIP $350

❑ **Mack Dump Truck**, Marx, silver cab, medium blue dump, wind-up, 12-3/4" long, 1936
EX $225   NM $355   MIP $525

❑ **Mack Dump Truck**, Marx, medium blue truck, wind-up, 13" long, 1934
EX $200   NM $300   MIP $525

❑ **Mack Dump Truck**, Marx, no driver, 19" long, 1930
EX $300   NM $450   MIP $650

❑ **Mack Dump Truck**, Marx, tin litho, wind-up, 13-1/2" long, 1926
EX $225   NM $350   MIP $575

❑ **Mack Dump Truck**, Marx, dark red cab, medium blue bed, wind-up, 10" long, 1928
EX $150   NM $225   MIP $475

❑ **Mack Railroad Express Truck #7**, Marx, tin, 1930s
EX $75   NM $125   MIP $450

❑ **Mack Towing Truck**, Marx, dark green cab, wind-up, 8" long, 1926
EX $175   NM $275   MIP $450

❑ **Mack U.S. Mail Truck**, Marx, black body, wind-up, 9-1/2" long
EX $250   NM $375   MIP $500

(Bob Smith)

❑ **Magnetic Crane and Truck**, Marx, 1950
EX $175   NM $275   MIP $350

❑ **Mammoth Truck Train**, Marx, truck w/five trailers, 1930s
EX $150   NM $250   MIP $450

❑ **Meadowbrook Dairy Truck**, Marx, 14" long, 1940
EX $150   NM $275   MIP $375

❑ **Mechanical Sand Dump Truck**, Marx, steel, 1940s
EX $100   NM $150   MIP $275

❑ **Medical Corps Ambulance Truck**, Marx, olive drab paint, 1940s
EX $100   NM $150   MIP $275

❑ **Merchants Transfer Mack Truck**, Marx, red open-stake truck, 10" long
EX $225   NM $350   MIP $450

(Bob Smith)

❑ **Merchants Transfer Mack Truck**, Marx, 13-1/3" long, 1928
EX $250   NM $375   MIP $600

❑ **Military Cannon Truck**, Marx, olive drab paint, cannon shoots marbles, 10" long, 1939
EX $125   NM $200   MIP $250

❑ **Milk Truck**, Marx, white truck, 4" long, 1940
EX $60   NM $90   MIP $120

❑ **Miniature Mayflower Moving Van**, Marx, operating lights
EX $60   NM $90   MIP $125

❑ **Motor Market Delivery**, Marx, 14" long, 1940s-1950s
EX $50   NM $90   MIP $150

VEHICLES

❏ **Motor Market Truck**, Marx, 10" long, 1939
EX $100   NM $175   MIP $225

❏ **Navy Jeep**, Marx, wind-up
EX $50   NM $75   MIP $100

❏ **North American Van Lines Tractor Trailer**, Marx, wind-up, 13" long, 1940s
EX $100   NM $175   MIP $225

❏ **Panel Wagon Truck**, Marx
EX $30   NM $55   MIP $75

(Toy Shop File Photo)

❏ **Pet Shop Truck**, Marx, plastic, six compartments w/six vinyl dogs, 11" long
EX $125   NM $200   MIP $250

❏ **Pickup Truck**, Marx, blue/yellow w/wood tires, 9" long, 1940s
EX $50   NM $75   MIP $150

(Toy Shop File Photo)

❏ **Polar Ice Co. Ice Truck**, Marx, 13" long, 1940s, stake body, picture of polar bear
EX $100   NM $175   MIP $275

❏ **Police Patrol Mack Truck**, Marx, wind-up, 10" long
EX $200   NM $300   MIP $475

❏ **Popeye Dippy Dumper Truck**, Marx, Popeye is celluloid, tin wind-up
EX $325   NM $500   MIP $800

❏ **Powerhouse Dump Truck**, Marx, pressed steel, plastic windshield, 19" long, 1960s
EX $25   NM $35   MIP $55

❏ **Pure Milk Dairy Truck**, Marx, glass bottles, pressed steel, 1940
EX $55   NM $80   MIP $250

❏ **Railway Express Agency Truck**, Marx, green closed van truck, 1940s
EX $90   NM $135   MIP $300

❏ **Range Rider**, Marx, tin wind-up, 1930s
EX $250   NM $375   MIP $500

❏ **Rapid Express Pickup**, Marx, wind-up, 9" long, 1940s
EX $125   NM $180   MIP $225

(Taylor's Toys John Taylor)

❏ **RCA Television Service Truck**, Marx, plastic Ford panel truck, 8-1/2" long, 1948-50
EX $150   NM $225   MIP $300

❏ **Reversing Road Roller**, Marx, tin wind-up
EX $60   NM $100   MIP $125

❏ **Road Builder Tank**, Marx, 1950
EX $125   NM $200   MIP $250

❏ **Rocker Dump Truck**, Marx, 17-1/2" long
EX $60   NM $90   MIP $120

❏ **Roy Rogers and Trigger Cattle Truck**, Marx, metal, 15" long, 1950s
EX $60   NM $100   MIP $225

❏ **Royal Oil Co. Mack Truck**, Marx, dark red cab, medium green tank, wind-up, 8-1/4" long, 1927
EX $200   NM $300   MIP $500

❏ **Royal Van Co. Mack Truck**, Marx, 1927
EX $250   NM $375   MIP $600

(Toy Shop File Photo)

❏ **Royal Van Co. Mack Truck**, Marx, red cab, tin litho and paint, wind-up, 9" long, 1928
EX $210   NM $315   MIP $550

❏ **Run Right To Read's Truck**, Marx, 14" long, 1940
EX $125   NM $200   MIP $250

❏ **Sand and Gravel Truck**, Marx, "Builder's Supply Co.," tin wind-up, 1920
EX $150   NM $225   MIP $400

❏ **Sand Truck**, Marx, tin litho, 12-1/2" long, 1940s
EX $125   NM $200   MIP $275

❏ **Sand Truck**, Marx, 9" long, 1948
EX $100   NM $150   MIP $200

❏ **Sand-Gravel Dump Truck**, Marx, blue cab, yellow dump w/"Gravel" on side, tin, 1930s
EX $140   NM $225   MIP $285

❏ **Sand-Gravel Dump Truck**, Marx, tin litho, 12" long, 1950
EX $150   NM $225   MIP $300

❏ **Sanitation Truck**, Marx, 1940s
EX $135   NM $200   MIP $270

❏ **Scoop & Dump Truck**, Marx, 17" long, 1940s
EX $50   NM $90   MIP $150

❏ **Searchlight Truck**, Marx, pressed steel, 9-3/4" long, 1930s
EX $160   NM $250   MIP $325

❏ **Side Dump Truck**, Marx, 1940
EX $90   NM $130   MIP $275

❏ **Side Dump Truck**, Marx, 10" long, 1930s
EX $140   NM $225   MIP $280

❏ **Side Dump Truck and Trailer**, Marx, 15" long, 1935
EX $150   NM $225   MIP $300

❏ **Sinclair Tanker**, Marx, tin, 14" long, 1940s
EX $150   NM $225   MIP $300

❏ **Stake Bed Truck**, Marx, red cab, green stake bed, 20" long, 1947
EX $100   NM $150   MIP $200

❏ **Stake Bed Truck**, Marx, medium blue cab, red stake bed, 10" long, 1940
EX $75   NM $130   MIP $185

❏ **Stake Bed Truck**, Marx, red cab, yellow and red trailer, 14" long
EX $100   NM $150   MIP $200

❏ **Stake Bed Truck**, Marx, red cab, blue stake bed, 6" long, 1930s
EX $75   NM $125   MIP $150

❏ **Stake Bed Truck**, Marx, rubber stamped chicken on one side of truck, bunny on other
EX $100   NM $150   MIP $200

❏ **Stake Bed Truck**, Marx, pressed steel, wooden wheels, 7" long, 1936
EX $60   NM $90   MIP $200

❏ **Stake Bed Truck and Trailer**, Marx, red truck, silver or blue stake bed, 18" long
EX $125   NM $200   MIP $250

❏ **Streamline Mechanical Hauler, Van, and Tank Truck Combo**, Marx, heavy gauge steel, 10 3/8" long, 1936
EX $170   NM $275   MIP $350

❏ **Sunshine Fruit Growers Truck**, Marx, red cab, yellow/white trailer w/blue roof, 14" long
EX $125   NM $175   MIP $250

❏ **Super Crane**, Marx, plastic and metal, battery-operated, 18" long truck body, 1960s
EX $100   NM $150   MIP $200

❏ **Tipper Dump Truck**, Marx, wind-up, 9-3/4" long, 1950
EX $75   NM $130   MIP $175

❏ **Tow Truck**, Marx, aluminum finish, wind-up, 6-1/4" long
EX $95   NM $150   MIP $190

❏ **Tow Truck**, Marx, 10" long, 1935
EX $125   NM $200   MIP $250

❏ **Tow Truck**, Marx, aluminum finsih, tin litho wind-up, 6-1/4" long
EX $75   NM $125   MIP $150

❏ **Tow Truck**, Marx, red cab, yellow towing unit, 6" long, 1930s
EX $137   NM $200   MIP $275

❏ **Toyland Dairy Truck**, Marx, 10" long
EX $140   NM $210   MIP $280

(Bob Smith)

❑ **Toyland's Farm Products Mack Milk Truck**, Marx, w/12 wooden milk bottles, 10-1/4" long, 1931
  EX $200   **NM** $300   **MIP** $400

❑ **Toytown Express Truck**, Marx, plastic cab
  EX $45   **NM** $70   **MIP** $95

❑ **Tractor Trailer with Dumpster**, Marx, blue/yellow hauler, tan dumpster
  EX $125   **NM** $200   **MIP** $250

❑ **Truck Train**, Marx, stake hauler and five trailers, 41" long, 1933
  EX $250   **NM** $400   **MIP** $525

❑ **Truck Train**, Marx, stake hauler and four trailers, 41" long, 1938
  EX $350   **NM** $550   **MIP** $725

❑ **Truck with Electric Lights**, Marx, battery-operated lights, 10" long, 1935
  EX $125   **NM** $200   **MIP** $375

❑ **Truck with Electric Lights**, Marx, 15" long, 1930s
  EX $110   **NM** $165   **MIP** $300

❑ **Truck with Searchlight**, Marx, toolbox behind cab, 10" long, 1930s
  EX $150   **NM** $225   **MIP** $400

❑ **U.S. Air Force Willy's Jeep**, Marx, tin body, plastic figures
  EX $70   **NM** $100   **MIP** $140

❑ **U.S. Army Jeep with Trailer**, Marx
  EX $100   **NM** $150   **MIP** $200

(Toy Shop File Photo)

❑ **U.S. Mail Truck**, Marx, metal, 14" long, 1950s
  EX $225   **NM** $350   **MIP** $450

❑ **U.S. Trucking Co. Mack Truck**, Marx, dark maroon cab, friction, 5-1/2" long, 1930
  EX $100   **NM** $150   **MIP** $200

❑ **Van Truck**, Marx, plastic, 10" long, 1950s
  EX $40   **NM** $60   **MIP** $80

❑ **Western Auto Truck**, Marx, steel, 25" long
  EX $60   **NM** $90   **MIP** $125

(Richard Jansen)

❑ **Willy's Jeep**, Marx, steel, 12" long, 1938
  EX $125   **NM** $200   **MIP** $250

❑ **Willy's Jeep and Trailer**, Marx, 1940s
  EX $100   **NM** $160   **MIP** $215

(RLM MacNary Collection)

❑ **Wrecker Truck**, Marx, 1930s
  EX $145   **NM** $225   **MIP** $290

VEHICLES

MATCHBOX

KING-SIZE

❑ **K1-1, Hydraulic Shovel,** 1960, Yellow body and front loader, no plastic windows, no interior, gray plastic wheels
EX $30   **NM** $65   **MIP** $95

(KP Photo by Dr. Douglas Sadecky)

❑ **K1-2, Foden Tipper Truck,** 1964, Red cab and chassis, orange dumper bed with "Hoveringham" decals or labels on sides, red plastic wheels with removable black plastic tires, blue plastic windows, no interior, axle suspension system to roll over bumps, silver metal horns on cab, 4-1/2"
EX $25   **NM** $45   **MIP** $70

❑ **K1-3, O & K Excavator,** 1970, Red body with silver excavator arm, red hubs with eight black plastic removable tires, "MH6", "O&K" and white stripe labels on sides, 4-15/16"
EX $15   **NM** $25   **MIP** $35

❑ **K2-1, Dumper Truck,** 1960, Blocky red body and chassis with open cab, gray or black plastic tires on green metal hubs, "Muir-Hill" decals
EX $25   **NM** $45   **MIP** $75

(KP Photo by Dr. Douglas Sadecky)

❑ **K2-2, KW-Dart Dump Truck,** 1964, Yellow articulated body with silver trim on engine and hood. Red hubs with removable black plastic tires, "KW-Dart" decals with arrow graphic, no window plastic, 5-5/8"
EX $30   **NM** $65   **MIP** $95

❑ **K2-3, Scammell Heavy Wreck Truck,** 1969, White or gold body with red plastic hubs and black removable wheels, silver metal hooks, red towing arm, silver horns on cab roof, "Esso" labels on doors, 4-3/4"
EX $22   **NM** $45   **MIP** $70

(KP Photo by Dr. Douglas Sadecky)

❑ **K3-1, Caterpillar Bulldozer,** 1960, Yellow body with green rubber treads and unpainted metal or yellow or red plastic roller wheels, cast tow hook, red-painted engine
EX $25   **NM** $50   **MIP** $80

(KP Photo by Dr. Douglas Sadecky)

❑ **K3-2, Hatra Tractor Shovel,** 1965, Orange-red body with articulating center and lifting loader. Blue-tinted plastic windows, "Hatra" decals on sides of cab, red hubs with black plastic removable tires, 6"
EX $36   **NM** $65   **MIP** $110

❑ **K3-3, Massey-Ferguson Tractor and Trailer,** 1970, Red cab and hood with gray engine and base, yellow hubs with removable black plastic tires, white grille, green plastic windows. Trailer with yellow chassis, red dumper bed, yellow hubs with black removable tires. Set measures 8"
EX $17   **NM** $28   **MIP** $55

(KP Photo)

❑ **K4-1, International Tractor,** 1960, Red body with "McCormick International" and "B-250" decals, green, red or orange hubs with black plastic removable tires, 2-7/8". Early versions with green metal hubs have approx. $80 MIP value
EX $25   **NM** $40   **MIP** $65

(KP Photo by Dr. Douglas Sadecky)

❑ **K4-2, GMC Tractor with Hopper Train,** 1967, Red tractor with two silver hopper trailers, red plastic hubs with black plastic removable wheels, opening chutes, "Fruehauf" decals on each trailer, set measures 11-1/4"
EX $55   **NM** $90   **MIP** $145

(KP Photo)

❑ **K4-3, Leyland Tipper,** 1969, Red cab and chassis, silver dumper bed, red hubs with black plastic removable tires, (duals in rear), "Wates" and "LE Transport" labels most common. Amber plastic windows, yellow plastic interior, 4-1/2". Some hard-to-find models with green cabs exist, but have approx. $300 MIP values. Other models include orange cabs with green dumper beds
EX $12   **NM** $20   **MIP** $45

(KP Photo by Dr. Douglas Sadecky)

❑ **K5-1, Tipper Truck,** 1961, Yellow body, silver-painted grille, silver metal or red plastic hubs with black tires, "Foden" decal on sides of hood, 4-1/4". First-version siver-hub models about $80 MIP
EX $25   **NM** $50   **MIP** $80

(KP Photo)

❑ **K5-2, Racing Car Transporter,** 1967, Medium-green body, cream plastic interior, clear plastic windows and skylights, red plastic hubs with black removable tires, decals on sides show racing car graphic with "Racing Transporter," "BP," and "LeMans, Sebring, Silverstone, Nurburgring." Silver metal base. Opening tailgate reveals tilting ramp and space for two racing cars, 5". This model entered the King-Size line, after being number M-6 in the Major Packs series
EX $25   **NM** $50   **MIP** $80

(KP Photo)

(KP Photo by Dr. Douglas Sadecky)

(KP Photo)

❏ **K5-2, Racing Car Transporter,** View of vehicle showing the ramp and car storage area

❏ **K6-1, Allis-Chalmers Earth Scraper,** 1961, Orange scraper with silver metal or red plastic hubs and black plastic tires. Adjustable scaper bed with springs (sometimes missing) "Allis-Chalmers" decals, 5-7/8"
EX $42   **NM** $75   **MIP** $130

(KP Photo)

❏ **K6-2, Mercedes-Benz "Binz" Ambulance,** 1967, White body with blue plastic windows and dome light, black base, red cross decal on hood and shield decals on opening doors, opening rear hatch with white plastic patient and red plastic blanket, silver hubs with black plastic tires, silver metal grille and bumpers, "True Guide" steering, 4-1/8"
EX $12   **NM** $25   **MIP** $55

(KP Photo by Dr. Douglas Sadecky)

❏ **K7-1, Curtiss-Wright Rear Dumper,** 1961, Yellow articulated body with silver metal hubs and black plastic tires, tilting dumper bed, "Curtiss-Wright" decals, red-painted engine block, 5-3/4"
EX $40   **NM** $85   **MIP** $135

❏ **K7-2, SD Refuse Truck,** 1967, Red cab & chassis, silver rear refuse unit, "Cleansing Service" decals or labels, red plastic wheels with black plastic tires, cream-colored plastic interior, clear plastic windows, 4-5/8"
EX $15   **NM** $25   **MIP** $45

❏ **K8-1, Prime Mover and Transporter with Caterpillar Tractor,** 1962, Orange body & trailer, yellow "Laing" decals, metal towhook, unpainted metal or red plastic wheels with black plastic tires, yellow tractor with green treads and no blade, set measures 12-1/2"
EX $125   **NM** $180   **MIP** $275

❏ **K8-2, Car Transporter,** 1967, Green or yellow cab, orange or yellow trailer, orange or red plastic wheels with black plastic tires, "Car Auction Collection" and "Farnborough Meashan" decals on trailer, 8-1/2"
EX $25   **NM** $45   **MIP** $70

❏ **K8-3, Caterpillar Traxcavator,** 1970, Various versions of shades of yellow cab, orange shovel & arms, figure, yellow or black wheels with green or black treads, "available mid-1970" in catalog, 4-1/4"
EX $15   **NM** $25   **MIP** $35

❏ **K9-1, Diesel Road Roller,** 1962, Green body, red metal rollers, gray or red driver, red "Aveling Barford" decals on sides with white reversed type, 3-3/4"
EX $35   **NM** $65   **MIP** $95

(KP Photo)

❏ **K9-2, Claas Combine Harvester,** 1967, Green or red body, red or yellow reels, "Claas" decals or labels, yellow plastic wheels with black plastic tires, 5-1/2"
EX $20   **NM** $40   **MIP** $60

❏ **K10-1, Aveling-Barford Tractor Shovel,** 1963, Light-blue body & shovel, red seat, with or without air filter, unpainted metal or red plastic wheels with black plastic tires, 4-1/8"
EX $30   **NM** $60   **MIP** $90

❏ **K10-2, Pipe Truck,** 1967, Yellow cab & trailer chassis, black house-shaped decal on cab doors, gray plastic pipes, red plastic wheels with black plastic tires, later issues had Superfast wheels and pink cab and chassis, 8"
EX $20   **NM** $40   **MIP** $75

❏ **K11-1, Fordson Tractor and Trailer,** 1963, Blue tractor body & trailer chassis, light-gray trailer bed, orange metal or plastic wheels with black plastic tires, 6-1/4"
EX $25   **NM** $45   **MIP** $70

❏ **K11-2, DAF Car Transporter,** 1969, Metallic blue cab with gold trailer or yellow cab with orange & yellow trailer, DAF labels, red plastic wheels with black plastic tires or Superfast Wheels, 9"
EX $20   **NM** $50   **MIP** $85

(KP Photo by Dr. Douglas Sadecky)

❏ **K12-1, Heavy Breakdown Wreck Truck,** 1963, Green body, yellow boom, with or without roof lights, unpainted metal or red plastic wheels with black plastic tires, 4-3/4"
EX $25   **NM** $50   **MIP** $75

(KP Photo)

❏ **K12-2, Scammell Crane Truck,** 1970, Yellow cab & crane, red plastic wheels with black plastic tires or orange body & crane with Superfast wheels, 6"
EX $20   **NM** $35   **MIP** $50

(KP Photo by Dr. Douglas Sadecky)

VEHICLES

K13-1, Ready-Mix Concrete Truck, 1963, Orange body & mixer with unpainted metal or red plastic wheels with black plastic tires, green plastic windows, no interior, "Readymix" or "RMC" decals on mixer barrel, 4-1/2"
EX $25   **NM** $50   **MIP** $75

(KP Photo by Dr. Douglas Sadecky)

K14-1, Taylor Jumbo Crane, 1964, Yellow body & crane, green windows, red or yellow weight box, red plastic wheels with black plastic tires, 5-1/4"
EX $25   **NM** $50   **MIP** $75

(KP Photo)

K15-1, Merryweather Fire Engine, 1964, Red body, gray extending ladder, red plastic wheels with black plastic tires or Superfast wheels, 6-1/8"
EX $25   **NM** $45   **MIP** $65

(KP Photo by Dr. Douglas Sadecky)

K16-1, Dodge Tractor with Twin Tippers, 1966, Green cab & trailer chassis, yellow dumps, Dodge Trucks decals, red plastic wheels with black plastic tires; later issues had yellow cab with blue dump & Superfast wheels, 11-7/8"
EX $70   **NM** $135   **MIP** $200

(KP Photo by Dr. Douglas Sadecky)

K17-1, Low Loader with Bulldozer, 1967, Green Ford cab & trailer, red plastic wheels with black plastic tires, red Case bulldozer body, yellow roof & blade, green treads, "Laing" or "Taylor Woodrow" decals or labels, later issues had Superfast wheels and lime-green cab and trailer, 9-1/2"
EX $65   **NM** $100   **MIP** $150

K18-1, Articulated Horse Box, 1967, Red Dodge cab with tan trailer, clear windows on trailer, gray ramp, four white horses, red plastic wheels with black plastic tires, later issues had Superfast wheels, 6-5/8"
EX $35   **NM** $55   **MIP** $90

K19-1, Scammell Tipper Truck, 1967, Red cab & yellow dump, red plastic wheels with black plastic tires or Superfast wheels, 4-3/4"
EX $20   **NM** $35   **MIP** $50

K20-1, Tractor Transporter, 1968, Red Ford cab & trailer, red plastic wheels with black plastic tires, green plastic windows, 3 blue tractors with yellow wheels, later issues had Superfast wheels, 9"
EX $65   **NM** $100   **MIP** $150

K21-1, Mercury Cougar, 1968, Gold body, red or white interior, unpainted metal wheels with black plastic tires, 4-1/8". Shown in blue in 1968 catalog, announcing model would be available mid-year
EX $25   **NM** $50   **MIP** $75

K22-1, Dodge Charger, 1969, Dark-blue body, light-blue interior, unpainted metal wheels with black plastic tires with "True Guide" steering, 4-1/2". Shown in 1969 catalog, announcing available mid-year
EX $25   **NM** $50   **MIP** $75

(KP Photo)

K23-1, Mercury Police Car, 1969, White body, red interior, blue dome lights, police labels, unpainted metal wheels with black plastic tires with "True Guide" steering or Superfast wheels, 4-3/8". Introduced in 1969 catalog as being available mid-year
EX $20   **NM** $35   **MIP** $50

K24-1, Lamborghini Miura, 1969, Red body, white interior, unpainted metal wheels with black plastic tires and "True Guide" steering, many color & wheel variations exist, 4"
EX $20   **NM** $35   **MIP** $50

MATCHBOX

REGULAR WHEELS

❏ **1-1RW, Road Roller,** 1953, One of the first Matchbox offerings, this model had a "steamroller"-style large-roofed cab that matched the large toy produced by Lesney. Green paint on body can vary in shade, red metal wheels and rollers
EX $40 　　**NM** $75 　　**MIP** $110

❏ **1-2RW, Diesel Road Roller,** 1955, Second in the series, but first with a smaller cab, roller attachment a little more snug than the first version, red metal wheels and roller, driver available in light and dark tan variations, gold-painted upright tow hook, 2-1/4"
EX $30 　　**NM** $45 　　**MIP** $85

❏ **1-3RW, Road Roller,** 1958, Third in the series, this casting kept the driver, but changed the tow hook at rear of the tractor. It still featured red metal wheels and rollers, 2-1/4"
EX $45 　　**NM** $70 　　**MIP** $90

(KP Photo)

❏ **1-4RW, Diesel Road Roller,** 1962, Green with orange/red plastic wheels, open window on cab behind driver, tow hook on back. 2-5/8", "Aveling Barford Road Roller" on base near rear wheels
EX $12 　　**NM** $35 　　**MIP** $60

(KP Photo, George Cuhaj collection)

❏ **1-5RW, Mercedes-Benz Truck,** 1968, Light pea-green, with orange or yellow plastic canopy, truck could be hitched to a matching trailer, released the same year, 3"
EX $5 　　**NM** $12 　　**MIP** $20

❏ **2-1RW, Dumper,** 1953, This first version featured a gold-painted front grille on a green body with red dump bed, 1-1/2"
EX $22 　　**NM** $40 　　**MIP** $90

(KP Photo by Dr. Douglas Sadecky)

❏ **2-2RW, Dumper,** 1957, Second casting is larger than first, with less painted detail. First issue with metal wheels, second with gray plastic wheels. Green body, red dumper bed, 2". Pictured here 2-3RW Muir-Hill Dumper
EX $20 　　**NM** $55 　　**MIP** $80

(KP Photo, George Cuhaj collection)

❏ **2-3RW, Dumper,** 1961, Short, blocky cab with "Laing" or "Muir-Hill" decal on right-hand door. Red cab with pea-green dumper bed, black plastic wheels, 2-1/8". Although the cab is different, this model is very similar to the K-2 dumper released one year earlier. "Muir-Hill" decal versions can have about $100 MIP value
EX $7 　　**NM** $12 　　**MIP** $30

(KP Photo, George Cuhaj collection)

❏ **2-3RW, Dumper,** 1961, Another view of 2-3RW, also simply called "Dumper" in Matchbox 1966 catalog
EX $7 　　**NM** $12 　　**MIP** $30

(KP Photo, George Cuhaj collection)

❏ **2-4RW, Mercedes-Benz Trailer,** 1968, Pea-green trailer released same year as Mercedes-Benz Truck, 1-5RW. Also came with orange or yellow canopy, 3-1/2"
EX $5 　　**NM** $10 　　**MIP** $20

(KP Photo by Dr. Douglas Sadecky)

❏ **3-1RW, Cement Mixer,** 1953, Another early Matchbox, this model mirrors one of Lesney's first larger die-cast toys. Variations seem to exist in castings, earlier models measure slightly larger at 1-3/4" length than the later ones, coming in at 1-1/2" length. Orange metal or gray plastic wheels
EX $25 　　**NM** $55 　　**MIP** $80

(KP Photo, Tom Michael collection)

❏ **3-2RW, Bedford Tipper Truck,** 1961, Available in red and maroon dumper variations, as well as gray and black plastic wheels, 2-1/2". Gray plastic wheeled version harder to find, about $120 MIP
EX $10 　　**NM** $20 　　**MIP** $45

(KP Photo)

❏ **3-3RW, Mercedes-Benz "Binz" Ambulance,** 1968, White or cream body with Red Cross label or decal and plastic patient on stretcher. This was a smaller version of the K-6 ambulance released one year earlier, 2-7/8". Unpainted base with textured surface along sides and near back tailgate
EX $6 　　**NM** $12 　　**MIP** $20

(KP Photo)

❑ **3-3RW, Mercedes-Benz "Binz" Ambulance,** 1968, Variation photo showing cream paint and decal version of Mercedes ambulance
EX $6   **NM** $12   **MIP** $20

❑ **4-1RW, Tractor,** 1954, Red Massey-Harris tractor body and fenders; a small version of larger Lesney Massey-Harris toy tractor
EX $35   **NM** $65   **MIP** $95

❑ **4-2RW, Massey-Harris Tractor,** 1957, Red with no fenders. An update on the previous model, this tractor was re-released painted green in 1994 as an anniversary issue. Metal wheel and gray plastic wheel variations, some casting variations with 1-1/2" and 1-3/4" lengths
EX $40   **NM** $75   **MIP** $135

(KP Photo, George Cuhaj collection)

❑ **4-3RW, Triumph Motorcycle w/Sidecar,** 1960, Light metallic blue with 24-spoke silver wheels and black tires, 2-1/8"
EX $17   **NM** $30   **MIP** $85

(KP Photo, George Cuhaj collection)

❑ **4-3RW, Triumph Motorcycle w/Sidecar,** 1960, Another view of the Triumph Motorcycle w/Sidecar
EX $17   **NM** $30   **MIP** $85

(KP Photo, George Cuhaj collection)

❑ **4-4RW, Dodge Stake Truck,** 1967, Yellow cab and body with green plastic stakes. A popular model, Matchbox made many toy trucks with this Dodge cab style, 2-7/8". Models with blue-green stakes, a very slight color difference, can have about $150 MIP value
EX $6   **NM** $9   **MIP** $19

❑ **5-1RW, Double Decker Bus,** 1954, First of Matchbox's London Buses, this one featured decals that read "Buy Matchbox Series" on the side, 2"
EX $15   **NM** $45   **MIP** $80

(KP Photo, Tom Michael collection)

❑ **5-2RW, Double Decker Bus,** 1958, Second London Bus, casting slightly larger, at 2-1/4" length. "No. 5" cast into front of bus, no interior. Available with metal and gray plastic wheels, with a variety of decals
EX $40   **NM** $80   **MIP** $120

❑ **5-3RW, Routemaster London Bus,** 1961, Red, with gray or black plastic wheels, "Visco-Static" decal most common. No interior in bus, major change from last model: a wider front grille, with cast headlights on front fenders
EX $20   **NM** $45   **MIP** $80

(KP Photo)

❑ **5-4RW, Routemaster London Bus,** 1965, Red body, white plastic interior-first Matchbox model bus to feature one. Like 5-3RW, the "Visco-Static" decals and labels are the most common, 2-3/4"
EX $6   **NM** $12   **MIP** $25

❑ **6-1RW, Quarry Truck,** 1954, Orange body with gray dumper bed. No interior. Most commonly seen with metal wheels, crimped or rounded axles, 2-1/4"
EX $20   **NM** $40   **MIP** $75

❑ **6-2RW, Quarry Truck,** 1959, Yellow body, black plastic wheels most common, red, white and black decal on cab doors, cab extends the full width of the front of truck, appears first in 1959 catalog with black plastic wheels
EX $12   **NM** $30   **MIP** $65

(KP Photo)

❑ **6-3RW, Euclid 10-Wheel Quarry Truck,** 1964, Yellow body, no decals, exposed engine shows on casting, partial cab does not extend across body of truck, 2-5/8"
EX $7   **NM** $15   **MIP** $30

(KP Photo, George Cuhaj collection)

❑ **6-4RW, Ford Pickup,** 1969, Red, with white plastic camper top and white or silver plastic front grille. Featured "Autosteer," a Matchbox innovation making its appearance in the 1969 catalog, that "turns the front wheels in either direction by simple pressure." 2-3/4"
EX $10   **NM** $20   **MIP** $30

(KP Photo by Dr. Douglas Sadecky)

❑ **7-1RW, Horse-Drawn Milk Float,** 1954, Orange wagon body, white painted driver, brown horse. Available with metal spoked or gray solid plastic wheels, 2-1/4". Quite a detailed little model
EX $45   **NM** $60   **MIP** $120

(KP Photo, George Cuhaj collection)

❑ **7-2RW, Ford Anglia,** 1961, Light blue body, no interior, gray, silver or black plastic wheels, silver painted grille, bumper and headlights, 2-5/8", black painted baseplate, tow hook. Gray plas-

tic wheel versions, about $90 MIP; silver plastic wheel versions, about $55 MIP
EX $15   **NM** $22   **MIP** $45

(KP Photo by Dr. Douglas Sadecky)

❏ **7-2RW, Ford Anglia,** 1961, A view of a gray-plastic-wheel version of the Ford Anglia, a harder-to-find variation
EX $20   **NM** $40   **MIP** $90

(KP Photo, Tom Michael collection)

❏ **7-3RW, Ford Refuse Truck,** 1967, Red body, gray and silver dumper section, tilts together when dumped, no interior, black plastic wheels, green window plastic, 3"
EX $7   **NM** $12   **MIP** $20

❏ **8-1RW, Caterpillar Tractor,** 1955, Yellow or orange with cast driver, silver painted grille. Unpainted roller wheels for treads, 1-1/2". Fully exposed engine under hood. Note: Orange variation harder to find, MIP value can reach over $200; yellow versions with painted drivers also about $200 MIP
EX $20   **NM** $40   **MIP** $85

❏ **8-2RW, Caterpillar Tractor,** 1959, Yellow, different casting with engine partially covered by hood, and cast "roller wheels" between two actual turning metal wheels. Driver cast with toy, 1-3/4", green or gray rubber treads
EX $25   **NM** $65   **MIP** $90

❏ **8-3RW, Caterpillar Crawler Tractor,** 1961, Yellow body with cast driver, metal or plastic tread wheels, very similar to previous casting, models with silver plastic roller wheels about $90 MIP
EX $20   **NM** $40   **MIP** $65

(KP Photo, Tom Michael collection)

❏ **8-4RW, Caterpillar Crawler Tractor,** 1965, Yellow, cast without driver, black plastic roller wheels, 2", gray or black rubber treads
EX $12   **NM** $22   **MIP** $30

(KP Photo, George Cuhaj collection)

❏ **8-5RW, Ford Mustang Fastback,** 1966, White, with red interior and tow hook. Black plastic tires on silver wheels. Unique steering lever on driver's side allows front wheels to turn left or right, 2-7/8", orange versions are quite rare, about $300 MIP
EX $12   **NM** $20   **MIP** $40

❏ **9-1RW, Fire Escape,** 1955, Red with cast driver, metal wheels, gold-painted trim, 2-1/4", no front bumper in casting
EX $20   **NM** $45   **MIP** $80

❏ **9-2RW, Fire Escape,** 1957, Red, cast with driver, metal wheels most common, versions with gray plastic wheels about $400 MIP, front bumper included in casting, 2-1/4"
EX $20   **NM** $45   **MIP** $80

(KP Photo)

❏ **9-3RW, Merryweather Marquis Fire Engine,** 1959, Red body with cab, gold ladder, black plastic wheels (first versions had gray plastic wheels), ladder colors can vary, 2-5/8", simply called "Fire Truck" in 1966 catalog
EX $20   **NM** $55   **MIP** $70

(KP Photo, Tom Michael collection)

❏ **9-4RW, Boat and Trailer,** 1967, Plastic blue and white boat with blue die-cast trailer, black plastic wheels. First time a stand-alone trailer makes appearance in regular wheels line
EX $7   **NM** $15   **MIP** $30

❏ **10-1RW, Mechanical Horse and Trailer,** 1955, Red, three-wheeled cab and gray stake-style trailer, metal wheels, 3"
EX $55   **NM** $70   **MIP** $95

(KP Photo by Dr. Douglas Sadecky)

❏ **10-2RW, Mechanical Horse and Trailer,** 1957, Second casting of Scammell Scarab, red three-wheeled cab and light-tan stake-style trailer with fenders. Grille can be painted or unpainted, metal wheels, 3". Appears first in 1957 catalog/flyer
EX $40   **NM** $60   **MIP** $95

(KP Photo, George Cuhaj collection)

❏ **10-3RW, Sugar Container Truck,** 1962, Blue Foden truck body with "Tate & Lyle" decal, with silver, gray, or black plastic wheels (shown). Popular Foden cab design, 2-5/8". Gray-wheeled models tend to have higher MIP values, up to $200
EX $15   **NM** $30   **MIP** $65

(KP Photo, George Cuhaj collection)

❏ **10-3RW, Sugar Container Truck,** 1962, Another view of 10-3RW, showing decal from back of truck

(KP Photo, John Brown Sr. collection)

❑ **10-4RW, Pipe Truck,** 1967, Red Leyland die-cast body, silver grille and baseplate, gray plastic pipes. "Ergomatic Cab" written on baseplate, 3". The Ergomatic cab was a new feature on large British trucks, including Leyland and AEC, beginning in the mid-sixties, so this model reflected the latest advance at time of release

EX $6 **NM** $12 **MIP** $20

❑ **11-1RW, Road Tanker,** 1955, Yellow or red ERF truck body, metal wheels, "Esso" decal on rear of tank, 2", painted side gas tanks, crimped axles

EX $40 **NM** $75 **MIP** $100

❑ **11-2RW, Road Tanker,** 1959, Red ERF truck body, metal wheels, gray or black plastic wheels, variations include silver painted side gas tanks and grilles, slightly larger casting, 2-1/2"

EX $35 **NM** $60 **MIP** $100

(KP Photo by Dr. Douglas Sadecky)

❑ **11-3RW, Jumbo Crane,** 1965, Yellow, red plastic hook, large black plastic wheels in front near cab, small in back-1966 catalog illustration looks more like King Size version, K-14, with what appears to be a die-cast hook. Some with red counterweights, 3". Shown here with 42-3RW Iron Fairy Crane

EX $8 **NM** $15 **MIP** $30

(KP Photo, John Brown Sr. collection)

❑ **11-4RW, Scaffold Truck,** mid-1969, Mercedes-Benz truck, silver body with yellow plastic scaffold sections in stake-style bed. "Builders Supply Company" decal on side, 2-5/8", released late in 1969, just before transition to Superfast

EX $8 **NM** $12 **MIP** $20

(KP Photo, John Brown Sr. collection)

❑ **12-1RW, Land Rover,** 1957, Dark green body with tan driver, metal wheels. No real windshield, just a low flat piece of the casting appearing where the base of a windshield would be. Slight casting variations, some 1-5/8" length, later editions, 1-3/4" length. Silver-painted grille

EX $8 **NM** $40 **MIP** $80

(KP Photo, George Cuhaj collection)

❑ **12-2RW, Land Rover,** 1960, Dark green, black or gray plastic wheels (black more common). Open cab, model shown has bent windshield. "Land-Rover Series II" on black baseplate

EX $15 **NM** $40 **MIP** $75

(KP Photo)

❑ **12-3RW, Safari Land Rover,** 1965, Dark green body, dark brown plastic luggage on top, white interior, white tow hook, black plastic baseplate. First issue of the Safari Land Rover, says "Land Rover Safari" on base, 2-3/4"

EX $8 **NM** $15 **MIP** $25

(KP Photo)

❑ **12-3RW, Safari Land Rover,** 1967, Medium-blue body, light reddish-brown plastic luggage, white plastic interior and tow hook, black plastic baseplate with "Land Rover Safari." Second issue of same casting in blue

EX $8 **NM** $15 **MIP** $25

(KP Photo, Tom Michael collection)

❑ **13-1RW, Wreck Truck,** 1955, Tan Bedford truck with red tow hook and scaffold, metal wheels, silver-painted grille and bumper, 2-1/4"

EX $35 **NM** $50 **MIP** $75

❑ **13-2RW, Wreck Truck,** 1958, Tan Bedford body, red boom section, metal or gray plastic wheels, no interior, slightly smaller than previous casting at 2"

EX $40 **NM** $60 **MIP** $90

(KP Photo, George Cuhaj collection)

❑ **13-3RW, Wreck Truck,** 1961, Red body with metal or plastic tow hook, and gray or black plastic wheels, decal on side of truck says "A.A. & R.A.C. Matchbox Garages Breakdown Service," silver trim on front grille

EX $18 **NM** $45 **MIP** $110

(KP Photo, George Cuhaj collection)

❑ **13-4RW, Wreck Truck,** 1966, Dodge Wreck Truck with yellow cab, green tow bed, red plastic hook, clear red plastic cab light, BP decals or labels, 3", black plastic wheels. Variations with colors reversed, (green cab and yellow body) are extremely rare. "Dodge Wreck Truck" on green base near rear wheels

EX $7 **NM** $12 **MIP** $30

❑ **14-1RW, Ambulance,** 1956, Cream painted body, metal wheels, Red Cross decal, word "Ambulance" cast in raised letters along side of vehicle, 2"

EX $20 **NM** $45 **MIP** $85

(KP Photo, John Brown Sr. collection)

❑ **14-2RW, Ambulance,** 1958, Daimler with cream or off-white body with metal or gray plastic wheels, Red Cross decal, slightly larger casting at 2-1/4", word "Ambulance" cast in raised letters

EX $18 **NM** $60 **MIP** $90

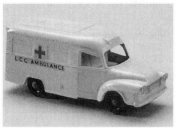

(KP Photo, George Cuhaj collection)

❏ **14-3RW, Lomas Ambulance,** 1962, White body with black plastic wheels and "LCC Ambulance" decals, 2-5/8", referred to simply as "Ambulance" in catalog. "LCC" is an abbreviation for the "London County Council," responsible for designing and building ambulances in the 1950s and 1960s to its own specifications, later adapted by Daimler and other companies
EX $10 **NM** $20 **MIP** $45

(KP Photo, George Cuhaj collection)

❏ **14-4RW, Iso Grifo,** 1968, Dark blue, almost purple body, light blue plastic interior and tow hook, opening doors, 3", in 1968 catalog, "available in early 1968," steering wheel on right-hand side, black tires on silver wheels, textured baseplate
EX $9 **NM** $17 **MIP** $25

(KP Photo, George Cuhaj collection)

❏ **14-4RW, Iso Grifo,** Detail photo: shows white tow hook and driver's side door open to British-style steering wheel arrangement

(KP Photo, George Cuhaj collection)

❏ **15-1RW, Prime Mover Truck,** 1956, Orange body, silver grille and trim, metal wheels. Harder to find editions: yellow body with metal wheels and orange with gray plastic wheels
EX $22 **NM** $45 **MIP** $70

❏ **15-2RW, Atlantic Prime Mover,** 1959, Orange body, black plastic wheels, spare tire in bed of truck, no interior
EX $25 **NM** $45 **MIP** $80

(KP Photo, George Cuhaj collection)

❏ **15-3RW, Dennis Refuse Truck,** 1963, Blue body, gray dumper section, red and white decals or labels say "Cleansing Service," and have cross-in-shield design at center. Black plastic knobby wheels, no interior, 2-1/2"
EX $7 **NM** $14 **MIP** $30

(KP Photo, George Cuhaj collection)

❏ **15-4RW, Volkswagen 1500 Saloon,** 1968, White Volkswagen Beetle body with "137" decals or labels, black plastic tires on silver wheels, 2-7/8"
EX $7 **NM** $12 **MIP** $25

❏ **16-1RW, Transporter Trailer,** 1956, Tan, flat bodied trailer with ramp and non-skid surface for vehicles, one axle and metal wheels in front near towbar, two axles with metal wheels on back near ramp, 3", ramp fold up onto trailer body
EX $17 **NM** $30 **MIP** $60

(KP Photo by Dr. Douglas Sadecky)

❏ **16-2RW, Atlantic Transporter,** 1960, Orange trailer body, black plastic wheels, 4 axles; two at front near drawbar, two at back near ramp, non-skid tire tracks on trailer, pictured here with 15-2RW Atlantic Prime Mover
EX $17 **NM** $40 **MIP** $75

(KP Photo, George Cuhaj collection)

❏ **16-3RW, "Mountaineer" Dump Truck w/Snowplough,** 1964, Gray cab and body with orange dumper section, snowplow on front with orange and white striped decal, black plastic wheels, 3", gray plastic wheel version about twice MIP value
EX $18 **NM** $30 **MIP** $50

(KP Photo, George Cuhaj collection)

❏ **16-3RW, "Mountaineer" Dump Truck w/Snowplough,** 1964, Another view of Mountaineer Dump Truck with raised dumper bed

(KP Photo, John Brown Sr. collection)

❏ **16-4RW, Case Bulldozer,** 1969, Red body with yellow blade and cab, "Available mid-1969" in 1969 1st issue catalog, 2-1/2"
EX $9 **NM** $18 **MIP** $32

❏ **17-1RW, Removals Van,** 1956, Green, blue or dark red body, metal wheels, "Matchbox Removals Service" decal, green more common color
EX $15 **NM** $60 **MIP** $100

(KP Photo by Dr. Douglas Sadecky)

17-2RW, Removals Van, 1958, Green body, with "Matchbox Removals Service" decal on sides, metal or gray plastic wheels
EX $35   NM $75   MIP $120

17-3RW, Metropolitan Taxi, 1960, Dark red with gray or silver plastic wheels, gray more common, silver can have $130+ MIP value, gray-wheel values shown
EX $25   NM $40   MIP $75

(KP Photo)

17-4RW, 8-Wheel Tipper, 1963, Red Foden body, orange dumper section, black plastic wheels, no interior, 3", "Hoveringham" decal on tipper. A "little brother" to the 8-Wheel Tipper K-1 in the King Size line
EX $9   NM $18   MIP $37

(KP Photo)

17-4RW, 8-Wheel Tipper, 1963, Another view of Foden 8-Wheel Tipper, with hinged gate at back opening when dumper section is tilted up
EX $9   NM $18   MIP $37

(KP Photo, George Cuhaj collection)

17-5RW, Horse Box, 1969, Red AEC (Associated Equipment Company) Ergomatic cab and truck body, green plastic box with gray door, two white plastic horses, black plastic wheels, 2-7/8", "Available mid-1969" in 1969 catalog, 1st edition
EX $8   NM $12   MIP $25

18-1RW, Bulldozer, 1956, Yellow body, tow hook, red blade, metal roller wheels, driver in hat cast as part of toy
EX $18   NM $35   MIP $85

18-2RW, Bulldozer, 1958, Yellow body, tow hook, yellow blade, driver cast into body, metal roller wheels. Engine partially covered on side
EX $25   NM $78   MIP $110

(KP Photo, John Brown Sr. collection)

18-3RW, Caterpillar Bulldozer, 1961, Yellow body, tow hook, yellow blade, driver cast into body, metal or black plastic rollers. Driver shown here is painted, but normally they were the same color as casting
EX $18   NM $40   MIP $80

18-4RW, Caterpillar Crawler Bulldozer, 1964, Yellow body, curving tow hook, no driver, black plastic roller wheels. Casting essentially the same as 18-3, but with flatter blade and no driver
EX $7   NM $18   MIP $40

(KP Photo, George Cuhaj collection)

18-5RW, Field Car, 1969, Yellow body, white plastic interior, generally red wheels with black plastic tires. Many collectors consider this vehicle to be an International Scout model, and in fact the side view bears close resemblance. However, the front grille also looks a bit like a French SINPAR Renault military vehicle (although they were produced in the 1970s). "Available mid-1969" in catalog. Auto-Steer model. 2-5/8"
EX $7   NM $11   MIP $18

(KP Photo, George Cuhaj collection)

18-5RW, Field Car, 1969, View of rear of Field Car, showing spare and tow hook

19-1RW, Sports Car, 1956, White or cream body with metal wheels, painted driver, silver grille
EX $45   NM $70   MIP $150

19-2RW, MG "A" Sports Car, 1958, White body, metal or gray plastic wheels, painted driver, can have rounded or crimped axles, silver-painted grille and headlights, 2-1/4"
EX $58   NM $85   MIP $150

19-3RW, Aston Martin Racer, 1961, Green body, white or gray driver, 24-spoke wheels with black plastic tires. Variable number decals on body
EX $45   NM $80   MIP $165

(KP Photo, Tom Michael collection)

19-4RW, Lotus Racing Car, 1966, Green or orange body, white plastic driver, yellow wheels with black plastic tires, No. "3" decal or label, 2-3/4". Green pictured in 1966 catalog, but orange variation included in G-4 Racetrack Set that same year. Driver missing in this photo
EX $11   NM $22   MIP $50

20-1RW, Heavy Lorry, 1956, Dark red ERF truck body, metal or gray plastic wheels, no interior, dropside stake bed appearance with fuel tanks along sides. Can have silver-painted grille, some casting variations, 2-1/4" and 2-5/8"
EX $18   NM $40   MIP $100

20-2RW, Transport Truck, 1959, ERF dropside truck with dark blue body, gray or black plastic wheels, "Ever Ready For Life" decal along stake sides, model also called "Heavy Lorry" in 1959 catalog
EX $18   NM $45   MIP $90

(KP Photo by Dr. Douglas Sadecky)

20-3RW, Taxi Cab, 1965, Chevrolet Impala Taxi Cab with yellow body, red or white plastic interior, (red is harder to find) black plastic wheels, 3"
EX $11   NM $18   MIP $30

(KP Photo, Colin Bruce collection)

❑ **21-1RW, Bedford Coach,** 1956, Light pea-green body with red and yellow "London to Glasgow" decals above windows, metal wheels
EX $22   **NM** $40   **MIP** $68

(KP Photo, George Cuhaj collection)

❑ **21-2RW, Bedford Coach,** 1958, Light pea-green body with red and yellow "London to Glasgow" decal above windows, metal or gray plastic wheels, "Bedford Duple Luxury Coach" on black base, 2-1/2", silver painted grille and front bumper, no interior
EX $25   **NM** $60   **MIP** $95

(KP Photo by Dr. Douglas Sadecky)

❑ **21-3RW, Milk Delivery Truck,** 1961, Commer truck with light green body, white or cream plastic cargo and gray or black plastic wheels, 2-1/4", cow or milk bottle decal on cab doors. Both variations shown here
EX $15   **NM** $35   **MIP** $65

(KP Photo, George Cuhaj collection)

❑ **21-4RW, Foden Concrete Truck,** 1969, Yellow Foden cab and plastic mixer with orange body, dark green plastic windows, eight black plastic wheels, 3". Worm-gear under second set of wheels turns mixer as truck rolls forward
EX $5   **NM** $9   **MIP** $22

❑ **22-1RW, Vauxhall Cresta,** 1956, Red body with white roof, no interior, metal wheels, silver painted grille and bumpers, tow hook
EX $22   **NM** $40   **MIP** $62

(KP Photo by Dr. Douglas Sadecky)

❑ **22-2RW, Vauxhall Cresta,** 1958, Different casting than previous version. Longer, more "Chevy-like" body with low tailfins and wraparound front and rear windshields. Many paint variations exist, some pushing MIP price well into the hundreds of dollars. Can have gray or black plastic wheels or metal wheels
EX $30   **NM** $72   **MIP** $150

(KP Photo, George Cuhaj collection)

❑ **22-3RW, Pontiac Grand Prix,** 1964, Red body, black plastic wheels, gray plastic interior & tow hook, 3", opening doors, "Pontiac G.P. Sports Coupe" on black painted baseplate
EX $12   **NM** $22   **MIP** $45

❑ **23-1RW, Caravan,** 1956, Pale blue body, metal wheels, 2-1/2"
EX $17   **NM** $30   **MIP** $75

❑ **23-2RW, Trailer,** 1958, Pale blue-green or lime-green body, metal or gray plastic wheels
EX $22   **NM** $40   **MIP** $75

(KP Photo by Dr. Douglas Sadecky)

❑ **23-3RW, Bluebird Dauphine Trailer,** 1960, Metallic tan or green body, opening door, no interior or plastic windows, black or gray plastic wheels. Variations with green bodies are hard to find, and can be quite valuable. More common tan variation prices given below
EX $25   **NM** $40   **MIP** $85

❑ **23-4RW, Trailer Caravan,** 1966, Yellow or pink body, black plastic wheels, white plastic interior, 3", pink more common beginning in 1968 and after. Yellow version about $45 MIP value
EX $9   **NM** $17   **MIP** $30

❑ **24-1RW, Hydraulic Excavator,** 1956, Yellow or orange body with metal wheels; larger two at rear and smaller at front, figure cast as part of body, front dumping bucket
EX $18   **NM** $40   **MIP** $75

❑ **24-2RW, Hydraulic Excavator,** 1959, Yellow body, black or gray plastic wheels, larger at rear or cab, smaller in front near dumper bucket. Figure cast in piece, 2-5/8"
EX $17   **NM** $28   **MIP** $45

(KP Photo, George Cuhaj collection)

❑ **24-3RW, Rolls-Royce Silver Shadow,** 1967, Deep red sedan body, white plastic interior, opening trunk, silver wheels with black plastic tires, clear plastic windshield and windows, unpainted silver metal grille, headlights and front bumper, 3". Black baseplate with "A" near front axle
EX $7   **NM** $11   **MIP** $25

(KP Photo, George Cuhaj collection)

❑ **24-3RW, Rolls-Royce Silver Shadow,** 1967, View of opening trunk on Rolls

❑ **25-1RW, Bedford Dunlop Van,** 1956, Dark blue Bedford panel van, with yellow "Dunlop" decals on sides, no interior or plastic windows
EX $18   **NM** $40   **MIP** $80

(KP Photo by Dr. Douglas Sadecky)

❑ **25-2RW, Volkswagen Sedan,** 1960, Volkswagen 1200 Sedan, blue-silver body, gray plastic wheels, opening rear engine hood, green or clear plastic windows, black base
EX $45   **NM** $65   **MIP** $100

(KP Photo, George Cuhaj collection)

❑ **25-3RW, Petrol Tanker,** 1964, Yellow Bedford cab, green body, white tanker with "BP" decal. Cab tilts to reveal white plastic interior. Black plastic wheels, 3". Called "B.P. Tanker" in 1966 catalog. Blue versions with "Aral" decals on tanker section harder to find, about $200 MIP
EX $8   **NM** $14   **MIP** $25

(KP Photo)

❑ **25-4RW, Ford Cortina,** 1968, Light brown body, cream-colored plastic interior and tow hook, black plastic wheels, "Auto-Steer," textured pattern on unpainted baseplate near front and rear axles, opening doors, 2-5/8". Interesting to note that its first catalog appearance in 1968 showed a blue car with the subhead "Available in mid-1968." The blue color wouldn't be used until the 1970 Superfast version was released. Yellow roof rack included in 1969 G-4 Race'n Rally Gift Set
EX $6   **NM** $9   **MIP** $17

(KP Photo, Tom Michael collection)

❑ **26-1RW, Ready Mixed Concrete Lorry,** 1957, Orange ERF cab and body with silver-painted grille and side gas tanks, metal or gray plastic wheels, 1-3/4", metal mixer section, four wheels
EX $18   **NM** $45   **MIP** $88

(KP Photo, George Cuhaj collection)

❑ **26-2RW, Ready-Mix Concrete Truck,** 1961, Orange die-cast Foden cab and body with plastic orange mixer section. Gray or black plastic wheels, 2-1/2". Six wheels, says "Foden Cement Mixer" on base
EX $9   **NM** $19   **MIP** $40

(KP Photo, George Cuhaj collection)

❑ **26-3RW, GMC Tipper Truck,** 1968, Red cab with green plastic windows, silver-gray tipper bed, green chassis, black plastic wheels with duals at rear, 2-5/8", 1968 catalog shows subhead "Available early 1968" and model with yellow tipper bed
EX $6   **NM** $10   **MIP** $18

(KP Photo, George Cuhaj collection)

❑ **26-3RW, GMC Tipper Truck,** 1968, View showing tilting cab and green engine block underneath

❑ **27-1RW, Bedford Low Loader,** 1956, Green Bedford cab with silver trim, tan trailer, metal wheels, 3", no windows or interior
EX $28   **NM** $48   **MIP** $90

❑ **27-2RW, Bedford Low Loader,** 1958, Green Bedford cab with silver trim, tan trailer, metal or gray plastic knobby wheels, slightly larger casting at 3-3/4" length. No windows or interior
EX $30   **NM** $75   **MIP** $140

(KP Photo, John Brown Sr. collection)

❑ **27-3RW, Cadillac Sixty Special,** 1960, Silver-gray or silver-purple Cadillac body with cream or pink colored roof, plastic windows, no interior and gray or black plastic wheels, red base, tow hook, red-painted taillights and silver-painted trim
EX $28   **NM** $45   **MIP** $90

(KP Photo, George Cuhaj collection)

❑ **27-4RW, Mercedes 230SL,** 1966, White Mercedes convertible with red plastic interior, opening doors, black plastic wheels, tow hook, 2-3/4", "Available early 1966" in catalog
EX $7   **NM** $13   **MIP** $25

(KP Photo, George Cuhaj collection)

❑ **27-4RW, Mercedes 230SL,** 1966, Rear view of Mercedes convertible showing opening doors and tow hook

(KP Photo by Dr. Douglas Sadecky)

❑ **28-1RW, Bedford Compressor Lorry,** 1956, Orange or yellow Bedford cab and chassis with Caterpillar-type compressor engine on back, painted-silver grille and trim, 1-3/4", metal wheels. Pictured here with 28-2RW Thames Compressor Truck
EX $20   **NM** $30   **MIP** $50

(KP Photo, John Brown Sr. collection)

❏ **28-2RW, Ford Thames Compressor Lorry,** 1959, Yellow Ford Thames truck cab and chassis with black plastic wheels, no interior or window plastic, silver headlights and grille
EX $25   **NM** $40   **MIP** $60

(KP Photo, George Cuhaj collection)

❏ **28-3RW, Mark Ten Jaguar,** 1964, Light metallic brown body with opening hood, black plastic wheels, black-painted base. Engine can be painted the same as body color or left unpainted, 2-3/4". White plastic interior, clear window plastic, tow hook
EX $12   **NM** $20   **MIP** $30

(KP Photo, George Cuhaj collection)

❏ **28-3RW, Mark Ten Jaguar,** 1964, View of opening hood on the Mark Ten Jaguar

(KP Photo, George Cuhaj collection)

❏ **28-4RW, Mack Dump Truck,** 1969, Orange Mack truck body with orange dumper bed, black plastic tires on orange or yellow wheels, 2-5/8", green window plastic, unpainted base
EX $7   **NM** $18   **MIP** $25

(KP Photo, George Cuhaj collection)

❏ **28-4RW, Mack Dump Truck,** 1969, View of operating dumper bed. This model first appears in the 1969 1st edition catalog

❏ **29-1RW, Bedford Milk Delivery Van,** 1956, Tan body with white plastic milk bottles and boxes, silver trim, metal or gray plastic wheels, no interior or window plastic, 2-1/4"
EX $18   **NM** $30   **MIP** $80

(KP Photo, George Cuhaj collection)

❏ **29-2RW, Austin A55 Cambridge,** 1961, Medium green body with light green roof, gray or black plastic wheels, green window plastic, no interior, black-painted base with tow hook, 2-1/2"
EX $17   **NM** $30   **MIP** $72

(KP Photo, John Brown Sr. collection)

❏ **29-3RW, Fire Pumper,** 1966, Red LaFrance fire engine body, white plastic ladders along sides, unpainted base and trim, green window plastic, no interior, blue dome light, black plastic wheels, 3". With or without "Denver" decal
EX $6   **NM** $11   **MIP** $22

(KP Photo, George Cuhaj collection)

❏ **30-1RW, Ford Prefect,** 1956, Light sage-green or light brown body with metal or gray plastic wheels, (light blue harder to find, $200 or more MIP). No window plastic or interior, silver-painted grille, headlights and bumpers, red-painted taillights. Tow hook, black-painted base, 2-3/8"
EX $15   **NM** $40   **MIP** $80

(KP Photo, George Cuhaj collection)

❏ **30-2RW, Magirus-Deutz Crane Truck,** 1961, Silver cab and truck body with orange boom section and gray or black plastic wheels. Hook can be metal or plastic. Black-painted baseplate under front cab section, 2-3/8"
EX $17   **NM** $30   **MIP** $72

(KP Photo, George Cuhaj collection)

❏ **30-3RW, 8-Wheel Crane,** 1965, Medium-dark green body with 8 black plastic wheels, orange crane section, yellow plastic hook, 3"
EX $5   **NM** $11   **MIP** $20

❏ **31-1RW, American Ford Station Wagon,** 1957, Yellow body with metal or gray plastic wheels, silver painted bumpers and headlights, no interior or window plastic, 2-5/8". Appears brown in 1957 leaflet catalog
EX $15   **NM** $40   **MIP** $78

(Photo by Dr. Douglas Sadecky)

❏ **31-2RW, Ford Fairlane Station Wagon,** 1960, Mint green with pink-white roof, gray or black plastic wheels, silver-painted trim, tow hook. Yellow-painted versions are harder to find, and can bring higher MIP values (up to $300). Two box variations shown
EX $22   **NM** $55   **MIP** $78

(KP Photo)

❏ **31-3RW, Lincoln Continental,** 1964, Dark blue or mint-green body, white plastic interior, clear window glass, opening trunk, 3". Metallic tan versions rare, over $1000 MIP at auction
EX $6 **NM** $10 **MIP** $22

(KP Photo by Dr. Douglas Sadecky)

❏ **32-1RW, Jaguar XK140 Coupe,** 1957, Cream body with metal or gray plastic wheels, 2-3/8", called "Fixed Head Coupe" in 1957 catalog/flyer. Silver-painted grille, red-painted taillights
EX $30 **NM** $45 **MIP** $70

(KP Photo, John Brown Sr. collection)

❏ **32-2RW, E-Type Jaguar,** 1962, Metallic red body, spoked wheels with gray or black tires, green or clear window plastic, 2-5/8", white plastic interior
EX $20 **NM** $40 **MIP** $80

❏ **32-2RW, Leyland Petrol Tanker,** 1968, Medium-green Ergomatic cab and chassis, eight black plastic wheels, white tanker section, "BP" decals or labels, silver or white plastic grille and bumper, 3". A blue and white version with "Aral" labels is harder to find, and can have $120 or more MIP value. "Available early 1968" in catalog
EX $4 **NM** $7 **MIP** $15

(KP Photo by Dr. Douglas Sadecky)

❏ **33-1RW, Ford Zodiac,** 1957, A variety of body colors exist for this model: blue, dark green, blue-green, silver, tan & orange and turquoise. Dark green and tan and orange models more common, with around $80-$90 MIP values. 2-5/8"
EX $20 **NM** $40 **MIP** $80

(KP Photo, George Cuhaj collection)

❏ **33-2RW, Ford Zephyr 6,** 1962, Blue-green body, white plastic interior, gray or black plastic wheels, silver front grille and headlights, slight tailfins, black painted base, 2-1/2". Some models with black wheels have a lighter blue-green color than earlier versions
EX $8 **NM** $15 **MIP** $30

(KP Photo, George Cuhaj collection)

❏ **33-3RW, Lamborghini Miura,** 1969, Yellow or gold body with red or cream plastic interior, 2-3/4", silver wheels with black plastic tires, opening doors. Gold cars with cream interiors (as shown in 1969 catalog) have high MIP values, around $200
EX $4 **NM** $12 **MIP** $25

(KP Photo, John Brown Sr. collection)

❏ **34-1RW, Volkswagen Microvan,** 1957, Blue panel van body, no interior, "Matchbox International Express" yellow type decal on sides, with silver-painted bumper and headlights, 2-1/4". Mostly found with metal or gray plastic wheels, decal on side with "Matchbox International Express" in yellow lettering
EX $30 **NM** $50 **MIP** $95

(KP Photo)

❏ **34-2RW, Volkswagen Camping Car,** 1962, Light sea-green body, gray or black plastic wheels, opening side doors, top window plastic, camper section interior, 2-5/8"
EX $20 **NM** $40 **MIP** $90

(KP Photo)

❏ **34-3RW, Volkswagen Camper,** 1967, Silver body with opening camper section doors, orange plastic interior, yellow window plastic, raised roof with windows and top window plastic, black plastic wheels, 2-5/8"
EX $10 **NM** $18 **MIP** $45

(KP Photo)

❏ **34-3RW, Volkswagen Camper,** 1967, Another view of the Volkswagen Camper
EX $10 **NM** $18 **MIP** $45

(KP Photo)

❏ **34-4RW, Volkswagen Camper,** 1969, Silver body, opening doors to camper section, slightly raised roof with window plastic on top but no windows, orange plastic interior, black plastic wheels. Interestingly, the size of this vehicle remained the same since the 1962 release at 2-5/8". Makes first appearance in 1969 catalog
EX $11 **NM** $17 **MIP** $35

(Photo by Dr. Douglas Sadecky)

❏ **35-1RW, Marshall Horse Box,** 1957, Red ERF cab with silver-painted grille and headlights, brown horse box with opening side door, metal and gray plastic wheels most common, 2-1/8". Silver plastic wheel version, about $180 MIP; black plastic wheel version, about $135 MIP
EX $15   **NM** $30   **MIP** $80

(Photo by Dr. Douglas Sadecky)

❏ **35-2RW, Snow-Trac Tractor,** 1964, Red body with unpainted base, six black tread roller wheels, green window plastic, 2-1/4". White or gray treads, some versions have "Snow-Trac" cast in side of tractor, (as seen in 1968 and 1969 catalogs) others have decal, and some variations have neither, (as seen in the 1966 catalog). Gray-tread models may have slightly higher MIP values, although decal models (based on the tenuous nature of decals) may start to become more desirable
EX $9   **NM** $17   **MIP** $40

(KP Photo)

❏ **35-2RW, Snow-Trac Tractor,** 1964, A plain-sided variation of the Snow-Trac in the condition many of us find them-without treads...

(KP Photo, George Cuhaj collection)

❏ **36-1RW, Austin A50,** 1957, Blue-green body, no interior, metal or gray plastic wheels, silver-painted grille, headlights and bumper, tow bar, 2-3/8"
EX $20   **NM** $35   **MIP** $75

(KP Photo, George Cuhaj collection)

❏ **36-3RW, Opel Diplomat,** 1966, Gold body, black-painted metal base, white plastic interior and tow hook, opening hood, silver or gray plastic motor, 2-3/4". Pictured in elusive sea-green in 1966 catalog with caption "Available mid 1966." These (possibly) first versions are rarely seen
EX $4   **NM** $10   **MIP** $20

(KP Photo, George Cuhaj collection)

❏ **36-1RW, Opel Diplomat,** 1966, A view of Opel Diplomat with open hood and silver engine

❏ **37-1RW, Coca-Cola Lorry,** 1956, Yellow-orange truck with Coca-Cola decals on sides and back of truck, metal or gray plastic wheels, 2-1/4", no step on the running board on cab, silver-painted trim on running boards, grille. Some versions have "uneven" loads of cast Coca-Cola cases (as seen in 1957 flyer) in the bed of the truck. These typically run about $150 MIP. "Even" load versions in gray plastic wheels comparable MIP price. Even-load metal wheel version prices shown below
EX $30   **NM** $55   **MIP** $95

(KP Photo by Dr. Douglas Sadecky)

❏ **37-2RW, Coca-Cola Lorry,** 1960, Yellow body, black baseplate, "even" cast crate load on bed, Coca-Cola decals on sides and back, 2-1/4", gray or black plastic wheels. Gray plastic wheel versions tend toward higher MIP values, about $110
EX $25   **NM** $40   **MIP** $80

(KP Photo, John Brown Sr. collection)

❏ **37-3RW, Cattle Truck,** 1966, Yellow Dodge cab and chassis, gray plastic cattle box, originally included two white plastic steers, 2-1/2". Introduced in 1966 catalog as a new model, but hadn't yet replaced the #37 Coca-Cola truck in the line-up
EX $4   **NM** $7   **MIP** $15

❏ **38-1RW, Refuse Wagon,** 1957, Silver-gray or dark-gray cab and almost tanker-truck shaped rounded-top bed and "Cleansing Department" decals. Metal or gray plastic wheels. 1957 flyer shows model painted green and without the decals. Casting variations must account for size difference: 2-1/8" and 2-1/2" lengths
EX $18   **NM** $45   **MIP** $85

❏ **38-2RW, Vauxhall Victor Estate Car,** 1963, Yellow station wagon with opening rear hatch, gray, silver or black plastic tires, red or green plastic interiors, clear plastic windows. 2-1/2"
EX $18   **NM** $32   **MIP** $60

(KP Photo, George Cuhaj collection)

❏ **38-3RW, Honda Motorcycle with Trailer,** 1967, Blue-silver Honda motorcycle with kickstand and orange or yellow trailer. Trailer may or may not included labels or decals. 3". As with many motorcycle-related toys, these fairly common models are increasing in value
EX $12   **NM** $25   **MIP** $40

(KP Photo, John Brown Sr. collection)

❏ **39-1RW, "Zodiac" Convertible,** 1957, Pink body, turquoise interior, driver, tow hook. Metal, gray or silver plastic wheels. Casting variations: Model can measure 2-5/8" or 2-1/2". Silver-painted grille, gray-painted headlights, red-painted taillights, light green baseplate

EX $27   **NM** $68   **MIP** $95

(KP Photo by Dr. Douglas Sadecky)

❑ **39-2RW, Pontiac Convertible,** 1962, Purple Pontiac convertible body with gray or silver plastic wheels; yellow body with gray, silver or black plastic wheels. Yellow with black plastic wheels is most common, around $55 MIP. Purple version with silver plastic wheels is hard to find (pictured above and in color section). 2-3/4". Yellow with gray or silver wheels prices shown below

EX $28   **NM** $55   **MIP** $95

(KP Photo)

❑ **39-3RW, Ford Tractor,** 1967, Blue Ford tractor body with yellow die-cast hood, yellow wheels with black plastic tires, 2-1/8", tow hook. Versions of this tractor exist in all-blue, being part of the King Size K-20 set

EX $7   **NM** $16   **MIP** $25

(KP Photo, John Brown Sr. collection)

❑ **40-1RW, Bedford 7-Ton Tipper,** 1957, Red Bedford cab and chassis, tan dumper bed, metal or gray plastic wheels, silver painted trim. Casting variations: Size varies between 2-1/8" and 2-1/4". Shown in all-green color in 1957 flyer

EX $15   **NM** $40   **MIP** $80

(KP Photo, Tom Michael collection)

❑ **40-2RW, Long Distance Bus,** 1961, Blue-silver coach body with tailfins at rear, 3", green window plastic, silver-painted grille. With gray, silver or black plastic wheels. (Gray or silver-wheel versions about $55 MIP value.) Black-wheel version values given below

EX $7   **NM** $15   **MIP** $28

(KP Photo)

❑ **40-3RW, Hay Trailer,** 1967, Blue die-cast trailer body with yellow die-cast stake-ends, often missing. Yellow plastic wheels with black plastic tires, 3-3/8"

EX $3   **NM** $8   **MIP** $12

(KP Photo by Dr. Douglas Sadecky)

❑ **41-1RW, "D" Type Jaguar,** 1957, Green D-type body, metal driver in later catalogs, but not in 1957 flyer, "41" decal, metal or gray plastic tires, 2-1/4". Photo shows 41-1RW and second release with a larger casting, 41-2R

EX $20   **NM** $45   **MIP** $70

❑ **41-2RW, Jaguar Racing Car ("D"-Type),** 1961, Second issue of car featured a green body and tan driver, but came in a variety of wheel types, from more common gray and silver plastic wheels to rare spoked versions and black plastic wheels

EX $25   **NM** $40   **MIP** $80

(KP Photo, George Cuhaj collection)

❑ **41-3RW, Ford G.T.,** 1966, Generally white Ford G.T. bodies with yellow plastic wheels and black plastic tires. Clear window plastic, blue rally stripe on hood with "6" or "9" reversed in white. Visible rear engine, 2-5/8". "Available early 1966" in 1966 catalog. Black base, red plastic interior. Versions with differ-

ently-colored wheels or bodies are hard to find

EX $5   **NM** $12   **MIP** $20

(KP Photo by Dr. Douglas Sadecky)

❑ **42-1RW, Bedford "Evening News" Van,** 1957, Mustard-yellow Bedford panel van body with die-cast billboard on roof and red decal "First With The News" in white type. "Evening News" on panel side of van and "Football Results" in red type decals on each door. Metal, gray or black plastic wheels, (gray and black shown). 2-1/4"

EX $17   **NM** $40   **MIP** $95

(KP Photo, George Cuhaj collection)

❑ **42-2RW, Studebaker Station Wagon,** 1965, Blue body with blue or light blue sliding roof, white plastic interior and tow hook, clear window plastic, white plastic dog and hunter figure included with original (often missing), 3"

EX $15   **NM** $30   **MIP** $65

❑ **42-2RW, Studebaker Station Wagon,** 1965, Another view, showing the sliding rear roof of the Studebaker Station Wagon, 42-2RW

(KP Photo, George Cuhaj collection)

❏ **42-3RW, Iron Fairy Crane,** 1969-70, Red body, yellow crane arm, yellow plastic hook and seat, black plastic wheels, 3". Introduced in 1970 catalog, as a "non-Superfast" toy

EX $4   **NM** $11   **MIP** $18

(KP Photo, George Cuhaj collection)

❏ **43-1RW, Hillman "Minx",** 1958, Blue body, light gray roof, no window plastic or interior, silver-painted grille, metal or gray plastic wheels, 2-1/2", first appears in 1958 catalog

EX $12   **NM** $40   **MIP** $75

(KP Photo, John Brown Sr. collection)

❏ **43-2RW, Aveling-Barford Tractor Shovel,** 1962, Yellow tractor body with cast yellow or red driver and yellow or red bucket, black wheels, 2-5/8". All yellow versions can have $140 MIP value. Model prices for yellow with red bucket and yellow with red driver shown

EX $15   **NM** $30   **MIP** $55

(KP Photo, George Cuhaj collection)

❏ **43-3RW, Pony Trailer,** 1968, Yellow body with clear window plastic on sides and top, gray/brown plastic door, black plastic wheels, 2 white plastic horses, 2-5/8"

EX $6   **NM** $11   **MIP** $25

(KP Photo, John Brown Sr. collection)

❏ **44-1RW, Rolls Royce Silver Cloud,** 1958, Blue metallic Rolls Royce body, metal, gray or silver plastic wheels, crimped axles, no interior, no window plastic, silver-painted grille and bumpers, 2-5/8"

EX $18   **NM** $35   **MIP** $80

(KP Photo, George Cuhaj collection)

❏ **44-2RW, Rolls Royce,** 1962, Metallic tan or metallic silver/gray body, opening trunk, black plastic wheels, white plastic interior, clear window plastic, black base, silver-painted grille, 2-7/8"

EX $12   **NM** $20   **MIP** $40

(KP Photo, George Cuhaj collection)

❏ **44-3RW, Refrigerator Truck,** 1967, Red GMC cab and chassis, green refrigerator box, green window plastic, black plastic wheels, opening rear door on box, 3"

EX $4   **NM** $7   **MIP** $13

(KP Photo, George Cuhaj collection)

❏ **44-3RW, Refrigerator Truck,** 1967, Another view showing box of refrigerator truck

(KP Photo, George Cuhaj collection)

❏ **45-1RW, Vauxhall "Victor",** 1958, Yellow body, silver-painted headlights and grille, can have no windows, clear or green plastic windows. No interior. Metal, gray, silver or black plastic wheels, 2-3/8"

EX $18   **NM** $40   **MIP** $85

(KP Photo by Dr. Douglas Sadecky)

❏ **45-1RW, Vauxhall "Victor",** 1958, Vauxhall Victor models can include green or clear plastic windows, as this one does

(KP Photo, George Cuhaj collection)

❏ **45-2RW, Ford Corsair,** 1965, Cream-yellow body, red plastic interior and tow hook, gray or black plastic wheels, silver-painted grille and headlights, green plastic roof rack and boat (not shown), 2-5/8". Gray-wheeled versions may have higher MIP values

EX $6   **NM** $12   **MIP** $30

❏ **46-1RW, Morris Minor 1000,** 1958, Dark blue or dark green body, metal or gray plastic wheels, black base, no interior, no plastic windows, 2". Dark blue with gray plastic wheels harder to find, with higher MIP values

EX $45   **NM** $65   **MIP** $100

(KP Photo by Dr. Douglas Sadecky)

❏ **46-2RW, Pickford's Removal Van,** 1960, Dark blue or green body, silver-painted grille, no interior, no plastic windows, gray, silver or black plastic wheels, 2-5/8". Decals can have 2 or 3 lines. Many variations of this model exist, although versions with 2-line decals seem hard to find, bumping up the MIP price from what is shown here
EX $30 **NM** $80 **MIP** $150

(KP Photo, George Cuhaj collection)

❏ **46-3RW, Mercedes 300SE,** 1968, Medium blue or green body, white plastic interior, opening doors and trunk, black plastic wheels, unpainted base extends to bumpers and front grille, 2-7/8"
EX $9 **NM** $18 **MIP** $25

(KP Photo)

❏ **46-3RW, Mercedes 300SE,** 1968, Another view of the 46-3RW Mercedes showing opening doors and trunk

(KP Photo by Dr. Douglas Sadecky)

❏ **47-1RW, Trojan "Brooke Bond" Van,** 1958, Red body, metal or gray plastic wheels, decals on van box read "Brooke Bond Tea," tea leaf decal on each door, silver-painted headlights, 2-1/4"
EX $18 **NM** $45 **MIP** $95

(KP Photo, John Brown Sr. collection)

❏ **47-2RW, Commer Ice Cream Van,** 1963, Blue, cream or metallic blue body with white plastic interior, clear plastic windows and black plastic wheels, 2-1/4". Color and decal variations change MIP values considerably. Metallic blue versions with square roof decals are more rare than cream-colored models with plain (non-striped) side decals (see color section)
EX $20 **NM** $45 **MIP** $75

(KP Photo, George Cuhaj collection)

❏ **47-3RW, DAF Tipper Container Truck,** 1969, Green or silver-gray cab and chassis, yellow tipper bed with removable gray top. Red plastic grille and baseplate under cab, black plastic wheels, 3". Makes first appearance in 1969 catalog. Green version higher MIP value, about $40
EX $3 **NM** $8 **MIP** $18

(KP Photo, George Cuhaj collection)

❏ **47-3RW, DAF Tipper Container Truck,** 1969, Another view of truck with raised tipper bed

(KP Photo, Tom Michael collection)

❏ **48-1RW, "Meteor" Sports Boat on Trailer,** 1958, Blue and yellow plastic boat with slight rise for windshield, black die-cast trailer, metal or gray plastic wheels, 2-3/4"
EX $25 **NM** $40 **MIP** $70

(KP Photo, George Cuhaj collection)

❏ **48-2RW, Sports-Boat and Trailer,** 1961, Plastic red and white boat with gold or silver outboard motor, blue die-cast trailer, gray or black plastic wheels, 3-1/2". Boat can come with red deck and white hull or white deck and red hull
EX $12 **NM** $25 **MIP** $60

(KP Photo, John Brown Sr. collection)

❏ **48-3RW, Dumper Truck,** 1967, Red Dodge cab, chassis and dumper bed, silver plastic baseplate, bumper and front grille, black plastic wheels, 3"
EX $3 **NM** $8 **MIP** $18

(KP Photo, George Cuhaj collection)

❏ **49-1RW, Army Half-Track,** 1958, Dark olive-green with star-in-circle U.S. insignia on hood, no interior, metal, gray or black plastic wheels and rollers, gray treads (often missing as they are here) 2-1/2". Known as Army Half-Track and Military Personnel Carrier, this toy stayed in the 1-75 lineup for many years
EX $18 **NM** $30 **MIP** $55

(KP Photo, George Cuhaj collection)

❏ **49-2RW, Mercedes Unimog,** 1967, Two color variations, one tan and blue and the other blue and red, green plastic windows, yellow plastic wheels with black plastic tires, silver-painted grille, tow hook cast, 2-1/2"

EX $8   **NM** $12   **MIP** $25

(KP Photo, George Cuhaj collection)

❏ **49-2RW, Mercedes Unimog,** 1967, Another view of the Mercedes Unimog, blue and red variation (also see color section)

(KP Photo, John Brown Sr. collection)

❏ **50-1RW, Commer Pickup,** 1958, Tan or red and gray body, with metal, gray or black plastic wheels, 2-1/2", silver-painted grille and headlights

EX $25   **NM** $45   **MIP** $60

(KP Photo by Dr. Douglas Sadecky)

❏ **50-1RW, Commer Pickup,** 1958, A view of the red and gray variation of the Commer Pickup with black plastic wheels

EX $40   **NM** $75   **MIP** $150

(KP Photo)

❏ **50-2RW, John Deere-Lanz Tractor,** 1964, Green body, yellow plastic wheels, gray or black plastic tires, cast tow hook, 2-1/8". After John Deere acquired the German manufacturer

Lanz in the 1950s, a variety of toy manufacturers, including Matchbox, produced models of this tractor. Photo shows black-tire version tractor with 51-2RW Tipping Trailer. Note: Gray-tire versions have slightly higher MIP value, about $55

EX $14   **NM** $20   **MIP** $35

(KP Photo, John Brown Sr. collection)

❏ **50-2RW, John Deere-Lanz Tractor,** 1964, A view of the gray-tire version of the John Deere-Lanz tractor-a very detailed model

❏ **50-3RW, Kennel Truck,** 1969, Dark green die-cast body, white or silver plastic grille, green window plastic, truck bed partitioned into four sections, to hold one plastic dog each (included), clear plastic canopy over truck bed, "Auto-Steer" front wheels, black plastic wheels, 2-3/4"

EX $9   **NM** $20   **MIP** $35

❏ **51-1RW, Albion "Portland Cement" Lorry,** 1958, Yellow Albion truck cab and chassis, two decal variations: "Portland Cement" and "Blue Circle Portland Cement." Metal, gray, silver or black plastic wheels, silver-painted trim, tan-painted cement bag load on flatbed, no interior, no window plastic, 2-1/2". Silver plastic wheel versions have about $150 MIP values

EX $18   **NM** $40   **MIP** $80

(KP Photo, George Cuhaj collection)

❏ **51-2RW, Tipping Trailer,** 1964, Green body, yellow wheels, tilting bed, black or gray plastic tires, three yellow barrels, 2-5/8"

EX $8   **NM** $12   **MIP** $25

(KP Photo, George Cuhaj collection)

❏ **51-3RW, 8-Wheel Tipper,** 1969, Orange or yellow Ergomatic AEC cab and chassis with silver-gray tipper bed, 8 black plastic wheels, green plastic windows, no interior, "Douglas" or "Pointer" labels on the sides of tipper bed, 3". Orange models with "Douglas" appear to have higher MIP values, about $40

EX $9   **NM** $16   **MIP** $28

(KP Photo, George Cuhaj collection)

❏ **51-3RW, 8-Wheel Tipper,** 1969, Another view of Tipper truck with bed tilted. As with all miniature construction toys, finding these models in pristine shape can be a bit of a hunt

(KP Photo by Dr. Douglas Sadecky)

❏ **52-1RW, Maserati 4CLT Racecar,** 1958, Yellow or red body with spoked wheels and black tires or solid black plastic wheels. Open cockpit with driver, mostly seen with "52" decal, 2-3/8", silver-painted grille

EX $20   **NM** $35   **MIP** $70

(KP Photo, George Cuhaj collection)

❏ **52-2RW, BRM Racing Car,** 1965, Blue or red body, white plastic driver, yellow wheels, black plastic tires, 2-3/4". Generally carries no. "5" decals on hood and sides

EX $7   **NM** $12   **MIP** $25

❏ **53-1RW, Aston Martin,** 1958, Light green, metal or gray plastic wheels, no interior, no plastic windows, 2-1/2", silver-painted grille

EX $18   **NM** $35   **MIP** $70

VEHICLES

(KP Photo, George Cuhaj collection)

❏ **53-2RW, Mercedes-Benz 220SE,** 1963, Red or maroon body, opening doors, white plastic interior, clear plastic windows, 2-3/4", silver, gray or black plastic wheels
EX $10   **NM** $30   **MIP** $55

(KP Photo, Tom Michael collection)

❏ **53-3RW, Ford Zodiac Mk. IV,** 1968, Blue-silver body, opening hood, white plastic interior, clear plastic windows, black plastic wheels, 2-3/4"
EX $3   **NM** $6   **MIP** $12

(KP Photo, Tom Michael collection)

❏ **53-3RW, Ford Zodiac Mk. IV,** 1968, View of Ford Zodiac with opened hood, showing silver plastic engine and a spare tire tucked in front! Opening doors and hoods were always favorite features

(KP Photo, George Cuhaj collection)

❏ **54-1RW, Army Saracen Carrier,** 1958, Olive-green "turtle-shaped" body, six black plastic wheels, rotating turret on top, 2-1/4". One of Matchbox's first military vehicle releases. Like rescue and construction vehicles, military toys tend

to be in rough shape, so finding mint or MIP examples can be a little tough
EX $8   **NM** $18   **MIP** $40

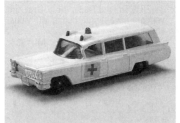

(KP Photo, George Cuhaj collection)

❏ **54-2RW, S&S Cadillac Ambulance,** 1965, White Cadillac ambulance body with red cross decal or label, blue plastic windows, detailed white plastic interior, black plastic interior, silver-painted grille, red plastic dome lights, 2-7/8"
EX $9   **NM** $18   **MIP** $40

(KP Photo)

❏ **55-1RW, D.U.K.W. Amphibian,** 1958, Olive-green body, metal, gray or black plastic wheels, 2-3/4", another in the early military grouping of Matchbox vehicles
EX $15   **NM** $35   **MIP** $60

(KP Photo by Dr. Douglas Sadecky)

❏ **55-2RW, Ford Fairlane Police Car,** 1963, Dark or light blue Ford Fairlane with white plastic interior, clear plastic windows, red dome light, silver-painted grille, black plastic wheels. Dark blue version is harder to find; about $300 MIP. Light blue values shown
EX $22   **NM** $40   **MIP** $85

(KP Photo, George Cuhaj collection)

❏ **55-3RW, Ford Galaxie Police Car,** 1966, White body, white plastic interior with molded figure, black plastic wheels, red, white and blue stars-in-shield decals, unpainted base, red dome light
EX $17   **NM** $25   **MIP** $40

(KP Photo)

❏ **55-4RW, Mercury Police Car,** 1969, White Mercury sedan with white plastic interior, featuring two officers, silver hubs with black plastic tires, blue dome light, clear plastic windows, unpainted base, "Auto-Steer" front wheels, 3-1/16". A new model, this police car was released at the same time as a Mercury station wagon, #73. Both share auto-steer feature and a baseplate, reading "55 or 73"
EX $16   **NM** $28   **MIP** $60

❏ **56-1RW, Trolley Bus,** 1958, Red double-decker body with sloped front, no interior; six metal, gray, or black plastic wheels, "Drink Peardrax" decals on sides, flat trolley poles on roof, "OXO" decal on front, 2-5/8". Note that MIP metal wheel versions have sold for $250. Common prices for gray and black wheel versions shown
EX $20   **NM** $45   **MIP** $70

(KP Photo, George Cuhaj collection)

❏ **56-2RW, Fiat 1500,** 1965, Pea-green Fiat 1500 sedan with dark or light brown plastic luggage on roof, red plastic interior, silver-painted grille and headlight details, black plastic wheels, 2-5/8", black plastic base. Red versions of this car were included with the G-1 Service Station Gift Set, and are tough to find, usually over $100 mint value. Standard green values shown
EX $4   **NM** $9   **MIP** $15

(KP Photo, George Cuhaj collection)

❏ **57-1RW, Wolseley 1500,** 1958, Pale green body, no plastic windows, no interior, silver-painted grille, bumpers and headlights, red-painted taillights, black-painted base, 2-1/8"
EX $20   **NM** $35   **MIP** $70

(KP Photo by Dr. Douglas Sadecky)

❏ **57-2RW, Chevrolet Impala,** 1961, Medium-blue body with light-blue top, cast tow hook, clear plastic windows, no interior, silver, gray or black plastic wheels
EX $25   **NM** $50   **MIP** $110

(KP Photo, George Cuhaj collection)

❏ **57-3RW, Land Rover Fire Truck,** 1966, Red Land Rover body with "Kent Fire Brigade" and fire dept. insignia decals on sides, blue plastic windows and dome light, white plastic ladder (removable) on top, black plastic wheels, 2-1/2"
EX $6   **NM** $11   **MIP** $25

❏ **58-1RW, British European Airways Coach,** 1958, Rounded metal blue bus body, no plastic windows, no interior, gray plastic wheels, "British European Airways" decals, 2-1/2"
EX $30   **NM** $50   **MIP** $85

(KP Photo, John Brown Sr. collection)

❏ **58-2RW, Drott Excavator,** 1962, Red or orange body, silver-painted motors on some red variations, orange motor on some orange models, 2-5/8"
EX $15   **NM** $35   **MIP** $60

(KP Photo, John Brown Sr. collection)

❏ **58-3RW, DAF Girder Truck,** 1968, Cream-colored cab and chassis, red plastic grille, green plastic windows, no interior, "Available mid-1968" in 1968 catalog, black plastic wheels, 12 red plastic girders, 3"
EX $4   **NM** $9   **MIP** $20

(KP Photo, John Brown Sr. collection)

❏ **59-1RW, Ford "Singer" Van,** 1958, Light green Ford Thames van with "Singer" decals on panel sides and "S" logo decals on doors. No plastic windows, no interior, silver-painted grille, gray plastic wheels, 2-1/8". Dark green models seem hard to find, about $250 MIP
EX $35   **NM** $55   **MIP** $100

❏ **59-2RW, Ford Fairlane Fire Chief Car,** Red Ford Fairlane casting (same as 55-2RW Ford Fairlane police car) black plastic wheels, white plastic interior, clear plastic windows
EX $25   **NM** $45   **MIP** $80

(KP Photo, Tom Michael collection)

❏ **59-3RW, Ford Galaxie Fire Chief Car,** 1966, Red Ford Galaxie body, white plastic interior with figure cast as part of interior (like police car version) unpainted base and metal grille and headlight section, fire chief decals or labels on side doors and hood, clear plastic windows, white plastic tow hook, blue plastic dome light, 2-7/8"
EX $9   **NM** $12   **MIP** $30

(KP Photo, George Cuhaj collection)

❏ **60-1RW, Morris J2 Pick-Up Truck,** 1958, Blue pick-up body, gray, silver or black plastic tires, "Builders Supply Company" decals on sides, silver-painted grille, no plastic windows, no interior, 2-1/4"
EX $18   **NM** $30   **MIP** $60

(KP Photo, George Cuhaj collection)

❏ **60-2RW, Site Hut Truck,** 1967, Blue Leyland Ergomatic cab and flatbed chassis, silver plastic grille and headlights, blue plastic windows, no interior, black plastic wheels, plastic yellow hut on back with green roof, 2-1/2"
EX $3   **NM** $6   **MIP** $12

(KP Photo, George Cuhaj collection)

❏ **61-1RW, Ferret Scout Car,** 1959, Olive-green, open-cockpit armored car body, tan-colored driver, four black plastic wheels, (one spare on side), 2-1/4"
EX $9   **NM** $12   **MIP** $30

(KP Photo, George Cuhaj collection)

❏ **61-2, Alvis Stalwart,** 1967, White body with green plastic windows and green or yellow wheels with black plastic tires. Plastic canopy over bed (not shown), no interior, 2-5/8". Yellow wheels are less common and have approx. $75 MIP values
EX $9   **NM** $17   **MIP** $30

VEHICLES

(KP Photo, George Cuhaj collection)

❑ **62-1RW, General Service Lorry,** 1959, Olive green body with six black plastic wheels, no plastic windows, no interior
EX $20 **NM** $32 **MIP** $60

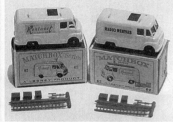

(KP photo by Dr. Douglas Sadecky)

❑ **62-2RW, TV Service Van,** 1963, Cream colored body with "Rentaset" or "Radio Rentals" decals on sides, red plastic accessories: antenna, 3 TV sets and ladder. No interior, 2-1/2"
EX $20 **NM** $50 **MIP** $110

(KP Photo)

❑ **62-3RW, Mercury Cougar,** 1969, Lime-green Mercury Cougar body with unpainted base, silver wheels with removable black plastic tires (like other Mercury models in the line), opening doors, red plastic interior, "auto-steer" front wheels, tow hook, 3"
EX $5 **NM** $8 **MIP** $15

(KP Photo, George Cuhaj collection)

❑ **63-2RW, Fire Fighting Crash Tender,** 1964, Block-shaped red body with white plastic ladder (missing in this photo) and white plastic lettering on sides. No plastic windows, no interior, black plastic wheels, 2-3/8"
EX $12 **NM** $30 **MIP** $50

(KP Photo, George Cuhaj collection)

❑ **63-2RW, Fire Fighting Crash Tender,** 1964, View of the detailed casting on rear of vehicle

(KP Photo, George Cuhaj collection)

❑ **63-3RW, Dodge Crane Truck,** 1969, Yellow Dodge cab and chassis, red or yellow plastic hook, black grille and headlights, green plastic windows, no interior, six black plastic wheels, swivelling crane section, 3"
EX $6 **NM** $10 **MIP** $18

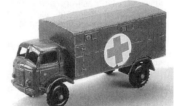

(KP Photo, George Cuhaj collection)

❑ **63-3RW, Service Ambulance,** 1959, Olive green truck-ambulance chassis, black plastic wheels, no interior, no plastic windows, red cross decals on sides
EX $8 **NM** $22 **MIP** $50

(KP Photo, George Cuhaj collection)

❑ **64-1RW, Scammell Breakdown Lorry,** 1959, Olive green body, box cab, green, silver or gray hook, six black plastic wheels
EX $25 **NM** $45 **MIP** $70

(KP Photo, George Cuhaj collection)

❑ **64-2RW, M.G. 1100,** 1966, Green car body, white plastic interior with driver in front and dog peeking out of rear window, clear plastic windows, black plastic wheels, unpainted base, white plastic tow hook, 2-5/8"
EX $3 **NM** $7 **MIP** $12

(KP Photo, George Cuhaj collection)

❑ **64-2RW, M.G. 1100,** 1966, View of the M.G. and collie peeking out from window. Matchbox included dogs in many later regular wheels models--a fun addition

(KP Photo by Dr. Douglas Sadecky)

❑ **65-RW, Jaguar 3.4 Litre,** 1959, Blue body, no interior, no plastic windows, gray plastic wheels, silver-painted grille. Shown here with 65-2RW Jaguar 3.8 Litre Sedan
EX $18 **NM** $35 **MIP** $60

(KP Photo, George Cuhaj collection)

❑ **65-2RW, Jaguar 3.8 Litre Sedan,** 1962, Red body, opening hood, silver-painted grille and headlights, gray, silver or black plastic wheels, green plastic windows, no interior, 2-5/8"
EX $11 **NM** $20 **MIP** $50

(KP Photo, George Cuhaj collection)

❑ **65-2RW, Jaguar 3.8 Litre Sedan,** 1962, View of gray-wheeled model with open hood-a favorite feature

(KP Photo)

❑ **65-3RW, Combine Harvester,** 1967, Red Claas combine with yellow plastic grain reel and yellow wheels with removable black plastic tires, 3". A popular casting for Matchbox, matching the King-Size model (K-9) version
EX $3   **NM** $7   **MIP** $12

(KP Photo by Dr. Douglas Sadecky)

❑ **66-1RW, Citroen DS19,** 1959, Yellow body, silver-painted grille, no window plastic, no interior, gray plastic wheels
EX $15   **NM** $32   **MIP** $55

(KP Photo by Dr. Douglas Sadecky)

❑ **66-2RW, Harley-Davidson Motorcycle with Sidecar,** 1962, Gold metallic body with spoked wheels, 2-5/8". This piece has escalated in value due to Matchbox and Harley-Davidson collector crossover
EX $65   **NM** $95   **MIP** $160

(KP Photo, George Cuhaj collection)

❑ **66-3RW, Greyhound Bus,** 1967, Silver-gray body, "Greyhound" decals or labels, yellow plastic windows, white plastic interior, black plastic wheels, 3"
EX $8   **NM** $12   **MIP** $25

(KP Photo, George Cuhaj collection)

❑ **67-1RW, Saladin Armoured Car,** 1959, Olive-green body, rotating turret (gun barrel in photo is broken, a common occurrence with these models) six black plastic wheels, 2-1/4"
EX $11   **NM** $18   **MIP** $30

(KP Photo, George Cuhaj collection)

❑ **67-2RW, Volkswagen 1600 TL,** 1967, Red body, white interior, unpainted base running up into headlights, clear window plastic, opening doors, 2-11/16". One version with snap-on plastic roof rack was included with Race'n Rally G-4 gift set, harder to find
EX $11   **NM** $17   **MIP** $25

(KP Photo, George Cuhaj collection)

❑ **67-2RW, Volkswagen 1600 TL,** 1967, Another view of the car showing opening doors and interior

(KP Photo, George Cuhaj collection)

❑ **68-1RW, Austin Mark II Radio Truck,** 1959, Olive-green body, no window plastic, no interior, black plastic wheels
EX $18   **NM** $35   **MIP** $65

❑ **68-2RW, Mercedes Coach,** 1966, White and blue-green or white and orange body, clear window plastic, white plastic interior, black plastic wheels, 2-7/8". Blue-green version harder-to-find with approx. $130 MIP values. More common orange-version values shown
EX $7   **NM** $11   **MIP** $15

(KP Photo by Dr. Douglas Sadecky)

❑ **69-1RW, Commer 30 CWT Nestlé's Van,** 1959, Dark red or red van with Nestlé's decals on panel sides, sliding doors, no window plastic, no interior, silver-painted grille, gray plastic wheels
EX $22   **NM** $40   **MIP** $90

❑ **69-2RW, Hatra Tractor Shovel,** 1965, Yellow or orange body with black plastic removable tires. Hubs can be yellow or red, 3-1/8". Models with red hubs seem to have higher MIP values, about $90-$125
EX $11   **NM** $17   **MIP** $30

(KP Photo, George Cuhaj collection)

❑ **70-1RW, Ford Thames Estate Car,** 1959, Pale blue and yellow van-shaped body with clear or green plastic windows, no interior, silver-painted grille. Gray, silver or black plastic wheels
EX $25 **NM** $40 **MIP** $70

(KP Photo, John Brown Sr. collection)

❑ **70-2RW, Grit Spreader,** 1966, Red Ford cab and chassis, yellow hopper section, green plastic windows, no interior, black plastic wheels, silver metal grille, gray or black plastic "pulls" that open bottom chute, 2-5/8"
EX $7 **NM** $9 **MIP** $20

❑ **71-1RW, Service Water Truck,** 1959, Olive-green truck chassis with water tank on back, black plastic wheels, spare black plastic tire behind cab, no plastic windows, no interior
EX $28 **NM** $40 **MIP** $75

(KP Photo, George Cuhaj collection)

❑ **71-2RW, Jeep Pick-Up Truck,** 1964, Red body, opening doors, black partial base, black plastic wheels, clear plastic windows, silver-painted grille, 2-5/8". Early models came with green plastic interior (shown in 1964 catalog) and are hard to find, about $175 MIP. White plastic interior more common; prices shown
EX $12 **NM** $22 **MIP** $40

(KP Photo, George Cuhaj collection)

❑ **71-2RW, Jeep Pick-Up Truck,** 1964, Another view of Jeep Pick-Up Truck showing opening doors

(KP Photo, George Cuhaj collection)

❑ **71-3RW, Ford Heavy Wreck Truck,** 1969, Red cab, green plastic windows and dome light, red plastic hook, black plastic wheels, "Esso" label, white grille extending from white base with "1968" date, 3". A nice, hefty model
EX $12 **NM** $20 **MIP** $40

(KP Photo by Dr. Douglas Sadecky)

❑ **72-1RW, Fordson Major Tractor,** 1959, Blue tractor with gray or black plastic tires, and orange hubs in rear and in variations, on front. Silver-painted grille, 2". Gray-tire version and black-tire version with box variations shown
EX $18 **NM** $30 **MIP** $75

(KP Photo, George Cuhaj collection)

❑ **72-1RW, Fordson Major Tractor,** 1959, Another variation of the Fordson tractor with orange hubs and black tires, front and rear. This is the version of the tractor that appeared in its last catalog appearance in 1966
EX $18 **NM** $30 **MIP** $75

(KP Photo, George Cuhaj collection)

❑ **72-2RW, Standard Jeep,** 1967, Yellow body with upright windshield, black base, red plastic interior and tow hook, black plastic removable tires over yellow hubs, spare tire on back, 2-3/8"
EX $12 **NM** $20 **MIP** $40

❑ **73-1RW, RAF Refueller Truck,** 1960, Blue body with RAF decal on top of truck behind cab, no plastic windows, no interior, gray plastic wheels
EX $20 **NM** $45 **MIP** $75

(KP Photo)

❑ **73-2RW, Ferrari Racing Car,** 1962, Red racing car body with "73" and Ferrari decals on sides, spoked wheels, white or gray plastic driver, 2-5/8"
EX $20 **NM** $35 **MIP** $80

(KP Photo)

❑ **73-3RW, Mercury Commuter,** 1969, Lime green body with clear plastic windows, white plastic interior (including two dogs peeking out of the back), black plastic removable tires with silver hubs, "Auto-Steer" front steering, 3-1/16"
EX $9 **NM** $12 **MIP** $25

(KP Photo)

❏ **73-3RW, Mercury Commuter,** 1969, Another view of the Mercury station wagon, showing the two dogs peeking out of the back window

❏ **74-1, Mobile Refreshment Bar,** 1960, Silver trailer body with opening sides and plastic interior, "Refreshments" decals below side openings, silver or gray plastic wheels, medium-blue base-plate models about $190 MIP, 2-5/8". Common prices with lighter blue bases shown below

EX $28   **NM** $45   **MIP** $95

(KP Photo, George Cuhaj collection)

❏ **74-2RW, Daimler Bus,** 1966, Cream, green or red bodies with white plastic interior, black plastic wheels, "Esso Extra Petrol" decals or labels, 3". First appears in 1966 catalog as new model, "Available mid 1966" with no series number

EX $7   **NM** $14   **MIP** $25

(KP Photo, John Brown Sr. collection)

❏ **74-2RW, Daimler Bus,** 1966, A view of the green variation of the 74-2RW Daimler Bus

(KP Photo by Dr. Douglas Sadecky)

❏ **75-1RW, Ford Thunderbird,** 1960, Pink and cream 1959 Ford Thunderbird body, green plastic windows, no interior, silver, gray or black plastic wheels

EX $20   **NM** $50   **MIP** $90

(KP Photo)

❏ **75-2RW, Ferrari Berlinetta,** 1965, Dark or light green body with white plastic interior and tow hook, clear plastic windows, spoked wheels or silver hubs, (with black plastic removable tires), 2-7/8". Red-colored versions of this model are very rare, about $750 MIP. Common prices shown below

EX $11   **NM** $18   **MIP** $40

VEHICLES

MATCHBOX

SUPERFAST

(KP Photo, George Cuhaj collection)

❏ **1-1SF, Mercedes Truck,** 1970, Gold-colored body, orange plastic tarp cover, green window plastic, narrow transitional Superfast wheels, silver plastic grille and half-baseplate, tow hook cast with body, 3"
EX $4   **NM** $8   **MIP** $18

(KP Photo, Tom Michael collection)

❏ **1-2SF, Mod Rod,** 1972, Yellow body, amber window plastic, exposed silver-plastic engine in back, red or black Superfast wheels, "wildcat" label on hood, 2-7/8"
EX $6   **NM** $12   **MIP** $25

(KP Photo)

❏ **1-3SF, Dodge Challenger,** 1976, Red or blue body, white or red plastic interior, black wheels, plastic air scoops on hood, blue-tinted windshield plastic, white plastic roof, 2-7/8"
EX $3   **NM** $5   **MIP** $10

(KP Photo)

❏ **1-4SF, Dodge Challenger,** 1982, Yellow body, gray base, "Toyman" tampos, black plastic roof

❏ **2-1SF, Mercedes Trailer,** 1970, Gold-colored body with orange plastic canopy, thin transitional wheels, 3-1/2"
EX $5   **NM** $9   **MIP** $20

❏ **2-2SF, Hot Rod Jeep,** 1972, Pink body, exposed silver plastic engine with black plastic exhaust pipes, white plastic seats, lime-green base and bumpers, 2-5/16"
EX $4   **NM** $7   **MIP** $12

(KP Photo)

❏ **2-3SF, Hovercraft,** 1976, Metallic-green hovercraft body with light brown plastic base and thin "hidden wheels" beneath, 3-1/6"
EX $1   **NM** $3   **MIP** $6

(KP Photo)

❏ **3-1SF, Mercedes-Benz "Binz" Ambulance,** 1970, White body with opening hatch and patient on stretcher, red cross labels, blue window plastic, white plastic interior, thin transitional wheels, (later issued with thicker wheels as part of TP-10 Two-Pack), 2-7/8"
EX $7   **NM** $11   **MIP** $25

(KP Photo)

❏ **3-1SF, Mercedes-Benz "Binz" Ambulance,** View of wider-wheel version without opening rear hatch, included as part of TP-10

(KP Photo)

❏ **3-2SF, Monterverdi Hai,** 1974, Orange body with number "3" label on hood, blue window plastic, thick black wheels, opening doors, 3"
EX $5   **NM** $7   **MIP** $15

(KP Photo)

❏ **3-2SF, Monterverdi Hai,** 1974, Another view of the Monterverdi Hai showing opening doors

(KP Photo, Tom Michael collection)

❏ **3-3SF, Porsche Turbo,** 1979, Charcoal-gray, red or white exterior with rally number "14," plastic interior can be yellow, tan or brown, plastic tow hook, opening doors
EX $1   **NM** $2   **MIP** $5

❏ **4-1SF, Stake Truck,** 1970, Yellow, or orange-yellow cab and chassis with green window plastic, no interior, green plastic stake-side cargo area, silver metal base, grille and headlights, 2-7/8"
EX $3   **NM** $8   **MIP** $15

(KP Photo, Tom Michael collection)

❏ **4-2SF, Gruesome Twosome,** 1972, Gold with cream interiors and pink or purple window plastic. Two exposed engines, unpainted base, 2-7/8"
EX $2   **NM** $4   **MIP** $9

(KP Photo, Tom Michael collection)

❏ **4-3SF, Pontiac Firebird,** 1976, Blue body with silver plastic interior, amber window plastic, unpainted base and bumpers, 2-7/8"
EX $1   NM $3   MIP $5

(KP Photo)

❏ **4-4SF, '57 Chevy,** 1981, Red or light purple with unpainted or black base, opening hood with silver plastic engine underneath
EX $1   NM $3   MIP $5

(KP Photo)

❏ **5-1SF, Lotus Europa,** 1970, Pink or blue body, white plastic interior, opening doors, 2-7/8", thin or thick Superfast wheels. Blue model shown in 1970 catalog, but pink was advertised afterward until model removed from lineup
EX $4   NM $9   MIP $20

(KP Photo, Tom Michael collection)

❏ **5-1SF, Lotus Europa,** 1970, The pink version of the Lotus Europa, here with thin wheels. This color variation also comes with wide wheels, and generally seems more common

(KP Photo, John Brown Sr. collection)

❏ **5-2SF, Seafire,** 1976, White body with "Seafire" label on front, blue base, blue or orange driver, exposed silver plastic engine with red plastic exhaust pipes. This casting has been used many times by Matchbox, returning in 5-Packs in the 1990s
EX $1   NM $3   MIP $5

(KP Photo)

❏ **6-1SF, Ford Pick-Up Truck,** 1970, Red body, white plastic camper top, silver or white plastic grille, 2-3/4", black or charcoal base
EX $8   NM $15   MIP $25

(KP Photo, Tom Michael collection)

❏ **6-2SF, Mercedes Tourer,** 1973, Orange or yellow 350SL body with black plastic top, amber windows, light yellow or cream plastic interior, 3", unpainted base. Later models in light or dark red with white plastic roof, or red or metallic blue with no roof
EX $3   NM $7   MIP $14

❏ **7-1SF, Ford Refuse Truck,** 1970, Red-orange cab with gray plastic and silver metal garbage dumper bed, 3". The same model as the old regular-wheels version, just with thin or thick Superfast wheels
EX $4   NM $8   MIP $12

(KP Photo, Tom Michael collection)

❏ **7-2SF, Hairy Hustler,** 1973, Bronze body, with amber windows, number "5" racing labels on front and side, or white body with checkered labels on hood and roof, and red stripes on fenders, black metal base
EX $2   NM $4   MIP $7

(KP Photo, John Brown Sr. collection)

❏ **7-3SF, Volkswagen Golf,** 1977, Lime green, dark green, yellow or red body, amber window plastic, black plastic, detachable surf boards on roof rack, yellow plastic interior, black or charcoal base, tow hook
EX $4   NM $7   MIP $12

❏ **8-1SF, Ford Mustang Fastback,** 1970, White, red or orange-red body, white or red plastic interior (red is harder-to-find), tow hook, 2-7/8". Red models with red plastic interiors are the most rare, selling for around $400 MIB
EX $65   NM $80   MIP $120

❏ **8-2SF, Wildcat Dragster,** 1971, Orange or pink body with silver engine protruding from hood, and "Wild Cat" labels on sides, tow hook, 2-7/8". This is the same casting used on the Mustang Fastback model 8-1SF
EX $3   NM $5   MIP $11

(KP Photo)

❏ **8-3SF, De Tomasa Pantera,** 1975, White body with "8" labels, blue base, red plastic interior, or blue body, tempo "17", black base, 3"
EX $2   NM $4   MIP $7

(KP Photo)

❏ **8-3SF, De Tomasa Pantera,** 1975, A view of the blue version of the Pantera with the "17" tempo

❏ **9-1SF, Boat and Trailer,** 1970, Blue die-cast boat trailer with thin Superfast wheels and plastic blue and white boat, 3-1/2"
EX $4   NM $9   MIP $20

VEHICLES

❑ **9-2SF, AMX Javelin,** 1972, Lime-green or blue body (blue included with Twin-Pack #3, Javelin and Pony Trailer), black or silver plastic air scoop, light yellow or white plastic interior, opening doors, tow hook, 3-1/16"
EX $3   **NM** $6   **MIP** $10

(KP Photo, Tom Michael collection)

❑ **9-3SF, Ford Escort RS 2000,** 1979, White body with Ford and Shell rally labels, clear window plastic, black base, tan plastic interior
EX $3   **NM** $5   **MIP** $8

❑ **10-1SF, Pipe Truck,** 1970, Red or orange cab and chassis, gray or yellow plastic pipes, thin or wide Superfast wheels, silver grille, green window plastic, 3". Red models about $35 MIB, orange model values shown below
EX $7   **NM** $14   **MIP** $23

(KP Photo, Tom Michael collection)

❑ **10-2SF, Piston Popper,** 1973, Blue or yellow Mustang Mach I body with silver Rola-Matic engine with red plastic pistons that move as car is rolled along. Yellow plastic interior, unpainted base, 2-7/8"
EX n/a   **NM** $5   **MIP** $10

(KP Photo)

❑ **10-3SF, Plymouth Gran Fury Police Car,** 1979, Black and white with "Metro Police" on doors and hood, blue police lights on roof, amber or blue window plastic, unpainted or silver base. Introduced in 1979/80 catalog, it hadn't yet replaced Piston Popper in the lineup
EX $1   **NM** $4   **MIP** $7

(KP Photo, George Cuhaj collection)

❑ **11-3SF, Scaffold Truck,** 1970, Silver Mercedes-Benz truck with red plastic base and grille, yellow plastic scaffold sections in back, "Builders Supply Company" labels on sides of truck, green window plastic, no interior, 2-5/8"
EX $4   **NM** $6   **MIP** $13

❑ **11-2SF, Flying Bug,** 1973, Red metallic Volkswagen Beetle with Iron Cross label on hood, oversized face with silver helmet peeking up from car, opaque windows, tailwing and yellow plastic jet engine section on back. Silver or unpainted base, 2-7/8"
EX $4   **NM** $9   **MIP** $16

(KP Photo)

❑ **11-3SF, Car Transporter,** 1978, Orange body with black base and light tan/cream car carrying section with red, yellow and blue plastic cars. Dark blue window plastic, no interior
EX $3   **NM** $5   **MIP** $9

(KP Photo, Tom Michael collection)

❑ **11-4SF, Cobra Mustang,** 1982, Orange body with opening hood, chrome interior, yellow windows, "The Boss" in white lettering on sides, number "5" on roof. Another in the many variations of the old "Boss Mustang" casting

(KP Photo)

❑ **12-1SF, Safari Land Rover,** 1970, Gold body with white plastic interior, red-brown plastic luggage, tow hook, thin Superfast wheels, 2-3/4". Blue versions of this model exist as Superfasts, but are extremely rare, so prices shown are for gold models only
EX $8   **NM** $14   **MIP** $25

(KP Photo, John Brown Sr. collection)

❑ **12-2SF, Setra Coach,** 1971, Metallic yellow and white or burgundy and white with clear or green window plastic, white plastic interior, unpainted base, 3"
EX $3   **NM** $6   **MIP** $14

(KP Photo, John Brown Sr. collection)

❑ **12-3SF, Big Bull,** 1975, Orange bulldozer body and rollers, green base and blade, silver plastic engine and trim, 2-1/2"
EX $1   **NM** $3   **MIP** $5

(KP Photo)

❑ **66-2SF, Citroen CX Station Wagon,** 1980, Blue body with cream or light yellow plastic interior, clear or blue window plastic, unpainted or silver base
EX $2   **NM** $5   **MIP** $10

❑ **13-1SF, Wreck Truck,** 1970, Yellow Dodge cab and tow boom with green bed. "BP" labels on sides, thin Superfast wheels, red window plastic and dome light, no interior, red plastic tow hook, 3". This is another transitional model that is becoming hard to find
EX $17   **NM** $30   **MIP** $48

(KP Photo, Tom Michael collection)

❑ **13-2SF, Baja Buggy,** 1972, Lime green body, orange plastic interior, no window plastic, thick Superfast wheels, flower label on hood, silver plastic engine with orange plastic exhaust pipes, 2-5/8"
EX $2   **NM** $4   **MIP** $8

(KP Photo)

❑ **13-3SF, Snorkel Fire Engine,** 1977, Red body with blue or amber window plastic, yellow or white snorkel section, unpainted metal base. Models with amber-colored window plastic tend to have higher MIP prices, about $15. This fire engine first appeared in the 1977 catalog with a white snorkel as a new model to watch for, not yet replacing Baha Buggy in the lineup
EX $1   **NM** $4   **MIP** $7

(KP Photo)

❑ **14-1SF, Iso Grifo,** 1970, Dark or medium blue with thin Superfast wheels, light blue or white plastic interior, unpainted base, 3"
EX $6   **NM** $12   **MIP** $25

❑ **14-2SF, Mini-Ha-Ha,** 1976, Red body with blue opaque window plastic, silver plastic rotary engine protruding through hood, large rear wheels, head with pilot's helmet showing through roof, circular British RAF side labels on doors
EX $3   **NM** $8   **MIP** $17

❑ **15-1SF, Volkswagen 1500,** 1970, White, cream or red body with white plastic interior, tow hook, unpainted base, "137" labels on doors, 2-7/8"
EX $7   **NM** $12   **MIP** $20

(KP Photo)

❑ **15-2SF, Fork Lift Truck,** 1973, Red body with larger wheels at front, gray or yellow plastic lifting forks on yellow metal or unpainted track, "Lansing Bagnall" or "Hi-Lift" side labels, unpainted, black or green base, 2-3/4"
EX $3   **NM** $6   **MIP** $9

(KP Photo)

❑ **15-3SF, Hi Ho Silver,** 1981, Silver Volkswagen Beetle (same casting as "Volks Dragon") with "Hi Ho Silver" and "31" tempo. Black base, clear window plastic, red plastic interior, 2-5/8". Having "31" on the roof is an interesting choice of graphic, considering it was the same vehicle casting as the 31-2SF
EX $4   **NM** $7   **MIP** $12

(KP Photo by Dr. Douglas Sadecky)

❑ **16-1SF, Case Bulldozer,** 1970, Red with yellow engine, cab and blade and green or black rubber tracks, 2-1/2". This model was released at the same time as the Superfast line-notice that the box has "speed lines" just like the other models
EX $5   **NM** $8   **MIP** $15

❑ **16-2SF, Badger,** 1974, Block, metallic bronze-red body with surface detail tools, ladders, etc., and plastic "Rola-Matic" radar. Green window plastic, no interior, six thick wheels, 2-3/4". Later editions in olive green were included as part of TP-14 Two-Pack
EX $4   **NM** $7   **MIP** $12

(KP Photo, Tom Michael collection)

❑ **16-3SF, Pontiac Firebird,** 1981, Metallic light or dark tan, Firebird tempo on hood, light tan plastic interior
EX n/a   **NM** $2   **MIP** $5

❑ **17-1SF, Horse Box,** 1971, Red or orange AEC Ergomatic cab with green or gray plastic horse box, gray or mustard door, and two white plastic horses, 2-7/8"
EX $3   **NM** $7   **MIP** $12

(KP Photo, John Brown Sr. collection)

❑ **17-2SF, The Londoner,** 1973, Red body with "Berger Paints" or "Swinging London Carnaby Street" side labels (most common). White plastic interior, no window plastic, 3". There are many color and label variations of this model, some limited runs that command MIP values over $200. However, prices shown are for the common red-colored "Berger" and "Swinging London" versions
EX $1   **NM** $3   **MIP** $5

(KP Photo, Tom Michael collection)

❑ **17-2SF, The Londoner,** 1973, The "Swinging London" version of the The Londoner bus

(KP Photo, Tom Michael collection)

VEHICLES

□ **18-1SF, Field Car,** 1970, Yellow body with tan plastic roof, white plastic interior, no window plastic, unpainted base, spare tire, tow hook, thin or thick wheels, 2-7/8". Other variations as part of Two-Packs in the 1970s, included orange with checked hood label and black plastic roof, olive green with light-tan plastic roof and hood label, red with light-tan plastic roof and "44" hood label-almost all with black plastic interiors. White editions are harder to find, about $250-300 in MIP condition. Prices shown reflect the more common models listed
EX $7   **NM** $12   **MIP** $25

(KP Photo, Tom Michael collection)

□ **18-1SF, Field Car,** Variation with dark yellow-orange body, black interior, base and roof. Part of Two Pack (TP-8), with Honda motorcycle

□ **18-2SF, Hondarora,** 1975, Red or orange body with silver or black forks and black seat are the most common, some with gas-tank labels, some without. Olive-drab military models were part of the TP-11 set with the olive-drab field car. 2-1/2"
EX n/a   **NM** $2   **MIP** $5

□ **19-1SF, Lotus Racing Car,** 1970, Dark metallic purple, white plastic driver, wide Superfast wheels, "3" decal on sides, 2-3/4"
EX $9   **NM** $20   **MIP** $48

(KP Photo, Tom Michael collection)

□ **19-2SF, Road Dragster,** 1971, Red or metallic pink body with unpainted base, exposed silver plastic engine, white plastic interior, wide wheels, clear window plastic, "8" labels on hood and roof, 3". Some models have "Wynns" or scorpion labels and are pink or orange-red and harder to find, about $80 MIP
EX $2   **NM** $5   **MIP** $10

(KP Photo)

□ **19-3SF, Cement Truck,** 1977, Red cab and chassis, unpainted metal base, green window plastic, no interior, yellow plastic mixer, with or without black or red stripes, 3"
EX $1   **NM** $3   **MIP** $6

(KP Photo)

□ **20-1SF, Lamborghini Marzal,** 1970, Pink or dark red with amber window plastic, white plastic interior and thin wheels; or pink or orange-pink with thick wheels, 2-3/4"
EX $4   **NM** $9   **MIP** $18

□ **20-2SF, Police Patrol,** 1975, White Range Rover with orange stripe "Police" label, frosted window plastic and blue or orange revolving police light (part of the Rola-Matics series). 2-7/8". Other models include orange Site Engineer from Gift Pack #13, olive-drab military ambulance model, and orange Paris-Dakar model, each with approx. $25-$35 MIP value. Common white model values given below
EX $1   **NM** $4   **MIP** $8

(KP Photo, Tom Michael collection)

□ **20-2SF, Police Patrol: Site Engineer,** 1977, Orange body with rotating orange dome light, "Site Engineer" labels on doors, plain metal base. Part of #13 Construction Gift Pack
EX $5   **NM** $8   **MIP** $14

(KP Photo)

□ **20-2SF, Police Patrol: Paris-Dakar Rallye,** 1983, Gold body with black and white checkered label and "Securitie-Rallye Paris Dakar 83" on sides, black base, red rotating dome light
EX $5   **NM** $9   **MIP** $13

(KP Photo)

□ **20-2SF, Police Patrol: County Sheriff,** 1982, White body with blue doors and roof, star design on hood and doors, "County Sheriff" in blue type on sides, blue rotating dome light
EX $3   **NM** $5   **MIP** $8

□ **20-2SF, Police Patrol: British Police,** 1983, White body with yellow and black/white checkered "Police" labels on sides. Blue rotating dome light, black base
EX $4   **NM** $8   **MIP** $12

□ **21-1SF, Foden Concrete Truck,** 1971, Yellow cab, orange truck bed with yellow plastic mixer, eight thin wheels, 3"
EX $8   **NM** $12   **MIP** $25

(KP Photo)

□ **21-2SF, Rod Roller,** 1973, Yellow body with red plastic seat, star and flames label on hood, (later editions without black plastic roller wheels, some with red or metallic red hubs on rear, black plastic steering lever, 2-1/2". Prices for metallic red hub versions about $45 MIP
EX $3   **NM** $8   **MIP** $17

(KP Photo)

❏ **21-3SF, Renault 5TL,** 1979, Yellow, blue, white or silver-gray body, clear or amber window plastic, tan or red plastic interior, tow hook, 2-1/2". Some yellow models have "Le Car" tempo
EX $2   **NM** $6   **MIP** $10

❏ **22-1SF, Pontiac Grand Prix,** 1970, Purple body, thin wheels, silver grille and black base, 3"
EX $12   **NM** $22   **MIP** $55

(KP Photo, Tom Michael collection)

❏ **22-2SF, Freeman Inter-City Commuter,** 1971, Purple-red body with white plastic interior, clear window plastic, unpainted base, some with side labels, 3"
EX $2   **NM** $4   **MIP** $8

(KP Photo)

❏ **22-3SF, Blaze Buster,** 1976, Red body with yellow or black plastic ladder, silver plastic interior, amber window plastic, black or silver base, 3-1/16". Black-ladder versions about $25 MIP value
EX $2   **NM** $4   **MIP** $7

(KP Photo)

❏ **22-4SF, 4 x 4 Big Foot,** 1982, Silver body, white plastic camper top, blue window plastic, black base, "Big Foot" and "26" tempos on sides and hood
EX $2   **NM** $5   **MIP** $12

❏ **23-1SF, Volkswagen Camper,** 1970, Blue or orange body with plastic orange lift-up top reveals white plastic interior, amber or clear window plastic. Some models with sailboat labels on sides, 2-5/8". Military olive-drab versions without lift-up camper top were included as ambulances with TP-12 Two-Pack
EX $9   **NM** $22   **MIP** $45

(KP Photo)

❏ **23-2SF, Atlas Tipper,** 1976, Blue body with orange or silver tipper section, wide wheels, amber or clear window plastic, silver or gray plastic interior, 2-3/4". Later versions available with red body
EX $1   **NM** $3   **MIP** $7

(KP Photo, Tom Michael collection)

❏ **23-3SF, Ford Mustang GT-350,** 1981, White body, blue Shelby stripes, exposed engine in front, "GT 350" on sides
EX $3   **NM** $6   **MIP** $14

(KP Photo)

❏ **24-1SF, Rolls-Royce Silver Shadow,** 1970, Metallic-red body, white plastic interior, clear window plastic, opening trunk, silver metal grille and headlights, black or silver base, 3"
EX $5   **NM** $9   **MIP** $20

(KP Photo, Tom Michael collection)

❏ **24-2SF, Team Matchbox,** 1973, Metallic green, red or orange body, "8" or "44" label (included with TP-9, Field Car and Racing Car Two-Pack), white plastic driver, 2-7/8". Metallic green version, about $35 MIP, orange version about $85 MIP. Values for red shown
EX $1   **NM** $4   **MIP** $9

(KP Photo, John Brown Sr. collection)

❏ **24-3SF, Diesel Shunter,** 1979, Dark green and red or yellow and red body, no window plastic, labels read "Rail Freight" or "D1496-RF"
EX n/a   **NM** $2   **MIP** $5

(KP Photo)

❏ **25-1SF, Ford Cortina GT,** 1970, Metallic tan or blue body, white plastic interior, opening doors, tow hook, 2-5/8". Metallic tan versions, the first of the transitional Superfast models, are harder-to-find and have approx. $70-$80 MIP values
EX $8   **NM** $12   **MIP** $25

(KP Photo)

❏ **25-2SF, Mod Tractor,** 1973, Metallic purple body, black base, some with "V" cast on fenders, some without, silver plastic exposed engine, yellow plastic seat, 2-1/4". Harder to find editions have headlights cast in rear fender, about $60 MIP

EX $1   **NM** $3   **MIP** $7

(KP Photo, John Brown Sr. collection)

❏ **25-3SF, Flat Car and Container,** 1979, Black or charcoal flat car with tan or red plastic container with "NYK Worldwide Service" labels

EX $1   **NM** $3   **MIP** $5

❏ **26-1SF, GMC Tipper Truck,** 1970, Red tipping cab, green engine and base, silver dump bed, green window plastic, no interior, 2-5/8"

EX $5   **NM** $9   **MIP** $20

(KP Photo, Tom Michael collection)

❏ **26-2SF, Big Banger,** 1973, Red with dark-blue window plastic, no interior, large silver plastic engine and exhaust pipes, "Big Banger" side labels, 3". Later versions were brown with "Brown Sugar" side labels or white with "Cosmic Blues" tempo

EX $4   **NM** $9   **MIP** $18

(KP Photo, Tom Michael collection)

❏ **26-2SF, Brown Sugar,** 1973, The "Brown Sugar" version of the Big Banger with brown body, large silver engine with black scoop and yellow and red "Brown Sugar" labels

❏ **26-3SF, Site Dumper,** 1977, Yellow body with yellow or red dumper bed, or orange body with silver-gray dumper bed, no window plastic, black or brown base, black plastic interior

EX $2   **NM** $4   **MIP** $7

(KP Photo)

❏ **27-1SF, Mercedes 230SL,** 1970, Yellow convertible body with black plastic interior, or white body with red plastic interior, clear window plastic, silver base, thin wheels, 2-3/4"

EX $8   **NM** $12   **MIP** $25

(KP Photo, Tom Michael collection)

❏ **27-2SF, Lamborghini Countach,** 1973, Pale-orange body with "3" label on hood, or red-orange with "8" tempo and stripes, silver or gray plastic interior, amber or blue window plastic, opening rear hood, 3"

EX $3   **NM** $7   **MIP** $12

(KP Photo, John Brown Sr. collection)

❏ **28-1SF, Mack Dump Truck,** 1970, Light-green body and dumper bed, silver base, wide wheels, no interior, amber window plastic, 2-5/8". Olive-drab versions were released with Case bulldozer in TP-16 Two-Pack

EX $6   **NM** $10   **MIP** $22

(KP Photo)

❏ **28-2SF, Stoat,** 1973, Metallic bronze-tan body with rotating (Rola-Matic) soldier holding binoculars. Black base, wide wheels, 2-5/8". Olive-green versions with all-black wheels were included in TP-13 Two-Pack along with an olive version of 73-2SF Weasel armored vehicle

EX $2   **NM** $6   **MIP** $12

(KP Photo, Tom Michael collection)

❏ **28-3SF, Lincoln Continental Mk V,** 1979, Red body, white plastic roof, light-yellow or gray interior, silver base. First introduced in the 1979/80 catalog, this model had not yet replaced the Stoat in the lineup, but was due to be "available in your shops later this year"

EX $3   **NM** $6   **MIP** $12

❏ **29-1SF, Fire Pumper,** 1970, Red body, blue window plastic and dome light, white plastic ladders and reels, silver base, thin wheels, 3"

EX $12   **NM** $32   **MIP** $70

(KP Photo, Tom Michael collection)

❏ **29-2SF, Racing Mini,** 1971, Orange-red body with yellow "29" labels, clear window plastic, white plastic interior, unpainted silver-gray base and grille, 2-1/4". Also included with TP-6 Two-Pack

EX $5   **NM** $8   **MIP** $16

(KP Photo)

❏ **29-3SF, Shovel-Nose Tractor,** 1977, Yellow body with silver or black plastic engine and interior, shovel can be red or black plastic, 2-7/8". Lime green models with yellow plastic shovels are harder to find, about $65 MIP value. Models with yellow body, black plastic and stripes (as shown) were included in the G-5 Giftset in the 1979/80 catalog. Orange models with red plastic shovels, also about $65 MIP value

EX $5   **NM** $8   **MIP** $16

VEHICLES

(KP Photo)

❏ **30-1SF, 8-Wheel Crane,** 1970, Red with gold crane section, red plastic hook, no window plastic, yellow plastic hook, 3"

EX $10   **NM** $20   **MIP** $45

(KP Photo, Tom Michael collection)

❏ **30-2SF, Beach Buggy,** 1971, Pink body with yellow "spatter paint," white or yellow plastic interior and side tanks, no window plastic, 2-9/16". White interior versions have approx. $20 MIP value

EX $4   **NM** $7   **MIP** $12

(KP Photo)

❏ **30-3SF, Swamp Rat,** 1977, Squared-boat body with olive-green deck, tan plastic hull, rotating striped army gunner (Rola-Matic), "Swamp Rat" labels, 3-1/16"

EX $3   **NM** $7   **MIP** $9

❏ **31-1SF, Lincoln Continental,** 1970, Lime-green body with thin wheels, opening trunk, clear window plastic, white plastic interior, 3"

EX $12   **NM** $21   **MIP** $38

❏ **31-2SF, Volksdragon,** 1972, Red Volkswagen Beetle body with clear window plastic, white or yellow plastic interior, silver plastic engine, "eyes" label, unpainted base, 2-5/8"

EX $6   **NM** $10   **MIP** $16

(KP Photo, John Brown Sr. collection)

❏ **31-3SF, Caravan,** 1978, White body with amber or blue window plastic, some with orange stripe with white reversed bird graphic label, unpainted base, light-yellow plastic interior, 2-3/4"

EX $1   **NM** $3   **MIP** $6

(KP Photo)

❏ **32-1SF, Leyland Petrol Tanker,** 1970, Green cab and chassis, white tank, "BP" labels, thin wheels, blue or amber window plastic, no interior, chrome plastic base, 3"

EX $6   **NM** $10   **MIP** $22

(KP Photo, Tom Michael collection)

❏ **32-2SF, Maserati Bora,** 1973, Magenta body with yellow plastic interior, clear window plastic, opening doors, "8" stripe label on hood, lime green, dark green or unpainted base, 3"

EX $3   **NM** $7   **MIP** $13

(KP Photo)

❏ **32-3SF, Field Gun,** 1978, Olive-green with black plastic barrel that fired shells attached to sprue on tan plastic base with soldiers, 3". An interesting piece, in that it included a diarama with the toy. Field Gun was removable from base

EX $3   **NM** $6   **MIP** $11

(KP Photo, George Cuhaj collection)

❏ **33-1SF, Lamborghini Miura,** 1970, Gold body, opening doors, white plastic interior, thin wheels, unpainted base, 2-3/4"

EX $7   **NM** $12   **MIP** $22

❏ **33-2SF, Datsun 126X,** 1973, Yellow body with silver plastic interior, orange base, opening rear hood, amber window plastic, 3". Some versions have black and red flame tempo detail on hood and roof

EX $1   **NM** $4   **MIP** $8

❏ **33-3SF, Police Motorcycle,** 1978, White motorcycle with blue plastic policeman rider, silver plastic engine, "Police" on saddlebags, silver or black wire spoked wheels, 2-7/8". Models included with the K-71 Porsche Polizei set had green plastic riders and detailing

EX $1   **NM** $4   **MIP** $7

❏ **34-1SF, Formula 1 Racing Car,** 1970, Magenta or yellow body, white plastic driver, silver plastic engine, wide wheels, "16" striped label on hood, clear windshield plastic, 2-7/8"

EX $5   **NM** $8   **MIP** $14

(KP Photo, Tom Michael collection)

❏ **34-2SF, Vantastic,** 1976, Modified orange Ford Mustang body, white plastic interior, blue window plastic, early models with large silver plastic engine, later models with closed hood, white base, 2-7/8"

EX $2   **NM** $6   **MIP** $12

(KP Photo, Tom Michael collection)

❏ **34-2SF, Vantastic,** 1976, Earlier and harder-to-find release without the exposed engine. Number "34" appears on hood

VEHICLES

(KP Photo, George Cuhaj collection)

❑ **35-1SF, Merryweather Marquis Fire Engine,** 1970, Red body, blue window plastic, gray plastic reels and instrument panel, white plastic ladder, blue dome lights, "London Fire Service" labels, narrow or wide tires, 3". This model was also included with TP-2 Two-Pack (900 Range). A modified casting was later used for 63-5SF Snorkel Fire Engine

EX $4   NM $7   MIP $12

(KP Photo, Tom Michael collection)

❑ **35-2SF, Fandango,** 1975, White body with red plastic interior, "35" label with stripe on hood, rotating (Rola-Matic) fan behind driver, clear window plastic, 3". Also red body with red or white plastic interiors, a later release. Versions with white body and red interior and a number "6" label are harder to find, and about $40 MIP

EX $1   NM $3   MIP $8

(KP Photo, Tom Michael collection)

❑ **36-1SF, Opel Diplomat,** 1970, Metallic green-gold color, opening hood, thin wheels, 2-3/4"

EX $6   NM $11   MIP $20

(KP Photo, Tom Michael collection)

❑ **36-2SF, Hot Rod Draguar,** 1971, Metallic pink or purple body with white or light yellow plastic interior, clear bubble window plastic, large silver engine, wide wheels, 2-7/8"

EX $5   NM $8   MIP $18

(KP Photo, Tom Michael collection)

❑ **36-3SF, Formula 5000,** 1977, Orange with blue label number "3" and blue plastic driver, or red with "Texaco" and "Champion" labels and yellow plastic driver, 2-7/8"

EX $1   NM $4   MIP $8

❑ **37-1SF, Cattle Truck,** 1970, Yellow Dodge cab and chassis, green plastic windows, no interior, gray-brown plastic stake-side bed with two white plastic cows, 2-1/2"

EX $6   NM $11   MIP $20

(KP Photo, Tom Michael collection)

❑ **37-2SF, Scoopa Coopa,** 1973, Blue or pink body with yellow plastic interior, amber plastic windshield, unpainted base, 2-7/8". Pink models have a daisy-shaped sticker on the roof section, and were shown first in the 1976 catalog

EX $1   NM $3   MIP $8

(KP Photo)

❑ **37-3SF, Skip Truck,** 1977, Red cab and chassis, clear or amber plastic windows, yellow bucket, white plastic interior, 2-3/4"

EX $2   NM $4   MIP $6

❑ **38-1SF, Honda Motorcycle with Trailer,** 1970, Yellow motorcycle trailer with thin wheels and "Honda" labels. Green or pink motorcycle, silver spokes, 3"

EX $7   NM $11   MIP $19

❑ **38-2SF, Stingeroo,** 1973, Purple chopper-style bike with cream-colored plastic horse head on seat, two wide wheels in rear, one solid wheel in front, purple plastic forks, silver plastic engine, 3-1/8"

EX $6   NM $10   MIP $22

❑ **38-3SF, Armored Jeep,** 1977, Dark olive-drab with white star emblem on hood, black base and grille, black plastic gun on back (swivels), all-black wide wheels

EX $4   NM $7   MIP $10

(KP Photo)

❑ **39-1SF, Ford Tractor,** 1970, Blue body with yellow hood and wheels or all-blue body (included with K-20 Tractor Transporter), 2-1/8". This was another regular-wheels holdover into the Superfast era

EX $7   NM $16   MIP $25

(KP Photo)

❑ **39-2SF, Clipper,** 1973, Metallic magenta body with light metallic green base, yellow plastic interior, flip-up cockpit, and "clicking" exhaust pipes that moved up and down as the car rolled along. One of the first in the Rola-Matics series, 3"

EX $1   NM $4   MIP $9

(KP Photo)

❑ **39-4SF, Rolls-Royce Mark II,** 1979, Silver body with red plastic interior or metallic red body with yellow plastic interior. Clear window plastic, opening doors, unpainted base, silver grille and headlights. Introduced in the 1979/80 catalog, but had not replaced Clipper in the 1-75 lineup

EX $2   NM $5   MIP $9

(KP Photo)

❏ **40-1SF, Hay Trailer**, 1970, Blue with yellow wheels and stakeside attachments, 3-3/8". Another holdover from the regular wheels series, this model was replaced in 1972 with the Superfast Guildsman
EX $3   **NM** $8   **MIP** $12

(KP Photo, Tom Michael collection)

❏ **40-2SF, Guildsman**, 1972, Pink with white plastic interior and light-green window plastic, star and flames label on hood; or, red body with white plastic interior with amber window plastic and "40" label on hood (first appears in 1976 catalog), 3"
EX $4   **NM** $8   **MIP** $16

(KP Photo, John Brown Sr. collection)

❏ **40-3SF, Horse Box**, 1978, Orange cab and chassis, no interior, green window plastic, cream-colored plastic box with light-brown door, two white plastic horses, 2-7/8". This model was reissued in the 1990s with green and blue color variations
EX $2   **NM** $6   **MIP** $10

❏ **41-1SF, Ford GT**, 1970, White or red with red plastic interior, blue stripe and number "6" label on hood, thin or wide wheels
EX $8   **NM** $15   **MIP** $28

(KP Photo, Tom Michael collection)

❏ **41-2SF, Siva Spyder**, 1973, Red body with cream-colored plastic interior, black segment wraps behind cabin, wide wheels, clear window plastic, 3". Blue versions with stars and stripes label motif available in 1976 catalog
EX $3   **NM** $7   **MIP** $12

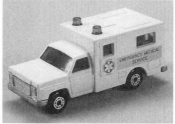

(KP Photo, John Brown Sr. collection)

❏ **41-3SF, Ambulance**, 1979, White body, blue window plastic and dome lights, opening rear doors, unpainted base, white plastic interior, "Emergency Medical Service" or "Ambulance" with red cross labels, 2-1/2"
EX $3   **NM** $6   **MIP** $12

❏ **42-1SF, Iron Fairy Crane**, 1971, Red with open cab (no window plastic) yellow plastic interior, yellow crane section with yellow plastic hook, wide wheels, 3". Continued as a regular wheels model, but only for the 1970 catalog, then converted to Superfast
EX $15   **NM** $25   **MIP** $45

(KP Photo, Tom Michael collection)

❏ **42-2SF, Tyre Fryer**, 1973, Light or dark-blue body, open cockpit, yellow plastic seat, large silver plastic engine behind driver, large Superfast wheels in rear, wide wheels in front, 3"
EX $2   **NM** $6   **MIP** $12

(KP Photo, John Brown Sr. collection)

❏ **42-3SF, Mercedes Container Truck**, 1978, Red cab and chassis, blue window plastic, no interior, unpainted or black base, plastic container with "SeaLand," "NYK" or "Matchbox" labels, 3"
EX $1   **NM** $3   **MIP** $6

(KP Photo)

❏ **42-4SF, '57 T-Bird**, 1981, Red body, white interior, clear windshield, silver metal base
EX $1   **NM** $3   **MIP** $6

(KP Photo)

❏ **42-4SF, '57 T-Bird**, 1982, Later version with black body, red interior, yellow windshield, plain base
EX $1   **NM** $3   **MIP** $7

(KP Photo)

❏ **43-1SF, Pony Trailer**, 1970, Yellow body with green base, clear window plastic, two white plastic horses, narrow wheels, brown plastic door, 2-5/8". Orange version with horse label included with TP-3 Two-Pack
EX $5   **NM** $8   **MIP** $15

(KP Photo, Tom Michael collection)

❏ **43-2SF, Dragon Wheels**, 1973, Green Volkswagen Beetle funny-car body hinged to silver plastic and metal base, "Dragon Wheels" labels on sides, 2-7/8"
EX $4   **NM** $7   **MIP** $14

VEHICLES

(KP Photo, John Brown Sr. collection)

❑ **43-3SF, Steam Loco,** 1979, Red and black body, red base, "4345" labels on sides, 2-11/16"

EX $1   **NM** $3   **MIP** $6

(KP Photo, Tom Michael collection)

❑ **44-1SF, Refrigerator Truck,** 1970, Yellow GMC cab and chassis with red refrigeration box, green window plastic, 3". The first release in 1970 was painted like the regular wheels version with red cab and chassis and green refrigeration box. These are hard to find and command approx. $145 MIP values

EX $6   **NM** $11   **MIP** $18

❑ **44-2SF, Boss Mustang,** 1973, Yellow body with opening black hood, silver plastic interior, amber plastic window, unpainted base, 3"

EX $3   **NM** $6   **MIP** $12

(KP Photo, John Brown Sr. collection)

❑ **44-3SF, Passenger Coach,** 1979, Red body, cream-colored plastic top, green window plastic, black base, "431 & 432" or "GWR" labels, 2-7/8"

(KP Photo, Tom Michael collection)

❑ **45-1SF, Ford Group Six,** 1970, Metallic green body with white plastic interior, silver plastic engine, clear window plastic and number "7" label; or red body with amber-colored windows and number "45" labels, (a later version, first appearing in 1973), 3"

EX $4   **NM** $10   **MIP** $22

(KP Photo)

❑ **45-2SF, B.M.W. 3.0 CSL,** 1975, Orange body with opening doors, yellow plastic interior, amber or blue plastic windows, silver base, "BMW" label on hood, 2-7/8"

EX $3   **NM** $7   **MIP** $15

(KP Photo)

❑ **46-1SF, Mercedes 300SE,** 1970, Gold or blue body, white plastic interior, opening trunk, (some early models with opening doors, too) thin wheels, unpainted base, grille and headlights, 2-7/8". Blue models are hard to find and may command MIP values of $100 or more. Olive-drab staff car versions as part of TP-14 Two-Pack set, about $15 in NM condition

EX $4   **NM** $8   **MIP** $16

(KP Photo, Tom Michael collection)

❑ **46-2SF, Stretcha Fetcha,** 1973, White with blue windows, white plastic interior, red base, "Ambulance" red cross labels, wide wheels, opening rear hatch, 2-3/4"

EX $2   **NM** $4   **MIP** $8

(KP Photo)

❑ **46-3SF, Ford Tractor & Harrow,** 1979, Blue Ford tractor with cab, no window plastic, gray engine block and base, black wheels with or without orange-yellow painted hubs, yellow plastic disk or harrow included (not shown). Also included with hay trailer in TP-11 Two-Pack

EX $1   **NM** $6   **MIP** $14

(KP Photo)

❑ **46-4SF, Hot Chocolate,** 1982, Metallic brown and black funny car body with white stripe. This car was an update on the "Dragon Wheels" funny car

EX $2   **NM** $5   **MIP** $8

❑ **47-1SF, DAF Tipper Container Truck,** 1970, Silver-green cab and chassis, plastic tipping box with removable top, red plastic grille and partial base, green plastic windows, no interior, 3". A Superfast update of the regular wheels model

EX $6   **NM** $10   **MIP** $22

(KP Photo, Tom Michael collection)

❑ **47-2SF, Beach Hopper,** 1973, Blue with pink "spatter" paint, brown plastic interior, tan plastic driver that "hops" as car moves along (a Rola-Matic model), wide wheels, sun label on hood, 2-5/8"

EX $2   **NM** $5   **MIP** $9

(KP Photo)

❏ **47-3SF, Pannier Locomotive,** 1979, Green body, "GWR" labels, metallic brown base. This model had not yet replaced the Beach Hopper in the 1-75 catalog lineup, but was introduced as being available later in the year
EX $2   NM $5   MIP $8

(KP Photo)

❏ **47-4SF, Jaguar SS,** 1982, Red body, silver grille, headlights and windshield, light-brown plastic interior, wide wheels
EX $1   NM $4   MIP $7

❏ **48-1SF, Dumper Truck,** 1970, Blue Dodge cab and chassis, yellow dumper bed, green plastic windows, no interior, silver plastic grille, bumper and partial base, 3". A Superfast version of the 48-3RW regular wheels model
EX $10   NM $18   MIP $32

(KP Photo, John Brown Sr. collection)

❏ **48-2SF, Pi-Eyed Piper,** 1973, Blue body, oversized plastic engine on hood, number "8" label on roof, silver exhaust pipes along sides, no interior, blue plastic windows, 2-1/2"
EX $5   NM $8   MIP $20

❏ **48-3SF, Sambron Jack Lift,** 1978, Yellow body with yellow plastic lifting forks, no window plastic, 3-1/16"
EX $2   NM $4   MIP $7

(KP Photo, Tom Michael collection)

❏ **49-1SF, Unimog,** 1970, Blue or metallic blue-green with red base, green plastic windows, wide wheels, 2-1/2". Another update of a regular wheels model, in the 1-75 lineup until 1973. An olive-drab version with a plastic container for artil-

lery shells in the bed was part of the TP-13 Two-Pack in 1979
EX $7   NM $12   MIP $25

❏ **49-2SF, Chop Suey,** 1973, Magenta seat, red plastic fork, yellow plastic bull's head on handlebars, silver plastic engine, black roller-style wheels, 2-7/8"
EX $5   NM $9   MIP $17

❏ **49-3SF, Crane Truck,** 1977, Yellow body with swiveling crane section, extendable crane arm, red plastic hook, six wide wheels, 3"
EX $3   NM $6   MIP $12

❏ **50-1SF, Kennel Truck,** 1970, Dark-green Ford truck body, with four white plastic dogs and clear plastic canopy over bed. Green plastic window, no interior, thin wheels, 2-3/4"
EX $8   NM $17   MIP $40

(KP Photo, Tom Michael collection)

❏ **50-2SF, Articulated Truck,** 1973, Short yellow cab with green plastic windows and blue trailer with yellow plastic chassis, wide wheels, 3". Some have arrow labels, some do not. Notice the difference in the wheels on the trailer.
EX $1   NM $4   MIP $7

(KP Photo, George Cuhaj collection)

❏ **51-1SF, 8-Wheel Tipper,** 1971, Yellow AEC cab and chassis, silver tipper bed, green plastic windows, no interior, "Pointer" labels, silver grille and headlights and partial base, 3"
EX $8   NM $18   MIP $40

(KP Photo)

❏ **51-2SF, Citroen SM,** 1973, Dark red metallic body, opening doors, unpainted base, white plastic interior

and tow hook, clear plastic windows, 2-7/8". In 1976, the paint scheme changed to blue with a red stripe and number "8" on roof
EX $4   NM $7   MIP $12

(KP Photo)

❏ **51-3SF, Combine Harvester,** 1979, Red with yellow reel and auger, black Superfast wheels, Superfast wheels with yellow hubs or regular wheels, 2-7/8"
EX $1   NM $3   MIP $7

(KP Photo)

❏ **52-1SF, Dodge Charger Mk III,** 1970, Metallic red or metallic lime-green body with black plastic interior, lift-up canopy, wide wheels, 3". Early red models also featured "hood scoop" labels
EX $4   NM $7   MIP $18

(KP Photo)

❏ **52-2SF, Police Launch,** 1977, White body with blue plastic base and two blue plastic officers, labels on sides read "Police," silver metal horns on cabin roof, dark-blue plastic windows, thin wheels, 3-1/16"
EX $1   NM $4   MIP $7

(KP Photo, Tom Michael collection)

VEHICLES

□ **53-1SF, Ford Zodiac Mk IV,** 1970, Metallic green body, opening hood, silver engine with spare tire, white plastic interior, clear plastic windows, 2-3/4"
EX $7   **NM** $10   **MIP** $22

(KP Photo, Tom Michael collection)

□ **53-2SF, Tanzara,** 1973, Orange body, amber plastic windows, opening rear hood shows silver plastic engine, wide wheels, silver plastic interior, unpainted base, 3". Models in 1976 had a bicentennial color scheme; white with red and blue stripes and number "53" on hood
EX $2   **NM** $4   **MIP** $7

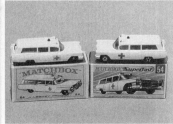

(KP Photo)

□ **53-3SF, CJ6 Jeep,** 1978, Red body, tan plastic roof, yellow plastic interior, unpainted metal base
EX $3   **NM** $7   **MIP** $12

(KP Photo by Dr. Douglas Sadecky)

□ **54-1SF, Cadillac Ambulance,** 1970, White body, blue plastic windows, white plastic interior, red cross labels, white or silver-painted grille, narrow wheels, 2-7/8". Shown here with its regular wheels predecessor
EX $12   **NM** $22   **MIP** $40

(KP Photo, Tom Michael collection)

□ **54-2SF, Ford Capri,** 1971, Red with black hood or all pink with white plastic interior, unpainted base, opening hood, wide wheels, 2-7/8". All-red models were included with boat and trailer in TP-5 Two-Pack starting in 1977
EX $2   **NM** $5   **MIP** $11

(KP Photo)

□ **54-3SF, Personnel Carrier,** 1978, Olive-green with tan plastic troops and gun, black base, wide wheels, 3"
EX $3   **NM** $7   **MIP** $12

(KP Photo, Tom Michael collection)

□ **55-1SF, Police Car,** 1970, White Mercury sedan, clear windows, white plastic interior with molded figures, police label on hood, shield labels on doors, blue or red dome light, thin wheels, 3-1/16"
EX $8   **NM** $17   **MIP** $30

□ **55-2SF, Mercury Police Car,** 1971, White station wagon body with blue or red dome lights, thin or wide wheels, unpainted base and grille, clear plastic windows, 3-1/16". Early versions had shield labels on doors and "Police" label on hood. Versions from 1973 to 1975 had only arrow-shaped red "Police" label. This car was a minor casting variation of the Mercury Commuter 73-1SF
EX $7   **NM** $15   **MIP** $27

(KP Photo, Tom Michael collection)

□ **55-3SF, Hellraiser,** 1976, White body with red plastic interior, silver plastic rear engine, clear windshield, wide wheels, stars and stripes label on hood. Or, blue body and white plastic interior, stars and stripes label, 3"
EX $2   **NM** $5   **MIP** $12

(KP Photo, Tom Michael collection)

□ **55-4SF, Ford Cortina 1600 GL,** 1979, Metallic gold with clear plastic windows, opening doors, unpainted base, red plastic interior. Introduced in 1979/80 catalog, but not yet part of the 1-75 lineup
EX $2   **NM** $6   **MIP** $12

(KP Photo, George Cuhaj collection)

□ **56-1SF, BMC 1800 Pininfarina,** 1970, Metallic gold or orange body, thin or wide wheels, opening doors, clear plastic windows, unpainted base, white plastic interior, 2-3/4". Later models modified the casting of the rear wheel wells to accommodate the wider Superfast wheels that became standard by 1973. This was a new model in the 1-75 lineup, not an adapted regular wheels casting like many others in 1970. Orange body versions about $16 MIP
EX $4   **NM** $7   **MIP** $12

(KP Photo)

□ **56-2SF, Hi-Tailer,** 1975, White body with yellow or blue plastic driver, silver plastic rear engine, red, white and blue striped label with "5, Team Matchbox and MB," 3"
EX $2   **NM** $4   **MIP** $9

□ **56-3SF, Mercedes 450 SEL,** 1979, Blue body, opening doors, light-yellow plastic interior, clear plastic windows, unpainted base. Introduced in 1979/80 catalog, had not yet replaced Hi-Tailer in the 1-75 lineup
EX $1   **NM** $3   **MIP** $6

❏ **57-1SF, Eccles Caravan,** 1970, Cream or light-yellow trailer body with four thin wheels, stripe and flower label on sides, red or orange plastic roof, green or light-yellow plastic interior, 3-1/16". Like many models, the Eccles Caravan continued on in a Two-Pack set, the TP-4 Holiday Set
EX $4　　**NM** $7　　**MIP** $16

❏ **57-2SF, Wild Life Truck,** 1973, Yellow body, red plastic windows, "Ranger" label on hood with elephant illustration, silver plastic grille, wide wheels, red plastic lion circles in truck bed as it is pushed along (Rola-Matic), no interior, clear plastic canopy over truck bed
EX $4　　**NM** $7　　**MIP** $14

❏ **58-1SF, DAF Girder Truck,** 1970, Off-white or lime-green cab and chassis, red plastic girders, red plastic grille and partial base, green window plastic, no interior, 3". Off-white versions aren't real common and have approx. $65 MIP value
EX $6　　**NM** $11　　**MIP** $20

(KP Photo, Tom Michael collection)

❏ **58-2SF, Woosh-N-Push,** 1973, Yellow body with open cockpit, red plastic interior, silver plastic exhaust, number "2" label on back of roof; or metallic red body, cream plastic interior, number "8" label with stars and stripes on roof (1976 version), 3"
EX $2　　**NM** $4　　**MIP** $8

(KP Photo)

❏ **58-3SF, Faun Dumper,** 1977, Yellow body and dumper bed, black base, red plastic windows, 2-3/4"
EX $1　　**NM** $3　　**MIP** $5

(KP Photo, Tom Michael collection)

❏ **59-1SF, Ford Galaxie Fire Chief Car,** 1970, Red body, white plastic interior and tow hook, clear plastic windows, thin wheels, shield labels on doors, blue dome light, 2-7/8". Oddly, this model dropped from the lineup for one year and returned, briefly, for 1972
EX $12　　**NM** $22　　**MIP** $45

❏ **59-1SF, Mercury Fire Chief Car,** 1971, Red sedan body with white plastic interior (early versions with two figures), unpainted base, blue dome light, thin or wide wheels, shield and fire chief labels or fire helmet labels, also included in TP-10 Two-Pack with a dual dome light arrangement
EX $4　　**NM** $8　　**MIP** $16

(KP Photo, Tom Michael collection)

❏ **59-3SF, Planet Scout,** 1976, Metallic green with lime-green or red with yellow body, silver plastic interior, yellow plastic windows, wide wheels, 2-3/4"
EX $2　　**NM** $4　　**MIP** $8

❏ **60-1SF, Truck with Site Office,** 1970, Blue Leyland truck with Ergomatic cab, yellow plastic hut with green plastic roof, thin wheels, green plastic windows, silver plastic grille and partial base, 2-1/2"
EX $6　　**NM** $10　　**MIP** $22

❏ **60-2SF, Lotus Super Seven,** 1972, Orange or yellow body with unpainted base, black plastic interior, clear plastic windshield, ghost and flame label on hood, or checker pattern with "60" along length of car, 2-7/8"
EX $5　　**NM** $9　　**MIP** $16

❏ **60-3SF, Holden Pick-Up,** 1978, Red with yellow plastic motorcycles in bed and yellow plastic interior, unpainted base, checkered label with "500" on hood, 3-1/16"
EX $4　　**NM** $7　　**MIP** $14

❏ **60-4SF, Piston Popper,** 1982, Yellow body with "Piston Popper" on hood and number "60" on sides. Unpainted metal base, red Rola-Matic pistons like the earlier version

(KP Photo, George Cuhaj collection)

❏ **61-1SF, Alvis Stalwart,** 1970, White body, with yellow plastic canopy (not shown) green plastic wheels with removable black tires, "BP Exploration" labels on sides, 2-5/8". Olive-green versions were included with TP-16 Two-Pack in 1979
EX $9　　**NM** $17　　**MIP** $30

(KP Photo)

❏ **61-2SF, Blue Shark,** 1972, Blue body with unpainted base, white plastic driver, silver plastic rear engine, black plastic exhaust pipes, clear plastic windshield, "86" or Scorpion label (harder to find, about $50 MIP), 3"
EX $3　　**NM** $8　　**MIP** $15

❏ **61-3SF, Wreck Truck,** 1979, Red truck body, black base, red plastic windows and dome lights, no interior, white towing arms with red plastic hooks
EX $3　　**NM** $6　　**MIP** $10

(KP Photo)

❏ **62-1SF, Mercury Cougar,** 1970, Lime-green body with red plastic interior and tow hook, opening doors, 3"
EX $9　　**NM** $16　　**MIP** $30

❏ **62-2SF, Rat Rod Dragster,** 1971, Light-green body, clear plastic windows, red plastic interior, exposed engine through hood, "Rat Rod" labels on sides, 3". A reworking of the Mercury Cougar casting
EX $5　　**NM** $8　　**MIP** $18

(KP Photo, Tom Michael collection)

❏ **62-2SF, Renault 17TL,** 1974, Red body with opening doors, white plastic interior, blue plastic windows, some with stripe and number "6" label, some without, 3". A version with "Fire" labels was included in the G-12 Rescue Gift Set in the 1977 catalog
EX $2　　**NM** $5　　**MIP** $12

VEHICLES

(KP Photo, Tom Michael collection)

❑ **62-3SF, Chevy Corvette,** 1982, Black body with yellow and orange stripes running from hood to trunk, white plastic interior, plain base with side-pipes
EX $2   **NM** $5   **MIP** $8

❑ **62-1SF, Dodge Crane Truck,** 1970, Yellow body with rotating crane section, yellow plastic hook, black base, green plastic windows, no interior, 3"
EX $6   **NM** $11   **MIP** $20

(KP Photo)

❑ **63-2SF, Freeway Gas Tanker,** 1974, Short red cab with black base and wide wheels, white plastic tanker trailer with red chassis, "Burmah" labels on tanker section, 3-1/8". Also available in yellow and white Shell versions, blue and white Aral versions and red and white Chevron version (part of TP-17 Two-Pack). As with regular wheels editions, the German-issue Aral version is harder to find, about $25 MIP. There is also an olive-green version with TP-14 with "High Octane" labels on the sides
EX $2   **NM** $4   **MIP** $8

(KP Photo, Tom Michael collection)

❑ **63-2SF, Freeway Gas Tanker,** 1974, A view showing the more popular edition with the "Burmah" labels and red cab

❑ **64-1SF, MG 1100,** 1970, Blue body, white plastic interior with dog and driver, tow hook, thin wheels, silver base, 2-5/8"
EX $9   **NM** $22   **MIP** $40

(KP Photo, Tom Michael collection)

❑ **64-2SF, Slingshot Dragster,** 1972, Pink or blue body with dual silver plastic engines and red exhaust pipes, label on hood with number "9" and flames, white plastic driver, 3"
EX $4   **NM** $7   **MIP** $15

(KP Photo, Tom Michael collection)

❑ **64-3SF, Fire Chief Car,** 1976, Red body with blue plastic windows, silver air scoops on hood, silver base, "Fire Chief" labels with shield on sides, 3"
EX $3   **NM** $5   **MIP** $12

(KP Photo)

❑ **64-4SF, Caterpillar Bulldozer,** 1981, Yellow die-cast body with yellow plastic blade and unpainted base and engine. Cab can be tan or black, and later models have "CAT" and "C" logos on sides near cab
EX $2   **NM** $4   **MIP** $7

(KP Photo, John Brown Sr. collection)

❑ **64-4SF, Caterpillar Bulldozer,** The black cab and "CAT" logos appeared on later versions of the bulldozer

(KP Photo)

❑ **65-1SF, Combine Harvester,** Red with yellow plastic reel and front wheels with removable black plastic tires, 3". This model was another holdover from the regular wheels lineup, first introduced in 1967, but remaining until 1973
EX $3   **NM** $7   **MIP** $12

❑ **65-2SF, Saab Sonnet,** 1974, Blue body with plastic lift-up rear hatch, light-yellow plastic interior, wide wheels, unpainted base, 2-7/8"
EX $4   **NM** $7   **MIP** $15

(KP Photo, Tom Michael collection)

❑ **65-3SF, Airport Coach,** 1978, Metallic blue body, white roof, yellow plastic windows, off-white interior, "British Airways," "American Airlines" or "Lufthansa" labels on sides are most common, 3-1/16". German versions with "Schulbus" labels are harder to find, about $45 MIP. Other variations include: Red body, white top with "TWA" or "Qantas" labels
EX $4   **NM** $6   **MIP** $9

(KP Photo, Tom Michael collection)

❑ **65-3SF, Airport Coach,** 1978, Version with red body, white top and "TWA" labels

(KP Photo, Tom Michael collection)

❏ **65-3SF, Airport Coach,** 1978, Version with red body, white top and "Qantas" labels

(KP Photo by Dr. Douglas Sadecky)

❏ **66-1SF, Greyhound Bus,** 1971, Silver with yellow plastic windows, thin wheels, blue and white Greyhound labels on sides, 3". Shown here in an interesting blister-pack/box combo that Matchbox tried out in the late 1960s and early 1970s. MIP value approx $60 for this combo, regular MIP values shown
EX $9   **NM** $16   **MIP** $30

(KP Photo, Tom Michael collection)

❏ **66-2SF, Mazda RX 500,** 1972, Early releases were orange with white base, opening rear engine hood, silver plastic interior with purple windows, 2-7/8". Later versions were red with white base and racing tempo "77" on hood with yellow windows
EX $3   **NM** $5   **MIP** $9

(KP Photo)

❏ **66-3SF, Ford Transit,** 1978, Orange truck with dropside bed and plastic cargo crates, unpainted base, blue/green plastic windows, light-yellow plastic interior, 2-3/4"
EX $4   **NM** $7   **MIP** $12

(KP Photo)

❏ **67-1SF, Volkswagen 1600 TL,** 1970, Pink or purple body, opening doors, white plastic interior, clear windows, unpainted base, thin or wide wheels (wide wheels version included in G-2 Transporter Gift Set), 2-11/16"
EX $8   **NM** $17   **MIP** $32

(KP Photo, Tom Michael collection)

❏ **67-2SF, Hot Rocker,** 1973, Ford Capri body with open hood and oversized "hopping" engine (part of Rola-Matics series). Wide wheels, unpainted base. Available in lime-green and red paint variations, 3"
EX $3   **NM** $5   **MIP** $9

(KP Photo, Tom Michael collection)

❏ **67-3SF, Datsun 260Z,** 1979, Pinkish-red or silver body with yellow plastic or red interior, opening doors, black base, 3". Silver model has red and black stripes on sides and hood with "Datsun 2+2" in black type
EX $3   **NM** $6   **MIP** $10

(KP Photo, Tom Michael collection)

❏ **68-1SF, Porsche 910,** 1970, Red body with thin or wide wheels, cream or light-yellow plastic interior, clear windows, number "68" label on hood, 3"
EX $4   **NM** $8   **MIP** $17

(KP Photo)

❏ **68-2SF, Cosmobile,** 1976, Blue or red body, silver plastic trim and interior, yellow base, wide wheels, 2-7/8"
EX $2   **NM** $5   **MIP** $8

❏ **68-3SF, Chevy Van,** 1979, Orange with blue and red stripes along sides, blue plastic windows, silver base. Introduced in the 1979/80 catalog, but hadn't yet replaced the Cosmobile in the 1-75 lineup
EX $1   **NM** $4   **MIP** $7

(KP Photo, George Cuhaj collection)

❏ **69-1SF, Rolls-Royce Coupe,** 1970, Blue body, clear windshield, brown plastic interior, thin wheels, opening trunk, tow hook, 3-1/16"
EX $6   **NM** $11   **MIP** $20

(KP Photo, Tom Michael collection)

❏ **69-2SF, Turbo Fury,** 1973, Red body, clear windshield, number "69" label on hood, white plastic driver, fans on rear of car rotate when pushed (Rola-Matics series), and front of vehicle same style as Blue Shark, 3"
EX $1   **NM** $4   **MIP** $7

(KP Photo, Tom Michael collection)

❏ **69-3SF, Security Truck,** 1979, Red armored truck with white "Wells Fargo" type on sides, blue windows and dome light, unpainted base, wide wheels, white roof, 2-7/8"
EX $5   **NM** $9   **MIP** $14

❏ **70-1SF, Grit Spreader,** 1971, Red Ford cab and chassis, yellow hopper section, no interior, thin wheels, green windows, 2-5/8"
EX $5   **NM** $10   **MIP** $18

VEHICLES

(KP Photo)

❑ **70-2SF, Dodge Dragster,** 1972, Pink funny-car Dodge Charger body, silver engine, black or unpainted base, red plastic struts to hold body, snake labels along sides, 3". A preview drawing of this model is seen in the 1971 catalog under the heading "watch out for these 4 new models"
EX $6   **NM** $11   **MIP** $20

❑ **70-3SF, Self-Propelled Gun,** 1977, Green with black plastic gun that fires and recoils while rolled along (Rola-Matics series). Tan treads, black roller wheels, 2-5/8"
EX n/a   **NM** n/a   **MIP** $8

(KP Photo, Tom Michael collection)

❑ **70-4SF, Ferrari 308 GTB,** 1981, Red, may or may not have "Ferrari" on sides and emblem on hood, black base

❑ **71-1SF, Ford Heavy Wreck Truck,** 1970, Red cab and towing crane, red plastic hook, white bed with "Esso" labels on sides, green windows and dome light, white grille, 3". Olive-green versions with all-black wheels were included in 1978's TP-16 Two-Pack
EX $11   **NM** $17   **MIP** $32

❑ **71-2SF, Jumbo Jet,** 1973, Motorcycle with blue seat and handlebars, black roller-style wheels, silver plastic engine, red elephant head on handlebars, 2-3/4"
EX $6   **NM** $9   **MIP** $18

(KP Photo, Tom Michael collection)

❑ **71-3SF, Cattle Truck,** 1978, Red or metallic gold with plastic yellow or cream stake bed, black plastic cattle, blue or green windows, 2-7/8". Also

included in the 1979 TP-19 Two-Pack in red with a matching trailer and plastic cattle
EX $2   **NM** $5   **MIP** $8

❑ **72-1SF, Standard Jeep,** 1970, Yellow body with red plastic seats, black bumpers, spare tire on back, 2-3/8". An update of the 72-2RW Standard Jeep, but in this case the spare couldn't actually be used
EX $8   **NM** $12   **MIP** $30

(KP Photo)

❑ **72-2SF, SRN Hovercraft,** 1972, White top with black plastic base and "SRN6" with British flag labels on sides, red plastic propeller, thin wheels in underside of hull, blue plastic windows, 3-1/16"
EX $1   **NM** $2   **MIP** $5

❑ **72-3SF, Bomag Road Roller,** 1979, Yellow body with red plastic interior and engine, black plastic roller, silver or yellow hubs. Introduced in 1979/80 catalog, but hadn't yet replaced the SRN Hovercraft in the 1-75 lineup
EX $1   **NM** $4   **MIP** $7

(KP Photo)

❑ **72-4SF, Maxi Taxi,** 1982, Yellow Ford Capri body with Rola-Matic engine that hops when car is moved, an update of the Hot Rocker model. Checkered taxi tampos and rates on sides, "Maxi Taxi" on roof, black base

(KP Photo)

❑ **73-1SF, Mercury Commuter,** 1970, Metallic lime-green body with thin wheels, clear windows, white plastic interior with dogs looking out the back, unpainted base, 3-1/16". By 1972, this

car had changed to red with a bull's head label on the hood and luggage rack grooves on the roof, with approx. $16 MIP value. Prices for green model shown
EX $6   **NM** $14   **MIP** $25

(KP Photo)

❑ **73-1SF, Mercury Commuter,** View showing back of car, with dogs still making an appearance out the back window

(KP Photo, Tom Michael collection)

❑ **73-1SF, Mercury Commuter,** 1973, View of red model, with roof rack grooves, red paint scheme, wide wheels and label on hood

❑ **73-2SF, Weasel,** 1973, Medium metallic-green armored vehicle with black turret that turns as the car is rolled (Rola-Matics series), wide wheels, all-black or with silver hubs, 2-7/8". Olive-green versions were issued as part of TP-13 Two-Pack
EX $2   **NM** $5   **MIP** $8

❑ **74-1SF, Daimler Bus,** 1970, Red or pink body, white plastic interior, thin or wide wheels, "Esso Extra Petrol" and Esso logo labels on sides, 3"
EX $5   **NM** $11   **MIP** $20

(KP Photo, Tom Michael collection)

❑ **74-2SF, Toe Joe,** 1974, Metallic lime-green body with green plastic towing arms and red plastic hooks, yellow windows, unpainted base, 3". Versions with yellow bodies and red towing arms with black plastic hooks were included with the Racing Mini in TP-6 Two-Pack
EX $3   **NM** $6   **MIP** $12

(KP Photo, Tom Michael collection)

❏ **74-3SF, Mercury Cougar Villager,**
1979, Lime-green or blue body, pale yellow interior, unpainted base, opening tailgate, 3-1/16"
EX $2   **NM** $5   **MIP** $11

❏ **75-1SF, Ferrari Berlinetta,** 1970, Red with white plastic interior, thin wheels, unpainted base, 2-7/8". Some early models were produced in green, echoing the regular wheels editions, but they are rare and can have $350 MIP values
EX $12   **NM** $22   **MIP** $40

❏ **75-2SF, Alfa Carabo,** 1971, Pink with yellow or white base, models in 1976 had yellow stripes running across top of car. White plastic interior, clear windows, 3"
EX $2   **NM** $5   **MIP** $11

(KP Photo)

❏ **75-3SF, Seasprite Helicopter,** 1977, White body, red base, blue windows, regular wheels landing gear, black plastic rotor, "Rescue" labels on tail section, 2-7/8"
EX $4   **NM** $6   **MIP** $9

VEHICLES

NYLINT

CARS & VANS

❏ **Baja Van**, black, opening rear doors, 11-1/2" long, late 1970s
EX $8   NM $12   MIP $17

❏ **Howdy Doody Pump Mobile**, 8-1/2" long
EX $255   NM $455   MIP $660

❏ **Pillsbury Hummer**, battery-operated, 11" long, 1990s
EX $8   NM $12   MIP $17

(Thomas G. Nefos Photo)

❏ **Vacationer Bronco and Travel Trailer,** 1960s, Blue open-top Ford Bronco with blue and white camper trailer. Bronco featured whitewall tires and fold-down windshield. 20" overall length
EX $105   NM $155   MIP $210

EMERGENCY VEHICLES

❏ **Aerial Hook-N-Ladder**, cab with roof opening and chromed grille, name on ladder, 33" long, 1980s
EX $10   NM $15   MIP $22

❏ **Aerial Hook-N-Ladder**, turbine cab, "Nylint Fire Dept.," extra ladders on sides, 29-5/8" long, early 1970s
EX $20   NM $30   MIP $50

❏ **Giant Aerial Hook-N-Ladder**, turbine cab, 30-1/4" long, late 1970s
EX $10   NM $15   MIP $22

❏ **Ladder Truck**, post war, 30" long
EX $100   NM $175   MIP $250

FARM AND CONSTRUCTION EQUIPMENT

(Toy Shop File Photo)

❏ **Michigan Shovel**, bright yellow, bucket tips automatically when raised to boom, boom raises and lowers, ten wheels, steerable front wheels, Model No. 2200
EX $150   NM $225   MIP $280

(Calvin Chausee Photo)

❏ **Payloader**, bright red, 3-3/4" rubber tires, 18" long, 1955, Model No. 1600
EX $125   NM $187   MIP $250

❏ **Road Grader**, sturdy blade can be raised, lowered, or tilted; tandem-pivoted rear wheels, 3-3/4" steel wheels, 19-1/4" long, 1955, Model No. 1400
EX $100   NM $180   MIP $225

❏ **Speed Swing Pettibone**, orange, raise or lower bucket and tip to dump, steerable wheels, 3-3/4" rubber tires, "Pettibone" decal on sides, 19" long, Model No. 2000
EX $200   NM $300   MIP $400

❏ **Street Sweep**, wind-up, 8-1/4" long, Model No. 1100
EX $175   NM $275   MIP $350

❏ **Tournahopper**, huge hopper, pull lever at rear opens wide clamshell jaws for bottom dumping, 3-3/4" rubber-tired steel wheels, 22-1/2" long,, Model No. 1500
EX $100   NM $150   MIP $200

❏ **Tournarocker**, oversize hopper, crank action hoist, 3-3/4" rubber-tired steel wheels, 18" long, 1955, Model No. 1300
EX $75   NM $125   MIP $175

❏ **Tournatractor**, yellow, big powerful adjustable blade on front, pivoted towbar on rear, 14-3/4" long, 1955, Model No. 1900
EX $100   NM $150   MIP $200

❏ **Traveloader**, orange, synchronized feeders, buckets, and rubber conveyor belt, hand crank, steel wheels w/3-3/4" rubber tires, 30" long,, Model No. 1800
EX $200   NM $310   MIP $400

TRACTOR-TRAILERS

❏ **Bandag**, display box, "Bandag, Your Tire ReSource" on side
EX $5   NM $10   MIP $20

❏ **Case**, display box
EX $17   NM $33   MIP $48

❏ **Cross Country Sears Van**, blue, 22" long, 1970s
EX $20   NM $30   MIP $50

❏ **Hooters NASCAR**, GMC 18-Wheeler series, Alan Kulwicki, 1992
EX $25   NM $50   MIP $80

(Toy Shop File Photo)

❏ **Horse Van Truck & Trailer**, Bronze and white finish, side and rear tailgates on trailer, includes two plastic horses and two plastic colts, Model No. 6300
EX $45   NM $65   MIP $110

❏ **Meineke**, GMC 18-Wheeler series, display box
EX $15   NM $25   MIP $60

❏ **Mobile Home**, turquoise, #6600, 30" long, 1960s
EX $105   NM $160   MIP $210

❏ **Moose Express**, GMC 18-Wheeler series, display box
EX $12   NM $25   MIP $40

❏ **Nutrena Feeds**, Sound Machine Semi series, display box, 20" long
EX $10   NM $20   MIP $35

❏ **Timber Toter**, log truck, 21-1/2" long, late 1970s
EX $12   NM $17   MIP $20

❏ **Wal-Mart**, "Wal-Mart/Sam's," 21" long
EX $10   NM $20   MIP $30

❏ **Winter Olympics**, 20" long, 1980
EX $10   NM $20   MIP $30

TRUCKS

❏ **Big Haul Dump Truck**, yellow, 17" long, 1970s
EX $10   NM $15   MIP $22

❏ **Dump Truck**, white cab, rear dump bed, 1960s
EX $60   NM $85   MIP $120

❏ **Ford Bronco N-8200 w/Sportsman Trailer**, open-topped Bronco; blue and white trailer w/"Sportsman" decal
EX $50   NM $72   MIP $95

❏ **Ford Bronco Safari Set**, Bronco, trailer with cage, plastic animals
EX $150   NM $250   MIP $350

❏ **Ford Econoline w/camper**, turquoise, 12'1/2" long, 1960s
EX $32   NM $62   MIP $105

❏ **Jumbo Dump**, yellow, opening cab, 19-3/4" long, 1970s
EX $12   NM $17   MIP $25

❏ **Jumbo Michigan Shovel**, 20" long, 40" high with boom extended, 1970s
EX $10   NM $14   MIP $20

❏ **Missile Launcher**, rotating radar and launcher, late 1950s, Model No. 2600
EX $80   NM $135   MIP $180

(Toy Shop File Photo)

❏ **Pepsi Truck,** 1962, Red, white and blue Pepsi truck features plastic cases of Pepsi bottles, steel dolly, whitewall tires, Model No. 5500
EX $190   NM $365   MIP $500

(Thomas G. Nefos Photo)

❑ **Ranch Truck, Chase & Sanborn Special,** 1961, Light blue and white truck with silver hubs, whitewall tires, removeable stake sides, Chase & Sanborn boxes, Model No. 4500
EX $52   **NM** $76   **MIP** $100

❑ **Roamer**, turbine cab pickup w/camper,
EX $10   **NM** $15   **MIP** $25

❑ **Tournahauler**, dark green, tractor w/enclosed cab, platform trailer, slid-out ramps, 41-1/2" long w/ramp extended, 1955, Model No. 1700
EX $125   **NM** $150   **MIP** $250

❑ **Tow Truck**, futuristic cab, 1970s
EX $18   **NM** $30   **MIP** $45

❑ **True Value Pickup**, red and white, 1970s
EX $50   **NM** $85   **MIP** $130

(Toy Shop File Photo)

❑ **U-Haul Chevy Truck,** 1975, Orange and white cab, silver box, opening rear door, Model No. 8411
EX $80   **NM** $115   **MIP** $155

❑ **U-Haul Ford Truck and Trailer**, w/twin I-Beam suspension
EX $125   **NM** $190   **MIP** $250

VEHICLES

SMITH-MILLER

EMERGENCY VEHICLES

❑ **"L" Mack Aerial Ladder**, Smith-Miller, red w/gold lettering; polished aluminum surface, SMFD decals on hood and trailer sides, six-wheeler, 1950
EX $375　　**NM** $475　　**MIP** $795

TRUCKS

❑ **"B" Mack Associated Truck Lines**, Smith-Miller, red cab, polished aluminum trailer, decals on trailer sides, six-wheel tractor, eight-wheel trailer, 1954
EX $500　　**NM** $850　　**MIP** $1200

❑ **"B" Mack Blue Diamond Dump**, Smith-Miller, all white truck w/blue decals, hydraulic piston, ten-wheeler, 1954
EX $600　　**NM** $950　　**MIP** $1300

❑ **"B" Mack Lumber Truck**, Smith-Miller, yellow cab and timber deck, three rollers, loading bar and two chains, six-wheeler, load of nine timbers, 1954
EX $450　　**NM** $650　　**MIP** $1000

❑ **"B" Mack Orange Dump Truck**, Smith-Miller, construction orange all over, no decals, hydraulic piston, ten-wheeler, 1954
EX $650　　**NM** $1150　　**MIP** $1650

❑ **"B" Mack P.I.E.**, Smith-Miller, red cab, polished trailer, six-wheel tractor, eight-wheel trailer, 1954
EX $375　　**NM** $600　　**MIP** $850

❑ **"B" Mack Searchlight**, Smith-Miller, dark red paint schemes, fully rotating and elevating searchlight, battery-operated, 1954
EX $500　　**NM** $775　　**MIP** $1100

❑ **"B" Mack Silver Streak**, Smith-Miller, yellow cab, unpainted, unpolished trailer sides, "Silver Streak" decal on both sides, six-wheel tractor, eight-wheel trailer, 1954
EX $450　　**NM** $775　　**MIP** $1050

❑ **"B" Mack Watson Bros.**, Smith-Miller, yellow cab, polished aluminum trailer, decals on trailer sides and cab doors, 10-wheel tractor, eight-wheel trailer, 1954
EX $650　　**NM** $1100　　**MIP** $1500

❑ **"L" Mack Army Materials Truck**, Smith-Miller, Army green, flatbed w/dark green canvas, ten-wheeler, load of three wood barrels, two boards, large and small crate, 1952
EX $375　　**NM** $500　　**MIP** $750

❑ **"L" Mack Army Personnel Carrier**, Smith-Miller, all Army green, wood sides, Army seal on door panels, military star on roof, ten-wheeler, 1952
EX $375　　**NM** $500　　**MIP** $750

❑ **"L" Mack Bekins Van**, Smith-Miller, white, covered w/"Bekins" decals, six-wheel tractor, four-wheel trailer, 1953
EX $1000　　**NM** $1650　　**MIP** $2000

❑ **"L" Mack Blue Diamond Dump**, Smith-Miller, white cab, white dump bed, blue fenders and chassis, hydraulically operated, ten-wheeler, 1952
EX $425　　**NM** $750　　**MIP** $1050

❑ **"L" Mack International Paper Co.**, Smith-Miller, white tractor cab, "International Paper Co." decals, six wheel tractor, four wheel trailer, 1952
EX $375　　**NM** $650　　**MIP** $900

❑ **"L" Mack Lyon Van**, Smith-Miller, silver gray cab, dark blue fenders and frame, silver gray van box w/blue "Lyon" decal, six-wheeler, 1950
EX $425　　**NM** $800　　**MIP** $1100

❑ **"L" Mack Material Truck**, Smith-Miller, light metallic green cab, dark green fenders and frame, wood flatbed, six-wheeler, load of two barrels and six timbers, 1950
EX $400　　**NM** $600　　**MIP** $875

❑ **"L" Mack Merchandise Van**, Smith-Miller, red cab, black fenders and frame, "Smith-Miller" decals on both sides of van box, double rear doors, six-wheeler, 1951
EX $425　　**NM** $695　　**MIP** $1000

❑ **"L" Mack Mobil Tandem Tanker**, Smith-Miller, all red cab, "Mobilgas" and "Mobiloil" decals on tank sides, six-wheel tractor, six-wheel trailer, 1952
EX $450　　**NM** $725　　**MIP** $1000

❑ **"L" Mack Orange Hydraulic Dump**, Smith-Miller, orange cab, orange dump bed, hydraulic, ten-wheeler, may or may not have "Blue Diamond" decals, 1952
EX $850　　**NM** $1500　　**MIP** $1950

❑ **"L" Mack Orange Materials Truck**, Smith-Miller, all orange, flatbed w/canvas, ten-wheeler, load of three barrels, two boards, large and small crate, 1952
EX $400　　**NM** $650　　**MIP** $900

❑ **"L" Mack P.I.E.**, Smith-Miller, all red tractor, polished aluminum trailer, "P.I.E." decals on sides and front, six wheel tractor, eight-wheel trailer, 1950
EX $395　　**NM** $550　　**MIP** $850

❑ **"L" Mack Sibley Van**, Smith-Miller, dark green cab, black fenders and frame, dark green van box w/"Sibley's" decal in yellow on both sides, six-wheeler, 1950
EX $850　　**NM** $1375　　**MIP** $1850

❑ **"L" Mack Tandem Timber**, Smith-Miller, red/black cab, six-wheeler, load of six wood lumber rollers, two loading bars, four chains and eighteen or twenty-four boards, 1950
EX $400　　**NM** $550　　**MIP** $725

❑ **"L" Mack Tandem Timber**, Smith-Miller, two-tone green cab, six-wheeler, load of six wood lumber rollers, two loading bars, four chains, and 18 timbers, 1953
EX $400　　**NM** $550　　**MIP** $725

❑ **"L" Mack Telephone Truck**, Smith-Miller, all dark or two-tone green truck, "Bell Telephone System" decals on truck sides, six-wheeler, 1952
EX $475　　**NM** $750　　**MIP** $975

❑ **"L" Mack West Coast Fast Freight**, Smith-Miller, silver w/red/black or silver cab and chassis, "West Coast-Fast Freight" decals on sides of box, six-wheeler, 1952
EX $475　　**NM** $775　　**MIP** $1000

❑ **Chevrolet Arden Milk Truck**, Smith-Miller, red cab, white wood body, four-wheeler, 1945
EX $275　　**NM** $465　　**MIP** $800

❑ **Chevrolet Bekins Van**, Smith-Miller, blue die-cast cab, all white trailer, fourteen-wheeler, 1945
EX $275　　**NM** $350　　**MIP** $750

❑ **Chevrolet Coca-Cola Truck**, Smith-Miller, red cab, wood body painted red, four-wheeler, 1945
EX $300　　**NM** $600　　**MIP** $850

❑ **Chevrolet Flatbed Tractor-Trailer**, Smith-Miller, unpainted wood trailer, unpainted polished cab, fourteen-wheeler, 1945
EX $250　　**NM** $300　　**MIP** $500

❑ **Chevrolet Heinz Grocery Truck**, Smith-Miller, yellow cab, load of four waxed cases, 1946
EX $225　　**NM** $325　　**MIP** $475

❑ **Chevrolet Livestock Truck**, Smith-Miller, polished, unpainted tractor cab and trailer, 1946
EX $175　　**NM** $275　　**MIP** $375

❑ **Chevrolet Lumber**, Smith-Miller, green cab, load of 60 polished boards and two chains, 1946
EX $150　　**NM** $195　　**MIP** $275

❑ **Chevrolet Lyons Van**, Smith-Miller, blue cab, silver trailer, 1946
EX $165　　**NM** $325　　**MIP** $500

❑ **Chevrolet Material Truck**, Smith-Miller, green cab, no side rails, load of three barrels, two cases and eighteen boards, 1946
EX $135　　**NM** $185　　**MIP** $225

❑ **Chevrolet Stake**, Smith-Miller, yellow tractor cab
EX $185　　**NM** $250　　**MIP** $425

❑ **Chevrolet Transcontinental Vanliner**, Smith-Miller, blue tractor cab, white trailer, "Bekins" logos and decals on trailer sides, 1946
EX $200　　**NM** $350　　**MIP** $495

❑ **Chevrolet Union Ice Truck**, Smith-Miller, blue cab, white body, load of eight waxed blocks of ice, 1946
EX $300　　**NM** $495　　**MIP** $800

❑ **Ford Bekins Van**, Smith-Miller, red sand-cast tractor, gray sheet metal trailer, fourteen-wheeler, 1944
EX $275　　**NM** $500　　**MIP** $750

❑ **Ford Coca-Cola Truck**, Smith-Miller, red sandcast cab, wood body painted red, four-wheeler, 1944
EX $400　　**NM** $650　　**MIP** $900

❑ **GMC Arden Milk Truck**, Smith-Miller, red cab, white painted wood body w/red stakes, four-wheeler, 1947
EX $200　　**NM** $425　　**MIP** $650

❑ **GMC Bank of America Truck**, Smith-Miller, dark brownish green cab and box, 'Bank of America' decal on box sides, four-wheeler, 1949
EX $115 **NM** $165 **MIP** $275

❑ **GMC Be Mac Tractor-Trailer**, Smith-Miller, red cab, plain aluminum frame, "Be Mac Transport Co." in white letters on door panels, fourteen-wheeler, 1949
EX $250 **NM** $350 **MIP** $700

❑ **GMC Bekins Vanliner**, Smith-Miller, blue cab, metal trailer painted white, fourteen-wheeler, 1947
EX $175 **NM** $275 **MIP** $425

❑ **GMC Coca-Cola Truck**, Smith-Miller, red cab, yellow wood body, four-wheeler, load of 16 Coca-Cola cases, 1947
EX $400 **NM** $675 **MIP** $895

❑ **GMC Coca-Cola Truck**, Smith-Miller, all yellow truck, red Coca-Cola decals, five spoke hubs, four-wheeler, load of six cases each w/24 plastic bottles, 1954
EX $275 **NM** $450 **MIP** $750

❑ **GMC Drive-O**, Smith-Miller, red cab, red dump body, runs forward and backward w/handturned control at end of 5-1/2 ft. cable, six-wheeler, 1949
EX $175 **NM** $300 **MIP** $450

❑ **GMC Dump Truck**, Smith-Miller, all red truck, six-wheeler, 1950
EX $150 **NM** $200 **MIP** $285

❑ **GMC Emergency Tow Truck**, Smith-Miller, white cab, red body and boom, 'Emergency Towing Service' on body side panels, four-wheeler, 1953
EX $185 **NM** $250 **MIP** $400

❑ **GMC Furniture Mart**, Smith-Miller, blue cab, off-white body, "Furniture Mart, Complete Home Furnishings" markings on body sides, four-wheeler, 1953
EX $135 **NM** $275 **MIP** $295

❑ **GMC Heinz Grocery Truck**, Smith-Miller, yellow cab, wood body, six-wheeler, 1947
EX $250 **NM** $325 **MIP** $450

❑ **GMC Highway Freighter Tractor-Trailer**, Smith-Miller, red tractor cab, hardwood bed on trailer w/full length wood fences, "Fruehauf" decal on trailer, fourteen-wheeler, 1948
EX $150 **NM** $210 **MIP** $325

❑ **GMC Kraft Foods**, Smith-Miller, yellow cab, yellow steel box, large "Kraft" decal on both sides, four-wheeler, 1948
EX $200 **NM** $300 **MIP** $450

❑ **GMC Lumber Tractor-Trailer**, Smith-Miller, metallic blue cab and trailer, three rollers and two chains, fourteen-wheeler, 1949
EX $185 **NM** $250 **MIP** $350

❑ **GMC Lumber Truck**, Smith-Miller, green cab, six-wheeler, 1947
EX $165 **NM** $215 **MIP** $300

❑ **GMC Lyons Van Tractor-Trailer**, Smith-Miller, blue tractor cab, "Lyons Van"

decals on both sides, fold down rear door, fourteen-wheeler, 1948
EX $165 **NM** $250 **MIP** $400

❑ **GMC Machinery Hauler**, Smith-Miller, construction orange, two loading ramps, ten-wheeler, 1953
EX $200 **NM** $295 **MIP** $425

❑ **GMC Machinery Hauler**, Smith-Miller, construction orange cab and lowboy trailer, "Fruehauf" decal on gooseneck, thirteen-wheeler, 1949
EX $150 **NM** $225 **MIP** $335

❑ **GMC Machinery Hauler**, Smith-Miller, construction orange cab and lowboy trailer, "Fruehauf" decal on gooseneck, thirteen-wheeler, 1949
EX $150 **NM** $225 **MIP** $335

❑ **GMC Marshall Field's & Company Tractor-Trailer**, Smith-Miller, dark green cab and trailer, double rear doors, never had Smith-Miller decals, ten-wheeler, 1949
EX $295 **NM** $395 **MIP** $500

❑ **GMC Material Truck**, Smith-Miller, green cab, wood body, six-wheeler, load of three barrels, three cases and eighteen boards, 1947
EX $115 **NM** $150 **MIP** $250

❑ **GMC Material Truck**, Smith-Miller, yellow cab, natural finish hardwood bed and sides, four-wheeler, load of four barrels and two timbers, 1949
EX $125 **NM** $175 **MIP** $265

❑ **GMC Mobilgas Tanker**, Smith-Miller, red cab and tanker trailer, large "Mobilgas", "Mobiloil" emblems on sides and rear panel of tanker, fourteen-wheeler, 1949
EX $135 **NM** $225 **MIP** $400

❑ **GMC Oil Truck**, Smith-Miller, orange cab, rear body unpainted, six-wheeler, load of three barrels, 1947
EX $115 **NM** $185 **MIP** $265

❑ **GMC P.I.E.**, Smith-Miller, red cab, polished aluminum box trailer, double rear doors, "P.I.E." decals on sides and front panels, fourteen-wheeler, 1949
EX $150 **NM** $265 **MIP** $350

❑ **GMC People's First National Bank and Trust Company**, Smith-Miller, dark brownish green cab and box, "People's First National Bank and Trust Co." decals on box sides, 1951
EX $165 **NM** $250 **MIP** $385

❑ **GMC Rack Truck**, Smith-Miller, red or yellow cab, natural finish wood deck, red stake sides, six-wheeler, 1948
EX $135 **NM** $200 **MIP** $325

❑ **GMC Redwood Logger Tractor-Trailer**, Smith-Miller, green or maroon cab, unpainted aluminum trailer w/four hardwood stakes, load of three cardboard logs, 1948
EX $365 **NM** $585 **MIP** $700

❑ **GMC Rexall Drug Truck**, Smith-Miller, orange cab and closed steel box body,

"Rexall" logo on both sides and on front panel of box, four-wheeler, 1948
EX $500 **NM** $750 **MIP** $1000

❑ **GMC Scoop Dump**, Smith-Miller, rack and pinion dump w/a scoop, five spoke wheels, six-wheeler, 1954
EX $275 **NM** $350 **MIP** $575

❑ **GMC Searchlight Truck**, Smith-Miller, four wheel truck pulling four wheel trailer, color schemes vary, "Hollywood Film Ad" on truck body side panels, 1953
EX $300 **NM** $415 **MIP** $695

❑ **GMC Silver Streak**, Smith-Miller, unpainted polished cab and trailer, wrap around sides and shield, some had tail gate, 1950
EX $140 **NM** $200 **MIP** $300

❑ **GMC Sunkist Special Tractor-Trailer**, Smith-Miller, cherry/maroon tractor cab, natural mahogany trailer bed, four-teen-wheeler, 1947
EX $165 **NM** $275 **MIP** $475

❑ **GMC Super Cargo Tractor-Trailer**, Smith-Miller, silver gray tractor cab, hardwood bed on trailer w/red wrap-around side rails, fourteen-wheeler, load of ten barrels, 1948
EX $150 **NM** $225 **MIP** $395

❑ **GMC Timber Giant**, Smith-Miller, green or maroon cab, unpainted aluminum trailer w/four hardwood stakes, load of three cardboard logs, 1948
EX $175 **NM** $285 **MIP** $495

❑ **GMC Tow Truck**, Smith-Miller, white cab, red body and boom, five spoke cast hubs, "Emergency Towing Service" on body side panels, four-wheeler, 1954
EX $95 **NM** $135 **MIP** $200

❑ **GMC Transcontinental Tractor-Trailer**, Smith-Miller, red tractor cab, hardwood bed on trailer w/full length wood fences, "Fruehauf" decal on trailer, fourteen-wheeler, 1948
EX $150 **NM** $210 **MIP** $325

❑ **GMC Triton Oil Truck**, Smith-Miller, blue cab, mahogany body unpainted, six-wheeler, load of three Triton Oil drums (banks) and side chains, 1947
EX $115 **NM** $185 **MIP** $265

❑ **GMC U.S. Treasury Truck**, Smith-Miller, gray cab and box, "U.S. Treasury" insignia and markings on box sides, four-wheeler, 1952
EX $235 **NM** $325 **MIP** $475

VEHICLES

STRUCTO

❑ **10 Pc. Truck Assortment,** 1955, 2 cabs plus one each #702, #706, #714, cattle trailer, Model No. 725
EX $225 NM $495 MIP $695

❑ **12 Pc. US Highway Set,** 1958, Orange, dump, grader, maintenance, pick-up plus 8 road signs, Model No. 550
EX $195 NM $245 MIP $425

❑ **15 Pc. Farm Set,** 1958, Various, caddy, dump, pick-up/horse trailer, 6 wheel transport, Model No. 93
EX $125 NM $175 MIP $225

❑ **17 Pc. Coast To Coast Fleet,** 1956-57, Various, 2 cars plus lumber trailer, #175, #935, #950; 2 cars, Model No. 925
EX $175 NM $295 MIP $495

❑ **17 Pc. USA Combat Convoy Set,** 1958, Green, transport, searchlight and missle trucks w/soldiers, Model No. 520
EX $155 NM $205 MIP $375

❑ **3 Pc. Truck Assortment,** 1954, One each: #75, #76, #77, Model No. 91
EX $125 NM $175 MIP $255

❑ **3 Pc. Truck Assortment,** 1955, One each: #105, #201, $300, Model No. 325
EX $175 NM $225 MIP $345

❑ **3 Pc. Truck Assortment,** 1956-57, Various, one each: #106, #201, #300, Model No. 326
EX $175 NM $225 MIP $345

❑ **3 Pc. Truck Assortment W/Garage,** 1956-57, One each: #75, #76, #77 with garage storage box, Model No. 92
EX $155 NM $195 MIP $295

❑ **3 Pc. Truck Assortment W/Garage,** 1958, Various, one each; dump, log and stake truck, Model No. 94
EX $155 NM $195 MIP $295

❑ **32 Pc. Big Job Transcontinental Set,** 1956-57, Various, 2 cabs plus one each #702, #706, #714, cattle trailer, Model No. 726
EX $225 NM $495 MIP $695

❑ **4 Pc. Truck Assortment,** 1954, One each: #21, #30, #40, #50, Model No. 90
EX $95 NM $125 MIP $175

❑ **5 Pc. Highway Builder Set,** 1958, Various, one each: #106, #201, #300 plus 2 metal road signs, Model No. 510
EX $175 NM $225 MIP $395

❑ **5 Pc. Turnpike Builder Set,** 1956-57, Various, one each: #321, #340, #404 combo, Model No. 327
EX $195 NM $275 MIP $395

❑ **6 Pc. Fire Department,** 1958, Red and white, pumper, hook & ladder, ambulance, road signs, Model No. 570
EX $175 NM $225 MIP $395

❑ **8-Wheel Transport Truck,** 1954, Orange, 7.25Lx2.5Wx2.25H, also in 1957 as 6 wheeled, red version in farm set, Model No. 40
EX $25 NM $55 MIP $75

❑ **Aerial Fire Truck,** 1948, Red, 24Lx6.75Wx6.25H, 1 raising/2 side ladders & bell on hood, Model No. 250
EX $115 NM $175 MIP $255

❑ **Aerial Fire Truck,** 1949, Red, 24Lx6.75Wx6.25H, 1 raising, 2 side ladders & bell on hood, Model No. 250
EX $115 NM $175 MIP $255

❑ **Aerial Fire Truck,** 1950, Red, 24Lx6.75Wx6.25H, 1 raising/2 side ladders & bell on hood, Model No. 250
EX $115 NM $175 MIP $255

❑ **Aerial Fire Truck,** 1951, Red, 24Lx6.75Wx6.25H, with plastic fireball motor under the hood, Model No. 250
EX $115 NM $175 MIP $255

❑ **Aerial Fire Truck,** 1952, Red, 24Lx6.75Wx6.25H, with plastic fireball motor under the hood, Model No. 250
EX $115 NM $175 MIP $255

❑ **Aerial Hook & Ladder,** 1961, Red, 30.75Lx6.25Wx6.25H, two metal ladders, crank operated lift ladder, Model No. 902
EX $65 NM $115 MIP $145

❑ **Aerial Hook & Ladder,** 1962, Red, 30.75Lx6.25Wx6.25H, two metal ladders, crank operated lift ladder, Model No. 902
EX $65 NM $115 MIP $155

❑ **Aerial Hook & Ladder,** 1963, Red and red, 30.75Lx6.25Wx6.25H, two metal ladders, crank operated lift ladder, Model No. 902
EX $65 NM $105 MIP $145

❑ **Aerial Hook & Ladder,** 1964, Red and red, 30.75Lx6.25Wx6.25H, two metal ladders, crank operated lift ladder, Model No. 902
EX $55 NM $95 MIP $135

❑ **Aerial Hook & Ladder,** 1965, Red and red, 30.75Lx6.25Wx6.25H, two metal ladders, crank operated lift ladder, Model No. 900
EX $55 NM $95 MIP $135

❑ **Aerial Hook & Ladder,** 1966, Red and white, 29.25Lx6.25Wx6.25H, two metal ladders, crank operated lift ladder, Model No. 901
EX $55 NM $85 MIP $125

❑ **Aerial Hook & Ladder,** 1967, Red and red, 29.25Lx6.25Wx6.25H, two metal ladders, crank operated lift ladder, Model No. 381
EX $55 NM $85 MIP $125

❑ **Aerial Hook & Ladder,** 1968, Red and red, 29.25Lx6.25Wx6.25H, two metal ladders, crank lift ladder "9" decal on side, Model No. 381
EX $55 NM $85 MIP $115

❑ **Aerial Hook & Ladder,** 1969, Red and red, 30.25Lx5.5Wx7H, typhoons design with crank operated extension ladder, Model No. 381
EX $35 NM $45 MIP $55

❑ **Aerial Hook & Ladder,** 1972, Red and red, 17.5Lx6Wx7.25H, typhoon design

with 2 ladders and extension ladder, Model No. 381
EX $35 NM $45 MIP $55

❑ **Air Force Anti-Aircraft Set,** 1959, Red and blue, scarce, canvas covered truck, missile launcher, searchlight, Model No. 506
EX $115 NM $195 MIP $245

❑ **Air Force Radar Truck,** 1959, Blue and red, 12Lx5.25Wx12.5H, scarce, radar dish on roof of box, 2 plastic soldiers, Model No. 102
EX $55 NM $95 MIP $125

❑ **Air Force Truck,** 1958, Blue and red, 17.25Lx7.25Wx8H, includes soldiers and canvas top, spare tires on side, Model No. 212
EX $115 NM $155 MIP $195

❑ **Air Force Truck,** 1968, Blue, 8.75Lx3.5Wx4H, scarce, Kom-pak design with clear cover on bed, 4 blue soldiers, Model No. 175
EX $45 NM $75 MIP $115

❑ **Air Terminal Service Set,** 1962, Red and white, includes #195, #303, #307, Model No. 908
EX $115 NM $135 MIP $175

❑ **Airlines Lift Truck,** 1961, Copper and white, 12.5Lx5.25Wx7H, lever lifts cargo box with scissors lift mechanism, Model No. 303
EX $55 NM $75 MIP $95

❑ **All Steel Dump Truck,** 1966, Grey and orange, 8.75Lx3.5Wx4H, Kom-pak design, Model No. 125
EX $15 NM $25 MIP $45

❑ **All-In-One Wild Animal Set,** 1960, Pink, blue, yellow, 5.5Lx4Wx2H, smaller animals fit inside larger animals, Model No. 105
EX $15 NM $25 MIP $35

❑ **American Airlines Sky Chef,** 1962, Blue and white, 12.5Lx5.25Wx7H, lever lifts cargo box with scissors lift mechanism, Model No. 303
EX $75 NM $95 MIP $125

❑ **American Rev-O-Lution,** 1972, White and black, 10Lx4.5Wx5H, sport model design with american flag on doors, Model No. 775
EX $25 NM $35 MIP $45

❑ **American Rev-O-Lution,** 1973, White and black, 10Lx4.5Wx5H, sport model design with american flag on doors, Model No. 775
EX $25 NM $35 MIP $45

❑ **Animal Set,** 1969, Yellow and green, 2 pc. set contains #837 and #870, Model No. 961
EX $35 NM $55 MIP $75

❑ **Army Engineers Dump & Sand Loader,** 1964, Army green, 21.5Lx5.5Wx8.25H, includes 4 plastic soldiers, Model No. 411
EX $55 NM $75 MIP $95

❑ **Army Engineer's Set,** 1963, Army green, includes #190, #400, #409, all in army green, Model No. 915
EX $115 NM $135 MIP $175

❑ **Army Troop Carrier,** 1966, Army green, 8.75Lx3.5Wx4H, Kom-pak design with clear plastic cover $2 soldiers, Model No. 115
EX $15   **NM** $25   **MIP** $45

❑ **Army Troop Transport,** 1959, Green, 18.75Lx6.75Wx9H, canvas top with "USA" printed. 4 plastic soldiers, Model No. 412
EX $55   **NM** $75   **MIP** $95

❑ **Auto Elevator,** 1960, Red and yellow, 9Lx3.5Wx9H, scarce, plastic parking garage, crank release car down ramp, Model No. 111
EX $75   **NM** $95   **MIP** $115

❑ **Auto Haulaway,** 1955, Blue and orange, 25Lx4.5Wx6.5H, with two cars, loading ramp and "S" grill cab, Model No. 175
EX $105   **NM** $175   **MIP** $195

❑ **Auto Haulaway,** 1956-57, Blue and orange, 25Lx4.5Wx6.5H, with two cars, loading ramp and "S" grill cab, Model No. 175
EX $105   **NM** $175   **MIP** $195

❑ **Auto Haulaway,** 1958, Yellow and red, 21.5Lx4.5Wx6.5H, smaller model with 2 cars and loading ramp, Model No. 946
EX $75   **NM** $115   **MIP** $155

❑ **Auto Transport,** 1954, White and red, 27Lx5.5Wx6.75H, with 4 die cast cars and loading ramp, Model No. 706
EX $95   **NM** $155   **MIP** $205

❑ **Auto Transport,** 1960, Met. green, 22Lx5.5Wx6.5H, 4 metal cars plus loading ramp, Model No. 402
EX $55   **NM** $75   **MIP** $95

❑ **Auto Transport,** 1961, Copper, 22Lx5.5Wx7H, includes one car and one truck plus loading ramp, Model No. 502
EX $35   **NM** $65   **MIP** $95

❑ **Auto Transport,** 1962, Yellow and green, 22Lx5.5Wx7H, two metal cars, one metal truck plus loading ramp, Model No. 502
EX $75   **NM** $115   **MIP** $155

❑ **Auto Transport,** 1963, Met. gold, 22Lx5.5Wx7H, one metal car, one metal truck plus loading ramp, Model No. 402
EX $35   **NM** $55   **MIP** $75

❑ **Auto Transport,** 1964, Red and yellow, 22Lx5.5Wx7H, includes 1 metal car and 1 metal truck & loading ramp, Model No. 402
EX $55   **NM** $75   **MIP** $95

❑ **Auto Transporter,** 1967, Red and yellow, 28.25Lx5.75Wx5.5H, large, open car carrier, ramps adjust, 3 plastic cars, Model No. 492
EX $85   **NM** $125   **MIP** $155

❑ **Auto Transporter,** 1968, Red and yellow, 28.25Lx5.75Wx5.5H, large, open car carrier, ramps adjust, 3 plastic cars, Model No. 492
EX $85   **NM** $125   **MIP** $155

❑ **Automatic Dump Truck,** 1964, Copper, 8.75Lx3.5Wx4H, spring dump mechanism, Model No. 125
EX $15   **NM** $25   **MIP** $55

❑ **Automatic Dump Truck,** 1965, Green and yellow, 8.75Lx3.5Wx4H, spring dump mechanism, Model No. 125
EX $15   **NM** $25   **MIP** $55

❑ **Automatic Under Counter Dishwasher,** 1959, Pink and grey, 7Lx7.75Wx13H, works with water, battery operated, Model No. 10
EX $15   **NM** $55   **MIP** $75

❑ **Barrel Truck,** 1951, Red and blue, 12.75Lx5.5Wx5H, wind-up motor and two oil can banks, Model No. 811
EX $135   **NM** $195   **MIP** $255

❑ **Barrel Truck,** 1952, Red and blue, 12.75Lx5.5Wx5H, wind-up motor and two oil can banks, Model No. 811
EX $135   **NM** $195   **MIP** $255

(Randy Prasse Photo)

❑ **Barrel Truck,** 1953, Red and blue, 12.75Lx5.5Wx5H, wind-up motor and oil can bank, Model No. 811
EX $135   **NM** $195   **MIP** $255

❑ **Barrel Truck,** 1954, White and red, 12.75Lx5.5Wx5H, rare, made only in 1954. Replaced #811, no wind-up, Model No. 609
EX $115   **NM** $175   **MIP** $205

❑ **Barrel Truck,** 1955, Yellow and red, 12.75Lx5.5Wx5H, non-wind-up model, no oil can bank, Model No. 913
EX $75   **NM** $115   **MIP** $175

❑ **Barrel Truck,** 1956-57, Yellow and red, 12.75Lx5.5Wx5H, non-wind-up model, no oil can bank, Model No. 913
EX $75   **NM** $115   **MIP** $175

❑ **Big 2-Dozen Assortment,** 1972, 17.75Lx14.75Wx16.5H, all 3 weird wheels designs in a store display - 24 cars total, Model No. 265
EX n/a   **NM** n/a   **MIP** $250

❑ **Big 2-Dozen Assortment,** 1973, 17.75Lx14.75Wx16.5H, all 3 weird wheels designs in a store display - 24 cars total, Model No. 265
EX n/a   **NM** n/a   **MIP** $250

❑ **Big Job Transcontinental Fleet,** 1958, Various, 2 cabs plus 1 each trailers: steel, auto, freight, cattle, Model No. 540
EX $225   **NM** $495   **MIP** $695

❑ **Blacktop Bandit,** 1972, Plum and black, 10Lx4.5Wx5H, sport model design with dragster styling, Model No. 780
EX $25   **NM** $35   **MIP** $45

❑ **Blacktop Bandit,** 1973, Yellow and black, 10Lx4.5Wx5H, sport model design with dragster styling, Model No. 780
EX $25   **NM** $35   **MIP** $45

❑ **Boat With Outboard Motor,** 1959, Red and white, 13.25Lx4Wx3.25H, boat

only, from #601 set, convertible boat and motor, Model No. 803
EX $55   **NM** $75   **MIP** $95

❑ **Boat With Play Motor,** 1959, Red and white, 9.5Lx3Wx2.5H, boat only, from #206 set, convertible boat and motor, Model No. 802
EX $35   **NM** $55   **MIP** $75

❑ **Boog-A-Loo,** 1969, Pink and white, 9.5Lx4.5Wx5H, sport model design with 5" blond doll, Model No. 766
EX $25   **NM** $35   **MIP** $45

❑ **Boog-A-Loo,** 1970, Pink and white, 9.5Lx4.5Wx5H, sport model design with 5" blond doll, Model No. 766
EX $25   **NM** $35   **MIP** $45

❑ **Boon Dock'r,** 1972, Red and green, 23Lx5.5Wx5.25H, sport model design with buggy towing boat & trailer, Model No. 758
EX $25   **NM** $35   **MIP** $45

❑ **Boon Dock'r,** 1973, Orange and green, 23Lx5.5Wx5.25H, sport model design with buggy towing boat & trailer, Model No. 758
EX $25   **NM** $35   **MIP** $45

❑ **Bottom Dump,** 1953, Orange, 21.5Lx6.5Wx6.5H, with plastic fireball motor under the hood, Model No. 320
EX $75   **NM** $105   **MIP** $155

❑ **Bottom Dump,** 1953, Orange, 21.5Lx6.5Wx6.5H, with plastic fireball motor under the hood, Model No. 320
EX $75   **NM** $105   **MIP** $155

❑ **Brain Barrel,** 1972, Brown, 2.75Lx3.5Wx3H, 2 wheeled design with brown "Wooden" barrel & bald driver, Model No. 250
EX $10   **NM** $15   **MIP** $20

❑ **Brain Barrel,** 1973, Brown, 2.75Lx3.5Wx3H, 2 wheeled design with brown "Wooden" brrel & bald driver, Model No. 250
EX $10   **NM** $15   **MIP** $20

❑ **Bridge Set,** 1970, Yellow and white, 22.25Lx3.5Wx5.5H, road tow'ds design with stake truck, 2 trailers & 4 pc. Bridge, Model No. 290
EX $15   **NM** $25   **MIP** $35

❑ **Bridge Set,** 1972, Yellow and white, 22.25Lx3.5Wx5.5H, road tow'ds design with stake truck, 2 trailers & 4 pc. Bridge, Model No. 290
EX $15   **NM** $25   **MIP** $35

❑ **Built-In Cooking Range,** 1959, Pink and grey, 7Lx7.75Wx13H, plastic burners on top, cabinets open, pots and pans, Model No. 4
EX $15   **NM** $35   **MIP** $55

❑ **Built-In Double Oven,** 1959, Pink and grey, 7.25Lx7.75Wx13H, battery operated, rotisserie in top oven unit, Model No. 14
EX $15   **NM** $35   **MIP** $55

❑ **Built-In Double Sink,** 1959, Pink and grey, 7Lx7.75Wx13H, works with water, battery operated, Model No. 8
EX $15   **NM** $55   **MIP** $75

VEHICLES

❏ **Bulldozer,** 1959, Copper and cream, 11.75Lx7Wx6.75H, cream blade, yellow wheels and motor, also on #502 set, Model No. 205
EX $35   NM $55   MIP $75

❏ **Bulldozer,** 1960, Yellow, 11.75Lx7Wx6.75H, black tires and motor, blade tips up, Model No. 210
EX $35   NM $55   MIP $75

❏ **Bulldozer,** 1961, Yellow, 11Lx6.5Wx6.5H, rubber tracks, Model No. 206
EX $35   NM $75   MIP $95

❏ **Bulldozer & Earth Mover,** 1966, Green and yellow, 25.5Lx7.5Wx7H, combination bulldozer towing bottom dump earth mover unit, Model No. 460
EX $55   NM $75   MIP $95

❏ **Bulldozer & Earth Mover,** 1967, Green and yellow, 24.5Lx6.5Wx5.75H, combination bulldozer towing bottom dump earth mover unit, Model No. 574
EX $45   NM $65   MIP $85

❏ **Bulldozer & Earth Mover,** 1968, Green and yellow, 24.5Lx6.5Wx5.75H, combination bulldozer towing bottom dump earth mover unit, Model No. 574
EX $45   NM $65   MIP $85

❏ **Bulldozer & Scraper,** 1966, Green and yellow, 25.5Lx7.5Wx7H, combination bulldozer towing scraper unit, Model No. 461
EX $55   NM $75   MIP $95

❏ **Buzzin' Bugggy,** 1972, Yellow, 2.75Lx3.5Wx3H, 2 wheeled design with open dune buggy style, Model No. 218
EX $10   NM $15   MIP $20

❏ **Buzzin' Buggy,** 1971, Yellow, 2.75Lx3.5Wx3H, 2 wheeled design with open dune buggy style, Model No. 218
EX $10   NM $15   MIP $20

❏ **Buzzin' Buggy,** 1973, Yellow, 2.75Lx3.5Wx3H, 2 wheeled design with open dune buggy style, Model No. 218
EX $10   NM $15   MIP $20

❏ **Cabin Cruiser,** 1960, Red and white, 12Lx4Wx3H, plastic hull, wooden deck and cabin, battery op motor, Model No. 212
EX $55   NM $95   MIP $125

❏ **Caddy Sedan,** 1954, Various, 6.25Lx2.5Wx2H, same scale as appear on auto transport set, Model No. 20
EX $15   NM $25   MIP $35

❏ **Camper,** 1960, Teal and red, 23.25Lx4.5Wx6.5H, red and white canvas over truck bed, boat and trailer, Model No. 211
EX $55   NM $95   MIP $125

❏ **Camper,** 1961, Met. green, 21.5Lx4.5Wx5H, rampside truck towing boat and trailer, Model No. 202
EX $45   NM $65   MIP $85

❏ **Camper,** 1962, Green and yellow, 10.5Lx4.5Wx6.5H, rampside truck with plastic camper in bed of truck, Model No. 203
EX $55   NM $75   MIP $95

❏ **Camper,** 1963, Teal, 10.5Lx4.5Wx6.5H, rampside truck with plastic camper in bed of truck, Model No. 203
EX $55   NM $75   MIP $95

❏ **Camper,** 1964, Teal and teal, 10.5Lx4.5Wx6.5H, plastic camper in truck bed, Model No. 203
EX $35   NM $65   MIP $85

❏ **Camper,** 1965, Teal and white, 10.5Lx4.5Wx6.5H, plastic camper in truck bed, Model No. 203
EX $35   NM $65   MIP $85

❏ **Camper,** 1966, Lt. blue and white, 10.5Lx4.5Wx6.5H, plastic camper in truck bed, Model No. 203
EX $25   NM $55   MIP $75

❏ **Camper Truck,** 1967, Lt. blue and dk. blue, 10.5Lx4.5Wx6.5H, dk. blue rampside truck with lt blue plastic cover, Model No. 235
EX $25   NM $55   MIP $75

❏ **Camper Truck,** 1968, Lt. blue and Dk. blue, 10.5Lx4.5Wx6.5H, Dk. blue rampside truck with Lt. blue plastic camper, Model No. 235
EX $25   NM $55   MIP $75

❏ **Camper Truck,** 1969, Gold and white, 10.5Lx5Wx6.5H, typhoons design with white plastic camper in bed, Model No. 235
EX $25   NM $35   MIP $45

❏ **Camper Truck,** 1970, Lime green and white, 9.25Lx4.25Wx5H, hurricane design with white plastic camper, Model No. 835
EX $15   NM $25   MIP $35

❏ **Camper Truck,** 1972, Orange and white, 9.25Lx4.25Wx5H, hurricanes design, Model No. 835
EX $10   NM $20   MIP $30

❏ **Camper Truck,** 1973, Orange and white, 9.25Lx4.25Wx5H, hurricanes design, Model No. 835
EX $10   NM $20   MIP $30

❏ **Camper With Boat & Trailer,** 1965, Teal and red, 20Lx4.5Wx6.5H, #203 with plastic boat on trailer, Model No. 304
EX $45   NM $85   MIP $105

❏ **Car Carrier,** 1965, Teal and teal, 22Lx6Wx7H, new, 2 plastic cars (T-Birds) and loading ramp, Model No. 413
EX $55   NM $75   MIP $95

❏ **Car Carrier,** 1966, Grey and yellow, 22.25Lx6Wx7H, 3 plastic cars (Mustangs & T-Birds) loading ramp, Model No. 418
EX $45   NM $65   MIP $85

❏ **Car Carrier,** 1967, Red and yellow, 22.25Lx6Wx7H, 3 plastic cars (Mustangs & T-Birds) loading ramp, Model No. 331
EX $45   NM $65   MIP $85

❏ **Car Carrier,** 1968, Red and yellow, 22.25Lx6Wx7H, 3 plastic cars (Mustangs & T-Birds) loading ramp, Model No. 331
EX $45   NM $65   MIP $85

❏ **Car Carrier,** 1969, Red and yellow, 22.5Lx5.5Wx5.5H, typhoons design with 3 plastic cars (Mustangs/T-Birds) ramp, Model No. 331
EX $35   NM $45   MIP $55

❏ **Car Carrier,** 1970, Red and yellow, 22.5Lx5.5Wx5.5H, typhoons design with 3 plastic cars (Mustangs/T-Birds) ramp, Model No. 331
EX $35   NM $45   MIP $55

❏ **Car Carrier,** 1972, Red and yellow, 22.5Lx5.5Wx6H, typhoon design with 3 plastic cars and ramp, Model No. 330
EX $45   NM $55   MIP $65

❏ **Cattle Trailer,** 1953, White and red, 21.5Lx5.5Wx7.5H, no loading ramp or animals, Model No. 708
EX $95   NM $155   MIP $205

❏ **Cattle Trailer,** 1954, White and red, 21.5Lx5.5Wx7.5H, no loading ramp or animals, Model No. 708
EX $95   NM $155   MIP $205

❏ **Cattle Trailer,** 1955, Green and orange, 21Lx5Wx7.75H, new pressed steel cab design, Model No. 960
EX $75   NM $135   MIP $195

❏ **Cattle Transport,** 1956-57, Green and orange, 21Lx5Wx7.75H, Model No. 960
EX $75   NM $135   MIP $195

❏ **Cattle Transport,** 1958, Green and orange, 21Lx5Wx7.5H, with plastic farm animals, Model No. 961
EX $75   NM $115   MIP $155

❏ **Cattle Transport,** 1959, Red and white, 21.25Lx5.25Wx7.5H, structo farms decals on white trailer, Model No. 304
EX $45   NM $65   MIP $85

❏ **Cattle Transport,** 1960, Red and white, 21.25Lx5.5Wx7.5H, plastic mirrors, windshield wipers and horn, Model No. 403
EX $45   NM $65   MIP $85

❏ **Cattle Transport,** 1961, Green and white, 23.5Lx6.5Wx8H, white trailer with green doors, Model No. 503
EX $35   NM $65   MIP $95

❏ **Cattle Transport,** 1962, Yellow and green, 23.5Lx5.5Wx8H, green trailer with yellow doors, Model No. 503
EX $55   NM $75   MIP $95

❏ **Cattle Transport,** 1963, Red and red, 22.25Lx6.5Wx8H, new cab - over design, plus steering wheel and seat detail, Model No. 503
EX $35   NM $65   MIP $95

❏ **Cattle Transport,** 1964, Red and red, 22.25Lx6.5Wx8H, Model No. 503
EX $45   NM $75   MIP $95

❏ **Cattle Truck,** 1965, Green and white, 16.5Lx4Wx5H, white plastic insert panels in side of trailer, Model No. 150
EX $25   NM $45   MIP $75

❏ **Cattle Truck,** 1966, Teal and white, 16.5Lx4Wx5.25H, Kom-pak design white insert panels in side of trailer, Model No. 150
EX $25   NM $45   MIP $75

❑ **Cement Mixer,** 1965, Grey and orange, 14Lx6.75Wx5.25H, axle driven gear operates barrel, Model No. 450
EX $45   **NM** $65   **MIP** $85

❑ **Cement Mixer,** 1965, Red and white, 8.75Lx3.5Wx5H, axle driven gear operates barrel, Model No. 136
EX $15   **NM** $35   **MIP** $65

❑ **Cement Mixer,** 1966, Grey and orange, 9.75Lx4Wx4.5H, Kom-pak design with dumping barrel, Model No. 136
EX $15   **NM** $25   **MIP** $45

❑ **Cement Mixer,** 1966, Grey and orange, 15.5Lx6.75Wx5.25H, axle driven gear operates barrel, POW-R-R-R sound, Model No. 450
EX $45   **NM** $65   **MIP** $85

❑ **Cement Mixer,** 1967, Grey and orange, 9.75Lx4Wx4.5H, Kom-pak design with dumping barrel, Model No. 153
EX $15   **NM** $25   **MIP** $45

❑ **Cement Mixer,** 1967, Grey and orange, 16.5Lx6.5Wx7.5H, axle driven gear operates barrel, POW-R-R-R sound, Model No. 432
EX $45   **NM** $65   **MIP** $85

❑ **Cement Mixer,** 1968, Red and yellow, 16.5Lx6.5Wx7.5H, axle driven gear operates barrel, Model No. 270
EX $35   **NM** $55   **MIP** $75

❑ **Cement Mixer,** 1968, Grey and orange, 9.75Lx4Wx4.5H, Kom-pak design with dumping barrel, Model No. 153
EX $15   **NM** $25   **MIP** $45

❑ **Cement Mixer,** 1969, Red and yellow, 14.5Lx7Wx7.5H, typhoons design with axle driven barrel, Model No. 270
EX $25   **NM** $35   **MIP** $45

❑ **Cement Mixer,** 1969, Dk. orange and white, 12.25Lx7Wx7H, thunderbolt design with steer-o-matic front wheels, Model No. 632
EX $25   **NM** $35   **MIP** $45

❑ **Cement Mixer,** 1969, Dk. orange and white, 9.5Lx4Wx4.25H, hurricanes design with axle driven barrel, Model No. 853
EX $15   **NM** $25   **MIP** $35

❑ **Cement Mixer,** 1970, Dk. orange and white, 9.5Lx4Wx4.25H, hurricanes design with axle driven barrel, Model No. 853
EX $15   **NM** $25   **MIP** $35

❑ **Cement Mixer,** 1970, Red and yellow, 14.5Lx7Wx7.5H, typhoons design with axle driven barrel, Model No. 270
EX $25   **NM** $35   **MIP** $45

❑ **Clam Bucket,** 1956-57, Yellow and green, 16.75Lx7Wx7.25H, Model No. 101
EX $75   **NM** $105   **MIP** $125

❑ **Clam Bucket and Machinery Truck,** 1956-57, Yellow and green, 32Lx7.25Wx13.75H, with plastic fireball motor under the hood, Model No. 404
EX $105   **NM** $175   **MIP** $205

❑ **Combination,** 1958, Green and orange, 32Lx7.5Wx6.75H, #106 power shovel and machinery hauling low-boy, Model No. 405
EX $75   **NM** $135   **MIP** $195

❑ **Combination Refrigerator/Freezer,** 1959, Pink and grey, 7.25Lx7.75Wx13H, swing out shelves, freezer drawer, plastic food, Model No. 12
EX $15   **NM** $35   **MIP** $55

❑ **Combination With Two Trailers,** 1951, Blue cast cab with #702 and 704 trailers, Model No. 706
EX $155   **NM** $215   **MIP** $275

❑ **Combination With Two Trailers,** 1952, Blue cast cab with #702 and 704 trailers, Model No. 706
EX $155   **NM** $215   **MIP** $275

❑ **Concrete Mixer,** 1960, Copper and yellow, 6.25Lx5.5Wx13.25H, scarce, plastic cement mixer with clear barrel w/marbels, Model No. 114
EX $75   **NM** $95   **MIP** $115

❑ **Construction And Paving Set,** 1961, Varies, 4 pc. set includes #309, #609, #700 plus barricade, Model No. 907
EX $95   **NM** $135   **MIP** $175

❑ **Contractor Set,** 1965, Varies, 3 pc. set includes #125, #136, #140, Model No. 180
EX $55   **NM** $85   **MIP** $125

❑ **Contractor Set,** 1966, Grey and orange, 3 pc. Kom-pak set includes #125, #136, #140, Model No. 180
EX $55   **NM** $85   **MIP** $125

❑ **Contractor Set,** 1967, Grey and orange, 3 pc. set includes #141, #153, #183, Model No. 192
EX $55   **NM** $85   **MIP** $125

❑ **Contractor Set,** 1972, Yellow, combination of #579 set and #184 set plus 10 street signs, Model No. 967
EX $35   **NM** $55   **MIP** $75

❑ **Contractor Set,** 1973, Yellow and orange, combination of #580 set and #184 set plus 10 street signs, Model No. 967
EX $35   **NM** $55   **MIP** $75

❑ **Corner Counter-Top Cabinet,** 1959, Pink and grey, 12Lx9.75Wx13H, 2 lazy susan shelves, drawer opens, pots and pans, Model No. 6
EX $15   **NM** $35   **MIP** $55

❑ **Counter-Top Cabinet,** 1959, Pink and grey, 7Lx7.75Wx13H, cabinet doors open, includes pots and pans, Model No. 2
EX $15   **NM** $35   **MIP** $55

❑ **Cub Pick-Up,** 1963, Lt. blue, 10.75Lx5Wx5H, white plastic convertible roof, doors open, Model No. 250
EX $35   **NM** $55   **MIP** $75

❑ **Cub Pick-Up,** 1964, Blue and white, 20.75Lx5Wx6H, white plastic convertible roof covers cab, doors open, Model No. 250
EX $25   **NM** $55   **MIP** $75

❑ **Cub Pick-Up,** 1965, Blue and white, 20.75Lx5Wx6H, white plastic convertible roof covers cab, doors open, Model No. 250
EX $25   **NM** $55   **MIP** $75

❑ **Cub Station Wagon,** 1963, Teal and white, 10.75Lx5Wx5H, same body as #250 but white plastic roof cover whole body, Model No. 325
EX $55   **NM** $75   **MIP** $95

❑ **Cub Station Wagon,** 1964, Teal and white, 10.75Lx5Wx5H, white plastic convertible roof cover body, doors open, Model No. 325
EX $25   **NM** $55   **MIP** $75

❑ **Cub Station Wagon,** 1965, Teal and white, 10.75Lx5Wx5H, white plastic convertible roof cover body, doors open, Model No. 325
EX $25   **NM** $45   **MIP** $65

❑ **Cub Station Wagon & Horse Trailer,** 1963, Teal and white, 20.5Lx5.25Wx6H, same as #190 plus 2 wheel horse trailer and 2 horses, Model No. 403
EX $75   **NM** $95   **MIP** $115

❑ **Cub Station Wagon With Horse Trailer,** 1964, Teal and white, 20.5Lx5.25Wx6H, #325 cub station wagon & trailer, 2 plastic horses, Model No. 403
EX $45   **NM** $75   **MIP** $95

❑ **Deluxe Auto Transport,** 1955, Chrome and yellow, 27Lx6Wx6.75H, with 4 die cast cars and loading ramp, Model No. 706
EX $75   **NM** $135   **MIP** $195

❑ **Deluxe Auto Transport,** 1956-57, Chrome and yellow, 27Lx6Wx6.75H, with 4 die cast cars and loading ramp, Model No. 706
EX $75   **NM** $135   **MIP** $195

❑ **Deluxe Auto Transport,** 1958, Chrome and yellow, 27Lx6Wx6.75H, with 2 cars, 1 truck and loading ramp, Model No. 707
EX $75   **NM** $135   **MIP** $195

❑ **Deluxe Auto Transport,** 1959, Green and yellow, 31.5Lx5.5Wx6.75H, two cars, one truck with loading ramp, plastic "S" grille, Model No. 401
EX $65   **NM** $95   **MIP** $125

❑ **Deluxe Camper,** 1960, Gold, 27.5Lx6Wx6.5H, #207 truck plus #212 boat on trailer, Model No. 602
EX $55   **NM** $95   **MIP** $125

❑ **Deluxe Camper,** 1962, Green and yellow, 21.5Lx4.5Wx6.5H, #203 plus boat and trailer, Model No. 304
EX $75   **NM** $105   **MIP** $135

❑ **Deluxe Camper,** 1963, Blue and white, 20Lx5Wx5H, same as #190 plus boat and trailer, Model No. 404
EX $65   **NM** $95   **MIP** $125

❑ **Deluxe Cattle Transport,** 1955, Chrome and green, 24Lx6Wx8.5H, with loading ramp and metal farm animals, Model No. 712
EX $75   **NM** $155   **MIP** $195

(Randy Prasse Photo)

❑ **Deluxe Cattle Transport,** 1956-57, Chrome and green, 24Lx6Wx8.5H, with loading ramp and metal farm animals, Model No. 712
EX $75   **NM** $155   **MIP** $195

❑ **Deluxe Cattle Transport,** 1958, Yellow and brown, 25.75Lx6.25Wx8.5H, includes plastic farm animals, Model No. 275
EX $95   **NM** $155   **MIP** $205

❑ **Deluxe Dump Truck,** 1961, Met. green, 11.75Lx5.5Wx5.75H, lever operates dump box, Model No. 309
EX $35   **NM** $65   **MIP** $85

❑ **Deluxe Dump Truck,** 1962, Yellow and red, 11.75Lx5.5Wx5.75H, lever operates dump box, Model No. 309
EX $35   **NM** $65   **MIP** $85

❑ **Deluxe Earth Mover,** 1958, Orange, 22Lx6.5Wx6.5H, with plastic fireball motor under the hood, Model No. 322
EX $65   **NM** $105   **MIP** $125

❑ **Deluxe Hydraulic Dumper,** 1959, Copper and yellow, 20.5Lx8Wx7H, hydraulic cylinder controls dump box, Model No. 500
EX $65   **NM** $95   **MIP** $125

❑ **Deluxe Kitchen-Laundry Ensemble,** 1960, Pink and grey, 7 pc. set, includes #8, #12, #4, #10, #14, #16, #2- 1959 models, Model No. 27
EX $115   **NM** $155   **MIP** $195

(Randy Prasse Photo)

❑ **Deluxe Moving Van,** 1955, Chrome and yellow, 24Lx6Wx8.5H, with loading ramp, Model No. 710
EX $105   **NM** $175   **MIP** $205

❑ **Deluxe Moving Van,** 1956-57, Chrome and blue, 24Lx6Wx8.5H, with loading ramp and mini grocery freight, Model No. 710
EX $105   **NM** $165   **MIP** $205

❑ **Deluxe Moving Van,** 1958, Chrome and blue, 31Lx6Wx8.5H, with loading ramp and mini grocery freight, Model No. 710
EX $105   **NM** $165   **MIP** $205

❑ **Deluxe Moving Van,** 1959, Yellow and red, 26.25Lx6Wx8.5H, red cab with bulb horn on roof, Model No. 504
EX $55   **NM** $95   **MIP** $125

❑ **Deluxe Power Wrecker,** 1959, Blue and white, 23Lx7Wx9.25H, battery operated winch & lights, Model No. 702
EX $75   **NM** $125   **MIP** $175

❑ **Deluxe Road Grader,** 1958, Orange, 18.75Lx7.25Wx7.5H, with plastic fireball motor under the hood, Model No. 301
EX $55   **NM** $95   **MIP** $115

❑ **Deluxe Road Grader,** 1959, Copper and yellow, 18.75Lx7.25Wx7.5H, copper with yellow wheels and engine, Model No. 301
EX $35   **NM** $55   **MIP** $75

❑ **Deluxe Rocker Dump,** 1958, Orange, 20.25Lx6.25Wx6.5H, with plastic fireball motor under the hood, Model No. 312
EX $65   **NM** $105   **MIP** $125

❑ **Deluxe Rocker Dump,** 1959, Copper and cream, 20.25Lx6.25Wx6.5H, bronze dump, cream tractor with yellow wheels & motor, Model No. 312
EX $45   **NM** $75   **MIP** $95

❑ **Deluxe Transport,** 1961, Red and white, 23.5Lx6.5Wx8H, North American Van-lines decals on trailer, Model No. 504
EX $55   **NM** $95   **MIP** $155

❑ **Deluxe Van Truck,** 1962, Blue and white, 25.5Lx6.5Wx8.5H, structo express with rocketship on decals, Model No. 600
EX $75   **NM** $115   **MIP** $135

❑ **Deluxe Van Truck,** 1963, Red and white, 25.5Lx6.5Wx8.5H, white trailer with red doors, Model No. 601
EX $55   **NM** $85   **MIP** $105

❑ **Deluxe Van Truck,** 1964, Red and white, 25.5Lx6.5Wx8.5H, white trailer with red doors, Model No. 601
EX $55   **NM** $85   **MIP** $105

❑ **Deluxe Van Truck,** 1965, Red and white, 25.5Lx6Wx8.75H, white trailer with red doors, Model No. 601
EX $55   **NM** $85   **MIP** $105

❑ **Deluxe Van Truck,** 1966, Red and silver, 24Lx6Wx8.75H, unpainted steel trailer with "Structo Freught Lines" decal, Model No. 609
EX $45   **NM** $65   **MIP** $85

❑ **Die-Cast Dump Truck,** 1961, Varies, 7.25Lx2.5Wx2.25H, packaged on bubble pack for in-store display, Model No. 79
EX $35   **NM** $55   **MIP** $75

❑ **Dig 'N Dump Set,** 1970, Orange and white, 20Lx3.25Wx4.25H, road tow'ds design with shovel & dual dump boxes in tow, Model No. 280
EX $15   **NM** $25   **MIP** $35

❑ **Dig'n Dump,** 1972, Orange and white, 20Lx3.25Wx4.25H, road tow'ds design with shovel & dual dump boxes in tow, Model No. 280
EX $15   **NM** $25   **MIP** $35

❑ **Dirt Tracker,** 1972, White and black, 10Lx4.5Wx5H, sport model design with

dual wheels #1 logo & flags on doors, Model No. 770
EX $25   **NM** $35   **MIP** $45

❑ **Dirt Tracker,** 1973, Yellow and black, 10Lx4.5Wx5H, sport model design with dual wheels #1 logo & flags on doors, Model No. 770
EX $25   **NM** $35   **MIP** $45

❑ **Dispatch Truck,** 1961, Met. green, 13Lx5.25Wx5H, similar to 1950's barrel truck, plastic mirrors, wipers & horns, Model No. 208
EX $55   **NM** $75   **MIP** $95

❑ **Display For Farm Set,** 1966, Rare, boxed set for dealer trade show & store display, Model No. 9371
EX $155   **NM** $195   **MIP** $245

❑ **Display For Highway Set,** 1966, Rare, boxed set for dealer trade show & store display, Model No. 9101
EX $155   **NM** $195   **MIP** $245

❑ **Display For State Fair Set,** 1966, Rare, boxed set for dealer trade show & store display, Model No. 9521
EX $155   **NM** $195   **MIP** $245

❑ **Double Hydraulic Load & Dump,** 1958, Black and yellow, 24.5Lx7.75Wx7H, hydraulic dump lift arm on dump box & front bucket, Model No. 252
EX $125   **NM** $165   **MIP** $205

❑ **Double Hydraulic Load & Dump,** 1959, Copper and yellow, 23.75Lx7.75Wx6.75H, yellow bucket dumps over top into dump box, Model No. 252
EX $55   **NM** $75   **MIP** $95

❑ **Duluxe Camper With Boat & Trailer,** 1959, Red and white, 29Lx6Wx6H, red truck with white roof, battery op boat motor, Model No. 601
EX $75   **NM** $125   **MIP** $175

❑ **Dump Truck,** 1948, Red, 20L x 6.75W x 6.25H, long bullet headlights, Model No. 200
EX $95   **NM** $155   **MIP** $225

❑ **Dump Truck,** 1949, Red, 20Lx6.75Wx6.25H, long bullet headlights, Model No. 200
EX $95   **NM** $155   **MIP** $225

❑ **Dump Truck,** 1950, Red, 20Lx6.75Wx6.25H, long bullet headlights, Model No. 200
EX $95   **NM** $155   **MIP** $225

❑ **Dump Truck,** 1951, Red, 20Lx6.75Wx6.25H, with plastic fireball motor under the hood, Model No. 200
EX $75   **NM** $135   **MIP** $195

❑ **Dump Truck,** 1952, Red, 20Lx6.75Wx6.25H, with plastic fireball motor under the hood, Model No. 200
EX $75   **NM** $135   **MIP** $195

❑ **Dump Truck,** 1953, Red, 20Lx6.75Wx6.25H, with plastic fireball motor under the hood, Model No. 200
EX $65   **NM** $105   **MIP** $155

❑ **Dump Truck,** 1953, Red, 20Lx6.75Wx6.25H, with plastic fireball motor under the hood, Model No. 200
EX $65 **NM** $105 **MIP** $155

❑ **Dump Truck,** 1954, Green and orange, 8.25Lx2.5Wx2.5H, spring dump action, Model No. 50
EX $35 **NM** $65 **MIP** $95

❑ **Dump Truck,** 1954, Green and orange, 10.25Lx3.25Wx3.5H, spring dump action, Model No. 75
EX $35 **NM** $55 **MIP** $75

❑ **Dump Truck,** 1955, Yellow and red, 20Lx6.75Wx6.25H, spring dump action, Model No. 201
EX $55 **NM** $95 **MIP** $125

❑ **Dump Truck,** 1956-57, Gold and blue, 10.25Lx3.25Wx3.5H, spring dump action, Model No. 75
EX $35 **NM** $55 **MIP** $75

❑ **Dump Truck,** 1956-57, Green and orange, 20Lx6.75Wx6.25H, spring dump action, Model No. 201
EX $55 **NM** $95 **MIP** $125

❑ **Dump Truck,** 1959, Blue and yellow, 9Lx3.5Wx3.5H, Model No. 75
EX $35 **NM** $55 **MIP** $75

❑ **Dump Truck,** 1959, Black and yellow, 15.75Lx6.75Wx6.75H, red roof and plastic "S" grille, no windshield, Model No. 201
EX $55 **NM** $95 **MIP** $115

❑ **Dump Truck,** 1959, Copper and cream, 10.75Lx4.5Wx4.5H, Model No. 70
EX $55 **NM** $75 **MIP** $95

❑ **Dump Truck,** 1963, Green, 11.75Lx5.5Wx5.75H, new cab - over design, plus steering wheel and seat detail, Model No. 300
EX $35 **NM** $65 **MIP** $85

❑ **Dump Truck,** 1964, Green, 11.75Lx5.5Wx5.75H, cab-over design, plus steering wheel and seat detail, Model No. 300
EX $35 **NM** $65 **MIP** $85

❑ **Dump Truck,** 1965, Met. green, 11.75Lx5.5Wx5.75H, cab - over design, plus steering wheel and seat detail, Model No. 300
EX $35 **NM** $65 **MIP** $85

❑ **Dump Truck,** 1966, Red, 11.75Lx5.5Wx5.75H, spring dump mechanism, Model No. 300
EX $25 **NM** $45 **MIP** $65

❑ **Dump Truck,** 1966, Green and yellow, 13.5Lx5.5Wx5.75H, lever action dump box, Model No. 316
EX $25 **NM** $45 **MIP** $65

❑ **Dump Truck,** 1967, Red, 13.5Lx5.5Wx5.75H, lever controls dump action, Model No. 303
EX $25 **NM** $45 **MIP** $65

❑ **Dump Truck,** 1968, Red, 13.5Lx5.5Wx5.75H, lever controls dump action, Model No. 303
EX $25 **NM** $45 **MIP** $65

❑ **Dump Truck,** 1969, Grey and orange, 13Lx5.5Wx6H, typhoons design with spring action dump box, Model No. 311
EX $25 **NM** $35 **MIP** $45

❑ **Dump Truck,** 1969, Red, 13.5Lx6Wx5.5H, typhoons design with lever action dump box, Model No. 303
EX $25 **NM** $35 **MIP** $45

❑ **Dump Truck,** 1969, Dk. orange and white, 10.5Lx4Wx4.25H, hurricanes design, Model No. 841
EX $15 **NM** $25 **MIP** $35

❑ **Dump Truck,** 1970, Red, 13.5Lx6Wx5.5H, typhoons design with lever action dump box, Model No. 303
EX $25 **NM** $35 **MIP** $45

❑ **Dump Truck,** 1970, Dk. orange and white, 10.5Lx4Wx4.25H, hurricanes design, Model No. 841
EX $15 **NM** $25 **MIP** $35

❑ **Dump Truck,** 1972, Yellow, 13.5Lx6Wx5.5H, typhoon design, Model No. 303
EX $15 **NM** $25 **MIP** $35

❑ **Dump Truck,** 1973, Gold and white, 10.75Lx4Wx4.25H, "Structo 841" stencilled on side of dump box, Model No. 841
EX $10 **NM** $20 **MIP** $30

❑ **Dump Truck and Sandloader,** 1962, Yellow and red, 21.5Lx5.5Wx8.25H, crank operated conveyer belt takes sand up to truck, Model No. 501
EX $55 **NM** $85 **MIP** $115

❑ **Dump Truck and Sandloader,** 1963, Green and chartreuse, 21.5Lx5.5Wx8.25H, crank operated conveyer belt takes sand up to truck, Model No. 409
EX $55 **NM** $85 **MIP** $115

❑ **Dump With Front-End Loader,** 1958, Yellow and blue, 23Lx6.75Wx6.25H, spring loaded dump with front loader bucket, Model No. 202
EX $105 **NM** $135 **MIP** $175

❑ **Dumper,** 1960, Copper, 11.5Lx5.5Wx6H, whitewall tires, plastic horn on roof, Model No. 209
EX $45 **NM** $75 **MIP** $95

❑ **Earth Mover,** 1955, Orange, 21.5Lx6.5Wx6.5H, with plastic fireball motor under the hood, Model No. 320
EX $75 **NM** $105 **MIP** $155

❑ **Earth Mover,** 1956-57, Orange, 22Lx6.5Wx6.5H, same tractor as #311, bottom panels open to dump, Model No. 321
EX $95 **NM** $125 **MIP** $155

❑ **Earth Mover,** 1960, Yellow, 21.5Lx6.5Wx6H, black tires and motor, Model No. 322
EX $35 **NM** $55 **MIP** $75

❑ **Emergency Fire Patrol Searchlight Unit,** 1959, White and red, 19.5Lx5.75Wx7.5H, white trailer with red battery operated searchlight unit, Model No. 303
EX $55 **NM** $95 **MIP** $125

❑ **End Loader,** 1953, Orange, 15.25Lx6.25Wx6.75H, with plastic fireball motor under the hood, Model No. 340
EX $65 **NM** $95 **MIP** $145

❑ **End Loader,** 1954, Orange, 15.25Lx6.25Wx6.75H, with plastic fireball motor under the hood, Model No. 340
EX $65 **NM** $95 **MIP** $145

❑ **End Loader,** 1955, Orange, 15.25Lx6.25Wx6.75H, with plastic fireball motor under the hood, Model No. 340
EX $65 **NM** $95 **MIP** $145

❑ **End Loader,** 1956-57, Green, 15.25Lx6Wx6.75H, with plastic fireball motor under the hood, Model No. 340
EX $65 **NM** $95 **MIP** $145

❑ **Explorer Vanguard Tracking Station,** 1959, Red, 7.75Lx4.5Wx10H, scarce, various buttons, globe revolves in TV screen, Model No. 801
EX $95 **NM** $155 **MIP** $195

❑ **Farm Pick-Up And Trailer,** 1959, Yellow and blue, 27.5Lx6.25Wx6H, 7 plastic animals included, Model No. 213
EX $95 **NM** $95 **MIP** $125

❑ **Farm Set,** 1962, Varies, includes #507, pick-up and trailer similar to nationwide set, Model No. 914
EX $115 **NM** $135 **MIP** $175

❑ **Farm Set,** 1963, Teal and white, includes #314 with trailer and #403, Model No. 914
EX $115 **NM** $135 **MIP** $175

❑ **Farm Set,** 1964, Teal and white, 5 pc. set includes #314 & trailer, #250 cub pick-up & trailer, Model No. 914
EX $95 **NM** $125 **MIP** $155

❑ **Farm Set,** 1965, Teal and white, 5 pc. set includes #310 & trailer, #250 cub pick-up & trailer, Model No. 914
EX $95 **NM** $125 **MIP** $155

❑ **Farm Set,** 1966, Green and yellow, 5 pc. set includes #194 & trailer, #310 & trailer, 4 animals, Model No. 937
EX $95 **NM** $125 **MIP** $155

❑ **Farm Set Showcase Display,** 1965, Rare, boxed set for dealer trade show & store display, Model No. 9140
EX $155 **NM** $195 **MIP** $245

❑ **Farm Stake Truck & Horse Trailer,** 1962, Red and white, 23.25Lx6.25Wx6H, same as #312 plus tow behind trailer and 4 animals, Model No. 507
EX $75 **NM** $95 **MIP** $125

❑ **Farm Trailer Truck,** 1958, Blue and red, 20.5Lx5.5Wx5.5H, with plastic animals and loading ramp, Model No. 945
EX $75 **NM** $115 **MIP** $155

❑ **Farm Truck,** 1958, Green and red, 13Lx5.75Wx4.5H, with plastic farm animals, Model No. 938
EX $65 **NM** $95 **MIP** $125

VEHICLES

❏ **Farm Truck & Trailer,** 1958, Blue and yellow, 28Lx6Wx6.25H, pick-up with pick-up box trailer & plastic farm animals, Model No. 213
EX $115　　NM $155　　MIP $195

❏ **Fire Department Set,** 1959, Red and white, 3 piece set, includes #701, #901, #303 (minus searchlight unit), Model No. 975
EX $125　　NM $195　　MIP $275

❏ **Fire Rescue Truck,** 1961, Red, 12Lx5.75Wx5.25H, plastic hose reel with braided hose, two ladders, Model No. 307
EX $35　　NM $65　　MIP $95

❏ **Fire Rescue Truck,** 1962, Red, 12Lx5.75Wx5.25H, plastic hose reel with braided hose, two ladders, Model No. 307
EX $35　　NM $65　　MIP $95

❏ **Fire Rescue Truck,** 1963, Red, 12Lx5.75Wx5.25H, plastic hose reel with braided hose, two ladders, Model No. 307
EX $35　　NM $65　　MIP $95

❏ **Fire Rescue Truck,** 1964, Red, 12Lx5.75Wx5.25H, plastic hose reel with braided hose, two ladders, Model No. 307
EX $35　　NM $65　　MIP $95

❏ **Fire Rescue Truck,** 1964, Red, 8.75Lx3.5Wx3.5H, 2 plastic ladders, Model No. 105
EX $15　　NM $35　　MIP $65

❏ **Fire Rescue Truck,** 1965, Red, 8.75Lx3.5Wx3.5H, 2 plastic ladders, Model No. 105
EX $25　　NM $45　　MIP $65

❏ **Fire Rescue Truck,** 1965, Red, 13.25Lx5.75Wx5.75H, red light on roof (non-operable), 2 metal ladders, Model No. 308
EX $45　　NM $75　　MIP $105

❏ **Fire Rescue Truck,** 1966, Red, 12.75Lx5.75Wx5.75H, red light on roof (non-operable) 3 ladders , sim. hose reel, Model No. 313
EX $45　　NM $65　　MIP $95

❏ **Fire Rescue Truck,** 1966, Red, 8.75Lx3.5Wx3.5H, Kom-pak design with 2 ladders, Model No. 105
EX $25　　NM $45　　MIP $65

❏ **Fire Rescue Truck,** 1967, Red, 12.75Lx5.75Wx5.75H, turbine cab. lever operated ladder, Model No. 453
EX $55　　NM $75　　MIP $95

❏ **Fire Rescue Truck,** 1967, Red, 8.75Lx3.5Wx3.5H, Kom-pak design with 2 ladders, Model No. 121
EX $25　　NM $45　　MIP $65

❏ **Fire Rescue Truck,** 1968, Red, 12.75Lx5.75Wx5.75H, turbine cab. lever operated ladder, Model No. 453
EX $55　　NM $75　　MIP $95

❏ **Fire Rescue Truck,** 1968, Red, 8.75Lx3.5Wx3.5H, Kom-pak design with 2 ladders, Model No. 121
EX $25　　NM $45　　MIP $65

❏ **Fire Rescue Truck,** 1969, Red and white, 12.5Lx6Wx6.5H, thunderbolt design with steer-o-matic front wheels, Model No. 653
EX $25　　NM $35　　MIP $45

❏ **Fisherman,** 1962, Blue, 21.5Lx4.5Wx5H, rampside truck towing boat and trailer, Model No. 202
EX $45　　NM $65　　MIP $85

❏ **Fisherman,** 1963, Teal, 21.5Lx4.5Wx5H, rampside truck towing boat and trailer, Model No. 204
EX $45　　NM $65　　MIP $85

❏ **Fisherman,** 1964, Teal and red, 20Lx4.5Wx6H, rampside pick-up towing plastic boat on trailer, Model No. 204
EX $35　　NM $65　　MIP $85

❏ **Fisherman,** 1965, Teal and red, 20Lx4.5Wx5H, rampside pick-up towing plastic boat on trailer, Model No. 204
EX $35　　NM $65　　MIP $85

❏ **Fisherman,** 1966, Lt. blue and red, 20Lx4.5Wx5H, rampside pick-up towing plastic boat on trailer, Model No. 204
EX $35　　NM $65　　MIP $85

❏ **Fisherman,** 1967, White and red, 20Lx5Wx4.75H, jeep towing plastic boat & trailer, no doors on jeep, Model No. 210
EX $45　　NM $65　　MIP $85

❏ **Fleetside Pick-Up,** 1959, Copper and cream, 14.5Lx6Wx6H, 6 mini grocery box play freight, Model No. 202
EX $45　　NM $75　　MIP $95

❏ **Freight Hauler,** 1956-57, Blue and yellow, 20.5Lx5.25Wx5.5H, with grocery freight, Model No. 935
EX $75　　NM $105　　MIP $155

❏ **Freight Trailer,** 1954, Red and red, 17.75Lx5Wx4.5H, new pressed steel cab design, Model No. 930
EX $115　　NM $155　　MIP $195

❏ **Freight Trailer,** 1955, Yellow and red, 17.75Lx5Wx4.5H, Model No. 930
EX $115　　NM $155　　MIP $195

❏ **Gasoline Truck,** 1951, Red and red, 13.5Lx5.5Wx5H, wind-up motor, Model No. 866
EX $135　　NM $195　　MIP $255

❏ **Gasoline Truck,** 1952, Red and red, 13.5Lx5.5Wx5H, wind-up motor, Model No. 866
EX $135　　NM $195　　MIP $255

❏ **Gasoline Truck,** 1953, Red and red, 13.5Lx5.5Wx5H, wind-up motor, Model No. 866
EX $135　　NM $195　　MIP $255

❏ **Gasoline Truck,** 1954, Red and red, 13.5Lx5.5Wx5H, wind-up motor, Model No. 866
EX $135　　NM $195　　MIP $255

❏ **Gasoline Truck,** 1955, Red and yellow, 13.5Lx5Wx4.5H, non-wind-up model, Model No. 912
EX $75　　NM $115　　MIP $175

❏ **Gasoline Truck,** 1956-57, Blue and yellow, 13.5Lx5Wx4.5H, Model No. 912
EX $75　　NM $115　　MIP $175

❏ **Gasoline Truck,** 1958, Blue and yellow, 13.5Lx5Wx4.5H, Model No. 912
EX $75　　NM $115　　MIP $175

❏ **Giant 24-Pack Assortment,** 1972, 17.75Lx16.5Wx16.5H, all 4 weird wheels designs in a store display - 24 cars total, Model No. 219
EX n/a　　NM n/a　　MIP $250

❏ **Giant 24-Pack Assortment,** 1973, 17.75Lx16.5Wx16.5H, all 4 weird wheels designs in a store display - 24 cars total, Model No. 219
EX n/a　　NM n/a　　MIP $250

❏ **Giant Bulldozer,** 1962, Orange, 11.5Lx7Wx5H, levers operate blade, rubber tracks, Model No. 405
EX $55　　NM $75　　MIP $95

❏ **Giant Bulldozer,** 1963, Chartreuse, 11.5Lx7Wx5H, scarce chartreuse color - only used in 1963 production year, Model No. 405
EX $55　　NM $75　　MIP $95

❏ **Giant Bulldozer,** 1964, Orange and black, 11.5Lx7Wx5H, blade raises and lowers with lever controls, Model No. 405
EX $45　　NM $65　　MIP $85

❏ **Giant Bulldozer,** 1965, Orange and black, 11.5Lx7Wx5H, blade raises and lowers with lever controls, Model No. 405
EX $45　　NM $65　　MIP $85

❏ **Giant Bulldozer,** 1966, Orange and black, 11.5Lx7Wx5H, blade raises and lowers with lever controls, Model No. 405
EX $45　　NM $65　　MIP $85

❏ **Giant Bulldozer,** 1967, Orange and black, 11.5Lx7Wx5H, blade raises and lowers with lever controls, Model No. 514
EX $45　　NM $65　　MIP $85

❏ **Giant Bulldozer,** 1968, Orange and black, 11.5Lx7Wx5H, blade raises and lowers with lever controls, Model No. 514
EX $45　　NM $65　　MIP $85

❏ **Giant Bulldozer,** 1969, Red and yellow, 12Lx6.75Wx7H, blade raises and lowers with lever controls, Model No. 514
EX $25　　NM $35　　MIP $55

❏ **Giant Bulldozer,** 1970, Lime green and yellow, 12Lx6.75Wx7H, blade raises and lowers with lever controls, Model No. 514
EX $25　　NM $35　　MIP $55

❏ **Giant Bulldozer,** 1972, Yellow, 12Lx6.75Wx7H, blade raises and lowers with lever controls, Model No. 514
EX $25   **NM** $35   **MIP** $55

❏ **Giant Bulldozer,** 1973, Yellow, 12Lx6.75Wx7H, "Structo 11" stencilled in black on blade, Model No. 514
EX $25   **NM** $35   **MIP** $55

❏ **Giant Bulldozer Truck & Trailer,** 1962, Orange, 29Lx7.25Wx6.25H, structo construction company on decals, Model No. 850
EX $95   **NM** $135   **MIP** $175

❏ **Giant Gantry Crane,** 1972, Yellow, 32.5Lx12.25Wx14H, hand crank pulley system with crane mechanism, Model No. 555
EX $25   **NM** $35   **MIP** $45

❏ **Giant Gantry Crane,** 1973, Yellow, 32.5Lx12.25Wx14H, hand crank pulley system with crane mechanism, Model No. 555
EX $25   **NM** $35   **MIP** $45

(Randy Prasse Photo)

❏ **Gold Plated Cadillac,** 1958, Gold, 6.75Lx2.25Wx2H, same as used on car carriers. 50th Anniversary decal on roof
EX $175   **NM** $225   **MIP** $300

❏ **Grading Service Set,** 1962, Yellow and red, 25Lx6Wx5.75H, same truck as in #501 set plus #207 bulldozer on trailer, Model No. 701
EX $75   **NM** $105   **MIP** $135

❏ **Grain Trailer,** 1953, White and orange, 20.75Lx5.5Wx5.5H, replaced freight trailer, sliding rear door, Model No. 704
EX $95   **NM** $155   **MIP** $205

❏ **Grain Trailer,** 1954, White and orange, 20.75Lx5.5Wx5.5H, sliding rear door, Model No. 704
EX $95   **NM** $155   **MIP** $205

❏ **Grain Trailer,** 1955, White and orange, 20.75Lx5.5Wx5.5H, shown in catalog with green cab but have not seen, Model No. 704
EX $95   **NM** $155   **MIP** $205

❏ **Green Beret Truck,** 1967, Green, 8.75Lx3.5Wx4H, Kom-pak design with clear plastic cover $2 soldiers, Model No. 126
EX $15   **NM** $25   **MIP** $45

❏ **Guided Missile Launcher,** 1959, Red and silver, 12.25Lx5.25Wx10.25H, plastic missile launcher on bed, metal "S" grille, Model No. 203
EX $75   **NM** $95   **MIP** $125

❏ **Hammer Tower,** 1960, Yellow and red, 6.5Lx4.75Wx9H, scarce, hammer button and marbles shoot up through tower, Model No. 110
EX $35   **NM** $55   **MIP** $75

❏ **Heavy Construction Set,** 1967, Red and yellow, 4 pc. set includes #303, #432, #514 and barricade, Model No. 941
EX $65   **NM** $95   **MIP** $135

❏ **Heavy Construction Set,** 1968, Red and yellow, 4 pc. set includes #270, #303, #514 and barricade, Model No. 941
EX $65   **NM** $95   **MIP** $135

❏ **Heavy Duty Dump Truck,** 1958, Blue and orange, 20Lx6.75Wx6.25H, spring dump action plus red light on roof, Model No. 200
EX $75   **NM** $105   **MIP** $135

❏ **Heavy Duty Steam Shovel,** 1948, Blue, 21.5L x 6.25W x 7.75H, rubber tracks, Model No. 105
EX $75   **NM** $135   **MIP** $195

❏ **Heavy Duty Steam Shovel,** 1949, Blue, 21.5Lx6.25Wx7.75H, rubber tracks, Model No. 105
EX $75   **NM** $135   **MIP** $195

❏ **Heavy Duty Steam Shovel,** 1950, Blue, 21.5Lx6.25Wx7.75H, rubber tracks, Model No. 105
EX $75   **NM** $135   **MIP** $195

❏ **Heavy Duty Steam Shovel,** 1951, Blue, 21.5Lx6.25Wx7.75H, Model No. 105
EX $65   **NM** $125   **MIP** $175

❏ **Heavy Duty Steam Shovel,** 1952, Blue, 21.5Lx6.25Wx7.75H,, Model No. 105
EX $65   **NM** $125   **MIP** $175

❏ **Heavy Duty Steam Shovel,** 1956-57, Green and orange, 26.5Lx7Wx6.75H, 2 cranks and rubber tracks, Model No. 106
EX $55   **NM** $95   **MIP** $125

❏ **Highway Builder Set,** 1959, Varies, 11 pc. set includes #201, #205, #302, road signs, plastic workers, Model No. 900
EX $95   **NM** $155   **MIP** $195

❏ **Highway Builder Set,** 1960, Copper, includes #209, #210, #305 plus road barricade, Model No. 903
EX $95   **NM** $135   **MIP** $175

❏ **Highway Builder Set,** 1961, Copper, includes #206, #305, #309 plus road barricade, Model No. 905
EX $95   **NM** $135   **MIP** $175

❏ **Highway Builder Set,** 1962, Varies, includes #207, #501 plus sand hopper and one barricade, Model No. 913
EX $115   **NM** $135   **MIP** $175

❏ **Highway Builder Set,** 1963, Varies, includes #190 and #409, Model No. 913
EX $115   **NM** $135   **MIP** $175

❏ **Highway Builder Set,** 1964, Varies, includes #207, #300, sand hopper, sand loader & barricade, Model No. 913
EX $95   **NM** $125   **MIP** $155

❏ **Highway Builder Set,** 1965, Varies, includes #207, #300, sand hopper, sand loader & barricade, Model No. 913
EX $95   **NM** $125   **MIP** $155

❏ **Highway Builder Set,** 1966, Green and yellow, 4 pc. set, includes #207, #316, sand hopper & sand loader, Model No. 910
EX $95   **NM** $125   **MIP** $155

❏ **Highway Builder Set,** 1967, Green and yellow, 4 pc. set includes #183, #303, #501 and sand hopper, Model No. 909
EX $65   **NM** $85   **MIP** $115

❏ **Highway Builder Set,** 1968, Yellow and green, 4 pc. set includes #183, #306 set, #501, Model No. 932
EX $65   **NM** $85   **MIP** $115

❏ **Highway Builder Set,** 1969, Green and yellow, 4 pc. set includes #183, #306 set, #501, Model No. 932
EX $55   **NM** $75   **MIP** $105

❏ **Highway Builder Set,** 1970, Green and yellow, 4 pc. set includes #183, #306 set, #501, Model No. 932
EX $55   **NM** $75   **MIP** $105

❏ **Highway Builder Set Showcase Display,** 1965, Rare, boxed set for dealer trade show & store display, Model No. 9130
EX $155   **NM** $195   **MIP** $245

❏ **Highway Department Set,** 1967, Red and yellow, 4 pc. set includes emergency, dump, wrecker & pickup trucks, Model No. 197
EX $75   **NM** $105   **MIP** $155

(Randy Prasse Photo)

❏ **Highway Maintenance Service,** 1958, Orange and green, 12Lx4.5Wx7H, with lift/swivel boom arm, Model No. 939
EX $65   **NM** $95   **MIP** $125

❏ **Highway Truck Assortment,** 1959, Varies, 13 pc. set, includes #70, #76 plus 6-wheel truck, log truck & signs, Model No. 400
EX $115   **NM** $155   **MIP** $195

❏ **Hi-Lift Bulldozer,** 1962, Yellow, 11.25Lx5.75Wx3.75H, rubber tracks, lever controls bucket, Model No. 207
EX $25   **NM** $55   **MIP** $75

❏ **Hi-Lift Bulldozer,** 1963, Chartreuse, 11.25Lx5.75Wx4H, scarce chartreuse color - only used in 1963 production year, Model No. 207
EX $55   **NM** $75   **MIP** $95

❏ **Hi-Lift Bulldozer,** 1964, Yellow and black, 11.25Lx5.75Wx4H, metal levers operate the bucket, Model No. 207
EX $25   **NM** $45   **MIP** $75

❏ **Hi-Lift Bulldozer,** 1965, Yellow and black, 11.25Lx5.75Wx4H, metal levers operate the bucket, Model No. 207
EX $25   **NM** $45   **MIP** $75

VEHICLES

❑ **Hi-Lift Bulldozer,** 1966, Orange and black, 11.25Lx5.75Wx4H, metal levers operate the bucket, Model No. 207
EX $25 **NM** $45 **MIP** $75

❑ **Hi-Lift Bulldozer,** 1967, Orange and black, 11.25Lx5.75Wx4H, metal levers operate the bucket, Model No. 501
EX $25 **NM** $45 **MIP** $75

❑ **Hi-Lift Bulldozer,** 1968, Orange and black, 11.25Lx5.75Wx4H, metal levers operate the bucket, Model No. 501
EX $25 **NM** $45 **MIP** $75

❑ **Hi-Lift Bulldozer,** 1969, Orange and black, 12Lx6Wx6.5H, metal levers operate the bucket, Model No. 501
EX $25 **NM** $35 **MIP** $55

❑ **Hi-Lift Bulldozer,** 1970, Lime green and yellow, 12Lx6Wx6.5H, metal levers operate the bucket, Model No. 501
EX $25 **NM** $35 **MIP** $55

❑ **Hi-Lift Bulldozer,** 1972, Yellow, 12Lx6Wx6.5H, metal levers operate the bucket, Model No. 501
EX $25 **NM** $35 **MIP** $55

❑ **Hi-Lift Bulldozer,** 1973, Yellow, 12Lx6Wx6.5H, "Structo 11" stencilled in black on blade, Model No. 501
EX $25 **NM** $35 **MIP** $55

❑ **Hi-Lift Dump Truck,** 1951, Red and blue, 12.5Lx5.5Wx5.25H, wind-up motor with scissors lift box, Model No. 844
EX $105 **NM** $155 **MIP** $215

(Randy Prasse Photo)

❑ **Hi-Lift Dump Truck,** 1952, Red and blue, 12.5Lx5.5Wx5.25H, wind-up motor with scissors lift box, Model No. 844
EX $105 **NM** $155 **MIP** $215

❑ **Hi-Lift Dump Truck,** 1953, White and red, 12.5Lx5.5Wx5.25H, wind-up motor with scissors lift box, Model No. 844
EX $105 **NM** $155 **MIP** $215

(Randy Prasse Photo)

❑ **Hi-Lift Dump Truck,** 1954, White and red, 12.5Lx5.5Wx5.25H, wind-up

motor with scissors lift box, Model No. 844
EX $105 **NM** $155 **MIP** $215

❑ **Hi-Lift Dump Truck,** 1955, Chrome and green, 12.5Lx6Wx5H, same as #844 from past years. Mag wheels, Model No. 644
EX $115 **NM** $195 **MIP** $225

❑ **Hi-Lift Dump Truck,** 1956-57, Chrome and blue, 12.5Lx6Wx5H, same as #644 from 1955 only blue dump box, Model No. 644
EX $115 **NM** $195 **MIP** $225

❑ **Hi-Lift Dump Truck,** 1958, Blue and yellow, 12Lx5.25Wx5.75H, with scissors lift mechanism, Model No. 914
EX $65 **NM** $95 **MIP** $125

❑ **Hook and Ladder Truck,** 1955, Red, 33.25Lx6.75Wx7H, with raising & two ladders, cast metal siren on roof, Model No. 260
EX $95 **NM** $155 **MIP** $205

❑ **Hook and Ladder Truck,** 1956-57, Red, 33.25Lx6.75Wx7H, with raising & two ladders, cast metal siren on roof, Model No. 260
EX $95 **NM** $155 **MIP** $205

❑ **Hook and Ladder Truck,** 1958, Red, 33.5Lx6Wx7H, with raising & two ladders, cast metal siren on roof, Model No. 261
EX $95 **NM** $155 **MIP** $205

❑ **Hurricane Construction Set,** 1970, Orange and white, 3 pc. set including #841, sand hopper & 10 pc. Road sign set, Model No. 965
EX $65 **NM** $85 **MIP** $105

❑ **Hurricane Contractor Set,** 1969, Dk orange and white, 2 pc. set contains #841 and #853 plus sand hopper and signs, Model No. 965
EX $35 **NM** $55 **MIP** $75

❑ **Hydraulic Cement Mixer,** 1968, Green and yellow, 16.5Lx6.5Wx7.5H, same as #270 but with hydraulic dump action on barrel, Model No. 271
EX $45 **NM** $65 **MIP** $85

❑ **Hydraulic Dump Trailer,** 1958, Yellow and green, 20.5Lx5.5Wx5.75H, with hydraulic lift arm on trailer dump, Model No. 941
EX $115 **NM** $155 **MIP** $195

❑ **Hydraulic Dump Truck,** 1965, Red, 14Lx5.5Wx6.25H, hydraulic cylinder controls dump box, Model No. 401
EX $35 **NM** $55 **MIP** $75

❑ **Hydraulic Dump Truck,** 1965, Grey and orange, 14Lx5.5Wx6.25H, hydraulic cylinder controls dump box, Model No. 425
EX $45 **NM** $65 **MIP** $85

(ToyShop File Photo)

❑ **Hydraulic Dump Truck,** 1966, Met. blue, 13.75Lx5.5Wx6.25H, same body style as #316 but with hydraulic dump control, Model No. 419
EX $35 **NM** $55 **MIP** $75

❑ **Hydraulic Dump Truck,** 1966, Grey and orange, 13.75Lx5.5Wx6.25H, hydraulic cylinder dumps box, POW-R-R-R sound, Model No. 425
EX $45 **NM** $65 **MIP** $85

❑ **Hydraulic Dump Truck,** 1967, Yellow and green, 12Lx6Wx6H, turbine cab. hydraulic controlled dump, Model No. 319
EX $35 **NM** $55 **MIP** $75

❑ **Hydraulic Dump Truck,** 1967, Red and yellow, 13.5Lx5.5Wx6.25H, hydraulic controlled dump box, Model No. 309
EX $35 **NM** $55 **MIP** $75

❑ **Hydraulic Dump Truck,** 1967, Grey and yellow, 12.75Lx6Wx6H, hydraulic dump box, POW-R-R-R sound, Model No. 423
EX $45 **NM** $65 **MIP** $85

❑ **Hydraulic Dump Truck,** 1968, Red and yellow, 13.5Lx5.5Wx6.25H, hydraulic controlled dump box, Model No. 309
EX $35 **NM** $55 **MIP** $75

❑ **Hydraulic Dump Truck,** 1968, Grey and orange, 12.75Lx6Wx6H, hydraulic dump box, POW-R-R-R sound, Model No. 423
EX $45 **NM** $65 **MIP** $85

❑ **Hydraulic Dump Truck,** 1968, Yellow and green, 12Lx6Wx6H, turbine cab. hydraulic controlled dump, Model No. 319
EX $35 **NM** $55 **MIP** $75

❑ **Hydraulic Dump Truck,** 1969, Yellow and green, 13Lx6Wx6H, typhoons design with hydraulic dump box, Model No. 319
EX $25 **NM** $35 **MIP** $45

❑ **Hydraulic Dump Truck,** 1969, Dk. orange and white, 12.25Lx5.5Wx6.25H, thunderbolt design with steer-o-matic front wheels, Model No. 626
EX $25 **NM** $35 **MIP** $45

❑ **Hydraulic Dump Truck,** 1970, Yellow and green, 13Lx6Wx6H, typhoons design with hydraulic dump box, Model No. 319
EX $25 **NM** $35 **MIP** $45

❑ **Hydraulic Dumper,** 1960, Met. green, 14.75Lx6.25Wx6.5H, plastic mirrors,

windshield wipers and horn, Model
No. 404
EX $35 **NM** $55 **MIP** $75

❑ **Hydraulic Dumper,** 1961, Met. green,
13.75Lx5.5Wx6.25H, hydraulic cylinder
controls dump box, Model No. 407
EX $35 **NM** $65 **MIP** $85

❑ **Hydraulic Dumper,** 1962, Green,
13.75Lx5.5Wx6.25H, hydraulic cylinder
controls dump box, Model No. 407
EX $35 **NM** $55 **MIP** $75

(Randy Prasse Photo)

❑ **Hydraulic Dumper,** 1963, Red,
13.75Lx5.5Wx6.25H, hydraulic cylinder
controls dump box, Model No. 401
EX $35 **NM** $55 **MIP** $75

❑ **Hydraulic Dumper,** 1964, Copper,
13.75Lx5.5Wx6.25H, hydraulic cylinder
controls dump box, Model No. 401
EX $35 **NM** $55 **MIP** $75

❑ **Hydraulic Hook & Ladder,** 1959, Red
and red, 31Lx6.25Wx7.25H, open cab,
plastic "S" grille, metal ladders, Model
No. 901
EX $75 **NM** $115 **MIP** $135

❑ **Hydraulic Hook & Ladder,** 1960, Red
and red, 31Lx6.25Wx7.25H, open cab,
two metal ladders, hydraulic lift ladder,
Model No. 901
EX $75 **NM** $125 **MIP** $175

❑ **Hydraulic Hook & Ladder Truck,** 1958,
Red, 33.25Lx6.75Wx7H, with raising &
two ladders, red flashing light on roof,
Model No. 266
EX $95 **NM** $175 **MIP** $215

❑ **Hydraulic Lift Dump Truck,** 1955,
Green and orange, 21Lx8Wx7H,
hydraulic dump lift arm on dump box,
Model No. 250
EX $95 **NM** $155 **MIP** $205

❑ **Hydraulic Lift Dump Truck,** 1956-57,
Yellow and green, 21Lx8Wx7H, hydrau-
lic dump lift arm on dump box, Model
No. 250
EX $95 **NM** $155 **MIP** $205

❑ **Hydraulic Lift Dump Truck,** 1958,
Orange and green, 21Lx8Wx7H,
hydraulic dump lift arm on dump box,
Model No. 250
EX $125 **NM** $165 **MIP** $205

❑ **Hydraulic Sanitation Truck,** 1959, Blue
and white, 18Lx6Wx7.5H, hydraulic cylinder controls dump box, Model
No. 454
EX $65 **NM** $95 **MIP** $125

❑ **Hydraulic Sanitation Truck,** 1961,
White, 18Lx6Wx8H, all white design,
Model No. 606
EX $55 **NM** $95 **MIP** $115

❑ **Hydraulic Sanitation Truck,** 1962, Grey
and white, 18Lx6Wx8H, with manual lift
arm that dumps into body, Model
No. 606
EX $75 **NM** $105 **MIP** $125

(ToyShop File Photo)

❑ **Hydraulic Sanitation Truck,** 1963, Blue
and white, 18Lx6Wx8H, with manual lift
arm that dumps into body, Model
No. 602
EX $75 **NM** $105 **MIP** $125

❑ **Hydraulic Sanitation Truck,** 1964, Grey
and white, 18Lx6Wx8H, with manual lift
arm that dumps into body, Model
No. 602
EX $75 **NM** $105 **MIP** $125

❑ **Hydraulic Sanitation Truck,** 1965, Grey
and white, 18Lx6Wx8H, with manual lift
arm that dumps into body, Model
No. 604
EX $55 **NM** $75 **MIP** $95

❑ **Hydraulic Sanitation Truck,** 1966, Grey
and white, 18Lx6Wx8H, manual lift
bucket dumps into body, POW-R-R-R
sound, Model No. 604
EX $55 **NM** $75 **MIP** $95

❑ **Hydraulic Sanitation Truck,** 1967, Grey
and white, 16.5Lx5.75Wx7.75H, manual lift bucket dumps into body, POW-
R-R-R sound, Model No. 474
EX $55 **NM** $75 **MIP** $95

❑ **Hydraulic Sanitation Truck,** 1968, Grey
and white, 16.5Lx5.75Wx7.75H, manual lift bucket dumps into body, Model
No. 268
EX $45 **NM** $65 **MIP** $85

❑ **Hydraulic Trailer Dump,** 1963, Chartreuse, 20.75Lx6.25Wx5.75H, scarce
chartreuse color - only used in 1963 production year, Model No. 603
EX $65 **NM** $95 **MIP** $125

❑ **Hydraulic Trailer Dump Truck,** 1964,
Grey and orange,
20.75Lx6.25Wx5.75H, also available as
"Scotch-O-Lass" private label-add $50,
Model No. 603
EX $55 **NM** $75 **MIP** $95

❑ **Hydraulic Trailer Dump Truck,** 1965,
Grey and orange,
20.75Lx5.75Wx5.75H, also available as
"Scotch-O-Lass" private label - add $50,
Model No. 603
EX $55 **NM** $75 **MIP** $95

❑ **Hydraulic Trailer Dump Truck,** 1966,
Grey and orange, 21.5Lx5.75Wx5.75H,

turbine cab, hydraulic controlled dump,
Model No. 610
EX $45 **NM** $65 **MIP** $85

❑ **Ice Cream Truck,** 1966, White and teal,
12Lx6Wx6.5H, scarce, bell rings as
truck moves, built-in coolers & detail,
Model No. 712
EX $75 **NM** $115 **MIP** $155

❑ **Jack And Jill Pump,** 1960, Copper and
yellow, 8Lx4.25Wx11.25H, scarce,
plastic marble toy, structo pre-school
series, Model No. 112
EX $75 **NM** $95 **MIP** $115

❑ **Kennel Truck,** 1966, Teal and white,
8.75Lx3.5Wx4H, Kom-pak design with
clear cover and 6 dogs, Model No. 130
EX $15 **NM** $35 **MIP** $55

❑ **Kennel Truck,** 1967, Yellow,
8.75Lx3.5Wx4H, Kom-pak design with
clear cover and 6 dogs, Model No. 137
EX $15 **NM** $35 **MIP** $55

❑ **Kennel Truck,** 1968, Yellow,
8.75Lx3.5Wx4H, Kom-pak design with
clear cover and 6 dogs, Model No. 137
EX $15 **NM** $35 **MIP** $55

❑ **Kenya Karryall,** 1967, Green and yellow, 9.25Lx4.25Wx4.25H, scarce, Kom-
pak design, 4 cages with 4 hand-painted
wild animals, Model No. 176
EX $45 **NM** $75 **MIP** $115

❑ **Kenya Karryall,** 1968, Green and yellow, 9.25Lx4.25Wx4.25H, scarce, Kom-
pak design, 4 cages with 4 hand-painted
wild animals, Model No. 176
EX $45 **NM** $75 **MIP** $105

❑ **Kitchen Ensemble,** 1960, Pink and
grey, individual appliances still available, see 1959 for values
EX $15 **NM** $35 **MIP** $55

❑ **Kitchen Ensemble,** 1960, Pink and
grey, 3 pc. set, includes #8, #12, #4-
1959 models, Model No. 23
EX $75 **NM** $125 **MIP** $155

❑ **Kitchen-Laundry Ensemble,** 1959,
Pink and grey, 9 piece 1/4 scale set,
Model No. 50
EX $95 **NM** $155 **MIP** $195

❑ **Kitchen-Laundry Ensemble,** 1960,
Pink and grey, 5 pc. set, includes #8,
#12, #4, #10, #16- 1959 models, Model
No. 25
EX $95 **NM** $155 **MIP** $175

❑ **Kom-pak Animal Set,** 1968, Teal and
white, 4 pc. set includes #137, #163, 6
dogs, 4 ponies & fence coral, Model
No. 196
EX $55 **NM** $85 **MIP** $115

❑ **Kompak Assortment,** 1965, Varies, 3
pc. set includes #100, #105, #110,
Model No. 170
EX $55 **NM** $85 **MIP** $125

❑ **Kom-pak Contractor Set,** 1968, Green
and yellow, 4 pc. set includes #153,
#183, #184, Model No. 193
EX $55 **NM** $85 **MIP** $115

VEHICLES

❑ **Kom-pak Pony Van,** 1968, Teal and teal, 16.5Lx3.5Wx4.5H, clear roof on trailer with coral & 3 ponies, Model No. 163
EX $35   NM $55   MIP $75

❑ **Kom-pak Sandy,** 1968, Green and yellow, 8.75Lx3.5Wx3.5H, Kom-pak design with plastic sand hopper, Model No. 184
EX $25   NM $45   MIP $65

❑ **Kom-pak Sandy,** 1969, Green and yellow, 9Lx5.25Wx8.5H, Kom-pak design, Model No. 184
EX $25   NM $35   MIP $45

❑ **Kom-pak Sandy,** 1970, Green and yellow, 9Lx5.25Wx8.5H, Kom-pak design, Model No. 184
EX $25   NM $35   MIP $45

❑ **Kom-pak Sandy,** 1972, Yellow, 9Lx5.25Wx8.5H, sand hopper and dump truck, Model No. 184
EX $15   NM $25   MIP $35

❑ **Kom-pak Sandy,** 1973, Yellow and orange, 8.5Lx5.5Wx9.5H, sand hopper and dump truck, Model No. 184
EX $15   NM $25   MIP $35

❑ **Lad-A-Bout,** 1970, Lime green and white, 9.5Lx4.5Wx5.25H, sport model design with 5" black male doll, Model No. 769
EX $35   NM $45   MIP $55

❑ **Litter Picker,** 1972, Chrome and orange, 2.75Lx3.5Wx3H, 2 wheeled design with trash can style, Model No. 252
EX $10   NM $15   MIP $20

❑ **Litter Picker,** 1973, White and orange, 2.75Lx3.5Wx3H, 2 wheeled design with trash can style with propeller, Model No. 252
EX $10   NM $15   MIP $20

❑ **Little Miss Structo Washer/Dryer,** 1962, Teal, 7.25Lx8Wx10H, washes & spins, battery operated, Model No. 16
EX $15   NM $25   MIP $55

❑ **Little Miss Structo Washer/Dryer,** 1963, Teal, 7.25Lx8Wx10H, washes & spins, battery operated, Model No. 16
EX $15   NM $25   MIP $55

❑ **Livestock Set,** 1965, Teal and white, 22.25Lx6.5Wx8H, white insert panels in side of trailer, 5 pc. fence & 4 animals, Model No. 505
EX $45   NM $65   MIP $85

❑ **Livestock Truck,** 1960, Red and white, 14.75Lx6Wx7.25H, white plastic stake panels and 2 plastic animals, Model No. 306
EX $35   NM $55   MIP $75

❑ **Livestock Truck,** 1961, Red and white, 14.5Lx6.25Wx7.5H, stake truck with 2 plastic animals, Model No. 306
EX $35   NM $65   MIP $85

❑ **Livestock Truck,** 1962, Red and white, 14.75Lx6.25Wx5.5H, white metal stake panels, Model No. 312
EX $55   NM $75   MIP $95

❑ **Livestock Truck,** 1964, Blue and white, 14.75Lx6.25Wx5.5H, white metal stake panels, 2 plastic cows, Model No. 314
EX $55   NM $75   MIP $95

❑ **Livestock Truck,** 1965, Blue and white, 14.75Lx6.25Wx5.5H, white stakes, 5 pc. plastic fence, 4 animals, Model No. 310
EX $55   NM $75   MIP $95

❑ **Livestock Truck,** 1967, Red and yellow, 14.75Lx3.25Wx5.5H, yellow metal panels, Model No. 260
EX $25   NM $45   MIP $65

❑ **Livestock Truck,** 1968, Red and yellow, 14.75Lx3.25Wx5.5H, yellow metal panels, Model No. 260
EX $25   NM $45   MIP $65

❑ **Livestock Truck,** 1969, Teal and white, 9.5Lx4.25Wx4H, hurricanes design with white stake panels and 5 animals, Model No. 870
EX $15   NM $25   MIP $35

❑ **Livestock Truck,** 1970, Green and white, 9.5Lx4.25Wx4H, hurricanes design with white stake panels and 5 animals, Model No. 870
EX $15   NM $25   MIP $35

❑ **Livestock Truck,** 1972, Blue and white, 9.5Lx4.25Wx4H, hurricanes design with white panels and 5 animals, Model No. 870
EX $10   NM $20   MIP $30

❑ **Livestock Truck,** 1973, Blue and white, 9.5Lx4.25Wx4H, hurricanes design with white panels and 5 animals, Model No. 870
EX $10   NM $20   MIP $30

❑ **Livestock Truck Set,** 1966, Teal and white, 14.75Lx6.25Wx5.5H, white stakes, 5 pc. plastic fence, 2 plastic cows, Model No. 310
EX $35   NM $65   MIP $85

❑ **Livestock Van,** 1966, Teal and white, 22.25Lx6.5Wx8H, white insert panels in side of trailer, 5 pc. fence & 4 animals, Model No. 505
EX $45   NM $65   MIP $85

❑ **Livestock Van,** 1967, Teal and white, 21.25Lx7.75Wx5.75H, turbine cab, white panels on side of trailer, Model No. 344
EX $55   NM $75   MIP $95

❑ **Livestock Van,** 1968, Teal and white, 21.25Lx7.75Wx5.75H, turbine cab, white panels on side of trailer, Model No. 344
EX $55   NM $75   MIP $95

❑ **Livestock Van,** 1969, Teal and white, 21.75Lx5.5Wx7.5H, typhoons design with fifth wheel detail, Model No. 344
EX $25   NM $35   MIP $45

❑ **Livetstock Truck,** 1963, Blue and white, 14.75Lx6.25Wx5.5H, white metal stake panels, Model No. 314
EX $55   NM $75   MIP $95

❑ **Log Trailer,** 1954, Orange and orange, 17.75Lx5Wx4.5H, with five wooden logs, Model No. 940
EX $115   NM $155   MIP $195

❑ **Log Trailer,** 1955, Green and orange, 17.75Lx5Wx4.5H, with five wooden logs, Model No. 940
EX $115   NM $155   MIP $195

❑ **Loonie Looper,** 1972, Yellow and orange, 2.75Lx3.5Wx3H, 2 wheeled design with airplane styling including propeller, Model No. 251
EX $10   NM $15   MIP $20

❑ **Loonie Looper,** 1973, Yellow and orange, 2.75Lx3.5Wx3H, 2 wheeled design with airplane styling including propeller, Model No. 251
EX $10   NM $15   MIP $20

❑ **Lumber Truck,** 1954, Red and blue, 10.5Lx3.5Wx3.25H, with five wooden logs, Model No. 77
EX $35   NM $55   MIP $75

❑ **Lumber Truck,** 1956-57, Red and blue, 10.5Lx3.5Wx3.25H, with five wooden logs, Model No. 77
EX $35   NM $55   MIP $75

❑ **Machinery Hauler,** 1960, Copper, 19.5Lx7.5Wx6.5H, includes #210 dozer, Model No. 509
EX $55   NM $75   MIP $95

❑ **Machinery Hauling Truck,** 1954, Red and yellow, 12.5Lx5.5Wx4H, flatbed with winch and "S" grill cab, Model No. 151
EX $75   NM $125   MIP $155

❑ **Machinery Hauling Truck,** 1956-57, Red and yellow, 12.5Lx5.5Wx4H, flatbed with winch and "S" grill cab, Model No. 151
EX $75   NM $125   MIP $155

(Randy Prasse Photo)

❑ **Machinery Truck,** 1951, orange and blue, 12.75Lx5.5Wx5H, with loading ramp and chain winch, Model No. 607
EX $95   NM $155   MIP $205

❑ **Machinery Truck,** 1952, Orange and blue, 12.75Lx5.5Wx5H, with loading ramp and chain winch, Model No. 607
EX $95   NM $155   MIP $205

❑ **Machinery Truck,** 1954, White and blue, 12.75Lx5.5Wx5H, rare, made only in 1954. Hubcaps, loading ramp, Model No. 607
EX $95   NM $155   MIP $205

❑ **Machinery Truck & Steam Shovel,** 1948, Orange and blue, 21.5Lx6.75Wx6.25H, comes 2/#105 steam shovel & loading ramp, Model No. 402
EX $115   NM $175   MIP $245

❏ **Machinery Truck & Steam Shovel,** 1949, Orange and blue, 21.5Lx6.75Wx6.25H, comes w/#105 steam shovel & loading ramp, Model No. 402
  EX $115   **NM** $175   **MIP** $245

❏ **Machinery Truck & Steam Shovel,** 1950, Orange and blue, 21.5Lx6.75Wx6.25H, comes w/#105 steam shovel & loading ramp, Model No. 402
  EX $115   **NM** $175   **MIP** $245

❏ **Machinery Truck & Steam Shovel,** 1951, Orange and blue, 21.5Lx6.75Wx6.25H, with plastic fire-ball motor under the hood, Model No. 402
  EX $100   **NM** $155   **MIP** $195

❏ **Machinery Truck & Steam Shovel,** 1952, Orange and blue, 21.5Lx6.75Wx6.25H, with plastic fire-ball motor under the hood, Model No. 402
  EX $100   **NM** $155   **MIP** $195

❏ **Machinery Truck & Steam Shovel,** 1953, Orange and blue, 21.5Lx6.75Wx6.25H, comes w/#105 steam shovel & loading ramp, Model No. 402
  EX $95   **NM** $155   **MIP** $195

❏ **Machinery Truck & Steam Shovel,** 1954, Orange and blue, 26.5Lx6.75Wx14.25H, comes w/#105 steam shovel & loading ramp, Model No. 402
  EX $95   **NM** $155   **MIP** $195

❏ **Mechanical Hydraulic Dump,** 1959, Red and white, 12.25Lx5.25Wx5.5H, scarce, hydraulic cylinder controls dump box, Model No. 204
  EX $75   **NM** $115   **MIP** $135

❏ **Merry-Go-Round,** 1969, Yellow and red, 9.5Lx4.25Wx5.75H, hurricanes design with carousel, Model No. 874
  EX $25   **NM** $35   **MIP** $45

❏ **Minuteman Tow Truck,** 1969, Dk. orange, 9.25Lx4Wx4H, hurricanes design with crank operated tow rope, Model No. 812
  EX $15   **NM** $25   **MIP** $35

❏ **Minuteman Tow Truck,** 1970, Dk. orange, 9.25Lx4Wx4H, hurricanes design with crank operated tow rope, Model No. 812
  EX $15   **NM** $25   **MIP** $35

❏ **Mobile Anti-Missile Unit,** 1959, Blue and yellow, 27Lx7.5Wx11.25H, scarce, battery op spotlight & missile launcher on trailer, Model No. 620
  EX $85   **NM** $115   **MIP** $175

❏ **Mobile Communications Center,** 1958, Red and blue, 20Lx6.25Wx6.25H, includes antenna tower & morse code buttons, Model No. 270
  EX $115   **NM** $155   **MIP** $195

❏ **Mobile Crane,** 1959, Green and yellow, 19.25Lx6.25Wx7.25H, battery operated boom and cab, Model No. 902
  EX $85   **NM** $135   **MIP** $195

❏ **Mobile Crane,** 1960, Copper and yellow, 19.25Lx6.25Wx7.25H, half-track with single-driver cab, Model No. 800
  EX $75   **NM** $115   **MIP** $135

❏ **Mobile Crane,** 1961, Yellow, 15.5Lx6.5Wx7.25H, double cranks control crane arm and clam bucket, Model No. 700
  EX $55   **NM** $95   **MIP** $115

❏ **Mobile Crane,** 1962, Yellow, 15.5Lx6.5Wx7.25H, double cranks control crane arm and clam bucket, Model No. 800
  EX $55   **NM** $95   **MIP** $115

❏ **Mobile Crane,** 1963, Chartreuse, 15.5Lx6.5Wx7.25H, scarce chartreuse color - only used in 1963 production year, Model No. 801
  EX $75   **NM** $105   **MIP** $155

❏ **Mobile Crane,** 1964, Orange, 15.5Lx6.5Wx7.25H, cranks control the boom and clam bucket, swivels, Model No. 801
  EX $75   **NM** $95   **MIP** $125

❏ **Mobile Crane,** 1965, Orange, 16.5Lx5.5Wx7H, cranks control the boom and clam bucket, swivels, Model No. 801
  EX $75   **NM** $95   **MIP** $125

❏ **Mobile Crane,** 1966, Orange, 16.5Lx5.5Wx7H, cranks control the boom and clam bucket, swivels, Model No. 801
  EX $75   **NM** $95   **MIP** $125

❏ **Mobile Merry-Go-Round Truck,** 1967, Yellow and red, 9.25Lx4.25Wx5.75H, scarce, Kom-pak design, circus carousel spins when truck moves, Model No. 174
  EX $55   **NM** $85   **MIP** $125

❏ **Mobile Merry-Go-Round Truck,** 1968, Yellow and red, 9.25Lx4.25Wx5.75H, scarce, Kom-pak design, circus carousel spins when truck moves, Model No. 174
  EX $55   **NM** $85   **MIP** $125

❏ **Mobile Outer Space Launcher,** 1959, Red and blue, 19.5Lx6Wx12.75H, scarce, 2 plastic missiles launch. Launcher swivels, Model No. 503
  EX $95   **NM** $135   **MIP** $195

❏ **Mobile Power Shovel Unit,** 1958, Green and yellow, 32.5Lx6.75Wx8H, half-track truck with steam shovel on back, Model No. 272
  EX $95   **NM** $155   **MIP** $205

❏ **Mobile Steam Shovel Unit,** 1956-57, Green and yellow, 32.5Lx6.75Wx8H, half-track truck with steam shovel on back, Model No. 272
  EX $95   **NM** $155   **MIP** $205

❏ **Monster Machine,** 1971, Green, 2.75Lx3.5Wx3H, 2 wheeled design with exposed "Chrome" engine, Model No. 215
  EX $10   **NM** $15   **MIP** $20

❏ **Monster Machine,** 1972, Green, 2.75Lx3.5Wx3H, 2 wheeled design with exposed "Chrome" engine, Model No. 215
  EX $10   **NM** $15   **MIP** $20

❏ **Monster Machine,** 1973, Green, 2.75Lx3.5Wx3H, 2 wheeled design with exposed "Chrome" engine, Model No. 215
  EX $10   **NM** $15   **MIP** $20

(Randy Prasse Photo)

❏ **Motor Express Truck,** 1951, Grey and orange, 12.75Lx5.5Wx5H, cast cab "Freeport Motor Express" decals, Model No. 601
  EX $75   **NM** $125   **MIP** $195

❏ **Motor Express Truck,** 1952, Grey and orange, 12.75Lx5.5Wx5H, cast cab "Freeport Motor Express" decals, Model No. 601
  EX $75   **NM** $125   **MIP** $195

❏ **Motor Express Truck,** 1953, White and red, 12.75Lx5.5Wx5H, cast cab "Freeport Motor Express" decals, Model No. 601
  EX $75   **NM** $125   **MIP** $195

❏ **Motor Express Truck,** 1954, Yellow and blue, 12.5Lx5.25Wx4.5H, stake truck with "S" grill cab, Model No. 150
  EX $75   **NM** $125   **MIP** $155

❏ **Motor Express Truck,** 1956-57, Yellow and blue, 12.5Lx5.25Wx4.5H, stake truck with "S" grill cab, Model No. 150
  EX $75   **NM** $125   **MIP** $155

❏ **Motorized Giant Gantry Crane,** 1973, Blue and yellow, 32.5Lx12.25Wx14H, motor operates all action, battery operated, Model No. 558
  EX $35   **NM** $45   **MIP** $55

❏ **Nationwide Rental Truck & Trailer,** 1962, Green and yellow, 21Lx5.75Wx5.5H, scarce, same design as #311 plus tow behind trailer, Model No. 500
  EX $75   **NM** $125   **MIP** $155

❏ **Nationwide Rental Truck & Trailer,** 1963, Green and yellow, 21Lx5.75Wx5.5H, scarce, same design as #311 plus tow behind trailer, Model No. 500
  EX $75   **NM** $125   **MIP** $155

❏ **Nationwide Rental Truck & Trailer Set,** 1962, Green and yellow, scarce, same as #500 set plus larger open trailer, Model No. 904
  EX $115   **NM** $155   **MIP** $195

❏ **Nationwide Rental Truck & Trailer Set,** 1963, Green and yellow, scarce, same as #500 set plus larger open trailer, Model No. 904
  EX $115   **NM** $155   **MIP** $195

VEHICLES

☐ **Overland Freight Trailer,** 1951, Blue and orange, 20.75Lx5.5Wx5.5H, blue cast cab with orange stake trailer, Model No. 704
EX $115   **NM** $175   **MIP** $225

(Randy Prasse Photo)

☐ **Overland Freight Trailer,** 1952, Blue and orange, 20.75Lx5.5Wx5.5H, blue cast cab with orange stake trailer, Model No. 704
EX $115   **NM** $175   **MIP** $225

(Calvin Chaussee Photo)

☐ **Package Delivery Truck,** 1951, Orange and green, 13Lx5.5Wx5H, cast cab, tail gate with chain, Model No. 603
EX $75   **NM** $125   **MIP** $195

☐ **Package Delivery Truck,** 1952, Orange and green, 13Lx5.5Wx5H, cast cab, tail gate with chain, Model No. 603
EX $75   **NM** $125   **MIP** $195

☐ **Package Delivery Truck,** 1953, White and orange, 13Lx5.5Wx5H, cast cab, tail gate with chain, w/hubcaps, Model No. 603
EX $75   **NM** $125   **MIP** $195

(Randy Prasse Photo)

☐ **Package Delivery Truck,** 1954, White and orange, 13Lx5.5Wx5H, cast cab, tail gate with chain, w/hubcaps, Model No. 603
EX $75   **NM** $125   **MIP** $195

☐ **Package Delivery Truck,** 1955, Yellow and green, 13Lx5.5Wx4.75H, with tailgate and chains, Model No. 911
EX $55   **NM** $95   **MIP** $155

☐ **Package Delivery Truck,** 1956-57, Blue and yellow, 13Lx5.5Wx4.75H, with tailgate and chains, Model No. 911
EX $55   **NM** $95   **MIP** $155

☐ **Panic Panel,** 1971, Orange, 2.75Lx3.5Wx3H, 2 wheeled design with panel wagon sides, Model No. 216
EX $10   **NM** $15   **MIP** $20

☐ **Panic Panel,** 1972, Orange, 2.75Lx3.5Wx3H, 2 wheeled design with panel wagon sides, Model No. 216
EX $10   **NM** $15   **MIP** $20

☐ **Panic Panel,** 1973, Orange, 2.75Lx3.5Wx3H, 2 wheeled design with panel wagon sides, Model No. 216
EX $10   **NM** $15   **MIP** $20

☐ **Parcel Service Truck,** 1958, Yellow and green, 12.25Lx5.25Wx7H, with mini grocery freight, Model No. 942
EX $75   **NM** $115   **MIP** $155

☐ **Paving Department,** 1962, Varies, same as #913 but #408 replaces sand loader trailer, Model No. 916
EX $125   **NM** $155   **MIP** $195

☐ **Paving Department,** 1963, Varies, includes #190, #305, #400, #401, #408, Model No. 916
EX $115   **NM** $135   **MIP** $175

☐ **Pickup,** 1964, Red and yellow, 8.75Lx3.5Wx3.5H, metal with rubber tires, Model No. 100
EX $15   **NM** $25   **MIP** $55

☐ **Pickup,** 1967, Green, 8.75Lx3.5Wx3.5H, Kom-pak design, Model No. 101
EX $15   **NM** $25   **MIP** $45

☐ **Pickup,** 1968, Teal, 8.75Lx3.5Wx3.5H, Kom-pak design, Model No. 101
EX $15   **NM** $25   **MIP** $45

☐ **Pickup And Delivery,** 1960, Met. green, 14Lx5.75Wx6.5H, whitewall tires, plastic horn on roof, Model No. 207
EX $45   **NM** $75   **MIP** $95

☐ **Pickup Truck,** 1966, Teal, 8.75Lx3.5Wx3.5H, Kom-pak design, Model No. 100
EX $15   **NM** $25   **MIP** $45

☐ **Pick-Up Truck,** 1954, Various, 6.5Lx2.5Wx2.25H, same scale as appear on auto transport set, Model No. 21
EX $15   **NM** $25   **MIP** $35

☐ **Pick-Up Truck,** 1958, Red and yellow, 19.25Lx6.5Wx6H, includes mini grocery freight, Model No. 210
EX $95   **NM** $125   **MIP** $155

☐ **Pick-Up Truck,** 1963, Red, 13.25Lx5.25Wx5.5H, Model No. 311
EX $35   **NM** $65   **MIP** $85

☐ **Pick-Up Truck,** 1964, Red, 13.25Lx5.25Wx5.5H, plastic window, yellow interior, whitewall tires, Model No. 311
EX $55   **NM** $75   **MIP** $95

☐ **Pick-Up Truck,** 1965, Teal and white, 8.75Lx3.5Wx3.5H, metal with rubber tires, Model No. 100
EX $15   **NM** $25   **MIP** $55

☐ **Pick-Up Truck With Horse Van,** 1958, Blue and yellow, 10.5Lx2.5Wx3H, includes 2 plastic horses, Model No. 100
EX $55   **NM** $85   **MIP** $105

☐ **Pipe-Layer Set,** 1970, Blue and white, 20Lx3.25Wx4.25H, road tow'ds design with grab bucket & dual trailers in tow, Model No. 285
EX $15   **NM** $25   **MIP** $35

☐ **Pipe-Layer Set,** 1972, Blue and white, 20Lx3.25Wx4.25H, road tow'ds design with grab bucket & dual trailers in tow, Model No. 285
EX $15   **NM** $25   **MIP** $35

☐ **Police Emergency Truck,** 1966, Blue and white, 12Lx6Wx7.5H, bell rings as truck moves, 3 ladders, hose reel, Model No. 716
EX $55   **NM** $95   **MIP** $125

☐ **Police Emergency Truck,** 1967, Blue and white, 12Lx6Wx7.5H, bell rings as truck moves, 3 ladders, hosse reel, Model No. 727
EX $55   **NM** $95   **MIP** $125

☐ **Police Emergency Truck,** 1968, Blue and white, 12Lx6Wx7.5H, bell rings as truck moves, 3 ladders, hose reel, Model No. 727
EX $55   **NM** $95   **MIP** $125

☐ **Pony Van,** 1969, Lime green, 16.5Lx3.25Wx5H, Kom-pak design with clear roof on trailer and 3 colts, Model No. 163
EX $25   **NM** $35   **MIP** $45

☐ **Pony Van,** 1970, Lime green, 16.5Lx3.25Wx5H, Kom-pak design with clear roof on trailer and 3 colts, Model No. 163
EX $25   **NM** $35   **MIP** $45

☐ **Power Shovel,** 1958, Orange, 26.5Lx7Wx6.75H, 2 cranks and rubber tracks, Model No. 106
EX $55   **NM** $95   **MIP** $115

☐ **Power Shovel,** 1959, Copper, 26.5Lx7Wx6.75H, rubber tracks, Model No. 302
EX $35   **NM** $55   **MIP** $75

☐ **Power Shovel,** 1960, Yellow, 26.5Lx7Wx6.75H, black rubber tracks, Model No. 305
EX $35   **NM** $55   **MIP** $75

☐ **Power Shovel,** 1961, Yellow, 26.5Lx7.5Wx7H, rubber tracks, Model No. 305
EX $35   **NM** $55   **MIP** $75

☐ **Power Shovel,** 1962, Yellow, 26.5Lx7.5Wx7H, rubber tracks, Model No. 305
EX $35   **NM** $55   **MIP** $75

☐ **Power Shovel,** 1963, Chartreuse, 26.5Lx7.25Wx7H, scarce chartreuse color - only used in 1963 production year, Model No. 305
EX $55   **NM** $75   **MIP** $95

☐ **Power Shovel,** 1964, Yellow, 26.5Lx7.25Wx7H, rubber tracks, 2 cranks operate boom and bucket, Model No. 305
EX $35   **NM** $65   **MIP** $85

☐ **Power Shovel,** 1965, Orange, 26.5Lx7.25Wx7H, rubber tracks, 2 cranks operate boom and bucket, Model No. 305
EX $35   **NM** $55   **MIP** $75

☐ **Power Shovel,** 1966, Orange, 26.5Lx7.25Wx7H, rubber tracks, 2 cranks operate boom and bucket, Model No. 305
EX $35   **NM** $55   **MIP** $75

❑ **Power Wrecker,** 1960, Blue and white, 23Lx7Wx9.25H, battery operated winch & lights, Model No. 802
EX $75   **NM** $125   **MIP** $175

❑ **Propur-T,** 1973, Blue and white, 10Lx4.5Wx5.75H, new design for 1973, Model No. 768
EX $25   **NM** $35   **MIP** $45

❑ **Pumper,** 1960, White, 19.75Lx7.25Wx6H, scarce, open cab, operating water tank and hose, Model No. 603
EX $95   **NM** $125   **MIP** $175

❑ **Pumper,** 1961, Red, 19.5Lx7.25Wx6.5H, operating water tank and hose, two ladders, Model No. 708
EX $55   **NM** $95   **MIP** $125

❑ **Pumper,** 1962, Red, 19.5Lx7.25Wx6.5H, operating water tank and hose, two ladders, Model No. 708
EX $55   **NM** $95   **MIP** $125

❑ **Pumper Fire Truck,** 1959, Red and red, 20Lx7.25Wx6H, open cab, plastic "S" grille, sprays water through hose, Model No. 701
EX $55   **NM** $95   **MIP** $155

❑ **Pumper Fire Truck W/Light,** 1958, Red, 22.75Lx7.25Wx7H, pumps water through truck & hydrant, flashing light, Model No. 262
EX $105   **NM** $165   **MIP** $205

❑ **Race-A-Roo,** 1970, Gold and white, 9.5Lx4.5Wx5H, sport model design with 5" white male doll, Model No. 760
EX $25   **NM** $35   **MIP** $45

❑ **Rampside Pick-Up,** 1961, Copper, 10.5Lx4.5Wx5H, plastic bed liner and drop-down door in side of bed, Model No. 195
EX $35   **NM** $55   **MIP** $75

❑ **Rampside Pick-Up,** 1962, Red, 10.5Lx4.5Wx5H, plastic bed liner and drop-down door in side of bed, Model No. 195
EX $35   **NM** $55   **MIP** $75

❑ **Rampside Pick-Up,** 1963, Red, 10.5Lx4.5Wx5H, plastic bed liner and drop-down door in side of bed, Model No. 194
EX $35   **NM** $55   **MIP** $75

❑ **Rampside Pick-Up,** 1964, Copper, 10.5Lx4.5Wx5H, plastic bed liner and drop-down door in side of bed, Model No. 194
EX $25   **NM** $55   **MIP** $75

❑ **Rampside Pick-Up,** 1965, Copper, 10.5Lx4.5Wx5H, plastic bed liner and drop-down door in side of bed, Model No. 194
EX $25   **NM** $55   **MIP** $75

❑ **Rampside Pick-Up,** 1966, Red, 10.5Lx4.5Wx5H, plastic bed liner and drop-down door in side of bed, Model No. 194
EX $25   **NM** $45   **MIP** $65

❑ **Rampside Pick-Up,** 1967, Red, 10.5Lx4.5Wx5H, plastic bed liner and drop-down door in side of bed, Model No. 230
EX $25   **NM** $45   **MIP** $65

❑ **Rampside Pick-Up,** 1968, Red, 10.5Lx4.5Wx5H, plastic bed liner and drop-down door in side of bed, Model No. 230
EX $25   **NM** $45   **MIP** $65

❑ **Rampside Pick-Up,** 1969, Gold and white, 10.5Lx4.75W5.25H, typhoons design with white plastic bed liner, Model No. 230
EX $25   **NM** $35   **MIP** $45

❑ **Ready Mix Concrete Truck,** 1956-57, Red and yellow, 21.5Lx7.5Wx9.25H, with gear on barrel, driven by axle, Model No. 271
EX $75   **NM** $105   **MIP** $155

❑ **Ready Mix Concrete Truck,** 1958, Green and orange, 21.5Lx7.5Wx9.25H, with gear on barrel, driven by axle, Model No. 271
EX $75   **NM** $105   **MIP** $175

❑ **Ready Mix Concrete Truck,** 1960, Teal and white, 16Lx7.5Wx9H, axle driven gear operates barrel, Model No. 604
EX $55   **NM** $75   **MIP** $95

❑ **Ready Mix Concrete Truck,** 1962, Red and white, 15.5Lx6.75Wx7.25H, axle driven gear operates barrel, Model No. 408
EX $35   **NM** $55   **MIP** $75

❑ **Ready-Mix Concrete Truck,** 1959, Copper and cream, 20.75Lx7.5Wx9.25H, gear powered barrel, runs off axle, Model No. 700
EX $55   **NM** $85   **MIP** $125

❑ **Ready-Mix Concrete Truck,** 1961, Red and white, 15.5Lx7.75Wx9H, axle driven gear operates barrel, Model No. 609
EX $55   **NM** $95   **MIP** $115

❑ **Ready-Mix Concrete Truck,** 1963, Green and chartreuse, 15.5Lx6.75Wx7.25H, axle driven gear operates barrel, Model No. 408
EX $35   **NM** $55   **MIP** $75

❑ **Ready-Mix Concrete Truck,** 1964, Red and yellow, 15.5Lx6.75Wx7.25H, axle driven gear operates barrel, Model No. 408
EX $35   **NM** $55   **MIP** $75

❑ **Refrigerated Express Truck,** 1958, Yellow and brown, 21Lx5Wx7.5H, transport trailer with refrigerator unit on front, Model No. 951
EX $95   **NM** $155   **MIP** $195

❑ **Ride 'Em Air Force Jeep,** 1958, Blue and red, 25.5Lx11Wx14.5H, with steering wheel and fold-down windshield, Model No. 995
EX $105   **NM** $175   **MIP** $215

❑ **Ride 'Em Dump Truck,** 1958, Blue and yellow, 20.5Lx7.75Wx10.25H, with seat and steering wheel, Model No. 990
EX $95   **NM** $155   **MIP** $195

❑ **Ride-er Air Force Jeep,** 1959, Blue and red, 25.75Lx10.25Wx18H, missile launcher and missiles on hood, trunk opens, Model No. 950
EX $75   **NM** $115   **MIP** $175

❑ **Ride-er Chief's Car,** 1966, Red and white, 25.5Lx10.25Wx12.75H, bell rings when string is pulled, Model No. 921
EX $75   **NM** $105   **MIP** $155

❑ **Ride-er Doodle Bug,** 1963, Yellow, 25.5Lx10.25Wx12.75H, same as ride-er fire truck from 1962, Model No. 925
EX $75   **NM** $105   **MIP** $135

❑ **Ride-er Doodle Bug,** 1964, Yellow, 25.5Lx10.25Wx12.75H, Model No. 925
EX $75   **NM** $105   **MIP** $135

❑ **Ride-er Doodle Bug,** 1965, Teal and white, 25.5Lx10.25Wx12.75H, Model No. 925
EX $75   **NM** $105   **MIP** $135

❑ **Ride-er Dump Truck,** 1959, Blue and yellow, 20Lx7.75Wx10H, metal seat in dump box, bulb horn on steering wheel, Model No. 505
EX $55   **NM** $95   **MIP** $125

❑ **Ride-er Dump Truck,** 1960, Blue and white, 20Lx7.75Wx10H, metal seat in dump box and bulb horn on steering wheel, Model No. 605
EX $55   **NM** $75   **MIP** $95

❑ **Ride-er Dump Truck,** 1963, Red and white, 20Lx7.75Wx10.25H, metal seat in dump box, Model No. 605
EX $75   **NM** $105   **MIP** $135

❑ **Ride-er Dump Truck,** 1964, Red and white, 20Lx7Wx10.25H, metal seat in dump box, Model No. 605
EX $75   **NM** $105   **MIP** $135

❑ **Ride-er Dump Truck,** 1965, Teal and white, 20Lx7Wx10.25H, metal seat in dump box, Model No. 605
EX $75   **NM** $105   **MIP** $135

❑ **Ride-er Dump Truck,** 1966, White and green, 20Lx7Wx10.25H, metal seat in dump box, Model No. 605
EX $55   **NM** $85   **MIP** $115

❑ **Ride-er Fire Truck,** 1959, Red and white, 25.5Lx10.5Wx12.75H, crank siren on hood, trunk opens, Model No. 925
EX $75   **NM** $115   **MIP** $155

❑ **Ride-er Fire Truck,** 1960, Red and white, 25.5Lx10.5Wx12.75H, crank siren on hood, trunk opens, Model No. 925
EX $75   **NM** $115   **MIP** $155

❑ **Ride-er Fire Truck,** 1961, Red and white, 25.5Lx10.5Wx12.75H, crank siren on hood, trunk opens, Model No. 925
EX $75   **NM** $105   **MIP** $135

❑ **Ride-er Fire Truck,** 1962, Red and white, 25.5Lx10.5Wx12.75H, crank siren on hood, trunk opens, Model No. 925
EX $75   **NM** $105   **MIP** $135

❑ **Ride-er Wrecker Truck,** 1961, Copper and white, 23.5Lx7.75Wx10.25H, metal seat and crank operated boom in box, Model No. 607
EX $55 **NM** $95 **MIP** $125

❑ **Ride-er Wrecker Truck,** 1962, Red and yellow, 23.5Lx7.5Wx10.25H, metal seat and crank operated tow boom in box, Model No. 607
EX $55 **NM** $95 **MIP** $125

❑ **Riding Academy,** 1965, Teal and teal, 20Lx4.75Wx6H, #250 cub pick-up plus horse trailer, 2 plastic horses, Model No. 252
EX $55 **NM** $75 **MIP** $95

❑ **Riding Academy,** 1966, Teal and teal, 18Lx4.75Wx6H, #194 rampside pick-up plus horse trailer, 2 plastic horses, Model No. 254
EX $55 **NM** $75 **MIP** $95

❑ **Road Boss Car Carrier,** 1972, Orange, 22.5Lx5.5Wx5.5H, with chrome stacks and air horn detail plus 3 cars, Model No. 335
EX $35 **NM** $45 **MIP** $55

❑ **Road Boss Car Carrier,** 1973, Blue and yellow, 22.5Lx5.5Wx5.5H, with chrome stacks and air horn detail plus 3 cars, Model No. 335
EX $35 **NM** $45 **MIP** $55

❑ **Road Boss Hydraulic Dump,** 1972, Orange, 13.25Lx5.25Wx6.25H, with chrome stacks and air horn detail, Model No. 327
EX $25 **NM** $35 **MIP** $45

❑ **Road Boss Hydraulic Dump,** 1973, Blue and yellow, 13.25Lx5.5Wx6.25H, with chrome stacks and air horn detail, Model No. 327
EX $25 **NM** $35 **MIP** $45

❑ **Road Boss Pipeline Transport,** 1973, Blue and yellow, 21.75Lx5.5Wx6.5H, with chrome stacks and air horn detail, same as #328, Model No. 323
EX $25 **NM** $35 **MIP** $45

❑ **Road Boss Timber Toter,** 1972, Orange, 21.75Lx5.5Wx6.5H, with chrome stacks and air horn detail, Model No. 328
EX $35 **NM** $45 **MIP** $55

❑ **Road Boss Timber Toter,** 1973, Blue and yellow, 21.75Lx5.5Wx6.5H, with chrome stacks and air horn detail, same as #323, Model No. 328
EX $35 **NM** $45 **MIP** $55

❑ **Road Boss Tractor Trailer Truck,** 1972, Orange, 22Lx5.5Wx8H, with chrome stacks and air horn detail, Model No. 329
EX $35 **NM** $45 **MIP** $55

❑ **Road Boss Tractor Trailer Truck,** 1973, Blue and yellow, 22Lx5.5Wx8H, with chrome stacks and air horn detail, Model No. 329
EX $35 **NM** $45 **MIP** $55

❑ **Road Boss Vista Dome Horse Van,** 1972, Orange, 22Lx5.5Wx6H, with chrome stacks and air horn detail plus 4 black horses, Model No. 324
EX $35 **NM** $45 **MIP** $55

❑ **Road Boss Vista-Dome Horse Van,** 1973, Blue and yellow, 22Lx5.5Wx6H, with chrome stacks and air horn detail, 4 black horses, Model No. 324
EX $25 **NM** $35 **MIP** $45

❑ **Road Builder Set,** 1962, Red and yellow, same as #913 set plus #400, Model No. 915
EX $125 **NM** $155 **MIP** $195

❑ **Road Grader,** 1951, Orange, 18Lx7Wx7.5H, with plastic fireball motor under the hood, Model No. 300
EX $55 **NM** $85 **MIP** $105

❑ **Road Grader,** 1952, Orange, 18Lx7Wx7.5H, with plastic fireball motor under the hood, Model No. 300
EX $55 **NM** $85 **MIP** $105

❑ **Road Grader,** 1953, Orange, 18Lx7Wx7.5H, with plastic fireball motor under the hood, Model No. 300
EX $55 **NM** $85 **MIP** $105

❑ **Road Grader,** 1953, Orange, 18Lx7Wx7.5H, with plastic fireball motor under the hood, Model No. 300
EX $55 **NM** $85 **MIP** $105

❑ **Road Grader,** 1955, Orange, 18Lx7Wx7.5H, with plastic fireball motor under the hood, Model No. 300
EX $55 **NM** $85 **MIP** $105

❑ **Road Grader,** 1956-57, Green, 18Lx7Wx7.5H, with plastic fireball motor under the hood, Model No. 300
EX $55 **NM** $85 **MIP** $105

❑ **Road Grader,** 1960, Yellow, 18.75Lx7.25Wx7.5H, black tires and motor, scraper blade lifts with levers, Model No. 301
EX $35 **NM** $55 **MIP** $75

❑ **Road Grader,** 1961, Yellow, 18.75Lx7Wx7.5H, plastic tires, Model No. 301
EX $25 **NM** $45 **MIP** $65

❑ **Road Grader,** 1962, Yellow, 19Lx7.5Wx8H, covered cab, plated blade, black plastic tires, Model No. 400
EX $55 **NM** $75 **MIP** $95

❑ **Road Grader,** 1963, Chartreuse, 19Lx7.5Wx8H, scarce chartreuse color - only used in 1963 production year, Model No. 400
EX $55 **NM** $75 **MIP** $95

❑ **Road Grader,** 1964, Orange, 19Lx7.5Wx8.25H, plated scraper blade, black plastic wheels & engine, Model No. 400
EX $45 **NM** $65 **MIP** $85

❑ **Road Grader,** 1965, Orange and black, 11.75Lx4Wx4H, new z-z-z sound when unit rolls, no batteries, Model No. 140
EX $15 **NM** $35 **MIP** $65

❑ **Road Grader,** 1965, Orange, 19Lx7.5Wx8.25H, plated scraper blade, black plastic wheels & engine, Model No. 400
EX $45 **NM** $65 **MIP** $85

❑ **Road Grader,** 1966, Orange, 19Lx7.5Wx8.25H, plated scraper blade, black plastic wheels & engine, Model No. 400
EX $35 **NM** $55 **MIP** $75

❑ **Road Grader,** 1966, Orange, 11.75Lx5Wx4.75H, Kom-pak design, Model No. 140
EX $15 **NM** $25 **MIP** $45

❑ **Road Grader,** 1967, Orange, 19Lx7.5Wx8H, plated scraper blade, black plastic wheels & engine, Model No. 527
EX $35 **NM** $55 **MIP** $75

❑ **Road Grader,** 1967, Orange, 11.75Lx5Wx4.75H, Kom-pak design, Model No. 183
EX $15 **NM** $25 **MIP** $45

❑ **Road Grader,** 1968, Orange, 11.75Lx5Wx4.75H, Kom-pak design, Model No. 183
EX $15 **NM** $25 **MIP** $45

❑ **Road Grader,** 1968, Orange, 19Lx7.5Wx8H, plated scraper blade, black plastic wheels & engine, Model No. 527
EX $35 **NM** $55 **MIP** $75

❑ **Road Grader,** 1969, Orange, 11.75Lx5Wx6H, black plastic wheels and motor, Model No. 183
EX $15 **NM** $25 **MIP** $45

❑ **Road Grader,** 1969, Orange, 19Lx7.5Wx8H, plated scraper blade, black plastic wheels & engine, Model No. 527
EX $25 **NM** $35 **MIP** $55

❑ **Road Grader,** 1970, Lime green and yellow, 11.75Lx5Wx6H, black plastic wheels and motor, Model No. 183
EX $15 **NM** $25 **MIP** $35

❑ **Road Grader,** 1972, Yellow, 11.75Lx5Wx6H, black plastic wheels and motor, Model No. 183
EX $15 **NM** $25 **MIP** $35

❑ **Road Grader,** 1973, Yellow, 11.75Lx5Wx6H, "Structo 11" stencilled in black on blade, Model No. 183
EX $15 **NM** $25 **MIP** $35

❑ **Roadbuilder Set,** 1968, Yellow and green, #580 set and #303 dump truck, Model No. 905
EX $55 **NM** $75 **MIP** $95

❑ **Roadbuilder Set,** 1969, Yellow and green, #580 set and #303 dump truck, Model No. 905
EX $45 **NM** $65 **MIP** $85

❑ **Rocker,** 1953, Red, 20Lx6.25Wx.6.5H, with plastic fireball motor under the hood, Model No. 310
EX $75 **NM** $105 **MIP** $155

❑ **Rocker,** 1953, Red, 20Lx6.25Wx6.5H, with plastic fireball motor under the hood, Model No. 310
EX $75 **NM** $105 **MIP** $155

❑ **Rocker,** 1955, Green, 20Lx6.25Wx6.5H, with plastic fireball motor under the hood, Model No. 310
EX $75 **NM** $105 **MIP** $155

❑ **Rocker Dump,** 1956-57, Green, 20Lx6Wx6.5H, rubber tracks on tractor, dumps to the rear, Model No. 311
EX $95 **NM** $125 **MIP** $155

❏ **Rough Rider Pickup,** 1970, Yellow, 9.25Lx4Wx4H, hurricanes design with open bed, Model No. 801
EX $15   **NM** $25   **MIP** $35

❏ **Rough Rider Pickup,** 1972, Yellow, 9.25Lx4Wx4H, hurricanes design, Model No. 801
EX $10   **NM** $20   **MIP** $30

❏ **Rough Rider Pickup,** 1973, Yellow, 9.25Lx4Wx4H, hurricanes design, Model No. 801
EX $10   **NM** $20   **MIP** $30

❏ **Rough Rider Pick-Up Truck,** 1969, Yellow, 9.25Lx4Wx4H, hurricanes design with open bed, Model No. 801
EX $15   **NM** $25   **MIP** $35

❏ **Sand Hopper,** 1963, Chartreuse, 8.25Lx6Wx12H, goes with construction sets, Model No. 190
EX $15   **NM** $25   **MIP** $35

❏ **Sand Loader,** 1972, Yellow, 9.5Lx5Wx9.5H, small sand hopper with conveyor, Model No. 560
EX $10   **NM** $15   **MIP** $20

❏ **Sand Master Set,** 1968, Yellow, 17.5Lx9Wx15H, plastic sand hopper with rubber conveyor belt, Model No. 580
EX $15   **NM** $25   **MIP** $35

❏ **Sand Master Set,** 1969, Yellow, 17.5Lx9Wx15H, plastic sand hopper with rubber conveyor belt, Model No. 580
EX $15   **NM** $25   **MIP** $35

❏ **Sand Master Set,** 1970, Yellow, 17.5Lx9Wx15H, plastic sand hopper with rubber conveyor belt, Model No. 580
EX $15   **NM** $25   **MIP** $35

❏ **Sand Master Set,** 1972, Yellow, 14.5Lx4.5Wx15H, plastic sand hopper with rubber conveyor belt, Model No. 580
EX $15   **NM** $25   **MIP** $35

❏ **Sand Master Set,** 1973, Yellow and orange, 14.5Lx4.5Wx15H, plastic sand hopper with rubber conveyor belt, Model No. 580
EX $15   **NM** $25   **MIP** $35

❏ **Sand Set,** 1972, Yellow, 9.75Lx5Wx9.5H, #560 unit plus sand hopper unit, Model No. 579
EX $15   **NM** $25   **MIP** $35

❏ **Sand-Grenade Dune Buggy,** 1970, Red and black, 9.5Lx4.5Wx5H, sport model design with dual rear mag wheels, Model No. 777
EX $25   **NM** $35   **MIP** $45

❏ **Sand-Grenade Dune Buggy,** 1972, Red and black, 9.5Lx4.5Wx5H, sport model design with dual rear mag wheels, Model No. 777
EX $25   **NM** $35   **MIP** $45

❏ **Sanitation Truck,** 1967, Grey and white, 11.5Lx3.5Wx5H, Kom-pak design, bucket dumps into body, Model No. 178
EX $25   **NM** $45   **MIP** $65

❏ **Sanitation Truck,** 1967, Green and white, 18Lx6Wx8H, lever action trash bucket dumps into box, Model No. 266
EX $45   **NM** $65   **MIP** $85

❏ **Sanitation Truck,** 1968, Grey and white, 11.5Lx3.5Wx5H, Kom-pak design, bucket dumps into body, Model No. 178
EX $25   **NM** $45   **MIP** $65

❏ **Sanitation Truck,** 1968, Green and white, 18Lx6Wx8H, lever action trash bucket dumps into box, Model No. 266
EX $45   **NM** $65   **MIP** $85

❏ **Sanitation Truck,** 1969, Grey and white, 16.5Lx6Wx7.5H, typhoons design with lever action, Model No. 269
EX $25   **NM** $35   **MIP** $45

❏ **Scamp,** 1969, Gold and white, 9.5Lx4.5Wx5.25H, sport model design with 5" blond doll, Model No. 744
EX $25   **NM** $35   **MIP** $45

❏ **Scamp Sportster,** 1970, Gold and white, 9.5Lx4.5Wx5.25H, sport model design with 5" blond female doll, Model No. 744
EX $25   **NM** $35   **MIP** $45

❏ **School Bus,** 1960, Yellow, 5.5Lx4Wx12H, scarce, plastic, hinged school bus with blocks. Pull toy, Model No. 115
EX $75   **NM** $95   **MIP** $115

❏ **School Bus,** 1962, Yellow, 10.5Lx4.75Wx5H, steel body, plastic mirrors, wipers and horn, Model No. 196
EX $55   **NM** $75   **MIP** $95

❏ **School Bus,** 1963, Yellow, 10.5Lx4.75Wx5H, steel body, plastic mirrors, wipers and horn, Model No. 196
EX $55   **NM** $75   **MIP** $95

❏ **Scorpion,** 1973, Pink and white, 10Lx4.5Wx5.75H, new design for 1973, Model No. 763
EX $25   **NM** $35   **MIP** $45

❏ **Scraper,** 1953, Red, 22Lx7Wx6.5H, with plastic fireball motor under the hood, Model No. 330
EX $75   **NM** $105   **MIP** $155

❏ **Scraper,** 1953, Red, 22Lx7Wx6.5H, with plastic fireball motor under the hood, Model No. 330
EX $75   **NM** $105   **MIP** $155

❏ **Scraper,** 1955, Red, 22Lx7Wx6.5H, with plastic fireball motor under the hood, Model No. 330
EX $75   **NM** $105   **MIP** $155

❏ **Scraper,** 1956-57, Orange, 22Lx7Wx6.5H, with plastic fireball motor under the hood, Model No. 330
EX $75   **NM** $105   **MIP** $155

❏ **Sea Sprite,** 1968, White and red, 23.5Lx5Wx5.25H, jeep towing "Johnson Reveler" model boat on trailer, Model No. 211
EX $45   **NM** $65   **MIP** $85

❏ **Sea Sprite,** 1969, Blue and red, 23Lx5.5Wx5.25H, sport model design

❏ **Sea Sprite,** 1969, Blue and red, 23Lx5.5Wx5.25H, sport model design with "Johnson Reveler" boat in tow, Model No. 755
EX $25   **NM** $35   **MIP** $45

❏ **Sea Sprite,** 1970, Blue and red, 23Lx5.5Wx5.25H, sport model design with "Johnson Reveler" boat in tow, Model No. 755
EX $25   **NM** $35   **MIP** $45

❏ **Semi Trailer Freight Truck,** 1955, Yellow and red, 17Lx4.5Wx4.5H, same trailer as #930 with "S" grill cab, Model No. 155
EX $95   **NM** $155   **MIP** $175

❏ **Semi Trailer Freight Truck,** 1956-57, Yellow and red, 17Lx4.5Wx4.5H, same trailer as #930 with "S" grill cab, Model No. 155
EX $95   **NM** $155   **MIP** $175

❏ **Semi Trailer Lumber Truck,** 1955, Green and orange, 17Lx4.5Wx4.5H, with three wooden logs and "S" grill cab, Model No. 156
EX $95   **NM** $155   **MIP** $175

❏ **Shovel Dump Truck,** 1951, Orange and blue, 12.75Lx5.5Wx5H, cast cab, dump box, Model No. 605
EX $75   **NM** $125   **MIP** $195

❏ **Shovel Dump Truck,** 1952, Orange and blue, 12.75Lx5.5Wx5H, cast cab, dump box, Model No. 605
EX $75   **NM** $125   **MIP** $195

❏ **Shovel Dump Truck,** 1953, White and blue, 12.75Lx5.5Wx5H, cast cab, dump box, w/hubcaps, Model No. 605
EX $75   **NM** $125   **MIP** $195

❏ **Shovel Dump Truck,** 1954, White and blue, 12.75Lx5.5Wx5H, cast cab, dump box, w/hubcaps, Model No. 605
EX $75   **NM** $125   **MIP** $195

❏ **Shovel Dump Truck,** 1955, Chrome and orange, 12.75Lx6Wx6.25H, same as #605 from past years. Mag wheels, Model No. 606
EX $105   **NM** $175   **MIP** $205

❏ **Shovel Dump Truck,** 1956-57, Green and yellow, 12.75Lx6Wx5H, with mag wheels, Model No. 606
EX $75   **NM** $155   **MIP** $195

❏ **Snorkel Fire Truck,** 1967, Red, 21Lx6.5Wx8H, same design as #380, Model No. 466
EX $65   **NM** $95   **MIP** $125

❏ **Snorkel Fire Truck,** 1968, Red, 21Lx6.5Wx8H, same design as #380, Model No. 466
EX $65   **NM** $95   **MIP** $125

❏ **Snorkel Fire Truck,** 1969, Red and white, 9.5Lx4Wx5.25H, hurricanes design with white plastic snorkel arm & bucket, Model No. 878
EX $15   **NM** $25   **MIP** $35

❏ **Snorkel Fire Truck,** 1969, Red, 17.5Lx5.75Wx9H, typhoons design, Model No. 385
EX $35   **NM** $45   **MIP** $55

VEHICLES

❏ **Snorkel Fire Truck,** 1970, Red, 17.5Lx5.75Wx9H, typhoons design, Model No. 385
EX $35　　NM $45　　MIP $55

❏ **Snorkel Fire Truck,** 1970, Red and white, 9.5Lx4Wx5.25H, hurricanes design with white plastic snorkel arm & bucket, Model No. 878
EX $15　　NM $25　　MIP $35

❏ **Snorkel Utility Truck,** 1967, Green and yellow, 21Lx6.5Wx5.5H, hydraulic snorkel book and plastic bucket, outriggers, Model No. 380
EX $65　　NM $95　　MIP $125

❏ **Snorkel Utility Truck,** 1968, Green and yellow, 21Lx6.5Wx5.5H, hydraulic snorkel book and plastic bucket, outriggers, Model No. 380
EX $65　　NM $95　　MIP $125

❏ **Snorkel Utility Truck,** 1969, Green and yellow, 17.5Lx6Wx9H, typhoons design with white boom and plastic bucket, Model No. 380
EX $35　　NM $45　　MIP $55

❏ **Snorkel Utility Truck,** 1970, Green and yellow, 17.5Lx6Wx9H, typhoons design with white boom and plastic bucket, Model No. 380
EX $35　　NM $45　　MIP $55

❏ **Speedway Ambulance,** 1973, White, 9.25Lx4Wx4H, similar to hurricane design with first aid decals, Model No. 855
EX $25　　NM $35　　MIP $45

❏ **Speedway Midget Race Hauler,** 1973, Red and black, 10.5Lx4Wx4H, flatbed with race car, Model No. 842
EX $25　　NM $35　　MIP $45

❏ **Speedway Pacer,** 1973, Green, 9.25Lx4Wx4H, same as hurricane design #801 with speedway decals, Model No. 865
EX $25　　NM $35　　MIP $45

❏ **Speedway Series Ambulance,** 1972, White, 9.25Lx4Wx4H, similar to hurricane design with first aid decals, Model No. 855
EX $25　　NM $35　　MIP $45

❏ **Speedway Series Pacer,** 1972, Green, 9.25Lx4Wx4H, same as hurricane design #801 with speedway decals, Model No. 865
EX $25　　NM $35　　MIP $45

❏ **Speedway Series Wrecker,** 1972, Purple, 9.25Lx4Wx4H, same as hurricane design #428 with speedway decals, Model No. 845
EX $25　　NM $35　　MIP $45

❏ **Speedway Water Tanker,** 1973, Blue and white, 9.25Lx4Wx4.5H, white plastic water tank on back, Model No. 868
EX $25　　NM $35　　MIP $45

❏ **Speedway Wrecker,** 1973, Purple, 9.25Lx4Wx4H, same as hurricane design #428 with speedway decals, Model No. 845
EX $25　　NM $35　　MIP $45

❏ **Sportsman,** 1962, Red and white, 13.25Lx5.25Wx5.5H, scarce, white plastic "Sportsman" camper top, Model No. 311
EX $75　　NM $115　　MIP $155

❏ **Stake Truck,** 1954, Green and orange, 9.25Lx3.25Wx3.25H, removable stake panels, Model No. 76
EX $35　　NM $55　　MIP $75

❏ **Stake Truck,** 1956-57, Gold and green, 9.25Lx3.25Wx3.25H, removable stake panels, Model No. 76
EX $35　　NM $55　　MIP $75

❏ **Stake Truck,** 1959, Copper and cream, 9.25Lx3.25Wx3H, Model No. 76
EX $35　　NM $55　　MIP $75

❏ **Standard Steam Shovel,** 1948, Orange, 20.5L x 6.25W x 7.75H, wooden wheels without tracks, Model No. 100
EX $55　　NM $115　　MIP $175

❏ **Standard Steam Shovel,** 1949, Orange, 20.5Lx6.25Wx7.75H, wooden wheels w/o tracks, Model No. 100
EX $55　　NM $115　　MIP $175

❏ **Standard Steam Shovel,** 1950, Orange, 20.5Lx6.25Wx7.75H, wooden wheels w/o tracks, Model No. 100
EX $55　　NM $115　　MIP $175

❏ **State Fair Set,** 1966, Met. blue, 4 pc. set includes #203, #310, #417, 6 animals, Model No. 952
EX $95　　NM $125　　MIP $155

❏ **Station Wagon,** 1966, Teal and white, 10.75Lx5Wx5H, white plastic convertible roof cover body, doors open, Model No. 325
EX $25　　NM $45　　MIP $65

❏ **Station Wagon With Boat & Trailer,** 1964, Blue and red, 20Lx5Wx5H, cub station wagon (#325) towing plastic boat on trailer, Model No. 404
EX $35　　NM $65　　MIP $85

❏ **Station Wagon With Boat & Trailer,** 1965, Blue and red, 20Lx5Wx5H, cub station wagon (#325) towing plastic boat on trailer, Model No. 404
EX $35　　NM $65　　MIP $85

❏ **Steam Shovel,** 1953, Blue, 26.5Lx6.5Wx8H, 2 cranks and rubber tracks, Model No. 105
EX $55　　NM $95　　MIP $125

❏ **Steam Shovel,** 1955, Orange, 26.5Lx6.5Wx8H, 2 cranks and rubber tracks, Model No. 105
EX $55　　NM $75　　MIP $115

❏ **Steam Shovel & Machinery Truck,** 1955, Green and orange, 26.5Lx6.5Wx14.25H, with plastic fireball motor under the hood, Model No. 403
EX $95　　NM $155　　MIP $195

❏ **Steam Shovel (New Design),** 1953, Blue, 26.5Lx6.5Wx8H, new design, 2 cranks, Model No. 105
EX $55　　NM $95　　MIP $125

❏ **Steel Cargo Trailer,** 1951, Blue and red, 20.75Lx5.5Wx5.5H, blue cast cab with red trailer, no hubcaps, Model No. 702
EX $95　　NM $135　　MIP $195

(Randy Prasse Photo)

❏ **Steel Cargo Trailer,** 1952, Blue and red, 20.75Lx5.5Wx5.5H, blue cast cab with red trailer, no hubcaps, Model No. 702
EX $95　　NM $135　　MIP $195

❏ **Steel Cargo Trailer,** 1953, White and red, 20.75Lx5.5Wx5.5H, w/hubcaps & loading ramp, Model No. 702
EX $75　　NM $125　　MIP $175

❏ **Steel Cargo Trailer,** 1954, White and red, 20.75Lx5.5Wx5.5H, w/hubcaps & loading ramp, Model No. 702
EX $75　　NM $125　　MIP $175

❏ **Steel Cargo Trailer,** 1955, White and red, 25.5Lx5.5Wx5.5H, shown in catalog with yellow cab but have not seen, Model No. 702
EX $75　　NM $125　　MIP $175

❏ **Steel Dump Truck,** 1967, Grey and orange, 8.75Lx3.5Wx4H, Kom-pak design, Model No. 141
EX $15　　NM $25　　MIP $45

❏ **Steel Dump Truck,** 1968, Red and yellow, 8.75Lx3.5Wx4H, Kom-pak design, Model No. 141
EX $15　　NM $25　　MIP $45

❏ **Steerable Camper Truck,** 1972, Red and white, 9.25Lx4.25Wx5H, steerable stormers design with white plastic camper, Model No. 435
EX $15　　NM $25　　MIP $35

❏ **Steerable Cement Mixer,** 1970, Orange and white, 12.25Lx7Wx7.5H, steerable thunderbolt design, Model No. 632
EX $15　　NM $25　　MIP $35

❏ **Steerable Cement Mixer Truck,** 1972, Gold and white, 12.25Lx7Wx7.5H, thunderbolt design, axle drives barrel, Model No. 634
EX $15　　NM $25　　MIP $35

❏ **Steerable Dump Truck,** 1970, Gold and white, 10.5Lx4Wx4.25H, steerable stormers design, Model No. 441
EX $15　　NM $25　　MIP $35

❏ **Steerable Dump Truck,** 1972, Gold and white, 10.5Lx4Wx4.25H, steerable stormers design, Model No. 441
EX $15　　NM $25　　MIP $35

❏ **Steerable Fire Rescue Truck,** 1970, Red, 12.5Lx6Wx6.5H, steerable thunderbolt design, Model No. 653
EX $15　　NM $25　　MIP $35

❏ **Steerable Fire Rescue Truck,** 1972, Red, 12.5Lx6Wx6.5H, thunderbolt design, with 2 ladders and extension ladder, Model No. 653
EX $15　　NM $25　　MIP $35

❏ **Steerable Hook & Ladder Truck,** 1970, Red and red, 17.5Lx6Wx7.25H, steerable thunderbolt design, Model No. 681
EX $25   **NM** $45   **MIP** $55

❏ **Steerable Hydraulic Dump Truck,** 1970, Orange and white, 13.25Lx5.5Wx6.25H, steerable thunderbolt design, Model No. 626
EX $15   **NM** $25   **MIP** $35

❏ **Steerable Hydraulic Dump Truck,** 1970, Blue and white, 13.25Lx5.5Wx6.25H, steerable thunderbolt design, Model No. 640
EX $15   **NM** $25   **MIP** $35

❏ **Steerable Hydraulic Dump Truck,** 1972, Blue and white, 13.25Lx5.5Wx6.25H, thunderbolt design, Model No. 640
EX $15   **NM** $25   **MIP** $35

❏ **Steerable Livestock Truck,** 1970, Gold and white, 9.5Lx4.25Wx4.25H, steerable stormers design with stake sides & 4 animals, Model No. 471
EX $15   **NM** $25   **MIP** $35

❏ **Steerable Minuteman Wrecker,** 1970, Lime green and white, 9.25Lx4Wx4H, steerable stormers design with white metal boom, Model No. 428
EX $15   **NM** $25   **MIP** $35

❏ **Steerable Minuteman Wrecker,** 1972, Lime green and white, 9.25Lx4Wx4H, steerable stormers design with white metal boom, Model No. 428
EX $15   **NM** $25   **MIP** $35

❏ **Steerable Rough Rider Pickup,** 1970, Blue and white, 9.25Lx4Wx4H, steerable stormers design, Model No. 420
EX $15   **NM** $25   **MIP** $35

❏ **Steerable Rough Rider Pickup,** 1972, Blue and white, 9.25Lx4Wx4H, steerable stormers design, Model No. 420
EX $15   **NM** $25   **MIP** $35

❏ **Steerable Snorkel Truck,** 1970, Red and white, 9.5Lx4Wx5.5H, steerable stormers design with white plastic snorkel, Model No. 478
EX $15   **NM** $25   **MIP** $35

❏ **Steerable Stormer Construction Set,** 1970, Yellow, #441 steer-o-matic dump, sand hopper & 10 pc. road sign set, Model No. 955
EX $35   **NM** $45   **MIP** $55

(ToyShop File Photo)

❏ **Steerable Stubby Wrecker,** 1970, Gold and white, 11Lx5.5Wx7H, steerable thunderbolt design with "Road Tug" decal on side, Model No. 615
EX $15   **NM** $35   **MIP** $55

❏ **Steerable Stubby Wrecker,** 1972, Gold and white, 11Lx5.5Wx7H, thunderbolt design, with black tow boom, Model No. 615
EX $15   **NM** $25   **MIP** $35

❏ **Steerable Stubby Wrecker,** 1973, Gold and white, 11Lx5.5Wx7H, thunderbolt design, with black tow boom, Model No. 615
EX $15   **NM** $25   **MIP** $35

❏ **Steerable Timber Toter,** 1970, Lime green and white, 21.75Lx5.5Wx6.5H, steerable thunderbolt design with 6 wooden logs & chains, Model No. 661
EX $25   **NM** $45   **MIP** $55

❏ **Steerable Tractor Trailer,** 1970, Orange and orange, 22Lx5.5Wx8H, steerable thunderbolt design, Model No. 673
EX $25   **NM** $45   **MIP** $55

❏ **Steerable Waggin' Wagon,** 1970, Blue and white, 9.25Lx4Wx4H, steerable stormers design with clear kennel & 6 dogs, Model No. 437
EX $15   **NM** $25   **MIP** $35

❏ **Steerable Waggin' Wagon,** 1972, Blue and white, 9.25Lx4Wx4H, steerable stormers design with waggin' wagon treatment, Model No. 437
EX $15   **NM** $25   **MIP** $35

❏ **Stock Farm Set,** 1959, Red and white, 15Lx6Wx7.25H, stake truck with cattle loading ramp and 4 plastic horses, Model No. 501
EX $55   **NM** $85   **MIP** $115

❏ **Stock Farm Set,** 1960, Red and white, 14.75Lx6Wx7.25H, stake truck with cattle loading ramp and 4 plastic horses, Model No. 510
EX $55   **NM** $85   **MIP** $115

❏ **Super Sandy Set,** 1968, Yellow and green, 13.5Lx5.5Wx5.75H, dump truck and large plastic sand hopper, Model No. 306
EX $55   **NM** $75   **MIP** $95

❏ **Super Sandy Set,** 1969, Green and yellow, 13.5Lx9.5Wx13H, #303 dump truck plus plastic sand hopper, Model No. 306
EX $25   **NM** $35   **MIP** $45

❏ **Super Sandy Set,** 1970, Green and yellow, 13.5Lx9.5Wx13H, #303 dump truck plus plastic sand hopper, Model No. 306
EX $25   **NM** $35   **MIP** $45

❏ **Telephone Truck (Fix-It),** 1954, Green, 12Lx5.5Wx5.25H, with mini tool set, new pressed steel cab design, Model No. 920
EX $75   **NM** $105   **MIP** $155

❏ **Telephone Truck (Fix-It),** 1955, Green, 12Lx5.5Wx5.25H, with mini tool set, Model No. 920
EX $75   **NM** $105   **MIP** $155

❏ **Telephone Truck (Fix-It),** 1956-57, Blue, 12Lx5.5Wx5.25H, with mini tool set, Model No. 920
EX $75   **NM** $105   **MIP** $155

❏ **The Army Cub,** 1963, Army green, 10.75Lx5Wx4.75H, windshield and tailgate raise & lower, yellow seat, no doors, Model No. 200
EX $25   **NM** $55   **MIP** $75

❏ **The Army Cub,** 1964, Army green, 10.75Lx5Wx4.75H, tailgate and windshield raises and lowers, Model No. 200
EX $25   **NM** $55   **MIP** $75

❏ **The Army Cub,** 1965, Army green, 10.75Lx5Wx4.75H, tailgate and windshield raises and lowers, Model No. 200
EX $25   **NM** $55   **MIP** $75

❏ **The Army Cub,** 1966, Army green, 10.75Lx5Wx4.75H, tailgate and windshield raises and lowers, Model No. 200
EX $25   **NM** $45   **MIP** $65

❏ **The Camper,** 1959, Red and white, 21.75Lx4.5Wx6.75H, canvas cover on truck, convertible boat & trailer, Model No. 206
EX $55   **NM** $95   **MIP** $125

❏ **The Cub Set,** 1963, Teal and white, 10.75Lx5Wx5H, converts to three variations with #250 and #325 roofs, Model No. 350
EX $55   **NM** $75   **MIP** $95

❏ **The Cub Set,** 1964, Teal and white, 10.75Lx5Wx5H, converts to three variations with #250 and #325 roofs, Model No. 350
EX $55   **NM** $75   **MIP** $95

❏ **Tilt-Top Trailer Truck With Dozer,** 1959, Yellow and green, 20.25Lx7.5Wx6H, dozer is copper with yellow plastic wheels and engine, Model No. 502
EX $55   **NM** $75   **MIP** $95

❏ **Timber Toter,** 1955, Chrome and green, 21Lx6Wx6H, with six wooden logs and chains, Model No. 714
EX $65   **NM** $135   **MIP** $175

(Randy Prasse Photo)

❏ **Timber Toter,** 1956-57, Chrome and green, 21Lx6Wx6H, with six wooden logs and chains, Model No. 714
EX $65   **NM** $135   **MIP** $175

❏ **Timber Toter,** 1958, Chrome and blue, 21Lx6Wx6.25H, with six wooden logs and chains, Model No. 714
EX $65   **NM** $135   **MIP** $175

❏ **Timber Toter,** 1959, Red and blue, 21.5Lx4.75Wx5.25H, 5 wooden logs and load chains, Model No. 714
EX $55   **NM** $75   **MIP** $95

❏ **Timber Toter,** 1960, Copper, 20.75Lx5.5Wx5.5H, plastic mirrors and horn, 5 wooden logs and chains, Model No. 323
EX $45   **NM** $65   **MIP** $85

❑ **Timber Toter,** 1961, Met. green, 23Lx5.5Wx6H, six wooden logs and chains, Model No. 406
EX $55 **NM** $75 **MIP** $95

❑ **Timber Toter,** 1962, Red, 23Lx5.5Wx6H, six wooden logs and chains, Model No. 406
EX $55 **NM** $75 **MIP** $95

❑ **Timber Toter,** 1963, Red, 23Lx5.5Wx6H, six wooden logs and chains, Model No. 406
EX $55 **NM** $75 **MIP** $95

❑ **Timber Toter,** 1965, Red and red, 23Lx6Wx5H, 5 wooden logs plus chains, Model No. 406
EX $55 **NM** $75 **MIP** $95

❑ **Timber Toter,** 1966, Red and red, 23Lx6Wx5H, 6 wooden logs & chains, Model No. 406
EX $55 **NM** $75 **MIP** $95

❑ **Timber Toter,** 1967, Red and red, 20.75Lx6.5Wx5.5H, turbine cab., 5 wooden logs and chains, Model No. 360
EX $55 **NM** $75 **MIP** $95

❑ **Timber Toter,** 1968, Blue and blue, 20.75Lx6.5Wx5.5H, turbine cab, 5 wooden logs and chains, Model No. 360
EX $45 **NM** $65 **MIP** $85

❑ **Timber Toter,** 1969, Red and red, 21.75Lx5.5Wx6.5H, typhoons design with 6 wooden logs and chain, Model No. 361
EX $25 **NM** $35 **MIP** $45

❑ **Top Chopper,** 1973, Lime green and orange, 10Lx4.5Wx5.75H, new design for 1973, Model No. 765
EX $25 **NM** $35 **MIP** $45

❑ **Tow Truck (Fix-It),** 1954, Red and red, 11.75Lx5.5Wx6H, with mini tool set. New pressed steel cab design, Model No. 910
EX $75 **NM** $105 **MIP** $155

❑ **Tow Truck (Fix-It),** 1955, Red and red, 11.75Lx5.5Wx6H, with mini tool set, Model No. 910
EX $75 **NM** $105 **MIP** $155

❑ **Tow Truck (Fix-It),** 1956-57, Blue and blue, 11.75Lx5.5Wx6H, with mini tool set, Model No. 910
EX $75 **NM** $105 **MIP** $155

❑ **Towing & Service Truck,** 1958, Green and orange, 17.5Lx6Wx7.5H, same as #210 but with tow set-up and red light on roof, Model No. 214
EX $105 **NM** $135 **MIP** $175

❑ **Tractor Trailer Truck,** 1967, Red and silver, 16.5Lx4Wx5.25H, Kom-pak design, no decals on trailer, Model No. 160
EX $25 **NM** $45 **MIP** $65

❑ **Tractor Trailer Truck,** 1967, Red and red, 21.25Lx7.75Wx5.75H, turbine cab. red, white & blue "Structo" decal on trailer, Model No. 483
EX $55 **NM** $75 **MIP** $95

❑ **Tractor Trailer Truck,** 1968, Red and silver, 16.5Lx4Wx5.25H, Kom-pak

design, with "National Freight Lines" decal on trailer, Model No. 160
EX $25 **NM** $45 **MIP** $65

❑ **Tractor Trailer Truck,** 1968, Red and red, 21.25Lx7.75Wx5.75H, turbine cab. red, white & blue "Structo" decal on trailer, Model No. 483
EX $55 **NM** $75 **MIP** $95

❑ **Tractor Trailer Truck,** 1969, White and red, 16.5Lx4.25Wx5.5H, Kom-pak design with red trailer & white doors, Model No. 160
EX $25 **NM** $35 **MIP** $45

❑ **Tractor Trailer Truck,** 1969, Red and red, 22Lx5.5Wx8H, typhoons design, Model No. 373
EX $25 **NM** $35 **MIP** $45

❑ **Tractor Trailer Truck,** 1970, White and red, 16.5Lx4.25Wx5.5H, Kom-pak design with red trailer & white doors, Model No. 160
EX $25 **NM** $35 **MIP** $45

❑ **Tractor-Trailer Truck,** 1972, Blue and silver, 16.5Lx4.25Wx5.5H, hurricanes design with structo van lines on trailer, Model No. 861
EX $15 **NM** $25 **MIP** $35

❑ **Tractor-Trailer Truck,** 1973, Blue and silver, 16.5Lx4.25Wx5.5H, hurricanes design with structo van lines on trailer, Model No. 861
EX $15 **NM** $25 **MIP** $35

❑ **Trailer Truck,** 1956-57, Chrome and red, 24.5Lx6Wx5.5H, same as #702 but with chrome cab and lift gate, Model No. 705
EX $95 **NM** $155 **MIP** $205

❑ **Trailer W/Mechanical Lift,** 1958, Blue and yellow, 50.75Lx5.5Wx5.75H, mechanical lift gate with mini grocery freight, Model No. 936
EX $95 **NM** $155 **MIP** $195

❑ **Transcontinental Express Fleet,** 1960, Varies, 20 pc. set includes auto transport, express, steel trailer, Model No. 904
EX $115 **NM** $155 **MIP** $195

❑ **Transcontinental Express Fleet,** 1961, Varies, 25 pc. set includes auto transport, express, cattle trailers, Model No. 906
EX $125 **NM** $155 **MIP** $195

❑ **Transcontinental Express Semi,** 1960, Blue and silver, 26Lx6Wx8.5H, unpainted aluminum trailer with blue decals, Model No. 905
EX $55 **NM** $95 **MIP** $125

❑ **Transport Trailer,** 1951, Blue and red, 21.5Lx5.5Wx7.5H, blue cast cab with red trailer, no hubcaps, Model No. 700
EX $95 **NM** $135 **MIP** $205

❑ **Transport Trailer,** 1952, Blue and red, 21.5Lx5.5Wx7.5H, blue cast cab with red trailer, no hubcaps, Model No. 700
EX $95 **NM** $135 **MIP** $205

❑ **Transport Trailer,** 1953, White and red, 21.5Lx5.5Wx7.5H, w/hubcaps, Model No. 700
EX $75 **NM** $125 **MIP** $195

❑ **Transport Trailer,** 1954, White and red, 21.5Lx5.5Wx7.5H, w/hubcaps, Model No. 700
EX $75 **NM** $125 **MIP** $195

❑ **Transport Trailer,** 1955, Yellow and red, 21Lx5Wx7.5H, new pressed steel cab design, Model No. 950
EX $75 **NM** $135 **MIP** $195

❑ **Transport Truck,** 1956-57, Red and yellow, 21Lx5Wx7.5H, Model No. 950
EX $75 **NM** $105 **MIP** $135

❑ **Tree Trimming Truck,** 1959, Copper and green, 12Lx4.25Wx12.5H, green boom arm and basket, Model No. 939
EX $35 **NM** $55 **MIP** $75

❑ **Triple Terrific 3 Pack,** 1972, 14Lx5Wx5H, one each #215, #216, #217 in a 3 pack store display box, Model No. 220
EX n/a **NM** n/a **MIP** $150

❑ **Triple Terrific 3 Pack,** 1972, 14Lx5Wx5H, one each #250, #251, #252 in a 3 pack store display box, Model No. 262
EX n/a **NM** n/a **MIP** $150

❑ **Triple Terrific 3 Pack,** 1973, 14Lx5Wx5H, one each #250, #251, #252 in a 3 pack store display box, Model No. 262
EX n/a **NM** n/a **MIP** $150

❑ **Triple Terrific 3 Pack,** 1973, 14Lx5Wx5H, one each #215, #216, #217 in a 3 pack store display box, Model No. 220
EX n/a **NM** n/a **MIP** $150

❑ **Typhoon Car Carrier,** 1973, Red and yellow, 22.5Lx5.5Wx6H, typhoon design with 3 plastic cars and ramp, Model No. 330
EX $45 **NM** $55 **MIP** $65

❑ **Typhoon Cement Mixer,** 1973, Blue and white, 13.5Lx6.75Wx7.5H, typhoon design with turbine cab, Model No. 325
EX $15 **NM** $25 **MIP** $35

❑ **Typhoon Construction Set,** 1969, Grey and orange, 3 pc. set including #270, #311, #501, Model No. 966
EX $65 **NM** $85 **MIP** $105

❑ **Typhoon Dump Truck,** 1973, Yellow, 13.5Lx6Wx5.5H, typhoon design, Model No. 303
EX $15 **NM** $25 **MIP** $35

❑ **Typhoon Emergency Truck,** 1973, White, 12.5Lx6Wx6.5H, typhoon design with 1 red ladder on top, Model No. 358
EX $25 **NM** $35 **MIP** $45

❑ **Typhoon Fire Rescue Truck,** 1973, Red, 12.5Lx6Wx6.5H, typhoon design with 3 ladders, Model No. 353
EX $25 **NM** $35 **MIP** $45

❑ **Typhoon Hydraulic Dump,** 1973, Blue and white, 13Lx6Wx6H, typhoon design with turbine cab, Model No. 311
EX $15 **NM** $25 **MIP** $35

❏ **U.S. Army Combat Set,** 1964, Army green, includes #315 & searchlight, #410, 8 plastic soldiers, Model No. 920
EX $105   NM $155   MIP $195

❏ **U.S. Army Combat Set,** 1965, Army green, includes #315 & searchlight, #410, 8 plastic soldiers, Model No. 920
EX $105   NM $155   MIP $195

❏ **U.S. Army Combat Set Showcase Display,** 1965, Rare, boxed set for dealer trade show & store display, Model No. 9201
EX $175   NM $215   MIP $275

❏ **U.S. Army Missile Launcher,** 1964, Army green, 17.25Lx6.5Wx7H, missile launcher on back, 3 missiles, 2 outriggers, Model No. 410
EX $45   NM $65   MIP $95

❏ **U.S. Army Missile Launcher,** 1965, Army green, 17.25Lx6.5Wx7H, missile launcher on back, 3 missiles, 2 outriggers, Model No. 410
EX $45   NM $65   MIP $95

❏ **U.S. Mail Van,** 1965, White and blue, 12Lx5.75Wx6.5H, includes 2 plastic mail bags, Model No. 710
EX $65   NM $85   MIP $105

❏ **U.S. Mail Van,** 1966, Blue and white, 12Lx5.75Wx6.5H, includes 2 cloth mail bags, Model No. 710
EX $65   NM $85   MIP $105

❏ **US Main Truck,** 1958, Blue and red, 12.25Lx5.25Wx6.5H, Model No. 943
EX $95   NM $125   MIP $175

❏ **USA Guided Missile Launcher,** 1958, Green, 12.75Lx5.25Wx6H, with 2 plastic missiles, Model No. 906
EX $65   NM $105   MIP $155

❏ **USA Searchlight Truck,** 1958, Green, 12.75Lx5.25Wx7.25H, with battery operated searchlight, Model No. 907
EX $75   NM $115   MIP $175

❏ **USA Transport Truck,** 1958, Green, 12.5Lx5.25Wx7.5H, with canvas top, Model No. 905
EX $55   NM $95   MIP $135

❏ **Utility (Garbage) Truck,** 1951, Red and blue, 21.5Lx6.5Wx7.5H, with plastic fireball motor under the hood, Model No. 500
EX $95   NM $155   MIP $205

❏ **Utility (Garbage) Truck,** 1952, Red and blue, 21.5Lx6.5Wx7.5H, with plastic fireball motor under the hood, Model No. 500
EX $95   NM $155   MIP $205

❏ **Utility (Garbage) Truck,** 1953, Red and white, 21.5Lx6.5Wx7.5H, with plastic fireball motor under the hood, Model No. 500
EX $95   NM $155   MIP $205

❏ **Utility (Garbage) Truck,** 1954, Red and white, 21.5Lx6.5Wx7.5H, with plastic fireball motor under the hood, Model No. 500
EX $95   NM $155   MIP $205

❏ **Utility (Garbage) Truck,** 1955, Blue and grey, 21.5Lx6.5Wx7.5H, with plastic fireball motor under the hood, Model No. 500
EX $95   NM $155   MIP $205

❏ **Utility (Garbage) Truck,** 1956-57, Blue and grey, 21.5Lx6.5Wx7.5H, with plastic fireball motor under the hood, Model No. 500
EX $95   NM $155   MIP $205

❏ **Vacation Set,** 1973, Orange and green, 22Lx5.75Wx10H, includes #758 and #835, Model No. 962
EX $25   NM $35   MIP $45

❏ **Van Truck,** 1965, Red and white, 22Lx6.5Wx8H, red structo van line decals on side, Model No. 506
EX $45   NM $65   MIP $85

❏ **Van Truck,** 1965, Red and white, 16.5Lx4Wx5H, red structo van line decals on side, Model No. 145
EX $25   NM $45   MIP $65

❏ **Van Truck,** 1966, Red and white, 16.5Lx4Wx5.25H, Kom-pak design, Model No. 145
EX $25   NM $45   MIP $65

❏ **Van Truck,** 1966, Dk. blue and lt. blue, 22Lx6.5Wx8H, scarce 2 tone blue color combination, Model No. 506
EX $55   NM $75   MIP $95

❏ **Vista Dome Army Truck,** 1964, Army green, 8.75Lx3.5Wx4H, clear plastic cover over bed, 2 plastic soldiers, Model No. 115
EX $15   NM $25   MIP $55

❏ **Vista Dome Army Truck,** 1965, Army green, 8.75Lx3.5Wx4H, clear plastic cover over bed, 2 plastic soldiers, Model No. 115
EX $15   NM $25   MIP $55

❏ **Vista Dome Horse Van,** 1964, Met. gold, 21.75Lx5.5Wx6H, ramp on side and back of trailer, 4 plastic horses, Model No. 412
EX $45   NM $65   MIP $85

❏ **Vista Dome Horse Van,** 1965, Teal and teal, 21.75Lx5.5Wx6H, ramp on side and back of trailer, 4 pc. fence, 4 plastic horses, Model No. 412
EX $45   NM $65   MIP $85

❏ **Vista Dome Horse Van,** 1966, Met. blue and met. blue, 21.75Lx6Wx6H, 2 ramp doors and 2 horses, 2 colts, Model No. 417
EX $45   NM $65   MIP $85

❏ **Vista Dome Horse Van,** 1967, Met. gold, 21.75Lx6Wx6H, 2 ramp doors and 2 horses, 2 colts, Model No. 322
EX $45   NM $65   MIP $85

❏ **Vista Dome Horse Van,** 1968, Met. gold, 21.75Lx6Wx6H, 2 ramp doors and 2 horses, 2 colts, Model No. 322
EX $45   NM $65   MIP $85

❏ **Vista Dome Horse Van,** 1969, Met. gold, 22Lx5.5Wx6.5H, typhoons design with 4 horses, Model No. 322
EX $35   NM $45   MIP $55

❏ **Vista Dome Horse Van,** 1970, Met. gold, 22Lx5.5Wx6.5H, typhoons design with 4 horses, Model No. 322
EX $35   NM $45   MIP $55

❏ **Vista Dome Horse Van,** 1972, Met. gold, 22Lx5.5Wx6H, typhoon design with 4 plastic horses, Model No. 320
EX $35   NM $45   MIP $55

❏ **Vista Dome Horse Van,** 1973, Met. gold, 22Lx5.5Wx6H, typhoon design with 4 plastic horses, Model No. 320
EX $35   NM $45   MIP $55

❏ **Vista Dome Kennel Truck,** 1964, Teal and yellow, 8.75Lx3.5Wx4H, clear plastic cover over bed, 6 plastic dogs, Model No. 130
EX $15   NM $35   MIP $65

❏ **Vista Dome Kennel Truck,** 1965, Blue and white, 8.75Lx3.5Wx4H, clear plastic cover over bed, 6 plastic dogs, Model No. 130
EX $15   NM $35   MIP $65

❏ **Vista Dome Livestock Truck,** 1964, Blue and yellow, 8.75Lx3.5Wx4H, clear plastic cover over bed, 2 plastic animals, Model No. 120
EX $15   NM $35   MIP $65

❏ **Vista Dome Troop Carrier,** 1964, Army green, 13.25Lx5.25Wx5.5H, clear plastic cover over bed, 8 plastic soldiers, Model No. 315
EX $55   NM $75   MIP $95

❏ **Vista Dome Troop Carrier,** 1965, Army green, 13.25Lx5.25Wx5.75H, clear plastic cover over bed, 8 plastic soldiers, Model No. 315
EX $55   NM $75   MIP $95

❏ **Vista Dome Troop Carrier,** 1966, Army green, 13.25Lx5.25Wx5.75H, clear plastic cover over bed, 6 plastic soldiers, Model No. 315
EX $55   NM $75   MIP $95

❏ **Waggin' Wagon,** 1972, Lime green and white, 9.25Lx4Wx4H, hurricanes design with clear cover & 6 dogs, Model No. 837
EX $10   NM $20   MIP $30

❏ **Waggin' Wagon,** 1973, Lime green and white, 9.25Lx4Wx4H, hurricanes design with clear cover & 6 dogs, Model No. 837
EX $10   NM $20   MIP $30

❏ **Waggin' Wagon Kennel Truck,** 1969, Yellow, 9.25Lx4Wx4H, hurricanes design with clear kennel and 6 dogs, Model No. 837
EX $15   NM $25   MIP $35

❏ **Waggin' Wagon Kennel Truck,** 1970, Yellow, 9.25Lx4Wx4H, hurricanes design with clear kennel and 6 dogs, Model No. 837
EX $15   NM $25   MIP $35

❏ **Washer-Dryer Combination,** 1959, Pink and grey, 7.25Lx8Wx10H, washes & spins, battery operated, Model No. 16
EX $15   NM $55   MIP $75

Weekender, 1965, Teal and white, 12Lx5.75Wx7H, canvas awning, white plastic interior, Model No. 700
EX $55   **NM** $75   **MIP** $95

Weekender, 1966, Teal and white, 12Lx5.75Wx7H, canvas awning, white plastic interior, Model No. 700
EX $55   **NM** $75   **MIP** $95

Weekender, 1967, Teal, 12Lx5.75Wx6.5H, molded built-in refrigerator & sink detail, Model No. 708
EX $55   **NM** $75   **MIP** $95

Weird Wagon, 1971, Red, 2.75Lx3.5Wx3H, 2 wheeled design with WV bug style, Model No. 217
EX $10   **NM** $15   **MIP** $20

Weird Wagon, 1972, Red, 2.75Lx3.5Wx3H, 2 wheeled design with WV bug style, Model No. 217
EX $10   **NM** $15   **MIP** $20

Weird Wagon, 1973, Red, 2.75Lx3.5Wx3H, 2 wheeled design with WV bug style, Model No. 217
EX $10   **NM** $15   **MIP** $20

Western Auto Moving Van, 1956-57, Chrome and white, 24Lx6Wx8.5H, private label. Same body as #710 deluxe moving van. Red doors, Model No. 711
EX $125   **NM** $185   **MIP** $225

Wrecker, 1961, White, 12Lx5.75Wx6.5H, crank operated winch, plastic mirrors, wipers & horns, Model No. 302
EX $55   **NM** $75   **MIP** $95

Wrecker, 1962, White, 12Lx5.75Wx6.5H, crank operated winch, plastic mirrors, wipers & horns, Model No. 302
EX $55   **NM** $75   **MIP** $95

Wrecker, 1963, White, 13Lx5.25Wx5.5H, door windows and interior detail, black metal boom arm, Model No. 301
EX $55   **NM** $75   **MIP** $95

Wrecker, 1964, White and black, 13.25Lx5.25Wx5.5H, door windows and interior detail, black metal boom arm, Model No. 301
EX $55   **NM** $75   **MIP** $95

Wrecker, 1966, White and red, 12.5Lx5.25Wx6.25H, red light on roof (non-operable), red interior & boom, Model No. 312
EX $45   **NM** $65   **MIP** $95

Wrecker Truck, 1951, Red and grey, 12.25Lx5.5Wx5.25H, wind-up motor and chain winch, Model No. 822
EX $95   **NM** $125   **MIP** $175

Wrecker Truck, 1952, Red and grey, 12.25Lx5.5Wx5.25H, wind-up motor and chain winch, Model No. 822
EX $95   **NM** $125   **MIP** $175

Wrecker Truck, 1953, White and orange, 12.25Lx5.5Wx5.25H, wind-up motor and chain winch, Model No. 822
EX $115   **NM** $155   **MIP** $195

Wrecker Truck, 1954, Various, 7.5Lx2.5Wx2.25H, same scale #21 pick-up but with cast tow boom arm, Model No. 30
EX $25   **NM** $55   **MIP** $75

Wrecker Truck, 1954, White and orange, 12.25Lx5.5Wx5.25H, wind-up motor and chain winch, Model No. 822
EX $115   **NM** $155   **MIP** $195

Wrecker Truck, 1955, White and orange, 12Lx5.5Wx5.25H, shown in catalog with green cab but have not seen, Model No. 822
EX $115   **NM** $155   **MIP** $195

Wrecker Truck, 1956-57, White and orange, 12Lx5.5Wx5.25H, wind-up, Model No. 822
EX $115   **NM** $155   **MIP** $195

Wrecker Truck, 1964, White and grey, 9.25Lx3.5Wx3.5H, with metal tow boom and hook, Model No. 110
EX $15   **NM** $25   **MIP** $55

Wrecker Truck, 1965, White and red, 12.5Lx5.25Wx6.25H, red light on roof (non-operable), red metal boom arm, Model No. 302
EX $55   **NM** $75   **MIP** $95

Wrecker Truck, 1965, Red and white, 9.25Lx3.5Wx3.5H, with metal tow boom and hook, Model No. 110
EX $15   **NM** $25   **MIP** $55

Wrecker Truck, 1965, White and red, 10.75Lx4.75Wx5.75H, red convertible roof, seats and metal boom arm, Model No. 251
EX $55   **NM** $75   **MIP** $95

Wrecker Truck, 1966, Yellow and red, 9.25Lx3.5Wx3.5H, Kom-pak design with red boom arm, Model No. 110
EX $15   **NM** $25   **MIP** $45

Wrecker Truck, 1966, White and black, 10.75Lx4.75Wx5.75H, black convertible roof and boom, red seat, Model No. 251
EX $35   **NM** $55   **MIP** $75

Wrecker Truck, 1967, White and black, 10.75Lx4.75Wx5.75H, black convertible roof and boom, red seat, Model No. 205
EX $45   **NM** $65   **MIP** $85

Wrecker Truck, 1967, White and grey, 9.25Lx3.5Wx3.5H, Kom-pak design with red boom arm, Model No. 112
EX $15   **NM** $25   **MIP** $45

Wrecker Truck, 1967, White, 12.5Lx5.25Wx6.25H, red light (non-operable) on roof, POW-R-R-R sound, Model No. 415
EX $45   **NM** $65   **MIP** $95

Wrecker Truck, 1968, Red, 15Lx5.5Wx6.25H, white boom arm, red light (non-operable) on roof, Model No. 264
EX $45   **NM** $65   **MIP** $85

Wrecker Truck, 1968, White and black, 10.75Lx4.75Wx5.75H, black convert-

ible roof and boom, red seat, Model No. 205
EX $45   **NM** $65   **MIP** $85

Wrecker Truck, 1968, White, 12.5Lx5.25Wx6.25H, red light (non-operable) on roof, POW-R-R-R sound, Model No. 415
EX $45   **NM** $65   **MIP** $95

Wrecker Truck, 1968, White and red, 9.25Lx3.5Wx3.5H, Kom-pak design with red boom arm, Model No. 112
EX $15   **NM** $25   **MIP** $45

Wrecker Truck, 1969, Yellow and red, 12.5Lx6Wx6.25H, typhoons design with red tow boom & crank winch, Model No. 277
EX $25   **NM** $35   **MIP** $45

TONKA

❏ **3-in-1 Hi-way Service Truck,** 1957, w/two snowblades, 13" long
EX $275   NM $400   MIP $700

❏ **Aerial Ladder Truck,** 1957
EX $200   NM $300   MIP $500

❏ **Allied Van Lines,** 1955
EX $150   NM $275   MIP $500

❏ **Big Mike Dual Hydraulic Dump Truck,** 1957, 14" long
EX $325   NM $595   MIP $1000

❏ **Dump,** 1955
EX $100   NM $150   MIP $350

❏ **Farm Stake Truck,** 1957
EX $190   NM $375   MIP $480

❏ **Freighter,** 1955
EX $90   NM $135   MIP $280

❏ **Gasoline Truck,** 1957, 15" long
EX $350   NM $525   MIP $1000

❏ **Green Giant Semi Reefer,** 1956
EX $155   NM $350   MIP $600

❏ **Hook and Ladder,** 1955
EX $100   NM $300   MIP $450

❏ **Jolly Green Giant Special,** 1960, white, green stake racks
EX $375   NM $450   MIP $850

❏ **Livestock Truck,** 1955
EX $110   NM $200   MIP $350

❏ **Loboy and Shovel,** 1955
EX $150   NM $300   MIP $450

(KP Photo)

❏ **No. 0001 Service Truck,** 1959, 12-3/4" long. Blue body, square box bed with "Tonka Service" decals, whitewall tires, solid silver hubs, removeable ladder, plastic windshield
EX $100   NM $150   MIP $350

❏ **No. 0001 Service Truck,** 1960, Blue body, square box bed with removeable ladder. "Tonka Service" decals, whitewall tires, plastic windshield
EX $100   NM $150   MIP $350

(ToyShop File Photo)

❏ **No. 0002 Pickup,** 1960, Gold body, whitewall tires, solid silver hubs, opening tailgate, trailer hitch, plastic windshield
EX $100   NM $200   MIP $375

❏ **No. 0002 Pickup,** 1961
EX $100   NM $190   MIP $320

❏ **No. 0002 Pickup Truck,** 1958 Next Generation Cars, Dark blue body, opening tailgate, trailer hitch
EX $100   NM $150   MIP $300

❏ **No. 0003 Utility Truck,** 1958 Next Generation Cars, Red cab, white flatbed
EX $100   NM $150   MIP $300

❏ **No. 0004 Farm Stake,** 1961
EX $85   NM $175   MIP $370

❏ **No. 0004 Farm Stake Truck,** 1958 Next Generation Cars, "Tonka Farms" bull decal on sides, white removeable stake panels
EX $100   NM $150   MIP $300

❏ **No. 0004 Farm Stake Truck,** 1960, Whitewall tires, five-spoke silver hubs, removeable stack sections, windshield plastic
EX $100   NM $200   MIP $325

(KP Photo)

❏ **No. 0005 Sportsman,** 1959, Tan body, camper top, whitewall tires, solid silver hubs, white plastic boat attaches to topper with rubber straps
EX $100   NM $175   MIP $350

❏ **No. 0005 Sportsman Pickup w/Topper,** 1958 Next Generation Cars, 12-3/4" long, dark blue body with camper topper, opening tailgate
EX $150   NM $225   MIP $450

❏ **No. 0006 Dump,** 1961
EX $75   NM $100   MIP $250

❏ **No. 0006 Dump Truck,** 1958 Next Generation Cars, Red cab, two-position tailgate on dumper bed
EX $100   NM $150   MIP $300

❏ **No. 0006 Dump Truck,** 1960, Silver five-spoke hubs, red cab, windshield plastic, opening tailgate on dumper bed
EX $75   NM $125   MIP $290

❏ **No. 0008 Logger,** 1960, Red cab, includes square and round sanded "logs,"
EX $150   NM $225   MIP $300

(KP Photo)

❏ **No. 0012 Road Grader,** 1958 Next Generation Cars, Orange body with rotating and tilting blade, working steering, floating rear wheels
EX $75   NM $112   MIP $150

❏ **No. 0014 Dragline,** 1959, 20" long. Rolling treads, working scoop that rotates on base, bucket actually scoops. Black nylon cord "cables" control the bucket
EX $100   NM $175   MIP $375

❏ **No. 0014 Dragline,** 1961, yellow
EX $100   NM $150   MIP $250

❏ **No. 0016 Air Express,** 1959, Dark blue body, square box bed, whitewall tires, "Air Express" decals on sides, plastic windshield
EX $350   NM $425   MIP $700

❏ **No. 0018 Wrecker,** 1960, white sidewalls
EX $100   NM $150   MIP $375

❏ **No. 0018 Wrecker,** 1961
EX $100   NM $250   MIP $400

❏ **No. 0018 Wrecker Truck,** 1958 Next Generation Cars, White body, "Triple A" decal on sides, dual rear wheels, red dome light, working winch for towing
EX $100   NM $250   MIP $450

❏ **No. 0020 Hydraulic Dump,** 1960, Dark gold body, working dumper with lever and hydraulic lifter, two-position tailgate on dumper
EX $75   NM $150   MIP $300

(KP Photo)

❏ **No. 0020 Hydraulic Dump,** 1961
EX $75   NM $110   MIP $250

❏ **No. 0020 Hydraulic Dump Truck,** 1958 Next Generation Cars
EX $125   NM $175   MIP $275

❏ **No. 0022 Deluxe Sportman,** 1961
EX $100   NM $200   MIP $450

❏ **No. 0022 Deluxe Sportsman,** 1959, Blue pickup truck with white cab roof, whitewall tires, silver rims, boat trailer with plastic boat,
EX $150   NM $325   MIP $500

VEHICLES

No. 0022 Deluxe Sportsman, 1960, Blue pickup truck with white cab roof, whitewall tires, silver rims, boat trailer with plastic boat,
EX $100   NM $250   MIP $400

(ToyShop File Photo)

No. 0028 Pickup & Trailer, 1960, Bronze/gold truck towing stakeside trailer with white plastic steer in back. End panel in trailer lifts out
EX $100   NM $150   MIP $300

No. 0028 Pickup with Stake Trailer and Animal, 1958 Next Generation Cars, Standard dark blue pickup, red stake trailer, plastic livestock animal, stake tailgate on trailer lifts for loading and unloading
EX $125   NM $175   MIP $350

No. 0029 Sportsman Truck w/Box Trailer, 1958 Next Generation Cars, Dark blue Sportsman edition pickup, dark blue trailer with opening tailgate
EX $150   NM $225   MIP $400

No. 0030 Tandem Platform Stake, 1959, 28-1/4" long
EX $240   NM $450   MIP $800

No. 0032 Stock Rack Truck, 1958 Next Generation Cars, White cab and chassis, tall, removeable red stake sections
EX $175   NM $300   MIP $500

No. 0033 Gasoline Truck, 1958 Next Generation Cars, hinged back door, hose and nozzle
EX $350   NM $500   MIP $900

No. 0034 Deluxe Sportsman with Boat Trailer, 1958 Next Generation Cars, 22-3/4" long. Red truck with white cab roof, red trailer with plastic fishing boat and attachable motor
EX $150   NM $325   MIP $750

(KP Photo)

No. 0035 Farm Stake, 1958 Next Generation Cars, w/two-horse trailer, 21-3/4" long. Trailer includes two plastic horses
EX $125   NM $250   MIP $450

No. 0035 Farm Stake and Horse Trailer, 1960
EX $125   NM $180   MIP $350

No. 0035 Farm Stake Truck and Horse Trailer, 1961
EX $100   NM $180   MIP $350

No. 0036 Livestock Van, 1958 Next Generation Cars, Red cab and trailer with opening rear ramp and floating suspension
EX $175   NM $250   MIP $450

No. 0037 Thunderbird Express, 1958 Next Generation Cars, White cab and freight trailer with fold-down wheels and opening rear doors
EX $150   NM $300   MIP $600

No. 0037 Thunderbird Express, 1960, Red cab with white roof, red trailer with white stripe and "Thunderbird" decal. Floating tandem dual wheels on trailer
EX $150   NM $350   MIP $550

(KP Photo)

No. 0039 Allied Van, 1961, Orange cab and trailer with "Allied Van Lines" decals. Black bumper on cab, blackwall tires on cab and trailer
EX $120   NM $250   MIP $450

No. 0039 Nationwide Moving Van, 1958 Next Generation Cars, 24-1/4" long, white cab and trailer with full-width doors
EX $250   NM $475   MIP $800

No. 0040 Car Carrier, 1960, Yellow cab with trailer includes three plastic 1960 Ford Falcon cars. Moveable ramp for loading and unloading
EX $100   NM $225   MIP $450

No. 0040 Car Carrier, 1961
EX $100   NM $250   MIP $450

No. 0041 Boat Transport, 1960, 38" long. Blue truck with semi-trailer that stacks four plastic boats virtually upright, with a bar at the front for storing the outboard motors
EX $250   NM $450   MIP $850

No. 0041 Boat Transport Truck, 1961
EX $150   NM $300   MIP $650

(KP Photo)

No. 0041 Hi-Way Service Truck, 1958 Next Generation Cars, Orange dump truck with two-position tailgate, drop side bed, scraper blade and plastic road signs
EX $100   NM $200   MIP $400

No. 0043 Shovel & Carry-All Trailer, 1958 Next Generation Cars, Orange cab and trailer, steam shovel with black rubber treads
EX $200   NM $300   MIP $500

No. 0044 Dragline & Trailer, 1959, 26-1/4" long
EX $150   NM $275   MIP $400

No. 0045 Big Mike Dual Hydraulic Dump Truck, 1958 Next Generation Cars, with "V" snow plow, and "twin hydraulic action"
EX $375   NM $675   MIP $1000

(Harvey K Rainess)

No. 0046 Suburban Pumper, 1958 Next Generation Cars, Bright red truck with miniature hydrant that could be hooked up to a garden hose
EX $175   NM $225   MIP $450

(Harvey K Rainess)

No. 0046 Suburban Pumper, 1960
EX $100   NM $250   MIP $350

No. 0048 Aerial Ladder, 1960
EX $125   NM $250   MIP $350

No. 0048 Aerial Ladder, 1961
EX $125   NM $200   MIP $450

No. 0048 Hydraulic Aerial Ladder, 1958 Next Generation Cars, Bright red cab and trailer with extending ladder to 36"
EX $100   NM $250   MIP $450

No. 005 Sportsman, 1960
EX $100   NM $275   MIP $400

No. 005 Sportsman, 1961
EX $100   NM $150   MIP $375

No. 0065 Trailer, 1955, stake side
EX $30   NM $45   MIP $60

No. 0086 Mini-Tonka Van, 1964, 16" long. Blue "new style" cab with white trailer. Opening rear doors on trailer. This cab style became common for many of Tonka's "mini" series of vehicles
EX $36   NM $54   MIP $72

No. 0090 Mini-Tonka Livestock Van, 1964, 16" long. New-style semi cab (cabover with large windshield), stake sided, closed-top trailer with opening rear door
EX $50   NM $75   MIP $100

No. 0096 Mini-Tonka Carrier, 1964, 18-1/2" long, two plastic Corvette Stingray cars
EX $50   NM $75   MIP $150

No. 0100 Bulldozer, 1960, 8-7/8" long, plated roller wheels only in 1960. Black rubber treads, 3-position blade
EX $75   NM $125   MIP $200

No. 0100 Steam Shovel, 1947, 20-3/4" long
EX $135   NM $200   MIP $350

❑ **No. 0100 Stearn Shovel Deluxe**, 1949, 22" long
EX $100   NM $250   MIP $400

❑ **No. 0105 Rescue Squad**, 1960, 13-3/4" long. White truck body with square box bed. Silver siren on driver's side of hood, red dome light, Civil Defence "CD" decals on doors, "Rescue Squad" with red cross decals on back, red plastic boat attached with rubber straps on top, removeable ladder
EX $100   NM $250   MIP $450

❑ **No. 0110 Fisherman Pick-up**, 1960, 14" long. Blue and white two-tone body and topper. Opening tailgate, topper with "Fisherman" decal
EX $100   NM $175   MIP $375

❑ **No. 0115 Power Boom Loader**, 1960, 1960 only, 18-1/2" long. Blue flatbed truck with working clamp and winch to pick up logs, pipe, etc. Whitewall tires, plastic windshield
EX $300   NM $650   MIP $1000

❑ **No. 0116 Dump Truck with Sand-loader**, 1961, 23-1/4" long
EX $100   NM $175   MIP $395

❑ **No. 0117 Boat Service Truck**, 1961, 1961 only. Included blue fleetside pickup truck with white cab roof, silver hubs, whitewall tires, blue trailer with three plastic boats stacked horizontally
EX $100   NM $250   MIP $450

❑ **No. 0118 Giant Dozer**, 1961, 12-1/2" long. A king-sized version of the regular dozer,
EX $70   NM $100   MIP $250

❑ **No. 012 Road Grader**, 1961, 17" long. Yellow cab and body with steerable front wheels, tilting and rotating scraper blade, and floating rear wheels
EX $75   NM $100   MIP $200

(KP Photo)

❑ **No. 0120 Cement Mixer**, 1960, 15-1/2" long. Red body, plastic mixer and hopper, tilting bed, blackwall tires
EX $100   NM $150   MIP $300

❑ **No. 0120 Cement Mixer**, 1961, 15-1/2" long. Red body, plastic mixer and hopper, tilting bed, adjustable chute for cement. Mixer geared to turn as truck moves
EX $100   NM $150   MIP $300

❑ **No. 0120 Shovel and Carry-All (Lo Boy)**, 1956, 33" long total
EX $188   NM $280   MIP $475

❑ **No. 0120 Tractor and Carry-All Trailer**, 1949, w/No. 50 Steam Shovel.
EX $155   NM $280   MIP $475

❑ **No. 0125 Lowboy and Bulldozer**, 1960, 26-1/4" long. Light green cab, trailer, and bulldozer. Solid rubber tires without hubs on rear of trailer. Bulldozer with 3-position blade
EX $190   NM $375   MIP $675

❑ **No. 0125 Tractor & Carry-All Trailer**, 1949, w/No. 100 Steam Shovel
EX $150   NM $250   MIP $550

❑ **No. 0130 Deluxe Fisherman**, 1960, New boat and trailer for this year (trailer stayed in lineup until the 1970s). Blue "Fisherman" pickup with white cab roof and white topper, larger white and red plastic boat on blue trailer with working winch
EX $150   NM $350   MIP $550

❑ **No. 0130 Deluxe Fisherman**, 1961, 27-5/8" long in toto. Same as previous year's model, that is, a fleetside pickup with topper, but this time in red and white rather than blue and white
EX $150   NM $350   MIP $550

❑ **No. 0130 Tractor-Carry-All Trailer**, 1949, 30-1/2" long
EX $100   NM $150   MIP $350

❑ **No. 0134 Grading Service Truck, Trailer and Bulldozer**, 1961, 25-1/2" long total. Includes yellow dump truck with red dumper bed, yellow trailer and bulldozer with 3-position blade
EX $100   NM $150   MIP $350

❑ **No. 0135 Mobile Dragline**, 1960, Orange cab, flatbed section and crane cab with black boom and bucket. Bucket operates with cords and levers, and swivels on base attached to truck
EX $100   NM $250   MIP $450

❑ **No. 0135 Mobile Dragline**, 1961
EX $100   NM $250   MIP $450

❑ **No. 0136 Houseboat Set**, 1961, 29" long total. Includes red and white "Fisherman" pickup with red tilt-bed boat trailer and plastic (floating) houseboat
EX $200   NM $400   MIP $800

(KP Photo)

❑ **No. 0140 Sanitary Truck**, 1960
EX $350   NM $550   MIP $900

(Patrick O'Neil)

❑ **No. 0140 Sanitary Truck**, 1961, 19-1/2" long. White cab and rounded garbage section. Swinging rear door, hopper bucket raises up to drop garbage in truck
EX $400   NM $700   MIP $1500

(KP Photo)

❑ **No. 0140 Tonka Toy Transport Van**, 1949, 22-1/4" long
EX $150   NM $300   MIP $500

❑ **No. 0142 Mobile Clam**, 1961, 27-1/4" long. Orange cab, flatbed section and crane cab. Floating rear wheels, operating "clam" style bucket (still in use on later "Mighty Tonka" models), that tripped open when pulled to top of crane boom
EX $100   NM $250   MIP $450

❑ **No. 0145 Steel Carrier Semi**, 1950, 22" long
EX $125   NM $200   MIP $350

(KP Photo)

❑ **No. 0145 Steel Carrier Truck**, 1954
EX $100   NM $185   MIP $380

❑ **No. 0145 Tanker**, 1960, first Tonka w/major use of plastic, 28" long
EX $100   NM $250   MIP $450

(Harvey K Rainess)

❑ **No. 0145 Tanker**, 1961
EX $100   NM $250   MIP $350

❑ **No. 0150 Crane and Clam**, 1947, 24" long
EX $135   NM $200   MIP $350

❑ **No. 0170 Tractor & Carry-All Trailer**, 1949, w/No. 150 Crane and Clam
EX $200   NM $300   MIP $525

❑ **No. 0175 Utility Hauler**, 1950, 12" long
EX $100   NM $150   MIP $300

(KP Photo)

VEHICLES

❑ **No. 0180 Dump Truck,** 1949, 12" long
EX $100   NM $175   MIP $375

❑ **No. 0180 Dump Truck,** 1956, 13" long
EX $100   NM $150   MIP $350

❑ **No. 0185 Express Truck,** 1950, 13-1/2" long
EX $200   NM $450   MIP $900

❑ **No. 0190 Loading Tractor,** 1949, 10-1/2" long
EX n/a   NM n/a   MIP n/a

❑ **No. 0200 Jeep Dispatcher,** 1962, 9-3/4" long
EX $50   NM $75   MIP $100

❑ **No. 0200 Jeep Dispatcher,** 1963
EX $30   NM $50   MIP $75

❑ **No. 0200 Lift Truck and Trailer,** 1948
EX $200   NM $350   MIP $600

❑ **No. 0201 Servi-I-Cae,** 1963
EX $55   NM $82   MIP $110

❑ **No. 0201 Serv-I-Car,** 1962, 9-1/8" long
EX $75   NM $125   MIP $200

(KP Photo)

❑ **No. 0249 Jeep Universal,** 1962
EX $75   NM $125   MIP $175

❑ **No. 0250 Military Tractor,** 1964, black seat
EX $55   NM $70   MIP $100

❑ **No. 0250 Tractor,** 1962, 8-5/8" long
EX $50   NM $75   MIP $100

❑ **No. 0250 Tractor,** 1963, yellow w/red seat
EX $75   NM $112   MIP $150

❑ **No. 0250 Wrecker Truck,** 1949, 12-1/2" long
EX $125   NM $250   MIP $375

❑ **No. 0251 Military Jeep Universal,** 1963, 10-1/2" long
EX $25   NM $38   MIP $50

❑ **No. 0251 Military Jeep Universal,** 1964
EX $35   NM $55   MIP $75

❑ **No. 0300 Bulldozer,** 1962
EX $50   NM $75   MIP $100

❑ **No. 0300 Bulldozer,** 1963
EX $55   NM $82   MIP $110

❑ **No. 0301 Utility Dump,** 1962, 12-1/2" long, revised Golf Club Tractor, 1961 only
EX $100   NM $150   MIP $300

(ToyShop File Photo)

❑ **No. 0302 Pickup,** 1962, Red body with silver hubs, white cab roof, opening tailgate
EX $95   NM $150   MIP $250

❑ **No. 0302 Pickup,** 1963
EX $35   NM $52   MIP $70

(KP Photo)

❑ **No. 0302 Pickup,** 1967, All red body, opening tailgate, five-spoke silver hubcaps, 12-3/4" long
EX $35   NM $55   MIP $76

❑ **No. 0304 Jeep Commander,** 1964, canvas top, 10-1/2" long
EX $30   NM $50   MIP $75

❑ **No. 0308 Stake Pickup,** 1962, 12-5/8" long
EX $50   NM $100   MIP $200

❑ **No. 0308 Stake Pickup,** 1963
EX $50   NM $95   MIP $150

❑ **No. 0315 Dump Truck,** 1964, 13-1/2" long
EX $40   NM $60   MIP $90

❑ **No. 0350 Jeep Surrey,** 1963
EX $50   NM $75   MIP $100

❑ **No. 0350 Jeep Surrey, fringe top,** 1962, 10-1/2" long
EX $75   NM $125   MIP $200

❑ **No. 0352 Loader,** 1963
EX $40   NM $60   MIP $80

❑ **No. 0354 Style-Side Pickup,** 1963, 14" long
EX $40   NM $60   MIP $125

❑ **No. 0375 Jeep Wrecker,** 1964, 11" long
EX $75   NM $130   MIP $200

❑ **No. 0380 Troop Carrier,** 1964, 14" long
EX $70   NM $100   MIP $150

❑ **No. 0384 Military Jeep & Box Trailer,** 1964, 19-3/8" overall
EX $50   NM $75   MIP $150

❑ **No. 0400 Allied Van Lines Semi,** 1950, 23-1/2" long
EX $175   NM $260   MIP $400

❑ **No. 0402 Loader,** 1962, yellow and green
EX $40   NM $60   MIP $80

❑ **No. 0404 Farm Stake Truck,** 1962
EX $50   NM $95   MIP $150

❑ **No. 0404 Farm Stake Truck,** 1963
EX $60   NM $90   MIP $150

❑ **No. 0404 Stake Truck,** 1964, red
EX $70   NM $120   MIP $170

❑ **No. 0405 Sportsman,** 1962
EX $75   NM $100   MIP $200

❑ **No. 0406 Dump Truck,** 1962
EX $75   NM $150   MIP $275

❑ **No. 0406 Dump Truck,** 1963
EX $45   NM $68   MIP $90

❑ **No. 0410 Jet Delivery Truck,** 1962, 14" long, 1962 only
EX $200   NM $350   MIP $850

❑ **No. 0420 Airlines Luggage Service,** 1962, 16-5/8 long
EX $100   NM $250   MIP $400

❑ **No. 0422 Back Hoe,** 1963, 17-1/8" long
EX $100   NM $175   MIP $350

❑ **No. 0425 Jeep Pumper,** 1963, 10-3/4" long
EX $100   NM $175   MIP $400

❑ **No. 0425 Jeep Pumper,** 1964, black steering wheel
EX $100   NM $150   MIP $275

(KP Photo)

❑ **No. 0500 Livestock Hauler Semi,** 1952, 22-1/4" long
EX $100   NM $150   MIP $350

❑ **No. 0504 Stake Pickup & Trailer,** 1964, 21-5/8" long
EX $50   NM $75   MIP $185

❑ **No. 0512 Road Grader,** 1962
EX $45   NM $68   MIP $90

❑ **No. 0512 Road Grader,** 1963, red clearance lights
EX $80   NM $120   MIP $160

❑ **No. 0514 Drag,** 1963
EX $60   NM $90   MIP $120

❑ **No. 0514 Dragline,** 1962
EX $150   NM $225   MIP $300

❑ **No. 0516 Jeep Runabout,** 1963, trailer and boat
EX $75   NM $150   MIP $300

(ToyShop File Photo)

❑ **No. 0516 Jeep Runabout, trailer, boat,** 1962, 25-5/8" long total. Jeep shown here, missing removeable canopy, and obviously, the boat and trailer
EX $75   NM $175   MIP $350

❑ **No. 0518 Wrecker,** 1962
EX $75   NM $175   MIP $325

(KP Photo)

❑ **No. 0518 Wrecker,** 1963
EX $45   NM $75   MIP $150

❑ **No. 0520 Hydraulic Dump,** 1962
EX $75   NM $100   MIP $220

❑ **No. 0520 Hydraulic Dump Truck,** 1963
EX $45   NM $68   MIP $90

(ToyShop File Photo)

❑ **No. 0520 Hydraulic Dump Truck,** 1965, Blue cab with white roof, blue dumper bed, 13-3/8" long
EX $35   NM $60   MIP $82

❑ **No. 0522 Style-Side Pickup & Stake Trailer,** 1963, 22-3/4" long total
EX $75   NM $125   MIP $250

❑ **No. 0524 Dozer Packer,** 1962, 18-1/4" long total, Packer has eleven tires, sold only in 1962
EX $100   NM $250   MIP $400

❑ **No. 0524 Dozer Packer,** 1963, yellow
EX $200   NM $300   MIP $400

❑ **No. 0525 Jeep & Horse Trailer,** 1964, 19-1/4" long total, two horses
EX $45   NM $68   MIP $135

❑ **No. 0528 Pickup & Trailer,** 1962
EX $50   NM $75   MIP $150

❑ **No. 0530 Camper,** 1962, 14" long
EX $75   NM $150   MIP $250

❑ **No. 0530 Camper,** 1963
EX $25   NM $38   MIP $50

(KP Photo)

❑ **No. 0534 Trencher,** 1963, 18-1/4" long
EX $40   NM $75   MIP $150

❑ **No. 0536 Giant Dozer,** 1963
EX $110   NM $160   MIP $225

❑ **No. 0550 Grain Hauler Semi,** 1952, 22-1/4" long
EX $125   NM $180   MIP $350

❑ **No. 0550-6 Tonka "Cargo King",** 1956, 23-1/2" long. Red cab, open-top silver trailer, opening rear door
EX $145   NM $230   MIP $355

❑ **No. 0575 Logger Semi,** 1953, 22-1/4" long
EX $125   NM $180   MIP $350

❑ **No. 0575 Logger Semi,** 1953, wood flat bed
EX $125   NM $180   MIP $350

❑ **No. 0575-6 Tonka Logger,** 1956, 13-1/2" long. Red cab, logging trailer includes 9 sanded dowel logs. Silver five-hole hubs
EX $130   NM $240   MIP $360

❑ **No. 0600 Grader,** 1955
EX $75   NM $125   MIP $200

❑ **No. 0600 Road Grader,** 1953, 17" long
EX $50   NM $75   MIP $100

❑ **No. 0600-6 Road Grader,** 1956, 17" long. Steerable front wheels, tilting and rotating blade, floating rear wheels
EX $75   NM $125   MIP $200

❑ **No. 0616 Dump Truck & Sand Loader,** 1963, yellow
EX $100   NM $150   MIP $235

❑ **No. 0616 Dump Truck & Sandloader,** 1964, orange and yellow
EX $75   NM $125   MIP $175

❑ **No. 0616 Dump Truck and Sand Loader,** 1962
EX $75   NM $125   MIP $240

❑ **No. 0618 Giant Dozer,** 1962
EX $100   NM $150   MIP $200

❑ **No. 0620 Cement Mixer,** 1962
EX $85   NM $150   MIP $300

❑ **No. 0620 Cement Mixer,** 1963
EX $75   NM $125   MIP $250

❑ **No. 0625 Stake Pickup & Horse Trailer,** 1963, 21-3/4" long overall
EX $75   NM $125   MIP $175

❑ **No. 0640 Ramp Hoist,** 1963, 19-1/4" long, red and white
EX $175   NM $350   MIP $550

❑ **No. 0640 Ramp Hoist,** 1964, park green and white, very rare
EX $300   NM $650   MIP $900

❑ **No. 0650 Green Giant Transport Semi,** 1953, 22-1/4" long. White cab and trailer with Green Giant logo decals
EX $150   NM $300   MIP $500

❑ **No. 0675 Trailer Fleet Set,** 1953, two tractors (five interchangeable trailers), per set
EX $450   NM $680   MIP $975

❑ **No. 0700 Aerial Ladder,** 1956, 32-1/2" long. Red cab and ladder section, 36" fully extendable aluminum ladder, rotating base, 2 extra ladders
EX $150   NM $300   MIP $450

(Harvey K Rainess)

❑ **No. 0700 Aerial Ladder Semi Fire Truck,** 1954, 32-1/2" long
EX $175   NM $260   MIP $450

❑ **No. 0720 Terminal Train,** 1963, 33-5/8" long, total, fifteen suitcases
EX $105   NM $175   MIP $300

(KP Photo)

❑ **No. 0725 Minute Maid Orange Juice Van,** 1955, 14-1/2" long. White truck with Minute Maid graphics and opening rear doors
EX $275   NM $650   MIP $950

❑ **No. 0725 Star Kist Van,** 1954, 14-1/2" long
EX $250   NM $575   MIP $950

❑ **No. 0735 Farm Stake and Horse Trailer,** 1962
EX $75   NM $125   MIP $225

❑ **No. 0739 Allied Van,** 1962
EX $125   NM $250   MIP $350

❑ **No. 0739 Allied Van,** 1963
EX $118   NM $175   MIP $235

❑ **No. 0739 Allied Van Lines,** 1964, black knob on door
EX $75   NM $125   MIP $175

❑ **No. 0750 Carnation Milk Delivery Van,** 1955, White with Carnation milk decals on panel sides, sliding front door, opening rear door
EX $200   NM $400   MIP $600

VEHICLES

(Mark McManus)

❑ **No. 0750 Carnation Milk Step Van,** 1954, 11-3/4" long
EX $200   NM $400   MIP $600

❑ **No. 0750 Parcel Delivery Van,** 1954, 11-3/4" long
EX $200   NM $300   MIP $500

❑ **No. 0775 Road Builder Set,** 1954, Road Grader, Semi T&T Crane and Dump Truck, five pieces
EX $350   NM $525   MIP $900

❑ **No. 0834 Grading Service Truck,** 1962
EX $70   NM $100   MIP $150

❑ **No. 0840 Car Carrier,** 1962
EX $100   NM $150   MIP $300

❑ **No. 0840 Car Carrier,** 1963
EX $42   NM $63   MIP $85

❑ **No. 0850 Lumber Truck,** 1955, six-wheel
EX $175   NM $260   MIP $400

❑ **No. 0860 Stake Truck,** 1955, six-wheel
EX $175   NM $360   MIP $500

(KP Photo)

❑ **No. 0880 Pickup Truck,** 1956, 13-3/4" long. Dark blue body, opening tailgate with securing chain
EX $150   NM $350   MIP $650

❑ **No. 0880 Pick-up Truck,** 1955
EX $125   NM $280   MIP $450

❑ **No. 0900 Mighty Tonka Dump Truck,** 1964, one of the most popular Tonka vehicles ever made; there were 9,655,000 sold between 1964 and 1983
EX $65   NM $100   MIP $230

❑ **No. 0925-6 Farm Stake Truck,** 1956, 13-1/2" long. White cab and flatbed section with blue removeable stake sections
EX $125   NM $260   MIP $410

❑ **No. 0926 Pumper,** 1963
EX $60   NM $90   MIP $120

❑ **No. 0926 Pumper Truck,** 1962
EX $100   NM $150   MIP $300

❑ **No. 0942 Mobile Clam,** 1962
EX $100   NM $150   MIP $320

❑ **No. 0942 Mobile Clam,** 1963
EX $75   NM $112   MIP $150

❑ **No. 0942 Mobile Clam,** 1964, yellow
EX $50   NM $75   MIP $100

(Mark McManus)

❑ **No. 0950 Pumper,** 1956, 17" long. Includes toy hydrant that attaches to garden hose with 6" hose (two included with MIB examples). Also includes removeable ladder
EX $150   NM $275   MIP $450

❑ **No. 0960 Wrecker,** 1956, 12" long. White body, silver five-hole hubs, red dome light, "triple A" decal on sides, working winch
EX $100   NM $300   MIP $600

(KP Photo)

❑ **No. 0980 Hi-Way Dump Truck,** 1956, 13" long
EX $130   NM $280   MIP $395

❑ **No. 0991 Farm Stake Truck,** 1956, 13" long
EX $150   NM $250   MIP $460

(KP Photo)

❑ **No. 0992 Aerial Sand Loader Set,** 1955, Loader and Dump Truck
EX $275   NM $425   MIP $875

❑ **No. 0996 Wrecker,** 1956, white, 12" long, rare
EX $390   NM $525   MIP $800

❑ **No. 0998 Aerial Ladder,** 1964, two auxiliary ladders
EX $50   NM $75   MIP $100

❑ **No. 0998 Lumber Truck,** 1956, 18-3/4" long
EX $130   NM $225   MIP $360

❑ **No. 1001 Trencher & LoBoy,** 1963, 28-1/2" long total
EX $75   NM $112   MIP $150

❑ **No. 1050 Mini-Tonka Jeep pickup,** 1963, 9-1/8" long. In various colors, red seems to be the most common. Working tailgate, white hubs, rubber tires
EX $35   NM $52   MIP $70

❑ **No. 1056 Mini-Tonka Stake Truck,** 1963, 9-3/4" long. Jeep truck cab with tipping stake side bed and dual rear wheels
EX $35   NM $52   MIP $70

❑ **No. 1060 Mini-Tonka Dump,** 1963, 9-1/2" long. Red Jeep truck cab with yellow tipping bed and dual rear wheels
EX $30   NM $50   MIP $75

❑ **No. 1068 Mini-Tonka Wrecker,** 1963, 9-1/2" long. White Jeep pickup body, red towing boom, working winch and metal hook for towing
EX $30   NM $50   MIP $75

(KP Photo)

❑ **No. 1070 Camper,** 1968, Jeep Gladiator truck body, magenta, with white camper top. The pattern for these trucks is the same as the No. 70 models dating from 1963, but color changes and line expansion forced Tonka to add more two more digits to the stock number
EX $15   NM $30   MIP $50

❑ **No. 1070 Mini-Tonka Camper,** 1963, 9-1/2" long. Jeep pickup cab, metal camper section with sliding rear window and opening door
EX $75   NM $112   MIP $150

❑ **No. 1077 Mini-Tonka Mixer,** 1964, 9-5/8" long. Jeep truck cab, rotating plastic mixer section and hopper, tilting bed
EX $30   NM $50   MIP $75

❑ **No. 1348 Aerial Ladder,** 1962
EX $100   NM $150   MIP $350

❑ **No. 1348 Aerial Ladder Truck,** 1963
EX $100   NM $150   MIP $200

❑ **No. 2100 Airport Service Set,** 1963
EX $150   NM $225   MIP $300

(KP Photo)

❑ **No. 2445 Dune Buggy,** 1968, Red body, white interior, removeable white plastic top, fold-down windshield. Originally came with chain for towing, expeditions, etc. 10-7/8" long
EX $22   **NM** $38   **MIP** $60

(ToyShop File Photo)

❑ **No. 2460 Jeepster with Boat & Trailer,** 1974, Blue jeep body with white interior, blue trailer, blue and white plastic boat
EX $40   **NM** $75   **MIP** $92

(ToyShop File Photo)

❑ **No. 402 Air Force Ambulance,** 1965, Dark blue with "troop carrier" canopy over bed, red cross decal on hood, "U.S.A.F." decals on doors. 14" long
EX $160   **NM** $325   **MIP** $650

(KP Photo)

❑ **No. 64 Hi-Way Patrol,** 1965, Jeep Wagoneer body, black with white roof, red dome light, opening tailgate, "Hi-Way Patrol" decals on doors, 9-1/4" long
EX $20   **NM** $40   **MIP** $80

(KP Photo)

❑ **No. 68 Wrecker,** 1963, White Jeep Gladiator truck body, red tow boom, black cord and silver hook. Part of the "Mini-Tonkas" range
EX $12   **NM** $25   **MIP** $50

(KP Photo)

❑ **No. 82 Pickup and Horse Trailer,** 1965, Blue Jeep Gladiator truck with white horse trailer with clear plastic dome roof. Includes two plastic horses. 14-3/4" long
EX $30   **NM** $55   **MIP** $110

(ToyShop File Photo)

❑ **No. 840 Car Carrier,** 1965, Yellow cabover truck and trailer with three plastic vehicles, 27" long. Makes first appearance in 1965 catalog
EX $80   **NM** $170   **MIP** $365

❑ **Parcel Delivery Van,** 1957, 12" long
EX $200   **NM** $350   **MIP** $500

❑ **Pickup with Stake Trailer,** 1957, 20-1/2" long
EX $150   **NM** $250   **MIP** $400

❑ **Rescue Squad Van,** 1956, 11-3/4" long
EX $225   **NM** $400   **MIP** $850

❑ **Rescue Van,** 1955
EX $200   **NM** $450   **MIP** $800

❑ **Sanitary Truck,** 1959, square back
EX $450   **NM** $700   **MIP** $1000

❑ **Stake Trailer,** 1957
EX $30   **NM** $45   **MIP** $75

❑ **Standard Oil Company Wrecker Special,** 1960
EX $400   **NM** $600   **MIP** $1200

❑ **Stock Rack Truck with Animals,** 1957, 16-1/4" long
EX $175   **NM** $365   **MIP** $650

❑ **Tandem No. 36 Tandem Air Express,** 1959, w/trailer, 24" long
EX $325   **NM** $650   **MIP** $1000

❑ **Tandem No. 40 Car Carrier,** 1959
EX $100   **NM** $300   **MIP** $500

❑ **Tandem No. 41 Boat Transport,** 1959, 38" long
EX $250   **NM** $350   **MIP** $700

❑ **Tandem No. 42 Hydraulic Land Rover,** 1959, 15" long
EX $550   **NM** $825   **MIP** $1700

❑ **Thunderbird Express Semi,** 1957, 24" long
EX $150   **NM** $400   **MIP** $600

❑ **Utility Truck,** 1954
EX $110   **NM** $275   **MIP** $425

❑ **Wrecker,** 1953
EX $125   **NM** $200   **MIP** $350

❑ **Wrecker,** 1954
EX $100   **NM** $300   **MIP** $500

❑ **Wrecker,** 1957
EX $100   **NM** $300   **MIP** $500

TOOTSIETOY (POSTWAR)

'47 INTERNATIONAL K5 TRACTOR-TRAILERS

☐ **Auto Transporter**, scaled to match 6" vehicles
EX $30   NM $42   MIP $55

☐ **Machinery Hauler**, scaled to match 6" vehicles
EX $30   NM $42   MIP $55

☐ **Shipping Van**, "Tootsietoy Trucking," scaled to match 6" vehicles
EX $27   NM $37   MIP $50

☐ **Utility Truck**, scaled to match 6" vehicles
EX $27   NM $37   MIP $50

'47 MACK L-LINE TRACTOR-TRAILERS (1954)

☐ **Hook and Ladder**, scaled to match 6" vehicles
EX $35   NM $55   MIP $75

☐ **Log Hauler**, scaled to match 6" vehicles
EX $35   NM $55   MIP $75

☐ **Machinery Hauler**, scaled to match 6" vehicles
EX $35   NM $55   MIP $75

☐ **Oil Tanker**, scaled to match 6" vehicles
EX $32   NM $50   MIP $70

☐ **Oil Tanker**, Tootsietoy Line, scaled to match 6" vehicles
EX $50   NM $75   MIP $125

☐ **Pipe Truck**
EX $35   NM $55   MIP $75

☐ **Shipping Van**, Tootsietoy Coast to Coast, scaled to match 6" vehicles
EX $37   NM $57   MIP $80

☐ **Shipping Van**, Tootsietoy Line, scaled to match 6" vehicles
EX $50   NM $50   MIP $75

☐ **Stake Truck**, open sides, scaled to match 6" vehicles
EX $50   NM $70   MIP $115

☐ **Stake Truck**, closed sides, scaled to match 6" vehicles
EX $35   NM $55   MIP $75

'55 MACK B-LINE TRACTOR-TRAILERS (1960)

☐ **Auto Transport**, scaled to match 6" vehicles
EX $30   NM $42   MIP $65

☐ **Boat Transport**, scaled to match 6" vehicles
EX $28   NM $40   MIP $60

☐ **Hook and Ladder**, scaled to match 6" vehicles
EX $28   NM $40   MIP $60

☐ **Log Hauler**, scaled to match 6" vehicles
EX $28   NM $40   MIP $60

☐ **Machinery Hauler**, scaled to match 6" vehicles
EX $28   NM $40   MIP $60

☐ **Oil Tanker**, "Mobil," scaled to match 6" vehicles
EX $32   NM $50   MIP $70

☐ **Oil Tanker**, "Tootsietoy Line," scaled to match 6" vehicles
EX $40   NM $60   MIP $80

☐ **Pipe Truck**, scaled to match 6" vehicles
EX $28   NM $40   MIP $60

☐ **Shipping Van**, scaled to match 6" vehicles
EX $28   NM $40   MIP $60

☐ **Stake Truck**, closed sides, scaled to match 6" vehicles
EX $28   NM $40   MIP $60

☐ **Utility Truck**, scaled to match 6" vehicles
EX $25   NM $35   MIP $55

'58 INTERNATIONAL RC180 TRACTOR-TRAILERS (1962)

☐ **Auto Transport**, metal trailer scaled to match 6" vehicles
EX $42   NM $65   MIP $85

☐ **Auto Transport**, plastic trailer, scaled to match 6" vehicles
EX $24   NM $32   MIP $45

☐ **Boat Transport**, plastic trailer, scaled to match 6" vehicles
EX $24   NM $32   MIP $45

☐ **Machinery Hauler**, scaled to match 6" vehicles
EX $25   NM $35   MIP $55

☐ **Shipping Van**, "Dean Van Lines," plastic trailer, scaled to match 6" vehicles
EX $40   NM $60   MIP $80

'59 CHEVROLET TRACTOR-TRAILERS (1965)

☐ **Auto Transport**, scaled to match 6" vehicles
EX $50   NM $75   MIP $125

☐ **Hook and Ladder**, scaled to match 6" vehicles
EX $50   NM $75   MIP $125

☐ **Log Hauler**, scaled to match 6" vehicles
EX $45   NM $70   MIP $100

☐ **Machinery Hauler**, scaled to match 6" vehicles
EX $45   NM $70   MIP $100

☐ **Oil Tanker**, scaled to match 6" vehicles
EX $45   NM $70   MIP $100

AIRPLANES

☐ **Beechcraft Bonanza**, 1948
EX $8   NM $16   MIP $25

☐ **Boeing 707**, 1958
EX $18   NM $35   MIP $55

☐ **Coast Guard Seaplane**, 1950
EX $50   NM $100   MIP $150

☐ **F-86 Sabre Jet**, 1950, two-casting body
EX $8   NM $16   MIP $25

☐ **F-86 Sabre Jet**, 1956, single casting
EX $7   NM $13   MIP $20

☐ **Lockheed Constellation**, 1951
EX $45   NM $90   MIP $135

☐ **P-38 Fighter**, 1950, twin boom, twin engine
EX $40   NM $75   MIP $110

☐ **P-39 Fighter**, 1947
EX $50   NM $100   MIP $150

☐ **P-80 Shooting Star**, 1948
EX $10   NM $20   MIP $30

☐ **Twin-Engine Convair**, 1950, twin engine
EX $35   NM $65   MIP $95

CLASSIC SERIES (1960)

☐ **1906 Cadillac Coupe**, w/plastic wheels
EX $8   NM $12   MIP $18

☐ **1907 Stanley Steamer Runabout**, w/plastic wheels
EX $8   NM $12   MIP $18

☐ **1912 Ford Model T Touring Car**, w/plastic wheels
EX $8   NM $12   MIP $18

☐ **1919 Stutz Bearcat**, w/plastic wheels
EX $8   NM $12   MIP $18

☐ **1921 Mack Dump Truck**, w/plastic wheels
EX $10   NM $15   MIP $25

☐ **1929 Ford Model A Coupe**, w/plastic wheels
EX $8   NM $12   MIP $18

HO POCKET SERIES (1960)

☐ **Cadillac**
EX $8   NM $15   MIP $20

☐ **Dump Truck**
EX $10   NM $15   MIP $22

☐ **Ford Sunliner Convertible**, w/midget racer Trailer
EX $12   NM $22   MIP $35

☐ **Ford Sunliner Convertible**, w/boat trailer
EX $10   NM $18   MIP $30

☐ **Ford Wrecker Truck**
EX $10   NM $15   MIP $22

☐ **Metro Van**, Railway Express
EX $10   NM $17   MIP $25

☐ **Metro Van**, various
EX $8   NM $15   MIP $20

☐ **Rambler Station Wagon**, w/U-Haul trailer
EX $10   NM $18   MIP $30

☐ **Township School Bus**
EX $10   NM $17   MIP $25

LITTLE TOUGHS/MIDGET SERIES (1970)

☐ **American La France Aerial Ladder Truck**
EX $5   NM $8   MIP $12

☐ **American La France Ladder Truck**
EX $4   NM $6   MIP $10

(KP Photo, John Brown Sr. collection)

❏ **Auto Transport Semi-Cab and Trailer**, Red Ford cab, yellow trailer, black plastic wheels. Includes three cars. Raised cast lettering on trailer reads, "tootsietoy turnpike transport"
EX $15   **NM** $20   **MIP** $32

(KP Photo, John Brown Sr. collection)

❏ **Auto Transport Semi-Cab and Trailer**, Red Chevy cab, yellow trailer, black plastic wheels. Includes three cars. Raised cast lettering on trailer reads, "tootsietoy turnpike transport"
EX $12   **NM** $17   **MIP** $25

❏ **Cement Truck**
EX $6   **NM** $8   **MIP** $12

❏ **Coast to Coast Shipping Semi-cab and Van**
EX $12   **NM** $17   **MIP** $25

❏ **Dump Truck**
EX $6   **NM** $8   **MIP** $12

❏ **Heavy duty Hydraulic Crane**
EX $8   **NM** $12   **MIP** $17

❏ **Logging Semi-cab and Trailer**
EX $6   **NM** $8   **MIP** $12

❏ **Mobil Semi-cab and Tanker**
EX $10   **NM** $15   **MIP** $20

❏ **Shipping Semi-cab and Van**
EX $6   **NM** $8   **MIP** $12

❏ **Shuttle Truck**, 1967
EX $2   **NM** $3   **MIP** $4

MACK FIRE TRUCK SERIES (1937), 4" VEHICLES

(KP Photo, John Brown Sr. collection)

❏ **Hook and Ladder**, A re-release of pre-war version 1040, note the wheel covers (over black wheels) added to the casting, and less paint variety overall, Model No. 1040
EX $30   **NM** $45   **MIP** $65

MISCELLANEOUS POSTWAR TOOTSIETOYS

(KP Photo, John Brown Sr. collection)

❏ **1931 Ford B Hot Rod**, 1960, Red body, black wheels, sharp casting
EX $8   **NM** $12   **MIP** $20

❏ **1938 Buick Y Experimental Convertible**
EX $20   **NM** $30   **MIP** $40

❏ **1940 Ford Special Deluxe Convertible**, 1960
EX $20   **NM** $30   **MIP** $401

❏ **1940 Ford V-8 Hot Rod**, 1960
EX $15   **NM** $22   **MIP** $30

❏ **1941 Chrysler Windsor Convertible**
EX $20   **NM** $30   **MIP** $40

❏ **1941 International Army Ambulance**
EX $24   **NM** $34   **MIP** $50

❏ **1941 International K1 Panel Truck**
EX $22   **NM** $32   **MIP** $45

(KP Photo, John Brown Sr. collection)

❏ **1941 White Army Half Track**, Dark green body covering black rubber wheels. Cast raised lettering on sides, "USA W-60118"
EX $10   **NM** $16   **MIP** $25

❏ **1942 Chrysler Thunderbolt Experimental Roadster**
EX $22   **NM** $32   **MIP** $40

❏ **1946 International K11 Oil Tanker**, Texaco
EX $25   **NM** $40   **MIP** $65

❏ **1946 International K11 Oil Tanker**, Sinclair
EX $25   **NM** $35   **MIP** $55

❏ **1946 International K11 Oil Tanker**, Shell
EX $25   **NM** $40   **MIP** $65

❏ **1946 International K11 Oil Tanker**, Standard
EX $25   **NM** $35   **MIP** $55

❏ **1947 Chevrolet Fleetmaster Coupe**
EX $13   **NM** $19   **MIP** $25

❏ **1947 Hudson Streamlined Pickup**
EX $22   **NM** $32   **MIP** $45

❏ **1947 Kaiser Sedan**
EX $28   **NM** $37   **MIP** $50

❏ **1947 Mack L-Line Dump Truck**
EX $14   **NM** $25   **MIP** $35

❏ **1947 Mack L-Line Fire Pumper**
EX $25   **NM** $40   **MIP** $65

❏ **1947 Mack L-Line Stake Truck**
EX $22   **NM** $32   **MIP** $45

❏ **1947 Mack L-Line Wrecker**
EX $14   **NM** $25   **MIP** $35

❏ **1947 Offenhauser Race Car**
EX $13   **NM** $19   **MIP** $25

❏ **1947 Offenhauser Race Car, on trailer**
EX $15   **NM** $22   **MIP** $30

(KP Photo, John Brown Sr. collection)

❏ **1947 Studebaker Champion Coupe**, Assorted colors, casting covers black wheels. A rare find in these postwar models
EX $25   **NM** $35   **MIP** $55

(KP Photo, Johnn Brown Sr. collection)

❏ **1947 Willys Jeepster**, 1949, Yellow body, black wheels, wheel covers over rear wheels
EX $10   **NM** $15   **MIP** $20

❏ **1948 Buick Super Estate Wagon**
EX $27   **NM** $42   **MIP** $65

❏ **1948 Cadillac 60 Special Four-door Sedan**
EX $18   **NM** $26   **MIP** $35

❏ **1948 GMC 3751 Greyhound Diesel Bus**
EX $25   **NM** $35   **MIP** $55

❏ **1949 Buick Roadmaster Four-door Sedan**
EX $20   **NM** $34   **MIP** $45

❏ **1949 Ford Custom Convertible**
EX $10   **NM** $15   **MIP** $25

❑ **1949 Ford Custom Four-door Sedan**
EX $10   NM $15   MIP $25

(KP Photo, John Brown Sr. collection)

❑ **1949 Ford F1 Pickup**, Assorted colors, casting fits over black plastic wheels
EX $10   NM $15   MIP $25

❑ **1949 Ford F6 Oil Tanker**
EX $13   NM $19   MIP $25

❑ **1949 Ford F6 Oil Tanker**, Shell
EX $25   NM $35   MIP $55

❑ **1949 Ford F6 Stake Truck**
EX $15   NM $22   MIP $30

❑ **1949 Indianapolis No. 3 Race Car**
EX $10   NM $15   MIP $25

❑ **1949 Mercury Fire Chief Sedan**
EX $22   NM $32   MIP $45

❑ **1949 Mercury Four-door Sedan**
EX $15   NM $24   MIP $35

❑ **1949 Oldsmobile 88 Convertible**
EX $20   NM $30   MIP $40

❑ **1950 Chevrolet Army Ambulance**
EX $15   NM $24   MIP $35

❑ **1950 Chevrolet Deluxe Panel**
EX $14   NM $21   MIP $28

❑ **1950 Chevrolet Deluxe Panel Truck**
EX $10   NM $15   MIP $25

(KP Photo, John Brown Sr. collection)

❑ **1950 Chevrolet Fleetline Deluxe Sedan**, Two door model. Casting covers black wheels, assorted colors
EX $10   NM $15   MIP $25

❑ **1950 Chrysler Windsor Convertible**
EX $70   NM $95   MIP $125

❑ **1950 Dodge Pickup**
EX $15   NM $22   MIP $30

❑ **1950 Ford F6 Oil Tanker**, Sinclair
EX $25   NM $35   MIP $55

(KP Photo, John Brown Sr. collection)

❑ **1950 Jeep CJ3**, Civilian model in a variety of colors. Shown here next to military version in green. Both have black wheels, civilian model without treads, earlier edition
EX $5   NM $7   MIP $14

❑ **1950 Jeep CJ3 Army**
EX $9   NM $15   MIP $22

(KP Photo, John Brown Sr. collection)

❑ **1950 Plymouth Special Deluxe Sedan**, Four door model, assorted colors, black wheels
EX $10   NM $15   MIP $25

❑ **1950 Pontiac Cheftain Deluxe Coupe Sedan**
EX $20   NM $30   MIP $40

❑ **1950 Pontiac Fire Chief Chieftain Sedan**
EX $22   NM $32   MIP $45

❑ **1950 Twin Coach Bus**, Red body, casting covers black wheels
EX $14   NM $23   MIP $34

❑ **1951 Buick Le Sabre Experimental Roadster**
EX $25   NM $38   MIP $55

❑ **1951 Ford F6 Oil Tanker**, Standard
EX $25   NM $35   MIP $55

❑ **1952 Ford F6 Oil Tanker**, Texaco
EX $25   NM $35   MIP $55

❑ **1952 Ford Mainline Four-door Sedan**
EX $12   NM $21   MIP $32

❑ **1952 Lincoln Capri Two-door Hardtop**
EX $28   NM $37   MIP $50

❑ **1952 Mercury Custom Sedan**, four door
EX $15   NM $22   MIP $30

❑ **1953 Chrysler New Yorker Sedan**, four door
EX $18   NM $28   MIP $45

❑ **1954 American La France Pumper**
EX $10   NM $15   MIP $25

❑ **1954 Buick Century Estate Wagon**
EX $20   NM $34   MIP $45

❑ **1954 Buick Special Experimental Coupe**
EX $23   NM $38   MIP $50

❑ **1954 Cadillac 62 Sedan**, four door
EX $20   NM $30   MIP $40

❑ **1954 Ford Ranch Wagon**
EX $8   NM $12   MIP $20

❑ **1954 Ford Ranch Wagon**
EX $15   NM $24   MIP $35

❑ **1954 Jaguar XK120 Roadster**
EX $8   NM $12   MIP $20

❑ **1954 MG Roadster**
EX $10   NM $20   MIP $30

❑ **1954 MG Roadster**
EX $8   NM $12   MIP $20

(KP Photo, John Brown Sr. collection)

❑ **1954 Nash Metropolitan Convertible**, Assorted colors, casting covers black wheels
EX $30   NM $40   MIP $55

❑ **1954-55 Chevrolet Corvette Roadster**
EX $15   NM $22   MIP $30

(KP Photo, John Brown Sr. collection)

❑ **1955 Chevrolet Bel Air Sedan**, Four door casting, assorted colors, black wheels
EX $8   NM $12   MIP $20

(KP Photo, John Brown Sr. collection)

❑ **1955 Ford Customline V-8 Sedan**, Two door model, assorted colors, black plastic wheels
EX $8   NM $12   MIP $20

(KP Photo, John Brown Sr. collection)

❑ **1955 Ford Thunderbird Coupe**, Assorted colors, black plastic wheels
EX $7   NM $11   MIP $18

❑ **1955 Ford Thunderbird Coupe**
EX $20   NM $30   MIP $40

❑ **1955 Mack B-Line Cement Mixer**
EX $22   NM $32   MIP $45

❑ **1955 Mack B-Line Cement Mixer**, axle-driven drum
EX $30   NM $40   MIP $55

❑ **1955 Mack L-Line Stake Truck**, 1958, w/"Tootsietoy" tin cover
EX $50   NM $75   MIP $100

❑ **1955 Oldsmobile 98 Holiday Hardtop**, two-door
EX $15   NM $24   MIP $35

❑ **1956 Austin-Healey 100-5 Roadster**
EX $20   NM $30   MIP $40

❑ **1956 Caterpillar Bulldozer**
EX $20   NM $30   MIP $40

❑ **1956 Caterpillar Road Scraper**
EX $18   NM $26   MIP $35

❑ **1956 Chevrolet Cameo Pickup**
EX $13   NM $19   MIP $25

❑ **1956 Dodge D100 Panel Truck**
EX $23   NM $38   MIP $50

❑ **1956 Ferrari Racer**
EX $18   NM $28   MIP $45

❑ **1956 Ford C600 Oil Tanker**
EX $8   NM $12   MIP $20

❑ **1956 Jaguar XK140 Coupe**
EX $15   NM $22   MIP $30

❑ **1956 Lancia Racer**
EX $18   NM $27   MIP $45

❑ **1956 Mercedes 190SL Coupe**
EX $10   NM $20   MIP $30

❑ **1956 Packard Patrician Sedan**, four door
EX $28   NM $37   MIP $50

❑ **1956 Porsche Spyder Roadster**
EX $10   NM $20   MIP $30

❑ **1956 Triumph TR3 Roadster**
EX $7   NM $11   MIP $18

(KP Photo, John Brown Sr. collection)

❑ **1957 Ford F100 Styleside Pickup**, Assorted colors, orange most common. Black plastic wheels
EX $5   NM $7   MIP $14

❑ **1957 Ford Fairlane 500 Convertible**
EX $8   NM $12   MIP $20

❑ **1957 GMC Greyhound Scenicruiser Bus**
EX $22   NM $32   MIP $45

❑ **1957 Jaguar Type D**
EX $8   NM $12   MIP $20

(KP Photo, John Brown Sr. collection)

❑ **1957 Plymouth Belvedere**, Two-door hardtop model, assorted colors, black wheels
EX $8   NM $12   MIP $20

❑ **1959 Ford Country Sedan Station Wagon**
EX $10   NM $20   MIP $30

❑ **1959 Oldsmobile Dynamic 88 Convertible**
EX $14   NM $25   MIP $35

❑ **1959 Pontiac Star Chief Sedan**, four door
EX $10   NM $16   MIP $25

❑ **1960 Chevrolet El Camino Pickup**, w/camper and boat
EX $17   NM $32   MIP $50

❑ **1960 Chevrolet El Camino Pickup**
EX $12   NM $22   MIP $30

❑ **1960 Chrysler Windsor Convertible**
EX $13   NM $19   MIP $25

❑ **1960 Ford Country Sedan Station Wagon**
EX $8   NM $12   MIP $20

(KP Photo)

❑ **1960 Ford Falcon Sedan**, Two-door body, black wheels
EX $5   NM $8   MIP $15

❑ **1960 International Metro Van**, rare
EX $100   NM $125   MIP $150

❑ **1960 Jeep CJ5**
EX $9   NM $18   MIP $25

❑ **1960 Jeep CJ5**, w/snow-plow
EX $25   NM $35   MIP $55

❑ **1960 Rambler Super Cross-Country Wagon**
EX $15   NM $24   MIP $35

❑ **1960 Studebaker Lark Custom Convertible**
EX $9   NM $16   MIP $22

❑ **1960 Volkswagen 113**
EX $10   NM $20   MIP $30

❑ **1960 Volkswagen Bug**
EX $7   NM $11   MIP $18

❑ **1962 Ford C600 Oil Tanker Truck**
EX $20   NM $30   MIP $40

❑ **1962 Ford Country Sedan Station Wagon**
EX $8   NM $18   MIP $25

❑ **1962 Ford Econoline Pickup**
EX $20   NM $30   MIP $40

❑ **1969 Ford LTD Hardtop**, two door, last of the larger-size die-cast Tootsietoys
EX $13   NM $19   MIP $25

(KP Photo, John Brown Sr. collection)

❑ **Army Cannon**, Four wheel version. Dark green body, black wheels, trailer hookups at both ends
EX $10   NM $15   MIP $25

❑ **Army Cannon**, six wheel
EX $12   NM $21   MIP $30

❑ **U-Haul Trailer**
EX $4   NM $6   MIP $8

❑ **U-Haul Trailer**
EX $5   NM $10   MIP $15

TOOTSIETOY (PREWAR)

5091 FUNNIES SERIES (1932)

❑ **Andy Gump Roadster**, Axles set so Andy Gump "bobs" as he drives, Model No. 5101X
EX $175   NM $265   MIP $350

❑ **Andy Gump Roadster**, Model No. 5101
EX $225   NM $340   MIP $450

❑ **Kayo Ice Wagon**, mechanical, Model No. 5105X
EX $225   NM $340   MIP $450

❑ **Kayo Ice Wagon**, Model No. 5105
EX $175   NM $265   MIP $350

❑ **Moon Mullins Police Wagon**, Mechanical toy, Moon moves as car is pushed along, Model No. 5104X
EX $225   NM $340   MIP $450

❑ **Moon Mullins Police Wagon**, Model No. 5104
EX $175   NM $265   MIP $350

❑ **Smitty Motorcyle**, Model No. 5103
EX $175   NM $265   MIP $350

❑ **Smitty Motorcyle**, mechanical, Model No. 5103X
EX $225   NM $340   MIP $450

❑ **Uncle Walt Roadster**, Model No. 5102
EX $225   NM $340   MIP $450

(KP Photo, John Brown Sr. collection)

❏ **Uncle Walt Roadster**, Green body, red painted rims, gold grille, black painted tires, silver painted cast figure of Walt moves as car is pushed along, Model No. 5102X
EX $175   NM $265   MIP $350

❏ **Uncle Willie rowboat**, Mechanical toy, Uncle Willie and Mamie move as boat is pushed along, Model No. 5106X
EX $225   NM $340   MIP $450

❏ **Uncle Willie rowboat**, Model No. 5106
EX $175   NM $265   MIP $350

AIRPLANES

❏ **Aerodawn**, 1928, metal tires, Model No. 4660
EX $30   NM $60   MIP $85

❏ **Aerodawn**, 1928, rubber tires, Model No. 4660
EX $30   NM $55   MIP $80

❏ **Army DC-4 Transport**, 1941
EX $40   NM $75   MIP $110

❏ **Autogyro**, 1934, Model No. 4659
EX $40   NM $80   MIP $120

❏ **Biplane**, 1926, open-spoke tires, Model No. 4650
EX $45   NM $85   MIP $125

❏ **Bleriot Plane**, 1910, Model No. 4482
EX $40   NM $80   MIP $120

❏ **Crusader**, 1937, twin boom, twin engine, Model No. 719
EX $35   NM $70   MIP $100

❏ **Curtis P-40 Pursuit**, 1941, silver, Model No. 721
EX $70   NM $140   MIP $200

❏ **Dive-Bomber Waco Biplane**, 1937
EX $50   NM $95   MIP $140

❏ **Ford Tri-Motor**, 1932, Model No. 4649
EX $45   NM $85   MIP $125

❏ **Lockheed Electra**, 1937, twin-engine, Model No. 125
EX $25   NM $50   MIP $75

❏ **TWA DC-2**, 1937, Model No. 717
EX $30   NM $60   MIP $90

❏ **U.S. Army Northrup Alpha Pursuit Plane**, 1936, Model No. 119
EX $25   NM $50   MIP $75

❏ **U.S. Navy Waco C-Model Biplane**, 1937, Model No. 718
EX $45   NM $85   MIP $125

❏ **United DC-4 Supre Mainliner**, 1941
EX $35   NM $65   MIP $95

❏ **USN Los Angeles Dirigible**, 1937, Model No. 1030
EX $45   NM $85   MIP $125

CAMELBACK DELIVERY VAN SERIES (1937), 3" VEHICLES

❏ **Lewis's**, Model No. 123
EX $135   NM $205   MIP $275

❏ **McLeans**, Model No. 123
EX $145   NM $215   MIP $285

❏ **Miller & Rhoads**, Model No. 123
EX $145   NM $215   MIP $285

❏ **Shepards**, Model No. 123
EX $145   NM $215   MIP $285

(KP Photo, John Brown Sr. collection)

❏ **Special Delivery**, Silver-painted body, white rubber wheels, "Special Delivery" in script type cast on panel sides, Model No. 123
EX $25   NM $38   MIP $50

❏ **Wieboldt's**, Model No. 123
EX $145   NM $215   MIP $285

DEPRESSION-YEARS MINIATURES (1931)

❏ **Bluebird Dayton Racer**, 1932, Model No. 110
EX $25   NM $40   MIP $55

❏ **Buick Marquette Coupe**, 1931
EX $10   NM $15   MIP $20

❏ **Buick Marquette Roadster**, Model No. 102
EX $13   NM $19   MIP $25

❏ **Buick Marquette Sedan**, 1931
EX $10   NM $15   MIP $20

❏ **Caterpillar tractor w/tread**, 1932, Model No. 108
EX $23   NM $34   MIP $45

❏ **Ford Stake Truck**, 1932, Model No. 109
EX $20   NM $30   MIP $40

❏ **High Wing Monoplane**, 1932, w/propeller, tin wings, Model No. 107
EX $35   NM $55   MIP $70

❏ **Low Wing Monoplane**, 1932, w/propeller, tin wings, Model No. 106
EX $35   NM $55   MIP $70

❏ **Mack Insurance Patrol Fire Truck**, 1931
EX $25   NM $35   MIP $45

❏ **Mack Tank Truck**, 1932, Model No. 105
EX $25   NM $40   MIP $55

FEDERAL DELIVERY VAN SERIES (1924)

❏ **Bakery**, Model No. 4631
EX $50   NM $80   MIP $105

❏ **Florist**, rarest in series, Model No. 4635
EX $95   NM $175   MIP $225

❏ **Grocery**, Model No. 4630
EX $35   NM $55   MIP $85

❏ **Laundry**, Model No. 4633
EX $45   NM $65   MIP $95

❏ **Market**, Model No. 4632
EX $35   NM $60   MIP $75

❏ **Milk**, most common in series, Model No. 4634
EX $25   NM $40   MIP $55

FORD V8 SERIES (1935), 3" VEHICLES

❏ **'34 Convertible Coupe**, Model No. 114
EX $40   NM $60   MIP $80

❏ **'34 Convertible Sedan**, Model No. 115
EX $40   NM $60   MIP $80

❏ **'34 Coupe**, Model No. 112
EX $33   NM $49   MIP $65

❏ **'34 Sedan**, Model No. 111
EX $30   NM $45   MIP $60

(KP Photo, John Brown Sr. collection)

❏ **'34 Wrecker**, 1934-35, Earlier model with separately-cast bumper and grill, gray hubs with white tires, assorted color body, Model No. 113
EX $40   NM $60   MIP $75

❏ **'35 Convertible Coupe**, Model No. 114
EX $30   NM $45   MIP $60

❏ **'35 Convertible Sedan**, Model No. 115
EX $30   NM $45   MIP $60

❏ **'35 Coupe**, Model No. 112
EX $18   NM $26   MIP $35

❏ **'35 Roadster**, Model No. 116
EX $23   NM $34   MIP $45

❏ **'35 Roadster Fire Chief Car**, Model No. 117
EX $50   NM $75   MIP $100

❏ **'35 Sedan**, Model No. 111
EX $15   NM $23   MIP $30

(KP Photo, John Brown Sr. collection)

❏ **'35 Wrecker**, 1935-36, Later model with single-piece cab (bumper and grille part of casting) and different hook configuration. Also, all-rubber white wheels

rather than the tires and hubs of the previous model, Model No. 113
EX $35   **NM** $50   **MIP** $68

(KP Photo, John Brown Sr. collection)

❑ **DeSoto Airflow Sedan**, Four-door model, assorted colors, white rubber tires, Model No. 118
EX $27   **NM** $40   **MIP** $55

GM SERIES (1927)

❑ **Buick Brougham**, Model No. 6003
EX $28   **NM** $41   **MIP** $55

❑ **Buick Coupe**, Model No. 6002
EX $28   **NM** $41   **MIP** $55

❑ **Buick Roadster**, Model No. 6001
EX $30   **NM** $45   **MIP** $60

❑ **Buick Screenside Delivery truck**, Model No. 6006
EX $35   **NM** $53   **MIP** $70

❑ **Buick Sedan**, Model No. 6004
EX $28   **NM** $41   **MIP** $55

❑ **Buick Touring Car**, Model No. 6005
EX $50   **NM** $75   **MIP** $100

❑ **Cadillac Brougham**, Model No. 6103
EX $40   **NM** $60   **MIP** $80

❑ **Cadillac coupe**, Model No. 6102
EX $40   **NM** $60   **MIP** $80

❑ **Cadillac Roadster**, Model No. 6101
EX $40   **NM** $60   **MIP** $80

❑ **Cadillac Screenside Delivery Truck**, Model No. 6106
EX $48   **NM** $71   **MIP** $95

❑ **Cadillac Sedan**, Model No. 6104
EX $40   **NM** $60   **MIP** $80

❑ **Cadillac Touring Car**, Model No. 6105
EX $60   **NM** $90   **MIP** $120

❑ **Chevrolet Brougham**, Model No. 6203
EX $33   **NM** $50   **MIP** $65

❑ **Chevrolet Coupe**, Model No. 6202
EX $33   **NM** $50   **MIP** $65

❑ **Chevrolet Roadster**, Model No. 6201
EX $33   **NM** $50   **MIP** $65

❑ **Chevrolet Screenside Delivery Truck**, Model No. 6206
EX $35   **NM** $53   **MIP** $70

❑ **Chevrolet Sedan**, Model No. 6204
EX $33   **NM** $50   **MIP** $65

❑ **Chevrolet Touring Car**, Model No. 6205
EX $55   **NM** $83   **MIP** $110

❑ **No-Name Brougham**, Model No. 6403
EX $55   **NM** $83   **MIP** $110

❑ **No-Name Coupe**, Model No. 6402
EX $55   **NM** $83   **MIP** $110

❑ **No-Name Roadster**, Model No. 6401
EX $55   **NM** $83   **MIP** $110

❑ **No-Name Screenside Delivery Truck**, Model No. 6406
EX $65   **NM** $95   **MIP** $125

❑ **No-Name Sedan**, Model No. 6404
EX $55   **NM** $83   **MIP** $110

❑ **No-Name Touring Car**, Model No. 6405
EX $75   **NM** $113   **MIP** $150

❑ **Oldsmobile Brougham**, Model No. 6303
EX $35   **NM** $53   **MIP** $70

❑ **Oldsmobile Coupe**, Model No. 6302
EX $35   **NM** $53   **MIP** $70

❑ **Oldsmobile Roadster**, Model No. 6301
EX $38   **NM** $55   **MIP** $75

❑ **Oldsmobile Screenside Delivery Truck**, Model No. 6306
EX $45   **NM** $68   **MIP** $90

❑ **Oldsmobile Sedan**, Model No. 6304
EX $35   **NM** $53   **MIP** $70

❑ **Oldsmobile Touring Car**, Model No. 6305
EX $55   **NM** $83   **MIP** $110

GRAHAM SERIES (1933), 4" VEHICLES

(KP Photo, John Brown Sr. collection)

❑ **Ambulance**, White body, fenders and running boards, raised and painted red cross symbol on sides, silver grille, Model No. 809
EX $75   **NM** $110   **MIP** $150

(KP Photo, John Brown Sr. collection)

❑ **Army Ambulance**, Light and dark green camouflage pattern on body, dark green fenders and running boards, white tires, painted and raised (cast) red cross symbol on sides, silver grille and headlights, Model No. 809
EX $75   **NM** $110   **MIP** $150

(KP Photo, John Brown Sr. collection)

❑ **Bild-A-Car Coupe**, 1933, Four wheel model--part of an innovative set containing 60 pieces, including bodys, chassis, tires and axles that allowed kids to invent their own car combinations
EX $65   **NM** $95   **MIP** $130

(KP Photo, John Brown Sr. collection)

❑ **Bild-A-Car Roadster**, 1933, Four wheel model. Part of Grahams set of interchangeable pieces, including body styles, chassis' colors, tires and axles. Vehicle shown has no spare tires on either trunk or sides
EX $85   **NM** $130   **MIP** $175

❑ **Bild-A-Car Sedan**, four wheel
EX $65   **NM** $95   **MIP** $130

(KP Photo, John Brown Sr. collection)

❑ **Commercial Tire & Supply Co. Van**, Mustard tan body with dark brown fenders and running boards, white rubber tires, "Commercial Tire & Supply Co." in script raised type along panel sides
EX $80   **NM** $115   **MIP** $160

❑ **Convertible Coupe**, six wheel, Model No. 614
EX $80   **NM** $120   **MIP** $160

(KP Photo, John Brown collection)

❑ **Convertible Coupe,** 1933, Five wheel model (one spare on trunk). A "convertible" by right of the differently-painted roof, the color range for this model is: Red, black and khaki, Light blue, dark blue and khaki, Light brown, dark brown and khaki, and green, red and khaki. White rubber tires, nickeled grille, headlights and bumper, Model No. 514
EX $80   **NM** $120   **MIP** $160

❑ **Convertible Sedan,** six wheel, Model No. 615
EX $80   **NM** $120   **MIP** $160

(KP Photo, John Brown Sr. collection)

❑ **Convertible Sedan,** 1933, Five wheel model (trunk-mounted spare). Color variations inlcude: red, black and khaki, light blue, dark blue and khaki, dark brown, light brown and khaki, green, red and khaki. Nickeled grille, headlights and front bumper. Again, a "convertible" model because of its khaki-painted roof, Model No. 515
EX $80   **NM** $120   **MIP** $160

❑ **Coupe,** five wheel, Model No. 512
EX $70   **NM** $110   **MIP** $145

(KP Photo, John Brown Sr. collection)

❑ **Coupe,** 1933, Six wheel model (spares on both sides). The coupe differed from the six wheel convertible (0614) in that it had a solid color for the roof and body. White rubber tires. Colors include: red and black, light and dark green, light and dark blue, yellow and brown, Model No. 612
EX $72   **NM** $110   **MIP** $145

(KP Photo, John Brown Sr. collection)

❑ **Roadster,** 1933, Five wheel model with trunk-mounted spare. Color variations include: red and black, light and dark blue, light and dark green, yellow and brown. White rubber tires, nickeled grille, headlights and front bumper, Model No. 511
EX $80   **NM** $125   **MIP** $165

(KP Photo, John Brown Sr. collection)

❑ **Roadster,** 1933, Six wheel model with two side-mounted spares. Color variations include: orange-yellow and brown, red and black, light and dark blue, light and dark green. Nickeled grille, bumper and headlights, white rubber tires, Model No. 611
EX $80   **NM** $125   **MIP** $165

(KP Photo, John Brown Sr. collection)

❑ **Sedan,** 1933, Six wheel model (spares on both sides). Colors include: Light and dark blue, red and black, light and dark green, or yellow and brown. Nickeled grille, headlights and bumpers, Model No. 613
EX $70   **NM** $110   **MIP** $145

(KP Photo, John Brown Sr. collection)

❑ **Sedan,** 1933, Five wheel model (trunk-mounted spare). Color variations include: red and black, light and dark blue, light and dark green, yellow and brown. White rubber tires, nickeled grille and headlights, Model No. 513
EX $75   **NM** $115   **MIP** $150

(KP Photo, John Brown Sr. collection)

❑ **Tootsietoy Dairy Delivery Van,** 1933, Cream-white body, black fenders and running boards, white rubber tires, raised lettering on panel sides, "Tootsietoy Dairy," silver grille, Model No. 808
EX $75   **NM** $110   **MIP** $150

❑ **Towncar,** five wheel, Model No. 516
EX $88   **NM** $130   **MIP** $175

(KP Photo, John Brown Sr. collection)

❑ **Towncar,** 1933, Six wheel model (spares on each side). Color variations include: blue with darker blue fenders, green with darker green fenders, and red and black. Nickeled grille and headlights, white rubber tires, Model No. 616
EX $80   **NM** $120   **MIP** $160

(KP Photo, John Brown Sr. collection)

❑ **Wrecker,** 1933, Body colors in white, red or yellow. Black fenders, running boards and chassis. White rubber tires, nickeled grille, headlights and bumper, Model No. 806
EX $75   **NM** $110   **MIP** $150

JUMBO SERIES (1936), 6" VEHICLES

❑ **Auburn Torpedo Roadster,** Model No. 1016
EX $23   **NM** $34   **MIP** $45

❑ **Greyhound Bus,** w/tin bottom, Model No. 1045
EX $55   **NM** $50   **MIP** $70

❑ **Torpedo Coupe,** Model No. 1017
EX $20   **NM** $30   **MIP** $40

❑ **Torpedo Cross-Country Greyhound Bus**
EX $25   **NM** $55   **MIP** $80

☐ **Torpedo Pickup Truck**, Model No. 1019
EX $20   NM $30   MIP $40

☐ **Torpedo Sedan**, Model No. 1018
EX $20   NM $30   MIP $40

☐ **Torpedo Wrecker**, Model No. 1027
EX $23   NM $34   MIP $45

☐ **Trans-America Bus**, 1941, sold only in sets, Model No. 1045
EX $90   NM $130   MIP $175

LASALLE SERIES (1935), 4" VEHICLES

☐ **Convertible Coupe**, Model No. 714
EX $125   NM $205   MIP $265
(KP Photo, John Brown Sr. collection)

☐ **Convertible Sedan**, 1935, Khaki-painted roof differentiates this model as a convertible. Separate grille and headlight casting, separate fenders and running boards. White rubber tires on hubs, Model No. 715
EX $125   NM $205   MIP $265

(KP Photo, John Brown Sr. collection)

☐ **Coupe**, 1935, Nicely detailed castings, separate grille and headlights, separate running boards and fenders. Like the Grahams series, convertible models were defined by khaki roofs, Model No. 712
EX $115   NM $180   MIP $240

(KP Photo, John Brown Sr. collection)

☐ **Sedan**, 1935, Sharply detailed castings. One color for body, another for separately cast fenders and running boards, Model No. 713
EX $115   NM $180   MIP $240

LINCOLN SERIES (1935), 4" VEHICLES

(KP Photo, John Brown Sr. collection)

☐ **Briggs-Lincoln prototype ("Doodle-bug")**, Very close to the Zephyr casting, but no trace of a wind-up motor. Separate grille, bumper and headlight casting. Hubs with white rubber tires, Model No. 716
EX $75   NM $95   MIP $125

☐ **Wrecker**, Model No. 6016
EX $250   NM $230   MIP $350

(KP Photo, John Brown Sr. collection)

☐ **Zephyr**, Non-wind-up model. Still has the same hubs with white rubber tires, but you can see a place in the casting for the wind-up key, Model No. 6015
EX $165   NM $245   MIP $325

(KP Photo, John Brown Sr. collection)

☐ **Zephyr**, 1937, Detail view showing wind-up motor underneath car, Model No. 6015
EX $285   NM $375   MIP $500

(KP Photo, John Brown Sr. collection)

☐ **Zephyr**, 1937, Featured a unique wind-up motor, white rubber tires, silver grille and bumper, Model No. 6015
EX $285   NM $375   MIP $500

(KP Photo, John Brown Sr. collection)

☐ **Zephyr and Roamer House Trailer**, Includes wind-up Zephyr and Roamer Trailer (1044) with opening door (often missing). The only motorized Tootsietoy of the period, Model No. 180
EX $680   NM $890   MIP $1200

☐ **Zephyr and Roamer House Trailer**, Non wind-up version, Model No. 180
EX $555   NM $740   MIP $925

☐ **Zephyr Wrecker**, An unusual car and a rare find with a wind-up motor, Model No. 6016
EX $350   NM $525   MIP $700

MACK DELIVERY TRUCKS AND VANS (1933), 4" VEHICLES

(KP Photo, John Brown Sr. collection)

☐ **City Fuel Company Coal Truck**, 1933, This ten-wheel version is more common. Rubber tires, black fenders and running boards, Model No. 804
EX $75   NM $115   MIP $150

(KP Photo, John Brown Sr. collection)

☐ **City Fuel Company Coal Truck**, 1937, This rare four wheel version has white rubber tires, Model No. 804
EX $60   NM $95   MIP $130

☐ **Commercial Tire & Supply Co. Van**, Model No. 810
EX $112   NM $168   MIP $225

☐ **Delivery Motorcycle**, adapted from 5103, Model No. 807
EX $85   NM $125   MIP $175

(KP Photo, John Brown Sr. collection)

☐ **Railway Express Co., Wrigley's Gum**, Earlier, two-piece cab version. Dark green cab, lighter green body with black fenders and running boards, Wrigley's advertisement on truck bed, white rubber tires, Model No. 810
EX $80   NM $120   MIP $175

(KP Photo, John Brown Sr. collection)

❑ **Railway Express Co., Wrigley's Gum,** 1935, One-piece cab (later) version. Dark green body with Wrigley's advertisment on truck bed. White rubber tires, Model No. 810
EX $75   **NM** $110   **MIP** $160

MACK FIRE TRUCK SERIES (1937), 4" VEHICLES

(KP Photo, John Brown Sr. collection)

❑ **Hook and Ladder,** Red body, silver grille, white rubber tires, three gold-painted ladders, Model No. 1040
EX $35   **NM** $50   **MIP** $70

(KP Photo, John Brown Sr. collection)

❑ **Hose Car,** Red body, silver-painted grille and fire hose. Nozzle on swivelling base, white rubber tires, blue painted driver, Model No. 1041
EX $35   **NM** $55   **MIP** $75

❑ **Insurance Patrol,** With ladder and rear fireman, Model No. 1042
EX $35   **NM** $55   **MIP** $75

(KP Photo, John Brown collection)

❑ **Insurance Patrol,** Open end red body with silver grille, fenders and truck bed. Blue painted driver, white rubber tires, Model No. 1042
EX $30   **NM** $45   **MIP** $60

MACK TRACTOR-TRAILERS, 1:43-SCALE (1931)

❑ **Auto Transport,** one-piece cab, three '35 Fords, Model No. 198
EX $125   **NM** $200   **MIP** $275

❑ **Auto Transport,** two-piece cab, three '35 Fords, Model No. 198
EX $150   **NM** $250   **MIP** $350

(KP Photo, John Brown collection)

❑ **Auto Transport,** 1941, Yellow cab and trailer holds three 1940s Buicks in tilted position, Model No. 187
EX $275   **NM** $415   **MIP** $550

❑ **Auto Transport four-car Hauler,** 1933, w/101-103 Buicks and 109 Ford, Model No. 190X
EX $115   **NM** $170   **MIP** $225

(KP Photo, John Brown Sr. collection)

❑ **Auto Transport three-car Hauler,** 1931, Red cab and trailer with three cars. (Originally, three Buicks. The Ford Stake truck was standard with the 190X transporter). White rubber tires, Model No. 190
EX $115   **NM** $145   **MIP** $180

(KP Photo, John Brown Sr. collection)

❑ **Contractor Set,** 1933, Red cab Mack AC hauling three spoke-wheeled tipper trailers. The original packaging for this model was an 11-1/2" box! Cab shown just hauling one of the three included with set, Model No. 191
EX $75   **NM** $100   **MIP** $150

❑ **Domaco Tank Semi-Trailer,** two-piece cab, Model No. 802
EX $90   **NM** $120   **MIP** $150

(KP Photo, John Brown Sr. collection)

❑ **Domaco Tank Semi-Trailer,** 1935, Orange-red one-piece cab towing tanker trailer with light green tank and red-orange chassis. Black type on tanker reads, "Domaco Gasoline and Oils", Model No. 802
EX $60   **NM** $90   **MIP** $120

(KP Photo, John Brown Sr. collection)

❑ **Express Stake Semi-Trailer,** 1933, Two-piece cab with black chassis and black paint on "Express" lettering on trailer. Colors range from orange, red, sand or green. Also features dual wheels, dropped from the later versions, Model No. 801
EX $80   **NM** $105   **MIP** $135

(KP Photo, John Brown Sr. collection)

❑ **Express Stake Semi-Trailer,** 1935, Later editions featured a one-piece cab and single wheels all-around. No paint on the raised letters, "Express" as the earlier version, Model No. 801
EX $55   **NM** $80   **MIP** $105

(KP Photo, John Brown Sr. collection)

❑ **Long Distance Hauling Semi-Trailer,** 1933, Two-piece cab with trailer, rubber dual wheels on cab and trailer. Colors range from orange, sand, red and green. All have black fenders, running boards and chassis. Raised "Long Distance Hauling" type on trailer painted black, Model No. 803
EX $85   **NM** $130   **MIP** $175

❑ **Tootsietoy Dairy Semi-Trailer,** single tires, Model No. 805
EX $60   **NM** $90   **MIP** $120

❑ **Tootsietoy Dairy Semi-Trailer,** 1933, dual tires, Model No. 805
EX $70   **NM** $105   **MIP** $140

(KP Photo, John Brown Sr. collection)

❑ **Tootsietoy Dairy Tanker,** All-yellow one-piece cab, three trailers with white tanks, yellow chassis and "Tootsietoy Dairy" in black lettering. Shown with one of three included trailers. Additional trailers could be purchased separately from toy stores, Model No. 192
EX $85   **NM** $125   **MIP** $175

❑ **Tootsietoy Dairy Tanker,** 1933, Yellow two-piece cab with black fenders and running boards, three trailers with white tanks, yellow chassis, Model No. 192
EX $120   **NM** $160   **MIP** $200

MACK TRUCKS, 1:72-SCALE (1925)

❑ **A&P Trailer Truck,** 1929, Model No. 4670
EX $100   **NM** $150   **MIP** $200

❑ **American Railway Express Trailer Truck,** 1929, Model No. 4670
EX $115   **NM** $170   **MIP** $225

(KP Photo, John Brown Sr. collection)

❑ **Anti-Aircraft Gun Army Truck,** 1931, Another in the Mack truck line, the gun rotates on a swivel base, Model No. 4643
EX $25   **NM** $38   **MIP** $50

(KP Photo, John Brown Sr. collection)

❑ **Coal Truck,** Assorted colors, rubber or metal tires, Model No. 4639
EX $25   **NM** $40   **MIP** $55

❑ **Interchangeable Truck Set,** Model No. 170
EX $50   **NM** $65   **MIP** $80

❑ **Overland Bus Lines,** 1929, Model No. 4680
EX $45   **NM** $65   **MIP** $95

❑ **Searchlight Army Truck,** 1931, This Mack truck was available with or without rubber tires. The searchlight, cleverly done, was a mirror, Model No. 4644
EX $25   **NM** $40   **MIP** $55

(KP Photo, John Brown Sr. collection)

❑ **Stake Truck,** Assorted colors, rubber or black metal tires, Model No. 4638
EX $23   **NM** $34   **MIP** $45

(KP Photo, John Brown Sr. collection)

❑ **Tank Truck,** Assorted colors, with or without rubber wheels, Model No. 4640
EX $25   **NM** $40   **MIP** $55

❑ **US Mail Air Mail Service,** 1931, Model No. 4645
EX $35   **NM** $55   **MIP** $75

MIDGET SERIES/CRACKER JACKS (1936), 1" VEHICLES

(KP Photo, John Brown Sr. collection)

❑ **Armored Car,** Model No. 1667
EX $6   **NM** $9   **MIP** $12

(KP Photo, John Brown Sr. collection)

❑ **Army Tank,** Assorted colors, Model No. 1666
EX $4   **NM** $6   **MIP** $8

❑ **Boxed Set,** twelve piece, Model No. 610
EX $100   **NM** $150   **MIP** $200

❑ **Boxed Set,** ten piece set, Model No. 510
EX $90   **NM** $130   **MIP** $175

❑ **Boxed Set,** eight piece, Model No. 510
EX $75   **NM** $100   **MIP** $150

(KP Photo, John Brown Sr. collection)

❑ **Bus,** Like others in the series, wheels are part of casting. The open windows are a nice touch, though, Model No. 1628
EX $8   **NM** $12   **MIP** $19

(KP Photo, John Brown Sr. collection)

❑ **Delivery Van,** Assorted colors body, Model No. 1635
EX $6   **NM** $9   **MIP** $12

(KP Photo, John Brown Sr. collection)

❑ **DeSoto Airflow Sedan,** Assorted colors, Model No. 1631
EX $5   **NM** $7   **MIP** $10

(KP Photo, John Brown Sr. collection)

❑ **Fire Engine**, Red body, cast driver, Model No. 1634
EX $7   **NM** $10   **MIP** $14

(KP Photo, John Brown Sr. collection)

❑ **Ford Pickup Truck**, 1936, Assorted colors, white rubber wheels, Model No. 121
EX $18   **NM** $26   **MIP** $35

(KP Photo, John Brown Sr. collection)

❑ **Racer**, Blue car, a tiny version of the Large Bluebird Racer, Model No. 1630
EX $5   **NM** $7   **MIP** $10

(KP Photo, John Brown Sr. collection)

❑ **Stake Truck**, Ford V-8-looking front grille and stake sides to truck bed. Assorted colors
EX $10   **NM** $15   **MIP** $20

(KP Photo, John Brown Sr. collection)

❑ **Wrecker**, Model No. 1629
EX $7   **NM** $10   **MIP** $14

(KP Photo, John Brown Sr. collection)

❑ **Zephyr Railcar**, Assorted colors, modelled after the larger Zephyr Railcar, #117, Model No. 1632
EX $7   **NM** $10   **MIP** $14

MINIATURE SHIPS

❑ **Fleet,** 1941, nine-piece carded battleship assortment: USS Idaho, USS Indiana, USS Tennessee, USS Texas, USS New Mexico, USS Maryland, USS Arizona, USS New York, USS Pennsylvania, Model No. 1405
EX $50   **NM** $75   **MIP** $100

❑ **Naval Defense,** 1941, fourteen-piece carded assortment, Model No. 1408
EX $70   **NM** $105   **MIP** $140

❑ **Sea Champions,** 1946, five-piece carded set contains two No. 1638 battleships, one No. 1618 submarine, one No. 1619 destroyer, and one No. 1620 aero carrier, Model No. 1811
EX $30   **NM** $45   **MIP** $60

MISCELLANEOUS PREWAR TOOTSIETOYS

(KP Photo, John Brown collection)

❑ **'38 Ford Paneled Station Wagon,** 1940, Reddish-brown body, silver grille, silver roof, black wheels. Despite the release date, item was re-issued during postwar period, Model No. 239
EX $20   **NM** $30   **MIP** $40

(KP Photo, John Brown collection)

❑ **'38 Ford Paneled Station Wagon,** 1947, Orange body, casting covers white rubber wheels, no separate colors for grille or wood panels, postwar re-issue, Model No. 239
EX $12   **NM** $22   **MIP** $30

(KP Photo, John Brown Sr. collection)

❑ **Armored Car**, 1938, Dark green body, black rubber wheels, (white on prewar model) silver-painted machine gun, "US Army" in raised cast lettering on sides, Model No. 4635
EX $33   **NM** $50   **MIP** $65

❑ **Army Long-Range Cannon,** 1931, Model No. 4642
EX $13   **NM** $18   **MIP** $25

❑ **Army Supply Truck**, Model No. 4634
EX $33   **NM** $50   **MIP** $65

❑ **Bluebird Dayton Record Car,** 1932, Model No. 4666
EX $30   **NM** $45   **MIP** $55

(KP Photo, John Brown Sr. collection)

❑ **Boattail Roadster**, Assorted color body, casting covers white rubber tires. Despite the release date, item was re-issued during postwar period. Prewar version shown here, Model No. 233
EX $15   **NM** $20   **MIP** $30

(KP Photo, John Brown Sr. collection)

❑ **Boattail Roadster**, Assorted color body, casting covers black wheels. Despite the release date, item was re-issued during postwar period. Postwar version shown here, Model No. 233
EX $12   **NM** $18   **MIP** $27

❑ **Buick Coupe**, 1924, Model No. 4636
EX $23   **NM** $34   **MIP** $45

(KP Photo, John Brown Sr. collection)

❏ **Buick Roadmaster Touring Coupe**, Assorted color body, casting covers white rubber wheels. Silver painted headlights and grille. Despite the release date, item was re-issued during postwar period, Model No. 232
EX $15   **NM** $20   **MIP** $30

❏ **Buick Touring Car,** 1925, Model No. 464
EX $28   **NM** $42   **MIP** $55

(KP Photo, John Brown Sr. collection)

❏ **Caterpillar Tractor,** 1931, Body colors include: red, blue, green or yellow. Gray treads, cast driver, Model No. 4646
EX $30   **NM** $45   **MIP** $60

(KP Photo, John Brown Sr. collection)

❏ **Chevy Coupe**, Red body, casting covering white or black wheels. Despite the release date, item was re-issued during postwar period, Model No. 231
EX $15   **NM** $20   **MIP** $30

❏ **Fageol Safety Coach,** 1927, Model No. 4651
EX $30   **NM** $45   **MIP** $65

❏ **Farm Set,** 1928, w/Ford Truck and Tractor, Huber StarBox Trailer, and Huber Star Scraper-Raker, Model No. 7003
EX $135   **NM** $205   **MIP** $275

❏ **Farm Tractor**, Army Field Battery Set #5071, Model No. 4654
EX $58   **NM** $86   **MIP** $115

❏ **Ford Model A Coupe,** 1928, Model No. 4655
EX $20   **NM** $30   **MIP** $40

❏ **Ford Model A Delivery Van,** 1931, "US Mail," sold in sets only
EX $38   **NM** $56   **MIP** $75

❏ **Ford Model A Sedan,** 1929, Model No. 4665
EX $20   **NM** $30   **MIP** $40

❏ **Ford Model T Pickup,** 1916, Model No. 4610
EX $35   **NM** $50   **MIP** $70

❏ **Ford Model T Tourer,** 1914, Model No. 4570
EX $35   **NM** $50   **MIP** $65

(KP Photo, John Brown Sr. collection)

❏ **GMC Box Truck**, Red body, silver painted grille, headlights and bumper. Despite the release date, item was re-issued during postwar period. Prewar version shown here, Model No. 234
EX $20   **NM** $25   **MIP** $35

❏ **Hook & Ladder Fire Engine,** 1927, Model No. 4652
EX $39   **NM** $52   **MIP** $75

(KP Photo, John Brown Sr. collection)

❏ **Hook and Ladder Fire engine**, Red body with silver-painted grille, bumper and rear ladder section. Cast driver, white rubber tires. Despite the release date, item was re-issued during postwar period, Model No. 236
EX $20   **NM** $30   **MIP** $40

(KP Photo, John Brown Sr. collection)

❏ **Hose Wagon Fire Engine**, Red body, no silver-painted trim, white rubber tires. Despite the release date, item was re-issued during postwar period, Model No. 238
EX $20   **NM** $30   **MIP** $40

(KP Photo, John Brown Sr. collection)

❏ **Huber Star Farm Tractor,** 1927, Assorted-colored body, black chassis and engine, metal wheels, Model No. 4654
EX $40   **NM** $65   **MIP** $95

(KP Photo, John Brown Sr. collection)

❏ **Insurance Patrol Fire Engine**, Red body, silver-painted grille and rear nozzle section, white rubber tires. Despite the release date, item was re-issued during postwar period, Model No. 237
EX $15   **NM** $25   **MIP** $35

(KP Photo, John Brown Sr. collection)

❏ **Insurance Patrol Fire Engine**, Postwar re-issue: all-red body, black rubber tires, Model No. 237
EX $15   **NM** $25   **MIP** $35

(KP Photo, John Brown Sr. collection)

❏ **LaSalle Sedan**, Casting covers white wheels, silver-painted grille. Despite the release date, item was re-issued during postwar period. Prewar issue shown here, Model No. 230
EX $15   **NM** $25   **MIP** $35

(KP Photo, John Brown Sr. collection)

❑ **LaSalle Sedan**, Casting covers white or black wheels, no paint on grille or trim. Despite the release date, item was re-issued during postwar period. Postwar issue shown, Model No. 230
EX $15   **NM** $20   **MIP** $30

(KP Photo, John Brown Sr. collection)

❑ **Limousine**, 1911, This was the first car Tootsietoy produced, and was available in a variety of colors. Spoked wheels, Model No. 4528
EX $24   **NM** $32   **MIP** $40

❑ **Massey-Ferguson Farm Tractor**, 1941, w/driver, Model No. 1011
EX $200   **NM** $300   **MIP** $400

(KP Photo, John Brown Sr. collection)

❑ **Oil Tank Truck**, Both versions shown here: one with the silver trim and white wheels in pre-war issue and one without in postwar colors. Despite the release date, item was re-issued during postwar period, Model No. 235
EX $13   **NM** $18   **MIP** $25

(KP Photo, John Brown Sr. collection)

❑ **Oil Tank Truck**, 1936, Available in assorted colors, white wheels, Model No. 120
EX $23   **NM** $34   **MIP** $45

❑ **Paneled Station Wagon**, Model No. 1046
EX $43   **NM** $64   **MIP** $85

❑ **Racer w/Driver**, 1927, Model No. 23
EX $35   **NM** $60   **MIP** $80

❑ **Renault Tank**, 1931, w/treads, Model No. 4647
EX $23   **NM** $34   **MIP** $45

(KP Photo, John Brown Sr. collection)

❑ **Roamer House Trailer w/door and tin bottom**, 1937, Various colors available, blue shown here. Doors are often missing from play wear from these models, so finding one intact is quite nice. White rubber tires on hubs, tin trailer tongue, Model No. 1044
EX $275   **NM** $420   **MIP** $580

❑ **Sedan**, 1923, marked "Yellow Cab", Model No. 4629
EX $15   **NM** $25   **MIP** $60

❑ **Small Ford Sedan or Coupe**, 1937, 111 or 112, and Camping Trailer, Model No. 1043
EX $35   **NM** $53   **MIP** $70

❑ **Steamroller**, 1931, Model No. 4648
EX $65   **NM** $95   **MIP** $125

❑ **Water Tower Fire Engine**, 1927, Model No. 4653
EX $38   **NM** $56   **MIP** $75

❑ **Wrigley GMC Box Truck**, Model No. 1010
EX $55   **NM** $80   **MIP** $110

REO OIL TRUCK SERIES (1938), DISTINCTIVE 6" TRUCKS

❑ **Shell**, Model No. 1009
EX $40   **NM** $60   **MIP** $90

❑ **Sinclair**, Model No. 1007
EX $35   **NM** $55   **MIP** $80

❑ **Standard**, Model No. 1006
EX $35   **NM** $55   **MIP** $80

❑ **Texaco**, Model No. 1008
EX $35   **NM** $55   **MIP** $80

WYANDOTTE

AIRPLANES

❑ **Army Bombing Plane,** 1938, Wyandotte, 8-1/2" wingspan; rubber wheels
EX $25   **NM** $65   **MIP** $85

❑ **Autogyro Plane,** 1937, Wyandotte, 9-1/4" long; rubber wheels
EX $75   **NM** $190   **MIP** $300

❑ **China Clipper Airplane,** 1935, Wyandotte, 9-1/4" long; rubber wheels
EX $90   **NM** $200   **MIP** $300

❑ **Defense Bomber Airplane,** 1941, Wyandotte, 9-1/4" long; "U.S. Army" marked on wing
EX $70   **NM** $150   **MIP** $225

❑ **Stratoship Mystery Plane,** 1936, Wyandotte, 4-1/4" long
EX $10   **NM** $25   **MIP** $50

BOATS

❑ **Battleship,** 1940s, Wyandotte, 6" long, rubber wheels
EX $35   **NM** $55   **MIP** $70

❑ **S.S. America Boat,** 1940, Wyandotte, 12-1/2" long, wood wheels
EX $40   **NM** $75   **MIP** $100

CARS

❑ **Air Speed Coupe,** 1930s, Wyandotte, 5-7/8" long, rubber wheels, 1930s
EX $40   **NM** $75   **MIP** $95

❑ **Coupe,** 1933, Wyandotte, 6-1/2" long, wood or rubber wheels
EX $40   **NM** $75   **MIP** $90

❑ **Rocket Racer,** 1935, Wyandotte, 6" long
EX $50   **NM** $75   **MIP** $100

❑ **Soap Box Derby Racer,** 1940s, Wyandotte, 6-1/4"
EX $45   **NM** $100   **MIP** $150

❑ **Station Wagon,** 1940s, Wyandotte, woodgrain and passenger lithography; 21" long
EX $200   **NM** $300   **MIP** $450

❑ **Zephyr Racer,** 1937, Wyandotte, 10" long
EX $75   **NM** $125   **MIP** $150

❑ **Zephyr Roadster,** 1937, Wyandotte, 13-3/8" long; rubber wheels
EX $400   **NM** $600   **MIP** $750

EMERGENCY VEHICLES

❑ **Ambulance,** 1936, Wyandotte, 11-1/4" long; Red Cross and "Wyandotte Toys" on side
EX $75   **NM** $150   **MIP** $185

❑ **Ambulance,** 1939, Wyandotte, 6", wood wheels
EX $45   **NM** $70   **MIP** $90

MISCELLANEOUS

❑ **Auto Hauler Set,** 1933, Wyandotte, trailer, sedan, dump truck, wooden wheels; 18-1/2" long
EX $175   **NM** $325   **MIP** $375

❑ **Coast to Coast Bus Lines,** 1938, Wyandotte, 21" long; rubber wheels
EX $200   **NM** $300   **MIP** $450

❑ **Flash Strat-O-Wagon,** 1941, Wyandotte, 6" long; rubber wheels
EX $35   **NM** $65   **MIP** $90

❑ **Gasoline and Service Station,** 1938, Wyandotte, Shell station; w/two vehicles
EX $250   **NM** $550   **MIP** $800

❑ **Land Cruiser Auto Set,** 1937, Wyandotte, sedan w/trailer; 11-3/4" long
EX $50   **NM** $100   **MIP** $150

❑ **Sand Hopper Set,** 1938, Wyandotte, 7" high; w/shovel
EX $20   **NM** $35   **MIP** $50

❑ **Streamlined Wagon,** 1934, Wyandotte, 5-1/4" long, rubber wheels
EX $25   **NM** $35   **MIP** $50

TRUCKS

❑ **Circus Truck and Wagon,** 1937, Wyandotte, 19" long; red/yellow; w/cardboard animals
EX $650   **NM** $950   **MIP** $1400

❑ **Contractors' Truck,** 1941, Wyandotte, 11-1/4" long; metal wheels; w/miniature wheelbarrow
EX $70   **NM** $125   **MIP** $175

❑ **Engineer Corps Truck,** 1941, Wyandotte, 17-1/2" long; wood wheels; marked "Army Engineer Corps"
EX $75   **NM** $130   **MIP** $190

❑ **Gasoline Truck,** 1939, Wyandotte, 21" long; rubber wheels
EX $100   **NM** $200   **MIP** $300

❑ **Hook 'n Ladder Truck,** 1930s, Wyandotte, 10-1/4" long, detachable ladders, rubber wheels
EX $90   **NM** $130   **MIP** $160

❑ **Ice Truck,** 1938, Wyandotte, 11-1/2" long, wood wheels
EX $100   **NM** $190   **MIP** $250

❑ **Medical Corps Truck,** 1940, Wyandotte, 11-3/4" long; metal wheels; "U.S.A. Medical Corps" on side
EX $90   **NM** $175   **MIP** $250

❑ **Milk Truck,** 1938, Wyandotte, 11-1/2" long, wood wheels
EX $100   **NM** $190   **MIP** $250

❑ **Semi-Trailer Dump Truck,** 1939, Wyandotte, 17-3/8" long; rubber wheels
EX $60   **NM** $90   **MIP** $150

❑ **Stake Truck,** 1933, Wyandotte, 6-3/4" long, rubber or wood wheels
EX $35   **NM** $65   **MIP** $80

View-Master Reels

View-Master toys have been great escapist fun for generations.

View-Masters have been a staple of rainy Saturday afternoons for generations of kids, ever since they were introduced at the New York World's Fair in 1939.

During the 1940s and 1950s, the company mainly produced reels for various national parks and other scenic attractions. During World War II, View-Master produced millions of reels for the U.S. government to aid in airplane and ship identification and range estimation.

The company began producing reels for children with the development of their Fairy Tale series in the late 1940s. They went on to produce hundreds of other favorite cartoon characters. In 1951, View-Master purchased the competition, the Tru-Vue Company. Since Tru-Vue held the license to use Disney characters, this acquisition was a coup for View-Master.

Since 1939, the style and construction of the View-Master viewer has greatly changed. Originally made of black Bakelite, the first models were round. The Model "C," which debuted in 1946, was the first square viewer and became the model for all viewers produced since. This model is easily-found today and very affordable. Character viewers were added to the line in 1989 but have since been removed from the product line.

The new 3-D viewer—the Virtual Viewer—is available in five colors and has been available for several years.

Tyco Toys purchased View-Master in 1989. In 1996, Mattel Toys acquired Tyco, bringing the View-Master name under its umbrella.

This Star Trek reel set is just one of many with a television or movie tie-in. Mint value, $25.

In pricing reels, the important thing to remember is condition. Three-reel packets consist of the reels, a book (if indicated on the packet reverse side), and the outer envelope with full-color picture. If any element is missing, the overall price drops dramatically. Also, if any part is torn or damaged in any way, the price should be adjusted accordingly.

Prices listed are for reels Mint in Package (MIP). Those in Excellent condition command about 85 percent of the MIP price.

Trends

Prices for View-Master reels have risen consistently over the past several years, but the market appears to have topped off. Scenic and travel titles continue to be modestly priced, but the demand for character reels, mostly by crossover character toy collectors, has resulted in a higher demand for these items. World's Fair titles never seem to go out of style.

Note: **All packages listed have three reels unless otherwise noted.**

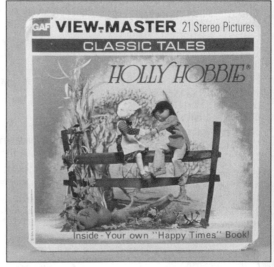

Character toy tie-ins like Holly Hobbie have a real following among both serious and casual collectors who just want to recapture part of their childhood. Obviously, Disney-related character items are in even higher demand. Mint value, $13.

VIEW-MASTER

❏ **$1,000,000 Duck**, Model No. B506
EX n/a   **NM** $7   **MIP** $10

❏ **101 Dalmatians**, Model No. B532
EX n/a   **NM** $3   **MIP** $5

❏ **101 Dalmatians**, Model No. 3014
EX n/a   **NM** $3   **MIP** $5

❏ **1939 New York World's Fair (single reel)**, Model No. 89
EX n/a   **NM** $5   **MIP** $25

❏ **1939 New York World's Fair (single reel)**, Model No. 86
EX n/a   **NM** $10   **MIP** $35

❏ **1939 New York World's Fair (single reel)**, Model No. 87
EX n/a   **NM** $10   **MIP** $35

❏ **1939 New York World's Fair (single reel)**, Model No. 88
EX n/a   **NM** $5   **MIP** $25

❏ **1940 Golden Gate International Expo (single reel)**, Model No. 57
EX n/a   **NM** $12   **MIP** $35

❏ **1940 Golden Gate International Expo (single reel)**, Model No. 58
EX n/a   **NM** $5   **MIP** $25

❏ **1940 Golden Gate International Expo (single reel)**, Model No. 56
EX n/a   **NM** $12   **MIP** $35

❏ **1940 Golden Gate International Expo (single reel)**, Model No. 59
EX n/a   **NM** $5   **MIP** $25

❏ **1962 Seattle World's Fair (four reels)**, Model No. A272
EX n/a   **NM** $20   **MIP** $40

❏ **1962 Seattle World's Fair (single reel)**, Model No. A2726
EX n/a   **NM** $7   **MIP** $15

❏ **1962 Space Needle U.S.A. (single reel)**, Model No. A2725
EX n/a   **NM** $7   **MIP** $15

❏ **1970s America's Cup (ABC's WW/Sports)**, Model No. B937
EX n/a   **NM** $45   **MIP** $50

(KP Photo)

❏ **20,000 Leagues Under the Sea**, 1954, Model No. B370
EX n/a   **NM** $7   **MIP** $15

❏ **Adam & the Ants**, Model No. BD199
EX n/a   **NM** $15   **MIP** $20

❏ **Adam-12**, Model No. B593
EX n/a   **NM** $10   **MIP** $12

❏ **Addams Family**, Model No. B486
EX n/a   **NM** $75   **MIP** $125

❏ **Adventures of Morph**, Model No. BD205
EX n/a   **NM** $7   **MIP** $8

❏ **Aladdin**, Model No. 3088
EX n/a   **NM** $3   **MIP** $4

❏ **Alex**, Model No. BD265
EX n/a   **NM** $9   **MIP** $10

❏ **ALF**, Model No. 4082
EX n/a   **NM** $5   **MIP** $10

❏ **An American Tail II**, Model No. 4111
EX n/a   **NM** $5   **MIP** $6

❏ **Annie**, Model No. N3
EX n/a   **NM** $5   **MIP** $6

❏ **Annie Oakley**, Model No. B470
EX n/a   **NM** $12   **MIP** $25

❏ **Apple's Way**, Model No. B558
EX n/a   **NM** $14   **MIP** $16

❏ **Archie**, Model No. B574
EX n/a   **NM** $7   **MIP** $8

❏ **Arena (Movie Preview Reel)**
EX n/a   **NM** $75   **MIP** $125

❏ **Aristocats, The,** 1970s, Model No. B365
EX n/a   **NM** $5   **MIP** $6

❏ **Astrix & Cleopatra**, Model No. B457
EX n/a   **NM** $21   **MIP** $25

❏ **A-Team**, Model No. 4045
EX n/a   **NM** $6   **MIP** $12

❏ **Auto Racing, Phoenix 200 (ABC's WW/Sports)**, Model No. B948
EX n/a   **NM** $35   **MIP** $50

❏ **Babes in Toyland**, Model No. B375
EX n/a   **NM** $21   **MIP** $25

❏ **Bad News Bears in "Breaking Training"**, 1977, Model No. H77
EX n/a   **NM** $7   **MIP** $8

❏ **Banana Splits**, Model No. B502
EX n/a   **NM** $10   **MIP** $20

❏ **Bananaman**, Model No. BD239
EX n/a   **NM** $9   **MIP** $10

❏ **Barbie and the Rockers**, Model No. 4071
EX n/a   **NM** $7   **MIP** $10

❏ **Barbie Prom Date**, Model No. 35428
EX n/a   **NM** $3   **MIP** $5

❏ **Barbie Special Pink Viewer set; regular viewer in Barbie pink**, Model No. 1998
EX n/a   **NM** $7   **MIP** $10

❏ **Barbie Special Pink Viewer set; Supershow viewer in Barbie pink; Target Exc**, Model No. 1998
EX n/a   **NM** $12   **MIP** $20

❏ **Barbie's Around the World Trip**, Model No. B500
EX n/a   **NM** $20   **MIP** $25

❏ **Barbie's Great American Photo Race**, Model No. B576
EX n/a   **NM** $20   **MIP** $35

❏ **Batman - The Animated Series (blister pack)**, blister pack, three reel, Model No. 3086
EX n/a   **NM** $2   **MIP** $4

❏ **Batman (Adam West)**, original envelope package, three reel, Model No. B492
EX n/a   **NM** $9   **MIP** $10

❏ **Batman (Adam West), (blister pack)**, blister pack, three reel, Model No. BB492
EX n/a   **NM** $13   **MIP** $15

❏ **Batman (blister pack)**, Model No. 1086
EX n/a   **NM** $5   **MIP** $8

❏ **Batman Returns (blister pack)**, blister pack, three reel, Model No. 4137
EX n/a   **NM** $7   **MIP** $8

❏ **Batman, The Perfect Crime (blister pack)**, 1976, blister pack, three reel, Model No. 4011
EX n/a   **NM** $7   **MIP** $8

❏ **Battle Beyond the Stars**, original envelope package, three reel, Model No. L16
EX n/a   **NM** $12   **MIP** $22

❏ **Battle of the Planets (blister pack)**, blister pack, three reel, Model No. BD185
EX n/a   **NM** $13   **MIP** $15

❏ **Beauty & the Beast (blister pack)**, blister pack, three reel, Model No. 3079
EX n/a   **NM** $2   **MIP** $4

❏ **Bedknobs & Broomsticks**, original envelope package, three reel, Model No. B366
EX n/a   **NM** $5   **MIP** $10

❏ **Beetlejuice (blister pack)**, blister pack, three reel, Model No. 1074
EX n/a   **NM** $5   **MIP** $6

❏ **Benji, Superstar (blister pack)**, blister pack, three reel, Model No. 4018
EX n/a   **NM** $5   **MIP** $6

❏ **Benji's Very Own Christmas**, original envelope package, three reel, Model No. J51
EX n/a   **NM** $7   **MIP** $8

❏ **Bertha**, blister pack, three reel, Model No. BD259
EX n/a   **NM** $7   **MIP** $8

❏ **Beverly Hillbillies**, 1963, original envelope package, three reel, Model No. B570
EX n/a   **NM** $12   **MIP** $28

❏ **Big Blue Marble**, original envelope package, three reel, Model No. B587
EX n/a   **NM** $10   **MIP** $12

❏ **Black Beauty**, original envelope package, three reel, Model No. D135
EX n/a   **NM** $9   **MIP** $10

❏ **Black Hole**, blister pack, three reel, Model No. BK035
EX n/a   **NM** $7   **MIP** $12

❑ **Black Hole,** 1979, original envelope package, three reel, Model No. K35
EX n/a   **NM** $15   **MIP** $18

❑ **Bollie & Billie,** blister pack, three reel, Model No. BD207
EX n/a   **NM** $7   **MIP** $8

❑ **Bonanza,** blister pack, three reel, Model No. BB487
EX n/a   **NM** $10   **MIP** $20

❑ **Bonanza,** original envelope package, three reel, Model No. B471
EX n/a   **NM** $10   **MIP** $20

❑ **Bonanza (w/o Pernell Roberts),** original envelope package, three reel, Model No. B487
EX n/a   **NM** $30   **MIP** $35

❑ **Bozo,** blister pack, three reel, Model No. BD1484
EX n/a   **NM** $13   **MIP** $15

❑ **Brady Bunch,** original envelope package, three reel, Model No. B568
EX n/a   **NM** $17   **MIP** $20

❑ **Brave Eagle,** original envelope package, three reel, Model No. B466
EX n/a   **NM** $21   **MIP** $25

❑ **Bravestar,** blister pack, three reel, Model No. BD272
EX n/a   **NM** $9   **MIP** $10

❑ **Buck Rogers,** 1979, original envelope package, three reel, Model No. L15
EX n/a   **NM** $7   **MIP** $8

❑ **Buckaroo Banzai,** blister pack, three reel, Model No. 4056
EX n/a   **NM** $10   **MIP** $12

❑ **Buffalo Bill, Jr.,** original envelope package, three reel, Model No. B464
EX n/a   **NM** $21   **MIP** $25

❑ **Buffalo Bill, Jr.,** 1955, original envelope package, three reel, Model No. 965abc
EX n/a   **NM** $21   **MIP** $25

❑ **Bugs Bunny,** 1959, original envelope package, three reel, Model No. B531
EX n/a   **NM** $9   **MIP** $10

❑ **Bugs Bunny & Tweety,** blister pack, three reel, Model No. 1077
EX n/a   **NM** $2   **MIP** $3

❑ **Bugs Bunny and Elmer Fudd (single reel),** 1951, original envelope package, one reel, Model No. 800
EX n/a   **NM** $7   **MIP** $8

❑ **Bugs Bunny, Big Top Bunny,** original envelope package, three reel, Model No. B549
EX n/a   **NM** $5   **MIP** $6

❑ **Bugs Bunny/Road Runner Show,** original envelope package, three reel, Model No. M10
EX n/a   **NM** $3   **MIP** $4

(KP Photo)

❑ **Bullwinkle,** original envelope package, three reel, Model No. B515
EX n/a   **NM** $12   **MIP** $15

❑ **Button Moon,** blister pack, three reel, Model No. BD212
EX n/a   **NM** $7   **MIP** $8

❑ **Can't Stop the Music,** original envelope package, three reel, Model No. L1
EX n/a   **NM** $17   **MIP** $20

❑ **Captain America,** original envelope package, three reel, Model No. H43
EX n/a   **NM** $4   **MIP** $5

❑ **Captain Kangaroo,** original envelope package, three reel, Model No. 755abc
EX n/a   **NM** $14   **MIP** $16

❑ **Captain Kangaroo,** original envelope package, three reel, Model No. B560
EX n/a   **NM** $10   **MIP** $12

❑ **Captain Kangaroo Show,** original envelope package, three reel, Model No. B565
EX n/a   **NM** $10   **MIP** $12

❑ **Care Bears,** blister pack, three reel, Model No. BD264
EX n/a   **NM** $5   **MIP** $6

❑ **Cartoon Carnival with Supercar,** original envelope package, three reel, Model No. B521
EX n/a   **NM** $50   **MIP** $75

❑ **Casimir Costureiro,** blister pack, three reel, Model No. BD171
EX n/a   **NM** $7   **MIP** $8

❑ **Casper the Friendly Ghost,** original envelope package, three reel, Model No. B533
EX n/a   **NM** $5   **MIP** $6

❑ **Casper the Friendly Ghost,** 1988, blister pack, three reel, Model No. BB533
EX n/a   **NM** $5   **MIP** $6

❑ **Cat from Outer Space,** 1970s, original envelope package, three reel, Model No. J22
EX n/a   **NM** $7   **MIP** $8

❑ **Centurions,** blister pack, three reel, Model No. 1057
EX n/a   **NM** $3   **MIP** $4

❑ **Charge at Feather River, The (Movie Preview Reel),** Movie Preview Reel
EX n/a   **NM** $128   **MIP** $150

❑ **Charlie Brown, Bon Voyage,** original envelope package, three reel, Model No. L2
EX n/a   **NM** $4   **MIP** $6

❑ **Charlie Brown, It's a Bird,** original envelope package, three reel, Model No. B556
EX n/a   **NM** $4   **MIP** $5

❑ **Charlie Brown, It's Your First Kiss,** 1980s, blister pack, three reel, Model No. 1039
EX n/a   **NM** $9   **MIP** $10

❑ **Charlotte's Web,** original envelope package, three reel, Model No. B321
EX n/a   **NM** $5   **MIP** $6

❑ **Chip 'n Dale Rescue Rangers,** blister pack, three reel, Model No. 3075
EX n/a   **NM** $4   **MIP** $5

❑ **CHiPs,** 1980, original envelope package, three reel, Model No. L14
EX n/a   **NM** $13   **MIP** $15

❑ **Cinderella (single reel),** 1953, original envelope package, one reel, Model No. FT5
EX n/a   **NM** $1   **MIP** $2

❑ **Cisco Kid (single reel),** original envelope package, one reel, Model No. 960
EX n/a   **NM** $2   **MIP** $4

❑ **City Beneath the Sea,** original envelope package, three reel, Model No. B496
EX n/a   **NM** $15   **MIP** $30

❑ **Close Encounters of the Third Kind,** original envelope package, three reel, Model No. J47
EX n/a   **NM** $10   **MIP** $15

(Toy Shop File Photo)

❑ **Cowboy Stars,** original envelope package, three reel, Model No. B461
EX n/a   **NM** $21   **MIP** $25

❑ **Curiosity Shop,** original envelope package, three reel, Model No. B564
EX n/a   **NM** $10   **MIP** $12

❑ **Daktari,** original envelope package, three reel, Model No. B498
EX n/a   **NM** $13   **MIP** $15

❑ **Dale Evans,** original envelope package, three reel, Model No. 944abc
EX n/a   **NM** $26   **MIP** $33

❑ **Dale Evans,** original envelope package, three reel, Model No. B463
EX n/a   **NM** $23   **MIP** $30

❑ **Danger Mouse**, blister pack, three reel, Model No. BD214
EX n/a   NM $15   MIP $18

❑ **Dangerous Mission (Movie Preview Reel)**, Movie Preview Reel
EX n/a   NM $128   MIP $150

❑ **Daniel Boone**, original envelope package, three reel, Model No. B479
EX n/a   NM $15   MIP $20

❑ **Dark Crystal**, blister pack, three reel, Model No. 4036
EX n/a   NM $7   MIP $10

❑ **Dark Shadows**, original envelope package, three reel, Model No. B503
EX n/a   NM $30   MIP $60

❑ **Davy Crockett**, original envelope package, three reel, Model No. 935abc
EX n/a   NM $64   MIP $75

❑ **Dempsey & Makepeace**, blister pack, three reel, Model No. BD244
EX n/a   NM $7   MIP $8

❑ **Dennis the Menace**, blister pack, three reel, Model No. 1065
EX n/a   NM $2   MIP $3

❑ **Dennis the Menace**, original envelope package, three reel, Model No. B539
EX n/a   NM $3   MIP $4

❑ **Deputy Dawg**, original envelope package, three reel, Model No. B519
EX n/a   NM $30   MIP $50

❑ **Devil's Canyon (Movie Preview Reel)**, Movie Preview Reel
EX n/a   NM $128   MIP $150

❑ **Dick Tracy**, 1990, blister pack, three reel, Model No. 4105
EX n/a   NM $7   MIP $8

❑ **Dick Turpin**, blister pack, three reel, Model No. BD188
EX n/a   NM $9   MIP $10

❑ **Dinosaurs (Disney TV show)**, blister pack, three reel, Model No. 4138
EX n/a   NM $4   MIP $7

(KP Photo)

❑ **Discovery Channel Space Images**, 1997, In plastic case/envelope with relief of Shuttle and planet Saturn
EX n/a   NM $3   MIP $7

❑ **Disneyland, Adventureland**, Model No. A177
EX n/a   NM $6   MIP $20

❑ **Disneyland, Fantasyland**, Model No. A178
EX n/a   NM $6   MIP $20

❑ **Disneyland, Frontierland**, Model No. A176
EX n/a   NM $6   MIP $20

❑ **Disneyland, Main Street U.S.A.**, Model No. A175
EX n/a   NM $6   MIP $20

❑ **Disneyland, New Orleans Square**, Model No. A180
EX n/a   NM $6   MIP $20

❑ **Disneyland, Tomorrowland**, Model No. A179
EX n/a   NM $6   MIP $20

❑ **Donald Duck**, 1973, original envelope package, three reel, Model No. B525
EX n/a   NM $7   MIP $8

❑ **Dr. Shrinker & Wonderbug**, original envelope package, three reel, Model No. H2
EX n/a   NM $10   MIP $14

❑ **Dr. Who**, blister pack, three reel, Model No. BD187
EX n/a   NM $35   MIP $75

❑ **Dr. Who**, blister pack, three reel, Model No. BD216
EX n/a   NM $35   MIP $75

❑ **Dracula**, 1976, original envelope package, three reel, Model No. B324
EX n/a   NM $13   MIP $15

❑ **Drums of Tahiti (Movie Preview Reel)**, Movie Preview Reel
EX n/a   NM $128   MIP $150

❑ **Duck Tales**, blister pack, three reel, Model No. 3055
EX n/a   NM $4   MIP $5

❑ **Dukes of Hazzard**, original envelope package, three reel, Model No. L17
EX n/a   NM $7   MIP $8

❑ **Dukes of Hazzard #2**, original envelope package, three reel, Model No. M19
EX n/a   NM $6   MIP $7

❑ **Dukes of Hazzard 2**, blister pack, three reel, Model No. 4000
EX n/a   NM $6   MIP $7

❑ **Dumbo**, blister pack, three reel, Model No. BD1474
EX n/a   NM $9   MIP $10

❑ **Dumbo**, original envelope package, three reel, Model No. J60
EX n/a   NM $7   MIP $8

❑ **Dune**, blister pack, three reel, Model No. 4058
EX n/a   NM $7   MIP $12

❑ **E.T. (reissued)**, blister pack, three reel, Model No. 4117
EX n/a   NM $3   MIP $6

❑ **E.T. The Extra-Terrestrial**, 1982, original envelope package, three reel, Model No. N7
EX n/a   NM $15   MIP $18

❑ **E.T., More Scenes from**, blister pack, three reel, Model No. 4001
EX n/a   NM $15   MIP $18

❑ **Eight is Enough**, original envelope package, three reel, Model No. K76
EX n/a   NM $13   MIP $15

❑ **Electra Woman & Dyna Girl**, 1977, original envelope package, three reel, Model No. H3
EX n/a   NM $7   MIP $10

❑ **Elmo Wants to Play**, blister pack, three reel, Model No. 4125
EX n/a   NM $2   MIP $3

❑ **Emergency**, original envelope package, three reel, Model No. B597
EX n/a   NM $10   MIP $12

❑ **Emil**, blister pack, three reel, Model No. BD122
EX n/a   NM $10   MIP $12

❑ **Expo 67 Montreal**, Model No. A071
EX n/a   NM $12   MIP $25

❑ **Expo 67 Montreal**, Model No. A073
EX n/a   NM $12   MIP $25

❑ **Expo 67 Montreal**, Model No. A074
EX n/a   NM $12   MIP $25

❑ **Expo 70 Osaka**
EX n/a   NM $20   MIP $40

❑ **Expo 74 Spokane**
EX n/a   NM $5   MIP $10

❑ **Fabeltjes Krant**, blister pack, three reel, Model No. BD251
EX n/a   NM $10   MIP $12

❑ **Family Affair**, original envelope package, three reel, Model No. B571
EX n/a   NM $21   MIP $25

❑ **Family Matters**, blister pack, three reel, Model No. 4118
EX n/a   NM $4   MIP $8

❑ **Fang Face**, original envelope package, three reel, Model No. K66
EX n/a   NM $5   MIP $6

❑ **Fantastic Four**, 1979, blister pack, three reel, Model No. K36
EX n/a   NM $9   MIP $10

❑ **Fantastic Voyage**, 1968, original envelope package, three reel, Model No. B546
EX n/a   NM $10   MIP $20

❑ **Fat Albert & Cosby Kids**, original envelope package, three reel, Model No. B554
EX n/a   NM $5   MIP $6

❑ **Ferdy**, blister pack, three reel, Model No. BD269
EX n/a   NM $9   MIP $10

❑ **Fiddler on the Roof**, original envelope package, three reel, Model No. B390
EX n/a   NM $21   MIP $25

❑ **Flash Gordon in the Planet Mongo**, 1963, original envelope package, three reel
EX n/a   NM $21   MIP $25

❏ **Flight to Tangier (Movie Preview Reel)**, Movie Preview Reel
EX n/a   **NM** $128   **MIP** $150

❏ **Flintstone Kids**, blister pack, three reel, Model No. 1066
EX n/a   **NM** $2   **MIP** $4

❏ **Flintstones**, blister pack, three reel, Model No. 1080
EX n/a   **NM** $2   **MIP** $3

(KP Photo)

❏ **Flintstones**, 1962, original envelope package, three reel, Model No. L6
EX n/a   **NM** $10   **MIP** $12

(KP Photo)

❏ **Flintstones: Pebbles and Bamm-Bamm**, 1964, Original picture envelope, three reel
EX n/a   **NM** $7   **MIP** $14

❏ **Flipper**, blister pack, three reel, Model No. BB480
EX n/a   **NM** $10   **MIP** $12

❏ **Flipper**, original envelope package, three reel, Model No. B485
EX n/a   **NM** $10   **MIP** $12

❏ **Flying Kiwi**, blister pack, three reel, Model No. BD189
EX n/a   **NM** $10   **MIP** $12

❏ **Flying Nun**, original envelope package, three reel, Model No. B495
EX n/a   **NM** $21   **MIP** $25

❏ **Fonz, The**, blister pack, three reel, Model No. BJ013
EX n/a   **NM** $7   **MIP** $8

❏ **For the Love of Benji**, original envelope package, three reel, Model No. H54
EX n/a   **NM** $7   **MIP** $8

❏ **Fort Ti (Movie Preview Reel)**, Movie Preview Reel
EX n/a   **NM** $128   **MIP** $150

❏ **Fox & Hound**, original envelope package, three reel, Model No. L29
EX n/a   **NM** $7   **MIP** $8

❏ **Fox & the Hound, The (Disney)**, 1980, blister pack, three reel, Model No. 3000
EX n/a   **NM** $4   **MIP** $5

❏ **Fraggle Rock**, blister pack, three reel, Model No. 1067
EX n/a   **NM** $4   **MIP** $5

❏ **Fraggle Rock**, blister pack, three reel, Model No. 4053
EX n/a   **NM** $4   **MIP** $5

❏ **Frankenstein**, 1976, original envelope package, three reel, Model No. B323
EX n/a   **NM** $13   **MIP** $15

❏ **French Line, The (Movie Preview Reel)**, Movie Preview Reel
EX n/a   **NM** $128   **MIP** $150

❏ **Full House**, blister pack, three reel, Model No. 4119
EX n/a   **NM** $3   **MIP** $6

❏ **G.I. Joe**, 1974, original envelope package, three reel, Model No. B585
EX n/a   **NM** $13   **MIP** $15

❏ **Garfield**, original envelope package, three reel, Model No. L28
EX n/a   **NM** $3   **MIP** $4

❏ **Gene Autry (single reel)**, original envelope package, one reel, Model No. 950
EX n/a   **NM** $2   **MIP** $3

❏ **Gene Autry, "The Kidnapping" (single reel)**, 1953, original envelope package, one reel, Model No. 951
EX n/a   **NM** $2   **MIP** $3

❏ **Ghostbusters, The Real**, blister pack, three reel, Model No. 1062
EX n/a   **NM** $4   **MIP** $6

❏ **Gil & Julie**, blister pack, three reel, Model No. BD225
EX n/a   **NM** $7   **MIP** $8

❏ **Glass Web (Movie Preview Reel)**, Movie Preview Reel
EX n/a   **NM** $128   **MIP** $150

❏ **Godzilla**, 1978, blister pack, three reel, Model No. J23
EX n/a   **NM** $13   **MIP** $15

❏ **Gold Cup Hydroplane Races (ABC's WW/Sports)**, original envelope package, three reel, Model No. B945
EX n/a   **NM** $34   **MIP** $40

❏ **Goldilocks and the Three Bears (single reel)**, 1946, original envelope package, one reel, Model No. FT6
EX n/a   **NM** $1   **MIP** $2

❏ **Goonies**, blister pack, three reel, Model No. 4064
EX n/a   **NM** $7   **MIP** $8

❏ **Great Muppet Caper**, original envelope package, three reel, Model No. M7
EX n/a   **NM** $4   **MIP** $5

❏ **Green Hornet**, original envelope package, three reel, Model No. B488
EX n/a   **NM** $30   **MIP** $60

❏ **Gremlins**, blister pack, three reel, Model No. 4055
EX n/a   **NM** $7   **MIP** $12

❏ **Grizzly Adams**, original envelope package, three reel, Model No. J10
EX n/a   **NM** $9   **MIP** $10

❏ **Gun Fury (Movie Preview Reel)**, Movie Preview Reel
EX n/a   **NM** $128   **MIP** $150

❏ **Gunsmoke**, original envelope package, three reel, Model No. B589
EX n/a   **NM** $21   **MIP** $25

❏ **Hair Bear Bunch**, original envelope package, three reel, Model No. B552
EX n/a   **NM** $7   **MIP** $8

❏ **Hammerman**, blister pack, three reel, Model No. 1081
EX n/a   **NM** $3   **MIP** $6

❏ **Hannah Lee (Movie Preview Reel)**, Movie Preview Reel
EX n/a   **NM** $128   **MIP** $150

❏ **Happy Days**, original envelope package, three reel, Model No. J13
EX n/a   **NM** $7   **MIP** $8

❏ **Happy Days**, 1974, original envelope package, three reel, Model No. B586
EX n/a   **NM** $9   **MIP** $10

❏ **Happy Days**, 1981, blister pack, three reel, Model No. BB586
EX n/a   **NM** $7   **MIP** $8

❏ **Hardy Boys**, original envelope package, three reel, Model No. B547
EX n/a   **NM** $9   **MIP** $12

❏ **Hawaii Five-O**, 1972, original envelope package, three reel, Model No. B590
EX n/a   **NM** $17   **MIP** $20

❏ **Herbie Rides Again**, original envelope package, three reel, Model No. B578
EX n/a   **NM** $7   **MIP** $8

❏ **Here's Lucy**, original envelope package, three reel, Model No. B588
EX n/a   **NM** $43   **MIP** $50

(KP Photo)

❏ **Holly Hobbie**, 1976, "Classic Tales" series, picture envelope and booklet, three reels
EX n/a   **NM** $6   **MIP** $13

❑ **Hopalong Cassidy (single reel)**, original envelope package, one reel, Model No. 956
EX n/a   **NM** $2   **MIP** $3

❑ **Hopalong Cassidy (single reel)**, original envelope package, one reel, Model No. 955
EX n/a   **NM** $2   **MIP** $3

❑ **House of Wax (Movie Preview Reel)**, Movie Preview Reel
EX n/a   **NM** $213   **MIP** $250

❑ **Howard the Duck**, blister pack, three reel, Model No. 4073
EX n/a   **NM** $7   **MIP** $10

❑ **Huckleberry Finn**, original envelope package, three reel, Model No. B343
EX n/a   **NM** $5   **MIP** $8

❑ **Huckleberry Hound & Yogi Bear,** 1960, original envelope package, three reel, Model No. B512
EX n/a   **NM** $4   **MIP** $5

❑ **I Go Pogo**, original envelope package, three reel, Model No. L32
EX n/a   **NM** $7   **MIP** $15

❑ **Inferno (Movie Preview Reel)**, Movie Preview Reel
EX n/a   **NM** $128   **MIP** $150

❑ **Inspector Gadget**, blister pack, three reel, Model No. BD232
EX n/a   **NM** $7   **MIP** $10

❑ **International Moto-Cross (ABC's WW/Sports)**, original envelope package, three reel, Model No. B946
EX n/a   **NM** $15   **MIP** $30

❑ **International Swimming & Diving Meet (ABC's WW/Sports)**, original envelope package, three reel, Model No. B936
EX n/a   **NM** $60   **MIP** $70

❑ **Ironman**, original envelope package, three reel, Model No. H44
EX n/a   **NM** $3   **MIP** $5

❑ **Isis,** 1976, original envelope package, three reel, Model No. T100
EX n/a   **NM** $10   **MIP** $12

❑ **Island at Top of the World**, original envelope package, three reel, Model No. B367
EX n/a   **NM** $21   **MIP** $25

❑ **It Came From Outer Space (Movie Preview Reel)**, Movie Preview Reel
EX n/a   **NM** $213   **MIP** $250

❑ **Jack and the Beanstalk (single reel),** 1951, original envelope package, one reel, Model No. FT3
EX n/a   **NM** $1   **MIP** $2

❑ **James Bond, Live & Let Die**, original envelope package, three reel, Model No. B393
EX n/a   **NM** $12   **MIP** $20

❑ **James Bond, Live & Let Die,** 1973, blister pack, three reel, Model No. BB393
EX n/a   **NM** $17   **MIP** $20

❑ **James Bond, Moonraker,** 1979, original envelope package, three reel, Model No. K68
EX n/a   **NM** $13   **MIP** $15

❑ **Jaws 3-D**, blister pack, three reel, Model No. 4041
EX n/a   **NM** $4   **MIP** $6

❑ **Jem,** 1986, blister pack, three reel, Model No. 1059
EX n/a   **NM** $6   **MIP** $7

❑ **Jesse James vs. The Daltons (Movie Preview Reel)**, Movie Preview Reel
EX n/a   **NM** $128   **MIP** $150

❑ **Jetsons**, original envelope package, three reel, Model No. L27
EX n/a   **NM** $5   **MIP** $6

❑ **Jim Henson's Muppet Movie**, original envelope package, three reel, Model No. K27
EX n/a   **NM** $4   **MIP** $5

❑ **Jimbo and the Jet Set**, blister pack, three reel, Model No. BD261
EX n/a   **NM** $7   **MIP** $8

❑ **Joe 90**, original envelope package, three reel, Model No. B456
EX n/a   **NM** $70   **MIP** $95

❑ **Joe Forrester**, original envelope package, three reel, Model No. BB454
EX n/a   **NM** $9   **MIP** $10

❑ **Johnny Mocassin**, original envelope package, three reel, Model No. B468
EX n/a   **NM** $21   **MIP** $25

❑ **Johnny Mocassin,** 1960s, original envelope package, three reel, Model No. 937abc
EX n/a   **NM** $21   **MIP** $25

❑ **Julia**, original envelope package, three reel, Model No. B572
EX n/a   **NM** $15   **MIP** $25

❑ **Jurassic Park**, blister pack, three reel, Model No. 4150
EX n/a   **NM** $7   **MIP** $10

❑ **King Kong**, original envelope package, three reel, Model No. B392
EX n/a   **NM** $7   **MIP** $8

❑ **Kiss Me Kate (Movie Preview Reel)**, Movie Preview Reel
EX n/a   **NM** $128   **MIP** $150

❑ **Knight Rider**, blister pack, three reel, Model No. 4054
EX n/a   **NM** $5   **MIP** $6

❑ **Korg 70,000 B.C.**, original envelope package, three reel, Model No. B557
EX n/a   **NM** $10   **MIP** $12

❑ **Kung Fu**, original envelope package, three reel, Model No. B598
EX n/a   **NM** $13   **MIP** $15

❑ **Lancelot Link Secret Chimp**, original envelope package, three reel, Model No. B504
EX n/a   **NM** $21   **MIP** $25

❑ **Land of the Giants**, original envelope package, three reel, Model No. B494
EX n/a   **NM** $25   **MIP** $50

❑ **Land of the Lost,** 1977, original envelope package, three reel, Model No. B579
EX n/a   **NM** $9   **MIP** $15

❑ **Land of the Lost 2**, original envelope package, three reel, Model No. H1
EX n/a   **NM** $9   **MIP** $15

❑ **Larry the Lamb**, blister pack, three reel, Model No. BD190
EX n/a   **NM** $7   **MIP** $8

❑ **Lassie & Timmy**, original envelope package, three reel, Model No. B472
EX n/a   **NM** $13   **MIP** $15

❑ **Lassie Look Homeward**, original envelope package, three reel, Model No. B480
EX n/a   **NM** $9   **MIP** $10

❑ **Lassie Rides the Log Flume**, original envelope package, three reel, Model No. B489
EX n/a   **NM** $13   **MIP** $15

❑ **Last Starfighter, The**, blister pack, three reel, Model No. 4057
EX n/a   **NM** $5   **MIP** $10

❑ **Laugh-In**, original envelope package, three reel, Model No. B497
EX n/a   **NM** $13   **MIP** $15

❑ **Laverne & Shirley**, original envelope package, three reel, Model No. J20
EX n/a   **NM** $5   **MIP** $6

❑ **Legend of Indiana Jones**, blister pack, three reel, Model No. 4092
EX n/a   **NM** $5   **MIP** $6

❑ **Legend of the Lone Ranger**, original envelope package, three reel, Model No. L26
EX n/a   **NM** $7   **MIP** $8

❑ **Legend of the Lone Ranger**, blister pack, three reel, Model No. 4033
EX n/a   **NM** $6   **MIP** $8

❑ **Les Maitres Du Temps**, blister pack, three reel, Model No. BD203
EX n/a   **NM** $7   **MIP** $8

❑ **Little League World Series (ABC's WW/Sports)**, original envelope package, three reel, Model No. B940
EX n/a   **NM** $43   **MIP** $50

❑ **Little Mermaid**, blister pack, three reel, Model No. 3078
EX n/a   **NM** $2   **MIP** $3

❑ **Little Mermaid - TV Show**, blister pack, three reel, Model No. 3089
EX n/a   **NM** $2   **MIP** $3

❑ **Little Red Hen/Thumbelina/Pied Piper,** 1957, original envelope package, three reel, Model No. B319
EX n/a   **NM** $7   **MIP** $8

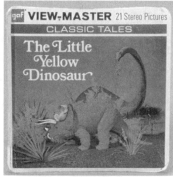

(KP Photo)

❑ **Little Yellow Dinosaur, The,** 1971, Original picture envelope, three reel
EX n/a NM $6 MIP $11

❑ **Lone Ranger,** original envelope package, three reel, Model No. B465
EX n/a NM $21 MIP $25

❑ **Lone Ranger, The,** original envelope package, three reel, Model No. 962abc
EX n/a NM $21 MIP $25

(KP Photo)

❑ **Lone Ranger, The Legend,** Tie-in with the movie, original picture envelope, three reels
EX n/a NM $10 MIP $17

❑ **Lost in Space,** original envelope package, three reel, Model No. B482
EX n/a NM $40 MIP $6

❑ **Lost Treasures of the Amazon (Movie Preview Reel),** Movie Preview Reel
EX n/a NM $128 MIP $150

❑ **Love Bug, The,** 1968, original envelope package, three reel, Model No. B501
EX n/a NM $9 MIP $10

❑ **Lucky Luke vs. The Daltons,** original envelope package, three reel, Model No. B455
EX n/a NM $21 MIP $25

❑ **M*A*S*H,** blister pack, three reel, Model No. BJ011
EX n/a NM $9 MIP $10

❑ **M*A*S*H,** original envelope package, three reel, Model No. J11
EX n/a NM $9 MIP $10

❑ **Magic Roundabout, The,** original envelope package, three reel, Model No. B441
EX n/a NM $13 MIP $15

❑ **Maja the Bee,** blister pack, three reel, Model No. BD182
EX n/a NM $7 MIP $8

❑ **Man from U.N.C.L.E.,** original envelope package, three reel, Model No. B484
EX n/a NM $25 MIP $35

❑ **Mannix,** original envelope package, three reel, Model No. BB450
EX n/a NM $21 MIP $25

❑ **Mary Poppins,** blister pack, three reel, Model No. BB372
EX n/a NM $7 MIP $8

❑ **Mary Poppins,** 1964, original envelope package, three reel, Model No. B376
EX n/a NM $7 MIP $8

❑ **Mask,** blister pack, three reel, Model No. 1056
EX n/a NM $4 MIP $5

❑ **Maze, The (Movie Preview Reel),** Movie Preview Reel
EX n/a NM $128 MIP $150

❑ **Metal Mickey,** blister pack, three reel, Model No. BD217
EX n/a NM $7 MIP $8

❑ **Meteor,** original envelope package, three reel, Model No. K46
EX n/a NM $9 MIP $10

❑ **Michael,** original envelope package, three reel, Model No. D122
EX n/a NM $26 MIP $30

❑ **Michael Jackson's Thriller,** blister pack, three reel, Model No. 4047
EX n/a NM $6 MIP $8

❑ **Mickey Mouse,** 1958, original envelope package, three reel, Model No. B528
EX n/a NM $5 MIP $10

❑ **Mickey Mouse - Clock Cleaners,** original envelope package, three reel, Model No. B551
EX n/a NM $9 MIP $30

❑ **Mickey Mouse Club,** original envelope package, three reel, Model No. 865abc
EX n/a NM $21 MIP $25

❑ **Mickey Mouse Club Mouseketeers,** 1956, original envelope package, three reel, Model No. B524
EX n/a NM $21 MIP $25

❑ **Mickey Mouse Jubilee,** 1980s, blister pack, three reel, Model No. J29
EX n/a NM $9 MIP $10

❑ **Mighty Mouse,** 1958, original envelope package, three reel, Model No. B526
EX n/a NM $17 MIP $20

❑ **Mighty Mouse,** 1970s, blister pack, three reel, Model No. BB526
EX n/a NM $4 MIP $5

❑ **Miss Sadie Thompson (Movie Preview Reel),** Movie Preview Reel
EX n/a NM $128 MIP $150

❑ **Mission Impossible,** original envelope package, three reel, Model No. B505
EX n/a NM $15 MIP $18

❑ **Mod Squad,** original envelope package, three reel, Model No. B478
EX n/a NM $16 MIP $20

❑ **Money From Home (Movie Preview Reel),** Movie Preview Reel
EX n/a NM $128 MIP $150

❑ **Monkees,** original envelope package, three reel, Model No. B493
EX n/a NM $12 MIP $25

❑ **Mork & Mindy,** 1978, original envelope package, three reel, Model No. K67
EX n/a NM $7 MIP $8

❑ **Movie Stars I (single reel),** original envelope package, one reel, Model No. 740
EX n/a NM $13 MIP $15

❑ **Movie Stars II (single reel),** original envelope package, one reel, Model No. 741
EX n/a NM $13 MIP $15

❑ **Movie Stars III (single reel),** original envelope package, one reel, Model No. 742
EX n/a NM $13 MIP $15

❑ **Mr. Magoo,** 1977, original envelope package, three reel, Model No. H56
EX n/a NM $6 MIP $10

❑ **Munch Bunch,** blister pack, three reel, Model No. BD197
EX n/a NM $7 MIP $8

❑ **Munsters,** original envelope package, three reel, Model No. B481
EX n/a NM $105 MIP $200

❑ **Muppet Movie, Scenes From The,** blister pack, three reel, Model No. 4005
EX n/a NM $4 MIP $5

❑ **Muppets Go Hawaiian, The,** original envelope package, three reel, Model No. L25
EX n/a NM $4 MIP $5

❑ **Muppets, Meet Jim Henson's,** original envelope package, three reel, Model No. K26
EX n/a NM $4 MIP $5

❑ **Muppets, The,** blister pack, three reel, Model No. BK026
EX n/a NM $4 MIP $5

❑ **Nanny & The Professor,** original envelope package, three reel, Model No. B573
EX n/a NM $30 MIP $35

❑ **NCAA Track & Field Championships (ABC's WW/Sports),** original envelope package, three reel, Model No. B935
EX n/a NM $50 MIP $75

❑ **Nebraskan, The (Movie Preview Reel),** Movie Preview Reel
EX n/a NM $128 MIP $150

❑ **New Mickey Mouse Club,** original envelope package, three reel, Model No. H9
EX n/a NM $5 MIP $6

❏ **New Zoo Revue**, original envelope package, three reel, Model No. B566
EX n/a   NM $13   MIP $15

❏ **New Zoo Revue 2**, original envelope package, three reel, Model No. B567
EX n/a   NM $13   MIP $15

❏ **Old Surehand**, original envelope package, three reel, Model No. B443
EX n/a   NM $43   MIP $50

❏ **One of Our Dinosaurs Is Missing**, original envelope package, three reel, Model No. B377
EX n/a   NM $10   MIP $12

❏ **Oregon Centennial Exposition (1959)**, Model No. A0250
EX n/a   NM $30   MIP $50

❏ **Orm & Cheap**, blister pack, three reel, Model No. BD266
EX n/a   NM $10   MIP $12

❏ **Partridge Family**, blister pack, three reel, Model No. BB5924
EX n/a   NM $17   MIP $20

❏ **Partridge Family**, 1971, original envelope package, three reel, Model No. B569
EX n/a   NM $17   MIP $20

(KP Photo)

❏ **Partridge Family**, 1971, Talking View-Master reels, original envelope package, three reel
EX n/a   NM $22   MIP $27

❏ **Pee-Wee's Playhouse**, 1988, blister pack, three reel, Model No. 4074
EX n/a   NM $9   MIP $10

❏ **Pendelton Round-Up (ABC's WW/Sports)**, original envelope package, three reel, Model No. B943
EX n/a   NM $30   MIP $35

❏ **Perishers, The**, blister pack, three reel, Model No. BD184
EX n/a   NM $6   MIP $8

❏ **Peter Pan, Disney's**, original envelope package, three reel
EX n/a   NM $5   MIP $6

❏ **Pete's Dragon**, original envelope package, three reel, Model No. H38
EX n/a   NM $7   MIP $8

❏ **Pink Panther**, original envelope package, three reel, Model No. J12
EX n/a   NM $5   MIP $6

❏ **Pink Panther,** 1970s, blister pack, three reel, Model No. BJ012
EX n/a   NM $4   MIP $5

❏ **Pinky Lee's 7 Days (single reel)**, original envelope package, one reel, Model No. 750
EX n/a   NM $21   MIP $25

❏ **Pippi Longstocking**, original envelope package, three reel, Model No. B322
EX n/a   NM $13   MIP $15

❏ **Pippi Longstocking**, original envelope package, three reel, Model No. D113
EX n/a   NM $13   MIP $15

❏ **Planet of the Apes**, blister pack, three reel, Model No. BB507
EX n/a   NM $30   MIP $35

❏ **Planet of the Apes,** 1967, original envelope package, three reel, Model No. B507
EX n/a   NM $30   MIP $35

❏ **Pluto**, blister pack, three reel, Model No. BB529
EX n/a   NM $4   MIP $7

❏ **Pluto**, blister pack, three reel, Model No. 3013
EX n/a   NM $4   MIP $7

❏ **Pluto**, original envelope package, three reel, Model No. B529
EX n/a   NM $9   MIP $10

❏ **Polly in Portugal**, original envelope package, three reel, Model No. B442
EX n/a   NM $26   MIP $30

❏ **Polly in Venice**, original envelope package, three reel, Model No. D100
EX n/a   NM $17   MIP $20

❏ **Popeye,** 1962, original envelope package, three reel, Model No. B516
EX n/a   NM $6   MIP $8

❏ **Popeye Talking View-Master Set,** 1983, original envelope package, three reel
EX n/a   NM $9   MIP $10

❏ **Popeye's Fun**, original envelope package, three reel, Model No. B527
EX n/a   NM $7   MIP $8

❏ **Portland Bill**, blister pack, three reel, Model No. BD226
EX n/a   NM $10   MIP $12

❏ **Poseidon Adventure**, original envelope package, three reel, Model No. B391
EX n/a   NM $21   MIP $25

❏ **Postman Pat**, blister pack, three reel, Model No. BD218
EX n/a   NM $7   MIP $8

❏ **Pumcki**, blister pack, three reel, Model No. BD220
EX n/a   NM $7   MIP $8

❏ **Punky Brewster,** 1984, blister pack, three reel, Model No. 4068
EX n/a   NM $7   MIP $8

❏ **Puppets Audition Night**, blister pack, three reel, Model No. 4003
EX n/a   NM $4   MIP $5

❏ **Puppets Audition Night, The**, original envelope package, three reel, Model No. L9
EX n/a   NM $4   MIP $5

❏ **Red Riding Hood (single reel),** 1950, original envelope package, one reel, Model No. FT1
EX n/a   NM $2   MIP $3

❏ **Rescuers, The**, blister pack, three reel, Model No. BH026
EX n/a   NM $5   MIP $6

❏ **Rescuers, The**, original envelope package, three reel, Model No. H26
EX n/a   NM $5   MIP $6

❏ **Return to Witch Mountain**, original envelope package, three reel, Model No. J25
EX n/a   NM $5   MIP $6

(Toy Shop File Photo)

❏ **Rin-Tin-Tin**, original envelope package, three reel, Model No. B467
EX n/a   NM $13   MIP $15

❏ **Rin-Tin-Tin,** 1955, original envelope package, three reel, Model No. 930abc
EX n/a   NM $13   MIP $15

❏ **Robin Hood,** 1954, original envelope package, three reel
EX n/a   NM $21   MIP $25

❏ **Robin Hood Meets Friar Tuck,** 1956, original envelope package, three reel, Model No. B373
EX n/a   NM $17   MIP $20

❏ **Rocketeer, The**, blister pack, three reel, Model No. 4115
EX n/a   NM $7   MIP $8

❏ **Roland Rat Superstar**, blister pack, three reel, Model No. BD240
EX n/a   NM $7   MIP $8

❏ **Romper Room**, original envelope package, three reel, Model No. K20
EX n/a   NM $7   MIP $8

❏ **Rookies, The,** 1975, original envelope package, three reel, Model No. BB452
EX n/a   NM $13   MIP $15

(KP Photo)

❑ **Roy Rogers**, original envelope package, three reel, Model No. B475
EX n/a **NM** $21 **MIP** $25

❑ **Roy Rogers**, original envelope package, three reel, Model No. 948abc
EX n/a **NM** $21 **MIP** $25

❑ **Roy Rogers**, original envelope package, three reel, Model No. B462
EX n/a **NM** $21 **MIP** $25

❑ **Roy Rogers (single reel)**, original envelope package, one reel, Model No. 945
EX n/a **NM** $2 **MIP** $3

(KP Photo)

❑ **Rudolph the Red-Nosed Reindeer**, 1955, Definitely based on the Golden Book, the puppets even look like the illustrations. Interesting, considering these reels were created about ten years before the Rankin/Bass animated special. Includes picture envelope and three reels
EX n/a **NM** $10 **MIP** $17

❑ **Run Joe Run**, 1974, original envelope package, three reel, Model No. B594
EX n/a **NM** $13 **MIP** $15

❑ **Rupert the Bear**, blister pack, three reel, Model No. BD109
EX n/a **NM** $12 **MIP** $15

❑ **S.W.A.T.**, 1975, original envelope package, three reel, Model No. BB453
EX n/a **NM** $10 **MIP** $12

❑ **Sangaree (Movie Preview Reel)**, Movie Preview Reel
EX n/a **NM** $128 **MIP** $150

❑ **Scooby Doo**, blister pack, three reel, Model No. 1079
EX n/a **NM** $2 **MIP** $3

❑ **Scooby Doo**, original envelope package, three reel, Model No. B553
EX n/a **NM** $4 **MIP** $5

❑ **Search**, original envelope package, three reel, Model No. B591
EX n/a **NM** $17 **MIP** $20

❑ **Sebastian**, original envelope package, three reel, Model No. B452
EX n/a **NM** $26 **MIP** $30

❑ **Sebastian**, original envelope package, three reel, Model No. D101
EX n/a **NM** $26 **MIP** $30

❑ **Second Chance (Movie Preview Reel)**, Movie Preview Reel
EX n/a **NM** $128 **MIP** $150

❑ **Secret Squirrel & Atom Ant**, original envelope package, three reel, Model No. B535
EX n/a **NM** $9 **MIP** $12

❑ **Secret Valley**, blister pack, three reel, Model No. BD208
EX n/a **NM** $10 **MIP** $12

❑ **Sesame Street - Follow That Bird**, blister pack, three reel, Model No. 4066
EX n/a **NM** $4 **MIP** $5

❑ **Sesame Street - People in Your Neighborhood**, blister pack, three reel, Model No. 4049
EX n/a **NM** $4 **MIP** $5

❑ **Sesame Street - People in Your Neighborhood**, original envelope package, three reel, Model No. M12
EX n/a **NM** $4 **MIP** $5

❑ **Sesame Street Alphabet**, blister pack, three reel, Model No. 4051
EX n/a **NM** $2 **MIP** $3

❑ **Sesame Street Baby Animals**, blister pack, three reel, Model No. 4072
EX n/a **NM** $4 **MIP** $5

❑ **Sesame Street Circus Fun**, blister pack, three reel, Model No. 4097
EX n/a **NM** $4 **MIP** $5

❑ **Sesame Street Counting**, blister pack, three reel, Model No. 4050
EX n/a **NM** $4 **MIP** $5

❑ **Sesame Street Goes on Vacation**, blister pack, three reel, Model No. 4077
EX n/a **NM** $4 **MIP** $5

❑ **Sesame Street Goes Western**, blister pack, three reel, Model No. 4085
EX n/a **NM** $4 **MIP** $5

❑ **Sesame Street Nursery Rhymes**, blister pack, three reel, Model No. 4083
EX n/a **NM** $4 **MIP** $5

❑ **Sesame Street Shapes, Colors**, blister pack, three reel, Model No. 4052
EX n/a **NM** $4 **MIP** $5

❑ **Sesame Street Visits the Zoo**, blister pack, three reel, Model No. 4017
EX n/a **NM** $4 **MIP** $5

❑ **Shaggy D.A.**, original envelope package, three reel, Model No. b368
EX n/a **NM** $10 **MIP** $12

❑ **Shazam**, original envelope package, three reel, Model No. B550
EX n/a **NM** $5 **MIP** $7

❑ **Shoe People, The**, blister pack, three reel, Model No. BD270
EX n/a **NM** $10 **MIP** $12

❑ **Sigmund & the Sea Monsters (correct issue numbers)**, original envelope package, three reel, Model No. B595
EX n/a **NM** $15 **MIP** $18

❑ **Sigmund & the Sea Monsters (wrong issue number)**, original envelope package, three reel, Model No. B559
EX n/a **NM** $15 **MIP** $18

❑ **Silverhawks**, blister pack, three reel, Model No. 1058
EX n/a **NM** $4 **MIP** $5

❑ **Six Million Dollar Man**, 1974, original envelope package, three reel, Model No. B556
EX n/a **NM** $13 **MIP** $15

❑ **Sleeping Beauty, Disney's**, original envelope package, three reel, Model No. B308
EX n/a **NM** $4 **MIP** $5

❑ **Smith Family, The**, original envelope package, three reel, Model No. B490
EX n/a **NM** $10 **MIP** $30

❑ **Smuggler**, blister pack, three reel, Model No. BD194
EX n/a **NM** $7 **MIP** $8

❑ **Smurf, Baby**, blister pack, three reel, Model No. BD246
EX n/a **NM** $7 **MIP** $8

❑ **Smurf, Flying**, original envelope package, three reel, Model No. N1
EX n/a **NM** $4 **MIP** $5

❑ **Smurf, Traveling**, original envelope package, three reel, Model No. N2
EX n/a **NM** $4 **MIP** $5

❑ **Smurfs**, blister pack, three reel, Model No. BD172
EX n/a **NM** $5 **MIP** $6

❑ **Snoopy and the Red Baron**, 1980s, blister pack, three reel, Model No. B544
EX n/a **NM** $7 **MIP** $8

❑ **Snorkes**, blister pack, three reel, Model No. BD250
EX n/a **NM** $8 **MIP** $10

❑ **Snow White & the Seven Dwarfs**, original envelope package, three reel, Model No. K69
EX n/a **NM** $7 **MIP** $8

❑ **Snow White (single reel)**, 1946, original envelope package, one reel, Model No. FT4
EX n/a **NM** $3 **MIP** $4

❑ **Snowman**, blister pack, three reel, Model No. BD262
EX n/a **NM** $7 **MIP** $8

❑ **Son of Sinbad (Movie Preview Reel)**, Movie Preview Reel
EX n/a **NM** $128 **MIP** $150

VIEW-MASTER

❑ **Space Mouse**, original envelope package, three reel, Model No. B509
EX n/a   **NM** $10   **MIP** $20

❑ **Space: 1999**, blister pack, three reel, Model No. BD150
EX n/a   **NM** $21   **MIP** $25

❑ **Space: 1999**, 1975, original envelope package, three reel, Model No. BB451
EX n/a   **NM** $21   **MIP** $25

❑ **Spider-Man**, original envelope package, three reel, Model No. K31
EX n/a   **NM** $9   **MIP** $10

❑ **Spider-Man**, 1978, original envelope package, three reel, Model No. H11
EX n/a   **NM** $10   **MIP** $12

❑ **Spider-Man**, 1980s, blister pack, three reel, Model No. BH011
EX n/a   **NM** $7   **MIP** $8

❑ **Star Trek - The Motion Picture**, original envelope package, three reel, Model No. K57
EX n/a   **NM** $10   **MIP** $12

❑ **Star Trek - The Next Generation**, blister pack, three reel, Model No. 4095
EX n/a   **NM** $7   **MIP** $8

❑ **Star Trek - Wrath of Khan**, original envelope package, three reel, Model No. M38
EX n/a   **NM** $10   **MIP** $12

❑ **Star Trek (Cartoon Series)**, original envelope package, three reel, Model No. B555
EX n/a   **NM** $9   **MIP** $10

(KP Photo)

❑ **Star Trek (TV Series), "Omega Glory"**, 1968, original envelope package, three reel, Model No. B499
EX n/a   **NM** $21   **MIP** $25

❑ **Steve Canyon**, 1959, original envelope package, three reel, Model No. B582
EX n/a   **NM** $64   **MIP** $75

❑ **Stranger Wore a Gun, The (Movie Preview Reel)**, Movie Preview Reel
EX n/a   **NM** $128   **MIP** $150

❑ **Superman**, blister pack, three reel, Model No. BJ78
EX n/a   **NM** $5   **MIP** $6

❑ **Superman**, blister pack, three reel, Model No. 1064
EX n/a   **NM** $4   **MIP** $5

❑ **Superman - The Movie**, original envelope package, three reel, Model No. J78
EX n/a   **NM** $10   **MIP** $20

❑ **Superman (cartoon)**, original envelope package, three reel, Model No. B584
EX n/a   **NM** $4   **MIP** $5

❑ **Superman II**, original envelope package, three reel, Model No. L46
EX n/a   **NM** $17   **MIP** $25

❑ **Superman III**, blister pack, three reel, Model No. 4044
EX n/a   **NM** $7   **MIP** $15

❑ **Superstar Barbie**, Model No. J070
EX n/a   **NM** $7   **MIP** $15

❑ **Tailspin**, blister pack, three reel, Model No. 3081
EX n/a   **NM** $4   **MIP** $5

❑ **Tarzan**, original envelope package, three reel, Model No. B580
EX n/a   **NM** $9   **MIP** $10

❑ **Tarzan (single reel)**, original envelope package, one reel, Model No. 975
EX n/a   **NM** $4   **MIP** $5

❑ **Tarzan Finds a Son (single reel)**, 1955, original envelope package, one reel, Model No. 976A
EX n/a   **NM** $3   **MIP** $4

❑ **Tarzan of the Apes,** 1955, original envelope package, three reel, Model No. 976abc
EX n/a   **NM** $21   **MIP** $25

❑ **Taza, Son of Cochise (Movie Preview Reel)**, Movie Preview Reel
EX n/a   **NM** $128   **MIP** $150

❑ **Teenage Mutant Ninja Turtles**, blister pack, three reel, Model No. 1073
EX n/a   **NM** $2   **MIP** $3

❑ **Teenage Mutant Ninja Turtles - Movie II**, blister pack, three reel, Model No. 4114
EX n/a   **NM** $3   **MIP** $4

❑ **Teenage Mutant Ninja Turtles - Movie III**, blister pack, three reel, Model No. 4149
EX n/a   **NM** $2   **MIP** $3

❑ **Teenage Mutant Ninja Turtles - The Movie**, blister pack, three reel, Model No. 4109
EX n/a   **NM** $3   **MIP** $5

❑ **Telecat**, blister pack, three reel, Model No. BD243
EX n/a   **NM** $7   **MIP** $8

❑ **Terrahawks**, blister pack, three reel, Model No. BD230
EX n/a   **NM** $10   **MIP** $20

❑ **They Called Him Hondo (Movie Preview Reel)**, Movie Preview Reel
EX n/a   **NM** $128   **MIP** $150

❑ **Thomas the Tank Engine**, blister pack, three reel, Model No. BD238
EX n/a   **NM** $6   **MIP** $10

❑ **Thor**, original envelope package, three reel, Model No. H39
EX n/a   **NM** $2   **MIP** $5

❑ **Those Redheads from Seattle (Movie Preview Reel)**, Movie Preview Reel
EX n/a   **NM** $128   **MIP** $150

❑ **Thunderbirds**, original envelope package, three reel, Model No. B453
EX n/a   **NM** $43   **MIP** $50

❑ **Time Tunnel,** 1966, original envelope package, three reel, Model No. B491
EX n/a   **NM** $20   **MIP** $35

❑ **Tiny Toon Adventures**, blister pack, three reel, Model No. 1076
EX n/a   **NM** $2   **MIP** $3

❑ **Tiswas**, blister pack, three reel, Model No. BD205
EX n/a   **NM** $7   **MIP** $8

(KP Photo)

❑ **Toby Tyler**, original envelope package, three reel, Model No. B476
EX n/a   **NM** $30   **MIP** $35

❑ **Tom & Jerry (single reel)**, 1956, original envelope package, three reel, Model No. 810
EX n/a   **NM** $2   **MIP** $3

❑ **Tom & Jerry, Two Musketeers**, 1956, original envelope package, three reel, Model No. B511
EX n/a   **NM** $9   **MIP** $10

❑ **Tom Corbett, Secret from Space**, original envelope package, three reel, Model No. B581
EX n/a   **NM** $21   **MIP** $25

❑ **Tom Corbett, Space Cadet**, 1954, original envelope package, three reel, Model No. 970abc
EX n/a   **NM** $21   **MIP** $25

❑ **Tom Sawyer**, original envelope package, three reel, Model No. B340
EX n/a   **NM** $7   **MIP** $8

❑ **Tom Thumb**, original envelope package, three reel, Model No. D123
EX n/a   **NM** $13   **MIP** $15

❑ **Top Cat**, original envelope package, three reel, Model No. B513
EX n/a   **NM** $13   **MIP** $15

❑ **Top Cat**, blister pack, three reel, Model No. BB513
EX n/a   **NM** $13   **MIP** $15

❑ **Tournament of Thrills (ABC's WW/Sports)**, original envelope package, three reel, Model No. B947
EX n/a   **NM** $30   **MIP** $35

❏ **Tripods, The**, blister pack, three reel, Model No. BD242
EX n/a   **NM** $10   **MIP** $12

❏ **Tron**, original envelope package, three reel, Model No. M37
EX n/a   **NM** $8   **MIP** $10

❏ **TV Shows at Universal Studios**, original envelope package, three reel, Model No. B477
EX n/a   **NM** $26   **MIP** $30

❏ **TV Stars I (single reel)**, original envelope package, one reel, Model No. 745
EX n/a   **NM** $17   **MIP** $20

❏ **TV Stars II (single reel)**, original envelope package, one reel, Model No. 746
EX n/a   **NM** $17   **MIP** $20

❏ **TV Stars III (single reel)**, original envelope package, one reel, Model No. 747
EX n/a   **NM** $17   **MIP** $20

❏ **Tweety & Sylvester**, blister pack, three reel, Model No. BD1161
EX n/a   **NM** $7   **MIP** $8

❏ **Tweety & Sylvester**, original envelope package, three reel, Model No. J28
EX n/a   **NM** $3   **MIP** $4

❏ **Twice Upon a Time**, blister pack, three reel, Model No. 4043
EX n/a   **NM** $3   **MIP** $4

❏ **U.F.O.**, original envelope package, three reel, Model No. B417
EX n/a   **NM** $38   **MIP** $45

❏ **Ulysses 31**, blister pack, three reel, Model No. BD198
EX n/a   **NM** $7   **MIP** $8

❏ **Victor & Maria**, blister pack, three reel, Model No. BD224
EX n/a   **NM** $7   **MIP** $10

❏ **Voyage to the Bottom of the Sea**, original envelope package, three reel, Model No. B483
EX n/a   **NM** $10   **MIP** $12

❏ **Waltons, The**, blister pack, three reel, Model No. BB596
EX n/a   **NM** $10   **MIP** $12

❏ **Waltons, The**, 1972, original envelope package, three reel, Model No. B596
EX n/a   **NM** $10   **MIP** $12

❏ **Welcome Back Kotter**, original envelope package, three reel, Model No. J19
EX n/a   **NM** $10   **MIP** $12

❏ **Who Framed Roger Rabbit**, blister pack, three reel, Model No. 4086
EX n/a   **NM** $8   **MIP** $16

(KP Photo)

❏ **Wild Animals of Africa,** 1960, Original picture envelope showing giraffes, three reel set
EX n/a   **NM** $5   **MIP** $11

❏ **Wild Bill Hickcock & Jingles**, original envelope package, three reel, Model No. B473
EX n/a   **NM** $26   **MIP** $30

❏ **Willo the Wisp**, blister pack, three reel, Model No. BD215
EX n/a   **NM** $7   **MIP** $8

❏ **Wind in the Willows**, blister pack, three reel, Model No. BD231
EX n/a   **NM** $7   **MIP** $8

❏ **Wind in the Willows**, blister pack, three reel, Model No. 4084
EX n/a   **NM** $7   **MIP** $10

❏ **Wings of the Hawk (Movie Preview Reel)**, Movie Preview Reel
EX n/a   **NM** $128   **MIP** $150

❏ **Winnetou**, blister pack, three reel, Model No. BB731
EX n/a   **NM** $21   **MIP** $25

❏ **Winnetou**, original envelope package, three reel, Model No. B728
EX n/a   **NM** $26   **MIP** $30

❏ **Winnetou**, blister pack, three reel, Model No. BB7284
EX n/a   **NM** $21   **MIP** $25

❏ **Winnetou & Halfblood Apache**, original envelope package, three reel, Model No. B728
EX n/a   **NM** $26   **MIP** $30

❏ **Winnie the Pooh & The Blustery Day**, original envelope package, three reel, Model No. K37
EX n/a   **NM** $7   **MIP** $8

❏ **Wiz, The**, 1978, original envelope package, three reel, Model No. J14
EX n/a   **NM** $17   **MIP** $20

❏ **Wizard of Oz**, blister pack, three reel, Model No. BD267
EX n/a   **NM** $7   **MIP** $8

❏ **Wizard of Oz**, 1957, original envelope package, three reel, Model No. FT45abc
EX n/a   **NM** $13   **MIP** $15

❏ **Wombles, The**, original envelope package, three reel, Model No. D131
EX n/a   **NM** $13   **MIP** $15

❏ **Wombles, The**, blister pack, three reel, Model No. BD131
EX n/a   **NM** $7   **MIP** $8

(KP Photo)

❏ **Wonderful World of Disney**, Includes three reels: Pinocchio, Lady & The Tramp, Snow White
EX n/a   **NM** $8   **MIP** $15

❏ **Woody Woodpecker,** 1955, original envelope package, three reel, Model No. B522
EX n/a   **NM** $13   **MIP** $15

❏ **Woody Woodpecker Pony Express Ride (single reel)**, 1951, original envelope package, one reel, Model No. 820
EX n/a   **NM** $3   **MIP** $4

❏ **World Bobsled Championships (ABC's WW/Sports)**, original envelope package, three reel, Model No. B949
EX n/a   **NM** $60   **MIP** $80

❏ **Worzel Gummidge**, blister pack, three reel, Model No. BD185
EX n/a   **NM** $7   **MIP** $8

❏ **Wrestling Superstars**, blister pack, three reel, Model No. 4067
EX n/a   **NM** $8   **MIP** $10

❏ **Young Indiana Jones Chronicles**, blister pack, three reel, Model No. 4140
EX n/a   **NM** $6   **MIP** $8

(KP Photo)

❏ **Zorro,** 1958, original envelope package, three reel, Model No. B469
EX n/a   **NM** $34   **MIP** $40

Index

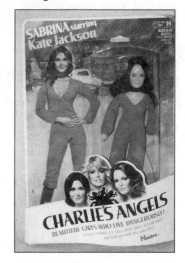

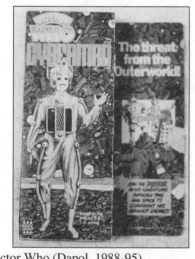

INDEX

Barbie Dolls 130

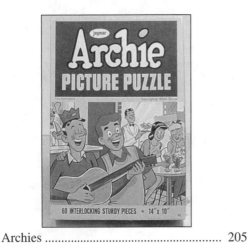

INDEX

OPEN SUNDAY ONLY

*Bargains Galore on New & Vintage Items – **You Can ORDER ONLINE!***

5pm to 10pm central

CLOSEOUTS – CLEARANCE – DISCONTINUED – OVERSTOCKS

www.adkinsstore.com

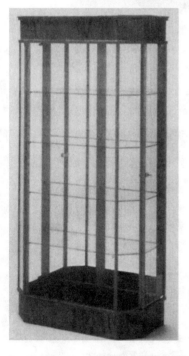

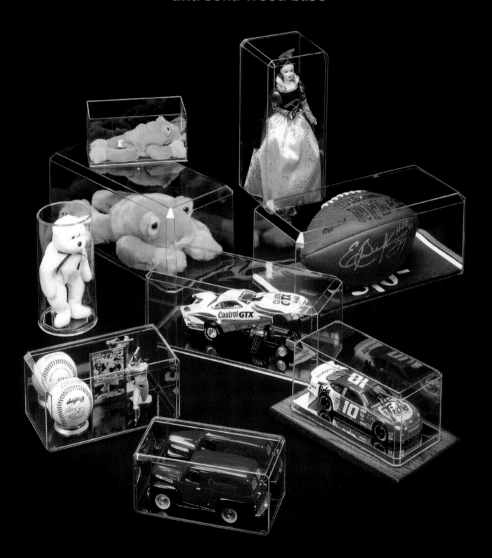

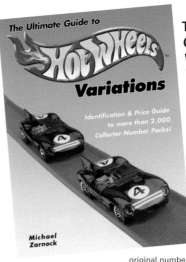

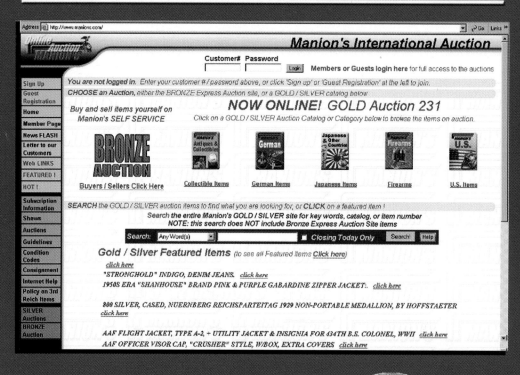